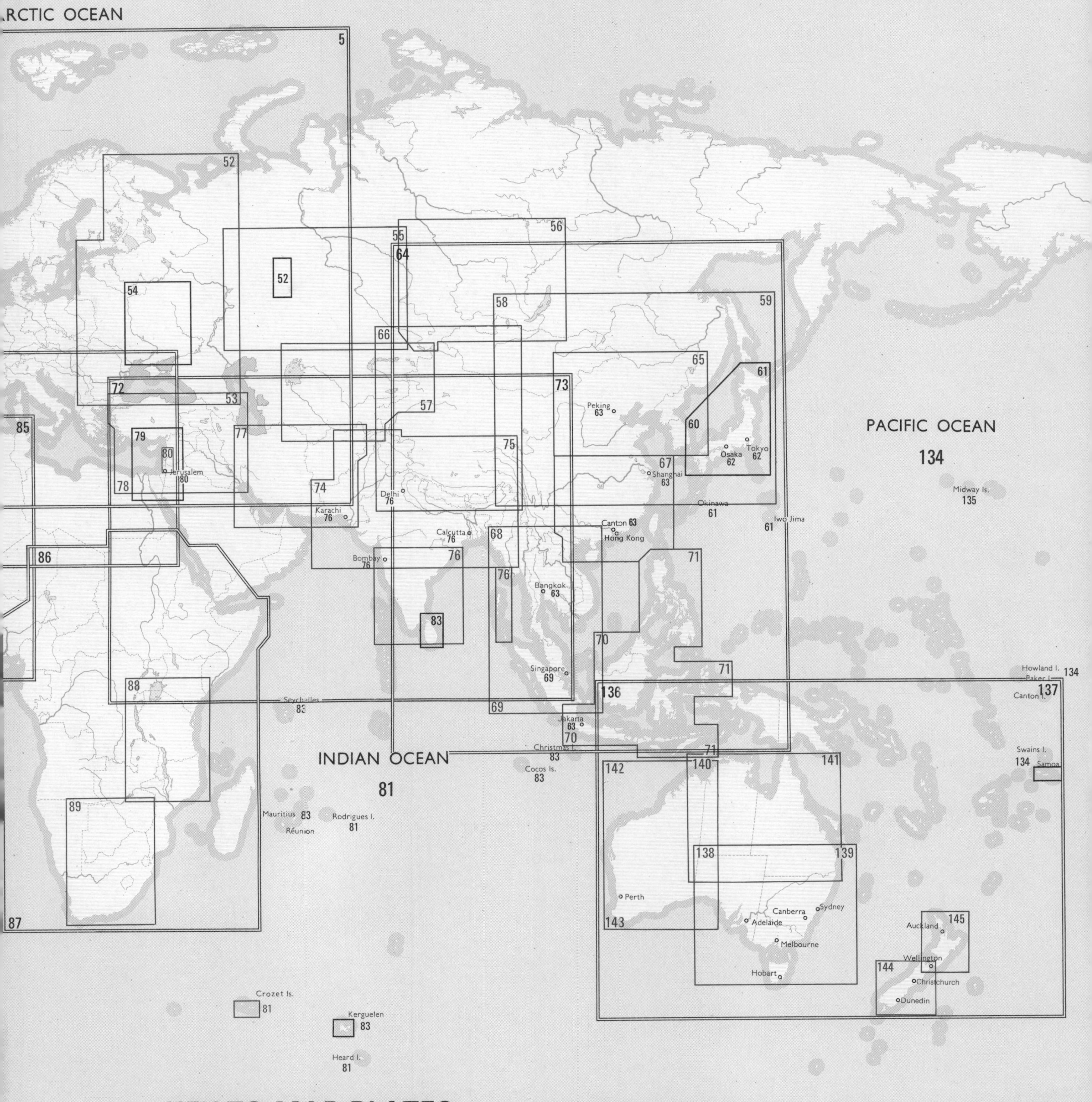
ARCTIC OCEAN
PACIFIC OCEAN
134
INDIAN OCEAN
81
5
52
52
54
55
64
56
58
59
65
61
60
66
57
72
53
73
85
79
80
77
75
67
78
74
Jerusalem 80
Peking 63
Osaka 62
Tokyo 62
Shanghai 63
Karachi 76
Delhi 76
Okinawa 61
Iwo Jima 61
Midway Is. 135
Calcutta 76
Canton 63
Hong Kong
86
68
71
76
Bombay 76
76
Bangkok 63
83
70
Singapore 69
71
Howland I. 134
Baker I.
Canton I.
137
136
88
Seychelles 83
69
Jakarta 63
70
Christmas I. 83
Cocos Is. 83
71
140
141
142
Swains I. 134
Samoa
89
Mauritius 83
Réunion
Rodrigues I. 81
138
139
Perth
Canberra
Sydney
Adelaide
Melbourne
143
145
Auckland
87
Wellington
Hobart
144
Christchurch
Dunedin
Crozet Is. 81
Kerguelen 83
Heard I. 81

KEY TO MAP PLATES

excluding larger scales in North America and Europe *(see other end-paper)*

Plate	Scale
114	1:12 000 000 and smaller
83	1:3 000 000
116	1:6 000 000
80	1:1 000 000 and larger

Inset maps of islands, cities, etc. are named

General Maps

World Topics (Introductory Section)

THE TIMES

CONCISE ATLAS OF THE WORLD

Times Books

Contributors

John C Bartholomew
Editorial Director
John Bartholomew & Son Limited

Hugh Clayton
Agricultural Correspondent
The Times London

Charles Cotter
Department of Maritime Studies, Uwist
Cardiff

F W Dunning
Curator
The Geological Museum, London

John Gribbin
Science Policy Research Unit
University of Sussex

H A G Lewis OBE
Geographical Consultant

Kenneth Mellanby
Monks Wood Experimental Station
Institute of Terrestrial Ecology

Eric Rawstron
Professor of Geography
Queen Mary College
University of London

Ian Ridpath
Editor
Encyclopedia of Astronomy and Space

Alan Smith
Department of Geology
University of Cambridge

Peter J Smith
Department of Earth Sciences
The Open University

David Tennant
Travel Correspondent
Thomson Regional Newspapers, London

Roger Vielvoye
Formerly Energy Correspondent
The Times, London

Editorial direction
Barry Winkleman
Paul Middleton

Maps prepared and printed
in Great Britain by
John Bartholomew & Son Limited, Edinburgh

Conurbation maps compiled and drawn by
Fairey Surveys Limited, Maidenhead;
A W Gatrell; and Hunting Surveys Limited

Artwork by Ivan and Robin Dodd, Key Graphics
and Donald Shewan

Preliminary section cartography by
Fairey Surveys Limited, Maidenhead
and filmset by
Crawley Composition Ltd, Crawley, Sussex

Index prepared by
Geographical Research Associates, Maidenhead

Index data processing by
Computer Data Processing Ltd, Haywards Heath

Index set by Computaprint, London

Index printed by The Anchor Press Limited, England

Books bound by Bookbinders Brandt, Holland

First published 1972 by
Times Books Limited, 16 Golden Square, London W1, the book publishing subsidiary of
Times Newspapers Limited, New Printing House Square,
London WC1 8EZ

Reprinted with revisions 1973, 1974
Revised edition 1975
Reprinted 1976, 1978
Revised edition 1978
Reprinted with revisions 1979
Revised edition 1980

Copyright © Times Newspapers Limited and
John Bartholomew & Son Limited
1972, 1973, 1974, 1975, 1976, 1978, 1979, 1980

British Library Cataloguing in Publication Data:
'The times' concise atlas of the world
—3rd ed.
1. Atlases, British
912 G1019
ISBN 0 7230 0238 X

All rights reserved including the right to reproduce
this book or parts thereof in any form.

Contents

Acknowledgements

Academy of Sciences of the USSR and the National Atlas Committee, Moscow
Aeronautical Chart and Information Center, United States Air Force, St Louis, Missouri
American Geographical Society, New York
The British Petroleum Company Ltd, London
British Tourist Authority, London
Ceskoslovenské Akademie Ved, Prague
Department of Lands and Survey, Wellington, New Zealand
The Department of the Environment, London
Food & Agriculture Organization of the United Nations, Rome
French Railways, London
Freytag-Berndt und Artaria, Vienna
Mr P. J. M. Geelan
General Drafting Company Inc, Convent Station, New Jersey
Dr R. Habel, VEB Hermann Haack, Geographisch-Kartographische Anstalt, Gotha, East Germany
The Controller, H.M. Stationery Office, London
Institut Géographique Militaire, Brussels
Le Directeur de l'Institut Géographique National, Paris
Instituto Brasiliero de Geografia e Estatistica, Rio de Janeiro
International Hydrographic Bureau, Monaco
International Road Federation, London
International Union of Official Travel Organizations, Geneva
Professor P. E. James, Syracuse University, New York
Mr P. Laffitte, Ecole des Mines, Paris
Dr E. Meynen, Bad Godesberg, West Germany
National Aeronautical and Space Administration, Washington DC
National Geographic Society, Washington DC
National Library of Scotland, Edinburgh
Director of National Mapping, Department of National Development, Canberra
Director-General, Ordnance Survey, Southampton
Palomar Observatory, California Institute of Technology
Petroleum Information Bureau, London
Dr B. B. Roberts, Antarctic Place-Names Committee, London
Mr P. Rouveyrol, Bureau de Recherches Géologiques et Minières, Paris
Royal Geographical Society, London
Royal Observatory, Edinburgh
Royal Scottish Geographical Society, Edinburgh
The Scientific American, San Francisco
Dr John Paxton, The Editor, The Statesman's Year Book, London
Dr H. J. Störig, Lexikon-Redaktion, Munich
The Trigonometrical Survey Office, Pretoria
Touring Club Italiano, Milan
Under-Secretary of State, Foreign and Commonwealth Office, London
Surveys and Mapping Branch, Department of Energy, Mines, and Resources, Ottawa
United States Army Topographic Command, Washington DC
United States Board on Geographic Names, Washington DC
United States Department of State, Washington DC
United States Embassy Press Office, London

Introduction

In presenting a further revision of an atlas which has proved to be extremely popular, we draw attention to an important change in this edition. Place-names in China are given in their Pinyin spellings, a step likewise taken in our larger atlas, the Comprehensive Edition. More is said on the subject below.

The preliminary section of the atlas is concerned with geography in its widest sense: as a science that has much to contribute to the understanding of the contemporary world. In these pages we first describe the origin and geology of the Earth and its physical nature, its resources of climate, vegetation and minerals. Then we examine major features of the geography of man, particularly his settlements and population patterns, his trade and industry, his use of energy, the development of tourism, and the effect of all these activities on the balance of his natural environment. The complex techniques of navigation, which have been central to the development of human history, are described, and the Earth as a whole is placed into its context in the expanding Universe. The present state of our knowledge of the Universe is described; two pages are devoted to maps of the Moon and one to star charts.

In the main body of the atlas the maps, with the exception of those covering the conurbation areas, have been compiled by John Bartholomew & Son Limited of Edinburgh, who have been associated with *The Times* in atlas-publishing since 1922. Several map projections are used, each for its own special properties. Without some adaptation the surface of the spherical earth cannot be transferred to a flat sheet of paper, any more than an orange can be wrapped in a sheet of paper without cutting and folding. Map projections are the means of adapting the round globe to the flat map.

How best to spell place-names, a matter of great complexity, has always been considered carefully in the preparation of atlases published by *The Times*. Difficulties arise from the diversity of writing systems in use in the world and the great number of languages, hundreds of which are inadequately written or have no writing system. In the absence of a uniform and internationally accepted method of recording and writing geographical names, conventional spellings established by long usage furnish us with Athens (English), Athènes (French), Azine (Spanish), etc. *The Times Concise Atlas* gives transliterations in English, e.g. Athinai, with the English conventional name, where appropriate, in parentheses: Athinai (Athens). In general, *The Times Concise Atlas* follows the rules recommended by the United States Board on Geographical Names and the Permanent Committee on Geographical Names for British Official Use.

In all previous editions names in China have been transcribed in terms of the Wade-Giles readings of Chinese characters. With increasing use of Pinyin within China as a roman alphabet equivalent of the Han characters and the reçent availability of sufficient sources for names, the publishers decided to replace Wade-Giles by Pinyin in mainland China. In Taiwan, Wade-Giles is still in use and so is retained in this atlas. Neither is Pinyin applicable in Hong Kong where a local system is in use. A special section on the Transcription of Chinese Place-Names has been added to this edition (p.88).

With regard to the sensitive political implications of maps, *The Times Atlas* has always considered its task to be to show facts as they are and not to pass judgements. When delineating a frontier this atlas shows which authority is administering the area at the time the map goes to press. Our wish is to help the traveller, businessman, student or teacher who we hope will buy it. It also follows that place-names are, as far as possible, spelt according to the usage of those administering the region concerned. An atlas can show where a frontier is disputed, but it strays beyond its proper sphere if it tries to adjudicate between the rights and wrongs of the dispute rather than to set down the facts as they are.

The index section contains over 90,000 entries. Not every name on the maps appears in that index, but all towns and physical features other than the smallest are indexed. Place-names and their descriptions (such as Lake or River) are listed in strict alphabetical order, so that Haig L. (Lake) does not immediately follow the town of Haig, but is interrupted by Haiger. Each name is accompanied by its country or location and by the page number and grid reference by letter and numeral.

The information on states and territories which precedes the index section has been revised to accord with the latest information available.

It is with pleasure that we issue this, our latest edition, and we hope the reader will find equal interest and pleasure from its use.

The Earth

The origin of the Earth

The Earth originated as part of the solar system about 4,700 million years ago, probably by the accretion of particles from a cloud of gas and dust (see *The origin of the planets*). Certainly it must have formed in a fairly cold state, for otherwise many of the more volatile elements still present in the Earth would never have been able to condense. On the other hand, the Earth must have warmed up quickly as it increased in size, heat being produced in three ways – by conversion of kinetic energy of the particles coming to rest on the surface of the new planet as the result of great compression in the body's interior, and from decay of radioactive elements.

This heat, which was produced more rapidly than it could escape, had a profound effect on the new Earth's structure. Without it, the Earth would have become a homogeneous globe of silicon compounds, iron and magnesium oxides and smaller quantities of all naturally-occurring elements. As it was, the planet very soon warmed up sufficiently to allow the separation of elements and compounds, to begin. The heavier materials such as iron sank towards the Earth's centre whereas the lighter ones, chiefly silicon compounds, rose towards the surface.

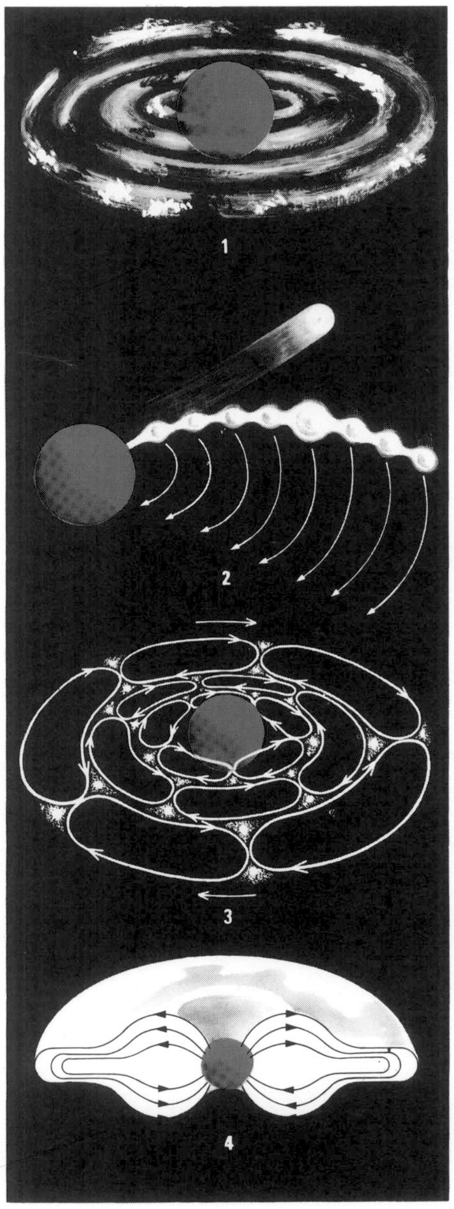

The origin of the planets

Most of the theories about the origin of the planets in the solar system may be divided into two broad types – those which attribute the creation of a solar system to gradual evolutionary processes and those which see it as the result of a catastrophic action.

Kant and Laplace *Nebular Theory*

The earliest theory of the first type was put forward in 1755 by Kant, who suggested that the solar system originated as a spinning disc of material which later separated out into the Sun and the planets. In 1796 this basic idea was developed by Laplace into the nebular theory. Laplace proposed that the Sun was originally a rotating gaseous nebula (1) which gradually contracted under gravitational forces and rotated more and more rapidly until gaseous material was thrown off at the edges to form a series of rings. Each ring then condensed into a separate planet.

Moulton, Chamberlin and Jeans *Tidal Theory*

By 1900 Laplace's theory in its original form had been abandoned, partly because it had proved to be inconsistent with the Sun's observed period of rotation and partly because scientists had shown that Laplace's rings would be too stable to coalesce into planets. So in 1905 Moulton and Chamberlin suggested a return to Buffon's idea of about 200 years before, namely, that the solar system resulted from the collision of the Sun with another body. Thirteen years later this proposal was modified by Jeans, who envisaged not a collision but a close encounter between the Sun and a star (2). As the star passed by the Sun its gravitational attraction drew out from the Sun's surface a long filament of gaseous matter which, being unstable, broke into separate zones. Each zone cooled and contracted into a planet.

Von Weizsäcker's Theory

By the 1930s, however, it had become clear that the sort of filament suggested by Jeans would be so unstable that it would be dispersed into space within a few hours. Moreover, planets such as the Earth are so different from the Sun in composition that they are unlikely to have formed directly from it. So in 1944 von Weizsäcker returned to, and modified, the nebular theory. He suggested that the Sun passed through a vast dense cloud of interstellar dust and gas which it attracted to itself in the form of a disc. The particles in the disc then gradually aggregated into larger and larger lumps which became the planets (3).

Hoyle's Theory

Although the broad outlines of von Weizsäcker's theory are now quite widely accepted, the theory is not entirely satisfactory in detail and so other scientists have proposed variations or even completely different theories. One of the most interesting of modern suggestions was put forward by Hoyle, who drew attention to the role of magnetism. Hoyle proposed that magnetic forces between the Sun and the dust-gas disc gradually move the disc outwards (4). As the disc spread away from the Sun it was capable of carrying smaller and smaller particles and so the larger particles gradually get left behind. This segregation into sizes also implies segregation into different compositions, which quite neatly explains why, when the particles aggregate into planets, the compositions of the planets vary considerably right across the solar system.

The position of the Earth in the Universe

The Earth is the third planet from the Sun and the largest of the group of inner, or terrestrial, planets, the other members of which are Mercury, Venus and Mars. The Sun, the inner planets and the group of outer planets (Jupiter, Saturn, Uranus, Neptune and Pluto – all of which, with the exception of Pluto, are much larger than the Earth) together make up most of the solar system. The solar system is completed by over 400,000 or so asteroids, or minor planets, most of whose orbits lie between Mars and Jupiter and the largest of which is Ceres with a diameter of 730 km. All the planets revolve around the Sun in the same direction and, with the exception of Pluto, their elliptical orbits lie almost in one plane.

Pluto, the outermost planet, is about 5,900 million kilometres, or about 5 light hours, away from the Sun. Yet vast as this distance is, the Sun and planets are but a speck in the universe. For a start, the solar system is but a very small part of the Milky Way, a lens-shaped galaxy which contains some 100,000 million stars like the Sun and vast clouds of hydrogen, helium and dust. The diameter of the Milky Way is about 100,000 light years and the Sun lies about two-thirds of the way from the centre.

The Milky Way, in turn, is only one of many thousands of millions of galaxies scattered throughout the universe. Galaxies tend to cluster; the Milky Way, for example, is but one galaxy in a local group of about 20 and is only about half the size of the largest galaxy in the group. The group itself has a spread of about 5 million light years.

Outside the local group, the furthest known ordinary galaxy is more than 8,000 million light years away, but beyond that are radio galaxies and quasars. Radio galaxies emit vast quantities of radio energy (more than a million times than that emitted by the Milky Way) and are believed to be the sites of gigantic explosions, possibly representing an early stage of galaxy formation. Quasars are very brilliant, but much smaller objects (less than 1 light year across), which are powerful emitters of radio waves and may be the nuclei of distant galaxies. The furthest known object, quasar OQ 172, lies 18,000 million light years away, at the very edge of the detectable universe.

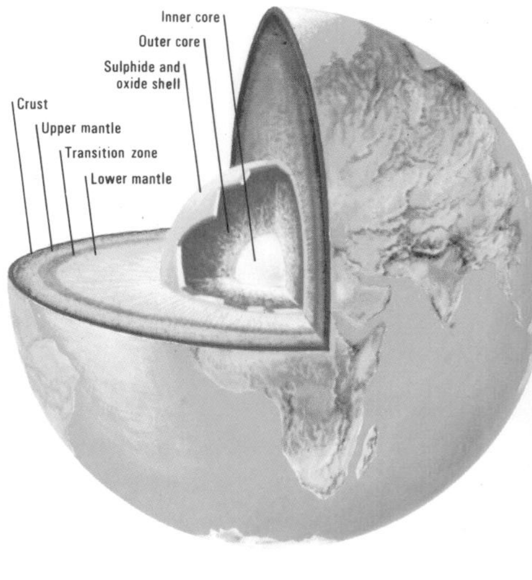

Structure of the solid Earth

The solid Earth consists of three shells: crust, mantle and core. The thin outer shell, the crust, is made up of different types of rock. Under continents it is about 40 km thick and is mostly granitic in composition. Under mountain ranges it may be thicker than 70 km. The oceanic crust is about 8 km thick and is basaltic. The mean crustal density is 2·8 (water = 1·0), and it is about 0·4% of the total mass of the Earth.

The base of the crust is marked by the Mohorovicic discontinuity (Moho or M—). At this level the velocity of the fastest seismic waves sent out by earthquakes rises rapidly from 6 km/sec to 8 km/sec. Below the Moho lies the mantle. Solid rocks brought up from the mantle by lava flows suggest that it is much less varied than the crust and consists mostly of the rock peridotite. The mantle has a thickness of 2,900 km, density of 4·5, and makes up 67·2% of the Earth's mass. The increase in pressure with depth causes the minerals in peridotite (mainly olivine and pyroxene) to change through a transition zone to new dense minerals unknown at the surface.

The innermost Earth shell is the core. The outer core, 2,200 km thick, is fluid. Motions in the fluid generate the Earth's magnetic field. The inner core, radius 1,270 km, is solid. The core density is 11·0 and contains 32·4% of the Earth's mass. Both cores are probably made of nickel-iron.

Physical characteristics of the Earth

The Earth is not perfectly spherical but has the shape of a spheroid, a sphere flattened at the poles. The average polar radius of 6,357 km is thus smaller than the average equatorial radius of 6,378 km. The overall average radius is 6,371 km, which is the radius of the sphere that has the same volume as the Earth.

The mass of the Earth is 6×10^{24} kg and its average density is about 5·5 grams/cm^3. But the average density of the surface rocks is only about 2·8 grams/cm^3. There must therefore be an increase in density towards the Earth's centre where the pressure exceeds that of 3½ million atmospheres. The temperature at the centre is uncertain; but is probably no more than about 5,000°C.

More than 70 per cent of the Earth's surface is covered by ocean. Indeed, the Pacific Ocean alone, which with its adjacent seas accounts for more than 35 per cent of the Earth's surface, covers a larger area than that of all the continents combined. More than 65 per cent of the continental area lies in the northern hemisphere, although at the poles themselves this imbalance is reversed.

Metal-bearing rocks deep inside the Earth, contain crystals of ferro-magnetic materials revealed by production of local anomalous magnetism. As the rocks cooled and solidified, the magnetised molecules were aligned like small magnets in the direction of the magnetic poles, thus preserving as 'frozen magnetism' a permanent record of the magnetism at the place and time of their solidification.

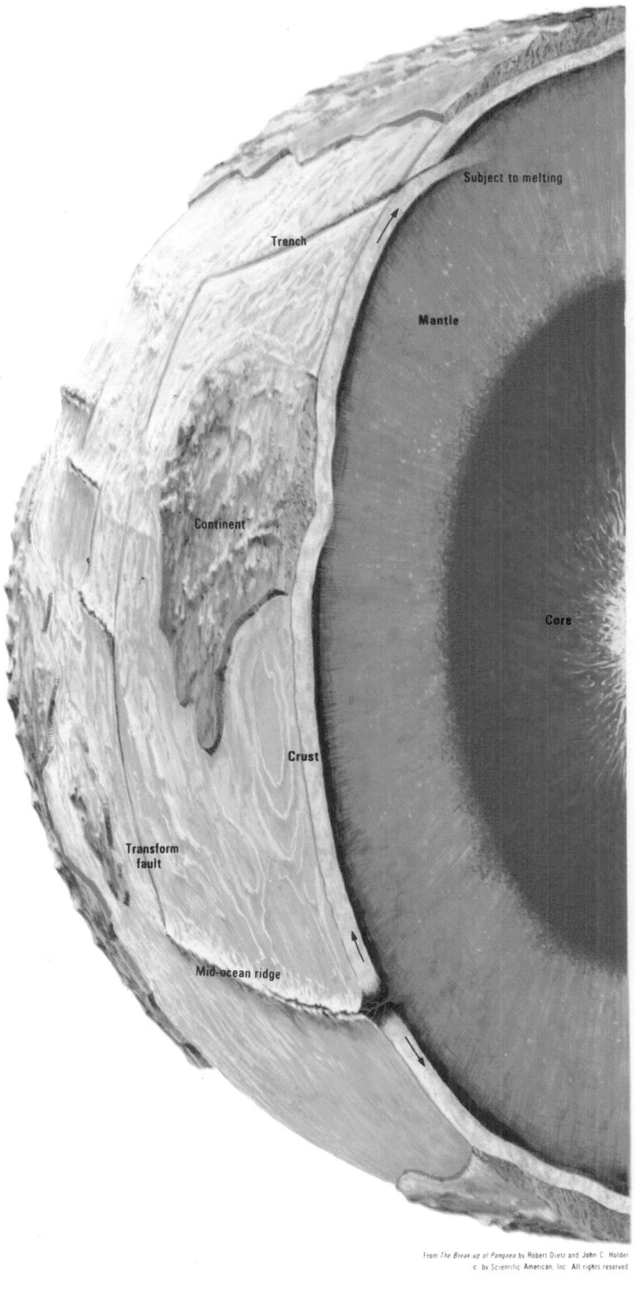

From *The Break-up of Pangaea* by Robert Dietz and John C. Holder

The magnetosphere

Ionized gas, or plasma, streams from the Sun in all directions, and is known as the 'solar wind'. The Earth's fluid iron-nickel core produces a magnetic field which extends beyond the Earth's surface into space. Where the solar wind comes into contact with this magnetic field there is a mutual interaction.

On the side of the Earth facing the Sun the solar wind compresses the Earth's magnetic field, whereas on the side of the Earth away from the Sun the field is greatly elongated. The field is thus confined to a zone known as the magnetosphere, the boundary of which is called the magnetopause. The position of the magnetopause changes a little as the intensity of the solar wind varies, but in the solar direction it lies at an average distance of about 10 Earth radii from the centre of the Earth, whilst in the anti-solar direction, it extends out to very large distances of at least 60 Earth radii.

The solar wind is travelling at almost 1000 km per second when it encounters the Earth's magnetic field. A shock wave is formed several Earth radii from the magnetopause in the direction of the Sun.

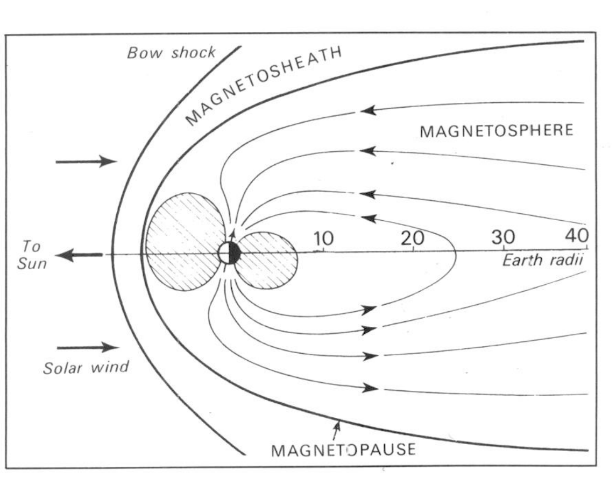

The region between the magnetopause and the shock wave front is known as the magnetosheath, or transition region of the magnetosphere.

Earthquakes

An earthquake is a sudden release of strain energy at a point – or, more accurately, within a small zone – in the Earth's crust or upper mantle. Because many shallow earthquakes are obviously related to sudden fault movements, it was once thought that they were responsible for all earthquakes. But it seems likely that at depths greater than a few tens of kilometres the pressure would be too great to allow any fault slippage, whereas earthquakes are known to occur down to depths of about 700 km. The cause of the deeper shocks remains unknown.

Whatever their basic cause, however, most earthquakes are clearly related to plate tectonic processes and occur along plate boundaries – oceanic ridges, oceanic trenches and transform faults. The most intense belt of seismic activity lies around the margin of the Pacific Ocean where 75 per cent of all shallow earthquakes (0–70 km depth), 90 per cent of all intermediate earthquakes (70–300 km) and almost all deep earthquakes (greater than 300 km) occur. Most of the remaining large earthquakes take place along the Alpine-Himalayan chain. Earthquakes are also concentrated along the oceanic ridge system, but most of these are shallow and comparatively small.

There are two ways of specifying the size of an earthquake – by magnitude and intensity. Magnitude is denoted by a number on a logarithmic scale ranging up to about 9·0. It is an absolute measure of the energy released by the earthquake, and so each earthquake is specified by a single magnitude number. Intensity, on the other hand, is denoted by numbered grades on the Modified Mercalli Scale and is based on the damage caused by the earthquake at the Earth's surface as well as on people's reaction to the shock. As these effects decrease with distance from the focus, an earthquake is described by a series of decreasing intensity grades with the highest grade corresponding to the area immediately above the focus.

Earthquake waves

When an earthquake occurs, the shock gives rise to vibrations, or seismic waves, which radiate outwards in all directions from the earthquake's focus. Some of the waves, known as body waves, pass through the Earth's interior; but others, surface waves, travel close to the Earth's surface.

There are two distinct types of body wave. In P, or longitudinal waves the particles of the Earth vibrate backwards and forwards along the direction in which the wave is travelling. In S, or transverse waves the Earth particles move up and down at right angles to the direction of wave travel. Both P and S waves travel along the same paths, except that S waves do not pass through fluids. S waves therefore do not enter the Earth's fluid outer core. In solid materials, however, P waves travel about twice as fast as S waves; so where both P and S waves arrive at a distant measuring station, the P waves arrive first.

The velocities of body waves depend on the physical and chemical state of the material through which they are passing and they generally increase with depth in the Earth. Within any given zone (the mantle, for example), waves are refracted along curved paths which ultimately bring them to the surface. But where the physical properties in the Earth suddenly change, the waves change velocity and are refracted equally abruptly. This occurs chiefly at the crust-mantle and mantle-core boundaries at which there are sharp chemical changes; indeed, these discontinuities were first recognized from the study of seismic waves. The combined effect of refraction and the inability of S waves to travel through the outer core is to prevent most P and S waves reaching the Earth's surface at angles of 105°–142° from the earthquake, a region known as the "shadow zone"

Surface waves are slower than body waves, but they are responsible for most of the ground motion and hence most of the earthquake damage to buildings.

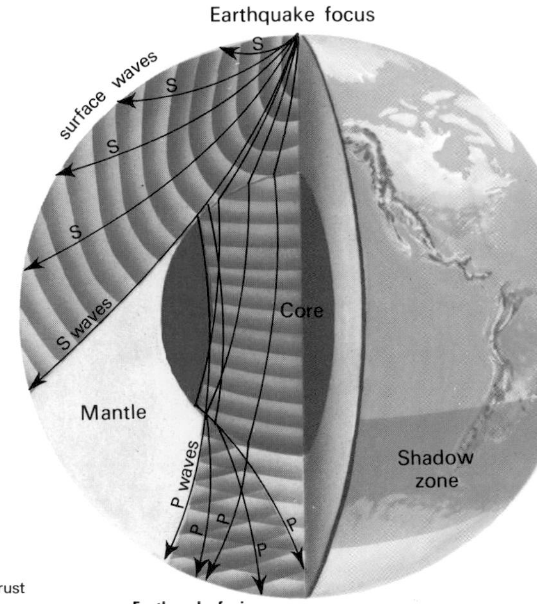

Seismic waves
Body waves, both Primary (P) and Secondary (S), pass through the interior of the Earth. Long waves are the slowest and the most damaging of waves, passing along the surface of the crust. The amplitude or strength of the waves is used to determine the magnitude of the earthquake. Magnitude is graded according to the Richter Scale which is logarithmic: a magnitude of 5 emits waves with a strength ten times that of 4 and one hundred times that of 3 etc.

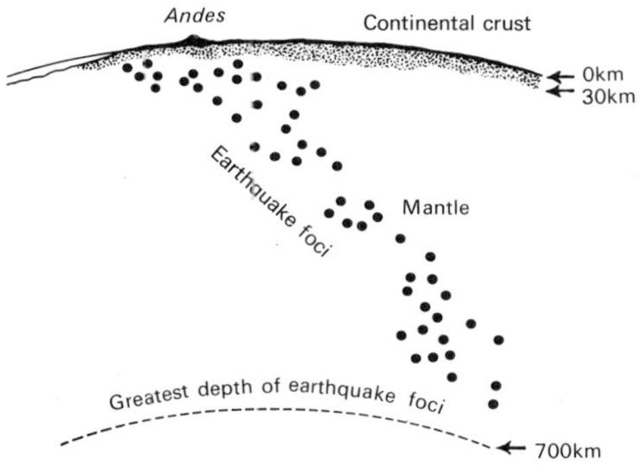

Earthquake foci
The focus of an earthquake is the small zone from which the seismic waves and energy are released. More than 70 per cent of all foci lie within the Earth's upper 70 km, but some earthquakes occur down to depths of about 700 km. Along deep ocean trenches, where the ocean plate descends into the mantle, the downward path of the plate may be traced by plotting the positions of the associated earthquake foci. Along other types of plate boundary the foci are usually much shallower; along the San Andreas fault, for example, they all lie in the upper 20 km or so.

Modified Mercalli Earthquake Intensity Scale
The 12-point scale designed in 1935 grades shocks according to the degree of disturbance felt by ordinary citizens. The numerals I to XII define the categories.

- I Shock not felt except by a few people under special circumstances.
- II Shock felt by few people at rest. Delicately suspended objects swing.
- III Shock felt noticeably indoors. Stationary cars may rock.
- IV Shock felt generally indoors. People awakened, cars rock and windows rattle.
- V Shock felt generally. Some plaster falls, dishes and windows break and pendulum clocks stop.
- VI Shock felt by all. Many frightened, chimneys and plaster damaged, furniture moves and objects upset.
- VII Shock felt in moving cars. People run outdoors. Moderate damage to buildings.
- VIII General alarm, shock very destructive. Damage to weak structures, but little to well-built structures. Furniture overturned.
- IX Panic. Total destruction of weak structures and considerable damage to well-built structures, foundations damaged, underground pipes break and ground fissures and cracks.
- X Panic. All but the very strongest buildings destroyed, foundations ruined, rails bend and water slops over river banks.
- XI Panic. Few buildings survive, broad fissures form and underground pipes out of service.
- XII Panic. Total destruction, waves seen in ground and objects thrown in air.

Volcanoes

There are about 500 active volcanoes situated on tectonic plate margins (see page 8 Plate tectonics). Volcanic belts are of two major types; those at the crest of mid-ocean ridges and those at the convergence of plate boundaries. The most recent eruptions include an eruption at Tristan Da Cunha (1956), the birth of a volcanic island at Surtsey near Iceland (1963), and eruption at Eldfjell, Heimaey in Iceland (1973). Other volcanoes are continuously active but with less dramatic results. They include Cotopaxi and Chimborazo in Ecuador, Popocatepetl in Mexico, and Lassen Peak and Katmai in the USA.

Cinder cone

This is the simplest form of volcano. Material is ejected through the central pipe and each eruption produces new deposits to overlay preceding layers. Gradually the cone is built up with larger fragments remaining near the summit at the steepest angle, around 30 degrees, and the smaller deposits moving to the base of the cone where the angle of rest may be as low as 10 degrees. Cinder cones rarely develop more than a kilometre in diameter.

Shield volcano

If much liquid or viscous lava is produced then deposits slowly build up a shallow-sloped volcano which may stretch up to 20 kilometres across. The gentle slopes are rarely steeper than 10 degrees.

Composite cone

This is the most common type of volcano formed by the vent emitting both rocks and lava at different times. The deposits therefore alternate to form a strong bonded structure resistant to erosion. Examples are Etna in Sicily, Vesuvius by Naples and Fujiyama in Japan.

Caldera

Calderas are formed either as the result of eruptions when the upper part of the cone is destroyed, or else by the collapse of the unsupported rim following the ejection of large quantities of lava. The cone is reduced in height but increased in circumference. Collapse occurs when the reservoir of molten magma issues through a side fissure instead of the central vent. The unsupported floor collapses with the crater rim, considerably enlarging the crater. Crater Lake, Oregon, 6–10 km in diameter, is an example of a caldera.

Flood basalt

Long narrow fissures in the Earth's crust may leak lava and heated rocks spreading them over a vast area. Fissure eruptions have produced the Deccan in India which covers half a million square kilometres.

Gas emission

In periods between eruptions, volcanoes release steam and various gases. As volcanic extinction approaches, lava and ashes are no longer ejected, the leaking gases are not under sufficient pressure to cause a fracture of the lava crust. This is called the solfatara stage after the large crater near Naples in Italy. The gases include sulphuretted hydrogen, sulphur dioxide, carbon dioxide, hydrochloric acid and ammonium chloride.

Explosive volcanoes sometimes eject material mixed with hot gas and this is known as *nuée ardente* or glowing cloud emission.

Volcanoes which emit chiefly steam are called fumaroles. The best example is the Valley of Ten Thousand Smokes near Katmai Volcano in Alaska. Carbon dioxide emitting volcanoes are termed mofettes.

Geysers and mud volcanoes

In certain parts of the world volcanic eruption expresses itself by the ejection of water at a high temperature. Geysers consist of clear water emission, but are called mud volcanoes if the water has a high content of solid matter. Both these mark the terminal phase of volcanic activity. The Waimangu geyser in New Zealand, active until 1904, had a jet fountain 500 feet high.

Volcanic prediction

The monitoring and prediction of volcanic activity is linked to earthquake detection on the site of recently active volcanoes. Most of those close to populated areas have permanently staffed observatories, such as at Mt Etna in Sicily and Mauna Loa in Hawaii. Transportable seismometers at selected locations record the small movements of the magma within the volcano which precede an eruption. The probable point of eruption can then be calculated. Tiltmeters and distance measuring equipment are used to map the changes to the landscape during and after an eruption. On many volcanoes, the slopes tilt downwards after an eruption and then build up slowly towards the next peak of activity. Volcanic movement sometimes produces a change in the local magnetic field caused by a rise in temperature of the underlying magma.

Cross-section through composite volcano

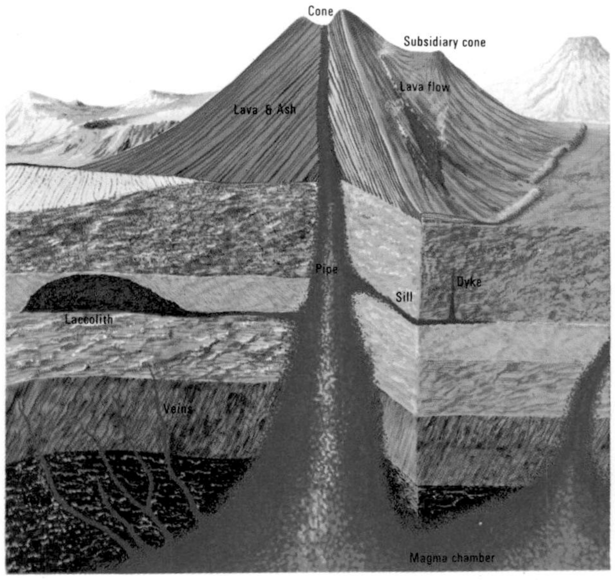

Volcanic activity
Volcanoes are formed when magma or molten material from the mantle or atmosphere, is extruded through weak or fractured points in the Earth's crust. Magma reaches the surface from the magma chamber through a volcanic pipe, but in some instances side vents leak magma through horizontal sills and vertical dykes. When magma reaches the surface it may be in liquid, solid or gaseous form. A lacolith is sometimes formed where molten rock is unable to reach the surface but is under enough pressure before solidifying to distort the overlying strata into a dome.

Caldera

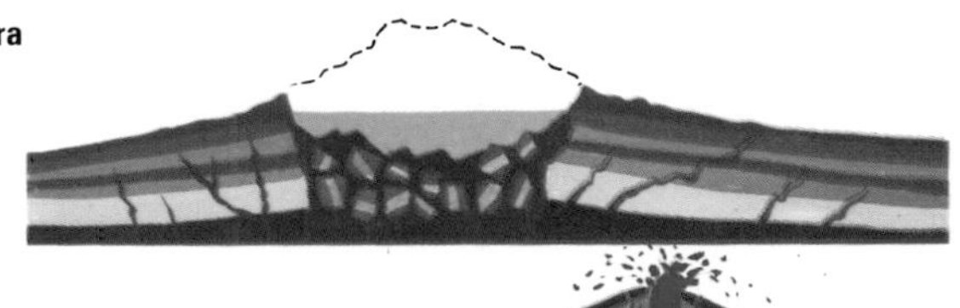

Calderas are large, basin-shaped depressions bounded by steep cliffs, like Crater Lake, Oregon, USA. They are usually formed when the magma chamber cannot support the cone above.

Shield volcano

Shield volcanoes, like Kilauea, Hawaii, repeatedly erupt highly fluid basalt lava that spreads out sometimes tens of kilometres.

Flood basalt

Flood basalt is an outflow of fluid lava from long and narrow fissures. The lava may spread out over vast areas to form extensive plateaux, like the Deccan in central India.

Nuée ardente

Nuée ardente (glowing cloud) eruptions are violent explosions of gas mixed with rock fragments which are ejected, sometimes to a considerable height, as at Mont Pelée in Martinique in 1902.

Plate tectonics

Earthquakes originate in well-defined zones of the Earth where rocks are actively being deformed. Earthquake zones separate large rigid areas free from active deformation known as tectonic plates. There are at least twelve such plates composing the Earth's outer shell, the lithosphere, and seven of them occupy a very large area, over 40 million square kilometres (see below Relative motions of tectonic plates). The lithosphere averages about 100 km in thickness and rests upon the asthenosphere, the semi-molten upper layer of the mantle. The detailed mechanism of plate movement is unknown but it is probably related to the transfer of heat energy deep within the Earth.

The idea of continual creation and destruction of the crust is seen in the movement of the ocean-floor plates forming mid-ocean ridges and deep trenches at the plate margins. Molten material from below the crust rises to the surface at the oceanic ridge where it forms new crust. To compensate for this additional material the leading edge of the moving plate is deflected downwards back into the mantle.

The theory of ocean-floor plate movement has been substantiated by dating of rock-core samples and comparison between magnetised rocks from either side of median ocean ridges. Deep ocean drilling has revealed that the oldest rock samples are in fact furthest away from the ocean ridge. Similarly, magnetised rock samples taken at an identical distance either side of a ridge show the same pattern of magnetic reversals. The oldest age of the rock samples appear to be about 200 million years, consistent with the estimate of the time when the Pangaea started to break up (see Continental drift).

There are three basic types of plate boundary identified by the differing movements of the plates in relation to one another.

Extensional plate boundary

At an extensional plate boundary new ocean floor is continuously created by the welling up of an oceanic ridge of hot basaltic crustal material from the underlying mantle. This material adheres to the plate edges as they move outwards from the median ridge. This process is known as ocean-floor spreading. The 40,000 km world-wide submarine mountain chain formed by ocean-floor spreading is the longest chain on Earth, but is visible only where exceptionally intense vulcanism, as in Iceland and Tristan da Cunha, raises it above sea-level. The usual ridge height is up to 5 km but widths may extend as far as 4,000 km. The forces of tension between the two diverging plates, cause rifts and transform faults where the fractured margins break up.

San Andreas fault

The fault is situated at the western margin of the North American plate which is sliding past the Pacific plate at an average speed of about 6 cms per year and setting up considerable stresses. In 1906, this vertical transform fault on a Translational plate boundary released its accumulated stress energy by a sudden sideways movement resulting in the San Francisco earthquake. Since 1906 the stresses have again been building up. Serious movement may again occur when the strength of the bonding of the two plates is exceeded by the stress.

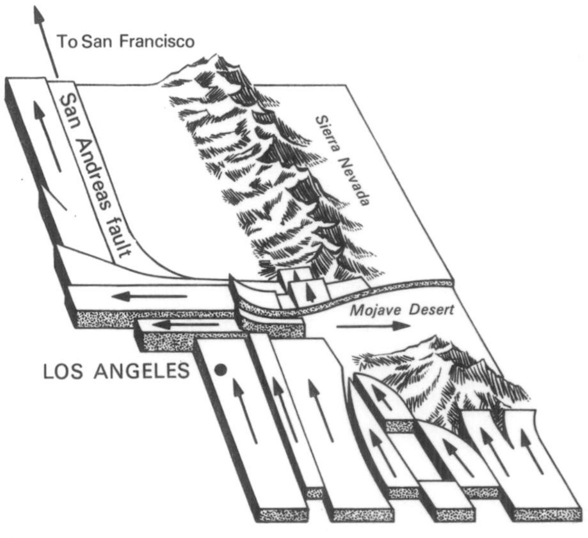

As the new ocean floor cools it acquires a weak magnetism. The older ocean floor moves away from the ridge at rates of between one and ten centimetres per year (see map below). The polarity of the Earth's magnetic field changes with time. Thus older ocean floors may be weakly magnetised in a differing direction to the present. The successive polarity changes or reversals, which occur at irregular intervals of a few hundred thousand years, give rise to a magnetic striping on the ocean floor by which older floors may be dated and the history of the oceans interpreted.

Translational plate boundaries

Crust is neither created nor destroyed at translational plate boundaries. The plates slide past each other along vertical faults or fractures known as transform or transcurrent faults. Best known as the San Andreas Fault in California (see diagram) and the Alpine Fault of New Zealand. Seismic activity is considerable along the numerous fracture zones which traverse the ocean ridge transform faults.

Compressional plate boundary

At compressional plate boundaries the older ocean floor sinks into the mantle at a subduction zone or steep zone of underthrust. This type of boundary is marked by ocean trenches where the edges of the crustal plates drop steeply into the mantle and become re-absorbed into the asthenosphere at depths of up to 600 or 700 km. Either plate could be pushed or subducted under the other, but usually, the less rigid and more flexible ocean-floor plate is deflected downwards by the continental plate. The descending plate carries crust material back into the under-lying mantle where it melts and breaks up. As it is less dense than the mantle it rises either towards the oceanic ridge and island arc or towards the continental lithosphere where it causes lava eruptions in a chain of volcanoes. The Aleutian, Japanese and Marianas islands are examples of such island arcs, and the South America Andes is an example of a subduction zone beneath a continental landmass. The sinking rate of one plate beneath its neighbour appears to be between 2 and 10 cm per year, resulting in intense seismic activity. The Earthquake foci in the subduction zone may be as deep as 700 km but they follow the subducted plate margin and give rise to severe disturbance.

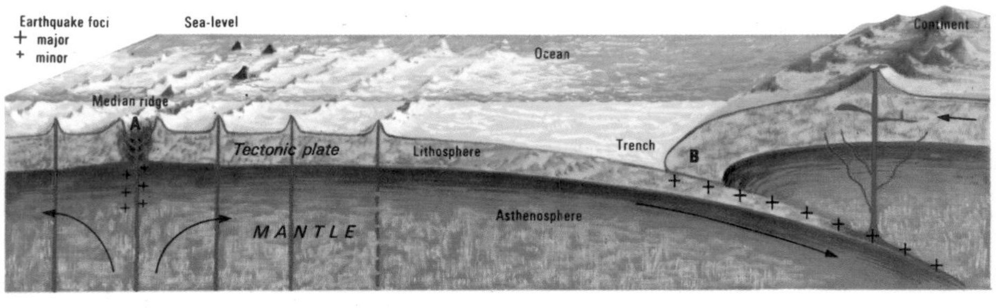

Volcanic activity and earthquakes are associated with plate tectonics. At A, an extensional boundary, magma from the upper mantle forms two parallel ridges. The rift between them broadens and new ridges are formed. At a compressional plate boundary, B, the ocean crust descends to perhaps 700 km, at which depth melting takes place.

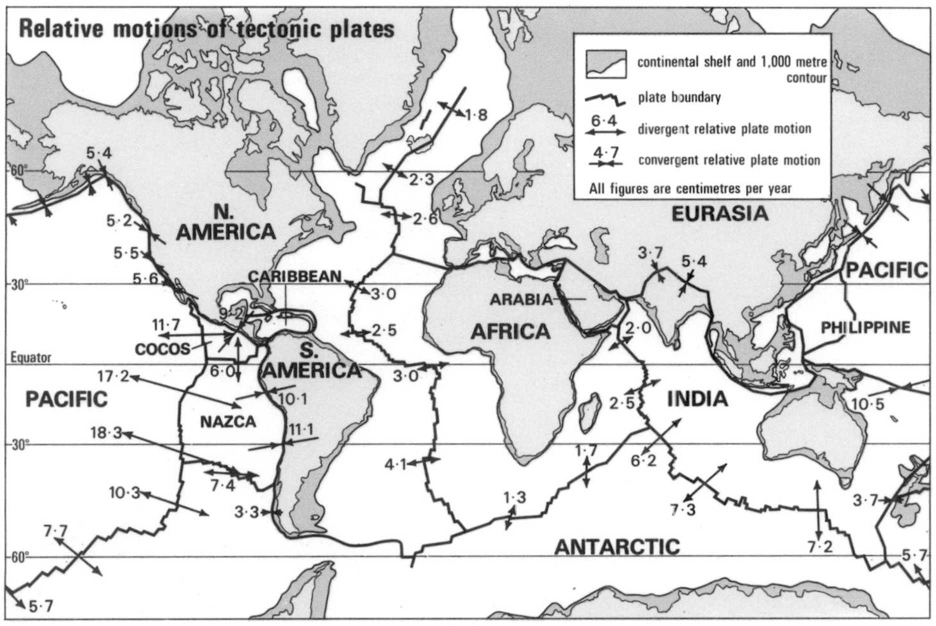

At mid-ocean ridges, plates are diverging at up to 18 centimetres per year. Where a continental plate meets an ocean plate the less dense continental material "floats" over the descending ocean plate and is pushed up to form a mountain range. Where two continental plates converge the continental material of both plates is forced upwards.

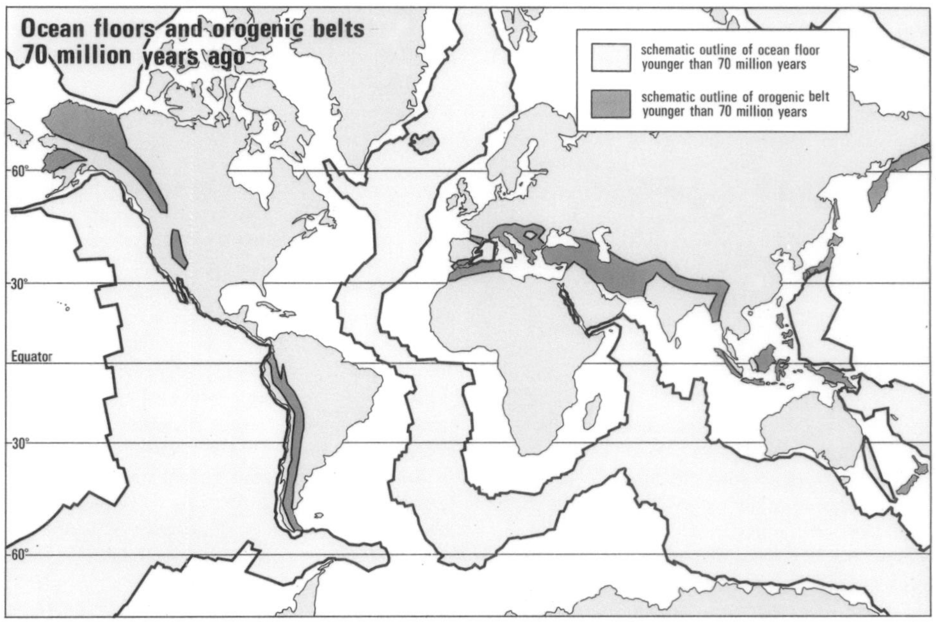

Ocean-floor spreading during the last 70 million years has been particularly apparent in the eastern Pacific and in the mid-Atlantic ridge which extends east of Africa across the south Indian Ocean. In the Americas the active orogenic belts are close up against the spreading plate boundaries. The mid-Atlantic ridge is passive in comparison.

Plate movement

Crustal plate movement occurs continuously in all parts of the globe but varies in type and rate of movement. This movement is generated by the complex interaction of a number of elements; the continental lithosphere plates themselves; the mid-ocean plate boundary ridges; micro-continental plates; island arcs; small enclosed ocean basins; and inland seas.

Present-day plates

Plate	*Area* (millions of sq.km)	*Continental area* (millions of sq.km)
Pacific	108	1·9
Eurasia	68	59·4
N. America	58·8	35·0
S. America	42·7	25·6
India	61	21·7
Africa	78·4	35·4
Antarctic	59·9	17·9
Nazca	16·4	
Cocos	3·1	
Philippine	5·7	
Caribbean	3·5	1·4
Arabia	4·9	4·2

A variety of movements are therefore possible. The fastest rate of movement is the divergence of the Pacific plate from the Cocos, Nazca and Antarctic plates with a figure of 18·3 cms per year at latitude 30° South (see map above). The Mid-Atlantic Ridge marks the boundary between the American, African and Eurasian plates. This divergence remains fairly constant at between 2 and 4 cms per year. The African, Indian and Antarctic plates are diverging from each other at a rate between 2 and 7 cms per year.

The above map shows that convergent plate motion involves an ocean plate and a continental plate or two continental plates, but rarely two ocean plates. The fastest rate of convergence is between the Cocos and the Caribbean plate in Central America where the Guatemala Trench marks the edge where the Cocos plate is sliding downwards at over 9 cms per year. The Himalayas mark a collision zone between the Eurasian and the Indian plates; the rate of crustal compression here is over 5 cms per year.

Mountain building

Orogeny is the geological process of mountain-building. The two most important agents of orogeny are deformation of Earth's crust (diastrophism), which includes faulting and folding; and vulcanism. Orogeny usually occurs along narrow belts of the Earth's surface and can involve the uplift and deformation of great thicknesses of sedimentary and volcanic rocks. This process is called the orogenic cycle and is associated with the movement of an oceanic plate against a continental land-mass (see Compressional plate boundary above). At this margin many layers of sedimentary and volcanic rock deposited over millions of years become uplifted and deformed. Until recently mountain-building was thought to be more associated with ascending and descending currents within crustal rocks.

The Earth's orogenic belts lie between the stable continental plates and an ocean or inland sea (see map of orogenic belts above). The Andes and Rocky Mountains lie between the American plates and the Pacific Ocean; the Himalayas lie between the stable Eurasian plate and the Indian sub-continent.

The uplifted and deformed rocks formed as a result of plate collision may be mixed with molten igneous rock rising from the mantle as a result of the melting subducted crust. Youngerfold mountains less than 500 million years old consist of these rocks thrust upward and over-folded as in the Alps, or simply uplifted as the central Andes. The rate of uplift may be as much as one centimetre a year. Over-fold mountain ranges are the remnants of earlier folding cycles which have been stranded away from active plate collision margins.

The map above was computed from the relative positions of dated sedimentary and metamorphic rocks plotted with reference to the trapped magnetism fields within them. Latest research reveals over one hundred and fifty magnetic field reversals during the last 70 million years. It is clear that the Earth's major orogenic belts have changed little during that time but the ocean floor areas have spread considerably.

Folding and faulting
When the Earth's crust bends under compression, folds develop. The simplest of these is the monocline, a one-sided fold, although downfolds (synclines) and upfolds (anticlines) are more usual. Increasing pressure steepens the side facing the pressure until one side is pushed under the other, forming a recumbent fold. Finally the fold may break along its axis, one limb being thrust over the other. Mountain chains often demonstrate intense folding, when sediments are crushed between converging plates.
Faults occur when the Earth's crust breaks, often causing earthquakes. When tension stretches the crust normal faulting occurs and the rocks on one side of the fault-plane override those on the other.
A horst is a block of the crust thrust up between faults; the reverse is called a graben or rift valley. Repeated horst and graben forms give basin and range topography as in Nevada, USA.
The upward movement of a roughly circular plug of salt, some thousands of feet in depth, may force up strata and the surface layers to form a salt dome. These are often associated with oil and gas.

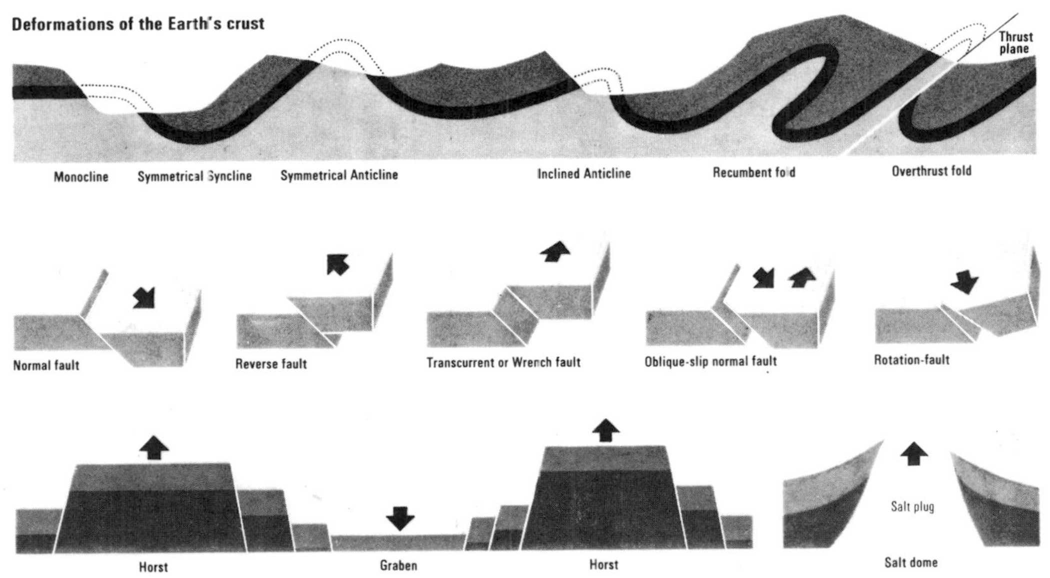

Deformations of the Earth's crust
Thrust plane
Monocline
Symmetrical Syncline
Symmetrical Anticline
Inclined Anticline
Recumbent fold
Overthrust fold
Normal fault
Reverse fault
Transcurrent or Wrench fault
Oblique-slip normal fault
Rotation-fault
Horst
Graben
Horst
Salt plug
Salt dome

Continental crust
A cross-section through the continental crust typically shows the following features: continental margins, younger and older-fold mountain chains, platforms and shields. The continental margin will either be passive as are most Atlantic margins, or active, as are the Pacific margins. Younger-fold mountains formed during the last 500 million years, such as the Rockies and Andes of America, and the Himalayas of Asia, mark the younger subduction zones and occur along most of the active continental margins. Older-fold mountains, like the Appalachians of eastern America and the Caledonian system of Britain and Scandinavia, are nearer to the older subduction zones across which two continents have been joined together. Platforms are areas on which flat-lying sediments have been laid down as in the central United States, Saharan Africa and the Arabian peninsula. Underneath the platforms are highly deformed pre-Cambrian rocks that emerge at the surface as shields. Most of north Canada, central Africa, South America east of the Andes, and Antarctica are shield areas.

The internal structure of the continental crust is known from monitoring seismic activity and from echo-sounding experiments. In most places the crust consists of an upper layer of less dense material over-lying a lower, more dense layer. The boundary between the two is termed the Conrad Discontinuity. The upper layer is 92 per cent igneous and metamorphic and 8 per cent sedimentary in composition. The lower layer is probably basaltic in character or a product of metamorphism called amphibolite, and is derived from partial melting of the mantle. The zone of transition between the continental crust and the underlying magma is called the Mohorovičić Discontinuity.

In comparison with the oceanic crust, the continental crust is less dense with a value of 2·7 as against 3·0; thicker reaching down to a depth of 70 km below mountain belts as opposed to 6 km; and older with some parts aged 3,500 million years and much over 1,500 million years compared with a maximum of 200 million years for the most ancient regions of the submerged oceanic crust.

Folding and faulting

In unstable regions of the Earth's crust stresses may cause folding, fracturing and distortion of sedimentary and volcanic rocks. This is termed crust deformation and is most apparent in the European Alps, South American Andes and the Himalayas. The causes of instability are multiple. Orogenesis or mountain-building deforms the crust, but larger more gentle movements may be caused by isostasy or natural adjustment of crustal levels. A basin accumulating sedimentary deposits may slowly sink under their weight, and weathering may lighten a mountain chain causing it to rise.

The processes and extent of folding and faulting depend on the type and magnitude of the stress; fast or slow, regular or irregular application of stress; the period of time of the stress; the constituency and type of rock or rocks; and relationship with adjacent rock strata. The interrelationships of these factors are so complex that the deformation may range from micro-scopic waves to vast folds tens of kilometres across, and from displacement of single crystals to giant faults.

Folding
Folds are of many types, classified according to the severity and shape of the fold. Basically a fold consists of two limbs or sides with a bisecting axis. If the limbs dip in opposite directions and are divided into two equal halves, the fold is symmetrical; if the axis does not bisect the fold it is asymmetric. An overturned fold has one limb lying partly under the other, and a fold is termed recumbent where one limb is wholly under the other. Folds are usually formed well below the surface and are only exposed by erosion. Anticlinal or synclinal stumps are typical of eroded folds – the ridges of the Appalachian Mountains in the eastern USA are the exposed limbs of folds.

Faulting
A fault is a fracture of the Earth's crust in which the rock on one side of the fracture moves in a different direction to the rock on the opposing side. The fracture and movement along the plane of the fault may be vertical, inclined or horizontal. A normal fault has the inclined plane of fracture exposed as one part of the crust slips downwards and away from another. A reverse fault occurs when compression causes a slab of the crust to slide under an adjacent block. Faults with horizontal rock movement are termed transcurrent or wrench faults, the best-known example of which is the San Andreas fault (see page 8). A combination of movements can produce a highly complex fault structure which creates problems of interpretation for the geologist. The block on one side of a normal fault may slip sideways as well as downwards, it may rotate about a fixed point, or both blocks may move in the same direction but one faster than the other.

Rift valleys or grabens, are caused by the subsidence of elongated blocks of crust sometimes on such a scale that they are marked by chains of volcanoes. The East African Rift Valley System stretches from the coast of Africa opposite Madagascar northwards to the Red Sea and the Mediterranean. Crustal movements upwards produce horst scenery of uplifted blocks; typical examples are the Tien Shan mountains of central Asia, now heavily eroded, and the ranges of Nevada, USA.

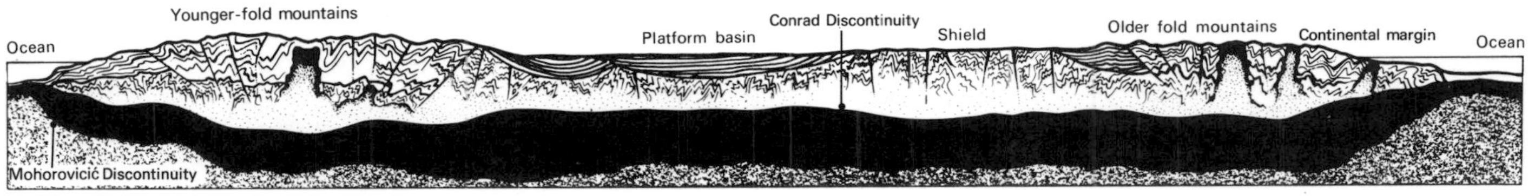

Younger-fold mountains
Ocean
Conrad Discontinuity
Platform basin
Shield
Older fold mountains
Continental margin
Ocean
Mohorovičić Discontinuity

Continental crust
The chemical composition of the crust down to 16 kilometres is: oxygen 46 per cent, silicon 28 per cent, aluminium 8 per cent, iron 5 per cent, calcium 4 per cent, sodium 3 per cent, potassium 2 per cent and magnesium 2 per cent.

Continental drift

Continental drift is a term used to describe the relative motions of the continents.

The relative positions of the continents as far back as 200 million years may be found from the magnetic anomaly maps of the Atlantic and Indian Oceans. The position of the geographic pole of past time may be found from studies of ancient magnetism on continents. From a knowledge of the relative positions and the geographic pole a map of the former positions of continents may be drawn.

Four such maps, drawn by computer, are shown opposite; the Earth 50, 100, 150 and 200 million years ago. By comparing the maps against each other one can see how the Atlantic and Indian Oceans shrank in size as the continents came closer together. As they shrank, a space opened between Eurasia on the one hand and Africa, Arabia, Iran and India on the other. This space is assumed to represent an old ocean, known as the Tethys, that has been completely subducted in the region east of the Mediterranean. The Alpine-Himalayan mountain chain is assumed to represent the final phases of a plate tectonic cycle involving the collision of continents that once bordered the Tethyan Ocean.

About 80 million years ago, Eurasia, Greenland and North America formed a single continent known as Laurasia. One hundred and forty million years ago the southern continents were joined together to form a single continent known as Gondwanaland. About 180 million years ago all the major continents formed a single super-continent known as Pangaea, first postulated by Wegener over half-a-century ago. Pangaea was itself formed some 250–300 million years ago by the collision of Gondwanaland with Laurasia west of the Urals and of Asia east of the Urals. It is not yet possible to draw maps of the continents prior to about 350 million years ago because the distance between the fragments that collided to form Pangaea prior to their collision cannot be estimated.

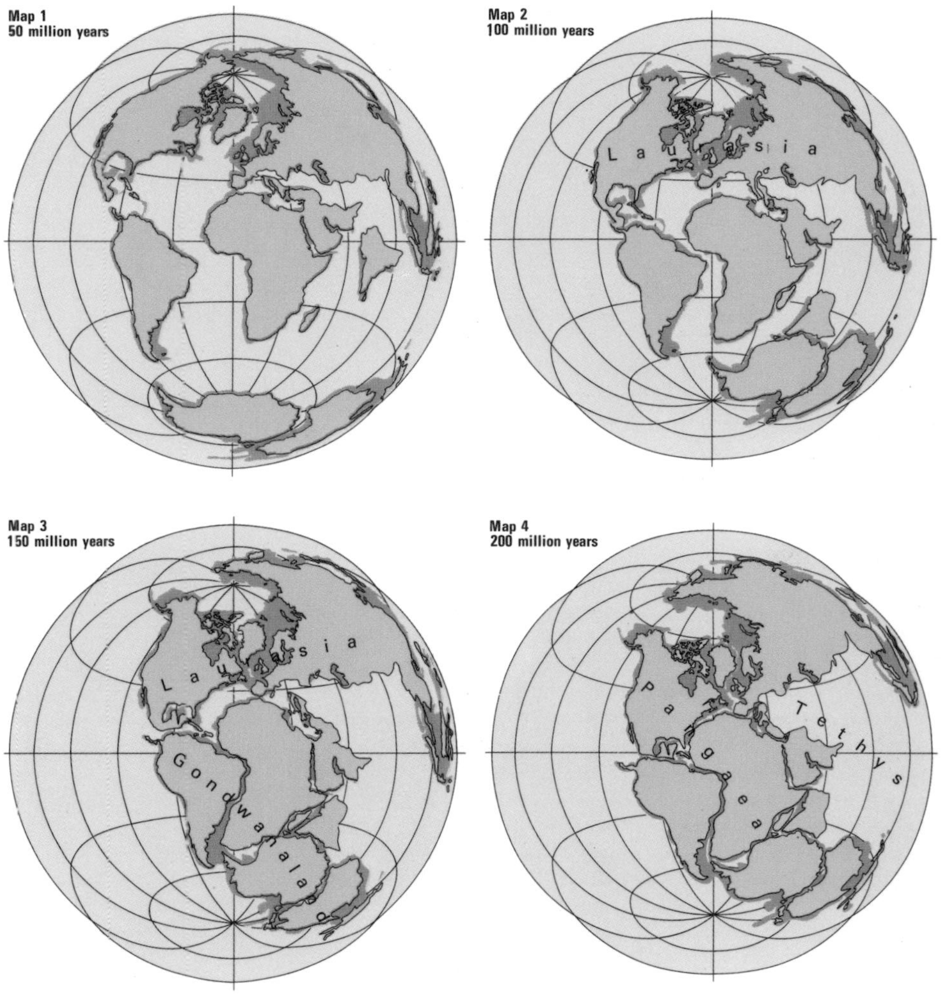

Map 1
50 million years
Map 2
100 million years
L a u r a s i a
Map 3
150 million years
L a u r a s i a
G o n d w a n a l a n d
Map 4
200 million years
P a n g a e a
T e t h y s

Continental drift
Early evidence of break-up and drift of the continents away from the single Pangaea landmass, has been confirmed by recent studies of ancient magnetism. The evidence consisted of matching continental shapes, for example the 'bulge' of Brazil fits closely to the coast of West Africa; and the joining of geological strata across the fit, for example the coal deposits of Uruguay and South Africa. The distribution of certain species of flora and fauna worldwide in the Palaeozoic and Mesozoic eras can only be satisfactorily explained by supporting the theory of continental drift. Animal fossils from Antarctica match those discovered in Argentina and South Africa, and climatic changes to the British Isles during the last 200 million years can be explained by continental movement.

Land and sea forms

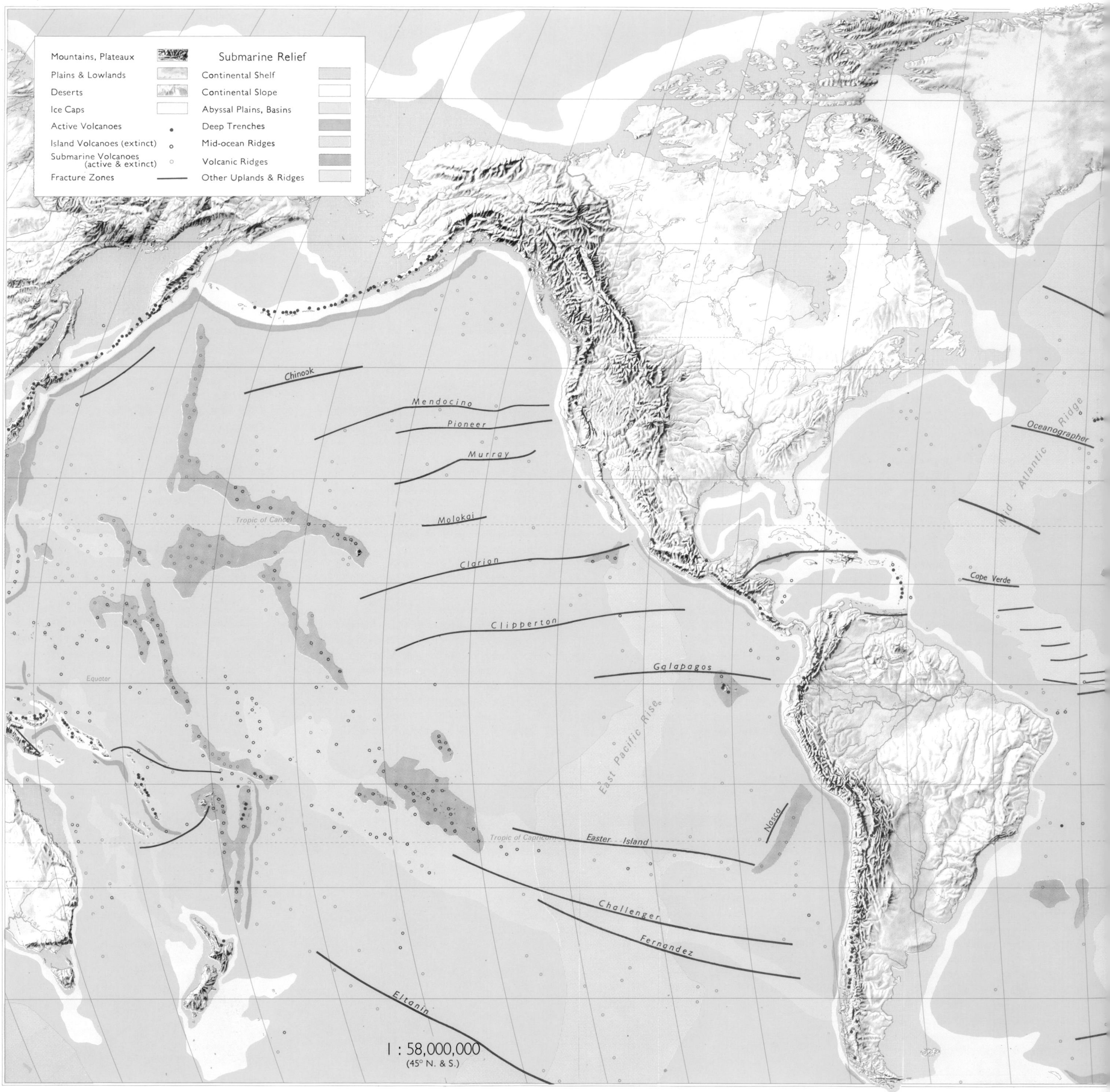

Mountains, Plateaux
Plains & Lowlands
Deserts
Ice Caps
Active Volcanoes
Island Volcanoes (extinct)
Submarine Volcanoes (active & extinct)
Fracture Zones
Submarine Relief
Continental Shelf
Continental Slope
Abyssal Plains, Basins
Deep Trenches
Mid-ocean Ridges
Volcanic Ridges
Other Uplands & Ridges
Chinook
Mendocino
Pioneer
Murray
Molokai
Clarion
Clipperton
Galapagos
Tropic of Cancer
Equator
East Pacific Rise
Nasca
Easter Island
Tropic of Capricorn
Challenger
Fernandez
Eltanin
Oceanographer
Mid-Atlantic Ridge
Cape Verde
1 : 58,000,000
(45° N. & S.)

The simplest division of the surface of the Earth is into continents and oceans. All the evidence confirms that the ocean basins were never part of the continental areas and the oldest continental blocks were never part of the true ocean floor.

The rocks of the old continental blocks are markedly different from the young folded mountains. The former are the original blocks, granitic and among the oldest rocks formed in Pre-Cambrian times. The margins of the continents have been repeatedly covered by the sea and the true limit of the continents is the edge of the continental shelf, the physiography of the continents therefore consists basically of the old stable mountain masses, young folded mountain ranges and the coastal plains and continental shelf.

The fundamental difference between the physiography of the oceans and that of the continents arises from distinct geological processes involved in their formation. The granite rocks of the continental masses are lighter than the silica and magnesia (sima) rocks on which they rest, and thus 'float' on them. The floor of the ocean is therefore composed of material denser than that of the surface rocks of the continents.

Different chemical processes operate in the continental and ocean rocks because of their different composition and also because of the atmospheric as opposed to the aqueous environment. The continents are subjected to the severe erosional forces of the weather and to more rapid chemical processes resulting from direct contact with the atmosphere. A wide temperature fluctuation ranging from intense heat to extreme cold has transformed the land forms; but of all the meteorological factors rain is the most destructive.

The Earth's surface features are produced by the interaction of internal and external forces. The former include mountain building, faulting, uplift, vulcanicity, and resistance, of the rocks. The external forces include the physical and chemical reactions that weather the surface rocks, and the main agents of erosion: running water, ice, sea and wind. Each of these gives rise to distinctive land forms, so that we can, for example, identify glaciated landscapes or desert landscapes, but always reflects the interaction of structure and the erosional process.

Running water is the most important sculptor of land forms, and the results of its work can be seen even in desert areas. Valleys are the work of the rivers that flow, or have flowed, through them. Most river systems flow into the sea but some empty into interior lakes, such as the Dead Sea, where water is lost by evaporation.

Glacier ice produced very distinctive land forms, such as trough-shaped valleys, pyramidal peaks and moraines; in the Pleistocene period glaciers were much more widespread than now.

The wind is most effective in areas of sparse or absent vegetation. Only about 25 per cent of the area of the world's deserts are dune-covered. The rest is rocky or gravelly.

The oceans are not subject to the violent effects of heat and frost, wind and rain, only to the quiet forces of sedimentation and gravity. Near the continents the sediments are at their thickest; over the rest of the ocean floor they are seldom more than a few hundred metres thick.

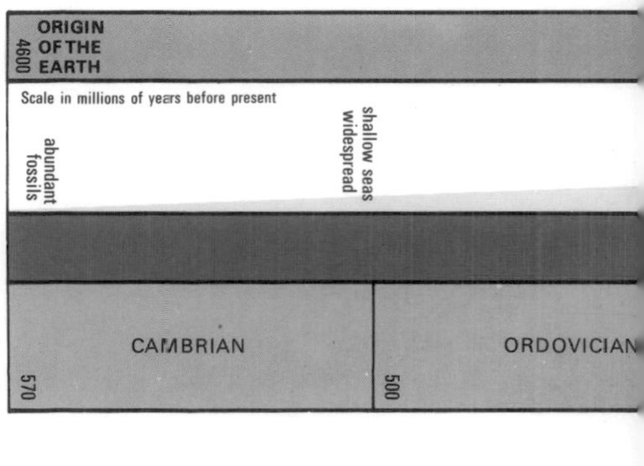

4600
ORIGIN OF THE EARTH
Scale in millions of years before present
abundant fossils
shallow seas widespread
CAMBRIAN
ORDOVICIAN
570
500

Like the continents, the oceans can be divided into main physiographic categories: continental shelf and slope, continental rises, abyssal plains, ocean ridges and rises and trenches. If we exclude the continental shelf and part of the continental slopes the area of the oceans at 2,000 metres below sea level is about 320 million sq km.

The abyssal plains extend over almost half this area and are below 2,500 metres. At this depth, temperature is never higher than 4°C (39°F).

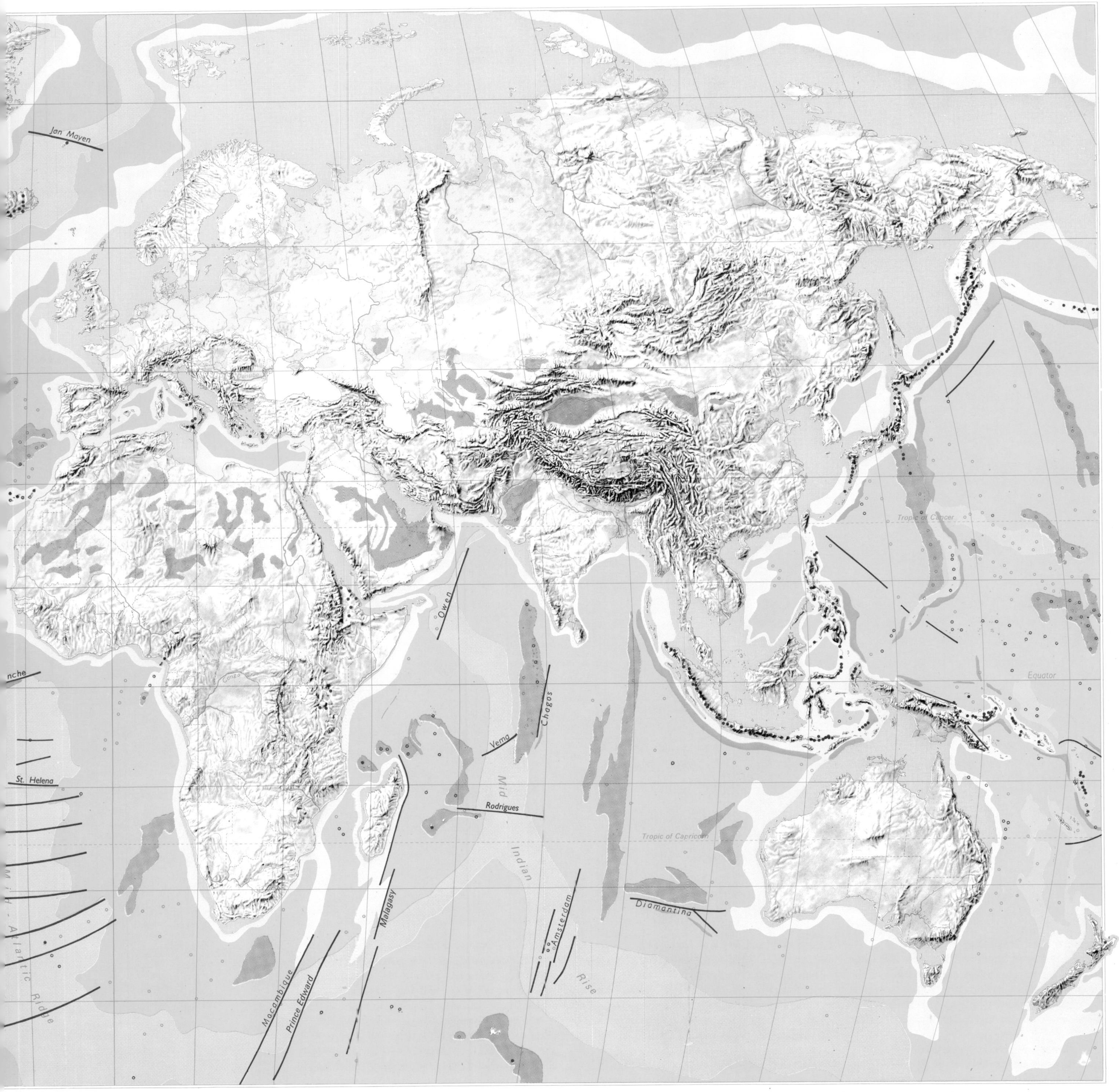

Jan Mayen
nche
St. Helena
Owen
Chagos
Verma
Mid
Rodrigues
Indian
Malagasy
Amsterdam
Rise
Diamantina
Moçambique
Prince Edward
Tropic of Cancer
Equator
Tropic of Capricorn
Congo

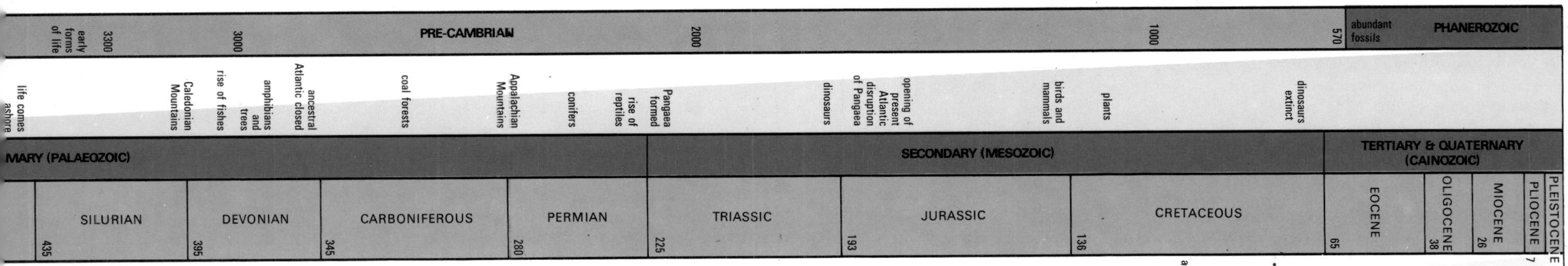

early forms of life
3300
3000
PRE-CAMBRIAN
2000
1000
570
abundant fossils
PHANEROZOIC
life comes ashore
Caledonian Mountains
rise of fishes
amphibians and trees
ancestral Atlantic closed
coal forests
Appalachian Mountains
conifers
Pangaea formed
rise of reptiles
dinosaurs
opening of present Atlantic
disruption of Pangaea
birds and mammals
plants
dinosaurs extinct
MARY (PALAEOZOIC)
SECONDARY (MESOZOIC)
TERTIARY & QUATERNARY (CAINOZOIC)
SILURIAN
435
DEVONIAN
395
CARBONIFEROUS
345
PERMIAN
280
TRIASSIC
225
JURASSIC
193
CRETACEOUS
136
EOCENE
65
OLIGOCENE
38
MIOCENE
26
PLIOCENE
7
PLEISTOCENE

Geological periods and the emergence of Man

Modern man has inhabited the Earth for less than one millionth of the total period of its existence, now known to approach some 5,000 million years. Much of this enormous span of time (see top column) was the almost barren and relatively unknown Pre-Cambrian period. For only one eighth of its history has the Earth borne abundant life: the second column shows this Phanerozoic divided into stratigraphic periods, based originally on fossil evidence. The third column details the last two and a half million years, marked by at least seven ice ages and the period when many of the Earth's land forms were shaped. *Homo sapiens* appears only recently, and though he became a cultivator and developed urban living quite early in this final period covering the last 10,000 years, only in the last 250 years has he harnessed the world's power and mineral resources.

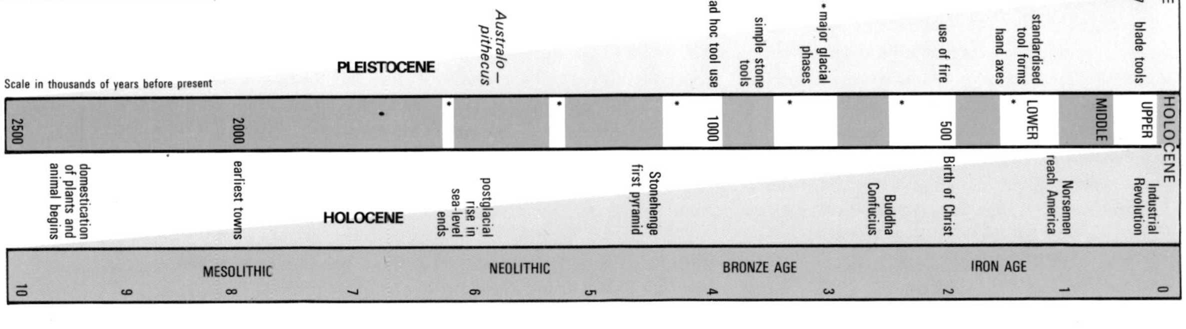

PLEISTOCENE
Australopithecus
ad hoc tool use
simple stone tools
major glacial phases
use of fire
standardised tool forms hand axes
blade tools
Scale in thousands of years before present
2500
2000
1000
500
LOWER
MIDDLE
UPPER
HOLOCENE
domestication of plants and animal begins
earliest towns
HOLOCENE
postglacial rise in sea-level ends
Stonehenge first pyramid
Buddha Confucius
Birth of Christ
Norsemen reach America
Industrial Revolution
MESOLITHIC
NEOLITHIC
BRONZE AGE
IRON AGE
10
9
8
7
6
5
4
3
2
1
0

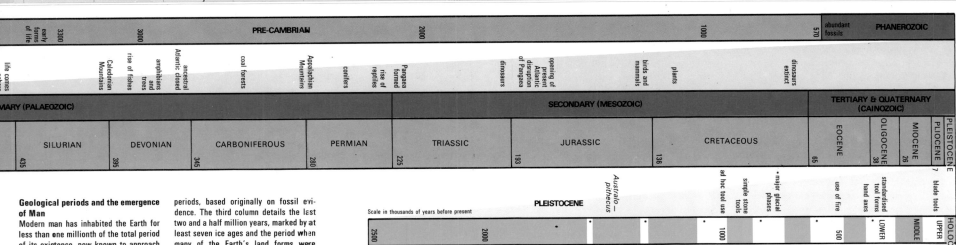

Atmosphere and climate

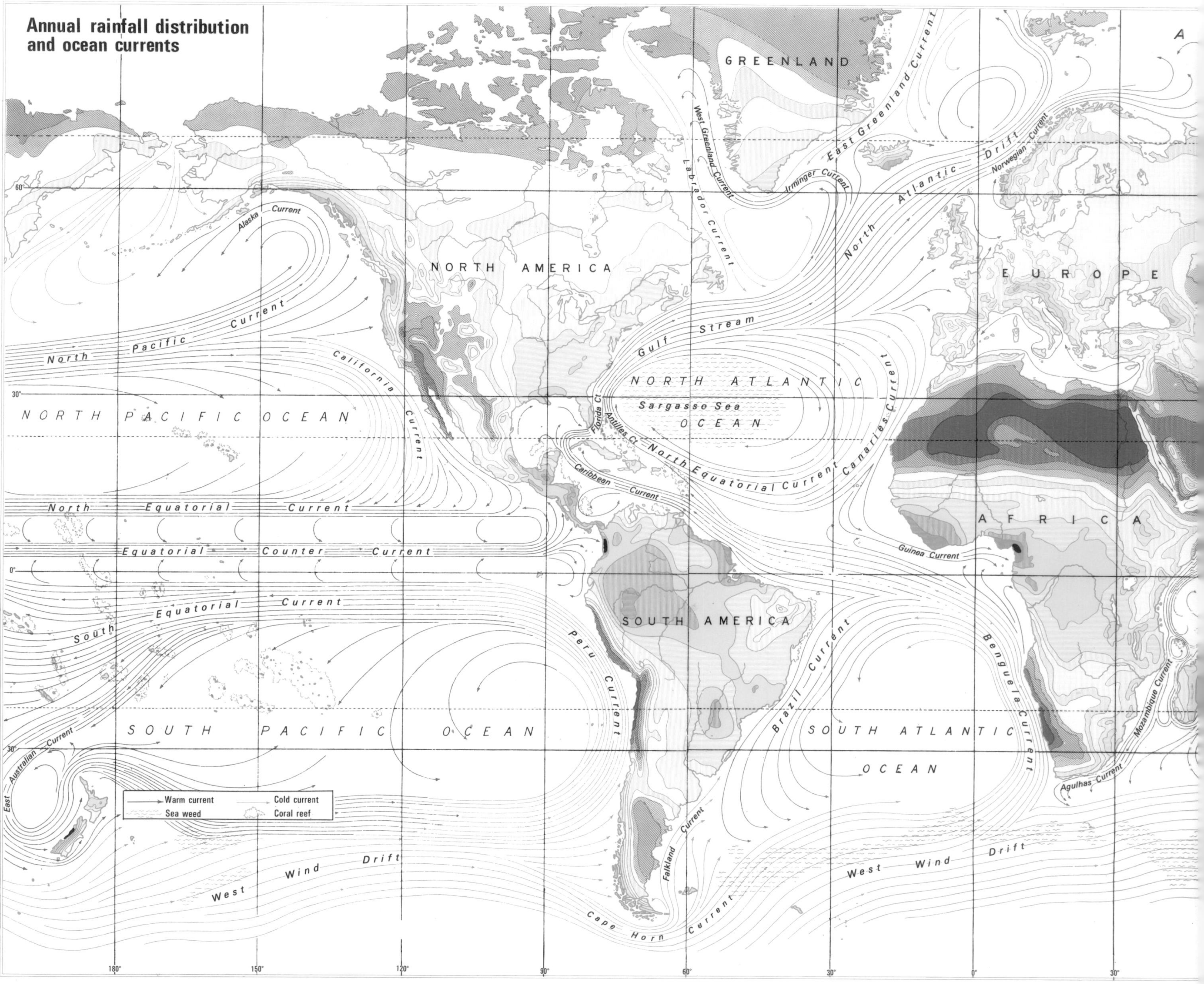

Evolution of the atmosphere

The Earth has an atmosphere because it is large enough for its gravitational pull to retain the gases surrounding it. Our present atmosphere is not the first. Most of the gases and probably all of the water in the oceans are the result of volcanic activity.

As the atmosphere lacks certain of the heavy gases it has been suggested that the Earth's original atmosphere was boiled away by a tremendous increase in the Sun's heat. At the same time the water and water vapour then present would also have evaporated. Studies of Mars from the Mariner and Viking spacecraft suggest that the same process happened there too, confirming the validity of this theory.

The Earth's atmosphere once largely consisted of hydrogen, combined with methane and ammonia. The hydrogen was gradually lost and free oxygen was slowly added.

In Cambrian times, between 570 and 500 million years ago, a much greater proportion of carbon dioxide was present in the atmosphere. Since life first appeared, the plants and rocks both on land and in the seas have competed for the carbon dioxide and the free oxygen. There is now a greater quantity of oxygen and carbon dioxide locked up in the rocks of the Earth than is to be found in the whole atmosphere. The balance of the atmosphere today is maintained by the constant erosion of limestone rocks and the decay of vegetable matter.

The composition by volume of the atmosphere is: nitrogen 78·09%, oxygen 20·95%, argon 0·93%, carbon dioxide, 0·03%, and smaller quantities of helium, krypton and hydrogen, 0·2% water vapour, traces of other gases and atmospheric dust.

Exactly what composition is necessary to support life and how far terrestial species can adapt by evolution to great changes in the composition of the atmosphere is not known. The basic essentials are oxygen, nitrogen, carbon dioxide and water.

The protective atmosphere

Apart from the atmosphere's role as the source of the gases necessary to life, it acts as a great shield against a perpetual bombardment of meteors and deadly rays and particles. Friction with the atmosphere causes all except the largest meteorites to burn themselves out before reaching the surface. Ultra-violet rays are absorbed in a layer of ozone present in the Stratosphere. Charged particles are prevented from reaching the Earth. Their contact with the atmosphere produces the aurora borealis and the aurora australis. Cosmic rays originating either from the Sun or from the outer reaches of space are likewise kept out.

Divisions of the atmosphere

For the first 80 kilometres above the Earth's surface the composition of the atmosphere is constant. Density decreases with height: at 16 kilometres it is only one-tenth of the density at sea level; at 32 kilometres it is one-tenth as dense as at 16 kilometres, and so on.

The terms Troposphere, Stratosphere, Mesosphere, Thermosphere and Exosphere have been used to describe the divisions of the atmosphere.

The Troposphere is the lowest division. Within it takes place nearly all the processes that produce weather and climate; evaporation, precipitation, movement of winds and air currents and the formation of the many types of storm etc.

Above 80 kilometres, oxygen and nitrogen molecules cannot remain associated and tend first to separate into atoms and then to be ionised into charged particles (ions) by the strong solar radiation. At the outermost limits of the atmosphere ionised helium and hydrogen dominate the very tenuous plasma (ionised gas), which, because of its electric charge, is controlled more by the Earth's magnetic field than by gravity.

The Ionosphere is the region of electrification which extends from the upper limit of the Stratosphere as far as the Thermosphere. It consists of a number of belts of radiation designated D, E, F_1 and F_2 which reflect radio waves back to Earth.

The outermost regions are now more commonly termed the Magnetosphere, the region dominated by magnetic fields. Beyond the Magnetosphere interplanetary space is dominated by the Sun's magnetic field and charged particles from the Sun – the solar wind.

Ultra-violet radiation produces concentrations of charged particles which are at their maximum in the upper part of the F_1 layer and the lower part of the F_2 layer.

The electrification belts are not fixed at particular altitudes: light and darkness and other physical factors cause them to move up or down. At night the F layers combine to form a single layer.

Atmosphere and the weather

Climate of the Troposphere close to the Earth's surface may be affected by changing influences high in the atmosphere. The amount of energy that penetrates the Stratosphere appears to follow the Sun's 11 year cycle of activity by altering the percentage of ozone in the Stratosphere. It is probable that energy in the form of ultra-violet waves from the Sun produces a swing in the ozone balance changing the effectiveness of heat absorption by the atmosphere.

At 3,000 and 15,000 kilometres, the two Van Allen radiation belts consist of electrically charged particles which occasionally migrate into the atmosphere. These particles react with atmospheric gases to produce the auroras. There is a strong likelihood that weather patterns are thus affected in the polar latitudes.

Changes in climate have been observed to coincide with changes in the Earth's magnetic field. The nature of the relationship is not known, but the extinction of species of fauna and changes in flora appear to have coincided with abrupt magnetic changes. These are identified by analysis of the direction of the magnetic field trapped within rocks on their formation.

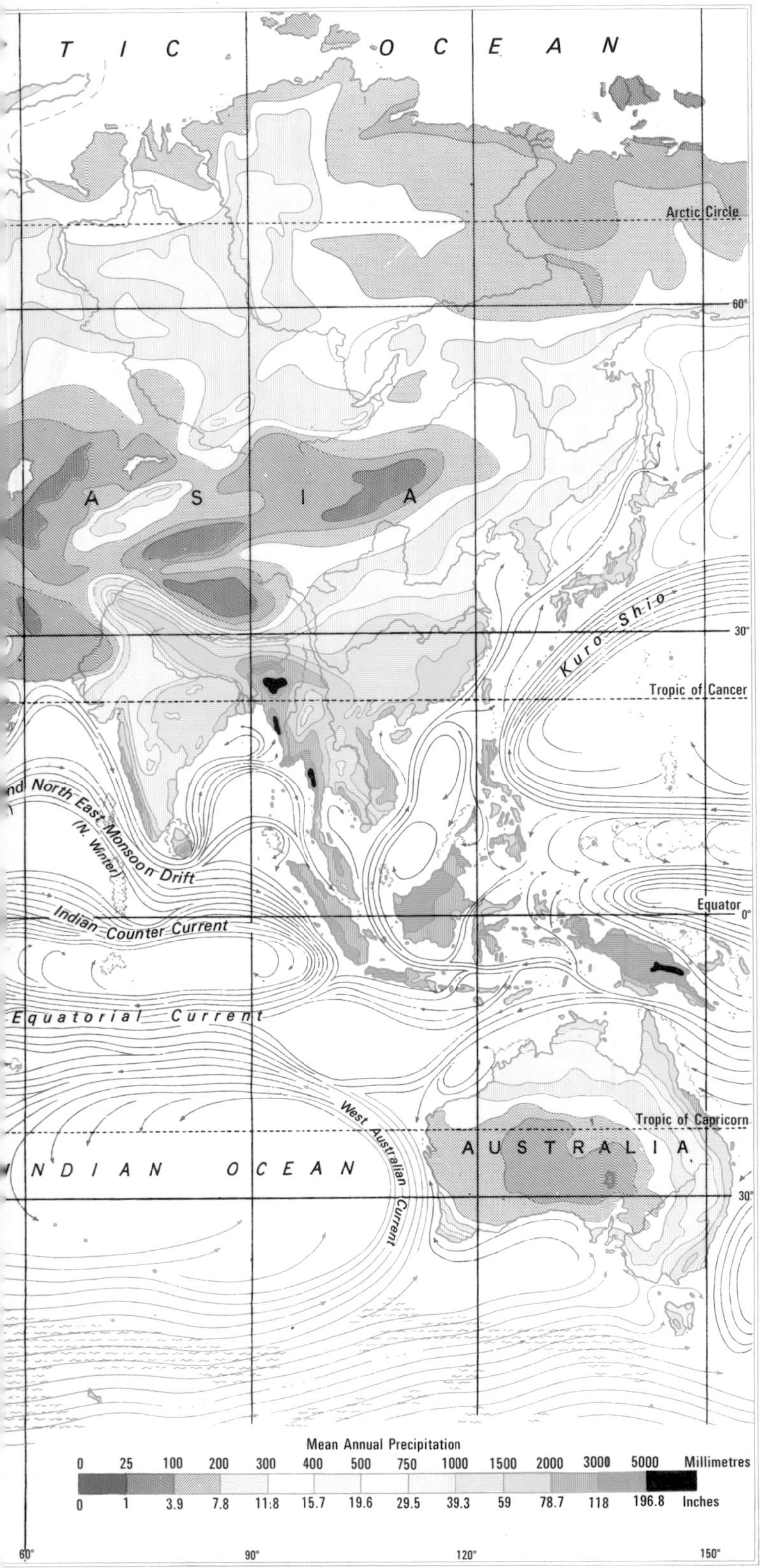

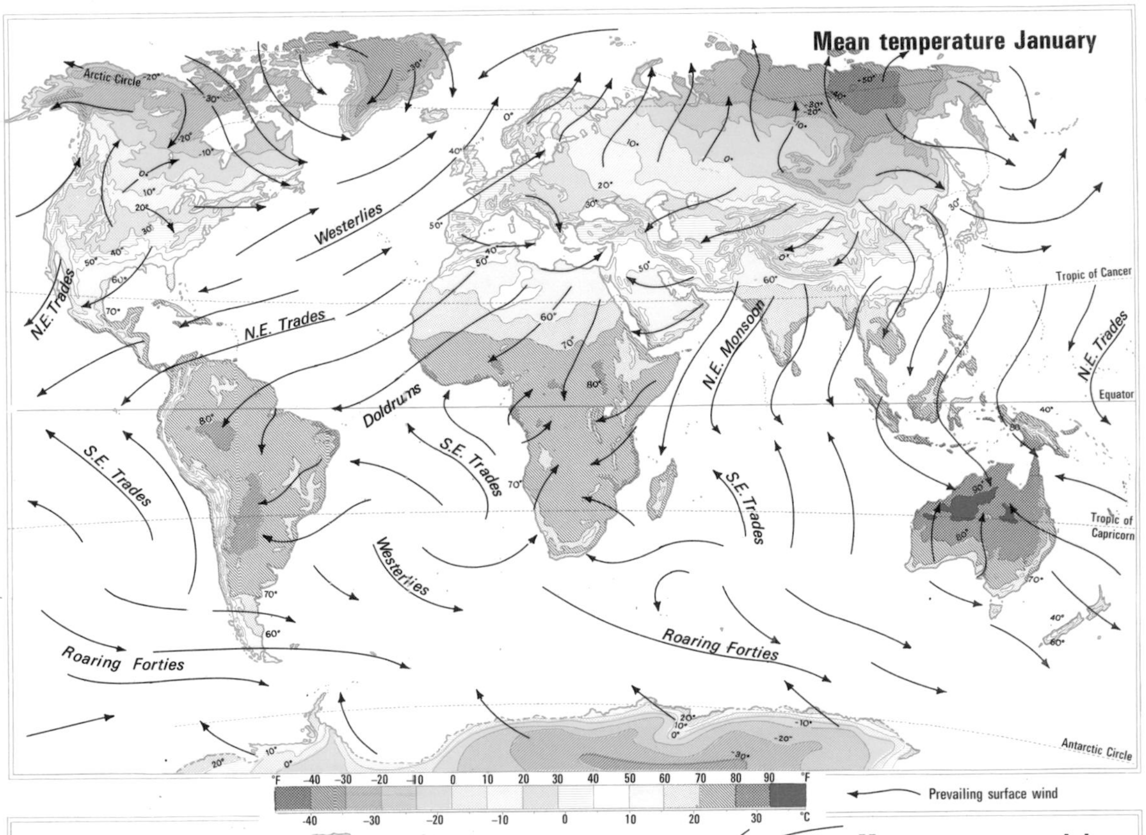

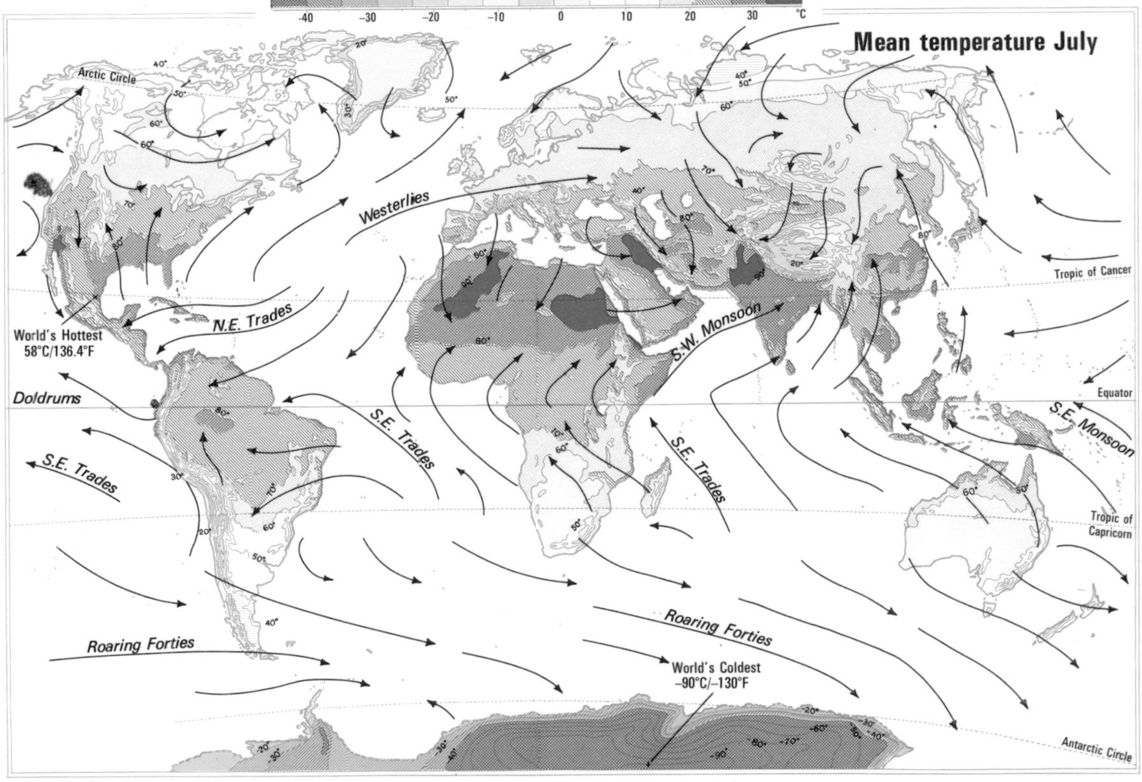

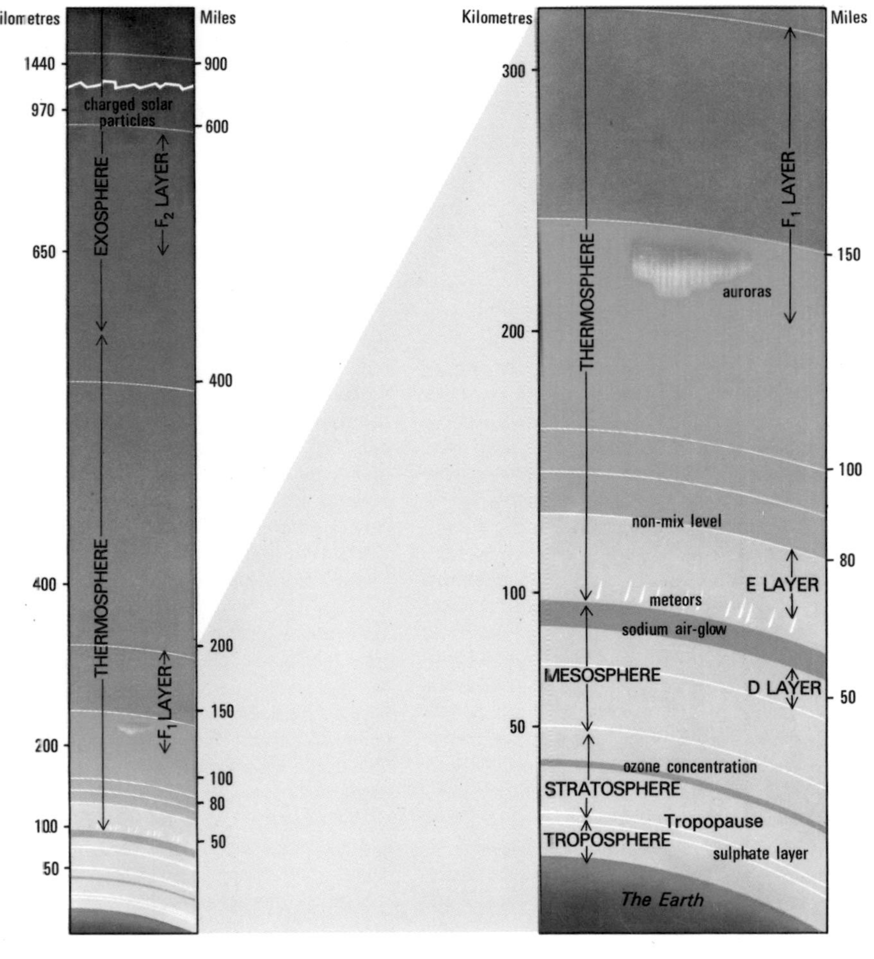

Monitoring the World's weather

International meteorology has made great advances in the last twenty-five years profiting from technological enterprise, notably artificial satellites, high-speed computers and methods of statistical analysis.

In 1961 the United Nations recommended that the World Meteorological Organisation (WMO), undertake a study of two measures. To advance the state of atmospheric science and technology so as to provide greater knowledge of basic physical forces affecting climate and the possibility of large-scale weather modification; and to develop existing weather-forecasting capabilities and to help Member States make effective use of such capabilities through regional meteorological centres. The WMO quickly produced a report on the advance of the atmospheric sciences and application in view of space developments. After four years of discussion and study this report was accepted in the form of the World Weather Watch plan.

The idea of monitoring a global weather system requires world-wide data collection on the condition of the atmosphere and associated geophysical phenomena, its processing to establish likely future weather activity, and a telecommunications network for collection and distribution of processed information. The WMO therefore set up the Global Observing System (GOS), the Global Data-processing System (GDPS), and the Global Telecommunications System (GTS) to carry out these functions.

Details of the activities of these organisations are impressive. In 24 hours the GOS makes about 110,000 observations from 9,000 land stations, 3,000 aircraft and 7,000 merchant ships throughout the world. In remote areas automatic weather stations are being built, and special-purpose ships are being constructed to traverse data-sparse areas. The GDPS has developed its System to manage this huge amount of input information. Giant computers are installed at Melbourne, Moscow and Washington DC, and a model of global weather for the following 24 hours is produced twice a day. These analyses and forecasts are distributed visually and digitally to the 23 Regional Meteorological Centres and 100 National Met. Centres. The GTS uses telegraph, telephone, radio, cable and landlines to distribute the material at speeds of up to 7,200 words per second.

The WMO has also instigated a Global Atmospheric Research Programme (GARP), to extend the scope and accuracy of weather forecasts, and to better understand the physical basis of climate and climatic fluctuations. To do this GARP has set up a series of regional experiments, such as the Atlantic Tropical, Air-Mass Transformation, Monsoon and Polar Experiments. In late 1978 the largest experimental programme will start. Named the First GARP Global Experiment (FGGE), it will monitor the atmospheric condition of the entire globe for one year, and apply world-wide tests of existing climatic models.

Polar-orbiting and geostationary satellites will be used to collect the extensive data for this global experiment.

Water resources and vegetation

Water is essential not only to practically all forms of life but is required in enormous quantities to support our modern industrial society. The average daily consumption for each individual in the UK is about 1 cubic metre, and in the USA the figure approaches ten times this quantity. Domestic use accounts for 20 per cent of this total in the UK and 10 per cent in the US. The need to husband water supplies is obvious in arid climates, but it is only in recent years that the need to conserve water resources in areas of more abundant rainfall, has been appreciated.

Hydrological cycle

Fresh water forms only 2 per cent of the water available on the Earth's surface. Even so, this amount would be more than adequate were not the greatest reserves locked, inaccessibly, in the polar ice caps. The problem therefore, is to provide water where and when it is needed and to ensure that it is not used faster than it can be replaced. The oceans are nature's reservoirs. From them water is evaporated to fall as rain or snow over the land. From the land it returns, mostly through rivers, to the sea. This process is known as the 'hydrological' cycle (see diagram). The maximum water potentially available is therefore dependent on the amount precipitated on the land. Water conservation aims to preserve for subsequent use as much of this water as possible.

Water conservation

When rain falls over land a proportion is quickly evaporated back into the atmosphere. Apart from limited and local measures, not a great deal can be done to conserve this water, nor that which is taken up by plants and returned to the atmosphere by transpiration. Some water 'runs off' and finds its way into rivers. Here control can be exercised, by adopting agricultural methods that will prevent too rapid run-off of surface water, retaining it in the soil for the benefit of crops, or alternatively by constructing drainage channels, dams and reservoirs in which water can be stored for later use. The remainder of the rainfall will sink deep into the earth, where a proportion will be held in rock strata. Rocks with a capacity to hold water are known as 'aquifers'; water is recovered by sinking wells to them.

Elementary though these measures are, they provide the foundation of proper control of water resources. Modern treatments increase the water supply still further by providing for water to be re-used. Water taken for industry can be cleansed and returned to the river from which it came. Further downstream it may be taken into the public water supply, and so into a sewage system from which it is discharged clean for further use.

Simple water conservation techniques can assure adequate supplies for large cities situated on rivers or lakes. Thus London, Washington and Chicago rarely suffer from water shortage. For other cities, not so fortunately situated, methods must be found to bring water from elsewhere. Birmingham in the UK, for example, is supplied with water from central Wales. New York City cannot use the brackish water of the Hudson estuary, but relies on supplies from catchment areas in New York State, some of which are over 160 km (100 miles) away. This water is brought to the metropolis from 27 reservoirs through 640 km (400 miles) of aqueducts and tunnels.

Techniques similar to those used to reclaim land allow arms of the sea to be isolated for conversion into freshwater lakes.

Further possibilities of increasing the water supply bring some hope for the arid regions of the world. For many decades rain has been induced by 'seeding' clouds with silver iodide crystals. This technique has achieved success, but it is extremely costly and uncertain. It cannot succeed unless there are clouds (i.e. water vapour) in the air. More promising are schemes to obtain fresh water from the sea by desalination and this is most commonly done by distillation and freezing. Distillation plants are currently in commercial use, particularly in the Middle East, but the cost is high and the quantity of water produced is small. The use of solar energy to support distillation processes is attractive in that fuel costs are abolished. However, while solar stills have proved successful on a small scale, larger versions have not worked efficiently. Experimental desalination plants based on freezing processes are in operation in the United States, and in Britain a pilot plant of this type is to be constructed in East Anglia.

Oil-rich but arid states have also considered seriously the possibility of towing icebergs from Antarctica to serve as a water supply. Recent estimates show this operation to be comparable in cost with desalination processes.

The Hydrological Cycle

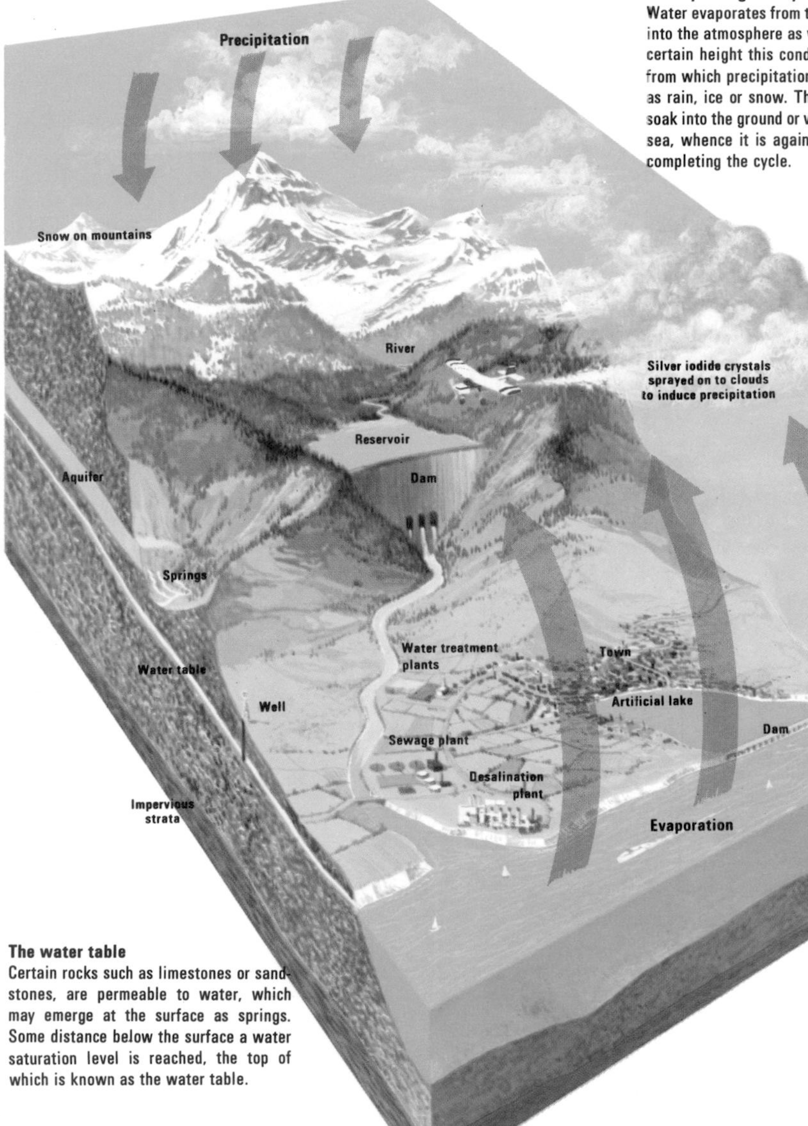

The Hydrological Cycle
Water evaporates from the sea and passes into the atmosphere as water vapour. At a certain height this condenses into clouds from which precipitation falls to the earth as rain, ice or snow. This will evaporate, soak into the ground or via rivers reach the sea, whence it is again evaporated, thus completing the cycle.

The water table
Certain rocks such as limestones or sandstones, are permeable to water, which may emerge at the surface as springs. Some distance below the surface a water saturation level is reached, the top of which is known as the water table.

Natural vegetation

A remarkable feature of the earth's land surface is the extent to which it is covered with plant life. Though there are inhospitable areas – such as the peaks of great mountain ranges and polar ice caps – where plant life all but disappears, for the most part vegetation exists in great abundance. Natural vegetation means the type of plant cover that would occur naturally without man's interference. In western Europe, man's activities have over the centuries so altered the natural plant cover that practically nowhere does it exist in its original form. Yet there is no difficulty in defining the broad categories of plants that flourish in the conditions that prevail locally.

The map on this page displays the major categories of natural vegetation, each characterized by important features which transcend differences between individual species. These vegetation zones are in essence a response to climatic conditions, for although local conditions of soil, relief and micro-climate are all important in determining local particulars of plant cover, the temperature and rainfall conditions of climatic regions exercise substantial control over the nature of plant cover. Thus, since latitude largely determines climate, the vegetation regions north and south of the Equator tend to be a mirror image one of the other. The close relationship between climate and vegetation has provided geographers with a convenient division of the world into major regions, since the particular features of plant life of each region are distinctive.

Vegetation regions

Near the Equator climate varies little throughout the year with rainfall and temperature consistently high. The absence of seasons means that plants do not undergo a resting period, while the abundance of warmth and moisture ensures a particularly luxuriant growth. Thus the characteristic vegetation of areas such as the Amazon and Zaire basins and the islands of Indonesia is dense, almost impenetrable forest, with trees competing for light attaining great heights.

Further away from the Equator lie the tropical

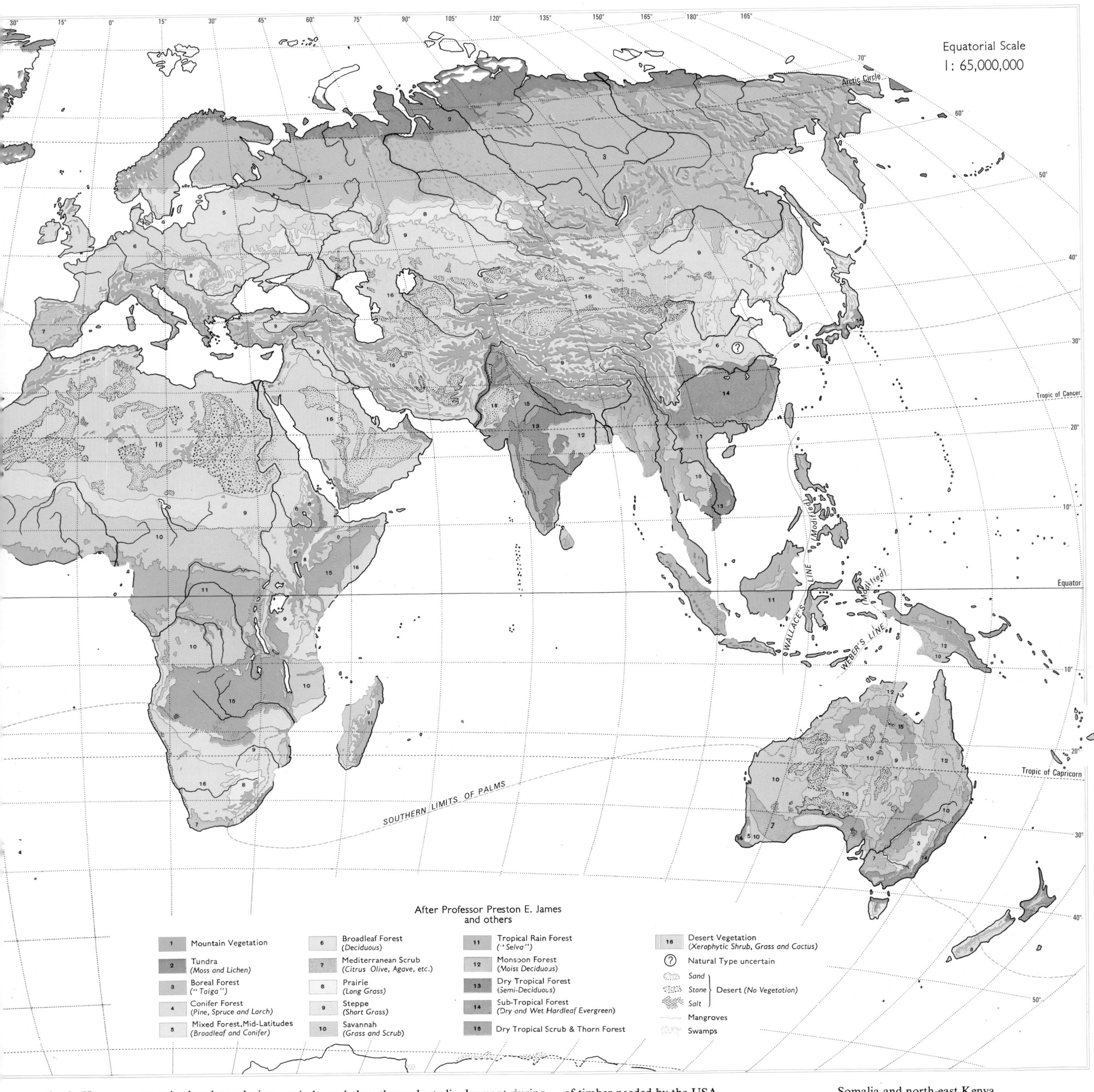
Equatorial Scale
1: 65,000,000
Arctic Circle
Tropic of Cancer
Equator
Tropic of Capricorn
WALLACE'S LINE (Modified)
WEBER'S LINE (Modified)
SOUTHERN LIMITS OF PALMS
After Professor Preston E. James and others
1 Mountain Vegetation
2 Tundra (Moss and Lichen)
3 Boreal Forest ("Taiga")
4 Conifer Forest (Pine, Spruce and Larch)
5 Mixed Forest, Mid-Latitudes (Broadleaf and Conifer)
6 Broadleaf Forest (Deciduous)
7 Mediterranean Scrub (Citrus Olive, Agave, etc.)
8 Prairie (Long Grass)
9 Steppe (Short Grass)
10 Savannah (Grass and Scrub)
11 Tropical Rain Forest ("Selva")
12 Monsoon Forest (Moist Deciduous)
13 Dry Tropical Forest (Semi-Deciduous)
14 Sub-Tropical Forest (Dry and Wet Hardleaf Evergreen)
15 Dry Tropical Scrub & Thorn Forest
16 Desert Vegetation (Xerophytic Shrub, Grass and Cactus)
? Natural Type uncertain
Sand
Stone
Salt
Desert (No Vegetation)
Mangroves
Swamps

grasslands. Here grass grows in abundance during the rainy season only to be withered by the sun in the ensuing drought. The sparse plant life of the world's deserts shows particular adaptations to drought conditions. Some species develop seeds which lie dormant for long periods and then, when rainfall comes, grow and complete their life cycle in the brief period in which moisture is retained in the soil. Many, including the cactus species' so typical of the arid regions of the western United States, are able to store water efficiently with little loss through transpiration.

The characteristic vegetation of much of Europe, including the British Isles, and the eastern half of the United States, is broad-leaved deciduous forest. In response to the clear climatic differences between summer and winter, trees have adapted to take fullest advantage of the favourable growing season. The broad leaf structure which allows maximum exposure to light and air means that the tree is an efficient starch-producing organ. This same adaptation renders the plant extremely sensitive to low temperatures and high winds, and thus these plants lie dormant during winter months. So precise is their adaptation that their activity is not dependent on average climatic conditions but on the likely variations from this average. In Britain the oak and ash are not tempted to unfold their leaves early in a mild spring yet imported species like the horse chestnut will do so. Most cultivated plants are imported or are 'artificial' cross-breeds and lack precise adaptation to prevailing climatic conditions. They need protection by shelter or irrigation or removal of other competitive plants if they are to flourish.

North of the regions of the broad-leaved deciduous forest flourish the conifer forests. In the United States they are developed particularly well in the north-western states. The trees that form these forests are much better adapted to withstanding unfavourable conditions and include the world's most magnificent specimens, in particular the giant redwood trees, which grow to greater heights than any other tree except the eucalyptus. These forests are of substantial economic importance and provide over 30 per cent of timber needed by the USA.

Climatic variations

We are now in an interglacial period within which minor climatic variations have occurred. Some 3,000 to 4,000 years ago climate in the British Isles was drier, with greater temperature variations between summer and winter so that hazel and birch flourished more than they do now. There is considerable evidence that land bordering the Sahara desert is drier now than it was 2,000 or so years ago, for plants grew more abundantly then, and in north Africa wheat was grown for the Roman Empire in regions which are now semi-desert. Some of this decline is undoubtably due to unwise farming methods, which have resulted in the loss of topsoil, or to clearance of the natural plant cover to grow crops. A wealth of evidence now shows that both Sahara and Gobi deserts spread towards the Equator when the climate cools slightly – as it has since the 1950s. This, plus overgrazing, is the cause of recent droughts in the Sahel (the region bordering the Sahara to the south), in Ethiopia, and in Somalia and north-east Kenya.

Although we are concerned mainly with the broad characteristics of the plant life of the major vegetation zones, we should not ignore the strange variations that occur, as species adapt to local conditions. The vegetation of the Everglades in Florida displays a remarkable adaption to the swampy conditions that prevail there, while along tropical coasts mangroves grow and with their preponderance of stilt-like roots keep a firm hold on the shifting ground beneath. These roots, the upper parts of which are exposed at low tide, have pores through which the plant can take oxygen, since there is little oxygen in the muddy water below, where organic matter is decomposing.

Precise adaptation of particular species to local conditions has been turned to economic advantage. A few species flourish abnormally well where certain minerals are present, and by study of these 'indicator plants', deposits of copper and other ores have been traced in many parts of the world.

Minerals and their uses

Gold

Precious metal and principal international reserve asset underwriting the means of exchange. Used in manufacture, medicine and fabrication for its special corrosive resistant properties. It does not tarnish and is unaffected by most acids. It weighs about two and a half times as much as steel and is very malleable and ductile. Thus it can be hammered to an extremely thin sheet or drawn into the finest of metal wires. Gold is an excellent conductor of electricity. Applications vary from jewellery and coinage to dentistry and electronic circuitry. Over 70 per cent of free world production comes from South Africa. Other producers include North America, USSR, Australia and central Africa. Non-communist output totals over 1,027,000 kilograms annually. For every million parts of ore about 13 parts of gold are extracted.

Silver

Precious metal of wide industrial usage and re-usage. Mine production is around 9,230 tonnes of new silver, to serve both speculative and industrial markets, which include photography and the decorative arts as well as coinage. Main producers include North America, Mexico, Peru and Australia.

Platinum

Often a by-product of copper-nickel mining, a precious metal of catalytic properties in, e.g., making nitric acid. Provides long-lasting protective coatings which are used in chemical, electrical, petroleum, glass and electronic industries. Main producer is South Africa, with 70 per cent of output, in meeting world demand of 1·4m troy oz. USSR and Canada also substantial producers. Platinum metals include Iridium, Rhodium, Palladium, Osmium, Ruthenium. Future demand may be affected by anti-pollution use in reforming petroleum.

Diamond

Precious stone of pure carbon formed at depth under pressure and temperature and then extruded in Kimberlitic rock pipes and dykes – coveted for rarity and qualities such as hardness, cutting and abrasive properties. World output of diamonds for industrial purposes 32,400 metric carats. Gemstone production is just over 13,500 metric carats. Over twenty countries produce diamonds with the bulk of output coming from Zaire, South Africa and the USSR. World synthetic diamond output is over 45 million metric carats.

Copper

One of the oldest known and most exploited metals, the mineral in refined form is used widely through the whole spectrum of industry, half going to electrical and telecommunication sectors. Other big areas of consumption are in general engineering and building components. Its main properties are its capacity as a conductor of heat or electricity, its ductile nature which allows it to be drawn into fine wire, and its value in alloys with zinc and tin. Bronzes are largely copper-tin alloys. Brasses are alloys of copper, zinc and tin. Copper deposits occur in the oceans and promise to extend the life of copper when continental deposits are nearing exhaustion. Total refined output varies because of volatile market conditions, but is now nearly 8 million tonnes. Top producers are USA, USSR, Chile, Zambia, Canada, Zaire, Peru and Australia, with about 20 other significant sources.

Tin

Soft silver-white corrosion-resistant metal used primarily as a coating for steel sheets used in food canning; has strong resistance to atmospheric tarnishing. Widely used in alloys, notably the brasses and bronzes, brazing materials and solder. World consumption is 197 million tonnes, mainly by USA, Japan, UK, Germany and France. Main sources are Malaysia, Bolivia, Thailand and Indonesia. Also mined in Australia, Nigeria, Zaire and Brazil. Total mined output is 181 million tonnes. Prices are subject to international marketing agreements because of importance of material (8 industrial countries account for 80 per cent of consumption).

Lead and Zinc

Major metals smelted from mines to meet consumption of more than 5·5 million tonnes of zinc and over 3·4 million tonnes of lead. Large stocks are kept in Europe, North America and USSR. Zinc is used in die castings for cars, and for brass and galvanizing iron and steel. Also used as a pigment in paints, chemical manufacture and metallurgical processes. Non-ferrous lead goes into production of batteries, and as additive for gasoline; main producers of refined lead are in North America and Europe, while mine production is led by the Americas, Oceania, USSR and Africa. Zinc production is dominated by North America, Europe and socialist countries.

Steel Metals

These include nickel, manganese, chromium, cobalt, molybdenum, tungsten, vanadium, columbium and tantalum, all offering specific qualities and properties for making special steels. Nickel, for example, is essential for making high quality stainless steel, which takes 40 per cent of consumption. Chromium is also necessary for the production of stainless steel. Tungsten is added to steel to produce high grade steels which can be hardened in air instead of water. Manganese is added to iron to produce castings which are not brittle. Base material of steel is iron ore, production of which rises steadily and in 1974 reached 507 million tonnes. The world's biggest producer of iron ore is USSR with around 123 million tonnes. Other big suppliers are Australia, Brazil, China, France, India, Liberia, Sweden and North America (90m tonnes). Ore is sold in lump, sinter and pellet forms for transportation to blast furnaces.

Aluminium

Primary aluminium (which, with titanium and magnesium, is a principal light weight metal) depends on production of bauxite amounting to 78 million tonnes annually. Nearly a fifth of bauxite comes from Jamaica. Other major sources are Australia, USSR, Surinam, Guyana, France, Guinea and Hungary. The USA accounts for about half of the Free World consumption; most primary aluminium goes into fabrication of industrial products made from plate, strip and wire. Alloyed with manganese or titanium, it offers tensile properties combined with lightness. World primary aluminium output is over 13 million tonnes led by North America, USSR, Japan and Norway.

Nuclear Metals

The most important of these is uranium. They include thorium, beryllium, zirconium and hafnium, caesium and ribidium, and rare earths. Development of nuclear power and related industries has expanded the search for and production of the various metals. Uranium production is around 18,500 tonnes a year.

Mercury

Liquid metal with volatile properties, known as quicksilver, derived from cinnabar. Mercury is used in scientific instruments and in chemicals, particularly in the production of chlorine and caustic soda. World mine output is 92 million tonnes. Leading sources are Spain, North America, Italy, Mexico, China, USSR and Yugoslavia.

Cadmium

A soft silvery-white metal occurs together with zinc. Mainly used in plating processes, as a pigment for plastics, for television phosphors and for nickel-cadmium batteries. It is also used for control rods in atomic nuclear reactors. The largest commercial producer is the USA. Total output is well over 10m lbs a year.

Rhenium

Derived from copper ores with molybdenite, this metal has a melting point exceeded only by tungsten. Its outstanding ductility, high temperature strength and corrosion resistance makes it an alternative for platinum as a petrochemical catalyst. Used for camera flash bulb filaments and for alloys. Main sources are Chile, USA, USSR and Sweden. Other electronic metals and minerals are indium, selenium, tellurium and mica.

Phosphate Rock

Universally mined phosphoric material with widespread usage in chemical processes. Output is in excess of 117 million tonnes.

Potash

An alkaline substance used for fertilizers and other chemical synthesis. World production is 24·2 million tonnes, with North America, USSR, Germany and France the leading sources.

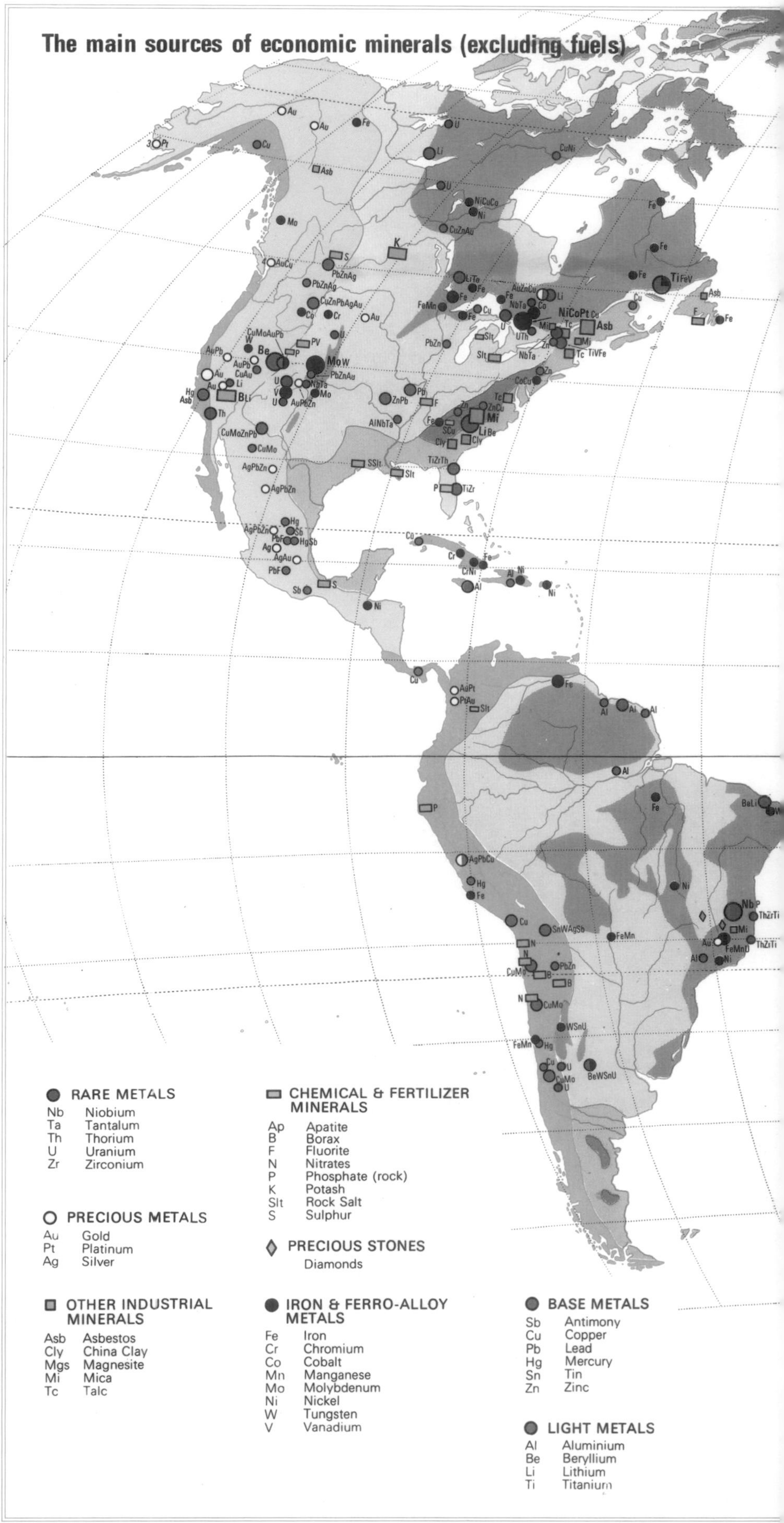

The main sources of economic minerals (excluding fuels)

● RARE METALS		▥ CHEMICAL & FERTILIZER MINERALS	
Nb	Niobium	Ap	Apatite
Ta	Tantalum	B	Borax
Th	Thorium	F	Fluorite
U	Uranium	N	Nitrates
Zr	Zirconium	P	Phosphate (rock)
		K	Potash
○ PRECIOUS METALS		Slt	Rock Salt
Au	Gold	S	Sulphur
Pt	Platinum		
Ag	Silver	◆ PRECIOUS STONES	
			Diamonds

▣ OTHER INDUSTRIAL MINERALS		● IRON & FERRO-ALLOY METALS		● BASE METALS	
Asb	Asbestos	Fe	Iron	Sb	Antimony
Cly	China Clay	Cr	Chromium	Cu	Copper
Mgs	Magnesite	Co	Cobalt	Pb	Lead
Mi	Mica	Mn	Manganese	Hg	Mercury
Tc	Talc	Mo	Molybdenum	Sn	Tin
		Ni	Nickel	Zn	Zinc
		W	Tungsten		
		V	Vanadium	● LIGHT METALS	
				Al	Aluminium
				Be	Beryllium
				Li	Lithium
				Ti	Titanium

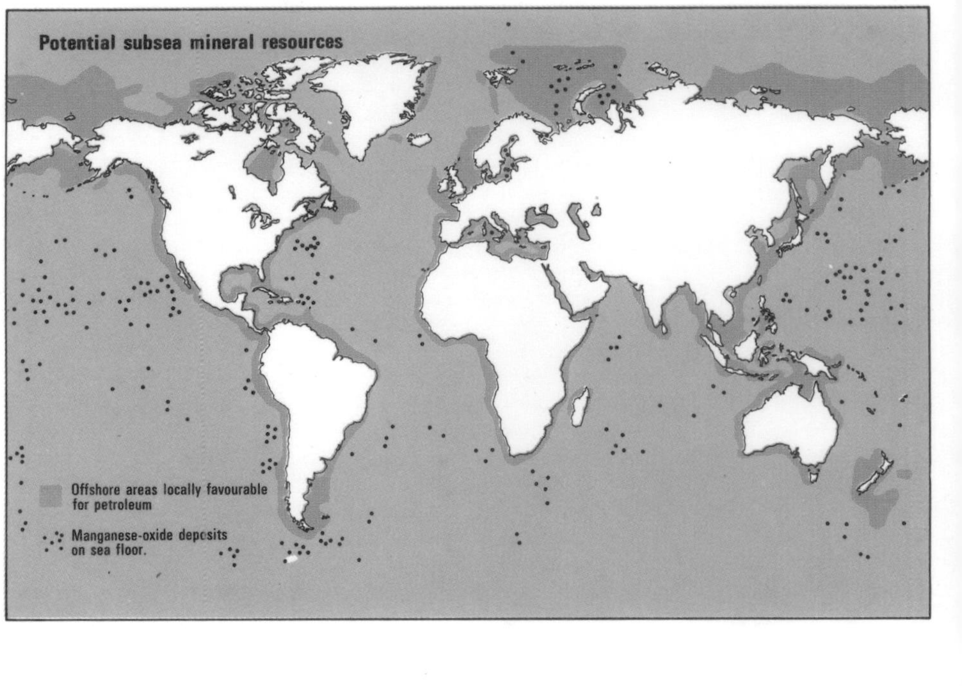

Potential subsea mineral resources

Offshore areas locally favourable for petroleum

Manganese-oxide deposits on sea floor.

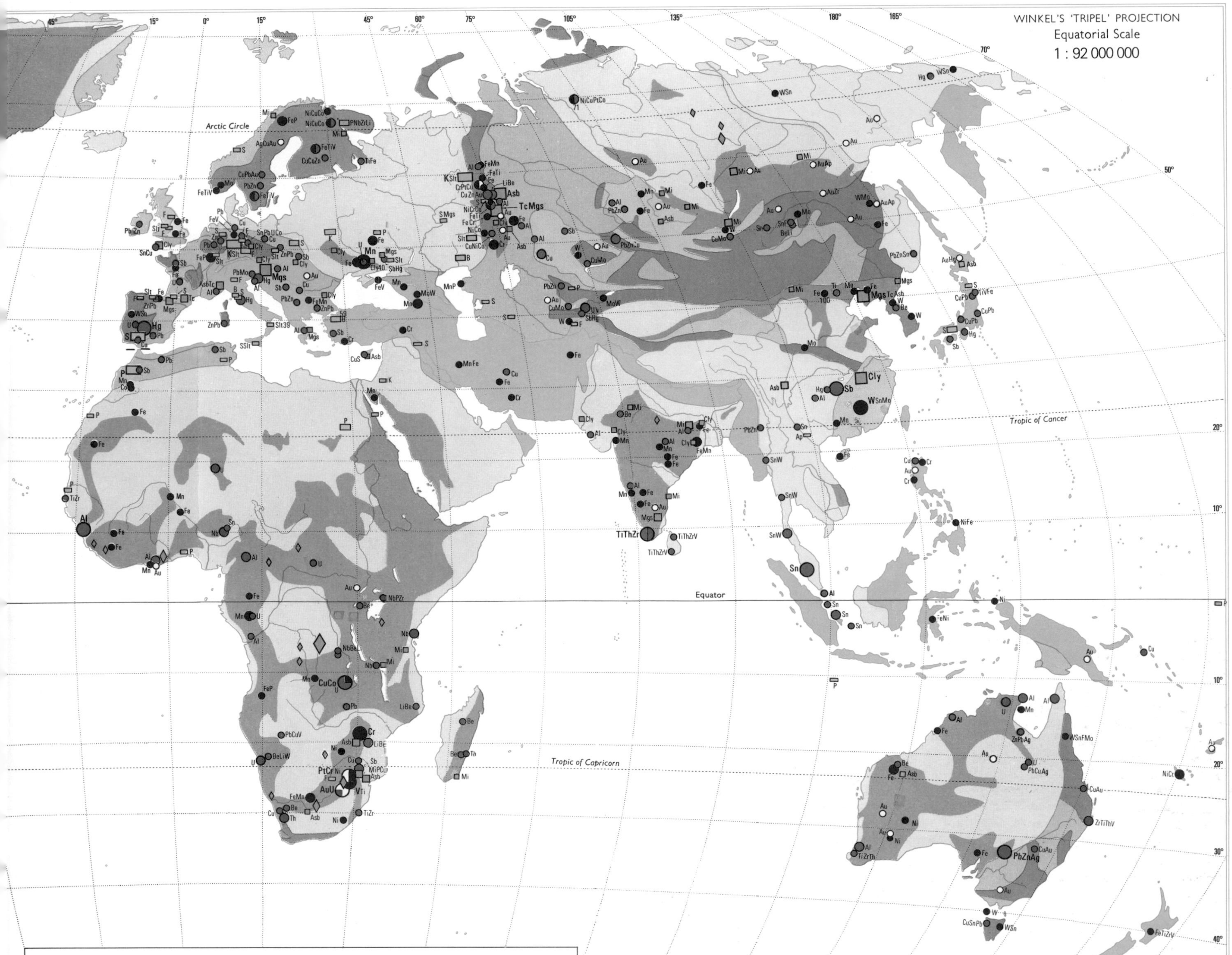

WINKEL'S 'TRIPEL' PROJECTION
Equatorial Scale
1 : 92 000 000
Arctic Circle
Tropic of Cancer
Equator
Tropic of Capricorn
IMPORTANCE OF SITES
over 20 per cent
5 — 20 per cent
1 — 5 per cent
World yield and known reserves of each mineral
STRUCTURAL REGIONS
Pre-Cambrian (exposed)
Pre-Cambrian (overlaid)
Caledonian
Hercynian (exposed)
Hercynian (overlaid)
Mesozoic
Alpine

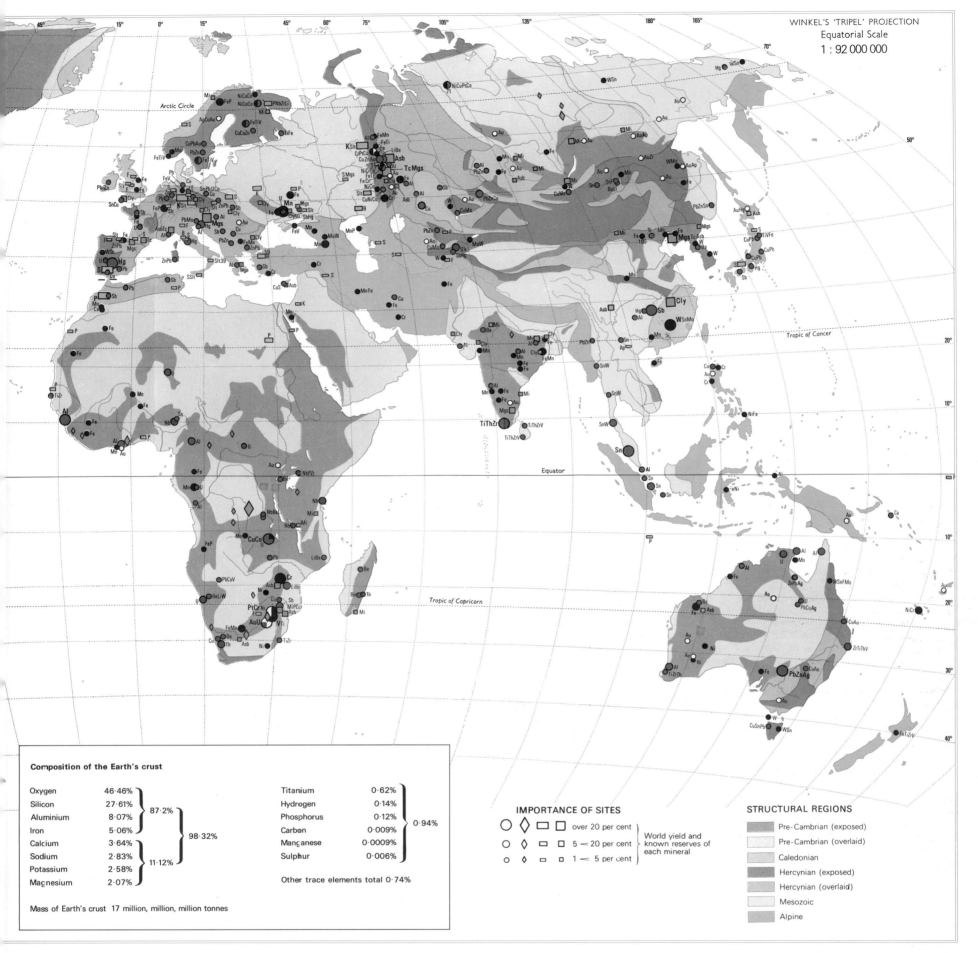

Composition of the Earth's crust

Oxygen	46·46%	87·2%	98·32%	
Silicon	27·61%			
Aluminium	8·07%			
Iron	5·06%			
Calcium	3·64%	11·12%		
Sodium	2·83%			
Potassium	2·58%			
Magnesium	2·07%			
Titanium	0·62%	0·94%		
Hydrogen	0·14%			
Phosphorus	0·12%			
Carbon	0·009%			
Manganese	0·0009%			
Sulphur	0·006%			

Other trace elements total 0·74%

Mass of Earth's crust 17 million, million, million tonnes

Sulphur

Pale yellow non-metallic element used for making sulphuric acid, gunpowder, matches and vulcanite. Also known as brimstone, the primary rock from which various sulphurs are recovered. World brimstone output is around 25 million tonnes. Derived also from natural gas, oil refining and iron pyrites. Chemicals industries are major consumers.

Lithium

Lightest metallic element produced from ore or natural brine in USA, USSR and Brazil for use in chemicals production.

Bismuth

Greyish-white metal mainly supplied by Peru, Bolivia, Mexico, USA, USSR and China. Important catalyst and is often recovered for secondary usage from other mining or smelting operations.

Barytes

The sulphate of barium; produced in 40 countries with output totalling 4 million tonnes. Usually used as weighting agent in drilling through mud for oil and gas. Also goes into making barium chemicals. USA is the largest producer.

Antimony

World output totals over 71,000 tonnes of this brittle metal substance derived from ores and concentrates. Leading suppliers are South Africa, Bolivia, China, Mexico, USSR and Yugoslavia, Thailand and Turkey. Used in battery, paint and oxide manufacture.

Boron

Dark brown non-metallic substance used to make fibreglass, vitreous enamel, heat-resistant glass, detergents and ceramics. Main source is USA borate mines; other supplies from Turkey, Argentina, France and Spain.

Fluorspar

Fusible gem-like mineral of varying quality needed for steel-making, aluminium, and fluorine based chemicals. World output is over 4 million tonnes. Leading producer is Mexico, but major sources also include USA, Argentina, Brazil, Chile, Europe, USSR, South Africa, Far and Middle East (Thailand dominant with China and North Korea).

Asbestos

A mined fibre which is best known of insulant and refractory materials, which also include perlite, sillimanite, vermiculite, graphite and magnesite. Over 5·2 million tonnes are produced annually mainly from Canada, Rhodesia, USSR, South Africa, China, Italy and USA.

Abrasives

A range of natural materials, apart from diamonds, used for abrasive and polishing purposes. Most common are emery (main sources Turkey, USA, Greece, USSR), corundum (USSR and Rhodesia), garnet (USA), tripoli (USA), pumice (USA, Germany and Italy). Finely ground and calcined clays are also used with lime, talc, feldspar and whiting. World usage of abrasives is beyond estimate.

Nickel

Element used for steel and other alloys. World consumption 750,500 tonnes, led by main steel producing countries. Main sources: Canada, New Caledonia, Australia, Rhodesia, USA, USSR, S. Africa and Japan. Latin America is a growing supplier. Biggest single use is in stainless steel.

Cobalt

Much used, like nickel, in special steels and alloys. World output is well over 22,000 million tonnes of ore bodies, often associated with copper deposits. Leading sources are Congo, Zambia, Canada, Finland and Germany.

Chromium

Chromium is derived from the ore chromite. Its main usages are in metallurgical (particularly stainless steel), refractory and chemicals industries. Output is 3·3 million tonnes. Largest producers are Rhodesia, South Africa, USSR, Turkey, Iran, Philippines, Albania and India.

Food and nutrition

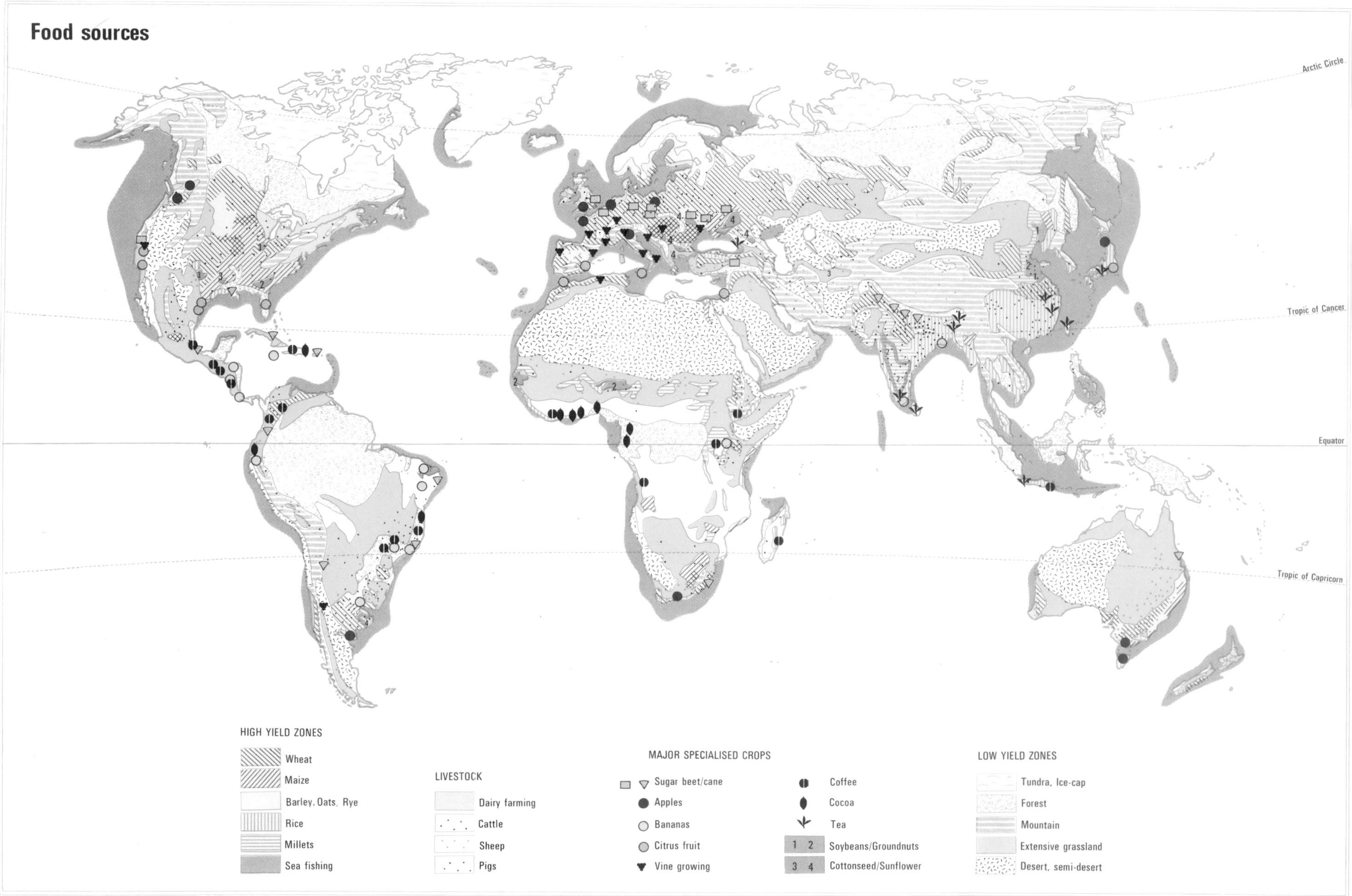

Food sources
Arctic Circle
Tropic of Cancer
Equator
Tropic of Capricorn
HIGH YIELD ZONES
Wheat
Maize
Barley, Oats, Rye
Rice
Millets
Sea fishing
LIVESTOCK
Dairy farming
Cattle
Sheep
Pigs
MAJOR SPECIALISED CROPS
Sugar beet/cane
Apples
Bananas
Citrus fruit
Vine growing
Coffee
Cocoa
Tea
1 2 Soybeans/Groundnuts
3 4 Cottonseed/Sunflower
LOW YIELD ZONES
Tundra, Ice-cap
Forest
Mountain
Extensive grassland
Desert, semi-desert

The provision of food from farms and factories depends on the most complex of all economic chains of supply. Basic foodstuffs pass from continent to continent, from temperate to tropical zones and vice versa. Foods are frozen, chilled, dehydrated, cooked and canned, pulped, or distributed fresh. Yet, in spite of better methods of preservation, storage and distribution, there is still not enough to go round. The greatest challenge to mankind is to cultivate and to process enough food to keep pace with the growth of world population, and to contrive efficient means of distribution world wide.

Poor harvests, natural disasters and civil disturbances complicate the task of agricultural scientists and economic planners who try to ease the worst problems. Their job, involving international collaboration, is formidable. In 1975 the world consumed 15,200 billion (i.e. thousand million) calories each day, but by the year 2050 the need will be 73,500 billion, with virtually all the increase concentrated on the regions of the world less well developed economically.

While the demand for food in less prosperous areas is based on grain, the raising of standards of living brings a demand for a higher consumption of animal foods. This implies great pressure to improve land crops, for only about 40 per cent of the world's crops are eaten directly by humans. The rest is fed to animals or represents waste. According to calculations, this means that six out of every seven calories are used to keep animals alive. As over half the Earth's fertile soil available for agriculture is devoted to the raising of animals, the supply of foodstuff to a world population of possibly 16 billion people by 2050 will require new sources for food if a diet comparable to that of the richer nations is to be attained.

World consumption and production patterns
Roughly 98 per cent of all human food is produced by agriculture, including horticulture; the remaining 2 per cent comes from the oceans. To avoid excessive price increases and rationing, agricultural output must continually be expanded, demanding suitable land, capital, labour and scientific knowledge. The factors of production vary according to region; plant production (i.e. crops) representing the basis of agriculture. The raw materials for raising animals come from plant production, for livestock transforms plants into finished or semi-finished products in a way similar to that of other processing industries.

Food consumption
All supply depends upon the world-wide production of basic foodstuffs, essential for either direct consumption or processing. Among the most important primary agricultural products are grains, used for both human and animal consumption, the animals being reared both for human food (meat and drink) and for their by-products such as wool or hides. Present diets, inadequate in large parts of the world, annually require up to 350 million tonnes of wheat, 176 million tonnes of barley, over 300 million tonnes of maize, and about 265 million tonnes of rice.

Food production
In tonnage terms, the world produces 424 million tonnes of milk, 84 million tonnes of meat (including poultry) and something like 23 million tonnes of eggs per year. Coffee output fluctuates around 5 million tonnes and wine near 32 million tonnes, while tea and cocoa production total about 3 million tonnes. To these must be added 38 million tonnes of vegetable oils and oil-seeds, and over 100 million tonnes of fresh fruit.

The United States slaughters around 39 million head of cattle annually to feed herself and others. Another 7 million sheep and lambs add to this huge supply of meat. Argentina, producing about 60 million head of cattle in 1976, is a major meat exporter, selling to Europe great quantities of chilled and frozen beef and various canned meats. Australian slaughterings of sheep amount to about 35 million head annually, some 5 million ahead of New Zealand which sells large quantities of lamb to Europe, beef to the USA and mutton to Japan. Nearly 8 million pigs form the stock for the famous Danish bacon industry.

The great dairy industry of Western Europe, is based on an average herd ranging from 5 head per herd in Italy to 22 in the Netherlands and 37 in the UK. With the trend to bigger farms the average herd size is growing each year.

Over the period 1967–77 the trend of food production per capita in the developing countries of the Far East (the world's most concentrated food deficit zone) and the Near East did not keep pace with the rise in population. There was a barely perceptible rise in Latin America, and a slight fall for the developing areas of Africa.

The introduction of new varieties of wheat has made Mexico virtually self-sufficient in this food commodity. Cereal yields have also advanced markedly in the Far East and India. The rising volume of world agricultural exports, up about 10 per cent annually, reflects the growing interdependence of all nations in exchanging surplus food or co-operating to ease the impact of crop failures. The operation of various international commodity agreements and markets is intended to assist marketing of food.

Changes in food supply
Fishing is a vital industry. The economies of Peru and the Philippines have benefited greatly from substantial landings. In Japan, fish still provides two-thirds of animal protein and in south-east Asia fish is more commonly eaten than meat. About one-third of fish landings round the world go to the production of fish meal to feed poultry and cattle. Over the last three decades many new fishing grounds have been intensively developed, including the Bering Sea (exploited by Japan and the Soviet Union), the north-east Pacific, the north-west Atlantic, many areas around South America, and south-east Asia.

Drought, cyclone and civil disturbance are not the only factors to alter the geographical patterns of food supply year by year; political and economic difficulties sometimes arise as well. National farm policies and subsidies to food industries, have become important elements in the world economy. A decision taken in Europe to restrict imports of a certain food in order to expand indigenous production may have a profound effect on the populations of other continents. The European Community's common agricultural policy and the United States' farm support programmes are of constant importance to the distribution of world food production.

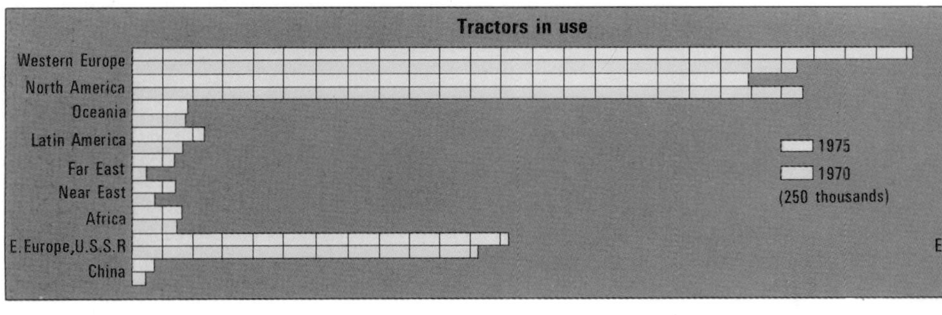

Tractors in use
Western Europe
North America
Oceania
Latin America
Far East
Near East
Africa
E. Europe,U.S.S.R
China
1975
1970
(250 thousands)

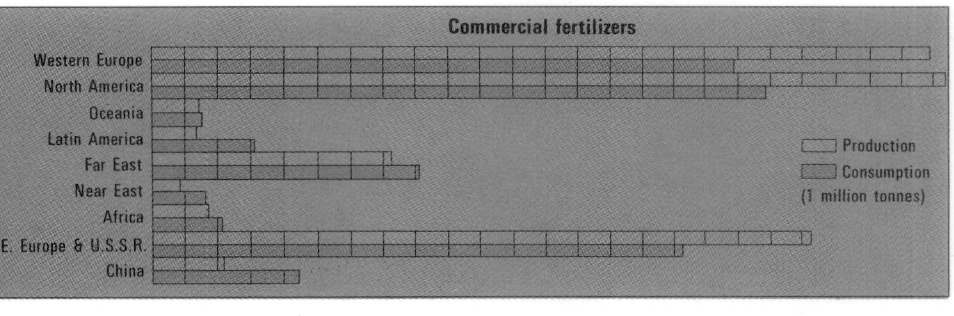

Commercial fertilizers
Western Europe
North America
Oceania
Latin America
Far East
Near East
Africa
E. Europe & U.S.S.R.
China
Production
Consumption
(1 million tonnes)

Calorie and protein consumption

Differences in calories and protein intake by different national populations need to be treated with caution. The average per capita difference in calorie intake between Canada and Brazil, for example, is around 550 calories and 35 grams of protein, yet the difference between income groups in urban areas within Brazil itself can be as high as 1,500 calories and 70 gms of protein. Some examples of calories per head per day are United States 3,330; Netherlands 3,320; West Germany 3,220; France 3,210; Italy 3,180; United Kingdom 3,180; Canada 3,180; and Japan 2,460.

To sustain their nutritional standards, nations vary greatly in their levels of consumption. Germany needs 92 kg per head per year of potatoes, compared with 36 kg for the United States. Japan consumes per head annually 90 kg of husked rice; in the UK the rice consumption is 2 kg. France and Italy drink between 100 and 105 litres of wine per head annually, whereas the consumption in the Netherlands is only 10 litres.

The importance of fish and rice in Japanese diets is demonstrated by the consumption of 25 kg per head per year of meat (measured by carcase weight) compared with 70 kg for the United Kingdom and 105 kg for the United States. The latter two nations are leading consumers of eggs in shell at 14 to 17 kg per head per year. Per capita, Finland consumes 258 kg of liquid milk annually, against 118 kg for the USA and 25 kg for Japan. Consumption of fats per head per year is 25 kg in Western Europe and North America, but in Japan the intake is 11 kg – half the level of consumption in Italy.

Innovations in food production

In recent years agricultural technologists have achieved profound changes to increase land yields by biological engineering in one form or another. Developed countries have contributed scientific skills to developing varieties of higher-yielding seed, precision fertilizers, and chemicals for pest control. As well as the 'Green Revolution', as this has become known, progress takes many other forms, such as conditioning the plants and animals of temperate zones to tropical agriculture. Desalination of sea water holds great promise for irrigation, while products unpalatable for human consumption are now being used for the enrichment of foodstuffs or for animal feeds.

There are twelve main categories of innovation in food production:

- high-yielding varieties of certain grains
- developing protein rich plants
- developing animal husbandry in less developed regions
- breeding plants and animals with high inbuilt resistance to pests and diseases
- providing more water
- providing more land
- new methods of getting food from the sea
- cultivation of algae
- producing single-cell protein
- getting food or feed from leaves
- extracting food or feed from wood
- synthetic industrial food production

Innovation in food production is taking an exciting new path in non-agricultural sectors. Fish and other sea foods offer valuable proteins. Their potential contribution to solving the world's food problems is beyond estimate. Fish protein concentrates can be used for either human or animal consumption. Mariculture in shallow waters of certain sea foods represents a major area of new research. The cultivation of algae, rich in proteins, in artificial surroundings to supplement the supply of animal feeding stuffs holds considerable promise.

One of the most dramatic recent developments has been the production of proteins by feeding single-cell organisms either bacteria or yeast on a petroleum base. The waste from various other materials or plants is being used to feed organisms. In the future, the greatest radical innovation is to produce food or feed, without the use of plants. The use of solar or other energy sources will allow amino-acids to be produced on an industrial scale, to be used to fortify foodstuffs. The consequence of the development of food without the use of plants could be enormous, reducing the world's total dependence on agriculture by a factor depending on the degree of scientific progress and scale of commercial exploitation.

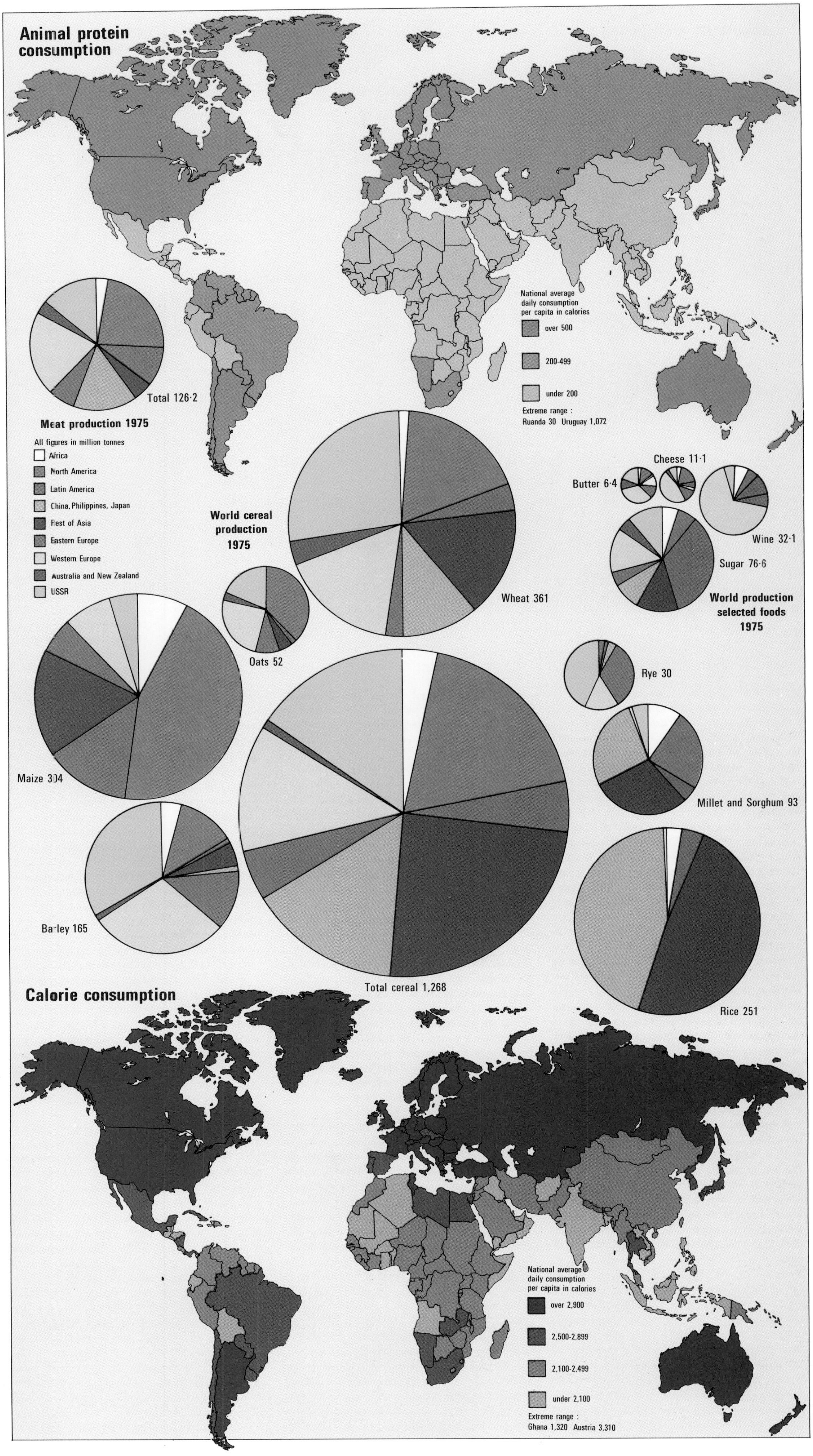

Animal protein consumption
National average daily consumption per capita in calories
over 500
200-499
under 200
Extreme range : Ruanda 30 Uruguay 1,072
Total 126·2
Meat production 1975
All figures in million tonnes
Africa
North America
Latin America
China, Philippines, Japan
Rest of Asia
Eastern Europe
Western Europe
Australia and New Zealand
USSR
World cereal production 1975
Wheat 361
Oats 52
Maize 304
Barley 165
Total cereal 1,268
Rye 30
Millet and Sorghum 93
Rice 251
Cheese 11·1
Butter 6·4
Wine 32·1
Sugar 76·6
World production selected foods 1975
Calorie consumption
National average daily consumption per capita in calories
over 2,900
2,500-2,899
2,100-2,499
under 2,100
Extreme range : Ghana 1,320 Austria 3,310

Population variations

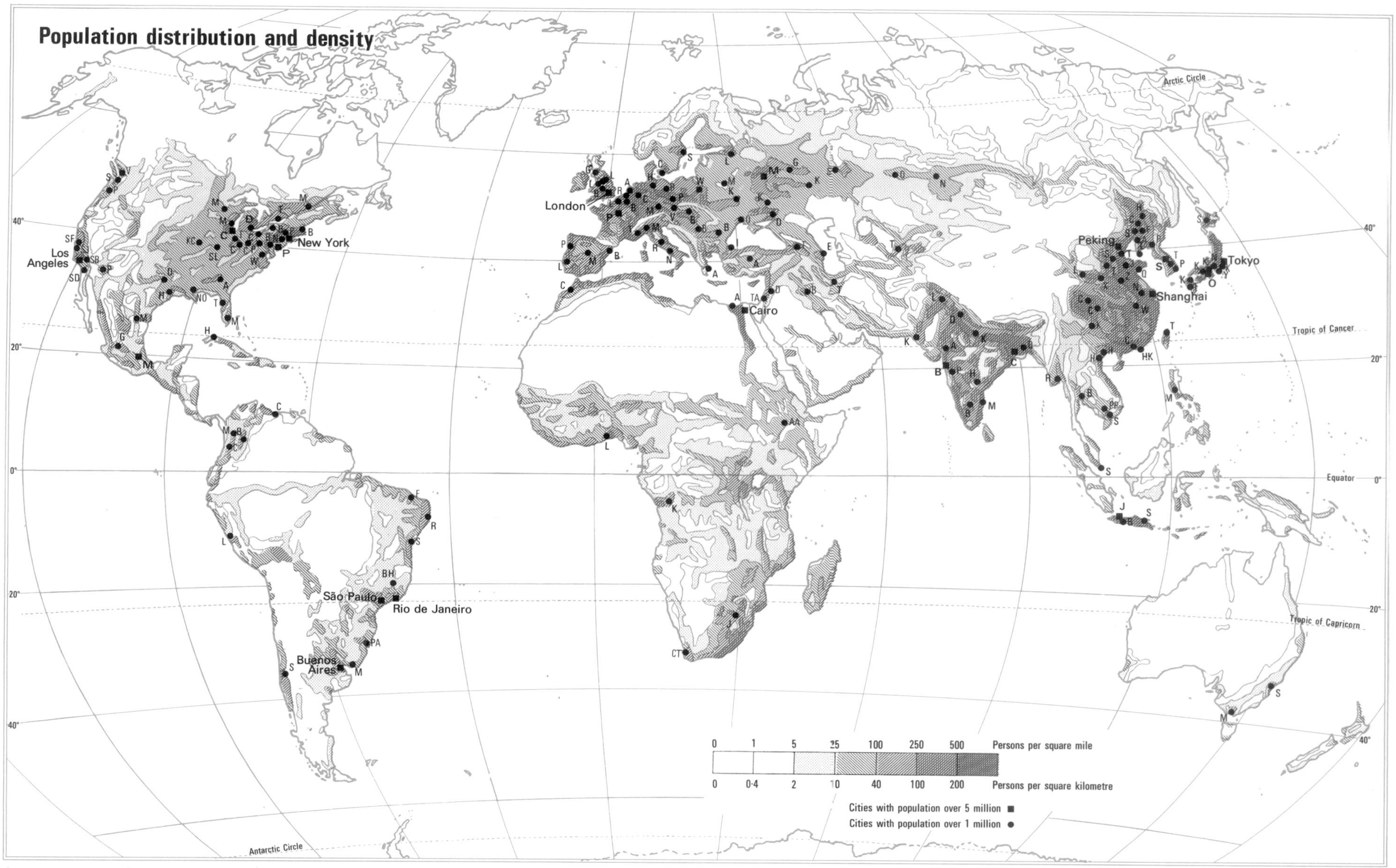

In the first 17 centuries AD world population increased by a mere 500 million. Then, largely through reduction in the death-rate rather than increase in fertility, the rate of growth accelerated so that by 1850 a further 500 million had been added, the population then being 1,300 million. A further 400 million was added to this figure in the next 50 years bringing the population in 1900 to 1,700 million.

Between 1930 and the beginning of 1975 the population of the world virtually doubled to about 3,900 million. If the growth rate of the last few decades (1·9%) were to continue there would be over 7,500 million people by AD 2010 representing an increase of 1,100 million in the decade following the end of the century. By 2050 this figure would have risen to 16,000 million and would attain 25,500 million by 2075. At this rate of growth the population doubles every 37 years.

Density and distribution

The mean density of population in 1975 was some 28 per square kilometre (about 73 per square mile). In other words each human being could have 9½ acres (or very nearly 4 hectares) to live on if the population were evenly distributed over all the land surface of the globe. But about 70 per cent of the land is either too cold or too high, too aird or too wet or else infertile and so presents mankind with conditions unfavourable for settlement by more than a very small proportion of even the world's present population. It is no wonder then, that the population is not evenly distributed over the Earth.

To this uneven distribution of population; imposed largely by nature, must be added maldistribution in relation to resources. Much of the land area (one third of the total) that could possibly be cultivated fairly intensively remains virtually unused. Economic efficiency in the actual areas under production varies greatly from one place to another. Less than 10 per cent (13,500,000 square km or 5,200,000 square miles) of the non-polar land surface is occupied by more than 95 per cent of the world's population. Within this proportionately small area, the patterns of distribution and density of population vary very greatly in response to many factors, none of which remains constant in its effect upon mankind save over areas where the pattern of human culture itself is the same. Thus the map on this page shows a pattern which cannot be interpreted in global terms simply with reference either to the density of population or to the distribution of cities.

Asia

The greatest concentration of people is to be found in monsoon Asia, especially in China, India, Japan and Java. Here, apart from Japan and small localities such as Hong Kong, Singapore, and Shanghai, people are dependent for their livelihood mainly upon agriculture. When the scarcity of cultivable land in monsoon Asia and its huge agricultural population (certainly more than 1,000 million) are taken jointly into account, the distinctive feature of the population distribution over the area is seen to be the prevalence of high rural, agrarian, densities. Farms become small holdings, often of no more than one hectare (two and a half acres) in size; farms larger than ten hectares are very rare indeed, and rural densities of population of 500 per square km (1,300 per square mile) are commonplace. Such densities as these are to be found in, for example, the Ganges plain; the valleys of southern China; much of the Great Plain of China; the Yangtse basin; the rice lands of Honshu, and in Java. Similar rural densities could have developed in the Mississippi lowlands following the discovery of the New World had the Chinese settled there and not the Europeans. Instead it can be seen that neither in North nor South America are extensive Asian-type rural densities to be found. Likewise in Europe agrarian densities are far lower than in monsoon Asia because farms are larger. It should be noted, on the other hand, that agrarian densities in the fertile parts of Europe generally exceed those of similar areas in North America because farm sizes in the mainland of western Europe are small in comparison with those of North America, and are smaller even than those of the United Kingdom.

Europe

The second great concentration of population is to be found in Europe, as is seen from a comparison of maps C and D opposite. Agriculture first led to the dense settlement of population in many areas in Europe but the growth of manufacturing, mining and service industries augmented those densities and led to further concentrations of people in areas not previously densely settled, e.g. the Ruhr and Lancashire. Unlike monsoon Asia, therefore, western Europe has become densely populated through urban growth and is now predominantly a land of town-dwellers, or town-workers. Nowhere is this fact more plainly visible than in Britain.

N.E. United States

The third great concentration comprises the north-eastern quarter of the USA and the adjacent strip of Canada. The total population of this highly urbanized area slightly exceeds that of Japan and is about equal to that of Indonesia. It is, therefore, much smaller than that of western Europe and is minute in comparison with the concentration in monsoon Asia. Yet this third concentration produces at least as much wealth as Western Europe and considerably more wealth than the whole of monsoon Asia (map E opposite).

In the rest of the world, population density is generally low but there are local pockets of high density in, for example, the Nile Valley of Egypt; California; some coastal areas of South America; central Mexico; parts of western and southern Africa, and in metropolitan Australia. The paramount fact of human geography is, therefore, the emptiness of the Earth. Very little of it is densely populated. Very little of it is overpopulated. Most of it is underpopulated.

Expectation of life

Lack of space may prove less of a problem than how to ensure a more uniform life-expectancy throughout the world. As map B on the opposite page shows, there is a large area including most of Africa, Arabia, Afghanistan, India, Bangladesh, Indo-China and Indonesia where the expectation of life at birth is less than 50 years, whereas in the United States, Canada, Cuba, Jamaica, most of Europe, Japan, and Australasia it is over 70 years. Latin America contrasts sharply with North America, but worst of all is the expectation of less than 40 years indicated for Bangladesh, Madagascar and several other African countries.

These and the other wide variations in life-expectancy illustrated on the map merit more immediate international concern than mere numbers of people or the numerical increase. Although effective measures to reduce the birth rate will contribute to the lowering of the death rate, some nations with high rate of birth oppose reduction in national birth-rate. As with density of population, problems arising from life-expectancy are not the same the world over; nor can they be solved solely by global strategies; they are regional and local in occurrence and for the most part demand regional and local treatment.

Increase of population

Increase of population is a matter of world concern because of its impact on life-expectancy, the quality of life and local living conditions. The rate of increase (shown on map A above) is highest in parts of Africa and Latin America, and almost tropical and sub-tropical countries have rates greater than the mean (1·9 per cent) for the world as a whole. It should be noted, however, that whereas rates of increase generally diminished a little in a large part of South America during the decade to 1975 the converse is probably true for Africa. Temperate lands of the northern hemisphere show low increases in the period up to 1975 while several, including England and Wales, have more recently recorded small decreases. The trend is towards a numerically static population, the birth rate equating to the death rate.

Rates of change, whether up or down, are less crucial to human well-being and political action than absolute changes represented by the differences between birth-rate and death-rate. China and, even more so, the Indian subcontinent, face the greatest problems of population increase. Their natural resources including availability of land are modest in relation to the total number of people added annually. In India alone, the increase exceeds that in the whole of the Americas. China's population growth is greater than that of Europe and the USSR combined. Mexico's annual increase now exceeds that of the United States and by AD 2000 the population will approach half that of the USA in a land only one-fifth of the area. Indonesia's absolute increase exceeds those of all countries except China and India.

Absolute increase in the population of a given area is caused either by the birth rate exceeding the death rate or by immigration. Large-scale migration occurs where there is disparity between two areas. In the past it was towards areas where agriculture offered better prospects. Today it is towards countries of high technology

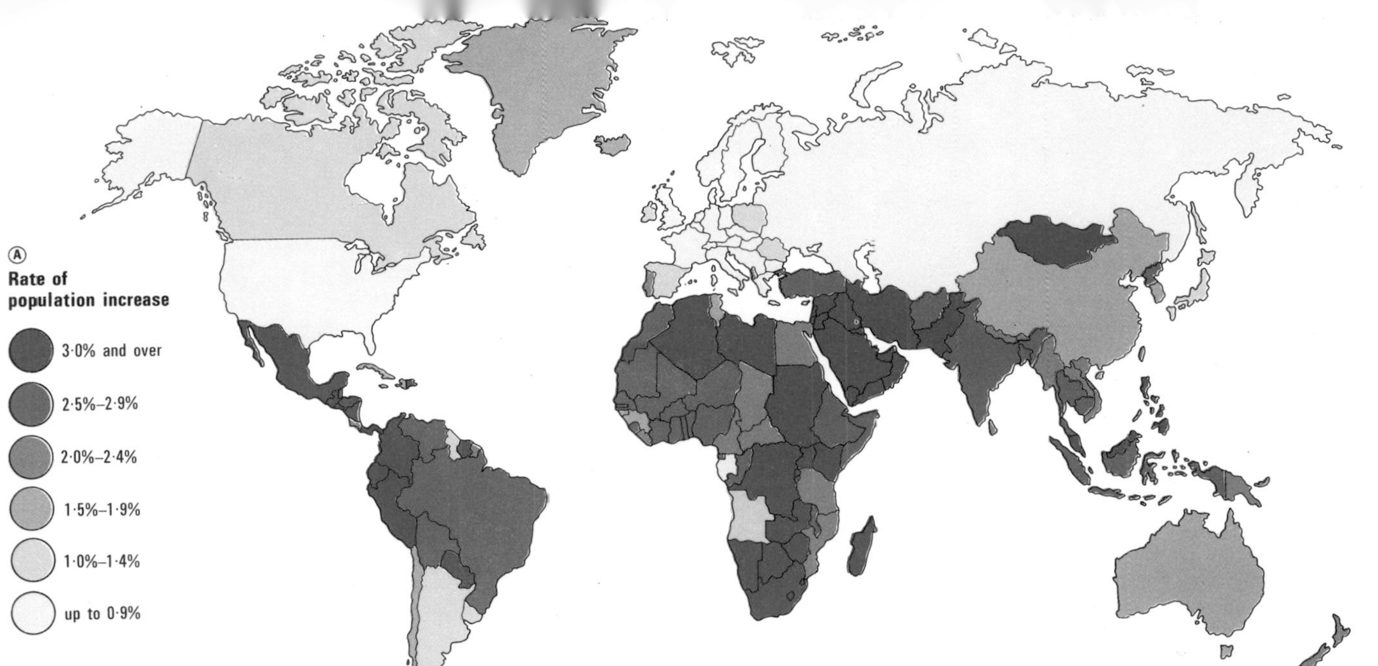

Rate of population increase
The rate of increase is very high in much of Latin America, Africa and south-eastern Asia with rates greater than the world mean of 1·9 per cent. In the 1960s Latin America, particularly Mexico, experienced up to 3·5 per cent increase; the trend in the 1970s appears to be a gradually diminishing rate of increase. The opposite trend is true for Africa. The temperate lands of America, Europe and Asia have nearly static population growth.

Life expectation
The relationship between rate of population increase and life expectation is clear by comparing maps A and B. Reduction of the birth rate would affect the death rate and improve life expectation but certain economies demand a high growth of population.

Area, population and GDP
How countries contrast in size depends upon the characteristic that is measured and upon the method of its portrayal. The maps below show how countries and continents vary greatly in size of Land area (map C); Total population (map D), and Gross Domestic Product (map E). Each country is represented on each map by a rectangle or a square. The sizes of these are made proportional to whatever may be the amount of each characteristic that a given country possesses. Thus, for example, the area (map C) of Australia requires a large square whereas its population appears on map D as a small square. Brazil is seen to have a large area on map C, far larger than that of France; but on map E Brazil's gross domestic product is seen to be much smaller than that of France. Study of these maps reveals many striking contrasts.

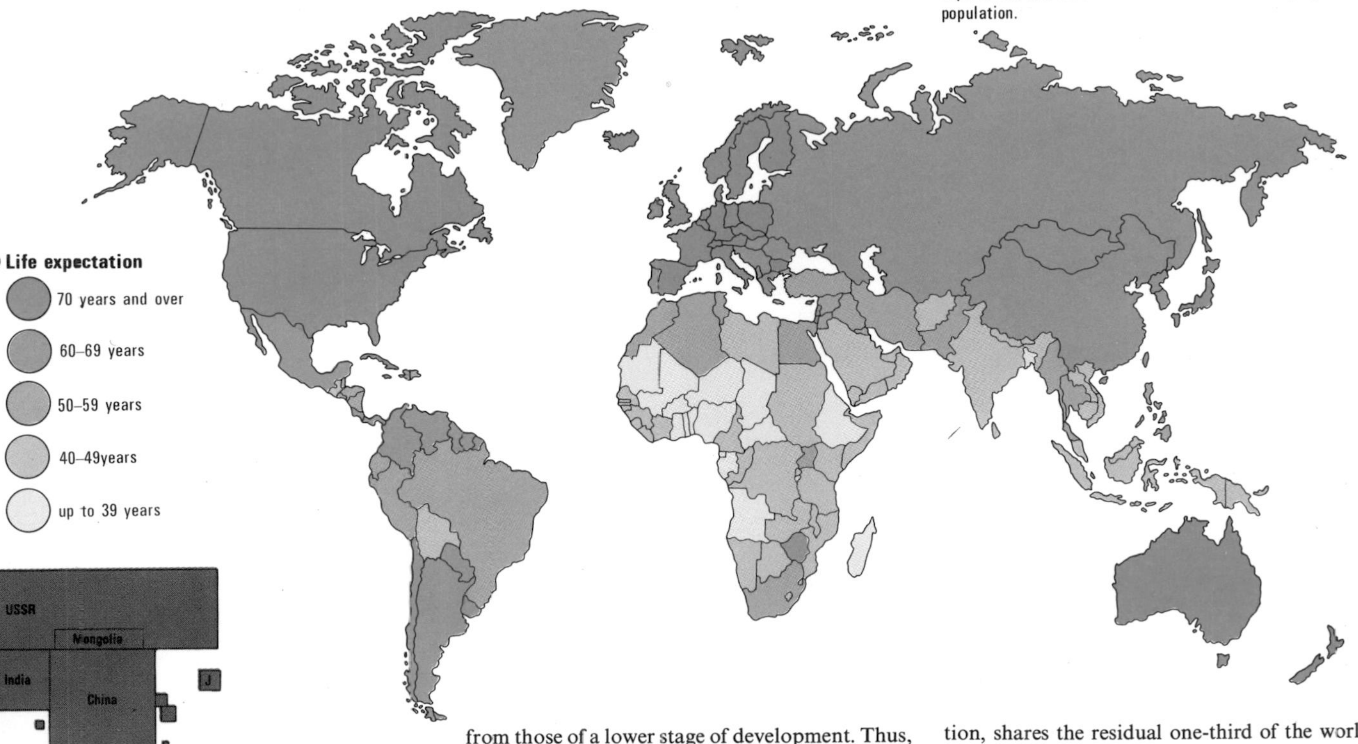

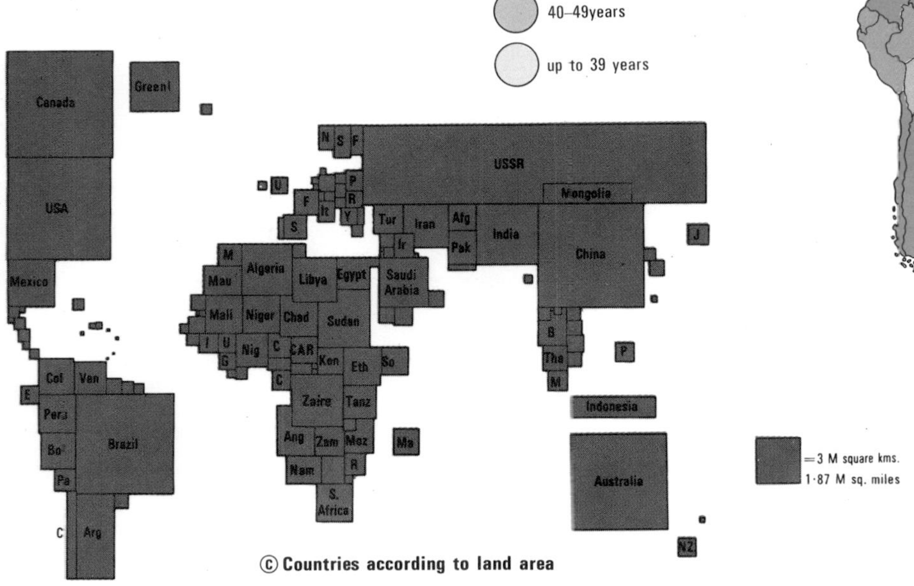

Ⓒ Countries according to land area

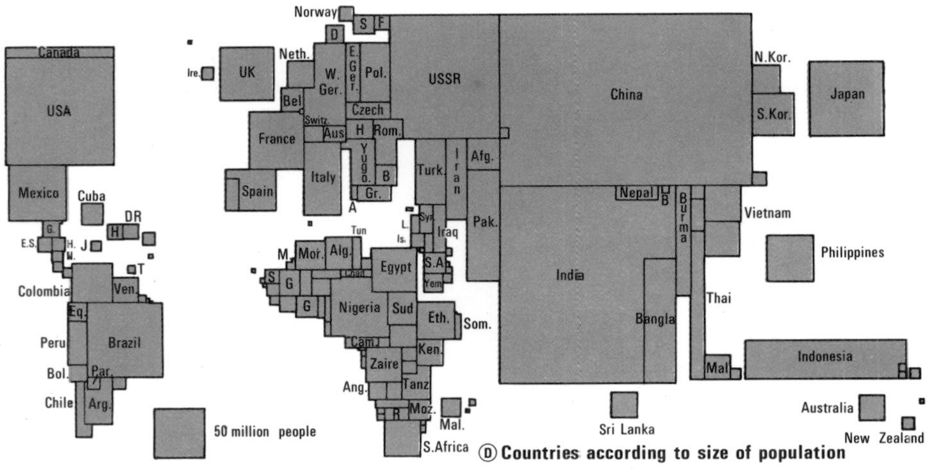

Ⓓ Countries according to size of population

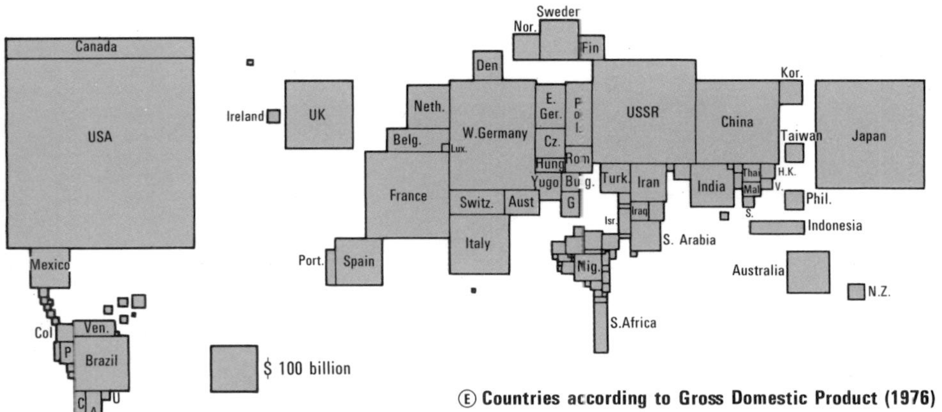

Ⓔ Countries according to Gross Domestic Product (1976)

from those of a lower stage of development. Thus, the flow of people from the Old World to the New has virtually ceased. Instead people migrate from the developing world to the developed unless political barriers prevent it. The flow over the past few decades has been from the New World excluding the USA and Canada to the Old World (Europe). Except for Norway, for example, Scandinavia has a birth-rate too low to maintain its population. Immigration is responsible for the increase which has taken place. Birth tends to be higher among the immigrant population from whatever source the immigrants came, e.g. Italians in the USA. Ireland alone amongst the western nations has an anomalously high birth rate.

Economic wealth
The two great powers and western Europe and Japan are areas with low rate of increase of population – Japan's birth rate was halved in a decade – but are of special interest on account of their enormous economic wealth. Map E on this page is an attempt to express this economic power visually and to put the countries of the world into approximate economic perspective. 'Approximate' is a very necessary reservation in any comparison of Gross Domestic Product, because the data for any two countries are seldom collected to exactly the same formula. Furthermore the value of subsistence production and unpaid family labour, far more important in some states than in others, is hard to assess. Also, the efficiency of data-collecting services varies between one country and another. Conversion of monetary data into a standard currency (in this instance into US dollars) adds a further source of inaccuracy. Nevertheless, map E probably shows the right order of wealth and is so different from normal atlas maps in the size it ascribes to particular countries and continents that it invites examination in some detail.

The outstanding feature is the pre-eminence of North America, with about 40 per cent of the gross global product. Next comes Western Europe with about 25 per cent. These two areas, together with Japan, produces annually at least two-thirds of the world's wealth. The rest of the world, comprising about five-sixths of the total population, shares the residual one-third of the world's output of products. Even this share is unequally allocated because half is accounted for by the USSR, the East European Community and China which together number about 1,200,000,000 people. Over 1,800,000,000 people in the third world, or almost half the global population, thus share only about 16 per cent of the total gross product. Given these statistics it comes as less of a shock to learn that Canada earns more annually than the whole of Africa; that West Germany earns more than the continent of South America; that the GDP of India is about the same as that of Australia and the Netherlands, and that the Netherlands with the same population as Sri Lanka (Ceylon) has 30 times Sri Lanka's gross domestic product.

If there is a worldwide demographic problem more striking than others today, it is this great imbalance in the distribution of wealth and the inequalities in the well-being of mankind that map E so graphically expresses. Pressure of population, poor life-expectancy and scarcity of resources are subsidiary and, for the most part, local and regional components of that larger problem. Maldistribution inevitably demands different remedial measures in different areas, for it has differing local causes and effects.

There is no single measure which could quickly increase equally effectively the wealth and well-being of countries as different, for example, as India and Brazil. Only concerted and co-operative international action might reconcile the needs and remedies in different areas. To ascertain the true needs, a detailed inventory-survey of human geography would be necessary, for detailed, objective knowledge of much of the world is still lacking.

Brazil is sparsely peopled, undeveloped and quite capable of absorbing a large number of immigrants provided they were used to develop and exploit the resources of the interior. India is, in contrast, densely populated, intensely but inefficiently developed and quite unsuited to receiving large numbers of immigrants. In Brazil, the key problem is how to organize development; in India, how to undertake redevelopment. Immigration could help Brazil. Emigration would help India.

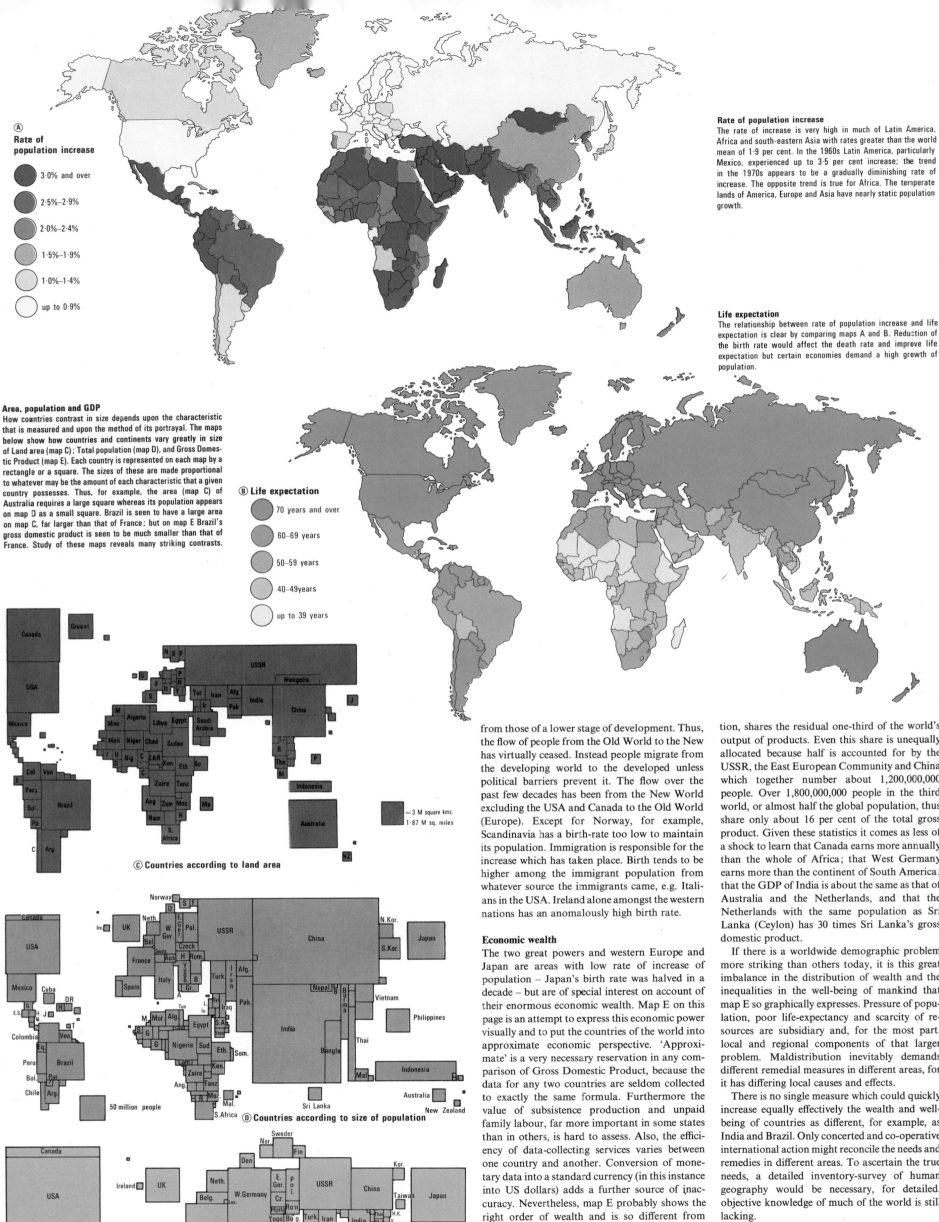

Patterns of human settlement

1
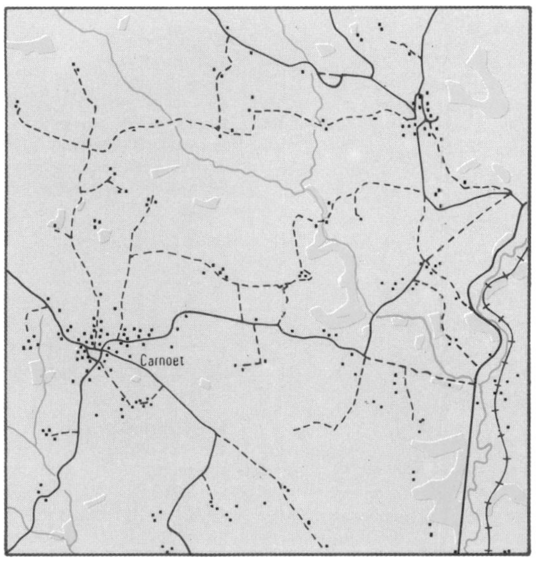

2

3
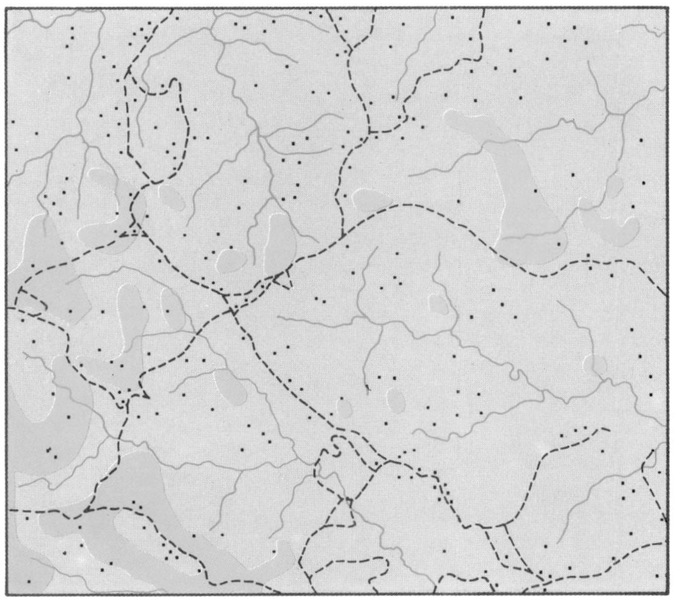

4
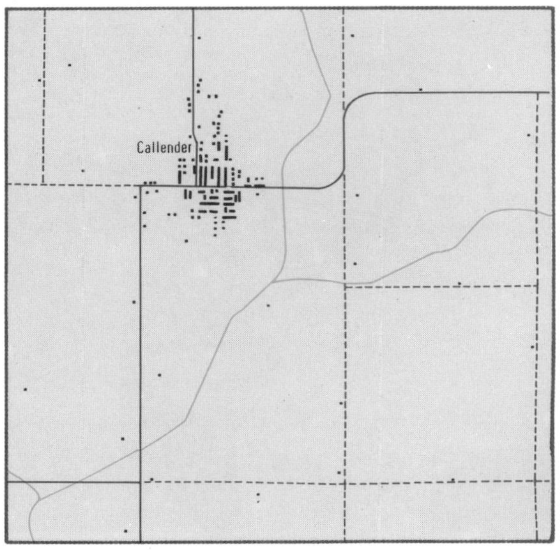

5
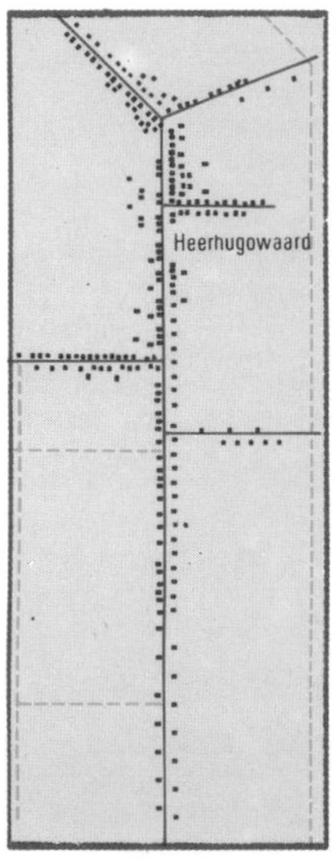

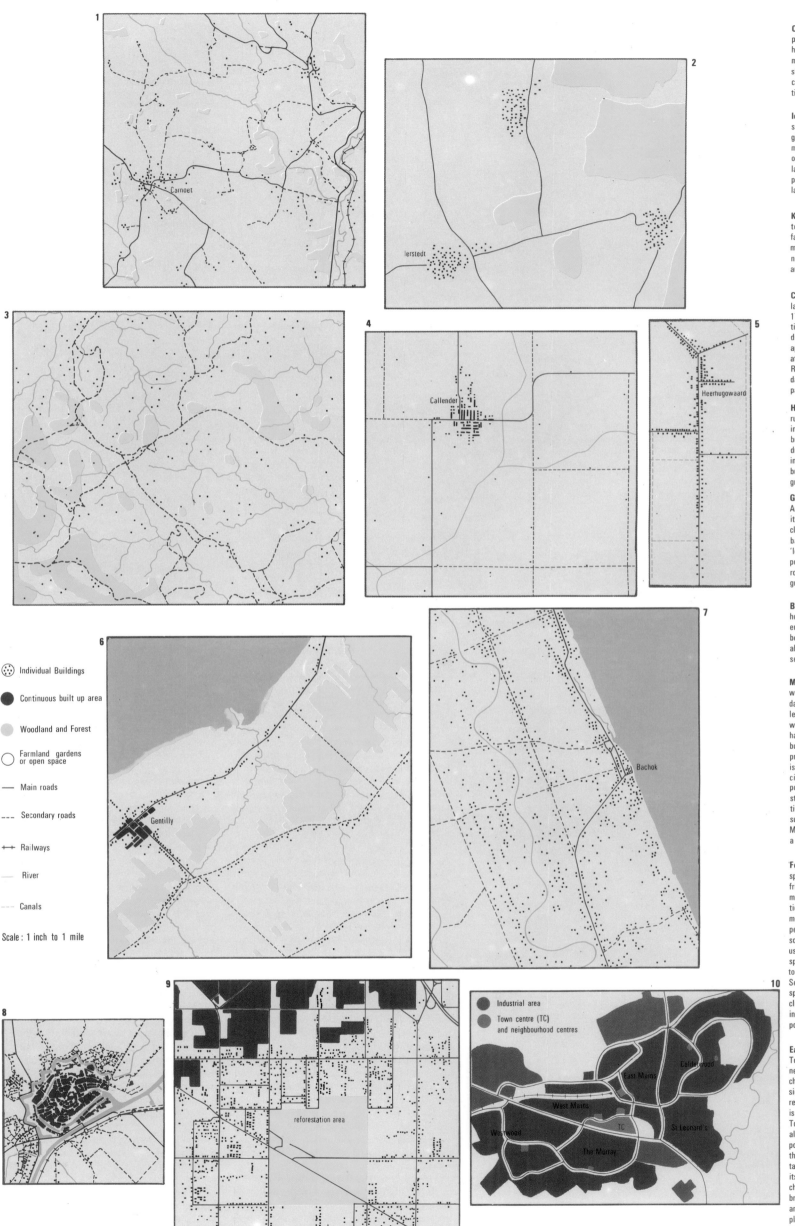

Individual Buildings

Continuous built up area

Woodland and Forest

Farmland gardens or open space

Main roads

Secondary roads

Railways

River

Canals

Scale: 1 inch to 1 mile

6
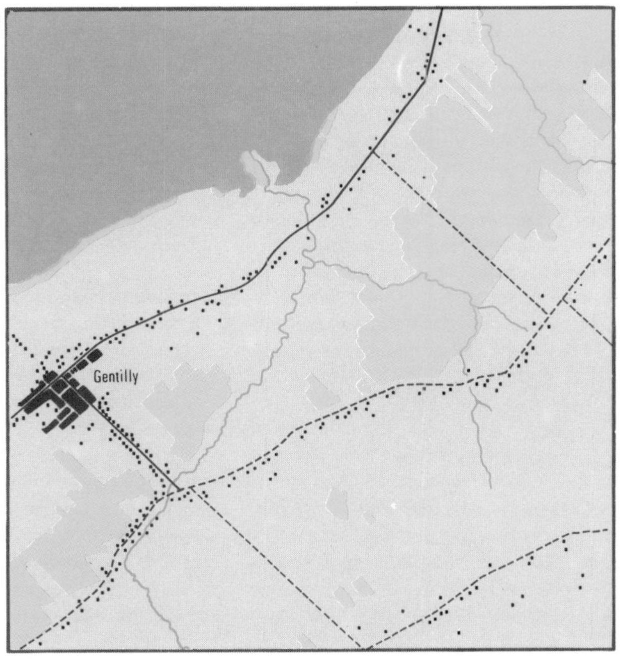

7
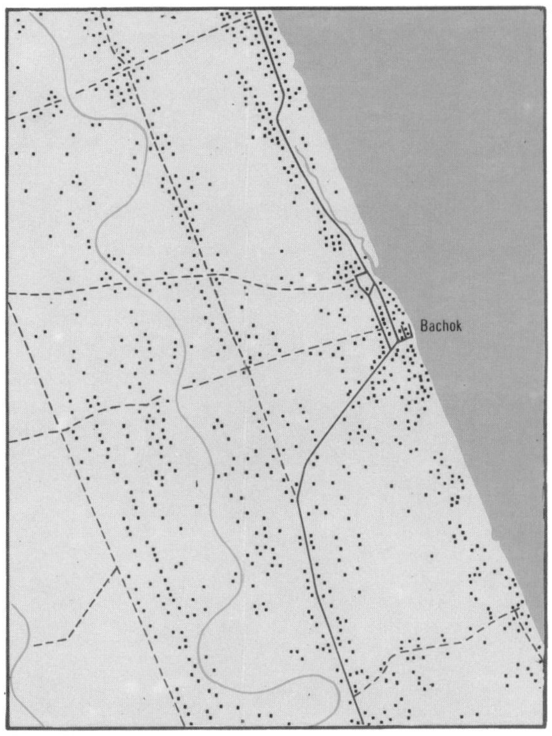

8

9
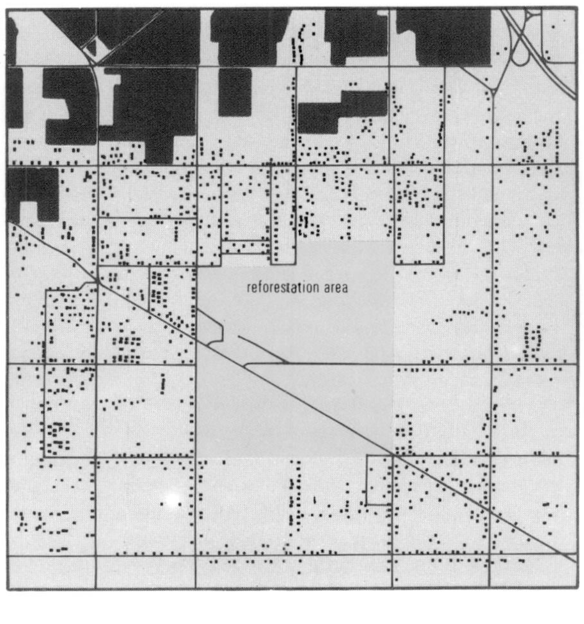

10
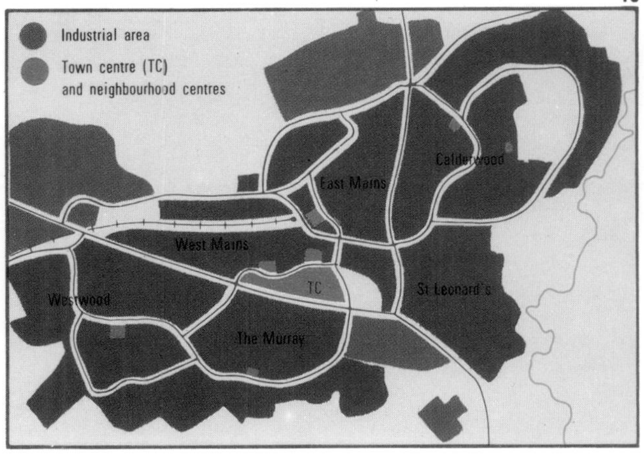

1

Carnoet, France Farmsteads are widely dispersed on compact holdings, with scattered hamlets and small villages containing community facilities like churches, schools and shops. In western Europe such a pattern occurs especially in regions where Celtic traditions survive.

2

Ierstedt, Germany Highly nucleated rural settlement, associated historically with regions of post-Roman Europe settled by Germanic tribes. Even today few farmsteads occur outside the large, rather formless villages, because traditionally farms are composed of separate scattered strips, although land consolidation is now widespread.

3

Kangundo, Kenya Moderately dense pattern of dispersed settlement in a tribal farming economy. Community facilities like markets and schools stand on isolated sites, not having formed, here at least, nuclei around which villages have evolved.

4

Callender, Iowa, USA To dispose of public land to settlers, US government surveys after 1785 created 1-mile square farm units ('sections'), though many have since been subdivided. Dispersed rural settlement thus appeared from the outset, with small nucleated villages at intervals throughout the area. Roads were built along most section boundaries, giving a characteristic checkerboard pattern.

5

Heerhugowaard, Holland Strongly linear rural settlement at high density in a region of intensive farming. Land reclamation confines building to the elevated dikes that line major drainage canals. Villages are large, extending considerable distances along roadsides, but with little opportunity for compact growth.

6

Gentilly, Québec French colonists in North America divided land into narrow plots, initially running back from rivers, with farms close together for safety, and along the river banks for access to water transport. This 'long lot' system later developed to incorporate other rows (rangs) of farms along roads, often parallel to the rivers. Villages grew up especially around churches.

7

Bachok, Malaya This linear arrangement of houses and villages has been strongly influenced by the existence of parallel sandy beach ridges. These are elevated slightly above the flat intervening tracts that are seasonally flooded for padi (rice) cultivation.

8

Middelburg, Holland Medieval towns in western Europe were small by modern standards and compact. Winding, narrow streets led to a central market square, around which were the town's chief public buildings (town hall, guildhall, the main church – in Middelburg, a 12th century abbey). Walls usually protected the town, but when later demolished, their line is often shown by roughly circular streets. In Middelburg, typical post-medieval fortifications were also constructed with moats and geometrical bastions. Many present-day large cities have such medieval towns as a historic core, but Middleburg has not expanded greatly due to a restricted economic basis.

9

Fort Mann, BC, Canada The characteristic sprawl of the North American 'rural-urban fringe'. Without tight control on development, and often with intense land speculation, sporadic growth of this kind occurs commonly around American cities. Housing appears in small clusters, or along roads, or on scattered individual lots. Non-residential uses develop, especially those needing ample space, e.g. shopping centres, modern factories, motels, drive-in cinemas or schools. Set among all these are recreational open spaces such as golf courses and country clubs. What is left of earlier farmsteads (often in a rundown condition) forms another component in this highly diversified area.

10

East Kilbride, Scotland The British New Towns, all established since 1946, are planned urban communities drawing population chiefly from conurbations (London and Clydeside especially), for which by intention they relieve housing pressures. Local employment is simultaneously created to make each New Town as independent as possible economically and socially. Earlier New Towns are composed of several neighbourhood units around the town centre, each neighbourhood containing facilities for the everyday needs of its residents (primary schools, shops, churches, doctors, meeting halls, etc.). East Kilbride (designated 1947) is an excellent example. Since 1952 somewhat more flexible plans are utilized, but all New Towns have segregated industrial areas and also sophisticated internal circulation systems, emphasising the separation of pedestrians from vehicular traffic.

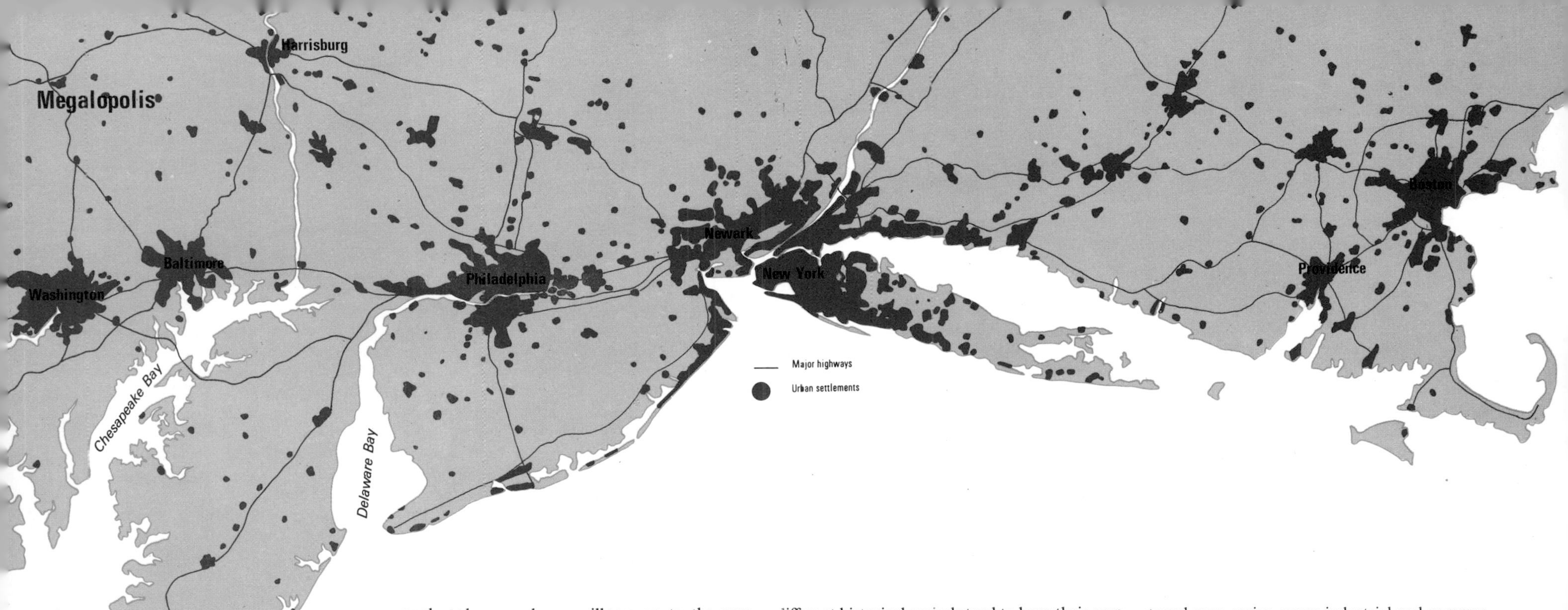

The distribution of homes and other buildings, constituting the settlement pattern of a region, is affected by a complex interplay of factors.

Rural settlement

Considering rural regions first, there are great differences in the *density* of settlement depending largely upon the carrying capacity of the land in terms of the particular types of agriculture practised, and upon the length of time the region has been settled. The disposition of buildings over the area, or the *form* of settlement, can vary from almost total dispersion to virtually complete clustering, though more often there will be a mixture of scattered farms and small nucleations (i.e. groupings of buildings). Such differences in form stem from variations in, for example, cultural tradition, land ownership systems, types of farming, the technological status of the society or the need for protection from external dangers, either human or environmental. Where an area has been occupied for very considerable periods, there are likely to be changes through time in some or all of these influences and thus the rural settlement pattern itself changes in response: for example, the enclosure movements that led to the consolidation of the earlier strip-field holdings into compact farm units over much of lowland Britain between the 16th and 18th centuries permitted farmers to move their homes from the highly nucleated pre-enclosure villages on to the new compact units, thereby creating the present mixed form of rural settlement that characterizes this region. Thus a *primary*, or original, settlement pattern changes into a *secondary* one.

The rural nucleations, villages and hamlets exhibit a morphology, or layout, which also varies considerably throughout the world. Linear types, e.g. along roadsides or riversides, are extremely common, but so too are compact but irregular groupings, of which the French and German examples are but two types. More regular shapes occur in many regions, e.g. rectangular and roughly circular villages are found in several parts of central and eastern Europe, and a grid plan is normal in Anglo-America.

Urban settlement

The regional or national economy develops and elaborates itself by the expansion of trade and the growth of industry. Both activities require, and create, more sophisticated types of settlement than the village, and towns and cities evolve, supported by an intensifying network of routes. The *degree of urbanisation* in a country is measured by the proportion of its population that live in towns and cities, and this is high (generally well over 60%) in advanced countries.

Urban settlements act as service centres where increasingly specialised activities locate themselves as the towns become larger, and people from usually extensive areas nearby will depend on them to provide goods and services that are unobtainable in smaller settlements, especially the villages. Towns and cities, too, will exhibit their distinctive morphologies, influenced in their case by factors such as the age of the town (for different historical periods tend to have their own characteristic standards and forms of street and building patterns) and by the cultural context in which the town has developed: compare, for example, the medieval and modern sections of European cities, or cities in Europe and India.

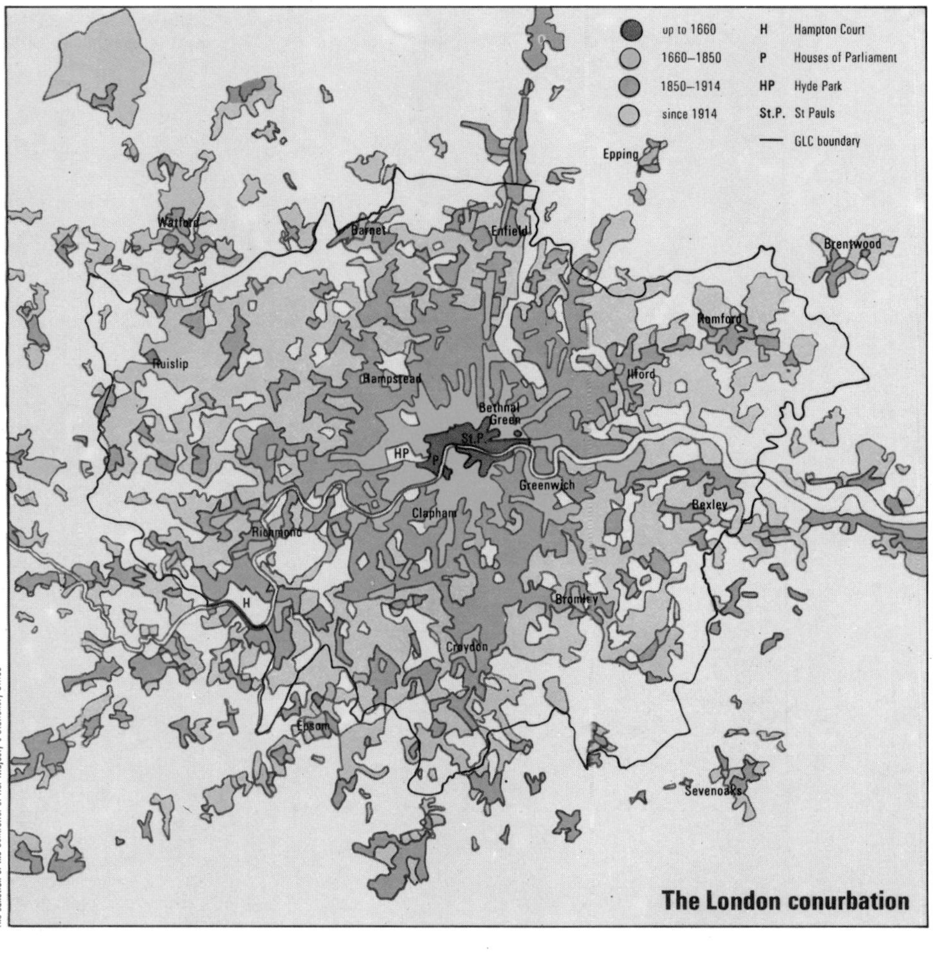

The London conurbation

based on a map compiled by the Department of the Environment and used with the sanction of the Controller of Her Majesty's Stationery Office

Conurbations

During the 19th century in advanced industrial nations, and especially on coalfields with their close grouping of thriving mining and manufacturing towns, continued growth produced the *conurbation*. Economic expansion was accompanied by increase in both population and the built-up areas of the towns, the latter outpacing the former very markedly by the late 1800s. Many urban activities came to require more spacious sites than their earlier counterparts (a trend that has become even more intense during the present century), housing in particular: the increasingly affluent populations in these countries demanded better standards in housing, and the drop in average family size generated an additional component since more homes were now required for a given size of population than when larger families were the rule.

Thus where these expansionist trends occurred in closely neighbouring towns, frequently the built-up areas of each merged with one another, obliterating most of the open spaces which had once separated them. This, then, was the conurbation, dominated by one main city, but composed of many towns, some at least quite sizeable entities in their own right. Generally, however, civic identity is retained for local administration and, especially, for local loyalties among the populace. In Britain, the West Midlands and South Lancashire (see page 11) are examples, and in Germany the Ruhr (see page 35), but all advanced nations contain conurbations.

London

London represents a rather different kind of conurbation, the 'super-city' (other examples being New York, Paris, Tokyo). This results from the surge of growth in one pre-eminent city, overwhelming in its expansion a very large number of villages and small towns which had always been completely overshadowed in size by comparison with the main urban centre.

Up to 1850, as the map shows, London was still reasonably compact, with its chief development on the north bank of the Thames: the paucity of crossing places had hampered development south of the river, away from London's Roman and medieval nucleus (which coincided approximately with the present City of London). Beyond the built-up area in 1850 were small communities which in some cases had already become the homes of wealthy commuters. During the next sixty years, however, growth was extensive.

London's rôle as capital of nation and empire added several millions to its population in this period. But the physical expansion which this necessitated was no longer compact. An intensifying network of railways attracted growth around suburban stations, and the beginnings of the Underground system towards the turn of the century added to these trends. Other forms of surface public transport were also improving, and larger segments of the city's population were becoming able to afford not inconsiderable daily journeys to their work. After 1918 motor buses and cars made travel even easier, many industrial and commercial activities moved to the suburbs from congested inner city locations (generating residential development around their new sites), slum clearance and re-housing programmes created vast new low-density municipal estates at increasing distances from central London, and private housing developments also added great increments to the total built-up area. Meanwhile, dormitory communities were attaching themselves to many outlying towns and villages, before they too became absorbed by the constant progress of urban sprawl. Checks were introduced by the creation of the Green Belt in 1935, by the effects of the Town and Country Planning Acts after the Second World War, and by the establishment of New Towns after 1946, but the conurbation still possesses remarkable economic and social vitality, largely frustrating attempts to constrain it.

Megalopolis

The north-eastern seaboard of the USA, first landfall of most European colonists, became the country's chief centre of economic activity and urbanisation from the outset. Despite subsequent developments elsewhere, this seaboard region between Boston and Washington DC has retained its dominance, to such an extent that though it comprises less than one-twentieth of the area of the USA it contains approximately 42 million people, one in five of the nation's population.

In terms of settlements, it is characterised first by a series of great conurbations, but there is also a dense scatter of other cities of all sizes, as the map shows. What the scale of the map does not allow, however, is to show the smaller communities, quasi-rural in nature, that act essentially as dormitories for the urban centres due to the ease of communication conferred by a complex, highly developed network of roads and, in places, commuter railway services. But the map does indicate that within the boundaries of this region vast tracts of non-urban land occur. Some of these are agricultural, with intensive and prosperous farming, for the most part geared to serving the needs of the region's urban dwellers (especially in milk and fresh vegetables and fruit); but much of the rest of the open land in Megalopolis is devoted to the recreational needs of the region's population, particularly the extensive forested areas of the central and northern Appalachians.

It is the extremely large territorial extent that exhibits such intimate and complicated integration between town and country that led Professor J. Gottmann to identify the whole region as a new and special phenomenon of urbanisation, and to use the word *Megalopolis* to denote it. Yet similar characteristics have by now emerged elsewhere: Chicago – Detroit – Buffalo – Toronto; south-east England – the Midlands – South Lancashire – West Riding of Yorkshire; and Tokyo – Nagoya – Osaka are but three other examples where megalopolitan features are clearly recognisable. The phenomenon cannot fail to multiply, because its essential bases continue to emerge; even planned decentralisation policies will not halt the process, as the dispersion of population and economic activities from major cities and conurbations only relocates them at no great distance away, promoting growth in the smaller urban constituents of a proto-megalopolis or, by creating New Towns, introducing new urban settlements into the open spaces of the region.

Fuel and energy

The relentless increase in the demand of all nations for fuel and power raises important questions about the future security of world energy supplies. Energy consumption accelerates from decade to decade, driven onwards by the world's rising population, the industrialisation of more economies and improvements in living standards.

In the 30 years from 1970 the energy-producing industries will, on conservative estimates, be required to raise their output to four times the total world consumption from the start of the industrial era to the present day. Extra energy resources are almost as vital to world populations as the requirements for food. Indeed, increase in food production calls for increase in energy resources. Maintenance of present rates of economic growth necessitate increased supply of energy.

Energy output

Over the past two decades the increase in world output of energy has reflected both the dominant economic progress of the great industrialised countries and greater utilisation of mineral fuels and electrical power by developing nations.

Using the standard measure of million metric tons of coal equivalent (mtce), total world energy output in 1950 was a little over 2,600 mtce. Coal was the major primary energy source ahead of crude oil and natural gas. All three, supplemented by hydroelectric power, were used to make electricity. By the mid 1970s production had reached over 8,000 mtce and crude oil had taken over from coal as the most important energy source. Nuclear power and tiny amounts of geothermal power had been introduced into the electricity generating systems. Most expert forecasters now project a global requirement of around 11,000 mtce by 1980 rising to over 20,000 mtce by the year 2000.

Energy consumption

The United States with her massive economic machine, is the largest single consumer of energy, aided by large resources of indigenous fossil fuels and the application of advanced technology to power production. By far the greater part of world energy resources is consumed by North America, the Soviet Union and Western Europe. In more recent years Japan has emerged as a leading consumer, multiplying her requirements six times since 1950 (see map).

Together, these areas account for over 80 per cent of world energy consumption but contain only 25 per cent of world population (see map on page 20). This imbalance, due to the concentration of manufacturing industry has occured over a long period during which the supply of fuel for energy has been relatively abundant.

Energy consumption per capita varies widely from country to country. Increasing industrialisation and application of new techniques to agriculture in the developing countries was, before 1974, beginning to disturb traditional patterns of energy use. However, the rapid increase in oil costs in the mid 1970s had made it difficult for the poorer nations to sustain the use of these new techniques.

Coal, oil, natural gas and water power are not always available in the areas where they are most needed. The result has been that fossil fuels have had to be transported both within and between continents. This availability of fuel as an export commodity depends on those with indigenous resources – particularly crude oil – selling their surpluses.

Except for short periods of political crisis in the Middle East, supplies of crude oil have always matched or exceeded demand. By the mid-1980s, oil supply from the Middle East and Africa will have reached its peak. Unless the energy-importing nations develop alternative sources of power, an energy crisis with soaring prices could drastically reduce world economic growth.

Nearly all the large industrial countries are dependent on imported oil. The United States which was self-sufficient in the 1950s, imports half of its oil requirements. Higher energy costs make it economically feasible to explore for oil in the deep oceans and the polar regions and to develop the more expensive alternatives such as solar power, tidal and wind power and to consider the extraction of the oil locked in shale rocks and tar sands. The discovery of new sources of oil and the development of alternative forms of energy will not alone be enough to meet energy requirements. Nuclear power and coal are the only sources of energy which can serve as an alternative to oil in the 1980s should supply fall short of world demand.

Oil

The organic remains of the earliest plant, marine and animal life that existed between 400 million and 40 million years ago are the sources of the crude oil deposits now tapped by man to meet over 40 per cent of the world's total energy requirements. Early civilisations made use of bitumen and lubricants, but it was not until the middle of the 19th century that the first oil wells were drilled.

Total world production of crude oil and natural gas liquids in 1976 amounted to 2,936 million tonnes, the equivalent of 59,555,000 barrels a day. The map of oil supply shows that the western hemisphere accounts for 26·3 per cent of total output compared with 73·7 per cent for the eastern hemisphere (including the 21 per cent share accounted for by the Soviet Union, Eastern Europe and China).

The Middle East, North America, Africa and the Soviet Union are the major producing regions. In recent years, a succession of discoveries has begun to widen the basis of supply. The newer sources of oil include Arctic Alaska, the northern part of the North Sea, the Spanish sector of the Mediterranean, Ecuador, Mexico, Australia, Indonesia, Turkey and parts of South America.

The present estimate of proven reserves is 90,066 million tonnes. The ratio between these reserves and annual production is falling as the rate of discovery of new oil reservoirs around the world slows down. Of the proven quantity, 56 per cent is in the Middle East, nearly 9 per cent in Africa, over 16 per cent in the USSR, Eastern Europe and China, and 6 per cent in North America. Western Europe, because of the oil discoveries in the North Sea, now has nearly 4 per cent of the total. The geographic balance of the proven reserves is 12 per cent for the western hemisphere and 88 per cent for the eastern.

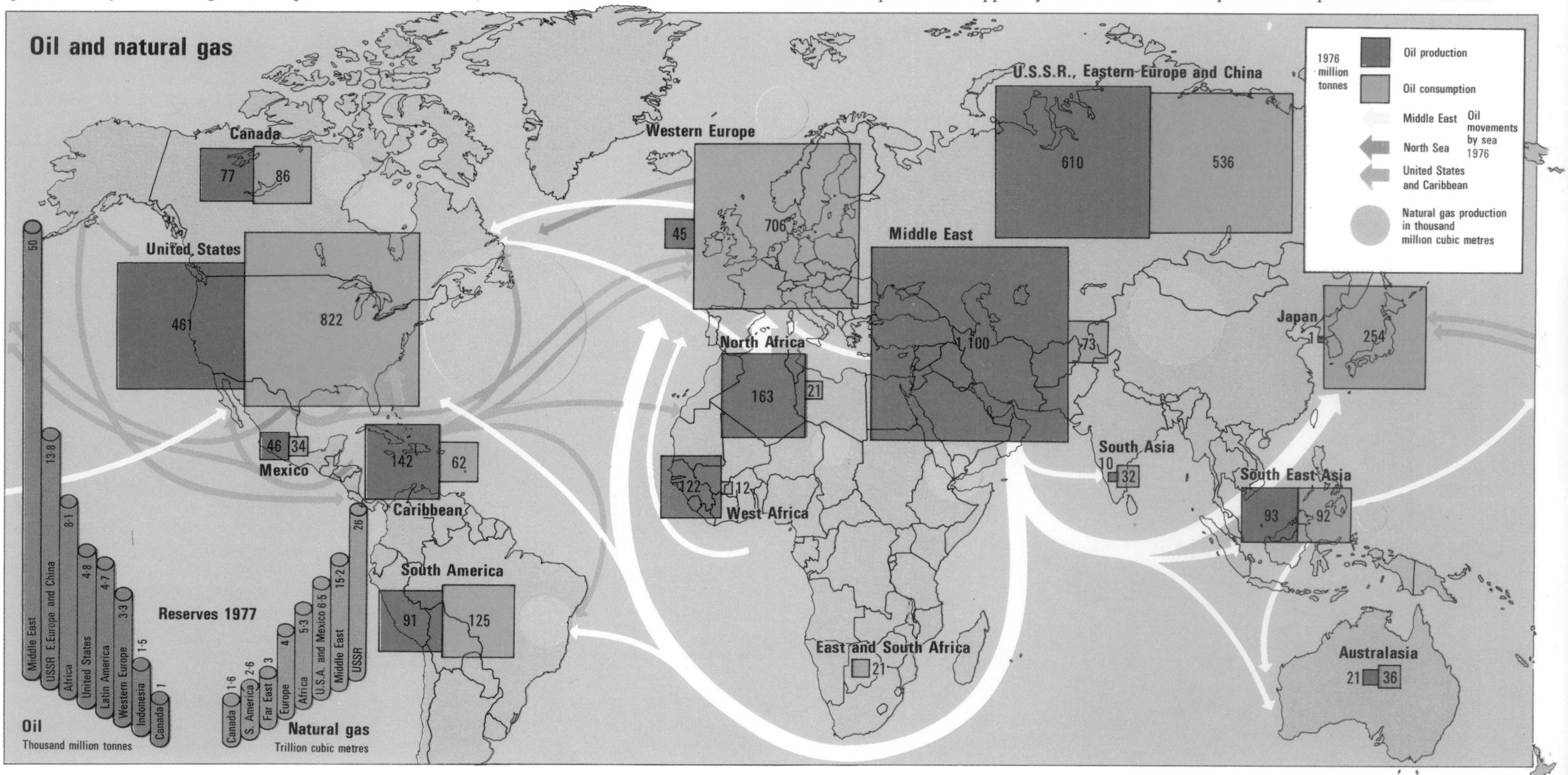

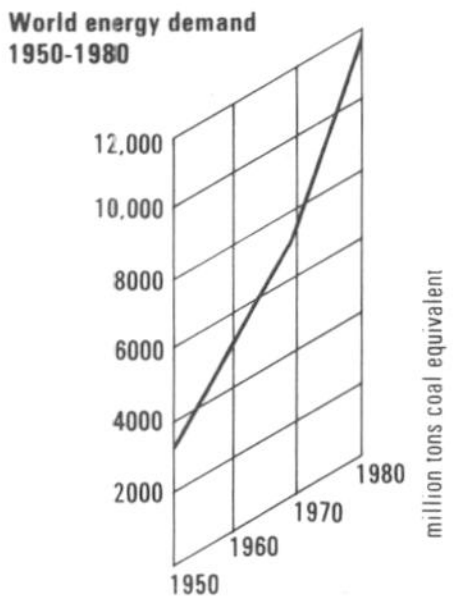

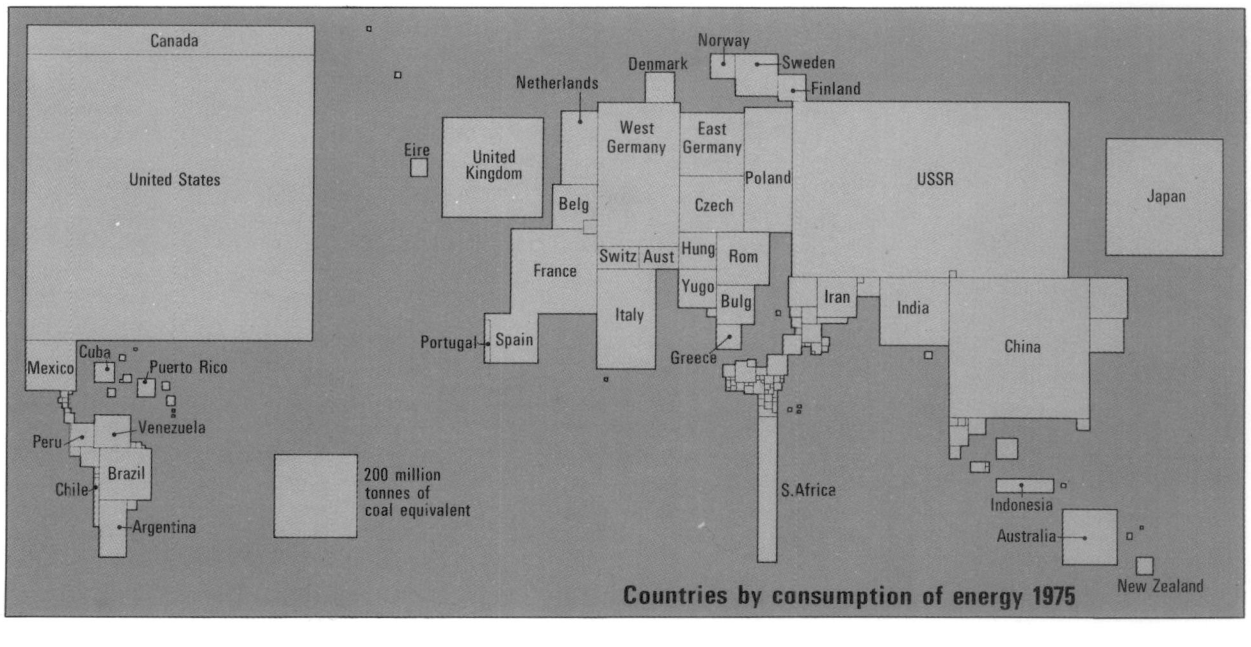

Energy consumption

Expressed in the standard measure of tonnes of coal equivalent, the world's demand for primary energy has attained a level of at least 7,000 million tce.

On current trends, projected future growth indicates a need for 11,000 million tce by the end of the present decade. All forms of energy will be required to make a high contribution, though oil is expected to remain the leading source. As the map illustrating the importance of oil to the world economy shows, annual consumption has reached over 2,936 million tonnes, and output more than 2,994 million tonnes; the balance represents stocks. This requires large-scale movements of crude oil and oil products between continents by sea and by pipeline.

More than $550,000 million will be required by the world oil industry in the coming decade to pay for exploration and development. The search for new sources ranges from the Arctic to the Yellow Sea, South China Sea and from north Africa to offshore south America. The emergence of economic nationalism in the Middle East, and the use of the price of oil as a political weapon that has disturbed traditional marketing, has coincided with the transformation of the United States from the status of oil exporter to oil importer. As unlimited oil imports into the 1980s cannot be assured, the United States is trying to reduce its imports from 9 million barrels a day in 1977 to 6 million a day in 1985, by stimulating domestic production and converting from oil to coal in many power stations. Without these measures imports of over 12 million barrels a day would be required in the 1980s to meet a demand of about 20 million barrels a day. In Western Europe demand could also double over the same period to a similar amount and Japanese oil requirements could increase from under 4 million barrels a day to over 10 million barrels a day.

Coal

World output of coal amounts to over 2,200 million tonnes a year. The leading industrialised countries of Western Europe produce over 300 million tonnes a year – equivalent to the total power station requirements of the United States where coal production totals about 550 million tonnes a year. Production of lignite, is nearly 867,000 tonnes a year. The main producers are East and West Germany and the USSR.

Coal is the fuel on which the industrial base of Europe and America was built. Cheap oil supplies in the 1950s and 1960s brought a sharp decline in production particularly in the older mining areas of Europe and North America. The prospect of a shortfall in oil supplies, coupled with difficulties in the development of nuclear power has brought new life to the coal industry. Fresh reserves are being developed in the United States and Europe. There are massive reserves of coal in the Soviet Union, North America and China.

These coal reserves are extremely large and sufficient to sustain international needs for at least 250 years on present projections of productive activity. Known economic reserves amount to one million million tonnes of which about 430,000 million tonnes could be mined under the prices and technology that are likely to exist in the 1970s and 1980s. Rates of extraction could be stepped up by improvements in mining techniques.

Only deposits that have been drilled and sampled are included in known reserves. Estimates do not include coal possibly existing in areas geologically favourable for the presence of coal. Ultimate global coal reserves probably exceed eight million million tonnes.

Natural gas

Natural gas, of which methane is the main constituent, is a highly efficient fuel now making an increasing contribution to energy resources. It produces twice the heat of town gas, is generally free of sulphur, and offers clean combustion.

Natural gas was first used in the United States in centres of population close to the gas fields. In Europe most gas was manufactured from coal. The change-over to natural gas came in the 1950s and 1960s with the discovery of reserves in France, Italy and in Holland. Britain is supplied from fields off the coast of East Anglia and from reserves in the northern part of the North Sea.

For decades large quantities of gas produced in association with oil was burned off because there was no way of moving it to the industrial centres. Development of long distance pipelining techniques and the movement of gas in liquefied form has opened up a small world trade in gas.

At the end of 1976 it was estimated that natural gas reserves round the world amounted to 2,325 million million cubic feet, with heavy concentrations in North America, the USSR and Asia.

Nuclear power

High hopes have been placed in the development of nuclear energy to provide the world with a new source of cheap and abundant power. Problems associated with the initial heavy costs of proving the first nuclear power stations against stiff competition from coal and oil have been overcome. Development is now being checked by opposition from environmentalists concerned at the safety aspects of reactors and the possibility that wider sales of nuclear power stations and their associated fuel enrichment and reprocessing facilities could lead to the proliferation of nuclear weapons.

Opposition is strongest in the United States and is reflected in the long delays in obtaining the necessary Government permits for new reactors. In 1977 there were 66 reactors operating in the USA with a capacity of 41,544 megawatts (9·4 per cent of total capacity). There are a further 142 reactors either under construction or planned.

France has one of the most ambitious nuclear power programmes. It plans to augment its network of 11 reactors producing 9 per cent of the nation's electricity, with 26 new reactors to produce over 70 per cent by 1985.

Development of nuclear power requires new techniques of production and control and fresh supplies of uranium. In non-Communist bloc countries, annual demand for uranium could reach 53,500 tonnes by 1980, roughly in line with production facilities. Reserves are two million tonnes reasonably capable of being recovered on present estimates of prices and demand.

Hydro-Electricity

The building of great dams, tidal barriers and other forms of man-made controls over sea and fresh waters have assisted in the slow but steady development of hydro-electrical generation. Areas well endowed with water resources have already benefited from one of the cheapest sources of power but opportunities for new hydro-electrical projects are limited.

The world's hydro-electricity represents one quarter of total electrical energy supplied – nearly twice as much as output from nuclear power stations. The big producers are North America and the Soviet Union, but within Europe hydro-electric stations are a major source of electricity. Scandinavia and Switzerland have the most highly developed water-power resources, followed by Italy and France.

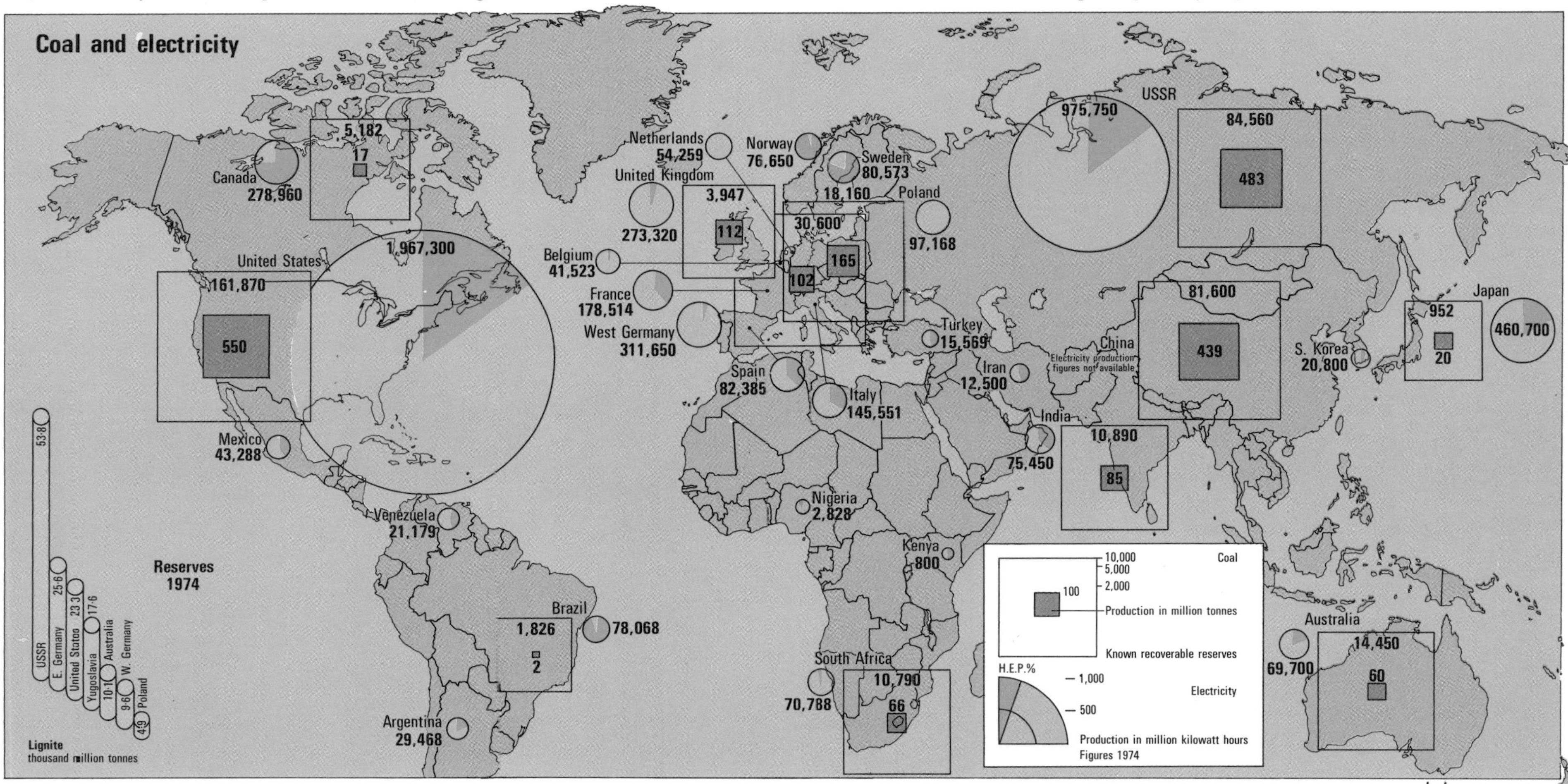

Nuclear energy

In 1977 there were 192 nuclear reactors in operation in 21 countries throughout the world with a capacity of 93,261 megawatts. A further seven countries have plans to become nuclear power producers. A total of 306 new reactors are either under construction or planned.

The quest for new forms of energy has also re-awakened interest in using geothermal power – hot steam from great depths below the earth's surface – to produce electricity. Italy leads the world in this field and has geothermal power stations with a capacity of 2,503 megawatts. There are also geothermal developments in the United States, Mexico, Japan and Iceland.

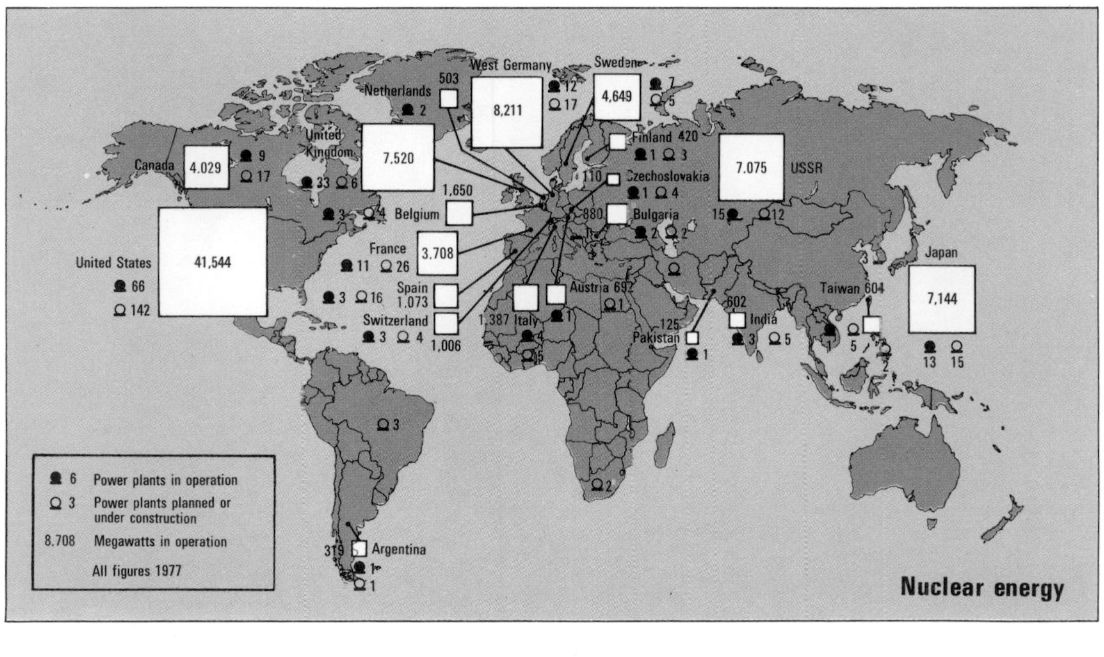

New needs, new sources

Great emphasis is now being placed on development of alternative sources of energy such as solar power, wind power and harnessing the energy contained in the tides. Although cheap to operate, the cost of developing efficient renewable energy systems is high and these sources are unlikely to make a significant contribution until the beginning of the next century.

Scientists are also working on prototype nuclear reactors that 'breed' more nuclear fuel than they consume, which would extend the life of world uranium reserves. Research is under way into the production of oil from coal, shale rocks and heavy tar sands, and into more effective and cleaner ways of burning coal in industry and in power stations. Even further into the future, scientists are working on ways to release energy from the hydrogen in sea water by the process of nuclear fusion. There is also a method of collecting solar energy by artificial satellite and transmitting it to Earth in the form of micro-waves.

Manufacturing industry

The wealth and economic influence of the world's richest nation, the United States of America, is derived from her factories and process plant. Although Europe has been the cradle of the industrial revolution, the New World has produced fresh concepts of manufacturing and the organisation of labour, establishing a chain of production and supply to which all advancing nations aspire, to raise their standards of material well-being. Whole new technologies have resulted from the constant application of the sciences to manufacturing. The consequence has been a worldwide urge to extract more materials to feed by mining or cultivation the industrial machines of all nations seeking to generate the economic wealth required to sustain their populations.

In the 20th century the determinents of economic power have been transformed. This transformation has been greatly affected by two world wars and periodic economic recessions. In the past few decades the rapid expansion in demand for material welfare and economic prosperity have brought an increase in world output of primary and secondary products to levels that have changed the living standards of whole populations. Wherever and however far back the roots of manufacturing, the fastest growth of production has taken place since the mid-fifties as nations embraced more productive concepts, selling their goods to each other and often specialising according to their indigenous skills or resources.

Manufacturing areas

The geographic concentration of world manufacturing power is well illustrated by the selected maps, which include crude steel production and motor vehicle engineering. The most striking development has been a significant shift of manufacturing power towards the Far East, related to the growth of industry in Japan and south-east Asia as well as the industrialisation of mainland China. However, this trend towards a wider distribution of industry has yet to show itself in Africa, the Middle East and to most of South America, areas which largely remain, in industrial terms, that of suppliers of raw materials and food.

Other important features reflected by the maps and in the closely related sections on world trade and energy supply are the re-emergence of Western Europe in the second half of this century, challenging the dominance of North America in global industry, and the establishment of the Soviet Union as a major industrialised nation. In steel manufacture, the Soviet Union and Japan have become main producers, though the former has yet to develop a substantial motor industry.

Textiles, electrical assembly, steel manufacturing, shipbuilding, and car production are now firmly established in the Far East, where output of certain goods has assumed dimensions of world importance in terms both of volume and commercial competitiveness.

Manufacturing growth

The most spectacular growth of production has taken place since the start of the 1960s, for by 1970 manufacturing output on a world basis had expanded by over 50 per cent, that for extractive industries by over 40 per cent, and these are to be compared with around 20 per cent for agricultural production.

Powering this industrial advance have been the factories and plant of North America, Western Europe and Japan. The installations grouped within the western trading nations have consequently lifted the gross domestic product by an average of nearly 5 per cent a year between 1960 and 1970.

The Western Nations, along with the Soviet Union, have made the major contribution to the world's increasing manufacturing capacity. That capacity, as reflected by actual output between 1960 and 1970, shows the following percentage rises in volume terms: light manufacturing 43 per cent; heavy manufacturing 58 per cent; food and drink 48 per cent; textiles 44 per cent; clothing and footwear 27 per cent; furniture and timber products 30 per cent; paper and printing 30 per cent; chemicals and fuel 95 per cent; basic metals 70 per cent; metal products 81 per cent.

Material possessions are greatest in the most industrialised nations. Using the measure of 1,000 inhabitants (taking no account of family groupings), there are over 523 telephones for this unit of population in the United States, 408 in Canada, and well over 200 in Japan and the United Kingdom, whereas Portugal has around 70 and Turkey only 12. With the same unit, there are around 400 television sets for the United States, over 260 for the United Kingdom, 200 in Japan and about 300 in Sweden, which enjoys one of the highest material standards of living.

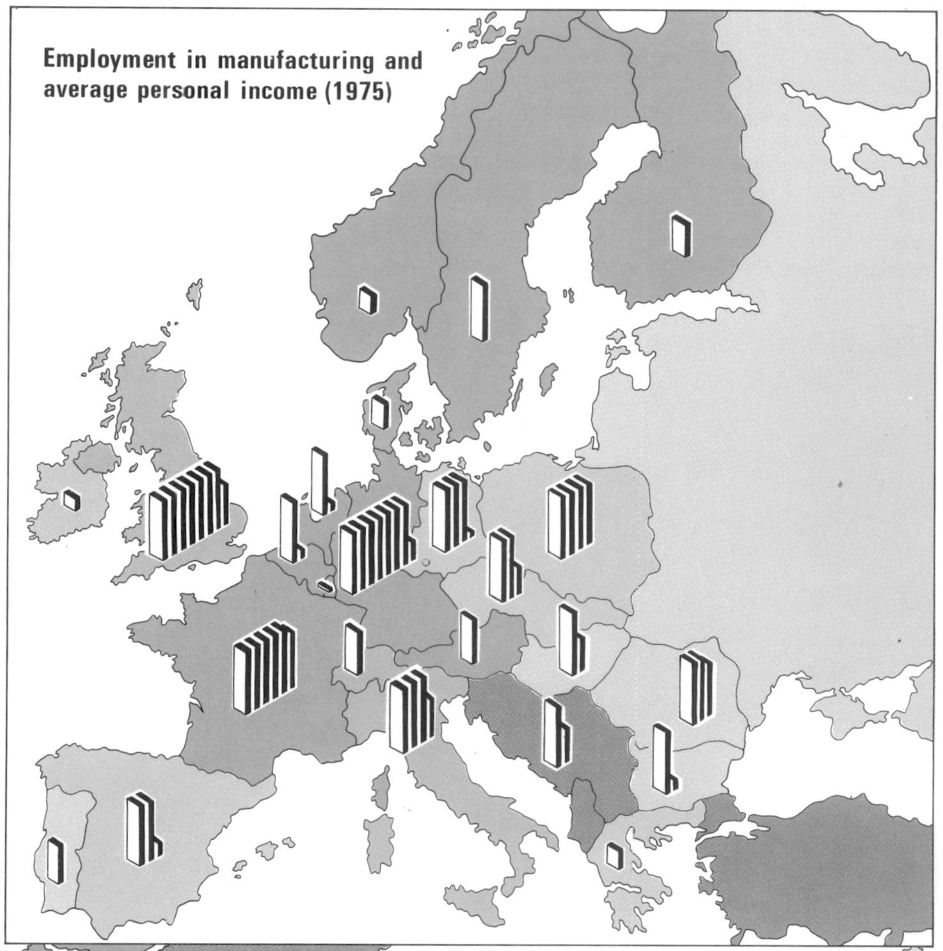
Employment in manufacturing and average personal income (1975)

The motor industry

The desire to own cars and replace them with new models has created one of the greatest and most economically important industries in the world, consuming vast quantities of steel and other materials and providing the backbone to satellite engineering industries. World car output is now over 25 million units with North America's huge assembly lines producing nearly a quarter and Western Europe and Japan much of the remainder. Assembly plants using imported vehicle components have sprung up in the developing world where demand has yet to be matched by the personal affluence needed to attain widespread ownership.

The significance of the motor manufacturing industry is reflected in the fact that many of the production companies have become the biggest corporations in the world. The second largest, General Motors of America, commands sales of over 35 billion dollars per year and has assets worth $21 billion. The largest of all is an oil and petroleum refining group, the Exxon Corporation whose supplies of oil to manufacturing industry are as important as the petrol needed to power car engines. United States motorists buy over 8 million new cars each year attracting imports from Western Europe and Japan, which has now built itself into the second largest manufacturer in the world, and the largest exporter. Overseas sales by Japanese manufacturers in 1974 totalled 1·8 million vehicles worth $3·5 billion. Japan now dominates the market for the small and medium car in most developing countries and has begun to make similar inroads into the European markets. Japanese dominance of the motor cycle industry is even more pronounced and in some European countries domestic producers have gone out of business in the face of Japanese imports.

In addition to passenger cars, commercial vehicles of all kinds from giant railer trucks and earth-moving equipment to farm tractors and delivery vans are produced in growing quantities. Annually the United States alone makes over 6,700,000 passenger cars and over two million vehicles other than cars. In Western Europe, France was the largest producer of passenger cars in 1975 with 2,951,000 units.

Steel

Like motor manufacturing, steel is an industry that is largely confined to the developed countries of the world. Three countries, the USA, the USSR and Japan, account for over half world production which in 1976 topped 661 million tonnes. Most European countries have steel industries. In Japan the growth of the steel industry

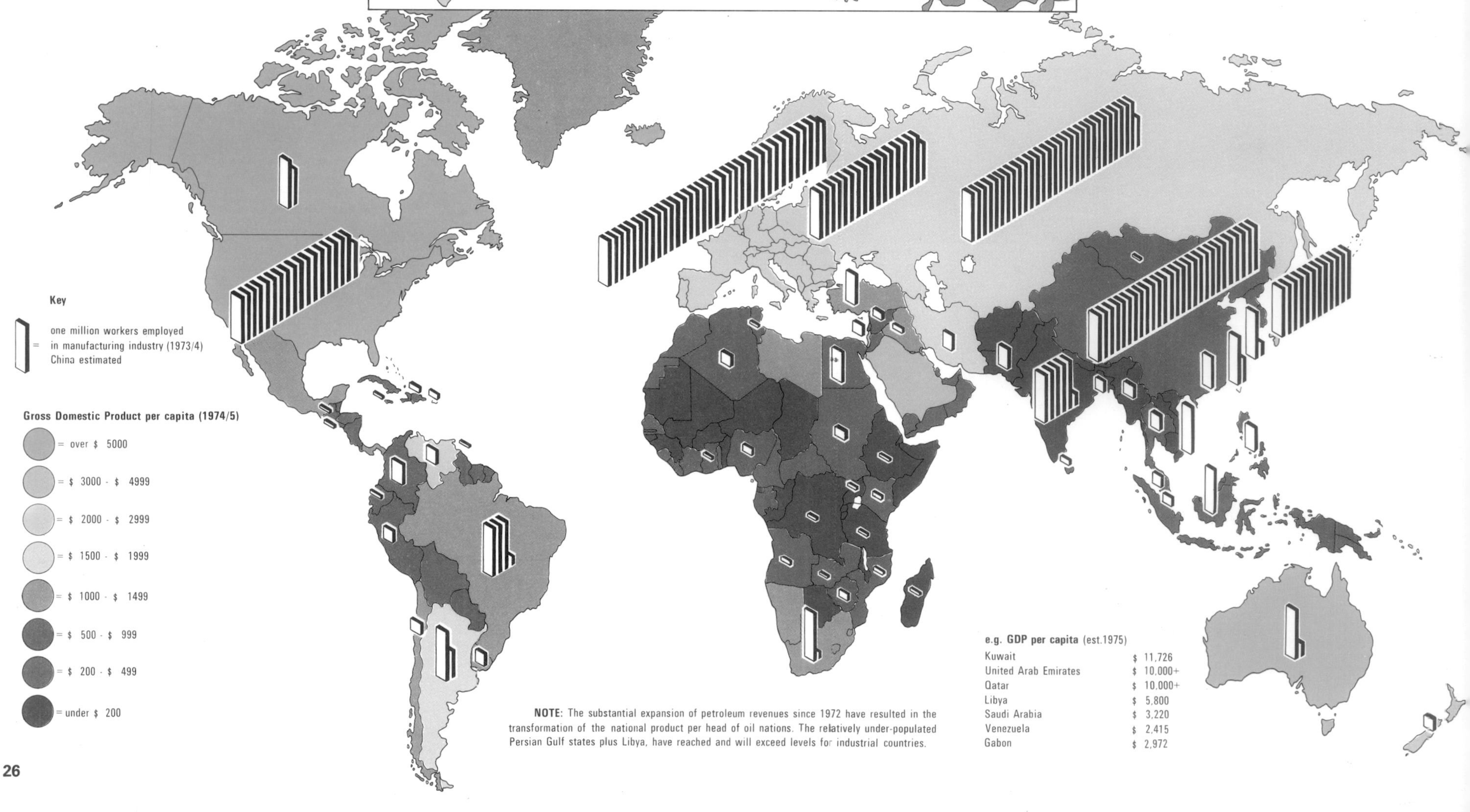
Key
= one million workers employed in manufacturing industry (1973/4) China estimated
Gross Domestic Product per capita (1974/5)
= over $ 5000
= $ 3000 - $ 4999
= $ 2000 - $ 2999
= $ 1500 - $ 1999
= $ 1000 - $ 1499
= $ 500 - $ 999
= $ 200 - $ 499
= under $ 200
NOTE: The substantial expansion of petroleum revenues since 1972 have resulted in the transformation of the national product per head of oil nations. The relatively under-populated Persian Gulf states plus Libya, have reached and will exceed levels for industrial countries.
e.g. GDP per capita (est.1975)
Kuwait $ 11,726
United Arab Emirates $ 10,000+
Qatar $ 10,000+
Libya $ 5,800
Saudi Arabia $ 3,220
Venezuela $ 2,415
Gabon $ 2,972

has paralleled that of its motor manufacturers. Since 1960 Japan has more than trebled its steel output using the very latest giant, continuous process mills and modern furnaces to make products so cheaply that they can be sold across oceans at prices keenly competitive with locally produced steel.

During the period 1970 to 1975 the regional share of world production changed significantly. North America's share decreased by 3½%, and that of Western Europe by 4%. Despite Japanese growth, Asia's share of world production increased by only 2½% during the five years. The greatest increase was that of the USSR and Eastern Europe with over 7% growth.

World trade in steel products of all kinds has risen more than five-fold since the beginning of the 1950s with the pattern of supply shifting according to competitive conditions as well as to such factors as deep water ports to take the largest bulk ore carriers. These are now being constructed in many parts of the world.

Shipbuilding

Japanese shipbuilders have also benefitted from the availability of cheap steel just as a well organised steel industry led to the building of a thriving motor industry. Launchings from Japanese yards in 1973 totalled well over 16·5 million tonnes of shipping compared with about three million tonnes by each of the other main shipbuilding nations, Germany, Sweden and Norway. The fortunes of the world's shipbuilders were based on an apparently unending demand for more and larger oil tankers. But after oil prices quadrupled in 1973 and 1974 the world demand for oil declined sharply. Millions of tonnes of tankers left without cargoes were laid up indefinitely. The flow of orders for new tonnage practically ceased. As a response to these changing forces shipbuilders have drastically pruned their work forces and production facilities and are looking carefully at a variety of new uses for the shipyards such as building oil platforms or even prefabricated houses.

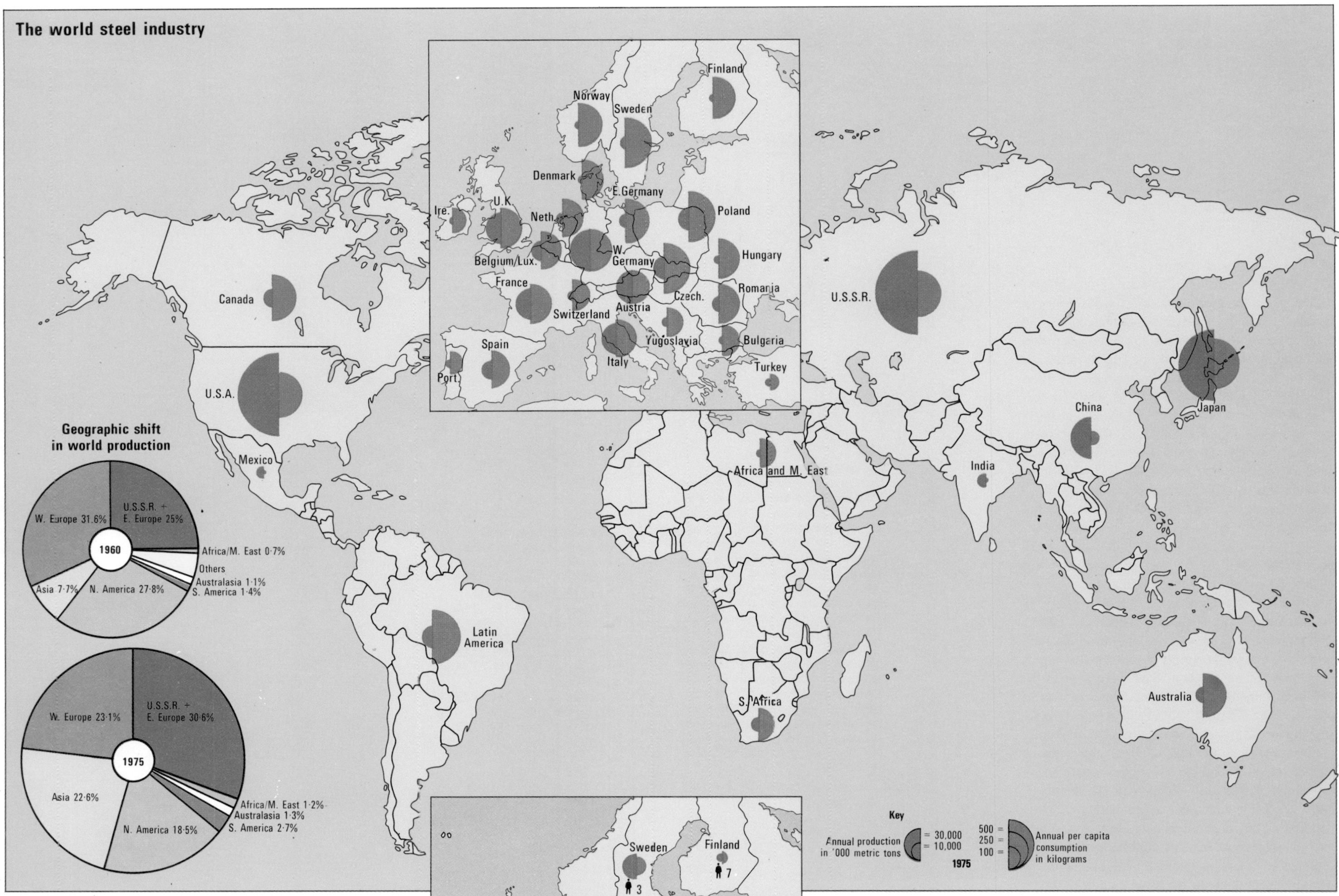

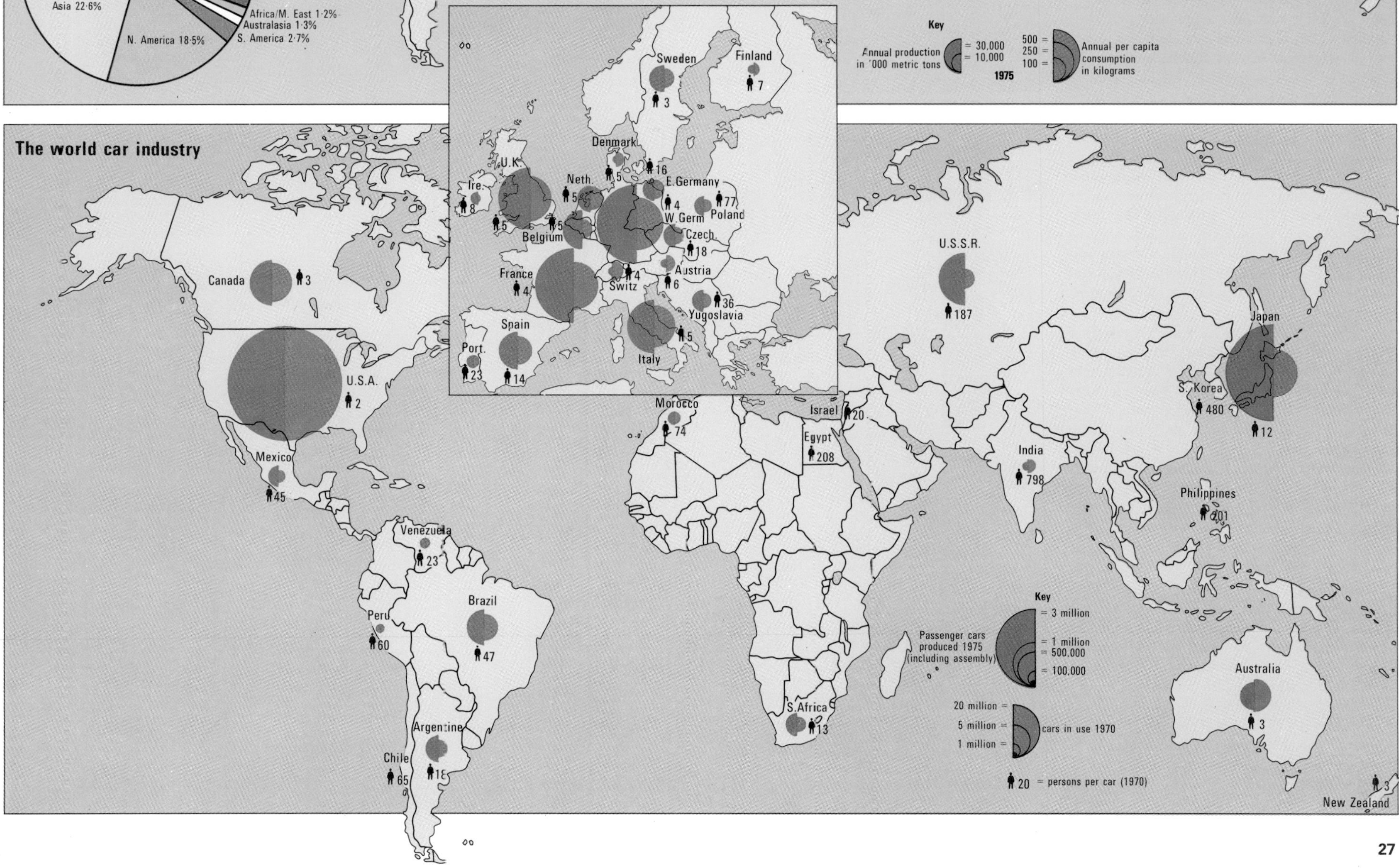

Patterns of world trade

The trade of the U.S.A.

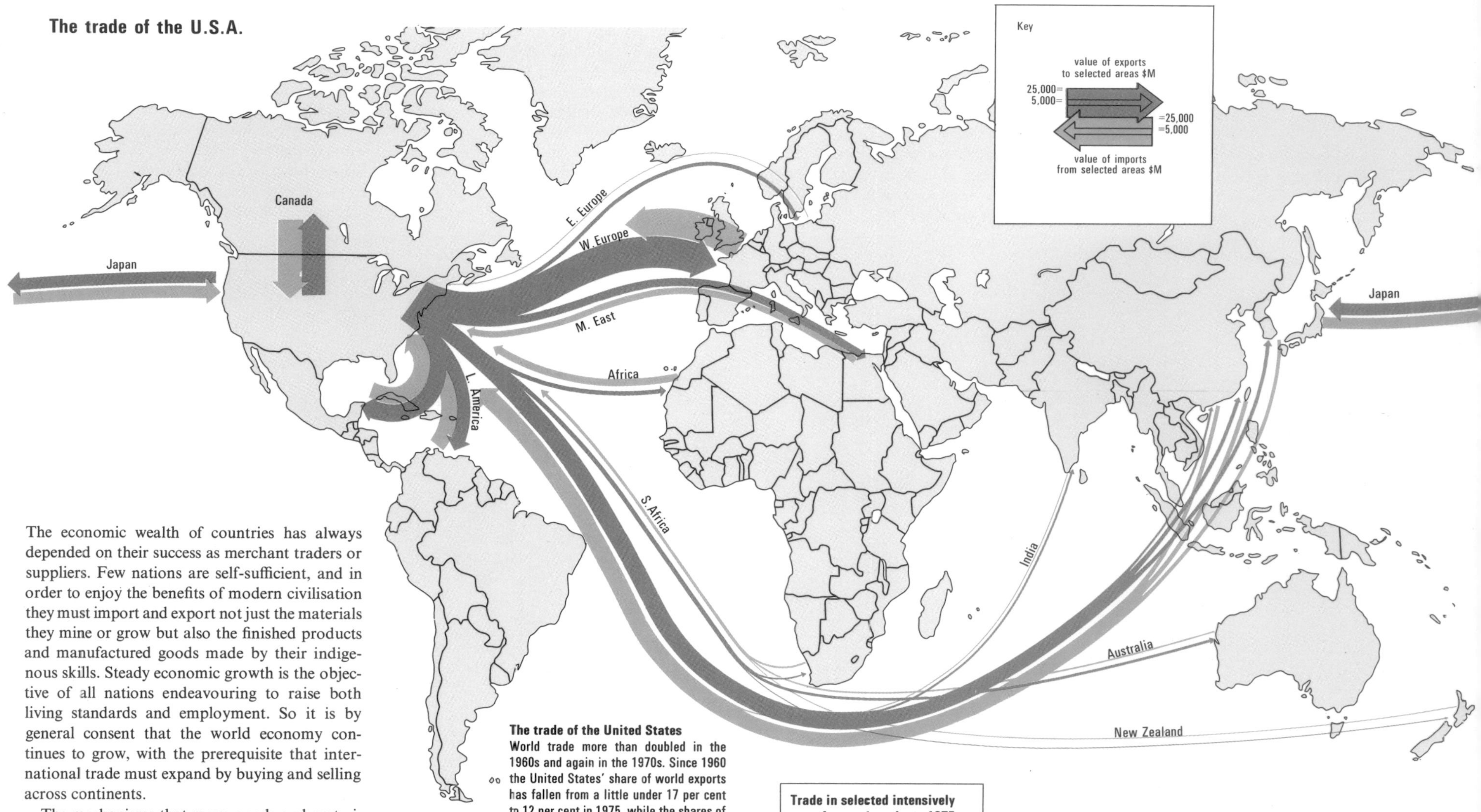

The trade of the United States
World trade more than doubled in the 1960s and again in the 1970s. Since 1960 the United States' share of world exports has fallen from a little under 17 per cent to 12 per cent in 1975, while the shares of Western Europe and Japan virtually doubled in the same period. Those of the developing countries declined heavily (their trade depends on foodstuffs and raw materials, for which demand rises only slowly).

Nearly one third of United States exports, as indicated by the maps, is shipped to Western Europe, another 20 per cent is moved across the border to Canada, and nearly 9 per cent goes to Japan. In return, some 20 per cent of United States imports come from Western Europe, 11 per cent from Japan, and 26 per cent from Canada.

Trade in selected intensively manufactured products 1975
(all figures in $M)

Product	*Export*	*Import*
Food beverages and tobacco	16,800	9,130
Crude materials excluding fuels	10,730	5,750
Mineral fuels	4,470	27,670
Chemicals	8,710	3,570
Machinery and transport	45,710	24,290
Other manufactured goods	16,610	22,750

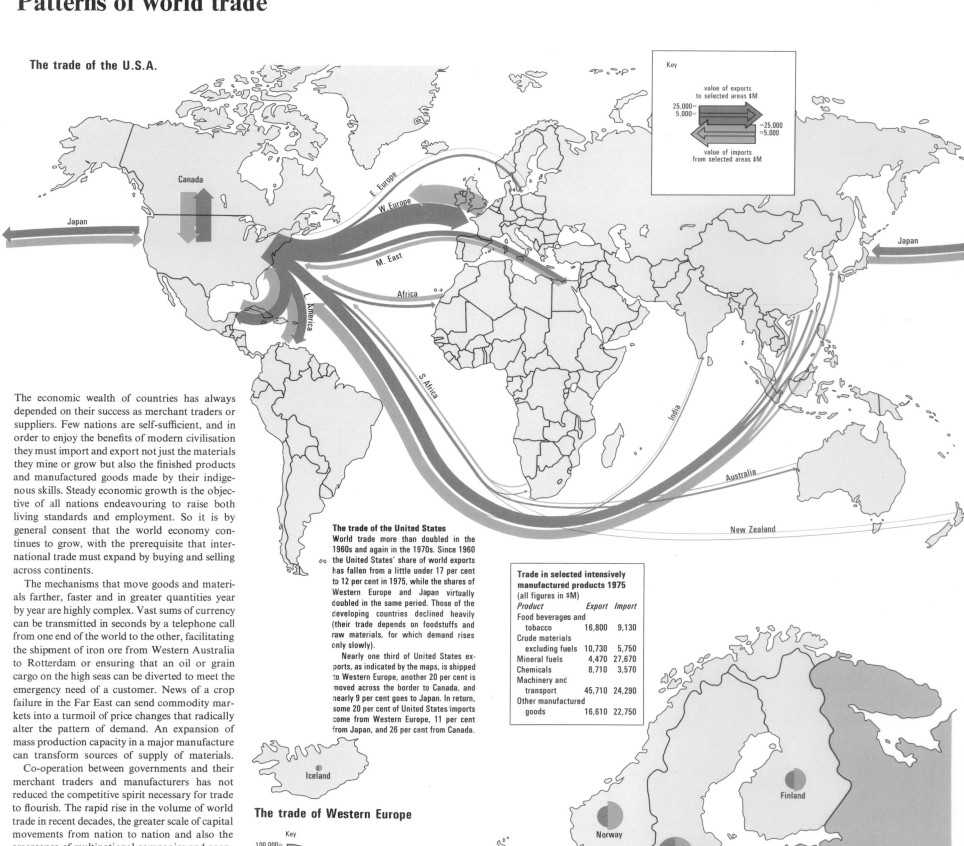

The economic wealth of countries has always depended on their success as merchant traders or suppliers. Few nations are self-sufficient, and in order to enjoy the benefits of modern civilisation they must import and export not just the materials they mine or grow but also the finished products and manufactured goods made by their indigenous skills. Steady economic growth is the objective of all nations endeavouring to raise both living standards and employment. So it is by general consent that the world economy continues to grow, with the prerequisite that international trade must expand by buying and selling across continents.

The mechanisms that move goods and materials farther, faster and in greater quantities year by year are highly complex. Vast sums of currency can be transmitted in seconds by a telephone call from one end of the world to the other, facilitating the shipment of iron ore from Western Australia to Rotterdam or ensuring that an oil or grain cargo on the high seas can be diverted to meet the emergency need of a customer. News of a crop failure in the Far East can send commodity markets into a turmoil of price changes that radically alter the pattern of demand. An expansion of mass production capacity in a major manufacture can transform sources of supply of materials.

Co-operation between governments and their merchant traders and manufacturers has not reduced the competitive spirit necessary for trade to flourish. The rapid rise in the volume of world trade in recent decades, the greater scale of capital movements from nation to nation and also the emergence of multinational companies and agencies have, nevertheless, made national economies more interdependent. Political sovereignty often masks the dependence of countries one on another as traders or suppliers. Technology, worldwide standardisation of man's material needs, a growing demand for the Earth's natural resources and the application of new agricultural and industrial methods have served to promote the expansion in world trade.

The capacity of nations to import to meet the requirements of their citizens, rises as living standards – measured in material possessions and services – improve. But nations that buy must have means to pay: an acceptable form of payment may be goods for barter or money that is convertible according to the importer's economic strength. All international trading nations need to balance their books, and the task of central bankers in keeping international trade flowing is crucial. The financial systems are as vital as communications. Their effectiveness is the preoccupation of economists and bankers round the world.

Industrialisation

The rebuilding of economies after the second world war has been characterised by rapid industrialisation, much under United States leadership, and the wider spread of economic nationalism created with the birth of many new nations once heavily dependent on American, British or French mercantile power and political rule. Efficiency in mass production and technological competence have a profound effect on the nature and routing of world trade. The rebuilding of

The trade of Western Europe

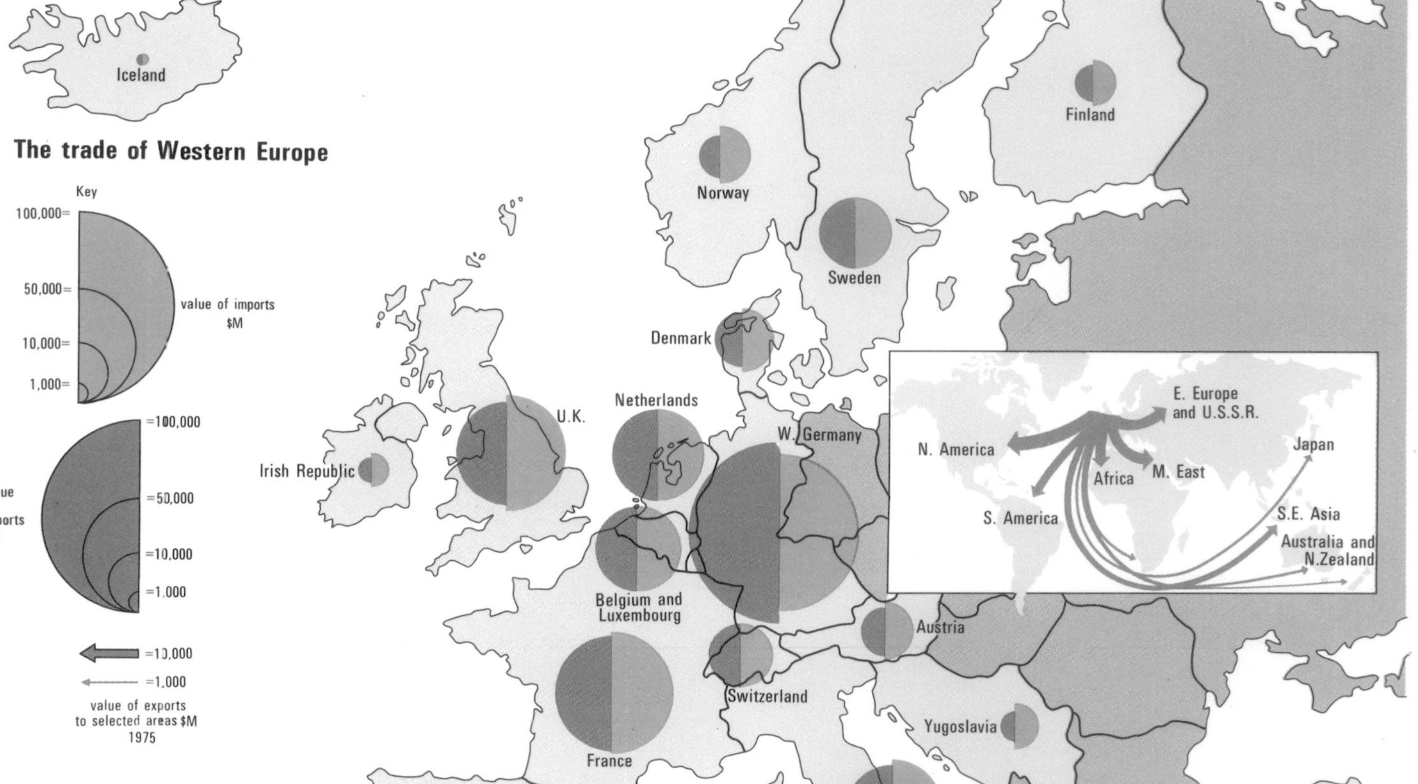

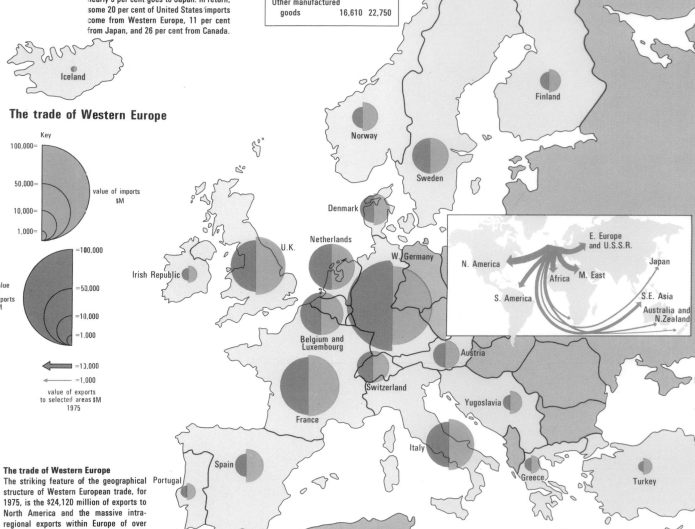

The trade of Western Europe
The striking feature of the geographical structure of Western European trade, for 1975, is the $24,120 million of exports to North America and the massive intra-regional exports within Europe of over $364,930 million. The scale of internal European exporting is due to the development of the European Economic Community (EEC) and the European Free Trade Area (EFTA). The United Kingdom has maintained preferential trade agreements with her Commonwealth.

the Japanese and German economies has been accomplished by each country devoting a high proportion of its national efforts to selling their goods in world markets.

While the United States still accounts for 40 per cent of the non-communist world's production, the European Economic Community and Japan have become major centres of economic power and pace-setters for competition in international markets. Half the world's seaborne tanker and dry cargo shipments are now unloaded in Western Europe, and more than a quarter discharges in the Far East, with Japan at the centre of activity.

Japan

If present patterns of growth stay as they are, the Japanese may surpass the Soviet Union's output in the next 25 years and draw close to that of the United States. In the 15 years from 1960 she has doubled her share of world exports to reach over 7 per cent. Her rate of growth in world trade is about twice as fast as the international average. A substantial competitive endeavour in world markets – she is a leading exporter of ships, electrical goods, fish and motor vehicles – is vital to pay for heavy imports. Japan has to buy half her raw materials abroad to fuel her growth.

United States

With the largest economy in the world and a currency essential for the effective financing of continent-to-continent trade, the USA contributed a vast sum of her national wealth to rebuilding the war-torn countries of the western world. This has required running a balance of payments deficit in virtually every year since the end of the forties. These deficits are now growing to unmanageable proportions. Unlike the industrial countries of Europe and Japan, the United States until the late 1960s, had been self-sufficient in crude oil. The entry of the USA into the world oil markets has helped to trigger the huge increases in oil prices. With over 40 per cent of US oil requirements met from foreign sources in 1977, the true deficit suddenly rose to $40 billion from only $5 billion in the previous year.

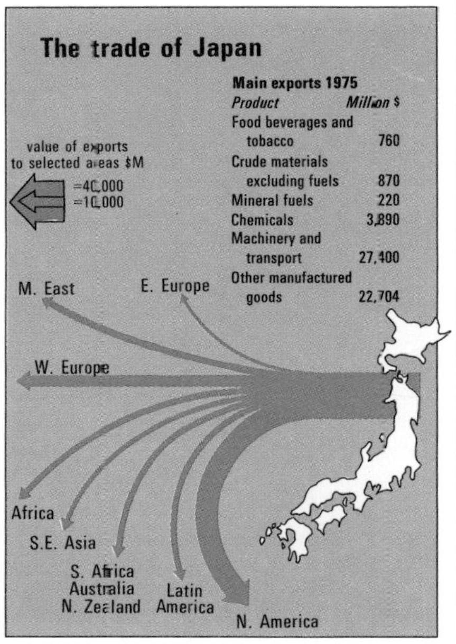

The geographical distribution of Japan's exports is an interesting feature of contemporary world trade. She maintains a firm relationship with industrialised markets and developing regions.

About 22 per cent of Japanese exports by value were sent to the USA and Canada in 1975. A further 14·5 per cent went to the markets of South East Asia and the Middle East, 8 per cent to Africa and 8·5 per cent to Latin America. Western Europe took 14·5 per cent of her exports, while Australasia received 1·5 per cent, and Eastern Europe 4 per cent.

Japan's exports in 1975 were $55,844 million compared with $19,318 million in 1970 and $4,050 million in 1960.

In the 15 years from 1960 to 1975 United States imports from Japan surged from just over one billion dollars to over 11 billion dollars. Initially Japanese imports of US goods lagged well behind but now US exports in 1975 totalled $9·35 billion – halving the deficit of a few years previously.

For 35 years the USA has sought to reduce artificial barriers to international trade, culminating in the famous Kennedy Round of tariff reductions of the sixties. Her gross domestic product is now annually exceeding $1,000 billion, making the nation the richest in the world. Exports in 1976 totalled over $107 billion. Huge sums are transferred every year to developing countries in aid and investment along with human skills and technology. Additionally, the world's most powerful single economy carries a disproportionate share of western defence costs. The attainment of American accord with China and further development of trade with the USSR are seen as the most encouraging factors for the future of international economic co-operation.

Western Europe

The nations of Western Europe are the most potent force in world mercantile trade. Their exports have risen from $52 billion in 1960 to $295 billion by 1976, led during this period by the EEC founder members and the nations of the former European Free Trade Area.

Enlargement of the EEC to 9 nations has provided an economic grouping with a GDP of around $1,000 billion, fast approaching that of the United States ($1,295 billion in 1973). EEC exports in 1973, including intra-area trade, were valued as $210 billion, $149 billion going to countries outside the Community. Her merchant fleet is four times the size of the USA's, and vehicle output is nearly 10 million units annually.

The growth of European exporting power has been equally spectacular, assisted greatly by American-inspired reductions in import tariffs, direct financial aid for industrial reconstruction, and the transfer of technological know-how.

The result has been a transformation of monetary power as well as industrial strength. This has reduced the role of the American dollar and the British pound sterling in supplying the foreign exchange for the finance of world trade. The dollar, of course, remains the standard common currency for the convertibility of money. But this has required new alignments of exchange values to ensure that national monies reflect the strength of nations as international traders as well as the size of their gross national product and stocks of gold.

World trade

An International Monetary Fund helps central bankers to keep money working as hard as the aircraft and ships that ply between markets. United Nations agencies, organisations set up for economic co-operation, and a network of commodity arrangements framed for orderly marketing of essential materials have all been the means for averting chaos and correcting the economic disruption that market forces may create. Whatever the periodic difficulties, such as monetary and materials crises or unfair trade practices, the overall achievement has been the expansion of the volume of world trade by 10 per cent every year to the end of the sixties.

This growth, the aid to international economic development, has not corrected the imbalance between rich and poor countries. In the sixties, the export trade of industrialised countries grew by about 164 per cent, that of developing nations by only 99 per cent. This disparity reflects the rapid growth of trade between developed countries due to the creation of special groups of countries with mutually advantageous arrangements for economic expansion. The EEC and EFTA have been prime examples where intra-group exports have risen sharply.

Prior to enlargement, the EEC was assessed as supplying 29 per cent of world exports, but in fact, half the trade was conducted between the member nations. The disparity can be illustrated by the fact that trade among the main industrial countries of the world grew from $54 billion in 1960 to $161 billion in 1970, while that between developing countries and the industrial countries went up from $19 billion to $40 billion.

Record rates of inflation, higher oil payments and the demise of fixed exchange rates cast their shadow over world trade midway through the seventies. The total value of world exports in 1975 was $567 billion compared with $312 billion in 1970 and $128 billion in 1960. This impressive figure must be treated with caution, for it reflects a sustained world-wide rise in prices, in particular the huge increase in oil bills.

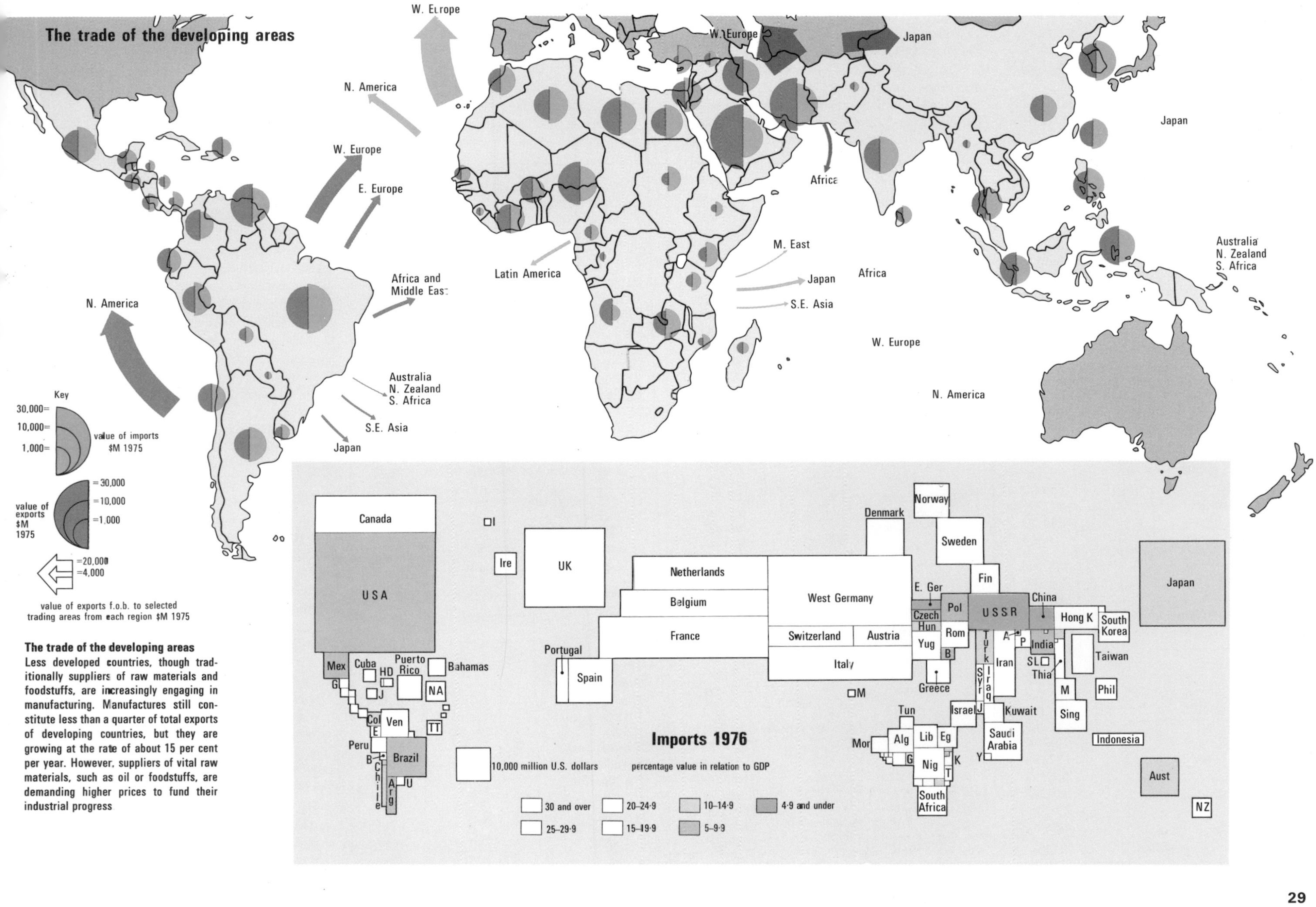

The trade of the developing areas
Less developed countries, though traditionally suppliers of raw materials and foodstuffs, are increasingly engaging in manufacturing. Manufactures still constitute less than a quarter of total exports of developing countries, but they are growing at the rate of about 15 per cent per year. However, suppliers of vital raw materials, such as oil or foodstuffs, are demanding higher prices to fund their industrial progress

World Tourism

Travelling for pleasure provides the vast majority of people with their only experience of other countries. The number of such travellers is increasing so much that the tourist trade – which transports, accommodates, feeds and entertains them – is now one of the world's largest industries and is growing internationally at a very fast rate. By 1985, it is calculated that 320 million people will be travelling abroad for pleasure, spending approximately $60,000 million in the process.

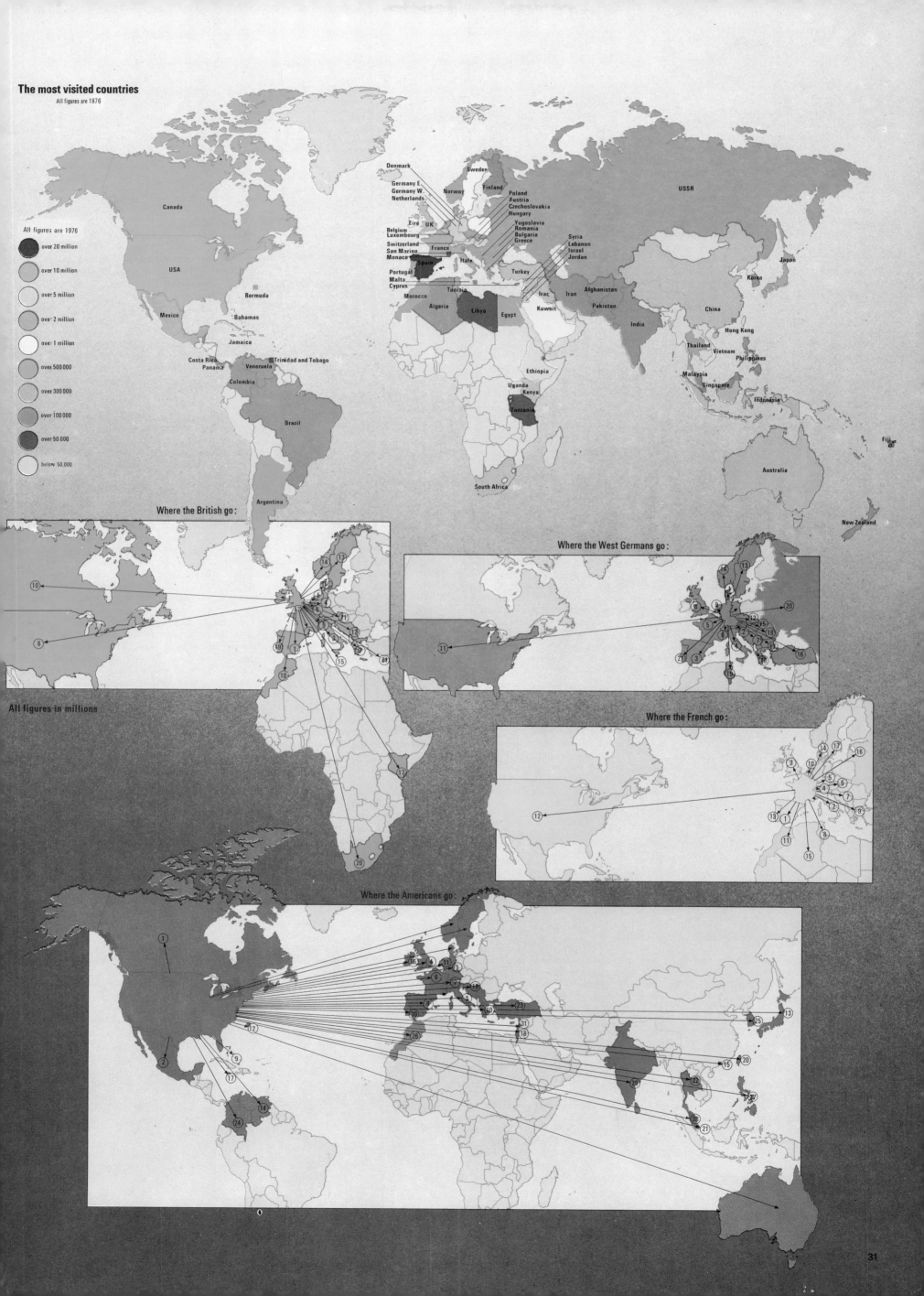

Already, income from tourism is vital to the national economies of scores of countries. Spain, the most visited land, earned $3,083 million from her foreign visitors in 1976. Tourism has become the leading foreign currency earner for Kenya, bringing in more funds ($68·50 million) than the export of coffee. Canada earns more ($1,930 million) from tourism than from wheat exports.

The growth of tourism

For most of the last thirty years world tourism has grown steadily, other than where wars or major civil commotion has intervened. In 1973 some 200 million tourists grossed around $30,000 million. This fell in 1974 but by 1976 the recovery world-wide was complete and the numbers had risen to 222 million, grossing $45,000 million. That recovery has been maintained, and in many countries accelerated. Portugal is a good example of a country whose tourism was very badly affected by the political events of 1974 (and 1975) but by 1977 it had substantially recovered.

The maps which accompany these notes show clearly which countries receive most holiday visitors and, to a certain extent, who goes where. They cannot show why such pleasure journeys are made – why Spain stands well above all others, for example. One can appreciate that France and Italy are popular, but it takes more than guesswork to establish how Britain has managed to build up its tourist industry to such an extent that it now exceeds that of Switzerland, which has a much longer tradition in tourism.

Contemporary tourism

To some extent the present situation is a reflection of the past – those days of the Grand Tour when no man of substance could consider himself educated without the experience of that journey round selected European cities. It is reflected, too, from those times when travellers discovered the medicinal benefits of certain spas, or the climatic benefits of wintering on the French Riviera. There are small traces, in today's pattern, of those first organized holidays from Britain to the continent which bore the stamp of Mr Thomas Cook well over a century ago.

The current map of world tourist movement has, however, mainly been drafted by the post-war development of the travel industry, particularly within and from Europe. It is an industry which in the main sets out to sell a low cost 'package' of holiday pleasures, and the huge attraction of Spain is the most obvious symbol of its success. This overall success has continued in spite of the slump from the record breaking total of 30 million tourists of 1973 which resulted from the fuel and economic crises and of the political changes, which were followed by steep inflation. The upward curve was once more noticeable in 1976–77.

Spain's success as Europe's main tourist country stemmed from its low cost of living in the 1960s and early 1970s, its high sunshine record, its cheapness of land and subsequent building costs, an availability of inexpensive labour and the active encouragement of tourist investment by the government. The French provide the largest number of visitors to Spain, most coming on camping or caravan holidays, with the West Germans in second place, having overtaken the British in third place. However, holidaymakers from the UK constitute the largest number of foreigners visiting the country by air and indeed it was the British who 'invented' the air package holiday in the 1950s. Even with the rapidly increased costs in Spain which started in 1976 and accelerated in 1977, it remains the most popular country if for no other reason than that it is the only nation in Europe which can cope with the millions who seek the sun mostly on modest budgets.

Canadian tourism

The reasons behind Canada's high position in tourism tables are rather different. In 1976 some 32·2 million visitors (including a high proportion of day visitors) came from the USA. Although this was a drop from the previous year of about 2·4 million they actually brought in more money, largely because of rising costs, the total being $1,346 million. The proximity of the USA, the minimal border formalities and the lack of a language problem (even with the strong French-Canadian movement) 'sold' Canada to the leisure traveller from south of the 49th parallel.

Why do other nationals visit Canada? The next largest number (408,176) crossed the Atlantic from the UK, and clearly demonstrates the importance of historic ties as well as 'family' tourism. Travelling for a holiday with relatives, visiting sons or daughters who have married and moved away, usually means that one remains, in effect, within one's own country. In the case of the UK and countries such as Canada, Australia or New Zealand – and to a lesser extent the USA – such journeys show up on the international statistical tables.

United States tourism

Apart from its 'cross border' neighbours Canada and Mexico, which in 1976 accounted for over 12 million visitors to the country, the USA has only moved into the big international tourism league in the last ten years or so, largely due to two things – the development of cheap air travel and the active promotion of both government and private enterprise (the airlines in particular) to encourage foreigners to visit there. But the air fares motivation has been the greater, coupled with the increased affluence of Europe – and Japan. The USA is still well 'in the red' on her tourism account as her citizens in 1976 spent $1,076 million more on holidays and travel outside the country than incoming tourists earned for her.

A small example of how patterns can change is to be seen in the Caribbean, where for some time the tourist scene has been dominated by visitors from the USA and Canada. In Barbados for instance, nearly 130,000 of the island's 224,314 visitors in 1976 came from those two countries. However, the increasing availability of moderately-priced package holidays based on charter flights, from Britain and West Germany, are bringing more of a European influence to bear and changing the established tourist situation.

European tourism

The popularity of France and Italy lies in the history and cultural tradition of those countries and their great cities. Art treasures, architectural masterpieces and religious buildings are tremendous attractions, as are the gastronomic and wine-growing traditions. Italy and France have also sought to attract the mass market tourists, with such developments as the resorts of the Italian Adriatic coast and the grander projects in the south-west of France.

The UK has only comparatively recently achieved a high place in the list of 'Most visited countries' but in 1976 earned about $3,600 million from foreign visitors. This figure is over $500 million more than the total tourist income for Spain in the same year in spite of the fact that the number of visitors to that country was nearly 26 million while to the UK it was just over 10 million. In tourism, numbers alone do not by any means indicate the true economic effect.

One must keep in mind the fact that international tourism includes travel within the same region. A breakdown of statistics supplied by various European countries shows how large a part their immediate neighbours play in the flow of visitors. Such regional movements account for 88 per cent of the total international tourist traffic in Europe. The detailed 'Who goes where' statistics illustrate this vividly: the British travelling to Spain, France, Ireland, Italy and Germany; the French and the Germans preferring similar European destinations.

Motivation and fulfilment

Overall, the simple desire to take a holiday in totally different surroundings, preferably at low cost and quite often to some large resort on the sea coast, lies behind most tourist journeys. This is the basic reason why people go where they do. Although large functional and to some extent 'artificial' resorts will continue to be very popular and account for the majority of holiday destinations, there is a definite trend away from this by the more discriminating (and often the more frequently travelled) holidaymaker to seek his or her vacation in more genuine surroundings. And the younger generation are much less inclined to be 'packaged' than were the holidaymakers of the expansionist 1960s. Mass travel will undoubtedly continue to grow but along with it will be an increasing desire for independence and less regimentation.

It is clear that tourist travel will do more to shape the way we explore our world than anything else. It will also do more to shape the world we explore. Its future can be predicted, for the forces that control it are known. First, an increase in available leisure time will be matched by an increase of per capita income as well as improvements in transportation systems. Increased leisure time is already having an effect on the lives of the workers in the developed industrial societies. Throughout Europe, as well as North America, the growth of second holidays has been very rapid. As automation of the productive processes becomes more widespread one must pay great heed to predictions such as those of Herman Kahn of the Hudson Institute, who sees the post-industrial society requiring its citizens to work on just 147 days in a year – with a four-day working week and 13 weeks of annual holidays. Leisure in the form of earlier retirement is another inevitability.

Transport developments

Improvements in transport systems are already having an effect on tourism. The importance of the motoring holidaymaker is clearly appreciated by those responsible for the long-term planning of tourist facilities. In Europe one can point to the enormous growth in car ferry services between the UK and the continent as evidence of the importance of motoring, and to the highway construction programmes designed to speed holiday motorists to the pleasure areas.

Railway and road systems carry the largest amount of traffic on short and medium distances, and are being re-organized and expanded to cope with the demands of the next 20 years.

The next 20 years

The development and expansion of air transport will continue to be the most important influencing factor. The increasing use of larger aircraft purely for leisure travel will continue in spite of greatly increased fuel costs. The blurring of the lines between 'scheduled' and 'charter' services will accelerate and it could well be that by the mid-1980s the difference between the two, other than on certain business routes, will be academic.

The last 25 years have seen the industry of tourism grow in size and strength and, at the same time, a greater involvement by governments in the regulation of tourism. The day of 'laissez faire' in tourism is past. The World Tourism Organisation with its HQ in Madrid will increase its influence particularly with the developing nations. Without proper planning and safeguards for the environment in its widest sense, tourism can be a blight. But with the full co-operation on both governmental and private enterprise levels tourism can be of immense benefit financially, commercially, psychologically and also to understanding better the ways and nature of people the world over.

Where the British go

1	Spain	2,170,000
2	France	2,036,000
3	Italy	690,000
4	West Germany	673,000
5	Netherlands	531,000
6	Belgium	472,000[1]
7	Greece	356,000
8	United States	346,000
9	Switzerland	252,000
10	Canada	200,000
11	Austria	197,000
12	Yugoslavia	196,000
13	Sweden	160,000
14	Norway	150,000
15	Malta	125,000
16	Denmark	109,000
17	Kenya	105,000
18	Morocco	95,000
19	Portugal	85,000
20	South Africa	55,000[2]
21	Cyprus	34,000

Where the Americans go

1	Canada	11,641,000
2	Mexico	2,715,000
3	Italy	1,845,000
4	United Kingdom	1,490,000
5	West Germany	1,232,000
6	France	1,055,000
7	Switzerland	845,000
8	Spain	793,000
9	The Bahamas	667,000
10	Greece	493,000
11	Netherlands	424,000
12	Bermuda	391,000
13	Japan	277,000
14	Venezuela	266,000
15	Hong Kong	238,000
16	Ireland	231,000
17	Jamaica	229,000
18	Israel	214,000
19	Yugoslavia	189,000
20	Taiwan	125,000[3]
21	Singapore	122,000
22	Thailand	116,000
23	Turkey	114,000
24	Colombia	103,000
25	Korea	102,000
26	Morocco	97,000
27	Philippines	93,000
28	Malaysia	68,000
29	India	62,000
30	Portugal	56,000

Where the French go

1	Spain	9,476,000
2	Italy	1,678,000
3	United Kingdom	1,171,000
4	Switzerland	644,000
5	West Germany	579,000
6	Austria	385,000
7	Yugoslavia	380,000
8	Tunisia	371,000
9	Greece	311,000
10	Netherlands	251,000
11	Morocco	225,000
12	United States	217,000
13	Portugal	114,000
14	Denmark	107,000
15	Algeria	83,000
16	USSR	71,000
17	Sweden	59,000

Where the West Germans go

1	Denmark	13,307,000[4]
2	Austria	7,369,000
3	Spain	3,885,000
4	Italy	3,595,000
5	France	2,890,000
6	Switzerland	1,589,000
7	Yugoslavia	1,546,000
8	United Kingdom	1,104,000
9	Netherlands	683,000
10	Greece	519,000
11	United States	365,000
12	Czechoslovakia	325,000
13	Sweden	324,000
14	Norway	320,000
15	Hungary	275,000
16	Turkey	197,000
17	Bulgaria	162,000
18	Romania	149,000
19	Tunisia	139,000
20	USSR	129,000
21	Portugal	105,000

1976 figures in millions rounded to nearest thousand

1 also includes Luxembourg
2 provisional
3 rough estimate
4 includes all frontier crossings

Income from international tourism

1976 figures expressed in $US millions

United States	5,755
France	3,613
United Kingdom	3,600
West Germany	3,211
Austria	3,131
Spain	3,083
Italy	2,525
Switzerland	1,643
Canada	1,641
Netherlands	1,061
Belgium/Luxembourg	959
Greece	824
Portugal	317
Japan	312

The most visited countries

All figures are 1976

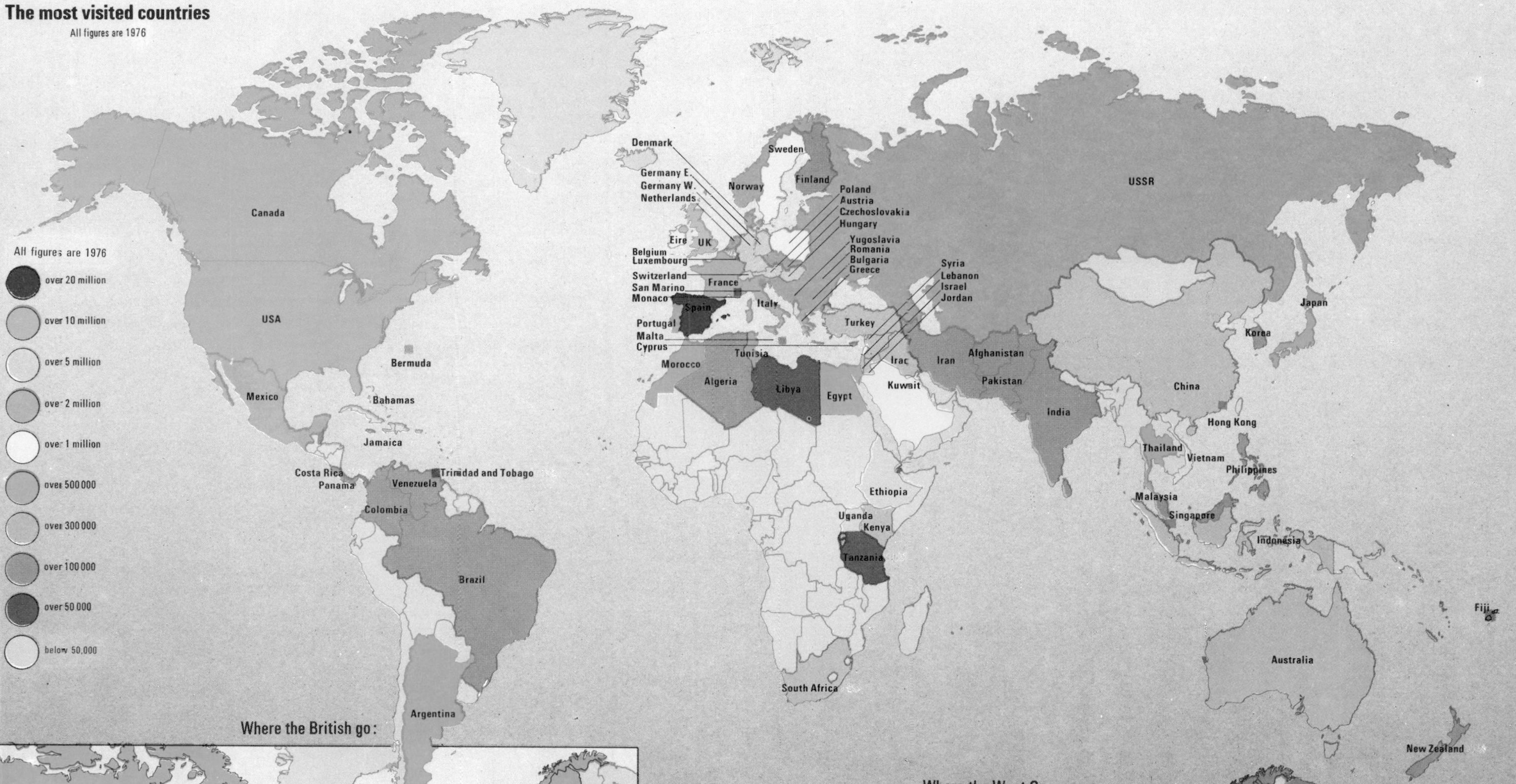
All figures are 1976
over 20 million
over 10 million
over 5 million
over 2 million
over 1 million
over 500 000
over 300 000
over 100 000
over 50 000
below 50,000
Canada
USA
Mexico
Bermuda
Bahamas
Jamaica
Costa Rica
Panama
Venezuela
Trinidad and Tobago
Colombia
Brazil
Argentina
Denmark
Germany E.
Germany W.
Netherlands
Norway
Sweden
Finland
Poland
Austria
Czechoslovakia
Hungary
Yugoslavia
Romania
Bulgaria
Greece
Eire
UK
Belgium
Luxembourg
Switzerland
San Marino
Monaco
France
Italy
Spain
Portugal
Malta
Cyprus
Syria
Lebanon
Israel
Jordan
Turkey
Tunisia
Morocco
Algeria
Libya
Egypt
Iraq
Iran
Kuwait
Afghanistan
Pakistan
India
USSR
China
Japan
Korea
Hong Kong
Thailand
Vietnam
Philippines
Malaysia
Singapore
Indonesia
Ethiopia
Uganda
Kenya
Tanzania
South Africa
Australia
New Zealand
Fiji

Where the British go:

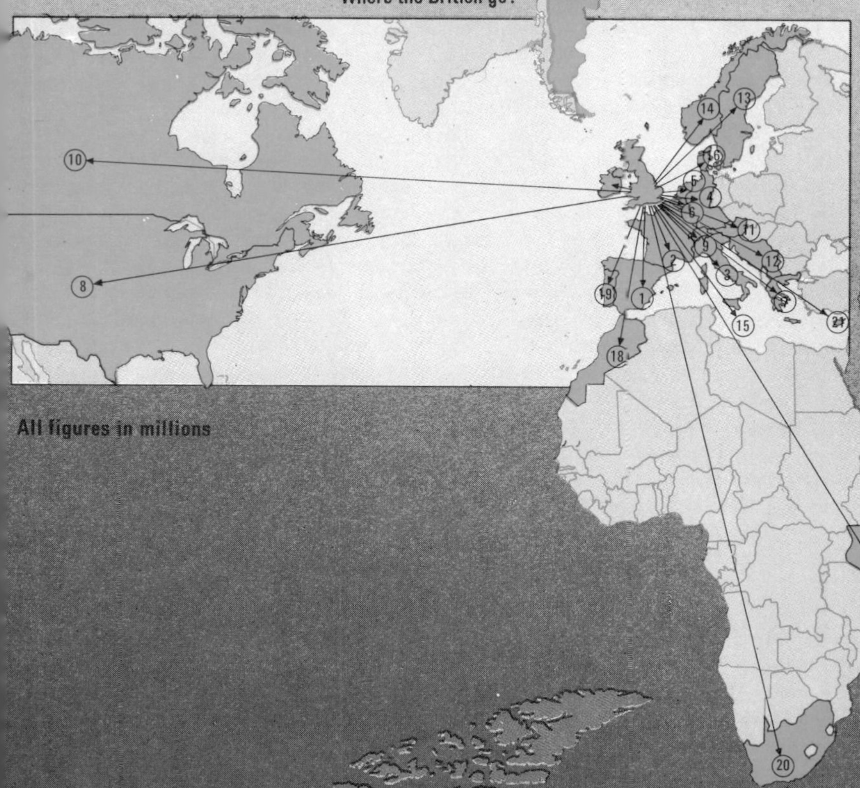

All figures in millions

Where the West Germans go:

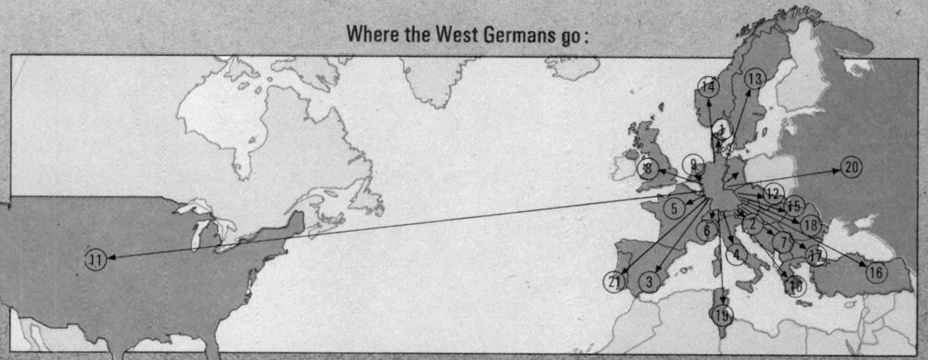

Where the French go:

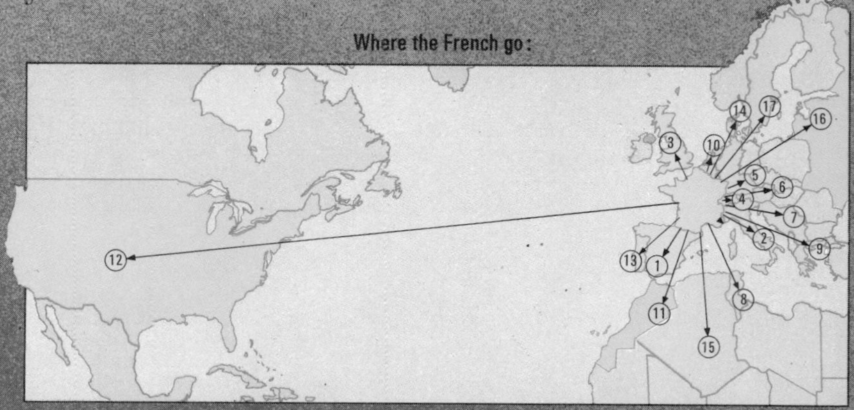

Where the Americans go:

The balance of man's environment

The natural balance – gradual change

During the thousands of millions of years of its existence the Earth has undergone many changes. At first it had no atmosphere, then some gases were released from the interior. These were mainly carbon dioxide and water vapour, with a small amount of nitrogen and no free oxygen. The atmosphere's composition changed as the water vapour condensed to form the ocean, and as the carbon dioxide was taken up into carbonate rocks and as a constituent of growing plants. Ultimately some of the carbon was locked up in the fossil fuels produced from this vegetation, and it has remained so stored for millions of years until today, when it is being widely exploited by man. The oxygen in the atmosphere arose mainly as a result of the photosynthesis which reduced the carbon dioxide levels.

Thus throughout geological time the proportions of these gases have varied from epoch to epoch. Our present atmosphere is one stage in this process. Today the Earth is surrounded by a mixture of gases, consisting mainly of some four-fifths of nitrogen and one-fifth of oxygen, with other substances at much lower levels. These include the surprisingly small amount of carbon dioxide – only 0·03 to 0·04 per cent – on which all green plants depend, a varying amount of water vapour, small quantities of helium and other inert gases, and various additions and pollutants arising from man's activities as well as from natural processes. The balance of the atmosphere is maintained mainly by Earth's 'green mantle'. The vast areas of natural forest sustain the level of oxygen required by animal life. Any profound changes in vegetation would ultimately affect the atmosphere, and so affect all animal life also.

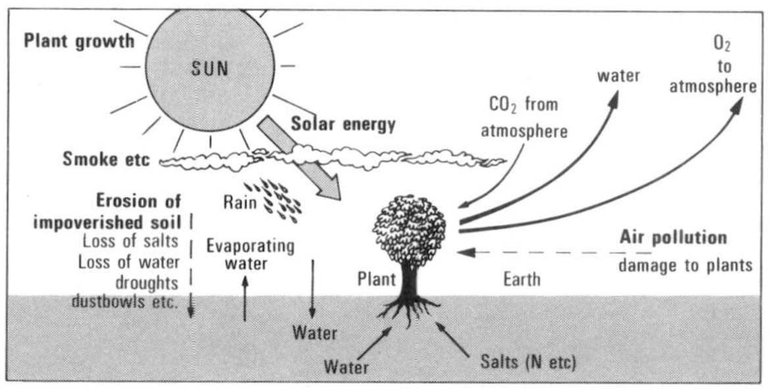

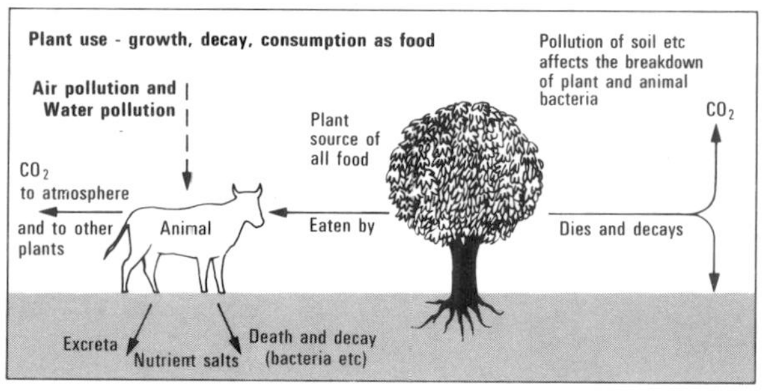

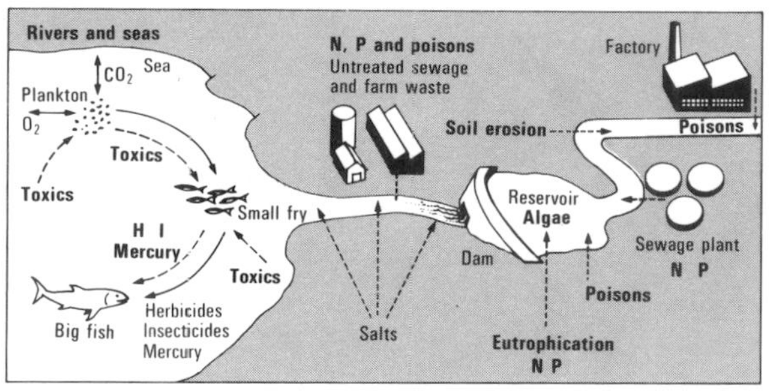

The essential cycles
All life on Earth depends on the essential cycle of energy, water and chemicals depicted here. The source of energy is radiation from the Sun. This radiation covers a wide range of wavelengths, some of which are essential for life, others harmful. The atmosphere filters out the most harmful rays, and admits those which are beneficial. Any atmospheric change alters the proportions of the various types of solar radiation which reach the Earth and the amounts which are lost. Any pollutant affects this balance.
Water, carbon dioxide and oxygen all go through these cycles. The rain falls on the land and sea alike. On land some is taken up by the soil, and is then absorbed by plant roots. A little of this water is used and retained by the plants, more is evaporated ('transpired') into the air. Water is also evaporated from the soil, and from the surface of streams, lakes and, most important, the sea. Solar energy is again involved in this evaporation. The water vapour eventually forms clouds and is deposited again as rain – and so the cycle continues.
The cycle in water is similar to that on land, except that aquatic animals are particularly susceptible to pollution. Pollutants are discharged into rivers, some of which run into lakes where excessive amounts of nutrient salts cause eutrophication. Poisons accumulate in the sea, are taken up by fish and other organisms and passed on (and concentrated) as predators eat their prey.

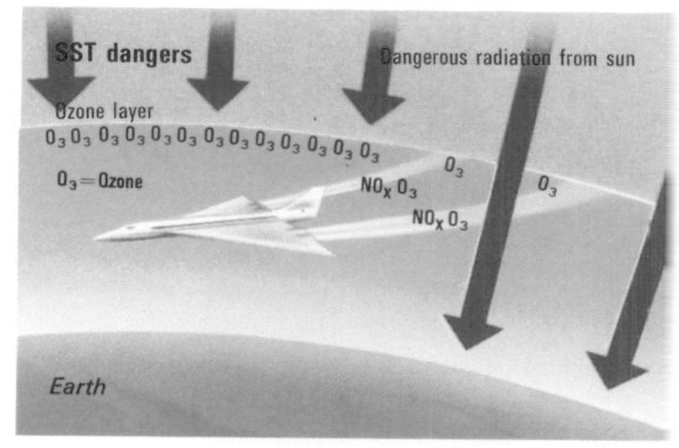

Exhausts from SST in the stratosphere may destroy the ozone layer which shields the earth from dangerous ultraviolet radiation

The scale of problems arising from interference by man with large natural regimes or ecosystems is perhaps well illustrated by the dilemma over the Brazilian rain forests. For some time there have been investigations and proposals to clear vast tracts of forest for agricultural development or the exploitation of potential mineral reserves. Latin America could certainly benefit socio-economically by some such successful development. Yet there is no clear understanding of what would happen to the climate and the fertility of the soil if a drastic change was attempted. Indeed, there is reason to believe that the decimation of the forests could easily lead to the creation of sterile deserts.

Effects of agriculture

The food for all animals is made by plants, which build up large molecules from the carbon dioxide in the air and water absorbed from the soil, using solar energy in the process. This process of photosynthesis is clearly vulnerable to direct and drastic alterations in the composition of the atmosphere, which in turn could interfere with the hydrological part of the natural cycle. Air pollution can screen radiation from the Sun, thus damaging plant life by reducing or inhibiting photosynthesis.

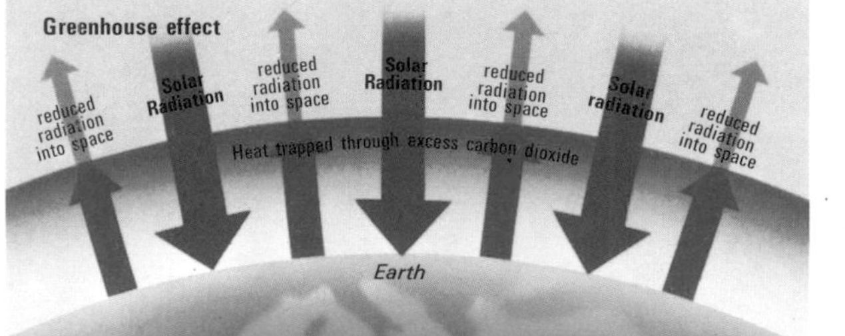

The Greenhouse Effect
Radiation from the Sun passes through space until it reaches the outer atmosphere of the Earth. Much of it is absorbed by the Earth's surface, causing the temperature to rise. The heat is then re-radiated. If the amount of CO_2 in the atmosphere increases, a larger amount of this radiation is trapped as in a glasshouse, instead of being lost into outer space. In the last fifty years the increase in the level of CO_2 in the Earth's atmosphere caused by the burning of fossil fuels has not been enough to raise the Earth's temperature.

The changing oceans

Today land covers only about a third of the surface of the Earth; the rest is covered by the oceans. This enormous mass of water, weighing 1,428,000,000,000,000,000 tonnes, plays a big part in stabilizing the conditions of man's environment. Water temperatures fluctuate much less than those of air, and the oceans form a reservoir not only of water but also of carbon dioxide and oxygen, the gases on which life depends. The plant life in the oceans – the phytoplankton – makes an essential contribution to the balance of these gases, producing vast quantities of oxygen by its photosynthesis. The area and the composition of the seas have changed slowly over the whole period of the world's existence.

We tend to accept the world as it is now, or rather as it was before man had noticeably affected it, as the ideal environment both for man and for all animal and plant life. We forget that change has always occurred, and is likely to continue to occur whether or not man dominates the globe. If such changes are gradual, life will survive, and man may even be able to adapt. Man is now so powerful, however, that he could himself suddenly upset the whole balance, changing the climate and the composition of the atmosphere. If there were drastic changes, life in some form, would almost certainly survive. New forms suited to the new conditions would evolve, but man, ingenious as he is, might not be the species most able to adapt.

Man made changes

Man is the only animal to modify not only his immediate environment but also the appearance and the economy of the whole globe. He can cut down vast areas of natural forest and replace them with arable crops and, sometimes, by man-made desert. He drains the wet places, and irrigates the dry. His industry could alter the whole balance of the atmosphere and the climate of the Earth. He also consumes the Earth's resources, and moves substances from one place to another. The misuse of his powers, and the subsequent release of harmful substances, we call pollution. We must discover which forms of pollution are a danger to man's environment, and control them before they upset the natural balance irreversibly.

Air pollution

Natural catastrophes, as well as human actions, can upset the balance. In 1883 Krakatoa blew up, and put so much dust into the atmosphere that the heat from the Sun was excluded and the average temperature of the Earth was significantly lowered for many months. Today man is polluting the air with dust and smoke, notwithstanding striking local improvements in Pittsburgh and other American cities and in Britain in places where the Clean Air Acts are operative. Air pollution, uncontrolled, could reduce sunlight at ground level and affect the world's climate, making it colder. An opposite effect, a warming of the Earth, could result from the increase in the level of carbon dioxide in the atmosphere. Carbon stored in fossil fuels (coal, oil, natural gas) is released as carbon dioxide gas when the fuels are burned; the levels of CO_2 in the atmosphere are rising slightly each year. This may produce the so-called 'greenhouse effect' (see diagram), and make the world warmer.

Such changes in climate would affect all forms of life. They would also affect the levels of the oceans. In former (natural) ice ages, so much water was immobilised as ice that the levels of the seas fell, to rise again and flood low-lying areas in the next warm epoch. A further rise in the temperature of the Earth could drown many of our cities and much of our most productive agricultural land. Scientists are not agreed on the probabilities of these changes, or on the magnitude of the likely effects, but they do agree that thorough monitoring of the atmosphere and climate is needed to detect the dangers at an early stage. The more optimistic scientists do also suggest that man-made changes in climate are likely to be less significant than the natural and inevitable fluctuations of temperature.

Green plants renew the supply of atmospheric oxygen. The destruction of forests may reduce the speed of renewal; the pollution of the oceans may affect the phytoplankton, which is equally important. This reduction in renewal is, at least in the short term, unlikely to endanger our oxygen supplies, which are probably sufficient for several hundred years, but the long-term composition of the atmosphere probably is being significantly affected, and will need to be safeguarded.

The atmosphere contains toxic gases, perhaps the most important being sulphur dioxide. Two thirds of the output of this gas is from natural sources, particularly the decay of vegetation in swamps, and from volcanoes. This natural SO_2 is just as toxic as that produced by man. It is harmful locally, but global levels are too low to have much effect. Man also raises the level of SO_2 in cities and where he is most numerous, often damaging trees and other plants which are particularly susceptible. These include lichens, mosses and liverworts, which are often absent from cities and from rural areas on the leeward side of cities. SO_2 pollution is at present seldom serious enough to harm man, except when its effects are combined with those of smoke. Among other damaging gases produced by industry is fluorine, which harms vegetation and is particularly dangerous to cattle.

Automobiles and aircraft also pollute the atmosphere. Exhausts from internal combustion engines contain many potentially dangerous substances, including carbon dioxide (CO_2), carbon monoxide (CO), oxides of nitrogen (NO), unburned hydrocarbons and lead. All these pollute the air of cities, often to a dangerous extent. In some areas where this pollution is already serious its effects are exacerbated by climatic factors. A temperature inversion traps the concentrated pollution near to the ground, and if combined with bright sunlight a photochemical reaction produces a toxic smog as seen in California and Tokyo.

Aircraft cause ground level pollution similar to that of automobiles. Supersonic planes (SST) flying in the thin atmosphere of the stratosphere may impose a greater threat. The amount of water vapour and of substances like oxides of nitrogen is likely to exceed, at least locally, the mass of the natural atmosphere, and some scientists are concerned that this may upset the existing conditions. One risk is that levels of ozone (O_3) may be reduced. The ozone in these high levels acts as a filter to the dangerous radiation from the Sun; if the ozone layer is reduced, too much radiation could reach the surface of the Earth. If too much ultraviolet radiation did penetrate to Earth living things would die. Calculations from measurements from rockets fired into the atmosphere indicate the amount of ozone that has to be present. Removal of ozone would come through jet exhausts: nitrous and hydrocarbon substances would modify the rate at which the chemical reaction takes place encouraging the separated two- and one-atom molecules to recombine to reform ozone. These substances would also steal some of the oxygen to form other compounds. The risk of this is probably small, but is one reason why environmentalists have opposed the operation of SST until the whole subject has been thoroughly studied.

In fact the possible changes of flying too many aircraft too high in the stratosphere is open to endless speculation, and will continue to be so until very much more knowledge of the upper atmosphere is obtained from scientific satellite exploration and allied investigations. Influences from the conditions 15 to 30 kilometres high have little direct bearing on the short-term weather forecast. Hence the amount of investigation of atmospheric conditions at these rarified heights has been small.

A potentially greater threat to the ozone layer would be widespread use throughout the world of fluoro-carbide aerosol sprays. The effect of these sprays can be studied directly and there are ample grounds for concern.

Energy and the environment

Human civilisation depends on an increasing supply of energy. At present most of this comes from burning fossil fuels: man is using at a fast rate the stored energy produced over millions of years by photosynthesis. Even with economies, oil reserves will be used up in a hundred years and

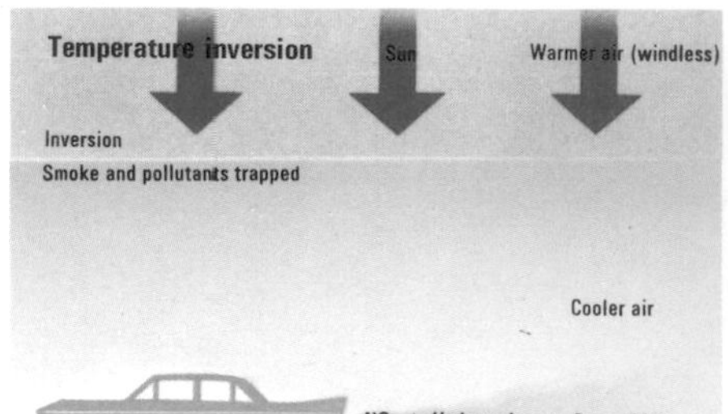

A toxic smog is produced by car exhaust when climatic factors trap the pollution at ground level.

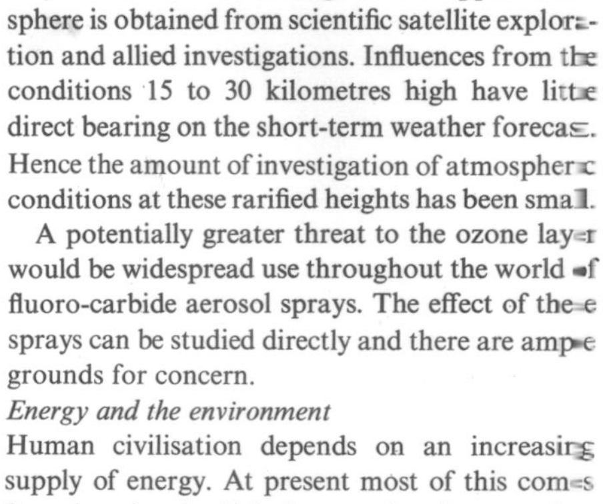

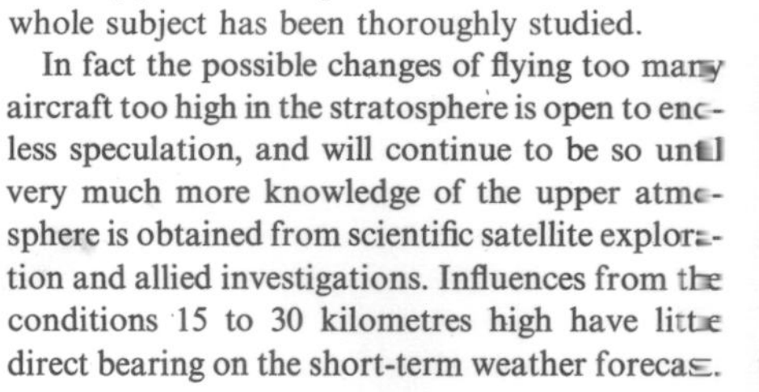

Traffic in Los Angeles

coal in two hundred. This will at least remove certain types of atmospheric pollution. Hydro-electric power is clean, but the amount attainable is limited. The energy of the Sun (solar energy) may be trapped directly and may make some contribution, but most future plans assume that nuclear power will play a greater, and ultimately a predominating, part in supplying man's needs. There are fears, however, concerning radiation hazards in spite of safeguards. Nuclear power stations are today very carefully controlled so that little radiation escapes to pollute the air or the sea, but as they increase in numbers the risk must grow. The greatest danger, however, is from the increasing amounts of radioactive waste, which are difficult to dispose of safely. Atmospheric testing of nuclear weapons imposes a further radiation risk whilst nuclear warfare of a global kind could lead to radiation levels so high as to threaten the existence of mankind.

Much of the energy man produces is lost as wasted heat. This too could eventually upset the climatic balance of the Earth. Already our large cities have a local climate measurably warmer than that of the surrounding country, though global effects are at present negligible. More serious 'thermal pollution' can occur locally when water from rivers and lakes is used for cooling purposes in industry as in large electrical generators, whether using fossil fuels or nuclear fuel. Water effluents from such power stations may be so hot that fish and invertebrates are killed; and even when heat pollution is less serious the water may be de-oxygenated so that aquatic life is asphyxiated. However, most electrical generating authorities are aware of the problem and try to guard against such damage to life.

Fresh water pollution

Rivers, lakes and the sea are all polluted by man. Limited amounts of sewage and other substances are disposed of by the process of self-purification in which nutrient salts are removed and used by living organisms – the normal process of biological cycling. Overloading prevents this from happening, and encourages organisms suited to living under polluted conditions. Man can reverse these processes by proper treatment of urban and industrial effluents but even in these, nutrient salts can cause damage by 'eutrophication', or excessive fertilisation of the water. Fortunately technology has developed methods – the tertiary treatment of effluents – which can obviate this danger, but only at a high cost. In Lake Tahoe in the USA, once very badly polluted, the problem has been overcome in this way.

In modern agriculture, with 'factory farming' where livestock is kept indoors in vast numbers, the animals' excreta, when not used as manure on the land, is often a source of pollution. Inorganic chemical fertilisers may also cause pollution when leached from the land into rivers and lakes.

Pesticides

Modern agriculture depends on chemical pesticides, particularly herbicides (weed-killers) and insecticides. These substances have contributed enormously to solving the problem of world starvation. Unfortunately some pesticides have also become contaminants, not usually at dangerous levels but sometimes in sufficient amounts to have harmful ecological effects locally. The organochlorine insecticides, including DDT and dieldrin, are of special concern. Although the dangers have often been exaggerated, there are many cases of contamination by those substances. DDT and dieldrin are very stable, long-lasting substances, which is a great advantage in, for example, protecting a house from disease-bearing mosquitoes. However, this very property makes them dangerous because they become concentrated in a particular food chain: a predator like a hawk can eat a number of pigeons or voles containing small amounts of DDT, and retain the DDT until a dangerous level is reached. Fish and other aquatic animals can also cause the concentration of pesticides in rivers, by a factor of as much as 10,000 times. Scientists are trying to replace the more dangerous pesticides with other substances and to develop non-chemical methods of control. This will take time but, although chemical pesticides will be used for many years, with care global pollution will be avoided.

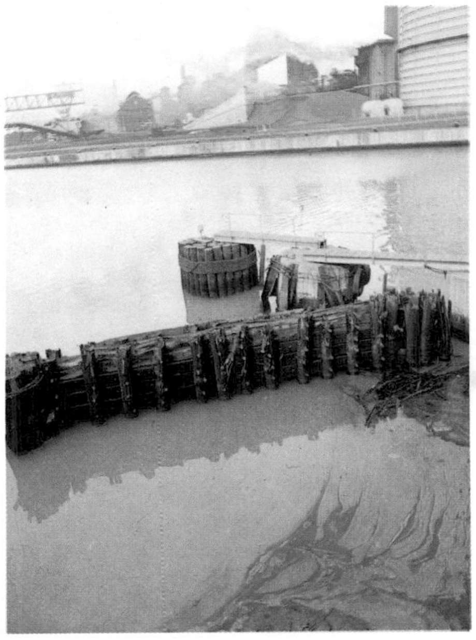

A river in Detroit, showing the effects of pollution.

Some quantities of pesticides ultimately end up in the sea. Levels in estuaries and coastal areas can be high enough to damage fish and marine arthropods and even to affect plant life. In the open ocean, however, levels are very low, and there is at present no evidence that the phytoplankton is in danger of being damaged. Some scientists have suggested that levels are likely to increase in the future to danger point, but this does not seem to be happening yet. In fact levels in many marine fish and in the sea birds which eat them are decreasing and not increasing because better controls have been introduced in many countries.

Salt water pollution

The importance of the oceans in sustaining the natural balance cannot be over-stated; pollution of the oceans is therefore a very serious matter. The most obvious pollutant is oil including waste oil discharged by ships, or spilled when oil tankers ships are damaged or wrecked. Some oil is also spilled at terminals where it is pumped ashore from tankers. Leaks from underwater oil wells are difficult to control and can cause pollution more serious than that from the sinking of the largest tanker. Oil is dangerous because it floats on the surface of the ocean and most life, particularly plant life, is found near the surface. Fortunately the most toxic substances in oil are relatively volatile, and evaporate from the ocean's surface, but the tarry residues can damage fish and interfere with the life and photosynthesis of the phytoplankton.

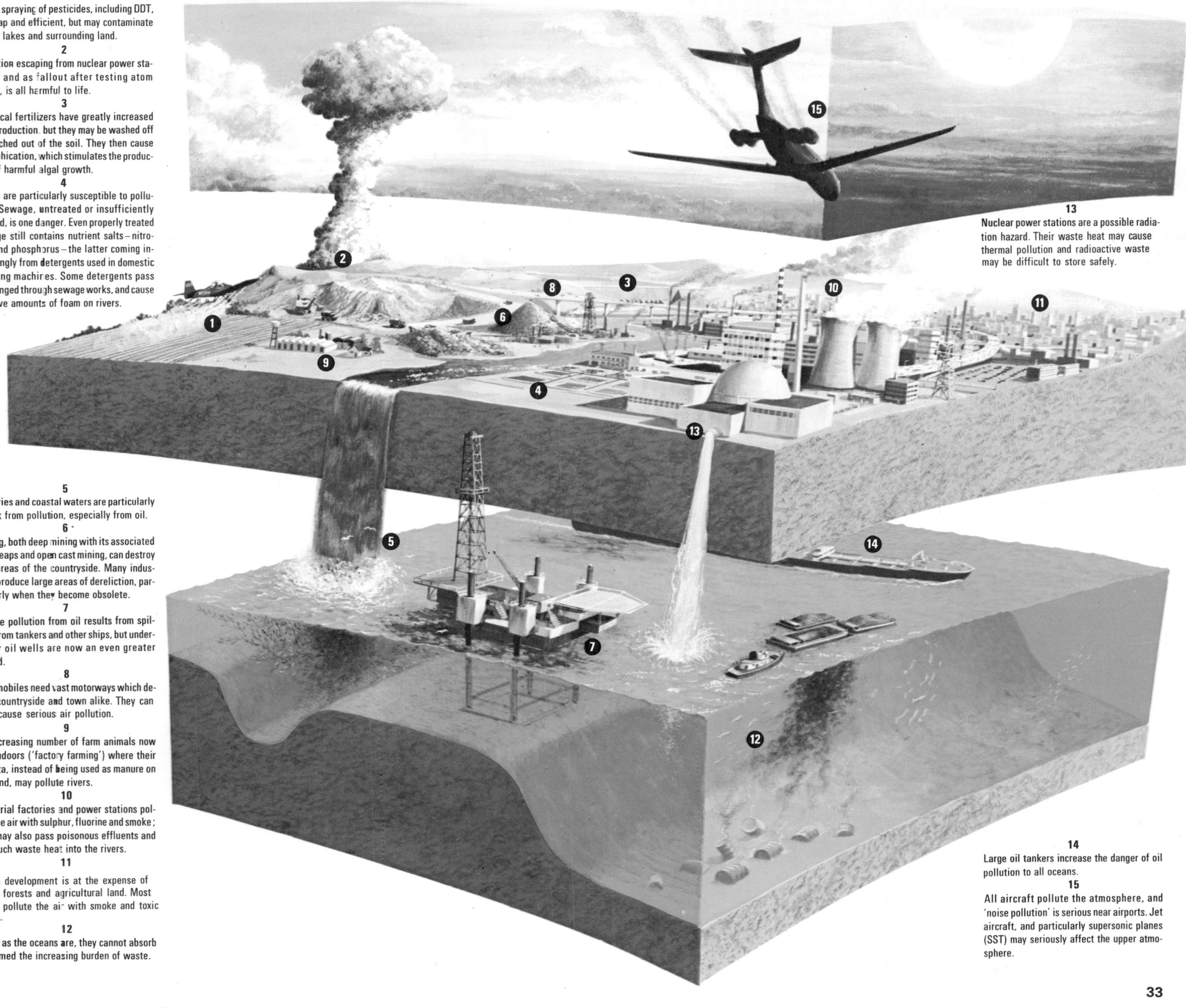

1
Aerial spraying of pesticides, including DDT, is cheap and efficient, but may contaminate rivers, lakes and surrounding land.

2
Radiation escaping from nuclear power stations, and as fallout after testing atom bombs, is all harmful to life.

3
Chemical fertilizers have greatly increased crop production, but they may be washed off or leached out of the soil. They then cause eutrophication, which stimulates the production of harmful algal growth.

4
Rivers are particularly susceptible to pollution. Sewage, untreated or insufficiently treated, is one danger. Even properly treated sewage still contains nutrient salts – nitrogen and phosphorus – the latter coming increasingly from detergents used in domestic washing machines. Some detergents pass unchanged through sewage works, and cause massive amounts of foam on rivers.

5
Estuaries and coastal waters are particularly at risk from pollution, especially from oil.

6
Mining, both deep mining with its associated slag heaps and open cast mining, can destroy vast areas of the countryside. Many industries produce large areas of dereliction, particularly when they become obsolete.

7
Marine pollution from oil results from spillage from tankers and other ships, but underwater oil wells are now an even greater hazard.

8
Automobiles need vast motorways which deface countryside and town alike. They can also cause serious air pollution.

9
An increasing number of farm animals now live indoors ('factory farming') where their excreta, instead of being used as manure on the land, may pollute rivers.

10
Industrial factories and power stations pollute the air with sulphur, fluorine and smoke; they may also pass poisonous effluents and too much waste heat into the rivers.

11
Urban development is at the expense of living forests and agricultural land. Most cities pollute the air with smoke and toxic gases.

12
Large as the oceans are, they cannot absorb unharmed the increasing burden of waste.

13
Nuclear power stations are a possible radiation hazard. Their waste heat may cause thermal pollution and radioactive waste may be difficult to store safely.

14
Large oil tankers increase the danger of oil pollution to all oceans.

15
All aircraft pollute the atmosphere, and 'noise pollution' is serious near airports. Jet aircraft, and particularly supersonic planes (SST) may seriously affect the upper atmosphere.

Techniques of navigation

Early maps were designed to show the spatial relationship between local geographical features, territorial boundaries, and routes. The early use of maps for finding the way (the essence of navigation) has persisted, first for travellers on land, later for mariners, and more recently for airmen and space travellers. Among the necessary instruments of marine navigation the chart – the seaman's name for a map – is important. In addition to the chart, the other basic navigational tools are 'sailing directions' which, in early times were passed down orally from master to apprentice, but which are now in printed form; the log, or device for measuring the speed of a ship; and, the most important instrument of all, the compass.

The Greeks

Anaximander of Miletus (6th century BC) is credited with having drawn the first map. Anaximander's map, which must have been crude and highly conjectural, marked an important epoch in the history of geography and navigation in particular, and in human progress in general. The first rectangular map was constructed by Democritus (5th century BC) who claimed that the habitable world was one and a half times as long in the east–west direction as it was broad in the north–south direction. It was this concept that led to the use of the terms 'latitude' and 'longitude', meaning respectively breadth and length, for defining terrestrial positions. Dicaearchus (4th century BC) constructed a map on which the first parallel of latitude was drawn through the Pillars of Hercules at the entrance to the Mediterranean Sea and the Island of Rhodes. Eratosthenes (3rd century BC), who made the first scientific attempt at measuring the Earth's size, constructed a map (according to the geographer Strabo) on which seven parallels of latitude and seven meridians or lines passing through the poles and any given place, irregularly spaced, were drawn; but the principles of Eratosthenes' division are not known. Hipparchus (2nd century BC) demanded that the positions of places to be mapped should be verified using astronomical observations. He suggested that parallels of latitude and meridians drawn on maps should be equidistantly spaced, and that to determine relative longitudes meridians should be regulated from eclipse observations.

Ptolemy of Alexandria (c AD 90–168), the 'Prince of Ancient Geographers', was the founder of scientific cartography. His monumental *Geographia* contains detailed explanations of mathematical geography and map projections. Ptolemy suggested that the Earth should be divided on the basis of climatic zones and that longitudes should be measured eastwards from a prime meridian through the 'Fortunate Isles' which he believed to be the westernmost part of the habitable globe. Ptolemy referred to Marinus, a Tyrian cartographer who employed a simple cylindrical projection for his maps.

Medieval navigation

The earliest charts extant are medieval maps of the Mediterranean world: the first record of a chart being used on a ship dating from 1270. By that time the Genoese, Venetians and Pisans had gained control of the maritime trade of the Mediterranean, and significant improvements in nautical science took place during the ascendancy of the Italian City States.

Portolan chart

The renaissance of scientific map-making began with the portolan charts of the thirteenth century to meet the needs of seamen. These charts were hand-drawn, each on a complete skin. The earlier examples are of the Mediterranean and Black Sea regions, but by the seventeenth century they embraced the whole of the known world, A characteristic feature of the portolan chart is the maze of intersecting straight lines which cover the sea area. These are systems of rhumb lines, each radiating from the centre of one of a series of compass roses. It is argued that each system of rhumb lines on a portolan chart denotes a magnetic compass, and that such charts, therefore, were based on compass bearings. If this be so, they must have made their first appearance after the invention of the magnetic compass.

There is no contemporary explanation of how the rhumb lines on a portolan chart were used; but it seems obvious that they were employed for finding the magnetic course to steer from one place to another. To find the course the navigator would place a straight-edge joining the plotted positions of departure and destination; and then, by means of dividers, he would seek the rhumb line most nearly parallel to the straight-edge. By tracing this line to the centre of the appropriate compass rose, he would readily ascertain the compass course to steer.

Magnetic compass

There is no strong evidence to suggest that the magnetic compass was not invented independently in the Mediterranean region; it is likely that it was invented in China perhaps before it made its first appearance, in the 12th century, in the Mediterranean. The 'natural' compass is the horizon of an observer, and in very early times, the horizon was divided into four quadrants by two rectangular diameters to indicate the four principal directions, North, East, South and West. The horizontal angle between the direction of North (or South) and that in which the ship is heading is the 'Course' of the ship. It is easy to see that when a ship is heading in a fixed direction on any given course, the line she traces out on the sea is one that cuts all meridians at the same angle. Such a line is a rhumb line, and because of the convenience of not having to change the ship's course when sailing from one given place to another, the normal navigational practice, especially for short distances, is to sail along a rhumb line.

The Golden Age of Discovery

When western Europeans first embarked on Atlantic voyages during the early phase of the Golden Age of Discovery, the need for scientifically constructed charts was pressing. Within the confines of the enclosed Mediterranean, where sailing distances between ports were relatively short, the portolan charts sufficed. But for ocean navigation, in which east–west distances of thousands of miles were common, something better was vitally necessary.

Although seamen must always have known that the Earth is spherical, the charts used by the Portuguese and Spanish mariners during the Age of Discoveries were based on the assumption that the Earth's surface was plane. The graticules or network of grid-lines drawn on the charts were simple rectangular networks in which equidistant parallels of latitude and meridians on the Earth were each projected as equidistant parallel lines forming a 'plane' projection. On such a map of the world every parallel of latitude is projected as a straight line of constant length. On the globe, however, the length of the parallels of latitude diminish from a maximum at the equator in latitude 0° to zero at either pole in latitude 90°.

Mercator chart

The most important step forward on the development of the navigational chart coincided with the publication of a world map in 1569 by the Flemish cartographer Gerhard Kremer, better known as Mercator. This map is the prototype of the modern chart.

On Mercator's world map equidistantly spaced meridians on the Earth are projected as equidistant parallel straight lines, and equidistantly spaced parallels of latitude are projected as parallel straight lines which cut the meridians at right angles. The graticule therefore, is rectangular like that of the 'plane' chart. The important difference is that the spacing of the parallels on a Mercator chart increases polewards in exactly the same proportion as the distortion of the east–west spacing of the meridians. In technical terms the Mercator projection is such that every line on the chart is distorted proportionally and therefore the projection is orthomorphic. In a cartographic sense, this means that angles are not distorted so that lines of constant course, or rhumb lines, are projected as straight lines. A mariner wishing to find the rhumb line course to steer from one place to another simply measures on a Mercator chart the angle which the rhumb line makes with any of the projected meridians.

Gnomonic chart

It was soon realised by early ocean navigators that long voyages could be substantially shortened, when wind and currents allowed, by practising what became known as 'Great Circle Sailing' instead of 'Rhumb Line Sailing'.

A great circle is a circle on a sphere on whose plane the centre of the sphere lies. The shortest route along the surface of a sphere between two points is along the shorter arc of the great circle on which the two points lie. In practising rhumb line sailing, although the navigator benefits in that a constant course is steered, his ship travels a greater distance than would be the case by practising great circle sailing. A major disadvantage of the latter however, is that the course along a great circle route constantly changes. Nevertheless, in the interests of economy of fuel and time, great circle sailing is commonly practised.

On a Mercator chart a great circle is projected as a relatively complex curve. To plot a great circle route on a chart, a navigator employs a chart constructed on the gnomonic projection as an auxiliary to the Mercator chart. Unlike the conventional Mercator projection, the mathematical principles of which were first given by the eminent Elizabethan mathematician Edward Wright, the gnomonic projection is a geometrical or perspective projection in which points on a spherical surface are projected onto a plane touching the surface, by straight lines of projection which emanate from the centre of the sphere. It is clear that on a gnomonic projection great circle arcs are projected as straight lines. To plot a great circle route on a gnomonic chart the navigator simply joins the plotted positions of the points of departure and destination with a straight line. To transfer the great circle route onto a Mercator chart merely involves lifting positions of a series of points on the route as projected on the gnomonic chart and transferring them to the Mercator chart. A fair curve through these points delineates the great circle route on the Mercator chart. The navigator practising great circle sailing sails along a series of short rhumb lines which collectively approximate to the great circle arc described above.

Mercator's projection shows all parallels of latitude as if equal in length to the Equator, although on the globe they are obviously progressively shorter towards the poles. Mercator increased his North–South scale on the meridians to match the increase in East–West scale, so that at any one point scale is equal in both directions and away from that point increases or decreases in equal proportions. Angles from the North–South meridians (i.e. bearings) can therefore be measured with a protractor without distortion. A straight line (rhumb line) thus has a constant bearing, but is not the shortest distance between its two end points The Gnomonic chart has scale distortion cutwards from its centre point, but the shortest distance between two points is the straight line joining them. The route required is therefore first plotted as a straight line on the Gnomonic chart and is then transferred to the Mercator chart as a series of straight lines, the bearing of each being measured with a protractor. A ship or aircraft does not follow the true Great Circle route, which would require continuous slow alteration of bearing, but steers on a constant bearing for a period of time and then changes to the new bearing at the next junction point along the series of straight lines drawn on the chart.

The Mercator map shows Great Circle routes and rhumb lines for three shipping routes and one air route. The latter is also shown on the Gnomonic map. The Great Circle route always lies on the poleward side of the rhumb line between the same points.

The Mercator chart need not be based on the Equator, but can be drawn at right-angles in the Transverse form, based on any meridian. This allows the polar areas to be charted, which is important for air routes although not for shipping. Likewise, the Gnomonic chart need not be centred on a pole but can be drawn centred on any point.

The navigator is, of course, constrained by many factors in laying out his route: the sailor may have to plan his voyage as a series of different Great Circle segments in order to avoid land, shallow water or ice hazards; sailing ships require routes planned with consideration of prevailing and seasonal winds and of ocean currents.

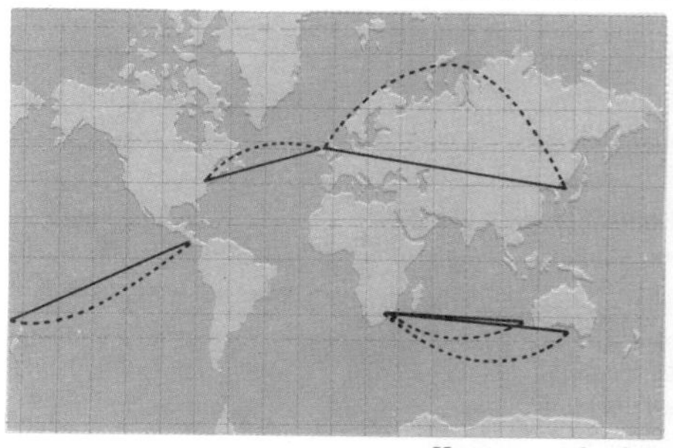

Mercator projection

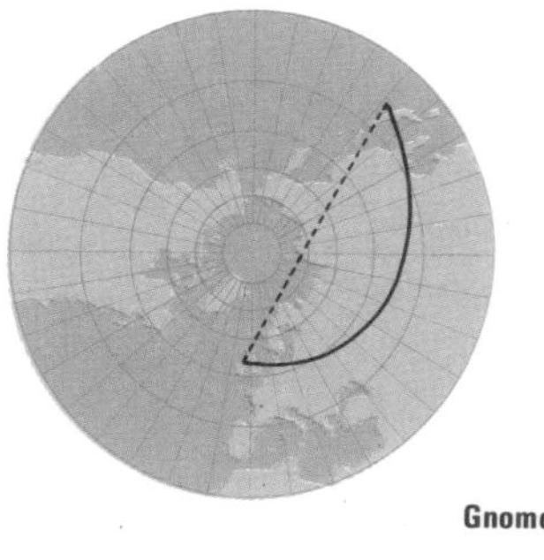

Gnomonic projection

Nautical Astronomy

A system of navigation in which the navigator relies wholly on compass and log to determine direction and distance travelled is known as 'Dead Reckoning' or 'DR Navigation'. Because compass and log are not without errors, and because their errors are cumulative, DR Navigation is unreliable and imperfect. It becomes necessary, in the interests of safety, for a navigator to be able to check his progress by some means other than by DR Navigation.

The defects of DR Navigation led to the development of 'Nautical Astronomy' by which a navigator may find his latitude and longitude from astronomical observations. The basic tools of a nautical astronomer are a *Nautical Almanac*, a sextant and a chronometer. The *Nautical Almanac* gives the celestial positions of the sun, moon, planets and stars used in nautical astronomy, against Greenwich Mean Time or GMT. The sextant is the instrument by which the navigator measures the elevations above his horizon of the sun, moon, planet or star he observes. The chronometer is merely an accurate timekeeper from which the GMT of an astronomical observation on 'sight' is obtained.

In the open sea a navigator may find his latitude from a sight of a celestial body on the celestial sphere bearing due north or south at which time the body reaches its greatest altitude during the day. Such an observation is known as a 'meridian altitude' sight. The celestial sphere is an imaginary sphere surrounding the Earth, on which celestial bodies are assumed to lie. The astronomical navigator constructs a network of guidelines on the celestial sphere like lines of latitude and longitude on the Earth. The equivalent of latitude is declination and that of longitude is called right ascension.

A mariner may find his ship's longitude from an observation of a celestial body provided that the observer knows his latitude. To find longitude it is necessary to solve a spherical triangle at the apexes of which are located, respectively, the celestial pole, the observer's zenith, and the observed body.

Radio and electronic navigation

The application of radio and electronic principles during the 20th century has revolutionised navigation. In the early decades of the century 'radio time signals' were made available for checking chronometers. Later, medium frequency radio direction finding (MF/DF) enabled a navigator to find his ship's position, even in fog when visual observations of the land or the celestial bodies rendered the traditional methods of navigation useless. This method of 'fixing' a position is exactly analogous to the method of taking bearings of lighthouses or other visible landmarks. Later still, the introduction of radar techniques facilitated coastal navigation in low visibility as well as providing efficient means for avoiding collision in fog. Radar, a contraction of 'radio detection and ranging' was developed between 1935 and 1940 independently in a number of countries. Range, direction and velocity are all displayed visually by means of a cathode-ray tube. After the Second World War refinements to radar techniques led in the direction of hyperbolic navigation.

Hyperbolic navigation

During the Second World War the need for sophisticated navigational systems for fast-flying military aircraft led to the introduction of hyper-

bolic navigation.

Hyperbolic navigation is based on the accurate measurement of the difference in times taken by simultaneous signals, transmitted from each of two fixed transmitting stations, to reach an observer.

If an observer receives radio signals transmitted simultaneously from each of two stations then he is able to measure the intervals of time taken for the radio energy to travel from the two stations to his position. Knowing the speed at which radio energy travels he can translate the difference of the two time intervals into a corresponding distance-difference. The position of constant distance-difference relative to the two stations is a hyperbola, which has the stations at its focal points. Such a hyperbola plotted on a chart gives the navigator a line somewhere on which his position is located. By plotting the second hyperbola from observations of a second pair of stations, the observer then locates his position at the point of intersection of the two hyperbolae. Systems of this nature, include the Decca Navigator, Loran and Omega, all of which are extensively used on aircraft and ships (see opposite for description of Decca Navigator System).

To facilitate hyperbolic navigation specially prepared charts, overprinted with families of hyperbolae, are used. Such a chart is called a 'lattice chart'. An example of a Decca Lattice Chart is illustrated.

The sophisticated technology of the Space Age has had a significant impact on navigation of ships and aeroplanes.

Inertial navigation

The system known as 'Inertial Navigation' is essentially, a sophisticated DR system in which the motion of an aircraft or ship is sensed, without compass or log, so that the position of the craft relative to its starting position is at all times known. It is a self-contained system that functions independently of weather conditions that can hamper the nautical astronomer, and of radio signals which may suffer natural or man-made interference. For this latter reason inertial navigation is of particular importance to naval vessels, especially nuclear submarines which attempt to avoid detection.

Satellite, VOR and DME navigation

Another advanced navigational technique of the Space Age is that which employs Earth satellites. By this system position finding to an accuracy of 0·1 miles is possible.

If a satellite is placed in polar orbit and can be tracked and plotted accurately, at a given instant of time its exact latitude, longitude and height is known. The distance of the satellite from a ship is obtained by utilising the Doppler principle that electromagnetic waves are modified by the motion of the source. As the satellite approaches the ship, its rapid motion shortens the wavelength of the signals. More waves therefore reach the ship per second than would be received from a stationary source. The wavelength lengthens as the satellite moves away from the ship and fewer waves per second are received. From the change in the number of signals received during transit of the satellite, range can be calculated.

A ship in motion fixes its position from more than one pass of a satellite; if stationary a greater number of fixes can be taken – these are called geodetic fixes and are often used by oil rigs and other off-shore installations such as large navigation beacons and lightships.

The navigation of aircraft is facilitated by VOR (VHF Omnidirectional Range) and DME (Distance Measuring Equipment). VOR allows an airman to navigate from any position directly towards or away from a fixed radio beacon, and DME enables him to measure the distance between his aircraft and the beacon using radio techniques.

Other electronic aids include the radio altimeter to measure the distance above ground, and the ground-speed indicator which uses the Doppler shift in reflected radio waves. Computers convert data to information capable of being instantly read by the pilot, and they are also capable of carrying out position-determining (dead-reckoning) by monitoring all speed and course changes of the aircraft. The automatic pilot can therefore carry out all the tasks necessary for piloting the aircraft.

Navigation, as has been stated, is essentially concerned with finding the way, but in certain instances, of more importance is the avoidance of collision. This becomes crucial in the vicinity of busy airports and seaways. The application of the concept of modern traffic control, in which aircraft are segregated and ships are routed, has marked an important epoch in the recent history of navigation. As far as the airman is concerned the role of the land-based traffic controller is vitally important in the navigation process. The Air Traffic Controller ensures that all the aircraft in his area follow carefully planned and prearranged routes. For certain defined points on these routes the controller identifies the height of each aircraft approaching it and the aircraft's arrival time at the point. By radio communication the controller is able to give directions to the pilots to ensure safe landings. The data for each aircraft is given on a 'flight strip', and it is the computerising of these data that will ultimately relieve controllers of much of their present onerous workload. (See Approach and Landing Chart for Heathrow Airport, and en route chart below).

The air and sea navigator is no longer limited to a small number of charts for use during a flight or voyage. He now has a wide variety at differing scales to back up his electronic aids. Coastal and land areas in particular are well mapped, and high-speed and multi-colour printing and symbol standardisation has now ensured that the navigator has information more readily available and more accurate than ever before.

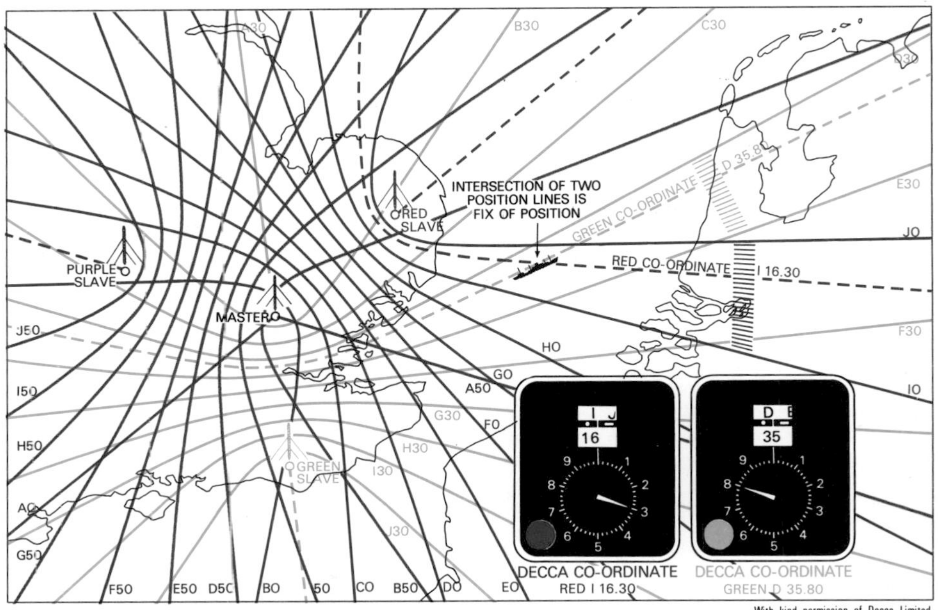

With kind permission of Decca Limited.

The Decca Navigator Sysytem fixes position using continuous radio waves from two transmitters. In the south-east of England the master transmitter is augmented by purple, red and green slave transmitters. The fix is given by the intersection of two hyperbolic position lines, and is obtained from the readings of two Decometer Indicators.

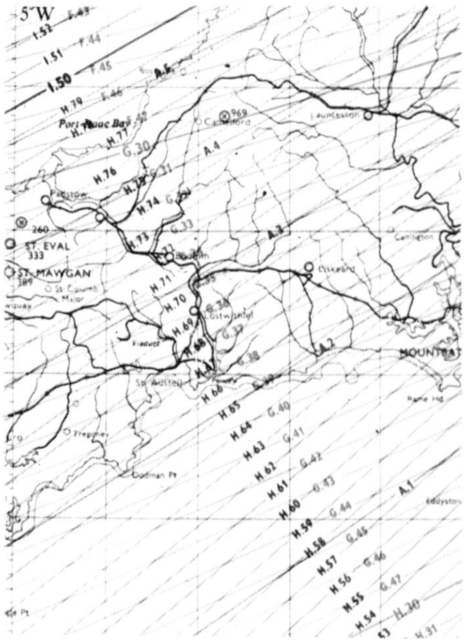

A Decca Lattice Chart used for location of aircraft position. The map shows only coast and rivers, railways, beacons and airfields (with their heights above sea level). The important part of the chart is the system of coloured lines, in purple, red and green, each colour representing directional signals from a fixed transmitter. It is possible to determine the aircraft's position on a line from each transmitter and so fix it on the map by the intersection of the corresponding coloured lines. For example, in the Bristol Channel a good fix can be obtained using the green transmitter with either the red or the purple; using only the latter two colours would give an uncertain fix.

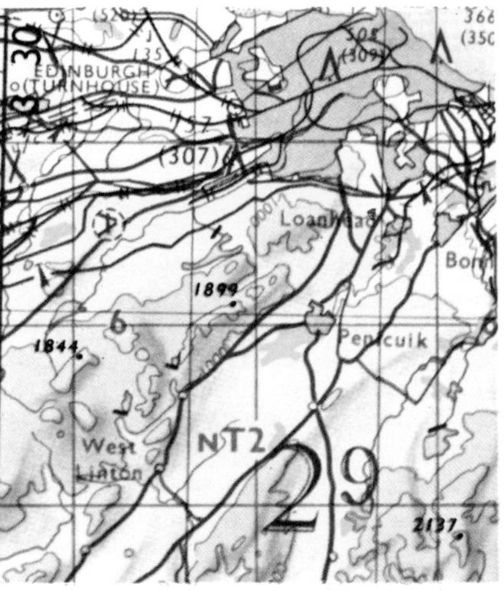

Part of an aeronautical topographical chart. The relief of the land is shown by generalised contours at a 500-foot Vertical Interval, with layer-tinting to assist a quick appreciation of land form. Spot heights are given for the highest summits, which must obviously be avoided. Railways, main roads, towns and major settlements are shown, as these are easily identified from an aircraft. The pattern of runways on the airfield is shown diagrammatically to avoid confusion; note the second airport to the south of Edinburgh (Turnhouse) which has a distinctly different pattern of runways. Direction beacons and flashing lights are marked for night flights. More detailed charts than this one are used for approach and take-off, and for restricted areas or directed flight paths.

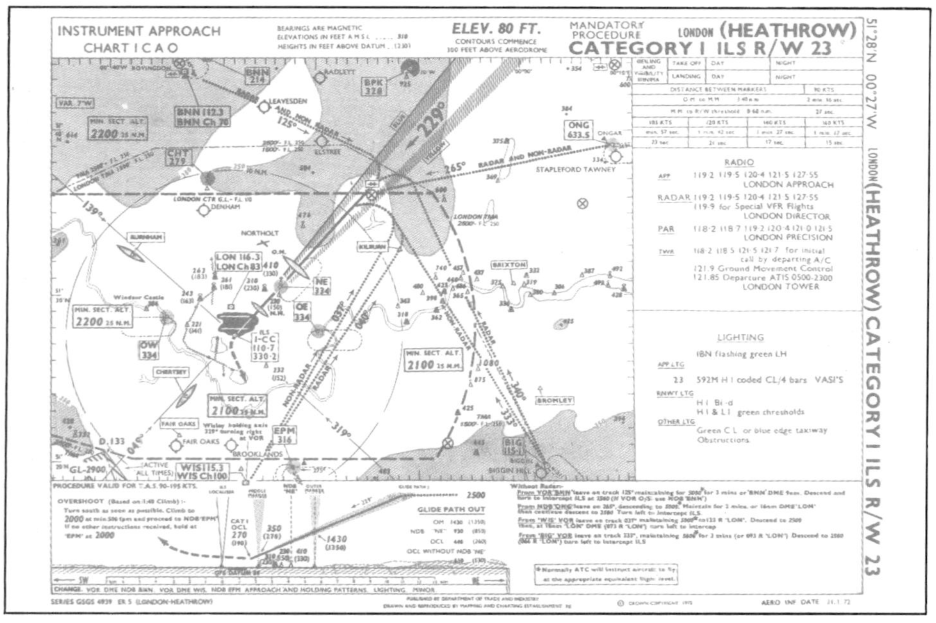

The Approach and Landing Chart for London (Heathrow) Airport illustrates the complexity of operation at a busy international centre. The higher land in the area is colour-tinted, and spot heights of topographical features and of towers, pylons and other obstructions are given not only above sea level but also above airfield altitude as aircraft altimeters can be set to read height above the runway. Beacons, lights, radar information, etc., is given in detail, with routes for visual and instrumental approaches.

An en route chart gives the pilot the bearings and distances along his route from beacon to beacon, which allows a dead reckoning passage by compass and air-speed indicator, suitably corrected for wind strength and direction. The chart also indicates information such as the aircraft control zones, radar transmitters, and lines of latitude and longitude. This is a specialised chart intended solely for aerial navigation purposes, and needs constant revision.

The Universe

No one knows how large the Universe is, or if indeed it has any limits. It stretches as far as our largest telescopes can see. Even a beam of light, which travels at the fastest known speed in the Universe, 186,000 miles per second, (i.e. the speed of light), takes 10,000 million years to reach the Earth from the remotest visible objects. Space is so vast that ordinary units of distance become insignificant. Distances in astronomy are usually described in light years, the distance that a beam of light covers in one year. This is equivalent to about six million million miles. The nearest star to our Sun, called Alpha Centauri, is 4·3 light years away, which means that we see it as it appeared 4·3 years ago. The remotest visible objects in the Universe are over 10,000 million light years away, which means that we see them as they appeared before the Earth was born.

Star magnitudes

The stars we see at night are relatively close to us in space. They are among the nearest of the estimated 100,000 million stars that make up our whirling star system called the Galaxy, the densest part of which is visible as the faint hazy band called the Milky Way. Stars appear different in brightness because some are genuinely bigger and hotter than others and also because they are all at different distances from the Earth. Astronomers grade star brightness in steps called magnitudes. The brightest-appearing stars are termed first magnitude, and the faintest visible to the naked eye are sixth magnitude. Still fainter stars, visible only through telescopes, are given progressively larger magnitude numbers. Each magnitude step corresponds to a change in brightness of approximately 2½ times.

The beginnings of the Universe

Astronomers speculate that originally the Universe was compressed into a single point from which it began to expand. The event which set off this expansion, and therefore marked the origin of the Universe as we know it, is termed the Big Bang. In this Big Bang, all the matter in the Universe was flung outwards in the form of a dense gas, which has since condensed into giant globules to form galaxies of stars, all of which continue to rush rapidly outwards as space expands.

When did the Big Bang occur? According to current measurements of the rate of expansion of the Universe, all the matter that we now see in space must have been compressed together into a superdense globule between 10,000 million and 20,000 million years ago – about two to four times the age of the Earth. Therefore, modern astronomy allows us to date the Creation with a fair degree of accuracy.

If this view is correct, we should be able to see the Universe as it appeared shortly after it was born by looking deep into space. This is equivalent to looking back in time, because we see objects whose light has taken thousands of millions of years to reach us. Certainly, as we look ever further into space, the Universe begins to change in appearance. Instead of normal-looking galaxies like our own or the Andromeda spiral, astronomers find strange galaxies with brilliant cores known as Seyfert galaxies. Most remote of all are the mysterious quasars, intense sources of light and radio waves which are believed to represent the violent birth of a galaxy. Seyfert galaxies mark a more recent stage than quasars in the evolution of galaxies.

Further confirmation of the Big Bang origin of the Universe has come in recent years with the discovery by radio astronomers of a weak background warmth pervading the Universe. This background radiation is believed to be heat left over from the intense fireball of the Big Bang, and it means that space is not entirely cold, but has a temperature 2·7° above absolute zero on the Centigrade scale.

What will happen to the Universe in the future? One possibility is that the expansion will slow down and the Universe will start to contract again until a further Big Bang. According to one theory, the Universe might continue with endless cycles of expansion and contraction. Astronomers can find no sign that the expansion of the Universe is markedly slowing down. They now think that the Universe will continue to expand forever, slowly thinning out, until all the stars are extinguished and the Universe runs down into eternal darkness.

Composition and structure of the Sun and planets

The **Sun** is a giant gaseous ball of hydrogen and helium with traces of heavier elements such as iron, carbon, calcium and sodium. There is uncertainty about the nature of its internal structure, but there is probably a large core in which thermonuclear reactions produce vast quantities of heat which is transmitted upwards by radiation and convection to the photosphere, the Sun's visible surface. Hydrogen is converted into helium and in the process 4,000,000 tons of matter are lost to the Sun every second. In spite of this staggering loss the supply of hydrogen at the core is sufficient for another 1,500 million years.

Mercury, Venus, Earth and **Mars,** the so-called terrestrial planets, consist largely of silicates (compounds of silicon and oxygen with various metals) and iron. They also include simpler compounds, such as oxides, some of which contain heat-producing radioactive elements. All four planets have undergone differentiation at some stage, with the heavier elements and compounds falling towards the centre. Thus each has a metallic core surrounded by a silicate mantle and topped with a crust of lighter silicates, although the relative sizes of these zones vary from planet to planet. The atmosphere of the Earth consists largely of oxygen and nitrogen, but those of Venus and Mars are predominantly carbon dioxide. Mercury has no atmosphere. The Moon has a composition similar to that of the terrestrial planets but with smaller concentrations of the more volatile elements.

The **Asteroids**, the thousands of small bodies revolving around the Sun mostly between Mars and Jupiter, vary in composition. About 80 per cent of them consist of silicates, 6–10 per cent are made of metal (chiefly iron with some nickel), and the rest are silicate-metal mixtures. Ceres, 429 miles in diameter, is the largest and Pallas (281 miles), is the second largest.

Jupiter is the largest of the planets, having a mass of about two and a half times greater than that of all the other planets combined. Because of its low density it must consist largely of light elements such as hydrogen and helium, although it probably also has a very small rocky core of silicates and iron. Surrounding this hypothetical core is a shell comprising mainly liquid atomic hydrogen, and above that is a surface layer of liquid molecular hydrogen. The atmosphere of Jupiter consists chiefly of hydrogen, helium, ammonia, methane and water. Apart from its great size, Jupiter is remarkable for the Red Spot and bands of clouds which sweep across its face.

Saturn, Uranus and **Neptune** are smaller than Jupiter but also have low densities and are similar in general composition and structure. Their rocky iron-silicate cores are proportionately larger, however, especially in the cases of Uranus and Neptune. All three planets have atmospheres in which the most abundant gas is hydrogen but in which there is little or no ammonia. Methane, on the other hand, is much more abundant than in the atmosphere of Jupiter. Titan, one of the 10 satellites of Saturn, is the largest satellite in the solar system (being larger even than the planet Mercury) and the only one known to have an atmosphere (mainly methane and hydrogen). It also appears to have a unique composition, for it comprises a rocky core surrounded by a wet rocky mantle, a layer of ammonia-water solution, and finally a surface layer of ice and methane. The rings of Saturn probably consist of small ice particles.

Pluto is an anomoly among the outer planets, although very little is really known about it. It is definitely very small, but its precise mass and density are uncertain. It would appear to have no atmosphere.

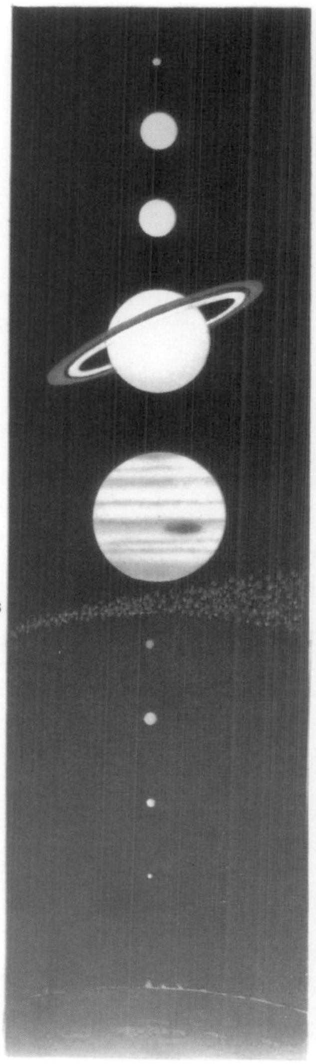

Pluto
Neptune
Uranus
Saturn
Jupiter
The asteroids
Mars
Earth
Venus
Mercury
The Sun

Planetary data	Mercury	Venus	Earth	Mars	Jupiter	Saturn	Uranus	Neptune	Pluto
Orbital revolution	87 days 23 hours	224 days 17 hours	365 days 6 hours	1 year 322 days	10 years 318 days	29 years 168 days	84 years 4 days	164 years 292 days	249 years 330 days
Distance from Sun in miles	36M	67M	92M	141M	465M	886M	1,783M	2,791M	3,671M
Orbital inclination	7°	3°24′	0°	1°48′	1°18′	2°30′	0°48′	1°48′	17°12′
Equatorial diameter in miles	3,025	3,526	7,926·4	4,200	88,700	75,000	29,300	31,200	3,700
Rotation	59 days	243 days	23 hours 56 mins	24 hours 10 mins	9 hours 50 mins	10 hours 14 mins	10 hours 48 mins	14 hours	153 hours
Satellites	0	0	1	2	14	10	5	2	0
Orbital velocity in miles per second	29·8	21·8	18·5	15	8·1	6	4·2	3·4	3

Big Bang theory

Following initial explosion of exceedingly dense matter dispersal outward continues with simultaneous formation of galaxies. This event is estimated to have taken place between 10 and 20,000 million years ago.

Steady State theory

The Universe did not originate at any one instant in time but all galaxies appear to be continually receding from each other. New matter is created to fill the spaces left and this forms new galaxies. There is strong evidence, particularly observational, against the theory.

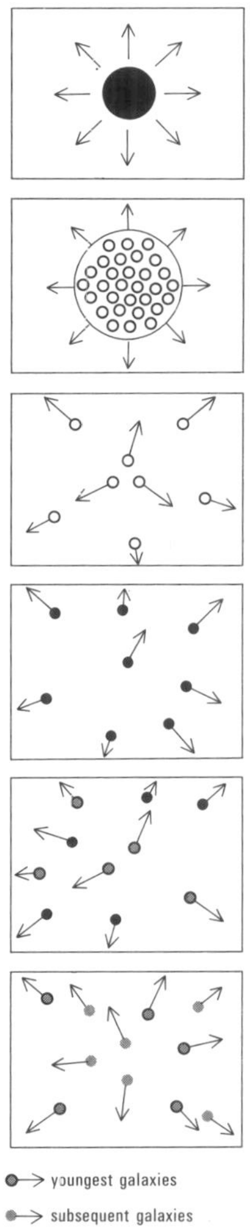

galaxies
oldest galaxies
youngest galaxies
subsequent galaxies

Bode's Law

If 4 is added to the sequence 0, 3, 6, 12, etc., the resulting numbers give the relative distances of the seven nearest planets to the Sun. The Law, first published in 1772 does not appear valid for Neptune and Pluto at the outer reaches of the solar system.

Mercury	Venus	Earth	Mars	Ceres (Asteroid)	Jupiter	Saturn	Uranus
0	3	6	12	24	48	96	192
4	4	4	4	4	4	4	4
4	7	10	16	28	52	100	196

Stars and galaxies

Stars are born from giant clouds of gas and dust in a galaxy. A typical cloud is the famous nebula in the constellation of Orion. The Orion nebula is lit up by stars that have formed within it during the past few million years. Such a cloud can eventually give rise to a whole cluster of perhaps a hundred stars or more, like the Pleiades cluster in Taurus (see photograph).

As the cloud collapses under the inward pull of its own gravity, it breaks up into smaller clumps from which individual stars will form. Each clump continues to get smaller and denser until the pressure and temperature at its centre becomes so extreme that nuclear reactions start to make the gas ball a true, self-luminous star. Sometimes two, three, or more stars come into being close to each other, and remain linked by gravity throughout their lives as a double or multiple star. In some cases, a star may be surrounded by a disc of material left over from its formation, from which a planetary system may grow. Planets are cold and non-luminous and shine only by reflecting the light of their parent stars.

Stars differ in size and temperature depending on how much matter they contain. The Sun, 865,000 miles in diameter, is an average star in its size and temperature. Some stars are smaller and cooler than the Sun; these are known as red dwarfs, and they are so faint that even the nearest is invisible without a telescope. Other stars are larger and hotter than the Sun, so they appear white like Sirius or even blue like Rigel. A star is powered throughout most of its active life by nuclear reactions that turn hydrogen into helium, as the process in a hydrogen bomb. Stars consist mostly of hydrogen, which is by far the most abundant element in the Universe, and of which gas clouds such as the Orion nebula are mostly made.

As a star ages, it begins to run out of hydrogen at its centre. The nuclear fires then move outwards into the layers surrounding the core, generating more energy as they do so. In response to this the star begins to swell up into a red giant, perhaps 100 times its former size. Stars several times heavier than the Sun then undergo a runaway series of nuclear reactions at their core, leading to their eventual eruption in a nuclear holocaust called a supernova. When a star erupts as a supernova, its brightness increases by millions of times for a few days or weeks before it fades away into obscurity.

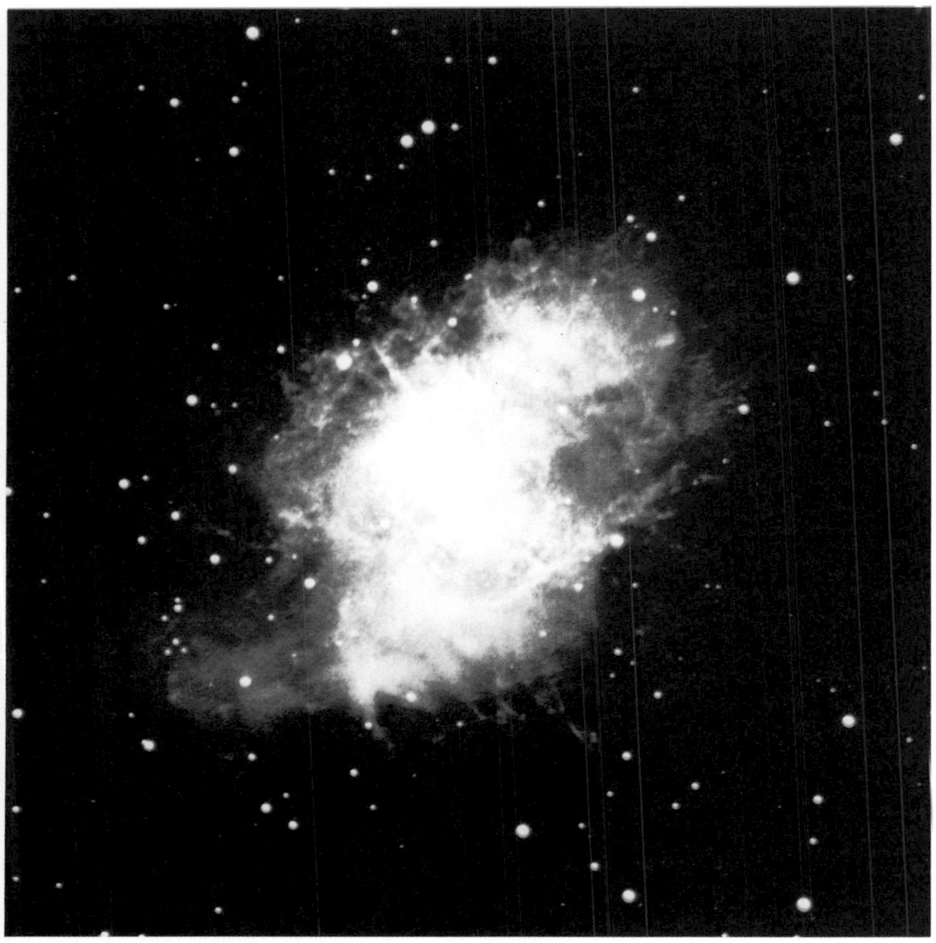

Crab Nebula
The supernova which was expanded to give the Crab Nebula occurred about 4,000 years ago. What we see today is the stage of development after only 920 years. A supernova explosion follows the collapse of a star at very high temperatures, and the rate of ejection of material is very rapid indeed; for about two weeks the radiation may be 200 times that of the Sun. The Nebula is 6,000 light years away in the constellation Taurus.

Pleiades
This cluster of 200 stars is about 130 parsecs distant from the Earth or 425 light years. The cluster is less than 100 million years old and is visible to the naked eye.

Andromeda Galaxy (below)
Sometimes called the Great Galaxy of Andromeda it is a flat, spiral galaxy containing about 100,000,000,000 stars, with two smaller satellite galaxies. Andromeda is 2·2 million light years from Earth.

A supernova explosion throws the star's outer layers off into space, producing an object like the Crab nebula in Taurus (see photograph) which is the remains of a supernova observed by Oriental astronomers in AD1054. During a supernova explosion the erupting star's central core is compressed into a small, dense object known as a neutron star, about 10 miles in diameter. Neutron stars were first detected by radio astronomers in 1967 as the rapidly flashing radio sources known as pulsars. Pulsars are actually fast-spinning neutron stars which emit a flash of energy every time they revolve.

Black holes

If the remnant core of a star weighs more than about three times the Sun, then the inward pull of its own gravity is so strong that it cannot remain as a neutron star. It continues to shrink ever smaller and denser until it vanishes from sight in a black hole. A black hole is formed once the object has reached a certain small size and high density and its gravitational pull is so great that nothing can escape, not even light. The centre of the black hole, the point where all matter is compressed to infinite density and zero volume is termed a 'singularity'. The hole therefore becomes truly black, and cannot be seen from outside. However, matter can fall into a black hole, and this gives a clue to the object's existence. Gas falling into the intense gravitational field around a black hole heats up to many millions of degrees, emitting X-rays which can be detected by satellites orbiting Earth. In this way, astronomers believe they have detected at least one black hole, known as the X-ray source Cygnus X-I, orbiting a visible star catalogued HDE 226868 in the constellation Cygnus about 6,500 light years distant.

Death of the Sun

An ordinary star such as the Sun dies much more quietly. The Sun is nearly 5,000 million years old, which means that it is halfway through its expected life. In about another 5,000 million years it will run out of hydrogen at the core and start to burn helium. It will then swell to 250 times its present size into a red giant star like Arcturus. As it does so it will engulf the planets Mercury, Venus, and perhaps also the Earth. Long before then, life on our planet will have become extinct. At its death, the Earth will be consumed by fire.

The nebulous outer layers of the red giant Sun will then slowly disperse into space, forming a giant smoke ring. This stage will last some fifty thousand years. The Sun's hot core will be left behind as a white dwarf star, about the size of the Earth. Over millions upon millions of years this white dwarf will slowly cool into invisibility by slowly releasing energy from its outer layers. Any charred remains of the Earth will be engulfed by ice as the white dwarf Sun fades away like a dying ember, leaving only memories of the human civilisation that once flourished around it.

Galaxies and the Universe

The Milky Way Galaxy in which the Solar System is situated probably started to form about 15,000 million years ago; the age of the oldest stars. This Galaxy is about 100,000 light years in diameter; the Sun and its system of nine planets lie about two-thirds of the way from the centre to the limit of the arm of the spiral. Large telescopes reveal countless other galaxies dotted throughout space. One of the nearest of these galaxies is the giant spiral in the constellation Andromeda (see photo) which lies over two million light years from the Earth. If we could see our own Galaxy from the outside, it would probably look much like Andromeda. All the Milky Way stars are orbiting around the centre of the Galaxy; the Sun takes 225 million years to complete the circuit.

Our own Galaxy and the Andromeda spiral are the two largest members of a cluster of about 30 galaxies called the Local Group. Many other galaxies are also bunched into groups like this, although there are plenty of individual galaxies dotted through space.

Two small galaxies, 160,000 light years away, are visible in the Southern Hemisphere. These are known as the Magellanic Clouds and are linked to our own Galaxy through a common envelope of hydrogen gas. Most galaxies are spiral in shape, but some are elliptical. The largest galaxies of all are giant ellipticals, containing a hundred times as many stars as our Milky Way.

As astronomers probed deep into the Universe with large telescopes half a century ago, they found an amazing fact: all galaxies, either individually or in groups, seemed to be rushing away from each other, as though the space between them was expanding. This fact was deduced from the red shift, or lengthening of the wavelength of light received from the galaxies, which would be caused by such a recession. The light waves are stretched out by the Doppler effect and at a given wavelength move towards the red end of the spectrum. The amount of the red shift is measured by the movement of the dark absorption line. This reveals the speed of recession of the galaxy and therefore its distance can be computed. Astronomers therefore began to compare the Universe to a continually inflating balloon. This provided a vital clue to the possible origin of the Universe, (see Big Bang theory).

Future scientific exploration of the centre of our Galaxy will rely on infra-red and radio observations which can penetrate the interstellar dust.

The Moon

The Moon is by far our nearest natural neighbour in space. It orbits the Earth every month at an average distance of 240,000 miles. The Moon is 2,160 miles in diameter, or roughly one-quarter the size of the Earth. No other natural satellite in the solar system is so close in size to its parent body, so astronomers often regard the Earth–Moon pairing as a double planet.

Rocks returned by American astronauts and Soviet automatic landers have confirmed that the Moon was born at the same time as the Earth, approximately 4,700 million years ago. Probably the two objects formed side by side, although it is possible that the Moon formed elsewhere in the solar system and was later captured. Most astronomers now think it unlikely that the Moon split away from the Earth.

The Moon's surface is pitted with craters of varying sizes, from vast basins more than 100 miles in diameter to microscopic pits. Astronomers argued over the origin of these for centuries, but it is now generally agreed that the majority of them were formed by the impact of meteorites long ago in the history of the solar system. This theory has been strengthened by the discovery that similar craters pockmark the surface of other bodies in the solar system, notably the planets Mercury and Mars.

Early in its history the Moon partially melted so that a rocky crust solidified at its surface. This crust has since been buffeted by meteorites which have produced the jumbled highlands. Several particularly large bodies have gouged out lowland basins which have since been flooded with dark lava. These dark lowlands are called the *maria*, or seas.

Unmanned space probes orbiting the Moon have made a complete photographic map of its front and back surface. As the Moon spins on its own axis in the same time as it takes to orbit the Earth (termed a *captured* rotation) no man had seen the far side of the Moon until the first space probes were sent to investigate. It has been found that there are no large *mare* regions on the far side of the Moon, evidently because the Moon's crust is about 25 miles thicker on the far side than on the Earth-turned hemisphere.

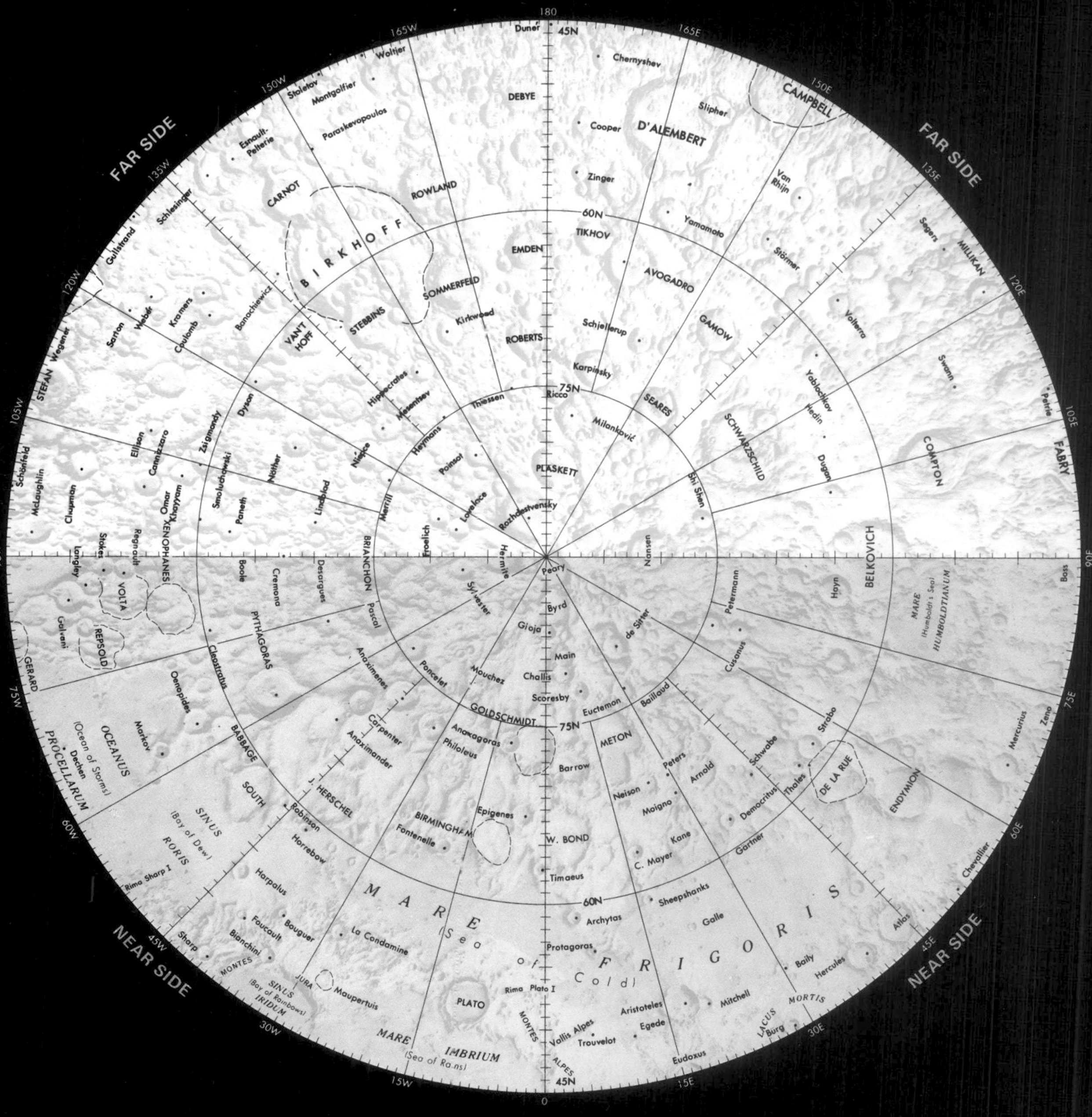

NORTH POLAR REGION

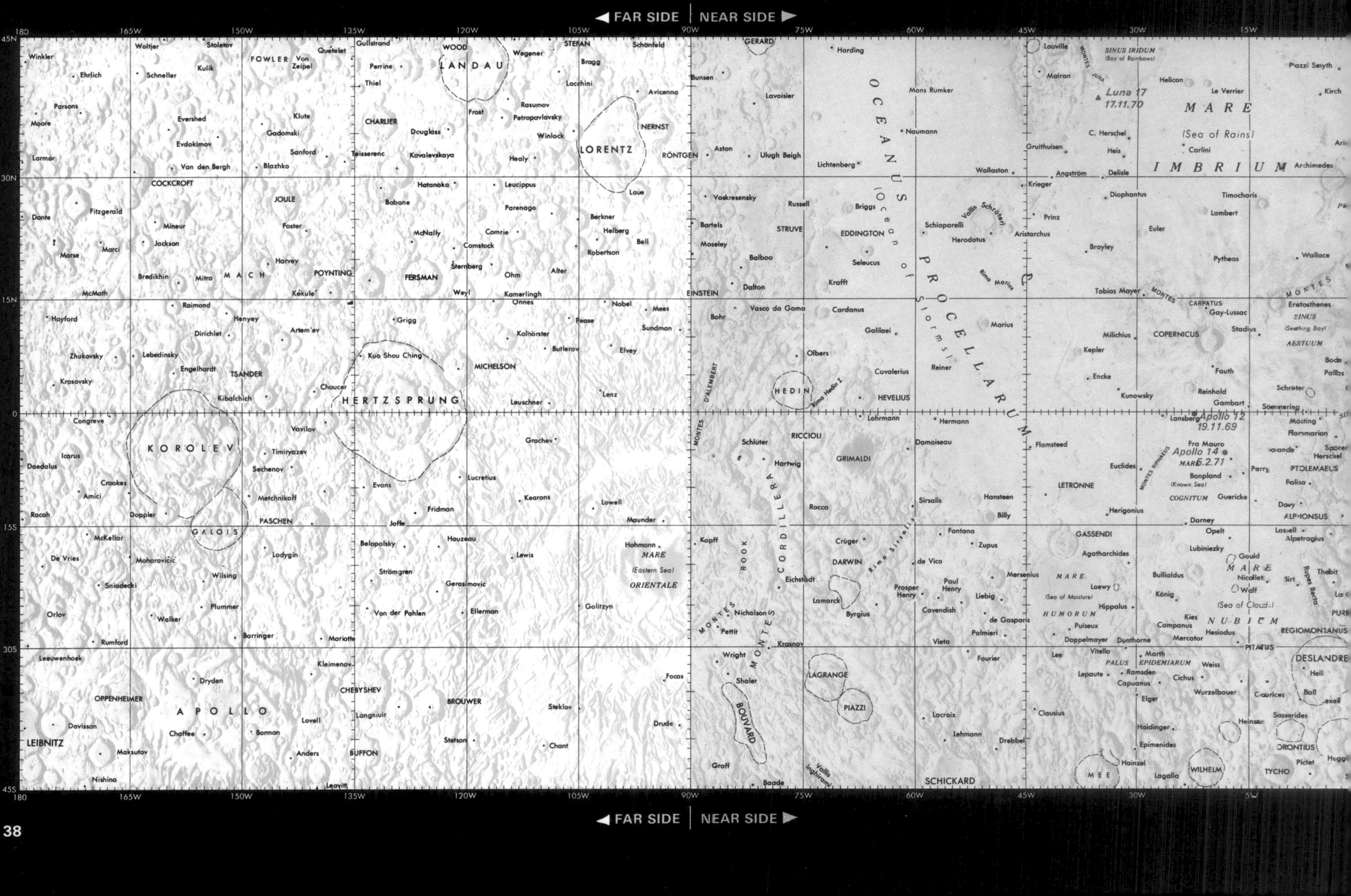

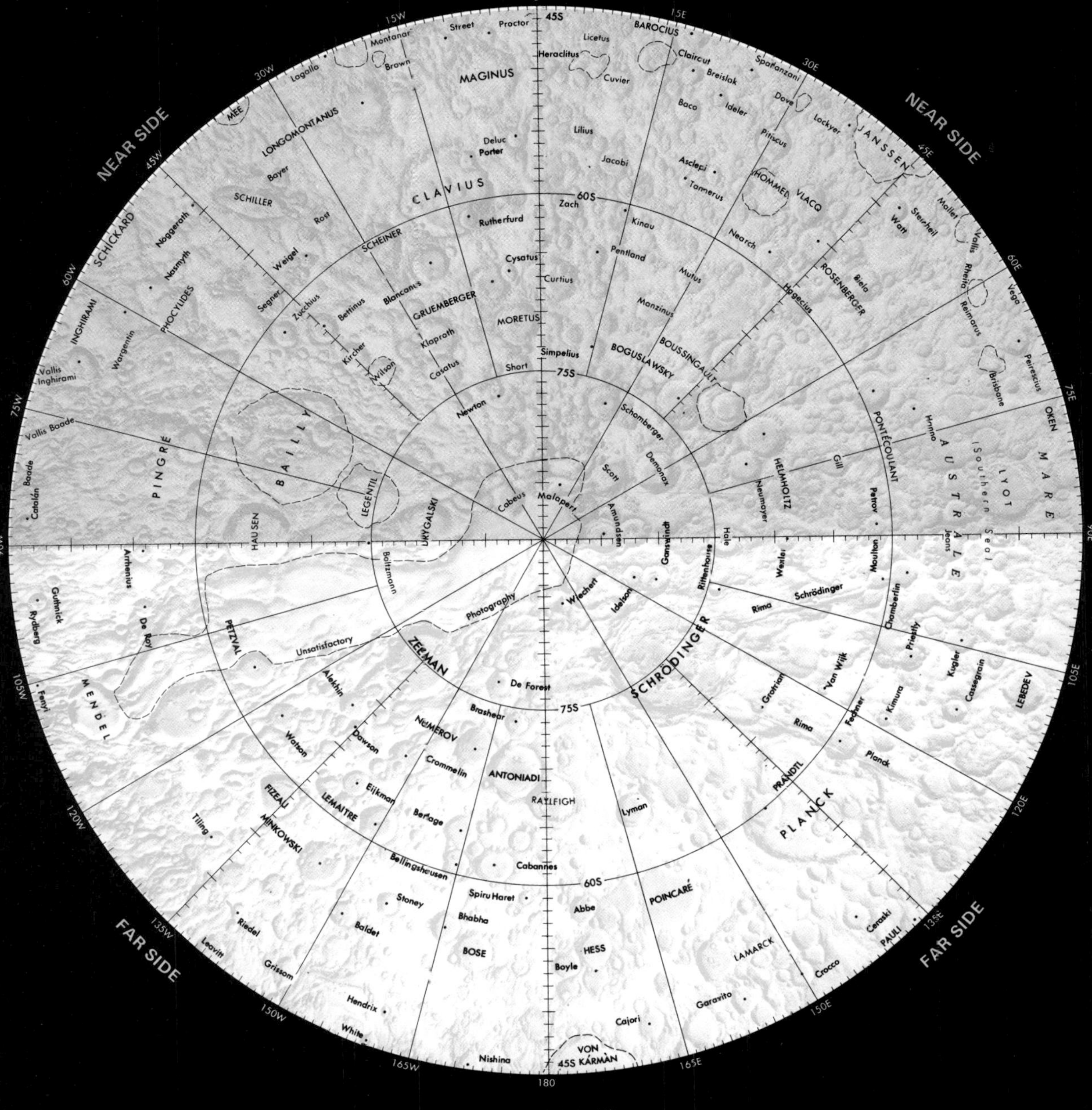

SOUTH POLAR REGION

LUNAR DATA

Earth/Moon Mass Ratio	M_e/M_m 81·3015
Density (mean)	3·34g/(cm)^3
Synodic Month (new Moon to new Moon)	29·530, 588d
Sidereal Month (fixed star to fixed star)	27·321, 661d
Inclination of Lunar orbit to eclipse	5°8′43″
Inclination of equator to eclipse	1°40′32″
Inclination of Lunar orbit to Earth's equator	18°·5 to 28°·5
Distance from Moon to Earth (mean)	238·328M (384,400km)
Optical libration in longitude	±7°·6
Optical libration in latitude	±6°·7
Magnitude (mean of full Moon)	−12·7
Temperature	−244°F to +273°F (120°K to 407°K)
Escape velocity	1·48mi/sec (2·38km/sec)
Diameter of Moon	2,160mi (3,476km)
Surface gravity	162·2 cm/sec^2
Orbital velocity	0·64mi/sec (Moon) 1·024km/sec 18·5mi/sec (Earth) 29·6km/sec

▲ *Landing site of Soviet Moon vehicle "Lunokhod"*
● *Manned Spacecraft landing site*

◀ NEAR SIDE | FAR SIDE ▶

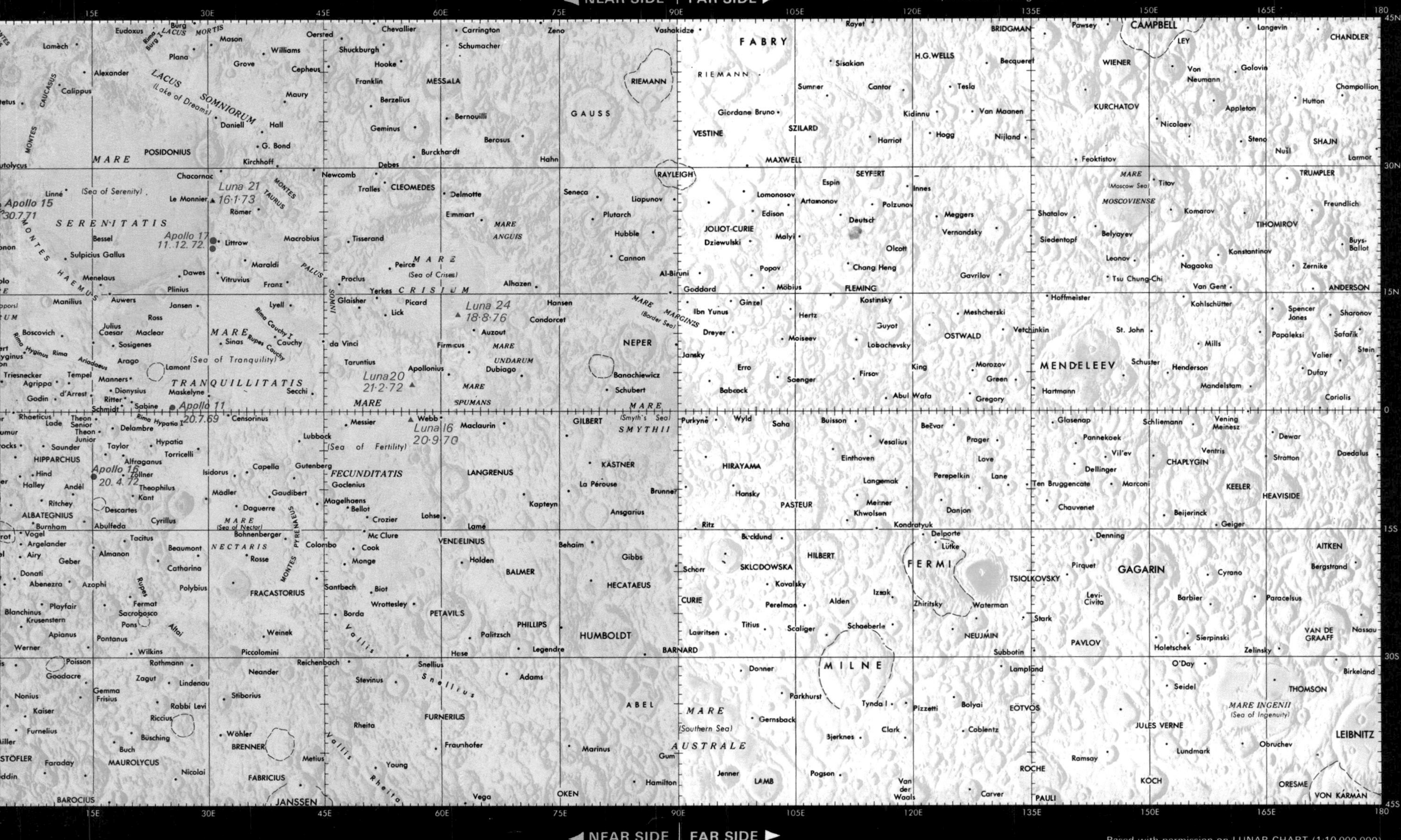

◀ NEAR SIDE | FAR SIDE ▶

Based with permission on LUNAR CHART (1:10,000,000) by the Aeronautical Chart and Information Centre.

The Stars

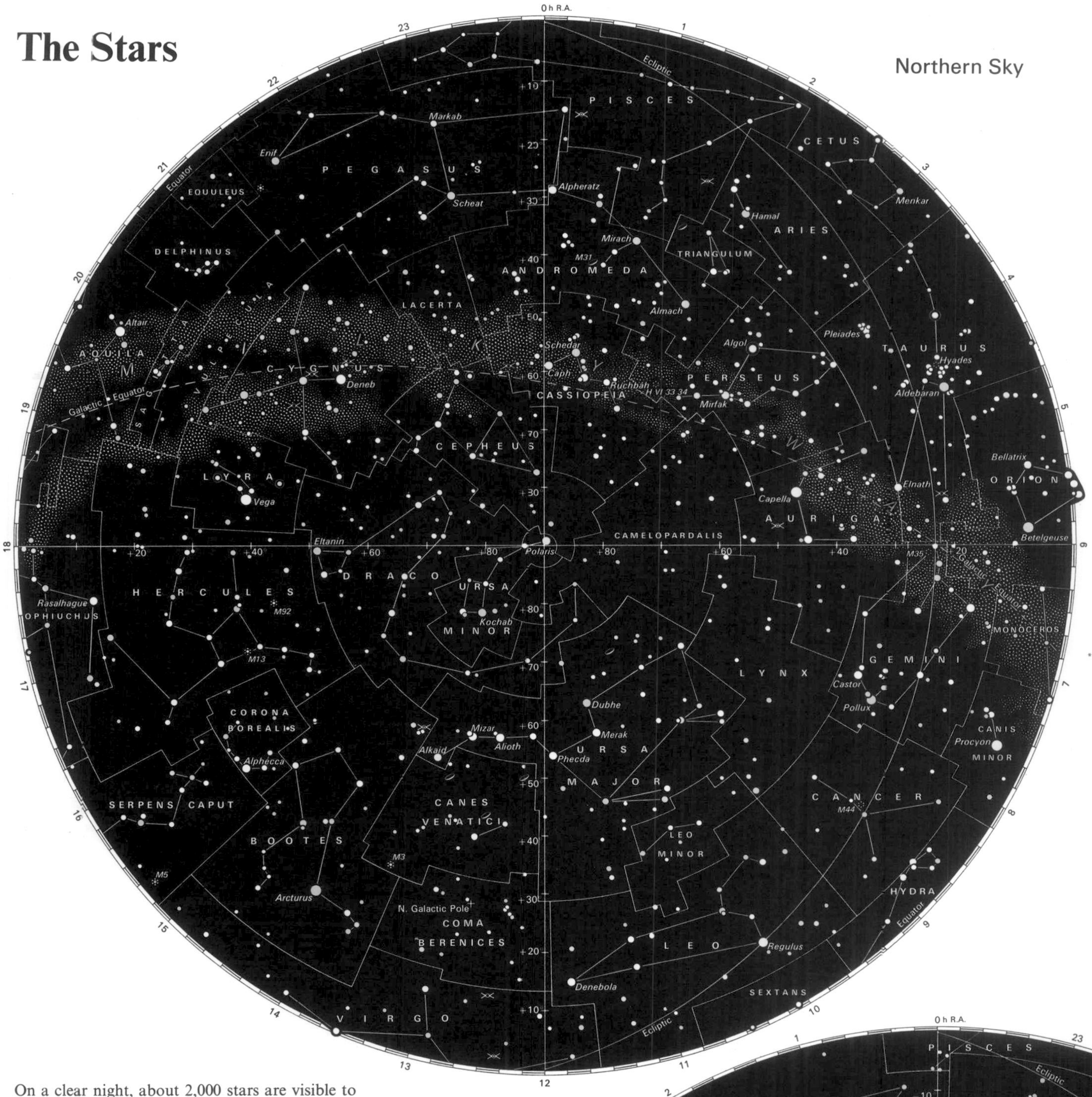

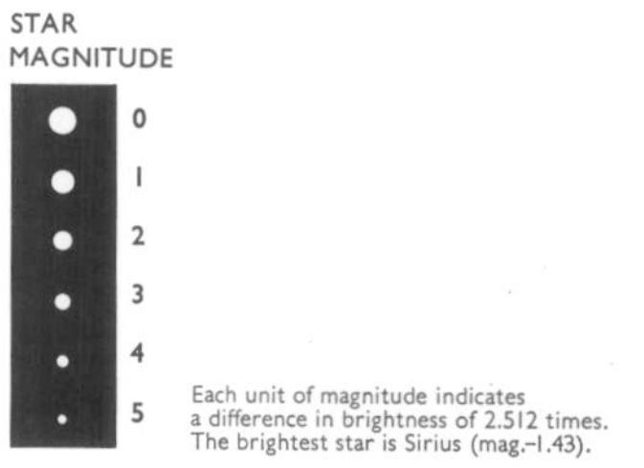

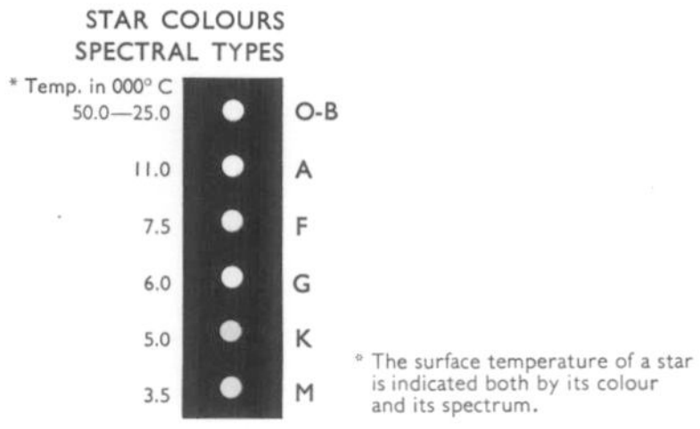

On a clear night, about 2,000 stars are visible to the naked eye at any one time. Countless thousands of others become visible with modest optical aid such as a pair of binoculars or a small telescope. The charts on this page show the main stars of the northern and southern hemisphere of the sky, along with the constellations into which they are grouped. Unless an observer is situated at the north or south pole, he will see some stars in both hemispheres. How far he sees into the opposite hemisphere depends on how close he is to the equator. The number of stars visible depends on the time and the season.

Some constellation figures go back thousands of years to ancient Mediterranean peoples, who placed their mythical beasts and heroes among the stars. Since then, more constellations have been added, particularly in the southern hemisphere which was invisible from the Mediterranean, so that a total of 88 constellations now cover the entire sky. They are useful for indicating the approximate locations of celestial objects. Precise locations are given by the celestial equivalents of longitude and latitude – Right Ascension (R.A., measured in hours, minutes, and seconds) and Declination (measured in degrees).

The size of the star images on the maps represents the perceived brightness of each star. Star brightnesses are measured in magnitudes, with the brightest stars first magnitude, and the faintest stars visible to the naked eye the sixth magnitude. A first magnitude star is 100 times brighter than a sixth magnitude star. Objects brighter than first magnitude are given increasingly large negative magnitudes, such as Sirius −1·47, the planet Venus at its brightest −4·4, the full Moon −12·7, and the Sun −26·8. Objects fainter than sixth magnitude are given progressively larger positive magnitudes. The faintest objects so far detected are around magnitude 24.

Although all stars appear white they are different colours, depending on their temperatures. The stars with coolest surface temperatures appear red, like the red giant Arcturus, while the hottest stars such as Sirius appears white or blue. The temperature of a star can be deduced from an examination of its spectrum; this classification is known as a star's spectral type.

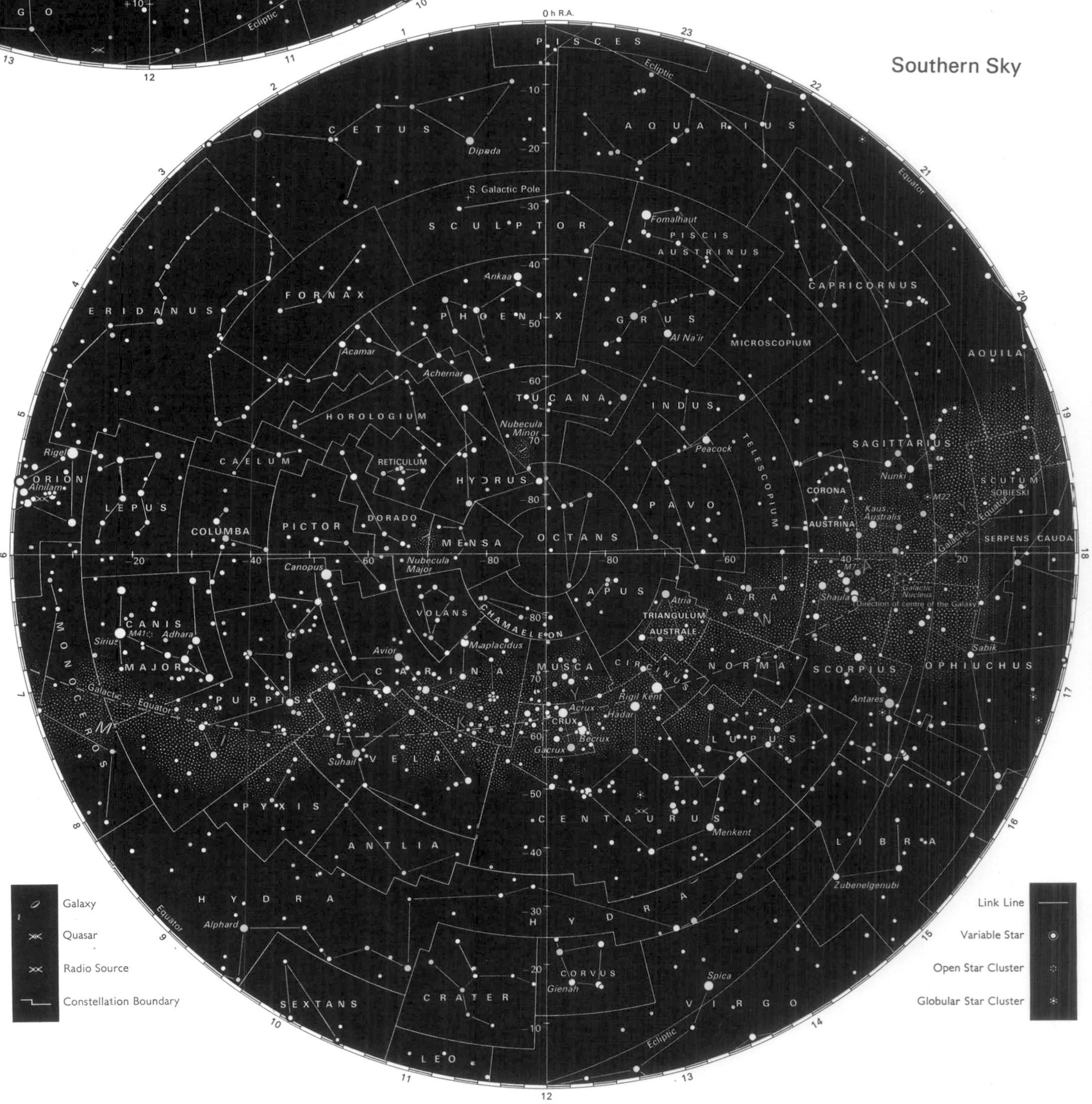

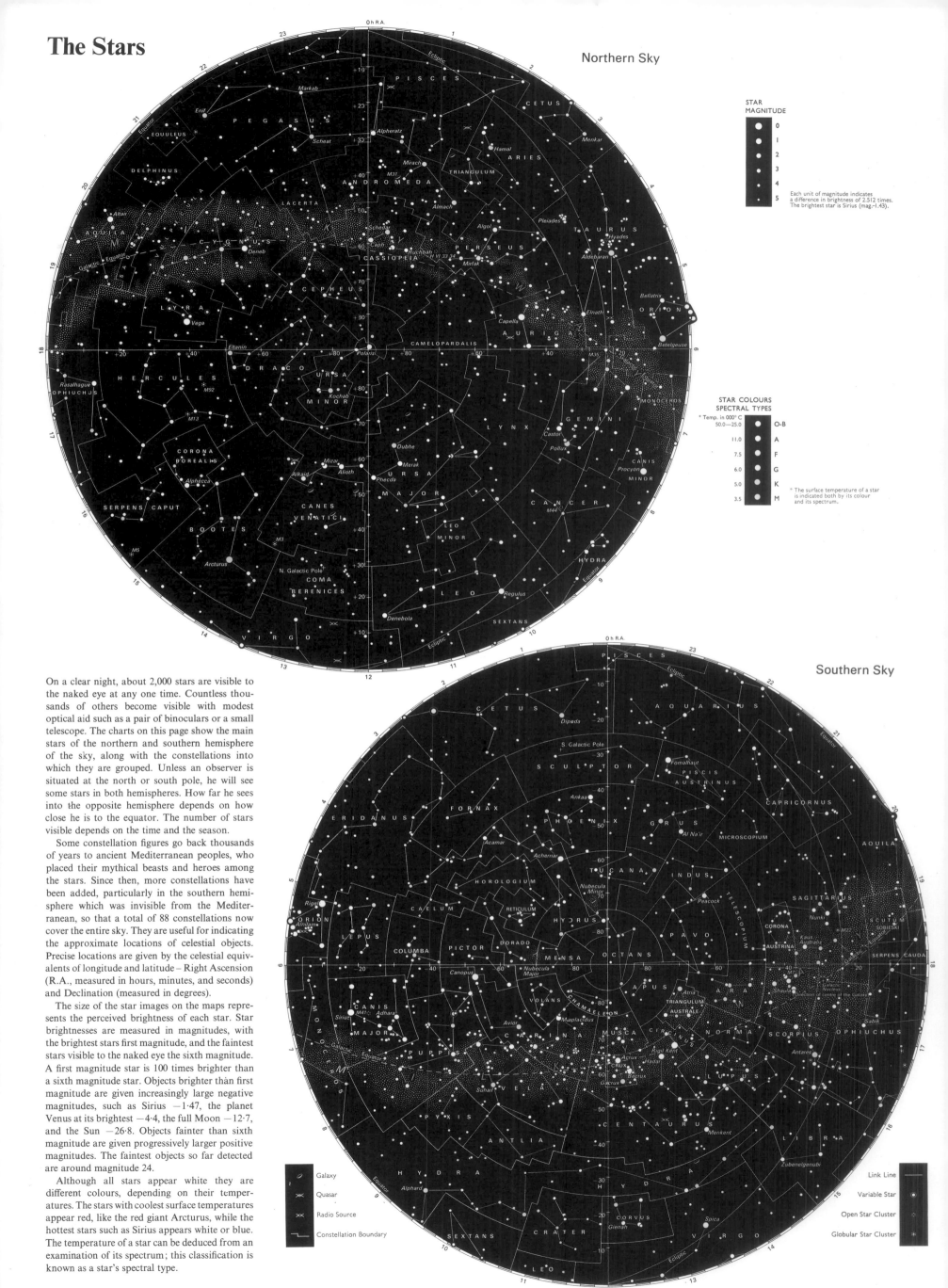

BOUNDARIES

- International
- International, Undefined or Alignment Uncertain
- Limits of Sovereignty across Water Areas
- Autonomous, Federal State
- Main Administrative
- Other Administrative
- Offshore Administrative
- Armistice, Cease-Fire Line
- Demilitarised Zone
- National Park
- Reserve, Reservation

COMMUNICATIONS

- Main Railways
- Other Railway
- Light Railway
- Projected Railways
- Railway Tunnels
- Road Tunnel
- Special Highway (Projected)
- Main Road (Projected)
- Other Road (Projected)
- Tracks
- Car Ferries
- Rail Ferries
- Navigable Canals (Locks)
- Projected or Disused Canal
- Drainage or Irrigation Canal
- Canal Tunnel
- Tunnel Aqueduct

LAKE TYPES

- Fresh-water
- Reservoir (Dam)
- Seasonal Fresh
- Seasonal Brackish
- Salt-lake, Lagoon
- Perennial Salt-lake
- Seasonal Salt-lake
- Saline Mud-flat
- Salt-flat

LANDSCAPE FEATURES

- Ice-field and Glaciers
- Ice-cap, Ice-sheet
- Lava-fields
- Lava-fields
- Sand Desert, Dunes
- Saline Marsh, Salt Desert
- Marsh, Swamp
- Swamp, Flood-area
- Mangrove Swamp
- Tidal Area
- Atoll

OTHER FEATURES

- River, Stream
- Seasonal Watercourses
- Seasonal Flood-plain
- Undefined Course of River
- Pass; Gorges
- Waterfalls, Rapids
- Dam, Barrage
- Escarpments
- Flood Dyke
- Limits of Ice-shelf
- Reefs
- Rocks
- Spot Depth (· 9650)
- Lighthouse
- Lightship; Beacon
- Waterhole, Well
- Active Volcano
- Summit, Peak
- Oil Wells
- Oil or Natural Gas Pipeline
- Mine
- Site of Battle
- Historic Site
- Historic Ruin
- Ancient Walls
- Mosque, Sheikh's Tomb
- Cathedral, Monastery, Church
- International or Main Airport
- Airport, Airfield

CITY MAPS

- State Boundary
- County, Department Boundary
- City Limits
- Borough, District Boundary
- Main Railways (Station)
- Other Railways (Bridge)
- Projected Railways
- Underground Railway (Station)
- Special Highway (Projected)
- Main Road
- Secondary Road
- Other Road, Street
- Track
- Road Tunnel
- Bridge; Flyover
- Seaway (Locks)
- Canals
- Drainage Canal
- Waterfalls, Rapids
- Historic Walls
- Airports
- Racecourses
- Stadium
- Cemetery; Churches
- Woodland, Park
- Built-up Area

STYLES OF LETTERING

TOGO	Country Name	*M O A B*	Historic Region
ALBERTA	Administrative Divisions -Major	*D E C C A N*	Physical Regions
KENT CHER	Administrative Divisions -Other	*S I N A I*	Physical Regions
PARIS Bern	National Capitals	*Mato Grosso*	Physical Regions
Omsk	Administrative Centres	*ATLAS Nile*	Physical Features
Denver	Administrative Centres	*Mt Blanc Thames*	Physical Features
Krakow	Administrative Centres	*BASIN Ridge*	Ocean Bottom Features
GANDER Gatwick	Airports	*M A S A I*	Tribal Name

PRINCIPAL MAP ABBREVIATIONS

A.	1. Alp, Alpen, Alpi. 2. Alt
Abb^{e}	Abbaye
A.C.T.	Australian Capital Territory
Aig.	Aiguille
Akr.	Ákra, Akrotírion
Anch.	Anchorage
A.O.	Avtonómnaya Oblast'
App^{no}	Appennino
Aqued.	Aqueduct
Ar.	Arroyo
Arch.	Archipel, Archipelago, Archipiélago
Arr.	Arrecife
A.S.S.R.	Avtonómnaya Sovétskaya Sotsialistícheskaya Respúblika
Ay.	Ayia, Áyioi, Áyion, Ayios
B.	1. Baai, Bahía, Baía, Baie, Baja, Bay, Bucht, Bukhta, Bukt. 2. Bad, 3. Ban. 4. Barazh, Barrage, Barragem 5. Bayou. 6. Bír. 7. Boeloe, Bonto, Bulu
B^{c}	Banc
B^{ca}	Boca
Bel.	Belgium, Belgian
Bg.	Berg
Bgt.	Bight, Bugt
B^{i}	Bani, Beni
B^{j}	Burj
B^{k}	Bank
Bk.	Boekoe, Buku
B^{n}	Basin
Bol.	Bol'shoy
Bos.	Bosanski
Br.	1. Branch. 2. Bredning. 3. Bridge, Brücke. 4. Britain, British. 5. Burun
Bt.	Bukit
Bü.	Büyük
Bukh.	Bukhta
C.	1. Cabo, Cap, Cape. 2. Cay. 3. Česká, -é, -y. 4. Col.
Cach.	Cachoeira, -o
Can.	1. Canal. 2. Canale. 3. Canavese. 4. Cañon, Canyon
Cas.	Castle
Cat.	1. Cataract. 2. Catena (Sardinia)
Cath.	Cathedral
C^{ca}	Cabeça, -o (Azores)
C^{d}	Ciudad
Cerv.	Červená, -é, -ý
Ch.	1. Chapel, Chapelle, Church. 2. Chaung. 3. Chott.
Chan.	Channel
Ch^{au}	Château
Ch^{e}	Chaine
Ch^{lle}	Chapelle
C^{ma}	Cima
C^{no}	Corno
C^{o}	Cerro
Const^{n}	Construction
Cord.	Cordillera
Cr.	Creek
Cuch.	Cuchilla
Cuc^{ru}	Cuccuru (Sardinia)
Cy.	City
Czo.	Cozzo
D.	1. Da, Dag, Dagh, Dağı, Dağları. 2. Darreh. 3. Daryācheh
-d.	dake
D.C.	District of Columbia
Den.	Denmark
Dists.	Districts
Div.	Division
Dj.	Djebel
Dns.	Downs
Dz.	Dzong
E.	East
E.D.	Existence doubtful
Eil.	Eiland, Eilanden
Escarp.	Escarpment
Est.	Estacion
E^{tg}	Etang
F.	Firth
F.D.	Federal District
Fj.	1. Fjell. 2. Fjord, Fjörður
F^{k}	Fork
Fl.	Fleuve
Fr.	France, French
Ft.	Fort
F.T.A.I.	Fr. Ter. of Afars & Issas
Fy.	Ferry
G.	1. Gawa. 2. Gebel. 3. Ghedir. 4. Göl, Gölü, Gōl. 5. Golfe, Golfo, Gulf. 6. Gompa. 7. Gora, Gory. 8. Guba. 9. Gunung
G.D.&D.	Goa, Daman & Diu
G^{d}	Grand
G^{de}	Grande
Geb.	Gebergte, Gebirge
Geog^{l}	Geographical
Gez.	Gezira
Ghub.	Ghubba
Gl.	1. Gamle, Gammel. 2. Glacier
Gp.	Group
Gr.	1. Graben. 2. Gross, -e
G^{r}	Gasr
Gr^{tes}	Grottes
Gt.	Great, Groot, -e
H.	1. Hawr. 2. Hill. 3. Hoch. 4. Hora, Hory
Halv.	Halvöy
Har.	Harbour
H^{d}	Head
H.E.P.	Hydro-Electric Power
H^{g}	Hegység
H^{gts}	Heights
H^{i}	Hasi, Hasy
Hist.	Historic
H^{n}	Horn
Hosp.	1. Hospice, Hospiz 2. Hospital
Ht.	Haut
Hte.	Haute
H^{ter}	Hinter
H^{y}	Highway
I.	Île, Ilha, Insel, Isla, Island, Isle, Isola, Isole
IJ.	IJssel
im.	imeni
In.	1. Inder, Indre, Inner, Inre. 2. Inlet
IND.	India
Inf.	Inferior, -e, Inférieure
Int.	International
I^{s}	Îles, Ilhas, Islands, Islas, Isles
ISR.	Israel
Isth.	Isthmus
J.	1. Jabal, Jebel, Jibāl. 2. Järvi, Jaure, Jazira, Jezero, Jezíoro. 3. Jökull
Jap.	Japan, Japanese
Jct.	Junction
K.	1. Kaap, Kap, Kapp. 2. Kaikyo. 3. Kato. 4. Kerang, Kering. 5. Kiang. 6. Kirke. 7. Ko. 8. Koh, Kūh, Kūhha. 9. Kolpos. 10. Kopf. 11. Kuala. 12. Kyst
Kan.	Kanal, Kanaal
Kap.	Kapelle
Kep.	Kepulauan
Kg.	Kampong, Kompong Kong
Kh.	1. Khawr. 2. Khirbet, Khīābān, -e. 3. Khowr
Khr.	Khrebet
Kl.	1. Kechil. 2. Klein, -e
Kör.	Körfez, -i
Kr.	Kangar
Kü.	Küçük
L.	1. Lac, Lago, Lagôa, Lake, Liman, Limni, Liqen, Loch, Lough. 2. Lam
Lag.	Lagoon, Laguna, -e
L^{d}	Land
Ldg.	Landing
L.H.	Light House
Lit.	Little
Ll.	Lille
M.	1. Mae, Me. 2. Meer. 3. Muang. 4. Muntil 5. Muong. 6. Mys
m.	metre/s
Mal.	Malyy
Mem.	Memorial
Mex.	Mexico, Mexican
M^{f}	Massif
M^{gna}	Montagna
M^{gne}	Montagne
Mkt.	Markt
Mon.	Monasterio, Monastery
Mont.	Monument
Mt.	Mont, Mount, Mountain
Mte.	Monte
M^{tes}	Montes
Mti.	Monti, Munti
Mts.	Monts, Mountains
N.	1. Nam. 2. Neu, Ny. 3. Nevado, Nudo, 4. Noord, Nord, Nörre, Nørre, North. 5. Nos
N^{a}	Nuestra
Nat.	National
Nats. Okr.	Natsionalnyy Okrug
N.D.	Notre Dame
N^{dr}	Neder, Nieder
N.E.	North East
Neth.	Netherlands
Nizh.	Nizhne, Nizhniy
Nizm.	Nizmennost
N.O.	Noord Oost, Nord Ost
Nor.	Norway, Norwegian
N^{os}	Nudos
Nov.	Novyy
N^{r}	Nether
N.T.	Neutral Territory
N.W.	North West
N.Z.	New Zealand
O.	1. Old. 2. Oost, Ost. 3. Ostrov
Ö.	1. Östre. 2. Öy
Ø.	1. Østre. 2. Øy
Ob.	Ober
O^{de}	Oude
O^{et}	Oguilet
Ogl.	Oglat
O.L.V.	Onze Lieve Vrouw
Or.	Ori, Oros
Orm.	Ormos
Ot.	Olet
Öv.	Över, Övre
O^{va}	Ostrova
Oz.	Ozero
P.	1. Pass. 2. Pic, Pico, Piz. 3. Pulau
Pal.	Palace, Palacio, Palais
Pass.	Passage
Peg.	Pegunungan
Pen.	Peninsula, Penisola
Per.	Pereval
P^{gio}	Poggio
Pk.	1. Park. 2. Peak, Pik
Pkwy.	Parkway
Pl.	1. Planina, Planinski. 2. Plei
P^{la}	Playa
Plat.	Plateau
Plosk.	Ploskogor'ye
P^{ro}	Pantano
P^{rte}	Pointe
Por.	Porog
Port.	Portugal, Portuguese
P^{ov}	Poluostrov
Pr.	1. Proliv. 2. Przyladek 3. Prince
Prom^{y}	Promontory
Prop.	Proposed
PROT.	Protectorate
PROV.	Provincial
P^{so}	Passo
Pt.	1. Point. 2. Pont
P^{t}	1. Petit. 2. Point. 3. Pont
P^{ta}	1. Ponta, Punta. 2. Puerta
P^{te}	1. Pointe. 2. Ponte, Puente
P^{to}	1. Porto, Puerto. 2. Ponto, Punto
P^{zo}	Pizzo
Q.	1. Qala, Qara, Qarn. 2. Quang
R.	1. Reka, Río, River, Rivière, Rud, Rzeka. 2. Ria
Ra.	Range
Rap.	Rapids
R^{ca}	Rocca
R^{d}	Road
REC.	Recreation
Res.	Reservoir
R^{f}	Reef
R^{ge}	Ridge
Rib^{a}	Ribeira
R^{k}	Rock
Rly.	Railway
R.S.F.S.R.	Rossíyskaya Sovétskaya Federatívnaya Sotsialistícheskaya Respúblika
R^{te}	Route
Rom.	Romania, Romanian
S.	1. Salar, Salina. 2. San. 3. Saw. 4. See. 5. Seto. 6. Sjö. 7. Sör, South, Syd. 8. Sung. 9. sur
S^{a}	Serra, Sierra
Sab.	Sabkhat
Sc.	Scoglio (Sardinia)
S^{d}	Sound, Sund
S.E.	South East
Seb.	Sebjet, Sebkhat, Sebkra
Sev.	Sever, Severnaya
S^{gno}	Stagno (Sardinia)
Sh.	1. Sh'aīb. 2. Sharif. 3. Shatt. 4. Shima
S^{i}	Sidi
S^{knoll}	Seaknoll
S^{kt}	Sankt
Sl.	Slieve
S^{mt}	Seamount
Snr^{a}	Senhora
Snr^{o}	Senhoro
Sp.	1. Spain, Spanish. 2. Spitze
S^{pk}	Seapeak
Spr.	Spring
S^{r}	Sönder, Sønder
Sr.	Sredniy
S.S.R.	Sovétskaya Sotsialísticheskaya Respúblika
S^{t}	Saint, Sint, Staryy
St.	1. State. 2. Stor, Store
Sta	Santa
Sta.	Station
Stby.	Staby, Statsjonsby
S^{te}	Sainte
Ste.	Store
Sten.	Stenon, Stenos
S^{to}	Santo
Str.	Strait
S^{tu}	Stuvina (Sardinia)
Sv.	Svaty, Sveti
S.W.	South West
T.	1. Tal. 2. Tal, Tall, Tell. 3. Tepe, Tepesi
Talsp.	Talsperre
Tel.	Teluk
Terr.	Terrace
Terr^{y}	Territory
Tg.	Tanjung
Thwy.	Throughway, Thruway
Tk.	Teluk
T^{mt}	Tablemount
T^{o}	Tando
Tpk.	Turnpike
Tr.	Trench, Trough
T^{re}	Torre
Tun.	Tunnel
U.	Uad
U.A.E.	United Arab Emirates
Ug.	Ujung
U.K.	United Kingdom
Unt.	Unter
Up^{r}	Upper
U.S.A.	United States of America
U.S.S.R.	Union of Soviet Socialist Republics
V.	1. Val, Valle, 2. Väster, Vest, Vester. 3. Vatn. 4. Ville. 5. Vorder
V^{a}	Vila
Vdkhr.	Vodokhranilishche
Vel.	Velikiy
Ven.	Venezuela, Venezuelan
Verkh.	Verkhniy
Vol.	Volcán, Volcano, Vulkán
Vost.	Vostochnyy
Vozv.	Vozvyshennost'
W.	1. Wadi. 2. Wald. 3. Wan. 4. Water. 5. Well. 6. West
W^{r}	Wester
Y.	Yama
Y^{t}	Ytre, Ytter, Ytri
Yuzh.	Yuzhnaya, Yuzhno, Yuzhnyy
Z.	Zaliv
Zal.	Zaliv
Zap.	Zapadnyy, -aya, -o, -oye
Zem.	Zemlya

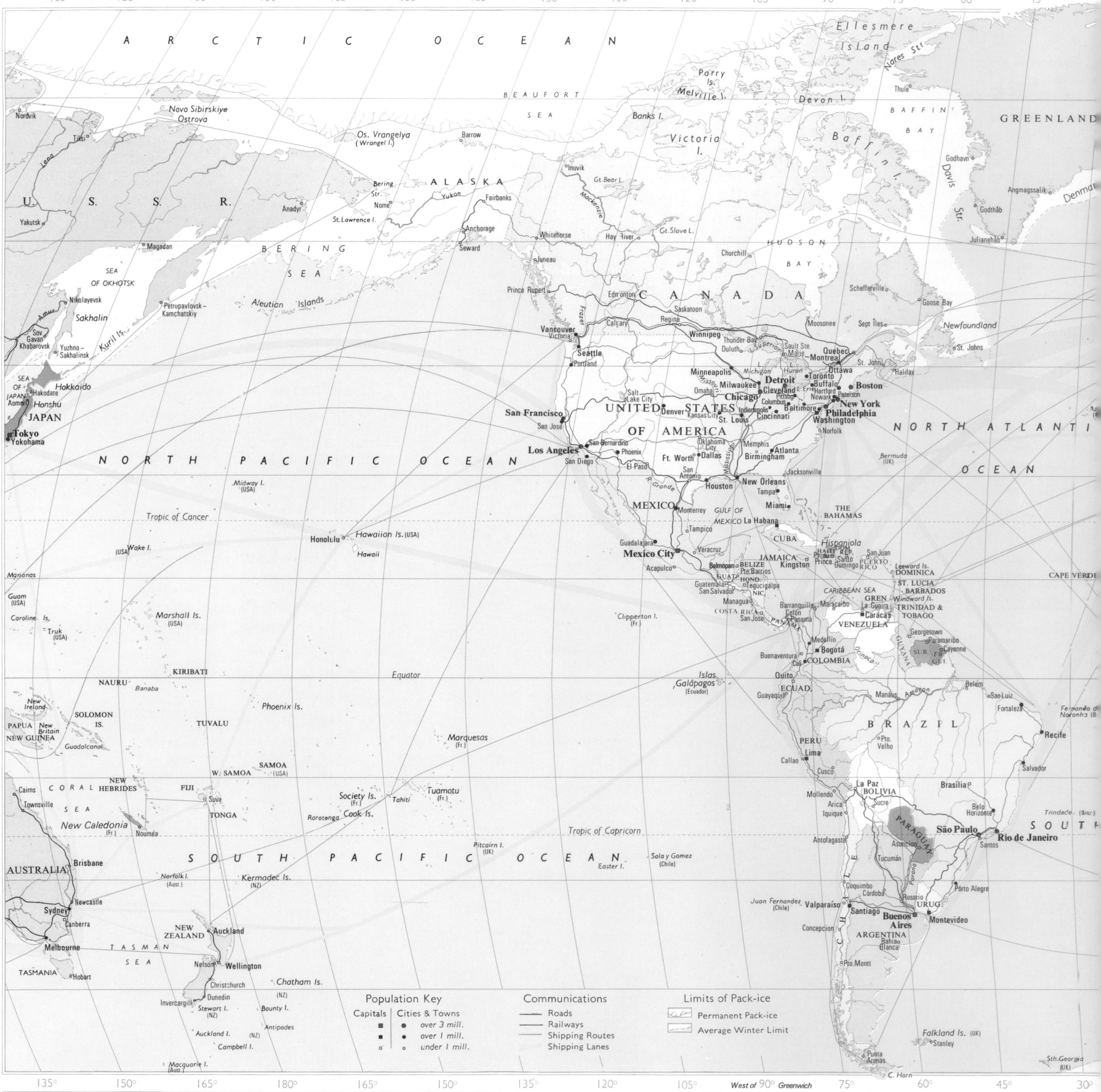
ARCTIC OCEAN
BEAUFORT SEA
Ellesmere Island
Nares Str.
Parry Is.
Melville I.
Devon I.
Banks I.
Victoria I.
BAFFIN BAY
Baffin I.
Davis Str.
GREENLAND
Thule
Godhavn
Godthåb
Angmagssalik
Julianehåb
Denmark
Novo Sibirskiye Ostrova
Nordvik
Tiksi
Lena
U. S. S. R.
Yakutsk
Magadan
SEA OF OKHOTSK
Nikolayevsk
Amur
Sakhalin
Sov. Gavan
Khabarovsk
Yuzhno-Sakhalinsk
Kuril Is.
Petropavlovsk-Kamchatskiy
Anadyr
Os. Vrangelya (Wrangel I.)
Barrow
Bering Str.
Nome
ALASKA
Yukon
Fairbanks
St. Lawrence I.
Anchorage
Seward
BERING SEA
Aleutian Islands
Inuvik
Gt. Bear L.
Mackenzie
Whitehorse
Juneau
Hay River
Gt. Slave L.
Churchill
HUDSON BAY
Schefferville
Goose Bay
Prince Rupert
Edmonton
CANADA
Saskatoon
Regina
Calgary
Vancouver
Victoria
Fraser
Winnipeg
Thunder Bay
Duluth
Superior
Sault Ste. Marie
Moosonee
Sept Îles
Quebec
Montreal
Newfoundland
St. Johns
St. John
Halifax
Ottawa
Huron
Toronto
Buffalo
Boston
Michigan
Detroit
Cleveland
Hartford
Paterson
Newark
New York
Philadelphia
Baltimore
Washington
Norfolk
Pittsburg
Columbus
Cincinnati
Indianapolis
Seattle
Portland
Minneapolis
Milwaukee
Chicago
Omaha
Salt Lake City
Denver
Kansas City
St. Louis
UNITED STATES OF AMERICA
San Francisco
San Jose
Los Angeles
San Bernardino
San Diego
Phoenix
El Paso
Oklahoma City
Ft. Worth
Dallas
Memphis
Atlanta
Birmingham
Mississippi
San Antonio
Houston
New Orleans
Jacksonville
Tampa
Miami
R. Grande
Bermuda (UK)
NORTH ATLANTIC OCEAN
THE BAHAMAS
MEXICO
Monterrey
GULF OF MEXICO
La Habana
CUBA
Tampico
Guadalajara
Mexico City
Veracruz
Acapulco
Hispaniola
HAITI
Port au Prince
DOM. REP.
Santo Domingo
San Juan
PUERTO RICO
JAMAICA
Kingston
Belmopan
BELIZE
Pto. Barrios
GUAT.
HOND.
Tegucigalpa
Guatemala
San Salvador
NIC.
Managua
COSTA RICA
San José
PAN.
Panama
Colón
Barranquilla
Maracaibo
CARIBBEAN SEA
GREN.
La Guaira
Caracas
Leeward Is.
DOMINICA
ST. LUCIA
BARBADOS
Windward Is.
TRINIDAD & TOBAGO
VENEZUELA
Orinoco
GUYANA
Georgetown
Paramaribo
Cayenne
SUR.
FR. GUI.
Medellin
Bogotá
COLOMBIA
Buenaventura
Quito
ECUAD.
Guayaquil
Islas Galápagos (Ecuador)
Manaus
Amazon
Belem
São Luiz
Fortaleza
Fernando de Noronha
BRAZIL
PERU
Lima
Callao
Pto. Velho
Recife
Salvador
Cusco
La Paz
BOLIVIA
Sucre
Mollendo
Arica
Iquique
Brasília
Belo Horizonte
Trindade
Antofagasta
PARAGUAY
Asunción
São Paulo
Santos
Rio de Janeiro
Tucumán
Paraná
CHILE
Coquimbo
Córdoba
Rosario
Porto Alegre
Juan Fernandez (Chile)
Valparaiso
Santiago
Buenos Aires
URUG.
Montevideo
Concepcion
ARGENTINA
Bahia Blanca
Pto. Montt
Falkland Is. (UK)
Stanley
Punta Arenas
C. Horn
Sth. Georgia (UK)
CAPE VERDE
SOUTH
NORTH PACIFIC OCEAN
Midway I. (USA)
Tropic of Cancer
Hawaiian Is. (USA)
Honolulu
Hawaii
(USA) Wake I.
Marianas
Guam (USA)
Caroline Is.
Truk (USA)
Marshall Is. (USA)
Clipperton I. (Fr.)
KIRIBATI
NAURU
Banaba
Equator
Phoenix Is.
New Ireland
PAPUA NEW GUINEA
New Britain
SOLOMON IS.
Guadalcanal
TUVALU
Marquesas (Fr.)
W. SAMOA
SAMOA (USA)
NEW HEBRIDES
FIJI
Suva
TONGA
Cairns
Townsville
CORAL SEA
New Caledonia (Fr.)
Nouméa
Society Is. (Fr.)
Tahiti
Tuamotu (Fr.)
Rarotonga
Cook Is.
Tropic of Capricorn
Pitcairn I. (UK)
AUSTRALIA
Brisbane
SOUTH PACIFIC OCEAN
Easter I.
Sala y Gomez (Chile)
Norfolk I. (Aust.)
Kermadec Is. (NZ)
Newcastle
Sydney
Canberra
Melbourne
TASMAN SEA
NEW ZEALAND
Auckland
Wellington
Nelson
Christchurch
Dunedin
Invercargill
Stewart I. (NZ)
TASMANIA
Hobart
Chatham Is. (NZ)
Bounty I.
Antipodes
Auckland I. (NZ)
Campbell I.
Macquarie I. (Aust.)
Tokyo
Yokohama
JAPAN
Honshu
Hokkaido
Hakodate
Aomori
SEA OF JAPAN
Population Key
Capitals | Cities & Towns
over 3 mill.
over 1 mill.
under 1 mill.
Communications
Roads
Railways
Shipping Routes
Shipping Lanes
Limits of Pack-ice
Permanent Pack-ice
Average Winter Limit
West of 90° Greenwich

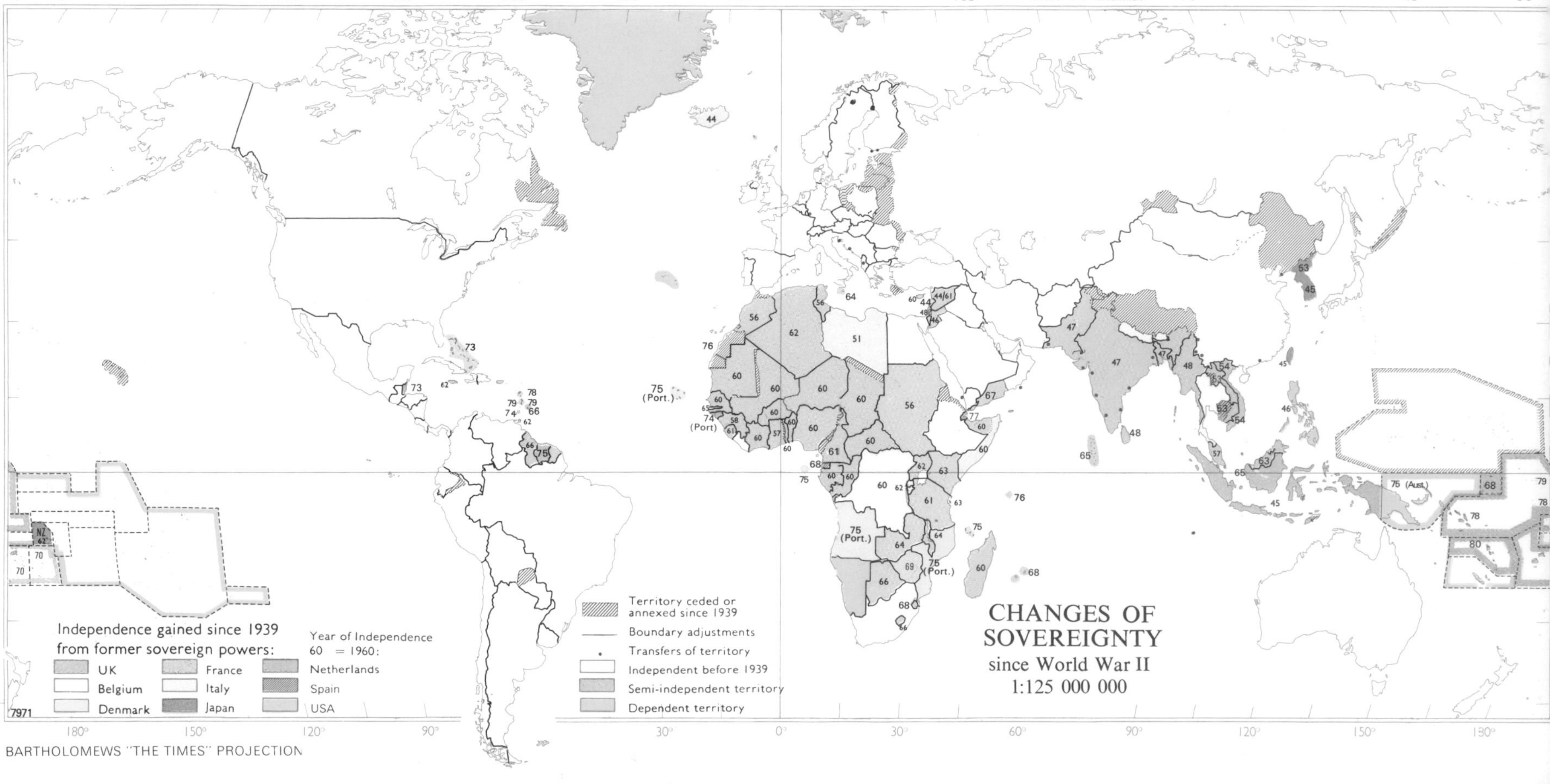
CHANGES OF SOVEREIGNTY
since World War II
1:125 000 000
Independence gained since 1939 from former sovereign powers:
UK
Belgium
Denmark
France
Italy
Japan
Netherlands
Spain
USA
Year of Independence 60 = 1960:
Territory ceded or annexed since 1939
Boundary adjustments
Transfers of territory
Independent before 1939
Semi-independent territory
Dependent territory
75 (Port.)
74 (Port)
75 (Aust.)
7971

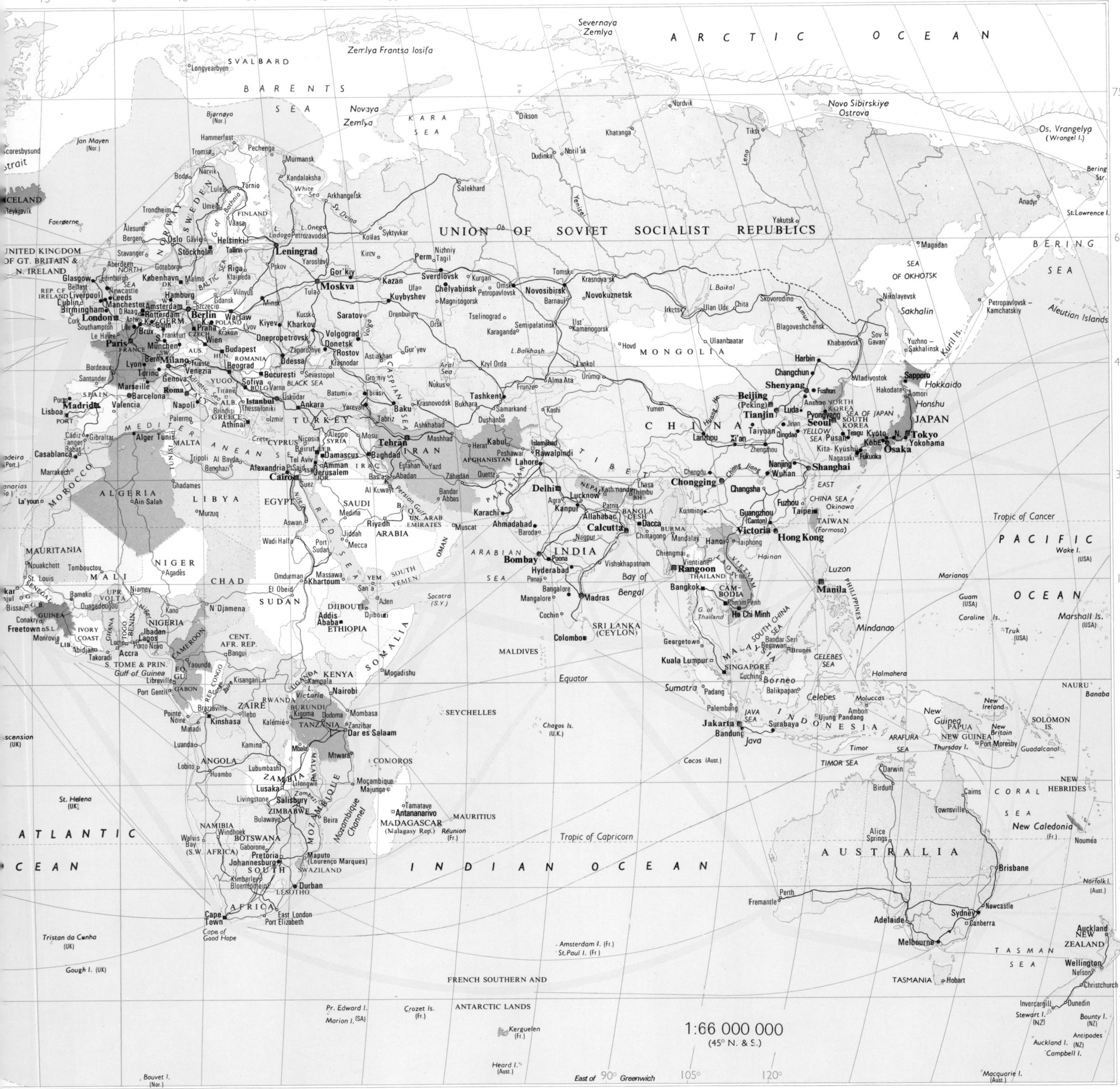
ARCTIC OCEAN
Severnaya Zemlya
Zemlya Frantsa Iosifa
SVALBARD
Longyearbyen
BARENTS SEA
Novaya Zemlya
KARA SEA
Novo Sibirskiye Ostrova
Os. Vrangelya (Wrangel I.)
Jan Mayen (Nor.)
ICELAND
Reykjavik
UNITED KINGDOM OF GT. BRITAIN & N. IRELAND
REP. OF IRELAND
London
Paris
Madrid
Lisboa
Roma
Berlin
Wien
Warsaw
Stockholm
Oslo
Helsinki
Leningrad
Moskva
UNION OF SOVIET SOCIALIST REPUBLICS
MONGOLIA
Ulaanbaatar
CHINA
Beijing (Peking)
Shanghai
Chongqing
Wuhan
Tianjin
Shenyang
Harbin
JAPAN
Tokyo
Osaka
Sapporo
Hokkaido
Honshu
Seoul
Pyongyang
NORTH KOREA
SOUTH KOREA
SEA OF JAPAN
SEA OF OKHOTSK
Sakhalin
Kuril Is.
BERING SEA
Aleutian Islands
TURKEY
Ankara
Istanbul
Tehran
IRAN
Baghdad
AFGHANISTAN
Kabul
PAKISTAN
Karachi
INDIA
Delhi
Bombay
Calcutta
Madras
NEPAL
Kathmandu
BANGLADESH
Dacca
BURMA
Rangoon
THAILAND
Bangkok
CAMBODIA
VIETNAM
Ho Chi Minh
Hanoi
Hong Kong
Victoria
TAIWAN (Formosa)
Taipei
Manila
PHILIPPINES
SRI LANKA (CEYLON)
Colombo
MALDIVES
MALAYSIA
Kuala Lumpur
SINGAPORE
Borneo
Sumatra
Java
Jakarta
INDONESIA
Celebes
New Guinea
PAPUA NEW GUINEA
Port Moresby
SOLOMON IS.
NEW HEBRIDES
New Caledonia (Fr.)
AUSTRALIA
Darwin
Perth
Adelaide
Melbourne
Sydney
Canberra
Brisbane
TASMANIA
Hobart
NEW ZEALAND
Auckland
Wellington
Christchurch
TASMAN SEA
CORAL SEA
PACIFIC OCEAN
Tropic of Cancer
Tropic of Capricorn
Equator
INDIAN OCEAN
ATLANTIC OCEAN
ARABIAN SEA
Bay of Bengal
SOUTH CHINA SEA
EAST CHINA SEA
YELLOW SEA
BLACK SEA
CASPIAN SEA
MEDITERRANEAN SEA
RED SEA
Persian Gulf
SAUDI ARABIA
Riyadh
OMAN
SOUTH YEMEN
YEMEN
UNITED ARAB EMIRATES
EGYPT
Cairo
LIBYA
ALGERIA
MOROCCO
MAURITANIA
MALI
NIGER
CHAD
SUDAN
Khartoum
ETHIOPIA
Addis Ababa
DJIBOUTI
SOMALIA
Mogadishu
KENYA
Nairobi
TANZANIA
Dar es Salaam
ZAIRE
Kinshasa
ANGOLA
ZAMBIA
Lusaka
ZIMBABWE
Salisbury
MOZAMBIQUE
Maputo (Lourenço Marques)
NAMIBIA (S.W. AFRICA)
BOTSWANA
SOUTH AFRICA
Johannesburg
Pretoria
Durban
Cape Town
Cape of Good Hope
LESOTHO
SWAZILAND
MADAGASCAR (Malagasy Rep.)
Antananarivo
MAURITIUS
Réunion (Fr.)
COMOROS
SEYCHELLES
NIGERIA
Lagos
CAMEROON
GABON
CENT. AFR. REP.
Gulf of Guinea
Accra
IVORY COAST
GHANA
Freetown
Dakar
St. Helena (UK)
Ascension (UK)
Tristan da Cunha (UK)
Gough I. (UK)
Bouvet I. (Nor.)
Pr. Edward I.
Marion I. (SA)
Crozet Is. (Fr.)
FRENCH SOUTHERN AND ANTARCTIC LANDS
Kerguelen (Fr.)
Heard I. (Aust.)
Amsterdam I. (Fr.)
St. Paul I. (Fr.)
Chagos Is. (U.K.)
Cocos (Aust.)
Macquarie I. (Aust.)
1:66 000 000
(45° N. & S.)
East of 90° Greenwich

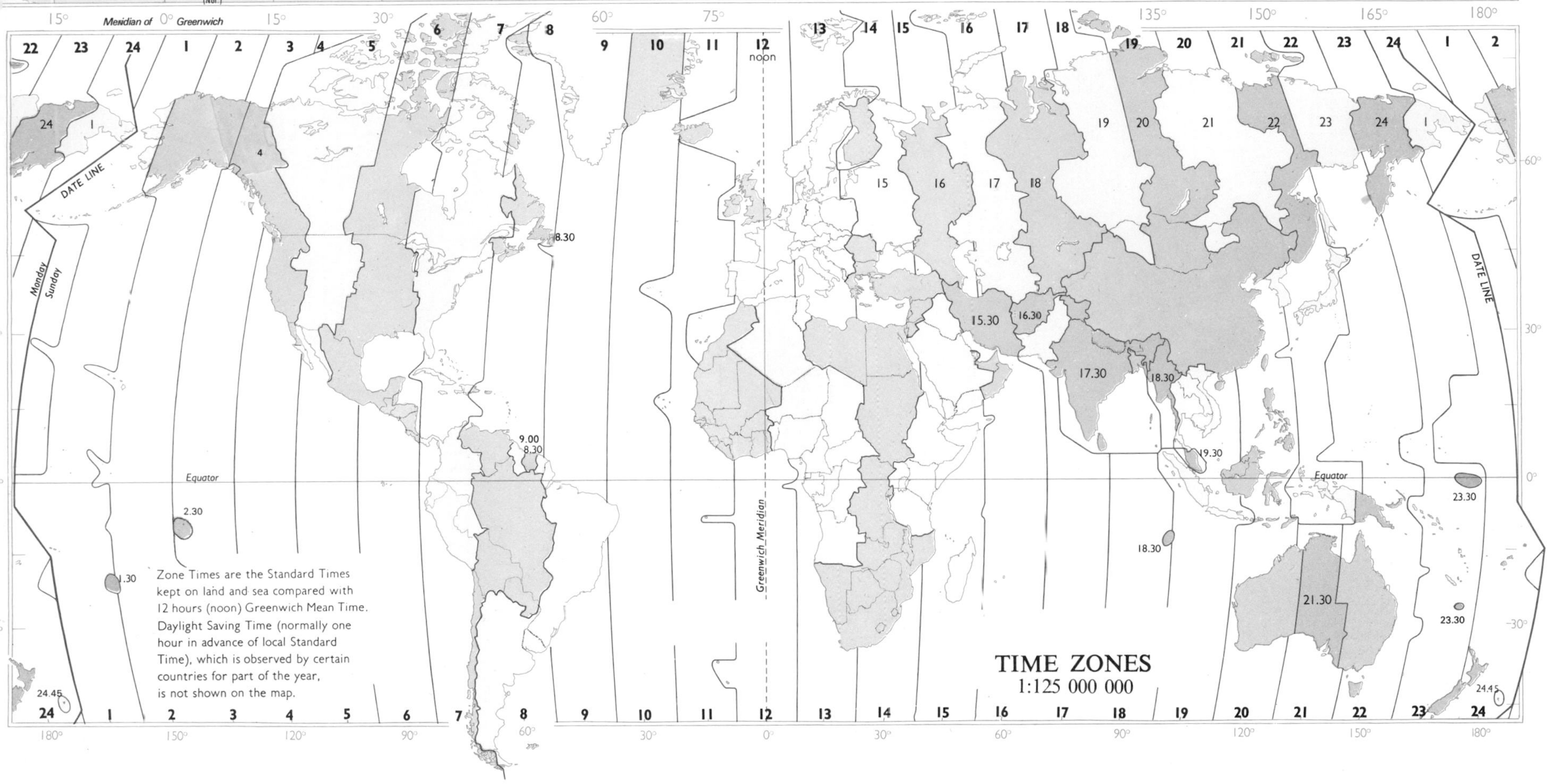
Meridian of 0° Greenwich
12 noon
DATE LINE
Monday
Sunday
Equator
Greenwich Meridian
Zone Times are the Standard Times kept on land and sea compared with 12 hours (noon) Greenwich Mean Time. Daylight Saving Time (normally one hour in advance of local Standard Time), which is observed by certain countries for part of the year, is not shown on the map.
TIME ZONES
1:125 000 000
22 23 24 1 2 3 4 5 6 7 8 9 10 11 12 13 14 15 16 17 18 19 20 21 22 23 24 1 2
8.30
9.00
15.30
16.30
17.30
18.30
19.30
21.30
23.30
24.45
2.30
1.30

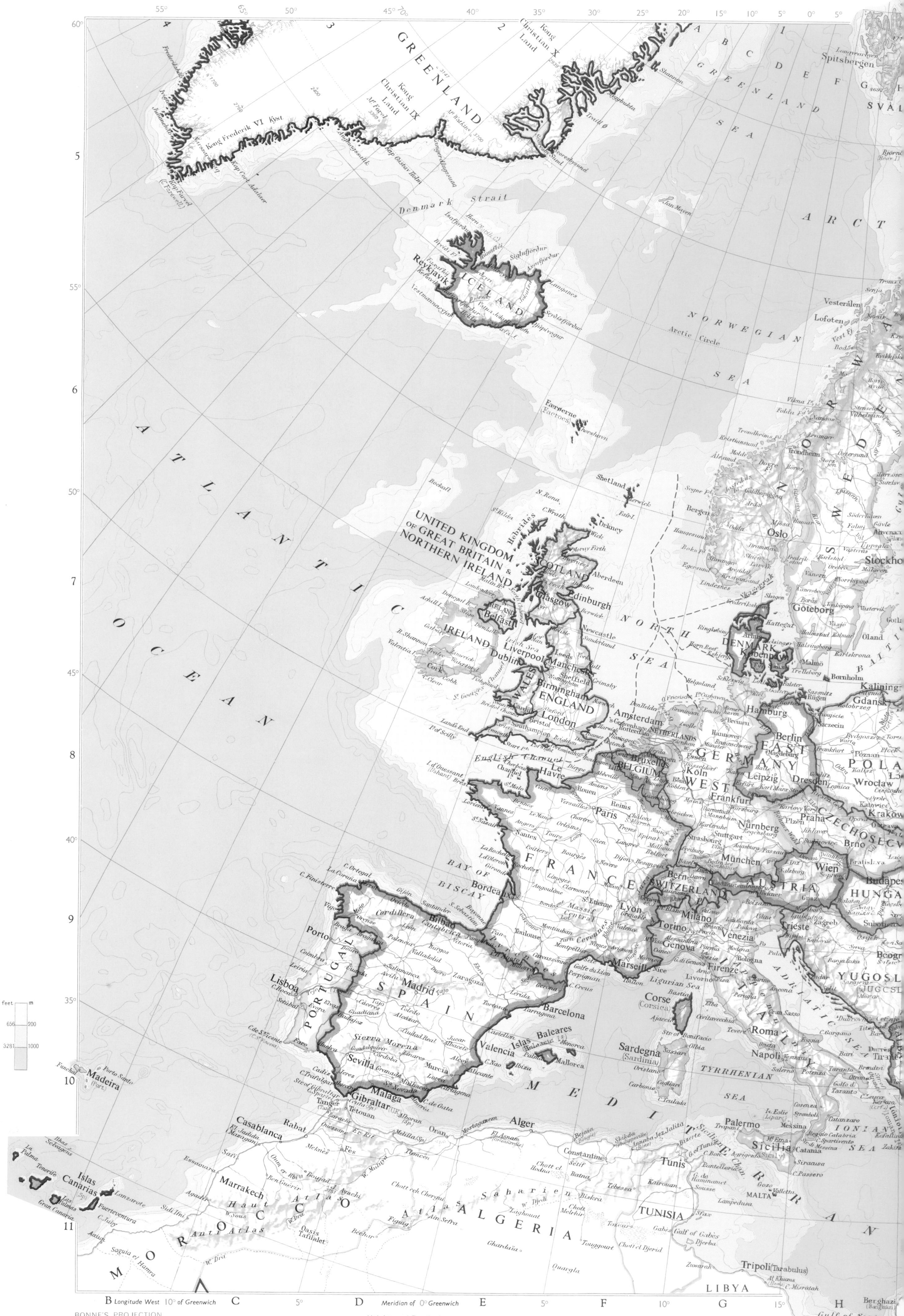

BONNE'S PROJECTION

Heights and Depths in metres

BARENTS SEA
OCEAN
Novaya Zemlya
KARA SEA
Zemlya Frantsa-Iosifa (Franz Joseph Land)
Nordaustlandet (North East Land)
FINLAND
ESTONIA
LATVIA
LITHUANIA
WHITE RUSSIA
UKRAINE
ROMANIA
BULGARIA
GREECE
TURKEY
GEORGIA
ARMENIA
AZERBAIJAN
SYRIA
IRAQ
IRAN (PERSIA)
LEBANON
ISRAEL
JORDAN
SAUDI ARABIA
KUWAIT
EGYPT
CYPRUS
UNION OF SOVIET SOCIALIST REPUBLICS
RUSSIAN SOVIET FEDERAL SOCIALIST REPUBLIC
KAZAKHSTAN
UZBEKISTAN
TURKMENISTAN
BLACK SEA
CASPIAN SEA
Azovskoye More (Sea of Azov)
Aral'skoye More (Aral Sea)
PERSIAN GULF
Beloye More (White Sea)
Kol'skiy Poluostrov
Ural'skiy Khrebet
Bol'shoy Kavkaz
Elburz
Syrian Desert
Leningrad
Helsinki
Tallinn
Riga
Moskva
Kiyev
Kharkov
Minsk
Odessa
Sevastopol
Volgograd
Astrakhan
Rostov
Kazan
Gor'kiy
Kuybyshev
Saratov
Sverdlovsk
Magnitogorsk
Omsk
Novosibirsk
Orenburg
Arkhangel'sk
Tbilisi
Baku
Tabriz
Tehran
Esfahan
Baghdad
Basra
Aleppo
Damascus
Beirût
Jerusalem
Ankara
Istanbul
Izmir
Athinai
Sofiya
Bucureşti
Thessaloníki
Kriti (Crete)
Ródhos (Rhodes)
Lésvos
Alexandria
Cairo
Port Said
Longitude East 45° of Greenwich
1:15M
km
miles

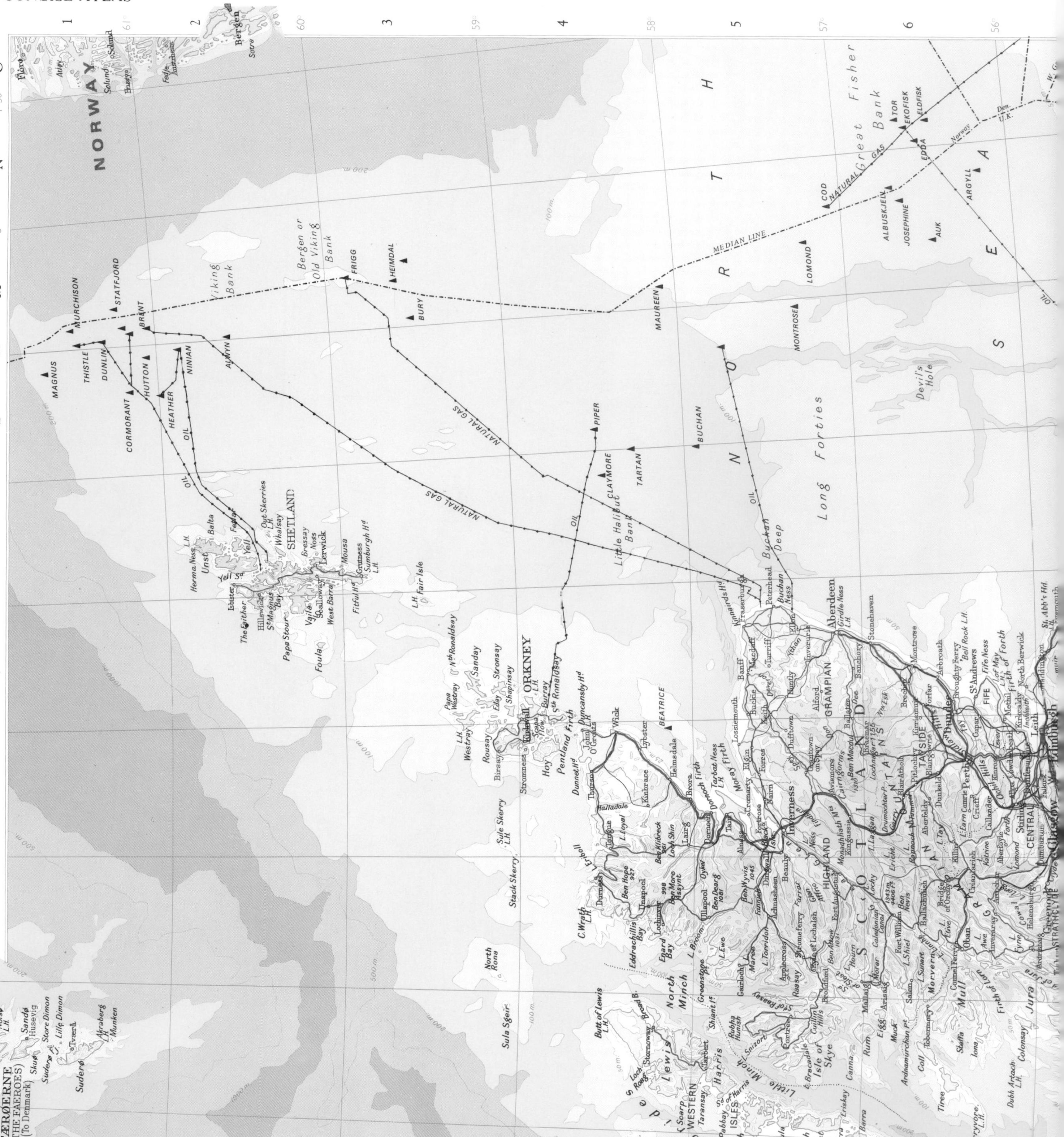
NORWAY
SHETLAND
ORKNEY
FÆRØERNE
(THE FAEROES)
(To Denmark)
Faeroe Bank
Bill Baileys Bank
Rosemary Bank
Outer Bailey or Lousy Bank
Rockall Bank
Long Forties
Viking Bank
Bergen or Old Viking Bank
Great Fisher Bank
MEDIAN LINE
NATURAL GAS
OIL
Aberdeen
Inverness
Dundee
Edinburgh
Glasgow
GRAMPIAN
HIGHLAND
TAYSIDE
CENTRAL
FIFE
STRATHCLYDE
WESTERN ISLES
Outer Hebrides
North Minch
Little Minch
Isle of Skye
Lewis
Harris
St Kilda
North Rona
Sula Sgeir
Sule Skerry
Stack Skerry
Fair Isle
Foula
Bergen
MAGNUS
THISTLE
DUNLIN
MURCHISON
STATFJORD
BRENT
CORMORANT
HUTTON
HEATHER
NINIAN
ALWYN
FRIGG
HEIMDAL
BURY
PIPER
CLAYMORE
TARTAN
BEATRICE
BUCHAN
MAUREEN
MONTROSE
LOMOND
COD
ALBUSKJELL
JOSEPHINE
AUK
ARGYLL
EDDA
EKOFISK
ELDFISK
TOR

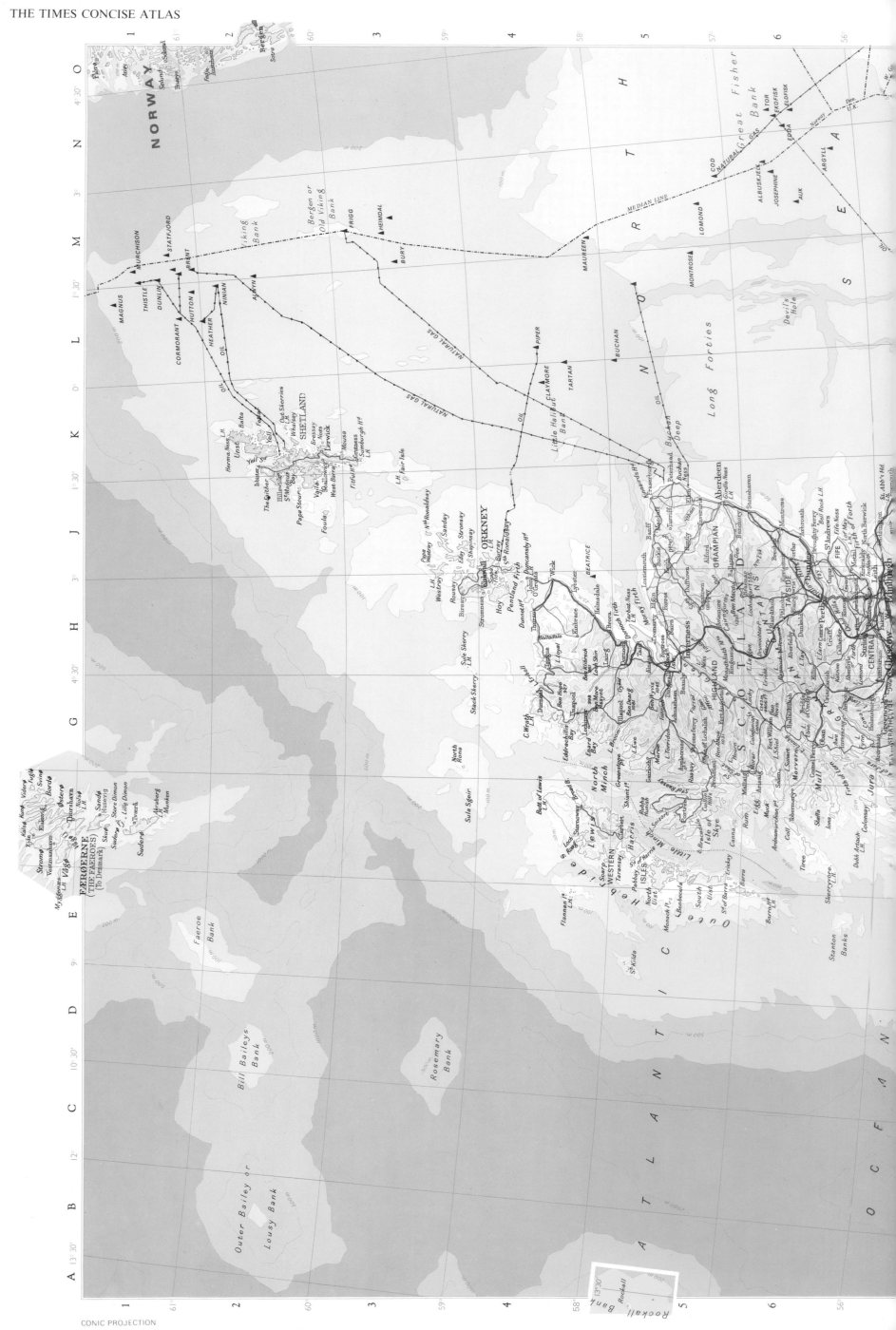

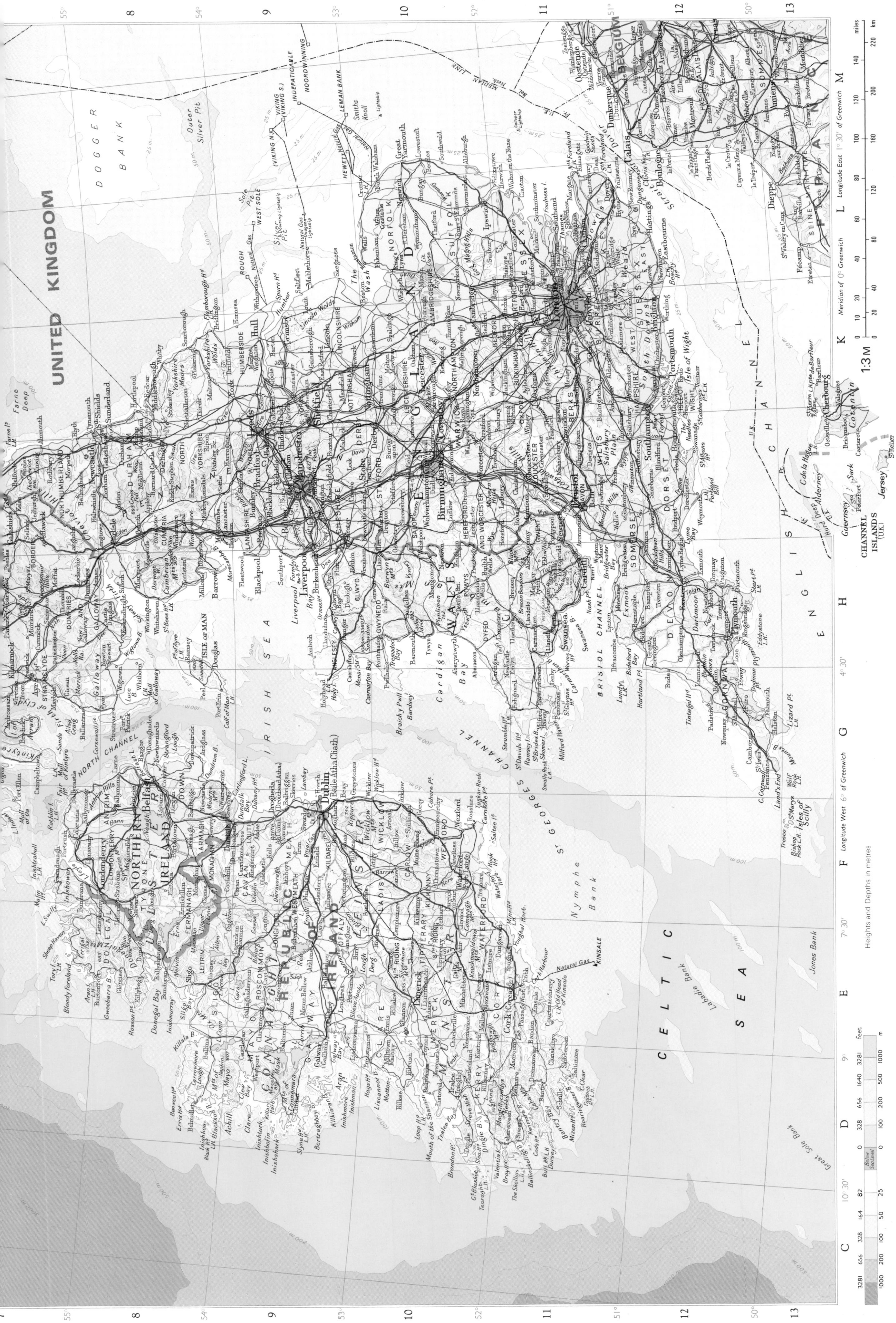
UNITED KINGDOM
DOGGER BANK
IRISH SEA
NORTH CHANNEL
CELTIC SEA
ENGLISH CHANNEL
BRISTOL CHANNEL
ST GEORGE'S CHANNEL
BELGIUM
FRANCE
CHANNEL ISLANDS (U.K.)
1:3M
Heights and Depths in metres
Longitude West 6° of Greenwich
Longitude East 1°30' of Greenwich
Meridian of 0° Greenwich

WALES
ANGLESEY
GWYNEDD
CLWYD
POWYS
DYFED
WEST GLAMORGAN
MID GLAMORGAN
SOUTH GLAMORGAN
GWENT
SALOP
HEREFORD AND WORCESTER
CHESHIRE
MERSEYSIDE
AVON
SOMERSET
DEVON
CORNWALL
DORSET
CARDIGAN BAY
BRISTOL CHANNEL
Caernarfon Bay
Tremadoc Bay
St. Brides Bay
Carmarthen Bay
Bideford Bay
Bridgwater Bay
Lyme Bay
Holyhead
Bangor
Llandudno
Colwyn Bay
Rhyl
Liverpool
Birkenhead
Chester
Wrexham
Shrewsbury
Aberystwyth
Cardigan
Fishguard
Haverfordwest
Pembroke
Carmarthen
Llanelli
Swansea
Neath
Port Talbot
Bridgend
Cardiff
Newport
Bristol
Bath
Weston super-mare
Hereford
Ilfracombe
Barnstaple
Bideford
Exeter
Plymouth
Torquay
Truro
Falmouth
Penzance
St. Ives
Lundy
to Dun Laoghaire
to Rosslare
to Cork
to Channel Islands
Longitude West 3° of Greenwich
CONIC PROJECTION
m feet
609 2000
304 1000
152 500
76 250
0 0
Below Sea Level

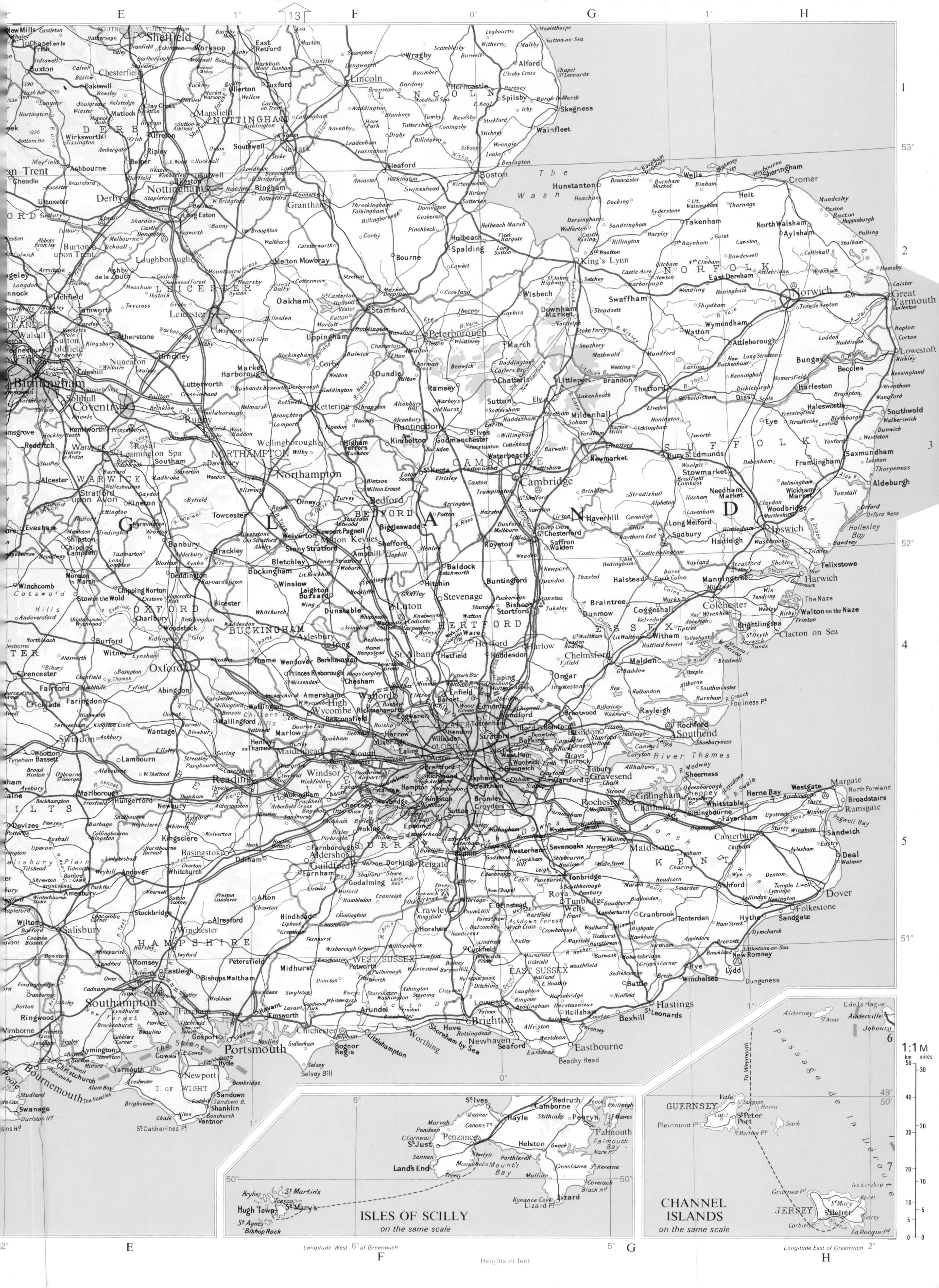
E
F
G
H
1
2
3
4
5
6
7
13
53°
52°
51°
49°
50°
1°
0°
2°
6°
5°
Sheffield
Lincoln
Nottingham
Derby
Leicester
Birmingham
Coventry
Northampton
Peterborough
Cambridge
Norwich
Great Yarmouth
Ipswich
Colchester
Oxford
Reading
Swindon
LONDON
Southend
Canterbury
Dover
Folkestone
Brighton
Portsmouth
Southampton
Bournemouth
Hastings
Eastbourne
Salisbury
Winchester
L I N C O L N
N O T T I N G H A M
D E R B Y
L E I C E S T E R
N O R F O L K
S U F F O L K
E S S E X
K E N T
S U R R E Y
H A M P S H I R E
WEST SUSSEX
EAST SUSSEX
B U C K I N G H A M
H E R T F O R D
O X F O R D
B E D F O R D
W A R W I C K
N O R T H A M P T O N
C A M B R I D G E
E N G L A N D
The Wash
River Thames
The Solent
I. OF WIGHT
ISLES OF SCILLY
on the same scale
CHANNEL ISLANDS
on the same scale
GUERNSEY
JERSEY
Passage de la Déroute
1:1M
km
miles
Longitude West of Greenwich
Longitude East of Greenwich
Heights in feet

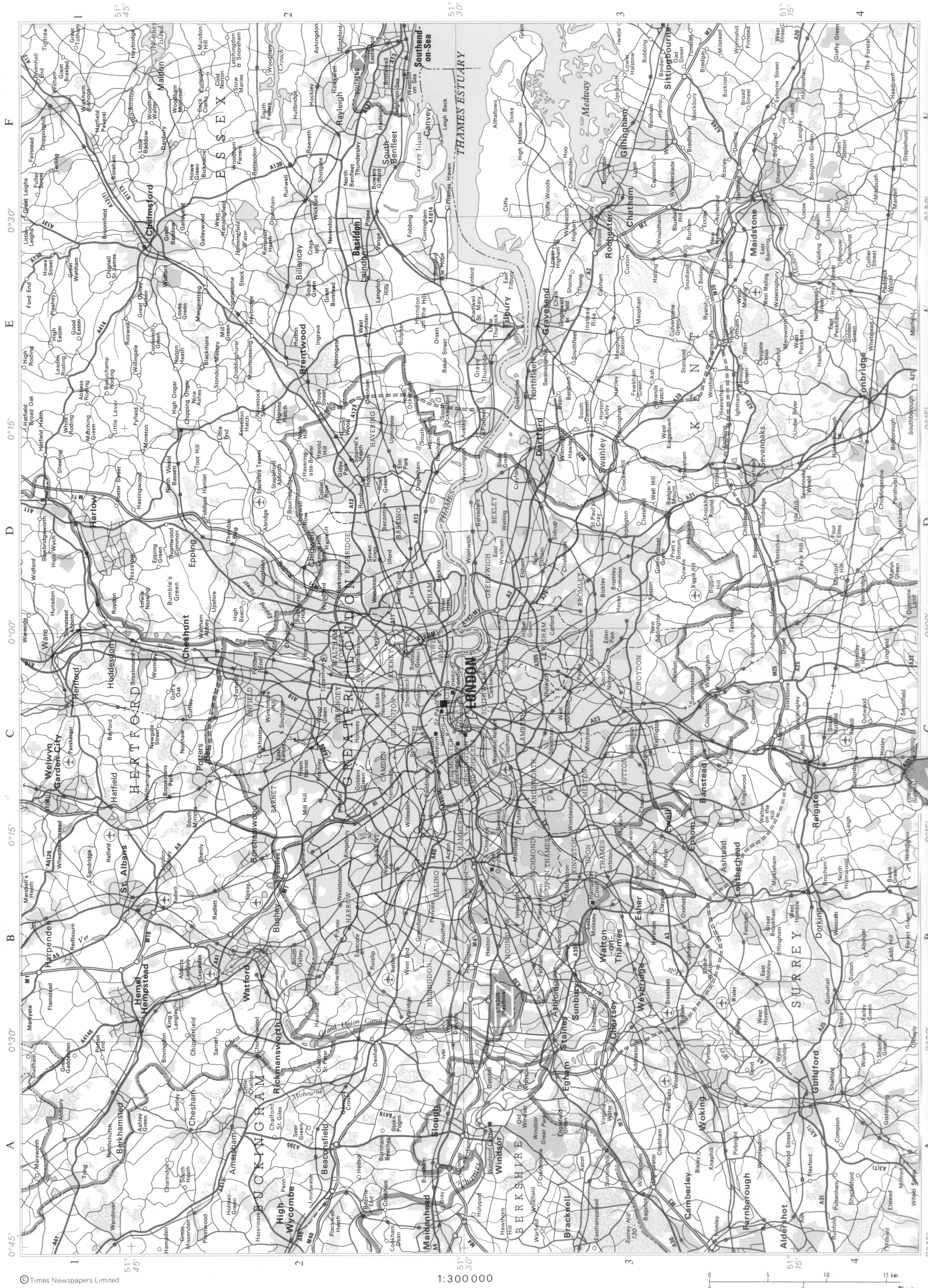

© Times Newspapers Limited

1:300 000

0 5 10 15 km
0 5 10 miles

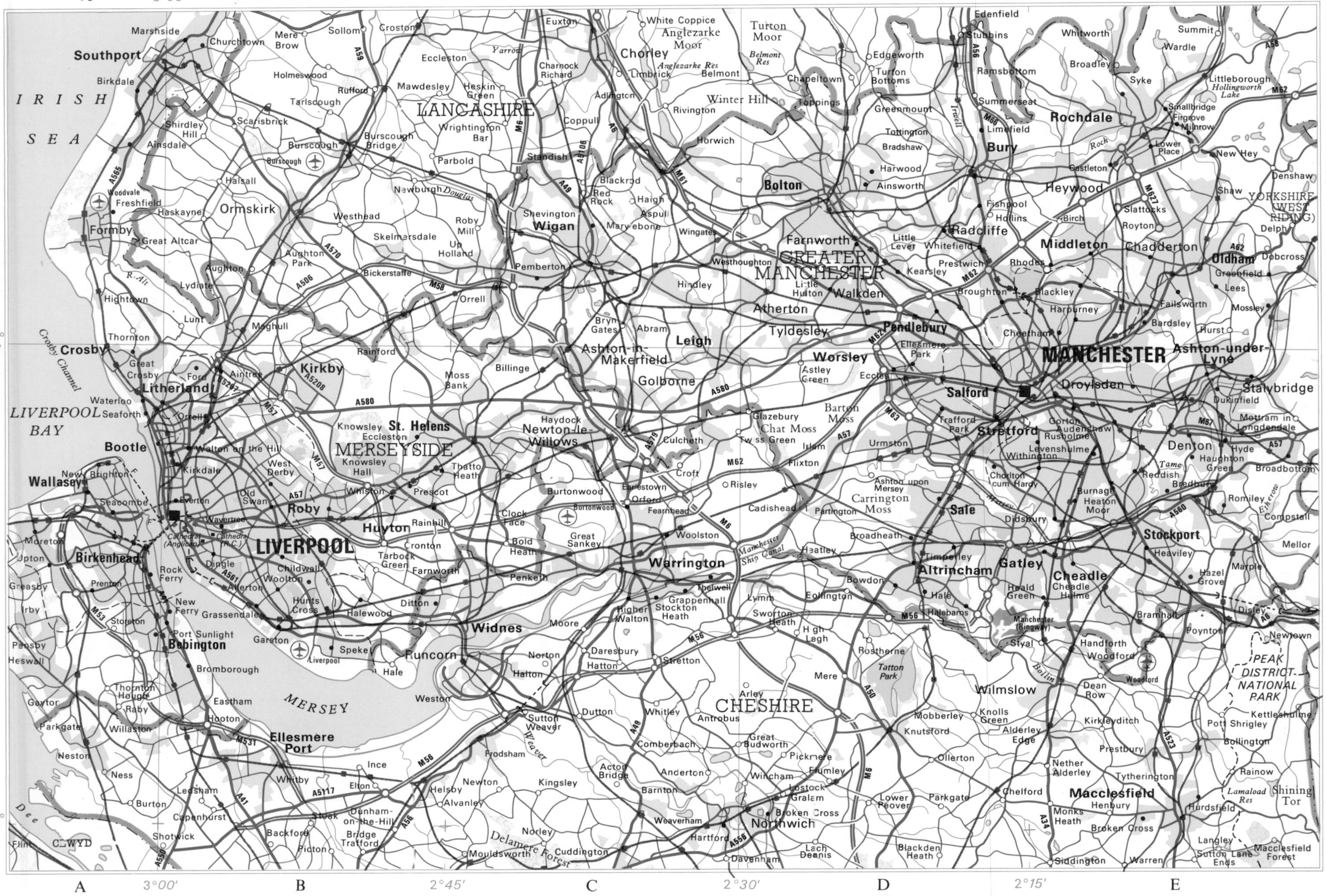
IRISH SEA
LIVERPOOL BAY
LANCASHIRE
MERSEYSIDE
GREATER MANCHESTER
CHESHIRE
CLWYD
YORKSHIRE WEST RIDING
PEAK DISTRICT NATIONAL PARK
MERSEY
Southport
Ormskirk
Wigan
Bolton
Bury
Rochdale
Heywood
Middleton
Oldham
Chorley
St. Helens
Liverpool
Birkenhead
Wallasey
Bootle
Crosby
Kirkby
Huyton
Widnes
Runcorn
Warrington
Leigh
Salford
MANCHESTER
Stockport
Altrincham
Sale
Stretford
Wilmslow
Macclesfield
Northwich
Ellesmere Port

WEST MIDLANDS

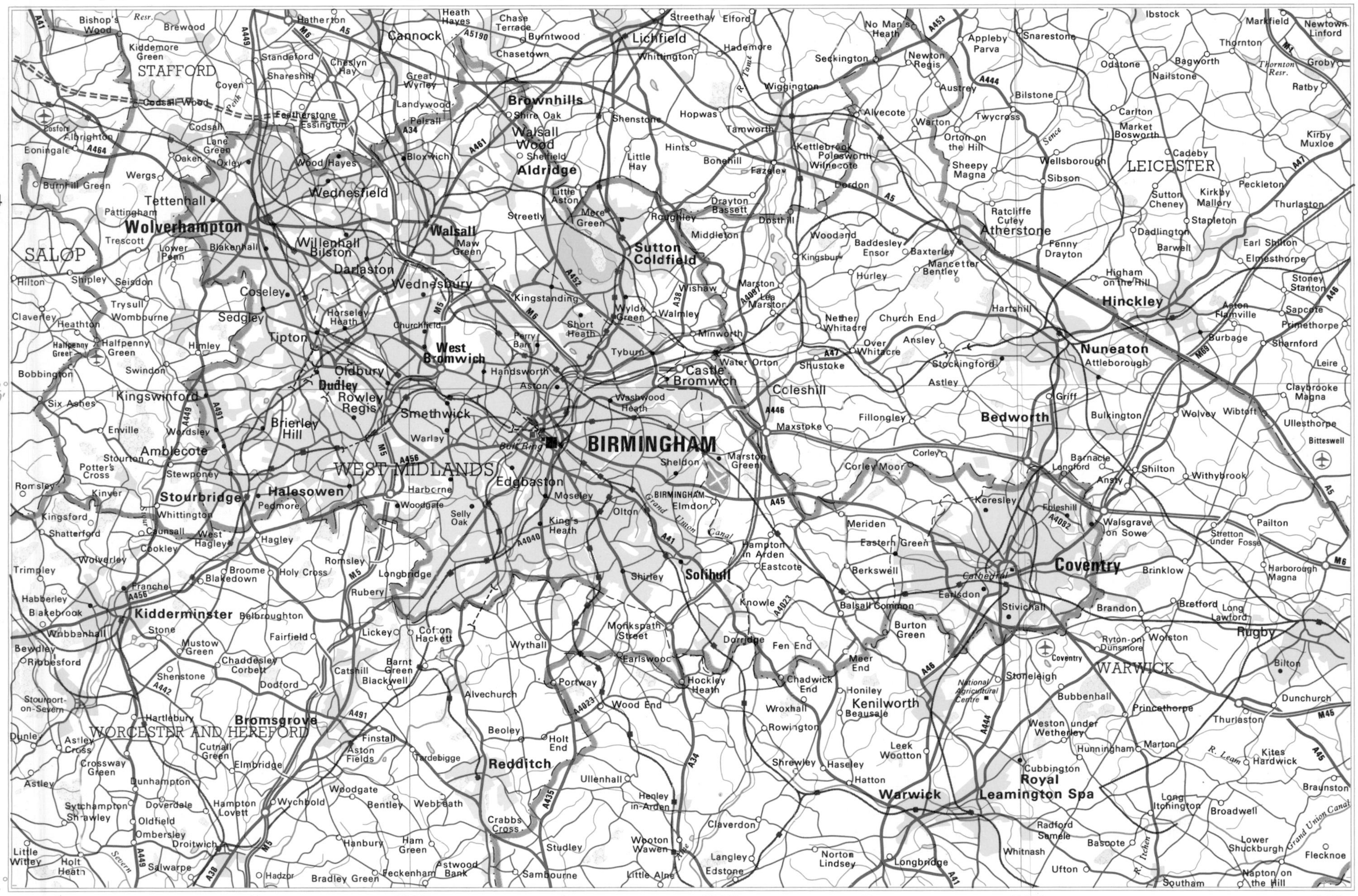
STAFFORD
SALOP
LEICESTER
WEST MIDLANDS
WORCESTER AND HEREFORD
WARWICK
Cannock
Lichfield
Brownhills
Walsall
Wolverhampton
Aldridge
Sutton Coldfield
West Bromwich
Dudley
BIRMINGHAM
Solihull
Halesowen
Stourbridge
Kidderminster
Bromsgrove
Redditch
Tamworth
Atherstone
Nuneaton
Hinckley
Bedworth
Coventry
Rugby
Kenilworth
Warwick
Royal Leamington Spa

1:300 000

© Times Newspapers Limited

NORTH CHANNEL
IRISH SEA
NORTHERN IRELAND
IRELAND
SCOTLAND
LONDONDERRY
ANTRIM
TYRONE
DOWN
ARMAGH
MONAGHAN
CAVAN
LOUTH
MEATH
DUBLIN
STRATHCLYDE
CENTRAL
TAYSIDE
DUMFRIES AND
ISLE OF MAN
MULL
JURA
ISLAY
ARRAN
KINTYRE
BELFAST
DUBLIN (BAILE ATHA CLIATH)
Londonderry
Glasgow
Oban
Stirling
Falkirk
Paisley
Greenock
Kilmarnock
Ayr
Irvine
Troon
Prestwick
Girvan
Stranraer
Newton Stewart
Wigtown
Whithorn
Kirkcudbright
Dumfries
Castle Douglas
Campbeltown
Lochgilphead
Inveraray
Tarbert
Rothesay
Brodick
Lamlash
Coleraine
Portrush
Ballymena
Larne
Antrim
Carrickfergus
Bangor
Newtownards
Lisburn
Lurgan
Craigavon
Portadown
Armagh
Banbridge
Newry
Downpatrick
Dundalk
Drogheda
Omagh
Cookstown
Dungannon
Strabane
Enniskillen
Monaghan
Cavan
Kells
Navan
Trim
Mullingar
Swords
Malahide
Howth
Dun Laoghaire
Dalkey
Douglas
Ramsey
Peel
Castletown
Holyhead
Amlwch
Workington
Whitehaven
Maryport
Mull of Kintyre
Mull of Galloway
Firth of Clyde
Firth of Lorn
Sound of Jura
Loch Fyne
Lough Neagh
Lough Foyle
Belfast Lough
Strangford L.
Dundalk Bay
Luce Bay
Wigtown Bay
Solway Firth
Mourne Mountains
Sperrin Mts
Rathlin I.
Lambay I.
Holy I.
Malin Hd
Fair Head
Giants Causeway
Colonsay
Oronsay
Iona
Gigha I.
Ailsa Craig
The Maidens
Calf of Man
Snaefell 2034
56°
55°
54°
7°
6°
5°
4°
A
B
C
D
E
1
2
3
4
5
6
15
14
8
m
feet
609
2000
304
1000
152
500
76
250
0
0
Below Sea Level

CONIC PROJECTION

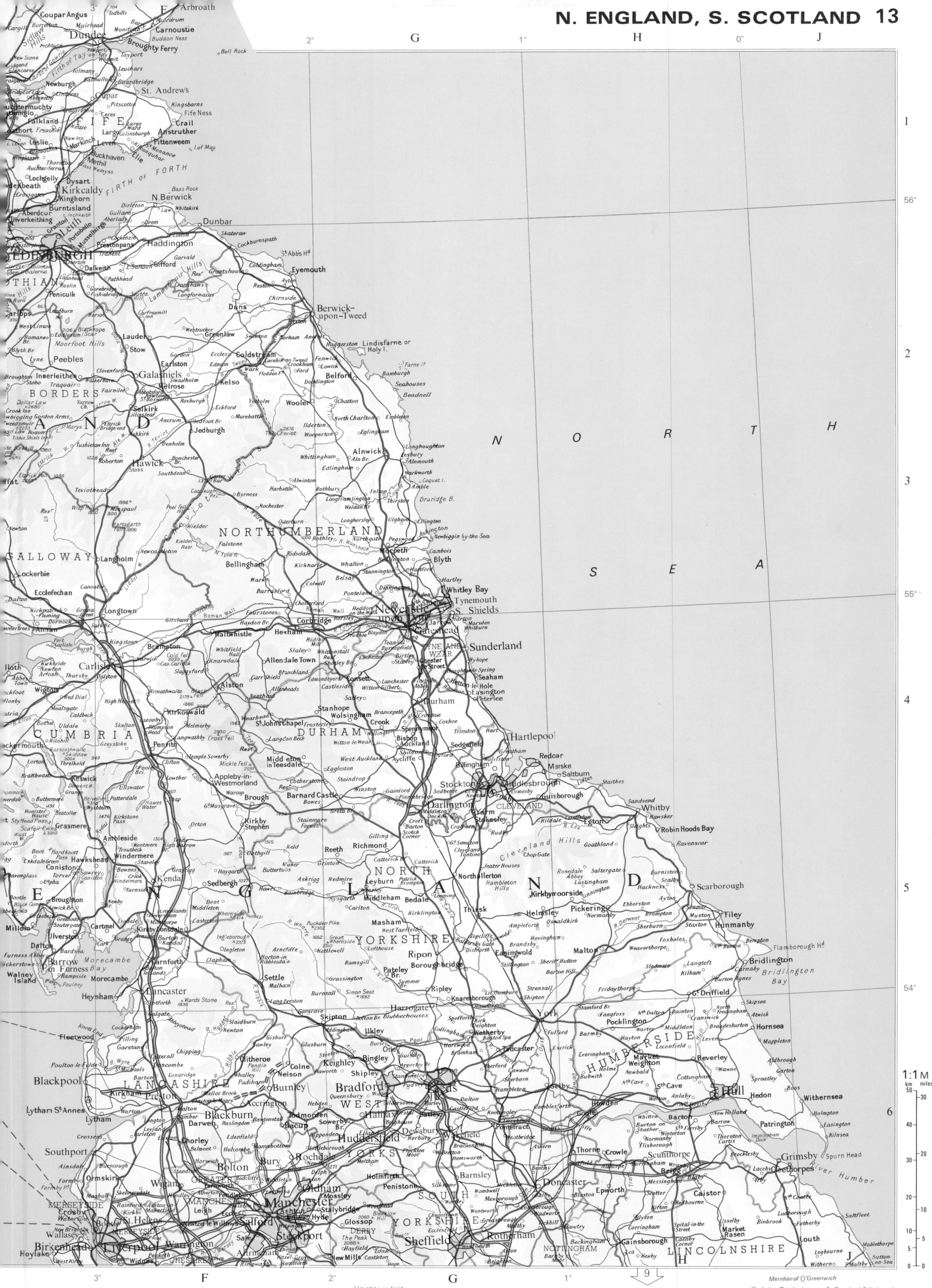
NORTH SEA
NORTHUMBERLAND
DURHAM
CUMBRIA
NORTH YORKSHIRE
WEST YORKS
SOUTH YORKSHIRE
LANCASHIRE
GREATER MANCHESTER
MERSEYSIDE
HUMBERSIDE
CLEVELAND
TYNE AND WEAR
LINCOLNSHIRE
NOTTINGHAM
DERBY
BORDERS
FIFE
LOTHIAN
GALLOWAY
ENGLAND
Edinburgh
Dundee
St. Andrews
Kirkcaldy
Firth of Forth
Firth of Tay
Dunbar
Haddington
N. Berwick
Eyemouth
Berwick-upon-Tweed
Lindisfarne or Holy I.
Galashiels
Peebles
Kelso
Jedburgh
Hawick
Langholm
Carlisle
Penrith
Kendal
Lancaster
Morecambe
Blackpool
Preston
Blackburn
Burnley
Bolton
Wigan
Southport
Liverpool
Birkenhead
Manchester
Salford
Stockport
Oldham
Rochdale
Huddersfield
Halifax
Bradford
Leeds
Wakefield
Barnsley
Sheffield
Rotherham
Doncaster
York
Harrogate
Ripon
Skipton
Scarborough
Whitby
Bridlington
Filey
Hull
Grimsby
Cleethorpes
Scunthorpe
Gainsborough
Louth
Middlesbrough
Stockton
Darlington
Hartlepool
Sunderland
Durham
Newcastle
Gateshead
Tynemouth
S. Shields
Whitley Bay
Blyth
Morpeth
Alnwick
Hexham
Flamborough Hd
Spurn Head
River Humber
Bridlington Bay
Morecambe Bay
Meridian of 0° Greenwich
Heights in feet
1:1M

© John Bartholomew & Son Ltd Edinburgh

A B C D E F
10° 9° 8° 7° 6°

Heights and Depths in metres

m	200	100	50	0	50	100	200	500	1000
feet	660	330	160	0	160	330	660	1640	3280

Longitude West of Greenwich

CONIC PROJECTION

1:1.5M

0 10 20 40 60 80 km
0 5 10 20 30 40 50 miles

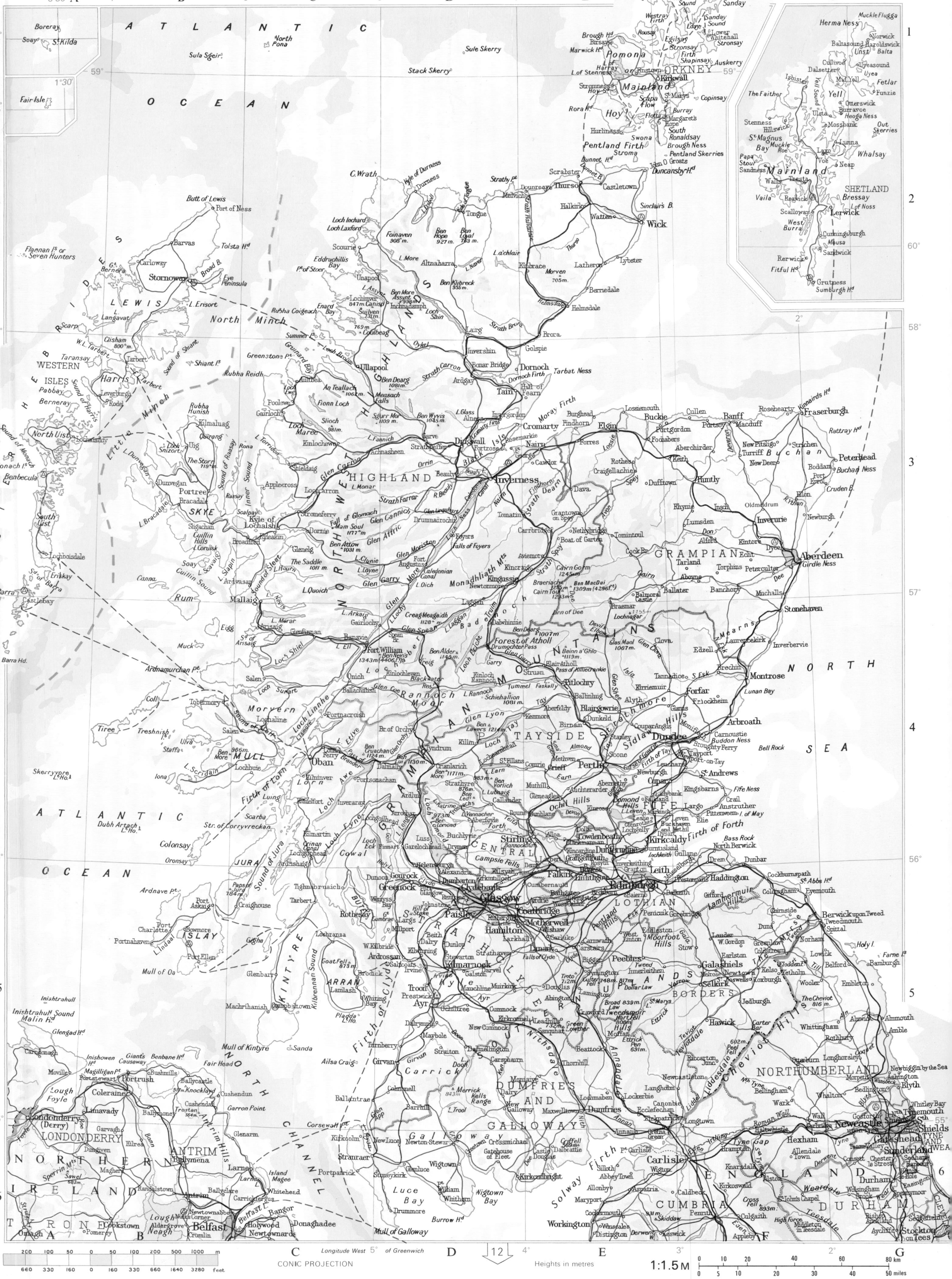

CONIC PROJECTION

Heights in metres

1:1.5 M

0 10 20 40 60 80 km
0 5 10 20 30 40 50 miles

200 100 50 0 50 100 200 500 1000 m
660 330 160 0 160 330 660 1640 3280 feet

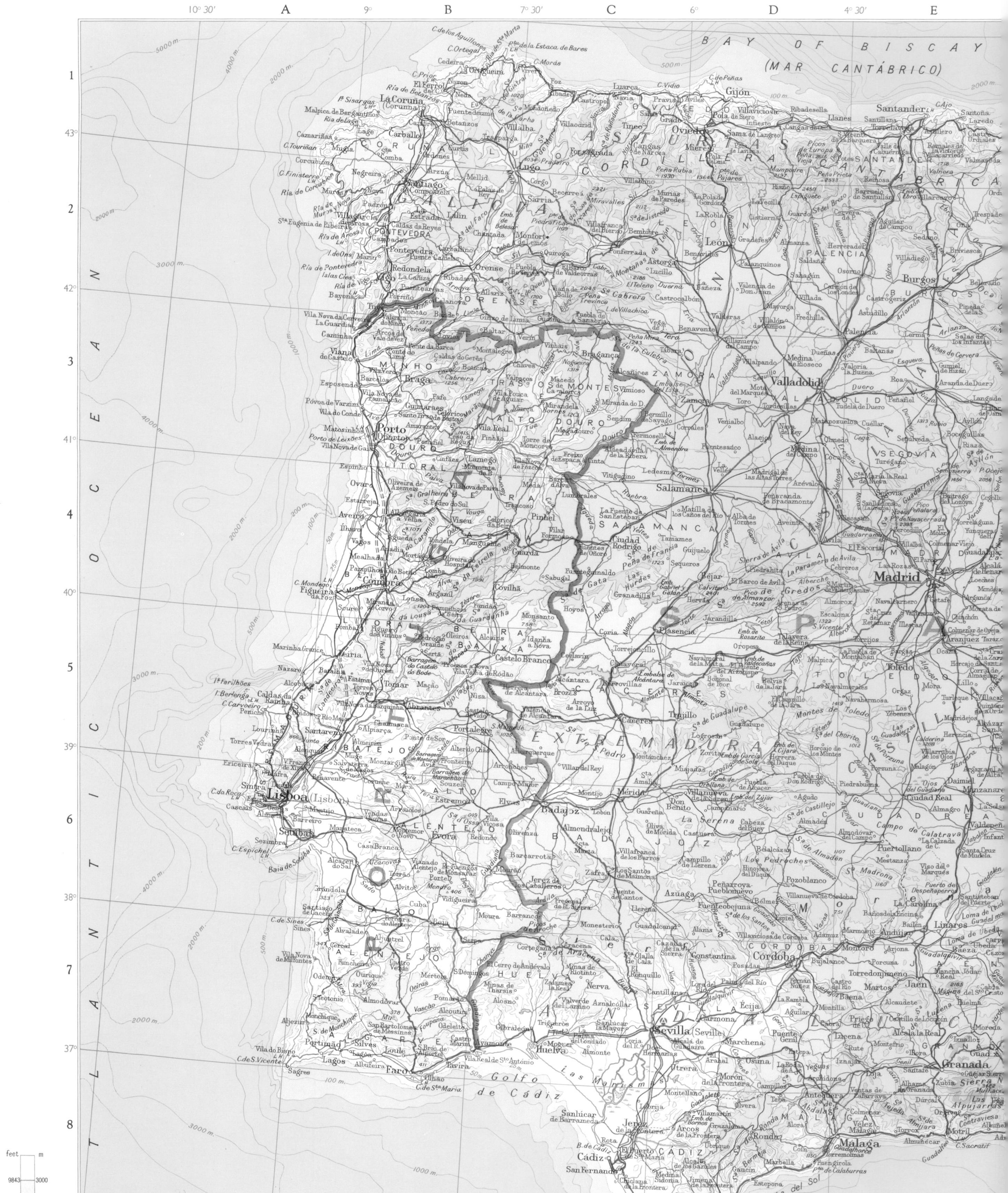

SECANT CONIC PROJECTION

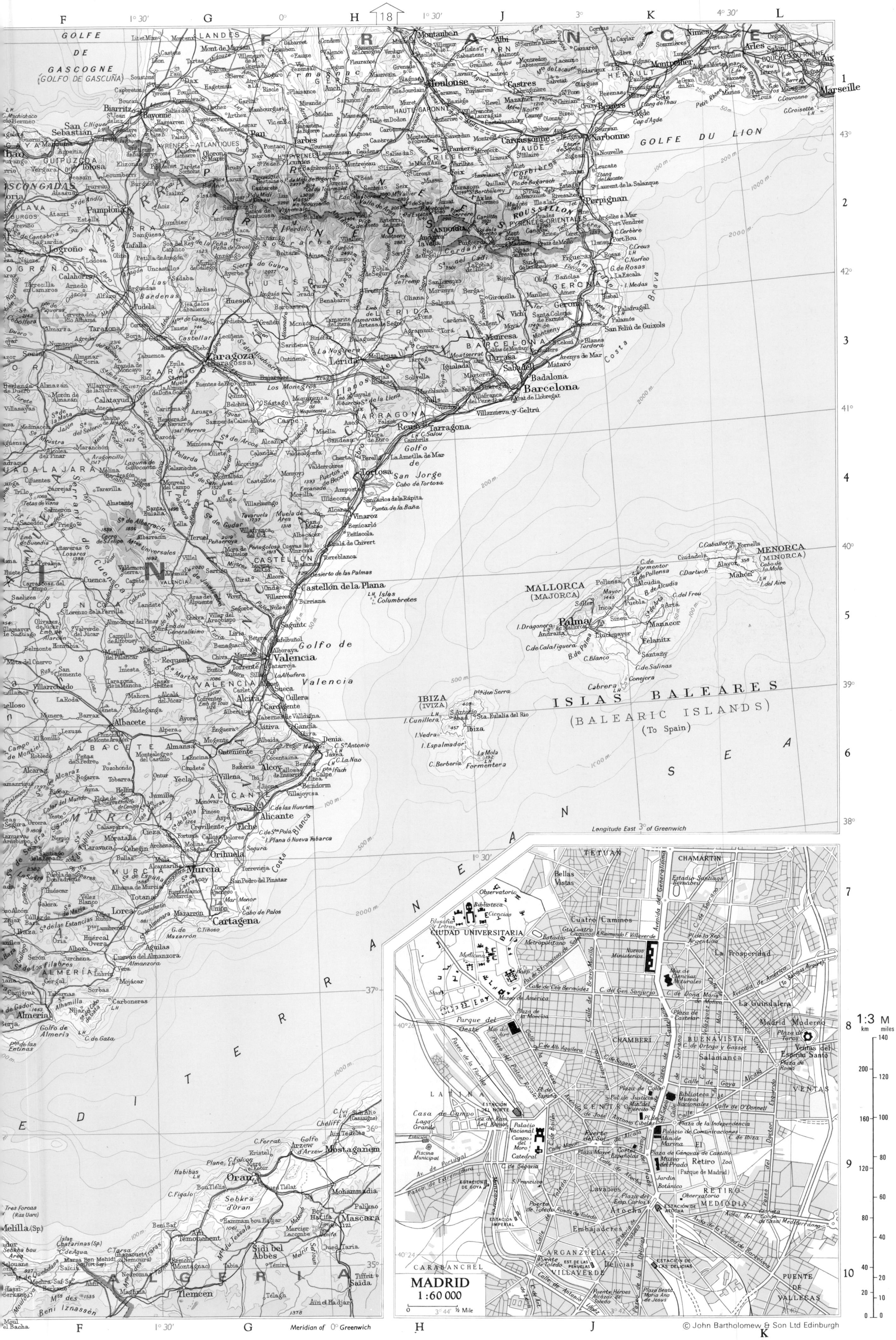
FRANCE
GOLFE DE GASCOGNE (GOLFE DE GASCUÑA)
GOLFE DU LION
PYRÉNÉES
ANDORRA
ROUSSILLON
Toulouse
Carcassonne
Narbonne
Perpignan
Montpellier
Nîmes
Arles
Marseille
Béziers
Bayonne
Biarritz
San Sebastián
Pamplona
Logroño
Tudela
Tarazona
Zaragoza (ZARAGOSSA)
Huesca
Lérida
Gerona
Manresa
Barcelona
Sabadell
Tarrasa
Badalona
Tarragona
Reus
Tortosa
Vinaroz
Teruel
Cuenca
Castellón de la Plana
Sagunto
Valencia
Golfo de Valencia
Alcira
Játiva
Gandía
Albacete
Almansa
Alcoy
Alicante
Elche
Orihuela
Murcia
Cartagena
Lorca
Almería
Golfo de Almería
Costa Brava
Costa Blanca
MALLORCA (MAJORCA)
Palma
MENORCA (MINORCA)
Mahón
Ciudadela
IBIZA (IVIZA)
Ibiza
Formentera
ISLAS BALEARES (BALEARIC ISLANDS) (To Spain)
MEDITERRANEAN SEA
ALGERIA
Oran
Mostaganem
Tlemcen
Sidi bel Abbès
Mascara
Melilla (Sp.)
Longitude East 3° of Greenwich
Meridian of 0° Greenwich
MADRID 1:60 000
CIUDAD UNIVERSITARIA
CHAMARTIN
TETUAN
Cuatro Caminos
CHAMBERÍ
BUENAVISTA
Salamanca
La Prosperidad
La Guindalera
Madrid Moderno
Ventas del Espíritu Santo
VENTAS
Casa de Campo
Palacio Nacional
Catedral
Plaza Mayor
Puerta del Sol
Retiro
Lavapiés
Atocha
Embajadores
ARGANZUELA
Delicias
CARABANCHEL
PUENTE DE VALLECAS
RETIRO MEDIODÍA
LATINA
1:3 M
km
miles

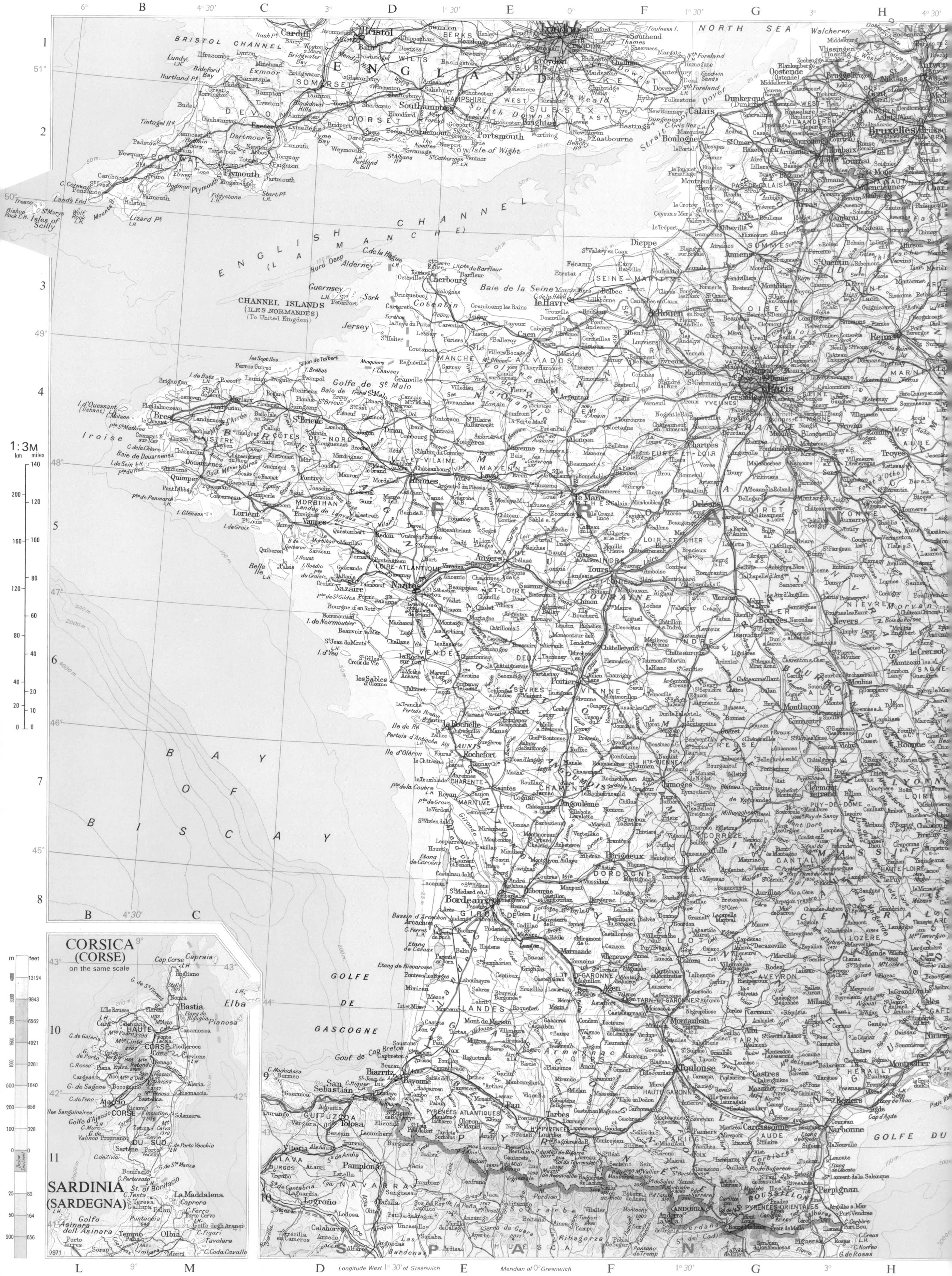
NORTH SEA
BRISTOL CHANNEL
ENGLAND
ENGLISH CHANNEL
(LA MANCHE)
CHANNEL ISLANDS
(ILES NORMANDES)
(To United Kingdom)
Baie de la Seine
Golfe de St Malo
BAY OF BISCAY
GOLFE DE GASCOGNE
GOLFE DU
London
Bristol
Cardiff
Plymouth
Portsmouth
Southampton
Brighton
Dover
Calais
Boulogne
Dunkerque
Lille
Bruxelles
Antwerpen
Amiens
Dieppe
le Havre
Rouen
Cherbourg
Caen
Reims
Paris
Versailles
Chartres
le Mans
Rennes
St Brieuc
Brest
Quimper
Lorient
Vannes
Nantes
St Nazaire
Angers
Tours
Orléans
Troyes
Bourges
Nevers
Poitiers
la Rochelle
Rochefort
Limoges
Angoulême
Clermont Ferrand
Bordeaux
Périgueux
Agen
Montauban
Toulouse
Biarritz
Bayonne
Pau
Tarbes
Carcassonne
Narbonne
Perpignan
Béziers
Montpellier
ANDORRA
PYRÉNÉES
SPAIN
CORSICA
(CORSE)
on the same scale
Bastia
Ajaccio
SARDINIA
(SARDEGNA)
1:3M
Longitude West 1° 30′ of Greenwich
Meridian of 0° Greenwich

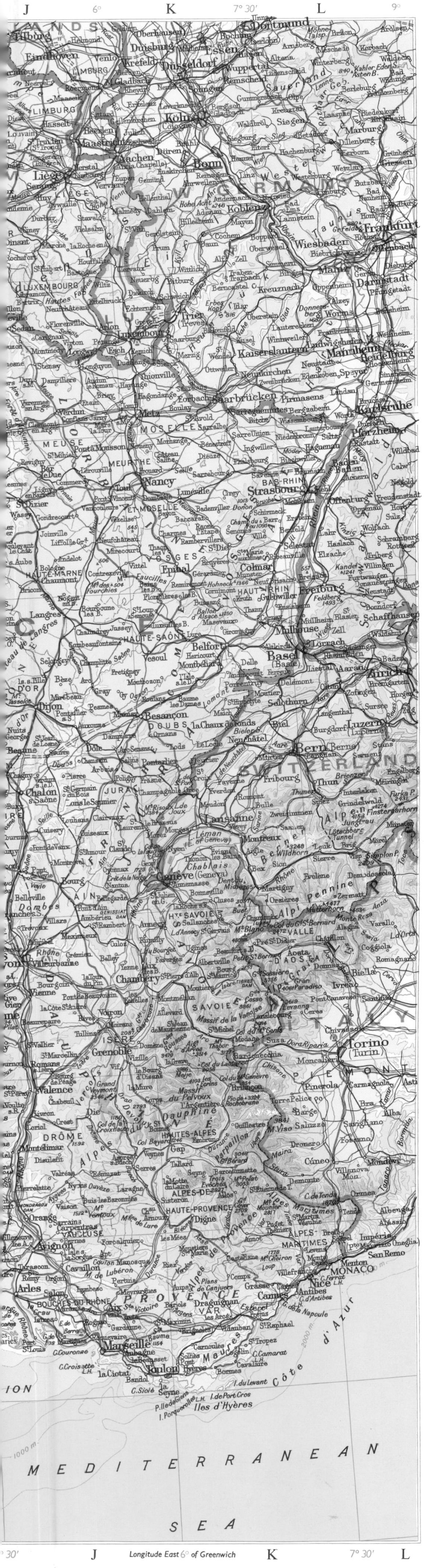
MEDITERRANEAN
SEA
Longitude East 6° of Greenwich

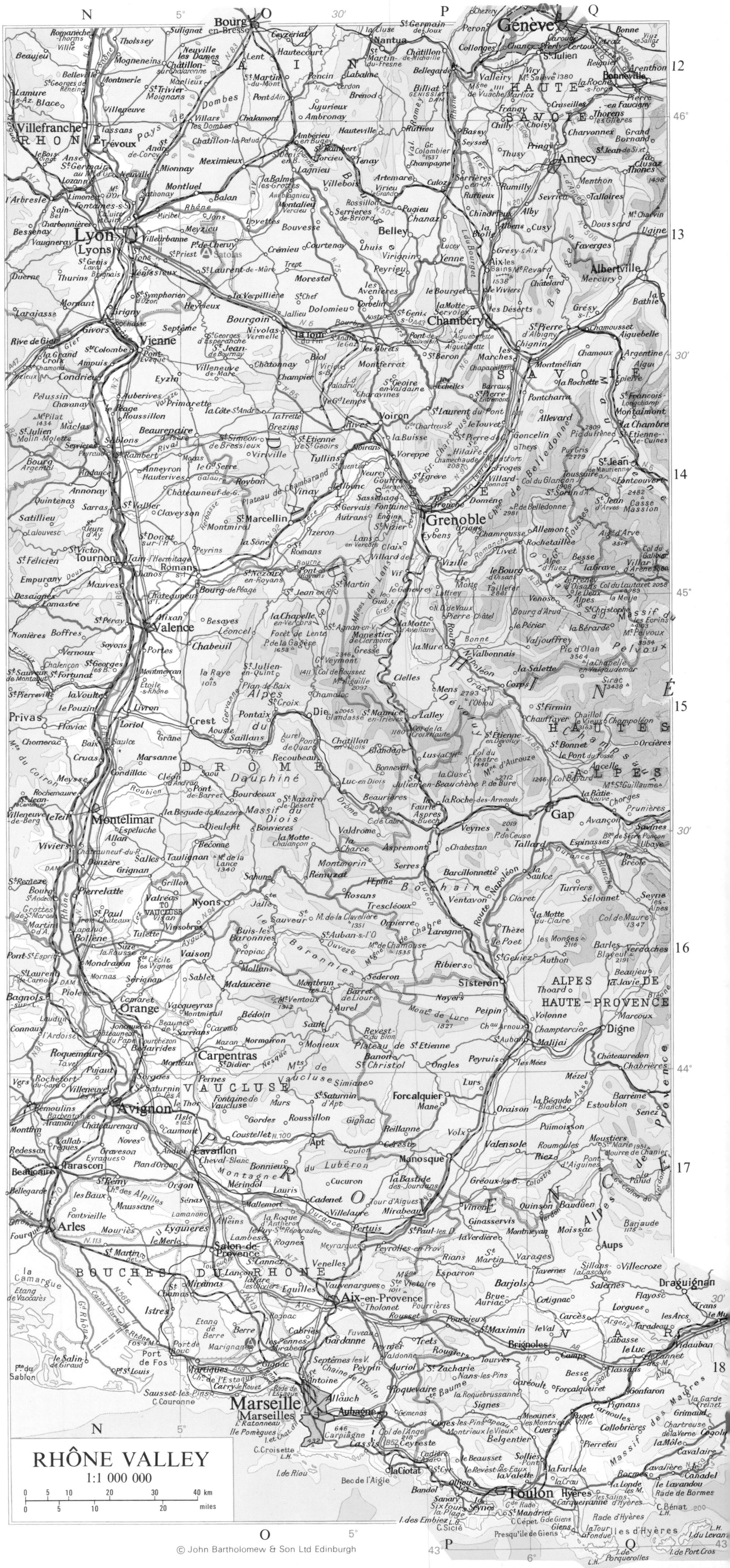
RHÔNE VALLEY
1:1 000 000
km
miles

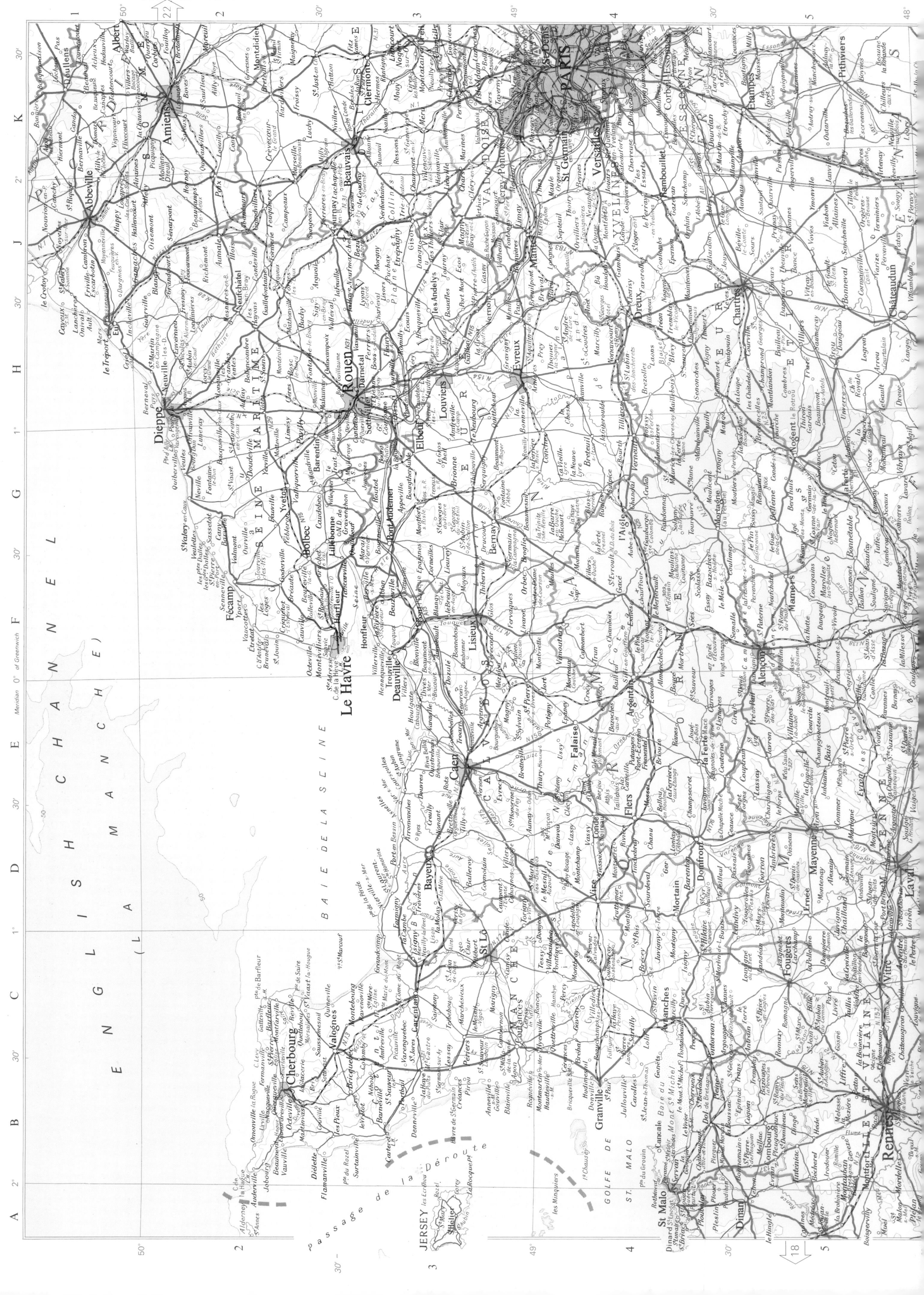
ENGLISH CHANNEL
(LA MANCHE)
BAIE DE LA SEINE
GOLFE DE ST. MALO
Passage de la Déroute
PARIS
St Denis
Versailles
St Germain
Amiens
Abbeville
Beauvais
Rouen
Dieppe
Le Havre
Caen
Cherbourg
Évreux
Chartres
Rennes
Laval
Alençon
Lisieux
Bayeux
St Lô
Granville
Avranches
Fougères
Vitré
St Malo
Dinan
Dinard
Falaise
Flers
Vire
Mamers
Dreux
Rambouillet
Étampes
Pithiviers
Châteaudun
Nogent le Rotrou
Mayenne
Domfront
Argentan
Bernay
Louviers
Elbeuf
Fécamp
Bolbec
Yvetot
Honfleur
Deauville
Trouville
Valognes
Carentan
Coutances
Mantes
Pontoise
Clermont
Doullens
Montdidier
Albert
Gisors
Corbeil
Étretat
Coulommiers
JERSEY
St Helier
Alderney
Meridian 0° of Greenwich

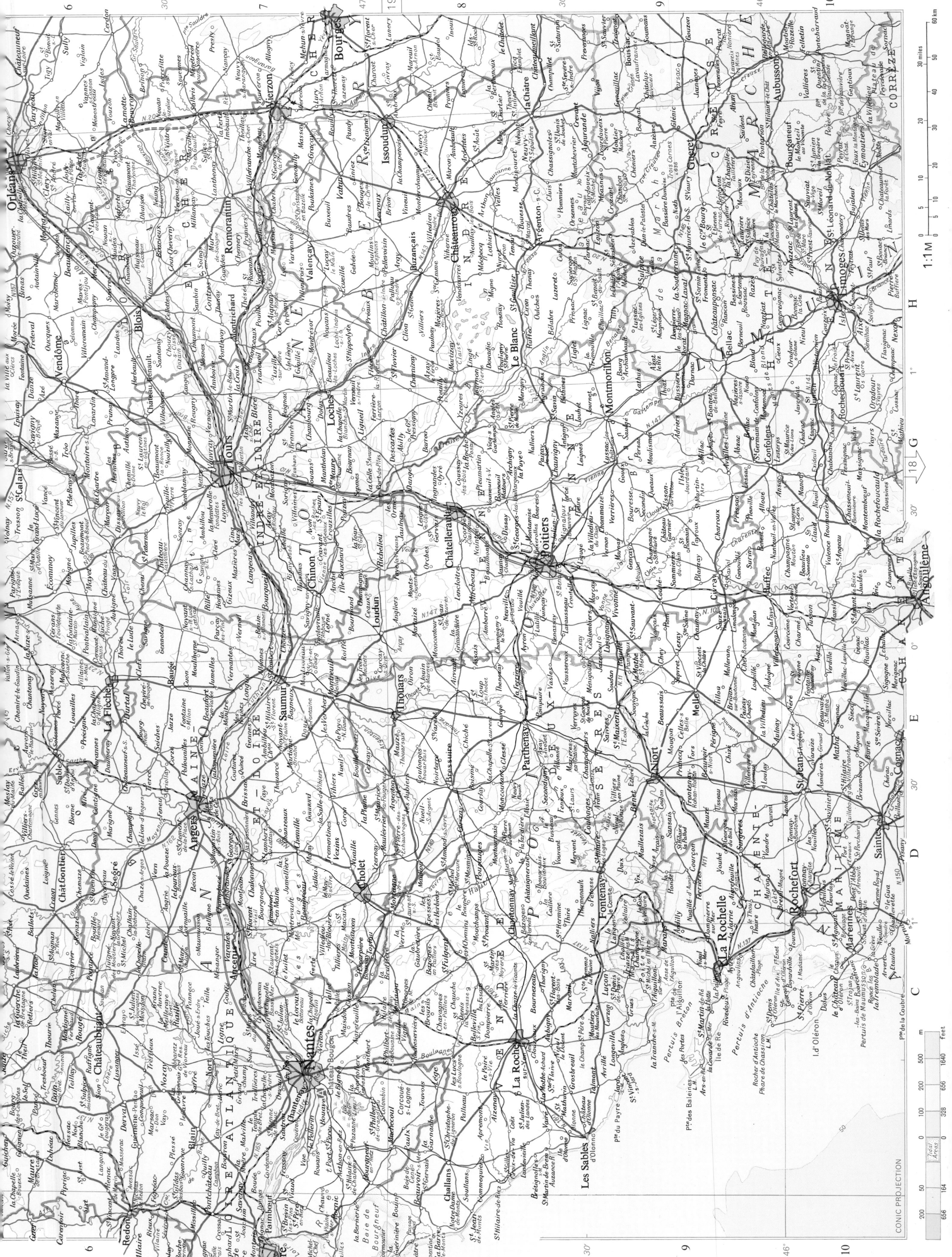
Orléans
Vierzon
Bourges
Issoudun
Châteauroux
Romorantin
Blois
Vendôme
Tours
Loches
Le Blanc
Montmorillon
Limoges
Guéret
Aubusson
Angers
Saumur
Chinon
Loudun
Châtellerault
Poitiers
Angoulême
Cognac
Saintes
Rochefort
La Rochelle
Niort
Parthenay
Fontenay
Cholet
Nantes
St Nazaire
La Roche-sur-Yon
Les Sables d'Olonne
Châteaubriant
Redon
La Flèche
Sablé
Thouars
Bressuire
Confolens
Ruffec
St Jean d'Angély
Marennes
Ancenis
Luçon
1:1M
CONIC PROJECTION

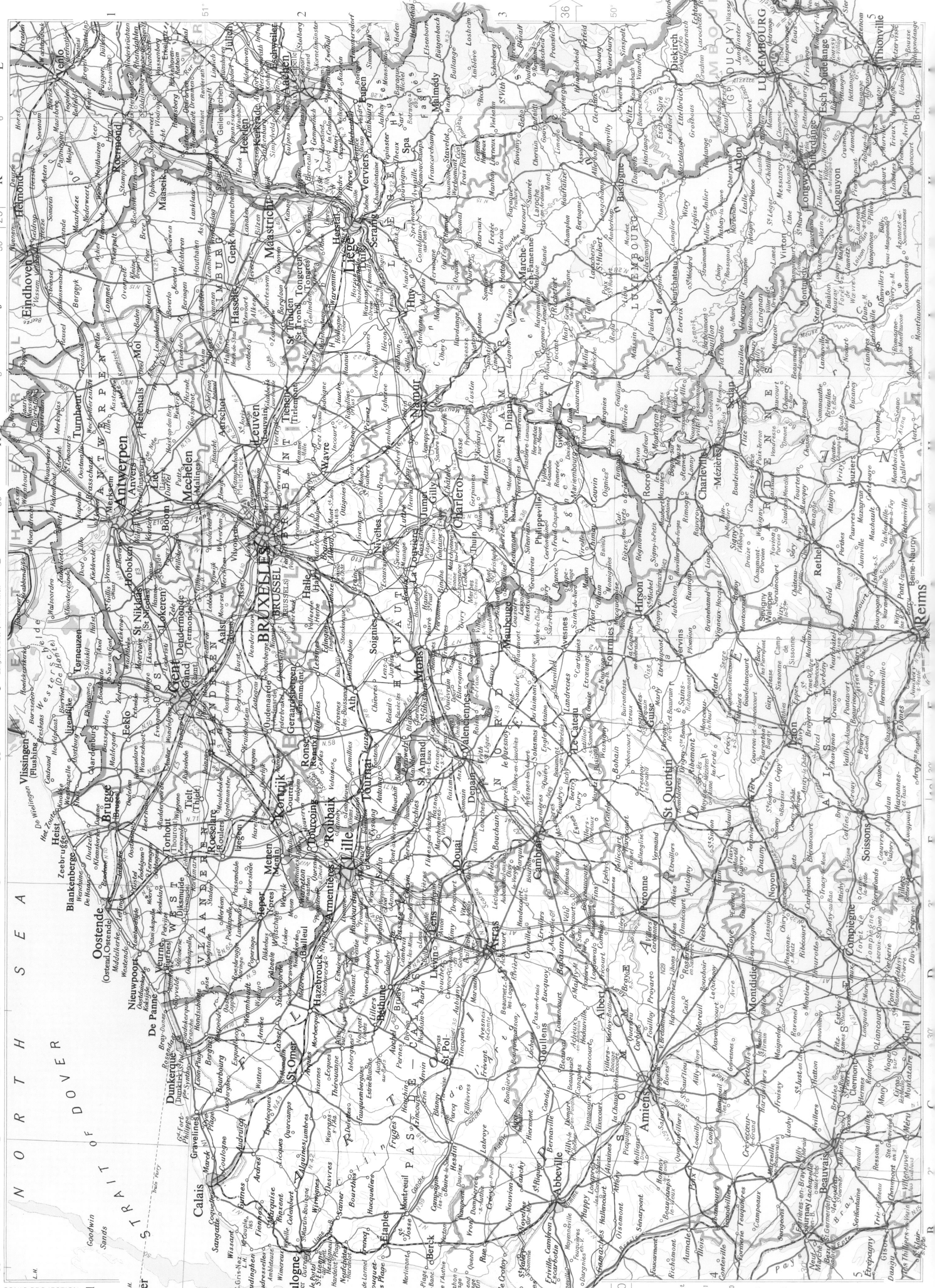

CONIC PROJECTION
Heights and Depths in metres
1:1M
0 10 20 30 40 50 miles
0 10 20 30 40 50 60 70 80 km

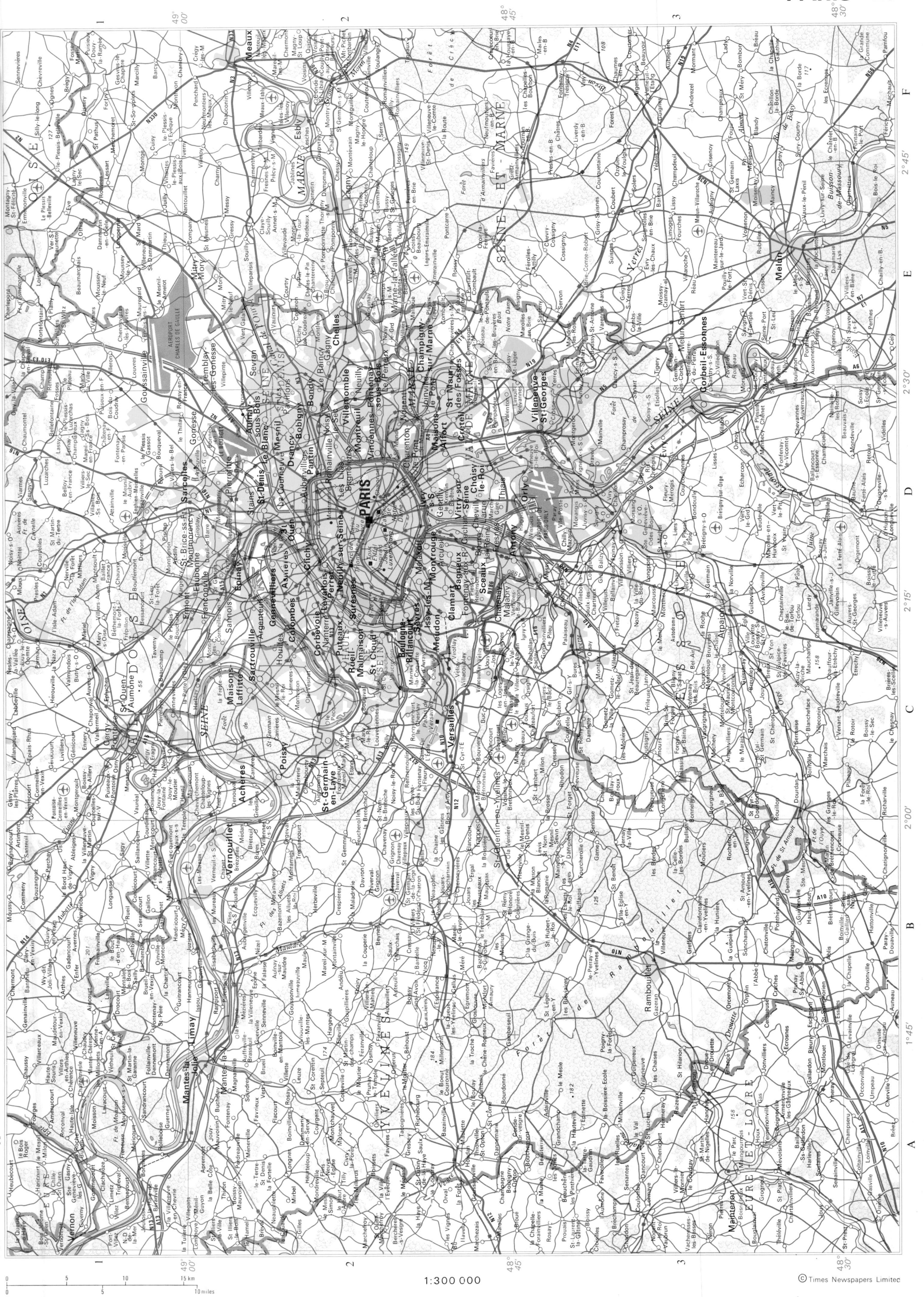
PARIS
Versailles
Melun
Meaux
St-Germain-en-Laye
Rambouillet
Corbeil-Essonnes
Mantes-la-Jolie
SEINE-ET-MARNE
YVELINES
ESSONNE
VAL-D'OISE
AEROPORT CHARLES DE GAULLE

1:300 000

AMSTERDAM / THE HAGUE

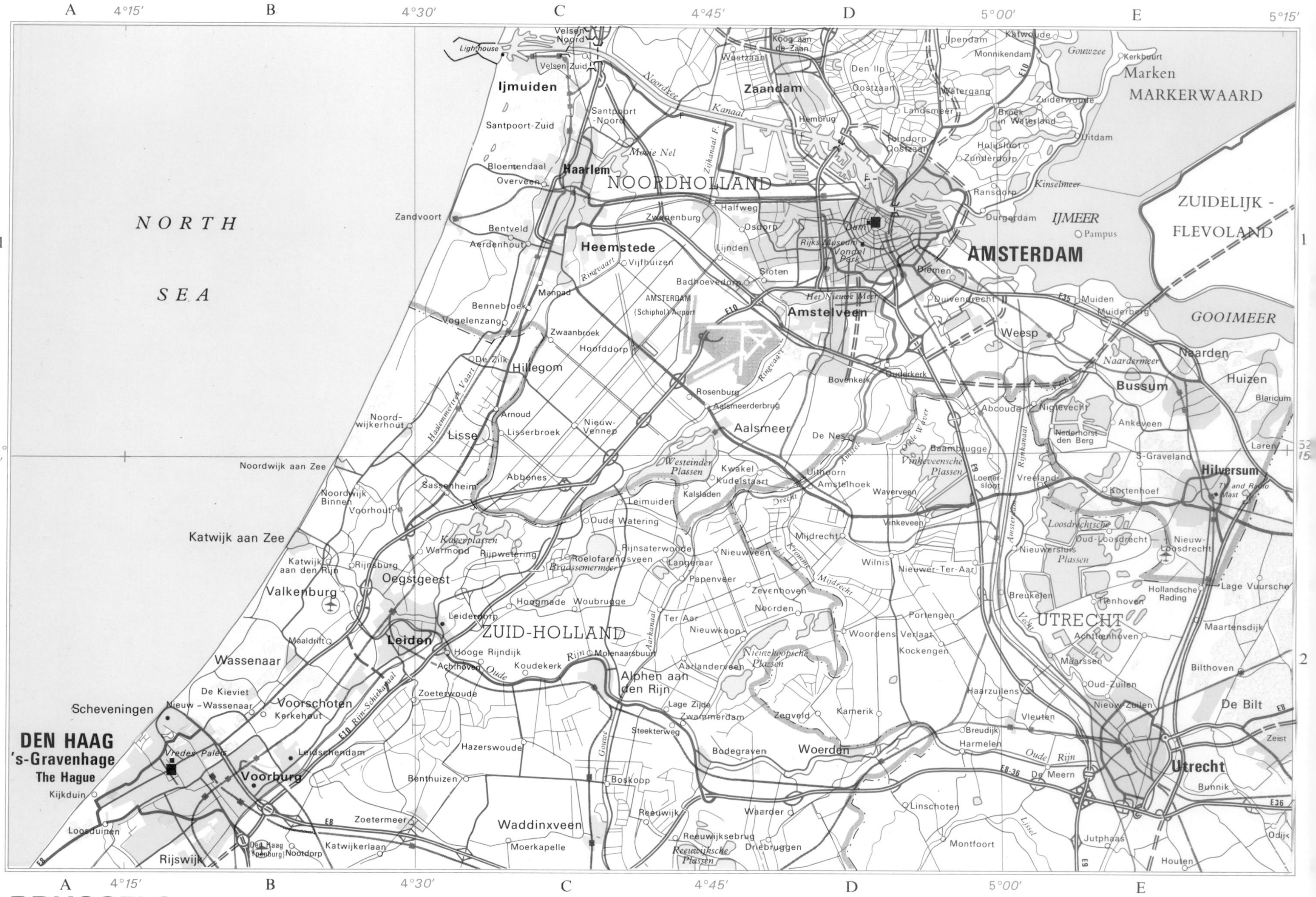
NORTH SEA
NOORDHOLLAND
ZUID-HOLLAND
UTRECHT
ZUIDELIJK - FLEVOLAND
MARKERWAARD
IJMEER
GOOIMEER
AMSTERDAM
DEN HAAG
's-Gravenhage
The Hague
Ijmuiden
Zaandam
Haarlem
Heemstede
Amstelveen
Hillegom
Lisse
Aalsmeer
Leiden
Oegstgeest
Wassenaar
Scheveningen
Voorschoten
Voorburg
Rijswijk
Alphen aan den Rijn
Woerden
Waddinxveen
Boskoop
Weesp
Naarden
Bussum
Huizen
Hilversum
Utrecht
Zandvoort
Katwijk aan Zee
Noordwijk aan Zee
Valkenburg
Kijkduin
Zoetermeer
Mijdrecht
Abcoude
Maarssen
Bilthoven
De Bilt
Nieuwegein
Vleuten
Kamerik
Bodegraven
Montfoort
Houten

BRUSSELS

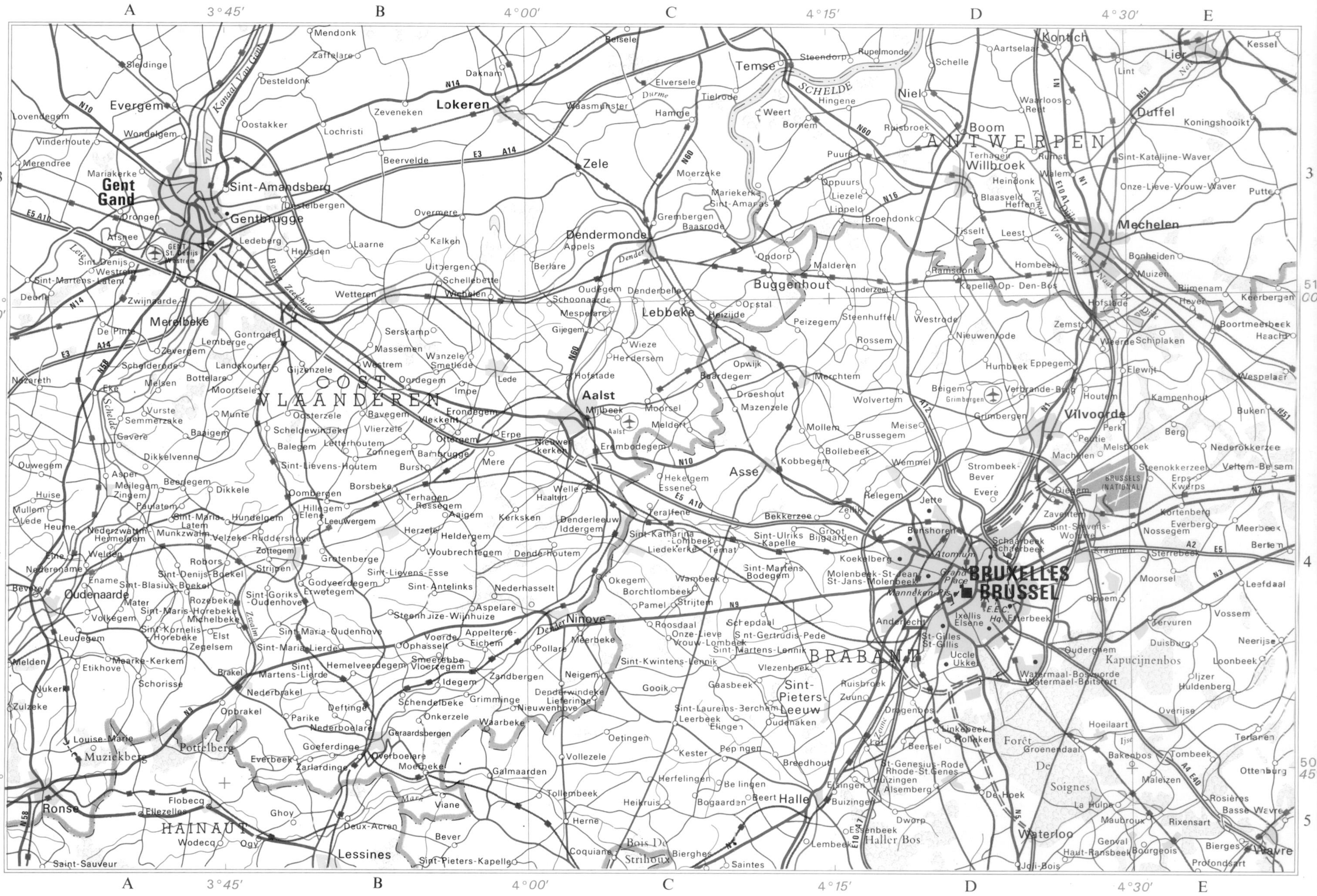
ANTWERPEN
OOST VLAANDEREN
BRABANT
HAINAUT
BRUXELLES
BRUSSEL
Gent
Gand
Lokeren
Temse
Niel
Boom
Willbroek
Mechelen
Lier
Duffel
Zele
Dendermonde
Buggenhout
Lebbeke
Aalst
Asse
Vilvoorde
Ninove
Oudenaarde
Ronse
Lessines
Halle
Waterloo
Wavre
Sint-Pieters-Leeuw
Merelbeke
Evergem
Sint-Amandsberg
Gentbrugge
Wetteren
Zottegem
Geraardsbergen
Muizen

© Times Newspapers Limited

1:300 000

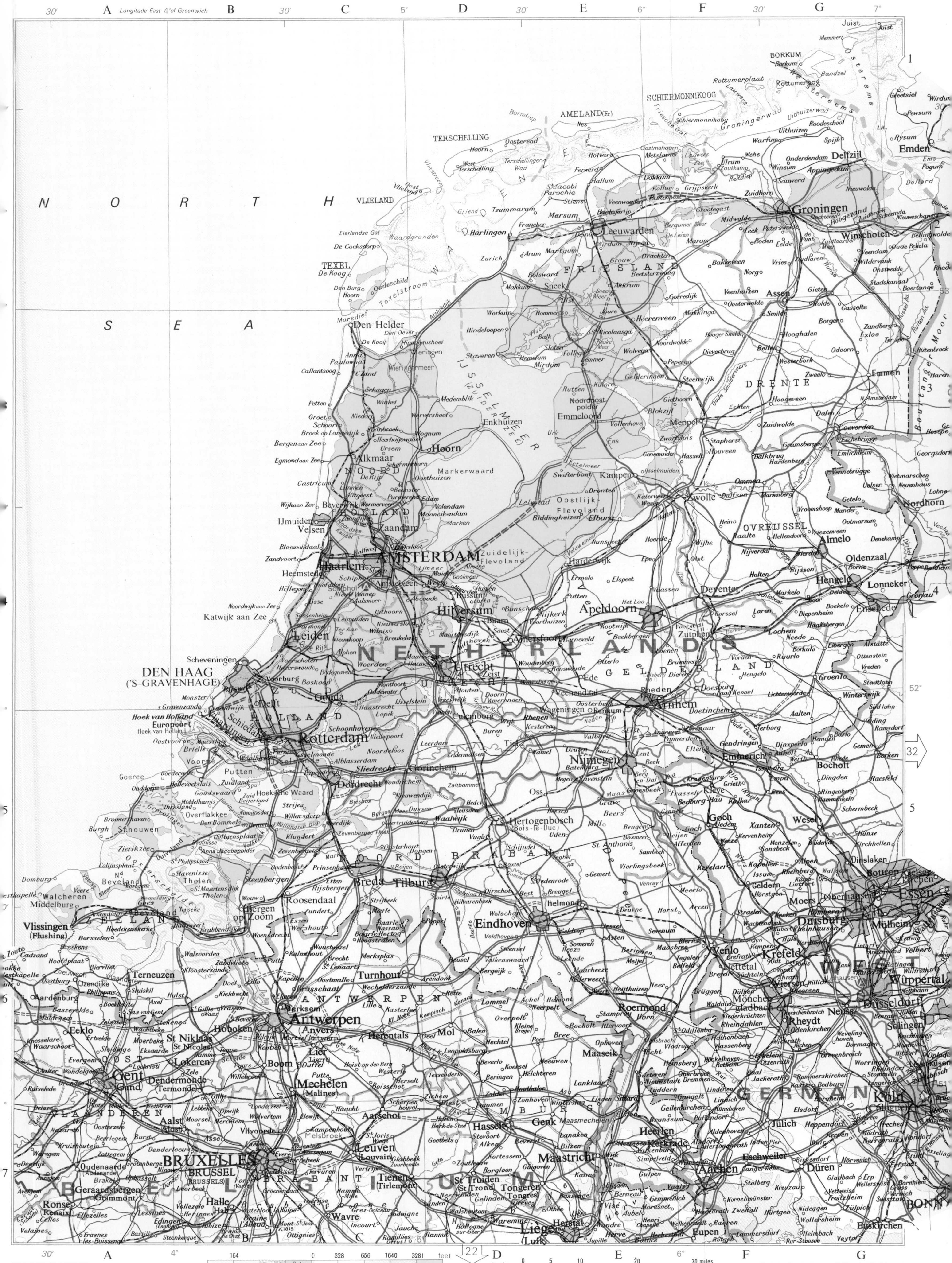
A
B
C
D
E
F
G
Longitude East 4° of Greenwich
30'
5°
6°
7°
52°
NORTH
SEA
NETHERLANDS
BELGIUM
GERMANY
FRIESLAND
DRENTE
OVERIJSSEL
GELDERLAND
NOORD HOLLAND
ZUID HOLLAND
UTRECHT
NOORD BRABANT
ZEELAND
LIMBURG
ANTWERPEN
OOST VLAANDEREN
BRABANT
IJSSELMEER
WADDENZEE
Markerwaard
Oostelijk-Flevoland
Zuidelijk-Flevoland
Noordoost polder
TEXEL
VLIELAND
TERSCHELLING
AMELAND
SCHIERMONNIKOOG
BORKUM
Juist
AMSTERDAM
Rotterdam
DEN HAAG
('S-GRAVENHAGE)
Utrecht
Haarlem
Leiden
Groningen
Leeuwarden
Den Helder
Alkmaar
Hoorn
Zaandam
Hilversum
Amersfoort
Apeldoorn
Arnhem
Nijmegen
Zwolle
Kampen
Deventer
Almelo
Hengelo
Enschede
Emmen
Assen
Delfzijl
Emden
Harlingen
Dordrecht
Gouda
Breda
Tilburg
Hertogenbosch
(Bois-le-Duc)
Eindhoven
Helmond
Venlo
Roermond
Maastricht
Heerlen
Kerkrade
Aachen
Vlissingen
(Flushing)
Middelburg
Bergen op Zoom
Roosendaal
Antwerpen
Anvers
(Antwerp)
Gent
Gand
Mechelen
(Malines)
Leuven
(Louvain)
BRUXELLES
BRUSSEL
(BRUSSELS)
Liège
(Luik)
Hasselt
Genk
Krefeld
Duisburg
Essen
Düsseldorf
Wuppertal
Köln
Cologne
BONN
Mönchengladbach
Neuss
Düren
Emmerich
Kleve
Wesel
32
22

CONIC PROJECTION

164			0	328	656	1640	3281	feet
50	Tidal Areas	Below Sea Level	0	100	200	500	1000	m

1:1M

0 5 10 20 30 miles

0 5 10 20 30 40 50 60 km

© John Bartholomew & Son Ltd Edinburgh

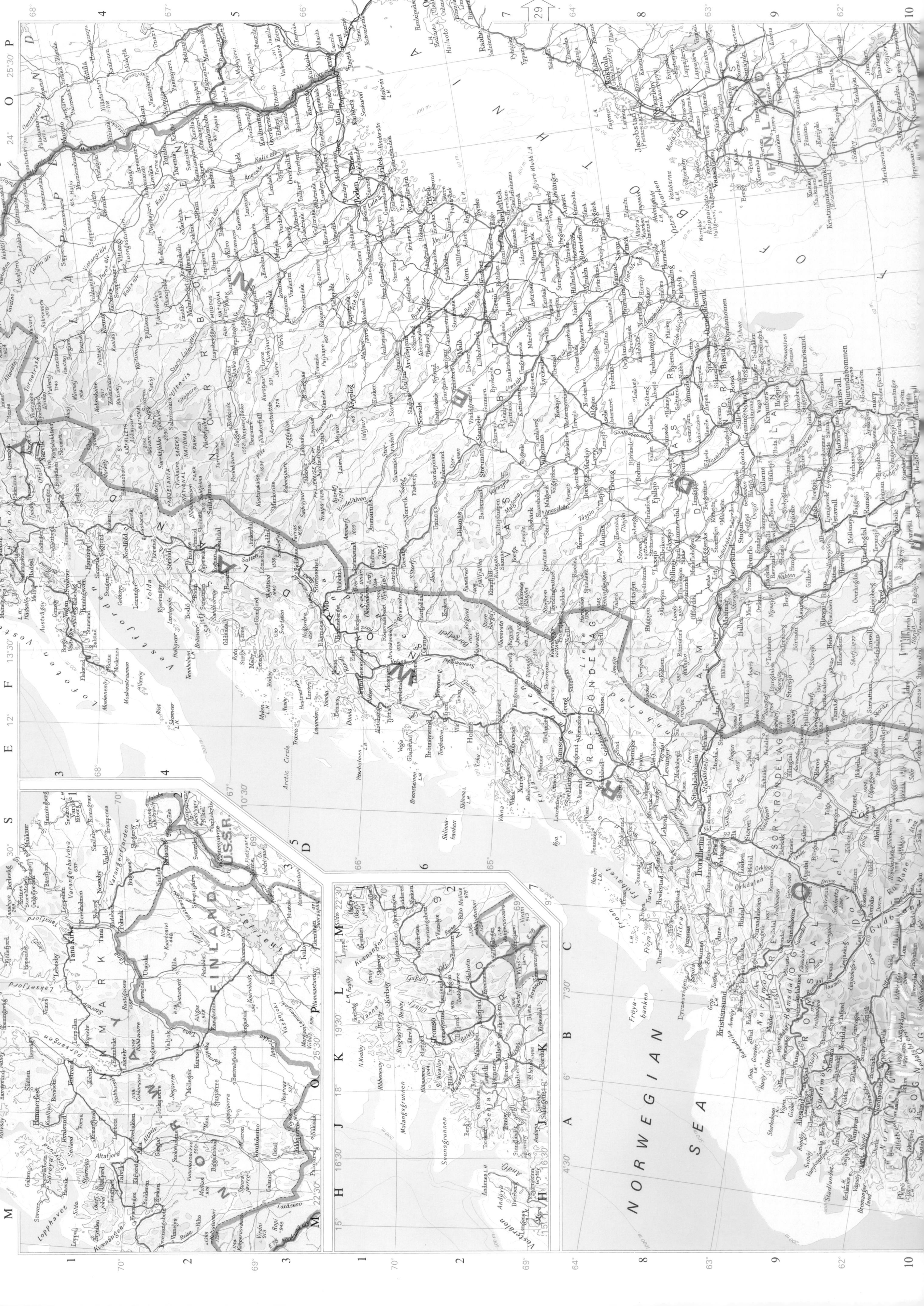
29
NORWEGIAN
SEA
Arctic Circle
FINLAND
U.S.S.R.
Trondheim
Kristiansund
Ålesund
Östersund
Sundsvall
Härnösand
Umeå
Skellefteå
Luleå
Oulu
Kokkola
Vaasa
Jakobstad
Bodø
Narvik
Tromsø
Hammerfest
NORWEGIAN SEA

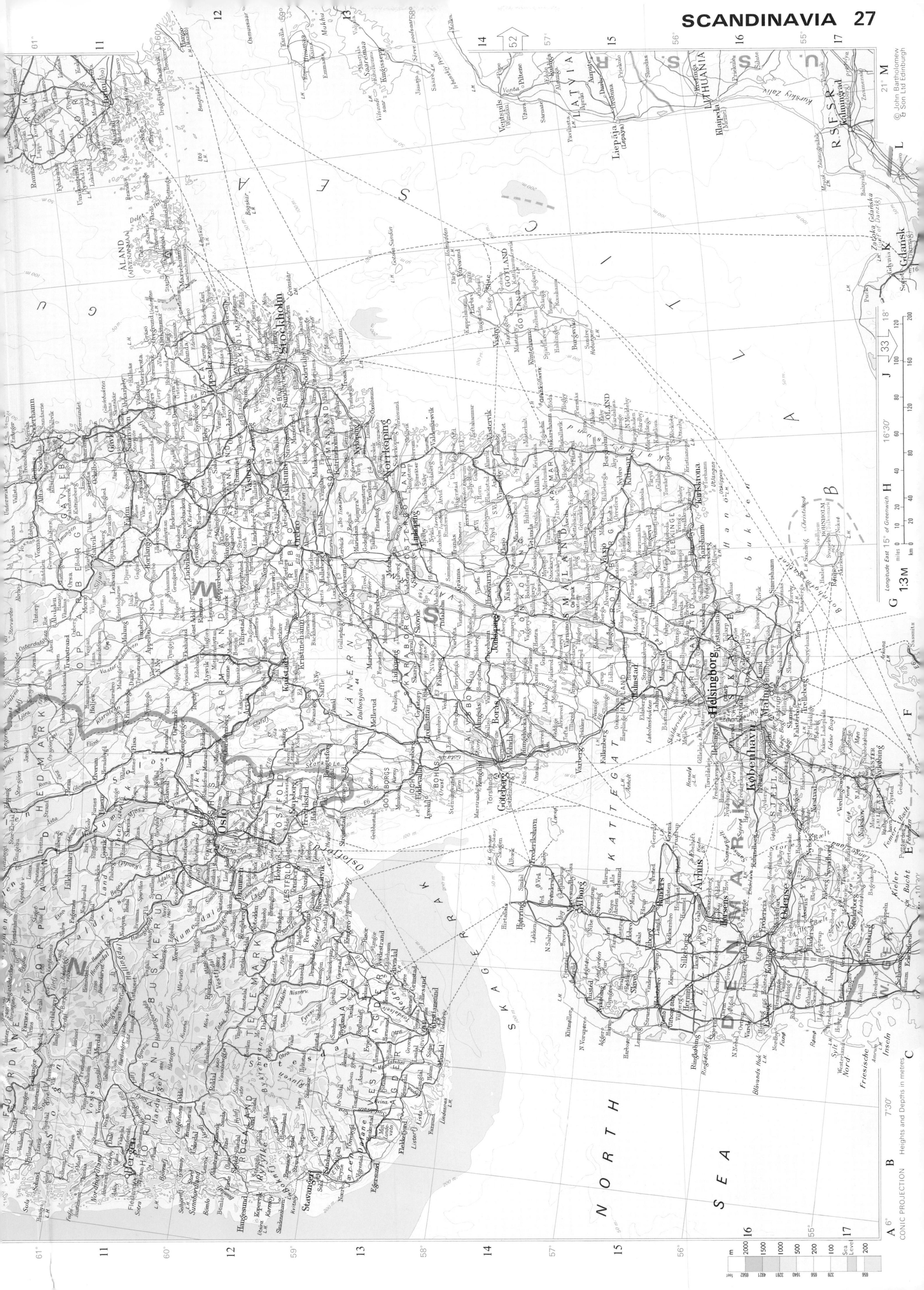
CONIC PROJECTION
Heights and Depths in metres
© John Bartholomew & Son Ltd Edinburgh
1:3M
Longitude East 15° of Greenwich
NORTH SEA
SKAGERRAK
KATTEGAT
BALTIC SEA
GULF OF BOTHNIA
NORWAY
SWEDEN
DENMARK
LATVIA
LITHUANIA
R.S.F.S.R.
Oslo
Stockholm
København
Göteborg
Malmö
Bergen
Stavanger
Gdańsk
Kaliningrad
Klaipeda (Memel)
Liepāja (Lepaya)
Ventspils (Windau)
Åland (Ahvenanmaa)
Gotland
Öland
Bornholm

SKAGERRAK
KATTEGAT
DENMARK
JYLLAND
JUTLAND
SJÆLLAND
ZEALAND
FYN
FÜNEN
LOLLAND
FALSTER
ALS
MORS
ÆRØ
LANGELAND
WEST GERMANY
NORDFRIESISCHE INSELN
ICELAND
Skagen
Frederikshavn
Hjørring
Hirtshals
Løkken
Brønderslev
Ålborg
Nørresundby
Limfjorden
Thisted
Nykøbing
Skive
Viborg
Hobro
Randers
Grenå
Århus
Silkeborg
Herning
Holstebro
Lemvig
Struer
Ringkøbing
Skjern
Skanderborg
Horsens
Vejle
Fredericia
Kolding
Esbjerg
Varde
Ribe
Haderslev
Åbenrå
Sønderborg
Tønder
Flensburg
Odense
Nyborg
Svendborg
Fåborg
Assens
Middelfart
Kalundborg
Holbæk
Slagelse
Korsør
Næstved
Vordingborg
Nakskov
Maribo
Læsø
Anholt
Samsø
Jammerbugt
Ålborg Bugt
Store Bælt
Lille Bælt
Sylt
Westerland
Fanø
Rømø
Fehmarn
1:1M
Longitude East 10° of Greenwich

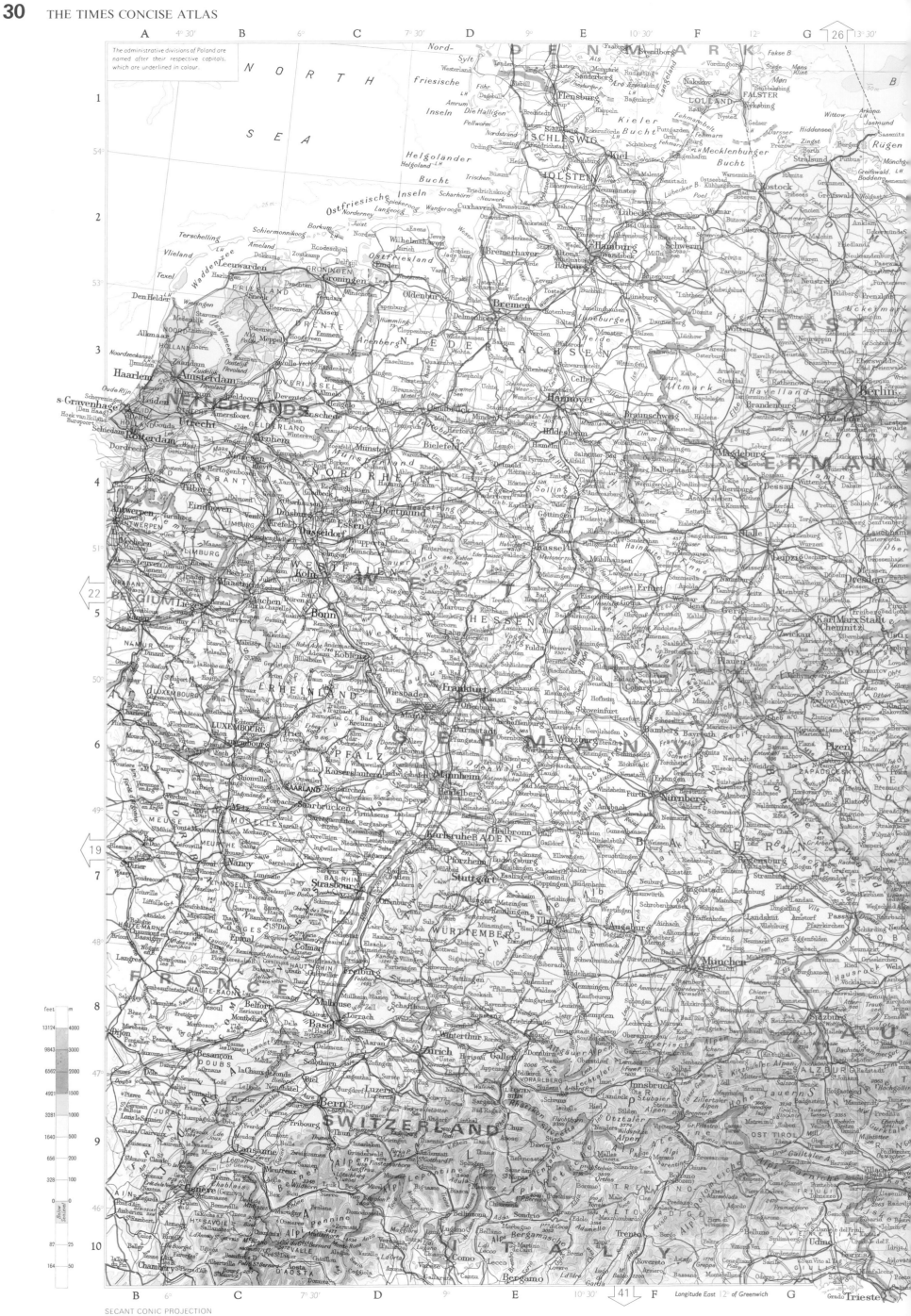

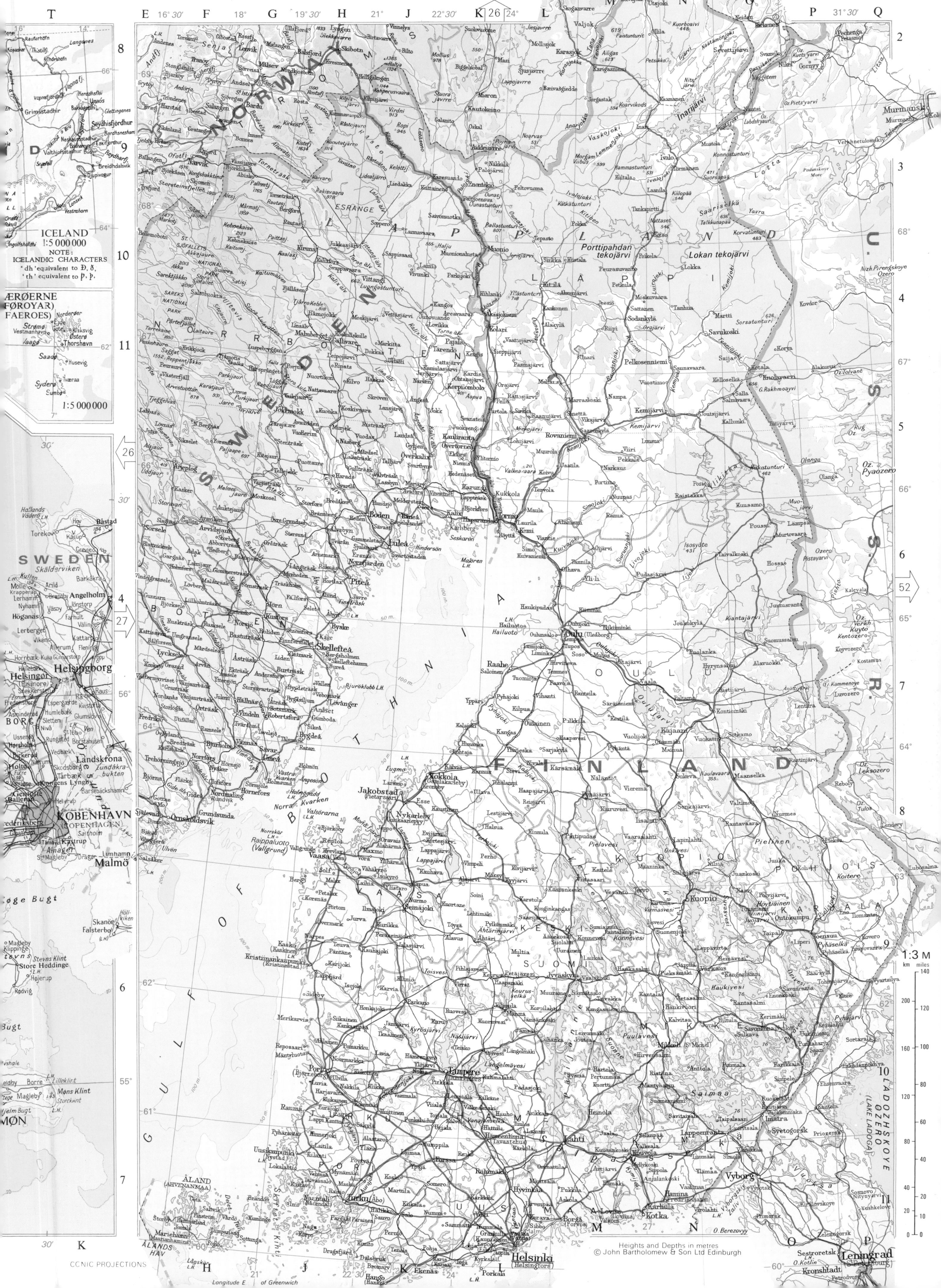
ICELAND
1:5 000 000
NOTE:
ICELANDIC CHARACTERS
'dh' equivalent to Ð, ð,
'th' equivalent to Þ, þ.
ÆRØERNE
(FØROYAR)
FAEROES
1:5 000 000
SWEDEN
KØBENHAVN
(COPENHAGEN)
Malmö
Helsingborg
NORWAY
SWEDEN
FINLAND
U. S. S. R.
LAPPI
LAPLAND
NORRBOTTEN
OULU
VAASA
KUOPIO
KESKI SUOMI
GULF OF BOTHNIA
Helsinki
(Helsingfors)
Tampere
Turku (Åbo)
Oulu (Uleåborg)
Rovaniemi
Vyborg
Leningrad
Murmansk
ÅLAND
(AHVENANMAA)
LADOZHSKOYE OZERO
(LAKE LADOGA)
1:3 M
km miles
Heights and Depths in metres
© John Bartholomew & Son Ltd Edinburgh
CONIC PROJECTIONS
Longitude E. of Greenwich

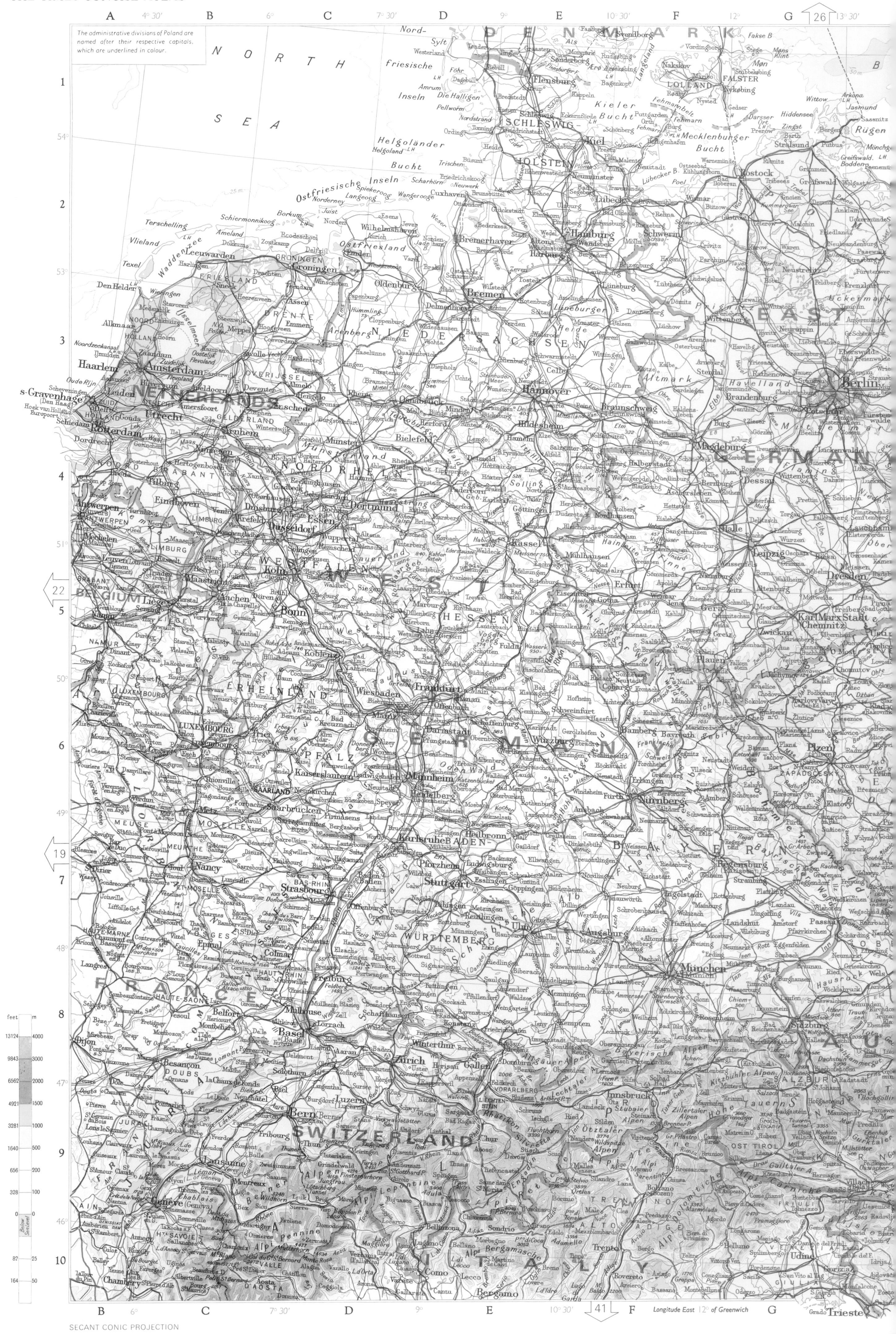

SECANT CONIC PROJECTION

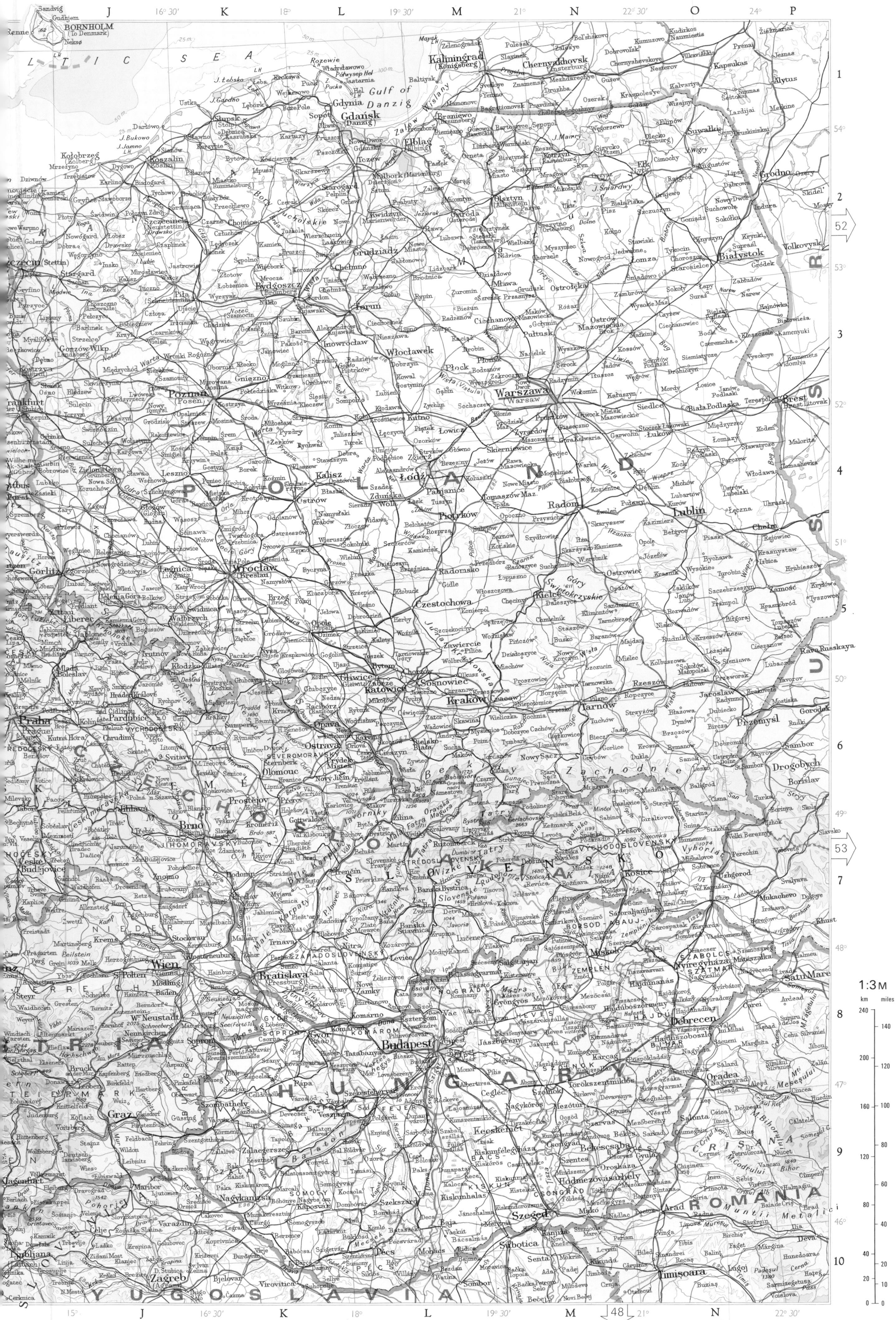
BALTIC SEA
Gulf of Danzig
BORNHOLM (To Denmark)
POLAND
CZECHOSLOVAKIA
HUNGARY
AUSTRIA
YUGOSLAVIA
ROMANIA
U.S.S.R.
Kaliningrad (Königsberg)
Gdańsk (Danzig)
Gdynia
Szczecin (Stettin)
Poznań (Posen)
Bydgoszcz (Bromberg)
Toruń
Warszawa (Warsaw)
Łódź
Wrocław (Breslau)
Kraków
Katowice
Lublin
Białystok
Grodno
Brest
Praha
Brno
Ostrava
Bratislava (Pressburg)
Wien
Graz
Budapest
Debrecen
Szeged
Košice
Zagreb (Agram)
Ljubljana
Oradea
Arad
Timişoara
J K L M N O P
1 2 3 4 5 6 7 8 9 10
52
53
48
1:3M
km
miles

© John Bartholomew & Son Ltd Edinburgh

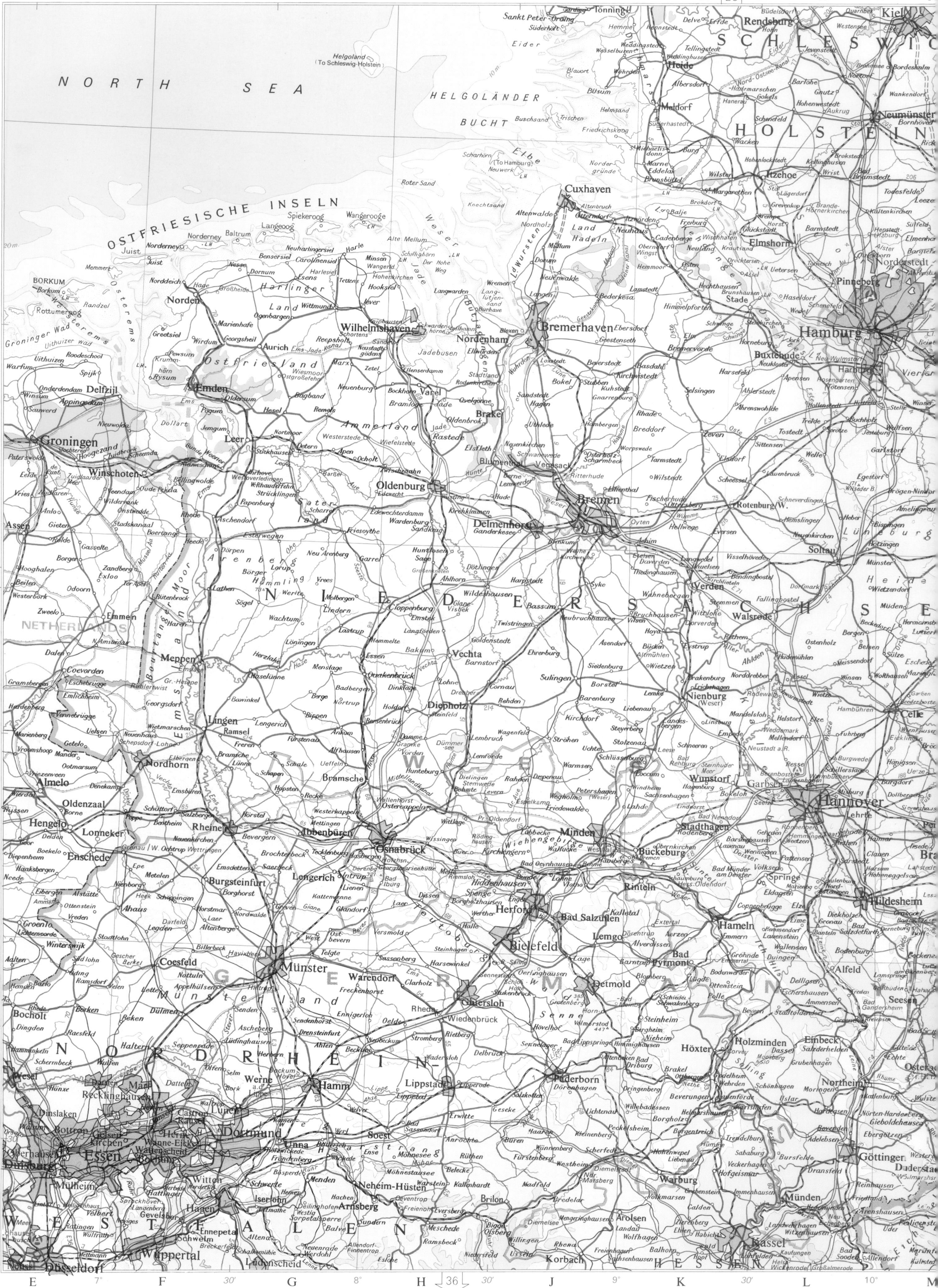

NOTE: 'ß'-German equivalent to 'ss'

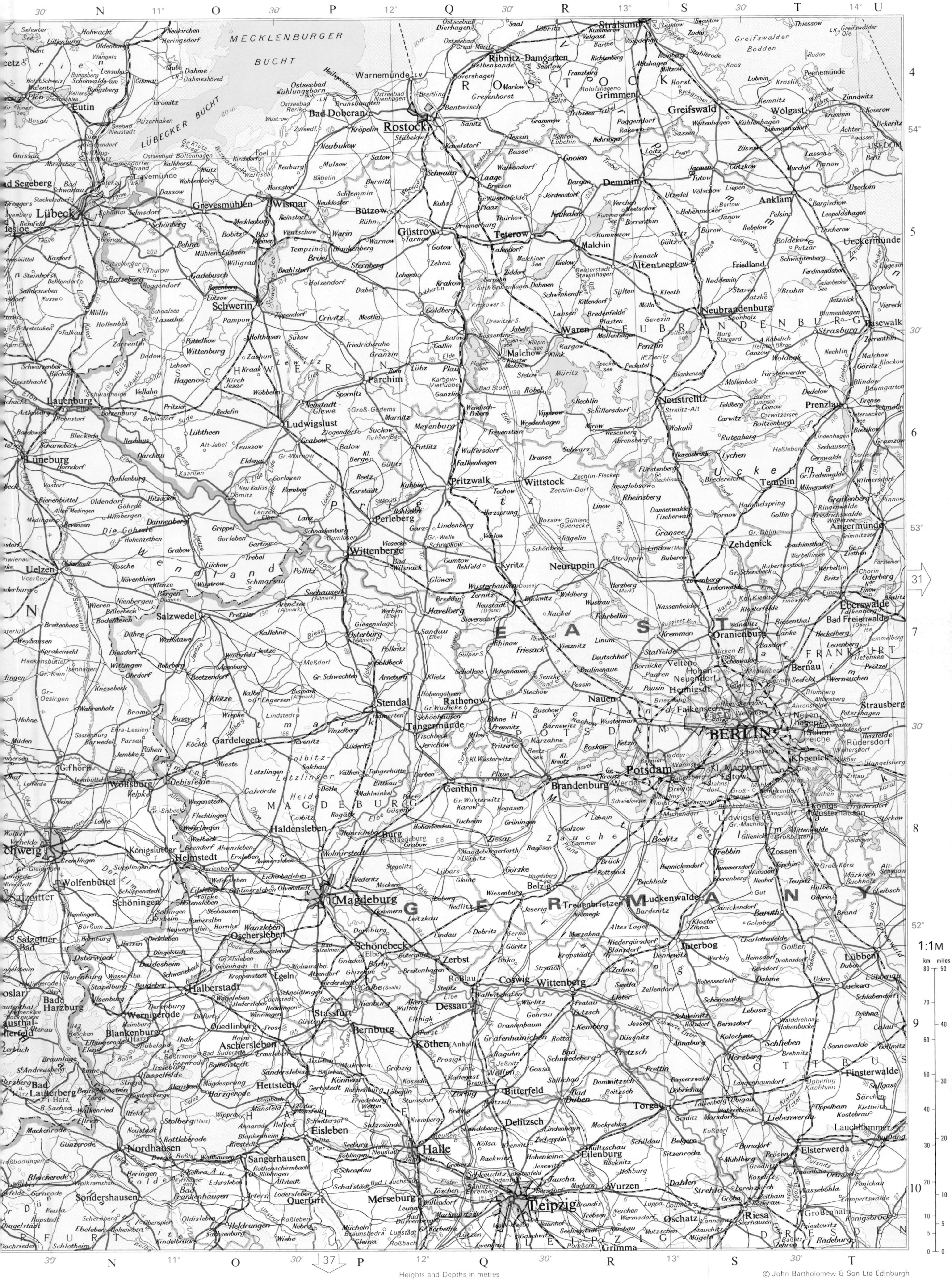
MECKLENBURGER BUCHT
LÜBECKER BUCHT
ROSTOCK
NEUBRANDENBURG
SCHWERIN
EAST GERMANY
POTSDAM
FRANKFURT
MAGDEBURG
HALLE
LEIPZIG
COTTBUS
DRESDEN
Uckermark
Prignitz
Altmark
Wendland
Stralsund
Greifswald
Rostock
Wismar
Lübeck
Schwerin
Güstrow
Neubrandenburg
Neustrelitz
Wittenberge
Stendal
Berlin
Potsdam
Brandenburg
Magdeburg
Dessau
Halle
Leipzig
Wittenberg
Frankfurt
1:1M
31
37

Heights and Depths in metres

© John Bartholomew & Son Ltd Edinburgh

HAMBURG

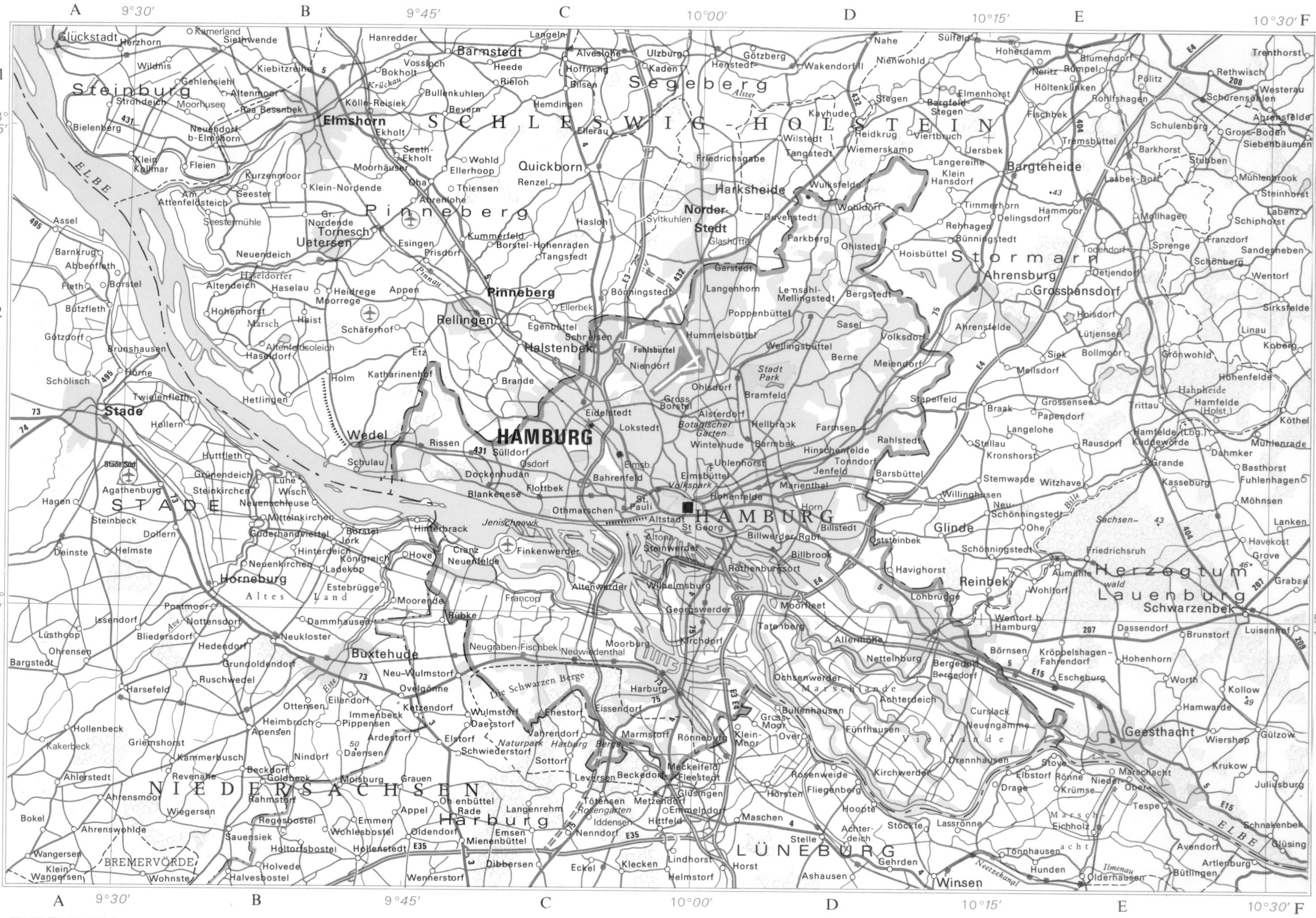

A
B
C
D
E
F
9°30'
9°45'
10°00'
10°15'
10°30'
53° 45'
53° 30'
Glückstadt
Steinburg
Elmshorn
Barmstedt
Segeberg
SCHLESWIG-HOLSTEIN
Quickborn
Pinneberg
Uetersen
Norder Stedt
Harksheide
Stormarn
Ahrensburg
Grosshansdorf
Bargteheide
Rellingen
Halstenbek
Fuhlsbüttel
Wedel
Stade
STADE
HAMBURG
Blankenese
Altona
St. Pauli
St. Georg
Wandsbek
Bergedorf
Reinbek
Glinde
Herzogtum Lauenburg
Schwarzenbek
Geesthacht
Buxtehude
Harburg
Wilhelmsburg
Finkenwerder
Horneburg
Altes Land
NIEDERSACHSEN
LÜNEBURG
Winsen
ELBE
BREMERVÖRDE

BERLIN

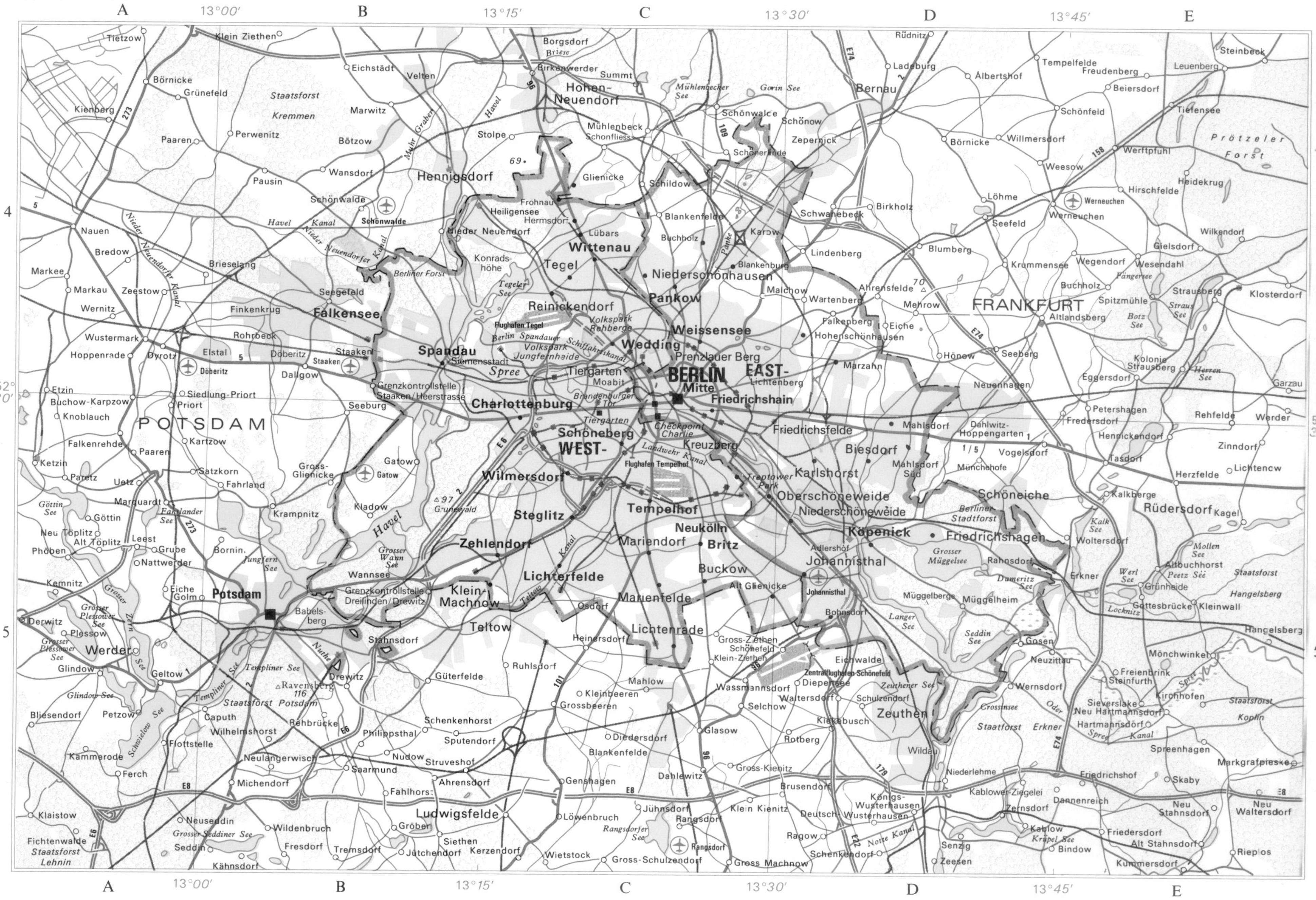

A
B
C
D
E
13°00'
13°15'
13°30'
13°45'
52° 30'
Oranienburg
Hennigsdorf
Bernau
Nauen
Falkensee
Spandau
Tegel
Wittenau
Reinickendorf
Pankow
Weissensee
Wedding
Tiergarten
Charlottenburg
BERLIN
EAST-
WEST-
Mitte
Friedrichshain
Kreuzberg
Schöneberg
Wilmersdorf
Steglitz
Zehlendorf
Tempelhof
Neukölln
Lichtenberg
Köpenick
Treptow
Marzahn
Biesdorf
Karlshorst
FRANKFURT
Strausberg
Rüdersdorf
POTSDAM
Potsdam
Werder
Teltow
Kleinmachnow
Lichtenrade
Zeuthen
Ludwigsfelde

© Times Newspapers Limited

1:300 000

0 5 10 15 km
0 5 10 miles

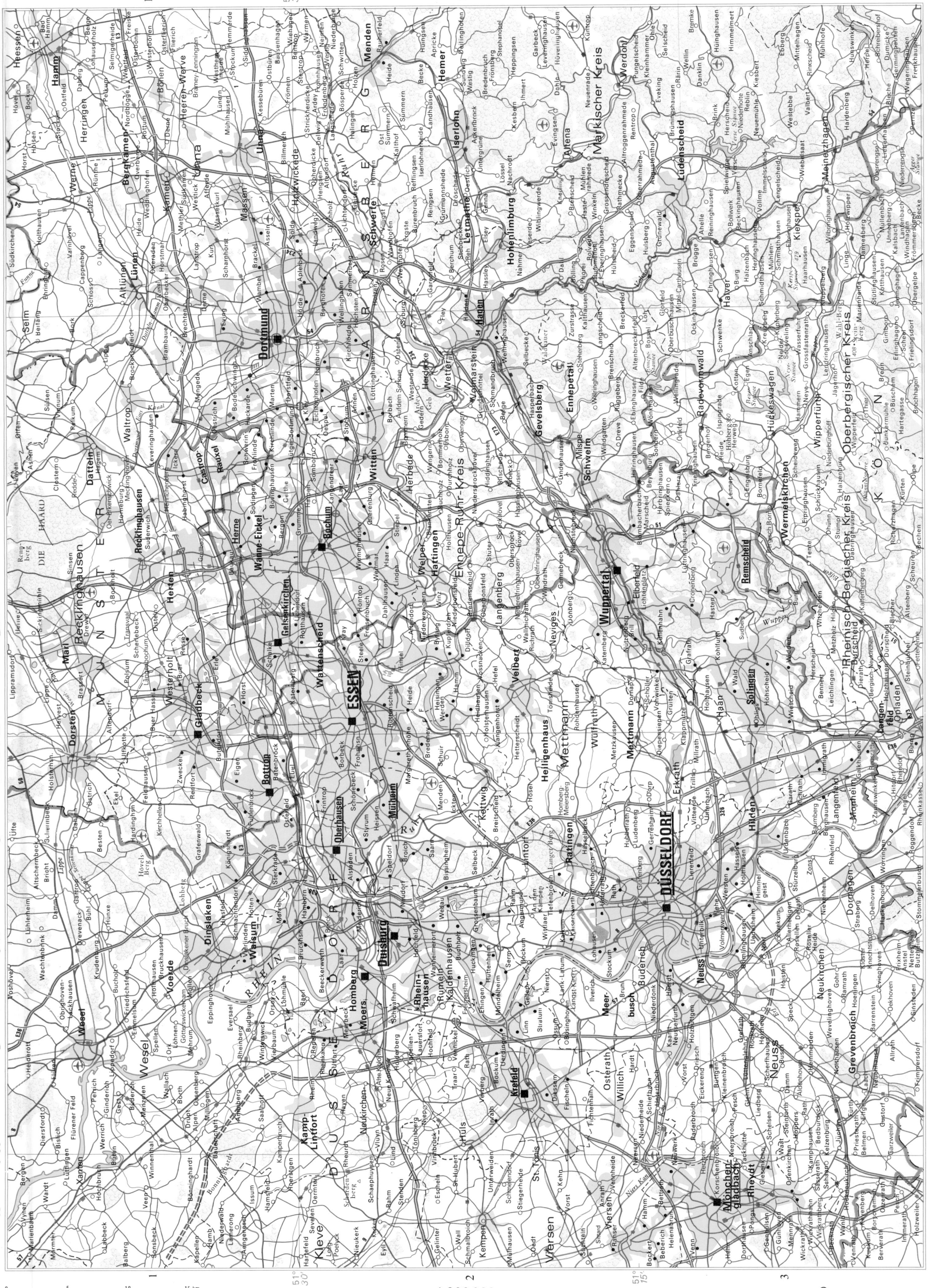

0 5 10 15 km
0 5 10 miles

1:300 000

© Times Newspapers Limited

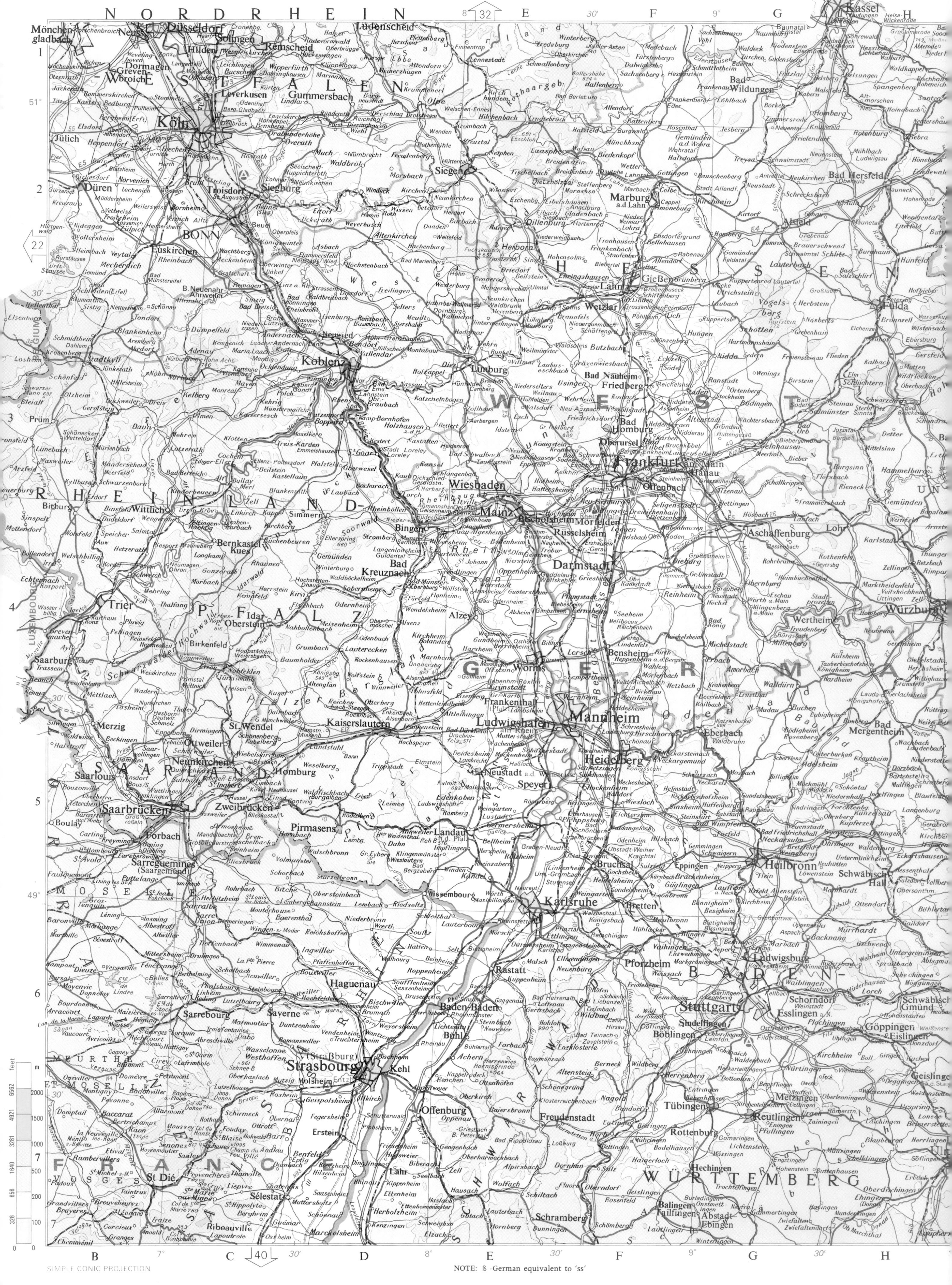
NORDRHEIN
WESTFALEN
HESSEN
RHEINLAND-PFALZ
SAARLAND
BADEN-WÜRTTEMBERG
FRANCE
LUXEMBOURG
BELGIUM
GERMANY
Köln
Bonn
Düsseldorf
Kassel
Koblenz
Frankfurt am Main
Wiesbaden
Mainz
Mannheim
Heidelberg
Karlsruhe
Stuttgart
Strasbourg
Saarbrücken
Trier
Würzburg
Heilbronn
Darmstadt
Kaiserslautern
Tübingen
32
22
40

SIMPLE CONIC PROJECTION

NOTE: ß -German equivalent to 'ss'

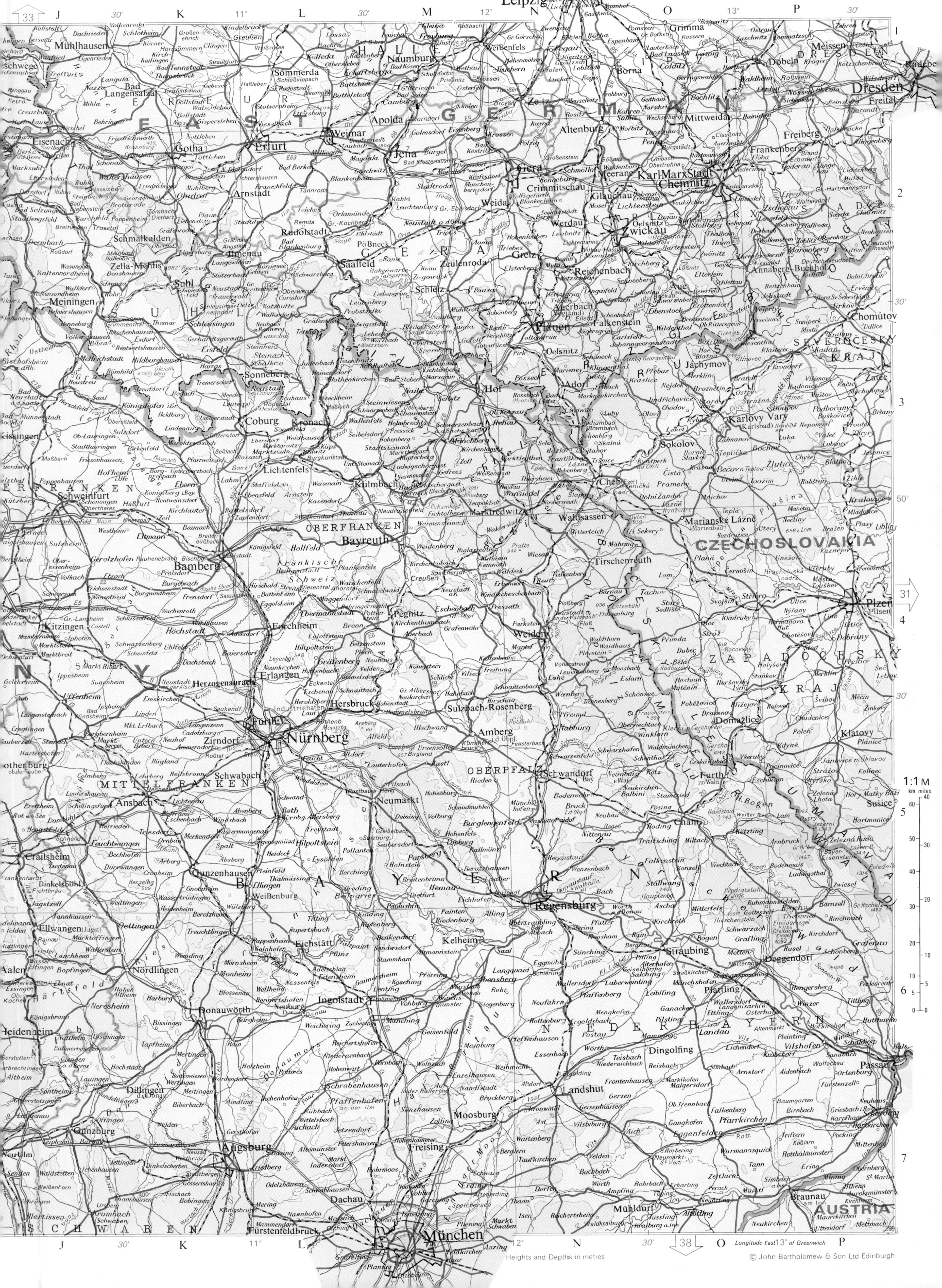
EAST GERMANY
HALLE
LEIPZIG
ERFURT
GERA
KARL-MARX-STADT
DRESDEN
CZECHOSLOVAKIA
SEVEROČESKÝ KRAJ
ZÁPADOČESKÝ KRAJ
AUSTRIA
OBERFRANKEN
MITTELFRANKEN
OBERPFALZ
NIEDERBAYERN
SCHWABEN
BAYERN
Leipzig
Dresden
Karl Marx Stadt (Chemnitz)
Erfurt
Weimar
Jena
Gera
Zwickau
Plauen
Hof
Bayreuth
Bamberg
Coburg
Schweinfurt
Würzburg
Nürnberg
Fürth
Erlangen
Ansbach
Regensburg
Ingolstadt
Augsburg
München
Landshut
Passau
Straubing
Amberg
Weiden
Cheb
Karlovy Vary
Plzeň (Pilsen)
Mariánské Lázně
Chomutov
Klatovy
Domažlice
Braunau
1:1M
km miles
Heights and Depths in metres
Longitude East 13° of Greenwich
31
33
38

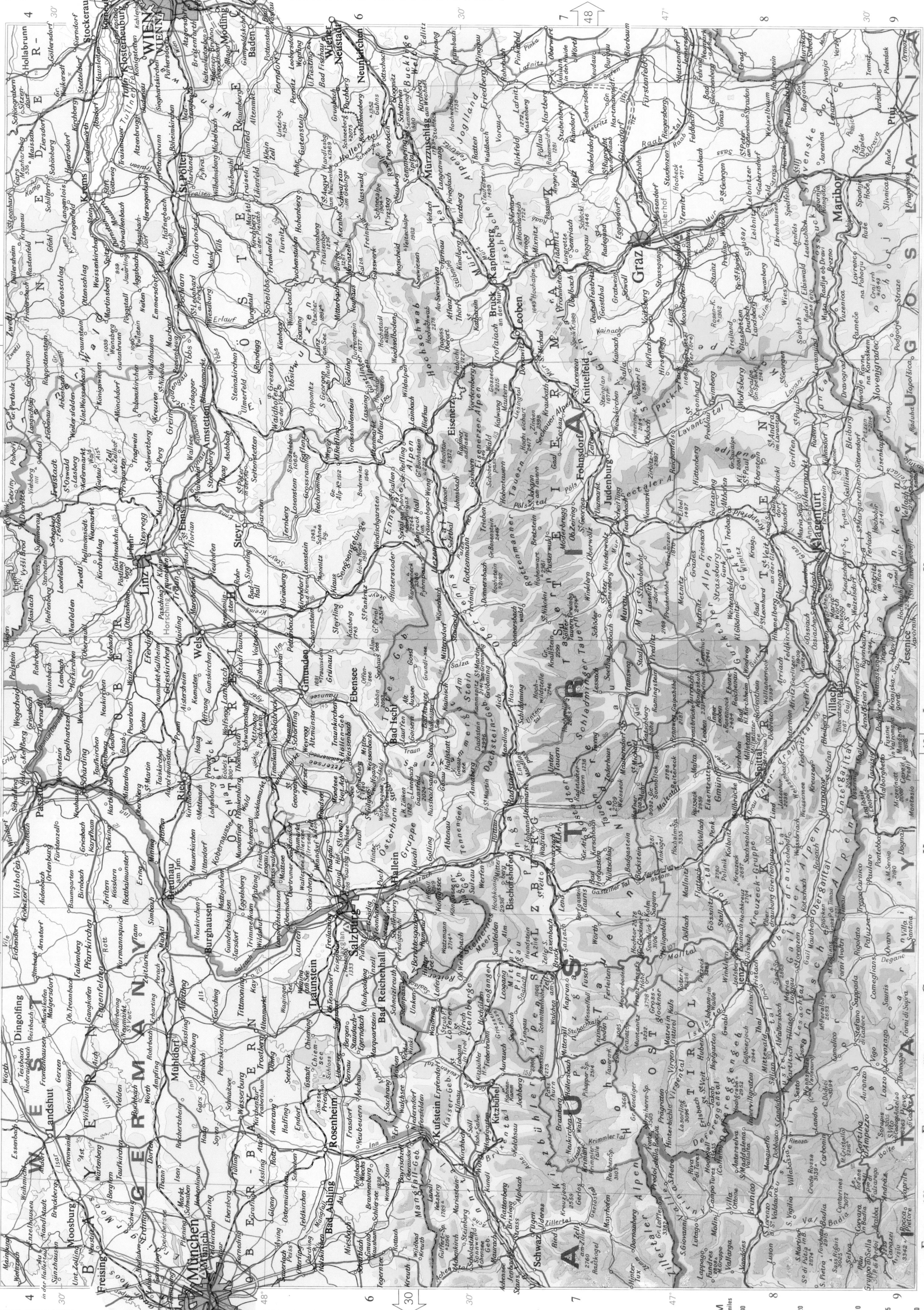

CONIC PROJECTION

Heights in metres

1:1M

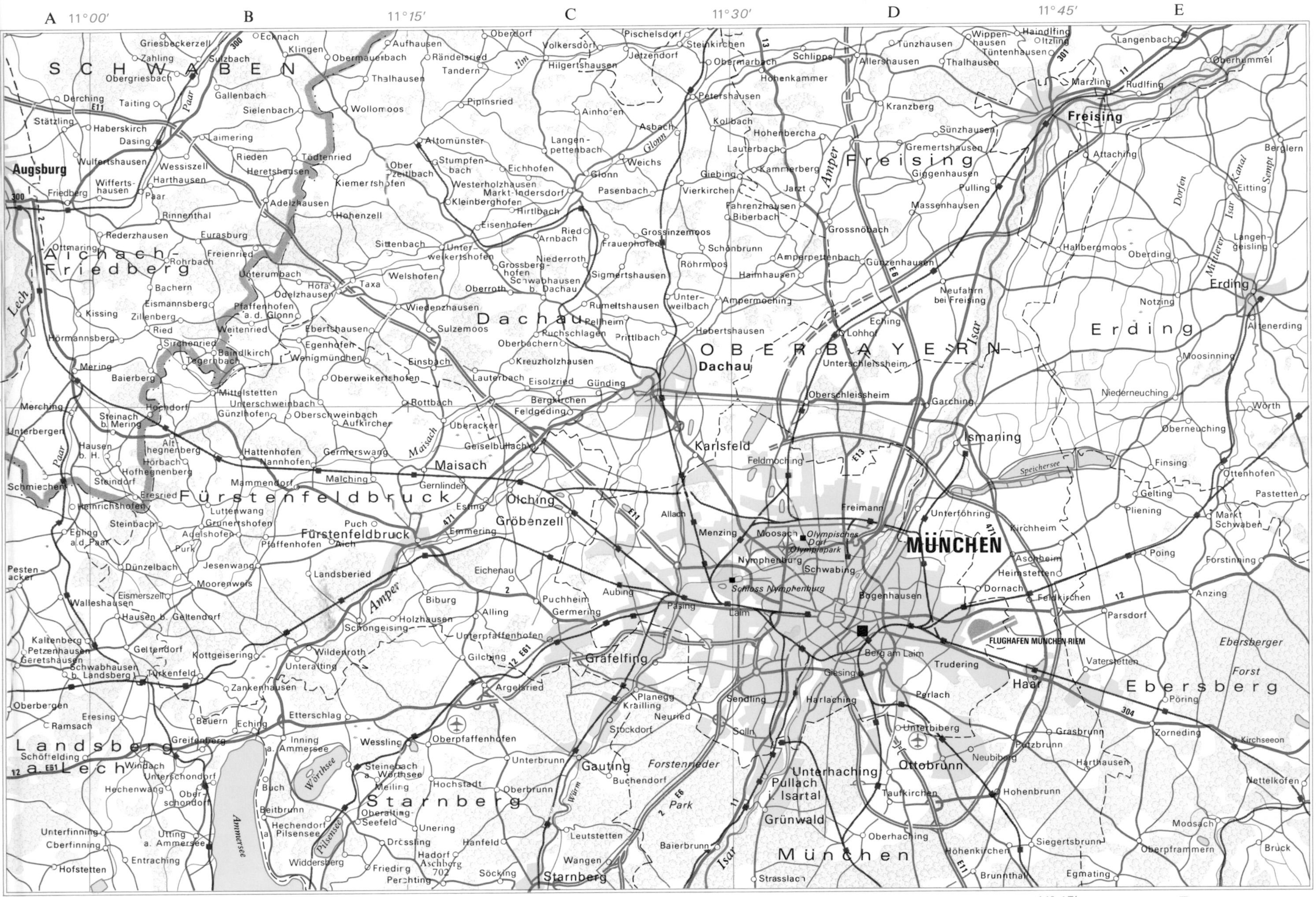

MILAN

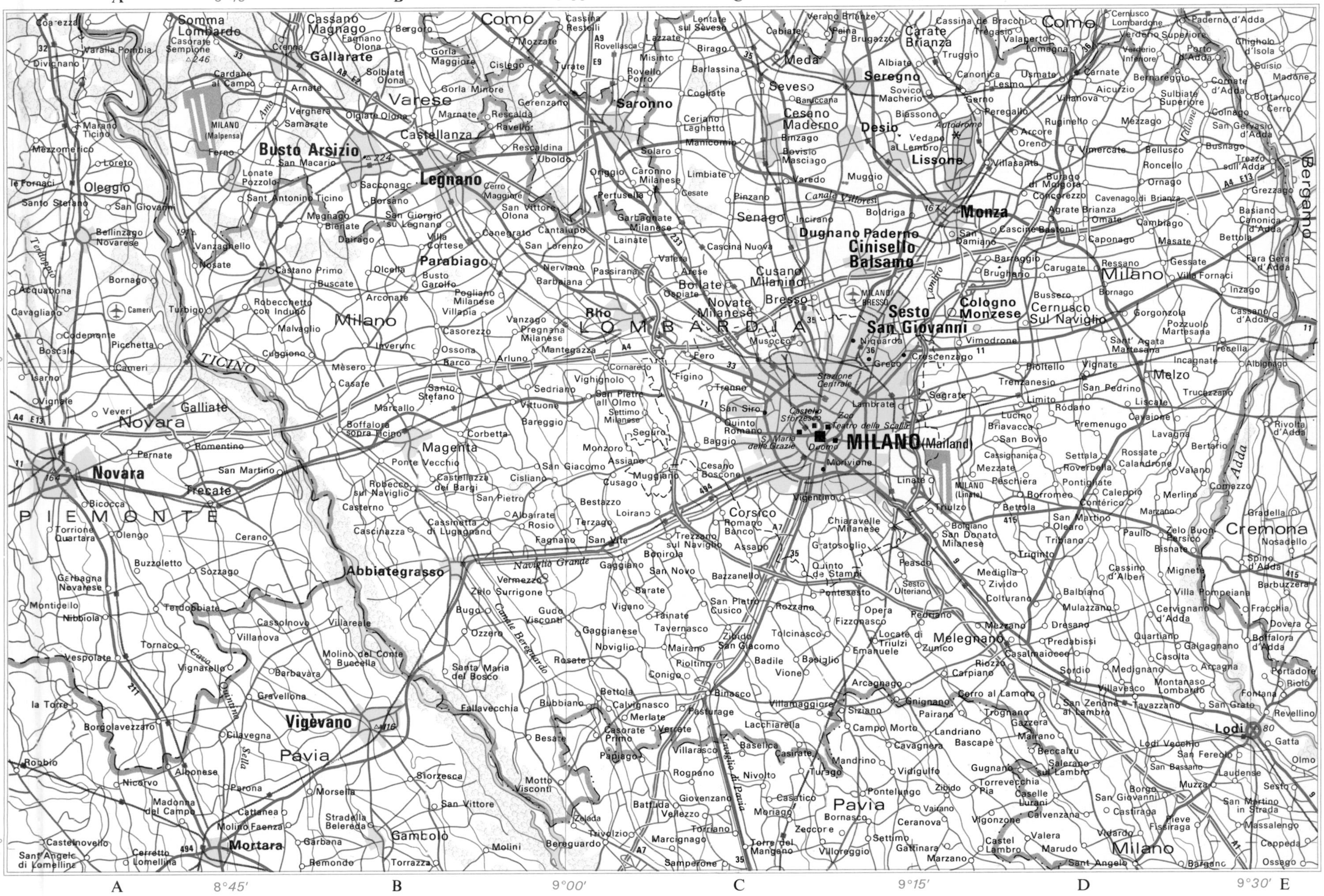

1:300 000

© Times Newspapers Limited

CONIC PROJECTION

0	328	656	1640	1381	4921	6562	9843	13124		feet
0	100	200	500	1000	1500	2000	3000	4000		m

Heights and Depths in metres

G E R M A N Y
S C H W A B E N
A U S T R I A
VORARLBERG
T I R O L
S W I T Z E R L A N D
G R A U B Ü N D E N
T I C I N O
L O M B A R D I A
T R E N T I N O
A L T O - A D I G E
I T A L Y
München
Zürich
Konstanz
Bodensee
Bregenz
Innsbruck
St. Gallen
Chur
Davos
St. Moritz
Bellinzona
Locarno
Lugano
Como
Lecco
Bergamo
Milano
Brescia
Verona
Trento
Bolzano
Merano
Novara
Pavia
Mantova
Varese
Sondrio
38
45
Longitude East 9° of Greenwich
1:1M
km
miles

© John Bartholomew & Son Ltd Edinburgh

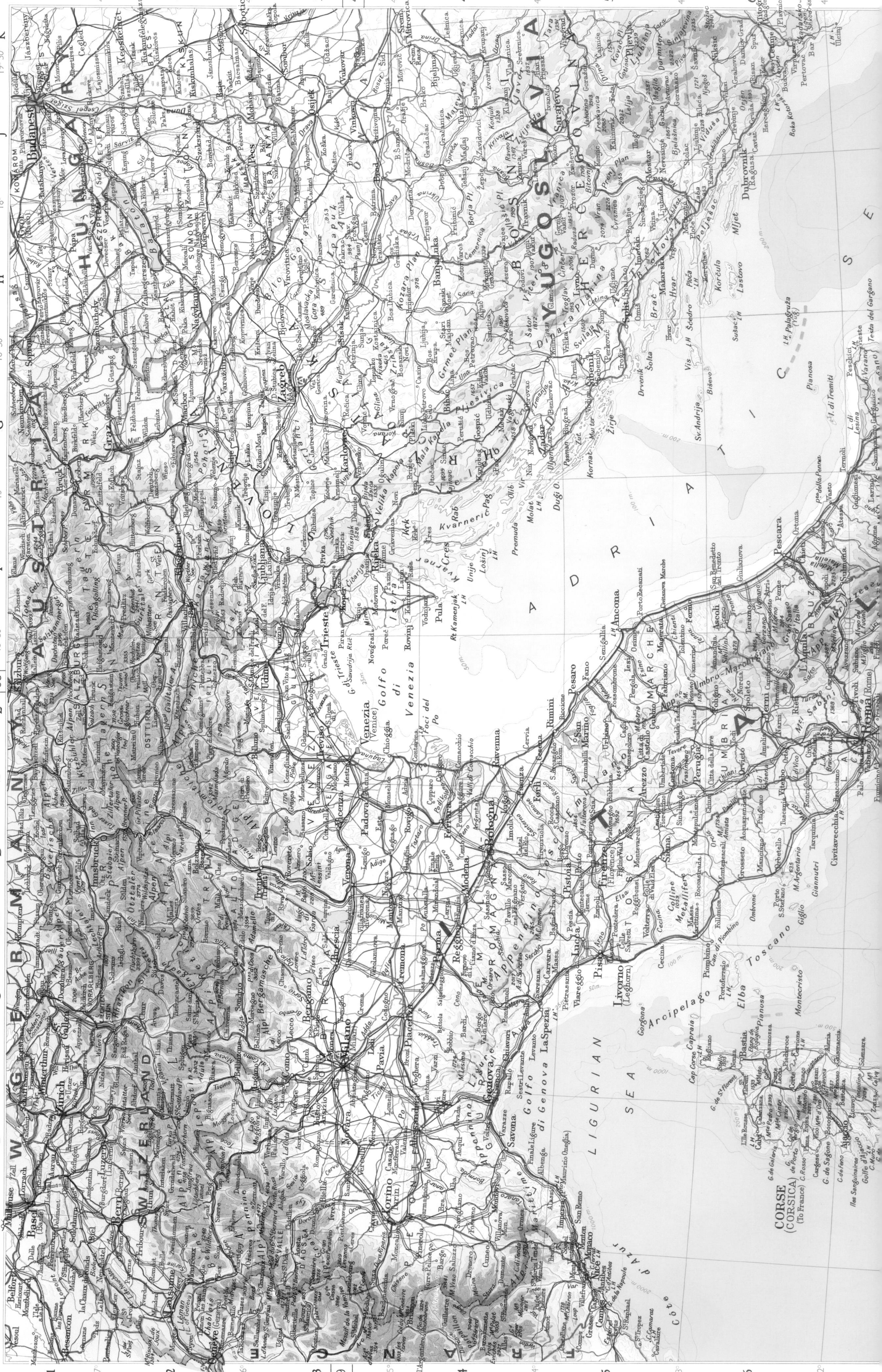
48
38
19
AUSTRIA
SWITZERLAND
HUNGARY
YUGOSLAVIA
GERMANY
ADRIATIC SEA
LIGURIAN SEA
Budapest
Zagreb
Ljubljana
Sarajevo
Dubrovnik
Venezia (Venice)
Trieste
Milano
Torino (Turin)
Genova
Bologna
Firenze (Florence)
Roma (Rome)
Pescara
Ancona
Livorno (Leghorn)
Bern
Zürich
Innsbruck
Graz
Osijek
Rijeka
Elba
CORSE (CORSICA) (To France)
Golfo di Venezia
Golfo di Genova

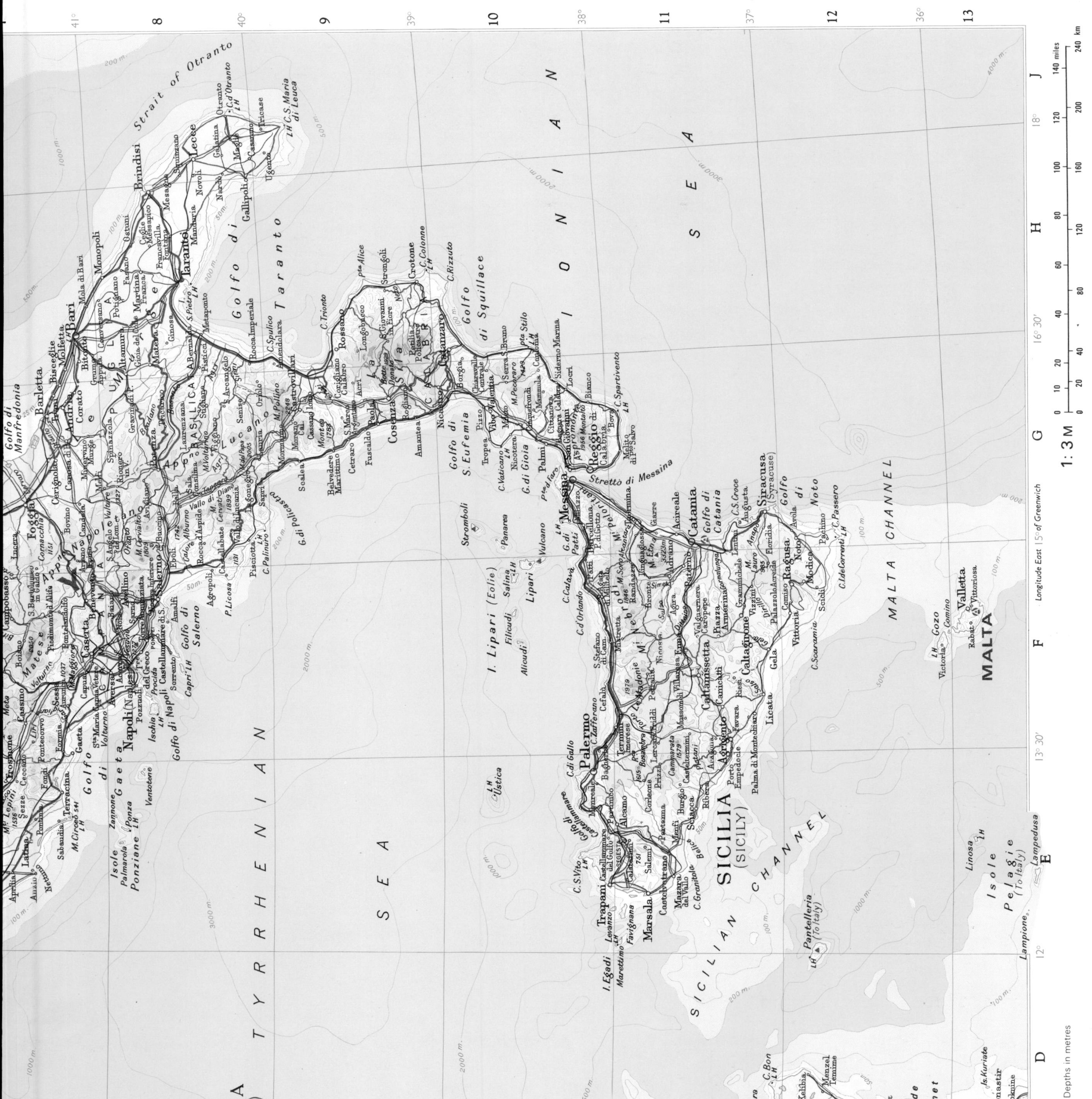
TYRRHENIAN SEA
IONIAN SEA
SARDEGNA (SARDINIA) (To Italy)
SICILIA (SICILY)
MALTA
MALTA CHANNEL
SICILIAN CHANNEL
TUNISIA
ALGERIA
Strait of Otranto
Golfo di Taranto
Golfo di Squillace
Stretto di Messina
Strait of Bonifacio
Isole Pelagie (To Italy)
I. Lipari (Eolie)
Isole Ponziane
Napoli
Palermo
Messina
Catania
Siracusa
Cagliari
Sassari
Bari
Taranto
Tunis
Valletta
1:3M
Longitude East 15° of Greenwich
Heights and Depths in metres

© John Bartholomew & Son Ltd Edinburgh

40
19
FRANCE
MONACO
Torino
(Turin)
Milano
Milan
Genova
(Genoa)
Alessandria
Asti
Novara
Vercelli
Pavia
Piacenza
Cremona
Savona
Sanremo
Imperia
Nice
Menton
Monte-Carlo
La Spezia
Carrara
Massa
Viareggio
Livorno
Leghorn
Cuneo
Pinerolo
Alba
Tortona
Chiavari
Rapallo
Albenga
GOLFO
DI GENOVA
LIGURIAN
SEA
RIVIERA DI PONENTE
RIVIERA DI LEVANTE
Cote d'Azur

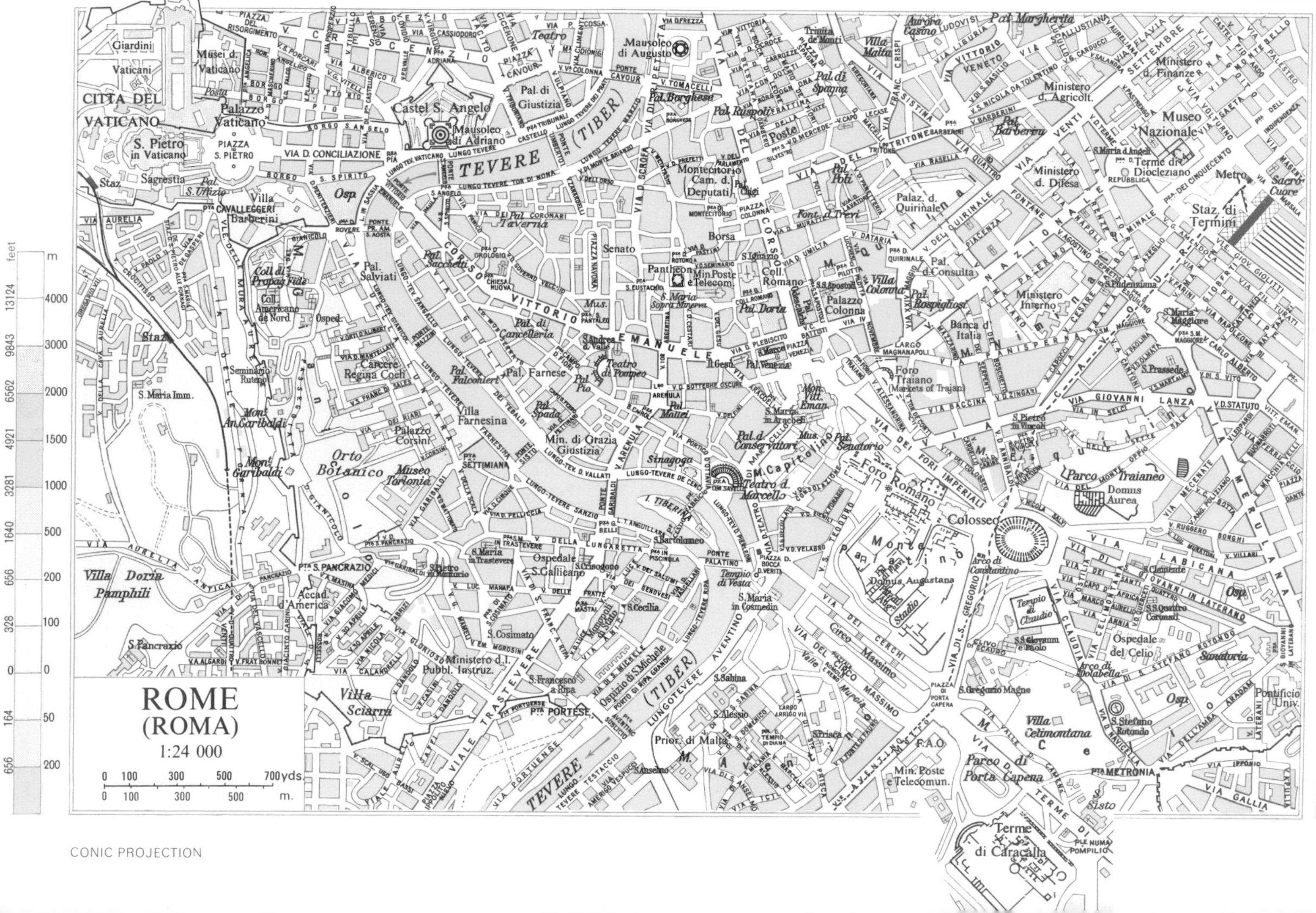
CITTA DEL VATICANO
S. Pietro in Vaticano
Castel S. Angelo
TEVERE
(TIBER)
Pantheon
Foro Romano
Colosseo
Staz. Termini
Villa Doria Pamphili
Terme di Caracalla
ROME
(ROMA)
1:24 000
0 100 300 500 700 yds
0 100 300 500 m.
feet
m

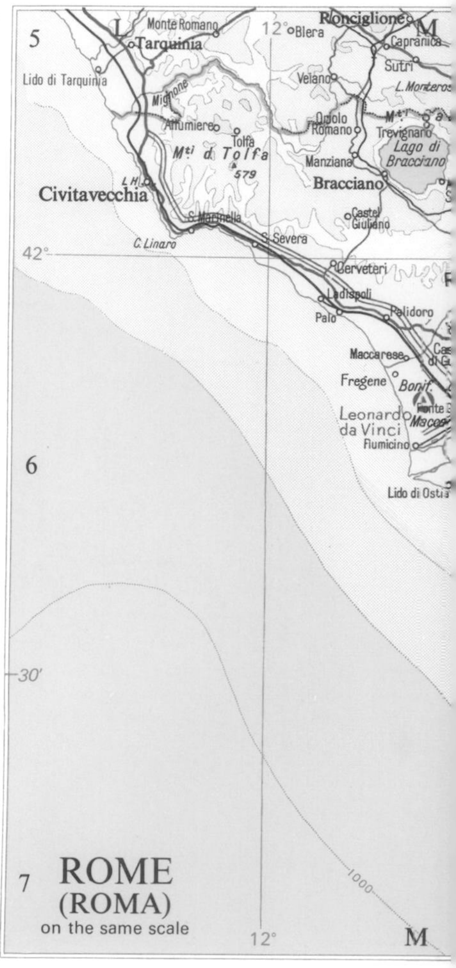
Civitavecchia
Tarquinia
Bracciano
Lago di Bracciano
Fiumicino
Lido di Ostia
ROME
(ROMA)
on the same scale

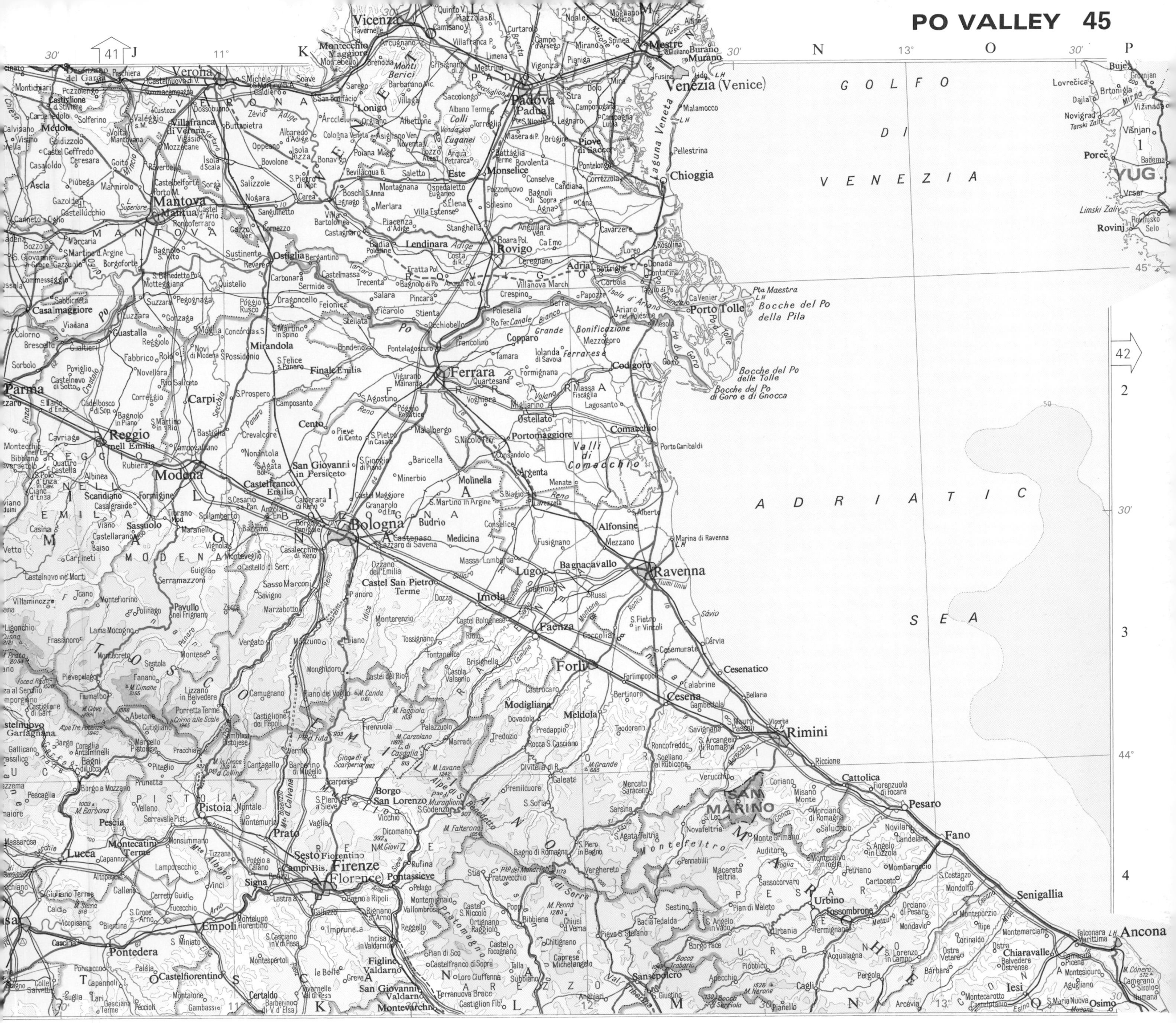

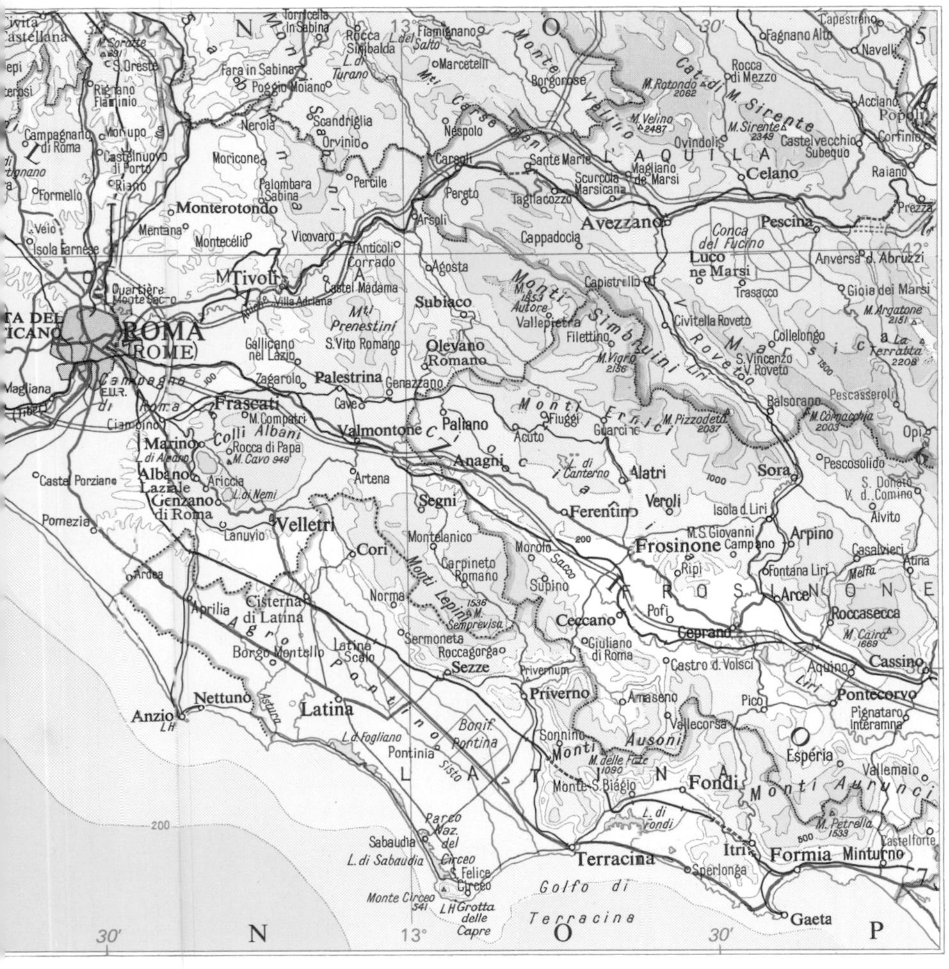

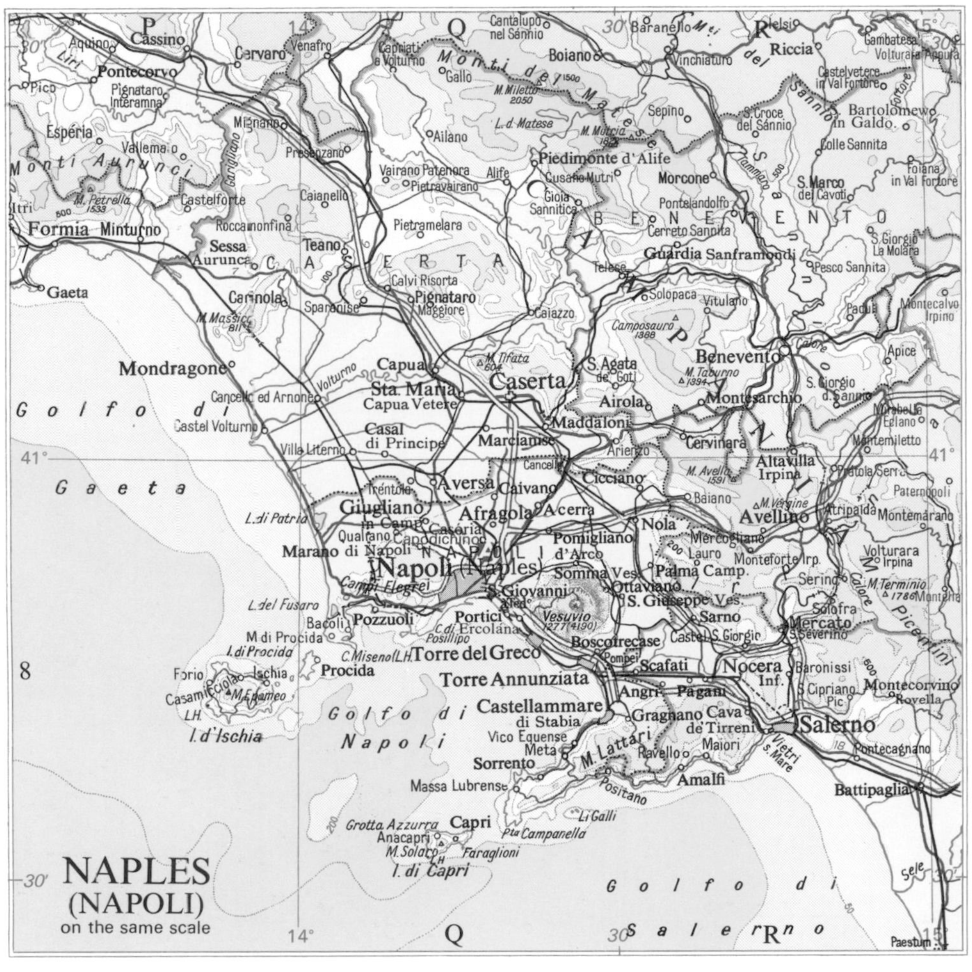

1:1M

km	miles
80	50
70	40
60	
50	30
40	20
30	
20	10
10	5
0	0

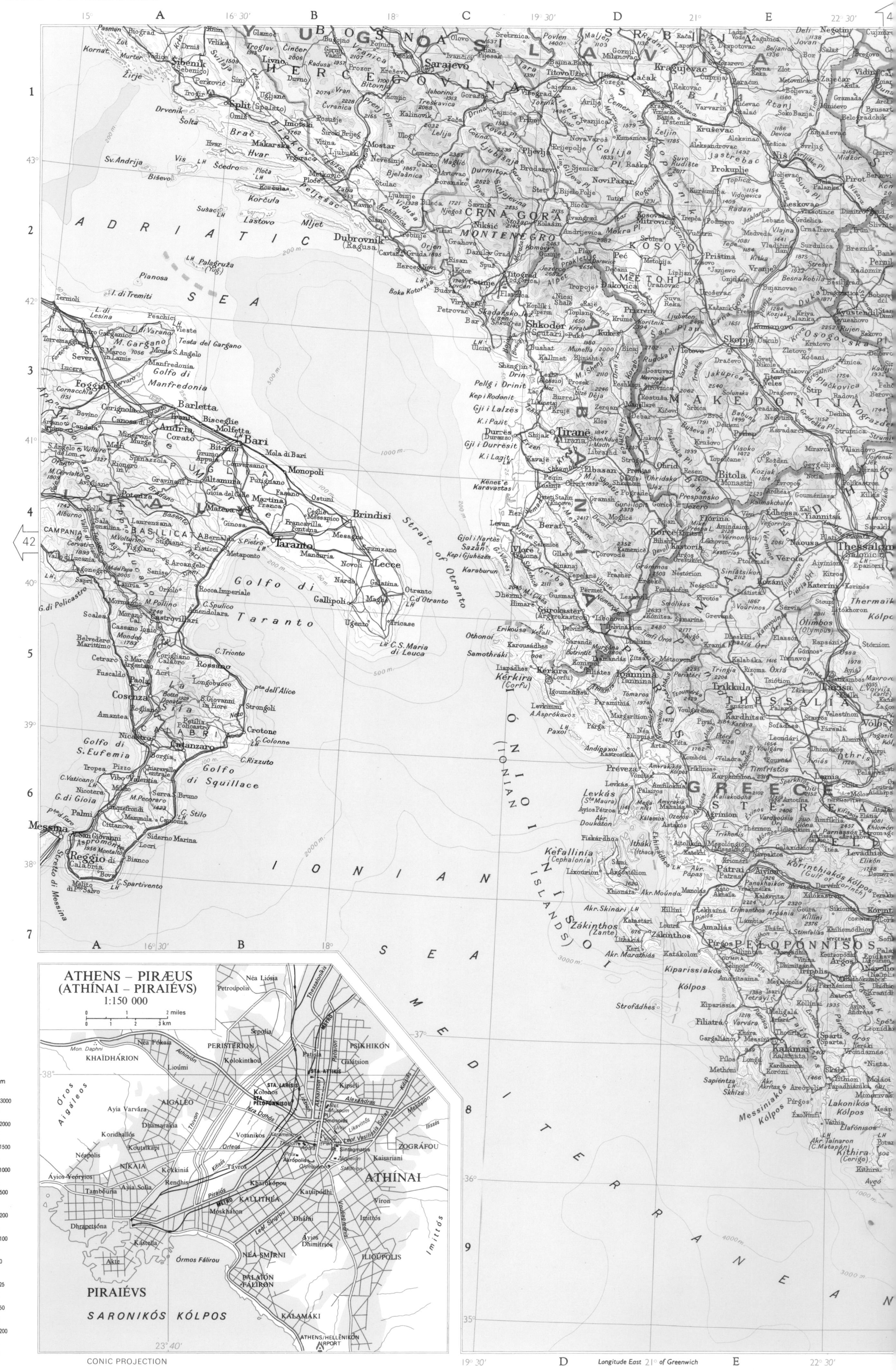
ADRIATIC SEA
IONIAN SEA
MEDITERRANEAN SEA
Strait of Otranto
Golfo di Taranto
Golfo di Manfredonia
Golfo di Squillace
Golfo di S.Eufemia
YUGOSLAVIA
HERCEGOVINA
CRNA GORA
MONTENEGRO
SRBIJA
KOSOVO
METOHIJA
MAKEDONIJA
ALBANIA
GREECE
THESSALÍA
STEREÁ ELLÁS
PELOPÓNNISOS
ITALIA
PUGLIA
BASILICATA
CALABRIA
CAMPANIA
IÓNIOI NÍSOI (IONIAN ISLANDS)
Sarajevo
Split (Spalato)
Dubrovnik (Ragusa)
Titograd
Skopje
Tiranë
Shkodër (Scutari)
Durrës (Durazzo)
Vlorë (Valona)
Bari
Brindisi
Taranto
Lecce
Foggia
Potenza
Cosenza
Catanzaro
Reggio di Calabria
Messina
Thessaloníki (Salonica)
Ioánnina
Kérkira (Corfu)
Pátrai (Patras)
Lamía
Lárisa
Kalamáta
Trípolis
42
ATHENS – PIRÆUS (ATHÍNAI – PIRAIÉVS)
1:150 000
ATHÍNAI
PIRAIÉVS
SARONIKÓS KÓLPOS
ATHENS/HELLENIKON AIRPORT
feet
m
9843 3000
6562 2000
4921 1500
3281 1000
1640 500
656 200
328 100
0 0
82 25
164 50
656 200
CONIC PROJECTION
Longitude East 21° of Greenwich

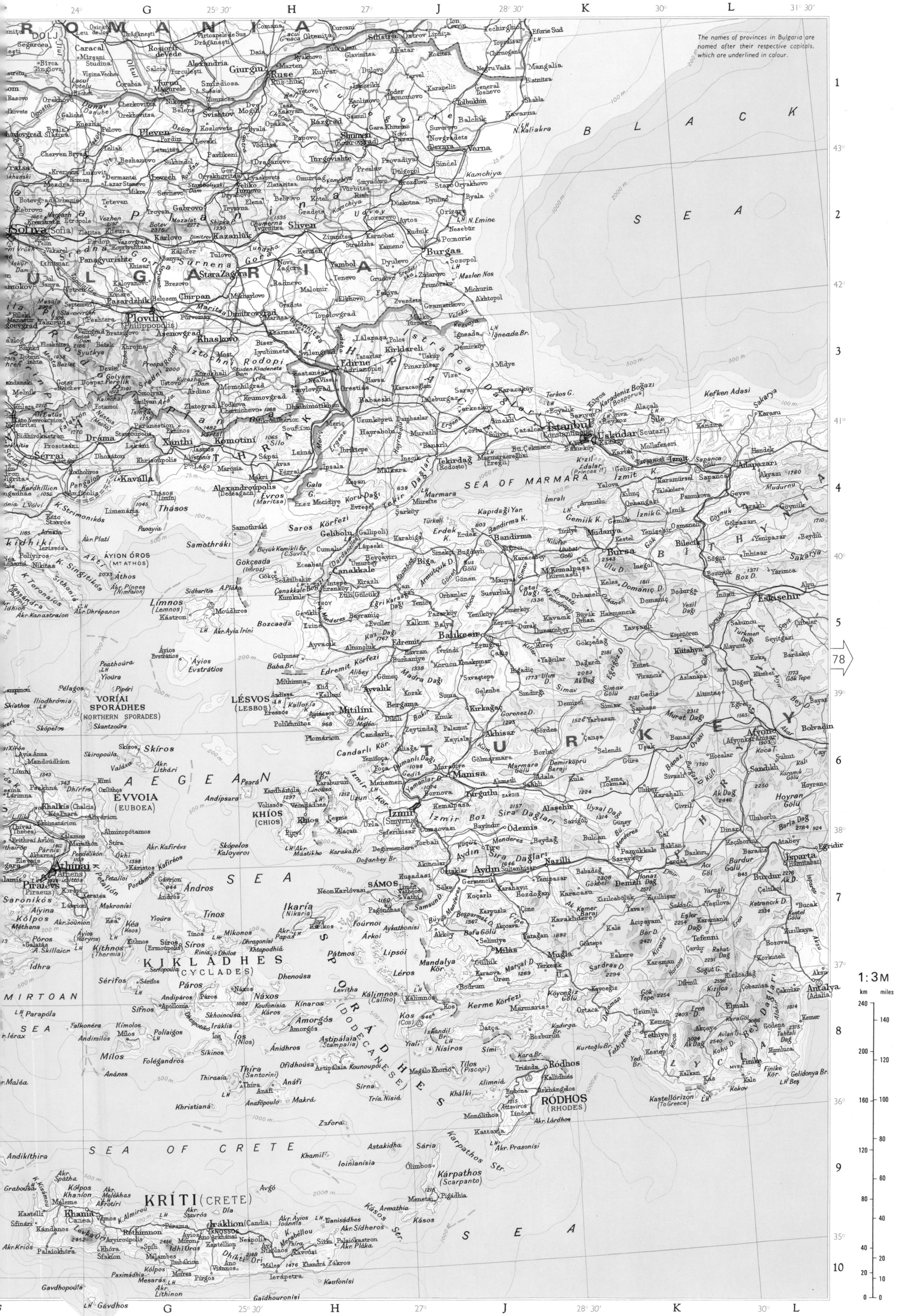

Heights and Depths in metres

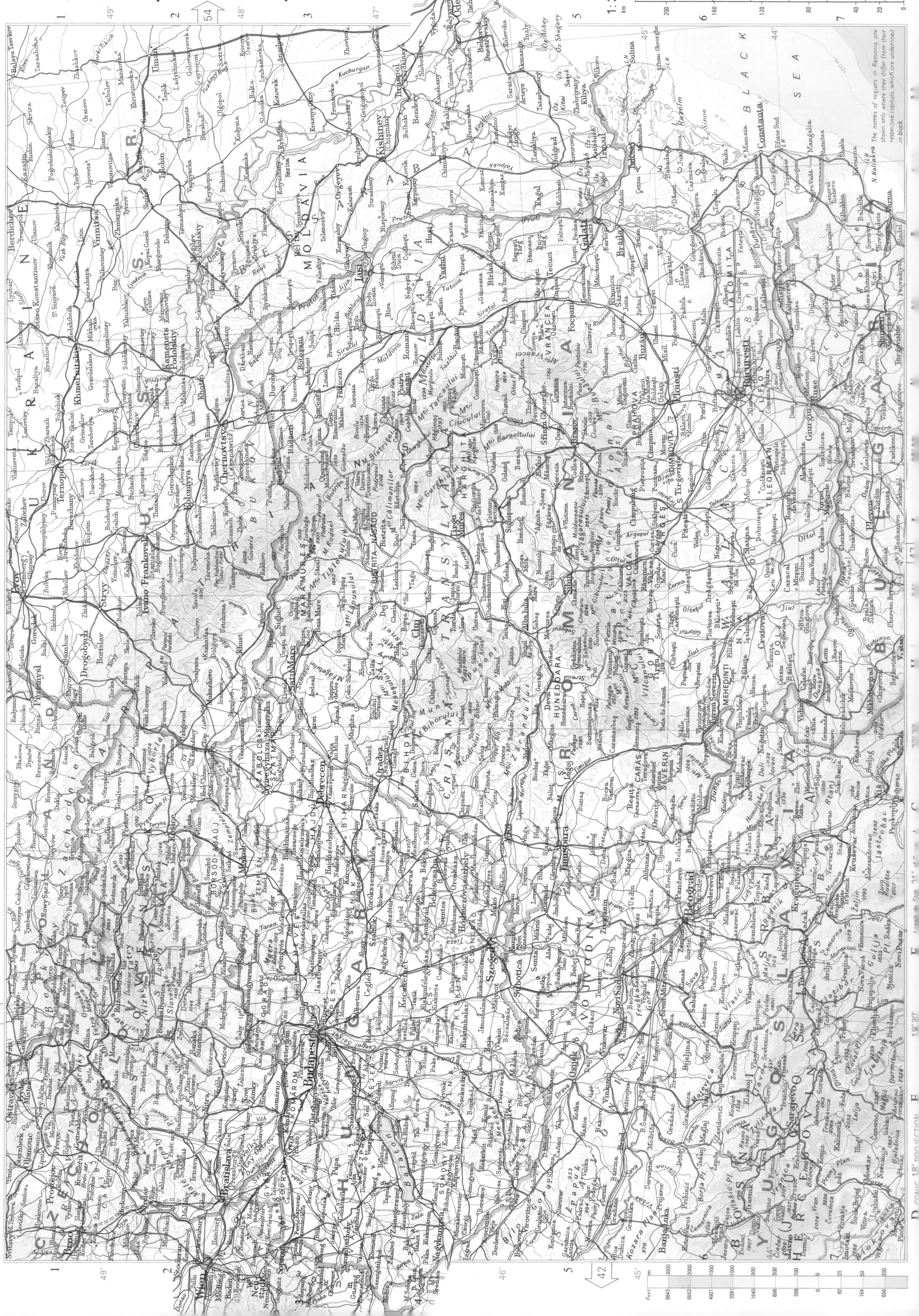
1:3M
The names of regions in Romania are shown only where they differ from their respective capitals, which are underlined in black
BLACK SEA
HUNGARY
ROMANIA
YUGOSLAVIA
BULGARIA
U.S.S.R.
CZECHOSLOVAKIA
Budapest
Bucureşti
Beograd
Wien
Sofia
54
31
42

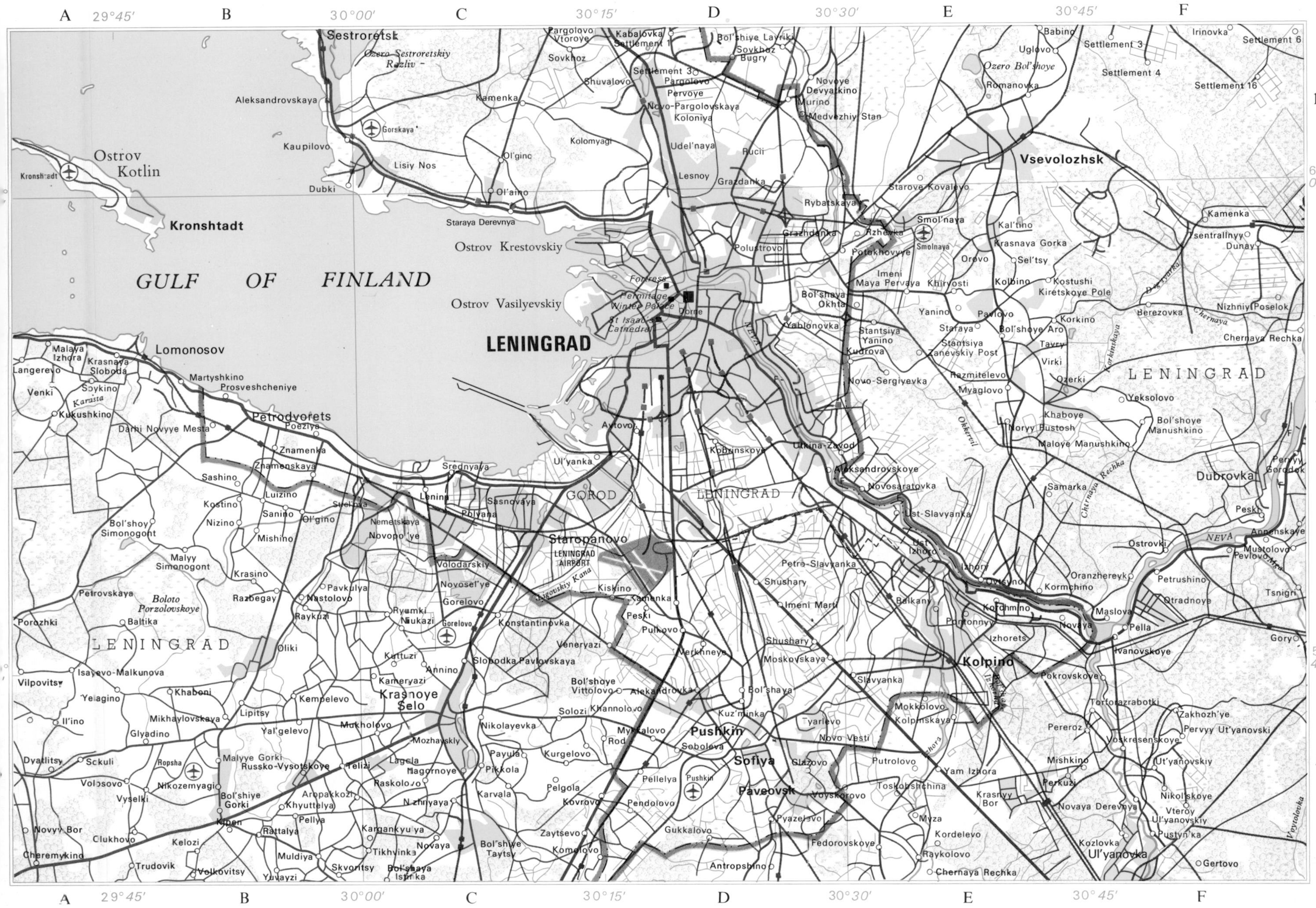
A
B
C
D
E
F
29°45'
30°00'
30°15'
30°30'
30°45'
60° 00'
59° 45'
1
2
3
GULF OF FINLAND
LENINGRAD
Ostrov Kotlin
Kronshtadt
Sestroretsk
Ostrov Krestovskiy
Ostrov Vasilyevskiy
Lomonosov
Petrodvorets
Vsevolozhsk
Kolpino
Pushkin
Krasnoye Selo
Pavlovsk
NEVA
GOROD
LENINGRAD AIRPORT

MOSCOW

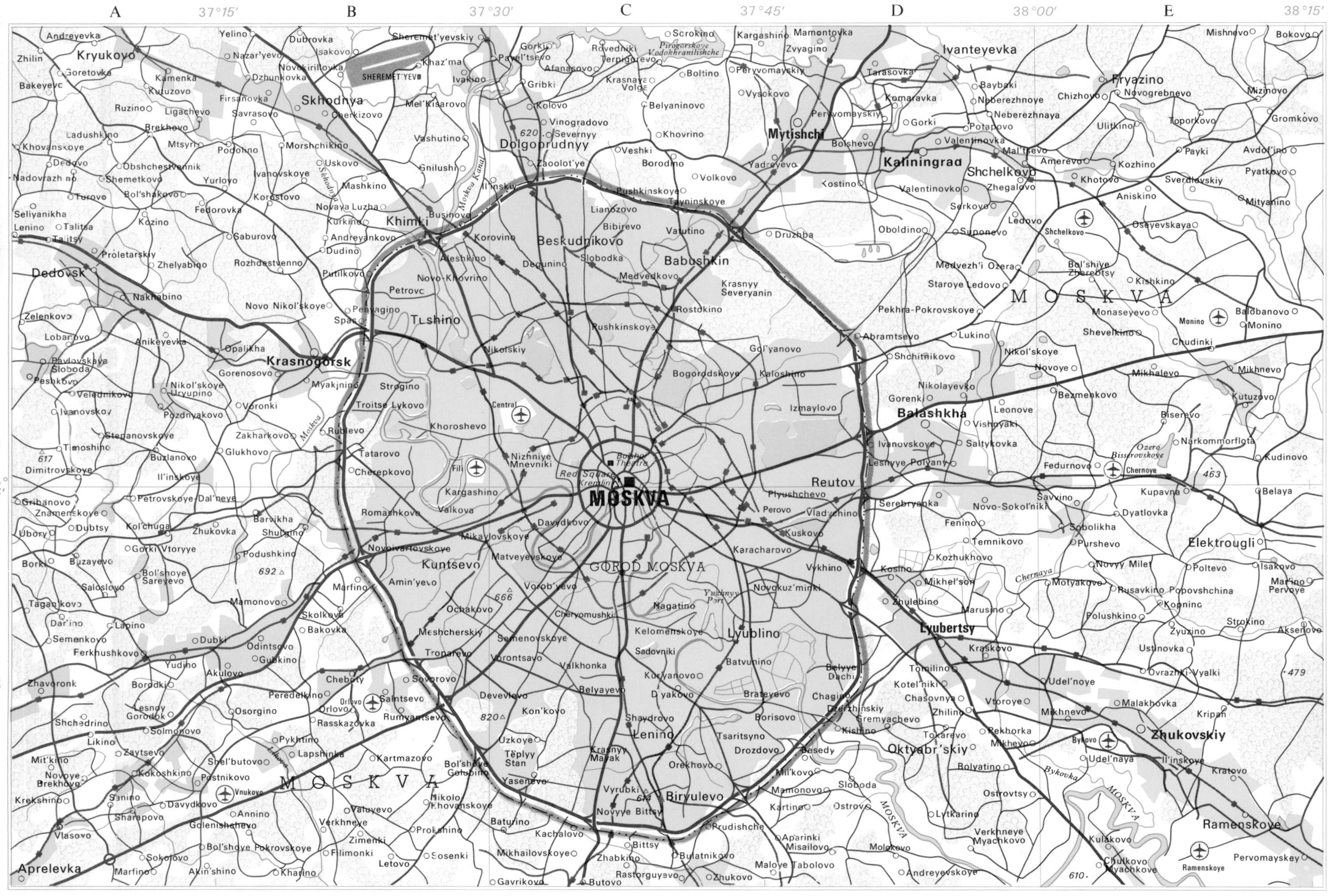
A
B
C
D
E
37°15'
37°30'
37°45'
38°00'
38°15'
55° 45'
4
5
MOSKVA
GOROD MOSKVA
M O S K V A
Mytishchi
Kaliningrad
Shchelkovo
Balashikha
Reutov
Lyubertsy
Zhukovskiy
Ramenskoye
Krasnogorsk
Khimki
Dolgoprudnyy
Ivanteyevka
Fryazino
Elektrougli
Dedovsk
Aprelevka
SHEREMET'YEVO

0 5 10 15 km
0 5 10 miles

1:300 000

© Times Newspapers Limited

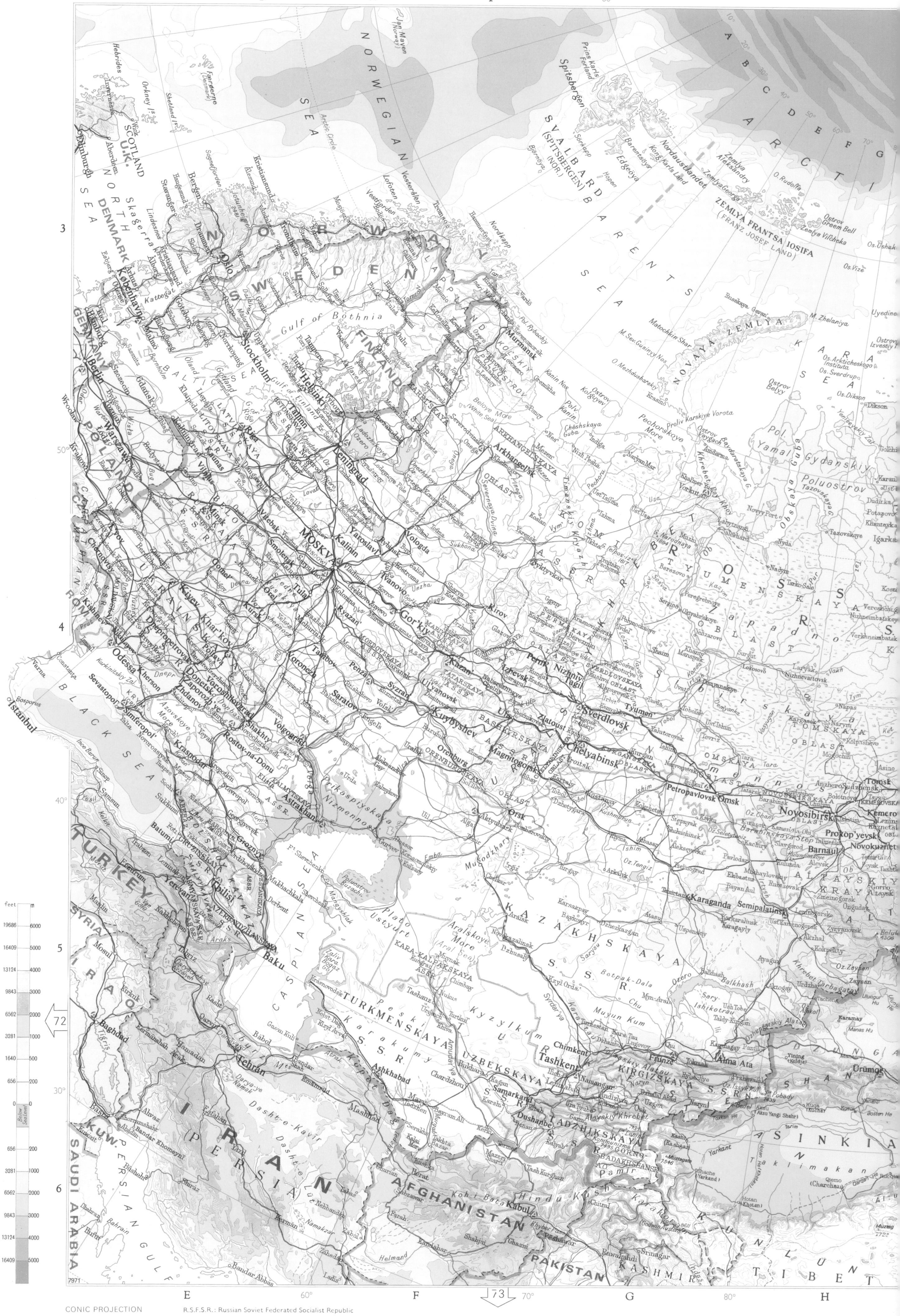

CONIC PROJECTION   R.S.F.S.R.: Russian Soviet Federated Socialist Republic

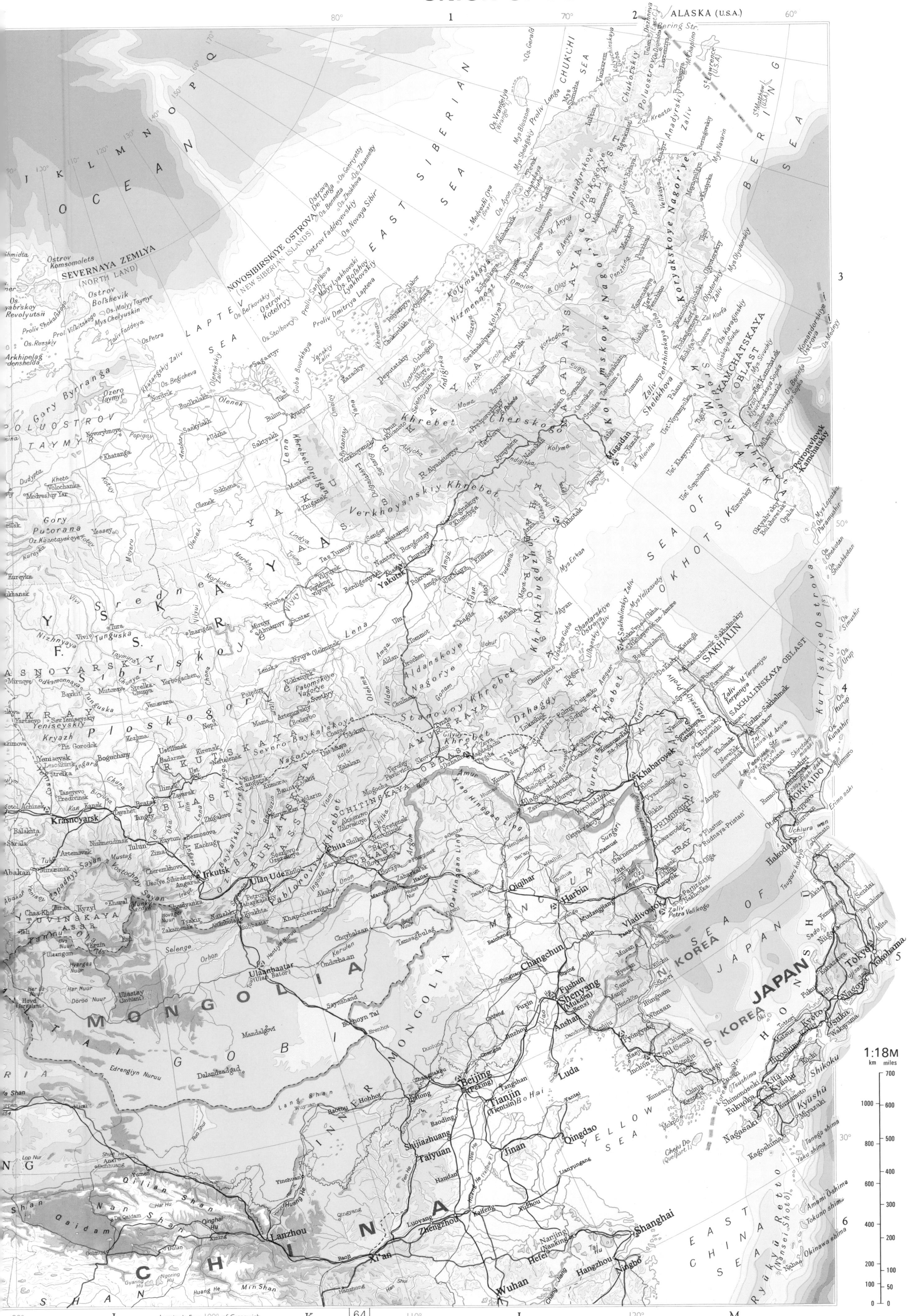

64

Heights and Depths in metres

© John Bartholomew & Son Ltd Edinburgh

INDUSTRIAL URALS
Central Area
1:3 000 000
FINLAND
Leningrad
Moskva
Arkhangel'sk
Murmansk
Helsinki
Sverdlovsk
Chelyabinsk

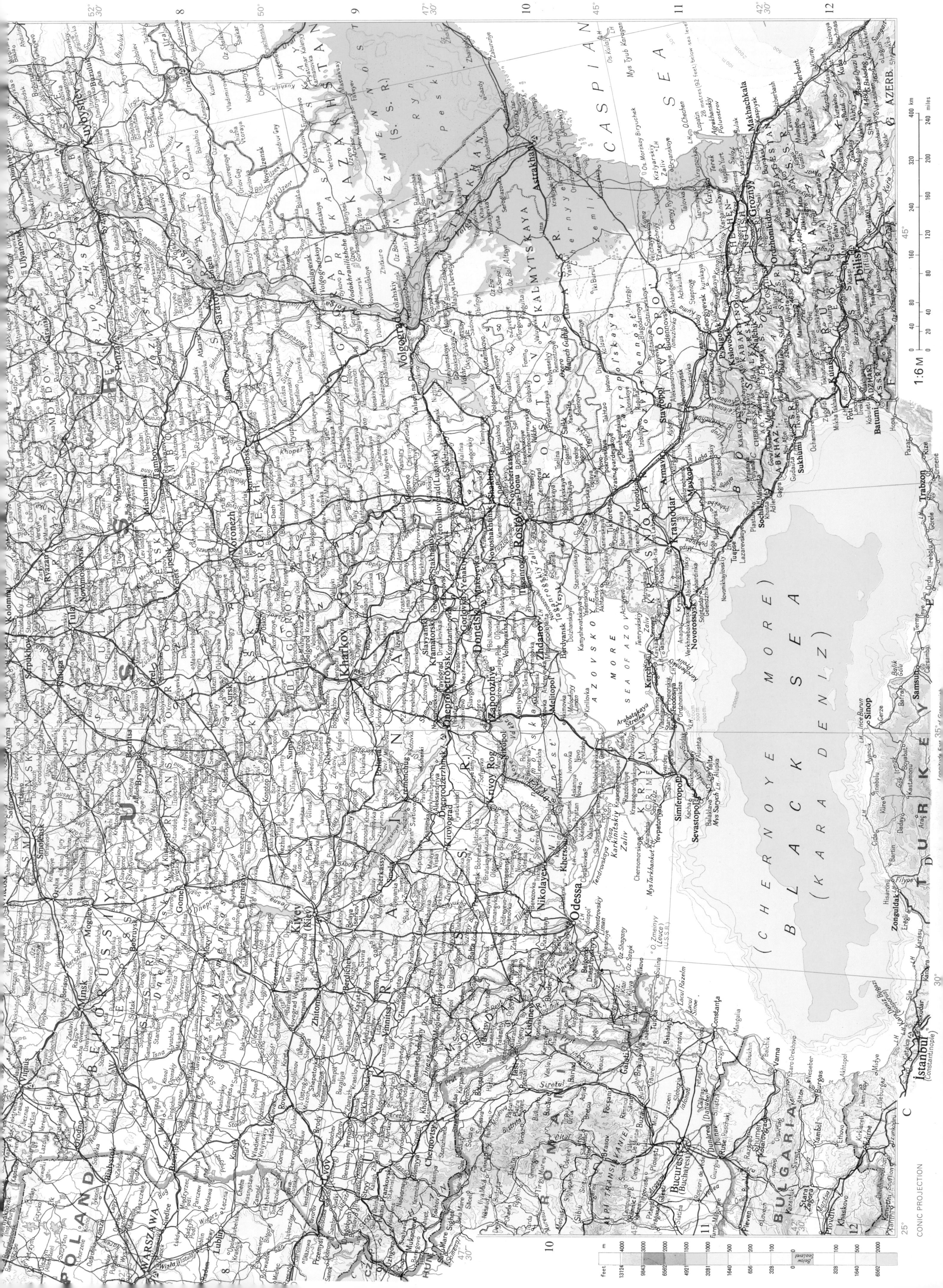
CASPIAN SEA
BLACK SEA
(CHERNOYE MORE)
(KARADENIZ)
AZOVSKOYE MORE
SEA OF AZOV
TURKEY
ROMANIA
BULGARIA
POLAND
1:6M
CONIC PROJECTION

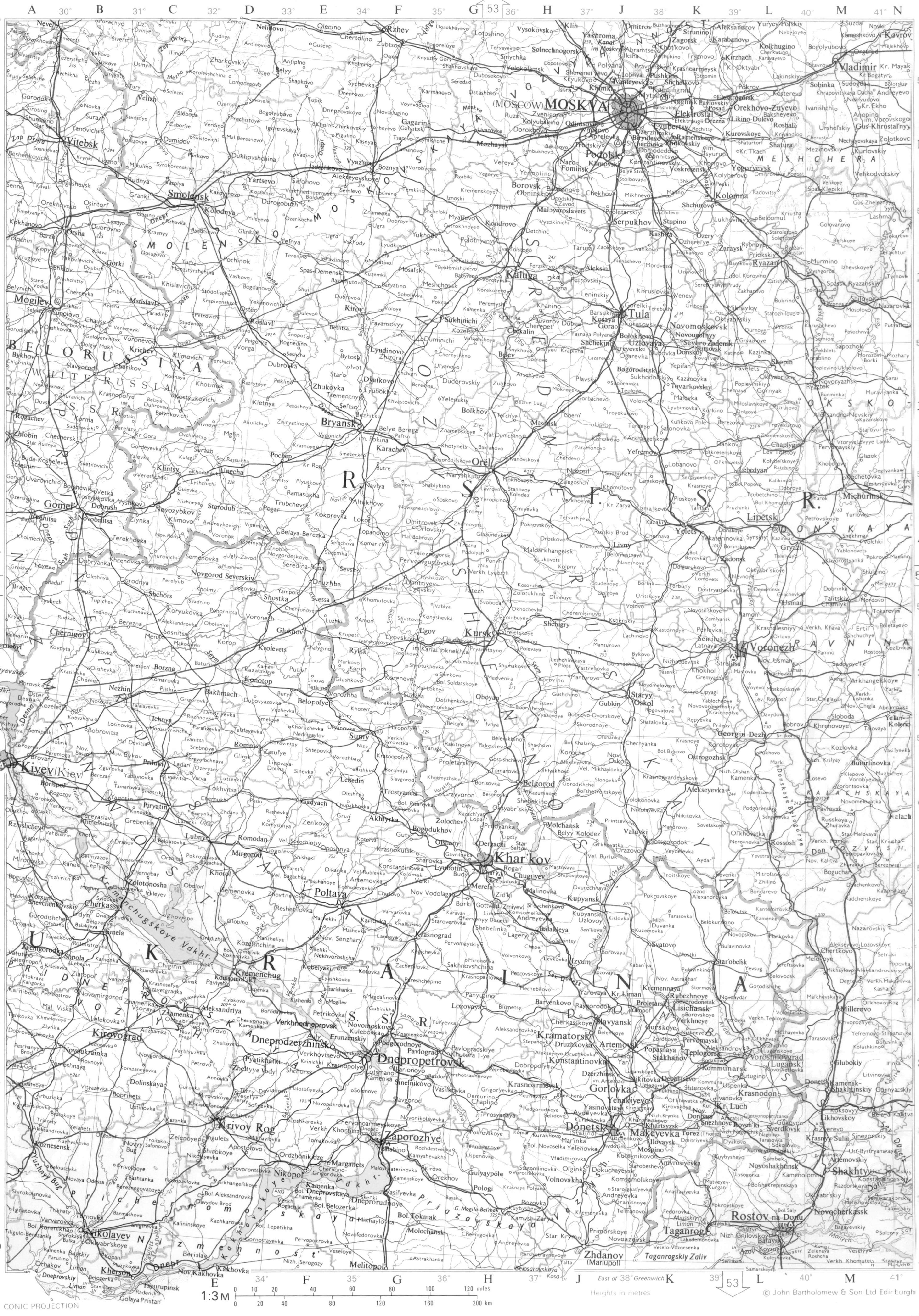
MOSKVA
(MOSCOW)
Kiyev (Kiev)
Khar'kov
Dnepropetrovsk
Zaporozh'ye
Donetsk
Rostov-na-Donu
Voronezh
Kursk
Orël
Tula
Bryansk
Smolensk
Vitebsk
Mogilev
Gomel'
Chernigov
Poltava
Kremenchug
Kirovograd
Krivoy Rog
Nikolayev
Kherson
Zhdanov
(Mariupol)
Taganrog
Lipetsk
Ryazan'
Kaluga
Belgorod
Sumy
Vladimir
BELORUSSIYA
WHITE RUSSIA
S.S.R.
R.S.F.S.R.
UKRAINA S.S.R.
SMOLENSK
MOSKOVSKAYA
DONSKAYA
KALACHSKAYA
MESHCHERA
Kremenchugskoye Vdkhr.
Kakhovskoye Vdkhr.
Taganrogskiy Zaliv
CONIC PROJECTION
1:3M
Heights in metres
East of 38° Greenwich
© John Bartholomew & Son Ltd Edinburgh
0 10 20 40 60 80 100 120 miles
0 20 40 80 120 160 200 km
53

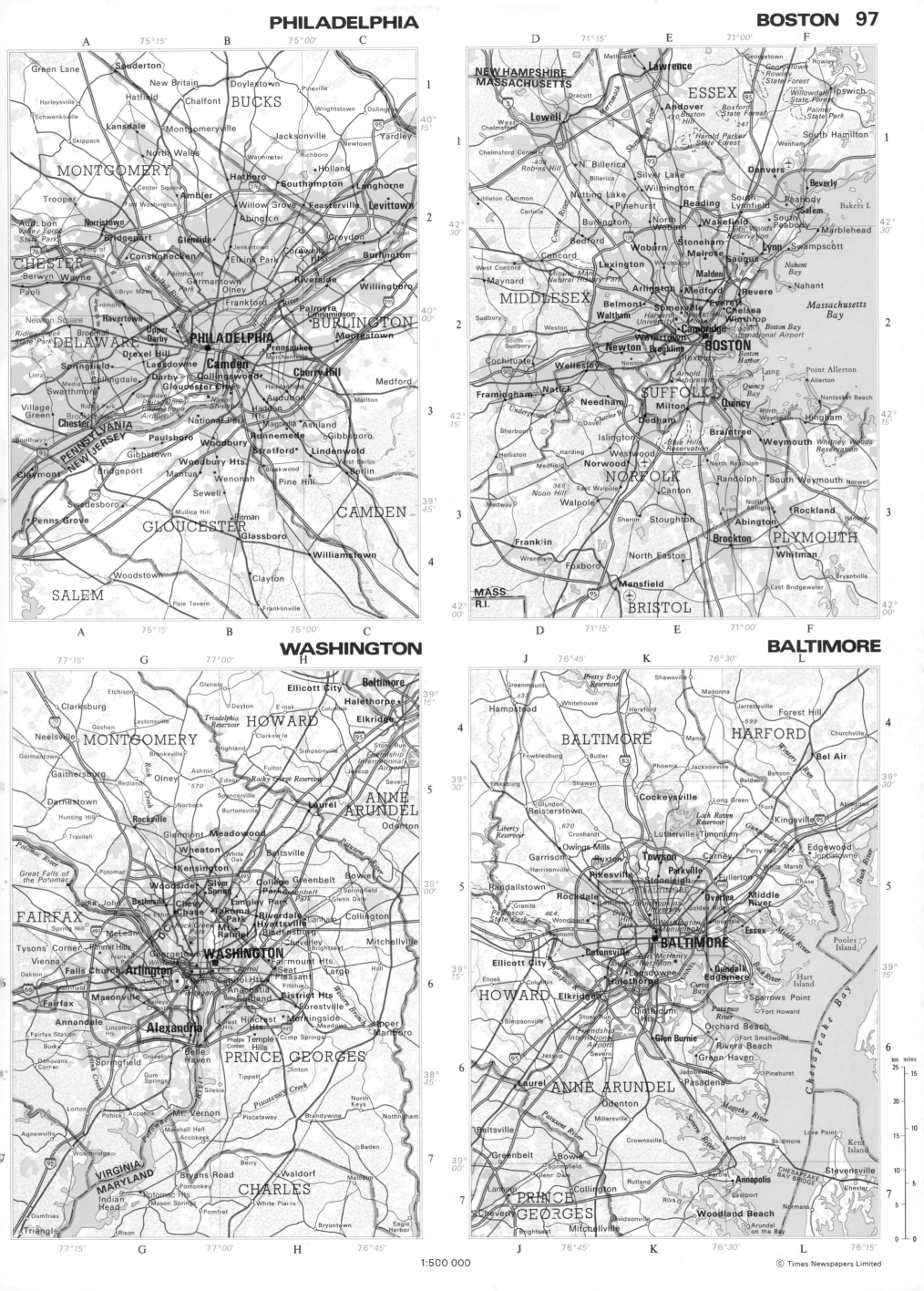

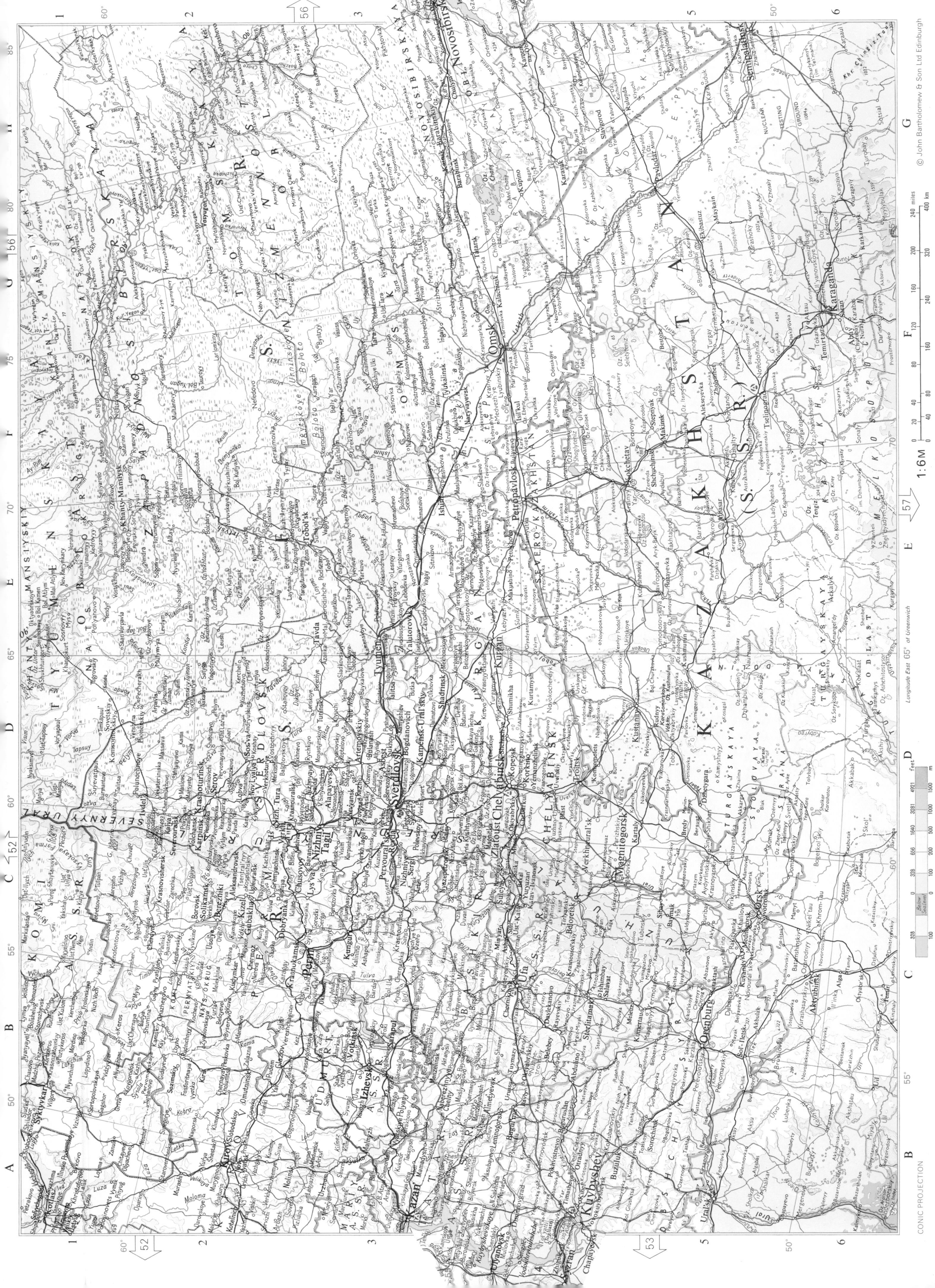
1:6M
CONIC PROJECTION
Longitude East 65° of Greenwich
© John Bartholomew & Son Ltd Edinburgh

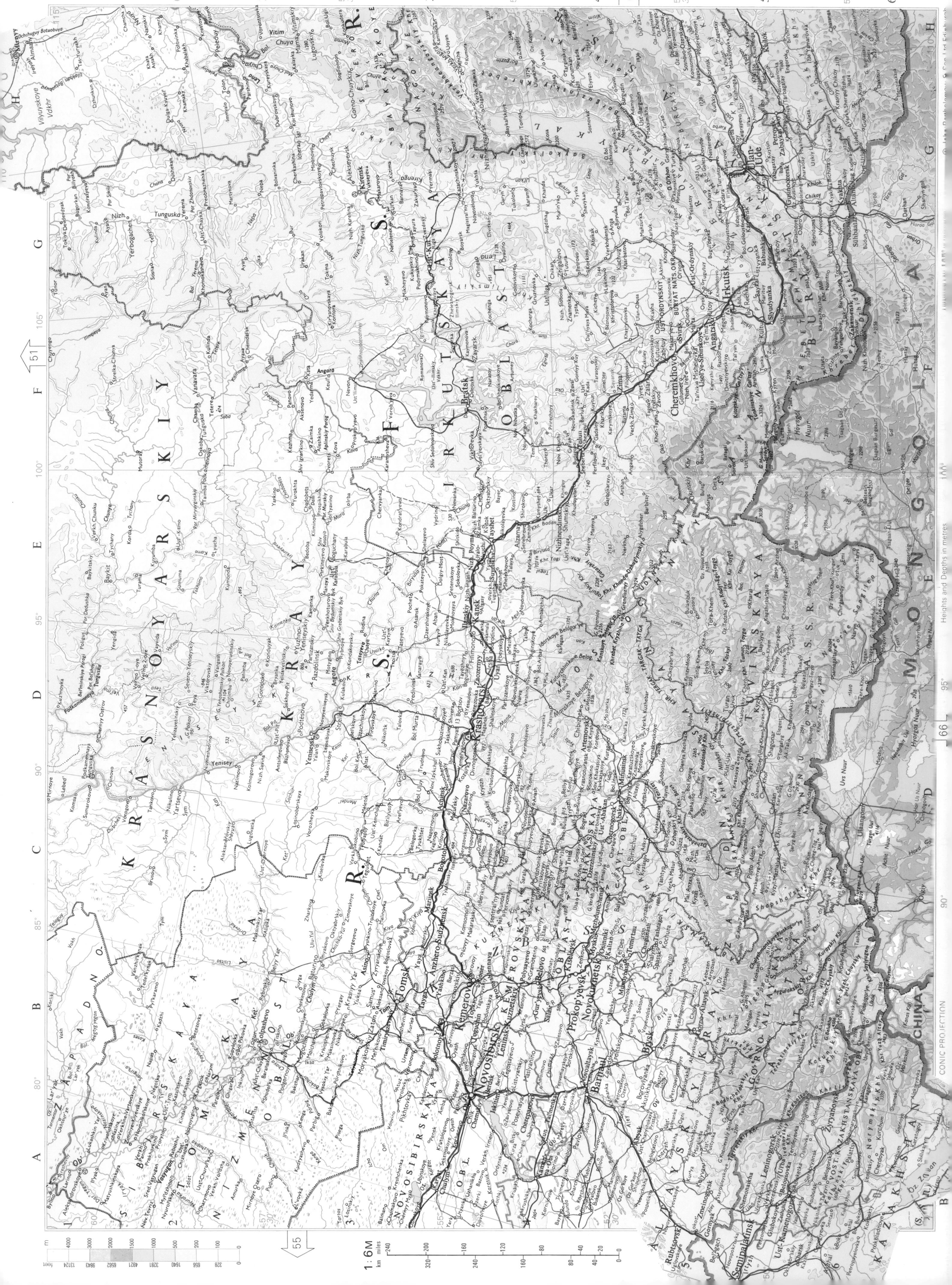
KRASNOYARSKIY KRAY
IRKUTSKAYA OBLAST
TOMSKAYA OBLAST
NOVOSIBIRSKAYA OBL.
KEMEROVSKAYA OBLAST
ALTAYSKIY KRAY
TUVINSKAYA A.S.S.R.
BURYATSKAYA A.S.S.R.
MONGOLIA
CHINA
KAZAKHSTAN
CONIC PROJECTION
Heights and Depths in metres
1:6M

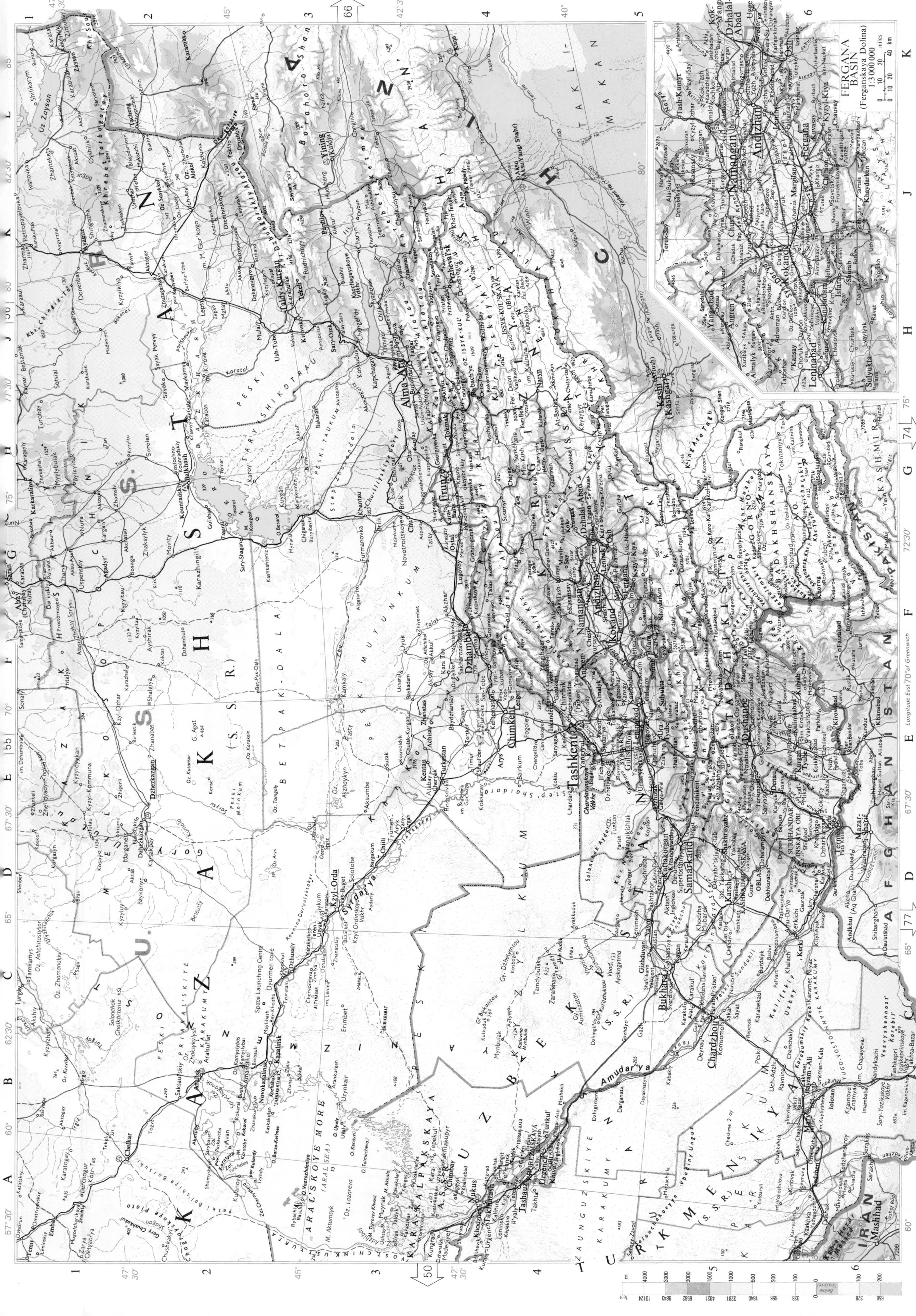
FERGANA BASIN
(Ferganskaya Dolina)
1:3 000 000
Heights and Depths in metres
1:6M
Longitude East 70° of Greenwich
CONIC PROJECTION
Tashkent
Samarkand
Bukhara
Alma-Ata
Frunze
Dushanbe
Chardzhou
Kzyl-Orda
Nukus
Mashhad
Kashi (Kashgar)
Andizhan
Namangan
Fergana
ARAL'SKOYE MORE (ARAL SEA)
AFGHANISTAN
IRAN

© John Bartholomew & Son Ltd Edinburgh

56

U. S. S. R.
MONGOLIA
GOBI
CHINA
IRKUTSKAYA OBLAST'
BURYAT A.S.S.R.
TUVINSKAYA A.S.S.R.
CHITINSKAYA OBLAST'
XINJIANG UYGUR ZIZHIQU
(SINKIANG)
QINGHAI
(TSINGHAI)
NEI MONGOL
(INNER MONGOLIA)
NINGXIA
GANSU
SHAANXI
SHANXI
HEBEI
HENAN
SHANDONG
ANHUI
HUBEI
SICHUAN
INDIA
BURMA
Irkutsk
Ulan-Ude
Chita
ULAANBAATAR
(ULAN BATOR)
BEIJING
(PEKING)
Tianjin
Hohhot
Baotou
Lanzhou
Xining
Yinchuan
Xi'an
Taiyuan
Shijiazhuang
Zhengzhou
Jinan
Nanjing
Wuhan
Chengdu
Chongqing
(Chungking)
ALBERS CONIC PROJECTION

66

67

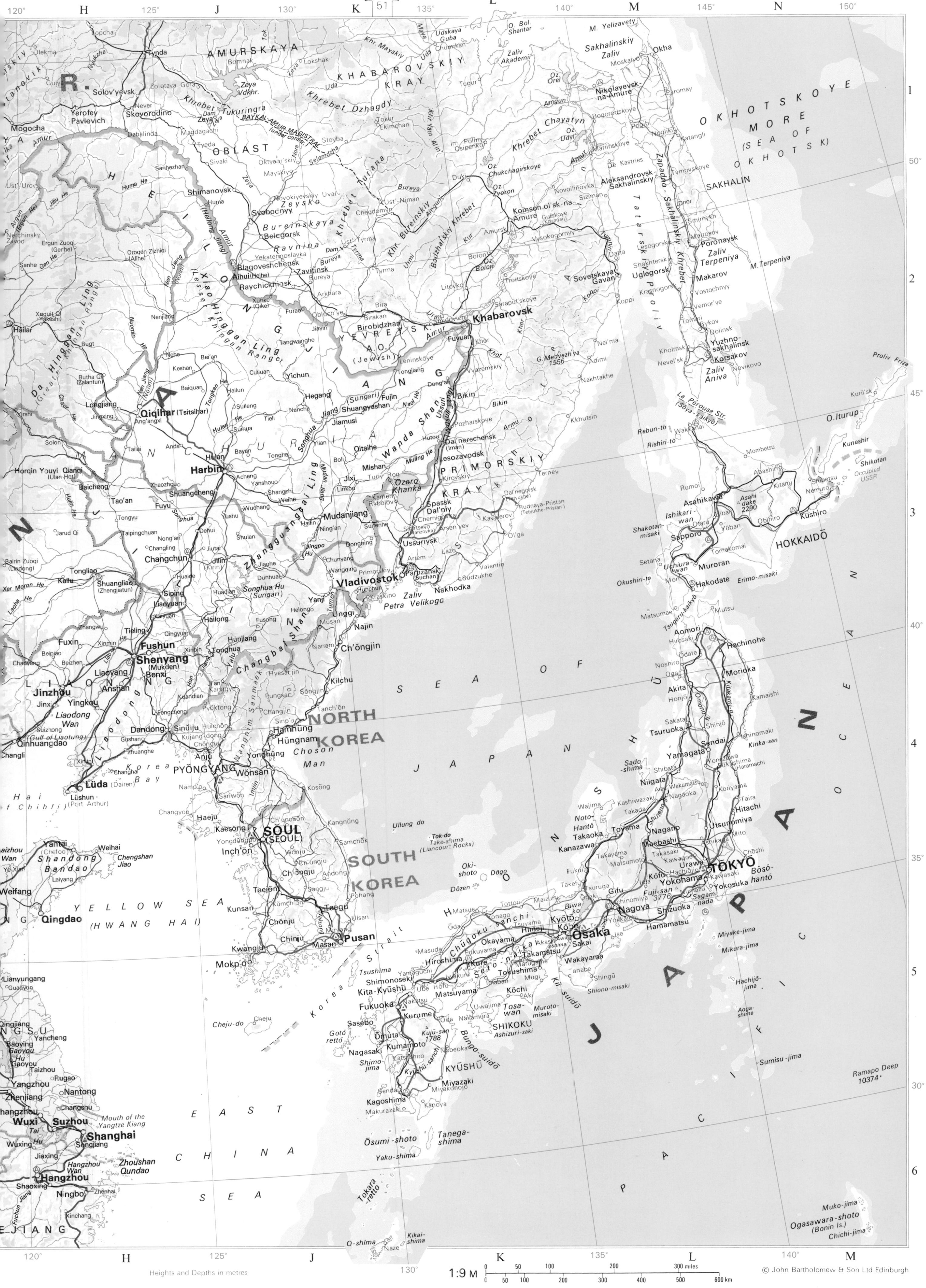
51
AMURSKAYA
OBLAST
KHABAROVSKIY
KRAY
YEVREYSKAYA A.O. (Jewish)
PRIMORSKIY
KRAY
HEILONGJIANG
JILIN
LIAONING
NORTH KOREA
SOUTH KOREA
JAPAN
HOKKAIDŌ
HONSHŪ
SHIKOKU
KYŪSHŪ
SAKHALIN
OKHOTSKOYE MORE
(SEA OF OKHOTSK)
SEA OF JAPAN
YELLOW SEA
(HWANG HAI)
EAST CHINA SEA
PACIFIC OCEAN
Khabarovsk
Vladivostok
Harbin
Qiqihar (Tsitsihar)
Changchun
Jilin
Shenyang (Mukden)
Fushun
Anshan
Jinzhou
Dandong
Lüda (Dairen)
Lüshun (Port Arthur)
Blagoveshchensk
Komsomol'sk-na-Amure
Nikolayevsk-na-Amure
Yuzhno-sakhalinsk
Korsakov
Nakhodka
Mudanjiang
Jiamusi
Hegang
P'YŎNGYANG
SŎUL (SEOUL)
Inch'ŏn
Pusan
Taegu
Kwangju
Taejŏn
Qingdao
Yantai (Chefoo)
Shanghai
Suzhou
Wuxi
Hangzhou
Ningbo
Sapporo
Asahikawa
Kushiro
Hakodate
Muroran
Aomori
Hachinohe
Morioka
Akita
Sendai
Niigata
Yamagata
Tōkyō
Yokohama
Kawasaki
Nagoya
Kyōto
Ōsaka
Kōbe
Hiroshima
Okayama
Kitakyūshū
Fukuoka
Kumamoto
Nagasaki
Kagoshima
Miyazaki
Kanazawa
Toyama
Shizuoka
Hamamatsu
Fuji-san 3776
La Pérouse Str. (Sōya-kaikyō)
Tsugaru-kaikyō
Korea Strait
Tatarskiy Proliv
Proliv Friza
Zaliv Petra Velikogo
Korea Bay
Liaodong Wan
Hai Chihli
Ramapo Deep 10374
Ogasawara-shoto (Bonin Is.)
Occupied USSR
Khrebet Dzhagdy
Khrebet Tukuringra
BAYKAL-AMUR MAGISTRAL (under constr.)
Zeyskoye Vdkhr.
Da Hinggan Ling (Greater Khingan Range)
Xiao Hinggan Ling (Lesser Khingan Range)
Changbai Shan
Ozero Khanka
Amur
Ussuri
Songhua Jiang
Heights and Depths in metres
1:9 M
50 100 200 300 miles
0 50 100 200 300 400 500 600 km

© John Bartholomew & Son Ltd Edinburgh

SEA OF OKHOTSK
SEA OF JAPAN
Continuation on the same scale
U.S.S.R.
Occupied U.S.S.R.
HOKKAIDO
Sapporo
Asahikawa
Hakodate
Muroran
Otaru
Kushiro
Obihiro
Abashiri
Wakkanai
Sōya-misaki
Shiretoko misaki
Nemuro
Tsugaru kaikyō
Aomori
Mutsu-wan
SOUTH KOREA
Pusan
KOREA STRAIT
Nishi-suidō (Chōsen-kaikyō)
Higashi-suidō
Tsushima
Oki shotō
Tottori
Matsue
Okayama
Hiroshima
Yamaguchi
Kita-Kyūshū
Fukuoka
Sasebo
Nagasaki
Kumamoto
Beppu
Ōita
Nobeoka
Miyazaki
Kagoshima
Matsuyama
Kōchi
Tokushima
Kōbe
Himeji
Sakai
Suō-nada
Iyo-nada
Tosa-wan
Muroto-misaki
Ashizuri-misaki
Ōsumi hantō
Sata-misaki
Koshiki-rettō
Gotō-rettō
Iki
HYŌGO
SHIKOKU
KYŪSHŪ
J A P A N
CONIC PROJECTION
feet m
9843 3000
6562 2000
4921 1500
3281 1000
1640 500
656 200
328 100
0 0
656 200
6562 2000
13124 4000
26248 8000

PACIFIC OCEAN
SEA OF JAPAN
TOKYO
Yokohama
Nagoya
Sendai
Niigata
Aomori
Akita
Morioka
Fukushima
Hachinohe
Hirosaki
Yamagata
Kanazawa
Toyama
Nagano
Matsumoto
Gifu
Shizuoka
Hamamatsu
Utsunomiya
Mito
Maebashi
Takasaki
Kofu
Chiba
Hitachi
Koriyama
Sado-shima
Noto-hantō
Izu-shotō
Ō-shima
Miyake-jima
Hachijō-jima
IWO JIMA
1:300 000
OKINAWA
1:1 200 000
Naha
1:3M
km miles
Long. East 136° of Greenwich

© John Bartholomew & Son Ltd Edinburgh

TOKYO

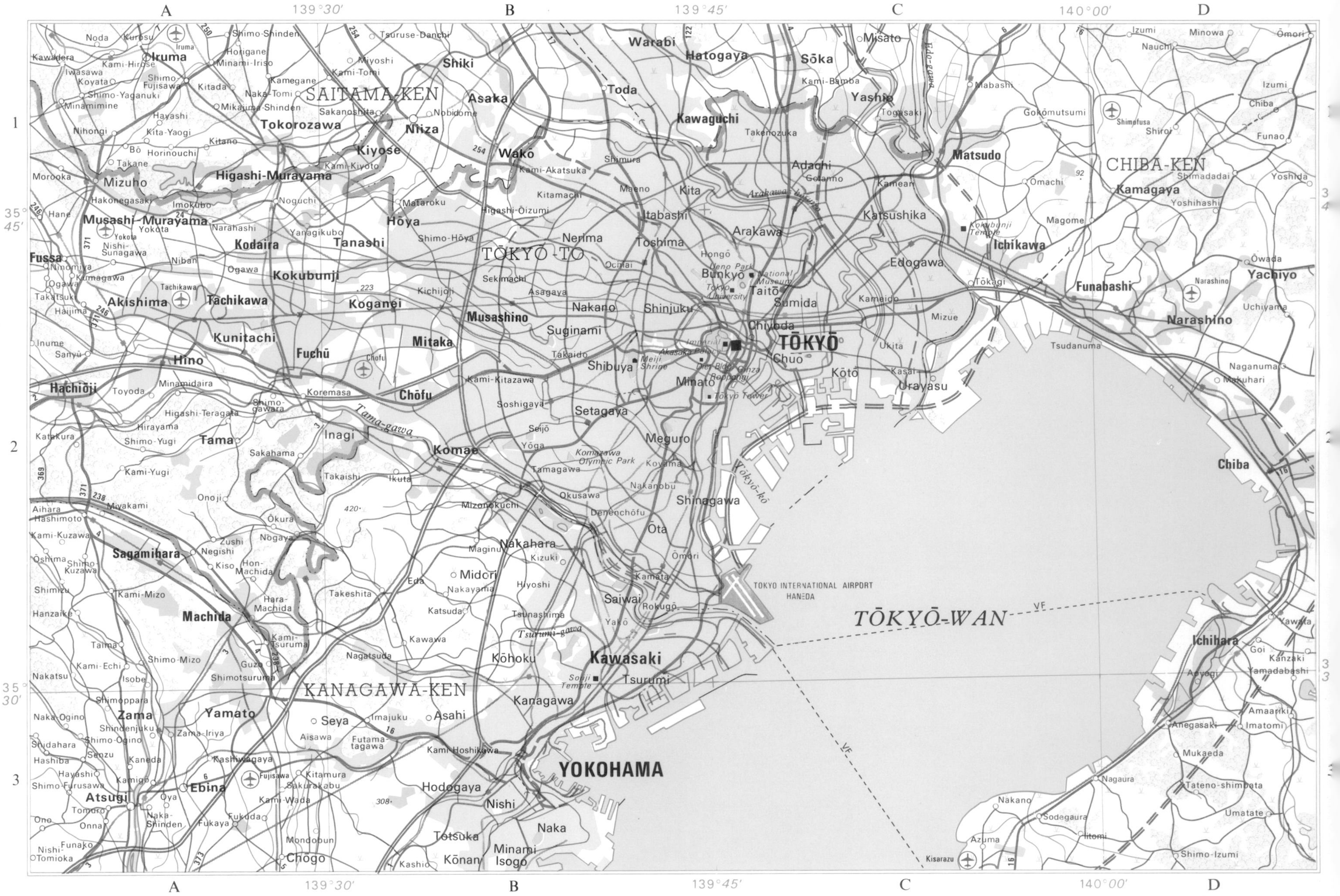

OSAKA

1:300 000

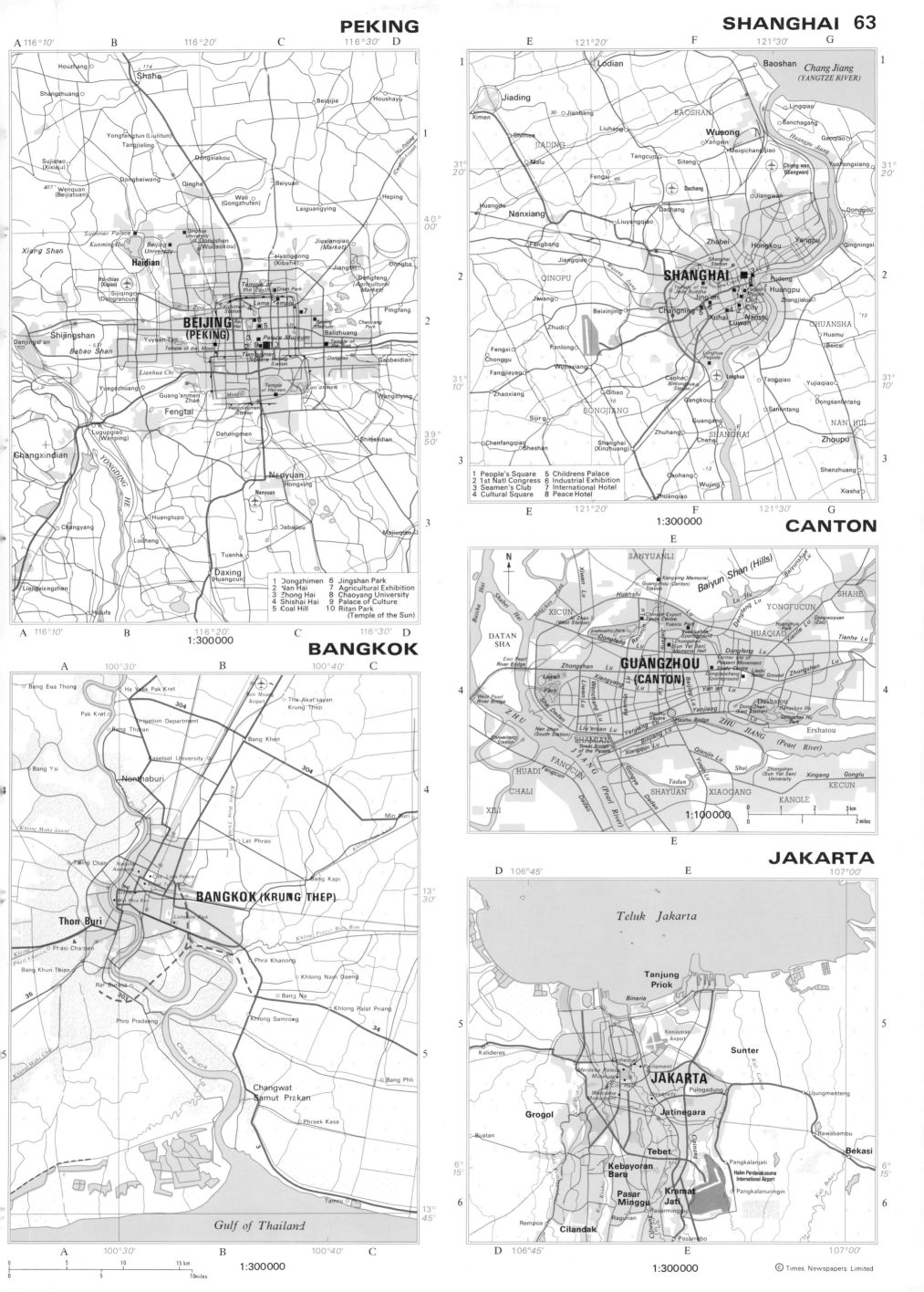

© Times Newspapers Limited

PEKING

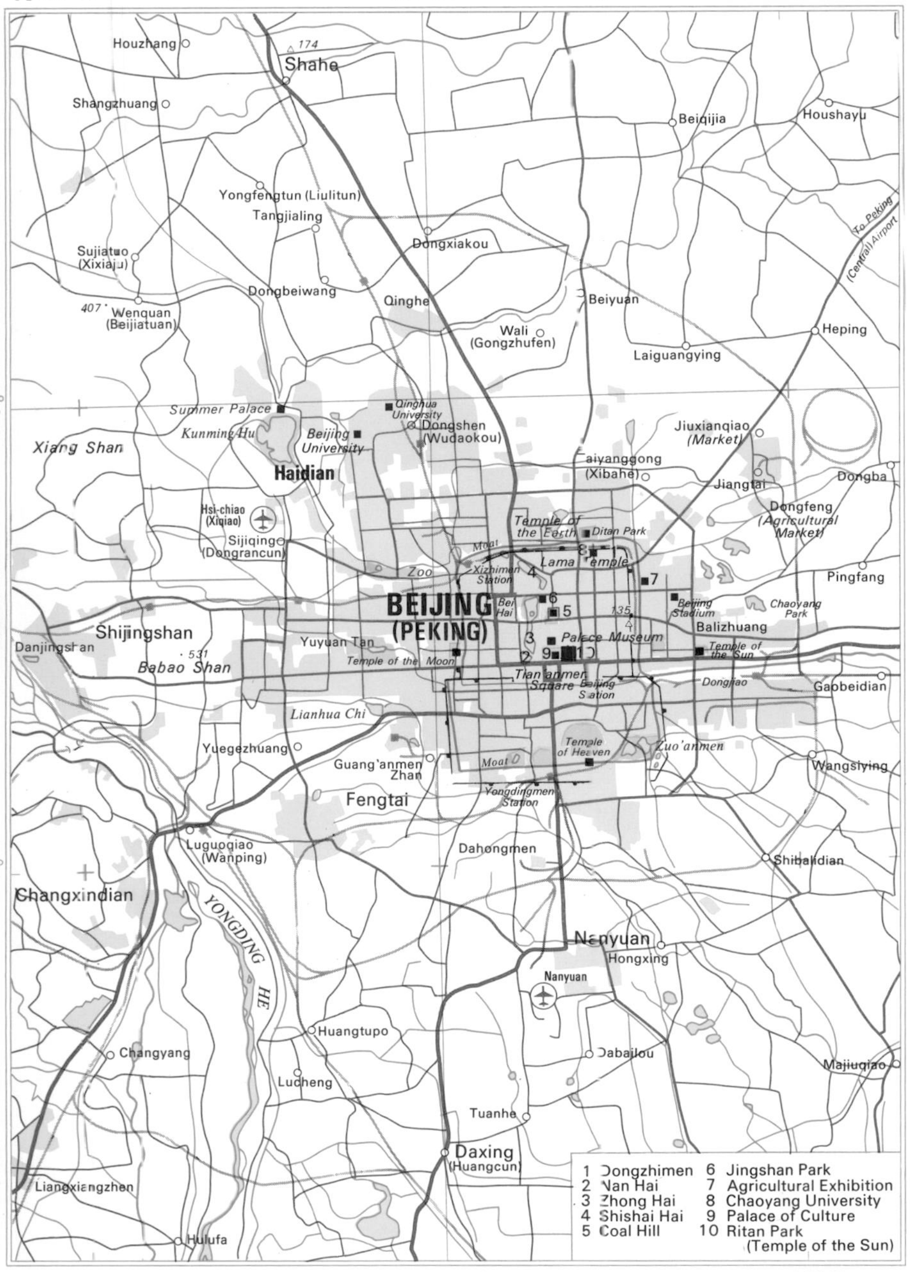

BEIJING (PEKING)
Houzhang
Shahe
Shangzhuang
Beiqijia
Houshayu
Yongfengtun (Liulitun)
Tangjialing
Sujiatuo (Xixiaju)
Dongxiakou
To Peking (Central) Airport
Dongbeiwang
Qinghe
Beiyuan
Wenquan (Beijiatuan)
Wali (Gongzhufen)
Heping
Laiguangying
Summer Palace
Qinghua University
Kunming Hu
Beijing University
Dongshen (Wudaokou)
Jiuxianqiao (Market)
Xiang Shan
Haidian
Jiangtai
Dongba
Hsi-chiao (Xijiao)
Sijiqing (Dongrancun)
Temple of the Earth
Ditan Park
Dongfeng (Agricultural Market)
Moat
Lama Temple
Pingfang
Shijingshan
Danjingshan
Babao Shan
Yuyuan Tan
Temple of the Moon
Beijing Stadium
Chaoyang Park
Balizhuang
Palace Museum
Temple of the Sun
Tian'anmen Square
Beijing Station
Dongjiao
Gaobeidian
Lianhua Chi
Yuegezhuang
Guang'anmen Zhan
Temple of Heaven
Zuo'anmen
Wangsiying
Fengtai
Yongdingmen Station
Luguoqiao (Wanping)
Dahongmen
Shibalidian
Changxindian
YONGDING HE
Nanyuan
Hongxing
Huangtupo
Changyang
Dabailou
Majiuqiao
Ludheng
Tuanhe
Daxing (Huangcun)
Liangxiangzhen
Hulufa
1 Dongzhimen
2 Nan Hai
3 Zhong Hai
4 Shishai Hai
5 Coal Hill
6 Jingshan Park
7 Agricultural Exhibition
8 Chaoyang University
9 Palace of Culture
10 Ritan Park (Temple of the Sun)

1:300000

SHANGHAI

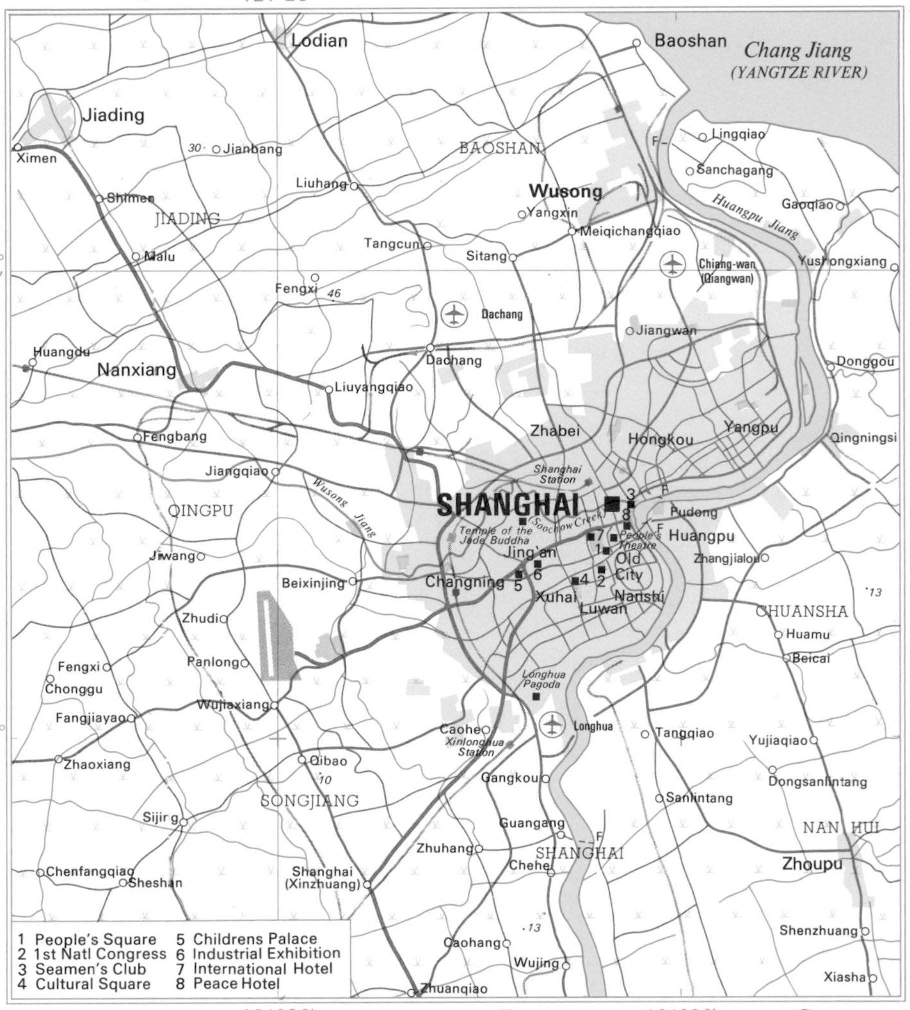

SHANGHAI
Lodian
Baoshan
Chang Jiang (YANGTZE RIVER)
Jiading
Ximen
Jianbang
BAOSHAN
Lingqiao
Sanchagang
Liuhang
Wusong
Yangxin
Meiqichanggiao
Gaoqiao
Shimen
JIADING
Huangpu Jiang
Malu
Tangcun
Sitang
Chiang-wan (Jiangwan)
Yushongxiang
Fengxi
Dachang
Huangdu
Jiangwan
Donggou
Nanxiang
Dachang
Liuyangqiao
Fengbang
Zhabei
Hongkou
Yangpu
Qingningsi
Jiangqiao
Wusong Jiang
Shanghai Station
QINGPU
Temple of the Jade Buddha
Pudong
Huangpu
Jing'an
Old City
Zhangjialou
Jiwang
Beixinjing
Changning
Xuhai
Nanshi
Luwan
CHUANSHA
Huamu
Zhudi
Beicai
Panlong
Fengxi
Chonggu
Longhua Pagoda
Wujiaxiang
Fangjiayao
Caohe
Xinlonghua Station
Longhua
Tangqiao
Yujiaqiao
Zhaoxiang
Qibao
Gangkou
Dongsanlintang
SONGJIANG
Sanlintang
Sijing
Guangang
NAN HUI
Zhuhang
Chehe
SHANGHAI
Zhoupu
Chenfangqiao
Sheshan
Shanghai (Xinzhuang)
Shenzhuang
Caohang
Wujing
Xiasha
Zhuanqiao
1 People's Square
2 1st Natl Congress
3 Seamen's Club
4 Cultural Square
5 Childrens Palace
6 Industrial Exhibition
7 International Hotel
8 Peace Hotel

1:300000

CANTON

GUANGZHOU (CANTON)
SANYUANLI
Kangying Memorial
Guangzhou (Canton) Station
Baiyun Shan (Hills)
Baiyunshan Lu
Huanshi
Lu Hu
YONGFUCUN
SHAHE
XICUN
Xi Zhan (West Station)
Chinese Export Trade Centre
Yuexiu Park
Dongwuyuan (Zoo)
DATAN SHA
Liuhuahu Park
Dongfeng Lu
Yuexiushan Sportsground
Zhongshan (Sun Yat Sen) Memorial Hall
HUAQIAO
Tianhe Lu
East Pearl River Bridge
Zhongshan Lu
Former site of Peasant Movement Study Centre
Dongjiaochang Sportsground
Lieshi Burial Ground
Zhongshan Lu
Liuyan Park
West Pearl River Bridge
Xiangyang Lu
Yan'an Lu
Dashatou
Haizhu Square
Haizhu Bridge
Yanjiang Lu
Dong Zhan (East Station)
Donghan Hu
ZHU JIANG (Pearl River)
Nan Zhan (South Station)
Liu'ersan Lu
SHAMIAN
Great Bridge of the People
Shiweitang Station
Ershatou
Xiangqun Lu
Qianjin Lu
Shui
HUADI
FANGCUN
Zhongshan (Sun Yat Sen) University
Xingang
Gongfu
KECUN
CHALI
Yadun
SHAYUAN
XIAOGANG
KANGLE
XILI
0 1 2 3 km
0 1 2 miles

1:100000

BANGKOK

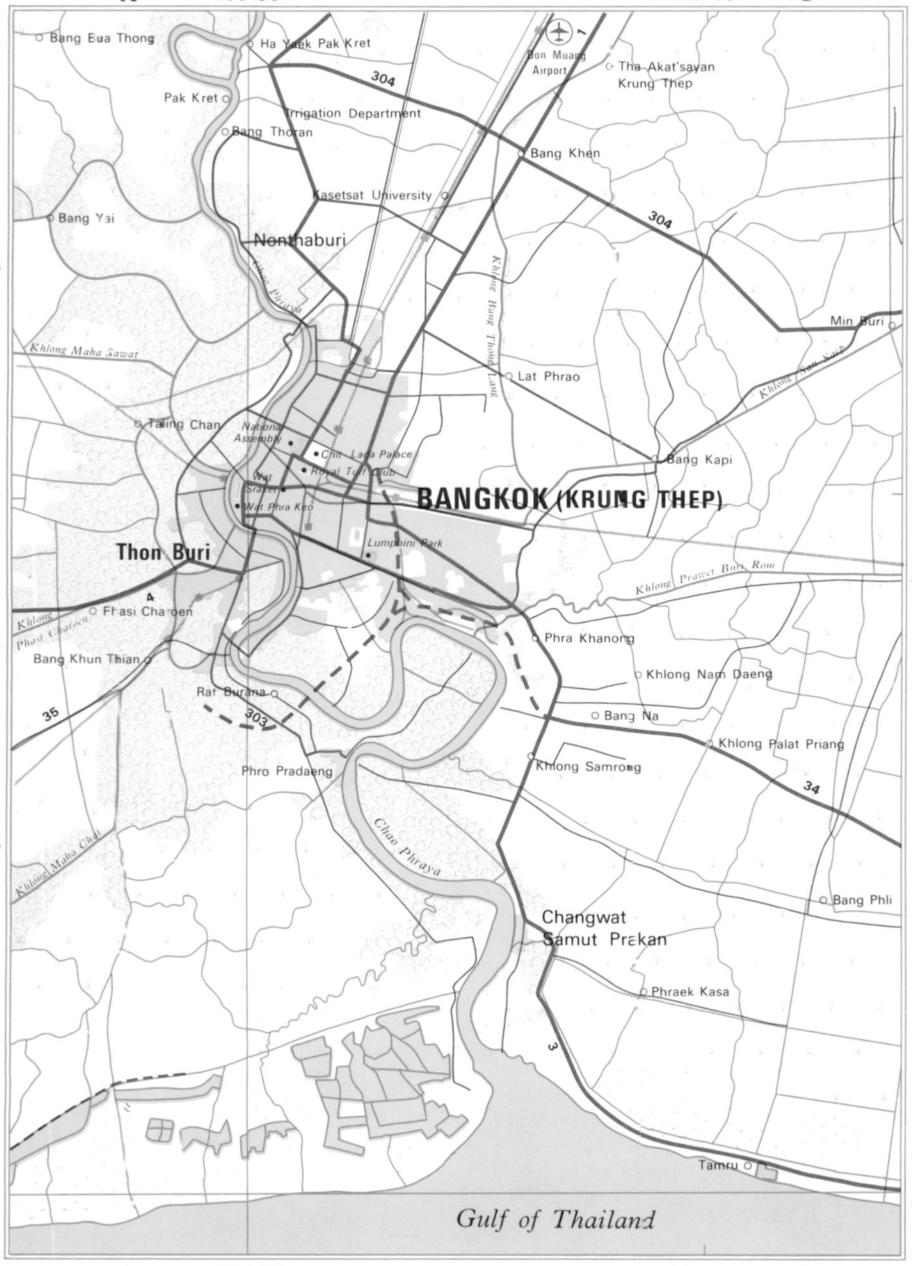

BANGKOK (KRUNG THEP)
Bang Bua Thong
Ha Yaek Pak Kret
Don Muang Airport
Tha Akat'sayan Krung Thep
Pak Kret
Irrigation Department
Bang Thoran
Bang Khen
Kasetsat University
Bang Yai
Nonthaburi
Chao Phraya
Min Buri
Khlong Maha Sawat
Lat Phrao
Taling Chan
National Assembly
Chitr Lada Palace
Royal Turf Club
Bang Kapi
Wat Phra Keo
Lumpini Park
Thon Buri
Khlong Prawet Buri Rom
Phasi Charoen
Phra Khanong
Bang Khun Thian
Khlong Nam Daeng
Rat Burana
Bang Na
Khlong Palat Priang
Phro Pradaeng
Khlong Samrong
Chao Phraya
Bang Phli
Changwat Samut Prakan
Phraek Kasa
Tamru
Gulf of Thailand
0 5 10 15 km
0 5 10 miles

1:300000

JAKARTA

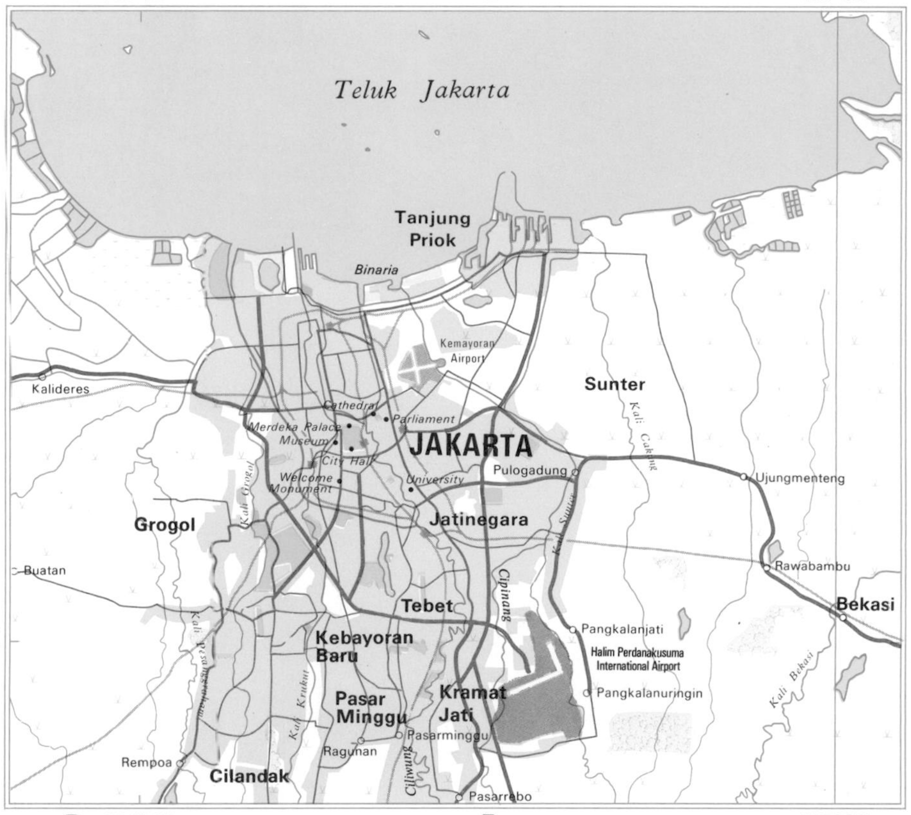

JAKARTA
Teluk Jakarta
Tanjung Priok
Binaria
Kemayoran Airport
Sunter
Kalideres
Cathedral
Parliament
Merdeka Palace
Museum
City Hall
Welcome Monument
University
Pulogadung
Ujungmenteng
Grogol
Jatinegara
Buaran
Rawabambu
Tebet
Bekasi
Pangkalanjati
Halim Perdanakusuma International Airport
Kebayoran Baru
Pasar Minggu
Kramat Jati
Pangkalanuringin
Pasarminggu
Ragunan
Rempoa
Cilandak
Pasarrebo
Cipinang

1:300000

© Times Newspapers Limited

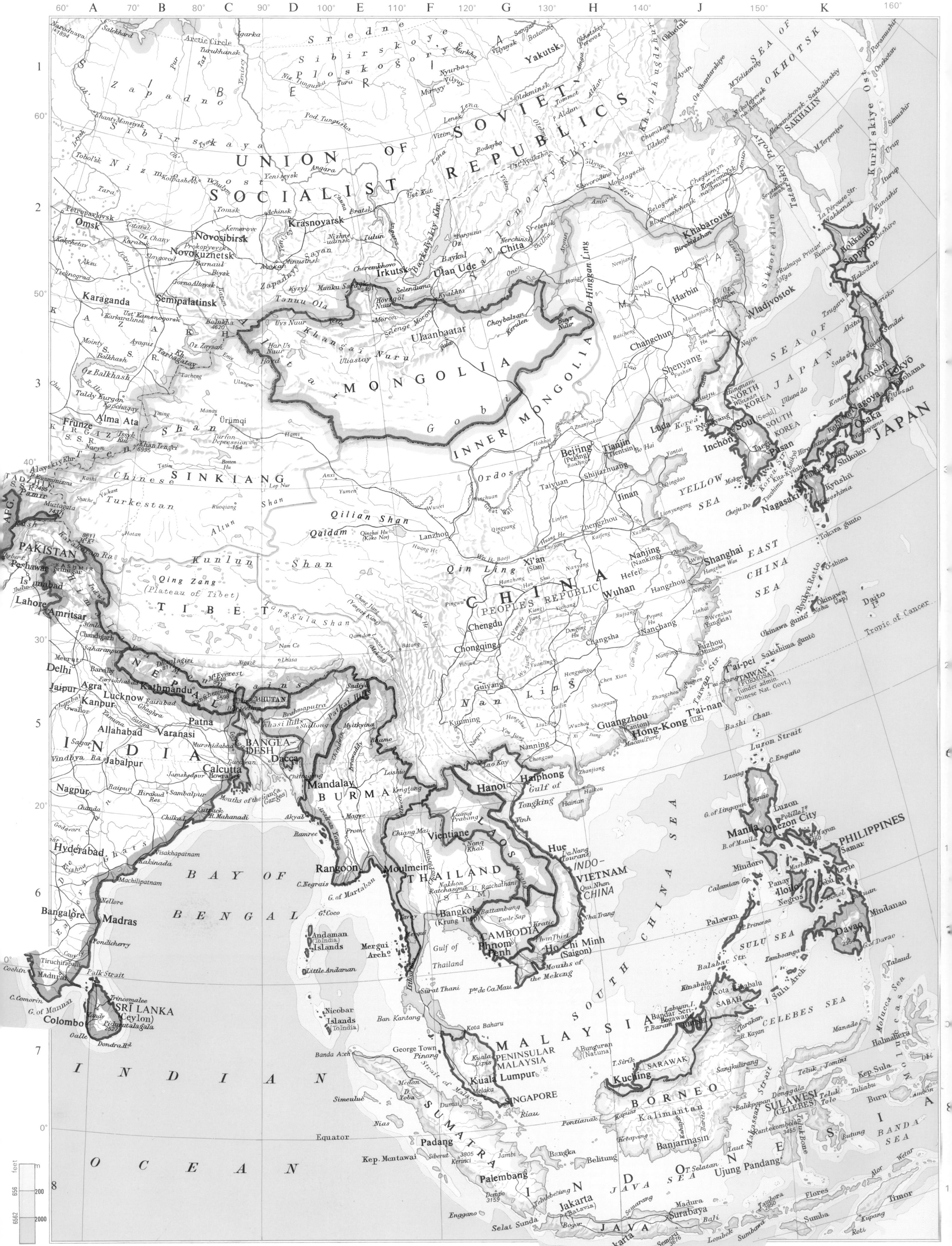
UNION OF SOVIET SOCIALIST REPUBLICS
MONGOLIA
INNER MONGOLIA
MANCHURIA
SINKIANG
TIBET
CHINA
(PEOPLES REPUBLIC)
NORTH KOREA
SOUTH KOREA
JAPAN
SEA OF JAPAN
SEA OF OKHOTSK
YELLOW SEA
EAST CHINA SEA
SOUTH CHINA SEA
PAKISTAN
INDIA
NEPAL
BHUTAN
BANGLA-DESH
BURMA
THAILAND
(SIAM)
LAOS
CAMBODIA
VIETNAM
MALAYSIA
PENINSULAR MALAYSIA
SINGAPORE
SRI LANKA
(Ceylon)
PHILIPPINES
TAIWAN
(FORMOSA)
INDONESIA
BORNEO
SUMATRA
JAVA
SULAWESI
(CELEBES)
BAY OF BENGAL
INDIAN OCEAN
SULU SEA
CELEBES SEA
JAVA SEA
BANDA SEA
Gulf of Thailand
Gulf of Tongking
Gobi
Qilian Shan
Kunlun Shan
Qing Zang
(Plateau of Tibet)
Tanggula Shan
Qin Ling
Nan Ling
Da Hinggan Ling
Tien Shan
Altun Shan
Ordos
Turkestan
Omsk
Novosibirsk
Novokuznetsk
Krasnoyarsk
Irkutsk
Ulan Ude
Chita
Yakutsk
Khabarovsk
Vladivostok
Karaganda
Semipalatinsk
Alma Ata
Frunze
Ulaanbaatar
Ürümqi
Harbin
Changchun
Shenyang
Beijing
(Peking)
Tianjin
(Tientsin)
Taiyuan
Shijiazhuang
Jinan
Lanzhou
Xi'an
(Sian)
Zhengzhou
Nanjing
(Nanking)
Shanghai
Hangzhou
Hefei
Wuhan
Nanchang
Changsha
Chengdu
Chongqing
Guiyang
Kunming
Nanning
Guangzhou
(Canton)
Hong-Kong
(UK)
Fuzhou
T'ai-pei
T'ai-nan
Lhasa
Seoul
Inchon
Pusan
Sapporo
Tokyo
Yokohama
Nagoya
Osaka
Nagasaki
Kathmandu
Delhi
Lahore
Amritsar
Jaipur
Agra
Kanpur
Lucknow
Allahabad
Varanasi
Patna
Calcutta
Dacca
Jabalpur
Nagpur
Hyderabad
Bangalore
Madras
Madurai
Colombo
Mandalay
Rangoon
Moulmein
Hanoi
Haiphong
Vientiane
Hue
Bangkok
(Krung Thep)
Phnom Penh
Ho Chi Minh
(Saigon)
Kuala Lumpur
Kuching
Palembang
Jakarta
(Batavia)
Surabaya
Padang
Banjarmasin
Ujung Pandang
Manila
Quezon City
Davao
Mindanao
Luzon
Equator
Tropic of Cancer
Arctic Circle

LAMBERT AZIMUTHAL EQUAL-AREA PROJECTION
1:24 M
Longitude East 100° of Greenwich

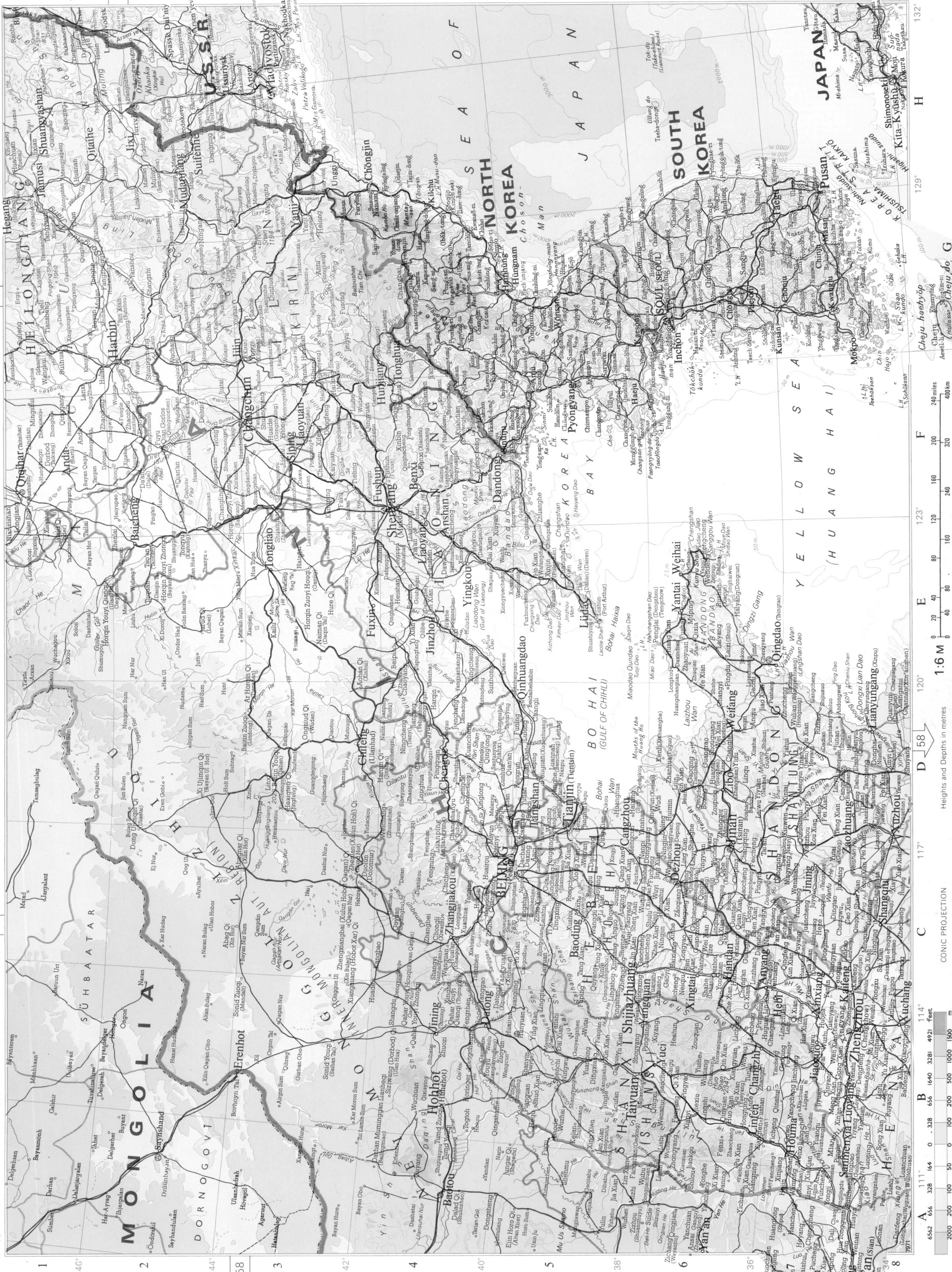
MONGOLIA
SÜHBAATAR
DORNOGOVĬ
U.S.S.R.
HEILONGJIANG
JILIN (KIRIN)
LIAONING
HEBEI
SHANXI
SHANDONG
HENAN
NEI MONGOL ZIZHIQU (INNER MONGOLIAN AUT. REGION)
NORTH KOREA
SOUTH KOREA
JAPAN
SEA OF JAPAN
YELLOW SEA (HUANG HAI)
KOREA BAY
BO HAI (GULF OF CHIHLI)
BEIJING
Tianjin
Harbin
Changchun
Shenyang
Pyongyang
Soul (Seoul)
Vladivostok
Pusan
1:6 M
CONIC PROJECTION
Heights and Depths in metres
Feet 6562 656 328 164 0 328 656 1640 3281 4921
m 2000 200 100 50 0 100 200 500 1000 1500
0 20 40 80 120 160 240 miles
0 20 40 80 120 160 200 240 320 400 km
59
58

Heights in metres

Below Sea Level	0	200	500	1000	2000	3000	4000	5000	6000 m
	0	656	1640	3281	6562	9843	13124	16409	19686 feet

ALBERS CONIC PROJECTION

1:9 M

0 50 100 200 300 miles

0 50 100 200 300 400 500 km

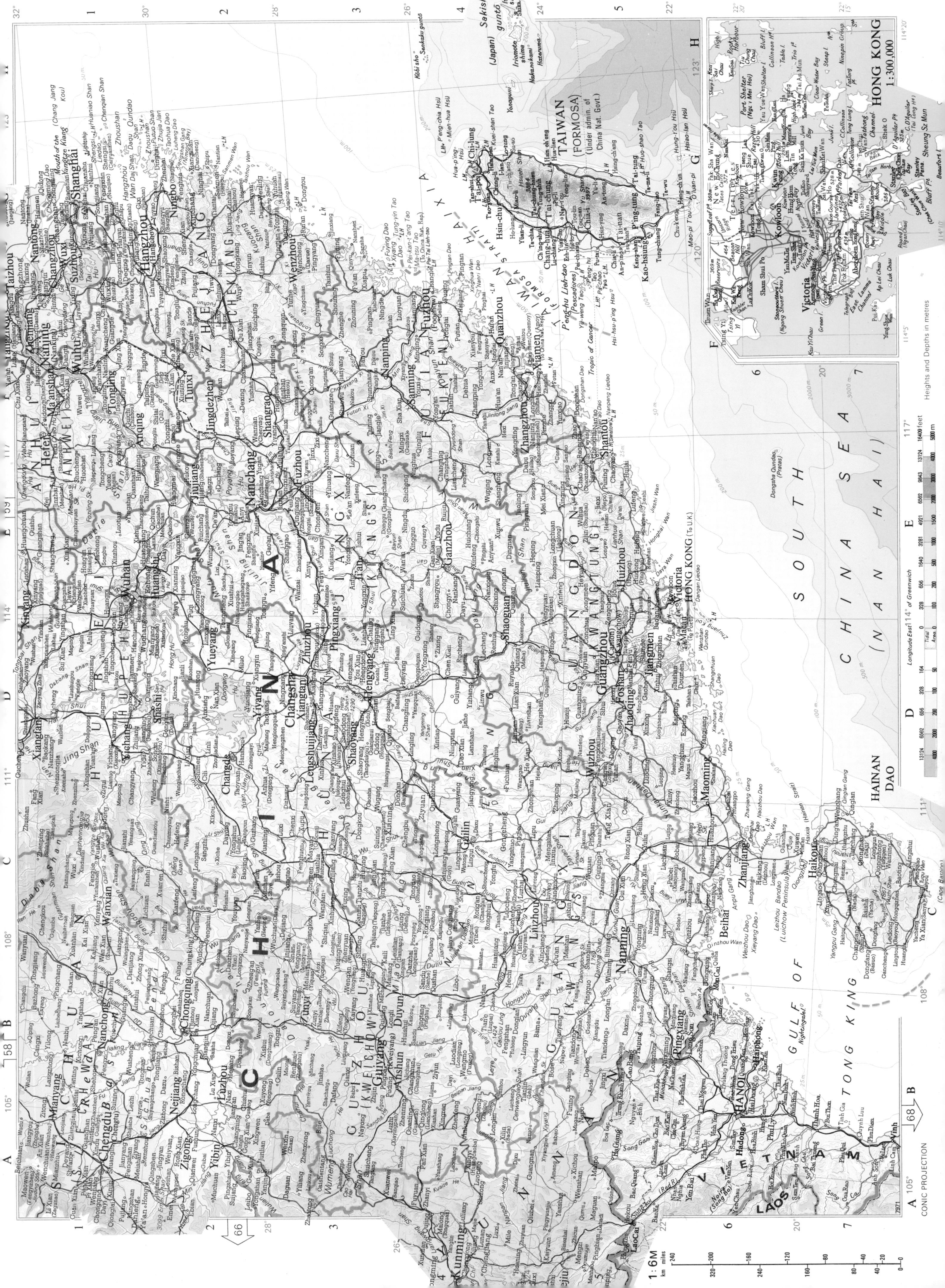
HONG KONG
1:300,000
SOUTH CHINA SEA
GULF OF TONG KING
TAIWAN (FORMOSA)
CONIC PROJECTION
Heights and Depths in metres
1:6M

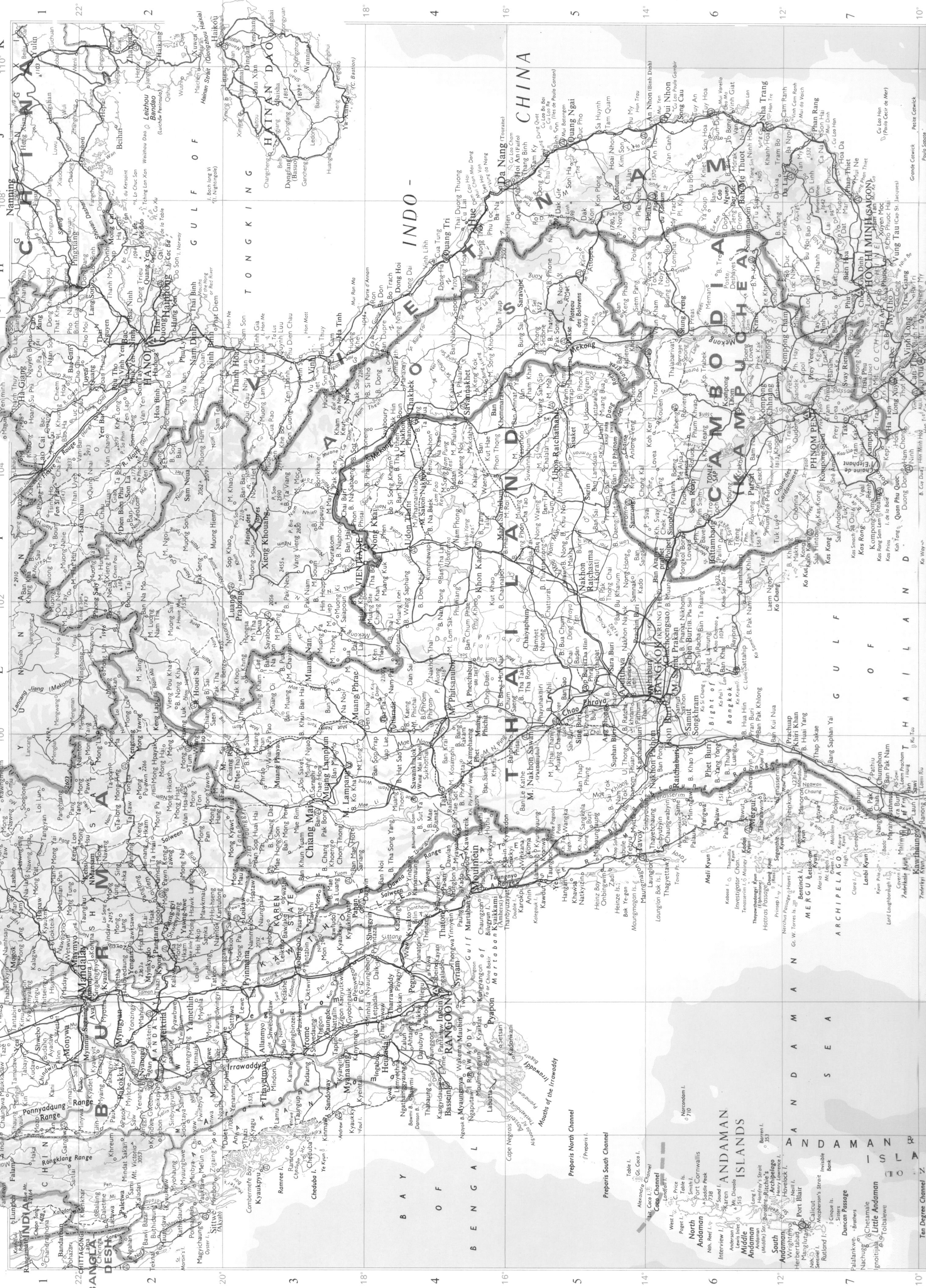
BURMA
THAILAND
CAMBODIA (KAMPUCHEA)
LAOS
VIETNAM
INDO-CHINA
CHINA
INDIA
BANGLADESH
HAINAN DAO
GULF OF TONGKING
GULF OF THAILAND
BAY OF BENGAL
ANDAMAN SEA
ANDAMAN ISLANDS
MERGUI ARCHIPELAGO
HANOI
BANGKOK (KRUNG THEP)
RANGOON
VIENTIANE
PHNOM PENH
HO CHI MINH (SAIGON)
Mandalay
Moulmein
Da Nang
Haiphong
Hue
Luang Prabang
Chiang Mai
Ten Degrees Channel
Preparis North Channel
Preparis South Channel
Coco Channel
Mouths of the Irrawaddy

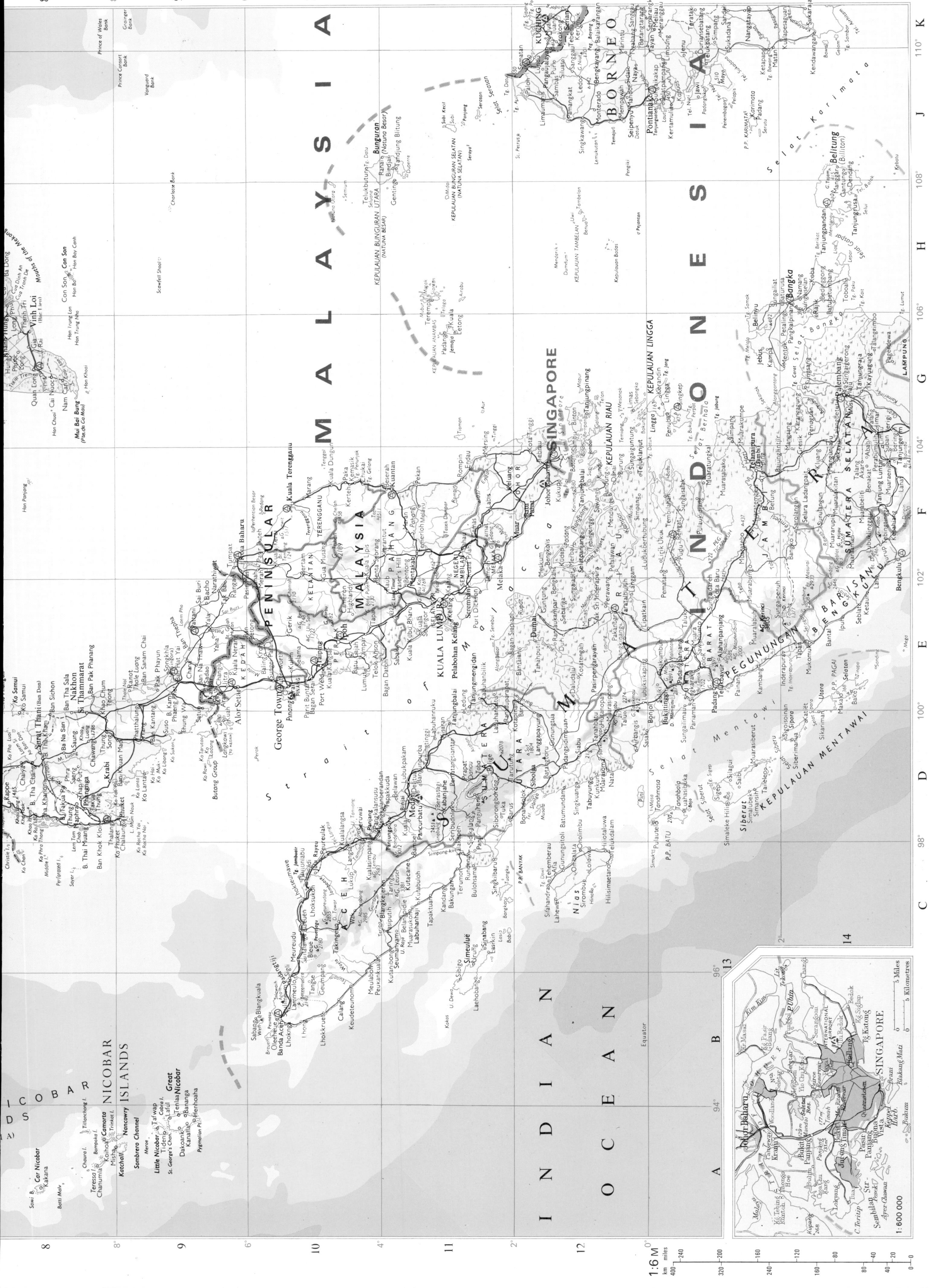

Heights and Depths in metres

© John Bartholomew & Son Ltd Edinburgh

MERCATOR PROJECTION

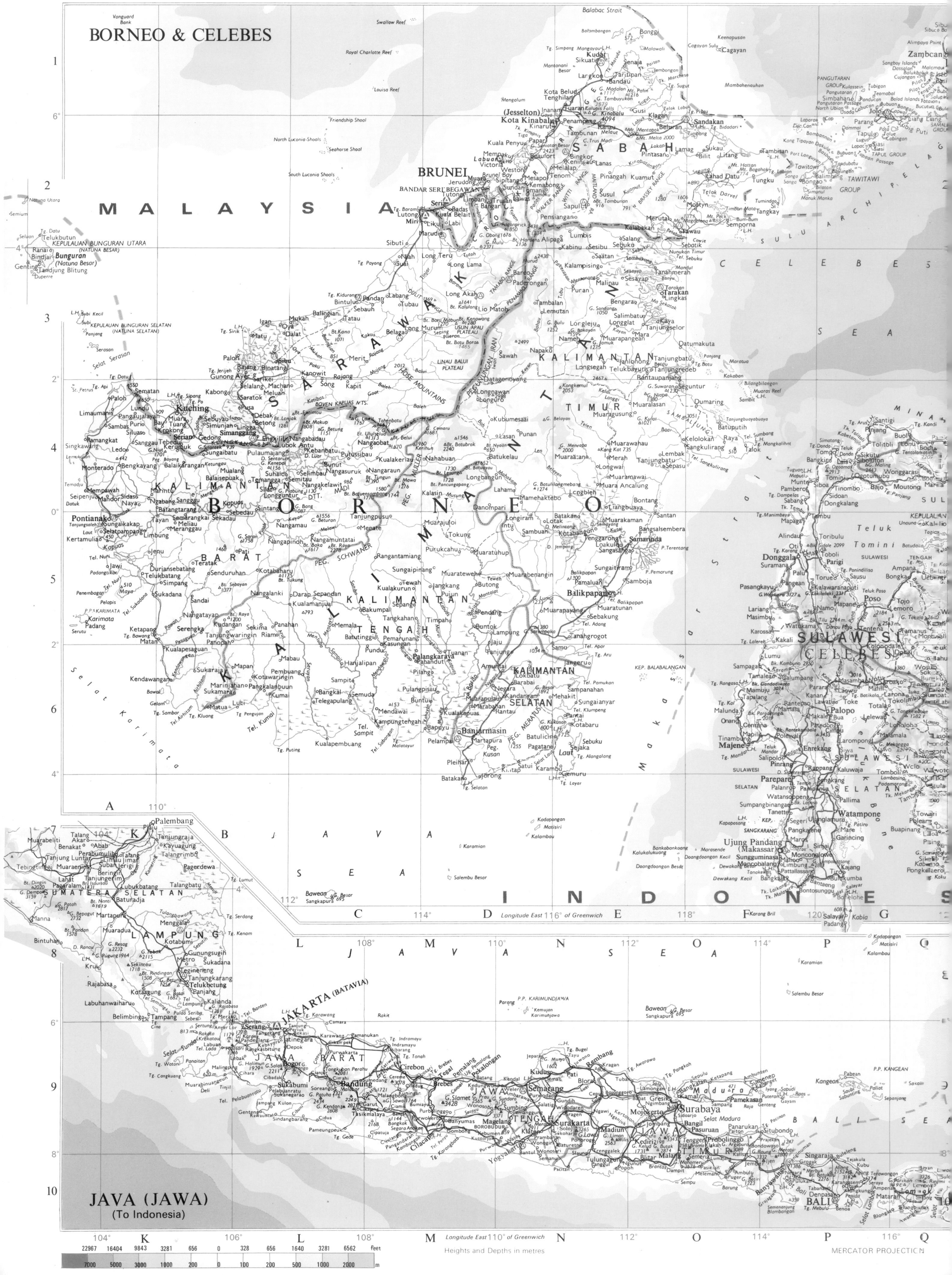
BORNEO & CELEBES
MALAYSIA
BRUNEI
SABAH
SARAWAK
BORNEO
KALIMANTAN BARAT
KALIMANTAN TENGAH
KALIMANTAN TIMUR
KALIMANTAN SELATAN
SULAWESI (CELEBES)
CELEBES SEA
JAVA SEA
INDONESIA
SULU ARCHIPELAGO
Makassar Strait
Selat Karimata
Teluk Tomini
SUMATERA SELATAN
LAMPUNG
JAWA BARAT
JAWA TENGAH
JAWA TIMUR
BALI
JAKARTA (BATAVIA)
Kuching
Pontianak
Banjarmasin
Samarinda
Balikpapan
Kota Kinabalu
Sandakan
Ujung Pandang (Makassar)
Surabaya
Bandung
Semarang
Palembang
JAVA (JAWA)
(To Indonesia)
Longitude East 116° of Greenwich
Longitude East 110° of Greenwich
Heights and Depths in metres
MERCATOR PROJECTION
22967 16404 9843 3281 656 0 328 656 1640 3281 6562 Feet
7000 5000 3000 1000 200 0 100 200 500 1000 2000 m

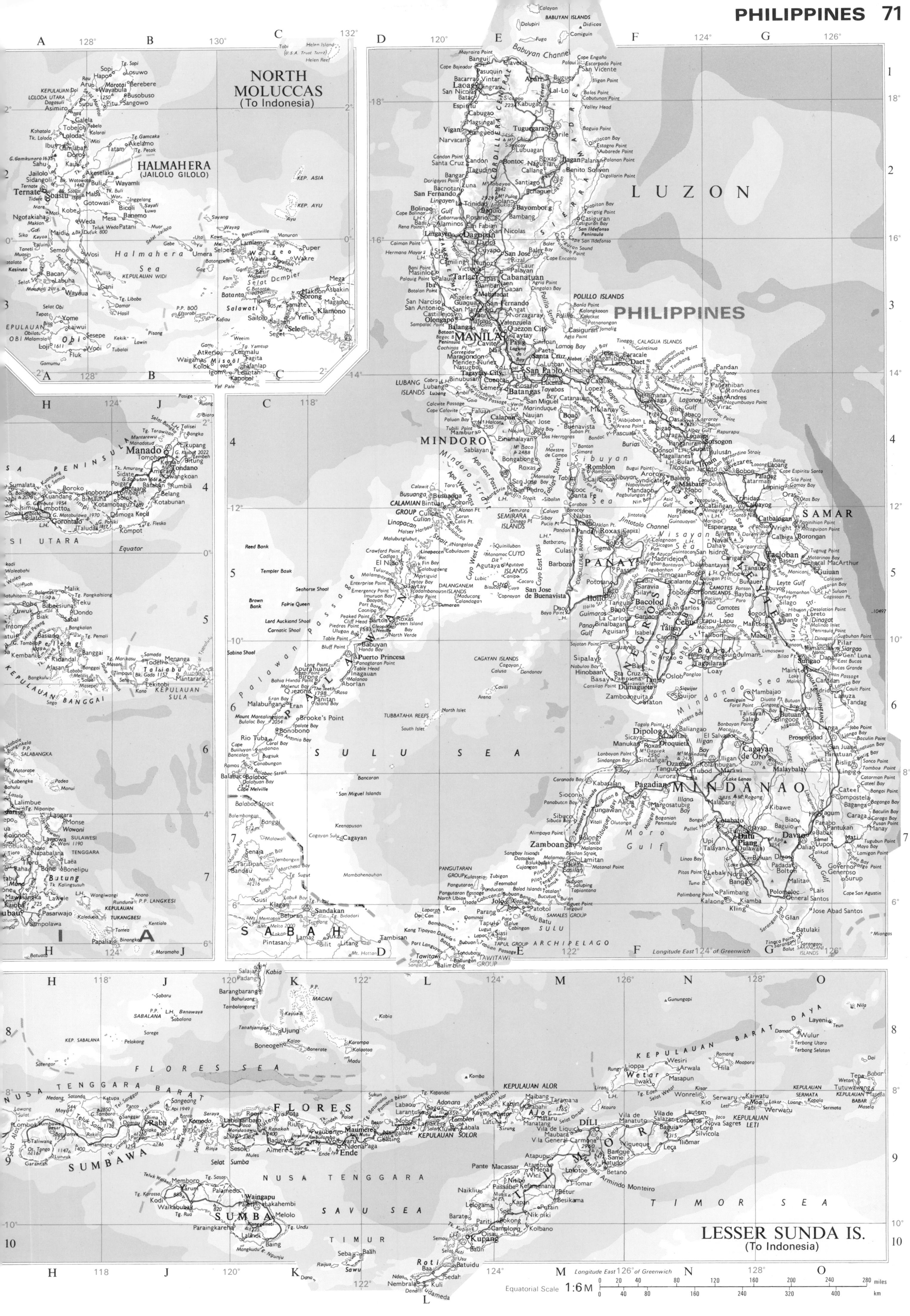
NORTH MOLUCCAS
(To Indonesia)
HALMAHERA
(JAILOLO GILOLO)
Halmahera Sea
LUZON
PHILIPPINES
MINDORO
PANAY
SAMAR
MINDANAO
SULU SEA
SABAH
SULU ARCHIPELAGO
MANILA
FLORES SEA
FLORES
SUMBAWA
SUMBA
NUSA TENGGARA
SAVU SEA
TIMOR SEA
LESSER SUNDA IS.
(To Indonesia)
Longitude East 124° of Greenwich
Longitude East 126° of Greenwich
Equatorial Scale 1:6M

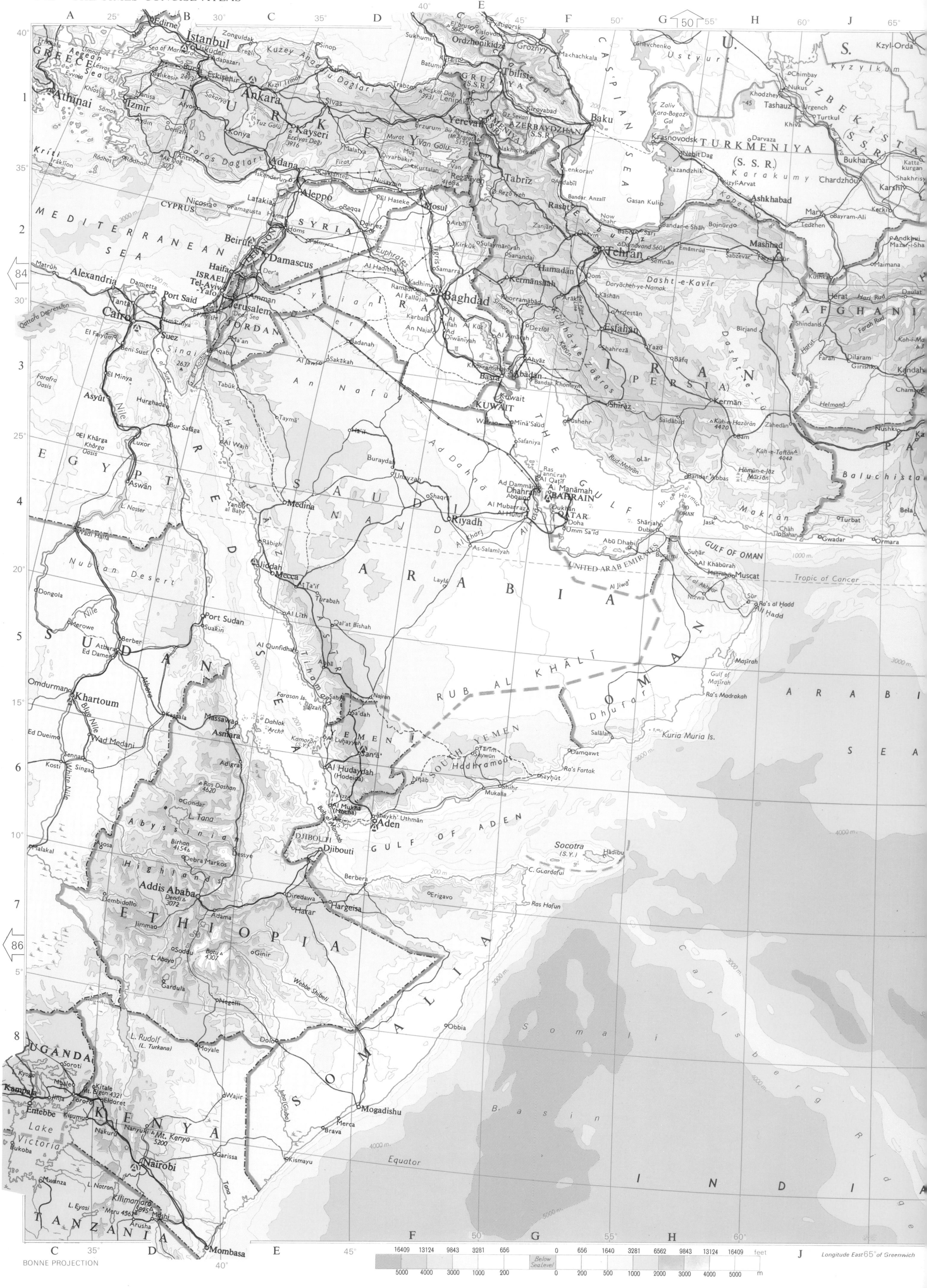
MEDITERRANEAN SEA
GREECE
TURKEY
CYPRUS
SYRIA
LEBANON
ISRAEL
JORDAN
IRAQ
IRAN (PERSIA)
KUWAIT
BAHRAIN
QATAR
UNITED ARAB EMIRATES
OMAN
GULF OF OMAN
THE GULF
SAUDI ARABIA
YEMEN
SOUTH YEMEN
DJIBOUTI
GULF OF ADEN
ARABIAN SEA
EGYPT
SUDAN
ETHIOPIA
SOMALIA
KENYA
UGANDA
TANZANIA
AFGHANISTAN
U.S.S.R.
TURKMENIYA (S.S.R.)
UZBEKISTAN S.S.R.
AZERBAYDZHAN (S.S.R.)
CASPIAN SEA
INDIAN OCEAN
Somali Basin
Carlsberg Ridge
Rub al Khālī
An Nafūd
Syrian Desert
Nubian Desert
Abyssinian Highlands
Tropic of Cancer
Equator
İstanbul
Ankara
Athínai
İzmir
Adana
Aleppo
Beirut
Damascus
Baghdad
Tehrān
Alexandria
Cairo
Port Said
Suez
Jerusalem
Tel-Aviv-Yafo
Amman
Mosul
Basra
Kuwait
Riyadh
Medina
Mecca
Jiddah
Doha
Muscat
Aden
Ṣan'ā'
Khartoum
Port Sudan
Djibouti
Addis Ababa
Mogadishu
Nairobi
Mombasa
Kampala
Baku
Tbilisi
Yerevan
Mashhad
Eşfahān
Shīrāz
Socotra
Lake Victoria
BONNE PROJECTION
Longitude East 65° of Greenwich

1:15M
0 100 200 400 600 800 1000 1200 1400 km
0 50 100 200 300 400 500 600 700 800 miles

Heights and Depths in metres

© John Bartholomew & Son Ltd Edinburgh

U.S.S.R.
AFG
CHINA
PAK
KASHMIR
Continued on the same scale
AFGHANISTAN
PAKISTAN
BALUCHISTAN
SIND
N.W. FRONTIER PROV.
PUNJAB
JAMMU AND KASHMIR
NORTHERN AREAS
HIMACHAL PRADESH
HARYANA
RAJASTHAN
GUJARAT
MADHYA PRADESH
MAHARASHTRA
UTTAR PRADESH
ANDHRA
INDIA
THAR OR INDIAN DESERT
Rann of Kutch
Tropic of Cancer
Gulf of Kutch
Gulf of Cambay (Khambat)
Aravalli Range
Malwa Plateau
Satpura Range
Mahadeo Hills
Satmala Hills
Gir Hills
Karakoram Range
Ladakh Range
Pir Panjal Range
Salt Range
Sulaiman Range
Mouths of the Indus
ISLAMABAD
DELHI
Kandahar
Quetta
Peshawar
Rawalpindi
Srinagar
Jammu
Lahore
Amritsar
Multan
Faisalabad
Hyderabad
Karachi
Sukkur
Jacobabad
Bahawalpur
Bikaner
Jodhpur
Jaipur
Ajmer
Agra
Gwalior
Lucknow
Kanpur
Bhopal
Indore
Ujjain
Jabalpur
Nagpur
Ahmadabad
Vadodara (Baroda)
Rajkot
Surat
Bombay
Poona
Nasik
Aurangabad
Sholapur
Secunderabad
Hyderabad
Diu (Goa Daman & Diu)
Daman (G.D. & D.)
Dadra & Nagar Haveli
K2 8611 (Godwin Austen)
Nanga Parbat 8126
Rakaposhi 7788
Kamet 7756
Nanda Devi 7817
IRAN
AFGHAN.
BALUCHISTAN
PAKISTAN
Continued on the same scale
77
76
ALBERS CONIC PROJECTION
1000 200 0 200 500 1000 1500 3000 4500 6000 m
3281 656 0 656 1640 3281 4921 9843 14763 19686 feet

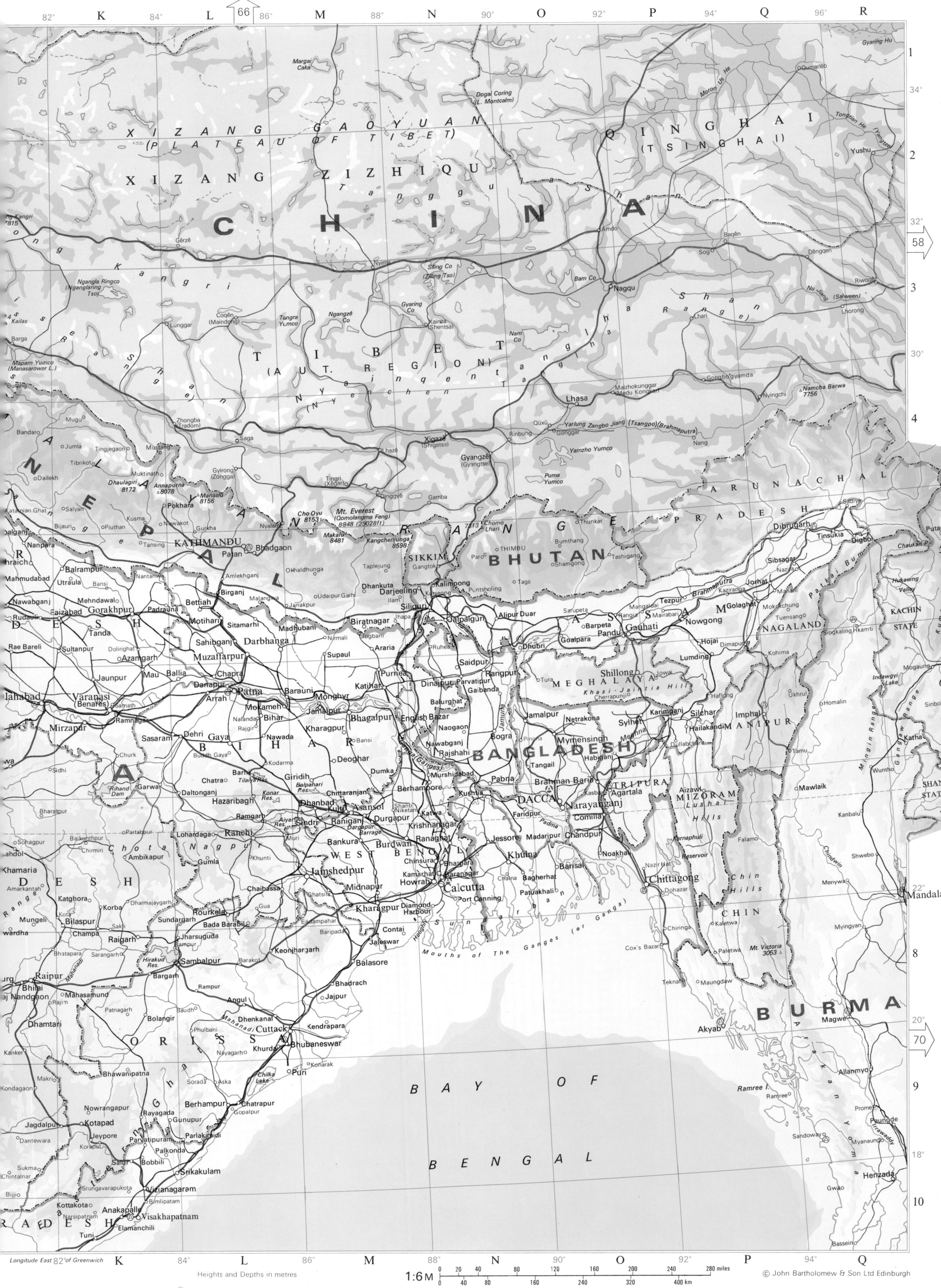
X I Z A N G G A O Y U A N
(P L A T E A U O F T I B E T)
X I Z A N G Z I Z H I Q U
C H I N A
Q I N G H A I
(T S I N G H A I)
T I B E T
(A U T. R E G I O N)
Lhasa
Nagqu
Xigazê
Gyangzê
Mt. Everest
KATHMANDU
N E P A L
SIKKIM
Gangtok
BHUTAN
THIMBU
A R U N A C H A L P R A D E S H
Dibrugarh
Gauhati
Shillong
M E G H A L A Y A
NAGALAND
MANIPUR
Imphal
MIZORAM
TRIPURA
Agartala
BANGLADESH
DACCA
Chittagong
Khulna
Calcutta
WEST BENGAL
B I H A R
Patna
Ranchi
Jamshedpur
O R I S S A
Cuttack
Bhubaneswar
Puri
Varanasi
(Benares)
Gorakhpur
Visakhapatnam
Mouths of The Ganges (or Ganga)
B A Y O F B E N G A L
B U R M A
Mandalay
Akyab
Henzada
KACHIN STATE
SHAN STATE
Mt. Victoria 3053
58
70
66

© John Bartholomew & Son Ltd Edinburgh

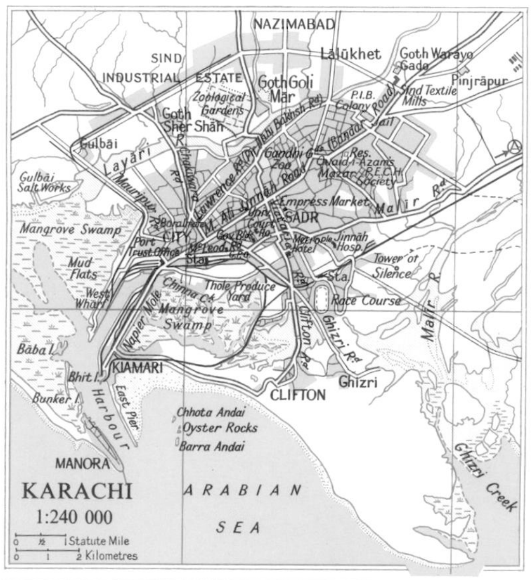
KARACHI
1:240 000
ARABIAN SEA
NAZIMABAD
SADR
CLIFTON
KIAMARI
MANORA
Mangrove Swamp
Chhota Andai Oyster Rocks
Barra Andai
Ghizri Creek

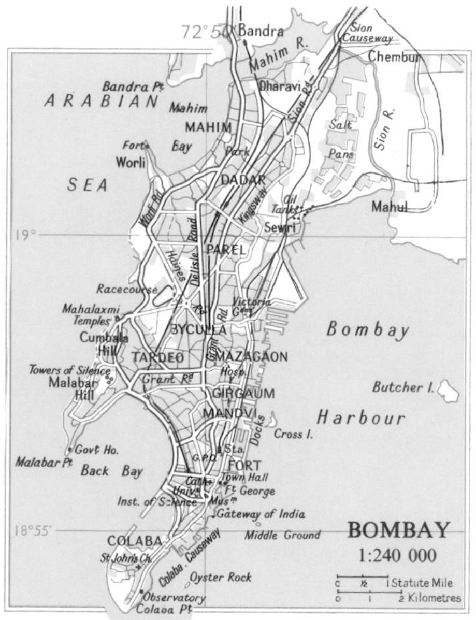
BOMBAY
1:240 000
ARABIAN SEA
Bombay Harbour
Back Bay
MAHIM
DADAR
PAREL
BYCULLA
MAZAGAON
FORT
COLABA
Butcher I.
Cross I.
Gateway of India
Chembur

DELHI
1:240 000
NEW DELHI
Shakurpur
Madipur
Shastrinagar
Karol Bagh
New Cantonment
Palam International Airport
Wazirabad

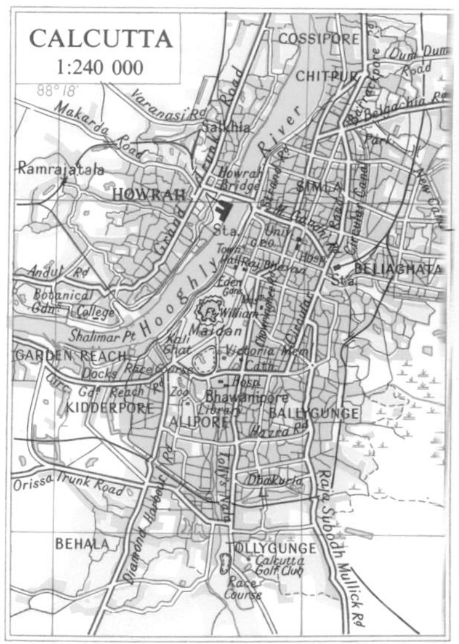
CALCUTTA
1:240 000
HOWRAH
COSSIPORE
CHITPUR
SIMLA
BELIAGHATA
GARDEN REACH
KIDDERPORE
ALIPORE
BEHALA
TOLLYGUNGE

MADHYA PRADESH
ORISSA
MAHARASHTRA
KARNATAKA
ANDHRA PRADESH
TAMIL NADU
KERALA
Bombay
Poona
Hyderabad
Secunderabad
Bangalore
Madras
Mysore
Madurai
Coimbatore
Cochin
Trivandrum
Vijayawada
Visakhapatnam
Cuttack
Bhubaneswar
Nagpur
Sholapur
Kolhapur
Belgaum
Hubli
Mangalore
Calicut
Tiruchirapalli
Salem
Pondicherry
Nellore
Guntur
Kakinada
Rajahmundry
Goa
Panaji
LAKSHADWEEP (Laccadive Islands)
Laccadive, Minicoy and Amindivi Islands (India)
Nine Degree Channel
Eight Degree Channel
MALDIVES
SRI LANKA (CEYLON)
COLOMBO
Kandy
Jaffna
Trincomalee
Palk Strait
Gulf of Manaar
Cape Comorin
ANDAMAN ISLANDS
NICOBAR ISLANDS
North Andaman
Middle Andaman
South Andaman
Port Blair
Little Andaman
Ten Degree Channel
Car Nicobar
Great Nicobar
on the same scale
1:6M

Heights and Depths in metres

ALBERS CONIC PROJECTION

© John Bartholomew & Son Ltd Edinburgh

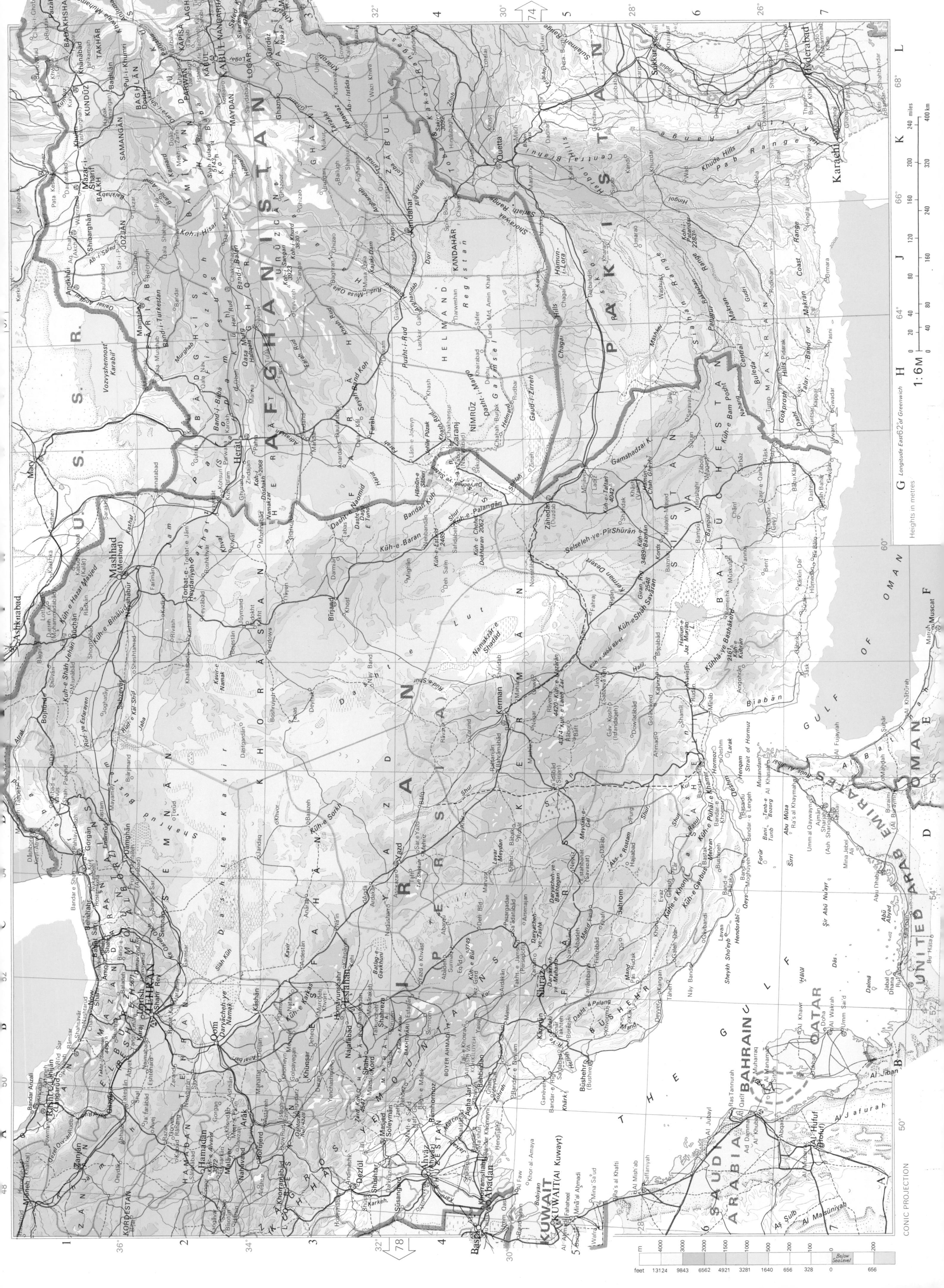
AFGHANISTAN
IRAN
PAKISTAN
U. S. S. R.
KUWAIT
SAUDI ARABIA
BAHRAIN
QATAR
UNITED ARAB EMIRATES
OMAN
GULF OF OMAN
THE GULF
TEHRAN
Mashhad (Meshed)
Herāt
Kandahār
Kabul
Quetta
Karachi
Hyderabad
Eşfahān
Shīrāz
Kerman
Zāhedān
Yazd
Dasht-e Kavīr
Dasht-e Lut
1:6M
Heights in metres
Longitude East 62° of Greenwich
CONIC PROJECTION
m 4000 3000 2000 1500 1000 500 200 100 0 Below Sea Level 200
feet 13124 9843 6562 4921 3281 1640 656 328 0 656
0 40 80 120 160 200 240 miles
0 20 40 80 160 240 320 400 km
74
78

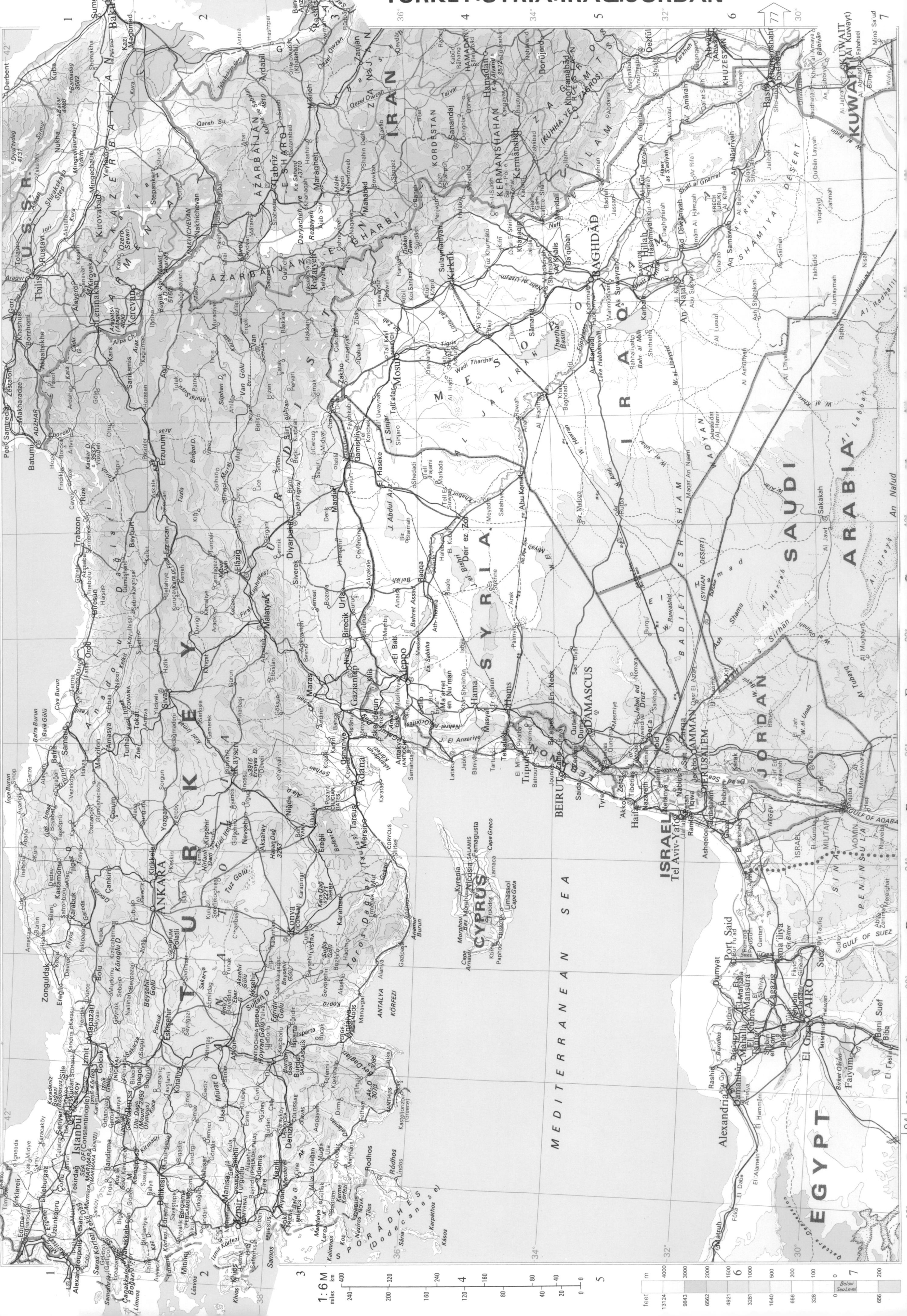
TURKEY
SYRIA
IRAQ
JORDAN
ISRAEL
SAUDI ARABIA
EGYPT
IRAN
U.S.S.R.
KUWAIT
CYPRUS
MEDITERRANEAN SEA
ANKARA
BAGHDAD
DAMASCUS
AMMAN
JERUSALEM
BEIRUT
CAIRO
Istanbul
Izmir
Adana
Aleppo
Mosul
Kirkuk
Homs
Hama
Tel Aviv-Yafo
Alexandria
Port Said
Suez
GULF OF AQABA
GULF OF SUEZ
1:6M

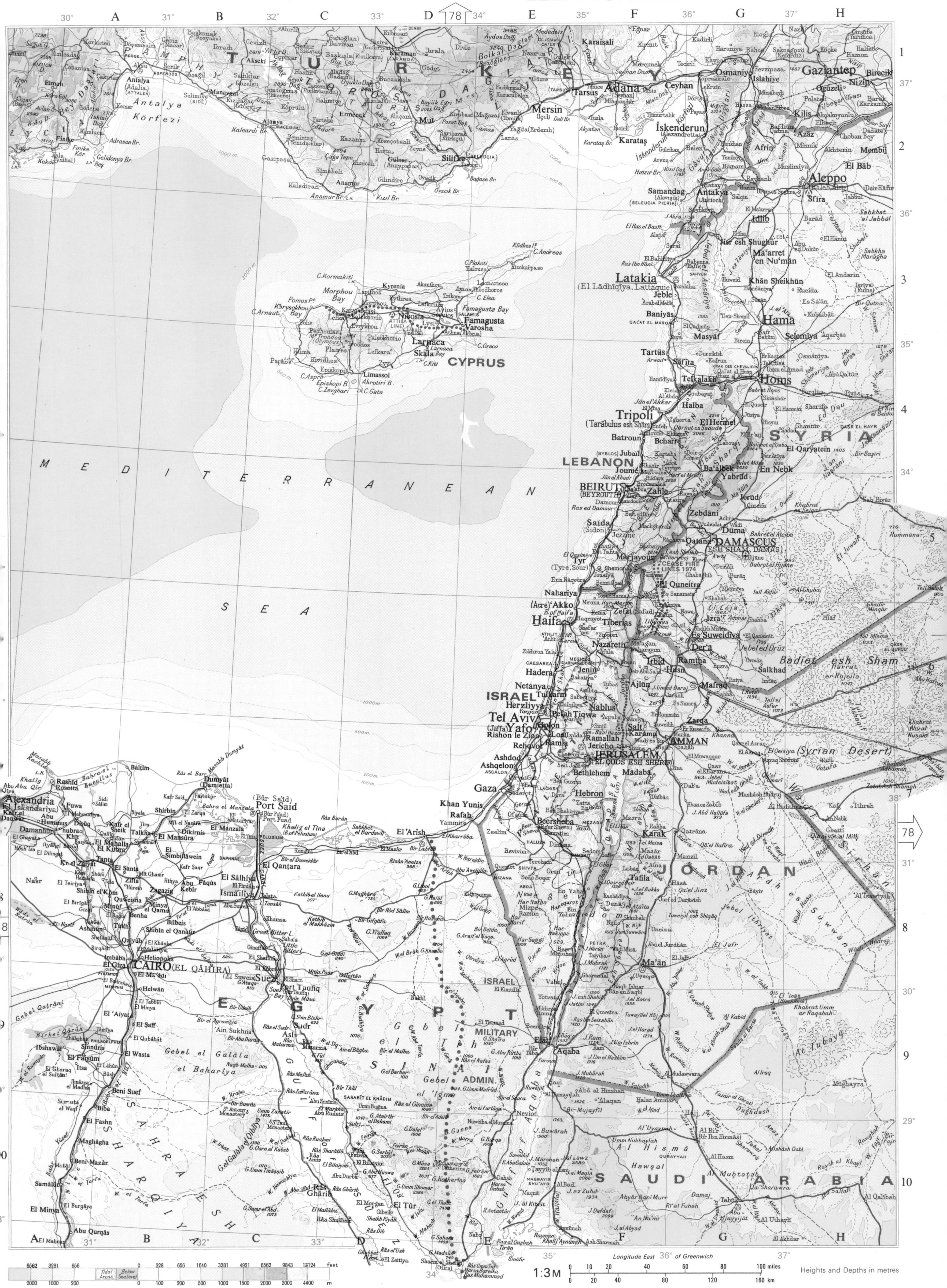
MEDITERRANEAN SEA
TURKEY
CYPRUS
LEBANON
SYRIA
ISRAEL
JORDAN
EGYPT
SAUDI ARABIA
Antalya Körfezi
Gulf of Suez
Gulf of Aqaba
Dead Sea
Sinai
Badiet esh Sham
Adana
Mersin
Tarsus
Antalya
Iskenderun
Antakya
Aleppo
Gaziantep
Latakia
Hama
Homs
Tripoli
Beirut
Saida
Tyr
Damascus
Haifa
Akko
Nazareth
Tiberias
Tel Aviv Yafo
Jerusalem
Amman
Gaza
Beersheba
Hebron
Ma'an
Aqaba
Elat
Port Said
Ismâ'ilîya
Suez
Cairo
Alexandria
Nicosia
Famagusta
Larnaca
Limassol
Kyrenia
El 'Arish
Tabuk
ISRAEL MILITARY ADMIN.
CEASE FIRE LINES 1974
Longitude East 36° of Greenwich
1:3M
Heights and Depths in metres
Tidal Areas
Below Sea Level
0 10 20 40 60 80 100 miles
0 20 40 80 120 160 km
6562 3281 656 0 328 656 1640 3281 4921 6562 9843 13124 feet
2000 1000 200 0 100 200 500 1000 1500 2000 3000 4000 m

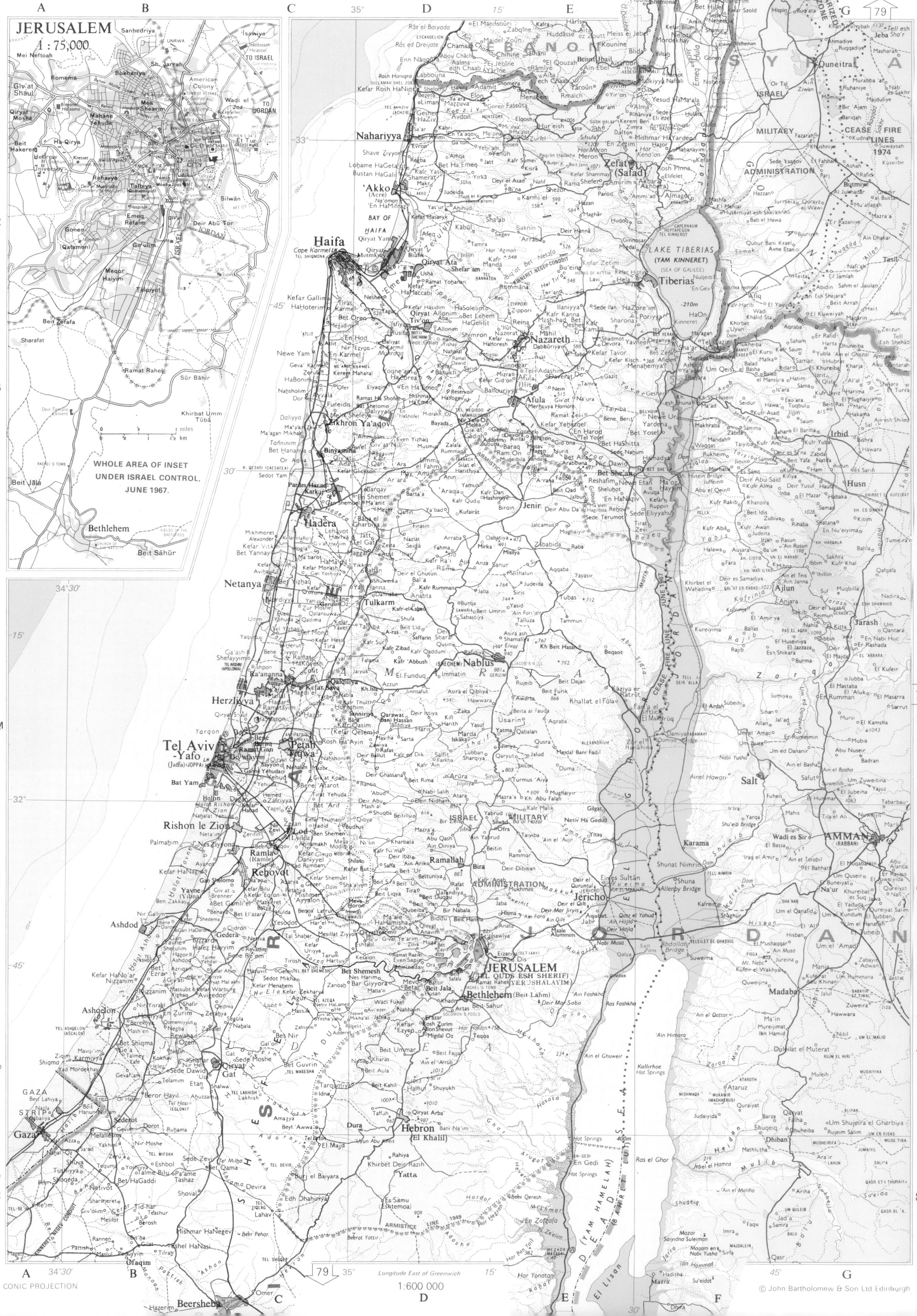
JERUSALEM
1 : 75,000
WHOLE AREA OF INSET UNDER ISRAEL CONTROL, JUNE 1967.
Bethlehem
LEBANON
SYRIA
DEMILITARIZED ZONE
ISRAEL MILITARY ADMINISTRATION
CEASE FIRE LINES 1974
Nahariyya
'Akko (Acre)
BAY OF HAIFA
Haifa
Zefat (Safad)
LAKE TIBERIAS (YAM KINNERET) (SEA OF GALILEE)
Tiberias
Nazareth
Afula
Irbid
Hadera
Netanya
Tulkarm
Nablus
Herzliyya
Tel Aviv -Yafo (Jaffa) (JOPPA)
Bat Yam
Rishon le Zion
Ramla
Rehovot
Ashdod
Ashqelon
GAZA STRIP
Gaza
Jericho
Salt
AMMAN (RABBAH)
Madaba
JERUSALEM (EL QUDS ESH SHERIF) (YERUSHALAYIM)
Bethlehem (Beit Lahm)
Hebron (El Khalil)
Beersheba
JORDAN
DEAD SEA (YAM HAMELAH) (BAHRET LUT)
ISRAEL MILITARY ADMINISTRATION
ARMISTICE LINE 1949
1:0.6M
miles km
feet m
CONIC PROJECTION
Longitude East of Greenwich
1:600 000
79
© John Bartholomew & Son Ltd Edinburgh

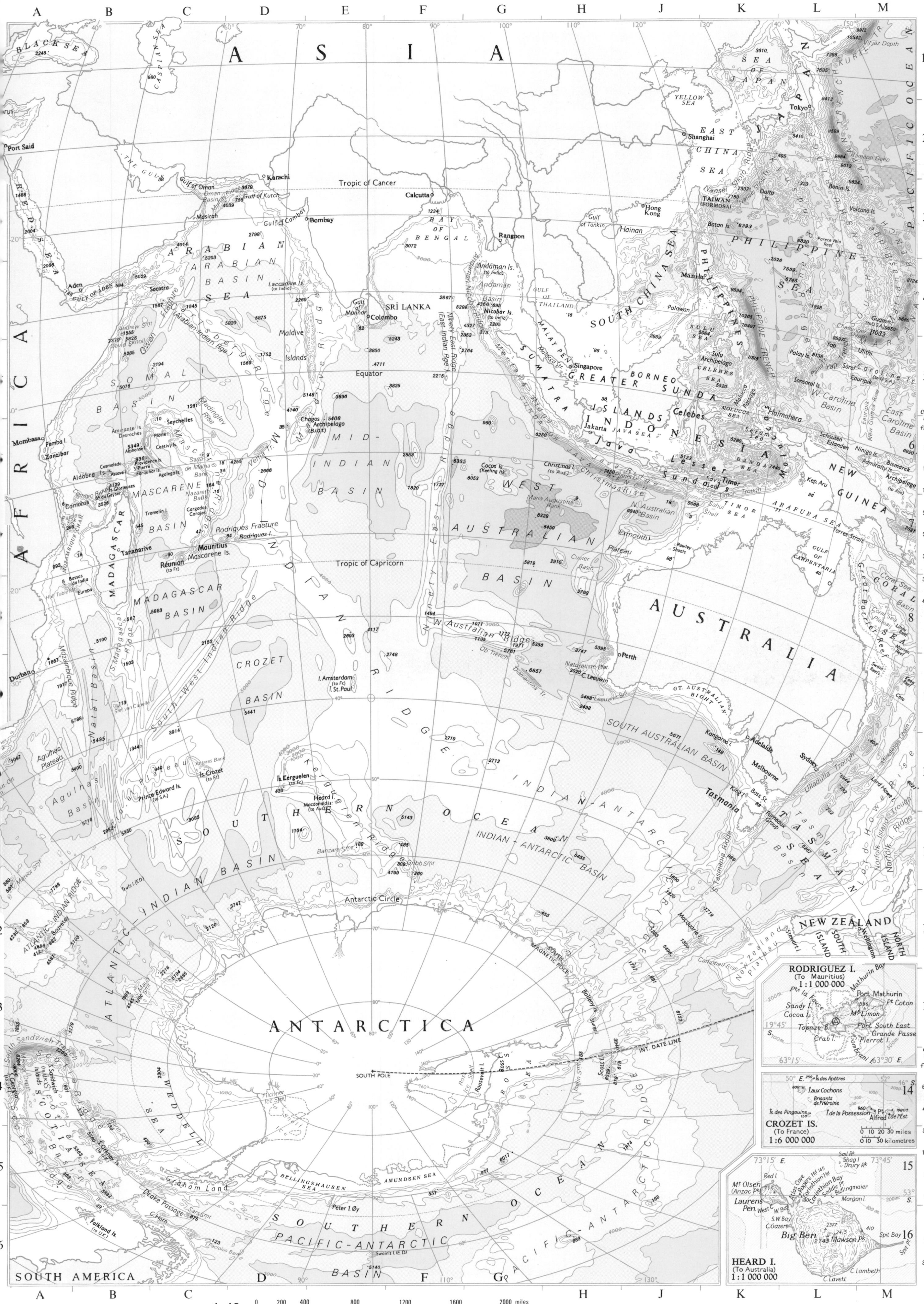

OBLIQUE AZIMUTHAL EQUAL AREA PROJECTION 1:48M 0 200 400 800 1200 1600 2000 miles 0 400 800 1600 2400 3200 km

Heights and Depths in metres

A
B
C
D
E
F
G
1
2
3
4
5
6
7
20°
10°
0°
30°
40°
MEDITERRANEAN SEA
GULF OF GUINEA
Equator
SOUTH ATLANTIC OCEAN
Tropic of Cancer
Tropic of Capricorn
SAHARA
LIBYAN DESERT
KALAHARI DESERT
MOROCCO
ALGERIA
TUNISIA
LIBYA
EGYPT
MAURITANIA
MALI
NIGER
CHAD
SUDAN
SENEGAL
THE GAMBIA
GUINEA-BISSAU
GUINEA
SIERRA LEONE
LIBERIA
IVORY COAST
UPPER VOLTA
GHANA
TOGO
BENIN
NIGERIA
CAMEROON
CENTRAL AFRICAN REPUBLIC
EQUAT. GUINEA
GABON
CONGO
ZAIRE
UGANDA
KENYA
RWANDA
BURUNDI
TANZANIA
ANGOLA
ZAMBIA
MALAWI
MOZAMBIQUE
ZIMBABWE (RHODESIA)
BOTSWANA
NAMIBIA (S.W. AFRICA)
REPUBLIC OF SOUTH AFRICA
LESOTHO
SWAZI.
ETHIOPIA
ERITREA
SPAIN
PORTUGAL
ITALY
GREECE
TURKEY
SYRIA
IRAQ
JORDAN
LEBANON
CYPRUS
BULGARIA
ALB.
YUG.
SAUDI ARABIA
SAO TOME & PRINCIPE
Madeira (Port.)
Funchal
Las Palmas
ISLAS CANARIAS (Sp.)
Ascension (UK)
ST. HELENA (UK)
Lisboa
Madrid
Barcelona
Valencia
Córdoba
Sevilla
Málaga
Tanger (Tangier)
Tétouan
Gibraltar (UK)
Rabat
Casablanca
Fès
Meknès
Marrakech
Sidi Ifni
Alger
Oran
Constantine
Annaba
Bizerte
Tunis
Sousse
Sfax
Roma
Napoli
Palermo
SICILIA
SARDEGNA
CORSE
MALTA
KRITI
Athínai
Istanbul
Izmir
Ankara
Antalya
Adana
Rodhos
Nicosia
Beirut (Beyrouth)
Damascus
Haifa
Tel-Aviv Yafo
Jerusalem
Amman
Aleppo
Mosul
Baghdad
Tripoli (Tarābulus)
Benghāzi
Al Bayḍā
Alexandria
Cairo
Pt Said
Suez
El Faiyûm
Asyût
Aswân
Medina
Jiddah
Mecca
Pt Sudan
Atbara
Ed Damer
Kassala
Omdurman
Khartoum
Wad Medani
El Obeid
El Fasher
Nyala
Muglad
Malakal
Wau
Juba
Asmara
Massawa
Gondar
Dessye
Diredawa
Addis Ababa
Jimma
Dakhla
Nouadhibou (Port Etienne)
Nouakchott
St Louis
Dakar
Banjul
Bissau
Conakry
Freetown
Monrovia
Buchanan
Kayes
Bamako
Ségou
Tombouctou
Bobo Dioulasso
Ouagadougou
Niamey
Zinder
Agadès
Tamanrasset
HOGGAR
In Salah
Ghudāmis
Ghat
Sabhah
Marzūq
Zelten
TIBESTI
Emi Koussi
L. Chad
N'Djamena
Sarh
Kano
Kaduna
Maiduguri
Nguru
Kaura Namoda
Parakou
Ilorin
Ogbomosho
Ibadan
Lagos
Porto Novo
Lomé
Accra
Kumasi
Tamale
Takoradi
Abidjan
Bouaké
Onitsha
Enugu
Pt Harcourt
Douala
Yaoundé
Ngaoundere
Bouar
Bangui
Bambari
Malabo
Bata
Libreville
Port Gentil
Lambaréné
Brazzaville
Kinshasa
Pointe Noire
Cabinda
Boma
Matadi
Mbandaka
Kisangani
Isiro
Bunia
Bandundu
Ilebo
Kananga
Lusambo
Kindu
Bukavu
Goma
Bujumbura
Kigoma
Kalémie
Kamina
Likasi
Lubumbashi
L. Albert
L. Edward
Lake Victoria
L. Kivu
Lake Tanganyika
L. Mweru
L. Bangweulu
L. Rudolf
Kampala
Entebbe
Gulu
Kisumu
Nairobi
Mt Kenya
Mt Elgon
Kilimanjaro
Arusha
Mwanza
Tabora
Dodoma
Mombasa
Tanga
Zanzibar
Dar es Salaam
Mbeya
Mbala
Lindi
Luanda
Uige
Malanje
Lobito
Benguela
Huambo
Bié
Moçâmedes
Lubango
Ndola
Kabwe
Lusaka
Kariba
Lake Kariba
Chipata
Lilongwe
Zomba
Blantyre
Limbe
Lichinga
Lake Nyasa
Nampula
Quelimane
Beira
Livingstone
Victoria Falls
Wankie
Salisbury
Umtali
Gwelo
Bulawayo
Francistown
Serowe
Gaborone
Mafeking
Pietersburg
Pretoria
Germiston
Johannesburg
Krugersdorp
Vereeniging
Springs
Kroonstad
Welkom
Kimberley
Bloemfontein
Maseru
Ladysmith
Pietermaritzburg
Durban
Maputo (Lourenço Marques)
Mbabane
Inhambane
Windhoek
Walvis Bay
Tsumeb
Etosha Pan
Lüderitz
Keetmanshoop
Beaufort West
GREAT KAROO
Queenstown
East London
Grahamstown
Port Elizabeth
Oudtshoorn
Mosselbaai
Worcester
Cape Town
Bassas da India (Reunion)
Europa (Reunion)
Nile
Niger
Benue
Zaire
Kasai
Cuanza
Cubango
Kunene
Orange
Limpopo
Zambezi
Ruvuma
feet
m
3281
1000
656
200
0
1:24 M
miles
km
960
1600
800
1280
640
960
480
640
320
320
160
160
80
0
7971
Meridian of 0° Greenwich

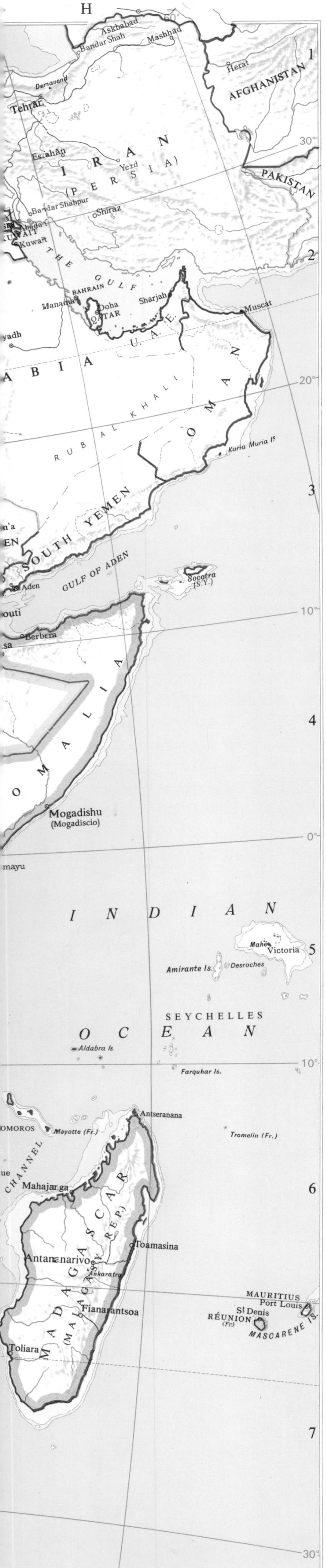

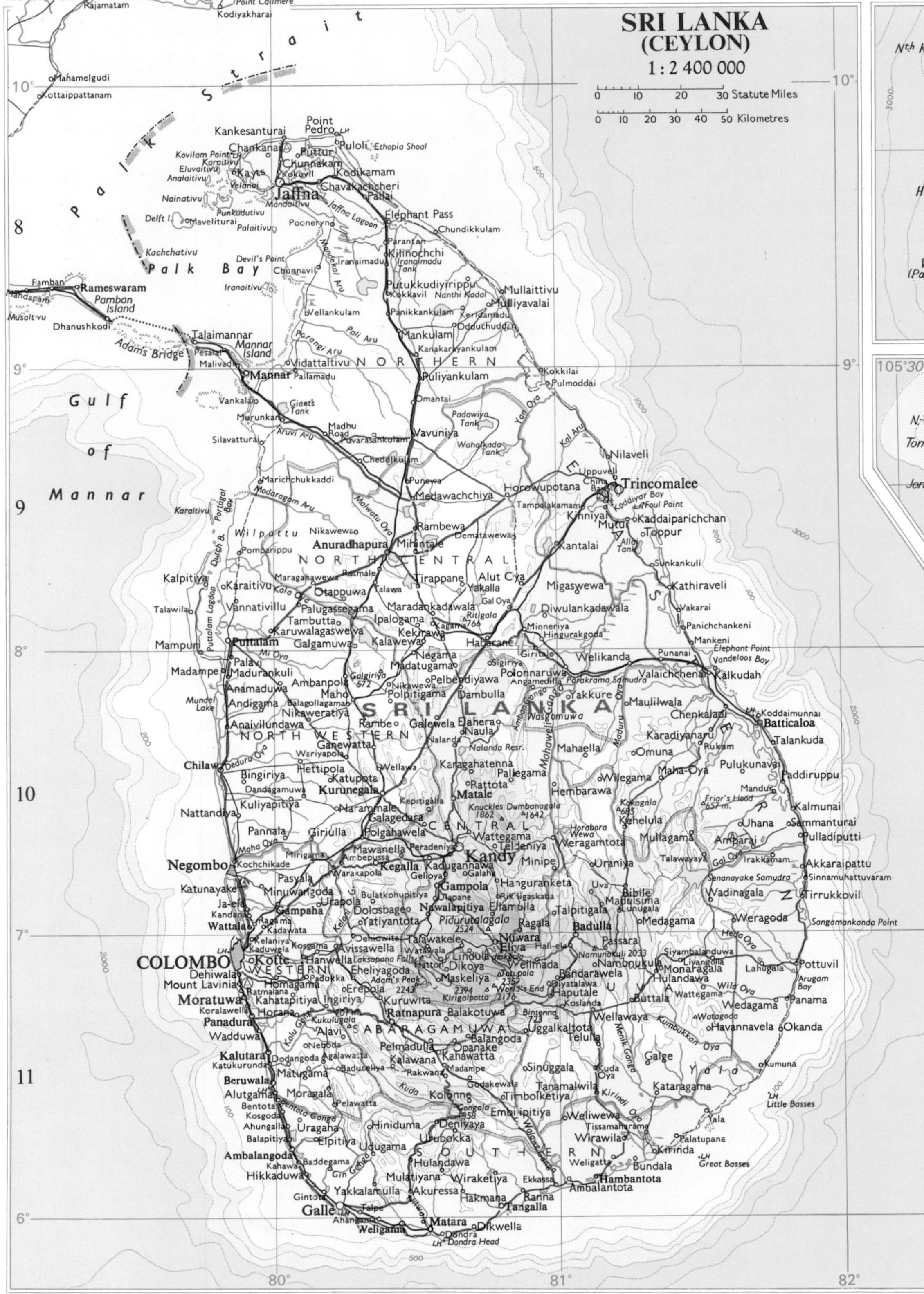

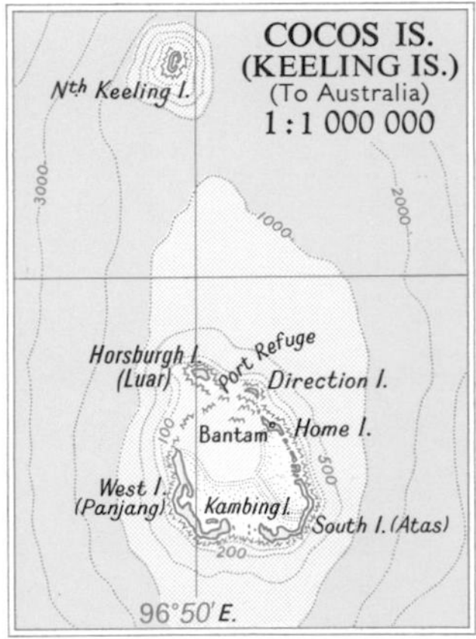

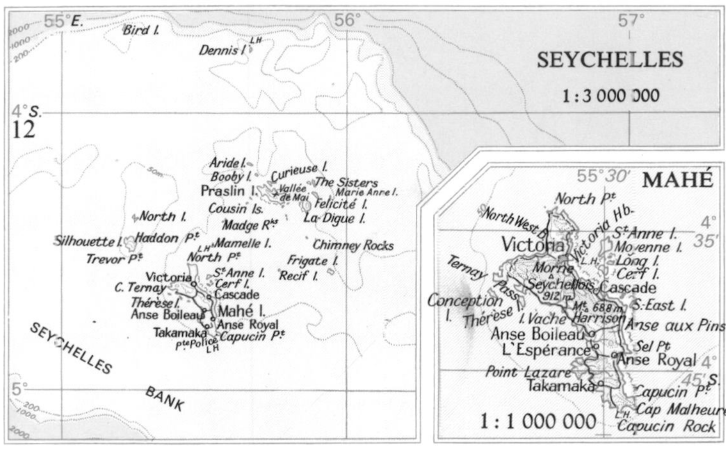

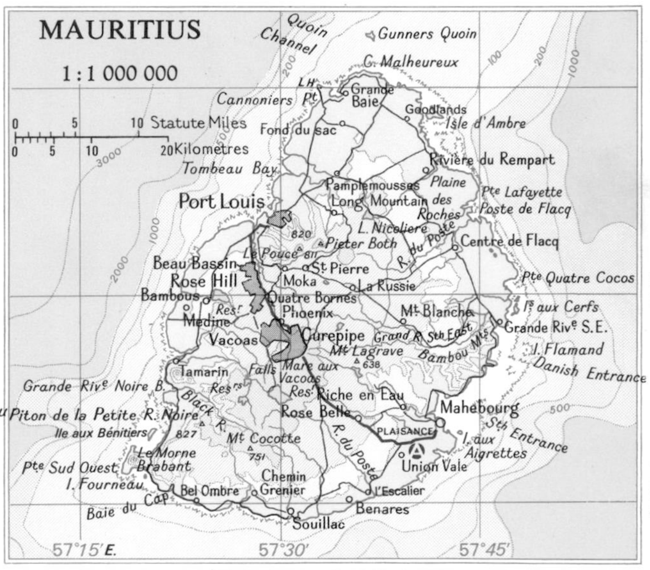

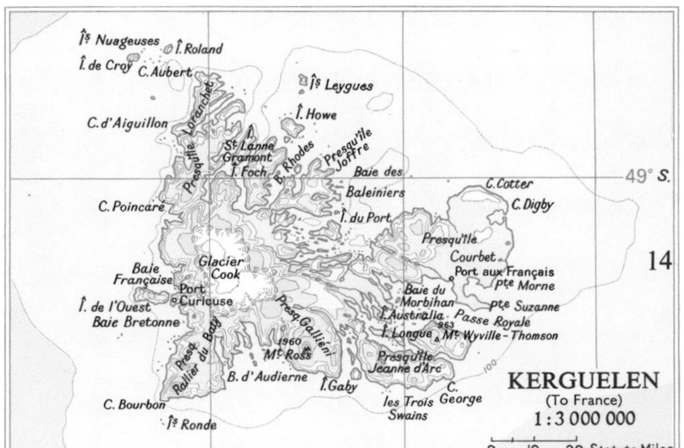

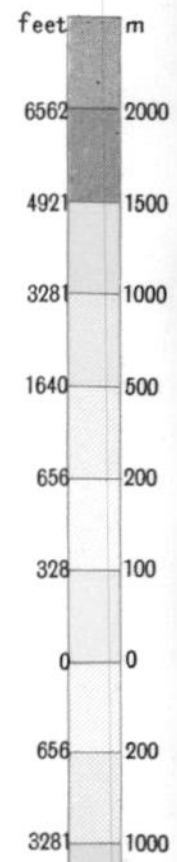

Heights in metres

© John Bartholomew & Son Ltd Edinburgh

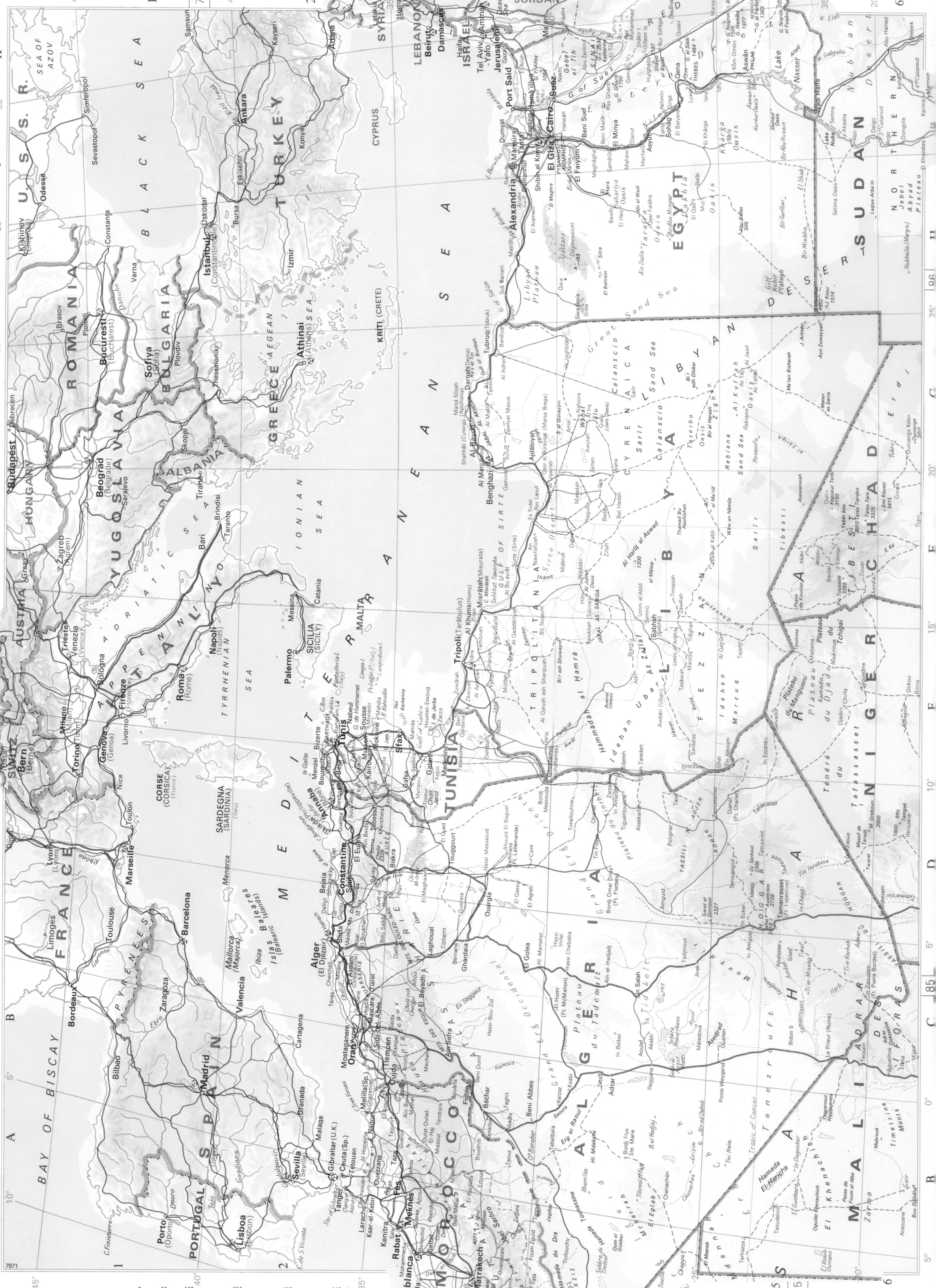

Heights in metres 1:12 M 0 80 160 320 480 640 km 0 40 80 160 240 320 400 miles

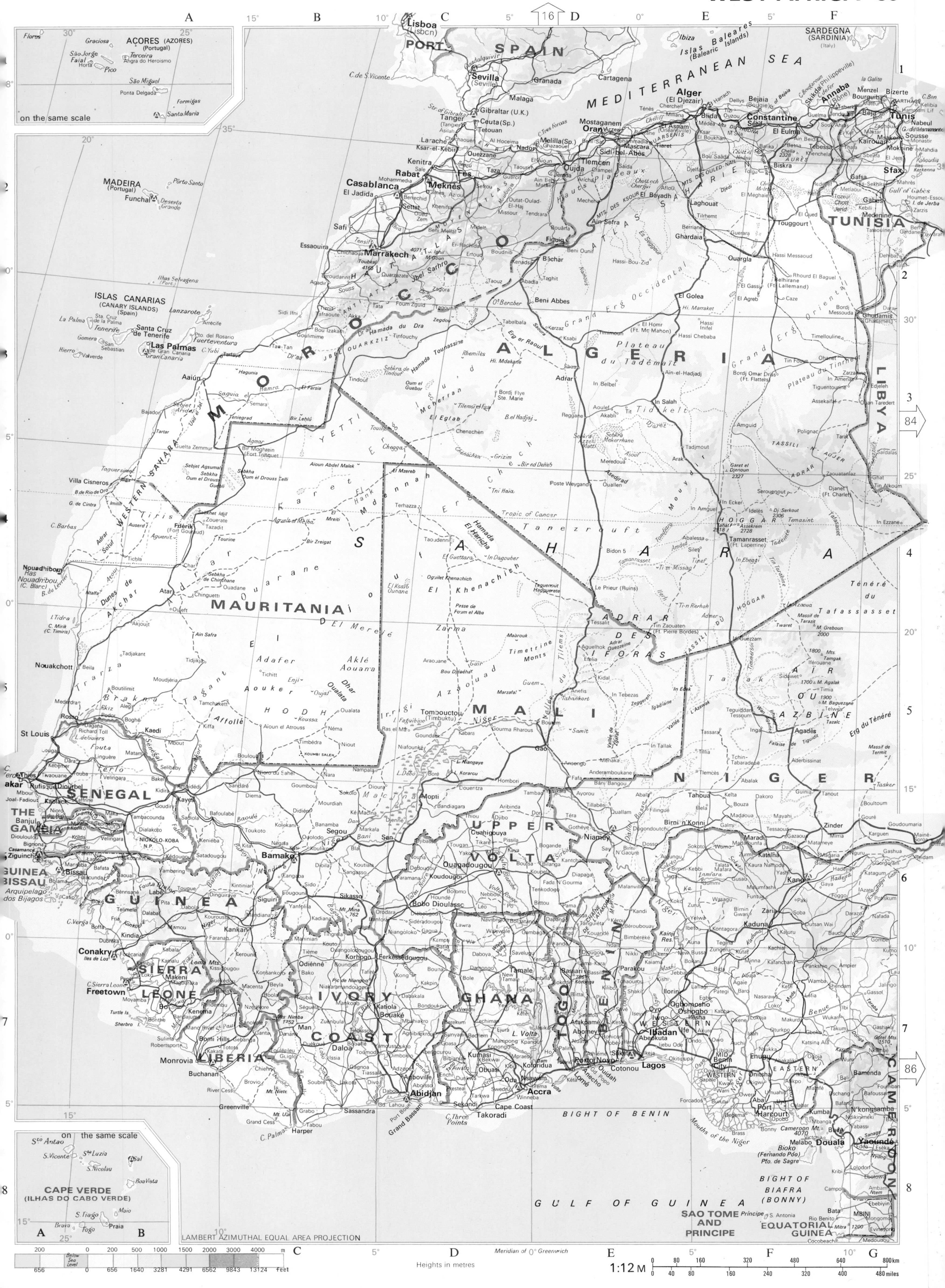
ACORES (AZORES) (Portugal)
on the same scale
MADEIRA (Portugal)
ISLAS CANARIAS (CANARY ISLANDS) (Spain)
Las Palmas
Santa Cruz de Tenerife
SPAIN
PORT.
Lisboa
Sevilla
Granada
Malaga
Gibraltar (U.K.)
MEDITERRANEAN SEA
Alger (El Djezair)
Oran
Constantine
Tunis
TUNISIA
LIBYA
Tanger
Rabat
Casablanca
Meknès
Fès
Marrakech
MOROCCO
ALGERIA
SAHARA
WESTERN SAHARA
MAURITANIA
MALI
NIGER
SENEGAL
THE GAMBIA
GUINEA BISSAU
GUINEA
SIERRA LEONE
LIBERIA
IVORY COAST
UPPER VOLTA
GHANA
TOGO
BENIN
NIGERIA
CAMEROON
Grand Erg Occidental
Grand Erg Oriental
Tanezrouft
HOGGAR
ADRAR DES IFORAS
AÏR OU AZBINE
Ténéré du Tafassasset
Tropic of Cancer
Nouakchott
St Louis
Dakar
Banjul
Bissau
Conakry
Freetown
Monrovia
Bamako
Ouagadougou
Niamey
Tombouctou (Timbuktu)
Abidjan
Accra
Lomé
Porto Novo
Lagos
Ibadan
Kano
Kaduna
Douala
Yaoundé
BIGHT OF BENIN
BIGHT OF BIAFRA (BONNY)
GULF OF GUINEA
SAO TOME AND PRINCIPE
EQUATORIAL GUINEA
CAPE VERDE (ILHAS DO CABO VERDE)
on the same scale
LAMBERT AZIMUTHAL EQUAL AREA PROJECTION
Meridian of 0° Greenwich
Heights in metres
1:12 M
84
86
16

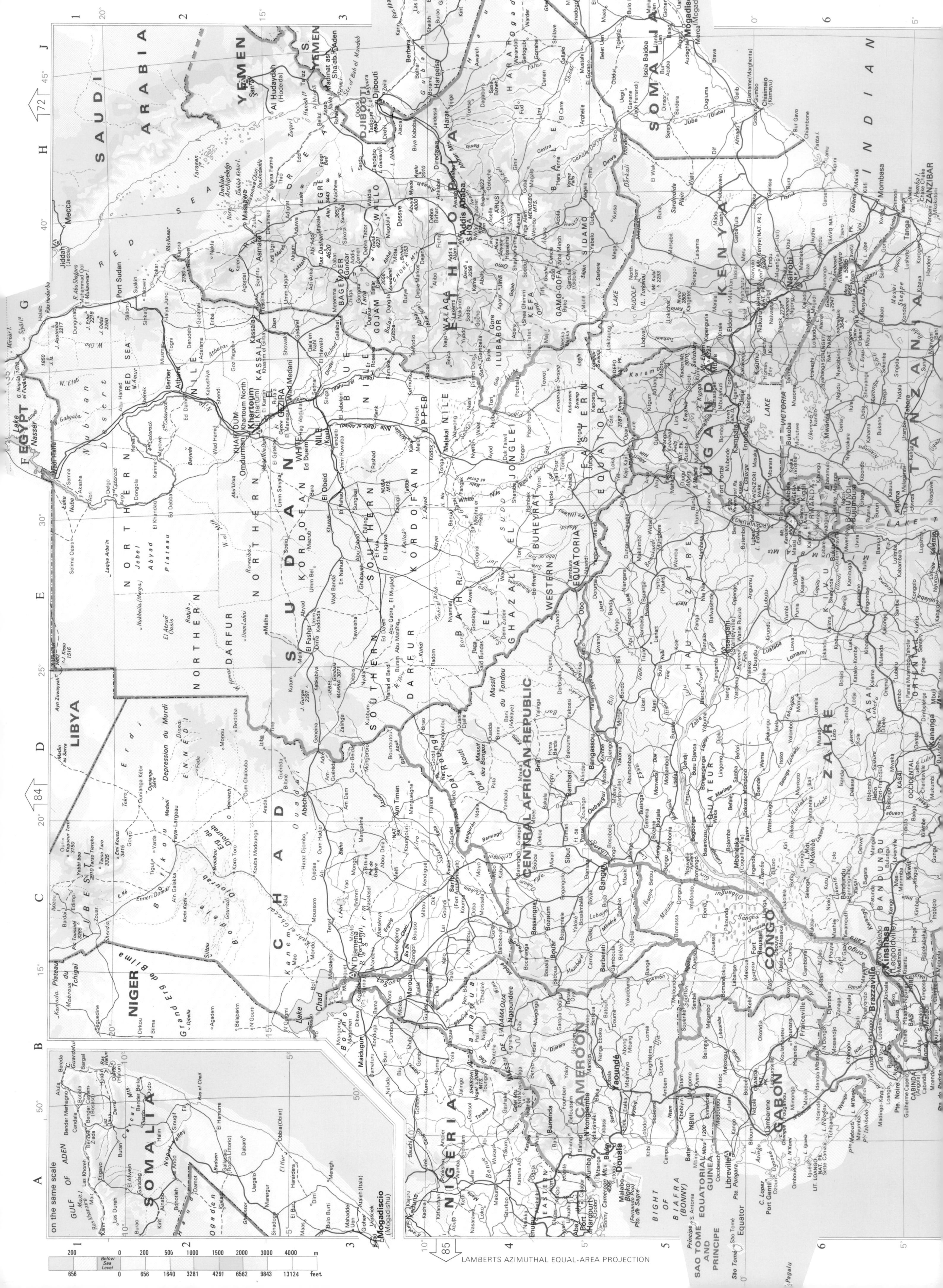
SAUDI ARABIA
YEMEN
EGYPT
LIBYA
NIGER
NIGERIA
CHAD
SUDAN
ETHIOPIA
DJIBOUTI
SOMALIA
KENYA
UGANDA
TANZANIA
RWANDA
BURUNDI
ZAIRE
CONGO
GABON
CAMEROON
CENTRAL AFRICAN REPUBLIC
EQUATORIAL GUINEA
SAO TOME AND PRINCIPE
RED SEA
GULF OF ADEN
INDIAN
Khartoum
Addis Ababa
Mogadiscio (Mogadishu)
Nairobi
Kampala
Kinshasa (Léopoldville)
Brazzaville
Bangui
N'Djamena (Fort Lamy)
Yaoundé
Libreville
Djibouti
Mecca
Jiddah (Jedda)
Port Sudan
Mombasa
ZANZIBAR
on the same scale
LAMBERTS AZIMUTHAL EQUAL-AREA PROJECTION
72
84
85
200 0 200 500 1000 1500 2000 3000 4000 m
Below Sea Level
656 0 656 1640 3281 4291 6562 9843 13124 feet

Heights in metres

1:12M 0 80 160 320 480 640 800 960 km
0 40 80 160 240 320 400 480 560 miles

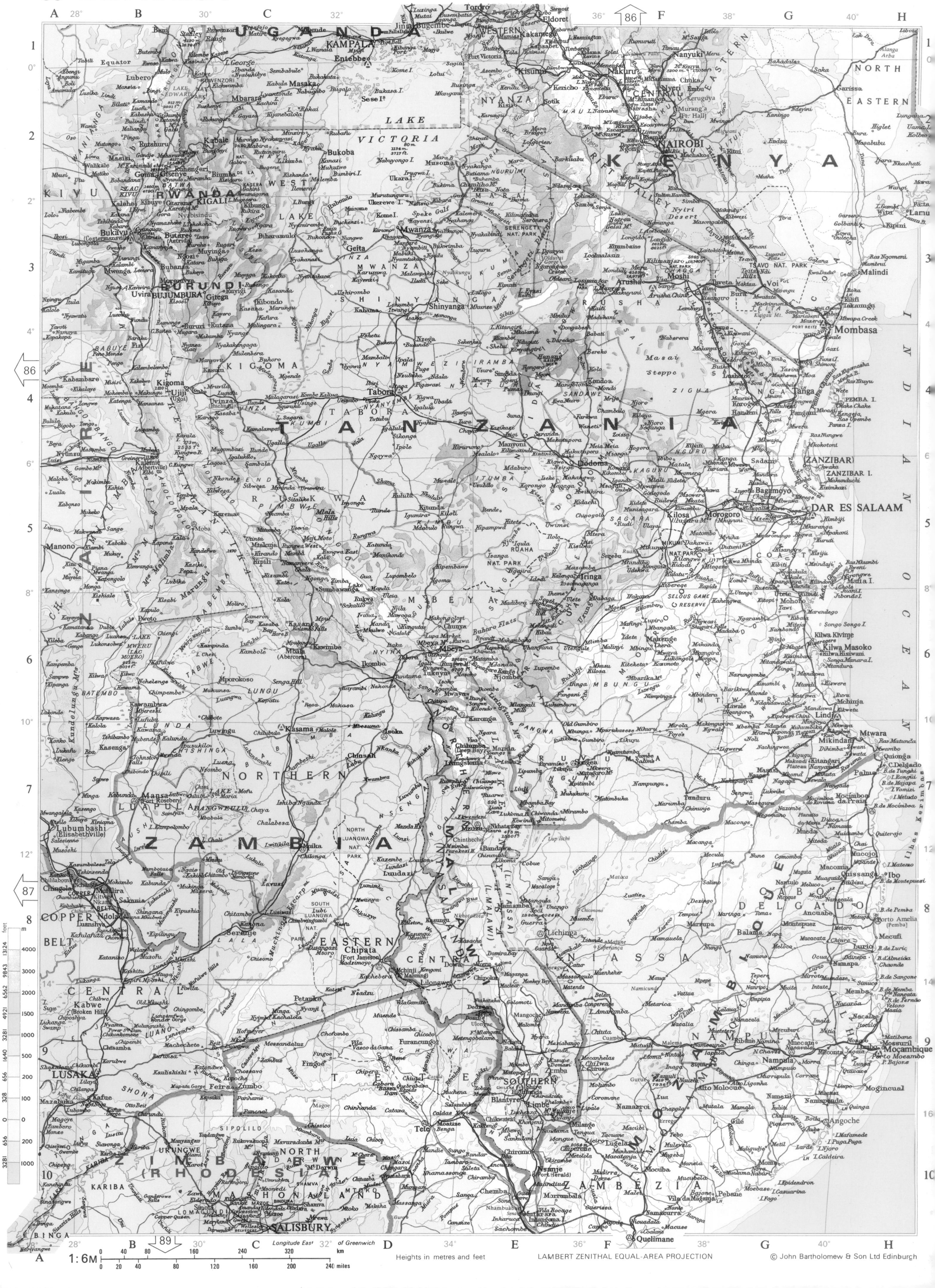
UGANDA
KENYA
TANZANIA
ZAMBIA
MALAWI
MOÇAMBIQUE
ZIMBABWE (RHODESIA)
RWANDA
BURUNDI
ZAÏRE
INDIAN OCEAN
LAKE VICTORIA
KAMPALA
Entebbe
NAIROBI
Mombasa
Tanga
Malindi
Dodoma
DAR ES SALAAM
ZANZIBAR
Morogoro
Tabora
Kigoma
Mwanza
Arusha
Moshi
Iringa
Mbeya
Lindi
Mtwara
KIGALI
BUJUMBURA
Bukavu
LUSAKA
Kabwe
Ndola
Lubumbashi (Elisabethville)
Kasama
Mansa (Fort Rosebery)
Chipata (Fort Jameson)
Lilongwe
Blantyre
Zomba
Tete
Quelimane
Nampula
Moçambique
SALISBURY
Heights in metres and feet
LAMBERT ZENITHAL EQUAL-AREA PROJECTION
© John Bartholomew & Son Ltd Edinburgh

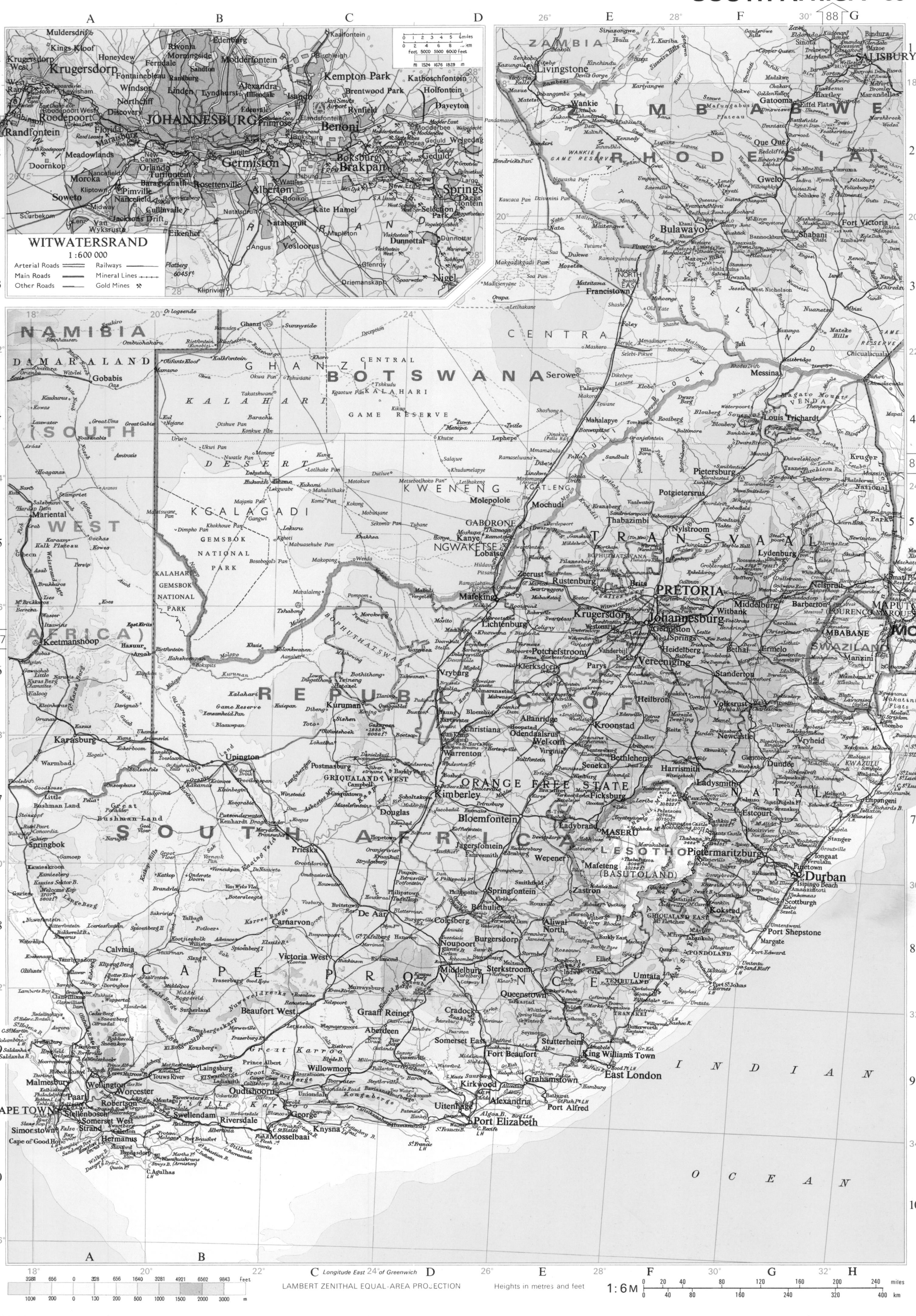
WITWATERSRAND
1:600 000
Arterial Roads
Main Roads
Other Roads
Railways
Mineral Lines
Gold Mines
JOHANNESBURG
Krugersdorp
Roodepoort
Randfontein
Germiston
Benoni
Boksburg
Brakpan
Springs
Kempton Park
Alberton
Soweto
Nigel
NAMIBIA
(SOUTH WEST AFRICA)
BOTSWANA
ZIMBABWE (RHODESIA)
ZAMBIA
REPUBLIC OF SOUTH AFRICA
TRANSVAAL
ORANGE FREE STATE
NATAL
CAPE PROVINCE
LESOTHO (BASUTOLAND)
SWAZILAND
MBABANE
MASERU
PRETORIA
Johannesburg
Bloemfontein
Kimberley
Durban
Pietermaritzburg
East London
Port Elizabeth
CAPE TOWN
SALISBURY
Bulawayo
Gaborone
MAPUTO (LOURENCO MARQUES)
KALAHARI DESERT
INDIAN OCEAN
Longitude East of Greenwich
LAMBERT ZENITHAL EQUAL-AREA PROJECTION
Heights in metres and feet
1:6M

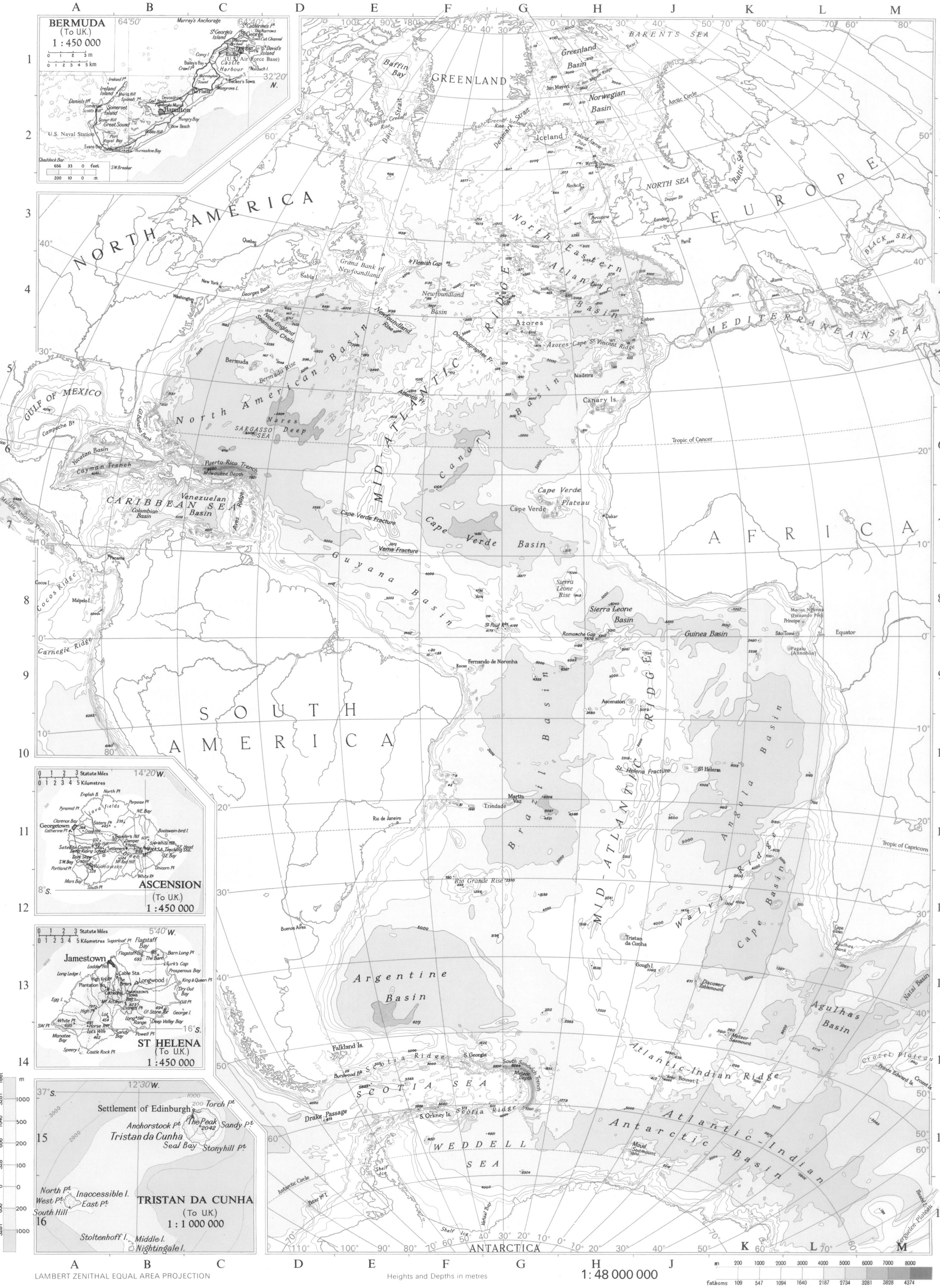

LAMBERT ZENITHAL EQUAL AREA PROJECTION

Heights and Depths in metres

1: 48 000 000

U.S.S.R.
ARCTIC OCEAN
North Pole
Severnaya Zemlya
Novosibirskiye Ostrova
Novaya Zemlya
Zemlya Frantsa Iosifa
Os. Vrangelya
SVALBARD (Nor.)
Moskva
BERING SEA
Bering Str.
ALEUTIAN ISLANDS
BEAUFORT SEA
QUEEN ELIZABETH ISLANDS
BAFFIN BAY
BAFFIN ISLAND
Davis Str.
Thule
GREENLAND
Søndre Strømfjord
Godthåb
Kap Farvel
Reykjavik
ICELAND
Jan Mayen
Arctic Circle
EUROPE
London
Paris
Madrid
Lisboa
U.S.A.
ALASKA
Yukon
Fairbanks
Mt. McKinley
Anchorage
GULF OF ALASKA
Juneau
Whitehorse
Mackenzie
Gt. Bear Lake
Yellowknife
Gt. Slave Lake
Prince Rupert
Queen Charlotte Is.
ROCKY MOUNTAINS
CANADA
Peace
Athabasca
Churchill
HUDSON BAY
Edmonton
Calgary
Saskatchewan
Nelson
Vancouver Island
Victoria
Vancouver
Regina
Winnipeg
L. Winnipeg
Goose Bay
NEWFOUNDLAND
Gander
St John's
C. Race
Seattle
Portland
Columbia
NORTH AMERICA
C. Mendocino
Snake
L. Superior
Quebec
Ottawa
St. Lawrence
Saint John
Halifax
Minneapolis
St Paul
Michigan
L. Huron
Montreal
San Francisco
Sacramento
UNITED STATES
Salt Lake City
Milwaukee
Hamilton
Toronto
L. Ontario
Detroit
Chicago
Buffalo
L. Erie
Boston
Mt. Whitney
Denver
Mt. Elbert
Kansas City
Colorado
Missouri
Cincinnati
Ohio
Pittsburgh
New York
Philadelphia
Baltimore
Washington
Norfolk
Los Angeles
San Diego
St. Louis
Arkansas
Phoenix
Memphis
Mississippi
Red
Atlanta
Ciudad Juárez
El Paso
Rio Grande
Dallas
Guadalupe (Mex.)
Bermuda (U.K.)
Houston
New Orleans
Jacksonville
Tampa
Monterrey
Torreón
GULF OF MEXICO
Miami
THE BAHAMAS
Nassau
C. Falso
MEXICO
Tropic of Cancer
Guadalajara
León
Tampico
Habana
Islas Revilla Gigedo (Mex.)
Mexico
Veracruz
Puebla
Mérida
CUBA
WEST INDIES
Acapulco
Santiago de Cuba
HAITI
DOM. REP.
San Juan
PUERTO RICO (U.S.)
Belize
BELIZE
Belmopan
Kingston
JAMAICA
Port au Prince
Santo Domingo
Guadeloupe (Fr.)
DOMINICA
Martinique (Fr.)
Guatemala
GUAT.
HOND.
EL SAL.
NICA.
Managua
CARIBBEAN SEA
ST. LUCIA
BARBADOS
GRENADA
Clipperton (Fr.)
CENTRAL AMERICA
Aruba
Curaçao (Neth.)
TRINIDAD & TOBAGO
Caracas
Barranquilla
Maracaibo
COSTA RICA
San José
Panama Canal
PANAMA
Orinoco
Georgetown
Paramaribo
Cayenne
GUYANA
SUR.
FR. GUI.
VENEZUELA
Medellín
Bogotá
COLOMBIA
Cali
Buenaventura
I. del Coco (C.R.)
I. de Malpelo (Col.)
PACIFIC OCEAN
Equator
São Pedro e São Paulo (Braz.)
Macapá
Belém
São Luís
Fortaleza
I. Fernando de Noronha (Braz.)
C. São Roque
João Pessoa
Recife
Maceió
Quito
ECUADOR
Guayaquil
Islas Galápagos (Ecu.)
Negro
Amazonas
Manaus
Santarém
Tocantins
Xingu
Tapajós
Madeira
Purus
Iquitos
Talara
Pta. Aguja
Pôrto Velho
São Francisco
Salvador
Ilhéus
PERU
Callao
Lima
Cuzco
Arequipa
SOUTH AMERICA
BRAZIL
Brasília
Cuiabá
La Paz
Cochabamba
BOLIVIA
Sucre
Arica
Iquique
Corumba
Belo Horizonte
Vitória
Campos
Juiz de Fora
Rio de Janeiro
Trindade (Braz.)
Tropic of Capricorn
PARAGUAY
Concepción
Asunción
Paraná
São Paulo
Santos
Curitiba
Antofagasta
Sala y Gómez
Easter I. (I. de Pascua) (Chi.)
I. San Félix (Chi.)
San Miguel de Tucumán
Corrientes
Porto Alegre
Viña del Mar
Valparaíso
Santiago
Córdoba
Santa Fé
Rosario
Mendoza
Co. Aconcagua
Paysandú
URUGUAY
Montevideo
Islas Juan Fernández (Chi.)
Buenos Aires
La Plata
Talca
Concepción
ARGENTINA
Bahía Blanca
Mar del Plata
Valdivia
CHILE
Comodoro Rivadavia
Falkland Is. (U.K.)
Punta Arenas
C. de Hornos
Drake Passage
SCOTIA SEA
South Georgia (U.K.)
South Shetland Is.
South Orkney Is. (U.K.)
NORTH ATLANTIC OCEAN
Açores (Port.)
Madeira (Port.)
Islas Canarias (Sp.)
Cape Verde
SOUTH ATLANTIC OCEAN
1:45 M
miles
km
The sea contour is drawn at 200 metres
Longitude West 90° of Greenwich
LAMBERT ZENITHAL EQUAL-AREA PROJECTION
© John Bartholomew & Son Ltd Edinburgh

CANADA
BRITISH COLUMBIA
ALBERTA
SASKATCHEWAN
MANITOBA
UNITED STATES
WASHINGTON
OREGON
CALIFORNIA
NEVADA
IDAHO
MONTANA
WYOMING
UTAH
COLORADO
ARIZONA
NEW MEXICO
NORTH DAKOTA
SOUTH DAKOTA
NEBRASKA
KANSAS
OKLAHOMA
TEXAS
MINNESOTA
IOWA
MISSOURI
ARKANSAS
LOUISIANA
MEXICO
BAJA CALIFORNIA
Golfo de California
SIERRA MADRE OCCIDENTAL
SIERRA MADRE ORIENTAL
Sierra Madre del Sur
PACIFIC OCEAN
GULF OF MEXICO
Bahía de Campeche
Golfo de Tehuantepec
ISLAS REVILLA GIGEDO (To Mex)
Tropic of Cancer
GUATEMALA
Vancouver
Seattle
Portland
San Francisco
Sacramento
Los Angeles
San Diego
Las Vegas
Salt Lake City
Phoenix
Tucson
Denver
Albuquerque
El Paso
Ciudad Juárez
Dallas
Fort Worth
Houston
San Antonio
Austin
Oklahoma City
Kansas City
Omaha
Minneapolis
St Paul
Winnipeg
Regina
Calgary
Chihuahua
Monterrey
Guadalajara
MEXICO
Puebla
Veracruz
Acapulco
Oaxaca
Mérida
Projection by courtesy of the National Geographic Society, Washington, D.C.
Longitude West 100° of Greenwich
feet 16409 13124 9843 6562 3281 1640 656 0 656 6562
m 5000 4000 3000 2000 1000 500 200 0 Below Sea Level 200 2000

ATLANTIC OCEAN
CARIBBEAN SEA
WEST INDIES
GREATER ANTILLES
LESSER ANTILLES
LEEWARD ISLANDS
WINDWARD ISLANDS
THE BAHAMAS
BERMUDA (To U.K.)
CUBA
HISPANIOLA
HAITI
DOMINICAN REPUBLIC
PUERTO RICO (To U.S.A.)
JAMAICA
BELIZE
HONDURAS
NIC.
VEN
NETHERLANDS ANTILLES
TRINIDAD & TOBAGO
BARBADOS
ST. LUCIA
DOMINICA
GRENADA
NEW YORK
PENNSYLVANIA
VIRGINIA
WEST VIRGINIA
NORTH CAROLINA
SOUTH CAROLINA
GEORGIA
ALABAMA
FLORIDA
KENTUCKY
MAINE
NEW BRUNSWICK
NOVA SCOTIA
PRINCE EDWARD I.
QUEBEC
ONTARIO
New York
Philadelphia
WASHINGTON D.C.
Boston
Montreal
OTTAWA
Toronto
Detroit
Chicago
Quebec
Halifax
Atlanta
Miami
HABANA (HAVANA)
Kingston
Santo Domingo
Port au Prince
San Juan
Caracas
Tegucigalpa
Gulf of Saint Lawrence
Straits of Florida
Tropic of Cancer
1:12.5M
miles km
Heights in feet Depths in metres

feet	3281	656	0	300	600	1500	3000	6000
m	1000	200	0	91	183	457	914	1829

CONFORMAL CONIC PROJECTION

121

Continued on Inset

Heights in feet Depths in metres

ATLANTIC OCEAN
Long Island Sound
Long Island
CONNECTICUT
NEW YORK
NEW JERSEY
NEW HAVEN
FAIRFIELD
PUTNAM
WESTCHESTER
ROCKLAND
ORANGE
SUSSEX
PASSAIC
MORRIS
BERGEN
ESSEX
HUDSON
UNION
SOMERSET
MIDDLESEX
MONMOUTH
STATEN ISLAND
BRONX
QUEENS
BROOKLYN
MANHATTAN
NASSAU
SUFFOLK
NEW YORK
Newark
Jersey City
Elizabeth
Paterson
Yonkers
Stamford
Bridgeport
New Haven
Long Beach
Fire Island
Jones Island

1:500 000

PHILADELPHIA

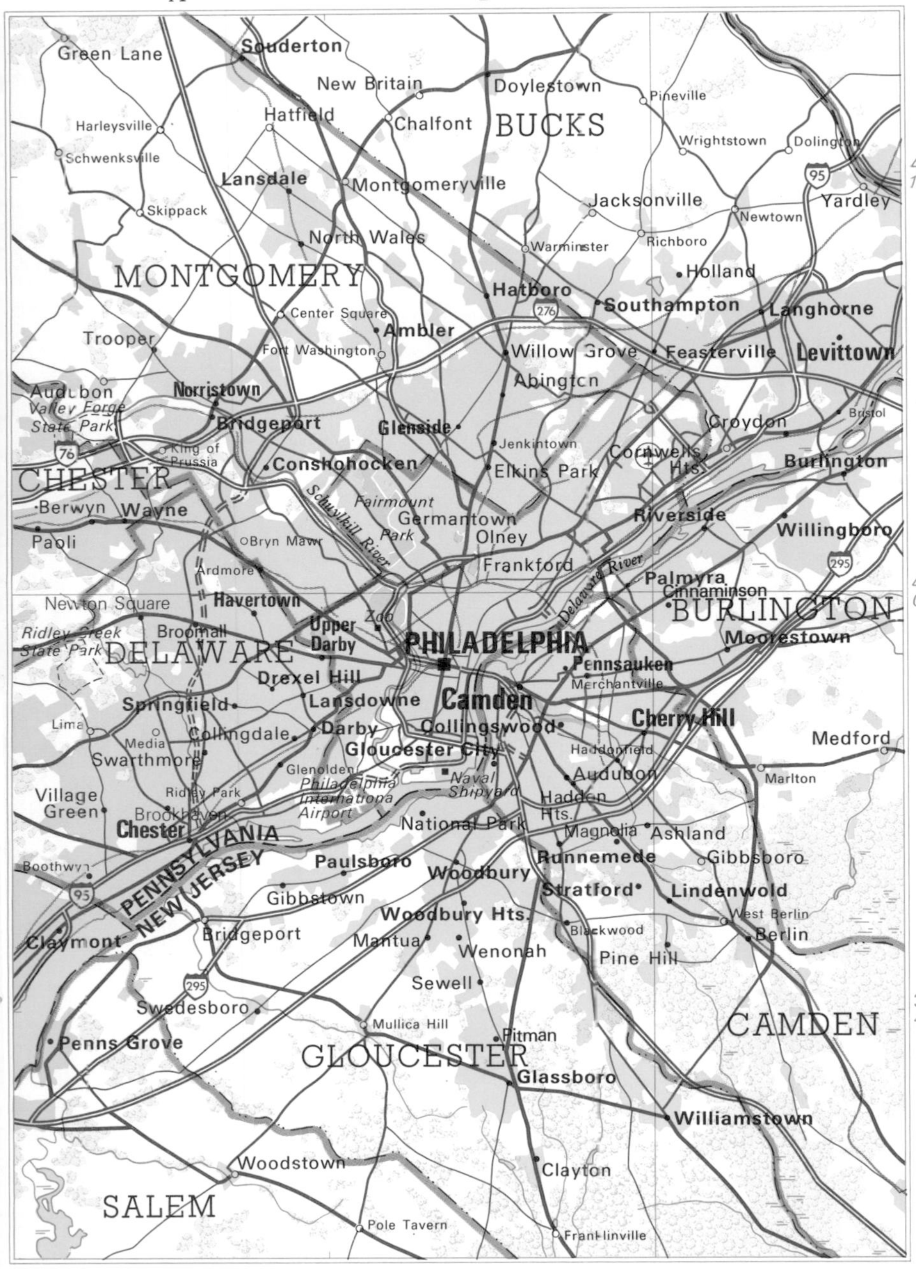

BOSTON

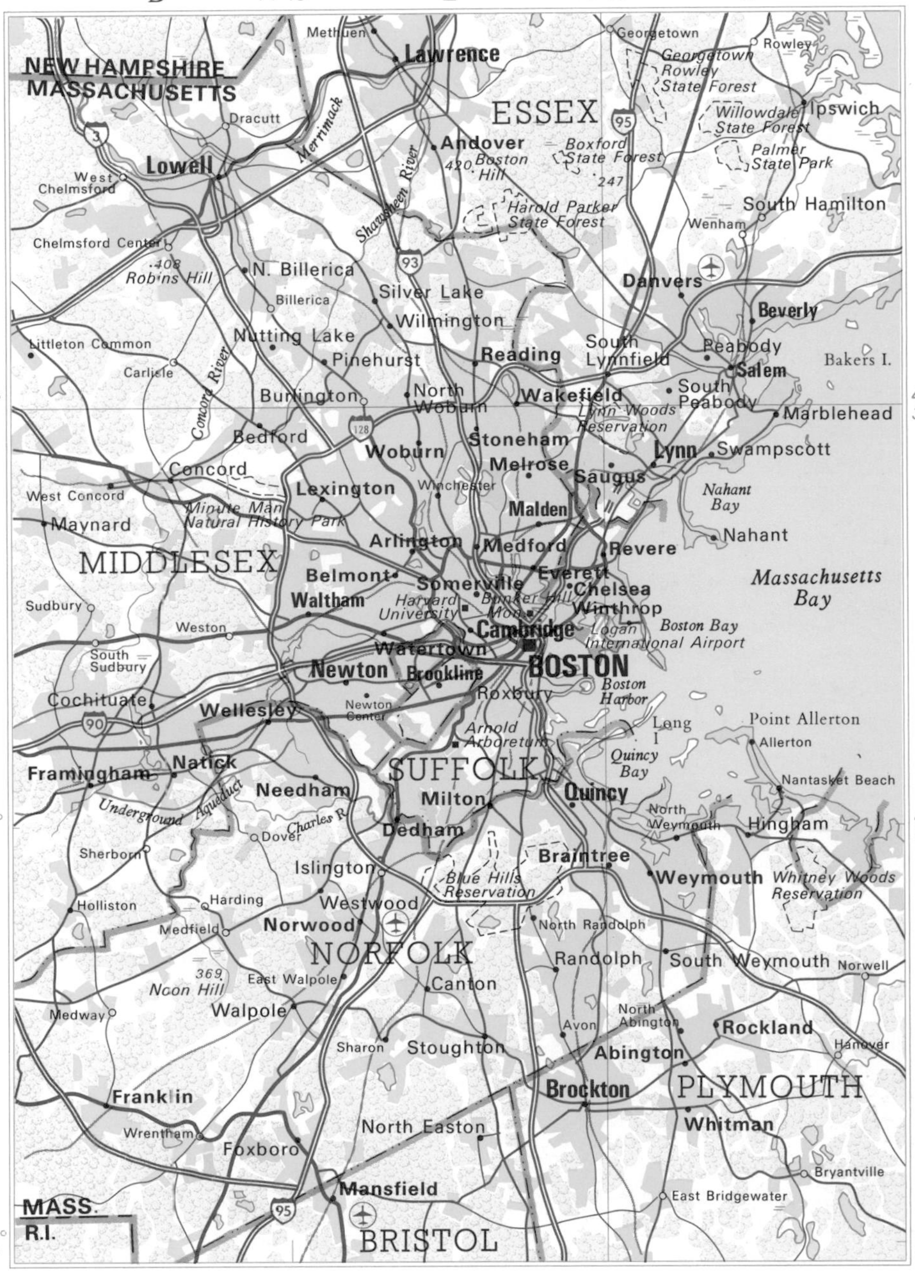

WASHINGTON

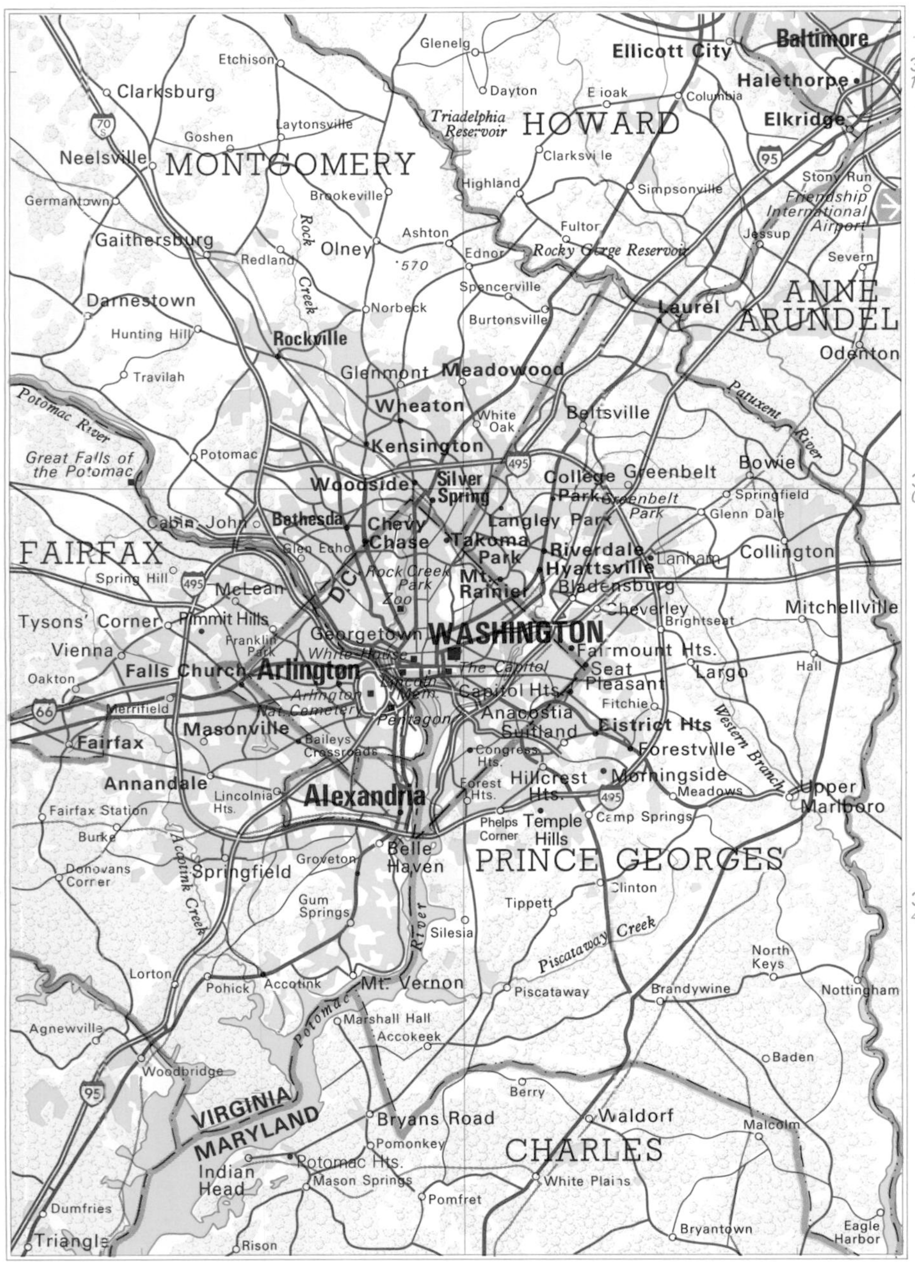

BALTIMORE

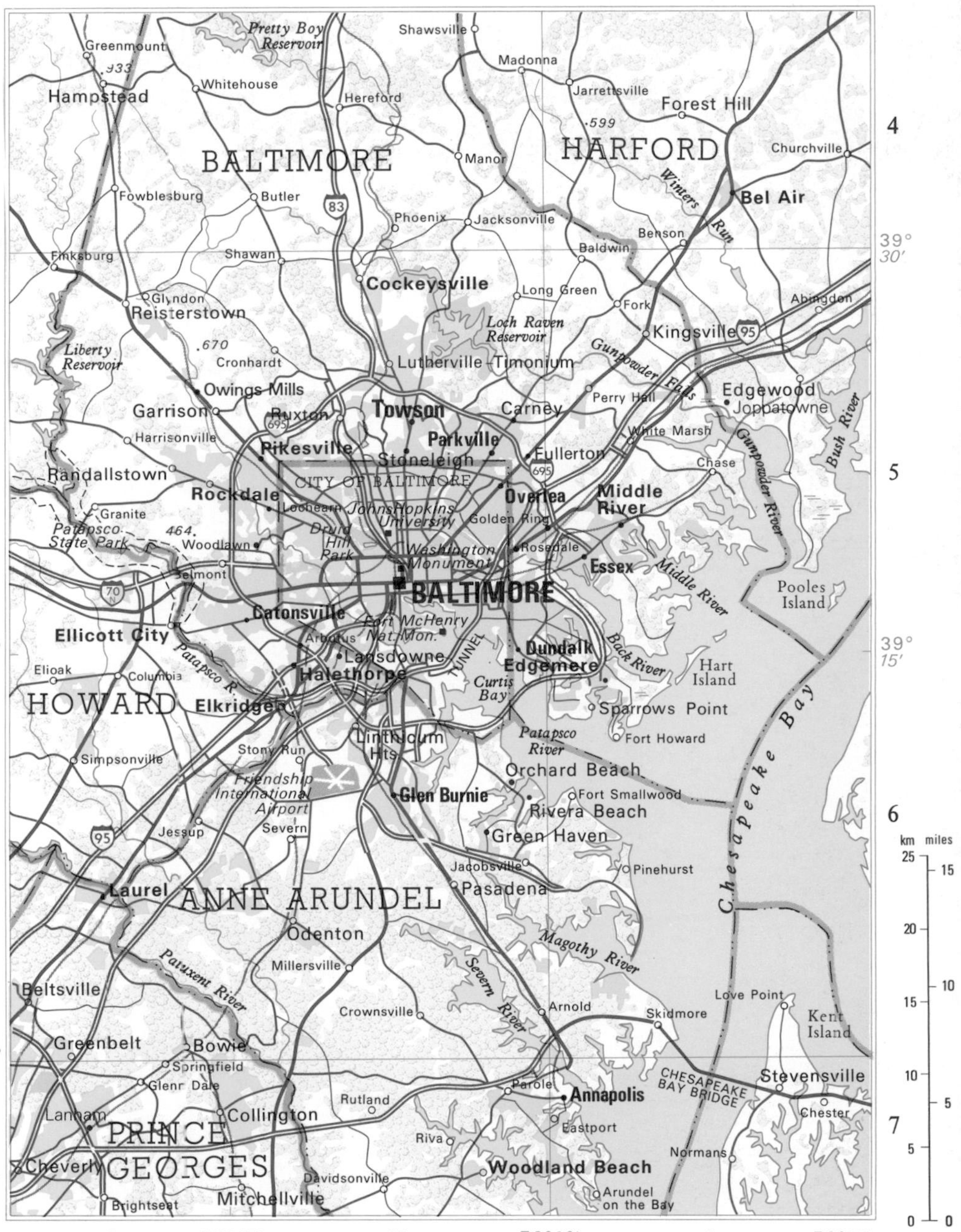

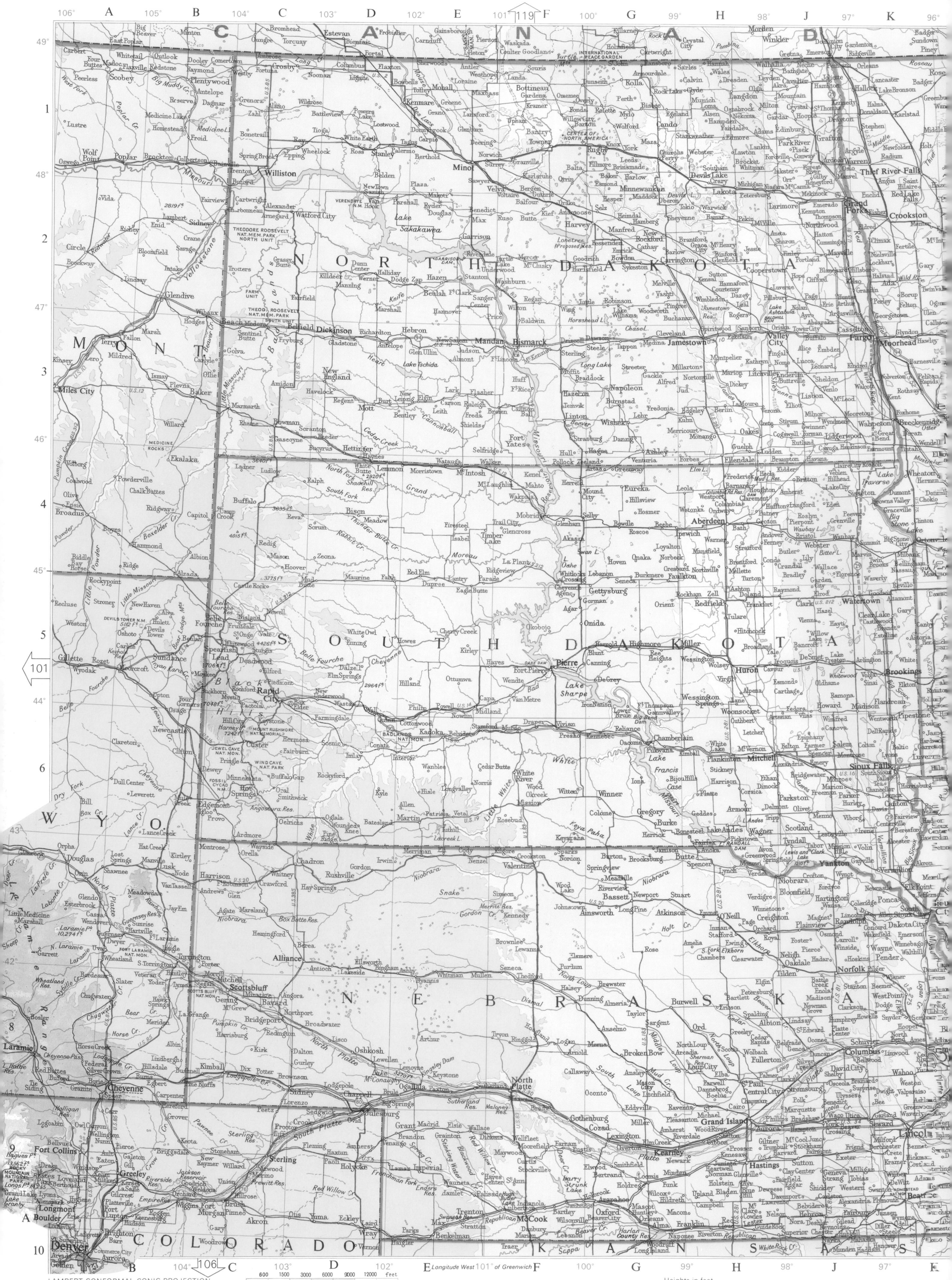
CANADA
NORTH DAKOTA
SOUTH DAKOTA
NEBRASKA
MONTANA
WYOMING
COLORADO
KANSAS
Bismarck
Fargo
Minot
Williston
Grand Forks
Jamestown
Aberdeen
Pierre
Rapid City
Sioux Falls
Huron
Mitchell
Yankton
Watertown
Brookings
Scottsbluff
North Platte
Grand Island
Kearney
Hastings
Lincoln
Norfolk
Columbus
McCook
Cheyenne
Laramie
Fort Collins
Greeley
Denver
Boulder
Sterling
Miles City
Glendive
Lake Sakakawea
Lake Oahe
Black Hills
Missouri
Platte
Niobrara
Yellowstone
119
101
106

LAMBERT CONFORMAL CONIC PROJECTION

Longitude West 101° of Greenwich

Heights in feet

feet	600	1500	3000	6000	9000	12000
m	183	457	914	1829	2743	3658

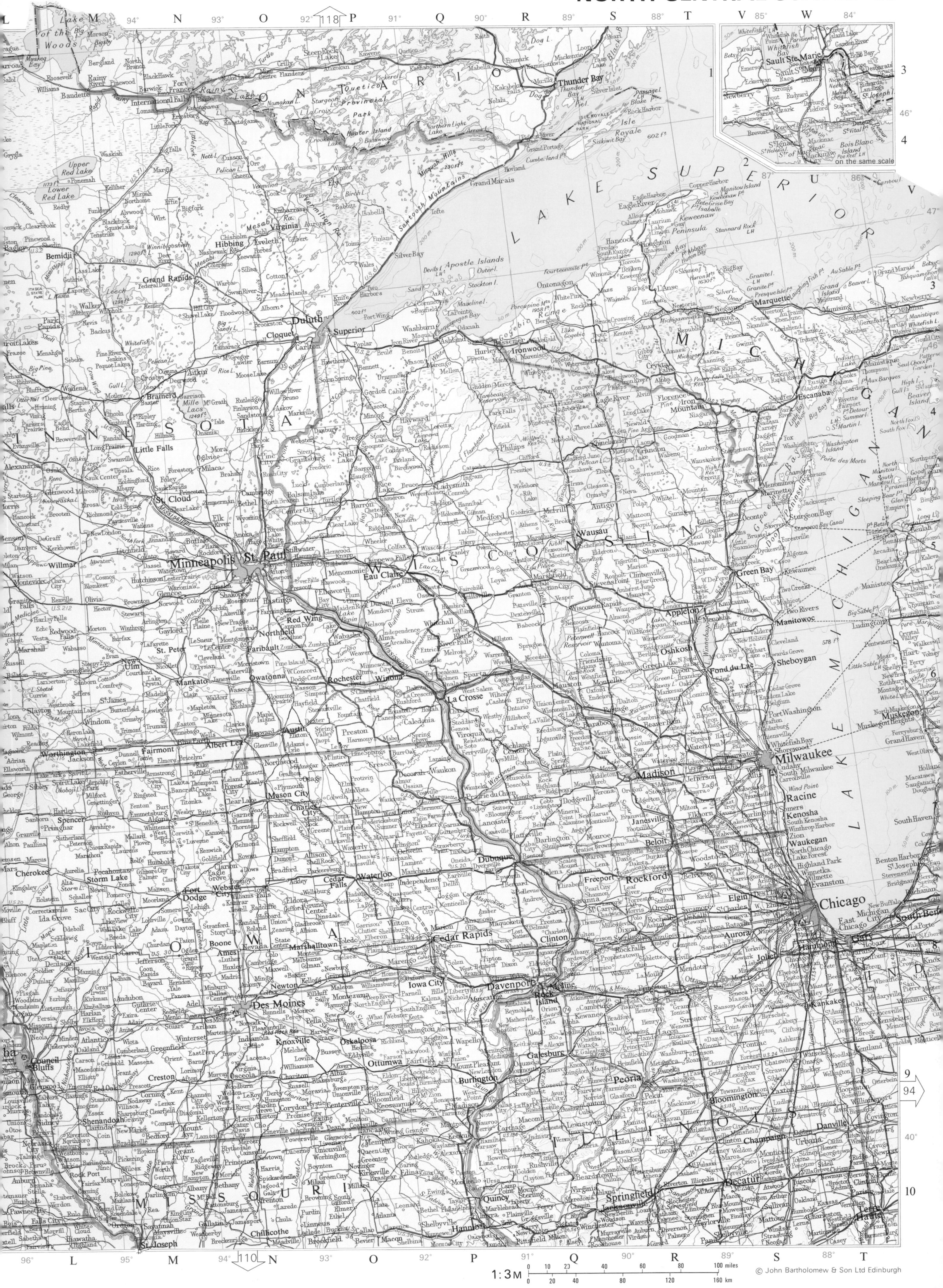
MINNESOTA
WISCONSIN
MICHIGAN
IOWA
ILLINOIS
MISSOURI
ONTARIO
LAKE SUPERIOR
LAKE MICHIGAN
Minneapolis
St. Paul
Duluth
Superior
Thunder Bay
Milwaukee
Chicago
Madison
Green Bay
Des Moines
Cedar Rapids
Davenport
Peoria
Springfield
Rockford
Dubuque
La Crosse
Eau Claire
Rochester
Sault Ste Marie
on the same scale
1:3M
100 miles
160 km
© John Bartholomew & Son Ltd Edinburgh

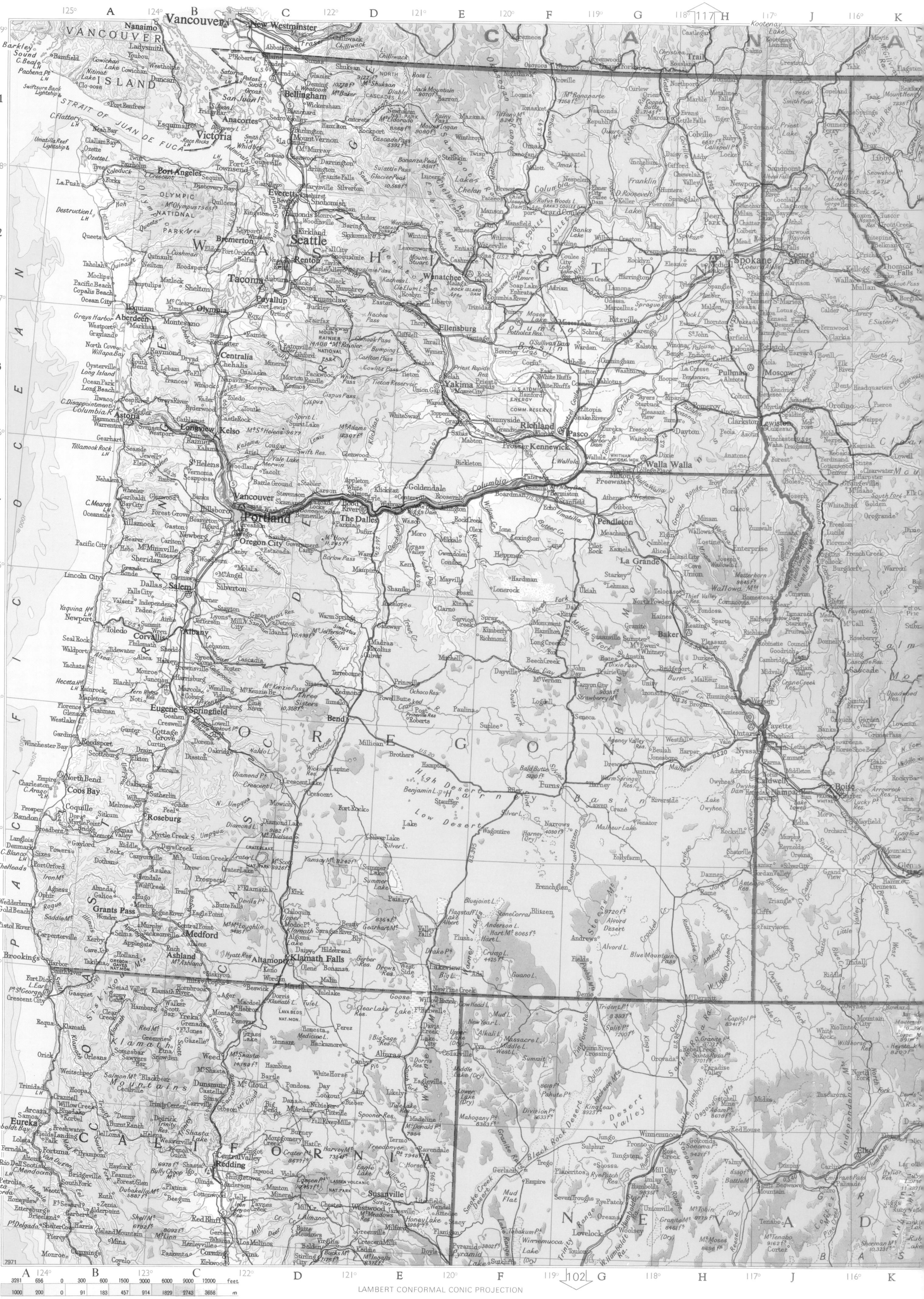
CANADA
WASHINGTON
OREGON
IDAHO
CALIFORNIA
NEVADA
PACIFIC OCEAN
VANCOUVER ISLAND
STRAIT OF JUAN DE FUCA
Vancouver
Victoria
Seattle
Tacoma
Olympia
Everett
Bellingham
Spokane
Yakima
Richland
Kennewick
Pasco
Walla Walla
Aberdeen
Astoria
Longview
Portland
Salem
Eugene
Springfield
Corvallis
Albany
Bend
The Dalles
Pendleton
La Grande
Baker
Medford
Grants Pass
Klamath Falls
Roseburg
Coos Bay
North Bend
Eureka
Redding
Susanville
Winnemucca
Lewiston
Moscow
Boise
Nampa
Caldwell
Elko
Columbia
Snake
Harney Basin
Klamath Mountains
Black Rock Desert
Desert Valley
Lambert Conformal Conic Projection
117
102

MONTANA
IDAHO
WYOMING
UTAH
COLORADO
ALBERTA
SASK.
Great Falls
Havre
Helena
Butte
Missoula
Kalispell
Bozeman
Billings
Lewistown
Miles City
Glasgow
Sheridan
Casper
Rawlins
Laramie
Rock Springs
Idaho Falls
Pocatello
Twin Falls
Ogden
Salt Lake City
Provo
Logan
Brigham City
Great Salt Lake
Yellowstone National Park
Fort Peck Reservoir
Bighorn Mountains
Wind River Range
Snake River Plain
Great Salt Lake Desert
Uinta Mountains
98
103
Heights in feet
Depths in metres
1:3M
Long West 114° of Greenwich

100
NEVADA
PACIFIC OCEAN
San Francisco
Oakland
Berkeley
Sacramento
Stockton
Modesto
Fresno
Bakersfield
Los Angeles
San Diego
Reno
Carson City
San Jose
Santa Barbara
Pasadena
Long Beach
Tijuana
Ensenada
Monterey
Salinas
Santa Cruz
Merced
Visalia
Redding
Eureka
Ukiah
Santa Rosa
Napa
Vallejo
Richmond
Susanville
Chico
Oroville
Marysville
Yuba City
Lodi
Madera
Hanford
Tulare
Delano
San Luis Obispo
Santa Maria
Ventura
Oxnard
Glendale
Riverside
San Bernardino
Barstow
Oceanside
Tonopah
Bishop
Goldfield
YOSEMITE NATIONAL PARK
SEQUOIA NATIONAL PARK
KINGS CANYON NATIONAL PARK
DEATH VALLEY
MOJAVE DESERT
CHANNEL ISLANDS
Santa Barbara Channel
GULF OF SANTA CATALINA
OAHU
(HONOLULU COUNTY)
Honolulu
Pearl City
Kaneohe
Kailua
Wahiawa
Waipahu
Ewa
1:1M
HAWAIIAN ISLANDS
(To U.S.A.)
1:9 000 000
KAUAI
NIIHAU
MOLOKAI
LANAI
MAUI
KAHOOLAWE
HAWAII
Hilo
Tropic of Cancer
Necker I.
Nihoa
also on page 135
Longitude West 117° of Greenwich

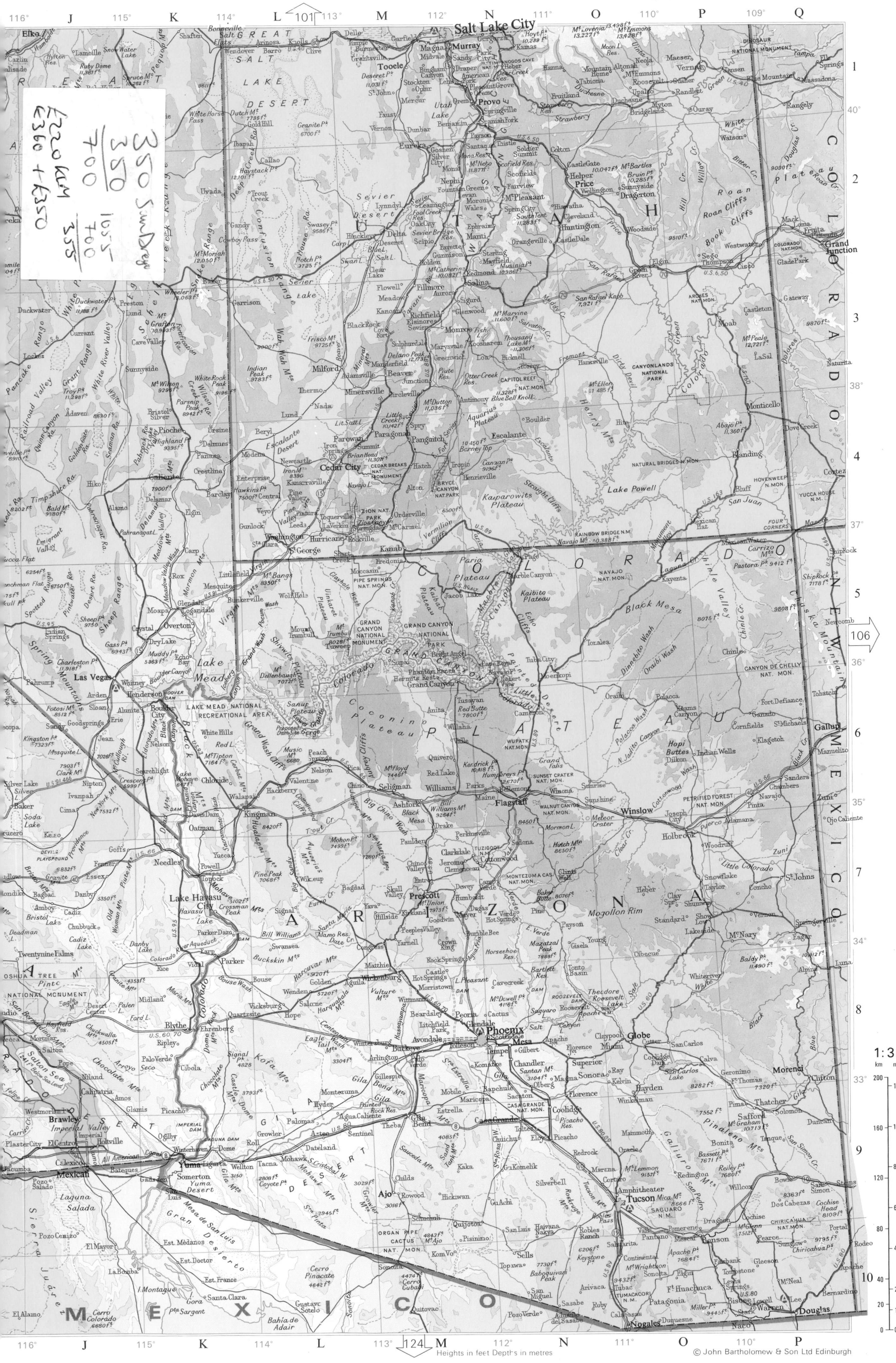

Heights in feet Depths in metres

© John Bartholomew & Son Ltd Edinburgh

SAN FRANCISCO

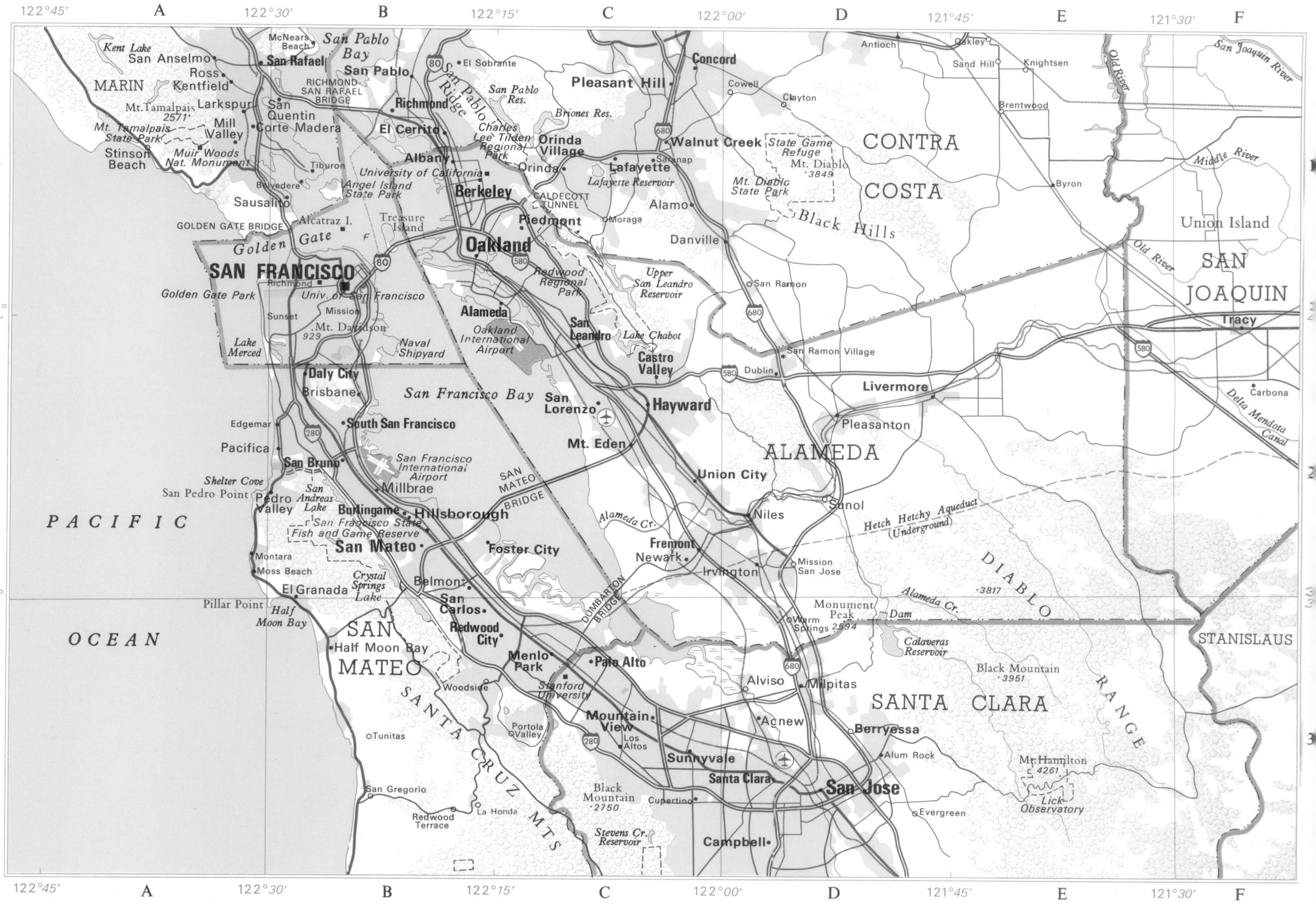

LOS ANGELES

1:500 000

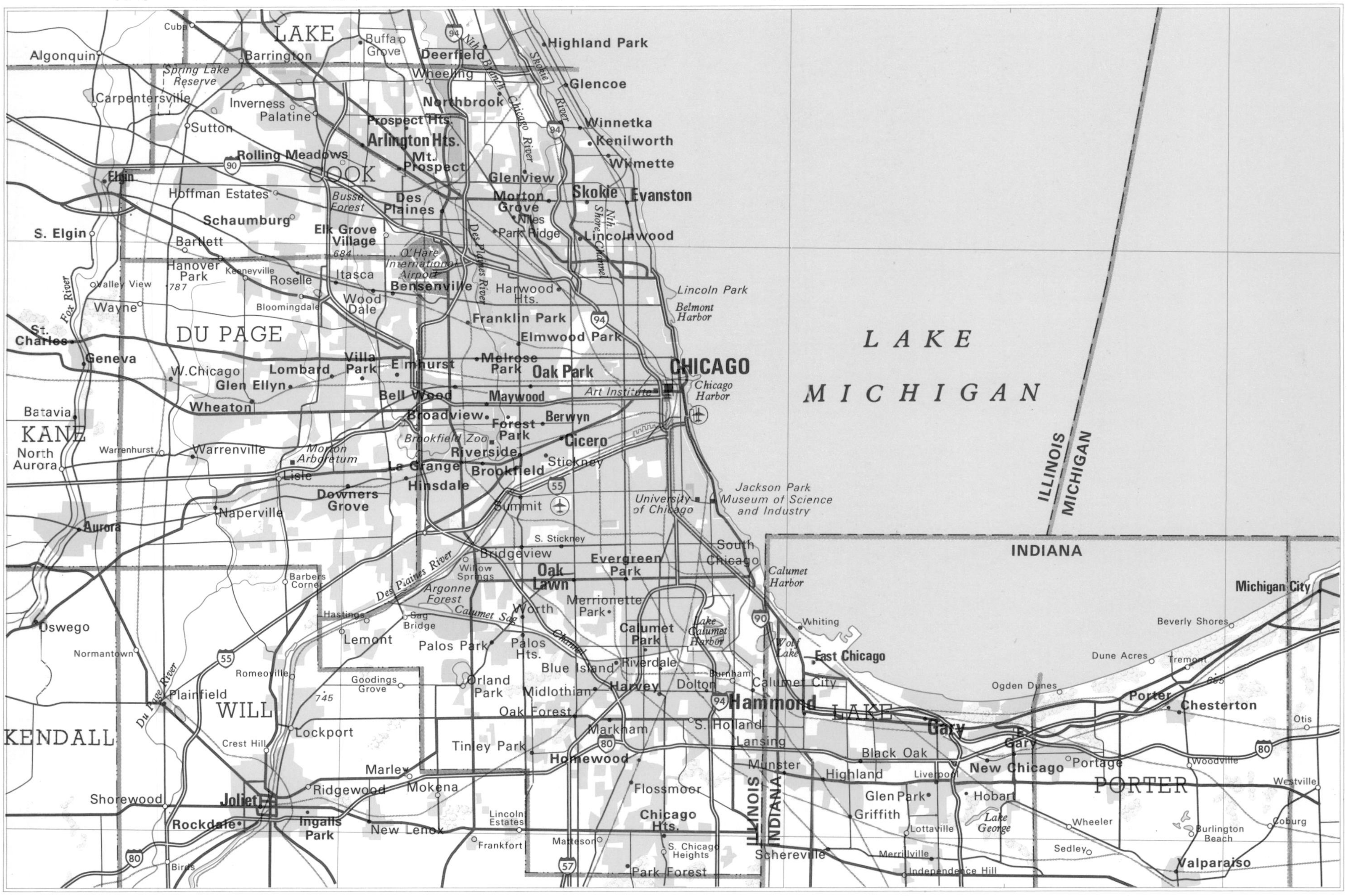
88°15′ A 88°00′ B 87°45′ C 87°30′ D 87°15′ E 87°00′
LAKE
COOK
DU PAGE
KANE
WILL
KENDALL
LAKE
PORTER
INDIANA
ILLINOIS
MICHIGAN
LAKE MICHIGAN
CHICAGO
Chicago Harbor
Art Institute
Jackson Park Museum of Science and Industry
University of Chicago
Lincoln Park
Belmont Harbor
Calumet Harbor
Lake Calumet Harbor
O'Hare International Airport
Morton Arboretum
Brookfield Zoo
Argonne Forest
Algonquin
Cuba
Barrington
Buffalo Grove
Deerfield
Highland Park
Wheeling
Glencoe
Spring Lake Reserve
Carpentersville
Inverness
Palatine
Northbrook
Winnetka
Kenilworth
Wilmette
Sutton
Prospect Hts.
Arlington Hts.
Rolling Meadows
Mt. Prospect
Glenview
Elgin
Hoffman Estates
Busse Forest
Des Plaines
Morton Grove
Niles
Park Ridge
Skokie
Evanston
Lincolnwood
Schaumburg
Elk Grove Village
S. Elgin
Bartlett
Hanover Park
Keeneyville
Itasca
Roselle
Bensenville
Harwood Hts.
Wood Dale
Valley View
Wayne
Bloomingdale
Franklin Park
Elmwood Park
St. Charles
Geneva
Villa Park
Elmhurst
Melrose Park
Oak Park
W. Chicago
Lombard
Glen Ellyn
Bell Wood
Maywood
Wheaton
Broadview
Forest Park
Berwyn
Cicero
Batavia
Warrenville
Riverside
Brookfield
Stickney
North Aurora
Warrenhurst
Lisle
La Grange
Hinsdale
Downers Grove
Summit
Naperville
Aurora
S. Stickney
Bridgeview
Willow Springs
Oak Lawn
Evergreen Park
South Chicago
Barbers Corner
Merrionette Park
Worth
Oswego
Hastings
Sag Bridge
Lemont
Palos Park
Palos Hts.
Calumet Park
Whiting
Wolf Lake
East Chicago
Michigan City
Beverly Shores
Normantown
Romeoville
Goodings Grove
Blue Island
Riverdale
Burnham
Calumet City
Dune Acres
Tremont
Plainfield
Orland Park
Midlothian
Harvey
Dolton
Ogden Dunes
Porter
Chesterton
Oak Forest
Hammond
Crest Hill
Lockport
Markham
S. Holland
Gary
Otis
Tinley Park
Lansing
Homewood
Munster
Black Oak
New Chicago
Portage
Woodville
Marley
Ridgewood
Mokena
Highland
Liverpool
Westville
Shorewood
Joliet
Flossmoor
Glen Park
Hobart
Lake George
Griffith
Rockdale
Ingalls Park
New Lenox
Lincoln Estates
Chicago Hts.
Lottaville
Wheeler
Burlington Beach
Coburg
Frankfort
Matteson
S. Chicago Heights
Merrillville
Sedley
Schererville
Valparaiso
Birds
Park Forest
Independence Hill
Fox River
Des Plaines River
Du Page River
Calumet Sag Channel
Chicago River
Skokie River
42° 00′
41° 45′
41° 30′
1
2
3

ST. LOUIS

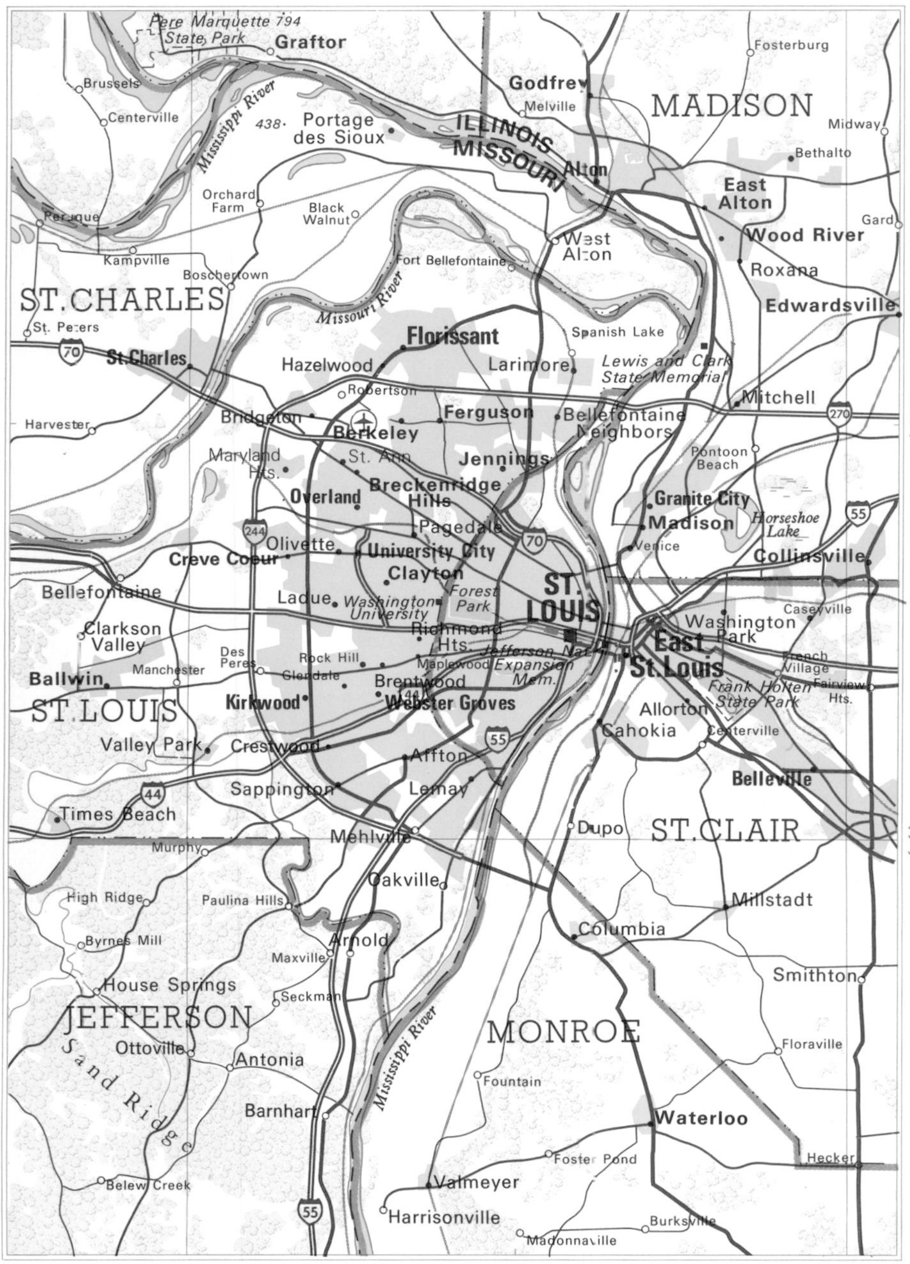
F 90°30′ G 90°15′ H 90°00′
Pere Marquette State Park
Grafton
Fosterburg
Godfrey
Melville
MADISON
Brussels
Centerville
Portage des Sioux
ILLINOIS
MISSOURI
Alton
Midway
Bethalto
Orchard Farm
Black Walnut
East Alton
Gard
West Alton
Wood River
Kampville
Boschertown
Fort Bellefontaine
Roxana
ST. CHARLES
Edwardsville
St. Peters
Missouri River
Mississippi River
Florissant
Spanish Lake
St. Charles
Hazelwood
Larimore
Lewis and Clark State Memorial
Robertson
Mitchell
Harvester
Bridgeton
Ferguson
Bellefontaine Neighbors
Berkeley
St. Ann
Jennings
Maryland Hts.
Pontoon Beach
Overland
Breckenridge Hills
Granite City
Pagedale
Madison
Horseshoe Lake
Olivette
University City
Venice
Collinsville
Creve Coeur
Clayton
Forest Park
ST. LOUIS
Bellefontaine
Ladue
Washington University
East St. Louis
Washington Park
Caseyville
Clarkson Valley
Richmond Hts.
Jefferson Nat. Expansion Mem.
Frank Holten State Park
Fairview Hts.
Manchester
Des Peres
Rock Hill
Glendale
Brentwood
Ballwin
Kirkwood
Webster Groves
Allorton
Centerville
Cahokia
ST. LOUIS
Valley Park
Crestwood
Belleville
Affton
Sappington
Lemay
Times Beach
Dupo
ST. CLAIR
Mehlville
Murphy
Oakville
High Ridge
Paulina Hills
Millstadt
Byrnes Mill
Columbia
Arnold
Maxville
Smithton
House Springs
Seckman
JEFFERSON
Ottoville
Antonia
MONROE
Floraville
Sand Ridge
Fountain
Barnhart
Waterloo
Foster Pond
Hecker
Belew Creek
Valmeyer
Harrisonville
Burksville
Madonnaville
38° 45′
38° 30′
4
5
6

ATLANTA

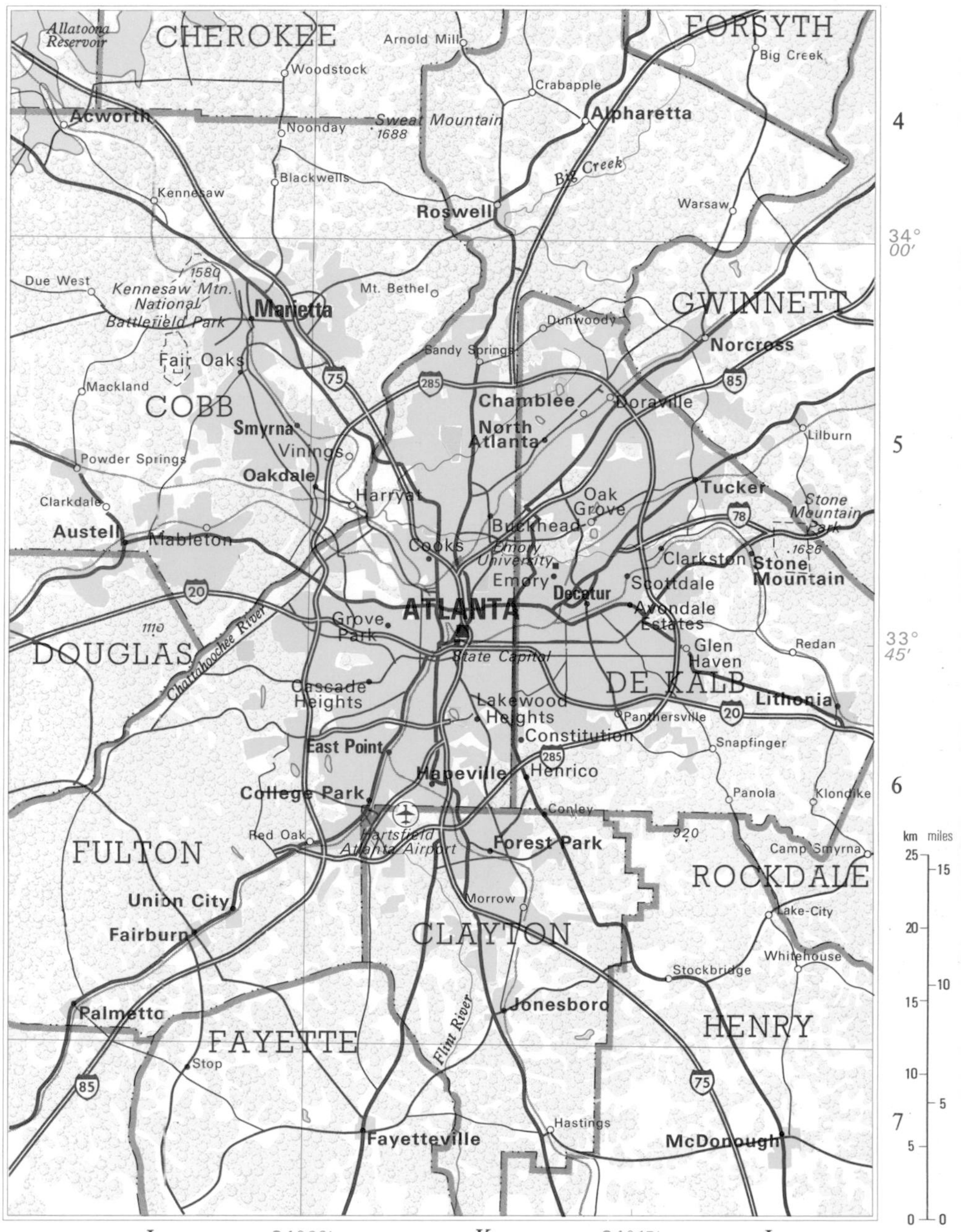
J 84°30′ K 84°15′ L
Allatoona Reservoir
CHEROKEE
Arnold Mill
FORSYTH
Big Creek
Woodstock
Crabapple
Acworth
Noonday
Sweat Mountain
Alpharetta
Blackwells
Big Creek
Kennesaw
Warsaw
Roswell
Due West
Kennesaw Mtn. National Battlefield Park
Marietta
Mt. Bethel
GWINNETT
Dunwoody
Fair Oaks
Sandy Springs
Norcross
Mackland
COBB
Chamblee
Doraville
Smyrna
Vinings
North Atlanta
Lilburn
Powder Springs
Oakdale
Tucker
Clarkdale
Harryat
Oak Grove
Stone Mountain Park
Austell
Mableton
Buckhead
Clarkston
Stone Mountain
Cooks
Emory University
Emory
Scottdale
DOUGLAS
Chattahoochee River
Grove Park
ATLANTA
Decatur
Avondale Estates
Glen Haven
Redan
State Capitol
Cascade Heights
DE KALB
Lithonia
Panthersville
Lakewood Heights
Constitution
Snapfinger
East Point
Hapeville
Henrico
Panola
Klondike
College Park
Conley
Red Oak
Hartsfield Atlanta Airport
Forest Park
Camp Smyrna
FULTON
ROCKDALE
Union City
Morrow
Lake City
Fairburn
CLAYTON
Whitehouse
Stockbridge
Palmetto
Flint River
Jonesboro
FAYETTE
HENRY
Stop
Hastings
Fayetteville
McDonough
34° 00′
33° 45′
33° 30′
4
5
6
7
km
miles

1:500 000

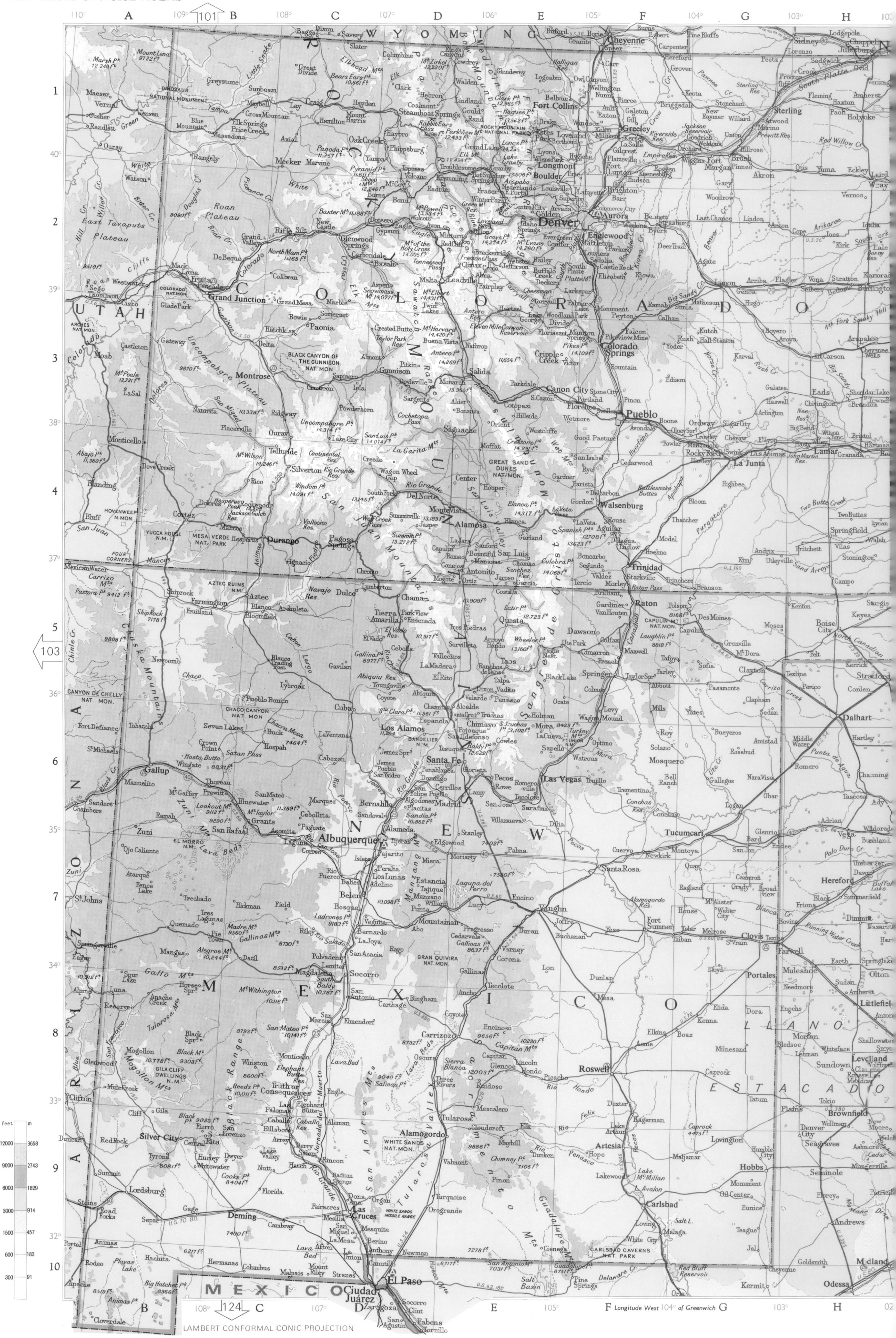

LAMBERT CONFORMAL CONIC PROJECTION

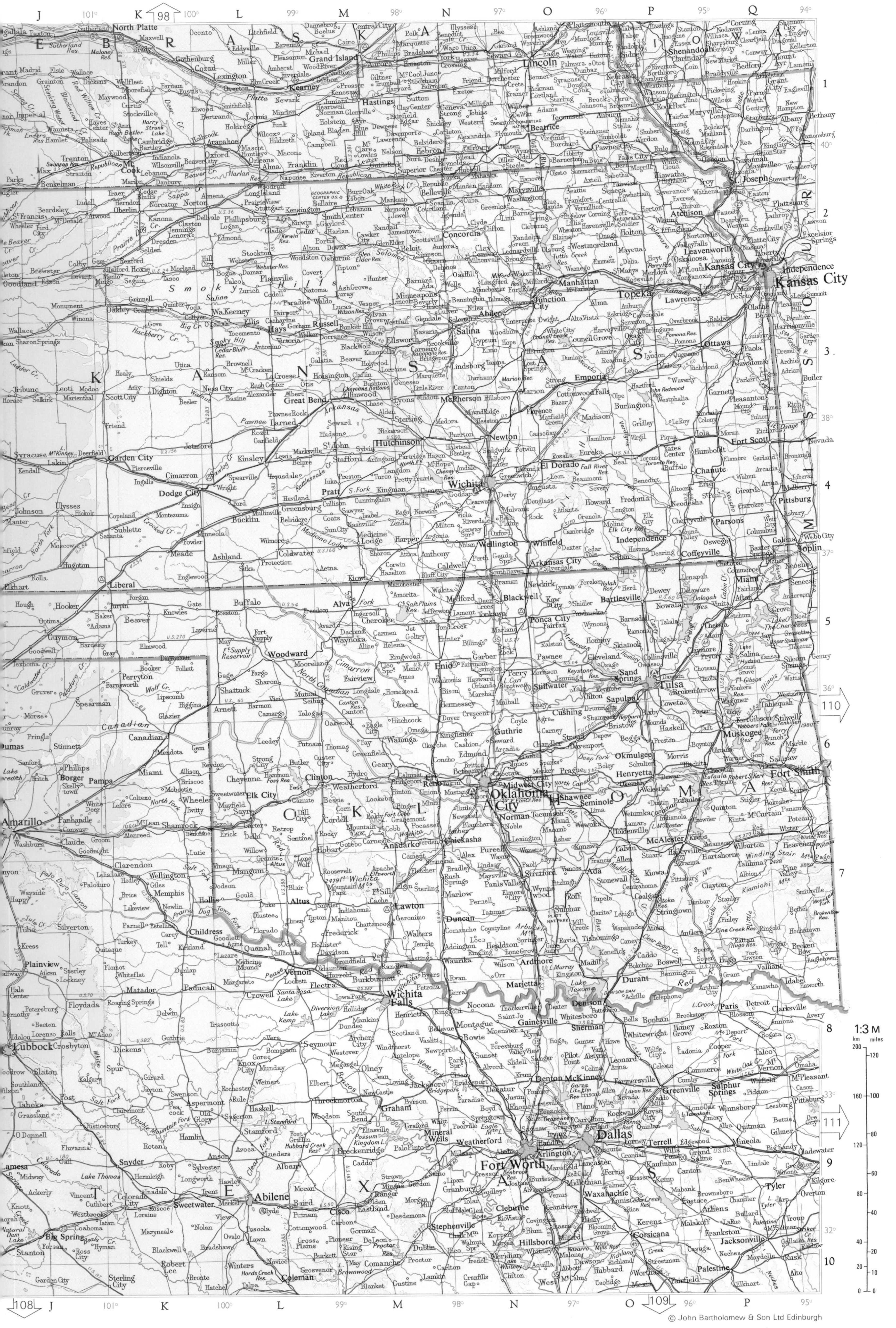
NEBRASKA
IOWA
KANSAS
MISSOURI
OKLAHOMA
TEXAS
Lincoln
Grand Island
Kearney
Hastings
North Platte
McCook
St. Joseph
Kansas City
Topeka
Lawrence
Manhattan
Salina
Hutchinson
Wichita
Dodge City
Garden City
Liberal
Emporia
Joplin
Tulsa
Oklahoma City
Enid
Lawton
Muskogee
Fort Smith
McAlester
Amarillo
Lubbock
Wichita Falls
Abilene
Fort Worth
Dallas
Denison
Sherman
Tyler
Smoky Hills
Lake Texoma
1:3 M
km
miles
98
110
111
108
109

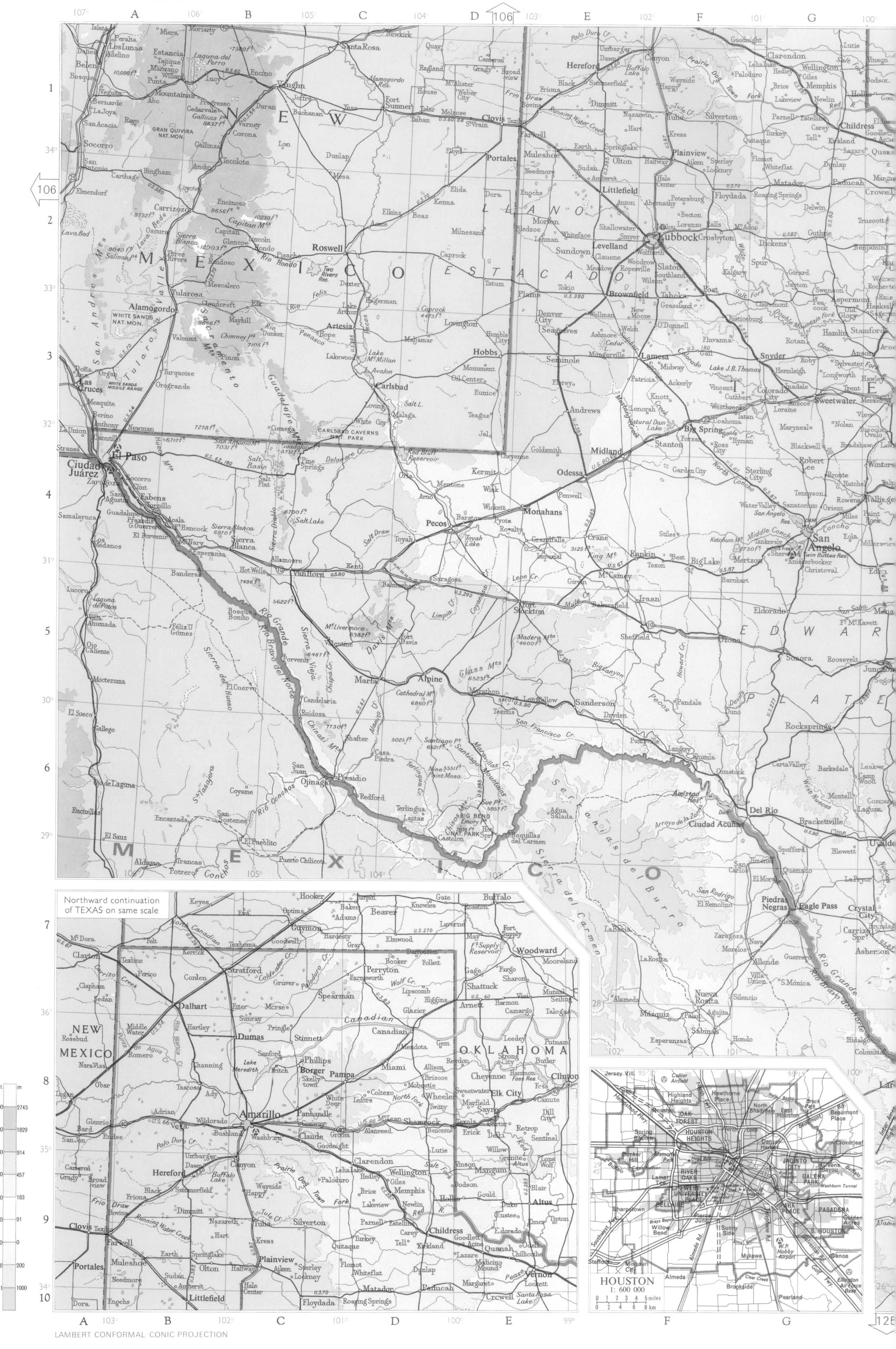
NEW MEXICO
LLANO ESTACADO
EDWARDS PLATEAU
MEXICO
Northward continuation of TEXAS on same scale
OKLAHOMA
NEW MEXICO
HOUSTON
1: 600 000
El Paso
Ciudad Juárez
Roswell
Carlsbad
Lubbock
Midland
Odessa
San Angelo
Del Rio
Ciudad Acuña
Piedras Negras
Eagle Pass
Amarillo
Clovis
Alamogordo
Las Cruces
Pecos
Alpine
Presidio
Ojinaga
Big Spring
Sweetwater
Dalhart
Pampa
Borger
Hereford
Plainview
Childress
Woodward
Guymon
Elk City
Clinton
White Sands Nat. Mon.
Carlsbad Caverns Nat. Park
Big Bend Nat. Park
Gran Quivira Nat. Mon.
Rio Grande
Pecos
feet
m
LAMBERT CONFORMAL CONIC PROJECTION

Heights in feet
Depths in metres

© John Bartholomew & Son Ltd Edinburgh

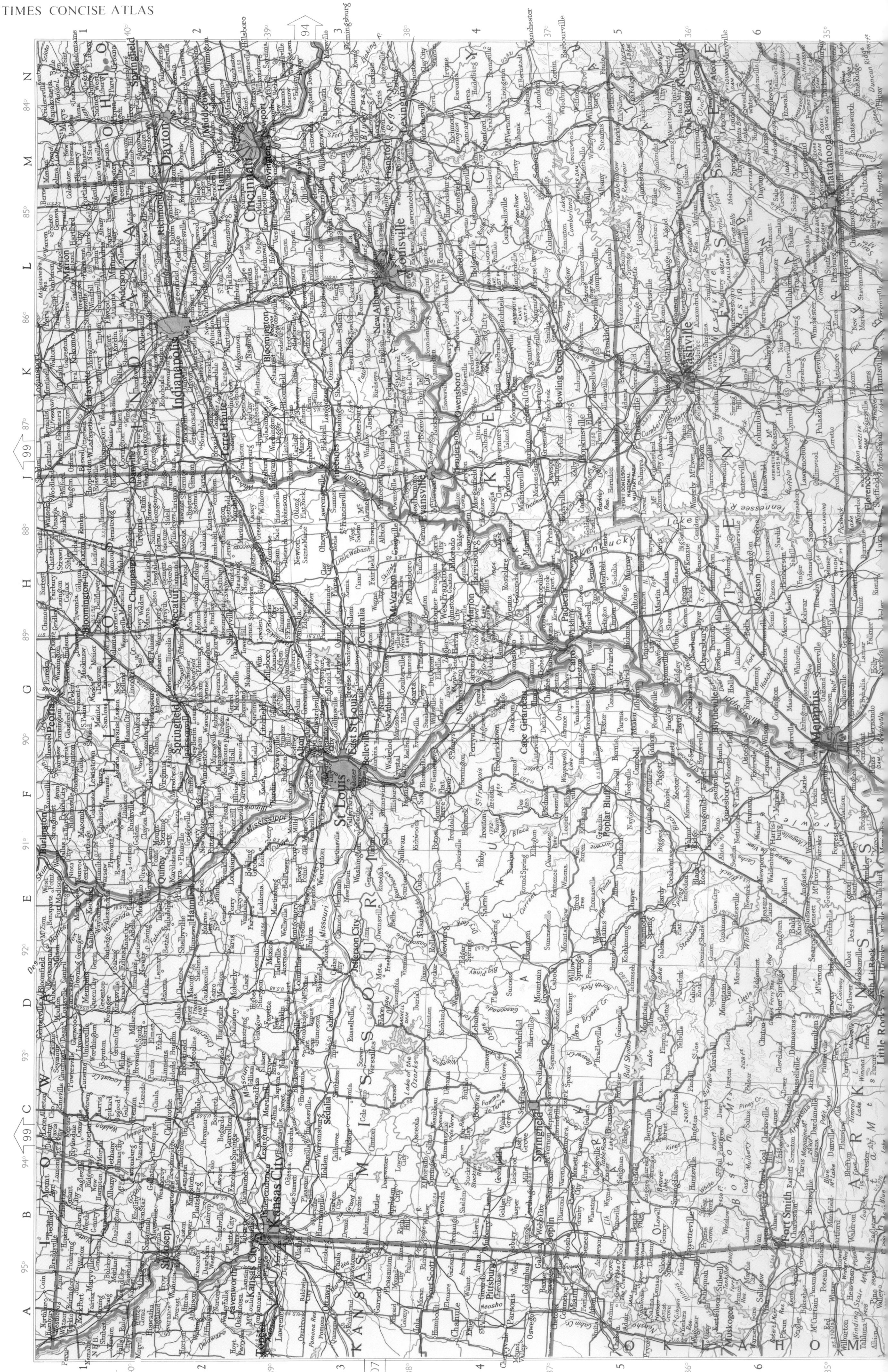
ILLINOIS
INDIANA
OHIO
KENTUCKY
TENNESSEE
MISSOURI
ARKANSAS
KANSAS
OKLAHOMA
St Louis
Indianapolis
Cincinnati
Louisville
Nashville
Memphis
Kansas City
Springfield
Evansville
Knoxville
Chattanooga
Little Rock
Fort Smith
Dayton
Lexington
Peoria
Terre Haute
Decatur
Jefferson City
Paducah
Joplin
St Joseph
Topeka
Burlington
Quincy
Hannibal
Bloomington
Champaign
Danville
Owensboro
Bowling Green
Cape Girardeau
Poplar Bluff
Jonesboro
Jackson
Pittsburg
Sedalia
94
99
107

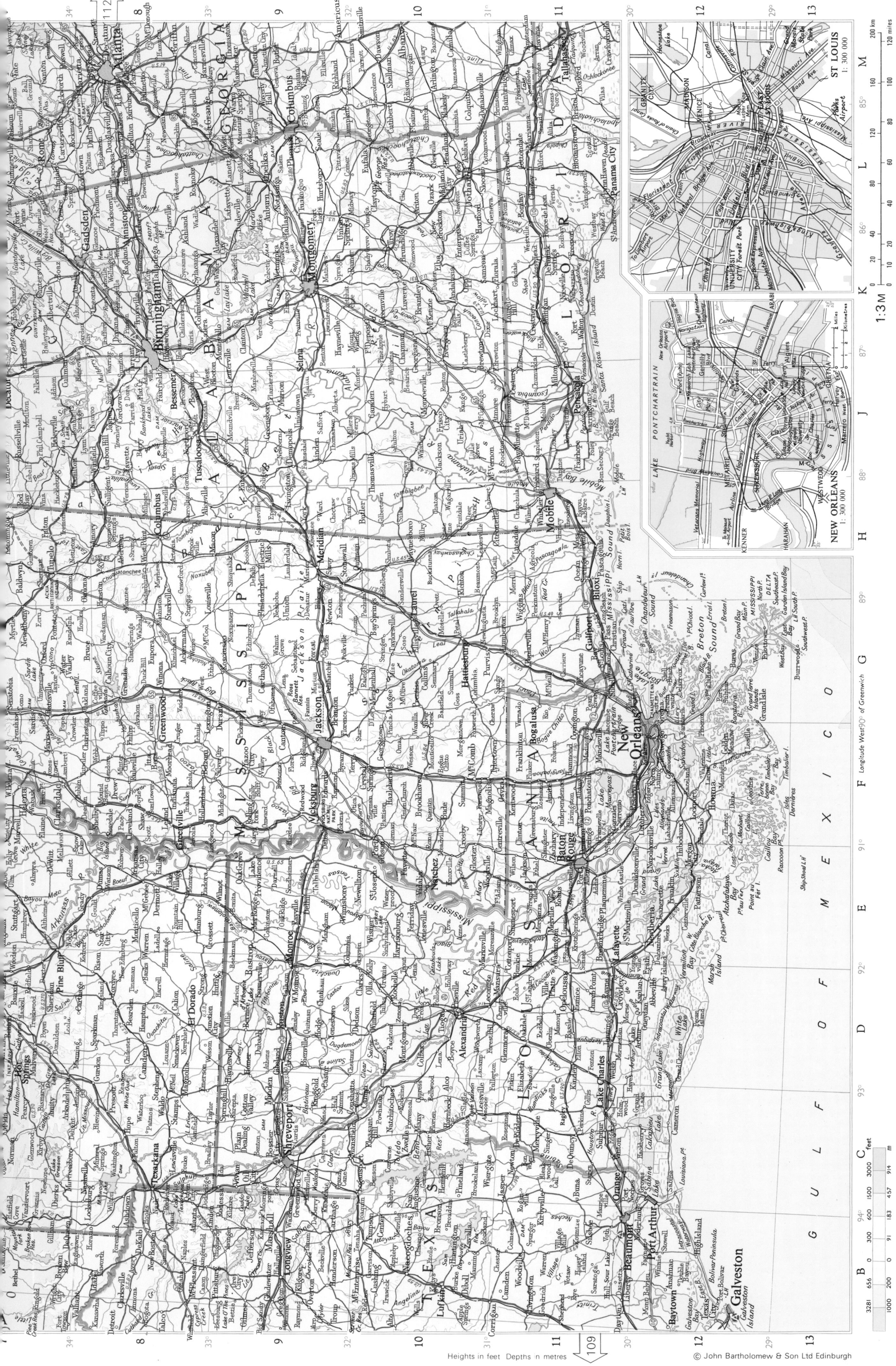
GULF OF MEXICO
ST LOUIS
1: 300 000
NEW ORLEANS
1: 300 000
1:3M
Longitude West of Greenwich

Heights in feet Depths in metres

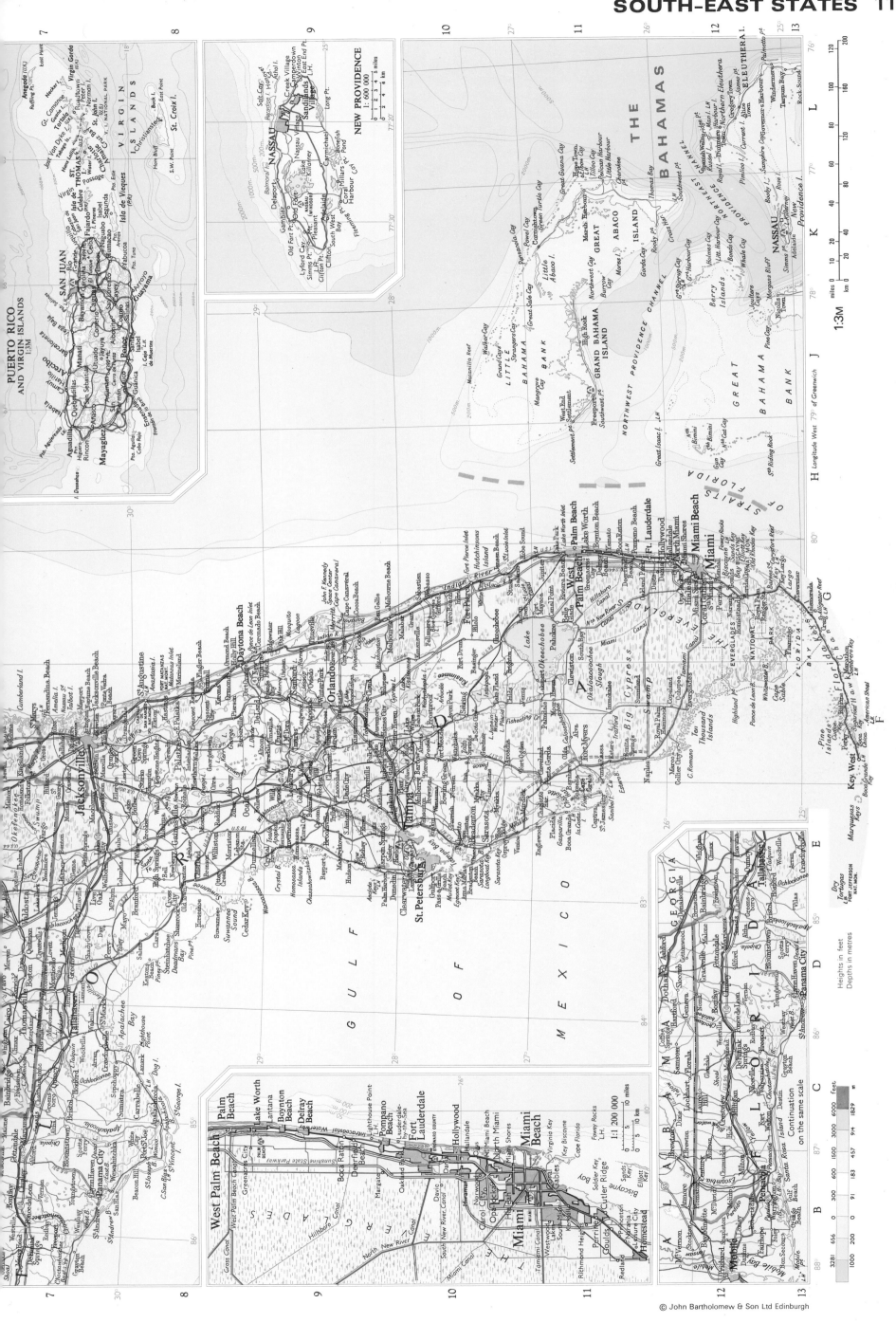

© John Bartholomew & Son Ltd Edinburgh

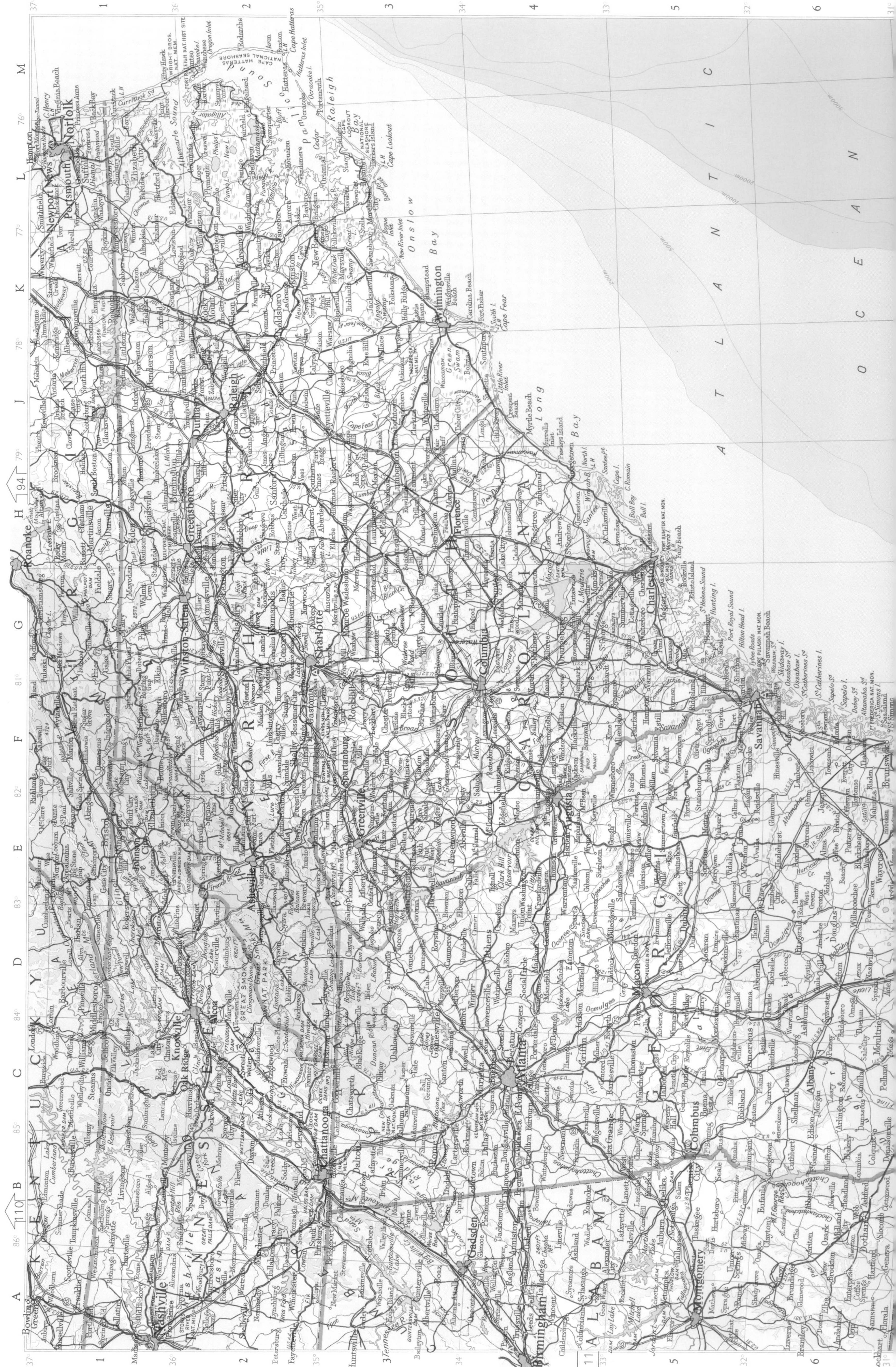

LAMBERT CONFORMAL CONIC PROJECTION

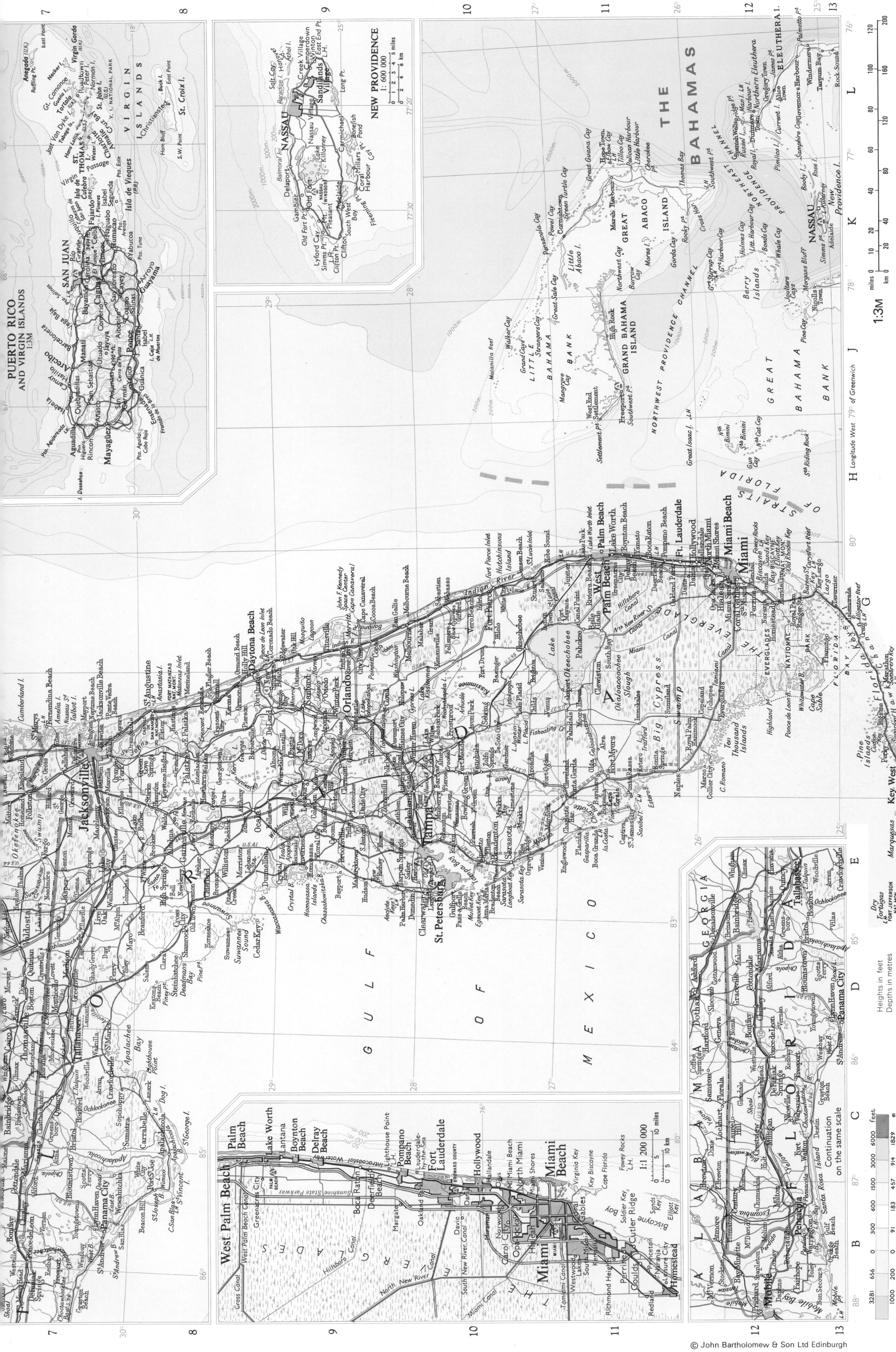
PUERTO RICO AND VIRGIN ISLANDS
1:3M
NEW PROVIDENCE
1: 600 000
THE BAHAMAS
GULF OF MEXICO
Jacksonville
Orlando
Tampa
St. Petersburg
Miami
Miami Beach
Key West
NASSAU
SAN JUAN
1:1 200 000
Continuation on the same scale
Heights in feet
Depths in metres
1:3M

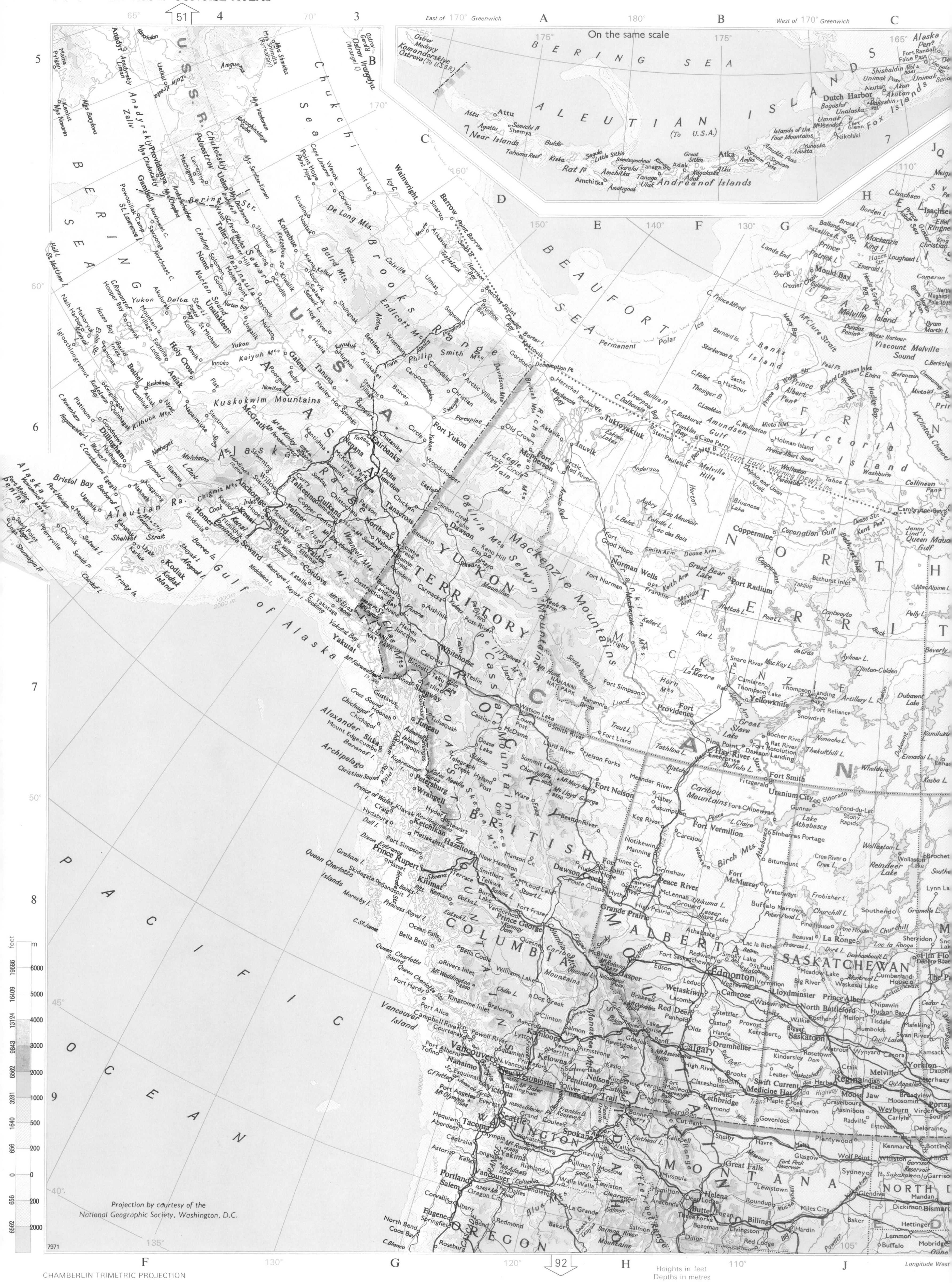
51
92
On the same scale
East of 170° Greenwich
West of 170° Greenwich
BERING SEA
ALEUTIAN ISLANDS
(To U.S.A.)
Near Islands
Rat Is
Andreanof Islands
Fox Islands
Dutch Harbor
U.S.S.R.
Chukchi Sea
BERING SEA
BEAUFORT SEA
Brooks Range
U.S.A.
ALASKA
Alaska Range
Aleutian Ra.
Kuskokwim Mountains
Gulf of Alaska
Anchorage
Fairbanks
Juneau
Kodiak Island
Bristol Bay
YUKON TERRITORY
Whitehorse
Dawson
Mackenzie Mountains
NORTHWEST TERRITORIES
MACKENZIE
Great Bear Lake
Great Slave Lake
Yellowknife
Victoria Island
Banks Island
Inuvik
BRITISH COLUMBIA
ROCKY MOUNTAINS
Alexander Archipelago
Queen Charlotte Islands
Vancouver Island
Vancouver
Victoria
Prince Rupert
Prince George
Kamloops
ALBERTA
Edmonton
Calgary
SASKATCHEWAN
Saskatoon
Regina
WASHINGTON
Seattle
Spokane
Portland
OREGON
IDAHO
MONTANA
NORTH DAKOTA
PACIFIC OCEAN
Projection by courtesy of the National Geographic Society, Washington, D.C.
feet
m
19686
16409
13124
9843
6562
3281
1640
656
0
656
6562
6000
5000
4000
3000
2000
1000
500
200
0
200
2000
7971

CHAMBERLIN TRIMETRIC PROJECTION

Heights in feet
Depths in metres

Longitude West

GREENLAND (DENMARK)
ICELAND
Reykjavík
Akureyri
DENMARK STRAIT
BAFFIN BAY
DAVIS STRAIT
Baffin Island
Devon Island
Ellesmere Island
FOXE BASIN
HUDSON STRAIT
LABRADOR SEA
ATLANTIC OCEAN
NEWFOUNDLAND
Island of Newfoundland
HUDSON BAY
James Bay
Ungava Bay
CANADA
QUEBEC
ONTARIO
LABRADOR
MANITOBA
MINNESOTA
MICHIGAN
WISCONSIN
NEW YORK
NEW BRUNSWICK
NOVA SCOTIA
PRINCE EDWARD I.
Gulf of St Lawrence
Cabot Str.
LAKE SUPERIOR
LAKE HURON
LAKE ONTARIO
LAKE ERIE
Ottawa
Montreal
Québec
Toronto
Winnipeg
Halifax
St John's
Boston
New York
Detroit
Buffalo
Duluth
Churchill
Thule
Godthåb
Frobisher Bay
Fort Chimo
Goose Bay
Schefferville
Sept-Iles
Gander
Corner Brook
Charlottetown
Sydney
Arctic Circle
1:12.5M
km
miles
93
of Greenwich

© John Bartholomew & Son Ltd Edinburgh

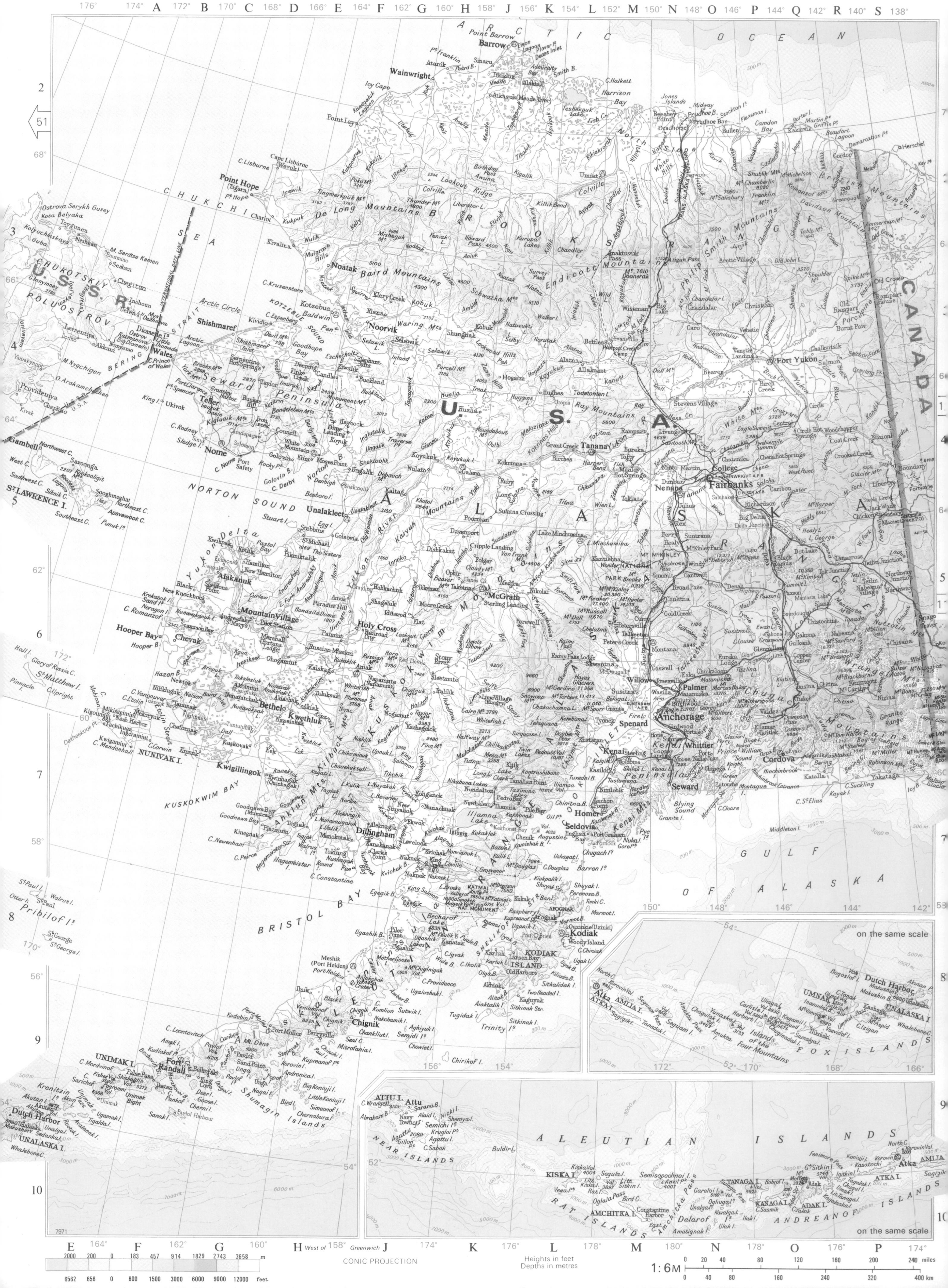
ARCTIC OCEAN
CHUKCHI SEA
BERING STRAIT
KOTZEBUE SOUND
NORTON SOUND
BRISTOL BAY
KUSKOKWIM BAY
GULF OF ALASKA
U. S. S. R.
CHUKOTSKIY POLUOSTROV
U. S. A.
ALASKA
CANADA
INTERNATIONAL DATE LINE
Arctic Circle
BROOKS RANGE
De Long Mountains
Baird Mountains
Endicott Mountains
Philip Smith Mountains
Seward Peninsula
Yukon Delta
Kuskokwim Mountains
ALASKA RANGE
Kilbuck Mts.
Ahklun Mts.
ALEUTIAN RANGE
Chugach Mts.
Wrangell Mts.
Kenai Mts.
Kenai Peninsula
ALASKA PENINSULA
Barrow
Point Barrow
Wainwright
Point Hope
Point Lay
Kotzebue
Shishmaref
Wales
Teller
Nome
Noatak
Noorvik
Unalakleet
Tanana
Fairbanks
College
Nenana
Fort Yukon
Anchorage
Palmer
Seward
Whittier
Kenai
Homer
Seldovia
Kodiak
Cordova
Valdez
Dillingham
Bethel
McGrath
Holy Cross
Mountain Village
Alakanuk
Chevak
Hooper Bay
Kwethluk
Kwigillingok
Chignik
Fort Randall
Dutch Harbor
Spenard
Mt. McKinley
Mt. Foraker
Mt. Hunter
Mt. Spurr
Mt. Wrangell
Mt. Sanford
Mt. Blackburn
Mt. Drum
Mt. Hayes
Mt. Deborah
Mt. St. Elias
Yukon
Kuskokwim
Koyukuk
Tanana
Colville
Noatak
Kobuk
Porcupine
Copper
Susitna
ST. LAWRENCE I.
NUNIVAK I.
St. Matthew I.
Pribilof Is.
St. Paul
St. George
UNIMAK I.
UNALASKA I.
KODIAK ISLAND
AFOGNAK
Shumagin Islands
Trinity Is.
Semidi Is.
Chirikof I.
Middleton I.
on the same scale
FOX ISLANDS
Islands of the Four Mountains
UMNAK I.
ATKA I.
AMLIA I.
ALEUTIAN ISLANDS
ANDREANOF ISLANDS
RAT ISLANDS
NEAR ISLANDS
ATTU I.
Attu
KISKA I.
AMCHITKA I.
ADAK I.
KANAGA I.
TANAGA I.
Adak
Atka
West of Greenwich
CONIC PROJECTION
Heights in feet
Depths in metres
1:6M
miles
km
7971

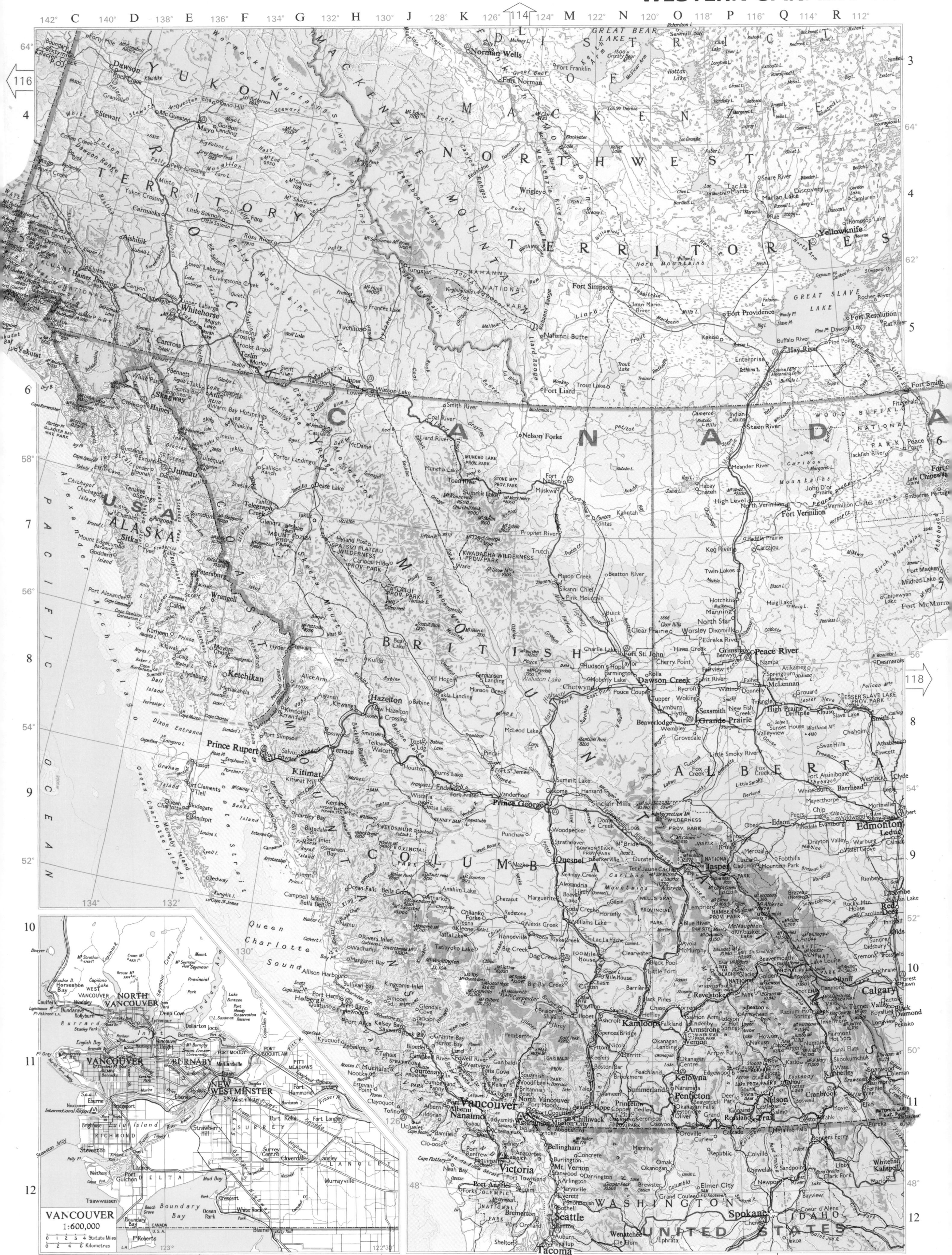

Heights in feet
Depths in metres

6562	656	0	600	1500	3000	6000	9000	12000 feet
2000	200	0	183	457	914	1829	2743	3658 m

1:6M 0 20 40 80 120 160 200 240 miles; 0 40 80 160 240 320 400 km

CONIC PROJECTION

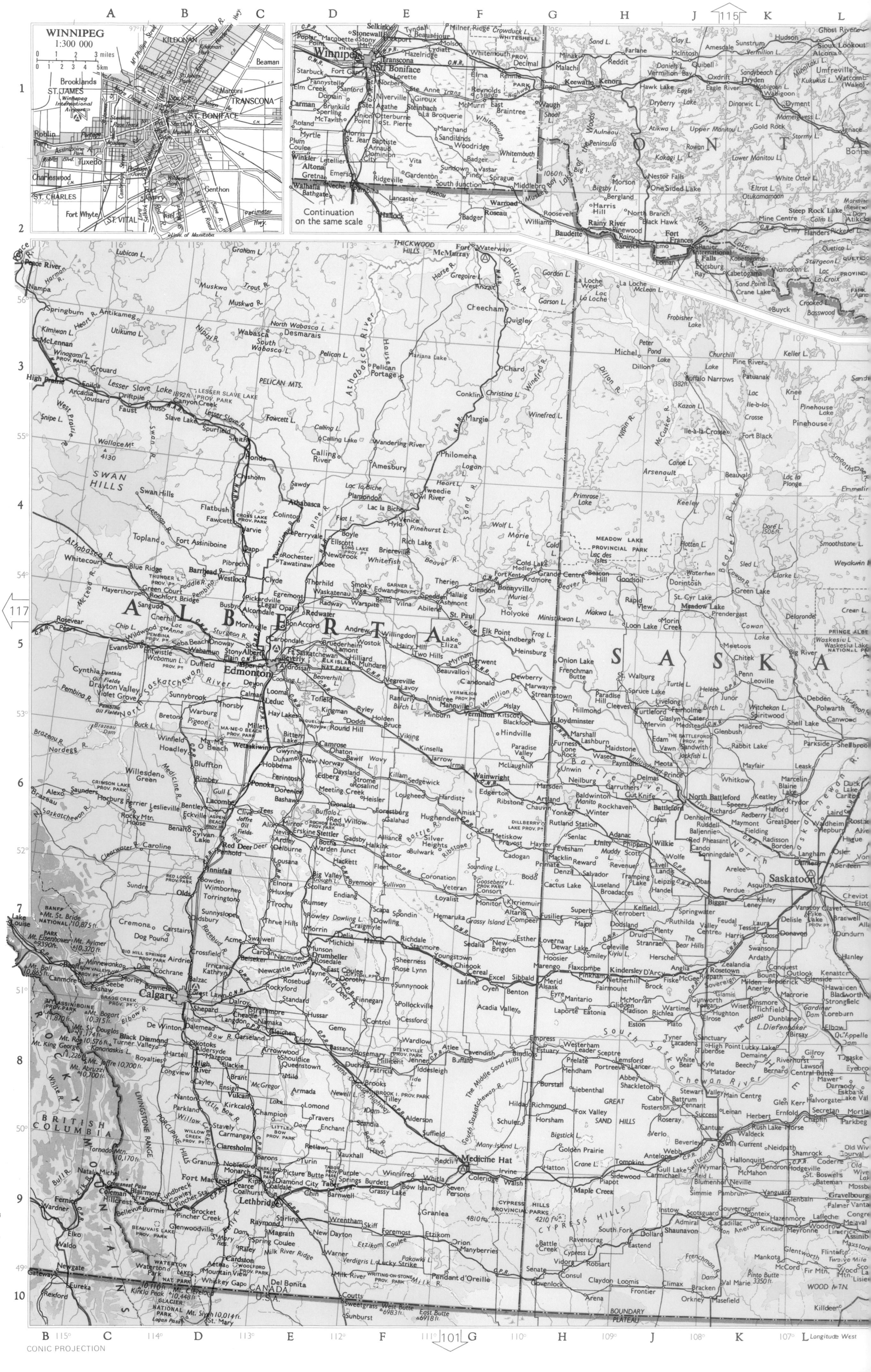
WINNIPEG
1:300 000
Continuation on the same scale
ALBERTA
SASKA
BRITISH COLUMBIA
ROCKY MOUNTAINS
Edmonton
Calgary
Saskatoon
Winnipeg
Lethbridge
Medicine Hat
Red Deer
Swift Current
Lloydminster
North Battleford
CANADA
U.S.A.
CYPRESS HILLS
GREAT SAND HILLS
SWAN HILLS
117
115
101
CONIC PROJECTION
Longitude West

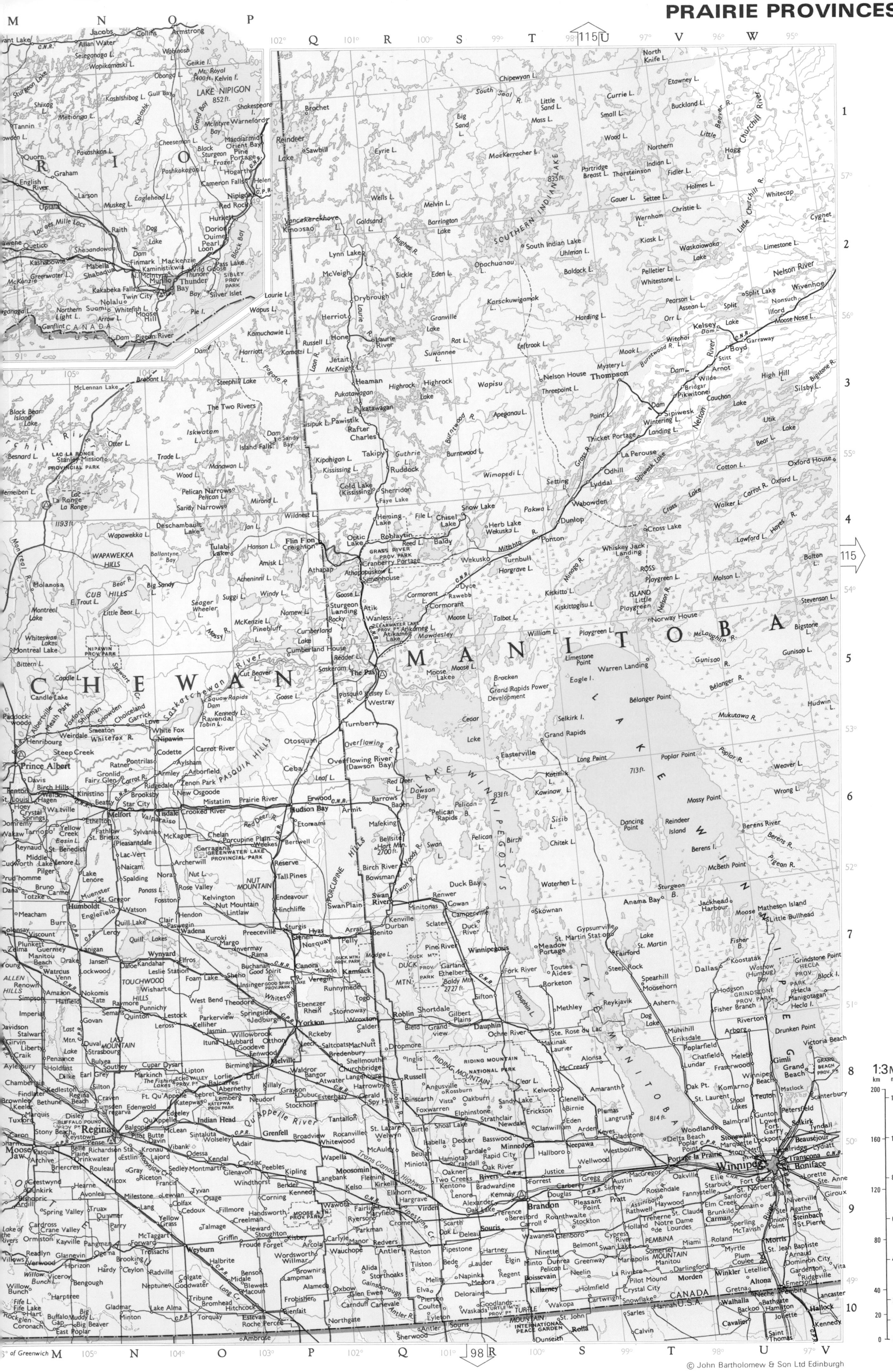
M A N I T O B A
LAKE WINNIPEG
LAKE WINNIPEGOSIS
LAKE MANITOBA
LAKE NIPIGON
SOUTHERN INDIAN LAKE
CHEWAN
Winnipeg
Brandon
Regina
Moose Jaw
Prince Albert
Thompson
Flin Flon
The Pas
Dauphin
Portage la Prairie
Yorkton
Melville
Thunder Bay
Nelson River
Churchill River
CANADA
U.S.A.
1:3M
115
98
Greenwich

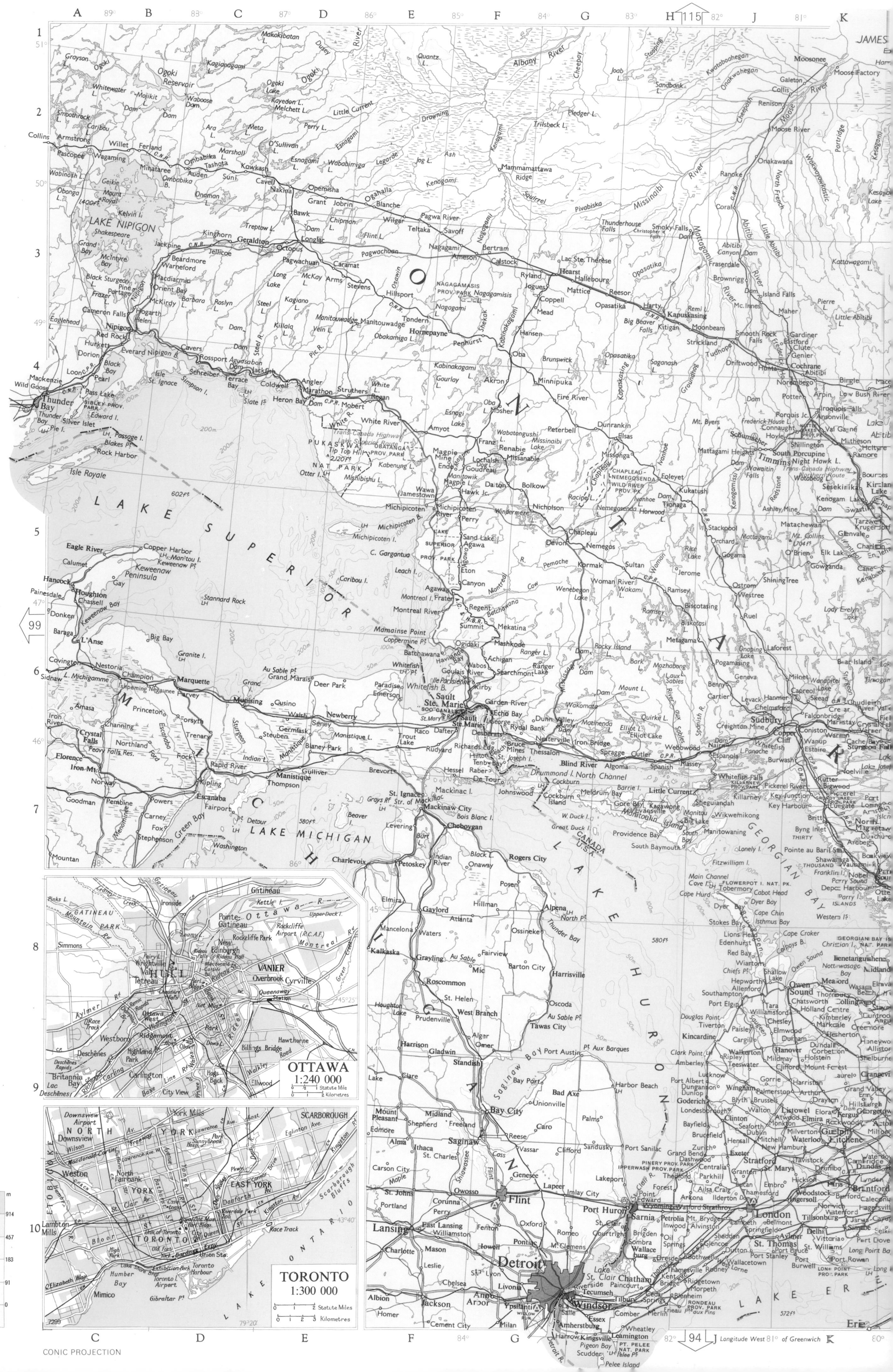

ONTARIO
LAKE SUPERIOR
LAKE MICHIGAN
LAKE HURON
GEORGIAN BAY
LAKE ERIE
MICHIGAN
LAKE NIPIGON
Isle Royale
Keweenaw Peninsula
Thunder Bay
Nipigon
Geraldton
Longlac
Hearst
Kapuskasing
Timmins
Cochrane
Moosonee
Moose Factory
Wawa
Chapleau
Sault Ste. Marie
Sudbury
Marquette
Houghton
Escanaba
Manistique
Mackinaw City
Cheboygan
St. Ignace
Alpena
Bay City
Saginaw
Flint
Lansing
Detroit
Windsor
Sarnia
Port Huron
London
Stratford
Kitchener
Guelph
Owen Sound
Chatham
Leamington
Blind River
Manitoulin Island
Drummond I.
Albany River
Moose River
Kenogami
Ogoki Reservoir
PUKASKWA NAT. PARK
LAKE SUPERIOR PROV. PARK
SIBLEY PROV. PARK
CANADA
U.S.A.
OTTAWA
1:240 000
Statute Mile
Kilometres
HULL
VANIER
Gatineau
Ottawa
Rockcliffe Park
Rockcliffe Airport (R.C.A.F.)
Carlington
Westboro
Britannia Bay
Aylmer
TORONTO
1:300 000
Statute Miles
Kilometres
NORTH YORK
YORK
EAST YORK
SCARBOROUGH
ETOBICOKE
Downsview Airport
Weston
Lambton Mills
Mimico
Humber Bay
Toronto Harbour
LAKE ONTARIO
Scarborough Bluffs
CONIC PROJECTION
Longitude West 81° of Greenwich
99
115
94

Heights in feet

Depths in metres

© John Bartholomew & Son Ltd Edinburgh

QUEBEC
NEW BRUNSWICK
PRINCE EDWARD ISLAND
MAINE
U.S.A.
NOVA SCOTIA
GASPÉ PENINSULA
ST. LAWRENCE (ST-LAURENT)
Shickshock Mountains
NOTRE DAME MOUNTAINS
ANTICOSTI
JACQUES-CARTIER PASSAGE
HONGUEDO PASSAGE
BAIE DES CHALEURS
BAY OF FUNDY
Northumberland Strait
Manicouagan Reservoir
Québec
Chicoutimi
Jonquière
Sept Iles
Baie Comeau
Rimouski
Matane
Gaspé
Campbellton
Bathurst
Chatham
Newcastle
Moncton
Fredericton
Saint John
Charlottetown
Summerside
Halifax
Dartmouth
Truro
Yarmouth
Digby
Bangor
Augusta
Portland
Lewiston
Waterville
Houlton
Presque Isle
Edmundston
Rivière du Loup
Thetford Mines
Sherbrooke
Mt Katahdin
Moosehead L.
BAXTER STATE PARK
ACADIA NAT. PARK
FUNDY NAT. PARK
Mingan Islands
115
121
A B C D E F G H J
1 2 3 4 5 6 7 8 9 10

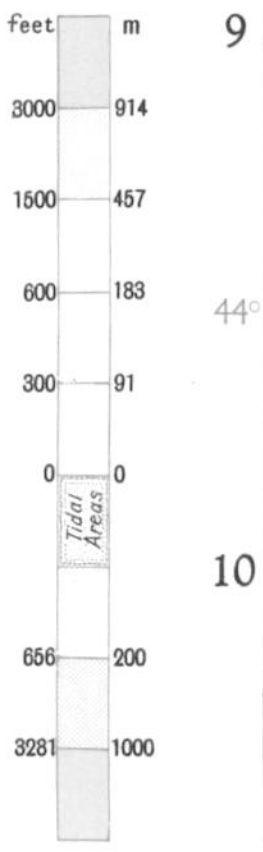
feet
m
3000
914
1500
457
600
183
300
91
0
0
656
200
3281
1000
Tidal Areas

L A B R A D O R
NEWFOUNDLAND
N E W F O U N D L A N D
ATLANTIC OCEAN
G U L F O F
S T. L A W R E N C E
CABOT STRAIT
CAPE BRETON ISLAND
SAINT-PIERRE & MIQUELON (To France)
ILES DE LA MADELEINE (Magdalen Islands) (To Quebec)
LONG RANGE MOUNTAINS
STRAIT OF BELLE ISLE
SABLE ISLAND BANK
Port Hope Simpson
Alexis R.
Francis Harbour
Seal Bight
Fox Harbour
Mary's Harbour
Battle Harbour
Cape Charles
Saint Peter Bay
Henley Harbour
York Pt.
Northeast Pt.
Belle Isle
Belle Isle Landing
White Point
Pinware R.
Barge Bay
Red Bay
Pinware Bay
West St. Modiste
L'Anse au Loup
Anse-Amour
Forteau
Blanc Sablon
Bradore Bay
Salmon Bay
Baie du Milieu
Old Fort Bay
Lac Fourneil
L. du Rocher
Coxipi Lake
Whole Bonne Espérance
Peril Rock
Bayfield I.
Saint Augustin Bay
Outer I.
St. Augustin
Saglenay
Lac Robertson
L. Nesle
Ha Ha Bay
Arabian I.
La Tabatière
Great Mecatina I.
Mutton Bay
Tête à la Baleine
Lac Triquet
Little Mecatina I.
Harrington Harbour
Black Rocks
Pointe-à-Maurier
Saint Mary Is.
Etamamu
Saint Mary Reefs
Wolf Bay
Gethsémani
Washikuti
Coacoachou
Lac du Feu
Musquaro L.
Lac de la Chapelle
Musquaro
Kegaska
Natashquan
Old Post Point
Curlew Point
Cloudberry Point
Lac Fontenedu
Lac Chenil
L. Vitré
Lac Le Tort
Lac Bastille
Lac Briconnet
Lac Verton
Lac Ferru
Lac Montcevelles
L. Boucher
Lac Cormier
Lac Boulain
Lac Durocher
Lac Gayelle
Lac Gaudreault
Lac Costebelle
Minipi L.
Dominion L.
Atiquipi L.
L. Gallet
Lac Poincaré
Kennedy L.
Cuff L.
St. Lewis R.
St. Paul R.
Cape Bauld
Quirpon Island
Quirpon
St. Lunaire
St. Lunaire Bay
Great Brehat
Little Brehat
St. Anthony
Goose Cove
Cook's Harbour
Raleigh
Pistolet
Hare Bay
Main Brook
Fichot I.
Grardois
Croque
Conche
Groais I.
Grey Islands
Bell I.
Grey Islands Harbour
Roddickton
Englee
Canada Bay
Hooping Harbour
Williamsport
Eddies Cove
Flower's Cove
St. Genevieve Bay
Bird Cove
Ten Mile Lake
St. Margaret B.
Ferolle Pt.
Bartlett's Harbour
St. John Bay
St. John I.
Eddies Cove West
Riche Point
Port Saunders
River of Ponds
Bellburns
Daniel's Cove
Portland Creek Pond
Parson's Pond
Gros Pate 2115ft
Harbour Deep
Little Harbour Deep
White Bay
Horse Islands
Partridge Pt.
Fleur de Lys
Confusion Bay
C. St. John
La Scie
Shoe Cove
Round Harbour
Pacquet
Baie Verte
Burlington
Notre Dame Bay
Coney Arm
Seal Cove
Cow Head
St. Pauls Inlet
Jackson's Arm
Sop's Arm
Silver Mt. 1500ft
Westport
Wild Bight
Chimney Cove
GROS MORNE
Gros Morne 2650ft
Bonne Bay
Norris Point
Woody Point
Trout River
NATIONAL PARK
Lomond
Glenburnie
Mt. St. Gregory 2225 ft
North Head
Rattling Brook
Hampden
Springdale
Little Bay Islands
Beaumont
Pilley's I.
Robert's Arm
Twillingate
Charge Islands
New World Island
Herring Neck
Summerford
Boyd's Cove
Fogo
Fogo I.
C. Fogo
Joe Batt's Arm
Tilting
Seldom
Wadham Islands
Sir Charles Hamilton Sound
Doting Cove
Carmanville
Funk I.
Brenton Rock
Lumsden
C. Freels
Newtown
Wesleyville
Greenspond
Indian Bay
Gander Bay
Campbellton
Loon Bay
Little Burnt Bay
Point Leamington
South Twin Lake
Lewisporte
North Twin L.
South Brook
Cormack
Sandy Lake
Trans Canada Highway
Deer Lake
Upper Humber R.
Howley
Main Topsail 1822ft
Millertown Junction
Hodges Hill 1868
Bishop's Falls
Botwood
Peterview
Norris Arm
Glenwood
Gander
Gander R.
Wellington
Trinity
Bonavista Bay
Cottel Island
St. Brendan's
Bonavista
Elliston
Newman's Co
Catalina
Port Union
Salvage
Blackhead Bay
Keels
Plate Cove
Summerville
Port Rexton
Trinity
Glovertown
TERRA NOVA NAT. PARK
Terra Nova
Gambo
Hare Bay
Maccles Lake
Bay of Islands
Lark Harbour
York Harbour
Frenchman's Cove
Cox's Cove
Summerside
Humbermouth
Curling
Corner Brook
Grand Lake
Hinds L.
Hinds Hill 2158ft
Badger
Windsor
Exploits
Grand Falls
Buchans
Buchans Jct.
Millertown
Red Indian L.
Long Pt.
Port-au-Port Bay
Lewis Hills 2673
Glover I.
Lourdes
Three Rock Cove
Port-au-Port Peninsula
Boswarlos
Port-au-Port
Piccadilly
Spruce Brook
Cape St. George
Jardin
Stephenville
Stephenville Crossing
St. George's Bay
St. George's
Flat Bay
Heatherton
Robinson's
St. David's
St. Fintan's
Codroy Pond
St. Andrew's
Cape Anguille
Codroy
Searston
Table Mt. 1700ft
Cape Ray
Channel Port aux Basques
Isle aux Morts
Rose Blanche
La Poile B.
Grand Bruit
North Bay
Blue Hills of Couteau
Burgeo
Ramea Islands
Ramea
Cape La Hune
François
Annieopsquotch Mountains
Victoria L.
Victoria R.
Granite L.
Meelpaeg Lake
Puddops
Noel Paul's Brook
Island Lake
Mt. Cormack 1200ft
Crooked L.
Great Burnt L.
Partridgeberry Hills
Round Pond
Middle Ridge
Kaegudeck L.
Jubilee L.
Deer Pond
St. John L.
Eastern Meelpaeg
Mt. Sylvester 1250ft
Port Blandford
Shoal Harbour
Clarenville
Meta Pond
Koskaecodde L.
Swift Current
Gisburn L.
Milltown
St. Alban's
Bay d'Espoir
Bay du Nord
Rencontre East
Terrenceville
Harbour Mille
Caultois
Hermitage
Belle Bay
Bay L'Argent
Pushthrough
Hermitage Bay
Pass Islands
Harbour Breton
Belleoram
English Harbour West
Fortune Bay
Brunette I.
Garnish
Fortune
Grand Bank
Cap du Nid à l'Aigle
Miquelon
Grande Miquelon
Langlade
Pointe du Ouest
St. Pierre
I. St. Pierre
Burin Peninsula
Creston
Marystown
Burin
Corbin Head
St. Lawrence
Lawn
Lamaline
Jude I.
PLACENTIA BAY
Ship Cove
Argentia
Placentia
Merasheen
Merasheen Island
Long Harbour
Red Island
Dunville
Mount Carmel
St. Bride's
Cape St. Mary's
Branch
St. Mary's Bay
St. Vincent's
Colinet
St. Joseph's
Riverhead
St. Mary's
Salmonier
Trepassey
Cape Race
St. Shott's
Cape Pine
Trepassey Bay
Renews
Cape Broyle
Ferryland
Witless Bay
Bay Bulls
Petty Harb.
Holyrood
Long Pond
St. John's
Conception Bay
Whitbourne
Harbour Grace
Carbonear
Spaniard's Bay
Bay Roberts
Brigus
Heart's Delight
Heart's Content
Victoria
Sunnyside
Winterton
Southern Harbour
Northern Bight
Random I.
Hickman's Harbour
Southport
Trinity
Old Perlican
Bay de Verde
Grate's Cove
New Burnt Cove
Lethbridge
Musgravetown
Lower Island Cove
Bay de Verde
Lance Cove
C. St. Francis
Pouch Cove
Portugal Cove
Torbay
Bell Island
Wabana
Brion I.
Bird Rocks
Grosse I.
East Pt.
Wolf I.
East I.
Coffin I.
Alright I.
Fatima
Étang-du-Nord
House Harbour
Grindstone Island
Grindstone I.
Amherst I.
Southwest Cape
Entry I.
L'Entrée
Havre Aubert
St. Paul Island
Cape St. Lawrence
Cape North
Capstick
Aspy Bay
Dingwall
South Harbour
Neil's Harbour
Pleasant Bay
CAPE BRETON HIGHLANDS NATIONAL PARK
1750ft
Petit Étang
Ingonish
Smoky Cape
Chéticamp
Grand Étang
Briton Cove
East Point
Elmira
Souris
Margaree Harbour
Margaree I.
Margaree Valley
Indian Brook
St. Anns Bay
Sydney Mines
New Waterford
Dominion
Glace Bay
North Sydney
Sydney
Port Morien
North River Bridge
St. Anns
Bras d'Or
Inverness
Strathlorne
Baddeck
St. Andrews
Boisdale
Mira
Scatarie I.
Main-à-Dieu
C. Breton
Louisbourg
Gabarus Bay
Gabarouse
FORTRESS OF LOUISBURG NAT. HIST. PARK
East Bay
Big Pond
Mabou
Ainslie
Scottsville
Trans Canada Highway
Iona
Grand Narrows
Whycocomagh
Orangedale
Bras d'Or Lake
Murray Head
Cardigan Bay
Port Hood
C. George
Judique
Malignant Cove
Antigonish
Tracadie
Havre Boucher
George Bay
River Denys
Port Hastings
Mulgrave
Port Hawkesbury
Louisdale
L'Ardoise
St. Peters
Loch Lomond
Grand River
Fourchu
Madame I.
Arichat
Lincolnville
Boylston
South Lochaber
Guysborough
Strait of Canso
Chedabucto Bay
Canso
Cape Canso
Ogden
Queensport
Port Felix
Tor Bay
Caledonia
Melrose
Sherbrooke
Goldenville
Larry's River
Isaac's Harbour
Port Bickerton
Moser River
Ecum Secum
Port Dufferin
Sonora
East Point
West Point
Sable Island
Lismore
QUEBEC
1:120 000
Statute Miles
Kilometres
Charlesbourg
Giffard
Beauport
Everell
Île d'Orléans
North Channel
Ste.-Petronville
Boulevard Henri Bourassa
Monument
Hôpital St. Michel Archange
Boulevard Ste Anne
Boulevard Métropolitain
Boulevard Charest
Parc de l'Exposition
Limoilou
Pointe Lévis
Lauzon
Lauzon Dry Dock
St. Joseph de Lévis
Duberger
Vanier
Parc Victoria
Port Samson
Bassin Louise
Château Frontenac
Ferry
QUÉBEC
LÉVIS
Bienville
Guay
St. Charles
Airport 3 miles
Centre Industriel
Monument des Braves
Citadelle
Champ de Bataille
Cap Diamant
Quai des Transatlantiques
Notre Dame-de-Lévis
Villemay
Bergerville
Wolfe's Cove
Spencer Crique
Ste.-Foy
Univ.
Hospital
Chemin Ste-Foy
T.V. Sta.
Sillery
Pte. Pizeau
Hadlow Crique
St. David-de-Levis
St. Laurent
St. Lawrence
Union Crique
St. Romuald d'Etchemin
Auberivière
Rivière de la Scie
Henri Road
Le Pont de Québec
Neilsonville
Pont Etchemin
Pont Pierre Laporte
Pont de Québec
New Liverpool
Chaudière Bassin
Etchemin
Rivière Chaudière
1:3 M
km
miles
Long. West 62° of Greenwich
© John Bartholomew & Son Ltd Edinburgh

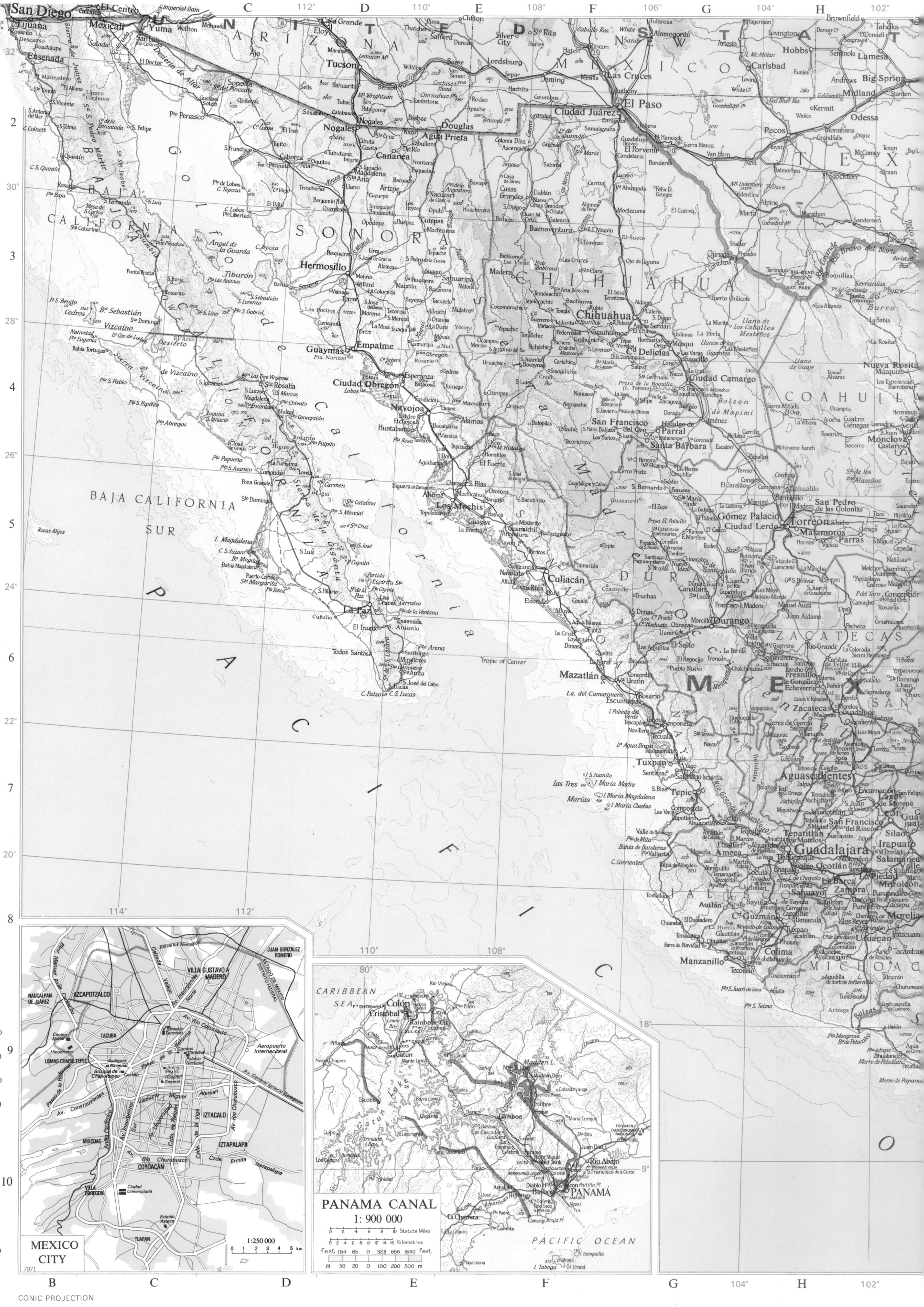
San Diego
Tijuana
Ensenada
Mexicali
Yuma
Tucson
Nogales
Douglas
Agua Prieta
Cananea
El Paso
Ciudad Juárez
Las Cruces
Hermosillo
Guaymas
Empalme
Ciudad Obregón
Navojoa
Los Mochis
Culiacán
Mazatlán
La Paz
Chihuahua
Delicias
Ciudad Camargo
Hidalgo del Parral
Torreón
Gómez Palacio
Ciudad Lerdo
Durango
Zacatecas
Aguascalientes
Tepic
Guadalajara
Colima
Manzanillo
SONORA
CHIHUAHUA
DURANGO
COAHUILA
ZACATECAS
BAJA CALIFORNIA
BAJA CALIFORNIA SUR
ARIZONA
NEW MEXICO
TEXAS
MEXICO
Golfo de California
PACIFIC
Tropic of Cancer
MEXICO CITY
1:250 000
PANAMA CANAL
1: 900 000
CARIBBEAN SEA
PACIFIC OCEAN
Colón
Cristóbal
PANAMÁ
Balboa
Gatun
Madden L.

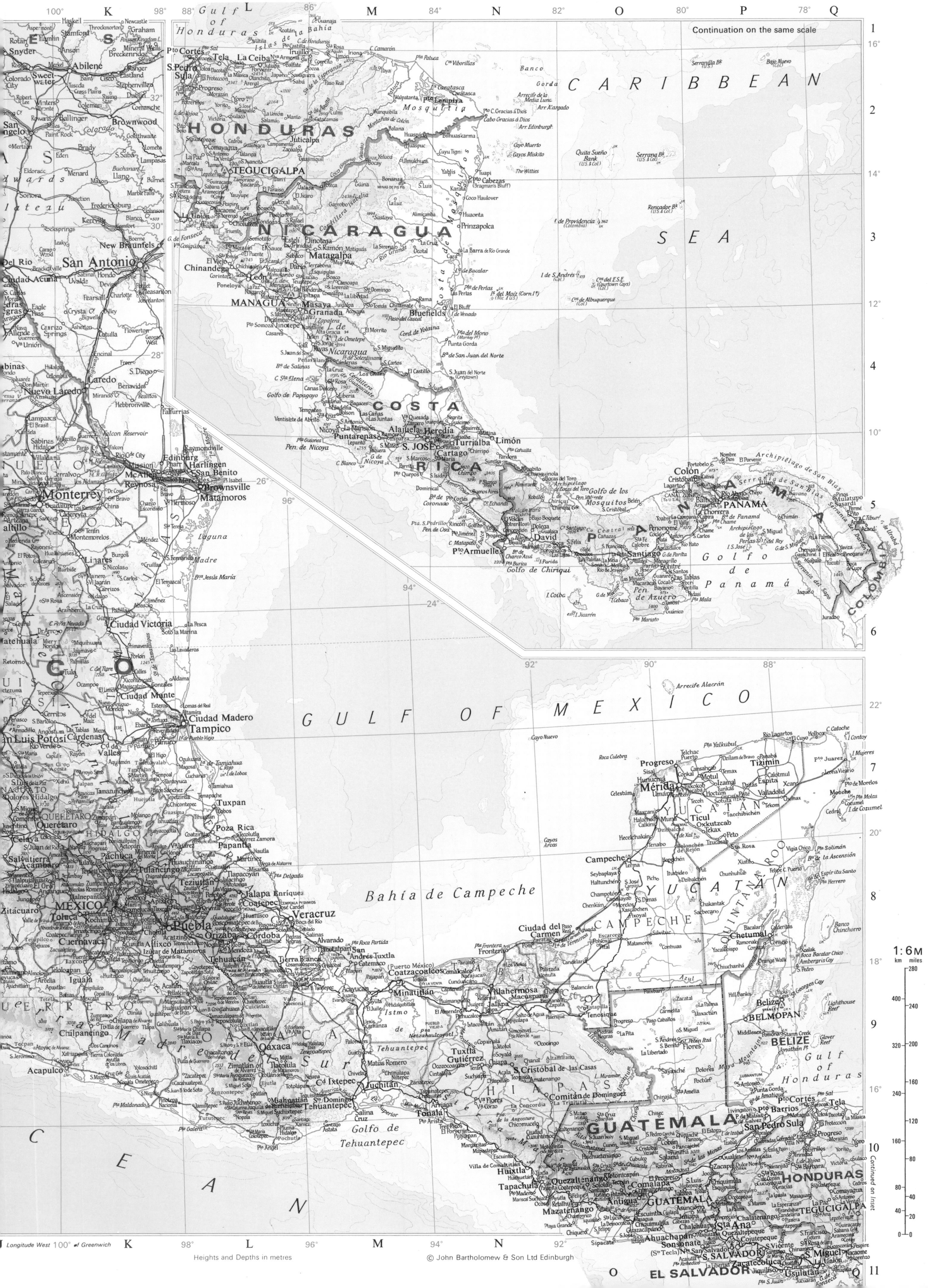
Continuation on the same scale
CARIBBEAN SEA
GULF OF MEXICO
Gulf of Honduras
HONDURAS
NICARAGUA
COSTA RICA
PANAMA
COLOMBIA
GUATEMALA
BELIZE
EL SALVADOR
MEXICO
YUCATAN
CAMPECHE
QUINTANA ROO
CHIAPAS
OAXACA
TEGUCIGALPA
MANAGUA
S. JOSE
BELMOPAN
S. SALVADOR
Bahía de Campeche
Golfo de Tehuantepec
Golfo de Panamá
Golfo de los Mosquitos
Golfo de Chiriquí
Golfo de Fonseca
Golfo de Papagayo
Pen. de Nicoya
Pen. de Azuero
Lago de Nicaragua
Sierra Madre del Sur
Istmo de Tehuantepec
Monterrey
San Antonio
Tampico
Veracruz
Puebla
Oaxaca
Mérida
Campeche
Villahermosa
Coatzacoalcos
Acapulco
Chetumal
Belize
San Pedro Sula
Tela
La Ceiba
Colón
Limón
Puntarenas
Bluefields
Matagalpa
Chinandega
León
Granada
Masaya
David
Santiago
Quezaltenango
Antigua
Mazatenango
Tapachula
Huixtla
Comitán de Domínguez
S. Cristóbal de las Casas
Tuxtla Gutiérrez
Juchitán
Tehuantepec
Salina Cruz
Ciudad Victoria
Ciudad Mante
Ciudad Madero
San Luis Potosí
Querétaro
Pachuca
Toluca
Cuernavaca
Orizaba
Córdoba
Jalapa Enríquez
Poza Rica
Papantla
Tuxpan
Reynosa
Matamoros
Brownsville
Nuevo Laredo
Laredo
Abilene
Sweetwater
Fredericksburg
Ciudad del Carmen
Progreso
Tizimin
Valladolid
Flores
Sonsonate
Ahuachapan
Sta Ana
S. Miguel
Chalatenango
Zacapa
Cobán
Puerto Barrios
Livingston
1:6M
km miles
Longitude West 100° of Greenwich
Continued on Inset

© John Bartholomew & Son Ltd Edinburgh

CONIC PROJECTION

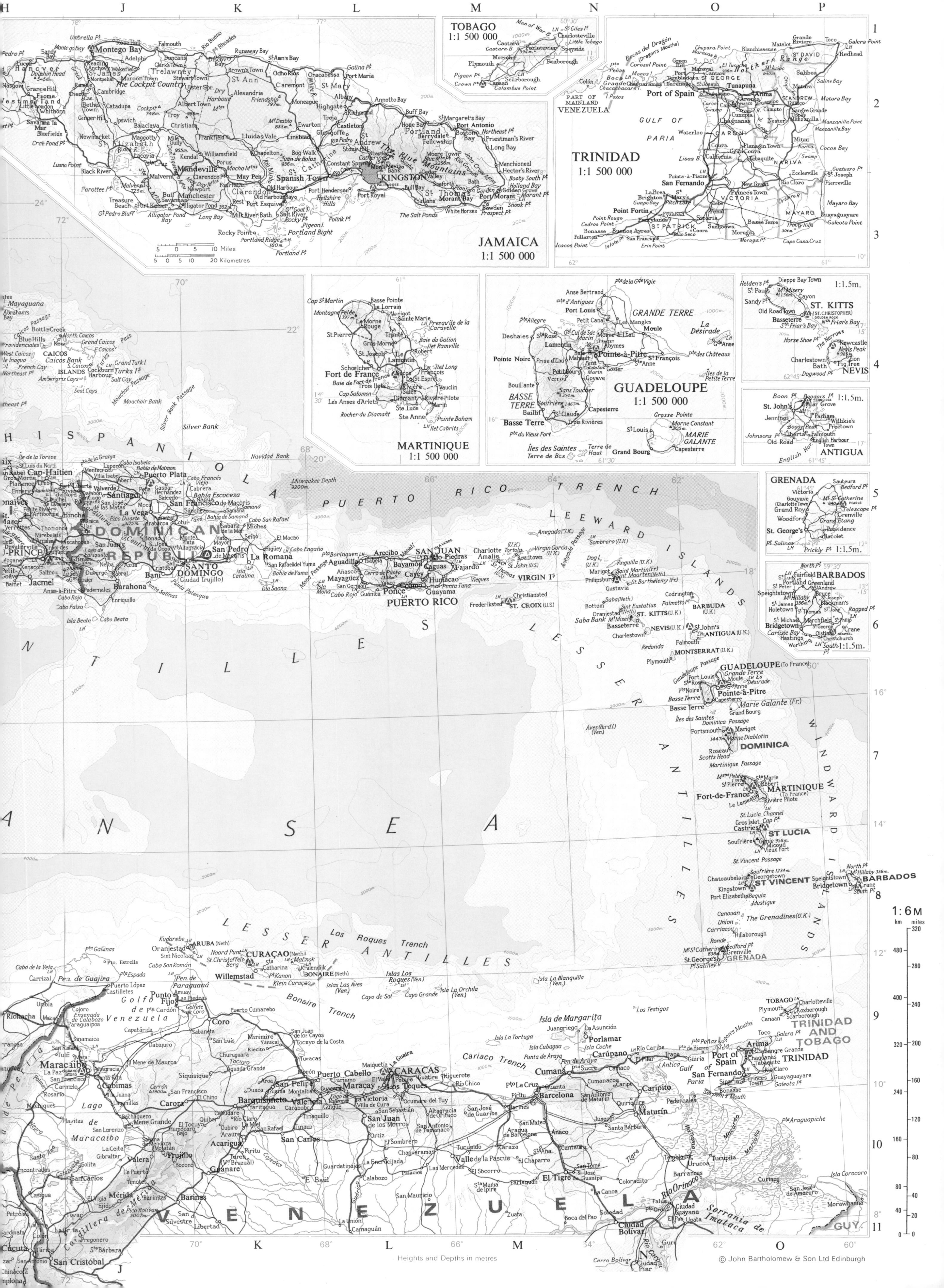
TOBAGO
1:1 500 000
TRINIDAD
1:1 500 000
PART OF MAINLAND VENEZUELA
GULF OF PARIA
Port of Spain
San Fernando
JAMAICA
1:1 500 000
Kingston
Montego Bay
Spanish Town
The Cockpit Country
The Blue Mountains
MARTINIQUE
1:1 500 000
Fort de France
GUADELOUPE
1:1 500 000
GRANDE TERRE
BASSE TERRE
MARIE GALANTE
Pointe-à-Pitre
ST. KITTS
1:1.5m.
NEVIS
ANTIGUA
1:1.5m.
GRENADA
1:1.5m.
BARBADOS
1:1.5m.
HISPANIOLA
DOMINICAN REPUBLIC
SANTO DOMINGO
Cap-Haïtien
PUERTO RICO TRENCH
SAN JUAN
PUERTO RICO
VIRGIN Is
ST. CROIX (U.S.)
LEEWARD ISLANDS
LESSER ANTILLES
WINDWARD ISLANDS
DOMINICA
MARTINIQUE
ST LUCIA
ST VINCENT
BARBADOS
GRENADA
TRINIDAD AND TOBAGO
ARUBA (Neth)
CURAÇAO (Neth)
BONAIRE (Neth)
Isla de Margarita
CARACAS
Maracaibo
Lago de Maracaibo
Golfo de Venezuela
Barcelona
Cumaná
Ciudad Bolívar
Ciudad Guayana
Río Orinoco
VENEZUELA
SEA
1:6M
Heights and Depths in metres
© John Bartholomew & Son Ltd Edinburgh

NICARAGUA
COSTA RICA
PANAMA
COLOMBIA
VENEZUELA
ECUADOR
PERU
BOLIVIA
CHILE
ARG.
SOUTH PACIFIC OCEAN
Bogotá
Caracas
Quito
Lima
La Paz
Medellín
Cali
Barranquilla
Guayaquil
Manaus
Porto Velho
Rio Branco
Iquitos
Cochabamba
Arequipa
Antofagasta
Port of Spain
ST LUCIA
ST VINCENT
BARBADOS
GRENADA
TRINIDAD & TOBAGO
GALAPAGOS ISLANDS
(ARCHIPIÉLAGO DE COLÓN)
(To Ecuador)
On the same scale
Tropic of Capricorn
125
127
133

LAMBERT AZIMUTHAL EQUAL AREA PROJECTION

Heights in metres

G
55°
H
Longitude West 50° of Greenwich
J
45°
K
40°
L
35°
M
N O R T H A T L A N T I C
O C E A N
Equator
SURINAME
FRENCH GUIANA
Paramaribo
Cayenne
Macapá
Belém
São Luís
Fortaleza (Ceará)
Natal
João Pessoa
Recife (Pernambuco)
Maceió
Aracaju
Salvador (Bahia)
Teresina
Brasília
Goiânia
Belo Horizonte
Vitória
Rio de Janeiro
São Paulo
Santos
Campinas
Cuiabá
Corumbá
Campo Grande
Fernando de Noronha (To Brazil)
I. Trindade (To Brazil)
I. Martin Vaz
1:12 M
km
miles

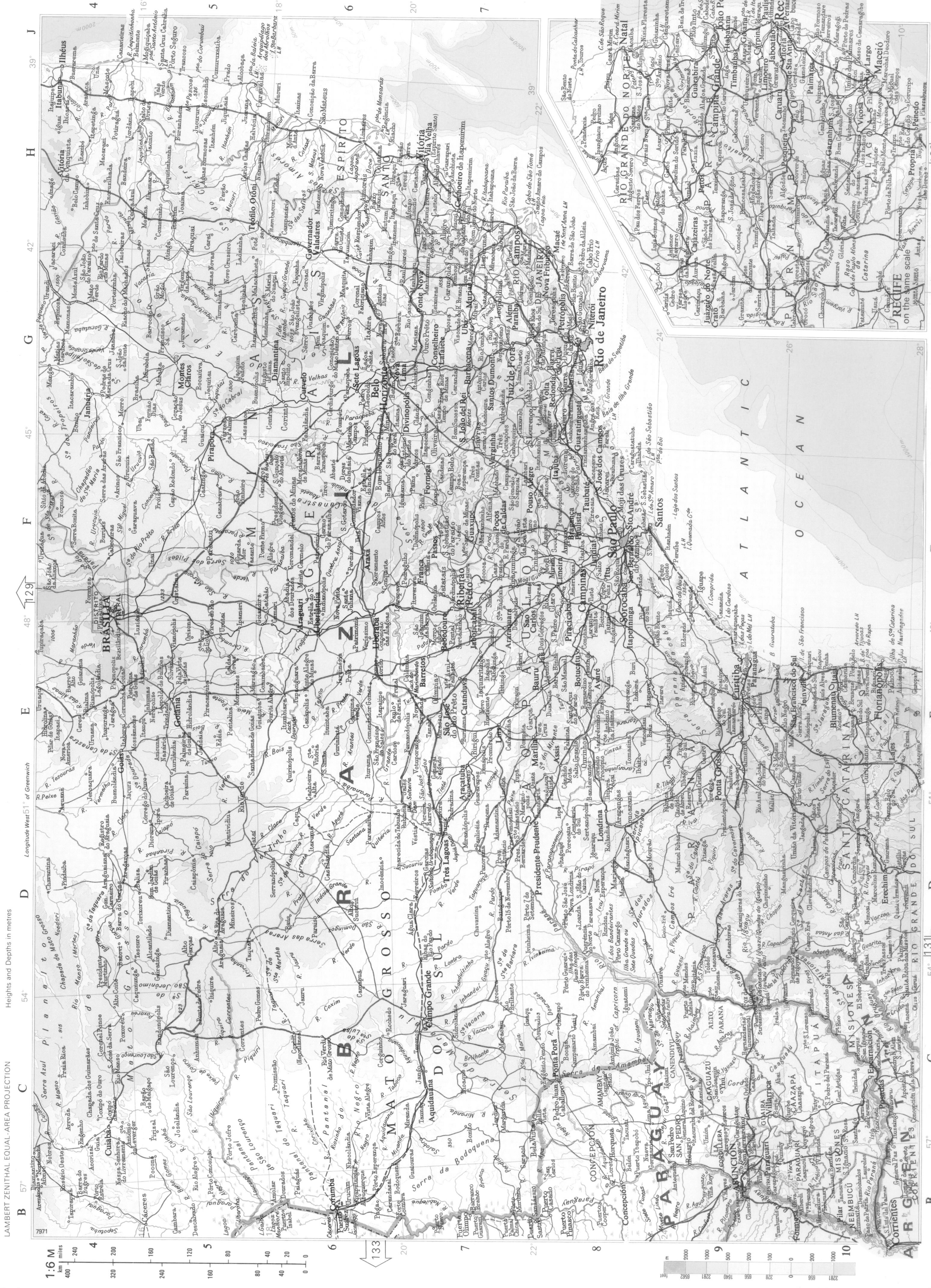

LAMBERT ZENITHAL EQUAL-AREA PROJECTION
Heights and Depths in metres
1:6 M
Longitude West 51° of Greenwich
B R A Z I L
MATO GROSSO DO SUL
MINAS GERAIS
SÃO PAULO
PARANÁ
SANTA CATARINA
ESPÍRITO SANTO
RIO DE JANEIRO
PARAGUAY
ARGENTINA
ATLANTIC OCEAN
BRASÍLIA
Rio de Janeiro
São Paulo
Belo Horizonte
Curitiba
Campo Grande
Goiânia
Vitória
Santos
Florianópolis
Asunción
RECIFE on the same scale
Natal
Recife
João Pessoa
Maceió

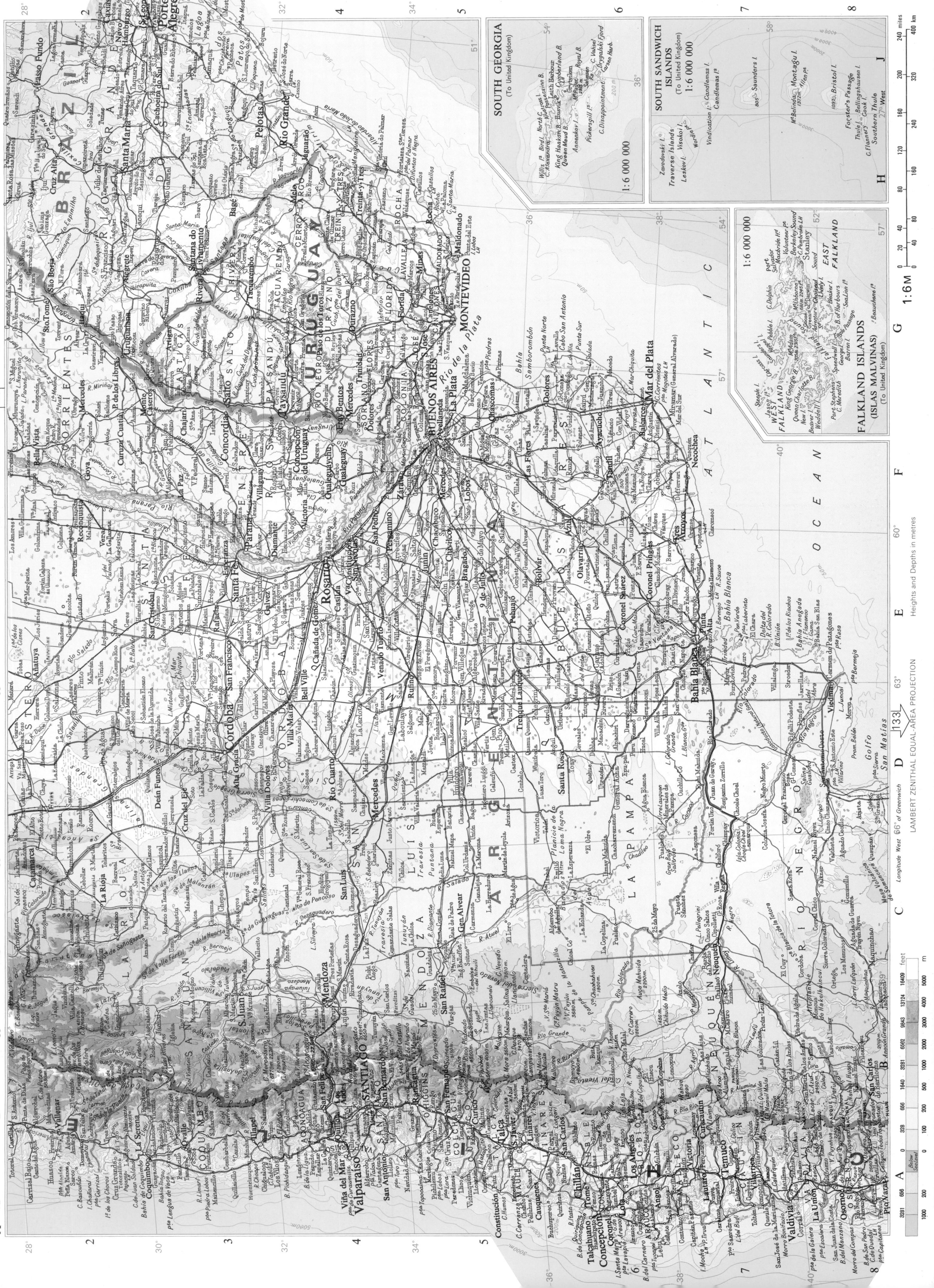
SOUTH GEORGIA
(To United Kingdom)
1:6 000 000
SOUTH SANDWICH ISLANDS
(To United Kingdom)
1:6 000 000
FALKLAND ISLANDS
(ISLAS MALVINAS)
(To United Kingdom)
1:6 000 000
WEST FALKLAND
EAST FALKLAND
Stanley
1:6M
LAMBERT ZENITHAL EQUAL-AREA PROJECTION
Heights and Depths in metres
ATLANTIC OCEAN
URUGUAY
MONTEVIDEO
BUENOS AIRES
SANTIAGO
Valparaíso
Córdoba
Rosario
Mendoza
Bahía Blanca
Mar del Plata
Concepción
Río de la Plata
133

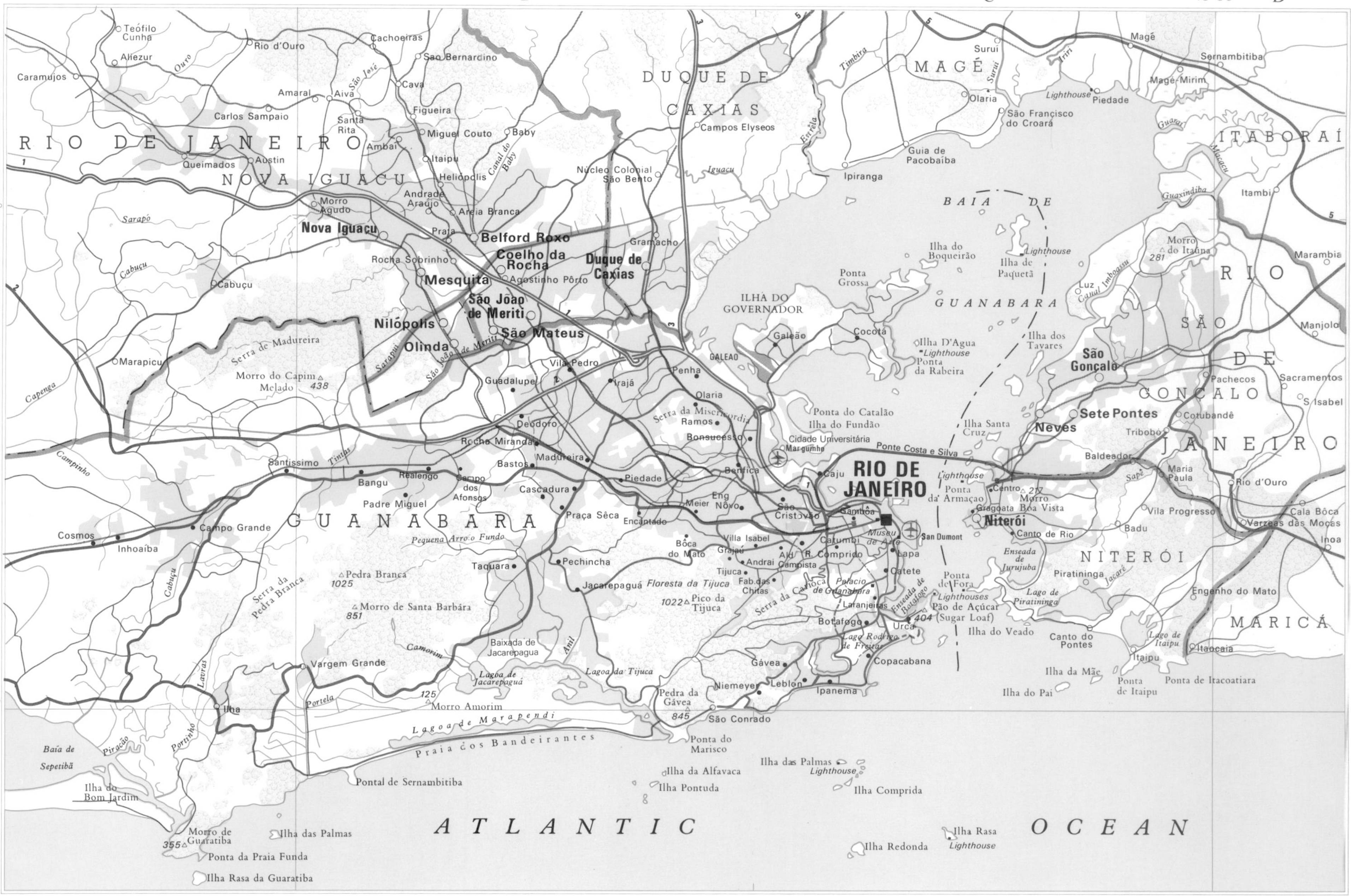
A
B
C
D
43°30′
43°15′
43°00′
22° 45′
23° 00′
1
2
3
RIO DE JANEIRO
NOVA IGUAÇU
DUQUE DE CAXIAS
MAGÉ
ITABORAÍ
RIO DE JANEIRO
GUANABARA
NITERÓI
SÃO GONÇALO
MARICÁ
BAIA DE GUANABARA
ATLANTIC OCEAN
Teófilo Cunha
Aliezur
Caramujos
Rio d'Ouro
Cachoeiras
São Bernardino
Cava
Amaral
Aiva
Figueira
Carlos Sampaio
Santa Rita
Miguel Couto
Baby
Ambai
Queimados
Austin
Itaipu
Heliópolis
Núcleo Colonial São Bento
Campos Elyseos
Morro Agudo
Andrade Araújo
Areia Branca
Nova Iguaçu
Belford Roxo
Coelho da Rocha
Duque de Caxias
Gramacho
Rocha Sobrinho
Mesquita
Agostinho Pôrto
São João de Meriti
Nilópolis
São Mateus
Olinda
Cabuçu
Marapicu
Serra de Madureira
Morro do Capim Melado
438
Guadalupe
Vila Pedro
Irajá
Penha
Olaria
Ramos
Bonsucesso
Deodoro
Rocha Miranda
Madureira
Bastos
Santíssimo
Bangu
Realengo
Padre Miguel
Campo dos Afonsos
Cascadura
Piedade
Praça Sêca
Encantado
Meier
Eng Novo
São Cristóvão
Benfica
Cosmos
Inhoaíba
Campo Grande
Pequena Arro o Fundo
Taquara
Pechincha
Boca do Mato
Villa Isabel
Grajaú
Andrai
Tijuca
Fab. das Chitas
Jacarepaguá
Floresta da Tijuca
Pico da Tijuca
1022
Pedra Branca
1025
Serra da Pedra Branca
Morro de Santa Bárbara
851
Camorim
Baixada de Jacarepagua
Lagoa de Jacarepaguá
Lagoa da Tijuca
Vargem Grande
Ilha
Morro Amorim
125
Lagoa de Marapendi
Praia dos Bandeirantes
Pedra da Gávea
845
São Conrado
Gávea
Leblon
Niemeyer
Ipanema
Copacabana
Lago Rodrigo de Freitas
Botafogo
Urca
404 Pão de Açúcar (Sugar Loaf)
Laranjeiras
Flamengo
Catete
Lapa
Gamboa
RIO DE JANEIRO
Caju
Cidade Universitária
Ponta do Catalão
Ilha do Fundão
Galeão
Cocotá
ILHA DO GOVERNADOR
Ponta Grossa
Ilha do Boqueirão
Ilha de Paquetá
Lighthouse
Ilha D'Agua
Ponta da Rabeira
Ilha dos Tavares
Ilha Santa Cruz
Ponte Costa e Silva
San Dumont
Niterói
Gragoatá
Boa Vista
Canto de Rio
Enseada de Jurujuba
Ponta de Fora
Lighthouses
Ilha do Veado
Canto do Pontes
Piratininga
Lago de Piratininga
Itaipu
Itacoaia
Ponta de Itaipu
Ponta de Itacoatiara
Ilha da Mãe
Ilha do Pai
Neves
Sete Pontes
São Gonçalo
Pachecos
Sacramentos
S Isabel
Tribobó
Colubandê
Baldeador
Maria Paula
Rio d'Ouro
Vila Progresso
Badu
Cala Bôca
Varzeas das Moças
Inoa
Engenho do Mato
Manjolo
Marambia
Itambi
Surui
Olaria
São Francisco do Croará
Piedade
Magé
Mage-Mirim
Sernambitiba
Guia de Pacobaíba
Ipiranga
Baía de Sepetiba
Ilha do Bom Jardim
Pontal de Sernambitiba
Morro de Guaratiba
355
Ilha das Palmas
Ponta da Praia Funda
Ilha Rasa da Guaratiba
Ponta do Marisco
Ilha da Alfavaca
Ilha Pontuda
Ilha das Palmas
Ilha Comprida
Ilha Redonda
Ilha Rasa

BUENOS AIRES

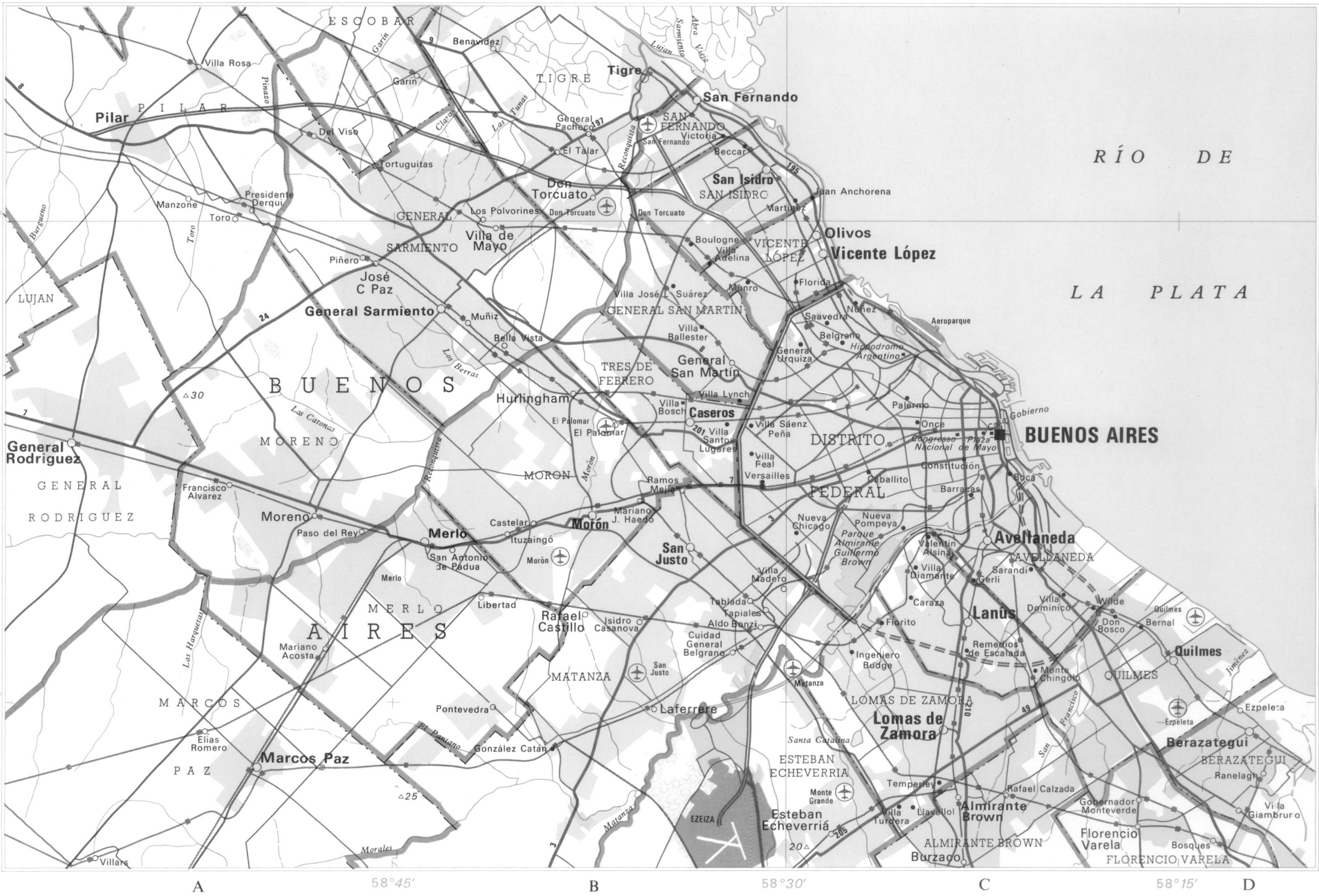
A
B
C
D
58°45′
58°30′
58°15′
34° 30′
34° 45′
4
5
6
ESCOBAR
PILAR
TIGRE
SAN FERNANDO
SAN ISIDRO
VICENTE LÓPEZ
GENERAL SARMIENTO
GENERAL SAN MARTÍN
TRES DE FEBRERO
LUJAN
BUENOS
AIRES
MORENO
MORON
MERLO
MATANZA
GENERAL RODRIGUEZ
MARCOS PAZ
DISTRITO FEDERAL
AVELLANEDA
QUILMES
LOMAS DE ZAMORA
ESTEBAN ECHEVERRIA
ALMIRANTE BROWN
FLORENCIO VARELA
BERAZATEGUI
RÍO DE LA PLATA
Villa Rosa
Pilar
Benavidez
Garín
Tigre
San Fernando
Victoria
Beccar
General Pacheco
El Talar
Del Viso
Tortuguitas
San Isidro
Juan Anchorena
Martínez
Presidente Derqui
Manzone
Toro
Don Torcuato
Los Polvorines
Villa de Mayo
Olivos
Vicente López
Boulogne
Villa Adelina
Piñero
José C Paz
Munro
Florida
Villa José L Suárez
General Sarmiento
Muñiz
Bella Vista
Saavedra
Núñez
Aeroparque
Belgrano
Hipódromo Argentino
Villa Ballester
General Urquiza
General San Martín
Hurlingham
Villa Lynch
Villa Bosch
Caseros
Palermo
El Palomar
Villa Santos Lugares
Villa Sáenz Peña
Villa Real
Versailles
Once
Congreso Plaza Nacional de Mayo
Constitución
Caballito
BUENOS AIRES
Boca
Barracas
General Rodríguez
Francisco Alvarez
Moreno
Paso del Rey
Merlo
San Antonio de Padua
Castelar
Ituzaingó
Morón
Mariano J. Haedo
Ramos Mejía
San Justo
Nueva Chicago
Nueva Pompeya
Parque Almirante Guillermo Brown
Valentín Alsina
Avellaneda
Villa Diamante
Sarandí
Gerli
Libertad
Rafael Castillo
Isidro Casanova
Tablada
Tapiales
Aldo Bonzi
Villa Madero
Caraza
Lanús
Villa Domínico
Wilde
Don Bosco
Bernal
Quilmes
Mariano Acosta
Cuidad General Belgrano
Florito
Remedios de Escalada
Ingeniero Budge
Monte Chingolo
Lomas de Zamora
Laferrere
Pontevedra
González Catán
Elias Romero
Marcos Paz
Santa Catalina
Monte Grande
Esteban Echeverría
EZEIZA
Temperley
Villa Turdera
Llavallol
Almirante Brown
Rafael Calzada
Burzaco
Gobernador Monteverde
Florencio Varela
Bosques
Berazategui
Ranelagh
Villa Giambruno
Ezpeleta
Villars
Río de la Plata

0 5 10 15 km
0 5 10 miles

1:300 000

© Times Newspapers Limited

SOUTH PACIFIC OCEAN
SOUTH ATLANTIC OCEAN
ARGENTINA
BOLIVIA
PARAGUAY
BRAZIL
URUGUAY
FALKLAND ISLANDS
(ISLAS MALVINAS)
(To U.K.)
West Falkland
East Falkland
Tierra del Fuego
Tropic of Capricorn
Buenos Aires
Montevideo
Santiago
Valparaiso
Asunción
Córdoba
Rosario
Mendoza
Bahía Blanca
Mar del Plata
Porto Alegre
São Paulo
Curitiba
Antofagasta
Punta Arenas
Río Gallegos
Ushuaia
C. de Hornos
(C. Horn)
on the same scale
Islas Juan Fernández
(To Chile)
Alejandro Selkirk
(Mas Afuera)
Robinson Crusoe
(Mas Atierra)
Sta Clara
San Félix
San Ambrosio
(To Chile)
South Georgia
(To U.K.)
Shag Rocks
(To U.K.)
Clerke Rocks
C. Disappointment
Below Sea Level
feet
m
LAMBERT AZIMUTHAL EQUAL AREA PROJECTION
Heights in metres
1:12 M
miles
km

LAMBERT ZENITHAL EQUAL-AREA PROJECTION

Heights and Depths in metres

© John Bartholomew & Son Ltd Edinburgh.

64
INDONESIA
MOLUCCAS
SULAWESI (Celebes)
Teluk Tomini
Kep. Togian
Peleng
Kep. Banggai
Kep. Sula
Taliabu
Obi
Bacan
Misoöl
Sorong
Manokwari
Cendrawasih
Teluk Cendrawasih
Biak
Numfoor
Yapen
Tg. d'Urville
Sarmi
Jayapura
IRIAN JAYA
Pegunungan Maoke
Pk. Jaya 4508
CERAM SEA
Seram
Buru 5280 m.
Ambon
Namlea
Bula
Piru
Fakfak
Kaimana
Kokonau
Kep. Banda
BANDA SEA
Kep. Kai
Dobo
Kep. Aru
7440 m.
Kep. Tanimbar
Saumlaki
Kep. Babar
Kep. Barat Daya
Damar
Romang
Wetar
Alor
Dili
TIMOR
Kep. Leti
Kep. Sermata
Atambua
Kupang
Roti
Sawu
Sumba
Waingapu
Flores
Ende
Lomblen
FLORES SEA
5121 m.
Sumbawa
Raba
Mataram
Memboro
Ujung Pandang
Bonthain
Kabaena
Baubau
Butung
Muna
Kendari
Kolaka
Palopo
Rantekombola 3455
Majene
Parepare
Watampone
Teluk Bone
Danau Towuti
Danau Poso
Poso
Donggala
Samarinda
Balikpapan
Makassar Strait
Sabang
Lokilalaki 3311
Kep. Tukangbesi
Kabia
P.P. Macan
Tg. Flamingo
Tg. de Jong
Dolak
Tg. Vals
Digul
Merauke
Tanamerah
NEW GUINEA
Wewak
Aitape
Central Ra.
Mt. Wilhelm 4508
Mt. Hagen
Mendi
Bismarck Ra.
Madang
Goroka
Karkar
Long I.
Schouten Is.
Manam
BISMARCK SEA
Bismarck Archipelago
Manus
Admiralty Is.
Hermit Is.
Mussau
Wuvulu
PAPUA NEW GUINEA
Bulolo
Lae
Wau
Morobe
Kerema
Kikori
Fly
Gulf of Papua
Mt. Victoria 4073
Popondetta
Kokoda
Owen Stanley Ra.
Port Moresby
Abau
Tufi
Daru
Saibai I.
Great N.E. Channel
Torres Strait
Thursday I.
Pr. of Wales I.
Banks I.
C. York
Somerset
ARAFURA SEA
Timor Trough
Timor Shelf
Sahul Shelf
TIMOR SEA
Java Trough
Hibernia Reef
Ashmore Reef
Cartier I.
Seringapatam Reef
Scott Reef
Browse I.
INDIAN OCEAN
C. Van Diemen
Bathurst I.
Melville I.
Dundas Str.
Van Diemen G.
Croker I.
Cobourg Pen.
Clarence Str.
Darwin
Rum Jungle
Adelaide River
Burrundie
Pine Creek
Katherine
Daly
Arnhem Land
Wessel Is.
C. Arnhem
Gove Pen
Nhulunbuy
Groote Eylandt
Gulf of Carpentaria
Limmen Bight
Roper
Sir Edward Pellew Group
Borroloola
Mornington I.
Wellesley Is.
Karumba
Burketown
Normanton
Croydon
Gilbert
Mitchell
Mitchell River
Duifken Pt.
Cape York Peninsula
Iron Range
Weipa
C. Grenville
Direction
Princess Charlotte B.
C. Melville
Cook's Passage
C. Flattery
Cooktown
Laura
Port Douglas
Cairns
Innisfail
Ravenshoe
Tully
Ingham
Palm Is.
Halifax Bay
Flinder's Passage
Townsville
Ayr
Charters Towers
Bowen
Proserpine
Repulse B.
Mackay
Sarina
Northumberland Is.
St. Lawrence
Clermont
Rockhampton
Emerald
Mount Morgan
Gladstone
Dawson
Theodore
Taroom
Great Barrier Reef
Coral Sea
CORAL ISLANDS
Willis Group
Coringa Is.
Coral Sea Plateau
4718 m.
C. Londonderry
Joseph Bonaparte Gulf
Admiralty G.
Queen's Chan.
York Sd.
Brunswick B.
Collier B.
King Sound
C. Lévêque
Rowley Shoals
Mermaid Reef
Imperieuse Reef
Black Rocks
Dampier Land
Derby
Broome
Fitzroy
Fitzroy Crossing
King Leopold Ra.
Mt. Ord
Kimberley Plateau
Ord River
Hall's Creek
Wyndham
Ord
Victoria
Victoria River Downs
Birdum
Daly Waters
Mt. Wallaston
Newcastle Waters
Anthony Lagoon
Wave Hill
L. Woods
Powell Creek
NORTHERN TERRITORY
Barkly Tableland
Tennant Creek
Sturt Cr.
Tanami
The Granites
Camooweal
Mount Isa
Kajabbi
Cloncurry
Richmond
Hughenden
Selwyn
Selwyn Ra.
Dajarra
Georgina
Boulia
Leichhardt
Flinders
Gregory Ra.
Forsayth
Winton
QUEENSLAND
Aramac
Blair Athol
Barcaldine
Longreach
Isisford
Jericho
Springsure
Blackall
Tambo
Yaraka
Barcoo
Thomson
Diamantina
Windorah
Bedi Ra.
GREAT DIVIDING RANGE
Expedition Ra.
Charleville
Roma
Miles
Mitchell
Darling Downs
Toowoomba
Dalby
Quilpie
McGregor Ra.
Grey Range
Warrego
Paroo
Thargomindah
Cunnamulla
St. George
Goondiwindi
Dirranbandi
Mungindi
Stanthorpe
Tenterfield
Moree
Inverell
Walgett
Brewarrina
Bourke
Narrabri
Coonamble
Armidale
Tamworth
Cobar
Wilcannia
Darling
Menindee
Broken Hill
NEW SOUTH WALES
Dubbo
Mudgee
Orange
Bathurst
Maitland
Cessnock
Newcastle
Sydney
Penrith
Parkes
Condobolin
Ivanhoe
Lachlan
Griffith
Hay
Campbelltown
Wollongong
Goulburn
Cootamundra
Wagga Wagga
Deniliquin
Riverina
Murrumbidgee
CANBERRA
A.C.T.
Nowra
Albury
Cooma
Bombala
Kosciusko
Australian Alps
Wentworth
Mildura
Balranald
Swan Hill
Murray
Echuca
Shepparton
Wangaratta
Bendigo
Castlemaine
Maryborough
VICTORIA
Horsham
Ararat
Ballarat
Geelong
Melbourne
Yallourn
Sale
Bairnsdale
Traralgon
Yarram
C. Howe
Hamilton
Portland
Port Fairy
Warrnambool
Colac
Wonthaggi
C. Otway
Wilson's Prom.
King I.
Bass Strait
Flinders I.
Furneaux Group
C. Barren I.
Banks Str.
C. Grim
Smithton
Burnie
Devonport
Scottsdale
Launceston
Queenstown
Mt. Ossa 1617
St. Mary's
Macquarie Harb.
Oyster B.
Hobart
Geeveston
TASMANIA
South West C.
South East C.
969 m.
Naracoorte
Kingston
Beachport
Mount Gambier
Pinnaroo
Nhill
Murray Bridge
Victor Harb.
Encounter Bay
Kangaroo I.
Investigator Str.
St. Vincent G.
Yorke Pen.
Adelaide
Elizabeth
Gawler
Renmark
Wallaroo
Port Pirie
Peterborough
Port Augusta
Quorn
Whyalla
Iron Knob
Spencer Gulf
Eyre Pen.
Cummins
Port Lincoln
Flinders I.
Streaky B.
Ceduna
Fowler's B.
Penong
Gawler Ranges
L. Gairdner
L. Everard
Tarcoola
Ooldea
Maralinga
Woomera
L. Torrens
Flinders Ra.
St. Mary Pk 1189
Leigh Cr.
L. Frome
L. Callabonna
Marree
Milparinka
SOUTH AUSTRALIA
Coober Pedy
Strangways Sprs.
Stuart Ra.
L. Eyre
Oodnadatta
Lake Eyre Basin
Cooper Cr.
Birdsville
Eyre Cr.
Simpson Desert
Finke
Musgrave Ra.
Mt. Woodroffe 1440
Mt. Aloysius 987
Tomkinson Ra.
Petermann Ra.
Giles
L. Amadeus
James Range
Macdonnell Ranges
Mt. Ziel
Alice Springs
Truer Ra.
Barrow Creek
Jervois Ra.
AUSTRALIA
WESTERN AUSTRALIA
Great Sandy Desert
Eighty Mile Beach
La Grange
Wallal
Stansmore Ra.
L. Mackay
Gibson Desert
L. Disappointment
L. Carnegie
L. Wells
Great Victoria Desert
Nullarbor Plain
Eucla
Forrest
Rawlinna
Eyre
Great Australian Bight
Port Samson
Dampier Arch.
Roebourne
Port Hedland
De Grey
Marble Bar
Nullagine
Monte Bello Is.
Barrow I.
Fortescue
Onslow
Wittenoom
Hamersley Ra.
Mt. Bruce 1226
Ashburton
North West C.
Exmouth G.
Barlee Ra.
Teano Ra.
Mt. Augustus
L. McLeod
Lyons
Carnarvon
Gascoyne
Geographe Chan.
Shark B.
Dirk Hartog I.
Murchison
Meekatharra
Wiluna
Big Bell
Cue
Sandstone
Mt. Magnet
Leonora
Laverton
Gantheaume B.
Northampton
Mullewa
Houtman Abrolhos
Geraldton
Dongara
L. Barlee
Menzies
L. Moore
Kalannie
Kalgoorlie
Boulder
Coolgardie
Bencubbin
Bullfinch
Southern Cross
Merredin
Moora
Goomalling
Northam
Perth
Fremantle
Pinjarra
Pingelly
Corrigin
Narrogin
L. Cowan
Norseman
Collie
Bunbury
C. Naturaliste
Busselton
Augusta
C. Leeuwin
Wagin
Pingrup
Katanning
Kojonup
Manjimup
Bluff Knoll 1110
C. Knob
Albany
King George Sd.
Esperance
C. Pasley
Arch. of the Recherche
Leeuwin Sill
SOUTH AUSTRALIAN BASIN
148 m.
feet
m.
9843 3000
6562 2000
3281 1000
1640 500
656 200
0
Below Sea Level
656 200
3281 1000
9843 3000
13124 4000
16409 5000
19686 6000
26248 8000
7971
East of Greenwich

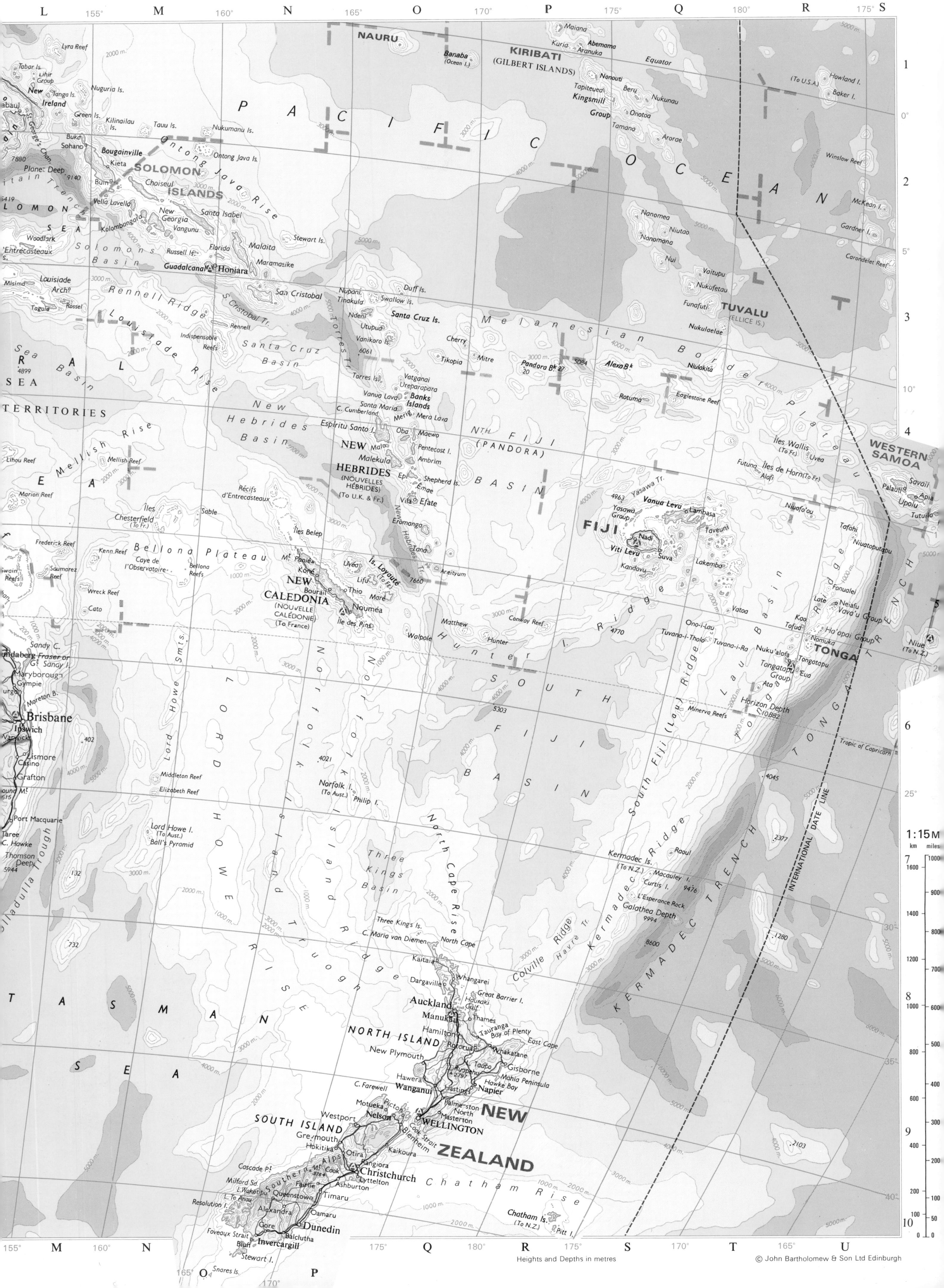
PACIFIC OCEAN
NAURU
KIRIBATI
(GILBERT ISLANDS)
Banaba
(Ocean I.)
Maiana
Abemama
Kuria
Aranuka
Equator
Nonouti
Tapiteuea
Beru
Nukunau
Kingsmill
Group
Onotoa
Tamana
Arorae
Howland I.
Baker I.
(To U.S.A.)
Winslow Reef
McKean I.
Gardner I.
Carondelet Reef
Nanomea
Niutao
Nanomana
Nui
Vaitupu
Nukufetau
Funafuti
TUVALU
(ELLICE IS.)
Nukulaelae
Niulakita
Eaglestone Reef
Rotuma
Alexa Bk.
Pandora Bk.
Melanesian Border Plateau
Lyra Reef
Tabar Is.
Lihir Group
New Ireland
Tanga Is.
Nuguria Is.
Green Is.
Kilinailau Is.
Tauu Is.
Nukumanu Is.
Ontong Java Is.
Ontong Java Rise
St George's Chan.
Buka
Sohano
Bougainville
Kieta
SOLOMON ISLANDS
Choiseul
Planet Deep
9140
7880
Buin
Vella Lavella
Kolombangara
New Georgia
Vangunu
Santa Isabel
SOLOMON SEA
Woodlark
D'Entrecasteaux Is.
Solomons Basin
Russell Is.
Florida
Malaita
Maramasike
Stewart Is.
Guadalcanal
Honiara
Louisiade Archᵒ
Misima
Tagula
Rossel
Rennell Ridge
San Cristobal
S. Cristobal Tr.
Rennell
Indispensable Reefs
Louisiade Rise
Santa Cruz Basin
Nupani
Tinakula
Duff Is.
Swallow Is.
Ndeni
Santa Cruz Is.
Utupua
Vanikoro Is.
Torres Tr.
6061
Cherry
Tikopia
Mitre
Torres Is.
Vatganai
Ureparapara
Banks Islands
Vanua Lava
Santa Maria
C. Cumberland
Merig
Mera Lava
Espiritu Santo I.
Oba
Maewo
Malo
Pentecost I.
Malekula
Ambrim
NEW HEBRIDES
(NOUVELLES HÉBRIDES)
(To U.K. & Fr.)
Epi
Shepherd Is.
Emae
Vila
Efate
Eromanga
Tana
Aneityum
New Hebrides Tr.
NTH FIJI (PANDORA) BASIN
New Hebrides Basin
Mellish Rise
Mellish Reef
Lihou Reef
CORAL SEA
TERRITORIES
Marion Reef
Récifs d'Entrecasteaux
Îles Chesterfield
(To Fr.)
Sable
Îles Belep
Frederick Reef
Kenn Reef
Bellona Plateau
Caye de l'Observatoire
Bellona Reefs
Saumarez Reef
Wreck Reef
Cato
Mt Panié
Koné
Bourail
NEW CALEDONIA
(NOUVELLE CALÉDONIE)
(To France)
Nouméa
Île des Pins
Is. Loyauté
Uvéa
Lifu
Maré
Thio
7660
Matthew
Hunter
Walpole
Conway Reef
Hunter Ridge
Yasawa Tr.
Yasawa Group
Vanua Levu
Lambasa
Taveuni
FIJI
Nadi
Viti Levu
Suva
Kandavu
Lakemba
4963
Vatoa
Lau Ridge
Lau Basin
Ono-i-Lau
Tuvana-i-Tholo
Tuvana-i-Ra
4770
Îles Wallis
(To Fr.)
Uvea
Futuna
Îles de Horn (To Fr.)
Alofi
Niuafo'ou
WESTERN SAMOA
Savaii
Apia
Upolu
Palauli
Tutuila
Tafahi
Niuatoputapu
Fonualei
Late
Neiafu
Vava'u Group
Kao
Tofua
Ha'apai Group
Nomuka
Niue
(To N.Z.)
TONGA
Nuku'alofa
Tongatapu
Tongatapu Group
'Eua
Ata
Tonga Ridge
TONGA TRENCH
Horizon Depth
10,882
Minerva Reefs
SOUTH FIJI BASIN
5303
South Fiji (Lau) Ridge
Tropic of Capricorn
INTERNATIONAL DATE LINE
4045
2377
Raoul
Kermadec Is.
(To N.Z.)
Macauley I.
Curtis I.
9476
L'Esperance Rock
Galathea Depth
9994
8600
Kermadec Ridge
KERMADEC TRENCH
Havre Tr.
Colville Ridge
1280
2103
Sandy C.
Bundaberg
Fraser or Gᵗ Sandy I.
Maryborough
Gympie
Moreton B.
Brisbane
Ipswich
Warwick
Lismore
Casino
Grafton
Port Macquarie
Taree
C. Hawke
Thomson Deep
5944
Lord Howe Smts.
Lord Howe Rise
Middleton Reef
Elizabeth Reef
Lord Howe I.
(To Aust.)
Ball's Pyramid
Norfolk I.
(To Aust.)
Philip I.
4021
Norfolk Island Ridge
Norfolk Island Trough
Three Kings Basin
North Cape Rise
Three Kings Is.
C. Maria van Diemen
North Cape
Kaitaia
Whangarei
Dargaville
Great Barrier I.
Hauraki Gulf
Auckland
Manukau
Thames
Hamilton
Tauranga
Bay of Plenty
East Cape
NORTH ISLAND
Rotorua
Whakatane
New Plymouth
Taupo
Gisborne
Ruapehu
Mahia Peninsula
Hawera
Hawke Bay
Wanganui
Hastings
Napier
C. Farewell
Palmerston North
Masterton
Motueka
Picton
Nelson
Westport
WELLINGTON
NEW ZEALAND
SOUTH ISLAND
Greymouth
Blenheim
Cook Strait
Hokitika
Otira
Kaikoura
Cascade Pt.
Mt Cook
Southern Alps
Kangiora
Christchurch
Lyttelton
Milford Sd.
L. Wakatipu
Fairlie
Ashburton
Queenstown
Timaru
Resolution I.
L. Te Anau
Alexandra
Oamaru
Gore
Dunedin
Foveaux Strait
Balclutha
Bluff
Invercargill
Stewart I.
Snares Is.
Chatham Rise
Chatham Is.
(To N.Z.)
Pitt I.
TASMAN SEA
Dampier Tr.
Ulladulla Trough
1:15M
km
miles

Heights and Depths in metres

© John Bartholomew & Son Ltd Edinburgh

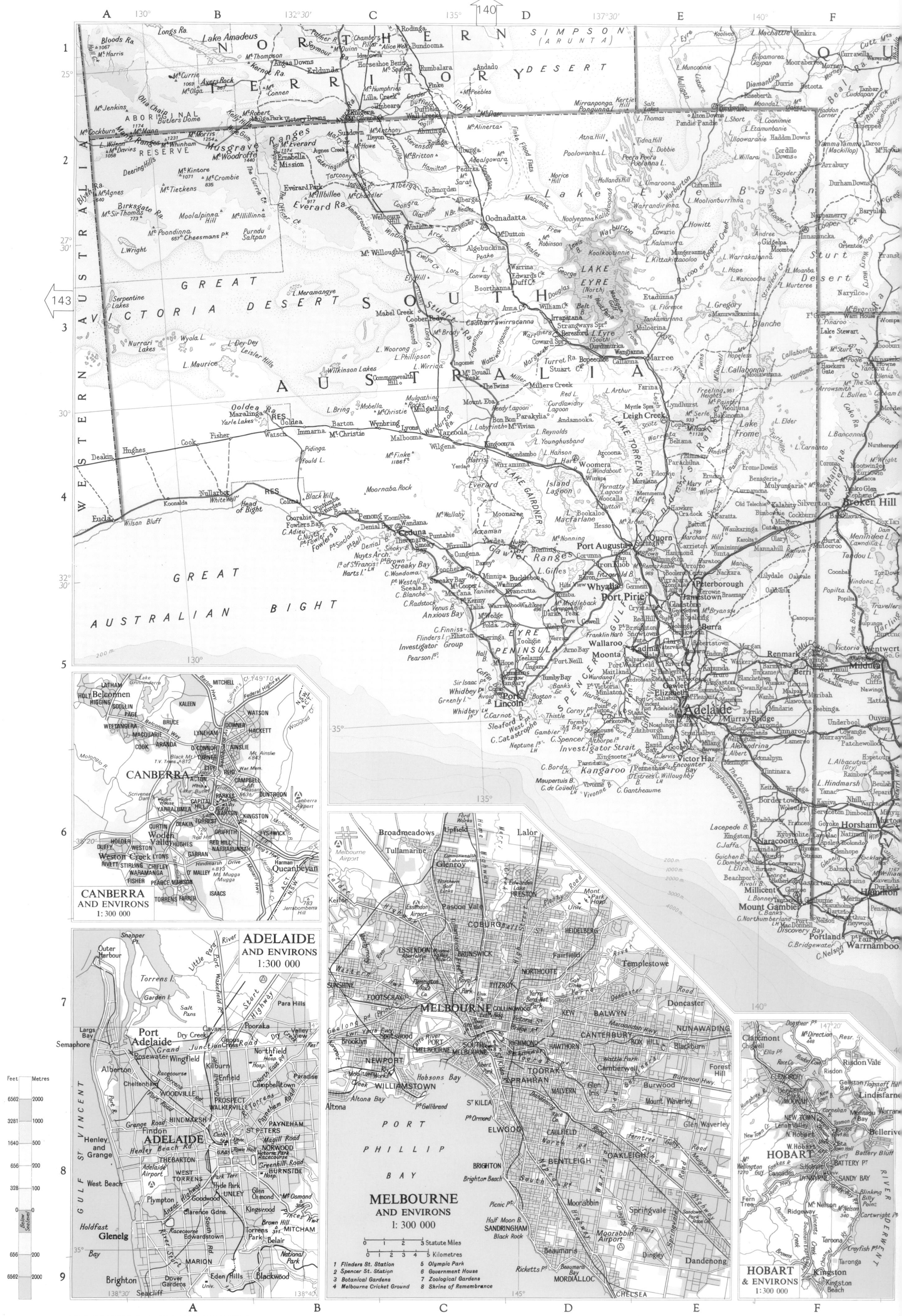
140
143
NORTHERN TERRITORY
SIMPSON (ARUNTA) DESERT
SOUTH AUSTRALIA
WESTERN AUSTRALIA
GREAT VICTORIA DESERT
GREAT AUSTRALIAN BIGHT
Lake Eyre Basin
Sturt Desert
LAKE EYRE (North)
L. Eyre (South)
LAKE TORRENS
LAKE GAIRDNER
Lake Frome
Gawler Ranges
EYRE PENINSULA
SPENCER GULF
Investigator Strait
Kangaroo I.
Musgrave Ranges
ABORIGINAL RESERVE
Oodnadatta
Coober Pedy
Woomera
Port Augusta
Whyalla
Port Pirie
Port Lincoln
Ceduna
Broken Hill
Peterborough
Adelaide
Renmark
Mildura
Horsham
Naracoorte
Mount Gambier
Portland
Warrnambool
Victor Har.
Murray Bridge
CANBERRA AND ENVIRONS
1: 300 000
CANBERRA
Queanbeyan
ADELAIDE AND ENVIRONS
1:300 000
ADELAIDE
Port Adelaide
Glenelg
GULF ST VINCENT
MELBOURNE AND ENVIRONS
1: 300 000
MELBOURNE
PORT PHILLIP BAY
Statute Miles
Kilometres
1 Flinders St. Station
2 Spencer St. Station
3 Botanical Gardens
4 Melbourne Cricket Ground
5 Olympic Park
6 Government House
7 Zoological Gardens
8 Shrine of Remembrance
HOBART & ENVIRONS
1:300 000
HOBART
RIVER DERWENT
Feet
Metres
6562
2000
3281
1000
1640
500
656
200
328
100
0
Below Sea Level

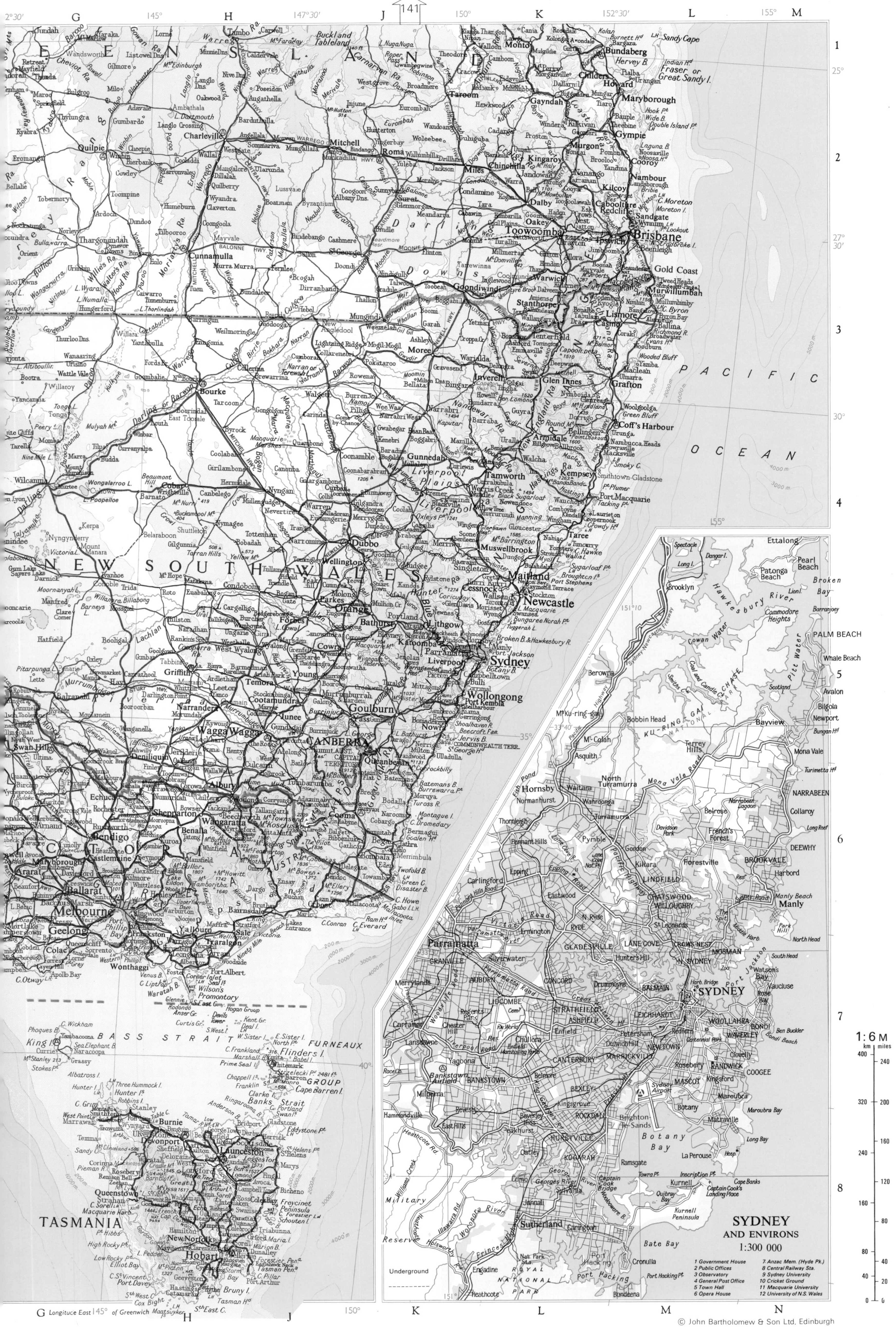
NEW SOUTH WALES
TASMANIA
BASS STRAIT
PACIFIC
OCEAN
Brisbane
Sydney
Canberra
Melbourne
Hobart
Newcastle
Wollongong
Toowoomba
Bundaberg
Maryborough
Gympie
Gold Coast
Lismore
Grafton
Coff's Harbour
Port Macquarie
Tamworth
Armidale
Dubbo
Orange
Bathurst
Goulburn
Wagga Wagga
Albury
Bendigo
Ballarat
Geelong
Launceston
Devonport
Burnie
Bourke
Charleville
Roma
Mitchell
Cunnamulla
Moree
Goondiwindi
Griffith
Mildura
Swan Hill
Echuca
Shepparton
Wangaratta
Cooma
Bega
Sale
Traralgon
Queenstown
SYDNEY
AND ENVIRONS
1:300 000
1 Government House
2 Public Offices
3 Observatory
4 General Post Office
5 Town Hall
6 Opera House
7 Anzac Mem. (Hyde Pk.)
8 Central Railway Sta.
9 Sydney University
10 Cricket Ground
11 Macquarie University
12 University of N.S. Wales
Parramatta
Manly
Botany Bay
Hornsby
Bankstown
Sutherland
1:6 M
km miles
Longitude East 145° of Greenwich

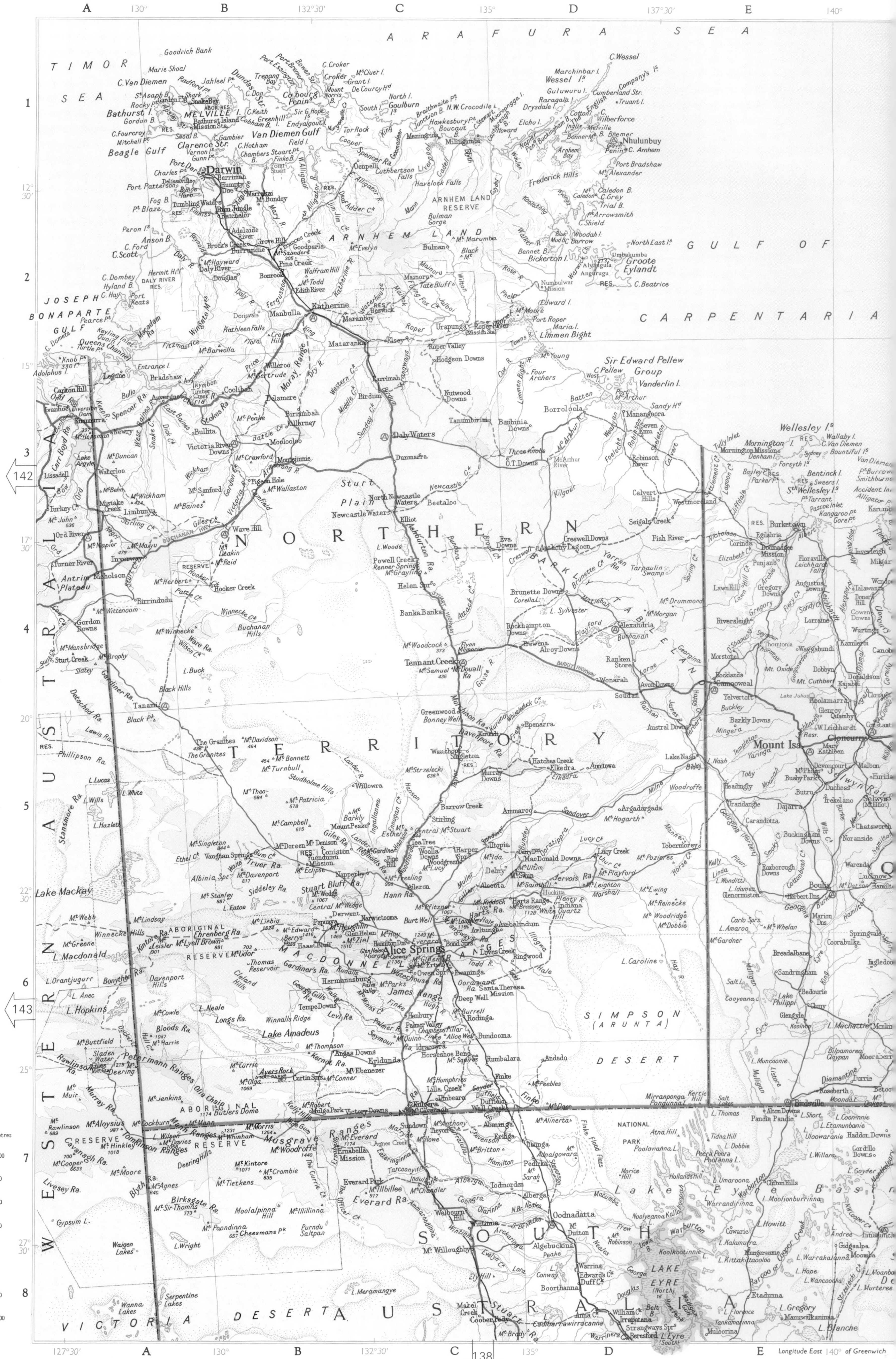

LAMBERT ZENITHAL EQUAL AREA PROJECTION

BRISBANE
1:300 000
Statute Miles
Kilometres
C O R A L S E A
G R E A T B A R R I E R R E E F
Q U E E N S L A N D
N E W S O U T H W A L E S
G R E A T D I V I D I N G R A N G E
CAPE YORK PENINSULA
Torres Strait
Gulf Country
Capricorn Channel
Tropic of Capricorn
Cooktown
Cairns
Gordonvale
Mareeba
Atherton
Innisfail
Tully
Ingham
Townsville
Ayr
Charters Towers
Bowen
Proserpine
Mackay
Hughenden
Winton
Longreach
Barcaldine
Emerald
Rockhampton
Yeppoon
Gladstone
Biloela
Bundaberg
Maryborough
Gympie
Nambour
Caboolture
Brisbane
Ipswich
Toowoomba
Dalby
Warwick
Stanthorpe
Goondiwindi
Roma
Charleville
Cunnamulla
Quilpie
Blackall
Mitchell
Miles
Chinchilla
Kingaroy
Gold Coast
Murwillumbah
Lismore
Casino
Croydon
Normanton
Clermont
Collinsville
Taroom
1:6 M
km
miles
Heights and Depths in metres

© John Bartholomew & Son Ltd, Edinburgh

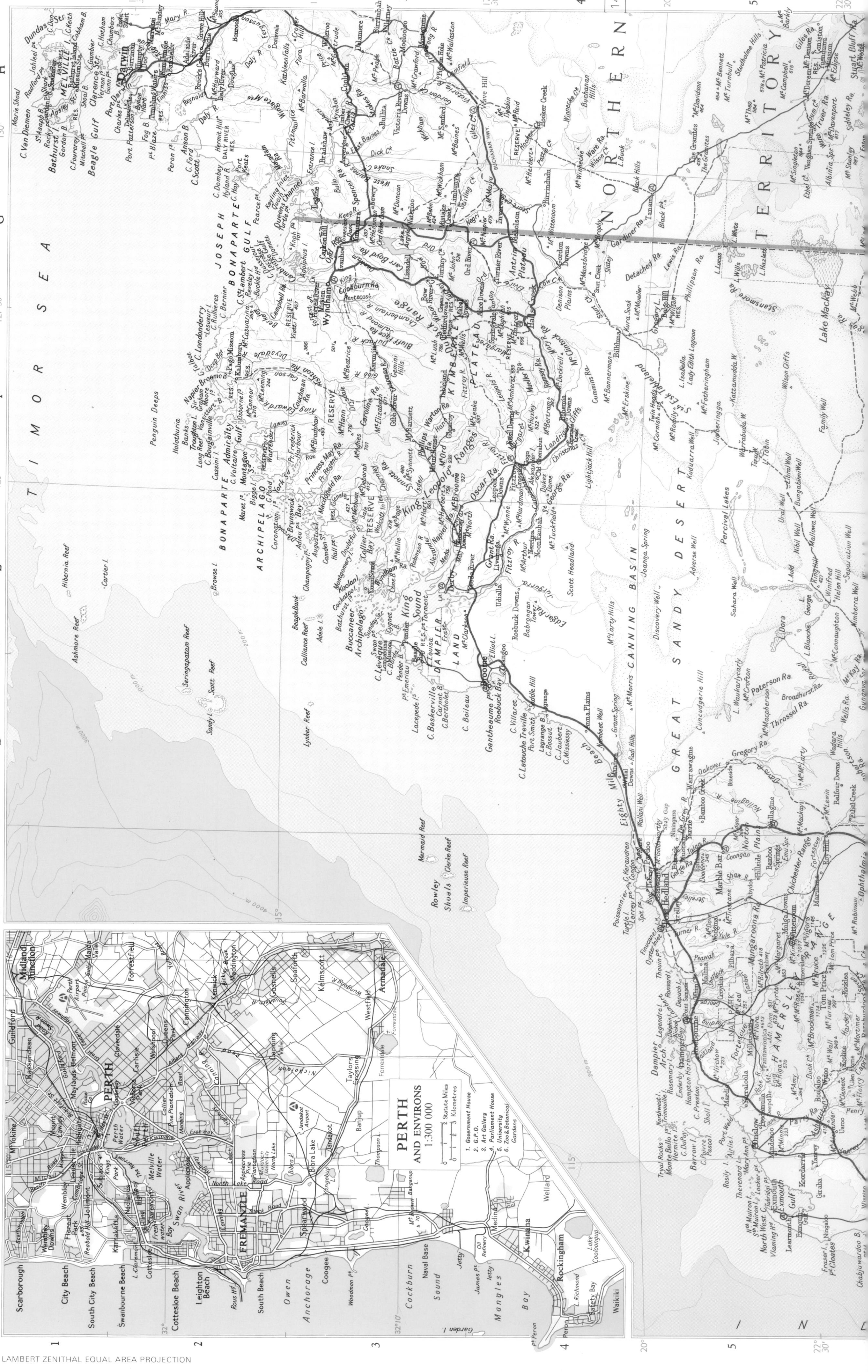
TIMOR SEA
JOSEPH BONAPARTE GULF
BONAPARTE ARCHIPELAGO
NORTHERN TERRITORY
GREAT SANDY DESERT
CANNING BASIN
KIMBERLEY PLATEAU
DAMPIER LAND
HAMERSLEY RANGE
Darwin
Wyndham
Derby
Broome
Port Hedland
King Sound
Eighty Mile Beach
Lake Mackay
PERTH
AND ENVIRONS
1:300 000
FREMANTLE
Rottnest I.
Rockingham
Kwinana
Cockburn Sound
Owen Anchorage
Armadale
Midland Junction
Guildford
1. Government House
2. G.P.O.
3. Art Gallery
4. Parliament House
5. University
6. Zoo & Botanical Gardens

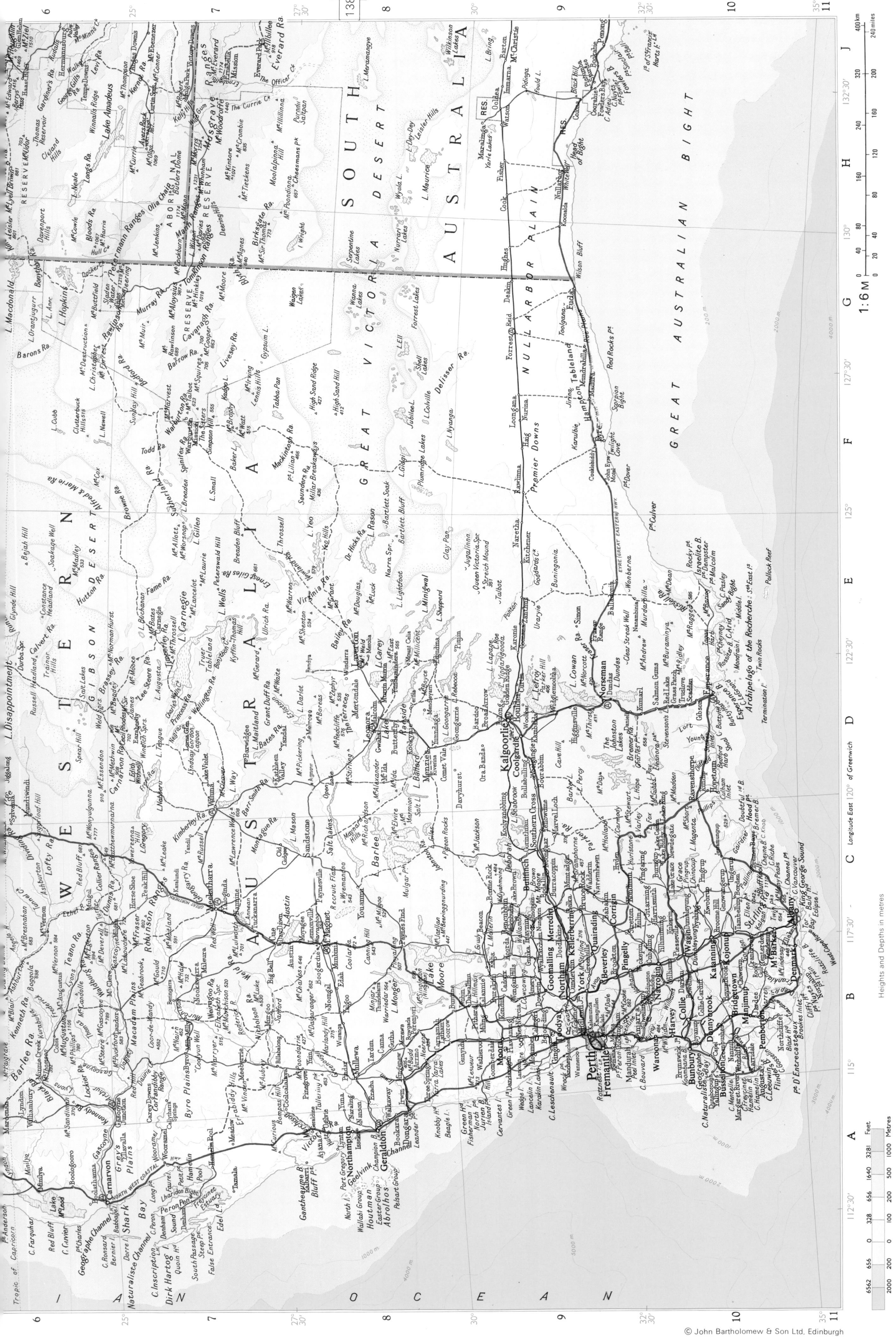
WESTERN AUSTRALIA
SOUTH AUSTRALIA
GREAT VICTORIA DESERT
GIBSON DESERT
NULLARBOR PLAIN
GREAT AUSTRALIAN BIGHT
INDIAN OCEAN
ABORIGINAL RESERVE
Perth
Fremantle
Kalgoorlie
Coolgardie
Geraldton
Carnarvon
Northampton
Bunbury
Albany
Esperance
Norseman
Meekatharra
Wiluna
Laverton
Leonora
Menzies
Southern Cross
Merredin
Northam
York
Narrogin
Katanning
Collie
Busselton
Manjimup
Denmark
Eucla
Forrest
Cook
Musgrave Ranges
Petermann Ranges
Warburton Ra.
Lake Carnegie
L. Disappointment
Lake Moore
Lake Barlee
Shark Bay
Dirk Hartog I.
Houtman Abrolhos
Archipelago of the Recherche
Heights and Depths in metres
Longitude East 120° of Greenwich
1:6M
Feet
Metres

© John Bartholomew & Son Ltd, Edinburgh

CHRISTCHURCH
AND ENVIRONS
1:300 000
Statute Miles
Kilometres
PEGASUS BAY
CHRISTCHURCH
LYTTELTON HARBOUR
Lyttelton
Sumner
NEW BRIGHTON
Riccarton
TASMAN
SOUTH ISLAND
SEA
PACIFIC
OCEAN
NELSON
MARLBOROUGH
CANTERBURY
WESTLAND
OTAGO
SOUTHLAND
FIORDLAND NATIONAL PARK
MT. ASPIRING NAT. PARK
Christchurch
Dunedin
Invercargill
Nelson
Blenheim
Greymouth
Timaru
Oamaru
Queenstown
FOVEAUX STRAIT
STEWART ISLAND
CANTERBURY BIGHT
TASMAN BAY
PEGASUS BAY
Karamea Bight
Banks Peninsula
DUNEDIN
AND ENVIRONS
1:300 000
OTAGO HARBOUR
OTAGO PENINSULA
Port Chalmers
Longitude East 170° of Greenwich
CONIC PROJECTION
3281 656 0 656 1640 3281 6562 9843 Feet
1000 200 0 200 500 1000 2000 3000 Metres

Great I.
Three Kings Is
AUCKLAND
AND ENVIRONS
1:300 000
NORTHLAND
Kaitaia
Russell
Kaikohe
Whangarei
Dargaville
CENTRAL
AUCKLAND
Helensville
Takapuna
Auckland
Papatoetoe
Manukau
Papakura
HAURAKI GULF
Great Barrier I
Coromandel Peninsula
Thames
Pukekohe
Waiuku
Paeroa
Waihi
SOUTH AUCKLAND-
BAY OF PLENTY
Te Aroha
Huntly
Morrinsville
Hamilton
Cambridge
Matamata
Tauranga
Mount Maunganui
Te Awamutu
Putaruru
Whakatane
Opotiki
Rotorua
Kawerau
Tokoroa
Te Kuiti
Taupo
EAST
COAST
Gisborne
Wairoa
Mahia Peninsula
HAWKE BAY
Napier
Hastings
Havelock North
HAWKE'S BAY
P A C I F I C
O C E A N
T A S M A N
S E A
NORTH ISLAND
North Taranaki Bight
Waitara
New Plymouth
Inglewood
TARANAKI
Stratford
Eltham
Hawera
Patea
South Taranaki Bight
Taumarunui
Ohakune
Taihape
Wanganui
WELLINGTON
Marton
Feilding
Palmerston North
Dannevirke
Waipukurau
Waipawa
Pahiatua
Foxton
Levin
Otaki
Masterton
Carterton
Greytown
Featherston
Porirua
Upper Hutt
Lower Hutt
Petone
Eastbourne
WELLINGTON
C. Palliser
COOK STRAIT
TASMAN BAY
Motueka
Nelson
Richmond
Picton
Blenheim
MARLBOROUGH
NELSON
WELLINGTON
AND ENVIRONS
1:300 000
Johnsonville
Tawa
Petone
LOWER HUTT
Wainuiomata
Eastbourne
Port Nicholson

Heights in feet
Depths in metres

Longitude East 174° of Greenwich

© John Bartholomew & Son Ltd, Edinburgh

1:2.5 M — 0 10 20 40 60 80 100 miles; 0 10 20 40 60 80 100 120 140 160 km

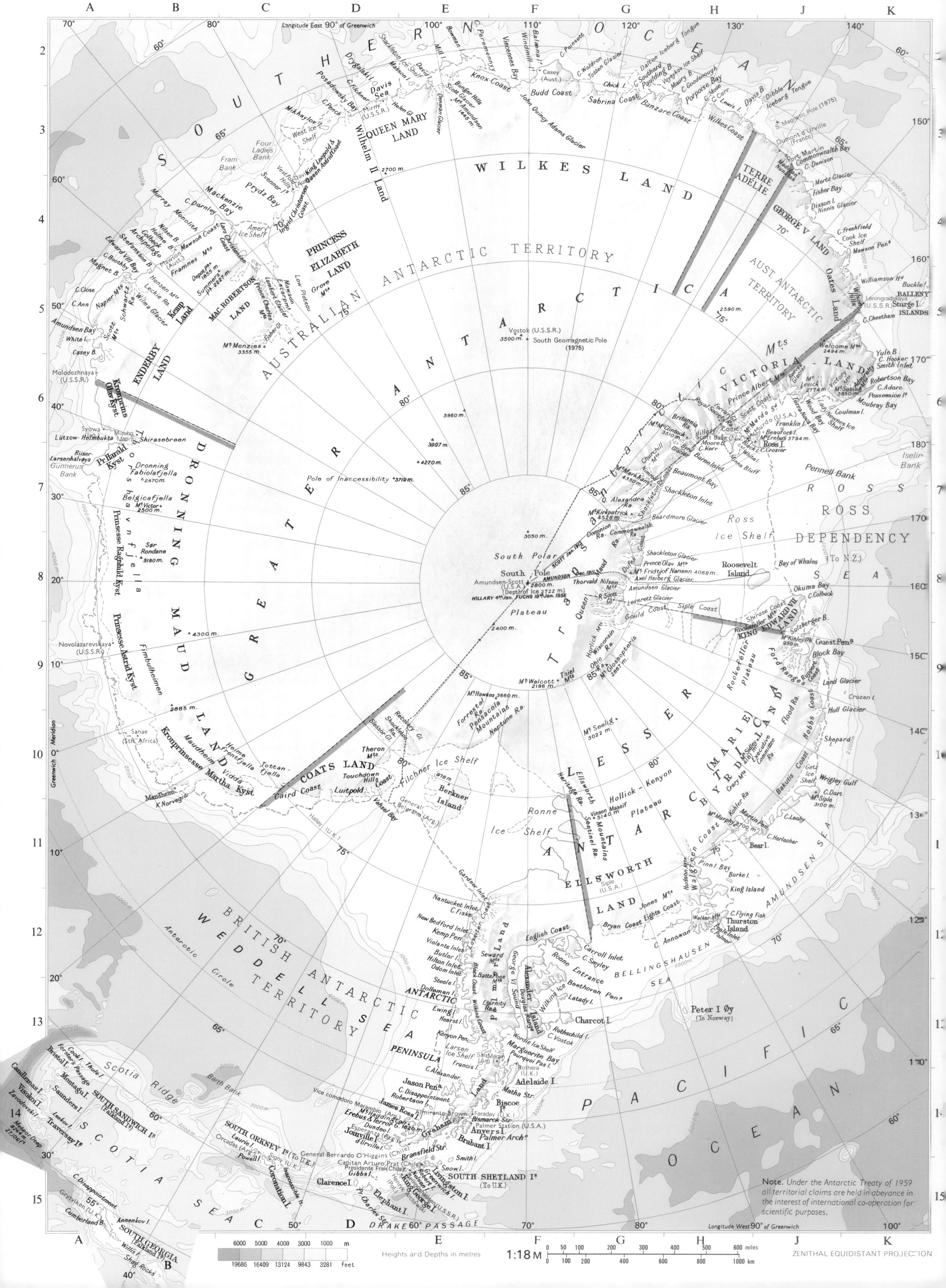
SOUTHERN OCEAN
WILKES LAND
GREATER ANTARCTICA
AUSTRALIAN ANTARCTIC TERRITORY
AUST ANTARCTIC TERRITORY
TERRE ADÉLIE
GEORGE V LAND
Oates Land
BALLENY ISLANDS
VICTORIA LAND
Transantarctic Mts
ROSS SEA
ROSS DEPENDENCY (To N.Z.)
Ross Ice Shelf
Roosevelt Island
KING EDWARD VII LAND
MARIE BYRD LAND
LESSER ANTARCTICA
ELLSWORTH LAND
AMUNDSEN SEA
BELLINGSHAUSEN SEA
Peter I Øy (To Norway)
Charcot I.
Alexander Island
ANTARCTIC PENINSULA
Palmer Land
BRITISH ANTARCTIC TERRITORY
WEDDELL SEA
Ronne Ice Shelf
Filchner Ice Shelf
Berkner Island
COATS LAND
DRONNING MAUD LAND
ENDERBY LAND
Kemp Land
MAC.ROBERTSON LAND
PRINCESS ELIZABETH LAND
Wilhelm II Land
QUEEN MARY LAND
Davis Sea
Pryde Bay
Amery Ice Shelf
Vostok (U.S.S.R.)
South Geomagnetic Pole (1975)
South Polar Plateau
South Pole
Amundsen-Scott (U.S.A.)
Pole of Inaccessibility 3719 m.
Vinson Massif 5140 m.
SOUTH SHETLAND Is (To U.K.)
SOUTH ORKNEY Is (To U.K.)
SOUTH SANDWICH Is (Falkland Is)
SOUTH GEORGIA (Falkland Is)
SCOTIA SEA
Scotia Ridge
DRAKE PASSAGE
PACIFIC OCEAN
Antarctic Circle
Longitude East 90° of Greenwich
Longitude West 90° of Greenwich
Greenwich Meridian
Note. Under the Antarctic Treaty of 1959 all territorial claims are held in abeyance in the interest of international co-operation for scientific purposes.
6000 5000 4000 3000 1000 m
19686 16409 13124 9843 3281 feet
Heights and Depths in metres
1:18 M
0 50 100 200 300 400 500 600 miles
0 100 200 400 600 800 1000 km
ZENITHAL EQUIDISTANT PROJECTION

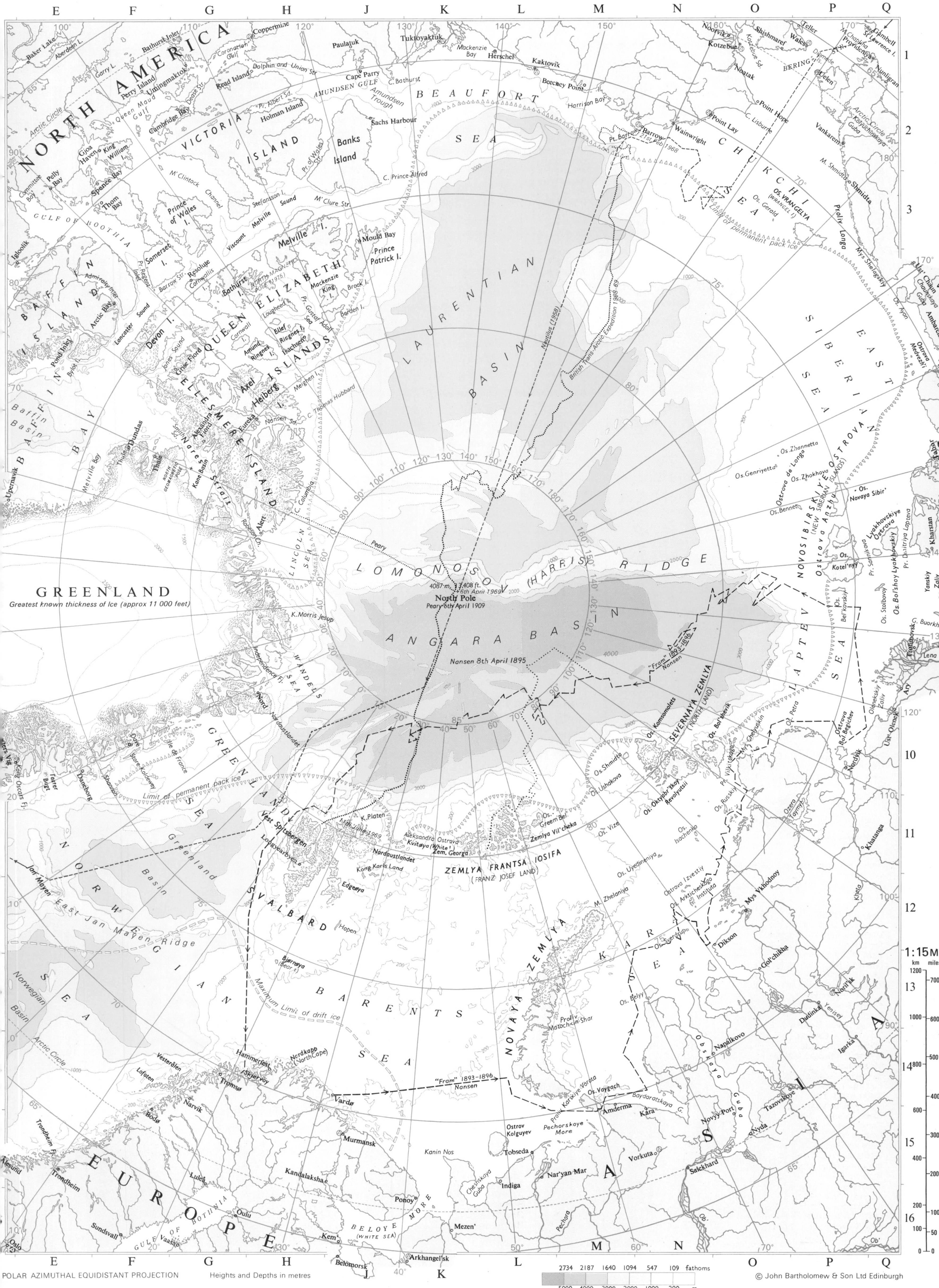
NORTH AMERICA
VICTORIA ISLAND
Banks Island
BEAUFORT SEA
AMUNDSEN GULF
QUEEN ELIZABETH ISLANDS
Melville I.
Prince Patrick I.
Bathurst I.
Devon I.
Axel Heiberg I.
ELLESMERE ISLAND
BAFFIN ISLAND
BAFFIN BAY
Baffin Basin
GULF OF BOOTHIA
Prince of Wales I.
Somerset I.
King William I.
GREENLAND
Greatest known thickness of Ice (approx 11 000 feet)
LINCOLN SEA
WANDELS SEA
GREENLAND SEA
Greenland Basin
NORWEGIAN SEA
Norwegian Basin
East Jan Mayen Ridge
Jan Mayen
LAURENTIAN BASIN
LOMONOSOV (HARRIS) RIDGE
ANGARA BASIN
North Pole
Peary 6th April 1909
4087 m. 13,408 ft.
Nansen 8th April 1895
"Fram" 1893–1896 Nansen
Nautilus (1958)
British Trans-Arctic Expedition 1968-69
Pt. Barrow 21st Feb 1968
Limit of permanent pack ice
Maximum Limit of drift ice
CHUKCHI SEA
Os. VRANGELYA (WRANGEL I.)
BERING STR.
EAST SIBERIAN SEA
NOVOSIBIRSKIYE OSTROVA (NEW SIBERIAN ISLANDS)
LAPTEV SEA
SEVERNAYA ZEMLYA (NORTH LAND)
KARA SEA
NOVAYA ZEMLYA
ZEMLYA FRANTSA IOSIFA (FRANZ JOSEF LAND)
SVALBARD
Vest Spitsbergen
Nordaustlandet
BARENTS SEA
Bjørnøya (Bear I.)
ASIA
EUROPE
Hammerfest
Tromsø
Murmansk
Arkhangel'sk
BELOYE MORE (WHITE SEA)
GULF OF BOTHNIA
Vorkuta
Salekhard
Dikson
Norilsk
Dudinka
Igarka
Khatanga
Tiksi
Barrow
Point Hope
Kotzebue
Tuktoyaktuk
Thule
Alert
1:15M
POLAR AZIMUTHAL EQUIDISTANT PROJECTION
Heights and Depths in metres
2734 2187 1640 1094 547 109 fathoms
5000 4000 3000 2000 1000 200 m

© John Bartholomew & Son Ltd Edinburgh

Geographical comparisons

Populations (estimated) of largest metropolitan areas

New York - N.E. New Jersey	16,678,818
Mexico City Mexico	11,943,050
Tokyo Japan	11,540,283
Shanghai China	11,300,000
Los Angeles - Long Beach Calif., USA	10,350,362
São Paulo Brazil	10,041,132
Paris France	9,878,524
Buenos Aires Argentina	8,925,000
Rio de Janeiro Brazil	8,328,800
Osaka Japan	8,279,000
Beijing (Peking) China	8,000,000
Moscow USSR	7,819,000
Seoul South Korea	7,800,000
Calcutta India	7,700,000
Chicago Illinois - N.W. Indiana, USA	7,658,335
Bombay India	7,450,000
London England, UK	7,110,000
Tianjin (Tientsin) China	7,000,000
Cairo Egypt	6,588,000
Chongqing (Chungking) China	6,000,000
Jakarta Indonesia	5,849,000
Philadelphia, Penn. - New Jersey USA	5,643,223
Guangzhou (Canton) China	5,000,000
Bangkok (Krung Thep) Thailand	4,870,509
Delhi - New Delhi India	4,700,000
Detroit Michigan, USA	4,669,106
San Francisco - Oakland Calif., USA	4,591,928
Hong Kong	4,514,000
Manila Philippines	4,500,000
Tehran Iran	4,498,159
Leningrad USSR	4,425,000
Shenyang (Mukden) China	4,400,000
Madras India	4,100,000
Karachi Pakistan	4,000,000
Santiago Chile	3,899,495
Istanbul Turkey	3,864,493
Boston Massachusetts, USA	3,553,203
Ho Chi Minh (Saigon) Vietnam	3,500,000
Wuhan China	3,500,000
Lima Peru	3,302,000
Madrid Spain	3,206,100
Baghdad Iraq	3,206,000
Washington DC, USA	3,021,801
Rome Italy	2,914,640
Cleveland Ohio, USA	2,902,461
Bogota Colombia	2,855,065
Montreal Canada	2,798,000
Sydney Australia	2,765,040
Toronto Canada	2,741,000
Birmingham England, UK	2,730,000
Manchester England, UK	2,675,000
Ankara Turkey	2,600,000
Athens-Piraeus Greece	2,540,241
Melbourne Australia	2,479,225
St. Louis Missouri - Illinois, USA	2,366,542
Pittsburgh Pennsylvania, USA	2,322,224
Alexandria Egypt	2,320,000
Singapore	2,308,000
Budapest Hungary	2,089,000
Kiev USSR	2,079,000
Bucharest Romania	1,934,025
Berlin W. Germany	1,909,706
Havana Cuba	1,861,442
Barcelona Spain	1,809,722
Casablanca Morocco	1,753,000
Johannesburg S. Africa	1,748,000
Glasgow Scotland, UK	1,727,625
Hamburg W. Germany	1,699,000

Lake Areas

Areas are average and some are subject to seasonal variations

	Sq. Miles	Sq. Km
Caspian USSR – Iran (salt)	143,240	371,000
Superior USA – Canada	32,150	83,270
Victoria Kenya – Uganda – Tanzania	26,560	68,800
Aral USSR (salt)	25,300	65,500
Huron USA – Canada	23,430	60,700
Michigan USA	22,400	58,020
Tanganyika Tanzania – Zambia – Zaire – Burundi	12,700	32,900
Great Bear Canada	12,270	31,790
Baykal USSR	11,800	30,500
Great Slave Canada	10,980	28,440
Erie USA – Canada	9,910	25,680
Winnipeg Canada	9,460	24,510
Nyasa (Malawi) Malawi – Mozambique	8,680	22,490
Ontario USA-Canada	7,430	19,230
Ladoga USSR	7,100	18,390
Balkhash USSR	6,700	17,400
Maracaibo Venezuela	6,300	16,300
Chad Nigeria – Niger – Chad – Cameroon	4-10,000	10-26,000
Onega USSR	3,710	9,600
Eyre Australia	0-3,430	0-8,900
Titicaca Peru – Bolivia	3,220	8,340
Nicaragua Nicaragua	3,190	8,270
Rudolf Kenya-Ethiopia	2,470	6,410
Torrens Australia	2,230	5,780
Vänern Sweden	2,160	5,580
Manitoba Canada	1,820	4,710
Loch Lomond Scotland, UK	27	70
Windermere England, UK	10	26

River Lengths

	Miles	Km
Nile Africa	4,160	6,695
Amazon South America	4,080	6,570
Yangtze Asia	3,964	6,380
Mississippi - Missouri N. America	3,740	6,020
Ob-Irtysh Asia	3,360	5,410
Huang He (Yellow) Asia	3,010	4,840
Zaïre (Congo) Africa	2,880	4,630
Paraná South America	2,795	4,500
Irtysh Asia	2,760	4,440
Amur Asia	2,745	4,416
Lena Asia	2,730	4,400
Mackenzie North America	2,630	4,240
Mekong Asia	2,600	4,180
Niger Africa	2,550	4,100
Yenisey Asia	2,540	4,090
Missouri North America	2,466	3,969
Mississippi North America	2,348	3,779
Murray-Darling Australia	2,330	3,750
Volga Europe	2,292	3,688
Madeira South America	2,013	3,240
Indus Asia	1,980	3,180
St Lawrence North America	1,900	3,058
Rio Grande North America	1,880	3,030
Yukon North America	1,870	3,020
Brahmaputra Asia	1,840	2,960
Danube Europe	1,770	2,850
Salween Asia	1,750	2,820
São Francisco South America	1,730	2,780
Ganges Asia	1,678	2,700
Zambezi Africa	1,650	2,650
Nelson - Saskatchewan North America	1,600	2,570
Euphrates Asia	1,510	2,430
Arkansas North America	1,450	2,330
Colorado North America	1,450	2,330
Dnepr Europe	1,370	2,200
Irrawaddy Asia	1,300	2,090
Orinoco South America	1,280	2,060
Negro South America	1,240	2,000
Don Europe	1,160	1,870
Orange Africa	1,155	1,859
Pechora Europe	1,118	1,799
Marañón South America	1,000	1,609
Dnestr Europe	876	1,410
Rhine Europe	820	1,320
Donets Europe	735	1,183
Elbe Europe	720	1,159
Gambia Africa	680	1,094
Yellowstone North America	671	1,080
Vistula Europe	630	1,014
Tagus Europe	625	1,006
Oder Europe	565	909
Seine Europe	473	761
Thames England, UK	209	336
Liffey Ireland	50	80

Populations 1978

China	975,230,000
India	638,388,000
USSR	260,700,000
USA	218,060,000
Indonesia	141,600,000
Brazil	116,400,000
Japan	115,100,000
Bangladesh	84,655,000
Pakistan	75,600,000
Nigeria	72,220,000
Mexico	66,944,000
West Germany	61,327,000
Italy	56,828,500
United Kingdom	55,836,000
France	53,373,000
Vietnam	50,000,000
Philippines	46,351,000
Thailand	45,100,000
Turkey	43,210,000
Egypt	39,939,000
Spain	37,109,000
South Korea	37,019,000
Iran	35,213,000
Poland	34,945,000
Burma	32,205,000

Mountain Heights

	Feet	Metres
Everest Tibet - Nepal	29,028	8,848
K2 (Godwin Austen) Kashmir - Sinkiang	28,250	8,611
Kangchenjunga Nepal - Sikkim	28,168	8,586
Makalu Tibet - Nepal	27,805	8,475
Dhaulagiri Nepal	26,810	8,172
Nanga Parbat Jammu/Kashmir	26,660	8,126
Annapurna Nepal	26,504	8,078
Gasherbrum Kashmir	26,470	8,068
Gosainthan (Xixabangma Feng) Tibet	26,291	8,013
Nanda Devi India	25,645	7,817
Rakaposhi Jammu/Kashmir	25,550	7,780
Kamet India - Tibet	25,447	7,756
Namcha Barwa Tibet	25,447	7,756
Gurla Mandhata Tibet	25,355	7,728
Ulugh Muztagh Tibet - Sinkiang	25,338	7,723
Kungur (Kongur Shan) Sinkiang	25,325	7,719
Tirich Mir Pakistan	25,230	7,690
Minya Konka (Gongga Shan) China	24,903	7,590
Muztagh Ata Sinkiang	24,757	7,546
Pik Kommunizma USSR	24,590	7,495
Pik Pobedy (Tomur Feng) USSR - Sinkiang	24,407	7,439
Chomo Lhari Bhutan - Tibet	23,993	7,313
Pik Lenina USSR	23,406	7,134
Ojos del Salado Chile - Argentina	23,240	7,084
Ancohuma Bolivia	23,012	7,014
Aconcagua Argentina	22,834	6,960
Bonete Argentina	22,541	6,870
Tupungato Argentina - Chile	22,310	6,800
Mercedario Argentina	22,211	6,770
Huascarán Peru	22,205	6,768
Llullaillaco Argentina - Chile	22,057	6,723
Kailas Tibet	22,028	6,714
Yerupaja Peru	21,765	6,634
Sajama Bolivia	21,463	6,542
Illampu Bolivia	21,276	6,485
Nudo Coropuna Peru	21,079	6,425
Illimani Bolivia	21,004	6,402
Chimborazo Ecuador	20,702	6,310
Mt McKinley USA	20,320	6,194
Logan Canada	19,850	6,050
Kilimanjaro Tanzania	19,340	5,895
Citlaltepetl Mexico	18,700	5,700
El'bruz USSR	18,510	5,642
Popocatepetl Mexico	17,887	5,452
Mt Kenya Kenya	17,058	5,200
Mt Ararat Turkey	16,946	5,165
Vinson Massif Antarctica	16,864	5,140
Stanley Zaire/Uganda	16,763	5,110
Jaya (Carstensz)	16,500	5,030
Mont Blanc France	15,781	4,810
Matterhorn Switzerland - Italy	14,688	4,477
Zugspitze Germany	9,721	2,963
Ben Nevis Scotland	4,406	1,343
Snowdon Wales	3,560	1,085
Carrantuohill Ireland	3,414	1,041
Scafell Pike England, UK	3,210	978

Areas

	Sq. Miles	Sq. Km
USSR	8,600,000	22,271,000
Canada	3,851,809	9,976,185
China	3,691,500	9,560,985
USA	3,615,123	9,363,169
Brazil	3,286,488	8,511,978
Australia	2,967,909	7,686,884
India	1,269,346	3,287,590
Argentina	1,072,067	2,776,654
Sudan	967,491	2,505,802
Algeria	919,591	2,381,741
UK	94,500	244,755

Oceans and Seas

Areas and greatest depths

	Sq. Miles	Sq. Km	Feet	Metres
Pacific Ocean	63,855,000	165,384,000	36,198	11,033
Atlantic Ocean	31,744,000	82,217,000	27,498	8,381
Indian Ocean	28,371,000	73,481,000	26,400	8,047
Arctic Ocean	5,427,000	14,056,000	17,880	5,450
Mediterranean Sea	967,000	2,505,000	15,900	4,846
South China Sea	895,000	2,318,000	18,090	5,514
Bering Sea	876,000	2,269,000	16,800	5,121
Caribbean Sea	750,000	1,943,000	24,580	7,492
Gulf of Mexico	596,000	1,544,000	14,360	4,377
Sea of Okhotsk	590,000	1,528,000	11,400	3,475
East China Sea	482,000	1,248,000	9,840	2,999
Yellow Sea	480,000	1,243,000	300	91
Hudson Bay	476,000	1,233,000	850	259
Sea of Japan	389,000	1,008,000	12,280	3,743
North Sea	222,000	575,000	2,170	661
Black Sea	178,000	461,000	7,360	2,243
Red Sea	169,000	438,000	7,370	2,246
Baltic Sea	163,000	422,000	1,400	439

Countries of the World

Country	Status or title	Capital	Area Sq. km.	Area Sq. miles	Population	Languages	Currency	Page numbers
Afghanistan	Democratic Republic	Kabul	650,090	(251,000)	15,108,000 (1978)	Pushtu, Dari Persian	Afghani (Afs)	77
Albania	People's Socialist Republic	Tirana	28,752	(11,101)	2,608,000 (1978)	Albanian (Gheg, Tosk)	Lek	46
Algeria	Democratic and Popular Republic	Algiers	2,381,741	(919,591)	18,515,000 (1978)	Arabic, French, Berber	Algerian dinar (DA)	85
Andorra	Co-principality under French/Spanish sovereignty	Andorra la Vella	453	(175)	30,000 (1978)	Catalan, French, Spanish	French franc, Spanish peseta	17
Angola	People's Republic	Luanda	1,246,699	(481,351)	6,732,000 (1978)	Portuguese, tribal dialects	Kwanza	87
Argentina	Republic	Buenos Aires	2,776,653	(1,072,067)	26,393,000 (1978)	Spanish	Arg. new peso	130–3
Australia	Commonwealth Nation	Canberra	7,686,884	(2,967,909)	14,418,200 (1979)	English	Australian dollar (A$)	136, 138–40
Austria	Republic	Vienna	83,849	(32,374)	7,497,000 (1979)	German	Schilling (Sch)	38, 41
Bahamas	Commonwealth Nation	Nassau	11,406	(4,404)	225,000 (1978)	English	Bahamian dollar	113, 126
Bahrain	State (sheikhdom)	Manama	598	(231)	345,000 (1978)	Arabic, English	Bahrain dinar (BD)	77
Bangladesh	People's Republic. Commonwealth Nation *formerly East Pakistan*	Dacca	142,776	(55,126)	84,655,000 (1978)	Bengali, Bihari, Hindi, English	Taka (Tk)	75
Barbados	Commonwealth Nation	Bridgetown	430	(166)	250,000 (1978)	English	Barbados dollar (BDS$)	127
Belgium	Kingdom	Brussels	30,513	(11,781)	9,841,000 (1978)	French, Dutch, German	Belgian franc	22
Belize	UK Dependent Territory *formerly British Honduras*	Belmopan	22,963	(8,866)	153,000 (1978)	English, Spanish, Maya	Belize dollar (BZ$)	125
Benin	People's Republic *formerly Republic of Dahomey*	Porto Novo	115,763	(44,696)	3,377,000 (1978)	French, tribal languages	CFA franc	85
Bhutan	Kingdom	Thimphu	46,620	(18,000)	1,240,000 (1978)	Dzong-Kha	Ngultrum, Indian rupee	75
Bolivia	Republic	La Paz	1,098,579	(424,162)	5,137,000 (1978)	Spanish, Quechua, Aymará	Bolivian peso ($b)	128, 133
Botswana	Republic. Commonwealth Nation	Gaborone	569,800	(220,000)	726,000 (1978)	Setswana, English	Pula (P)	87, 89
Brazil	Federative Republic	Brasília	8,512,001	(3,286,487)	116,400,000 (1978)	Portuguese	Cruzeiro (Cr$)	128–131
Brunei	Commonwealth State	Bandar Seri Begawan	5,765	(2,226)	201,000 (1978)	Malay, English, Chinese	Brunei dollar	70
Bulgaria	People's Republic	Sofia	110,912	(42,823)	8,814,000 (1978)	Bulgarian	Lev	47
Burma	Socialist Republic of the Union of Burma	Rangoon	678,034	(261,789)	32,205,000 (1978)	Burmese	Kyat (K)	68
Burundi	Republic	Bujumbura	27,731	(10,707)	4,256,000 (1978)	French, Kirundi, Swahili	Burundi franc	88
Cambodia	Democratic Kampuchea *formerly the Khmer Republic*	Phnom Penh	181,036	(69,898)	8,574,000 (1978)	Khmer	Riel	68–9
Cameroon	United Republic	Yaoundé	475,501	(183,591)	8,058,000 (1978)	English, French	CFA franc	86
Canada	Commonwealth Nation	Ottawa	9,976,185	(3,851,809)	23.742,000 (1979)	English, French	Canadian dollar (C$)	115, 117–123
Cape Verde	Republic	Praia	4,033	(1,557)	314,000 (1978)	Portuguese Creole	Cape Verde escudo	85
Central African Rep	Republic (1979) *formerly Empire*	Bangui	622,999	(240,540)	2 600,000 (1974)	French, Sangho	CFA franc	86
Chad	Republic	N'Djamena	1,270,998	(490,733)	4,309,000 (1978)	French, Arabic	CFA franc	86
Chile	Republic	Santiago	756,946	(292,257)	10,857,000 (1978)	Spanish	Chilean peso	128, 131, 133
China	People's Republic	Beijing (Peking)	9,560,985	(3,691,500)	975,230,000 (1978)	Mandarin Chinese, regional languages	Renminbi or yuan	65–7
Colombia	Republic	Bogotá	1,138,911	(439,734)	25,645,000 (1978)	Spanish, Indian languages	Colombian peso	126, 128
Comoros	Federal and Islamic Republic	Moroni	2,274	(878)	320,000 (1978)	French, Comoran	CFA franc	87
Congo	People's Republic	Brazzaville	349,000	(134,749)	1,459,000 (1978)	French, Lingala, Monokutuba	CFA franc	86
Costa Rica	Republic	San José	50,899	(19,652)	2,111,000 (1978)	Spanish	Colon (₡)	125
Cuba	Republic	Havana	114,525	(44,218)	9,728,000 (1978)	Spanish	Cuban peso	126
Cyprus	Republic. Commonwealth Nation	Nicosia	9,251	(3,572)	616,000 (1978)	Greek, Turkish, English	Cyprus pound	79
Czechoslovakia	Federal Socialist Republic	Prague	127,871	(49,371)	15,199,000 (1979)	Czech, Slovak	Koruna (Kčs)	31, 37, 48
Dahomey	*see Benin*							
Denmark	Kingdom	Copenhagen	43,030	(16,614)	5,112,000 (1979)	Danish	Krone (Kr)	28–9
Djibouti	Republic (1977) *formerly French Territory of Afars and Issas*	Djibouti	21,699	(8,378)	113,000 (1978)	French, Somali, Dankali, Arabic	Djibouti franc	86
Dominica	Commonwealth Nation (1978)	Roseau	751	(290)	81,000 (1978)	English, French patois	E Caribbean dollar ($EC)	127
Dominican Republic	Republic	Santo Domingo	48,441	(18,703)	5,124,000 (1978)	Spanish	Dominican peso	127
Ecuador	Republic	Quito	455,451	(175,850)	7,814,000 (1978)	Spanish, Quechua, other Indian languages	Sucre	128
Egypt	Arab Republic	Cairo	1,000,253	(386,198)	39,939,000 (1978)	Arabic, Berber, Nubian, English, French	Egyptian pound (£E)	79, 84
Eire	*see Irish Republic*							
El Salvador	Republic	San Salvador	20,865	(8,056)	4,354,000 (1978)	Spanish	Colon	125
Equatorial Guinea	Republic	Malabo	45,392	(17,526)	346,000 (1978)	Spanish, Fang, Bubi, other tribal languages	Guinea peseta or Ekpwele	85–6
Ethiopia	Socialist Republic	Addis Ababa	1,221,900	(471,776)	29,705,000 (1978)	Amharic, English, Arabic	Birr	86
Fiji	Commonwealth Nation	Suva	18,316	(7,072)	601,485 (1977)	Fijian, English, Hindustani	Fiji dollar ($F)	137
Finland	Republic	Helsinki	360,318	(139,119)	4,759,000 (1978)	Finnish, Swedish	Markka	29
Formosa	*see Taiwan*							
France	Republic	Paris	549,621	(212,209)	53,373,000 (1978)	French	French franc	18–22, 40
Gabon	Republic	Libreville	265,001	(102,317)	538,000 (1978)	French, Bantu dialects	CFA franc	86
Gambia, The	Republic. Commonwealth Nation	Banjul	10,367	(4,003)	569,000 (1978)	English, Madinka	Dalasi	85
Germany, East	German Democratic Republic	East Berlin	107,861	(41,645)	16,756,000 (1978)	German	Mark of the GDR (M)	30, 32–3, 36–7
Germany, West	Federal Republic of Germany	Bonn	248,529	(95,957)	61,327,000 (1978)	German	Deutschmark (DM)	30, 32–9
Ghana	Republic. Commonwealth Nation	Accra	237,873	(91,843)	10,969,000 (1978)	English, tribal languages	Cedi (₵)	85
Gilbert Islands	*see Kiribati*							
Great Britain	*see United Kingdom*							
Greece	The Hellenic Republic	Athens	131,990	(50,948)	9,360,000 (1978)	Greek	Drachma (Dr)	46–7
Grenada	Commonwealth Nation	St George's	344	(133)	97,000 (1978)	English	E Caribbean dollar (EC$)	127
Guatemala	Republic	Guatemala City	108,889	(42,042)	6,621,000 (1978)	Spanish, Indian languages	Quetzal (Q)	125
Guinea	Republic	Conakry	245,856	(94,925)	4,763,000 (1978)	French, Soussou, Manika	Syli	85
Guinea-Bissau	Republic	Madina do Boé	36,125	(13,948)	553,000 (1978)	Portuguese, Guinean Creole	Peso	85
Guyana	Cooperative Republic. Commonwealth Nation	Georgetown	214,970	(83,000)	820,000 (1978)	English, Hindi, Urdu, Amerindian dialects	Guyana dollar (G$)	128–9
Haiti	Republic	Port-au-Prince	27,749	(10,714)	4,833,000 (1978)	French, Creole	Gourde, US dollar ($)	126–7
Honduras	Republic	Tegucigalpa	112,087	(43,277)	3,439,000 (1978)	Spanish, Indian dialects	Lempira (lp) or peso	125
Hungary	People's Republic	Budapest	93,030	(35,919)	10,703,000 (1979)	Hungarian	Forint	48
Iceland	Republic	Reykjavík	102,828	(39,702)	224,000 (1978)	Icelandic	Icelandic króna	115
India	Republic and Union of States. Commonwealth Nation	New Delhi	3,287,606	(1,269,346)	638,388,000 (1978)	Hindi, English, regional languages	Rupee	73–6
Indonesia	Republic	Jakarta	1,919,270	(741,031)	141,600,000 (1978)	Bahasa Indonesia	Rupiah (Rp)	69–71
Iran	Islamic Republic (1979) *formerly Empire*	Teheran	1,648,190	(636,367)	35,213,000 (1978)	Farsi, Kurdish, Arabic, Baluchi	Rial	77
Iraq	Republic	Baghdad	434,001	(167,568)	12,327,000 (1978)	Arabic, Kurdish	Iraqi dinar (ID)	78
Irish Republic	The Republic of Ireland	Dublin	70,282	(27,136)	3,221,000 (1978)	Irish, English	Punt	14
Israel	The State of Israel. Republic	Jerusalem	20,702	(7,993)	3,709,000 (1978)	Hebrew, Arabic	Shekel	79–80
Italy	Republic	Rome	301,191	(116,290)	56,828,511 (1978)	Italian	Lira (Lr)	41–5
Ivory Coast	Republic	Abidjan	319,821	(123,483)	7,613,000 (1978)	French, tribal languages	CFA franc	85
Jamaica	Commonwealth Nation	Kingston	11,424	(4,411)	2,133.000 (1978)	English	Jamaican dollar (J$)	127
Japan	Democratic State with Emperor	Tokyo	369,699	(142,741)	116,050 000 (1979)	Japanese	Yen (Yn)	60–1
Jordan	Hashemite Kingdom	Amman	97,739	(37,737)	2,984,000 (1978)	Arabic	Jordanian dinar (JD)	80
Kampuchea, Democratic	*see Cambodia*							
Kenya	Republic. Commonwealth Nation	Nairobi	582,646	(224,960)	14,856,000 (1978)	Swahili, English, Kikuyu, other tribal langs	Kenya pound (K£)	86, 88
Khmer Republic	*see Cambodia*							
Kiribati	Republic (1979). Commonwealth Nation *formerly Gilbert Is UK Dependent Territory*	Tarawa	684	(264)	56,452 (1978)	Gilbertese, English	Australian dollar (A$)	137
Korea, North	Democratic People's Republic of Korea	Pyŏnyang	121,248	(46,814)	17,072,000 (1978)	Korean	Won	65
Korea, South	Republic of Korea	Seoul	99,591	(38,452)	37,019,000 (1978)	Korean	Won	65
Kuwait	State	Kuwait	20,150	(7,780)	1,199,000 (1978)	Arabic, English	Kuwait dinar (KD)	77
Laos	Lao People's Democratic Republic	Vientiane	236,799	(91,428)	3,546,000 (1978)	Lao, French, tribal langs	Kip (K)	68
Lebanon	Republic	Beirut	10,399	(4,015)	3,012,000 (1978)	Arabic, French, English, Armenian	Lebanese pound (£Leb)	79
Lesotho	Kingdom. Commonwealth Nation	Maseru	30,344	(11,716)	1,279,000 (1978)	English, Lesotho	South African rand (R)	89
Liberia	Republic	Monrovia	111,370	(43,000)	1,742,000 (1978)	English, tribal languages	Liberian dollar (L$)	85
Libya	Socialist People's Libyan Arab Jamahiriya	Tripoli	1,759,537	(679,358)	2,748,000 (1978)	Arabic, Italian	Libyan dinar (LD)	84
Liechtenstein	Principality	Vaduz	161	(62)	25,000 (1978)	Alemannish, German	Swiss franc	41
Luxembourg	Grand Duchy	Luxembourg Ville	2,587	(999)	356,000 (1978)	Luxembourgish, French, German	Luxembourg franc, Belgian franc	22
Madagascar	Democratic Republic	Tananarive	587,044	(226,658)	8,289,000 (1978)	Malagasy, French	Malagasy franc (FMG)	87
Malawi	Republic. Commonwealth Nation	Lilongwe	94,527	(36,497)	5,669,000 (1978)	Chichewa, English	Malawi kwacha (K)	88
Malaysia	Federation of States. Commonwealth Nation (comprising Peninsular Malaysia, Sabah and Sarawak)	Kuala Lumpur	332,318	(128,308)	12,960,000 (1978)	Bahasa Malaysia, English, Chinese, Tamil	Malaysian dollar (M$)	69–70
Maldives	Republic	Malé	298	(115)	143,046 (1978)	Divehi	Maldivian rupee	73
Mali	Republic	Bamako	1,204,026	(464,875)	6,290,000 (1978)	French, native languages	Mali franc (MF)	85

Country	Status or title	Capital	Area Sq. km.	Area Sq. miles	Population	Languages	Currency	Page numbers
Malta	Republic. Commonwealth Nation	Valletta	316	(122)	340,000 (1978)	Maltese, English	Maltese pound (£M)	43
Mauritania	Islamic Republic	Nouakchott	1,118,608	(431,895)	1,544,000 (1978)	Arabic, French	Ouguiya	85
Mauritius	Commonwealth Nation	Port Louis	1,865	(720)	924,000 (1978)	English, French, Creole	Mauritius rupee (R)	83
Mexico	The United Mexican States. Federal Republic	Mexico City	1,972,363	(761,530)	66,944,000 (1978)	Spanish	Mexican peso	125
Monaco	Principality	Monaco-Ville	1.5	(0.6)	26,000 (1978)	French, Monégasque	French franc	44
Mongolia	People's Republic	Ulaanbaatar	1,565,007	(604,250)	1,576,000 (1978)	Mongolian	Tugrik	58
Morocco	Kingdom	Rabat	622,014	(240,160)	18,906,000 (1978)	Arabic, French, Spanish	Dirham (DH)	85
Mozambique	People's Republic	Maputo	784,964	(303,075)	9,935,000 (1978)	Portuguese, tribal langs	Mozambique escudo	87–8
Namibia	United Nations Trust Territory	Windhoek	824,296	(318,261)	852,000 (1974)	Afrikaans, German, English	South African rand (R)	87, 89
Nauru	Republic with special membership of the Commonwealth	Nauru	21	(8)	8,000 (1978)	Nauruan, English	Australian dollar (A$)	137
Nepal	Kingdom	Kathmandu	141,414	(54,600)	13,421,000 (1978)	Nepali	Nepalese rupee (NR)	75
Netherlands	Kingdom	Amsterdam/ The Hague	36,175	(13,967)	13,986,000 (1979)	Dutch	Guilder or florin (fl)	25
New Hebrides	*see Vanduaatu*							
New Zealand	Commonwealth Nation	Wellington	268,676	(103,736)	3,145,900 (1978)	English, Maori	New Zealand dollar ($NZ)	144–5
Nicaragua	Republic	Managua	148,006	(57,145)	2,395,000 (1978)	Spanish	Córdoba (C$)	125
Niger	Republic	Niamey	1,188,999	(459,073)	4,994,000 (1978)	French, native languages	CFA franc	85
Nigeria	Federal Republic. Commonwealth Nation	Lagos	923,773	(356,669)	72,217,000 (1978)	English, Hausa, Yoruba, Ibo	Naira (₦)	85–6
Norway	Kingdom	Oslo	324,219	(125,181)	4,068,000 (1979)	Norwegian, (Bokmål and Landsmål), Lappish	Norwegian krone (Kr)	26–7
Oman	Sultanate	Muscat	212,380	(82,000)	839,000 (1978)	Arabic, English	Rial Omani (RO)	72, 77
Pakistan	Islamic Republic	Islamabad	803,944	(310,403)	75,600,000 (1978)	Punjabi, Sindhi, Urdu, Pushto	Pakistan rupee (R)	74, 77
Panama	Republic	Panama City	75,649	(29,208)	1,826,000 (1978)	Spanish, English	Balboa (B)	125
Papua New Guinea	Independent State. Commonwealth Nation	Port Moresby	461,693	(178,260)	2,959,800 (1978)	Pidgin English, native languages	Kina (K)	136
Paraguay	Republic	Asunción	406,752	(157,047)	2,888,000 (1978)	Spanish, Guaraní	Guaraní (G)	130
Peru	Republic	Lima	1,285,220	(496,224)	16,819,000 (1978)	Spanish, Quechua, Aymará	Sol	128
Philippines	Republic	Quezon City	299,767	(115,740)	46,351,000 (1978)	Filipino, Tagalog, English, Spanish	Philippine (P)	71
Poland	People's Republic	Warsaw	311,701	(120,348)	34,945,000 (1978)	Polish	Zloty	31
Portugal	Republic	Lisbon	91,971	(35,510)	9,798,000 (1978)	Portuguese	Escudo (Esc)	16
Puerto Rico	Self governing commonwealth associated with the USA	San Juan	8,891	(3,435)	3,317,000 (1978)	English, Spanish	US dollar ($)	127
Qatar	State	Doha	10,360	(4,000)	201,000 (1978)	Arabic, English	Qatar riyal (QR)	77
Rhodesia	*see Zimbabwe*							
Romania	Socialist Republic	Bucharest	237,500	(91,699)	21,855,000 (1978)	Romanian, Magyar, German	Leu (plural Lei)	48
Rwanda	Republic	Kigali	26,338	(10,169)	4,508,000 (1978)	French, tribal languages, Kinyarwanda (Bantu)	Rwanda franc	88
St Lucia	Independent State (1979). Commonwealth Nation	Castries	616	(238)	113,000 (1978)	English, French patois	E Caribbean dollar ($EC)	127
St Vincent	Independent State (1979). Commonwealth Nation	Kingstown	389	(150)	113,000 (1979)	English	E Caribbean dollar ($EC)	127
San Marino	Republic	San Marino	60	(23)	21,000 (1978)	Italian	Italian lira and Papal coinage	45
São Tomé and Principe	Democratic Republic	São Tomé	963	(372)	83,000 (1978)	Portuguese	Portuguese escudo	86
Saudi Arabia	Kingdom	Riyadh	2,263,587	(873,972)	7,012,642 (1974)	Arabic	Saudi riyal (SR)	72, 86
Senegal	Republic	Dakar	197,161	(76,124)	5,381,000 (1978)	French, native languages	CFA franc	85
Seychelles	Republic. Commonwealth Nation	Victoria	443	(171)	62,000 (1978)	English, French	Seychelles rupee (R)	83
Sierra Leone	Republic. Commonwealth Nation	Freetown	72,326	(27,925)	3,470,000 (1977)	English, (also Krio, Temne, Mende)	Leone (Le)	85
Singapore	Republic. Commonwealth Nation	Singapore	596	(230)	2,334,000 (1978)	Malay, Chinese (Mandarin), Tamil, English	Singapore dollar (S$)	69
Solomon Islands	Independent State (1978). Commonwealth Nation	Honiara	27,556	(10,639)	221,000 (1979)	English, native langs	Solomon Islands dollar	137
Somalia	The Somali Democratic Republic	Mogadishu	637,541	(246,155)	3,443,000 (1978)	Somali, Arabic, English, Italian	Somali shilling (Som. Sh.)	86
South Africa	Republic	Pretoria	1,221,042	(471,445)	27,700,000 (1978)	Afrikaans, English, various African langs	Rand (R)	87, 89
South West Africa	*see Namibia*							
South Yemen	The People's Democratic Republic of Yemen	Aden	290,274	(112,075)	1,853,000 (1978)	Arabic	South Yemeni dinar (YD)	72
Spain	The Spanish State. Kingdom	Madrid	504,747	(194,883)	37,109,000 (1978)	Spanish, Catalan, Basque	Peseta	16–7
Sri Lanka	Democratic Socialist Republic. Commonwealth Nation *formerly Ceylon*	Colombo	65,610	(25,332)	14,346,000 (1978)	Sinhala, Tamil, English	Sri Lanka rupee (R)	83
Sudan	Democratic Republic	Khartoum	2,505,802	(967,491)	17,376,000 (1978)	Arabic, tribal languages	Sudanese pound (£S)	86
Suriname	Republic	Paramaribo	163,820	(63,251)	374,000 (1978)	Dutch, native languages	Suriname guilder	129
Swaziland	Kingdom. Commonwealth Nation	Mbabane	17,366	(6,705)	544,000 (1978)	English, SiSwati	Lilangeni and South African rand (R)	89
Sweden	Kingdom	Stockholm	449,792	(173,665)	8,285,000 (1979)	Swedish, Finnish, Lappish	Swedish krona (Kr)	26–7
Switzerland	Republic. Confederation	Berne	41,287	(15,941)	6,298,000 (1978)	German, French, Italian, Romansch	Swiss franc	40-1
Syria	Arab Republic	Damascus	185,180	(71,498)	8,088,000 (1978)	Arabic	Syrian pound (£Syr)	78–80
Taiwan (Formosa)	Republic of China	Taipei	35,989	(13,895)	17,136,000 (1978)	Mandarin Chinese	New Taiwan dollar (NT$)	67
Tanzania	United Republic. Commonwealth Nation	Dar es Salaam (new capital Dodoma)	939,766	(362,844)	16,553,000 (1978)	Swahili, English, tribal languages	Tanzanian shilling (sh)	88
Thailand	Kingdom	Bangkok (Krung Thep)	513,519	(198,270)	45,100,000 (1978)	Thai	Baht	68
Togo	Republic	Lomé	56,591	(21,850)	2,409,000 (1978)	French, tribal languages	CFA franc	85
Tonga	Kingdom. Commonwealth Nation	Nuku'alofa	699	(270)	93,000 (1978)	Tongan, English	Pa'anga (Tongan $)	137
Trinidad and Tobago	Republic. Commonwealth Nation	Port of Spain	5,128	(1,980)	1,133,000 (1978)	English	Trinidad and Tobago dollar (TT$)	127
Tunisia	Republic	Tunis	164,149	(63,378)	6,077,000 (1978)	Arabic, French	Tunisian dinar (TD)	85
Turkey	Republic	Ankara	780,579	(301,382)	43,210,000 (1978)	Turkish, Arabic, Kurdish	Turkish lira (TL)	47,78
Tuvalu	Independent State (1978). Commonwealth Nation *formerly Ellice Islands*	Funafuti	24.5	(9.5)	10,000 (1976)	Tuvaluan, English	Australian dollar (A$)	134
Uganda	Republic. Commonwealth Nation	Kampala	236,037	(91,134)	12,780,000 (1978)	English, tribal languages	Uganda shilling (sh)	86, 88
USSR	Union of Soviet Socialist Republics	Moscow	22,402,200	(8,647,249)	260,020,000 (1978)	Russian, regional languages	Rouble	49–59
United Arab Emirates	Federal union of seven emirates *formerly Trucial States*	Abū Dhabi	86,449	(33,378)	711,000 (1978)	Arabic, English	UAE dirham (UD)	77
United Kingdom	United Kingdom of Great Britain and Northern Ireland. Commonwealth Nation	London	244,755	(94,500)	55,836,000 (1978)	English, Welsh, Gaelic	Pound Sterling (£)	8–15
United States of America	Federal Republic	Washington; DC	9,363,168	(3,615,123)	219,530,000 (1979)	English	US dollar ($)	91–116
Upper Volta	Republic	Ouagadougou	274,123	(105,839)	6,554,000 (1978)	French, native languages	CFA franc	85
Uruguay	Republic	Montevideo	186,925	(72,172)	2,864,000 (1978)	Spanish	Uruguayan new peso (Ur N)	131, 133
Vanduaatu	Independence May 1980 *formerly Anglo-French Condominium of The New Hebrides*	Vila	14,763	(5,700)	99,000 (1977)	English, French, many Melanesian languages and dialects	Australian dollar and New Hebrides franc	137
Vatican City	Ecclesiastical State	Vatican City	0.44	(0.17)	723 (1977)	Italian, Latin	Italian lira and Papal coinage	44
Venezuela	Republic	Caracas	912,050	(352,143)	13,122,000 (1978)	Spanish	Bolívar (Bs)	127–8
Vietnam	Socialist Republic	Hanoi	334,333	(129,086)	49,890,000 (1978)	Vietnamese, French, Chinese	Dong	65
Western Sahara	Ceded to Morocco and Mauritania (1976) (disputed) *formerly Spanish Sahara*							
Western Samoa	Independent State. Commonwealth Nation	Apia	2,841	(1,097)	154,000 (1978)	English, Samoan	Tala or dollar (WS$)	137
Yemen	Yemen Arab Republic	San'a	195,001	(75,290)	5,642,000 (1978)	Arabic	Riyal	72
Yemen, South	*see South Yemen*							
Yugoslavia	Socialist Federal Republic	Belgrade	255,804	(98,766)	22,083,000 (1979)	Serbo-Croat, Macedonian, Slovenian, Albanian	New Yugoslavian dinar	42, 46, 48
Zaire	Republic	Kinshasa	2,344,113	(905,063)	27,745,000 (1978)	French, numerous native languages	Zaire	86
Zambia	Republic. Commonwealth Nation	Lusaka	752,620	(290,587)	5,472,000 (1978)	English, African languages	Kwacha (K)	87–8
Zimbabwe	Republic 18 April 1980. Unilaterally independent as Rhodesia 1965-1980 *formerly self-governing UK territory of Southern Rhodesia.* Commonwealth Nation	Salisbury (Harare)	389,362	(150,333)	6,930,000 (1978)	English, native languages	Zimbabwe dollar (Z$)	88–9

INDEX

Abbreviations used in the Index

Afghan	Afghanistan
Afr	Africa, African
Ala	Alabama
Amer	America, American
Anc mon	Ancient monument
Anc site	Ancient site
Arch	Archipel, archipelago, archipiélago
Arg	Argentina
Ariz	Arizona
Ark	Arkansas
A.S.S.R.	Autonomous Soviet Socialist Republic
Aust	Australia
Aut	Autonomous
B	Bay
Berks	Berkshire
Br	British
Br Col	British Columbia
C	Cape
Cal	California
Can	Canal
Cat(s)	Cataract(s)
Cent	Central
Chan	Channel
Co	County
Coastal reg	Coastal region
Colo	Colorado
Conn	Connecticut
Czech	Czechoslovakia
Den	Denmark
Dep	Département, department
Des	Desert
Dist	District
Div	Division
E	East
Equat	Equatorial
Est	Estuary
Fed	Federal, federation
Fj	Fjord
Fr	French
G	Gulf
Ger	Germany
Gla	Glacier
Gt	Great
Hbr	Harbor, harbour
Hd	Head
H.E.	Hydro-electricity
Hist reg	Historical region
I, isld	Island
Ind	Indian
Is, islds	Islands
Isld king	Island kingdom
Isth	Isthmus
Jct, junc, junct	Junction
L	Lake
Lincs	Lincolnshire
Lt Ho	Light House
Madhya Prad	Madhya Pradesh
Man	Manitoba
Mich	Michigan
Minn	Minnesota
Miss	Mississippi
Mon	Monument
Mont	Montana
Moz	Mozambique
Mt, Mte	Mountain
Mts	Mountains
Mt ra	Mountain range
N	North
Nether	Netherlands
Nev	Nevada
New Bruns	New Brunswick
New Hamps	New Hampshire
Nex Mex	New Mexico
Nfld	Newfoundland
Notts	Nottinghamshire
N Scotia	Nova Scotia
N.S.W.	New South Wales
Oc	Ocean
Old prov	Old province
Pass	Passage
Pen	Peninsula
Penn	Pennsylvania
People's Rep	People's Republic
Physical reg	Physical region
Pk	Peak
Port	Portuguese
Pt, Pta, Pto	Point
Prefect	Prefecture
Princ	Principality
Prot	Protectorate
Prov	Province
Qnsld	Queensland
R	Rio, River
Ra	Range
Rdg	Ridge
Reg	Region
Rep	Republic
Res	Reservoir
River mth	River mouth
S	South
Sa	Serra, Sierra
Salt des	Salt desert
Sand des	Sand desert
Sask	Saskatchewan
Sd	Sound
Sk	Shuiku (reservoir)
Spr	Spring
S.S.R.	Soviet Socialist Republic
St, Ste	Saint, Sainte
Sta	Station
Staffs	Staffordshire
Stat Area	Statistical Area
Stony des	Stony desert
Str	Strait
Swtz	Switzerland
Terr	Territory
Tex	Texas
Tribal dist	Tribal district
U.A.E.	United Arab Emirates
U.K.	United Kingdom
Union Terr	Union Territory
U.S.A.	United States of America
U.S.S.R.	Union of Soviet Socialist Republics
V	Valley
Ven	Venezuela
Vict	Victoria
Virg	Virginia
Vol	Volcano
W	West
Wash	Washington
Wilts	Wiltshire

Aa — Aiguillon

83 L13 Aiguillon,C d' Kerguelen Indian Oc
21 I9 Aigurande France
59 J1 Aihui China
61 M7 Aikawa Japan
112 F4 Aiken S Carolina
45 Q7 Ailano Italy
140 C6 Aileron N Terr Aust
22 E5 Ailette R France
29 M2 Ailigas mt Finland
19 Q18 Aille R France
40 D2 Aillevillers France
20 J1 Ailly-le-Haut-Clocher France
20 G2 Ailly,Pte.d' France
20 K2 Ailly-sur-Noye France
120 J9 Ailsa Craig Ontario
12 C3 Ailsa Craig isld Scotland
51 N3 Aim U.S.S.R.
71 K9 Aimere Indonesia
129 K7 Aimores Brazil
129 K7 Aimores,Serra dos mts Brazil
40 B5 Ain dep France
40 B6 Ain R France
86 A2 Ainabo Somalia
78 G3 Ainaisa Syria
52 B5 Ainaži U.S.S.R.
43 A13 Aïn Beïda Algeria
85 F1 Ain Beida Algeria
85 D2 Ain Beni Mathar Morocco
20 J3 Aincourt France
84 H4 'Ain Dalla Egypt
37 K7 Aindling W Germany
43 B12 Aïn Draham Tunisia
80 E1 Aïn Ebel Lebanon
79 H4 'Ain el Beida, El Syria
80 G3 Ain el Ghazal Jordan
80 E7 'Ain el Ghuweir Jordan
85 E3 Aïn-el-Hadjadj Algeria
17 H10 Ain el Hadjar Algeria
84 H4 Aïn el Wadi Egypt
80 G3 Ain esh Shilaq Jordan
86 C2 Aïn Galakka Chad
68 B2 Ainggyi Burma
80 G4 Ain Janna Jordan
43 B12 Aïn-Kerma Algeria
43 C13 Ain Mestour Tunisia
80 E6 Ain Qilt Jordan
17 H2 Ainsa Spain
85 B5 Ain Safra Mauritania
Ain Salah see In Salah
13 E6 Ainsdale England
85 D2 Aïn Sefra Algeria
123 L7 Ainslie,L C Breton I, N Scotia
79 C9 'Ain Sukhna Egypt
98 G7 Ainsworth Nebraska
17 H9 Ain Tédèles Algeria
17 G9 Ain Témouchent Algeria
Aïn Touta see El Homr
60 H11 Aioi Japan
60 R2 Aioi Japan
85 C4 Aïoun Abdel Malek Mauritania
85 C5 Aïoun el Atrouss Mauritania
128 E7 Aiquile Bolivia
69 H11 Airabu isld Indonesia
20 J2 Airaines France
128 F4 Airao Brazil
69 D12 Airbangis Sumatra
118 C7 Airdrie Alberta
12 D2 Airdrie Scotland
22 C2 Aire France
17 K5 Aire,I.del Balearic Is
20 C3 Airel France
13 G6 Aire,R England
18 E9 Airè sur L'Adour France
115 M4 Air Force I N W Terr
65 B3 Airgin Sum China
100 B5 Airlie Oregon
142 B5 Airlie I W Australia
45 R7 Airola Italy
85 F5 Aïr ou Azbine mt reg Niger
12 E1 Airth Scotland
37 K4 Aisch R W Germany
86 H3 Aiscia Ethiopia
133 C7 Aisén prov Chile
114 F5 Aishihik Yukon Terr
22 F5 Aisne dep France
22 H5 Aisne R France
40 D3 Aissey France
80 E1 Aïta ech Chaab Lebanon
136 J2 Aitape Papua New Guinea
37 O6 Aiterhofen W Germany
144 A7 Aitken, Mt New Zealand
99 N3 Aitkin Minnesota
46 E6 Aitolikón Greece
55 B4 Aitova U.S.S.R.
48 H4 Aiud Romania
18 E6 Aix isld France
18 G5 Aix d'Angillon,les France
19 O18 Aix-en-Provence France
21 H10 Aixe-sur-Vienne France
Aix-la-Chapelle see Aachen
117 J8 Aiyansh Br Col
79 B9 'Aiyat,El Egypt
47 F7 Aíyina isld Greece
46 F4 Aiyínion Greece
46 E6 Aíyion Greece
47 G4 Áiyon Óros Greece
46 F7 Áiyos Andréas Greece
47 H9 Áiyos Ioánnis, Akr C Crete Greece
75 P7 Aizawl India
87 C10 Aizeb R Namibia
21 B8 Aizenay France
27 M15 Aizpute U.S.S.R.
61 N8 Aizu-Takada Japan
61 N8 Aizu-Wakamatsu Japan
78 L3 Ajab Shir Iran
18 L11 Ajaccio Corsica
74 J6 Ajaigarh India
128 D3 Ajaju R Colombia
80 G3 'Ajami Syria
143 A8 Ajana W Australia
115 M9 Ajax Ontario
101 M4 Ajax Mt Idaho/Montana
144 D5 Ajax, Mt New Zealand
84 G3 Ajdābiyah Libya
42 F3 Ajdovščina Yugoslavia
61 O5 Ajigasawa Japan
61 N10 Ajiro Japan
61 P7 Aji-shima isld Japan
48 D3 Ajka Hungary
80 G4 Ajlun Jordan
74 F5 Ajmer India
103 M9 Ajo Arizona
16 E1 Ajo,C Spain
129 G3 Ajoewa Suriname
103 M9 Ajo,Mt Arizona
71 C2 Aju isld W Irian
128 E4 Ajuana R Brazil
125 J8 Ajuchitlán Mexico
71 F5 Ajuy Philippines
85 E3 Akabli Algeria
59 L1 Akademii, Zaliv B U.S.S.R.
61 M8 Akadomari Japan
61 M10 Akaishi-dake peak Japan
74 G10 Akalkot India
60 S2 Akan Japan
79 D3 Akanthou Cyprus
60 G12 Akaoka Japan
47 L6 Akar R Turkey
61 P12 Akarie-Ue Okinawa
144 D5 Akaroa New Zealand
27 G15 Åkarp, N Sweden
60 G10 Akasaki Japan
86 F1 Akasha Sudan
60 H11 Akashi Japan
29 K4 Äkäsjoki R Finland
29 K4 Äkäsjokisuu Finland
98 F4 Akaska S Dakota
61 N8 Akatani Japan
26 J4 Akavare mt Sweden
80 F2 'Akbara Israel
57 G1 Akbaur U.S.S.R.
55 F5 Akbent U.S.S.R.
55 C5 Akbulak U.S.S.R.
78 F2 Akçadağ Turkey
78 G3 Akçakale Turkey
47 K8 Akçay Turkey
85 A4 Akchar,Dunes de l' Mauritania
57 G1 Akchatau U.S.S.R.
57 H3 Akchi U.S.S.R.
47 J7 Akçoava Turkey
47 K5 Ak Dağ mt Turkey
47 K6 Ak Dağ mt Turkey
47 K8 Ak Dağ mt Turkey
78 E2 Akdağmadeni Turkey
56 D5 Ak Dovurak U.S.S.R.
61 L10 Akechi Japan
71 B2 Akelamo Halmahera Indonesia
9 F3 Akeley England
99 M2 Akeley Minnesota
27 B13 Åkernes Norway
27 K12 Åkersberga Sweden
27 E12 Akershus county Norway
26 G8 Åkersjön Sweden
27 J12 Akers-styckebruk Sweden
71 B2 Akeselaka Halmahera Indonesia
57 B2 Akespe U.S.S.R.
53 F12 Akhalkalaki U.S.S.R.
53 F12 Akhaltsikhe U.S.S.R.
47 F6 Akharnaí Greece
80 F2 'Akhbera Israel
84 G3 Akhdar, Jabal al mts Libya
46 E5 Akhelóös R Greece
116 K8 Akhiok Alaska
78 A2 Akhisar Turkey
84 J4 Akhmim Egypt
Akhna see Athna
79 H2 Akhterin Syria
53 C12 Akhtopol Bulgaria
53 G9 Akhtubinsk U.S.S.R.
53 G12 Akhty U.S.S.R.
53 D8 Akhtyrka U.S.S.R.
60 G12 Aki Japan
116 G6 Akiak Alaska
52 H3 Akim U.S.S.R.
58 G1 Akima U.S.S.R.
115 L7 Akimiski I N W Terr
53 E10 Akimovka U.S.S.R.
60 F11 Aki-nada sea Japan
47 J7 Akıncılar Turkey
27 G16 Akirkeby Denmark
61 O6 Akita Japan
145 F4 Akitio New Zealand
56 G3 Akitkan, Khrebet mts U.S.S.R.
85 B5 Akjoujt Mauritania
80 G4 'Akka Jordan
85 C3 Akka Morocco
55 D6 Akkabak U.S.S.R.
26 J4 Akkajaure L Sweden
57 A3 Akkala, Mys C U.S.S.R.
116 B4 Akkani U.S.S.R.
55 D5 Akkarga U.S.S.R.
80 D2 'Akko Israel
57 H2 Akkol' U.S.S.R.
47 J7 Akköy Turkey
55 B6 Akkozinskiy U.S.S.R.
25 E2 Akkrum Netherlands
46 F7 Akladhókambos Greece
114 F4 Aklavik N W Terr
85 C5 Aklé Aouana reg Mauritania
48 M5 Akmangit U.S.S.R.
52 B6 Akmene U.S.S.R.
52 C6 Akniste U.S.S.R.
86 F4 Akobo R Ethiopia/Sudan
74 G8 Akola India
116 F6 Akolmiut Alaska
74 G8 Akot India
56 C5 Ak-Oyuk, Gora mt U.S.S.R.
115 N5 Akpatok I N W Terr
57 J4 Akqi China
98 J1 Akra N Dakota
27 B12 Åkrafjorden inlet Norway
46 E6 Akráta Greece
46 E8 Akrítas, Akra C Greece
28 D6 Åkrog Bugt B Denmark
111 J9 Akron Alabama
98 C9 Akron Colorado
94 A5 Akron Indiana
98 K7 Akron Iowa
94 D3 Akron Michigan
94 J3 Akron New York
94 F5 Akron Ohio
120 F4 Akron Ontario
95 L6 Akron Pennsylvania
47 G9 Akrotíri Crete Greece
79 D4 Akrotiri B Cyprus
74 H1 Aksai Chin L Kashmir
55 B4 Aksakovo U.S.S.R.
78 E2 Aksaray Turkey
57 F3 Aksay U.S.S.R.
57 H4 Aksay R U.S.S.R.
78 C2 Akşehir Turkey
78 C2 Aksehir Gölü L Turkey
55 B4 Aksenovo U.S.S.R.
58 G1 Aksenovo-Zilovskoye U.S.S.R.
77 D5 Aks-e Rostam R Iran
51 L3 Aksha U.S.S.R.
55 B6 Akshatau U.S.S.R.
57 C1 Akshiy U.S.S.R.
78 K1 Akstafa U.S.S.R.
53 G12 Akstata U.S.S.R.
66 C3 Aksu China
47 L8 Aksu Turkey
47 L7 Aksu R Turkey
57 J2 Aksu R U.S.S.R.
55 D5 Aksuat U.S.S.R.
52 H7 Aksubayevo U.S.S.R.
57 J4 Aksu He R China
86 G3 Aksum Ethiopia
57 E3 Aksumbe U.S.S.R.
Aksu Yangi Shahr see Aksu
52 H6 Aktanysh U.S.S.R.
57 D1 Aktas U.S.S.R.
56 C5 Aktash U.S.S.R.
57 D5 Aktash U.S.S.R.
55 D5 Aktasty U.S.S.R.
55 F5 Aktau U.S.S.R.
47 G4 Akti Greece
57 B1 Aktogay U.S.S.R.
57 J2 Aktogay U.S.S.R.
57 H5 Aktu China
57 A3 Aktumsyk, Mys C U.S.S.R.
55 C5 Aktyubinsk U.S.S.R.
53 D7 Akulichi U.S.S.R.
60 D13 Akune Japan
116 E9 Akun I Aleutian Is
85 F7 Akure Nigeria
115 S4 Akureyri Iceland
116 D9 Akutan I Aleutian Is
116 D9 Akutan Pass Aleutian Is
56 B5 Akutikha U.S.S.R.
Akyab see Sittwe
55 C5 Ak'yar U.S.S.R.
47 L4 Akyazı Turkey
50 H4 Akzhal U.S.S.R.
57 L1 Akzhar U.S.S.R.
57 E3 Akzhaykin, Ozero L U.S.S.R.
27 C11 Ål Norway
41 O6 Ala Italy
111 K8 Alabama state U.S.A.
111 J10 Alabama R Alabama
94 D2 Alabaster Michigan
144 B6 Alabaster, L New Zealand
71 F3 Alabat isld Luzon Philippines
79 F4 Al 'Abde Lebanon
55 E4 Alabota, Oz L U.S.S.R.
78 E1 Alaca Turkey
47 K3 Alaçah Turkey
47 H6 Alaçatı Turkey
113 E8 Alachua Florida
84 G3 Al'Adhem Libya
16 D3 Alaejos Spain
53 F11 Alagir U.S.S.R.
40 G6 Alagna Italy
18 H7 Alagnon R France
130 J9 Alagoa Grande Brazil
130 H10 Alagoas state Brazil
129 L6 Alagoinhas Brazil
17 G3 Alagón Spain
16 C4 Alagón R Spain
71 G7 Alah Mindanao Philippines
69 E13 Alahanpanjang Sumatra
29 K8 Alahärmä Finland
77 A5 Al Ahmadi Kuwait
79 F3 Alaja Syria
29 K8 Alajärvi Finland
79 G3 'Ala,Jebel el mts Syria
86 G3 Alaji mt Ethiopia
125 M4 Alajuela Costa Rica
47 L8 Alakır R Turkey
57 K2 Alakol', Ozero L U.S.S.R.
29 P5 Alakurtti U.S.S.R.
29 L4 Alakylä Finland
80 G3 'Al'al Jordan
135 T3 Alalakeiki Chan Hawaiian Is
128 F4 Alalaú R Brazil
101 N7 Alameda Idaho
124 H3 Alameda Mexico
106 D6 Alameda New Mexico
119 P9 Alameda Sask
71 D2 Alaminos Luzon Philippines
124 D3 Alamito Mexico
108 C6 Alamito Creek Texas
124 H4 Alamítos, Sa. de los ra Mexico
112 E5 Alamo Georgia
98 C1 Alamo N Dakota
103 J4 Alamo Nevada
110 G6 Alamo Tennessee
109 J9 Alamo Texas
103 J9 Alamo R California
106 E9 Alamogordo New Mexico
106 F7 Alamogordo Res New Mexico
43 C8 Ala, Monti di Sardinia
103 L7 Alamo Res Arizona
124 E4 Alamos Mexico
106 E4 Alamosa Colorado
124 F2 Alamos de Peña Mexico
76 D3 Alampor India
26 H7 Alanäs Sweden
74 G10 Aland India
27 J12 Åland Sweden
29 H11 Åland isld Finland
33 P7 Aland R E Germany
26 J9 Ålandsbro Sweden
29 H11 Ålands Hav Finland/Sweden
88 H1 Alanga Bay Kenya
70 E6 Alangalang Tg Kalimantan
69 G13 Alangangtang isld Sumatra
29 L6 Alaniemi Finland
108 D8 Alanreed Texas
87 H11 Alaotra, L Madagascar
112 D6 Alapaha R Georgia
50 F3 Alapayevsk U.S.S.R.
80 G2 'Alaq R Syria
17 F5 Alarcón, Embalse de Spain
71 H5 Alasan Indonesia
78 B2 Alaşehir Turkey
56 C5 Alash R U.S.S.R.
116 Alaska state U.S.A.
116 O7 Alaska,G.of Alaska
135 L2 Alaska Pen Alaska
70 Q10 Alas,Selat Indonesia
44 D3 Alassio Italy
29 K11 Alastaro Finland
57 C5 Alat U.S.S.R.
116 L3 Alatna Alaska
45 O6 Alatri Italy
52 G7 Alatyr' U.S.S.R.
17 F2 Alava prov Spain
78 K1 Alaverdi U.S.S.R.
29 O7 Alavuokki Finland
29 K9 Alavus Finland
138 F5 Alawoona S Australia
17 K5 Alayor Menorca
57 F5 Alayskiy Khrebet mts U.S.S.R.
47 L5 Alayunt Turkey
78 L1 Alazan R U.S.S.R.
109 K8 Alazan Bay Texas
53 G12 Alazani R U.S.S.R.
51 P2 Alazeya R U.S.S.R.
40 H2 Alb R W Germany
44 D2 Alba Italy
94 C2 Alba Michigan
109 M3 Alba Texas
17 F5 Albacete Spain
17 F6 Albacete prov Spain
138 F6 Albacutya,L Victoria
16 D4 Alba de Tormes Spain
28 E1 Albæk Denmark
56 C5 Albagan, Gora mt U.S.S.R.
17 G6 Albaida Spain
48 H4 Alba Iulia Romania
144 B6 Alba, Mt New Zealand
121 S4 Albanel Quebec
46 D2 Albania rep S Europe
42 E7 Albani,Colli hills Italy
45 N6 Albano L Italy
45 N6 Albano Laziale Italy
45 J4 Albano, Mte Italy
111 M10 Albany Georgia
99 O8 Albany Illinois
110 L1 Albany Indiana
127 L2 Albany Jamaica
110 L5 Albany Kentucky
111 F11 Albany Louisiana
110 B1 Albany Missouri
95 O4 Albany New York
94 E7 Albany Ohio
100 B5 Albany Oregon
109 H3 Albany Texas
95 P2 Albany Vermont
143 C10 Albany W Australia
101 T8 Albany Wyoming
141 J7 Albany Downs Queensland
133 D4 Albardón Argentina
45 K1 Albaredo d'Adige Italy
40 B6 Albarine R France
17 F4 Albarracín, Sa. de mt Spain
141 F2 Albatross B Queensland
126 G6 Albatross Bank Caribbean
141 F1 Albatross Bay Queensland
32 K9 Albaxen W Germany
71 F4 Albay Gulf Luzon Philippines
40 H2 Albbruck W Germany
112 G2 Albemarle N Carolina
112 L1 Albemarle Sound N Carolina
44 D3 Albenga Italy
100 J1 Albeni Falls Dam Idaho
16 E4 Alberche R Spain
130 B10 Alberdi Paraguay
18 G10 Albéres mts France
138 D2 Alberga S Australia
16 B4 Albergaria a Valha Portugal
17 G5 Alberique Spain
117 L11 Alberni Br Col
32 K4 Albersdorf W Germany
22 D3 Albert France
107 L3 Albert Kansas
122 H8 Albert New Brunswick
140 E4 Albert R Queensland
111 J9 Alberta Alabama
118 D5 Alberta Canada
94 K10 Alberta Virginia
114 H7 Alberta prov Canada
117 P9 Alberta,Mt Alberta
48 F3 Albertirsa Hungary
22 J1 Albert Kanaal Belgium
100 E7 Albert, L Oregon
138 E6 Albert, L S Australia
86 F5 Albert, L Uganda/Zaire
86 F5 Albert Nile R Uganda
122 H7 Alberton Pr Edward I
127 K2 Albert Town Jamaica
126 G3 Albert Town Long Cay Bahamas
Albertville see Kalémié
40 D6 Albertville France
119 M5 Albertville Sask
48 L6 Albeşti Romania
36 B6 Albestroff France
45 L1 Albettone Italy
18 G9 Albi France
99 O8 Albia Iowa
98 B8 Albin Wyoming
129 H2 Albina Suriname
45 J2 Albinea Italy
140 B5 Albinia Spring N Terr Aust
102 A2 Albion California
101 M7 Albion Idaho
110 H3 Albion Illinois
94 B5 Albion Indiana
99 O7 Albion Iowa
94 C4 Albion Michigan
98 B4 Albion Montana
98 H8 Albion Nebraska
94 J3 Albion New York
110 A7 Albion Oklahoma
94 G5 Albion Pennsylvania
44 D3 Albissola-Marina Italy
25 C5 Alblasserdam Netherlands
17 H4 Albocácer Spain
27 J15 Alböke Sweden
43 C8 Albo,M Sardinia
17 G5 Alboraya Spain
28 D2 Ålborg Denmark
Ålborg co see Nordjylland
99 O3 Alborn Minnesota
17 F7 Albox Spain
117 O9 Albreda Br Col
8 D2 Albrighton England
141 H6 Albro Queensland
16 B7 Albufeira Portugal
17 G5 Albufera L Spain
41 L4 Albula Pass Switzerland
37 J1 Albungen W Germany
16 E8 Albuñol Spain
130 B6 Albuquerque Brazil
106 D6 Albuquerque New Mexico
95 O2 Alburg Vermont
43 G8 Alburno mt Italy
16 C5 Alburquerque Spain
144 C6 Albury New Zealand
139 H6 Albury Victoria
6 M6 Albuskjell oil rig North Sea
19 Q13 Alby France
26 H9 Alby Sweden
16 B6 Alcacer do Sal Portugal
17 H4 Alcalá de Chivert Spain
16 D7 Alcalá de Guadaira Spain
17 G5 Alcalá del Júcar Spain
16 D8 Alcalá de los Gazules Spain
16 E7 Alcala la Real Spain
131 B2 Alcalde, Pta C Chile
43 E11 Alcamo Sicily
17 G3 Alcanadre R Spain
17 H4 Alcanar Spain
16 C3 Alcañices Spain
17 G3 Alcañiz Spain
16 C5 Alcántara Spain
16 C5 Alcántara, Embalse de res Spain
17 G7 Alcantarilla Spain
130 D5 Alcantilado Brazil
17 F6 Alcaraz Spain
17 F6 Alcaraz, Sa. de mts Spain
16 E7 Alcaudete Spain
16 E5 Alcázar de San Juan Spain
9 E3 Alcester England
98 K6 Alcester S Dakota
17 G5 Alcira Spain
111 C10 Alco Louisiana
112 D2 Alcoa Tennessee
129 L7 Alcobaça Brazil
16 B5 Alcobaca Portugal
17 F3 Alcolea del Pinar Spain
112 G4 Alcolu S Carolina
118 D5 Alcomdale Alberta
118 L1 Alcona Ontario
9 F3 Alconbury Hill England
140 C6 Alcoota N Terr Aust
17 G4 Alcora Spain
17 G4 Alcorisa Spain
101 T7 Alcova Wyoming
17 G6 Alcoy Spain
17 G3 Alcubbiere, Sa. de mt Spain
81 B6 Aldabra I Indian Oc
124 G3 Aldama Mexico
51 M3 Aldan U.S.S.R.
51 M3 Aldanskoye Nagorye U.S.S.R.
9 E5 Aldbourne England
13 H6 Aldbrough England
16 C3 Aldeadávila de la Ribera Spain
9 H3 Aldeburgh England
107 M3 Alden Kansas
94 B2 Alden Michigan
94 J4 Alden New York
25 F7 Aldenhoven W Germany
106 D3 Alder Colorado
9 H3 Alde,R England
101 N4 Alder Montana
14 E2 Aldergrove N Ireland
100 C3 Alder L Washington
9 E5 Aldermaston England
145 F2 Aldermen Is, The New Zealand
20 A2 Alderney isld Channel Is
102 C6 Alder Pk California
101 M4 Alder Pk Montana
102 A1 Alderpoint California
9 F5 Aldershot England
28 D4 Alderslyst Denmark
118 F8 Alderson Alberta
94 G9 Alderson W Virginia
118 D8 Aldersyde Alberta
8 D1 Aldford England
9 E4 Aldsworth England
28 D5 Åle Denmark
99 Q8 Aledo Illinois
109 K3 Aledo Texas
85 B5 Aleg Mauritania
130 B5 Alegra R Brazil
130 F6 Alegre Brazil
133 F3 Alegrete Brazil
106 B7 Alegros Mt New Mexico
133 A9 Alejandro Selkirk isld Juan Fernández Is Pacific Oc
116 H7 Aleknagik Alaska
147 K11 Aleksandra Ostrova U.S.S.R.
54 E8 Aleksandriya U.S.S.R.
54 M3 Aleksandro-Nevskiy U.S.S.R.
52 E6 Aleksandrov U.S.S.R.
48 G6 Aleksandrovac Yugoslavia
53 G8 Aleksandrov Gay U.S.S.R.
52 J5 Aleksandrovsk U.S.S.R.
58 G1 Aleksandrovskiy Zavod U.S.S.R.
53 F11 Aleksandrovskoye U.S.S.R.
59 M1 Aleksandrovsk Sakhalinskiy U.S.S.R.
31 L4 Aleksandrów Poland
31 L3 Aleksandrów Kujawski Poland
50 G3 Alekseyevka U.S.S.R.
56 G2 Alekseyevsk U.S.S.R.
53 F8 Alekseyevskaya U.S.S.R.
54 F1 Alekseyevskoye U.S.S.R.
53 F8 Aleksikovo U.S.S.R.
54 J2 Aleksin U.S.S.R.
46 E1 Aleksinac Yugoslavia
27 F14 Älekulla Sweden
27 H15 Ålem Sweden
106 C9 Aleman New Mexico
133 D3 Alemania Argentina
129 K8 Alem Paraíba Brazil
20 F5 Alençon France
129 H4 Alenquer Brazil
16 A5 Alenquer Portugal
102 V13 Alenuihaha Chan Hawaiian Is
76 C6 Aleppey India
79 H2 Aleppo Syria
115 N1 Alert N W Terr
128 D6 Alerta Peru
117 K10 Alert Bay Br Col
18 H8 Alès France
43 B9 Ales Sardinia
48 G3 Aleşd Romania
52 G2 Alëshki U.S.S.R.
26 K3 Alesjaure L Sweden
44 E2 Alessándria Italy
44 D1 Alessandria prov Italy
Alessio see Lezhë
28 C3 Ålestrup Denmark
26 B9 Ålesund Norway
18 G10 Alet France
116 L10 Aleutian Is Alaska
116 H8 Aleutian Ra Alaska
107 N7 Alex Oklahoma
137 Q4 Alexa Bank Pacific Oc
20 D5 Alexain France
80 C4 Alexander Israel
107 L3 Alexander Kansas
119 R9 Alexander Manitoba
98 C2 Alexander N Dakota
117 E7 Alexander Archipelago Alaska
87 C11 Alexander B S Africa
111 L9 Alexander City Alabama
146 F12 Alexander I Antarctica
142 F4 Alexander I W Australia
140 D2 Alexander, Mt N Terr Aust
141 G5 Alexander,Mt Queensland
142 B6 Alexander, Mt W Australia
143 D8 Alexander, Mt W Australia
144 B6 Alexandra New Zealand
140 F4 Alexandra R Queensland
133 J8 Alexandra,C S Georgia
117 P5 Alexandra Falls N W Terr
147 G6 Alexandra Fiord N W Terr
146 G7 Alexandra Ra Antarctica
117 M9 Alexandria Br Col
79 A7 Alexandria Egypt
84 H3 Alexandria Egypt
110 L1 Alexandria Indiana
127 K2 Alexandria Jamaica
110 M3 Alexandria Kentucky
111 D10 Alexandria Louisiana
99 L4 Alexandria Minnesota
110 E1 Alexandria Missouri
98 J9 Alexandria Nebraska
140 D4 Alexandria N Terr Australia
121 Q7 Alexandria Ontario
47 G1 Alexandria Romania
89 E9 Alexandria S Africa
12 D2 Alexandria Scotland
98 J6 Alexandria S Dakota
110 K5 Alexandria Tennessee
95 K8 Alexandria Virginia
95 M2 Alexandria Bay New York
144 C5 Alexandrina, L New Zealand
138 E6 Alexandrina, L S Australia
80 E5 Alexandrium Jordan
78 A1 Alexandroúpolis Greece
99 Q8 Alexis Illinois
115 O7 Alexis B Labrador
33 O9 Alexisbad E Germany
117 M9 Alexis Creek Br Col
123 P1 Alexis R Labrador
118 B6 Alexo Alberta
79 F5 'Aley Lebanon
56 B4 Aley R U.S.S.R.
56 B5 Aleysk U.S.S.R.
36 C3 Alf W Germany
36 B3 Alf R W Germany
17 G4 Alfambra R Spain
128 C4 Alfaro Ecuador
17 F2 Alfaro Spain
47 J1 Alfatar Bulgaria
32 L9 Alfeld W Germany
37 M5 Alfeld W Germany
130 F7 Alfenas Brazil
55 G4 Alferovka U.S.S.R.
32 G3 Alfhausen W Germany
45 M3 Alfonsine Italy
9 G1 Alford England
111 L11 Alford Florida
15 F3 Alford Scotland
26 A10 Ålfotbreen gla Norway
95 R3 Alfred Maine
98 G3 Alfred N Dakota
143 F6 Alfred and Marie Ra W Australia
130 H7 Alfredo Chaves Brazil
145 E4 Alfredton New Zealand
9 E1 Alfreton England
9 G6 Alfriston England
27 H10 Alfta Sweden
36 C2 Alfter W Germany
50 E4 Alga U.S.S.R.
27 A13 Algård Norway
133 D5 Algarrobo del Aguila Argentina
16 E7 Algarve prov Portugal
53 F7 Algasovo U.S.S.R.
57 F3 Algatart U.S.S.R.
138 D3 Algebuckina S Australia
16 D8 Algeciras Spain
85 E1 Alger Algeria
94 C2 Alger Michigan
94 D6 Alger Ohio
84 B4 Algeria rep N Africa
43 B8 Alghero Sardinia
27 H14 Älghult Sweden
Algiers see Alger
111 J12 Algiers New Orleans
17 G5 Alginet Spain
89 D9 Algoa B S Africa
130 H10 Algodões Brazil
106 D6 Algodones New Mexico
16 E5 Algodor R Spain
120 H6 Algoma Ontario
100 D7 Algoma Oregon
99 T5 Algoma Wisconsin
99 M6 Algona Iowa
121 M7 Algonquin Park Ontario
110 L5 Algood Tennessee
22 L5 Algrange France
26 J7 Älgsjön Sweden
68 B5 Alguada Reef Burma
17 F2 Alhama R Spain
17 F3 Alhama de Aragón Spain
16 E7 Alhama de Granada Spain
17 F7 Alhama de Murcia Spain
17 F8 Alhamilla, Sa mt Spain
16 E9 Al Hoceima Morocco
86 H3 Al Hudaydah N Yemen
79 E9 Al Humaydah Egypt
26 B10 Ålhus Norway
17 G4 Aliaga Spain
47 H6 Aliağa Turkey
46 E4 Aliákmon R Greece
74 E9 Alibagh India
48 M5 Alibey,Oz L U.S.S.R.
71 F4 Alibijaban Luzon Philippines
86 G4 Alibo Ethiopia
48 F5 Alibunar Yugoslavia
47 F3 Ali Butús mt Greece
124 F5 Alicama Mexico
17 G6 Alicante Spain
17 G6 Alicante prov Spain
98 J3 Alice N Dakota
141 H6 Alice Queensland
109 J8 Alice Texas
141 F3 Alice R Queensland
117 J8 Alice Arm Br Col
142 G4 Alice Downs W Australia
100 H4 Alicel Oregon
43 H9 Alice,Pta Italy
126 E6 Alice Shoal Caribbean
140 C6 Alice Springs N Terr Aust
126 E2 Alice Town Bimini Is Bahamas
111 H8 Aliceville Alabama
140 C6 Alice Well N Terr Aust
110 E6 Alicia Arkansas
71 F7 Alicia Mindanao Philippines
141 F5 Alick R Queensland
43 F10 Alicudi isld Italy
119 Q9 Alida Sask
45 Q7 Alife Italy
74 H5 Aligarh India
77 A3 Aligudarz Iran
Alihe see Oroqen Zizhiqi
59 H1 A-li-ho China
77 L3 Ali Khel Afghanistan
52 G6 Alikovo U.S.S.R.
86 B6 Alima R Congo
125 M3 Alimicamba Nicaragua
47 J8 Alimniá isld Greece
71 F5 Alimodian Philippines
71 E7 Alimpaya Pt Mindanao Philippines
86 D4 Alindao Cent Afr Republic
70 F5 Alindau Sulawesi Indonesia
107 M5 Aline Oklahoma
138 D2 Alinerta,Mt S Australia
77 L2 Alingar R Afghanistan
66 C5 Aling Kangri mt China
27 F14 Alingsås Sweden
70 E2 Alipaga Sabah
75 N5 Alipur Duar India
94 G6 Aliquippa Pennsylvania
102 C5 Alisal California
124 D2 Alisos R Mexico
47 F3 Alistáti Greece
116 K8 Alitak B Alaska
47 G6 Alivérion Greece
89 E8 Aliwal North S Africa
118 D6 Alix Alberta
80 G7 Aliyan Jordan
16 E9 Ali-Youssef-ou-Ali Morocco
16 B7 Aljezur Portugal
80 G2 Al Jukhadar Syria
16 B7 Aljustrel Portugal
100 F8 Alkali L Nevada
22 J2 Alken Belgium
25 C3 Alkmaar Netherlands
95 R6 Allagash Maine
95 R7 Allagash L Maine
75 J6 Allahabad India
20 J5 Allaines France
20 J5 Allainville France
21 A6 Allaire France
83 L9 Allai Tank L Sri Lanka
103 J9 All American Can California
108 C4 Allamoore Texas
19 N16 Allan France
118 L7 Allan Sask
80 G2 'Allan R Syria
68 B3 Allanmyo Burma
83 M9 Allan Pt Christmas I Indian Oc
89 E6 Allanridge S Africa
84 J5 Allaqi,Radi Egypt
121 N3 Allard R Quebec
122 G6 Allardville New Brunswick
16 B2 Allariz Spain
36 C7 Allarmont France
112 C3 Allatoona Res Georgia
22 H4 Alle Belgium
94 B4 Allegan Michigan
94 J4 Allegany New York
94 H5 Allegheny R Pennsylvania
94 E10 Allegheny Mts U.S.A.
127 M4 Allegre, Pte Guadeloupe W I
19 O17 Alleins France
111 F12 Allemands Louisiana
89 E7 Allemanskraal Dam res S Africa
19 Q14 Allemont France
94 E9 Allen Kentucky
98 K7 Allen Nebraska
109 L1 Allen Oklahoma
71 G4 Allen Philippines
98 E6 Allen S Dakota
109 L2 Allen Texas
14 D3 Allen, Bog of Irish Rep
112 F4 Allendale S Carolina
13 F4 Allendale Town England
125 J3 Allende Mexico
32 G10 Allendorf W Germany
32 L10 Allendorf W Germany
36 F1 Allendorf W Germany
36 F2 Allendorf W Germany
120 J8 Allenford Ontario
13 F4 Allenheads England
119 M7 Allen Hills Saskatchewan
14 C2 Allen,L Irish Rep
116 Q5 Allen,Mt Alaska
144 A7 Allen, Mt New Zealand
106 E1 Allens Park Colorado
31 J7 Allensteig Austria
Allenstein see Olsztyn
95 Q3 Allenstown New Hampshire
110 J5 Allensville Kentucky
95 M6 Allentown Pennsylvania
33 M7 Aller R W Germany
22 K3 Allerborn Luxembourg
36 E6 Allerheiligen W Germany
37 L5 Allersberg W Germany
28 J6 Allerslev Denmark
110 C1 Allerton Iowa
28 K4 Allerum Sweden
20 J2 Allery France
40 D7 Allevard France
127 K3 Alley,The Jamaica
109 L6 Alleyton Texas
41 M3 Allgäuer Alpen mts W Ger/Austria
8 D1 Allgreave England
9 G5 Allhallows England
118 F6 Alliance Alberta
98 D7 Alliance Nebraska
94 F6 Alliance Ohio
18 H6 Allier dep France
18 H6 Allier R France
145 E4 Alligator Headland New Zealand
127 J3 Alligator Pond Jamaica
112 L2 Alligator R N Carolina
140 C2 Alligator R., E N Terr Aust
113 G13 Alligator Reef Florida
28 D4 Alling Denmark
37 M6 Alling W Germany
28 E4 Alling Å R Denmark
28 E4 Allingåbro Denmark
99 O7 Allison Iowa
117 K10 Allison Harbour Br Col
12 E1 Alloa Scotland
13 E4 Allonby England
80 D3 Allonim Israel
20 K3 Allonne France
20 J5 Allonnes France
21 E7 Allonnes France
80 D7 Allon Shevut Jordan
141 K8 Allora Queensland
143 E7 Allott, Mt W Australia
99 S2 Allouez Michigan
12 D3 Alloway Scotland
33 O10 Allstedt E Germany
121 N7 Allumette I Quebec
121 R4 Ally Quebec
38 G7 Alm Austria
38 J6 Alm R Austria
110 B6 Alma Arkansas
106 D2 Alma Colorado
112 E6 Alma Georgia
107 O2 Alma Kansas
94 C3 Alma Michigan
110 C2 Alma Missouri
98 G9 Alma Nebraska
122 H8 Alma New Brunswick
121 T4 Alma Quebec
99 P5 Alma Wisconsin
57 H3 Alma-Ata U.S.S.R.
16 A6 Almada Portugal
141 G3 Almaden Queensland
16 D6 Almadén Spain
16 D6 Almadén, Sa. de mts Spain
80 F2 Almagor Israel
71 G5 Almagro isld Philippines
57 E4 Almalyk U.S.S.R.
102 C1 Almanor, L California
17 G6 Almansa Spain
16 D2 Almanza Spain
117 K7 Alma Peak Br Col
17 F3 Almarza Spain
130 E4 Almas, R das Brazil
48 H3 Almasul R Romania
48 G6 Almasului Muntii mt Romania
17 F3 Almazán Spain
27 H12 Almby Sweden
32 J9 Alme R W Germany
27 H15 Älmeboda Sweden
100 B7 Almeda Oregon
129 H4 Almeirim Brazil
16 B5 Almeirim Portugal
25 G4 Almelo Netherlands
107 L2 Almena Kansas
129 K7 Almenara Brazil
17 F7 Almenara, Sa. de mt Spain
17 F3 Almenar de Soria Spain
16 C3 Almendra, Embalse de res Spain
16 C6 Almendralejo Spain
20 F4 Alménêches France
55 D4 Al'menevo U.S.S.R.
8 D6 Almer England
98 G8 Almeria Nebraska
17 F8 Almería Spain
17 F7 Almería prov Spain
17 F8 Almería,G.de Spain
52 H7 Al'met'yevsk U.S.S.R.
27 G15 Älmhult Sweden
16 E8 Almijara, Sierra de mts Spain
28 C5 Almind Vejle Denmark
28 C4 Almind Viborg Denmark
100 G2 Almira Washington
130 E9 Almirante Tamandaré Brazil
47 G6 Almiropótamos Greece
46 F5 Almirós Greece
47 G9 Almiroú Kólpos gulf Crete Greece
101 M7 Almo Idaho
16 B7 Almodôvar Portugal
16 E6 Almodóvar del Campo Spain
17 F5 Almodóvar del Pinar Spain
133 D3 Almogasta Argentina
94 K4 Almond New York
99 R5 Almond Wisconsin
15 E4 Almond,R Scotland
8 D4 Almondsbury England
106 D3 Almont Colorado
94 D4 Almont Michigan
98 E3 Almont N Dakota
121 O7 Almonte Ontario
16 C5 Almonte R Spain
74 H4 Almora India
16 E4 Almorox Spain
100 H3 Almota Washington
79 F9 Al Mudawwara Jordan
86 H3 Al Mukhā Yemen
27 G15 Almundsryd Sweden
16 E8 Almuñécar Spain
27 H14 Almvik Sweden
101 P8 Almy Wyoming
111 E7 Almyra Arkansas
13 G3 Aln Br England
15 D3 Alness Scotland
13 G3 Alnmouth England
26 J9 Alnö Sweden
13 G3 Alnwick England
137 R4 Alofi isld Îles de Horn Pacific Oc
94 C1 Aloha Michigan
68 B1 Alon Burma
71 E5 Alonon Pt Philippines
119 T8 Alonsa Manitoba
71 M9 Alor isld Indonesia
16 D8 Alora Spain
71 M8 Alor,Kep isld Indonesia
71 L9 Alor,Selat Indonesia
69 E9 Alor Setar Malaysia
16 C7 Alosno Spain
Alost see Aalst
143 G7 Aloysius, Mt W Australia
52 D2 Alozero U.S.S.R.
133 E5 Alpachiri Argentina
38 E7 Alpbach Austria
19 Q14 Alpe d'Huez mt France
110 C5 Alpena Arkansas
94 D1 Alpena Michigan
98 H5 Alpena S Dakota
94 H8 Alpena W Virginia
17 G6 Alpera Spain
129 J5 Alpercatas, Serra das mts Brazil
19 O15 Alpes du Dauphiné mts France
46 D2 Alpet mt Albania
44 C3 Alpet mt Italy
99 Q8 Alpha Illinois
95 M6 Alpha New Jersey
141 H6 Alpha Queensland
94 J9 Alpha Virginia
25 C4 Alphen Netherlands
81 C6 Alphonse I Indian Oc
16 B5 Alpiarça Portugal
103 P8 Alpine Arizona
108 D5 Alpine Texas
36 E7 Alpirsbach W Germany
16 B7 Alportel,S Braz de Portugal
4 F7 Alps, The mt ra Europe
47 L5 Alpu Turkey
22 B2 Alquines France
9 E5 Alresford England
123 L6 Alright I Madeleine Is, Quebec
28 E5 Alrø isld Denmark
140 D4 Alroy Downs N Terr Aust
28 E3 Als Denmark
28 D7 Als isld Denmark
19 K4 Alsace prov France
118 H7 Alsask Sask
17 F2 Alsasua Spain
25 F7 Alsdorf W Germany
100 B5 Alsea Oregon
117 E6 Alsek R Br Columbia
98 H1 Alsen N Dakota
36 D4 Alsenz W Germany
110 F2 Alsey Illinois
36 G2 Alsfeld W Germany
28 D6 Als Fjord inlet Denmark
36 E4 Alsheim W Germany
26 J5 Alsjaur L Sweden
33 P9 Alsleben E Germany
28 A5 Alslev Denmark
28 C6 Alslevkro Denmark
28 F4 Ålsø Denmark
26 F6 Alstahaug Norway
32 E8 Alstätte W Germany
95 P3 Alstead New Hampshire
26 F6 Alsten isld Norway
32 M5 Alster R W Germany
13 F4 Alston England
27 M15 Alsunga U.S.S.R.
101 L4 Alta Montana
26 N2 Alta Norway
26 N2 Altaelv R Norway
26 N1 Altafjord inlet Norway
131 D3 Alta Gracia Argentina
127 J9 Altagracía Venezuela
128 E2 Altagracia de Orituco Venezuela
109 L6 Altair Texas
128 E7 Altamachí Bolivia
112 E6 Altamaha R Georgia
133 E4 Alta Melincué Argentina
129 H4 Altamira Brazil
125 N9 Altamirano Mexico
102 C4 Altamont California
110 H2 Altamont Illinois
100 D7 Altamont Oregon
98 K5 Altamont S Dakota
110 L6 Altamont Tennessee
101 P8 Altamont Wyoming
144 B6 Alta, Mt New Zealand
43 H8 Altamura Italy
65 B2 Altan Bulag China
124 D2 Altar Mexico
118 G7 Altario Alberta
124 F5 Altata Mexico
45 R7 Altavilla Irpina Italy
99 O6 Alta Vista Iowa
107 O3 Alta Vista Kansas
94 H9 Altavista Virginia
66 D2 Altay China
58 C2 Altay Mongolia
56 C5 Altay mts U.S.S.R.
56 B5 Altayskiy Kray terr U.S.S.R.
37 N6 Altdorf Niederbayern W Germany
41 J4 Altdorf Switzerland
37 L5 Altdorf W Germany
17 G6 Altea Spain
33 O6 Alte Elde R E Germany
32 H5 Alte Mellum W Germany
36 B3 Altenahr W Germany
33 M9 Altenau W Germany
32 J9 Altenbeken W Germany
32 F8 Altenberge W Germany
32 J5 Altenbruch W Germany
37 N2 Altenburg E Germany
37 M7 Altenerding W Germany
36 C4 Altenglan W Germany
36 E1 Altenhundem W Germany
36 D2 Altenkirchen W Germany
38 L6 Altenmarkt Ober Österreich Austria
38 H7 Altenmarkt Salzburg Austria
37 P6 Altenmarkt W Germany
33 N6 Alten Medingen W Germany
36 H6 Altenstadt Baden-Württemberg W Germany

36 F3 **Altenstadt** Hessen W Germany
36 F6 **Altensteig** W Germany
33 S5 **Altentreptow** E Germany
32 J5 **Altenwalde** W Germany
16 B5 **Alter do Chão** Portugal
33 R8 **Altes Lager** E Germany
26 K3 **Altevatn** *L* Norway
111 L11 **Altha** Florida
37 J6 **Altheim** W Germany
111 E7 **Altheimer** Arkansas
38 K8 **Althofen** Austria
9 G4 **Althorne** England
13 H6 **Althorpe** England
138 D6 **Althorpe Is** S Australia
139 G3 **Altiboullin, L** New S Wales
45 M1 **Altino** Italy
47 L5 **Altıntaş** Turkey
33 O6 **Alt-Jabel** E Germany
19 K5 **Altkirch** France
33 T7 **Altlandsberg** E Germany
36 E5 **Altleiningen** W Germany
37 M6 **Altmannstein** W Germany
95 L3 **Altmar** New York
33 O7 **Altmark** *reg* E Germany
36 H1 **Altmorschen** W Germany
37 K5 **Altmühl** *R* W Germany
32 K7 **Altmühlen** W Germany
15 D2 **Altnaharra** Scotland
111 A10 **Alto** Texas
16 B6 **Alto Alentejo** *prov* Portugal
130 D5 **Alto Araguaia** Brazil
126 G4 **Alto Cedro** Cuba
130 C4 **Alto Coité** Brazil
130 D5 **Alto Garças** Brazil
87 C8 **Alto Hama** Angola
87 G9 **Alto Molocue** Mozambique
44 D3 **Alto,Monte** Italy
37 L7 **Altomünster** W Germany
102 A1 **Alton** California
9 F5 **Alton** Hampshire England
110 F3 **Alton** Illinois
95 L3 **Alton** New York
103 M4 **Alton** Utah
99 Q8 **Altona** Illinois
118 D1 **Altona** Manitoba
101 P9 **Altonah** Utah
138 E2 **Alton Downs** S Australia
111 K7 **Altoona** Alabama
113 F9 **Altoona** Florida
107 P4 **Altoona** Kansas
94 J6 **Altoona** Pennsylvania
128 G8 **Alto Paraguay** *dep* Paraguay
130 C9 **Alto Paraná** *dep* Paraguay
129 J5 **Alto Parnaiba** Brazil
45 J4 **Altopascio** Italy
129 H7 **Alto Sucuriú** Brazil
38 G5 **Altötting** W Germany
129 J4 **Alto Turi** Brazil
130 C10 **Alto Uruguai** Brazil
126 A1 **Alto Vista** *hill* Aruba W I
13 F6 **Altrincham** England
33 R7 **Altruppin** E Germany
33 T8 **Alt-Schadow** E Germany
54 F4 **Altukhovo** U.S.S.R.
78 K4 **Altun Köprü** Iraq
47 H5 **Altunoluk** Turkey
66 C4 **Altun Shan** *mts* China
99 O5 **Altura** Minnesota
100 E8 **Alturas** California
113 F10 **Alturas** Florida
107 L7 **Altus** Oklahoma
41 M2 **Altusried** W Germany
36 B6 **Altwiller** France
57 C2 **Altynasar** U.S.S.R.
55 D3 **Altynay** U.S.S.R.
52 C6 **Alūksne** U.S.S.R.
86 B1 **Alula** Somalia
28 D4 **Alum** Denmark
9 E6 **Alum Bay** England
133 C5 **Aluminé** Argentina
26 M6 **Ålund** Sweden
27 K11 **Alunda** Sweden
103 K6 **Alunite** Nevada
76 C3 **Alur** India
53 D11 **Alushta** U.S.S.R.
17 F4 **Alustante** Spain
83 J11 **Alutgama** Sri Lanka
83 K9 **Alut Oya** Sri Lanka
113 F11 **Alva** Florida
94 D10 **Alva** Kentucky
107 M5 **Alva** Oklahoma
12 E1 **Alva** Scotland
98 B5 **Alva** Wyoming
16 B4 **Alva** *R* Portugal
16 B7 **Alvalade** Portugal
125 M8 **Alvarado** Mexico
109 K3 **Alvarado** Texas
128 F4 **Alvaraes** Brazil
26 E9 **Alvdal** Norway
118 L6 **Alvena** Sask
33 O8 **Alvensleben** E Germany
32 K8 **Alverdissen** W Germany
117 D5 **Alverstone Mt** Alaska/Yukon Terr
27 A11 **Alversund** Norway
27 G15 **Alvesta** Sweden
8 D4 **Alveston** England
27 G10 **Älvho** Sweden
110 J1 **Alvin** Illinois
109 M6 **Alvin** Texas
99 S4 **Alvin** Wisconsin
45 P6 **Alvito** Italy
16 B6 **Alvito** Portugal
27 J11 **Älvkarleby** Sweden
98 K9 **Alvo** Nebraska
109 K2 **Alvord** Texas
100 G7 **Alvord L** Oregon
26 F10 **Älvros** Sweden
27 F14 **Älvsborg** *reg* Sweden
26 M6 **Älvsbyn** Sweden
27 F14 **Älvsered** Sweden
99 M2 **Alvwood** Minnesota
87 E12 **Alwal Nth** S Africa
74 G5 **Alwar** India
76 C5 **Alwaye** India
13 F3 **Alwinton** England
110 C7 **Aly** Arkansas
140 D2 **Alyangula** N Terr Aust
51 N2 **Alyaskitovyy** U.S.S.R.
55 E2 **Alymka** *R* U.S.S.R.
15 E4 **Alyth** Scotland
31 P1 **Alytus** U.S.S.R.
38 G5 **Alz** *R* W Germany
98 B4 **Alzada** Montana
36 G3 **Alzenau** W Germany
22 L4 **Alzette** *R* Luxembourg
36 E4 **Alzey** W Germany
128 F2 **Amacuro Delta** Venezuela
140 B6 **Amadeus,L** N Terr Aust
86 F4 **Amadi** Sudan
115 M4 **Amadjuak L** N W Terr
60 J11 **Amagasaki** Japan
28 K5 **Amager** *isld* Denmark
60 D12 **Amagi** Japan
61 N11 **Amagi-san** *mt* Japan
22 G5 **Amagne** France
20 F4 **Amain,Mt.d'** France
116 F9 **Amak I** Alaska
60 C13 **Amakusa-nada** *sea* Japan
60 D13 **Amakusa-shotō** *islds* Japan
84 G4 **Amal** Libya
27 F12 **Åmål** Sweden
76 F2 **Amalapuram** India
43 F8 **Amalfi** Italy
46 E7 **Amaliás** Greece
16 C5 **Amalia,Sta** Spain
74 F8 **Amalner** India
129 G8 **Amambai** Brazil
130 C8 **Amambaí, Serra de** *mts* Brazil/Paraguay
130 C8 **Amambay** *dep* Paraguay
133 F2 **Amambay, Sa. de** *mts* Brazil/Paraguay
128 F4 **Amaná,L** Brazil
40 D2 **Amance** France
40 D3 **Amancey** France
94 E7 **Amanda** Ohio
42 E6 **Amandola** Italy
55 E6 **Amangel'dy** U.S.S.R.
55 D4 **Amankaragay** U.S.S.R.
60 J10 **Amano-hashidate** *inlet* Japan
43 G9 **Amantea** Italy
87 F12 **Amanzimtoti** S Africa
129 H3 **Amapa** Brazil
72 F2 **Amārah, Al** Iraq
88 F9 **Amaramba,L** Mozambique
129 K5 **Amarante** Brazil
119 T8 **Amaranth** Manitoba
68 C2 **Amarapura** Burma
102 H5 **Amargosa Ra** California
106 D5 **Amarilla** New Mexico
108 C8 **Amarillo** Texas
131 B4 **Amarillo,Cerro** *peak* Argentina
75 J7 **Amarkantah** India
129 J6 **Amaro Leite** Brazil
140 E6 **Amaroo,L** Queensland
61 N7 **Amarume** Japan
99 S3 **Amasa** Michigan
45 O7 **Amaseno** Italy
78 D1 **Amasra** Turkey
78 F1 **Amasya** Turkey
128 E4 **Amataura** Brazil
125 N9 **Amatenango** Mexico
87 F11 **Amatikulu** S Africa
124 H7 **Amatitán** Mexico
125 L8 **Amatlan** Mexico
124 G7 **Amatlán de Cañas** Mexico
22 J2 **Amay** Belgium
119 M7 **Amazon** Sask
Amazon *R* *see* **Amazonas** *R*
128 C5 **Amazonas** *dep* Peru
128 D4 **Amazonas** *div* Colombia
129 H4 **Amazonas** *R* S America
128 E4 **Amazonas** *state* Brazil
128 E3 **Amazonas** *state* Venezuela
110 B2 **Amazonia** Missouri
129 J3 **Amazon,Mouths of the** Brazil
80 C7 **Amazya** Israel
74 E1 **Amb** Pakistan
74 G9 **Ambajogai** India
74 G3 **Ambala** India
83 J11 **Ambalangodo** Sri Lanka
87 H12 **Ambalavao** Madagascar
140 C6 **Ambalindum** N Terr Aust
85 G8 **Ambam** Cameroon
83 K10 **Amban Ganga** *R* Sri Lanka
87 H10 **Ambanje** Madagascar
70 N9 **Ambarawa** Java
51 Q2 **Ambarchik** U.S.S.R.
18 E8 **Ambarès et Lagrave** France
52 D2 **Ambarnyy** U.S.S.R.
139 H2 **Ambathala** Queensland
128 C4 **Ambato** Ecuador
87 H11 **Ambato-Boeny** Madagascar
87 H11 **Ambatolampy** Madagascar
131 C2 **Ambato,Sa** *ra* Argentina
18 F7 **Ambazac** France
107 N6 **Amber** Oklahoma
100 H2 **Amber** Washington
116 J8 **Amber B** Alaska
37 M5 **Amberg** W Germany
99 T4 **Amberg** Wisconsin
9 E1 **Ambergate** England
127 H4 **Ambergris Cays** *islds* Turks & Caicos Is
19 O13 **Ambérieu-en-Bugey** France
144 D5 **Amberley** New Zealand
120 J8 **Amberley** Ontario
22 K3 **Amberloup** Belgium
18 H7 **Ambert** France
18 G9 **Ambialet** France
85 B6 **Ambidédi** Mali
75 K7 **Ambikapur** India
71 E4 **Ambil** *isld* Philippines
21 F7 **Ambillou** France
87 H10 **Ambilobe** Madagascar
117 H7 **Ambition,Mt** Br Columbia
20 K3 **Amblainville** France
13 G3 **Amble** England
116 J3 **Ambler** *R* Alaska
13 F5 **Ambleside** England
22 B2 **Ambleteuse** France
22 L3 **Amblève** Belgium
141 G6 **Ambo** Queensland
87 H12 **Amboasary** Madagascar
87 H11 **Ambodifototra** Madagascar
87 H12 **Ambohimahasoa** Madagascar
21 H7 **Amboise** France
136 F2 **Ambon** Moluccas Indonesia
87 H12 **Amborompotsy** Madagascar
86 G6 **Amboseli, L** Kenya
87 H12 **Ambositra** Madagascar
87 H13 **Ambovombe** Madagascar
103 J7 **Amboy** California
99 R8 **Amboy** Illinois
95 N6 **Amboy,S** New Jersey
21 I8 **Ambrault** France
87 H10 **Ambre, Cap d'** Madagascar
94 G6 **Ambridge** Pennsylvania
20 D5 **Ambrières** France
137 O5 **Ambrim** *isld* New Hebrides
87 B7 **Ambriz** Angola
112 D6 **Ambrose** Georgia
98 C1 **Ambrose** N Dakota
71 E2 **Ambuklao Dam** Luzon Philippines
71 K9 **Ambulombo Vol** Indonesia
70 O10 **Ambulu** Java
70 O9 **Ambunten** Java
76 D4 **Ambur** India
141 J7 **Amby** Queensland
27 C12 **Åmdal** Norway
86 D3 **Am Dam** Chad
85 E4 **Amded** *watercourse* Algeria
50 F2 **Amderma** U.S.S.R.
75 O2 **Amdo** China
86 G3 **Amedamit** *mt* Ethiopia
102 D1 **Amedee** California
25 E2 **Ameland** *isld* Netherlands
42 E6 **Amelia** Italy
98 H7 **Amelia** Nebraska
94 K9 **Amelia** Virginia
113 F7 **Amelia I** Florida
32 M6 **Amelinghausen** W Germany
43 H9 **Amendolara** Italy
67 A5 **Ameng** China
17 J2 **Amer** Spain
102 D2 **American** *R* California
130 F8 **Americana** Brazil
101 N7 **American Falls** Idaho
103 N1 **American Fork** Utah
134 E1 **American Samoa** *islds* Pacific Oc
113 F13 **American Shoal** *lt ho* Florida
112 C5 **Americus** Georgia
25 D4 **Amerongen** Netherlands
25 D4 **Amersfoort** Netherlands
9 F4 **Amersham** England
143 B9 **Amery** W Australia
99 O4 **Amery** Wisconsin
146 C4 **Amery Ice Shelf** Antarctica
99 N7 **Ames** Iowa
98 K8 **Ames** Nebraska
107 M5 **Ames** Oklahoma
118 E3 **Amesbury** Alberta
9 E5 **Amesbury** England
95 R4 **Amesbury** Massachusetts
118 J1 **Amesdale** Ontario
120 F3 **Ameson** Ontario
94 F7 **Amesville** Ohio
122 J8 **Amet Sound** Nova Scotia
46 F6 **Amfíklia** Greece
46 E6 **Amfilokhía** Greece
47 F4 **Amfípolis** Greece
46 E6 **Ámfissa** Greece
20 C3 **Amfreville** France
20 G3 **Amfreville-la-Campagne** France
51 N2 **Amga** U.S.S.R.
51 M3 **Amga** *R* U.S.S.R.
58 G2 **Amgalang Bulag** China
51 N3 **Amgan** *R* U.S.S.R.
51 N4 **Amgu** U.S.S.R.
86 D3 **Am Guéréda** Chad
85 F3 **Amguid** Algeria
59 K1 **Amgun** *R* U.S.S.R.
86 G3 **Amhara** *reg* Ethiopia
Amherst *see* **Kyaikkami**
106 H1 **Amherst** Colorado
95 T2 **Amherst** Maine
95 P4 **Amherst** Massachusetts
98 G9 **Amherst** Nebraska
95 Q4 **Amherst** New Hampshire
115 N8 **Amherst** Nova Scotia
94 E5 **Amherst** Ohio
98 J4 **Amherst** S Dakota
94 H9 **Amherst** Virginia
120 G10 **Amherstburg** Ontario
94 F9 **Amherstdale** W Virginia
123 K6 **Amherst I** Madeleine Is, Quebec
121 O8 **Amherst I** Ontario
99 R5 **Amherst Junction** Wisconsin
142 F4 **Amherst, Mt** W Australia
42 D6 **Amiata,Monte** Italy
98 C3 **Amidon** N Dakota
20 K2 **Amiens** France
141 K8 **Amiens** Queensland
78 H5 **Amij,Wadi** Iraq
46 E4 **Amíndaion** Greece
73 L6 **Amindivi Is** Lakshadweep Indian Ocean
60 H10 **Amino** Japan
87 C10 **Aminuis** Namibia
79 F4 **Amioune** Lebanon
80 F1 **'Amir** Israel
83 H5 **Amirante Is** Indian Oc
113 F6 **Amisk** Alberta
119 P4 **Amisk L** Sask
106 G6 **Amistad** New Mexico
108 F6 **Amistad Res** Mexico
111 F11 **Amite** Louisiana
111 C7 **Amity** Arkansas
95 O6 **Amityville** Long I, N Y
75 L5 **Amlekhganj** Nepal
27 C13 **Amli** Norway
8 B1 **Amlwch** Wales
80 G6 **'Amman** Jordan
8 C4 **Ammanford** Wales
26 H5 **Ammarfjallet** *mt* Sweden
26 H6 **Ammarnäs** Sweden
140 D5 **Ammaroo** N Terr Aust
28 E4 **Ammelhede** Denmark
33 P10 **Ammendorf** E Germany
32 L9 **Ammensen** W Germany
41 O2 **Ammer** *R* W Germany
41 N2 **Ammer Gebirge** *mt* W Germany
41 O2 **Ammerland** W Germany
32 G6 **Ammerland** *reg* W Germany
116 R2 **Ammerman Mt** Yukon Terr
37 K5 **Ammerndorf** W Germany
41 O1 **Ammer See** *L* W Germany
80 F2 **'Ammi 'ad** Israel
101 O6 **Ammon** Idaho
Amne Machin *see* **A'nyêmaqên Shan**
77 C1 **Āmol** Iran
130 B6 **Amolar** Brazil
109 N9 **Amon Carter Airfield** Texas
36 F2 **Amöneburg** W Germany
36 G4 **Amorbach** W Germany
131 F2 **Amores** *R* Argentina
47 H8 **Amorgós** *isld* Greece
107 M5 **Amorita** Oklahoma
111 H8 **Amory** Mississippi
103 J8 **Amos** California
115 M8 **Amos** Quebec
28 G5 **Åmose Å** *R* Denmark
27 H11 **Åmot** Sweden
27 D12 **Amot Akershus** Norway
27 C12 **Åmotsdal** Norway
Amoy *see* **Xiamen**
70 G5 **Ampana** Sulawesi Indonesia
87 G12 **Ampanihy** Madagascar
130 F8 **Amparo** Brazil
128 D7 **Ampato, Cord. de** *mts* Peru
70 Q10 **Ampenan** Indonesia
37 M7 **Amper** *R* W Germany
37 N7 **Ampfing** W Germany
103 O9 **Amphitheater** Arizona
85 F7 **Ampier** Nigeria
13 G5 **Ampleforth** England
17 H4 **Amposta** Spain
9 F3 **Ampthill** England
19 N14 **Ampuis** France
17 J2 **Ampurdán** *dist* Spain
80 D2 **'Amqa** Israel
122 E5 **Amqui** Quebec
74 G8 **Amravati** India
74 D8 **Amreli** India
74 F3 **Amritsar** India
30 D1 **Amrum** *isld* W Germany
26 K7 **Åmsele** Sweden
38 J7 **Am Stein** *mt* Austria
25 C4 **Amstelveen** Netherlands
113 C7 **Amsterdam** Georgia
101 L7 **Amsterdam** Idaho
25 C4 **Amsterdam** Netherlands
95 N4 **Amsterdam** New York
94 G6 **Amsterdam** Ohio
24 **Amsterdam** *conurbation* Netherlands
81 E9 **Amsterdam,I** Indian Oc
38 L5 **Amstetten** Austria
27 F12 **Åmtervik, V** Sweden
86 D3 **Am Timan** Chad
28 E2 **Amtoft** Denmark
41 L2 **Amtzell** W Germany
127 J9 **Amuay** Venezuela
57 D5 **Amu-Dar'ya** U.S.S.R.
57 B4 **Amudar'ya** *R* U.S.S.R.
147 H5 **Amund Ringness I** N W Terr
146 A5 **Amundsen B** Antarctica
146 G8 **Amundsen Glacier** Antarctica
147 J1 **Amundsen Gulf** N W Terr
146 E3 **Amundsen, Mt** Antarctica
146 J11 **Amundsen Sea** Antarctica
147 J2 **Amundsen Trough** Arctic Oc
27 H10 **Amungen** *L* Sweden
70 D3 **Amuntai** Kalimantan
51 N3 **Amur** *R* U.S.S.R.
59 J1 **Amur** *reg* U.S.S.R.
71 J4 **Amurang** Sulawesi Indonesia
71 J4 **Amurang Teluk** *B* Sulawesi Indonesia
144 D5 **Amuri Pass** New Zealand
17 F1 **Amurrio** Spain
59 L1 **Amursk** U.S.S.R.
51 M3 **Amurskaya Oblast'** *prov* U.S.S.R.
55 C4 **Amurskiy** U.S.S.R.
46 E6 **Amvrakía, L** Greece
46 D6 **Amvrakikós Kólpos** *gulf* Greece
54 K9 **Amvrosiyevka** U.S.S.R.
107 K3 **Amy** Kansas
56 D4 **Amyl** *R* U.S.S.R.
142 B6 **Amy, Mt** W Australia
120 F4 **Amyot** Ontario
16 E9 **Amzoughen-Khémis-Mrapten** Morocco
68 B3 **An** Burma
138 F5 **Ana Branch** *R* New S Wales
80 D4 **Anabta** Jordan
102 E7 **Anacapa Is** California
45 Q8 **Anacapri** Italy
127 M10 **Anaco** Venezuela
111 C10 **Anacoco** Louisiana
114 H8 **Anaconda** Montana
101 M4 **Anaconda Range** Montana
100 C1 **Anacortes** Washington
107 M6 **Anadarko** Oklahoma
130 H10 **Anadia** Brazil
16 B4 **Anadia** Portugal
78 F1 **Anadolu Dağlari** *mt* Turkey
51 R2 **Anadyr** U.S.S.R.
51 R2 **Anadyrskoye Ploskogor'ye** *tableland* U.S.S.R.
47 H8 **Anáfi** *isld* Greece
26 F9 **Anafjället** *mt* Sweden
47 H8 **Anafópoulo** *isld* Greece
130 H4 **Anagé** Brazil
45 O6 **Anagni** Italy
117 L9 **Anahim Lake** Br Columbia
135 O1 **Anahola** Hawaiian Is
125 J4 **Anáhuac** Mexico
111 B12 **Anahuac** Texas
102 R11 **Anahulu** *R* Hawaiian Is
76 C5 **Anaimalai Hills** India
75 K10 **Anakapalle** India
141 J6 **Anakie** Queensland
116 M2 **Anaktuvuk Pass** Alaska
87 H10 **Analalava** Madagascar
128 F4 **Anama** Brazil
119 T7 **Anama Bay** Manitoba
126 E4 **Ana Maria, Cayos de** *islds* Cuba
69 G11 **Anambas, Kep** *isld* Indonesia
61 L8 **Anamizu** Japan
98 F2 **Anamoose** N Dakota
129 G3 **Anamu** *R* Brazil
78 D3 **Anamur** Turkey
60 H12 **Anan** Japan
47 G8 **Anánes** *isld* Greece
71 J7 **Anano** *isld* Indonesia
76 C3 **Anantapur** India
74 F2 **Anantnag** Kashmir
48 M3 **Anan'yev** U.S.S.R.
53 E11 **Anapa** U.S.S.R.
43 G11 **Anapo** *R* Sicily
129 J7 **Anápolis** Brazil
129 H4 **Anapú** *R* Brazil
77 D4 **Anār** Iran
77 C3 **Anārak** Iran
77 G3 **Anardarra** Afghanistan
26 F8 **Anaris Fjällen** *mt* Sweden
26 O3 **Anarjokka** *R* Norway/Finland
127 L5 **Añasco** Puerto Rico
26 M7 **Ånäset** Sweden
113 F8 **Anastasia I** Florida
78 D2 **Anatolia** *reg* Turkey
100 H3 **Anatone** Washington
29 O7 **Änättijärvi** *L* Finland
131 E2 **Añatuya** Argentina
128 F3 **Anauá** *R* Brazil
69 G8 **An Bien** Vietnam
128 C5 **Ancash** *dep* Peru
9 F2 **Ancaster** England
101 O4 **Anceney** Montana
21 C7 **Ancenis** France
21 F7 **Anché** France
130 H7 **Anchieta** Brazil
106 E8 **Ancho** New Mexico
116 N6 **Anchorage** Alaska
94 B8 **Anchorage** Kentucky
94 E4 **Anchor Bay** Michigan
144 A6 **Anchor I** New Zealand
116 M7 **Anchor Point** Alaska
127 J2 **Anchovy** Jamaica
65 C5 **Anci** China
121 T6 **Ancienne Lorette** *airport* Quebec
113 E9 **Anclote Keys** *islds* Florida
128 E7 **Ancohuma** *mt* Bolivia
128 C6 **Ancón** Peru
45 O4 **Ancona** Italy
128 C3 **Ancon de Sardinas B.de** Ecuador
95 O4 **Ancram** New York
22 D4 **Ancre** *R* France
13 F2 **Ancroft** England
13 F3 **Ancrum** Scotland
88 G8 **Ancuabe** Mozambique
133 C6 **Ancud** Chile
59 J2 **Anda** China
65 F1 **Anda** China
133 C5 **Andacollo** Argentina
140 D7 **Andado** N Terr Aust
128 D6 **Andahuaylas** Peru
107 N4 **Andale** Kansas
133 D3 **Andalgala** Argentina
26 C9 **Åndalsnes** Norway
16 D7 **Andalucia** *reg* Spain
111 K10 **Andalusia** Alabama
68 A6 **Andaman Islands** Bay of Bengal
138 D4 **Andamooka** S Australia
52 G5 **Andanga** U.S.S.R.
129 K6 **Andaria** Brazil
67 B5 **Ande** China
41 K4 **Andeer** Switzerland
28 N1 **Andefjord** Faeroes
52 H1 **Andeg** U.S.S.R.
20 H3 **Andelle** *R* France
19 J4 **Andelot** France
20 H3 **Andelys,les** France
22 J3 **Andenne** Belgium
85 E5 **Anderamboukane** Mali
41 J4 **Andermatt** Switzerland
36 C3 **Andernach** W Germany
36 C3 **Andernach-Land** W Germany
57 F6 **Anderov** U.S.S.R.
26 L7 **Andersfors** Sweden
100 C9 **Anderson** California
94 B6 **Anderson** Indiana
110 B5 **Anderson** Missouri
112 E3 **Anderson** S Carolina
114 G4 **Anderson** *R* N W Terr
139 H8 **Anderson Bay** Tasmania
68 A6 **Anderson I** Andaman Is
100 F7 **Anderson L** Oregon
101 K6 **Anderson Ranch Res** Idaho
112 C5 **Andersonville** Georgia
110 L2 **Andersonville** Indiana
27 G14 **Anderstorp** Sweden
95 N4 **Andes** New York
133 D3 **Andes, Cordillera de los** *mts* S America
98 H6 **Andes,L** S Dakota
87 H11 **Andevoranto** Madagascar
26 H2 **Andfjord** *inlet* Norway
76 D2 **Andhra Pradesh** *prov* India
17 F2 **Andía,Sierra de** *mt* Spain
83 J10 **Andigama** Sri Lanka
47 F9 **Andikíthira** *isld* Greece
87 H11 **Andilamena** Madagascar
47 G8 **Andimilos** *isld* Greece
47 G7 **Andipáros** *isld* Greece
46 D5 **Andipaxoi** *isld* Greece
47 H6 **Andipsara** *isld* Greece
78 F3 **Andirin** Turkey
66 C4 **Andirlangar** China
47 H5 **Ándissa** Greece
53 G12 **Andiyskoye Koysu** *R* U.S.S.R.
57 F4 **Andizhan** U.S.S.R.
77 J1 **Andkhūi** Afghanistan
36 C7 **Andlau** France
40 F1 **Andolsheim** France
52 E4 **Andomskiy Pogost** U.S.S.R.
65 G6 **Andong** S Korea
65 D7 **Andongwei** China
141 F1 **Andoom** Queensland
44 D4 **Andora** Italy
26 J3 **Andörja** *isld* Norway
17 J2 **Andorra** Pyrenees
17 H2 **Andorra la Vella** Andorra
20 D5 **Andouille** France
9 E5 **Andover** England
95 R2 **Andover** Maine
122 E7 **Andover** New Brunswick
95 Q3 **Andover** New Hampshire
95 N6 **Andover** New Jersey
94 K4 **Andover** New York
94 G5 **Andover** Ohio
98 J4 **Andover** S Dakota
9 E4 **Andoversford** England
26 H2 **Andöya** *isld* Norway
130 D7 **Andradina** Brazil
116 F5 **Andreafsky** Alaska
116 O10 **Andreanof Is** Aleutian Is
52 D6 **Andreapol'** U.S.S.R.
12 D5 **Andreas** I of Man U.K.
79 E3 **Andreas,C** Cyprus
87 H11 **Andreba** Madagascar
138 F2 **Andree,L** S Australia
115 R3 **Andrée Land** Greenland
130 G7 **Andre lándia** Brazil
118 E5 **Andrew** Alberta
99 Q7 **Andrew** Iowa
68 B3 **Andrew B** Burma
143 E10 **Andrew, Mt** W Australia
94 B6 **Andrews** Indiana
112 D2 **Andrews** N Carolina
98 C7 **Andrews** Nebraska
100 G7 **Andrews** Oregon
112 H4 **Andrews** S Carolina
108 E3 **Andrews** Texas
53 H8 **Andreyevka** U.S.S.R.
54 N1 **Andreyevo** U.S.S.R.
53 D9 **Andreyevo-Ivanovka** U.S.S.R.
55 E2 **Andreyevskoye, Oz** *L* U.S.S.R.
53 D8 **Andreykovichi** U.S.S.R.
43 G7 **Andria** Italy
46 D2 **Andrijevica** Yugoslavia
46 E7 **Andrítsaina** Greece
106 G4 **Andrix** Colorado
87 G12 **Androka** Madagascar
116 G9 **Andronica I** Alaska
126 E2 **Andros** *isld* Bahamas
47 G7 **Ándros** *isld* Greece
95 R2 **Androscogg** *R* New Hamps/Maine
53 G7 **Androsovka** U.S.S.R.
126 F2 **Andros Town** Andros Bahamas
73 L6 **Androth I** Lakshadweep Indian Oc
53 C8 **Andrushevka** U.S.S.R.
31 L6 **Andrychów** Poland
55 D2 **Andryushino** U.S.S.R.
26 K2 **Andselv** Norway
16 E6 **Andújar** Spain
87 C8 **Andulo** Angola
18 H8 **Anduze** France
27 G14 **Aneby** Sweden
85 E7 **Anecho** Togo
143 G6 **Anec, L** W Australia
131 B8 **Anecón Grande** *peak* Argentina
85 E5 **Anefis** Mali
113 L7 **Anegada** *isld* Virgin Is
133 E6 **Anegado, B** Argentina
137 O6 **Aneityum** *isld* New Hebrides
118 K7 **Anerley** Sask
118 K9 **Aneroid** Sask
20 H4 **Anet** France
98 J2 **Aneta** N Dakota
67 E3 **Anfu** China
140 B3 **Angalarri** *R* N Terr Aust
133 C2 **Angamos, Pta** *C* Chile
125 J8 **Angangue** Mexico
59 H2 **Ang'angxi** China
147 K8 **Angara Basin** Arctic Oc
56 F4 **Angarsk** U.S.S.R.
140 B7 **Angas Downs** N Terr Aust
142 G6 **Angas Ra** W Australia
138 E5 **Angaston** S Australia
71 E3 **Angat** Luzon Philippines
130 E8 **Angatuba** Brazil
26 H9 **Ånge** Sweden
26 H10 **Ängebo** Sweden
124 C3 **Angel de la Guarda** *isld* Mexico
71 E3 **Angeles** Luzon Philippines
128 F2 **Angel Falls** *waterfall* Venezuela
27 F15 **Ängelholm** Sweden
94 J4 **Angelica** New York
111 B10 **Angelina** *R* Texas
141 H7 **Angellala** Queensland
28 D7 **Angeln** *reg* W Germany
43 G8 **Angelo de Lom,S** Italy
27 H12 **Ängelsberg** Sweden
102 D3 **Angels Camp** California
38 N7 **Anger** Austria
41 J6 **Angera** Italy
26 K9 **Ångermanälven** *isld* Sweden
26 J8 **Ångermanälven** *R* Sweden
32 E10 **Angermund** W Germany
21 D7 **Angers** France
26 G10 **Ängersjö** Sweden
20 J5 **Angerville** France
26 M5 **Ängeså** Sweden
26 N5 **Ängesan** *R* Sweden
26 L8 **Ängesön** *isld* Sweden
70 G7 **Anggowala, Bk** *mt* Sulawesi Indonesia
45 M4 **Anghiari** Italy
112 J2 **Angier** N Carolina
115 K5 **Angikuni L** N W Terr
8 A4 **Angle** Wales
144 A7 **Anglem, Mt** New Zealand
120 D4 **Angler** Ontario
Anglesey *co see* **Gwynedd**
Anglesey *isld see* **Môn**
18 D9 **Anglet** France
109 M6 **Angleton** Texas
118 J7 **Anglia** Sask
21 F8 **Angliers** France
21 H8 **Anglin** *R* France
115 Q4 **Angmagssalik** Greenland
88 G10 **Angoche** Mozambique
77 E6 **Angohrān** Iran
131 A6 **Angol** Chile
87 C8 **Angola** Africa
94 B5 **Angola** Indiana
94 H4 **Angola** New York
90 K11 **Angola Basin** Atlantic Oc
112 K3 **Angola Swamp** N Carolina
117 F7 **Angoon** Alaska
98 C8 **Angora** Nebraska
124 E5 **Angostura** Mexico
125 J6 **Angostura** Mexico
128 D3 **Angostura I, Salto** *cataract* Colombia
124 E2 **Angostura, Presa de la** *res* Mexico
125 N9 **Angostura, Psa. de la** *res* Mexico
98 C6 **Angostura Reserve** S Dakota
18 F7 **Angoulême** France
18 F7 **Angoumois** *prov* France
129 K8 **Angra dos Reis** Brazil
45 R8 **Angri** Italy
21 D6 **Angrie** France
37 L2 **Angstedt-Gräfinau** E Germany
68 E5 **Ang Thong** Thailand
17 G2 **Angués** Spain
126 E3 **Anguila Isles** Bahamas
127 N5 **Anguilla** *isld* Lesser Antilles
45 L1 **Anguillara Ven** Italy
123 N6 **Anguille, C** Newfoundland
75 L8 **Angul** India
86 E6 **Angumu** Zaïre
65 C5 **Anguo** China
140 D2 **Angurugu** Northern Territory
98 K1 **Angus** Minnesota
Angus *co see* **Tayside** *reg*
119 Q8 **Angusville** Manitoba
88 C10 **Angwa** *R* Zimbabwe
129 H8 **Anhandui** *R* Brazil
28 R3 **Anholt** Denmark
28 H3 **Anholt** *isld* Denmark
68 G3 **Anh Son** Vietnam
67 D2 **Anhua** China
58 G5 **Anhui** *prov* China
Anhwei *prov see* **Anhui**
61 O5 **Aniai** Japan
116 H6 **Aniak** Alaska
116 H8 **Aniakchak Vol. Crater** Alaska
22 E3 **Aniche** France
130 E5 **Anicuns** Brazil
47 H8 **Ánidhros** *isld* Greece
85 E7 **Anié** Togo
45 N6 **Aniene** *R* Italy
18 E10 **Anie, Pic d'** *mt* Spain/France
55 D5 **Anikhovka** U.S.S.R.
52 F5 **Anikovo** U.S.S.R.
106 B10 **Animas** New Mexico
106 C4 **Animas** *R* Colorado
124 C3 **Animas,Pta Las** *C* Mexico
68 C5 **Anin** Burma
48 G5 **Anina** Romania
103 M6 **Anita** Arizona
99 M8 **Anita** Iowa
71 G5 **Anitaguipan Pt** Philippines
130 E10 **Anitápolis** Brazil
116 J2 **Aniuk** *R* Alaska
59 M2 **Aniva, Zaliv** *B* U.S.S.R.
99 R4 **Aniwa** Wisconsin
22 E4 **Anizy-le-Chât** France
29 M11 **Anjalankoski** Finland
74 D7 **Anjar** India
80 G4 **'Anjara** Jordan
70 K9 **Anjer-Lor** Java
67 F1 **Anji** China
65 G2 **Anjia** China
Anjiang *see* **Qianyang**
Anjiangying *see* **Luanping**
61 L11 **Anjō** Japan
21 C7 **Anjou** *prov* France
87 G10 **Anjouan** *isld* Comoros
87 H11 **Anjozorobe** Madagascar
59 J4 **Anjŭ** N Korea
77 L2 **Anjuman** *reg* Afghanistan
58 E5 **Ankang** China
78 D2 **Ankara** Turkey
87 H11 **Ankaratra** *mt* Madagascar
27 H14 **Ankarsrum** Sweden
26 J6 **Ankarsund** Sweden
87 G12 **Ankazoabo** Madagascar
99 N8 **Ankeny** Iowa
33 T5 **Anklam** E Germany
74 E8 **Anklesvar** India
86 G4 **Ankober** Ethiopia
16 D10 **Ankod** Morocco
38 H7 **Ankogel** *mt* Austria
87 E7 **Ankoro** Zaïre
52 E6 **An'kovo** U.S.S.R.
32 G7 **Ankum** W Germany
13 H6 **Anlaby** England
67 E3 **Anle** China
22 K4 **Anlier** Belgium
68 H7 **An Loc** Vietnam
67 B4 **Anlong** China
68 G5 **Anlong Veng** Cambodia
58 F5 **Anlu** China
26 F8 **Ånn** Sweden
110 G4 **Anna** Illinois
25 C3 **Anna** Netherlands
94 C6 **Anna** Ohio
109 L2 **Anna** Texas
53 F8 **Anna** U.S.S.R.
85 F1 **Annaba** Algeria
38 H7 **Annaberg** Austria
37 P2 **Annaberg-Buchholz** E Germany
33 S9 **Annaburg** E Germany
138 D3 **Anna Creek** S Australia
128 G3 **Annai** Guyana
25 B5 **Anna Jacobapolder** Netherlands
61 M9 **Annaka** Japan
68 G3 **Annam** *reg* Vietnam
113 E10 **Anna Maria** Florida
13 E4 **Annan** Scotland
99 M4 **Annandale** Minnesota
141 J5 **Annandale** Queensland
15 E5 **Annandale** Scotland
13 E3 **Annan Water** Scotland
133 C7 **Anna Pink, B** Chile
142 D4 **Anna Plains** W Australia
95 L8 **Annapolis** Maryland
122 G9 **Annapolis R** Nova Scotia
75 K4 **Annapurna** *mt* Nepal
94 D4 **Ann Arbor** Michigan
33 O9 **Annarode** E Germany
78 L7 **An Nāsirīyah** Iraq
99 R8 **Annawan** Illinois
146 H12 **Annawan,C** Antarctica
146 A5 **Ann,C** Antarctica
143 C7 **Annean, L** W Australia
20 F3 **Annebault** France
19 Q13 **Annecy** France
40 D6 **Annecy,L.d'** France
146 A15 **Annenkov I** Antarctica
133 J8 **Annenkov Is** S Georgia
141 K2 **Annerley** *dist* Brisbane, Qnsld
117 H8 **Annette I** Alaska
20 B3 **Anneville-sur-Mer** France
19 N14 **Anneyron** France
68 J6 **An Nhon** Vietnam
141 G2 **Annie** *R* Queensland
123 P5 **Annieopsquotch Mts** Newfoundland
58 D6 **Anning He** *R* China
28 J5 **Annisse** Denmark
111 L8 **Anniston** Alabama
140 D5 **Annitowa** N Terr Aust
40 G5 **Anniviers Val d'** Switzerland
Annobón *isld see* **Pagalu** *isld*
22 D2 **Annœulin** France
109 N2 **Annona** Texas
19 N14 **Annonay** France
127 L2 **Annotto Bay** Jamaica
36 D5 **Annweiler** W Germany
47 G9 **Áno Arkhánai** Crete Greece
99 N4 **Anoka** Minnesota
98 H7 **Anoka** Nebraska
54 M1 **Anopino** U.S.S.R.
22 G4 **Anor** France
36 B7 **Anould** France
47 G9 **Áno Viánnos** Crete Greece
68 J7 **An Phuoc** Vietnam
65 C5 **Anping** China
67 C6 **Anpu** China
67 C6 **Anpu Gang** *B* China
58 G5 **Anqing** China
65 D6 **Anqiu** China
25 F6 **Anrath** W Germany
67 D3 **Anren** China
32 H9 **Anröchte** W Germany
22 K2 **Ans** Belgium
21 G10 **Ansac-sur-Vienne** France
28 B5 **Ansager** Denmark
65 A6 **Ansai** China
79 G3 **Ansārīye, Jebel el** *mts* Syria
37 K5 **Ansbach** W Germany
40 A6 **Anse** France
127 H5 **Anse-à-Galets** Haiti
127 J5 **Anse-à-Pitre** Haiti
122 H5 **Anse-au-Griffon** Quebec
126 H5 **Anse-à-Veau** Haiti
127 N4 **Anse Bertrand** Guadeloupe W I
126 G5 **Anse d'Hainault** Haiti
98 G8 **Anselmo** Nebraska
22 H3 **Anseremme** Belgium
139 H7 **Anser Gr** *islds* Tasmania
122 B5 **Anse St.Jean,L'** Quebec
127 L4 **Anses d'Arlets, Les** Martinique W I
59 H3 **Anshan** China
67 B3 **Anshun** China
131 B3 **Ansilta** *peak* Argentina
131 B3 **Ansilta, Cord. de** *ra* Argentina
109 P3 **Ansley** Louisiana
98 G8 **Ansley** Nebraska
140 B2 **Anson B** N Terr Aust
85 E5 **Ansongo** Mali
94 C6 **Ansonia** Ohio
112 G2 **Ansonville** N Carolina
115 L8 **Ansonville** Ontario
28 C6 **Anst** Denmark
94 F8 **Ansted** W Virginia
15 F4 **Anstruther** Scotland
128 D6 **Anta** Peru
78 C3 **Antalya** Turkey
87 H11 **Antananarivo** Madagascar
87 H11 **Antanifotsy** Madagascar
87 H12 **Antanimora** Madagascar
90 D16 **Antarctic Circle**
146 E13 **Antarctic Pen** Antarctica
81 C10 **Antares Bank** Indian Oc
130 H11 **Antas** Brazil
130 D10 **Antas,R das** Brazil
15 C3 **An Teallach** *mt* Scotland
98 B1 **Antelope** Montana
98 D3 **Antelope** N Dakota
118 J8 **Antelope** Sask
109 J2 **Antelope** Texas
101 Q9 **Antelope** Utah
100 H7 **Antelope Cr** Oregon
130 H9 **Antenor Navarro** Brazil
16 D7 **Antequera** Spain
130 B9 **Antequera,Pto** Paraguay
106 D3 **Antero Pk** Colorado
106 E3 **Antero Res** Colorado
38 F8 **Anterselva** Italy
107 N4 **Anthony** Kansas
106 D9 **Anthony** New Mexico
108 A3 **Anthony** New Mex/Tex
136 H5 **Anthony Lagoon** N Terr Australia
138 C2 **Anthony,Mt** S Australia
85 C3 **Anti Atlas** *mts* Morocco
44 B4 **Antibes** France
44 B4 **Antibes,C.d'** France
127 N9 **Antica, I** Venezuela
45 N5 **Anticoli Corrado** Italy
122 J4 **Anticosti I** Quebec
20 F2 **Antifer,C.d'** France
123 K8 **Antigonish** Nova Scotia
125 O10 **Antigua** Guatemala
127 P4 **Antigua** *isld* Lesser Antilles
127 N4 **Antigues Pte. d'** Guadeloupe W I
118 B3 **Antikameg** Alberta
133 C5 **Antilhue** Chile
126 G4 **Antilla** Cuba
103 N3 **Antimony** Utah
102 C3 **Antioch** California
99 S7 **Antioch** Illinois
98 D7 **Antioch** Nebraska
21 C9 **Antioche, Pertuis d'** *str* France
43 B9 **Antioco, S** Sardinia
43 B9 **Antioco,S** *isld* Sardinia
128 C2 **Antioquia** *div* Colombia
80 C5 **Antipatris** Israel
52 D6 **Antipovo** U.S.S.R.
128 C4 **Antisana** *mt* Ecuador
98 E1 **Antler** N Dakota
119 Q9 **Antler** Sask
107 P7 **Antlers** Oklahoma
133 C2 **Antofagasta** Chile
133 D3 **Antofagasta de la Sierra** Argentina
133 D3 **Antofalla** *vol* Argentina
109 O1 **Antoine** Arkansas
22 E2 **Antoing** Belgium
44 F2 **Antola,Monte** Italy
106 G2 **Anton** Colorado
108 E2 **Anton** Texas
87 J11 **Antongil, B.d'** Madagascar
87 G12 **Antongo** Madagascar
130 E9 **Antonina** Brazil
107 L3 **Antonino** Kansas
48 K1 **Antoniny** U.S.S.R.
129 K7 **Antônio** *R* Brazil
130 G7 **Antônio Carlos** Brazil
130 G6 **Antônio Dias** Brazil
Antonio Enes *see* **Angoche**
130 C8 **Antônio João** Brazil
106 D4 **Antonito** Colorado
126 D3 **Antón Recio** Cuba
140 D4 **Antony Lagoon** N Terr Aust
20 C5 **Antrain** France
52 C4 **Antrea** U.S.S.R.
36 G5 **Antrefftal** W Germany
95 P3 **Antrim** New Hampshire
14 E2 **Antrim** N Ireland
95 K5 **Antrim** Pennsylvania
14 E2 **Antrim** *co* N Ireland
14 E2 **Antrim Hills** N Ireland
142 G4 **Antrim Plat** W Australia
87 G11 **Antsalova** Madagascar
87 H10 **Antserañana** Madagascar
52 D5 **Antsiferovo** U.S.S.R.
87 H11 **Antsirabe** Madagascar
52 C5 **Antsla** U.S.S.R.
87 H10 **Antsohihy** Madagascar
29 N10 **Anttola** Finland
65 G3 **Antu** China
68 J6 **An Tuc** Vietnam
Antwerp *see* **Antwerpen**
95 M2 **Antwerp** New York
94 C5 **Antwerp** Ohio
22 H1 **Antwerpen** Belgium
14 E3 **An Uaimh** Irish Rep
116 F6 **Anukslak L** Alaska
26 K8 **Anundsjö** Sweden
74 E4 **Anupgarh** India
83 K9 **Anuradhapura** Sri Lanka
Anvers *see* **Antwerpen**
45 P6 **Anversa degli Abruzzi** Italy
146 E14 **Anvers I** Antarctica
116 G5 **Anvik** Alaska
121 P3 **Anvilla** Quebec
22 C3 **Anvin** France
58 C3 **Anxi** China
67 F4 **Anxi** China
67 A1 **An Xian** China
67 D2 **Anxiang** China
65 C5 **Anxin** China
138 C5 **Anxious B** S Australia
58 F4 **Anyang** China
58 C5 **A'nyêmaqên Shan** *mts* China
65 B7 **Anyi** China
67 E2 **Anyi** China
67 D7 **Anyou** China
117 J8 **Anyox** Br Col
67 E4 **Anyuan** China
52 J3 **An'yudin** U.S.S.R.
67 B1 **Anyue** China
51 Q2 **Anyuy** *R* U.S.S.R.
42 B3 **Anza** *R* Italy
118 F2 **Anzac** Alberta
17 G2 **Anzánigo** Spain
40 H6 **Anzasca, Valle** Italy
18 F10 **Anzat** France
65 B6 **Anze** China
22 E2 **Anzegem** Belgium
21 I9 **Anzème** France
56 C3 **Anzhero-Sudzhensk** U.S.S.R.
147 P7 **Anzhu Os** *isld* U.S.S.R.
22 E3 **Anzin** France
38 E5 **Anzing** W Germany
45 N7 **Anzio** Italy
128 F2 **Anzoátegui** *state* Venezuela
45 K2 **Anzola dell'Emilia** Italy
59 L5 **Aoga-shima** *isld* Japan
65 D3 **Aohan Qi** China
18 E10 **Aoiz** Spain
61 O5 **Aomori** Japan
60 N3 **Aonae** Japan
145 E4 **Aorangi Mts** New Zealand
145 D4 **Aorere R** New Zealand
68 D7 **Ao Sawi** *B* Thailand
40 F6 **Aosta** Italy
145 E3 **Aotea Harbour** New Zealand
85 C5 **Aouker** *reg* Mauritania
85 E3 **Aoulef** Algeria
67 B3 **Aoxi** China
60 G10 **Aoya** Japan
86 C1 **Aozou** Chad
103 P10 **Apache** Arizona
109 J1 **Apache** Oklahoma
106 B8 **Apache Creek** New Mexico
103 N8 **Apache Junct** Arizona
103 O10 **Apache Pk** Arizona
113 C7 **Apalachee B** Florida
112 C2 **Apalachia Dam** N Carolina
113 C8 **Apalachicola** Florida
128 D3 **Apaporis** *R* Colombia
130 B8 **Apa.R** Brazil/Paraguay
130 D7 **Aparecida do Tabuado** Brazil
144 B7 **Aparima R** New Zealand
71 E1 **Aparri** Luzon Philippines
70 E6 **Apar, Teluk** *B* Kalimantan
48 E5 **Apatin** Yugoslavia
52 D1 **Apatity** U.S.S.R.
124 H8 **Apatzingán** Mexico
116 C5 **Apavawook C** St. Lawrence I, Alaska
52 C5 **Ape** U.S.S.R.
45 M4 **Apecchio** Italy
119 S3 **Apeganau L** Manitoba
25 E4 **Apeldoorn** Netherlands
32 G6 **Apen** W Germany
33 O7 **Apenburg** E Germany
32 L6 **Apensen** W Germany
128 E6 **Apere** *R* Bolivia
112 J2 **Apex** N Carolina
41 L1 **Apfingen** W Germany
101 L1 **Apgar** Montana

80 C5 **Aphek** Israel
116 E6 **Aphrewn** *R* Alaska
86 E5 **Api** Zaïre
137 S4 **Apia** W Samoa
129 G5 **Apiacás,Serra dos** *mts* Brazil
130 E9 **Apiaí** Brazil
45 R7 **Apice** Italy
71 J9 **Api,Gunung** *vol* Indonesia
130 B10 **Apipe Grande** *isld* Argentina
106 F4 **Apishapa** *R* Colorado
70 G5 **Api,Tg** *C* Sulawesi Indonesia
145 E3 **Apiti** New Zealand
125 K8 **Apizaco** Mexico
124 H5 **Apizolaya** Mexico
56 F2 **Aplinskiy Porog** *falls* U.S.S.R.
129 L5 **Apodi** *R* Brazil
71 E4 **Apo East Pass** Philippines
37 M1 **Apolda** E Germany
Apollonia *see* **Marsá Sūsah**
47 G8 **Apollonía** Greece
128 E6 **Apolo** Bolivia
113 F9 **Apopka** Florida
113 F9 **Apopka,L** Florida
133 G1 **Aporé** *R* Brazil
129 H3 **Aporema** Brazil
99 Q2 **Apostle Is** Michigan
133 F3 **Apostoles** Argentina
54 E9 **Apostolovo** U.S.S.R.
128 G3 **Apoteri** Guyana
71 E4 **Apo West Pass** Philippines
94 E10 **Appalachia** Virginia
94 F10 **Appalachian Mts** U.S.A.
27 G11 **Äppelbo** Sweden
32 F9 **Appelhülsen** W Germany
28 B7 **Appelland** *isld* W Germany
44 D3 **Appenino Ligure** *mt* Italy
42 E5 **Appennino Umbro-Marchigiano** *mts* Italy
36 D6 **Appenweier** W Germany
41 K3 **Appenzell** *canton* Switzerland
13 G6 **Apperley Br** England
20 G3 **Appeville** France
25 G2 **Appingedam** Netherlands
109 N4 **Appleby** Texas
13 F4 **Appleby-in-Westmorland** England
142 A2 **Applecross** *dist* Perth, W Aust
8 B5 **Appledore** England
102 D3 **Applegate** California
100 B7 **Applegate** Oregon
122 H8 **Apple River** Nova Scotia
109 N4 **Apple Springs** Texas
95 S2 **Appleton** Maine
100 D4 **Appleton** Washington
99 S5 **Appleton** Wisconsin
110 B3 **Appleton City** Missouri
94 J9 **Appomattox** Virginia
54 J1 **Aprelevka** U.S.S.R.
22 J5 **Apremont** France
27 M15 **Apriki** U.S.S.R.
43 E7 **Aprilia** Italy
53 E11 **Apsheronsk** U.S.S.R.
121 M8 **Apsley** Ontario
138 F6 **Apsley** Victoria
140 B1 **Apsley Str** N Terr Aust
19 O17 **Apt** France
45 H3 **Apuane** Italy
135 V6 **Apua Pt** Hawaiian Is
130 D8 **Apucarana** Brazil
130 D8 **Apucarana, Serra Da** *mts* Brazil
71 D6 **Apurauan** Philippines
128 E2 **Apure** *state* Venezuela
128 D6 **Apurímac** *dep* Peru
48 H4 **Apuseni Muntii** *mt* Romania
88 D6 **Apwa** Tanzania
79 F9 **'Aqaba** Jordan
84 J4 **Aqaba,G.of** Red Sea
77 J1 **Aq Chah** Afghanistan
66 D4 **Aqqikkol Hu** *L* China
80 G3 **'Aqraba** Jordan
103 L7 **Aquarius Mts** Arizona
103 N4 **Aquarius Plat** Utah
130 B8 **Aquidabán,R** Paraguay
130 C7 **Aquidauana** Brazil
130 C6 **Aquidauana,R** Brazil
124 G3 **Aquiles Serdán** Mexico
109 K4 **Aquilla** Texas
126 H5 **Aquin** Haiti
45 P7 **Aquino** Italy
17 G2 **Ara** *R* Spain
80 F3 **Arab** *R* Jordan
53 E10 **Arabatskaya Strelka** *spit* U.S.S.R.
38 E8 **Arabba** Italy
112 D6 **Arabi** Georgia
111 K12 **Arabi** New Orleans
123 N3 **Arabian L** Quebec
84 H3 **Arabs Gulf** Egypt
78 D1 **Araç** Turkey
128 F3 **Araçá** *R* Brazil
129 L6 **Aracaju** Brazil
130 C9 **Aracanguy, Mt de** Paraguay
126 G9 **Aracataca** Colombia
129 L4 **Aracati** Brazil
130 E7 **Araçatuba** Brazil
16 C7 **Aracena** Spain
16 C7 **Aracena, Sa. de** *mts* Spain
130 G5 **Araçuaí** Brazil
48 G4 **Arad** Romania
86 D2 **Arada** Chad
56 D5 **Aradanskiy Khrebet** *mts* U.S.S.R.
81 L7 **Arafura Sea** Aust/New Guinea
129 H7 **Aragarças** Brazil
78 J1 **Aragats** *mt* U.S.S.R.
61 M9 **Ara-gawa** *R* Japan
100 A6 **Arago,Cape** Oregon
17 G2 **Aragón** *R* Spain
17 G4 **Aragon** *reg* Spain
43 F11 **Aragona** Sicily
17 F4 **Aragoncillo** *mt* Spain
128 E2 **Aragua** *state* Venezuela
129 J6 **Araguaçu** Brazil
128 F2 **Aragua de Barcelona** Venezuela
129 J7 **Araguari** Brazil
129 H3 **Araguari** *R* Brazil
133 H1 **Araguari** *R* Brazil
129 J5 **Araguatins** Brazil
53 F12 **Aragvi** *R* U.S.S.R.
144 C5 **Arahura** New Zealand
61 M8 **Arai** Japan
79 E8 **Araif el Naqa** *mt* Egypt
80 G8 **Ara'ir** Jordan
85 E3 **Arak** Algeria
77 A2 **Arāk** Iran
78 G4 **Arak** Syria
61 N8 **Arakai-yama** *mt* Japan
128 G2 **Arakaka** Guyana
116 A4 **Arakamchechen, Ostrov** *isld* U.S.S.R.
68 A2 **Arakan** *prov* Burma
68 B2 **Arakan Yoma** *ra* Burma
46 F6 **Arákhova** Greece
46 D5 **Árakhthos** *R* Greece
120 C2 **Ara L** Ontario
57 B2 **Aral'sk** U.S.S.R.
57 A3 **Aral'skoye More** *sea* U.S.S.R.
55 B6 **Aralsor, Oz** *L* U.S.S.R.
26 A9 **Åram** Norway
141 H6 **Aramac** Queensland
141 G6 **Aramac** *R* Queensland
125 K5 **Aramberri** Mexico
19 N17 **Aramon** France
16 E3 **Aranda de Duero** Spain
17 F3 **Aranda de Moncayo** Spain
87 B10 **Arandis** Namibia
145 D1 **Aranga** New Zealand
128 E7 **Arani** Bolivia
14 C1 **Aran I** Irish Rep
16 E4 **Aranjuez** Spain
89 A5 **Aranos** Namibia
109 L7 **Aransas B** Texas
109 K8 **Aransas Pass** Texas
130 E6 **Arantes,R** Brazil
137 P1 **Aranuka** *isld* Kiribati
85 D5 **Araouane** Mali
106 E1 **Arapaho** *mt* Colorado
106 H3 **Arapahoe** Colorado
98 G9 **Arapahoe** Nebraska
101 R7 **Arapahoe** Wyoming
128 E7 **Arapa,L** Peru
145 E4 **Arapawa I** New Zealand
133 F4 **Arapey** Uruguay
130 H10 **Arapiraca** Brazil
78 G2 **Arapkir** Turkey
130 D8 **Arapongas** Brazil
145 E3 **Arapuni** New Zealand
130 E10 **Araquari** Brazil
80 D4 **'Ar'Ara** Israel
133 H3 **Araranguá** Brazil
129 J8 **Araraquara** Brazil
130 F8 **Araras** São Paulo Brazil
130 D6 **Araras,Serra das** Mato Grosso Brazil
130 D9 **Araras, Serra das** *mts* Paraná Brazil
139 G6 **Ararat** Victoria
Ararat,Mt *see* **Bügük Ağri**
129 K4 **Arari** Brazil
75 M5 **Araria** India
130 G8 **Araruama L.de** Brazil
78 H6 **Arar,Wadi** Saudi Arabia
80 D5 **A-ras** Jordan
78 J1 **Aras** *R* Turkey
17 G5 **Aras de Alpuente** Spain
126 A1 **Arasji** Aruba W I
145 D2 **Aratapu** New Zealand
145 F3 **Aratiatia** New Zealand
61 O7 **Arato** Japan
128 F5 **Araua** *R* Brazil
128 D2 **Arauca** Colombia
133 C5 **Arauco** Chile
127 K10 **Araure** Venezuela
80 E2 **'Arav** Israel
74 E6 **Aravalli Range** India
144 B6 **Arawata R** New Zealand
129 J7 **Araxá** Brazil
128 F1 **Araya,P.de** Venezuela
61 P14 **Ara-zaki** *C* Okinawa
17 G3 **Arba** *R* Spain
86 G4 **Arba Minch** Ethiopia
43 C9 **Arbatax** Sardinia
52 G5 **Arbazh** U.S.S.R.
40 C2 **Arbecey** France
37 K5 **Arberg** W Germany
27 H12 **Arboga** Sweden
27 H12 **Arbogaån** *R* Sweden
40 C4 **Arbois** France
101 N7 **Arbon** Idaho
41 K2 **Arbon** Switzerland
119 O5 **Arborfield** Sask
9 F5 **Arborfield Cross** England
119 U8 **Arborg** Manitoba
99 R4 **Arbor Vitae** Wisconsin
27 H10 **Arbrå** Sweden
13 F1 **Arbroath** Scotland
102 B2 **Arbuckle** California
113 F10 **Arbuckle,L** Florida
109 K1 **Arbuckle Mts** Oklahoma
110 F5 **Arbyrd** Missouri
19 J5 **Arc** France
19 O18 **Arc** *R* France
18 E8 **Arcachon** France
94 J4 **Arcade** New York
118 A3 **Arcadia** Alberta
113 F10 **Arcadia** Florida
94 A6 **Arcadia** Indiana
107 Q4 **Arcadia** Kansas
111 D9 **Arcadia** Louisiana
99 U5 **Arcadia** Michigan
110 F4 **Arcadia** Missouri
98 G8 **Arcadia** Nebraska
94 D5 **Arcadia** Ohio
107 N6 **Arcadia** Oklahoma
99 P5 **Arcadia** Wisconsin
95 T2 **Arcadia Nat. Park** Maine
43 G8 **Arcangelo,S** Italy
94 C7 **Arcanum** Ohio
102 G3 **Arc Dome** *mt* Nevada
45 P6 **Arce** Italy
125 J8 **Arcelia** Mexico
25 F6 **Arcen** Netherlands
45 N4 **Arcévia** Italy
46 F1 **Archar** Bulgaria
95 M5 **Archbald** Pennsylvania
94 C5 **Archbold** Ohio
112 H2 **Archdale** N Carolina
113 E8 **Archer** Florida
141 F2 **Archer** *R* Queensland
109 J2 **Archer City** Texas
141 K2 **Archerfield Airfield** Brisbane, Qnsld
141 H3 **Archer Pt** Queensland
119 O6 **Archerwill** Sask
40 E1 **Arches** France
103 P3 **Arches Nat.Mon** Utah
110 B3 **Archie** Missouri
21 G8 **Archigny** France
119 M8 **Archive** Sask
106 C5 **Archuleta** New Mexico
18 H4 **Arcis sur Aube** France
138 C2 **Arckaringa** *R* S Australia
101 M6 **Arco** Idaho
98 K5 **Arco** Minnesota
99 S10 **Arcola** Illinois
111 F8 **Arcola** Mississippi
119 P9 **Arcola** Sask
45 K1 **Árcole** Italy
18 H6 **Arconce** *R* France
138 D4 **Arcoona** S Australia
131 B7 **Arco, Paso de** Arg/Chile
130 F7 **Arcos** Brazil
16 D8 **Arcos de la Frontera** Spain
16 B3 **Arcos de Vale de Vez** Portugal
17 G3 **Arcos,Sierra de** *mt* Spain
76 D4 **Arcot** India
130 H10 **Arcoverde** Brazil
19 J5 **Arc-Senans** France
147 F4 **Arctic Bay** N W Terr
90 J2 **Arctic Circle**
116 D4 **Arctic Lagoon** Alaska
147 **Arctic Ocean**
114 F4 **Arctic Red River** N W Terr
116 P2 **Arctic Village** Alaska
45 L1 **Arcugnano** Italy
22 E5 **Arcy-Ste. Restitue** France
44 G2 **Arda** *R* Italy
78 M2 **Ardabīl** Iran
38 L5 **Ardagger** Austria
78 J1 **Ardahan** Turkey
77 C3 **Ardakan** Esfahān Iran
77 C4 **Ardakan** Fārs Iran
77 B4 **Ardal** Iran
27 C10 **Årdal** Opland Norway
27 B12 **Årdal** Rogaland Norway
14 C2 **Ardara** Irish Rep
118 K7 **Ardath** Sask
52 F6 **Ardatov** U.S.S.R.
120 K7 **Ardbeg** Ontario
12 B2 **Ardbeg** Scotland
45 N6 **Ardea** Italy
48 H3 **Ardead** Romania
18 H8 **Ardèche** *dep* France
14 E3 **Ardee** Irish Rep
119 S8 **Arden** Manitoba
103 J5 **Arden** Nevada
121 O8 **Arden** Ontario
138 E4 **Arden Mt** S Australia
22 H4 **Ardennes** France
21 I8 **Ardentes** France
12 D1 **Ardentinny** Scotland
77 C3 **Ardestān** Iran
15 D3 **Ardgay** Scotland
14 F2 **Ardglass** N Ireland
46 E4 **Ardhéa** Greece
16 C6 **Ardila,R** Spain
119 M9 **Ardill** Sask
124 H6 **Ardilla, Cerro La** *peak* Mexico
47 G3 **Ardino** Bulgaria
18 E10 **Ardisa** Spain
70 P9 **Ardjasa** Java
70 O9 **Ardjuna,G** *mt* Java
145 F3 **Ardkeen** New Zealand
118 D6 **Ardley** Alberta
15 D4 **Ardlui** Scotland
12 C2 **Ardminish** Scotland
139 H6 **Ardmona** Victoria
118 G4 **Ardmore** Alberta
107 N7 **Ardmore** Oklahoma
98 C6 **Ardmore** S Dakota
110 K6 **Ardmore** Tennessee
14 D5 **Ardmore B** Irish Rep
15 B4 **Ardnamurchan Pt** Scotland
15 B5 **Ardnave Pt** Scotland
98 J1 **Ardoch** N Dakota
141 G7 **Ardoch** Queensland
22 B2 **Ardres** France
12 C1 **Ardrishaig** Scotland
118 D5 **Ardrossan** Alberta
138 E5 **Ardrossan** S Australia
15 D5 **Ardrossan** Scotland
14 F2 **Ards Pen** N Ireland
12 B2 **Ardtalla** Scotland
15 C3 **Ardvasar** Scotland
53 F7 **Ardym** U.S.S.R.
26 F8 **Åre** Sweden
26 N4 **Areavaara** Sweden
127 L5 **Arecibo** Puerto Rico
131 F5 **Areco** *R* Argentina
129 L4 **Areia Branca** Brazil
45 Q7 **Areinzo** Italy
118 K6 **Arelee** Sask
27 E12 **Aremark** Norway
36 B3 **Aremberg** W Germany
95 N4 **Arena** New York
71 E6 **Arena** Philippines
118 H9 **Arena** Sask
133 C7 **Arenales** *mt* Chile
130 C4 **Arenápolis** Brazil
71 F4 **Arena Pt** Luzon Philippines
124 E6 **Arena, Pta** *C* Mexico
16 D4 **Arenas de S.Pedro** Spain
128 D8 **Arenas,Pta** *C* Chile
32 F7 **Arenberg** *reg* W Germany
27 C13 **Arendal** Norway
22 J1 **Arendonk** Belgium
33 O7 **Arendsee** E Germany
32 L10 **Arenshausen** E Germany
19 Q12 **Arenthon** France
28 D2 **Arentsminde** Denmark
17 J3 **Arenys de Mar** Spain
46 E8 **Areópolis** Greece
128 D7 **Arequipa** Peru
129 H4 **Arere** Brazil
18 E8 **Arés** France
16 D3 **Arévalo** Spain
42 D5 **Arezzo** Italy
46 E7 **Arfará** Greece
17 F2 **Arga** *R* Spain
140 D5 **Argadargada** N Terr Aust
16 E5 **Argamasilla de Alba** Spain
16 E4 **Arganda** Spain
16 B4 **Arganil** Portugal
71 F6 **Argao** Philippines
45 P6 **Argatone, M** *mt* Italy
55 D3 **Argayash** U.S.S.R.
55 D3 **Argazi** *L* U.S.S.R.
55 D3 **Argazi, Oz** U.S.S.R.
18 H10 **Argelès sur Mer** France
41 L2 **Argen** *R* W Germany
20 E3 **Argences** France
19 Q18 **Argens** *R* France
117 P10 **Argenta** Br Columbia
45 L2 **Argenta** Italy
101 N4 **Argenta** Montana
20 E4 **Argentan** France
42 D6 **Argentario,Monte** Italy
18 G7 **Argentat** France
44 B3 **Argentera Mt** Italy
20 K4 **Argenteuil** France
123 S6 **Argentia** Newfoundland
40 E6 **Argentières** France
44 C4 **Argentina** *R* Italy
131 D5 **Argentina** *rep* S America
90 E13 **Argentine Basin** Atlantic Oc
133 C8 **Argentino,L** Argentina
21 E7 **Argenton** *R* France
21 I8 **Argenton-sur-Creuse** France
122 C3 **Argent,R à l'** Quebec
20 D5 **Argentré** France
20 C5 **Argentré-du-Plessis** France
18 G5 **Argent sur Sauldre** France
48 J5 **Argeş** *reg* Romania
48 J5 **Argeşul** *R* Romania
77 J4 **Arghandab** *R* Afghanistan
77 K4 **Arghastan** *R* Afghanistan
86 H4 **Argheile** Ethiopia
84 J6 **Argo** Sudan
46 F7 **Argolikós Kólpos** *B* Greece
107 N4 **Argonia** Kansas
99 S4 **Argonne** Wisconsin
22 J5 **Argonne** *reg* France
70 O9 **Argopura G** *mt* Java
101 N5 **Argora** Idaho
46 F7 **Argos** Greece
94 A5 **Argos** Indiana
46 E4 **Árgos Orestikón** Greece
20 C4 **Argouges** France
18 D10 **Arguedas** Spain
20 J2 **Argueil** France
Argun *R* China *see* **Ergun He**
51 L3 **Argun** *R* U.S.S.R.
85 E6 **Argungu** Nigeria
102 G6 **Argus Ra** California
98 J2 **Argusville** N Dakota
112 E6 **Argyle** Georgia
94 E3 **Argyle** Michigan
98 K1 **Argyle** Minnesota
122 G10 **Argyle** Nova Scotia
99 R7 **Argyle** Wisconsin
140 A3 **Argyle, L** W Australia
Argyll *co see* **Strathclyde and Highland** *regions*
6 M6 **Argyll** *oil rig* North Sea
Argyrokastron *see* **Gjirokastër**
65 E3 **Ar Horquin Qi** China
28 E4 **Århus** Denmark
28 D4 **Århus** *co* Denmark
145 E3 **Aria** New Zealand
139 H5 **Ariah Pk** New S Wales
60 D13 **Ariake-kai** *gulf* Japan
87 C11 **Ariamsvlei** Namibia
43 G7 **Ariano Irpino** Italy
45 M2 **Ariano Nel Polésine** Italy
128 D3 **Ariari** *R* Colombia
73 L8 **Ari Atoll** Maldives
85 D6 **Aribinda** Upper Volta
128 D7 **Arica** Chile
128 D4 **Arica** Colombia
45 N6 **Ariccia** Italy
123 M8 **Arichat** C Breton I, N Scotia
60 J11 **Arida** Japan
60 J11 **Arida-gawa** *R* Japan
143 E10 **Arid, C** W Australia
83 J12 **Aride I** Seychelles
Arid I *see* **Rakitu I**
18 G9 **Ariège** *dep* France
18 G10 **Ariège** *R* France
100 C4 **Ariel** Washington
48 H4 **Arieşul** *R* Romania
80 G8 **Ariha** Jordan
106 H2 **Arikaree** *R* Colorado
60 C13 **Arikawa** Japan
28 K4 **Arild** Sweden
48 F7 **Arilje** Yugoslavia
128 F5 **Arima** Brazil
60 J11 **Arima** Japan
127 O2 **Arima** Trinidad
101 N7 **Arimo** Idaho
128 G3 **Arinda** Guyana
129 J7 **Arinos** Brazil
129 G6 **Arinos** *R* Brazil
101 M9 **Arinosa** Utah
99 L8 **Arion** Iowa
127 P1 **Aripo, Mt** Trinidad
128 D2 **Ariporo** *R* Colombia
128 F5 **Aripuana** *R* Brazil
128 F5 **Ariquemes** Brazil
130 D5 **Ariranha** *R* Brazil
15 C4 **Arisaig** Scotland
79 D7 **'Arîsh, El** Egypt
117 J9 **Aristazabal I** Br Columbia
133 D7 **Aristizábal, C** Argentina
111 L10 **Ariton** Alabama
43 C9 **Aritzo** Sardinia
103 N10 **Arivaca** Arizona
87 H11 **Arivonimamo** Madagascar
17 F3 **Ariza** Spain
18 F9 **Arize** *R* France
133 D5 **Arizona** Argentina
103 M7 **Arizona** *state* U.S.A.
124 D2 **Arizpe** Mexico
27 F12 **Årjäng** Sweden
26 J5 **Arjeplog** Sweden
128 D1 **Arjona** Colombia
16 E7 **Arjona** Spain
51 O2 **Arka** U.S.S.R.
53 F8 **Arkadak** U.S.S.R.
109 O1 **Arkadelphia** Arkansas
50 F3 **Arkalyk** U.S.S.R.
110 C6 **Arkansas** *R* Arkansas
109 O1 **Arkansas** *state* U.S.A.
111 E8 **Arkansas City** Arkansas
107 O4 **Arkansas City** Kansas
84 G5 **Arkanu Jebel** *mt* Libya
66 D4 **Arkatag** *mts* China
117 F5 **Arkell,Mt** Yukon Terr
27 G15 **Arkelstorp** Sweden
47 J8 **Arkhángelos** Rhodes Greece
52 F3 **Arkhangel'sk** U.S.S.R.
53 F11 **Arkhangel'skoye** U.S.S.R.
59 K2 **Arkhara** U.S.S.R.
53 D7 **Arkhipovka** U.S.S.R.
53 D8 **Arkino** U.S.S.R.
14 E4 **Arklow** Irish Rep
47 H7 **Árkoi** *isld* Greece
30 H1 **Arkona** E Germany
120 J9 **Arkona** Ontario
76 D4 **Arkonam** India
27 J13 **Arkösund** Sweden
94 K4 **Arkport** New York
52 H6 **Arkul'** U.S.S.R.
95 N4 **Arkville** New York
27 J12 **Ärla** Sweden
18 H7 **Arlanc** France
16 E2 **Arlanza** *R* Spain
41 M3 **Arlberg** *pass* Austria
101 L2 **Arlee** Montana
19 N17 **Arles** Bouches du Rhône France
18 G10 **Arles** Pyrénées-Orientales France
22 E3 **Arleux** France
100 J5 **Arling** Idaho
8 D4 **Arlingham** England
103 M8 **Arlington** Arizona
102 G8 **Arlington** California
106 G3 **Arlington** Colorado
113 F7 **Arlington** Florida
112 C6 **Arlington** Georgia
99 P7 **Arlington** Iowa
107 M4 **Arlington** Kansas
110 G5 **Arlington** Kentucky
99 M5 **Arlington** Minnesota
98 K8 **Arlington** Nebraska
94 D6 **Arlington** Ohio
100 E4 **Arlington** Oregon
98 J5 **Arlington** S Dakota
110 G6 **Arlington** Tennessee
109 N9 **Arlington** Texas
95 O3 **Arlington** Vermont
117 M11 **Arlington** Washington
101 T8 **Arlington** Wyoming
99 S7 **Arlington Heights** Illinois
110 E4 **Arlington Res** Missouri
22 K4 **Arlon** Belgium
140 C6 **Arltunga** N Terr Aust
107 Q4 **Arma** Kansas
118 E8 **Armada** Alberta
12 E2 **Armadale** Scotland
143 B9 **Armadale** W Australia
14 E2 **Armagh** N Ireland
122 B7 **Armagh** Quebec
14 E2 **Armagh** *co* N Ireland
18 F9 **Armagnac** *reg* France
18 H5 **Armançon** *R* France
47 H9 **Armathia** *isld* Greece
13 F4 **Armathwaite** England
53 F10 **Armavir** U.S.S.R.
128 C3 **Armenia** Colombia
78 K1 **Armenia** *reg* U.S.S.R.
48 G5 **Armeniş** Romania
20 G4 **Armentières** Eure France
22 D2 **Armentières** France
101 P2 **Armington** Montana
101 S6 **Arminto** Wyoming
119 Q6 **Armit** Sask
9 E2 **Armitage** England
55 E3 **Armizonskoye** U.S.S.R.
119 N5 **Armley** Sask
98 H6 **Armour** S Dakota
98 G1 **Armourdale** N Dakota
120 D3 **Arms** Ontario
36 E4 **Armsheim** W Germany
101 N5 **Armstead** Montana
114 H7 **Armstrong** Br Columbia
99 T9 **Armstrong** Illinois
99 M6 **Armstrong** Iowa
110 D2 **Armstrong** Missouri
109 K9 **Armstrong** Texas
140 B3 **Armstrong** *R* N Terr Aust
59 L2 **Armu** *R* U.S.S.R.
74 H9 **Armur** India
47 J4 **Armutçuk Dağ** *mt* Turkey
47 K4 **Armutlu** Turkey
53 D10 **Armyansk** U.S.S.R.
28 B7 **Arnå** *R* Denmark
28 M2 **Árnafjall** *mt* Faeroes
47 F4 **Arnaía** Greece
118 D1 **Arnaud** Manitoba
115 M6 **Arnaud,R** Quebec
79 C3 **Arnauti, C** Cyprus
18 J5 **Arnay le Duc** France
28 B4 **Arnborg** Denmark
37 P5 **Arnbruck** W Germany
33 Q7 **Arneburg** E Germany
18 D10 **Arnedo** Spain
28 O9 **Arnefjord** Faeroes
98 C2 **Arnegard** N Dakota
22 C2 **Arneke** France
26 M6 **Arnemark** Sweden
25 A6 **Arnemuiden** Netherlands
27 E11 **Årnes** Norway
107 L5 **Arnett** Oklahoma
94 F9 **Arnett** W Virginia
25 E5 **Arnhem** Netherlands
140 D1 **Arnhem,C** N Terr Aust
140 C2 **Arnhem Land** *reg* N Terr Aust
140 C2 **Arnhem Land Res** N Terr Aust
20 H4 **Arnières** France
45 H4 **Arno** *R* Italy
138 D5 **Arno Bay** S Australia
102 D3 **Arnold** California
98 F8 **Arnold** Nebraska
94 H6 **Arnold** Pennsylvania
99 L6 **Arnolds Park** Iowa
38 J8 **Arnoldstein** Austria
21 J7 **Arnon** *R* France
119 V3 **Arnot** Manitoba
26 L1 **Arnöy** Norway
16 B2 **Arnoya** *R* Spain
12 D1 **Arnprior** Scotland
32 G10 **Arnsberg** W Germany
13 F5 **Arnside** England
37 K2 **Arnstadt** E Germany
37 L3 **Arnstein** W Germany
37 O6 **Arnstorf** W Germany
Arnswalde *see* **Choszczno**
121 L4 **Arntfield** Quebec
28 B6 **Arnum** Denmark
128 F2 **Aro** *R* Venezuela
127 K9 **Aroa** Venezuela
87 C11 **Aroab** Namibia
46 E7 **Aroánia** *mt* Greece
124 H4 **Arocha** Mexico
130 C7 **Aroeira** Brazil
32 K10 **Arolsen** W Germany
55 E3 **Aromashevo** U.S.S.R.
20 D5 **Aron** France
20 D5 **Aron** *R* France
42 B3 **Arona** Italy
122 E7 **Aroostook** New Brunswick
95 S7 **Aroostook** *R* Maine
116 E6 **Aropuk L** Alaska
137 Q2 **Arorae** *isld* Kiribati
71 F4 **Aroroy** Philippines
28 D6 **Arøsund** Denmark
127 O2 **Arouca** Trinidad
145 F3 **Arowhana** *mt* New Zealand
106 G3 **Aroya** Colorado
109 M3 **Arp** Texas
57 G4 **Arpa** U.S.S.R.
18 G8 **Arpajon** France
20 K4 **Arpajon** France
48 J5 **Arpasu de Jos** Romania
55 D1 **Arpavla** U.S.S.R.
120 K4 **Arpin** Ontario
45 P6 **Arpino** Italy
45 L1 **Arquà Petrarca** Italy
45 L1 **Arquà Polesine** Italy
22 C2 **Arques** Pas-de-Calais France
20 H2 **Arques-la-Bataille** France
80 E2 **'Arraba** Israel
138 F2 **Arrabury** Queensland
141 F7 **Arrabury** Queensland
36 B6 **Arracourt** France
131 D2 **Arraga** Argentina
16 C4 **Arrago** *R* Spain
75 L6 **Arrah** India
129 J6 **Arraias** Brazil
16 B6 **Arraiolos** Portugal
14 C4 **Arra Mts** Irish Rep
111 M11 **Arran** Florida
119 Q7 **Arran** Sask
15 C5 **Arran** *isld* Scotland
80 E4 **'Arrana** Jordan
117 H8 **Arrandale** Br Col
22 D3 **Arras** Pas-de-Calais France
18 F9 **Arrats** *R* France
28 B5 **Arre** Denmark
18 F10 **Arreau** France
128 E3 **Arrecifal** Colombia
85 B3 **Arrecife** Canary Is
18 C4 **Arrée,Mgnes.d'** *mts* France
28 J5 **Arresø** *L* Denmark
106 C9 **Arrey** New Mexico
45 L4 **Arrezzo** *reg* Italy
38 J8 **Arriach** Austria
125 N9 **Arriaga** Mexico
106 G2 **Arriba** Colorado
141 G6 **Arrilalah** Queensland
28 B6 **Arrild** Denmark
9 F3 **Arrington** England
143 B8 **Arrino** W Australia
12 D1 **Arrochar** Scotland
133 G4 **Arroio Grande** Brazil
20 D3 **Arromanches** France
16 C5 **Arronches** Portugal
44 M6 **Arrone** *R* Italy
18 F9 **Arros** *R* France
20 H5 **Arrou** France
18 H6 **Arroux** *R* France
101 Q2 **Arrow Cr** Montana
117 P10 **Arrowhead** Br Col
14 C2 **Arrow,L** Irish Rep
119 Q2 **Arrow L** Ontario
117 O10 **Arrow Park** Br Col
110 D2 **Arrow Rock** Missouri
100 K6 **Arrowrock Res** Idaho
138 F4 **Arrowsmith Mt** New S Wales
144 C5 **Arrowsmith, Mt** New Zealand
140 D2 **Arrowsmith Pt** N Terr Aust
144 E6 **Arrowtown** New Zealand
118 D8 **Arrow Wood** Alberta
16 C5 **Arroyo de la Luz** Spain
108 F6 **Arroyo de la Zorra** *R* Mexico
102 D6 **Arroyo Grande** California
131 F6 **Arroyo Grande** *R* Argentina
106 E5 **Arroyo Hondo** New Mexico
131 F4 **Arroyo Negro** *R* Uruguay
103 J8 **Arroyo Seco** *R* California
128 F6 **Arroyos,L de Los** Bolivia
130 B9 **Arroyos-y-Esteros** Paraguay
130 C4 **Arruda** Brazil
28 D3 **Års** Denmark
77 C5 **Arsenajan** Iran
118 J3 **Arsenault L** Sask
117 Q3 **Arseno L** N W Terr
59 K3 **Arsen'yev** U.S.S.R.
55 C3 **Arshinskoye** U.S.S.R.
41 O6 **Arsiero** Italy
76 C4 **Arsikere** India
52 G6 **Arsk** U.S.S.R.
26 J9 **Årskogen** Sweden
45 O5 **Arsoli** Italy
19 K3 **Ars-sur-Moselle** France
27 J11 **Årsunda** Sweden
22 D5 **Arsy** France
46 D5 **Árta** Greece
17 K5 **Artá** Majorca
80 D7 **Artas** Jordan
98 G4 **Artas** S Dakota
17 K5 **Artá,Sierra de,Mt** Majorca
124 H8 **Arteaga** Mexico
59 K3 **Artem** U.S.S.R.
126 C3 **Artemisa** Cuba
51 J3 **Artemovak** U.S.S.R.
54 G7 **Artemovka** U.S.S.R.
56 D4 **Artemovsk** U.S.S.R.
53 F9 **Artemovskiy** U.S.S.R.
45 N6 **Artena** Italy
20 J5 **Artenay** France
33 O10 **Artern** E Germany
17 H3 **Artesa de Segre** Spain
Artesia *see* **Mosomane**
111 H8 **Artesia** Mississippi
98 J5 **Artesian** S Dakota
109 H7 **Artesia Wells** Texas
26 G6 **Artfjallet** *mt* Sweden
121 T6 **Arthabaska** Quebec
18 E9 **Arthez** France
110 H2 **Arthur** Illinois
98 J2 **Arthur** N Dakota
98 E8 **Arthur** Nebraska
139 H8 **Arthur** *R* Tasmania
109 M2 **Arthur City** Texas
138 E4 **Arthur,L** S Australia
139 H8 **Arthur,L** Tasmania
145 D4 **Arthur, Mt** New Zealand
142 E4 **Arthur, Mt** W Australia
141 K5 **Arthur Pt** Queensland
143 B6 **Arthur, R** W Australia
144 C5 **Arthur's Pass** New Zealand
126 G2 **Arthur's Town** Cat I Bahamas
55 C3 **Arti** U.S.S.R.
133 F4 **Artigas** Uruguay
114 J5 **Artillery L** N W Terr
29 M11 **Artjärvi** Finland
118 H6 **Artland** Sask
33 M6 **Artlenburg** W Germany
102 B2 **Artois** California
22 C3 **Artois** *prov* France
22 D3 **Artois Collines d'** France
46 E6 **Artotína** Greece
78 F1 **Artova** Turkey
Artsakan Nor *see* **Qagan Nur**
48 M5 **Artsyz** U.S.S.R.
87 C8 **Artur de Paiva** Angola
66 B4 **Artux** China
71 B1 **Aru** Halmahera Indonesia
86 F5 **Aru** Zaïre
129 H6 **Aruanã** Brazil
123 A2 **Aruba** *isld* W Indies
13 E9 **Arudy** France
80 E8 **Arugot** *R* Jordan
136 G3 **Aru,Kep** *islds* Moluccas Indonesia
25 D2 **Arum** Netherlands
128 F4 **Arumá** Brazil
61 Q12 **Arume** *B* Okinawa
75 Q4 **Arunachal Pradesh** *prov* India
9 F6 **Arundel** England
144 C5 **Arundel** New Zealand
9 F5 **Arun,R** England
28 E6 **Årup** Denmark
76 D6 **Aruppukkottai** India
80 D5 **'Arūra** Jordan
88 F3 **Arusha** Tanzania
86 G4 **Arusi** *prov* Ethiopia
70 G4 **Arus,Tg** *C* Sulawesi Indonesia
70 B5 **Arut** *R* Kalimantan
70 E6 **Aru,Tg** *C* Kalimantan
83 K9 **Aruvi Aru** *R* Sri Lanka
86 D5 **Aruwimi** *R* Zaïre
106 E2 **Arvada** Colorado
101 T5 **Arvada** Wyoming
26 K7 **Arvån** Sweden
58 D2 **Arvayheer** Mongolia
40 D5 **Arve** *R* France
26 K5 **Arvestuottar** *mt* Sweden
74 H8 **Arvi** India
115 M8 **Arvida** Quebec
26 K6 **Arvidsjaur** Sweden
27 F12 **Arvika** Sweden
102 F6 **Arvin** California
94 J9 **Arvonia** Virginia
65 E1 **Arxan** China
147 Q9 **Ary** U.S.S.R.
55 C3 **Aryazh** U.S.S.R.
47 G9 **Aryiroúpolis** Crete Greece
55 E4 **Aryk-Balyk** U.S.S.R.
57 E4 **Arys'** U.S.S.R.
57 E4 **Arys'** *R* U.S.S.R.
57 D2 **Arys,Ozero** *L* U.S.S.R.
18 D5 **Arz** *R* France
52 F6 **Arzamas** U.S.S.R.
37 N3 **Arzberg** W Germany
37 L5 **Arzberg** *mt* W Germany
32 K8 **Ärzen** W Germany
85 D1 **Arzew** Algeria
36 B3 **Arzfeld** W Germany
53 F10 **Arzgir** U.S.S.R.
41 O6 **Arzignano** Italy
41 N3 **Arzl** Austria
16 B2 **Arzúa** Spain
22 K1 **As** Belgium
37 N3 **Aš** Czechoslovakia
26 E8 **Ås** Norway
28 E2 **Aså** Denmark
27 F14 **Åsa** Sweden
87 C11 **Asab** Namibia
74 D1 **Asadabad** Afghanistan
69 D11 **Asahan** *R* Sumatra
61 O10 **Asahi** Chiba Japan
60 G10 **Asahi** *R* Japan
60 Q2 **Asahi-dake** *mt* Japan
61 N7 **Asahi-dake** *mt* Japan
60 Q2 **Asahikawa** Japan
61 M9 **Asama yama** *vol* Japan
65 G6 **Asan Man** *B* S Korea
75 M7 **Asansol** India
26 G9 **Åsarna** Sweden
84 F5 **Asawanwah** Libya
36 C2 **Asbach** W Germany
71 C3 **Asbakin** W Irian
55 D3 **Asbest** U.S.S.R.
121 T7 **Asbestos** Quebec
89 C7 **Asbestos Mts** S Africa
107 Q4 **Asbury** Kansas
110 B4 **Asbury** Missouri
128 F7 **Ascensión** Bolivia
124 E2 **Ascensión** Chihuahua Mexico
126 A1 **Ascension** Curaçao W I
90 B12 **Ascension** *isld* Atlantic Oc
37 O6 **Ascha** W Germany
38 L5 **Aschbach** Austria
32 G9 **Ascheberg** Nordrhein-Westfalen W Germany
33 M4 **Ascheberg** W Germany
32 F6 **Aschendorf** W Germany
20 J5 **Aschères-le Marche** France
33 O9 **Aschersleben** E Germany
17 H3 **Asco** Spain
12 C2 **Ascog** Scotland
42 F6 **Ascoli Piceno** Italy
9 F5 **Ascot** England
141 K1 **Ascot** *dist* Brisbane, Qnsld
133 D2 **Ascotán** Chile
27 H14 **Åseda** Sweden
85 E4 **Asedjrad** *hills* Algeria
53 H7 **Asekeyevo** U.S.S.R.
26 J7 **Åsele** Sweden
86 G4 **Aselle** Ethiopia
26 E8 **Åsen** Norway
27 G10 **Åsen** Sweden
32 K7 **Asendorf** W Germany
47 G3 **Asenovgrad** Bulgaria
27 B13 **Åseral** Norway
22 G5 **Asfeld-la-ville** France
27 D12 **Asgårdstr** Norway
55 C3 **Asha** U.S.S.R.
52 J5 **Ashan** U.S.S.R.
80 C8 **Ashan** *R* Israel
55 C3 **Ashap** U.S.S.R.
77 A4 **Ashar** Iran
9 E1 **Ashbourne** England
112 D6 **Ashburn** Georgia
8 C6 **Ashburton** England
144 C5 **Ashburton** New Zealand
142 B6 **Ashburton R** W Australia
143 C6 **Ashburton, R** W Australia
140 C4 **Ashburton Ra** N Terr Aust
9 E4 **Ashbury** England
95 N6 **Ashbury Park** New Jersey
99 L3 **Ashby** Minnesota
9 E2 **Ashby de la Zouch** England
57 D2 **Ashchikol', Ozero** *L* U.S.S.R.
57 C1 **Ashchitastysor, Ozero** *L* U.S.S.R.
114 G7 **Ashcroft** Br Columbia
80 B6 **Ashdod** Israel
109 N2 **Ash Down** Arkansas
9 G5 **Ashdown Forest** England
112 H2 **Asheboro** N Carolina
107 O7 **Asher** Oklahoma
119 T7 **Ashern** Manitoba
108 H7 **Asherton** Texas
112 E2 **Asheville** N Carolina
110 E5 **Ash Flat** Arkansas
113 D11 **Ashford** Alabama
9 G5 **Ashford** Kent England
100 C3 **Ashford** Washington
9 E5 **Ashford Hill** England
103 M6 **Ashfork** Arizona
107 M2 **Ash Grove** Kansas
110 C4 **Ash Grove** Missouri
141 K1 **Ashgrove** *dist* Brisbane, Qnsld
145 E4 **Ashhurst** New Zealand
60 Q2 **Ashibetsu** Japan
61 N9 **Ashikaga** Japan
9 F6 **Ashington** W Sussex England
61 N9 **Ashio** Japan
52 G6 **Ashit** *R* U.S.S.R.
60 J11 **Ashiya** Japan
60 G13 **Ashizuri-misaki** *C* Japan
77 D4 **Ashkazar** Iran
77 F1 **Ashkhabad** Iran
50 E5 **Ashkhabad** U.S.S.R.
13 F3 **Ashkirk** Scotland
99 T9 **Ashkum** Illinois
111 L8 **Ashland** Alabama
110 F2 **Ashland** Illinois
107 L4 **Ashland** Kansas
94 E8 **Ashland** Kentucky
95 S7 **Ashland** Maine
101 T4 **Ashland** Montana
98 K8 **Ashland** Nebraska
95 Q3 **Ashland** New Hampshire
94 E6 **Ashland** Ohio
100 C7 **Ashland** Oregon
95 L6 **Ashland** Pennsylvania
94 K9 **Ashland** Virginia
99 Q3 **Ashland** Wisconsin
110 J5 **Ashland City** Tennessee
110 G3 **Ashley** Illinois
94 C3 **Ashley** Michigan
98 G3 **Ashley** N Dakota
144 D5 **Ashley** New Zealand
120 K4 **Ashley Mine** Ontario
55 E3 **Ashlyk** *R* U.S.S.R.
118 F4 **Ashmont** Alberta
108 E3 **Ashmore** Texas
142 E1 **Ashmore Reef** Timor Sea
79 A8 **Ashmûn** Egypt
80 F1 **Ashmura** Syria
95 N5 **Ashokan Res** New York
60 R2 **Ashorobuto** Japan
80 B7 **Ashqelon** Israel
78 J4 **Ash Sharqat** Iraq
94 G5 **Ashtabula** Ohio
98 J2 **Ashtabula,L** N Dakota
74 F9 **Ashti** India
77 A2 **Ashtiān** Iran
101 O5 **Ashton** Idaho
99 R8 **Ashton** Illinois
94 B3 **Ashton** Michigan
121 O7 **Ashton** Ontario
98 H5 **Ashton** S Dakota
142 F3 **Ashton Ra** W Australia
13 F6 **Ashton-under-Lyne** England
115 N7 **Ashuanipi,L** Labrador
121 R3 **Ashuapmuchuan** *R* Quebec
78 J4 **Ashur** Iraq
78 J6 **Ashuriyah, Al** Iraq
111 K8 **Ashville** Alabama
79 G3 **'Āsi** *R* Syria/Lebanon
42 D3 **Asiago** Italy
71 C2 **Asia Pulau Pulau** *islds* Indonesia
71 F4 **Asid Gulf** Philippines
124 H6 **Asientos** Mexico
45 K1 **Asigliano Ven** Italy
85 C1 **Asilah** Morocco
71 A1 **Asimiro** Halmahera Indonesia
43 B7 **Asinara** *isld* Sardinia
43 B7 **Asinara, Golfo dell'** Sardinia
56 C3 **Asino** U.S.S.R.
75 L9 **Aska** India
53 D10 **Askaniya Nova** U.S.S.R.
55 C4 **Askarovo** U.S.S.R.
14 C4 **Askeaton Adare** Irish Rep
27 D12 **Asker** Norway
13 G6 **Askern** England
27 G13 **Askersund** Sweden
83 H1 **Askhabad** Iran
26 J7 **Åskilje** Sweden
27 E12 **Askim** Norway
112 K2 **Askin** N Carolina
55 C3 **Askino** U.S.S.R.
28 G7 **Askø** Denmark
29 M11 **Askola** Finland
65 J3 **Askol'd, O** *isld* U.S.S.R.
28 C6 **Askov** Denmark
99 O3 **Askov** Minnesota
13 F5 **Askrigg** England
27 A10 **Askvoll** Norway
79 C9 **Asl** Egypt
47 K5 **Aslanapa** Turkey
74 D1 **Asmar** Afghanistan
86 G2 **Asmara** Ethiopia
28 K5 **Asminderød** Denmark
28 G5 **Asnæs** Denmark
28 F5 **Asnæs** *pen* Denmark
85 E1 **Asnam, El** Algeria
20 D3 **Asnelles** France
27 G15 **Åsnen** Sweden
27 E11 **Åsnes** Norway
129 G3 **Asoenangka** Brazil
45 J1 **Asola** Italy
60 E13 **Aso Nat. Park** Japan
86 F3 **Asosa** Ethiopia
86 G1 **Asoteriba, Jebel** *mt* Sudan
100 H3 **Asotin** Washington
85 E3 **Asouf** *watercourse* Algeria
60 C11 **Asō-wan** *B* Japan
60 E13 **Aso zan** *vol* Japan
36 G6 **Aspach** W Germany
48 C3 **Aspang** Austria
26 G8 **Aspås** Sweden
13 E4 **Aspatria** England
17 G6 **Aspe** Spain
26 J8 **Aspeå** Sweden
106 D2 **Aspen** Colorado
101 P8 **Aspen** Wyoming
118 D6 **Aspen Beach Prov. Park** Alberta
36 G6 **Asperg** W Germany
28 D6 **Asperup** Denmark
144 B6 **Aspiring, Mt** New Zealand
19 P16 **Aspremont** France
46 D5 **Asprókavos, Akr** *C* Greece
43 G10 **Aspromonte** *mts* Italy
123 M7 **Aspy B** C Breton I, N Scotia
118 K6 **Asquith** Sask
86 H3 **Assab** Ethiopia
74 D1 **Assad-Abad** Afghanistan
86 H3 **Assale, L** Ethiopia
75 O5 **Assam** *prov* India
95 M8 **Assateague I** Maryland
22 G2 **Asse** Belgium
19 Q17 **Asse** *R* France
119 V2 **Assean L** Manitoba
89 G6 **Assegai** *R* Swaziland
85 F3 **Assekaifaf** Algeria
85 F4 **Assekreme** *mt* Algeria
32 K5 **Assel** W Germany
20 E5 **Asse-la-Boisne** France
22 K3 **Asselborn** Luxembourg
25 G3 **Assen** Netherlands
36 F3 **Assenheim** W Germany
28 E3 **Assens** Århus Denmark
28 D6 **Assens** Fyn Denmark
22 J3 **Assesse** Belgium
122 G2 **Assigny,L** Quebec
118 L9 **Assinboia** Sask
28 B4 **Assing** Denmark
114 J8 **Assiniboia** Sask
114 H7 **Assiniboine,Mt** Br Col/Alberta
119 Q8 **Assiniboine R** Manitoba/Sask
46 F4 **Ássiros** Greece
129 H8 **Assis** Brazil
42 E5 **Assisi** Italy
36 D3 **Assmannshausen** W Germany
41 K6 **Asso** Italy
110 G2 **Assumption** Illinois
87 H9 **Assumption** *isld* Seychelles
78 K5 **As Suwayrah** Iraq
36 C5 **Assweiler** W Germany
37 N7 **Ast** W Germany
27 E10 **Asta** *R* Norway
18 F8 **Astaffort** France
47 H9 **Astakidha** *isld* Greece
46 E6 **Astakós** Greece
77 A1 **Astaneh** Iran
28 E2 **Åsted** Nordjylland Denmark
28 B3 **Åsted** Viborg Denmark
25 E6 **Asten** Netherlands
77 C1 **Asterabad** Iran
44 D2 **Asti** Italy
16 E1 **Astillero** Spain
Astin Tagh *mt ra see* **Altun Shan**
47 H8 **Astipálaia** *isld* Greece
9 E1 **Aston** England
8 D3 **Aston Cross** England
74 F1 **Astor** Kashmir
16 C2 **Astorga** Spain
99 Q9 **Astoria** Illinois
114 G8 **Astoria** Oregon
98 K5 **Astoria** S Dakota
27 F15 **Åstorp** Sweden
121 L6 **Astorville** Ontario
87 H10 **Astove** *isld* Br Indian Oc Terr
53 G10 **Astrakhan'** U.S.S.R.
55 E5 **Astrakhanka** U.S.S.R.
26 L7 **Åsträsk** Sweden
46 F7 **Astros** Greece
28 E6 **Åstrup** Fyn Denmark
28 B5 **Åstrup** Ribe Denmark
28 D6 **Åstrup** Sønderjylland Denmark
28 D5 **Åstrup** Vejle Denmark
28 J7 **Åstrup** *isld* Storstrøm Denmark
16 E2 **Astudillo** Spain
45 N7 **Astura** *R* Italy
16 C1 **Asturias** *reg* Spain
9 F3 **Astwood** England
28 E6 **Åsum** Denmark
133 F3 **Asunción** Paraguay
27 H14 **Asunden** *L* Sweden
28 E5 **As Vig** *B* Denmark
84 J5 **Aswân** Egypt
84 J5 **Aswan High Dam** Egypt
84 J4 **Asyût** Egypt
48 E3 **Aszód** Hungary
137 R6 **Ata** *isld* Pacific Oc

57 E3 Atabay U.S.S.R.
47 L7 Atabey Turkey
133 C3 Atacama reg Chile
123 E8 Atacama, Des de Chile
133 D3 Atacama, Puna de plat Argentina
48 L2 Ataki U.S.S.R.
85 E7 Atakpamé Togo
130 J10 Atalaia Brazil
46 F6 Atalándi Greece
128 D6 Atalaya Peru
86 J5 Ataleh Somalia
130 H6 Ataléia Brazil
71 M9 Atambua Timor Indonesia
61 N10 Atami Japan
115 O5 Atangmik Greenland
55 F4 Atansor, Oz L U.S.S.R.
71 M9 Atapupo Timor Indonesia
79 C9 'Ataqa, G mt Egypt
85 B4 Atar Mauritania
80 D5 'Atara Jordan
80 F7 Ataroth Jordan
106 B7 Atarque New Mexico
80 F7 Ataruz Jordan
Atas isld see South I
102 D6 Atascadero California
109 J6 Atascosa R Texas
57 F1 Atasu U.S.S.R.
68 C4 Atatano R Burma
17 F2 Atauri Spain
71 M9 Atauro isld Indonesia
86 F2 Atbara Sudan
86 G2 Atbara R Sudan
50 F3 Atbasar Kazakhstan U.S.S.R.
57 H4 At-Bash U.S.S.R.
111 E12 Atchafalaya Bay Louisiana
107 P2 Atchison Kansas
116 G5 Atchueelinguk R Alaska
112 C3 Atco Georgia
95 N7 Atco New Jersey
17 F3 Ateca Spain
79 G5 Ateibe, Bahret el L Syria
58 E4 A-t'eng-hsi-lien China
124 G7 Atenguillo Mexico
61 O7 Aterazawa Japan
42 F6 Aterno R Italy
42 D2 Atesine,Alpi Italy
42 F6 Atessa Italy
22 F2 Ath Belgium
114 H7 Athabasca Alberta
114 J6 Athabasca, L Alberta/Sask
119 Q4 Athapap Manitoba
119 Q4 Athapapuskow L Manitoba
28 C4 Atheden reg Denmark
110 B1 Athelstan Iowa
100 G4 Athena Oregon
14 C3 Athenry Irish Rep
112 D4 Athens Georgia
Athens Greece see Athínai
99 R10 Athens Illinois
109 O3 Athens Louisiana
95 S2 Athens Maine
94 B4 Athens Michigan
94 E7 Athens Ohio
121 P8 Athens Ontario
95 L5 Athens Pennsylvania
112 C2 Athens Tennessee
109 M3 Athens Texas
99 Q4 Athens Wisconsin
121 L8 Atherley Ontario
9 E2 Atherstone England
13 F6 Atherton England
141 H3 Atherton Queensland
141 H3 Atherton Plateau Queensland
85 E7 Athiémé Benin
22 F4 Athies Aisne France
22 D4 Athies Somme France
47 F7 Athínai Greece
20 K4 Athis Essonne France
20 E4 Athis Orne France
14 C3 Athleague Irish Rep
14 D3 Athlone Irish Rep
79 D3 Athna Cyprus
76 B2 Athni India
100 J2 Athol Idaho
95 P4 Athol Massachusetts
144 B6 Athol New Zealand
113 L9 Athol I New Providence I Bahamas
122 F6 Atholville New Brunswick
47 G4 Áthos mt Greece
Athos, Mt see Áyion Óros
78 G4 Ath-Thawra Syria
22 K4 Athus Belgium
14 E4 Athy Irish Rep
86 C3 Ati Chad
145 F3 Atiamuri New Zealand
130 F8 Atibaia Brazil
128 D7 Atico Peru
123 N2 Aticonipi L Quebec
17 F3 Atienza Spain
119 Q4 Atik Manitoba
117 Q8 Atikameg Alberta
119 R4 Atikameg Lake Manitoba
115 K8 Atikokan Ontario
115 N7 Atikonak, L Labrador
122 H1 Atikonal L Labrador
118 J1 Atikwa L Ontario
71 E3 Atimonan Philippines
45 P6 Atina Italy
76 D5 Atirampattinam India
116 P9 Atka Aleutian Is
51 P2 Atka U.S.S.R.
53 F3 Atkarsk U.S.S.R.
116 J1 Atkasuk Alaska
71 B3 Atkerio W Irian
110 D6 Atkins Arkansas
99 Q8 Atkinson Illinois
112 J3 Atkinson N Carolina
98 G7 Atkinson Nebraska
111 M8 Atlanta Georgia
101 K6 Atlanta Idaho
110 G1 Atlanta Illinois
94 A6 Atlanta Indiana
107 O4 Atlanta Kansas
110 D2 Atlanta Missouri
95 K4 Atlanta New York
109 N2 Atlanta Texas
105 Atlanta conurbation Georgia
99 L8 Atlantic Iowa
112 L3 Atlantic N Carolina
95 N7 Atlantic City New Jersey
101 R7 Atlantic City Wyoming
95 N6 Atlantic Highlands New Jersey
90 J15 Atlantic-Indian Basin Southern Oc
90 J14 Atlantic-Indian Ridge S Atlantic Oc
128 D1 Atlántico div Colombia
90 Atlantic Oc
90 E5 Atlantis Fracture Atlantic Oc
94 D4 Atlas Michigan
85 C2 Atlas, Haut mts Morocco
85 C2 Atlas, Moyen mts Morocco
85 E2 Atlas Saharien mts Algeria
118 G8 Atlee Alberta
114 F6 Atlin Br Columbia
80 C3 'Atlit Israel
125 K8 Atlixco Mexico
26 A10 Atlöy isld Norway
76 D3 Atmakur India
113 B11 Atmore Alabama
138 D2 Atna Hill S Australia
117 L9 Atnarko Br Columbia
26 D10 Atnasjö L Norway
55 E2 Atnis U.S.S.R.
87 H12 Atofinandrahana Madagascar
107 O7 Atoka Oklahoma
102 G6 Atolia California
101 N6 Atomic City Idaho
124 H7 Atotonilco el Alto Mexico
77 E1 Atrak R Iran
27 F14 Atran Sweden
26 L7 Åträsk Sweden
128 C2 Atrato R Colombia
42 F6 Atri Italy
45 R8 Atripaida Italy
61 N10 Atsugi Japan
61 N7 Atsumi Japan
61 L11 Atsumi-hantō pen Japan
61 L11 Atsumi wan B Japan
140 C4 Attack Cr N Terr Aust
111 K7 Attalla Alabama
47 J8 Attaviros mt Rhodes Greece
115 L7 Attawapiskat Ontario
36 D1 Attendorn W Germany
38 J6 Attersee Austria
110 J1 Attica Indiana
107 M4 Attica Kansas
94 D3 Attica Michigan
94 J4 Attica New York
94 E5 Attica Ohio
22 E5 Attichy France
40 B5 Attignat France
22 H5 Attigny France
95 Q5 Attleboro Massachusetts
9 H2 Attleborough England
9 H2 Attlebridge England
26 J9 Attmar Sweden
68 H5 Attopeu Laos
109 N4 Attoyac Bayou R Texas
116 J9 Attu Aleutian Is
76 D5 Attur India
133 D5 Atuel R Argentina
131 C6 Atuel, Banados del swamps Argentina
27 H13 Åtvid Sweden
27 H13 Åtvidaberg Sweden
102 D4 Atwater California
99 M4 Atwater Minnesota
119 P8 Atwater Sask
13 H6 Atwick England
106 G1 Atwood Colorado
110 H2 Atwood Illinois
107 J2 Atwood Kansas
94 F6 Atwood Res Ohio
53 G7 Atyashevo U.S.S.R.
38 N5 Atzenbrugg Austria
33 P9 Atzendorf E Germany
36 D2 Au Rheinland-Pfalz W Germany
128 E4 Auati-Paraná R Brazil
135 S3 Auau Chan Hawaiian Is
37 J4 Aub W Germany
19 P18 Aubagne France
22 K4 Aubange Belgium
71 F2 Aubarede Pt Luzon Philippines
18 H4 Aube dep France
18 H4 Aube R France
22 K2 Aubel Belgium
22 E3 Aubencheul-Au-Bac France
22 G4 Aubenton France
83 L13 Aubert,C Kerguelen Indian Ocean
20 G4 Aube-sur-Risle France
18 F7 Aubeterre France
21 E9 Aubigné Deux-Sèvres France
21 F6 Aubigné Sarthe France
21 C8 Aubigny France
22 D3 Aubigny Pas-de-Calais France
18 G5 Aubigny sur Nère France
18 G8 Aubin France
18 H8 Aubrac, Mts d' France
103 M6 Aubrey Cliffs Arizona
143 B7 Aubrey, Mt W Australia
114 G4 Aubry L N W Terr
111 L9 Auburn Alabama
102 C3 Auburn California
110 G2 Auburn Illinois
94 B5 Auburn Indiana
107 P3 Auburn Kansas
110 K5 Auburn Kentucky
95 R2 Auburn Maine
94 C3 Auburn Michigan
99 L9 Auburn Nebraska
95 L4 Auburn New York
138 E5 Auburn S Australia
117 M12 Auburn Washington
141 K7 Auburn R Queensland
113 F9 Auburndale Florida
99 R5 Auburndale Wisconsin
141 K7 Auburn Ra Queensland
18 G7 Aubusson France
133 D5 Auca Mahuida,Sa mt Argentina
52 B6 Auce U.S.S.R.
18 F9 Auch France
22 C3 Auchel France
12 E4 Auchencairn Scotland
12 D4 Auchenmalg Scotland
85 F7 Auchi Nigeria
12 D3 Auchinleck Scotland
12 E1 Auchterarder Scotland
13 E1 Auchterderran Scotland
13 E1 Auchtermuchty Scotland
22 C2 Auchy-au-Bois France
113 D7 Aucilla R Florida
145 F1 Auckland New Zealand
68 D6 Auckland B Burma
18 G9 Aude dep France
18 G9 Aude R France
18 G10 Aude R France
86 H5 Audeghle Somalia
115 L7 Auden Ontario
Audenarde see Oudenaarde
18 E8 Audenge France
20 B2 Auderville France
18 B4 Audierne France
83 L14 Audierne,B Kerguelen Indian Ocean
40 E3 Audincourt France
22 B2 Audinghen France
45 N4 Auditore Italy
8 D2 Audlem England
22 B2 Audresselles France
22 C2 Audruicq France
99 M8 Audubon Iowa
19 J3 Audun le Roman France
37 O2 Aue E Germany
32 G6 Aue R W Germany
84 E4 Auenat Uennin Libya
36 G5 Auenstein W Germany
37 N2 Auerbach E Germany
36 F4 Auerbach Hessen W Germany
41 N2 Auer Berg mt W Germany
37 O2 Auerswalde E Germany
111 E12 Au Far, Point Louisiana
20 H2 Auffay France
141 H7 Augathella Queensland
14 E2 Aughnacloy N Ireland
87 D11 Aughrabies Falls S Africa
14 E4 Aughrim Irish Rep
115 O3 Augpilagtoq Greenland
94 D2 Au Gres Michigan
37 K7 Augsburg W Germany
110 E6 Augusta Arkansas
112 E4 Augusta Georgia
110 F1 Augusta Illinois
107 O4 Augusta Kansas
94 C8 Augusta Kentucky
95 S2 Augusta Maine
94 B4 Augusta Michigan
101 N2 Augusta Montana
43 G11 Augusta Sicily
143 B10 Augusta W Australia
99 P5 Augusta Wisconsin
143 E7 Augusta, L W Australia
116 R6 Augusta,Mt Yukon Terr
94 H8 Augusta Springs Virginia
116 L7 Augustine I Alaska
130 G6 Augusto de Lima Brazil
130 H8 Augusto Severo Brazil
31 O2 Augustów Poland
140 E4 Augustus Downs Queensland
142 E3 Augustus Island W Australia
143 B6 Augustus, Mt W Australia
37 M6 Au in der Hallertau W Germany
40 B2 Aujon R France
32 L4 Aukrug W Germany
26 K6 Auktsjaur Sweden
112 K1 Aulander N Carolina
142 E5 Auld, L W Australia
21 E9 Aulnay France
18 E6 Aulnay de Saintonge France
20 K5 Aulnay-la-Rivière France
18 C4 Aulne R France
118 H1 Aulneau Pen Ontario
22 F3 Aulnoye France
106 F1 Ault Colorado
20 H1 Ault France
15 C3 Aultbea Scotland
54 F8 Auly U.S.S.R.
37 M2 Auma E Germany
37 M2 Auma R E Germany
20 J2 Aumale France
18 G6 Aumance R France
22 K5 Aumetz France
57 C4 Auminzatau,Gory mt U.S.S.R.
40 C4 Aumont France
18 H8 Aumont Lozère France
33 M5 Aumühle W Germany
20 D3 Aunay-sur-Odon France
74 F10 Aundh India
21 F6 Aune R France
20 J5 Auneau France
20 K3 Auneuil France
28 E4 Auning Denmark
18 E6 Aunis prov France
21 C10 Aunis reg France
87 C11 Auob R Namibia
71 J5 Auponhia Moluccas Indonesia
19 Q17 Aups France
69 G11 Aur isld Malaysia
29 K11 Aura Finland
26 C9 Aura R Norway
37 K4 Aurach R W Germany
74 H5 Auraiya India
29 K11 Aurajoki R Finland
74 F9 Aurangabad India
18 C5 Auray France
26 C8 Aure Norway
20 D3 Aure R France
19 O16 Aurel France
99 L7 Aurelia Iowa
85 F1 Aurès mts Algeria
32 F6 Aurich W Germany
130 E5 Aurilândia Brazil
18 G8 Aurillac France
19 P18 Auriol France
27 B11 Aurland Norway
130 H9 Aurora Brazil
106 F2 Aurora Colorado
99 S8 Aurora Illinois
94 C7 Aurora Indiana
107 N2 Aurora Kansas
110 C5 Aurora Missouri
112 L2 Aurora N Carolina
98 H9 Aurora Nebraska
121 L9 Aurora Ontario
103 N3 Aurora Utah
19 P15 Aurouze, Mt d' France
26 C9 Aursjöen L Norway
27 E12 Aurskog Norway
26 E9 Aursunden L Norway
141 F2 Aurukun Queensland
45 P7 Aurunci Monti Italy
87 C11 Aus Namibia
94 C2 Au Sable R Michigan
95 O2 Ausable Forks New York
94 D2 Au Sable Pt Michigan
128 D6 Ausangate mt Peru
80 F4 Ausara Jordan
85 B4 Auserd Mauritania
88 B7 Aushi Zambia
15 F1 Auskerry Scotland
45 O7 Ausoni, Monti mt Italy
41 K3 Ausser-Rhoden dist Switzerland
8 D4 Aust England
27 C13 Austad Norway
27 C13 Aust Agder Fylker Norway
112 C4 Austell Georgia
Austerlitz see Slavkov
119 T9 Austin Manitoba
99 O6 Austin Minnesota
101 N3 Austin Montana
100 G5 Austin Oregon
94 J5 Austin Pennsylvania
109 K5 Austin Texas
143 C8 Austin W Australia
143 C8 Austin, L W Australia
109 M4 Austonio Texas
140 E5 Austral Downs N Terr Aust
136 Australia
139 J6 Australian Alps New S Wales/Victoria
146 C6 Australian Antarctic Territory Antarctica
135 M11 Austral Ridge Pacific Oc
26 D8 Austråt Norway
27 A11 Austrheim Norway
33 E7 Austria rep
26 G3 Austvågöy isld Norway
109 L7 Austwell Texas
21 H6 Autainville France
128 G4 Autazes Brazil
22 K4 Autelbas Belgium
18 G9 Auterive France
123 L3 Auteuil, L. d' Quebec
22 C3 Authie R France
121 M4 Authier Quebec
21 E7 Authion R France
21 G6 Authon France
20 G5 Authon-du-Perche France
20 J5 Authon-la-Plaine France
124 G8 Autlán de Navarro Mexico
45 O6 Autore, M mt Italy
99 U3 Au Train Michigan
19 P14 Autrans France
20 K5 Autruy-sur-Juine France
22 H5 Autry France
18 H6 Autun France
140 B3 Auvergne N Terr Aust
18 H7 Auvergne prov France
21 E6 Auvers-le-Hamon France
20 K3 Auvers-sur-Oise France
18 F7 Auvezère R France
22 G4 Auvillers-les-Forges France
94 E2 Aux Barques, Pt Michigan
18 H5 Auxerre France
20 K1 Auxi-le-Château France
40 B3 Auxonne France
110 E2 Auxvasse Missouri
128 F2 Auyán Tepui mt Venezuela
18 G6 Auzances France
68 B2 Ava Burma
110 G4 Ava Illinois
110 D5 Ava Missouri
26 M5 Avafors Sweden
18 F6 Availles-Limouzine France
116 H1 Avalik R Alaska
18 H5 Avallon France
102 F8 Avalon California
111 F8 Avalon Mississippi
95 N7 Avalon New Jersey
108 C3 Avalon, L New Mexico
115 O8 Avalon Pen Nfld
124 J5 Avalos Mexico
131 F2 Avalos R Argentina
57 B2 Avan U.S.S.R.
19 Q15 Avançon France
53 G12 Avar R U.S.S.R.
107 M5 Avard Oklahoma
129 J8 Avaré Brazil
47 H4 Ávas Greece
116 E9 Avatanak I Aleutian Is
26 H7 Avaträsk Sweden
26 L5 Avaudden Sweden
26 K6 Avaviken Sweden
102 H6 Avawatz Mts California
54 J8 Avdeyevka U.S.S.R.
9 E5 Avebury England
16 D4 Aveinte Spain
129 G4 Aveiro Brazil
16 B4 Aveiro Portugal
77 A2 Avej Iran
22 E2 Avelgem Belgium
94 G6 Avella Pennsylvania
133 F4 Avellaneda Argentina
45 R8 Avellino Italy
102 D6 Avenal California
40 F4 Avenches Switzerland
95 Q4 Aver Massachusetts
28 E6 Avernak By B Denmark
26 B8 Averöy isld Norway
45 Q8 Aversa Italy
100 K2 Avery Idaho
99 O8 Avery Iowa
109 N2 Avery Texas
111 E12 Avery Island Louisiana
22 F3 Avesnes France
22 D3 Avesnes le Comte France
22 E3 Avesnes-les-Aubert France
90 C7 Aves Ridge Atlantic Oc
27 H11 Avesta Sweden
28 O9 Avevig Faeroes
18 G8 Aveyron dep France
18 F8 Aveyron R France
45 O5 Avezzano Italy
46 F8 Avgó isld Greece
47 H9 Avgó isld Greece
46 E5 Avgó mt Greece
133 E3 Aviá Terai Argentina
15 E3 Aviemore Scotland
144 C6 Aviemore Dam New Zealand
115 P5 Avigait Greenland
80 B7 Avigedor Israel
43 G8 Avigliano Italy
19 N17 Avignon France
16 D4 Avila prov Spain
16 D4 Ávila, Sa. de mts Spain
16 D1 Avilés Spain
40 D3 Avilley France
109 N3 Avinger Texas
141 H6 Avington Queensland
22 D3 Avion France
95 K5 Avis Pennsylvania
41 O5 Avisio R Italy
80 E1 Avivim Israel
16 B5 Aviz Portugal
47 K8 Avlan Gölü L Turkey
47 F6 Avlón Greece
28 B4 Avlum Denmark
80 G2 Avne Etan Syria
28 H6 Avnø Fjord inlet Denmark
28 F6 Avnslev Denmark
14 E4 Avoca Irish Rep
94 E3 Avoca Michigan
95 K4 Avoca New York
144 C5 Avoca New Zealand
108 H3 Avoca Texas
139 G6 Avoca Victoria
14 E4 Avoca,Vale of Irish Rep
138 D5 Avoid B S Australia
117 O10 Avola Br Columbia
43 G12 Avola Sicily
106 D2 Avon Colorado
95 P5 Avon Connecticut
110 F1 Avon Illinois
99 M4 Avon Minnesota
101 N3 Avon Montana
112 M2 Avon N Carolina
94 K4 Avon New York
94 E5 Avon Ohio
98 H6 Avon S Dakota
8 D5 Avon co England
15 E3 Avon R Scotland
103 M8 Avondale Arizona
106 F3 Avondale Colorado
110 B2 Avondale Missouri
141 K6 Avondale Queensland
109 L8 Avondale Texas
140 D4 Avon Downs N Terr Aust
141 H5 Avon Downs Queensland
94 E5 Avon Lake Ohio
119 M8 Avonlea Sask
94 H6 Avonmore Pennsylvania
8 D4 Avonmouth England
113 F10 Avon Park Florida
9 E3 Avon, R Warwicks England
143 B9 Avon, R W Australia
9 E5 Avon, R Wilts/Hants England
130 E10 Avoredo It ho Brazil
40 D3 Avoudrey France
20 C4 Avranches France
20 H4 Avre R Eure France
36 B6 Avricourt France
48 J5 Avrig Romania
22 K5 Avril France
21 C9 Avrillé France
48 E7 Avtovac Yugoslavia
80 F4 Avuqa Israel
61 P12 Awa Okinawa
60 H11 Awaji-shima isld Japan
145 E3 Awakino New Zealand
84 E4 Awâl watercourse Libya
70 Q10 Awang Indonesia
145 D1 Awanui New Zealand
86 H4 Awarch Ethiopia
144 B6 Awarua Bay New Zealand
86 H4 Awash Ethiopia
61 N7 Awa-shima isld Japan
85 D7 Awaso Ghana
57 K4 Awat China
86 G4 Awata R Ethiopia
145 E4 Awatere R New Zealand
84 E4 Awbāri Libya
12 C1 Awe,L Scotland
112 H4 Awendaw S Carolina
144 B6 Awful, Mt New Zealand
84 G4 Awjilah Libya
70 G6 Awo R Sulawesi Indonesia
117 Q4 Awry L N W Terr
116 J2 Awuna R Alaska
86 G4 Awusa, L Ethiopia
8 D5 Axbridge England
25 A6 Axel Netherlands
27 F14 Axelfors Sweden
146 G8 Axel Heiberg Gl Antarctica
147 H5 Axel Heiberg I N W Terr
106 C1 Axial Colorado
128 G4 Axinim Brazil
18 G10 Ax-les-Thermes France
8 D6 Axminster England
112 E6 Axson Georgia
107 O2 Axtell Kansas
27 G13 Axvall Sweden
18 H3 Ay France
128 C4 Ayabaca Peru
60 J10 Ayabe Japan
133 F5 Ayacucho Argentina
128 D6 Ayacucho Peru
68 B1 Ayadaw Burma
57 K1 Ayaguz U.S.S.R.
57 D4 Ayakkuduk U.S.S.R.
66 D4 Ayakkum Hu L China
16 C7 Ayamonte Spain
78 E1 Ayancik Turkey
80 C6 Ayanot Israel
126 G10 Ayapel Colombia
78 D1 Ayaş Turkey
128 D6 Ayaviri Peru
13 G4 Aycliffe England
55 E4 Aydabul' U.S.S.R.
54 L8 Aydar R U.S.S.R.
112 K2 Ayden N Carolina
47 J7 Aydın Turkey
78 A3 Aydin Turkey
47 J7 Aydın Sıra Dağları mts Turkey
55 C5 Aydrlinskiy U.S.S.R.
86 H3 Ayelu mt Ethiopia
40 G5 Ayer Switzerland
17 G2 Ayerbe Spain
100 G3 Ayers Washington
140 C7 Ayers Ra N Terr Aust
140 B7 Ayers Rock mt N Terr Aust
55 F3 Ayev R U.S.S.R.
19 O16 Aygues R France
56 C5 Aygulaskiy Khrebet mts U.S.S.R.
46 F5 Ayiá Greece
47 F6 Ayía Ánna Greece
47 G5 Ayía Iríni Akra C Greece
47 H5 Ayiássos Greece
47 G4 Áyion Óros mt Greece
47 F7 Áyios isld Greece
47 G5 Áyios Evstrátios isld Greece
47 G9 Áyios Míron Crete Greece
47 H9 Ayios Nikólaos Crete Greece
46 D6 Ayios Pétros Greece
79 D3 Ayios Seryios Cyprus
79 E3 Ayios Theodhoros Cyprus
116 L2 Ayiyak R Alaska
47 H7 Aykathonisi isld Greece
47 H7 Ay Kírikos Greece
36 B4 Ayl W Germany
121 N7 Aylen,L Ontario
9 F4 Aylesbury England
144 D5 Aylesbury New Zealand
119 M8 Aylesbury Sask
122 H8 Aylesford Nova Scotia
9 H5 Aylesham England
117 D6 Aylesworth, Mt Br Col/Alaska
16 E3 Ayllón Spain
16 E3 Ayllón, Sa. de mts Spain
121 P7 Aylmer Quebec
114 J5 Aylmer L N W Terr
118 B7 Aylmer,Mt Alberta
9 H2 Aylsham England
119 O5 Aylsham Sask
121 O7 Aylwin Quebec
17 F6 Ayna Spain
9 E3 Aynho England
112 H4 Aynor S Carolina
84 G5 Ayn Zuwayyah Libya
147 C4 Ayon,Ostrov isld U.S.S.R.
17 G5 Ayora Spain
85 E6 Ayorou Niger
55 G2 Aypolovo U.S.S.R.
98 J2 Ayr N Dakota
98 H9 Ayr Nebraska
141 H4 Ayr Queensland
12 D3 Ayr Scotland
Ayr co see Strathclyde reg
21 F3 Ayron France
99 M6 Ayrshire Iowa
141 G5 Ayrshire Downs Queensland
55 F4 Aysary U.S.S.R.
13 G5 Aysgarth England
57 F1 Ayshirak U.S.S.R.
13 H5 Ayton N Yorks England
141 H3 Ayton Queensland
13 F2 Ayton Scotland
47 J2 Aytos Bulgaria
57 C4 Aytym U.S.S.R.
61 P7 Ayukawahama Japan
65 C2 Ayulhai China
124 G7 Ayutla Mexico
68 E5 Ayutthaya Thailand
78 A2 Ayvacik Turkey
47 H5 Ayvalık Turkey
78 A2 Ayvalik Turkey
22 K3 Aywaille Belgium
100 B7 Azalea Oregon
61 P13 Azama Okinawa
75 K5 Azamgarh India
55 C3 Azangulovo U.S.S.R.
55 D2 Azanka U.S.S.R.
22 J5 Azannes-et-Soumazannes France
78 K2 Āzārbāijān-e Gharbi Iran
78 L2 Āzārbāijān-e Sharqi Iran
85 G6 Azare Nigeria
52 E5 Azatskoye, Oz L U.S.S.R.
21 F7 Azay-le-Rideau France
21 G7 Azay-sur-Cher France
21 E8 Azay-sur-Thouet France
79 H2 A'zāz Syria
Azbine reg Niger see Aïr ou Azbine
21 H6 Azé France
40 G7 Azeglio Italy
78 L1 Azerbaijan U.S.S.R.
50 D4 Azerbaydzhanskaya S.S.R U.S.S.R.
19 N13 Azergues R France
53 F7 Azeyevo U.S.S.R.
55 G4 Azhbulat, Oz L U.S.S.R.
56 C5 Azho-Tayga, Gora mt U.S.S.R.
22 C3 Azincourt France
86 A6 Azingo, L Gabon
95 R1 Aziscoos L Maine
84 E3 Aziziyan, Al Libya
16 C7 Aznàlcóllar Spain
128 C4 Azogues Ecuador
52 G2 Azopol'ye U.S.S.R.
Azores islds see Açores
90 G5 Azores-Cape St Vincent Ridge Atlantic Oc
86 D3 Azoum R Chad
54 L9 Azov U.S.S.R.
Azov,Sea of see Azovskoye More
54 L9 Azovskiy Kanal U.S.S.R.
53 E10 Azovskoye More U.S.S.R.
17 F1 Azpeitia Spain
85 C2 Azrou Morocco
103 L9 Aztec Arizona
106 C5 Aztec New Mexico
106 B5 Aztec Ruins Nat.Mon New Mexico
127 J5 Azua Dominican Rep
16 D6 Azuaga Spain
17 G3 Azuara Spain
128 C4 Azuay prov Ecuador
17 F6 Azuer R Spain
125 O6 Azuero,Pen.de Panama
131 B3 Azufre, P. del Chile
133 F5 Azul Argentina
131 B5 Azul peak Chile
125 P9 Azul R Mexico
131 B8 Azul, Cerro peak Neuquén Argentina
130 E7 Azul Paulista, Mte Brazil
130 C4 Azul,Serra mts Mato Grosso Brazil
61 O8 Azuma-yama mt Japan
80 B8 Azza Israel
84 E4 Az Zallaf Libya
71 L10 Baa Indonesia
79 F5 Ba'abda Lebanon
41 M3 Baad Austria
71 K10 Baäh Indonesia
70 E4 Baai R Kalimantan
25 F6 Baal W Germany
79 G4 Ba'albek Lebanon
25 C6 Baarle-Hertog Netherlands
25 C6 Baarle Nassau Netherlands
25 D4 Baarn Netherlands
70 K8 Baati, G mt Sumatra Indonesia
60 D14 Baba Japan
46 E4 Baba mt Yugoslavia
47 H5 Baba Burun C Turkey
48 M6 Babadag Romania
47 J3 Babaeski Turkey
128 C4 Babahoyo Ecuador
71 G7 Babak Philippines
143 C9 Babakin W Australia
77 K2 Bābā, Koh-i- mts Afghanistan
72 E6 Bab al Mandab str Arabia/Djibouti
67 B5 Babao China
71 O8 Babar isld Indonesia
71 O9 Babar,Kep islds Indonesia
70 O9 Babat Java
57 E5 Babatag, Khr mts U.S.S.R.
88 E4 Babati Tanzania
80 G7 Babayir et Tiwal Jordan
101 M1 Babb Montana
116 S2 Babbage R Yukon Terr
143 A6 Babbage I W Australia
99 P2 Babbitt Minnesota
99 Q5 Babcock Wisconsin
79 H2 Bāb, El Syria
33 P5 Bäbelin E Germany
88 C7 Babemba tribe Zambia
88 C5 Babemba tribe Zaïre
36 F4 Babenhausen Hessen W Germany
79 G3 Babenna Syria
69 C11 Babi isld Indonesia
31 M6 Babia Góra mts Czech/Poland
124 E3 Babícora Mexico
124 F3 Babícora, L. de Mexico
141 H3 Babinda Queensland
114 G7 Babine L Br Columbia
117 K8 Babine Ra Br Columbia
136 G2 Babo W Irian
48 D4 Babócsa Hungary
77 C1 Bābol Iran
103 N10 Baboquivari Pk Arizona
142 E4 Babrongan Tower mt W Australia
113 F10 Babson Park Florida
36 G5 Babstadt W Germany
16 D9 Bab Taza Morocco
67 B3 Babu China
46 E3 Babuna mt Yugoslavia
56 G5 Babushkin U.S.S.R.
71 D6 Babuyan Philippines
71 E1 Babuyan islds Philippines
71 E1 Babuyan Ch Philippines
124 E4 Baca Mexico
124 E4 Bacabáche Mexico
129 G5 Bacabal Brazil
129 H4 Bacaja R Brazil
71 A3 Bacan Halmahera Indonesia
124 E3 Bacanora Mexico
71 E1 Bacarra Philippines
48 K4 Bacău Romania
68 G1 Bac Can Vietnam
19 K4 Baccarat France
122 G10 Baccaro Pt Nova Scotia
45 L1 Bacchiglione R Italy
41 H5 Baceno Italy
48 L4 Băcești Romania
94 D3 Bach Michigan
37 N5 Bach W Germany
127 J10 Bachaquero Venezuela
36 D3 Bacharach W Germany
115 M2 Bache Pen N W Terr
124 F3 Bachiniva Mexico
68 J2 Bach Long Vi isld Vietnam
69 E9 Bacho Thailand
37 L1 Bachra E Germany
57 J5 Bachu China
115 K4 Back R N W Terr
48 E5 Backa reg Yugoslavia
27 G14 Bäckaby Sweden
48 E5 Bačka Palanka Yugoslavia
48 F5 Bačka Petrovo Selo Yugoslavia
48 F5 Bačka Topola Yugoslavia
95 L10 Back Bay Virginia
117 J4 Backbone Ranges N W Terr
27 F13 Bäckefors Sweden
27 G12 Bäckhammar Sweden
36 G6 Backnang W Germany
119 U10 Backoo N Dakota
138 E6 Backstaiys Pass S Australia
26 H6 Bäckstrand Sweden
99 M3 Backus Minnesota
Bac Lieu see Vinh Loi
68 H2 Bac Ninh Vietnam
71 E2 Bacnotan Luzon Philippines
127 P5 Bacolet Grenada
45 Q8 Bacoli Italy
71 F5 Bacolod Philippines
71 E4 Baco, Mt Philippines
112 C6 Baconton Georgia
68 G1 Bac Quang Vietnam
20 G2 Bacqueville-en-Caux France
48 E4 Bácsalmás Hungary
48 E4 Bács-Kiskun co Hungary
9 H2 Bacton England
124 F5 Bacubirito Mexico
71 G7 Baculin Bay Mindanao Philippines
13 F6 Bacup England
129 J4 Bacuri,I de Brazil
98 F5 Bad R S Dakota
Bada see Xilin
68 D7 Bada isld Burma
75 L7 Bada Barabil India
37 N6 Bad Abbach W Germany
76 B5 Badagara India
38 E6 Bad Aibling W Germany
129 J4 Badajós Brazil
16 C6 Badajoz Spain
16 C6 Badajoz prov Spain
128 F4 Badajoz, L Brazil
77 L1 Badakhshan Afghanistan
17 J3 Badalona Spain
76 B3 Badami India
75 M7 Badampahar India
72 E2 Badanah Saudi Arabia
56 E3 Badan, Khrebet mts U.S.S.R.
65 H3 Badaohe China
Badaojiang see Hunjiang
124 F5 Badariguato Mexico
70 D2 Badas Brunei
69 H12 Badas,Kep isld Indonesia
38 J6 Bad Aussee Austria
94 E3 Bad Axe Michigan
32 G7 Badbergen W Germany
36 D5 Bad Bergzabern W Germany
37 L2 Bad Berka E Germany
36 E1 Bad Berleburg W Germany
37 M3 Bad Berneck W Germany
36 B3 Bad Bertrich W Germany
37 M1 Bad Bibra Halle E Germany
37 L2 Bad Blankenburg E Germany
37 J3 Bad Bocklet W Germany
32 L5 Bad Bramstedt W Germany
123 M7 Baddeck C Breton I, N Scotia
32 M8 Baddeckenstedt W Germany
26 M2 Badderen Norway
33 P4 Bad Doberan E Germany
32 K9 Bad Driburg W Germany
33 R9 Bad Düben E Germany
36 E5 Bad Dürkheim W Germany
33 Q10 Bad Dürrenberg E Germany
37 N3 Bad Elster E Germany
36 D3 Bad Ems W Germany
48 C2 Baden Austria
119 Q6 Baden Manitoba
94 G6 Baden Pennsylvania
41 H3 Baden Switzerland
36 E6 Baden-Baden W Germany
15 D4 Badenoch Scotland
19 K4 Badenviller France
36 G6 Baden-Württemberg W Germany
45 P1 Baderna Yugoslavia
33 U7 Bad Freienwalde E Germany
36 G5 Bad Friedrichshall W Germany
32 M9 Bad Gandersheim W Germany
102 E5 Badger California
118 F1 Badger Manitoba
98 K1 Badger Minnesota
123 Q5 Badger Nfld
101 Q5 Badger Basin Wyoming
77 H2 Bādghīs Afghanistan
38 N8 Bad Gleichenberg Austria
36 C2 Bad Godesberg W Germany
30 H5 Bad Gottleuba E Germany
32 M9 Bad Grund W Germany
38 K5 Bad Hall Austria
33 N9 Bad Harzburg W Germany
36 E6 Bad Herrenalb W Germany
36 H2 Bad Hersfeld W Germany
38 H7 Bad Hofgastein Austria
36 F3 Bad Homburg W Germany
36 C2 Bad Honnef W Germany
45 K1 Badia Polesine Italy
45 M4 Badia Tedalda Italy
32 H8 Bad Iburg W Germany
79 H6 Badiet esh Sham des Jordan/Syria
112 G2 Badin N Carolina
74 C6 Badin Pakistan
112 G2 Badin L N Carolina
38 J6 Bad Ischl Austria
71 K9 Badjawa Flores Indonesia
70 G4 Badjo Sulawesi Indonesia
37 J3 Bad Kissingen W Germany
33 O5 Bad Kleinen E Germany
37 M2 Bad Klosterlausnitz E Germany
37 M1 Bad Kösen E Germany
36 D4 Bad Kreuznach W Germany
98 C2 Bad Lands reg N Dakota
98 E6 Badlands Nat.Mon S Dakota
37 K1 Bad Langensalza E Germany
33 P10 Bad Lauchstädt E Germany
37 O1 Bad Lausik E Germany
33 M9 Bad Lauterberg W Germany
38 K8 Bad Leonhard Austria
37 K2 Bad Liebenstein E Germany
36 F6 Bad Liebenzell W Germany
32 J9 Bad Lippspringe W Germany
32 J9 Bad Meinberg W Germany
36 H5 Bad Mergentheim W Germany
32 K8 Bad Münder am Deister W Germany
36 D4 Bad Münster W Germany
36 B2 Bad Münstereifel W Germany
36 F3 Bad Nauheim W Germany
32 K8 Bad Nenndorf W Germany
36 C2 Bad Neuenahr W Germany
36 C2 Bad Neuenahr-Ahrweiler W Germany
37 J3 Bad Neustadt W Germany
32 J8 Bad Oeynhausen W Germany
33 M5 Bad Oldersloe W Germany
68 H4 Ba Don Vietnam
67 C1 Badong China
69 H8 Ba Dong Vietnam
36 B6 Badonviller France
36 G3 Bad Orb W Germany
65 D6 Badou China
36 E7 Bad Peterstal W Germany
32 K9 Bad Pyrmont W Germany
36 G5 Bad Rappenau W Germany
38 G6 Bad Reichenhall W Germany
36 E7 Bad Rippoldsau W Germany
32 M8 Bad Salzdetfurth W Germany
33 P8 Bad Salzelmen E Germany
36 H2 Bad Salzschlirf W Germany
32 J8 Bad Salzuflen W Germany
37 J2 Bad Salzungen E Germany
32 H9 Bad Sassendorf W Germany
33 R9 Bad Schmiedeberg E Germany
36 E3 Bad Schwalbach W Germany
33 N5 Bad Schwartau W Germany
33 M5 Bad Segeberg W Germany
36 E3 Bad Soden W Germany
32 L10 Bad Sooden W Germany
37 M3 Bad Steben W Germany
33 Q6 Bad Stuer E Germany
33 O9 Bad Suderode E Germany
37 M1 Bad Sulza E Germany
33 R4 Bad Sülze E Germany
36 F6 Bad Teinach-Zavelstein W Germany
37 K1 Bad Tennstedt E Germany
41 P2 Bad Tölz W Germany
86 A2 Baduen Somalia
83 L10 Badulla Sri Lanka
36 F3 Bad Vilbel W Germany
38 O6 Bad Voslau Austria
102 H5 Badwater L California
36 G1 Bad Wildungen W Germany
33 P7 Bad Wilsnack E Germany
36 G5 Bad Wimpfen W Germany
37 J5 Bad Windsheim W Germany
59 K1 Badzhal'skiy Khrebet mt U.S.S.R.
26 O2 Baeivašgiedde Norway
28 C5 Bække Denmark
28 A4 Bækmarksbro Denmark
28 E3 Bælum Denmark
16 E7 Baena Spain
36 D6 Baerenthal France
128 C4 Baeza Ecuador
16 E7 Baeza Spain
47 J7 Bafa Gölü L Turkey
86 B4 Bafang Cameroon
85 B6 Bafata Guinea-Bissau
109 K8 Baffin B Texas
147 E6 Baffin Basin Arctic Oc
115 N3 Baffin Bay Greenland/Canada
90 E2 Baffin-Greenland Rise Atlantic Oc
115 M3 Baffin I N W Terr
141 K6 Baffle Creek Queensland
86 B5 Bafia Cameroon
85 B6 Bafing R Guinea/Mali
79 H2 Bafliūn Syria
85 B6 Bafoulabé Mali
86 B4 Bafoussam Cameroon
77 D4 Bāfq Iran
78 E1 Bafra Turkey
86 E5 Bafwasende Zaïre
58 D3 Baga Bogd Uul mt Mongolia
71 E3 Bagac Bay Luzon Philippines
76 B2 Bagalkot India
88 G5 Bagamoyo Tanzania
71 G7 Baganga Mindanao Philippines
71 F7 Baganian Peninsula Mindanao Philippines
69 E10 Bagan Serai Malaysia
142 A3 Baganup L W Australia
44 H2 Baganza R Italy
57 K1 Bagar R U.S.S.R.
55 D3 Bagaryak U.S.S.R.
103 J7 Bagbad California
32 G6 Bagband W Germany
103 L7 Bagdad Arizona
110 L3 Bagdad Kentucky
109 K10 Bagdad Mexico
51 L3 Bagdarin U.S.S.R.
58 F1 Bagdarino U.S.S.R.
131 G3 Bagé Brazil
86 G3 Bagemder prov Ethiopia
28 F7 Bagenkop Denmark
101 S8 Baggs Wyoming
78 K5 Baghdād Iraq
77 A4 Bāgh-e Malek Iran
75 N7 Bagherhat Bangladesh
43 F10 Bagheria Sicily
77 E4 Baghin Iran
77 L1 Baghlān Afghanistan
77 J3 Baghran Afghanistan
Baghrash Köl see Bosten Hu
14 E4 Baginbun Hd Irish Rep
99 L2 Bagley Minnesota
99 P7 Bagley Wisconsin
116 Q6 Bagley Icefield Alaska
45 L3 Bagnacavallo Italy
110 D3 Bagnell Dam Missouri
18 F9 Bagnères de Bigorre France
18 F10 Bagnères de Luchon France
40 F6 Bagnes,Val De Switzerland
21 E7 Bagneux France
45 J3 Bagni di Lucca Italy
41 L5 Bagni di Masino Italy
45 K4 Bagno A Ripoli Italy
45 L4 Bagno di Romagna Italy
20 E4 Bagnoles-de-l'Orne France
45 L1 Bagnoli di Sopra Italy
45 L1 Bagnolo di Po Italy
45 J2 Bagnolo in Piano Italy
44 H1 Bagnolo Mella Italy
45 J1 Bagnolo San Vito Italy

19 N16 Bagnols-sur-Cèze France
28 D6 Bågø isld Denmark
85 C6 Bagoe R Ivory Co/Mali
Bagong see Sansui
121 U4 Bagotville Quebec
31 M1 Bagrationovsk U.S.S.R.
9 F5 Bagshot England
65 E3 Bag Tal China
128 C5 Bagua Peru
85 F5 Baguezane, Mt Niger
71 N9 Baguia Timor Indonesia
71 E2 Baguio Luzon Philippines
71 G7 Baguio Mindanao Philippines
71 F2 Baguio Pt Luzon Philippines
86 C3 Baguirmi dist Chad
126 E2 Bahama Bank,Great Bahamas
126 F1 Bahama Bank, Little Bahamas
126 F2 Bahamas, The W Indies
127 M4 Baham, Pte Martinique W I
86 G3 Bahar Dar Ethiopia
84 H4 Baharîya Oasis Egypt
70 D3 Bahau R Sarawak
74 E4 Bahawalnagar Pakistan
74 D4 Bahawalpur Pakistan
71 H5 Baheësiuna Sulawesi Indonesia
88 E4 Bahi Tanzania
129 K6 Bahia state Brazil
131 E7 Bahia Blanca Argentina
125 L1 Bahía, Islas de la Honduras
124 C3 Bahia Kino Mexico
133 D7 Bahía Laura Argentina
133 C6 Bahia Pargua Chile
124 B4 Bahía Tortugas Mexico
48 L3 Bahluiul R Romania
48 J4 Bahnea Romania
88 B5 Baholoholo tribe Zaïre
69 H8 Ba,Hon isld Vietnam
79 A7 Baḥra el Burullus lagoon Egypt
79 B7 Baḥra el Manzala lagoon Egypt
75 J5 Bahraich India
77 B6 Bahrain sheikhdom The Gulf
86 C4 Bahr Aouk R Cent Afr Republic
86 D3 Bahr Aouk R Chad
86 F3 Bahr el Abiad R Sudan
86 E4 Bahr el Arab watercourse Sudan
86 F3 Bahr el Azraq R Sudan
86 E4 Bahr el Ghazal prov Sudan
86 E4 Bahr el Ghazal R Sudan
78 G4 Bahret Assad L Syria
86 F4 Bahr ez Zeraf R Sudan
77 G7 Bāhu Kālat Iran
71 H6 Bahulu isld Sulawesi Indonesia
71 K8 Bahuluang isld Indonesia
70 G6 Bahu-Mbelu Sulawesi Indonesia
129 J4 Baiâ Brazil
48 H6 Baia de Aramă Romania
48 H6 Baia de Cris Romania
16 B6 Baia de Setúbal Portugal
87 B9 Baia doz Tigres Angola
128 F7 Baia Grande,L Brazil
48 H3 Baia Mare Romania
45 R8 Baiano Italy
48 H3 Baia Spriei Romania
77 D3 Baiazeh Iran
86 C4 Baïbokoum Chad
65 H3 Baicaogou China
57 K4 Baicheng China
65 F2 Baicheng China
48 K5 Băicoi Romania
121 N5 Baie Carrière Quebec
115 N8 Baie-Comeau Quebec
21 A7 Baie de Bourgneuf France
126 H5 Baie de Henne Haiti
122 E5 Baie de Sables Quebec
123 P2 Baie-du-Milieu Quebec
115 M7 Baie-du-Poste Quebec
122 G6 Baie du Vin New Brunswick
68 F7 Baie,I.de la Cambodia
122 K3 Baie Johan Beetz Quebec
127 N4 Baie Mahault Guadeloupe W I
36 E7 Baiersbronn W Germany
122 C5 Baie Ste.Catherine Quebec
122 H4 Baie Ste.Clair Quebec
122 B6 Baie St.Paul Quebec
122 E4 Baie Trinité Quebec
122 J7 Baie Verte New Brunswick
123 Q4 Baie Verte Newfoundland
67 D3 Baifang China
Baiguan see Shangyu
74 J7 Baihar India
58 F5 Baihe China
65 B6 Baijiazhuang China
Baikal L see Baykal,Ozero L
75 K7 Baikunthpur India
65 E1 Bailang China
Baile Átha see Dublin
48 G6 Băile Herculane Romania
16 E6 Bailén Spain
48 H6 Băileşti Romania
22 G3 Baileux Belgium
106 E2 Bailey Colorado
112 J2 Bailey N Carolina
143 D8 Bailey Ra W Australia
111 K7 Baileyton Alabama
95 U1 Baileyville Maine
14 D3 Bailieborough Irish Rep
67 D3 Bailin China
129 H3 Bailique, I Brazil
20 H5 Bailleau-le-Pin France
22 D2 Bailleul France
20 E4 Bailleul Orne France
22 D3 Bailleul-Sire-Berthoult France
115 K2 Baillie Hamilton I N W Terr
114 G3 Baillie Is N W Terr
127 M4 Baillif Guadeloupe W I
77 K3 Bailugh Afghanistan
48 L4 Baimakliya U.S.S.R.
111 M11 Bainbridge Georgia
95 M4 Bainbridge New York
94 D7 Bainbridge Ohio
21 B6 Bain-de-Brét France
140 B3 Baines, Mt N Terr Aust
127 H5 Bainet Haiti
71 K10 Baing Indonesia
Baini see Yuqing
19 K4 Bains-les-Bains France
13 H6 Bainton England
98 B1 Bainville Montana
59 J2 Baiquan China
109 H3 Baird Texas
116 E6 Baird Inlet Alaska
116 G3 Baird Mts Alaska
65 D3 Bairin Youqi China
58 G3 Bairin Zuoqi China
139 J7 Bairnsdale Victoria
101 S7 Bairoil Wyoming
21 C6 Bais France
20 E5 Bais Mayenne France
18 F8 Baïse R France
Baisha see Jiande
65 B7 Baisha China
67 B2 Baisha China
67 C7 Baisha China
65 B7 Baisha Shuiku res China
67 E3 Baishi Feng mt China
65 A7 Baishui China
58 D5 Baishui Jiang R China
22 E2 Baisieux France
45 J3 Baiso Italy
52 B6 Baisogala U.S.S.R.
74 J4 Baitadi Nepal
68 G3 Bai Thoung Vietnam
19 N15 Baix France
65 C6 Baixiang China
65 A3 Baixingt China
65 E3 Baixingt China
16 B6 Baixo Alentejo prov Portugal
130 H6 Baixo Guandu Brazil
87 C9 Baixo Longa Angola
65 C5 Baiyang Dian L China
67 C1 Baiyangping China
Baiyashi see Dong'an
58 D4 Baiyin China
86 F2 Baiyuda Sudan
67 E3 Baiyun Shan mt China
58 E4 Baiyu Shan mts China
67 B1 Baizi China
48 E4 Baja Hungary
124 B3 Baja California state Mexico
70 Q10 Bajan Indonesia
124 J4 Baján Mexico
124 B3 Baja, Pta C Mexico
48 F7 Bajina Bašta Yugoslavia
48 E5 Bajmok Yugoslavia
71 J9 Bajo Sumbawa Indonesia
128 C2 Bajo Baudo Colombia
126 E7 Bajo Nuevo Caribbean
141 K6 Bajool Queensland
28 C7 Bajstrup Denmark
48 D4 Bak Hungary
70 E3 Bakajan, G mt Kalimantan
55 C4 Bakal U.S.S.R.
86 D4 Bakala Cent Afr Republic
57 H3 Bakanas U.S.S.R.
57 J2 Bakanas R U.S.S.R.
56 B3 Bakchar R U.S.S.R.
69 E14 Bake Indonesia
85 B6 Bakel Senegal
103 H6 Baker California
101 M4 Baker Idaho
98 B3 Baker Montana
98 G1 Baker N Dakota
103 K2 Baker Nevada
100 H5 Baker Oregon
94 J7 Baker W Virginia
133 C7 Baker R Chile
103 N7 Baker Butte mt Arizona
117 G8 Baker I Alaska
137 R1 Baker I Pacific Oc
95 R7 Baker L Maine
115 K5 Baker Lake N W Terr
143 F7 Baker Lake W Australia
100 D1 Baker,Mt Washington
125 P9 Bakers Belize
102 F6 Bakersfield California
112 E1 Bakersfield N Carolina
108 E5 Bakersfield Texas
95 P2 Bakersfield Vermont
9 E1 Bakewell England
77 G2 Bakharz reg Iran
53 D11 Bakhchisaray U.S.S.R.
54 D5 Bakhmach U.S.S.R.
77 B4 Bakhtiyāri Iran
47 J5 Bakır R Turkey
47 K4 Bakırköy Turkey
25 F2 Bakkeveen Netherlands
47 K7 Baklan Turkey
86 G4 Bako Ethiopia
85 C7 Bako Ivory Coast
48 D4 Bakony mts Hungary
86 D4 Bakouma Cent Afr Republic
85 C6 Bakoye R Guinea/Mali
54 L1 Baksheyevo U.S.S.R.
26 K6 Baktsjaure Sweden
50 D4 Baku U.S.S.R.
71 G6 Bakulin Pt Mindanao Philippines
32 H7 Bakum W Germany
70 C5 Bakumpai Kalimantan
69 G12 Bakung isld Indonesia
69 C11 Bakungan Sumatra
142 J10 Bakutis Coast Antarctica
80 D4 Bal'a Jordan
121 L7 Bala Ontario
78 D2 Bâlâ Turkey
8 C2 Bala Wales
71 C7 Balabac Str Borneo/Philippines
70 E6 Balabalangan, Kep islds Indonesia
71 H8 Balabalangan Pulau Pulau islds Indonesia
54 H1 Balabanovo U.S.S.R.
71 C7 Balabec isld Palawan Philippines
54 G9 Balabino U.S.S.R.
128 E6 Bala,Cerros de mts Bolivia
48 H6 Bălăciţa Romania
127 J2 Balaclava Jamaica
138 F4 Balaclava New S Wales
86 J5 Balad Somalia
77 B1 Baladeh Iran
80 F3 Balad el Basha Jordan
80 F3 Balad el Mansura Jordan
146 F2 Balæna Is Antarctica
74 J8 Balaghat India
17 H3 Balaguer Spain
68 A2 Balaing Burma
70 B4 Balaisepuac Kalimantan
138 E5 Balaklava S Australia
54 H7 Balakleya U.S.S.R.
8 C2 Bala, L Wales
87 G8 Balama Mozambique
77 H2 Bala Murghab Afghanistan
40 B6 Balan France
125 O9 Balancán Mexico
71 E3 Balanga Luzon Philippines
71 H5 Balantak, G mt Sulawesi Indonesia
71 F5 Balaring Negros Philippines
86 G3 Balas R Ethiopia
75 M8 Balasore India
48 E2 Balassagyarmat Hungary
84 H4 Balât Egypt
99 L5 Balaton Minnesota
48 D4 Balaton L Hungary
48 D4 Balatonfüred Hungary
48 D4 Balatonszentgyörgy Hungary
71 L9 Balaurin Flores Indonesia
124 F10 Balboa Panama Can Zone
14 E3 Balbriggan Irish Rep
141 H8 Balbuna Queensland
13 G6 Balby England
144 D5 Balcairn New Zealand
138 E4 Balcanoona S Australia
131 F6 Balcarce Argentina
119 O8 Balcarres Sask
48 H6 Bălceşti Romania
47 J1 Balchik Bulgaria
109 O9 Balch Springs Texas
144 B7 Balclutha New Zealand
9 F5 Balcombe England
100 F6 Bald Butte mt Oregon
94 K6 Bald Eagle Mt Pennsylvania
41 H3 Baldegg See L Switzerland
143 C11 Bald Hd W Australia
110 E6 Bald Knob Arkansas
94 F9 Bald Knob W Virginia
101 L5 Bald Mt Idaho
103 J4 Bald Mt Nevada
9 F4 Baldock England
119 T2 Baldock L Manitoba
42 D3 Baldo,Monte Italy
113 F7 Baldwin Florida
110 A3 Baldwin Kansas
94 B3 Baldwin Michigan
98 F2 Baldwin N Dakota
99 O5 Baldwin Wisconsin
102 H7 Baldwin L California
116 F3 Baldwin Pen Alaska
118 H6 Baldwinton Sask
95 P4 Baldwinville Massachusetts
95 R3 Baldwin, W Maine
111 H7 Baldwyn Mississippi
119 R7 Baldy Mt Manitoba
103 P8 Baldy Pk Arizona
106 E6 Baldy Pk New Mexico
86 H4 Bale prov Ethiopia
Balearic Is see Islas Baleares
70 C4 Baleh R Sarawak
130 H5 Baleia, Pta da C Brazil
115 N6 Baleine,à la R Quebec
83 L14 Baleiniers, Baie des Kerguelen Indian Oc
71 C7 Balembangan isld Sabah
22 J1 Balen Belgium
48 K6 Bâleni Romîni Romania
71 E3 Baler Luzon Philippines
71 E3 Baler Bay Luzon Philippines
15 E5 Balerno Scotland
51 L3 Baley U.S.S.R.
58 G1 Baley U.S.S.R.
141 H5 Balfe's Creek Queensland
48 D4 Bal Földvár Hungary
26 K7 Bålforsen Sweden
117 P11 Balfour Br Columbia
98 F2 Balfour N Dakota
144 B6 Balfour New Zealand
142 D6 Balfour Downs W Australia
12 D1 Balfron Scotland
77 F1 Bālgirān Iran
142 G5 Balgo Hill W Australia
119 N8 Balgonie Sask
32 K10 Balhorn W Germany
86 B4 Bali Cameroon
70 P10 Bali isld Indonesia
71 F6 Baliangao Mindanao Philippines
69 D11 Balige Sumatra
31 N6 Baligród Poland
65 D4 Balihan China
47 J5 Balıkesir Turkey
70 E5 Balikpapan Kalimantan
86 C3 Bal Illi R Chad
70 G2 Balimbing Tawitaw isld Philippines
69 E10 Baling Malaysia
70 C3 Balingian Sarawak
70 C3 Balingian R Sarawak
65 D3 Balinqiao China
48 G5 Balint Romania
70 P9 Bali Sea Indonesia
70 P10 Bali,Selat Bali/Java
70 G2 Baliungan Tawitawi Philippines
130 D5 Baliza Brazil
32 K5 Balje W Germany
118 K6 Baljennie Sask
25 E3 Balk Netherlands
48 G3 Balkány Hungary
55 C4 Balkany U.S.S.R.
55 E4 Balkashino U.S.S.R.
25 F3 Balkbrug Netherlands
77 K1 Balkh Afghanistan
57 G2 Balkhash U.S.S.R.
57 G2 Balkhash, Ozero L U.S.S.R.
74 H9 Balkonda India
87 E10 Balla Balla Zimbabwe
15 C4 Ballachulish Scotland
143 E9 Balladonia W Australia
14 C3 Ballaghaderreen Irish Rep
20 K4 Ballancourt-sur-Essonne France
141 K8 Ballandean Queensland
26 J3 Ballangen Norway
101 R4 Ballantine Montana
15 C5 Ballantrae Scotland
114 J7 Ballantyne Bay Sask
114 H2 Ballantyne Str N W Terr
43 C9 Ballao Sardinia
102 G5 Ballarat California
139 G6 Ballarat Victoria
143 D8 Ballard, L W Australia
80 F4 Ballas Jordan
15 E3 Ballater Scotland
12 D5 Ballaugh I of Man U.K.
28 F4 Balle Denmark
21 E6 Ballée France
28 F5 Ballen Denmark
133 C3 Ballena,Pta C Chile
33 O9 Ballenstedt E Germany
146 K5 Balleny I Antarctica
20 D3 Balleroy France
28 K5 Ballerup Denmark
112 C3 Ball Ground Georgia
75 L6 Ballia India
14 B2 Ballina Irish Rep
14 C3 Ballinasloe Irish Rep
14 C3 Ballindine Irish Rep
28 B3 Balling Denmark
14 C4 Ballingarry Irish Rep
108 H4 Ballinger Texas
15 E4 Ballinluig Scotland
14 B3 Ballinrobe Irish Rep
14 A5 Ballinskelligs B Irish Rep
37 J6 Ballmertshofen W Germany
118 B7 Ball,Mt Alberta
12 D1 Balloch Scotland
20 F5 Ballon France
19 K5 Ballon d'Alsace mt France
21 C6 Ballots France
137 M8 Ball's Pyramid isld Pacific Oc
37 K1 Ballstädt E Germany
95 O4 Ballston Spa New York
28 B6 Ballum Denmark
14 E2 Ballybay Irish Rep
14 D2 Ballybofey Irish Rep
14 B4 Ballybunnion Irish Rep
14 B2 Ballycastle Irish Rep
14 E1 Ballycastle N Ireland
14 E2 Ballyclare N Ireland
14 D2 Ballyconnell Irish Rep
14 D5 Ballycotton B Irish Rep
14 C4 Ballyduff Irish Rep
14 C3 Ballygar Irish Rep
14 D2 Ballygawley N Ireland
12 B2 Ballygrant Scotland
14 D2 Ballyhaise Irish Rep
14 C3 Ballyhaunis Irish Rep
14 C4 Ballyhoura Hills Irish Rep
14 D3 Ballyjamesduff Irish Rep
14 D3 Ballymahon Irish Rep
14 E2 Ballymena N Ireland
14 E1 Ballymoney N Ireland
14 C2 Ballymote Irish Rep
14 F2 Ballynahinch N Ireland
14 F2 Ballyquintin Pt N Ireland
14 D4 Ballyragget Irish Rep
14 C2 Ballyshannon Irish Rep
14 E3 Ballytore Irish Rep
14 B3 Ballyvaghan Irish Rep
12 D3 Balmaclellan Scotland
12 D1 Balmaha Scotland
95 M2 Balmat New York
48 G3 Balmazújváros Hungary
40 F7 Balme Italy
40 G5 Balmhorn mt Switzerland
119 U8 Balmoral Manitoba
144 D5 Balmoral New Zealand
138 F6 Balmoral Victoria
141 K1 Balmoral dist Brisbane, Qnsld
15 E3 Balmoral Castle Scotland
113 L9 Balmoral I isld New Providence I Bahamas
108 D5 Balmorhea Texas
13 F1 Balmullo Scotland
139 J2 Balonne R Queensland
141 J8 Balonne R Queensland
55 D2 Balotovskoye U.S.S.R.
74 E6 Balotra India
33 P6 Balow E Germany
12 D1 Balquhidder Scotland
75 K5 Balrampur India
48 J6 Balş Romania
99 O4 Balsam L Wisconsin
121 M8 Balsam Lake Ontario
129 J5 Balsas Brazil
124 H8 Balsas R Mexico
26 K2 Balsfjord Norway
26 K2 Balsfjord inlet Norway
45 P6 Balsorano Italy
26 G3 Balstad Norway
98 F1 Balta N Dakota
48 M3 Balta U.S.S.R.
16 E3 Baltanás Spain
16 B3 Baltar Spain
133 F4 Baltasar Brum Uruguay
98 K6 Baltic S Dakota
27 H16 Baltic Sea N Europe
79 B7 Baltîm Egypt
14 B5 Baltimore Irish Rep
95 L7 Baltimore Maryland
87 E10 Baltimore S Africa
97 Baltimore conurbation Maryland
14 E4 Baltinglass Irish Rep
Baltit see Hunza
31 M1 Baltiysk U.S.S.R.
32 F5 Baltrum W Germany
80 G8 Balu Jordan
80 G8 Balu R Jordan
77 G6 Balūchestān va Sīstān Iran
74 A4 Baluchistan reg Pakistan
70 C3 Balui R Sarawak
71 E7 Balukbaluk isld Philippines
75 N6 Balurghat India
71 G8 Balut isld Philippines
32 G10 Balve W Germany
52 C6 Balvi U.S.S.R.
47 J5 Balya Turkey
84 J4 Balyana,El Egypt
56 H4 Bal Yeravnoye, Oz L U.S.S.R.
56 C4 Balyksa U.S.S.R.
56 E5 Balyktyg Khem R U.S.S.R.
118 C7 Balzac Alberta
77 F5 Bam Iran
67 B4 Bama China
86 B3 Bama Nigeria
141 F1 Bamaga Queensland
85 C6 Bamako Mali
128 C5 Bambamarca Peru
71 E3 Bamban Luzon Philippines
71 E2 Bambang Luzon Philippines
71 E8 Bambannan isld Philippines
86 D4 Bambari Cent Afr Republic
141 H4 Bambaroo Queensland
69 C11 Bambel Sumatra
13 F6 Bamber Br England
112 F4 Bamberg S Carolina
37 K4 Bamberg W Germany
86 E5 Bambesa Zaïre
86 E5 Bambili Zaïre
86 C5 Bambio Cent Afr Republic
27 D13 Bamble Norway
142 D5 Bamboo Creek W Australia
142 C5 Bamboo Springs W Australia
83 M13 Bambou Mt Mauritius
130 F7 Bambui Brazil
13 G2 Bamburgh England
66 E5 Bam Co L China
86 B4 Bamenda Cameroon
117 L11 Bamfield Br Col
77 K2 Bamian Afghanistan
67 C4 Bamian China
65 F3 Bamiancheng China
Bamiantong see Muling
86 C4 Bamingui R Cent Afr Republic
77 K2 Bāmīyān Afghanistan
68 G6 Bam Nak Cambodia
68 E5 Bamnet Narong Thailand
124 E5 Bamoa Mexico
69 A8 Bampoka I Nicobar Is
77 H6 Bam Posht, Kūh-e mts Iran
8 C6 Bampton England
9 E4 Bampton Oxon England
77 G6 Bampūr Iran
77 G6 Bampur R Iran
68 H4 Ba Na Vietnam
137 O1 Banaba isld Pacific Oc
129 L5 Banabuiu Açude res Brazil
14 D3 Banagher Irish Rep
71 E4 Banahao, Mt Luzon Philippines
86 E5 Banalia Zaïre
68 G7 Banam Cambodia
85 C6 Banamba Mali
124 D2 Banámichi Mexico
68 G5 Ban Amnat Thailand
141 K6 Banana Queensland
129 H6 Bananal, Ilha do Brazil
113 G9 Banana R Florida
130 J9 Bananeiras Brazil
76 G7 Bananga Nicobar Is
68 F6 Ban Aranyaprathet Thailand
47 J3 Banarlı Turkey
69 D8 Ba Na San Thailand
48 F6 Banat Novo Selo Yugoslavia
15 C4 Banavie Scotland
71 J8 Banawaja isld Indonesia
78 B2 Banaz Turkey
68 E4 Ban Bang Mun Nak Thailand
68 E4 Ban Bang Rakam Thailand
71 G6 Banbayan Pt Mindanao Philippines
69 E10 Ban Betong Thailand
68 J6 Ban Bik Vietnam
14 E2 Banbridge N Ireland
68 E5 Ban Bua Chum Thailand
68 F5 Ban Bua Yai Thailand
68 E5 Ban Bu Khanum Thailand
68 H5 Ban Bung Sai Laos
9 E3 Banbury England
71 C6 Bancalan Palawan Philippines
138 F4 Bancannia, L New S Wales
68 D3 Ban Chang Khoeng Thailand
68 F4 Ban Channabot Thailand
68 D3 Ban Chiang Dao Thailand
15 F3 Banchory Scotland
68 E4 Ban Chum Phae Thailand
125 Q8 Banco Chinchorro isld Mexico
71 D7 Bancoron isld Philippines
101 O7 Bancroft Idaho
99 M6 Bancroft Iowa
121 N7 Bancroft Ontario
98 J5 Bancroft S Dakota
48 J4 Band Romania
74 J6 Banda India
69 B10 Banda Aceh Sumatra
69 C11 Bandahara, Gunung mt Sumatra
61 N7 Bandai-Asahi Nat.Pk Japan
61 O8 Bandai-san mt Japan
85 B7 Bandajuma Sierra Leone
27 C12 Bandak L Norway
136 G2 Banda, Kep. isld Indonesia
85 C7 Bandama R Ivory Coast
77 G4 Bandan Kuh mt Iran
Bandar see Machilipatnam
77 J2 Bandar Afghanistan
87 F9 Bandar Mozambique
75 J4 Bandar Nepal
77 E6 Bandar 'Abbās Iran
77 A1 Bandar Anzalī Iran
77 B4 Bandar-e Deylam Iran
77 D6 Bandar-e Khoemir Iran
77 D6 Bandar-e Lengeh Iran
77 A4 Bandar-e Ma'shūr Iran
77 B5 Bandar-e Rīg Iran
77 D1 Bandar-e Shah Iran
77 A4 Bandar Khomeynī Iran
70 D2 Bandar Seri Begawan Brunei
83 H1 Bandar Shah Iran
136 F3 Banda Sea Indonesia
71 C7 Bandau Sabah
88 E7 Bandawe Malawi
22 J3 Bande Belgium
16 B2 Bande Spain
129 K8 Bandeira mt Brazil
130 H7 Bandeira mt Brazil
130 E8 Bandeirantes Brazil
130 D8 Bandeirantes, I. dos Brazil
87 B8 Bandeira, Sa da Angola
106 D6 Bandelier Nat.Mon New Mexico
77 D6 Band-e Moghūyeh Iran
109 H6 Bandera Texas
108 B4 Banderas Mexico
124 G7 Banderas,B de Mexico
28 G7 Bandholm Denmark
85 D6 Bandiagara Mali
77 K2 Band-i-Amur R Afghanistan
77 J2 Band-i-Balan mts Afghanistan
78 B1 Bandirma Turkey
47 J4 Bandirma Körfezi gulf Turkey
77 J2 Band-i-Turkestan mts Afghanistan
70 M9 Bandjar Java
70 D6 Bandjarmasin Kalimantan
70 M9 Bandjarnegara Java
19 P18 Bandol France
Ban Don see Surat Thani
14 C5 Bandon Irish Rep
100 A6 Bandon Oregon
68 H6 Ban Don Vietnam
14 C5 Bandon R Irish Rep
68 G4 Ban Dong Laos
68 F4 Ban Don Khi Thailand
74 E9 Bandra India
86 C6 Bandundu Zaïre
70 L9 Bandung Java
69 F12 Bandung Sumatra
68 G4 Ban Dupre Laos
94 F9 Bandy Virginia
143 D8 Bandya W Australia
48 K6 Băneasa Romania
48 L5 Băneasa Romania
78 K4 Baneh Iran
71 B2 Banema Halmahera Indonesia
17 G6 Bañeras Spain
126 G4 Banes Cuba
118 B7 Banff Alberta
15 F3 Banff Scotland
Banff co see Grampian reg
85 D6 Banfora Upper Volta
86 D7 Banga Zaïre
71 F7 Bangaan Mindanao Philippines
71 G7 Bangai Pt Mindanao Philippines
71 E7 Bangalao isld Philippines
76 C4 Bangalore India
71 E2 Bangar Luzon Philippines
70 D2 Bangar Sarawak
27 H12 Bångbro Sweden
86 C5 Bangé Cameroon
110 E4 Bangert Missouri
70 C4 Bang,G mt Kalimantan
71 H6 Banggai, Kep islds Indonesia
71 C7 Banggi isld Sabah
68 G4 Bang Hieng R Laos
70 O9 Bangil Java
71 J4 Bangka Sulawesi Indonesia
69 G14 Bangka isld Indonesia
70 C8 Bangkal Kalimantan
70 F7 Bangkala Sulawesi Indonesia
70 O9 Bangkalan Java
69 C11 Bangkaru isld Sumatra
69 G14 Bangka,Selat str Sumatra
70 G4 Bangkir Sulawesi Indonesia
69 F14 Bangko Sumatra
68 E6 Bangkok Thailand
63 Bangkok conurbation China
68 E6 Bangkok,Bight of Thailand
71 H5 Bangkulu Sulawesi Indonesia
75 N6 Bangladesh rep S Asia
68 E6 Bang Lamung Thailand
68 J7 Ba Ngoi Vietnam
66 B5 Bangong Co L China
95 T2 Bangor Maine
94 A4 Bangor Michigan
14 F2 Bangor N Ireland
95 M6 Bangor Pennsylvania
119 P8 Bangor Sask
8 B1 Bangor Wales
86 C4 Bangoran R Cent Afr Republic
109 H4 Bangs Texas
70 E5 Bangsalsembera Kalimantan
68 D7 Bang Saphan Yai Thailand
28 F2 Bangsbostrand Denmark
103 L5 Bangs,Mt Arizona
26 E7 Bangsund Norway
71 E2 Bangued Luzon Philippines
86 C5 Bangui Cent Afr Republic
71 E1 Bangui Luzon Philippines
69 D11 Bangunpurba Sumatra
88 B7 Bangweulu, L Zambia
68 F3 Ban Hai Laos
68 D4 Ban Hat Sao Thailand
69 E9 Ban Hat Yai Thailand
68 F3 Ban Hin Heup Laos
68 J6 Ban Ho Vietnam
68 E2 Ban Houei Sai Laos
68 D6 Ban Hua Hin Thailand
68 F3 Ban Huai Kho Thailand
68 D7 Ban Huai Yang Thailand
116 L7 Ban I Alaska
86 D4 Bani Cent Afr Republic
127 J5 Baní Dominican Rep
71 D2 Bani Luzon Philippines
85 C6 Bani R Mali
85 E5 Bani Bangou Niger
127 J5 Bánica Dominican Rep
31 H2 Banie Poland
71 D3 Bani Pt Luzon Philippines
94 H10 Banister R Virginia
77 D6 Bani Tunb isld Iran
84 E3 Banī Walīd Libya
79 F3 Bāniyās Syria
80 F1 Bāniyās Syria
48 E6 Banja Koviljača Yugoslavia
42 H4 Banja Luka Yugoslavia
68 H6 Ban Jeng Drom Vietnam
85 A6 Banjul The Gambia
70 M9 Banjumas Java
142 B3 Banjup dist Perth, W Aust
70 P10 Banjuwangi Java
140 C4 Banka Banka N Terr Aust
68 G5 Ban Kadiene Laos
68 E4 Ban Kaeng Thailand
69 E9 Ban Kam Phaeng Phet Thailand
69 D9 Ban Kantang Thailand
89 D9 Bankberg mts S Africa
12 E3 Bankend Scotland
68 H5 Ban Keng Phao Cambodia
68 F2 Ban Keo Lom Vietnam
68 E6 Ban Khai Thailand
68 F1 Ban Khang Kha Vietnam
68 D6 Ban Khao Yoi Thailand
111 J8 Bankhead L Alabama
68 G4 Ban Khemmarat Thailand
68 E3 Ban Khing Laos
68 F6 Ban Khlung Thailand
69 D8 Ban Khok Kloi Thailand
69 D9 Ban Khuan Mao Thailand
68 E3 Ban Khun Ban Hai Thailand
68 F5 Ban Khu Noi Thailand
68 C3 Ban Khun Yuam Thailand
68 J6 Ban Kniet Vietnam
70 E7 Bankobankoang isld Indonesia
68 D4 Ban Krai Thailand
100 J5 Banks Idaho
100 B4 Banks Oregon
138 F7 Banks,C S Australia
138 D5 Bank's Group isld S Australia
117 H9 Banks I Br Columbia
147 J2 Banks I N W Terr
141 F1 Banks I Queensland
100 F2 Banks L Washington
144 D5 Banks Peninsula New Zealand
139 K7 Bankstown Airfield Sydney, New S Wales
68 D6 Ban Kui Nua Thailand
75 M7 Bankura India
68 G4 Ban Kut Hae Thailand
46 F2 Bankya Bulgaria
68 F5 Ban Lamduan Thailand
71 F3 Banla Pt Philippines
68 D5 Ban Le Kathe Thailand
68 E5 Ban Len Thailand
68 C3 Ban Mae La Luang Thailand
68 D3 Ban Mae Mo Thailand
68 D4 Ban Mae Ramat Thailand
68 C3 Ban Mae Sariang Thailand
68 D4 Ban Mae Sot Thailand
68 D3 Ban Mae Suai Thailand
68 D3 Ban Mae Thalop Thailand
68 J6 Ban Me Thout Vietnam
68 D3 Ban Mong Pong Thailand
68 E3 Ban Muang Thailand
68 F6 Ban Muang Thailand
68 F5 Ban Muang Phon Thailand
14 E4 Bann R Irish Rep
14 E2 Bann R N Ireland
71 E1 Banna Luzon Philippines
69 D8 Ban Na Thailand
68 F4 Ban Na Baek Thailand
68 H4 Ban Nabo Laos
101 N4 Bannack Montana
68 G4 Ban Na Kae Thailand
68 E3 Ban Na Kon Thailand
68 E2 Ban Na Mo Laos
68 E4 Ban Nam Pong Thailand
68 F1 Ban Nam Sau Vietnam
68 E3 Ban Na Noi Thailand
68 F3 Ban Naphong Laos
68 F3 Ban Na Sabaeng Thailand
69 E9 Ban Na Thawi Thailand
142 F4 Bannerman, Mt W Australia
126 F2 Bannerman Town Eleuthera Bahamas
68 F4 Ban Ngon Thailand
102 H8 Banning California
Banningville see Bandundu
40 H6 Bannio Italy
144 B6 Bannockburn New Zealand
121 N8 Bannockburn Ontario
12 E1 Bannockburn Scotland
101 M5 Bannock Pass Idaho/Montana
101 N7 Bannock Ra Idaho
68 C4 Ban Noi Thailand
68 E2 Ban Nong Kha Laos
68 F5 Ban Nong Makha Thailand
68 H5 Ban Nong Met Laos
68 F5 Ban Nong Waeng Thailand
74 D2 Bannu Pakistan
17 J2 Bañolas Spain
19 P16 Banon France
124 H6 Bañón Mexico
31 L7 Bánovce Czechoslovakia
68 F3 Ban Pacpeup Laos
68 D3 Ban Pak Bong Thailand
68 D7 Ban Pak Chan Thailand
68 D6 Ban Pak Khlong Thailand
68 D7 Ban Pak Nam Thailand
68 E6 Ban Pak Nam Thailand
68 E3 Ban Pak Neun Laos
69 E8 Ban Pak Phanang Thailand
68 F5 Ban Pak Thong Chai Thailand
68 E5 Ban Phachi Thailand
68 G4 Ban Phaeng Thailand
68 F5 Ban Phai Thailand
68 E6 Ban Phanat Nikhom Thailand
68 H5 Ban Phone Laos
68 G5 Ban Phon Ngam Thailand
68 F4 Ban Phon Thong Thailand
68 D5 BanPhot Phisai Thailand
68 D4 Ban Phran Katai Thailand
68 E4 Ban Phrom Phirom Thailand
68 F5 Ban Phutthaisong Thailand
Ban Pla Soi see Chon Buri
68 D6 Ban Pong Thailand
67 A3 Banqiao China
65 D7 Banquan China
68 D4 Ban Saen To Thailand
68 E2 Ban Sai Laos
68 F5 Ban Sai Thailand
68 D5 Ban Sai Yok Thailand
69 E9 Ban Sanam Chai Thailand
68 F5 Ban Sangae Thailand
68 E5 Ban Sao Thailand
68 D3 Ban Saraphi Chae Hom Thailand
68 E6 Ban Sattahip Thailand
68 D7 Ban Sawi Thailand
74 E8 Bansda India
75 K5 Bansi India
69 E8 Ban Sichon Thailand
68 E6 Ban Si Racha Thailand
31 L7 Banská Bystrica Czechoslovakia
31 L7 Banská Stiavnica Czechoslovakia
47 F3 Bansko Bulgaria
68 D3 Ban Sop Huai Hai Thailand
68 D4 Ban Sop Prap Thailand
68 G3 Ban Sot Laos
68 D4 Ban Sut Ta Thailand
74 F7 Banswara India
71 J9 Banta isld Sumbawa Indonesia
70 F7 Bantaeng Sulawesi Indonesia
69 E12 Bantaian Sumatra
68 E5 Ban Ta Khli Thailand
69 D8 Ban Takua Pa Thailand
69 E13 Bantal Sumatra
68 F5 Ban Tan Thailand
68 F6 Ban Ta Ruang Thailand
68 H4 Ban Taup Laos
68 F3 Ban Ta Viang Laos
71 F5 Bantayan isld Philippines
32 L8 Banteln W Germany
70 L9 Banten Java
69 D8 Ban Tha Chang Thailand
69 D8 Ban Thai Muang Thailand
69 D8 Ban Tha Kham Thailand
68 F4 Ban Tha Lat Thailand
68 G5 Ban Tham Khae Thailand
68 D5 Ban Thap Phung Thailand
69 E8 Ban Tha Sala Thailand
68 D4 Ban Tha Song Yang Thailand
68 E5 Ban Tha Tako Thailand
68 H5 Ban Thateng Laos
68 G4 Ban Tha Uthen Thailand
69 E9 Ban Thepha Thailand
22 J5 Bantheville France
68 D6 Ban Thung Luang Thailand
71 F4 Banton isld Philippines
68 H6 Ban Treo Cambodia
14 B5 Bantry Irish Rep
98 F1 Bantry N Dakota
14 B5 Bantry B Irish Rep
70 N9 Bantul Java
74 D8 Bantva India
76 B4 Bantval India
68 F4 Ban Waeng Noi Thailand
68 E4 Ban Wang Saphong Thailand
68 G4 Ban Wang Ta Mua Thailand
8 D5 Banwell England
47 G2 Banya Bulgaria
69 C11 Banyak, Kep. isld Indonesia
68 F4 Ban Yang Talat Thailand
68 D6 Ban Yang Yong Thailand
68 H6 Ban Ya Soup Vietnam
86 B4 Banyo Cameroon
141 K1 Banyo dist Brisbane, Qnsld
69 G14 Banyuasin R Sumatra
37 L3 Banz W Germany
146 G3 Banzare Coast Antarctica
81 E11 Banzare Seamount Southern Oc
67 B4 Bao'an China
67 E5 Bao'an China
58 F4 Baode China
65 D5 Baodi China
58 G4 Baoding China
65 B7 Baofeng China
67 A5 Bao Ha Vietnam
65 D4 Bao He R China
58 E5 Baoji China
67 C2 Baojing China
Baokang see Horqin Zouyi Zhongqi
67 D1 Baokang China
68 G1 Bao Lac Vietnam
65 F3 Baolizhen China
68 H7 Bao Loc Vietnam
65 J1 Baoqing China
67 G1 Baoshan China
68 J3 Baoting China
58 E3 Baotou China
85 C6 Baoulé R Mali
59 G5 Baoying China
Baoyou see Ledong
76 E3 Bapatla India
22 D3 Bapaume France
103 N8 Bapchule Arizona
121 M7 Baptiste Ontario
Bapu see Liucheng
70 D6 Bapuju Kalimantan
80 D4 Bāqa el Gharbiya Israel
66 E5 Baqên China
79 F9 Bāqir, J mt Jordan
78 K5 Ba'Qūbah Iraq
80 F3 Baqura Jordan
48 L1 Bar U.S.S.R.
42 J6 Bar Yugoslavia
22 H4 Bar R France
86 F3 Bara Sudan
70 D6 Barabai Kalimantan
55 G3 Barabinsk U.S.S.R.
50 G3 Barabinskaya Step' U.S.S.R.
141 G5 Barabon Queensland
99 R6 Baraboo Wisconsin
122 H5 Barachois Quebec
126 G4 Baracoa Cuba
47 L7 Baradis Turkey
99 S3 Baraga Michigan
86 G5 Baragoi Kenya
127 J5 Barahona Dom Rep
57 F6 Barak Afghanistan
88 B4 Baraka Zaïre
75 L8 Barakot India
141 K7 Barakula Queensland
141 J6 Baralaba Queensland
80 E1 Bar'am Israel
70 D3 Baram R Sarawak
128 G2 Barama R Guyana
74 F9 Baramati India
141 K7 Barambah R Queensland
70 C2 Baram,Tg C Sarawak
74 G6 Baran India
54 B2 Baran' U.S.S.R.
75 N7 Baranagar India
55 C2 Baranchinskiy U.S.S.R.
45 R6 Baranello Italy
86 E5 Baranga Zaïre
71 K8 Barangbarang Indonesia
21 J7 Barangeon R France
77 G4 Baran, Kūh-e- mts Iran
126 G9 Baranoa Colombia
117 F7 Baranof I Alaska
31 N5 Baranów Poland
48 E5 Baranya co Hungary
129 G6 Barao de Capenema Brazil
130 C5 Barão de Melgaço Mato Grosso Brazil
48 K4 Baraolt Romania
48 K4 Baraoltului Munti mt Romania
22 K3 Baraque-le Fraiture Belgium
22 L2 Baraque Michel Belgium
70 L9 Barat Java
70 B5 Barat Kalimantan
111 F12 Barataria Louisiana
111 G12 Barataria B Louisiana
71 N8 Barat Daya, Kep islds Philippines
71 L9 Barate Indonesia
138 E4 Baratta S Australia
75 M6 Barauni India
130 G7 Barbacena Minas Gerais Brazil
128 C3 Barbacoas Colombia
78 M1 Barbadag mt U.S.S.R.
127 P6 Barbados Lesser Antilles
130 G9 Barbalha Brazil
45 O4 Bárbara Italy
120 C3 Barbara L Ontario
45 L1 Barbarano Vicentino Italy
85 A4 Barbas,C Mauritania
21 A8 Barbâtre France
122 D2 Barbel,L Quebec
100 J6 Barber Idaho
45 K3 Barberino di Mugello Italy
45 K4 Barberino di Val d'Elsa Italy
102 R12 Barbers Pt Hawaiian Is
94 F5 Barberton Ohio
89 G5 Barberton S Africa
113 F8 Barberville Florida
18 E7 Barbezieux France
45 J4 Barbona, M mt Italy
128 D2 Barbosa Colombia
48 L5 Barbosi Romania
94 J8 Barboursville Virginia
110 N5 Barbourville Kentucky
127 O6 Barbuda isld Lesser Antilles
33 P9 Barby E Germany
16 C4 Barca d'Alva Portugal
126 A2 Barcadera Aruba W I
126 A2 Barcadera Bonaire W I
141 H6 Barcaldine Queensland
16 C6 Barcarrota Spain
17 J3 Barcelona Spain
127 M9 Barcelona Venezuela
17 J3 Barcelona prov Spain
128 F4 Barcelos Brazil
16 B3 Barcelos Portugal
37 J2 Barchfeld E Germany
19 P16 Barcillonnette France
31 K3 Barcin Poland
103 K4 Barclay Nevada
112 L1 Barco N Carolina
136 J6 Barcoo R Queensland
141 G6 Barcoo Cr Queensland/S Aust
141 H6 Barcoorah, L Queensland
48 D5 Barcs Hungary
106 G6 Bard New Mexico
84 F5 Bardaï Chad
47 L5 Bardakçi Turkey
31 N6 Bardejov Czechoslovakia
33 R8 Bardenitz E Germany
86 H5 Bardera Somalia
28 M2 Bardhidh C Faeroes
139 J4 Bardine New S Wales
84 G3 Bardīyah Libya
9 F1 Bardney England
143 D9 Bardoc W Australia
41 N6 Bardolino Italy
122 E2 Bardoux,L Quebec
33 M6 Bardowick W Germany
13 E5 Bardsea England
8 B2 Bardsey isld Wales
110 L4 Bardstown Kentucky
26 K3 Bardu Norway
26 K3 Barduelv R Norway
141 H7 Barduthulla Queensland
110 G5 Bardwell Kentucky
109 L3 Bardwell Texas
145 F3 Bare I New Zealand
74 H4 Bareilly India
32 J7 Barenburg W Germany
37 O3 Bärenstein E Germany
20 G2 Barentin France
20 D4 Barenton France
22 F4 Barenton-Bugny France
50 B1 Barentsöya isld Spitzbergen
147 J13 Barents Sea Arctic Oc
86 G2 Barentu Ethiopia
70 D3 Bareo Sarawak
20 C2 Barfleur France
20 C2 Barfleur, Pte. de France
9 E3 Barford Warwicks England
9 E5 Barford Wilts England
66 C5 Barga China
45 H3 Barga Italy
86 B1 Bargal Somalia
141 K6 Bargara Queensland
75 K8 Bargarh India
16 E5 Bargas Spain
44 B2 Barge Italy
123 Q2 Barge B Labrador
33 T5 Bargischow E Germany
32 M5 Bargteheide W Germany
56 H3 Barguzin R U.S.S.R.
56 G4 Barguzinskiy Khrebet mts U.S.S.R.
56 G4 Barguzinskiy Zaliv gulf U.S.S.R.
95 T2 Bar Harbor Maine
75 L6 Barhi India
74 G5 Bari India
43 H7 Bari Italy
86 D4 Bari R Cent Afr Republic
128 E3 Baria R Venezuela
45 L2 Baricella Italy

74 H4 Barielly India
44 G2 Barigazzo Monte Italy
85 F1 Barika Algeria
128 F2 Barima,Pta C Venezuela
127 J10 Barinas Venezuela
128 D2 Barinas Venezuela
110 D1 Baring Missouri
100 D2 Baring Washington
143 B6 Baring Downs W Australia
143 E10 Baring, Mt W Australia
28 D5 Båring Vig B Denmark
127 J10 Barinitas Venezuela
75 M8 Baripada India
130 E8 Bariri Brazil
84 J5 Bârîs Egypt
22 E4 Barisis France
70 D5 Barito R Kalimantan
19 Q17 Barjaude mt France
19 P17 Barjols France
84 E4 Barjuj watercourse Libya
28 K4 Barkåkra Sweden
58 D5 Barkam China
27 H11 Barken,N L Sweden
94 J3 Barker New York
143 D9 Barker L W Australia
117 N9 Barkerville Br Columbia
94 H5 Barkeyville Pennsylvania
9 G4 Barking England
120 H6 Bark L Ontario
110 J5 Barkley Res Kentucky
100 A1 Barkley Sound Br Columbia
140 E5 Barkly Downs Queensland
140 D4 Barkly Highway rd N Terr Aust
140 E5 Barkly, Mt N Terr Aust
136 H5 Barkly Tableland Qnsld/N Terr
89 D7 Barkly West S Africa
66 E3 Barkol China
99 T4 Bark River Michigan
108 G6 Barksdale Texas
47 L6 Barla Dağ mt Turkey
9 E1 Barlborough England
19 J4 Bar le Duc France
143 C8 Barlee L W Australia
143 B6 Barlee Ra W Australia
8 C5 Barle, R England
19 Q16 Barles France
43 G7 Barletta Italy
22 D3 Barlin France
31 J3 Barlinek Poland
27 K14 Barlingbo isld Gotland Sweden
32 E9 Barlo W Germany
32 L4 Barlohe W Germany
98 G2 Barlow N Dakota
100 D4 Barlow Pass Oregon
57 L2 Barlyk, Khr mts U.S.S.R.
13 H6 Barmby England
139 H5 Barmedman New S Wales
74 D3 Barmer India
138 F5 Barmera S Australia
8 B2 Barmouth Wales
32 L5 Barmstedt W Germany
122 G7 Barnaby River New Brunswick
74 F7 Barnagar India
107 N2 Barnard Kansas
98 H4 Barnard S Dakota
13 G4 Barnard Castle England
117 E6 Barnard,Mt Br Col/Alaska
37 N4 Bärnau W Germany
56 B4 Barnaul U.S.S.R.
56 B4 Barnaulka R U.S.S.R.
139 H8 Barn Bluff mt Tasmania
9 E1 Barnby Moor England
95 N7 Barnegat New Jersey
146 H7 Barne Inlet Antarctica
107 O2 Barnes Kansas
94 J6 Barnesboro Pennsylvania
115 M3 Barnes Icecap N W Terr
113 G12 Barnes Sd Florida
98 K9 Barneston Nebraska
112 C4 Barnesville Georgia
98 K3 Barnesville Minnesota
9 F4 Barnet England
25 E4 Barneveld Netherlands
20 B3 Barneville France
33 R7 Barnewitz E Germany
99 M8 Barney Iowa
103 N4 Barney Top mt Utah
108 F4 Barnhart Texas
33 T7 Barnim reg E Germany
122 F5 Barn Mtn Quebec
107 O5 Barnsdall Oklahoma
13 G6 Barnsley England
95 R5 Barnstable Massachusetts
8 B5 Barnstaple England
8 C6 Barnstaple Cross England
95 Q3 Barnstead New Hampshire
32 H7 Barnstorf W Germany
32 K9 Barntrup W Germany
99 O3 Barnum Minnesota
118 E9 Barnwell Alberta
112 F4 Barnwell S Carolina
37 P6 Bärnzell W Germany
85 F7 Baro Nigeria
86 F4 Baro R Ethiopia
Baroda see Vadodara
145 D4 Barometer mt New Zealand
22 K5 Baroncourt France
45 R8 Baronissi Italy
19 O16 Baronnies, Les reg France
118 D9 Barons Alberta
143 F6 Baron's Ra W Australia
36 B6 Baronville France
87 D8 Barotseland reg Zambia
75 O5 Barpeta India
80 D4 Barqay Israel
99 U4 Barques, Pt. Aux Michigan
127 K9 Barquisimeto Venezuela
98 B10 Barr Colorado
19 K4 Barr France
12 D3 Barr Scotland
129 K6 Barra Brazil
15 A3 Barra isld Scotland
130 E8 Barra Bonita Brazil
130 G5 Barracão Brazil
128 G5 Barracão do Barreto Brazil
89 B10 Barracouta,C S Africa
129 K6 Barra da Estiva Brazil
124 G8 Barra de Navidad Mexico
130 H8 Barra de sã João Brazil
130 B4 Barra do Bugres Brazil
129 J5 Barra do Corda Brazil
130 H6 Barra do Cuieté Brazil
87 B7 Barra do Dande Angola
130 D4 Barra do Garças Brazil
130 F6 Barra do Paraopeba Brazil
130 G8 Barra do Pirai Brazil
129 G5 Barra do São Manuel Brazil
87 G10 Barra Falsa,Pta.da Mozambique
16 B5 Barragem de Maranhão res Portugal
16 B5 Barragem de Montargil Res Portugal
16 B5 Barragem do Castello do Bode Portugal
138 E6 Barrages S Australia
15 A4 Barra Head Scotland
129 K8 Barra Mansa Brazil
128 C4 Barranca Peru
128 D2 Barrancabermeja Colombia
127 H9 Barrancas Colombia
127 N10 Barrancas Venezuela
131 F2 Barrancas R Corrientes Argentina
131 B6 Barrancas,R Mendoza Argentina
130 B7 Barranco Branco Brazil
16 C6 Barrancos Portugal
133 F3 Barranqueras Argentina
126 G9 Barranquilla Colombia
13 F3 Barrasford England
121 N4 Barraute Quebec
19 P14 Barraux France
17 F5 Barrax Spain
95 P4 Barre Massachusetts
95 P2 Barre Vermont
20 G4 Barre-en-Ouche,la France
129 K6 Barreiras Brazil
129 G4 Barreirinha Brazil
129 K4 Barreirinhas Brazil
16 A6 Barreiro Portugal
130 D4 Barreiro R Brazil
130 J10 Barreiros Brazil
110 K5 Barren R Kentucky
68 A6 Barren I Andaman Is
116 L7 Barren Is Alaska
19 P16 Barret de Lioure France
129 J8 Barretos Brazil
102 H9 Barrett L California
142 F4 Barrett, Mt W Australia
118 C4 Barrhead Alberta
12 D2 Barrhead Scotland
15 D5 Barrhill Scotland
8 C5 Barri Wales
115 M9 Barrie Ontario
120 H7 Barrie I Ontario
145 E2 Barrier, C New Zealand
117 N10 Barrière Br Columbia
99 S7 Barrington Illinois
141 H8 Barrington New S Wales
122 G10 Barrington Nova Scotia
119 R1 Barrington L Manitoba
141 H8 Barringun New S Wales
129 L6 Barris R Brazil
28 D5 Barrit Denmark
101 M9 Barro Utah
130 E4 Barro Alto Brazil
100 E1 Barron Washington
99 P4 Barron Wisconsin
99 P4 Barronett Wisconsin
141 H3 Barron Falls & Gorge Queensland
109 J8 Barroso Texas
124 J4 Barroterán Mexico
21 G8 Barrou France
116 J1 Barrow Alaska
133 E5 Barrow Argentina
14 E4 Barrow R Irish Rep
140 D2 Barrow, C N Terr Aust
140 C5 Barrow Creek N Terr Aust
142 B5 Barrow I W Australia
13 E5 Barrow-in-Furness England
147 M2 Barrow,Pt Alaska
141 G2 Barrow Pt Queensland
143 F7 Barrow Ra W Australia
119 Q6 Barrows Manitoba
115 K3 Barrow Str N W Terr
143 D7 Barr Smith Ra W Australia
16 E2 Barruelo de Santullán Spain
110 E2 Barry Illinois
13 F1 Barry Scotland
121 N7 Barrys Bay Ontario
94 B3 Barryton Michigan
144 C5 Barrytown New Zealand
95 N5 Barryville New York
28 H6 Bårse Denmark
28 K5 Barsebäckshamn Sweden
76 B1 Barsi India
32 K8 Barsinghausen W Germany
28 D6 Barsø isld Denmark
32 G6 Barssel W Germany
102 G7 Barstow California
108 D4 Barstow Texas
54 J2 Barsuki U.S.S.R.
19 J4 Bar-sur-Aube France
18 H4 Bar-sur-Seine France
80 D4 Barta'a Jordan
36 H5 Bartenstein W Germany
116 Q1 Barter I Alaska
30 G1 Barth E Germany
146 B14 Barth Bank Antarctica
33 R4 Barthe R E Germany
81 B15 Barth Seamount S Atlantic Oc
122 G6 Bartibog New Brunswick
128 G2 Bartica Guyana
78 D1 Bartin Turkey
100 D8 Bartle California
141 H3 Bartle Frere,Mt Queensland
103 O2 Bartles,Mt Utah
107 P5 Bartlesville Oklahoma
98 H8 Bartlett Nebraska
95 Q2 Bartlett New Hampshire
109 K5 Bartlett Texas
143 E8 Bartlett Bluff W Australia
117 O4 Bartlett L N W Terr
103 N8 Bartlett Res Arizona
123 P3 Bartlett's Harbour Nfld
143 E8 Bartlett Soak L W Australia
98 F9 Bartley Nebraska
117 G8 Bartolome, C Alaska
87 G10 Bartolomeu Dias Mozambique
13 H6 Barton Humberside England
13 F6 Barton Lancs England
98 F1 Barton N Dakota
71 D5 Barton Palawan Philippines
138 C4 Barton S Australia
95 P2 Barton Vermont
94 D2 Barton City Michigan
9 G3 Barton Mills England
31 M1 Bartoszyce Poland
121 N4 Bartoville Quebec
33 S5 Bartow E Germany
113 F10 Bartow Florida
112 E5 Bartow Georgia
126 G9 Barú, I. de Colombia
69 E12 Barumun R Sumatra
70 O10 Barung isld Java
69 D11 Barus Sumatra
33 S8 Baruth E Germany
58 F2 Baruun Urt Mongolia
15 B2 Barvas Scotland
22 J3 Barvaux Belgium
54 J8 Barvenkovo U.S.S.R.
74 G7 Barwah India
74 F7 Barwani India
33 N7 Barwedel W Germany
113 D7 Barwick Georgia
99 N1 Barwick Ontario
143 D7 Barwidgee W Australia
140 B2 Barwolla, Mt N Terr Aust
141 F7 Baryulah Queensland
80 F7 Barza Jordan
77 D6 Basaidu Iran
106 D2 Basalt Colorado
101 N6 Basalt Idaho
102 F3 Basalt Nevada
141 H4 Basalt R Queensland
86 C5 Basankusu Zaïre
48 L6 Basarabi Romania
57 G2 Basaral, Ozero L U.S.S.R.
71 F6 Basay Negros Philippines
71 E8 Basbas Philippines
131 B2 Bascuñán,C Chile
32 K6 Basdahl W Germany
33 S7 Basdorf E Germany
22 F2 Basècles Belgium
40 G2 Basel Switzerland
40 G3 Baselland canton Switzerland
43 G8 Basento R Italy
48 K2 Başeul R Romania
71 G5 Basey Samar Philippines
77 F6 Bashākerd, Kūhhā-ye mts Iran
118 E6 Bashaw Alberta
56 B5 Bashchelakskiy Khrebet mts U.S.S.R.
89 F9 Bashee R S Africa
57 C5 Bashir U.S.S.R.
56 C5 Bashkaus R U.S.S.R.
50 E3 Bashkirskaya ASSR U.S.S.R.
71 F3 Basiad Bay Luzon Philippines
71 H5 Basiano Sulawesi Indonesia
71 F7 Basilan isld Mindanao Philippines
71 F7 Basilan Str Mindanao Philippines
9 G4 Basildon England
111 D11 Basile Louisiana
43 G8 Basilicata prov Italy
101 N3 Basin Montana
101 R5 Basin Wyoming
113 F10 Basinger Florida
9 E5 Basingstoke England
119 M6 Basin L Sask
95 U1 Baskahegan L Maine
78 K2 Båskâle Turkey
121 P6 Baskatong, Rés Quebec
142 D3 Baskerville, C W Australia
Basle see Basel
9 E1 Baslow England
26 G5 Båsmoen Norway
41 H5 Basodino mt Switzerland
86 D5 Basoko Zaïre
86 D6 Basongo Zaïre
126 A2 Basora,Pt Aruba W I
77 A4 Basra Iran
83 G1 Basra Iraq
36 D6 Bas Rhin dep France
118 E8 Bassano Alberta
42 D3 Bassano Italy
85 E7 Bassari Togo
81 A8 Bassas da India isld Mozambique Chan
33 R5 Basse E Germany
22 D3 Bassée, la France
68 B4 Bassein Burma
76 A1 Bassein India
142 B1 Bassendean dist Perth, W Aust
22 K2 Bassenge Belgium
13 E4 Bassenthwaite L England
127 L4 Basse Pointe Martinique W I
127 M4 Basse Terre Guadeloupe W I
127 P4 Basseterre St Kitts W I
127 O3 Basse Terre Trinidad
98 G7 Bassett Nebraska
103 O9 Bassett Pk Arizona
22 F1 Bassevelde Belgium
111 G10 Bassfield Mississippi
85 E7 Bassila Benin
22 F2 Bassilly Belgium
102 E4 Bass Lake California
33 T10 Basslitz E Germany
122 J8 Bass River Nova Scotia
15 F4 Bass Rock Scotland
139 H7 Bass Strait Tasmania
32 J7 Bassum W Germany
119 R8 Basswood Manitoba
99 P1 Basswood L Ontario
19 P13 Bassy France
27 F15 Båstad Sweden
77 D6 Bastak Iran
77 D1 Bastam Iran
18 M10 Bastia Corsica
45 J2 Bastiglia Italy
123 M2 Bastille,L Quebec
22 K3 Bastogne Belgium
112 E4 Bastonville Georgia
111 E9 Bastrop Louisiana
109 K5 Bastrop Texas
26 L7 Bastuträsk Sweden
Basuo see Dongfang
Basutoland see Lesotho
55 D2 Bas'yanovskiy U.S.S.R.
86 B7 Bas Zaïre prov Zaïre
86 A5 Bata Equat Guinea
85 F8 Bata Mbini Eq Guinea
71 E3 Bataan Penin Luzon Philippines
126 C3 Batabanó, G. de Cuba
71 E1 Batac Luzon Philippines
71 G4 Batag isld Philippines
130 D7 Bataguaçu Brazil
47 G3 Batak Bulgaria
70 E5 Batakan Kalimantan
47 G3 Batak Dam Bulgaria
74 F3 Batala India
16 B5 Batalha Portugal
51 M2 Batamay U.S.S.R.
71 G4 Batan isld Philippines
58 C5 Batang China
70 M9 Batang Java
86 C4 Batangafo Cent Afr Republic
71 E4 Batangas Luzon Philippines
71 C3 Batangpele Waigeo Indonesia
69 D12 Batangtoru Sumatra
71 C3 Batanta isld W Irian
48 E4 Bataszék Hungary
130 F7 Batatais Brazil
Batavia see Jakarta
133 D4 Batavia Argentina
99 S8 Batavia Illinois
94 J3 Batavia New York
110 M2 Batavia Ohio
54 L9 Bataysk U.S.S.R.
71 E5 Batbatan Panay Philippines
120 F6 Batchawana Ontario
140 B2 Batchelor N Terr Aust
69 B10 Bateemucica, Gunung mt Sumatra
88 B6 Batembo Zaïre
61 P13 Baten Okinawa
25 E5 Batenburg Netherlands
56 D4 Batenevskiy Kryazh ridge U.S.S.R.
103 J9 Bateques Mexico
101 O6 Bates Idaho
100 G5 Bates Oregon
112 F4 Batesburg S Carolina
98 D6 Batesland S Dakota
143 E7 Bates,Mt W Australia
143 D7 Bates Ra W Australia
110 E6 Batesville Arkansas
110 L2 Batesville Indiana
111 G7 Batesville Mississippi
109 H7 Batesville Texas
52 D5 Batetskiy U.S.S.R.
8 D5 Bath England
110 F1 Bath Illinois
127 M3 Bath Jamaica
95 S3 Bath Maine
112 L2 Bath N Carolina
127 P4 Bath Nevis W I
122 E7 Bath New Brunswick
95 K4 Bath New York
112 F4 Bath S Carolina
98 H4 Bath S Dakota
86 C3 Batha R Chad
68 G6 Batheay Cambodia
98 J1 Bathgate N Dakota
12 E2 Bathgate Scotland
122 G6 Bathurst New Brunswick
139 J5 Bathurst New S Wales
Bathurst The Gambia see Banjul
141 G2 Bathurst Bay Queensland
114 G3 Bathurst,C N W Terr
136 G4 Bathurst I N Terr Australia
115 K2 Bathurst I N W Terr
114 J4 Bathurst Inlet N W Terr
142 E3 Bathurst Is W Australia
140 B1 Bathurst Island Mission Sta N Terr Aust
85 D7 Batié Upper Volta
70 G6 Batikala,Tg B Sulawesi Indonesia
48 E5 Batina Yugoslavia
78 L7 Batin, Wadi al Iraq
121 S6 Batiscan Quebec
121 T5 Batiscan,L Quebec
77 C3 Batlag-e-Gavkhuni Iran
13 G6 Batley England
85 F1 Batna Algeria
71 F4 Bato,L Luzon Philippines
111 E11 Baton Rouge Louisiana
86 B5 Batouri Cameroon
130 D4 Batovi Brazil
68 H7 Ba Tri Vietnam
42 H3 Batrina Yugoslavia
79 F4 Batroun Lebanon
26 R1 Båtsfjord Norway
80 D3 Bat Shelomo Israel
45 L1 Battáglia Terme Italy
68 F6 Battambang Cambodia
140 D3 Batten R N Terr Aust
36 F1 Battenberg W Germany
146 F12 Batterbee Mts Antarctica
143 C6 Batthewmurnarna mt W Aust
83 L10 Batticaloa Sri Lanka
22 K2 Battice Belgium
69 A8 Batti Malv isld Nicobar Is
45 R8 Battipaglia Italy
9 G6 Battle England
100 J7 Battle Cr Idaho
101 Q1 Battle Cr Montana
98 J8 Battle Cr Nebraska
140 B3 Battle Cr N Terr Aust
94 B4 Battle Creek Michigan
118 H9 Battle Creek Sask
118 J6 Battleford Sask
118 J5 Battlefords Prov.Park,The Sask
100 C4 Battle Ground Washington
115 O7 Battle Harbour Labrador
102 G1 Battle Mt Nevada
118 F6 Battle R Alberta
118 H6 Battle R Sask
98 D1 Battleview N Dakota
48 G4 Battonya Hungary
118 J8 Battrum Sask
70 D4 Batuajau, Bt mt Kalimantan
71 H8 Batuata isld Indonesia
69 H14 Batubetumbang Indonesia
70 D3 Batu Bora mt Sarawak
70 D4 Batubrok, Bt mt Kalimantan
70 G5 Batudaka Indonesia
70 C4 Batuensambang mt Kalimantan
69 E10 Batu Gajah Malaysia
71 H5 Batuhitam,Tg C Sulawesi Indonesia
71 L10 Batuidu Roti Indonesia
70 D4 Batuilangmebang, G mt Kalimantan
70 D4 Batukelau Kalimantan
70 P10 Batukou, Bt mt Bali Indonesia
70 D6 Batulitjin Kalimantan
70 D3 Batu Mabun mt Sarawak
78 H1 Batumi U.S.S.R.
69 D12 Batumundam Sumatra
69 F12 Batu Pahat Malaysia
69 C13 Batu,Pulaupulau isld Indonesia
70 F4 Batuputih Kalimantan
70 K8 Baturadja Sumatra Indonesia
70 N9 Baturetno Java
52 D6 Baturino U.S.S.R.
129 L4 Baturité Brazil
69 H14 Baturusa Indonesia
70 F3 Batu Tg B Kalimantan
70 C5 Batutinggi Kalimantan
80 B5 Bat Yam Israel
18 C4 Batz,I.de France
71 H7 Baubau Sulawesi Indonesia
86 A3 Bauchi Nigeria
18 C5 Baud France
75 L8 Baudh India
128 C2 Baudo, Sa. de mts Colombia
21 I7 Baudres France
19 Q17 Bauduen France
21 E6 Baugé France
19 Q13 Bauges dist France
140 D3 Bauhinia Downs N Terr Aust
141 J6 Bauhinia Downs Queensland
70 G7 Baula Sulawesi Indonesia
123 R2 Bauld,C Nfld
18 D5 Baule,la France
21 B6 Baulon France
41 J3 Bauma Switzerland
9 F1 Baumber England
19 K5 Baume les Dames France
33 T6 Baumgarten E Germany
37 O7 Baumgarten W Germany
36 C4 Baumholder W Germany
71 L10 Baun Timor Indonesia
37 K4 Baunach W Germany
37 K3 Baunach R W Germany
58 F1 Baunt U.S.S.R.
141 L7 Bauple Queensland
128 F6 Baures Bolivia
130 E8 Bauru Brazil
130 D6 Baús Brazil
52 B6 Bauska U.S.S.R.
31 H4 Bautzen E Germany
109 P1 Bauxite Arkansas
21 I8 Bauzanne R France
126 E10 Bavano L. Panama
107 N3 Bavaria Kansas
22 F3 Bavay France
89 C9 Baviaanskloofberge mts S Africa
124 E2 Bavispe Mexico
9 H2 Bawdeswell England
9 H3 Bawdsey England
70 O8 Bawean isld Java
32 F7 Bawinkel W Germany
84 H4 Bawîti Egypt
120 D3 Bawk Ontario
85 D6 Bawku Ghana
68 C3 Bawlake Burma
118 E6 Bawlf Alberta
68 A2 Bawli Bazar Burma
68 B4 Bawmi Burma
13 G6 Bawtry England
68 F1 Ba Xat Vietnam
58 G4 Ba Xian China
67 B2 Ba Xian China
66 D4 Baxkorgan China
112 E6 Baxley Georgia
99 N8 Baxter Iowa
99 M3 Baxter Minnesota
101 S10 Baxter Mt Colorado
110 B4 Baxter Springs Kansas
122 C7 Baxter State Park Maine
80 D3 Bayada Israel
126 F4 Bayamo Cuba
127 L5 Bayamón Puerto Rico
59 J2 Bayan China
58 E2 Bayan Mongolia
58 E2 Bayanchandman Mongolia
56 G4 Bayanday U.S.S.R.
Bayan Gol see Dengkou
58 C5 Bayan Har Shan China
58 D2 Bayanhongor Mongolia
65 E1 Bayan Hot China
65 A3 Bayan Hure China
Bayan Huxu see Horqin Youyi Zhongqi
58 E2 Bayanmönh Mongolia
65 C3 Bayan Nur Sum China
58 E3 Bayan Obo China
58 C3 Bayan-Öndör Mongolia
Bayan Qagan see Qahar Youyi Houqi
65 A1 Bayan Qagan China
65 E2 Bayan Qagan China
58 E2 Bayantsogt Mongolia
113 F7 Bayard Florida
99 M8 Bayard Iowa
98 C8 Bayard Nebraska
94 H7 Bayard W Virginia
19 Q15 Bayard, Col pass France
47 L6 Bayat Turkey
71 F6 Bayawan Negros Philippines
71 G5 Baybay Leyte Philippines
112 L2 Bayboro N Carolina
123 U6 Bay Bulls Nfld
78 H1 Bayburt Turkey
69 H8 Bay Canh, Hon isld Vietnam
94 D3 Bay City Michigan
100 B4 Bay City Oregon
109 M7 Bay City Texas
99 O5 Bay City Wisconsin
84 G3 Bayda,Al Libya
50 F2 Baydaratskaya Guba gulf U.S.S.R.
123 U5 Bay de Verde Nfld
123 R6 Bay du Nord Nfld
57 E3 Baydzhansay U.S.S.R.
37 P5 Bayer-Eisenstein W Germany
41 O2 Bayerische Alpen mt W Germany
37 K5 Bayern land W Germany
20 D3 Bayeux France
120 J9 Bayfield Ontario
99 Q3 Bayfield Wisconsin
123 O2 Bayfield I Quebec
122 E5 Bayfield Mtn Quebec
57 D3 Baygakum U.S.S.R.
55 D4 Baygara U.S.S.R.
98 A4 Bay Horse Montana
47 J6 Bayindir Turkey
55 D3 Baykalovo U.S.S.R.
56 G4 Baykal,Ozero L U.S.S.R.
56 G4 Baykal'skiy Khrebet mts U.S.S.R.
57 C2 Bay-Khozha U.S.S.R.
55 C3 Baykibashevo U.S.S.R.
56 E1 Baykit U.S.S.R.
57 D1 Baykonyr U.S.S.R.
71 E3 Bay, Laguna de Luzon Philippines
123 R6 Bay l'Argent Nfld
140 E3 Bayley Pt Queensland
55 C4 Baymak U.S.S.R.
111 J11 Bay Minette Alabama
9 E4 Baynard's Green England
71 E2 Bayombong Luzon Philippines
19 K4 Bayon France
16 B2 Bayona Spain
18 E9 Bayonne France
71 E5 Bayo Pt Panay Philippines
111 E7 Bayou Bartholomew R Arkansas
111 D9 Bayou D'Arbonne Louisiana
110 E6 Bayou de View R Arkansas
111 H11 Bayou La Batre Alabama
111 F12 Bayou Lafourche R Louisiana
111 E9 Bayou Macon R Louisiana
111 E7 Bayou Meto R Arkansas
111 F9 Bayou Pierre R Mississippi
128 B5 Bayovar Peru
113 E9 Bayport Florida
94 D3 Bay Port Michigan
99 O5 Bayport Minnesota
117 K10 Bay Pt Br Col
71 D5 Bay Pt Philippines
47 H5 Bayramiç Turkey
37 M4 Bayreuth W Germany
37 N5 Bayrischer Wald mts W Germany
123 T6 Bay Roberts Nfld
58 F1 Baysa U.S.S.R.
111 G11 Bay St.Louis Mississippi
113 F11 Bayshore Florida
95 O6 Bay Shore Long I, N Y
112 E1 Bays Mt Tennessee
111 G10 Bay Springs Mississippi
Baytag Bogdo see Baytik Shan
9 G3 Baythorn End England
66 E2 Baytik Shan mt ra China/Mongolia
109 N6 Baytown Texas
117 P12 Bayview Idaho
145 F3 Bay View New Zealand
17 F7 Baza Spain
48 K1 Bazaliya U.S.S.R.
22 G5 Bazancourt France
107 O3 Bazar Kansas
87 G10 Bazaruto, I Mozambique
18 E8 Bazas France
17 F7 Baza,Sierra de Spain
22 J4 Bazeilles France
67 B1 Bazhong China
48 G6 Baziaş Romania
18 G9 Baziége France
121 Q5 Bazin R Quebec
107 L3 Bazine Kansas
77 G5 Bazmān, Kūh-e mt Iran
77 F6 Bazman Iran
20 G5 Bazoche-Gouet,la France
22 F5 Bazoches France
20 E4 Bazoches-au-Houlme France
20 K5 Bazoches-les-Gallerandes France
20 F4 Bazoches-sur-Hoëne France
20 F5 Bazoge,la France
21 C8 Bazoges-en-Paillers France
20 D5 Bazougers France
20 B5 Bazouges la Perouse France
45 K3 Bazzano Italy
79 F4 Bcharre Lebanon
112 E6 Beach Georgia
98 C3 Beach N Dakota
95 N7 Beach Haven New Jersey
138 E6 Beachport S Australia
95 N7 Beachwood New Jersey
9 G6 Beachy Head England
95 O5 Beacon New York
143 C9 Beacon W Australia
113 B8 Beacon Hill Florida
118 H4 Beacon Hill Sask
9 F4 Beaconsfield England
139 H8 Beaconsfield Tasmania
13 G2 Beadnell England
142 E3 Beagle Bank W Australia
142 E3 Beagle Bay W Australia
133 D8 Beagle, Canal str Chile/Arg
140 A1 Beagle G N Terr Aust
143 A8 Beagle I W Australia
87 H10 Bealanana Madagascar
117 L11 Beale,C Br Col
94 K8 Bealeton Virginia
141 F7 Beal Ra Queensland
108 F3 Beals Cr Texas
118 C1 Beaman Manitoba
8 D6 Beaminster England
100 J4 Bear Idaho
101 O7 Bear R Idaho etc
111 J7 Bear Cr Alabama
107 J4 Bear Cr Kansas
99 S5 Bear Cr Wisconsin
98 B8 Bear Cr Wyoming
101 Q4 Bearcreek Montana
95 M5 Bear Cr.Res Pennsylvania
111 D8 Bearden Arkansas
120 C3 Beardmore Ontario
146 G7 Beardmore Gl Antarctica
139 J3 Beardmore Res. Queensland
103 M8 Beardsley Arizona
107 J2 Beardsley Kansas
110 F1 Beardstown Illinois
123 K4 Bear Head Anticosti I, Quebec
118 J7 Bear Hills,The Sask
90 H1 Bear I Arctic Oc
14 B5 Bear I Irish Rep
115 L7 Bear I N W Terr
120 K6 Bear Island Ontario
101 O7 Bear L Idaho/Utah
119 V3 Bear L Manitoba
117 K7 Bear Lake Br Col
94 A2 Bear Lake Michigan
98 B5 Bear Lodge Mts Wyoming
101 M3 Bearmouth Montana
121 M4 Béarn Quebec
18 E9 Béarn prov France
101 Q1 Bear Paw Mt Montana
119 N4 Bear R Sask
101 N8 Bear R.City Utah
12 D2 Bearsden Scotland
101 S9 Bears Ears Pk Colorado
115 K7 Bearskin L Ontario
74 F3 Beas R India
18 D9 Beasain Spain
17 F6 Beas de Segura Spain
127 J6 Beata, I Dom Rep
40 G4 Beatenberg Switzerland
117 P10 Beaton Br Col
111 J10 Beatrice Alabama
98 K9 Beatrice Nebraska
6 H4 Beatrice oil rig North Sea
140 D2 Beatrice,C Aust
142 F3 Beatrice,Mt W Australia
107 O2 Beattie Kansas
15 E5 Beattock Scotland
117 N7 Beatton River Br Col
102 H5 Beatty Nevada
100 D7 Beatty Oregon
119 N6 Beatty Sask
94 D9 Beattyville Kentucky
115 M8 Beattyville Quebec
19 N17 Beaucaire France
20 J2 Beaucamps-le-Vieux France
121 L3 Beaucanton Quebec
122 B7 Beauceville Quebec
20 C4 Beauchamps France
133 F8 Beauchene Is Falkland Is
121 M6 Beauchêne, Lac Quebec
141 L8 Beaudesert Queensland
121 L4 Beaudry Quebec
20 F5 Beaufay France
40 E6 Beaufort France
22 L4 Beaufort Luxembourg
112 L3 Beaufort N Carolina
70 D2 Beaufort Sabah
112 G5 Beaufort S Carolina
21 E7 Beaufort-en-Vallée France
146 J6 Beaufort I Antarctica
112 L3 Beaufort Inlet N Carolina
116 R2 Beaufort Lag Alaska
147 K2 Beaufort Sea Arctic Oc
89 B9 Beaufort West S Africa
21 I6 Beaugency France
121 R7 Beauharnois Quebec
121 Q7 Beauharnois Power Canal Quebec
19 N12 Beaujeu France
19 Q16 Beaujeu France
18 H6 Beaujolais, Mts du France
95 S6 Beau L Maine/New Brunswick
9 E6 Beaulieu England
21 H7 Beaulieu-lès-Loches France
15 D3 Beauly Scotland
15 D3 Beauly, R Scotland
8 B1 Beaumaris Wales
22 D3 Beaumetz-les-Loges France
22 G3 Beaumont Belgium
102 H8 Beaumont California
107 O4 Beaumont Kansas
111 H10 Beaumont Mississippi
144 B6 Beaumont New Zealand
123 R4 Beaumont Nfld
111 B11 Beaumont Texas
146 H7 Beaumont B Antarctica
18 F9 Beaumont de Lomogne France
18 F8 Beaumont de Périgord France
22 J4 Beaumont-en-Argonne France
20 F3 Beaumont-en-Auge France
22 E3 Beaumont-en-Cambrésis France
20 B2 Beaumont-Hague France
21 G6 Beaumont la-Ronce France
20 G3 Beaumont-le-Roger France
20 G5 Beaumont-les-Autels France
20 K3 Beaumont-sur-Oise France
20 F5 Beaumont-sur-Sarthe France
19 J5 Beaune France
18 G4 Beaune la Rolande France
21 D7 Beaupréau France
20 K1 Beauquesne France
22 H3 Beauraing Belgium
40 B7 Beaurepaire d'Isère France
19 P15 Beaurières France
22 F5 Beaurieux France
118 E1 Beausejour Manitoba
21 E9 Beaussais France
139 H6 Beauty,Mt Victoria
20 K3 Beauvais France
118 C9 Beauvais Lake Prov. Park Alberta
21 E10 Beauvais sur Matha France
20 K1 Beauval France
118 K3 Beauval Sask
118 F5 Beauvallon Alberta
21 B8 Beauvoir-sur-Mer France
116 O3 Beaver Alaska
107 M3 Beaver Kansas
108 D7 Beaver Oklahoma
100 B4 Beaver Oregon
94 G6 Beaver Pennsylvania
103 M3 Beaver Utah
114 H7 Beaver R Alberta
98 F3 Beaver R N Dakota
103 L3 Beaver R Utah
117 L5 Beaver R Yukon Terr/Br Col
122 J9 Beaverbank Nova Scotia
122 G6 Beaver Brook New Brunswick
98 G9 Beaver City Nebraska
116 O4 Beaver Cr Alaska
106 G2 Beaver Cr Colorado
101 N5 Beaver Cr Idaho
107 J2 Beaver Cr Kansas
110 D5 Beaver Cr Missouri
98 B3 Beaver Cr Montana
98 F9 Beaver Cr Nebraska
98 B6 Beaver Cr Wyoming
114 E5 Beaver Creek Yukon Terr
117 C4 Beaver Creek Yukon Terr
98 J9 Beaver Crossing Nebraska
110 K4 Beaver Dam Kentucky
99 S6 Beaver Dam Wisconsin
117 O11 Beaverdell Falls Br Col
94 G6 Beaver Falls Pennsylvania
101 N4 Beaverhead R Montana
101 M4 Beaverhead Ra Idaho/Montana
118 E5 Beaverhill L Alberta
99 V4 Beaver I Michigan
123 N2 Beaver Island L Quebec
99 U3 Beaver L Michigan
117 N9 Beaver Lake Br Col
117 O8 Beaverlodge Alberta
117 P10 Beavermouth Br Col
116 J5 Beaver Mts Alaska
118 F4 Beaver R Alberta
118 H4 Beaver R Sask
118 K4 Beaver R Sask
110 C5 Beaver Res Arkansas
95 M3 Beaver R.Flow New York
94 C3 Beaverton Michigan
121 L8 Beaverton Ontario
100 C4 Beaverton Oregon
95 K6 Beavertown Pennsylvania
99 T9 Beaverville Illinois
74 F5 Beawar India
133 D4 Beazley Argentina
131 C4 Bebedero, Salina Argentina
129 J8 Bebedouro Brazil
36 G6 Bebenhausen W Germany
129 L4 Beberibe Brazil
36 H2 Bebra W Germany
47 H2 Bebrovo Bulgaria
9 H3 Beccles England
48 F5 Bečej Yugoslavia
48 K5 Beceni Romania
16 C2 Becerreá Spain
126 C7 Becerro,Cayos reefs Caribbean
85 D2 Béchar Algeria
116 J8 Becharof L Alaska
85 D7 Bechem Ghana
144 C5 Beche, Mt de la New Zealand
20 B5 Bécherel France
47 G1 Bechet Romania
116 F9 Bechevin B Alaska
37 K5 Bechhofen W Germany
Bechuanaland Prot see Botswana
31 H6 Bechyně Czechoslovakia
32 M7 Beckedorf W Germany
13 E4 Beckfoot England
9 E5 Beckhampton England
36 B5 Beckingen W Germany
8 D5 Beckington England
94 F9 Beckley W Virginia
144 B6 Becks New Zealand
32 H9 Beckum W Germany
109 N3 Beckville Texas
102 D2 Beckwourth California
48 J3 Beclean Romania
21 D7 Bécon France
19 O16 Béconne France
9 G4 Becontree England
37 O3 Bečov nad Teplou Czechoslovakia
108 F2 Becton Texas
31 K6 Bečva R Czechoslovakia
84 F4 Beda Libya
13 G5 Bedale England
18 H9 Bédarieux France
19 N16 Bedarrides France
36 B1 Bedburg W Germany
8 B1 Beddgelert Wales
9 G6 Beddingham England
119 R9 Bede Manitoba
20 B5 Bédée France
28 E4 Beder Denmark
32 J5 Bederkesa W Germany
55 C3 Bedeyeva Polyana U.S.S.R.
9 F3 Bedford England
110 K3 Bedford Indiana
99 M9 Bedford Iowa
94 B8 Bedford Kentucky
95 Q4 Bedford New Hampshire
122 J9 Bedford Nova Scotia
94 J6 Bedford Pennsylvania
121 S7 Bedford Quebec
94 H9 Bedford Virginia
101 P7 Bedford Wyoming
141 H3 Bedford C Queensland
142 F3 Bedford Downs W Australia
143 D10 Bedford Harb W Australia
127 P5 Bedford Pt Grenada
143 F7 Bedford Ra W Australia
9 F3 Bedfordshire co England
74 D7 Bedi India
69 H14 Bedinggong Indonesia
13 G3 Bedlington England
19 O16 Bédoin France
41 O5 Bedollo Italy
140 E6 Bedourie Queensland
8 A7 Bedruthan Steps England
28 C6 Bedsted Denmark
98 J8 Bee Nebraska
110 E6 Beebe Arkansas
98 G4 Beebe S Dakota
141 H7 Beechal R Queensland
94 K5 Beech Cr Pennsylvania
110 J4 Beech Creek Kentucky
100 F5 Beech Creek Oregon
99 T8 Beecher Illinois
110 H2 Beecher City Illinois
116 N1 Beechey Point Alaska
110 L4 Beech Fork R Kentucky
110 K2 Beech Grove Indiana
99 S3 Beechwood Michigan
139 H6 Beechworth Victoria
118 K8 Beechy Sask
32 M7 Beedenbostel W Germany
100 C9 Beegum California
25 E5 Beek Gelderland Netherlands
25 E4 Beekbergen Netherlands
111 E9 Beekman Louisiana
107 K3 Beeler Kansas
33 R8 Beelitz E Germany
98 K8 Beemer Nebraska
33 O8 Beendorf E Germany
141 L8 Beenleigh Queensland
37 K2 Beerberg mt E Germany
33 S8 Beeren E Germany
36 F4 Beerfelden W Germany
113 E10 Bee Ridge Florida
143 C8 Beeringgnurding, Mt W Aust
22 F2 Beerlegem Belgium
79 F8 Beer Menuha Israel
22 E1 Beernem Belgium
79 E9 Beer Ora Israel
80 C8 Be'er Pehar Israel
25 E5 Beers Netherlands
80 C8 Beersheba Israel
25 D6 Beerze R Netherlands
31 H3 Beeskow E Germany
87 E11 Beestekraal S Africa
9 E2 Beeston England
140 C3 Beetaloo N Terr Aust
146 G13 Beethoven Pen Antarctica
25 F2 Beetsterzwaag Netherlands
33 O7 Beetzendorf E Germany
33 R8 Beetz-see L E Germany
109 K7 Beeville Texas
86 D5 Befale Zaïre
87 H11 Befandriana Madagascar
86 D5 Befori Zaïre
18 C4 Begard France
8 B4 Begelly Wales
127 P4 Beggars Pt Antigua W I
107 O6 Beggs Oklahoma
51 L1 Begicheva, Ostrov isld U.S.S.R.
27 D11 Begna R Norway
57 E4 Begovat U.S.S.R.
28 E4 Begtrup Vig B Denmark
19 N15 Begude-de-Mazenc, la France
77 B4 Behbedān Iran
33 N5 Behlendorf W Germany
117 H8 Behm Can Alaska
140 A3 Behn, Mt N Terr Aust
22 L3 Beho Belgium
33 R4 Behren-Lübchin E Germany
37 L4 Behringersmühle W Germany
77 C1 Behshahr Iran
59 J2 Bei'an China
26 G4 Beiarn Norway
67 B2 Beibei China
86 F4 Beica Ethiopia
67 A1 Beichuan China
65 A6 Beichuan He R China
65 D5 Beidaihehaibin China
32 M10 Beienrode W Germany
37 O2 Beierfeld E Germany
68 J2 Beihai China
36 G6 Beihingen W Germany
67 D4 Bei Jiang R China
63 Beijing conurbation China
85 A5 Beila Mauritania
25 G3 Beilen Netherlands
68 J3 Beili China
68 K1 Beiliu China
37 L5 Beilngries W Germany
36 G5 Beilstein Baden-Württemberg W Germany
36 E2 Beilstein Hessen W Germany
36 C3 Beilstein Rheinland-Pfalz W Germany
86 H3 Beilul Ethiopia
67 B6 Beilun Ai pass China
36 H7 Beimerstetten W Germany
22 G5 Beine France
36 E6 Beinheim France
15 E4 Beinn a' Ghlo mt Scotland
40 H3 Beinwil Switzerland
67 B4 Beipan Jiang R China
65 E4 Beipiao China
Beira see Sofala
16 B4 Beira Alta prov Portugal
16 B5 Beira Baixa prov Portugal
16 B4 Beira Litoral prov Portugal
79 F5 Beirut Lebanon
118 D7 Beiseker Alberta
65 F2 Beitaolaizhao China
87 E10 Beitbridge Zimbabwe
79 F5 Beit ed Dīne Lebanon
15 D5 Beith Scotland
80 D6 Beit Haninā Jordan
80 F4 Beit Idis Jordan
80 D7 Beit Jala Jordan
80 D7 Beit Kahil Jordan
80 A7 Beit Lahiya Israel
80 D7 Beit Lahm Jordan
80 G3 Beit Ras Jordan
80 D7 Beit Sahur Jordan
26 E7 Beitstad Norway
26 E8 Beitstadfjord inlet Norway
48 G4 Beius Romania
67 G2 Beiyandang Shan mt China
65 D6 Beizhen China
65 E4 Beizhen China
16 B6 Beja Portugal
43 C12 Beja Tunisia
143 E6 Bejah Hill W Australia
85 E1 Bejaia Algeria
16 D4 Béjar Spain
77 F2 Bejestān Iran
143 B9 Bejoording W Australia
70 L9 Bekasi Java
48 G4 Békés Hungary
48 F4 Békés co Hungary
48 G4 Békéscsaba Hungary
85 D7 Bekwai Ghana
Bela see Villach
74 B5 Bela Pakistan

86 B2 **Bélabérim** Niger
86 B4 **Bélabo** Cameroon
48 G6 **Bela Crkva** Yugoslavia
56 B5 **Bel'Agach** U.S.S.R.
95 L7 **Bel Air** Maryland
70 D4 **Belajan** *R* Kalimantan
70 D4 **Belajan, G** *mt* Kalimantan
16 D6 **Belalcázar** Spain
74 H9 **Belampalli** India
37 O4 **Bělá nad Radbuzou** Czechoslovakia
71 J4 **Belang** Sulawesi Indonesia
119 U5 **Bélanger Pt** Manitoba
119 U5 **Bélanger R** Manitoba
69 C11 **Belangpidie** Sumatra
46 E1 **Bela Palanka** Yugoslavia
139 H4 **Belaraboon** New S Wales
87 C8 **Bela Vista** Angola
129 G8 **Bela Vista** Brazil
133 F2 **Bela Vista** Brazil
87 F11 **Bela Vista** Mozambique
130 C8 **Bela Vista** Paraguay
130 E5 **Bela Vista de Goiás** Brazil
69 D11 **Belawan** Sumatra
54 E4 **Belaya-Berezka** U.S.S.R.
54 M8 **Belaya-Kalitva** U.S.S.R.
48 N1 **Belaya Tserkov** U.S.S.R.
44 D2 **Belbo** *R* Italy
48 L3 **Belceşti** Romania
115 K2 **Belcher Chan** N W Terr
115 M6 **Belcher, Les Iles** N W Terr
17 G3 **Belchite** Spain
14 D2 **Belcoo** N Ireland
121 N4 **Belcourt** Quebec
102 C1 **Belden** California
98 D1 **Belden** N Dakota
94 B3 **Belding** Michigan
52 D5 **Belebelka** U.S.S.R.
55 B4 **Belebey** U.S.S.R.
129 J4 **Belém** Brazil
129 L5 **Belém de São Francisco** Brazil
128 C3 **Belén** Colombia
108 A1 **Belen** New Mexico
129 G8 **Belén** Paraguay
131 G3 **Belén,Cuchilla de** *mt* Uruguay
124 H7 **Belén del Refugio** Mexico
47 G1 **Belene** Bulgaria
137 N5 **Belep,Îles** New Caledonia
16 B2 **Belesar, Embalse de** *res* Spain
86 J5 **Belet Uen** Somalia
57 D2 **Beleutty** *R* U.S.S.R.
54 H3 **Belev** U.S.S.R.
86 C5 **Bélézé** Cent Afr Republic
100 C2 **Belfair** Washington
95 S2 **Belfast** Maine
144 B4 **Belfast** New Zealand
14 F2 **Belfast** N Ireland
122 K7 **Belfast** Pr Edward I
25 F6 **Belfeld** Netherlands
98 C3 **Belfield** N Dakota
86 F3 **Belfodio** Ethiopia
13 G2 **Belford** England
19 K5 **Belfort** France
40 E2 **Belfort, Terr De** France
101 Q4 **Belfry** Montana
76 B3 **Belgaum** India
19 P18 **Belgentier** France
33 S10 **Belgern** E Germany
146 B7 **Belgicafjella** Antarctica
22 E2 **Belgium**
99 T6 **Belgium** Wisconsin
54 H6 **Belgorod** U.S.S.R.
48 N4 **Belgorod Dnestrovskiy** U.S.S.R.
Belgrade *see* **Beograd**
98 H8 **Belgrade** Nebraska
133 F5 **Belgrano** Argentina
131 E7 **Belgrano,Pto** Argentina
145 D4 **Belgrove** New Zealand
112 L2 **Belhaven** N Carolina
84 F4 **Bel Hedam** Libya
85 F2 **Belhirane** Algeria
20 H5 **Belhomert** France
43 E11 **Belice** *R* Sicily
78 G4 **Belikh** *R* Syria
47 H1 **Beli Lom** *R* Bulgaria
48 E5 **Beli Manastir** Yugoslavia
70 K8 **Belimbing** Indonesia
18 E8 **Belin** France
94 H7 **Belington** W Virginia
69 G13 **Belinyu** Indonesia
69 J14 **Belitung** *isld* Indonesia
125 P9 **Belize** Belize
125 P9 **Belize** Cent America
48 G6 **Beljanića** *mt* Yugoslavia
143 C9 **Belka** W Australia
99 O9 **Belknap** Iowa
100 K2 **Belknap** Montana
147 P8 **Bel'kovskiy Os** *isld* U.S.S.R.
113 E8 **Bell** Florida
141 K7 **Bell** Queensland
121 N3 **Bell** *R* Quebec
114 G7 **Bella Bella** Br Col
18 F6 **Bellac** France
133 F4 **Bellaco** Uruguay
117 K9 **Bella Coola** Br Col
107 M2 **Bellaire** Kansas
94 B2 **Bellaire** Michigan
94 G6 **Bellaire** Ohio
141 G7 **Bellalie** Queensland
42 C2 **Bellano** Italy
76 C3 **Bellary** India
40 G5 **Bella Tola** *mt* Switzerland
131 F2 **Bella Vista** Argentina
128 C4 **Bellavista** Loreto Peru
128 C5 **Bellavista** San Martin Peru
139 J8 **Bell B** Tasmania
145 E3 **Bell Block** New Zealand
141 K5 **Bell Cay** *isld* Gt Barrier Reef Aust
110 E3 **Belle** Missouri
123 R6 **Belle B** Nfld
33 P9 **Belleben** E Germany
94 D6 **Belle Center** Ohio
40 E7 **Bellecôte** *mt* France
19 P14 **Belledonne, Pic de** *mt* France
94 D6 **Bellefontaine** Ohio
94 K6 **Bellefonte** Pennsylvania
98 C5 **Belle Fourche** S Dakota
98 A5 **Belle Fourche** *R* Wyoming
18 G5 **Bellegarde** France
19 P12 **Bellegarde** France
21 J10 **Bellegarde en-Marche** France
113 G11 **Belle Glade** Florida
40 E3 **Belleherbe** France
18 C5 **Belle Ile** *isld* France
115 O7 **Belle Isle** Nfld
18 C4 **Belle Isle en Terre** France
123 R2 **Belle Isle Landing** Belle I, Nfld
123 Q2 **Belle Isle,Strait of** Labrador/Nfld
20 G5 **Bellême** France
110 K5 **Belle Meade** Tennessee
103 N6 **Bellemont** Arizona
20 H2 **Bellencombre** France
141 H3 **Bellenden Ker Ra** Queensland
22 E4 **Bellenglise** France
123 R6 **Belleoram** Nfld
99 O8 **Belle Plaine** Iowa
107 N4 **Belle Plaine** Kansas
99 N5 **Belle Plaine** Minnesota
119 M8 **Belle Plaine** Sask
110 H3 **Belle Rive** Illinois
139 H9 **Bellerive** Tasmania
121 T4 **Belle-Rivière,Lac de la** Quebec
121 M5 **Belleterre** Quebec
94 F7 **Belle Valley** Ohio
40 E5 **Bellevaux** France
40 B4 **Bellevesvre** France
113 E8 **Belleview** Florida
110 G3 **Belleville** Illinois
107 N2 **Belleville** Kansas
95 L3 **Belleville** New York
115 M9 **Belleville** Ontario
94 K6 **Belleville** Pennsylvania
99 R7 **Belleville** Wisconsin
94 F7 **Belleville** W Virginia
21 C8 **Belleville-sur-Vie** France
118 C9 **Bellevue** Alberta
101 L6 **Bellevue** Idaho
99 Q7 **Bellevue** Iowa
94 B4 **Bellevue** Michigan
94 E5 **Bellevue** Ohio
141 G3 **Bellevue** Queensland
109 J2 **Bellevue** Texas
19 P13 **Belley** France
110 H1 **Bellflower** Illinois
110 E2 **Bellflower** Missouri
36 E5 **Bellheim** W Germany
123 T6 **Bell I** Newfoundland
115 O7 **Bell I** Nfld
22 E4 **Bellicourt** France
21 D7 **Belligne** France
13 F3 **Bellingham** England
98 K4 **Bellingham** Minnesota
114 G8 **Bellingham** Washington
146 G12 **Bellingshausen Sea** Antarctica
25 H2 **Bellingwolde** Netherlands
41 K5 **Bellinzona** Switzerland
118 E4 **Bellis** Alberta
36 F2 **Bellnhausen** W Germany
12 C2 **Bellochantuy** Scotland
137 M6 **Bellona Plateau** Coral Sea
102 C3 **Bellota** California
95 P3 **Bellows Falls** Vermont
20 K3 **Belloy** France
115 L5 **Bell Pen** N W Terr
138 C4 **Bell,Pt** S Australia
106 F6 **Bell Ranch** New Mexico
13 F1 **Bell Rock** Scotland
110 G6 **Bells** Tennessee
109 L2 **Bells** Texas
119 Q6 **Bellsite** Manitoba
42 E2 **Belluno** Italy
131 D4 **Bell Ville** Argentina
94 E6 **Bellville** Ohio
109 L6 **Bellville** Texas
106 E1 **Bellvue** Colorado
111 C10 **Bellwood** Louisiana
98 J8 **Bellwood** Nebraska
94 J6 **Bellwood** Pennsylvania
118 D9 **Belly R** Alberta
55 F2 **Belly Yar** U.S.S.R.
95 N6 **Belmar** New Jersey
16 D6 **Bélmez** Spain
56 D1 **Bel'minskiye Porogi** *falls* U.S.S.R.
99 N7 **Belmond** Iowa
119 S9 **Belmont** Manitoba
112 F2 **Belmont** N Carolina
102 H3 **Belmont** Nevada
95 Q3 **Belmont** New Hampshire
94 K4 **Belmont** New York
122 J8 **Belmont** Nova Scotia
120 J10 **Belmont** Ontario
109 K6 **Belmont** Texas
94 K8 **Belmont** Virginia
99 Q7 **Belmont** Wisconsin
142 B1 **Belmont** *dist* Perth, W Aust
129 L7 **Belmonte** Brazil
16 C4 **Belmonte** Portugal
17 F5 **Belmonte** Spain
125 P9 **Belmopan** Belize
141 F4 **Belmore** *R* Queensland
14 A2 **Belmullet** Irish Rep
130 H4 **Belo Campo** Brazil
51 M3 **Belogorsk** U.S.S.R.
55 E1 **Belogorye** U.S.S.R.
46 F1 **Belogradchik** Bulgaria
87 G13 **Beloha** Madagascar
129 K7 **Belo Horizonte** Brazil
147 J16 **Belohorsk** U.S.S.R.
107 M2 **Beloit** Kansas
99 R7 **Beloit** Wisconsin
130 H10 **Belo Jardim** Brazil
129 H4 **Belo Monte** Brazil
52 D3 **Belomorsk** U.S.S.R.
54 L2 **Beloomut** U.S.S.R.
54 F5 **Belopol'ye** U.S.S.R.
16 E2 **Belorado** Spain
55 C4 **Beloretsk** U.S.S.R.
54 B3 **Belorussiya** *rep* U.S.S.R.
114 G4 **Belot,L** N W Terr
87 G11 **Belo-Tsiribihina** Madagascar
56 B5 **Belousovka** U.S.S.R.
56 C4 **Belovo** U.S.S.R.
52 E2 **Beloye More** U.S.S.R.
47 G2 **Belozem** Bulgaria
55 C4 **Belozerka** U.S.S.R.
55 E3 **Belozerskoye** U.S.S.R.
9 E1 **Belper** England
107 L4 **Belpre** Kansas
13 G3 **Belsay** England
32 L7 **Belsen** W Germany
101 P2 **Belt** Montana
138 E4 **Beltana** S Australia
138 D3 **Belt B** S Australia
103 H4 **Belted Ra** Nevada
129 G4 **Belterre** Brazil
110 B3 **Belton** Missouri
101 M1 **Belton** Montana
138 E4 **Belton** S Australia
112 E3 **Belton** S Carolina
109 K4 **Belton** Texas
109 K4 **Belton Res** Texas
131 E2 **Beltrán,L** Argentina
48 L3 **Bel'tsy** U.S.S.R.
14 D2 **Belturbet** Irish Rep
116 M6 **Beluga L** Alaska
70 C4 **Belui, Bt** *mt* Kalimantan
56 C6 **Belukha,Gora** *mt* U.S.S.R.
71 C8 **Beluran** Sabah
31 L6 **Beluša** Czechoslovakia
43 G9 **Belvedere Marittimo** Italy
45 O4 **Belvedere Ostrense** Italy
18 F8 **Belvès** France
99 S7 **Belvidere** Illinois
107 L4 **Belvidere** Kansas
112 L1 **Belvidere** N Carolina
98 J9 **Belvidere** Nebraska
95 M6 **Belvidere** New Jersey
98 E6 **Belvidere** S Dakota
16 D5 **Belvis de la Jara** Spain
80 F3 **Belvoir** Israel
141 H5 **Belyando** *R* Queensland
48 N4 **Belyayevka** U.S.S.R.
54 F3 **Belye Berega** U.S.S.R.
54 A3 **Belynichi** U.S.S.R.
52 D6 **Belyy** U.S.S.R.
54 J6 **Belyy Kolodez'** U.S.S.R.
50 F1 **Belyy, Ostrov** *isld* U.S.S.R.
31 O5 **Bełżec** Poland
33 R8 **Belzig** E Germany
111 F8 **Belzoni** Mississippi
31 N4 **Bełżyce** Poland
87 B7 **Bembe** Angola
16 D6 **Bembézar** *R* Spain
89 F2 **Bembezi** *R* Zimbabwe
16 C2 **Bembibre** Spain
9 E6 **Bembridge** England
99 M2 **Bemidji** Minnesota
110 H6 **Bemis** Tennessee
36 G6 **Bempflingen** W Germany
13 H5 **Bempton** England
94 H4 **Bemus Point** New York
88 E6 **Bena** Tanzania
17 H2 **Benabarre** Spain
86 D6 **Bena Dibele** Zaïre
138 F4 **Benagerie** S Australia
17 G5 **Benaguacil** Spain
21 H9 **Benaixe** *R* France
69 F14 **Benakat** Sumatra
15 D4 **Ben Alder** *mt* Scotland
118 C6 **Benalto** Alberta
Benares *see* **Varanasi**
16 D2 **Benarides** Spain
19 Q18 **Bénat,C** France
15 C3 **Ben Attow** *mt* Scotland
16 B6 **Benavente** Portugal
16 D2 **Benavides** Spain
109 J8 **Benavides** Texas
14 E1 **Benbane Hd** N Ireland
15 A3 **Benbecula** *isld* Scotland
109 L9 **Benbrook** Texas
109 K3 **Benbrook Res** Texas
14 C2 **Benbulbin** *mt* Irish Rep
14 B3 **Benbury** *mt* Irish Rep
68 H7 **Ben Cat** Vietnam
Bencheng *see* **Luannan**
144 B7 **Bench I** New Zealand
101 P2 **Benchland** Montana
109 L5 **Benchley** Texas
15 C4 **Ben Cruachan** *mt* Scotland
143 C9 **Bencubbin** W Australia
114 G9 **Bend** Oregon
109 J4 **Bend** Texas
15 D3 **Ben Dearg** *mt* Scotland
116 F4 **Bendeleben Mts** Alaska
88 C5 **Bende Pimbwe** Tanzania
119 P8 **Bender** Sask
86 B2 **Bender Beila** Somalia
86 A1 **Bender Cassim** Somalia
86 B1 **Bender Merhagno** Somalia
48 M4 **Bendery** U.S.S.R.
86 A1 **Bender Ziada** Somalia
138 E4 **Bendieuta** *R* S Australia
139 G6 **Bendigo** Victoria
32 K7 **Bendingbostel** W Germany
36 D3 **Bendorf** W Germany
44 C2 **Bene** Italy
80 C5 **Bene'Atarot** Israel
80 C5 **Bene Beraq** Israel
45 L4 **Benedetto Alpe di S** *mt* Italy
107 P4 **Benedict** Kansas
95 L8 **Benedict** Maryland
98 E2 **Benedict** N Dakota
98 J8 **Benedict** Nebraska
41 O2 **Benediktenwand** *mt* W Germany
129 K5 **Beneditinos** Brazil
87 H12 **Benenitra** Madagascar
31 H6 **Benešov** Czechoslovakia
19 K4 **Bénéstroff** France
18 G6 **Bénévent L'Abbaye** France
43 F7 **Benevento** Italy
112 C6 **Benevolence** Georgia
94 J5 **Benezett** Pennsylvania
80 C5 **Bene Ẕiyyon** Israel
19 L4 **Benfeld** France
75 N9 **Bengal, Bay of** S Asia
70 E3 **Bengara** Kalimantan
85 G2 **Ben Gardane** Tunisia
58 G5 **Bengbu** China
84 F3 **Benghazi** Libya
65 D7 **Beng He** *R* China
69 F12 **Bengkalis** Sumatra
69 J12 **Bengkayang** Indonesia
119 M9 **Bengough** Sask
27 F12 **Bengtsfors** Sweden
27 M12 **Bengtskär** *lt ho* Finland
87 B8 **Benguela** Angola
84 J3 **Benha** Egypt
68 H5 **Ben Hien** Vietnam
145 D4 **Benhope** New Zealand
15 D2 **Ben Hope** *mt* Scotland
88 B1 **Beni** Zaïre
128 E6 **Beni** *dep* Bolivia
85 D2 **Beni Abbes** Algeria
117 R4 **Beniah L** N W Terr
17 H4 **Benicarló** Spain
17 G6 **Benidorm** Spain
79 A10 **Beni Mazâr** Egypt
85 C2 **Beni Mellal** Morocco
85 E8 **Benin,Bight of** W Africa
85 F7 **Benin City** Nigeria
36 B5 **Bening** France
9 G1 **Benington** England
85 E7 **Benin, Rep. of** W Africa
85 D2 **Beni Ounif** Algeria
17 G9 **Beni Saf** Algeria
79 B9 **Beni Suef** Egypt
103 N1 **Benjamin** Utah
128 D4 **Benjamin Constant** Brazil
124 D2 **Benjamín Hill** Mexico
100 E6 **Benjamin L** Oregon
60 O3 **Benkei Misaki** *C* Japan
98 E9 **Benkelman** Nebraska
15 D2 **Ben Klibreck** *mt* Scotland
42 G4 **Benkovac** Yugoslavia
15 D4 **Ben Lawers** *mt* Scotland
15 D4 **Ben Ledi** *mt* Scotland
141 G6 **Benlidi** Queensland
15 D4 **Ben Lomond** *mt* Scotland
15 D2 **Ben Loyal** *mt* Scotland
15 D4 **Ben Lui** *mt* Scotland
15 E3 **Ben Macdhui** *mt* Scotland
43 B12 **Ben Mehidi** Algeria
15 D4 **Ben More** *mt* Central Scotland
15 B4 **Ben More** *mt* Highland Scotland
15 D2 **Ben More Assynt** *mt* Scotland
144 C6 **Benmore Dam** New Zealand
144 C6 **Benmore Pk** *mt* New Zealand
33 N9 **Benneckenstein** E Germany
98 K9 **Bennet** Nebraska
140 D2 **Bennet B** N Terr Australia
114 F6 **Bennett** Br Col
99 P8 **Bennett** Iowa
99 P3 **Bennett** Wisconsin
51 P1 **Bennetta, Ostrov** *isld* U.S.S.R.
117 F6 **Bennett L** Br Col
140 B5 **Bennett,Mt** N Terr Aust
144 D5 **Bennetts** New Zealand
112 H3 **Bennettsville** S Carolina
144 B6 **Ben Nevis** *mt* New Zealand
15 D4 **Ben Nevis** *mt* Scotland
145 E3 **Benneydale** New Zealand
101 O7 **Bennington** Idaho
107 N2 **Bennington** Kansas
95 Q3 **Bennington** New Hampshire
107 O7 **Bennington** Oklahoma
95 O4 **Bennington** Vermont
85 B6 **Bénnsané** Guinea
80 E1 **Bennt Jbail** Lebanon
120 J6 **Benny** Ontario
70 P10 **Benoa** Bali Indonesia
144 C6 **Ben Ohau Range** New Zealand
99 P3 **Benoit** Wisconsin
87 E11 **Benoni** S Africa
107 K6 **Benonine** Oklahoma
86 B4 **Bénoué** *R* Cameroon
20 E3 **Bénouville** France
36 B1 **Benrath** W Germany
36 C2 **Bensberg** W Germany
32 G5 **Bensersiel** W Germany
37 K2 **Benshausen** E Germany
36 F4 **Bensheim** W Germany
103 O10 **Benson** Arizona
9 E4 **Benson** England
99 R9 **Benson** Illinois
111 C10 **Benson** Louisiana
99 L4 **Benson** Minnesota
112 J2 **Benson** N Carolina
119 O9 **Benson** Sask
68 H7 **Ben Suc** Vietnam
77 F6 **Bent** Iran
32 F8 **Bentheim** W Germany
68 G3 **Ben Thuy** Vietnam
16 E9 **Ben Tib** Morocco
68 C7 **Bentinck I** Burma
140 E3 **Bentinck I** Queensland
86 E4 **Bentiu** Sudan
118 C6 **Bentley** Alberta
107 N4 **Bentley** Kansas
98 D3 **Bentley** N Dakota
13 G6 **Bentley** S Yorks England
94 G6 **Bentleyville** Pennsylvania
130 B5 **Bento Gomes,R** Brazil
133 G3 **Bento Gonçalves** Brazil
111 K9 **Benton** Alabama
118 G7 **Benton** Alberta
111 D7 **Benton** Arkansas
102 F4 **Benton** California
113 E7 **Benton** Florida
110 H3 **Benton** Illinois
110 H5 **Benton** Kentucky
109 O3 **Benton** Louisiana
110 G4 **Benton** Missouri
122 E8 **Benton** New Brunswick
95 L5 **Benton** Pennsylvania
99 Q7 **Benton** Wisconsin
69 E11 **Bentong** Malaysia
99 U7 **Benton Harbor** Michigan
111 F9 **Bentonia** Mississippi
110 B5 **Bentonville** Arkansas
33 Q4 **Bentwisch** E Germany
69 H12 **Benua** *isld* Indonesia
86 A4 **Benue** *R* Nigeria
12 D1 **Ben Venue** *mt* Scotland
15 D4 **Ben Vorlich** *mt* Scotland
14 B2 **Benwee Hd** Irish Rep
109 M3 **Ben Wheeler** Texas
15 D3 **Ben Wyvis** *mt* Scotland
20 D4 **Bény Bocage,le** France
33 U5 **Benz** E Germany
80 B6 **Ben Zakkay** Israel
99 U5 **Benzonia** Michigan
48 F5 **Beočin** Yugoslavia
48 F6 **Beograd** Yugoslavia
70 K8 **Bepagut, G** *mt* Sumatra Indonesia
60 E12 **Beppu** Japan
80 E5 **Beqaot** Jordan
80 C6 **Beqoa' Latrun** Israel
37 M5 **Beratzhausen** W Germany
70 E3 **Berau** *R* Kalimantan
86 F2 **Berber** Sudan
86 H3 **Berbera** Somalia
86 C5 **Berberati** Cent Afr Republic
37 L5 **Berching** W Germany
57 A1 **Berchogur** U.S.S.R.
38 G6 **Berchtesgaden** W Germany
22 B3 **Berck** France
22 B3 **Berck Plage** France
109 K7 **Berclair** Texas
56 B4 **Berd'** *R* U.S.S.R.
20 G5 **Berd'huis** France
48 M1 **Berdichev** U.S.S.R.
51 M2 **Berdigestyakh** U.S.S.R.
86 D2 **Berdoba** Chad
56 B4 **Berdsk** U.S.S.R.
55 C3 **Berdyaush** U.S.S.R.
55 E3 **Berdyuzh'ye** U.S.S.R.
98 D7 **Berea** Nebraska
94 F5 **Berea** Ohio
71 B1 **Berebere** Halmahera Indonesia
86 B1 **Bereda** Somalia
48 J2 **Beregomet** U.S.S.R.
48 H2 **Beregovo** U.S.S.R.
85 D7 **Berekum** Ghana
32 L8 **Berenbostel** W Germany
102 D4 **Berenda** California
84 J5 **Berenice** Egypt
119 U6 **Berens I** Manitoba
115 K7 **Berens River** Manitoba
8 D6 **Bere Regis** England
119 R9 **Beresford** Manitoba
122 G6 **Beresford** New Brunswick
138 D3 **Beresford** S Australia
98 K6 **Beresford** S Dakota
48 L4 **Beresti Târg** Romania
48 G3 **Berettyo** *R* Hungary
48 G3 **Berettyóújfalu** Hungary
48 J1 **Berezhany** U.S.S.R.
54 C5 **Berezna** U.S.S.R.
52 J5 **Berezniki** U.S.S.R.
55 C2 **Berezovka** U.S.S.R.
50 F2 **Berezovo** U.S.S.R.
56 C3 **Berezovskiy** U.S.S.R.
29 N11 **Berezovyy,Ostrov** *isld* U.S.S.R.
26 J2 **Berg** Norway
26 G9 **Berg** Sweden
37 N2 **Berga** E Germany
17 J2 **Berga** Spain
27 G15 **Berga** Sweden
27 H14 **Berga** Sweden
78 A2 **Bergama** Turkey
42 C2 **Bergamasche,Alpi** Italy
42 C3 **Bergamo** Italy
45 K1 **Bergantino** Italy
32 G7 **Berge** W Germany
32 M6 **Bergedorf** W Germany
25 D6 **Bergeijk** Netherlands
98 F1 **Bergen** N Dakota
121 N9 **Bergen** New York
27 A11 **Bergen** Norway
32 L7 **Bergen** W Germany
25 C3 **Bergen aan Zee** Netherlands
6 M2 **Bergen Bank** North Sea
25 E5 **Berg-en-Dal** Netherlands
25 B6 **Bergen op Zoom** Netherlands
18 F8 **Bergerac** France
26 L3 **Bergfors** Sweden
36 C1 **Berg. Gladbach** W Germany
145 D1 **Berghan Pt** New Zealand
36 C7 **Bergheim** France
36 B2 **Bergheim** W Germany
94 G6 **Bergholz** Ohio
27 H15 **Bergkvara** Sweden
99 R3 **Bergland** Michigan
99 M1 **Bergland** Ontario
37 M7 **Berglern** W Germany
26 K5 **Bergnäs, N** Sweden
36 D1 **Bergneustadt** W Germany
29 J9 **Bergö** Finland
94 G8 **Bergoo** W Virginia
37 J3 **Bergrheinfeld** W Germany
25 C5 **Bergse Maas** *R* Netherlands
27 K12 **Bergshamra** Sweden
26 J10 **Bergsjö** Sweden
37 N6 **Bergstorf** W Germany
37 J4 **Bergtheim** W Germany
22 C2 **Bergues** France
25 F2 **Bergumer Meer** *L* Netherlands
41 L4 **Bergün** Switzerland
75 N6 **Berhampore** India
75 L9 **Berhampur** India
45 L1 **Berici,Monti** Italy
143 B7 **Beringarra** W Australia
22 J1 **Beringen** Belgium
25 E6 **Beringen** Netherlands
116 Q6 **Bering Glacier** Alaska
70 K7 **Beringin** Indonesia
116 P6 **Bering L** Alaska
114 B5 **Bering Sea**
116 C4 **Bering Strait** U.S.S.R./Alaska
106 D9 **Berino** New Mexico
54 E10 **Berislav** U.S.S.R.
17 F8 **Berja** Spain
20 E4 **Berjou** France
26 D9 **Berkåk** Norway
25 F4 **Berkel** *R* Netherlands
32 F9 **Berkel** *R* W Germany
102 B4 **Berkeley** California
8 D4 **Berkeley** England
114 J3 **Berkeley,C** N W Terr
142 G2 **Berkeley, R** W Australia
133 F8 **Berkeley Sd** Falkland Is
9 F4 **Berkhamsted** England
146 E10 **Berkner I** Antarctica
46 F1 **Berkovitsa** Bulgaria
9 E5 **Berkshire** *co* England
95 O4 **Berkshire Hills** Massachusetts
22 F3 **Berlaimont** France
117 P8 **Berland** *R* Alberta
110 K6 **Berland Plateau** Tennessee
17 F3 **Berlanga de Duero** Spain
16 A5 **Berlenga** *isld* Portugal
26 R1 **Berlevåg** Norway
30 G3 **Berlin** Germany
95 M8 **Berlin** Maryland
98 H3 **Berlin** N Dakota
95 Q2 **Berlin** New Hampshire
94 J7 **Berlin** Pennsylvania
99 S6 **Berlin** Wisconsin
34 **Berlin** *conurbation* Germany
115 L3 **Berlinguet Inlet** N W Terr
94 G6 **Berlin Res** Ohio
144 C4 **Berlins** New Zealand
133 E6 **Bermeja,Pta** Argentina
16 D8 **Bermeja, Sa** *mt* Spain
124 H5 **Bermejillo** Mexico
128 F8 **Bermejo** *R* Argentina
133 D4 **Bermejo** *R* Argentina
131 E7 **Bermejo, I** Argentina
17 F1 **Bermeo** Spain
16 C3 **Bermillo de Sayago** Spain
90 A1 **Bermuda** *isld* Atlantic Oc
90 D5 **Bermuda Rise** Atlantic Oc
99 L10 **Bern** Kansas
40 G4 **Bern** Switzerland
43 H8 **Bernalda** Italy
106 D6 **Bernalillo** New Mexico
99 Q7 **Bernard** Iowa
118 K8 **Bernard** Sask
103 P10 **Bernardino** Arizona
130 E8 **Bernardino de Campos** Brazil
114 G3 **Bernard Is** N W Terr
122 J3 **Bernard,L** Quebec
119 M3 **Bernard L** Sask
130 D10 **Bernardo de Irigoyen** Argentina
133 E5 **Bernasconi** Argentina
33 T7 **Bernau** E Germany
20 K1 **Bernaville** France
20 G3 **Bernay** Eure France
20 E5 **Bernay** Sarthe France
33 P9 **Bernburg** E Germany
38 O6 **Berndorf** Austria
Berne *see* **Bern**
110 M1 **Berne** Indiana
32 H6 **Berne** W Germany
22 K2 **Berneau** Belgium
36 F6 **Berneck** W Germany
15 A3 **Berneray** *isld* Scotland
40 G4 **Berner Oberland** *reg* Switzerland
16 D2 **Bernesga** *R* Spain
20 H2 **Berneval** France
111 D9 **Bernice** Louisiana
110 G5 **Bernie** Missouri
115 L3 **Bernier B** N W Terr
143 A6 **Bernier I** W Australia
41 L5 **Bernina, Passo del** Switzerland
22 F3 **Bernissart** Belgium
33 P5 **Bernitt** E Germany
36 C4 **Bernkastel-Kues** W Germany
33 S9 **Bernsdorf** E Germany
95 L6 **Bernville** Pennsylvania
37 K5 **Berolzheim** W Germany
80 B7 **Beror Ḥayil** Israel
87 H12 **Beroroha** Madagascar
80 B8 **Berosh** Israel
85 E6 **Béroubouay** Benin
30 H6 **Beroun** Czechoslovakia
30 H6 **Berounka** *R* Czechoslovakia
46 F3 **Berovo** Yugoslavia
45 L2 **Berra** Italy
40 F4 **Berra** *mt* Switzerland
43 A12 **Berrahall** Algeria
19 O18 **Berre** France
85 C2 **Berrechid** Morocco
19 O18 **Berre, Etang de** France
36 B2 **Berrenrath** W Germany
138 F5 **Berri** S Australia
85 E2 **Berriane** Algeria
15 E2 **Berriedale** Scotland
99 U8 **Berrien Springs** Michigan
139 H6 **Berrigan** New S Wales
140 B1 **Berrimah** N Terr Aust
22 G5 **Berru** France
111 J8 **Berry** Alabama
110 M3 **Berry** Kentucky
21 H7 **Berry** *prov* France
22 F5 **Berry-au-Bac** France
127 M2 **Berrydale** Jamaica
102 B3 **Berryessa,L** California
110 K5 **Berry Ford** Tennessee
8 C7 **Berry Head** England
113 K12 **Berry Is** Bahamas
140 B6 **Berrys Pass** N Terr Aust
110 C5 **Berryville** Arkansas
94 K7 **Berryville** Virginia
87 C11 **Berseba** Namibia
22 E3 **Bersée** France
32 G7 **Bersenbrück** W Germany
48 M2 **Bershad** U.S.S.R.
22 G3 **Bersillies** Belgium
122 E5 **Bersimis, Les Lacs** Quebec
55 D4 **Bersuat** U.S.S.R.
69 F10 **Bertam** Malaysia
122 D3 **Berté,L** Quebec
121 R6 **Berthierville** Quebec
98 E1 **Berthold** N Dakota
98 A9 **Berthoud** Colorado
141 F1 **Bertiehaugh** Queensland
22 D3 **Bertincourt** France
45 M3 **Bertinoro** Italy
22 K3 **Bertogne** Belgium
86 B5 **Bertoua** Cameroon
14 B3 **Bertraghboy B** Irish Rep
120 F3 **Bertram** Ontario
109 J5 **Bertram** Texas
142 F4 **Bertram,Mt** W Australia
98 G9 **Bertrand** Nebraska
36 B7 **Bertrichamps** France
22 H4 **Bertrix** Belgium
22 E3 **Bertry** France
119 P6 **Bertwell** Saskatchewan
128 F4 **Beruri** Brazil
83 J11 **Beruwala** Sri Lanka
137 Q2 **Berv** *isld* Kiribati
20 F3 **Berville-sur-Mer** France
95 R3 **Berwick** Maine
122 H8 **Berwick** Nova Scotia
95 L5 **Berwick** Pennsylvania
139 H6 **Berwick** Victoria
Berwick *co see* **Borders** *reg*
13 G2 **Berwick-upon-Tweed** England
117 P7 **Berwyn** Alberta
7 H10 **Berwyn Mts** Wales
103 L4 **Beryl** Utah
22 G3 **Berzee** Belgium
48 D4 **Berzence** Hungary
47 L8 **Beş** *isld* Turkey
87 G11 **Besalampy** Madagascar
19 K5 **Besançon** France
71 L9 **Besar** Flores Indonesia
70 O8 **Besar, G** *mt* Java
70 D6 **Besar, G** *mt* Kalimantan
69 E10 **Besar,Gunung** Malaysia
69 E11 **Besar Hantu** *mt* Malaysia
19 O15 **Besayes** France
43 B12 **Besbes** Algeria
116 G4 **Besboro I** Alaska
18 H6 **Besbre** *R* France
69 F11 **Beserah** Malaysia
54 A1 **Beshenkovichi** U.S.S.R.
36 G5 **Besigheim** W Germany
71 M9 **Besikama** Timor Indonesia
71 C3 **Besir** W Irian
78 H3 **Beşiri** Turkey
31 L6 **Beskidy Zachodnie** *reg* Poland
46 E2 **Besna Kobila** *mt* Yugoslavia
57 G1 **Besoba** U.S.S.R.
47 J7 **Beşparmak Dağ** *mt* Turkey
26 D7 **Bessaker** Norway
48 L2 **Bessarabia** *old prov* U.S.S.R.
48 M4 **Bessarabka** U.S.S.R.
19 Q14 **Besse** Isère France
19 Q18 **Besse** Var France
18 H8 **Bessèges** France
111 K8 **Bessemer** Alabama
99 Q3 **Bessemer** Michigan
121 N7 **Bessemer** Ontario
94 G6 **Bessemer** Pennsylvania
112 F2 **Bessemer City** N Carolina
19 N13 **Bessenay** France
36 G4 **Bessenbach** W Germany
28 F5 **Besser** Denmark
21 G6 **Bessé-sur-Braye** France
107 M6 **Bessie** Oklahoma
141 G6 **Bessie's Castle** Queensland
20 D3 **Bessin** *reg* France
18 F6 **Bessines sur Gartempe** France
25 D5 **Best** Netherlands
57 J1 **Bestamak** U.S.S.R.
28 A3 **Bested** Denmark
55 F4 **Bestobe** U.S.S.R.
100 C8 **Beswick** California
140 C2 **Beswick** N Terr Aust
87 H11 **Betafo** Madagascar
126 D3 **Betancourt,P** Cuba
71 M9 **Betano** Timor
16 B1 **Betanzos** Spain
16 B1 **Betanzos, Ría de** Spain
17 G5 **Bétara** Spain
86 B4 **Betaré Oya** Cameroon
80 C6 **Bet 'Arif** Israel
122 C4 **Betchie L** Quebec
99 T2 **Bete Grise Bay** Michigan
80 C7 **Bet Guvrin** Israel
80 D2 **Bet Ha'Emeq** Israel
80 B8 **Bet Ha Gaddi** Israel
89 F6 **Bethal** S Africa
80 C3 **Bet Ḥananya** Israel
87 C11 **Bethanie** Namibia
110 B1 **Bethany** Missouri
107 N6 **Bethany** Oklahoma
95 M8 **Bethany Beach** Delaware
116 G6 **Bethel** Alaska
95 O5 **Bethel** Connecticut
95 M8 **Bethel** Delaware
95 R2 **Bethel** Maine
99 N4 **Bethel** Minnesota
99 O10 **Bethel** Missouri
112 K2 **Bethel** N Carolina
110 M3 **Bethel** Ohio
87 E11 **Bethel** S Africa
95 P3 **Bethel** Vermont
127 J2 **Bethel Town** Jamaica
22 G5 **Bétheniville** France
95 K7 **Bethesda** Maryland
94 F6 **Bethesda** Ohio
80 F1 **Bet Hillel** Israel
22 D5 **Béthisy-St.Pierre** France
80 D7 **Bethlehem** Jordan
95 Q2 **Bethlehem** New Hampshire
95 M6 **Bethlehem** Pennsylvania
89 F7 **Bethlehem** S Africa
122 A2 **Béthoulet, L** Quebec
110 K5 **Bethpage** Tennessee
89 D8 **Bethulie** S Africa
106 H2 **Bethune** Colorado
22 D2 **Béthune** France
119 M8 **Bethune** Sask
112 G3 **Bethune** S Carolina
20 H2 **Béthune** *R* France
130 G6 **Betim** Brazil
87 G12 **Betioky** Madagascar
70 O10 **Betiri, G** Java
80 D2 **Bet Ke'rem** Israel
80 D3 **Bet Leḥem** Israel
8 D1 **Betley** England
80 C7 **Bet Nir** Israel
70 B4 **Betong** Sarawak
138 F2 **Betoota** Queensland
140 F7 **Betoota** Queensland
80 D3 **Bet Oren** Israel
86 C5 **Betou** Congo
57 E3 **Betpak-Dala** *region* U.S.S.R.
80 C8 **Bet Qama** Israel
87 H12 **Betroka** Madagascar
80 E3 **Bet She'an** Israel
80 B7 **Bet Shiqma** Israel
115 N8 **Betsiamites** Quebec
122 C4 **Betsiamites, R** Quebec
87 H11 **Betsiboka** *R* Madagascar
99 U5 **Betsie, Pt** Michigan
99 V3 **Betsy L** Michigan
22 K4 **Bettembourg** Luxembourg
75 L5 **Bettiah** India
109 N3 **Bettie** Texas
116 M3 **Bettles** Alaska
27 J13 **Bettna** Sweden
20 B5 **Betton** France
74 G8 **Betul** India
71 M9 **Betun** Timor Indonesia
69 F13 **Betung** Sumatra
70 C4 **Betung, G** *mt* Kalimantan
70 C5 **Beturan, G** *mt* Kalimantan
73 M3 **Betwa** *R* India
8 C1 **Betws-y-Coed** Wales
80 C4 **Bet Yannay** Israel
80 C4 **Bet Yizḥaq** Israel
80 F3 **Bet Yosef** Israel
36 D2 **Betzdorf** W Germany
37 L4 **Betzenstein** W Germany
41 O2 **Beuerberg** W Germany
25 E5 **Beugen** Netherlands
119 Q8 **Beulah** Manitoba
99 V5 **Beulah** Michigan
98 E2 **Beulah** N Dakota
100 G6 **Beulah** Oregon
8 C3 **Beulah** Wales
98 B5 **Beulah** Wyoming
112 K3 **Beulaville** N Carolina
9 G5 **Beult,R** England
36 B4 **Beurig** W Germany
22 D4 **Beuvraignes** France
21 I6 **Beuvron** *R* France
20 E3 **Beuvron-en-Auge** France
20 F3 **Beuzeville** France
20 F2 **Beuzeville-la-Grenier** France
33 N6 **Bevensen** W Germany
32 G8 **Bever** *R* W Germany
22 G1 **Beveren** Oost Vlanderen Belgium
32 G8 **Bevergern** W Germany
41 K4 **Beverin,Piz** *mt* Switzerland
13 H6 **Beverley** England
118 K8 **Beverley** Sask
100 F3 **Beverley** Washington
143 B9 **Beverley** W Australia
141 J5 **Beverley Grp** *islds* Queensland
116 H7 **Beverley,L** Alaska
22 J1 **Beverlo** Belgium
118 D5 **Beverly** Alberta
107 N2 **Beverly** Kansas
95 R4 **Beverly** Massachusetts
94 F7 **Beverly** Ohio
94 H8 **Beverly** W Virginia
114 J5 **Beverly L** N W Terr
100 C2 **Beverly Park** Washington
32 L9 **Bevern** W Germany
22 J2 **Beverst** Belgium
32 J6 **Beverstedt** W Germany
32 K9 **Beverungen** W Germany
25 C4 **Beverwijk** Netherlands
99 O10 **Bevier** Missouri
45 K1 **Bevilacqua Boschi** Italy
20 J5 **Béville-le-Comte** France
28 C6 **Bevtoft** Denmark
128 C7 **Beware,Pta** *C* Peru
8 D3 **Bewdley** England
40 F5 **Bex** Switzerland
9 G6 **Bexhill** England
144 D5 **Bexley** New Zealand
47 H4 **Beyçayırı** Turkey
47 J6 **Beydağ** Turkey
78 C3 **Bey Daglari** Turkey
47 L4 **Beydili** Turkey
47 K3 **Beykoz** Turkey
85 C7 **Beyla** Guinea
20 J4 **Beynes** France
78 B1 **Beyoglu** Turkey
78 C1 **Beypazari** Turkey
76 B5 **Beypore** India
Beyrouth *see* **Beirut**
78 C3 **Beyşehir** Turkey
80 C7 **Beyt 'Awwa** Jordan
48 E5 **Bezdan** Yugoslavia
37 O4 **Bezdružice** Czechoslovakia
19 J5 **Bèze** France
80 F4 **Bezeq** *R* Israel
52 C6 **Bezhanitsy** U.S.S.R.
47 G1 **Bezhanovo** Bulgaria
18 H9 **Béziers** France
47 F3 **Bezlet** *mt* Bulgaria
20 J3 **Bezu-la-Forêt** France
75 L5 **Bhadgaon** Nepal
75 M8 **Bhadrach** India
76 E2 **Bhadrachalam** India
76 B4 **Bhadravati** India
74 B4 **Bhag** Pakistan
75 M6 **Bhagalpur** India
74 G9 **Bhainsa** India
76 E1 **Bhairamgarh** India
74 D3 **Bhakkar** Pakistan
74 G9 **Bhalki** India
79 F5 **Bḥamdoun** Lebanon
76 E1 **Bhamragarh** India
74 H8 **Bhandara** India
75 J7 **Bharatpur** India
74 E8 **Bharuch** India
74 F3 **Bhatinda** India
76 B4 **Bhatkal** India
75 N7 **Bhatpara** India
74 E2 **Bhaun** Pakistan
76 C5 **Bhavani** India
74 E8 **Bhavnagar** India
75 K9 **Bhawanipatna** India
74 E2 **Bhera** Pakistan
75 J8 **Bhilai** India
74 F6 **Bhilwara** India
73 M5 **Bhima** *R* India
76 E2 **Bhimavaram** India
74 H5 **Bhind** India
74 G4 **Bhiwani** India
74 H10 **Bhongir** India
74 G7 **Bhopal** India
76 E1 **Bhopalpatnam** India
74 E9 **Bhor** India
75 L8 **Bhubaneswar** India
74 C7 **Bhuj** India
68 D4 **Bhumiphol Dam** Thailand
74 F8 **Bhusawal** India
75 N5 **Bhutan** *kingdom* S Asia
77 E6 **Biabān** *coastal reg* Iran
85 F8 **Biafra,Bight of** W Africa
71 H5 **Biak** Sulawesi Indonesia
136 H2 **Biak** *isld* W Irian
31 N2 **Biała Piska** Poland
31 O3 **Biała Podlaska** Poland
31 M4 **Białobrzegi** Poland
31 J1 **Białogard** Poland
31 K2 **Biały Bór** Poland
31 O2 **Białystok** Poland
44 G3 **Bianca,P** *C* Italy
43 G10 **Bianco** Italy
45 L2 **Bianco, Canale** Italy
65 F4 **Bianmen** China
Bianzhuang *see* **Cangshan**
71 G7 **Biao** Mindanao Philippines
73 R5 **Bia,Pou** *mt* Laos
77 D1 **Biārjmand** Iran
71 J4 **Biaro** *isld* Indonesia
18 D9 **Biarritz** France
71 H4 **Biau** Sulawesi Indonesia
55 G3 **Biaza** U.S.S.R.
79 A10 **Biba** Egypt
42 D5 **Bibbiena** Italy
140 E5 **Bibby** *R* N Terr Aust
41 L1 **Biberach** W Germany
37 K5 **Bibert** *R* W Germany
16 C2 **Bibey,R** Spain
85 D7 **Bibiania** Ghana
36 E4 **Biblis** W Germany
37 J3 **Bibra** Suhl E Germany
142 A3 **Bibra Lake** *dist* Perth, W Aust
9 E4 **Bibury** England
122 D5 **Bic** Quebec
46 D3 **Bicaj** Albania
130 G7 **Bicas** Brazil
48 K4 **Bicaz** Romania
9 E4 **Bicester** England
41 O2 **Bichl** W Germany
41 N3 **Bichlbach** Austria
122 D5 **Bic, I. du** Quebec
140 D2 **Bickerton I** N Terr Aust
8 C6 **Bickington** England
8 C6 **Bickleigh** England
100 E3 **Bickleton** Washington
142 B2 **Bickley Brook** Perth, W Aust
94 F8 **Bickmore** W Virginia
110 J3 **Bicknell** Indiana
103 N3 **Bicknell** Utah
48 E3 **Bicske** Hungary
85 F7 **Bida** Nigeria
76 C2 **Bidar** India
95 R3 **Biddeford** Maine
80 D6 **Biddu** Jordan
8 D1 **Biddulph** England
8 B5 **Bideford** England
Bidon 5 *see* **Poste Maurice Cortier**
85 E4 **Bidon 5** Algeria
94 E8 **Bidwell** Ohio
87 C8 **Bié** Angola
100 D8 **Bieber** California
36 G3 **Bieber** W Germany
36 G3 **Biebergemünd** W Germany
36 D5 **Biebermühle** W Germany
36 F2 **Biebertal** W Germany
36 E3 **Biebrich** W Germany
31 O2 **Biebrza** *R* Poland
31 N6 **Biecz** Poland
36 F2 **Biedenkopf** W Germany
33 P8 **Biederitz** E Germany
40 G1 **Biegel** W Germany
60 Q2 **Biei** Japan
40 F3 **Biel** Switzerland
119 Q7 **Bield** Manitoba
32 J8 **Bielefeld** W Germany
41 M4 **Bielerhöhe** *pass* Austria
40 F3 **Bieler See** *L* Switzerland
42 B3 **Biella** Italy
17 H2 **Bielsa** Spain
31 L6 **Bielsko-Biała** Poland
31 O3 **Bielsk Podlaski** Poland
36 C2 **Bielstein** W Germany
33 M6 **Bienenbüttel** W Germany
119 P9 **Bienfait** Sask
68 H7 **Bien Hoa** Vietnam
Bienne *see* **Biel**
45 J4 **Bientina** Italy
67 C2 **Bi'er** China
141 H7 **Bierbank** Queensland
36 F7 **Bieringen** W Germany
21 D6 **Bierne** France
28 D2 **Biersted** Denmark
25 A6 **Biervliet** Netherlands
33 P7 **Biese** *R* E Germany
33 T7 **Biesenthal** W Germany
40 B1 **Biesles** France
36 E6 **Bietigheim** W Germany
36 G6 **Bietigheim** W Germany
33 T6 **Bietikow** E Germany
22 J4 **Bièvre** Belgium
20 K4 **Bievres** France
31 M3 **Bieżun** Poland
43 F7 **Biferno** *R* Italy
86 B6 **Bifoum** Gabon
116 K5 **Big** *R* Alaska
78 A1 **Biga** Turkey
47 J5 **Bigadiç** Turkey
101 L2 **Big Arm** Montana
Big B *see* **Awarua B**
101 P2 **Big Baldy Mt** Montana
117 M10 **Big Bar Creek** Br Col
99 T3 **Big Bay** Michigan
102 H7 **Big Bear City** California
109 N8 **Big Bear Cr** Texas
102 G7 **Big Bear L** California
119 M9 **Big Beaver** Sask
120 H3 **Big Beaver Falls** Ontario
115 L7 **Big Beaver House** Ontario
143 C7 **Big Bell** W Australia
101 O3 **Big Belt Mts** Montana
100 D8 **Big Bend** California
106 H3 **Big Bend** Colorado
108 D6 **Big Bend Nat.Pk** Texas
111 G8 **Big Black** *R* Mississippi
112 G3 **Big Black Cr** S Carolina
94 E10 **Big Black Mt** Kentucky/Virg
8 C7 **Bigbury B** England
8 C7 **Bigbury-on-Sea** England
108 E5 **Big Canyon** *R* Texas
122 E3 **Big Caotibi L** Quebec
103 M6 **Big Chino Wash** Arizona
110 K4 **Big Clifty** Kentucky
107 K3 **Big Cr** Kansas
117 M10 **Big Creek** Br Col
94 F8 **Big Creek** W Virginia
113 F11 **Big Cypress Swamp** Florida
116 O4 **Big Delta** Alaska
101 T2 **Big Dry Cr** Montana
99 Q5 **Big Eau Pleine Res** Wisconsin
101 O6 **Big Elk Mt** Idaho
107 O2 **Bigelow** Kansas
99 N1 **Big Falls** Minnesota
99 N2 **Bigfork** Minnesota
101 L1 **Bigfork** Montana
109 M9 **Big Fossil Cr** Texas
114 J7 **Biggar** Sask
12 E2 **Biggar** Scotland
36 D1 **Bigge** *R* W Germany
142 F2 **Bigge I** W Australia
26 N2 **Biggeluobbal** Norway
141 K7 **Biggenden** Queensland
32 H10 **Bigge-Olsberg** W Germany
117 E6 **Bigger,Mt** Br Col

113 F5 **Biggers** Arkansas
9 F3 **Biggleswade** England
102 C2 **Biggs** California
100 E4 **Biggs** Oregon
99 Q9 **Biggsville** Illinois
106 B10 **Big Hatchet Pk** New Mexico
118 C7 **Big Hill Sp.Prov.Pk** Alberta
101 N4 **Big Hole** *R* Montana
101 M4 **Big Hole Battlefield Nat. Mon** Montana
114 J8 **Big Horn** *R* Montana
101 S4 **Bighorn** *R* Wyo/Mont
101 S5 **Bighorn Mts** Wyo/Mont
126 G3 **Bight of Acklins** Bahamas
126 G2 **Bight,The** Cat I Bahamas
111 E8 **Big I** Arkansas
115 M5 **Big I** N W Terr
118 H1 **Big I** Ontario
94 H9 **Big Island** Virginia
117 F4 **Big Kalzas L** Yukon Terr
116 H9 **Big Koniuji I** Alaska
95 U1 **Big L** Maine
117 R3 **Big L** N W Terr
100 E7 **Big L** Oregon
116 N3 **Big Lake** Alaska
108 F4 **Big Lake** Texas
95 K7 **Biglerville** Pennsylvania
144 A7 **Big Moggy I** New Zealand
95 N3 **Big Moose** New York
110 G4 **Big Muddy** *R* Illinois
98 B1 **Big Muddy Cr** Montana
119 N9 **Big Muddy L** Sask
44 C4 **Bignone,Monte** Italy
94 H9 **Big Otter** *R* Virginia
102 F4 **Big Pine** California
99 L3 **Big Pine L** Minnesota
102 E7 **Big Pine Peak** California
101 P7 **Big Piney** Wyoming
110 D4 **Big Piney** *R* Missouri
123 M8 **Big Pond** C Breton I, N Scotia
94 B3 **Big Rapids** Michigan
99 Q4 **Big Rib** *R* Wisconsin
114 J7 **Big River** Sask
99 U5 **Big Sable Pt** Michigan
100 E8 **Big Sage Res** California
117 F5 **Big Salmon** *R* Yukon Terr
119 S1 **Big Sand L** Manitoba
101 P1 **Big Sandy** Montana
109 M3 **Big Sandy** Texas
101 Q7 **Big Sandy** Wyoming
103 L7 **Big Sandy** *R* Arizona
106 H3 **Big Sandy Cr** Colorado
99 N3 **Big Sandy L** Minnesota
119 N4 **Big Sandy L** Sask
118 H1 **Bigsby I** Ontario
98 K5 **Big Sioux** *R* S Dakota
102 G3 **Big Smoky Valley** Nevada
101 Q3 **Big Snowy Mt** Montana
144 A7 **Big South Cape I** New Zealand
108 F3 **Big Spring** Texas
101 O5 **Big Springs** Idaho
98 G8 **Big Springs** Nebraska
118 H8 **Bigstick L** Sask
98 K4 **Big Stone City** S Dakota
94 E10 **Big Stone Gap** Virginia
119 W5 **Bigstone L** Manitoba
98 K4 **Big Stone L** Minnesota
119 W3 **Bigstone** *R* Manitoba
102 C5 **Big Sur** California
109 M5 **Big Thicket L** Texas
101 Q4 **Bigtimber** Montana
101 S6 **Bigtrails** Wyoming
115 L7 **Big Trout Lake** Ontario
130 E10 **Biguaçú** Brazil
118 E6 **Big Valley** Alberta
109 H7 **Big Wells** Texas
111 L7 **Big Wills Cr** Alabama
120 K6 **Bigwood** Ontario
101 L6 **Big Wood** *R* Idaho
42 G4 **Bihac** Yugoslavia
75 L6 **Bihar** *prov* India
48 G4 **Bihor** *reg* Romania
48 G4 **Bihorului Muntii** *mts* Romania
67 F2 **Bihu** China
85 A6 **Bijagós, Arquipélago dos** Guinea-Bissau
74 G5 **Bijaipur** India
76 G2 **Bijapur** India
77 A2 **Bijar** Iran
75 K4 **Bijauri** Nepal
42 F3 **Bijela Lasica** *mt* Yugoslavia
48 E6 **Bijeljina** Yugoslavia
46 D1 **Bijelo Polje** Yugoslavia
67 B3 **Bijie** China
76 E1 **Bijji** India
77 F6 **Bijnābād** Iran
74 H4 **Bijnor** India
98 G6 **Bijou Hills** S Dakota
74 E4 **Bikaner** India
79 F5 **Bikfaya** Lebanon
51 N4 **Bikin** U.S.S.R.
65 J1 **Bikin** U.S.S.R.
59 L2 **Bikin** *R* U.S.S.R.
134 G7 **Bikini** *atoll* Marshall Is Pacific Oc
31 L6 **Bílá** Czechoslovakia
71 G6 **Bilaa Pt** Mindanao Philippines
85 E6 **Bilanga** Upper Volta
70 F3 **Bilangbilangen** Kalimantan
74 E5 **Bilara** India
74 G3 **Bilaspur** India
70 F2 **Bilatan** *isld* Philippines
71 H4 **Bilato** Sulawesi Indonesia
68 D5 **Bilauktaung Range** Burma/Thailand
17 F1 **Bilbao** Spain
79 B8 **Bilbeis** Egypt
42 J5 **Bileća** Yugoslavia
78 B1 **Bilecik** Turkey
48 F5 **Biled** Romania
48 D2 **Bilé Karpaty** Czechoslovakia
31 O5 **Biłgoraj** Poland
125 N2 **Bilhuaskarma** Nicaragua
86 E5 **Bili** Zaïre
68 C4 **Bilin** Burma
30 H5 **Bílina** *R* Czechoslovakia
71 D3 **Bilit** Sabah
67 E5 **Biliu He** *R* China
98 A3 **Bill** Wyoming
143 B7 **Billabalong** W Australia
6 D2 **Bill Baileys Bank** N Atlantic Oc
20 C5 **Billé** France
33 M5 **Bille** *R* W Germany
32 F9 **Billerbeck** W Germany
9 G4 **Billericay** England
9 F2 **Billesdon** England
19 P12 **Billiat** France
36 G5 **Billigheim** W Germany
143 B9 **Billiluna** W Australia
9 F2 **Billingborough** England
27 F16 **Billinge** Sweden
9 F1 **Billinghay** England
114 J8 **Billings** Montana
107 N5 **Billings** Oklahoma
9 F5 **Billingshurst** England
8 D3 **Billingsley** England
Billiton *see* **Belitung** *I*
18 H7 **Billom** France
46 E8 **Billum** Denmark
28 C5 **Billund** Denmark
103 M6 **Bill Williams Mt** Arizona
56 G1 **Billyakh Porog** *falls* U.S.S.R.
22 K5 **Billy-sous-Mangiennes** France
86 B2 **Bilma** Niger
141 K6 **Biloela** Queensland
42 H3 **Bilo Gora** *dist* Yugoslavia
111 H11 **Biloxi** Mississippi
140 E7 **Bilpamorea Claypan** Queensland
142 C5 **Bilroth,Mt** W Australia
36 E1 **Bilstein** W Germany
25 D4 **Bilthoven** Netherlands
86 D3 **Biltine** Chad
26 M2 **Bilto** Norway
68 C4 **Bilugyun** *isld* Burma
22 K2 **Bilzen** Belgium
71 J9 **Bima,Teluk** *B* Sumbawa Indonesia
85 E6 **Bimbéréké** Benin
138 F4 **Bimbowrie** S Australia
126 E2 **Bimini Is** Bahamas
75 K10 **Bimlipatam** India
71 F5 **Binalbagan** Negros Philippines
77 F1 **Binālūd, Kūh-e-** *mts* Iran
70 B3 **Binatang** Sarawak
141 J5 **Binbee** Queensland
13 H6 **Binbrook** England
22 G3 **Binche** Belgium
141 J7 **Bindango** Queensland
28 C5 **Bindeballe** Denmark
139 H3 **Bindebango** Queensland
28 D3 **Binderup** Denmark
69 J11 **Bindjai** Indonesia
141 J8 **Bindle** Queensland
118 G8 **Bindloss** Alberta
89 G1 **Bindura** Zimbabwe
17 H3 **Binéfar** Spain
98 H2 **Binford** N Dakota
87 E9 **Binga** Zimbabwe
87 F9 **Binga,Mt** Mozambique/Zimbabwe
141 G8 **Bingara** Queensland
36 D4 **Bingen** W Germany
107 M6 **Binger** Oklahoma
9 F2 **Bingham** England
95 S1 **Bingham** Maine
99 V5 **Bingham** Michigan
108 A2 **Bingham** New Mexico
101 N9 **Bingham Canyon** Utah
95 M4 **Binghamton** New York
70 E2 **Bingkor** Sabah
120 K4 **Bingle** Ontario
13 G6 **Bingley** England
Bingmei *see* **Congjiang**
78 H2 **Bingol** Turkey
78 H2 **Bingol D** Turkey
9 G2 **Binham** England
Binh Dinh *see* **An Nhon**
68 G7 **Binh Minh** Vietnam
68 J5 **Binh Son** Vietnam
69 J11 **Binjai** Indonesia
69 D11 **Binjai** Sumatra
71 J7 **Binongka** *isld* Indonesia
119 Q8 **Binscarth** Manitoba
144 C5 **Binser, Mt** New Zealand
36 B4 **Binsfeld** W Germany
69 G12 **Bintan** *isld* Indonesia
71 H4 **Bintauna** Sulawesi Indonesia
71 E4 **Bintuan** Philippines
70 C3 **Bintulu** Sarawak
71 E4 **Binubusan** Philippines
58 G4 **Bin Xian** China
65 G2 **Bin Xian** China
80 C3 **Binyamina** Israel
65 C5 **Binyang** China
Binzhou *see* **Bin Xian**
133 C5 **Bio-Bio** *prov* Chile
46 D2 **Bioča** Yugoslavia
42 G5 **Biograd** Yugoslavia
85 F8 **Bioko** *isld* Eq Guinea
19 O14 **Biol** France
40 E5 **Biot, le** France
32 G7 **Bippen** W Germany
94 B6 **Bippus** Indiana
80 E2 **Biq'at Bet Netofa** Israel
74 F9 **Bir** India
80 D6 **Bira** Jordan
48 L3 **Bira** Romania
59 K2 **Bira** U.S.S.R.
84 J5 **Bir Abu Husein** Egypt
84 H4 **Bir Abu Minqar** Egypt
71 E2 **Birac** Philippines
52 K2 **Birakan** U.S.S.R.
86 D3 **Birao** Cent Afr Republic
84 E4 **Bi'r Ash Shuwayrif** Libya
75 M5 **Biratnagar** Nepal
77 F7 **Bir Bālo** Iran
78 G4 **Bir Btaiman** Syria
47 F1 **Birca Ginglova** Romania
116 P3 **Birch Cr** Alaska
116 L4 **Birches** Alaska
145 D4 **Birch Hill** New Zealand
119 M5 **Birch Hills** Sask
119 S6 **Birch I** Manitoba
9 H5 **Birchington** England
48 G5 **Birchiş** Romania
118 F5 **Birch L** Alberta
99 P2 **Birch L** Minnesota
117 P4 **Birch L** N W Terr
118 J5 **Birch L** Sask
114 H6 **Birch Mts** Alberta
117 R6 **Birch** *R* Alberta
119 Q6 **Birch River** Manitoba
110 E5 **Birch Tree** Missouri
116 N6 **Birchwood** Alaska
144 A6 **Birchwood** New Zealand
99 P4 **Birchwood** Wisconsin
31 N6 **Bircza** Poland
115 K6 **Bird** Manitoba
107 J2 **Bird City** Kansas
119 H9 **Bird I** Alaska
83 J12 **Bird I** Seychelles
89 E9 **Bird I** *lt ho* S Africa
8 D4 **Birdlip** England
123 L6 **Bird Rocks** *lt ho* Madeleine Is, Quebec
110 K3 **Birdseye** Indiana
140 E7 **Birdsville** Queensland
140 C3 **Birdum** N Terr Aust
140 C3 **Birdum** *R* N Terr Aust
85 D3 **Bir ed Deheb** Algeria
79 G3 **Bireín** Syria
85 D3 **Bir el Hadjaj** Algeria
69 C10 **Bireuën** Sumatra
79 H10 **Bi'r Fajr** Saudi Arabia
75 L5 **Birganj** Nepal
37 M5 **Birgland** W Germany
27 E11 **Biri** Norway
71 G4 **Biri** *isld* Philippines
89 G1 **Biri** *R* Zimbabwe
130 F7 **Birigüí** Brazil
56 D4 **Birikchul'** U.S.S.R.
141 H6 **Biringan** Queensland
86 D4 **Birini** Cent Afr Republic
77 F3 **Birjand** Iran
28 B6 **Birkelev** Denmark
28 D2 **Birkelse** Denmark
36 B4 **Birkenau** W Germany
41 H2 **Birkendorf** W Germany
27 C13 **Birkenes** Norway
36 C4 **Birkenfeld** W Germany
13 E6 **Birkenhead** England
33 S7 **Birkenwerder** E Germany
28 K5 **Birkerød** Denmark
36 B2 **Birkesdorf** W Germany
28 G7 **Birket** Denmark
79 A9 **Birket Qârûn** *L* Egypt
38 N7 **Birkfeld** Austria
41 O3 **Birkkar Sp** Austria
28 D7 **Birknack** C W Germany
138 A2 **Birksgate Ra** S Australia
48 L4 **Birlad** Romania
48 L4 **Birladul** *R* Romania
79 D7 **Bir Lahfân** Egypt
85 C3 **Bir Lehlú** Morocco
78 K5 **Bir Meloza** Iraq
111 K8 **Birmingham** Alabama
9 E3 **Birmingham** England
99 P9 **Birmingham** Iowa
94 D4 **Birmingham** Michigan
119 P8 **Birmingham** Sask
11 C5 **Birmingham** *conurbation* England
84 H5 **Bir Misâha** Egypt
85 B3 **Bir Moghrein** Mauritania
51 E4 **Birnam** Scotland
37 P7 **Birnbach** W Germany
101 T4 **Birney** Montana
134 K8 **Birnie I** Phoenix Is Pacific Oc
85 E6 **Birni N'Gaouré** Niger
85 F6 **Birnin Gwari** Nigeria
85 E6 **Birnin-Kebbi** Nigeria
85 F6 **Birni n'Konni** Niger
51 N3 **Birobidzhan** U.S.S.R.
71 D6 **Birong** Palawan Philippines
14 D3 **Birr** Irish Rep
140 B3 **Birrimbah** N Terr Aust
140 A4 **Birrindudu** N Terr Aust
118 K7 **Birsay** Sask
50 E3 **Birsk** U.S.S.R.
13 G6 **Birstal** W Yorks England
36 G3 **Birstein** W Germany
26 L2 **Birtavarre** Norway
141 G2 **Birthday Mt** Queensland
116 J2 **Birthday Pass** Alaska
13 G4 **Birtley** England
66 E5 **Biru** China
56 E3 **Biryusa** *R* U.S.S.R.
52 B6 **Biržai** U.S.S.R.
85 C4 **Bir Zreigat** Mauritania
88 C8 **Bisa** Zambia
61 K10 **Bisai** Japan
74 H4 **Bisalpur** India
103 P10 **Bisbee** Arizona
18 C7 **Biscay,B of** France/Spain
113 G12 **Biscayne Nat. Mon** Florida
43 G7 **Bisceglie** Italy
37 K4 **Bischberg** W Germany
36 H1 **Bischhausen** W Germany
36 D6 **Bischheim** France
37 M3 **Bischofsgrün** W Germany
37 J3 **Bischofsheim** W Germany
38 H7 **Bischofshofen** Austria
31 H4 **Bischofswerda** E Germany
19 L4 **Bischwiller** France
112 H2 **Biscoe** N Carolina
146 F14 **Biscoe I** Antarctica
115 L8 **Biscotasing** Ontario
61 P12 **Bise** Okinawa
45 K4 **Bisenzio** *R* Italy
47 H3 **Biser** Bulgaria
55 C2 **Biser** U.S.S.R.
55 C3 **Biserť** U.S.S.R.
42 G6 **Biševo** *isld* Yugoslavia
61 P12 **Bise-zaki** *C* Okinawa
67 A5 **Bisezhai** China
67 B2 **Bishan** China
102 F4 **Bishop** California
112 D4 **Bishop** Georgia
95 M8 **Bishop** Maryland
109 K8 **Bishop** Texas
144 A7 **Bishop and Clerks Is** New Zealand
13 G4 **Bishop Auckland** England
12 D2 **Bishopbriggs** Scotland
101 L8 **Bishop Creek Res** Nevada
117 P3 **Bishop L** N W Terr
119 M8 **Bishopric** Sask
9 E7 **Bishop Rock** Isles of Scilly England
8 D3 **Bishops Castle** England
123 R4 **Bishop's Falls** Nfld
8 C5 **Bishops Lydeard** England
9 G4 **Bishops Stortford** England
9 E3 **Bishops Tachbrook** England
9 E6 **Bishops Waltham** England
112 G3 **Bishopville** S Carolina
80 G3 **Bishra** Jordan
35 F2 **Biskra** Algeria
31 M2 **Biskupiec** Poland
28 D3 **Bislev** Denmark
9 F5 **Bisley** England
71 G6 **Bislig** Mindanao Philippines
71 G6 **Bislig Bay** Mindanao Philippines
111 C7 **Bismarck** Arkansas
99 T9 **Bismarck** Illinois
110 F4 **Bismarck** Missouri
98 F3 **Bismarck** N Dakota
136 K2 **Bismarck Archipelago** Papua New Guinea
136 J3 **Bismarck Range** Papua New Guinea
136 K2 **Bismarck Sea** Papua New Guinea
146 E14 **Bismarck Str** Antarctica
33 P7 **Bismark** E Germany
78 H3 **Bismil** Turkey
107 N5 **Bison** Oklahoma
98 D4 **Bison** S Dakota
117 P7 **Bison L** Alberta
77 A2 **Bīsotūn** Iran
26 B6 **Bisping** France
32 L6 **Bispingen** W Germany
85 A6 **Bissau** Guinea-Bissau
115 K7 **Bissett** Manitoba
37 K6 **Bissingen** W Germany
116 H6 **Bistcho L** Alberta
47 F1 **Bistretu** Romania
48 J3 **Bistrița** Romania
48 J3 **Bistrița Năsăud** *reg* Romania
48 K3 **Bistrițel, Muntii** *mt* Romania
71 E5 **Bisucay** *isld* Philippines
31 M1 **Bisztynek** Poland
85 B5 **Bitam** Gabon
36 B4 **Bitburg** W Germany
19 K3 **Bitche** France
80 B8 **Bit'ha** Israel
47 L4 **Bithynia** Turkey
71 B2 **Bitjoli** Halmahera Indonesia
86 C3 **Bitkine** Chad
73 H2 **Bitlis** Turkey
46 E3 **Bitola** Yugoslavia
43 H7 **Bitonto** Italy
43 H5 **Bitovnja** *mt* Yugoslavia
112 D6 **Bitter Creek** Wyoming
103 P2 **Bitter Cr** Utah
101 R8 **Bitter Creek** Wyoming
33 Q9 **Bitterfeld** E Germany
87 C12 **Bitterfontein** S Africa
84 J3 **Bitter L** Egypt
98 J4 **Bitter L** S Dakota
9 E6 **Bitterne** England
144 C6 **Bitterness, Mt** New Zealand
119 M5 **Bittern L** Sask
118 D5 **Bittern Lake** Alberta
101 L3 **Bitterroot** *R* Montana
114 H8 **Bitterroot Ra** Mont/Idaho
43 C8 **Bitti** Sardinia
33 P8 **Bittkau** E Germany
85 D6 **Bittou** Upper Volta
71 J4 **Bitung** Sulawesi Indonesia
86 B3 **Biu** Nigeria
61 L10 **Biwa** Japan
48 K3 **Bivolari** Romania
48 K3 **Bivolu** *mt* Romania
59 L4 **Biwa Ko** *L* Japan
110 E4 **Bixby** Missouri
107 P6 **Bixby** Oklahoma
86 H3 **Biya Kaboba** Ethiopia
56 C4 **Biysk** U.S.S.R.
18 G9 **Bize** France
85 G1 **Bizerte** Tunisia
43 C11 **Bizerte, Lac de** Tunisia
28 J6 **Bjæverskov** Denmark
27 H13 **BJärka-Säby** Sweden
27 J13 **Bjarköy** Norway
26 K8 **Bjästa** Sweden
27 E7 **Bjelašnica** *mt* Yugoslavia
27 E13 **Bjelland** Norway
42 H3 **Bjelovar** Yugoslavia
28 E1 **Bjergby** Denmark
28 G6 **Bjergby** Denmark
28 G5 **Bjerge** Denmark
28 G5 **Bjergsted** Denmark
27 G11 **Bjørkelangen** Norway
27 A10 **Bjordal** Norway
27 B11 **Bjoreia** *R* Norway
26 D9 **Björgan** Norway
27 E12 **Björkelangen** Norway
27 F14 **Björketorp** Sweden
27 G11 **Björkfjäll** *mt* Sweden
26 H6 **Björkfors** Sweden
27 J11 **Björkliden** Sweden
27 K12 **Björklinge** Sweden
27 K12 **Björkö** Sweden
27 G12 **Björköby** Finland
26 J8 **Björksele** Sweden
26 K7 **Björksele** Sweden
26 K8 **Björna** Sweden
27 M10 **Björneborg** Finland
27 G12 **Björneborg** Sweden
115 L2 **Bjorne Pen** N W Terr
27 C11 **Bjørnesfjord** *L* Norway
28 E6 **Bjørnø** *isld* Denmark
147 H13 **Björnöya** *isld* Arctic Oc
26 C3 **Björnsholm Å** *R* Denmark
26 H3 **Björnskinn** Norway
28 E5 **Bjørnsknude** *C* Denmark
27 H13 **Björsäter** Sweden
26 J10 **Bjuråker** Sweden
26 K8 **Bjurholm** Sweden
27 H11 **Bjursås** Sweden
27 G12 **Bjurtjärn** Sweden
26 K7 **Bjurträsk** Sweden
85 C6 **Bla** Mali
28 A5 **Blåbjerg** *hill* Denmark
9 E2 **Blaby** England
19 N12 **Blace** France
122 C3 **Blache,L.de la** Quebec
100 B5 **Blachly** Oregon
111 J8 **Black** *R* Alabama
116 R3 **Black** *R* Alaska/Yukon Terr
103 P8 **Black** *R* Arizona
110 F5 **Black** *R* Arkansas
111 E10 **Black** *R* Louisiana
94 C3 **Black** *R* Michigan
111 H11 **Black** *R* Mississippi
110 F4 **Black** *R* Missouri
112 H4 **Black** *R* N Carolina
112 J3 **Black** *R* S Carolina
99 Q5 **Black** *R* Wisconsin
141 H6 **Blackall** Queensland
144 C5 **Blackball** New Zealand
119 P2 **Black Bay** Ontario
100 B8 **Blackbear** California
119 M3 **Black Bear Island L** Sask
111 H8 **Black Belt** Miss/Ala
8 D2 **Blackbrook** England
141 F4 **Blackbull** Queensland
13 F6 **Blackburn** England
12 E2 **Blackburn** Scotland
116 Q6 **Blackburn,Mt** Alaska
103 K6 **Black Canyon** Nevada
106 C3 **Black Canyon of the Gunnison Nat.Mon** Colorado
146 E12 **Black Coast** Antarctica
103 P6 **Black Creek** Arizona
99 S5 **Black Creek** Wisconsin
118 C8 **Black Diamond** Alberta
100 C2 **Black Diamond** Washington
117 K9 **Black Dome** *mt* Br Col
121 O7 **Black Donald Mines** Ontario
141 G3 **Blackdown** Queensland
8 C6 **Blackdown Hills** England
99 M2 **Blackduck** Minnesota
101 O2 **Black Eagle** Montana
94 E9 **Blackey** Kentucky
13 F4 **Black Fell** England
118 D7 **Blackfalds** Alberta
101 N6 **Blackfoot** Idaho
101 N1 **Blackfoot** Montana
101 O6 **Blackfoot** *R* Idaho
12 E1 **Blackford** Scotland
118 J2 **Black Hawk** Ontario
14 B3 **Black Head** Irish Rep
145 F4 **Black Head** New Zealand
123 T5 **Blackhead B** Nfld
139 K5 **Blackheath** New S Wales
138 B4 **Black Hill** S Australia
140 A4 **Black Hills** N Terr Aust
98 C5 **Black Hills** S Dakota
146 H7 **Black I** Antarctica
119 V7 **Black I** Manitoba
15 D3 **Black I** Scotland
118 D6 **Blackie** Alberta
116 H8 **Black L** Alaska
111 C9 **Black L** Louisiana
94 C1 **Black L** Michigan
112 J3 **Black L** N Carolina
95 M2 **Black L** New York
106 E5 **Black Lake** New Mexico
121 T6 **Black Lake** Quebec
101 N1 **Blackleaf** Montana
127 P6 **Blackman's** Barbados
103 M6 **Black Mesa** *plat* Arizona
112 E2 **Black Mountain** N Carolina
102 G6 **Black Mt** California
118 B1 **Black Mt** New Mexico
140 C2 **Black Mt** N Terr Aust
103 K6 **Black Mts** Arizona
122 E6 **Black Mts** Quebec
8 C3 **Black Mts** Wales/England
101 M7 **Black Pine Pk** Idaho
117 N10 **Black Pines** Br Col
106 B9 **Black Pk** New Mexico
140 C2 **Black Pk** N Terr Aust
117 N10 **Black Pool** Br Col
13 E6 **Blackpool** England
83 L13 **Black R** Mauritius
143 B6 **Black Ra** W Australia
106 C8 **Black Range** New Mexico
94 D2 **Black River** Michigan
99 Q5 **Black River Falls** Wisconsin
110 E5 **Black Rock** Arkansas
103 M3 **Black Rock** Utah
100 F9 **Black Rock Desert** Nevada
112 G3 **Blacksburg** S Carolina
94 G9 **Blacksburg** Virginia
53 D11 **Black Sea** S E Europe
101 P8 **Blacks Fork** *R* Utah/Wyoming
122 F8 **Blacks Hbr** New Brunswick
112 E6 **Blackshear** Georgia
112 D6 **Blackshear, L** Georgia
14 A2 **Blacksod B** Irish Rep
106 B8 **Black Springs** New Mexico
27 H14 **Blackstad** Sweden
14 E4 **Blackstairs Mts** Irish Rep
112 F3 **Blackstock** S Carolina
94 J9 **Blackstone** Virginia
120 B3 **Black Sturgeon L** Ontario
94 G7 **Blacksville** W Virginia
94 H6 **Blackwick** Pennsylvania
122 G7 **Blackville** New Brunswick
112 G4 **Blackville** S Carolina
14 E4 **Blackwater** Irish Rep
110 D3 **Blackwater** Missouri
141 J6 **Blackwater** Queensland
113 C12 **Blackwater** *P* Florida
14 C3 **Blackwater** *R* Irish Rep
110 C3 **Blackwater** *R* Missouri
141 J7 **Blackwater** *R* Queensland
12 C3 **Blackwaterfoot** Scotland
117 M3 **Blackwater L** N W Terr
141 J7 **Blackwater,R** England
9 G4 **Blackwater Reservoir** Scotland
107 N5 **Blackwell** Oklahoma
109 H3 **Blackwell** Texas
107 M3 **Black Wolf** Kansas
98 E9 **Blackwood Cr** Nebraska
143 B10 **Blackwood, R** W Australia
112 F6 **Bladen** Georgia
98 H9 **Bladen** Nebraska
112 K3 **Bladenboro** N Carolina
118 L7 **Bladworth** Sask
8 C2 **Blaenau-Ffestiniog** Wales
8 C4 **Blaenavon** Wales
8 C4 **Blaenporth** Wales
28 C3 **Blære** Denmark
28 C5 **Blagdon** England
18 F9 **Blagnac** France
47 F2 **Blagoevgrad** Bulgaria
51 M3 **Blagoveshchensk** U.S.S.R.
28 M5 **Blåhøj** Denmark
21 B7 **Blain** France
94 K6 **Blain** Pennsylvania
118 A9 **Blaine** Kansas
102 O2 **Blaine** Minnesota
117 M11 **Blaine** Washington
94 H7 **Blaine** W Virginia
119 M5 **Blaine Lake** Sask
20 B3 **Blainville** France
98 K8 **Blair** Nebraska
107 L7 **Blair** Oklahoma
99 P5 **Blair** Wisconsin
94 F9 **Blair** W Virginia
141 H6 **Blair Athol** Queensland
15 E4 **Blair Atholl** Scotland
15 E4 **Blairgowrie** Scotland
102 G3 **Blair Junction** Nevada
12 D1 **Blairmore** Scotland
143 B6 **Blair,Mt** W Australia
102 D2 **Blairsden** California
112 D3 **Blairsville** Georgia
94 H6 **Blairsville** Pennsylvania
94 H6 **Blaise** *R* Eure France
48 H4 **Blaj** Romania
112 C6 **Blakely** Georgia
9 H2 **Blakeney** England
99 S1 **Blake Pt** Michigan
99 O9 **Blakesburg** Iowa
26 K2 **Blåmannen** *mt* Norway
26 H4 **Blåmannsisen** *mt* Norway
36 B6 **Blâmont** France
43 C11 **Blanc** *C* Tunisia
131 E7 **Blanca,B** Argentina
106 G7 **Blanca Cr** New Mex/Tex
131 D7 **Blanca Grande,L** Argentina
133 C8 **Blanca,L** Chile
106 E4 **Blanca Pk** Colorado
106 E8 **Blanca, Sa** *mt* New Mexico
100 J1 **Blanchard** Idaho
94 E3 **Blanchard** Michigan
98 J2 **Blanchard** N Dakota
107 N6 **Blanchard** Oklahoma
120 E2 **Blanche** Ontario
121 F7 **Blanche** Quebec
138 C5 **Blanche,C** S Australia
138 F3 **Blanche,L** S Australia
142 E5 **Blanche, L** W Australia
94 D7 **Blanchester** Ohio
138 E5 **Blanchetown** S Australia
127 C1 **Blanchisseuse** Trinidad
13 F4 **Blanchland** England
106 C5 **Blanco** New Mexico
109 J5 **Blanco** Texas
128 F7 **Blanco** *R* Bolivia
128 D5 **Blanco** *R* Peru
114 G9 **Blanco,C** Oregon
128 B4 **Blanco,C** Peru
115 O7 **Blanc-Sablon** Quebec
94 F9 **Bland** Virginia
43 B12 **Blandan** Algeria
8 D6 **Blandford** England
103 P4 **Blanding** Utah
99 Q9 **Blandinsville** Illinois
17 J3 **Blanes** Spain
112 G3 **Blaney** S Carolina
99 V3 **Blaney Park** Michigan
69 C11 **Blangkejeren** Sumatra
69 B10 **Blangkuala** Sumatra
20 J2 **Blangy** France
20 F3 **Blangy-le-Château** France
22 C3 **Blangy-sur-Ternoise** France
30 H6 **Blanice** *R* Czechoslovakia
33 P5 **Blankenberg** E Germany
22 E1 **Blankenberge** Belgium
33 N9 **Blankenburg** E Germany
37 L2 **Blankenhain** Erfurt E Germany
37 N2 **Blankenhain** Karl-Marx-Stadt E Germany
33 O9 **Blankenheim** E Germany
36 B3 **Blankenheim** W Germany
36 C3 **Blankenrath** W Germany
33 S6 **Blankensee** E Germany
109 J4 **Blanket** Texas
9 F1 **Blankney** England
31 K6 **Blansko** Czechoslovakia
87 G9 **Blantyre** Malawi
12 D2 **Blantyre** Scotland
21 F9 **Blanzay** France
22 F3 **Blaregnies** Belgium
94 J4 **Blasdell** New York
26 G7 **Blåsjön** *L* Sweden
31 L4 **Błaszki** Poland
40 F3 **Blatnitsa** Bulgaria
37 P3 **Blatno** Czechoslovakia
22 F3 **Blaton** Belgium
32 G6 **Blattnicksele** Sweden
36 H7 **Blaubeuren** W Germany
36 H5 **Blaufelden** W Germany
32 J4 **Blaustein** W Germany
18 C5 **Blavet** *R* France
13 H6 **Blaxton** England
13 G4 **Blaydon** England
18 E7 **Blaye** France
142 C5 **Blaze,Mt** W Australia
140 B2 **Blaze Pt** N Terr Aust
31 N6 **Błażowa** Poland
33 N6 **Bleckede** W Germany
42 F2 **Bled** Yugoslavia
8 C3 **Bleddfa** Wales
31 J3 **Bledzew** Poland
27 D12 **Blefjell** *mt* Norway
22 E3 **Bleharies** Belgium
36 B3 **Bleialf** W Germany
38 L8 **Bleiburg** Austria
33 N10 **Bleicherode** E Germany
37 M3 **Bleilochsperre** *res* E Germany
27 H15 **Blekinge** *reg* Sweden
99 L8 **Blencoe** Iowa
145 D4 **Blenheim** New Zealand
120 J10 **Blenheim** Ontario
21 G7 **Bléré** France
25 F6 **Blerick** Netherlands
19 J4 **Blesmes** France
109 L7 **Blessing** Texas
14 E3 **Blessington** Irish Rep
9 E4 **Bletchingdon** England
9 F3 **Bletchley** England
40 B4 **Bletterans** France
69 C1C **Blewe** Sumatra
121 M6 **Bleu,L** Quebec
111 C8 **Blevins** Arkansas
20 H4 **Blévy** France
119 O9 **Blewett** Sask
108 G6 **Blewett** Texas
117 H2 **Blexen Falls L** N Scotia
32 J5 **Blexen** W Germany
85 E1 **Blida** Algeria
27 L12 **Blidö** Sweden
27 F14 **Blidsberg** Sweden
36 C5 **Blies** *R* W Germany
36 C5 **Blieskastel** W Germany
116 O6 **Bligh I** Alaska
38 L5 **Blindenmarkt** Austria
33 T6 **Blindow** E Germany
120 H6 **Blind River** Ontario
46 D3 **Blinisht** Albania
138 E4 **Blinman** S Australia
101 L7 **Bliss** Idaho
94 D5 **Blissfield** Michigan
9 F3 **Blisworth** England
70 O10 **Blitar** Java
85 E7 **Blitta** Togo
100 F7 **Blitzen** Oregon
37 O5 **Blížejov** Czechoslovakia
146 J9 **Block B** Antarctica
95 Q5 **Block I** Rhode I
117 L10 **Bloedel** Br Col
25 C4 **Bloemendaal** Netherlands
87 E4 **Bloemfontein** S Africa
87 E11 **Bloemhof** S Africa
21 H6 **Blois** France
32 L4 **Blokhus** Denmark
32 K9 **Blomberg** W Germany
99 L5 **Blomkest** Minnesota
18 F4 **Blond** France
21 G10 **Blond, Monts de** *mts* France
115 R4 **Blönduos** Iceland
70 Q10 **Blongas** Indonesia
31 M3 **Błonie** Poland
33 R9 **Blönsdorf** E Germany
17 F3 **Blonville** France
140 A6 **Bloods Ra** N Terr Aust
14 C1 **Bloodsworth I** Maryland
14 C1 **Bloody Foreland** Irish Rep
106 G4 **Bloom** Colorado
94 C1 **Bloom** Kansas
99 P4 **Bloomer** Wisconsin
110 K2 **Bloomfield** Indiana
110 D1 **Bloomfield** Iowa
110 G5 **Bloomfield** Kentucky
110 G5 **Bloomfield** Missouri
98 B2 **Bloomfield** Montana
98 J7 **Bloomfield** Nebraska
106 C5 **Bloomfield** New Mexico
121 N9 **Bloomfield** Ontario
95 Q2 **Bloomfield** Vermont
109 L3 **Blooming Grove** Texas
99 N6 **Blooming Prairie** Minnesota
101 O7 **Bloomington** Idaho
99 S9 **Bloomington** Illinois
110 K2 **Bloomington** Indiana
109 L7 **Bloomington** Texas
99 R5 **Bloomington** Wisconsin
95 L6 **Bloomsburg** Pennsylvania
141 J5 **Bloomsbury** Queensland
110 F3 **Bloomsdale** Missouri
95 N4 **Bloomville** New York
94 D5 **Bloomville** Ohio
70 N9 **Blora** Java
37 K6 **Blossenau** W Germany
95 K5 **Blossburg** Pennsylvania
115 R4 **Blosseville Kyst** *coast* Greenland
109 M2 **Blossom** Texas
51 R2 **Blossom Mys** *C* U.S.S.R.
111 L11 **Blountstown** Florida
126 F6 **Blower Rock** Caribbean
112 F1 **Blowing Rock** N Carolina
9 E3 **Bloxham** England
95 M9 **Bloxom** Virginia
13 G6 **Blubberhouses** England
41 L3 **Bludenz** Austria
103 P8 **Blue** *R* Arizona
106 D2 **Blue** *R* Colorado
107 O7 **Blue** *R* Oklahoma
103 N3 **Blue Bell Knoll** *peak* Utah
117 N7 **Blueberry** *R* Br Col
144 C6 **Blue Cliffs** New Zealand
101 N8 **Blue Creek** Utah
113 G10 **Blue Cypress L** Florida
94 D9 **Blue Diamond** Kentucky
99 M6 **Blue Earth** Minnesota
99 M6 **Blue Earth** *R* Minnesota
110 C5 **Blue Eye** Missouri
94 F9 **Bluefield** W Virginia/Virg
125 N3 **Bluefields** Nicaragua
110 M3 **Bluegrass Reg** Kentucky
95 T2 **Blue Hill** Maine
98 H9 **Blue Hill** Nebraska
127 H4 **Blue Hills** Turks & Caicos Is
123 O6 **Blue Hills of Couteau** Nfld
100 F7 **Bluejoint L** Oregon
94 J6 **Blue Knob** *mt* Pennsylvania
103 M2 **Blue L** Utah
100 B9 **Blue Lake** California
99 T8 **Blue Lake** Illinois
94 K7 **Bluemont** Virginia
110 G2 **Blue Mound** Illinois
106 B1 **Blue Mountain** Colorado
110 B7 **Blue Mt** Arkansas
94 K6 **Blue Mt** Pennsylvania
95 L6 **Blue Mt** Pennsylvania
110 C6 **Blue Mt,L** Arkansas
95 N3 **Blue Mt. Lake** New York
100 H7 **Blue Mt. Pass** Oregon
127 M2 **Blue Mt.Pk** Jamaica
144 B6 **Blue Mts** New Zealand
114 G8 **Blue Mts** Oregon/Wash
127 L2 **Blue Mts, The** Jamaica
140 D2 **Blue Mud B** N Terr Aust
86 F3 **Blue Nile** *prov* Sudan
Blue Nile *R see* **Bahr el Azraq**
114 H4 **Bluenose L** N W Terr
117 J6 **Blue** *R* Br Col
107 O2 **Blue Rapids** Kansas
118 B4 **Blue Ridge** Alberta
112 C3 **Blue Ridge** Georgia
94 G10 **Blue Ridge** *mts* Virginia
112 C3 **Blue Ridge L** Georgia
117 O9 **Blue River** Br Col
100 C5 **Blue River** Oregon
121 O6 **Blue Sea Lake** Quebec
14 C2 **Blue Stack Mt** Irish Rep
106 C6 **Bluewater** New Mexico
144 B7 **Bluff** New Zealand
103 P4 **Bluff** Utah
107 N4 **Bluff City** Kansas
112 E1 **Bluff City** Tennessee
109 J3 **Bluffdale** Texas
141 H4 **Bluff Downs** Queensland
142 F3 **Bluff Face Ra** W Australia
143 C10 **Bluff Knoll** *mt* W Australia
71 D6 **Bluff Pt** Palawan Philippines
143 A8 **Bluff Pt** W Australia
110 F2 **Bluffs** Illinois
126 F2 **Bluff, The** Eleuthera Bahamas
118 C7 **Bluffton** Alberta
110 C6 **Bluffton** Arkansas
112 C6 **Bluffton** Georgia
94 B6 **Bluffton** Indiana
99 L3 **Bluffton** Minnesota
94 D6 **Bluffton** Ohio
112 G5 **Bluffton** S Carolina
109 K3 **Blum** Texas
130 E10 **Blumenau** Brazil
33 O8 **Blumenberg** E Germany
33 T5 **Blumenhagen** E Germany
118 K8 **Blumenhof** Sask
32 J6 **Blumenthal** W Germany
36 B3 **Blumenthal** W Germany
40 G4 **Blümlisalp** *mt* Switzerland
98 G5 **Blunt** S Dakota
100 D7 **Bly** Oregon
89 C9 **Blyde Berg** *mt* S Africa
116 N7 **Blying Sound** Alaska
13 G3 **Blyth** England
120 J9 **Blyth** Ontario
140 C1 **Blyth** *R* N Terr Aust
13 E2 **Blyth Br** Scotland
9 H3 **Blythburgh** England
110 A2 **Blythedale** Missouri
142 A5 **Blythe Ra** W Australia
110 A2 **Blytheville** Arkansas
143 G7 **Blyth Ra** S/W Australia
13 H6 **Blyton** England
55 G3 **Blyudtsy** U.S.S.R.
26 G3 **Bo** Norway
85 B7 **Bo** Sierra Leone
27 H13 **Bo** Sweden
71 E4 **Boac** *isld* Philippines
125 M3 **Boaco** Nicaragua
130 F7 **Bôa Esperança** Brazil
65 B7 **Bo'ai** China
120 K7 **Boakview** Ontario
67 D7 **Bo'ao** China
61 L1 **Boara Polesine** Italy
49 B2 **Boardman** *R* Michigan
141 H7 **Boatman** Queensland
138 E3 **Boat of Garten** Scotland
128 F3 **Boa Vista** Brazil
71 D5 **Boayan** *isld* Palawan Philippines
111 K7 **Boaz** Alabama
106 G8 **Boaz** New Mexico
68 J1 **Bobai** China
41 J4 **Bobawaba** Queensland
75 K9 **Bobbili** India
44 F2 **Bobbio** Italy
121 M8 **Bobcaygeon** Ontario
36 E4 **Bobenheim-Roxheim** W Germany
37 K7 **Böbingen** W Germany
33 O5 **Bobitz** E Germany
36 F6 **Böblingen** W Germany
85 D6 **Bobo Dioulasso** Upper Volta
31 K2 **Bobolice** Poland
71 G4 **Bobon** Philippines
128 C4 **Bobonaza** Ecuador
46 F2 **Bobov Dol** Bulgaria
41 J3 **Bóbr** *R* Poland
54 D8 **Bobrinets** U.S.S.R.
48 J1 **Bobrka** U.S.S.R.
54 M5 **Bobrov** U.S.S.R.
52 C5 **Bobrovitsa** U.S.S.R.
31 H4 **Bobrowice** Poland
94 H7 **Bobtown** Pennsylvania
109 K10 **Boca Chica** Texas
113 F13 **Boca Chica** *isld* Florida
127 M10 **Boca del Pao** Venezuela
128 F4 **Bôca do Acre** Brazil
128 E5 **Bôca do Curuquetê** Brazil
128 E5 **Bôca do Jari** Brazil
128 E5 **Bôca do Moaca** Brazil
21 D6 **Bocages** *reg* France
113 E11 **Boca Grande** Florida
127 N1 **Boca Grande** *chan* Trinidad/Ven
113 F13 **Boca Grande Key** *isld* Florida
129 K7 **Bocaiúva** Brazil
130 E9 **Bocaiúva do Sul** Brazil
110 K5 **Bocajá** Brazil
113 G11 **Boca Raton** Florida
127 N1 **Bocas del Dragon** *chan* Trinidad
125 M2 **Bocay** Nicaragua
45 M2 **Bocche del Po Della Pila** Italy
45 M2 **Bocche del Po Delle Tolle** Italy
45 M2 **Bocche del Po di Goro e di Gnocca** Italy
16 E3 **Boceguillas** Spain
19 P16 **Bochaine** *reg* France
121 R3 **Bochart** Quebec
31 M6 **Bochnia** Poland
22 K1 **Bocholt** Belgium
32 E9 **Bocholt** W Germany
37 P3 **Bochov** Czechoslovakia
32 F10 **Bochum** W Germany
37 O3 **Bockau** E Germany
32 M8 **Bockenem** W Germany
32 H6 **Bockhorn** W Germany
31 O3 **Bocki** Poland
38 H7 **Böckstein** Austria
33 T10 **Bockwitz** E Germany
127 J10 **Boconó** Venezuela
124 F4 **Bocoyna** Mexico
48 G5 **Bocsa Vasiovei** Romania
86 C5 **Boda** Cent Afr Republic
27 H10 **Böda** Sweden
27 J14 **Böda** Sweden
27 G14 **Bodafors** Sweden
143 C9 **Bodallin** W Australia
51 L3 **Bodaybo** U.S.S.R.
15 G3 **Boddam** Scotland
97 M8 **Bode** Iowa
102 A3 **Bodega Head** California
86 C2 **Bodele** *dist* Chad
32 H7 **Bodelschwingh** W Germany
26 M6 **Boden** Sweden
12 L8 **Bodenburg** W Germany
36 E4 **Bodenheim** W Germany
37 J3 **Bodenlaube** W Germany
37 P5 **Bodenmais** W Germany
41 K2 **Bodensee** *L* Switzerland
33 N7 **Bodenteich** W Germany
32 L9 **Bodenwerder** W Germany
38 L6 **Bodenwies** *mt* Austria
37 N5 **Bodenwöhr** W Germany
14 C3 **Boderg,L** Irish Rep
102 F6 **Bodfish** California
74 G9 **Bodhan** India
70 G4 **Bodi** Sulawesi Indonesia
36 G5 **Bödigheim** W Germany
76 C5 **Bodinayakkanur** India
8 B7 **Bodinnick** England
70 O9 **Bodjonegoro** Java
7 B7 **Bodmin** England
8 B6 **Bodmin Moor** England
118 G6 **Bodo** Alberta
26 G4 **Bodö** Norway
25 C4 **Bodograven** Netherlands
130 C6 **Bodoquena** Brazil
78 A3 **Bodrum** Turkey
26 G9 **Bodsjö** Sweden
68 H7 **Bo Duc** Vietnam
26 H8 **Bodum** Sweden
48 F2 **Bodva** *R* Hungary
31 M3 **Bodzanów** Poland
40 D5 **Boëge** France
25 G4 **Boekelo** Netherlands
22 F1 **Boekhoute** Belgium
98 H8 **Boelus** Nebraska
18 H7 **Boën** France
86 D6 **Boende** Zaïre
68 G6 **Boeng Lovea** Cambodia
68 G6 **Boeng Me Alpa** Cambodia
109 J6 **Boerne** Texas
25 H2 **Boertange** Netherlands
28 G6 **Boeslunde** Denmark
111 E8 **Boeuf** *R* Arkansas
83 K14 **Bœuf, Nez de** *peak* Réunion
85 B6 **Boffa** Guinea
14 D3 **Bofin,L** Irish Rep
68 B4 **Bogale** Burma
68 B5 **Bogale** *R* Burma
111 F11 **Bogalusa** Louisiana
85 D6 **Bogande** Upper Volta
86 C4 **Bogangolo** Cent Afr Republic
141 H6 **Bogantungan** Queensland
17 F6 **Bogarra** Spain
118 B8 **Bogart,Mt** Alberta
109 M2 **Bogata** Texas
55 C3 **Bogatoye** U.S.S.R.
31 H5 **Bogatynia** Poland
86 C5 **Bogbonge** Zaïre
55 D3 **Bogdanovich** U.S.S.R.
66 D3 **Bogda Shan** *mts* China
27 K14 **Boge** *isld* Gotland Sweden
55 F4 **Bogembay** U.S.S.R.
37 O6 **Bogen** W Germany
87 C11 **Bogenfels** Namibia
28 E5 **Bogense** Denmark
14 C4 **Boggeragh Mts** Irish Rep
143 C6 **Boggola** *mt* W Australia
26 H8 **Boggsjö** Sweden
85 B5 **Boghé** Mauritania
141 J5 **Bogie** *R* Queensland
9 F6 **Bognor Regis** England
22 H4 **Bogny-sur-Meuse** France
71 F5 **Bogo** Cebu Philippines
28 J7 **Bogø** Denmark
54 G6 **Bogodukhov** U.S.S.R.
70 P9 **Bogor** Java
48 J2 **Bogorodchany** U.S.S.R.
51 O3 **Bogorodskoy** U.S.S.R.
128 D3 **Bogotá** Colombia
111 A8 **Bogota** Texas
56 C3 **Bogotol** U.S.S.R.
75 N6 **Bogra** Bangladesh
27 L12 **Bogskär** *lt ho* Finland
56 E2 **Boguchany** U.S.S.R.
54 M7 **Boguchar** U.S.S.R.
55 E4 **Bogudukhovka** U.S.S.R.
107 L2 **Bogue** Kansas
111 F10 **Bogue Chitto** Mississippi
112 K3 **Bogue Inlet** N Carolina
54 B2 **Bogushevsk** U.S.S.R.
54 B7 **Boguslav** U.S.S.R.
31 J5 **Boguszów** Poland
127 L2 **Bog Walk** Jamaica
65 D5 **Bo Hai** *gulf* China
65 E6 **Bohai Haixia** *str* China
22 E4 **Bohain** France
65 D5 **Bohai Wan** *B* China
119 M8 **Boharm** Sask
38 N5 **Böheimkirchen** Austria
30 H6 **Bohemia** *old region* Czech
142 F4 **Bohemia Downs** W Australia
85 E7 **Bohicon** Benin
42 F2 **Bohiniska Bistrica** Yugoslavia
37 N1 **Böhlen** W Germany
37 K7 **Böhmen** W Germany
37 N4 **Böhmer Wald** *mts* W Germany
32 H8 **Bohmte** W Germany
33 Q7 **Böhne** E Germany
71 G6 **Bohol** *isld* Philippines
71 F6 **Bohol Str** Philippines
16 D5 **Bohonal de Ibor** Spain
48 D4 **Bőhönye** Hungary
86 J4 **Bohotleh** Somalia
80 B8 **Bohu** Israel
128 F4 **Boiaçu** Brazil
43 F7 **Boiano** Italy
122 F7 **Boiestown** New Brunswick
122 K5 **Boigneville** France
122 B5 **Boileau** Quebec
130 C9 **Boi Preto,Serra de** *mts* Brazil
130 J8 **Boi, Pta. do** *C* Brazil
129 J7 **Bois** *R* Brazil
94 C1 **Bois Blanc I** Michigan
123 M7 **Boisdale** C Breton I, N Scotia
40 D4 **Bois d' Amont** France
18 H5 **Bois du Roi** *mt* France
106 H5 **Boise City** Oklahoma
20 A5 **Boisgervilly** France
20 H3 **Bois-Guillaume** France
114 G4 **Bois, Lac Des** *L* N W Terr
Bois-le-Duc *see* **'s-Hertogenbosch**
18 H7 **Bois Noirs** *hills* France
22 H1 **Boisschot** Belgium
119 R9 **Boissevain** Manitoba
20 G4 **Boissy-les-Perche** France
20 G5 **Boissy-Maugis** France
38 F9 **Boite** *R* Italy

130 F8 Boituva Brazil
33 T6 Boitzenburg E Germany
33 N6 Boize *R* E Germany
33 N6 Boizenburg E Germany
85 B3 Bojador Morocco
46 C3 Bojana *R* Albania
28 E6 Bøjden Denmark
71 E1 Bojeador,C Luzon Philippines
77 E1 Bojnūrd Iran
69 D13 Bojo *isld* Indonesia
48 F5 Boka Yugoslavia
42 J6 Boka Kotorska *B* Yugoslavia
85 F7 Bokani Nigeria
85 B6 Boké Guinea
113 E11 Bokeelia Florida
32 J6 Bokel W Germany
32 K8 Bokeloh W Germany
68 H6 Bo Kheo Cambodia
89 A8 Bokkeveld Berg *mt* S Africa
27 A12 Boknfjorden *inlet* Norway
56 B6 Boko Kazakhstan U.S.S.R.
86 C3 Bokoro Chad
107 Q6 Bokoshe Oklahoma
86 D6 Bokote Zaïre
59 H2 Bo-ko-tu China
68 D7 Bokpyin Burma
86 D6 Bokungu Zaïre
68 C5 Bok Ye-gan *isld* Burma
70 G5 Bolaäng Sulawesi Indonesia
71 J4 Bolaang Sulawesi Indonesia
86 D6 Bolaiti Zaïre
85 A6 Bolama Guinea-Bissau
75 K8 Bolangir India
124 H7 Bolaños Mexico
67 C5 Bolao China
20 F2 Bolbec France
55 E2 Bolchary U.S.S.R.
99 M9 Bolckow Missouri
48 E4 Bölcske Hungary
33 T5 Boldekow E Germany
28 C6 Bolderslev Denmark
48 K5 Boldeşti Romania
66 C3 Bole China
85 D7 Bole Ghana
101 N2 Bole Montana
48 H1 Bolekhov U.S.S.R.
86 D6 Boleko Zaïre
71 L9 Boleng,Selat Flores Indonesia
100 J4 Boles Idaho
31 J4 Bolesławiec Poland
107 O6 Boley Oklahoma
85 D6 Bolgatanga Ghana
121 O4 Bolger Quebec
48 M5 Bolgrad U.S.S.R.
59 K2 Boli China
86 C6 Bolia Zaïre
26 L7 Boliden Sweden
111 H9 Boligee Alabama
71 D2 Bolinao,C Luzon Philippines
48 K6 Bolintin Vale Romania
71 H4 Boliohutu,Gunung *mt* Sulawesi Indonesia
131 E6 Bolivár Argentina
128 C3 Bolivar Colombia
110 C4 Bolivar Missouri
94 J4 Bolivar New York
110 H6 Bolivar Tennessee
128 D2 Bolivar *div* Colombia
128 C4 Bolivar *prov* Ecuador
128 E2 Bolivar *state* Venezuela
128 F2 Bolivar,Cerro *mt* Venezuela
109 N6 Bolivar Pen Texas
112 J3 Bolivia N Carolina
128 E7 Bolivia *rep* S America
46 E1 Boljevac Yugoslavia
78 E3 Bolkar Dağları *mts* Turkey
27 D12 Bolkesjö Norway
120 G4 Bolkow Ontario
31 J5 Bolków Poland
36 H6 Boll W Germany
41 H2 Boll W Germany
45 K4 Bolle,Le Italy
36 B4 Bollendorf W Germany
19 N16 Bollène France
40 G4 Bolligen Switzerland
28 B5 Bølling Denmark
8 D1 Bollington England
27 H10 Bollnäs Sweden
141 H8 Bollon Queensland
27 G15 Bolmen *L* Sweden
9 F6 Bolney England
71 F5 Bolo Panay Philippines
86 C6 Bolobo Zaïre
71 E7 Bolod Islands Philippines
42 D4 Bologna Italy
19 J4 Bologne France
52 D6 Bologovo U.S.S.R.
54 J2 Bolokhovo U.S.S.R.
86 C5 Bolomba Zaïre
86 D6 Bolombo Zaïre
59 L2 Bolon U.S.S.R.
125 P7 Bolonchén de Rejón Mexico
71 F7 Bolong Mindanao Philippines
59 L2 Bolon,Oz *L* U.S.S.R.
71 F1 Bolos Pt Luzon Philippines
43 B8 Bolotana Sardinia
56 B3 Bolotnoye U.S.S.R.
68 H5 Bolovens, Plateau des Laos
131 C2 Bolsa,Cerro *peak* Argentina
42 D6 Bolsena,L.di Italy
31 N1 Bol'shakovo U.S.S.R.
54 F9 Bolshaya Belozerka U.S.S.R.
55 F3 Bol'shaya Tava *R* U.S.S.R.
56 G1 Bol'shaya Yerema *R* U.S.S.R.
55 F3 Bol'sherech'ye U.S.S.R.
51 P3 Bol'sheretsk U.S.S.R.
55 C3 Bolshe-ustikinskoye U.S.S.R.
54 B4 Bol'shevik U.S.S.R.
51 K1 Bol'shevik, Ostrov *isld* U.S.S.R.
55 F3 Bolshiye Uki U.S.S.R.
56 B1 Bolshoi Megtyg'yegan *R* U.S.S.R.
54 G9 Bolshoi Tokmak U.S.S.R.
48 J1 Bolshovtsy U.S.S.R.
55 E1 Bol'shoy Atlym U.S.S.R.
55 F1 Bol'shoy Balyk *R* U.S.S.R.
147 P10 Bol'shoy Begichev,Os *isld* U.S.S.R.
56 H2 Bol'shoy Chuya *R* U.S.S.R.
55 E3 Bol'shoye Sorokino U.S.S.R.
55 G4 Bol'shoye Topol'noye, Oz *L* U.S.S.R.
55 G4 Bol'shoye Yaravoye, Oz *L* U.S.S.R.
55 E1 Bol'shoy Kamen U.S.S.R.
55 F2 Bol'shoy Kun'yak U.S.S.R.
55 D3 Bol'shoy Kuyash U.S.S.R.
51 O1 Bolshoy Lyakhovskiy,O *isld* U.S.S.R.
56 D2 Bol'shoy Pit *R* U.S.S.R.
55 F1 Bolshoy Salym *R* U.S.S.R.
59 L1 Bol'shoy Shantar,Oz *isld* U.S.S.R.
55 E1 Bol'shoy Tap *R* U.S.S.R.
52 C5 Bol'shoy Tyuters, Os. *isld* U.S.S.R.
55 F3 Bol'shoy Uvat, Oz *L* U.S.S.R.
56 D5 Bolshoy Yenisey *R* U.S.S.R.
55 F2 Bol'shoy Yugan *R* U.S.S.R.
25 E2 Bolsward Netherlands
17 H2 Boltaña Spain
8 C7 Bolt Head England
13 F6 Bolton England
112 J3 Bolton N Carolina
121 L9 Bolton Ontario
13 G6 Bolton Br England
119 W4 Bolton L Manitoba
13 F5 Bolton le-Sands England
78 C1 Bolu Turkey
66 E4 Boluntay China
14 A5 Bolus Hd Irish Rep
54 F3 Bolva *R* U.S.S.R.
47 L6 Bolvadin Turkey
78 C2 Bolvadin Turkey
8 B6 Bolventor England
141 G4 Bolwarra Queensland
48 E5 Bóly Hungary
42 D2 Bolzano Italy
86 B7 Boma Zaïre
22 K3 Bomal Luxembourg/Belgium
86 B5 Bomandjokou Congo
109 H2 Bomarton Texas
86 C5 Bomassa Congo
74 E9 Bombay India
145 E2 Bombay New Zealand
87 H11 Bombetoka,B.de Madagascar
86 F5 Bombo Uganda
86 C5 Bomboma Zaïre
130 H10 Bom Conselho Brazil
129 J7 Bom Despacho Brazil
27 J11 Bomhus Sweden
85 B7 Bomi Hills Liberia
130 J9 Bom Jardim Brazil
130 D5 Bom Jardim de Goiás Brazil
128 E5 Bom Jardin Brazil
129 K5 Bom Jesus Brazil
129 K5 Bom Jesus da Gurgueia, Serra *mts* Brazil
129 K6 Bom Jesus da Lapa Brazil
130 H7 Bom Jesus do Itabapoana Brazil
130 H7 Bom Jesus do Norte Brazil
27 A12 Bömlafjorden *inlet* Norway
27 A12 Bömlo Norway
51 M3 Bomnak U.S.S.R.
86 E5 Bomokandi *R* Zaïre
86 C5 Bomongo Zaïre
143 B7 Bompas Hill W Australia
130 E10 Bom Retiro Brazil
130 G7 Bom Sucesso Brazil
118 D5 Bon Accord Alberta
94 K9 Bon Air Virginia
127 K8 Bonaire *isld* Lesser Antilles
127 K9 Bonaire Trench Caribbean
116 R6 Bona,Mt Alaska
69 D12 Bonandolok Sumatra
106 D3 Bonanza Colorado
125 M3 Bonanza Nicaragua
100 D7 Bonanza Oregon
127 J5 Bonao Dom Rep
99 P9 Bonaparte Iowa
142 E2 Bonaparte Arch W Australia
100 F1 Bonaparte,Mt Washington
15 D3 Bonar Bridge Scotland
121 N8 Bonarlaw Ontario
116 G5 Bonasila Dome *mt* Alaska
127 N3 Bonasse Trinidad
44 G3 Bonassola Italy
122 G5 Bonaventure Quebec
122 H5 Bonaventure I Quebec
115 O8 Bonavista Nfld
40 C3 Bonboillon France
138 D4 Bon Bon S Australia
85 G1 Bon,C Tunisia
106 F4 Boncarbo Colorado
20 J5 Bonce France
13 F3 Bonchester Br Scotland
9 E6 Bonchurch England
101 T10 Bond Colorado
28 C7 Bonden Au *R* W Germany
45 K2 Bondeno Italy
86 D5 Bondo Zaïre
71 F4 Bondoc Penin Luzon Philippines
71 F4 Bondoc Pt Luzon Philippines
36 F6 Bondorf W Germany
85 D7 Bondoukou Ivory Coast
70 O9 Bondowoso Java
126 F2 Bonds Cay *isld* Bahamas
144 C5 Bonds Peak *mt* New Zealand
140 C6 Bond Springs N Terr Aust
99 S5 Bonduel Wisconsin
101 P6 Bondurant Wyoming
Bône *see* Annaba
101 O6 Bone Idaho
113 L9 Bonefish Pond New Providence I Bahamas
71 H7 Bonelipu Indonesia
70 G7 Bonelohe Indonesia
68 G4 Boneng Laos
71 K8 Boneogeh Indonesia
71 K8 Bonerate *isld* Indonesia
26 K3 Bones Norway
15 E5 Boness Scotland
98 H6 Bonesteel S Dakota
131 C2 Bonete,Cerro *peak* Argentina
70 G7 Bone, Teluk *B* Sulawesi Indonesia
98 C1 Bonetraill N Dakota
121 L6 Bonfield Ontario
71 E4 Bongabong Philippines
86 D5 Bongandanga Zaïre
70 F2 Bongao Philippines
70 G5 Bongka Sulawesi Indonesia
70 M9 Bongkok *mt* Java
71 G7 Bongo *isld* Mindanao Philippines
86 C3 Bongor Chad
109 L2 Bonham Texas
118 L1 Bonheur Ontario
12 D2 Bonhill Scotland
36 C7 Bonhomme, Col du *pass* France
43 B7 Bonifacio,Str.of Corsica/Sardinia
111 L11 Bonifay Florida
Bonin Is *see* Ogasawara-shoto
103 P9 Bonita Arizona
111 E9 Bonita Louisiana
113 F11 Bonita Springs Florida
130 C7 Bonito Brazil
69 E13 Bonjol Sumatra
36 C2 Bonn W Germany
18 G6 Bonnat France
19 Q12 Bonne France
19 P15 Bonne *R* France
123 P4 Bonne Bay Nfld
20 F3 Bonnebosq France
22 G3 Bonne Esperance Belgium
123 P2 Bonne Espérance Quebec
20 K4 Bonnelles France
20 B5 Bonnemain France
101 M3 Bonner Montana
140 D1 Bonner Mt N Terr Aust
114 H8 Bonners Ferry Idaho
110 B2 Bonner Springs Kansas
28 A3 Bonnet Denmark
20 F5 Bonnétable France
110 F4 Bonne Terre Missouri
20 K2 Bonneuil-les-Eaux France
20 H5 Bonneval Eure-et-Loir France
40 F7 Bonneval-sur-Arc France
40 D4 Bonnevaux France
19 Q12 Bonneville France
100 D4 Bonneville Oregon
101 R6 Bonneville Wyoming
20 H3 Bonneville,la France
101 N7 Bonneville Pk Idaho
101 L9 Bonneville Salt Flats Utah/Nev
138 F6 Bonney,L S Australia
140 C5 Bonney Well N Terr Aust
20 K1 Bonnières Pas-de-Calais France
20 J3 Bonnières Yvelines France
143 C9 Bonnie Rock W Australia
19 O17 Bonnieux France
36 G5 Bönnigheim W Germany
36 H3 Bonnland W Germany
18 G5 Bonny France
85 F8 Bonny Nigeria
Bonny, Bight Of *see* Biafra, Bight Of
106 H2 Bonny Res Colorado
122 F8 Bonny River New Brunswick
118 G4 Bonnyville Alberta
110 F6 Bono Arkansas
43 C8 Bono Sardinia
71 C6 Bonobond Palawan Philippines
60 D14 Bōno-misaki *C* Japan
68 H7 Bonom Mhai *mt* Vietnam
43 B8 Bonorva Sardinia
140 B2 Bonrook N Terr Aust
111 J11 Bon Secour Alabama
70 E4 Bontang Kalimantan
89 A9 Bonteberg *mts* S Africa
85 B7 Bonthe Sierra Leone
71 E2 Bontoc Luzon Philippines
70 G7 Bontosunggu Sulawesi
109 O5 Bon Wier Texas
48 E4 Bonyhád Hungary
143 G6 Bonython Ra N Terr/W Aust
113 K12 Booby I Bahamas
141 F1 Booby I Queensland
127 M3 Booby South Pt Jamaica
36 D7 Boofzheim France
141 H8 Boogah Queensland
143 C8 Boogardie W Australia
138 C4 Bookabie S Australia
138 D4 Bookaloo,L S Australia
143 A8 Bookara W Australia
103 P2 Book Cliffs Utah
108 D7 Booker Texas
85 C7 Boola Guinea
142 B6 Boolaloo W Australia
143 A6 Boolathanna W Australia
138 E5 Booleroo Centre S Australia
143 A6 Boologooro W Australia
22 G1 Boom Belgium
94 B2 Boon Michigan
141 L8 Boonah Queensland
106 F3 Boone Colorado
99 N7 Boone Iowa
112 F1 Boone N Carolina
94 H9 Boones Mill Virginia
110 C6 Booneville Arkansas
110 N4 Booneville Kentucky
94 D9 Booneville Res Kentucky
141 H6 Boongoondoo Queensland
127 P4 Boon Pt Antigua W I
94 K7 Boonsboro Maryland
58 C2 Bööntsagaan Nuur *L* Mongolia
102 A2 Boonville California
110 J3 Boonville Indiana
110 D3 Boonville Missouri
95 M3 Boonville New York
71 B3 Boo,Pulau Pulau *islds* W Irian
143 D9 Boorabbin W Australia
138 D3 Boorthanna S Australia
20 H3 Boos-sur-Andelle France
13 E5 Boot England
146 A4 Boothby,C Antarctica
147 E3 Boothia, Gulf of N W Terr
115 K3 Boothia Pen N W Terr
111 J8 Boothton Alabama
13 E5 Bootle England
13 F6 Bootle England
37 J6 Bopfingen W Germany
89 C6 Bophuthatswana *reg* S Africa
65 C6 Boping China
36 D3 Boppard W Germany
129 K6 Boqueirão, Serra do *mts* Brazil
128 F8 Boquerón *dep* Paraguay
124 G4 Boquilla de Conchos Mexico
37 O4 Bor Czechoslovakia
86 E4 Bo R Sudan
78 E3 Bor Turkey
48 G6 Bor Yugoslavia
135 M10 Bora-Bora *isld* Society Is Pac Oc
101 M5 Borah Pk Idaho
86 H4 Borama Somalia
27 F14 Borås Sweden
77 B5 Borāzjān Iran
128 G4 Borba Brazil
28 B4 Borbjerg Denmark
71 G5 Borbon Cebu Philippines
130 H9 Borborema, Planalto da *plat* Brazil
48 K3 Borca Romania
48 L6 Borcea *R* Romania
78 H1 Borçka Turkey
138 D6 Borda,C S Australia
47 K7 Bor Dağı *mt* Turkey
18 E8 Bordeaux France
98 B8 Bordeaux Wyoming
122 J7 Borden Pr Edward I
118 K6 Borden Sask
143 C10 Borden W Australia
114 H2 Borden I N W Terr
115 L3 Borden Pen N W Terr
95 N6 Bordentown New Jersey
15 F5 Borders *reg* Scotland
138 F6 Bordertown S Australia
32 M4 Bordesholm W Germany
44 C4 Bordighera Italy
85 D3 Bordj Flye Ste Marie Algeria
85 F2 Bordj Messouda Algeria
85 F3 Bordj Omar Driss Algeria
28 O9 Bordø *isld* Faeroes
57 H4 Bordunskiy U.S.S.R.
85 D5 Boré Mali
143 D8 Boreas,Mt W Australia
31 K4 Borek Poland
29 M11 Borgå Finland
115 R5 Borgarnes Iceland
26 G3 Borge Norway
26 G6 Börgefjell *mt* Norway
32 K9 Borgentreich W Germany
25 G3 Borger Netherlands
108 C8 Borger Texas
32 G7 Börger W Germany
32 K9 Borgholz W Germany
32 H8 Borgholzhausen W Germany
32 F8 Borghorst W Germany
43 H10 Borgia Italy
28 N3 Borgin Faeroes
22 J2 Borgloon Belgium
28 D2 Børglum Denmark
40 G5 Borgne *R* Switzerland
41 O5 Borgo Italy
45 J4 Borgo a Mozzano Italy
45 J1 Borgoforte Italy
45 N6 Borgo Montello Italy
44 F1 Borgonovo Val Tidone Italy
45 M4 Borgo Pace Italy
45 K2 Borgo Panigale Italy
45 O5 Borgorose Italy
42 D5 Borgo S. Lorenzo Italy
41 J6 Borgoticino Italy
44 G3 Borgo Val di Taro Italy
42 D2 Borgo Valsugana Italy
41 H7 Borgo Vercelli Italy
26 H9 Borgsjö Sweden
27 F14 Borgstena Sweden
12 D4 Borgue Scotland
26 B9 Borgund Norway
27 C10 Borgund Norway
26 H8 Borgvattnet Sweden
98 B8 Borie Wyoming
68 F3 Borikhane Laos
31 O6 Borinya U.S.S.R.
26 S2 Boris Gleb U.S.S.R.
31 O6 Borislav U.S.S.R.
57 E3 Borisovka U.S.S.R.
55 F4 Borisovskiy U.S.S.R.
54 B6 Borispol U.S.S.R.
130 C9 Borja Paraguay
17 F3 Borja Spain
42 H4 Borja Planina Yugoslavia
17 H3 Borjas Blancas Spain
26 M6 Börjelslandet Sweden
32 F9 Bork W Germany
32 E9 Borken W Germany
36 G1 Borken W Germany
54 H7 Borki U.S.S.R.
28 D5 Børkop Denmark
86 C2 Borkou *dist* Chad
52 C6 Borkovichi U.S.S.R.
25 G4 Borkulo Netherlands
32 E5 Borkum W Germany
27 H11 Borlänge Sweden
47 J6 Borlu Turkey
44 D3 Bormida di Millésimo *R* Italy
44 D3 Bormida di Spigno *R* Italy
42 C2 Bormio Italy
37 O1 Borna E Germany
25 E2 Borndiep Netherlands
25 G4 Borne Netherlands
70 B4 Borneo *isld* E Indies
16 C3 Bornes *mt* Portugal
36 B2 Bornheim W Germany
27 H16 Bornholm *isld* Denmark
27 G16 Bornholmsgattet *str* Sweden/Denmark
32 M4 Bornhöved W Germany
33 R7 Börnicke E Germany
33 R8 Bornim E Germany
86 B3 Borno *prov* Nigeria
16 D8 Bornos, Embalse de *res* Spain
86 E4 Boro *R* Sudan
48 K3 Boroaia Romania
70 M9 Borobudur *ruins* Java
71 E5 Borocay *isld* Panay Philippines
51 N2 Borogontsy U.S.S.R.
57 L3 Borohoro Shan *mt ra* China
71 H4 Boroko Sulawesi Indonesia
85 D6 Boromo Upper Volta
102 G6 Boron California
141 K6 Bororen Queensland
13 G5 Boroughbridge England
56 B5 Borovlyanka U.S.S.R.
55 F4 Borovoye U.S.S.R.
54 H1 Borovsk U.S.S.R.
55 E3 Borovskiy U.S.S.R.
55 D4 Borovskoye U.S.S.R.
27 G16 Borrby Sweden
28 K6 Borre Denmark
33 R5 Borrenthin E Germany
138 E5 Borrika S Australia
28 B5 Borris Denmark
14 E4 Borris Irish Rep
14 D4 Borrisoleigh Irish Rep
140 D3 Borroloola N Terr Aust
27 J13 Börrum Sweden
48 J3 Borşa Romania
58 G1 Borsch Chovochnyy Khrebet *mt* U.S.S.R.
33 R10 Borsdorf E Germany
26 P1 Börselv Norway
48 H2 Borshava *R* U.S.S.R.
48 K2 Borshchev U.S.S.R.
48 F2 Borsod-Abaúj Zemplén Hungary
25 A6 Borsselen Netherlands
33 N8 Börssum W Germany
28 K5 Borstahusen Sweden
32 J7 Borstel W Germany
57 K3 Bortala He *R* China
8 B3 Borth Wales
18 G7 Bort-les-Orgues France
26 G9 Börtnan Sweden
58 F1 Borto U.S.S.R.
77 B4 Borūjen Iran
77 A3 Borūjerd Iran
28 E4 Borum Denmark
28 H5 Borup Denmark
98 K2 Borup Minnesota
56 D4 Borus,Khrebet *mts* U.S.S.R.
31 K2 Bory Tucholskie *forest* Poland
31 M5 Borzęcin Poland
78 J1 Borzhomi U.S.S.R.
54 D5 Borzna U.S.S.R.
51 L3 Borzya U.S.S.R.
58 G1 Borzya *R* U.S.S.R.
57 G1 Bosaga U.S.S.R.
Bosaso *see* Bender Cassim
33 M4 Bosau W Germany
8 B6 Boscastle England
95 Q3 Boscawen New Hampshire
45 K1 Boschi Santa Anna Italy
20 H2 Bosc-le-Hard France
99 Q6 Boscobel Wisconsin
9 E6 Boscombe England
45 Q8 Boscotrecase Italy
67 B5 Bose China
38 K7 Bosenstein,Gross *mt* Austria
65 D6 Boshan China
55 F5 Boshchekul' U.S.S.R.
89 D7 Boshof S Africa
77 E3 Boshruyeh Iran
46 E2 Bosiljgrad Yugoslavia
68 G4 Bo Si Song Khram Thailand
27 G12 Bosjön Sweden
25 C4 Boskoop Netherlands
98 A8 Bosler Wyoming
8 D1 Bosley England
42 H4 Bosna *R* Yugoslavia
86 C5 Bosobolo Zaïre
61 O10 Bōsō-hantō *pen* Japan
32 G10 Bösperde W Germany
Bosporus Turkey *see* Karadeniz Boğazı
106 D7 Bosque New Mexico
124 G2 Bosque Bonito Mexico
86 C4 Bossangoa Cent Afr Republic
86 C4 Bossèmbélé Cent Afr Republic
86 C4 Bossemtele Cent Afr Republic
111 C9 Bossier City Louisiana
86 B3 Bosso Niger
66 D3 Bosten Hu *L* China
9 F2 Boston England
113 D7 Boston Georgia
95 Q4 Boston Massachusetts
97 Boston *conurbation* Massachusetts
138 D5 Boston B S Australia
117 N11 Boston Bar Br Col
127 M2 Boston Bay Jamaica
110 C6 Boston Mts Arkansas
13 G6 Boston Spa England
28 F6 Bøstrup Fyn Denmark
28 D4 Bøstrup Viborg Denmark
48 E5 Bosut *R* Yugoslavia
123 O5 Boswarlos Nfld
117 P11 Boswell Br Col
99 T9 Boswell Indiana
107 P7 Boswell Oklahoma
94 H6 Boswell Pennsylvania
110 C2 Bosworth Missouri
74 D7 Botad India
139 K5 Botany B New S Wales
26 J8 Boteå Sweden
47 G2 Botev *mt* Bulgaria
47 F2 Botevgrad Bulgaria
118 E6 Botha Alberta
9 F1 Bothamsall England
87 E11 Bothaville S Africa
13 E4 Bothel England
117 M12 Bothell Washington
26 L8 Bothnia,Gulf of Sweden/Finland
120 J10 Bothwell Ontario
12 D2 Bothwell Scotland
139 H8 Bothwell Tasmania
86 B1 Botiala Somalia
16 B3 Boticas Portugal
87 D10 Botletle *R* Botswana
9 E6 Botley England
48 M4 Botna *R* U.S.S.R.
28 H7 Bøtø Denmark
71 D3 Botolan Pt Luzon Philippines
48 K3 Botoşani Romania
68 H4 Bo Trach Vietnam
22 L3 Botrange *mt* Belgium
26 L7 Botsmark Sweden
89 C4 Botswana *rep* Africa
43 G9 Botte Donato *mt* Italy
89 A8 Botter Kloof Pass S Africa
9 F2 Bottesford England
114 J8 Bottineau N Dakota
9 G3 Bottisham England
127 N6 Bottom Saba W I
9 E1 Bottom House England
45 M1 Bottrighe Italy
32 E9 Bottrop W Germany
47 F1 Botunya *R* Bulgaria
115 O8 Botwood Nfld
43 A12 Bou Aci Algeria
85 C7 Bouaflé Ivory Coast
20 H3 Bouafles France
85 D7 Bouaké Ivory Coast
86 C4 Bouala Cent Afr Republic
86 C4 Bouar Cent Afr Republic
85 D2 Bouârfa Morocco
21 B7 Bouaye France
30 H6 Boubín *mt* Czechoslovakia
86 C4 Bouca Cent Afr Republic
18 D9 Boucau France
140 C1 Boucaut B N Terr Aust
20 E4 Boucé France
22 E3 Bouchain France
22 D4 Bouchavesnes France
43 B12 Bouchegouf Algeria
123 N2 Boucher,L Quebec
19 N17 Bouches-du-Rhône *dep* France
121 P6 Bouchette Quebec
22 D4 Bouchoir France
85 D5 Bou Djébéha Mali
84 A3 Boudnib Morocco
40 A2 Boudreville France
40 E4 Boudry Switzerland
21 B7 Bouée France
122 E3 Bouffard,L Quebec
137 M3 Bougainville *isld* Solomon Is
142 F2 Bougainville, C W Australia
141 H3 Bougainville Reef Gt Barrier Reef Aust
71 C2 Bougainville,Selat W Irian
85 F1 Bougaroun,C Algeria
21 I7 Bouges-le-Château France
Bougie *see* Bejaia
85 C6 Bougouni Mali
43 C11 Bouhairet Benzart *gulf* Tunisia
17 G9 Bou Hanifa Algeria
17 G9 Bou Hanifa, Barrage de Algeria
127 M4 Bouillante Guadeloupe W I
20 G3 Bouille,la France
21 E7 Bouillé-Loretz France
21 D6 Bouillé-Ménard France
22 J4 Bouillon Belgium
85 C3 Bou Izakam Morocco
123 L3 Boulain,L Quebec
19 K3 Boulay France
98 A9 Boulder Colorado
101 N3 Boulder Montana
103 N4 Boulder Utah
143 D9 Boulder W Australia
101 Q7 Boulder Wyoming
103 K5 Boulder Can Nevada
103 K6 Boulder City Nevada
102 B4 Boulder Cr California
100 J7 Boulder Cr Idaho
121 N5 Bouleau, L. au Quebec
102 H9 Boulevard California
136 H6 Boulia Queensland
140 E6 Boulia Queensland
22 B2 Boulogne France
21 G6 Bouloire France
85 C5 Boulouli Mali
85 D6 Boulsa Upper Volta
22 H5 Boult-aux-Bois France
85 G6 Boultoum Niger
22 H4 Boulzicourt France
86 C5 Boumba *R* Cameroon
85 D7 Bouna Ivory Coast
117 C3 Boundary Alaska
116 R4 Boundary Yukon Terr
102 F4 Boundary Pk Nevada
118 J9 Boundary Plateau Mont/Sask
114 G7 Boundary Ranges Br Col
85 C7 Boundiali Ivory Coast
68 H6 Boung Long Cambodia
68 E2 Boun Neua Laos
106 E4 Bountiful Colorado
140 E3 Bountiful Is Queensland
118 K7 Bounty Sask
20 K1 Bouquemaison France
28 M2 Bøur Faeroes
110 E3 Bourbeuse *R* Missouri
94 A5 Bourbon Indiana
110 E3 Bourbon Missouri
83 L14 Bourbon,C Kerguelen Indian Oc
18 H6 Bourbon-Lancy France
18 H6 Bourbon l'Archambault France
18 H6 Bourbonnais *prov* France
40 C2 Bourbonne les Bains France
18 G7 Bourboule,la France
19 J5 Bourboune les Bassigny France
22 C2 Bourbourg France
19 O13 Bourbre *R* France
19 O15 Bourdeaux France
36 B6 Bourdonnay France
16 E10 Boured Morocco
85 D5 Bourem Mali
18 E7 Bourg Gironde France
20 G3 Bourg-Achard France
21 I10 Bourganeuf France
21 H9 Bourg Archambault France
18 H7 Bourg Argental France
19 Q15 Bourg d'Arud France
19 O14 Bourg-de-Péage France
21 B6 Bourg-des-Comptes France
20 G2 Bourg Dun France
19 O12 Bourg-en-Bresse Ain France
18 G5 Bourges France
22 F5 Bourg et Comin France
40 C6 Bourget,L.du France
20 K4 Bourget,le France
18 G10 Bourg-Madame France
21 D7 Bourgneuf Maine-et-Loire France
21 E6 Bourg-Neuf Maine-et-Loire France
21 B7 Bourgneuf-en-Retz France
20 D5 Bourgneuf,le France
22 G5 Bourgogne France
19 O13 Bourgoin France
40 E6 Bourg-St-Maurice France
20 G3 Bourgtheroulde France
20 E3 Bourguébus France
21 F7 Bourgueil France
120 K4 Bourkes Ontario
121 N4 Bourlamaque Quebec
22 E3 Bourlon France
40 C1 Bourmont France
121 P4 Bourmont Quebec
21 G7 Bournan France
21 F7 Bournand France
9 F2 Bourne England
115 K1 Bourne,C N W Terr
9 F4 Bourne End England
9 E6 Bournemouth England
20 G3 Bourneville France
21 C8 Bournezeau France
18 E8 Bourriot Bergonce France
32 F7 Bourtanger Moor W Germany
20 G4 Bourth France
22 B2 Bourthes France
8 D5 Bourton England
86 D3 Bourtoutou Chad
22 L4 Bous Luxembourg
85 E1 Bou Saâda Algeria
43 E12 Bou Salem Tunisia
103 K8 Bouse Arizona
103 K8 Bouse Wash *R* Arizona
36 B5 Bous/Saar W Germany
21 J9 Boussac France
20 B5 Boussac, la France
21 C7 Boussay France
22 L5 Bousse France
86 C3 Bousso Chad
20 K5 Boutigny France
85 B5 Boutilimit Mauritania
21 E9 Boutonne *R* France
143 B10 Bouvard,C W Australia
19 O13 Bouvesse France
90 J14 Bouvet *isld* S Atlantic Oc
81 A12 Bouvetøy *isld* S Atlantic Oc
21 B7 Bouvron France
36 C6 Bouxwiller France
85 F6 Bouza Niger
36 B5 Bouzonville France
28 C7 Bov Denmark
43 G11 Bova Italy
32 L9 Bovenden W Germany
70 C4 Boven Kapuas *mts* Sarawak
28 F6 Bovense Denmark
26 C10 Böverdal Norway
20 K2 Boves France
44 C3 Boves Italy
8 C6 Bovey Tracey England
22 K3 Bovigny Belgium
100 J3 Bovill Idaho
43 G7 Bovino Italy
28 A4 Bøvlingbjerg Denmark
45 L1 Bovolenta Italy
45 K1 Bovolone Italy
8 C6 Bow England
98 D1 Bowbells N Dakota
113 F7 Bowden Florida
127 M3 Bowden Jamaica
98 G4 Bowdle S Dakota
101 S1 Bowdoin,L Montana
112 B4 Bowdon Georgia
98 G2 Bowdon N Dakota
143 B10 Bowelling W Australia
110 E1 Bowen Illinois
141 J5 Bowen Queensland
141 J5 Bowen *R* Queensland
141 H5 Bowen Downs Queensland
117 M11 Bowen I Br Col
140 B1 Bowen Str N Terr Aust
95 M7 Bowers Delaware
94 D7 Bowersville Ohio
101 L5 Bowery Pk Idaho
13 F5 Bowes England
143 B8 Bowgada W Australia
103 P9 Bowie Arizona
106 C3 Bowie Colorado
141 H5 Bowie Queensland
109 K2 Bowie Texas
118 F9 Bow Island Alberta
78 L3 Bowkan Iran
12 D2 Bowling Scotland
113 F10 Bowling Green Florida
110 J2 Bowling Green Indiana
110 K4 Bowling Green Kentucky
110 E2 Bowling Green Missouri
94 D5 Bowling Green Ohio
95 K8 Bowling Green Virginia
141 H4 Bowling Green,C Queensland
112 D3 Bowman Georgia
98 C3 Bowman N Dakota
121 M9 Bowmanville Ontario
15 B5 Bowmore Scotland
118 C7 Bowness Alberta
13 F5 Bowness England
118 C7 Bow R Alberta
142 G3 Bow River W Australia
117 N9 Bowron Lake Prov. Park Br Columbia
117 J7 Bowser L Br Columbia
119 Q6 Bowsman Manitoba
118 B7 Bow Valley Prov. Park Alberta
36 H5 Boxberg W Germany
98 C7 Box Butte Res Nebraska
98 A6 Box Cr Wyoming
101 P1 Box Elder Montana
98 C5 Box Elder S Dakota
106 F2 Box Elder Cr Colorado
98 B4 Boxelder Cr Montana
101 R2 Boxelder Cr Montana
9 F5 Box Hill England
27 H13 Boxholm Sweden
58 G5 Bo Xian China
65 D6 Boxing China
25 E5 Boxmeer Netherlands
138 F4 Box Tank New S Wales
25 D5 Boxtel Netherlands
78 E1 Boyabat Turkey
128 D2 Boyacá *div* Colombia
86 C4 Boyali Cent Afr Republic
47 K3 Boyalık Turkey
58 G6 Boyang China
143 B10 Boyanup W Australia
111 D10 Boyce Louisiana
94 J7 Boyce Virginia
143 D8 Boyce,Mt W Australia
115 K6 Boyd Manitoba
101 Q4 Boyd Montana
109 K2 Boyd Texas
123 S4 Boyd's Cove Newfoundland
94 J10 Boydton Virginia
65 C5 Boye China
99 L7 Boyer Iowa
99 L7 Boyer *R* Iowa
106 G3 Boyero Colorado
95 M6 Boyertown Pennsylvania
98 A4 Boyes Montana
95 K10 Boykins Virginia
118 E4 Boyle Alberta
14 C3 Boyle Irish Rep
111 F8 Boyle Mississippi
123 L8 Boylston Nova Scotia
14 E3 Boyne *R* Irish Rep
141 K6 Boyne *R* Queensland
94 C1 Boyne City Michigan
94 C1 Boyne Falls Michigan
20 K5 Boynes France
110 C1 Boynton Missouri
107 P6 Boynton Oklahoma
113 G11 Boynton Beach Florida
86 E5 Boyoma Falls Zaire
101 R6 Boysen Res Wyoming
143 B10 Boyup Brook W Australia
47 J8 Bozburun Turkey
47 H5 Bozcaada *isld* Turkey
47 L5 Boz Dağ *mt* Turkey
47 J7 Bozdoğan Turkey
114 H8 Bozeman Montana
Bozen *see* Bolzano
86 C5 Bozene Zaïre
31 K1 Boże Pole Poland
65 C5 Bozhen China
37 O3 Boží Dar Czechoslovakia
78 D3 Bozkir Turkey
54 F1 Boznya U.S.S.R.
78 G3 Bozova Turkey
48 G6 Bozovici Romania
45 J1 Bozzolo Italy
44 C2 Bra Italy
22 G2 Brabançonne *prov* Belgium
22 G2 Brabant *prov* Belgium
146 E14 Brabant I Antarctica
119 O2 Brabant L Sask
28 E4 Brabrand Denmark
28 H6 Bråby Denmark
42 H5 Brač *isld* Yugoslavia
15 B3 Bracadale Scotland
129 H6 Braça Menor *R* Brazil
44 M5 Bracciano Italy
42 E6 Bracciano,Lago di Italy
44 M5 Bracciano, Lago di Italy
121 L7 Bracebridge Ontario
84 E4 Brach Libya
21 I6 Bracieux France
26 H9 Bräcke Sweden
118 J9 Bracken Sask
109 J6 Bracken Texas
36 G5 Brackenheim W Germany
13 G6 Brackenhill England
119 S5 Bracken L Manitoba
108 G6 Brackettville Texas
9 E3 Brackley England
9 F5 Bracknell England
32 J9 Brackwede W Germany
12 E1 Braco Scotland
43 G8 Bradano *R* Italy
98 F3 Braddock N Dakota
94 H6 Braddock Pennsylvania
99 L9 Braddyville Iowa
113 E10 Bradenton Florida
113 E10 Bradenton Beach Florida
28 B7 Braderup W Germany
110 E6 Bradford Arkansas
8 D5 Bradford England
13 G6 Bradford England
99 R8 Bradford Illinois
99 N7 Bradford Iowa
95 T1 Bradford Maine
95 P3 Bradford New Hampshire
94 C6 Bradford Ohio
121 L8 Bradford Ontario
94 J5 Bradford Pennsylvania
95 Q5 Bradford Rhode I
94 B9 Bradfordsville Kentucky
111 C8 Bradley Arkansas
102 D6 Bradley California
99 T8 Bradley Illinois
107 N7 Bradley Oklahoma
110 D5 Bradleyville Missouri
94 D5 Bradner Ohio
123 P2 Bradore Bay Quebec
123 P2 Bradore Hills Quebec
98 J9 Bradshaw Nebraska
140 B3 Bradshaw N Terr Aust
142 F3 Bradshaw,Mt W Australia
119 R9 Bradwardine Manitoba
9 G4 Bradwell England
118 L7 Bradwell Sask
98 F8 Brady Nebraska
109 H4 Brady Texas
117 E6 Brady Glacier Alaska
138 C3 Brady,Mt S Australia
28 D5 Brædstrup Denmark
138 E5 Braemar S Australia
15 E3 Braemar Scotland
15 E3 Braeriach *mt* Scotland
142 D5 Braeside W Australia
16 B3 Braga Portugal
131 E5 Bragado Argentina
129 J4 Bragança Brazil
16 C3 Bragança Portugal
130 F8 Bragança Paulista Brazil
112 E6 Braganza Georgia
110 G5 Bragg City Missouri
118 C7 Bragg Creek Prov. Park Alberta
54 B5 Bragin U.S.S.R.
99 N4 Braham Minnesota
33 N6 Brahlstorf Schwerin E Germany
75 O7 Brahmanbaria Bangladesh
75 P5 Brahmaputra *R* S Asia
32 L4 Brahmsee *L* W Germany
77 K5 Brahui,Cen *reg* Pakistan
99 S8 Braidwood Illinois
48 L5 Brăila Romania
9 E2 Brailsford England
98 J8 Brainard Nebraska
22 F5 Braine France
22 G2 Braine L'Alleud Belgium
22 G2 Braine-le Château Belgium
22 G2 Braine-le Comte Belgium
99 M3 Brainerd Minnesota
21 F7 Brain-sur-Allonnes France
9 G4 Braintree England
13 E4 Braithwaite England
111 G12 Braithwaite Louisiana
140 C1 Braithwaite Pt N Terr Aust
22 J2 Braives Belgium
89 F4 Brak *R* S Africa
32 H6 Brake W Germany
22 F2 Brakel Belgium
32 K9 Brakel W Germany
85 B5 Brakna *reg* Mauritania
57 D1 Brali U.S.S.R.
114 G7 Bralorne Br Columbia
107 N5 Braman Oklahoma
Brambach *see* Radiumbad-Brambach
38 F7 Bramberg Austria
13 G6 Bramham England
32 H6 Bramloge W Germany
28 B6 Bramming Denmark
44 B3 Bram,Monte Italy
26 J9 Brämö *isld* Sweden
9 H3 Brampton England
98 J3 Brampton N Dakota
141 J5 Brampton I Queensland
32 G8 Bramsche W Germany
141 G1 Bramwell Queensland
94 F9 Bramwell W Virginia
9 G2 Brancaster England
13 G4 Brancepeth England
99 U6 Branch Michigan
123 T7 Branch Nfld
95 K4 Branchport New York
112 G4 Branchville S Carolina
130 B7 Branco *R* Mato Grosso Brazil
128 F3 Branco *R* Roraima Brazil
130 J9 Branco,Cabo Brazil
131 B2 Branco,R Argentina
41 L3 Brand Austria
37 O3 Brand Czechoslovakia
87 B10 Brandberg *mt* Namibia
26 H9 Brändbo Sweden
28 C5 Brande Denmark
32 L5 Brande-Hörnerkirchen W Germany
101 T4 Brandenberg Montana
33 R8 Brandenburg E Germany
110 K4 Brandenburg Kentucky
37 P2 Brand-Erbisdorf E Germany
28 C6 Branderup Denmark
21 G9 Brandes *reg* France
13 H6 Brandesburton England
89 E7 Brandfort S Africa
33 R10 Brandis E Germany
29 J11 Brändö Finland
106 H3 Brandon Colorado
9 G3 Brandon England
119 S9 Brandon Manitoba
98 E9 Brandon Nebraska
141 H4 Brandon Queensland
95 O3 Brandon Vermont
99 S6 Brandon Wisconsin
14 A4 Brandon B Irish Rep
14 A4 Brandon Hd Irish Rep
14 A4 Brandon Mt Irish Rep
95 N3 Brandreth New York
13 G5 Brandsby England
133 F5 Brandsen Argentina
28 D6 Brandsø *isld* Denmark
110 E5 Brandsville Missouri
98 K5 Brandt S Dakota
27 F11 Brandval Norway
87 D12 Brandvlei S Africa
94 K8 Brandy Virginia
95 L8 Brandywine Maryland
48 K6 Braneşti Romania
95 P5 Branford Connecticut
113 E8 Branford Florida
31 M1 Braniewo Poland
27 L17 Braniewo U.S.S.R.
31 M6 Branisko *mts* Czechoslovakia
18 E8 Branne France
47 H3 Brannitsa Bulgaria
141 F8 Bransby Queensland
102 A2 Branscomb California
146 E14 Bransfield Str Antarctica
106 G4 Branson Colorado
110 C5 Branson Missouri
9 F1 Branston England
118 D8 Brant Alberta
70 O9 Brantas Java
70 O10 Brantas *R* Java
98 H2 Brantford N Dakota
115 L9 Brantford Ontario
111 K10 Brantley Alabama
18 F7 Brantôme France
138 F7 Branxholme Victoria
115 N8 Bras d'or L Nova Scotia
99 O9 Brashear Missouri
128 E6 Brasiléia Brazil
129 J7 Brasília Brazil
129 G4 Brasilia Legal Brazil
52 C6 Braslav U.S.S.R.
48 K5 Brasov Romania
85 F8 Brass Nigeria
22 G1 Brasschaat Belgium
140 C6 Brassey Mt N Terr Aust
143 D6 Brassey Ra W Australia
70 E2 Brassey Ra *mts* Sabah
139 G5 Brassi New S Wales
28 D4 Brassø *L* Denmark
95 R1 Brassua L Maine
48 H4 Bratca Romania
48 L5 Brates, L Romania
31 K7* Bratislava Czechoslovakia
47 G3 Bratsigovo Bulgaria
56 F3 Bratsk U.S.S.R.
48 M2 Bratslav U.S.S.R.

95 P4 **Brattleboro** Vermont
32 M8 **Brau** W Germany
36 D3 **Braubach** W Germany
36 G2 **Brauerschwend** W Germany
38 H5 **Braunau** Austria
36 E3 **Braunfels** W Germany
33 N9 **Braunlage** W Germany
33 P10 **Braunsbedra** E Germany
Braunsberg *see* **Braniewo**
8 B5 **Braunton** England
36 B2 **Brauweiler** W Germany
86 H5 **Brava** Somalia
131 D4 **Brava, L. la** Argentina
94 G7 **Brave** Pennsylvania
27 H13 **Bråviken** *L* Sweden
131 D2 **Bravo,Sa** *mt* Argentina
14 E3 **Bray** Irish Rep
22 D1 **Bray-Dunes** France
22 E5 **Braye** France
21 G6 **Braye** *R* France
20 J3 **Bray-et-Lû** France
8 C5 **Brayford** England
14 A5 **Bray Hd** Irish Rep
115 M4 **Bray I** N W Terr
110 C2 **Braymer** Missouri
18 H4 **Bray sur Seine** France
21 H5 **Bray-sur-Somme** France
118 A6 **Brazeau** Alberta
118 B6 **Brazeau Dam** Alberta
110 J2 **Brazil** Indiana
128 F6 **Brazil** *rep* S America
90 G11 **Brazil Basin** Atlantic Oc
109 M6 **Brazoria** Texas
109 L4 **Brazos** *R* Texas
86 C6 **Brazzaville** Congo
48 E6 **Brčko** Yugoslavia
31 K2 **Brda** *R* Poland
48 D1 **Brdo** *mt* Czechoslovakia
140 E6 **Breadalbane** Queensland
143 E7 **Breaden Bluff** *hill* W Australia
143 F7 **Breaden,L** W Australia
141 K1 **Breakfast Creek** *dist* Brisbane, Qnsld
144 A6 **Breaksea I** New Zealand
144 B7 **Breaksea Is** New Zealand
141 L6 **Breaksea Spit** Queensland
20 B5 **Bréal-s-M** France
8 D4 **Bream** England
145 E1 **Bream Bay** New Zealand
27 F15 **Breared** Sweden
20 F2 **Bréaute** France
111 E11 **Breaux Bridge** Louisiana
70 M9 **Brebes** Java
70 M9 **Brebes,Tg** *C* Java
121 U4 **Brébeuf, L** Quebec
122 B5 **Brébeuf,L** Quebec
20 C4 **Brécey** France
36 E3 **Brechen** W Germany
121 L8 **Brechin** Ontario
15 F4 **Brechin** Scotland
22 H1 **Brecht** Belgium
106 D2 **Breckenridge** Colorado
98 K3 **Breckenridge** Minnesota
110 C2 **Breckenridge** Missouri
109 J3 **Breckenridge** Texas
133 C8 **Brecknock, Pen** Chile
31 K7 **Břeclav** Czechoslovakia
8 C4 **Brecon** Wales
8 C4 **Brecon Beacons** *mts* Wales
Breconshire *co see* **Powys, Gwent, Mid Glamorgan** *counties*
99 M7 **Breda** Iowa
25 C5 **Breda** Netherlands
26 M6 **Bredåker** Sweden
27 H15 **Bredåkra** Sweden
27 G14 **Bredaryd** Sweden
87 D12 **Bredasdorp** S Africa
33 Q7 **Breddin** E Germany
32 K6 **Breddorf** W Germany
28 B6 **Brede** Denmark
9 G6 **Brede** England
28 B6 **Brede Å** *R* Denmark
28 B6 **Bredebro** Denmark
32 J10 **Bredelar** W Germany
22 E1 **Bredene** Belgium
28 E5 **Bredenfelde** E Germany
119 P8 **Bredenbury** Sask
33 S6 **Bredereiche** E Germany
28 C7 **Bredevad** Denmark
27 G12 **Bredsjö** Sweden
30 E1 **Bredstedt** W Germany
28 C5 **Bredsten** Denmark
26 K8 **Bredträsk** Sweden
55 D4 **Bredy** U.S.S.R.
22 K1 **Bree** Belgium
89 A9 **Breede** *R* S Africa
110 G3 **Breese** Illinois
33 Q5 **Breesen** E Germany
46 E3 **Bregalnica** *R* Yugoslavia
41 H2 **Brege** *R* W Germany
41 L2 **Bregenz** Austria
41 L3 **Bregenzer Ache** *R* Austria
41 L3 **Bregenzer Wald** *mt* Austria
28 G5 **Bregninge** Denmark
48 H6 **Bregovo** Bulgaria
20 C4 **Bréhal** France
18 C4 **Bréhat, I** France
122 B1 **Bréhat, L** Quebec
33 Q9 **Brehna** E Germany
33 T9 **Brehnitz** E Germany
36 E2 **Breidenbach** W Germany
98 E3 **Breien** N Dakota
20 G5 **Breil-sur-Mérize, le** France
26 B10 **Breim** Norway
40 G1 **Breisach** W Germany
37 M5 **Breitenbrunn** W Germany
33 Q10 **Breitenfeld** E Germany
37 K4 **Breitengüssbach** W Germany
33 P9 **Breitenhagen** E Germany
33 M7 **Breitenhees** W Germany
37 O3 **Breitenhof** E Germany
33 S6 **Breiter Luzinsee** *L* E Germany
40 G5 **Breithorn** *mt* Switzerland
33 O4 **Breitling** E Germany
37 J2 **Breitungen** W Germany
26 M1 **Breivikbotn** Norway
28 F4 **Brejning** Denmark
129 K4 **Brejo** Brazil
94 C3 **Brekenridge** Michigan
26 E9 **Brekken** Norway
26 D8 **Brekstad** Norway
26 A10 **Bremangerland** *isld* Norway
41 L6 **Brembana, Val** Italy
41 L6 **Brembo** *R* Italy
112 B4 **Bremen** Georgia
94 A5 **Bremen** Indiana
94 E7 **Bremen** Ohio
32 J6 **Bremen** W Germany
140 D1 **Bremer** *isld* N Terr Aust
143 C10 **Bremer Bay** W Australia
143 D10 **Bremer Ra** W Australia
117 M12 **Bremerton** Washington
32 K6 **Bremervörde** W Germany
41 H3 **Bremgarten** Switzerland
116 Q6 **Bremner** *R* Alaska
109 L4 **Bremond** Texas
26 E6 **Bremsteinen** *It ho* Norway
139 H3 **Brenda** New S Wales
141 H8 **Brenda** Queensland
28 D6 **Brenderup** Denmark
45 K1 **Brendola** Italy
8 C5 **Brendon Hills** England
109 L5 **Brenham** Texas
21 G7 **Brenne** *R* France
41 O3 **Brenner** Austria
101 M5 **Brenner** Montana
41 O4 **Brennero** Italy
41 O3 **Brenner Pass** Austria/Italy
41 M6 **Breno** Italy
42 C3 **Breno** Italy
19 P12 **Brénod** France
36 C5 **Brenschelbach** W Germany
111 J9 **Brent** Alabama
121 M6 **Brent** Ontario
42 D3 **Brenta** *R* Italy
41 N5 **Brenta, Gruppa di** *mt* Italy
9 F5 **Brentford** England
98 H4 **Brentford** S Dakota
123 T4 **Brenton Rock** Nfld
102 C4 **Brentwood** California
9 G4 **Brentwood** England
37 J6 **Brenz** *R* W Germany
9 G5 **Brenzett** England
45 J2 **Brescello** Italy
41 M6 **Brescia** Italy
25 A6 **Breskens** Netherlands
Breslau *see* **Wrocław**
20 J2 **Bresle** *R* France
20 K3 **Bresles** France
143 C6 **Bresnahan,Mt** W Australia
41 P4 **Bressanone** Italy
21 E8 **Bressuire** France
18 B4 **Brest** France
31 O3 **Brest** U.S.S.R.
18 D5 **Brest** *R* France
18 C4 **Bretagne** *prov* France
83 J14 **Bretagne, Pnte de** Réunion Indian Oc
48 K4 **Breţcu** Romania
18 G8 **Bretenoux** France
20 G4 **Breteuil-sur-Iton** France
20 K2 **Breteuil-sur-Noye** France
20 K4 **Bretigny** France
118 C5 **Breton** Alberta
20 G5 **Bretoncelles** France
111 G12 **Breton I** Louisiana
20 K2 **Bretonneux,V** France
21 C9 **Breton, Pertuis** *str* France
95 N6 **Breton Woods** New Jersey
38 K7 **Bretstein** Austria
145 E1 **Brett, C** New Zealand
36 F5 **Bretten** W Germany
20 E3 **Bretteville** France
20 D3 **Bretteville l'Orgueilleuse** France
37 J5 **Brettheim** W Germany
36 G5 **Bretzfeld** W Germany
36 G4 **Breuberg** W Germany
69 B10 **Breueh** *isld* Sumatra
25 E5 **Breugel** Netherlands
20 F3 **Breuil-en-Auge,le** France
20 H4 **Breuilpont** France
25 D4 **Breukelen** Netherlands
40 C1 **Breuvannes** France
20 J4 **Bréval** France
112 E2 **Brevard** N Carolina
129 H4 **Breves** Brazil
27 D12 **Brevik** Norway
95 T2 **Brewer** Maine
95 L3 **Brewerton** New York
113 E10 **Brewster** Florida
107 J2 **Brewster** Kansas
98 G8 **Brewster** Nebraska
95 O5 **Brewster** New York
94 F6 **Brewster** Ohio
117 O11 **Brewster** Washington
144 B6 **Brewster, Mt** New Zealand
111 J10 **Brewton** Alabama
25 F6 **Breyell** W Germany
19 O14 **Brezins** France
46 F2 **Breznik** Bulgaria
48 F2 **Brezno** Czechoslovakia
38 M8 **Brezno** Yugoslavia
20 H4 **Brezolles** France
16 D2 **Brezo, Sa. del** *mts* Spain
46 F3 **Brezovo** Bulgaria
86 D4 **Bria** Cent Afr Republic
103 M4 **Brian Head** Utah
18 G5 **Briare** France
141 L7 **Bribie I** Queensland
108 G1 **Brice** Texas
99 N6 **Bricelyn** Minnesota
48 L2 **Brichany** U.S.S.R.
110 F7 **Brickeys** Arkansas
19 J4 **Bricon** France
123 M2 **Briconnet,L** Quebec
20 B3 **Bricquebec** France
20 B4 **Bricqueville-sur-Mer** France
12 D5 **Bride** I of Man U.K.
14 C4 **Bride** *R* Irish Rep
8 B3 **Bridell** Wales
8 B6 **Bridestowe** England
119 U3 **Bridge** Manitoba
101 M7 **Bridge** Idaho
117 M10 **Bridge** *R* Br Columbia
112 D6 **Bridgeboro** Georgia
12 B2 **Bridgend** Islay Scotland
13 E1 **Bridgend** Tayside Scotland
8 C5 **Bridgend** Wales
12 E1 **Bridge of Allan** Scotland
12 D3 **Bridge of Doon** Scotland
12 D2 **Bridge of Weir** Scotland
102 E3 **Bridgeport** California
95 O5 **Bridgeport** Connecticut
107 N3 **Bridgeport** Kansas
98 C8 **Bridgeport** Nebraska
100 H5 **Bridgeport** Oregon
100 F2 **Bridgeport** Washington
102 E3 **Bridgeport Res** California
113 L12 **Bridge Pt** Bahamas
101 R4 **Bridger** Montana
101 P4 **Bridger Pk** Montana
101 S8 **Bridger Pk** Wyoming
112 K2 **Bridgeton** N Carolina
95 M7 **Bridgeton** New Jersey
127 P6 **Bridgetown** Barbados
122 H9 **Bridgetown** Nova Scotia
143 B10 **Bridgetown** W Australia
100 B9 **Bridgeville** California
122 K8 **Bridgeville** Nova Scotia
95 S7 **Bridgewater** Maine
95 R5 **Bridgewater** Massachusetts
115 N9 **Bridgewater** Nova Scotia
98 J6 **Bridgewater** S Dakota
94 J8 **Bridgewater** Virginia
138 F7 **Bridgewater,C** Victoria
94 A5 **Bridgman** Michigan
8 D2 **Bridgnorth** England
95 R2 **Bridgton** Maine
8 C5 **Bridgwater** England
13 H5 **Bridlington** England
13 H5 **Bridlington Bay** England
8 D6 **Bridport** England
139 H8 **Bridport** Tasmania
18 G4 **Brie** *reg* France
Brieg *see* **Brzeg**
25 B5 **Brielle** Netherlands
112 F4 **Brier Creek** Georgia
119 M8 **Briercrest** Sask
118 F4 **Brierreville** Alberta
122 F9 **Brier I** Nova Scotia
22 H5 **Brieulles-sur-Bar** France
22 K5 **Briey** France
40 G5 **Brig** Switzerland
41 H3 **Brigach** *R* W Germany
120 H10 **Brigden** Ontario
13 H6 **Brigg** England
109 K5 **Briggs** Texas
106 G3 **Briggsdale** Colorado
98 B9 **Brigham City** Utah
13 G6 **Brighouse** England
13 E6 **Brightsone** England
103 M5 **Bright Angel Pt** Arizona
9 H4 **Brightlingsea** England
98 B10 **Brighton** Colorado
9 F6 **Brighton** England
113 F10 **Brighton** Florida
110 F2 **Brighton** Illinois
99 P8 **Brighton** Iowa
94 D4 **Brighton** Michigan
120 J8 **Brighton** Ontario
138 D6 **Brighton** S Australia
138 F6 **Brighton** Victoria
141 F6 **Brighton Downs** Queensland
145 D4 **Brightwater** New Zealand
18 C4 **Brignogan** France
123 T6 **Brigus** Nfld
17 F4 **Brihuega** Spain
26 G4 **Brikserver** *isld* Norway
130 C7 **Brilhante,R** Brazil
21 G9 **Brillac** France
106 F5 **Brilliant** New Mexico
99 S5 **Brillion** Wisconsin
99 R9 **Brimfield** Illinois
83 H8 **Brindisi** Italy
138 C4 **Bring,L** S Australia
94 E6 **Brinkhaven** Ohio
110 E7 **Brinkley** Arkansas
9 G3 **Brinkley** England
9 E3 **Brinklow** England
32 J6 **Brinkum** W Germany
138 E5 **Brinkworth** S Australia
21 J6 **Brinon-sur-Sauldre** France
98 G1 **Brinsmade** N Dakota
113 C7 **Brinson** Georgia
123 L6 **Brion I** Madeleine Is, Quebec
20 G3 **Brionne** France
18 H7 **Brioude** France
21 E9 **Brioux-sur-Boutonne** France
20 E4 **Briouze** France
141 L8 **Brisbane** Queensland
141 L7 **Brisbane R** Queensland
108 D8 **Briscoe** Texas
45 L3 **Brisighella** Italy
21 E7 **Brissac** France
41 J4 **Bristenstock** *mt* Switzerland
106 H3 **Bristol** Colorado
95 P5 **Bristol** Connecticut
8 D5 **Bristol** England
113 C7 **Bristol** Florida
112 E6 **Bristol** Georgia
94 B5 **Bristol** Indiana
122 E7 **Bristol** New Brunswick
95 Q3 **Bristol** New Hampshire
95 M6 **Bristol** Pennsylvania
121 O7 **Bristol** Quebec
95 Q5 **Bristol** Rhode I
98 J4 **Bristol** S Dakota
95 P2 **Bristol** Vermont
94 E10 **Bristol** Virginia/Tenn
116 G8 **Bristol B** Alaska
8 C5 **Bristol Chan** England/Wales
146 A13 **Bristol I** Antarctica
103 J7 **Bristol L** California
103 J7 **Bristol Mts** California
113 K3 **Bristol Silver** Nevada
107 O6 **Bristow** Oklahoma
117 M11 **Britannia Beach** Br Col
146 H6 **Britannia Ra** Antarctica
146 C12 **British Antarctic Territory** Antarctica
117 L8 **British Columbia** *prov* Canada
115 L1 **British Empire Ra** N W Terr
British Guiana *see* **Guyana**
British Honduras *see* **Belize**
83 H5 **British Ind.Oc.Terr** *colony* Indian Oc
114 F4 **British Mts** Alaska/Yukon Terr
British N. Borneo *see* **Sabah**
British Solomon Is *see* **Solomon Is.**
123 M7 **Briton Cove** C Breton I, N Scotia
8 C4 **Briton Ferry** Wales
87 E11 **Brits** S Africa
87 D12 **Britstown** S Africa
99 N6 **Britt** Iowa
120 K7 **Britt** Ontario
27 G14 **Brittatorp** Sweden
107 N6 **Britton** Oklahoma
98 J4 **Britton** S Dakota
138 C2 **Britton,Mt** S Australia
33 T7 **Britz** E Germany
18 G7 **Brive** France
16 E2 **Briviesca** Spain
20 B2 **Brix** France
38 F7 **Brixental** *V* Austria
8 C7 **Brixham** England
141 G6 **Brixton** Queensland
48 D1 **Brno** Czechoslovakia
27 F12 **Bro** Sweden
12 D3 **Broad** *R* Georgia
112 F3 **Broad** *R* S Carolina
118 J6 **Broadacres** Sask
95 N3 **Broadalbin** New York
143 D9 **Broad Arrow** W Australia
115 M7 **Broadback** *R* Quebec
15 B2 **Broad Bay** Scotland
100 B7 **Broadbent** Oregon
109 N4 **Broaddus** Texas
15 C3 **Broadford** Scotland
14 B2 **Broad Haven** Irish Rep
8 A4 **Broad Haven** Wales
9 E5 **Broad Hinton** England
71 G5 **Broadhurst Ra** W Australia
98 H5 **Broadland** S Dakota
15 E5 **Broad Law** Scotland
141 J7 **Broadmere** Queensland
116 N5 **Broad Pass** Alaska
141 J5 **Broad Sound** Queensland
141 K5 **Broad Sound Chan** Queensland
141 J6 **Broadsound Ra** Queensland
9 H5 **Broadstairs** England
98 A4 **Broadus** Montana
101 R3 **Broadview** Montana
106 C7 **Broadview** New Mexico
119 P8 **Broadview** Sask
9 F6 **Broadwater** England
98 D8 **Broadwater** Nebraska
9 E3 **Broadway** England
8 D6 **Broadway** England
8 D6 **Broadwindsor** England
145 D1 **Broadwood** New Zealand
126 C3 **Broa, Ensenada de la** *B* Cuba
28 D7 **Broager** Denmark
28 E6 **Broby** Denmark
27 G15 **Broby** Sweden
119 Q1 **Brochet** Manitoba
122 C4 **Brochet,L.au** Quebec
32 G8 **Brochterbeck** W Germany
121 Q4 **Brochu,L** Quebec
99 L9 **Brock** Nebraska
118 J7 **Brock** Sask
32 L6 **Brockel** W Germany
33 N9 **Brocken** *mt* E Germany
9 E6 **Brockenhurst** England
118 D9 **Brocket** Alberta
98 H1 **Brocket** N Dakota
114 H2 **Brock I** N W Terr
13 H6 **Brocklesby** England
142 E6 **Brockman,Mt** W Australia
94 K3 **Brockport** New York
98 G7 **Brocksburg** Nebraska
140 B2 **Brock's Creek** N Terr Aust
95 C4 **Brockton** Massachusetts
98 A1 **Brockton** Montana
121 P8 **Brockville** Ontario
98 A4 **Brockway** Montana
94 J5 **Brockway** Pennsylvania
110 J2 **Brocton** Illinois
94 H4 **Brocton** New York
46 D1 **Brod** Yugoslavia
48 F7 **Brodarevo** Yugoslavia
118 F7 **Broderick** Sask
11 L3 **Brodeur Pen** N W Terr
99 R7 **Brodhead** Wisconsin
98 G5 **Brodica** Yugoslavia
12 C2 **Brodick** Scotland
94 K10 **Brodnax** Virginia
31 L2 **Brodnica** Poland
55 D3 **Brodokalmak** U.S.S.R.
25 C3 **Broek op Langedijk** Netherlands
100 H5 **Brogan** Oregon
20 G3 **Broglie** France
20 K5 **Brohinière,la** France
36 C3 **Brohl-Lützing** W Germany
33 T5 **Brohm-Cosa** E Germany
33 M8 **Brokstedt** W Germany
31 N2 **Brok** Poland
99 R4 **Brokaw** Wisconsin
36 K5 **Brokdorf** W Germany
107 P6 **Broken Arrow** Oklahoma
139 K5 **Broken Bay** New S Wales
98 G8 **Broken Bow** Nebraska
107 Q7 **Broken Bow** Oklahoma
138 F4 **Broken Hill** New S Wales
Broken Hill Zambia *see* **Kabwe**
129 G3 **Brokopondomeer** *L* Suriname
29 K12 **Bromarv** Finland
Bromberg *see* **Bydgoszcz**
33 N7 **Brome** W Germany
8 D3 **Bromfield** England
98 C1 **Bromhead** Sask
9 G5 **Bromley** England
27 D11 **Bromma** Norway
28 G5 **Brommes** Denmark
70 O9 **Bromo** *mt* Java
13 H5 **Brompton** England
99 O9 **Brompton** Iowa
8 D3 **Bromsgrove** England
8 D3 **Bromyard** England
110 B4 **Bronaugh** Missouri
28 D2 **Brønderslev** Denmark
28 A5 **Brøndum** Denmark
8 C3 **Bronllys** Wales
37 L4 **Bronn** W Germany
27 G15 **Brönnestad** Sweden
55 E2 **Bronnikovo** U.S.S.R.
26 F6 **Brønnøysund** Norway
36 H2 **Bronnzell** W Germany
28 B6 **Brøns** Denmark
113 E8 **Bronson** Florida
94 B5 **Bronson** Michigan
109 N4 **Bronson** Texas
121 L9 **Bronte** Ontario
43 F11 **Bronte** Sicily
108 G4 **Bronte** Texas
139 H8 **Bronte Park** Tasmania
95 O6 **Bronx** New York
41 O5 **Bronzolo** Italy
122 E3 **Brooch L** Quebec
99 T9 **Brook** Indiana
94 K8 **Brooke** Virginia
109 O4 **Brookeland** Texas
113 E8 **Brooker** Florida
71 C6 **Brooke's Pt** Palawan Philippines
110 C2 **Brookfield** Missouri
122 J8 **Brookfield** Nova Scotia
111 F10 **Brookhaven** Mississippi
119 N9 **Brooking** Sask
100 A7 **Brookings** Oregon
98 K5 **Brookings** S Dakota
141 H4 **Brook Is.Lt.Ho** Queensland
9 G6 **Brookland** England
95 K5 **Brookland** Pennsylvania
112 F5 **Brooklet** Georgia
121 M9 **Brooklin** Ontario
95 Q4 **Brookline** Massachusetts
110 K2 **Brooklyn** Indiana
99 O8 **Brooklyn** Iowa
94 C4 **Brooklyn** Michigan
111 G10 **Brooklyn** Mississippi
95 O6 **Brooklyn** New York
95 M5 **Brooklyn** Pennsylvania
117 N11 **Brookmere** Br Columbia
94 H10 **Brookneal** Virginia
99 N4 **Brook Park** Minnesota
110 H4 **Brookport** Illinois
114 H7 **Brooks** Alberta
95 S2 **Brooks** Maine
101 Q2 **Brooks** Montana
117 G5 **Brooks Brook** Yukon Terr
119 N5 **Brooksby** Sask
109 M6 **Brookshire** Texas
116 D4 **Brooks Mt** Alaska
116 M5 **Brooks,Mt** Alaska
116 H2 **Brooks Range** Alaska
99 O3 **Brookston** Minnesota
109 M2 **Brookston** Texas
113 E9 **Brooksville** Florida
95 U1 **Brookton** Maine
143 B9 **Brookton** W Australia
95 L4 **Brooktondale** New York
110 M2 **Brookville** Indiana
107 N3 **Brookville** Kansas
111 H8 **Brookville** Mississippi
94 H5 **Brookville** Pennsylvania
141 H5 **Brookville** Queensland
111 J8 **Brookwood** Alabama
141 L7 **Brooloo** Queensland
123 K4 **Broom B** Anticosti I, Quebec
142 D4 **Broome** W Australia
143 C10 **Broome Hill** W Australia
142 F3 **Broome, Mt** W Australia
18 D4 **Broons** France
99 L4 **Brooten** Minnesota
142 G4 **Brophy,Mt** W Australia
143 F7 **Brophy,Mt** W Australia
15 E2 **Brora** Scotland
28 B5 **Brørup** Denmark
27 G16 **Brösarp** Sweden
14 D3 **Brosna** *R* Irish Rep
83 L14 **Brossard** Réunion Indian Oc
100 D6 **Brothers** Oregon
68 A7 **Brothers** *islds* Andaman Is
145 F4 **Brothers, The** New Zealand
84 K4 **Brothers,The** *islds* Red Sea
37 J2 **Brotterode** E Germany
20 H5 **Brou** France
13 F4 **Brough** England
15 E1 **Brough Hd** Orkney Scotland
15 F2 **Brough Ness** Scotland
13 E5 **Broughton** Cumbria England
110 H4 **Broughton** Illinois
107 N2 **Broughton** Kansas
9 F3 **Broughton** Northants England
141 G5 **Broughton** Queensland
13 E5 **Broughton** Scotland
121 T6 **Broughton Station** Quebec
12 F6 **Broughty Ferry** Scotland
86 C2 **Broulkou** Chad
79 F5 **Broummana** Lebanon
36 B7 **Brouvelieures** France
25 A5 **Brouwershaven** Netherlands
40 E4 **Brove** *R* Switzerland
85 C7 **Brovio** Liberia
28 D2 **Brovst** Denmark
99 L3 **Browerville** Minnesota
71 C5 **Brown Bank** Palawan Philippines
94 E3 **Brown City** Michigan
107 L3 **Brownell** Kansas
143 F7 **Browne Ra** W Australia
108 E2 **Brownfield** Texas
110 B2 **Browning** Missouri
101 M1 **Browning** Montana
119 P9 **Browning** Sask
144 C5 **Browning Pass** New Zealand
143 C9 **Brown,L** W Australia
106 F7 **Brownlee** Nebraska
119 M8 **Brownlee** Sask
138 E4 **Brown,Mt** S Australia
143 B6 **Brown,Mt** S Australia
142 A3 **Brown,Mt** W Australia
138 C4 **Brown Pt** S Australia
141 G3 **Brown** *R* Queensland
120 J3 **Brownrigg** Ontario
110 G3 **Browns** Illinois
144 B7 **Browns** New Zealand
99 M3 **Brownsboro** Texas
110 K2 **Brownsburg** Indiana
121 Q7 **Brownsburg** Quebec
126 E2 **Browns Cay** *isld* Bahamas
145 G1 **Browns I** New Zealand
118 C8 **Brownson** Alberta
94 A8 **Brownstown** Indiana
127 K2 **Brown's Town** Jamaica
97 N6 **Browns Valley** Minnesota
110 L2 **Brownsville** Indiana
110 K4 **Brownsville** Kentucky
100 C5 **Brownsville** Oregon
94 H6 **Brownsville** Pennsylvania
110 G6 **Brownsville** Tennessee
109 K10 **Brownsville** Texas
99 R7 **Browntown** Wisconsin
111 J8 **Brownville** Alabama
99 L9 **Brownville** Nebraska
95 M2 **Brownville** New York
95 S1 **Brownville Junc** Maine
109 J4 **Brownwood** Texas
109 J4 **Brownwood, L** Texas
136 E4 **Browse I** Australia
142 E3 **Browse I** Indian Ocean
140 D2 **Broxburn** Scotland
15 E6 **Broxton** Georgia
112 E6 **Brozas** Spain
16 C5 **Brozzi** Italy
16 C4 **Brozas** Spain
45 L4 **Brozzi** Italy
45 P1 **Brtonigla** Yugoslavia
22 D3 **Bruay** France
22 F3 **Bruay-sur-l'Escaut** France
118 C6 **Bruce** Alberta
127 P6 **Bruce** Barbados
111 G7 **Bruce** Mississippi
145 E4 **Bruce** New Zealand
99 P4 **Bruce** Wisconsin
144 B5 **Bruce Bay** New Zealand
99 R3 **Bruce Crossing** Michigan
120 J9 **Brucefield** Ontario
142 C6 **Bruce,Mt** W Australia
120 J7 **Bruce Pen** Ontario
143 C9 **Bruce Rock** W Australia
110 H5 **Bruceton** Tennessee
109 K4 **Bruceville** Texas
19 K4 **Bruche** *R* France
32 K7 **Bruchhausen-Vilsen** W Germany
36 F3 **Bruchköbel** W Germany
36 F5 **Bruchsal** W Germany
31 K7 **Bruck** Austria
37 L4 **Bruck** Bayern W Germany
33 R8 **Brück** E Germany
38 M7 **Bruck-an-der-Mur** Austria
37 M6 **Bruckberg** W Germany
33 L8 **Brückl** Austria
38 J8 **Brückl** Austria
20 E3 **Brucourt** France
19 P18 **Brue-Auriac** France
118 E5 **Bruederheim** Alberta
33 P5 **Brüel** E Germany
14 C4 **Bruff** Irish Rep
Bruges *see* **Brugge**
40 H3 **Brugg** Switzerland
22 E1 **Brugge** Belgium
36 D1 **Brügge** W Germany
25 F6 **Brüggen** W Germany
45 L1 **Brugine** Italy
44 F2 **Brugnato, L. di** Italy
36 B2 **Brühl** W Germany
94 H5 **Bruin** Pennsylvania
103 O2 **Bruin Pt** Utah
117 P9 **Brûlé** Alberta
98 E8 **Brule** Nebraska
99 P3 **Brule** Wisconsin
121 N6 **Brûlé, L** Quebec
121 M7 **Brûlé Lake** Ontario
21 E6 **Brûlon** France
22 J4 **Brûly** Belgium
129 K6 **Brumado** Brazil
25 F4 **Brummen** Netherlands
45 Q7 **Bruncu Spina** *mt* Sardinia
108 H7 **Brundage** Texas
111 L10 **Brundidge** Alabama
100 K7 **Bruneau** Idaho
22 G4 **Brunehamel** France
70 D2 **Brunei** *state* Borneo
70 D2 **Brunei** B Brunei
Brunei Town *see* **Bandar Seri Begawan**
140 D4 **Brunette Downs** N Terr Aust
123 Q6 **Brunette I** Nfld
20 F2 **Bruneval** France
26 G8 **Brunflo** Sweden
109 J8 **Bruni** Texas
42 D2 **Brunico** Italy
118 D1 **Brunkild** Manitoba
Brünn *see* **Brno**
37 N2 **Brunn** E Germany
28 K4 **Brunnby** Sweden
41 J3 **Brunnen** Switzerland
144 C5 **Brunner** New Zealand
99 O3 **Brunno** Minnesota
119 M6 **Bruno** Sask
32 K5 **Brunsbüttelkoog** W Germany
33 M8 **Brunschwig** W Germany
32 L5 **Brunshausen** W Germany
25 E7 **Brunssum** Netherlands
Brunswick *see* **Braunschweig**
112 F6 **Brunswick** Georgia
95 S3 **Brunswick** Maine
94 K7 **Brunswick** Maryland
94 F5 **Brunswick** Ohio
142 E3 **Brunswick B** W Australia
143 B10 **Brunswick Junction** W Australia
120 G3 **Brunswick L** Ontario
133 C8 **Brunswick, Pen. de** Chile
31 K6 **Bruntál** Czechoslovakia
139 H9 **Bruny I** Tasmania
26 G6 **Brurskanken** *mt* Norway
46 F1 **Brusartsi** Bulgaria
106 G1 **Brush** Colorado
95 N2 **Brushton** New York
112 F1 **Brushy Mts** N Carolina
130 E10 **Brusque** Brazil
Brussels *see* **Bruxelles**
120 J9 **Brussels** Ontario
99 T5 **Brussels** Wisconsin
8 D5 **Bruton** England
22 G2 **Bruxelles** Belgium
24 **Bruxelles** *conurbation* Belgium
19 K4 **Bruyères** France
20 B5 **Bruz** France
128 E2 **Bruzual** Venezuela
22 F3 **Bry** France
94 C5 **Bryan** Ohio
109 L5 **Bryan** Texas
101 Q8 **Bryan** Wyoming
138 E5 **Bryan,Mt** S Australia
54 F3 **Bryansk** U.S.S.R.
109 P1 **Bryant** Arkansas
110 M1 **Bryant** Indiana
110 D5 **Bryant Cr** Missouri
95 R2 **Bryant Pond** Maine
22 C3 **Bryas** France
103 M4 **Bryce Canyon Nat. Park** Utah
144 B7 **Brydone** New Zealand
8 F7 **Bryher** *isld* Isles of Scilly England
8 C4 **Bryn-amman** Wales
8 C3 **Bryn-crug** Wales
8 B3 **Bryneglwys** Wales
26 M1 **Brynilen** Norway
8 C4 **Bryn Mawr** Wales
48 L2 **Brynzen** U.S.S.R.
28 D2 **Brysup** Denmark
112 E2 **Bryson City** N Carolina
121 N6 **Bryson,L** Quebec
48 G6 **Brza Palanka** Yugoslavia
31 K5 **Brzeg** Poland
31 M6 **Brzesko** Poland
31 L4 **Brzeziny** Poland
31 M4 **Brzeznie** Poland
31 N6 **Brzozów** Poland
20 J4 **Bû** France
70 G6 **Bua** Sulawesi Indonesia
88 E8 **Bua** *R* Malawi
70 G7 **Buapinang** Sulawesi Indonesia
84 F3 **Bu Ayrat,Al** Libya
33 S7 **Buberow** E Germany
89 F2 **Bubi** *R* Zimbabwe
77 A5 **Bubiyan** *isld* Kuwait
71 F7 **Bubuan** *isld* Mindanao Philippines
13 H6 **Bubwith** England
87 F10 **Bubye** *R* Zimbabwe
47 L7 **Bucak** Turkey
128 D2 **Bucaramanga** Colombia
71 G6 **Bucas Grande** Philippines
111 H10 **Bucatunna** Mississippi
142 E3 **Buccaneer Arch** W Australia
43 G8 **Buccino** Italy
48 K3 **Buceea** Romania
47 K3 **Bü Çekmece** Turkey
48 J1 **Bachach** U.S.S.R.
15 F3 **Buchan** *dist* Scotland
6 L5 **Buchan** *oil rig* North Sea
112 B4 **Buchanan** Georgia
85 B7 **Buchanan** Liberia
99 U8 **Buchanan** Michigan
98 G2 **Buchanan** N Dakota
106 F7 **Buchanan** New Mexico
119 P7 **Buchanan** Sask
94 H9 **Buchanan** Virginia
140 D4 **Buchanan** *R* N Terr Aust
140 C5 **Buchanan Dam** Texas
109 J5 **Buchanan Dam** Texas
140 C5 **Buchanan Hills** N Terr Aust
141 H5 **Buchanan,L** Queensland
143 E7 **Buchanan,L** W Australia
109 J5 **Buchanan Res** Texas
115 M3 **Buchan Gulf** N W Terr
15 G3 **Buchan Ness** Scotland
115 O8 **Buchans** Nfld
123 Q5 **Buchans Jnct** Nfld
133 E4 **Buchardo** Argentina
Bucharest *see* **Bucureşti**
37 N7 **Buchbach** W Germany
36 G4 **Buchen** W Germany
36 C4 **Buchenbeuren** W Germany
37 L1 **Buchenwald** E Germany
33 R8 **Buchholz** E Germany
32 L6 **Buchholz** W Germany
41 N2 **Buching** W Germany
41 N1 **Buchloe** W Germany
15 D4 **Buchlyvie** Scotland
41 K3 **Buchs** Switzerland
20 H2 **Buchy** France
106 C6 **Buck** New Mexico
9 F3 **Buckden** England
32 K8 **Bückeburg** W Germany
32 K7 **Bücken** W Germany
103 M8 **Buckeye** Arizona
94 E7 **Buckeye Lake** Ohio
95 K7 **Buckeystown** Maryland
8 C7 **Buckfastleigh** England
94 G8 **Buckhannon** W Virginia
15 E4 **Buckhaven & Methil** Scotland
98 C5 **Buckhorn** Wyoming
15 E3 **Buckie** Scotland
9 E3 **Buckingham** England
121 P7 **Buckingham** Quebec
94 J9 **Buckingham** Virginia
140 D1 **Buckingham B** N Terr Aust
140 E5 **Buckingham Downs** Queensland
118 C5 **Buck L** Alberta
140 B4 **Buck,L** N Terr Aust
116 G4 **Buckland** Alaska
119 V1 **Buckland L** Manitoba
145 G1 **Bucklands Beach** New Zealand
141 J6 **Buckland Tableland** Queensland
146 K5 **Buckle I** Antarctica
110 H1 **Buckley** Illinois
94 B2 **Buckley** Michigan
100 C2 **Buckley** Washington
140 E5 **Buckley** *R* Queensland
38 O6 **Bucklige Welt** *reg* Austria
107 L4 **Bucklin** Kansas
110 D2 **Bucklin** Missouri
Buckner Bay *see* **Nakagusuku-wan**
102 C2 **Bucks** California
103 L7 **Buckskin Mts** Arizona
102 C2 **Bucks Mt** California
95 T2 **Bucksport** Maine
33 Q7 **Bückwitz** E Germany
31 K6 **Bucovice** Czechoslovakia
86 B6 **Buco Zau** Angola
22 D3 **Bucquoy** France
122 H7 **Buctouche** New Brunswick
48 K6 **Bucureşti** Romania
71 F7 **Bucutua** *isls* Philippines
71 E4 **Bucy-lès-Pierrepont** France
98 D3 **Bucyrus** N Dakota
26 B9 **Bud** Norway
109 K5 **Buda** Texas
48 E3 **Budafok** Hungary
54 B4 **Buda-Koshelevo** U.S.S.R.
68 B1 **Budalin** Burma
48 E3 **Budapest** Hungary
74 H4 **Budaun** India
9 E1 **Budby** England
146 F3 **Budd Coast** Antarctica
53 F10 **Buddennovsk** U.S.S.R.
143 B8 **Budd,Mt** W Australia
15 F4 **Buddon Ness** Scotland
8 B6 **Bude** England
14 L2 **Büdelsdorf** W Germany
32 G9 **Büderich** W Germany
22 K4 **Budersheid** Luxembourg
48 K6 **Budeşti** Romania
131 A7 **Budi,L.del** Chile
36 G3 **Büdingen** W Germany
86 C5 **Budjala** Zaïre
8 C6 **Budleigh Salterton** England
45 L2 **Budrio** Italy
42 J6 **Budva** Yugoslavia
54 H7 **Budy** U.S.S.R.
86 A5 **Buéa** Cameroon
19 P16 **Buech** *R* France
20 H4 **Buéil** France
102 D7 **Buellton** California
128 C3 **Buenaventura** Colombia
106 C8 **Buena Vista** Colorado
112 C5 **Buena Vista** Georgia
71 G6 **Buenavista** Mindanao Philippines
71 E4 **Buenavista** Philippines
94 H9 **Buena Vista** Virginia
126 E3 **Buena Vista, B. de** Cuba
17 F4 **Buendia, Embalse de** Spain
Buene *R see* **Bojana**
131 A8 **Bueno** *R* Chile
130 E4 **Buenolândia** Brazil
129 K7 **Buenópolis** Brazil
128 D4 **Buenos Aires** Colombia
132 **Buenos Aires** *conurbation* Argentina
131 E6 **Buenos Aires** *prov* Argentina
133 C7 **Buenos Aires,L** Chile/Arg
127 N3 **Buenos Ayres** Trinidad
133 D7 **Buen Pasto** Argentina
133 D8 **Buen Tiempo,C** Argentina
130 H4 **Buerarema** Brazil
40 E5 **Buet,Mt** France
107 P4 **Buffalo** Kansas
110 L4 **Buffalo** Kentucky
99 N4 **Buffalo** Minnesota
110 C4 **Buffalo** Missouri
101 Q3 **Buffalo** Montana
94 J4 **Buffalo** New York
107 L5 **Buffalo** Oklahoma
112 F3 **Buffalo** S Carolina
98 C4 **Buffalo** S Dakota
101 T5 **Buffalo** Wyoming
117 Q6 **Buffalo** *R* Alberta/N W Terr
110 C5 **Buffalo** *R* Arkansas
98 K3 **Buffalo** *R* Minnesota
89 G8 **Buffalo** *R* S Africa
110 J6 **Buffalo** *R* Tennessee
99 P5 **Buffalo** *R* Wisconsin
101 Q5 **Buffalo Bill Dam** Wyoming
101 Q5 **Buffalo Bill Res** Wyoming
99 N6 **Buffalo Center** Iowa
106 E2 **Buffalo Creek** Colorado
119 M9 **Buffalo Gap** Sask
98 C6 **Buffalo Gap** S Dakota
118 E6 **Buffalo, L** Alberta
114 H5 **Buffalo L** N W Terr
108 E1 **Buffalo L** Texas
139 H6 **Buffalo,Mt** Victoria
114 J6 **Buffalo Narrows** Sask
119 M8 **Buffalo Pound Prov Park** Sask
127 L2 **Buff Bay** Jamaica
112 C3 **Buford** Georgia
98 D1 **Buford** N Dakota
101 S8 **Buford** Wyoming
48 K6 **Buftea** Romania
31 O4 **Bug** *R* Poland/U.S.S.R.
128 C3 **Buga** Colombia
18 G10 **Bugarach, Pic de** *mt* France
58 G1 **Bugarikhta** U.S.S.R.
48 J1 **Bugaz** U.S.S.R.
47 J4 **Buğdaylı** Turkey
70 N9 **Bugel,Tg** Java
40 B6 **Bugey** *dist* France
Buggs Island Lake *see* **Kerr Lake**
88 D1 **Bugiri** Uganda
26 R2 **Bugøynes** Norway
54 C10 **Bugskiy Liman** *lagoon* U.S.S.R.
71 C6 **Bugsuk** *isld* Palawan Philippines
59 H2 **Bugt** China
18 F8 **Bugue,Le** France
71 E1 **Buguey** Luzon Philippines
78 K2 **Bügük Ağri** *mt* Turkey
87 F9 **Buhera** Zimbabwe
58 C4 **Buh He** *R* China
71 F4 **Buhi** Luzon Philippines
101 L7 **Buhl** Idaho
99 O2 **Buhl** Minnesota
36 E6 **Bühl** W Germany
36 E6 **Bühlerhöhe** W Germany
36 E6 **Bühlertal** W Germany
36 H5 **Bühlertann** W Germany
88 E6 **Buhoro Flats** Tanzania
78 J3 **Bühtan** *R* Turkey
48 K4 **Buhuşi** Romania
117 N7 **Buick** British Columbia
25 C4 **Buiksloot** Netherlands
8 C3 **Builth Wells** Wales
137 M3 **Buin** Bougainville I Solomon Is
41 M4 **Buin,Piz** *mt* Switz/Austria
130 H10 **Buique** Brazil
36 B2 **Buir** W Germany
22 B3 **Buire-le-Sec** France
22 F4 **Buironfosse** France
19 O16 **Buis-les-Baronnies** France
25 F2 **Buitenpost** Netherlands
67 B7 **Bui Thon** Vietnam
122 J2 **Buit,L** Quebec
16 E7 **Bujalance** Spain
21 I10 **Bujaleuf** France
46 E2 **Bujanovac** Yugoslavia
17 G3 **Bujaraloz** Spain
42 F3 **Buje** Yugoslavia
41 L5 **Bujor Târg** Romania
88 B3 **Bujumbura** Burundi
48 D3 **Bük** Hungary
137 L3 **Buka** *isld* Solomon Is
88 D2 **Bukakata** Uganda
87 E7 **Bukama** Zaïre
66 C5 **Buka Mangna Range** China
88 D2 **Bukasa I** Uganda
88 B3 **Bukavu** Zaïre
88 C2 **Bukene** Tanzania
57 C5 **Bukhara** U.S.S.R.
69 E13 **Bukittinggi** Sumatra
48 F2 **Bükk** *mt* Hungary
79 F8 **Bukka, J. el** *mt* Jordan
48 D4 **Bükkösd** Hungary
33 Q9 **Buko** E Germany
88 C2 **Bukoba** Tanzania
48 J2 **Bukovina** *old prov* U.S.S.R.
31 J1 **Bukowo,Jezioro** *L* Poland
136 G2 **Bula** Moluccas Indonesia
41 J2 **Bülach** Switzerland
65 D2 **Bulag** Sum China
71 E5 **Bulalacao** Calamian Grp Philippines
71 E4 **Bulalacao** Philippines
71 F4 **Bulan** Philippines
71 E7 **Bulan** *isld* Philippines
55 D3 **Bulanash** U.S.S.R.
55 C4 **Bulanovo** U.S.S.R.
89 F3 **Bulawayo** Zimbabwe
55 F3 **Bulayevo** U.S.S.R.
28 C2 **Bulbjerg** *hill* Denmark
48 K3 **Bulboki** U.S.S.R.
47 K6 **Buldan** Turkey
74 G8 **Buldana** India
77 H6 **Buleda** *reg* Pakistan
70 P10 **Buleleng** Bali Indonesia
9 E5 **Bulford** England
58 B2 **Bulgan** Mongolia
58 D2 **Bulgan** Mongolia
47 F2 **Bulgaria**
40 C1 **Bulgnéville** France
141 G7 **Bulgroo** Queensland
86 H3 **Bulhar** Somalia
71 B2 **Buli** Halmahera Indonesia
71 C6 **Buliluyan,C** Palawan Philippines
141 K1 **Bulimba** *dist* Brisbane, Qnsld
71 L2 **Bulimba Cr** Brisbane, Qnsld
67 B4 **Buliu He** *R* China
117 K8 **Bulkley** *R* Br Col
143 D9 **Bullabulling** W Australia
22 L3 **Bullange** Belgium
16 B4 **Bullaque** *R* Spain
109 M3 **Bullard** Texas
27 E13 **Bullaren S** *L* Sweden
17 F6 **Bullas** Spain
119 G3 **Bullawarra,L** Queensland
37 M3 **Bullay** W Germany
127 J3 **Bull Bay** Jamaica
112 H5 **Bull Bay** S Carolina
40 F4 **Bulle** Switzerland
138 F4 **Bullea,L** New S Wales
116 O1 **Bullen** Alaska
126 A1 **Bullen Baai** *B* Curaçao
145 D4 **Buller** *R* New Zealand
143 C9 **Bullfinch** W Australia
141 H5 **Bull I** S Carolina
102 H7 **Bullion Mts** California
140 B3 **Bullita** N Terr Aust
101 Q5 **Bull Mts** Montana
141 G5 **Bullock** *R* Queensland
141 G4 **Bullock Creek** Queensland
141 G8 **Bulloo** *R* Queensland
141 G8 **Bulloo Downs** Queensland
141 F8 **Bulloo, L** Queensland
118 B9 **Bull** *R* Br Col
145 E4 **Bulls** New Zealand
127 J3 **Bull Savannah** Jamaica
110 D5 **Bull Shoals Lake** Missouri
22 D3 **Bully** France
100 C9 **Bully Choop Mt** California
140 C2 **Bulman** N Terr Aust
140 C2 **Bulman Gorge** N Terr Aust
86 J5 **Bulo Berti** Somalia
69 C11 **Bulohsama** Sumatra
139 G6 **Buloke,L** Victoria
77 L2 **Bulola** Afghanistan
136 K3 **Bulolo** Papua New Guinea
143 D9 **Bulong** W Australia
138 F5 **Bulpunga** New S Wales
74 E8 **Bulsar** India
87 E11 **Bultfontein** S Africa
71 G7 **Buluan** Mindanao Philippines
70 E3 **Bulu, G** *mt* Kalimantan
51 M1 **Bulun** U.S.S.R.
86 D7 **Bulungu** Zaïre
71 G4 **Bulusan** Luzon Philippines
118 F6 **Bulwark** Alberta
9 F2 **Bulwell** England
141 L1 **Bulwer I** Brisbane, Qnsld
141 H8 **Bulwer, L** Queensland
9 F2 **Bulwick** England
119 N8 **Bulyea** Sask
86 D5 **Bumba** Zaïre
48 H5 **Bumbeşti Jiu** Romania
103 M7 **Bumble Bee** Arizona
70 G4 **Bumbulan** Sulawesi Indonesia
70 F2 **Bum-Bum** Sabah
70 M9 **Bumiaju** Java
66 F6 **Bumkhang** Burma
100 D3 **Bumping L** Washington
40 F4 **Bümpliz** Switzerland
74 F6 **Bundi** India
109 O5 **Buna** Texas
87 G7 **Bunawan** Mindanao Philippines
84 G3 **Bunbah,Gulf of** Libya
143 B10 **Bunbury** W Australia
36 B7 **Bunch** Oklahoma
14 E4 **Bunclody** Irish Rep
14 D1 **Buncrana** Irish Rep
141 K6 **Bundaberg** Queensland
141 F5 **Bunda Bunda** Queensland
141 H8 **Bundaleer** Queensland
140 C4 **Bundara** *creek* N Terr Aust
32 F6 **Bünde** W Germany
32 J8 **Bünde** W Germany
140 D5 **Bundey** *R* N Terr Aust
143 D7 **Bundey,Mt** W Australia
111 C11 **Bundick** L Louisiana
111 C11 **Bundicks Cr** Louisiana
140 C6 **Bundooma** N Terr Aust
14 C2 **Bundoran** Irish Rep
68 J6 **Bun Duc** Vietnam
12 B1 **Bunessan** Scotland
71 G7 **Bunga** *R* Mindanao Philippines
142 F5 **Bungabinni Well** W Australia
9 H3 **Bungay** England

146 E3 Bunger Hills Antarctica
141 J7 Bungil R Queensland
71 H6 Bunginkela isld Sulawesi Indonesia
70 G6 Bungku Sulawesi Indonesia
87 C7 Bungo Angola
60 G2 Bungo-suidō str Japan
69 J11 Bunguran Selatan Kep islds Indonesia
69 H10 Bunguran Utara, Kep isld Indonesia
86 B3 Buni Nigeria
86 F5 Bunia Zaïre
143 E9 Buningonia W Australia
70 E3 Bunju isld Kalimantan
110 E4 Bunker Missouri
141 K6 Bunker Grp islds Gt Barrier Reef Aust
116 E4 Bunker Hill Alaska
110 G2 Bunker Hill Illinois
110 K1 Bunker Hill Indiana
107 M3 Bunker Hill Kansas
103 K5 Bunkerville Nevada
87 E8 Bunkeya Zaïre
111 D11 Bunkie Louisiana
113 F8 Bunnell Florida
9 E2 Bunny England
145 E4 Bunnythorpe New Zealand
68 H7 Bu Noi Vietnam
17 G5 Buñol Spain
25 D4 Bunschoten Netherlands
143 B8 Buntine W Australia
9 F4 Buntingford England
70 D5 Buntok Kalimantan
70 D6 Buntui Kalimantan
84 E3 Bū Nujaym Libya
70 C4 Bunut Kalimantan
141 K1 Bunyaville dist Brisbane, Qnsld
68 E3 Bun Yun Thailand
70 G4 Buol Sulawesi Indonesia
51 L1 Buolkalakh U.S.S.R.
51 N1 Buorkhaya,Guba gulf U.S.S.R.
28 A4 Bur Denmark
88 G3 Bura Kenya
77 D7 Buraimi U.A.E.
143 B9 Burakin W Australia
86 E3 Buram Sudan
143 E10 Buraminya,Mt W Australia
86 A1 Buran Somalia
141 K2 Buranda dist Brisbane, Qnsld
75 J3 Burang China
130 H5 Buranhaém Brazil
45 M1 Burano Italy
86 J4 Burao Somalia
111 G12 Buras Louisiana
71 G5 Burauen Leyte Philippines
72 E3 Buraydah Saudi Arabia
55 C3 Burayevo U.S.S.R.
36 E2 Burbach W Germany
9 E5 Burbage England
102 F7 Burbank California
98 K9 Burchard Nebraska
139 H5 Burcher New S Wales
99 N6 Burchinal Iowa
57 C5 Burdalyk U.S.S.R.
141 H5 Burdekin R Queensland
141 H5 Burdekin Falls Queensland
117 M7 Burden,Mt Br Col
118 F9 Burdett Alberta
95 L4 Burdett New York
48 K3 Burdujeni Romania
78 C3 Burdur Turkey
47 L7 Burdur Gölü L Turkey
75 M7 Burdwan India
90 E14 Burdwood Bank Atlantic Oc
26 M7 Bureå Sweden
121 P4 Bureau, L Quebec
86 G4 Burei Ethiopia
51 N4 Bureinskiy Khrebet mts U.S.S.R.
25 D5 Buren Netherlands
32 J9 Büren W Germany
51 N4 Bureya U.S.S.R.
59 K1 Bureya R U.S.S.R.
9 E4 Burford England
33 P8 Burg E Germany
32 K5 Burg W Germany
36 D5 Burgalben W Germany
77 A5 Burgān Kuwait
47 J2 Burgas Bulgaria
38 O7 Burgau Austria
37 J7 Burgau W Germany
86 H6 Bur Gavo Somalia
112 J3 Burgaw N Carolina
47 K6 Burgaz Dağ mt Turkey
37 J5 Burgbernheim W Germany
100 K4 Burgdorf Idaho
40 G3 Burgdorf Switzerland
32 M8 Burgdorf W Germany
37 K4 Burgebrach W Germany
37 M2 Bürgel E Germany
48 C3 Burgenland prov Austria
123 P6 Burgeo Nfld
87 E12 Burgersdorp S Africa
9 F6 Burgess Hill England
95 L9 Burgess Store Virginia
13 E4 Burgh England
25 A5 Burgh Netherlands
36 H2 Burghaun W Germany
38 G5 Burghausen W Germany
37 L6 Burgheim W Germany
9 G1 Burgh-le-Marsh England
43 E11 Burgio Sicily
36 H3 Burgjoss W Germany
37 L3 Burgkunstadt W Germany
37 N5 Burglengenfeld W Germany
16 E2 Burgos Spain
16 E2 Burgos prov Spain
37 K3 Burgpreppach W Germany
36 H3 Burgsinn W Germany
37 O2 Burgstädt E Germany
36 G4 Bürgstadt W Germany
33 S6 Burg Stargard E Germany
32 F8 Burgsteinfurt W Germany
27 K14 Burgsvik Sweden
17 G2 Burguete Spain
36 F2 Burgwald W Germany
32 L7 Burgwedel W Germany
37 K4 Burgwindheim W Germany
47 H5 Burhaniye Turkey
32 H5 Burhave W Germany
130 E8 Buri Brazil
71 F4 Burias isld Philippines
71 F4 Burias Pass Luzon Philippines
123 R6 Burin Nfld
55 D3 Burino U.S.S.R.
68 F5 Buriram Thailand
130 E7 Buritama Brazil
128 G6 Buriti R Brazil
130 E6 Buriti Alegre Brazil
129 K5 Buriti Bravo Brazil
130 F4 Buritis Brazil
80 C8 Burj el Baiyara Jordan
28 C7 Burkal Denmark
109 J1 Burkburnett Texas
100 K2 Burke Idaho
98 G6 Burke S Dakota
109 N4 Burke Texas
140 E6 Burke R Queensland
140 F5 Burke R Queensland
117 K9 Burke Chan Br Col
146 H11 Burke I Antarctica
144 C6 Burke Pass New Zealand
110 L5 Burkesville Kentucky
140 E4 Burketown Queensland
109 H4 Burkett Texas
94 J9 Burkeville Virginia
37 O2 Burkhardtsdorf E Germany
98 G4 Burkmere S Dakota
121 L7 Burk's Falls Ontario
55 G4 Burla U.S.S.R.
36 G7 Burladingen W Germany
141 G5 Burleigh Queensland
109 K3 Burleson Texas
13 G6 Burley England
101 M7 Burley Idaho
8 D3 Burley Gate England
55 D4 Burli U.S.S.R.
102 B4 Burlingame California
107 P3 Burlingame Kansas
106 H2 Burlington Colorado
99 P9 Burlington Iowa
107 P3 Burlington Kansas
112 H1 Burlington N Carolina
95 N6 Burlington New Jersey
123 Q4 Burlington Nfld
121 L9 Burlington Ontario
95 O2 Burlington Vermont
117 M11 Burlington Washington
101 R5 Burlington Wyoming
110 A1 Burlington Junction Missouri
8 D2 Burlton England
57 J2 Burlyu-Tobe U.S.S.R.
80 G5 Burma Jordan
68 B2 Burma rep S E Asia
139 H6 Burmah Forest Victoria
55 D1 Burmantovo U.S.S.R.
101 N9 Burmester Utah
118 C9 Burmis Alberta
144 D5 Burnbrae New Zealand
109 J5 Burnet Texas
141 K7 Burnett R Queensland
141 K6 Burnett Hd Queensland
100 D9 Burney California
143 C10 Burngup W Australia
8 C5 Burnham England
9 G4 Burnham Essex England
95 S2 Burnham Maine
144 D5 Burnham New Zealand
94 K6 Burnham Pennsylvania
9 G2 Burnham Deepdale England
9 G2 Burnham Market England
40 F2 Burnhaupt France
139 H8 Burnie Tasmania
13 H5 Burniston England
13 F6 Burnley England
13 G4 Burnopfield England
57 F3 Burnoye U.S.S.R.
101 T10 Burns Colorado
100 F6 Burns Oregon
98 B8 Burns Wyoming
13 G5 Burnsall England
110 M5 Burnside Kentucky
94 J6 Burnside Pennsylvania
114 G7 Burns Lake Br Col
98 G3 Burnstad N Dakota
112 E2 Burnsville N Carolina
122 G6 Burnsville New Brunswick
94 G8 Burnsville W Virginia
101 P8 Burntfork Wyoming
126 G3 Burnt Ground Long I Bahamas
13 E1 Burntisland Scotland
122 J1 Burnt L Labrador
116 Q3 Burnt Paw Alaska
100 H5 Burnt R Oregon
100 B9 Burnt Ranch California
121 M8 Burnt River Ontario
119 R3 Burntwood L Manitoba
33 S5 Burow E Germany
66 D2 Burqin China
119 M6 Burr Sask
138 E5 Burra S Australia
143 C9 Burracoppin W Australia
99 P6 Burr Oak Iowa
107 M2 Burr Oak Kansas
94 B5 Burr Oak Michigan
94 E7 Burr Oak Res Ohio
15 F2 Burray Scotland
46 D3 Burrel Albania
140 C6 Burrell,Mt N Terr Aust
13 E1 Burrelton Scotland
139 J5 Burrendong Res. New South Wales
17 G5 Burriana Spain
13 H6 Burringham England
124 J3 Burro Mexico
103 L7 Burro Cr Arizona
108 E6 Burro, Serranias del mts Mexico
113 K11 Burrow Cay Bahamas
140 F3 Burrowes, Pt Queensland
15 D6 Burrow Head Scotland
107 N3 Burrton Kansas
140 B2 Burrundie N Terr Aust
133 E3 Burruyacú Argentina
111 G13 Burrwood Louisiana
8 B4 Burry Port Wales
78 B1 Bursa Turkey
84 J4 Bur Safâga Egypt
36 C1 Burscheid W Germany
13 F6 Burscough England
32 L9 Bursfelde W Germany
8 D1 Burslem England
28 G7 Bursø Denmark
22 F2 Burst Belgium
118 H8 Burstall Sask
99 M6 Burt Iowa
98 D3 Burt N Dakota
138 F4 Burta New S Wales
94 C1 Burt L Michigan
9 E6 Burton England
98 G7 Burton Nebraska
109 L5 Burton Texas
8 B4 Burton Wales
13 H5 Burton Agnes England
13 F5 Burton-in-Kendal England
112 D3 Burton L Georgia
14 C2 Burtonport Irish Rep
9 E2 Burton upon Trent England
26 L7 Burträsk Sweden
122 F7 Burtts Corner New Brunswick
138 F5 Burtundy New S Wales
140 C6 Burt Well N Terr Aust
136 F2 Buru isld Moluccas Indonesia
84 J3 Burullus L Egypt
88 B3 Burundi rep Cent Africa
69 F12 Burung Sumatra
88 B3 Bururi Burundi
85 F7 Burutu Nigeria
8 D3 Burwarton England
9 G6 Burwash England
9 G1 Burwell England
98 G8 Burwell Nebraska
33 S10 Burxdorf E Germany
13 F6 Bury Greater Manchester England
121 T7 Bury Quebec
9 F6 Bury W Sussex England
56 F5 Buryatskaya U.S.S.R.
9 G3 Bury St.Edmunds England
43 E11 Busambra, Rca mt Sicily
71 F7 Busan B Mindanao Philippines
87 D7 Busango Zaïre
118 D5 Busby Alberta
101 T4 Busby Montana
44 B2 Busca Italy
33 R7 Buschow E Germany
32 J4 Buschsand isld W Germany
46 E3 Buševa Planina mt Yugoslavia
46 D3 Bushat Albania
77 B5 Būshehr Iran
88 C2 Bushenyi Uganda
95 M5 Bushkill Pennsylvania
108 B8 Bushland Texas
113 E9 Bushnell Florida
110 F1 Bushnell Illinois
98 C8 Bushnell Nebraska
121 L6 Bushnell Ontario
107 M3 Bushton Kansas
140 E5 Bushy Park Queensland
89 F1 Busi R Zimbabwe
88 E1 Busia Uganda
22 E3 Busigny France
86 D5 Businga Zaïre
86 C6 Busira R Zaïre
48 J1 Busk U.S.S.R.
27 C11 Buskerud reg Norway
31 M5 Busko Poland
37 P3 Buškovice Czechoslovakia
55 D4 Buskul' U.S.S.R.
71 B1 Busobuso Halmahera Indonesia
19 K5 Bussang France
40 E2 Bussang,Col.de pass France
143 B10 Busselton W Australia
44 H2 Busseto Italy
99 O8 Bussey Iowa
21 G9 Bussiere Poitevine France
41 N7 Bussolengo Italy
25 D4 Bussum Netherlands
57 C4 Bustan U.S.S.R.
77 D6 Bustaneh Iran
80 D2 Bustan Ha Galil Israel
141 K6 Bustard Hd Queensland
48 K5 Bustenari Romania
42 B3 Busto Arsizio Italy
71 D4 Busuanga Philippines
86 D5 Busu Djanoa Zaïre
32 J4 Büsum W Germany
86 D5 Buta Zaïre
131 G2 Butai R Brazil
70 O9 Butak, G mt Java
69 D9 Butang Group isld Thailand
133 D5 Buta Ranquil Argentina
88 B3 Butare Rwanda
71 F3 Butaunan isld Philippines
138 E5 Bute S Australia
Bute co see Strathclyde reg
15 C5 Bute isld Scotland
117 J9 Butedale Br Col
117 L10 Bute Inlet Br Col
88 B1 Butembo Zaïre
22 L3 Bütgenbach Belgium
59 H2 Butha Qi China
68 A2 Buthidaung Burma
86 F5 Butiaba Uganda
32 H5 Butjadingen reg W Germany
55 D3 Butka U.S.S.R.
68 B3 Butle R Burma
111 H9 Butler Alabama
112 C5 Butler Georgia
94 C5 Butler Indiana
110 M3 Butler Kentucky
110 B3 Butler Missouri
95 N6 Butler New Jersey
94 E6 Butler Ohio
107 L6 Butler Oklahoma
94 H6 Butler Pennsylvania
98 J4 Butler S Dakota
146 E12 Butler I Antarctica
138 B2 Butlers Dome mt N Terr Australia
80 G2 Butmiye Syria
70 D5 Butong Kalimantan
46 D5 Butrintit, Liqen i L Albania
140 E5 Butru Queensland
41 K3 Bütschwil Switzerland
45 K1 Buttapietra Italy
114 H8 Butte Montana
98 F2 Butte N Dakota
98 H7 Butte Nebraska
100 C7 Butte Falls Oregon
37 L1 Buttelstedt E Germany
102 C1 Butte Meadows California
36 G7 Buttenhausen W Germany
37 L4 Buttenheim W Germany
37 K6 Buttenwiesen W Germany
100 F4 Butter Cr Oregon
99 M6 Butterfield Minnesota
143 D8 Butterfly W Australia
13 E5 Buttermere England
87 E12 Butterworth S Africa
14 C4 Buttevant Irish Rep
143 G6 Buttfield, Mt W Australia
27 K14 Buttle Sweden
117 L11 Buttle L Br Col
15 B2 Butt of Lewis Scotland
115 K6 Button B Manitoba
115 N5 Button Is N W Terr
102 E6 Buttonwillow California
37 L1 Buttstädt E Germany
143 D10 Butty Harb W Australia
98 J3 Buttzville N Dakota
71 G6 Butuan Mindanao Philippines
71 G6 Butuan B Mindanao Philippines
71 H7 Butung isld Sulawesi Indonesia
54 M6 Buturlinovka U.S.S.R.
68 H6 Bu Tu Suay Vietnam
36 F3 Butzbach W Germany
33 P5 Bützow E Germany
26 E9 Buvika Norway
79 E10 Buwārah, J mt Saudi Arabia
21 I7 Buxeuil France
32 L6 Buxtehude W Germany
9 E1 Buxton England
112 M2 Buxton N Carolina
19 J6 Buxy France
55 C3 Buy R U.S.S.R.
58 G2 Buyr Nuur L Mongolia
47 H4 Büyük Kemikli Br C Turkey
47 J7 Büyük Menderes R Turkey
47 K5 Büyük Orhan Turkey
21 H8 Buzançais France
22 H5 Buzancy France
48 K5 Buzău Romania
48 K5 Buzăul R Romania
48 K5 Buzăului Muntii mt Romania
55 B4 Buzdyak U.S.S.R.
60 E12 Buzen Japan
87 F9 Buzi Mozambique
48 G5 Buziaş Romania
55 C4 Buzov'yazy U.S.S.R.
95 R5 Buzzards B Massachusetts
8 C4 Bwlch Wales
27 H11 By Sweden
47 H1 Byala Bulgaria
47 F1 Byala Slatina Bulgaria
114 J2 Byam Martin I N W Terr
109 K1 Byars Oklahoma
Byblos see Jubail
31 O4 Bychawa Poland
31 L4 Byczyna Poland
31 K2 Bydgoszcz Poland
106 F2 Byers Colorado
109 J1 Byers Texas
141 G3 Byerstown Queensland
94 F7 Byesville Ohio
9 E3 Byfield England
9 F5 Byfleet England
26 L7 Bygdeå Sweden
26 L7 Bygdeträsk Sweden
27 C10 Bygdin L Norway
26 L7 Bygdsiljum Sweden
28 D5 Bygholm Å R Denmark
27 C13 Bygland Norway
27 C13 Byglandsfj Norway
141 F8 Bygrave, Mt Queensland
54 B3 Bykhov U.S.S.R.
27 B12 Bykle Norway
27 B12 Bykleheiane Norway
59 M2 Bykov U.S.S.R.
28 C7 Bylderup Denmark
57 H1 Bylkyldak U.S.S.R.
115 M3 Bylot I N W Terr
140 F4 Bynoe R Queensland
140 B2 Bynoe Harbour N Terr Aust
101 N2 Bynum Res Montana
111 F9 Byram Mississippi
146 H7 Byrd Gl Antarctica
121 O5 Byrd,L Quebec
13 F3 Byrness England
143 B7 Byro W Australia
112 D5 Byromville Georgia
102 C4 Byron California
99 R7 Byron Illinois
95 R2 Byron Maine
101 R5 Byron Wyoming
139 L3 Byron Bay New S Wales
143 B7 Byro Plains W Australia
51 J1 Byrranga,Gory mt U.S.S.R.
109 J2 Byrson Texas
28 F2 Byrum Denmark
26 M7 Byske Sweden
26 L6 Byske älv R Sweden
48 F1 Bystra mt Czechoslovakia
55 F2 Bystryy U.S.S.R.
31 K5 Bystrzyca Kłodzka Poland
51 N2 Bytantay R U.S.S.R.
31 L6 Bytča Czechoslovakia
31 L5 Bytom Poland
54 F3 Bytosh U.S.S.R.
31 K1 Bytów Poland
141 J7 Byzantium Queensland
31 M3 Bzura R Poland
130 B9 Caacupé Paraguay
133 F3 Caaguazu Paraguay
130 C9 Caaguazú dep Paraguay
130 C9 Caaguazú, Cord de mts Paraguay
130 B10 Caapucú Paraguay
130 C8 Caarapó Brazil
130 F5 Caatinga Brazil
130 C10 Caazapá Paraguay
129 G7 Cabacal R Brazil
130 H9 Cabaceiras Brazil
126 E3 Cabaiguán Cuba
71 E3 Cabalantian Luzon Philippines
71 G5 Cabalian Leyte Philippines
106 C9 Caballo New Mexico
128 D4 Caballococha Peru
106 C9 Caballo Res New Mexico
124 G3 Caballos Mesteños, Llano de los Mexico
71 E3 Cabanatuan Luzon Philippines
122 D6 Cabano Quebec
71 E2 Cabarruyan isld Luzon Philippines
19 Q18 Cabasse France
141 K7 Cabawin Queensland
141 K1 Cabbage Tree Cr Brisbane, Qnsld
16 B2 Cabe R Spain
130 F4 Cabeceiras Brazil
130 J9 Cabedelo Brazil
99 S8 Cabery Illinois
16 D6 Cabeza del Buey Spain
128 F7 Cabezas Bolivia
106 C6 Cabezon New Mexico
71 F6 Cabilao isld Philippines
127 J9 Cabimas Venezuela
107 P5 Cabin Creek Oklahoma
86 B7 Cabinda Angola
100 J1 Cabinet Gorge Dam Idaho
100 J1 Cabinet Mts Idaho
71 E8 Cabingan isld Philippines
99 P3 Cable Wisconsin
133 D7 Cabo Blanco Argentina
17 F8 Cabo de Gata,Sierra del Spain
88 G8 Cabo Delgado dist Mozambique
130 G8 Cabo Frio Brazil
115 M8 Cabonga, Rés Quebec
110 D4 Cabool Missouri
141 L7 Caboolture Queensland
88 D9 Cabora Bassa Dam Mozambique
133 D6 Cabo Raso Argentina
110 E6 Cabot Arkansas
120 J7 Cabot Head C Ontario
115 O8 Cabot Str Nfld/Nova Scotia
20 E3 Cabourg France
85 A8 Cabo Verde, Ilhas do islds Atlantic Oc
71 E4 Cabra isld Philippines
16 E7 Cabra del Santo Cristo Spain
69 A9 Cabra I Nicobar Is
127 J5 Cabral Dominican Rep
130 G5 Cabral,Serra do mts Brazil
43 B9 Cabras Sardinia
19 P15 Cabre, Col de pass France
16 B3 Cabreira mt Portugal
127 K5 Cabrera Dominican Rep
17 J5 Cabrera isld Balearic Is
16 C2 Cabrera R Spain
126 F4 Cabreras R Cuba
16 C2 Cabrera,Sierra mt Spain
118 J8 Cabri Sask
17 F5 Cabriel R Spain
19 O18 Cabriès France
102 G9 Cabrillo Nat Mon California
127 M4 Cabrits, I Martinique W I
130 G10 Cabrobó Brazil
128 E2 Cabruta Venezuela
71 E7 Cabucan isld Philippines
71 E2 Cabugao Luzon Philippines
71 E5 Cabulauan isld Philippines
124 E2 Cabullona Mexico
71 G8 Caburan Mindanao Philippines
128 E1 Cabure Venezuela
71 F1 Cabutunan Pt Luzon Philippines
133 G3 Caçador Brazil
46 D1 Čačak Yugoslavia
122 F3 Cacaoui L Quebec
130 F8 Cacapava Brazil
133 G4 Caçapava do Sul Brazil
94 J7 Cacapon R W Virginia
68 H2 Cac Ba isld Vietnam
43 B8 Caccia,C Sardinia
133 G3 Cacequi Brazil
129 G7 Cáceraes Brazil
130 B5 Cáceres Brazil
16 C5 Cáceres Spain
16 C5 Cáceres prov Spain
107 M7 Cache Oklahoma
110 E6 Cache R Arkansas
110 G4 Cache R Illinois
120 K6 Cache Bay Ontario
102 B3 Cache Cr California
85 A6 Cacheu Guinea-Bissau
129 G5 Cachimbo, Serra do mts Brazil
133 D2 Cachinal Chile
87 C8 Cachingues Angola
129 L6 Cachoeira Brazil
130 E6 Cachoeira Alta Brazil
130 E5 Cachoeira de Goiás Brazil
131 H3 Cachoeira do Sul Brazil
130 F8 Cachoeira Paulista Brazil
130 H7 Cachoeiro de Itapemirim Brazil
102 E7 Cachuma, L California
16 E7 Cacín R Spain
42 H3 Čačinci Yugoslavia
71 D5 Cacnipa isld Philippines
87 C8 Cacolo Angola
87 C8 Caconda Angola
122 C6 Cacouna Quebec
103 M8 Cactus Arizona
109 H8 Cactus Texas
118 H6 Cactus Lake Sask
102 H4 Cactus Ra Nevada
130 D6 Caçu Brazil
87 B9 Caculavar R Angola
129 K6 Caculé Brazil
130 D5 Caçununga Brazil
141 K7 Çadarga Queensland
31 L6 Čadca Czechoslovakia
107 O7 Caddo Oklahoma
109 J3 Caddo Texas
111 C7 Caddo R Arkansas
111 B9 Caddo L Texas
109 L2 Caddo Mills Texas
45 J2 Cadelbosco di Sopra Italy
111 F12 Cade,L.de Louisiana
140 C1 Cadell R N Terr Aust
141 F5 Cadell R Queensland
128 D6 Cadena del Pantiacolla Peru
32 K5 Cadenberge W Germany
19 O17 Cadenet France
125 K5 Cadereyta Mexico
8 C2 Cader Idris mt Wales
112 H4 Cades S Carolina
138 D3 Cadibarrawirracanna,L S Australia
71 F3 Cadig Mts Philippines
18 E8 Cadillac France
94 B2 Cadillac Michigan
121 M4 Cadillac Quebec
118 K9 Cadillac Sask
18 G10 Cadi, Sierra del mts Spain
103 J7 Cadiz California
110 J5 Cadiz Kentucky
71 F5 Cadiz Negros Philippines
94 G6 Cadiz Ohio
16 C8 Cádiz Spain
16 D8 Cádiz prov Spain
16 C8 Cádiz, B. de Spain
103 J7 Cadiz L California
118 G6 Cadogan Alberta
117 P9 Cadomin Alberta
38 F9 Cadore reg Italy
99 P5 Cadott Wisconsin
117 P7 Cadotte R Alberta
143 B9 Cadoux W Australia
8 C5 Cadoxton Wales
41 N6 Cadria,Monte Italy
45 L1 Ca Emo Italy
20 E3 Caen France
13 H6 Caenby Corner England
8 C1 Caergwrle Wales
8 B1 Caergybi Wales
8 D4 Caerleon Wales
8 B1 Caernarvon Wales
Caernarvon co see Gwynedd
8 C4 Caerphilly Wales
8 C3 Caersws Wales
8 D4 Caerwent Wales
80 C3 Caesarea Israel
80 F1 Caesarea Philippi Syria
112 E2 Caesars Head S Carolina
130 G6 Caete Brazil
129 K6 Caetite Brazil
130 E7 Cafelândia Brazil
83 K14 Cafres,Pl.des Réunion Indian Oc
129 G3 Cafuini R Brazil
71 D7 Cagayan Philippines
71 E1 Cagayan R Luzon Philippines
71 G6 Cagayan de Oro Mindanao Philippines
71 E6 Cagayan Is Philippines
47 J5 Çağiş Turkey
42 E5 Cagli Italy
43 C9 Cagliari Sardinia
43 C9 Cagliari,G.di Sardinia
44 B4 Cagnes France
71 F4 Cagraray isld Philippines
127 L5 Caguas Puerto Rico
111 J9 Cahaba R Alabama
20 D3 Cahagnes France
14 B5 Caha Mts Irish Rep
14 D4 Caher Irish Rep
14 A5 Cahirsiveen Irish Rep
14 E4 Cahore Pt Irish Rep
18 G8 Cahors France
87 G9 Caia Mozambique
129 G6 Caiabis, Serra dos Brazil
87 D8 Caianda Angola
45 Q7 Caianello Italy
129 H7 Caiapó R Brazil
130 D5 Caiapónia Brazil
130 D5 Caiapo, Serra do mts Brazil
45 Q7 Caiazzo Italy
126 E3 Caibarién Cuba
68 H7 Cai Be Vietnam
128 E2 Caicara Bolívar Venezuela
130 J9 Caicará Brazil
128 F2 Caicara Monagas Venezuela
129 L5 Caico Brazil
127 H4 Caicos Is W Indies
Caidian see Hanyang
122 E1 Cailleteau,L Quebec
128 D7 Cailloma Peru
111 E12 Caillou B Louisiana
126 G5 Caimanera Cuba
71 D3 Caiman Pt Luzon Philippines
109 J5 Cain City Texas
87 B9 Cainde Angola
133 D1 Caine R Bolivia
122 G7 Cains R New Brunswick
99 N9 Cainsville Missouri
69 G8 Cai Nuoc Vietnam
45 P6 Caira, M mt Italy
146 C10 Caird Coast Antarctica
12 C1 Cairnbaan Scotland
94 J6 Cairnbrook Pennsylvania
139 G6 Cairn Curran Dam Victoria
15 E3 Cairn Gorm mt Scotland
116 K6 Cairn Mt Alaska
12 C4 Cairn Ryan Scotland
141 H3 Cairns Queensland
15 E3 Cairn Toul mt Scotland
79 B3 Cairo Egypt
113 C7 Cairo Georgia
110 G4 Cairo Illinois
44 D3 Cairo Italy
110 D2 Cairo Missouri
98 H8 Cairo Nebraska
95 N4 Cairo New York
94 C6 Cairo Ohio
94 F7 Cairo W Virginia
67 A3 Caishenfang China
67 F1 Caishi China
9 H2 Caister England
13 H6 Caistor England
Caithness co see Highland reg
87 E8 Caitou Angola
87 C9 Caiundo Angola
48 K4 Căiuţi Romania
45 Q8 Caivano Italy
141 G8 Caiwarro Queensland
22 D4 Caix France
Caiyuanzhen see Shengsi
67 F1 Caizi Hu China
128 C5 Cajamarca Peru
128 C5 Cajamarca dep Peru
18 G8 Cajarc France
130 H9 Çajàzeiras Brazil
48 F7 Čajetina Yugoslavia
71 F4 Cajidiocan Philippines
48 E7 Čajniče Yugoslavia
130 F7 Cajuru Brazil
47 L8 Çakırlar Turkey
47 K6 Çal Turkey
16 C7 Cala Spain
85 F7 Calabar Nigeria
103 O10 Calabasas Arizona
121 O7 Calabogie Ontario
127 L10 Calabozo Venezuela
43 G9 Calabria prov Italy
71 D5 Calabugdong Philippines
16 D8 Calaburras, Pta. de Spain
128 E7 Calacoto Bolivia
46 F1 Calafat Romania
133 C8 Calafate Argentina
71 F5 Calagnaan isld Philippines
71 F3 Calagua islds Philippines
17 F2 Calahorra Spain
22 B2 Calais France
95 T8 Calais Maine
115 N8 Calais New Brunswick
Calais,Pas de see Dover,Str.of
128 F5 Calama Brazil
133 D2 Calama Chile
126 G9 Calamar Colombia
71 D4 Calamian Group islds Philippines
99 Q7 Calamine Wisconsin
22 L2 Calamine,la Belgium
128 F4 Calanaque Brazil
17 G4 Calanda Spain
41 K4 Calanda mt Switzerland
71 E5 Calandagan isld Philippines
69 B10 Calang Sumatra
84 G4 Calanscio Sand Sea Libya
71 E4 Calapan Philippines
100 C5 Calapooia R Oregon
48 L6 Călăraşi Romania
43 B9 Calasetta Sardinia
17 F6 Calasparra Spain
43 E11 Calatafimi Sicily
17 F3 Calatayud Spain
48 H4 Călăţele Romania
33 T9 Calau E Germany
71 F4 Calauag Philippines
43 F10 Calavà, C Sicily
102 C4 Calaveras Res California
71 E4 Calavite,Cape Philippines
71 E1 Calayan isld Luzon Philippines
71 G4 Calbayog Philippines
33 P9 Calbe E Germany
71 G5 Calbiga Samar Philippines
131 A8 Calbuco peak Chile
129 L5 Calcanhar, Pta. do C Brazil
111 C12 Calcasieu L Louisiana
128 B4 Calceta Ecuador
133 E3 Calchaqui Argentina
45 J4 Calci Italy
45 J1 Calcinato Italy
129 H3 Calcoene Brazil
75 N7 Calcutta India
128 C2 Caldas div Colombia
16 A5 Caldas da Rainha Portugal
17 J3 Caldas de Montbuy Spain
16 B2 Caldas de Reyes Spain
16 B3 Caldas do Gerês Portugal
130 E5 Caldas Novas Brazil
13 E4 Caldbeck England
88 G10 Caldeira isld Mozambique
32 K10 Calden W Germany
117 G7 Calder Alaska
100 J2 Calder Idaho
133 C3 Caldera Chile
45 K2 Calderara di Reno Italy
12 E2 Caldercruix Scotland
12 E5 Calder Hall England
16 E5 Calderina mt Spain
141 H7 Caldervale Queensland
8 D4 Caldicot Wales
100 J6 Caldwell Idaho
107 N4 Caldwell Kansas
94 F7 Caldwell Ohio
109 L5 Caldwell Texas
8 B4 Caldy I Wales
89 A10 Caledon S Africa
89 E8 Caledon R S Africa
94 B4 Caledonia Michigan
99 P6 Caledonia Minnesota
94 K4 Caledonia New York
122 G9 Caledonia Nova Scotia
94 E6 Caledonia Ohio
15 D3 Caledonian Canal Scotland
140 D2 Caledon,Mt N Terr Aust
141 J5 Calen Queensland
111 K8 Calera Alabama
124 G3 Calera Mexico
124 H6 Calera Victor Rosales Mexico
128 D7 Caleta Buena Chile
133 D8 Caleta Coig est Argentina
133 D7 Caleta Olivia Argentina
131 B8 Caleufu R Argentina
103 J9 Calexico California
114 H7 Calgary Alberta
106 F2 Calhan Colorado
111 M7 Calhoun Georgia
110 J4 Calhoun Kentucky
111 G8 Calhoun City Mississippi
112 E3 Calhoun Falls S Carolina
128 C3 Cali Colombia
47 K4 Çalı Turkey
71 G5 Calicoan isld Samar Philippines
110 D5 Calico Rock Arkansas
68 A7 Calicut Andaman Is
76 B5 Calicut India
102 F6 Caliente California
103 K4 Caliente Nevada
110 D3 California Missouri
94 H6 California Pennsylvania
127 O2 California Trinidad
102 C1 California state U.S.A.
124 D4 California,G.de Mexico
102 F6 California Hot Springs California
48 J3 Călimanilor Muntii mt Romania
76 D5 Calimere,Pt India
48 J5 Călinaneşti Romania
48 J5 Călinesti Romania
133 D4 Calingasta Argentina
143 B9 Calingiri W Australia
Calino isld see Kálimnos I
111 D8 Calion Arkansas
103 J8 Calipatria California
100 H1 Calispell Peak Washington
71 E5 Calis Pt Philippines
102 B3 Calistoga California
87 D12 Calitzdorp S Africa
71 E4 Calivite Passage Philippines
109 O5 Call Texas
138 F3 Callabonna R S Australia
18 C4 Callac France
86 H4 Callafo Ethiopia
113 F7 Callahan Florida
14 D4 Callan Irish Rep
121 L6 Callander Ontario
12 D1 Callander Scotland
71 E2 Callang Luzon Philippines
138 E3 Callanna S Australia
25 C3 Callantsoog Netherlands
99 O10 Callao Missouri
128 C6 Callao Peru
103 L2 Callao Utah
95 L9 Callao Virginia
98 G8 Callaway Nebraska
43 B12 Calle, la Algeria
125 K6 Calles Mexico
142 E3 Calliance Reef W Australia
141 K6 Callide Queensland
109 J7 Calliham Texas
118 D3 Calling L Alberta
118 E3 Calling River Alberta
8 B7 Callington England
141 K6 Calliope Queensland
117 H6 Callison Ranch Br Col
17 G6 Callosa de Ensarriá Spain
143 B7 Callytharra Springs W Australia
118 D5 Calmar Alberta
99 P6 Calmar Iowa
36 F6 Calmbach W Germany
118 L2 Calm L Ontario
9 E5 Calne England
71 G4 Calolbon Philippines
71 F6 Calolot Mindanao Philippines
113 F11 Caloosahatchee R Florida
43 G8 Calore R Italy
17 H6 Calpe Spain
101 P7 Calpet Wyoming
102 D2 Calpine California
125 K8 Calpulálpam Mexico
120 F3 Calstock Ontario
43 F11 Caltagirone Sicily
43 F11 Caltanissetta Sicily
87 C7 Caluango Angola
87 C8 Calucinga Angola
87 B8 Calulo Angola
99 S2 Calumet Michigan
107 M6 Calumet Oklahoma
121 Q7 Calumet Quebec
87 B8 Caluquembe Angola
71 E6 Calusa isld Philippines
40 G7 Caluso Italy
71 E5 Caluya isld Philippines
103 O8 Calva Arizona
20 E3 Calvados dep France
45 K4 Calvana,Monte Della Italy
9 E1 Calver England
111 H10 Calvert Alabama
109 L5 Calvert Texas
140 D3 Calvert R N Terr Aust
110 H4 Calvert City Kentucky
140 D3 Calvert Hills N Terr Aust
117 J10 Calvert I Br Col
94 K8 Calverton Virginia
143 E6 Calvert Ra W Australia
124 H7 Calvillo Mexico
119 T10 Calvin N Dakota
107 O7 Calvin Oklahoma
89 A8 Calvinia S Africa
45 Q7 Calvi Risorta Italy
45 J1 Calvisano Italy
16 D4 Calvitero mt Spain
33 O8 Calvörde E Germany
36 F6 Calw-Hirsau W Germany
112 J2 Calypso N Carolina
87 C7 Camabatela Angola
129 L7 Camacá Brazil
124 H5 Camache Mexico
121 O5 Camachigama,L Quebec
127 L10 Camaguán Venezuela
126 F4 Camagüey Cuba
126 E3 Camagüey, Arch. de islds Cuba
128 G5 Camaitu R Brazil
126 E3 Camajuaní Cuba
128 D7 Camaña Peru
71 G5 Camandag Samar Philippines
100 C1 Camano I Washington
130 C6 Camapuã Mato Grosso Brazil
133 G4 Camaquã Rio Grande do Sul Brazil
131 H3 Camaquã,R Brazil
128 F4 Camara Brazil
128 G6 Camarare R Brazil
17 H3 Camarasa,Embalse de Spain
18 G9 Camarès France
18 B4 Camaret sur Mer France
107 L5 Camargo Oklahoma
19 N17 Camargue, La reg France
102 E7 Camarillo California
16 A1 Camariñas Spain
124 F6 Camaronero, L. del Mexico
133 D6 Camarones Argentina
101 N5 Camas Idaho
100 C4 Camas Washington
101 L6 Camas Cr Idaho
100 B6 Camas Valley Oregon
Ca Mau, Pte De see Mui Bai Bung
87 C7 Camaxilo Angola
16 B2 Cambados Spain
130 B5 Cambara Brazil
Cambay, G. of see Khambat, G. of
8 B6 Cambeak England
20 C3 Cambe,la France
36 E3 Camberg W Germany
20 C3 Cambernon France
68 F6 Cambodia rep S E Asia
13 G3 Cambois England
18 E9 Cambo les B France
141 K7 Camboon Queensland
130 E10 Camboriú Brazil
8 A7 Camborne England
22 E3 Cambrai France
16 B1 Cambre Spain
20 F3 Cambremer France
102 C6 Cambria California
99 R6 Cambria Wisconsin
7 H10 Cambrian Mts Wales
144 B6 Cambrians New Zealand
9 G3 Cambridge England
100 J5 Cambridge Idaho
99 Q8 Cambridge Illinois
99 N8 Cambridge Iowa
127 J2 Cambridge Jamaica
107 O4 Cambridge Kansas
95 L8 Cambridge Maryland
95 Q4 Cambridge Massachusetts
99 N4 Cambridge Minnesota
98 F9 Cambridge Nebraska
95 O3 Cambridge New York
145 E2 Cambridge New Zealand
94 F6 Cambridge Ohio
120 K9 Cambridge Ontario
Cambridge and I of Ely co see Cambridgeshire
114 J4 Cambridge Bay N W Terr
141 G5 Cambridge Downs Queensland
142 G2 Cambridge G W Australia
9 F3 Cambridgeshire co England
94 G5 Cambridge Springs Pennsylvania
17 H3 Cambrils Spain
22 D3 Cambrin France
130 F7 Cambuquira Brazil
37 M1 Camburg E Germany
12 D2 Cambuslang Scotland
111 J10 Camden Alabama
111 D8 Camden Arkansas
95 M7 Camden Delaware
95 S2 Camden Maine
94 C5 Camden Michigan
95 N7 Camden New Jersey
139 K5 Camden New S Wales
95 M3 Camden New York
112 G3 Camden S Carolina
110 H5 Camden Tennessee
111 B11 Camden Texas
116 P1 Camden B Alaska
94 G8 Camden on Gauley W Virginia
142 E3 Camden Sd W Australia
110 D3 Camdenton Missouri
87 D8 Cameia,Parque Nacional da Angola
8 B6 Camelford England
8 B7 Camel,R England
145 E2 Camels Back mt New Zealand
87 B7 Camembe Angola
20 F4 Camembert France
45 O4 Camerano Italy
45 O4 Camerata Picena Italy
42 E5 Camerino Italy
103 N6 Cameron Arizona
99 Q9 Cameron Illinois
111 C12 Cameron Louisiana
110 B2 Cameron Missouri
101 O4 Cameron Montana
112 H2 Cameron N Carolina
106 G7 Cameron New Mexico
95 K4 Cameron New York
94 J5 Cameron Pennsylvania
109 L5 Cameron Texas
99 P4 Cameron Wisconsin
94 G7 Cameron W Virginia
88 C6 Cameron B Zambia
141 G5 Cameron Downs Queensland
120 B3 Cameron Falls Ontario
69 E10 Cameron Highlands Malaysia
117 O6 Cameron Hills Alberta
114 J2 Cameron I N W Terr
144 A7 Cameron Mts New Zealand
86 B4 Cameroon rep Africa
85 F8 Cameroon Mt Cameroon
129 J4 Cameta Brazil
140 B3 Camfield R N Terr Aust
71 E1 Camiguin isld Luzon Philippines
71 G6 Camiguin isld Philippines
71 E3 Camiling Luzon Philippines
111 M10 Camilla Georgia
133 D1 Camiña Chile
16 B3 Caminha Portugal
102 D3 Camino California
129 J4 Camiranga Brazil
133 E2 Camiri Bolivia
128 D6 Camisea R Peru
117 R4 Camlaren N W Terr
95 K5 Cammal Pennsylvania
43 F11 Cammarata mt Sicily
33 R8 Cammer E Germany
124 E4 Camoa Mexico
125 M3 Camoapa Nicaragua
129 K4 Camocim Brazil
41 K5 Camoghe mt Switzerland
44 F3 Camogli Italy
41 M6 Camonica,Val Italy
141 G6 Camoola Queensland
140 E4 Camooweal Queensland
129 H3 Camopi Fr Guiana
69 A8 Camorta Nicobar Is
71 G5 Camotes Islands Philippines
71 G5 Camotes Sea Philippines
124 G8 Camotlán de Miraflores Mexico
41 M6 Camowiche,Alpi mt Italy
42 E7 Campagna reg Italy
45 M1 Campagna Lupia Italy
45 M5 Campagnano di Roma Italy
20 F5 Campagne d'Alençon reg France

45 J1 Castel Goffredo Italy
18 F8 Casteljaloux France
109 J5 Castell Texas
37 J4 Castell W Germany
100 C8 Castella California
43 F8 Castellabate Italy
43 E10 Castellammare del Golfo Sicily
45 Q8 Castellammare di Stabia Italy
40 G7 Castellamònte Italy
45 J2 Castellarano Italy
133 F5 Castelli Argentina
45 K3 Castello di Serravalle Italy
17 G4 Castellón prov Spain
17 G5 Castellón de la Plana Spain
17 G4 Castellote Spain
45 J1 Castellucchio Italy
45 N6 Castel Madama Italy
45 K2 Castel Maggiore Italy
45 K1 Castelmassa Italy
18 G9 Castelnaudary France
18 E7 Castelnau de Médoc France
18 F8 Castelnau de Montratier France
18 F9 Castelnau-Magnoac France
45 J2 Castelnovo di Sotto Italy
45 H3 Castel novo ne'Monti Italy
45 H3 Castelnuovo di Garfagnana Italy
45 N5 Castelnuovo di Porto Italy
45 J1 Castelnuovo di Verona Italy
130 H7 Castelo Brazil
16 C5 Castelo de Vide Portugal
45 O4 Castelplanio Italy
45 M6 Castel Porziano Italy
45 R8 Castel San Giorgio Italy
45 L4 Castel San Niccolo Italy
45 L3 Castel San Pietro Terme Italy
18 F8 Castelsarrasin France
44 F1 Castel S.Giov Italy
43 F11 Casteltermini Sicily
45 P5 Castelvecchio Subequo Italy
43 E11 Castelvetrano Sicily
45 P7 Castel Volturno Italy
45 K3 Castenaso Italy
41 M7 Castenedolo Italy
138 F6 Casterton Victoria
18 E9 Castets France .
122 F7 Castigan Mts New Brunswick
45 K3 Castiglione dei Pepoli Italy
45 J1 Castiglione delle Stiviere Italy
45 H3 Castiglione di Garfagnana Italy
45 L4 Castiglion Fibocchi Italy
42 D5 Castiglion Fiorentino Italy
94 K4 Castile New York
133 C3 Castilla Chile
16 D4 Castilla Lavieja reg Spain
71 E3 Castillejos Luzon Philippines
16 D6 Castillejo, Sa. de mts Spain
127 J9 Castilletes Venezuela
133 C7 Castillo mt Chile
131 B4 Castillo,Cerro del peak Argentina
113 F8 Castillo de San Marcos Nat. Mon Florida
124 H3 Castillón Mexico
18 F8 Castillon et Capitourlan France
18 F8 Castillonnés France
133 D7 Castillo,Pampa del plain Argentina
133 G4 Castillos Uruguay
95 T2 Castine Maine
9 G2 Castle Acre England
14 B3 Castlebar Irish Rep
15 A4 Castlebay Scotland
14 E3 Castlebellingham Irish Rep
111 J10 Castleberry Alabama
14 E2 Castleblayney Irish Rep
9 E3 Castle Bromwich England
13 F4 Castle Carrock England
8 D5 Castle Cary England
14 D4 Castlecomer Irish Rep
100 J7 Castle Cr Idaho
103 N2 Castle Dale Utah
14 D2 Castlederg N Ireland
14 E4 Castledermot Irish Rep
103 K8 Castle Dome Mts Arizona
9 E2 Castle Donington England
12 E4 Castle Douglas Scotland
12 E3 Castlefern Scotland
13 G6 Castleford England
101 L7 Castleford Idaho
100 H1 Castlegar Br Col
103 O2 Castle Gate Utah
90 C1 Castle Harbour Bermuda
112 K3 Castle Hayne N Carolina
103 M8 Castle Hot Sp Arizona
126 G3 Castle I Bahamas
14 B4 Castleisland Irish Rep
14 B4 Castlemaine Irish Rep
139 G6 Castlemaine Victoria
14 C5 Castlemartyr Irish Rep
102 D6 Castle Mt California
101 L5 Castle Peak Idaho
145 F4 Castlepoint New Zealand
14 D3 Castlepollard Irish Rep
14 C3 Castlerea Irish Rep
139 J4 Castlereagh R New S Wales
140 D1 Castlereagh B N Terr Aust
9 G2 Castle Rising England
106 F2 Castle Rock Colorado
98 C5 Castle Rock S Dakota
101 O8 Castle Rock Utah
100 C3 Castle Rock Washington
99 R6 Castle Rock Res Wisconsin
13 G4 Castleside England
9 E1 Castleton England
127 L2 Castleton Jamaica
103 P3 Castleton Utah
95 O3 Castleton Vermont
95 O4 Castleton on Hudson New York
12 D5 Castletown I of Man U.K.
14 B5 Castletown Bere Irish Rep
14 F2 Castlewellan N Ireland
98 J5 Castlewood S Dakota
108 D6 Castolon Texas
118 F6 Castor Alberta
111 C9 Castor Louisiana
111 D9 Castor R Louisiana
95 M3 Castorland New York
20 B3 Castre,Mt France
18 G9 Castres France
25 C3 Castricum Netherlands
127 O7 Castries St Lucia
133 C6 Castro Chile
16 D2 Castrocalbón Spain
45 L3 Castrocaro Italy
45 O6 Castro dei Volsci Italy
16 E2 Castrogeriz Spain
16 C1 Castropol Spain
32 F9 Castrop-Rauxel W Germany
16 E1 Castro Urdiales Spain
16 B7 Castro Verde Portugal
43 G9 Castrovillari Italy
102 C5 Castroville California
109 J6 Castroville Texas
16 D6 Castuera Spain
88 G10 Casuarina isld Mozambique
142 G2 Casuarina, Mt W Australia
116 N6 Caswell Alaska
144 A6 Caswell Sd New Zealand
48 E3 Čata Czechoslovakia
127 J2 Catadupa Jamaica
130 G7 Cataguases Brazil
111 D10 Catahoula L Louisiana
71 F4 Cataiñgan Philippines
78 J2 Çatak Turkey
130 F6 Catalão Brazil
47 J3 Çatalca Turkey
47 J5 Çatal Dağı mt Turkey
127 K5 Catalina, I Dominican Rep
139 H9 Catamaran Tasmania
131 D2 Catamarca Argentina
133 D3 Catamarca prov Argentina
71 F4 Catanauan Philippines
87 F9 Catandica Mozambique
71 G4 Catanduanes isld Philippines
130 E7 Catanduva Brazil
130 D9 Catanduvas Brazil
43 G11 Catania Sicily
43 G11 Catania,Golfo di Sicily
43 H10 Catanzaro Italy
111 F12 Cataouatche,L Louisiana
110 K2 Cataract L Indiana
71 G4 Catarman Philippines
71 G7 Catarman Pt Mindanao Philippines
17 G5 Catarroja Spain
95 M6 Catasauqua Pennsylvania
138 D6 Catastrophe, C S Australia
128 D2 Catatumbo R Venezuela/Colombia
111 M9 Cataula Georgia
129 G4 Catavara Brazil
99 Q4 Catawba Wisconsin
112 F2 Catawba L S Carolina
95 L6 Catawissa Pennsylvania
87 F9 Cataxa Mozambique
71 G5 Catbalogan Samar Philippines
126 E2 Cat Cays islds Bahamas
101 R2 Cat Creek Montana
22 F3 Cateau,Le France
71 G7 Cateel Mindanao Philippines
9 G6 Catel Channel Is
22 E3 Catelet, le France
125 M8 Catemaco Mexico
45 P5 Catena di Monte Sirente Italy
130 J10 Catende Brazil
118 J5 Cater Sask
9 F5 Caterham England
87 B7 Catete Angola
107 L3 Catharine Kansas
98 G2 Cathay N Dakota
139 J6 Cathcart New S Wales
87 E12 Cathcart S Africa
108 D5 Cathedral Mt Texas
109 P1 Catherine,L Arkansas
103 M2 Catherine, Mt Utah
127 L2 Catherine's Peak Jamaica
89 F7 Cathkin Pk mt Lesotho
100 B3 Cathlamet Washington
94 D1 Cathro Michigan
126 G2 Cat I Bahamas
111 G11 Cat I Mississippi
22 F3 Catillon-sur-Sambre France
85 A6 Catio Guinea-Bissau
128 F3 Catisimiña Venezuela
115 K7 Cat Lake Ontario
94 E8 Catlettsburg Kentucky
99 T9 Catlin Illinois
144 B7 Catlins R New Zealand
95 L3 Cato New York
137 M6 Cato isld Coral Sea
94 K7 Catoctin Mt Maryland/Virg
130 H9 Catolé do Rocha Brazil
42 E5 Catria,Monte Italy
133 E5 Catrilo Argentina
128 F3 Catrimani Brazil
95 O4 Catskill New York
95 N4 Catskill Mts New York
94 J4 Cattaraugus New York
22 L5 Cattenom France
13 F6 Catterall England
13 G5 Catterick England
45 N4 Cattolica Italy
87 F11 Catuane Mozambique
133 D4 Catuna Argentina
128 E3 Cauaburi R Brazil
45 M1 Cauárzera Italy
129 J4 Cauaxi R Brazil
71 F6 Cauayan Negros Philippines
128 C3 Cauca div Colombia
126 G10 Cauca,R Colombia
72 E1 Caucasus mt ra U.S.S.R.
119 V3 Cauchon L Manitoba
95 R7 Caucomgomoc L Maine
20 G2 Caudebec France
20 H3 Caudebec-les-Elbeuf France
17 G6 Caudete Spain
22 E3 Caudry France
88 C9 Cauese Mts Mozambique
121 R7 Caughnawaga Quebec
71 G6 Cauit Pt Philippines
20 A5 Caulnes France
43 G10 Caulonia Italy
19 N17 Caumont France
20 D3 Caumont-l'Eventé France
126 E4 Caunao R Cuba
18 G9 Caunes France
87 C7 Caungulu Angola
131 A5 Cauquenes Chile
133 C5 Cauquenes Chile
128 F2 Caura R Venezuela
122 E5 Causapscal Quebec
18 G8 Caussade France
128 F6 Cautário R Brazil
18 E10 Cauterets France
131 A7 Cautin prov Chile
126 F4 Cauto Cuba
76 D5 Cauvery R India
20 F2 Cauville France
45 R8 Cava Italy
16 B3 Cavado R Portugal
40 H7 Cavaglia Italy
19 O17 Cavaillon France
19 Q18 Cavalaire France
129 J6 Cavalcante Brazil
41 O5 Cavalese Italy
98 J1 Cavalier N Dakota
119 U10 Cavalier N Dakota
145 D1 Cavalli Is New Zealand
109 L7 Cavallo, Pass Texas
85 C7 Cavally R Ivory Co/Liberia
14 D3 Cavan Irish Rep
14 D3 Cavan co Irish Rep
143 G7 Cavanagh Ra W Australia
47 K7 Çavdır Turkey
45 N6 Cave Italy
144 C6 Cave New Zealand
110 E6 Cave City Arkansas
94 B9 Cave City Kentucky
103 N8 Cavecreek Arizona
143 D9 Cave Hill W Australia
110 H4 Cave in Rock Illinois
130 E10 Caveiras,R Brazil
100 B7 Cave Junction Oregon
120 C2 Cavell Ontario
118 J6 Cavell Sask
138 C2 Cavenagh,Mt N Terr Australia
118 G8 Cavendish Alberta
9 G3 Cavendish England
138 F6 Cavendish Victoria
45 M2 Ca Venier Italy
131 G3 Cavera R Brazil
131 G3 Cavera, Serra do mts Brazil
68 C7 Cavern I Burma
130 D9 Cavernoso, Serra do mts Brazil
120 C4 Cavers Ontario
9 F5 Caversham England
111 L7 Cave Spring Georgia
103 K3 Cave Valley Nevada
129 H3 Caviana isld Brazil
18 E7 Cavignac France
71 E6 Cavili Philippines
71 E3 Cavite Luzon Philippines
45 N6 Cavo, M mt Italy
44 B2 Cavour Italy
98 H5 Cavour S Dakota
45 J2 Cavriago Italy
42 J6 Cavtat Yugoslavia
15 E3 Cawdor Scotland
107 M2 Cawker City Kansas
138 F4 Cawndilla L New S Wales
Cawnpore see Kanpur
13 G6 Cawood England
121 P7 Cawood Low Quebec
9 H2 Cawston England
130 G7 Caxambu Brazil
128 D4 Caxias Amazonas Brazil
129 K4 Caxias Brazil
131 H2 Caxias do Sul Brazil
87 B7 Caxito Angola
9 F3 Caxton England
9 F3 Caxton Gibbet England
47 L6 Çay Turkey
128 C3 Cayambe vol Ecuador
112 F4 Cayce S Carolina
68 F8 Cay Dua B Vietnam
78 H1 Cayeli Turkey
129 H3 Cayenne Fr Guiana
20 H1 Cayeux-sur-Mer France
127 L5 Cayey Puerto Rico
18 H9 Caylar, le France
118 D8 Cayley Alberta
18 G8 Caylus France
126 E5 Cayman Brac isld W Indies
126 D5 Cayman, Grand isld W Indies
126 D5 Cayman, Little isld W Indies
90 A6 Cayman Trench Caribbean
68 G7 Cay Mit Vietnam
125 P9 Cayo Belize
127 P4 Cayon St Kitts W I
126 D3 Cay Sal Bank Bahamas
102 D6 Cayucos California
99 T10 Cayuga Indiana
98 J3 Cayuga N Dakota
109 M4 Cayuga Texas
95 L4 Cayuga L New York
16 D7 Cazalla de la Sierra Spain
48 L6 Căzănești Romania
18 E9 Cazaubon France
18 E8 Cazaux, Etang de L France
85 F2 Caze Algeria
95 M4 Cazenovia New York
18 F9 Cazères France
42 G4 Çazin Yugoslavia
42 H3 Čazma Yugoslavia
87 D8 Cazombo Angola
16 E7 Cazorla Spain
87 F9 Cazula Mozambique
16 D2 Cea R Spain
48 K3 Ceahlau Romania
48 K4 Ceahlău mt Romania
14 E3 Ceanannus Mór Irish Rep
130 J8 Ceará Mirim Brazil
20 D5 Ceauce France
21 F7 Ceaux France
119 P5 Ceba Sask
125 O6 Cebaco,I Panama
124 G4 Ceballos Mexico
106 D5 Cebolla New Mexico
133 D3 Cebollar Argentina
133 G4 Cebollati R Uruguay
17 F3 Cebollera mt Spain
106 C6 Cebollita New Mexico
16 E4 Cebreros Spain
71 F5 Cebu Philippines
71 F7 Cebuano Barracks Mindanao Philippines
43 E7 Ceccano Italy
48 E4 Cece Hungary
94 C5 Cecil Ohio
99 S5 Cecil Wisconsin
141 K8 Cecil Plains Queensland
143 D7 Cecil Rhodes, Mt mt W Australia
95 M7 Cecilton Maryland
100 B8 Cecilville California
42 D5 Cecina Italy
16 C5 Ceclavín Spain
107 M2 Cedar Kansas
99 O7 Cedar R Iowa
94 C2 Cedar R Michigan
98 H8 Cedar R Nebraska
111 H8 Cedarbluff Mississippi
94 F9 Cedar Bluff Virginia
107 L3 Cedar Bluff Res Kansas
107 K2 Cedar Bluffs Kansas
98 K8 Cedar Bluffs Nebraska
103 M4 Cedar Breaks Nat.Mon Utah
99 T6 Cedarburg Wisconsin
98 E6 Cedar Butte S Dakota
110 D3 Cedar City Missouri
103 L4 Cedar City Utah
98 D3 Cedar Cr N Dakota
109 K5 Cedar Creek Texas
109 O9 Cedar Crest Texas
101 L7 Cedar Cr.Res Idaho
109 L3 Cedar Cr.Res Texas
99 O7 Cedar Falls Iowa
127 P4 Cedar Grove Antigua W I
99 T6 Cedar Grove Wisconsin
94 F8 Cedar Grove W Virginia
112 L2 Cedar I N Carolina
95 M9 Cedar I Virginia
113 D8 Cedar Key Florida
119 R5 Cedar L Manitoba
108 E3 Cedar L Texas
99 T8 Cedar Lake Indiana
109 M7 Cedar Lane Texas
102 G3 Cedar Mts Nevada
94 D5 Cedar Pt Ohio
99 P8 Cedar Rapids Iowa
98 H8 Cedar Rapids Nebraska
95 K5 Cedar Run Pennsylvania
94 B3 Cedar Springs Michigan
120 H10 Cedar Springs Ontario
111 L7 Cedartown Georgia
107 O4 Cedar Vale Kansas
106 E7 Cedarvale New Mexico
127 L2 Cedar Valley Jamaica
100 E8 Cedarville California
95 M7 Cedarville New Jersey
110 N2 Cedarville Ohio
106 F4 Cedarwood Colorado
94 K8 Cedon Virginia
119 O9 Cedoux Sask
43 C8 Cedrino R Sardinia
130 G9 Cedro Brazil
124 E4 Cedros Mexico
124 B3 Cedros isld Mexico
127 N3 Cedros Pt Trinidad
138 C4 Ceduna S Australia
43 F10 Cefalù Sicily
16 E3 Cega R Spain
48 F3 Cegléd Hungary
43 H8 Ceglie Messapico Italy
17 F6 Cehegin Spain
67 B4 Ceheng China
48 H3 Cehu Silvaniei Romania
48 G4 Ceica Romania
128 E3 Cejal Colombia
87 C8 Cela Angola
45 P5 Celano Italy
16 B2 Celanova Spain
125 J7 Celaya Mexico
Celebes isld see Sulawesi
70 G3 Celebes Sea Indonesia
109 L2 Celeste Texas
94 C6 Celina Ohio
110 M1 Celina Ohio
94 B10 Celina Tennessee
109 L2 Celina Texas
17 G4 Cella Spain
48 D3 Celldömölk Hungary
32 M7 Celle W Germany
22 E2 Celles Belgium
21 H6 Cellettes France
16 B3 Celorico de Basto Portugal
7 E12 Celtic Sea British Isles/France
47 L7 Çeltikçi Turkey
41 O5 Cembra Italy
107 M7 Cement Oklahoma
94 C4 Cement City Michigan
46 D1 Čemerna Planina mt Yugoslavia
42 H4 Čemernica mt Yugoslavia
48 E7 Čemerno Yugoslavia
8 B1 Cemlyn B Wales
8 B1 Cemmaes Wales
17 F6 Cenajo,Embalso de res Spain
8 B3 Cenarth Wales
86 G4 Cencia Ethiopia
136 G2 Cendrawasih pen W Irian
44 G2 Ceno R Italy
133 C6 Cenoa R Argentina
86 C4 Cent.Afr.Rep Equat Africa
130 D8 Centenario do Sul Brazil
112 H3 Centenary S Carolina
101 T8 Centennial Wyoming
103 L8 Centennial Wash R Arizona
106 D4 Center Colorado
110 E2 Center Missouri
98 E2 Center N Dakota
111 B10 Center Texas
94 E6 Centerburg Ohio
99 O4 Center City Minnesota
95 L9 Center Cross Virginia
113 F9 Center Hill Florida
110 L5 Center Hill Res Tennessee
95 P6 Center Moriches Long I, N Y
95 Q3 Center Ossipee New Hampshire
109 H6 Center Point Texas
111 J9 Centerville Alabama
110 D1 Centerville Iowa
111 E12 Centerville Louisiana
94 H6 Centerville Pennsylvania
98 K6 Centerville S Dakota
110 J6 Centerville Tennessee
109 M4 Centerville Texas
101 O9 Centerville Utah
100 E4 Centerville Washington
124 H3 Centinela, Pico del mt Mexico
42 D4 Cento Italy
44 G3 Cento Croci, Passo di Italy
107 O7 Centrahoma Oklahoma
109 L1 Centrahoma Oklahoma
116 P4 Central Alaska
106 B9 Central New Mexico
112 E3 Central S Carolina
103 L4 Central Utah
130 B9 Central dep Paraguay
89 D3 Central dist Botswana
15 D4 Central reg Scotland
145 E2 Central Auckland stat area New Zealand
118 L8 Central Butt Sask
106 E2 Central City Colorado
99 P7 Central City Iowa
110 J4 Central City Kentucky
98 H8 Central City Nebraska
94 J6 Central City Pennsylvania
95 Q5 Central Falls Rhode I
110 G3 Centralia Illinois
107 O2 Centralia Kansas
110 D2 Centralia Missouri
100 C3 Centralia Washington
94 G8 Centralia W Virginia
94 B1 Central Lake Michigan
140 C5 Central Mt. Stewart N Terr Aust
100 C7 Central Point Oregon
136 J2 Central Ra Papua New Guinea
56 Central Siberia
95 L3 Central Square New York
102 B1 Central Valley California
111 L7 Centre Alabama
144 A7 Centre I New Zealand
95 L7 Centreville Maryland
94 B5 Centreville Michigan
111 E10 Centreville Mississippi
122 E7 Centreville New Brunswick
122 F9 Centreville Nova Scotia
111 J11 Century Florida
94 G7 Century W Virginia
67 B4 Cenwanglao Shan mt China
67 C5 Cenxi China
19 P18 Cépet,C France
Cephalonia isld Greece see Kefallinia /
44 C4 Ceppo Monte mt Italy
45 O6 Ceprano Italy
136 F2 Ceram Sea Indonesia
21 F6 Cérans-Foulletourte France
128 E2 Cerbatana, Sa. de la mts Venezuela
103 K6 Cerbat Mts Arizona
18 H10 Cerbère, C France
16 B7 Cercal Portugal
16 E4 Çercedilla Spain
37 O5 Čerchov mt Czechoslovakia
20 J6 Cercottes France
18 H6 Cercy la Tour France
18 G10 Cerdaña dist Spain
21 J6 Cerdon France
21 H7 Cere France
18 G8 Cère R France
45 K1 Cerea Italy
118 G7 Cereal Alberta
45 L1 Ceregnano Italy
20 C4 Cérences France
130 E4 Ceres Brazil
102 C4 Ceres California
40 F7 Ceres Italy
87 C12 Ceres S Africa
13 F1 Ceres Scotland
45 J1 Ceresara Italy
40 F7 Ceresole Reale Italy
18 G10 Céret France
126 G10 Cereté Colombia
87 J9 Cerf isld Br Indian Oc Terr
83 J12 Cerf I Mahé I Indian Oc
121 P6 Cerf. L du Quebec
22 G3 Cerfontaine Belgium
20 K3 Cergy-Pontoise France
44 D3 Ceriale Italy
43 G7 Cerignola Italy
Cerigo isld Greece see Kíthira /
18 G6 Cerilly France
20 D3 Cerisy-la Forêt France
20 C3 Cerisy-la-Salle France
47 J3 Çerkesköy Turkey
42 F3 Čerknica Yugoslavia
48 G4 Cermei Romania
48 L5 Cerna Romania
48 H5 Cerna R Romania
48 L6 Cernavodă Romania
19 K5 Cernay France
8 D6 Cerne Abbas England
42 H3 Çernik Yugoslavia
37 O4 Černošin Czechoslovakia
109 H9 Cerralvo Mexico
124 E5 Cerralvo isld Mexico
45 J4 Cerreto Guidi Italy
44 H3 Cerreto, Passo di Italy
45 R7 Cerreto Sannita Italy
8 C1 Cerrigydrudion Wales
46 D3 Cerrik Albania
106 D6 Cerrillos New Mexico
125 J6 Cerritos Mexico
130 E9 Cêrro Azul Brazil
128 C6 Cerro de Pasco Peru
127 L5 Cerro de Punta peak Puerto Rico
110 H2 Cerro Gordo Illinois
131 G4 Cerro Largo dep Uruguay
127 J9 Cerrón mt Venezuela
124 F4 Cerro Prieto Mexico
21 E7 Cersay France
45 K4 Certaldo Italy
143 B9 Cervantes I W Australia
45 P7 Cervaro Italy
43 G7 Cervaro R Italy
43 G8 Cervati, M mt Italy
44 H2 Cervellino mt Italy
17 H3 Cervera Spain
17 F2 Cervera del Rio Alhama Spain
16 D2 Cervera de P Spain
42 E4 Cervia Italy
43 G8 Cervialto, M mt Italy
45 R7 Cervinara Italy
44 D4 Cervo Italy
41 H7 Cervo R Italy
128 D2 César div Colombia
126 H10 César,R Colombia
42 E4 Cesena Italy
45 M3 Cesenatico Italy
52 C6 Cēsis U.S.S.R.
37 O5 Česká Kubice Czechoslovakia
31 H5 Česká Lípa Czechoslovakia
31 H7 Ceské Budějovice Czechoslovakia
31 H6 Českézemé reg Czechoslovakia
31 J6 Českomoravská Vysočina mts Czechoslovakia
31 H5 Český Brod Czechoslovakia
31 H7 Český Krumlov Czechoslovakia
37 O4 Český les Sumava mts Czechoslovakia
48 E1 Český Těšin Czechoslovakia
78 A2 Çesme Turkey
47 H6 Çeşnıe Turkey
139 K5 Cessnock New S Wales
48 H6 Cetate Romania
42 H5 Cetina R Yugoslavia
42 J6 Cetinje Yugoslavia
20 G5 Ceton France
43 G9 Cetraro Italy
19 P15 Ceuse, Pic de mt France
16 D9 Ceuta Spain
85 C1 Ceuta Span exclave Morocco
41 N5 Cevedale mt Italy
18 H8 Cevennes mts France
78 G3 Ceylânpinar Turkey
99 M6 Ceylon Minnesota
119 N9 Ceylon Sask
Ceylon rep see Sri Lanka Rep
19 P18 Ceyreste France
57 B6 Chaacha U.S.S.R.
21 G10 Chabanais France
19 P16 Chabestan France
19 O15 Chabeuil France
142 A6 Chabjuwardoo B W Australia
18 H5 Chablis France
19 P16 Chabre, Mt de France
19 Q16 Chabrières France
21 I7 Chabris France
133 C1 Chaca Chile
131 E5 Chacabuco Argentina
127 N1 Chacachacare I Trinidad
133 D2 Chacance Chile
133 C6 Chacao, Canal de Chile
133 D6 Chacays, Sa. de los mts Argentina
131 C6 Chachahuen,Sa mt Argentina
128 D7 Chachani mt Peru
128 C5 Chachapoyas Peru
68 E6 Chachoengsao Thailand
74 D6 Chachro Pakistan
128 F8 Chaco dep Paraguay
133 E3 Chaco prov Argentina
133 E3 Chaco Austral reg Argentina
128 F8 Chaco Boreal plain Paraguay
133 E2 Chaco Boreal reg Paraguay
106 B5 Chaco Canyon Nat. Mon New Mexico
133 E2 Chaco Central reg Argentina
117 H3 Chacon,C Pr of Wales I, Alaska
129 G5 Chacorãco, Cachoeira do waterfall Brazil
106 C5 Chacra Mesa mt New Mexico
86 C3 Chad rep Equat Africa
56 D5 Chadan U.S.S.R.
112 J3 Chadbourn N Carolina
131 C6 Chadileo,R Argentina
133 D5 Chadileuvú R Argentina
86 B3 Chad,L Equat Africa
56 F2 Chadobets R U.S.S.R.
98 D7 Chadron Nebraska
99 R7 Chadwick Illinois
48 M4 Chadyr Lunga U.S.S.R.
110 G4 Chaffee Missouri
94 J4 Chaffee New York
74 A4 Chagai Pakistan
77 H5 Chagai Hills Pakistan
53 H8 Chagan R U.S.S.R.
51 N3 Chagda U.S.S.R.
8 C6 Chagford England
55 E4 Chaglinka R U.S.S.R.
40 A4 Chagny France
52 E5 Chagoda U.S.S.R.
52 E5 Chagodoshcha R U.S.S.R.
81 E6 Chagos Arch Indian Oc
57 A2 Chagrayskoye Plato U.S.S.R.
94 F5 Chagrin Falls Ohio
127 O2 Chaguanas Trinidad
127 M1 Chaguaramas Trinidad
127 L10 Chaguaramas Venezuela
77 H4 Chahah Burjak Afghanistan
77 G7 Chāh Bahār Iran
77 G5 Chah Ghevhī, Hamún-e L Iran
77 L1 Chāh-i-Ghab Afghanistan
78 K4 Chah-I-Surkh Iraq
78 K2 Chai Iran
68 E5 Chai Badan Thailand
75 L7 Chaibassa India
68 F3 Chai Buri Thailand
Chaigoubu see Huai'an
20 D5 Chailland France
19 P14 Chaine de Belledonne mts France
85 E6 Chaîne de l'Atakora mts Benin
19 N17 Chaine des Alpilles mts France
18 H7 Chaise Dieu, la France
69 D8 Chaiya Thailand
68 E5 Chaiyaphum Thailand
131 F3 Chajari Argentina
116 L6 Chakachamna L Alaska
74 F2 Chak Amru Pakistan
88 G4 Chake Chake Tanzania
77 H4 Chakhansur Afghanistan
77 J2 Chakhcharan Afghanistan
74 E2 Chakwal Pakistan
128 D7 Chala Peru
87 F8 Chalabesa Zambia
40 C4 Chalain,L.de France
59 H2 Cha-lan-t'un China
128 D7 Chala,Pta Peru
125 P10 Chalatenango Honduras
69 D9 Chalaung Thailand
124 H6 Chalchihuites Mexico
125 P11 Chalchuapa El Salvador
Chalcis Greece see Khalkís
9 E6 Chale England
122 G6 Chaleurs, Baie des Quebec/New Bruns
128 D6 Chalhuanca Peru
133 C7 Chalía R Argentina
88 B7 Chali,L Zambia
19 J5 Chalindrey France
67 D3 Chaling China
74 F8 Chalisgaon India
9 G5 Chalk England
98 B4 Chalk Buttes Montana
109 K3 Chalk Mountain Texas
121 N6 Chalk River Ontario
144 A7 Chalky Inlet New Zealand
116 Q3 Chalkyitsik Alaska
21 C6 Challain-la-Potherie France
21 B8 Challans France
133 D1 Challapata Bolivia
115 M1 Challenger Mts N W Terr
22 H5 Challerange France
101 L5 Challis Idaho
111 G12 Chalmette Nat. Hist. Park Louisiana
52 E2 Chal'mny Varre U.S.S.R.
75 N7 Chalna Bangladesh
52 D4 Chalna U.S.S.R.
21 D7 Chalonnes France
18 H4 Chalons-sur-Marne France
19 J6 Chalon-sur-Saône France
65 J3 Chaluhe China
18 F7 Châlus France
57 B4 Chalysh U.S.S.R.
37 O5 Cham W Germany
37 O5 Cham R W Germany
106 E4 Chama Colorado
106 D5 Chama New Mexico
69 E10 Chamah, Gunung Malaysia
74 B3 Chaman Pakistan
68 E6 Chamao,Khao mt Thailand
106 D5 Chama, R New Mexico
128 C5 Chamaya R Peru
74 G2 Chamba India
73 M3 Chambal Madhya Prad/Rajasthan India
40 B7 Chambaran, Plat. de France
126 E3 Chambas Cuba
119 M8 Chamberlain Sask
98 G6 Chamberlain S Dakota
95 R7 Chamberlain L Maine
142 G3 Chamberlain R W Australia
116 P2 Chamberlin,Mt Alaska
103 P6 Chambers Arizona
98 H7 Chambers Nebraska
140 B1 Chambers B N Terr Aust
94 K7 Chambersburg Pennsylvania
99 T4 Chambers I Wisconsin
138 C1 Chambers Pillar peak N Terr Australia
19 P13 Chambéry France
88 C7 Chambeshi R Zambia
128 C4 Chambira R Peru
20 K3 Chambly France
20 F4 Chambois France
18 H7 Chambon, le Loire France
121 S4 Chambord Quebec
21 G7 Chambourg-sur-Indre France
66 E5 Chamdo prov China
124 G8 Chamela Mexico
77 B4 Cham-e Zeydun Iran
77 B3 Chamgordan Iran
133 D4 Chamical Argentina
106 D5 Chamita New Mexico
110 E3 Chamois Missouri
86 G4 Chamo, L Ethiopia
74 H3 Chamoli India
40 E6 Chamonix France
19 P16 Chamouse,Mt.de France
75 K7 Champa India
21 C9 Champagné Vendée France
89 F7 Champagne Castle mt Lesotho
21 F10 Champagne-Mouton France
40 C4 Champagnole France
142 E3 Champagny Is W Australia
99 S9 Champaign Illinois
131 D3 Champaqui peak Argentina
121 N4 Champcoeur Quebec
21 E9 Champdeniers France
36 C7 Champ du Feu mt France
20 E5 Champgeneteux France
19 O14 Champier France
21 D6 Champigné France
21 H6 Champigny France
21 F7 Champigny-sur-Veude France
21 J8 Champillet France
118 D8 Champion Alberta
22 J3 Champion Belgium
99 T3 Champion Michigan
94 G5 Champion Heights Ohio
95 O2 Champlain New York
121 R8 Champlain New York
121 S6 Champlain Quebec
95 O3 Champlain Canal New York
19 J5 Champlitte France
40 B2 Champlitte France
121 N4 Champneuf Quebec
40 G6 Champorcher Italy
20 H5 Champrond France
20 D4 Champsecret France
21 D7 Champtocé France
21 C7 Champtoceaux France
76 C5 Chamrajnagar India
19 P14 Chamrousse France
16 B5 Chamusca Portugal
69 E9 Chana Thailand
18 H8 Chanac France
133 C3 Chañaral Chile
131 B2 Chañaral R Chile
131 B2 Chañaral, I Chile
98 K6 Chancellor S Dakota
133 C5 Chanco Chile
116 N3 Chandalar Alaska
116 P2 Chandalar R Alaska
111 G11 Chandeleur Sound Louisiana
103 N8 Chandler Arizona
107 O6 Chandler Oklahoma
122 H5 Chandler Quebec
109 M3 Chandler Texas
116 M2 Chandler R Alaska
116 L2 Chandler L Alaska
138 C2 Chandler,Mt S Australia
99 Q9 Chandlerville Illinois
128 D6 Chandless R Peru/Brazil
75 O7 Chandpur Bangladesh
74 H9 Chandrapur India
77 G6 Chānf Iran
Chang'an see Rong'an
65 A7 Chang'an China
87 F9 Changara Mozambique
65 G4 Changbai China
65 G4 Changbai Shan mt ra China
67 B1 Changchi China
65 F3 Changchun China
65 F2 Changchunling China
67 F1 Changdang Hu L China
67 D2 Changde China
123 S4 Change I Nfld
65 B7 Changge China
65 E5 Changhai China
58 F5 Chang Hu L China
67 F1 Changhua China
67 G4 Chang-hua Taiwan
67 C7 Changhua Jiang R China
67 A4 Changjiang China
68 J3 Changjiang China
67 C1 Chang Jiang R China
67 E2 Chang Jiang R Jiangxi China
Chang Jiang Kou see Mouth of the Yangtze Kiang
65 G4 Changjin Res N Korea
68 F6 Chang,Ko isld Thailand
65 D6 Changle China
67 F4 Changle China
67 G2 Changle China
65 D5 Changli China
59 H3 Changling China
69 E9 Changlun Malaysia
67 A2 Changning China
67 D3 Changning China
65 C4 Changping China
Changpuzhen see Suining
65 C6 Changqing China
65 F5 Changsan-got C N Korea
67 D2 Changsha China
67 F2 Changshan China
65 E5 Changshan Qundao islds China
65 D4 Changshanyu China
67 B2 Changshou China
67 G1 Changshu China
67 B3 Changshun China
67 F4 Changtai China
65 G2 Changting China
67 E4 Changting China
65 F3 Changtu China
65 G2 Changwu China
67 F1 Changxing China
65 E5 Changxing Dao isld China
67 D1 Changyang China
65 D6 Changyi China
59 H4 Changyon N Korea
65 C7 Changyuan China
Changzhai see Changshun
65 B6 Changzhi China
67 G1 Changzhou Jiangsu China
67 E1 Changzhuyuan China
83 J8 Chankanai Sri Lanka
116 H8 Chankluit I Alaska
69 C8 Chan,Ko isld Thailand
21 F7 Channay-sur-Lathan France
145 E2 Channel I New Zealand
102 E8 Channel Is California
9 H7 Channel Is English Chan
123 N6 Channel Port aux Basques Nfld
143 C10 Channel Pt W Australia
126 F3 Channel Rock Bahamas
22 B1 Channel Tunnel
76 C4 Channiapatna India
99 S3 Channing Michigan
108 B8 Channing Texas
119 P4 Channing airfield Manitoba
16 B2 Chantada Spain
21 B7 Chantenay Loire-Atlantique France
21 E6 Chantenay Sarthe France
68 F6 Chanthaburi Thailand
18 G3 Chantilly France
21 C8 Chantonnay France
115 K4 Chantrey Inlet N W Terr
20 D4 Chanu France
69 A8 Chanumla Nicobar Is
107 P4 Chanute Kansas
110 A4 Chanute Kansas
55 G3 Chany U.S.S.R.
21 D7 Chanzeaux France
17 G10 Chanzy Algeria
67 E5 Chao'an China
65 C6 Chaocheng China
16 D9 Chaoen Morocco
58 G5 Chao Hu L China
128 C5 Chao, I Peru
68 E5 Chao Phraya Ra Thailand
65 E1 Chaor He R China
58 E5 Chaotianyi China
67 F1 Chao Xian China
Chaoyang see Huinan
59 K2 Ch'ao-Yang China
67 E5 Chaoyang Guangdong China
65 E4 Chaoyang Liaoning China
65 A7 Chaoyi China
Chaozhou see Chao'an
68 F1 Cha Pa Vietnam
129 J5 Chapada das Mangabeiras mts Brazil
129 K6 Chapada Diamantina mts Brazil
129 K5 Chapada do Araripe mts Brazil
130 C4 Chapada dos Guimarães Brazil
129 K4 Chapadinha Brazil
121 Q3 Chapais Quebec
124 H7 Chapala,L.de Mexico
129 K8 Chaparao,Serra do mts Brazil
126 F4 Chaparra Cuba
57 C6 Chapayeva, Imeni U.S.S.R.
53 G7 Chapayevsk U.S.S.R.
121 N7 Chapeau Quebec
130 D10 Chapecó Brazil
130 D10 Chapecózinho R Brazil
9 E1 Chapel en le Frith England
112 H2 Chapel Hill N Carolina
110 K6 Chapel Hill Tennessee
20 E5 Chapelle-au-Riboul,la France
18 G5 Chapelle d' Angillon,la France
22 J4 Chapelle, la France
123 L3 Chapelle,L. de la Quebec
20 E4 Chapelle Moche,la France
20 D5 Chapelle-Rainsouin,la France
20 H5 Chapelle-Royale France
9 G1 Chapel St Leonards England
127 K2 Chapelton Jamaica
13 G6 Chapeltown England
99 Q10 Chapin Illinois
110 F2 Chapin Illinois
115 L8 Chapleau Ontario
120 G4 Chapleau R Ontario
120 H4 Chapleau-Nemecosenda Wild R. Prov. Pk Ontario
118 L8 Chaplin Sask
147 P1 Chaplina,Mys C U.S.S.R.
54 H8 Chaplino U.S.S.R.
54 L3 Chaplygin U.S.S.R.
111 K10 Chapman Alabama
107 N3 Chapman Kansas
101 R1 Chapman Montana
98 H8 Chapman Nebraska
117 O10 Chapman,Mt Br Col
142 F3 Chapman R W Australia
109 K8 Chapman Ranch Texas
94 E9 Chapmanville W Virginia
52 E2 Chapoma U.S.S.R.
98 D8 Chappell Nebraska
109 L5 Chappell Hill Texas
139 J8 Chappell Is Tasmania
75 L6 Chapra India
95 L8 Chaptico Maryland
18 E7 Chapus, le France
120 K4 Chaput Ontario
128 E7 Chaqui Bolivia
133 D1 Chaqui Bolivia
74 G2 Char Kashmir
85 B4 Char Mauritania
51 L3 Chara U.S.S.R.
133 E1 Charagua Bolivia
124 E4 Charay Mexico
98 C2 Charbonneau N Dakota
40 C3 Charcenne France
20 E5 Charchigné France
109 K7 Charco Texas
146 F13 Charcot I Antarctica
118 G3 Chard Alberta
8 D6 Chard England
57 E4 Chardara U.S.S.R.
57 E4 Chardarinskoye Vdkhr res U.S.S.R.
94 F5 Chardon Ohio
126 G5 Chardonnière Haiti
57 C5 Chardzhou U.S.S.R.
21 E10 Charente dep France
21 D10 Charente R France
18 E7 Charente-Maritime dep France
20 G3 Charentonne R France
86 C3 Chari R Chad
77 L2 Charikar Afghanistan
9 G5 Charing England
116 D2 Chariot Alaska
18 H5 Charité, la France
99 N8 Chariton Iowa
99 N9 Chariton R Iowa
110 D2 Chariton R Missouri
128 G2 Charity Guyana
52 H2 Charkayuvom U.S.S.R.
74 H6 Charkhari India
57 F5 Charku U.S.S.R.
9 E4 Charlbury England
22 H3 Charleroi Belgium
94 H6 Charleroi Pennsylvania
119 Q3 Charles Manitoba
121 T6 Charlesbourg Quebec
95 M9 Charles,C Virginia
99 O6 Charles City Iowa
115 M5 Charles I N W Terr
143 B8 Charles,Mt W Australia
143 D10 Charles Pk W Australia
140 B1 Charles Pt N Terr Australia
144 A6 Charles Sd New Zealand
110 B6 Charleston Arkansas
99 S10 Charleston Illinois
111 F7 Charleston Mississippi
110 G5 Charleston Missouri
144 C4 Charleston New Zealand
100 A6 Charleston Oregon
112 H5 Charleston S Carolina
112 C2 Charleston Tennessee
94 F8 Charleston W Virginia
103 J5 Charleston Pk Nevada
94 B8 Charlestown Indiana
14 C3 Charlestown Irish Rep
127 P4 Charlestown Nevis W I
95 P3 Charlestown New Hampshire

94 K7 Charles Town W Virginia
86 D7 Charlesville Zaïre
118 A1 Charles Wood Manitoba
Charlet,Ft *see* Djanet
20 H3 Charleval France
141 H7 Charleville Queensland
22 H4 Charleville-Mézières France
94 B1 Charlevoix Michigan
94 B1 Charlevoix,L Michigan
116 Q4 Charley *R* Alaska
117 N7 Charlie Lake Br Col
18 H6 Charlieu France
94 C4 Charlotte Michigan
112 G2 Charlotte N Carolina
109 J7 Charlotte Texas
127 M5 Charlotte Amalie Virgin Is
113 E11 Charlotte Harbor Florida
117 L9 Charlotte L Br Col
27 F12 Charlottenberg Sweden
33 S7 Charlottenburg W Berlin
33 S9 Charlottenfelde E Germany
94 J8 Charlottesville Virginia
Charlotte Town Grenada *see* Gouyave
115 N8 Charlottetown Pr Edward I
127 N1 Charlotteville Tobago
120 K5 Charlton Ontario
139 G6 Charlton Victoria
115 M7 Charlton I N W Terr
21 F10 Charmé France
19 K4 Charmes France
40 F4 Charmey Switzerland
40 F3 Chärmoille Switzerland
8 D6 Charmouth England
142 F3 Charnley,R W Australia
121 T6 Charny Quebec
60 R2 Charo-gawa *R* Japan
18 H6 Charolles France
21 J8 Charost France
52 E4 Charozero U.S.S.R.
122 J2 Charpeney,L Quebec
21 F9 Charroux France
20 J3 Chars France
74 D1 Charsadda Pakistan
57 D5 Charshanga U.S.S.R.
56 B6 Charsk U.S.S.R.
99 L7 Charter Oak Iowa
141 H5 Charters Towers Queensland
122 A8 Chartierville Quebec
20 H5 Chartres France
57 F4 Charvakskoye Vdkhr. U.S.S.R.
19 Q13 Charvin, Mt France
19 Q13 Charvonnex France
56 B5 Charysh *R* U.S.S.R.
131 F5 Chascomas Argentina
117 O10 Chase Br Columbia
107 M3 Chase Kansas
99 P6 Chaseburg Wisconsin
94 J10 Chase City Virginia
98 G3 Chase L N Dakota
55 D3 Chashi U.S.S.R.
57 B5 Chashkent U.S.S.R.
99 N5 Chaska Minnesota
144 B7 Chaslands Mistake New Zealand
117 N10 Chasm Br Columbia
144 B6 Chasm P New Zealand
52 E3 Chasovenskaya U.S.S.R.
52 H4 Chasovo U.S.S.R.
54 J8 Chasov Yar U.S.S.R.
113 E9 Chassahowitzka B Florida
99 S2 Chassell Michigan
18 F7 Chasseneuil France
18 H8 Chassezac *R* France
21 I8 Chassignoles France
20 E5 Chassille France
55 E3 Chastoozerskoye U.S.S.R.
52 H6 Chastyye U.S.S.R.
116 O4 Chatanika Alaska
121 L10 Chatauqua L New York
127 O8 Chateaubelair St Vincent
20 C5 Châteaubourg France
21 C6 Châteaubriant France
18 H5 Château Chinon France
19 O18 Château d'If *isld* France
21 F6 Château-du Loir France
20 H5 Châteaudun France
20 K4 Châteaufort France
95 N2 Chateaugay New York
20 B5 Châteaugiron France
21 D6 Château Gontier France
21 F6 Château-la Vallière France
18 E7 Château, le France
18 C4 Châteaulin France
21 J8 Châteaumeillant France
19 N14 Châteauneuf-de-Galaure France
20 B4 Châteauneuf-d'Ille-et-Vilaine France
18 C4 Châteauneuf du Faou France
20 H4 Chateauneuf-en-Thymerais France
21 I10 Chateauneuf la Forêt France
18 E7 Châteauneuf-sur-Charente France
18 G5 Châteauneuf sur Loire France
21 E6 Chateauneuf-sur-Sarthe France
21 H9 Châteauponsac France
22 G4 Château-Porcien France
19 Q16 Châteauredon France
19 N17 Châteaurenard France
21 G6 Château Renault France
122 A7 Chateau Richer Quebec
21 I8 Châteauroux France
19 K4 Château Salins France
18 H3 Château-Thierry France
145 E3 Château Tongariro New Zealand
121 R5 Chateauvert, L Quebec
127 O4 Châteaux, Pte. des Guadeloupe W I
117 O6 Chateh Alberta
21 C9 Châtelaillon-Plage France
22 H3 Châtelet Belgium
20 H5 Châtelets,les France
18 H7 Chatelguyon France
40 A2 Chatellenot France
21 F8 Châtellerault France
21 I10 Châtelus le Marcheix France
21 J9 Châtelus-Malvaleix France
36 C7 Chatenois France
99 O6 Chatfield Minnesota
117 F7 Chatham Alaska
9 G5 Chatham England
99 R10 Chatham Illinois
110 G2 Chatham Illinois
111 D9 Chatham Louisiana
95 S5 Chatham Massachusetts
122 G6 Chatham New Brunswick
95 O4 Chatham New York
120 H10 Chatham Ontario
94 H10 Chatham Virginia
137 R10 Chatham Is Pacific Oc
117 H8 Chatham Sd Br Col
133 C8 Chatham Stokes *mt* Chile
22 K4 Châtillon Belgium
40 G6 Châtillon Italy
18 G5 Châtillon-Coligny France
19 P12 Châtillon de Michaille France
20 C5 Châtillon-en-Vendelais France
19 O13 Chatillon-la-Palud France
21 H8 Châtillon-sur-Indre France
18 G5 Châtillon-sur-Loire France
57 F4 Chatkal *R* U.S.S.R.
57 F4 Chatkal'skiy Khr *mts* U.S.S.R.
111 H10 Chatom Alabama
75 L6 Chatra India
75 L9 Chatrapur India
112 C3 Chatsworth Georgia
110 H1 Chatsworth Illinois
95 N7 Chatsworth New Jersey
120 K8 Chatsworth Ontario
140 F5 Chatsworth Queensland
111 M11 Chattahoochee Florida
111 L8 Chattahoochee *R* Georgia/Alabama
112 B2 Chattanooga Tennessee
100 H2 Chattaroy Washington
94 E9 Chattaroy W Virginia
9 G3 Chatteris England
144 B6 Chatto Cr New Zealand
13 G2 Chatton England
111 L7 Chattooga *R* Georgia/Alabama
112 D3 Chattooga *R* S Carolina/Georgia
68 E5 Chatturat Thailand
112 D2 Chatuge L N Carolina
57 H4 Chatyrkel', Ozero *L* U.S.S.R.
18 H8 Chaudes-Aigues France
22 K2 Chaudfontaine Belgium
Chau Doc *see* Chau Phu
21 D7 Chaudron-en-Maine France
22 E5 Chaudun France
116 H6 Chauekuktuli L Alaska
19 Q15 Chauffayer France
68 B2 Chauk Burma
75 R5 Chaukan Pass Burma/India
22 D4 Chaulnes France
40 B4 Chaumergy France
19 J4 Chaumont Haute-Marne France
40 D3 Chaumont *mt* France
22 G4 Chaumont-Porcien France
21 H7 Chaumont-sur-Loire France
21 I6 Chaumont sur Tharonne France
21 F9 Chaunay Vienne France
94 E7 Chauncey Ohio
68 D6 Chaungwabyin Burma
68 C4 Chaungzon Burma
51 Q2 Chaunskaya Guba *gulf* U.S.S.R.
22 E4 Chauny France
68 G7 Chau Phu Vietnam
69 A8 Chaura I Nicobar Is
20 B4 Chausey, I France
20 K2 Chaussée Tirancourt, la France
19 J6 Chaussin France
54 B3 Chausy U.S.S.R.
94 H4 Chautauqua New York
94 H4 Chautauqua L New York
57 F4 Chauvay U.S.S.R.
21 H6 Chauvigny France
21 G8 Chauvigny Vienne France
118 G6 Chauvin Alberta
19 K5 Chaux de Fonds, la France
40 E3 Chaux de Fonds, La Switzerland
21 C8 Chavagnes-en-Paillers France
19 N14 Chavanay France
52 E2 Chavan'ga U.S.S.R.
130 D4 Chavantina Brazil
130 D7 Chavantina Brazil
16 C3 Chaves Portugal
94 D9 Chavies Kentucky
22 F5 Chavignon France
87 D8 Chavuma Zambia
69 D8 Chawang Thailand
9 F5 Chawton England
56 G2 Chaya *R* U.S.S.R.
88 C7 Chaya, L Zambia
57 E3 Chayan U.S.S.R.
57 G4 Chayek U.S.S.R.
52 H6 Chaykovskiy U.S.S.R.
66 F6 Ch'a-yü China
21 D6 Chazé-sur-Argos France
52 H4 Chazhegovo U.S.S.R.
133 E4 Chazon Argentina
95 O2 Chazy New York
118 D7 Cheadle Alberta
8 E2 Cheadle England
111 L8 Cheaha Mt Alabama
94 H7 Cheat *R* W Virginia
110 J5 Cheatham L Tennessee
37 N3 Cheb Czechoslovakia
55 D4 Chebarkul' U.S.S.R.
52 G6 Cheboksary U.S.S.R.
94 C1 Cheboygan Michigan
52 E5 Chebsara U.S.S.R.
53 G11 Chechen-Ingush U.S.S.R.
54 B4 Chechersk U.S.S.R.
31 M5 Chęciny Poland
107 P6 Checotah Oklahoma
21 J6 Checy France
123 L8 Chedabucto B Nova Scotia
8 D5 Cheddar England
68 A3 Cheduba Burma
68 A3 Cheduba *isld* Burma
68 A3 Cheduba Str Burma
118 G2 Cheecham Alberta
120 J2 Cheepash *R* Ontario
120 G1 Cheepay *R* Ontario
141 G7 Cheepie Queensland
119 O1 Cheeseman L Ontario
106 E2 Cheesman,L Colorado
138 B2 Cheesmans Pk S Australia
146 K5 Cheetham,C Antarctica
111 G11 Chef Menteur Louisiana
Chefoo *see* Yantai
116 E6 Chefornak Alaska
121 R3 Chef,R.du Quebec
51 N3 Chegdomyn U.S.S.R.
85 C3 Chegga Mauritania
116 A3 Chegitun *R* U.S.S.R.
100 C3 Chehalis Washington
100 B3 Chehalis *R* Washington
67 B4 Chehe China
87 F8 Cheif Serenje Zambia
21 F7 Cheillé France
59 J5 Cheju S Korea
65 G8 Cheju do *isld* S Korea
65 G8 Cheju haehyŏp *str* S Korea
54 H2 Chekalin U.S.S.R.
52 H7 Chekan U.S.S.R.
54 J1 Chekhov U.S.S.R.
Chekiang *prov see* Zhejiang
55 G2 Chekino U.S.S.R.
51 N3 Chekunda U.S.S.R.
52 E3 Chekuyevo U.S.S.R.
69 F10 Chelah *mt* Malaysia
119 O6 Chelan Sask
100 F2 Chelan Washington
100 E1 Chelan,L Washington
100 E1 Chelan Range Washington
116 M5 Chelatna L Alaska
133 D5 Chelforó Argentina
85 F1 Chelia *mt* Algeria
85 E1 Chéliff *R* Algeria
55 C3 Chelkakovo U.S.S.R.
57 A1 Chelkar U.S.S.R.
31 O4 Chełm Poland
31 L2 Chełmno Poland
9 G4 Chelmsford England
120 J6 Chelmsford Ontario
52 E3 Chelmuzhi U.S.S.R.
31 L2 Chełmża Poland
99 O8 Chelsea Iowa
94 C4 Chelsea Michigan
107 P5 Chelsea Oklahoma
95 P3 Chelsea Vermont
8 D4 Cheltenham England
17 G5 Chelva Spain
55 D3 Chelyabinsk U.S.S.R.
50 F3 Chelyabinskaya Oblast' *prov* U.S.S.R.
94 F8 Chelyan W Virginia
51 K1 Chelyuskin,Mys *C* U.S.S.R.
117 M11 Chemainus Br Col
100 C4 Chemawa Oregon
21 D6 Chemazé France
87 F9 Chemba Mozambique
57 B6 Chemen-i-Bit U.S.S.R.
22 H4 Chémery-sur-Bar France
21 D7 Chemillé France
21 G6 Chemillé-sur-Dême France
40 B4 Chemin France
21 E6 Chemiré-le-Gaudin France
Chemnitz *see* Karl-Marx-Stadt
95 R7 Chemquasabamticook L Maine
56 B4 Chemskiy U.S.S.R.
95 K4 Chemung *R* New York
116 O4 Chena *R* Alaska
74 D3 Chenab *R* Pakistan
85 D3 Chenachèn Algeria
116 O4 Chena Hot Springs Alaska
95 M4 Chenango *R* New York
22 K2 Chênée Belgium
18 G6 Chénérailles France
121 P7 Chénéville Quebec
107 N4 Cheney Kansas
100 H2 Cheney Washington
111 D10 Cheneyville Louisiana
65 C6 Cheng'an China
67 B4 Chengbihe Shuiku *res* China
67 C3 Chengbu China
65 A7 Chengcheng China
Chengchow *see* Zhengzhou
65 D4 Chengde China
67 E1 Chengdong Hu *L* China
67 A1 Chengdu China
67 A4 Chenggong China
67 E5 Chenghai China
65 D5 Chengkou China
67 C1 Chengkou China
67 C7 Chengmai China
65 E6 Chengshan Jiao *pen* China
Chengtu *see* Chengdu
65 C7 Chengwu China
65 E6 Chengyang China
67 F2 Chengyang China
65 E5 Chengzitan China
121 O6 Chenier Quebec
123 N2 Chenil,L Quebec
36 B7 Cheniménil France
65 D7 Cheniu Shan *isld* China
65 D7 Chenjiagang China
65 C7 Chenliu China
110 H1 Chenoa Illinois
21 H7 Chenonceaux France
67 G1 Chenqian Shan *isld* China
21 F6 Chenu France
67 C2 Chenxi China
67 D4 Chen Xian China
Chenying *see* Wannian
68 G5 Cheom Ksan Cambodia
67 F3 Chepan China
128 C5 Chepén Peru
133 D4 Chepes Argentina
8 D4 Chepstow Wales
99 Q3 Chequamegon B Wisconsin
18 G5 Cher *dep* France
21 G7 Cher *R* France
21 J7 Cher *reg* France
22 K3 Cherain Belgium
44 C2 Cherasco Italy
106 G3 Cheraw Colorado
111 G10 Cheraw Mississippi
112 H3 Cheraw S Carolina
20 B2 Cherbourg France
85 E1 Cherchell Algeria
52 J4 Cherdyn' U.S.S.R.
21 B6 Chère *R* France
56 F4 Cheremkhovo U.S.S.R.
48 J2 Cheremosh *R* U.S.S.R.
55 D3 Cheremshanka U.S.S.R.
55 D1 Cheremukhovo U.S.S.R.
56 E4 Cherepanovo U.S.S.R.
54 H2 Cherepet' U.S.S.R.
52 E5 Cherepovets U.S.S.R.
52 D5 Chereptsovo U.S.S.R.
118 C5 Cherhill Alberta
54 C3 Cherikov U.S.S.R.
20 H4 Cherisy France
54 J8 Cherkasskoye U.S.S.R.
53 F11 Cherkessk U.S.S.R.
47 G1 Cherkovitsa Bulgaria
55 F4 Cherlak U.S.S.R.
52 J5 Chermoz U.S.S.R.
141 K1 Chermside *dist* Brisbane, Qnsld
116 H9 Chernabura I Alaska
55 D2 Chernaya *R* U.S.S.R.
52 H5 Chernaya Kholunitsa U.S.S.R.
47 H3 Chernichevo Bulgaria
54 C5 Chernigov U.S.S.R.
59 K3 Chernigovka U.S.S.R.
116 F9 Cherni I Alaska
55 C4 Chernikovsk U.S.S.R.
47 H1 Cherni Lom *R* Bulgaria
47 F2 Cherni Vrŭkh *mt* Bulgaria
56 D4 Chernogorsk U.S.S.R.
55 C2 Chernoistochinsk U.S.S.R.
55 G4 Chernoretskoye U.S.S.R.
55 F4 Chernousovka U.S.S.R.
52 G6 Chernovskoye U.S.S.R.
48 K2 Chernovtsy U.S.S.R.
55 E2 Chernoye U.S.S.R.
55 E3 Chernoye, Oz *L* U.S.S.R.
55 C3 Chernushka U.S.S.R.
52 G3 Chernut'yevo U.S.S.R.
31 N1 Chernyakhovsk U.S.S.R.
58 G1 Chernyshevsk U.S.S.R.
31 O1 Chernyshevskoye U.S.S.R.
53 G10 Chernyye Zemli U.S.S.R.
55 C5 Chernyy Otrog U.S.S.R.
126 F1 Cherokee Great Abaco I Bahamas
99 L7 Cherokee Iowa
107 Q4 Cherokee Kansas
107 M5 Cherokee Oklahoma
109 J5 Cherokee Texas
112 D1 Cherokee Dam Tennessee
94 D10 Cherokee L Tennessee
111 B9 Cherokee,L Texas
113 K11 Cherokee Pt Bahamas
110 B5 Cherokees, L O'The Oklahoma
55 E2 Cherpiya U.S.S.R.
75 O6 Cherrapunji India
20 B4 Cherrueix France
137 O4 Cherry *isld* Santa Cruz Is
103 K2 Cherry Cr Nevada
98 E5 Cherry Cr S Dakota
94 H4 Cherry Creek New York
103 K1 Cherry Cr.Mt Nevada
95 U2 Cherryfield Maine
117 O7 Cherry Point Alberta
107 P4 Cherryvale Kansas
95 N4 Cherry Valley New York
112 F2 Cherryville N Carolina
56 G3 Cherskogo,Gora *mt* U.S.S.R.
51 O2 Cherskogo,Khrebet *mts* U.S.S.R.
17 H4 Cherta Spain
54 M7 Chertkovo U.S.S.R.
54 E1 Chertolino U.S.S.R.
9 F5 Chertsey England
144 C5 Chertsey New Zealand
52 F6 Cherusti U.S.S.R.
19 O13 Cheruy,Pt.de France
52 G4 Cherva U.S.S.R.
54 G9 Chervonoarmeyskoye U.S.S.R.
48 N3 Chervonoz-namenka U.S.S.R.
9 E3 Cherwell,R England
94 C3 Chesaning Michigan
94 E8 Chesapeake Ohio
95 L10 Chesapeake Virginia
95 L8 Chesapeake B U.S.A.
95 L8 Chesapeake Beach Maryland
95 M7 Chesapeake City Maryland
9 F4 Chesham England
95 O4 Cheshire Massachusetts
8 D1 Cheshire *co* England
52 G2 Chëshskaya Guba *B* U.S.S.R.
88 B6 Chesi,L Zambia
8 D6 Chesil Bank England
120 J8 Chesley Ontario
55 D4 Chesma U.S.S.R.
112 F2 Chesnee S Carolina
22 H5 Chesne, le Ardennes France
20 G4 Chesne,le Eure France
110 B6 Chester Arkansas
100 D9 Chester California
95 P5 Chester Connecticut
8 D1 Chester England
101 O5 Chester Idaho
110 G4 Chester Illinois
95 P4 Chester Massachusetts
101 P1 Chester Montana
98 J9 Chester Nebraska
122 H9 Chester Nova Scotia
95 M6 Chester Pennsylvania
112 F3 Chester S Carolina
109 N5 Chester Texas
95 P3 Chester Vermont
94 K9 Chester Virginia
95 L7 Chester *R* Maryland
122 H9 Chester Basin Nova Scotia
9 E1 Chesterfield England
101 O7 Chesterfield Idaho
110 F2 Chesterfield Illinois
112 G3 Chesterfield S Carolina
94 K9 Chesterfield Virginia
137 M5 Chesterfield, Îles Coral Sea
115 K5 Chesterfield Inlet N W Terr
94 F7 Chesterhill Ohio
9 F2 Chesterton England
99 T8 Chesterton Indiana
95 L7 Chestertown Maryland
95 O3 Chestertown New York
121 P7 Chesterville Ontario
109 O3 Chestnut Louisiana
94 H6 Chestnut Ridge Pennsylvania
144 D5 Chest Pk New Zealand
95 R7 Chesuncook L Maine
95 M7 Cheswold Delaware
56 C3 Chet' *R* U.S.S.R.
68 A7 Chetamale Andaman Is
99 P4 Chetek Wisconsin
123 L7 Cheticamp C Breton I, N Scotia
73 L6 Chetlat *isld* Lakshadweep Indian Oc
107 P4 Chetopa Kansas
125 P8 Chetumal Mexico
145 E4 Chetwode Is New Zealand
117 N8 Chetwynd Br Col
116 E6 Chevak Alaska
19 O17 Cheval-Blanc France
20 J5 Chevilly France
144 D5 Cheviot New Zealand
118 L6 Cheviot Sask
13 F3 Cheviot Hills England/Scotland
141 G7 Cheviot Ra Queensland
139 G2 Cheviot Rge Queensland
21 E6 Cheviré-le-Rouge France
18 B4 Chèvre, Cap de la *C* France
111 E12 Chevreuil, Point Louisiana
20 K4 Chevreuse France
40 E7 Chevril,L France
88 D9 Chewa Mozambique
100 H1 Chewelah Washington
21 E9 Chey France
107 L6 Cheyenne Oklahoma
108 D4 Cheyenne Texas
98 B8 Cheyenne Wyoming
98 D5 Cheyenne *R* S Dakota
98 F5 Cheyenne Agency S Dakota
107 M3 Cheyenne Bottoms Kansas
98 A8 Cheyenne Pass Wyoming
106 H3 Cheyenne Wells Colorado
18 H8 Cheylard, le France
143 C10 Cheyne B W Australia
143 E10 Cheyney.Pt W Australia
117 M9 Chezacut Br Col
21 J8 Chezal-Benoit France
74 H6 Chhatarpur India
68 G6 Chhlong Cambodia
68 H6 Chhlong *R* Cambodia
68 G7 Chhuk Cambodia
116 H9 Chiachi I Alaska
67 G5 Chia-i Taiwan
66 D5 Chia-jen Ts'o *L* China
40 F7 Chialamberto Italy
66 D5 Chia-man-t'e-k'a-mu Hu *L* China
86 H6 Chiambone Somalia
87 B9 Chiange Angola
68 D3 Chiang Mai Thailand
68 E2 Chiang Saen Thailand
42 E6 Chiani *R* Italy
125 N9 Chiapa del Corzo Mexico
45 O4 Chiaravalle Italy
43 G10 Chiaravalle Centrale Italy
41 L5 Chiareggio Italy
41 L6 Chiari Italy
125 K8 Chiautla Mexico
44 F3 Chiavari Italy
41 K5 Chiavenna Italy
61 O10 Chiba Japan
61 O10 Chiba *prefect* Japan
61 P13 Chibana Okinawa
121 Q3 Chibougamau Quebec
121 P3 Chibougamau *R* Quebec
121 R3 Chibougamau,Parc de Quebec
88 B8 Chibuluma Zambia
60 G9 Chiburi-shima *isld* Japan
87 F10 Chibuto Mozambique
87 E8 Chibwe Zambia
99 T8 Chicago Illinois
105 Chicago *conurbation* Illinois
99 T8 Chicago Heights Illinois
122 F5 Chic-Chocs,Parc des Quebec
117 E7 Chichagof I Alaska
85 C2 Chichaoua Morocco
65 C4 Chicheng China
125 P7 Chichén Itza *ruins* Mexico
9 F6 Chichester England
142 C5 Chichester Ra W Australia
61 N10 Chichibu Japan
61 M9 Chichibu Nat. Park Japan
56 C3 Chichka-Yul *R* U.S.S.R.
95 K9 Chickahominy *R* Virginia
112 B3 Chickamauga Georgia
112 B2 Chickamauga Dam Tennessee
111 H10 Chickasawhay *R* Mississippi
107 N6 Chickasha Oklahoma
116 R4 Chicken Alaska
146 G2 Chick I Antarctica
8 D5 Chicklade England
16 C8 Chiclana de la Frontera Spain
128 C5 Chiclayo Peru
102 C2 Chico California
100 H4 Chico Oregon
109 K2 Chico Texas
133 D6 Chico *R* Argentina
71 E2 Chico *R* Luzon Philippines
133 D3 Chicoana Argentina
121 M4 Chicobi,L Quebec
87 F10 Chicomo Mozambique
125 K7 Chicontepec Mexico
87 D7 Chicopa *R* Angola
95 P4 Chicopee Massachusetts
121 T4 Chicoutimi Quebec
121 T5 Chicoutimi *R* Quebec
122 B5 Chicoutimi, Parc des Quebec
89 G4 Chicualacuala Mozambique
76 D5 Chidambaram India
9 F5 Chiddingfold England
109 O2 Chidester Arkansas
115 N5 Chidley,C Quebec
100 F1 Chief Joseph Dam Washington
113 E8 Chiefland Florida
120 J8 Chiefs Pt Ontario
85 C7 Chiehn Liberia
67 B5 Chiem Hoa Vietnam
87 E7 Chiengi Zambia
42 F5 Chienti *R* Italy
57 L2 Chierh Shan *mts* U.S.S.R.
44 C1 Chieri Italy
22 K5 Chiers *R* France
41 L5 Chiesa Italy
41 M5 Chiese *R* Italy
42 F6 Chieti Italy
22 F2 Chièvres Belgium
130 H5 Chifre,Serra do *mts* Brazil
57 G2 Chiganak U.S.S.R.
61 N10 Chigasaki Japan
116 J8 Chiginigak Vol., Mt Alaska
54 D7 Chigirin U.S.S.R.
116 L6 Chigmit Mts Alaska
122 H8 Chignecto B Nova Scotia/New Bruns
116 H8 Chignik Alaska
19 Q13 Chignin France
121 R3 Chigoubiche, L Quebec
87 F10 Chigubo Mozambique
66 E6 Chigu Co *L* China
9 G4 Chigwell England
Chihli, Gulf of *see* Bo Hai
124 F3 Chihuahua Mexico
131 B7 Chihuido Medio *peak* Argentina
57 D3 Chiili U.S.S.R.
67 C6 Chikan China
107 N5 Chikaskia *R* Okla/Kansas
76 C4 Chik Ballapur India
52 C6 Chikhachevo U.S.S.R.
60 O3 Chikiu-misaki *C* Japan
76 C3 Chikjaju India
76 B4 Chikmagalur India
56 G5 Chikoy *R* U.S.S.R.
68 G6 Chikreng *R* Cambodia
60 D12 Chikugo Japan
60 D12 Chikugo *R* Japan
61 M9 Chikuma *R* Japan
116 H6 Chikuminuk L Alaska
61 N11 Chikura Japan
88 E10 Chikwawa Malawi
68 A2 Chi-kyaw Burma
117 L9 Chilanko Forks Br Columbia
74 F1 Chilas Kashmir
83 J10 Chilaw Sri Lanka
128 C6 Chilca, Pta. de *point* Peru
102 D2 Chilcoot California
117 M10 Chilcotin *R* Br Col
141 K3 Chilcott I Gt Barrier Reef Aust
141 K7 Childers Queensland
111 K8 Childersburg Alabama
108 G1 Childress Texas
103 M9 Childs Arizona
113 F10 Childs Florida
133 C6 Chile *rep* S America
128 C5 Chilete Peru
86 G3 Chilga Ethiopia
9 G5 Chilham England
110 C3 Chilhowee Missouri
94 F10 Chilhowie Virginia
55 B5 Chilik U.S.S.R.
116 K6 Chilikadrotna *R* Alaska
87 E8 Chililabombwe Zambia
88 A8 Chililabombwe Zambia
59 H1 Chi-liu Ho *R* China
75 L9 Chilka Lake India
117 F6 Chilkat *R* Alaska
117 M10 Chilko *R* Br Col
117 F6 Chilkoot Alaska
141 G3 Chillagoe Queensland
131 A6 Chillán Chile
20 K5 Chilleurs-aux-Bois France
99 R9 Chillicothe Illinois
110 C2 Chillicothe Missouri
94 D7 Chillicothe Ohio
109 H1 Chillicothe Texas
139 G6 Chillingollah Victoria
100 D1 Chilliwack Br Col
19 P13 Chilly France
101 M5 Chilly Idaho
116 J6 Chilnuk Mts Alaska
133 C6 Chiloé *prov* Chile
135 R14 Chiloe, I. de Chile
88 C8 Chilonga Zambia
87 F8 Chilongazi Zambia
100 D7 Chiloquin Oregon
125 K9 Chilpancingo Mexico
139 H6 Chiltern Victoria
9 F4 Chiltern Hills England
99 S5 Chilton Wisconsin
88 E7 Chilumba Malawi
67 G4 Chi-lung Taiwan
87 G9 Chilwa,L Malawi
88 F9 Chilwa,L Mozambique
9 E6 Chilworth England
125 M9 Chimalapa Mexico
87 F10 Chimanimani Nat. Park Zimbabwe
22 G3 Chimay Belgium
106 E6 Chimayo New Mexico
57 A3 Chimbay U.S.S.R.
128 C4 Chimborazo *mt* Ecuador
128 C5 Chimbote Peru
88 C8 Chimbwin-gombi *mt* Zambia
55 E3 Chimeyevo U.S.S.R.
57 F4 Chimion U.S.S.R.
48 M4 Chimishliya Moldavia U.S.S.R.
57 E4 Chimkent U.S.S.R.
123 P4 Chimney Cove Nfld
108 B3 Chimney Peak New Mexico
106 E9 Chimney Pk New Mexico
83 J12 Chimney Rocks Seychelles
87 F9 Chimoio Mozambique
118 E9 Chin Alberta
65 F7 Chin *isld* S Korea
95 S2 China Maine
58 D4 China *People's Rep* E Asia
68 C4 China Bakir *R* Burma
124 G5 Chinacates Mexico
112 G2 China Grove N Carolina
102 G6 China L California
125 L3 Chinandega Nicaragua
102 F9 China Pt California
109 K4 China Spring Texas
108 C6 Chinati Mts Texas
120 J7 Chin, Cape Ontario
128 C6 Chincha Alta Peru
117 O6 Chinchaga *R* Alberta
128 C6 Chincha, Is Peru
141 K7 Chinchilla Queensland
17 F6 Chinchilla de Monte Aragón Spain
128 C4 Chinchipe *R* Ecuador/Peru
16 E4 Chinchón Spain
95 M9 Chincoteague Virginia
95 M8 Chincoteague B Maryland
87 G9 Chinde Mozambique
73 P4 Chindwin *R* Burma
61 P14 Chinen Okinawa
88 E8 Chinengue Mozambique
66 B4 Chinese Turkestan *reg* Xinjiang Uygur Zizhiqu China
67 D1 Ching-Chiang Res China
Chinghai *see* Qinghai
Chinghai *prov see* Qinghai
57 J1 Chingiz-Tau, Khr *mts* U.S.S.R.
76 E4 Chingleput India
88 A8 Chingola Zambia
87 B8 Chingoroi Angola
87 C8 Chinguai Angola
73 P4 Chin Hills Burma
116 L8 Chiniak,C Alaska
Chining *see* Jining
74 E3 Chiniot Pakistan
124 E4 Chinipas Mexico
116 L7 Chinitna B Alaska
65 G7 Chinju S Korea
86 D4 Chinko *R* Cent Afr Republic
103 P5 Chinle Arizona
103 P5 Chinle Cr Arizona
103 P5 Chinle V Arizona
67 F4 Chin-men Taiwan
65 F5 Chinnamp'o N Korea
103 M6 Chino Arizona
143 C10 Chinocup, L W Australia
21 F7 Chinon France
118 G7 Chinook Alberta
101 Q1 Chinook Montana
100 D3 Chinook Pass Washington
103 M7 Chino Valley Arizona
87 F8 Chinsali Zambia
88 D7 Chinsali Zambia
76 E1 Chintalnar India
88 E7 Chintheche Malawi
126 G10 Chinú Colombia
22 J4 Chiny Belgium
55 G3 Chinyavino U.S.S.R.
42 E3 Chioggia Italy
Chios *isld* Greece *see* Khíos I
88 D8 Chipata Zambia
87 E9 Chipepo Zambia
88 D9 Chipera Mozambique
88 E10 Chiperone *mt* Mozambique
119 T1 Chipewyan,L Manitoba
117 R7 Chipewyan Lake Alberta
87 E8 Chipili Zambia
65 C6 Chiping China
87 F10 Chipinga Zimbabwe
117 Q9 Chip Lake Alberta
111 L11 Chipley Florida
111 M9 Chipley Georgia
74 E10 Chiplun India
122 G7 Chipman New Brunswick
120 D3 Chipman L Ontario
88 E8 Chipoka Malawi
111 L11 Chipola *R* Florida
88 A9 Chiposhya, L Zambia
68 G7 Chi Pou Cambodia
121 L9 Chippawa Ontario
8 D5 Chippenham England
99 L4 Chippewa *R* Minnesota
99 P5 Chippewa Falls Wisconsin
99 P4 Chippewa Lake Wisconsin
13 F6 Chipping England
9 E3 Chipping Campden England
9 E4 Chipping Norton England
8 D4 Chipping Sodbury England
46 F1 Chiprovtsi Bulgaria
128 C6 Chiquian Peru
128 D2 Chiquinquirá Colombia
131 F6 Chiquita, L. Mar Buenos Aires Argentina
128 F7 Chiquitos, Llanos de Bolivia
128 B4 Chira *R* Peru
76 E3 Chirala India
87 F9 Chiramba Mozambique
128 C3 Chirambirá, Pta *point* Colombia
77 J2 Chiras Afghanistan
57 E4 Chirchik U.S.S.R.
87 F10 Chiredzi Zimbabwe
89 G3 Chiredzi *R* Zimbabwe
109 N4 Chireno Texas
111 B10 Chireno Texas
84 E5 Chirfa Niger
103 P9 Chirica Hua Nat.Mon Arizona
103 P10 Chiricahua Pk Arizona
126 H10 Chiriguaná Colombia
116 K9 Chirikof I Alaska
75 P8 Chiringa Bangladesh
125 N5 Chiriqui,G.de Panama
75 K7 Chirmiri India
47 J1 Chirnogeni Romania
15 F5 Chirnside Borders Scotland
13 F2 Chirnside Scotland
88 E10 Chiromo Malawi
47 G2 Chirpan Bulgaria
Chirua, L *see* Chilwa, L
87 E9 Chirundu Zimbabwe
22 D4 Chiry-Ourscamps France
88 B9 Chisamba Zambia
116 R5 Chisana Alaska
116 Q6 Chisana Glacier Alaska
44 B2 Chisane *R* Italy
119 R4 Chisel Lake Manitoba
88 D6 Chisenga Malawi
55 C4 Chishmy U.S.S.R.
118 C4 Chisholm Alberta
95 R2 Chisholm Maine
99 O2 Chisholm Minnesota
74 E4 Chishtian Mandi Pakistan
67 B2 Chishui China
67 F4 Chishui China
67 B3 Chishui He *R* China
88 B7 Chisi *isld* Zambia
86 H6 Chisimaio Somalia
87 F8 Chisimba Falls Zambia
Chişinău *see* Kishinev
48 G4 Chişineu Criş Romania
108 D6 Chisos Mts Texas
108 C5 Chispa Cr Texas
116 P5 Chistochina Alaska
55 G4 Chisto-ozernoye U.S.S.R.
52 H6 Chistopol U.S.S.R.
55 E4 Chistopol'ye U.S.S.R.
55 G4 Chistovo U.S.S.R.
55 F4 Chistyakovka U.S.S.R.
88 E8 Chisumulu *isld* Mozambique
51 L3 Chita U.S.S.R.
87 B9 Chitado Angola
116 L4 Chitanana *R* Alaska
58 C5 Chi-t'ang China
61 K11 Chita wan *gulf* Japan
52 G4 Chitayevo U.S.S.R.
118 K5 Chitek Sask
119 S6 Chitek L Manitoba
87 C8 Chitembo Angola
45 L4 Chitignano Italy
116 P6 Chitina Alaska
116 Q6 Chitina *R* Alaska
51 L3 Chitinskaya Oblast' *prov* U.S.S.R.
60 P3 Chitose Japan
76 C3 Chitradurga India
74 J6 Chitrakut India
74 D1 Chitral Pakistan
125 O6 Chitré Panama
75 O7 Chittagong Bangladesh
75 M7 Chittaranjan India
74 F6 Chittaurgarh India
76 D4 Chittoor India
76 C5 Chittur India
88 F8 Chiulézi *R* Mozambique
87 D9 Chiume Angola
42 D2 Chiusa Italy
42 D5 Chiusi Italy
45 L4 Chiusi di Verna Italy
87 G8 Chiuta, L Malawi
88 E9 Chiuta,L Mozambique
17 G5 Chiva Spain
40 G7 Chivasso Italy
124 C4 Chívato,Pta *C* Mexico
128 D7 Chivay Peru
87 B9 Chivemba Angola
131 E5 Chivilcoy Argentina
106 H3 Chivington Colorado
22 F4 Chivy France
67 D6 Chixi China
125 O10 Chixoy *R* Guatemala
21 E9 Chizé France
52 F2 Chizha U.S.S.R.
Chizhou *see* Guichi
60 H10 Chizu Japan
55 F4 Chkalovo U.S.S.R.
57 H6 Chkalovsk U.S.S.R.
103 K6 Chloride Arizona
31 J5 Chlumec nad Cidlinou Czechoslovakia
31 M5 Chmielnik Poland
65 F5 Cho *isld* N Korea
65 G7 Ch'o *isld* S Korea
131 B3 Choapo,R Chile
9 F5 Chobham England
68 G2 Cho Bo Vietnam
31 J5 Choceň Czechoslovakia
121 O5 Chochocouane *R* Quebec
67 B6 Cho Chu Vietnam
31 J4 Chocianów Poland
128 C2 Chocó *div* Colombia
103 K8 Chocolate Mts Arizona
103 J8 Chocolate Mts California
95 Q3 Chocorua New Hampshire
112 K2 Chocowinity N Carolina
107 N6 Choctaw Oklahoma
111 K11 Choctawhatchee B Florida
37 O3 Chodov Czechoslovakia
31 K3 Chodzież Poland
133 D5 Choele Choel Argentina
88 C9 Chofombo Mozambique
68 H7 Cho Giua Vietnam
119 N5 Choiceland Sask
137 M3 Choiseul *isld* Solomon Is
133 F8 Choiseul Sd Falkland Is
19 Q12 Choisy France
22 D5 Choisy-au-Bac France
20 K4 Choisy-le-Roi France
124 E4 Choix Mexico
31 H3 Chojna Poland
31 K2 Chojnice Poland
31 J4 Chojnów Poland
61 O6 Chōkai-san *mt* Japan
86 G3 Choke Mts Ethiopia
98 K4 Chokio Minnesota
57 G3 Choknar U.S.S.R.
57 H4 Choktal U.S.S.R.
51 O1 Chokurdakh U.S.S.R.
102 D6 Cholame California
102 D6 Cholame Cr California
133 C4 Cholchagua *prov* Chile
21 D7 Cholet France
13 F3 Chollerford England
68 H7 Cho Lon Vietnam
57 H4 Cholpon U.S.S.R.
57 H4 Cholpon-Ata U.S.S.R.
125 K8 Cholula Mexico
125 L3 Choluleca Honduras
87 E9 Choma Zambia
68 F7 Chomna Cambodia
68 G2 Cho Moi Vietnam
75 N5 Chomo Lhari *mt* Bhutan/Xizang Zizhiqu
68 D3 Chom Thong Thailand
37 P3 Chomutov Czechoslovakia
56 H1 Chona *R* U.S.S.R.
68 E6 Chon Buri Thailand
68 E4 Chon Daen Thailand
128 B4 Chone Ecuador
67 F3 Chong'an China
67 G1 Chongde China
65 H4 Ch'ŏngjin N Korea
65 G6 Ch'ŏngju S Korea
68 F6 Chong Kal Cambodia
65 C4 Chongli China
67 G1 Chongming China
67 G1 Chongming Dao *isld* China
67 A1 Chongqing China
67 B2 Chongqing China
67 E3 Chongren China
67 E4 Chongshi China
88 B9 Chongwe *R* Zambia
67 E2 Chongyang China
67 F3 Chongyang Xi *R* China
67 E4 Chongyi China
56 D5 Chongyz-Tayga, Gora *mt* U.S.S.R.
68 H1 Chongzuo China
65 G7 Chŏnju S Korea
133 C6 Chonos,Arch.de los *islds* Chile
68 H7 Chon Thanh Vietnam
75 M4 Cho Oyu *peak* Xizang Zizhiqu/Nepal
48 G2 Chop U.S.S.R.
13 G5 Chop Gate England
68 H7 Cho Phuoc Hai Vietnam
130 D9 Chopim, R Brazil
130 D9 Chopimzinho Brazil
95 M8 Choptank *R* Maryland
68 G1 Cho Ra Vietnam
56 F3 Chora *R* U.S.S.R.
33 T7 Chorin E Germany
16 E5 Chorito, Sa. del *mts* Spain
13 F6 Chorley England
78 H1 Chorokh *R* Turkey
131 B2 Choros *R* Chile
131 B2 Choros,I.de los Chile
31 O2 Choroszcz Poland
141 G6 Chorregon Queensland
128 C6 Chorrillos Peru
130 G10 Chorrochó Brazil
48 K1 Chortkov U.S.S.R.
31 M2 Chorzele Poland
31 L5 Chorzów Poland
61 O10 Chōshi Japan
133 C5 Chos Malal Argentina
65 G5 Choson-Man *B* N Korea
31 J2 Choszczno Poland
128 C5 Chota Peru
75 K7 Chota Nagpur *reg* India
74 F7 Chota Udaipur India
101 N2 Choteau Montana
107 P5 Choteau Oklahoma
31 J6 Chotěbor Czechoslovakia
37 P4 Chotěšov Czechoslovakia
85 E2 Chott ech Chergui *salt lake* Algeria
85 E1 Chott et Hodna *marsh* Algeria
85 F2 Chott Jerid *salt flats* Tunisia
85 F2 Chott Melrhir *salt flats* Algeria
21 F7 Chouzé-sur-Loire France
21 H7 Chouzy-sur-Cisse France
112 L1 Chowan *R* N Carolina
102 D4 Chowchilla California
143 B10 Chowerup W Australia
138 F5 Chowilla Dam S Australia
117 O9 Chown,Mt Alberta
58 F2 Choybalsan Mongolia
40 C3 Choye France
48 D1 Chřiby Czechoslovakia
31 K6 Chřiby *dist* Czechoslovakia
109 L5 Chriesman Texas
99 T10 Chrisman Illinois
144 D5 Christabel, L New Zealand
9 E6 Christchurch England
144 B4 Christchurch New Zealand
127 P6 Christchurch *parish* Barbados
116 P3 Christian Alaska
127 K2 Christiana Jamaica
95 L7 Christiana Pennsylvania
89 D6 Christiana S Africa
115 N3 Christian,C N W Terr
120 K8 Christian I Ontario
94 C6 Christiansburg Ohio
110 M1 Christiansburg Ohio
94 G9 Christiansburg Virginia
28 C6 Christiansfeld Denmark
115 O4 Christianshåb Greenland
28 C4 Christianshede Denmark
27 H16 Christiansø *isld* Denmark
127 M6 Christiansted Virgin Is
69 C8 Christie I Burma
119 V2 Christie L Manitoba
101 Q2 Christina Montana
118 G3 Christina,L Alberta
100 G1 Christina L Br Col
144 B6 Christina, Mt New Zealand
118 G2 Christina R Alberta
109 J7 Christine Texas
142 F4 Christmas Creek W Australia
83 M9 Christmas I Indian Oc
135 U10 Christmas I Pacific Oc
120 H2 Christopher Falls Ontario
143 G6 Christopher, L W Australia
108 G4 Christoval Texas
131 H3 Christovão Pereira,Pte Brazil
106 D4 Chromo Colorado
31 J6 Chrudim Czechoslovakia
31 L5 Chrzanow Poland
79 F5 Chtaura Lebanon
57 G3 Chu U.S.S.R.
57 F3 Chu *R* U.S.S.R.
125 O10 Chuacús,Sa.de *ra* Guatemala
67 F2 Chuankeng China
67 G1 Chuansha China
57 J1 Chubartau U.S.S.R.
103 J7 Chubbuck California
61 L9 Chūbu Sangaku Nat. Park Japan
133 D6 Chubut *prov* Argentina
133 D6 Chubut *R* Argentina
Chuchow *see* Zhuzhou
103 J8 Chuckwalla Mts California
133 E4 Chucul Argentina
37 P5 Chudenice Czechoslovakia
55 D4 Chudinovo U.S.S.R.
8 C6 Chudleigh England
141 G4 Chudleigh Park Queensland
120 K6 Chudleigh River Valley Ontario
52 D5 Chudovo U.S.S.R.

52 C5 **Chudskoye, Ozero** *L* U.S.S.R.
116 M7 **Chugach Is** Alaska
116 O6 **Chugach Mts** Alaska
60 F11 **Chūgoku sanchi** *mts* Japan
Chuguchak *see* **Tacheng**
56 C4 **Chugunash** U.S.S.R.
55 F3 **Chugunly** U.S.S.R.
54 H7 **Chuguyev** U.S.S.R.
98 B8 **Chugwater** Wyoming
98 B8 **Chugwater Cr** Wyoming
103 N9 **Chuichu** Arizona
57 G3 **Chu-Iliyskiye Gory** *mts* U.S.S.R.
69 F10 **Chukai** Malaysia
59 L1 **Chukchagirskoye, Oz** *L* U.S.S.R.
147 O3 **Chukchi Sea** Arctic Oc
52 F5 **Chukhloma** U.S.S.R.
52 F5 **Chukhlomskoye, Oz** *L* U.S.S.R.
116 A3 **Chukotskiy Poluostrov** U.S.S.R.
112 D6 **Chula** Georgia
99 N10 **Chula** Missouri
94 K9 **Chula** Virginia
56 G2 **Chula** *R* U.S.S.R.
68 J5 **Chu Lai** Vietnam
57 E3 **Chulak-Kurgan** U.S.S.R.
52 G3 **Chulasa** U.S.S.R.
102 G9 **Chula Vista** California
116 N5 **Chulitna** *R* Alaska
51 M3 **Chulman** U.S.S.R.
8 C6 **Chulmleigh** England
128 B5 **Chulucanas** Peru
58 D2 **Chuluut Gol** *R* Mongolia
56 B3 **Chulym** U.S.S.R.
56 D3 **Chulym** *R* U.S.S.R.
56 C5 **Chulyshman** *R* U.S.S.R.
56 C5 **Chulyshmunskiy Khrebet** *mts* U.S.S.R.
74 H2 **Chumar** Kashmir
133 D3 **Chumbicha** Argentina
47 H2 **Chumerna** *mt* Bulgaria
59 L1 **Chumikan** U.S.S.R.
68 D7 **Chumphon** Thailand
68 E5 **Chum Saeng** Thailand
111 J11 **Chumuckla** Florida
56 B4 **Chumysh** *R* U.S.S.R.
56 E2 **Chuna** *R* U.S.S.R.
67 F2 **Chun'an** China
65 G6 **Ch'unch'ŏn** S Korea
111 H11 **Chunchula** Alabama
Chungking *see* **Chongqing**
66 C6 **Chung-pa** China
68 K3 **Chung-yüan** China
65 A7 **Chunhua** China
65 H3 **Chunhua** China
56 E1 **Chunku** *R* U.S.S.R.
58 D6 **Chün-lien** China
67 C1 **Chunmuying** China
83 K8 **Chunnakam** Sri Lanka
88 D6 **Chunya** Tanzania
56 E1 **Chunya** *R* U.S.S.R.
59 J3 **Chunyang** China
69 G8 **Chuoi,Hon** *isld* Vietnam
52 D2 **Chupa** U.S.S.R.
127 O1 **Chupara Pt** Trinidad
128 D6 **Chuquibambilla** Peru
133 D2 **Chuquicamata** Chile
133 E2 **Chuquisaca** *dep* Bolivia
41 L4 **Chur** Switzerland
52 H6 **Chur** U.S.S.R.
52 J5 **Churaki** U.S.S.R.
51 N2 **Churapcha** U.S.S.R.
55 C3 **Churayevo** U.S.S.R.
119 Q8 **Churchbridge** Sask
95 L8 **Church Creek** Maryland
94 E10 **Church Hill** Tennessee
8 D5 **Churchill** England
101 M7 **Churchill** Idaho
115 K6 **Churchill** Manitoba
115 N7 **Churchill** *R* Labrador
114 J6 **Churchill** *R* Sask
95 R7 **Churchill L** Maine
114 J6 **Churchill L** Sask
146 G7 **Churchill Mts** Antarctica
114 G6 **Churchill Pk** Br Columbia
119 W1 **Churchill R** Manitoba
8 C6 **Churchingford** England
111 D11 **Church Point** Louisiana
122 F9 **Church Pt** Nova Scotia
98 G1 **Churchs Ferry** N Dakota
8 D2 **Church Stretton** England
94 K3 **Churchville** New York
94 H8 **Churchville** Virginia
99 M7 **Churdan** Iowa
56 D5 **Chureg-Tag,Gora** *mt* U.S.S.R.
41 K3 **Churfirsten** *mt* Switzerland
75 K6 **Churk** India
52 F3 **Churkino** U.S.S.R.
74 F4 **Churu** India
94 B5 **Churubusco** Indiana
128 E1 **Churuguara** Venezuela
52 F4 **Chushevitsy** U.S.S.R.
57 A2 **Chushkakyl'** U.S.S.R.
106 B5 **Chuska Mts** Ariz/New Mex
55 C2 **Chusovaya** *R* U.S.S.R.
50 E3 **Chusovoy** U.S.S.R.
52 J4 **Chusovskoy** U.S.S.R.
57 F4 **Chust** U.S.S.R.
122 D4 **Chute-aux-Outardes** Quebec
122 A4 **Chute-des-Passes** Quebec
52 J4 **Chuval** U.S.S.R.
67 F1 **Chu Xian** China
61 N9 **Chūzenji-ko** *L* Japan
37 P3 **Chyše** Czechoslovakia
88 F3 **Chyulu Ra** Kenya
45 N6 **Ciampino** Italy
42 C4 **Ciano d'Enza** Italy
103 O7 **Cibecue** Arizona
48 H5 **Cibinului,Munţii** *mts* Romania
103 K8 **Cibola** Arizona
124 D2 **Cibuta** Mexico
42 F3 **Čičarija** *mt* Yugoslavia
45 R8 **Cicciano** Italy
94 A6 **Cicero** Indiana
95 L3 **Cicero** New York
129 L6 **Cicero Dantas** Brazil
46 E1 **Ćićevac** Yugoslavia
67 G1 **Cicheng** China
17 F2 **Cidacos** *R* Spain
78 D1 **Cide** Turkey
31 J5 **Cidlina** *R* Czechoslovakia
31 M3 **Ciéchanow** Poland
31 N3 **Ciechanowiec** Poland
31 L3 **Ciechocinek** Poland
126 E4 **Ciego de Avila** Cuba
128 D1 **Ciénaga** Colombia
126 G10 **Ciénaga de Oro** Colombia
106 E9 **Cienega** New Mexico
124 H5 **Ciénega del Carmen** Mexico
124 H5 **Cieneguilla** Mexico
124 D3 **Cieneguita** Mexico
126 D3 **Cienfuegos** Cuba
22 J3 **Ciergnon** Belgium
31 O5 **Cieszanow** Poland
31 L6 **Cieszyn** Poland
21 H10 **Cieux** France
17 G6 **Cieza** Spain
31 M6 **Ciężkowice** Poland
47 L5 **Çifteler** Turkey
17 F4 **Cifuentes** Spain
40 H7 **Cigliano** Italy
78 D2 **Cihanbeyli** Turkey
124 G8 **Cihuatlán** Mexico
16 D5 **Cijara, Embalse de** *res* Spain
46 D4 **Çikës, Mal i** *mt* Albania
78 J1 **Çildir G** *L* Turkey
67 D2 **Cili** China
8 C3 **Cilycwm** Wales
103 J6 **Cima** California
106 C3 **Cimarron** Colorado
107 K4 **Cimarron** Kansas
106 F5 **Cimarron** New Mexico
107 M5 **Cimarron** *R* Okla/Kansas
31 O2 **Cimochy** Poland
42 D4 **Cimone, M** *mt* Italy
48 H4 **Cîmpia Turzii** Romania
48 K5 **Cîmpina** Romania
48 J5 **Cîmpulung** Romania
48 K3 **Cîmpulung Moldovenesc** Romania
48 K4 **Cîmpuri** Romania
128 E2 **Cinaruco** *R* Venezuela
18 F10 **Cinca** *R* Spain
42 H5 **Činčer** *mt* Yugoslavia
99 O9 **Cincinnati** Iowa
94 C7 **Cincinnati** Ohio
95 M4 **Cincinnatus** New York
116 H8 **Cinder** *R* Alaska
8 D4 **Cinderford** England
48 K5 **Cîndeşti** Romania
48 H5 **Cîndrelu** *mt* Romania
47 J7 **Çine** Turkey
47 J7 **Çine** *R* Turkey
22 J3 **Ciney** Belgium
16 B3 **Cinfães** Portugal
21 F7 **Cinq Mars** France
68 A7 **Cinque I** Andaman Is
129 J5 **Cinta,Serra da** *mts* Brazil
85 A4 **Cintra, G.de** Mauritania
48 L6 **Cioara Doiceşti** Romania
45 O6 **Ciociaria** Italy
48 J6 **Ciolăneşti** Romania
67 E3 **Ciping** China
20 E5 **Ciral** France
17 G4 **Cirat** Spain
43 E7 **Circeo, M** *lt ho* Italy
43 E7 **Circeo, M** *mt* Italy
116 P4 **Circle** Alaska
98 A2 **Circle** Montana
94 E7 **Circleville** Ohio
103 M3 **Circleville** Utah
9 E4 **Cirencester** England
20 K3 **Cires-les-Mello** France
19 K4 **Cirey** France
36 B6 **Cirey-sur-Vezouse** France
44 C1 **Ciriè** Italy
18 E8 **Ciron** *R* France
44 G3 **Cisa, Passo di** Italy
99 S9 **Cisco** Illinois
109 J3 **Cisco** Texas
103 P3 **Cisco** Utah
48 K5 **Cislău** Romania
33 N4 **Cismar** W Germany
31 N6 **Cisna** Poland
48 J5 **Cisnadie** Romania
110 H3 **Cisne** Illinois
128 C2 **Cisneros** Colombia
133 C6 **Cisnes** *R* Chile
100 D3 **Cispus** *R* Washington
100 D3 **Cispus Pass** Washington
37 O3 **Čistá** Czechoslovakia
109 K6 **Cistern** Texas
45 N6 **Cisterna di Latina** Italy
16 D2 **Cistierna** Spain
129 G3 **Citare** *R* Brazil
113 E8 **Citra** Florida
111 H10 **Citronelle** Alabama
87 C12 **Citrusdal** S Africa
42 D3 **Cittadella** Italy
42 E6 **Citta della Pieve** Italy
42 E5 **Citta di Castello** Italy
43 G10 **Cittanova** Italy
142 A1 **City Beach** *dist* Perth, W Aust
113 G9 **City Point** Florida
48 K5 **Ciucas** *mt* Romania
48 H4 **Ciucea** Romania
48 K4 **Ciucului Muntii** *mt* Romania
108 G6 **Ciudad Acuña** Mexico
125 J8 **Ciudad Altamirano** Mexico
128 F2 **Ciudad Bolívar** Venezuela
109 J9 **Ciudad Camargo** Mexico
124 G4 **Ciudad Camargo** Mexico
125 O8 **Ciudad del Carmen** Mexico
124 G3 **Ciudad Delicias** Mexico
127 N10 **Ciudad Guayana** Venezuela
124 F3 **Ciudad Guerrero** Mexico
124 H8 **Ciudad Guzmán** Mexico
106 D10 **Ciudad Juárez** Mexico
124 H5 **Ciudad Lerdo** Mexico
125 L6 **Ciudad Madero** Mexico
125 K6 **Ciudad Mante** Mexico
124 E4 **Ciudad Obregón** Mexico
128 F2 **Ciudad Piar** Venezuela
16 E6 **Ciudad Real** Spain
16 E6 **Ciudad Real** *prov* Spain
16 C4 **Ciudad Rodrigo** Spain
Ciudad Trujillo *see* **Santo Domingo**
125 K6 **Ciudad Victoria** Mexico
48 L6 **Ciulniţa** Romania
48 G4 **Ciumeghiu** Romania
48 L5 **Ciuşlea** Romania
42 E2 **Cividale del F** Italy
42 E6 **Civita Castellana** Italy
42 F5 **Civitanova Marche** Italy
44 L5 **Civitavecchia** *lt ho* Italy
45 L3 **Civitella di Romagna** Italy
45 O6 **Civitella Roveto** Italy
44 B1 **Civrari Monte** Italy
21 F9 **Civray** France
47 K6 **Çivril** Turkey
67 G1 **Cixi** China
65 C6 **Ci Xian** China
78 J3 **Cizre** Turkey
12 C2 **Clachan** Scotland
100 C4 **Clackamas** *R* Oregon
143 B9 **Clackline** W Australia
Clackmannon *co see* **Central** *reg*
9 H4 **Clacton on Sea** England
12 C1 **Cladich** Scotland
107 M3 **Claflin** Kansas
100 J1 **Clagstone** Idaho
18 F6 **Clain** *R* France
119 N6 **Clair** Sask
68 G1 **Claire** *R* Vietnam
98 J4 **Claire City** S Dakota
114 H6 **Claire,L** Alberta
108 G2 **Clairemont** Texas
94 H6 **Clairton** Pennsylvania
19 J6 **Clairvaux** France
21 H8 **Claise** *R* France
100 A1 **Clallam Bay** Washington
18 H5 **Clamecy** France
102 G2 **Clan Alpine Mts** Nevada
144 C6 **Clandeboye** New Zealand
118 F5 **Clandonald** Alberta
9 E4 **Clanfield** England
111 K9 **Clanton** Alabama
119 S8 **Clanwilliam** Manitoba
87 C12 **Clanwilliam** S Africa
12 C2 **Claonaig** Scotland
9 F5 **Clapham** London England
106 G5 **Clapham** New Mexico
13 F5 **Clapham** N Yorks England
44 B3 **Clapier, Mt** France
113 D8 **Clara** Florida
14 D3 **Clara** Irish Rep
141 F4 **Clara** *R* Queensland
141 H7 **Clara** *R* Queensland
99 L5 **Clara City** Minnesota
68 C7 **Clara I** Burma
141 F4 **Claraville** Queensland
9 G3 **Clare** England
99 M7 **Clare** Iowa
94 C3 **Clare** Michigan
138 E5 **Clare** S Australia
14 C4 **Clare** *co* Irish Rep
14 C3 **Clare** *R* Irish Rep
14 C4 **Clarecastle** Irish Rep
139 G5 **Clare Corner** New S Wales
14 A3 **Clare I** Irish Rep
127 K2 **Claremont** Jamaica
95 P3 **Claremont** New Hampshire
98 H4 **Claremont** S Dakota
139 H8 **Claremont** Tasmania
142 A2 **Claremont** *dist* Perth, W Aust
141 G2 **Claremont Is** Gt Barrier Reef Australia
14 C3 **Claremorris** Irish Rep
99 P8 **Clarence** Iowa
99 O10 **Clarence** Missouri
144 D5 **Clarence** New Zealand
139 L3 **Clarence** *R* New S Wales
110 D2 **Clarence Cannon Res** Missouri
133 C8 **Clarence,I** Chile
146 D15 **Clarence I** S Shetland Is
117 G8 **Clarence Str** Alaska
140 B1 **Clarence Str** N Terr Aust
126 G3 **Clarence Town** Long I Bahamas
110 E7 **Clarendon** Arkansas
121 O8 **Clarendon** Ontario
94 H5 **Clarendon** Pennsylvania
108 G1 **Clarendon** Texas
127 K3 **Clarendon** *parish* Jamaica
115 O8 **Clarenville** Nfld
114 H7 **Claresholm** Alberta
19 P16 **Claret** France
98 B6 **Clareton** Wyoming
32 H9 **Clarholz** W Germany
141 F4 **Clarina** *R* Queensland
99 L9 **Clarinda** Iowa
127 M10 **Clarines** Venezuela
94 H5 **Clarington** Pennsylvania
99 N7 **Clarion** Iowa
94 H5 **Clarion** Pennsylvania
94 H5 **Clarion** *R* Pennsylvania
126 H4 **Clarion Bank** Bahamas
107 O7 **Clarita** Oklahoma
101 T9 **Clark** Colorado
110 D2 **Clark** Missouri
98 J5 **Clark** S Dakota
101 Q5 **Clark** Wyoming
102 H8 **Clark** *L* California
101 N4 **Clark Canyon Res** Montana
103 M7 **Clarkdale** Arizona
141 G4 **Clarke** *R* Queensland
122 F3 **Clarke City** Quebec
139 J8 **Clarke I** Tasmania
118 K4 **Clarke L** Sask
141 J5 **Clarke Ra** Queensland
141 H4 **Clarke River** Queensland
112 D3 **Clarkesville** Georgia
98 L5 **Clarkfield** Minnesota
100 J1 **Clark Fork** Idaho
117 Q12 **Clark Fork** *R* Idaho
112 E4 **Clark Hill Dam** Georgia
112 E4 **Clark Hill Res** Georgia
100 J2 **Clarkia** Idaho
116 K6 **Clark,L** Alaska
103 J6 **Clark Mt** California
117 M3 **Clark,Mt** N W Terr
106 E1 **Clark Pk** Colorado
120 J8 **Clark Pt** Ontario
111 D9 **Clarks** Louisiana
98 J8 **Clarks** Nebraska
110 H6 **Clarksburg** Tennessee
94 G7 **Clarksburg** W Virginia
111 F7 **Clarksdale** Mississippi
99 N6 **Clarks Grove** Minnesota
122 G10 **Clark's Harbour** Nova Scotia
110 K1 **Clarks Hill** Indiana
144 C6 **Clarks Junction** New Zealand
98 J8 **Clarkson** Nebraska
121 L9 **Clarkson** Ontario
142 E4 **Clarkson, Mt** W Australia
116 H7 **Clarks Point** Alaska
94 D4 **Clarkston** Michigan
101 O3 **Clarkston** Montana
100 H3 **Clarkston** Washington
127 K2 **Clark's Town** Jamaica
110 C6 **Clarksville** Arkansas
110 F2 **Clarksville** Illinois
99 O7 **Clarksville** Iowa
94 B4 **Clarksville** Michigan
144 B7 **Clarksville** New Zealand
110 J5 **Clarksville** Tennessee
109 M2 **Clarksville** Texas
94 J10 **Clarksville** Virginia
112 J3 **Clarkton** N Carolina
109 K8 **Clarkwood** Texas
100 E5 **Clarno** Oregon
129 H7 **Claro** *R* Brazil
22 E3 **Clary** France
108 C8 **Claude** Texas
141 H6 **Claude** *R* Queensland
130 G7 **Cláudio** Brazil
32 M8 **Clauen** W Germany
37 O2 **Claussnitz** E Germany
33 M9 **Clausthal-Zellerfeld** W Germany
71 E1 **Claveria** Luzon Philippines
141 H7 **Claverton** Queensland
118 L8 **Clavet** Sask
40 A7 **Claveyson** France
112 F5 **Claxton** Georgia
102 C3 **Clay** California
110 J4 **Clay** Kentucky
109 L5 **Clay** Texas
94 F8 **Clay** W Virginia
107 N2 **Clay Center** Kansas
98 H9 **Clay Center** Nebraska
110 H3 **Clay City** Illinois
110 J2 **Clay City** Indiana
110 N4 **Clay City** Kentucky
9 E1 **Clay Cross** England
9 H3 **Claydon** England
118 J9 **Claydon** Sask
18 H6 **Clayette, la** France
103 L5 **Clayhole Wash** *creek* Arizona
118 J1 **Clay L** Ontario
107 P5 **Claymore** Oklahoma
117 L11 **Clayoquot** Br Col
103 O8 **Claypool** Arizona
103 O7 **Clay Springs** Arizona
94 G6 **Claysville** Pennsylvania
111 L10 **Clayton** Alabama
9 F6 **Clayton** England
112 D3 **Clayton** Georgia
101 L5 **Clayton** Idaho
99 Q9 **Clayton** Illinois
110 K2 **Clayton** Indiana
107 K2 **Clayton** Kansas
112 J2 **Clayton** N Carolina
106 G5 **Clayton** New Mexico
95 L2 **Clayton** New York
107 P7 **Clayton** Oklahoma
138 E3 **Clayton** *R* S Australia
95 R7 **Clayton Lake** Maine
13 F6 **Clayton-le-Moors** England
94 G9 **Claytor Lake** Virginia
95 M4 **Clayville** New York
131 F4 **Clé** *R* Argentina
107 O7 **Clear Boggy Cr** Oklahoma
99 L2 **Clearbrook** Minnesota
144 C6 **Clearburn** New Zealand
14 B5 **Clear,C** Irish Rep
94 G8 **Clearco** W Virginia
101 T5 **Clear Cr** Wyoming
103 O7 **Clear Cr** *R* Arizona
100 B8 **Clear Creek** California
116 O7 **Cleare,C** Alaska
99 M9 **Clearfield** Iowa
94 J5 **Clearfield** Pennsylvania
101 N8 **Clearfield** Utah
108 G3 **Clear Fork** *R* Texas
117 O7 **Clear Hills** Alberta
14 B5 **Clear I** Irish Rep
102 B2 **Clear L** California
99 N6 **Clear L** Iowa
109 P4 **Clear L** Louisiana
119 S8 **Clear L** Manitoba
99 N4 **Clear L** Minnesota
121 N7 **Clear, L** Ontario
98 K5 **Clear L** S Dakota
103 M2 **Clear L** Utah
99 O4 **Clear L** Wisconsin
100 D8 **Clear L. Res** California
101 T5 **Clearmont** Wyoming
117 O7 **Clear Prairie** Alberta
143 D10 **Clear Streak Well** W Australia
117 N10 **Clearwater** Br Col
113 E10 **Clearwater** Florida
100 K3 **Clearwater** Idaho
107 N4 **Clearwater** Kansas
98 H7 **Clearwater** Nebraska
100 J3 **Clearwater** *R* Idaho
119 Q4 **Clearwater L. Prov. Park** Manitoba
114 H8 **Clearwater Mts** Idaho
118 B6 **Clearwater R** Alberta
110 F4 **Clearwater Res** Missouri
99 L2 **Clearwter** *R* Minnesota
143 D7 **Cleaver, Mt** W Australia
107 O2 **Cleburne** Kansas
109 K3 **Cleburne** Texas
20 E4 **Clécy** France
8 B4 **Cleddau, R** Wales
8 D3 **Clee Hill** England
100 D2 **Cle Elum L** Washington
13 H6 **Cleethorpes** England
118 H5 **Cleeves** Sask
40 B1 **Clefmont** France
21 E6 **Clefs** France
109 J7 **Clegg** Texas
140 B6 **Cleland Hills** N Terr Aust
22 K4 **Clemency** Luxembourg
142 B6 **Clement, Mt** W Australia
102 C3 **Clements** California
115 N1 **Clements Markham Inlet** N W Terr
122 G9 **Clementsport** Nova Scotia
122 G9 **Clementsvale** Nova Scotia
94 F8 **Clendenin** W Virginia
94 F6 **Clendening Res** Ohio
71 D5 **Cleopatra Needle** *mt* Philippines
107 M5 **Cleo Springs** Oklahoma
20 H2 **Clères** France
121 M4 **Cléricy** Quebec
142 C3 **Clerke Reef** Indian Oc
133 J9 **Clerke Rocks** S Georgia
113 F9 **Clermont** Florida
99 P6 **Clermont** Iowa
20 K3 **Clermont** Oise France
94 J5 **Clermont** Pennsylvania
122 B6 **Clermont** Quebec
141 J6 **Clermont** Queensland
19 J3 **Clermont en Argonne** France
18 H7 **Clermont Ferrand** France
18 H9 **Clermont l'Herault** France
40 D3 **Clerval** France
121 L4 **Clerval** Quebec
22 L3 **Clervaux** Luxembourg
20 J3 **Cléry-en-Vexin** France
21 I6 **Cléry-St. André** France
22 D4 **Clery-sur-Somme** France
42 D2 **Cles** Italy
21 E8 **Clessé** France
138 D5 **Cleve** S Australia
8 D5 **Clevedon** England
110 D6 **Cleveland** Arkansas
113 F11 **Cleveland** Florida
112 D3 **Cleveland** Georgia
101 O7 **Cleveland** Idaho
99 N5 **Cleveland** Minnesota
111 F8 **Cleveland** Mississippi
101 Q1 **Cleveland** Montana
112 G2 **Cleveland** N Carolina
98 G3 **Cleveland** N Dakota
95 M3 **Cleveland** New York
94 F5 **Cleveland** Ohio
107 O5 **Cleveland** Oklahoma
112 E2 **Cleveland** S Carolina
112 C2 **Cleveland** Tennessee
109 M5 **Cleveland** Texas
103 O2 **Cleveland** Utah
99 T6 **Cleveland** Wisconsin
13 G4 **Cleveland** *co* England
141 H4 **Cleveland, C** Queensland
13 G4 **Cleveland Hills** England
130 D10 **Clevelândia** Brazil
101 M1 **Cleveland,Mt** Montana
139 H8 **Cleveland,Mt** Tasmania
113 G11 **Clewiston** Florida
9 H2 **Cley** England
14 A3 **Clifden** Irish Rep
144 A7 **Clifden** New Zealand
106 B9 **Cliff** New Mexico
100 D3 **Cliffdell** Washington
71 D5 **Cliff Head** Philippines
101 O5 **Cliff Lake** Montana
109 K8 **Cliff Maus** *airport* Texas
94 D3 **Clifford** Michigan
98 J2 **Clifford** N Dakota
94 H9 **Clifford** Virginia
99 Q4 **Clifford** Wisconsin
100 H7 **Cliffs** Idaho
112 F2 **Cliffside** N Carolina
103 P8 **Clifton** Arizona
8 D5 **Clifton** England
99 T9 **Clifton** Illinois
107 N2 **Clifton** Kansas
95 N6 **Clifton** New Jersey
113 K9 **Clifton** New Providence I Bahamas
141 K8 **Clifton** Queensland
98 B6 **Clifton** Wyoming
94 H9 **Clifton Forge** Virginia
138 E2 **Clifton Hills** S Australia
113 K9 **Clifton Pt** New Providence I **Bahamas**
106 D2 **Climax** Colorado
111 M11 **Climax** Georgia
94 B4 **Climax** Michigan
98 K2 **Climax** Minnesota
118 J9 **Climax** Sask
112 C2 **Clinch** *R* Tennessee
112 E1 **Clinch** *R* Tennessee
94 E10 **Clinch** *R* Tenn/Virg
94 E9 **Clinchco** Virginia
94 E10 **Clinch Mts** Tenn/Virg
94 E10 **Clinchport** Virginia
117 P9 **Cline, Mt** Alberta
37 K1 **Clingen** E Germany
112 D2 **Clingmans Dome** Tennessee
108 A4 **Clint** Texas
110 D6 **Clinton** Arkansas
117 N10 **Clinton** Br Columbia
95 P5 **Clinton** Connecticut
99 S9 **Clinton** Illinois
99 T10 **Clinton** Indiana
99 Q8 **Clinton** Iowa
110 H5 **Clinton** Kentucky
111 E11 **Clinton** Louisiana
95 S2 **Clinton** Maine
95 Q4 **Clinton** Massachusetts
94 D4 **Clinton** Michigan
98 K4 **Clinton** Minnesota
111 F9 **Clinton** Mississippi
110 C3 **Clinton** Missouri
101 M3 **Clinton** Montana
95 M3 **Clinton** New York
144 B7 **Clinton** New Zealand
107 M6 **Clinton** Oklahoma
120 J9 **Clinton** Ontario
112 F3 **Clinton** S Carolina
112 C1 **Clinton** Tennessee
99 S7 **Clinton** Wisconsin
114 J5 **Clinton-Colden L** N W Terr
114 E5 **Clinton Creek** Yukon Terr
99 S5 **Clintonville** Wisconsin
103 N7 **Clints Well** Arizona
110 C1 **Clio** Iowa
94 D3 **Clio** Michigan
112 H3 **Clio** S Carolina
135 Q7 **Clipperton** *atoll* Pacific Oc
15 B3 **Clisham Mt** Lewis Scotland
13 F6 **Clitheroe** England
118 D6 **Clive** Alberta
145 F3 **Clive** New Zealand
101 M9 **Clive** Utah
117 O4 **Clive L** N W Terr
118 J6 **Cloan** Sask
14 D3 **Cloghan** Irish Rep
14 D2 **Clogher** N Ireland
14 E3 **Clogher Hd** Irish Rep
140 F5 **Clonagh** Queensland
14 C5 **Clonakilty** Irish Rep
14 C5 **Clonakilty B** Irish Rep
140 F5 **Cloncurry** Queensland
140 F4 **Cloncurry** *R* Queensland
14 E3 **Clondalkin** Irish Rep
14 E4 **Clonegal** Irish Rep
14 D2 **Clones** Irish Rep
59 J4 **Clŏngiu** N Korea
59 J3 **Clŏngjin** N Korea
14 D4 **Clonmel** Irish Rep
99 L4 **Clontarf** Minnesota
117 L11 **Clo-oose** Br Columbia
9 F3 **Clophill** England
32 H7 **Cloppenburg** W Germany
99 O3 **Cloquet** Minnesota
130 B9 **Clorinda** Argentina
12 E3 **Closeburn** Scotland
146 A5 **Close,C** Antarctica
123 L3 **Cloudberry Pt** Quebec
106 E9 **Cloudcroft** New Mexico
101 S5 **Cloud Pk** Wyoming
145 E4 **Cloudy Bay** New Zealand
116 J5 **Cloudy Mt** Alaska
21 G9 **Clouère** *R* France
121 L4 **Cloutier** Quebec
121 P4 **Clova** Quebec
15 E4 **Clova** Scotland
8 B5 **Clovelly** England
13 F2 **Clovenfords** Scotland
112 F2 **Clover** S Carolina
94 J10 **Clover** Virginia
102 A3 **Cloverdale** California
110 K2 **Cloverdale** Indiana
106 B10 **Cloverdale** New Mexico
110 K4 **Cloverport** Kentucky
106 G7 **Clovis** New Mexico
8 D3 **Clows Top** England
20 H5 **Cloyes** France
14 C5 **Cloyne** Irish Rep
48 H4 **Cluj** Romania
8 C3 **Clun** England
139 G7 **Clunes** Victoria
118 E3 **Cluny** Alberta
140 E5 **Cluny** Queensland
102 H1 **Cluro** Nevada
40 E5 **Cluses** France
41 L6 **Clusone** Italy
120 J3 **Clute** Ontario
144 B6 **Clutha R** New Zealand
144 B7 **Clutha R** New Zealand
99 O7 **Clutier** Iowa
117 P3 **Clut L** N W Terr
143 F6 **Clutterbuck Hills** W Australia
8 C1 **Clwyd** *co* Wales
8 C1 **Clwyd** *R* Wales
113 D7 **Clyattville** Georgia
8 C4 **Clydach** Wales
118 D4 **Clyde** Alberta
107 N2 **Clyde** Kansas
98 H1 **Clyde** N Dakota
95 L3 **Clyde** New York
144 B6 **Clyde** New Zealand
115 N3 **Clyde** N W Terr
94 E5 **Clyde** Ohio
109 H3 **Clyde** Texas
12 D2 **Clydebank** Scotland
12 D3 **Clyde,Firth of** Scotland
121 O7 **Clyde Forks** Ontario
101 P4 **Clyde Park** Montana
122 G10 **Clyde R** Nova Scotia
12 D2 **Clyde,R** Scotland
144 B7 **Clydevale** New Zealand
99 S6 **Clyman** Wisconsin
94 H6 **Clymer** Pennsylvania
8 B1 **Clynnog-Fawr** Wales
8 C3 **Clyro** Wales
8 C6 **Clyst Honiton** England
16 C4 **Coa** *R* Portugal
123 M3 **Coacoachou L** Quebec
108 F3 **Coahoma** Texas
124 H4 **Coahuila** *state* Mexico
117 K5 **Coal** *R* Br Col/Yukon Terr
94 F8 **Coal** *R* W Virginia
99 S8 **Coal City** Illinois
124 H8 **Coalcomán de Matamoros** Mexico
144 B6 **Coal Cr** New Zealand
116 Q4 **Coal Creek** Alaska
118 E9 **Coaldale** Alberta
102 G3 **Coaldale** Nevada
144 C5 **Coalgate** New Zealand
107 O7 **Coalgate** Oklahoma
94 E8 **Coal Grove** Ohio
110 C6 **Coal Hill** Arkansas
144 A7 **Coal I** New Zealand
102 D5 **Coalinga** California
101 T9 **Coalmont** Colorado
94 J6 **Coalport** Pennsylvania
117 K6 **Coal River** Br Columbia
94 E7 **Coalton** Ohio
9 E2 **Coalville** England
101 O9 **Coalville** Utah
98 A4 **Coalwood** Montana
127 L5 **Coamo** Puerto Rico
128 F4 **Coari** Brazil
114 F6 **Coast Mts** Br Columbia
141 K7 **Coast Ra** Queensland
139 K2 **Coast Ra** *mts* Queensland
100 B9 **Coast Range** *mts* U.S.A.
102 A1 **Coast Rge** California
12 E2 **Coatbridge** Scotland
125 L8 **Coatepec** Mexico
95 M6 **Coatesville** Pennsylvania
121 T7 **Coaticook** Quebec
107 M4 **Coats** Kansas
112 J2 **Coats** N Carolina
115 L5 **Coats I** N W Terr
146 D10 **Coats Land** Antarctica
110 D1 **Coatsville** Iowa
125 M8 **Coatzacoalcos** Mexico
101 L4 **Cobalt** Idaho
121 L5 **Cobalt** Ontario
125 O10 **Cobán** Guatemala
47 L8 **Çobanisa** Turkey
139 H4 **Cobar** New S Wales
139 J6 **Cobargo** New S Wales
99 Q7 **Cobb** Wisconsin
139 J6 **Cobberas,Mt** Victoria
143 F6 **Cobb, L** W Australia
9 E6 **Cobblers Corner** England
145 D4 **Cobb River** New Zealand
110 G4 **Cobden** Illinois
121 O7 **Cobden** Ontario
139 G7 **Cobden** Victoria
122 J8 **Cobequid B** Nova Scotia
122 J8 **Cobequid Mts** Nova Scotia
14 C5 **Cóbh** Irish Rep
140 B1 **Cobham B** N Terr **Aust**
138 F4 **Cobham L** New S Wales
128 E6 **Cobija** Bolivia
95 N4 **Cobleskill** New York
121 M8 **Coboconk** Ontario
121 M9 **Cobourg** Ontario
140 B1 **Cobourg Pen** N Terr Aust
136 G4 **Cobourg Pen** N Terr Australia
143 B6 **Cobra** W Australia
139 H6 **Cobram** New S Wales
101 L8 **Cobre** Nevada
127 L2 **Cobre, R** Jamaica
87 F8 **Cobue** Mozambique
100 B5 **Coburg** Oregon
37 K3 **Coburg** W Germany
115 M2 **Coburg I** N W Terr
16 D3 **Coca** Spain
128 D7 **Cocachacra** Peru
128 D6 **Cocamá** Peru
42 C2 **Coca, Pzo. di** Italy
45 M3 **Coccolia** Italy
17 G6 **Cocentaina** Spain
128 E7 **Cochabamba** Bolivia
128 C3 **Cocha, L** Colombia
127 N9 **Coche, I** Venezuela
106 D3 **Cochetopa Pass** Colorado
76 C6 **Cochin** India
68 G7 **Cochin** *reg* Vietnam
128 E8 **Cochinoca** Argentina
126 D3 **Cochinos, B. de** Cuba
103 P9 **Cochise** Arizona
103 P9 **Cochise Head** *mt* Arizona
112 D5 **Cochran** Georgia
118 C7 **Cochrane** Alberta
120 J3 **Cochrane** Ontario
133 C7 **Cochrane, L** Chile/Arg
94 G5 **Cochranton** Pennsylvania
33 O9 **Cochstedt** E Germany
142 E3 **Cockatoo I** W Australia
15 E3 **Cock Bridge** Scotland
138 F4 **Cockburn** S Australia
141 G3 **Cockburn** *R* Queensland
133 C8 **Cockburn, Canal** *str* Chile
127 H4 **Cockburn Harbour** Turks & Caicos Is
120 G7 **Cockburn I** Ontario
140 A7 **Cockburn, Mt** N Terr Aust
142 G3 **Cockburn Ra** W Australia
142 A3 **Cockburn Sd** W Australia
13 F2 **Cockburnspath** Scotland
126 G2 **Cockburn Town** San Salvador **Bahamas**
13 F2 **Cockenzie** Scotland
13 F6 **Cockerham** England
13 E4 **Cockermouth** England
95 L7 **Cockeysville** Maryland
143 F9 **Cocklebiddy** W Australia
127 J2 **Cockpit** *peak* Jamaica
127 J2 **Cockpit Country, The** *reg* Jamaica
109 N9 **Cockrell Hill** Texas
15 F5 **Cocksburnpath** Scotland
89 D9 **Cockscomb** *mt* S Africa
129 J5 **Côco** *R* Brazil
125 M2 **Coco** *R* Honduras/Nicaragua
113 G9 **Cocoa** Florida
113 G9 **Cocoa Beach** Florida
126 E3 **Coco, Cayo** *isld* Cuba
111 F12 **Cocodrie** Louisiana
100 J1 **Cocolalla** Idaho
103 M6 **Coconino Plat** Arizona
139 H5 **Cocoparra Rge** New S Wales
71 E5 **Cocoro** *isld* Philippines
127 P2 **Cocos B** Trinidad
81 G6 **Cocos I** Indian Oc
90 A8 **Cocos I** Pacific Oc
90 A8 **Cocos Ridge** Pacific Oc
83 L13 **Cocotte, Mt** Mauritius
124 H7 **Cocula** Mexico
43 C8 **Coda Cavallo, C** Sardinia
48 L4 **Codăeşti** Romania
128 F4 **Codajas** Brazil
107 L2 **Codell** Kansas
118 L8 **Coderre** Sask
119 N5 **Codette** Sask
144 A7 **Codfish I** New Zealand
115 N6 **Cod I** Labrador
9 F4 **Codicote** England
42 E4 **Codigoro** Italy
48 J5 **Codlea** Romania
129 K4 **Codó** Brazil
44 G1 **Codogna** Italy
127 N6 **Codrington** Barbuda **W I**
123 N6 **Codroy** Nfld
123 O5 **Codroy Pond** Nfld
48 G4 **Codrului Muntii** *mts* Romania
98 E7 **Cody** Nebraska
122 G8 **Cody** New Brunswick
101 Q5 **Cody** Wyoming
94 E10 **Coeburn** Virginia
121 N8 **Coe Hill** Ontario
141 G2 **Coen** Queensland
141 F2 **Coen** *R* Queensland
32 F9 **Coesfeld** W Germany
81 C6 **Coëtivy I** Indian Oc
100 J2 **Coeur d'Alene** Idaho
22 E5 **Coeuvres et Valsery** France
25 G3 **Coevorden** Netherlands
20 E5 **Coëvrons, les** *hills* France
112 E6 **Coffee** Georgia
101 P2 **Coffee Creek** Montana
117 D4 **Coffee Creek** Yukon Terr
110 G2 **Coffeen** Illinois
111 L10 **Coffee Springs** Alabama
111 G8 **Coffeeville** Mississippi
107 P4 **Coffeyville** Kansas
138 D5 **Coffin B** S Australia
123 L6 **Coffin I** Madeleine Is, Quebec
139 L4 **Coff's Harbour** New S Wales
17 G5 **Cofrentes** Spain
48 M6 **Cogealac** Romania
9 G4 **Coggeshall** England
42 B3 **Coggiola** Italy
99 P7 **Coggon** Iowa
43 B8 **Coghinas** *R* Sardinia
43 C8 **Coghinas, L.d** Sardinia
142 G4 **Coghlan, Mt** W Australia
140 C7 **Coglin** *R* N Terr/S Aust
21 E10 **Cognac** France
40 F6 **Cogne, V.de** Italy
44 E3 **Cogoleto** Italy
16 E4 **Cogolludo** Spain
41 N5 **Cógolo** Italy
98 J3 **Cogswell** N Dakota
101 T2 **Cohagen** Montana
94 K4 **Cohocton** New York
95 K4 **Cohocton** *R* New York
95 O4 **Cohoes** New York
139 G6 **Cohuna** Victoria
112 C3 **Cohutta** Georgia
125 O6 **Coiba, I** Panama
133 C8 **Coig** *R* Argentina
20 J4 **Coignières** France
133 C7 **Coihaique** Chile
76 C5 **Coimbatore** India
129 G7 **Coimbra** Brazil
16 B4 **Coimbra** Portugal
110 A1 **Coin** Iowa
16 D8 **Coin** Spain
128 E7 **Coipasa, L** Bolivia
Coire *see* **Chur**
19 N15 **Coiron, Mts du** France
128 E2 **Cojedes** *state* Venezuela
128 B3 **Cojimies** Ecuador
48 H4 **Cojocna** Romania
127 J9 **Cojoro** Venezuela
133 D7 **Cojudo Blanco** *mt* Argentina
99 M4 **Cokato** Minnesota
94 G6 **Cokeburg** Pennsylvania
101 P7 **Cokeville** Wyoming
26 O2 **Cokkarassa** *mt* **Norway**
138 F4 **Coko Ra** New S Wales
144 A7 **Colac** New Zealand
139 G7 **Colac** Victoria
131 B2 **Colanguil, Cerro de** *mt* Argentina
130 H6 **Colatina** Brazil
36 F2 **Cölbe** W Germany
146 B4 **Colbeck Arch** Antarctica
146 J8 **Colbeck, C** Antarctica
100 H2 **Colbert** Washington
33 P8 **Colbitz** E Germany
33 P8 **Colbitz-Letzlinger Heide** E Germany
121 N8 **Colborne** Ontario
107 J2 **Colby** Kansas
99 Q5 **Colby** Wisconsin
128 D7 **Colca** *R* Peru
95 P5 **Colchester** Connecticut
9 G4 **Colchester** England
99 Q9 **Colchester** Illinois
8 D5 **Cold Ashton** England
116 F9 **Cold B** Alaska
44 B2 **Col de Longet** France
94 J4 **Colden** New York
13 F4 **Cold Fell** *mt* England
13 F2 **Coldingham** Scotland
37 O1 **Colditz** E Germany
118 G4 **Cold L** Alberta
119 Q3 **Cold L** Manitoba
99 M4 **Cold Spring** Minnesota
109 M5 **Coldspring** Texas
13 F2 **Coldstream** Scotland
107 L4 **Coldwater** Kansas
94 C5 **Coldwater** Michigan
110 M1 **Coldwater** Ohio
121 L8 **Coldwater** Ontario
111 F7 **Coldwater** *R* Mississippi
108 C7 **Coldwater Cr** Texas/Okla
120 D4 **Coldwell** Ontario
121 T8 **Colebrook** New Hampshire
139 H8 **Colebrook** Tasmania
110 C3 **Cole Camp** Missouri
116 Q2 **Coleen** *R* Alaska
8 D4 **Coleford** England
94 J5 **Colegrove** Pennsylvania
118 C9 **Coleman** Alberta
113 E9 **Coleman** Florida
94 C3 **Coleman** Michigan
109 H4 **Coleman** Texas
141 F2 **Coleman** *R* Queensland
22 B2 **Colembert** France
99 N2 **Coleraine** Minnesota
14 E1 **Coleraine** N Ireland
121 T7 **Coleraine** Quebec
138 F6 **Coleraine** Victoria
118 G9 **Coleridge** Alberta
98 J7 **Coleridge** Nebraska
139 J8 **Coles B** Tasmania
89 D8 **Colesberg** S Africa
8 E4 **Colesborne** England
9 E2 **Coleshill** England
128 D7 **Coles, Pta** *C* Peru
102 E3 **Coleville** California
118 H7 **Coleville** Sask
102 D2 **Colfax** California
110 H1 **Colfax** Illinois
110 K1 **Colfax** Indiana
99 N8 **Colfax** Iowa
111 D10 **Colfax** Louisiana
106 F5 **Colfax** New Mexico
119 O9 **Colfax** Sask
100 H3 **Colfax** Washington
99 P4 **Colfax** Wisconsin
119 O9 **Colgate** Sask
133 D7 **Colhué Huapí, L** Argentina
131 B5 **Coliauco** Argentina
131 B7 **Colico, L** Chile
25 A5 **Colijnsplaat** Netherlands
124 H8 **Colima** Mexico
129 K5 **Colinas** Brazil
13 F1 **Colinsburgh** Scotland
118 D4 **Colinton** Alberta
13 E2 **Colinton** Scotland
12 C2 **Colintraive** Scotland
15 B4 **Coll** *isld* Scotland
139 H4 **Collabah** New S Wales
139 J3 **Collarenebri** New S Wales
106 C2 **Collbran** Colorado
42 D5 **Colle di Vald Elsa** Italy
116 O4 **College** Alaska
110 M2 **College Corner** Indiana
110 K6 **College Grove** Tennessee
111 M8 **College Park** Georgia
95 L7 **College Park** Maryland
100 G3 **College Place** Washington
109 L5 **College Station** Texas
45 P6 **Collelongo** Italy
139 H3 **Collerina** New S Wales
42 C5 **Colle Salvetti** Italy
45 R7 **Colle Sannita** Italy
109 N9 **Colleyville** Texas
45 N6 **Colli Albani** Italy
139 J4 **Collie** New S Wales
143 B10 **Collie** W Australia
143 B10 **Collie Cardiff** W Australia
142 E3 **Collier B** W Australia
113 F12 **Collier City** Florida
143 C6 **Collier Ras** *mts* W Australia
110 G6 **Collierville** Tennessee
12 E3 **Collin** Scotland
45 J3 **Collina, Passo di** Italy
20 C4 **Collines de Normandie** *reg* France
9 E5 **Collingbourne Kingston** England
9 F1 **Collingham** England
13 G6 **Collingham** England
95 N7 **Collingswood** New Jersey
145 D4 **Collingwood** New Zealand
120 K8 **Collingwood** Ontario
141 F5 **Collingwood** Queensland
112 E5 **Collins** Georgia
111 G10 **Collins** Mississippi
110 C4 **Collins** Missouri
101 O2 **Collins** Montana
94 J4 **Collins** New York
114 J3 **Collinson Pen** N W Terr
111 E9 **Collinston** Louisiana
14 E3 **Collinstown** Irish Rep
111 L7 **Collinsville** Alabama
110 G3 **Collinsville** Illinois
107 P5 **Collinsville** Oklahoma
141 J5 **Collinsville** Queensland
110 J6 **Collinwood** Tennessee
41 M6 **Collio** Italy
120 J1 **Collis** Ontario
37 Q1 **Cölln** E Germany
19 Q18 **Collobrières** France
131 B8 **Collon Cura** *R* Argentina
14 C2 **Collooney** Irish Rep
107 K2 **Collyer** Kansas
40 F1 **Colmar** France
37 J5 **Colmberg** W Germany
133 E3 **Colmena** Argentina
16 E8 **Colmenar** Spain
16 E4 **Colmenar de Oreja** Spain
16 E4 **Colmenar Vieja** Spain
109 N5 **Colmesneil** Texas
12 D3 **Colmonell** Scotland
20 D5 **Colmont** *R* France
106 F5 **Colmor** New Mexico
13 F6 **Colne** England
9 G4 **Colne, R** England
124 A2 **Colnett, C** Mexico
99 N7 **Colo** Iowa
139 K5 **Colo** *R* New S Wales
41 O7 **Cologna** Italy
45 K1 **Cologna Veneta** Italy
Cologne *see* **Köln**
99 N5 **Cologne** Minnesota
94 A4 **Coloma** Michigan
99 R5 **Coloma** Wisconsin
20 E3 **Colombelles** France
40 A1 **Colombey les Deux Églises** France
129 J8 **Colombia** Brazil
108 H8 **Colombia** Mexico
128 C3 **Colombia** *rep* S America
90 B6 **Colombian Basin** Atlantic Oc
121 N4 **Colombiere** Quebec
83 J11 **Colombo** Sri Lanka
20 B3 **Colomby** France
98 G6 **Colome** S Dakota
133 E4 **Colón** Argentina
126 D3 **Colón** Cuba
94 B5 **Colon** Michigan
125 P5 **Colón** Panama
138 B4 **Colona** S Australia
126 G3 **Colonel Hill** Crooked I Bahamas
131 F5 **Colonia** Uruguay
133 D5 **Colonia Catriel** Argentina
131 D7 **Colonia Choele Choel** *isld* Argentina
133 F4 **Colonia del Sac** Uruguay
124 E2 **Colonia Díaz** Mexico
133 D7 **Colonia las Heras** Argentina
95 K8 **Colonial Beach** Virginia
94 K9 **Colonial Heights** Virginia
95 L9 **Colonial Nat. Hist. Park** Virginia
130 H4 **Colônia, R** Brazil
125 M2 **Colón, Montañas de** *ra* Honduras
43 H9 **Colonne, C** Italy
119 M7 **Colonsay** Sask
15 B4 **Colonsay** *isld* Scotland
107 P3 **Colony** Kansas
131 D7 **Colorada Grande, L** Argentina
127 N10 **Coloradito** Venezuela
103 L5 **Colorado** *R* Arizona
131 B5 **Colorado** *R* Chile
106 B2 **Colorado** *R* Colorado etc
109 J4 **Colorado** *R* Texas
106 B2 **Colorado** *state* U.S.A.
103 J10 **Colorado, Cerro** *peak* Mexico
108 G3 **Colorado City** Texas
131 E7 **Colorado, Delta del R** Argentina
106 B2 **Colorado Nat.Mon** Colorado
103 N5 **Colorado Plat** Arizona
103 K7 **Colorado R.Aqueduct** California
106 F3 **Colorado Springs** Colorado
16 C4 **Colorico da Beira** Portugal
45 H2 **Colorno** Italy
19 Q17 **Colostre** *R* France
125 L10 **Colotepec** Mexico
124 H6 **Colotlán** Mexico
120 K8 **Colpoys B** Ontario
133 D1 **Colquechaca** Bolivia
111 M10 **Colquitt** Georgia
9 F2 **Colsterworth** England
101 T4 **Colstrip** Montana
108 D8 **Coltexo** Texas
9 H2 **Coltishall** England
102 G7 **Colton** California
95 L8 **Colton** Maryland
95 N2 **Colton** New York
98 K6 **Colton** S Dakota
103 O2 **Colton** Utah
100 H3 **Colton** Washington
111 L10 **Columbia** Alabama
113 E7 **Columbia** Florida
110 F3 **Columbia** Illinois
94 B9 **Columbia** Kentucky
111 D9 **Columbia** Louisiana

95 L7 Columbia Maryland
111 G10 Columbia Mississippi
110 D3 Columbia Missouri
112 L2 Columbia N Carolina
95 L6 Columbia Pennsylvania
112 F3 Columbia S Carolina
98 H4 Columbia S Dakota
110 J6 Columbia Tennessee
94 J9 Columbia Virginia
117 O10 Columbia R Br Columbia
117 O11 Columbia R Wash/Br Col
100 E4 Columbia R Wash/Oregon
100 F2 Columbia Basin reg Washington
115 N1 Columbia, C N W Terr
94 B5 Columbia City Indiana
95 L8 Columbia, Dist. of (D.C.) U.S.A.
101 L1 Columbia Falls Montana
116 O6 Columbia Glacier Alaska
117 Q10 Columbia Lake Br Columbia
117 F9 Columbia, Mt Br Col/Alberta
114 G7 Columbia Mts Br Columbia
111 K8 Columbiana Alabama
94 G6 Columbiana Ohio
100 E2 Columbia River Washington
98 H4 Columbia Road Res S Dakota
95 C4 Columbiaville New York
106 D1 Columbine Colorado
101 T6 Columbine Wyoming
89 A9 Columbine, C S Africa
17 H5 Columbretes, I Spain
141 J5 Columbria Queensland
111 M9 Columbus Georgia
110 L2 Columbus Indiana
107 O4 Columbus Kansas
111 H8 Columbus Mississippi
101 Q4 Columbus Montana
98 D1 Columbus N Dakota
98 J8 Columbus Nebraska
106 C10 Columbus New Mexico
94 D7 Columbus Ohio
109 L6 Columbus Texas
99 R6 Columbus Wisconsin
126 G3 Columbus Bank Bahamas
99 P8 Columbus Junction Iowa
126 G2 Columbus Mon San Salvador Bahamas
126 G2 Columbus Pt Cat I Bahamas
127 M2 Columbus Pt Tobago
102 B2 Colusa California
12 E4 Colvend Scotland
94 J6 Colver Pennsylvania
145 E2 Colville New Zealand
100 H1 Colville Washington
116 L2 Colville R Alaska
114 G4 Colville L N W Terr
143 F8 Colville, Lake W Australia
137 Q8 Colville Ridge sea feature Pacific Oc
13 F3 Colwell England
99 O6 Colwell Iowa
8 C1 Colwyn Bay Wales
8 C6 Colyford England
45 M2 Comacchio Italy
125 O10 Comalapa Guatemala
125 N8 Comalcalco Mexico
131 B8 Comallo R Argentina
48 K6 Comana Romania
107 N7 Comanche Oklahoma
109 J4 Comanche Texas
133 D7 Comandante Luis Piedrabuena Argentina
133 D4 Comandante Salas Argentina
48 K4 Comănești Romania
125 L2 Comayagua Honduras
16 B4 Comba Dão Portugal
112 G5 Combahee R S Carolina
133 C4 Combarbala Chile
40 C2 Combeaufontaine France
8 B5 Combe Martin England
14 F2 Comber N Ireland
120 H10 Comber Ontario
121 N7 Combermere Ontario
68 A3 Combermere B Burma
109 K9 Combes Texas
22 D3 Combles France
20 B5 Combourg France
139 L4 Comboyne New S Wales
20 H5 Combres France
94 D9 Combs Kentucky
131 D4 Comechingones, Sa. de ra Argentina
38 G8 Comeglians Italy
38 G8 Comelico Italy
130 E6 Comendador Gomes Brazil
111 L9 Comer Alabama
112 D3 Comer Georgia
14 D4 Comeragh Mts Irish Rep
130 H5 Comercinho Brazil
98 B1 Comertown Montana
141 J6 Comet Queensland
141 J6 Comet R Queensland
141 J6 Comet Downs Queensland
143 D8 Comet Vale W Australia
109 J6 Comfort Texas
99 M5 Comfrey Minnesota
75 O7 Comilla Bangladesh
22 E2 Comines France
43 F12 Comino isld Malta
43 C8 Comino, C Sardinia
94 C2 Comins Michigan
43 F12 Comiso Sicily
125 N9 Comitán de Domínguez Mexico
121 L7 Commanda Ontario
18 G6 Commentry France
20 D5 Commer France
112 D3 Commerce Georgia
107 P5 Commerce Oklahoma
109 M2 Commerce Texas
106 F2 Commerce City Colorado
19 J4 Commercy France
45 J1 Commessaggio Italy
121 S4 Commissaires, Lac des Quebec
115 L4 Committee B N W Terr
146 J3 Commonwealth B Antarctica
138 C3 Commonwealth Hill S Australia
146 G7 Commonwealth Ra Antarctica
139 K6 Commonwealth Terr New S Wales
106 E2 Como Colorado
41 K6 Como Italy
111 G7 Como Mississippi
133 D7 Comodoro Rivadavia Argentina
41 K5 Como, Lago di Italy
124 D4 Comondú Mexico
125 J7 Comonfort Mexico
76 C6 Comorin, C India
81 B7 Comoro Ridge Indian Oc
87 G10 Comoros islds, rep Indian Oc
118 G7 Compeer Alberta
22 D5 Compiègne France
22 D5 Compiègne, Forêt de France
124 G7 Compostela Mexico
71 G7 Compostela Mindanao Philippines
21 H10 Compreignac France
130 F9 Comprida, I São Paulo Brazil
102 A2 Comptche California
102 F8 Compton California
99 R8 Compton Illinois
12 E1 Comrie Scotland
95 O3 Comstock New York
108 F6 Comstock Texas
45 O4 Cona Italy
66 E5 Co Nag L China
85 B7 Conakry Guinea
133 D6 Cona Niyeo Argentina
139 J8 Conara Junct Tasmania
112 C3 Conasauga R Georgia
98 D6 Conata S Dakota
45 N4 Conca R Italy
45 P5 Conca del Fucino Italy
108 H6 Concan Texas
18 C5 Concarneau France
130 H9 Conceição Paraíba Brazil
130 H6 Conceição da Barra Brazil
130 E6 Conceiçao das Alagoas Brazil
129 J5 Conceiçao do Araguaia Brazil
130 G6 Conceição do Mato Dentro Brazil
133 D3 Concepción Argentina
128 E6 Concepcion Beni Bolivia
131 A6 Concepcion Chile
130 B8 Concepción Paraguay
128 F7 Concepción Santa Cruz Bolivia
130 B8 Concepcion dep Paraguay
124 C2 Concepcion R Mexico
131 A6 Concepción, B. del Chile
133 B8 Concepción, Can str Chile
130 C10 Concepción de la Sierra Argentina
124 J5 Concepción del Oro Mexico
131 F4 Concepción del Uruguay Argentina
128 F7 Concepción, L Bolivia
124 D4 Concepción, Pta C Mexico
99 M9 Conception Missouri
87 B10 Conception B Namibia
123 U6 Conception B Nfld
123 T6 Conception Harb Nfld
126 G3 Conception I Bahamas
83 K12 Conception I Mahé I Indian Oc
124 G6 Concha Mexico
130 E8 Conchas Brazil
106 F6 Conchas New Mexico
106 F6 Conchas Res New Mexico
20 G4 Conches France
133 D2 Conchi Chile
103 P7 Concho Arizona
124 G4 Concho Mexico
107 N6 Concho Oklahoma
108 G4 Concho R Texas
108 B7 Conchos, Rio Mexico
102 B4 Concord California
111 M8 Concord Georgia
94 C4 Concord Michigan
112 G2 Concord N Carolina
98 K7 Concord Nebraska
95 Q3 Concord New Hampshire
95 Q2 Concord Vermont
131 F3 Concordia Argentina
130 D10 Concórdia Brazil
107 N2 Concordia Kansas
124 F6 Concordia Mexico
110 C3 Concordia Missouri
45 J2 Concórdia sulla Secchia Italy
100 D1 Concrete Washington
68 G3 Con Cuong Vietnam
101 O7 Conda Idaho
141 K7 Condamine Queensland
141 K7 Condamine R Queensland
18 G7 Condat en Féniers France
129 L6 Conde Brazil
98 H4 Conde S Dakota
88 E9 Condédzi R Mozambique
125 L3 Condega Nicaragua
20 G5 Condé-sur-Huisne France
22 F3 Condé-sur-l'Escaut France
20 D4 Condé-sur-Noireau France
20 J4 Condé-sur-Vesgre France
20 C3 Condé-sur-Vire France
130 H4 Condeúba Brazil
139 H5 Condobolin New S Wales
18 F9 Condom France
100 E4 Condon Oregon
142 C5 Condon Creek B W Australia
128 C4 Condor, Cord. del mts Ecuador/Peru
12 D2 Condorrat Scotland
19 N14 Condrieu France
22 J3 Condroz Belgium
111 K10 Conecuh R Alabama
42 E3 Conegliano Italy
17 J5 Conejera isld Balearic Is
106 D4 Conejos Colorado
94 H6 Conemaugh R Pennsylvania
45 O4 Cónero, M mt Italy
131 E6 Conesa Argentina
94 K4 Conesus L New York
99 P8 Conesville Iowa
94 F6 Conesville Ohio
123 Q4 Coney Arm Nfld
90 C1 Coney I Bermuda
95 O6 Coney Island New York
40 D2 Conflans France
19 J3 Conflans-Jarny France
20 K3 Conflans-Ste. Honorine France
94 H7 Confluence Pennsylvania
21 G9 Confolens France
103 L2 Confusion Range Utah
130 B9 Confuso, R Paraguay
14 B3 Cong Irish Rep
112 G4 Congaree R S Carolina
67 D5 Conghua China
67 C4 Congjiang China
13 G6 Congleton England
82 D5 Congo rep W Africa
Congo (Brazzaville) rep see Congo Rep
Congo (Kinshasa) rep see Zaire Rep
130 G7 Congonhas Brazil
8 D5 Congresbury England
103 M7 Congress Arizona
118 L9 Congress Sask
133 C6 Cónico mt Chile/Arg
20 G5 Conie R France
106 E2 Conifer Colorado
9 F1 Coningsby England
13 G6 Conisbrough England
13 E5 Coniston England
140 B5 Coniston N Terr Aust
120 K6 Coniston Ontario
141 G4 Conjuboy Queensland
118 F3 Conklin Alberta
108 B7 Conlen Texas
20 E5 Conlie France
40 C4 Conliège France
14 B3 Conn L Irish Rep
14 B3 Connacht prov Irish Rep
120 K7 Connaught Ontario
142 E6 Connaughton, Mt W Australia
19 N16 Connaux France
94 G5 Conneaut Ohio
94 G5 Conneautville Pennsylvania
95 P3 Connecticut R U.S.A.
95 O5 Connecticut state U.S.A.
15 C4 Connel Ferry Scotland
100 G3 Connell Washington
94 H6 Connellsville Pennsylvania
141 F6 Connemara Queensland
14 B3 Connemara dist Irish Rep
101 L4 Conner Montana
140 B7 Conner, Mt N Terr Aust
138 B2 Conner, Mt N Terr Australia
20 G5 Connerre France
94 B7 Connersville Indiana
14 B2 Conn, L Irish Rep
142 F2 Connor, Mt W Australia
122 D6 Connors New Brunswick
141 J5 Connors Ra mts Queensland
128 C4 Cononaco R Ecuador
112 F2 Conover N Carolina
99 R3 Conover Wisconsin
33 S6 Conow E Germany
118 K7 Conquest Sask
18 B4 Conquet, le France
130 F6 Conquista Brazil
101 Q2 Conrad Montana
139 J7 Conran, C Victoria
99 Q4 Conrath Wisconsin
109 M5 Conroe Texas
109 M5 Conroe, L Texas
45 L2 Consandolo Italy
121 N9 Consecon Ontario
130 G7 Conselheiro Lafaiete Brazil
45 L3 Conselice Italy
45 L1 Conselve Italy
22 J5 Consenvoye France
13 G4 Consett England
95 M6 Conshohocken Pennsylvania
22 H4 Cons-la-Grandville France
126 C3 Consolación del Sur Cuba
69 H8 Con Son Vietnam
69 H8 Con Son isld Vietnam
118 G6 Consort Alberta
95 M3 Constableville New York
Constance see Konstanz
143 E6 Constance Headland hill W Aust
Constance, L see Bodensee
128 F5 Constância dos Baetas Brazil
48 M6 Constanța Romania
16 D7 Constantina Spain
85 F1 Constantine Algeria
94 B5 Constantine Michigan
113 H7 Constantine, C Alaska
117 C5 Constantine, Mt Yukon Terr
Constantinople Turkey see İstanbul
127 N4 Constant, Morne hill Guadeloupe W I
127 L2 Constant Spring Jamaica
131 A5 Constitución Chile
141 J6 Consuelo Queensland
118 H9 Consul Sask
101 L8 Contact Nevada
130 G7 Contagalo Brazil
75 M8 Contai India
128 D5 Contamana Peru
128 F3 Contão Brazil
131 D4 Contara R Argentina
45 M1 Contarina Italy
129 K6 Cóntas R Brazil
20 J2 Conteville France
40 F5 Conthey Switzerland
103 O10 Continental Arizona
94 C5 Continental Ohio
106 C4 Continental Res Colorado
95 Q3 Contoocook New Hampshire
125 Q7 Contoy, I Mexico
16 E8 Contraviesa, Sa mts Spain
121 R7 Contrecoeur Quebec
133 C8 Contreras, I Chile
21 H7 Contres France
22 H5 Contreuve France
40 C1 Contrexéville France
130 G6 Contria Brazil
118 F7 Control Alberta
36 C5 Contwig W Germany
114 J4 Contwoyto L N W Terr
20 K2 Conty France
126 H10 Convención Colombia
43 H8 Conversano Italy
94 B6 Converse Indiana
111 C10 Converse Louisiana
94 C6 Convoy Ohio
110 D6 Conway Arkansas
99 M9 Conway Iowa
110 D4 Conway Missouri
112 K1 Conway N Carolina
98 J1 Conway N Dakota
95 Q3 Conway New Hampshire
112 H4 Conway S Carolina
141 J5 Conway, C Queensland
110 D6 Conway, L Arkansas
138 D3 Conway, L S Australia
140 C6 Conway, Mt N Terr Aust
95 Q2 Conway, N New Hampshire
144 D5 Conway R New Zealand
137 P6 Conway Reef Pacific Oc
107 N4 Conway Springs Kansas
8 B4 Conwil Elvet Wales
8 C1 Conwy Wales
112 C4 Conyers Georgia
22 K3 Coo Belgium
138 C3 Coober Pedy S Australia
9 G6 Cooden England
142 A3 Coogee dist Perth, W Aust
142 A3 Coogee L W Australia
141 J7 Coogoon Queensland
139 J2 Coogoon R Queensland
99 O2 Cook Minnesota
99 K9 Cook Nebraska
138 B4 Cook S Australia
133 C9 Cook, B.de Chile
117 K10 Cook, C Br Col
101 Q4 Cooke Montana
143 B9 Cooke, Mt W Australia
94 B10 Cookeville Tennessee
9 F4 Cookham England
146 A13 Cook I Antarctica
146 K4 Cook Ice Shelf Antarctica
118 D5 Cooking L Alberta
116 L7 Cook Inlet Alaska
117 D5 Cook, Mt Alaska/Yukon Terr
144 C5 Cook, Mt New Zealand
99 U4 Cooks Michigan
123 Q2 Cook's Hbr Nfld
121 T7 Cookshire Quebec
141 H2 Cook's Passage Queensland
106 C9 Cooks Pk New Mexico
14 E2 Cookstown N Ireland
121 L8 Cookstown Ontario
145 E4 Cook Strait New Zealand
141 H3 Cooktown Queensland
141 H7 Cooladdi Queensland
139 J4 Coolah New S Wales
139 H5 Coolamon New S Wales
143 C8 Coolarda hill W Australia
142 A2 Coolbellup, L W Australia
143 B8 Coolcalalaya W Australia
112 G2 Cooleemee N Carolina
143 D9 Coolgardie W Australia
140 B3 Coolibah N Terr Aust
103 N9 Coolidge Arizona
112 D6 Coolidge Georgia
109 L4 Coolidge Texas
127 P4 Coolidge airport Antigua W I
103 O8 Coolidge Dam Arizona
100 J1 Coolin Idaho
141 K8 Coolmunda Dam Queensland
142 A4 Cooloongup, L W Australia
94 F7 Coolville Ohio
143 B7 Coolyun Well W Australia
139 J6 Cooma New S Wales
14 A5 Coomacarrea mt Irish Rep
9 E5 Coombe Bissett England
8 D4 Coombe Hill England
143 B9 Coomberdale W Australia
139 J4 Coonabarabran New S Wales
138 F6 Coonalpyn S Australia
139 J4 Coonamble New S Wales
143 E9 Coonana W Australia
138 F6 Coonawarra S Australia
138 F5 Coonbah New S Wales
138 D4 Coondambo S Australia
76 B4 Coondapoor India
142 C5 Coongan, R W Australia
141 H8 Coongoola Queensland
138 C2 Coongra R S Australia
138 F2 Cooninnie, L S Australia
76 C5 Coonoor India
99 M8 Coon Rapids Iowa
129 G8 Cooper Paraguay
109 M2 Cooper Texas
140 C1 Cooper R N Terr Aust
141 F7 Cooper Cr Qnsld/S Aust
138 F2 Cooper Cr Queensland
144 A6 Cooper I New Zealand
138 C5 Cooper, Mt S Australia
143 G7 Cooper, Mt W Australia
139 L4 Coopernook New S Wales
141 K2 Coopers Plains dist Brisbane, Qnsld
126 F1 Coopers Town Great Abaco I Bahamas
98 H2 Cooperstown N Dakota
95 M4 Cooperstown New York
94 B3 Coopersville Michigan
127 O3 Coora Trinidad
138 B4 Coorabie S Australia
140 F6 Coorabulka Queensland
143 B7 Coor-de-Wandy mt W Australia
138 E6 Coorong, The L S Australia
143 B8 Coorow W Australia
141 L7 Cooroy Queensland
111 L7 Coosa R Alabama
112 C3 Coosawattee R Georgia
112 F5 Coosawhatchie R S Carolina
100 A6 Coos Bay Oregon
139 J5 Cootamundra New S Wales
14 E2 Cootehill Irish Rep
141 K7 Cooyar Queensland
140 E6 Cooyeana Queensland
133 C5 Copahue mt Chile/Arg
131 B6 Copahué peak Chile
100 A2 Copalis Beach Washington
109 K7 Copano B Texas
100 C8 Copco California
106 H2 Cope Colorado
128 F4 Copea, Paraná R Brazil
113 F12 Copeland Florida
100 J1 Copeland Idaho
107 K4 Copeland Kansas
94 B2 Copemish Michigan
Copenhagen see København
95 M3 Copenhagen New York
133 E5 Copetonas Argentina
139 K3 Copeton Res. New South Wales
133 C3 Copiapó Chile
15 F2 Copinsay Scotland
138 E4 Copley S Australia
128 D6 Coporaque Peru
45 L2 Copparo Italy
120 G3 Coppell Ontario
109 N8 Coppell Texas
129 G2 Coppename R Suriname
32 L8 Coppenbrügge W Germany
116 P5 Copper R Alaska
109 K4 Copperas Cove Texas
100 G1 Copper Butte mt Washington
116 P6 Copper Center Alaska
120 J6 Copper Cliff Ontario
141 J6 Copperfield Queensland
99 T2 Copper Hbr Michigan
114 H4 Coppermine N W Terr
120 F6 Coppermine Pt C Ontario
117 N11 Copper Mt Br Col
100 K8 Copper Mt Nevada
117 Q5 Copp L N W Terr
48 J4 Copșa Mică Romania
131 B6 Copulhue, Paso del Arg/Chile
75 L3 Coqên China
22 B2 Coquelles France
13 G3 Coquet I England
13 G3 Coquet, R England
Coquilhatville see Mbandaka
100 A6 Coquille Oregon
131 B2 Coquimbo Chile
101 P7 Cora Wyoming
47 G1 Corabia Romania
130 G5 Coração de Jesus Brazil
139 L3 Coraki New S Wales
120 J2 Coral Ontario
71 C6 Coral B Palawan Philippines
113 L9 Coral Harbour New Providence I Bahamas
115 L5 Coral Harbour N W Terr
137 K4 Coral Sea Islands Terr Australasia
99 P8 Coralville Res Iowa
101 L1 Coram Montana
139 G7 Corangamite, L Victoria
129 G3 Corantijn R Suriname
94 G6 Coraopolis Pennsylvania
43 G7 Corato Italy
20 K4 Corbeil-Essonnes France
19 P13 Corbelin France
22 F5 Corbény France
120 K8 Corbetton Ontario
20 K2 Corbie France
9 H7 Corbiere Channel Is
18 G10 Corbières reg France
18 H5 Corbigny France
94 C10 Corbin Kentucky
123 R7 Corbin Hd Nfld
45 M1 Córbola Italy
16 D7 Corbones R Spain
13 F4 Corbridge England
9 F2 Corby Lincs England
9 F2 Corby Northants England
Corcaigh see Cork
36 B7 Corcieux France
102 E5 Corcoran California
21 B8 Corcoué-sur-Logne France
133 C6 Corcovado mt Chile
133 C6 Corcovado, Golfo Chile
16 A2 Corcubion Spain
112 D6 Cordele Georgia
107 M6 Cordell Oklahoma
18 G8 Cordes France
129 J5 Cordilheiras, Serra das mts Brazil
16 D1 Cordillera Cantábrica mts Spain
128 C3 Cordillera Central mts Colombia
127 J5 Cordillera Central mts Dom Rep
71 E2 Cordillera Central mts Luzon Philippines
125 O5 Cordillera Central mts Panama
128 C5 Cordillera Central mts Peru
127 J10 Cordillera de Mérida mts Venezuela
128 C3 Cordillera Occidental mts Colombia
128 D2 Cordillera Oriental mts Colombia
71 F5 Cordilleras Ra Panay Philippines
138 F2 Cordillo Downs S Australia
130 G6 Cordisburgo Brazil
131 D3 Córdoba Argentina
125 L8 Cordoba Mexico
16 D7 Córdoba Spain
128 C2 Córdoba div Colombia
131 D4 Cordoba prov Argentina
16 D7 Córdoba prov Spain
131 D3 Cordoba, Sierra de ra Argentina
111 J8 Cordova Alabama
116 P6 Cordova Alaska
99 Q8 Cordova Illinois
128 C6 Córdova Peru
121 N8 Cordova Mines Ontario
116 P6 Cordova Pk Alaska
45 J3 Coreglia Antelminelli Italy
140 F4 Corella R Queensland
140 D4 Corella L N Terr Aust
141 G5 Corfield Queensland
45 P5 Corfinio Italy
94 J4 Corfu New York
100 F3 Corfu Washington
Corfu isld Greece see Kérkira I
16 C2 Corgo Spain
130 C6 Corguinho Brazil
45 N6 Cori Italy
16 C5 Coria Spain
16 C7 Coria del R Spain
45 N4 Coriano Italy
121 O3 Coribelle Quebec
139 K5 Coricudgy mt New S Wales
43 H9 Corigliano Calabro Italy
45 O4 Corinaldo Italy
140 E4 Corinda Queensland
141 K2 Corinda dist Brisbane, Qnsld
136 L5 Coringa Is Coral Sea
141 K3 Coringa Is Gt Barrier Reef Aust
139 H8 Corinna Tasmania
101 N8 Corinne Utah
Corinth see Kórinthos
101 S4 Corinth Montana
95 O3 Corinth New York
Corinth, Gulf of Greece see Korinthiakós Kólpos
143 C9 Corinthian W Australia
130 G6 Corinto Brazil
130 C6 Corixinha, R Brazil
14 C5 Cork Irish Rep
14 C5 Cork co Irish Rep
18 C4 Corlay France
43 E11 Corleone Sicily
47 J3 Çorlu Turkey
123 P4 Cormack Nfld
123 Q5 Cormack mt Nfld
20 J5 Cormainville France
20 F3 Cormeilles France
21 G7 Cormery France
22 F5 Cormicy France
123 L2 Cormier, L Quebec
20 D3 Cormolain France
119 R4 Cormorant Manitoba
123 L4 Cormorant Pt Anticosti I, Quebec
107 M6 Corn Oklahoma
41 M6 Corna Italy
45 P6 Cornacchia, M mt Italy
32 H7 Cornau W Germany
112 D3 Cornelia Georgia
133 G2 Cornélio Procópio Brazil
99 S9 Cornell Illinois
99 P4 Cornell Wisconsin
123 P5 Corner Brook Nfld
139 H7 Corner Inlet Victoria
110 K6 Cornersville Tennessee
111 D9 Corney L Louisiana
103 P6 Cornfields Arizona
13 F2 Cornhill-on-Tweed England
20 C5 Cornille France
40 E2 Cornimont France
110 F5 Corning Arkansas
99 M9 Corning Iowa
107 O2 Corning Kansas
99 L9 Corning Missouri
95 K4 Corning New York
94 E7 Corning Ohio
119 P9 Corning Sask
141 G5 Cornish R Queensland
95 P3 Cornish Flat New Hampshire
142 F5 Cornish, Mt W Australia
113 K11 Cornishtown Bahamas
45 J3 Corno alle Scale mt Italy
42 F6 Corno, M mt Italy
100 H4 Cornucopia Oregon
99 P3 Cornucopia Wisconsin
18 H9 Cornus France
121 Q7 Cornwall Ontario
8 B7 Cornwall co England
115 K2 Cornwallis I N W Terr
138 D5 Corny Pt S Australia
127 K9 Coro Venezuela
130 G6 Coroaci Brazil
129 K4 Coroatá Brazil
87 B9 Coroca R Angola
128 E7 Corocoro Bolivia
128 E7 Coroico Bolivia
130 F6 Coromandel Brazil
145 E2 Coromandel New Zealand
76 E5 Coromandel Coast India
145 E2 Coromandel Peninsula New Zealand
71 E4 Coron Philippines
102 G8 Corona California
106 E7 Corona New Mexico
138 F4 Corona N S Wales
119 M9 Coronach Sask
102 G9 Coronado California
71 F7 Coronado B Mindanao Philippines
125 N5 Coronado, B.de Costa Rica
113 G8 Coronado Beach Florida
118 F6 Coronation Alberta
114 H4 Coronation G N W Terr
146 C14 Coronation I S Orkney Is
142 E2 Coronation Is W Australia
71 E5 Coron B Philippines
71 E5 Coron Delian isld Philippines
131 A6 Coronel Chile
133 E5 Coronel Dorrego Argentina
130 G6 Coronel Fabriciano Brazil
130 C9 Coronel Oviedo Paraguay
130 C4 Coronel Ponce Brazil
131 E6 Coronel Pringles Argentina
131 E6 Coronel Suárez Argentina
133 F5 Coronel Vidal Argentina
144 B6 Coronet Pk New Zealand
128 D7 Coropuna mt Peru
46 D4 Çorovodë Albania
139 H6 Corowa New S Wales
126 G10 Corozal Colombia
127 O1 Corozal Pt Trinidad
130 C10 Corpus Argentina
109 K8 Corpus Christi Texas
133 D1 Corque Bolivia
101 L6 Corral Idaho
16 E5 Corralde Almaguer Spain
124 G5 Corrales Mexico
16 D3 Corrales Spain
133 F4 Corrales Uruguay
126 D3 Corralilla Cuba
124 F2 Corralitos Mexico
143 B7 Corrandibby Ra mts W Australia
14 B3 Corraun Irish Rep
14 B3 Corraun Pen Irish Rep
99 L7 Correctionville Iowa
71 E3 Corregidor Luzon Philippines
130 E5 Córrego do Ouro Brazil
129 J6 Corrente Brazil
130 D6 Corrente, R Goiás Brazil
43 F12 Correnti, C.I. de Sicily
129 K6 Correntina Brazil
106 C7 Correo New Mexico
21 I10 Corrèze dep France
18 G7 Corrèze R France
45 K1 Correzzo Italy
45 M1 Corrézzola Italy
14 B3 Corrib, L Irish Rep
12 C2 Corrie Scotland
130 B10 Corrientes Argentina
131 F2 Corrientes prov Argentina
133 F3 Corrientes R Argentina
128 C4 Corrientes R Peru
133 F5 Corrientes, C Argentina
126 B4 Corrientes, C Cuba
124 G7 Corrientes, C Mexico
109 N5 Corrigan Texas
143 C9 Corrigin W Australia
139 K5 Corrimal New S Wales
13 H6 Corringham England
14 B4 Corrofin Irish Rep
94 H5 Corry Pennsylvania
139 J6 Corryong Victoria
12 C1 Corryvreckan, Str.of Scotland
18 L11 Corse-du-Sud dep Corsica
12 C3 Corsewall Pt Scotland
8 D5 Corsham England
18 L10 Corsica France
98 H6 Corsica S Dakota
18 L10 Corsica isld Medit Sea
109 L3 Corsicana Texas
12 E3 Corsock Br Scotland
8 D5 Corston England
13 E2 Corstorphine Scotland
115 P5 Cort Adelaer, Kap C Greenland
103 N9 Cortaro Arizona
16 C7 Cortegana Spain
130 J10 Cortês Brazil
106 B4 Cortez Colorado
102 H1 Cortez Nevada
38 F8 Cortina d'Ampezzo Italy
98 K9 Cortland Nebraska
95 L4 Cortland New York
94 G5 Cortland Ohio
9 H2 Corton England
42 D5 Cortona Italy
85 B6 Corubal R Guinea/Guinea-Bissau
16 B6 Coruche Portugal
78 H1 Çoruh R Turkey
15 B3 Coruisk, L Scotland
78 E1 Çorum Turkey
130 B6 Corumbá Brazil
130 E4 Corumbá de Goiás Brazil
130 E6 Corumbaíba Brazil
130 E5 Corumbá, R Brazil
130 H5 Corumbaú, Pta. do C Brazil
128 F6 Corumbiara R Brazil
128 F2 Corumo R Venezuela
16 B1 Coruña prov Spain
16 B1 Coruña, Lá Spain
Corunna see Lá Coruña
94 C4 Corunna Michigan
138 D4 Corunna S Australia
130 H11 Coruripe Brazil
101 L3 Corvallis Montana
100 B5 Corvallis Oregon
38 E8 Corvara in Badia Italy
32 K9 Corvey W Germany
8 C2 Corwen Wales
107 M4 Corwin Kansas
116 E7 Corwin, C Alaska
101 P4 Corwin Springs Montana
94 A8 Corydon Indiana
99 N9 Corydon Iowa
110 J4 Corydon Kentucky
94 J5 Corydon Pennsylvania
9 G5 Coryton England
21 E6 Corzé France
Cos isld see Kos isld
124 F5 Cosalá Mexico
125 M8 Cosamaloapan Mexico
43 G9 Cosenza Italy
9 E6 Cosham England
94 F6 Coshocton Ohio
81 B6 Cosmoledo I Indian Oc
99 M5 Cosmos Minnesota
18 G5 Cosne France
18 G6 Cosne-d'Allier France
102 G5 Coso Junction California
133 E4 Cosquin Argentina
21 I6 Cosson R France
109 K6 Cost Texas
17 G7 Costa Blanca Spain
17 K3 Costa Brava Spain
45 L1 Costa di Rovigo Italy
113 E11 Costa I, La Florida
102 G8 Costa Mesa California
124 C2 Costa Rica Mexico
125 M4 Costa Rica rep Cent America
123 K3 Costebelle, L Quebec
94 J5 Costello Pennsylvania
Costermansville see Bukavu
48 J6 Costești Romania
95 T1 Costigan Maine
106 E5 Costilla New Mexico
33 Q9 Coswig E Germany
71 G7 Cotabato Mindanao Philippines
128 E8 Cotagaita Bolivia
128 D7 Cotahuasi Peru
102 B3 Cotati California
130 H6 Cotaxé, R Brazil
121 Q7 Côteau Station Quebec
118 K7 Coteau, The Sask
126 G5 Coteaux Haiti
20 G4 Coteaux-du-Perche reg France
111 E12 Cote Blanche B Louisiana
44 B4 Côte d'Azur France
19 J5 Côte d'Or France
20 B3 Cotentin reg France
18 C4 Côtes-du-Nord mts France
13 F4 Cotherstone England
141 J6 Cotherstone Queensland
19 Q18 Cotignac France
45 L3 Cotignola Italy
48 E7 Cotina R Yugoslavia
128 F3 Cotinga R Brazil
85 E7 Cotonou Benin
106 E3 Cotopaxi Colorado
128 C4 Cotopaxi vol Ecuador
9 E4 Cotswold Hills England
100 B6 Cottage Grove Oregon
112 G5 Cottageville S Carolina
94 F8 Cottageville W Virginia
31 H4 Cottbus E Germany
33 S9 Cottbus reg E Germany
123 T5 Cottel I Nfld
9 G3 Cottenham England
110 D5 Cotter Arkansas
83 M14 Cotter, C Mauritius
142 A2 Cottesloe Beach dist Perth, W Aust
9 F2 Cottesmore England
129 H3 Cottica Suriname
13 H6 Cottingham England
99 O2 Cotton Minnesota
140 E6 Cottonbush Cr Queensland
111 J8 Cottondale Alabama
111 L11 Cottondale Florida
140 D1 Cotton I N Terr Aust
119 V3 Cotton L Manitoba
110 E6 Cotton Plant Arkansas
111 D11 Cottonport Louisiana
109 O3 Cotton Valley Louisiana
111 L10 Cottonwood Alabama
103 N7 Cottonwood Arizona
100 C9 Cottonwood California
100 J3 Cottonwood Idaho
98 E6 Cottonwood S Dakota
109 H3 Cottonwood Texas
99 M5 Cottonwood R Minnesota
103 L6 Cottonwood Cliffs Arizona
107 O3 Cottonwood Falls Kansas
103 O6 Cottonwood Wash R Arizona
127 J5 Cotuí Dom Rep
109 H7 Cotulla Texas
21 C10 Coubre, Pte. de la France
142 F3 Couchman Ra W Australia
22 E4 Coucy-le-Château Auffrique France
21 H7 Couddes France
22 C1 Coudekerque-Branche France
99 P4 Couderay Wisconsin
94 J5 Coudersport Pennsylvania
20 J3 Coudray St. Germer, le France
20 G6 Coudrecieux France
20 H4 Coudres France
122 B6 Coudres, I.aux Quebec
138 D6 Couëdic, C.de S Australia
20 D5 Couesmes France
20 C5 Couesnon R France
21 C7 Couffé France
100 C3 Cougar Washington
18 F6 Couhé France
14 A5 Coulagh B Irish Rep
20 F5 Coulans France
15 C2 Coulbeag Mt Scotland
100 F2 Coulee City Washington
100 G1 Coulee Dam Washington
20 F5 Coulimer France
146 J6 Coulman I Antarctica
21 I6 Coulmiers France
22 B2 Coulogne France
21 F9 Coulombiers France
20 J4 Coulombs France
121 O6 Coulonge R Quebec
21 D9 Coulonges France
21 E8 Coulonges-Thouarsais France
20 C4 Coulouvray-Boisbenâtre France
119 R9 Coulter Manitoba
102 D4 Coulterville California
110 G3 Coulterville Illinois
116 F4 Council Alaska
100 J5 Council Idaho
99 L8 Council Bluffs Iowa
107 O3 Council Grove Kansas
8 D2 Cound England
107 N7 Countyline Oklahoma
15 E4 Coupar Angus Scotland
100 C1 Coupeville Washington
109 K5 Coupland Texas
22 B2 Couple, Mt France
20 E5 Couptrain France
117 S3 Courageous L N W Terr
20 K5 Courances France
122 B8 Courcelles Quebec
20 F5 Courcemont France
21 H7 Cour Cheverny France
20 E5 Courcité France
21 F10 Courcôme France
21 D9 Courçon France
20 F5 Courgains France
18 H7 Courpière France
22 D3 Courrières France
18 H9 Coursan France
20 E3 Courseulles France
18 H5 Courson les Carrières France
20 H5 Courtalain France
40 F3 Courtelary Switzerland
114 G8 Courtenay Br Columbia
98 H2 Courtenay N Dakota
18 G7 Courtine, la France
107 N2 Courtland Kansas
99 M5 Courtland Minnesota
95 K10 Courtland Virginia
14 C5 Courtmacsherry Irish Rep
109 L5 Courtney Texas
20 F4 Courtomer France
Courtrai see Kortrijk
22 H2 Court Saint-Etienne Belgium
118 L8 Courval Sask
20 H5 Courville France
109 O3 Coushatta Louisiana
83 J12 Cousin I Seychelles
22 G3 Cousolre France
87 D9 Coutada do Mucusso Angola
20 C3 Coutances France
20 E5 Couterne France
22 J2 Couthuin Belgium
18 E7 Coutras France
101 N1 Coutts Alberta
127 O2 Couva Trinidad
20 B2 Couville France
22 H3 Couvin Belgium
22 F4 Couvron-et-Aumencourt France
48 K5 Covasna Romania
109 N1 Cove Arkansas
100 H4 Cove Oregon
112 K2 Cove City N Carolina
103 M3 Cove Fort Utah
100 B10 Covelo California
94 K7 Cove Mt Pennsylvania
126 G10 Coveñas Colombia
9 E3 Coventry England
95 L8 Cove Point Maryland
107 M2 Covert Kansas
94 A4 Covert Michigan
94 J9 Covesville Virginia
16 B4 Covilhã Portugal
116 K7 Coville, L Alaska
112 D4 Covington Georgia
99 T9 Covington Indiana
94 C7 Covington Kentucky
111 F11 Covington Louisiana
99 S3 Covington Michigan
94 C6 Covington Ohio
107 N5 Covington Oklahoma
110 G6 Covington Tennessee
109 K3 Covington Texas
94 G9 Covington Virginia
120 G5 Cow R Ontario
15 C4 Cowal Scotland
139 J5 Cowal, L New S Wales
119 R6 Cowan Manitoba
110 K6 Cowan Tennessee
140 E4 Cowan Downs Queensland
138 F6 Cowangie Victoria
118 K4 Cowan L Sask
143 D9 Cowan, Lake W Australia
101 P4 Cowan, Mt Montana
121 S7 Cowansville Quebec
138 D3 Coward Springs S Australia
138 E2 Cowarie S Australia
9 F2 Cowbit England
103 L2 Cowboy Pass Utah
8 C5 Cowbridge Wales
143 B9 Cowcowing,L W Australia
100 G2 Cow Cr Washington
110 H2 Cowden Illinois
13 E1 Cowdenbeath Scotland
101 T9 Cowdrey Colorado
138 D5 Cowell S Australia
94 G8 Cowen W Virginia
9 E6 Cowes England
139 H7 Cowes Victoria
107 P6 Coweta Oklahoma
9 F6 Cowfold England
123 P4 Cow Head Nfld
100 E8 Cow Head L California
100 A1 Cowichan L Br Col
70 E2 Cowie Harb Kalimantan
140 A6 Cowle, Mt N Terr Australia
98 H9 Cowles Nebraska
106 E6 Cowles New Mexico
118 D9 Cowley Alberta
141 G7 Cowley Queensland
101 R5 Cowley Wyoming
100 C3 Cowlitz R Washington
100 D3 Cowlitz Pass Washington
94 H8 Cowpasture R Virginia
112 F2 Cowpens S Carolina
112 F2 Cowpens Nat.Bat.Site S Carolina
139 J5 Cowra New S Wales
130 G4 Coxa, R Brazil
139 H9 Cox Bight Tasmania
13 G4 Coxhoe England
130 C4 Coxibó do Ouro Brazil
130 C6 Coxim Brazil
123 O2 Coxipi L Quebec
130 C4 Coxipó da Ponté Brazil
143 F6 Cox,Mt W Australia
140 D3 Cox R N Terr Australia
95 O4 Coxsackie New York
75 O8 Cox's Bazar Bangladesh
123 P4 Cox's Cove Nfld
108 B6 Coyame Mexico
108 D5 Coyanosa Cr Texas
20 K3 Coye-la-Forêt France
107 N6 Coyle Oklahoma
102 C4 Coyote California
106 E8 Coyote New Mexico
102 H6 Coyote L California
102 F5 Coyote Peak California
103 L9 Coyote Pk Arizona
124 D5 Coyote, Pta C Mexico
124 F6 Coyotitán Mexico
98 G9 Cozad Nebraska
44 B2 Cozie Alpi mt Italy
124 C2 Cozón, Cerro mt Mexico
125 Q7 Cozumel, I.de Mexico
100 F3 Crab Cr Washington
141 F1 Crab I Queensland
139 J4 Craboon New S Wales
94 C9 Crab Orchard Kentucky
112 C2 Crab Orchard Tennessee
110 G4 Crab Orchard L Illinois
127 H2 Crab Pond Pt Jamaica
139 H7 Crab Pt Victoria
8 B6 Crackington Haven England
8 D2 Crackleybank England
Cracow see Kraków
141 K7 Cracow Queensland
139 H8 Cradle, Mt Tasmania
89 D9 Cradock S Africa
138 E4 Cradock S Australia
117 G8 Craig Alaska
101 S9 Craig Colorado
113 G13 Craig Florida
99 L9 Craig Missouri
101 O2 Craig Montana
98 K8 Craig Nebraska
15 E3 Craigellachie Scotland
13 E1 Craigend Scotland
15 C5 Craighouse Scotland
12 D2 Craigie Scotland
144 C5 Craigieburn New Zealand
100 J3 Craigmont Idaho
116 R6 Craig, Mt Alaska
118 E7 Craigmyle Alberta
13 E1 Craigrothie Scotland
141 K7 Craigs Ra mts Queensland
94 H8 Craigsville Virginia
14 D4 Craiguenamanagh Irish Rep
119 M7 Craik Sask
13 F1 Crail Scotland
37 J5 Crailsheim W Germany
48 H6 Craiova Romania

13 E2 Cramond Scotland
85 D2 Crampel Algeria
86 C4 Crampel Cent Afr Republic
121 Q8 Cranberry, L New York
119 Q4 Cranberry Portage Manitoba
9 E6 Cranborne England
114 H8 Cranbrook Br Columbia
9 G5 Cranbrook England
143 C10 Cranbrook W Australia
119 R8 Crandall Manitoba
98 J4 Crandall S Dakota
109 L3 Crandall Texas
99 S4 Crandon Wisconsin
127 P6 Crane Barbados
110 C5 Crane Missouri
98 B2 Crane Montana
100 G6 Crane Oregon
108 E4 Crane Texas
100 J5 Crane Cr.Res Idaho
118 H8 Crane L Sask
119 M9 Crane Valley Sask
109 K4 Cranfills Gap Texas
9 F5 Cranleigh England
100 A8 Crannell California
13 F2 Cranshaws Scotland
95 Q5 Cranston Rhode I
13 H6 Cranswick England
21 D6 Craon France
22 F5 Craonne France
139 K2 Craoow Queensland
18 H7 Craponne-sur-Arzon France
98 H1 Crary N Dakota
146 H10 Crary Mts Antarctica
48 L4 Crasna Romania
48 H3 Crasna R Romania
48 H3 Crasnei, Muntii mt Romania
100 C7 Crater L Oregon
100 C7 Crater Lake Nat. Park Oregon
100 D9 Crater Peak mt California
101 M6 Craters of the Moon Nat.Mon Idaho
43 G9 Crati R Italy
130 G9 Crato Brazil
21 F7 Cravant les Coteaux France
119 N8 Craven Sask
130 F7 Cravinhos Brazil
128 D2 Cravo Norte R Colombia
112 D4 Crawford Georgia
111 H8 Crawford Mississippi
98 C7 Crawford Nebraska
12 E3 Crawford Scotland
109 K4 Crawford Texas
12 E3 Crawfordjohn Scotland
140 B3 Crawford,Mt N Terr Australia
95 Q2 Crawford Notch New Hampshire
71 D5 Crawford Pt Philippines
110 K1 Crawfordsville Indiana
111 M11 Crawfordville Florida
112 E4 Crawfordville Georgia
9 F5 Crawley England
8 C4 Cray Wales
9 G5 Crayford England
116 P4 Crazy Mts Alaska
101 P3 Crazy Mts Montana
101 P4 Crazy Pk Montana
101 T5 Crazy Woman Cr Wyoming
15 D4 Creag Meagaidh mt Scotland
20 B3 Créances France
118 L4 Crean L Sask
40 A5 Crêches France
22 B3 Crécy-en-Pontieu France
22 F4 Crécy-sur-Serre France
8 C6 Crediton England
12 D4 Cree Bridge Scotland
106 D4 Creede Colorado
112 J1 Creedmoor N Carolina
101 R9 Creek Colorado
94 H6 Creekside Pennsylvania
113 L9 Creek Village New Providence I Bahamas
124 F4 Creel Mexico
114 J6 Cree L Sask
119 O9 Creelman Sask
120 K8 Creemore Ontario
114 J6 Cree River Saskatchewan
12 D4 Creetown Scotland
37 J5 Creglingen W Germany
98 H7 Creighton Nebraska
119 P4 Creighton Sask
120 J6 Creighton Mine Ontario
44 G1 Crema Italy
19 O13 Crémieu France
118 C7 Cremona Alberta
44 G1 Cremona Italy
111 F7 Crenshaw Mississippi
18 E8 Créon France
48 F5 Crepaja Yugoslavia
129 G5 Crepori R Brazil
22 D5 Crépy-en-Valois France
120 K6 Crerar Ontario
42 F4 Cres Yugoslavia
98 G4 Cresbard S Dakota
107 N6 Crescent Oklahoma
112 J4 Crescent Beach S Carolina
100 A8 Crescent City California
113 F8 Crescent L Florida
100 D6 Crescent L Oregon
100 B1 Crescent, L Washington
100 E9 Crescent Mills California
103 J6 Crescent Pk Nevada
99 O6 Cresco Iowa
45 L2 Crespino Italy
8 B4 Cresselly Wales
109 K3 Cresson Texas
139 H8 Cressy Tasmania
139 G7 Cressy Victoria
19 O15 Crest France
103 K4 Crestline Nevada
94 E6 Crestline Ohio
100 J1 Creston Br Col
99 M8 Creston Iowa
101 L1 Creston Montana
123 R6 Creston Nfld
100 G2 Creston Washington
101 S8 Creston Wyoming
106 E3 Crestone Pk Colorado
111 K11 Crestview Florida
110 J6 Crestview Tennessee
119 M8 Crestwynd Sask
112 L2 Creswell N Carolina
100 B6 Creswell Oregon
115 K3 Creswell B N W Terr
140 D4 Creswell Downs N Terr Australia
139 G7 Creswick Victoria
19 J6 Crêt de la Neige mt France
99 T8 Crete Illinois
98 H3 Crete N Dakota
98 K9 Crete Nebraska
Crete isld Greece see Kriti I
47 G9 Crete, Sea of Greece
20 D3 Creully France
17 K2 Creus, C Spain
21 I9 Creuse dep France
18 G6 Creuse R France
37 M4 Creussen W Germany
37 J1 Creuzburg E Germany
43 K2 Crevalcore Italy
20 F3 Crèvecoeur France
20 K2 Crèvecoeur-le-Grand France
17 G6 Crevillente Spain
41 H5 Crevola Italy
8 D1 Crewe England
94 J9 Crewe Virginia
8 D6 Crewkerne England
12 D1 Crianlarich Scotland
8 B2 Criccieth Wales
8 E1 Crich England
118 K9 Crichton Sask
133 H3 Criciuma Brazil
9 E3 Crick England
8 C4 Crickhowell Wales
9 E4 Cricklade England
94 C6 Cridersville Ohio
12 E1 Crieff Scotland
20 H1 Criel-sur-Mer France
15 E6 Criffell mt Scotland
42 F3 Crikvenica Yugoslavia
117 E6 Crillon, Mt Alaska
99 O1 Crilly Ontario
Crimea see Krym
37 N2 Crimmitschau E Germany
12 C1 Crinan Scotland
15 C4 Crinan Canal Scotland
106 E3 Cripple Creek Colorado
116 J5 Cripple Landing Alaska
9 G6 Cripps's Corner England
20 F2 Criquetot-l'Esneval France
48 G4 Crişana Romania
130 F5 Cristalina Brazil
129 H6 Cristalino R Brazil
38 F8 Cristallo mt Italy
126 H10 Cristóbal Colón, Pico mt Colombia
48 J4 Cristuru Secuiesc Romania
48 G4 Crişul Alb R Romania
48 G4 Crişul Negru R Romania
48 H4 Crişul Repede R Romania
94 C8 Crittenden Kentucky
33 P5 Crivitz E Germany
99 S4 Crivitz Wisconsin
38 L9 Črna Yugoslavia
46 E3 Crna R Yugoslavia
46 E2 Crna Gora mt Yugoslavia
46 E2 Crna Trava Yugoslavia
46 D3 Crni Drim R Yugoslavia
38 M9 Crni-vrh mt Yugoslavia
14 B3 Croagh Patrick Mt Irish Rep
Croatia see Hrvatska
41 O5 Croce, C mt Italy
43 G11 Croce, S., C Sicily
110 D4 Crocker Missouri
70 D2 Crocker Ra Borneo
12 D5 Crocketford Scotland
109 M4 Crockett Texas
9 G5 Crockham Hill England
20 E4 Crocy France
38 F8 Croda Rossa mt Italy
110 J4 Crofton Kentucky
98 J7 Crofton Nebraska
142 D5 Crofton,Mt W Australia
95 M3 Croghan New York
19 O18 Croisette, C France
20 B5 Croisic, le France
18 D3 Croisilles France
145 D4 Croisilles Harbour New Zealand
127 H5 Croix des Bouquets Haiti
19 P15 Croix Haute, Col de la pass France
20 C5 Croixille, la France
122 B2 Croix, Là la Quebec
122 E8 Croix R New Brunswick
20 H3 Croix-St.Leufroy, la France
22 D3 Croix-St.Ouen, la France
120 K8 Croker, Cape Ontario
140 B2 Croker Hill N Terr Australia
140 C1 Croker I N Terr Australia
15 D3 Cromarty Scotland
15 D3 Cromarty Firth Scotland
138 B2 Crombie, Mt S Australia
9 H2 Cromer England
119 Q9 Cromer Manitoba
99 O3 Cromwell Minnesota
144 B6 Cromwell New Zealand
144 C5 Cronadun New Zealand
37 K5 Cronheim W Germany
98 D9 Crook Colorado
13 F5 Crook Cumbria England
13 G4 Crook Durham England
107 K4 Crooked Cr Kansas
100 G7 Crooked Cr Oregon
126 G3 Crooked I Bahamas
126 G3 Crooked I.Passage Bahamas
113 F10 Crooked L Florida
123 Q5 Crooked L Nfld
117 M8 Crooked R Br Columbia
100 E5 Crooked R Oregon
119 O6 Crooked River Sask
13 F2 Crookham England
14 B5 Crookhaven Irish Rep
109 M2 Crook, L Texas
13 F5 Crooklands England
12 E1 Crook of Devon Scotland
98 K2 Crookston Minnesota
98 F7 Crookston Nebraska
94 E7 Crooksville Ohio
139 J5 Crookwell New S Wales
13 E9 Croom Florida
14 C4 Croom Irish Rep
139 K3 Croppa Cr New S Wales
123 R2 Croque Nfld
141 G3 Crosbie R Queensland
99 N3 Crosby Minnesota
111 E10 Crosby Mississippi
98 C1 Crosby N Dakota
109 M6 Crosby Texas
108 F2 Crosbyton Texas
8 D5 Cross England
85 F7 Cross R Nigeria
21 A7 Crossac France
12 C2 Crossaig Scotland
87 B10 Cross, C Namibia
113 D7 Cross City Florida
13 F6 Cross Fell England
118 C7 Crossfield Alberta
13 E1 Crossgates Scotland
8 C3 Cross Gates Wales
8 B4 Cross Hands Wales
113 K12 Cross Harbour Bahamas
14 C5 Crosshaven Irish Rep
112 F3 Cross Hill S Carolina
12 D3 Crosshill Scotland
111 C9 Cross L Louisiana
113 O2 Cross L Ontario
119 U4 Cross Lake Manitoba
144 D5 Crossley, Mt New Zealand
117 P5 Cross L. Prov. Park Alberta
14 B3 Crossmaglen N Ireland
103 K7 Crossman Pk Arizona
12 E4 Crossmichael Scotland
14 C3 Crossmolina Irish Rep
112 C1 Cross Mountain Colorado
109 H3 Cross Plains Texas
94 B1 Cross Village Michigan
110 L6 Crossville Tennessee
116 P5 Crosswind L Alaska
45 J2 Crostolo R Italy
110 L3 Crothersville Indiana
43 H9 Crotone Italy
20 J1 Crotoy, le France
37 O3 Crottendorf E Germany
100 K5 Crouch Idaho
9 G3 Crouch, R England
21 F8 Croutelle France
22 E5 Crouy France
27 F7 Crouzilles France
101 S4 Crow Agency Montana
139 H4 Crowal R New S Wales
9 G5 Crowborough England
8 C5 Crowcombe England
106 F1 Crow Cr Colorado
111 F7 Crowder Mississippi
107 P6 Crowder Oklahoma
118 F1 Crowduck L. Manitoba
99 L4 Crowdy Hd New S Wales
109 H2 Crowell Texas
139 G7 Crowes Victoria
101 Q6 Crowheart Wyoming
139 H4 Crowl R New S Wales
9 F2 Crowland England
13 H6 Crowle England
106 F2 Crowley Colorado
111 D11 Crowley Louisiana
102 F4 Crowley, L California
94 E8 Crown City Ohio
103 M7 Crown King Arizona
106 B6 Crown Point New Mexico
95 O3 Crown Point New York
115 L4 Crown Prince Frederick I N W Terr
99 T8 Crown Pt Indiana
127 M2 Crown Pt Tobago
101 O3 Crow Peak Montana
141 K7 Crow's Nest Queensland
118 C9 Crowsnest Pass Alberta/Br Col
99 M3 Crow Wing R Minnesota
13 G4 Croxdale England
8 B5 Croyde England
9 F5 Croydon England
144 B7 Croydon New Zealand
141 F4 Croydon Queensland
142 C5 Croydon W Australia
83 L13 Croy, Í de Kerguelen Indian Oc
21 I9 Crozant France
94 J8 Crozet Virginia
81 D9 Crozet Basin Indian Oc
81 C10 Crozet, Is Indian Oc
81 B10 Crozet Plateau Indian Oc
146 J7 Crozier, C Antarctica
114 G2 Crozier Chan N W Terr
18 B4 Crozon France
19 N15 Crus France
103 H6 Crucero California
130 D3 Cruces Cuba
128 C2 Cruces, Pta point Colombia
22 L4 Cruchten Luxembourg
94 H7 Crucible Pennsylvania
15 G3 Cruden B Scotland
8 D2 Crudgington England
8 D4 Crudwell England
111 F8 Cruger Mississippi
20 G4 Crulai France
14 E2 Crumlin N Ireland
100 F7 Crump L Oregon
22 K5 Crusnes France
133 E4 Cruz Argentina
133 G3 Cruz Alta Brazil
131 D3 Cruz del Eje Argentina
130 G8 Cruzeiro Brazil
133 G2 Cruzeiro do Oeste Brazil
128 D5 Cruzeiro do Sul Brazil
146 K9 Cruzen I Antarctica
133 C3 Cruz Grande Chile
128 C3 Cruz, La Colombia
18 G9 Cruzy France
117 M8 Crysdale, Mt Br Columbia
98 J1 Crystal N Dakota
103 K5 Crystal Nevada
106 C2 Crystal R Colorado
113 E9 Crystal B Florida
138 E5 Crystal Bridge S Australia
119 T9 Crystal City Manitoba
108 H7 Crystal City Texas
99 S3 Crystal Falls Michigan
99 S7 Crystal L Illinois
99 U5 Crystal L Michigan
99 N6 Crystal Lake Iowa
113 E9 Crystal River Florida
111 F9 Crystal Springs Mississippi
119 M6 Crystal Springs Sask
99 U6 Crystal Valley Michigan
48 F4 Csanytelek Hungary
48 E3 Csepel Sziget R Hungary
48 F4 Csongrád Hungary
48 F4 Csongrád co Hungary
48 D3 Csorna Hungary
48 D4 Csorvas Hungary
48 E3 Csóványos mt Hungary
48 D4 Csurgó Hungary
127 L9 Cúa Venezuela
88 F9 Cuambo Mozambique
87 D9 Cuando R Angola
87 C9 Cuangar Angola
87 C7 Cuango Angola
86 C7 Cuango Zaïre
87 B7 Cuanza R Angola
67 A7 Cua Rao Vietnam
133 F4 Cuareim Brazil
131 F3 Cuaro R Uruguay
133 E4 Cuatro R Argentina
124 H4 Cuatro Ciénegas de Carranza Mexico
68 H4 Cua Tung Vietnam
124 F3 Cuauhtémoc Mexico
124 G8 Cuautitlán Mexico
125 K8 Cuautla Mexico
110 F1 Cuba Illinois
107 N2 Cuba Kansas
110 E3 Cuba Missouri
106 D5 Cuba New Mexico
94 J4 Cuba New York
16 B6 Cuba Portugal
126 D4 Cuba rep W Indies
103 M10 Cubabi, Cerro peak Mexico
99 Q7 Cuba City Wisconsin
127 M9 Cubagua, I Venezuela
143 B10 Cuballing W Australia
87 C9 Cubango R Angola
78 G1 Cubatão Brazil
119 N4 Cub Hills Sask
127 K10 Cubiro Venezuela
48 J6 Cuca Romania
133 C6 Cucao, B.de Chile
133 F4 Cuchilla de Haedo hills Uruguay
9 F5 Cuckfield England
9 E1 Cuckney England
94 K9 Cuckoo Virginia
87 C8 Cucumbi Angola
124 D2 Cucurpe Mexico
128 D2 Cúcuta Colombia
99 T7 Cudahy Wisconsin
76 D5 Cuddalore India
76 D5 Cuddapah India
141 F7 Cuddapan,L Queensland
102 G6 Cuddeback L California
113 F13 Cudjoe Key isld Florida
119 M6 Cudworth Sask
143 C7 Cue W Australia
16 E3 Cuéllar Spain
128 C4 Cuenca Ecuador
71 E4 Cuenca Philippines
17 F4 Cuenca Spain
17 F5 Cuenca prov Spain
124 H5 Cuencamé de Ceniceros Mexico
17 F4 Cuenca, Serrania de Spain
125 K8 Cuernavaca Mexico
109 K6 Cuero Texas
19 Q18 Cuers France
106 F6 Cuervo New Mexico
102 D6 Cuesta Pass California
126 G4 Cueto Cuba
17 F7 Cuevas del Almanzora Spain
133 E2 Cuevo Bolivia
43 E5 Cuffies France
123 N2 Cuff L Quebec
19 P18 Cuges-les-Pins France
43 B8 Cuglieri Sardinia
131 G2 Cuguen France
130 C4 Cuiabá Brazil
14 D2 Cuilcagh mt N Ireland
15 B3 Cuillin Hills Scotland
87 C9 Cuilo R Angola
59 J2 Cuilian China
87 B8 Cuima Angola
22 D2 Cuinchy France
36 B4 Cuint W Germany
22 E5 Cuise-la-Motte France
130 H9 Cuité Brazil
130 H6 Cuité, R Brazil
87 C9 Cuito R Angola
87 C9 Cuito Cuanavale Angola
128 F4 Cuiuni R Brazil
110 E2 Cuivre R Missouri
71 E7 Cujangan isld Philippines
48 H6 Cujmiru Romania
68 J7 Cukurca Turkey
68 H4 Cu Lai Vietnam
18 G6 Culan France
68 J5 Cu Lao Bo Bai isld Vietnam
68 J5 Cu Lao Chàm isld Vietnam
68 J7 Cu Lao Hon isld Vietnam
68 J5 Cu Lao Re isld Vietnam
71 F5 Culasi Panay Philippines
98 B1 Culbertson Montana
98 F9 Culbertson Nebraska
139 H6 Culcairn New S Wales
22 G4 Cul-des-Sarts Belgium
106 F4 Culebra Pk Colorado
16 C3 Culebra, Sa de la mts Spain
25 D5 Culemborg Netherlands
87 C9 Culevai Angola
141 H8 Culgoa R N S W/Qnsld
139 H3 Culgoa, R Australia
124 F5 Culiacán Mexico
124 F5 Culiacancito Mexico
71 D5 Culion Philippines
129 H6 Culiseu R Brazil
17 F7 Cúllar de Baza Spain
139 J5 Cullarin Rge New S Wales
15 F3 Cullen Scotland
17 G5 Cullera Spain
107 M4 Cullison Kansas
111 K7 Cullman Alabama
141 G5 Culloden R Queensland
8 C6 Cullompton England
125 M2 Culmi Honduras
8 D3 Culmington England
19 P13 Culoz France
94 J8 Culpeper Virginia
128 A7 Culpepper isld Galapagos Is
15 E5 Culter Fell Scotland
139 G4 Cultowa New S Wales
129 H6 Culuene R Brazil
99 U8 Culver Indiana
107 N3 Culver Kansas
100 D5 Culver Oregon
144 D5 Culverden New Zealand
143 E10 Culver,Pt W Australia
87 C8 Cuma Angola
129 K4 Cuma, B.de Brazil
47 H4 Cumali Turkey
128 F1 Cumana Venezuela
127 N9 Cumanacoa Venezuela
47 J6 Cumaovası Turkey
130 E6 Cumari Brazil
117 L11 Cumberland Br Columbia
99 M8 Cumberland Iowa
94 D9 Cumberland Kentucky
94 J7 Cumberland Maryland
94 F7 Cumberland Ohio
94 J9 Cumberland Virginia
99 O4 Cumberland Wisconsin
Cumberland co see Cumbria
110 J5 Cumberland R Tennessee
146 A15 Cumberland B Antarctica
137 O4 Cumberland, C New Hebrides
110 J5 Cumberland City Tennessee
94 D10 Cumberland Gap Tenn/Virg
119 P5 Cumberland House Sask
113 F7 Cumberland I Georgia
141 J5 Cumberland Is Queensland
94 B10 Cumberland, L Kentucky
110 L5 Cumberland, L Kentucky
119 P4 Cumberland L Sask
94 D10 Cumberland Mts Tennessee etc
115 N4 Cumberland Pen N W Terr
99 R2 Cumberland Pt Michigan
94 D10 Cumberland R Kentucky
94 J7 Cumberland Res Pennsylvania
115 N4 Cumberland Sound N W Terr
140 D1 Cumberland Str N Terr Australia
12 E2 Cumbernauld Scotland
139 J3 Cumborah New S Wales
133 C7 Cumbrera mt Chile
13 E4 Cumbria co England
76 D3 Cumbum India
109 M2 Cumby Texas
44 B2 Cumiana Italy
129 G4 Cumina R Brazil
129 G3 Cuminapanema R Brazil
13 E4 Cummertrees Scotland
102 C3 Cummings California
98 J2 Cummings N Dakota
138 D5 Cummins S Australia
142 F4 Cummins Ra W Australia
139 J5 Cumnock New S Wales
12 D3 Cumnock Scotland
48 J5 Cumpăna Romania
124 E2 Cumpas Mexico
78 D3 Çumra Turkey
124 E3 Cumuripa Mexico
130 H5 Cumuruxatiba Brazil
127 O2 Cumuto Trinidad
126 E3 Cunagua Cuba
129 H3 Cunani Brazil
126 E6 Cuñaño Mexico
131 G3 Cuñapiru R Uruguay
133 C5 Cunco Chile
142 D5 Cuncudgerie Hill W Australia
143 B9 Cunderdin W Australia
128 D3 Cundinamarca div Colombia
87 B9 Cunene R Angola
44 B3 Cuneo Italy
138 C4 Cungena S Australia
17 H6 Cunillera isld Balearic Is
18 H7 Cunlhat France
141 H8 Cunnamulla Queensland
107 M4 Cunningham Kansas
100 G3 Cunningham Washington
127 O2 Cunupia Trinidad
21 E7 Cuon France
107 N8 Cupar Sask
12 E1 Cupar Scotland
128 C2 Cupica, G.de Colombia
46 E1 Cuprija Yugoslavia
101 J4 Cuprum Idaho
124 D5 Cupula, P Mexico
129 G7 Curabá R Brazil
129 L5 Curaçá Brazil
126 B1 Curaçao isld W Indies
131 B7 Curacautín Chile
131 B7 Curaco, R Argentina
131 E6 Cura Malal, Cerro peak Argentina
133 C5 Curanilahue Chile
128 C4 Curaray R Peru/Ecuador
131 B4 Curaumilla, Pta de C Chile
139 H4 Curban New S Wales
48 K6 Curcani Romania
21 E7 Curcay-sur-Dive France
138 D3 Curdimurka S Australia
15 F3 Curdlawidny Lagoon S Australia
9 E2 Curdworth England
18 H5 Cure R France
83 M13 Curepipe Mauritius
87 G12 Curepipe Mauritius
133 C5 Curepto Chile
131 B5 Curico Chile
131 B5 Curicó, L Argentina
128 E4 Curicuriari R Brazil
83 J12 Curieuse I Seychelles
131 B5 Curimatai R Brazil
130 J3 Curious,Mt W Australia
143 A7 Curiplaya Colombia
128 D3 Curitiba Brazil
130 E10 Curitibanos Brazil
100 G1 Curlew Washington
141 J5 Curlew I Queensland
111 H12 Curlew Is Louisiana
139 K4 Curlews New S Wales
116 F5 Curlew L Alaska
123 L3 Curlew Pt Quebec
123 O5 Curling Nfld
138 E4 Curnamona S Australia
44 F2 Curone R Italy
139 K4 Currabubula New S Wales
130 H9 Currais Novas Brazil
138 E4 Curralulla R S Australia
94 D2 Curran Michigan
121 Q7 Curran Ontario
103 J3 Currant Nevada
139 G4 Curranyalpa New S Wales
141 F7 Currawilla Queensland
110 E4 Current R Missouri
113 L12 Current I Bahamas
126 F2 Current, The Eleuthera Bahamas
99 L5 Currie Minnesota
112 J3 Currie N Carolina
103 K1 Currie Nevada
13 E2 Currie Scotland
139 G7 Currie Tasmania
138 B2 Currie Cr., The S Australia
119 U1 Currie L Manitoba
140 B7 Currie,Mt N Terr Australia
112 L1 Currituck N Carolina
112 M1 Currituck Sound N Carolina
139 K6 Currockbilly, Mt New S Wales
110 E2 Curryville Missouri
37 L2 Cursdorf E Germany
45 L1 Curtarolo Italy
48 J5 Curtea de Argeş Romania
100 B6 Curtin Oregon
143 D9 Curtin W Australia
140 B7 Curtin Springs N Terr Aust
111 C9 Curtis Louisiana
99 V3 Curtis Michigan
98 F9 Curtis Nebraska
16 B1 Curtis Spain
141 L6 Curtis Chan Gt Barrier Reef Australia
139 H7 Curtis Group islds Tasmania
137 R8 Curtis I Kermadec Is Pacific Oc
141 K6 Curtis I Queensland
94 D2 Curtisville Michigan
129 G4 Curuá Brazil
129 H5 Curuaés R Brazil
129 H3 Curuá, I Brazil
129 G3 Curuapanema R Brazil
129 J4 Curuçá Brazil
128 D5 Curuçá R Brazil
133 F2 Curuguaty Paraguay
129 J4 Cururupu Brazil
131 F2 Curuzú Cuatiá Argentina
129 K7 Curvelo Brazil
94 H6 Curwensville Pennsylvania
14 E3 Cushendall N Ireland
14 E3 Cushendun N Ireland
99 M3 Cushing Minnesota
107 O5 Cushing Oklahoma
111 B10 Cushing Texas
110 E6 Cushman Arkansas
101 O3 Cushman Montana
100 A3 Cushman Oregon
100 B2 Cushman, L Washington
124 F3 Cusihuiráchic Mexico
45 H3 Cusna, Mt Italy
18 H6 Cusset France
12 C5 Cusseta Georgia
99 C1 Cusson Minnesota
144 D5 Cust New Zealand
101 S3 Custer Montana
98 C6 Custer S Dakota
101 S4 Custer Battlefield Montana
107 M6 Custer City Oklahoma
45 J1 Custoza Italy
138 F4 Cutana S Australia
101 N1 Cut Bank Montana
117 O8 Cutbank R Alberta
119 P5 Cut Beaver L Sask
111 A8 Cuthand Cr Texas
112 C6 Cuthbert Georgia
98 H6 Cuthbert S Dakota
108 F3 Cuthbert Texas
140 E4 Cuthbert, Mt Queensland
45 J3 Cutigliano Italy
118 H6 Cut Knife Sask
102 E5 Cutler California
95 T9 Cutler Maine
120 H6 Cutler Ontario
116 H3 Cutler R Alaska
14 C3 Cuts, L Irish Rep
133 E4 Cutts France
139 H3 Cuttaburra R New S Wales
75 L8 Cuttack India
103 O8 Cutter Arizona
141 F7 Cutts Mts Queensland
81 H7 Cuvier Basin Indian Oc
142 A5 Cuvier,C W Australia
145 E2 Cuvier I New Zealand
87 C8 Cuvo R Angola
32 J5 Cuxhaven W Germany
68 H2 Cu Xu isld Vietnam
94 F5 Cuyahoga R Ohio
94 F5 Cuyahoga Falls Ohio
102 E6 Cuyama R California
71 E3 Cuyapo Luzon Philippines
71 E5 Cuyo isld Philippines
71 E5 Cuyo East Passage Philippines
71 E5 Cuyo West Passage Philippines
99 N3 Cuyuna Minnesota
128 G2 Cuyuni R Guyana
128 N2 Cuyu Tigni Nicaragua
128 D6 Cuzco Peru
128 E8 Cuzco mt Bolivia
42 H5 Čvrsnica mt Yugoslavia
8 C4 Cwmbran Wales
88 B3 Cyangugu Rwanda
31 H3 Cybinka Poland
Cyclades islds see Kiklàdhes Is
139 H9 Cygnet Tasmania
119 W2 Cygnet L Manitoba
118 E5 Cynthia Alberta
110 M3 Cynthiana Kentucky
110 G4 Cypress Illinois
111 C10 Cypress Louisiana
109 M6 Cypress Texas
111 A8 Cypress Cr Texas
109 N3 Cypress Cr., L Texas
118 H9 Cypress Hills Sask
118 G9 Cypress Hills Prov. Park Alberta
113 F9 Cypress L Florida
119 S9 Cypress River Manitoba
79 D4 Cyprus rep Mediterranean Sea
84 G4 Cyrenaica reg Libya
Cyrene see Shahhat
115 N5 Cyrus Field B N W Terr
22 E2 Cysoing France
31 H2 Czaplinek Poland
118 G6 Czar Alberta
31 M4 Czarna R Poland
31 K2 Czarne Poland
31 L3 Czarnków Poland
31 M6 Czarny Dunajec Poland
31 M6 Czchów Poland
31 J6 Czechoslovakia rep Europe
31 K3 Czempin Poland
31 O3 Czeremcha Poland
Czernowitz see Chernovtsy
31 K2 Czersk Poland
31 J3 Czerwiensk Poland
31 L5 Czestochowa Poland
31 J2 Człopa Poland
31 K2 Człuchów Poland
31 N3 Czyżew Poland
36 D2 Daaden W Germany
35 F2 Da'an China
71 F5 Daanbantayan Cebu Philippines
122 B7 Daaquam Quebec
59 H3 Daba China
79 F7 Dabab, J. Ed mt Jordan
127 J9 Dabajuro Venezuela
85 D7 Dabakala Ivory Coast
58 D4 Daban Shan mt China
86 A2 Dabaro Somalia
58 D5 Daba Shan mts China
86 G3 Dabat Ethiopia
128 C2 Dabeiba Colombia
68 C4 Dabein Burma
33 P5 Dabel E Germany
74 E7 Dabhoi India
18 H2 Dabie Poland
58 D4 Dabie Shan mts China
36 C6 Dabo France
85 B6 Dabola Guinea
85 D7 Dabou Ivory Coast
85 D7 Daboya Ghana
36 C1 Dabringhausen W Germany
31 O2 Dąbrowa Poland
31 M2 Dąbrówno Poland
65 D7 Dabu China
67 E4 Dabu China
65 F2 Dabusu Pao L China
75 O7 Dacca Bangladesh
65 C5 Dachang China
37 L7 Dachau W Germany
37 L7 Dachauer Moos marshes W Germany
37 K4 Dachsbach W Germany
38 J7 Dachstein mt Austria
38 J7 Dachstein-Gebirge mts Austria
31 J6 Dačice Czechoslovakia
107 M5 Dacoma Oklahoma
128 G3 Dadanawa Guyana
79 H2 Dādāte Syria
78 D1 Daday Turkey
113 E9 Dade City Florida
111 L9 Dadeville Alabama
74 B4 Dadhar Pakistan
65 D7 Dadian China
65 G3 Dadianzi China
71 C3 Dadi, Tg C W Irian
68 J1 Dadong China
18 G9 Dadou R France
27 H11 Dådran Sweden
74 E8 Dadra & Nagar Haveli Union Terr India
74 G4 Dadri India
74 B5 Dadu Pakistan
68 H7 Da Dung R Vietnam
48 L6 Dăeni Romania
65 C4 Da'erhao China
140 D7 Daer,Mt N Terr Australia
71 F3 Daet Philippines
58 G5 Dafang China
80 F1 Dafna Israel
119 N7 Dafoe Sask
83 B4 Daga R Burma
86 H4 Dagabur Ethiopia
27 C11 Dagali Norway
85 A5 Dagana Senegal
47 K5 Dagardı Turkey
71 A1 Dagasuli Indonesia
30 D1 Dagebüll W Germany
9 G4 Dagenham England
53 G11 Dagestan A.S.S.R U.S.S.R.
102 H7 Daggett California
99 T4 Daggett Michigan
78 K3 Daghgharah, Al Iraq
27 G12 Daglösen Sweden
98 B1 Dagmar Montana
25 D5 Dagu China
67 A3 Daguan China
71 E2 Dagupan Luzon Philippines
94 J5 Dagus Mines Pennsylvania
68 A2 Dagwin Burma
141 G4 Dagworth Queensland
66 E6 Dagzê China
79 E10 Dahab Egypt
117 L4 Dahadinni R N W Terr
67 D5 Dahao Dao isld China
65 J1 Dahezhen China
59 H2 Da Hinggan Ling mt ra China
86 H2 Dahlak Arch Ethiopia
86 H2 Dahlak Kebir I Ethiopia
32 G10 Dahle W Germany
36 B3 Dahlem W Germany
33 R10 Dahlen E Germany
33 N6 Dahlenburg W Germany
33 S8 Dahlewitz E Germany
95 K8 Dahlgren Virginia
112 C3 Dahlonega Georgia
33 S9 Dahme E Germany
33 O4 Dahme W Germany
33 T8 Dahme R E Germany
33 R5 Dahmen E Germany
33 O4 Dahmeshöved W Germany
36 D5 Dahn W Germany
72 F3 Dahnā, Ad reg Saudi Arabia
78 J3 Dahok Iraq
Dahomey rep see Benin, Rep. of
66 B4 Dahongliutan China
65 E4 Dahongqi China
67 D1 Dahong Shan mts China
84 F4 Dāhra Libya
33 N7 Dähre E Germany
78 J3 Dahuk Iraq
65 E4 Dahushan China
139 G5 Dahwilly New S Wales
71 O8 Dai isld Indonesia
48 K7 Daia Romania
65 C5 Daicheng China
65 B4 Dai Hai L China
68 C4 Daik-U Burma
75 J4 Dailekh Nepal
121 T3 Daillebout, L Quebec
60 G9 Daimanji-san mt Japan
16 E5 Daimiel Spain
109 N2 Daingerfield Texas
61 K10 Dainichiga-take peak Japan
66 F5 Dainkog China
143 B9 Daintree W Australia
141 H3 Daintree Queensland
141 H3 Daintree R Queensland
61 K11 Daiō Japan
66 E5 Daiqin Tal China
126 G5 Daiquiri Cuba
Dairen see Lüda
84 J4 Dairût Egypt
100 D7 Dairy Oregon
60 G10 Daisen mt Japan
60 G10 Dai sen-Oki Nat. Park Japan
109 N5 Daisetta Texas
67 G1 Dai Shan isld China
129 K5 Dais Irmaos, Serra mts Brazil
100 G1 Daisy Washington
58 F4 Dai Xian China
Daiyue see Shanyin
67 D4 Daiyun Shan mts China
127 J5 Dajabón Dom Rep
140 E5 Dajarra Queensland
58 D5 Dajin Chuan R China
67 G2 Dajing China
48 E5 Daja Yugoslavia
70 D5 Daju Kalimantan
85 A6 Dakar Senegal
67 D4 Dakengkou China
67 D4 Dakengkou China
68 H5 Dak Gle Vietnam
85 A4 Dakhla Mauritania
84 A4 Dakhla Western Sahara
84 H4 Dakhla Oasis Egypt
68 H5 Dak Kon Vietnam
69 A9 Dakoank Nicobar Is
85 F6 Dakoro Niger
99 R7 Dakota Illinois
99 P6 Dakota Minnesota
99 M7 Dakota City Iowa
98 K7 Dakota City Nebraska
46 E2 Dakovica Yugoslavia
48 E5 Dakovo Yugoslavia
28 D3 Dal Denmark
27 E11 Dal Norway
87 D8 Dala Angola
27 J11 Dalå L Sweden
41 L3 Dalaas Tal Austria
85 B6 Dalaba Guinea
65 A4 Dalad Qi China
Dalai see Da'an
Dalai Nor L see Hulun Nur
58 G3 Dalai Nur L China
65 C3 Dalai Nur L China
27 G11 Dala-Järna Sweden
78 B3 Dalaman R Turkey
58 D3 Dalandzadgad Mongolia
71 E5 Dalanganem islds Philippines
58 E2 Dalanjargalan Mongolia
85 C6 Dalarö Sweden
70 B3 Dalat Sarawak
68 J7 Da Lat Vietnam
74 B5 Dalbandin Pakistan
15 E6 Dalbeattie Scotland
27 F13 Dalbosjön L Sweden
28 F5 Dalby Denmark
12 D5 Dalby I of Man U.K.
141 K7 Dalby Queensland
27 F11 Dalby Sweden
28 E3 Dalbyneder Denmark
28 E3 Dalbyover Denmark
110 K3 Dale Indiana
27 A10 Dale Norway
27 A11 Dale Norway
100 G5 Dale Oregon
94 J6 Dale Pennsylvania
109 K6 Dale Texas
8 A4 Dale Wales
118 D8 Dalemead Alberta
143 B9 Dale,Mt W Australia
25 G3 Dalen Netherlands
28 B7 Daler Denmark
28 F6 Daleszyce Poland
68 A3 Dalet Burma
68 A2 Dalet R Burma
68 A2 Daletme Burma
110 L1 Daleville Indiana
27 H10 Dalfors Sweden
25 F4 Dalfsen Netherlands
143 B8 Dalgaranger,Mt W Australia
139 J6 Dalgety New S Wales
12 E1 Dalginross Scotland
141 F5 Dalgonally Queensland
108 B7 Dalhart Texas
114 G3 Dalhousie, C N W Terr
65 A7 Dali China
Dalian see Lüda
58 D6 Daliang Shan China
65 E5 Dalian Wan B China
71 G7 Daliao Philippines
106 D7 Dalies New Mexico
65 A6 Dali He R China
Dalinghe see Jin Xian
80 D3 Daliyat el Karmil Israel
65 G4 Dalizi China
48 E5 Dalj Yugoslavia
15 E5 Dalkeith Scotland
14 E3 Dalkey Irish Rep
141 K7 Dallarnil Queensland
111 M8 Dallas Georgia
119 U7 Dallas Manitoba
100 B5 Dallas Oregon
109 N10 Dallas Texas
99 P4 Dallas Wisconsin
94 E6 Dallas Center Iowa
99 P9 Dallas City Illinois
95 L7 Dallastown Pennsylvania
102 D4 Dallas Warner Res California
100 D4 Dalles, The Oregon
117 G8 Dall I Alaska
116 F6 Dall L Alaska
116 N3 Dall Mt Alaska
85 E6 Dallol Bosso watercourse Niger
77 C7 Dalmā isld U.A.E.
133 E4 Dalmacio Velez Sarsfield Argentina
12 D1 Dalmally Scotland
42 G4 Dalmatia reg Yugoslavia
55 D3 Dalmatovo U.S.S.R.
12 D3 Dalmellington Scotland
118 L6 Dalmeny Sask
28 G6 Dalmose Denmark
12 D2 Dalmuir Scotland
59 L3 Dal'negorsk U.S.S.R.
52 F6 Dal'ne-Konstantinovo U.S.S.R.
59 K2 Dal'nerechensk U.S.S.R.
52 E1 Dal'niye Zelentsy U.S.S.R.
85 C7 Daloa Ivory Coast
67 C5 Dalongdong Shuiku res China
67 B3 Dalou Shan mt ra China
121 M4 Dalquier Quebec
118 D7 Dalroy Alberta
15 D5 Dalry Dumfries & Galloway Scotland
15 D5 Dalry Strathclyde Scotland
141 H4 Dalrymple Queensland
15 D5 Dalrymple Scotland
141 J5 Dalrymple,Mt Queensland
29 K11 Dalsbruk Finland
13 F4 Dalston England
112 C3 Dalton Georgia
95 O4 Dalton Massachusetts
98 D8 Dalton Nebraska
120 F4 Dalton Ontario
95 M5 Dalton Pennsylvania
13 E3 Dalton Scotland
75 L6 Daltonganj India
146 G2 Dalton Iceberg Tongue Antarctica
115 R4 Dalton, Kap C Greenland
69 E12 Daludalu Sumatra
65 F5 Dalu Dao isld China
28 E6 Dalum Denmark
68 E2 Daluo China
65 H2 Daluolemi China
65 G1 Daluozhen China
71 G4 Dalupiri Philippines
71 E1 Dalupiri isld Philippines
141 K8 Dalveen Queensland
12 E3 Dalveen P Scotland
143 B9 Dalwallinu W Australia
15 D4 Dalwhinnie Scotland
37 M6 Dalwigksthal W Germany
136 G4 Daly R N Terr Australia
140 B2 Daly R N Terr Aust
140 B2 Daly River N Terr Aust
140 B3 Daly Waters N Terr Aust
98 D5 Dalzell S Dakota
74 E8 Daman India
79 A7 Damanhûr Egypt
65 C4 Damaqun Shan mt ra China
107 L2 Damar Kansas
71 B3 Damar isld Indonesia
71 O8 Damar isld Indonesia
86 C5 Damara Cent Afr Republic
87 C10 Damaraland reg Namibia
95 S2 Damariscotta L Maine
Damas see Damascus
110 D6 Damascus Arkansas
95 K7 Damascus Maryland
79 G5 Damascus Syria
94 F10 Damascus Virginia
131 B5 Damas, Paso de las Chile/Arg
86 B3 Damaturu Nigeria
77 C2 Damavand Iran
87 C7 Damba Angola
72 C2 Dambach France
36 C7 Dambach France
83 K10 Dambulla Sri Lanka
126 G5 Dame Marie Haiti
77 D1 Dāmghān Iran
28 A4 Dammhus Å R Denmark
65 D3 Damiao China
48 L4 Dămieneşti Romania
20 F5 Damigni France
65 C3 Daming China
67 C5 Daming Shan mts China
80 F5 Damiya Jordan
80 F5 Damiya Br Jordan
71 E8 Dammai isld Philippines
72 D3 Dammam, Ad Saudi Arabia
20 J5 Dammarie France
18 G3 Dammartin-en-Goële France
22 E1 Damme Belgium
32 H7 Damme W Germany
74 H4 Damoh India
109 M6 Damon Texas
85 D7 Damongo Ghana
86 A2 Damot Ethiopia
79 F5 Damour Lebanon
70 F4 Dampelas, Tg C Celebes
22 K4 Dampicourt Belgium
142 B5 Dampier W Australia
142 B5 Dampier Arch W Australia
142 E3 Dampier Land pen W Australia
40 C2 Dampierre-sur-Saône France
71 C3 Dampier, Selat str W Irian
70 O10 Dampit Java
28 J7 Damsholte Denmark
19 J3 Damvillers France
20 H4 Damville France

22 J5 Dâmvillers France
112 H1 Dan *R* N Carolina
94 J10 Dan *R* Virginia
99 S9 Dana Illinois
110 J2 Dana Indiana
79 F8 Danā Jordan
119 M6 Dana Sask
71 K10 Dana *isld* Indonesia
69 F12 Danai Sumatra
86 H3 Danakil *tribal dist* Ethiopia
86 H4 Danan Ethiopia
85 C7 Danané Ivory Coast
68 J4 Da Nang Vietnam
75 L6 Danapur India
116 G9 Dana Vol Alaska
58 D5 Danba China
95 O5 Danbury Connecticut
98 F9 Danbury Nebraska
95 Q3 Danbury New Hampshire
109 M6 Danbury Texas
99 O4 Danbury Wisconsin
103 J7 Danby California
103 J7 Danby L California
119 T6 Dancing Point Manitoba
143 E9 Dandaragan W Australia
74 J4 Dandel Dhura Nepal
76 E3 Dandeli India
139 H7 Dandenong Victoria
59 H3 Dandong China
74 E2 Dandot Pakistan
121 Q5 Dandurand, L Quebec
99 R6 Dane Wisconsin
147 E10 Daneborg Greenland
109 L6 Danevang Texas
65 A8 Danfeng China
67 E6 Dangan Liedao *isld* China
57 E5 Dangara U.S.S.R.
65 J2 Dangbizhen China
Dangcheng *see* Xiangshan
21 G8 Dangé France
20 H5 Dangeau France
89 A10 Danger Pt S Africa
20 F5 Dangeul France
66 F4 Dang He *R* China
86 G3 Dangila Ethiopia
68 G5 Dangrek, Chaine des *mts* Cambodia
65 C7 Dangshan China
67 F1 Dangtu China
20 J3 Dangu France
67 D1 Dangyang China
68 J7 Da Nhim *R* Vietnam
113 G11 Dania Florida
101 P7 Daniel Wyoming
42 E2 Daniele del Friuli, S Italy
122 D3 Daniel-Johnston Dam Quebec
143 D10 Daniell W Australia
144 D5 Daniells, L New Zealand
123 P3 Daniel's Cove Nfld
115 O7 Daniels Har Nfld
118 J1 Daniels L Ontario
95 Q5 Danielson Connecticut
112 D3 Danielsville Georgia
52 F5 Danilov U.S.S.R.
42 J6 Danilov Grad Yugoslavia
52 J3 Danilovka U.S.S.R.
55 F4 Danilovka U.S.S.R.
52 E3 Danilovo U.S.S.R.
58 F4 Daning China
67 C1 Daningchang China
Danjiang *see* Leishan
68 J6 Dankia Vietnam
67 A1 Danleng China
98 H8 Dannebrog Nebraska
115 Q4 Dannebrogs Ø *isld* Greenland
28 G7 Dannemare Denmark
95 O2 Dannemora New York
27 J11 Dannemora Sweden
33 O6 Dannenberg W Germany
33 S6 Dannenwalde E Germany
100 H7 Danner Oregon
145 F4 Dannevirke New Zealand
70 D4 Danompari Kalimantan
68 E4 Dan Sai Thailand
144 C6 Danseys Pass New Zealand
67 E5 Danshui China
68 B4 Danson B Burma
94 C4 Dansville Michigan
94 K4 Dansville New York
86 B1 Dante Somalia
94 E10 Dante Virginia
76 E1 Dantewara India
Dantu *see* Zhenjiang
Danube *R* Bulgaria/Yugoslavia *see* Dunav *R*
Danube *R* Czechoslovakia *see* Dunaj *R*
Danube *R* Hungary *see* Duna *R*
Danube *R* Romania *see* Dunărea *R*
Danube *R* W Germany/Austria *see* Donau *R*
68 B4 Danubyu Burma
110 G1 Danvers Illinois
99 L4 Danvers Minnesota
101 Q2 Danvers Montana
110 C6 Danville Arkansas
112 D5 Danville Georgia
99 T9 Danville Illinois
110 K2 Danville Indiana
95 R2 Danville Maine
94 E6 Danville Ohio
95 L6 Danville Pennsylvania
121 S7 Danville Quebec
95 P2 Danville Vermont
94 H10 Danville Virginia
94 F8 Danville W Virginia
20 D4 Danvou France
67 C7 Dan Xian China
67 F1 Danyang China
21 H6 Danzé France
67 B3 Danzhai China
67 C5 Danzhu China
Danzig *see* Gdańsk
98 G3 Danzig N Dakota
Danzig, G. of *see* Gdańska, Zatoka
71 E5 Dao Panay Philippines
16 B4 Dão *R* Portugal
67 B6 Dao Bach Long Vi *isld* Vietnam
Daokou *see* Hua Xian
21 D6 Daon France
74 G5 Daosa India
Daoud *see* Aïn Beïda
18 C4 Daoulas France
85 D3 Daoura *watercourse* Algeria/Morocco
67 D4 Dao Xian China
67 B2 Daozhen China
71 G6 Dapa Philippines
85 E6 Dapango Togo
111 J11 Daphne Alabama
71 F6 Dapiak, Mt Philippines
65 E4 Dapingfang China
71 F6 Dapitan Philippines
74 E10 Dapoli India
118 D4 Dapp Alberta
66 F4 Da Qaidam China
65 E5 Daqin Dao *isld* China
65 A4 Daqing Shan *mt ra* China
65 B4 Daqing Shan *mts* China
Daqin Tal *see* Naiman Qi
67 G1 Daqu Shan *isld* China
85 A5 Dara Senegal
77 D5 Dārāb Iran
48 K2 Dărăbani Romania
71 F5 Daraga Philippines
85 G2 Daraj Libya
71 G5 Daram *isld* Philippines
77 B3 Daran Iran
48 D5 Darány Hungary
70 C5 Darap Kalimantan
46 D2 Daravice *mt* Yugoslavia
85 G6 Darazo Nigeria
52 B6 Darbėnai U.S.S.R.
101 L3 Darby Montana
116 F4 Darby C Alaska
116 F4 Darby Mts Alaska
33 N6 Darchau E Germany
142 E3 D'Arcole Is W Australia
117 M10 D'Arcy Br Col
118 J7 D'Arcy Sask
110 C6 Dardanelle Arkansas
102 E3 Dardanelle California
Dardanelles Turkey *see* Çanakkale Boğazi
33 N9 Dardesheim E Germany
141 J8 Dareel Town Queensland
Dar el Beida *see* Casablanca
86 D4 Dar-el-Kouti *dist* Cent Afr Republic
88 G5 Dar es Salaam Tanzania
144 D5 Darfield New Zealand
Darfur *prov* Sudan *see* Northern and Southern Darfur *provs*
74 D1 Dargai Pakistan
57 B4 Darganata U.S.S.R.
145 D1 Dargaville New Zealand
20 J1 Dargnies France
139 H6 Dargo Victoria
33 R5 Dargun E Germany
58 E2 Darhan Mongolia
59 F3 Darhan Muminggan Lianheqi China
112 F6 Darien Georgia
126 F10 Darién, G.del Colombia/Panama
125 Q5 Darién, Serranía del *ra* Panama
71 E2 Darigayos Pt Luzon Philippines
125 L3 Darío Nicaragua
66 D6 Darjeeling India
143 B10 Darkan W Australia
138 D5 Darke Peak S Australia
77 A4 Darkhazineh Iran
138 F5 Darling *R* S Australia
139 J3 Darling Downs Queensland
141 J8 Darling Downs *reg* Queensland
119 T9 Darlingford Manitoba
115 M1 Darling Pen N W Terr
13 G5 Darlington England
101 M6 Darlington Idaho
99 M9 Darlington Missouri
112 H3 Darlington S Carolina
99 Q7 Darlington Wisconsin
139 H5 Darlington Pt New S Wales
143 D8 Darlot, L W Australia
31 J1 Darłowo Poland
48 K3 Dărmănești Romania
77 F3 Darmiān Iran
118 L8 Darmody Sask
36 F4 Darmstadt W Germany
84 G3 Darnah Libya
111 E9 Darnell Louisiana
20 H3 Darnetal France
139 G5 Darnick New S Wales
114 G4 Darnley B N W Terr
146 B4 Darnley, C Antarctica
17 G3 Daroda Spain
48 J1 Darokhov U.S.S.R.
52 G5 Darovskoye U.S.S.R.
141 G6 Darr Queensland
141 G6 Darr *R* Queensland
141 K2 Darra *sub* Brisbane, Qnsld
77 F1 Darreh Gaz Iran
100 D1 Darrington Washington
86 A1 Darror *R* Somalia
86 D4 Dar Rounga *reg* Cent Afr Republic
108 D7 Darrouzett Texas
76 D3 Darsi India
30 G1 Darsser Ort *C* E Germany
146 J10 Dart, C Antarctica
9 G5 Dartford England
138 F7 Dartmoor Victoria
8 C6 Dartmoor Forest England
8 C7 Dartmouth England
122 J9 Dartmouth Nova Scotia
141 H7 Dartmouth *L* Queensland
122 H4 Dartmouth R Quebec
8 C6 Dart, R England
14 C2 Dartry Mts Irish Rep
136 J3 Daru Papua New Guinea
66 E5 Darum Tso *L* China
42 H3 Daruvar Yugoslavia
15 D5 Darvel Scotland
70 F2 Darvel B Sabah
58 B2 Darvi Mongolia
13 F6 Darwen England
77 J4 Darweshan Afghanistan
102 G5 Darwin California
140 B1 Darwin N Terr Aust
88 C10 Darwin Zimbabwe
133 C7 Darwin, Can *str* Chile
77 G4 Daryacheh *L* Iran
56 A1 Dar'yegan *R* U.S.S.R.
77 C7 Dās *isld* U.A.E.
22 L3 Dasburg W Germany
67 C1 Dashennongjia *mt* China
65 A4 Dashetai China
Dashiqiao *see* Yingkou
65 E1 Dashizhai China
77 E1 Dasht Iran
77 H7 Dasht *R* Pakistan
77 C2 Dasht-e-Kavir Iran
77 G7 Dashtiari Iran
65 C3 Dashui Nur China
120 J9 Dashwood Ontario
37 L7 Dasing W Germany
71 E7 Dassalan *isld* Philippines
99 M4 Dassel Minnesota
32 L9 Dassel W Germany
33 N5 Dassow E Germany
77 E2 Dastgardān Iran
70 D4 Datagenojang Kalimantan
65 C4 Datan China
68 J1 Datang China
47 J8 Datça Turkey
9 F5 Datchet England
60 O3 Date Japan
103 L7 Date Cr Arizona
103 L9 Dateland Arizona
74 H6 Datia India
67 F4 Datian China
106 C7 Datil New Mexico
67 F1 Datong China
67 F1 Datong Heilongjiang China
65 B4 Datong Shanxi China
58 C4 Datong Shan *mt ra* China
140 F6 Datson,Mt Queensland
59 M2 Datta U.S.S.R.
32 F9 Datteln W Germany
70 E3 Datumakuta Kalimantan
65 J2 Daubikhe *R* U.S.S.R.
74 D2 Daud Khel India
32 K7 Dauelsen W Germany
115 N1 Daugaard Jensen Land Greenland
28 D5 Daūgård Denmark
52 C6 Daugav'pils U.S.S.R.
77 K1 Daulatabad Afghanistan
74 F9 Daulatabad India
77 J2 Daulat Yar Afghanistan
128 C4 Daule Ecuador
41 M3 Daumen *mt* W Germany
21 E6 Daumeray France
36 B3 Daun W Germany
68 C6 Daung Kyun *isld* Burma
119 R7 Dauphin Manitoba
95 L6 Dauphin Pennsylvania
19 O14 Dauphiné *prov* France
111 H11 Dauphin I Alabama
119 S7 Dauphin L Manitoba
85 F6 Daura Nigeria
15 E3 Dava Scotland
76 B3 Davangere India
71 G7 Davao Mindanao Philippines
71 G7 Davao Gulf Mindanao Philippines
12 C3 Davarr I Scotland
147 F10 Dave *isld* Greenland
121 S6 Daveluyville Quebec
22 D4 Davenescourt France
121 M4 Davengus Quebec
116 J5 Davenport Alaska
102 B4 Davenport California
113 F9 Davenport Florida
99 Q8 Davenport Iowa
98 J9 Davenport Nebraska
95 N4 Davenport New York
107 O6 Davenport Oklahoma
100 G2 Davenport Washington
141 F6 Davenport Downs Queensland
140 A6 Davenport Hills N Terr Aust
140 B5 Davenport,Mt N Terr Aust
140 C5 Davenport Ra N Terr Aust
9 E3 Daventry England
80 E3 Daverat Israel
32 K7 Daverden W Germany
125 N5 David Panama
146 E2 David *isld* Antarctica
98 J8 David City Nebraska
112 G2 Davidson N Carolina
107 L7 Davidson Oklahoma
119 M7 Davidson Sask
140 B5 Davidson,Mt N Terr Aust
116 Q2 Davidson Mts Alaska
8 B6 Davidstow England
113 G11 Davie Florida
138 A2 Davies, Mt S Australia
26 A10 Davik Norway
109 K5 Davilla Texas
119 N8 Davin Sask
102 C3 Davis California
99 R7 Davis Illinois
107 N7 Davis Oklahoma
119 M5 Davis Sask
98 K6 Davis S Dakota
94 H7 Davis W Virginia
146 H3 Davis B Antarctica
112 E5 Davisboro Georgia
99 N9 Davis City Iowa
100 E8 Davis Creek California
103 K6 Davis Dam Arizona
115 N6 Davis Inlet Labrador
94 H7 Davis, Mt Pennsylvania
108 C5 Davis Mts Texas
94 D3 Davison Michigan
146 D3 Davis Sea Antarctica
115 O4 Davis Str Greenland/Canada
110 E4 Davisville Missouri
55 C4 Davlekanovo U.S.S.R.
41 L4 Davos Switzerland
94 F9 Davy W Virginia
143 D9 Davyhurst W Australia
65 E4 Dawa China
65 F3 Dawa China
86 H5 Dawa *R* Ethiopia
65 C6 Dawenkou China
141 K6 Dawes Ra Queensland
68 D4 Dawlan Burma
8 C6 Dawlish England
110 C2 Dawn Missouri
108 E1 Dawn Texas
68 C4 Dawna Ra Burma
111 M10 Dawson Georgia
98 K5 Dawson Minnesota
98 G3 Dawson N Dakota
106 F5 Dawson New Mexico
107 P5 Dawson Oklahoma
109 L4 Dawson Texas
117 D3 Dawson Yukon Terr
141 J6 Dawson *R* Queensland
119 R6 Dawson Bay Manitoba
117 N8 Dawson Creek Br Columbia
114 H5 Dawson Landing N W Terr
117 Q5 Dawson Lodge N W Terr
117 P10 Dawson, Mt Br Columbia
117 D4 Dawson Range Yukon Terr
110 J4 Dawson Springs Kentucky
111 M7 Dawsonville Georgia
67 E1 Dawu China
18 E9 Dax France
67 B1 Da Xian China
68 H1 Daxin China
65 E6 Daxindian China
65 C5 Daxing China
59 J3 Daxinggou China
36 E5 Daxlanden W Germany
67 C4 Daxu China
67 C5 Daxuan China
Daxue *see* Wencheng
58 D4 Daxue Shan *mt ra* China
58 D5 Daxue Shan *mt* China
67 F3 Daxu Shan *pass* China
100 D8 Day California
113 D7 Day Florida
57 B4 Dayakhatyn U.S.S.R.
65 F4 Dayang He *R* China
67 C5 Dayao Shan *mts* China
67 E5 Daya Wan *B* China
143 C8 Day Dawn W Australia
67 E1 Daye China
67 A1 Dayi China
67 E4 Dayi China
Dayishan *see* Guanyun
139 G6 Daylesford Victoria
102 G5 Daylight Pass California
133 F4 Dayman *R* Uruguay
131 F3 Dayman, Cuchilla del *mts* Uruguay
143 D9 Day, Mt W Australia
67 C2 Dayong China
100 B7 Days Creek Oregon
118 E3 Daysland Alberta
99 M7 Dayton Iowa
94 J4 Dayton New York
94 C7 Dayton Ohio
94 H6 Dayton Pennsylvania
112 B2 Dayton Tennessee
109 N5 Dayton Texas
100 H3 Dayton Washington
101 S5 Dayton Wyoming
113 F8 Daytona Beach Florida
67 E4 Dayu China
67 E4 Dayu Ling *mt* China
100 F5 Dayville Oregon
98 H2 Dazey N Dakota
67 F4 Dazhang Xi *R* China
67 B1 Dazhu China
47 K7 Dazkırı Turkey
67 B2 Dazu China
89 D8 De Aar S Africa
99 T3 Dead *R* Michigan
116 N1 Deadhorse Alaska
101 Q5 Dead Indian Pk Wyoming
111 L11 Dead L Florida
103 H7 Deadman L California
113 D8 Deadmans B Florida
126 G3 Deadman's Cay Long I Bahamas
103 K6 Dead Mts Cal/Nev
95 R1 Dead R Maine
80 E8 Dead Sea Israel/Jordan
95 R8 Deadwater L Maine
98 C5 Deadwood S Dakota
100 K5 Deadwood Res Idaho
140 C2 Deaf Adder Cr N Terr Aust
143 G9 Deakin W Australia
140 B4 Deakin,Mt N Terr Aust
9 H5 Deal England
95 L8 Deale Maryland
139 H7 Deal I Tasmania
95 M8 Deal Island Maryland
58 G6 De'an China
110 D1 Dean Iowa
117 K9 Dean Ch Br Columbia
141 H5 Deane,Mt Queensland
8 D4 Dean, Forest of England
131 D3 Deán Funes Argentina
143 E10 Dean,Mt W Australia
117 L9 Dean R Br Columbia
95 M4 Deansboro New York
94 D4 Dearborn Michigan
110 B2 Dearborn Missouri
107 P4 Dearing Kansas
100 J3 Deary Idaho
114 G4 Dease Arm *B* N W Terr
116 K1 Dease Inlet Alaska
117 J6 Dease Lake Br Col
147 G2 Dease Str N W Terr
102 G5 Death Valley California
20 F3 Deauville France
101 R5 Deaver Wyoming
70 B4 Debak Sarawak
54 K8 Debal'tsevo U.S.S.R.
67 B5 Debao China
46 D3 Debar Yugoslavia
116 H4 Debauch Mt Alaska
84 J6 Debba, Ed Sudan
118 L5 Debden Sask
127 O3 Débé Trinidad
122 E7 Debec New Brunswick
9 H3 Debenham England
9 H3 Deben, R England
106 B2 De Beque Colorado
109 N3 De Berry Texas
52 H5 Debessy U.S.S.R.
31 N5 Dębica Poland
31 N4 Dęblin Poland
31 K1 Dębnica Kaszubska Poland
31 H3 Dębno Poland
85 D5 Débó, L Mali
143 C9 Deborah,L W Australia
116 O5 Deborah, Mt Alaska
142 F3 Deborah,Mt W Australia
100 K2 De Borgia Montana
86 G4 Debra Birhan Ethiopia
86 G3 Debra Markos Ethiopia
86 G3 Debra Tabor Ethiopia
48 F6 Debrc Yugoslavia
48 G3 Debrecen Hungary
71 E2 Debutunan Pt Luzon Philippines
86 G2 Decamere Ethiopia
46 D2 Dečani Yugoslavia
111 K7 Decatur Alabama
110 B5 Decatur Arkansas
111 M8 Decatur Georgia
99 S10 Decatur Illinois
110 H2 Decatur Illinois
94 C6 Decatur Indiana
99 N9 Decatur Iowa
94 B4 Decatur Michigan
111 G9 Decatur Mississippi
98 K7 Decatur Nebraska
109 K2 Decatur Texas
110 H6 Decaturville Tennessee
18 G8 Decazeville France
76 C4 Deccan *plat* India
121 M5 Decelles, Lac Quebec
115 M5 Déception Quebec
89 C3 Deception *watercourse* Botswana
Dechen Dzong *see* Dagzê
122 E2 Dechêne, L Quebec
110 K6 Decherd Tennessee
22 E3 Dechy France
118 F1 Decimal Manitoba
43 B9 Decimomannu Sardinia
31 H5 Děčín Czechoslovakia
117 F7 Decision, C Alaska
18 H6 Decize France
110 J3 Decker Indiana
119 R8 Decker Manitoba
101 T4 Decker Montana
106 E2 Deckers Colorado
25 C2 De Cocksdorp Netherlands
140 C1 De Courcy Hd N Terr Aust
48 E4 Decs Hungary
48 J4 Deda Romania
9 E4 Deddington England
Dedéagach *see* Alexandroúpolis
33 N8 Dedeleben E Germany
33 T6 Dedelow E Germany
99 M8 Dedham Iowa
46 E3 Dedino Yugoslavia
130 F9 Dedo de Deus *mt* Brazil
85 D6 Dedougou Upper Volta
52 C6 Dedovichi U.S.S.R.
100 B9 Dedrick California
83 J10 Deduru Oya *R* Sri Lanka
56 E1 Dedushka, Porog *falls* U.S.S.R.
88 E9 Dedza Malawi
15 F3 Dee *R* Scotland
141 K6 Deeford Queensland
14 C4 Deel *R* Irish Rep
112 H2 Deep *R* N Carolina
Deep Bay Malawi *see* Chilumba
122 G9 Deep Brook Nova Scotia
100 J7 Deep Cr Idaho
94 H7 Deep Creek L Maryland
103 L2 Deep Creek Ra Utah
142 B5 Deepdale Western Australia
107 O6 Deep Fork *R* Oklahoma
112 F1 Deep Gap N Carolina
95 P5 Deep River Connecticut
99 O8 Deep River Iowa
121 N6 Deep River Ontario
100 B3 Deep River Washington
102 G4 Deep Sp California
110 C3 Deepwater Missouri
139 K3 Deepwater New S Wales Australia
140 C6 Deep Well N Terr Aust
110 C6 Deer Arkansas
8 C1 Dee, R England/Wales
12 E4 Dee, R Scotland
100 D9 Deer Cr California
99 L3 Deer Cr Minnesota
98 F9 Deer Cr Nebraska
101 T7 Deer Cr Wyoming
107 N5 Deer Creek Oklahoma
103 N1 Deer Cr.Res Utah
107 J3 Deerfield Kansas
113 G11 Deerfield Beach Florida
116 F9 Deer I Alaska
95 T2 Deer I Maine
122 F9 Deer I New Brunswick
116 F3 Deering Alaska
98 E1 Deering N Dakota
138 A2 Deering Hills S Australia
143 G7 Deering,Mt W Australia
123 P4 Deer Lake Nfld
22 E2 Deerlijk Belgium
101 N3 Deer Lodge Montana
111 H10 Deer Park Alabama
100 H2 Deer Park Washington
117 O11 Deer Pk Br Columbia
123 S5 Deer Pond Nfld
99 N2 Deer River Minnesota
99 T3 Deerton Michigan
106 F2 Deer Trail Colorado
99 N3 Deerwood Minnesota
111 F7 Deeson Mississippi
100 K8 Deeth Nevada
Defeng *see* Liping
38 F8 Defereggengeb *mt* Austria
38 F8 Defereggental *V* Austria
95 M2 Deferiet New York
133 F5 Defferrari Argentina
99 L8 Defiance Iowa
94 C5 Defiance Ohio
111 K11 De Funiak Springs Florida
16 B6 Degebe *R* Portugal
85 F8 Degema Nigeria
27 G12 Degerfors Sweden
37 O6 Deggendorf W Germany
36 H6 Deggingen W Germany
47 J6 Degirmendere Turkey
99 L4 De Graff Minnesota
110 N1 Degraff Ohio
111 C7 De Gray Res Arkansas
98 G5 De Grey S Dakota
142 C5 De Grey W Australia
142 D5 De Grey R W Australia
55 D3 Degtyarsk U.S.S.R.
22 E1 De Haan Belgium
77 C4 Deh Bid Iran
74 E8 Dehej India
85 G2 Dehibat Tunisia
74 H3 Dehra Dun India
75 L6 Dehri India
36 E3 Dehrn W Germany
77 F4 Deh Salm Iran
67 F4 Dehua China
59 J3 Dehui China
36 E5 Deidesheim W Germany
86 E4 Deim Zubeir Sudan
37 M5 Deining W Germany
25 E2 Deinum Netherlands
22 F2 Deinze Belgium
80 F4 Deir Abu Said Jordan
79 G4 Deir el Ahmar Lebanon
80 F4 Deir es Samadiya Jordan
78 H4 Deir ez Zor Syria
80 D5 Deir Istiya Jordan
80 E6 Deir Mar Jiryis Jordan
80 D4 Deir Sharal Jordan
79 G3 Deir Shemil Syria
32 K8 Deister *hills* W Germany
48 H3 Dej Romania
46 D3 Déja *mt* Albania
71 B2 Dejailolo, Selat *str* Indonesia
28 A5 Dejbjerg Denmark
27 F12 Deje Sweden
86 G3 Dejen Ethiopia
67 C2 Dejiang China
99 S8 De Kalb Illinois
111 H9 De Kalb Mississippi
109 N2 De Kalb Texas
95 M2 De Kalb Junc New York
51 O3 De Kastri U.S.S.R.
59 M1 De Kastries U.S.S.R.
86 D6 Dekese Zaïre
86 C4 Dekoa Cent Afr Republic
25 C2 De Koog Netherlands
25 C3 De Kooij Netherlands
111 G12 Delacroix Louisiana
106 F4 Delagua Colorado
100 J6 Delamar Idaho
103 K4 Delamar Mts Nevada
140 B3 Delamere N Terr Aust
113 F8 De Land Florida
102 E6 Delano California
103 M3 Delano Peak Utah
113 L9 Delaport New Providence I Bahamas
118 K4 Delaronde L Sask
110 G1 Delavan Illinois
99 S7 Delavan Wisconsin
94 D6 Delaware Ohio
107 P5 Delaware Oklahoma
107 P2 Delaware *R* Kansas
95 N5 Delaware *R* U.S.A.
95 M7 Delaware *state* U.S.A.
145 D4 Delaware B New Zealand
95 M7 Delaware B U.S.A.
95 M7 Delaware City Delaware
108 C4 Delaware Cr Texas/New Mex
94 D6 Delaware Res Ohio
118 E9 Del Bonita Alberta
32 J9 Delbrück W Germany
118 D6 Delburne Alberta
111 E12 Delcambre Louisiana
106 F4 Delcarbon Colorado
46 F3 Delčevo Yugoslavia
87 E8 Delcommune, L Zaïre
25 G4 Delden Netherlands
119 R9 Deleau Manitoba
139 J6 Delegate New S Wales
25 F2 De Leien Netherlands
40 F3 Delémont Switzerland
109 J3 De Leon Texas
29 H11 Delet Teili *chan* Finland
22 C2 Delettes France
102 B2 Delevan California
94 J4 Delevan New York
130 F7 Delfinópolis Brazil
25 B5 Delfshaven Netherlands
25 B4 Delft Netherlands
83 J8 Delft *isld* Sri Lanka
25 G2 Delfzijl Netherlands
100 A9 Delgada, Pt California
133 E6 Delgada, Pta Argentina
88 H7 Delgado, C Mozambique
58 D2 Delgerhaan Mongolia
86 F1 Delgo Sudan
74 G4 Delhi India
99 P7 Delhi Iowa
111 E9 Delhi Louisiana
107 L6 Delhi Oklahoma
120 K10 Delhi Ontario
70 K9 Deli *isld* Java
118 E7 Delia Alberta
107 P2 Delia Kansas
129 H3 Delices Fr Guiana
109 O1 Delight Arkansas
77 B3 Delijan Iran
46 E1 Deli Jovan *mt* Yugoslavia
118 K7 Delisle Sask
140 B2 Delissaville N Terr Aust
143 F8 Delisser Ra W Australia
69 D11 Delitua Sumatra
33 Q9 Delitzsch E Germany
110 F6 Dell Arkansas
101 N5 Dell Montana
36 C2 Dellbrück W Germany
40 E2 Delle France
101 N9 Delle Utah
103 L5 Dellenbaugh, Mt Arizona
26 J10 Dellen, N *L* Sweden
32 L9 Delligsen W Germany
100 B9 Del Loma California
98 K6 Dell Rapids S Dakota
107 L2 Dellvale Kansas
85 E1 Dellys Algeria
102 G9 Del Mar California
99 Q7 Delmar Iowa
95 M8 Delmar Maryland
118 J6 Delmas Sask
32 J6 Delmenhorst W Germany
130 H10 Delmiro Gouveia Brazil
98 H6 Delmont S Dakota
103 K4 Delmues Nevada
42 F3 Delnice Yugoslavia
106 D4 Del Norte Colorado
140 C6 Delny N Terr Aust
116 F2 De Long Mts Alaska
119 R9 Deloraine Manitoba
139 H8 Deloraine Tasmania
13 F6 Delph England
46 E6 Delphi Greece
110 K1 Delphi Indiana
107 N2 Delphos Kansas
94 C6 Delphos Ohio
113 G11 Delray Beach Florida
124 D2 Del Río Mexico
108 G6 Del Rio Texas
26 J10 Delsbo Sweden
106 B3 Delta Colorado
110 G4 Delta Missouri
94 C5 Delta Ohio
95 L7 Delta Pennsylvania
103 M2 Delta Utah
119 T8 Delta Beach Manitoba
141 F3 Delta Downs Queensland
116 O4 Delta Junction Alaska
102 C4 Delta Mendota Canal California
95 M3 Delta Res New York
95 L9 Deltaville Virginia
94 B4 Delton Michigan
139 K3 Delungra New S Wales
74 D8 Delvada India
109 K5 Del Valle Texas
32 K4 Delve W Germany
46 D5 Delvinákion Greece
46 D5 Delvinë Albania
108 G2 Delwin Texas
48 J2 Delyatin U.S.S.R.
55 B4 Dema *R* U.S.S.R.
118 K8 Demaine Sask
70 N9 Demak Java
16 E2 Demando, S. de la *mts* Spain
116 R2 Demarcation Pt Alaska
86 D7 Demba Zaïre
86 D4 Dembia Cent Afr Republic
86 F4 Dembi Dolo Ethiopia
74 H2 Demchok India
48 G2 Demecser Hungary
22 J2 Demer *R* Belgium
Demerara *see* Georgetown Guyana
54 C1 Demidov U.S.S.R.
55 D3 Demina U.S.S.R.
106 C9 Deming New Mexico
100 C1 Deming Washington
128 F3 Demini *R* Brazil
47 K5 Demirci Turkey
47 J6 Demirköprü Baraji *L* Turkey
47 J3 Demirköy Turkey
33 S5 Demmin E Germany
128 F5 Democracia Brazil
111 J9 Demopolis Alabama
143 E10 Dempster, Pt W Australia
50 G3 Dem'yanka *R* U.S.S.R.
52 D5 Demyansk U.S.S.R.
50 F3 Dem'yanskoye U.S.S.R.
22 E3 Denain France
116 O5 Denali Alaska
114 J7 Denare Beach Saskatchewan
57 E5 Denau U.S.S.R.
121 N7 Denbigh Ontario
8 C1 Denbigh Wales
Denbigh *co see* Clwyd and Gwynedd *counties*
116 G4 Denbigh, C Alaska
25 B5 Den Bommel Netherlands
25 C2 Den Burg Netherlands
68 E4 Den Chai Thailand
69 J14 Dendang Indonesia
22 G2 Dender *R* Belgium
22 G2 Denderleeuw Belgium
22 G1 Dendermonde Belgium
25 D3 Den Dever Netherlands
86 G4 Dendi *mt* Ethiopia
118 K8 Dendron Sask
25 H4 Denekamp Netherlands
55 C1 Denezhkin Kamen', G *mt* U.S.S.R.
65 B7 Dengfeng China
58 E3 Dengkou China
75 Q3 Dêngqên China
58 F5 Deng Xian China
65 C4 Dengyoufang China
65 E6 Dengzhou China
24 A2 Den Haag *conurbation* Netherlands
9 F4 Denham England
143 A7 Denham W Australia
142 G3 Denham *R* W Australia
140 E3 Denham I Queensland
141 J5 Denham Ra Queensland
143 A7 Denham Sd W Australia
111 F11 Denham Springs Louisiana
25 C3 Den Helder Netherlands
118 K6 Denholm Sask
13 F3 Denholm Scotland
17 G7 Denia Spain
138 C4 Denial Bay S Australia
122 C6 Deniau Quebec
139 G6 Deniliquin New S Wales
100 G7 Denio Oregon
99 L7 Denison Iowa
109 L2 Denison Texas
146 J3 Denison, C Antarctica
107 O8 Denison Dam Oklahoma
116 K7 Denison, Mt Alaska
142 G4 Denison Plains W Australia
141 J4 Denison Pt Queensland
55 D4 Denisovka Kazakhstan U.S.S.R.
52 J2 Denisovka Komi U.S.S.R.
83 K11 Deniyaya Sri Lanka
47 K7 Denizli Turkey
37 L6 Denkendorf W Germany
139 K4 Denman New S Wales
146 E3 Denman Gl Antarctica
122 J8 Denmark Nova Scotia
100 A7 Denmark Oregon
112 F4 Denmark S Carolina
143 B10 Denmark W Australia
99 T5 Denmark Wisconsin
28 Denmark *kingdom* N W Europe
115 R4 Denmark Str Greenland/Iceland
20 B3 Denneville France
33 S9 Dennewitz E Germany
83 J12 Dennis I Seychelles
94 F6 Dennison Ohio
95 R5 Dennis Port Massachusetts
144 C4 Denniston New Zealand
94 H10 Denniston Virginia
100 B9 Denny California
12 E1 Denny Scotland
12 E2 Dennyloanhead Scotland
95 U2 Dennysville Maine
70 P10 Denpasar Bali Indonesia
13 F5 Dent England
100 J3 Dent Idaho
48 G5 Denta Romania
40 G5 Dent Blanche *mt* Switzerland
40 E5 Dent du Midi *mt* Switzerland
9 H5 Denton England
112 E6 Denton Georgia
94 E8 Denton Kentucky
95 M8 Denton Maryland
109 K2 Denton Texas
137 L3 D'Entrecasteaux Is Papua New Guinea
106 E2 Denver Colorado
100 J4 Denver Idaho
94 A6 Denver Indiana
99 O7 Denver Iowa
95 L6 Denver Pennsylvania
108 E3 Denver City Texas
118 H6 Denzil Sask
86 B4 Déo *R* Cameroon
74 G4 Deoband India
75 M6 Deogarh India
68 J4 Deo Hai Van Vietnam
74 E9 Deolali India
68 J6 Deo Ma Vietnam
22 D1 De Panne Belgium
25 E5 De Peel Netherlands
99 S5 De Pere Wisconsin
94 J4 Depew New York
107 O6 Depew Oklahoma
65 C6 Deping China
22 F2 De Pinte Belgium
70 L9 Depok Java
109 M2 Deport Texas
95 M4 Deposit New York
128 F3 Depósito Brazil
95 Q4 Depot New Hampshire
120 K7 Depot Harbour Ontario
146 B5 Depot Pk Antarctica
86 D2 Depression du Murdi Chad
9 E5 Deptford England
142 C5 Depuch I W Australia
99 R8 Depue Illinois
25 G2 De Punt Netherlands
51 O2 Deputatskiy U.S.S.R.
58 C6 Dêqên China
67 D5 Deqing China
67 G1 Deqing China
111 B7 De Queen Arkansas
111 C11 De Quincy Louisiana
77 L5 Dera Bugti Pakistan
74 D3 Dera Ghazi Khan Pakistan
74 D3 Dera Ismail Khan Pakistan
48 L1 Derazhnya U.S.S.R.
33 Q8 Derben E Germany
78 M1 Derbent U.S.S.R.
52 H6 Derbeshkinskiy U.S.S.R.
86 D4 Derbisaka Cent Afr Republic
95 O5 Derby Connecticut
9 E2 Derby England
99 N9 Derby Iowa
107 N4 Derby Kansas
139 J8 Derby Tasmania
109 H7 Derby Texas
142 E3 Derby W Australia
95 P2 Derby Center Vermont
9 E1 Derbyshire *co* England
16 D9 Derdara Morocco
48 G3 Derecske Hungary
33 N8 Der Elm *hills* W Germany
33 N9 Derenburg E Germany
52 D4 Derevyanka U.S.S.R.
14 D2 Derg *R* N Ireland
54 H6 Dergachi U.S.S.R.
14 D2 Derg, L Irish Rep
32 H5 Der Hohe Weg *sandbank* W Germany
111 C11 De Ridder Louisiana
25 C3 De Rijp Netherlands
86 H5 Derkali Kenya
54 L8 Derkul *R* U.S.S.R.
47 G1 Dermantsi Bulgaria
37 J2 Dermbach E Germany
111 E8 Dermott Arkansas
Derna *see* Darnah
87 C11 Dernberg, C Namibia
32 M8 Derneburg W Germany
111 F12 Dernieres, Is Louisiana
138 C2 De Rose Hill S Australia
20 B3 Déroute, Passage de la France
14 D3 Derravaragh, L Irish Rep
Derry *see* Londonderry
95 Q4 Derry New Hampshire
106 C9 Derry New Mexico
94 H6 Derry Pennsylvania
140 D5 Derry Downs N Terr Aust
14 C2 Derryveagh Mts Irish Rep
36 D1 Derschlag W Germany
9 G2 Dersingham England
86 G2 Derudeb Sudan
95 M4 De Ruyter New York
21 B6 Derval France
46 E6 Dervéni Greece
42 H4 Derventa Yugoslavia
118 F5 Derwent Alberta
140 B6 Derwent N Terr Aust
139 H8 Derwent *R* Tasmania
139 H8 Derwent Bridge Tasmania
12 E4 Derwent, R England
13 E4 Derwent Water *L* England
55 E5 Derzhavinsk U.S.S.R.
133 D4 Desaguadero *R* Argentina
131 B5 Desague, Cerro *peak* Argentina
110 E7 Des Arc Arkansas
110 F4 Des Arc Missouri
102 G2 Desatoya Mts Nevada
9 F3 Desborough England
130 B5 Descalvado Mato Grosso Brazil
130 F7 Descalvado São Paulo Brazil
102 H9 Descanso California
124 A1 Descanso Mexico
21 G8 Descartes France
121 S6 Deschaillons Quebec
100 E4 Deschutes *R* Oregon
109 J3 Desdemona Texas
45 M1 Dese *R* Italy
133 P7 Deseado Argentina
41 N7 Desenzano del Garda Italy
103 M2 Deseret Utah
101 N9 Deseret Pk Utah
121 N8 Deseronto Ontario
103 J8 Desert Center California
102 H8 Desert Hot Springs California
121 O6 Desért, L Quebec
101 M8 Desert Pk Utah
103 J5 Desert Ra Nevada
100 G8 Desert Valley Nevada
103 N5 Desert View Arizona
127 M4 Deshaies Guadeloupe W I
67 A3 Deshengpo China
98 J9 Deshler Nebraska
94 D5 Deshler Ohio
74 E5 Deshnoke India
77 H4 Deshu Afghanistan
124 B1 Desierto de Altar *des* Mexico
17 H4 Desierto de las Palmas Spain
98 E1 Des Lacs *R* N Dakota
118 D3 Desmarais Alberta
100 J2 Desmet Idaho
101 L3 De Smet Montana
98 J5 De Smet S Dakota
130 B10 Desmochados Paraguay
99 N8 Des Moines Iowa
106 G5 Des Moines New Mexico
99 M7 Des Moines *R* Iowa
99 L6 Des Moines *R* Minnesota
54 B6 Desna *R* U.S.S.R.
133 C8 Desolación, I Chile
71 G5 Desolation Pt Philippines
110 G4 De Soto Illinois
107 Q3 De Soto Kansas
110 F3 De Soto Missouri
99 P6 De Soto Wisconsin
113 F10 De Soto City Florida
16 E6 Despeñaperros, Pto. de Spain
99 T7 Des Plaines Illinois
48 G6 Despotovac Yugoslavia
83 H5 Desroches *isld* Seychelles
33 Q9 Dessau E Germany
40 E3 Dessoubre *R* France
86 G3 Dessye Ethiopia
111 K11 Destin Florida
31 K5 Deštná *mt* Poland
138 E6 D'Estrees, B S Australia
117 D5 Destruction Bay Yukon Terr
100 A2 Destruction I Washington
143 G6 Destruction,Mt W Australia
22 B2 Desvres France
48 G5 Deta Romania
142 G4 Detached Ra W Australia
32 G6 Detern W Germany
121 N7 Detlor Ontario
32 J9 Detmold W Germany
94 D1 Detour Michigan
94 D1 Detour Passage Michigan
99 U4 Detour, Pt Michigan
94 D4 Detroit Michigan
109 M2 Detroit Texas
122 H4 Détroit d'Honguedo Quebec
99 L3 Detroit Lakes Minnesota
94 D4 Detroit R Michigan
100 C5 Detroit Res Oregon
87 E9 Dett Zimbabwe
37 J4 Dettelbach W Germany
36 G6 Dettenhausen W Germany
36 H3 Detter W Germany
36 F7 Dettingen Baden-Württemberg W Germany
36 G3 Dettingen Bayern W Germany
36 C6 Dettwiller France
68 G5 Det Udom Thailand
48 E2 Detva Czechoslovakia
25 E6 Deurne Netherlands
37 Q2 Deutsch-Einsiedel E Germany
33 R7 Deutschhof E Germany
48 D3 Deutschkreutz Austria
37 P2 Deutsch-Neudorf E Germany
122 B2 Deux Décharges, L Quebec
121 M6 Deux Rivieres Ontario
21 E9 Deux-Sèvres *dep* France
48 H5 Deva Romania
16 D1 Deva *R* Spain
110 E7 De Valls Bluff Arkansas
48 F3 Dévaványa Hungary
48 D3 Devecser Hungary
78 E2 Develi Turkey
25 F4 Deventer Netherlands
143 C6 Deverell,Mt W Australia
112 D4 Devereux Georgia
15 F3 Deveron *R* Scotland
46 E1 Devica *mt* Yugoslavia
74 D5 Devikot India
20 H3 Deville France
116 E3 Devil Mt Alaska
102 E4 Devil Post Pile Nat.Mon California
145 D4 Devil River Pk New Zealand
108 F5 Devils *R* Texas
14 D4 Devilsbit Mt Irish Rep
8 C3 Devils Bridge Wales
102 E6 Devils Den California
15 E4 Devil's Elbow Scotland
116 K5 Devils Elbow *V* Alaska
102 E3 Devils Gate California
89 E1 Devil's Gorge Zambia
6 L6 Devil's Hole North Sea
99 Q2 Devils I Michigan
110 H4 Devil's Kitchen L Illinois
98 H1 Devils Lake N Dakota
100 K8 Devils L. Res Nevada
117 G6 Devils Paw *mt* Br Col/Alaska
100 C7 Devils Peak *mt* Oregon
102 E4 Devils Pk California
103 J7 Devils Playground *des* California
126 G2 Devil's Point Cat I Bahamas
101 O8 Devils Slide Utah
98 B5 Devils Tower Wyoming
139 H7 Devils Tower *isld* Tasmania
47 G3 Devin Bulgaria
109 J6 Devine Texas
80 C8 Devira Israel
9 E5 Devizes England
74 F6 Devli India

47 J1 Devnya Bulgaria
107 M7 Devol Oklahoma
46 D4 Devoll *R* Albania
118 D5 Devon Alberta
101 O1 Devon Montana
120 G5 Devon Ontario
8 C6 Devon *co* England
140 F5 Devoncourt Queensland
115 L2 Devon I N W Terr
8 B7 Devonport England
139 H8 Devonport Tasmania
80 E3 Devora Israel
78 D1 Devrez *R* Turkey
89 G2 Devuli *R* Zimbabwe
52 E4 Devyatiny U.S.S.R.
55 E2 Devyatkova U.S.S.R.
70 F7 Dewakang Besar *isld* Indonesia
70 F7 Dewakang Ketjil *isld* Indonesia
107 P6 Dewar Oklahoma
118 H7 Dewar Lake Sask
74 G7 Dewas India
69 B11 Dewa, Udjung *C* Indonesia
118 G5 Dewberry Alberta
98 H9 Deweese Nebraska
103 M7 Dewey Arizona
107 P5 Dewey Oklahoma
98 C6 Dewey S Dakota
94 E9 Dewey Res Kentucky
22 E1 De Wielingen Belgium/Neths
118 C8 De Winton Alberta
111 E7 De Witt Arkansas
94 C4 De Witt Michigan
110 C2 De Witt Missouri
98 K9 De Witt Nebraska
13 G6 Dewsbury England
67 F2 Dexing China
111 D7 Dexter Arkansas
99 M8 Dexter Iowa
107 O4 Dexter Kansas
95 S1 Dexter Maine
94 D4 Dexter Michigan
99 O6 Dexter Minnesota
110 G5 Dexter Missouri
108 C2 Dexter New Mexico
95 L2 Dexter New York
109 L2 Dexter Texas
113 F8 Dexter, L Florida
99 Q5 Dexterville Wisconsin
138 B3 Dey-Dey, L S Australia
22 L3 Deyfeldt Belgium
77 E3 Deyhuk Iran
57 C5 Deynau U.S.S.R.
77 B6 Deyyer Iran
117 E5 Dezadeash L Yukon Terr
72 F2 Dezfūl Iran
77 A3 Dezfūl Iran
77 B4 Dez Gerd Iran
65 C6 Dezhou China
78 L4 Dezh Shahpur Iran
41 M6 Dezzo Italy
46 E7 Dháfni Greece
79 G6 Dhahab, Wādī *watercourse* Syria
79 D3 Dhali Cyprus
75 J8 Dhamtari India
75 M7 Dhanbad India
74 J4 Dhangarhi Nepal
109 H6 D'Hanis Texas
75 M5 Dhankuta Nepal
76 D6 Dhanuskodi India
74 F7 Dhar India
76 C5 Dharapuram India
75 K7 Dharmajaygarh India
76 D4 Dharmapuri India
76 C3 Dharmavaram India
74 G2 Dharmsala India
85 C5 Dhar Oualata *plat* Mauritania
76 B3 Dharwar India
66 C6 Dhaulagiri *mt* Nepal
74 G5 Dhaulpur India
75 L8 Dhenkanal India
47 H7 Dhenoúsa *isld* Greece
46 D4 Dhërmi Albania
46 E5 Dheskáti Greece
47 G8 Dhespotikó *isld* Greece
40 A4 Dheune *R* France
80 G7 Dhiban Jordan
46 F7 Dhídhimoi Greece
47 H3 Dhidhimótikhon Greece
47 G9 Dhíkti Ori *mt* Crete Greece
47 G7 Dhílos *isld* Greece
46 E7 Dhimitsána Greece
80 F8 Dhira Jordan
47 F6 Dhírfis *mt* Greece
74 G5 Dholpur India
46 E5 Dhomokós Greece
74 F9 Dhond India
76 C3 Dhone India
74 D8 Dhoraji India
47 G3 Dhoxáton Greece
47 G7 Dhragonísi *isld* Greece
74 D7 Dhrangadhra India
47 F5 Dhrépanon, Ákr *C* Greece
46 D5 Dhrin *R* Albania
75 N5 Dhubri India
72 G5 Dhufar *prov* Oman
21 I6 Dhuison France
74 F8 Dhule India
74 E2 Dhulian Pakistan
47 G9 Día *isld* Crete Greece
129 H2 Diable, I.du Fr Guiana
40 F5 Diablerets *mt* Switzerland
100 D1 Diablo L Washington
127 K2 Diablo, Mt Jamaica
108 C4 Diablo, Sa *mts* Texas
127 O7 Diablotin, Morne *hill* Dominica
99 M9 Diagonal Iowa
85 B6 Dialakoto Senegal
131 E4 Diamante Argentina
133 D4 Diamante *R* Argentina
129 K7 Diamantina Brazil
130 G6 Diamantina Minas Gerais Brazil
141 F6 Diamantina *R* Queensland
141 F6 Diamantina Lakes Queensland
81 G9 Diamantina Trench Indian Oc
129 G6 Diamantino Brazil
130 C4 Diamantino Mato Grosso Brazil
130 D5 Diamantino Mato Grosso Brazil
110 B5 Diamond Missouri
118 E9 Diamond City Alberta
75 N7 Diamond Harb India
102 S12 Diamond Hd Hawaiian Is
141 K3 Diamond Islets Gt Barrier Reef Australia
100 C6 Diamond L Oregon
103 J2 Diamond Mts Nevada
100 C6 Diamond Peak *mt* Oregon
103 J2 Diamond Pk Nevada
102 D3 Diamond Springs California
101 P8 Diamondville Wyoming
94 G8 Diana W Virginia
141 J3 Diana Bank Gt Barrier Reef Aust
28 G5 Dianaland Denmark
67 C6 Dianbai China
Dianbu *see* Feidong
67 A4 Dian Chi *L* China
67 B1 Dianjiang China
44 D4 Diano Marina Italy
129 J6 Dianópolis Brazil
65 H2 Diaoling China
85 E6 Diapaga Upper Volta
71 F2 Diapitan B Luzon Philippines
46 F4 Diavata Greece
68 A6 Diavolo, Mt Andaman Is
65 A5 Dibabu China
87 D7 Dibaya Zaïre
86 D3 Dibbis Sudan
146 J3 Dibble Iceberg Tongue Antarctica
66 F6 Dibhuk Pass India/Burma
86 B4 Dibi Cameroon
109 N4 Diboll Texas
66 E6 Dibrugarh India
75 Q5 Dibrugarh India
71 E3 Dicapanisan Pt Luzon Philippines
Diciosânmârtin *see* Tîrnăveni
98 E9 Dickens Nebraska
108 G2 Dickens Texas
95 R6 Dickey Maine
98 H3 Dickey N Dakota
98 D3 Dickinson N Dakota
109 M6 Dickinson Texas
9 H3 Dickleburgh England
36 D3 Dickscheid-Geroldstein W Germany
110 J5 Dickson Tennessee
95 M5 Dickson City Pennsylvania
78 H3 Dicle *R* Turkey
45 L4 Dicomano Italy
71 F1 Didacas *isld* Luzon Philippines
9 E4 Didcot England
85 C6 Didiéni Mali
109 L8 Dido Texas
118 C7 Didsbury Alberta
74 F5 Didwana India
121 S4 Didyme Quebec
19 O15 Die France
89 G5 Die Berg *mt* S Africa
36 B5 Diebling France
85 D6 Diébougou Upper Volta
36 F4 Dieburg W Germany
118 K7 Diefenbaker, L Sask
33 N6 Die Göhrde *reg* W Germany
131 F3 Diego Lamas Uruguay
133 D9 Diego Ramírez, Is Chile
Diego Suarez *see* Antseranana
30 D1 Die Halligen *inlet* W Germany
32 L8 Diekholzen W Germany
22 L4 Diekirch Luxembourg
20 B2 Diélette France
32 H8 Dielingen W Germany
85 C6 Diema Mali
32 K9 Diemel *R* W Germany
36 C6 Diemeringen France
68 F2 Dien Bien Phu Vietnam
32 J8 Diepenau W Germany
25 G4 Diepenheim Netherlands
32 H7 Diepholz W Germany
20 H2 Dieppe France
127 P4 Dieppe Bay Town St Kitts W I
36 D2 Dierdorf W Germany
25 F4 Dieren Netherlands
33 Q4 Dierhagen E Germany
36 D2 Dieringhausen W Germany
109 N1 Dierks Arkansas
65 F2 Di'er Songhua Jiang *R* China
33 N7 Diesdorf E Germany
41 J2 Diessenhofen Switzerland
22 J2 Diest Belgium
110 H2 Dieterich Illinois
37 K3 Dietersdorf W Germany
37 M5 Dietfurt W Germany
41 H3 Dietikon Switzerland
101 L7 Dietrich Idaho
36 F3 Dietzenbach W Germany
19 O15 Dieulefit France
19 K4 Dieuze France
25 F3 Dieverbrug Netherlands
36 B2 Die Ville *reg* W Germany
36 E3 Diez W Germany
86 H5 Dif Somalia
65 D7 Difang China
22 K4 Differdange Luxembourg
131 H5 Difuntos ó Negra, L Uruguay
67 F1 Digang China
75 Q5 Digboi India
9 F1 Digby England
122 G9 Digby Nova Scotia
83 M14 Digby, C Kerguelen Indian Oc
122 F9 Digby Neck Nova Scotia
107 K3 Dighton Kansas
95 Q5 Dighton Massachusetts
94 B2 Dighton Michigan
74 G9 Diglur India
19 Q16 Digne France
20 H4 Digny France
18 H6 Digoin France
71 F2 Digollorin Pt Luzon Philippines
71 G7 Digos Mindanao Philippines
74 G8 Digras India
136 H3 Digul *R* W Irian
71 E5 Diit *isld* Philippines
22 H2 Dijle *R* Belgium
19 J5 Dijon France
86 C4 Dik Chad
26 H6 Dikanäs Sweden
86 H3 Dikhil Djibouti
47 H5 Dikili Turkey
79 B7 Dikirnis Egypt
22 D2 Dikkebus Belgium
67 F3 Dikou China
83 K11 Dikoya Sri Lanka
55 D2 Dikoye, Oz *L* U.S.S.R.
22 D1 Diksmuide Belgium
50 H1 Dikson U.S.S.R.
50 G1 Dikson, Ostrov *isld* U.S.S.R.
86 B3 Dikwa Nigeria
77 H3 Dilaram Afghanistan
71 M9 Dili Timor
106 E6 Dilia New Mexico
68 A6 Diligent Str Andaman Is
68 J7 Di Linh Vietnam
119 M8 Dilke Sask
103 O6 Dilkon Arizona
36 E2 Dill *R* W Germany
141 H7 Dillalah Queensland
118 G6 Dillberry L. Prov Park Alberta
141 G5 Dillcar Queensland
107 L6 Dill City Oklahoma
36 E2 Dillenburg W Germany
98 K9 Diller Nebraska
109 H7 Dilley Texas
86 E3 Dilling Sudan
36 B5 Dillingen W Germany
116 H7 Dillingham Alaska
106 D2 Dillon Colorado
101 N4 Dillon Montana
118 H3 Dillon Sask
112 H3 Dillon S Carolina
144 D5 Dillon Cone *mt* New Zealand
94 E6 Dillon Res Ohio
95 K6 Dillsburg Pennsylvania
94 J9 Dillwyn Virginia
87 D8 Dilolo Zaïre
75 P6 Dimapur India
124 F6 Dimas Mexico
86 D7 Dimbelenge Zaïre
85 D7 Dimbokro Ivory Coast
138 F6 Dimboola Victoria
48 J5 Dîmbo Viţa *R* Romania
141 H3 Dimbulah Queensland
54 E8 Dimitrova U.S.S.R.
47 G2 Dimitrov Dam Bulgaria
47 H2 Dimitrovgrad Bulgaria
53 G7 Dimitrovgrad U.S.S.R.
46 F1 Dimitrovgrad Yugoslavia
108 E1 Dimmitt Texas
98 H6 Dimock S Dakota
79 F7 Dimona Israel
71 G5 Dinagat *isld* Philippines
71 G5 Dinagat Sound Philippines
75 N6 Dinajpur Bangladesh
20 A5 Dinan France
22 H3 Dinant Belgium
47 L6 Dinar Turkey
42 G4 Dinara Planina Yugoslavia
20 A4 Dinard St Enogat France
86 F3 Dinder *R* Sudan
76 C5 Dindigul India
109 K7 Dinero Texas
86 C7 Dinga Zaïre
71 E3 Dingalan B Luzon Philippines
68 K3 Ding'an China
58 E4 Dingbian China
32 E9 Dingden W Germany
20 B5 Dingé France
33 M10 Dingelstädt E Germany
33 O9 Dingelstedt E Germany
48 K3 Dîngem Romania
75 M4 Dinggyê China
67 G1 Dinghai China
101 O7 Dingle Idaho
14 A4 Dingle B Irish Rep
67 E4 Dingnan China
141 J6 Dingo Queensland
37 O6 Dingolfing W Germany
71 E1 Dingras Luzon Philippines
65 C7 Dingtao China
85 B6 Dinguiraye Guinea
123 M7 Dingwall C Breton I, N S
15 D3 Dingwall Scotland
58 D4 Dingxi China
65 C5 Ding Xian China
65 B5 Dingxiang China
65 C5 Dingxing China
65 E6 Dingzi Gang *B* China
69 H8 Dinh An, Cua *river mth* Vietnam
67 B6 Dinh Lap Vietnam
25 H4 Dinkel *R* Netherlands
37 J5 Dinkelsbühl W Germany
37 K7 Dinkelscherben W Germany
32 H7 Dinklage W Germany
103 O5 Dinnebito Wash *creek* Arizona
13 G3 Dinnington England
87 E10 Dinokwe Botswana
118 K1 Dinorwic L Ontario
101 Q9 Dinosaur Nat.Mon Utah/Colo
32 E9 Dinslaken W Germany
113 F7 Dinsmore Florida
118 K7 Dinsmore Sask
86 H5 Dinsor Somalia
102 E5 Dinuba California
94 K9 Dinwiddie Virginia
25 F5 Dinxperlo Netherlands
27 G15 Diö Sweden
85 C6 Dioila Mali
116 C4 Diomede Is Bering Str
51 S2 Diomida, Ostrova *islds* U.S.S.R.
22 H3 Dion Belgium
86 D2 Diona Chad
130 D10 Dionisio Cerqueira Brazil
130 D5 Diorama Brazil
48 F2 Diósgyör Hungary
85 A6 Diouloulou Senegal
85 C6 Dioura Mali
85 A6 Diourbel Senegal
74 C6 Diplo Pakistan
71 F6 Dipolog Mindanao Philippines
22 L4 Dippach Luxembourg
12 C2 Dippen Scotland
12 C3 Dippin Scotland
144 B6 Dipton New Zealand
74 D1 Dir Pakistan
27 B13 Dirdal Norway
141 G2 Direction,C Queensland
83 M8 Direction I Cocos Is Indian Oc
86 H4 Diredawa Ethiopia
125 L4 Diriamba Nicaragua
87 D9 Dirico Angola
43 F11 Dirillo *R* Sicily
143 A7 Dirk Hartog I W Australia
84 E6 Dirkou Niger
25 B5 Dirksland Netherlands
13 F1 Dirleton Scotland
47 K8 Dirmil Turkey
36 C5 Dirmingen W Germany
86 E3 Dirra Sudan
141 J8 Dirranbandi Queensland
86 J5 Dirri Somalia
103 O3 Dirty Devil *R* Utah
102 T13 Disappearing I Hawaiian Is
146 E14 Disappointment, C Antarctica
133 J8 Disappointment, C S Georgia
100 A3 Disappointment, C Washington
135 N9 Disappointment Is Tuamotu Arch Pac Oc
143 E6 Disappointment,L W Australia
139 K6 Disaster B New S Wales
100 F1 Disautel Washington
37 J6 Dischingen W Germany
117 Q4 Discovery N W Terr
138 F7 Discovery B S Aust/Vict
127 K1 Discovery Bay Jamaica
100 C2 Discovery Bay Washington
100 C1 Discovery I Washington
90 K13 Discovery Tablemount S Atlantic Oc
142 E5 Discovery Well W Australia
41 J4 Disentis Switzerland
13 G5 Dishforth England
116 J5 Dishkakat Alaska
116 J5 Dishna *R* Alaska
80 F1 Dishon Israel
80 F1 Dishon *R* Israel
115 O4 Diskofjord Greenland
119 M8 Disley Sask
98 F8 Dismal *R* Nebraska
140 F4 Dismal *R* Queensland
95 L10 Dismal Swamp Virginia
52 C6 Disna U.S.S.R.
22 K2 Dison Belgium
95 K9 Disputanta Virginia
121 T7 Disraëli Quebec
9 H3 Diss England
21 F8 Dissay France
32 H8 Dissen W Germany
122 C4 Dissimieux, L Quebec
100 C6 Disston Oregon
95 L8 District of Columbia (D.C.) U.S.A.
79 A7 Disûq Egypt
9 F6 Ditchling England
33 O9 Ditfurt E Germany
32 K4 Dithmarschen *reg* W Germany
43 F11 Dittaino *R* Sicily
74 D8 Diu India
71 G6 Diuata Mts Mindanao Philippines
52 D5 Divenskaya U.S.S.R.
121 L6 Diver Ontario
110 G2 Divernon Illinois
142 G3 Diversion Dam W Australia
109 H2 Diversion L Texas
20 E3 Dives *R* France
20 E3 Dives-sur-Mer France
20 B2 Divette *R* France
26 L3 Dividal *R* Norway
106 E3 Divide Colorado
143 C6 Dividing Ra W Australia
141 H6 Dividing Range Queensland
71 F2 Divilacan B Luzon Philippines
87 F10 Divinhe Mozambique
130 G7 Divinópolis Brazil
22 C3 Divion France
100 F8 Division Peak *mt* Nevada
53 F10 Divnoye U.S.S.R.
85 C7 Divo Ivory Coast
78 G2 Divrigi Turkey
74 B5 Diwana Pakistan
72 F2 Diwāniyah, Ad Iraq
98 C8 Dix Nebraska
121 O4 Dix Quebec
95 R2 Dixfield Maine
111 K8 Dixiana Alabama
111 K10 Dixie Alabama
113 D7 Dixie Georgia
100 K4 Dixie Idaho
100 G3 Dixie Washington
100 G5 Dixie Pass Oregon
102 F2 Dixie Valley Nevada
121 Q5 Dix Milles, L.des Quebec
95 S2 Dixmont Maine
95 O2 Dix Mt New York
Dixmude *see* Diksmuide
102 C3 Dixon California
99 R8 Dixon Illinois
110 D4 Dixon Missouri
101 L2 Dixon Montana
98 K7 Dixon Nebraska
106 E5 Dixon New Mexico
101 S8 Dixon Wyoming
117 G8 Dixon Entrance *str* Br Col/Alaska
111 J9 Dixons Mills Alabama
117 P7 Dixonville Alberta
94 H6 Dixonville Pennsylvania
146 J4 Dixson I Antarctica
67 A4 Dixu China
121 T7 Dixville Quebec
65 H3 Diyingou China
74 B9 Diz Pakistan
67 C2 Dizhuang China
8 B6 Dizzard Pt England
86 B5 Dja *R* Cameroon
84 E5 Djado Niger
84 E5 Djado, Pl.du Niger
71 A2 Djailolo Halmahera Indonesia
Djailolo Gilolo *isld see* Halmahera *isld*
Djajapura *see* Jayapura
86 B6 Djambala Congo
69 F13 Djambi *prov* Sumatra
70 L9 Djampang-Kulon Java
85 F4 Djanet Algeria
70 E6 Djangeru Kalimantan
70 D5 Djangkang Kalimantan
70 E3 Djanlonong Kalimantan
85 E3 Djaret *watercourse* Algeria
70 M9 Djatibarang Java
70 L9 Djatinegara Java
70 M9 Djatiwangi Java
86 B2 Djbella Niger
69 G13 Djebus Indonesia
86 C3 Djédaa Chad
85 E2 Djedi *watercourse* Algeria
85 E2 Djelfa Algeria
70 O10 Djember Java
70 E5 Djempang *L* Kalimantan
70 F7 Djeneponto Sulawesi
70 N9 Djepara Java
Djerba, I de *see* Jerba, I de
86 B4 Djerem *R* Cameroon
Djezair, El *see* Alger
85 D6 Djibasso Upper Volta
85 D6 Djibo Upper Volta
86 H3 Djibouti Djibouti
86 H3 Djibouti *rep* N E Africa
86 D5 Djolu Zaïre
70 O9 Djombang Java
70 D7 Djorong Kalimantan
86 B6 Djoué *R* Congo
85 C5 Djouf, El *reg* Mauritania/Mali
85 E7 Djougou Benin
86 B5 Djoum Cameroon
86 C2 Djourab *dist* Chad
86 F5 Djugu Zaïre
115 S5 Djúpivogur Iceland
27 H11 Djura Sweden
27 K12 Djursholm Sweden
28 E4 Djursland *reg* Denmark
70 N9 Djuwono Java
111 G10 D'Lo Mississippi
51 O1 Dmitriya Lapteva, Proliv *str* U.S.S.R.
55 G3 Dmitriyevka U.S.S.R.
54 G4 Dmitriyev-L'govskiy U.S.S.R.
54 J1 Dmitrov U.S.S.R.
54 G4 Dmitrovsk-Orlovskiy U.S.S.R.
54 B4 Dnepr *R* U.S.S.R.
54 F8 Dneprodzerzhinsk U.S.S.R.
54 G8 Dnepropetrovsk U.S.S.R.
54 F9 Dneprorudnoye U.S.S.R.
53 C7 Dneprovskaya Nizmennost *lowland* U.S.S.R.
54 C10 Dneprovskiy Liman *lagoon* U.S.S.R.
53 C9 Dnestr *R* Europe
48 N4 Dnestrovskiy Liman *lagoon* Ukraine U.S.S.R.
Dnieper *R see* Dnepr *R*
Dniester *R see* Dnestr *R*
52 C5 Dno U.S.S.R.
77 K2 Doāb Mekh-i-Zarīn Afghanistan
122 F7 Doaktown New Brunswick
70 E7 Doangdoangan Besar *isld* Indonesia
70 E7 Doangdoangan Ketjil *isld* Indonesia
67 B6 Doan Hung Vietnam
86 C4 Doba Chad
33 Q5 Dobbertin E Germany
138 E2 Dobbie, L S Australia
140 E6 Dobbie,Mt N Terr Aust
109 M5 Dobbin Texas
140 E4 Dobbyn Queensland
31 M6 Dobczyce Poland
52 B6 Dobele U.S.S.R.
37 P1 Döbeln E Germany
33 T9 Doberlug Kirchhain E Germany
31 J3 Dobiegniew Poland
133 E5 Doblas Argentina
136 G3 Dobo Moluccas Indonesia
48 E6 Doboj Yugoslavia
112 F6 Doboy Sd Georgia
31 J2 Dobra Poland
37 M3 Döbraberg *mt* W Germany
37 P4 Dobřany Czechoslovakia
38 J8 Dobratsch *mt* Austria
31 M2 Dobre Miasto Poland
48 G4 Dobresti Romania
38 J8 Döbriach Austria
33 S9 Döbrichau E Germany
47 F3 Dobrinisnta Bulgaria
31 H6 Dobříš Czechoslovakia
31 L5 Dobrodzień Poland
31 O6 Dobromil U.S.S.R.
54 J8 Dobropol'ye U.S.S.R.
48 J6 Dobroteşti Romania
54 C4 Dobrush U.S.S.R.
54 C4 Dobryanka U.S.S.R.
31 L3 Dobrzyn Poland
48 F2 Dobšiná Czechoslovakia
112 G1 Dobson N Carolina
144 B6 Dobson *R* New Zealand
8 B7 Dobwalls England
127 N1 Docas del Dragón *chan* Trinidad/Ven
71 D7 Doc Can *isld* Sulu Arch Philippines
130 G6 Doce, R Brazil
143 G6 Docker Cr W Australia
9 G2 Docking England
26 H9 Dockmyr Sweden
142 F4 Dockrell, Mt W Australia
36 B3 Dockweiler W Germany
109 H10 Doctor Cos Mexico
143 E8 Doctor Hicks Ra W Australia
48 G4 Doctor Petru Croza Romania
121 P3 Doda, L Quebec
76 C4 Dod Ballapur India
13 F2 Doddington England
109 O2 Doddridge Arkansas
118 E5 Dodds Alberta
Dodecanese *see* Sporádhes *Is*
98 D2 Dodge N Dakota
98 K8 Dodge Nebraska
99 O5 Dodge Center Minnesota
107 K4 Dodge City Kansas
99 Q7 Dodgeville Wisconsin
8 B7 Dodman Pt England
88 E5 Dodoma Tanzania
33 O6 Dodow E Germany
118 J7 Dodsland Sask
109 P3 Dodson Louisiana
101 R1 Dodson Montana
47 K5 Dodurga Turkey
22 G1 Doel Belgium
112 D6 Doerun Georgia
25 F4 Doesburg Netherlands
25 F5 Doetinchem Netherlands
36 F6 Doffingen W Germany
66 D5 Dogai Coring *L* China
47 H6 Doğanbey Burun *C* Turkey
117 M10 Dog Creek Br Columbia
47 L5 Döğer Turkey
7 M8 Dogger Bank North Sea
113 C8 Dog I Florida
127 N5 Dog I Lesser Antilles
144 B7 Dog I New Zealand
119 T7 Dog L Manitoba
99 R1 Dog L Ontario
44 C2 Dogliani Italy
38 H9 Dogna Italy
60 G9 Dōgo *isld* Japan
85 E6 Dogondoutchi Niger
60 G10 Dōgo-yama *mt* Japan
118 C7 Dog Pound Alberta
126 E2 Dog Rocks Bahamas
78 K2 Doğubayazit Turkey
141 K7 Dogwood *R* Queensland
127 P4 Dogwood Pt Nevis W I
77 B7 Doha Qatar
74 F7 Dohad India
75 P7 Dohazar Bangladesh
121 S5 Doheny Quebec
33 N4 Döhnsdorf W Germany
71 A1 Doi Indonesia
68 D3 Doi Saket Thailand
22 H3 Doische Belgium
130 E8 Dois Córregos Brazil
21 D9 Doix France
46 F3 Dojran Yugoslavia
46 F3 Dojransko, Jez *L* Yugoslavia
27 D11 Dokka Norway
26 M4 Dokkas Sweden
28 E3 Dokkedal Denmark
25 E2 Dokkum Netherlands
54 J9 Dokuchayevsk U.S.S.R.
136 H3 Dolak *isld* W Irian
98 H5 Doland S Dakota
121 S4 Dolbeau Quebec
32 G9 Dolberg W Germany
20 B4 Dol-de-Bretagne France
19 J5 Dôle France
125 N5 Dolega Panama
8 C3 Dolfor Wales
8 C2 Dolgellau Wales
95 N3 Dolgeville New York
116 G9 Dolgoi I Alaska
48 H2 Dolgoye U.S.S.R.
43 C9 Dolianova Sardinia
48 H2 Dolina U.S.S.R.
59 M2 Dolinsk U.S.S.R.
54 D8 Dolinskaya U.S.S.R.
75 K5 Dolirighat India
47 F1 Dolj Romania
46 E1 Doljevac Yugoslavia
38 G8 Döllach Austria
12 E1 Dollar Scotland
118 J9 Dollard Sask
122 F3 Dollard, L Quebec
15 E5 Dollar Law *mt* Scotland
32 F6 Dollart *inlet* W Germany/Neths
32 M8 Dollbergen W Germany
33 P8 Dolle E Germany
146 E13 Dolleman I Antarctica
28 C4 Dollerup Denmark
37 L6 Dollnstein W Germany
20 G5 Dollon France
37 K1 Döllstädt E Germany
46 E3 Dolneni Yugoslavia
37 O2 Dolní Jiřetín Czechoslovakia
31 J6 Dolní Královice Czechoslovakia
37 O3 Dolní Žandov Czechoslovakia
86 H5 Dolo Ethiopia
45 M1 Dolo Italy
19 P13 Dolomieu France
42 D2 Dolomitiche, Alpi Italy
Dolonnur *see* Duolun
131 F6 Dolores Argentina
106 E4 Dolores Colorado
125 F9 Dolores Guatemala
17 G6 Dolores Spain
131 F4 Dolores Uruguay
106 B3 Dolores *R* Colorado
125 J7 Dolores Hidalgo Mexico
133 F8 Dolphin, C Falkland Is
87 B11 Dolphin Hd Namibia
127 H1 Dolphin Hd *hill* Jamaica
142 B5 Dolphin I W Australia
13 E2 Dolphinton Scotland
114 H4 Dolphin & Union Str N W Terr
38 G8 Dölsach Austria
31 K4 Dolsk Poland
21 G7 Dolus-le-Sec France
8 C1 Dolwyddelan Wales
136 H2 Dom *mt* W Irian
122 H2 Domagaya L Labrador
119 U9 Domain Manitoba
47 K5 Domaniç Turkey
47 K5 Domaniç Dağı *mt* Turkey
20 K1 Domart France
37 O5 Domažlice Czechoslovakia
50 E3 Dombarovskiy U.S.S.R.
26 D9 Dombås Norway
19 K4 Dombasle France
87 B8 Dombe Grande Angola
140 A2 Dombey,C N Terr Aust
138 E6 Dombey, C S Australia
48 E4 Dombóvár Hungary
48 G2 Dombrád Hungary
37 J5 Dombühl W Germany
25 A5 Domburg Netherlands
103 K9 Dome Arizona
117 N9 Dome Creek Br Col
40 E7 Dôme-de-Chasseforêt France
103 K8 Dome Rock Mts Arizona
144 C6 Domet, Mt New Zealand
144 D5 Domett New Zealand
145 D4 Domett, Mt New Zealand
36 B6 Domèvre France
20 D4 Domfront France
106 D6 Domingo New Mexico
127 O7 Dominica *isld* Lesser Antilles
127 J5 Dominican Rep W Indies
123 M7 Dominion C Breton I, N Scotia
115 M4 Dominion, C N W Terr
119 U9 Dominion City Manitoba
123 L1 Dominion L Labrador
146 G7 Dominion Ra Antarctica
115 O7 Domino Labrador
33 O6 Dömitz E Germany
20 C4 Domjean France
130 G6 Dom Joaquim Brazil
41 K4 Domleschg *R* Switzerland
18 F8 Domme France
25 D6 Dommel *R* Netherlands
33 R9 Dommitzsch E Germany
54 J1 Domodedovo U.S.S.R.
41 H5 Domodossola Italy
40 D1 Dompaire France
20 C5 Dompierre du-Chemin France
22 B3 Dompierre-sur-Authie France
21 C9 Dompierre-sur-Mer France
36 B7 Domptail France
71 J9 Dompu Sumbawa Indonesia
119 M6 Domremy Sask
26 K8 Domsjö Sweden
88 E9 Domue *peak* Mozambique
131 B6 Domuyo *peak* Argentina
139 K3 Domville *mt* Queensland
141 K8 Domville,Mt Queensland
46 F6 Domvraína Greece
42 F2 Domzale Yugoslavia
22 D2 Don France
124 E4 Don Mexico
21 B6 Don *R* France
141 J5 Don *R* Queensland
15 F3 Don *R* Scotland
54 L5 Don *R* U.S.S.R.
106 D9 Dona Ana New Mexico
45 M1 Donada Italy
14 F2 Donaghadee N Ireland
121 M8 Donald Ontario
139 G6 Donald Victoria
118 E6 Donalda Alberta
144 A6 Donald, Mt New Zealand
109 P1 Donaldson Arkansas
98 K1 Donaldson Minnesota
140 F4 Donaldson Queensland
111 E11 Donaldsonville Louisiana
112 C6 Donalsonville Georgia
14 E3 Donard Irish Rep
124 G5 Donato Guerra Mexico
38 L5 Donau *R* Austria
37 L6 Donau *R* W Germany
41 J2 Donaueschingen W Germany
37 L6 Donaumoos *reg* W Germany
37 K6 Donauried *reg* W Germany
37 N5 Donaustauf W Germany
37 K6 Donauwörth W Germany
118 K7 Donavon Sask
38 M7 Donawitz Austria
54 J8 Donbass (Donetskiy Ugol'nyy Basseyn) U.S.S.R.
16 D6 Don Benito Spain
140 B1 Don,C N Terr Aust
13 G6 Doncaster England
95 K8 Doncaster Maryland
22 H4 Donchery France
22 K4 Doncols Luxembourg
87 B7 Dondo Angola
87 F9 Dondo Mozambique
71 H5 Dondo Sulawesi
71 E6 Dondonay *isld* Philippines
70 G4 Dondo, Teluk *B* Sulawesi
70 G4 Dondo, Tg *C* Sulawesi
73 N7 Dondra Head *C* Sri Lanka
48 L2 Dondyushany U.S.S.R.
14 C2 Donegal Irish Rep
14 D2 Donegal *co* Irish Rep
14 B4 Donegal Pt Irish Rep
145 D1 Donelly's Crossing New Zealand
110 K5 Donelson Tennessee
14 C4 Doneraile Irish Rep
54 J8 Donetsk U.S.S.R.
53 E9 Donetskiy Kryazh *mts* U.S.S.R.
127 J2 Don Figuerero Mts Jamaica
86 B4 Donga *R* Nigeria
59 K2 Dong'an China
67 D3 Dong'an China
68 J5 Dong An Vietnam
143 A8 Dongara W Australia
74 J8 Dongargarh India
Dongchangshou *see* Xinle
Dongcun *see* Haiyang
68 H2 Dong Dang Vietnam
65 C6 Dong'e China
25 C5 Dongen Netherlands
67 C7 Dongfang China
68 J3 Dongfang China
65 J1 Dongfanghong China
65 F3 Dongfeng China
58 C4 Donggai Cona *L* China
70 F5 Donggala Sulawesi
136 D2 Donggala Sulawesi
67 D1 Donggong China
65 F4 Donggou China
67 E3 Donggu China
67 E5 Dongguan China
65 C6 Dongguang China
68 H4 Dong Ha Vietnam
65 D7 Donghai China
67 C6 Donghai Dao *isld* China
58 E4 Dong He *R* China
68 H4 Dong Hoi Vietnam
Donghuang *see* Xishui
70 G6 Dongi Sulawesi
67 C4 Dongjiang China
67 B4 Dong Jiang *R* China
65 H2 Dongjingcheng China
70 G4 Dongkalang Sulawesi
68 H1 Dong Khe Vietnam
67 C3 Dongkou China
67 B4 Donglan China
Dongliao *see* Liaoyuan
65 F3 Dongliao He *R* China
67 B5 Dongling China
67 E1 Dongliu China
65 C7 Dongming China
68 H7 Dong Nai *R* Vietnam
59 K2 Dongning China
87 C8 Dongo Angola
41 K5 Dongo Italy
86 C5 Dongo Zaïre
84 J6 Dongola Sudan
86 C5 Dongou Congo
68 E4 Dong Phraya Fai *ra* Thailand
68 E5 Dong Phraya Yen Thailand
Dongping *see* Anhua
65 C7 Dongping China
65 C6 Dongping Hu *L* China
68 H7 Dong Sai Vietnam
67 F5 Dongshan China
67 F5 Dongshan Dao *isld* China
67 E6 Dongsha Qundao *isld* China
65 A5 Dongsheng China
67 B2 Dongsheng China
67 D2 Dongting Hu *L* China
67 G3 Dongtou China
67 B6 Dong Trieu Vietnam
65 D2 Dong Ujimqin Qi China
68 G1 Dong Van Vietnam
87 D8 Dongwe *R* Zambia
67 B2 Dongxi China
67 E2 Dongxiang China
65 D7 Dongxi Lian Dao *isld* China
65 G1 Dongxing China
67 B6 Dongxing China
67 G2 Dongyang China
67 F1 Dongzhi China
109 L4 Donie Texas
9 F2 Donington England
110 F5 Doniphan Missouri
117 D4 Donjek *R* Yukon Terr
48 G6 Donji Milanovac Yugoslavia
42 H4 Donji Vakuf Yugoslavia
18 H6 Donjon, le France
99 S3 Donken Michigan
109 J9 Donna Texas
26 F5 Dönna *isld* Norway
121 T6 Donnacona Quebec
42 B3 Donnaz Italy
36 B6 Donnelay France
110 G2 Donnellson Illinois
117 P8 Donnelly Alberta
100 J5 Donnelly Idaho
98 K4 Donnelly Minnesota
145 D1 Donnelly's Crossing New Zealand
102 D2 Donner Pass California
38 K7 Donnersbach Austria
38 K7 Donnersbach Wald Austria
36 D4 Donnersberg *mt* W Germany
100 G6 Donner und Blitzen *R* Oregon
26 F5 Dönnes Norway
98 E1 Donnybrook N Dakota
143 B10 Donnybrook W Australia
19 K4 Donon *mt* France
36 C7 Donon, Col du *pass* France
94 H6 Donora Pennsylvania
140 F4 Donor's Hill Queensland
99 T9 Donovan Illinois
102 D4 Don Pedro Res California
13 G6 Don, R England
54 K3 Donskoy U.S.S.R.
54 L6 Donskoye Belogorye U.S.S.R.
28 B5 Donslund Denmark
68 C4 Donthami *R* Burma
20 B4 Donville France
36 H6 Donzdorf W Germany
18 G7 Donzenac France
19 N16 Donzère France
18 H5 Donzy France
143 C9 Doodlakine W Australia
109 H4 Doole Texas
142 C5 Dooleena *mt* W Australia
98 B1 Dooley Montana
121 O6 Doolittle, L Quebec
140 E4 Doomadgee Mission Queensland
141 J8 Doondi Queensland
116 M3 Doonerak, Mt Alaska
12 D3 Doon, L Scotland
25 D4 Doorn Netherlands
99 T5 Door Pen Wisconsin
111 J8 Dora Alabama
44 B1 Dora Italy
106 G8 Dora New Mexico
42 B3 Dora Baltea *R* Italy
124 G4 Dorado Mexico
142 E5 Dora,L W Australia
113 F9 Dora, Mt Florida
98 K3 Doran Minnesota
27 G15 Dörarp Sweden
18 F6 Dorat, le France
Dorbod *see* Siziwang Qi
65 F1 Dorbod China
8 D6 Dorchester England
9 E4 Dorchester England
98 J9 Dorchester Nebraska
122 H8 Dorchester New Brunswick
99 Q4 Dorchester Wisconsin
115 M4 Dorchester, C N W Terr
18 F7 Dordogne *dep* France
18 E8 Dordogne *R* France
25 C5 Dordrecht Netherlands
18 H7 Dore *R* France
118 K4 Doré L Sask
18 G7 Dore, Mont *mt* France
100 C6 Dorena Oregon
32 H8 Dörenberg *mt* W Germany
32 J9 Dörenhagen W Germany
118 E6 Dorenlee Alberta
32 J8 Dörentrup W Germany
130 F6 Dores do Indaiá Brazil
37 N7 Dorfen W Germany
32 L7 Dorfmark W Germany
33 R6 Dorf Zechlin E Germany
43 C8 Dorgali Sardinia
85 D6 Dori Upper Volta
77 J4 Dori *R* Afghanistan
89 A8 Doring *R* S Africa
118 J4 Dorintosh Sask
120 B4 Dorion Ontario
121 Q7 Dorion Quebec
140 B2 Dorisvale N Terr Aust
9 F5 Dorking England
36 B1 Dormagen W Germany
18 H3 Dormans France
19 N13 D'Or, Mt France
41 L3 Dornbirn Austria
36 E2 Dornburg W Germany
37 J2 Dorndorf E Germany
37 M1 Dorndorf E Germany
48 K3 Dorneşti Romania
36 F7 Dornhan W Germany
15 C3 Dornie Scotland
48 J3 Dornisoara Romania
33 Q8 Dörnitz E Germany
15 D3 Dornoch Scotland
15 D3 Dornoch Firth Scotland
13 E4 Dornock Scotland
65 A2 Dornogovĭ *prov* Mongolia
36 F7 Dornstetten W Germany
32 F5 Dornum W Germany
71 A2 Doro Indonesia
54 E2 Dorogobuzh U.S.S.R.
52 F2 Dorogorskoye U.S.S.R.
48 K3 Dorohoi Romania
54 H1 Dorokhovo U.S.S.R.
26 H7 Dorotea Sweden
118 E7 Dorothy Alberta
52 G5 Dorovitsa U.S.S.R.
32 F7 Dörpen W Germany
107 M3 Dorrance Kansas
143 A7 Dorre I W Australia
139 L4 Dorrigo New S Wales
8 D2 Dorrington England
100 D8 Dorris California
100 E8 Dorris Res California
94 G5 Dorset Ohio
121 M7 Dorset Ontario
95 O3 Dorset Vermont
8 D6 Dorset *co* England
32 E9 Dorsten W Germany
32 G9 Dortmund W Germany
32 J5 Dorum W Germany
86 E5 Doruma Zaïre
121 R7 Dorval Quebec
36 H5 Dörzbach W Germany
133 D6 Dos Bahías, C Argentina
125 P9 Dos Bocas Belize
103 P9 Dos Cabezas Arizona
77 G2 Doshakh, Koh-I *mt* Afghanistan
16 D7 Dos Hermanas Spain
71 E4 Dos Hermanas *isld* Philippines
77 L2 Doshi Afghanistan
68 H2 Do Son Vietnam
102 D5 Dos Palos California
47 G3 Dospat Bulgaria
121 T6 Dosquet Quebec
102 A2 Dos Rios California
109 H5 Doss Texas
33 R6 Dosse *R* E Germany
85 E6 Dosso Niger
45 J1 Dossobuono Italy
50 E4 Dossor U.S.S.R.
28 D3 Døstrup Denmark
94 K9 Doswell Virginia
111 L10 Dothan Alabama
100 B7 Dothan Oregon
123 T4 Doting Cove Nfld
116 P5 Dot Lake Alaska
32 H7 Dötlingen W Germany
101 S10 Dotsero Colorado
36 H5 Döttingen W Germany
22 E3 Douai France
86 A5 Douala Cameroon
18 C4 Douarnenez France
18 B4 Douarnenez,Baie de France
109 N6 Double Bayou Texas
126 D3 Double Headed Shot Cays *islds* Bahamas
68 C5 Double I Burma
141 L7 Double Island Pt Queensland
108 G2 Double Mountain Fork *R* Texas
102 F6 Double Mt California
116 L6 Double Peak Alaska
141 H4 Double Pt *C* Queensland
111 J7 Double Springs Alabama
31 J6 Doubrava *R* Czechoslovakia
40 D3 Doubs *dep* France
19 J6 Doubs *R* France
40 F3 Doubs *R* Switzerland
142 E3 Doubtful B W Australia
143 C10 Doubtful Island B W Australia
144 A6 Doubtful Sd New Zealand
145 D1 Doubtless B New Zealand
40 C4 Doucier France
20 G2 Doudeville France
99 O9 Douds Iowa
21 E7 Doué-la-Fontaine France
85 D6 Douentza Mali
144 A7 Doughboy Bay New Zealand
117 F6 Douglas Alaska
103 P10 Douglas Arizona
112 E6 Douglas Georgia
12 D5 Douglas I of Man U.K.
119 S9 Douglas Manitoba
99 U7 Douglas Michigan
98 E2 Douglas N Dakota
98 K9 Douglas Nebraska
140 B2 Douglas N Terr Aust
121 O7 Douglas Ontario
89 C7 Douglas S Africa
12 E3 Douglas Scotland
100 E2 Douglas Washington
98 A7 Douglas Wyoming
138 D3 Douglas *R* S Australia
117 J9 Douglas Chan Br Columbia
106 B2 Douglas Cr Colorado
112 D1 Douglas Dam Tennessee
94 C1 Douglas L Michigan
112 D2 Douglas L Tennessee
12 E2 Douglas Mill Scotland

143 E8 Douglas,Mount
W Australia
116 L7 Douglas, Mt Alaska
120 J8 Douglas Pt Ontario
146 F13 Douglas Ra Antarctica
107 O4 Douglass Kansas
122 G6 Douglastown
New Brunswick
122 H5 Douglastown Quebec
111 M8 Douglasville Georgia
22 F3 Doui Belgium
46 D6 Doukáton,Akr C Greece
19 J4 Doulevant le Château
France
20 K1 Doullens France
14 A5 Doulus Hd Irish Rep
86 B5 Doumé Cameroon
67 D5 Doumen China
67 A5 Doumuge China
12 D1 Doune Scotland
15 E2 Dounreay Scotland
85 C7 Douobé R Liberia
37 P3 Doupov Czechoslovakia
22 F3 Dour France
130 E6 Dourada, Cachoeira rapids
Brazil
129 J6 Dourada,Serra mts Brazil
130 E5 Dourada,Serra mts Brazil
130 B6 Dourados Brazil
130 C8 Dourados Brazil
133 F2 Dourados R Brazil
130 D8 Dourados,Serra dos mts
Brazil
20 K4 Dourdan France
18 G9 Dourdou R France
22 B3 Douriez France
16 C3 Douro R Portugal
16 B3 Douro Litoral prov Portugal
Doushi see Gong'an
19 Q13 Doussard France
20 C3 Douve R France
20 E3 Douvres France
19 N14 Doux R France
18 E9 Douze R France
22 J4 Douzy France
45 L3 Dovadola Italy
106 B4 Dove Creek Colorado
142 C5 Dove,Mt W Australia
110 C6 Dover Arkansas
95 M7 Dover Delaware
28 D4 Dover Denmark
9 E1 Dove,R England
9 H5 Dover England
113 E9 Dover Florida
112 F5 Dover Georgia
110 N3 Dover Kentucky
112 K2 Dover N Carolina
95 Q3 Dover New Hampshire
95 N6 Dover New Jersey
94 F6 Dover Ohio
107 N6 Dover Oklahoma
139 H9 Dover Tasmania
110 J5 Dover Tennessee
95 S1 Dover Foxcroft Maine
143 F10 Dover,Pt W Australia
22 C1 Dover,Str.of
France/England
38 J9 Dovje Yugoslavia
28 F7 Dovnsklint Denmark
26 D9 Dovre Norway
26 D9 Dovrefjell Norway
88 D8 Dowa Malawi
94 A5 Dowagiac Michigan
143 B9 Dowerin W Australia
Dow, L. see Xau, L.
8 C4 Dowlais Wales
77 E5 Dowlatābād Iran
118 F7 Dowling Alberta
14 F2 Down co N Ireland
99 T8 Downers Grove Illinois
101 N7 Downey Idaho
141 K1 Downfall Cr
Brisbane, Qnsld
9 G2 Downham Market
England
102 D2 Downieville California
99 O9 Downing Missouri
95 M6 Downingtown Pennsylvania
14 F2 Downpatrick N Ireland
14 B2 Downpatrick Hd Irish Rep
107 M2 Downs Kansas
101 Q6 Downs Mt Wyoming
95 M4 Downsville New York
9 E5 Downton England
117 L9 Downton,Mt Br Columbia
8 B6 Downtown England
99 N7 Dows Iowa
7 L9 Dowsing Lightship
North Sea
69 C12 Dowu, Tanjung C
Indonesia
102 D1 Doyle California
110 L6 Doyle Tennessee
144 D5 Doyleston New Zealand
95 M6 Doylestown Pennsylvania
106 D3 Doyleville Colorado
60 F9 Dozen islds Japan
59 K4 Dozen Nishi Jima isld
Japan
111 K10 Dozier Alabama
121 N5 Dozois, Rés Quebec
20 E3 Dozulé France
45 L3 Dozza Italy
85 C2 Dr'aa R Morocco/Algeria
36 C2 Drabenderhöhe
W Germany
28 F4 Dråby Denmark
19 P15 Drac R France
130 D7 Dracena Brazil
46 E3 Dračevo Yugoslavia
36 E5 Drachenfels mt
W Germany
25 F2 Drachten Netherlands
95 Q4 Dracut Massachusetts
28 F6 Dræby Denmark
26 H7 Dragan L Sweden
48 J6 Drăgănești Romania
47 H1 Draganovo Bulgaria
48 J6 Drăgășani Romania
103 O2 Dragerton Utah
46 E3 Dragoevo Yugoslavia
46 F2 Dragoman Bulgaria
45 K2 Dragoncello Italy
Dragon's Mouths chan see
Bocas del Dragon
103 O9 Dragoon Arizona
28 K5 Dragør Denmark
46 F2 Dragovistica Yugoslavia
29 J11 Dragsfjärd Finland
28 B3 Dragstrup Denmark
19 Q17 Draguignan France
33 T9 Drahnsdorf E Germany
100 B6 Drain Oregon
22 G4 Draize France
103 M7 Drake Arizona
98 A9 Drake Colorado
98 F2 Drake N Dakota
139 K3 Drake New S Wales
119 M7 Drake Sask
32 K7 Drakenburg W Germany
89 F8 Drakensberg mts S Africa
89 G5 Drakensberg Garden
S Africa
146 D15 Drake Passage
S Atlantic Oc
100 E7 Drake Peak mt Oregon
102 B4 Drakes Bay California
110 J4 Drakesboro Kentucky
94 J10 Drakes Branch Virginia
47 G3 Dráma Greece
27 D12 Drammen Norway
27 D12 Dramsfj inlet Norway
40 F5 Drance R Switzerland
48 L4 Drânceni Romania
27 D12 Drangedal Norway
33 R6 Dranse E Germany
40 E5 Dranse R France
32 L9 Dransfeld W Germany
28 C5 Drantum Denmark
112 H1 Draper N Carolina
98 F6 Draper S Dakota
101 O9 Draper Utah
117 D6 Draper, Mt Alaska
74 F1 Dras Kashmir
38 G8 Drau R Austria
38 N9 Drava R Yugoslavia
42 G2 Dravograd Yugoslavia
31 J2 Drawa R Poland
31 J2 Drawsko Poland
98 J1 Drayton N Dakota
141 K8 Drayton Queensland
118 B5 Drayton Val Alberta
37 O5 Draženov Czechoslovakia
43 B12 Drean Algeria
37 P2 Drebach E Germany
32 H7 Drebber W Germany
48 E2 Drégelypalánk Hungary
33 M5 Dreggers W Germany
36 F3 Dreieichenhain
W Germany
Dreihausen see
Ebsdorfergrund
38 F7 Dreiherrn-Spitze mt
Italy/Austria
36 B3 Dreis W Germany
40 G1 Dreisam R W Germany
37 P6 Dreitannenriegel mt
W Germany
28 E7 Drejø Denmark
13 F1 Drem Scotland
47 F2 Dren Bulgaria
33 T6 Drense E Germany
32 G9 Drensteinfurt W Germany
25 G3 Drente prov Netherlands
37 Q1 Dresden E Germany
107 K2 Dresden Kansas
98 H1 Dresden N Dakota
94 E6 Dresden Ohio
120 H10 Dresden Ontario
110 H5 Dresden Tennessee
33 T10 Dresden reg E Germany
52 C6 Dretun' U.S.S.R.
20 H4 Dreux France
26 F10 Drevsjö Norway
111 F8 Drew Mississippi
100 C7 Drew Oregon
33 Q5 Drewitzer See L
E Germany
100 G6 Drewsey Oregon
100 E7 Drews Res Oregon
110 B3 Drexel Missouri
52 E6 Drezna U.S.S.R.
54 K1 Drezna U.S.S.R.
36 E2 Driedorf W Germany
113 D7 Drifton Florida
118 B3 Driftpile Alberta
120 J3 Driftwood Ontario
94 J5 Driftwood Pennsylvania
101 O6 Driggs Idaho
141 J7 Drillham Queensland
46 D2 Drim R Yugoslavia
14 B5 Drimoleague Irish Rep
46 D2 Drin R Albania
48 E7 Drina R Yugoslavia
32 K9 Dringenberg W Germany
48 K2 Drinin U.S.S.R.
46 D3 Drinit, Pellg i B Albania
46 D3 Drin i zi R Albania
119 M8 Drinkwater Sask
109 J5 Dripping Springs Texas
109 K8 Driscoll Texas
52 C6 Drissa U.S.S.R.
26 D9 Driva R Norway
26 D9 Drivstua Norway
41 N6 Dro Italy
27 E12 Dröbak Norway
31 M3 Drobin Poland
55 F4 Drobyshevo U.S.S.R.
48 G4 Drocea mt Romania
32 K5 Drochtersen W Germany
22 D3 Drocourt France
32 M6 Drögen Nindorf
W Germany
14 E3 Drogheda Irish Rep
14 E3 Drogheda B Irish Rep
48 H1 Drogobych U.S.S.R.
31 O3 Drohiczyn Poland
8 D3 Droitwich England
48 L2 Drokiya U.S.S.R.
36 D1 Drolshagen W Germany
139 H7 Dromana Victoria
14 F2 Dromara N Ireland
19 O15 Drôme dep France
20 D3 Drome R France
139 K6 Dromedary,C New S Wales
33 O8 Dromling E Germany
14 D3 Dromod Irish Rep
14 D2 Dromore N Ireland
14 C2 Dromore West Irish Rep
44 B3 Dronero Italy
9 E1 Dronfield England
22 F1 Drongen Belgium
18 F7 Dronne R France
146 B7 Dronning Fabiolafjella
Antarctica
28 E2 Dronninglund Denmark
146 B7 Dronning Maude Ld
Antarctica
119 Q7 Dropmore Manitoba
18 F8 Dropt R France
31 J7 Drosendorf Austria
74 D1 Drosh Pakistan
28 G6 Drøsselbjerg Denmark
20 H5 Droué France
120 E2 Drowning R Ontario
37 N1 Droyssig E Germany
20 F3 Drucourt France
118 J7 Druid Sask
8 C2 Druid Wales
126 A1 Druif Aruba W Indies
36 C6 Drulingen France
118 E7 Drumheller Alberta
14 D4 Drum Hills Irish Rep
14 D3 Drumlish Irish Rep
101 M3 Drummond Montana
144 B7 Drummond New Zealand
99 P3 Drummond Wisconsin
94 D1 Drummond I Michigan
95 L10 Drummond,L Virginia
140 D4 Drummond,Mt N Terr Aust
141 H6 Drummond Ra Queensland
121 S7 Drummondville Quebec
12 D4 Drummore Luce Bay
Scotland
12 D4 Drummore Scotland
15 D3 Drumnadrochit Scotland
15 D4 Drumochter Pass Scotland
107 O6 Drumright Oklahoma
14 C2 Drumshanbo Irish Rep
12 D1 Drumvaich Scotland
25 D5 Drunen Netherlands
119 V8 Drunken Point C Manitoba
13 G3 Druridge B England
145 E2 Drury New Zealand
117 F4 Drury L Yukon Terr
36 D6 Drusenheim France
31 O1 Druskininkai U.S.S.R.
25 E5 Druten Netherlands
52 C6 Druya U.S.S.R.
54 E4 Druzhba U.S.S.R.
51 O2 Druzhina U.S.S.R.
55 C3 Druzhinino U.S.S.R.
54 J8 Druzhkovka U.S.S.R.
79 G6 Drūz, Jebel ed mts Syria
42 G4 Drvar Yugoslavia
42 G5 Drvenik isld Yugoslavia
100 B3 Dryad Washington
47 G2 Dryanovo Bulgaria
117 D6 Dry B Alaska
118 J1 Dryberry L Ontario
119 Q2 Drybrough Manitoba
101 R5 Dry Cr Wyoming
94 D4 Dryden Michigan
95 L4 Dryden New York
118 K1 Dryden Ontario
108 E5 Dryden Texas
110 E4 Dry Fork R Missouri
98 A6 Dry Fork R Wyoming
146 D2 Drygalski I Antarctica
8 C3 Drygarn Fawr mt Wales
127 K2 Dry Harbour Mts Jamaica
102 G6 Dry L California
102 G2 Dry L Nevada
122 F1 Drylake Labrador
103 K5 Dry Lake Nevada
103 K4 Dry Lake Valley Nevada
12 D1 Drymen Scotland
111 D10 Dry Prong Louisiana
141 G4 Dry R Queensland
140 D1 Drysdale I N Terr Aust
142 F2 Drysdale R W Australia
113 E13 Dry Tortugas islds Florida
85 G7 Dschang Cameroon
86 D5 Dua R Zaïre
127 K9 Duaca Venezuela
67 C4 Du'an China
Duancun see Wuxiang
95 N2 Duane New York
141 J6 Duaringa Queensland
127 J5 Duarte, Pico mt Dom Rep
130 E8 Duartina Brazil
130 D8 Duas Onças,Ilha das Brazil
109 P3 Dubach Louisiana
72 H3 Dubai U.A.E.
100 B9 Dubakella Mt California
114 J5 Dubawnt R N W Terr
139 J4 Dubbo New S Wales
56 C1 Dubches R U.S.S.R.
37 O4 Dubec Czechoslovakia
33 T9 Duben E Germany
55 C5 Dubenskiy U.S.S.R.
12 B1 Dubh Artach isld Scotland
48 G1 Dubiecko Poland
124 F2 Dublán Mexico
112 E5 Dublin Georgia
94 B7 Dublin Indiana
14 E3 Dublin Irish Rep
99 V5 Dublin Michigan
111 F7 Dublin Mississippi
94 D6 Dublin Ohio
120 J9 Dublin Ontario
109 J3 Dublin Texas
14 E3 Dublin co Irish Rep
54 H2 Dubna U.S.S.R.
52 E6 Dubna R U.S.S.R.
101 N5 Dubois Idaho
99 K9 Du Bois Nebraska
94 J5 Du Bois Pennsylvania
101 Q6 Dubois Wyoming
48 M3 Dubossary U.S.S.R.
54 K3 Dubovka U.S.S.R.
85 B7 Dubréka Guinea
54 E3 Dubrovka U.S.S.R.
42 J6 Dubrovnik Yugoslavia
54 B2 Dubrovno U.S.S.R.
55 E2 Dubrovnoye U.S.S.R.
119 P8 Dubuc Sask
99 Q7 Dubuque Iowa
52 G6 Dub'yazy U.S.S.R.
20 C4 Ducey France
67 E2 Duchang China
121 Q3 Ducharme Quebec
30 H5 Duchcov Czechoslovakia
33 T5 Ducherow E Germany
101 P9 Duchesne Utah
118 F8 Duchess Alberta
140 E5 Duchess Queensland
135 C11 Ducie I Pacific Oc
110 J5 Duck R Tennessee
119 R6 Duck Bay Manitoba
99 S5 Duck Cr Wisconsin
111 G8 Duck Hill Mississippi
118 L6 Duck Lake Sask
119 Q7 Duck Mt ra Manitoba
119 R7 Duck Mt. Prov. Park
Manitoba
112 C2 Ducktown Tennessee
103 J3 Duckwater Nevada
103 J3 Duckwater Pk Nevada
20 G3 Duclair France
102 E6 Ducor California
127 L4 Ducos Martinique W I
68 J5 Duc Pho Vietnam
9 F2 Duddington England
22 L5 Dudelange Luxembourg
36 B4 Dudeldorf W Germany
32 M9 Duderstadt W Germany
109 P3 Dudgemona R Louisiana
7 L9 Dudgeon Lightship
North Sea
50 H2 Dudinka U.S.S.R.
9 D3 Dudley England
112 D5 Dudley Georgia
110 F5 Dudley Missouri
86 B2 Dudo Somalia
54 G3 Dudorovskiy U.S.S.R.
36 C5 Dudweiler W Germany
51 J1 Dudypta R U.S.S.R.
22 E1 Dudzele Belgium
85 C7 Duékoué Ivory Coast
16 D3 Dueñas Spain
16 C2 Duerna R Spain
17 F3 Duero R Spain
112 E3 Due West S Carolina
146 G8 Dufek Coast Antarctica
119 O8 Duff Sask
138 D3 Duff Creek S Australia
22 H1 Duffel Belgium
118 C5 Duffield Alberta
140 C7 Duffield N Terr Aust
138 C2 Duffield R N Terr Australia
137 O3 Duff Is Santa Cruz Is
15 E3 Dufftown Scotland
122 F2 Dufresne,L Quebec
122 G2 Dufresne Lake Quebec
100 D4 Dufur Oregon
140 F5 Dugald R Queensland
103 N7 Dugas Arizona
111 D9 Dugdemona R Louisiana
110 J2 Dugger Indiana
42 F4 Dugi O Yugoslavia
86 H5 Dugiuma Somalia
54 H2 Dugna U.S.S.R.
141 G1 Dugong I Gt Barrier Reef
Aust
118 E6 Duhamel Alberta
131 D2 Duice, R Argentina
128 E3 Duida, Co mt Venezuela
141 F2 Duifken Pt Queensland
32 L8 Duingen W Germany
32 E10 Duisburg W Germany
25 A5 Duiveland Netherlands
67 C4 Dujiang China
46 E2 Dukat Yugoslavia
107 L7 Duke Oklahoma
117 H8 Duke I Alaska
141 K5 Duke Is Queensland
135 N10 Duke of Gloucester Is
Pacific Oc
142 F4 Dukes Dome mt
W Australia
86 F4 Duk Faiwil Sudan
72 G3 Dukhān Qatar
54 D1 Dukhovshchina U.S.S.R.
59 L1 Duki U.S.S.R.
31 N6 Dukla Poland
52 C6 Dukstas U.S.S.R.
111 F12 Dulac Louisiana
58 C4 Dulan China
58 C4 Dulansi China
8 B1 Dulas B Wales
71 G7 Dulawan Mindanao
Philippines
116 K4 Dulbi R Alaska
106 D5 Dulce New Mexico
141 F1 Dulcie R Queensland
80 G7 Duleilat el Muterat Jordan
51 N2 Dulgalakh R U.S.S.R.
47 J1 Dŭlgopol Bulgaria
141 F1 Dulhunty R Queensland
70 D3 Dulit Ra Sarawak
67 C4 Duliu Jiang R China
71 G5 Duljugan Pt Leyte
Philippines
25 F6 Dülken W Germany
75 P6 Dullabchara India
98 B6 Dull Center Wyoming
32 F9 Dülmen W Germany
67 A5 Dulong China
47 J1 Dulovo Bulgaria
99 O3 Duluth Minnesota
8 C5 Dulverton England
79 G5 Dūma Syria
71 F6 Dumaguete Negros
Philippines
69 E12 Dumai Sumatra
47 J6 Dumanlı Dağı mt Turkey
71 F7 Dumanquilas B Mindanao
Philippines
71 D5 Dumaran isld Philippines
139 K3 Dumaresq R Queensland
70 F4 Dumaring Kalimantan
111 E8 Dumas Arkansas
108 C8 Dumas Texas
83 K10 Dumbanagala mt
Sri Lanka
12 D2 Dumbarton Scotland
48 F2 Ďumbier mt
Czechoslovakia
143 C10 Dumbleyung W Australia
143 C10 Dumbleyung, L W Australia
86 B3 Dumboa Nigeria
48 J4 Dumbrăveni Romania
69 H12 Dumdum isld Indonesia
79 G5 Dumeir,Jebel mts Syria
12 E3 Dumfries Scotland
Dumfries co see
Dumfries and Galloway
reg
15 D5 Dumfries and Galloway
reg Scotland
54 G3 Duminichi U.S.S.R.
48 K5 Dumitrești Romania
75 M6 Dumka India
119 N9 Dummer Sask
32 H7 Dümmersee L W Germany
71 H4 Dumoga Ketjil Sulawesi
121 N6 Dumoine, L Quebec
98 K4 Dumont Minnesota
121 O6 Dumont,L Quebec
36 B3 Dümpelfeld W Germany
65 J1 Dumune China
79 B7 Dumyât Egypt
48 E4 Duna R Hungary
48 K2 Dunaevtsy U.S.S.R.
48 D3 Dunaj R Czechoslovakia
31 M6 Dunajec R Poland
14 E3 Dunany Pt Irish Rep
48 E4 Dunapataj Hungary
48 L6 Dunărea R Romania
48 E4 Dunaujváros Hungary
48 F5 Dunav R S Europe
144 C6 Dunback New Zealand
107 P7 Dunbar Oklahoma
141 F3 Dunbar Queensland
13 F1 Dunbar Scotland
101 N9 Dunbar Utah
99 S4 Dunbar Wisconsin
94 F8 Dunbar W Virginia
Dunbarton co see
Strathclyde reg
118 L7 Dunblane Sask
12 E1 Dunblane Scotland
14 E3 Dunboyne Irish Rep
103 P9 Duncan Arizona
100 B1 Duncan Br Columbia
98 J8 Duncan Nebraska
107 N7 Duncan Oklahoma
101 Q6 Duncan Wyoming
141 F1 Duncan Is Queensland
117 R4 Duncan L N W Terr
140 A3 Duncan, Mt N Terr Aust
14 E4 Duncannon Irish Rep
95 K6 Duncannon Pennsylvania
68 A7 Duncan Passage
Andaman Is
112 C3 Duncan Ridge Georgia
127 K1 Duncans Jamaica
15 E2 Duncansby Hd Scotland
126 G3 Duncan Town Bahamas
109 N10 Duncanville Texas
9 E3 Dunchurch England
13 F6 Duncombe England
9 F6 Duncton England
52 B6 Duncaga U.S.S.R.
14 E2 Dundalk Irish Rep
120 K8 Dundalk Ontario
14 E3 Dundalk B Irish Rep
115 N2 Dundas Greenland
147 F6 Dundas N W Terr
94 E7 Dundas Ohio
117 H8 Dundas I Br Columbia
143 D9 Dundas L W Australia
136 G4 Dundas Str N Terr
Australia
99 S7 Dundee Illinois
94 D5 Dundee Michigan
95 L4 Dundee New York
89 G7 Dundee S Africa
13 F1 Dundee Scotland
109 J2 Dundee Texas
146 D14 Dundee I Antarctica
26 G5 Dunderlands-dal V Norway
Dund Hot see Zhenlan Qi
141 G8 Dundoo Queensland
12 E4 Dundrennan Scotland
14 F2 Dundrum N Ireland
14 F2 Dundrum B N Ireland
118 L7 Dundurn Sask
113 E9 Dunedin Florida
144 C7 Dunedin New Zealand
139 J4 Dunedoo New S Wales
14 C1 Dunfanaghy Irish Rep
15 E4 Dunfermline Scotland
14 E2 Dungannon N Ireland
120 J9 Dungannon Ontario
74 E7 Dungarpur India
14 D4 Dungarvan Irish Rep
14 D4 Dungarvan Harb Irish Rep
66 D5 Dungbaree Range China
9 G6 Dungeness England
133 D8 Dungeness,Pta Arg/Chile
14 E2 Dungiven N Ireland
14 C2 Dungloe Irish Rep
139 K4 Dungog New S Wales
86 E5 Dungu Zaïre
86 G1 Dungunab Sudan
9 F1 Dunham England
59 J3 Dunhua China
58 B3 Dunhuang China
141 J7 Dunkeld Queensland
15 E4 Dunkeld Scotland
138 F6 Dunkeld Victoria
106 E9 Dunken New Mexico
22 C1 Dunkerque France
141 H4 Dunk I Queensland
Dunkirk see Dunkerque
110 L1 Dunkirk Indiana
101 O1 Dunkirk Montana
121 L10 Dunkirk New York
119 M8 Dunkirk Sask
86 G3 Dunkur Ethiopia
85 D7 Dunkwa Ghana
14 E3 Dún Laoghaire Irish Rep
99 L8 Dunlap Iowa
107 O3 Dunlap Kansas
106 F7 Dunlap New Mexico
108 G1 Dunlap Texas
14 E3 Dunlavin Irish Rep
109 J6 Dunlay Texas
14 E3 Dunleer Irish Rep
119 T4 Dunlop Manitoba
120 J9 Dunlop Ontario
12 D2 Dunlop Scotland
14 B5 Dunmanus B Irish Rep
14 B5 Dunmanway Irish Rep
140 C3 Dunmarra N Terr Aust
14 C3 Dunmore Irish Rep
95 M5 Dunmore Pennsylvania
113 L12 Dunmore Town Bahamas
126 F2 Dunmore Town Eleuthera
Bahamas
9 G4 Dunmow England
112 J2 Dunn N Carolina
98 D2 Dunn Center N Dakota
99 M6 Dunnell Minnesota
113 E8 Dunnellon Florida
15 E2 Dunnet B Scotland
15 E2 Dunnet Hd Scotland
98 F8 Dunning Nebraska
12 E1 Dunning Scotland
36 E7 Dunningen W Germany
143 C6 Dunns Ra W Australia
120 G6 Dunn Valley Ontario
121 L10 Dunnville Ontario
139 G6 Dunolly Victoria
12 D2 Dunoon Scotland
100 J9 Dunphy Nevada
84 J5 Dunqul Oasis Egypt
120 G4 Dunrankin Ontario
119 S9 Dunrea Manitoba
13 F2 Duns Scotland
144 D5 Dunsandel New Zealand
143 B10 Dunsborough W Australia
12 E3 Dunscore Scotland
98 G1 Dunseith N Dakota
100 C8 Dunsmuir California
9 F4 Dunstable England
144 B6 Dunstan Mts New Zealand
117 O9 Dunster Br Col
8 C5 Dunster England
31 K7 Dun Streda
Czechoslovakia
18 G6 Dun sur Auron France
22 J5 Dun-sur-Meuse France
144 C6 Duntroon New Zealand
120 K8 Duntroon Ontario
36 D6 Duntzenheim France
15 B3 Dunvegan Scotland
15 B3 Dunvegan,L Scotland
123 T6 Dunville Nfld
9 H3 Dunwich England
58 G3 Duolun China
68 F7 Duong Dong Vietnam
67 D4 Dupang Ling mts China
121 L4 Duparquet Quebec
69 J11 Duperre I Indonesia
94 B8 Dupont Indiana
95 M5 Dupont Pennsylvania
98 E4 Dupree S Dakota
121 L4 Dupuy Quebec
101 N1 Dupuyer Montana
87 C7 Duque de Braganca
Angola
130 G8 Duque de Caxias Brazil
133 B8 Duque de York,I Chile
103 O10 Duquesne Arizona
94 H6 Duquesne Pennsylvania
110 G3 Du Quoin Illinois
80 D7 Dura Jordan
41 M2 Durach W Germany
142 F3 Durack,R W Australia
142 F3 Durack Ra W Australia
78 E1 Durağan Turkey
139 K2 Durah Queensland
141 K7 Durah Queensland
47 J5 Durak Turkey
106 E7 Duran New Mexico
19 Q16 Durance R France
99 R7 Durand Illinois
94 D4 Durand Michigan
99 P5 Durand Wisconsin
106 C4 Durango Colorado
124 G5 Durango Mexico
18 D9 Durango Spain
111 G8 Durant Mississippi
107 O8 Durant Oklahoma
16 E3 Duratón R Spain
131 G4 Durazno Uruguay
131 G4 Durazno dep Uruguay
Durazzo see Durrës
89 G7 Durban S Africa
143 E6 Durba Spring W Australia
27 M15 Durbe U.S.S.R.
94 H8 Durbin W Virginia
22 J3 Durbuy Belgium
16 E8 Dúrcal Spain
79 G4 Dureikish Syria
36 B2 Düren W Germany
75 J8 Durg India
75 M7 Durgapur India
102 C2 Durham California
13 G4 Durham England
107 N3 Durham Kansas
112 J2 Durham N Carolina
95 R3 Durham New Hampshire
120 K8 Durham Ontario
121 S7 Durham Quebec
13 G4 Durham co England
122 F7 Durham Br New Brunswick
141 F7 Durham Downs
Queensland
12 E3 Durisdeer Scotland
100 H5 Durkee Oregon
36 E6 Durlach W Germany
9 E6 Durlston Hd England
36 E6 Durmersheim W Germany
42 J5 Durmitor mt Yugoslavia
15 D2 Durness Scotland
38 N5 Durnstein Austria
123 L3 Durocher,L Quebec
38 M6 Durrenstein mt Austria
46 C3 Durrës Albania
140 F7 Durrie Queensland
14 D4 Durrow Irish Rep
37 J5 Dürrwangen W Germany
14 A5 Dursey Hd Irish Rep
14 A5 Dursey I Irish Rep
8 D4 Dursley England
8 C5 Durston England
47 K5 Dursunbey Turkey
21 E6 Durtal France
Duru see Wuchuan
28 B3 Durup Denmark
145 D4 D'Urville New Zealand
77 J2 Durzab Afghanistan
120 D1 Dusey R Ontario
57 A6 Dushak U.S.S.R.
67 B4 Dushan China
57 E5 Dushanbe U.S.S.R.
65 C4 Dushikou China
95 L5 Dushore Pennsylvania
47 J2 Dŭskotna Bulgaria
144 A6 Dusky Sd New Zealand
32 E10 Düsseldorf W Germany
25 C5 Dussen Netherlands
41 J4 Düssist mt Switzerland
33 R9 Düssnitz E Germany
107 O6 Dustin Oklahoma
83 J9 Dutch B Sri Lanka
Dutch Guiana see
Surinam
116 D10 Dutch Harbor Aleutian Is
101 M9 Dutch Mt Utah
89 C4 Dutlwe Botswana
52 J3 Dutovo U.S.S.R.
85 F6 Dutsan Wai Nigeria
101 O2 Dutton Montana
120 J10 Dutton Ontario
141 G5 Dutton R Queensland
138 D4 Dutton,L S Australia
103 M3 Dutton,Mt Utah
119 N7 Duval Sask
127 H5 Duvalierville Haiti
121 N6 Duval,L Quebec
55 C3 Duvan U.S.S.R.
144 D5 Duvauchelle New Zealand
26 F8 Duved Sweden
127 J5 Duvergé Dominican Rep
52 D3 Duvogero U.S.S.R.
22 D5 Duvy France
95 R4 Duxbury Massachusetts
9 G3 Duxford England
67 B4 Duyang Shan mts China
68 C4 Duyinzeik Burma
67 B3 Duyun China
78 C1 Düzce Turkey
43 B12 Duzerville Algeria
47 H1 Dve Mogili Bulgaria
26 H2 Dverberg Norway
52 F3 Dvina, Severnyy R U.S.S.R.
52 E2 Dvinskaya Guba B
U.S.S.R.
54 C1 Dvin'ye,Oz L U.S.S.R.
31 K6 Dvorec Czechoslovakia
31 J5 Dvůr Králové
Czechoslovakia
88 D8 Dwangwa R Malawi
143 B10 Dwarda W Australia
74 C7 Dwarka India
89 E5 Dwars Berg mts S Africa
143 B10 Dwellingup W Australia
99 S8 Dwight Illinois
107 O3 Dwight Kansas
98 J8 Dwight Nebraska
94 F9 Dwight Virginia
106 C9 Dwyer New Mexico
98 B7 Dwyer Wyoming
54 F3 Dyat'kovo U.S.S.R.
28 D7 Dybbøl Denmark
28 A3 Dybe Kirke Denmark
28 H6 Dybsø Fjord inlet Denmark
119 R4 Dyce Manitoba
15 F3 Dyce Scotland
99 T5 Dyckesville Wisconsin
110 H5 Dyer Tennessee
114 G2 Dyer B N W Terr
120 J7 Dyer Bay Ontario
110 G5 Dyersburg Tennessee
99 P7 Dyersville Iowa
8 B3 Dyfed co Wales
8 B2 Dyfi R Wales
31 J1 Dygowo Poland
31 J7 Dyje R Czechoslovakia
22 H2 Dyle R Belgium
9 G5 Dymchurch England
118 K1 Dyment Ontario
8 D4 Dymock England
141 G8 Dynevor Downs
Queensland
31 N6 Dynów Poland
102 F4 Dyor Nevada
28 E6 Dyreborg Denmark
26 C8 Dyrnesvågen Norway
26 J2 Dyröy Norway
99 O7 Dysart Iowa
119 N8 Dysart Sask
13 E1 Dysart Scotland
47 J2 Dyulevo Bulgaria
47 J2 Dyulino Bulgaria
78 L1 Dyul'tydag mt U.S.S.R.
57 C2 Dyurmen'tove U.S.S.R.
58 C2 Dzag Mongolia
58 F3 Dzamïn Üüde Mongolia
87 H10 Dzaoudzi Comoros
58 C2 Dzavhan Gol R Mongolia
30 H5 Džban mt Czechoslovakia
54 J8 Dzerzhinsk U.S.S.R.
56 C4 Dzerzhinskiy U.S.S.R.
57 K2 Dzerzhinskoye U.S.S.R.
51 N3 Dzhagdy,Khrebet mts
U.S.S.R.
55 E5 Dzhaksy U.S.S.R.
56 D5 Dzhakul', Gora mt U.S.S.R.
57 G4 Dzhalal-Abad U.S.S.R.
59 H1 Dzhalinda U.S.S.R.
55 E5 Dzhaltyr U.S.S.R.
55 B5 Dzhambeyty U.S.S.R.
55 D5 Dzhambul U.S.S.R.
57 J2 Dzhansugurov U.S.S.R.
56 D5 Dzhebashskiy Khrebet mts
U.S.S.R.
55 D5 Dzhetygara U.S.S.R.
57 C4 Dzhetymtau, Gory mt
U.S.S.R.
57 E4 Dzhetysay U.S.S.R.
57 E1 Dzhezkazgan U.S.S.R.
56 G5 Dzhida R U.S.S.R.
56 F5 Dzhidinskiy,Khrebet mts
Mongolia/U.S.S.R.
57 B4 Dzhigirbent U.S.S.R.
57 E4 Dzhizak U.S.S.R.
56 D4 Dzhoyskiy Khrebet mts
U.S.S.R.
57 D5 Dzhuma U.S.S.R.
57 K2 Dzhungarskiy Alatau,
Khrebet mts U.S.S.R.
48 L2 Dzhurin U.S.S.R.
57 C2 Dzhusaly U.S.S.R.
31 M2 Działdowo Poland
31 M5 Działoszyce Poland
31 L4 Działoszyn Poland
31 L2 Dzierżgoń Poland
31 K5 Dzierżoniów Poland
125 O7 Dzitbalché Mexico
31 H1 Dziwnów Poland
52 B6 Džūkste U.S.S.R.
66 C3 Dzungaria reg China
66 C2 Dzungarian Gate pass
U.S.S.R./China
58 E3 Dzüünbayan Mongolia
106 H3 Eads Colorado
103 P7 Eagar Arizona
101 T10 Eagle Colorado
100 J6 Eagle Idaho
98 K9 Eagle Nebraska
99 S7 Eagle Wisconsin
101 R5 Eagle Wyoming
110 M3 Eagle R Kentucky
98 E4 Eagle Butte S Dakota
107 M6 Eagle City Oklahoma
102 G6 Eagle Crags California
121 O6 Eagle Depot Quebec
141 K1 Eagle Farm dist
Brisbane, Qnsld
99 N7 Eagle Grove Iowa
99 S2 Eagle Harbor Michigan
139 J9 Eaglehawk Neck Tasmania
119 O1 Eaglehead L Ontario
119 T5 Eagle I Manitoba
100 E9 Eagle L California
95 R7 Eagle L Maine
95 S6 Eagle L Maine
118 J1 Eagle L Ontario
113 F10 Eagle Lake Florida
109 L6 Eagle Lake Texas
109 K3 Eagle Mt. L Texas
103 J8 Eagle Mts California
106 E5 Eagle Nest New Mexico
108 G7 Eagle Pass Texas
114 F4 Eagle Plain Yukon Terr
100 C7 Eagle Point Oregon
99 S2 Eagle River Michigan
99 R4 Eagle River Wisconsin
94 H9 Eagle Rock Virginia
12 D2 Eaglesham Scotland
137 Q4 Eaglestone Reef Pacific Oc
116 O4 Eagle Summit Alaska
103 L8 Eagle Tail Mts Arizona
109 N1 Eagleton Arkansas
107 Q7 Eagletown Oklahoma
100 E8 Eagleville California
61 O7 Eai-gawa R Japan
68 H6 Ea Kan R Vietnam
9 F4 Ealing England
144 C6 Ealing New Zealand
143 D7 Earaheedy W Australia
8 D3 Eardisland England
117 L11 Ear Lakes Cove Br Col
110 F6 Earle Arkansas
99 M8 Earlham Iowa
102 E6 Earlimart California
99 L8 Earling Iowa
110 J4 Earlington Kentucky
100 A8 Earl,L California
144 A6 Earl Mts New Zealand
13 F2 Earlston Scotland
121 L5 Earlton Ontario
99 S8 Earlville Illinois
99 P7 Earlville Iowa
13 E1 Earn,Br.of Scotland
12 D1 Earn,L Scotland
117 F4 Earn L Yukon Terr
12 E1 Earn,R Scotland
144 B6 Earnslaw, Mt
New Zealand
103 K7 Earp California
13 G3 Earsdon England
9 F6 Easebourne England
13 G4 Easington Durham England
13 J6 Easington Humberside
England
13 G5 Easingwold England
112 E3 Easley S Carolina
110 F3 East Alton Illinois
121 T7 East Angus Quebec
123 M7 East B C Breton I, N Scotia
113 B7 East B Florida
111 G12 East B Louisiana
111 B12 East B Texas
112 G1 East Bend N Carolina
95 L7 East Berlin Pennsylvania
109 L6 East Bernard Texas
9 G6 Eastbourne England
145 G4 Eastbourne New Zealand
94 H6 East Brady Pennsylvania
8 D5 East Brent England
111 J10 East Brewton Alabama
71 G6 East Bucas Philippines
101 O1 East Butte mt Montana
145 G2 East Cape New Zealand
99 T8 East Chicago Indiana
64 G4 East China Sea
145 F3 East Coast stat area
New Zealand
145 E2 East Coast Bays
New Zealand
118 E7 East Coulee Alberta
9 G6 Eastdean England
9 G2 East Dereham England
99 Q7 East Dubuque Illinois
103 K2 East Ely Nevada
118 J9 Eastend Sask
143 A8 Easter Grp islds
W Australia
135 U16 Easter I Pacific Oc
141 F5 Eastern Creek Queensland
84 J4 Eastern Desert Egypt
86 F4 Eastern Equatoria prov
Sudan
76 C4 Eastern Ghats mts India
123 S5 Eastern Meelpaeg L Nfld
119 S5 Easterville Manitoba
122 E7 East Florenceville
New Brunswick
120 J3 Eastford Ontario
99 Q9 East Galesburg Illinois
102 G2 Eastgate Nevada
30 G2 East Germany
101 M1 East Glacier Park Montana
9 F5 East Grinstead England
95 P6 East Hampton Long I, N Y
95 P4 Easthampton
Massachusetts
101 O3 East Helena Montana
9 G6 East Hoathly England
123 L6 East I Madeleine Is, Quebec
9 E4 East Ilsley England
95 P4 East Jaffrey
New Hampshire
147 F12 East Jan Mayen Rdg
Norwegian Sea
122 J9 East Jeddore Nova Scotia
94 B1 East Jordan Michigan
122 G10 East Jordan Nova Scotia
9 G1 East Keal England
122 G9 East Kemptville
Nova Scotia
95 R6 East L Maine
99 U5 East Lake Michigan
109 J3 Eastland Texas
94 C4 East Lansing Michigan
9 E6 Eastleigh England
110 N1 East Liberty Ohio
13 F2 East Linton Scotland
94 G6 East Liverpool Ohio
89 E9 East London S Africa
East Lothian co see
Lothian reg
94 E8 East Lynn W Virginia
115 M7 Eastmain Quebec
112 D5 Eastman Georgia
141 H6 Eastmere Queensland
143 E8 East, Mt W Australia
8 D3 Eastnor England
99 R9 Easton Illinois
95 Q4 Easton Massachusetts
99 N6 Easton Minnesota
110 B2 Easton Missouri
95 M6 Easton Pennsylvania
100 D2 Easton Washington
112 G4 Eastover S Carolina
East Pakistan see
Bangladesh
113 F8 East Palatka Florida
94 G6 East Palestine Ohio
102 B2 East Park Res California
99 N8 East Peru Iowa
117 N8 East Pine Br Col
111 M8 East Point Georgia
94 E9 East Point Kentucky
123 L6 East Point
Madeleine Is, Quebec
121 L1 East Point Ontario
123 L7 East Point Pr Edward I
123 N10 East Point Sable I, N Scotia
119 M9 East Poplar Sask
106 E2 East Portal Colorado
110 G5 East Prairie Missouri
122 G10 East Pubnico Nova Scotia
94 G9 East Rainelle W Virginia
100 H9 East Range Nevada
9 F1 East Retford England
9 H5 Eastry England
110 F3 East St Louis Illinois
147 P5 East Siberian Sea
Arctic Oc
139 J7 East Sister I Tasmania
100 K2 East Sister Peak mt Idaho
9 F1 East Stoke England
8 D5 East Stour England
9 G6 East Sussex co England
94 D2 East Tawas Michigan
139 H4 East Toorale New S Wales
119 N4 East Trout L Sask
99 S7 East Troy Wisconsin
103 N7 East Verde R Arizona
95 M9 Eastville Virginia
13 E1 East Wemyss Scotland
9 E1 East Wood England
138 C2 Eateringinna Cr S Australia
98 B9 Eaton Colorado
110 L1 Eaton Indiana
110 M2 Eaton Ohio
118 H7 Eatonia Sask
140 B6 Eaton L N Terr Aust
94 C4 Eaton Rapids Michigan
9 F3 Eaton Socon England
112 D4 Eatonton Georgia
100 C3 Eatonville Washington
99 U7 Eau Claire Michigan
99 P5 Eau Claire Wisconsin
99 P5 Eau Claire R Wisconsin
122 G1 Eau-Claire, L. à l' Labrador
115 M6 Eau Claire, L. à l' Quebec
113 G9 Eau Gallie Florida
121 Q3 Eau-Jaune, L. a l' Quebec
20 H2 Eaulne R France
134 E7 Eauripik Rise Pac Oc
18 F9 Eauze France
141 G2 Ebagoola Queensland
125 K6 Ebano Mexico
43 B13 Ebba Ksour Tunisia
36 D1 Ebbe mts W Germany
13 H5 Ebberston England
28 D6 Ebberup Denmark
8 C4 Ebbw Vale Wales
86 B5 Ebebiyin Equat Guinea
33 N10 Ebeleben E Germany
28 F4 Ebeltoft Denmark
119 P7 Ebenezer Sask
99 U3 Eben Junction Michigan
94 J6 Ebensburg Pennsylvania
38 J6 Ebensee Austria
37 K3 Ebensfeld W Germany
36 G5 Eberbach W Germany
78 C2 Eber Gölü Turkey
32 M9 Ebergötzen W Germany
37 L4 Ebermannstadt
W Germany
37 K3 Ebern W Germany
36 D4 Ebernburg W Germany
110 M4 E Bernstadt Kentucky
36 H6 Ebersbach W Germany
36 H3 Ebersburg W Germany
37 L3 Ebersdorf W Germany
36 F4 Eberstadt W Germany
38 L8 Eberstein Austria
33 T7 Eberswalde E Germany
60 P2 Ebetsu Japan
55 F4 Ebeyty, Oz L U.S.S.R.
67 A2 Ebian China
36 G7 Ebingen W Germany
66 C3 Ebinur Hu L China
79 G3 Ebla anc site Syria
41 K3 Ebnat Switzerland
37 J6 Ebnat W Germany
86 D5 Ebola R Zaïre
43 G8 Eboli Italy
86 B5 Ebolowa Cameroon
37 K4 Ebrach W Germany
9 F2 E Bridgford England
44 F2 Ebro mt Italy
16 E2 Ebro R Spain
16 E2 Ebro, Embalse del res
Spain
36 E2 Ebschloh mt W Germany
36 F2 Ebsdorfergrund
W Germany
33 M6 Ebstorf W Germany
22 G2 Ecaussines Belgium
13 E3 Ecclefechan Scotland
13 F2 Eccles Scotland
94 F9 Eccles W Virginia
13 G6 Ecclesfield England
8 D2 Eccleshall England
127 P2 Ecclesville Trinidad
47 H4 Eceabat Turkey

40 E4 **Echallens** Switzerland
20 F4 **Echauffour** France
67 E1 **Echeng** China
101 U5 **Echeta** Wyoming
61 J10 **Echizen-misaki** *C* Japan
99 L5 **Echo** Minnesota
100 F4 **Echo** Oregon
101 O9 **Echo** Utah
103 K5 **Echo B** Nevada
120 G6 **Echo Bay** Ontario
103 N5 **Echo Cliffs** Arizona
139 H8 **Echo,L** Tasmania
121 P5 **Échouani L** Quebec
122 H4 **Echouerie, L'** Quebec
119 O8 **Echo Valley Prov. Park** Sask
25 E6 **Echt** Netherlands
15 F3 **Echt** Scotland
32 M9 **Echte** W Germany
25 F3 **Echten** Netherlands
36 G6 **Echterdingen** W Germany
22 L4 **Echternach** Luxembourg
139 G6 **Echuca** Victoria
36 F3 **Echzell** W Germany
16 D7 **Écija** Spain
36 H5 **Eckartshausen** W Germany
98 H3 **Eckelson** N Dakota
37 L4 **Eckental** W Germany
30 E1 **Eckernförde** W Germany
109 J5 **Eckert** Texas
13 F3 **Eckford** Scotland
9 E1 **Eckington** Derby England
8 D3 **Eckington** Hereford & Worcester England
12 C1 **Eck,L** Scotland
98 D9 **Eckley** Colorado
94 F9 **Eckman** W Virginia
118 C6 **Eckville** Alberta
32 H5 **Eckwarderhörne** W Germany
111 K9 **Eclectic** Alabama
143 C11 **Eclipse I** W Australia
140 B5 **Eclipse, Mt** N Terr Aust
115 M3 **Eclipse Sound** N W Terr
21 F6 **Écommoy** France
110 L2 **Economy** Indiana
121 O5 **Écorces,L.aux** Quebec
20 J3 **Ecos** France
20 E4 **Ecouché** France
20 H3 **Ecouls** France
20 F4 **Ecouves,Forêt d'** France
22 J4 **Ecouviez** Belgium
22 C2 **Ecques** France
20 A3 **Ecréhou,les** English Chan
111 G7 **Ecru** Mississippi
128 C4 **Ecuador** *rep* S America
21 H7 **Écueillé** France
123 K9 **Ecum Secum** Nova Scotia
143 B8 **Edah** W Australia
25 D3 **Edam** Netherlands
118 J5 **Edam** Sask
15 F1 **Eday** Scotland
118 E6 **Edberg** Alberta
109 K9 **Edcouch** Texas
86 H3 **Edd** Ethiopia
6 N6 **Edda** *oil rig* North Sea
86 E3 **Ed Da'ein** Sudan
86 F2 **Ed Damer** Sudan
86 F2 **Ed Debba** Sudan
32 K5 **Eddelak** W Germany
123 Q2 **Eddies Cove** Nfld
13 E2 **Eddleston** Scotland
15 C2 **Eddrachillis B** Scotland
86 F3 **Ed Dueim** Sudan
100 K2 **Eddy** Montana
109 K4 **Eddy** Texas
8 B7 **Eddystone Lt. Ho** English Chan
139 J8 **Eddystone Pt** Tasmania
99 O8 **Eddyville** Iowa
110 H4 **Eddyville** Kentucky
98 G8 **Eddyville** Nebraska
25 E4 **Ede** Netherlands
85 E7 **Ede** Nigeria
86 B5 **Edea** Cameroon
27 G11 **Edebäck** Sweden
27 K11 **Edebo** Sweden
130 E5 **Edéia** Brazil
143 A7 **Edel Land** *pen* W Australia
119 S8 **Eden** Manitoba
101 O2 **Eden** Montana
94 H10 **Eden** N Carolina
112 H1 **Eden** N Carolina
139 J6 **Eden** New S Wales
94 J4 **Eden** New York
98 J4 **Eden** S Dakota
108 H4 **Eden** Texas
101 O8 **Eden** Utah
99 S6 **Eden** Wisconsin
101 Q7 **Eden** Wyoming
9 G5 **Edenbridge** England
89 D7 **Edenburg** S Africa
144 B7 **Edendale** New Zealand
14 D3 **Edenderry** Irish Rep
13 F6 **Edenfield** England
138 F6 **Edenhope** Victoria
120 J8 **Edenhurst** Ontario
36 E5 **Edenkoben** W Germany
119 R2 **Eden L** Manitoba
9 G5 **Eden,R** England
71 N9 **Eden,Tg** *C* Indonesia
112 L1 **Edenton** N Carolina
141 G4 **Eden Vale** Queensland
94 C3 **Edenville** Michigan
119 N8 **Edenwold** Sask
138 E4 **Edeowie** S Australia
36 E1 **Eder** *R* W Germany
36 G1 **Edermünde** W Germany
33 O10 **Edersleben** E Germany
36 F1 **Ederstausee** *res* W Germany
36 G1 **Edertal** W Germany
27 F13 **Edet, L** Sweden
32 G6 **Edewecht** W Germany
32 G6 **Edewechterdamm** W Germany
101 R4 **Edgar** Montana
98 J9 **Edgar** Nebraska
111 F11 **Edgard** Louisiana
142 D5 **Edgar, Mt** W Australia
142 E4 **Edgar Ra** W Australia
110 E4 **Edgar Springs** Missouri
95 R5 **Edgartown** Massachusetts
109 M9 **Edgecliff** Texas
145 F2 **Edgecumbe** New Zealand
141 J5 **Edgecumbe B** Queensland
112 F4 **Edgefield** S Carolina
98 H3 **Edgeley** N Dakota
119 O8 **Edgeley** Sask
115 N5 **Edgell I** N W Terr
110 D6 **Edgemont** Arkansas
98 C6 **Edgemont** S Dakota
50 B1 **Edgeöya** *isld* Spitzbergen
109 O5 **Edgerly** Louisiana
118 G6 **Edgerton** Alberta
94 C5 **Edgerton** Ohio
99 R7 **Edgerton** Wisconsin
101 T6 **Edgerton** Wyoming
113 G9 **Edgewater** Florida
117 O11 **Edgewood** Br Col
110 H3 **Edgewood** Illinois
95 L7 **Edgewood** Maryland
106 D6 **Edgewood** New Mexico
109 M3 **Edgewood** Texas
9 F4 **Edgware** England
80 C8 **Edh Dhahiriya** Jordan
46 E4 **Édhessa** Greece
144 B6 **Edievale** New Zealand
36 C3 **Ediger-Eller** W Germany
84 F5 **Edimpi** Chad
94 G5 **Edinboro** Pennsylvania
99 R10 **Edinburg** Illinois
110 L2 **Edinburg** Indiana
111 G9 **Edinburg** Mississippi
98 J1 **Edinburg** N Dakota
109 J9 **Edinburg** Texas
94 J8 **Edinburg** Virginia
13 E2 **Edinburgh** Scotland
141 H7 **Edinburgh, Mt** Queensland
22 F2 **Edingen** Belgium
47 H3 **Edirne** Turkey
102 F6 **Edison** California
106 F3 **Edison** Colorado
111 M10 **Edison** Georgia
112 G4 **Edisto** *R* S Carolina
112 G5 **Edisto Island** S Carolina
138 E6 **Edithburgh** S Australia
117 P9 **Edith Cavell,Mt** Alberta
101 O3 **Edith, Mt** Montana
140 B2 **Edith River** N Terr Aust
143 D7 **Edith Withnell, L** W Australia
85 F3 **Edjeleh** Algeria
143 D8 **Edjudina** W Australia
13 G3 **Edlingham** England
38 O6 **Edlitz** Austria
95 M4 **Edmeston** New York
107 L2 **Edmond** Kansas
107 N6 **Edmond** Oklahoma
100 C2 **Edmonds** Washington
114 H7 **Edmonton** Alberta
9 F4 **Edmonton** England
94 C3 **Edmore** Michigan
98 H1 **Edmore** N Dakota
122 D6 **Edmundston** New Brunswick
109 L7 **Edna** Texas
13 F2 **Ednam** Scotland
27 J13 **Ed, O** Sweden
61 N10 **Edo-gawa** *R* Japan
27 M14 **Edole** U.S.S.R.
42 C2 **Edolo** Italy
26 C8 **Edoy** *isld* Norway
47 J5 **Edremit** Turkey
47 H5 **Edremit Körfezi** *B* Turkey
58 C3 **Edrengiyn Nuruu** *mt* Mongolia
109 K8 **Edroy** Texas
27 K12 **Edsbro** Sweden
27 H13 **Edsbruk** Sweden
27 H10 **Edsbyn** Sweden
26 J8 **Edsele** Sweden
Edsin Gol *see* **Ruo Shui**
58 D3 **Edsin Gol** China
114 H7 **Edson** Alberta
107 J2 **Edson** Kansas
27 J14 **Ed, V** Sweden
118 E4 **Edward** Alberta
139 G6 **Edward** *R* New S Wales
140 D2 **Edward I** N Terr Aust
120 B4 **Edward I** Ontario
88 B2 **Edward, L** Zaïre
140 B6 **Edward, Mt** N Terr Aust
141 F4 **Edward River** Queensland
102 G7 **Edwards** California
111 F9 **Edwards** Mississippi
95 M2 **Edwards** New York
99 Q8 **Edwards** *R* Illinois
94 A5 **Edwardsburg** Michigan
138 D3 **Edwards Creek** S Australia
144 B7 **Edwardson, C** New Zealand
144 A6 **Edwardson Sd** New Zealand
108 G5 **Edwards Plateau** Texas
110 G3 **Edwardsville** Illinois
146 A4 **Edward VIII B** Antarctica
15 F4 **Edzell** Scotland
117 H7 **Edziza, Mt** Br Col
22 F1 **Eeklo** Belgium
100 B9 **Eel** *R* California
94 B6 **Eel** *R* Indiana
25 G2 **Eelde** Netherlands
25 D4 **Eem** *R* Netherlands
25 D4 **Eem Meer** Netherlands
89 B6 **Eenzamheid Pan** *salt lake* S Africa
22 E1 **Eernegem** Belgium
137 O5 **Efate** *isld* New Hebrides
38 K5 **Eferding** Austria
99 N2 **Effie** Minnesota
110 H2 **Effingham** Illinois
107 P2 **Effingham** Kansas
78 D1 **Eflani** Turkey
48 M6 **Eforie Sud** Romania
71 B3 **Ef Torobi** *isld* W Irian
28 E4 **Egå** Denmark
18 D10 **Ega** *R* Spain
43 E10 **Egadi, I** Sicily
133 F5 **Egaña** Argentina
103 K2 **Egan Range** Nevada
121 N7 **Eganville** Ontario
85 F7 **Egbe** Nigeria
98 B8 **Egbert** Wyoming
28 H5 **Egebjerg** Denmark
115 O4 **Egedesminde** Greenland
116 J7 **Egegik B** Alaska
98 G1 **Egeland** N Dakota
33 O9 **Egeln** E Germany
36 F4 **Egelsbach** W Germany
28 D7 **Egen** Denmark
28 F4 **Egens** Denmark
28 E3 **Egense** Denmark
48 F3 **Eger** Hungary
37 J6 **Eger** *R* W Germany
28 D7 **Egernsund** Denmark
27 A13 **Egersund** Norway
143 C6 **Egerton, Mt** W Australia
32 M6 **Egestorf** W Germany
41 L3 **Egg** Austria
27 D11 **Eggedal** Norway
31 J7 **Eggenburg** Austria
37 O7 **Eggenfelden** W Germany
33 U5 **Eggesin** E Germany
28 G6 **Eggeslevmagle** Denmark
99 T4 **Egg Harbor** Wisconsin
95 N7 **Egg Harbor City** New Jersey
95 N7 **Egg Harbor, Gt** New Jersey
95 N7 **Egg Harbor, Little** New Jersey
116 G5 **Egg I** Alaska
13 G4 **Eggleston** England
37 N6 **Eggmühl** W Germany
37 L4 **Eggolsheim** W Germany
9 F5 **Egham** England
22 H2 **Eghezee** Belgium
28 G6 **Egholm** *isld* Denmark
28 D2 **Egholm** *isld* Nordjylland Denmark
140 E4 **Egilabria** Queensland
15 F1 **Egilsay** Scotland
142 C5 **Eginbah** W Australia
56 F3 **Egirta** *R* U.S.S.R.
85 D3 **Eglab,El** *reg* Algeria
18 G7 **Egletons** France
36 G1 **Egling** W Germany
13 G3 **Eglingham** England
144 B6 **Eglinton** *R* New Zealand
114 H2 **Eglinton I** N W Terr
41 J2 **Eglisau** Switzerland
37 L4 **Egloffstein** W Germany
25 C3 **Egmond aan Zee** Netherlands
122 H7 **Egmont B** Pr Edward I
113 E10 **Egmont Key** *isld* Florida
145 E3 **Egmont, Mt** New Zealand
28 J6 **Egøje** Denmark
118 D4 **Egremont** Alberta
47 L6 **Eğret** Turkey
47 L7 **Eğridir** Turkey
78 C2 **Egridir Gölü** Turkey
47 K5 **Egrigöz Dağı** *mt* Turkey
47 J5 **Eğri Karaağaç Dağı** *mt* Turkey
13 H5 **Egton** England
28 C5 **Egtved** Denmark
71 E7 **Eguet Pt** Philippines
19 O17 **Eguilles** France
28 C6 **Egvad** Denmark
48 F3 **Egyek** Hungary
112 F5 **Egypt** Georgia
111 H8 **Egypt** Mississippi
109 L6 **Egypt** Texas
84 H4 **Egypt** *rep* Africa
79 F4 **Ehdene** Lebanon
36 H7 **Ehingen** W Germany
33 Q8 **Ehle** *R* E Germany
32 K10 **Ehlen** W Germany
36 F6 **Ehningen** W Germany
33 N7 **Ehra-Lessien** W Germany
113 E9 **Ehren** Florida
103 K8 **Ehrenberg** Arizona
140 B6 **Ehrenberg Ra** N Terr Aust
36 D3 **Ehrenbreitstein** W Germany
32 J7 **Ehrenburg** W Germany
37 O2 **Ehrenfriedersdorf** E Germany
112 F4 **Ehrhardt** S Carolina
36 E2 **Ehringshausen** W Germany
60 D14 **Ei** Japan
36 E2 **Eibach** W Germany
36 E2 **Eibelshausen** W Germany
37 J4 **Eibelstadt** W Germany
37 O3 **Eibenstock** E Germany
25 G4 **Eibergen** Netherlands
38 M8 **Eibiswald** Austria
33 O8 **Eichenbarleben** E Germany
37 O6 **Eichendorf** W Germany
37 M5 **Eichhofen** W Germany
32 M10 **Eichsfeld** *mts* E Germany
37 L6 **Eichstätt** W Germany
40 G1 **Eichstetten** W Germany
36 F5 **Eichtersheim** W Germany
33 T8 **Eichwalde** E Germany
36 H2 **Eichzell** W Germany
32 M7 **Eicklingen** W Germany
27 D12 **Eidanger** Norway
26 B9 **Eide** Norway
32 J4 **Eider** W Germany
32 L4 **Eider** *R* W Germany
26 G3 **Eidsfjord** Norway
27 D12 **Eidsfoss** Norway
27 F11 **Eidskog** Norway
141 K7 **Eidsvold** Queensland
27 E11 **Eidsvoll** Norway
25 C2 **Eierlandse Gat** Netherlands
36 B3 **Eifel** *mts* W Germany
89 F2 **Eiffel Flats** Zimbabwe
37 J1 **Eigenrieden** E Germany
40 G4 **Eiger** *mt* Switzerland
15 B4 **Eigg** *isld* Scotland
146 G12 **Eights Coast** Antarctica
142 D4 **Eighty Mile Beach** W Australia
26 A10 **Eikefjord** Norway
27 D12 **Eikeren** *R* Norway
26 C9 **Eikesdalsvatn** *L* Norway
86 A2 **Eil** Somalia
139 H6 **Eildon** Victoria
33 R10 **Eilenburg** E Germany
129 G3 **Eilerts de Haan Geb** *mts* Suriname
33 O8 **Eilsleben** E Germany
32 L8 **Eime** W Germany
33 M7 **Eimke** W Germany
27 E11 **Eina** Norway
141 G4 **Einasleigh** Queensland
32 L9 **Einbeck** W Germany
25 D6 **Eindhoven** Netherlands
32 L4 **Einfeld** W Germany
68 B4 **Einme** Burma
36 C5 **Einöd** W Germany
37 P6 **Einödsriegel** *mt* W Germany
Einsiedel *see* **Deutsch-Einsiedel**
79 F8 **Ein Yahav** Israel
Eire *rep see* **Irish Republic**
120 G4 **Eire River** Ontario
128 E5 **Eirunepe** Brazil
22 L4 **Eisch** *R* Luxembourg
22 K2 **Eisden** Belgium
25 E7 **Eisden** Netherlands
36 C4 **Eisen** W Germany
37 J2 **Eisenach** E Germany
37 M2 **Eisenberg** E Germany
36 E4 **Eisenberg** W Germany
38 L6 **Eisenerz** Austria
38 L7 **Eisenerzer-Alpen** *mts* Austria
118 B7 **Eisenhower, Mt** Alberta
38 J8 **Eisenhut** *mt* Austria
31 H3 **Eisenhüttenstadt** E Germany
38 L8 **Eisenkappel** Austria
48 D3 **Eisenstadt** Austria
38 J8 **Eisentratten** Austria
38 L5 **Eisenwurzen** *reg* Austria
36 D2 **Eiserfeld** W Germany
37 K3 **Eisfeld** E Germany
33 P9 **Eisleben** E Germany
36 H6 **Eislingen** W Germany
37 L6 **Eitensheim** W Germany
36 H2 **Eiterfeld** W Germany
36 C2 **Eitorf** W Germany
28 M1 **Ejde** Faeroes
17 G2 **Ejea de los Caballeros** Spain
87 G12 **Ejeda** Madagascar
28 D5 **Ejer Bavnehøj** *hill* Denmark
28 B3 **Ejersiev** Denmark
127 J10 **Ejido** Venezuela
65 A5 **Ejin Horo Qi** China
65 C2 **Ej Nur** China
28 B3 **Ejsing** Denmark
28 C5 **Ejstrup** Denmark
85 D7 **Ejura** Ghana
98 B4 **Ekalaka** Montana
27 J15 **Ekby** Sweden
22 F2 **Eke** Belgium
29 K12 **Ekenäs** Finland
22 G1 **Ekeren** Belgium
145 E4 **Eketahuna** New Zealand
26 N5 **Ekfors** Sweden
46 D6 **Ekhinádhes** *isld* Greece
47 G3 **Ekhinos** Greece
55 G5 **Ekibastuz** U.S.S.R.
59 K1 **Ekimchan** U.S.S.R.
116 N6 **Eklutna** Alaska
27 J12 **Ekoln** *L* Sweden
22 F1 **Eksaarde** Belgium
27 G11 **Ekshärad** Sweden
27 G14 **Eksjö** Sweden
26 L7 **Ekträsk** Sweden
115 L7 **Ekwan** *R* Ontario
116 J7 **Ekwok** Alaska
68 C3 **Ela** Burma
El Aaiún *see* **La'youn**
46 F8 **Elafónisos** *isld* Greece
86 J4 **El Afweín** Somalia
111 F7 **Elaine** Arkansas
80 E5 **El 'Ajjaira** Jordan
103 H10 **El Alamo** Mexico
75 K10 **Elamanchili** India
99 R5 **Eland** Wisconsin
89 E5 **Elands** *R* S Africa
89 C8 **Elands Berg** *mt* S Africa
8 C3 **Elan Valley Reservoirs** Wales
43 B13 **El-Aouinet** Algeria
16 D7 **El Arahal** Spain
El Aràich *see* **Larache** Morocco
124 C4 **El Arco** Mexico
80 F5 **El Ardah** Jordan
141 H4 **El Arish** Queensland
46 E5 **Elassón** Greece
79 E9 **Elat** Israel
46 F6 **Elátia** Greece
86 E2 **El Atrun Oasis** Sudan
80 D7 **El 'Azar** Jordan
78 G2 **Elâzığ** Turkey
111 K10 **Elba** Alabama
101 M7 **Elba** Idaho
98 H8 **Elba** Nebraska
94 J3 **Elba** New York
42 C6 **Elba** *isld* Italy
79 F3 **El Bahlüliye** Syria
126 H10 **El Banco** Colombia
16 D4 **El Barco de Avila** Spain
46 D3 **Elbasan** Albania
127 K10 **El Baúl** Venezuela
32 J5 **Elbe** *est* W Germany
33 M6 **Elbe** *R* W Germany
33 N5 **Elbe-Lübeck Kanal** W Germany
79 G4 **El Beqa'a** *R* Lebanon
110 J3 **Elberfeld** Indiana
32 F8 **Elbergen** W Germany
99 O7 **Elberon** Iowa
109 J2 **Elbert** Texas
99 U5 **Elberta** Michigan
106 D2 **Elbert,Mt** Colorado
112 E3 **Elberton** Georgia
20 H3 **Elbeuf** France
Elbing *see* **Elblag**
33 N9 **Elbingerode** E Germany
78 F2 **Elbistan** Turkey
31 L1 **Elblag** Poland
17 F6 **El Bonillo** Spain
16 D9 **El Borck** Morocco
124 H6 **El Bordo** Mexico
118 L7 **Elbow** Sask
113 L11 **Elbow Cay** *isld* Bahamas
98 K4 **Elbow L** Minnesota
118 C8 **Elbow R** Alberta
124 J6 **El Bozal** Mexico
53 F11 **El'brus** *mt* U.S.S.R.
86 E4 **El Buheyrat** *prov* Sudan
86 A3 **El Bur** Somalia
25 E4 **Elburg** Netherlands
16 E3 **El Burgo de Osma** Spain
100 K9 **Elburz** Nevada
77 B1 **Elburz Mountains** Iran
102 H9 **El Cajon** California
128 F2 **El Callao** Venezuela
16 D5 **El Campillo de la Jara** Spain
109 L6 **El Campo** Texas
102 H9 **El Capitan Res** California
128 C2 **El Carmen** Colombia
86 H4 **El Carre** Ethiopia
124 G5 **El Casco** Mexico
17 G3 **El Castellar** Spain
103 J9 **El Centro** California
128 F7 **El Cerro** Bolivia
16 C7 **El Cerro de Andévalo** Spain
124 F3 **El Charco** Mexico
17 G6 **Elche** Spain
17 F6 **Elche de la Sierra** Spain
127 K9 **El Chino** Venezuela
99 R4 **Elcho** Wisconsin
140 D1 **Elcho I** N Terr Aust
133 E2 **El Chorro** Argentina
124 H5 **El Cobre** Mexico
128 D2 **El Cocuy** Colombia
126 C3 **El Cotorro** Cuba
126 G4 **El Cristo** Cuba
108 B5 **El Cuervo** Mexico
32 L8 **Eldagsen** W Germany
124 C2 **El Dátil** Mexico
33 Q6 **Elde** *R* E Germany
33 O6 **Eldena** E Germany
138 F4 **Elder,L** S Australia
99 R5 **Elderon** Wisconsin
126 G10 **El Difícil** Colombia
33 M7 **Eldingen** W Germany
124 G8 **El Divisadero** Mexico
128 C3 **El Diviso** Colombia
124 B2 **El Doctor** Mexico
99 O9 **Eldon** Iowa
110 D3 **Eldon** Missouri
100 B2 **Eldon** Washington
99 N7 **Eldora** Iowa
130 C10 **Eldorado** Argentina
109 P2 **El Dorado** Arkansas
130 E9 **Eldorado** Brazil
110 H4 **Eldorado** Illinois
107 O4 **El Dorado** Kansas
124 F5 **Eldorado** Mexico
114 J6 **Eldorado** Sask
108 G5 **Eldorado** Texas
128 F2 **El Dorado** Venezuela
89 G1 **Eldorado** Zimbabwe
100 D1 **Eldorado,Mt** Washington
103 K6 **Eldorado Mts** Nevada
110 B4 **El Dorado Springs** Missouri
88 E1 **Eldoret** Kenya
98 K2 **Eldred** Minnesota
95 N5 **Eldred** New York
94 J5 **Eldred** Pennsylvania
27 F15 **Eldsberga** Sweden
100 H2 **Eleanor** Washington
143 D10 **Eleanora Pk** W Australia
102 E3 **Eleanor, L** California
89 E4 **Elebe** *mt* Botswana
109 J1 **Electra** Texas
101 P5 **Electric Pk** Mont/Wyoming
135 O1 **Eleele** Hawaiian Is
52 B6 **Eleja** U.S.S.R.
48 G4 **Elek** Hungary
54 K1 **Elektrogorsk** U.S.S.R.
54 K1 **Elektrostal'** U.S.S.R.
22 J2 **Elemalle** Belgium
47 H2 **Elena** Bulgaria
128 D4 **El Encanto** Colombia
33 N9 **Elend** E Germany
106 C8 **Elephant Butte** New Mexico
106 C8 **Elephant Butte Res** New Mexico
68 G7 **Elephant, Chaine de l'** *mts* Cambodia
146 D15 **Elephant I** S Shetland Is
83 K8 **Elephant Pass** Sri Lanka
116 G3 **Elephant Point** Alaska
16 E4 **El Escorial** Spain
47 F3 **Eleshnitsa** Bulgaria
128 E3 **El Esmeralda** Venezuela
128 C3 **El Espinal** Colombia
84 J5 **Elet, Wadi** *watercourse* Sudan
84 C2 **El Eulma** Algeria
113 L12 **Eleuthera I** Bahamas
99 P5 **Eleva** Wisconsin
106 E3 **Eleven Mile Canyon Res** Colorado
110 E5 **Eleven Point** *R* Missouri
47 F6 **Elevsís** Greece
22 H2 **Elewijt** Belgium
80 G2 **El Fahham** Syria
43 C12 **El Fahs** Tunisia
86 E3 **El Fasher** Sudan
16 D9 **El Fendek** Morocco
16 B1 **El Ferrol del C** Spain
117 E6 **Elfin Cove** Alaska
119 O7 **Elfros** Sask
86 H4 **El Fud** Ethiopia
124 E4 **El Fuerte** Mexico
86 E3 **El Fula** Sudan
80 D5 **El Fundug** Jordan
26 E9 **Elgå** Norway
26 E9 **Elgepiggen** *mt* Norway
37 K2 **Elgersburg** E Germany
86 F3 **El Geteina** Sudan
86 F3 **El Gezira** *prov* Sudan
80 F5 **El Ghor** Jordan
103 O10 **Elgin** Arizona
99 S7 **Elgin** Illinois
99 P7 **Elgin** Iowa
119 R9 **Elgin** Manitoba
98 E3 **Elgin** N Dakota
98 H8 **Elgin** Nebraska
103 K4 **Elgin** Nevada
122 G8 **Elgin** New Brunswick
107 M7 **Elgin** Oklahoma
100 H4 **Elgin** Oregon
15 E3 **Elgin** Scotland
109 K5 **Elgin** Texas
103 O3 **Elgin** Utah
141 H5 **Elgin Downs** Queensland
86 F5 **Elgon, Mt** Uganda
86 H4 **El Goran** Ethiopia
17 H2 **El Grado** Spain
124 G8 **El Grullo** Mexico
128 D3 **El Guamo** Colombia
78 G5 **El Hamad** Saudi Arabia
86 A2 **El Hamurre** Somalia
84 H4 **El Harra** Egypt
86 F3 **El Hawata** Sudan
85 E3 **El Homr** Algeria
86 A2 **El Hur** Somalia
87 D7 **Elias Garcia** Angola
127 J5 **Elías Piña** Dom Rep
109 J3 **Eliasville** Texas
108 D2 **Elida** New Mexico
119 U9 **Elie** Manitoba
13 F1 **Elie** Scotland
46 F6 **Elikón** *mt* Greece
29 M11 **Elimäki** Finland
47 F2 **Elin Pelin** Bulgaria
95 R3 **Eliot** Maine
29 O10 **Elisenvaara** U.S.S.R.
129 K5 **Eliseu Martins** Brazil
53 F10 **Elista** U.S.S.R.
106 F2 **Elizabeth** Colorado
99 Q7 **Elizabeth** Illinois
109 P5 **Elizabeth** Louisiana
95 N6 **Elizabeth** New Jersey
94 F7 **Elizabeth** W Virginia
112 L1 **Elizabeth City** N Carolina
95 R5 **Elizabeth Is** Massachusetts
122 F6 **Elizabeth,Mt** New Brunswick
101 P9 **Elizabeth Mt** Utah
142 F3 **Elizabeth, Mt** W Australia
137 M7 **Elizabeth Reef** Pacific Oc
143 B7 **Elizabeth Spring** W Australia
94 E10 **Elizabethton** Tennessee
94 B7 **Elizabethtown** Indiana
94 B9 **Elizabethtown** Kentucky
112 J3 **Elizabethtown** N Carolina
95 O2 **Elizabethtown** New York
95 L6 **Elizabethtown** Pennsylvania
Elizabethville *see* **Lubumbashi**
95 L6 **Elizabethville** Pennsylvania
138 E6 **Eliza,L** S Australia
18 D9 **Elizondo** Spain
124 G4 **El Jaralito** Mexico
86 F3 **El Jebelein** Sudan
102 A2 **Elk** California
108 B3 **Elk** New Mexico
31 N2 **Ełk** Poland
101 P6 **Elk** Wyoming
110 B5 **Elk** *R* Missouri
95 M7 **Elk** *R* Penn/Maryland
110 K6 **Elk** *R* Tennessee
94 F8 **Elk** *R* W Virginia
99 P7 **Elkader** Iowa
86 F2 **El Kamlin** Sudan
101 R5 **Elk Basin** Wyoming
100 K4 **Elk City** Idaho
107 P4 **Elk City** Kansas
107 L6 **Elk City** Oklahoma
102 B2 **Elk Creek** California
140 D5 **Elkedra** N Terr Aust
43 B12 **El Kef** Tunisia
102 C3 **Elk Grove** California
86 F2 **El Khandaq** Sudan
79 E7 **El Kharrûba** Egypt
94 B5 **Elkhart** Indiana
107 J4 **Elkhart** Kansas
109 M4 **Elkhart** Texas
99 T6 **Elkhart Lake** Wisconsin
101 S9 **Elkhead Mts** Colorado
99 L8 **Elk Horn** Iowa
119 Q9 **Elkhorn** Manitoba
99 S7 **Elkhorn** Wisconsin
98 H7 **Elkhorn** *R* Nebraska
47 H2 **Elkhovo** Bulgaria
112 G1 **Elkin** N Carolina
118 E5 **Elk I. Nat. Park** Alberta
108 C2 **Elkins** New Mexico
94 H8 **Elkins** W Virginia
94 B2 **Elk L** Michigan
120 K5 **Elk Lake** Ontario
95 K4 **Elkland** Pennsylvania
106 D1 **Elk Mt** Colorado
101 T8 **Elk Mt** Wyoming
100 K1 **Elko** Br Col
100 K9 **Elko** Nevada
101 P8 **Elkol** Wyoming
101 N3 **Elk Park** Montana
112 F1 **Elk Park** N Carolina
118 G5 **Elk Point** Alberta
98 K7 **Elk Pt** S Dakota
118 C9 **Elk R** Br Col
99 N4 **Elk R** Minnesota
94 B2 **Elk Rapids** Michigan
43 C12 **El Krib** Tunisia
100 J3 **Elk River** Idaho
106 B1 **Elk Springs** Colorado
113 F8 **Elkton** Florida
110 J5 **Elkton** Kentucky
95 M7 **Elkton** Maryland
99 O6 **Elkton** Minnesota
100 B6 **Elkton** Oregon
98 K5 **Elkton** S Dakota
110 K6 **Elkton** Tennessee
94 J8 **Elkton** Virginia
79 E9 **El Kuntilla** Egypt
94 C10 **Elk Valley** Tennessee
110 G4 **Elkville** Illinois
79 G4 **El Laboue** Lebanon
86 E3 **El Lagowa** Sudan
83 K10 **Ellamulla** Sri Lanka
12 C1 **Ellanbeich** Scotland
13 G6 **Elland** England
143 A7 **Ellavalla** W Australia
113 D7 **Ellaville** Florida
111 M9 **Ellaville** Georgia
37 N3 **Ellefeld** W Germany
114 J2 **Ellef Ringnes I** N W Terr
143 C10 **Elleker** W Australia
95 O2 **Ellenburg** New York
95 M8 **Ellendale** Delaware
111 F12 **Ellendale** Louisiana
98 H3 **Ellendale** N Dakota
103 O3 **Ellen,Mt** Utah
95 P2 **Ellen,Mt** Vermont
143 C10 **Ellen Pk** W Australia
13 E4 **Ellen,R** England
114 G8 **Ellensburg** Washington
32 H6 **Ellenserdamm** W Germany
113 E10 **Ellenton** Florida
95 N5 **Ellenville** New York
36 C3 **Ellenz-Poltersdorf** W Germany
112 G2 **Eller** N Carolina
112 H2 **Ellerbe** N Carolina
113 E7 **Ellerbee** Florida
36 D4 **Ellerspring** *mt* W Germany
144 B6 **Ellery, L** New Zealand
139 J6 **Ellery,Mt** Victoria
8 D2 **Ellesmere** England
115 L2 **Ellesmere I** N W Terr
144 D5 **Ellesmere, L** New Zealand
8 D1 **Ellesmere Port** England
110 K2 **Ellettsville** Indiana
22 F2 **Ellezelles** Belgium
Ellice Is. *see* **Tuvalu** *islds state*
95 L7 **Ellicott City** Maryland
94 J4 **Ellicottville** New York
28 D3 **Ellidshøj** Denmark
112 C3 **Ellijay** Georgia
28 E2 **Elling** Denmark
28 F6 **Ellinge** Denmark
37 K5 **Ellingen** W Germany
13 G3 **Ellington** England
110 F4 **Ellington** Missouri
107 M3 **Ellinwood** Kansas
95 L8 **Elliot** Maryland
140 C3 **Elliot** N Terr Aust
89 E8 **Elliot** S Africa
112 G3 **Elliot** S Carolina
139 H9 **Elliot B** Tasmania
120 H6 **Elliot Lake** Ontario
142 E4 **Elliot Lake** W Australia
141 H4 **Elliot, Mt** Queensland
99 L8 **Elliott** Iowa
98 J3 **Elliott** N Dakota
113 G12 **Elliott Key** *isld* Florida
122 H4 **Ellis B** Quebec
101 N3 **Elliston** Montana
123 T5 **Elliston** Nfld
138 C5 **Elliston** S Australia
94 G9 **Elliston** Virginia
111 G10 **Ellisville** Mississippi
143 G8 **Ell, L** W Australia
38 F6 **Ellmau** Austria
36 F6 **Ellmendingen** W Germany
15 F3 **Ellon** Scotland
74 F8 **Ellora** India
112 G4 **Elloree** S Carolina
33 N9 **Ellrich** W Germany
118 E4 **Ellscott** Alberta
110 F5 **Ellsinore** Missouri
107 M3 **Ellsworth** Kansas
95 T2 **Ellsworth** Maine
99 L6 **Ellsworth** Minnesota
98 D7 **Ellsworth** Nebraska
99 O5 **Ellsworth** Wisconsin
109 J1 **Ellsworth,L** Oklahoma
146 G11 **Ellsworth Land** Antarctica
146 G10 **Ellsworth Mts** Antarctica
37 J6 **Ellwangen** W Germany
94 G6 **Ellwood City** Pennsylvania
32 H6 **Ellwürden** W Germany
41 K4 **Elm** Switzerland
32 K5 **Elm** W Germany
99 O6 **Elma** Iowa
100 B2 **Elma** Washington
79 G2 **El Ma'arra** Syria
133 C6 **El Maitén** Argentina
47 K8 **Elmalı** Turkey
78 B3 **Elmali** Turkey
86 F3 **El Manaquil** Sudan
124 A2 **El Maneadero** Mexico
124 G5 **El Martínez** Mexico
109 L7 **Elmaton** Texas
103 J9 **El Mayor** Mexico
79 D7 **El Mazâr** Egypt
112 K2 **Elm City** N Carolina
98 G9 **Elm Cr** Nebraska
118 D1 **Elm Creek** Manitoba
107 N6 **Elm Cr.Res.,E** Oklahoma
108 A2 **Elmendorf** New Mexico
127 J9 **El Mene de Mauroa** Venezuela
32 M5 **Elmenhorst** W Germany
99 O10 **Elmer** Missouri
95 M7 **Elmer** New Jersey
109 H1 **Elmer** Oklahoma
100 G1 **Elmer City** Washington
43 B13 **El Meskiana** Algeria
99 T8 **Elmhurst** Illinois
79 F4 **El Mīna** Lebanon
102 C3 **Elmira** California
94 C1 **Elmira** Michigan
95 L4 **Elmira** New York
123 K7 **Elmira** Pr Edward I
98 H4 **Elm L** S Dakota
109 K4 **Elm Mott** Texas
107 N3 **Elmo** Kansas
99 L9 **Elmo** Missouri
101 T8 **Elmo** Wyoming
16 E4 **El Molar** Spain
108 G7 **El Moral** Mexico
111 K9 **Elmore** Alabama
99 M6 **Elmore** Minnesota
94 D5 **Elmore** Ohio
139 G6 **Elmore** Victoria
109 K1 **Elmore City** Oklahoma
106 B6 **El Morro Nat.Mon** New Mexico
122 J9 **Elmsdale** Nova Scotia
32 L5 **Elmshorn** W Germany
98 D5 **Elm Springs** S Dakota
36 D5 **Elmstein** W Germany
122 J8 **Elmsvale** Nova Scotia
86 E3 **ElMuglad** Sudan
110 G1 **Elmwood** Illinois
107 K5 **Elmwood** Oklahoma
120 J8 **Elmwood** Ontario
99 O5 **Elmwood** Wisconsin
18 G10 **Elne** France
71 D5 **El Nido** Philippines
118 D7 **Elnora** Alberta
110 J3 **Elnora** Indiana
86 F3 **El Obeid** Sudan
111 G12 **Eloi Bay** Louisiana
80 D1 **Elon** Israel
110 K6 **Elora** Tennessee
125 J8 **El Oro** Mexico
128 C4 **El Oro** *prov* Ecuador
124 F6 **Elota** Mexico
103 N9 **Eloy** Arizona
124 G5 **El Palmito** Mexico
128 F2 **El Pao** Venezuela
16 E4 **El Pardo** Spain
99 R9 **El Paso** Illinois
108 A4 **El Paso** Texas
131 B4 **El Peñón** *peak* Chile
14 C3 **Elphin** Irish Rep
119 R8 **Elphinstone** Manitoba
141 J5 **Elphinstone** Queensland
127 N9 **El Pilar** Venezuela
133 E2 **El Pintado** Argentina
83 K11 **Elpitiya** Sri Lanka
102 E4 **El Portal** California
128 C5 **El Portugues** Peru
108 B4 **El Porvenir** Mexico
16 D5 **El Puente del Arzobispo** Spain
16 C8 **El Puerto de Sta. Maria** Spain
79 G3 **El Qadmūs** Syria
80 E1 **El Qouzah** Lebanon
131 B2 **Elqui** *R* Chile
79 E8 **El Quşeima** Egypt
79 G4 **El Quseir** Syria
79 F9 **El Quweira** Jordan
124 G6 **El Regocijo** Mexico
108 F7 **El Remolino** Mexico
125 J6 **El Retorno** Mexico
106 D5 **El Rito** New Mexico
98 J5 **Elrod** S Dakota
16 C7 **El Ronquillo** Spain
99 M4 **Elrosa** Minnesota
118 J7 **Elrose** Sask
99 Q6 **Elroy** Wisconsin
124 H6 **El Rucio** Mexico
109 K9 **Elsa** Texas
114 F5 **Elsa** Yukon Terr
42 D5 **Elsa** *R* Italy
124 G6 **El Salto** Mexico
71 G6 **El Salvador** Mindanao Philippines
125 P11 **El Salvador** *rep* Cent America
120 H4 **Elsas** Ontario
108 A6 **El Sauz** Mexico
109 J9 **El Sauz** Texas
25 E4 **Elsberg** *hill* Netherlands
110 F2 **Elsberry** Missouri
32 K6 **Elsdorf** W Germany
32 H8 **Else** *R* W Germany
28 F4 **Elsegørde** Denmark
22 L3 **Elsenborn** Belgium
36 F5 **Elsenz** *R* W Germany
140 C2 **Elsey** N Terr Aust
26 G5 **Elsfjord** Norway
32 H6 **Elsfleth** W Germany
98 E9 **Elsie** Nebraska
100 B4 **Elsie** Oregon
102 G8 **Elsinore** California
103 M3 **Elsinore** Utah
102 G8 **Elsinore L** California
25 E7 **Elsloo** Netherlands
98 F7 **Elsmere** Nebraska
107 P4 **Elsmore** Kansas
33 Q9 **Elsnigk** E Germany
130 C10 **El Soberbio** Argentina
127 M10 **El Socorro** Venezuela
127 L10 **El Sombrero** Venezuela
116 K1 **Elson Lagoon** Alaska
25 E4 **Elspeet** Netherlands
25 E5 **Elst** Netherlands
9 F5 **Elstead** England
33 R9 **Elster** E Germany
33 Q10 **Elster** *R* E Germany
37 N2 **Elsterberg** E Germany
33 T10 **Elsterwerda** E Germany
145 F3 **Elsthorpe** New Zealand
9 F4 **Elstree** England
108 A6 **El Sueco** Mexico
124 G8 **El Tabaco** Mexico
16 C2 **El Teleno** *mt* Spain
25 F5 **Elten** W Germany
37 O2 **Elterlein** E Germany
9 G5 **Eltham** England
145 E3 **Eltham** New Zealand
79 E9 **El Thamad** Egypt
128 F2 **El Tigre** Venezuela
9 F3 **Eltisley** England
37 K4 **Eltmann** W Germany
128 E2 **El Tocuyo** Venezuela
109 P5 **Elton** Louisiana
100 G3 **Eltopia** Washington
102 G8 **El Toro** California
133 C3 **El toro** Chile
133 C3 **El Tránsito** Chile
124 C2 **El Tren** Mexico
124 D6 **El Triunfo** Mexico
118 K1 **Eltrut L** Ontario
127 O2 **El Tucuche** *mt* Trinidad
133 C8 **El Turbio** Argentina
36 E3 **Eltville** W Germany
76 E2 **Eluru** India
119 Q9 **Elva** Manitoba
106 D5 **El Vado** New Mexico
128 C2 **El Valle** Colombia
127 L9 **El Valle** Venezuela
12 E3 **Elvanfoot** Scotland
27 E10 **Elvdal** Norway
26 N2 **Elvebakken** Norway
27 E11 **Elverum** Norway
125 L3 **El Viejo** Nicaragua
128 D2 **El Vigia** Venezuela
128 D5 **Elvira** Brazil
114 J3 **Elvira,C** N W Terr
142 B5 **Elvire, Mt** W Australia
143 C8 **Elvire, Mt** W Australia
142 G4 **Elvire, R** W Australia
44 D1 **Elvo** *R* Italy
133 C4 **El Volcán** Chile
86 H5 **El Wak** Kenya
99 S8 **Elwood** Illinois
94 B6 **Elwood** Indiana
110 B2 **Elwood** Missouri
98 G9 **Elwood** Nebraska
9 G3 **Ely** England
99 P8 **Ely** Iowa
99 P2 **Ely** Minnesota
103 K2 **Ely** Nevada
80 D3 **Elyaqim** Israel
138 C3 **Ely Hill** S Australia
99 N5 **Elysian** Minnesota
36 E3 **Elz** W Germany
40 H1 **Elz** *R* W Germany
36 E7 **Elzach** W Germany
124 G5 **El Zape** Mexico
32 L7 **Elze** W Germany
27 G10 **Emådalen** Sweden
137 O5 **Emae** *isld* New Hebrides
77 D1 **Emāmrūd** Iran
27 H14 **Emån** *R* Sweden
57 A1 **Emba** U.S.S.R.
50 E4 **Emba** *R* U.S.S.R.
122 G1 **Embar** Labrador
133 E2 **Embarcación** Argentina
110 H2 **Embarras** *R* Illinois
114 H6 **Embarras Portage** Alberta
99 O2 **Embarrass** Minnesota
98 J3 **Embden** N Dakota
60 P1 **Embetsu** Japan
128 D5 **Embira** *R* Brazil
101 R5 **Emblem** Wyoming
13 G3 **Embleton** England
47 J8 **Embóna** Rhodes Greece
121 P7 **Embrun** Ontario
88 F2 **Embu** Kenya
99 R9 **Emden** Illinois
32 F6 **Emden** W Germany
67 A2 **Emei** China
67 A2 **Emei Shan** *mt* China
80 F1 **Emeq Hula** Israel
80 D2 **'Emeq Zevulun** Israel
98 J2 **Emerado** N Dakota
141 J6 **Emerald** Queensland
114 H2 **Emerald I** N W Terr
71 D5 **Emergency Pt** Philippines
115 N7 **Emeril** Labrador
99 L8 **Emerson** Iowa
119 U9 **Emerson** Manitoba
98 K7 **Emerson** Nebraska
98 J6 **Emery** S Dakota
47 K5 **Emet** Turkey
101 P4 **Emigrant** Montana
102 D2 **Emigrant Gap** California
100 J9 **Emigrant Pass** Nevada
101 P4 **Emigrant Pk** Montana
103 J4 **Emigrant Valley** Nevada
86 C2 **Emi Koussi** *mt* Chad
42 D4 **Emilia-Romagna** *prov* Italy
40 F6 **Emilius, M** Italy
47 J2 **Emine,N** Bulgaria
94 B8 **Eminence** Kentucky
110 E4 **Eminence** Missouri
47 K7 **Emir** *R* Turkey
78 C2 **Emirdag** Turkey
139 J7 **Emita** Flinders I, Tasmania
94 H5 **Emlenton** Pennsylvania
32 E7 **Emlichheim** W Germany
27 H15 **Emmaboda** Sweden
126 B1 **Emmastad** Curaçao
27 N13 **Emmaste** U.S.S.R.
95 M6 **Emmaus** Pennsylvania
139 K3 **Emmaville** New S Wales
40 G4 **Emme** *R* Switzerland
118 L3 **Emmeline L** Sask
25 E3 **Emmeloord** Netherlands
25 G3 **Emmen** Netherlands
41 H3 **Emmen** Switzerland
40 G4 **Emmen Tal** Switzerland
25 F5 **Emmerich** W Germany
28 B7 **Emmerlev** Denmark
32 K8 **Emmern** W Germany
38 M5 **Emmersdorf** Austria
28 B7 **Emmerske** Denmark
32 K9 **Emmerthal** W Germany
100 J6 **Emmet** Idaho
98 H7 **Emmet** Nebraska
141 G6 **Emmet** Queensland
99 M6 **Emmetsburg** Iowa
107 O2 **Emmett** Kansas
76 C3 **Emmiganuru** India
95 K7 **Emmitsburg** Maryland
103 O1 **Emmons,Mt** Utah
99 N1 **Emo** Ontario
48 F3 **Emöd** Hungary
109 M3 **Emory** Texas
108 D6 **Emory Pk** Texas
124 D4 **Empalme** Mexico
89 G7 **Empangeni** S Africa
32 K7 **Empede** W Germany
133 F3 **Empedrado** Argentina
25 F5 **Empel** W Germany
112 D5 **Empire** Georgia
99 U5 **Empire** Michigan
100 F9 **Empire** Nevada
100 A6 **Empire** Oregon
106 F1 **Empire Res** Colorado
42 D5 **Empoli** Italy
107 O3 **Emporia** Kansas
94 K10 **Emporia** Virginia
94 J5 **Emporium** Pennsylvania
118 G8 **Empress** Alberta
22 J3 **Emptinne** Belgium
19 N14 **Empurany** France
98 G2 **Emrick** N Dakota
32 F6 **Ems** *R* W Germany
32 F8 **Emsbüren** W Germany
32 F9 **Emscher** *R* W Germany
121 L7 **Emsdale** Ontario
32 G8 **Emsdetten** W Germany
32 G6 **Ems-Jade Kanal** W Germany
37 K4 **Emskirchen** W Germany
32 F7 **Emslage** W Germany
36 G1 **Emstal** W Germany
32 H7 **Emstek** W Germany
9 F6 **Emsworth** England
65 G3 **Emu** China
141 F3 **Emu Ck** Queensland
142 C5 **Emu Spring** W Australia
61 L10 **Ena** Japan
27 J10 **Enånger** Sweden
80 C3 **'En Ayyala** Israel
101 T8 **Encampment** Wyoming
17 H4 **Encanade** *mt* Spain
108 B6 **Encantada** Mexico
124 B2 **Encantada, Cerro de la** Mexico
131 H3 **Encantadas,Sa** *mts* Brazil
124 C4 **Encantado, Cerro** *mt* Mexico
71 E3 **Encanto,C** Luzon Philippines
124 H7 **Encarnación** Mexico
130 C10 **Encarnación** Paraguay
118 E8 **Enchant** Alberta
85 D7 **Enchi** Ghana
109 H7 **Encinal** Texas
108 A6 **Encinillas** Mexico
102 G8 **Encinitas** California
108 B1 **Encino** New Mexico
108 B2 **Encinoso** New Mexico
128 D2 **Encontrados** Venezuela
138 E6 **Encounter B** S Australia
133 G4 **Encruzilhada do Sul** Brazil
117 L8 **Endako** Br Col
69 F11 **Endau** Malaysia
69 F11 **Endau** *R* Malaysia
71 K9 **Ende** *isld* Flores Indonesia
99 R6 **Endeavor** Wisconsin
141 H3 **Endeavour** Queensland
119 P6 **Endeavour** Sask
141 F1 **Endeavour Str** Queensland
108 A8 **Endee** New Mexico
28 E5 **Endelave** Denmark
134 K8 **Enderbury I** Phoenix Is Pacific Oc
117 O10 **Enderby** Br Col
142 B5 **Enderby I** W Australia
146 B6 **Enderby Land** Antarctica
98 J3 **Enderlin** N Dakota
98 E9 **Enders Res** Nebraska
118 E7 **Endiang** Alberta
95 L4 **Endicott** New York
100 H3 **Endicott** Washington
117 G7 **Endicott Arm** *pen* Alaska

116 L3 Endicott Mts Alaska
117 G4 End,Mt Yukon Terr
8 D1 Endon England
80 E3 'En Dor Israel
140 C1 Endyalgout I N Terr Aust
128 D6 Ene R Peru
47 H4 Enez Turkey
78 A1 Enez Turkey
79 F4 Enfeh Lebanon
43 C12 Enfida Tunisia
9 F4 Enfield England
110 H3 Enfield Illinois
112 K1 Enfield N Carolina
95 P3 Enfield New Hampshire
122 J9 Enfield Nova Scotia
127 K5 Engaño, C Dom Rep
71 E1 Engaño,C Luzon Philippines
60 R1 Engaru Japan
28 B7 Enge W Germany
80 E8 En Gedi Israel
41 H4 Engelberg Switzerland
112 M2 Engelhard N Carolina
38 J5 Engelhartszell Austria
53 G8 Engel's U.S.S.R.
36 C2 Engelskirchen W Germany
41 J2 Engen W Germany
130 C4 Engenho Brazil
138 D3 Engenina R S Australia
32 J8 Enger W Germany
26 E10 Engerdal Norway
27 F10 Engeren,L Norway
36 D3 Engers W Germany
89 G3 Engesi R Zimbabwe
28 C4 Engesvang Denmark
80 F2 'En Gev Israel
Enghien see Edingen
20 K4 Enghien France
117 F6 Engineer Br Columbia
22 J2 Engis Belgium
70 E4 Engkilili Sarawak
111 E7 England Arkansas
8 D3 England U.K.
106 C8 Engle New Mexico
123 Q3 Englee Nfld
119 N6 Englefield Sask
117 K10 Englewood Br Columbia
106 F2 Englewood Colorado
113 E11 Englewood Florida
107 L4 Englewood Kansas
112 C2 Englewood Tennessee
110 K3 English Indiana
116 L7 English Bay Alaska
122 E4 English Bay Quebec
75 N6 English Bazar India
20 D1 English Channel France/England
146 F12 English Coast Antarctica
140 D1 English Company's Is N Terr Aust
127 P4 English Harbour Town Antigua W I
123 R6 English Harbour W Nfld
119 N1 English River Ontario
52 D2 Engozero U.S.S.R.
36 G7 Engstingen W Germany
17 G6 Énguera Spain
52 B6 Engure U.S.S.R.
80 D3 'En Ha'Emeq Israel
80 D2 'En HaMifraz Israel
80 E3 'En Harod Israel
80 C3 'En Hod Israel
98 B2 Enid Montana
107 N5 Enid Oklahoma
111 G7 Enid L Mississippi
142 B5 Enid, Mt W Australia
118 A3 Enilda Alberta
36 G7 Eningen W Germany
60 P3 Eniwa dake mt Japan
134 G7 Eniwetok atoll Marshall Is Pacific Oc
85 C5 Enji Mauritania
80 C3 'En Karmel Israel
89 G2 Enkeldoorn Zimbabwe
36 D5 Enkenbach-Alsenborn W Germany
25 D3 Enkhuizen Netherlands
36 C4 Enkirch W Germany
27 J12 Enköping Sweden
128 G8 En Madrejón Paraguay
114 J5 Ennadai N W Terr
86 E3 En Nahud Sudan
79 G4 En Nebk Syria
86 D2 Ennedi plat Chad
14 D3 Ennell,L Irish Rep
32 F10 Ennepetal W Germany
127 H5 Ennery Haiti
139 H3 Enngonia New S Wales
32 H9 Ennigerloh W Germany
98 D5 Enning S Dakota
27 E13 Enningdal Norway
14 C4 Ennis Irish Rep
101 O4 Ennis Montana
109 L3 Ennis Texas
14 E4 Enniscorthy Irish Rep
14 D2 Enniskillen N Ireland
14 B4 Ennistimon Irish Rep
80 D1 Enn Nâqoûra Lebanon
38 K6 Ennstaler Alpen mts Austria
80 G4 En Nu'eiyima Jordan
140 C5 Ennugan Cr N Terr Aust
29 P9 Eno Finland
108 E2 Enochs Texas
141 K1 Enoggera dist Brisbane, Qnsld
98 J8 Enola Nebraska
29 O9 Enonkoski Finland
29 K3 Enontekiö Finland
112 F3 Enoree S Carolina
112 F3 Enoree R S Carolina
95 P2 Enosburg Falls Vermont
67 D5 Enping China
70 F6 Enrekang Sulawesi
71 E2 Enrile Luzon Philippines
127 J5 Enriquillo, Lago de Dom Rep
25 E3 Ens Netherlands
139 J6 Ensay Victoria
25 G4 Enschede Netherlands
36 B5 Ensdorf W Germany
32 H10 Ense W Germany
133 F4 Ensenada Argentina
124 A2 Ensenada Mexico
106 D5 Ensenada New Mexico
36 C5 Ensheim W Germany
80 D4 'En Shemer Israel
67 C1 Enshi China
118 D8 Ensign Alberta
107 K4 Ensign Kansas
99 U4 Ensign Michigan
19 K5 Ensisheim France
28 F4 Enslev Denmark
9 E4 Enstone England
86 F5 Entebbe Uganda
37 N4 Entenbühl mt W Germany
12 E3 Enterkinfoot Scotland
111 L10 Enterprise Alabama
107 N3 Enterprise Kansas
111 H9 Enterprise Mississippi
114 H5 Enterprise N W Terr
121 O8 Enterprise Ontario
100 H4 Enterprise Oregon
103 L4 Enterprise Utah
71 D5 Enterprise Pt Philippines
100 E2 Entiat Mts Washington
70 C4 Entimau, Bt mt Sarawak
17 F8 Entinas,Pta. De Las Spain
133 D8 Entrada,Pta Argentina
18 H5 Entrains France
20 D5 Entrammes France
140 A3 Entrance I N Terr Aust
18 G8 Entraygues France
143 B10 Entrecasteaux, Pt.d' W Australia
137 N5 Entrecasteaux, Récifs D' reefs New Caledonia
83 J14 Entre-Deux Réunion Indian Ocean
123 L6 Entré, I. d' Madeleine Is, Quebec
129 H5 Entre Rios Brazil
130 G7 Entre Rios de Minas Brazil
36 F6 Entringen W Germany
103 M7 Entro Arizona
118 C5 Entwistle Alberta
85 F7 Enugu Nigeria
100 D2 Enumclaw Washington
20 H2 Envermeu France
27 H11 Enviken Sweden
8 D3 Enville England
128 D5 Envira Brazil
79 F8 En Yahav Israel
67 B1 Enyang China
48 E4 Enying Hungary
144 C5 Enys, Mt New Zealand
36 F6 Enz R W Germany
45 H2 Enza R Italy
80 E8 'En Zafzafa Israel
61 M10 Enzan Japan
37 M6 Enzelhausen W Germany
36 E6 Enzklösterle W Germany
80 B7 En Zurim Israel
36 F6 Enzweihingen W Germany
111 D11 Eola Louisiana
110 E2 Eolia Missouri
20 F3 Epaignes France
45 P8 Epameo, M mt Italy
20 E4 Epaney France
46 F4 Epanomí Greece
25 E4 Epe Netherlands
32 F8 Epe W Germany
133 E5 Epecuén,L Argentina
22 E3 Epéhy France
140 D5 Epenarra N Terr Aust
22 C2 Éperlecques France
18 H3 Épernay France
87 B9 Epernbe Namibia
20 J4 Épernon France
111 H9 Epes Alabama
36 C7 Epfig France
103 N2 Ephraim Utah
95 L6 Ephrata Pennsylvania
100 F2 Ephrata Washington
137 O5 Epi isld New Hebrides
88 G10 Epidendron isld Mozambique
46 F7 Epídhavros Greece
20 J5 Epieds France
17 G3 Epila Spain
19 K4 Epinal France
20 B5 Epiniac France
98 J6 Epiphany S Dakota
79 C4 Episkopi Cyprus
20 J4 Epône France
36 B5 Eppelborn W Germany
37 P2 Eppendorf E Germany
22 F4 Eppes France
22 G3 Eppe-Sauvage France
9 G4 Epping England
98 C1 Epping N Dakota
95 Q3 Epping New Hampshire
36 F5 Eppingen W Germany
36 E3 Eppstein W Germany
98 A4 Epsie Montana
9 F5 Epsom England
21 G6 Epuisay France
87 C10 Epukiro Namibia
13 H6 Epworth England
99 Q7 Epworth Iowa
77 C4 Eqlid Iran
110 H4 Equality Illinois
86 D5 Equateur prov Zaïre
86 E4 Equatoria prov Sudan
73 L9 Equatorial Chan Maldives
85 F8 Equatorial Guinea rep W Africa
20 B2 Equeurdreville France
95 M5 Equmunk Pennsylvania
60 O4 Era Japan
86 E4 Era watercourse Sudan
141 H7 Erac R Queensland
143 B8 Eradu W Australia
71 C6 Eran Palawan Philippines
71 C6 Eran Bay Palawan Philippines
111 D12 Erath Louisiana
78 F1 Erbaa Turkey
36 H7 Erbach Baden-Württemberg W Germany
36 G4 Erbach Hessen W Germany
36 D5 Erbach R W Germany
86 G1 Erba, Jebel mt Sudan
37 N4 Erbendorf W Germany
135 N4 Erben Tablemount Pacific Oc
36 C4 Erbes Kopf mt W Germany
22 D4 Ercheu France
78 E2 Erciyas Dag Turkey
48 E3 Ercsi Hungary
48 E3 Erd Hungary
65 H2 Erdaohezi China
65 G3 Erdao Jiang R China
47 J4 Erdek Turkey
47 J4 Erdek Körfezi B Turkey
86 D2 Erdi dist Chad
37 M7 Erding W Germany
37 M7 Erdinger Moos marsh W Germany
9 E2 Erdington England
37 P2 Erdmansdorf E Germany
36 B3 Erdorf W Germany
21 C7 Erdre R France
128 F2 Erebato R Venezuela
146 J6 Erebus,Mt Antarctica
146 D14 Erebus & Terror G Antarctica
78 K6 Erech Iraq
130 D10 Erechim Brazil
58 G2 Ereentsav Mongolia
Ereğli see Marmaraereğlisi
78 C1 Ereğli Turkey
47 L7 Eren R Turkey
47 K8 Eren Dağ mt Turkey
65 D2 Eren Gobi China
65 B3 Erenhot China
Erenköy see İntepe
129 G4 Erepecu, L Brazil
16 D3 Eresma R Spain
47 H5 Eressós Greece
80 B7 Erez Israel
22 K3 Erezée Belgium
32 K4 Erfde W Germany
89 E7 Erfenis Dam res S Africa
65 A4 Erfenzi China
85 D2 Erfoud Morocco
36 B2 Erft R W Germany
36 B2 Erftstadt W Germany
37 L2 Erfurt E Germany
78 G2 Ergani Turkey
85 D4 Erg Chech des reg Mali/Algeria
86 C2 Erg du Djourab dist Chad
47 H3 Ergene R Turkey
85 D3 Erg er Raoul des reg Algeria
85 C3 Erg Iguid sand des Algeria/Mauritania
55 E1 Erginskiy Sor, Oz L U.S.S.R.
52 C6 Ergli U.S.S.R.
37 N6 Ergolding W Germany
37 N6 Ergoldsbach W Germany
65 G1 Ergu China
86 C3 Erguig R Chad
59 H1 Ergun Zuoqi China
37 O7 Erharting W Germany
16 D2 Eria R Spain
86 G2 Eriba Sudan
16 A6 Ericeira Portugal
32 K7 Erichshagen W Germany
107 L6 Erick Oklahoma
119 S8 Erickson Manitoba
122 G2 Eric L Quebec
99 N1 Ericsburg Minnesota
98 H8 Ericson Nebraska
98 A9 Erie Colorado
99 Q8 Erie Illinois
107 P4 Erie Kansas
94 D5 Erie Michigan
98 J2 Erie N Dakota
103 J6 Erie Nevada
94 G4 Erie Pennsylvania
120 J10 Erieau Ontario
120 K10 Erie, L Ontario/Mich
94 G4 Erie,L U.S.A./Canada
86 A1 Erigavo Somalia
46 D5 Erikoúsa isld Greece
119 T8 Eriksdale Manitoba
46 E7 Erímanthos mt Greece
57 C3 Erimbet U.S.S.R.
60 R4 Erimo-misaki C Japan
22 C3 Erin France
37 P7 Ering W Germany
27 H15 Eringsboda Sweden
127 N3 Erin Pt Trinidad
15 A3 Eriskay isld Scotland
9 G5 Erith England
47 F6 Erithraí Greece
36 G2 Eritrea prov Ethiopia
25 F6 Erkelenz W Germany
27 K12 Erken Sweden
33 T8 Erkner E Germany
36 G2 Erkowit Sudan
38 F6 Erl Austria
Erlangdiang see Dawu
37 L4 Erlangen W Germany
94 C7 Erlanger Kentucky
38 M5 Erlauf R Austria
37 N3 Erlbach E Germany
140 C7 Erldunda N Terr Aust
36 F3 Erlensee W Germany
111 C8 Erling,L Arkansas
65 G3 Erlong Shan mt China
38 F8 Erlsbach Austria
25 E4 Ermelo Netherlands
89 F6 Ermelo S Africa
78 D3 Ermenek Turkey
20 K4 Ermont France
Ermoúpolis see Síros
33 O9 Ermsleben E Germany
138 B2 Ernabella R S Australia
138 B2 Ernabella Mission S Australia
76 C6 Ernakulam India
36 E1 Erndtebrück W Germany
14 C2 Erne R Irish Rep
20 D5 Ernée France
20 D5 Ernée R France
14 D2 Erne,L.Lower N Ireland
14 D2 Erne,L.Upper N Ireland
143 E7 Ernest Giles Ra W Australia
144 A7 Ernest Is New Zealand
135 M12 Ernest Legouve Reef Pacific Oc
117 G8 Ernest Sd Alaska
118 L8 Ernfold Sask
45 O6 Ernici, Monti mt Italy
36 G4 Ernstthal W Germany
76 C5 Erode India
78 J2 Erois Turkey
141 G7 Eromanga Queensland
137 O5 Eromanga isld New Hebrides
111 D9 Eros Louisiana
36 B2 Erp W Germany
22 G3 Erquelinnes Belgium
18 D4 Erquy France
143 B7 Errabiddy Hills W Australia
85 C2 Er-Rachida Morocco
86 F3 Er Rahad Sudan
80 G6 Er Rajib Jordan
79 G4 Er Rastan Syria
88 F10 Errego Mozambique
14 C1 Errigal mt Irish Rep
28 G7 Errindlev Denmark
14 A2 Erris Hd Irish Rep
28 D5 Erritsø Denmark
111 G12 Errol I Louisiana
86 F3 Er Roseires Sudan
46 D4 Ersekë Albania
118 E6 Erskine Alberta
142 F4 Erskine, Mount W Australia
26 M6 Ersnäs Sweden
36 D7 Erstein France
19 L4 Ersteir France
36 H3 Erthal W Germany
54 M5 Ertil' U.S.S.R.
66 D2 Ertix He R China
47 J5 Ertugrul Turkey
22 F1 Ertvelde Belgium
145 E3 Erua New Zealand
138 E4 Erudina S Australia
27 H12 Ervalla Sweden
21 E6 Erve R France
37 Q2 Ervěnice Czechoslovakia
22 D3 Ervillers France
112 J2 Erwin N Carolina
112 E1 Erwin Tennessee
32 H9 Erwitte W Germany
119 P6 Erwood Sask
8 C3 Erwood Wales
33 O8 Erxleben E Germany
46 D3 Erzen R Albania
37 N3 Erzgebirge E Germany
56 E5 Erzin U.S.S.R.
78 G2 Erzincan Turkey
78 H2 Erzurum Turkey
52 B7 Erzvilkas U.S.S.R.
60 P4 Esan-misaki C Japan
20 D3 Esaue R France
28 A6 Esbjerg Denmark
107 M2 Esbon Kansas
17 G2 Esca R Spain
18 E10 Esca R Spain
130 J10 Escada Brazil
103 M4 Escalante Utah
103 M4 Escalante R Utah
103 L4 Escalante Des Utah
131 A8 Escalera,Pta Chile
124 G4 Escalón Mexico
16 E4 Escalona Spain
111 J11 Escambia R Florida
99 T4 Escanaba Michigan
99 T3 Escanaba R Michigan
125 Q8 Escárcega Mexico
22 E3 Escaut R France
22 L5 Esch Luxembourg
36 E3 Esch W Germany
36 G4 Eschau W Germany
36 F3 Eschborn W Germany
22 K4 Eschdorf Luxembourg
32 E7 Eschebrügge W Germany
32 M7 Eschede W Germany
37 L4 Eschenau W Germany
37 M4 Eschenbach W Germany
36 E2 Eschenberg W Germany
32 L9 Eschershausen W Germany
40 G4 Escholzmatt Switzerland
116 G3 Eschscholtz B Alaska
22 K4 Esch-sur-la-Sûre Luxembourg
37 J1 Eschwege W Germany
25 F7 Eschweiler W Germany
127 K5 Escocesa, B Dom Rep
130 H5 Escondido Brazil
102 G8 Escondido California
122 C6 Escoumins,R Quebec
20 K5 Escrennes France
13 G6 Escrick England
124 G6 Escuinapa de Hidalgo Mexico
122 F5 Escuminac Quebec
122 H6 Escuminac, Pt New Brunswick
86 B5 Eséka Cameroon
32 G5 Esens W Germany
17 H2 Esera R Spain
77 B3 Eşfahān Iran
80 B8 Eshbol Israel
80 B8 Eshel Ha Nasi Israel
9 F5 Esher England
87 F11 Eshowe S Africa
Esh Sham see Damascus
77 B2 Eshtehard Iran
80 D8 Eshtemoa Jordan
42 E5 Esino R Italy
141 K7 Esk Queensland
139 H8 Esk R Tasmania
116 N6 Eska Alaska
118 L8 Eskbank Sask
145 F3 Eskdale New Zealand
13 E5 Eskdale Green England
14 C2 Eske, L Irish Rep
47 K7 Eskere Turkey
115 S4 Eskifjördhur Iceland
28 H5 Eskildstrup Denmark
28 H7 Eskilstrup Denmark
27 H12 Eskilstuna Sweden
122 J3 Eskimo I Quebec
114 F4 Eskimo Lakes N W Terr
115 K5 Eskimo Point N W Terr
78 D1 Eskipazar Turkey
47 L5 Eskişehir Turkey
13 H5 Esk,R England
15 E5 Esk,R Scotland
107 O3 Eskridge Kansas
16 D2 Esla R Spain
16 D3 Esla, Embalse del res Spain
37 O4 Eslarn W Germany
47 K7 Eşler Dağı mt Turkey
32 H10 Eslohe W Germany
27 F16 Eslöv Sweden
121 O3 Oesmaraisville Quebec
47 K6 Esme Turkey
126 E4 Esmeralda Cuba
141 G4 Esmeralda Queensland
133 B7 Esmeralda, I Chile
128 C3 Esmeraldas Ecuador
98 G1 Esmond N Dakota
98 J5 Esmond S Dakota
120 D2 Esnagami L Ontario
120 F4 Esnagi L Ontario
22 J2 Esnaux Belgium
27 E11 Espa Norway
127 J8 Espada,Pta Colombia
18 G8 Espalion France
17 H6 Espalmador isld Balearic Is
113 F8 Espanola Florida
106 D6 Espanola New Mexico
120 J6 Espanola Ontario
128 B8 Española isld Galapagos Is
19 P17 Esparron France
102 B3 Esparto California
125 M5 Esparza Costa Rica
28 E6 Espe Denmark
27 D10 Espedals-vatn L Norway
32 J8 Espelkamp W Germany
116 E3 Espenberg,C Alaska
37 N1 Espenhain E Germany
88 F8 Esperança Mozambique
143 D10 Esperance W Australia
143 D10 Esperance B W Australia
131 E3 Esperanza Argentina
124 E4 Esperanza Mexico
108 B4 Esperanza Texas
108 F8 Esperanzas Mexico
125 M2 Esperanza, Sa. de la ra Honduras
28 K5 Espergærde Denmark
45 P7 Esperia Italy
16 A6 Espichel,C Portugal
16 D6 Espiel Spain
130 E10 Espigão,Serra do mts Brazil
16 D2 Espigüete mt Spain
128 D6 Espinar Peru
19 Q16 Espinasses France
124 J4 Espinazo Mexico
130 G6 Espinhaço,Serra,do mt Brazil
16 B4 Espinho Portugal
131 G2 Espinilho, Serra do ra Brazil
130 G4 Espinosa Brazil
130 H6 Espirito Santo state Brazil
124 D5 Espíritu Santo isld Mexico
125 Q8 Espíritu Santo, B. del Mexico
133 D8 Espíritu Santo,C Chile/Arg
71 G4 Espiritu Santo,C Philippines
137 O5 Espiritu Santo I New Hebrides
125 P7 Espita Mexico
123 R6 Espoir, B. d' Nfld
16 B3 Esposende Portugal
40 D2 Esprels France
87 F10 Espungabera Mozambique
100 F3 Esquatzel Coulee R Washington
124 E2 Esqueda Mexico
133 C6 Esquel Argentina
22 C2 Esquelbecq France
16 E3 Esqueva R Spain
100 B1 Esquimalt Br Columbia
117 M11 Esquimalt Br Columbia
133 F3 Esquina Argentina
28 K4 Esrum Sø L Denmark
55 D1 Ess R U.S.S.R.
80 F3 Es Samt Jordan
80 D8 Es Samu Jordan
85 C2 Essaouira Morocco
80 G3 Es Sarih Jordan
20 J4 Essarts,les France
20 F4 Essay France
29 K8 Esse Finland
85 E2 Es Seggeur watercourse Algeria
85 F1 Es-sekhina Tunisia
32 L7 Essel W Germany
22 G1 Essen Belgium
32 G7 Essen Niedersachsen W Germany
32 E10 Essen Nordrhein-Westfalen W Germany
37 N6 Essenbach W Germany
143 D6 Essendon, Mt W Australia
103 J7 Essex California
95 P5 Essex Connecticut
99 L9 Essex Iowa
101 M1 Essex Montana
95 O2 Essex New York
120 H10 Essex Ontario
9 G4 Essex co England
95 O2 Essex Junct Vermont
87 E10 Essexvale Zimbabwe
94 D3 Essexville Michigan
37 M6 Essing W Germany
37 J6 Essingen W Germany
36 G6 Esslingen W Germany
20 K4 Essonne dep France
20 K5 Essonne R France
52 D4 Essoyla U.S.S.R.
78 G4 Es Sukhne Syria
100 C4 Estacada Oregon
16 B1 Estaca de Bares, Pta. de la Spain
106 G8 Estacado, Llano plain New Mex/Tex
103 K10 Estacion Doctor Mexico
103 K10 Estacion France Mexico
103 K9 Estación Médanos Mexico
133 E8 Estados, I. de los Argentina
18 G10 Estagel France
71 F2 Estagno Pt Luzon Philippines
77 D5 Estahbānāt Iran
120 K6 Estaire Ontario
22 D2 Estaires France
129 L6 Estância Brazil
108 A1 Estancia New Mexico
17 F7 Estancias, Sierra de las mts Spain
77 G4 Estand, Kūh-e- mt Iran
125 O9 Estapilla Mexico
16 B4 Estarreja Portugal
18 F10 Estats, Pic d' mt Spain
40 E4 Estavayer le Lac Switzerland
87 J11 Est, C Madagascar
89 F7 Estcourt S Africa
42 D3 Este Italy
32 L6 Este R W Germany
125 L3 Estelí Nicaragua
18 D10 Estella Spain
98 K5 Estelline S Dakota
16 D5 Estena R Spain
16 D7 Estepa Spain
16 D8 Estepona Spain
133 G4 Este, Pta. del Uruguay
116 N4 Ester Alaska
98 A7 Esterbrook Wyoming
119 P8 Esterhazy Sask
18 H4 Esternay France
113 F11 Estero Florida
102 C6 Estero B California
133 C8 Estero Obstrucción Chile
125 K6 Esteros Mexico
133 E2 Esteros Paraguay
133 F3 Esteros del Iberá swamp Argentina
18 F10 Esterri de Aneu Spain
32 G6 Esterwegen W Germany
98 A9 Estes Pk Colorado
119 P9 Estevan Sask
117 J9 Estevan Group islds Br Columbia
117 K11 Estevan Point Br Columbia
118 G7 Esther Alberta
140 C5 Esther Mt N Terr Aust
99 M6 Estherville Iowa
112 F5 Estill S Carolina
18 H4 Estissac France
119 N8 Estlin Sask
118 J7 Eston Sask
52 B5 Estoniya S.S.R. U.S.S.R.
16 A6 Estoril Portugal
19 Q17 Estoublon France
22 C2 Estree Blanche France
22 D5 Estrées St. Denis France
133 G4 Estreíto Brazil
130 F6 Estrêla do Indaiá Brazil
130 F6 Estrêla do Sul Brazil
16 B4 Estrela, Sa. da mts Portugal
103 M9 Estrella Arizona
102 D6 Estrella R California
103 M8 Estrella,Sierra mt Arizona
129 K6 Estrelto, Serra do mts Brazil
16 A6 Estremadura prov Portugal
16 B6 Estremoz Portugal
129 J5 Estrondo, Serra do mts Brazil
28 E3 Estruplund Denmark
118 H8 Estuary Sask
28 B3 Estvad Denmark
48 E3 Esztergom Hungary
138 E3 Etadunna S Australia
115 M2 Etah Greenland
19 J3 Etain France
22 K4 Étalle Belgium
123 N3 Etamamiou,R Quebec
123 N3 Etamamu Quebec
123 N3 Etamamu R Quebec
20 K5 Étampes France
138 F2 Etamunbanie,L S Australia
80 B7 Etan Israel
18 H6 Étang France
123 L6 Étang-du-Nord Madeleine Is, Quebec
22 B2 Étaples France
74 H6 Etawa India
119 V1 Etawney L Manitoba
124 E4 Etchojoa Mexico
27 K14 Etelhem Gotland Sweden
85 E5 Etelia Mali
32 K7 Etelsen W Germany
122 B5 Eternité,L Quebec
146 F13 Eternity Ra Antarctica
98 H6 Ethan S Dakota
22 K4 Ethe Belgium
111 E11 Ethel Louisiana
111 G8 Ethel Mississippi
110 D2 Ethel Missouri
94 F9 Ethel W Virginia
119 R7 Ethelbert Manitoba
140 A5 Ethel Cr N Terr Aust
141 G3 Ethel Cr Queensland
142 D6 Ethel Creek W Australia
143 C6 Ethel R W Australia
111 H8 Ethelsville Alabama
119 N6 Ethelton Sask
141 G4 Etheridge R Queensland
101 R6 Ethete Wyoming
86 G4 Ethiopia,Empire of
101 N1 Ethridge Montana
47 H5 Etili Turkey
40 F5 Etivaz, l' L Switzerland
116 J2 Etivluk R Alaska
95 S2 Etna Maine
101 M8 Etna Utah
27 D10 Etna R Norway
43 F11 Etna, M Sicily
27 A12 Etne Norway
27 D11 Etnedal Norway
111 B10 Etoile Texas
116 D6 Etolin,C Alaska
117 G7 Etolin I Alaska
116 E6 Etolin Str Alaska
119 P6 Etomami Sask
9 F5 Eton England
22 K5 Eton France
120 F5 Eton Ontario
141 J5 Eton Queensland
87 C9 Etosha Pan Namibia
112 C2 Etowah Tennessee
112 B3 Etowah R Georgia
22 F4 Etreaupont France
20 K5 Etrechy France
22 E4 Etreillers France
20 J3 Étrépagny France
20 F2 Étretat France
22 F4 Etreux France
22 D3 Étricourt-Manancourt France
40 A4 Etrigny France
22 F3 Etrœungt France
47 F2 Etropole Bulgaria
22 L4 Ettelbrück Luxembourg
25 C5 Etten Netherlands
36 D7 Ettenheim W Germany
100 A9 Ettersburg California
37 L1 Ettersburg E Germany
37 J2 Etterwinden E Germany
9 E3 Ettington England
37 O6 Ettling W Germany
36 E6 Ettlingen W Germany
144 B6 Ettrick New Zealand
142 C5 Ettrick W Australia
99 P5 Ettrick Wisconsin
15 E5 Ettrick Pen mt Scotland
13 E3 Ettrick Water Scotland
80 G6 Et Tuneib Jordan
80 G3 Et Turra Jordan
9 E2 Etwall England
124 G7 Etzatlán Mexico
37 P1 Etzdorf E Germany
118 F9 Etzikom Alberta
118 F9 Etzikom Coulee R Alberta
20 H1 Eu France
137 S6 'Eua isld Tonga
139 H5 Euabalong New S Wales
94 C9 Eubank Kentucky
36 H4 Eubigheim W Germany
Euboea Greece see Évvoia
143 G9 Eucla W Australia
98 K2 Euclid Minnesota
94 F5 Euclid Ohio
139 J6 Eucumbene,L New S Wales
122 G3 Eudites,L.des Quebec
111 E8 Eudora Arkansas
138 E5 Eudunda S Australia
37 J3 Euerdorf W Germany
111 L10 Eufala Alabama
107 P6 Eufaula Oklahoma
107 P6 Eufaula Res Oklahoma
43 G10 Eufemia,S.,Golfo di Italy
45 L1 Euganei, Colli hills Italy
100 B5 Eugene Oregon
124 B4 Eugenia, Pta C Mexico
130 C8 Eugênio Penzo Brazil
29 K8 Eugmo isld Finland
139 J5 Eugowra New S Wales
37 O1 Eula R E Germany
109 N9 Euless Texas
141 H8 Eulo Queensland
112 F6 Eulonia Georgia
139 J4 Eumaungerie New S Wales
16 B1 Eume R Spain
111 D11 Eunice Louisiana
108 D3 Eunice New Mexico
22 L2 Eupen Belgium
78 J5 Euphrates R S W Asia
111 G8 Eupora Mississippi
27 M10 Eura Finland
29 J10 Eurajoki Finland
20 G3 Eure dep France
20 H3 Eure R France
20 H5 Eure-et-Loir dep France
100 A9 Eureka California
99 R9 Eureka Illinois
107 O4 Eureka Kansas
101 L1 Eureka Montana
103 J2 Eureka Nevada
115 L1 Eureka N W Terr
98 G4 Eureka S Dakota
101 N10 Eureka Utah
100 G3 Eureka Washington
116 O6 Eureka Lodge Alaska
117 O7 Eureka River Alberta
115 L2 Eureka Snd N W Terr
110 C5 Eureka Springs Arkansas
102 G4 Eureka Valley California
138 F4 Eurinilla R S Australia
138 F4 Euriowie New S Wales
139 H6 Euroa Victoria
141 J7 Eurombah Queensland
141 J7 Eurombah R Queensland
81 A8 Europa isld Mozambique Chan
25 B5 Europoort Netherlands
61 J11 Eushimi Japan
36 B2 Euskirchen W Germany
109 L3 Eustace Texas
113 F9 Eustis Florida
98 F9 Eustis Nebraska
139 G5 Euston New S Wales
111 J9 Eutaw Alabama
112 G4 Eutawville S Carolina
33 N4 Eutin W Germany
36 F7 Eutingen W Germany
114 G7 Eutsuk L Br Col
33 R9 Eutzsch E Germany
13 F6 Euxton England
111 E10 Eva Louisiana
108 C7 Eva Oklahoma
140 C4 Eva Downs N Terr Aust
87 C9 Evale Angola
99 M5 Evan Minnesota
139 H8 Evandale Tasmania
100 H1 Evans Washington
118 B5 Evansburg Alberta
115 L1 Evans,C N W Terr
94 G6 Evans City Pennsylvania
139 L3 Evans Hd New S Wales
115 M7 Evans,L Quebec
117 O9 Evans,Mt Alberta
106 E2 Evans,Mt Colorado
101 M3 Evans, Mt Montana
115 L5 Evans Str N W Terr
99 T7 Evanston Illinois
101 P8 Evanston Wyoming
116 M3 Evansville Alaska
110 G3 Evansville Illinois
110 J3 Evansville Indiana
99 L3 Evansville Minnesota
120 H7 Evansville Ontario
99 R7 Evansville Wisconsin
101 T7 Evansville Wyoming
109 J4 Evant Texas
94 B3 Evart Michigan
94 D10 Evarts Kentucky
18 G6 Evaux France
47 H5 Evciler Turkey
99 O2 Eveleth Minnesota
138 C3 Evelyn Ck S Australia
140 C2 Evelyn, Mt N Terr Aust
26 J3 Evenes Norway
110 E5 Evening Shade Arkansas
80 E1 Even Menahem Israel
80 C4 Even Yehuda Israel
141 G2 Eve Pk Queensland
22 G3 Evêque Belgium
120 B4 Everard Ontario
139 J7 Everard,C Victoria
138 D4 Everard,L S Australia
140 C6 Everard, Mt N Terr Aust
138 B2 Everard,Mt S Australia
138 C2 Everard Pk S Australia
138 C2 Everard Ra S Australia
28 H6 Everdrup Denmark
22 G2 Evere Belgium
107 P2 Everest Kansas
75 M5 Everest, Mt Xizang Zizhiqu/Nepal
94 J6 Everett Pennsylvania
100 C2 Everett Washington
112 F6 Everett City Georgia
95 O4 Everett, Mt Massachusetts
22 F1 Evergem Belgium
113 F12 Everglades Florida
113 G12 Everglades Nat. Park Florida
111 K10 Evergreen Alabama
106 E2 Evergreen Colorado
112 J3 Evergreen N Carolina
109 M10 Everman Texas
27 G16 Everöd Sweden
32 H10 Eversberg W Germany
32 K6 Eversen W Germany
9 E3 Evesham England
141 G6 Evesham Queensland
118 H6 Evesham Sask
29 K8 Evijärvi Finland
85 G8 Evinayong Mbini Eq Guinea
46 E6 Évinos R Greece
27 C13 Evje Norway
80 D2 Evlayim Israel
40 G5 Evolène Switzerland
16 B6 Évora Portugal
20 B5 Evran France
20 E3 Evrecy France
47 H4 Evreşe Turkey
20 H3 Évreux France
20 E5 Évron France
80 D2 Evron Israel
46 E3 Évropos Greece
47 H4 Évros R Greece
46 E7 Evrótas R Greece
79 C3 Evrykhou Cyprus
47 G6 Évvoia isld Greece
102 R12 Ewa Hawaiian Is
102 R12 Ewa Bch Hawaiian Is
141 H4 Ewan Queensland
100 H2 Ewan Washington
140 C6 Ewaninga N Terr Aust
116 P5 Ewan L Alaska
127 K2 Ewarton Jamaica
86 B6 Ewc Congo
9 F5 Ewell England
36 E2 Ewersbach W Germany
94 D8 Ewing Kentucky
99 P9 Ewing Missouri
98 H7 Ewing Nebraska
146 E13 Ewing I Antarctica
140 D6 Ewing, Mt N Terr Aust
128 E6 Exaltación Bolivia
118 G7 Excel Alberta
110 B2 Excelsior Missouri
102 E3 Excelsior Mt California
102 F3 Excelsior Mts Nevada
117 F6 Excursion Alaska
37 K3 Exdorf E Germany
146 J10 Executive Com.Ra Antarctica
99 P4 Exeland Wisconsin
8 C5 Exe,R England
102 E5 Exeter California
8 C6 Exeter England
110 C5 Exeter Missouri
98 J9 Exeter Nebraska
95 R4 Exeter New Hampshire
120 J9 Exeter Ontario
117 S3 Exeter L N W Terr
8 C5 Exford England
99 M8 Exira Iowa
99 O9 Exline Iowa
25 G3 Exloo Netherlands
20 F4 Exmes France
8 C6 Exminster England
8 C5 Exmoor Forest England
95 M9 Exmore Virginia
8 C6 Exmouth England
142 A5 Exmouth W Australia
142 A5 Exmouth Gulf W Australia
117 Q3 Exmouth L N W Terr
81 J7 Exmouth Plateau Indian Oc
46 E8 Éxo Nímfi Greece
141 J6 Expedition Ra Queensland
123 R5 Exploits R Nfld
118 B7 Exshaw Alberta
32 K8 Extertal W Germany
8 C5 Exton England
16 C5 Extremadura reg Spain
128 D6 Extremo Brazil
126 F2 Exuma Sd Bahamas
116 P6 Eyak Alaska
80 C5 Eyal Israel
88 E3 Eyasi,L Tanzania
19 P14 Eybens France
27 C13 Eydehamn Norway
9 F2 Eye England
9 H3 Eye Suffolk England
118 L8 Eyebrow Sask
13 F2 Eyemouth Scotland
18 G7 Eygurande France
18 F8 Eymet France
18 G7 Eymoutiers France
9 E4 Eynsham England
99 O6 Eyota Minnesota
118 H7 Eyre Sask
143 F9 Eyre W Australia
140 E6 Eyre R Queensland
14 C3 Eyrecourt Irish Rep
136 H7 Eyre Cr R Queensland
138 D3 Eyre,L (N) S Australia
138 D3 Eyre,L (S) S Australia
138 E4 Eyre,Mt S Australia
144 B6 Eyre Mts New Zealand
138 D5 Eyre Pen S Australia
119 R1 Eyrie L Manitoba
37 L5 Eysölden W Germany
28 O9 Eystnes C Faeroes
32 K7 Eystrup W Germany
19 N14 Eyzin France
48 J5 Ezeru mt Romania
47 H5 Ezine Turkey
77 A3 Ezna Iran
134 C12 Faaoné Tahiti I Pac Oc
45 J2 Fabbrico Italy
108 A4 Fabens Texas
27 D10 Fåberg Norway
117 P4 Faber L N W Terr
121 L5 Fabre Quebec
42 E5 Fabriano Italy
130 E9 Fábrica de Papel Brazil
48 L6 Făcăeni Romania
128 D3 Facatativa Colombia
144 A6 Facile Harb New Zealand
141 K6 Facing I Queensland
18 E8 Facture France
133 C7 Facundo Argentina
86 D2 Fada Chad
85 E6 Fada N'Gourma Upper Volta
51 K1 Faddeya,Zaliv gulf U.S.S.R.
51 O1 Faddeyevskiy Ostrov isld U.S.S.R.
73 L7 Fadippolu Atoll Maldives
42 D4 Faenza Italy
115 O5 Færingehavn Greenland
6 E1 Faeroe Bank N Atlantic Oc
28 M2 Færøerne islds N Atlantic Oc
Faeroes, The islds see Færøerne
85 E5 Fafa Mali
86 C4 Fafa R Cent Afr Republic
86 H4 Fafan watercourse Ethiopia
71 C3 Fafanlap W Irian
16 B3 Fafe Portugal
48 J5 Făgăraş Romania
48 J5 Făgarasului, Muntii mts Romania
26 G10 Fågelsjö Sweden
27 H14 Fagerhult Sweden
27 H12 Fagersta Sweden
48 G5 Făget Romania
48 H3 Făgetului, Muntii mts Romania
45 L3 Faggiola, M mt Italy
71 C3 Fagita W Irian
45 P5 Fagnano Alto Italy
133 D8 Fagnano, L Chile/Arg
22 G3 Fagnes Belgium
85 D5 Faguibine,L Mali
77 A5 Fahaheel Kuwait
77 F5 Fahraj Iran
41 J5 Faido Switzerland
Faifo see Hoi An
121 O4 Faillon,L Quebec
106 D9 Fairacres New Mexico
141 J6 Fairbairn Res Queensland
103 O10 Fairbank Arizona
99 O7 Fairbank Iowa
116 O4 Fairbanks Alaska
95 R2 Fairbanks Maine
109 M6 Fairbanks Texas
112 H3 Fair Bluff N Carolina
94 C7 Fairborn Ohio
111 M8 Fairburn Georgia
98 C6 Fairburn S Dakota
99 S9 Fairbury Illinois
98 J9 Fairbury Nebraska
94 H7 Fairchance Pennsylvania
99 Q5 Fairchild Wisconsin
98 H1 Fairdale N Dakota
144 C4 Fairdown New Zealand
111 L9 Fairfax Alabama
99 M5 Fairfax Minnesota
99 L9 Fairfax Missouri
144 B7 Fairfax New Zealand
107 O5 Fairfax Oklahoma
112 F5 Fairfax S Carolina
98 H6 Fairfax S Dakota
95 O2 Fairfax Vermont
100 C2 Fairfax Washington
111 K8 Fairfield Alabama
127 P6 Fairfield Barbados
102 B3 Fairfield California
95 O5 Fairfield Connecticut
101 L6 Fairfield Idaho
110 H3 Fairfield Illinois
99 P8 Fairfield Iowa
95 S2 Fairfield Maine
101 N2 Fairfield Montana
98 C2 Fairfield N Dakota
98 H9 Fairfield Nebraska
95 K7 Fairfield Pennsylvania
109 L4 Fairfield Texas
95 P2 Fairfield Vermont
100 H2 Fairfield Washington
9 E4 Fairford England
119 T7 Fairford Manitoba
110 C4 Fair Grove Missouri
95 R5 Fairhaven Massachusetts
95 L3 Fair Haven New York
95 O3 Fair Haven Vermont
100 B1 Fairholm Washington
118 J5 Fairholme Sask
113 B12 Fairhope Alabama
71 C5 Fairie Queen Philippines
107 Q5 Fairland Oklahoma
144 C6 Fairlie New Zealand
12 D2 Fairlie Scotland
144 B6 Fairlight New Zealand
141 G3 Fairlight Queensland
141 G5 Fairlight Queensland
119 Q9 Fairlight Sask
99 M6 Fairmont Minnesota
112 H3 Fairmont N Carolina
98 J9 Fairmont Nebraska
107 N5 Fairmont Oklahoma
94 G7 Fairmont W Virginia
117 Q10 Fairmont Hot Springs Br Columbia
111 M7 Fair Mount Georgia
94 B6 Fairmount Indiana
95 M8 Fairmount Maryland
98 K3 Fairmount N Dakota
118 H7 Fairmount Sask
115 M5 Fair Ness C N W Terr
13 F2 Fairnilee Scotland
110 E6 Fairoaks Arkansas
102 C3 Fair Oaks California
99 T8 Fair Oaks Indiana
106 E2 Fairplay Colorado
110 C4 Fair Play Missouri
107 L2 Fairport Kansas
99 U4 Fairport Michigan
95 K3 Fairport New York
95 L9 Fair Port Virginia
94 F5 Fairport Harbor Ohio
114 H6 Fairview Alberta
99 Q9 Fairview Illinois
107 P2 Fairview Kansas
94 C2 Fairview Michigan
98 B2 Fairview Montana
107 M5 Fairview Oklahoma
94 G4 Fairview Pennsylvania
141 G3 Fairview Queensland
98 K6 Fairview S Dakota
103 N2 Fairview Utah

94 G7 Fairview W Virginia
117 D6 Fairweather,C Alaska
117 E6 Fairweather,Mt Br Col/Alaska
119 N5 Fairy Glen Sask
74 E3 Faisalabad India
112 J2 Faison N Carolina
22 H4 Faissault France
98 D4 Faith S Dakota
79 A9 Faiyûm,El Egypt
57 F6 Faizabad Afghanistan
66 C6 Faizabad India
127 M5 Fajardo Puerto Rico
135 N10 Fakarava atoll Tuamotu Arch Pacific Oc
9 G2 Fakenham England
136 G2 Fakfak W Irian
47 J2 Fakiya Bulgaria
28 J6 Fakse Denmark
28 J6 Fakse Ladeplads Denmark
65 F3 Faku China
20 E4 Falaise France
117 P5 Falaise L N W Terr
47 F3 Falakrón mt Greece
68 A1 Falam Burma
80 D5 Falama Jordan
48 L4 Fălciu Romania
106 F3 Falcon Colorado
128 D1 Falcón state Venezuela
45 O4 Falconara Marittima Italy
120 K6 Falconbridge Ontario
17 G9 Falcon,C Algeria
43 B8 Falcone,C.del Sardinia
94 H4 Falconer New York
109 H9 Falcon Res Texas/Mexico
28 E6 Faldsled Denmark
85 B6 Falémé R Senegal/Mali
52 H5 Falenki U.S.S.R.
27 H13 Falerum Sweden
48 L3 Faleshty U.S.S.R.
109 J8 Falfurrias Texas
117 P8 Falher Alberta
100 A9 Falk California
33 S9 Falkenberg Cottbus E Germany
33 T7 Falkenberg Frankfurt E Germany
37 O7 Falkenberg Niederbayern W Germany
121 L7 Falkenberg Ontario
27 F15 Falkenberg Sweden
37 N4 Falkenberg W Germany
33 Q6 Falkenhagen E Germany
33 S7 Falkensee E Germany
37 N3 Falkenstein E Germany
37 O5 Falkenstein W Germany
12 E2 Falkirk Scotland
117 O10 Falkland Br Columbia
13 E1 Falkland Scotland
131 G8 Falkland Is Atlantic Oc
133 E8 Falkland Sd Falkland Is
47 F8 Falkonéra isld Greece
27 F13 Falköping Sweden
111 K7 Falkville Alabama
125 P9 Fallabón Guatemala
102 G8 Fallbrook California
100 D2 Fall City Washington
99 P5 Fall Creek Wisconsin
33 N8 Fallersleben W Germany
26 L6 Fällfors Sweden
28 E5 Falling Denmark
32 L7 Fallingbostel W Germany
15 C3 Fall of Glomach Scotland
98 A3 Fallon Montana
102 F2 Fallon Nevada
95 Q5 Fall River Massachusetts
100 D8 Fall River Mills California
107 O4 Fall R.Res Kansas
95 N5 Fallsburg, S New York
99 L9 Falls City Nebraska
100 B5 Falls City Oregon
109 J7 Falls City Texas
94 J5 Falls Cr Pennsylvania
15 E5 Falls of Clyde Scotland
15 D3 Falls of Foyers Scotland
72 E2 Fallūjah, Al Iraq
22 H3 Falmagne Belgium
9 F6 Falmer England
127 P4 Falmouth Antigua W I
8 A7 Falmouth England
127 J1 Falmouth Jamaica
94 C8 Falmouth Kentucky
95 R5 Falmouth Massachusetts
94 B2 Falmouth Michigan
94 K8 Falmouth Virginia
95 R3 Falmouth-Foreside Maine
8 B7 Fal,R England
89 A10 False B S Africa
116 F9 False Pass Aleutian Is
141 F2 False Pera Hd Queensland
94 D1 False Presque I Michigan
17 H3 Falset Spain
127 J5 Falso, C Dom Rep
124 E6 Falso,C Mexico
133 D9 Falso C. de Hornos Chile
28 H7 Falster isld Denmark
28 K6 Falsterbo Sweden
13 F3 Falstone England
42 D5 Falterona, M mt Italy
48 K3 Fălticeni Romania
27 H11 Falun Sweden
71 C3 Fam isld W Irian
79 D3 Famagusta Cyprus
86 F3 Famaka Sudan
133 D3 Famatina Argentina
133 D3 Famatina, Sa. de mts Argentina
22 J3 Famenne Belgium
143 E7 Fame Ra W Australia
143 F6 Family Well W Australia
28 N3 Fámjin Faeroes
102 E6 Famoso California
71 C2 Fan isld W Irian
14 D1 Fanad Hd Irish Rep
145 E1 Fanal I New Zealand
45 J3 Fanano Italy
67 F1 Fanchang China
110 H5 Fancy Farm Kentucky
87 H12 Fandriana Madagascar
86 F4 Fangak Sudan
58 F5 Fangcheng China
67 C6 Fangcheng China
67 C1 Fangdou Shan mts China
28 E6 Fangel Denmark
65 B5 Fanglan China
65 B6 Fangshan China
67 C1 Fang Xian China
65 G2 Fangzheng China
65 D6 Fangzi China
65 F3 Fanjiatun China
111 B12 Fannett Texas
111 G9 Fannin Mississippi
109 K7 Fannin Texas
135 U9 Fanning I atoll Pac Oc
77 F6 Fannuj Iran
117 L11 Fanny Bay Br Columbia
119 U9 Fannystelle Manitoba
42 E5 Fano Italy
28 A6 Fanø isld Denmark
65 B5 Fanshi China
68 F1 Fan Si Pan mt Vietnam
65 C7 Fan Xian China
18 C4 Faouët,le France
80 F8 Faqu Jordan
79 B8 Fâqûs Egypt
80 F4 Fara Jordan
141 H6 Faraday, Mt Queensland
86 E5 Faradje Zaïre
87 H12 Farafangana Madagascar
45 Q8 Faraglioni Italy
77 H3 Farāh Afghanistan
77 H3 Farah Rud R Afghanistan
45 N5 Fara in Sabina Italy
102 A4 Farallon Is California
85 D6 Faramana Upper Volta
85 B6 Faranah Guinea
86 H2 Farasan I Red Sea
84 J5 Farâyid,G.El mt Egypt
28 C4 Fårbæk Denmark
110 E2 Farber Missouri
26 J6 Fårberg Sweden
48 J3 Farcaului mt Romania
16 E7 Fardes R Spain
28 A4 Fåre Denmark
36 B5 Fareberswiller France
9 E6 Fareham England
28 H6 Farendløse Denmark
28 G5 Fårevejle Denmark
116 L5 Farewell Alaska
Farewell, C Greenland see Farvel,Kap
145 D4 Farewell, C New Zealand
98 K3 Fargo N Dakota
107 L5 Fargo Oklahoma
28 K4 Farhult Sweden
28 C7 Fårhus Denmark
77 J2 Fāriab Afghanistan
80 F5 Fari'a el Jiftlick Jordan
99 N5 Faribault Minnesota
121 Q3 Faribault Quebec
75 N7 Faridpur Bangladesh
84 G3 Farigh watercourse Libya
16 A5 Farilhões isld Portugal
26 H10 Färilla Sweden
85 A6 Farim Guinea-Bissau
138 E4 Farina S Australia
9 E4 Faringdon England
27 K12 Faringe Sweden
106 E4 Farista Colorado
27 H15 Färjestaden Sweden
80 D5 Farkha Jordan
118 H1 Farlane Ontario
141 J5 Farleigh Queensland
99 P7 Farley Iowa
106 F5 Farley New Mexico
121 O6 Farley Quebec
98 J6 Farmer S Dakota
99 S9 Farmer City Illinois
109 O8 Farmers Branch Texas
99 T10 Farmersburg Indiana
99 P7 Farmersburg Iowa
109 L2 Farmersville Texas
111 D9 Farmerville Louisiana
95 N6 Farmingdale New Jersey
98 D6 Farmingdale S Dakota
117 N8 Farmington Br Col
102 D4 Farmington California
99 Q9 Farmington Illinois
99 P9 Farmington Iowa
95 R2 Farmington Maine
99 N5 Farmington Minnesota
110 F4 Farmington Missouri
95 Q3 Farmington New Hampshire
106 B5 Farmington New Mexico
101 O9 Farmington Utah
100 H2 Farmington Washington
94 G7 Farmington W Virginia
94 B6 Farmland Indiana
98 C2 Farm Unit N Dakota
112 K2 Farmville N Carolina
94 J9 Farmville Virginia
98 F9 Farnam Nebraska
9 F5 Farnborough England
8 D1 Farndon England
13 G2 Farne Is England
112 C2 Farner Tennessee
27 C10 Farnes Norway
9 F5 Farnham England
94 H4 Farnham New York
121 S7 Farnham Quebec
117 P10 Farnham,Mt Br Col
9 G5 Farningham England
13 F6 Farnworth England
129 G4 Faro Brazil
16 B7 Faro Portugal
117 G4 Faro Yukon Terr
28 H7 Farø isld Denmark
27 K14 Fårö isld Gotland Sweden
71 G6 Farol Pt Philippines
43 G10 Faro,Pta d Sicily
86 B4 Faro R Cameroon
16 B2 Faro, Sa del mts Spain
27 K14 Fårösund Gotland Sweden
81 B7 Farquhar I Indian Oc
87 J10 Farquhar Is Br Indian Oc Terr
141 F6 Farrars Cr Queensland
26 H5 Farras mt Sweden
77 C5 Farrāshband Iran
94 G5 Farrell Pennsylvania
121 P7 Farrellton Quebec
8 D5 Farrington Gurney England
28 C6 Farris Denmark
77 C5 Fārs Iran
46 E5 Fársala Greece
77 H3 Farsi Afghanistan
85 C3 Farsia,El Morocco
28 C3 Farsø Denmark
99 O8 Farson Iowa
101 Q7 Farson Wyoming
27 B13 Farsund Norway
130 D10 Fartura,Serra da mts Brazil
28 D4 Fårvang Denmark
115 P6 Farvel,Kap C Greenland
94 C3 Farwell Michigan
98 H8 Farwell Nebraska
108 D1 Farwell Texas
77 C5 Fasā Iran
43 H8 Fasano Italy
109 J7 Fashing Texas
79 A10 Fashn,El Egypt
28 B5 Faster Denmark
28 C4 Fasterholt Denmark
14 B5 Fastnet Rock Irish Rep
74 F7 Fatehabad India
74 H5 Fatehgarh India
45 O7 Fate, Mt. delle Italy
54 G4 Fatezh U.S.S.R.
78 J4 Fathan,Al Iraq
121 P3 Father,L Quebec
123 L6 Fatima Madeleine Is, Quebec
16 B5 Fatina Portugal
78 F1 Fatsa Turkey
135 N9 Fatu Hiva isld Marquesas Is Pac Oc
86 C6 Fatunda Zaïre
110 B2 Faucett Missouri
40 D6 Faucigny dist France
19 K4 Faucilles, Mts France
45 J4 Fauglia Italy
40 G4 Faulhorn mt Switzerland
98 G4 Faulkton S Dakota
111 J9 Faunsdale Alabama
22 C2 Fauquembergues France
117 O11 Fauquier Br Col
48 L5 Făurei Romania
89 D7 Fauresmith S Africa
26 H4 Fauske Norway
118 B3 Faust Alberta
95 N2 Faust New York
101 N9 Faust Utah
20 G2 Fauville France
87 H13 Faux Cap Madagascar
43 F11 Favara Sicily
19 Q13 Faverges France
20 J4 Faverolles Eure France
9 G5 Faversham England
43 E11 Favignana isld Sicily
28 C4 Favrholt Denmark
77 A5 Faw, Al Iraq
118 C4 Fawcett Alberta
118 D3 Fawcett L Alberta
9 E6 Fawley England
115 L7 Fawn R Ontario
115 R5 Faxa Flói B Iceland
26 J8 Faxälven R Sweden
27 F10 Faxfj mt Norway
107 M6 Fay Oklahoma
Faya see Largeau
86 C2 Faya-Largeau Chad
54 F2 Fayansovyy U.S.S.R.
21 B7 Fay-de-Bret France
119 Q3 Faye Lake Manitoba
21 F8 Faye-la-Vineuse France
111 J8 Fayette Alabama
99 P7 Fayette Iowa
99 U4 Fayette Michigan
111 E10 Fayette Mississippi
110 D2 Fayette Missouri
94 C5 Fayette Ohio
103 N2 Fayette Utah
110 B5 Fayetteville Arkansas
111 M8 Fayetteville Georgia
112 J2 Fayetteville N Carolina
110 N2 Fayetteville Ohio
110 K6 Fayetteville Tennessee
109 L6 Fayetteville Texas
94 F8 Fayetteville W Virginia
22 F3 Fay le Franc Belgium
109 J9 Faysville Texas
80 G1 Fazarah Syria
74 F3 Fazilka India
85 B4 Fdérik Mauritania
14 B4 Feale R Irish Rep
102 C3 Feather R California
102 C2 Feather Falls California
145 E4 Featherston New Zealand
139 H6 Feathertop,Mt Victoria
101 K6 Featherville Idaho
144 A6 Febrero Pt New Zealand
20 F2 Fécamp France
40 F1 Fecht R France
133 F4 Federación Argentina
98 A8 Federal Wyoming
99 M2 Federal Dam Minnesota
95 M8 Federalsburg Maryland
27 A11 Fedje isld Norway
98 J5 Fedora S Dakota
14 B3 Feeagh,L Irish Rep
36 D7 Fegersheim France
28 B3 Feggesund chan Denmark
30 F1 Fehmarn isld W Germany
33 R7 Fehrbellin E Germany
38 O8 Fehring Austria
130 H8 Feia, Lagoa L Brazil
65 C6 Feicheng China
67 F1 Feidong China
65 C7 Fei Huang R China
128 D5 Feijó Brazil
67 D5 Feilai Xia R China
145 E4 Feilding New Zealand
88 C9 Feira Zambia
129 L6 Feira de Santana Brazil
38 J8 Feistritz Austria
38 K8 Feistritz-im-Ros Austria
67 F1 Feixi China
65 D7 Fei Xian China
65 C6 Feixiang China
129 K8 Feja, L Brazil
48 E3 Fejer co Hungary
28 G7 Fejø isld Denmark
48 D5 Fekete Viz R Hungary
17 K5 Felanitx Majorca
9 F5 Felbridge England
99 T3 Felch Michigan
36 G2 Feldatal W Germany
38 N8 Feldbach Austria
28 F4 Feldballe Denmark
33 S6 Feldberg E Germany
40 H2 Feldberg mt W Germany
28 C3 Feldingbjerg Denmark
41 L3 Feldkirch Austria
131 F3 Feliciano R Argentina
83 J12 Felicité I Seychelles
94 C8 Felicity Ohio
73 L8 Felidu Atoll Maldives
130 G6 Felixlândia Brazil
106 F8 Felix,R New Mexico
108 C3 Felix, Rio New Mexico
9 H4 Felixstowe England
108 B5 Félix U. Gómez Mexico
36 B4 Fell W Germany
36 G6 Fellbach W Germany
21 J10 Felletin France
13 G4 Felling England
102 E6 Fellows California
127 M2 Fellowship Jamaica
113 G10 Fellsmere Florida
45 K2 Felonica Italy
9 F6 Felpham England
36 G1 Felsberg W Germany
28 C7 Felsted Denmark
108 B7 Felt Oklahoma
102 B4 Felton California
13 G3 Felton England
111 L8 Felton Georgia
98 K2 Felton Minnesota
42 D2 Feltre Italy
28 F4 Femmøller Denmark
28 H7 Femø isld Denmark
28 G7 Femø Sund chan Denmark
87 G13 Fenambosy, Pte Madagascar
106 B7 Fence Lake New Mexico
65 B7 Fencheng China
121 M8 Fenelon Falls Ontario
36 B6 Fénétrange France
21 D6 Feneu France
59 H3 Fengcheng China
67 E2 Fengcheng China
67 D5 Fengchuan China
67 B2 Fengdu China
58 F4 Fengfeng China
67 B3 Fenggang China
67 G2 Fenghua China
67 C3 Fenghuang China
67 C1 Fengjie R China
67 D5 Fengkai China
65 F2 Fengle China
67 D1 Fengle China
67 E5 Fengliang China
65 A7 Fenglingdu China
65 D5 Fengnan China
65 C4 Fengning China
67 G2 Fengqiao China
65 C7 Fengqiu China
65 D5 Fengrun China
65 D4 Fengshan China
67 B4 Fengshan China
58 G4 Fengtai China
67 F4 Fengting China
67 B5 Fengwu China
65 C7 Feng Xian China
67 G1 Fengxian China
58 E5 Fengxiang China
67 E2 Fengxin China
Fengyi see Zheng'an
Fengyizhen see Maowen
65 B4 Fengzhen China
65 B6 Fen He R China
116 H2 Feniak L Alaska
14 B4 Fenit Irish Rep
100 J4 Fenn Idaho
103 J7 Fenner California
99 Q7 Fennimore Wisconsin
94 A4 Fennville Michigan
9 F3 Fenny Stratford England
87 H11 Fenoarivo Atsinanana Madagascar
28 H6 Fensmark Denmark
9 F3 Fenstanton England
109 P5 Fenton Louisiana
94 D4 Fenton Michigan
119 M6 Fenton Sask
95 L10 Fentress Virginia
135 L10 Fenua Ura isld Society Is Pacific Oc
13 G2 Fenwick England
121 L9 Fenwick Ontario
12 D2 Fenwick Strathclyde Scotland
94 G8 Fenwick W Virginia
119 O7 Fenwood Sask
99 Q5 Fenwood Wisconsin
65 B6 Fenxi China
65 B6 Fenyang China
67 E3 Fenyi China
22 H3 Fépin France
26 E9 Feragen L Norway
85 F1 Fer,C.de Algeria
100 J3 Ferdinand Idaho
110 K3 Ferdinand Indiana
33 T5 Ferdinandshof E Germany
18 H4 Fère-Champenoise France
22 E4 Fère,La France
26 E8 Feren L Norway
45 O6 Ferentino Italy
57 F4 Fergana U.S.S.R.
57 K6 Fergana Basin U.S.S.R.
57 G4 Ferganskiy Khr mts U.S.S.R.
101 Q2 Fergus Montana
98 K3 Fergus Falls Minnesota
140 B2 Fergusson R N Terr Aust
118 E6 Ferintosh Alberta
85 C7 Ferkéssédougou Ivory Coast
120 B2 Ferland Ontario
14 D2 Fermanagh co N Ireland
20 C2 Fermanville France
121 P6 Ferme Neuve Quebec
33 S9 Fermerswalde E Germany
45 N4 Fermignano Italy
42 F5 Fermo Italy
16 C3 Fermoselle Spain
14 C4 Fermoy Irish Rep
128 A8 Fernandina isld Galapagos Is
113 F7 Fernandina Beach Florida
90 G9 Fernando de Noronha isld Atlantic Oc
130 E7 Fernandópolis Brazil
Fernando Póo isld see Bioko
16 D7 Fernán Núñez Spain
130 G5 Fernão Dias Brazil
100 C1 Ferndale Washington
98 H4 Ferney S Dakota
9 F5 Fernhurst England
118 B9 Fernie Br Col
141 H8 Fernlee Queensland
102 E2 Fernley Nevada
41 N3 Fern Pass Austria
100 B5 Fern Ridge Res Oregon
14 E4 Ferns Irish Rep
144 D5 Fernside New Zealand
36 F2 Fernwald W Germany
100 J2 Fernwood Idaho
111 F10 Fernwood Mississippi
123 P2 Ferolle Pt Nfld
47 H4 Férrai Greece
42 D4 Ferrara Italy
146 H6 Ferrar Gl Antarctica
17 G9 Ferrat,C Algeria
44 B4 Ferrat,Cape France
43 C9 Ferrato,C Sardinia
79 F4 Ferraya Lebanon
16 B6 Ferreira do Alentejo Portugal
129 H3 Ferreira Gomes Brazil
130 D7 Ferreiros Brazil
20 C5 Ferré, le France
128 C5 Ferreñafe Peru
18 E8 Ferret,C France
40 F6 Ferret,Col pass Switz/Italy
19 K5 Ferreue France
111 E10 Ferriday Louisiana
118 C6 Ferrier Alberta
20 E4 Ferrière-aux-Étangs France
21 G7 Ferrière-Larçon France
18 G4 Ferrières France
20 J3 Ferrieres-en-Bray France
20 G4 Ferrière-sur-Risle, la France
28 A3 Ferring Denmark
28 A3 Ferring Sø Denmark
99 P9 Ferris Illinois
109 L3 Ferris Texas
95 O2 Ferrisburg Vermont
101 S7 Ferris Mts Wyoming
28 F6 Ferritslev Denmark
43 C7 Ferro,C Sardinia
130 G6 Ferros Brazil
123 N2 Ferru,L Quebec
94 G10 Ferrum Virginia
43 B8 Ferru, M mt Sardinia
116 N5 Ferry Alaska
99 U6 Ferry Michigan
13 G6 Ferrybridge England
123 U6 Ferryland Nfld
107 P5 Ferry Res Oklahoma
99 U6 Ferrysburg Michigan
8 B4 Ferryside Wales
99 P6 Ferryville Wisconsin
55 C4 Fershampenuaz U.S.S.R.
28 H5 Ferslev Denmark
20 G5 Ferté-Bernard, la France
20 G4 Ferté Fresnel, la France
18 H4 Ferté Gaucher,La France
22 F4 Ferté, la France
20 E4 Ferté-Macé, la France
18 H4 Ferté sur Jouarre, la France
20 G4 Ferté-Vidame, la France
98 K2 Fertile Minnesota
48 D3 Fertöszentmiklos Hungary
Fertö Tór see Neusiedler See
20 F3 Fervaques France
41 M3 Ferwall Gruppe mt Austria
25 E2 Ferwerd Netherlands
85 C2 Fès Morocco
86 C7 Feshi Zaïre
98 G2 Fessenden N Dakota
19 P15 Festre, Col du pass France
22 D2 Festubert France
110 F3 Festus Missouri
48 L6 Feteşti Romania
14 D4 Fethard Irish Rep
47 K8 Fethiye Turkey
47 K8 Fethiye Körfezi B Turkey
43 A12 Fetzara, L Algeria
37 L5 Feucht W Germany
41 N3 Feuchten Austria
37 J5 Feuchtwangen W Germany
118 K7 Feudal Sask
20 J3 Feuillie, la France
123 M3 Feu, L. du Quebec
20 J2 Feuquieres France
20 J1 Feuquières-en-Vimeu France
18 H7 Feurs France
77 F2 Feyzābād Iran
84 E4 Fezzan Libya
8 C2 Ffestiniog Wales
8 C4 Fforest Fawr hills Wales
86 H3 Fgogi Bad Ethiopia
133 D3 Fiambalá Argentina
45 O5 Fiamignano Italy
83 G7 Fianarantsoa Madagascar
86 C4 Fianga Chad
40 F7 Fiano Italy
48 G5 Fibiş Romania
45 K2 Ficarolo Italy
86 G4 Fiche Ethiopia
123 R2 Fichot I Nfld
37 M3 Fichtelberg W Germany
37 O3 Fichtelberg mt E Germany
37 M3 Fichtelfebirge mts W Germany
37 J5 Fichtenau W Germany
89 E7 Ficksburg S Africa
44 H2 Fidenza Italy
119 V1 Fidler L Manitoba
135 O4 Fieberling Table Mt Pacific Oc
106 C7 Field New Mexico
94 G10 Fieldale Virginia
140 B1 Field I N Terr Aust
118 K6 Fielding Sask
100 G7 Fields Oregon
100 A9 Fields Landing California
139 H8 Field West Mt Tasmania
22 B2 Fiennes France
46 D4 Fier Albania
19 P13 Fier R France
42 D2 Fiera di Primiero Italy
106 B9 Fierro New Mexico
109 H4 Fife Texas
13 E1 Fife reg Scotland
119 M9 Fife L Sask
13 F1 Fife Ness Scotland
139 J5 Fifield New S Wales
99 Q4 Fifield Wisconsin
101 R5 Fifteen Mile Cr Wyoming
17 G9 Figalo,C Algeria
43 C8 Figari,C Sardinia
18 G8 Figeac France
27 J14 Figeholm Sweden
45 K4 Figline Valdarno Italy
127 P4 Fig Tree Nevis W I
16 B4 Figuera da Foz Portugal
16 B5 Figuera dos Vinhos Portugal
18 G10 Figueras Spain
85 D2 Figuig Morocco
137 Q5 Fiji islds Pacific Oc
17 F7 Filabres, Sierra de los mts Spain
129 J5 Filadélfia Brazil
128 F8 Filadelfia Paraguay
48 F2 Filakovo Czechoslovakia
146 E10 Filchner Ice Shelf Antarctica
27 C10 Filefj mt Norway
119 R4 File L Manitoba
101 L7 Filer Idaho
45 O6 Filettino Italy
13 H5 Filey England
46 D5 Filiátes Greece
46 E7 Filiatrá Greece
43 F10 Filicudi isld Italy
85 E6 Filingué Niger
31 O1 Filipów Poland
27 G12 Filipstad Sweden
41 L4 Filisur Switzerland
48 H6 Fillaşi Romania
22 C3 Fillièvres France
102 F7 Fillmore California
98 G1 Fillmore N Dakota
94 J4 Fillmore New York
119 O9 Fillmore Sask
103 M3 Fillmore Utah
36 H6 Fils R W Germany
28 C5 Filskov Denmark
28 A5 Filsø Denmark
8 D4 Filton England
86 H4 Filtu Ethiopia
146 B9 Fimbulheimen ra Antarctica
42 D4 Finale Emilia Italy
44 D3 Finale Ligure Italy
17 F7 Fiñana Spain
94 H9 Fincastle Virginia
121 P7 Finch Ontario
9 F4 Finchley England
28 C4 Finderup Denmark
15 E3 Findhorn Scotland
15 E3 Findhorn R Scotland
119 M8 Findlater Sask
99 S10 Findlay Illinois
94 D5 Findlay Ohio
117 P10 Findlay,Mt Br Col
9 F6 Findon England
9 F3 Finedon England
98 J3 Fingal N Dakota
139 J8 Fingal Tasmania
110 H6 Finger Tennessee
115 K7 Finger L Ontario
95 L4 Finger Lakes New York
14 E3 Finglas Irish Rep
88 C9 Fingoe Mozambique
88 C9 Fingoe mt Mozambique
47 L8 Finike Turkey
18 C4 Finistère dep France
140 C7 Finke N Terr Aust
138 D2 Finke R N Terr Australia
138 D2 Finke Flood Flats S Australia
140 C6 Finke Gorge N Terr Aust
138 C4 Finke,Mt S Australia
140 D7 Finke, R N Terr Aust
99 P2 Finland Minnesota
29 L8 Finland N Europe
52 C5 Finland, Gulf of Finland/U.S.S.R.
114 G6 Finlay R Br Col
99 O3 Finlayson Minnesota
98 J2 Finley N Dakota
109 M1 Finley Oklahoma
119 O2 Finmark Ontario
14 D2 Finn R Irish Rep
12 D1 Finnart Scotland
118 E7 Finnegan Alberta
26 H4 Finneid Norway
36 D1 Finnentrop W Germany
16 A2 Finnesterre,C Spain
26 L7 Finnforsfallet Sweden
141 H3 Finnigan, Mt Queensland
140 B2 Finniss R N Terr Aust
138 C5 Finniss,C S Australia
26 O1 Finnmark county Norway
116 J6 Finn Mt Alaska
27 F11 Finnskog Norway
27 F11 Finnskoga,S Sweden
26 K2 Finnsnes Norway
26 M6 Finnträsk Sweden
33 T7 Finow E Germany
33 T7 Finowfurt E Germany
33 T7 Finow Kanal E Germany
27 H13 Finspång Sweden
40 H4 Finsteraarhorn mt Switzerland
33 T9 Finsterwalde E Germany
15 E1 Finstown Scotland
29 H11 Finström Finland
36 E4 Finthen W Germany
14 D2 Fintona N Ireland
12 D1 Fintry Scotland
142 C5 Finucane I W Australia
141 F5 Finucane Ra Queensland
40 F5 Fionnay Switzerland
15 C3 Fionn Loch L Scotland
12 E1 Fionphort Scotland
45 J2 Fiorano Modenese Italy
144 A6 Fiordland Nat. Park New Zealand
44 G2 Fiorenzuola d'Arda Italy
45 M4 Fiorenzuola di Focara Italy
88 C5 Fip Tanzania
78 G2 Firat R Turkey
102 D5 Firebaugh California
116 M6 Fire I Alaska
42 D5 Firenze Italy
42 D4 Firenzuola Italy
98 E4 Firesteel S Dakota
48 H3 Firiza de Jos Romania
133 E4 Firmat Argentina
18 H7 Firminy France
118 L9 Fir Mt Sask
74 H5 Firozabad India
77 H2 Firozkoh reg Afghanistan
74 F3 Firozpur India
112 F2 First R N Carolina
116 R2 Firth R Alaska/Yukon Terr
77 C5 Firūzābād Iran
37 K7 Fischach W Germany
36 C4 Fischbach W Germany
38 M7 Fischbacher Alpen mts Austria
33 Q7 Fischbeck E Germany
36 E2 Fischelbach W Germany
41 M3 Fischen W Germany
109 J6 Fischer Texas
32 K6 Fischerhude W Germany
33 S6 Fischerwall E Germany
89 A5 Fish watercourse Namibia
9 E6 Fishbourne England
102 E4 Fish Camp California
116 L1 Fish Cr Alaska
101 M6 Fish Cr.Res Idaho
113 F10 Fisheating Cr Florida
111 C10 Fisher Louisiana
98 K2 Fisher Minnesota
121 N4 Fisher Quebec
138 B4 Fisher S Australia
146 J4 Fisher B Antarctica
119 U7 Fisher Branch Manitoba
146 C5 Fisher Gl Antarctica
143 A9 Fisherman I W Australia
95 M9 Fishermans I Virginia
115 L5 Fisher Str N W Terr
116 E9 Fisher Vol Aleutian Is
8 B4 Fishguard Wales
95 L8 Fishing Creek Maryland
116 M4 Fish L Alaska
117 M4 Fish L N W Terr
103 N3 Fish L Utah
94 D3 Fish Pt Michigan
140 E4 Fish River N Terr Aust
102 A3 Fish Rock California
101 Q4 Fishtail Montana
101 M4 Fishtrap Montana
94 E9 Fishtrap Res Kentucky
46 D6 Fiskárdho Greece
28 C3 Fiskbæk Denmark
95 P4 Fiskdale Massachusetts
118 J7 Fiske Sask
146 E12 Fiske,C Antarctica
115 O5 Fiskenæsset Greenland
22 F5 Fismes France
95 Q4 Fitchburg Massachusetts
86 C3 Fitri, L Chad
28 C5 Fitting Denmark
9 F6 Fittleworth England
128 D6 Fitzcarrald Peru
114 H6 Fitzgerald Alberta
112 D6 Fitzgerald Georgia
109 L1 Fitzhugh Oklahoma
117 K10 Fitzhugh Sd Br Columbia
22 C5 Fitz James France
140 B2 Fitzmaurice R N Terr Aust
121 S5 Fitzpatrick Quebec
133 D7 Fitz Roy Argentina
133 C7 Fitz Roy mt Chile/Arg
141 K6 Fitzroy R Queensland
142 F4 Fitzroy Crossing W Australia
121 O7 Fitzroy Harbour Ontario
141 H3 Fitzroy I Queensland
142 E4 Fitzroy R W Australia
120 J7 Fitzwilliam I Ontario
42 E7 Fiuggi Italy
45 J3 Fiumalbo Italy
Fiume see Rijeka
42 E7 Fiumicino Italy
45 M3 Fiumi Uniti R Italy
144 A6 Five Fingers Pen New Zealand
122 H8 Five Islands Nova Scotia
101 R6 Fivemile Cr Wyoming
14 D2 Fivemiletown N Ireland
144 B6 Five Rivers New Zealand
88 B4 Fizi Zaïre
26 L4 Fjällåsen Sweden
26 G6 Fjällfjällen mt Sweden
26 F9 Fjällnäs Sweden
26 H8 Fjällsjö Sweden
28 H7 Fjelde Denmark
28 F3 Fjellerup Denmark
28 E6 Fjelsted Denmark
28 D6 Fjelstrup Denmark
28 C2 Fjerritslev Denmark
27 B10 Fjordane reg Norway
27 B13 Fjotland Norway
27 D11 Flå Norway
37 K5 Flachslanden W Germany
28 A3 Flade Sø Denmark
28 B6 Fladså R Denmark
37 J2 Fladungen W Germany
106 G2 Flagler Colorado
113 F8 Flagler Beach Florida
103 N6 Flagstaff Arizona
95 R1 Flagstaff L Maine
100 E7 Flagstaff L Oregon
100 K1 Flagstone Br Col
28 G6 Flakkebjerg Denmark
26 F3 Flakstad Norway
27 B11 Flåm Norway
20 B2 Flamanville France
99 Q4 Flambeau R Wisconsin
99 Q3 Flambeau Res Wisconsin
13 H5 Flamborough Hd England
133 C3 Flamenco Chile
131 E8 Flamenco, I Argentina
33 R9 Fläming reg E Germany
101 Q8 Flaming Gorge Res Utah/Wyoming
113 G12 Flamingo Florida
18 F10 Flamisell R Spain
36 C2 Flammersfeld W Germany
127 O2 Flanagin Town Trinidad
99 O1 Flanders Ontario
22 E3 Flandre France
22 D2 Flandre prov France
98 K5 Flandreau S Dakota
102 E1 Flanigan Nevada
38 H6 Flankenmarkt Austria
26 K8 Flärke Sweden
98 E3 Flasher N Dakota
26 H7 Flåsjön L Sweden
109 K4 Flat Texas
94 B3 Flat R Michigan
117 K5 Flat R N W Terr
123 O5 Flat Bay Nfld
118 C4 Flatbush Alberta
111 J8 Flat Creek Alabama
101 L2 Flathead L Montana
101 L1 Flathead Mts Montana
117 Q11 Flathead R Idaho
141 J5 Flat I Queensland
118 E4 Flat L Alberta
144 A6 Flat Mt New Zealand
109 K6 Flatonia Texas
110 F4 Flat River Missouri
110 J3 Flat Rock Illinois
94 B7 Flat Rock Indiana
141 H2 Flattery, C Queensland
100 A1 Flattery,C Washington
38 K8 Flattnitz Austria
94 F9 Flat Top W Virginia
101 R3 Flatwillow Montana
94 G8 Flatwoods W Virginia
41 O3 Flaurling Austria
27 C12 Flåv L Norway
28 E2 Flavanskjold Denmark
21 H10 Flavignac France
22 F4 Flavigny le Grd. et Beaurain France
22 E4 Flavy le Martel France
118 H7 Flaxcombe Sask
116 P1 Flaxsman I Alaska
98 D1 Flaxton N Dakota
98 A1 Flaxville Montana
33 O8 Flechtingen E Germany
113 K9 Fleeming Pt New Providence I Bahamas
118 F6 Fleet Alberta
9 G2 Fleet Hargate England
13 E6 Fleetwood England
95 M6 Fleetwood Pennsylvania
141 H5 Fleetwood Queensland
36 G5 Flein W Germany
95 N4 Fleischmanns New York
27 B13 Flekkefjord Norway
27 C13 Flekkeröy isld Norway
Flemhude see Quarnbek
98 D9 Fleming Colorado
119 Q8 Fleming Sask
94 D8 Flemingsburg Kentucky
95 N6 Flemington New Jersey
90 F4 Flemish Cap Atlantic Oc
28 E6 Flemløse Denmark
27 J12 Flen Sweden
28 K4 Fleninge Sweden
28 D7 Flensborg Fjord inlet Denmark/W Germany
28 C7 Flensburg W Germany
21 H7 Fléré-le-Rivière France
20 D4 Flers France
22 D3 Flers France
101 N2 Flesher Montana
120 K8 Flesherton Ontario
71 J4 Flesko,Tg C Sulawesi
112 E2 Fletcher N Carolina
107 M7 Fletcher Oklahoma
94 D2 Fletcher Pond Michigan
9 F2 Fletton England
18 F9 Fleurance France
123 Q3 Fleur de Lys Nfld
122 H2 Fleur-de-May,L Labrador
40 E4 Fleurier Switzerland
22 H3 Fleurus Belgium
20 H3 Fleury France
21 J6 Fleury les Aubrais France
68 G1 Fleuve Rouge R Vietnam
36 H3 Flieden W Germany
41 K4 Flims Switzerland
9 G5 Flimwell England
140 F4 Flinders R Queensland
143 B10 Flinders B W Australia
141 G2 Flinders Group islds Gt Barrier Reef Aust
139 J7 Flinders I Tasmania
136 K5 Flinder's Passage Australia
141 J4 Flinders Reefs Gt Barrier Reef Aust
138 E4 Flinders Rge S Australia
22 E3 Flines-le-Râches France
114 J7 Flin Flon Manitoba
20 J4 Flins France
94 D3 Flint Michigan
8 C1 Flint Wales
Flint co see Clwyd
111 M10 Flint R Georgia
107 O4 Flint Hills Kansas
135 M9 Flint I Pacific Oc
120 E3 Flint L Ontario
118 L9 Flintoft Sask
141 J8 Flinton Queensland
110 D5 Flippin Arkansas
112 C4 Flirt R Georgia
27 F11 Flisa Norway
27 H14 Fliseryd Sweden
17 H3 Flix Spain
13 H6 Flixborough England
20 K1 Flixecourt France
22 H4 Flize France
13 G6 Flockton Moor England
111 J11 Flomaton Florida
108 G1 Flomot Texas
36 E4 Flonheim W Germany
67 D1 Flood Basin L Hubei China
146 J10 Flood Ra Antarctica
99 O3 Floodwood Minnesota
110 H3 Flora Illinois
94 A6 Flora Indiana
111 F9 Flora Mississippi
100 H4 Flora Oregon
18 H8 Florac France
111 K10 Florala Alabama
113 E9 Floral City Florida
142 B5 Flora, Mt W Australia
141 H3 Flora Pass Gt Barrier Reef Aust
140 E4 Floraville Queensland
142 A1 Floreat Park dist Perth, W Aust
22 H3 Floreffe Belgium
Florence see Firenze
103 N8 Florence Arizona
106 E3 Florence Colorado
100 J4 Florence Idaho
107 O3 Florence Kansas
94 C8 Florence Kentucky
111 F9 Florence Mississippi
101 L3 Florence Montana
95 N6 Florence New Jersey
100 A6 Florence Oregon
112 H3 Florence S Carolina
98 J4 Florence S Dakota
109 K5 Florence Texas
99 S4 Florence Wisconsin
103 N8 Florence Junc Arizona
102 F4 Florence L California
128 F8 Florencia Argentina
128 C3 Florencia Colombia
22 H3 Florennes Belgium
22 J4 Florenville Belgium
130 H9 Flores Brazil
125 P9 Flores Guatemala
131 F4 Flores dep Uruguay
85 A1 Flores isld Azores Atlantic Oc
71 K9 Flores isld Indonesia
131 F5 Flores R Argentina
48 L3 Floreshty U.S.S.R.
117 K11 Flores I Br Col
71 J8 Flores Sea Indonesia
130 H10 Floresta Brazil
109 J6 Floresville Texas
108 E3 Florey Texas
129 K5 Floriano Brazil
128 E5 Floriano Peixoto Brazil
130 E10 Florianopólis Brazil
126 E4 Florida Cuba
106 C9 Florida New Mexico
94 C5 Florida Ohio
131 G5 Florida Uruguay
137 N3 Florida isld Solomon Is
113 B12 Florida state U.S.A.
113 G12 Florida B Florida
113 F13 Florida Keys islds Florida
113 H12 Florida,Str.of U.S.A./Bahamas
130 B10 Florida,V Paraguay
43 G11 Floridia Sicily
109 O4 Florien Louisiana
46 E4 Flórina Greece
99 O9 Floris Iowa
106 E3 Florissant Colorado
26 A10 Flörö Norway
142 B6 Florry, Mt W Australia
36 G3 Flörsbach W Germany
37 N4 Floss W Germany
37 N4 Flossenbürg W Germany
15 F2 Flotta Scotland
118 J4 Flotten L Sask
27 J12 Flottsund Sweden
103 M3 Flowell Utah
120 J7 Flowerpot I. Nat. Park Ontario
123 Q2 Flower's Cove Nfld
108 D1 Floyd New Mexico
98 K7 Floyd R Iowa
108 F2 Floydada Texas
103 M6 Floyd,Mt Arizona
27 D11 Fluberg Norway
41 L4 Flüela Pass Switzerland
25 E3 Fluessen R Netherlands
71 A3 Fluk Indonesia
111 F11 Fluker Louisiana
20 B5 Flume R France
17 G3 Flumen R Spain
43 B9 Fluminimaggiore Sardinia
36 F7 Fluorn W Germany
94 D3 Flushing Michigan
Flushing Netherlands see Vlissingen
94 F6 Flushing Ohio
108 F3 Fluvanna Texas
18 G10 Fluvia R Spain
28 C4 Fly Denmark
136 J3 Fly R Papua/W Irian
146 H12 Flying Fish,C Antarctica
83 M9 Flying Fish Cove Christmas I Ind Oc
140 C2 Flying Fox Cr N Terr Aust
28 A4 Flynder Kirke Denmark
28 B3 Flynder Sø L Denmark
109 L4 Flynn Texas
140 C4 Flynn Mem N Terr Aust
119 O7 Foam Lake Sask
73 L9 Foa Mulaku I Maldives
47 H6 Foça Turkey
22 J3 Focant Belgium
45 H3 Foce d. Radici mt Italy
15 E3 Fochabers Scotland
42 E4 Foci del Po Italy
48 L5 Focşani Romania
28 H6 Fodby Denmark
140 D3 Foelsche R N Terr Aust
67 D5 Fogang China
140 B2 Fog B N Terr Aust
43 G7 Foggia Italy
85 F6 Foggo Nigeria
42 E5 Foglia R Italy
45 N7 Fogliano L Italy
29 H11 Föglö Finland
123 S4 Fogo Nfld
88 G10 Fogo isld Mozambique
123 S4 Fogo,C Nfld
28 C4 Fogstrup Denmark
38 L7 Fohnsdorf Austria
28 A7 Föhr isld W Germany
45 R7 Foiana in Val Fortore Italy
14 A5 Foilclogh mt Irish Rep
15 D2 Foinaven,Mt Scotland
18 G10 Foix France
52 H6 Foki U.S.S.R.
54 F3 Fokina, imeni U.S.S.R.
26 D9 Fokstua Norway
26 G4 Folda inlet Norway
48 F4 Földeák Hungary
26 F7 Foldereid Norway
28 B6 Foldingbro Denmark
28 C6 Folding Kirke Denmark
28 B6 Fole Denmark
47 G8 Folégandros isld Greece
111 J11 Foley Alabama
89 E3 Foley Botswana
113 D7 Foley Florida
99 N4 Foley Minnesota
120 H4 Foleyet Ontario
115 M4 Foley I N W Terr
87 C9 Folgares Angola
27 B11 Folgefonna gla Norway
116 J5 Folger Alaska
42 E6 Foligno Italy
9 H5 Folkestone England
9 F2 Folkingham England
113 E7 Folkston Georgia
112 K3 Folkstone N Carolina
26 D9 Folla R Norway
26 D9 Folldal Norway
28 E4 Følle Denmark
25 E3 Follega Netherlands
28 G5 Føllenslev Denmark
20 C4 Folligny France
26 G8 Föllinge Sweden
27 E12 Follo Norway
42 D6 Follonica Italy
112 H5 Folly Beach S Carolina
100 G6 Follyfarm Oregon
102 C3 Folsom California
111 F11 Folsom Louisiana
106 G5 Folsom New Mexico
102 C3 Folsom L California

48 L5 **Folteşti** Romania
126 E3 **Fómento** Cuba
52 F6 **Fominki** U.S.S.R.
52 G2 **Fominskaya** U.S.S.R.
52 F5 **Fominskoye** U.S.S.R.
99 M7 **Fonda** Iowa
98 F1 **Fonda** N Dakota
95 N4 **Fonda** New York
114 J6 **Fond-du-Lac** Sask
99 S6 **Fond du Lac** Wisconsin
94 D10 **Fonde** Kentucky
43 E7 **Fondi** Italy
45 O7 **Fondi, L. di** Italy
26 E8 **Fongen** *mt* Norway
43 C8 **Fonni** Sardinia
16 C1 **Fonsagrada** Spain
28 D6 **Fønsskov** Denmark
22 G3 **Fontaine** Belgium
21 H6 **Fontaine** France
18 G4 **Fontainebleau** France
19 O17 **Fontaine-de-Vaucluse** France
40 B2 **Fontaine-Française** France
20 G3 **Fontaine-l'Abbé** France
20 H2 **Fontaine-le-Bourg** France
20 G2 **Fontaine-le-Dun** France
21 E7 **Fontaine Milon** France
133 C6 **Fontana,L** Argentina
112 D2 **Fontana L** N Carolina
45 P6 **Fontana Liri** Italy
45 L3 **Fontanelice** Italy
117 N6 **Fontas** Br Columbia
40 D7 **Fontcouvert** France
38 F7 **Fonte** Italy
128 E4 **Fonte Boa** Brazil
128 G6 **Fonte do Pau d'Água** Brazil
21 D9 **Fontenay-le Comte** France
20 J3 **Fontenay-St.Père** France
123 L2 **Fonteneau,L** Quebec
122 H5 **Fontenelle** Quebec
101 P7 **Fontenelle Fork** *R* Wyoming
22 E2 **Fontenoy** Belgium
21 F7 **Fontevrault-l'abbaye** France
8 D6 **Fontmell Magna** England
22 L5 **Fontoy** France
137 S5 **Fonualei** *isld* Tonga
48 D4 **Fonyód** Hungary
Foochow *see* **Fuzhou**
103 M2 **Fool Cr.Res** Utah
117 P9 **Foothills** Alberta
99 R7 **Footville** Wisconsin
41 H5 **Foppiano** Italy
27 J14 **Föra** Sweden
107 O5 **Foraker** Oklahoma
116 M5 **Foraker,Mt** Alaska
19 K3 **Forbach** France
36 E6 **Forbach** W Germany
99 O2 **Forbes** Minnesota
98 H4 **Forbes** N Dakota
139 J5 **Forbes** New S Wales
117 P10 **Forbes, Mt** Alberta
85 F7 **Forcados** Nigeria
19 Q18 **Forcalqueiret** France
19 P17 **Forcalquier** France
38 E8 **Forchetta** *mt* Italy
37 L4 **Forchheim** W Germany
36 H5 **Forchtenberg** W Germany
13 F2 **Ford** England
107 L4 **Ford** Kansas
94 C9 **Ford** Kentucky
99 T3 **Ford** *R* Michigan
140 A2 **Ford, C** N Terr Aust
102 E6 **Ford City** California
94 H6 **Ford City** Pennsylvania
26 A10 **Förde** Norway
145 E3 **Fordell** New Zealand
33 P9 **Förderstedt** E Germany
9 G3 **Fordham** England
9 E6 **Fordingbridge** England
103 J8 **Ford L** California
110 D4 **Fordland** Missouri
31 L2 **Fordon** Poland
146 J9 **Ford Rge** Antarctica
139 H3 **Ford's Br** New S Wales
110 K4 **Fordsville** Kentucky
109 K6 **Fordtran** Texas
98 J1 **Fordville** N Dakota
111 D8 **Fordyce** Arkansas
98 J7 **Fordyce** Nebraska
26 G5 **Fore** Norway
85 B7 **Forécariah** Guinea
8 C5 **Foreland,The** England
115 Q4 **Forel, Mt** Greenland
109 N2 **Foreman** Arkansas
118 F9 **Foremost** Alberta
22 G2 **Forest** Belgium
100 J3 **Forest** Idaho
111 G9 **Forest** Mississippi
94 D6 **Forest** Ohio
120 H9 **Forest** Ontario
141 F4 **Forest** *R* Queensland
118 E6 **Forestburg** Alberta
109 K2 **Forestburg** Texas
110 F6 **Forest City** Arkansas
99 N6 **Forest City** Iowa
112 F2 **Forest City** N Carolina
95 M5 **Forest City** Pennsylvania
95 O3 **Forest Dale** Vermont
142 B3 **Forestdale** *dist* Perth, W Aust
109 O1 **Forester** Arkansas
94 E3 **Forester** Michigan
100 B9 **Forest Glen** California
101 Q3 **Forestgrove** Montana
100 B4 **Forest Grove** Oregon
102 D2 **Foresthill** California
111 D10 **Forest Hill** Louisiana
109 M9 **Forest Hill** Texas
141 G4 **Forest Home** Queensland
139 J8 **Forestier, C** Tasmania
139 J9 **Forestier Pen** Tasmania
99 O4 **Forest Lake** Minnesota
118 D7 **Forest Lawn** Alberta
15 D4 **Forest of Atholl** Scotland
99 N4 **Foreston** Minnesota
95 M3 **Forestport** New York
98 J1 **Forest River** N Dakota
9 G5 **Forest Row** England
102 B3 **Forestville** California
94 E3 **Forestville** Michigan
94 H4 **Forestville** New York
122 C5 **Forestville** Quebec
122 C5 **Forestville, Parc de** Quebec
19 J3 **Forêt d'Argonne** France
20 K5 **Forêt Ste. Croix, la** France
18 H7 **Forez, Mts du** France
15 F4 **Forfar** Scotland
107 K5 **Forgan** Oklahoma
118 K7 **Forgan** Sask
20 J2 **Forges-les-Eaux** France
121 O4 **Forget** Quebec
119 P9 **Forget** Sask
41 N2 **Forggen See** *L* W Germany
45 P8 **Forio** Italy
110 G6 **Forked Deer** *R* Tennessee
119 R7 **Fork River** *R* Manitoba
100 A2 **Forks** Washington
144 C5 **Forks, The** New Zealand
94 J9 **Fork Union** Virginia
42 E4 **Forlì** Italy
45 M3 **Forlimpopoli** Italy
14 E4 **Forlorn Pt** Irish Rep
98 J3 **Forman** N Dakota
13 E6 **Formby** England
138 D6 **Formby B** S Australia
13 E6 **Formby Pt** England
45 M5 **Formello** Italy
17 H6 **Formentera** *isld* Balearic Is
20 J2 **Formerie** France
43 F7 **Formia** Italy
130 F7 **Formiga** Brazil
126 G5 **Formigas Bank** Caribbean
45 J2 **Formigine** Italy
45 L2 **Formignana** Italy
20 D3 **Formigny** France
26 F7 **Formofoss** Norway
Formosa *see* **Taiwan**
133 F3 **Formosa** Argentina
129 J7 **Formosa** Brazil
129 J6 **Formosa** *R* Brazil
129 J6 **Formosa do Rio Prêto** Brazil
129 G6 **Formosa, Serra** *mts* Brazil
130 F4 **Formoso** Brazil
107 M2 **Formoso** Kansas
28 F4 **Fornæs** *C* Denmark
17 K4 **Fornells** Menorca
38 G8 **Forni Avoltri** Italy
15 E3 **Forres** Scotland
99 S9 **Forrest** Illinois
119 S9 **Forrest** Manitoba
143 G9 **Forrest** W Australia
146 E10 **Forrestal Ra** Antarctica
117 G8 **Forrester I** Alaska
142 C2 **Forrestfield** *dist* Perth, W Aust
143 G8 **Forrest Lakes** W Australia
143 G6 **Forrest, Mt** W Australia
99 R7 **Forreston** Illinois
142 G3 **Forrest River Mission** W Aust
26 J9 **Fors** Sweden
26 J3 **Forsa** Norway
26 J10 **Forsa** Sweden
108 F3 **Forsan** Texas
27 B13 **Forsand** Norway
141 G4 **Forsayth** Queensland
27 J11 **Forsbacka** Sweden
27 F12 **Forshaga** Sweden
27 F13 **Forshem** Sweden
27 F15 **Förslöv** Sweden
27 K11 **Forsmark** Sweden
26 J8 **Forsmo** Sweden
26 K5 **Forsnäs** Sweden
26 C8 **Forsnes** Norway
29 K11 **Forssa** Finland
31 H4 **Forst** E Germany
139 L4 **Forster** New S Wales
146 A13 **Forster's Passage** Antarctica
112 D4 **Forsyth** Georgia
99 S10 **Forsyth** Illinois
101 T3 **Forsyth** Montana
121 O4 **Forsythe** Quebec
145 E4 **Forsyth I** New Zealand
140 E3 **Forsyth Is** Queensland
141 G6 **Forsyth Ra** Queensland
74 E4 **Fort Abbas** Pakistan
111 E10 **Fort Adams** Mississippi
115 L7 **Fort Albany** Ontario
129 L4 **Fortaleza** Brazil
128 E5 **Fortaleza de Ituxi** Brazil
122 G9 **Fort Anne Nat. Hist. Park** Nova Scotia
Fort Archambault *see* **Sarh**
94 J7 **Fort Ashby** W Virginia
118 C4 **Fort Assiniboine** Alberta
99 S7 **Fort Atkinson** Wisconsin
15 D3 **Fort Augustus** Scotland
87 E12 **Fort Beaufort** S Africa
122 H8 **Fort Beau Sejour Nat. Hist. Park** New Brunswick
101 R1 **Fort Belknap Agency** Montana
111 M9 **Fort Benning** Georgia
101 P2 **Fort Benton** Montana
100 E8 **Fort Bidwell** California
118 K3 **Fort Black** Sask
102 A2 **Fort Bragg** California
112 H2 **Fort Bragg** N Carolina
110 J3 **Fort Branch** Indiana
101 P8 **Fort Bridger** Wyoming
99 K8 **Fort Calhoun** Nebraska
Fort Carnot *see* **Ikongo**
Fort Charlet *see* **Djanet**
115 N6 **Fort Chimo** Quebec
114 H6 **Fort Chipewyan** Alberta
98 E2 **Fort Clark** N Dakota
107 M6 **Fort Cobb** Oklahoma
98 A9 **Fort Collins** Colorado
140 F5 **Fort Constantine** Queensland
121 O7 **Fort Coulonge** Quebec
95 N2 **Fort Covington** New York
Fort Dauphin *see* **Taolañaro**
111 L9 **Fort Davis** Alabama
108 D5 **Fort Davis** Texas
103 P6 **Fort Defiance** Arizona
127 L4 **Fort de France** Martinique W I
111 K10 **Fort Deposit** Alabama
100 A8 **Fort Dick** California
99 M7 **Fort Dodge** Iowa
110 J5 **Fort Donelson Nat Mil Park** Tennessee
113 G10 **Fort Drum** Florida
9 E3 **Fort Dunlop** England
123 P2 **Forteau** Labrador
130 B6 **Forte Coimbra** Brazil
44 H4 **Forte dei Marmi** Italy
121 L10 **Fort Erie** Ontario
142 B5 **Fortescue R** W Australia
142 C5 **Fortescue, R** W Australia
95 L9 **Fort Eustis** Virginia
95 T7 **Fort Fairfield** Maine
112 K4 **Fort Fisher** N Carolina
Fort Flatters *see* **Bordj Omar Driss**
99 N1 **Fort Frances** Ontario
114 G4 **Fort Franklin** N W Terr
114 G7 **Fort Fraser** Br Col
112 F6 **Fort Frederica Nat. Mon** Georgia
111 L10 **Fort Gaines** Georgia
Fort Garaud *see* **Fdérik**
106 E4 **Fort Garland** Colorado
118 B1 **Fort Garry** Manitoba
94 E8 **Fort Gay** W Virginia
115 M7 **Fort George** Quebec
15 D3 **Fort George** Scotland
107 P6 **Fort Gibson** Oklahoma
114 G4 **Fort Good Hope** N W Terr
113 F10 **Fort Green** Florida
138 F3 **Fort Grey** New S Wales
109 H3 **Fort Griffin** Texas
12 E2 **Forth** Scotland
Fort Hall *see* **Murango** Kenya
101 N6 **Fort Hall** Idaho
13 F1 **Forth, Firth of** Scotland
115 L7 **Fort Hope** Ontario
12 D1 **Forth, R** Scotland
103 O10 **Fort Huachuca** Arizona
121 S6 **Fortierville** Quebec
6 L5 **Forties** *oil rig* North Sea
122 H9 **Forties Settlement** Nova Scotia
103 K3 **Fortification Ra** Nevada
128 F8 **Fortin Carlos Antonio López** Paraguay
101 L1 **Fortine** Montana
128 G8 **Fortin Falcón** Paraguay
133 F2 **Fortin Gen. Caballero** Paraguay
128 F8 **Fortin General Eugenio Garay** Paraguay
128 F8 **Fortin Infante Rivarola** Paraguay
122 E3 **Fortin, L** Quebec
133 E3 **Fortin Lavalle** Argentina
128 F8 **Fortin Linares** Paraguay
133 F2 **Fortín Madrejón** Paraguay
128 F7 **Fortin Ravelo** Bolivia
128 G8 **Fortin Rojas Silva** Paraguay
128 F7 **Fortin Suárez Arana** Bolivia
128 G7 **Fortin Teniente Américo Picco** Paraguay
Fort Jameson Zambia *see* **Chipata**
113 E13 **Fort Jefferson Nat.Mon** Florida
Fort Johnston *see* **Mangoche**
100 C8 **Fort Jones** California
118 G4 **Fort Kent** Alberta
95 S6 **Fort Kent** Maine
100 C7 **Fort Klamath** Oregon
94 B9 **Fort Knox** Kentucky
Fort Lallemande *see* **Belhirane**
Fort Lamy *see* **N'Djamena**
Fort Laperrine *see* **Tamanrasset**
98 B7 **Fort Laramie** Wyoming
113 G11 **Fort Lauderdale** Florida
112 G3 **Fort Lawn** S Carolina
100 C2 **Fort Lewis** Washington
114 G5 **Fort Liard** N W Terr
127 J5 **Fort Liberté** Haiti
98 F3 **Fort Lincoln** N Dakota
112 C2 **Fort Loudon Lake** Tennessee
98 B9 **Fort Lupton** Colorado
106 G3 **Fort Lyon** Colorado
103 G5 **Fort McKavett** Texas
117 S7 **Fort MacKay** Alberta
101 S5 **Fort Mackenzie** Wyoming
118 D9 **Fort Macleod** Alberta
Fort McMahon *see* **El Homr**
118 F2 **Fort McMurray** Alberta
114 F4 **Fort McPherson** N W Terr
99 P9 **Fort Madison** Iowa
22 B3 **Fort Mahon Plage** France
Fort Manning *see* **Mchinji**
113 F8 **Fort Matanzas Nat.Mon** Florida
113 F10 **Fort Meade** Florida
112 G2 **Fort Mill** S Carolina
98 C9 **Fort Morgan** Colorado
106 G1 **Fort Morgan** Colorado
113 F11 **Fort Myers** Florida
114 G6 **Fort Nelson** Br Col
117 M6 **Fort Nelson** Br Col
114 G5 **Fort Norman** N W Terr
113 F10 **Fort Ogden** Florida
43 G7 **Fortore** *R* Italy
111 L7 **Fort Payne** Alabama
114 J8 **Fort Peck Res** Montana
113 G10 **Fort Pierce** Florida
98 F5 **Fort Pierre** S Dakota
Fort Pierre Bordes *see* **Tin Zaouaten**
95 N4 **Fort Plain** New York
86 F5 **Fort Portal** Uganda
114 H5 **Fort Providence** N W Terr
112 G5 **Fort Pulaski Nat. Mon** Georgia
119 O8 **Fort Qu' Appelle** Sask
112 M2 **Fort Raleigh Nat.Hist.Site** N Carolina
116 F9 **Fort Randall** Alaska
98 H6 **Fort Randall Dam** S Dakota
94 C6 **Fort Recovery** Ohio
114 J5 **Fort Reliance** N W Terr
114 H5 **Fort Resolution** N W Terr
101 Q5 **Fortress Mt** Wyoming
123 M8 **Fortress of Louisburg Nat. Hist. Park** C Breton I, N Scotia
98 F3 **Fort Rice** N Dakota
107 C2 **Fort Riley** Kansas
99 M3 **Fort Ripley** Minnesota
87 E10 **Fort Rixon** Zimbabwe
98 C7 **Fort Robinson** Nebraska
100 D6 **Fort Rock** Oregon
144 B7 **Fortrose** New Zealand
Fort Rosebery Zambia *see* **Mansa**
102 A3 **Fort Ross** California
86 C6 **Fort Rousset** Congo
121 M1 **Fort Rupert** Quebec
117 L8 **Fort St. James** Br Col
114 G6 **Fort St. John** Br Col
74 C3 **Fort Sandeman** Pakistan
114 H7 **Fort Saskatchewan** Alberta
107 Q4 **Fort Scott** Kansas
115 L6 **Fort Severn** Ontario
100 B9 **Fort Seward** California
107 M7 **Fort Sill** Oklahoma
114 G5 **Fort Simpson** N W Terr
107 Q6 **Fort Smith** Arkansas
114 H5 **Fort Smith** N W Terr
101 T8 **Fort Steele** Wyoming
108 E5 **Fort Stockton** Texas
108 C1 **Fort Sumner** New Mexico
112 H5 **Fort Sumter Nat.Mon** S Carolina
107 L5 **Fort Supply** Oklahoma
108 E7 **Fort Supply Res** Oklahoma
103 P8 **Fort Thomas** Arizona
98 G5 **Fort Thompson** S Dakota
107 P7 **Fort Towson** Oklahoma
27 C10 **Fortun** Norway
100 A9 **Fortuna** California
98 C1 **Fortuna** N Dakota
17 G6 **Fortuna** Spain
116 F6 **Fortuna Lodge** Alaska
123 R6 **Fortune** Nfld
106 E6 **Fort Union Nat.Mon** New Mexico
112 D5 **Fort Valley** Georgia
114 H6 **Fort Vermilion** Alberta
89 G3 **Fort Victoria** Zimbabwe
94 B7 **Fortville** Indiana
111 K11 **Fort Walton** Florida
101 R6 **Fort Washakie** Wyoming
94 B5 **Fort Wayne** Indiana
113 E8 **Fort White** Florida
118 A2 **Fort Whyte** Manitoba
15 C4 **Fort William** Scotland
109 M10 **Fort Worth** Texas
98 F3 **Fort Yates** N Dakota
116 R5 **Fortymile** *R* Alaska
116 P3 **Fort Yukon** Alaska
77 D6 **Forūr** *isld* Iran
22 J2 **Forville** Belgium
119 N9 **Forward** Sask
52 H5 **Fosforitnaya** U.S.S.R.
67 D5 **Foshan** China
115 L2 **Fosheim Pen** N W Terr
26 D8 **Fosna** Norway
26 E7 **Fosnes** Norway
107 L6 **Foss** Oklahoma
44 C2 **Fossano** Italy
22 H3 **Fosse** Belgium
100 E4 **Fossil** Oregon
101 P8 **Fossil** Wyoming
141 G4 **Fossilbrook** Queensland
98 C6 **Fossil Cycad Nat.Mon** S Dakota
142 F4 **Fossil Downs** W Australia
121 L6 **Fossmill** Ontario
42 E5 **Fossombrone** Italy
99 L2 **Fosston** Minnesota
119 O6 **Fosston** Sask
98 J7 **Foster** Nebraska
100 C5 **Foster** Oregon
121 S7 **Foster** Quebec
139 H7 **Foster** Victoria
147 E10 **Foster Bugt** Greenland
99 T4 **Foster City** Michigan
118 J8 **Fosterton** Sask
110 K6 **Fosterville** Tennessee
94 D5 **Fostoria** Ohio
109 M5 **Fostoria** Texas
67 F4 **Fotan** China
142 F5 **Fotheringham, Mt** W Australia
20 J2 **Foucarmont** France
36 C7 **Fouday** France
18 C5 **Fouesnant** France
86 B6 **Fougamou** Gabon
20 C5 **Fougères** France
83 K13 **Fougères,Pl.des** Réunion Indian Oc
20 D5 **Fougerolles-du-Plessis** France
20 K2 **Fouilloy** France
109 O2 **Fouke** Arkansas
68 B3 **Foul** *isld* Burma
84 K5 **Foul Bay** Egypt
9 G4 **Foulness Pt** England
13 E5 **Foulney** *isld* England
144 C4 **Foulwind, C** New Zealand
86 B4 **Foumban** Cameroon
85 C2 **Foum Zguid** Morocco
106 F3 **Fountain** Colorado
99 U5 **Fountain** Michigan
99 O6 **Fountain** Minnesota
112 K2 **Fountain** N Carolina
103 N2 **Fountain Grn** Utah
111 E8 **Fountain Hill** Arkansas
112 E3 **Fountain Inn** S Carolina
16 B7 **Foupana** *R* Portugal
140 D3 **Four Archers** *mt* N Terr Aust
18 E7 **Fouras** France
101 U1 **Four Buttes** Montana
20 G5 **Fourche, la** France
110 B7 **Fourche la Fave** *R* Arkansas
19 J4 **Fourchies, Mts des** France
123 M8 **Fourchu** C Breton I, N Scotia
103 P4 **Four Corners** Utah
98 B5 **Four Corners** Wyoming
140 A1 **Fourcroy, C** N Terr Aust
146 C3 **Four Ladies Bank** Antarctica
22 G3 **Fourmies** France
83 K14 **Fournaise, Piton de la** *vol* Réunion Indian Oc
46 E5 **Fournás** Greece
83 L13 **Fourneau** *isld* Mauritius
123 P2 **Fournel, L** Quebec
22 D2 **Fournes-en-Weppes** France
122 G2 **Fournier, L** Quebec
47 H7 **Foúrnoi** *isld* Greece
127 K3 **Four Paths** Jamaica
19 N17 **Fourques** France
13 F3 **Fourstones** England
99 R3 **Fourteenmile Pt** Michigan
85 B6 **Fouta Djalon** *mt reg* Guinea
85 B5 **Fouta Ferlo** *reg* Senegal
8 D5 **Fovant** England
144 A7 **Foveaux Strait** New Zealand
28 C3 **Fovlum** Denmark
8 B7 **Fowey** England
113 G12 **Fowey Rocks** Florida
126 F2 **Fowl Cay** *isld* Bahamas
106 F3 **Fowler** Colorado
99 T9 **Fowler** Indiana
107 K4 **Fowler** Kansas
94 C3 **Fowler** Michigan
101 O1 **Fowler** Montana
144 A6 **Fowler Pass** New Zealand
138 B4 **Fowler Pt** S Australia
138 B4 **Fowlers B** S Australia
109 J7 **Fowlerton** Texas
94 C4 **Fowlerville** Michigan
110 G6 **Fowlkes** Tennessee
111 M11 **Fowlstown** Georgia
77 A1 **Fowman** Iran
99 T4 **Fox** Michigan
100 F5 **Fox** Oregon
99 S8 **Fox** *R* Illinois
115 K6 **Fox** *R* Manitoba
99 U3 **Fox** *R* Michigan
99 P9 **Fox** *R* Missouri
99 S5 **Fox** *R* Wisconsin
123 L4 **Fox B** Anticosti I, Quebec
94 H5 **Foxburg** Pennsylvania
117 O8 **Fox Creek** Alberta
117 P8 **Fox Creek** Alberta
115 M4 **Foxe Basin** N W Terr
115 L4 **Foxe Chan** N W Terr
115 M5 **Foxe Pen** N W Terr
14 B3 **Foxford** Irish Rep
119 M5 **Foxford** Sask
123 R1 **Fox Harbour** Labrador
13 H5 **Foxholes** England
98 K3 **Foxhome** Minnesota
116 P8 **Fox Islands** *isld* Aleutian Is
143 C10 **Fox, L** W Australia
99 S6 **Fox Lake** Wisconsin
101 T8 **Foxpark** Wyoming
144 C5 **Fox Peak** *mt* New Zealand
123 L4 **Fox Pt** Anticosti I, Quebec
117 L7 **Fox R** Br Col
145 E4 **Foxton** New Zealand
118 H8 **Fox Valley** Sask
119 Q8 **Foxwarren** Manitoba
111 G10 **Foxworth** Mississippi
15 D3 **Foyers** Scotland
14 D2 **Foyle** *R* N Ireland
14 D1 **Foyle, L** Irish Rep
14 B4 **Foynes** Irish Rep
16 C1 **Foz** Spain
87 B9 **Foz do Cunene** Angola
128 D5 **Foz do Gregório** Brazil
130 C9 **Foz do Iguaçú** Brazil
128 F5 **Foz do Jamari** Brazil
128 D5 **Foz do Jordao** Brazil
128 E4 **Foz do Jutai** Brazil
128 E4 **Foz do Mamoriá** Brazil
128 D5 **Foz do Riozinho** Brazil
67 E1 **Foziling Shuiku** *res* China
128 E5 **Foz Tarauacá** Brazil
95 L6 **Frackville** Pennsylvania
8 B7 **Fraddon** England
17 H3 **Fraga** Spain
36 B7 **Fraize** France
146 C3 **Fram Bank** Antarctica
22 F3 **Frameries** Belgium
95 Q4 **Framingham** Massachusetts
9 H3 **Framlingham** England
36 G3 **Frammersbach** W Germany
146 B5 **Framnes Mts** Antarctica
31 O5 **Frampol** Poland
130 F7 **Franca** Brazil
43 H8 **Francavilla Fontana** Italy
18 **France** *rep* W Europe
20 K3 **France, Île de** *reg* France
147 G10 **France, Ile de** Greenland
138 F6 **Frances** S Australia
100 B3 **Frances** Washington
117 J5 **Frances** *R* Yukon Terr
140 B2 **Frances Creek** N Terr Aust
101 N1 **Frances, L** Montana
114 G5 **Frances L** Yukon Terr
127 K5 **Francés Viejo, C** Dominican Rep
99 U9 **Francesville** Indiana
86 B6 **Franceville** Gabon
19 J6 **Franche Comté** *prov* France
107 O7 **Francis** Oklahoma
119 O8 **Francis** Sask
146 E13 **Francis** *isld* Antarctica
98 G6 **Francis Case, L** S Dakota
128 D4 **Francisco de Orellana** Peru
124 H5 **Francisco I. Madero** Coahuila Mexico
124 G5 **Francisco I. Madero** Durango Mexico
130 C9 **Francisco, S** *R* Brazil
130 G5 **Francisco Sá** Brazil
123 R1 **Francis Harbour** Labrador
95 Q1 **Francis, L** New Hampshire
89 E3 **Francistown** Botswana
123 Q6 **François** Nfld
117 K8 **François L** Br Col
127 M4 **François, Le** Martinique W I
45 L2 **Francolino** Italy
22 K2 **Francorchamps** Belgium
101 Q6 **Francs Pk** Wyoming
21 H7 **Francueil** France
25 E2 **Franeker** Netherlands
118 C9 **Frank** Alberta
36 F1 **Frankenau** W Germany
36 F2 **Frankenbach** W Germany
37 P2 **Frankenberg** E Germany
36 F1 **Frankenberg/Eder** W Germany
37 J5 **Frankenhardt** W Germany
37 J5 **Frankenhöhe** *mts* W Germany
94 D3 **Frankenmuth** Michigan
36 D5 **Frankenstein** W Germany
36 E4 **Frankenthal** W Germany
37 M3 **Frankenwald** *mts* E & W Germany
127 K2 **Frankfield** Jamaica
110 E2 **Frankford** Missouri
121 N8 **Frankford** Ontario
94 G9 **Frankford** W Virginia
94 A6 **Frankfort** Indiana
107 O2 **Frankfort** Kansas
94 C8 **Frankfort** Kentucky
99 U5 **Frankfort** Michigan
95 M3 **Frankfort** New York
94 D7 **Frankfort** Ohio
98 H5 **Frankfort** S Dakota
33 T7 **Frankfurt** E Germany
36 F3 **Frankfurt am Main** W Germany
31 H3 **Frankfurt an der Oder** E Germany
37 K6 **Fränkische Alb** *mts* W Germany
37 L4 **Fränkische Schweiz** *reg* W Germany
139 J7 **Frankland, C** Tasmania
111 L8 **Franklin** Georgia
101 O7 **Franklin** Idaho
94 A7 **Franklin** Indiana
110 K5 **Franklin** Kentucky
111 E12 **Franklin** Louisiana
95 T2 **Franklin** Maine
95 Q4 **Franklin** Massachusetts
101 Q3 **Franklin** Montana
112 D2 **Franklin** N Carolina
98 H9 **Franklin** Nebraska
95 Q3 **Franklin** New Hampshire
95 N5 **Franklin** New Jersey
95 M4 **Franklin** New York
94 C7 **Franklin** Ohio
94 H5 **Franklin** Pennsylvania
110 K6 **Franklin** Tennessee
109 L4 **Franklin** Texas
95 L10 **Franklin** Virginia
94 H8 **Franklin** W Virginia
114 G3 **Franklin B** N W Terr
115 H3 **Franklin, Dist.of** N W Terr
100 G1 **Franklin D. Roosevelt L** Washington
99 R8 **Franklin Grove** Illinois
138 D5 **Franklin Harb** S Australia
146 J6 **Franklin I** Antarctica
120 K7 **Franklin I** Ontario
103 J1 **Franklin L** Nevada
116 P2 **Franklin Mts** Alaska
144 A6 **Franklin Mts** New Zealand
117 L3 **Franklin Mts** N W Terr
116 H1 **Franklin, Pt** Alaska
139 J8 **Franklin Snd** Tasmania
115 K3 **Franklin Str** N W Terr
111 F11 **Franklinton** Louisiana
112 J1 **Franklinton** N Carolina
112 H2 **Franklinville** N Carolina
94 J4 **Franklinville** New York
100 J6 **Franklin Whitney** *airport* Idaho
144 D5 **Franklyn, Mt** New Zealand
37 J3 **Fränk Saale** *R* W Germany
109 M3 **Frankston** Texas
139 H7 **Frankston** Victoria
99 T7 **Franksville** Wisconsin
144 B6 **Frankton** New Zealand
101 R5 **Frannie** Wyoming
87 B10 **Fransfontein** Namibia
9 G5 **Frant** England
37 N3 **Františkovy Lázně** Czechoslovakia
147 L11 **Frantsa Iosifa, Zemlya** Arctic Oc
115 L8 **Franz** Ontario
33 R4 **Franzburg** E Germany
144 C5 **Franz Josef Gla** New Zealand
Franz Josef Land *see* **Frantsa Iosifa, Zemlya**
38 G7 **Franz-Josefs Höhe** *mt* Austria
43 B9 **Frasca, C. d** Sardinia
42 E7 **Frascati** Italy
106 E2 **Fraser** Colorado
139 L2 **Fraser** *isld* Queensland
100 C1 **Fraser** *R* Br Col
87 D12 **Fraserburg** S Africa
15 F3 **Fraserburgh** Scotland
120 J3 **Fraserdale** Ontario
141 L7 **Fraser I** Queensland
142 A6 **Fraser I** W Australia
143 C7 **Fraser, Mt** W Australia
143 E9 **Fraser Range** W Australia
69 E11 **Fraser's Hill** Malaysia
145 F3 **Frasertown** New Zealand
119 U8 **Fraserwood** Manitoba
46 D4 **Frashër** Albania
48 K6 **Frasinet** Romania
19 K6 **Frasne** France
22 F2 **Frasnes-les-Buissenal** Belgium
25 F5 **Frasselt** W Germany
45 J3 **Frassinoro** Italy
120 F5 **Frater** Ontario
45 L1 **Fratta Polesine** Italy
41 J2 **Frauenfeld** Switzerland
33 S10 **Frauenhain** E Germany
37 O5 **Frauenstein** *mt* W Germany
37 K2 **Frauenwald** E Germany
28 E6 **Fraugde** Denmark
131 F4 **Fray Bentos** Uruguay
20 H5 **Frazé** France
99 L3 **Frazee** Minnesota
101 T1 **Frazer** Montana
120 B3 **Frazer L** Ontario
36 B2 **Frechen** W Germany
16 D2 **Frechilla** Spain
32 G9 **Freckenhorst** W Germany
99 S2 **Freda** Michigan
98 E3 **Freda** N Dakota
36 E1 **Fredeburg** W Germany
32 L9 **Freden** W Germany
28 K5 **Fredensborg** Denmark
94 C2 **Frederic** Michigan
99 O4 **Frederic** Wisconsin
95 M7 **Frederica** Delaware
28 D5 **Fredericia** Denmark
99 Q9 **Frederick** Illinois
95 K7 **Frederick** Maryland
107 L7 **Frederick** Oklahoma
98 H4 **Frederick** S Dakota
140 D2 **Frederick Hills** N Terr Aust
120 J3 **Frederick House** *R* Ontario
137 L6 **Frederick Reef** Coral Sea
99 O7 **Fredericksburg** Iowa
95 L6 **Fredericksburg** Pennsylvania
94 K8 **Fredericksburg** Virginia
117 F7 **Frederick Sd** Alaska
110 F4 **Fredericktown** Missouri
94 E6 **Fredericktown** Ohio
122 F8 **Fredericton** New Brunswick
122 F8 **Fredericton Junct** New Brunswick
28 C4 **Frederiks** Denmark
29 K5 **Frederiksberg** Denmark
28 C5 **Frederikshåb** Denmark
115 P5 **Frederikshåb** Greenland
28 F2 **Frederikshavn** Denmark
28 H5 **Frederikssund** Denmark
127 M5 **Frederiksted** Virgin Is
28 J5 **Frederiksværk** Denmark
103 M5 **Fredonia** Arizona
128 C2 **Fredonia** Colombia
107 P4 **Fredonia** Kansas
110 H4 **Fredonia** Kentucky
98 G3 **Fredonia** N Dakota
94 H4 **Fredonia** New York
109 J5 **Fredricksburg** Texas
26 K7 **Fredrika** Sweden
27 E12 **Fredrikstad** Norway
110 E3 **Freeburg** Missouri
95 K6 **Freeburg** Pennsylvania
100 J4 **Freedom** Idaho
110 K2 **Freedom** Indiana
107 L5 **Freedom** Oklahoma
100 E9 **Freedonyer Peak** *mt* California
95 N6 **Freehold** New Jersey
94 C3 **Freeland** Michigan
95 M5 **Freeland** Pennsylvania
138 E4 **Freeling Heights** *mt* S Australia
140 C6 **Freeling Mt** N Terr Aust
102 E3 **Freel Peak** California
123 T4 **Freels, C** Nfld
98 J6 **Freeman** S Dakota
118 B4 **Freeman** *R* Alberta
110 K1 **Freeman, L** Indiana
111 G12 **Freemason I** Louisiana
111 K11 **Freeport** Florida
113 J11 **Freeport** Grand Bahama I
99 R7 **Freeport** Illinois
95 R3 **Freeport** Maine
122 F9 **Freeport** Nova Scotia
94 F6 **Freeport** Ohio
94 H6 **Freeport** Pennsylvania
109 M7 **Freeport** Texas
109 J8 **Freer** Texas
99 U5 **Freesoil** Michigan
127 P4 **Freetown** Antigua W I
126 F2 **Freetown** Eleuthera Bahamas
94 A8 **Freetown** Indiana
122 J7 **Freetown** Pr Edward I
85 B7 **Freetown** Sierra Leone
95 L4 **Freeville** New York
100 G4 **Freewater** Oregon
101 T7 **Freezeout Mts** Wyoming
16 C6 **Fregenal de la Sierra** Spain
26 C8 **Frei** Norway
37 P2 **Freiberg** E Germany
36 G6 **Freiberg** W Germany
37 O1 **Freiberger Mulde** *R* E Germany
40 G1 **Freiburg** W Germany
32 K10 **Freienhagen** W Germany
32 H10 **Freienohl** W Germany
36 G3 **Freiensteinau** W Germany
37 M4 **Freihung** W Germany
36 D2 **Freilingen** W Germany
133 C3 **Freirina** Chile
36 C4 **Freisen** W Germany
37 M7 **Freising** W Germany
38 L4 **Freistadt** Austria
16 C3 **Freixo de Espada à Cinta** Portugal
28 D2 **Frejlev** Denmark
143 B9 **Fremantle** W Australia
94 C5 **Fremont** Indiana
99 V6 **Fremont** Michigan
112 K2 **Fremont** N Carolina
98 K8 **Fremont** Nebraska
94 D5 **Fremont** Ohio
103 O3 **Fremont** *R* Utah
101 N8 **Fremont I** Utah
101 Q7 **Fremont L** Wyoming
106 D2 **Fremont Pass** Colorado
101 Q6 **Fremont Pk** Wyoming
106 F5 **French** New Mexico
112 D2 **French Broad** *R* Tennessee
94 D9 **Frenchburg** Kentucky
94 G5 **French Cr** Pennsylvania
100 J4 **French Creek** Idaho
102 T13 **French Frigate Shoals** Hawaiian Is
100 G7 **Frenchglen** Oregon
129 H3 **French Guiana** S America
100 C9 **French Gulch** California
139 H7 **French I** Victoria
110 K3 **French Lick** Indiana
102 F2 **Frenchman** Nevada
95 T2 **Frenchman Bay** Maine
118 H5 **Frenchman Butte** Sask
139 H8 **Frenchman Cap** Tasmania
101 S1 **Frenchman Cr** Mont/Sask
103 J5 **Frenchman Flat** *dry lake* Nevada
98 E9 **Frenchman Fork** *R* Nebraska
118 J9 **Frenchman R** Sask
123 O4 **Frenchman's Cove** Nfld
14 C3 **Frenchpark** Irish Rep
145 D4 **French Pass** New Zealand
French Terr. of the Afars and the Issas (FTAI) *see* **Djibouti** *rep*
95 M6 **Frenchtown** New Jersey
22 B2 **Frencq** France
19 Q14 **Frêne, Pic du** *mt* France
20 G3 **Freneuse-sur-Risle** France
37 K4 **Frensdorf** W Germany
31 L6 **Frenštát** Czechoslovakia
32 G8 **Freren** W Germany
143 D7 **Frere Ra** W Australia
129 H5 **Fresco** *R* Brazil
146 K4 **Freshfield, C** Antarctica
14 D4 **Freshford** Irish Rep
144 B6 **Freshford Plain** New Zealand
100 A9 **Freshwater** California
9 E6 **Freshwater** England
20 F5 **Fresnay** France
20 F5 **Fresnaye-sur-Chédouet, la** France
40 C2 **Fresnes** France
22 F3 **Fresnes-sur-L'Escaut** France
124 H6 **Fresnillo de González Echeverría** Mexico
102 E5 **Fresno** California
102 E4 **Fresno** *R* California
101 P1 **Fresno Res** Montana
20 H2 **Fresnoy-Folny** France
22 E4 **Fresnoy-le-Grand** France
40 C4 **Fresse, Mt.de** France
20 J1 **Fressenneville** France
27 B10 **Fresvik** Norway
21 H6 **Fréteval** France
27 B11 **Fretheim** Norway
19 J5 **Fretigney** France
13 E1 **Freuchie** Scotland
36 G4 **Freudenberg** Baden-Württemberg W Germany
36 D2 **Freudenberg** Nordrhein-Westfalen W Germany
36 E7 **Freudenstadt** W Germany
22 C3 **Frévent** France
138 D2 **Frew** *R* S Australia
140 D4 **Frewena** N Terr Aust
94 H4 **Frewsburg** New York
37 M1 **Freyburg** E Germany
143 A10 **Freycinet, C** W Australia
143 A7 **Freycinet Estuary** *inlet* W Aust
139 J8 **Freycinet Pen** Tasmania
33 Q6 **Freyenstein** E Germany
36 B5 **Freyming** France
37 L5 **Freystadt** W Germany
30 H7 **Freyung** W Germany
85 B6 **Fria** Guinea
87 B9 **Fria, C** Namibia
102 E5 **Friant** California
102 E5 **Friant Dam** California
111 F7 **Friar Port** Mississippi
127 P4 **Friar's B., North** St Kitts W I
83 L10 **Friar's Hood** *mt* Sri Lanka
131 D2 **Frias** Argentina
40 F4 **Fribourg** Switzerland
36 E3 **Frickhofen** W Germany
22 D3 **Fricourt** France
100 B1 **Friday Harbour** Washington
141 F1 **Friday I** Queensland
13 H5 **Fridaythorpe** England
146 G8 **Fridtjof Nansen, Mt** Antarctica
38 O7 **Friedberg** Austria
37 K7 **Friedberg** Bayern W Germany
36 F3 **Friedberg** Hessen W Germany
33 P9 **Friedeburg** E Germany
38 M4 **Friedersbach** Austria
33 T8 **Friedersdorf** E Germany
33 T5 **Friedland** E Germany
32 L10 **Friedland** W Germany
37 K2 **Friedrichroda** E Germany
36 F3 **Friedrichsdorf** W Germany
33 T7 **Friedrichsfelde** E Germany
41 K2 **Friedrichshafen** W Germany
33 T8 **Friedrichshagen** E Germany
32 J4 **Friedrichskoog** W Germany
33 P5 **Friedrichsruhe** E Germany
30 E1 **Friedrichstadt** W Germany
33 T6 **Friedrichswalde** E Germany
37 K2 **Friedrichswerth** E Germany
36 G2 **Frielendorf** W Germany
107 K3 **Friend** Kansas
98 J9 **Friend** Nebraska
Friendly Is *see* **Tonga**
95 S3 **Friendship** Maine
94 J4 **Friendship** New York
94 D8 **Friendship** Ohio
99 R6 **Friendship** Wisconsin
127 K2 **Friendship** *peak* Jamaica
70 C2 **Friendship Shoal** S China Sea
94 H7 **Friendsville** Maryland
27 D12 **Frierfjord** *inlet* Norway
94 F10 **Fries** Virginia
38 K8 **Friesach** Austria
33 R7 **Friesack** E Germany
25 F2 **Friesche Gat** Netherlands
36 D7 **Friesenheim** W Germany
28 A7 **Friesische Inseln** *islds* W Germany
25 E2 **Friesland** Netherlands
32 G6 **Friesoythe** W Germany
83 J12 **Frigate** *isld* Seychelles
45 J3 **Frignano** Italy
9 H4 **Frinton** England
124 H6 **Frío** Mexico
109 J7 **Frio** *R* Texas
130 H8 **Frio, C** Brazil
15 F4 **Friockheim** Scotland
108 E1 **Frio Draw** *R* New Mex/Tex
36 F6 **Friolzheim** W Germany
22 L4 **Frisange** Luxembourg
109 L2 **Frisco** Texas
111 J10 **Frisco City** Alabama
103 L3 **Frisco Mt** Utah
108 C8 **Fritch** Texas
8 B6 **Frithelstock Stone** England
36 G1 **Fritzlar** W Germany
42 E2 **Friuli-Venezia-Giulia** *prov* Italy
20 J1 **Friville-Escarbotin** France
12 E5 **Frizington** England
26 D8 **Froan** *isld* Norway
119 P9 **Frobisher** Sask
115 N5 **Frobisher Bay** N W Terr
114 J6 **Frobisher L** Sask
19 P14 **Froges** France
118 G5 **Frog L** *L* Alberta
26 D8 **Frohavet** *inlet* Norway
37 O1 **Frohburg** E Germany
33 S7 **Frohnau** E Germany
33 P8 **Frohse** E Germany
98 B1 **Froid** Montana
22 G3 **Froid-Chapelle** Belgium
130 F5 **Fróis** Brazil
20 K2 **Froïssy** France
36 B2 **Froitzheim** W Germany
52 H4 **Frolovskaya** U.S.S.R.
55 E1 **Froly** U.S.S.R.
101 R4 **Fromberg** Montana
31 M1 **Frombork** Poland
8 D5 **Frome** England
127 H1 **Frome** Jamaica
141 G3 **Frome** Queensland
138 E3 **Frome** *R* S Australia
138 E4 **Frome Downs** S Australia
138 E4 **Frome, L** S Australia
22 D2 **Fromelles** France
32 G10 **Fröndenberg** W Germany
36 F2 **Fronhausen** W Germany
16 B5 **Fronteira** Portugal
18 E6 **Frontenay** France
21 D9 **Frontenay-Rohan-Rohan** France
37 O6 **Frontenhausen** W Germany
125 N8 **Frontera** Mexico
124 E2 **Fronteras** Mexico
118 J9 **Frontier** Sask
101 P8 **Frontier** Wyoming
18 H9 **Frontignan** France
106 E1 **Front Range** Colorado
94 J8 **Front Royal** Virginia
28 F6 **Frørup** Denmark
33 O9 **Frose** E Germany
43 E7 **Frosinone** Italy
28 B3 **Frøslev** Denmark
21 B7 **Frossay** France
109 L3 **Frost** Texas
26 E8 **Frosta** Norway
94 J7 **Frostburg** Maryland
113 F10 **Frostproof** Florida
28 B2 **Føstrup** Denmark
26 G7 **Frostviken** Sweden
37 K2 **Fröttstädt** E Germany
19 K4 **Frouard** France
119 O9 **Froude** Sask
27 H12 **Frövi** Sweden
9 E5 **Froxfield** England
26 C8 **Fröya** *isld* Norway
26 B8 **Fröyabanken** Norway
22 C3 **Fruges** France
106 B2 **Fruita** Colorado
111 H10 **Fruitdale** Alabama
98 C5 **Fruitdale** S Dakota
100 J5 **Fruitland** Idaho
106 B5 **Fruitland** New Mexico
101 P9 **Fruitland** Utah
144 B6 **Fruitlands** New Zealand
100 J5 **Fruitvale** Idaho
48 K3 **Frumuşica** Romania
57 G3 **Frunze** U.S.S.R.
54 F8 **Frunzenskiy** U.S.S.R.
48 M3 **Frunzovka** U.S.S.R.
48 F5 **Fruška Gora** *mt* Yugoslavia
130 E7 **Frutal** Brazil
40 G4 **Frutigen** Switzerland
102 B2 **Fruto** California
54 K1 **Fryanovo** U.S.S.R.
98 C3 **Fryburg** N Dakota
48 E1 **Frýdek Mistek** Czechoslovakia
95 R2 **Fryeburg** Maine
27 F11 **Fryksände** Sweden
46 E5 **Ftéri** *mt* Greece
67 F3 **Fu'an** China
45 J4 **Fucecchio** Italy
65 B7 **Fucheng** China
65 C6 **Fucheng** China
36 E2 **Fuchskauten** *mt* W Germany
60 G11 **Fuchū** Japan
67 D4 **Fuchuan** China
59 G6 **Fuchun Jiang** *R* China
42 F7 **Fucino, Alveo del L** Italy
61 P5 **Fudai** Japan
67 G3 **Fuding** China
16 D8 **Fuengirola** Spain
108 G7 **Fuente** Mexico
17 G7 **Fuente Alamo de Murcia** Spain
16 C6 **Fuente de Cantos** Spain
16 C4 **Fuenteguinaldo** Spain
16 D6 **Fuenteobejuna** Spain
16 D3 **Fuentesaúco** Spain
17 G3 **Fuentes de Ebro** Spain
16 C4 **Fuentes de Oñoro** Spain
130 B7 **Fuerte Olimpo** Paraguay
85 B3 **Fuerteventura** *isld* Canary Is
71 E1 **Fuga** *isld* Luzon Philippines
38 E7 **Fügen** Austria
28 M2 **Fuglebjærge** Faeroes
28 H6 **Fuglebjerg** Denmark
28 O9 **Fuglø** *isld* Faeroes
26 L1 **Fuglöy** *isld* Norway
28 F7 **Fuglsbølle** Denmark
65 C7 **Fugou** China
65 B5 **Fugu** China
Fuguo *see* **Zhanhua**
33 Q9 **Fuhne** *R* E Germany
32 L7 **Fuhrberg** W Germany
77 E7 **Fujayrah, Al** U.A.E.
67 B1 **Fu Jiang** *R* China
67 F3 **Fujian** *prov* China
61 M10 **Fuji Hakone Izu Nat. Park** Japan
61 M10 **Fuji-kawa** *R* Japan
59 K2 **Fujin** China
61 M10 **Fujinomiya** Japan
61 N9 **Fujioka** Japan
61 O5 **Fujisaki** Japan
59 L4 **Fuji San** *mt* Japan
61 M10 **Fuji-san** *vol* Japan
61 N10 **Fujisawa** Japan
61 M10 **Fujiyoshida** Japan
61 N5 **Fukaura** Japan
Fukien *prov see* **Fujian**
60 J10 **Fukuchiyama** Japan
60 B13 **Fukue** Japan
60 B13 **Fukue-jima** *isld* Japan
61 K9 **Fukui** Japan
60 D12 **Fukuma** Japan

98 E7 Gordon Cr Nebraska
140 B3 Gordon Cr N Terr Aust
142 G4 Gordon Downs W Australia
118 G2 Gordon, L Alberta
117 R4 Gordon L N W Terr
139 H8 Gordon L. Tasmania
117 F4 Gordon Landing Yukon Terr
94 B10 Gordonsville Tennessee
94 J8 Gordonsville Virginia
141 H3 Gordonvale Queensland
15 F5 Gordon W Scotland
86 C4 Goré Chad
86 G4 Gore Ethiopia
144 B7 Gore New Zealand
107 P6 Gore Oklahoma
144 D5 Gore Bay New Zealand
120 H7 Gore Bay Ontario
13 E2 Gorebridge Scotland
109 H2 Goree Texas
54 J2 Gorelki U.S.S.R.
95 Q2 Gore Mt Vermont
47 J5 Gorenez Dağı mt Turkey
116 M7 Gore Pt Alaska
139 E4 Gore Pt Queensland
106 D2 Gore Ra Colorado
110 H4 Goreville Illinois
9 H7 Gorey Channel Is
14 E4 Gorey Irish Rep
77 D1 Gorgān Iran
147 K11 Gorga, Zemlya isld U.S.S.R.
83 K14 Gorge R Réunion Indian Oc
142 C5 Gorge Ra W Australia
141 H4 Gorge Ra., The Queensland
128 C3 Gorgona isld Colombia
41 K6 Gorgonzola Italy
86 G3 Gorgora Ethiopia
85 G6 Gorgoram Nigeria
101 O9 Gorgoza Utah
107 L3 Gorham Kansas
95 R3 Gorham Maine
95 Q2 Gorham New Hampshire
95 K4 Gorham New York
53 F12 Gori U.S.S.R.
46 D4 Goricë Albania
99 O9 Gorin Missouri
25 C5 Gorinchem Netherlands
9 E4 Goring Oxon England
27 H10 Göringen Sweden
78 L2 Goris U.S.S.R.
52 E6 Goritsy U.S.S.R.
47 F3 Gorizia Italy
52 G3 Gorka U.S.S.R.
48 N1 Gorki Tikich R U.S.S.R.
52 F6 Gor'kiy U.S.S.R.
52 F6 Gor'kovskoye Vodokhranilishche res U.S.S.R.
33 O6 Gorleben W Germany
9 H2 Gorleston England
28 G5 Gørlev Denmark
31 N6 Gorlice Poland
52 F3 Gorlichevskaya U.S.S.R.
33 H4 Görlitz E Germany
28 J5 Gørløse Denmark
33 O6 Gorlosen E Germany
98 F5 Gorman S Dakota
109 J3 Gorman Texas
94 H7 Gormania Maryland
139 H8 Gormanston Tasmania
43 F11 Gornalunga R Sicily
47 H1 Gorna Oryakhovitsa Bulgaria
55 E2 Gornaya Subbota U.S.S.R.
46 D1 Gornji Milanovac Yugoslavia
42 H5 Gornji Vakuf Yugoslavia
56 C5 Gorno-Altaysk U.S.S.R.
56 C5 Gorno-Altayskaya U.S.S.R.
57 G5 Gorno Badakhshanskaya Oblast' prov U.S.S.R.
56 H2 Gorno-Chuyskiy U.S.S.R.
55 E2 Gorno Slinkina U.S.S.R.
52 G1 Gornostal'ya Guba B U.S.S.R.
54 M8 Gornyatskiy U.S.S.R.
29 P2 Gornyy U.S.S.R.
45 M2 Goro Italy
48 J2 Gorodenka U.S.S.R.
52 F6 Gorodets U.S.S.R.
54 C7 Gorodishche U.S.S.R.
52 D6 Gorodnya U.S.S.R.
54 A1 Gorodok U.S.S.R.
136 K3 Goroka Papua New Guinea
138 F6 Goroke Victoria
52 F6 Gorokhovets U.S.S.R.
87 F9 Gorongosa Mozambique
71 H4 Gorontalo Sulawesi
31 M1 Górowo Iławeckie Poland
86 H4 Gorrahei Ethiopia
25 F2 Gorredijk Netherlands
120 J9 Gorrie Ontario
20 D5 Gorron France
33 S9 Görsdorf E Germany
54 K8 Gorskoye U.S.S.R.
25 F4 Gorssel Netherlands
14 C3 Gort Irish Rep
14 B3 Gorumna I Irish Rep
130 G4 Gorutuba, R Brazil
57 A2 Gory Chushkakul' mt U.S.S.R.
53 C8 Goryn' R U.S.S.R.
31 M5 Góry Świętokrzyskie mts Poland
42 E6 Gorzano, M mt Italy
33 Q8 Görzke E Germany
31 L4 Gorzów Poland
31 J3 Gorzów Wielkopolski Poland
Gosainthan mt see Xixabangma Feng
9 F2 Gosberton England
37 M2 Göschwitz E Germany
61 N8 Gosen Japan
139 K5 Gosford New S Wales
102 E5 Goshen California
94 B5 Goshen Indiana
95 N5 Goshen New York
100 B6 Goshen Oregon
101 O10 Goshen Utah
94 H9 Goshen Virginia
61 O5 Goshogawara Japan
127 N4 Gosier Guadeloupe W I
33 M9 Goslar W Germany
20 C5 Gosné France
142 C2 Gosnells dist Perth, W Aust
42 G4 Gospić Yugoslavia
9 E6 Gosport England
110 K2 Gosport Indiana
111 G10 Goss Mississippi
33 Q9 Gossa E Germany
41 K3 Gossau Switzerland
22 G3 Gosselies Belgium
26 B9 Gossen isld Norway
140 C4 Gosse R N Terr Aust
86 E4 Gossinga Sudan
38 J6 Gossl Austria
38 H8 Gössnitz Austria
37 N2 Gössnitz E Germany
46 D3 Gostivar Yugoslavia
38 L6 Göstling Austria
38 L6 Göstlinger Alpen mts Austria
31 K4 Gostyn Poland
31 L3 Gostynin Poland
27 H13 Göta Kanal Sweden
28 N2 Gøte Faeroes
107 M6 Gotebo Oklahoma
27 E14 Göteborg Sweden
27 E13 Göteborgs Och Bohus county Sweden
85 G7 Gotel Mts Nigeria
61 M10 Gotemba Japan
37 K2 Gotha E Germany
27 K14 Gothem Gotland Sweden
98 F9 Gothenburg Nebraska
85 E6 Gothéye Niger
27 K14 Gotland county Sweden
27 K14 Gotland isld Sweden
27 H12 Götlunda Sweden
60 B12 Gotō-rettō islds Japan
71 B2 Gotowasi Indonesia
47 F3 Gotse Delchev Bulgaria
27 K13 Gotska Sandön isld Sweden
60 F10 Gōtsu Japan
44 G3 Gottero mt Italy
37 O6 Gotteszell W Germany
36 F2 Göttingen Hessen W Germany
32 L9 Göttingen Niedersachsen W Germany
26 K8 Gottne Sweden
117 M10 Gott Pk Br Columbia
28 C2 Gøttrup Denmark
54 H7 Gottvald U.S.S.R.
31 K6 Gottwaldov Czechoslovakia
41 L3 Götzis Austria
65 E4 Goubangzi China
25 C4 Gouda Netherlands
86 C4 Goudeï Chad
22 F4 Goudelancourt France
9 G5 Goudhurst England
85 B6 Goudiry Senegal
85 G6 Goudoumaria Niger
120 F4 Goudreau Ontario
25 B5 Goudswaard Netherlands
20 B4 Gouesnière, la France
112 E4 Gough Georgia
90 J13 Gough I S Atlantic Oc
118 E6 Gough L Alberta
40 D2 Gouhenans France
115 M8 Gouin, Rés Quebec
120 F6 Goulais River Ontario
139 J5 Goulburn New S Wales
139 K4 Goulburn R New S Wales
140 C1 Goulburn Is N Terr Aust
111 E8 Gould Arkansas
106 D1 Gould Colorado
107 L7 Gould Oklahoma
121 T7 Gould Quebec
99 V3 Gould City Michigan
146 G8 Gould Coast Antarctica
143 B7 Gould, Mt W Australia
85 B3 Goulimime Morocco
85 C6 Goumbou Mali
46 E4 Gouménissa Greece
40 E3 Goumois France
85 D5 Goundam Mali
86 C4 Goundi Chad
46 E7 Goúra Greece
86 C2 Gouradi Chad
18 F8 Gourdon France
85 G6 Gouré Niger
120 F4 Gourlay L Ontario
85 D5 Gourma Rharous Mali
20 J3 Gournay-en-Bray France
84 F6 Gouro Chad
12 D2 Gourock Scotland
139 J6 Gourock Rge New S Wales
95 M2 Gouverneur New York
118 K9 Gouverneur Sask
20 K3 Gouvieux France
20 B3 Gouville France
22 K3 Gouvy Belgium
127 P5 Gouyave Grenada
22 E3 Gouzeaucourt France
18 G6 Gouzon France
119 N7 Govan Sask
12 D2 Govan Scotland
107 K3 Gove Kansas
140 D1 Gove N Terr Australia
20 B5 Goven France
114 J8 Govenlock Sask
140 D1 Gove Pen N Terr Aust
48 J2 Goverla mt U.S.S.R.
130 H6 Governador Valadares Brazil
100 D4 Government Camp Oregon
71 G7 Governor Generoso Philippines
122 K8 Governor, L Nova Scotia
113 L12 Governor's Harbour Bahamas
145 D4 Gowanbridge New Zealand
94 J4 Gowanda New York
141 G6 Gowan Ra Queensland
144 D4 Gowan Valley New Zealand
110 B2 Gower Missouri
8 B4 Gower Inn Wales
120 K5 Gowganda Ontario
77 E5 Gowk Iran
14 D3 Gowna, L Irish Rep
99 M7 Gowrie Iowa
131 F2 Goya Argentina
127 N4 Goyave Guadeloupe W I
140 D2 Goyder R N Terr Aust
138 C2 Goyder R N Terr Australia
123 M3 Goyelle, L Quebec
128 C6 Goyllarisquizga Peru
47 L4 Göynük Turkey
61 P6 Goyō-zan mt Japan
86 D3 Goz-Beïda Chad
43 F12 Gozo isld Malta
86 G2 Goz Regeb Sudan
89 D9 Graaff Reinet S Africa
36 E5 Graben-Neudorf W Germany
85 C8 Grabo Ivory Coast
47 F9 Grabousa isld Crete Greece
55 F4 Grabovo U.S.S.R.
33 P8 Grabow Magdeburg E Germany
31 L4 Grabów Poland
33 P6 Grabow Schwerin E Germany
33 O6 Grabow W Germany
42 G4 Gračac Yugoslavia
48 E6 Gračanica Yugoslavia
21 I7 Graçay France
101 O7 Grace Idaho
98 H2 Grace City N Dakota
121 O6 Gracefield Quebec
122 G1 Grace L Labrador
143 C10 Grace, L W Australia
107 M6 Gracemont Oklahoma
111 L11 Graceville Florida
98 K4 Graceville Minnesota
141 K2 Graceville dist Brisbane, Qnsld
110 J5 Gracey Kentucky
38 O8 Grad Yugoslavia
48 E6 Gradačac Yugoslavia
129 H5 Gradaús, Serra dos mts Brazil
26 H5 Graddis Norway
16 D2 Gradefes Spain
46 E3 Gradeska Pl mt Yugoslavia
47 H2 Gradets Bulgaria
48 H5 Grădistea Muncelului Romania
33 S9 Graditz E Germany
70 P10 Gradjagan Java
42 E3 Grado Italy
16 C1 Grado Spain
46 E3 Gradsko Yugoslavia
141 J8 Gradule Queensland
111 E7 Grady Arkansas
108 D1 Grady New Mexico
28 A5 Grådyb chan Denmark
143 B9 Grady, L W Australia
102 D2 Graeagle California
28 C5 Grædstrup Denmark
28 H7 Grænge Denmark
28 J4 Græsted Denmark
99 M6 Graettinger Iowa
37 P6 Grafenau W Germany
37 L4 Gräfenberg W Germany
33 Q9 Gräfenhainichen E Germany
37 K2 Gräfenroda E Germany
38 M5 Grafenschlag Austria
37 L2 Gräfenthal E Germany
37 K1 Gräfentonna E Germany
37 M4 Grafenwöhr W Germany
38 N5 Grafenwörth Austria
36 D6 Graffenstaden W Germany
Gräfinau see Angstedt-Gräfinau
37 O6 Grafling W Germany
109 J3 Graford Texas
32 F10 Grafrath W Germany
36 C2 Grafschaft W Germany
110 F3 Grafton Illinois
98 J1 Grafton N Dakota
139 L3 Grafton New S Wales
95 O4 Grafton New York
94 E5 Grafton Ohio
99 T6 Grafton Wisconsin
94 G7 Grafton W Virginia
141 H3 Grafton, C Queensland
133 C8 Grafton, Is Chile
103 K3 Grafton, Mt Nevada
141 H3 Grafton Pass Gt Barrier Reef Australia
45 R8 Gragnano Italy
119 N1 Graham Ontario
109 J2 Graham Texas
117 M7 Graham R Br Columbia
114 F7 Graham I Br Columbia
115 K2 Graham I N W Terr
118 C2 Graham L Alberta
95 T2 Graham L Maine
146 E14 Graham Land Antarctica
103 P9 Graham, Mt Arizona
89 E9 Grahamstown S Africa
95 N5 Grahamsville New York
42 J6 Grahovo Yugoslavia
42 A3 Graie, Alpi Italy
14 E4 Graigue Irish Rep
107 K2 Grainfield Kansas
118 D7 Grainger Alberta
98 E9 Grainton Nebraska
129 J5 Grajau Brazil
31 N2 Grajewo Poland
52 H6 Grakhovo U.S.S.R.
16 B4 Gralheira, Sa mts Portugal
28 C6 Gram Denmark
46 F1 Gramada Bulgaria
18 G8 Gramat France
47 J2 Gramatikovo Bulgaria
32 H7 Gramke W Germany
43 F11 Grammichele Sicily
Grammont see Geraardsbergen
33 R4 Grammow E Germany
143 C9 Gramphorne, Mt W Australia
15 F3 Grampian reg Scotland
15 D4 Grampian Mt Scotland
138 F6 Grampians mts Victoria
25 G3 Gramsbergen Netherlands
46 D4 Gramsh Albania
33 U6 Gramzow E Germany
44 B3 Grana R Italy
126 G10 Granada Colombia
106 H3 Granada Colorado
125 M4 Granada Nicaragua
16 E7 Granada Spain
16 E7 Granada prov Spain
16 C4 Granadilla Spain
133 D7 Gran Altiplanicie Central plain Argentina
14 D3 Granard Irish Rep
45 K2 Granarolo dell'Emilia Italy
38 G7 Granat-Spitze mt Austria
133 D7 Gran Baja hills Argentina
131 C7 Gran Bajo Salitroso salt lake Argentina
109 K3 Granbury Texas
106 E1 Granby Colorado
110 B5 Granby Missouri
115 M8 Granby Quebec
98 A9 Granby, L Colorado
85 A3 Gran Canaria isld Canary Is
40 B2 Grancey France
133 E3 Gran Chaco reg Argentina
127 O2 Gran Couva Trinidad
111 E12 Grand R Louisiana
99 M9 Grand R Missouri
98 E4 Grand R S Dakota
21 C6 Grand Auverne France
119 P1 Grand B Ontario
113 J11 Grand Bahama isld Bahamas
115 O8 Grand Bank Nfld
90 E4 Grand Banks of Nfld Atlantic Oc
85 D8 Grand Bassam Ivory Coast
122 F8 Grand Bay New Brunswick
119 V8 Grand Beach Manitoba
119 V8 Grand Beach Prov. Park Manitoba
120 J9 Grand Bend Ontario
94 D4 Grand Blanc Michigan
19 Q13 Grand Bornand France
127 N5 Grand Bourg Guadeloupe W I
123 O6 Grand Bruit Nfld
20 C3 Grandcamp France
103 M5 Grand Can Arizona
65 D7 Grand Canal China
14 D3 Grand Canal Irish Rep
111 C9 Grand Cane Louisiana
19 Q17 Grand Cañon du Verdon France
113 J10 Grand Cays islds Bahamas
85 C8 Grand Cess Liberia
111 D12 Grand Cheniere Louisiana
19 P13 Grand Colombier mt France
100 F2 Grand Coulee Washington
20 H3 Grand Couronne France
20 J2 Grandcourt France
127 N4 Grand Cul de Sac Marin B Guadeloupe W I
128 C6 Grande R Peru
131 G3 Grande R Uruguay
127 O4 Grande Anse Guadeloupe W I
122 G6 Grande-Anse New Brunswick
133 D8 Grande, B Argentina
121 U4 Grande-Baie Quebec
45 M2 Grande Bonificazione Ferrarese Italy
21 A7 Grande Brière reg France
83 K14 Grande Brûlé Réunion Indian Oc
118 G4 Grande Centre Alberta
19 P14 Grande Chartreuse mts France
133 D5 Grande Colorado R Argentina
18 H8 Grande Combe, la France
87 G10 Grande Comore isld Comoros
131 H2 Grande, Coxilha mt Brazil
21 I9 Grande Creuse R France
131 G4 Grande, Cuchilla ra Uruguay
126 G4 Grande de Moa, C Cuba
129 G4 Grande do Curuai, L Brazil
122 H5 Grande Grève Quebec
129 K8 Grande, I Brazil
45 M3 Grande, M mt Italy
128 F7 Grande, Monte mts Bolivia
128 F7 Grande O'Guapay R Bolivia
114 H6 Grande Prairie Alberta
127 M2 Grande, R Jamaica
86 B2 Grand Erg de Bilma Niger
85 E2 Grand Erg Occidental des Algeria
122 H5 Grande Rivière Quebec
127 P1 Grande Riviere Trinidad
127 H5 Grande Rivière du Nord Haiti
100 H4 Grande Ronde R Oregon
21 J6 Grande Sauldre R France
122 C5 Grandes Bergeronnes Quebec
20 G2 Grandes Dalles, les France
129 K5 Grande, Serra mts Brazil
121 S6 Grandes Piles Quebec
20 H2 Grandes Ventes, les France
123 L7 Grand Etang C Breton I, N Scotia
127 P5 Grand Etang L Grenada
127 N4 Grande Terre isld Guadeloupe W I
122 G4 Grande Vallée Quebec
127 N3 Grande Vigie,Pte.de la Guadeloupe W I
103 N6 Grand Falls Arizona
115 N8 Grand Falls New Brunswick
115 O8 Grand Falls Nfld
108 E4 Grandfalls Texas
112 F1 Grandfather Mt N Carolina
107 M7 Grandfield Oklahoma
100 G1 Grand Forks Br Columbia
98 J2 Grand Forks N Dakota
22 C1 Grand Fort Philippe France
95 N4 Grand Gorge New York
127 J5 Grand Gosier Haiti
22 K3 Grand-Halleux Belgium
122 F9 Grand Harbour New Brunswick
99 U6 Grand Haven Michigan
111 G11 Grand I Louisiana
99 U3 Grand I Michigan
98 H9 Grand I Nebraska
121 M9 Grand I New York
113 F8 Grandin Florida
110 F5 Grandin Missouri
98 J2 Grandin N Dakota
117 O3 Grandin, Lac N W Terr
111 G12 Grand Isle Louisiana
95 O2 Grand Isle Vermont
99 M7 Grand Junct Iowa
106 B2 Grand Junction Colorado
94 A4 Grand Junction Michigan
110 G6 Grand Junction Tennessee
95 U1 Grand L Maine
94 D1 Grand L Michigan
122 E8 Grand L New Brunswick
123 P4 Grand L Nfld
94 C6 Grand L Ohio
122 F2 Grand Lac Germain Quebec
106 E1 Grand Lake Colorado
111 C11 Grand Lake Louisiana
95 S7 Grand Lakes L Maine
94 C4 Grand Ledge Michigan
28 H5 Grandløse Denmark
99 V3 Grand Marais Michigan
99 Q2 Grand Marais Minnesota
111 M13 Grand Marais State Park St Louis
121 S6 Grand-Mère Quebec
106 C2 Grand Mesa Colorado
122 E2 Grandmesnil, L Quebec
117 P10 Grand Mt Br Columbia
123 R2 Grandois Nfld
16 B6 Grândola Portugal
16 B6 Grândola, Sa. de mt Portugal
110 C2 Grand Pass Missouri
99 R2 Grand Portage Minnesota
109 N9 Grand Prairie Texas
22 H5 Grandpré France
20 H3 Grand Quevilly France
94 F5 Grand R Ohio
119 S5 Grand Rapids Manitoba
94 B4 Grand Rapids Michigan
99 N2 Grand Rapids Minnesota
22 G3 Grandrieu Belgium
18 H8 Grandrieu France
123 M8 Grand River C Breton I, N Scotia
99 N9 Grand River Iowa
100 B4 Grand Ronde Oregon
127 P5 Grand Roy Grenada
42 A3 Grand St. Bernard, Col du pass Switz/Italy
109 M3 Grand Saline Texas
129 H3 Grand Santi Fr Guiana
40 E4 Grandson Switzerland
111 G12 Grand Terre Is Louisiana
101 P6 Grand Teton mt Wyoming
101 P6 Grand Teton Nat. Park Wyoming
106 B2 Grand Valley Colorado
100 J7 Grand View Idaho
119 R7 Grandview Manitoba
109 K3 Grandview Texas
100 F3 Grandview Washington
94 B4 Grandville Michigan
36 B7 Grandvillers France
103 L5 Grand Wash creek Arizona
103 L6 Grand Wash Cliffs Arizona
19 N15 Grâne France
26 F6 Grane Norway
26 K7 Graned Sweden
17 G3 Grañén Spain
44 B2 Granero mt Italy
121 N5 Granet, L Quebec
14 C4 Graney, L Irish Rep
27 G11 Grangarde Sweden
27 H11 Grängeberg Sweden
127 H1 Grange Hill Jamaica
12 E1 Grangemouth Scotland
99 P9 Granger Missouri
109 K5 Granger Texas
100 E3 Granger Washington
101 Q8 Granger Wyoming
36 B7 Granges-sur-Vologne France
100 J4 Grangeville Idaho
26 J8 Graninge Sweden
107 L7 Granite Oklahoma
100 G5 Granite Oregon
98 A8 Granite Wyoming
117 L10 Granite Bay Br Columbia
110 F3 Granite City Illinois
111 M12 Granite City St Louis
99 L5 Granite Falls Minnesota
112 F2 Granite Falls N Carolina
100 D1 Granite Falls Washington
116 N7 Granite I Alaska
99 T3 Granite I Michigan
123 P5 Granite L Nfld
100 H9 Granite Mt Nevada
103 J7 Granite Mts California
102 H6 Granite Peak California
100 H8 Granite Peak mt Nevada
101 Q4 Granite Pk Montana
101 M9 Granite Pk Utah
101 R7 Granite Pk Wyoming
99 T3 Granite Pt Michigan
116 Q6 Granite Range Alaska
100 F9 Granite Range Nevada
140 B5 Granites, The peak N Terr Aust
112 F4 Graniteville S Carolina
130 G9 Granito Brazil
144 C4 Granity New Zealand
129 K4 Granja Brazil
127 J5 Granja, Pta. de la Dominican Rep
54 C2 Granki U.S.S.R.
29 L11 Grankulla Finland
27 J14 Grankullavik Sweden
133 D6 Gran Laguna Salada L Argentina
118 F9 Granlea Alberta
133 E6 Gran Lorenzo Argentina
26 G8 Granlunda Sweden
124 F3 Gran Morelos Mexico
27 G13 Gränna Sweden
111 B7 Grannis Arkansas
98 E1 Grano N Dakota
17 J3 Granollers Spain
42 A3 Gran Paradiso mt Italy
133 E5 Gran Pico Argentina
42 D2 Gran Pilastro mt Italy/Austria
133 E4 Gran Pinto Argentina
44 B2 Gran Queyron mt Italy/France
108 A1 Gran Quivira Nat.Mon New Mexico
133 D5 Gran Roca Argentina
42 F6 Gran Sasso d'Italia Italy
33 S6 Gransee E Germany
113 G10 Grant Florida
99 M8 Grant Iowa
94 B3 Grant Michigan
101 M4 Grant Montana
98 E9 Grant Nebraska
107 P8 Grant Oklahoma
120 D2 Grant Ontario
99 M9 Grant City Missouri
143 D7 Grant Duff Ra W Australia
9 F2 Grantham England
140 C1 Grant I N Terr Aust
117 P3 Grant L N W Terr
116 E4 Grantley Hbr Alaska
143 E8 Grant, Mt W Australia
120 J9 Granton Ontario
13 E2 Granton Scotland
99 Q5 Granton Wisconsin
15 E3 Grantown on Spey Scotland
103 J3 Grant Ra Nevada
142 E4 Grant Ra W Australia
26 K7 Grantråsk Sweden
116 M6 Grants Alaska
106 C6 Grants New Mexico
99 O4 Grantsburg Wisconsin
101 L3 Grantsdale Montana
13 F2 Grantshouse Scotland
100 B7 Grants Pass Oregon
142 D4 Grant Spring W Australia
101 N9 Grantsville Utah
94 F8 Grantsville W Virginia
111 M8 Grantville Georgia
20 B4 Granville France
99 R8 Granville Illinois
99 L7 Granville Iowa
98 F1 Granville N Dakota
95 O3 Granville New York
94 E6 Granville Ohio
94 K6 Granville Pennsylvania
122 G9 Granville Ferry Nova Scotia
133 E5 Gran Villegas Argentina
119 R2 Granville L Manitoba
33 P6 Granzin E Germany
130 G5 Grão Mogol Brazil
109 M4 Grapeland Texas
102 F7 Grapevine California
109 N8 Grapevine Texas
109 K3 Grapevine Res Texas
42 D3 Grappa mt Italy
126 G6 Grappler Bk Caribbean
27 H11 Gräsberg Sweden
32 M8 Grasdorf W Germany
87 F10 Graskop S Africa
114 H8 Gras,L.de N W Terr
13 E5 Grasmere England
27 K11 Gräsö Sweden
95 M2 Grass R New York
101 R6 Grass Creek Wyoming
44 B4 Grasse France
121 M3 Grasset, L Quebec
13 G5 Grassington England
100 C8 Grass Lake California
108 F2 Grassland Texas
145 E4 Grassmere, L New Zealand
143 D10 Grass Patch W Australia
119 T3 Grass R Manitoba
101 R2 Grassrange Montana
119 Q4 Grass River Prov. Park Manitoba
102 C2 Grass Valley California
100 E4 Grass Valley Oregon
139 G8 Grassy Tasmania
98 C2 Grassy Butte N Dakota
126 F3 Grassy Cr Andros Bahamas
118 G7 Grassy Island L Alberta
94 G3 Grassy Knob mt W Virginia
118 F9 Grassy Lake Alberta
28 D7 Gråsten Denmark
27 F13 Grästorp Sweden
26 J3 Gratangen Norway
123 U5 Grate's Cove Nfld
99 R7 Gratiot Wisconsin
94 C7 Gratis Ohio
26 L6 Gråträsk Sweden
28 D4 Grauballe Denmark
41 K4 Graubünden canton Switzerland
18 H9 Grau-du-Roi,le France
17 H2 Graus Spain
131 H2 Gravata Brazil
25 E5 Grave Netherlands
114 J3 Gravelbourg Sask
22 C2 Gravelines France
20 C5 Gravelle,la France
87 F10 Gravelotte S Africa
20 G3 Gravenchon, N.D. de France
121 L8 Gravenhurst Ontario
36 F3 Grävenwiesbach W Germany
101 L3 Grave Pk Idaho
18 E7 Grave, Pte de C France
9 G5 Gravesend England
139 K3 Gravesend New S Wales
19 N17 Graveson France
110 E5 Gravette Arkansas
20 H3 Gravigny France
20 F3 Graville France
43 G8 Gravina di Puglia Italy
99 M9 Gravity Iowa
28 D3 Gravlev Denmark
26 E7 Gravvik Norway
99 V5 Grawn Michigan
19 J5 Gray France
112 D4 Gray Georgia
95 R3 Gray Maine
108 D7 Gray Oklahoma
119 N8 Gray Sask
100 A3 Grayland Washington
94 C2 Grayling Michigan
117 L6 Grayling R Br Columbia
116 R3 Grayling Fk. R Alaska
140 C4 Grayling, Mt N Terr Aust
13 F5 Grayrigg England
100 A3 Grays Harbor Washington
101 O6 Grays L Idaho
99 S7 Grays Lake Illinois
94 E8 Grayson Kentucky
111 D9 Grayson Louisiana
119 P8 Grayson Sask
120 A2 Grayson L Ontario
106 E2 Grays Pk Colorado
94 B1 Grays Reef Michigan
100 B3 Grays River Washington
9 G5 Grays Thurrock England
111 K11 Grayton Beach Florida
110 H3 Grayville Illinois
54 G6 Grayvoron U.S.S.R.
38 M7 Graz Austria
16 D8 Grazalema Spain
46 E2 Grdelica Yugoslavia
48 K6 Greaca Lacul L Romania
13 G6 Greasbrough England
117 M4 Greasy L N W Terr
138 B5 Great Australian Bight Australia
9 G4 Great Baddow England
113 J12 Great Bahama Bank Bahamas
145 E2 Great Barrier I New Zealand
136 Great Barrier Reef Australia
95 O4 Great Barrington Massachusetts
103 H1 Great Basin Nevada
117 L3 Great Bear R N W Terr
114 H4 Great Bear L N W Terr
107 M3 Great Bend Kansas
98 K3 Great Bend N Dakota
89 A9 Great Berg R S Africa
15 B2 Great Bernera isld Scotland
14 A4 Great Blasket I. Irish Rep
122 F3 Great Boule I Quebec
123 R2 Great Brehat Nfld
8 D1 Great Budworth England
123 Q5 Great Burnt L. Nfld
89 A7 Great Bushman Land reg S Africa
94 J7 Great Cacapon W Virginia
9 F2 Great Casterton England
9 G3 Great Chesterford England
123 T7 Great Colinet I. Nfld
12 D2 Great Cumbrae isld Scotland
9 F2 Great Dalby England
118 K6 Great Deer Sask
101 S9 Great Divide Colorado
139 Great Dividing Ra Australia
13 H5 Great Driffield England
120 H7 Great Duck I. Ontario
Greater Khingan Range see Da Hinggan Ling
13 F6 Greater Manchester co England
145 D1 Great Exhibition Bay New Zealand
126 F3 Great Exuma isld Bahamas
114 H8 Great Falls Montana
112 G3 Great Falls S Carolina
110 L6 Great Falls Dam Tennessee
110 L6 Great Falls L Tennessee
89 E9 Great Fish R S Africa
6 N6 Great Fisher Bank North Sea
89 E9 Great Fish Pt. lt ho S Africa
145 E4 Greatford New Zealand
127 K3 Great Goat I Jamaica
9 F2 Great Gonerby England
113 K11 Great Guana Cay isld Bahamas
9 F5 Greatham England
126 F2 Great Harbour Cay isld Bahamas
144 A6 Great I New Zealand
145 D1 Great I New Zealand
126 H4 Great Inagua isld Bahamas
Great Indian Desert see Thar
113 H11 Great Isaac I Bahamas
89 A6 Great Karas Berg mts Namibia
89 C9 Great Karroo reg S Africa
89 E9 Great Kei R S Africa
141 K6 Great Keppel isld Queensland
112 K3 Great L N Carolina
139 H8 Great L Tasmania
8 D3 Great Malvern England
145 E2 Great Mercury I New Zealand
9 F4 Great Missenden England
87 C11 Great Namaland reg Namibia
136 J3 Great NE Channel Qnsld/Papua New Guinea
69 A9 Great Nicobar isld Nicobar Is
9 F4 Great Offley England
8 C1 Great Ormes Head Wales
95 P6 Great Peconic B Long I, N Y
127 J3 Great Pedro Bluff Jamaica
95 T2 Great Pond Maine
95 R5 Great Pt Massachusetts
122 G10 Great Pubnico L Nova Scotia
127 J2 Great R Jamaica
88 E5 Great Ruaha R Tanzania
113 J11 Great Sale Cay Bahamas
101 N8 Great Salt L Utah
101 M9 Great Salt L.Des Utah
107 M5 Great Salt Plains Res Oklahoma
106 E4 Great Sand Dunes Nat.Mon Colorado
118 H8 Great Sand Hills Sask
142 D5 Great Sandy Desert W Australia
141 L7 Great Sandy I Queensland
9 G3 Great Shelford England
89 G4 Great Shingwidzi R S Africa
114 H5 Great Slave L N W Terr
112 D2 Great Smoky Mts Tenn/N Carolina
117 L7 Great Snow Mt Br Columbia
7 D13 Great Sole Bank Atlantic Oc
95 O6 Great South Bay Long I, N Y
113 K12 Great Stirrup Cay isld Bahamas
8 B6 Great Torrington England
87 C10 Great Ums Namibia
138 B3 Great Victoria Desert S Australia
122 J8 Great Village Nova Scotia
9 G4 Great Waltham England
95 U2 Great Wass I Maine
139 H8 Great Western Tiers Tasmania
68 C7 Great West Torres I Burma
13 G5 Great Whernside mt England
9 H2 Great Yarmouth England
27 E13 Grebbestad Sweden
36 G2 Grebenau W Germany
36 G3 Grebenhain W Germany
54 D6 Grebenka U.S.S.R.
32 K10 Grebenstein W Germany
38 K7 Grebenzen mt Austria
85 F4 Greboun, Mt Niger
43 F8 Greco, Torre del Italy
37 L5 Greding W Germany
16 D4 Gredos, Sa. de mts Spain
28 B6 Gredstedbro Denmark
46 E6 Greece rep S Europe
98 B9 Greeley Colorado
98 H8 Greeley Nebraska
115 L1 Greely Fiord N W Terr
50 F1 Greem Bell, Ostrov isld U.S.S.R.
107 O2 Green Kansas
112 E2 Green R N Carolina
113 G11 Greenacres City Florida
95 M8 Greenbackville Maryland
99 T5 Green Bay Wisconsin
139 L4 Green Bluff New S Wales
94 G8 Greenbrier R W Virginia
94 D2 Greenbush Michigan
98 K1 Greenbush Minnesota
143 B10 Greenbushes W Australia
139 K6 Green Cape New S Wales
110 K2 Greencastle Indiana
94 K7 Greencastle Pennsylvania
126 F2 Green Cay isld Bahamas
99 O9 Green City Missouri
118 B4 Green Court Alberta
113 F8 Green Cove Springs Florida
99 O7 Greene Iowa
98 E1 Greene N Dakota
95 M4 Greene New York
32 L9 Greene W Germany
143 G6 Greene, Mt W Australia
112 E1 Greeneville Tennessee
102 C5 Greenfield California
110 F2 Greenfield Illinois
94 B7 Greenfield Indiana
99 M8 Greenfield Iowa
95 P4 Greenfield Massachusetts
110 C4 Greenfield Missouri
94 D7 Greenfield Ohio
107 M6 Greenfield Oklahoma
110 H5 Greenfield Tennessee
110 C5 Green Forest Arkansas
127 O2 Green Hill Trinidad
140 B1 Greenhill I N Terr Aust
144 B7 Greenhills New Zealand
143 B9 Greenhills W Australia
102 F6 Greenhorn Mts California
116 O6 Green I Alaska
144 B7 Green I New Zealand
123 Q2 Green I Nfld
141 H3 Green I Queensland
143 B9 Green I W Australia
121 Q4 Greening Quebec
137 L2 Green Is Solomon Is
127 H1 Green Island Jamaica
144 C7 Green Island New Zealand
71 D5 Green Island B Philippines
144 A7 Green Islets New Zealand
117 N10 Green L Br Columbia
99 S6 Green L Wisconsin
118 K4 Green Lake Sask
109 L7 Green Lake Texas
115 P2 Greenland
127 P6 Greenland Barbados
90 H1 Greenland Basin Arctic Oc
90 G2 Greenland-Iceland Rise N Atlantic Oc
144 B6 Greenland Res New Zealand
147 H10 Greenland Sea Arctic Oc
13 F2 Greenlaw Scotland
107 O2 Greenleaf Kansas
12 E1 Greenloaning Scotland
15 E5 Green Lowther mt Scotland
123 P2 Greenly I Quebec
138 C5 Greenly I S Australia
145 F3 Greenmeadows New Zealand
106 D2 Green Mt Res Colorado
95 O3 Green Mts Vermont
101 S7 Green Mts Wyoming
12 D2 Greenock Scotland
14 E2 Greenore Irish Rep
14 E4 Greenore Pt Irish Rep
116 R2 Greenough, Mt Alaska
112 G5 Green Pond S Carolina
95 P5 Greenport Long I, N Y
122 D6 Green R New Brunswick
101 Q8 Green River Wyoming
94 B9 Green R. Res Kentucky
111 J9 Greensboro Alabama
111 M11 Greensboro Florida
112 D4 Greensboro Georgia
112 H1 Greensboro N Carolina
95 P2 Greensboro Vermont
94 B7 Greensburg Indiana
107 L4 Greensburg Kansas
94 B9 Greensburg Kentucky
111 F11 Greensburg Louisiana
94 H6 Greensburg Pennsylvania
141 K2 Greenslopes dist Brisbane, Qnsld
123 T4 Greenspond Nfld
94 J7 Green Spring W Virginia
94 D5 Green Springs Ohio
139 J5 Greenthorpe New S Wales
99 O9 Greentop Missouri
94 B6 Greentown Indiana
113 K11 Green Turtle Cay isld Bahamas
110 H2 Greenup Illinois
141 H4 Greenvale Queensland
142 G3 Greenvale W Australia
111 K10 Greenville Alabama
100 E9 Greenville California
113 D7 Greenville Florida
110 G3 Greenville Illinois
110 J4 Greenville Kentucky
85 C8 Greenville Liberia
95 S1 Greenville Maine
94 B3 Greenville Michigan
111 E8 Greenville Mississippi
110 F4 Greenville Missouri
112 K2 Greenville N Carolina
95 Q4 Greenville New Hampshire
95 N4 Greenville New York
94 C6 Greenville Ohio
94 G5 Greenville Pennsylvania
112 E3 Greenville S Carolina
109 L2 Greenville Texas
94 H8 Greenville Virginia
119 N2 Greenwater L Ontario
119 O6 Greenwater L. Prov. Park Sask
119 S9 Greenway Manitoba
98 G4 Greenway S Dakota
9 G5 Greenwich England
107 N4 Greenwich Kansas
95 O3 Greenwich New York
94 E5 Greenwich Ohio
103 N3 Greenwich Utah
146 E15 Greenwich I S Shetland Is
110 B6 Greenwood Arkansas
100 G1 Greenwood Br Columbia
102 D3 Greenwood California
95 M8 Greenwood Delaware
94 A7 Greenwood Indiana
94 C10 Greenwood Kentucky
111 C9 Greenwood Louisiana
111 F8 Greenwood Mississippi
98 K9 Greenwood Nebraska
140 C5 Greenwood N Terr Aust
112 E3 Greenwood S Carolina
98 H7 Greenwood S Dakota
99 Q5 Greenwood Wisconsin
111 H8 Greenwood Springs Mississippi
100 J3 Greer Idaho
112 E3 Greer S Carolina
111 C7 Greeson, L Arkansas
32 F5 Greetsiel W Germany
20 G5 Greez France
25 F6 Grefrath W Germany
119 S9 Gregg Manitoba
111 B9 Greggton Texas
118 F2 Gregoire L Alberta
128 D5 Gregório R Brazil
98 G6 Gregory S Dakota
140 E4 Gregory Downs Queensland
142 G5 Gregory L W Australia
143 C7 Gregory, L W Australia
141 G4 Gregory Ra Queensland
142 D5 Gregory Ra W Australia
113 L12 Gregory Town Bahamas
38 H8 Greifenburg Austria
41 J3 Greifensee L Switzerland
33 T6 Greiffenberg E Germany
33 S4 Greifswald E Germany
33 T4 Greifswalder Bodden E Germany
33 T4 Greifswalder Oie isld E Germany
38 K7 Greimberg mt Austria
38 L5 Grein Austria
41 J4 Greina Pass Switzerland
38 M5 Greinerwald woods Austria
37 L5 Greisselbach W Germany
37 N2 Greiz E Germany
52 E1 Gremikha U.S.S.R.
33 N4 Gremsmühlen W Germany
28 F4 Grenå Denmark
100 C8 Grenada California
111 G8 Grenada Mississippi
127 P5 Grenada isld Lesser Antilles
18 E9 Grenade France
18 F9 Grenade sur Garonne France
127 O8 Grenadines, The islds Lesser Antilles
40 F3 Grenchen Switzerland
28 C5 Grene Denmark
28 F1 Grenen C Denmark
139 J5 Grenfell New S Wales
119 P8 Grenfell Sask
19 P14 Grenoble France
107 O4 Grenola Kansas
98 C1 Grenora N Dakota
26 S2 Grense/Jakobselv Norway
127 P5 Grenville Grenada
106 G5 Grenville New Mexico
98 J4 Grenville S Dakota
141 G1 Grenville C Queensland
117 J9 Grenville Chan Br Columbia
117 L10 Grenville, Mt Br Columbia
19 P17 Gréoux-les-Bains France
33 Q9 Greppin E Germany
33 Q4 Gresenhorst E Germany
100 C4 Gresham Oregon
70 O9 Gresik Java
69 F14 Gresik Sumatra
19 P15 Gresse France
19 Q13 Grésy-sur-Isère France
139 K5 Greta New S Wales
13 G5 Greta Br England
111 G12 Gretna Louisiana
119 U9 Gretna Manitoba
111 J13 Gretna New Orleans
94 H10 Gretna Virginia
13 E3 Gretna Green Scotland
37 K1 Greussen E Germany
45 K4 Greve Italy
25 A5 Grevelingen Netherlands
32 G8 Greven W Germany
46 E4 Grevená Greece
36 B1 Grevenbroich W Germany
32 L5 Grevenkop W Germany
33 O5 Grevesmühlen E Germany
27 F16 Grevie Sweden
29 K4 Grevie Sweden
28 H5 Grevinge Denmark
101 R5 Greybull Wyoming
140 D2 Grey, C N Terr Aust
101 Q4 Greycliff Montana
99 M4 Grey Eagle Minnesota
117 F4 Grey Hunter Pk Yukon Terr
123 R3 Grey I Nfld
123 R3 Grey Is Nfld
144 C5 Greymouth New Zealand
139 G7 Grey, Pt Victoria
123 Q5 Grey R Nfld
141 G8 Grey Ra Queensland/N S W
141 G8 Grey Range Queensland
101 P6 Greys R Wyoming
143 A7 Grey's Plains W Australia

13 F4 Greystoke England
101 R9 Greystone Colorado
14 E3 Greystones Irish Rep
145 E4 Greytown New Zealand
89 G7 Greytown S Africa
22 H2 Grez-Doiceau Belgium
21 E6 Grez-en-Bouère France
46 D4 Griba mt Albania
81 F11 Gribb Seamount Southern Oc
86 C4 Gribingui R Cent Afr Republic
52 D2 Gridino U.S.S.R.
102 C2 Gridley California
99 S9 Gridley Illinois
107 P3 Gridley Kansas
25 D2 Griend Netherlands
37 P7 Griesbach W Germany
36 F4 Griesheim W Germany
41 O3 Gries im Sellrain Austria
Griessen see Klettgau
25 F5 Grieth W Germany
38 L8 Griffen Austria
111 M8 Griffin Georgia
113 F9 Griffin, L Florida
116 Q1 Griffin Pt Alaska
139 H5 Griffith New S Wales
115 K3 Griffith I N W Terr
110 E6 Griffithville Arkansas
112 K2 Grifton N Carolina
99 Q10 Griggsville Illinois
41 K6 Grigna mt Italy
19 N16 Grignan France
18 E8 Grignols France
48 M3 Grigoriopol U.S.S.R.
25 F2 Grijpskerk Netherlands
48 K1 Grimailov U.S.S.R.
86 C4 Grimari Cent Afr Republic
19 C18 Grimaud France
139 G8 Grim, C Tasmania
102 C2 Grimes California
100 K5 Grimes Pass Idaho
33 R10 Grimma E Germany
33 S4 Grimmen E Germany
Grimmenthal see Obermassfeld-Grimmenthal
37 J2 Grimmenthal E Germany
33 T7 Grimnitzsee E Germany
13 H6 Grimsby England
121 L9 Grimsby Ontario
41 H4 Grimsel mt Switzerland
115 S4 Grimsey isld Iceland
114 H6 Grimshaw Alberta
27 C13 Grimstad Norway
28 B5 Grimstrup Denmark
40 H4 Grindelwald Switzerland
28 C3 Grinderslev Denmark
28 B5 Grindsted Å R Denmark
95 S8 Grindstone Maine
123 L6 Grindstone Island Quebec
119 U7 Grindstone Prov. Park Manitoba
119 V7 Grindstone Pt Manitoba
99 O8 Grinnell Iowa
107 K2 Grinnell Kansas
115 K2 Grinnell Pen N W Terr
42 F2 Grintavec mt Yugoslavia
13 G5 Grinton England
26 C8 Grip lt ho Norway
33 O6 Grippel W Germany
89 F8 Griqualand E reg S Africa
89 C7 Griqualand W reg S Africa
87 D11 Griquatown S Africa
40 F6 Grisanche, Val Italy
115 L2 Grise Fiord N W Terr
45 L1 Grisignano Italy
22 B2 Gris Nez, C France
18 F9 Grisolles France
27 K11 Grisslehamn Sweden
99 L8 Griswold Iowa
52 H4 Griva U.S.S.R.
20 K2 Grivesnes France
40 F6 Grivola mt Italy
33 P9 Grizeline E Germany
85 D3 Grizim Algeria
117 N3 Grizzly Bear Mt N W Terr
26 C9 Grjotli Norway
42 G4 Grmeč Plan Yugoslavia
123 R3 Groais I Nfld
33 S10 Gröba E Germany
33 Q10 Gröbers E Germany
27 M15 Grobina U.S.S.R.
9 E2 Groby England
33 P9 Gröbzig E Germany
31 O2 Gródek Poland
31 K5 Grodków Poland
33 S10 Grödlitz E Germany
31 O2 Grodno U.S.S.R.
31 J3 Grodzisk Poland
31 M3 Grodzisk Mazowiecki Poland
89 C8 Groen watercourse S Africa
22 G2 Groenendaal Belgium
25 G4 Groenlo Netherlands
109 L4 Groesbeck Texas
25 E5 Groesbeek Netherlands
25 C3 Groet Netherlands
70 P10 Grogak Bali Indonesia
32 K8 Grohnde W Germany
22 F3 Groise, la France
37 N1 Groitzsch E Germany
18 C5 Groix.I.de France
31 M4 Grójec Poland
43 C12 Grombalia Tunisia
28 C7 Grønå R Denmark
32 L8 Gronau Niedersachsen W Germany
32 F8 Gronau Nordrhein-Westfalen W Germany
28 B4 Grønbjerg Denmark
26 F7 Grong Norway
28 C4 Grønhøj Denmark
33 O9 Gröningen E Germany
25 G2 Groningen Netherlands
25 F2 Groningerwad Netherlands
119 N5 Gronlid Sask
115 P5 Grønnedal Greenland
26 F5 Grönöy Norway
27 K12 Grönskär lt ho Sweden
27 H14 Grönskåra Sweden
28 J7 Grønsund chan Denmark
89 D9 Groot R S Africa
89 B7 Groot Aughrabies Falls Orange R S Africa
140 D2 Groote Eylandt isld N Terr Aust
25 F2 Grootegast Netherlands
87 C9 Grootfontein Namibia
89 B3 Groot Laagte watercourse Namibia
89 B9 Groot Swartberge mts S Africa
89 C8 Groot Tafelberg mt S Africa
89 B7 Groot Vloer S Africa
87 D11 Grootvloer L S Africa
89 E9 Groot Winterberg mt S Africa
22 K4 Grosbous Luxembourg
127 O7 Gros Islet St Lucia
27 G14 Grosjö Sweden
127 H5 Gros Morne Haiti
127 L4 Gros Morne Martinique W I
122 G4 Gros Morne Quebec
123 P4 Gros Morne peak Nfld
123 P4 Gros Morne Nat. Park Newfoundland
19 J6 Grosne R France
9 H7 Grosnez Pt Channel Is
41 M5 Grosotto Italy
123 P3 Gros Pate peak Nfld
113 F7 Gross Florida
37 M4 Gross Albershof W Germany
40 H4 Gross Aletsch Gl Switzerland
32 L10 Grossalmerode W Germany
33 O9 Gross Alsleben E Germany
33 P8 Gross Ammensleben E Germany
37 P5 Gross Arber mt W Germany
33 S8 Grossbeeren E Germany
33 T8 Grossbesten E Germany
33 M10 Grossbodungen E Germany
37 O1 Gross Bothen E Germany
36 G5 Grossbottwar W Germany
37 L2 Gross-Breitenbach E Germany
33 T7 Gross-Dölln E Germany
37 M2 Gross Ebersdorf E Germany
123 L6 Grosse I Madeleine Is, Quebec
36 F2 Grossenbuseck W Germany
37 K1 Grossenehrich E Germany
33 O7 Gross Engersen E Germany
33 T10 Grossenhain E Germany
32 H7 Grossenkneten W Germany
37 N2 Grossenstein E Germany
127 N4 Grosse Pointe Guadeloupe W I
33 S10 Grosse Röder R E Germany
42 D6 Grosseto Italy
51 N4 Grossevichi U.S.S.R.
36 D5 Gross Eyberg mt W Germany
36 E3 Gross Feldberg mt W Germany
33 T6 Gross Fredenwalde E Germany
36 E4 Gross-Gerau W Germany
33 M8 Gross Gleidingen W Germany
38 G7 Gross-Glockner Austria
33 P6 Gross-Godems E Germany
37 N1 Gross Görschen E Germany
33 N5 Gross Gronau W Germany
33 M5 Gross Hansdorf W Germany
37 P2 Gross Hartmannsdorf E Germany
32 F5 Grossheide W Germany
37 M1 Gross Heringen E Germany
33 M7 Gross-Kain W Germany
36 E4 Gross Karlbach W Germany
33 O4 Gross Klützhöved E Germany
37 L2 Gross Kochberg E Germany
33 Q10 Gross Korbetha E Germany
33 T8 Gross Köris E Germany
33 R8 Gross Kreutz E Germany
37 N6 Gross Laaber R W Germany
37 J4 Gross-Langheim W Germany
36 H2 Grosslüder W Germany
33 S8 Gross-Machnow E Germany
37 M6 Grossmehring W Germany
33 M7 Gross-Oesingen W Germany
36 G4 Grossostheim W Germany
33 M4 Gross Plöner See L W Germany
37 P6 Gross Rachel mt W Germany
38 L6 Grossraming Austria
32 M9 Gross Rhüden W Germany
36 B5 Grossrosseln W Germany
37 L1 Gross Rudestedt E Germany
33 T7 Gross Schönebeck E Germany
33 P7 Gross Schwechten E Germany
33 T8 Gross Selchower See L E Germany
33 N8 Gross-Sisbeck W Germany
33 S6 Gross Stechlinsee L E Germany
36 H6 Gross Süssen W Germany
36 F4 Gross-Umstadt W Germany
37 P2 Gross Waltersdorf E Germany
33 P6 Gross-Warnow E Germany
33 Q6 Gross Welle E Germany
33 Q7 Gross Wudicke E Germany
33 R5 Gross Wüstenfelde E Germany
33 Q8 Gross Wusterwitz E Germany
33 T7 Gross Ziethen E Germany
36 F4 Gross-Zimmern W Germany
36 B6 Gros Tenquin France
42 F3 Grosuplje Yugoslavia
141 J5 Grosvenor Downs Queensland
116 K7 Grosvenor, L Alaska
101 P6 Gros Ventre Ra Wyoming
32 J9 Grotenberg mt W Germany
22 F2 Grotenberge Belgium
22 H1 Grote Nete R Belgium
95 Q5 Groton Connecticut
95 Q4 Groton Massachusetts
95 L4 Groton New York
98 H4 Groton S Dakota
95 P2 Groton Vermont
26 G4 Grötöy Norway
45 Q8 Grotta Azzurra Italy
45 O7 Grotta delle Capre Italy
22 J3 Grotte-de-Han Belgium
19 N16 Grottes de St. Marcel France
94 J8 Grottoes Virginia
36 F5 Grotzingen W Germany
114 H6 Grouard Alberta
20 B4 Grouin, Pte. du France
120 H4 Groundhog R Ontario
101 M6 Grouse Idaho
101 M8 Grouse Creek Utah
25 E2 Grouw Netherlands
27 C13 Grovane Norway
107 Q5 Grove Oklahoma
94 E7 Grove City Ohio
94 G5 Grove City Pennsylvania
117 O8 Grovedale Alberta
111 J10 Grove Hill Alabama
140 B2 Grove Hill N Terr Aust
28 C4 Grove Kirke Denmark
102 D4 Groveland California
26 F9 Grövelsjön Sweden
146 D5 Grove Mts Antarctica
98 B9 Grover Colorado
101 P7 Grover Wyoming
111 C12 Groves Texas
109 M4 Groveton Texas
95 Q2 Groveton Vermont
112 E4 Grovetown Georgia
145 D4 Grovetown New Zealand
101 P6 Grovont Wyoming
103 L9 Growler Arizona
103 L9 Growler Mts Arizona
47 J1 Grozd'ovo Bulgaria
45 P1 Groznjan Yugoslavia
57 F3 Groznoye U.S.S.R.
53 G11 Groznyy U.S.S.R.
41 J4 Gr. Scheerh mt Switzerland
33 O4 Grube W Germany
32 L9 Grubenhagen W Germany
42 H3 Grubišno Polje Yugoslavia
37 P6 Grubweg W Germany
20 F2 Gruchet-le-Valasse France
42 J6 Gruda Yugoslavia
47 J2 Grudovo Bulgaria
31 M2 Grudusk Poland
31 L2 Grudziadz Poland
128 D8 Gruesa, Pta C Chile
122 B6 Grues, I. aux Quebec
12 B2 Gruinart Scotland
109 J9 Grulla Texas
36 D4 Grumbach W Germany
43 H7 Grumo Appula Italy
27 F12 Grums Sweden
37 O2 Gruna E Germany
15 C3 Grunard Bay Scotland
33 T8 Grunau E Germany
87 C11 Grunau Namibia
36 G6 Grunbach W Germany
36 F2 Grünberg W Germany
36 G3 Gründau W Germany
Gründelhardt see Frankenhardt
26 K8 Grundsunda Sweden
26 J8 Grundtjärn Sweden
99 O7 Grundy Center Iowa
120 K7 Grundy Lake Prov. Park Ontario
28 D7 Grünholz W Germany
124 J5 Gruñidora Mexico
33 Q8 Grüningen E Germany
36 F2 Grüningen W Germany
36 H4 Grünsfeld W Germany
36 E4 Grünstadt W Germany
38 E8 Gruppo mt Italy
41 L4 Grüsch Switzerland
108 C7 Gruver Texas
40 F4 Gruyère, L. de la Switzerland
52 B6 Gruzdžiai U.S.S.R.
53 F12 Gruziya S.S.R. U.S.S.R.
54 L4 Gryazi U.S.S.R.
52 F5 Gryazovets U.S.S.R.
31 M6 Grybów Poland
27 H11 Grycksbo Sweden
31 J2 Gryfice Poland
31 H2 Gryfino Poland
99 L1 Grygla Minnesota
27 G12 Grythyttehed Sweden
26 H3 Grytöy L Norway
26 C9 Grytten Norway
133 J8 Grytviken S Georgia
31 J2 Grzmiąca Poland
41 O3 Gschnitz Austria
36 H6 Gschwend W Germany
40 F5 Gstaad Switzerland
40 F5 Gsteig Switzerland
19 P15 Guâ France
75 L7 Gua India
41 O7 Gua R Italy
128 D3 Guacamayas Colombia
126 F4 Guacanayabo, G.de Cuba
127 L9 Guacara Venezuela
103 M9 Gu Achi Arizona
128 D2 Guachiria R Colombia
130 C8 Guaçu Brazil
124 H7 Guadalajara Mexico
16 E4 Guadalajara Spain
17 F4 Guadalajara prov Spain
16 D6 Guadalcanal Spain
137 M3 Guadalcanal isld Solomon Is
16 E6 Guadalén R Spain
17 F7 Guadalentin R Spain
16 D8 Guadalete R Spain
16 E8 Guadalfeo R Spain
16 E8 Guadalhorce R Spain
16 E6 Guadalimar R Spain
17 F6 Guadalmena R Spain
16 D6 Guadalmez R Spain
16 D7 Guadalquivir R Spain
131 C5 Guadal, Sa. de Argentina
102 D7 Guadalupe California
71 F5 Guadalupe Cebu Philippines
108 A4 Guadalupe Mexico
124 H6 Guadalupe Mexico
109 J6 Guadalupe R Texas
108 B3 Guadalupe Mts New Mex/Tex
108 C4 Guadalupe Pk Texas
16 D5 Guadalupe, Sa de mts Spain
124 G5 Guadalupe Victoria Durango Mexico
124 F4 Guadalupe y Calvo Mexico
16 E4 Guadarrama, Sa. de mts Spain
17 F5 Guadazaón R Spain
127 N4 Guadeloupe islds Lesser Antilles
16 E6 Guadiana R Spain
126 B3 Guadiana, B.de Cuba
16 E7 Guadiano Menor R Spain
16 D6 Guadiato R Spain
17 F4 Guadiela R Spain
16 E7 Guadix Spain
133 C6 Guafo isld Chile
127 P2 Guaico Trinidad
130 C7 Guaicuras Brazil
128 F2 Guaina Venezuela
128 E3 Guainía R Colombia
130 C9 Guaíra Brazil
130 C9 Guaira Paraguay
133 C6 Guaitecas, Is Chile
126 F4 Guajaba, Cayo isld Cuba
128 E6 Guajará Mirim Brazil
128 E5 Guajarraã Brazil
128 F5 Guajaturaba Brazil
124 H4 Guaje, Llano de reg Mexico
125 L2 Guajiniquil Honduras
128 D1 Guajira div Colombia
128 D1 Guajira, Pena de pen Colombia
102 A3 Gualala California
42 E5 Gualdo Tadino Italy
131 F4 Gualeguay Argentina
131 F4 Gualeguay R Argentina
133 F4 Gualeguaychu Argentina
131 D3 Gualicho Salina salt pan Argentina
128 E7 Guallatiri mt Chile
45 J2 Gualtieri Italy
134 E6 Guam isld Mariana Is Pacific Oc
129 J4 Guamá Brazil
127 K9 Guama Venezuela
129 J4 Guamá R Brazil
133 B6 Guamblin, I Chile
133 E5 Guamini Argentina
124 E5 Guamúchil Mexico
69 E10 Gua Musang Malaysia
65 C5 Gu'an China
126 C3 Guanabacoa Cuba
130 G8 Guanabara Brazil
125 M4 Guanacaste, Cord. de ra Costa Rica
124 G5 Guanacevi Mexico
126 B3 Guanahacabibes, Pen. de Cuba
126 C3 Guanajay Cuba
124 J7 Guanajuato Mexico
129 K6 Guanambi Brazil
128 C5 Guañape, I Peru
127 O2 Guanapo Trinidad
128 E2 Guanarito Venezuela
65 B5 Guancen Shan mt ra China
67 C6 Guanchang China
133 D3 Guandacol Argentina
65 G3 Guandi China
67 C1 Guandiankou China
126 B3 Guane Cuba
67 B1 Guang'an China
67 E3 Guangchang China
67 F1 Guangde China
67 D5 Guangdong prov China
67 F2 Guangfeng China
67 A1 Guangfu China
67 A1 Guanghan China
58 F5 Guanghua China
65 B6 Guanghua China
67 E2 Guangji China
58 F4 Guangling China
65 E5 Guanglu Dao isld China
67 F1 Guangming Ding mt China
67 B4 Guangnan China
67 D5 Guangning China
65 C6 Guangping China
65 D6 Guangrao China
67 E1 Guangshan China
67 B5 Guangxi aut reg China
67 F1 Guangyang China
58 E5 Guangyuan China
67 F3 Guangze China
67 D5 Guangzhou China
65 C6 Guangzong China
130 G6 Guanhães Brazil
127 L5 Guánica Puerto Rico
128 F2 Guanipa R Venezuela
67 D3 Guanjiazui China
67 B4 Guanling China
67 C1 Guanmian Shan mts China
65 D7 Guannan China
100 F7 Guano L Oregon
65 G1 Guansongzhen China
Guansuo see Guanling
128 F1 Guanta Venezuela
126 G4 Guantánamo Cuba
126 G5 Guantánamo, B. de Cuba
65 C6 Guantao China
65 C4 Guanting Shuiku res China
65 C6 Guan Xian China
67 A1 Guan Xian China
67 D4 Guanyang China
65 D7 Guanyun China
130 F7 Guapé Brazil
128 C3 Guapi Colombia
133 G3 Guaporé Brazil
130 J9 Guarabira Brazil
130 D10 Guarama Brazil
130 F8 Guarantinguetá Brazil
130 H7 Guarapari Brazil
130 D9 Guarapuava Brazil
130 E9 Guaraqueçaba Brazil
130 E7 Guararapes Brazil
130 J10 Guararapes Brazil
17 G2 Guara, Sa. de Spain
18 E10 Guara, Sierra de mts Spain
130 E9 Guaratuba Brazil
45 O6 Guarcino Italy
16 C4 Guarda Portugal
86 B1 Guardafui, C Somalia
17 F7 Guardal R Spain
130 F5 Guarda Mor Brazil
127 L10 Guardatinajas Venezuela
13 F1 Guardbridge Scotland
133 E6 Guardia Mitre Argentina
133 D7 Guardián, C Argentina
45 R7 Guardia Sanframondi Italy
16 D2 Guardo Spain
16 B4 Guardunha Sa.da mts Portugal
128 F5 Guariba R Amazonas Brazil
127 L10 Guárico R Venezuela
128 E2 Guárico state Venezuela
130 D10 Guarita R Brazil
124 E5 Guasave Mexico
128 C3 Guascama, Pta point Colombia
125 K7 Guasima Mexico
130 C9 Guassú, R Brazil
42 D4 Guastalla Italy
125 O10 Guatemala Guatemala
125 O10 Guatemala rep Cent America
127 L9 Guatire Venezuela
128 E3 Guaviare R Colombia
126 F4 Guayabal Cuba
128 E2 Guayabal Venezuela
128 D3 Guayabero R Colombia
131 C3 Guayaguas, Sa. da ra Argentina
127 P3 Guayaguayare Trinidad
127 L5 Guayama Puerto Rico
128 C4 Guayaquil Ecuador
128 B4 Guayaquil, Golfo de Ecuador
128 E6 Guayaramerin Bolivia
128 B4 Guayas prov Ecuador
133 B7 Guayeco Arch islds Chile
124 D4 Guaymas Mexico
131 F3 Guayquiraró, R Argentina
130 F7 Guazupé Brazil
86 G5 Guba Ethiopia
87 E8 Guba Zaïre
67 A2 Gubai China
52 J5 Gubakha U.S.S.R.
86 H3 Guban dist Somalia
71 G4 Gubat Philippines
86 G3 Gubba Ethiopia
42 E5 Gubbio Italy
52 J4 Gubdor U.S.S.R.
65 D4 Gubeikou China
Guben see Wilhelm Pieck Stadt
31 H4 Gubin E Germany
54 J5 Gubkin U.S.S.R.
65 D6 Gucheng China
67 D1 Gucheng China
17 G4 Gudar, Sa. de mts Spain
28 F6 Gudbjerg Denmark
26 C9 Gudbrandsdalen Norway
28 D5 Gudenå R Denmark
36 G1 Gudensberg W Germany
36 F4 Gudernheim W Germany
28 D6 Guderup Denmark
27 G16 Gudhjem Denmark
28 F6 Gudme Denmark
77 J6 Gudri R Pakistan
65 B7 Gudui China
28 G6 Gudum Denmark
28 E3 Gudumholm Denmark
28 A3 Gudum Kirke Denmark
76 D3 Gudur India
27 B11 Gudvangen Norway
19 K5 Guebwiller France
133 C6 Guechucuicui, Pta Chile
20 G5 Gué-de-la-Chaîne, le France
20 J5 Gue-de-Longroi, le France
121 N4 Guéguen L Quebec
16 E7 Güéjar Sierra Spain
85 B7 Guékédou Guinea
86 C3 Guelengdeng Chad
85 F1 Guelma Algeria
98 H3 Guelph N Dakota
85 B3 Guelta Zemmur Morocco
85 D5 Guem Mali
36 C7 Guémar France
18 C4 Guémené France
21 B6 Guémene-Penfao France
121 P6 Guenette Quebec
133 C7 Guenguel R Argentina
21 B6 Guenroue France
21 A6 Guer France
16 C6 Guerañа Spain
18 D5 Guérande France
86 C3 Guéra, Pic de mt Chad
85 E2 Guerara Algeria
18 G6 Guerche-sur-l'Aubois, la France
86 D3 Guéréda Chad
21 I9 Gueret France
121 L5 Guerin Quebec
18 D9 Guernica Spain
119 M7 Guernsey Sask
98 B7 Guernsey Wyoming
9 G6 Guernsey isld Channel Is
98 B7 Guernsey Res Wyoming
20 G4 Gueroulde, la France
109 J9 Guerra Texas
20 J2 Guerville France
146 J9 Guest pen Antarctica
85 D4 Guettara, El Mali
18 H6 Gueugnon France
111 D12 Gueydan Louisiana
41 K4 Güferhorn mt Switzerland
38 E6 Güffert-Spitze mt Austria
86 G4 Gughe mt Ethiopia
42 F7 Guglionesi Italy
86 G4 Gugu mt Ethiopia
48 H5 Gugu mt Romania
33 R6 Gühlen-Glienecke E Germany
130 C4 Guia Brazil
21 B6 Guichen France
67 F1 Guichi China
125 M9 Guichicovi Mexico
86 B4 Guider Cameroon
98 H9 Guide Rock Nebraska
67 B3 Guiding China
45 J1 Guidizzolo Italy
67 D3 Guidong China
19 P13 Guiers R France
85 A5 Guiers, L. de Senegal
45 J3 Guiglia Italy
85 C7 Guiglo Ivory Coast
21 B6 Guignen France
22 J2 Guigoven Belgium
127 L9 Güigüi Venezuela
Guihua see Mingxi
87 F10 Guija Mozambique
67 C4 Gui Jiang R China
67 G2 Guiji Shan mts China
9 F5 Guildford England
143 B9 Guildford W Australia
95 Q2 Guildhall Vermont
65 E1 Guiler Gol R China
95 P5 Guilford Connecticut
95 S1 Guilford Maine
112 H1 Guilford Ct. Ho. Nat. Mil. Park N Carolina
86 B7 Guilherme Capelo Angola
67 C4 Guilin China
16 B3 Guimaraes Portugal
71 F5 Guimaras isld Philippines
71 F5 Guimaras Str Philippines
111 J8 Guin Alabama
125 M3 Güina Nicaragua
71 F5 Guinauayan isld Philippines
126 E3 Guinchos Cay isld Cuba
102 B3 Guinda California
71 G6 Guindulman Philippines
85 B6 Guinea rep W Africa
90 J8 Guinea Basin Atlantic Oc
85 A6 Guinea-Bissau rep W Africa
85 E8 Guinea, Gulf of W Africa
122 C3 Guinecourt, L Quebec
126 D3 Güines Cuba
22 B2 Guines France
18 C4 Guingamp France
85 F6 Guinia Niger
71 F5 Guintacan isld Philippines
71 F3 Guintinua isld Philippines
110 E6 Guion Arkansas
67 C5 Guiping China
17 F1 Guipúzcoa prov Spain
85 D5 Guir Mali
126 C3 Güira de Melena Cuba
130 D5 Guiratinga Brazil
129 H3 Guisanbourg Fr Guiana
13 G5 Guisborough England
22 E4 Guiscard France
22 F4 Guise France
13 G6 Guiseley England
9 G2 Guist England
71 G5 Guiuan Philippines
22 E4 Guivry France
67 F2 Guixi China
67 C5 Gui Xian China
67 B3 Guizhou prov China
74 D7 Gujarat prov India
74 F2 Gujranwala Pakistan
74 F2 Gujrat Pakistan
67 C1 Gujunba China
103 N9 Gu Komelik Arizona
54 L8 Gukovo U.S.S.R.
58 D4 Gulang China
139 J4 Gulargambone New S Wales
77 L2 Gulbahar Afghanistan
74 G10 Gulbarga India
52 C6 Gulbene U.S.S.R.
57 G4 Gul'cha U.S.S.R.
28 A5 Guldager Denmark
28 E5 Guldbjerg Denmark
28 H7 Guldborg Denmark
36 D4 Guldental W Germany
27 H12 Guldsmedshyttan Sweden
76 B2 Guledgarh India
27 A10 Gulen Norway
112 H2 Gulf N Carolina
111 J11 Gulf Beach Florida
141 G4 Gulf Highway rd Queensland
113 E10 Gulfport Florida
111 G11 Gulfport Mississippi
77 A5 Gulf, The S W Asia
26 R1 Gulgofjorden Norway
139 J4 Gulgong New S Wales
67 B2 Gulin China
57 E4 Gulistan U.S.S.R.
33 P6 Gülitz E Germany
116 P5 Gulkana Alaska
118 D6 Gull L Alberta
27 H15 Gullabo Sweden
13 F1 Gullane Scotland
119 O1 Gull Bay Ontario
28 D4 Gullev Denmark
99 V4 Gull I Michigan
99 V3 Gulliver Michigan
99 M3 Gull L Minnesota
118 J8 Gull Lake Sask
26 K6 Gullön Sweden
27 G13 Gullspång Sweden
26 M5 Gullträsk Sweden
47 J7 Güllük Turkey
65 F2 Gulong China
25 E7 Gulpen Netherlands
33 Q7 Gülper See L E Germany
47 H5 Gülpınar Turkey
77 G2 Gulran Afghanistan
78 E2 Gülşehir Turkey
26 J8 Gulsele Sweden
57 G2 Gul'shad U.S.S.R.
33 S5 Gültz E Germany
86 F5 Gulu Uganda
141 J7 Guluguba Queensland
140 D1 Guluwuru I N Terr Aust
59 H1 Gulya U.S.S.R.
54 H9 Gulyaypole U.S.S.R.
33 S4 Gülzow E Germany
141 G7 Gumbardo Queensland
26 M7 Gumboda Sweden
140 B5 Gum Cr N Terr Aust
85 F6 Gumel Nigeria
125 K6 Gümez Mexico
16 E3 Gumiel de Hizán Spain
75 L7 Gumla India
139 G5 Gum Lake L New S Wales
61 M9 Gumma prefect Japan
36 D1 Gummersbach W Germany
85 F6 Gummi Nigeria
71 E2 Gumotgong Luzon Philippines
69 C10 Gumpang R Sumatra
94 K9 Gum Spring Virginia
33 Q7 Gumtow E Germany
67 A5 Gumu China
78 G1 Gümüşhane Turkey
74 G6 Guna India
86 G3 Guna mt Ethiopia
142 E6 Gunanya Spring W Australia
139 H5 Gunbar New S Wales
113 H12 Gun Cay Bahamas
58 F1 Gunda U.S.S.R.
139 J6 Gundagai New S Wales
37 J6 Gundelfingen W Germany
36 G5 Gundelsheim W Germany
28 C3 Gundersted Denmark
36 E4 Gundheim W Germany
70 N9 Gundih Java
86 D5 Gundji Zaïre
28 H7 Gundslev Denmark
47 K6 Güney Turkey
119 N2 Gunflint Ontario
86 C7 Gungu Zaïre
119 V5 Gunisao L Manitoba
119 U5 Gunisao R Manitoba
103 L4 Gunlock Utah
114 J6 Gunnar Sask
26 J6 Gunnarn Sweden
141 H4 Gunnawarra Queensland
27 J14 Gunnebo Sweden
139 K4 Gunnedah New S Wales
146 A7 Gunnerus Bank Antarctica
139 J5 Gunning New S Wales
8 B7 Gunnislake England
106 D3 Gunnison Colorado
106 B3 Gunnison R Colorado
101 N8 Gunnison I Utah
140 B1 Gunn Pt N Terr Aust
70 B3 Gunong Ayer Sarawak
140 E4 Gunpowder R Queensland
101 N1 Gunsight Montana
76 C3 Guntakal India
100 B6 Gunter Oregon
109 L2 Gunter Texas
33 N9 Güntersberge E Germany
36 E4 Guntersblum W Germany
111 K7 Guntersville Alabama
119 U8 Gunton Manitoba
111 H7 Guntown Mississippi
69 E12 Guntung Sumatra
76 E2 Guntur India
71 N8 Gunungapi isld Indonesia
69 C12 Gunungsitoli Indonesia
70 K8 Gunungsugih Sumatra
69 D12 Gunungtua Sumatra
75 K9 Gunupur India
118 J7 Gunworth Sask
143 B9 Gunyidi W Australia
37 J7 Günz R W Germany
37 J7 Günzburg W Germany
37 K5 Gunzenhausen W Germany
33 N9 Günzerode E Germany
67 B5 Guohua China
65 C4 Guojiatun China
Guoluezhen see Lingbao
65 B5 Guoyangzhen China
65 D7 Gupei China
65 B3 Gurban Obo China
66 D2 Gurbantünggüt Shamo des China
138 E6 Gurchen B S Australia
74 F2 Gurdaspur India
111 C8 Gurdon Arkansas
47 K6 Güre Turkey
74 G4 Gurgaon India
86 D3 Gurgei, Jebel mt Sudan
129 K5 Gurgueia R Brazil
127 N11 Guri Venezuela
130 E6 Gurinhatã Brazil
46 D4 Gur-i-Topit mt Albania
38 J8 Gurk R Austria
75 L5 Gurkha Nepal
38 K8 Gurktal V Austria
38 J8 Gurktaler Alpen mts Austria
66 C5 Gurla Mandhata mt China
57 B4 Gurlen U.S.S.R.
98 D8 Gurley Nebraska
88 D10 Guro Mozambique
59 L1 Gurskoye U.S.S.R.
88 F9 Gurué Mozambique
48 K3 Guru Humorului Romania
78 F2 Gürün Turkey
129 H4 Gurupá Brazil
129 J6 Gurupi Brazil
129 J4 Gurupi R Brazil
129 J4 Gurupi, C Brazil
76 D2 Guruzala India
58 D3 Gurvan Sayhan Uul mt Mongolia
50 E4 Gur'yev U.S.S.R.
56 C4 Gur'yevsk U.S.S.R.
85 F6 Gusau Nigeria
33 P8 Güsen E Germany
31 N1 Gusev U.S.S.R.
59 H4 Gushan China
101 Q9 Gusher Utah
67 E1 Gushi China
61 P14 Gushikami Okinawa
61 P13 Gushikawa Okinawa
70 E1 Gusi Sabah
52 G7 Gusikha U.S.S.R.
46 D2 Gusinje Yugoslavia
56 G5 Gusinoozersk U.S.S.R.
56 G5 Gusinoye, Oz L U.S.S.R.
52 F6 Gus'Khrustal'nyy U.S.S.R.
46 D4 Gusmar Albania
67 B2 Gusong China
43 B9 Guspini Sardinia
48 C3 Güssing Austria
45 J1 Gussola Italy
27 G11 Gust Adolf Sweden
115 Q4 Gustav Holm, Kap C Greenland
127 N6 Gustavia Lesser Antilles
124 C2 Gustavo Sotelo Mexico
117 F6 Gustavus Alaska
33 P9 Güsten E Germany
36 E2 Gusternhain W Germany
102 C4 Gustine California
109 J4 Gustine Texas
33 S4 Gustow E Germany
33 Q5 Güstrow E Germany
27 H13 Gusum Sweden
48 K1 Gusyatin U.S.S.R.
36 E7 Gutach W Germany
56 E4 Gutarskiy Khrebet mts U.S.S.R.
38 L5 Gutau Austria
37 M3 Gutenfürst E Germany
38 N6 Gutenstein Austria
33 P9 Güterglück E Germany
32 H9 Gütersloh W Germany
143 B8 Gutha W Australia
110 J5 Guthrie Kentucky
99 M2 Guthrie Minnesota
98 F1 Guthrie N Dakota
107 N6 Guthrie Oklahoma
108 G2 Guthrie Texas
99 M8 Guthrie Center Iowa
119 R3 Guthrie L Manitoba
67 F3 Gutian China
Guting see Yutai
33 S8 Gut-Neuhof E Germany
33 Q5 Gutow E Germany
38 L8 Guttaring Austria
99 P7 Guttenberg Iowa
87 F9 Gutu Zimbabwe
54 G6 Guty U.S.S.R.
33 S5 Gützkow E Germany
80 C7 Guvrin R Israel
36 G1 Guxhagen W Germany
65 B6 Gu Xian China
65 C4 Guyan China
128 G3 Guyana rep S America
94 E8 Guyandotte R W Virginia
58 F3 Guyang China
65 A4 Guyang China
121 M4 Guyenne Quebec
18 E8 Guyenne prov France
9 G2 Guyhirn England
Guyi see Sanjiang
107 J5 Guymon Oklahoma
116 R6 Guyot Glacier Alaska
139 K4 Guyra New S Wales
123 L8 Guysborough Nova Scotia
112 F5 Guyton Georgia
67 C2 Guzhang China
58 G5 Guzhen China
Guzhou see Rongjiang
124 F2 Guzmán, L. de Mexico
48 K1 Gvardeiskoe U.S.S.R.
48 J2 Gvozdets U.S.S.R.
68 B4 Gwa Burma
139 J4 Gwabegar New S Wales
38 G8 Gwabl Austria
74 B10 Gwadar Pakistan
89 E2 Gwai R Zimbabwe
8 B1 Gwalchmai Wales
143 D8 Gwalia W Australia
74 H5 Gwalior India
141 J7 Gwambegwine Queensland
89 F3 Gwanda Zimbabwe
86 E5 Gwane Zaïre
8 B3 Gwbert-on-Sea Wales
68 B2 Gwebin Burma
14 C2 Gweebarra B Irish Rep
89 F2 Gwelo Zimbabwe
89 F2 Gwelo R Zimbabwe
100 E4 Gwendolen Oregon
8 D4 Gwent co Wales
99 T3 Gwinn Michigan
98 J3 Gwinner N Dakota
139 J3 Gwydir R New S Wales
8 B1 Gwynedd co Wales
118 D6 Gwynne Alberta
19 J5 Gy France
66 C5 Gyangrang China
Gyangtse see Gyangzê
66 D6 Gyangzê China
66 D5 Gyaring Co L China
58 C5 Gyaring Hu L China
50 G1 Gydanskiy Poluostrov pen U.S.S.R.
75 L4 Gyirong China
66 F5 Gyitang China
8 C2 Gylchedd mt Wales
115 P5 Gyldenløves Fjord Greenland
28 H5 Gyldenløves Høj hill Denmark
26 N5 Gyljen Sweden
28 E5 Gylling Denmark
28 E5 Gylling Næs Denmark
141 L7 Gympie Queensland
68 B3 Gyobingauk Burma
61 N9 Gyōda Japan
48 F4 Gyoma Hungary
48 F3 Gyöngyös Hungary
48 F3 Gyöngyös R Hungary
48 E4 Gyönk Hungary
48 D3 Györ Hungary
48 D3 Györ-Sopron Hungary
106 D2 Gypsum Colorado
107 N3 Gypsum Kansas
143 F7 Gypsum L W Australia
117 Q5 Gypsum Pt N W Terr
119 T7 Gypsumville Manitoba
28 H5 Gyrstinge Denmark
27 J11 Gysinge Sweden
46 F2 Gyueshovo Bulgaria
48 G4 Gyula Hungary
52 D6 Gzhat' R U.S.S.R.
Gzhatsk see Gagarin
22 H2 Haacht Belgium
37 M4 Haag W Germany
25 G4 Haaksbergen Netherlands
137 S5 Ha'apai Group islds Tonga
29 L8 Haapajärvi Finland
29 L9 Haapamäki Finland
29 L7 Haapavesi Finland
52 B5 Haapsalu U.S.S.R.
25 C4 Haarlem Netherlands
32 G9 Haarstrang W Germany
144 B5 Haast New Zealand
140 B6 Haast Bluff N Terr Aust
25 C5 Haastrecht Netherlands
80 G4 Habaka Jordan
126 C3 Habana Cuba
83 K9 Habarane Sri Lanka
86 G5 Habaswein Kenya
114 H6 Habay Alberta
22 K4 Habay-la-Neuve Belgium
78 J5 Habbamyah Iraq
32 K10 Habichtswald wood W Germany
75 O6 Habiganj Bangladesh
65 C3 Habirag China
80 G7 Habis R Jordan
80 C5 Habla Israel
27 K14 Hablingo Sweden
27 G14 Habo Sweden
80 C3 Ha Bonim Israel
60 P1 Haboro Japan
22 L3 Habscheid W Germany
61 N11 Habuminato Japan
131 B7 Hachado, Paso de Arg/Chile
32 G10 Hachen W Germany
36 D2 Hachenburg W Germany
59 L5 Hachijō Jima isld Japan
61 N5 Hachimori Japan
60 O2 Hachinai dake mt Japan
59 M3 Hachinohe Japan
59 L4 Hachiōjio Japan
106 B10 Hachita New Mexico
100 D8 Hackamore California
26 G9 Hackås Sweden
103 L6 Hackberry Arizona
111 C12 Hackberry Louisiana
107 K3 Hackberry Cr Kansas
118 E6 Hackett Alberta
110 B6 Hackett Arkansas
95 N6 Hackettstown New Jersey
111 J7 Hackleburg Alabama
138 E4 Hack, Mt S Australia
13 H5 Hackness England
87 C8 Haco Angola
68 H2 Ha Coi Vietnam
36 E3 Hadamar W Germany
80 C5 Hadar Israel
98 J7 Hadar Nebraska
72 H4 Hadd, Al Oman
107 N2 Haddam Kansas
9 G3 Haddenham England
13 F2 Haddington Scotland
146 D14 Haddington, Mt Antarctica
9 H2 Haddiscoe England
112 D4 Haddock Georgia
141 F7 Haddon Corner Qnsld/S Aust
138 F2 Haddon Downs S Australia
73 L8 Haddunmahti Atoll Maldives
85 F6 Hadejia R Nigeria
27 D11 Hadeland Norway
32 J5 Hadelner Kanal W Germany
32 K4 Hademarschen W Germany
141 K7 Haden Queensland
80 C4 Hadera Israel
80 C4 Hadera R Israel
38 N5 Hadersdorf Austria
28 C6 Haderslev Denmark
Haderslev co see Sønderjylland
28 B4 Haderup Denmark
72 F5 Hadhramaut reg S Yemen
72 G6 Hadiboh Socotra
72 E2 Hadithah, Al Iraq
9 G4 Hadleigh England
9 G3 Hadleigh Suffolk England
114 J3 Hadley B N W Terr
144 C6 Hadlow New Zealand
33 O9 Hadmersleben E Germany
26 G3 Hadsel Norway
26 G3 Hädselöy isld Norway
28 E4 Hadsten Denmark
28 E3 Hadsund Denmark
116 O3 Hadweenzic R Alaska
131 G3 Haedo, Cuchilla de ra Uruguay
65 F5 Haeju N Korea
80 C7 Ha-Ela Israel
28 E6 Hæsinge Denmark
41 O3 Hafelekar Sp mt Austria
80 C6 Hafez Ḥayyim Israel
33 N4 Haffkrug-Scharbeutz W Germany
115 N2 Haffners Bjerg mt Greenland
118 K6 Hafford Sask
43 C13 Haffouz Tunisia
78 F2 Hafik Turkey
74 E2 Hafizabad Pakistan
75 P6 Haflong India
38 H7 Hafner mt Austria
77 A4 Haft Gel Iran
77 H2 Haftqala R Afghanistan
Hafun see Dante Somalia
86 F3 Hag Abdullah Sudan
112 F5 Hagan Georgia
27 J11 Hagaström Sweden
32 F5 Hage W Germany
80 D3 Ha Gelilit Israel
33 R8 Hagelsberg mt E Germany
116 G7 Hagemeister I Alaska
119 M6 Hagen Sask
32 F10 Hagen W Germany
32 K8 Hagenburg W Germany
38 H6 Hagen-Gebirge mts Austria
33 O6 Hagenow E Germany
101 L7 Hagerman Idaho
106 F8 Hagerman New Mexico
27 H13 Hägerstad Sweden
94 B7 Hagerstown Indiana
94 K7 Hagerstown Maryland
120 K10 Hagersville Ontario
27 G11 Hagfors Sweden
26 G8 Häggenås Sweden
13 G2 Haggerston England
26 G8 Häggsjön Sweden
68 G1 Ha Giang Vietnam
48 K4 Hăgimaş mt Romania
61 L10 Hagiwara Japan
8 D3 Hagley England
19 K3 Hagondage France
112 G3 Hagood S Carolina
80 C5 Hagor Israel
80 F1 Ha Gosherim Israel
14 B4 Hags Hd Irish Rep
98 F3 Hague N Dakota
95 O3 Hague New York
118 L6 Hague Sask
20 B2 Hague, C. de la France

19 L4 Haguenau France
98 A9 Hagues Pk Colorado
Hague, The see Den Haag
18 E9 Haguetmau France
85 B3 Hagunia Morocco
123 O3 Haha Bay Quebec
122 B5 Ha Ha, L Quebec
80 D6 Ha Hamisha Jordan
113 D7 Hahira Georgia
37 M4 Hahnbach W Germany
36 D2 Hahnbei W Germany
33 M9 Hahnenklee-Bockswiese W Germany
80 C3 Ha Hoterim Israel
67 C6 Hai'an China
67 G1 Hai'an China
65 E4 Haicheng China
67 F4 Haicheng China
37 N5 Haidhof W Germany
43 B13 Haïdra Tunisia
37 O5 Haidstein mt W Germany
68 H2 Hai Duong Vietnam
22 J2 Haien Belgium
80 C2 Haifa Israel
80 D2 Haifa, Bay of Israel
67 E5 Haifeng China
143 F9 Haig W Australia
36 E2 Haiger W Germany
36 F7 Haigerloch W Germany
117 P7 Haig Lake Alberta
98 E10 Haigler Nebraska
65 D5 Hai He R China
67 C6 Haikang China
60 C12 Haiki Japan
69 D9 Hai,Ko isld Thailand
68 K2 Haikou China
135 T3 Haiku Hawaiian Is
75 P6 Hailakandi India
59 G2 Hailar China
101 L6 Hailey Idaho
115 M8 Haileybury Ontario
107 P7 Haileyville Oklahoma
59 J3 Hailin China
67 D6 Hailing Dao isld China
65 J3 Hailong China
9 G6 Hailsham England
59 J2 Hailun China
29 L6 Hailuoto isld Finland
32 M8 Haimar W Germany
67 G1 Haimen China
67 G2 Haimen China
67 D7 Hainan Dao isld China
68 D2 Hai-nang Burma
Hainan Strait see Qiongzhou Haixia
22 F2 Hainaut Belgium
22 F3 Hainaut France
31 K7 Hainburg Austria
117 F6 Haines Alaska
100 H5 Haines Oregon
22 G3 Haine-St-Paul Belgium
113 F9 Haines City Florida
114 F5 Haines Junct Yukon Terr
38 N5 Hainfeld Austria
68 B4 Haing R Burma
37 P2 Hainichen E Germany
67 G1 Haining China
33 N10 Hainleite E Germany
37 O2 Hainsberg E Germany
94 D4 Haintramck Michigan
68 H2 Haiphong Vietnam
118 F5 Hairy Hill Alberta
65 E3 Haisgai China
127 H5 Haiti rep W Indies
68 J3 Haitou China
65 F2 Haituo China
103 N9 Haivana Nakya Arizona
102 G5 Haiwee Res California
65 D5 Haixing China
86 G2 Haiya Junct Sudan
65 E6 Haiyang China
65 F5 Haiyang Dao isld China
Haiyou see Sanmen
67 B5 Haiyuan China
68 H1 Haiyuan China
48 G3 Hajdú-Bihar co Hungary
48 G3 Hajdúböszörmény Hungary
48 G3 Hajdúdorog Hungary
48 G3 Hajdúhadház Hungary
48 G3 Hajdúnánás Hungary
48 G3 Hajdúszoboszlo Hungary
61 M7 Hajiki-saki C Japan
79 G9 Hājj Saudi Arabia
31 O3 Hajnówka Poland
65 F7 Hajo isld S Korea
68 A1 Haka Burma
135 V5 Hakalou Hawaiian Is
80 G3 Hakama Jordan
87 E7 Hakansson mts Zaïre
27 F13 Håkantorp Sweden
144 A7 Hakapoua, L New Zealand
61 N8 Hakase-yama mt Japan
144 C6 Hakataramea New Zealand
60 G11 Hakata shima isld Japan
131 B8 Hakelhuincul, Altiplanicie de plat Argentina
78 J3 Hakkari Turkey
26 M5 Hakkas Sweden
61 O5 Hakköda san Japan
60 Q1 Hako dake mt Japan
59 M3 Hakodate Japan
60 O4 Hakodate wan B Japan
61 K9 Haku-san mt Japan
61 K9 Hakusan Nat. Park Japan
Hal see Halle
78 K4 Halabja Iraq
65 F2 Halahai China
86 G1 Halaib Sudan
79 D8 Halâl, G mt Egypt
48 G3 Halasto L Hungary
79 G9 Halat 'Ammar Saudi Arabia
48 K3 Hălăucești Romania
135 S2 Halawa Hawaiian Is Pacific Ocean
80 F4 Halawa Jordan
135 S2 Halawa, C Hawaiian Is
79 G4 Halba Lebanon
33 T8 Halbe E Germany
33 O9 Halberstadt E Germany
8 C6 Halberton England
119 O9 Halbrite Sask
145 E4 Halcombe New Zealand
71 E4 Halcon, Mt Philippines
117 P10 Halcyon Hot Springs Br Columbia
28 E3 Hald Århus Denmark
28 C3 Hald Viborg Denmark
28 H6 Haldagerlille Denmark
27 E12 Halden Norway
33 O8 Haldensleben E Germany
28 M1 Haldersvig Faeroes
28 C4 Hald Sø L Denmark
28 E4 Haldum Denmark
74 H4 Haldwani India
106 H2 Hale Colorado
94 D2 Hale Michigan
110 C2 Hale Missouri
140 D6 Hale R N Terr Aust
135 T3 Haleakala Crater Hawaiian Is
86 H3 Haleb I Red Sea
78 G4 Halebiye Syria
108 F1 Hale Center Texas
135 Q2 Haleiwa Hawaiian Is
143 B7 Hale, Mt W Australia
135 R2 Halena Hawaiian Is
112 B2 Hales Bar Dam Tennessee
9 D3 Halesowen England
9 G5 Hale Street England
9 H3 Halesworth England
111 J7 Haleyville Alabama
144 B7 Half Moon B New Zealand
9 E3 Halford England
107 K2 Halford Kansas
94 K7 Halfway Maryland
100 H5 Halfway Oregon
108 F1 Halfway Texas
117 M7 Halfway R Br Columbia
116 K6 Halfway Mt Alaska
25 C4 Halfweg Netherlands
80 B7 Halib Israel
121 M7 Haliburton Ontario
13 G6 Halifax England
112 K1 Halifax N Carolina
115 N9 Halifax Nova Scotia
95 L6 Halifax Pennsylvania
141 H4 Halifax Queensland
94 H10 Halifax Virginia
136 K5 Halifax B Queensland
141 H4 Halifax, Mt Queensland
29 K11 Halikko Finland
77 E5 Halil R Iran
79 G4 Halimet el Qabu mt Lebanon
70 L9 Halimun, G mt Java
86 A2 Halin Somalia
Haliut see Urad Zhonghou Lianheqi
76 B3 Haliyal India
26 N4 Halju mt Sweden
28 D6 Halk Denmark
116 L1 Halkett, C Alaska
118 E6 Halkirk Alberta
15 E2 Halkirk Scotland
26 O2 Halkkavarre mt Norway
101 M3 Hall Montana
26 J8 Hälla Sweden
9 G6 Halland England
26 F8 Hålland Sweden
27 F15 Halland county Sweden
113 G12 Hallandale Florida
27 F15 Hallandsås hills Sweden
28 K4 Hallands Väderö isld Sweden
138 D5 Hall B S Australia
115 N1 Hall Basin Canada/Greenland
119 S8 Hallboro Manitoba
22 G2 Halle Belgium
33 P10 Halle E Germany
32 H8 Halle W Germany
33 O9 Halle reg E Germany
27 H15 Hälleberga Sweden
120 G3 Hallebourg Ontario
28 G5 Halleby Å R Denmark
100 K9 Halleck Nevada
27 G12 Hällefors Sweden
38 H6 Hallein Austria
26 G8 Hallen Sweden
36 F1 Hallenberg W Germany
20 J2 Hallencourt France
28 F4 Hallendrup Denmark
26 H9 Hällesjö Sweden
109 L6 Hallettsville Texas
111 E8 Halley Arkansas
116 B6 Hall I Bering Sea
98 D2 Halliday N Dakota
98 A9 Halligan Res Colorado
27 D11 Hallingdalselv R Norway
27 C11 Hallingskarvet mt Norway
27 B11 Hallingskeid Norway
115 L4 Hall Lake L N W Terr
27 J11 Hållnäs Sweden
119 V10 Hallock Minnesota
118 K8 Hallonquist Sask
115 N5 Hall Pen N W Terr
110 G6 Halls Tennessee
8 C7 Hallsands England
27 H12 Hallsberg Sweden
142 G4 Halls Creek W Australia
37 K4 Hallstadt W Germany
27 H12 Hallstahammar Sweden
106 G3 Hall Station Colorado
38 J6 Hallstatt Austria
27 K11 Hallstavik Sweden
95 M5 Hallstead Pennsylvania
111 C9 Hall Summit Louisiana
110 D2 Hallsville Missouri
109 N3 Hallsville Texas
81 A8 Hall Table Mt Indian Oc
41 O3 Halltal Austria
94 J5 Hallton Pennsylvania
22 E2 Halluin France
25 E2 Hallum Netherlands
28 E2 Hallund Denmark
28 C5 Hallundbæk Denmark
26 H8 Hallviken Sweden
98 K1 Halma Minnesota
71 B2 Halmahera isld Indonesia
71 B3 Halmahera sea Indonesia
48 H3 Halmeu Romania
27 F15 Halmstad Sweden
43 C12 Halq el Oued Tunisia
28 E2 Hals Denmark
26 C8 Halsa Norway
37 P2 Halsbrucke E Germany
36 F2 Halsdorf W Germany
98 F8 Halsey Nebraska
100 B5 Halsey Oregon
71 D5 Halsey Harbour Philippines
28 H5 Halsnæs pen Denmark
28 G6 Halsskov Denmark
98 K2 Halstad Minnesota
9 G4 Halstead England
107 N4 Halstead Kansas
36 B5 Halstroff France
29 L8 Halsua Finland
26 E9 Haltdalen Norway
26 D7 Halten Norway
32 F9 Haltern W Germany
29 J2 Haltia mt Finland
109 M9 Haltom City Texas
13 F4 Haltwhistle England
77 C7 Hālūl isld Qatar
36 C1 Halver W Germany
118 L8 Halvorgate Sask
28 D2 Halvrimmen Denmark
141 K7 Haly, Mt Queensland
22 E4 Ham France
80 G3 Ham Jordan
60 F12 Hama Japan
79 G3 Hama Syria
60 F11 Hamada Japan
85 F3 Hamada de Tinrhert stony des Algeria
85 D4 Hamada El Haricha reg Mali
72 F2 Hamadān Iran
85 C3 Hamada Tounassine stony des Algeria
80 F3 Hamadya Israel
61 P13 Hamahika-jima isld Okinawa
61 L11 Hamakita Japan
60 P2 Hamamasu Japan
59 L5 Hamamatsu Japan
60 T2 Hamanaka Japan
61 L11 Hamana ko L Japan
80 C4 Ha Ma 'Pil Israel
98 H2 Hamar N Dakota
27 E11 Hamar Norway
26 H3 Hamaröy Norway
60 H10 Hamasaka Japan
84 J5 Hamâta, Gebel mt Egypt
80 F3 Hamat Gader Jordan
60 Q1 Hama-Tombetsu Japan
36 C5 Hambach France
83 L11 Hambantota Sri Lanka
98 G2 Hamberg N Dakota
32 J6 Hambergen W Germany
117 O9 Hamber Prov. Park Br Columbia
9 F5 Hambledon England
13 G6 Hambleton England
13 G5 Hambleton Hills England
100 D8 Hambone California
32 L7 Hambühren W Germany
111 E8 Hamburg Arkansas
100 B8 Hamburg California
99 L9 Hamburg Iowa
95 N5 Hamburg New Jersey
94 J4 Hamburg New York
95 M6 Hamburg Pennsylvania
34 Hamburg conurbation W Germany
20 C4 Hambye France
79 G3 Hamdānīya Syria
95 M4 Hamden New York
94 E7 Hamden Ohio
29 L10 Hame prov Finland
29 K10 Hämeenkyrö Finland
29 L11 Hämeenlinna Finland
143 A10 Hamelin B W Australia
143 A7 Hamelin Pool W Australia
32 K8 Hameln W Germany
101 N6 Hamer Idaho
33 O8 Hamersleben E Germany
142 C5 Hamersley W Australia
142 B5 Hamersley Ra W Australia
33 P7 Hamerten E Germany
65 G5 Hamhŭng N Korea
66 E3 Hami China
111 J7 Hamilton Alabama
90 B2 Hamilton Bermuda
101 S9 Hamilton Colorado
111 M9 Hamilton Georgia
99 P9 Hamilton Illinois
94 C5 Hamilton Indiana
107 O4 Hamilton Kansas
94 A4 Hamilton Michigan
114 H8 Hamilton Montana
119 U10 Hamilton N Dakota
95 M4 Hamilton New York
145 E2 Hamilton New Zealand
94 C7 Hamilton Ohio
115 M9 Hamilton Ontario
100 F5 Hamilton Oregon
140 F6 Hamilton Queensland
12 D2 Hamilton Scotland
139 H8 Hamilton Tasmania
109 J4 Hamilton Texas
138 F6 Hamilton Victoria
100 D1 Hamilton Washington
140 F6 Hamilton R Queensland
138 C2 Hamilton R S Australia
102 C2 Hamilton City California
101 R6 Hamilton Dome Wyoming
140 C6 Hamilton Downs N Terr Aust
115 O7 Hamilton Inlet Labrador
111 C7 Hamilton,L Arkansas
103 J2 Hamilton, Mt Nevada
29 N11 Hamina Finland
74 J6 Hamirpur India
Hamitabat see Isparta
94 C5 Hamler Ohio
94 A5 Hamlet Indiana
112 H3 Hamlet N Carolina
98 E9 Hamlet Nebraska
142 B6 Hamlet, Mt W Australia
138 E5 Hamley Bridge S Australia
94 K3 Hamlin New York
108 G3 Hamlin Texas
94 E8 Hamlin W Virginia
94 A2 Hamlin L Michigan
32 G9 Hamm W Germany
84 E4 Hammādah Al Hamrā plat Libya
17 G9 Hammam Bou Hadjar Algeria
43 D12 Hammamet Tunisia
85 G1 Hammamet, G de Tunisia
85 G1 Hammam Lif Tunisia
29 H11 Hammarland Finland
27 F11 Hammarsbyn Sweden
29 M3 Hammastunturi mt Finland
22 G1 Hamme Belgium
32 J6 Hamme R W Germany
28 D4 Hammel Denmark
36 H3 Hammelburg W Germany
28 C6 Hammelev Denmark
28 F4 Hammelev Denmark
33 S6 Hammelspring E Germany
22 H2 Hamme-Mille Belgium
26 H8 Hammerdal Sweden
147 H14 Hammerfest Norway
28 D3 Hammershøj Denmark
36 C3 Hammerstein W Germany
13 G6 Hammerton England
28 C4 Hammerum Denmark
100 K7 Hammett Idaho
32 E9 Hamminkeln W Germany
107 L6 Hammon Oklahoma
99 T8 Hammond Illinois
110 H2 Hammond Illinois
111 F11 Hammond Louisiana
98 B4 Hammond Montana
95 M2 Hammond New York
100 B3 Hammond Oregon
138 E4 Hammond S Australia
99 O5 Hammond Wisconsin
94 D1 Hammond B Michigan
141 F1 Hammond I Queensland
95 K4 Hammondsport New York
122 G8 Hammond Vale New Brunswick
102 C2 Hammonton California
95 N7 Hammonton New Jersey
26 O1 Hamnbukt Norway
26 L2 Hamneidet Norway
26 S1 Hamningberg Norway
68 G7 Ham Ninh Vietnam
121 T7 Ham Nord Quebec
26 L4 Håmojokk Sweden
22 K1 Hamont Belgium
86 G2 Hamoyet, Jebel mt Sudan
98 H1 Hampden N Dakota
144 C6 Hampden New Zealand
115 O8 Hampden Nfld
95 T2 Hampden Highlands Maine
28 C4 Hampen Denmark
36 B6 Hampont France
9 E5 Hampshire co England
95 K7 Hampstead Maryland
112 K3 Hampstead N Carolina
122 F8 Hampstead New Brunswick
111 D8 Hampton Arkansas
9 F5 Hampton England
113 E8 Hampton Florida
111 M8 Hampton Georgia
99 N7 Hampton Iowa
98 J9 Hampton Nebraska
122 G8 Hampton New Brunswick
95 R4 Hampton New Hampshire
100 E6 Hampton Oregon
112 F5 Hampton S Carolina
95 L9 Hampton Virginia
101 P8 Hampton Wyoming
95 P6 Hampton Bays Long I, N Y
142 B5 Hampton Harb W Australia
143 F9 Hampton Tableland W Australia
27 H10 Hamra Sweden
27 J11 Hamrånge Sweden
101 P7 Hams Fork R Wyoming
9 G5 Ham Street England
68 H7 Ham Tan Vietnam
135 T3 Hana Hawaiian Is
126 D3 Hanábana R Cuba
135 O1 Hanalei Hawaiian Is
135 T3 Hanamanioa, C Hawaiian Is
135 O1 Hanamaulu Hawaiian Is
135 O1 Hanapepe Hawaiian Is
61 N13 Hanare-iwa islds Japan
36 F3 Hanau W Germany
102 S12 Hanauma B Hawaiian Is
121 L5 Hanbury Ontario
111 K7 Hanceville Alabama
117 M10 Hanceville Br Col
58 F4 Hancheng China
67 D1 Hanchuan China
95 T2 Hancock Maine
94 J7 Hancock Maryland
99 S2 Hancock Michigan
99 L4 Hancock Minnesota
95 P4 Hancock New Hampshire
95 M5 Hancock New York
99 R5 Hancock Wisconsin
113 F10 Hancock, L Florida
61 K11 Handa Japan
58 F4 Handan China
28 B4 Handbjerg Denmark
9 F5 Handcross England
118 J6 Handel Sask
27 K12 Handen Sweden
88 G4 Handeni Tanzania
28 D3 Handest Denmark
70 C6 Handjalipan Kalimantan
109 K3 Handley Texas
119 P9 Handsworth Sask
32 K4 Hanerau W Germany
102 E5 Hanford California
100 F3 Hanford Washington
76 B3 Hangal India
68 C5 Hangan Burma
65 G6 Hangang R S Korea
145 F3 Hangaroa New Zealand
27 C11 Hangastöl Norway
145 E3 Hangatiki New Zealand
58 C2 Hangayn Nuruu mt Mongolia
Hangchow see Hangzhou
33 T8 Hangelsberg E Germany
27 G14 Hånger Sweden
58 E3 Hanggin Houqi China
94 E8 Hanging Rock Ohio
89 A10 Hangklip, C S Africa
100 H2 Hangman Cr Washington
29 K12 Hango Finland
65 D5 Hangu China
67 D4 Hanguang China
59 H5 Hangzhou China
59 H5 Hangzhou Wan B China
32 M7 Hänigsen W Germany
86 H3 Hanish I Red Sea
80 D1 Hanita Israel
Hanjiang see Yangzhou
67 F4 Hanjiang China
29 M9 Hankasalmi Finland
85 C4 Hank, El Mauritania
98 J3 Hankinson N Dakota
58 F5 Hankou China
103 O3 Hanksville Utah
8 D1 Hanley England
118 L7 Hanley Sask
99 L5 Hanley Falls Minnesota
144 D5 Hanmer Springs New Zealand
118 F7 Hanna Alberta
101 P9 Hanna Utah
101 T8 Hanna Wyoming
98 H2 Hannaford N Dakota
119 T10 Hannah N Dakota
120 K1 Hannah B Ontario
99 P10 Hannibal Missouri
99 Q4 Hannibal Wisconsin
28 A4 Hanning Kirke Denmark
142 F3 Hann, Mt W Australia
98 E2 Hannover N Dakota
32 L8 Hannover W Germany
140 C6 Hann Ra N Terr Aust
22 J2 Hannut Belgium
27 H16 Hanöbukten B Sweden
68 G2 Hanoi Vietnam
48 D4 Hanót Hungary
107 O2 Hanover Kansas
99 N4 Hanover Minnesota
101 Q2 Hanover Montana
95 P3 Hanover New Hampshire
120 J8 Hanover Ontario
89 D8 Hanover S Africa
127 H1 Hanover parish Jamaica
133 C8 Hanover, I Chile
48 E6 Han Pijesak Yugoslavia
48 D3 Hanság Hungary
117 N8 Hansard Br Columbia
98 G1 Hansboro N Dakota
120 F3 Hansen Ontario
146 B5 Hansen Mt Antarctica
67 F1 Hanshan China
67 D2 Hanshou China
58 E5 Han Shui R China
67 D1 Han Shui R China
74 F4 Hansi India
27 G10 Hansjö Sweden
140 C5 Hanson R N Terr Aust
119 P4 Hanson L Sask
138 D4 Hanson, L S Australia
28 D5 Hansted Vejle Denmark
28 B2 Hanstholm Havn C Denmark
65 D2 Han Sum China
22 J3 Han-sur-Lesse Belgium
25 B6 Hansweert Netherlands
Hantan see Handan
Hanting see Wei Xian
Hants co see Hampshire
122 H8 Hantsport Nova Scotia
36 C7 Hantz, Col du pass France
65 D2 Han Ul China
67 A1 Hanwang China
83 K11 Hanwella Sri Lanka
58 F5 Hanyang China
58 D6 Hanyuan China
58 E5 Hanzhong China
65 D7 Hanzhuang China
135 N10 Hao atoll Tuamotu Arch Pacific Oc
65 H1 Haolianghe China
80 F3 Ha On Israel
26 N6 Haparanda Sweden
71 B1 Hapo Halmahera Indonesia
9 H2 Happisburgh England
100 B8 Happy Camp California
140 E5 Happy Cr N Terr Aust
144 D5 Hapuku New Zealand
83 L11 Haputale Sri Lanka
79 E9 Haql Saudi Arabia
58 E2 Hara Mongolia
26 M5 Harads Sweden
86 H4 Hara Fanna Ethiopia
111 H12 Harahan New Orleans
26 B9 Haram Norway
59 M4 Haramachi Japan
86 H4 Harar Ethiopia
86 A3 Harardera Somalia
Harare see Salisbury Zimbabwe
58 E2 Har-ayrag Mongolia
86 C3 Haraz Djombo Chad
86 D3 Haraze Chad
80 E8 Har Ben Yai'r Israel
65 G2 Harbin China
27 J11 Harbo Sweden
77 K5 Harboi Hills Pakistan
28 J7 Hårbølle Denmark
22 D4 Harbonnières France
28 A3 Harboør Denmark
28 A3 Harboør Tange pen Denmark
100 A7 Harbor Oregon
94 E3 Harbor Beach Michigan
117 E6 Harbor Pt Alaska
94 B1 Harbor Springs Michigan
13 F3 Harbottle England
115 O8 Harbour Breton Nfld
123 S6 Harbour Buffett Nfld
113 K12 Harbour Cay, Little isld Bahamas
123 Q3 Harbour Deep Nfld
115 O8 Harbour Grace Nfld
113 L12 Harbour I Bahamas
123 S6 Harbour Mille Nfld
122 H8 Harbourville Nova Scotia
37 K6 Harburg Bayern W Germany
32 L6 Harburg Niedersachsen W Germany
28 E6 Hårby Denmark
122 G7 Harcourt New Brunswick
103 L7 Harcuvar Mts Arizona
74 G7 Harda India
27 B11 Hardanger Norway
27 B11 Hardanger-fjorden inlet Norway
27 C11 Hardangervidda plat Norway
89 A5 Hardap Dam Namibia
111 F9 Hardee Mississippi
112 F5 Hardeeville S Carolina
25 E2 Hardegarijp Netherlands
32 L9 Hardegsen W Germany
22 B2 Hardelot-Plage France
25 G3 Hardenberg Netherlands
70 D2 Harden, Bt mt Kalimantan
25 E4 Harderwijk Netherlands
107 J5 Hardesty Oklahoma
142 B6 Hardey, R W Australia
36 H4 Hardheim W Germany
110 F2 Hardin Illinois
110 C2 Hardin Missouri
114 J8 Hardin Montana
99 M3 Harding Minnesota
87 E12 Harding S Africa
116 M6 Harding Icefield Alaska
111 L9 Harding, L Georgia
119 T2 Harding L Manitoba
110 K4 Hardinsburg Kentucky
118 F6 Hardisty Alberta
117 P3 Hardisty L N W Terr
20 K2 Hardivillers France
100 F4 Hardman Oregon
142 E4 Hardman, Mt W Australia
80 D8 Hardof R Jordan
74 H4 Hardwar India
98 K6 Hardwick Minnesota
95 P2 Hardwick Vermont
8 D4 Hardwicke England
138 D5 Hardwicke B S Australia
110 E5 Hardy Arkansas
101 O2 Hardy Montana
119 N9 Hardy Sask
145 F2 Hardy, Mt New Zealand
133 D9 Hardy, Pen Chile
94 B3 Hardy Res Michigan
123 S5 Hare B Nfld
80 E4 Hare Gilboa Israel
26 B9 Hareid Norway
22 E2 Harelbeke Belgium
32 F7 Haren W Germany
115 O3 Hare Øen isld Greenland
9 F1 Hare Park England
13 G6 Harewood England
79 F5 Harf el Mreffi mt Lebanon
20 F3 Harfleur France
27 K1' Harg Sweden
36 B5 Hargarten aux Mines France
86 H4 Hargeisa Somalia
48 K4 Harghitei Muntii mt Romania
22 E4 Hargicourt France
109 J9 Hargill Texas
22 J3 Hargimont Belgium
22 H3 Hargnies France
119 Q9 Hargrave Manitoba
119 S4 Hargrave L Manitoba
79 E8 Har Hakippa mt Israel
79 E8 Har Harif Israel
80 D8 Har Hezron Israel
66 F4 Har Hu L China
61 M9 Hari Japan
76 B3 Harihar India
144 C5 Harihari New Zealand
60 H11 Harima-nada sea Japan
25 B5 Haringvliet Netherlands
74 E1 Haripur Pakistan
77 J2 Hari Rud R Afghanistan/Iran
79 G6 Harir, Wādi watercourse Syria
87 C10 Haris Namibia
26 G10 Härjån R Sweden
29 J10 Harjavalta Finland
26 F10 Härjehågna mt Sweden
80 F2 Har Kena'an peak Israel
112 L3 Harkers I N Carolina
99 L8 Harlan Iowa
107 M2 Harlan Kansas
94 D10 Harlan Kentucky
98 G9 Harlan Co. Res Nebraska
22 K4 Harlange Luxembourg
32 G5 Harle W Germany
8 B2 Harlech Wales
112 E4 Harlem Georgia
101 R1 Harlem Montana
32 L5 Harlesiel W Germany
9 H3 Harleston England
28 D4 Harlev Denmark
28 J6 Hårlev Denmark
112 G4 Harleyville S Carolina
25 D2 Harlingen Netherlands
109 K9 Harlingen Texas
32 G5 Harlinger Land W Germany
33 M9 Harlingerode W Germany
9 G4 Harlow England
98 G1 Harlow N Dakota
101 Q3 Harlowton Montana
94 H8 Harman W Virginia
47 K5 Harmancık Turkey
26 J10 Harmånger Sweden
25 C4 Harmelen Netherlands
80 E2 Har Meron peak Israel
107 L5 Harmon Oklahoma
118 A2 Harmon R Alberta
95 S2 Harmony Maine
99 O6 Harmony Minnesota
79 E8 Har Natha mt Israel
100 G6 Harney Oregon
100 F6 Harney Basin reg Oregon
113 F9 Harney, L Florida
100 F6 Harney L Oregon
98 C6 Harney Pk S Dakota
28 E6 Harnorup Denmark
26 J9 Härnösand Sweden
65 E2 Har Nur China
58 B2 Har Nuur L Mongolia
80 E3 Harod R Israel
26 B9 Haröy isld Norway
9 F4 Harpenden England
107 M4 Harper Kansas
85 C8 Harper Liberia
100 H6 Harper Oregon
109 H5 Harper Texas
116 L4 Harper Bend Alaska
117 Q6 Harper Cr Alberta
102 G6 Harper L California
116 Q4 Harper, Mt Alaska
144 C5 Harper Pass New Zealand
94 K7 Harpers Ferry W Virginia
140 C5 Harper Springs N Terr Aust
110 J5 Harpeth R Tennessee
8 C6 Harpford England
9 G2 Harpley England
27 F15 Harplinge Sweden
32 J7 Harpstedt W Germany
119 M9 Harptree Sask
65 D4 Harqin China
65 D4 Harqin Qi China
103 L8 Harquahala Mts Arizona
85 E1 Harrach, El Algeria
107 N6 Harrah Oklahoma
26 F7 Harran Norway
37 K3 Harras E Germany
28 B3 Harre Denmark
111 D8 Harrell Arkansas
144 D5 Harrelville New Zealand
115 M7 Harricana R Quebec
28 E3 Harridslev Denmark
94 B2 Harrietta Michigan
112 C2 Harriman Tennessee
95 M8 Harrington Delaware
95 U2 Harrington Maine
100 G2 Harrington Washington
115 O7 Harrington Harbour Quebec
119 P2 Harriot L Sask
100 B9 Harris California
99 N9 Harris Missouri
118 K7 Harris Sask
15 B3 Harris div Scotland
110 F6 Harrisburg Arkansas
110 H4 Harrisburg Illinois
98 C8 Harrisburg Nebraska
94 D7 Harrisburg Ohio
100 B5 Harrisburg Oregon
95 L6 Harrisburg Pennsylvania
93 K6 Harrisburg S Dakota
113 H2 Harris Hill Ontario
113 F9 Harris, L Florida
138 D4 Harris, L S Australia
89 F7 Harrismith S Africa
143 C10 Harrismith W Australia
140 A6 Harris, Mt N Terr Aust
144 B6 Harris Mts New Zealand
110 C5 Harrison Arkansas
112 E5 Harrison Georgia
100 J2 Harrison Idaho
94 C2 Harrison Michigan
101 O4 Harrison Montana
98 C7 Harrison Nebraska
98 H6 Harrison S Dakota
116 L1 Harrison B Alaska
111 E10 Harrisonburg Louisiana
94 J8 Harrisonburg Virginia
115 O7 Harrison, C Labrador
117 M11 Harrison L Br Columbia
83 K12 Harrison, Mt Mahé I Ind Oc
110 B3 Harrisonville Missouri
94 D2 Harrisville Michigan
95 M2 Harrisville New York
94 F7 Harrisville W Virginia
110 K2 Harrodsburg Indiana
94 C9 Harrodsburg Kentucky
13 G6 Harrogate England
98 G5 Harrold S Dakota
109 H1 Harrold Texas
9 F4 Harrow England
120 H10 Harrow Ontario
119 Q8 Harrowby Manitoba
26 H7 Harrsjön Sweden
27 F14 Härryda Sweden
98 F9 Harry Strunk L Nebraska
79 E8 Har Saggi mt Israel
32 K6 Harsefeld W Germany
32 H9 Harsewinkel W Germany
78 G1 Harsit Turkey
26 L5 Harsprånget Sweden
26 J3 Harstad Norway
32 L8 Harsum W Germany
28 A4 Harsyssel reg Denmark
13 G4 Hart England
99 U6 Hart Michigan
119 M9 Hart Sask
65 E3 Hartao China
89 B7 Hartbees watercourse S Africa
38 N7 Hartberg Austria
89 E5 Hartebeespoort Dam S Africa
27 B11 Hårteigen mt Norway
118 C8 Hartell Alberta
22 E5 Hartennes-et-Taux France
36 E2 Hartenrod W Germany
37 O2 Hartenstein E Germany
37 J5 Hartershofen W Germany
15 E5 Hart Fell Scotland
9 G5 Hartfield England
111 L10 Hartford Alabama
109 N1 Hartford Arkansas
95 P5 Hartford Connecticut
107 P3 Hartford Kansas
110 K4 Hartford Kentucky
94 A4 Hartford Michigan
94 E6 Hartford Ohio
112 D2 Hartford Tennessee
99 S6 Hartford Wisconsin
94 B6 Hartford City Indiana
95 P5 Hartford, E Connecticut
37 O1 Hartha E Germany
37 O2 Harthau E Germany
12 E2 Harthill Scotland
9 E1 Hartington England
98 J7 Hartington Nebraska
80 E2 Har Tir'an Israel
122 D2 Hart-jaune, R Quebec
138 D4 Hart, L S Australia
8 B6 Hartland England
95 S2 Hartland Maine
122 E7 Hartland New Brunswick
8 B5 Hartland Pt England
8 D3 Hartlebury England
13 G4 Hartlepool England
13 G3 Hartley England
99 L6 Hartley Iowa
108 B8 Hartley Texas
89 G2 Hartley Zimbabwe
117 J9 Hartley Bay Br Columbia
9 F5 Hartley Wintney England
100 F2 Hartline Washington
106 H3 Hartman Colorado
37 P5 Hartmanice Czechoslovakia
37 O2 Hartmannsdorf E Germany
36 G3 Hartmannshain W Germany
119 Q6 Hart Mt Manitoba
100 F7 Hart Mt Oregon
142 F3 Hart, Mt W Australia
119 R9 Hartney Manitoba
29 M10 Hartola Finland
13 G4 Harton England
106 E2 Hartsel Colorado
111 K7 Hartselle Alabama
37 J6 Härtsfeld mts W Germany
107 P7 Hartshorne Oklahoma
138 C4 Harts I S Australia
140 C6 Harts Range N Terr Aust
112 G3 Hartsville S Carolina
110 K5 Hartsville Tennessee
89 D6 Hartswater S Africa
80 C6 Hartuv Israel
110 D4 Hartville Missouri
98 B7 Hartville Wyoming
112 E3 Hartwell Georgia
112 D3 Hartwell Res S Carolina
120 H3 Harty Ontario
89 D6 Hartz R S Africa
84 F4 Harūj al Aswad, Al Libya
58 B2 Har Us Nuur L Mongolia
80 C7 Haruvit Israel
102 H7 Harvard California
100 J3 Harvard Idaho
99 S7 Harvard Illinois
98 H9 Harvard Nebraska
116 O6 Harvard Gl Alaska
106 D3 Harvard, Mt Colorado
143 F7 Harvest, Mt W Australia
99 T8 Harvey Illinois
99 O8 Harvey Iowa
98 F2 Harvey N Dakota
111 J13 Harvey New Orleans
143 B10 Harvey W Australia
102 C1 Harvey Mt California
122 F8 Harvey Stn New Brunswick
107 P3 Harveyville Kansas
110 F5 Harviell Missouri
9 E4 Harwell England
9 H4 Harwich England
109 K6 Harwood Texas
36 E4 Harxheim W Germany
74 F4 Haryana prov India
80 E8 Har Yonatan Israel
33 N9 Harz mts Germany
33 O9 Harzegerode E Germany
79 F8 Hāsā Jordan
72 F4 Hasā, Al reg Saudi Arabia
74 H9 Hasanparti India
80 E7 Hasasa R Jordan
79 F5 Hâsbaiya Lebanon
32 G8 Hasbergen W Germany
36 B5 Hasborn-Dautweiler W Germany
32 G7 Hase R W Germany
78 H3 Haseke, El Syria
37 K2 Hasel R E Germany
32 L5 Haseldorf W Germany
32 F7 Haselünne W Germany
80 D4 Hashimiye Jordan
61 J11 Hashimoto Japan
78 M2 Hashtpar Iran
77 A1 Hashtrūd Iran
71 B3 Hasil Indonesia
26 H8 Håsjö Sweden
111 D7 Haskell Arkansas
107 P6 Haskell Oklahoma
108 H2 Haskell Texas
38 K4 Haslach Austria
36 E7 Haslach W Germany
27 G16 Hasle Denmark
109 M8 Haslet Texas
28 H6 Haslev Denmark
13 F6 Haslingden England
41 H4 Hasli Tal Switzerland
28 E4 Haslund Denmark
28 E5 Hasmark Denmark
22 E3 Hasnon France
80 D3 Ha Solelim Israel
18 E9 Hasparren France
32 F10 Haspe W Germany
22 E3 Haspres France
76 C4 Hassan India
103 M8 Hassayampa R Arizona
37 K3 Hassberge mts W Germany
26 J9 Hassela Sweden
33 N9 Hasselfelde E Germany
115 K2 Hassel Sd N W Terr
22 J2 Hasselt Belgium
25 F3 Hasselt Netherlands
28 F4 Hassensør C Denmark
33 N9 Hasserode E Germany
37 K3 Hassfurt W Germany
85 E2 Hassi-Bou-Zid Algeria
85 E3 Hassi Chebaba Algeria
28 A3 Hassing Denmark
79 H3 Hass, Jebel el mts Syria
37 L3 Hasslach W Germany
33 T6 Hassleben E Germany
37 K1 Hassleben Erfurt E Germany
27 G15 Hässleholm Sweden
27 G13 Hasslerör Sweden
36 E5 Hassloch W Germany
22 H3 Hastière-Lavaux Belgium
127 P6 Hastings Barbados
9 G6 Hastings England
113 F8 Hastings Florida
99 L9 Hastings Iowa
94 B4 Hastings Michigan
99 O5 Hastings Minnesota
98 H9 Hastings Nebraska
145 F3 Hastings New Zealand
107 M7 Hastings Oklahoma
121 N8 Hastings Ontario
94 J6 Hastings Pennsylvania
139 H9 Hastings Tasmania
139 L4 Hastings R New S Wales
139 K4 Hastings Ra mts New S Wales
28 E6 Håstrup Denmark
27 G15 Hästveda Sweden
106 H3 Hasty Colorado
26 M1 Hasvik Norway
106 G3 Haswell Colorado
58 E3 Hatanbulag Mongolia
95 M6 Hatboro Pennsylvania
106 C9 Hatch New Mexico
103 M4 Hatch Utah
140 D5 Hatches Cr N Terr Aust
126 F2 Hatchet Bay Eleuthera Bahamas
110 G6 Hatchie R Tennessee
98 B7 Hat Cr Wyoming
100 D9 Hat Creek California
48 H5 Haţeg Romania
67 H4 Haterumashima Japan
111 B7 Hatfield Arkansas
9 F4 Hatfield Herts England
98 K6 Hatfield Minnesota
139 G5 Hatfield New S Wales
119 M7 Hatfield Sask
9 G4 Hatfield Peverel England
101 T3 Hathaway Montana
8 B6 Hatherleigh England
138 F6 Hatherleigh S Australia
9 E1 Hathersage England
74 H5 Hathras India
68 G7 Ha Tien Vietnam
80 G3 Hatim Jordan
68 G3 Ha Tinh Vietnam
127 K5 Hato Mayor Dominican Rep
56 C3 Hatskiy U.S.S.R.
60 F11 Hatsukaichi Japan
138 F5 Hattah Victoria
70 F2 Hattan, Mt Sabah
25 F4 Hattem Netherlands
36 D6 Hatten France
112 M2 Hatteras N Carolina
112 M2 Hatteras Inlet N Carolina
36 E3 Hattersheim W Germany
28 O9 Hattervig Faeroes
26 G6 Hattfjelldal Norway
111 G10 Hattiesburg Mississippi
36 B6 Hattigny France
28 D5 Hatting Denmark
32 F10 Hattingen W Germany
20 K3 Hatton France
98 J2 Hatton N Dakota
118 H8 Hatton Sask
100 G3 Hatton Washington
68 C6 Hattras Passage Burma
40 F1 Hattstatt France
29 L10 Hattula Finland
126 F4 Hatuey Cuba
145 F4 Hatuma New Zealand
48 F3 Hatvan Hungary
38 O8 Hatzendorf Austria
36 C3 Hatzenport W Germany
36 F2 Hatzfeld W Germany
68 J6 Hau Bon Vietnam
22 D2 Haubourdin France
86 A2 Haud reg Ethiopia
80 G4 Haufa Jordan
28 C4 Hauge Denmark
27 C10 Hauge Norway
99 P4 Haugen Wisconsin
27 A12 Haugesund Norway
111 C9 Haughton Louisiana
31 J7 Haugsdorf Austria
29 L10 Hauho Finland
145 E3 Hauhungaroa Ra New Zealand
27 B12 Haukeliseter Norway
29 L6 Haukipudas Finland
29 N9 Haukivesi L Finland
29 N9 Haukivuori Finland
145 F3 Haumoana New Zealand
36 H2 Haune R W Germany
36 H2 Hauneck W Germany
36 H2 Haunetal Hessen W Germany
37 K7 Haunstetten W Germany
144 C5 Haupiri, L New Zealand
37 O5 Hauptenberg mt W Germany
145 E2 Hauraki Gulf New Zealand
144 A6 Hauroko, L New Zealand
27 A11 Haus Norway
36 E7 Hausach W Germany
32 J8 Hausberge W Germany
101 O3 Hauser L. Dam Montana
38 H5 Hausruck mts Austria
Haussez Iles d' see Mercury Is
41 K4 Hausstock mt Switzerland
22 B3 Haut Banc, Pte du France
40 B2 Haut du Sec mt France
18 L10 Haute-Corse dep Corsica
18 F7 Hautefort France
18 F9 Haute-Garonne dep France
18 H7 Haute-Loire dep France
40 E6 Hauteluce France
19 J4 Haute-Marne dep France
121 Q4 Haute Mauricie, Parc de Quebec
122 D4 Hauterive Quebec
19 Q15 Hautes Alpes dep France
19 J5 Haute-Saône dep France
40 D6 Haute-Savoie dep France
22 L2 Hautes Fagnes Belgium
22 H4 Hautes Rivières France
21 D8 Hauteurs de Gâtine hills France
21 H9 Haute-Vienne dep France
36 B5 Haut-Hombourg France
95 T2 Haut, I. au Maine
22 F3 Hautmont France
19 K5 Haut-Rhin dep France
85 D2 Hauts Plateaux Morocco/Algeria
20 B4 Hautteville-sur-Mer France
86 E5 Haut-Zaïre prov Zaire
135 Q2 Hauula Hawaiian Is
145 E4 Hauwai New Zealand
110 C6 Havana Arkansas
Havana Cuba see Habana
111 M11 Havana Florida
99 R9 Havana Illinois
107 P4 Havana Kansas
98 J4 Havana N Dakota
9 F6 Havant England
103 K7 Havasu L Cal/Ariz
28 C3 Havbro Denmark
28 J5 Havdrup Denmark
33 R6 Havel E Germany
22 J3 Havelange Belgium
33 Q7 Havelberg E Germany
33 R7 Havelland reg E Germany
33 R7 Havelland Grosse Haupt-kanal E Germany
112 L3 Havelock N Carolina
98 D3 Havelock N Dakota
122 G8 Havelock New Brunswick
145 D4 Havelock New Zealand
121 N8 Havelock Ontario
140 C2 Havelock Falls N Terr Aust
68 A7 Havelock I Andaman Is
145 F3 Havelock North New Zealand
107 N4 Haven Kansas
107 O2 Havensville Kansas
8 B4 Haverfordwest Wales
9 G3 Haverhill England
95 Q4 Haverhill Massachusetts
95 Q3 Haverhill New Hampshire
76 B3 Haveri India
26 H9 Haverö Sweden
22 J3 Haversin Belgium
28 D3 Haverslev Nordjylland Denmark
95 N5 Haverstraw New York
107 L4 Haviland Kansas
94 C5 Haviland Ohio
120 F6 Haviland Bay Ontario

48 K2 Havirna Romania
31 J6 Havlíčkův Brod Czechoslovakia
28 D6 Havnbjerg Denmark
28 E3 Havndal Denmark
28 B6 Havneby Denmark
28 G5 Havnsø Denmark
28 B4 Havnstrup Denmark
26 O1 Havoysund Norway
47 J5 Havran Turkey
22 G3 Havre Belgium
114 J8 Havre Montana
123 L6 Havre Aubert Madeleine Is, Quebec
28 G6 Havrebjerg Denmark
123 L8 Havre Boucher Nova Scotia
95 L7 Havre de Grace Maryland
20 F3 Havre, Le France
115 N7 Havre-St-Pierre Quebec
137 Q8 Havre Trench sea feature Pacific Oc
28 A5 Havrvig Denmark
26 H7 Havsnäs Sweden
78 E1 Havza Turkey
135 U5 Hawaii isld Hawaiian Is
135 Hawaiian Is Pacific Oc
86 B3 Hawal R Nigeria
98 K6 Hawarden Iowa
144 D5 Hawarden New Zealand
118 L7 Hawarden Sask
8 C1 Hawarden Wales
138 F6 Hawdon, L S Australia
144 E6 Hawea Flat New Zealand
145 E3 Hawera New Zealand
102 G7 Hawes California
110 K4 Hawesville Kentucky
13 F5 Hawes Water England
135 U4 Hawi Hawaiian Is
13 F3 Hawick Scotland
144 B6 Hawkdun Range New Zealand
145 F3 Hawke Bay New Zealand
139 L4 Hawke, C New S Wales
138 E4 Hawker S Australia
138 F3 Hawker Gate New S Wales
145 F3 Hawke's Bay stat area New Zealand
141 F1 Hawkesbury I Queensland
140 C1 Hawkesbury Pt N Terr Aust
139 K5 Hawkesbury R New S Wales
146 F9 Hawkes, Mt Antarctica
9 G5 Hawkhurst England
103 L4 Hawkins Pk Utah
112 D5 Hawkinsville Georgia
120 F4 Hawk Junct Ontario
118 J1 Hawk Lake Ontario
110 E3 Hawk Point Missouri
94 D1 Hawks Michigan
126 F2 Hawksbill Cay isld Bahamas
13 E5 Hawkshead England
126 G2 Hawks Nest Pt Cat I Bahamas
98 B8 Hawk Springs Wyoming
141 K7 Hawkwood Queensland
106 G4 Hawley Colorado
98 K3 Hawley Minnesota
95 M5 Hawley Pennsylvania
108 H3 Hawley Texas
68 D2 Hawng Luk Burma
13 G6 Haworth England
107 Q8 Haworth Oklahoma
112 H2 Haw R N Carolina
78 H5 Hawran, Wadi Iraq
78 L5 Hawr as S'adiyah L Iraq
13 H5 Hawsker England
113 E8 Hawthorn Florida
102 F3 Hawthorne Nevada
99 P3 Hawthorne Wisconsin
80 D5 Hawwara Jordan
65 F2 Haxat China
65 B2 Haxat Hudag China
101 T2 Haxby Montana
98 D9 Haxtun Colorado
139 G5 Hay New S Wales
100 H3 Hay Washington
117 N6 Hay R Br Columbia
99 P4 Hay R Wisconsin
61 P6 Hayachine-san mt Japan
60 P3 Hayakita Japan
19 K3 Hayange France
60 E12 Hayasui-seto str Japan
101 T9 Haybro Colorado
103 O8 Hayden Arizona
101 S9 Hayden Colorado
100 J2 Hayden L Idaho
141 F4 Haydon Queensland
13 F4 Haydon Br England
20 B3 Haye-du-Puits, la France
20 H3 Haye, la France
20 C4 Haye-Pesnel, la France
111 D11 Hayes Louisiana
98 E5 Hayes S Dakota
115 K6 Hayes R Manitoba
20 G4 Haye St. Sylvestre, la France
98 E9 Hayes Center Nebraska
116 L6 Hayes Glaciers Alaska
115 N2 Hayes Halvø pen Greenland
68 C7 Hayes I Burma
116 O5 Hayes, Mt Alaska
112 D2 Hayesville N Carolina
13 G6 Hayfield England
99 O6 Hayfield Minnesota
103 J8 Hayfield Res Carolina
102 A1 Hayfork California
13 F5 Haygarth England
36 G7 Hayingen W Germany
117 O6 Hay L Alberta
118 D5 Hay Lakes Alberta
8 A7 Hayle England
9 F6 Hayling England
113 E7 Haylow Georgia
141 J5 Hayman I Queensland
94 K8 Haymarket Virginia
140 C6 Hay, Mt N Terr Aust
109 O3 Haynesville Louisiana
95 T8 Haynesville Maine
111 K9 Hayneville Alabama
20 H2 Hayons, les France
8 C3 Hay-on-Wye England
141 J5 Hay Point Queensland
140 D6 Hay R N Terr Aust
47 J3 Hayrabolu Turkey
47 J3 Hayrabolu R Turkey
114 H5 Hay River N W Terr
118 F8 Hays Alberta
107 L3 Hays Kansas
101 R1 Hays Montana
98 D7 Hay Springs Nebraska
100 K8 Haystack Mt Nevada
103 L2 Haystack Pk Utah
118 G6 Hayter Alberta
110 G5 Hayti Missouri
98 J5 Hayti S Dakota
13 H6 Hayton England
102 B4 Hayward California
99 N6 Hayward Minnesota
107 N5 Hayward Oklahoma
99 P4 Hayward Wisconsin
140 B2 Hayward, Mt N Terr Aust
9 F6 Haywards Heath England
119 T9 Haywood Manitoba
80 E2 Hazan Israel
57 F6 Hazara Afghanistan
77 J3 Hazarajat reg Afghanistan
94 D9 Hazard Kentucky
95 P4 Hazardville Connecticut
75 L7 Hazaribagh India
77 F1 Hazar Masjed, Kūh-e mts Iran
22 D2 Hazebrouck France
98 K1 Hazel Minnesota
98 J5 Hazel S Dakota
119 V9 Hazelridge Manitoba
117 K8 Hazelton Br Col
107 M4 Hazelton Kansas
98 F3 Hazelton N Dakota
110 E7 Hazen Arkansas
98 E2 Hazen N Dakota
102 E2 Hazen Nevada
116 E6 Hazen B Alaska
115 N1 Hazen, L N W Terr
118 K9 Hazenmore Sask
114 H2 Hazen Str N W Terr
80 B8 Hazerim Israel
25 C4 Hazerswoude Netherlands
79 F8 Hazeva Israel
112 E2 Hazewood N Carolina
112 E6 Hazlehurst Georgia
111 F10 Hazlehurst Mississippi
95 M6 Hazleton Pennsylvania
142 G5 Hazlett, L W Australia
37 N3 Hazlov Czechoslovakia
80 F2 Hazor Israel
80 F3 HaZore'im Israel
80 C7 He Israel
9 G2 Heacham England
9 G5 Headcorn England
14 B3 Headford Irish Rep
140 E5 Headingly Queensland
111 L10 Headland Alabama
144 B6 Headlong Pk New Zealand
138 B4 Head of Bight B S Australia
100 K3 Headquarters Idaho
83 M9 Headridge Hill Christmas I Indian Oc
100 A7 Heads, The C Oregon
99 R4 Heafford Junct Wisconsin
102 B3 Healdsburg California
109 K1 Healdton Oklahoma
139 H7 Healesville Victoria
116 N5 Healy Alaska
107 K3 Healy Kansas
116 P4 Healy R Alaska
116 P5 Healy L Alaska
119 Q3 Heaman Manitoba
9 E1 Heanor England
90 M16 Heard I Southern Oc
119 M8 Hearne Sask
109 L5 Hearne Texas
117 R4 Hearne L N W Terr
102 A2 Hearst California
115 L8 Hearst Ontario
146 E13 Hearst I Antarctica
98 D3 Heart R N Dakota
118 F3 Heart L Alberta
101 P5 Heart L Wyoming
118 A3 Heart R Alberta
123 T6 Heart's Content Nfld
123 T6 Heart's Delight Nfld
98 H9 Heartwell Nebraska
128 E6 Heath R Bolivia/Peru
139 G6 Heathcote Victoria
6 L2 Heather oil rig North Sea
123 O5 Heatherton Nfld
9 G6 Heathfield England
123 L4 Heath Pt Anticosti I, Quebec
9 F5 Heathrow Airport England
112 G3 Heath Springs S Carolina
122 F6 Heath Steel Mines New Brunswick
95 L9 Heathsville Virginia
107 Q7 Heavener Oklahoma
109 J8 Hebbronville Texas
13 F6 Hebden Br England
65 C5 Hebei prov China
103 O7 Heber Arizona
101 O9 Heber Utah
32 L6 Heber W Germany
110 D6 Heber Springs Arkansas
121 P3 Hébert, L Quebec
20 C3 Hébert, Pt France
121 T4 Hébertville Station Quebec
101 O5 Hebgen L Montana
65 C7 Hebi China
100 B4 Hebo Oregon
101 T9 Hebron Colorado
99 S7 Hebron Illinois
99 T8 Hebron Indiana
80 D7 Hebron Jordan
115 N6 Hebron Labrador
98 E3 Hebron N Dakota
98 J9 Hebron Nebraska
122 F10 Hebron Nova Scotia
94 E7 Hebron Ohio
27 J12 Heby Sweden
114 F7 Hecate Str Br Columbia
100 A5 Heceta Head Oregon
117 G8 Heceta I Alaska
67 C4 Hechi China
36 F7 Hechingen W Germany
22 J1 Hechtel Belgium
32 K5 Hechthausen W Germany
36 E4 Hechtsheim W Germany
67 B1 Hechuan China
33 T7 Heckelberg E Germany
9 F2 Heckington England
33 P9 Hecklingen E Germany
98 H4 Hecla S Dakota
114 H2 Hecla & Griper B N W Terr
119 V7 Hecla I Manitoba
119 V7 Hecla Prov. Park Manitoba
122 F9 Hectanooga Nova Scotia
102 H7 Hector California
99 M5 Hector Minnesota
144 C4 Hector New Zealand
145 E4 Hector mt New Zealand
117 P10 Hector, Mt Alberta
127 M2 Hector's River Jamaica
27 H12 Hed Sweden
61 M11 Heda Japan
27 D11 Hedal Norway
20 K1 Hedauville France
26 K6 Hedberg Sweden
27 D12 Heddal Norway
36 F4 Heddesheim W Germany
13 G3 Heddon on-the-Wall England
20 B5 Hédé France
26 G9 Hede Sweden
25 D5 Hedel Netherlands
27 H11 Hedemora Sweden
32 L10 Hedemunden W Germany
28 E6 Heden Denmark
26 M6 Heden Sweden
26 N5 Hedenäset Sweden
28 D5 Hedensted Denmark
33 O9 Hedersleben E Germany
27 J11 Hedesunda Sweden
26 G9 Hedeviken Sweden
144 B7 Hedgehope New Zealand
101 Q3 Hedgesville Montana
94 J7 Hedgesville W Virginia
67 C6 Hedi Shuiku res China
117 N11 Hedley Br Columbia
27 E11 Hedmark Norway
27 E10 Hedmark county Norway
61 Q12 Hedo Okinawa
13 H6 Hedon England
83 L11 Hedo Oya R Sri Lanka
61 Q12 Hedo-zaki C Okinawa
99 O8 Hedrick Iowa
28 A4 Hee Denmark
32 F7 Heede W Germany
33 T7 Heegermühle E Germany
32 F8 Heek W Germany
25 C4 Heemstede Netherlands
32 J8 Heepen W Germany
22 H3 Heer Belgium
25 E7 Heer Netherlands
25 F4 Heerde Netherlands
25 E3 Heerenveen Netherlands
25 C3 Heerhugo-waard Netherlands
25 E7 Heerlen Netherlands
25 E5 Heesch Netherlands
25 E6 Heeze Netherlands
67 F1 Hefei China
67 C2 Hefeng China
117 N10 Heffley Br Columbia
111 L8 Heflin Alabama
59 K2 Hegang China
65 H1 Hegang China
61 K8 Hegura-jima isld Japan
88 E5 Hehe Tanzania
26 D10 Heidal Norway
80 F8 Heidan R Jordan
32 K4 Heide W Germany
37 L5 Heideck W Germany
111 H10 Heidelberg Mississippi
87 E11 Heidelberg S Africa
36 F5 Heidelberg W Germany
110 N4 Heidelburg Kentucky
36 F5 Heidelsheim W Germany
37 M4 Heide Naab R W Germany
37 J6 Heidenheim W Germany
36 D3 Heidenrod W Germany
94 B2 Heights, The Michigan
60 F12 Heigun-tō isld Japan
Heihe see Aihui
59 J1 Hei-ho China
25 E6 Heijthuizsen Netherlands
87 E11 Heilbron S Africa
36 G5 Heilbronn W Germany
38 G7 Heiligenblut Austria
33 P4 Heiligendamm E Germany
30 F1 Heiligenhafen W Germany
32 M10 Heiligenstadt E Germany
37 L4 Heiligenstadt W Germany
65 D7 Heilin China
59 H1 Heilongjiang prov China
59 J1 Heilong Jiang R China
37 K5 Heilsbronn W Germany
Heilungkiang prov see Heilongjiang
36 B2 Heimbach W Germany
36 G4 Heimbuchenthal W Germany
33 N9 Heimburg E Germany
98 G2 Heimdal N Dakota
26 D8 Heimdal Norway
146 C10 Heimefrontfjella ra Antarctica
36 F6 Heimsheim W Germany
29 O9 Heinävesi Finland
36 H1 Heinebach W Germany
22 L3 Heinerscheid Luxembourg
37 L3 Heinersdorf E Germany
36 C5 Heinitz W Germany
25 F4 Heino Netherlands
29 M10 Heinola Finland
33 P8 Heinrichsburg E Germany
25 F6 Heinsberg W Germany
118 G5 Heinsburg Alberta
33 S9 Heinsdorf E Germany
68 C5 Heinz B Burma
68 C5 Heinze I Burma
65 E4 Heishan China
65 C3 Heishantou China
67 C2 Heishui China
118 E6 Heisler Alberta
22 E1 Heist Belgium
22 H1 Heist-op-den-Berg Belgium
80 G3 Heit Syria
80 G2 Heital Syria
79 D8 Heitân, G mt Egypt
40 G2 Heitersheim W Germany
65 F2 Heiyupao China
84 H4 Heiz, El Egypt
65 A5 Hejialiang China
67 B2 Hejiang China
67 C6 Hejiang China
67 D5 He Jiang R China
67 D4 Hejie China
65 A7 Hejin China
28 D6 Hejls Denmark
28 C6 Hejlsminde Denmark
28 B5 Hejnsvig Denmark
28 D6 Hejsager Denmark
145 F3 Hekerangi Pt New Zealand
115 S5 Hekla vol Iceland
Hekou see Yanshan
65 B4 Hekou China
67 D5 Hekou Guangdong China
67 A5 Hekou Yunnan China
31 L1 Hel Poland
80 E2 Hela Israel
26 F9 Helagsfjället mt Sweden
58 E4 Helan Shan mt ra China
37 K1 Helbe R E Germany
28 E3 Helberskov Denmark
33 O9 Helbra E Germany
22 J1 Helchteren Belgium
37 K3 Heldburg E Germany
36 F3 Heldenbergen W Germany
127 P3 Helden's Pt St Kitts W I
33 O10 Heldrungen E Germany
112 D3 Helen Georgia
111 K8 Helena Alabama
111 F7 Helena Arkansas
100 B9 Helena California
112 E5 Helena Georgia
114 H8 Helena Montana
107 M5 Helena Oklahoma
102 G7 Helendale California
118 J5 Helénè L Sask
146 D3 Helen Gl Antarctica
142 E6 Helen Hill W Australia
71 C1 Helen I Pacific Oc
119 P1 Helen L Ontario
141 F5 Helen, Mt Queensland
15 D4 Helensburgh Scotland
140 C4 Helen Springs N Terr Aust
145 E2 Helensville New Zealand
33 P10 Helfta E Germany
26 F6 Helgeland reg Norway
27 D12 Helgen Norway
32 G4 Helgoland isld W Germany
32 H4 Helgoländer Bucht W Germany
26 K1 Helgöy Norway
65 H1 Heli China
79 B8 Heliopolis Egypt
26 E8 Hell Norway
33 O7 Hellberg hills E Germany
28 K4 Hellebæk Denmark
77 B5 Helleh R Iran
26 J4 Hellemobotn Norway
25 F4 Hellendoorn Netherlands
36 B3 Hellenthal W Germany
28 K5 Hellerup Denmark
28 J6 Hellested Denmark
26 B9 Hellesylt Norway
28 E2 Hellevad Nordjylland Denmark
28 C6 Hellevad Sønderjylland Denmark
26 L2 Helligskogen Norway
26 G4 Helligvoer isld Norway
17 F6 Hellin Spain
Hell's Canyon see Snake River Canyon
127 L3 Hellshire Hills Jamaica
28 E2 Hellum Denmark
87 H10 Hell-Ville Madagascar
32 K6 Hellwege W Germany
102 D5 Helm California
72 J2 Helmand R Afghanistan
32 K9 Helmarshausen W Germany
37 M3 Helmbrechts W Germany
33 N10 Helme R E Germany
87 C11 Helmeringhausen Namibia
37 J2 Helmershausen E Germany
9 H3 Helmingham England
25 E6 Helmond Netherlands
32 J4 Helmsand sandbank W Germany
15 E2 Helmsdale Scotland
15 E2 Helmsdale R Scotland
13 G5 Helmsley England
36 F5 Helmstadt W Germany
33 O8 Helmstedt W Germany
101 N3 Helmville Montana
28 D6 Helnæs Denmark
28 E6 Helnæs Bugt B Denmark
26 P1 Helnes Norway
59 J3 Helong China
65 F2 Helong China
109 J6 Helotes Texas
103 O2 Helper Utah
33 T6 Helpter Berge peak E Germany
32 L10 Helsa-Wickenrode W Germany
29 K4 Helsingborg Sweden
28 J4 Helsinge Denmark
Helsingfors see Helsinki
28 K4 Helsingør Denmark
29 L11 Helsinki Finland
9 G6 Helston England
32 L7 Helstorf W Germany
28 O9 Heltnin Faeroes
110 K3 Heltonville Indiana
130 H5 Helvécia Brazil
14 D4 Helvick Hd Irish Rep
84 J4 Helwan Egypt
28 D4 Hem Vejle Denmark
28 B3 Hem Viborg Denmark
118 F7 Hemaruka Alberta
37 M5 Hemau W Germany
32 E9 Hemden W Germany
9 F4 Hemel Hempstead England
25 D3 Hemelum Netherlands
32 G10 Hemer W Germany
102 H8 Hemet California
36 B6 Héming France
98 C7 Hemingford Nebraska
119 Q4 Heming Lake Manitoba
112 H4 Hemingway S Carolina
141 L1 Hemmant dist Brisbane, Qnsld
32 J4 Hemme W Germany
28 F3 Hemmed Denmark
32 L8 Hemmendorf W Germany
28 A5 Hemmet Denmark
32 L8 Hemmingen W Germany
121 R7 Hemmingford Quebec
32 K5 Hemmoor W Germany
26 G5 Hemnesberget Norway
111 C10 Hemphill Texas
95 O6 Hempstead Long I, N Y
109 L5 Hempstead Texas
9 H2 Hemsby England
27 K14 Hemse isld Gotland Sweden
27 C11 Hemsedal Norway
27 C11 Hemsil R Norway
27 G15 Hemsjö Sweden
32 L6 Hemslingen W Germany
26 K9 Hemsö Sweden
13 G6 Hemsworth England
65 B7 Henan prov China
145 E1 Hen and Chicken Is New Zealand
16 E4 Henares R Spain
61 N5 Henashi-zaki C Japan
140 C6 Henbury N Terr Aust
18 D9 Hendaye France
22 D3 Hendecourt-lès Cagnicourt France
47 L4 Hendek Turkey
112 J1 Henderson N Carolina
103 K5 Henderson Nevada
95 L3 Henderson New York
110 H6 Henderson Tennessee
109 N3 Henderson Texas
94 E8 Henderson W Virginia
135 O11 Henderson I Pacific Oc
112 E2 Hendersonville N Carolina
77 A4 Hendījān Iran
9 F4 Hendon England
141 K8 Hendon Queensland
119 O6 Hendon Sask
77 C6 Hendorābī isld Iran
48 J4 Hendorf Romania
141 K1 Hendra dist Brisbane, Qnsld
98 K5 Hendricks Minnesota
94 H7 Hendricks W Virginia
129 G3 Hendrik Top mt Suriname
89 D8 Hendrik Verwoerd Dam S Africa
8 B4 Hendy Wales
101 O8 Henefer Utah
65 H2 Hengdaohezi China
65 G3 Hengdaozi China
67 D3 Hengdong China
58 C6 Hengduan Shan mts China
25 G4 Hengelo Netherlands
37 P6 Hengersberg W Germany
67 F2 Hengfeng China
67 A2 Heng Jiang R China
67 D2 Henglongqiao China
67 D3 Hengnan China
67 D3 Hengshan China
67 D3 Heng Shan mt China
58 G4 Hengshui China
37 J5 Hengstfeld W Germany
67 C5 Heng Xian China
69 A9 Henhoaha Nicobar Is
22 D3 Henin Lietard France
144 C6 Henley New Zealand
123 R2 Henley Hbr Labrador
9 E3 Henley in Arden England
9 F4 Henley-on-Thames England
100 C10 Henleyville California
9 F3 Henlow England
109 J5 Henly Texas
27 E12 Henmes Norway
61 P13 Henna Okinawa
26 H9 Hennan Sweden
28 A5 Henne Denmark
37 J3 Henneberg E Germany
18 C5 Hennebont France
36 C2 Hennef W Germany
37 K5 Hennenbach W Germany
99 R8 Hennepin Illinois
20 F3 Hennequeville France
107 N5 Hennessey Oklahoma
33 S8 Hennickendorf E Germany
33 S7 Hennigsdorf E Germany
95 Q3 Henniker New Hampshire
110 J1 Henning Illinois
99 L3 Henning Minnesota
110 G6 Henning Tennessee
26 G3 Henningsvaer Norway
32 K4 Hennstedt W Germany
20 K3 Hénonville France
77 D6 Henqam isld Iran
119 M5 Henribourg Sask
22 K2 Henri-Chapelle Belgium
109 J2 Henrietta Texas
115 L6 Henrietta Maria, C Ontario
103 N4 Henrieville Utah
117 L7 Henri, Mt Br Col
Henrique de Carvalho see Suarimo
101 O7 Henry Idaho
99 R8 Henry Illinois
95 M10 Henry, C Virginia
146 E15 Henryk Arckowski Poland
115 N4 Henry Kater Pen N W Terr
111 K8 Henry L Alabama
68 A6 Henry Lawrence I Andaman Is
100 K1 Henry, Mt Montana
103 O4 Henry Mts Utah
142 B6 Henry, R W Australia
101 O5 Henrys Fork R Idaho
110 L3 Henryville Indiana
120 J9 Hensall Ontario
110 H4 Henshaw Kentucky
102 H8 Henshaw, L California
12 E5 Hensingham England
142 G3 Hensman, Mt W Australia
32 L5 Henstedt-Ulzburg W Germany
8 D6 Henstridge England
58 E2 Hentiy Mongolia
58 E2 Hentiyn Nuruu mt Mongolia
139 H6 Henty New S Wales
68 B4 Henzada Burma
61 P13 Henza-jima isld Okinawa
118 L6 Hepburn Sask
67 E1 Hepeng China
112 E4 Hephzibah Georgia
Heping see Yanhe
67 E4 Heping China
Hepo see Jiexi
36 B2 Heppendorf W Germany
36 F4 Heppenheim W Germany
100 F4 Heppner Oregon
80 F2 Heptapegon Israel
68 J2 Hepu China
120 J8 Hepworth Ontario
65 B5 Hequ China
27 E11 Heradsbygd Norway
141 J3 Herald Cays islds Gt Barrier Reef Aust
72 J2 Herat Afghanistan
18 H9 Hérault R France
19 O14 Herbasse R France
21 H6 Herbault France
32 F10 Herbede W Germany
36 D3 Herberge, K mt W Germany
32 G9 Herbern W Germany
144 C6 Herbert New Zealand
114 J7 Herbert Sask
140 E5 Herbert R N Terr Aust
141 H4 Herbert R Queensland
68 A7 Herbertabad Andaman Is
140 E6 Herbert Downs Queensland
140 B4 Herbert, Mt N Terr Aust
142 F3 Herbert, Mt W Australia
141 H3 Herberton Queensland
145 F4 Herbertville New Zealand
22 K2 Herbesthal Belgium
22 J4 Herbeumont Belgium
21 A7 Herbignac France
36 C5 Herbitzheim France
119 S4 Herb L Manitoba
36 D7 Herbolzheim W Germany
36 E2 Herborn W Germany
36 G2 Herbstein W Germany
31 L5 Herby Poland
42 J6 Herceg Novi Yugoslavia
42 H5 Hercegovina reg Yugoslavia
115 K6 Herchmer Manitoba
36 H4 Herchsheim W Germany
107 O5 Herd Oklahoma
32 F10 Herdecke W Germany
125 M4 Heredía Costa Rica
98 B9 Hereford Colorado
8 D3 Hereford England
108 E1 Hereford Texas
Hereford co see Hereford and Worcester co
8 D3 Hereford and Worcester co England
145 D1 Herekino New Zealand
16 E5 Herencia Spain
40 F5 Herens, Val. d' Switzerland
22 H1 Herentals Belgium
144 B5 Heretaniwha Pt New Zealand
28 J6 Herfølge Denmark
32 J8 Herford W Germany
22 L2 Hergenrath Belgium
19 K5 Hericourt France
33 N10 Heringen E Germany
107 O3 Herington Kansas
22 G2 Herinnes Belgium
144 B6 Heriot New Zealand
13 F2 Heriot Scotland
117 L10 Heriot Bay Br Col
41 K3 Herisau Switzerland
146 F10 Heritage Rge Antarctica
22 J2 Herk-de-Stad Belgium
95 N3 Herkimer New York
121 Q9 Herkimer New York
146 J11 Herlacher, C Antarctica
37 N2 Herlasgrün E Germany
58 F2 Herlen Gol R Mongolia
58 G2 Herlen He R China
37 J1 Herleshausen W Germany
28 K5 Herlev Denmark
28 H6 Herlufmagle Denmark
9 H6 Herm isld Channel Is
38 H8 Hermagor Austria
99 S3 Herman Michigan
98 K4 Herman Minnesota
98 K8 Herman Nebraska
71 D3 Hermana Mayor isld Philippines
124 J4 Hermanas Mexico
106 C10 Hermanas New Mexico
110 E3 Hermann Missouri
32 M7 Hermannsberg W Germany
140 C6 Hermannsburg N Terr Aust
37 P4 Heřmanova Hut' Czechoslovakia
99 T4 Hermansville Michigan
89 A10 Hermanus S Africa
111 F10 Hermanville Mississippi
79 G4 Hermel, El Lebanon
20 K3 Hermes France
36 B4 Hermeskeil W Germany
22 H3 Hermeton-sur-Meuse Belgium
139 H4 Hermidale New S Wales
22 E3 Hermies France
100 F4 Hermiston Oregon
111 D8 Hermitage Arkansas
144 C5 Hermitage New Zealand
123 R6 Hermitage Nfld
123 Q3 Hermitage B Nfld
142 B5 Hermite I W Australia
133 D9 Hermite, Is Chile
140 B2 Hermit Hill N Terr Aust
136 K2 Hermit Is Bismarck Arch
103 M5 Hermits Rest Arizona
108 G3 Hermleigh Texas
Hermōn, Mt see Sheikh, J. esh
22 F5 Hermonville France
98 C6 Hermosa S Dakota
124 D3 Hermosillo Mexico
Hermsdorf see Ottendorf-Okrilla
130 C9 Hernandarias Paraguay
113 E9 Hernando Florida
102 E5 Herndon California
99 M8 Herndon Iowa
107 K2 Herndon Kansas
110 J5 Herndon Kentucky
95 L6 Herndon Pennsylvania
94 K8 Herndon Virginia
94 F9 Herndon W Virginia
32 F9 Herne W Germany
9 H5 Herne Bay England
28 B4 Herning Denmark
124 C2 Heroica Caborca Mexico
37 L4 Heroldsberg W Germany
22 J2 Héron Belgium
100 K1 Heron Montana
120 D4 Heron Bay Ontario
25 F6 Herongen W Germany
141 K6 Heron I Gt Barrier Reef Aust
99 L6 Heron L Minnesota
144 C5 Heron, L New Zealand
26 A9 Heroy Norway
42 F3 Herpelje Kozina Yugoslavia
130 B10 Herradura Argentina
16 D5 Herrara del Duque Spain
98 F4 Herreid S Dakota
36 F6 Herrenberg W Germany
36 E6 Herrenwies W Germany
133 E3 Herrera Argentina
17 G3 Herrera mt Spain
16 C5 Herrera de Alcántara Spain
17 G3 Herrera de los Navarros Spain
124 G5 Herreras Mexico
28 F6 Herrested Denmark
98 G6 Herrick S Dakota
139 J8 Herrick Tasmania
110 G4 Herrin Illinois
123 S4 Herring Neck Nfld
94 C9 Herrington L Kentucky
119 Q2 Herriot Manitoba
28 H7 Herritslev Denmark
36 H7 Herrlingen W Germany
27 F13 Herrljunga Sweden
36 E4 Herrnsheim W Germany
36 C4 Herrstein W Germany
18 G9 Hers R France
37 L5 Hersbruck W Germany
36 D1 Herscheid W Germany
118 J7 Herschel Sask
116 S2 Herschel Yukon Terr
99 S8 Herscher Illinois
37 J3 Herschfeld W Germany
22 H1 Herselt Belgium
94 B3 Hersey Michigan
95 L6 Hershey Pennsylvania
28 D5 Herslev Denmark
28 D3 Hersom Denmark
22 K2 Herstal Belgium
9 G6 Herstmonceux England
22 E2 Hertain Belgium
32 F9 Herten W Germany
9 F4 Hertford England
112 L1 Hertford N Carolina
9 F4 Hertfordshire co England
80 C5 Herut Israel
16 D4 Hervas Spain
22 K2 Herve Belgium
141 L7 Hervey B Queensland
121 S6 Hervey Junction Quebec
141 H4 Hervey Ra Queensland
36 E5 Herxheim W Germany
33 S9 Herzberg E Germany
33 M9 Herzberg W Germany
33 T8 Herzfelde E Germany
32 G7 Herzlake W Germany
80 C5 Herzliyya Israel
37 K4 Herzogenaurach W Germany
38 N5 Herzogenburg Austria
25 F7 Herzogenrath W Germany
33 Q6 Herzsprung E Germany
22 B2 Hesdigneul-lès-Boulogne France
22 C3 Hesdin France
32 G6 Hesel W Germany
67 D5 Heshui China
65 B6 Heshun China
27 B13 Heskestad Norway
98 G2 Hesper N Dakota
22 L4 Hesperange Luxembourg
102 G7 Hesperia California
94 A3 Hesperia Michigan
106 B4 Hesperus Colorado
106 B4 Hesperus Pk Colorado
117 G4 Hess R Yukon Terr
116 N4 Hess Cr Alaska
28 F6 Hesselager Denmark
37 K5 Hesselberg mt W Germany
28 H4 Hesselø isld Denmark
33 N8 Hessen E Germany
36 F2 Hessen land W Germany
36 F1 Hessenstein W Germany
36 H5 Hessenthal W Germany
36 H1 Hessisch Lichtenau W Germany
117 H4 Hess Mts Yukon Terr
138 D4 Hesso S Australia
107 N3 Hesston Kansas
28 J7 Hestehoved C Denmark
26 F5 Hestmannen isld Norway
28 N2 Hestø isld Faeroes
27 G14 Hestra, N Sweden
22 G3 Hestrud France
102 C4 Hetch Hetchy California
94 C2 Hetherton Michigan
25 E4 Het Loo Netherlands
68 J2 Hetou China
22 L5 Hettange Gde France
Hettenhausen see Ebersburg
36 E4 Hettenleidelheim W Germany
114 J8 Hettinger N Dakota
13 G4 Hetton-le-Hole England
33 P9 Hettstedt E Germany
36 F4 Hetzbach W Germany
36 B4 Hetzerath W Germany
22 E1 Het Zoute Belgium
36 H6 Heubach W Germany
41 J1 Heuberg dist W Germany
22 C3 Heuchin France
33 N9 Heudeber E Germany
140 B6 Heughlin, Mt N Terr Aust
36 C2 Heumar W Germany
20 H3 Heuqueville France
25 D5 Heusden Netherlands
37 J3 Heustreu W Germany
95 M2 Heuvelton New York
20 F3 Hève, C. de la France
80 E8 Hever R Jordan
13 F5 Heversham England
48 F3 Heves Hungary
28 E3 Hevring Å R Denmark
80 C8 Hevron R Israel
119 O9 Heward Sask
7 M9 Hewett sea rig North Sea
13 F4 Hexham England
67 F4 Hexi China
67 D4 He Xian China
67 F1 He Xian China
65 D3 Hexigten Qi China
109 H5 Hext Texas
65 A7 Heyang China
101 M7 Heyburn Idaho
107 O6 Heyburn Res Oklahoma
13 F5 Heysham England
8 D5 Heytesbury England
67 E5 Heyuan China
13 F6 Heywood England
138 F7 Heywood Victoria
65 C7 Heze China
113 G12 Hialeah Florida
112 D3 Hiawassee Georgia
107 P2 Hiawatha Kansas
103 O2 Hiawatha Utah
121 Q5 Hibbard Quebec
99 O2 Hibbing Minnesota
142 E1 Hibernia Reef Timor Sea
60 D11 Hibiki-nada sea Japan
71 G5 Hibuson isld Philippines
103 M9 Hickiwan Arizona
13 G6 Hickleton England
110 G5 Hickman Kentucky
98 K9 Hickman Nebraska
106 C7 Hickman New Mexico
123 T5 Hickman's Hbr Nfld
107 J4 Hickok Kansas
111 G9 Hickory Mississippi
112 F2 Hickory N Carolina
112 F2 Hickory, L N Carolina
110 G6 Hickory Valley Tennessee
109 M8 Hicks Texas
145 G2 Hick's Bay New Zealand
125 P9 Hicks Cays islds Belize
94 C5 Hicksville Ohio
109 J4 Hico Texas
48 H3 Hida Romania
60 Q3 Hidaka Japan
60 J12 Hidaka R Japan
60 R3 Hidaka-sammyaku mts Japan
124 G4 Hidalgo de Parral Mexico
32 J8 Hiddenhausen W Germany
30 G1 Hiddensee isld E Germany
141 H4 Hidden Valley Queensland
32 J9 Hiddesen W Germany
130 E5 Hidrolândia Brazil
130 E4 Hidrolina Brazil
20 K1 Hiermont France
85 A3 Hierro isld Canary Is
127 N9 Hierro, Pto. de Venezuela
61 O13 Higashi-iwa islds Japan
61 N9 Higashi-Matsuyama Japan
61 P13 Higashi-Onna Okinawa
61 J11 Higashiosaka Japan
60 C12 Higashi-suidō str Japan
110 D2 Higbee Missouri
94 C2 Higgins L Michigan
110 C2 Higginsville Missouri
143 D9 Higginsville W Australia
9 E1 Higham England
9 F3 Higham Ferrers England
8 B6 Highampton England
106 G4 Highbee Colorado
8 D5 Highbridge England
95 N6 High Bridge New Jersey
12 D3 High Br. of Ken Scotland
9 E5 Highclere England
99 S5 High Cliff Wisconsin
100 E6 High Desert Oregon
99 S4 High Falls Reservoir Wisconsin
9 G5 Highgate England
127 L2 Highgate Jamaica
142 B1 Highgate dist Perth, W Aust
13 F4 High Hesket England
119 W3 High Hill L Manitoba
99 V4 High I Michigan
109 N6 High Island Texas
102 G7 Highland California
110 G3 Highland Illinois
107 P2 Highland Kansas
99 Q6 Highland Wisconsin
15 C3 Highland reg Scotland
99 T7 Highland Park Illinois
94 D4 Highland Park Michigan
109 O9 Highland Park Texas
102 E3 Highland Peak California
103 K4 Highland Pk Nevada
112 D2 Highlands N Carolina
109 M6 Highlands Texas
95 K9 Highland Springs Virginia
117 P6 High Level Alberta
98 G5 Highmore S Dakota
141 K5 High Peak I Queensland
112 H2 High Point N Carolina
118 K8 High Point Sask
114 H6 High Prairie Alberta
114 H7 High River Alberta
113 J11 High Rock Grand Bahama I
119 R3 Highrock Manitoba
112 G2 High Rock L N Carolina
139 H9 High Rocky Pt Tasmania
143 F8 High Sand Hill W Australia
143 F8 High Sand Ridge W Australia
113 E8 High Springs Florida
95 N6 Hightstown New Jersey
99 S7 Highwood Illinois
101 P2 Highwood Montana
9 E4 Highworth England
9 F4 High Wycombe England
124 E5 Higuera de Zaragoza Mexico
17 F1 Higuer, C Spain
127 L9 Higuerote Venezuela
127 K5 Higüey Dom Rep
145 E3 Hihitahi New Zealand
27 N13 Hiiumaa isld U.S.S.R.
79 G5 Hijāne, Bahret el L Syria
17 G3 Hijar Spain
69 F14 Hijau, Gunung mt Sumatra
60 E12 Hiji Japan
71 G7 Hijo Philippines
60 E12 Hikari Japan
60 H11 Hiketa Japan
60 J12 Hiki R Japan
83 J11 Hikkaduwa Sri Lanka
103 J4 Hiko Nevada
61 K10 Hikone Japan
60 D12 Hiko-san mt Japan
145 E2 Hikuai New Zealand
145 E1 Hikurangi New Zealand
145 G2 Hikurangi mt New Zealand
145 E2 Hikutaia New Zealand
71 N8 Hila Indonesia
101 S6 Hiland Wyoming
36 E1 Hilchenbach W Germany
118 G8 Hilda Alberta
37 K3 Hildburghausen E Germany
100 D7 Hildebrand Oregon
36 B1 Hilden W Germany
37 J2 Hilders W Germany
32 L8 Hildesheim W Germany
98 G9 Hildreth Nebraska
101 Q2 Hilger Montana
69 C12 Hiliotaluwa Indonesia
69 C12 Hilisimaetano Indonesia
101 O1 Hill Montana
127 P6 Hillaby, Mt Barbados
78 K5 Hillah, Al Iraq
98 E5 Hilland S Dakota
27 F14 Hillared Sweden
146 H6 Hillary Coast Antarctica
125 P9 Hill Bank Belize
101 K6 Hill City Idaho
107 L2 Hill City Kansas
99 N3 Hill City Minnesota
98 C6 Hill City S Dakota
103 P2 Hill Cr Utah
118 C9 Hillcrest Alberta
117 Q11 Hillcrest Creek Alberta
25 C4 Hillegom Netherlands
32 J8 Hillegossen W Germany
28 J5 Hillerød Denmark
28 B2 Hillerslev Denmark
28 E6 Hillerslev Denmark
28 C7 Hillerup W Germany
36 B3 Hillesheim W Germany
26 K2 Hillesöy Norway
139 K4 Hillgrove New S Wales
144 C6 Hillgrove New Zealand
141 H4 Hill Grove Queensland
98 J4 Hillhead S Dakota
118 E5 Hilliard Alberta
113 F7 Hilliard Florida
9 G2 Hillington England
94 D1 Hillman Michigan
99 N3 Hillman Minnesota
143 B9 Hillman, L W Australia
118 H5 Hillmond Sask
15 E3 Hill of Fearn Scotland
15 D5 Hill of Stake mt Scotland
98 C9 Hillrose Colorado
99 P8 Hills Iowa
98 K6 Hills Minnesota
112 D4 Hillsboro Georgia
110 G2 Hillsboro Illinois
99 P9 Hillsboro Iowa
107 N3 Hillsboro Kansas
110 F3 Hillsboro Missouri
112 H1 Hillsboro N Carolina
98 J2 Hillsboro N Dakota
95 Q3 Hillsboro New Hampshire
106 C9 Hillsboro New Mexico
110 N2 Hillsboro Ohio
100 C4 Hillsboro Oregon
109 K3 Hillsboro Texas
94 G8 Hillsboro W Virginia
113 G11 Hillsboro Can Florida
122 H8 Hillsborough New Brunswick
122 J7 Hillsborough B Pr Edward I
141 J5 Hillsborough, C Queensland
36 D3 Hillscheid W Germany
94 C5 Hillsdale Michigan
121 L8 Hillsdale Ontario
98 B8 Hillsdale Wyoming
103 M7 Hillside Arizona
106 E3 Hillside Colorado
142 C5 Hillside W Australia
120 E3 Hillsport Ontario
139 H5 Hillston New S Wales
138 D5 Hills View Queensland
98 G4 Hillsview S Dakota
94 G10 Hillsville Virginia
112 F5 Hilltonia Georgia
110 F2 Hillview Illinois
102 D4 Hilmar California
102 V14 Hilo Hawaiian Is
113 G10 Hilolo Florida
37 L5 Hilpoltstein W Germany
36 F5 Hilsbach W Germany
8 B7 Hilsea Pt England
36 D7 Hilsenheim France
94 K3 Hilton New York
112 G5 Hilton Head I S Carolina
146 E12 Hilton Inlet Antarctica
37 L4 Hiltpoltstein W Germany
32 G9 Hiltrup W Germany
100 C8 Hilts California
29 N10 Hiltula Finland
25 D6 Hilvarenbeck Netherlands
25 D4 Hilversum Netherlands
74 G2 Himachal Pradesh prov India
74 F1 Himalayan Mt.Ra.,Great Asia
29 K7 Himanka Finland
46 D4 Himarë Albania
145 E4 Himatangi New Zealand
33 N6 Himbergen W Germany
60 H11 Himeji Japan
61 P6 Himekami dake mt Japan
101 R5 Himes Wyoming
60 E12 Hime-shima isld Japan
61 K9 Himi Japan
32 K5 Himmelpforten W Germany
32 K9 Himmighausen W Germany
71 F5 Himugaan Philippines
60 D13 Hinagu Japan
69 C12 Hinako isld Indonesia
145 E4 Hinakura New Zealand
71 G6 Hinatuan Philippines
127 J5 Hinche Haiti
116 O6 Hinchinbrook Entrance str Alaska
116 O6 Hinchinbrook I Alaska
141 H4 Hinchinbrook I Queensland
119 P6 Hinchliffe Sask
9 E2 Hinckley England
99 O3 Hinckley Minnesota
103 M2 Hinckley Utah
95 N3 Hinckley Res New York
74 G5 Hindaun India
41 M2 Hindelang W Germany
25 D3 Hindeloopen Netherlands
Hindenburg see Lindenhagen

28 A7 Hindenburg Damm causeway W Germany
26 N6 Hindersön isld Sweden
109 J7 Hindes Texas
9 F5 Hindhead England
13 F6 Hindley England
138 F6 Hindmarsh, L Victoria
8 D5 Hindon England
144 C6 Hindon New Zealand
144 C6 Hinds New Zealand
123 Q4 Hinds Hill peak Nfld
28 F5 Hindsholm Denmark
123 P5 Hinds L Nfld
74 B3 Hindubagh Pakistan
72 K1 Hindu Kush mts Afghanistan
76 C4 Hindupur India
118 G5 Hindville Alberta
68 G4 Hine Laos
95 O2 Hinesburg Vermont
117 O7 Hines Creek Alberta
112 F6 Hinesville Georgia
74 H8 Hinganghat India
28 D4 Hinge Denmark
101 P1 Hingham Montana
77 J7 Hinglaj Pakistan
20 A5 Hinglé, le France
77 K6 Hingol R Pakistan
74 G9 Hingoli India
102 G7 Hinkley California
143 G7 Hinkley, Mt W Australia
29 J11 Hinnerjoki Finland
28 E4 Hinnerup Denmark
26 H3 Hinnöy isld Norway
61 K9 Hino R Japan
71 F6 Hinoba-an Philippines
16 D6 Hinojosa del Duque Spain
60 E13 Hinokage Japan
60 F10 Hinomi saki C Japan
99 S8 Hinsdale Illinois
95 O4 Hinsdale Massachusetts
101 S1 Hinsdale Montana
94 J4 Hinsdale New York
8 D2 Hinstock England
38 F7 Hinterbichl Austria
36 E3 Hintermeilingen W Germany
41 K4 Hinterrhein Switzerland
41 O3 Hinter Riss Austria
38 K6 Hinterstoder Austria
41 P3 Hinter Tux Austria
36 D5 Hinter Weidenthal W Germany
9 H3 Hintlesham England
117 P9 Hinton Alberta
107 M6 Hinton Oklahoma
61 O9 Hi-numa Japan
129 J7 Hiocolândia Brazil
135 R2 Hio Pt Hawaiian Is
124 J5 Hipólito Mexico
25 C3 Hippolytushoef Netherlands
80 F2 Hippos Syria
60 C12 Hirado Japan
60 C12 Hirado-jima isld Japan
75 K8 Hirakud Res India
95 R3 Hiram Maine
60 C12 Hira shima isld Japan
60 F10 Hirata Japan
61 N10 Hiratsuka Japan
124 D5 Hiray Mexico
78 D2 Hirfanli Dam Turkey
48 K3 Hîrlău Romania
61 O8 Hirono Japan
60 R3 Hiroo Japan
61 O5 Hirosaki Japan
60 G10 Hirose Japan
60 F11 Hiroshima Japan
61 P7 Hirota-wan B Japan
36 F6 Hirsau W Germany
37 M4 Hirschau W Germany
Hirschberg see Jelenia Góra
37 M3 Hirschberg E Germany
38 L7 Hirschegg Austria
37 O6 Hirschenstein mt W Germany
36 F5 Hirschhorn W Germany
28 F2 Hirsholmene isld Denmark
22 G4 Hirson France
48 L6 Hîrşova Romania
28 D1 Hirtshals Denmark
29 M10 Hirvensalmi Finland
29 L7 Hirvineva Finland
8 C4 Hirwaun Wales
60 B13 Hisaka-shima isld Japan
74 F4 Hisar India
77 J2 Hisar, Koh-i- mts Afghanistan
80 F6 Hisban R Jordan
27 F15 Hishult Sweden
98 E6 Hisle S Dakota
80 E6 Hisma Jordan
127 J5 Hispaniola isld W Indies
80 G1 Hispin Syria
79 G4 Hisya Syria
78 J5 Hit Iraq
60 D12 Hita Japan
61 O9 Hitachi Japan
61 O9 Hitachi-Ōta Japan
60 C11 Hitakatsu Japan
9 G3 Hitcham England
107 M6 Hitchcock Oklahoma
119 O9 Hitchcock Sask
98 H5 Hitchcock S Dakota
109 M6 Hitchcock Texas
9 F4 Hitchin England
107 P6 Hitchita Oklahoma
103 O4 Hite Utah
60 D13 Hitoyoshi Japan
26 C8 Hitra Norway
32 L6 Hittfeld W Germany
33 O6 Hitzacker W Germany
61 N9 Hiuchi dake mt Japan
60 G11 Hiuchi-nada sea Japan
135 N9 Hiva Oa isld Pacific Oc
60 H12 Hiwasa Japan
112 C2 Hiwassee R N Carolina/Tenn
112 C2 Hiwassee Lake N Carolina
141 L5 Hixson Cay isld Gt Barrier Reef Aust
60 O3 Hiyama prefect Japan
78 J2 Hizan Turkey
28 E2 Hjallerup Denmark
27 H12 Hjälmaren L Sweden
28 C3 Hjarbæk Denmark
28 B2 Hjardemål Denmark
26 G6 Hjarfjell mt Norway
28 E5 Hjarnø isld Denmark
27 C12 Hjartdal Norway
28 C6 Hjarup Denmark
26 B10 Hjelle Norway
28 F4 Hjelm isld Denmark
28 K7 Hjelm Bugt B Denmark
27 B12 Hjelmeland Norway
26 O1 Hjelmsöy isld Norway
28 G5 Hjembæk Denmark
26 D9 Hjerkinn Norway
28 B4 Hjerm Denmark
28 C6 Hjerndrup Denmark
28 B6 Hjerpsted Denmark
28 A5 Hjerting Denmark
27 G13 Hjo Sweden
28 C4 Hjøllund Denmark
28 C6 Hjordkær Denmark
28 D2 Hjørring Denmark
Hjørring co see Nordjylland
28 E7 Hjortø Denmark
28 E4 Hjortshøj Denmark
28 C5 Hjortsvang Denmark
26 B9 Hjörundfjord Norway
27 D12 Hjuksebö Norway
68 D2 Hka R Burma
68 D2 Hkok R Burma
68 C4 Hlegu Burma
37 P3 Hlinec R Czechoslovakia
31 K7 Hlohovec Czechoslovakia
28 A5 Ho Denmark
85 E7 Ho Ghana
67 B6 Hoa Binh Vietnam
68 J7 Hoa Da Vietnam
118 C6 Hoadley Alberta
98 F8 Hoagland Nebraska
68 J5 Hoai Nhon Vietnam
68 G1 Hoang Su Phi Vietnam
87 B9 Hoanib R Namibia
60 E12 Hoashi Japan
101 P6 Hoback R Wyoming
101 P6 Hoback Pk Wyoming
99 T8 Hobart Indiana
107 L6 Hobart Oklahoma
138 F8 Hobart Tasmania
141 H6 Hobartville Queensland
108 D3 Hobbs New Mexico
146 J10 Hobbs Coast Antarctica
111 K7 Hobbs Island Alabama
113 G10 Hobe Sound Florida
112 K1 Hobgood N Carolina
22 G1 Hoboken Belgium
112 E6 Hoboken Georgia
Hobot Xar see Xianghuang Qi
28 D3 Hobro Denmark
101 Q3 Hobson Montana
145 E2 Hobson, Mt New Zealand
112 L2 Hobucken N Carolina
28 A5 Ho Bugt B Denmark
27 K15 Hoburgen lt ho Sweden
71 D5 Hoc isld Philippines
47 K6 Hocalar Turkey
111 B7 Hochatown Oklahoma
38 N8 Hocheck mt Austria
87 C10 Hochfeld Namibia
36 D6 Hochfelden France
38 G7 Hochfilzen Austria
38 F8 Hochgall mt Italy
37 K2 Hochheim E Germany
109 K6 Hochheim Texas
36 E3 Hochheim W Germany
68 H7 Ho Chi Minh Vietnam
38 K8 Hochobir mt Austria
41 N2 Hoch Platte mt W Germany
38 M6 Hochschwab mt Austria
36 D5 Hochspeyer W Germany
37 K4 Höchstadt W Germany
37 K6 Höchstädt W Germany
36 D2 Höchstenbach W Germany
144 C5 Hochstetter, L New Zealand
38 K9 Hochstuhl mt Yugoslavia
36 F5 Hockenheim W Germany
94 E7 Hocking R Ohio
94 F7 Hockingport Ohio
109 M5 Hockley Texas
9 E3 Hockley Heath England
9 F4 Hockliffe England
28 B5 Hodde Denmark
13 F6 Hodder, R England
9 F4 Hoddesdon England
Hodeida see Ḩudaydah, Al
111 D9 Hodge Louisiana
110 L4 Hodgenville Kentucky
98 B3 Hodges Montana
112 E3 Hodges S Carolina
123 Q4 Hodges Hill peak Nfld
102 G8 Hodges, L California
118 L8 Hodgeville Sask
119 U7 Hodgson Manitoba
140 C3 Hodgson Downs N Terr Aust
85 C5 Hodh reg Mauritania
80 B7 Hodiyya Israel
48 F4 Hódmezövásárhely Hungary
85 E1 Hodna, Mts. du Algeria
31 K7 Hodonín Czechoslovakia
48 C4 Hodos Yugoslavia
28 B4 Hodsager Denmark
116 N3 Hodzana, R Alaska
28 F4 Hoed Denmark
25 A6 Hoedekenskerke Netherlands
18 D5 Hoëdic, I France
106 F4 Hoehne Colorado
25 B5 Hoeksche Waard Netherlands
25 B5 Hoek van Holland Netherlands
119 M6 Hoey Sask
37 M3 Hof W Germany
36 H2 Hofbieber W Germany
Hofei see Hefei
36 F6 Höfen W Germany
37 J6 Hofen W Germany
98 L4 Hoffman Minnesota
112 H2 Hoffman N Carolina
32 K10 Hofgeismar W Germany
36 E3 Hofheim W Germany
37 K3 Hofheim W Germany
37 P6 Hofkirchen W Germany
115 S5 Höfn Iceland
60 E11 Hōfu Japan
28 K4 Höganäs Sweden
139 H7 Hogan Group islds Tasmania Australia
102 D3 Hogan Res California
111 M8 Hogansville Georgia
141 H7 Hoganthulla R Queensland
119 P1 Hogarth Ontario
140 D5 Hogarth, Mt N Terr Aust
116 K3 Hogatza Alaska
116 K3 Hogatza R R Alaska
101 N5 Hogback Mt Montana
27 F12 Högboda Sweden
27 J14 Högby Sweden
28 C7 Högel W Germany
101 R1 Hogeland Montana
27 H12 Högfors Sweden
85 F4 Hoggar mt reg Algeria
119 V1 Hogg L Manitoba
48 J5 Hoghiz Romania
94 B1 Hog I Michigan
95 M9 Hog I Virginia
28 B4 Høgild Denmark
80 C4 Hogla Israel
27 H14 Högsby Sweden
26 J9 Högsjö Sweden
126 H4 Hogsty Reef Bahamas
26 G5 Högtuvbre mt Norway
100 A2 Hoh R Washington
33 R10 Hohburg E Germany
36 C3 Hohe Acht mt W Germany
41 N3 Hohe Geige mt Austria
37 K6 Hohen-Altheim W Germany
38 N6 Hohenberg Austria
37 M3 Hohenberg W Germany
33 S9 Hohenbucke E Germany
37 M5 Hohenburg W Germany
33 N10 Hohenebra E Germany
32 M8 Hoheneggelsen W Germany
36 H1 Hoheneiche W Germany
41 L3 Hohenems Austria
37 M5 Hohenfels W Germany
33 Q7 Hohengöhren E Germany
36 G6 Hohenheim W Germany
37 M7 Hohenkammer W Germany
33 Q10 Hohenleina E Germany
37 N2 Hohenleuben E Germany
32 G10 Hohenlimburg W Germany
32 L5 Hohenlockstedt W Germany
33 S5 Hohenmocker E Germany
37 N1 Hohenmölsen E Germany
33 Q7 Hohennauen E Germany
36 H2 Hohenroda W Germany
33 Q8 Hohenseeden E Germany
33 S9 Hohenseefeld E Germany
36 E2 Hohensolms W Germany
36 H6 Hohenstaufen W Germany
36 G7 Hohenstein W Germany
37 O2 Hohenstein-Ernstthal E Germany
110 J6 Hohenwald Tennessee
37 L6 Hohenwart W Germany
32 K9 Hohenwepel W Germany
32 L4 Hohenwestedt W Germany
33 N6 Hohenzethen W Germany
36 F7 Hohenzollern W Germany
41 M3 Hoher Ifen mt Austria
41 M3 Hohes Licht mt Austria
37 J5 Hohe Steig mt W Germany
38 F7 Hohe Tauern Austria
58 F3 Hohhot China
36 E6 Hohloh mt W Germany
33 M7 Hohne W Germany
19 K4 Hohneck mt France
33 N6 Hohnstorf W Germany
116 J6 Hoholitna R Alaska
32 K4 Hohrr W Germany
66 E4 Hoh Sai Hu L China
33 N4 Hohwacht W Germany
36 C7 Hohwald France
66 D4 Hoh Xil Shan ra China
68 J5 Hoi An Vietnam
107 M3 Hoisington Kansas
66 F4 Hoit Taria China
67 B6 Hoi-Xuan Vietnam
75 P6 Hojai India
28 E6 Højby Denmark
28 C5 Højen Denmark
28 B7 Højer Denmark
28 K6 Højerup Denmark
60 F12 Hōjō Japan
28 B6 Højrup Denmark
28 C3 Højslev Denmark
68 D2 Hok R Burma
99 P6 Hokah Minnesota
Hokang see Hegang
27 K11 Hökhuvud Sweden
61 N9 Hōki R Japan
145 D1 Hokianga Harbour New Zealand
144 C5 Hokitika New Zealand
60 Q2 Hokkaido isld Japan
27 D12 Hokksund Norway
61 O9 Hokota Japan
61 K10 Hokunō Japan
61 K10 Hokuriku Tunnel Japan
27 C11 Hol Norway
27 E12 Höland Norway
28 E3 Holbæk Denmark
28 H5 Holbæk Denmark
Holbæk co see Vestjælland
9 G2 Holbeach England
117 K10 Holberg Br Col
28 C7 Holbøl Denmark
141 J4 Holborne I Queensland
103 O7 Holbrook Arizona
101 N7 Holbrook Idaho
98 F9 Holbrook Nebraska
139 H6 Holbrook New S Wales
13 F6 Holcombe England
99 P4 Holcombe Wisconsin
118 E5 Holden Alberta
95 Q4 Holden Massachusetts
110 C3 Holden Missouri
103 M2 Holden Utah
94 E9 Holden W Virginia
107 O6 Holdenville Oklahoma
119 M8 Holdfast Sask
99 M4 Holdingford Minnesota
32 H7 Holdorf W Germany
98 G9 Holdrege Nebraska
28 G7 Holeby Denmark
27 E12 Hölen Norway
76 C4 Hole Narsipur India
31 K6 Holešov Czechoslovakia
127 P6 Holetown Barbados
94 C5 Holgate Ohio
126 F4 Holguin Cuba
48 D2 Holíč Czechoslovakia
116 H5 Holikachuk Alaska
116 J6 Holitna R Alaska
27 F11 Höljes Sweden
119 T9 Holland Manitoba
99 U7 Holland Michigan
98 K5 Holland Minnesota
94 J4 Holland New York
100 B7 Holland Oregon
109 K5 Holland Texas
9 F2 Holland div England
111 F8 Hollandale Mississippi
127 M3 Holland B Jamaica
120 K8 Holland Centre Ontario
143 C9 Holland,Mt W Australia
141 K2 Holland Park dist Brisbane, Qnsld
25 C5 Hollandsch Diep Netherlands
138 E2 Hollands Hill S Australia
22 K4 Hollange Belgium
32 M8 Holle W Germany
33 N5 Hollenbek W Germany
32 L6 Hollenstedt W Germany
38 N6 Hollen-Tal V Austria
38 F7 Hollersbach Austria
9 H3 Hollesley B England
94 J3 Holley New York
37 L4 Hollfeld W Germany
146 G10 Hollick-Kenyon Pl Antarctica
109 J2 Holliday Texas
94 J6 Hollidaysburg Pennsylvania
107 L7 Hollis Oklahoma
102 C5 Hollister California
101 L7 Hollister Idaho
110 C5 Hollister Missouri
107 M7 Hollister Oklahoma
22 J2 Hollogne-sur-Geer Belgium
111 D10 Holloway Louisiana
28 K6 Höllviken C Sweden
106 H3 Holly Colorado
94 D4 Holly Michigan
111 F9 Holly Bluff Mississippi
144 B6 Hollyford R New Zealand
111 E7 Holly Grove Arkansas
113 F8 Holly Hill Florida
112 G4 Holly Hill S Carolina
112 K3 Holly Ridge N Carolina
113 G11 Hollywood Florida
95 L8 Hollywood Maryland
28 D6 Holm Denmark
26 F6 Holm Norway
26 J9 Holm Sweden
106 E5 Holman New Mexico
114 H3 Holman Island N W Terr
28 B5 Holme Å R Denmark
146 B4 Holme B Antarctica
99 P6 Holmen Wisconsin
113 K12 Holmes Cay isld Bahamas
8 D1 Holmes Chapel England
119 V1 Holmes L Manitoba
101 P5 Holmes, Mt Wyoming
141 J3 Holmes Reef Great Barrier Reef Aust
27 D12 Holmestr Norway
119 S9 Holmfield Manitoba
13 G6 Holmfirth England
26 K6 Holmfors Sweden
26 L8 Holmögadd lt ho Sweden
26 L8 Holmön Sweden
13 J6 Holmpton England
27 D12 Holmsbu Norway
26 J8 Holmsjö Sweden
26 H9 Holmsjön L Sweden
28 A4 Holmsland Klit sand spit Denmark
115 O3 Holms Ø isld Greenland
28 E6 Holmstrup Fyn Denmark
28 G5 Holmstrup Vestjælland Denmark
26 L8 Holmsund Sweden
27 K14 Holmudden lt ho Gotland Sweden
111 C11 Holmwood Louisiana
37 M5 Holnstein W Germany
27 J12 Hölö Sweden
88 C5 Holoholo Tanzania
80 C5 Holon Israel
87 C11 Holoog Namibia
113 F9 Holopaw Florida
80 B6 Holot Ashdod Israel
142 F2 Holothuria Banks W Australia
80 B6 Holot Yavne Israel
26 E9 Holöydal Norway
141 F2 Holroyd R Queensland
28 B4 Holstebro Denmark
28 B5 Holsted Denmark
99 L7 Holstein Iowa
98 H9 Holstein Nebraska
120 K8 Holstein Ontario
28 G6 Holsteinborg Denmark
115 O4 Holsteinsborg Greenland
112 E1 Holston R Tennessee
94 F10 Holston R Virginia
33 N4 Holst Schweiz W Germany
8 B6 Holsworthy England
111 J8 Holt Alabama
9 H2 Holt England
111 K11 Holt Florida
94 C4 Holt Michigan
98 K1 Holt Minnesota
8 D1 Holt Wales
98 G7 Holt Cr Nebraska
28 K5 Holte Denmark
33 O9 Holtemme R E Germany
25 F4 Holten Netherlands
101 O3 Holter L. Dam Montana
33 O5 Holthusen E Germany
94 B7 Holton Indiana
107 P2 Holton Kansas
94 B3 Holton Michigan
65 D2 Holt Sum China
28 C4 Holtum Å R Denmark
103 J9 Holtville California
120 K4 Holtyre Ontario
135 U5 Holualoa Hawaiian Is
27 C13 Holum Norway
25 E2 Holwerd Netherlands
116 H5 Holy Cross Alaska
Holyhead see Caergybi
Holy I see Lindisfarne
12 C3 Holy I Scotland
8 B1 Holy I Wales
118 G4 Holyoke Alberta
106 H1 Holyoke Colorado
95 P4 Holyoke Massachusetts
107 M3 Holyrood Kansas
123 T6 Holyrood Nfld
37 P4 Holýšov Czechoslovakia
8 D6 Holywell England
8 C1 Holywell Wales
14 F2 Holywood N Ireland
36 D3 Holzappel W Germany
33 S9 Holzdorf E Germany
33 P5 Holzendorf E Germany
32 H8 Holzhausen W Germany
36 D3 Holzhausen W Germany
37 K6 Holzheim W Germany
32 K9 Holzminden W Germany
32 G10 Holzwickede W Germany
28 H6 Høm Denmark
86 G6 Homa Bay Kenya
75 Q6 Homalin Burma
36 G1 Homberg W Germany
60 R2 Hombetsu Japan
22 E4 Homblières France
85 D5 Hombori Mali
Homburg see Nümbrecht
36 H4 Homburg Bayern W Germany
36 C5 Homburg Rheinland-Pfalz W Germany
115 N4 Home B N W Terr
100 J6 Homedale Idaho
141 H4 Home Hill Queensland
83 M8 Home I Cocos Is Indian Oc
116 M7 Homer Alaska
99 T9 Homer Illinois
111 C9 Homer Louisiana
94 C4 Homer Michigan
94 H6 Homer City Pennsylvania
9 H3 Homersfield England
144 A6 Homer Tun New Zealand
112 E6 Homerville Georgia
113 G12 Homestead Florida
99 P8 Homestead Iowa
98 B1 Homestead Montana
107 M5 Homestead Oklahoma
100 J4 Homestead Oregon
141 H5 Homestead Queensland
98 K9 Homestead Nat Mon Nebraska
111 K8 Homewood Alabama
145 E4 Homewood New Zealand
68 A6 Homfray's Str Andaman Is
107 O5 Hominy Oklahoma
26 E9 Hommelfjell mt Norway
26 E8 Hommelvik Norway
25 E3 Hommerts Netherlands
21 F7 Hommes France
74 G10 Homnabad India
89 H5 Homoine Mozambique
48 G6 Homoljske Planina mt Yugoslavia
71 G5 Homonhon Philippines
48 J4 Homorod Romania
113 E9 Homosassa Florida
Homs Libya see Khums, Al
79 G4 Homs Syria
60 F12 Honai Japan
Honan prov see Henan
76 B3 Honavar India
47 K7 Honaz Dağ mt Turkey
68 G7 Hon Chong Vietnam
102 C2 Honcut California
128 D2 Honda Colombia
71 D6 Honda B Palawan Philippines
118 D3 Hondo Alberta
60 D13 Hondo Japan
106 E8 Hondo New Mexico
109 H6 Hondo Texas
125 P8 Hondo R Belize
22 D2 Hondschoote France
125 L2 Honduras rep Cent America
119 Q2 Hone Manitoba
112 E3 Honea Path S Carolina
36 H2 Hönebach W Germany
27 D11 Hönefoss Norway
95 M5 Honesdale Pennsylvania
102 A1 Honeydew California
98 J1 Honeyford N Dakota
109 M2 Honey Grove Texas
109 N5 Honey Island Texas
100 E9 Honey L California
120 K8 Honeywood Ontario
20 F3 Honfleur France
28 G5 Høng Denmark
65 G2 Hongai China
68 H2 Hon Gai Vietnam
67 B6 Hon Gay Vietnam
67 E5 Honghai Wan B China
58 F5 Hong He R China
67 D2 Honghu China
67 C3 Hongjiang China
67 G6 Hong Kong colony E Asia
67 F4 Honglai China
68 G7 Hong Ngu Vietnam
Hongning see Wulian
58 F2 Hongor Mongolia
Hongqiao see Qidong
67 D7 Hongqizhen China
68 E3 Hongsa Laos
67 B4 Hongshui He R China
65 B6 Hongtong China
61 J12 Hongū Japan
122 H4 Honguedo Passage Canada
67 A2 Hongya China
58 G5 Hongze Hu L China
137 N3 Honiara Guadalcanal I Solomon Is
9 H2 Honingham England
8 C6 Honiton England
61 O6 Honjō Japan
29 J10 Honkajoki Finland
68 H3 Hon Matt isld Vietnam
68 G3 Hon Me isld Vietnam
76 B3 Honnali India
26 P1 Honningsvåg Norway
102 V13 Honokaa Hawaiian Is
135 S3 Honokahua Hawaiian Is
145 F2 Honokawa New Zealand
135 S3 Honokohau Hawaiian Is
102 S12 Honolulu Hawaiian Is
135 V5 Honomu Hawaiian Is
102 R12 Honouliuli Hawaiian Is
17 F5 Honrubia Spain
59 K4 Honshū isld Japan
28 H5 Hønsinge Denmark
135 U6 Honuapo Hawaiian Is
100 D4 Hood, Mt Oregon
143 C10 Hood Pt W Australia
141 G8 Hood Ra Queensland
100 D4 Hood River Oregon
100 B2 Hoodsport Washington
32 K10 Hoof W Germany
25 C4 Hoofddorp Netherlands
25 A6 Hoofdplaat Netherlands
25 F3 Hooger Smilde Netherlands
25 G3 Hoogeveen Netherlands
25 G2 Hoogezand Netherlands
25 G3 Hooghalen Netherlands
75 M8 Hooghly R India
22 D2 Hoogstade Belgium
22 H1 Hoogstraten Belgium
41 K2 Höohster mt W Germany
9 F5 Hook England
144 C6 Hook New Zealand
135 U5 Hookena Hawaiian Is
107 J5 Hooker Oklahoma
146 K6 Hooker, C Antarctica
140 B4 Hooker Creek N Terr Aust
14 E4 Hook Hd Irish Rep
141 J5 Hook I Queensland
141 L7 Hook Pt Queensland
141 J4 Hook Reef Gt Barrier Reef Aust
109 N2 Hooks Texas
95 Q3 Hooksett New Hampshire
32 H5 Hooksiel W Germany
102 V13 Hoolehua Hawaiian Is
117 F6 Hoonah Alaska
100 B8 Hoopa California
106 E4 Hooper Colorado
98 K8 Hooper Nebraska
101 N8 Hooper Utah
100 G3 Hooper Washington
116 D6 Hooper Bay Alaska
95 L8 Hooper I Maryland
99 T9 Hoopeston Illinois
123 Q3 Hooping Hbr Nfld
98 J1 Hoople N Dakota
89 D6 Hoopstad S Africa
27 G16 Höör Sweden
25 D3 Hoorn Noord Netherlands
25 C2 Hoorn Texel Netherlands
95 O4 Hoosick Falls New York
118 H7 Hoosier Sask
98 C4 Hoover S Dakota
103 K5 Hoover Dam Arizona
94 E6 Hoover Res Ohio
94 J6 Hooversville Pennsylvania
78 H1 Hopa Turkey
95 M5 Hop Bottom Pennsylvania
9 E4 Hopcrofts Holt England
103 L8 Hope Arizona
111 C8 Hope Arkansas
117 N11 Hope Br Col
94 B7 Hope Indiana
107 N3 Hope Kansas
98 J2 Hope N Dakota
127 M2 Hope Bay Jamaica
115 N6 Hopedale Labrador
Hopeh prov see Hebei
138 E3 Hope, L S Australia
138 E3 Hopeless, Mt S Australia
112 J3 Hope Mills N Carolina
138 D5 Hope, Mt S Australia
147 J12 Hopen isld Arctic Oc
144 D5 Hope Pass New Zealand
116 D2 Hope, Pt Alaska
138 F6 Hopetoun Victoria
143 D10 Hopetoun W Australia
113 L11 Hope Town Bahamas
89 D7 Hopetown S Africa
122 K8 Hopewell Nova Scotia
94 J6 Hopewell Pennsylvania
95 K9 Hopewell Virginia
115 M6 Hopewell Is N W Terr
103 O6 Hopi Buttes mt Arizona
67 E4 Ho-p'ing China
94 E4 Hopkins Michigan
99 M9 Hopkins Missouri
139 G7 Hopkins R Victoria
143 G6 Hopkins,L W Australia
144 B5 Hopkins, Mt New Zealand
110 J5 Hopkinsville Kentucky
102 A3 Hopland California
68 C2 Hopong Burma
33 T7 Hoppegarten E Germany
26 Q1 Hopseidet Norway
32 G8 Hopsten W Germany
9 H2 Hopton England
28 C6 Hoptrup Denmark
94 H7 Hopwood Pennsylvania
141 G5 Hopwood,Mt Queensland
114 G8 Hoquiam Washington
86 G4 Hora Abyata dist Ethiopia
107 J3 Horace Kansas
37 P2 Hora Svatého Šebastiána Czechoslovakia
37 P2 Hora Svaté Katering Czechoslovakia
111 B8 Horatio Arkansas
30 H6 Horaždovice Czechoslovakia
36 F7 Horb W Germany
28 J7 Horbelev Denmark
37 O7 Horbering W Germany
118 B6 Horburg Alberta
13 G6 Horbury England
28 D3 Hørby Nordjylland Denmark
28 E2 Hørby Nordjylland Denmark
27 G16 Hörby Sweden
16 D5 Horcajo de los Montes Spain
16 E5 Horcajo de Santiago Spain
124 G3 Horcasitas Mexico
36 E4 Horchheim W Germany
27 A11 Hordaland reg Norway
86 B1 Hordio Somalia
109 H4 Hords Cr. Res Texas
28 A3 Hørdum Denmark
8 B3 Horeb Wales
88 C6 Hore B Zambia
48 H5 Horezu Romania
48 F4 Horgos Yugoslavia
31 J5 Hořice Czechoslovakia
99 S6 Horicon Wisconsin
58 F3 Horinger China
22 J2 Horion Hozémont Belgium
119 M9 Horizon Sask
137 S6 Horizon Depth Pacific Oc
31 H4 Horka E Germany
9 F5 Horley England
146 G9 Horlick Mts Antarctica
28 E2 Hørmested Denmark
Hormo see Nyima
77 E6 Hormoz isld Iran
77 E6 Hormuz, Strait of Iran
31 J7 Horn Austria
25 E6 Horn Netherlands
27 H14 Horn Sweden
48 F2 Hornad R Czechoslovakia
26 J5 Hornavan L Sweden
36 C5 Hornbach W Germany
32 J9 Horn-Bad Meinog W Germany
28 K4 Hornbæk Denmark
111 C10 Hornbeck Louisiana
36 E7 Hornberg W Germany
27 G13 Hornborgasjön L Sweden
100 C8 Hornbrook California
33 N8 Hornburg W Germany
9 F1 Horncastle England
27 H11 Horndal Sweden
33 N6 Horndorf W Germany
28 D1 Horne Denmark
28 B5 Horne Ribe Denmark
32 L5 Horneburg W Germany
26 L8 Hörnefors Sweden
28 E6 Horneland Denmark
94 K4 Hornell New York
115 L8 Hornepayne Ontario
110 F5 Hornersville Missouri
27 C13 Hornesund Norway
28 G2 Hornfiskrøn isld Denmark
14 C1 Horn Hd Irish Rep
33 O8 Hornhsleben E Germany
111 H11 Horn I Mississippi
141 F1 Horn I Queensland
31 K6 Horni Benešov Czechoslovakia
137 R4 Horn, Îles de Îles Wallis Pacific Oc
124 E4 Hornillos Mexico
26 B10 Hornindal Norway
26 B10 Hornindalsvatn L Norway
36 E6 Hornisgrinde mt W Germany
37 O3 Horní Slavkov Czechoslovakia
41 J3 Hörnli mt Switzerland
116 H6 Horn Mts Alaska
114 G5 Horn Mts N W Terr
27 C13 Hornnes Norway
133 C6 Hornopiren mt Chile
124 H5 Hornos Mexico
133 D9 Hornos, C. de Chile
20 J2 Hornoy France
117 O4 Horn R N W Terr
139 K5 Hornsby New S Wales
110 H6 Hornsby Tennessee
8 B6 Horns Cross England
13 H6 Hornsea England
26 L8 Hörnsjö Sweden
28 E4 Hornslet Denmark
80 E2 Horns of Hittin Israel
37 K1 Hornsömmern E Germany
33 P5 Hornstorf E Germany
28 D5 Hornstrup Denmark
28 D5 Hornum Vejle Denmark
28 A7 Hørnum W Germany
33 S6 Horn Zieritz E Germany
60 T1 Horobetsu Japan
60 R3 Horoizumi Japan
60 Q1 Horonai Japan
145 E3 Horopito New Zealand
144 C5 Hororata New Zealand
60 Q3 Horoshiri-dake mt Japan
65 A5 Horo Sum China
30 H6 Hořovice Czechoslovakia
145 E4 Horowhenua Plain New Zealand
83 K9 Horowupotana Sri Lanka
20 E5 Horps, le France
59 H2 Horqin Youyi Qianqi China
65 E2 Horqin Youyi Zhongqi China
65 F2 Horqin Zouyi Zhongqi China
65 E3 Horqin Zuoyi Houqi China
129 G8 Horqueta Paraguay
133 F2 Horqueta Paraguay
28 H7 Horreby Denmark
27 F14 Horred Sweden
36 B2 Horrem W Germany
83 M8 Horsburgh I Cocos Is Indian Oc
37 J1 Hörschel E Germany
110 K4 Horse Branch Kentucky
9 G6 Horsebridge E Sussex England
94 B9 Horse Cave Kentucky
106 G3 Horse Cr Colorado
110 B4 Horse Cr Missouri
140 D6 Horse Cr N Terr Aust
98 A8 Horse Cr Wyoming
117 N9 Horsefly Br Col
98 F2 Horsehead L N Dakota
95 L4 Horseheads New York
123 R3 Horse Is Nfld
102 D1 Horse L California
37 J2 Hörsel R E Germany
37 J2 Hörsel Berge mt E Germany
28 D5 Horsens Vejle Denmark
28 E5 Horsens Fjord inlet Denmark
118 F2 Horse, R Alberta
113 D8 Horseshoe Florida
143 C7 Horse Shoe W Australia
100 J6 Horse Shoe Bend Idaho
140 C7 Horseshoe Bend N Terr Aust
138 C2 Horseshoe Bend N Terr Australia
127 P4 Horse Shoe Pt St Kitts W I
103 N7 Horseshoe Res Arizona
106 B8 Horse Springs New Mexico
9 F5 Horsham England
118 H8 Horsham Sask
138 F6 Horsham Victoria
28 K5 Hørsholm Denmark
13 G4 Horsley England
28 G7 Horslunde Denmark
37 O4 Horšovský Týn Czechoslovakia
33 S4 Horst E Germany
25 F6 Horst Netherlands
32 L5 Horst W Germany
32 G8 Hörstel W Germany
25 F6 Hörstgen W Germany
32 F8 Horstmar W Germany
48 E2 Hor Stubňa Czechoslovakia
27 D12 Horten Norway
112 F6 Hortense Georgia
26 M6 Hortlax Sweden
107 P2 Horton Kansas
114 G4 Horton R N W Terr
27 C10 Horungane Norway
28 C7 Hörup W Germany
28 G5 Hørve Denmark
27 G15 Hörvik Sweden
13 F6 Horwich England
120 H5 Horwood L Ontario
37 P5 Hory Matky Boží Czechoslovakia
31 J5 Hory Orlické mts Czechoslovakia
47 K7 Horzom R Turkey
36 G3 Hösbach W Germany
76 C4 Hosdurga India
70 C3 Hose Mts Sarawak
84 G5 Hosenofu Libya
77 A3 Hoseynābad Iran
111 M11 Hosford Florida
74 C10 Hoshab Pakistan
74 G7 Hoshangabad India
74 F3 Hoshiarpur India
98 J7 Hoskins Nebraska
98 G4 Hosmer S Dakota
60 E13 Hososhima Japan
106 C6 Hospah New Mexico
76 C3 Hospet India
14 C4 Hospital Irish Rep
131 G3 Hospital, Cuchilla del mt Uruguay
29 O6 Hossa Finland
86 G4 Hosseina Ethiopia
106 B6 Hosta Butte mt New Mexico
133 D9 Hoste, I Chile
18 E8 Hostens France
27 G13 Höstholmen Sweden
37 O4 Hostouň Czechoslovakia
28 A5 Hostrup Ribe Denmark
28 B7 Hostrup Sønderjylland Denmark
28 D7 Hostrup W Germany
28 C7 Hostrup Sø L Denmark
76 C4 Hosur India
26 G8 Hotagen Sweden
61 L9 Hotaka Japan
66 B4 Hotan China
66 C4 Hotan He R China
87 D11 Hotazel S Africa
117 P7 Hotchkiss Alberta
106 C3 Hotchkiss Colorado
102 H3 Hot Creek Ra Nevada
33 O8 Hötensleben E Germany
140 B1 Hotham,C N Terr Aust
116 F3 Hotham Inlet Alaska
139 H6 Hotham, Mt Victoria
26 H7 Hoting Sweden
111 C7 Hot Springs Arkansas
80 E8 Hot Springs Israel
101 L2 Hot Springs Montana
112 E2 Hot Springs N Carolina
98 C6 Hot Springs S Dakota
108 D6 Hot Springs Texas
94 H9 Hot Springs Virginia
109 O1 Hot Springs nat park Arkansas
106 D1 Hot Sulphur Springs Colorado
114 H4 Hottah L N W Terr
22 J3 Hotton Belgium
108 B5 Hot Wells Texas
32 L6 Hötzingen W Germany
28 E2 Hou Denmark
18 D5 Houat, I France
22 D3 Houdain France
20 J4 Houdan France
22 G3 Houdeng Belgium
18 E8 Houeillès France
22 K3 Houffalize Belgium
107 J5 Hough Oklahoma
99 S2 Houghton Michigan
94 J4 Houghton New York
98 H4 Houghton S Dakota
141 H4 Houghton R Queensland
94 C2 Houghton L Michigan
13 G4 Houghton-le-Spring England
145 D1 Houhora New Zealand
20 K4 Houilles France
144 B7 Houipapa New Zealand
20 E3 Houlgate France
111 G7 Houlka Mississippi
20 H3 Houlme, le France
95 T7 Houlton Maine
65 B7 Houma China
111 F12 Houma Louisiana
85 G2 Houmet Essoug Tunisia
85 D6 Houndé Upper Volta
9 F5 Hounslow England
18 E7 Hourtin France
95 O5 Housatonic R Connecticut
108 D1 House New Mexico
123 L6 House Hbr Madeleine Is, Quebec
12 D3 House o'-Hill Scotland
118 E3 House R Alberta
103 L2 House Ra Utah
117 K8 Houston Br Col
99 P6 Houston Minnesota
111 H8 Houston Mississippi
110 E4 Houston Missouri
109 F9 Houston Texas
110 C3 Houstonia Missouri
109 M5 Houston, L Texas
111 C11 Houston R Louisiana
89 F4 Hout R S Africa
89 A10 Hout B S Africa
25 D4 Houten Netherlands
22 J1 Houthalen Belgium
143 A8 Houtman Abrolhos arch W Aust
94 J6 Houtzdale Pennsylvania
22 J3 Houyet Belgium
28 E5 Hov Denmark
28 N3 Hov Faeroes
28 K4 Hov Sweden
27 G13 Hova Sweden
28 B5 Hovborg Denmark
58 B2 Hovd Mongolia
27 B12 Hovden Norway
26 H9 Hovdsjö Sweden
28 A3 Hove Denmark
9 F6 Hove England
28 G5 Høve Vestjælland Denmark
28 D5 Hovedgård Denmark
32 J9 Hövelhof W Germany
28 B5 Hoven Denmark
98 G4 Hoven S Dakota
103 P4 Hovenweep Nat. Mon Utah
28 A4 Hover Denmark
28 A4 Hover Å R Denmark
77 A4 Hoveyzeh Iran
99 R2 Hovland Minnesota
53 F9 Hovlya U.S.S.R.
28 C6 Hovslund Denmark
107 O4 Howard Kansas
94 E6 Howard Ohio
94 K5 Howard Pennsylvania
141 L7 Howard Queensland
98 J5 Howard S Dakota
94 B3 Howard City Michigan
108 F5 Howard Cr Texas
140 D1 Howard I N Terr Aust
99 M4 Howard L Minnesota
116 J2 Howard Pass Alaska
99 T6 Howards Grove Wisconsin
86 D2 Howar, Wadi watercourse Sudan
13 H6 Howden England
101 M6 Howe Idaho
94 B5 Howe Indiana
109 N1 Howe Oklahoma
109 L2 Howe Texas
139 J6 Howe, C New S Wales
83 L13 Howe, Î Indian Oc
94 D4 Howell Michigan
139 K3 Howell New S Wales
101 N8 Howell Utah
98 J8 Howells Nebraska
138 C2 Howe, Mt S Australia
15 F4 Howe of Mearns Scotland
98 D5 Howes S Dakota
117 M11 Howe Sound Br Col
145 E2 Howick New Zealand
121 R7 Howick Quebec
141 H2 Howick Group islds Gt Barrier Reef Aust
138 E2 Howitt, L S Australia
139 H6 Howitt, Mt Victoria
95 T1 Howland Maine
137 R1 Howland I Pacific Oc
123 P4 Howley Nfld
75 N7 Howrah India
117 P10 Howser Br Col
14 E3 Howth Irish Rep
110 F5 Hoxie Arkansas
107 K2 Hoxie Kansas
32 K9 Höxter W Germany
66 D2 Hoxtolgay China
15 E2 Hoy Scotland
32 K7 Hoya W Germany
31 H4 Hoyerswerda E Germany
8 C1 Hoylake England
26 F7 Höylandet Norway
120 J4 Hoyle Ontario
110 G3 Hoyleton Illinois
33 O9 Hoym E Germany
16 C4 Hoyos Spain
47 L6 Hoyran Turkey
15 E2 Hoy Snd Scotland
107 P2 Hoyt Kansas
122 F8 Hoyt New Brunswick
29 O9 Höytiäinen L Finland
101 O9 Hoyt Pk Utah
68 C2 Hpa Lai Burma
37 P4 Hracholuská Nádrž res Czechoslovakia
31 J5 Hradec Králové Czechoslovakia
37 P3 Hradiště mt Czechoslovakia
Hranice Czechoslovakia see Rossbach
31 K6 Hranice Czechoslovakia
48 F2 Hriňová Czechoslovakia
31 L7 Hron R Czechoslovakia
37 O3 Hroznetín Czechoslovakia
31 O5 Hrubieszów Poland
31 J7 Hrušovany Czechoslovakia
42 G4 Hrvatska reg Yugoslavia
68 C2 Hsa Mong Hkam Burma
68 C3 Hsataw Burma
66 D5 Hsia-ju Ts'o L China
67 G6 Hsiao-lan Hsü isld Taiwan
68 C2 Hsi Hkip Burma
68 C2 Hsi-hseng Burma
58 F4 Hsin-ch'iang China
67 G4 Hsin-chu Taiwan
59 H3 Hsin-min China
68 C1 Hsipaw Burma
66 D5 Hsi-tsang Kao-yüan reg China
68 C1 Hsumhsai Burma
67 F4 Hua'an China
128 C6 Huacho Peru
65 H1 Huachuan China
128 C5 Huacrachuco Peru
65 C4 Huade China
59 J3 Huadian China
67 G2 Huading Shan mt China
68 F5 Huai R Thailand
65 C4 Huai'an China
58 G5 Huaibei China
65 F3 Huaide China
65 F3 Huaidezhen China
58 F5 Huai He R China
67 C3 Huaihua China
67 D5 Huaiji China
65 C4 Huailai China
68 F4 Huai Luang R Thailand
58 G5 Huainan China
67 E1 Huaining China
58 F4 Huairen China

65 C4 Huairou China
68 F4 Huai Yang Res Thailand
67 C4 Huaiyuan China
125 L9 Huajuápan de León Mexico
103 L8 Hualapai Mts Arizona
67 E2 Hualin China
128 C5 Huallaga R Peru
128 C5 Huallanca Peru
65 H1 Huama China
65 H1 Huanan China
128 E7 Huanay Bolivia
128 C5 Huancabamba Pasco Peru
128 C5 Huancabamba Piura Peru
128 E7 Huancane Peru
128 C6 Huancavelica Peru
128 C6 Huancayo Peru
128 E8 Huanchaca Bolivia
128 F6 Huanchaca, Sa. de mts Bolivia
128 C5 Huanchaco Peru
Huang'an see Hong'an
67 G1 Huangang China
Huangcaoba see Xingyi
58 G5 Huangchuan China
67 E1 Huanggang China
65 D3 Huanggangliang mt China
67 F3 Huanggang Shan mt China
58 D4 Huang He R China
67 E1 Huang He R China
65 D5 Huang Ho, Mouths of the China
65 D5 Huanghua China
65 C7 Huangkou China
67 E2 Huanglaomen China
65 A7 Huangling China
68 J3 Huangliu China
65 A7 Huanglong China
65 C7 Huanglongsi China
67 E1 Huangmei China
67 C4 Huangmian China
65 G3 Huangnihe China
67 E1 Huangpi China
67 B3 Huangpin China
67 C6 Huangpo China
67 D5 Huangpu China
67 E2 Huangshagang China
67 F1 Huang Shan mts China
65 E6 Huangshanguan China
58 D4 Huang Shui R China
65 G3 Huangsongdian China
65 D4 Huangtuliangzi China
65 E6 Huang Xian China
67 G2 Huangyan China
67 D3 Huangyangsi China
Huangzhou see Huanggang
67 C7 Huangzhu China
67 G1 Huaniao Shan isld China
67 A4 Huaning China
67 C4 Huanjiang China
58 E4 Huan Jiang R China
65 F4 Huanren China
Huanshan see Yuhuan
58 G5 Huanshi China
128 D6 Huanta Peru
65 D6 Huantai China
128 C5 Huánuco Peru
128 D6 Huanzo, Cord. de mts Peru
125 N3 Huaonta Nicaragua
67 G4 Hua-p'ing Hsü isld Taiwan
128 E7 Huara Chile
128 C5 Huaraz Peru
128 C6 Huariaca Peru
128 C6 Huarmey Peru
67 D2 Huarong China
128 C5 Huascarán mt Peru
133 C3 Huasco Chile
131 B2 Huasco, R Chile
67 D3 Huashi China
125 M2 Huaspuc Honduras
124 E4 Huatabampo Mexico
65 E3 Hua Tugal China
125 L8 Huatusco Mexico
125 K7 Huauchinango Mexico
65 A7 Hua Xian China
65 C7 Hua Xian China
67 D5 Hua Xian China
65 C7 Huaxiancheng China
65 A7 Huayin China
67 B1 Huaying Shan mts China
58 E6 Huayuan China
67 C2 Huayuan China
67 E1 Huayuan China
67 C6 Huazhou China
65 F4 Huazi China
99 N7 Hubbard Iowa
119 O7 Hubbard Sask
109 L4 Hubbard Texas
109 H3 Hubbard Cr. Res Texas
94 D2 Hubbard L Michigan
117 D5 Hubbard, Mt Alaska/Yukon Terr
122 H9 Hubbards Nova Scotia
98 J9 Hubbell Nebraska
58 F5 Hubei prov China
121 Q7 Huberdeau Quebec
33 T7 Hubertusstock E Germany
76 B3 Hubli India
32 J6 Huchting W Germany
25 F6 Hückelhoven-Ratheim W Germany
36 C1 Hückeswagen W Germany
140 D6 Huckitta N Terr Aust
9 E1 Hucknall England
22 B2 Hucqueliers France
72 E6 Hudaydah, Al N Yemen
13 G6 Huddersfield England
27 J12 Huddinge Sweden
32 H6 Hude W Germany
32 L7 Hudemühlen W Germany
26 J10 Hudiksvall Sweden
20 B4 Hudimesnil France
106 F1 Hudson Colorado
113 E9 Hudson Florida
110 G1 Hudson Illinois
94 B5 Hudson Indiana
99 O7 Hudson Iowa
107 M3 Hudson Kansas
94 C5 Hudson Michigan
95 O4 Hudson New York
94 F5 Hudson Ohio
115 K7 Hudson Ontario
101 R7 Hudson Wyoming
133 C7 Hudson mt Chile
95 O3 Hudson R New York
115 L6 Hudson Bay Canada
114 J7 Hudson Bay Sask
95 O3 Hudson Falls New York
107 P5 Hudson, L. Oklahoma
146 H11 Hudson Mts Antarctica
114 G6 Hudson's Hope Br Columbia
115 M5 Hudson Str Canada
94 B4 Hudsonville Michigan
119 W5 Hudwin L Manitoba
68 H4 Hue Vietnam
16 C4 Huebra R Spain
131 B7 Huechulafquén, L Argentina
108 B4 Hueco Mts Texas
48 H4 Huedin Romania
124 G5 Huehueto, Cerro mt Mexico
125 K7 Huejutla Mexico
18 C4 Huelgoat France
16 E7 Huelma Spain
16 C7 Huelva Spain
16 C7 Huelva prov Spain
16 C7 Huelva R Spain
68 G4 Huen Laos
131 B3 Huentelauquén Chile
124 D3 Huépac Mexico
133 C6 Huequi, Pen Chile
17 F7 Huércal Overa Spain
106 F3 Huerfano R Colorado
131 C3 Huerta, Sa. de la ra Argentina
17 G6 Huertas, C. de las Spain
124 J5 Huertecillas Mexico
17 G3 Huerva R Spain
17 G2 Huesca Spain
17 G2 Huesca prov Spain
17 F7 Huéscar Spain
16 D7 Huesna R Spain
108 B5 Hueso, Sierra del mts Mexico
125 J8 Huétamo Mexico
17 F4 Huete Spain
98 F3 Huff N Dakota
36 G5 Hüffenhardt W Germany
98 H4 Huffton S Dakota
77 A7 Hufuf, Al Saudi Arabia
116 K4 Huggins I Alaska
98 F9 Hugh Butler L Nebraska
118 F6 Hughenden Alberta
141 G5 Hughenden Queensland
110 F7 Hughes Arkansas
121 L4 Hughes Ontario
138 A4 Hughes S Australia
119 R2 Hughes R Manitoba
109 N3 Hughes Springs Texas
110 C3 Hughesville Missouri
140 C6 Hugh R N Terr Aust
118 K7 Hughton Sask
9 F7 Hugh Town Isles of Scilly England
106 G2 Hugo Colorado
99 N4 Hugo Minnesota
107 P7 Hugo Oklahoma
100 B7 Hugo Oregon
107 J4 Hugoton Kansas
36 D7 Hugsweier W Germany
65 B6 Huguan China
Huhehot see Hohhot
58 F3 Huhehot China
67 F4 Hui'an China
145 F3 Huiarau Range New Zealand
67 E4 Huichang China
Huicheng see She Xian
124 H7 Huicholes, Sa. de los mts Mexico
59 J3 Huichŏn N Korea
67 E5 Huidong China
65 G2 Huifaheng China
128 C3 Huila div Colombia
58 G4 Huimin China
65 G3 Huinan China
67 B3 Huishui China
21 F7 Huismes France
20 G5 Huisne R France
21 I6 Huisseau-sur-Cosson France
65 C7 Huiting China
67 C3 Huitong China
29 K10 Huittinen Finland
125 K8 Huitzuco Mexico
65 B7 Hui Xian China
125 N10 Huixtla Mexico
Huiyang see Huizhou
25 D4 Huizen Netherlands
67 E5 Huizhou China
145 F3 Huka Falls New Zealand
145 E4 Hukanui New Zealand
144 C5 Hukarere New Zealand
75 R5 Hukawng Valley Burma
145 E1 Hukerenui New Zealand
67 E2 Hukou China
87 D10 Hukuntsi Botswana
107 O5 Hulah Oklahoma
59 J2 Hulan China
65 F1 Hulan Ergi China
65 G1 Hulan He R China
80 F1 Hulata Israel
98 B5 Hulett Wyoming
Huliao see Dabu
65 J2 Hulin China
65 E2 Hulin He R China
13 H6 Hull England
99 P10 Hull Illinois
98 K6 Hull Iowa
98 F3 Hull N Dakota
115 M8 Hull Quebec
109 N5 Hull Texas
140 A6 Hull Cr N Terr Aust
138 A1 Hull Cr N Terr Australia
146 J10 Hull Gl Antarctica
134 K9 Hull I Phoenix Is Pacific Oc
22 G2 Hulpe, la Belgium
28 E1 Hulsig Denmark
25 B6 Hulst Netherlands
27 H14 Hultsfred Sweden
65 E4 Huludao China
58 G2 Hulun Nur L China
59 J1 Huma China
127 M5 Humacao Puerto Rico
59 H1 Huma He R China
128 F5 Humaitá Brazil
130 B10 Humaitá Paraguay
87 D12 Humansdorp S Africa
110 C4 Humansville Missouri
128 C6 Humay Peru
87 C9 Humbe Angola
123 P5 Humbermouth Nfld
13 H6 Humber, R England
13 H6 Humberside co England
99 Q5 Humbird Wisconsin
28 F7 Humble Denmark
109 M6 Humble Texas
106 G9 Humble City New Mexico
103 M7 Humboldt Arizona
99 S10 Humboldt Illinois
99 M7 Humboldt Iowa
107 P4 Humboldt Kansas
102 F1 Humboldt Nevada
114 J7 Humboldt Sask
110 H6 Humboldt Tennessee
102 F1 Humboldt R Nevada
100 A9 Humboldt B California
115 N2 Humboldt Gletscher gla Greenland
102 F2 Humboldt L Nevada
144 D5 Humboldt, Mt New Zealand
144 B6 Humboldt Mts New Zealand
100 G9 Humboldt Range Nevada
102 F1 Humboldt Rge Nevada
102 G2 Humboldt Salt Marsh Nevada
94 J8 Hume Virginia
141 H7 Humeburn Queensland
77 F7 Hūmedān Iran
48 G2 Humenné Czechoslovakia
139 H6 Hume Res New S Wales
99 N9 Humeston Iowa
28 K5 Humlebæk Denmark
28 B3 Humlum Denmark
32 K9 Humme W Germany
95 L6 Hummelstown Pennsylvania
32 G7 Hümmling hills W Germany
144 C6 Hummock mt New Zealand
127 K10 Humocaro Bajo Venezuela
131 A5 Humos, C Chile
87 B9 Humpata Angola
111 E7 Humphrey Arkansas
101 N5 Humphrey Idaho
98 J8 Humphrey Nebraska
100 D2 Humphrey Washington
102 E5 Humphreys California
110 C1 Humphreys Missouri
103 N6 Humphreys Pk Arizona
140 C7 Humphries, Mt N Terr Aust
31 J6 Humpolec Czechoslovakia
29 K11 Humppila Finland
100 B2 Humptulips Washington
140 B2 Humpty Doo N Terr Aust
84 F4 Hūn Libya
115 R4 Huna Fjordhur Iceland
67 C3 Hunan prov China
65 H3 Hunchun China
144 D5 Hundalee New Zealand
28 A3 Hundborg Denmark
28 B6 Hunderup Denmark
28 H5 Hundested Denmark
117 N10 Hundred Mile House Br Col
26 M6 Hundsjö Sweden
28 E5 Hundslund Denmark
38 G7 Hundstein mt Austria
28 D2 Hune Denmark
48 H5 Hunedoara Romania
48 H5 Hunedoara reg Romania
36 H2 Hünfeld W Germany
36 E3 Hünfelden W Germany
48 D3 Hungary rep Europe
26 H9 Hunge Sweden
36 F3 Hungen W Germany
9 E5 Hungerford England
141 G8 Hungerford Queensland
65 G5 Hüngnam N Korea
101 L1 Hungry Horse Dam Montana
101 M1 Hungry Horse Res Montana
68 H2 Hung Yen Vietnam
65 B4 Hun He R China
65 E4 Hun He R China
65 G4 Hunjiang China
65 F4 Hun Jiang R China
13 H5 Hunmanby England
99 P10 Hunnewell Missouri
25 G2 Hunse R Netherlands
25 F7 Hünshoven W Germany
9 G2 Hunstanton England
28 B2 Hunstrup Denmark
76 C4 Hunsur India
65 E2 Hunt China
109 H5 Hunt Texas
120 J3 Hunta Ontario
32 H8 Hunte R W Germany
32 H8 Hunteburg W Germany
110 E6 Hunter Arkansas
107 M2 Hunter Kansas
98 J2 Hunter N Dakota
144 C6 Hunter New Zealand
107 N5 Hunter Oklahoma
109 J6 Hunter Texas
137 P6 Hunter isld Pacific Oc
139 K4 Hunter R New S Wales
117 J10 Hunter I Br Col
99 P1 Hunter I Ontario
139 G8 Hunter I Tasmania
116 M5 Hunter, Mt Alaska
144 A6 Hunter Mts New Zealand
144 B6 Hunter R New Zealand
122 J7 Hunter River Pr Edward I
100 G1 Hunters Washington
68 A3 Hunter's B Burma
141 F6 Hunter's Gorge Queensland
144 C6 Hunter's Hills, The New Zealand
12 D2 Hunterston Scotland
112 G2 Huntersville N Carolina
94 G8 Huntersville W Virginia
141 J7 Hunterton Queensland
94 B5 Huntertown Indiana
145 E3 Hunterville New Zealand
110 K3 Huntingburg Indiana
9 F3 Huntingdon England
94 J6 Huntingdon Pennsylvania
121 Q7 Huntingdon Quebec
110 H6 Huntingdon Tennessee
Huntingdon and Peterborough co see Cambridgeshire
122 J3 Hunting I Quebec
112 G5 Hunting I S Carolina
94 E6 Huntington Indiana
95 O6 Huntington Long I, N Y
100 H5 Huntington Oregon
111 E10 Huntington Texas
103 O2 Huntington Utah
94 E8 Huntington W Virginia
102 F8 Huntington Beach California
102 E4 Huntington L California
8 D4 Huntley England
101 R4 Huntley Montana
98 G9 Huntley Nebraska
98 B8 Huntley Wyoming
32 H7 Huntlosen W Germany
145 E2 Huntly New Zealand
15 F3 Huntly Scotland
114 C4 Hunt, Mt Yukon Terr
138 D3 Hunt Pen S Australia
101 S5 Hunts Mt Wyoming
122 H10 Hunts Pt Nova Scotia
110 C5 Huntsville Arkansas
110 D2 Huntsville Missouri
115 M8 Huntsville Ontario
109 M5 Huntsville Texas
101 O8 Huntsville Utah
32 E9 Hünxe W Germany
89 G1 Hunyani R Zimbabwe
88 C10 Hunyani Rge mts Zimbabwe
65 B5 Hunyuan China
66 A4 Hunza Kashmir
66 C3 Huocheng China
65 F1 Huodifangzi China
65 B7 Huojia China
139 H9 Huon R Tasmania
68 H4 Huong Hoa Vietnam
68 G3 Huong Khe Vietnam
68 H8 Huong My Vietnam
68 G3 Huong Son Vietnam
68 H4 Huong Thuy Vietnam
139 H9 Huonville Tasmania
67 E1 Huoshan China
65 B6 Huo Shan mt China
67 G5 Huo-shao Tao isld Taiwan
65 B6 Huo Xian China
Hupeh prov see Hubei
20 J1 Huppy France
33 M10 Hüpstedt E Germany
48 E3 Hurbanovo Czechoslovakia
27 E11 Hurdals L Norway
120 J7 Hurd, Cape Ontario
110 D1 Hurdland Missouri
98 F2 Hurdsfield N Dakota
65 E3 Hure Qi China
80 E1 Hurfeish Israel
84 J4 Hurghada Egypt
18 G6 Huriel France
119 P2 Hurkett Ontario
9 F4 Hurley England
111 H11 Hurley Mississippi
106 B9 Hurley New Mexico
98 J6 Hurley S Dakota
99 Q3 Hurley Wisconsin
12 D2 Hurlford Scotland
15 E2 Hurliness Scotland
95 M8 Hurlock Maryland
143 C10 Hurlstone, L W Australia
102 D5 Huron California
94 E5 Huron Ohio
98 H5 Huron S Dakota
99 S3 Huron B Michigan
94 E2 Huron City Michigan
94 E2 Huron, L U.S.A./Canada
99 T3 Huron Mts Michigan
103 L4 Hurricane Utah
94 E8 Hurricane W Virginia
112 E6 Hurricane Cr Georgia
126 E3 Hurricane Flats Bahamas
110 J6 Hurricane Mills Tennessee
9 E5 Hursley England
109 M9 Hurst Texas
9 E5 Hurstbourne Tarrant England
9 G5 Hurst Green England
9 F6 Hurstpierpoint England
131 B3 Hurtado R Chile
36 B2 Hürtgen W Germany
36 B2 Hürth W Germany
111 L9 Hurtsboro Alabama
144 D5 Hurunui R New Zealand
28 E3 Hurup Denmark
28 D7 Hurup W Germany
115 S4 Húsavík Iceland
9 E3 Husbands Bosworth England
28 A4 Husby Denmark
80 F3 Husein Br Jordan
28 O10 Husevig Faeroes
Hushan see Cixi
65 H2 Hushan China
48 L4 Huşi Romania
80 D3 Husifa Israel
27 G14 Huskvarna Sweden
116 J4 Huslia Alaska
80 G4 Husn Jordan
101 L2 Huson Montana
27 A10 Husöy Norway
118 E7 Hussar Alberta
26 B9 Hustadvika Norway
28 B6 Husum Denmark
28 N1 Husum Faeroes
30 E1 Husum W Germany
58 D2 Hutag Mongolia
69 D12 Hutanopan Sumatra
109 O10 Hutchins Texas
107 N3 Hutchinson Kansas
99 M5 Hutchinson Minnesota
113 G10 Hutchinsons I Florida
103 N7 Hutch Mt Arizona
68 D4 Huthi Burma
59 K2 Hutou China
110 J2 Hutsonville Illinois
38 H7 Hüttau Austria
20 F5 Hutte, la France
37 L4 Hüttenbach W Germany
38 L8 Hüttenberg Austria
36 G3 Hüttengesäss W Germany
37 P6 Hutthurm W Germany
111 D8 Huttig Arkansas
109 K5 Hutto Texas
141 J7 Hutton, Mt Queensland
143 E6 Hutton Ra W Australia
94 G8 Huttonsville W Virginia
40 G3 Huttwil Switzerland
58 F4 Hutuo He R China
73 L8 Huvadu Atoll Maldives
65 A7 Hu Xian China
118 D7 Huxley Alberta
116 R6 Huxley, Mt Alaska
144 B6 Huxley, Mt New Zealand
142 F4 Huxley, Mt W Australia
22 J3 Huy Belgium
Huzhou see Wuxing
27 E12 Hvaler isld Norway
28 C3 Hvalpsund Denmark
115 M2 Hval Sound Greenland
28 C3 Hvam Denmark
42 G5 Hvar Yugoslavia
42 H5 Hvar isld Yugoslavia
28 B3 Hvidbjerg Denmark
28 N2 Hvidenæs Faeroes
28 B6 Hviding Denmark
28 E4 Hvilsager Denmark
28 D3 Hvilsom Denmark
28 E4 Hvilsted Denmark
27 E12 Hvitsten Norway
27 D12 Hvittingfoss Norway
Hwainan see Huainan
Hwang-hai see Huang Hai
61 P14 Hyakuna Okinawa
101 P4 Hyalite Pk Montana
100 B9 Hyampom California
95 R5 Hyannis Massachusetts
98 E8 Hyannis Nebraska
58 B2 Hyargas Nuur L Mongolia
100 C7 Hyatt Res Oregon
95 L8 Hyattsville Maryland
101 S5 Hyattville Wyoming
111 J10 Hybart Alabama
121 N7 Hybla Ontario
27 H14 Hycklinge Sweden
117 G8 Hydaburg Alaska
13 F6 Hyde England
144 C6 Hyde New Zealand
94 D9 Hyden Kentucky
143 C9 Hyden W Australia
117 H8 Hyder Br Col/Alaska
74 H10 Hyderabad India
77 L7 Hyderabad Pakistan
Hydra isld see Ídhra I
109 J5 Hye Texas
20 C4 Hyenville France
19 Q18 Hyères France
59 J3 Hyesanjin N Korea
98 A9 Hygiene Colorado
117 J5 Hyland R Yukon Terr
114 G6 Hyland Post Br Col
28 D5 Hylke Denmark
28 G7 Hyllekrog C Denmark
27 A10 Hyllestad Norway
28 F4 Hyllested Denmark
118 E4 Hylo Alberta
27 B12 Hylsfjorden inlet Norway
110 J2 Hymera Indiana
138 F6 Hynam S Australia
12 E2 Hyndford Br Scotland
139 L4 Hyndland, Mt New S Wales
94 J7 Hyndman Pennsylvania
101 L6 Hyndman Peak Idaho
94 K5 Hyner Pennsylvania
60 J10 Hyōgo prefect Japan
86 D4 Hyrra Banda Cent Afr Republic
101 O8 Hyrum Utah
52 C3 Hyrynsalmi Finland
101 S3 Hysham Montana
114 H6 Hythe Alberta
9 E6 Hythe Hampshire England
9 H5 Hythe Kent England
60 E13 Hyūga Japan
29 L11 Hyvinkää Finland
68 J6 Ia Ayun R Vietnam
128 E6 Iaco R Brazil
48 J3 Iacobeni Romania
129 K6 Iaçu Brazil
94 F9 Iaeger W Virginia
36 B7 Iaintrux France
48 K6 Ialomiţa R Romania
113 C7 Iamonia, L Florida
48 L5 Ianca Romania
144 C5 Ianthe, L New Zealand
48 H4 Iara Romania
14 B3 Iar Connaught Irish Rep
129 H3 Iaripo Brazil
53 C10 Iasi Romania
47 G3 Íasmos Greece
111 D10 Iatt, L Louisiana
128 E3 Iauaretê Brazil
52 H4 Ib U.S.S.R.
71 D3 Iba Luzon Philippines
85 E7 Ibadan Nigeria
128 C3 Ibagué Colombia
130 E8 Ibaiti Brazil
101 M9 Ibapah Utah
46 D1 Ibar R Yugoslavia
60 G11 Ibara Japan
61 O9 Ibaraki prefect Japan
128 C3 Ibarra Ecuador
32 G8 Ibbenbüren W Germany
80 G4 Ibbin Jordan
86 C5 Ibenga R Congo
131 F2 Iberá, Esteros del marshes Argentina
131 F2 Iberá, L Argentina
110 D3 Iberia Missouri
121 R7 Iberville Quebec
26 J3 Ibestad Norway
85 F6 Ibeto Nigeria
85 F7 Ibi Nigeria
129 J7 Ibiá Brazil
130 G5 Ibiaí Brazil
129 K4 Ibiapaba, Serra da mts Brazil
131 G3 Ibicui da Cruz R Brazil
131 G2 Ibicuí, R Brazil
133 F4 Ibicuy Argentina
61 K10 Ibigawa Japan
80 D2 I'billin Israel
130 D8 Ibiporã Brazil
130 H6 Ibiraçu Brazil
130 E10 Ibirama Brazil
130 H5 Ibiranhém Brazil
131 G3 Ibirapuita R Brazil
130 E7 Ibitinga Brazil
17 H5 Ibiza isld Balearic Is
80 F8 Ibn Hammad Jordan
88 H8 Ibo Mozambique
129 K6 Ibotirama Brazil
86 D3 Ibra., Wadi watercourse Sudan
52 G6 Ibresi U.S.S.R.
47 H3 İbriktepe Turkey
79 A9 Ibshawâi Egypt
9 E6 Ibsley England
61 Q12 Ibu Okinawa
60 D14 Ibusuki Japan
128 C6 Ica Peru
128 E4 Içá R Brazil
128 F3 Icabaru R Venezuela
127 N3 Icacos Pt Trinidad
71 D5 Icadambanauan Philippines
131 G2 Icamaqua R Brazil
128 E3 Icana Brazil
103 K5 Iceberg Canyon Nev/Ariz
100 G3 Ice Harbor Dam Washington
115 S4 Iceland rep N Atlantic Oc
90 H2 Iceland-Faeroe Rise Atlantic Oc
56 B3 Icha R U.S.S.R.
76 B2 Ichalkaranji India
37 J7 Ichenhausen W Germany
60 G11 Ichi Japan
60 E13 Ichifusa-yama mt Japan
61 O10 Ichihara Japan
61 P5 Ichinohe Japan
59 L4 Ichinomiya Japan
54 D6 Ichnya U.S.S.R.
22 E1 Ichtegem Belgium
37 K2 Ichtershausen E Germany
130 H7 Iconha Brazil
Iconium see Konya
116 R6 Icy B Alaska
116 F1 Icy Cape Alaska
117 E6 Icy Pt Alaska
109 O3 Ida Louisiana
94 D5 Ida Michigan
109 N2 Idabel Oklahoma
99 L7 Ida Grove Iowa
85 F7 Idah Nigeria
101 M6 Idaho state U.S.A.
100 K6 Idaho City Idaho
101 N6 Idaho Falls Idaho
106 E2 Idaho Springs Colorado
106 H2 Idalia Colorado
140 E6 Idamea, L Queensland
140 C5 Ida, Mt N Terr Aust
143 D8 Ida, Mt W Australia
36 C4 Idar Oberstein W Germany
56 E4 Idarskoye Belogor'ye mts U.S.S.R.
36 C4 Idarwald mts W Germany
144 C6 Ida Valley New Zealand
27 E12 Idd Norway
118 F8 Iddesleigh Alberta
111 M9 Ideal Georgia
84 E5 Idehan Marzuq Libya
84 E4 Idehan Ubari Libya
52 D3 Idel' U.S.S.R.
85 F4 Idelès Algeria
86 B6 Idemba Gabon
28 H7 Idestrup Denmark
84 J5 Idfu Egypt
47 G9 Ídhi Óros mt Crete Greece
47 F7 Ídhra isld Greece
69 C10 Idi Sumatra
Idi Amin Dada, L see Edward, L
45 K3 Idice R Italy
116 H5 Iditarod Alaska
70 P10 Idjen Java
27 H11 Idkerberget Sweden
79 G3 Idlib Syria
80 C7 Idna Jordan
140 C6 Idracowra N Terr Aust
26 F10 Idre Sweden
102 D5 Idria California
84 E3 Idris Libya
52 C6 Idritsa U.S.S.R.
42 C3 Idro, L. d' Italy
36 E3 Idstein W Germany
28 A4 Idum Denmark
87 E12 Idutywa S Africa
61 P12 Ie-jima isld Okinawa
45 R6 Ielsi Italy
22 H3 Iemeppe Belgium
130 D8 Iepê Brazil
22 D2 Ieper Belgium
47 H9 Ierápetra Crete Greece
47 F8 Iérax, Akr C Greece
59 G2 I-erh-hsieh China
47 F4 Ierissós Greece
43 C9 Ierzu Sardinia
45 O4 Iesi Italy
61 P12 Ie-suidō str Okinawa
17 H6 Ifach, Pta Spain
87 H12 Ifanadiana Madagascar
85 E7 Ife Nigeria
85 F5 Iférouane Niger
141 F4 Iffley Queensland
138 B4 Ifould L S Australia
16 E10 Igé R Morocco
85 E5 Igadiane watercourse Mali
70 B3 Igan Sarawak
88 D1 Iganga Uganda
130 J9 Igaraçu Brazil
129 J4 Igarape-Açu Brazil
147 P14 Igarka U.S.S.R.
130 C9 Igatimi Paraguay
74 E9 Igatpuri India
71 F5 Igbon isld Philippines
20 G5 Igé France
36 B4 Igel W Germany
27 J10 Iggesund Sweden
85 C2 Ighil M'Goun, Jbel mt Morocco
133 D4 Iglesia Argentina
43 B9 Iglesias Sardinia
98 C6 Igloo S Dakota
147 E4 Igloolik N W Terr
41 O3 Igls Austria
79 D9 'Igma, Gebel el mts Egypt
115 K8 Ignace Ontario
106 C4 Ignacio Colorado
124 H5 Ignacio Allende Mexico
52 C6 Ignalina U.S.S.R.
47 J3 İğneada Turkey
68 A7 Ingoitijala Andaman Is
102 B1 Igo California
71 C3 Igom W Irian
87 F7 Igoma Tanzania
70 B3 Igon R Sarawak
46 D5 Igoumenitsa Greece
52 H5 Igra U.S.S.R.
130 E9 Iguaçu, R Brazil
130 H4 Iguai Brazil
125 K8 Iguala Mexico
17 J3 Igualda Spain
129 J8 Iguapé Brazil
130 D8 Iguaraçu Brazil
130 F7 Iguatama Brazil
130 C8 Iguatemi Brazil
129 L5 Iguatu Brazil
86 A6 Iguéla Gabon
116 K8 Igvak, C Alaska
87 H12 Ihosy Madagascar
68 F6 Ihr Cambodia
22 L3 Ihren W Germany
32 F6 Ihrhove W Germany
40 G1 Ihringen W Germany
58 D2 Ihtamir Mongolia
29 L6 Ii Finland
61 L10 Iida Japan
61 N8 Iide-san mt Japan
29 N2 Iijärvi L Finland
29 N6 Iijoki R Finland
52 C5 Iisaku U.S.S.R.
29 N9 Iisvesi Finland
61 O8 Iizaka Japan
60 D12 Iizuka Japan
71 K9 Ija isld Indonesia
70 P9 Ijang isld Indonesia
85 E7 Ijebu Ode Nigeria
25 E2 IJlst Netherlands
25 D4 IJmeer Netherlands
25 C4 IJmuiden Netherlands
25 F3 Ijonger R Netherlands
25 C4 Ijsel R Netherlands
25 F4 IJssel R Netherlands
25 D3 IJsselmeer Netherlands
25 C5 IJsselmonde Netherlands
25 E3 IJsselmuiden Netherlands
25 D4 IJsselstein Netherlands
133 G3 Ijuí Brazil
131 G2 Ijuí, R Brazil
25 A6 IJzendijke Netherlands
22 D2 Ijzer R Belgium
52 H6 Ik R U.S.S.R.
29 K10 Ikaalinen Finland
144 C5 Ikamatua New Zealand
115 O4 Ikamiut Greenland
86 D6 Ikanda Zaïre
47 H7 Ikaría isld Greece
28 C4 Ikast Denmark
56 H4 Ikatskiy Khrebet mts U.S.S.R.
145 F3 Ikawhenua Range New Zealand
60 J11 Ikeda Japan
60 G12 Ikegawa Japan
61 P13 Ikei-jima isld Okinawa
85 E7 Ikeja Nigeria
86 D6 Ikela Zaïre
115 O3 Ikerasak Greenland
47 F2 Ikhtiman Bulgaria
60 C12 Iki isld Japan
88 C2 Ikimba L Tanzania
60 C12 Iki-suidō str Japan
116 K8 Ikolik, C Alaska
85 F7 Ikom Nigeria
88 D6 Ikomba Tanzania
87 H12 Ikongo Madagascar
87 H11 Ikopa R Madagascar
116 K1 Ikpikpuk R Alaska
56 B3 Iksa R U.S.S.R.
54 J1 Iksha U.S.S.R.
88 C1 Ikulwe Uganda
60 H10 Ikuno Japan
60 R2 Ikutahara Japan
140 B3 Ikymbon R N Terr Aust
71 E2 Ilagan Philippines
78 L5 Ilam Iran
75 M5 Ilam Nepal
56 E3 Ilanskiy U.S.S.R.
41 K4 Ilanz Switzerland
85 E7 Ilaro Nigeria
31 M2 Iława Poland
28 E2 Ilbro Denmark
138 D2 Ilbunga S Australia
8 D5 Ilchester England
13 G3 Ilderton England
120 J9 Ilderton Ontario
118 J3 Ile-à-la Crosse Sask
118 K3 Ile-à-la-Crosse L Sask
48 H3 Ileanda Romania
83 L13 Ile aux Bénitiers Mauritius
86 D6 Ilebo Zaïre
21 C10 Ile d'Oléron France
25 E5 Ileijen Netherlands
55 B5 Ilek U.S.S.R.
85 E4 Ilerh watercourse Algeria
127 N5 Îles des Saintes Guadeloupe W I
85 F7 Ilesha Nigeria
52 G6 Ilet' R U.S.S.R.
33 N9 Ilfeld E Germany
9 G4 Ilford England
119 W2 Ilford Manitoba
8 B5 Ilfracombe England
141 G6 Ilfracombe Queensland
56 F4 Ilga R U.S.S.R.
78 D1 Ilgaz Dağ Turkey
88 H9 Ilha Mozambique
130 F8 Ilhabela Brazil
128 F4 Ilha Grande Brazil
130 G8 Ilha Grande, B. de Brazil
130 D7 Ilha Solteira Brazil
16 B4 Ílhavo Portugal
130 H4 Ilhéus Brazil
48 H5 Ilia Romania
116 K7 Iliamna L Alaska
71 L9 Ili Boleng vol Indonesia
48 N4 Ilichevsk U.S.S.R.
98 C9 Iliff Colorado
71 G6 Iligan Philippines
71 G6 Iligan B Philippines
71 F1 Iligan Pt Philippines
47 F6 Ilikí, L Greece
56 F3 Ilim R U.S.S.R.
56 F1 Ilimpeya R U.S.S.R.
56 F3 Ilimskiy, Khrebet mts U.S.S.R.
71 E4 Ilin isld Philippines
55 C6 Il'inka U.S.S.R.
52 F5 Il'inskoye U.S.S.R.
71 E4 Ilin Str Philippines
48 M1 Ilintsy U.S.S.R.
47 F5 Iliodhrómia isld Greece
95 M3 Ilion New York
42 F3 Ilirska Bistrica Yugoslavia
76 C3 Ilkal India
13 G6 Ilkley England
36 D7 Ill R France
128 E7 Illampu mt Bolivia
17 F4 Illana Spain
71 F7 Illana B Philippines
131 B3 Illapel Chile
131 B3 Illapel, R Chile
54 G8 Illarionovo U.S.S.R.
41 O7 Illasi Italy
41 O6 Illasi, Val d' Italy
138 C2 Illbillee, Mt S Australia
20 B5 Ille-et-Vilaine dep France
37 J7 Iller R W Germany
37 J7 Illertissen W Germany
16 E4 Illescas Spain
20 H5 Illiers France
128 E7 Illimani mt Bolivia
36 F6 Illingen W Germany
110 G1 Illinois R Illinois
110 B5 Illinois R Oklahoma
100 B7 Illinois R Oregon
99 R9 Illinois state U.S.A.
99 R8 Illinois & Mississippi Canal Illinois
110 G2 Illiopolis Illinois
128 G3 Illiwa R Guyana
36 D6 Illkirch France
110 G4 Illmo Missouri
140 D6 Illogwa R N Terr Aust
16 E7 Illora Spain
37 M5 Illschwang W Germany
28 E6 Illumø isld Denmark
37 M6 Ilm R W Germany
29 K9 Ilmajoki Finland
37 K2 Ilmenau E Germany
33 M6 Ilmenau R W Germany
52 D5 Il'men', Ozero L U.S.S.R.
8 D6 Ilminster England
128 D7 Ilo Peru
71 F5 Iloilo Philippines
29 P9 Ilomantsi Finland
85 E7 Ilorin Nigeria
54 K9 Ilovaysk U.S.S.R.
116 L7 Oil Pt Alaska
33 N8 Ilse R E Germany
33 N9 Ilsenburg E Germany
36 G5 Ilsfeld W Germany
36 H5 Ilshofen W Germany
28 C4 Ilskov Denmark
86 F4 Ilubabor prov Ethiopia
88 D3 Ilula Tanzania
48 J3 Ilva Mică Romania
100 A3 Ilwaco Washington
71 N8 Ilwaki Indonesia
52 J4 Ilych R U.S.S.R.
52 D6 Il'yino U.S.S.R.
31 N4 Iłża Poland
31 N4 Iłżanka R Poland
59 K5 Imabari Japan
60 O4 Imabetsu Japan
60 N9 Imaichi Japan
61 K10 Imajō Japan
124 F5 Imala Mexico
78 K6 Imām al Ḩamzah Iraq
57 B6 Imambaba U.S.S.R.
Iman see Dal'nerechensk
52 D1 Imandra U.S.S.R.
130 C10 Iman, Sa. del ra Argentina
55 E4 Imantau, Oz L U.S.S.R.
60 C12 Imari Japan
128 F2 Imataca, Sa de mts Venezuela
29 O10 Imatra Finland
61 J10 Imazu Japan
79 B8 Imbâba Egypt
128 C3 Imbabura prov Ecuador
127 J5 Imbert Dom Rep
133 H3 Imbituba Brazil
130 E9 Imbituva Brazil
100 H4 Imbler Oregon
110 E5 Imboden Arkansas
52 F5 Imeni-Babushkina U.S.S.R.
52 F5 Imeni Kalinina U.S.S.R.
128 E3 Imeri, Sa mts Venezuela
113 F7 Imeson airport Florida
55 F2 Imgyt R U.S.S.R.
86 H4 Imi Ethiopia
47 F7 Imittós mt Greece
65 G5 Imjin R N Korea
102 F1 Imlay Nevada
98 D6 Imlay S Dakota
94 D3 Imlay City Michigan
138 B4 Immarna S Australia
32 K10 Immenhausen W Germany
41 M2 Immenstadt W Germany
113 F11 Immokalee Florida
100 J4 Imnaha Oregon
99 L9 Imogene Iowa
45 L3 Imola Italy
42 H5 Imotski Yugoslavia
128 E5 Imperatriz Brazil
44 D4 Imperia Italy
103 J9 Imperial California
98 E9 Imperial Nebraska
119 M7 Imperial Sask
103 K9 Imperial Dam Cal/Ariz
103 J9 Imperial Valley California
142 C4 Imperieuse Reef W Australia
122 J9 Imperoyal Nova Scotia
36 E5 Impflingen W Germany
86 C5 Impfondo Congo
75 P6 Imphal India
18 H6 Imphy France
52 D4 Impilakhti U.S.S.R.
45 K4 Impruneta Italy
80 F8 Imra Jordan
47 K4 İmralı isld Turkey
İmroz isld see Gökçeada isld
41 N3 Imst Austria
124 D2 Imuris Mexico
71 D5 Imuruan B Philippines
116 D4 Imuruk Basin Alaska
116 F4 Imuruk L Alaska
61 L10 Ina Japan
31 J2 Ina R Poland
90 A16 Inaccessible I Atlantic Oc
146 C14 Inaccessible I S Orkney Is
71 D6 Inagauan Philippines
61 N8 Ina-gawa R Japan
127 H4 Inagua I., Little Bahamas
61 N12 Inamba-jima isld Japan
128 D6 Inambiri R Peru
85 F3 In Amenas Algeria
85 E4 In Amguel Algeria
70 E1 Inanam Sabah
144 C4 Inangahua Junction New Zealand
51 K2 Inarigda U.S.S.R.
29 N3 Inarijärvi L Finland
61 N11 Inatori Japan
61 O8 Inawashiro Japan
61 O8 Inawashiro ko L Japan
85 F4 In Azaoua Algeria
85 E3 In Belbel Algeria
133 D3 Incahuasi mt Chile/Arg
14 E4 Inch Irish Rep
100 G1 Inchelium Washington
37 L6 Inchenhofen W Germany
20 H1 Incheville France
13 E1 Inchkeith isld Scotland
15 D2 Inchnadamph Scotland
65 G6 Inch'ŏn S Korea
116 B3 Inchoun U.S.S.R.
13 E1 Inchture Scotland
22 E3 Inchy France
45 K4 Incisa in Valdarno Italy
89 H5 Incomati R Mozambique
22 H2 Incourt Belgium
12 B2 Indaal, L Scotland
85 D4 In Dagouber Mali
130 D6 Indaia Grande, R Brazil
26 J9 Indal Sweden
26 H8 Indalsälven R Sweden
68 C2 Indaw Burma
75 R6 Indawgyi Lake Burma
124 G5 Indé Mexico
7 M9 Indefatigable sea rig North Sea
102 F5 Independence California
99 P7 Independence Iowa
107 P4 Independence Kansas
111 F11 Independence Louisiana
110 B2 Independence Missouri
100 B5 Independence Oregon
94 F10 Independence Virginia
99 P5 Independence Wisconsin
147 H9 Independence Fj Greenland
100 J8 Independence Mts Nevada
69 F13 Inderagiri R Sumatra
69 E13 Inderapura Sumatra
69 E13 Inderapura, Tg C Sumatra
55 B6 Inderborskiy U.S.S.R.
26 E8 Inderöy Norway
55 B6 Inder, Oz L U.S.S.R.
100 D2 Index Washington
74 G10 Indi India
74 India rep S Asia
107 M7 Indiahoma Oklahoma
95 M2 Indian R New York
117 D4 Indian R Yukon Terr
140 D6 Indiana N Terr Aust
94 H6 Indiana Pennsylvania
94 B6 Indiana state U.S.A.
81 G11 Indian-Antarctic Basin Southern Oc
81 J11 Indian-Antarctic Ridge Southern Oc
94 A7 Indianapolis Indiana
123 T4 Indian B Nfld
123 M7 Indian Brook Nova Scotia
117 P6 Indian Cabins Alberta
115 O7 Indian Hbr Labrador
122 J9 Indian Hbr Nova Scotia
141 L7 Indian Hd Queensland
95 K8 Indian Head Maryland
114 J7 Indian Head Sask
115 K6 Indian L Manitoba
95 N3 Indian L New York
101 P7 Indian Mt Wyoming
81 Indian Ocean
83 Indian Ocean Islands
99 N8 Indianola Iowa
111 F8 Indianola Mississippi
98 F9 Indianola Nebraska
107 P6 Indianola Oklahoma
130 F6 Indianópolis Brazil
103 L3 Indian Peak Utah
101 Q5 Indian Pk Wyoming
113 G10 Indian R Florida
94 C1 Indian River Michigan
113 G9 Indian River City Florida
103 J5 Indian Sp Nevada
113 G10 Indian Town Florida
100 J5 Indian Valley Idaho
103 O6 Indian Wells Arizona
122 A2 Indicator L Quebec
52 G1 Indiga U.S.S.R.
147 L15 Indiga U.S.S.R.
51 O2 Indigirka R U.S.S.R.
52 G1 Indigskaya Guba B U.S.S.R.
48 F5 Indija Yugoslavia
117 Q3 Indin L N W Terr
103 H8 Indio California
109 K9 Indios Mexico
137 N4 Indispensable Reefs Pacific Oc
70 D7 Indonesia rep S E Asia
141 K2 Indooroopilly dist Brisbane, Qnsld
74 F7 Indore India
70 M9 Indramaju Java
73 N5 Indravati R India
21 H8 Indre dep France
21 H7 Indre R France
21 F7 Indre-et-Loire dep France
113 G10 Indrio Florida
21 H7 Indrois R France
138 C2 Indulkana R S Australia
31 O2 Indura U.S.S.R.
118 D8 Indus Alberta
73 L2 Indus R S W Asia
74 B6 Indus, Mouths of Pakistan
110 F1 Industry Illinois
109 L6 Industry Texas
89 E8 Indwe S Africa
85 F4 In Ebeggi Algeria
78 D1 Inebolu Turkey
47 J4 İnecik Turkey
85 F4 In Ecker Algeria
85 E5 In Edek Niger
78 B1 Inegöl Turkey

71 K9 Inerie mt Flores Indonesia
109 L7 Inez Texas
85 G4 In Ezzane Algeria
89 B10 Infanta, C S Africa
16 E6 Infantes Spain
128 F5 Infernão, Cach rapids Brazil
124 H8 Infiernillo, L Mexico
16 D1 Infiesto Spain
130 J9 Ingá Brazil
29 L11 Inga Finland
85 F5 Inga Niger
68 B4 Ingabu Burma
140 C5 Ingallanna R N Terr Aust
94 B7 Ingalls Indiana
107 K4 Ingalls Kansas
99 T4 Ingalls Michigan
100 E10 Ingalls, Mt California
55 F3 Ingaly U.S.S.R.
9 G4 Ingatestone England
36 H5 Ingelfingen W Germany
36 E4 Ingelheim W Germany
22 E2 Ingelmunster Belgium
86 C6 Ingende Zaïre
133 E5 Ingeniero Luiggi Argentina
131 E7 Ingeniero, Pto Argentina
117 L7 Ingenika R Br Col
116 E7 Ingeramuit Alaska
107 M5 Ingersoll Oklahoma
71 B2 Inggelang isld Halmahera Indonesia
141 H4 Ingham Queensland
83 K11 Ingiriya Sri Lanka
13 F5 Ingleborough mt England
140 F6 Ingledoon Queensland
115 N2 Inglefield Land Greenland
109 K8 Ingleside Texas
13 F5 Ingleton England
102 F8 Inglewood California
145 E3 Inglewood New Zealand
141 K8 Inglewood Queensland
139 G6 Inglewood Victoria
119 Q8 Inglis Manitoba
140 D1 Inglis isld N Terr Aust
116 G4 Inglutalik R Alaska
51 L3 Ingoda R U.S.S.R.
76 G5 Ingoitijala Andaman Is
118 F1 Ingolf Ontario
86 C7 Ingololo Zaïre
37 L6 Ingolstadt W Germany
101 S3 Ingomar Montana
138 C3 Ingomar S Australia
123 M7 Ingonish C Breton I, N Scotia
102 B1 Ingot California
26 N1 Ingöy Norway
109 H5 Ingram Texas
99 Q4 Ingram Wisconsin
122 J9 Ingramport Nova Scotia
21 D7 Ingrandes France
21 G8 Ingrandes France
117 P3 Ingray L N W Terr
146 C4 Ingrid Christensen Coast Antarctica
28 D2 Ingstrup Denmark
85 F5 In Guezzam Algeria
54 D9 Ingul R U.S.S.R.
54 E9 Ingulets U.S.S.R.
54 D10 Ingulets R U.S.S.R.
55 F1 Inguyagun R U.S.S.R.
19 K4 Ingwiller France
89 H6 Inhaca Pen Mozambique
87 G10 Inhambane Mozambique
130 C7 Inhandui, R Brazil
130 C7 Inhanduizinho, R Brazil
88 E10 Inhangoma I Mozambique
130 C10 Inhanhora R Brazil
130 G6 Inhapim Brazil
87 G10 Inharrime Mozambique
47 L4 İnhisar Turkey
130 H4 Inhobim Brazil
129 J7 Inhumas Brazil
116 L3 Iniakuk R Alaska
71 K9 Inielika mt Flores Indonesia
17 F5 Iniesta Spain
85 E3 Inifel, Hassi Algeria
27 M11 Iniö Finland
128 E3 Inírida R Colombia
14 A3 Inishark isld Irish Rep
14 A3 Inishbofin isld Irish Rep
14 C1 Inishbofin isld Irish Rep
14 B2 Inishcrone Irish Rep
14 B3 Inisheer isld Irish Rep
14 A2 Inishkea isld Irish Rep
14 B3 Inishmaan isld Irish Rep
14 B3 Inishmore isld Irish Rep
14 C2 Inishmurray isld Irish Rep
14 D1 Inishowen dist Irish Rep
14 E1 Inishowen Hd Irish Rep
14 D1 Inishtrahull isld Irish Rep
14 A3 Inishturk isld Irish Rep
65 D2 Injgan Sum China
141 J7 Injune Queensland
122 H6 Inkerman New Brunswick
141 F3 Inkerman Queensland
86 C7 Inkis R Zaïre
117 G6 Inklin Br Col
101 N7 Inkom Idaho
52 F5 Inkovo U.S.S.R.
98 J1 Inkster N Dakota
68 C2 Inle, L Burma
98 H7 Inman Nebraska
95 N2 Inman New York
112 E2 Inman S Carolina
41 O3 Inn R Austria
38 F6 Inn R W Germany
138 F2 Innamincka S Australia
15 E5 Innerleithen Scotland
Inner Mongolia see Nei Monggol Zizhiqu
Inner Mongolia aut reg see Nei Monggol Zizhiqu
41 K3 Inner-Rhoden dist Switzerland
15 C3 Inner Sound Scotland
32 M8 Innerste R W Germany
41 H4 Innertkirchen Switzerland
38 F8 Innervillgraten Austria
Innien see Aukrug
14 C5 Inniscarra Res Irish Rep
118 D6 Innisfail Alberta
141 H3 Innisfail Queensland
118 F5 Innisfree Alberta
116 J5 Innoko R Alaska
60 G11 Inno-shima Japan
41 O3 Innsbruck Austria
26 K3 Innset Norway
26 B10 Innvik Norway
116 A3 Innymney, Gora mt U.S.S.R.
71 H4 Inobonto Sulawesi
130 D6 Inocência Brazil
107 P5 Inola Oklahoma
47 L5 İnönü Turkey
141 G4 Inorunie Queensland
31 L3 Inowrocław Poland
128 E7 Inquisivi Bolivia
40 F3 Ins Switzerland
85 E3 In Salah Algeria
15 F3 Insch Scotland
143 A7 Inscription,C W Australia
68 B4 Insein Burma
37 J2 Inselsberg mt E Germany
119 O7 Insinger Sask
87 E9 Insiza Zimbabwe
89 F2 Insiza R Zimbabwe
31 J2 Insko Poland
36 B6 Insming France
Insterburg see Chernyakhovsk
8 B5 Instow England
118 J9 Instow Sask
48 L6 Insurăţei Romania
52 K2 Inta U.S.S.R.
98 B2 Intake Montana
85 E5 In Tebezas Mali
47 H4 İntepe Turkey
98 E6 Interior S Dakota
113 F8 Interlachen Florida
40 G4 Interlaken Switzerland
139 H8 Interlaken Tasmania
99 N1 International Falls Minnesota
119 R10 International Peace Gdn Canada/U.S.A.
117 O9 Intersection Mt Alberta/Br Col
68 A6 Interview I Andaman Is
48 K5 Intorsura Buzăului Romania
41 J5 Intragna Switzerland
32 G8 Intrup W Germany
52 F2 Intsy U.S.S.R.
70 D5 Intu Kalimantan
61 O10 Inubō saki Japan
115 O3 Inugsulik Bugt B Greenland
133 C8 Inútil, B Chile
114 F4 Inuvik N W Terr
128 D6 Inuya R Peru
52 J5 In'va R U.S.S.R.
15 C4 Inveraray Scotland
15 F4 Inverbervie Scotland
144 B7 Invercargill New Zealand
12 C2 Invercloy Scotland
139 K3 Inverell New S Wales
15 D3 Invergordon Scotland
15 E4 Inverkeithing Scotland
12 D2 Inverkip Scotland
140 F4 Inverleigh Queensland
12 D1 Inverlochlarig Scotland
119 O7 Invermay Sask
117 P10 Invermere Br Col
123 L7 Inverness C Breton I, N Scotia
113 E9 Inverness Florida
101 P1 Inverness Montana
121 T6 Inverness Quebec
15 D3 Inverness Scotland
Inverness co see Highland reg
15 D3 Invershin Scotland
15 F3 Inverurie Scotland
140 A4 Inverway N Terr Aust
68 C6 Investigator Chan Burma
138 C5 Investigator Group islds S Australia
138 D6 Investigator Str S Australia
68 A7 Invisible Bank Andaman Is
102 C1 Inwood California
120 J10 Inwood Ontario
56 B3 Inya R U.S.S.R.
98 B5 Inyan Kara Cr Wyoming
87 F9 Inyazura Zimbabwe
102 G6 Inyokern California
55 C4 Inzer U.S.S.R.
86 C7 Inzia R Zaïre
46 D5 Ioánnina Greece
47 H9 Ioinianísia isld Greece
52 E1 Iokanga U.S.S.R.
106 C3 Iola Colorado
107 P4 Iola Kansas
109 L5 Iola Texas
45 L2 Iolanda di Savoia Italy
57 B6 Iolotan' U.S.S.R.
123 M8 Iona C Breton I, N Scotia
101 O6 Iona Idaho
99 L6 Iona Minnesota
98 G6 Iona S Dakota
12 B1 Iona isld Scotland
47 J1 Ion Corvin Romania
102 G3 Ione Nevada
100 F4 Ione Oregon
100 H1 Ione Washington
48 J6 Ioneşti Romania
99 O6 Ionia Iowa
94 B3 Ionia Michigan
110 C3 Ionia Missouri
Ionian Is see Iónioi Nísoi
43 H10 Ionian Sea S Europe
46 D5 Iónioi Nísoi islds Greece
116 A4 Ioniveem R U.S.S.R.
78 K1 Iori R U.S.S.R.
47 G8 Íos isld Greece
52 H3 Iosser U.S.S.R.
61 N13 Iō tō isld Japan
111 C11 Iowa Louisiana
99 N7 Iowa R Iowa
99 N7 Iowa state U.S.A.
99 P8 Iowa City Iowa
99 N7 Iowa Falls Iowa
109 J2 Iowa Park Texas
124 G7 Ipala Mexico
83 K9 Ipalogama Sri Lanka
130 E5 Ipameri Brazil
130 H6 Ipanema Brazil
130 H10 Ipanema R Brazil
130 H8 Ipanguacu Brazil
99 Q9 Ipava Illinois
48 E2 Ipel' R Czechoslovakia
116 E2 Ipewik R Alaska
37 J4 Iphofen W Germany
128 C3 Ipiales Colombia
129 L6 Ipiau Brazil
Ipin see Yibin
128 E4 Ipiranga Amazonas Brazil
130 E9 Ipiranga Paraná Brazil
128 D5 Ipixuna Amazonas Brazil
128 F5 Ipixuna R Amazonas Brazil
69 E10 Ipoh Malaysia
130 J10 Ipojuca R Brazil
71 C6 Ipolote B Palawan Philippines
129 H7 Iporá Brazil
130 E9 Iporanga Brazil
120 J9 Ipperwash Prov. Park Ontario
37 J4 Ippesheim W Germany
86 D4 Ippy Cent Afr Republic
78 A1 Ipsala Turkey
9 H3 Ipswich England
127 J2 Ipswich Jamaica
95 R4 Ipswich Massachusetts
141 L8 Ipswich Queensland
98 G4 Ipswich S Dakota
129 K4 Ipu Brazil
54 C4 Iput' R U.S.S.R.
78 K2 Iğdir Turkey
128 D8 Iquique Chile
128 D4 Iquitos Peru
80 F6 'Ira Jordan
108 F5 Iraan Texas
61 L11 Irago-misaki Japan
130 D10 Irai Brazil
47 G8 Iráklia isld Greece
47 G9 Iráklion Crete
130 C9 Irala Paraguay
77 C4 Iran empire S W Asia
130 D10 Irani R Brazil
77 G6 Irānshahr Iran
128 F1 Irapa Venezuela
124 J7 Irapuato Mexico
78 H5 Iraq rep S W Asia
95 P2 Irasburg Vermont
129 H3 Iratapuru R Brazil
130 E9 Iratí Brazil
133 G3 Irati Brazil
17 G2 Irati R Spain
84 E4 Irāwan Libya
52 J3 Irayel' U.S.S.R.
27 M14 Irbenskiy Proliv str U.S.S.R.
80 G3 Irbid Jordan
50 F3 Irbit U.S.S.R.
55 D2 Irbit R U.S.S.R.
9 G1 Irby England
38 K7 Irdning Austria
54 C7 Irdyn' U.S.S.R.
109 K4 Iredell Texas
109 K4 Ireland Texas
90 A1 Ireland I Bermuda
14 Ireland, Rep of
14 E3 Ireland's Eye isld Irish Rep
55 C3 Iren R U.S.S.R.
98 J6 Irene S Dakota
98 K7 Ireton Iowa
57 B1 Irgiz R U.S.S.R.
85 F5 Irhazer Wan Agadez V Niger
86 D2 Iriba Chad
129 G3 Iricoumé, Serra mts Brazil
71 F4 Iriga Philippines
55 C5 Iriklinskiy U.S.S.R.
87 G7 Iringa Tanzania
67 H4 Iriomote-shima isld Japan
125 M2 Iriona Honduras
129 H5 Iriri R Brazil
14 C3 Irish Republic
139 H8 Irishtown Tasmania
47 K3 İriva Turkey
56 E2 Irkineyeva R U.S.S.R.
56 F5 Irkutsk U.S.S.R.
56 F3 Irkutskaya Oblast' U.S.S.R.
118 F6 Irma Alberta
99 R4 Irma Wisconsin
36 E2 Irmgarteichen W Germany
112 F3 Irmo S Carolina
20 B5 Irodouer France
18 B4 Iroise gulf France
86 C3 Iro, L Chad
138 D4 Iron Baron S Australia
8 D2 Ironbridge England
120 G6 Iron Bridge Ontario
100 C9 Iron Canyon Res California
110 J6 Iron City Tennessee
110 F4 Irondale Missouri
94 G6 Irondale Ohio
121 M8 Irondale Ontario
138 D4 Iron Knob S Australia
99 S4 Iron Mountain Michigan
100 A7 Iron Mt Oregon
103 L4 Iron Mt Utah
98 G5 Iron Nation S Dakota
141 G2 Iron Range Queensland
99 S6 Iron Ridge Wisconsin
99 S3 Iron River Michigan
99 P3 Iron River Wisconsin
94 B2 Irons Michigan
100 H5 Ironside Oregon
103 L4 Iron Sp Utah
94 B1 Ironton Michigan
110 F4 Ironton Missouri
94 E8 Ironton Ohio
99 Q3 Ironwood Michigan
98 J5 Iroquois S Dakota
99 T9 Iroquois R Illinois
120 K4 Iroquois Falls Ontario
71 G4 Irosin Philippines
61 M11 Irō zaki C Japan
45 R8 Irpinia Italy
138 D3 Irrapatana S Australia
68 B4 Irrawaddy prov Burma
68 B5 Irrawaddy R Burma
68 B5 Irrawaddy, Mouths of Burma
36 B4 Irrel W Germany
118 D7 Irricana Alberta
85 D5 Irrigi reg Mali/Mauritania
56 D3 Irsha U.S.S.R.
48 H2 Irshava U.S.S.R.
52 G4 Irta U.S.S.R.
13 F3 Irthing, R England
55 D3 Irtyash, Oz L U.S.S.R.
55 F4 Irtysh U.S.S.R.
55 E2 Irtysh R U.S.S.R.
55 F4 Irtyshsk U.S.S.R.
86 E5 Irumu Zaïre
18 D9 Irun Spain
17 F2 Irurzun Spain
18 D10 Irurzun Spain
128 E8 Iruya Argentina
52 G3 Irva R U.S.S.R.
118 G9 Irvine Alberta
110 N4 Irvine Kentucky
15 D5 Irvine Scotland
15 D5 Irvine R Scotland
141 H3 Irvinebank Queensland
14 D2 Irvinestown N Ireland
107 O2 Irving Kansas
109 N9 Irving Texas
143 F7 Irving, Mt W Australia
110 K4 Irvington Kentucky
95 L9 Irvington Virginia
94 J6 Irvona Pennsylvania
13 F6 Irwell, R England
101 O6 Irwin Idaho
99 L8 Irwin Iowa
98 D7 Irwin Nebraska
143 B8 Irwin W Australia
143 B11 Irwin, Pt W Australia
112 D5 Irwinton Georgia
141 J6 Isaac R Queensland
117 N9 Isaac L Br Col
123 L8 Isaacs Hbr Nova Scotia
17 G2 Isaba Spain
107 M4 Isabel Kansas
98 E4 Isabel S Dakota
71 F5 Isabela Negros Philippines
71 E7 Isabela Philippines
127 L5 Isabela Puerto Rico
128 A8 Isabela, Isla Galapagos Is
125 M3 Isabelia, Cord ra Nicaragua
102 F6 Isabella California
119 Q8 Isabella Manitoba
99 P2 Isabella Minnesota
142 F5 Isabella, L W Australia
147 N11 Isachenko, Ostrov isld U.S.S.R.
114 J2 Isachsen N W Terr
60 D13 Isahaya Japan
52 F3 Isakogorka U.S.S.R.
48 H6 Işalniţat Romania
86 D5 Isangi Zaïre
37 N7 Isar R W Germany
42 D2 Isarco R Italy
46 E7 Isari Greece
41 O2 Isar Tal W Germany
111 J7 Isbell Alabama
22 C2 Isbergues France
15 G1 Isbister Scotland
40 C1 Isches France
41 M3 Ischgl Austria
45 P8 Ischia Italy
86 H5 Iscia Baidoa Somalia
142 F3 Isdell,R W Australia
21 J6 Isdes France
59 L5 Ise Japan
28 H5 Isefjord inlet Denmark
41 O3 Isel Berg mt Austria
146 K7 Iselin Bank Antarctica
81 H14 Iselin Seamount Southern Oc
52 H6 Isenbayevo U.S.S.R.
36 D3 Isenburg W Germany
33 N8 Isenbüttel W Germany
33 N7 Isenhagen W Germany
28 C4 Isenvad Denmark
42 C3 Iseo Italy
42 C3 Iseo, L. d' Italy
19 P14 Isère dep France
19 O14 Isère R France
32 G10 Iserlohn W Germany
43 F7 Isernia Italy
61 K11 Ise shima Nat. Park Japan
55 E3 Isetskoye U.S.S.R.
61 K11 Ise-wan B Japan
85 E7 Iseyin Nigeria
61 N9 Isezaki Japan
Isfahan see Eşfahān
57 E5 Isfana U.S.S.R.
57 F4 Isfara U.S.S.R.
80 D3 Isfiya Israel
52 J4 Isherim, Gora mt U.S.S.R.
128 G3 Isherton Guyana
88 C7 Ishiba Ngandu Zambia
67 H4 Ishigaki Japan
67 H4 Ishigaki-shima isld Japan
61 K9 Ishika prefect Japan
60 P2 Ishikari Japan
60 R2 Ishikari dake mt Japan
59 M3 Ishikari-wan B Japan
50 F3 Ishim U.S.S.R.
55 C4 Ishimbay U.S.S.R.
55 F5 Ishimo R U.S.S.R.
55 F3 Ishimskaya Step steppe U.S.S.R.
55 E5 Ishimskoye U.S.S.R.
59 M4 Ishinomaki Japan
60 G12 Ishizuchi-san mt Japan
86 G6 Isiolo Kenya
87 F11 Isipingo Bch S Africa
86 E5 Isiro Zaire
141 G6 Isisford Queensland
86 G1 Is, Jebel mt Sudan
55 E3 Iska R U.S.S.R.
80 D5 Iskāka Jordan
57 E4 Iskander U.S.S.R.
47 J8 İskandil Burun C Turkey
78 F3 İskenderun Turkey
57 G4 Iski-Naukat U.S.S.R.
56 B4 Iskitim U.S.S.R.
47 G1 Iskŭr R Bulgaria
117 J7 Iskut Br Columbia
117 H7 Iskut R Br Col
119 O3 Iskwatam L Sask
15 E4 Isla R Scotland
78 F3 Islâhiye Turkey
74 E2 Islamabad Pakistan
113 G13 Islamorada Florida
110 J4 Island Kentucky
117 N5 Island R N W Terr
71 D6 Island B Palawan Philippines
100 H4 Island City Oregon
95 S7 Island Falls Maine
120 J3 Island Falls Ontario
119 P3 Island Falls Sask
141 K5 Island Hd Queensland
95 N7 Island Heights New Jersey
115 K7 Island L Manitoba
123 Q5 Island L Nfld
120 K7 Island L Ontario
138 D4 Island Lagoon S Australia
99 W3 Island Lake Ontario
100 B9 Island Mountain California
101 O5 Island Park Idaho
95 Q2 Island Pond Vermont
143 B9 Island Pt W Australia
145 E1 Islands, Bay of New Zealand
115 O8 Islands, Bay of Nfld
17 J5 Islas Baleares Spain
16 B2 Islas Cíes Spain
127 M5 Isla Verde airport Puerto Rico
118 G5 Islay Alberta
15 B5 Islay isld Scotland
21 H10 Isle France
99 N3 Isle Minnesota
18 F7 Isle R France
20 K3 Isle Adam, l' France
123 O6 Isle aux Morts Nfld
95 T2 Isleboro Maine
18 F9 Isle en Dodon, L' France
18 F9 Isle Jourdain, L' Gers France
18 F6 Isle Jourdain, L' Vienne France
118 H4 Isle, Lac des Sask
122 A5 Isle Maligne Quebec
112 F6 Isle of Hope Georgia
15 G2 Isle of Noss Scotland
12 D4 Isle of Whithorn Scotland
99 S1 Isle Royale Michigan
22 G5 Isles-sur-Suippes France
18 H5 Isle-sur-Serein, L' France
106 D7 Isleta New Mexico
102 C3 Isleton California
122 C5 Isle Verte Quebec
9 E4 Islip England
127 N3 Islote Pt Trinidad
133 D1 Isluga mt Chile
128 E7 Isluga vol Chile
131 F4 Ismael Cortinas Uruguay
84 J3 Ismâ'ilîya Egypt
37 M7 Ismaning W Germany
98 B3 Ismay Montana
78 A2 Ismir Körfezi Turkey
84 J4 Isna Egypt
87 H12 Isoanala Madagascar
29 J9 Isojoki Finland
87 F8 Isoka Zambia
29 J8 Isokyrö Finland
41 O7 Isola Italy
111 F8 Isola Mississippi
45 P6 Isola d. Liri Italy
45 M5 Isola Farnese Italy
87 H12 Isola, Massif de L' mts Madagascar
45 K1 Isola Rizza Italy
110 L5 Isoline Tennessee
45 J1 Isorella Italy
29 N6 Isosyöte mt Finland
78 C3 Isparta Turkey
47 H1 Isperikh Bulgaria
78 H1 Ispir Turkey
80 Israel rep S W Asia
143 E10 Israelite B W Australia
28 F4 Issehoved C Denmark
143 A8 Isseka W Australia
25 F5 Isselburg W Germany
85 C7 Issia Ivory Coast
18 H7 Issoire France
21 I8 Issoudun France
25 F5 Issum W Germany
57 H4 Issyk-Kul, Ozero L U.S.S.R.
57 J4 Issyk-Kul'skaya oblast U.S.S.R.
77 L2 Istalif Afghanistan
47 K3 İstanbul Turkey
120 J7 Isthmus Bay Ontario
46 F6 Istiaía Greece
78 H3 Istilil Turkey
128 C2 Istmina Colombia
54 H1 Istra U.S.S.R.
42 F3 Istra pen Yugoslavia
47 J3 Istranca Dağları mts Turkey
19 N18 Istres France
61 M11 Isu hantō pen Japan
55 C5 Isyangulovo U.S.S.R.
130 B9 Itá Paraguay
129 L6 Itabaiana Brazil
130 H7 Itabapoana Brazil
130 E8 Itaberá Brazil
130 E5 Itaberaí Brazil
129 K7 Itabira Brazil
130 G7 Itabirito Brazil
128 F4 Itaboca Brazil
129 L6 Itabuna Brazil
129 J5 Itacajá Brazil
129 H5 Itacajuna R Brazil
130 G4 Itacarambi Brazil
129 L6 Itacaré Brazil
128 G4 Itacoatiara Brazil
128 D5 Itacuai R Brazil
130 C9 Itacurubí del Rosario Paraguay
130 H6 Itaguaçu Brazil
130 D8 Itaguaje Brazil
129 J6 Itaguari R Brazil
130 E8 Itaí Brazil
130 E10 Itaiópolis Brazil
129 G4 Itaituba Brazil
130 E10 Itajai Acú, R Brazil
129 J8 Itajuba Brazil
130 H4 Itajuipe Brazil
61 O10 Itako Japan
Itala see Ataleh
109 L3 Italy Texas
42 Italy rep S Europe
130 G5 Itamarandiba Brazil
129 J4 Itamatare Brazil
130 H6 Itambacuri Brazil
129 K7 Itambé Brazil
130 G6 Itambe, P. de mt Brazil
60 J11 Itami Japan
130 F9 Itanhaém Brazil
129 K7 Itanhém R Brazil
129 H3 Itany R Suriname
130 H5 Itaobim Brazil
129 J6 Itapaci Brazil
130 E6 Itapajipe Brazil
130 H4 Itapebi Brazil
130 F7 Itapecerica Brazil
129 K4 Itapecuru Mirim Brazil
130 H7 Itapemirim Brazil
129 K8 Itaperuna Brazil
129 K7 Itapetinga Brazil
129 J8 Itapetininga Brazil
129 J8 Itapeva Brazil
129 G3 Itapi R Brazil
129 K5 Itapicura R Brazil
129 J5 Itapicuru, Serra do mts Brazil
128 F5 Itapinima Brazil
129 L4 Itapipoca Brazil
128 G4 Itapira Brazil
130 E10 Itapocu, R Brazil
130 E7 Itápolis Brazil
130 H9 Itaporanga Brazil
130 C10 Itapuá reg Paraguay
129 H7 Itapuranga Brazil
131 G2 Itaqui Brazil
133 F2 Itaquyry Paraguay
129 J8 Itararé Brazil
74 G7 Itarsi India
130 D6 Itarumá Brazil
109 K3 Itasca Texas
99 L2 Itasca State Park Minnesota
131 A6 Itata, R Chile
130 F8 Itatiba Brazil
131 F2 Itati, L Argentina
130 E8 Itatinga Brazil
128 F5 Itatuba Brazil
130 E5 Itauçu Brazil
130 G7 Itaúna Brazil
129 L7 Itaúnas Brazil
130 H6 Itaúnas Brazil
9 E5 Itchin, R England
55 F4 Itemgen, Oz L U.S.S.R.
94 C3 Ithaca Michigan
95 L4 Ithaca New York
Ithaca isld Greece see Itháki
46 D6 Itháki isld Greece
8 C3 Ithon, R Wales
86 D5 Itimbiri R Zaïre
130 H5 Itinga Brazil
129 H7 Itiquira Brazil
129 K5 Itiúba, Serra de mts Brazil
115 O4 Itivdleq Greenland
116 M2 Itkillik R Alaska
61 N11 Itō Japan
61 L3 Itoigawa Japan
86 D6 Itoko Zaïre
61 P14 Itoman Okinawa
20 H4 Iton R France
45 P7 Itri Italy
79 A9 Itsa Egypt
111 F8 Itta Bena Mississippi
25 E6 Ittervoort Netherlands
43 E8 Ittiri Sardinia
130 F8 Itu Brazil
131 G2 Itú R Brazil
129 J7 Ituiutaba Brazil
88 A3 Itula Zaïre
88 E5 Itumba Tanzania
129 J7 Itumbiara Brazil
119 O7 Ituna Sask
128 G2 Ituni Guyana
130 E10 Ituporanga Brazil
128 E8 Iturbe Argentina
130 C10 Iturbe Paraguay
59 N3 Iturup, Ostrov isld U.S.S.R.
130 F7 Ituverava Brazil
130 C10 Ituzaingo Argentina
37 K3 Itz R W Germany
32 L5 Itzehoe W Germany
32 K5 Itzwärden W Germany
88 D6 Iufira R Malawi
110 H3 Iuka Illinois
107 M4 Iuka Kansas
130 H7 Iúna Brazil
112 E3 Iva S Carolina
129 H8 Ivaí R Brazil
29 N3 Ivalo Finland
29 N3 Ivalojoki R Finland
48 E7 Ivančići Yugoslavia
46 D2 Ivangrad Yugoslavia
98 K5 Ivanhoe Minnesota
139 G5 Ivanhoe New S Wales
94 G10 Ivanhoe Virginia
142 G3 Ivanhoe W Australia
120 H4 Ivanhoe R Ontario
54 M1 Ivanishchi U.S.S.R.
48 F7 Ivanjica Yugoslavia
53 B9 Ivano-Frankovsk U.S.S.R.
48 L1 Ivanopol U.S.S.R.
55 G3 Ivanovka Omsk U.S.S.R.
55 B4 Ivanovka U.S.S.R.
52 F6 Ivanovo U.S.S.R.
103 J6 Ivanpah California
54 J1 Ivanteyvka U.S.S.R.
47 H3 Ivaylovgrad Bulgaria
55 D1 Ivdel' U.S.S.R.
33 R5 Ivenack E Germany
99 S10 Ivesdale Illinois
17 H8 Ivi, C Algeria
115 P5 Ivigtut Greenland
86 B5 Ivindo R Gabon
9 F4 Ivinghoe England
129 H8 Ivinheima R Brazil
116 N2 Ivishak R Alaska
Iviza see Ibiza
95 L10 Ivor Virginia
85 C7 Ivory Coast rep W Africa
27 G15 Ivösjön Sweden
54 F3 Ivot U.S.S.R.
42 B3 Ivrea Italy
47 J5 İvrindi Turkey
20 J4 Ivry-la-Bataille France
115 M5 Ivugivik Quebec
8 C7 Ivybridge England
94 F8 Ivydale W Virginia
61 O7 Iwadeyama Japan
61 O7 Iwai-gawa R Japan
61 P6 Iwaizumi Japan
61 O9 Iwaki Japan
61 O5 Iwaki R Japan
61 O5 Iwaki-san mt Japan
59 K5 Iwakuni Japan
60 P2 Iwamizawa Japan
70 D3 Iwan R Kalimantan
60 O3 Iwanai Japan
61 O7 Iwanuma Japan
61 O9 Iwase Japan
61 M9 Iwasuge-yama mt Japan
61 L11 Iwata Japan
61 P6 Iwate Japan
60 H11 Iwaya Japan
85 E7 Iwo Nigeria
Iwo Jima see Iō-tō
61 N13 Iwo Jima isld Japan
22 E3 Iwuy France
128 E6 Ixiamas Bolivia
125 M9 Ixtepec, Ciudad Mexico
124 H8 Ixtlahuacán Mexico
124 G7 Ixtlán del Río Mexico
9 G3 Ixworth England
56 F4 Iya R U.S.S.R.
55 E3 Iyevlevo U.S.S.R.
60 G12 Iyomishima Japan
60 F12 Iyo-nada sea Japan
48 J3 Iza R Romania
125 P10 Izabal, L. de Guatemala
17 G2 Izalzu Spain
116 F6 Izaviknek R Alaska
31 O5 Izbica Poland
54 E1 Izdeshkovo U.S.S.R.
22 E2 Izegem Belgium
19 O14 Izeron France
52 H6 Izhevsk U.S.S.R.
52 H2 Izhma U.S.S.R.
53 C10 Izmail U.S.S.R.
78 A2 Izmir Turkey
47 J6 İzmir Boz Sira Dağları mts Turkey
78 C1 Izmit Turkey
47 K4 İzmit Körfezi B Turkey
16 E7 Iznajar Spain
16 E7 Iznalloz Spain
78 B1 Iznik Turkey
78 B1 Iznik Gölü Turkey
128 F7 Izozog, Bañados de Bolivia
79 G6 Izra' Syria
48 E4 Izsák Hungary
47 G3 Iztochni Rodopi Bulgaria
60 C11 Izuhara Japan
60 D13 Izumi Japan
60 J11 Izumi-ōtsu Japan
60 F10 Izumo Japan
61 M8 Izumozaki Japan
55 D3 Izumrud U.S.S.R.
61 N11 Izu-shotō islds Japan
147 N12 Izvestiy, Os isld U.S.S.R.
50 H1 Izvestiy Tsik, Ostrova isld U.S.S.R.
48 K4 Izvorul Oltului Romania
57 A2 Izyndy U.S.S.R.
54 J7 Izyum U.S.S.R.
29 M10 Jaala Finland
29 L5 Jaatila Finland
77 E2 Jaba R Iran
84 G3 Jabal al Akhdar mts Libya
77 C7 Jabal Dhana U.A.E.
16 E6 Jabalón R Spain
74 H7 Jabalpur India
22 E1 Jabbeke Belgium
33 R5 Jabel E Germany
46 D3 Jablanica Albania
46 E2 Jablanica R Yugoslavia
31 J5 Jablonec nad Nisou Czechoslovakia
31 K7 Jablonica Czechoslovakia
31 L2 Jabłonowo Poland
31 L6 Jablunkov Czechoslovakia
129 M5 Jaboatão Brazil
129 J8 Jaboticabal Brazil
69 G13 Jabung, Tanjung C Sumatra
128 F5 Jaburu Brazil
17 G2 Jaca Spain
130 B6 Jacadigo L Brazil
130 G4 Jacaraci Brazil
129 K6 Jacaré R Brazil
130 F8 Jacareí Brazil
128 G5 Jacaretinga Brazil
130 E8 Jacarezinho Brazil
133 D4 Jachal Argentina
37 O3 Jáchymov Czechoslovakia
130 H5 Jacinto Brazil
109 M5 Jacinto, S R Texas
128 F5 Jaciparaná Brazil
120 D4 Jackfish Ontario
118 J5 Jackfish L Sask
117 R6 Jackfish River Alberta
119 U7 Jackhead Harbour Manitoba
115 N6 Jack Lane B Labrador
95 R1 Jackman Maine
100 E1 Jack Mt Washington
120 C3 Jackpine Ontario
141 G3 Jack R Queensland
112 C1 Jacksboro Tennessee
109 J2 Jacksboro Texas
94 K6 Jacks Mt Pennsylvania
111 J10 Jackson Alabama
102 D3 Jackson California
112 D4 Jackson Georgia
94 D9 Jackson Kentucky
111 E11 Jackson Louisiana
111 F9 Jackson Mississippi
110 G4 Jackson Missouri
101 M4 Jackson Montana
112 K1 Jackson N Carolina
94 E7 Jackson Ohio
141 J7 Jackson Queensland
112 F4 Jackson S Carolina
110 H6 Jackson Tennessee
101 P6 Jackson Wyoming
94 H8 Jackson R Virginia
117 L10 Jackson Bay Br Col
144 B5 Jackson Bay New Zealand
145 E4 Jackson, C New Zealand
110 M1 Jackson Cen Ohio
106 B4 Jackson Gulch Res Colorado
113 C7 Jackson, L Florida
112 D4 Jackson L Georgia
101 P6 Jackson L Wyoming
143 C9 Jackson, Mt W Australia
100 G8 Jackson Mts Nevada
99 T5 Jacksonport Wisconsin
111 G9 Jackson Prairie Mississippi
106 F1 Jackson Res Colorado
144 C5 Jacksons New Zealand
123 Q4 Jackson's Arm Nfld
111 L8 Jacksonville Alabama
110 D7 Jacksonville Arkansas
113 F7 Jacksonville Florida
99 Q10 Jacksonville Illinois
110 D2 Jacksonville Missouri
112 K3 Jacksonville N Carolina
100 C7 Jacksonville Oregon
109 M4 Jacksonville Texas
113 F7 Jacksonville Beach Florida
127 H5 Jacmel Haiti
124 G4 Jaco Mexico
71 N9 Jaco isld Timor
74 C4 Jacobabad Pakistan
129 K6 Jacobina Brazil
103 M5 Jacob L Arizona
80 E5 Jacob's Well Jordan
124 H8 Jacona Mexico
121 T9 Jacques Cartier Quebec
121 T5 Jacques Cartier, L Quebec
122 G4 Jacques Cartier, Mt Quebec
122 F6 Jacquet R New Brunswick
130 J9 Jacú R Brazil
130 F7 Jacuí Minas Gerais Brazil
131 H2 Jacui Rio Grande do Sul Brazil
131 H2 Jacui R Rio Grande do Sul Brazil
129 L6 Jacuípe R Brazil
103 H9 Jacumba California
129 J4 Jacundá Brazil
129 H4 Jacunda R Brazil
130 F9 Jacupiranga Brazil
129 E4 Jaçura Brazil
80 G8 Jad'a Jordan
48 E6 Jadar R Yugoslavia
32 H6 Jade W Germany
32 H6 Jade R W Germany
85 C2 Jadida, El Morocco
87 E8 Jadotville Zaïre
31 N3 Jadów Poland
17 F4 Jadraque Spain
84 E3 Jādū Libya
28 H5 Jægerspris Denmark
22 F3 Jaeibise Belgium
143 C8 Jaellan, Mt W Australia
71 E3 Jaen Luzon Philippines
16 E7 Jaén Spain
16 E7 Jaén prov Spain
27 A13 Jaeren R Norway
26 F7 Jaevsjo Norway
77 A2 Ja'farābād Iran
80 C5 Jaffa Israel
138 E6 Jaffa, C S Australia
83 K8 Jaffna Sri Lanka
75 K9 Jagdalpur India
87 E11 Jagersfontein S Africa
84 G4 Jaghbūb, Al Libya
116 Q2 Jago R Alaska
36 H5 Jagst R W Germany
37 J5 Jagstzell W Germany
74 H9 Jagtial India
129 K6 Jaguaquara Brazil
131 H4 Jaguarão Brazil
131 G2 Jaguari R Brazil
129 H8 Jaguariaiva Brazil
129 L5 Jaguaribe R Brazil
131 C2 Jagüe, R Argentina
126 D3 Jaguey Grande Cuba
140 B1 Jahleel Pt N Terr Aust
78 K7 Jahmah Iraq
48 E7 Jahorina mt Yugoslavia
77 C5 Jahrom Iran
74 G3 Jaijon Doaba India
74 F5 Jaipur India
74 D5 Jaisalmer India
42 H4 Jajce Yugoslavia
75 M8 Jajpur India
70 L9 Jakarta Java
63 Jakarta conurbation Indonesia
26 J5 Jäkkvik Sweden
26 S2 Jakobselv R Norway/U.S.S.R.
29 K8 Jakobstad Finland
46 E3 Jakupica Yugoslavia
106 G9 Jal New Mexico
77 H6 Jāla Iran
58 G2 Jalai Nur China
77 L2 Jalalabad Afghanistan
125 L3 Jalapa Nicaragua
125 L8 Jalapa Enríquez Mexico
29 K9 Jalasjärvi Finland
74 H5 Jalaun India
140 C2 Jalboi R N Terr Aust
86 H4 Jaldessa Ethiopia
130 E7 Jales Brazil
75 M8 Jaleswar India
74 F8 Jalgaon India
22 K2 Jalhay Belgium
78 L6 Jalibah Iraq
86 B4 Jalingo Nigeria
124 G8 Jalisco state Mexico
21 D7 Jallais France
74 F9 Jalna India
17 F3 Jalón R Spain
Jalo Oasis see Gialo
74 E6 Jalor India
124 H7 Jalostotitlán Mexico
124 H7 Jalpa Mexico
75 N5 Jalpaiguri India
124 K7 Jalpan Mexico
77 L2 Jalrez Afghanistan
84 G4 Jalu Libya
78 K4 Jalūlā Iraq
77 G2 Jam reg Iran
128 B4 Jama Ecuador
126 G4 Jamaica Cuba
95 P3 Jamaica Vermont
127 K2 Jamaica W I
126 G5 Jamaica Chan Caribbean
27 M13 Jämaja U.S.S.R.
75 N6 Jamalpur Bangladesh
75 M6 Jamalpur India
126 A2 Jamanota hill Aruba W I
129 G5 Jamanxim R Brazil
128 F5 Jamari Brazil
66 C2 Jamati China
139 K5 Jamberoo New S Wales
Jambi see Telanaipura
69 F13 Jambi dist Sumatra
141 K6 Jambin Queensland
69 C10 Jamboaye R Sumatra
122 F4 Jambon, Pte Quebec
69 C10 Jambuair, Tanjung C Sumatra
110 C5 James R Missouri
98 H3 James R N Dakota
98 J6 James R S Dakota
115 L7 James B Canada
95 N6 Jamesburg New Jersey
112 K2 James City N Carolina
94 J5 James City Pennsylvania
112 F2 James, L N Carolina
99 N9 Jameson Missouri
115 R3 Jameson Land Greenland
99 N10 Jamesport Missouri
113 L12 James Pt Bahamas
140 D5 James R N Terr Aust
95 L9 James R Virginia
140 C6 James Ra N Terr Aust
146 D14 James Ross I Antarctica
115 K4 James Ross Str N W Terr
110 K2 Jamestown Indiana
107 N2 Jamestown Kansas
94 B4 Jamestown Michigan
98 H3 Jamestown N Dakota
94 H4 Jamestown New York
94 D7 Jamestown Ohio
94 G5 Jamestown Pennsylvania
95 Q5 Jamestown Rhode I
90 A13 Jamestown St Helena
138 E5 Jamestown S Australia
112 H4 Jamestown S Carolina
94 C10 Jamestown Tennessee
95 L9 Jamestown Nat. Hist. Site Virginia
112 L2 Jamesville N Carolina
95 L4 Jamesville New York
22 J5 Jametz France
100 H5 Jamieson Oregon
29 K10 Jämijärvi Finland
125 L9 Jamilzepec Mexico
98 G7 Jamison Nebraska
76 B2 Jamkhandi India
74 F9 Jamkhed India
76 D3 Jammalamadugu India
28 C2 Jammerbugt B Denmark
28 F5 Jammerland Bugt B Denmark
74 F2 Jammu Kashmir
Jammu and Kashmir see Kashmir
74 G1 Jammu and Kashmir India
74 D7 Jamnagar India
31 J1 Jamno, Jezioro L Poland
22 J4 Jamoigne Belgium
74 D4 Jampur Pakistan
29 L10 Jämsä Finland
29 L10 Jämsänkoski Finland
75 M7 Jamshedpur India
26 F8 Jämtland Sweden
26 H8 Jämtl Sikås Sweden
71 C3 Jamtup, Tg C W Irian
70 E3 Jamuk, G mt Kalimantan
102 H9 Jamul California
75 N6 Jamuna R Bangladesh
128 C3 Jamundí Colombia
75 M5 Janakpur Nepal
129 K7 Janaúba Brazil
129 H3 Janaucu, I Brazil
130 E5 Jandaia Brazil
142 B3 Jandakot dist Perth, W Aust
142 B3 Jandakot, L W Australia
77 D2 Jandaq Iran
28 A5 Janderup Denmark
128 E5 Jandiatuba R Brazil
141 K7 Jandowae Queensland
94 G7 Jane Lew W Virginia
144 B6 Jane Pk New Zealand
100 E9 Janesville California
99 O7 Janesville Iowa
99 N5 Janesville Minnesota
99 R7 Janesville Wisconsin
130 D10 Jangada Brazil
130 C7 Jango Brazil
69 G13 Jang, Tanjung C Indonesia
33 S8 Jänickendorf E Germany
46 E2 Janjevo Yugoslavia
89 D6 Jan Kemp S Africa
119 P4 Jan L Sask
90 H1 Jan Mayen isld Arctic Oc
90 H1 Jan Mayen Ridge, E Arctic Oc
77 G2 Jannatabad Iran
124 E2 Janos Mexico
48 E4 Jánoshalma Hungary
48 D3 Jánosháza Hungary
37 P5 Janovice nad Uhlavou Czechoslovakia
33 S5 Janow E Germany
31 K3 Janowiec Poland
31 N5 Janów Lubelski Poland
31 O3 Janów Podlaski Poland
98 K9 Jansen Nebraska
119 N7 Jansen Sask
130 G4 Januária Brazil
20 J5 Janville France
21 C6 Janzé France
130 G5 Jaoquim Felício Brazil
74 F7 Jaora India
61 Japan empire E Asia
59 K3 Japan, Sea of E Asia
29 N9 Jäppilä Finland
128 E4 Japurá Brazil
127 J5 Jarabacoa Dom Rep
129 J7 Jaraguá Brazil
130 E10 Jaraguá do Sul Brazil
130 C7 Jaraguari Brazil
130 E10 Jaraguá Serra mts Brazil
16 D5 Jaraicejo Spain
16 E4 Jarama R Spain
133 D7 Jaramillo Argentina
16 D4 Jarandilla Spain
129 H4 Jarauçu R Brazil
100 K8 Jarbidge Nevada
100 K7 Jarbidge R Idaho
27 J11 Järbo Sweden
143 B10 Jardee W Australia
130 G9 Jardim Ceará Brazil
130 C7 Jardim Mato Grosso Brazil
130 H9 Jardim do Seridó Brazil
141 F1 Jardine R Queensland
122 E6 Jardine Brook New Brunswick
126 E4 Jardines de la Reina islds Cuba
130 E6 Jardinésia Brazil
130 F7 Jardinópolis Brazil
21 B9 Jard-sur-Mer France
27 H14 Järeda Sweden
27 E11 Jaren Norway
38 N8 Jarenina Yugoslavia
58 G2 Jargalant Mongolia
21 J6 Jargeau France
129 H3 Jari R Brazil
128 F4 Jari, L Brazil
33 S5 Jarmen E Germany

27 J12 Järna Sweden
18 E7 Jarnac France
27 H13 Järnlunden L Sweden
71 F5 Jaro Panay Philippines
31 K4 Jarocin Poland
31 J5 Jaroměř Czechoslovakia
31 J6 Jaroměřice Czechoslovakia
126 F4 Jaronu Cuba
31 O5 Jaroslaw Poland
106 E4 Jaroso Colorado
26 F8 Järpen Sweden
80 F8 Jarra R Jordan
94 K10 Jarratt Virginia
26 K5 Jarre mt Sweden
109 K5 Jarrell Texas
68 F3 Jarres, Plaine des Laos
118 F6 Jarrow Alberta
13 G4 Jarrow England
128 F6 Jaru Brazil
65 E2 Jarud Qi China
52 C5 Järva-Jaani U.S.S.R.
118 D4 Jarvie Alberta
134 B3 Jarvis I Pacific Oc
26 H10 Järvsö Sweden
21 E6 Jarzé France
48 F5 Jaša Tomic Yugoslavia
74 D7 Jasdan India
33 T8 Jasdorf E Germany
85 E7 Jasikan Ghana
77 E7 Jāsk Iran
31 N6 Jasło Poland
119 O7 Jasmin Sask
30 H1 Jasmund pen E Germany
133 E8 Jason Is Falkland Is
146 E14 Jason Pen Antarctica
110 J2 Jasonville Indiana
111 J8 Jasper Alabama
114 H7 Jasper Alberta
110 C5 Jasper Arkansas
106 D4 Jasper Colorado
113 E7 Jasper Florida
111 M7 Jasper Georgia
110 K3 Jasper Indiana
94 C5 Jasper Michigan
98 K6 Jasper Minnesota
110 B4 Jasper Missouri
94 K4 Jasper New York
121 P8 Jasper Ontario
112 B2 Jasper Tennessee
111 C11 Jasper Texas
117 O9 Jasper Nat. Park Alberta
118 D5 Jasper Place Alberta
78 K5 Jassan Iraq
Jassy see Iasi
31 L1 Jastarnia Poland
46 E1 Jastrebac mt Yugoslavia
31 K2 Jastrowie Poland
48 F3 Jászapáti Hungary
48 F3 Jászarokszállás Hungary
48 F3 Jászberény Hungary
48 F3 Jászfényszaru Hungary
48 F3 Jászladány Hungary
129 H7 Jataí Brazil
128 G4 Jatapu R Brazil
76 B2 Jath India
126 E4 Jatibonico Cuba
17 G6 Játiva Spain
129 H4 Jatobá Brazil
129 J4 Jatobal Brazil
80 D4 Jatt Israel
128 F5 Jatuarana Brazil
33 T5 Jatzke E Germany
33 T5 Jatznick E Germany
129 J8 Jaú Brazil
128 F4 Jaú R Brazil
128 F3 Jauaperi R Brazil
22 H2 Jauche Belgium
126 G4 Jauco Cuba
128 C6 Jauja Peru
21 F10 Jauldes France
128 G5 Jauna R Brazil
21 F8 Jaunay-Clan France
52 B6 Jaunjelgava U.S.S.R.
52 C6 Jaunpiebalga U.S.S.R.
75 K6 Jaunpur India
38 L8 Jauntal V Austria
129 G7 Jauru R Brazil
130 D6 Jauru, R Brazil
22 D5 Jaux France
Java isld Indonesia see Jawa
76 D4 Javadi Hills India
129 J6 Javaés, Serra dos mts Brazil
17 G4 Javalambre, Sierra de mts Spain
128 D4 Javari R Brazil/Peru
70 M8 Java Sea Indonesia
136 D4 Java Trough Indian Oc
17 H6 Jávea Spain
Javhlant see Uliastay
133 C7 Javier B Chile
48 E6 Javor mts Yugoslavia
48 E2 Javoria mt Czechoslovakia
38 K9 Javornik Yugoslavia
48 E1 Javorniky mt Czechoslovakia
26 M6 Jävre Sweden
20 E5 Javron France
80 G6 Jawa Jordan
70 Jawa isld Indonesia
84 G5 Jawf, Al Libya
69 J13 Jawi Indonesia
31 J4 Jawor Poland
31 L5 Jaworzno Poland
107 Q5 Jay Oklahoma
136 H2 Jaya Pk mt W Irian
136 J2 Jayapura W Irian
98 B7 Jay Em Wyoming
33 P7 Jayenitz E Germany
9 H4 Jaywick Sands England
78 H4 Jazirah, Al Iraq
124 J5 Jazminal Mexico
77 F6 Jaz Murian, Hamun-e L Iran
78 G4 Jdaide Syria
103 J6 Jean Nevada
109 J2 Jean Texas
111 E12 Jeanerette Louisiana
122 E1 Jean L Quebec
117 N5 Jean Marie River N W Terr
94 H6 Jeannette Pennsylvania
127 H5 Jean Rabel Haiti
13 G5 Jeater Houses England
80 G1 Jeba Syria
77 F5 Jebāl Bārez, Kūh-e mts Iran
85 E7 Jebba Nigeria
86 E2 Jebel Abyad Plateau Sudan
16 D9 Jebha Morocco
28 B3 Jebjerg Denmark
79 F3 Jeble Syria
88 E8 Jeci mt Mozambique
119 P7 Jedburgh Sask
13 F2 Jedburgh Scotland
Jedda see Jiddah
94 E3 Jeddo Michigan
43 C12 Jedeida Tunisia
13 F3 Jedfoot Br Scotland
31 M5 Jędrzejów Poland
31 N2 Jedwabne Poland
117 H9 Jedway Br Col
29 M4 Jeesiö Finland
33 O7 Jeetze E Germany
33 O6 Jeetze R W Germany
99 L5 Jeffers Minnesota
106 E2 Jefferson Colorado
112 D3 Jefferson Georgia
94 K7 Jefferson Maryland
94 G5 Jefferson Ohio
107 N5 Jefferson Oklahoma
100 C5 Jefferson Oregon
98 K7 Jefferson S Dakota
111 B9 Jefferson Texas
99 S6 Jefferson Wisconsin
110 D3 Jefferson City Missouri
101 N3 Jefferson City Montana
112 D1 Jefferson City Tennessee
101 O4 Jefferson Island Montana
100 D5 Jefferson, Mt Oregon
94 B8 Jeffersontown Kentucky
110 L3 Jeffersontown Kentucky
112 D5 Jeffersonville Georgia
94 B8 Jeffersonville Indiana
95 N5 Jeffersonville New York
94 D7 Jeffersonville Ohio
95 P2 Jeffersonville Vermont
101 S7 Jeffrey City Wyoming
71 C3 Jef Lio W Irian
85 E6 Jega Nigeria
28 B3 Jegindø isld Denmark
18 F9 Jegun France
77 G4 Jehile Pūzak L Iran
28 B7 Jejsing Denmark
130 C9 Jejui Guazú, R Paraguay
52 C6 Jékabpils U.S.S.R.
112 F6 Jekyll I Georgia
31 J5 Jelenia Góra Poland
52 B6 Jelgava U.S.S.R.
115 L8 Jellicoe Ontario
28 C5 Jelling Denmark
102 B1 Jelly California
31 L5 Jełowa Poland
27 E12 Jelöy isld Norway
28 C6 Jels Denmark
27 B12 Jelsa Norway
48 F2 Jelšava Czechoslovakia
69 G11 Jemaja Indonesia
22 F3 Jemappes Belgium
33 N8 Jembke W Germany
70 E1 Jembongan isld Sabah
85 G1 Jem, El Tunisia
22 J3 Jemelle Belgium
106 D6 Jemez R New Mexico
106 D6 Jemez Pueblo New Mexico
106 D6 Jemez Springs New Mexico
32 F6 Jemgum W Germany
43 D13 Jemmal Tunisia
31 J6 Jemnice Czechoslovakia
122 F8 Jemseg New Brunswick
37 M2 Jena E Germany
111 D10 Jena Louisiana
38 E7 Jenbach Austria
80 E4 Jenin Jordan
94 F9 Jenkinjones W Virginia
94 E9 Jenkins Kentucky
99 M3 Jenkins Minnesota
140 A7 Jenkins,Mt N Terr Aust
118 F8 Jenner Alberta
102 A3 Jenner California
127 O4 Jennings Antigua W I
113 D7 Jennings Florida
107 K2 Jennings Kansas
111 D11 Jennings Louisiana
107 O5 Jennings Oklahoma
117 H6 Jennings R Br Col
114 J4 Jenny Lind I N W Terr
139 K5 Jenolan Caves New S Wales
101 Q9 Jensen Utah
113 G10 Jensen Beach Florida
115 P5 Jensen Nunatakker peak Greenland
115 L4 Jens Munk I N W Terr
69 J13 Jenu Indonesia
138 F6 Jeparit Victoria
29 K8 Jeppo Finland
129 K6 Jequie Brazil
130 G5 Jequitai Brazil
129 K7 Jequitinhonha Brazil
85 D2 Jerada Morocco
69 F11 Jerantut Malaysia
85 G2 Jerba, I de Tunisia
126 G5 Jérémie Haiti
129 L6 Jeremoabo Brazil
124 H6 Jerez de García Salinas Mexico
16 C8 Jerez de la Frontera Spain
16 C6 Jerez de los Caballeros Spain
80 E6 Jericho Jordan
141 H6 Jericho Queensland
33 Q8 Jerichow E Germany
129 K4 Jericoaquara, Pta C Brazil
69 G14 Jerigi Sumatra
26 N5 Jerijärvi Sweden
70 B3 Jerijeh, Tg C Sarawak
139 H6 Jerilderie New S Wales
29 L4 Jerisjärvi L Finland
130 E4 Jeroaquara Brazil
103 M7 Jerome Arizona
101 L7 Jerome Idaho
120 H5 Jerome Ontario
129 H7 Jerônimo, Serra do mts Brazil
143 C10 Jerraymungup W Australia
9 H7 Jersey isld Channel Is
95 N6 Jersey City New Jersey
95 K5 Jersey Shore Pennsylvania
110 F2 Jerseyville Illinois
28 E2 Jerslev Denmark
28 C6 Jerstal Denmark
16 D4 Jerte R Spain
79 G5 Jerūd Syria
70 D2 Jerudong Brunei
129 K5 Jerumenha Brazil
28 E1 Jerup Denmark
80 D6 Jerusalem Israel
145 E3 Jerusalem New Zealand
136 H6 Jervais Ra N Terr Australia
139 K6 Jervis Bay New S Wales
138 E6 Jervis, C S Australia
117 M10 Jervis Inlet Br Col
140 D6 Jervois Ra N Terr Aust
33 N8 Jerxheim W Germany
36 G2 Jesberg W Germany
37 P3 Jesenice Czechoslovakia
42 F2 Jesenice Yugoslavia
31 K5 Jeseník Czechoslovakia
48 F2 Jesenské Czechoslovakia
33 Q8 Jeserig E Germany
33 R10 Jesewitz E Germany
Jesselton Sabah see Kota Kinabalu
27 E11 Jessheim Norway
98 H2 Jessie N Dakota
33 Q9 Jessnitz E Germany
113 F9 Jessup, L Florida
32 L6 Jesteburg W Germany
112 F6 Jesup Georgia
99 O7 Jesup Iowa
133 E4 Jesús María Argentina
124 H7 Jesús María Mexico
107 M5 Jet Oklahoma
119 Q2 Jetait Manitoba
94 J9 Jetersville Virginia
107 L3 Jetmore Kansas
37 J7 Jettingen W Germany
37 L7 Jetzendorf W Germany
22 G3 Jeumont France
32 L4 Jevenau R W Germany
32 L4 Jevenstedt W Germany
32 G5 Jever W Germany
48 D1 Jevičko Czechoslovakia
27 D11 Jevnaker Norway
98 C6 Jewel Cave Nat. Mon S Dakota
99 N7 Jewell Iowa
107 M2 Jewell Kansas
100 B4 Jewell Oregon
110 H2 Jewett Illinois
94 G6 Jewett Ohio
109 L4 Jewett Texas
95 Q5 Jewett City Connecticut
75 K9 Jeypore India
46 D2 Jezerce mt Albania
37 P5 Jezerni mt Czechoslovakia
42 H4 Jezero Yugoslavia
31 M2 Jeziorak, Jezioro L Poland
31 M2 Jeziorany Poland
31 P1 Jeznas U.S.S.R.
31 M4 Jeżów Poland
79 F5 Jezzine Lebanon
74 F7 Jhabua India
74 G4 Jhajjar India
74 G6 Jhalawar India
74 E3 Jhang Maghiana Pakistan
74 H6 Jhansi India
75 M5 Jhapa Nepal
74 E2 Jhelum India
74 E2 Jhelum R Pakistan
74 F4 Jhunjhuna India
65 E3 Jiade He R China
67 G1 Jiading China
67 C4 Jiagui China
67 D4 Jiahe China
Jiaji see Qionghai
67 A2 Jiajiang China
58 E5 Jialing Jiang R China
65 G4 Ji'an China
67 E3 Ji'an China
65 D4 Jianchang China
65 F4 Jianchang China
67 F2 Jiande China
67 B2 Jiang'an China
67 B2 Jiangbei China
68 E1 Jiangcheng China
67 C3 Jiangdong China
67 F1 Jiangdu China
67 C6 Jianghong China
67 D4 Jianghua China
67 B2 Jiangjin China
Jiangkou see Fengkai
67 C3 Jiangkou China
67 D1 Jiangkou China
67 F3 Jiangle China
67 D1 Jiangling China
67 D5 Jiangmen China
58 G5 Jiangsu prov China
67 E3 Jiangxi prov China
65 B7 Jiang Xian China
67 F1 Jiangxiang China
67 G1 Jiangyin China
67 D4 Jiangyong China
67 A1 Jiangyou China
67 C3 Jianhe China
Jianjun see Yongshou
67 D2 Jianli China
67 E3 Jianning China
67 F3 Jian'ou China
65 D4 Jianping China
65 D5 Jianping China
67 C1 Jianshi China
67 A5 Jianshui China
58 D5 Jianyang China
67 F3 Jianyang China
65 B6 Jiaocheng China
59 J3 Jiaohe China
65 C5 Jiaohe China
65 B6 Jiaokou China
67 E4 Jiaoling China
65 E7 Jiaonan China
65 D6 Jiao Xian China
58 F4 Jiaozuo China
65 G3 Jiapigou China
58 G5 Jiashan China
67 G1 Jiashan China
57 H5 Jiashi China
65 D7 Jiawang China
65 A5 Jia Xian China
65 B7 Jia Xian China
59 H5 Jiaxing China
67 C4 Jiaya China
59 K2 Jiayin China
67 D2 Jiayu China
58 C4 Jiayuguan China
65 E6 Jiazhou Wan B China
77 B7 Jiban, Al Saudi Arabia
129 J7 Jibao, Serra do mts Brazil
126 E4 Jibaro Cuba
88 G6 Jibondo isld Tanzania
48 H3 Jibou Romania
67 B3 Jichang China
31 J5 Jičín Czechoslovakia
86 G1 Jiddah Saudi Arabia
65 H2 Jidong China
Jiehu see Yinan
26 L2 Jiekkevarre mt Norway
67 E5 Jieshi China
67 E5 Jieshi Wan B China
26 O2 Jiesjavrre L Norway
67 E5 Jiexi China
65 B6 Jiexiu China
143 D6 Jiggalong W Australia
100 K9 Jiggs Nevada
67 E1 Jigong Shan mt China
79 H4 Jihar, Wādī el watercourse Syria
31 J6 Jihlava Czechoslovakia
31 H6 Jihočesky reg Czechoslovakia
31 J6 Jihomoravský reg Czechoslovakia
85 F1 Jijel Algeria
48 L3 Jijia R Romania
86 H4 Jijiga Ethiopia
80 G3 Jijjin Jordan
17 G6 Jijona Spain
59 H2 Jilin prov China
65 G3 Jilin China
65 F3 Jilin Hada Ling mt ra China
59 H1 Jiliu He R China
17 G4 Jiloca R Spain
116 M3 Jim R Alaska
86 G4 Jimā Ethiopia
69 G14 Jimar Sumatra
142 F5 Jimberingga W Australia
48 F5 Jimbolia Romania
141 L8 Jimboomba Queensland
16 D8 Jimena de la Frontera Spain
124 G4 Jiménez Mexico
140 C2 Jim Jim Cr N Terr Aust
65 E6 Jimo China
65 C6 Jinan China
65 B7 Jincheng China
139 J6 Jindabyne New S Wales
37 O3 Jindřichovice Czechoslovakia
31 J6 Jindřichův Hradec Czechoslovakia
67 E2 Jing'an China
67 F1 Jingde China
67 F2 Jingdezhen China
Jingfeng see Hexigten Qi
65 D5 Jinghai China
65 E6 Jinghaiwei China
66 C3 Jinghe China
58 E5 Jing He R China
68 E2 Jinghong China
67 G1 Jingjiang China
65 B5 Jingle China
67 D1 Jingmen China
Jingping see Pinglu
65 G2 Jingpo China
65 G3 Jingpo Hu L China
67 D1 Jingshan China
58 F5 Jing Shan mt ra China
58 D4 Jingtai China
65 C6 Jing Xian China
67 C3 Jing Xian China
67 F1 Jing Xian China
59 H2 Jingxing China
67 A2 Jingyan China
65 A7 Jingyang China
65 G3 Jingyu China
58 D4 Jingyuan China
Jingzhou see Jiangling
67 F2 Jinhua China
65 C7 Jining China
65 B4 Jining Nei Monggol Zizhiqu China
88 D1 Jinja-Bugembe Uganda
67 F4 Jinjiang China
67 C3 Jin Jiang R China
67 E2 Jin Jiang R China
67 D2 Jinjing China
65 E6 Jinkou China
67 E1 Jinkou China
67 F4 Jinlong Jiang R China
125 M3 Jinotega Nicaragua
125 L4 Jinotepe Nicaragua
67 C3 Jinping China
68 F1 Jinping China
Jinsha see Nantong
67 B3 Jinsha China
58 C6 Jinsha Jiang R China
Jinshan see Harqin Qi
67 G1 Jinshan China
67 D2 Jinshi China
67 F1 Jintan China
67 A1 Jintang China
67 C5 Jintian Shuiku res China
71 F5 Jintotolo isld Philippines
71 F5 Jintotolo Ch Philippines
59 H3 Jinxi China
67 B5 Jinxi China
67 E3 Jinxi China
67 F3 Jin Xi China
65 C5 Jin Xian China
65 E4 Jin Xian China
65 E5 Jin Xian China
67 E2 Jinxian China
65 C7 Jinxiang China
67 G3 Jinxiang China
67 C4 Jinxiu China
67 G2 Jinyun China
67 E1 Jinzhai China
65 E4 Jinzhou China
65 E5 Jinzhou Wan B China
128 B4 Jipijapa Ecuador
126 F4 Jiquaní Cuba
130 H5 Jiquitaia Brazil
143 F9 Jirina W Australia
65 D2 Jirin Gol China
37 P3 Jirkov Czechoslovakia
48 L5 Jirlău Romania
65 A7 Jishan China
67 C2 Jishou China
67 E3 Jishui China
79 G3 Jisr esh Shughūr Syria
16 C2 Jistredo, Sa. de mts Spain
143 C10 Jitarning W Australia
69 E9 Jitra Malaysia
Jiucheng see Wucheng
67 A1 Jiuding Shan mt China
58 G6 Jiujiang China
67 E2 Jiujiang China
67 D1 Jiukou China
48 H6 Jiul R Romania
67 E4 Jiulian Shan mts China
67 E2 Jiuling Shan mt ra China
58 C4 Jiuquan China
65 E6 Jiurongcheng China
59 J3 Jiutai China
67 C4 Jiuwan Dashan mts China
65 C5 Jiuwuqing China
65 C5 Jiuxincheng China
67 B4 Jiuxu China
67 F1 Jiuyuhang China
67 B4 Jiuzhou China
72 G4 Jiwā', Al oasis U.A.E.
77 G7 Jiwani Iran
74 B10 Jiwani Pakistan
65 H2 Jixi China
67 F1 Jixi China
65 A6 Ji Xian China
65 C6 Ji Xian China
65 C7 Ji Xian China
65 D4 Ji Xian China
65 D6 Jiyang China
65 B7 Jiyuan China
65 D5 Jiyun He R China
80 G7 Jiza Jordan
65 C6 Jize China
31 H5 Jizera R Czechoslovakia
60 G10 Jizō zaki C Japan
86 E1 J. Kissu mt Sudan
120 G1 Joab L Ontario
130 D10 Joaçaba Brazil
33 T7 Joachimsthal E Germany
130 H5 Joaíma Brazil
85 A6 Joal-Fadiout Senegal
142 E5 Joanna Spring W Australia
129 L5 Joao Camara Brazil
129 J4 João Coelho Brazil
87 B9 João de Almeid Angola
131 H4 João Maria, Albardão do Brazil
130 E10 João Paulo R Brazil
129 M5 João Pessoa Brazil
130 J9 João Pessoa Brazil
130 F5 João Pinheiro Brazil
111 B10 Joaquin Texas
126 F4 Jobabo Cuba
61 O9 Jōban Japan
71 G6 Jobo Pt Mindanao Philippines
20 B2 Jobourg France
102 F2 Job Pk Nevada
120 D2 Jobrin Ontario
38 F7 Jochberg Austria
16 E7 Jódar Spain
74 E5 Jodhpur India
74 D7 Jodiya Bandar India
22 H2 Jodoigne Belgium
123 S4 Joe Batt's Arm Nfld
29 O9 Joensuu Finland
106 H2 Joes Colorado
26 G6 Joeström Sweden
19 K3 Jœuf France
87 F10 Jofane Mozambique
106 E7 Joffre New Mexico
117 Q10 Joffre, Mt Br Col
61 L9 Joganji R Japan
75 M5 Jogbani India
65 C3 Jogdor China
52 C5 Jõgeva U.S.S.R.
122 H8 Joggins Nova Scotia
74 G3 Jogindernagar India
120 E2 Jog L Ontario
38 N7 Joglland Austria
61 K9 Jōhana Japan
32 J9 Johannaberg W Germany
102 G6 Johannesburg California
89 A1 Johannesburg S Africa
37 O3 Johanngeorgenstadt E Germany
115 M2 Johan Pen N W Terr
60 F13 Jōhen Japan
116 L3 John R Alaska
122 J8 John, C Nova Scotia
127 M2 John Crow Mts Jamaica
100 G5 John Day Oregon
100 E4 John Day R Oregon
117 Q6 John d'Or Prairie Alberta
143 F9 John Eyre Motel W Australia
113 G9 John F. Kennedy Space Center Florida
106 H3 John Martin Res Colorado
142 G3 John,Mt W Australia
15 E2 John O'Groats Scotland
146 F3 John Quincey Adams Gl Antarctica
107 P3 John Redmond Res Kansas
107 J4 Johnson Kansas
99 K9 Johnson Nebraska
94 J5 Johnsonburg Pennsylvania
95 M4 Johnson City New York
94 E10 Johnson City Tennessee
109 J5 Johnson City Texas
99 S6 Johnson Cr Wisconsin
117 G5 Johnsons Crossing Yukon Terr
127 P4 Johnsons Pt Antigua W I
112 H4 Johnsonville S Carolina
112 F4 Johnston S Carolina
8 A4 Johnston Wales
110 H4 Johnston City Illinois
15 D5 Johnstone Scotland
117 K10 Johnstone Str Br Col
88 B7 Johnston Falls Zambia
143 D9 Johnston Ls.,The W Australia
143 C8 Johnston Ra W Australia
14 E3 Johnstown Irish Rep
98 F7 Johnstown Nebraska
95 N4 Johnstown New York
94 E6 Johnstown Ohio
94 J6 Johnstown Pennsylvania
94 E9 John W Flannagan Res Virginia
61 P5 Jōhōji Japan
69 F12 Johor Malaysia
69 F12 Johor Baharo Malaysia
37 P2 Jöhstadt E Germany
52 C5 Jõhvi U.S.S.R.
18 H5 Joigny France
110 F6 Joiner Arkansas
130 E10 Joinville Brazil
19 J4 Joinville France
146 D14 Joinville I Antarctica
48 L5 Joita Romania
125 K8 Jojutla Mexico
26 N5 Jokk Sweden
26 L5 Jokkmokk Sweden
27 C10 Jokuleggi mt Norway
78 K2 Jolfa Iran
99 S8 Joliet Illinois
101 Q4 Joliet Montana
119 U10 Joliette N Dakota
115 M8 Joliette Quebec
142 A1 Jolimont dist Perth, W Aust
99 M7 Jolley Iowa
117 S3 Jolly L N W Terr
71 E7 Jolo Philippines
102 C6 Jolon California
26 B10 Jölstervatn L Norway
26 G7 Joma mt Norway
29 H11 Jomala Finland
71 F3 Jomalig isld Luzon Philippines
69 F12 Jombol isld Indonesia
66 F5 Jomda China
71 A3 Jome Indonesia
27 D13 Jomfruland isld Norway
52 B6 Jonava U.S.S.R.
22 F5 Jonchery-sur-Vesle France
7 E13 Jones Bank Atlantic Oc
110 F6 Jonesboro Arkansas
111 M8 Jonesboro Georgia
110 G4 Jonesboro Illinois
109 P3 Jonesboro Louisiana
95 U2 Jonesboro Maine
112 H2 Jonesboro N Carolina
100 H6 Jonesboro Oregon
112 E1 Jonesboro Tennessee
109 K4 Jonesboro Texas
116 N1 Jones Is Alaska
146 G12 Jones Mts Antarctica
95 U2 Jonesport Maine
83 M9 Jones Pt Christmas I Indian Oc
115 L2 Jones Sound N W Terr
111 F7 Jonestown Mississippi
94 B7 Jonesville Indiana
111 E10 Jonesville Louisiana
94 C5 Jonesville Michigan
112 F3 Jonesville S Carolina
94 D10 Jonesville Virginia
86 F4 Jonglei prov Sudan
52 B6 Joniskis U.S.S.R.
27 G14 Jönköping Sweden
27 G14 Jönköping county Sweden
115 M8 Jonquière Quebec
28 K4 Jönstorp Sweden
18 E7 Jonzac France
110 B4 Joplin Missouri
101 P1 Joplin Montana
110 H4 Joppa Illinois
80 B5 Joppa Israel
99 N5 Jordan Minnesota
101 T2 Jordan Montana
95 L3 Jordan New York
80 Jordan kingdom S W Asia
80 F1 Jordan R Israel/Jordan
100 H7 Jordan R Oregon
141 H6 Jordan R Queensland
129 K7 Jordânia Brazil
111 K9 Jordan L Alabama
122 G9 Jordan L Nova Scotia
48 F1 Jordanow Poland
100 H7 Jordan Valley Oregon
130 D9 Jordão, R Brazil
28 C3 Jordbro Å R Denmark
33 R5 Jördenstorf E Germany
27 F10 Jordet Norway
28 E6 Jordløse Denmark
28 C5 Jordrup Denmark
28 B6 Jordsand isld Denmark
26 P2 Jorgastak Norway
133 B8 Jorge Montt, I Chile
75 Q5 Jorhat India
32 L5 Jork W Germany
26 L6 Jörn Sweden
106 C9 Jornada del Muerto reg New Mexico
27 B12 Jörpeland Norway
20 E4 Jort France
85 F7 Jos Nigeria
71 G8 Jose Abad Santos Mindanao Philippines
133 C6 José de San Martín Argentina
129 J8 José dos Campos Brazil
130 C5 Joselândia Brazil
133 E5 José Maria Blanco Argentina
27 B12 Josenfjord inlet Norway
71 F3 Jose Pañganiban Philippines
100 J4 Joseph Idaho
100 H4 Joseph Oregon
142 G2 Joseph Bonaparte G Australia
136 F4 Joseph Bonaparte Gulf Australia
103 O7 Joseph City Arizona
115 N7 Joseph L Labrador
123 K4 Joseph Pt Anticosti I, Quebec
144 B6 Josephville New Zealand
61 M9 Jōshin-etsu Kogen Nat. Park Japan
109 K3 Joshua Texas
102 H7 Joshua Tree California
21 I6 Josnes France
36 H3 Jossatal W Germany
18 D5 Josselin France
26 E7 Jössund Nord-Tröndelag Norway
26 D8 Jössund Sör-Tröndelag Norway
26 B10 Jostedal Norway
26 B10 Jostedalsbreen gla Norway
48 F2 Josvafö Hungary
26 N2 Jotkajavrre Norway
27 C10 Jotunheimen mt Norway
79 F5 Jouaiya Lebanon
20 J4 Jouars France
20 E4 Joué-du-Bois France
21 G7 Joué les Tours France
21 C7 Joué sur Erdre France
29 N6 Joukokylä Finland
113 J12 Joulters Cays islds Bahamas
79 F5 Jounié Lebanon
109 J7 Jourdanton Texas
25 E3 Joure Netherlands
118 B3 Joussard Alberta
121 M3 Joutel Quebec
29 M10 Joutsa Finland
29 N5 Joutsijärvi Finland
40 D4 Joux, L.de Switzerland
20 J5 Jouy France
21 I6 Jouy-le Potier France
126 D3 Jovellanos Cuba
75 P6 Jowai India
14 B3 Joyce Country Irish Rep
117 G4 Joy, Mt Yukon Terr
60 O3 Jōzankei Japan
31 N4 Józefów Poland
77 J1 Jozjān Afghanistan
71 B3 Ju isld Indonesia
124 H5 Juan Aldama Mexico
65 C7 Juancheng China
141 J7 Juandah R Queensland
127 K2 Juan de Bolas peak Jamaica
114 G8 Juan de Fuca, Str. of Canada/U.S.A.
87 G11 Juan de Nova isld Madagascar
133 A9 Juan Fernández, Is Pacific Oc
127 N9 Juangriego Venezuela
88 G6 Juani isld Tanzania
128 C5 Juanjui Peru
29 N8 Juankoski Finland
44 B4 Juan les Pins France
124 E2 Juan M. Ortíz Mexico
131 B2 Juan Soldado, C.de Chile
133 B7 Juan Stuven, I Chile
133 F5 Juárez Argentina
103 J9 Juárez, Sa ra Mexico
129 K5 Juazeiro Brazil
130 G9 Juàzeiro do Norte Brazil
86 F5 Juba Sudan
86 H5 Juba R Somalia
79 F4 Jubail Lebanon
77 A6 Jubayl, Al Saudi Arabia
80 G5 Jubba Jordan
123 R5 Jubilee L Nfld
143 F8 Jubilee Lake W Australia
102 H6 Jubilee Peak California
20 E5 Jublains France
17 F5 Júcar R Spain
36 B1 Jüchen W Germany
124 H7 Juchipila Mexico
125 M9 Juchitán Mexico
124 H7 Juchitlán Mexico
129 K7 Jucurucú R Brazil
98 H3 Jud N Dakota
99 R7 Juda Wisconsin
80 B7 Judaea Israel
123 S6 Jude I Nfld
80 D2 Judeida Israel
37 L3 Judenbach E Germany
38 L7 Judenburg Austria
123 L8 Judique C Breton I, N S
101 Q2 Judith R Montana
101 Q2 Judith Basin reg Montana
101 Q3 Judith Gap Montana
98 E3 Judson N Dakota
Juegang see Rudong
28 E5 Juelsminde Denmark
130 H5 Juerana Brazil
128 F4 Jufari R Brazil
84 F4 Jufrah Oasis, Al Libya
143 E9 Jugalinna W Australia
18 D4 Jugon France
65 E4 Juhua Dao isld China
18 F7 Juillac France
32 F5 Juist W Germany
32 E5 Juist isld W Germany
129 K8 Juiz de Fora Brazil
65 D3 Jujinchang China
69 E13 Jujuhan R Sumatra
128 E8 Jujuy prov Argentina
26 L7 Juken Sweden
26 L4 Jukkasjärvi Sweden
67 D3 Jukoupu China
26 H6 Juktån R Sweden
128 E8 Julaca Bolivia
98 D9 Julesburg Colorado
128 E7 Julí Peru
141 F5 Julia R Queensland
128 D7 Juliaca Peru
141 F5 Julia Creek Queensland
100 J3 Juliaetta Idaho
102 H8 Julian California
115 P5 Julianehåb Greenland
14 E3 Julianstown Irish Rep
36 B2 Jülich W Germany
42 E2 Julijske A mts Yugoslavia
124 G3 Julimes Mexico
80 D2 Jūlis Israel
27 H12 Julita Sweden
140 E5 Julius L. Queensland
20 B4 Jullouville France
28 D4 Julsø L Denmark
65 C6 Julu China
69 C10 Julu Rayeu Sumatra
80 G8 Jumaiyil Jordan
117 P10 Jumbo Mt Br Col
21 E7 Jumelles France
22 G3 Jumet Belgium
20 G3 Jumièges France
17 G6 Jumilla Spain
75 K4 Jumla Nepal
74 G5 Jumna R India
74 D8 Junagadh India
65 D7 Junan China
65 D2 Jun Bulen China
124 D5 Juncal Mexico
131 D8 Juncal, L Argentina
108 H5 Junction Texas
103 M3 Junction Utah
140 C1 Junction B N Terr Australia
111 D8 Junction City Arkansas
111 M9 Junction City Georgia
107 O2 Junction City Kansas
94 C9 Junction City Kentucky
110 M4 Junction City Kentucky
100 B5 Junction City Oregon
99 R5 Junction City Wisconsin
141 G6 Jundah Queensland
65 C4 Jundu Shan mt ra China
117 F6 Juneau Alaska
99 S6 Juneau Wisconsin
139 J5 Junee New S Wales
113 F10 June in Winter, L Florida
102 E4 June Lake California
79 F4 Jūn el 'Akkar Lebanon
65 A5 Jungar Qi China
40 G4 Jungfrau mt Switzerland
40 G4 Jungfraujoch Switzerland
22 L4 Junglinster Luxembourg
100 G9 Jungo Nevada
98 H9 Juniata Nebraska
95 K6 Juniata R Pennsylvania
131 E5 Junin Argentina
128 D7 Junín Chile
128 C6 Junin Peru
133 C5 Junín de los Andes Argentina
94 H8 Junior W Virginia
95 T1 Junior L Maine
122 E7 Juniper New Brunswick
103 L6 Juniper Mts Arizona
102 C5 Junipero Sierra Pk California
61 O5 Jūni sho Japan
22 G5 Juniville France
116 O2 Junjik R Alaska
36 B3 Jünkerath W Germany
26 H5 Junkerdal Norway
67 A2 Junlian China
108 F5 Juno Texas
118 K5 Junor Sask
26 M4 Junosuando Sweden
26 J8 Junsele Sweden
67 E2 Junshan Hu L China
16 A5 Junto mt Portugal
65 A5 Juntuliang China
100 G6 Juntura Oregon
29 O6 Juntusranta Finland
29 O9 Juojärvi L Finland
26 N5 Juoksengi Sweden
130 H6 Juparaña, Lagoa L Brazil
130 D7 Jupia Brazil
130 D7 Jupia Dam Brazil
22 K2 Jupille Belgium
21 F6 Jupilles France
113 G11 Jupiter Florida
122 J4 Jupiter R Quebec
129 J8 Juquiá Brazil
86 E4 Jur R Sudan
15 C4 Jura Scotland
40 F3 Jura canton Switzerland
40 C4 Jura dep France
128 C2 Jurado Colombia
31 L5 Jura Krakowska reg Poland
130 G5 Juramento Brazil
52 B6 Jurbarkas U.S.S.R.
12 D5 Jurby I of Man U.K.
79 F8 Jurf ed Darāwish Jordan
142 E4 Jurgurra,R W Australia
65 E2 Jurh China
143 B9 Jurien B W Australia
48 M6 Jurilovca Romania
57 F6 Jurm Afghanistan
52 B6 Jurmala U.S.S.R.
67 F1 Jurong China
38 N9 Juršinci Yugoslavia
128 E4 Juruá Brazil
128 D5 Juruá R Brazil
128 G6 Juruena Brazil
129 G4 Juruti Brazil
29 J9 Jurva Finland
61 O5 Jūsan-ko L Japan
127 N10 Jusepín Venezuela
79 G4 Jūsiya Syria
19 J5 Jussey France
119 S8 Justice Manitoba
108 F2 Justiceburg Texas
109 K2 Justin Texas
133 D4 Justo Daract Argentina
128 E5 Jutaí Brazil
33 S9 Jüterbog E Germany
130 C8 Juti Brazil
125 L2 Juticalpa Honduras
26 J5 Jutis Sweden
Jutland see Jylland
26 E10 Jutulhugget pass Norway
29 O8 Juuka Finland
29 N10 Juva Finland
20 C5 Juvigné France
20 C4 Juvigny-le-Tertre France
20 E4 Juvigny-sous-Andaine France
20 K4 Juvisy France
28 B6 Juvre Denmark
79 H5 Juwaif, El Syria
65 D7 Ju Xian China
65 C7 Juye China
77 F2 Jūymand Iran
40 A1 Juzennecourt France
Jye Kundo see Yushu
28 B4 Jylland reg Denmark
29 M9 Jyväskylä Finland
66 B4 K2 mt Kashmir/China
85 E6 Ka R Nigeria
102 S11 Kaaawa Hawaiian Is
89 B7 Kaaing Veld plat S Africa
57 A5 Kaakhka U.S.S.R.
102 R11 Kaala peak Hawaiian Is
26 L4 Kaalasjarvi L Sweden
135 U6 Kaalualu Hawaiian Is
29 N2 Kaamanen Finland
89 C7 Kaap Plato S Africa
33 O6 Kaarssen E Germany
29 N9 Kaavi Finland
48 G3 Kaba Hungary
70 G7 Kabaena isld Sulawesi
85 B7 Kabala Sierra Leone
86 F5 Kabalega Falls Uganda
70 G5 Kabali Sulawesi
86 E7 Kabalo Zaïre
88 A4 Kabambare Zaïre
69 D11 Kabanjahe Sumatra
85 D5 Kabara Mali
53 F11 Kabardino Balkarskaya U.S.S.R.
88 B3 Kabare Zaïre
71 F7 Kabasalang Philippines
60 C13 Kaba shima isld Japan
68 C3 Kabaung R Burma
85 F7 Kabba Nigeria
26 G3 Kabelvåg lt ho Norway
120 E4 Kabenung L Ontario
70 G4 Kabetan. I Sulawesi
99 O1 Kabetogama Minnesota
99 N1 Kabetogama L Minnesota
71 L8 Kabia isld Indonesia
120 F3 Kabinakagami R Ontario
86 D7 Kabinda Zaïre
70 E2 Kabinu Kalimantan
71 M9 Kabir Indonesia
57 E5 Kabla U.S.S.R.
86 C4 Kabo Cent Afr Republic
87 D8 Kabompo R Zambia
70 B4 Kabong Sarawak
87 E7 Kabongo Zaïre
68 C6 Kabosa I. Burma
80 D1 Kabri Israel
77 F1 Kabūd Gonbad Iran
71 E2 Kabugao Philippines
77 L2 Kābul Afghanistan
80 D2 Kābūl Israel
88 C2 Kabula Uganda
88 B7 Kabunda Zambia
87 E8 Kabunda Zaïre
86 F2 Kabushiya Sudan
88 B9 Kabwe Zambia
55 F3 Kabyrdak U.S.S.R.
55 D5 Kabyrga R U.S.S.R.
46 E2 Kačanik Yugoslavia
87 F8 Kachalola Zambia
116 M7 Kachemak B Alaska
100 D2 Kachess L Washington
85 F7 Kachia Nigeria
75 R5 Kachin State prov Burma
55 G4 Kachiry U.S.S.R.
55 C2 Kachkanar U.S.S.R.
56 G4 Kachug U.S.S.R.
78 H1 Kackar D Turkey
60 J11 Kada Japan
68 C4 Kadaingti Burma
86 F5 Kadam Mt Uganda
37 P3 Kadaň Czechoslovakia
68 D6 Kadan Kyun isld Burma
70 D7 Kadapongan isld Indonesia
48 D4 Kadarkút Hungary
71 H7 Kadatuang isld Indonesia
41 H2 Kadelburg W Germany
61 P13 Kadena Okinawa
143 F7 Kadgo L W Australia
72 E2 Kadhimain Iraq
74 E7 Kadi India
85 C6 Kadiana Mali
46 F3 Kadijica mt Yugoslavia
47 K4 Kadıköy Turkey
138 E5 Kadina S Australia
74 F9 Kadirabad India
47 J8 Kadírga Burun C Turkey
76 D3 Kadiri India
78 F3 Kadirli Turkey
70 G7 Kadjang Sulawesi
77 F2 Kadkan Iran
73 L6 Kadmat isld Lakshadweep Indian Oc
52 F5 Kadnikov U.S.S.R.
68 C4 Kado Burma
60 E13 Kadogawa Japan
98 E6 Kadoka S Dakota
68 B5 Kadonkani Burma
46 E3 Kadrifakovo Yugoslavia
86 E3 Kadugli Sudan
86 A3 Kaduna Nigeria
76 C4 Kadur India
52 E5 Kaduy U.S.S.R.
56 E5 Kadyr-Egi-Tayga, Khrebet mts U.S.S.R.
52 F5 Kadyy U.S.S.R.
57 H4 Kadzhi-Say U.S.S.R.
85 B5 Kaedi Mauritania
123 R5 Kaegudeck L Nfld
86 B3 Kaélé Cameroon
145 D1 Kaeo New Zealand
28 D6 Kærum Denmark
65 G5 Kaesŏng N Korea
87 D7 Käfakumba Zaïre
85 F7 Kafanchan Nigeria
85 A6 Kaffrine Senegal
47 G7 Kafiréos, Porthmós str Greece
47 G6 Kafirévs, Akr C Greece
26 N2 Kåfjord Norway
26 L2 Kåfjord inlet Norway
80 D5 Kafr 'Abbush Jordan
80 D5 Kafr 'Ain Jordan
79 G3 Kafr Behūm Syria
80 F6 Kafrein R Jordan
79 A7 Kafr el Dauwâr Egypt
80 D4 Kafr-el-Labad Jordan
79 A7 Kafr el Sheik Egypt
79 A8 Kafr el Zaiyât Egypt
80 D2 Kafr Mandā Israel
80 D4 Kafr Qud Jordan
80 D4 Kafr Ra'i Jordan
80 D4 Kafr Rumman Jordan
79 G4 Kafrun Syria
80 D5 Kafr Zibad Jordan
88 B9 Kafue Zambia
87 E8 Kafue Nat. Park Zambia
87 E7 Kafulwe Zambia
55 C4 Kaga U.S.S.R.
60 G10 Kagami Japan
57 C5 Kagan U.S.S.R.
116 G7 Kagati L Alaska
60 G11 Kagawa prefect Japan
120 H7 Kagawong Ontario
26 M7 Kåge Sweden
88 C2 Kagera National Park Rwanda
28 J5 Kagerup Denmark
120 C2 Kagianagami L Ontario
120 D3 Kagiano L Ontario
78 J1 Kagizman Turkey
60 D14 Kagoshima Japan
48 L5 Kagul Moldavia U.S.S.R.
48 L5 Kagul, Ozero L U.S.S.R.
116 L8 Kaguyak Alaska
70 D6 Kahajan R Kalimantan
135 O1 Kahala Pt Hawaiian Is
102 S12 Kahaluu Hawaiian Is
88 D3 Kahama Tanzania
74 C4 Kahan Pakistan
102 S11 Kahana Hawaiian Is
145 F3 Kaharoa mt New Zealand
71 A2 Kahatola isld Halmahera Indonesia
87 C7 Kahemba Zaire

102 R12 **Kahe Pt** Hawaiian Is
144 A6 **Kaherekoau Mts** New Zealand
116 M5 **Kahiltna Gl** Alaska
36 G3 **Kahl** *R* W Germany
37 M2 **Kahla** E Germany
36 F1 **Kahler-Asten** *mt* W Germany
100 G3 **Kahlotus** Washington
117 N6 **Kahntah** Br Columbia
77 E6 **Kahnuj** Iran
110 E1 **Kahoka** Missouri
61 K9 **Kahoku-gata** *L* Japan
102 V13 **Kahoolawe** *isld* Hawaiian Is
29 J2 **Kahperusvaara** *mt* Finland
135 U4 **Kahua** Hawaiian Is
135 Q1 **Kahuku** Hawaiian Is
102 S11 **Kahuku Pt** Hawaiian Is
135 T3 **Kahului** Hawaiian Is
Kahutara Pt *see* **Table Cape**
85 E7 **Kaiama** Nigeria
144 D5 **Kaiapoi** New Zealand
119 O1 **Kaiashk** *R* Ontario
103 M5 **Kaibab Plat** Arizona
60 J10 **Kaibara** Japan
103 N5 **Kaibito Plat** Arizona
66 D3 **Kaidu He** *R* China
128 G2 **Kaieteur Falls** Guyana
65 C7 **Kaifeng** China
145 D1 **Kaihu** New Zealand
67 F2 **Kaihua** China
145 E3 **Kai-Iwi** New Zealand
67 B1 **Kaijiang** China
136 G3 **Kai, Kep** *islds* Moluccas Indonesia
145 D1 **Kaikohe** New Zealand
67 B3 **Kaikou** China
144 D5 **Kaikoura** New Zealand
144 D5 **Kaikoura Range** New Zealand
75 J3 **Kailas** *mt* Xizang Zizhiqu
Kailas Range *see* **Gangdisê Shan**
36 G4 **Kailbach** W Germany
67 B3 **Kaili** China
65 E3 **Kailu** China
102 S12 **Kailua** Hawaiian Is
135 R2 **Kailua** Hawaiian Is
135 T5 **Kailua** Hawaiian Is
145 E2 **Kaimai Ra** New Zealand
46 E4 **Kaïmakchalán** *mt* Greece
136 G2 **Kaimana** W Irian
145 E3 **Kaimanawa Mts** New Zealand
144 C5 **Kaimata** New Zealand
60 D14 **Kaimon-dake** *peak* Japan
135 V5 **Kaimu** Hawaiian Is
27 N13 **Käina** U.S.S.R.
38 M7 **Kainach** *R* Austria
135 U5 **Kainaliu** Hawaiian Is
60 J11 **Kainan** Japan
47 G3 **Kainchal** *mt* Greece
57 G3 **Kainda** U.S.S.R.
68 B2 **Kaing** Burma
145 F3 **Kaingaroa Forest** New Zealand
145 F3 **Kaingaroa Plat.** New Zealand
38 J6 **Kainisch** Austria
85 E6 **Kainji Res** Nigeria
55 G3 **Kainsk-Barabinskiy** U.S.S.R.
71 H7 **Kaioba** Indonesia
145 E2 **Kaipara Flats** New Zealand
103 N4 **Kaiparowits Plat** Utah
65 D5 **Kaiping** China
67 D5 **Kaiping** China
43 C13 **Kairouan** Tunisia
38 F6 **Kaiser-Gebirge** *mts* Austria
102 E4 **Kaiser Pk** California
36 C3 **Kaisersesch** W Germany
36 D5 **Kaiserslautern** W Germany
40 G1 **Kaiserstuhl** *mt* W Germany
32 E10 **Kaiserswerth** W Germany
60 F11 **Kaita** Japan
145 D1 **Kaitaia** New Zealand
144 B7 **Kaitangata** New Zealand
70 F6 **Kai, Tangjung** *C* Sulawesi
145 F3 **Kaitawa** New Zealand
145 D4 **Kaiteriteri** New Zealand
74 G4 **Kaithal** India
145 E4 **Kaitoki** New Zealand
Kaitong *see* **Tongyu**
26 K4 **Kaitumälven** *R* Sweden
26 K4 **Kaitumj** Sweden
26 L3 **Kaivare** *mt* Sweden
145 E2 **Kaiwaka** New Zealand
71 N9 **Kaiwatu** Indonesia
102 V13 **Kaiwi Ch** Hawaiian Is
67 C1 **Kai Xian** China
67 B3 **Kaiyang** China
59 H3 **Kaiyuan** China
67 A5 **Kaiyuan** China
116 H5 **Kaiyuh Mts** Alaska
60 J11 **Kaizuka** Japan
70 E3 **Kaja** Kalimantan
29 N7 **Kajaani** Finland
141 F5 **Kajabbi** Queensland
77 J3 **Kajaki Dam** Afghanistan
71 L9 **Kajan** *isld* Indonesia
69 E11 **Kajang** Malaysia
88 F2 **Kajiado** Kenya
61 M10 **Kajikazawa** Japan
60 D14 **Kajiki** Japan
71 A2 **Kajoa** *isld* Halmahera Indonesia
86 F5 **Kajo Kaji** Sudan
71 K8 **Kajuadi** *isld* Indonesia
85 F6 **Kajuru** Nigeria
103 M9 **Kaka** Arizona
86 F3 **Kaka** Sudan
70 F3 **Kakaban** *isld* Kalimantan
119 O2 **Kakabeka Falls** Ontario
118 J1 **Kakagi L** Ontario
145 E3 **Kakahi** New Zealand
71 G7 **Kakal** *R* Mindanao Philippines
70 F5 **Kakali** Sulawesi
87 D11 **Kakamas** S Africa
88 E1 **Kakamega** Kenya
69 A8 **Kakana** Nicobar Is
144 C6 **Kakanui** New Zealand
135 T3 **Kaka Pt** Hawaiian Is
145 E3 **Kakaramea** New Zealand
85 B7 **Kakata** Liberia
145 E3 **Kakatahi** New Zealand
117 G7 **Kake** Alaska
60 F11 **Kake** Japan
42 F3 **Kake** Yugoslavia
61 M11 **Kakegawa** Japan
56 E5 **Ka-Khem** *R* U.S.S.R.
116 K7 **Kakhonak** Alaska
54 E10 **Kakhovka** U.S.S.R.
54 E10 **Kakhovskoye Vdkhr** *res* U.S.S.R.
77 F2 **Kakht** Iran
77 B5 **Kākī** Iran
76 F2 **Kakinada** India
117 P5 **Kakisa L** N W Terr
61 M8 **Kakizaki** Japan
60 H11 **Kakogawa** Japan
55 E4 **Kak, Oz** *L* U.S.S.R.
85 D7 **Kakpin** Ivory Coast
116 Q1 **Kaktovik** Alaska
61 O8 **Kakuda** Japan
61 O6 **Kakumagawa** Japan
61 O6 **Kakunodate** Japan
70 C3 **Kakus** *R* Sarawak
86 E7 **Kakuyu** Zaïre
117 O8 **Kakwa** *R* Alberta
48 F3 **Kál** Hungary
43 D13 **Kalaa Kebira** Tunisia
43 B13 **Kalaat-es-Nam** *mt* Tunisia
71 M9 **Kalabahi** Indonesia
46 E5 **Kalabáka** Greece
70 E2 **Kalaban** Sabah
138 F4 **Kalabity** S Australia
87 D8 **Kalabo** Zambia
54 N6 **Kalach** U.S.S.R.
55 F3 **Kalachinsk** U.S.S.R.
53 F9 **Kalach-na-donu** U.S.S.R.
54 N6 **Kalachskaya Vozvyshennost'** *uplands* U.S.S.R.
68 A2 **Kaladan** Burma
121 N8 **Kaladar** Ontario
70 G6 **Kaladu** *R* Sulawesi
102 V14 **Kalae** Hawaiian Is
70 G6 **Kalaena** *R* Sulawesi
68 C1 **Kalagwe** Burma
89 B4 **Kalahari Desert** Botswana
89 B6 **Kalahari Game Res** S Africa
89 B5 **Kalahari Gemsbok Nat. Park** S Africa
76 D4 **Kalahasti** India
57 F5 **Kalai-Khumb** U.S.S.R.
57 B6 **Kalai-Mor** U.S.S.R.
29 K7 **Kalajoki** Finland
29 L8 **Kalajoki** *R* Finland
58 G1 **Kalakan** U.S.S.R.
69 C11 **Kalakepen** Sumatra
135 O1 **Kalalau** Hawaiian Is
74 E1 **Kalam** Pakistan
100 C3 **Kalama** Washington
46 E7 **Kalámai** Greece
Kalamata Greece *see* **Kalámai**
94 B4 **Kalamazoo** Michigan
70 D7 **Kalambau** *isld* Indonesia
87 F7 **Kalambo Falls** Tanzania
47 F6 **Kálamos** Greece
46 D6 **Kálamos** *isld* Greece
70 E3 **Kalampising** Kalimantan
143 B9 **Kalamunda** W Australia
138 E3 **Kalamurra, L** S Australia
143 B9 **Kalannie** W Australia
29 J11 **Kalanti** Finland
71 K8 **Kalao** *isld* Indonesia
71 G7 **Kalaong** Mindanao Philippines
71 K8 **Kalaotoa** *isld* Indonesia
83 K9 **Kala Oya** *R* Sri Lanka
58 G1 **Kalar** *R* U.S.S.R.
48 L3 **Kalarash** U.S.S.R.
26 H9 **Kälarne** Sweden
83 L9 **Kal Aru** *R* Sri Lanka
70 D4 **Kalasin** Kalimantan
74 B4 **Kalat** Pakistan
77 G6 **Kalateh-Masjed** Iran
135 S2 **Kalaupapa** Hawaiian Is
53 F10 **Kalaus** *R* U.S.S.R.
46 E6 **Kalávrita** Greece
68 C2 **Kalaw** Burma
70 F5 **Kalawaranaputi** Sulawesi
83 K9 **Kalawewa** Sri Lanka
36 H3 **Kalbach** W Germany
28 N2 **Kalbak** Faeroes
143 A8 **Kalbarri** W Australia
33 O7 **Kalbe** E Germany
56 B6 **Kalbinskiy Khrebet** *mts* U.S.S.R.
55 B5 **Kaldygayty** *R* U.S.S.R.
47 K7 **Kale** Turkey
78 D1 **Kalecik** Turkey
71 H7 **Kaledupa** *isld* Indonesia
68 C5 **Kalegauk I** Burma
52 H6 **Kalegino** U.S.S.R.
88 E6 **Kalehe** Zaïre
68 B3 **Kaleindaung** *inlet* Burma
86 D6 **Kalema** Zaïre
88 B4 **Kalémié** Zaïre
32 K7 **Kalenberg** *reg* W Germany
31 L5 **Kalety** Poland
94 B2 **Kaleva** Michigan
29 P6 **Kalevala** U.S.S.R.
52 E3 **Kalgachikha** U.S.S.R.
Kalgan *see* **Zhangjiakou**
58 G3 **Kalgan** China
143 C10 **Kalgan,R** W Australia
108 F2 **Kalgary** Texas
116 M6 **Kalgin I** Alaska
143 D9 **Kalgoorlie** W Australia
46 E4 **Kalí** Greece
47 L6 **Kalı** *R* Turkey
46 E6 **Kaliakoúdha** *mt* Greece
47 J1 **Kaliakra, N** Bulgaria
70 K8 **Kalianda** Sumatra
70 O9 **Kalianget** Indonesia
55 F4 **Kalibek, Oz** *L* U.S.S.R.
71 F5 **Kalibo** Philippines
94 C6 **Kalida** Ohio
86 E6 **Kalima** Zaïre
70 **Kalimantan** Borneo
70 B4 **Kalimantan Barat** Borneo
70 D6 **Kalimantan Selatan** Kalimantan
70 C5 **Kalimantan Tengah** Kalimantan
70 E3 **Kalimantan Timur** Kalimantan
47 H8 **Kálimnos** *isld* Greece
75 N5 **Kalimpong** India
71 H7 **Kalingsusuh Tk** *B* Indonesia
52 E6 **Kalinin** U.S.S.R.
57 E5 **Kalininabad** U.S.S.R.
27 L17 **Kaliningrad** U.S.S.R.
55 C3 **Kalinino** U.S.S.R.
53 F8 **Kalininsk** U.S.S.R.
48 E7 **Kalinovik** Yugoslavia
48 M1 **Kalinovka** U.S.S.R.
55 C6 **Kalinovka** U.S.S.R.
55 D3 **Kalinovo** U.S.S.R.
70 O10 **Kalisat** Java
101 L1 **Kalispell** Montana
31 L4 **Kalisz** Poland
53 F9 **Kalitva** *R* U.S.S.R.
88 C4 **Kaliua** Tanzania
26 N6 **Kalix** Sweden
26 N5 **Kalix älv** *R* Sweden
26 L4 **Kalixfors** Sweden
74 G3 **Kalka** India
141 G2 **Kalkah** Queensland
47 K8 **Kalkan** Turkey
25 F5 **Kalkar** W Germany
94 B2 **Kalkaska** Michigan
33 T8 **Kalkberge** E Germany
87 C10 **Kalkfeld** Namibia
87 D10 **Kalkfontein** Botswana
33 O5 **Kalkhorst** E Germany
47 J5 **Kalkım** Turkey
89 A5 **Kalk Plateau** Namibia
83 L10 **Kalkudah** Sri Lanka
138 D2 **Kallakoopah** *R* S Australia
52 C5 **Kallaste** U.S.S.R.
29 N9 **Kallavesi** *L* Finland
33 O7 **Kallehne** E Germany
32 H10 **Kallenhardt** W Germany
32 J8 **Kalletal** W Germany
37 P2 **Kallich** Czechoslovakia
47 J8 **Kallidhiés** Rhodes Greece
80 F7 **Kallirhoe Hot Sp** Jordan
46 D3 **Kallmet** Albania
37 M5 **Kallmünz** W Germany
47 H5 **Kalloní** Greece
47 H5 **Kallonís Kólpos** Greece
26 F8 **Kallsjön** Sweden
29 O5 **Kallunki** Finland
28 N1 **Kallur** Faeroes
27 H15 **Kalmar** Sweden
27 H14 **Kalmar** *county* Sweden
27 H15 **Kalmarsund** *chan* Sweden
36 E5 **Kalmit** *mt* W Germany
53 E10 **Kal'mius** U.S.S.R.
22 H1 **Kalmthout** Belgium
76 E7 **Kalmunai** Sri Lanka
55 B6 **Kalmykovo** U.S.S.R.
53 G9 **Kalmytskaya A.S.S.R** U.S.S.R.
48 E4 **Kalocsa** Hungary
47 G2 **Kalofer** Bulgaria
135 S3 **Kalohi Ch** Hawaiian Is
79 C3 **Kalokhorio** Cyprus
74 E7 **Kalol** India
70 G5 **Kalolio** Sulawesi
87 E9 **Kalomo** Zambia
47 F4 **Kalón** Greece
99 P8 **Kalona** Iowa
117 K9 **Kalone Peak** Br Col
71 F3 **Kalongkooan** *isld* Luzon Philippines
71 F3 **Kalotkot** *isld* Luzon Philippines
28 E4 **Kalø Vig** *B* Denmark
47 G2 **Kaloyanovc** Bulgaria
73 L6 **Kalpeni I** Lakshadweep Indian Oc
74 H5 **Kalpi** India
57 J4 **Kalpin** China
83 J9 **Kalpitiya** Sri Lanka
28 E5 **Kalsenakke** Denmark
77 E1 **Kāl-Shūr, Rūd-e** *R* Iran
28 N1 **Kalsø** *isld* Faeroes
116 H4 **Kaltag** Alaska
56 C4 **Kaltan** U.S.S.R.
41 M3 **Kalte Berg** *mt* Austria
37 M4 **Kaltenbrunn** W Germany
32 L5 **Kaltenkirchen** W Germany
37 J2 **Kaltennordheim** E Germany
37 J2 **Kaltensundheim** E Germany
54 H2 **Kaluga** U.S.S.R.
83 K11 **Kalu Ganga** *R* Sri Lanka
70 E7 **Kalukalukuang** *isld* Indonesia
70 D3 **Kalulong, Bt** *mt* Sarawak
87 E8 **Kalulushi** Zambia
142 F2 **Kalumburu** W Australia
28 G5 **Kalundborg** Denmark
28 F5 **Kalundborg Fjord** *inlet* Denmark
88 D6 **Kalungu** *R* Zambia
88 B6 **Kalungwishi** *R* Zambia
70 E1 **Kalupis Falls** Sabah
48 J1 **Kalush** U.S.S.R.
31 N3 **Kałuszyn** Poland
83 J11 **Kalutara** Sri Lanka
70 G6 **Kaluwadja** Sulawesi
31 O1 **Kalvariya** U.S.S.R.
28 J6 **Kalvehave** Denmark
29 K8 **Kälviä** Finland
29 N10 **Kalvitsa** Finland
29 L10 **Kalvola** Finland
28 B6 **Kalvslund** Denmark
38 L7 **Kalwang** Austria
55 C1 **Kal'ya** U.S.S.R.
74 E9 **Kalyan** India
76 C3 **Kalyandrug** India
74 G10 **Kalyani** India
68 B3 **Kama** Burma
55 G3 **Kama** Novosibirsk U.S.S.R.
55 D1 **Kama** Sverdlovsk U.S.S.R.
52 H5 **Kama** *R* U.S.S.R.
86 B1 **Kamada** Niger
60 E13 **Kamae** Japan
61 P6 **Kamaishi** Japan
61 N13 **Kama iwa** *islds* Iwo Jima Japan
135 S2 **Kamakou** *peak* Hawaiian Is
61 N10 **Kamakura** Japan
70 O9 **Kamal** Indonesia
74 E3 **Kamalia** Pakistan
135 S3 **Kamalo** Hawaiian Is
85 B7 **Kamalu** Sierra Leone
68 C4 **Kamamaung** Burma
78 D2 **Kaman** Turkey
56 F2 **Kamanga** *R* U.S.S.R.
87 D8 **Kamapanda** Zambia
72 E5 **Kamarān** *isld* S Yemen
77 K2 **Kamard** *reg* Afghanistan
74 H9 **Kamareddi** India
75 N7 **Kamarhati** India
74 B9 **Kamarod** Pakistan
101 O9 **Kamas** Utah
87 E9 **Kamativi** Zimbabwe
119 P2 **Kamatsi L** Sask
60 H11 **Kamatsushima** Japan
143 D9 **Kambalda** W Australia
52 G1 **Kambal'nitskiye Koshki, Ova** *islds* U.S.S.R.
76 C6 **Kambam** India
69 E13 **Kambang** Sumatra
70 M9 **Kambangan** *isld* Java
52 H6 **Kambarka** U.S.S.R.
85 B7 **Kambia** Sierra Leone
83 M8 **Kambing** *isld* Cocos Is Indian Oc
65 H4 **Kambo Ho** *mt* N Korea
70 F6 **Kambuno** *mt* Sulawesi
51 Q3 **Kamchatka Pen** U.S.S.R.
51 Q3 **Kamchatskaya Oblast'** *prov* U.S.S.R.
47 J1 **Kamchiya** *R* Bulgaria
52 F4 **Kamchuga** U.S.S.R.
61 N8 **Kameda** Japan
100 G4 **Kamela** Oregon
32 G9 **Kamen** W Germany
52 D6 **Kamenets** U.S.S.R.
48 K2 **Kamenets Podolskiy** U.S.S.R.
46 D4 **Kamenicë** Albania
42 F4 **Kamenjak. Rt** *C* Yugoslavia
52 F2 **Kamenka** U.S.S.R.
56 E2 **Kamenka** *R* U.S.S.R.
54 F9 **Kamenka-Dneprovskaya** U.S.S.R.
56 B4 **Kamen'na-Obi** U.S.S.R.
52 D3 **Kamennoye, Oz** *L* U.S.S.R.
47 J2 **Kameno** Bulgaria
54 M9 **Kamenolomni** U.S.S.R.
87 D8 **Kamenongue** Angola
59 K3 **Kamen Rybolov** U.S.S.R.
56 G5 **Kamensk** U.S.S.R.
55 E3 **Kamenskoye** U.S.S.R.
53 F9 **Kamensk-Shakhtinskiy** U.S.S.R.
55 D3 **Kamensk-Ural'skiy** U.S.S.R.
31 O3 **Kamenyuki** U.S.S.R.
30 H4 **Kamenz** E Germany
61 J10 **Kameoko** Japan
12 C2 **Kames** Scotland
54 N1 **Kameshkovo** U.S.S.R.
74 H3 **Kamet** *mt* India/Xizang Zizhiqu
61 K11 **Kameyama** Japan
100 J3 **Kamiah** Idaho
31 K2 **Kamien** Poland
31 J5 **Kamienna Góra** Poland
31 H2 **Kamień Pomorski** Poland
31 L4 **Kamieńsk** Poland
87 C12 **Kamieskroon** S Africa
89 A8 **Kamies Sektor Berg** *mt* S Africa
60 Q2 **Kami-Furano** Japan
60 Q2 **Kamikawa** *prefect* Japan
60 C14 **Kami koshiki jima** *isld* Japan
140 F4 **Kamileroi** Queensland
114 J5 **Kamilukuak L** N W Terr
87 D7 **Kamina** Zaïre
115 K5 **Kaminak L** N W Terr
99 R1 **Kaministikwia** Ontario
60 C11 **Kami no-shima** *isld* Japan
115 K5 **Kaminuriak L** N W Terr
61 L9 **Kamioka** Japan
116 L7 **Kamishak B** Alaska
60 R2 **Kami-Shihoro** Japan
88 B3 **Kamituga** Zaïre
61 O13 **Kamiyama jima** *isld* Okinawa
60 R1 **Kami-Yūbetsu** Japan
57 F3 **Kamkaly** U.S.S.R.
117 N10 **Kamloops** Br Col
29 P7 **Kammenoye, Oz** *L* U.S.S.R.
60 E12 **Kammon Kaikyō** *str* Japan
60 D12 **Kammon Tunnels** Japan
60 J10 **Kammuri shima** *isld* Japan
60 F11 **Kammuri-yama** *mt* Japan
42 F2 **Kamnik** Yugoslavia
61 M8 **Kamo** Japan
145 E1 **Kamo** New Zealand
78 K1 **Kamo** U.S.S.R.
56 E1 **Kamo** *R* U.S.S.R.
128 G3 **Kamoa Mts** Guyana
60 O2 **Kamoenai** Japan
60 H11 **Kamojima** Japan
122 C6 **Kamouraska** Quebec
38 N4 **Kamp** *R* Austria
69 G13 **Kampa** Indonesia
86 F5 **Kampala** Uganda
69 E12 **Kampar** *R* Sumatra
36 D3 **Kamp-Bornhofen** W Germany
25 E3 **Kampen** Netherlands
28 A7 **Kampen** W Germany
86 E6 **Kampene** Zaïre
22 H2 **Kampenhout** Belgium
38 M5 **Kamp, Gr** *R* Austria
68 D4 **Kamphaeng Phet** Thailand
88 B6 **Kampinda** Zambia
88 B7 **Kampolombo, L** Zambia
68 G7 **Kampot** Cambodia
74 H8 **Kamptee** India
85 D6 **Kampti** Upper Volta
Kampuchea *see* **Cambodia**
Kampuchea *rep see* **Cambodia**
70 C6 **Kampungtengah** Kalimantan
99 N7 **Kamrar** Iowa
119 Q7 **Kamsack** Sask
52 G6 **Kamskoye Ust'ye** U.S.S.R.
119 P2 **Kamuchawie L** Sask
60 Q3 **Kamui-dake** *mt* Japan
46 E4 **Kamvoúnia, Óri** *mts* Greece
53 G8 **Kamyshin** U.S.S.R.
55 D3 **Kamyshlov** U.S.S.R.
55 D5 **Kamyshnyy** U.S.S.R.
54 H9 **Kamysh-Zarya** U.S.S.R.
68 B1 **Kan** Burma
85 G6 **Kan** Nigeria
56 D3 **Kan** *R* U.S.S.R.
89 E2 **Kana** *R* Zimbabwe
115 M7 **Kanaaupscow** Quebec
103 M4 **Kanab** Utah
103 M5 **Kanab Cr** Arizona
70 C3 **Kana, Bt** *mt* Sarawak
61 O5 **Kanagi** Japan
42 F2 **Kanal** Yugoslavia
46 F5 **Kanália** Greece
69 A9 **Kanalla** Nicobar Is
70 G6 **Kanan** Sulawesi
118 C8 **Kananaskis L** Alberta
86 D7 **Kananga** Zaïre
55 C4 **Kananikol'skoye** U.S.S.R.
103 L4 **Kanarraville** Utah
52 G6 **Kanash** U.S.S.R.
47 F5 **Kanastraion, Ákr** *C* Greece
116 K8 **Kanatak** Alaska
52 H4 **Kanava** U.S.S.R.
99 N7 **Kanawha** Iowa
109 M2 **Kanawha** Texas
94 E8 **Kanawha** *R* W Virginia
94 F7 **Kanawha, Little** *R* W Virginia
61 M11 **Kanaya** Japan
61 K9 **Kanazawa** Japan
61 K9 **Kanazu** Japan
75 Q7 **Kanbalu** Burma
68 D5 **Kanchanaburi** Thailand
76 D4 **Kanchipuram** India
60 D12 **Kanda** Japan
74 B4 **Kanda** Pakistan
77 J4 **Kandahar** Afghanistan
119 N7 **Kandahar** Sask
52 D2 **Kandalaksha** U.S.S.R.
52 D2 **Kandalalakshskaya Guba** *B* U.S.S.R.
69 C11 **Kandang** Sumatra
70 D6 **Kandangan** Kalimantan
47 F9 **Kándanos** Crete Greece
52 B6 **Kandava** U.S.S.R.
137 Q5 **Kandavu** *isld* Fiji
85 E6 **Kandé** Togo
36 E5 **Kandel** W Germany
40 G2 **Kandern** W Germany
28 E1 **Kandestederne** Denmark
74 C4 **Kandhkot** Pakistan
85 E6 **Kandi** Benin
76 D2 **Kandi** India
77 K5 **Kandi** Pakistan
116 R4 **Kandik** *R* Alaska
47 L3 **Kandıra** Turkey
70 G4 **Kandi, Tg** *C* Sulawesi
139 J5 **Kandos** New S Wales
87 H11 **Kandreho** Madagascar
55 B4 **Kandry** U.S.S.R.
76 D3 **Kandukur** India
83 K10 **Kandy** Sri Lanka
110 F2 **Kane** Illinois
94 J5 **Kane** Pennsylvania
101 R5 **Kane** Wyoming
115 M2 **Kane Basin** Canada/Greenland
116 G7 **Kanektok** *R* Alaska
86 C3 **Kanem** *dist* Chad
102 S12 **Kaneohe** Hawaiian Is
102 S12 **Kaneohe Bay** Hawaiian Is
54 C7 **Kanev** U.S.S.R.
52 E2 **Kanevka** U.S.S.R.
61 O7 **Kaneyama** Japan
42 F3 **Kanfanar** Yugoslavia
87 D10 **Kang** Botswana
85 C6 **Kangaba** Mali
78 F2 **Kangal** Turkey
115 O4 **Kangâmiut** Greenland
77 C6 **Kangan** Iran
69 E9 **Kangar** Malaysia
138 D6 **Kangaroo I** S Australia
140 E4 **Kangaroo Pt** Queensland
29 L7 **Kangas** Finland
29 N9 **Kangaslampi** Finland
29 M9 **Kangasniemi** Finland
115 O4 **Kangâtsiaq** Greenland
77 A2 **Kangāvar** Iran
48 M4 **Kangaz** U.S.S.R.
65 C4 **Kangbao** China
75 N5 **Kangchenjunga** *mt* Nepal/India
58 D5 **Kangding** China
70 P9 **Kangean** *isld* Indonesia
115 N4 **Kangeeak Pt** N W Terr
115 Q4 **Kangerdlugssuaq** *inlet* Greenland
115 Q4 **Kangerdlugssvatsiaq** *inlet* Greenland
86 G5 **Kangetet** Kenya
59 J3 **Kanggye** N Korea
65 B5 **Kangjiahui** China
65 G1 **Kangjinjing** China
59 J4 **Kangnŭng** S Korea
86 B5 **Kango** Gabon
61 N13 **Kangoku-iwa** *islds* Iwo Jima Japan
26 N4 **Kangos** Sweden
65 F3 **Kangping** China
71 E8 **Kang Tipayan Dakula** *isld* Philippines
57 E5 **Kangurt** U.S.S.R.
Kan-hsien *see* **Ganzhou**
68 B1 **Kani** Burma
87 D7 **Kaniama** Zaïre
57 F4 **Kanibadam** U.S.S.R.
144 C5 **Kaniere** New Zealand
144 C5 **Kaniere, L** New Zealand
76 D3 **Kanigiri** India
52 F1 **Kanin Nos, Mys** *C* U.S.S.R.
52 F1 **Kanin, Poluostrov** *pen* U.S.S.R.
52 F1 **Kaninskiy Bereg** *coast* U.S.S.R.
61 O5 **Kanita** Japan
26 N5 **Kaniulasjärvi** Sweden
138 F6 **Kaniva** Victoria
48 F4 **Kanjiža** Yugoslavia
29 J10 **Kankaanpää** Finland
99 S8 **Kankakee** *R* Illinois
85 C6 **Kankan** Guinea
75 J8 **Kanker** India
83 J8 **Kankesanturai** Sri Lanka
29 L4 **Kankonen** Finland
74 E6 **Kankroli** India
76 D7 **Kanmaw Kyun** *isld* Burma
56 D5 **Kanmegirskiy Khrebet** *mts* U.S.S.R.
27 G15 **Kånna** Sweden
112 G2 **Kannapolis** N Carolina
61 P13 **Kanna-zaki** *C* Okinawa
22 K2 **Kanne** Belgium
74 G7 **Kannod** India
29 L9 **Kannonkoski** Finland
29 K8 **Kannus** Finland
60 E11 **Kano** Japan
85 F6 **Kano** Nigeria
71 J6 **Kano** *isld* Indonesia
107 K2 **Kanona** Kansas
55 G5 **Kanonerka** U.S.S.R.
60 G11 **Kanonji** Japan
126 B2 **Kanon, Pt** Curaçao
107 M3 **Kanopolis** Kansas
103 M3 **Kanosh** Utah
70 C3 **Kanowit** Sarawak
60 D14 **Kanoya** Japan
74 J5 **Kanpur** India
99 T10 **Kansas** Illinois
107 Q5 **Kansas** Oklahoma
107 P2 **Kansas** *R* Kansas
107 K3 **Kansas** *state* U.S.A.
107 Q2 **Kansas City** Kansas
110 B2 **Kansas City** Missouri
67 E4 **Kanshi** China
56 E3 **Kansk** U.S.S.R.
56 E4 **Kanskoye Belogor'ye** *mts* U.S.S.R.
88 A5 **Kansonge** Zaïre
Kansu *prov see* **Gansu**
57 G3 **Kant** U.S.S.R.
29 N9 **Kantala** Finland
68 G5 **Kantaralak** Thailand
85 E6 **Kantchari** Upper Volta
116 M4 **Kantishna** *R* Alaska
61 M10 **Kanto sanchi** *mts* Japan
68 C2 **Kantulong** Burma
14 C4 **Kanturk** Irish Rep
77 J5 **Kanuk** Afghanistan
102 S11 **Kanuku** Hawaiian Is
128 G3 **Kanuku Mts** Guyana
61 N9 **Kanuma** Japan
87 C11 **Kanus** Namibia
116 M3 **Kanuti** *R* Alaska
89 D5 **Kanye** Botswana
68 B3 **Kanyinngu** Burma
68 C3 **Kanyutkwin** Burma
38 J8 **Kanzel** *mt* Austria
87 E8 **Kanzenze** Zaïre
137 R5 **Kao** *isld* Tonga
87 E9 **Kaoko Veld** *reg* Namibia
85 A6 **Kaolack** Senegal
47 J1 **Kaolinovo** Bulgaria
87 D8 **Kaoma** Zambia
65 F2 **Kaoshan** China
102 V13 **Kapaa** Hawaiian Is
102 V13 **Kapaau** Hawaiian Is
74 E7 **Kapadvanj** India
57 J2 **Kapal** U.S.S.R.
71 O9 **Kapala** *isld* Indonesia
71 M9 **Kapan** Timor Indonesia
87 D7 **Kapanga** Zaïre
145 E3 **Kapara** New Zealand
87 F7 **Kapatu** Zambia
66 B3 **Kapchagay** U.S.S.R.
57 H3 **Kapchagayskoye Vdkhr.** *res* U.S.S.R.
22 G1 **Kapellen** Belgium
25 F5 **Kapellen** W Germany
86 G5 **Kapenguria** Kenya
38 M7 **Kapfenberg** Austria
47 J4 **Kapıdağı Yar** *pen* Turkey
70 G5 **Kapinju, Tg** *C* Sulawesi
87 E8 **Kapiri Mposhi** Zambia
77 L2 **Kāpīsā** Afghanistan
115 L7 **Kapiskau** Ontario
70 C4 **Kapit** Sarawak
145 E4 **Kapiti I** New Zealand
111 D11 **Kaplan** Louisiana
31 H7 **Kaplice** Czechoslovakia
69 D8 **Kapoe** Thailand
86 F5 **Kapoeta** Sudan
135 V5 **Kapoho** Hawaiian Is
145 E3 **Kaponga** New Zealand
70 F7 **Kapoposang** *isld* Indonesia
48 E4 **Kapos** *R* Hungary
48 D4 **Kaposvár** Hungary
71 C3 **Kapotjol** W Irian
74 B10 **Kappar** Pakistan
28 G7 **Kappel** Denmark
36 C3 **Kappel** W Germany
28 D7 **Kappeln** W Germany
36 E6 **Kappelrodeck** W Germany
27 K14 **Kappelshamn** *isld* Gotland Sweden
41 M3 **Kappl** Austria
38 G7 **Kaprun** Austria
31 O1 **Kapsukas** U.S.S.R.
88 C9 **Kapsuku** *mt* Zimbabwe
70 B4 **Kapuas** *R* Kalimantan
70 D5 **Kapuas** *R* Kalimantan
70 C4 **Kapuas Hulu, Peg** Kalimantan
138 E5 **Kapunda** S Australia
145 E3 **Kapuni** New Zealand
74 F3 **Kapurthala** India
120 H3 **Kapuskasing** Ontario
120 H4 **Kapuskasing** *R* Ontario
139 K4 **Kaputar** *mt* New S Wales
48 D3 **Kapuvár** Hungary
56 H4 **Kapylyushi, Oz** *L* U.S.S.R.
78 G2 **Kara** *R* Turkey
57 J1 **Karaaul** U.S.S.R.
57 G3 **Kara-Balty** U.S.S.R.
54 K1 **Karabanovo** U.S.S.R.
57 H2 **Karabas** U.S.S.R.
57 C5 **Karabekaul** U.S.S.R.
47 J4 **Karabiga** Turkey
57 C6 **Karabil', Vozvyshennost'** *uplands* U.S.S.R.
78 D1 **Karabuk** Turkey
46 C4 **Karaburun** Albania
47 H6 **Karaburun** Turkey
47 H6 **Kara Burun** *C* Turkey
55 D6 **Karabutak** U.S.S.R.
47 J4 **Karacabey** Turkey
47 J3 **Karacaköy** Turkey
47 J3 **Karacaoğlan** Turkey
47 K7 **Karacasu** Turkey
53 F11 **Karachayevo-Cherkesskaya Aut. Obl.** U.S.S.R.
54 F3 **Karachev** U.S.S.R.
74 B6 **Karachi** Pakistan
76 B2 **Karad** India
47 K3 **Karadeniz Boğazı** *str* Turkey
55 F2 **Karagach** U.S.S.R.
50 G3 **Karaganda** U.S.S.R.
50 G4 **Karagayly** U.S.S.R.
51 Q4 **Karaginskiy, Ostrova** *islds* U.S.S.R.
47 K8 **Kara Göl** *L* Turkey
47 K6 **Karahalh** Turkey
47 J7 **Karahayıt** Turkey
55 C3 **Karaidel'** U.S.S.R.
Kara Irtysh *R see* **Ertix He**
83 J9 **Karaitivu** Sri Lanka
77 B2 **Karaj** Iran
79 F7 **Karak** Jordan
47 H6 **Karaka Burun** *C* Turkey
57 A3 **Karakalpakskaya A.S.S.R** *prov* U.S.S.R.
57 C2 **Karaketken** U.S.S.R.
143 B9 **Karakin Ls** W Australia
57 E2 **Karakoin, Ozero** *L* U.S.S.R.
57 H4 **Karakolka** U.S.S.R.
74 F1 **Karakoram** *ra* Kashmir
74 G1 **Karakoram Pass** Kashmir
85 B5 **Karakoro** *R* Mauritania/Mali
58 D2 **Karakorum** Mongolia
55 G5 **Karakuduk** U.S.S.R.
55 F4 **Kara-Kuga** U.S.S.R.
57 C5 **Karakul'** U.S.S.R.
57 G4 **Kara-Kul'dzha** U.S.S.R.
52 H6 **Karakulino** U.S.S.R.
57 G5 **Kara-Kul', Ozero** *L* U.S.S.R.
55 D4 **Karakul'skoye** U.S.S.R.
57 C5 **Karakumskiy Kanal** U.S.S.R.
57 A5 **Karakumy, Peski** *des* U.S.S.R.
38 M8 **Karalpe** *mts* Austria
143 C7 **Karalundi** W Australia
70 F6 **Karam** *R* Sulawesi
80 F6 **Karama** Jordan
47 K7 **Karaman** Turkey
47 K7 **Karamanlı** Turkey
66 C2 **Karamay** China
70 E6 **Karambu** Kalimantan
145 D4 **Karamea** New Zealand
70 D7 **Karamian** *isld* Indonesia
47 L6 **Karamık Gölü** *L* Turkey
66 C4 **Karamiran He** *R* China
66 D4 **Karamiran Shankou** *pass* China
86 F5 **Karamoja** *dist* Uganda
47 K4 **Karamürsel** Turkey
78 L4 **Karand** Iran
69 G14 **Karangagung** Sumatra
144 B5 **Karangarua R** New Zealand
70 P10 **Karangasem** Indonesia
70 M9 **Karangboto Tg** *C* Java
70 F7 **Karang Bril** Indonesia
70 F5 **Karang, Tg** *C* Sulawesi
74 G8 **Karanja** India
47 J7 **Karaova** Turkey
57 D3 **Karaozek** U.S.S.R.
47 J1 **Karapelit** Bulgaria
78 D3 **Karapinar** Turkey
145 E2 **Karapiro** New Zealand
66 C4 **Karasay** China
57 J4 **Karasay** U.S.S.R.
89 A7 **Karasburg** Namibia
147 N12 **Kara Sea** Arctic Oc
55 G5 **Karashoky** U.S.S.R.
26 O2 **Karasjok** Norway
26 O2 **Karasjokka** *R* Norway
55 G5 **Karasor** U.S.S.R.
55 D5 **Karasu** Kustanay U.S.S.R.
55 F4 **Karasu** Makinsk U.S.S.R.
47 L3 **Karasu** Turkey
55 G4 **Karasuk** U.S.S.R.
56 B4 **Karasuk** *R* U.S.S.R.
61 O9 **Karasuyama** Japan
55 E2 **Karas'ye, Oz** *L* U.S.S.R.
57 H2 **Karatal** *R* U.S.S.R.
78 E3 **Karatas** Turkey
57 F3 **Kara Tau** U.S.S.R.
68 D7 **Karathuri** Burma
26 K5 **Karatjaur** *L* Sweden
55 B6 **Karatobe** U.S.S.R.
57 B2 **Karatobe, Mys** *C* U.S.S.R.
55 D5 **Karatomarskoye Vodokhranilishche** *res* U.S.S.R.
60 C12 **Karatsu** Japan
55 E6 **Karaturgay** *R* U.S.S.R.
57 A2 **Karatyup, Poluostrov** *pen* U.S.S.R.
Karaul *see* **Qongkol**
50 H1 **Karaul** U.S.S.R.
57 H4 **Karaultëbë** U.S.S.R.
60 D14 **Karauni** Japan
57 A3 **Kara-uzyak** U.S.S.R.
46 E5 **Karáva** *mt* Greece
57 F4 **Karavan** U.S.S.R.
46 C4 **Karavastas, Kënet'e** Albania
79 C4 **Karavostasi** Cyprus
70 L9 **Karawang** Java
70 L8 **Karawang Tg.** *cape* Java
38 K8 **Karawanken** *mt* Austria
57 F1 **Karazhal** U.S.S.R.
57 G2 **Karazhingil** U.S.S.R.
78 J5 **Karbala** Iraq
36 F3 **Karben** W Germany
26 H10 **Kårböle** Sweden
33 Q6 **Karbow-Vietlübbe** E Germany
28 B3 **Karby** Denmark
48 F3 **Karcag** Hungary
46 E8 **Kardhamíla** Greece
47 H6 **Kardhámila** Greece
46 E5 **Kardhítsa** Greece
26 N5 **Kardis** Sweden
52 B5 **Kärdla** U.S.S.R.
138 B2 **Karee** N Terr Australia
52 D3 **Karelskaya** *A.S.S.R.* U.S.S.R.
52 D3 **Karel'skaya Masel'ga** U.S.S.R.
87 F7 **Karema** Tanzania
76 G4 **Karen** Andaman Is
68 C3 **Karen State** Burma
52 J4 **Karepino** U.S.S.R.
85 C4 **Karet** Mauritania
145 F2 **Karewa I** New Zealand
57 G1 **Kargaly** U.S.S.R.
55 D3 **Kargapolye** U.S.S.R.
56 B3 **Kargat** *R* U.S.S.R.
Karghalik *see* **Yecheng**
52 E4 **Kargopol'** U.S.S.R.
33 R6 **Kargow** E Germany
31 J3 **Kargowa** Poland
85 G6 **Kargueri** Niger
117 G8 **Karheen** Alaska
29 M11 **Karhula** Finland
88 B10 **Kariba** Zimbabwe
88 B10 **Kariba Dam** Zimbabwe/Zambia
88 B10 **Kariba,L** Zimbabwe/Zambia
60 N3 **Kariba yama** *mt* Japan
87 C10 **Karibib** Namibia
89 C9 **Kariega** *watercourse* S Africa
29 M2 **Karigasniemi** Finland
29 J9 **Karijoki** Finland
76 D5 **Karikal** India
145 D1 **Karikari, C** New Zealand
86 F2 **Karima** Sudan
75 P6 **Karimganj** India
74 H9 **Karimnagar** India
70 N8 **Karimundjawa** *isld* Indonesia
70 N8 **Karimundjawa, Pulau Pulau** *islds* Indonesia
86 A1 **Karin** Somalia
145 E3 **Karioi** New Zealand
145 E2 **Karioi** *mt* New Zealand
29 K11 **Karis** Finland
28 J6 **Karise** Denmark
88 E6 **Karisimbi. Mt** Zaïre
47 G6 **Káristos** Greece
144 C6 **Karitane** New Zealand
76 B4 **Karkal** India
136 K2 **Karkar** *isld* Papua New Guinea
57 H1 **Karkaralinsk** U.S.S.R.
77 F7 **Kārkīn Dar** Iran
29 L11 **Karkkila** Finland
29 L11 **Kärkölä** Finland
Karlá *L see* **Voïvïïs** *L*
54 G5 **Karla Libknekhta** U.S.S.R.
57 G6 **Karla Marksa, Pik** *mt* U.S.S.R.
28 F4 **Karlby** Denmark
26 R1 **Karlebotn** Norway
28 J7 **Karleby** Denmark
31 J1 **Karlino** Poland
37 O2 **Karl-Marx-Stadt** E Germany
42 G4 **Karlobag** Yugoslavia
54 G7 **Karlovka** U.S.S.R.
47 G2 **Karlovo** Bulgaria
37 O3 **Karlovy Vary** Czechoslovakia
26 K8 **Karlsbäck** Sweden
36 E6 **Karlsbad** W Germany
29 K6 **Karlsberg** Sweden
27 G13 **Karlsborg** Sweden
37 L7 **Karlsfeld** W Germany
32 K9 **Karlshafen** W Germany
27 G15 **Karlshamn** Sweden
27 G12 **Karlskoga** Sweden
27 H15 **Karlskrona** Sweden
26 L1 **Karlsöy** Norway
98 F1 **Karlsruhe** N Dakota
36 E5 **Karlsruhe** W Germany
98 K1 **Karlstad** Minnesota
27 F12 **Karlstad** Sweden
36 H4 **Karlstadt** W Germany
116 K8 **Karluk L** Alaska
57 D5 **Karlyuk** U.S.S.R.
76 B1 **Karmala** India
52 E6 **Karmanovo** U.S.S.R.
80 C2 **Karmel, Cape** Israel
80 E2 **Karmi'el** Israel
80 B7 **Karmiyya** Israel
27 A12 **Karmöy** *isld* Norway
109 N3 **Karnack** Texas
110 H4 **Karnak** Illinois
74 G4 **Karnal** India
76 B3 **Karnataka** *prov* India
109 K7 **Karnes City** Texas
38 G8 **Karnische Alpen** *mts* Austria
47 H2 **Karnobat** Bulgaria
27 E13 **Kärnsj** *L* Sweden
38 H8 **Kärnten** Austria
87 E9 **Karoi** Zimbabwe
77 H2 **Karokh** Afghanistan
68 C5 **Karokpi** Burma
138 E4 **Karolta** S Australia
71 K8 **Karompa** *isld* Indonesia
128 G3 **Karona Fall** Guyana
88 D6 **Karonga** Malawi
143 D9 **Karonie** W Australia
138 E6 **Karoonda** S Australia
47 H8 **Káros** *isld* Greece
70 F5 **Karossa** Sulawesi Indonesia
71 J9 **Karossa, Tg** *C* Indonesia
46 D5 **Karousádhes** Greece
33 Q5 **Karow** E Germany
57 G2 **Karoy** U.S.S.R.
47 J9 **Kárpathos** *isld* Greece
47 J9 **Karpathos Str** Greece
46 E6 **Karpenision** Greece
41 K4 **Kärpf** *mt* Switzerland
37 P7 **Karpfham** W Germany
55 C2 **Karpinsk** U.S.S.R.
52 F3 **Karpogory** U.S.S.R.
55 C2 **Karpushikha** U.S.S.R.
47 J7 **Karpuzlu** Turkey
143 B9 **Karragullen** W Australia
142 A1 **Karrakatta** *dist* Perth, W Aust
115 O3 **Karrats Fjord** Greenland
28 H6 **Karrebæk** Denmark
28 H6 **Karrebæksminde** Denmark
28 G6 **Karrebæksminde Bugt** *B* Denmark
89 B8 **Karree Berge** *mts* S Africa
143 B10 **Karridale** W Australia
78 J1 **Kars** Turkey
57 D1 **Karsakpay** U.S.S.R.
119 S2 **Karsakuwigamak L** Manitoba
29 M8 **Kärsämäki** Finland
52 C6 **Kärsava** U.S.S.R.
57 D5 **Karshi** U.S.S.R.
57 D5 **Karshinskaya Step'** U.S.S.R.
50 E1 **Karskiye Vorota, Proliv** *str* U.S.S.R.
33 P6 **Karstädt** E Germany
28 B5 **Karstoft** Denmark
29 L9 **Karstula** Finland
26 H10 **Karsvall** Sweden
79 F4 **Kartaba** Lebanon
47 K4 **Kartal** Turkey
47 G3 **Kartál** *mt* Greece
50 F3 **Kartaly** U.S.S.R.
52 H3 **Kartayël** U.S.S.R.
94 J5 **Karthaus** Pennsylvania
36 B4 **Karthaus** W Germany
29 N9 **Karttula** Finland
31 L1 **Kartuzy** Poland
87 E9 **Karubwe** Zambia
61 M9 **Karuizawa** Japan
143 F9 **Karulbie** W Australia
140 F3 **Karumba** Queensland
77 A4 **Karun** *R* Iran
26 N5 **Karungi** Sweden
71 J9 **Karuni** Indonesia
142 G3 **Karunjie** W Australia
106 G3 **Karval** Colorado
29 K9 **Karvia** Finland
26 K2 **Kårvik** Norway
31 L6 **Karviná** Czechoslovakia
48 E1 **Karvina** Czechoslovakia
76 B3 **Karwar** India
41 O3 **Karwendel Geb** *mts* Austria
55 E1 **Karym** U.S.S.R.
55 C4 **Karzala** U.S.S.R.
28 D2 **Kås** Denmark
47 K8 **Kas** Turkey
56 C2 **Kas** *R* U.S.S.R.
88 C6 **Kasaba B** Zambia
86 D6 **Kasai** *prov* Zaïre
87 D7 **Kasai** *R* Zaïre
87 D8 **Kasaji** Zaïre
61 O9 **Kasama** Japan
88 C7 **Kasama** Zambia
88 C6 **Kasanga** Tanzania
57 F4 **Kasansay** U.S.S.R.
76 B4 **Kasaragod** India
75 O7 **Kasba** Bangladesh
114 J5 **Kasba L** N W Terr
27 G16 **Kåseberga** Sweden
60 D14 **Kaseda** Japan
116 F1 **Kasegaluk Lag** Alaska
87 E8 **Kasempa** Zambia
37 L3 **Kasendorf** W Germany
88 B7 **Kasenga** Zaïre
86 F5 **Kasenyi** Zaïre
77 B5 **Kāserūn** Iran
88 C1 **Kasese** Uganda
86 E6 **Kasese** Zaïre
119 N2 **Kashabowie** Ontario
77 B2 **Kāshān** Iran
Kashgar *see* **Kashi**
66 B4 **Kashi** China
61 J11 **Kashihara** Japan
60 D12 **Kashima** Japan
52 E6 **Kashin** U.S.S.R.
74 H4 **Kashipur** India
54 K2 **Kashira** U.S.S.R.
119 O1 **Kashishibog L** Ontario
61 M8 **Kashiwazaki** Japan
57 D5 **Kashkadar'in-skaya Oblast** U.S.S.R.
57 G2 **Kashkanteniz** U.S.S.R.
52 D4 **Kashkany** U.S.S.R.
52 E2 **Kashkarantsy** U.S.S.R.
57 H4 **Kashkasu** U.S.S.R.
77 F2 **Kāshmar** Iran
66 B5 **Kashmir** India/Pakistan
74 C4 **Kashmor** Pakistan
88 G3 **Kasigao Mt** Kenya
71 A3 **Kasiruta** *isld* Indonesia
110 G2 **Kaskaskia** *R* Illinois
26 K6 **Kasker** Sweden
29 J9 **Kaskö** Finland
68 F7 **Kas Kong** Cambodia
55 D3 **Kasli** U.S.S.R.
117 P11 **Kaslo** Br Col
86 E6 **Kasongo** Zaïre
87 C7 **Kasongo-Lunda** Zaïre
47 H9 **Kásos** *isld* Greece
47 H9 **Kásos Str** Greece
54 C1 **Kasplya** *R* U.S.S.R.
68 H6 **Kas Preas** Cambodia
68 F7 **Kas Prins** *isld* Cambodia
68 F7 **Kas Rong** *isld* Cambodia
68 F7 **Kas Rong Sam Lem** *isld* Cambodia
86 G2 **Kassala** Sudan
47 F4 **Kassándra** Greece
32 L10 **Kassel** W Germany
85 F1 **Kasserine** Tunisia
68 F7 **Kas Smach** *isld* Cambodia
99 O5 **Kasson** Minnesota
78 D1 **Kastamonu** Turkey
47 H3 **Kastanéai** Greece
28 E3 **Kastbjerg** Denmark
36 E3 **Kastel** W Germany
36 C3 **Kastellaun** W Germany
47 F9 **Kastélli** Crete Greece
47 G9 **Kastéllion** Crete Greece
47 K8 **Kastellórizon** *isld* Greece
36 B1 **Kaster** W Germany
22 H1 **Kasterlee** Belgium
37 M5 **Kastl** W Germany
27 H15 **Kastlösa** Sweden
33 N5 **Kastorf** W Germany
46 E4 **Kastoría** Greece
46 E4 **Kastorías, L** Greece
47 G5 **Kástron** Límnos I **Greece**
47 F4 **Kástron Nigrita** Greece
46 D5 **Kastrosikiá** Greece
28 K5 **Kastrup** Denmark
60 F10 **Kasubuchi** Japan
61 K10 **Kasugai** Japan
61 O9 **Kasumiga-ura** *L* Japan
70 C6 **Kasungan** Kalimantan
87 F8 **Kasungu** Malawi
88 E9 **Kasupe** Malawi
74 F3 **Kasur** Pakistan
71 H7 **Katabu** Indonesia
85 G6 **Katagum** Nigeria
95 S8 **Katahdin, Mt** Maine
86 D6 **Katako-Kombe** Zaïre
46 E7 **Katákolon** Greece
116 P2 **Katakturuk** *R* Alaska
116 P6 **Katalla** Alaska
86 D7 **Katanda** Zaïre
74 H8 **Katangi** India
59 M1 **Katangli** U.S.S.R.
143 C10 **Katanning** W Australia
75 J4 **Katarnian Ghat** India
46 D7 **Katastári** Greece

61 J10 **Katata** Japan
77 L3 **Katáwáz-Urgan** Afghanistan
55 D3 **Kataysk** U.S.S.R.
69 A9 **Katchall** *isld* Nicobar Is
38 J7 **Katchberg** Austria
116 H4 **Kateel** *R* Alaska
119 O8 **Katepwa** Sask
46 F4 **Katerini** Greece
25 F4 **Katerveer** Netherlands
114 F6 **Kates Needle** *mt* Br Col
75 K7 **Katghora** India
75 R6 **Katha** Burma
84 J4 **Katherina, Gebel** *hill* Egypt
140 B2 **Katherine** N Terr Aust
140 C2 **Katherine R** N Terr Aust
74 H4 **Kathgodam** India
74 D8 **Kathiawar** *reg* India
76 E6 **Kathiraveli** Sri Lanka
113 E9 **Kathleen** Florida
140 E2 **Kathleen Falls** N Terr Aust
143 D7 **Kathleen Valley** W Australia
75 L5 **Kathmandu** Nepal
118 D7 **Kathryn** Alberta
98 H3 **Kathryn** N Dakota
74 F2 **Kathwa** Kashmir
85 C6 **Kati** Mali
70 C4 **Katibas** *R* Sarawak
69 D14 **Katiët** Indonesia
75 M6 **Katihar** India
145 E2 **Katikati** New Zealand
87 D9 **Katima Mulilo** Namibia
119 S8 **Katimik L** Manitoba
85 C7 **Katiola** Ivory Coast
29 L3 **Kätkätunturi** *mt* Finland
89 A8 **Katkop Hills** S Africa
48 M5 **Katlabukh, Oz** *L* U.S.S.R.
32 M9 **Katlenburg** W Germany
116 K8 **Katmai B** Alaska
116 K7 **Katmai Nat. Monument** Alaska
116 K7 **Katmai Vol., Mt** Alaska
74 J7 **Katni** India
46 E6 **Káto Akhaïa** Greece
46 E6 **Katokhí** Greece
88 C9 **Katondwe** Zambia
47 F3 **Káto Nevrokópion** Greece
139 K5 **Katoomba** New S Wales
47 F4 **Káto Stavrós** Greece
31 L5 **Katowice** Poland
47 L7 **Katrancık Dağ** *mt* Turkey
27 H10 **Katrineberg** Sweden
27 H13 **Katrineholm** Sweden
12 D1 **Katrine, L** Scotland
85 F6 **Katsina** Nigeria
61 O9 **Katsuta** Japan
61 O10 **Katsuura** Japan
61 K9 **Katsuyama** Fukui Japan
61 N10 **Katsuyama** Japan
60 G10 **Katsuyama** Okayama Japan
57 D5 **Kattakurgan** U.S.S.R.
142 F5 **Kattamudda Well** W Australia
28 K4 **Kattarp** Sweden
47 J9 **Kattavía** Rhodes Greece
120 K3 **Kattawagami L** Ontario
28 E3 **Kattegat** *str* Denmark
32 G8 **Kattenvenne** W Germany
27 K14 **Katthammarsvik** *isld* Gotland Sweden
28 D5 **Kattrup** Denmark
88 A8 **Katue** *R* Zambia
87 E7 **Katumba** Zaïre
88 D7 **Katumbi** Malawi
56 C5 **Katun'** *R* U.S.S.R.
56 C6 **Katunskiy Khr** *mts* U.S.S.R.
71 J9 **Katupa** Sumbawa Indonesia
75 N7 **Katwa** India
88 B2 **Katwe** Uganda
25 B4 **Katwijk aan Zee** Netherlands
31 K4 **Katy Wrocł** Poland
36 G5 **Katzenbuckel** *mt* W Germany
36 D3 **Katzenelnbogen** W Germany
37 L2 **Katzhütte** E Germany
71 A2 **Kau** Halmahera Indonesia
102 V13 **Kauai** *isld* Hawaiian Is
102 V13 **Kauai Ch** Hawaiian Is
144 B7 **Kauana** New Zealand
36 D3 **Kaub** W Germany
135 U6 **Kau Desert** Hawaiian Is
41 N2 **Kaufbeuren** W Germany
41 N1 **Kaufering** W Germany
109 L3 **Kaufman** Texas
32 L10 **Kaufungen** W Germany
29 K8 **Kauhava** Finland
135 T3 **Kauiki Hd** Hawaiian Is
145 E2 **Kaukapakapa** New Zealand
99 S5 **Kaukauna** Wisconsin
102 U13 **Kaula** *isld* Hawaiian Is
102 U13 **Kaulakahi Ch** Hawaiian Is
135 U5 **Kauluoa Pt** Hawaiian Is
135 O1 **Kaumakani** Hawaiian Is
38 N5 **Kaumberg** Austria
135 R2 **Kaunakakai** Hawaiian Is
135 U6 **Kauna Pt** Hawaiian Is
53 B7 **Kaunas** U.S.S.R.
85 F6 **Kaura Namoda** Nigeria
48 M4 **Kaushany** U.S.S.R.
29 K8 **Kaustinen** Finland
22 L4 **Kautenbach** Luxembourg
71 A2 **Kau, Tk** *B* Halmahera Indonesia
26 N3 **Kautokeino** Norway
68 D7 **Kau-ye Kyun** *isld* Burma
47 K5 **Kavacık** Turkey
46 E3 **Kavadarci** Yugoslavia
46 D3 **Kavajë** Albania
47 J7 **Kavaklıdere** Turkey
59 K3 **Kavalerov** U.S.S.R.
76 E3 **Kavali** India
47 G4 **Kaválla** Greece
73 L6 **Kavaratti** *isld* Lakshadweep Indian Oc
47 J1 **Kavarna** Bulgaria
33 Q4 **Kavelstorf** E Germany
136 L2 **Kavieng** New Ireland
116 O2 **Kavik** *R* Alaska
27 F16 **Kävlinge** Sweden
47 H9 **Kavoúsi** Crete Greece
88 C5 **Kavu** *R* Tanzania
80 D2 **Kavul** Israel
129 H3 **Kaw** Fr Guiana
121 M7 **Kawagama L** Ontario
61 N10 **Kawagoe** Japan
61 N10 **Kawaguchi** Japan
60 H10 **Kawahara** Japan
61 M7 **Kawaharada** Japan
135 U4 **Kawaihae** Hawaiian Is
135 N1 **Kawaihoa Pt** Hawaiian Is
135 O1 **Kawaikini** *peak* Hawaiian Is
102 R11 **Kawailoa Bch** Hawaiian Is
61 M10 **Kawakami** Japan
145 E1 **Kawakawa** New Zealand
145 E2 **Kawakawa B** New Zealand
60 E13 **Kawakita** Japan
61 O8 **Kawamata** Japan
88 B6 **Kawambwa** Zambia
61 N11 **Kawana** Japan
71 J4 **Kawangkoan** Sulawesi
60 G11 **Kawanoe** Japan
144 B6 **Kawarau R** New Zealand
75 J7 **Kawardha** India
121 M8 **Kawartha Lakes** Ontario
61 N10 **Kawasaki** Japan
60 D11 **Kawashiri-misaki** *C* Japan
60 O4 **Kawauchi** Japan
145 E2 **Kawau I** New Zealand
107 O5 **Kaw City** Oklahoma
71 C2 **Kawe** *isld* Indonesia
102 E5 **Kaweah** *R* California
145 F3 **Kaweka** *mt* New Zealand
102 R11 **Kawela B** Hawaiian Is
145 F3 **Kawerau** New Zealand
145 E3 **Kawhia** New Zealand
102 H4 **Kawich Ra** Nevada
88 C6 **Kawimbe** Zambia
119 S6 **Kawinaw L** Manitoba
68 D4 **Kawkareik** Burma
68 C3 **Kawludo** Burma
68 D6 **Kawmapyin** Burma
68 D7 **Kawthaung** Burma
68 C3 **Kawthoolei** *prov* Burma
66 B4 **Kaxgar He** *R* China
52 H4 **Kay** U.S.S.R.
85 D6 **Kaya** Upper Volta
116 P7 **Kayak I** Alaska
68 C4 **Kayan** Burma
70 E3 **Kayan** *R* Kalimantan
76 C6 **Kayankulam** India
55 E4 **Kaybagar, Oz** *L* U.S.S.R.
101 T6 **Kaycee** Wyoming
120 D2 **Kayedon L** Ontario
103 O5 **Kayenta** Arizona
85 B6 **Kayes** Mali
94 F8 **Kayford** W Virginia
55 D5 **Kaygy** U.S.S.R.
47 J6 **Kayislar** Turkey
55 G4 **Kaymanachikha** U.S.S.R.
55 G2 **Kaymysovy** U.S.S.R.
37 N2 **Kayna** E Germany
48 M4 **Kaynary** U.S.S.R.
116 S2 **Kay Pt** Yukon Terr
129 G3 **Kayser Geb** *mts* Suriname
78 E2 **Kayseri** Turkey
101 O8 **Kaysville** Utah
69 G14 **Kayuagung** Sumatra
119 M9 **Kayville** Sask
121 P7 **Kazabazua** Quebec
78 K1 **Kazakh** U.S.S.R.
57 D1 **Kazakhskiy Melkosopochnik** *region* U.S.S.R.
57 **Kazakhstan** U.S.S.R.
57 B2 **Kazalinsk** U.S.S.R.
52 G6 **Kazan'** U.S.S.R.
115 K5 **Kazan** *R* N W Terr
52 G6 **Kazanka** *R* U.S.S.R.
47 G2 **Kazanlük** Bulgaria
54 K3 **Kazanovka** U.S.S.R.
55 E3 **Kazanskoye** U.S.S.R.
57 G4 **Kazarman** U.S.S.R.
48 M1 **Kazatin** U.S.S.R.
47 H5 **Kaz Dağı** *mt* Turkey
55 E5 **Kazgorodok** Kazakhstan U.S.S.R.
55 F4 **Kazgorodok** Kokchetav U.S.S.R.
52 H4 **Kazhim** U.S.S.R.
31 N4 **Kazimierz** Poland
48 F2 **Kazincbarcika** Hungary
54 L3 **Kazinka** U.S.S.R.
37 P4 **Kaznějov** Czechoslovakia
86 D7 **Kazumba** Zaïre
50 F2 **Kazym** *R* U.S.S.R.
56 D4 **Kazyr** *R* U.S.S.R.
77 G4 **Kbash** Afghanistan
31 K3 **Kcynia** Poland
37 P5 **Kdyně** Czechoslovakia
47 G7 **Kéa** *isld* Greece
135 V5 **Keaau** Hawaiian Is
14 E2 **Keady** N Ireland
135 T5 **Keahole Pt** Hawaiian Is
135 S3 **Kealaikahiki Pt** Hawaiian Is
102 V14 **Kealakekue B** Hawaiian Is
135 U5 **Kealia** Hawaiian Is
102 R11 **Keamapapa Pt** Hawaiian Is
103 O6 **Keams Canyon** Arizona
98 G9 **Kearney** Nebraska
121 L7 **Kearney** Ontario
102 F5 **Kearsarge Pass** California
109 O3 **Keatchie** Louisiana
100 H5 **Keating** Oregon
94 K5 **Keating** Pennsylvania
118 K6 **Keatley** Sask
113 D8 **Keatons Beach** Florida
135 V5 **Keaukaha** Hawaiian Is
70 L9 **Kebajoran** *R* Java
78 G2 **Keban** Turkey
68 H2 **Ke Bao, I de** Vietnam
85 A5 **Kébémer** Senegal
85 F2 **Kebili** Tunisia
79 F3 **Kebīr** *R* Syria/Lebanon
86 D3 **Kebkabiya** Sudan
26 K4 **Kebnekaise** Sweden
70 M9 **Kebumen** Java
48 E4 **Kecel** Hungary
60 C11 **Kechi** Japan
117 K6 **Kechika** *R* Br Col
47 L7 **Keçiborlu** Turkey
48 F4 **Kecskemet** Hungary
69 E9 **Kedah** *prov* Malaysia
52 B6 **Kėdainiai** U.S.S.R.
100 E9 **Keddie** California
80 F1 **Kedesh Naphtali** Israel
122 E6 **Kedgewick** New Brunswick
70 O9 **Kediri** Java
85 B6 **Kédougou** Senegal
111 D7 **Kedron** Arkansas
141 K1 **Kedron** *dist* Brisbane, Qnsld
141 K1 **Kedron Brook** Brisbane, Qnsld
55 D3 **Kedrovoye** U.S.S.R.
55 E1 **Kedrovyy** U.S.S.R.
70 M9 **Kedungwuni** Java
52 H3 **Kedva** U.S.S.R.
117 N10 **Keefers** Br Col
117 J4 **Keele Pk** Yukon Terr
119 M8 **Keeler** Sask
118 J4 **Keeley L** Sask
Keeling Is *see* **Cocos Is**
123 T5 **Keels** Nfld
71 D7 **Keenapusan** Philippines
102 F6 **Keene** California
95 P4 **Keene** New Hampshire
95 O2 **Keene** New York
111 L7 **Keener** Alabama
98 B9 **Keenesburg** Colorado
14 C4 **Keeper Hill** Irish Rep
141 F2 **Keer-weer,C** Queensland
95 O2 **Keeseville** New York
89 A6 **Keetmanshoop** Namibia
99 N2 **Keewatin** Minnesota
118 H1 **Keewatin** Ontario
115 K5 **Keewatin, Dist of** N W Terr
86 G4 **Kefa** *prov* Ethiopia
46 D6 **Kefallinía** *isld* Greece
71 M9 **Kefamenanu** Timor Indonesia
80 C6 **Kefar Bilu** Israel
80 F1 **Kefar Blum** Israel
80 C6 **Kefar Daniyyel** Israel
80 D7 **Kefar 'Ezyon** Jordan
80 C2 **Kefar Gallim** Israel
80 C6 **Kefar Habad** Israel
80 D2 **Kefar Ha Maccabi** Israel
80 B6 **Kefar Ha Nagid** Israel
80 F2 **Kefar HaNasi** Israel
80 B7 **Kefar Ha No'ar Nizzanim** Israel
80 C5 **Kefar Hess** Israel
80 C5 **Kefar Mallal** Israel
80 C7 **Kefar Menahem** Israel
80 D1 **Kefar Rosh HaNiqra** Israel
80 F4 **Kefar Ruppin** Israel
80 D6 **Kefar Rut** Jordan
80 C5 **Kefar Sava** Israel
80 F1 **Kefar Szold** Israel
80 E3 **Kefar Tavor** Israel
80 C6 **Kefar Uriyya** Israel
80 C4 **Kefar Vitkin** Israel
99 C4 **Kefar Ya'vetz** Israel
80 C4 **Kefar Yona** Israel
80 C7 **Kefar Zekharya** Israel
80 C4 **Kefer Monash** Israel
85 F7 **Keffi** Nigeria
47 L3 **Kefken Adasi** *isld* Turkey
115 R5 **Keflavík** Iceland
83 K10 **Kegalla** Sri Lanka
123 L3 **Kégashka, L** Quebec
123 L3 **Kegaska** Quebec
28 D7 **Kegnæs** Denmark
117 P7 **Keg River** Alberta
84 F5 **Kegueur Terbi** *mt* Chad
52 B6 **Ķegums** U.S.S.R.
9 E2 **Kegworth** England
32 K5 **Kehdingen Das Alte Ld** *reg* W Germany
84 J6 **Keheili** Sudan
77 C3 **Kehi** Iran
36 D6 **Kehl** W Germany
52 C5 **Kehra** U.S.S.R.
36 C3 **Kehrig** W Germany
13 G6 **Keighley** England
52 B5 **Keila** U.S.S.R.
86 E3 **Keilak, L** Sudan
85 F6 **Keïta** Niger
86 C4 **Keita** *R* Chad
29 M8 **Keitele** Finland
138 F6 **Keith** S Australia
117 M3 **Keith Arm** *B* N W Terr
117 N9 **Keithley Creek** Br Col
99 Q8 **Keithsburg** Illinois
109 O3 **Keithville** Louisiana
135 N1 **Kekaha** Hawaiian Is
145 E5 **Kekerenga** New Zealand
115 N4 **Kekertuk** N W Terr
48 F3 **Kékes** *mt* Hungary
71 B3 **Kekik** *isld* Indonesia
83 K9 **Kekirawa** Sri Lanka
47 K8 **Kekov** *isld* Turkey
74 F6 **Kekri** India
73 L7 **Kelai** *isld* Maldives
65 B5 **Kelan** China
69 E11 **Kelang** Malaysia
69 E10 **Kelantan** *prov* Malaysia
69 F9 **Kelantan** *R* Malaysia
70 F7 **Kelara** *R* Sulawesi
36 B3 **Kelberg** W Germany
33 O10 **Kelbra** E Germany
38 F7 **Kelchsau** Austria
13 F5 **Keld** England
52 F3 **Kel'da** *R* U.S.S.R.
28 K6 **Keldby** Denmark
80 C8 **Kelekh** *R* Israel
47 K5 **Keles** Turkey
57 E4 **Keles** U.S.S.R.
118 J7 **Kelfield** Sask
112 K1 **Kelford** N Carolina
37 M6 **Kelheim** W Germany
43 D12 **Kelibia** Tunisia
77 K1 **Kelif** U.S.S.R.
57 C5 **Kelifskiy Uzboy** U.S.S.R.
98 B9 **Kelim** Colorado
71 K9 **Keli Mutu** *mt* Flores Indonesia
36 E3 **Kelkheim** W Germany
78 G1 **Kelkit** Turkey
86 B6 **Kellé** Congo
95 M9 **Keller** Virginia
100 G1 **Keller** Washington
143 C9 **Kellerberrin** W Australia
117 N4 **Keller L** N W Terr
118 K2 **Keller L** Sask
33 N4 **Kellersee** W Germany
99 M9 **Kellerton** Iowa
114 G3 **Kellet, C** N W Terr
94 H5 **Kellettville** Pennsylvania
94 E5 **Kelleys I** Ohio
99 M2 **Kelliher** Minnesota
119 O7 **Kelliher** Sask
32 L5 **Kellinghusen** W Germany
41 M1 **Kellmünz** W Germany
100 J2 **Kellogg** Idaho
99 O8 **Kellogg** Iowa
29 O5 **Kelloselkä** Finland
15 D5 **Kells Range** Scotland
110 J5 **Kelly** Kentucky
111 D10 **Kelly** Louisiana
101 P6 **Kelly** Wyoming
116 F2 **Kelly** *R* Alaska
140 E6 **Kelly** *R* Queensland
140 B7 **Kelly Hills** N Terr Aust
117 K3 **Kelly L** N W Terr
9 F3 **Kelmarsh** England
52 B6 **Kelme** U.S.S.R.
48 K2 **Kelmentsy** U.S.S.R.
142 C3 **Kelmscott** *dist* Perth, W Aust
86 C4 **Kélo** Chad
26 M3 **Kelottijarvi** *L* Sweden
117 O11 **Kelowna** Br Col
8 D1 **Kelsall** England
36 F3 **Kelsberbach** W Germany
119 V2 **Kelsey** Manitoba
117 L10 **Kelsey Bay** Br Col
119 Q5 **Kelsey L** Manitoba
102 B3 **Kelseyville** California
103 J6 **Kelso** California
98 J2 **Kelso** N Dakota
144 B6 **Kelso** New Zealand
119 Q9 **Kelso** Sask
13 F2 **Kelso** Scotland
100 C3 **Kelso** Washington
9 E1 **Kelstedge** England
28 H5 **Kelstrup** Denmark
28 D6 **Kelstrupstrand** Denmark
101 M8 **Kelton** Utah
109 N4 **Keltys** Texas
69 F11 **Keluang** Malaysia
70 O9 **Kelud G** *mt* Java
9 G4 **Kelvedon** England
103 O8 **Kelvin** Arizona
119 O6 **Kelvington** Sask
119 P1 **Kelvin I** Ontario
119 S8 **Kelwood** Manitoba
52 D3 **Kem'** U.S.S.R.
71 J4 **Kema** Sulawesi
52 E4 **Kema** *R* U.S.S.R.
70 D2 **Kemabong** Sabah
78 G2 **Kemah** Turkey
78 G2 **Kemaliye** Turkey
47 J6 **Kemalpasa** Turkey
Kemalpaşa *R* Turkey *see* **Kirmasti** *R*
117 K9 **Kemano** Br Col
69 F10 **Kemasik** Malaysia
71 H5 **Kembani** Sulawesi
86 D5 **Kembe** Cent Afr Republic
33 R9 **Kemberg** E Germany
56 D3 **Kemchug** *R* U.S.S.R.
47 L8 **Kemer** Lycia Turkey
47 K8 **Kemer** Turkey
47 K7 **Kemer Baraji** *L* Turkey
56 C3 **Kemerovo** U.S.S.R.
56 C4 **Kemerovskaya Oblast'** *prov* U.S.S.R.
29 L6 **Kemi** Finland
29 N5 **Kemijärvi** Finland
29 M5 **Kemijoki** *R* Finland
101 P8 **Kemmerer** Wyoming
37 M4 **Kemnath** W Germany
119 R9 **Kemnay** Manitoba
33 T4 **Kemnitz** E Germany
109 L3 **Kemp** Texas
29 L7 **Kempele** Finland
25 F6 **Kempen** W Germany
36 C3 **Kempenich** W Germany
22 H1 **Kempenland** *reg* Belgium
36 C4 **Kempfeld** W Germany
22 J1 **Kempisch Kan** Belgium
109 H2 **Kemp, L** Texas
109 K4 **Kempner** Texas
146 E12 **Kemp Pen** Antarctica
126 F2 **Kemp's Bay** Andros Bahamas
139 L4 **Kempsey** New S Wales
36 D4 **Kempten** W Germany
41 M2 **Kempten** W Germany
121 Q5 **Kempt, L** Quebec
99 S9 **Kempton** Illinois
98 J2 **Kempton** N Dakota
139 H8 **Kempton** Tasmania
121 P7 **Kemptville** Ontario
70 N8 **Kemudjan** *isld* Indonesia
85 D2 **Kenadsa** Algeria
116 M6 **Kenai** Alaska
116 N6 **Kenai L** Alaska
116 N6 **Kenai Pen** Alaska
70 K8 **Kenam, Tg** *C* Sumatra
86 F4 **Kenamuke Swamp** Sudan
118 L7 **Kenaston** Sask
70 D3 **Kenawang, Bt** *mt* Sarawak
94 J10 **Kenbridge** Virginia
13 F5 **Kendal** England
127 K2 **Kendal** Jamaica
70 N9 **Kendal** Java
139 L4 **Kendal** New S Wales
119 O8 **Kendal** Sask
113 G12 **Kendall** Florida
107 J4 **Kendall** Kansas
94 J3 **Kendall** New York
141 F2 **Kendall** *R* Queensland
115 L5 **Kendall, C** N W Terr
145 D4 **Kendall, Mt** New Zealand
94 B5 **Kendallville** Indiana
71 H6 **Kendari** Sulawesi
143 C10 **Kendenup** W Australia
86 C3 **Kendigué** Chad
75 M8 **Kendrapara** Indiana
100 J3 **Kendrick** Idaho
103 N6 **Kendrick Pk** Arizona
57 L1 **Kendyrlik** U.S.S.R.
57 B3 **Kendyrli, Ozero** *L* U.S.S.R.
139 J4 **Kenebri** New S Wales
109 K7 **Kenedy** Texas
107 O7 **Kenefick** Oklahoma
98 F4 **Kenel** S Dakota
85 B7 **Kenema** Sierra Leone
70 B4 **Kenepai** *mt* Kalimantan
145 D4 **Kenepuru Sound** New Zealand
98 H9 **Kenesaw** Nebraska
56 B3 **Kenga** *R* U.S.S.R.
86 C6 **Kenge** Zaïre
57 A3 **Kenges** U.S.S.R.
26 N4 **Kengis** Sweden
68 G4 **Keng Kabao** Laos
68 G4 **Keng Kok** Laos
68 E2 **Keng Lap** Burma
68 D1 **Keng Lon** Burma
68 D2 **Keng Tawng** Burma
68 D2 **Kengtung** Burma
87 D11 **Kenhardt** S Africa
116 L6 **Kenibuna L** Alaska
85 B6 **Keniéba** Mali
9 E3 **Kenilworth** England
70 E2 **Keningau** Sabah
85 C2 **Kenitra** Morocco
12 D3 **Ken, L** Scotland
65 D6 **Kenli** China
112 J2 **Kenly** N Carolina
14 B5 **Kenmare** Irish Rep
98 E1 **Kenmare** N Dakota
14 A5 **Kenmare, R** Irish Rep
15 E4 **Kenmore** Scotland
141 K2 **Kenmore** *dist* Brisbane, Qnsld
108 D2 **Kenna** New Mexico
94 F8 **Kenna** W Virginia
95 R1 **Kennebago Lake** Maine
98 G6 **Kennebec** S Dakota
95 S2 **Kennebec** *R* Maine
95 R3 **Kennebunk** Maine
109 M10 **Kennedale** Texas
98 J1 **Kennedy** Minnesota
98 F7 **Kennedy** Nebraska
94 J4 **Kennedy** New York
119 P8 **Kennedy** Sask
115 N1 **Kennedy Channel** Canada/Greenland
141 G4 **Kennedy Highway** *rd* Queensland
119 P5 **Kennedy L** Sask
117 D5 **Kennedy, Mt** Yukon Terr
141 G3 **Kennedy R** Queensland
143 B6 **Kennedy Ra** W Australia
95 M7 **Kennedyville** Maryland
111 F11 **Kenner** Louisiana
111 H12 **Kenner** New Orleans
122 J8 **Kennetcook** Nova Scotia
143 B6 **Kenneth Ra** W Australia
9 E5 **Kennet, R** England
110 F5 **Kennett** Missouri
100 F3 **Kennewick** Washington
110 G1 **Kenney** Illinois
117 L9 **Kenney Dam** Br Col
116 Q6 **Kennicott** Alaska
9 H3 **Kenninghall** England
137 M6 **Kenn Reef** Coral Sea
100 D7 **Keno** Oregon
120 E2 **Kenogami** *R* Ontario
121 T4 **Kénogami L** *res* Quebec
120 J4 **Kenogamissi L** Ontario
117 F4 **Keno Hill** Yukon Terr
118 H1 **Kenora** Ontario
99 T7 **Kenosha** Wisconsin
94 E8 **Kenova** W Virginia
29 P7 **Kenozero** U.S.S.R.
52 E4 **Kenozero, Oz** *L* U.S.S.R.
98 H2 **Kensal** N Dakota
127 H5 **Kenscoff** Haiti
57 E2 **Kense** U.S.S.R.
110 E6 **Kensett** Arkansas
99 N6 **Kensett** Iowa
107 M2 **Kensington** Kansas
122 J7 **Kensington** Pr Edward I
95 O5 **Kent** Connecticut
99 M9 **Kent** Iowa
98 K3 **Kent** Minnesota
94 F5 **Kent** Ohio
100 E4 **Kent** Oregon
100 C2 **Kent** Washington
9 G5 **Kent** *co* England
57 E3 **Kentau** U.S.S.R.
120 H10 **Kent Bridge** Ontario
94 B3 **Kent City** Michigan
9 G3 **Kentford** England
139 H7 **Kent Gr** *islds* Tasmania
68 E4 **Ken Thao** Thailand
71 J7 **Kentiolo** *isld* Indonesia
122 G7 **Kent Junction** New Brunswick
99 T9 **Kentland** Indiana
13 F5 **Kentmere** England
119 R9 **Kenton** Manitoba
99 S3 **Kenton** Michigan
94 D6 **Kenton** Ohio
106 H5 **Kenton** Oklahoma
110 G5 **Kenton** Tennessee
114 J4 **Kent Pen** N W Terr
110 J4 **Kentucky** *state* U.S.A.
110 H5 **Kentucky L** Kentucky/Tenn
110 M3 **Kentucky R** Kentucky
122 H8 **Kentville** Nova Scotia
111 F11 **Kentwood** Louisiana
119 Q7 **Kenville** Manitoba
142 C2 **Kenwick** *dist* Perth, W Aust
86 G5 **Kenya** *rep* Africa
88 F2 **Kenya Mt** Kenya
88 F2 **Kenya National Park** Kenya
118 E9 **Kenyon** Alberta
61 N10 **Ken-zaki** *C* Japan
55 F6 **Kenzharyk'** U.S.S.R.
36 D7 **Kenzingen** W Germany
135 T3 **Keokea** Hawaiian Is
110 E1 **Keokuk** Iowa
102 S12 **Keolu Hills** Hawaiian Is
68 G3 **Keo Neua, Col de** *mt* Laos
75 L8 **Keonjhargarh** India
Keos *isld* Greece *see* **Kéa I**
110 D1 **Keosauqua** Iowa
98 B9 **Keota** Colorado
99 P8 **Keota** Iowa
107 Q6 **Keota** Oklahoma
68 G7 **Kep** Cambodia
52 D2 **Kepa** U.S.S.R.
57 A4 **Këpekli** U.S.S.R.
52 F2 **Kepina** U.S.S.R.
144 A6 **Kepler Mts** New Zealand
31 K4 **Kępno** Poland
133 E8 **Keppel** *isld* Falkland Is
141 K6 **Keppel B** Queensland
47 J5 **Kepsut** Turkey
69 D13 **Kepulauan Mentawai** *island gro* Indonesia
76 B5 **Kerala** *prov* India
69 G13 **Kerandin** Indonesia
139 G6 **Kerang** Victoria
47 F7 **Keratéa** Greece
142 C5 **Keraudren,C** W Australia
29 L11 **Kerava** Finland
100 B7 **Kerby** Oregon
53 E10 **Kerch'** U.S.S.R.
55 D2 **Kerchel'** U.S.S.R.
52 H4 **Kerchem'ya** U.S.S.R.
52 J5 **Kerchevskiy** U.S.S.R.
47 F4 **Kerdhíllion** *mt* Greece
136 K3 **Kerema** Papua New Guinea
100 F1 **Keremeos** Br Col
80 C3 **Kerem Maharal** Israel
86 G2 **Keren** Ethiopia
109 L3 **Kerens** Texas
145 E2 **Kerepehi** New Zealand
52 D2 **Keret'** U.S.S.R.
52 E2 **Kerets, Mys** *C* U.S.S.R.
52 G3 **Kerga** U.S.S.R.
90 M16 **Kerguelen-Gaussberg Ridge** Southern Oc
81 D10 **Kerguelen Ridge** Indian Oc
95 N5 **Kerhonkson** New York
46 D7 **Kerí** Greece
88 E2 **Kerichot** Kenya
145 D1 **Kerikeri** New Zealand
29 O10 **Kerimäki** Finland
69 E13 **Kerinci, Danau** *L* Sumatra
69 E13 **Kerinci, Gunung** *mt* Sumatra
48 D4 **Kerka** *R* Hungary
25 F6 **Kerken** W Germany
85 G2 **Kerkenna, Is** Tunisia
99 L4 **Kerkhoven** Minnesota
52 H3 **Kerki** U.S.S.R.
57 D5 **Kerkichi** U.S.S.R.
47 F3 **Kerkinítis, L** Greece
46 D5 **Kérkira** Greece
46 D5 **Kérkira** *isld* Greece
25 F7 **Kerkrade** Netherlands
137 R8 **Kermadec Is** Pacific Oc
102 D5 **Kerman** California
77 E4 **Kerman** Iran
77 F5 **Kerman Desert** Iran
78 L4 **Kermānshāh** Iran
78 A3 **Kerme Körfezi** Turkey
47 H2 **Kermen** Bulgaria
108 D4 **Kermit** Texas
94 E9 **Kermit** W Virginia
102 F6 **Kern** *R* California
36 B2 **Kernen** W Germany
112 G1 **Kernersville** N Carolina
140 B7 **Kernot Ra** N Terr Aust
102 F6 **Kernville** California
52 H4 **Keros** U.S.S.R.
85 C7 **Kerouné** Guinea
139 G4 **Kerpa** New S Wales
48 M4 **Kerpineny** U.S.S.R.
146 H7 **Kerr, C** Antarctica
12 C1 **Kerrera** *isld* Scotland
108 B7 **Kerrick** Texas
113 F8 **Kerr, L** Florida
94 J10 **Kerr L** N Carolina/Virg
118 H7 **Kerrobert** Sask
145 D1 **Kerr Pt** New Zealand
94 H9 **Kerrs Creek** Virginia
110 G6 **Kerrville** Tennessee
109 H5 **Kerrville** Texas
8 C3 **Kerry** Wales
14 A4 **Kerry** *co* Irish Rep
14 B4 **Kerry Hd** Irish Rep
68 J2 **Kersaint, I. du** Vietnam
106 F1 **Kersey** Colorado
112 G3 **Kershaw** S Carolina
69 F10 **Kerteh** Malaysia
28 F6 **Kerteminde** Denmark
140 E7 **Kertie Hill** N Terr Aust
70 O9 **Kertosono** Java
88 F2 **Keruguya** Kenya
Kerulen *R* *see* **Herlen He**
25 F5 **Kervenheim** W Germany
85 D3 **Kerzaz** Australia
36 H2 **Kerzell** W Germany
40 F4 **Kerzers** Switzerland
52 F6 **Kerzhenets** *R* U.S.S.R.
120 K2 **Kesagami L** Ontario
29 O10 **Kesälahti** Finland
78 A1 **Kesan** Turkey
41 L4 **Kesch, Piz** *mt* Switzerland
61 P7 **Kesennuma** Japan
59 J2 **Keshan** China
99 S5 **Keshena** Wisconsin
76 C3 **Kesigi** India
52 D4 **Keskozero** U.S.S.R.
52 E5 **Kesova Gora** U.S.S.R.
47 K4 **Kestel** Turkey
47 L7 **Kestel Gölü** *L* Turkey
52 D2 **Kesten'ga** U.S.S.R.
47 K8 **Kestep** Turkey
25 E5 **Kesteren** Netherlands
36 D3 **Kestert** W Germany
29 M7 **Kestilä** Finland
13 E4 **Keswick** England
122 F8 **Keswick Rdg** New Brunswick
48 D4 **Keszthely** Hungary
56 C2 **Ket'** *R* U.S.S.R.
85 E7 **Kéta** Ghana
70 O9 **Ketapang** Java
69 E13 **Ketaun** Sumatra
117 H8 **Ketchikan** Alaska
101 L6 **Ketchum** Idaho
107 P5 **Ketchum** Oklahoma
108 F4 **Ketchum Mt** Texas
85 D7 **Kété** Ghana
25 E3 **Ketelmeer** Netherlands
74 B6 **Keti Bandar** Pakistan
116 H2 **Ketik** *R* Alaska
66 C3 **Ketmen', Khr** *mts* U.S.S.R./China
85 E7 **Kétou** Benin
31 N1 **Kętrzyn** Poland
36 E3 **Kettenbach** W Germany
9 F3 **Kettering** England
28 D7 **Ketting** Denmark
28 H7 **Kettinge** Denmark
13 E1 **Kettle** Scotland
99 O3 **Kettle** *R* Minnesota
100 G1 **Kettle** *R* Washington
94 K5 **Kettle Cr** Pennsylvania
100 G1 **Kettle Falls** Washington
102 E5 **Kettleman City** California
100 G1 **Kettle R. Range** *mts* Washington
13 F5 **Kettlewell** England
9 F2 **Ketton** England
32 E10 **Kettwig** W Germany
70 B4 **Ketungau** *R* Kalimantan
33 R8 **Ketzin** E Germany
69 B10 **Keudeteunom** Sumatra
95 K4 **Keuka L** New York
33 N10 **Keula** E Germany
55 F2 **Keum** *R* U.S.S.R.
29 L9 **Keurusselkä** *L* Finland
55 E1 **Keushki** U.S.S.R.
25 F5 **Kevelaer** W Germany
110 H4 **Kevil** Kentucky
101 O1 **Kevin** Montana
121 M4 **Kewagama** Quebec
99 R8 **Kewanee** Illinois
111 H9 **Kewanee** Mississippi
94 A5 **Kewanna** Indiana
99 T5 **Kewaunee** Wisconsin
99 S3 **Keweenaw B** Michigan
99 S2 **Keweenaw Pen** Michigan
98 F6 **Keyapaha** S Dakota
98 F6 **Keya Paha** *R* S Dakota
119 S8 **Keyes** Manitoba
106 H5 **Keyes** Oklahoma
110 G3 **Keyesport** Illinois
98 B5 **Keyhole Res** Wyoming
120 K7 **Key Junction** Ontario
14 C2 **Key, L** Irish Rep
113 G12 **Key Largo** Florida
140 A2 **Keyling Inlet** N Terr Aust
95 K7 **Keymar** Maryland
8 D5 **Keynsham** England
100 C2 **Keyport** Washington
94 J7 **Keyser** W Virginia
99 O8 **Keystone** Iowa
98 E8 **Keystone** Nebraska
107 O5 **Keystone** Oklahoma
98 C6 **Keystone** S Dakota
94 F9 **Keystone** W Virginia
113 F8 **Keystone Heights** Florida
103 N10 **Keystone Pk** Arizona
119 M8 **Keystown** Sask
112 E4 **Keysville** Georgia
94 J9 **Keysville** Virginia
113 F13 **Key West** Florida
52 H5 **Kez** U.S.S.R.
95 R3 **Kezar Falls** Maine
95 R2 **Kezar L** Maine
31 M6 **Kežmarok** Czechoslovakia
89 B5 **Kgalagadi** *dist* Botswana
89 E5 **Kgatleng** *reg* Botswana
52 H2 **Khabarikha** U.S.S.R.
59 L2 **Khabarovsk** U.S.S.R.
55 E5 **Khabay** *R* U.S.S.R.
79 H5 **Khabrat es Seiqal** Syria
78 H4 **Khabur** *R* Syria
77 E7 **Khābūrah, Al** Oman
52 E3 **Khachela** U.S.S.R.
77 C5 **Khafr** Iran
77 H4 **Khairabad** Afghanistan
74 C5 **Khairpur** Pakistan
74 H6 **Khajurāho** *anc site* India
56 C4 **Khakasskaya Aut. Oblast'** U.S.S.R.
87 D10 **Khakhea** Botswana
57 C5 **Khalach** U.S.S.R.
77 A4 **Khalafābād** Iran
74 G1 **Khalatse** Kashmir
55 C5 **Khalilovo** U.S.S.R.
78 K5 **Khālis, Al** Iraq
46 F5 **Khálki** Greece
47 J8 **Khálki** *isld* Greece
47 F6 **Khalkís** Greece
80 E5 **Khallat El Fūla** Jordan
52 G5 **Khalturin** U.S.S.R.
75 J7 **Khamaria** India
74 E8 **Khambat, Gulf of** India
89 F2 **Khami** *R* Zimbabwe
47 H9 **Khamilí** *isld* Greece
68 G3 **Kham Keut** Laos
76 E2 **Khammam** India
68 H5 **Khampho** *R* Laos
56 E4 **Khamsara** *R* U.S.S.R.
77 A1 **Khamseh** Iran
57 F4 **Khamza** U.S.S.R.
77 L1 **Khānābād** Afghanistan
76 B3 **Khanapur** India
78 K4 **Khānaqin** Iraq
79 H4 **Khanāzīr, Jebel el** *mts* Syria
139 J6 **Khancoban** New S Wales
84 J6 **Khandaq, El** Sudan
47 H9 **Khandrá** Crete Greece
74 G8 **Khandwa** India
74 D3 **Khanewal** Pakistan
55 D1 **Khangokurt** U.S.S.R.
68 J6 **Khanh Hoa** Vietnam
69 G8 **Khanh Hung** Vietnam
47 G9 **Khaniá** Crete Greece
74 H6 **Khaniadhana** India
54 H2 **Khanino** U.S.S.R.
47 F9 **Khaníon, Kólpos** *B* Crete Greece
74 D4 **Khanpur** Pakistan
79 G3 **Khān Sheikhūn** Syria
57 G3 **Khantau** U.S.S.R.
50 H2 **Khantayka** U.S.S.R.
51 J2 **Khantayskoye, Ozero** *L* U.S.S.R.
66 C3 **Khan Tengri** U.S.S.R.
57 J4 **Khan Tengri, Pik** *mt* U.S.S.R.
55 E1 **Khanty-Mansiysk** U.S.S.R.
68 D4 **Khanu** Thailand
79 E7 **Khan Yunis** Egypt
80 F4 **Khanzira** Jordan
69 D8 **Khao Chum Thong** Thailand
74 G1 **Khapalu** Kashmir
58 F2 **Khapcheranga** U.S.S.R.
75 M6 **Kharagpur** India
77 J5 **Kharan** Pakistan
74 A4 **Kharan Kalat** Pakistan
84 J4 **Khârga, El** Egypt
84 J5 **Khârga Oasis** Egypt
56 H4 **Kharga, Oz** *L* U.S.S.R.
79 D8 **Kharîm, G** *mt* Egypt
72 F4 **Kharj, Al** *reg* Saudi Arabia
77 B5 **Khārk** *isld* Iran
54 H6 **Khar'kov** U.S.S.R.
52 E1 **Kharlovka** U.S.S.R.
52 D4 **Kharlu** U.S.S.R.
47 H3 **Kharmanli** Bulgaria
77 L3 **Kharoti** *reg* Afghanistan
52 F5 **Kharovsk** U.S.S.R.
147 Q7 **Kharstan** U.S.S.R.
86 F2 **Khartoum** Sudan
54 K8 **Khartsyzsk** U.S.S.R.
52 J2 **Kharutayuvam** U.S.S.R.
65 H3 **Khasan** U.S.S.R.
77 H4 **Khash** Afghanistan
77 G5 **Khāsh** Iran
86 G2 **Khashem el Girba** Sudan
77 H4 **Khash Rud** *R* Afghanistan
78 J1 **Khashusi** U.S.S.R.
46 E5 **Khasiá Óri** Greece
75 O6 **Khasi-Jaintia Hills** India
47 H3 **Khaskovo** Bulgaria
51 K1 **Khatanga** U.S.S.R.
51 L1 **Khatangskiy Zaliv** *gulf* U.S.S.R.
52 J2 **Khatayakha** U.S.S.R.
57 D5 **Khatyrchi** U.S.S.R.
57 D5 **Khaudag** U.S.S.R.
68 C5 **Khawsa** Burma
57 F5 **Khaydarken** U.S.S.R.
57 B4 **Khazar-Asp** U.S.S.R.
68 G3 **Khe Bo** Vietnam
74 E10 **Khed** India
68 G2 **Khe Long** Vietnam
52 D4 **Khelyulya** U.S.S.R.
56 D5 **Khemchik** *R* U.S.S.R.
56 D5 **Khemchikskiy, Khr** *mts* U.S.S.R.
85 D4 **Khenachich, El** *reg* Mali
85 F1 **Khenchela** Algeria
68 A2 **Khenkhar** Burma
53 D10 **Kherson** U.S.S.R.
51 J1 **Kheta** *R* U.S.S.R.
52 D2 **Khetolambina** U.S.S.R.
74 F5 **Khetri** India
68 E5 **Khiaw, Khao** *mt* Thailand
52 D1 **Khibiny** *mt* U.S.S.R.
29 O10 **Khiitola** U.S.S.R.
46 F7 **Khiliomódhion** Greece
56 H5 **Khilok** U.S.S.R.
56 G5 **Khilok** *R* U.S.S.R.
52 E6 **Khimki** U.S.S.R.
56 C5 **Khindiktig Khol', Oz** *L* U.S.S.R.
46 D6 **Khionáta** Greece
47 H6 **Khíos** *isld* Greece
80 D8 **Khirbet Deir Razih** Jordan
80 G4 **Khirbet el Kufeirat** Jordan
80 F4 **Khirbet el Wahadina** Jordan
80 G4 **Khirbet Harqala** Jordan
80 D5 **Khirbet Isla** Jordan
80 F4 **Khirbet Listib** Jordan
80 F4 **Khirbet Mar Ilyas** Jordan
47 G2 **Khisar** Bulgaria
57 B4 **Khiva** U.S.S.R.
46 F6 **Khlomón** *mt* Greece
48 L1 **Khmelnik** U.S.S.R.
48 K1 **Khmel'nitskiy** U.S.S.R.
Khmer Rep *see* **Cambodia**
69 G8 **Khoai, Hon** *isld* Vietnam
48 J1 **Khodorov** U.S.S.R.
57 D5 **Khodzha Mubarek** U.S.S.R.
57 A4 **Khodzheyli** U.S.S.R.
54 K5 **Khokhol** U.S.S.R.
52 D6 **Kholm** U.S.S.R.
52 F3 **Kholmogorskaya** U.S.S.R.
52 F3 **Kholmogory** U.S.S.R.
59 M2 **Kholmsk** U.S.S.R.
56 B5 **Kholzun, Khr** *mts* U.S.S.R.
77 A1 **Khoman** Iran
87 C10 **Khomas Hochland** *dist* Namibia
77 B3 **Khomeyn** Iran
87 F8 **Khondowe** Malawi
68 G5 **Khong** Laos
68 G5 **Khong Sedone** Laos
88 E10 **Khonjeni** Malawi
77 C6 **Khonj, Kūhe-e** *mt* Iran
68 F4 **Khon Kaen** Thailand
53 F8 **Khoper** *R* U.S.S.R.
59 L2 **Khor** U.S.S.R.
59 L2 **Khor** *R* U.S.S.R.
46 E7 **Khóra** Greece
77 E2 **Khorāsan** Iran
47 G9 **Khóra Sfakíon** Crete Greece
52 J2 **Khoreyver** U.S.S.R.
57 B4 **Khorezmskaya Oblast'** *prov* U.S.S.R.
Khorgos *see* **Huo ch eng**
57 C2 **Khorkhut** U.S.S.R.
54 K1 **Khorlovo** U.S.S.R.
57 F6 **Khorog** U.S.S.R.
54 E7 **Khorol** U.S.S.R.
54 E7 **Khorol** *R* U.S.S.R.
55 G4 **Khorosheye** U.S.S.R.
77 A3 **Khorramābād** Iran
77 A4 **Khorramshahr** Iran
52 J2 **Khoseda Khard** U.S.S.R.
77 F3 **Khosf** Iran
74 B3 **Khost** Pakistan
77 L3 **Khost** *reg* Afghanistan
Khotan *see* **Hotan**
54 D3 **Khotimsk** U.S.S.R.
48 K2 **Khotin** U.S.S.R.
54 K1 **Khot'kovo** U.S.S.R.
116 H4 **Khotol** *mt* Alaska
53 F12 **Khrami** *R* U.S.S.R.
52 F6 **Khrapovitskaya** U.S.S.R.
54 M5 **Khrenovoye** U.S.S.R.
68 A2 **Khreum** Burma
47 G4 **Khrisoúpolis** Greece
47 G8 **Khristianá** *isld* Greece
48 M2 **Khristinovka** U.S.S.R.
52 G4 **Khristoforovo** U.S.S.R.
47 G3 **Khrojna** Bulgaria
55 C5 **Khrom-Tau** U.S.S.R.
79 C3 **Khrysokhou B** Cyprus
47 H7 **Khtapodhiá** *isld* Greece
77 B6 **Khubar, Al** Saudi Arabia
77 K6 **Khude Hills** Pakistan
56 G5 **Khudunskiy Khr** *mts* U.S.S.R.
68 G5 **Khu Khan** Thailand
77 K1 **Khulm** Afghanistan
75 N7 **Khulna** Bangladesh
84 E3 **Khums, Al** Libya
Khungari *see* **Gurskoye**
74 F1 **Khunjerab Pass** China/India
77 B3 **Khunsar** Iran
75 L7 **Khunti** India
75 L8 **Khurda** India
77 J3 **Khurd, Koh-i-** *mt* Afghanistan
74 G4 **Khurja** India
74 E2 **Khushab** Pakistan
48 H2 **Khust** U.S.S.R.
86 E3 **Khuwei** Sudan
77 A4 **Khuzestan** Iran
56 G4 **Khuzhir** U.S.S.R.
77 G2 **Khvāf** Iran
77 D3 **Khvor** Iran
78 K2 **Khvoy** Iran
52 D5 **Khvoynaya** U.S.S.R.
77 L1 **Khwāja-i-Ghar** Afghanistan
77 L1 **Khwaja Muhammad Range** Afghanistan
74 D1 **Khyber Pass** Pakistan/Afghan
48 H1 **Khyrov** U.S.S.R.
139 K5 **Kiama** New S Wales
71 G7 **Kiamba** Mindanao Philippines
88 F2 **Kiambu** Kenya
107 P7 **Kiamichi Mts** Oklahoma
121 P6 **Kiamika** Quebec
Kiamusze *see* **Jiamusi**
141 K6 **Kianga** Queensland
Kiangsi *prov see* **Jiangxi**
Kiangsu *prov see* **Jiangsu**
29 O6 **Kiantajärvi** *L* Finland
119 U2 **Kiask L** Manitoba
28 B4 **Kibæk** Denmark
86 F5 **Kibanga** Uganda
86 B6 **Kibangou** Congo
71 G7 **Kibawe** Mindanao Philippines
88 F4 **Kibaya** Tanzania
26 S1 **Kiberg** Norway
85 D7 **Kibi** Ghana
87 G7 **Kibiti** Tanzania
86 E6 **Kibombo** Zaïre
88 C3 **Kibondo** Tanzania
79 E10 **Kibrīt, J. al** Saudi Arabia
88 C3 **Kibungu** Rwanda
46 D3 **Kičevo** Yugoslavia
86 C2 **Kichi Kichi** Chad
52 G4 **Kichmenga** *R* U.S.S.R.
52 G5 **Kichmengskiy Gorodok** U.S.S.R.
52 H7 **Kichuy** U.S.S.R.
99 Q6 **Kickapoo** *R* Wisconsin
117 P10 **Kicking Horse Pass** Br Col
85 E5 **Kidal** Mali
71 H5 **Kidandal** Indonesia
98 J4 **Kidder** S Dakota
8 D3 **Kidderminster** England
86 F5 **Kidepo Nat. Park** Kenya
85 B6 **Kidira** Senegal
9 E4 **Kidlington** England
145 F3 **Kidnappers, C** New Zealand
141 G4 **Kidston** Queensland
70 C3 **Kidurong, Tg** *C* Sarawak
8 B4 **Kidwelly** Wales
98 F2 **Kief** N Dakota
32 M4 **Kiel** W Germany
99 S6 **Kiel** Wisconsin
31 M5 **Kielce** Poland
13 F3 **Kielder** England
13 F3 **Kielder Res** England
22 G1 **Kieldrecht** Belgium
30 E1 **Kieler Bucht** *B* W Germany
138 D5 **Kielpa** S Australia
67 B6 **Kien An** Vietnam
69 G8 **Kien Hung** Vietnam
37 N1 **Kieritzsch** E Germany
36 D1 **Kierspe** W Germany
109 N9 **Kiest Park** Texas
Kiev *see* **Kiyev**
139 H6 **Kiewa** *R* Victoria
85 B5 **Kiffa** Mauritania
46 F6 **Kifissós** *R* Greece
78 K5 **Kifl, Al** Iraq
88 C2 **Kigali** Rwanda
116 K2 **Kigalik** *R* Alaska
116 E4 **Kigluaik Mts** Alaska
88 B4 **Kigoma** Tanzania
88 C4 **Kigoma** *dist* Tanzania
141 F7 **Kihee** Queensland
27 M13 **Kihelkonna** U.S.S.R.
145 E3 **Kihikihi** New Zealand
29 K4 **Kihlanki** Finland
29 K9 **Kihniö** Finland
102 V14 **Kiholo** Hawaiian Is
29 K11 **Kiikala** Finland
29 K10 **Kiikoinen** Finland
135 N1 **Kii Landing** Hawaiian Is
29 M6 **Kiiminki** Finland
61 K11 **Kii-Nagashima** Japan
61 J12 **Kii Sanchi** *mts* Japan
60 H12 **Kii suidō** *str* Japan
116 K6 **Kijik** Alaska
61 Q12 **Kijoka** Okinawa
59 J6 **Kikai-shima** *isld* Japan
116 L2 **Kikiakrorak** *R* Alaska
48 F5 **Kikinda** Yugoslavia
47 G7 **Kikladhes** *islds* Greece
52 G6 **Kiknur** U.S.S.R.
60 O4 **Kikonai** Japan
136 J3 **Kikori** Papua New Guinea
60 D13 **Kikuchi** Japan
89 D8 **Kikvors Berg** S Africa
121 M6 **Kikwissi, L** Quebec
86 C7 **Kikwit** Zaïre
27 F12 **Kil** Sweden
101 L1 **Kila** Montana
27 J13 **Kila** Sweden
27 J10 **Kilafors** Sweden
113 L9 **Kilarney, L** New Providence I **Bahamas**
135 O1 **Kilauea** Hawaiian Is
102 V14 **Kilauea Crater** Hawaiian Is
14 D3 **Kilbeggan** Irish Rep
12 C2 **Kilberry** Scotland
15 C5 **Kilbrennan Snd** Scotland
12 D2 **Kilbride** Scotland
116 G6 **Kilbuck Mts** Alaska
122 E7 **Kilburn** New Brunswick
12 C2 **Kilchattan** Scotland
12 B2 **Kilchoman** Scotland
12 C1 **Kilchrenan** Scotland
65 H4 **Kilchu** N Korea
13 F1 **Kilconquhar** Scotland
14 D3 **Kilcormac** Irish Rep
141 K7 **Kilcoy** Queensland
14 E3 **Kilcullen** Irish Rep
117 K9 **Kildala Arm** *R* Br Columbia
13 G5 **Kildale** England
14 E3 **Kildare** Irish Rep
109 N3 **Kildare** Texas
14 E3 **Kildare** *co* Irish Rep
122 J7 **Kildare, C** Pr Edward I
28 J5 **Kildebrønde** Denmark
52 D1 **Kil'din, Os** *isld* U.S.S.R.
117 L11 **Kildonan** Br Col
118 B1 **Kildonan** Manitoba
87 F9 **Kildonan** Zimbabwe
86 C7 **Kilembe** Zaïre

28 A3 Kilen L Denmark
14 B4 Kilfenora Irish Rep
12 C2 Kilfinan Scotland
14 C4 Kilfinnane Irish Rep
14 B5 Kilgarvan Irish Rep
101 O5 Kilgore Idaho
98 F7 Kilgore Nebraska
111 B9 Kilgore Texas
13 H5 Kilham England
85 E7 Kilibo Benin
88 G3 Kilifi Kenya
88 F3 Kilimanjaro mt Tanzania
137 M2 Kilinailau Is Solomon Is
47 K4 Kılınç Turkey
15 C4 Kilinelfort Scotland
52 B5 Kilingi-Nõmme U.S.S.R.
83 K8 Kilinochchi Sri Lanka
78 F3 Kilis Turkey
116 L8 Kiliuda B Alaska
48 M5 Kiliya U.S.S.R.
14 B4 Kilkee Irish Rep
14 F2 Kilkeel N Ireland
14 D4 Kilkenny Irish Rep
14 D4 Kilkenny co Irish Rep
12 C3 Kilkenzie Scotland
8 B6 Kilkhampton England
14 B3 Kilkieran B Irish Rep
46 F4 Kilkís Greece
141 K7 Kilkivan Queensland
14 E3 Kill Irish Rep
14 B2 Killala Irish Rep
14 B2 Killala B Irish Rep
120 D3 Killala L Ontario
14 C4 Killaloe Irish Rep
121 N7 Killaloe Ontario
119 P8 Killaly Sask
118 F6 Killam Alberta
14 B4 Killarney Irish Rep
119 S9 Killarney Manitoba
140 B3 Killarney N Terr Aust
120 J7 Killarney Ontario
141 K8 Killarney Queensland
120 J6 Killarney Prov. Park Ontario
14 A3 Killary Hbr Irish Rep
14 D2 Killashandra Irish Rep
98 D2 Killdeer N Dakota
118 L9 Killdeer Sask
99 O8 Killduff Iowa
12 D1 Killearn Scotland
109 K4 Killeen Texas
47 J5 Killer R Turkey
15 E4 Killiecrankie, Pass of Scotland
116 K2 Killik Bend Alaska
14 C3 Killimor Irish Rep
15 D4 Killin Scotland
26 E9 Killingdal Norway
46 E7 Killíni Greece
46 E7 Killini mt Greece
14 B4 Killorglin Irish Rep
14 C2 Killybegs Irish Rep
14 F2 Killyleagh N Ireland
14 C4 Kilmallock Irish Rep
15 B3 Kilmaluag Scotland
13 F1 Kilmany Scotland
12 D2 Kilmarnock Scotland
95 L9 Kilmarnock Virginia
12 C1 Kilmartin Scotland
52 H6 Kil'mez U.S.S.R.
111 G8 Kilmichael Mississippi
139 G6 Kilmore Victoria
12 C2 Kilmory Scotland
12 D1 Kilmun Scotland
13 E4 Kilnhill England
12 C1 Kilninver Scotland
13 J6 Kilnsea England
88 F6 Kilombero R Tanzania
88 F5 Kilosa Tanzania
29 H2 Kilpisjärvi Finland
29 L7 Kilpua Finland
29 Q2 Kilp'yavr U.S.S.R.
14 E2 Kilrea N Ireland
14 B4 Kilrush Irish Rep
9 E3 Kilsby England
12 D2 Kilsyth Scotland
14 C3 Kiltamagh Irish Rep
73 L6 Kiltan isld Lakshadweep Indian Oc
26 M5 Kilvo Sweden
87 E7 Kilwa Zaïre
88 B6 Kilwa isld Zambia
88 G6 Kilwa Kisiwani Tanzania
88 G6 Kilwa Kivinje Tanzania
88 G6 Kilwa Masoko Tanzania
12 D2 Kilwinning Scotland
47 K3 Kilyos Turkey
106 G4 Kim Colorado
101 M7 Kimama Idaho
70 D2 Kimanis B Sabah
138 D5 Kimba S Australia
98 C8 Kimball Nebraska
98 H6 Kimball S Dakota
94 F9 Kimball W Virginia
116 P5 Kimball, Mt Alaska
99 L8 Kimballton Iowa
86 C7 Kimbao Zaïre
117 Q11 Kimberley Br Col
120 K8 Kimberley Ontario
89 D7 Kimberley S Africa
141 H3 Kimberley,C Queensland
142 E3 Kimberley Downs W Australia
142 F3 Kimberley Plateau W Australia
143 C7 Kimberley Ra W Australia
101 L7 Kimberly Idaho
103 J2 Kimberly Nevada
99 S5 Kimberly Wisconsin
9 F3 Kimbolton England
145 E4 Kimbolton New Zealand
88 D5 Kimbu Tanzania
47 G6 Kimi Greece
29 K11 Kimito Finland
118 A3 Kimiwan Lake Alberta
110 F3 Kimmswick Missouri
47 G8 Kímolos isld Greece
61 M7 Kimpoku-san mt Japan
52 E6 Kimry U.S.S.R.
68 J5 Kim Son Vietnam
27 H13 Kimstad Sweden
52 F2 Kimzha U.S.S.R.
68 B1 Kin Burma
61 P13 Kin Okinawa
61 P13 Kina Okinawa
70 E1 Kinabalu mt Sabah
70 E2 Kinabatangan R Sabah
88 F2 Kinangop, Mt Kenya
47 H8 Kínaros isld Greece
70 D2 Kinarut Sabah
117 O10 Kinbasket Br Col
118 F8 Kinbrook I. Prov. Pk Alberta
107 P3 Kincaid Kansas
118 K9 Kincaid Sask
120 J8 Kincardine Ontario
12 E1 Kincardine Scotland
Kincardine co see Grampian reg
117 J8 Kincolith Br Col
15 E3 Kincraig Scotland
87 E7 Kinda Zaïre
94 E3 Kinde Michigan
33 O10 Kindelbrück E Germany
109 P5 Kinder Louisiana
36 C3 Kinderbeuern W Germany
118 J7 Kindersley Sask
85 B6 Kindia Guinea
98 J3 Kindred N Dakota
86 E6 Kindu Zaïre
116 G7 Kinegnak Alaska
53 H7 Kinelyu R U.S.S.R.
52 F6 Kineshma U.S.S.R.
140 C1 King R N Terr Aust
140 E6 King R Queensland
141 G2 King R Queensland
141 K7 Kingaroy Queensland
133 C6 King, Canal str Chile
114 J2 King Christian I N W Terr
102 C5 King City California
99 M9 King City Missouri
117 K10 Kingcome Inlet Br Col
116 F9 King Cove Alaska
142 F3 King Edward R W Australia
146 J8 King Edward V11 Land Antarctica
95 R2 Kingfield Maine
107 N6 Kingfisher Oklahoma
146 E15 King George 1 S Shetland Is
115 M6 King George Is N W Terr
135 N10 King George Is Tuamotu Arch Pacific Oc
118 B8 King George, Mt Br Col
117 D5 King George, Mt Yukon Terr
143 C11 King George Sd W Australia
133 J8 King Haakon B S Georgia
142 E6 King Hill W Australia
120 C3 Kinghorn Ontario
13 E1 Kinghorn Scotland
146 H11 King I Antarctica
117 K9 King I Br Col
73 Q6 King I Burma
139 G7 King I Tasmania
52 C5 Kingisepp U.S.S.R.
52 B5 Kingissepp U.S.S.R.
100 G8 King Lear mt Nevada
146 D3 King Leopold & Queen Astrid Coast Antarctica
142 E3 King Leopold Ra W Australia
118 E5 Kingman Alberta
103 K6 Kingman Arizona
107 M4 Kingman Kansas
95 T1 Kingman Maine
141 H7 King, Mt Queensland
108 E4 King Mt Texas
142 C5 King, Mt W Australia
86 E6 Kingombe Zaïre
138 D4 Kingoonya S Australia
139 H8 King, R Tasmania
142 G3 King, R W Australia
102 D5 Kings R California
100 G8 Kings R Nevada
116 J7 King Salmon Alaska
13 F1 Kingsbarns Scotland
8 C7 Kingsbridge England
102 E5 Kingsburg California
109 K6 Kingsbury Texas
106 D1 Kings Canyon Colorado
102 F4 Kings Canyon Nat Park California
9 E5 Kingsclere England
139 L3 Kingscliff-Fingal New S Wales
138 D6 Kingscote S Australia
14 E3 Kingscourt Irish Rep
145 E2 Kingseat New Zealand
9 G5 Kingsferry Bridge England
9 F5 Kingsfold England
109 P2 Kingsland Arkansas
113 F7 Kingsland Georgia
9 F4 Kings Langley England
99 L7 Kingsley Iowa
94 B2 Kingsley Michigan
98 E8 Kingsley Dam Nebraska
9 G2 King's Lynn England
137 P2 Kingsmill Group islds Kiribati
112 F2 Kings Mt N Carolina
95 O6 Kings Park Long I, N Y
101 P9 Kings Pks Utah
122 H8 Kingsport Nova Scotia
94 E10 Kingsport Tennessee
142 E3 Kings Sd W Australia
8 C6 Kingsteignton England
110 C5 Kingston Arkansas
9 F5 Kingston England
127 L3 Kingston Jamaica
110 B2 Kingston Missouri
95 R4 Kingston New Hampshire
95 N5 Kingston New York
144 B6 Kingston New Zealand
94 E7 Kingston Ohio
107 O7 Kingston Oklahoma
121 O8 Kingston Ontario
95 M5 Kingston Pennsylvania
138 E6 Kingston S Australia
139 H9 Kingston Tasmania
100 C2 Kingston Washington
94 F9 Kingston W Virginia
9 E4 Kingston Lisle England
103 J6 Kingston Pk California
13 F4 Kingstown England
127 O8 Kingstown St Vincent
112 H4 Kingstree S Carolina
94 G5 Kingsville Ohio
120 H10 Kingsville Ontario
109 K8 Kingsville Texas
8 C7 Kingswear England
8 C3 Kington England
86 C7 Kinguji Zaïre
15 D3 Kingussie Scotland
115 K4 King William I N W Terr
89 E9 King William's Town S Africa
94 H7 Kingwood W Virginia
87 E8 Kiniama Zaïre
47 J5 Kınık Turkey
119 M6 Kinistino Sask
61 P7 Kinka-san C Japan
87 H11 Kinkony, L Madagascar
122 J7 Kinkora Pr Edward I
145 E3 Kinleith New Zealand
118 K6 Kinley Sask
144 B6 Kinloch New Zealand
15 C3 Kinlochewe Scotland
15 D4 Kinlochleven Scotland
15 D4 Kinloch Rannoch Scotland
68 B3 Kinmaw Burma
61 P13 Kin-misaki C Okinawa
121 M8 Kinmount Ontario
110 H3 Kinmundy Illinois
27 F14 Kinna Sweden
117 P11 Kinnaird Br Col
15 F3 Kinnairds Hd Scotland
101 R6 Kinnear Wyoming
80 F3 Kinneret Israel
80 B8 Kinneret-Negev-Conduit Israel
83 L9 Kinniyai Sri Lanka
29 L8 Kinnula Finland
60 J11 Kino R Japan
61 K10 Kinomoto Japan
119 Q1 Kinoosa Manitoba
60 H10 Kinosaki Japan
13 E1 Kinqlassie Scotland
13 E1 Kinross Scotland
Kinross co see Tayside reg
14 C5 Kinsale Irish Rep
95 L8 Kinsale Virginia
7 E11 Kinsale oil rig Celtic Sea
14 C5 Kinsale, Old Hd of C Irish Rep
118 F5 Kinsella Alberta
101 U3 Kinsey Montana
86 C6 Kinshasa Zaïre
60 C11 Kin Shimo no-shima Japan
107 L4 Kinsley Kansas
94 G5 Kinsman Ohio
112 K2 Kinston N Carolina
107 P6 Kinta Oklahoma
70 P10 Kintamani, G mt Indonesia
70 D6 Kintap Kalimantan
85 C6 Kintinian Guinea
101 L1 Kintla Pk Montana
71 H5 Kintom Sulawesi
15 F3 Kintore Scotland
138 B2 Kintore, Mt S Australia
140 A6 Kintore Ra N Terr Aust
55 F1 Kintus U.S.S.R.
12 C2 Kintyre pen Scotland
68 B1 Kinu Burma
61 N9 Kinu R Japan
118 B3 Kinuso Alberta
14 C3 Kinvarra Irish Rep
61 P13 Kin wan B Okinawa
86 F5 Kinyeti mt Sudan
55 C6 Kinzhaly U.S.S.R.
36 D7 Kinzig R Baden-Württemberg W Germany
36 G3 Kinzig R Hessen W Germany
100 E5 Kinzua Oregon
94 J5 Kinzua Pennsylvania
71 N9 Kio Indonesia
100 F3 Kiona Washington
121 M6 Kiosk Ontario
106 F2 Kiowa Colorado
107 M4 Kiowa Kansas
107 P7 Kiowa Oklahoma
119 Q3 Kipahigan L Manitoba
135 T3 Kipahulu Hawaiian Is
46 E7 Kiparissia Greece
46 E7 Kiparissiakós Kolpos B Greece
121 M6 Kipawa Quebec
88 C5 Kipili Tanzania
86 H6 Kipini Kenya
119 P8 Kipling Sask
116 E7 Kipnuk Alaska
118 E9 Kipp Alberta
12 D1 Kippen Scotland
36 D7 Kippenheim W Germany
123 O5 Kippens Nfld
95 M9 Kiptopeke Virginia
87 E8 Kipushi Zaïre
60 H12 Kiragawa Japan
47 H4 Kirazh Turkey
Kirberg see Hünfelden
111 C7 Kirby Arkansas
9 H4 Kirby England
120 F6 Kirby Ontario
101 R6 Kirby Wyoming
111 C11 Kirbyville Texas
38 N8 Kirchbach Austria
38 M5 Kirchberg Austria
36 H5 Kirchberg Baden-Württemberg W Germany
37 O2 Kirchberg E Germany
36 C4 Kirchberg Rheinland-Pfalz W Germany
33 O5 Kirchdorf E Germany
37 P6 Kirchdorf W Germany
37 M4 Kirchenlaibach W Germany
37 M3 Kirchenlamitz W Germany
36 D2 Kirchen-Sieg W Germany
36 G6 Kirchentellinsfurt W Germany
37 M4 Kirchenthumbach W Germany
33 T9 Kirchhain E Germany
36 F2 Kirchhain W Germany
37 K1 Kirchheilingen E Germany
36 G5 Kirchheim W Germany
36 D4 Kirchheim Bolanden W Germany
32 E9 Kirchhellen W Germany
36 E1 Kirchhundem W Germany
33 O6 Kirch Jesar E Germany
32 H6 Kirchkimmen W Germany
37 K3 Kirchlauter W Germany
32 J8 Kirchlengern W Germany
32 K7 Kirchlinteln W Germany
38 K5 Kirchschlag Austria
32 J7 Kirchweyhe W Germany
32 J6 Kirchwistedt W Germany
47 J5 Kireç Turkey
33 Q5 Kireh Grubenhagen E Germany
56 G3 Kirenga R U.S.S.R.
47 K7 Kirenis R Turkey
56 G2 Kirensk U.S.S.R.
55 E6 Kirey R U.S.S.R.
54 J3 Kireyevsk U.S.S.R.
83 K11 Kirgalpotta mt Sri Lanka
55 G6 Kirgiziya U.S.S.R.
57 F4 Kirgiziya S.S.R rep U.S.S.R.
55 B4 Kirgiz-Miyaki U.S.S.R.
86 C6 Kiri Zaïre
78 F3 Kirikhan Turkey
78 D2 Kirikkale Turkey
145 E1 Kirikopuni New Zealand
29 O11 Kirillovskoye U.S.S.R.
Kirin see Jilin
Kirin prov see Jilin
83 L11 Kirindi Oya R Sri Lanka
145 E1 Kiripa New Zealand
52 D5 Kirishi U.S.S.R.
60 D14 Kirishima-yama mt Japan
86 A2 Kirit Somalia
136 L3 Kiriwina Is Papua New Guinea
106 H2 Kirk Colorado
98 C8 Kirk Nebraska
100 D7 Kirk Oregon
47 L5 Kırka Turkey
47 J5 Kırkağaç Turkey
12 E4 Kirkbean Scotland
13 E4 Kirkbride England
13 F5 Kirkby Lonsdale England
13 H5 Kirkbymoorside England
13 F5 Kirkby Stephen England
118 D8 Kirkcaldy Alberta
13 E1 Kirkcaldy Scotland
12 C4 Kirkcolm Scotland
12 D4 Kirkcowan Scotland
12 D4 Kirkcudbright Scotland
Kirkcudbright co see Dumfries and Galloway reg
12 D4 Kirkcudbright B Scotland
13 G6 Kirk Deighton England
28 N2 Kirkebø Faeroes
28 F6 Kirkeby Fyn Denmark
28 B6 Kirkeby Sønderjylland Denmark
28 G5 Kirke Helsinge Denmark
28 H5 Kirke Hvalsø Denmark
28 H5 Kirke Hyllinge Denmark
119 Q8 Kirkella Manitoba
36 C5 Kirkel-Neuhausel W Germany
26 R2 Kirkenes Norway
28 H5 Kirke Såby Denmark
28 G6 Kirke Stillinge Denmark
26 K3 Kirkestind mt Norway
12 E2 Kirkfieldbank Scotland
13 F6 Kirkham England
12 D4 Kirkinner Scotland
12 D2 Kirkintilloch Scotland
28 N2 Kirkjubønes Faeroes
103 M7 Kirkland Arizona
99 S7 Kirkland Illinois
12 E3 Kirkland Scotland
100 C2 Kirkland Washington
120 K4 Kirkland Lake Ontario
47 J3 Kirklareli Turkey
94 A6 Kirklin Indiana
9 F1 Kirklington Notts England
13 G5 Kirklington N Yorks England
12 E2 Kirkliston Scotland
144 C6 Kirkliston Range New Zealand
99 L8 Kirkman Iowa
12 D3 Kirkmichael Scotland
13 F4 Kirkoswald England
12 D3 Kirkoswald Scotland
13 E3 Kirkpatrick-Fleming Scotland
146 G7 Kirkpatrick, Mt Antarctica
13 F5 Kirkstone Pass England
110 D1 Kirksville Missouri
78 K4 Kirkūk Iraq
15 F2 Kirkwall Scotland
102 B2 Kirkwood California
95 M4 Kirkwood New York
89 D9 Kirkwood S Africa
98 E5 Kirley S Dakota
47 K5 Kirmasti R Turkey
12 D2 Kirn Scotland
36 C4 Kirn W Germany
54 F2 Kirov Kaluga U.S.S.R.
52 G5 Kirov Kirov U.S.S.R.
78 L1 Kirovabad Azerbaydzhan U.S.S.R.
57 E6 Kirovabad Tadzhik U.S.S.R.
78 K1 Kirovakan U.S.S.R.
55 D3 Kirovo U.S.S.R.
54 D8 Kirovograd U.S.S.R.
52 D1 Kirovsk U.S.S.R.
118 G7 Kirriemuir Alberta
15 E4 Kirriemuir Scotland
52 H5 Kirs U.S.S.R.
78 E2 Kirşehir Turkey
87 D11 Kirstonia S Africa
98 B7 Kirtley Wyoming
13 H6 Kirton England
9 F2 Kirton Holme England
36 G2 Kirtorf W Germany
26 L4 Kiruna Sweden
86 E6 Kirundu Zaïre
144 D5 Kirwee New Zealand
107 M2 Kirwin Kansas
61 N9 Kiryū Japan
54 K1 Kirzhach U.S.S.R.
27 H14 Kisa Sweden
61 N6 Kisakata Japan
87 G7 Kisaki Tanzania
47 F9 Kisámou, K B Crete Greece
86 E5 Kisangani Zaïre
71 N9 Kisar isld Indonesia
116 G6 Kisaralik R Alaska
69 D11 Kisaran Sumatra
61 N10 Kisarazu Japan
48 D3 Kisbér Hungary
119 P9 Kisbey Sask
56 C4 Kiselevsk U.S.S.R.
74 F5 Kishangarh India
85 E7 Kishi Nigeria
55 F4 Kishikaroy, Oz L U.S.S.R.
48 M3 Kishinev U.S.S.R.
60 J11 Kishiwada Japan
74 F2 Kishtwar Kashmir
Kisi see Jixi
88 G3 Kisigau Mt Kenya
88 E5 Kisigo R Tanzania
88 E2 Kisii Kenya
119 T4 Kiskittogisu L Manitoba
119 T4 Kiskitto L Manitoba
48 D4 Kiskomárom Hungary
48 E4 Kiskörei-viztárole L Hungary
48 F3 Kisköreiviztároló L Hungary
48 F4 Kiskundorozsma Hungary
48 F4 Kiskunfélegyháza Hungary
48 E4 Kiskunhalas Hungary
48 F4 Kiskunmajsa Hungary
53 F11 Kislovodsk U.S.S.R.
Kismayu see Chisimaio
61 L10 Kiso Japan
61 L10 Kiso-sammyaku mts Japan
48 E3 Kispest Hungary
117 J8 Kispiox R Br Col
28 H5 Kisserup Denmark
85 B7 Kissidougou Guinea
113 F9 Kissimmee Florida
113 F10 Kissimmee R Florida
119 Q3 Kississing L Manitoba
41 L2 Kisslegg W Germany
84 H5 Kissu, Jebel mt Sudan
26 L3 Kistefjell mt Norway
48 F4 Kistelek Hungary
48 F2 Kisterenye Hungary
26 O1 Kistrand Norway
48 F3 Kisújszállás Hungary
88 E2 Kisumu Kenya
48 G2 Kisvárda Hungary
50 E5 Kisyl Arvat U.S.S.R.
85 C6 Kita Mali
57 D5 Kitab U.S.S.R.
60 H12 Kitagawa Japan
61 O9 Kita-Ibaraki Japan
48 M5 Kitai, Ozero L U.S.S.R.
26 L5 Kitajaur Sweden
61 P6 Kitakami Japan
61 N8 Kitakata Japan
60 D12 Kita-Kyūshū Japan
86 G5 Kitale Kenya
60 R2 Kitami Japan
60 Q1 Kitami-sanchi mts Japan
88 G7 Kitangari Tanzania
61 N13 Kitano-hana C Japan
61 O9 Kita-ura L Japan
61 J12 Kitayama R Japan
106 H3 Kit Carson Colorado
115 L9 Kitchener Ontario
143 E9 Kitchener W Australia
112 E5 Kite Georgia
29 P9 Kitee Finland
86 F5 Kitgum Uganda
47 F6 Kithairón mt Greece
46 F8 Kíthira isld Greece
47 G7 Kíthnos isld Greece
120 H3 Kitigan Ontario
80 G4 Kitim Jordan
117 J8 Kitimat Br Col
117 J9 Kitimat Mill Alberta
29 M4 Kitinen R Finland
52 C1 Kitinen R Finland
46 E2 Kitka mt Yugoslavia
46 F4 Kítros Greece
118 G5 Kitscoty Alberta
48 K2 Kitsman U.S.S.R.
60 E12 Kitsuki Japan
61 O9 Kitsuregawa Japan
138 E3 Kittakittaooloo, L S Australia
94 H6 Kittanning Pennsylvania
95 N5 Kittatinny Mts New Jersey
33 R5 Kittendorf E Germany
95 R3 Kittery Maine
29 L4 Kittilä Finland
112 M1 Kitty Hawk N Carolina
88 G2 Kitui Kenya
88 D5 Kitunda Tanzania
117 J8 Kitwanga Br Col
88 B8 Kitwe-Nkana Zambia
38 F7 Kitzbühler Alpen mts Austria
37 J4 Kitzingen W Germany
27 M10 Kiukainen Finland
116 L7 Kiukpalik I Alaska
86 E7 Kiumbi Zaïre
29 M8 Kiuruvesi Finland
116 A4 Kivak U.S.S.R.
116 E3 Kivalina Alaska
116 E3 Kividlo Alaska
29 L8 Kivijärvi Finland
27 G17 Kivik Sweden
52 C5 Kiviõli U.S.S.R.
46 E4 Kivotós Greece
88 B2 Kivu, Lac Zaïre/Rwanda
145 D4 Kiwi New Zealand
56 C3 Kiya R U.S.S.R.
55 E6 Kiyakty, Oz L U.S.S.R.
61 O14 Kiyan Okinawa
61 O14 Kiyan-zaki C Okinawa
54 B6 Kiyev U.S.S.R.
55 F5 Kiyevka U.S.S.R.
54 B5 Kiyevskoy Vdkr res U.S.S.R.
47 L5 Kıyır R Turkey
118 H7 Kiyiu L Sask
55 E5 Kiyma U.S.S.R.
52 J5 Kizel U.S.S.R.
52 F4 Kizema U.S.S.R.
47 K4 Kızıl Adalar islds Turkey
47 K7 Kızılcabölük Turkey
47 K7 Kızılcadağ Turkey
47 K8 Kızılca Dağ mt Turkey
78 D1 Kizilcahamam Turkey
47 K7 Kızılhişar Turkey
78 E2 Kizil Irmak R Turkey
77 G2 Kizil Islam Afghanistan
47 L7 Kızılkaya Turkey
55 C5 Kizil'skoye U.S.S.R.
56 D4 Kizir R U.S.S.R.
53 G11 Kizlyar U.S.S.R.
26 M2 Kjaekan Norway
28 C4 Kjellerup Denmark
26 P1 Kjelvik Norway
26 G4 Kjerringöy Norway
26 Q1 Kjöllefjord Norway
71 J4 Klabat mt Sulawesi
48 E6 Kladanj Yugoslavia
30 H5 Kladno Czechoslovakia
48 H6 Kladovo Yugoslavia
37 O4 Kladruby Czechoslovakia
70 E2 Klagan Sabah
38 K8 Klagenfurt Austria
103 P6 Klagetoh Arizona
27 M16 Klaipeda U.S.S.R.
52 B6 Klaipėda U.S.S.R.
28 D5 Klakring Denmark
28 O9 Klaksvig Faeroes
100 A8 Klamath California
100 B8 Klamath R California
100 D7 Klamath Falls Oregon
100 B8 Klamath Mts California
100 C8 Klamath River California
71 C3 Klamono W Irian
117 J7 Klappan R Br Col
27 F12 Klarä R Sweden
27 F11 Klarabro Sweden
27 F11 Klarälven R Sweden
37 P3 Klášterec Czechoslovakia
70 N9 Klaten Java
37 P5 Klatovy Czechoslovakia
38 O5 Klausen-Leopoldsdorf Austria
41 J4 Klausen P mt Switzerland
117 G8 Klawak Alaska
31 K3 Kłecko Poland
31 L3 Kleczew Poland
122 J3 Kleczkowski L Quebec
117 L10 Kleena Kleene Br Col
101 S5 Kleenburn Wyoming
33 S5 Kleeth E Germany
25 F5 Klefe W Germany
79 F4 Kleiat Lebanon
101 R3 Klein Montana
33 P6 Kleinberge E Germany
22 J1 Kleine-Brogel Belgium
33 S9 Kleine Elster R E Germany
32 J9 Kleinenberg W Germany
22 H1 Kleine Nete R Belgium
33 R8 Klein Kreutz E Germany
37 N6 Klein Laaber R W Germany
36 F2 Klein Linden W Germany
89 B9 Klein Roggeveld Berge mts S Africa
89 B9 Klein Swartberge mts S Africa
33 N5 Klein Thurow E Germany
33 Q8 Klein Wusterwitz E Germany
38 N6 Klein Zell Austria
28 D3 Klejtrup Denmark
42 H4 Klekovača mt Yugoslavia
99 N6 Klemme Iowa
22 E1 Klemskerke Belgium
117 J9 Klemtu Br Col
48 F6 Klenak Yugoslavia
33 N7 Klenze W Germany
89 E6 Klerksdorp S Africa
116 G3 Klery Creek Alaska
54 E3 Kletnya U.S.S.R.
53 F9 Kletskiy U.S.S.R.
41 H2 Klettgau R W Germany
33 T9 Klettwitz E Germany
100 D3 Klickitat R Washington
79 E3 Klidhes Is Cyprus
33 Q7 Klietz E Germany
28 C2 Klim Denmark
31 N5 Klimontów Poland
54 C3 Klimovichi U.S.S.R.
52 H5 Klimovka U.S.S.R.
54 D4 Klimovo U.S.S.R.
54 J1 Klimovsk U.S.S.R.
26 G6 Klimpfjäll Sweden
54 H1 Klin U.S.S.R.
117 L10 Klinaklini R Br Col
112 F4 Kline S Carolina
71 G8 Kling Mindanao Philippines
37 Q2 Klingenberg E Germany
36 G4 Klingenberg W Germany
36 D5 Klingenmünster W Germany
37 N3 Klingenthal E Germany
70 B4 Klingkang Ra Sarawak
41 H2 Klingnau W Germany
33 R6 Klink E Germany
37 O3 Klínovec mt Czechoslovakia
28 E5 Klinte Denmark
27 K14 Klintehamn Sweden
54 D4 Klintsy U.S.S.R.
47 H5 Klió Greece
27 F15 Klippan Sweden
89 A8 Kliprug Berg mt S Africa
47 G2 Klisura Bulgaria
28 B2 Klitmøller Denmark
28 B7 Klixbüll W Germany
42 H4 Ključ Yugoslavia
31 L5 Kłobuck Poland
121 M6 Klock Ontario
33 U6 Klockow E Germany
31 L3 Kłodawa Poland
31 K5 Kłodzko Poland
27 E11 Klöfta Norway
103 H7 Klondike California
25 B6 Kloosterzande Netherlands
46 D3 Klos Albania
41 L3 Kloster R Austria
33 S7 Klosterfelde E Germany
28 A4 Klosterhede Plantage Denmark
41 M3 Klösterle Austria
33 Q6 Kloster Malchow E Germany
33 O9 Kloster Mansfeld E Germany
31 J7 Klosterneuburg Austria
36 E6 Klosterreichenbach W Germany
41 L4 Klosters Switzerland
33 S8 Kloster Zinna E Germany
27 H12 Kloten Sweden
36 C3 Klotten W Germany
33 O7 Klötze E Germany
28 C5 Klovborg Denmark
26 G9 Klövsjö Sweden
117 D5 Kluane Yukon Terr
117 D5 Kluane Nat. Park Yukon Terr
69 F14 Kluang Sumatra
31 L5 Kluczbork Poland
70 E6 Klumpeng, Teluk B Kalimantan
25 C5 Klundert Netherlands
70 P10 Klungkung Indonesia
36 C1 Kluppelberg W Germany
116 P6 Klutina L Alaska
26 L7 Klutmark Sweden
33 O5 Klütz E Germany
71 L9 Kluwang Indonesia
52 H7 Klyavlino U.S.S.R.
52 F6 Klyazma R U.S.S.R.
52 F2 Klyuchevaya U.S.S.R.
55 D2 Klyuchi U.S.S.R.
55 G4 Klyuchi U.S.S.R.
27 B13 Knabengruber Norway
38 J7 Knallstein, Gross mt Austria
99 O5 Knapp Wisconsin
13 G5 Knaresborough England
13 F4 Knarsdale England
37 M2 Knau E Germany
9 F4 Knebworth England
32 H5 Knechtsand sandbank W Germany
118 K3 Knee L Sask
33 N7 Knesebeck W Germany
22 E1 Knesselare Belgium
37 K4 Knetsgau W Germany
117 L9 Knewstubb L Br Col
47 G1 Knezha Bulgaria
98 D2 Knife R N Dakota
116 K7 Knife Pk Alaska
99 P3 Knife River Minnesota
101 P8 Knight Wyoming
116 O6 Knight I Alaska
117 K10 Knight Inlet Br Col
8 C3 Knighton Wales
94 B7 Knightstown Indiana
110 J2 Knightsville Indiana
42 G4 Knin Yugoslavia
32 H5 Kniphausen W Germany
109 H6 Knippa Texas
38 L7 Knittelfeld Austria
27 J12 Knivsta Sweden
46 E1 Knjaževac Yugoslavia
110 F5 Knobel Arkansas
142 G2 Knob Pk W Australia
14 B5 Knockboy mt Irish Rep
14 B5 Knockbrack mt Irish Rep
14 E1 Knocklayd mt N Ireland
14 D4 Knockmealdown Mts Irish Rep
14 B5 Knockowen mt Irish Rep
22 E1 Knokke Belgium
29 O5 Knolayarvi U.S.S.R.
101 M9 Knolls Utah
29 L10 Knorevesi Finland
28 E2 Knøsen hill Denmark
47 G9 Knossos Crete Greece
108 F3 Knott Texas
9 E3 Knowle England
107 K5 Knowles Oklahoma
121 S7 Knowlton Quebec
99 R5 Knowlton Wisconsin
99 U8 Knox Indiana
98 G1 Knox N Dakota
94 H5 Knox Pennsylvania
117 G8 Knox, C Graham I, Br Col
110 E1 Knox City Missouri
108 H2 Knox City Texas
146 F2 Knox Coast Antarctica
102 B3 Knoxville California
99 Q9 Knoxville Illinois
99 N8 Knoxville Iowa
111 E10 Knoxville Mississippi
94 K5 Knoxville Pennsylvania
112 C1 Knoxville Tennessee
83 K10 Knuckles mt Sri Lanka
115 R4 Knud Rasmussens Land Greenland
28 H6 Knudshoved C Denmark
36 G2 Knüllwald W Germany
8 D1 Knutsford England
52 D2 Knyazhaya Guba U.S.S.R.
52 F5 Knyazhevo U.S.S.R.
87 D12 Knysna S Africa
31 O2 Knyszyn Poland
29 M2 Koarvikods mt Finland
69 H14 Koba Indonesia
60 D14 Koba Japan
28 H6 Kobanke hill Denmark
42 F2 Kobarid Yugoslavia
60 D13 Kobayashi Japan
115 P5 Kobbermine Bugt B Greenland
28 C3 Kobberup Denmark
Kobdo Jargalant see Hovd
71 A2 Kobe Halmahera Indonesia
60 J11 Kōbe Japan
28 G7 Købelev Denmark
54 F7 Kobelyaki U.S.S.R.
89 A8 Kobe Mts S Africa
28 K5 København Denmark
38 H5 Kobernausser Wald reg Austria
36 C3 Kobern-Gondorf W Germany
67 H4 Kōbi-sho isld Japan
36 D3 Koblenz W Germany
86 F4 Kobowem Swamp Sudan
52 E5 Kobozha R U.S.S.R.
52 H5 Kobra R U.S.S.R.
61 M10 Kobuchizawa Japan
116 J3 Kobuk Alaska
116 H3 Kobuk R Alaska
31 K4 Kobylin Poland
47 K8 Koca R Turkey
47 J4 Kocabaş R Turkey
46 E3 Kočani Yugoslavia
47 J7 Koçarlı Turkey
47 L6 Koca Tepe mt Turkey
48 F6 Koceljevo Yugoslavia
42 F3 Kočevje Yugoslavia
73 R6 Ko Chang isld Thailand
52 F4 Kochen'ga U.S.S.R.
36 H5 Kocher R W Germany
54 M4 Kochetovka U.S.S.R.
52 H5 Kochevo U.S.S.R.
60 F11 Kōchi Japan
60 G12 Kōchi Japan
115 M4 Koch I N W Terr
60 G12 Kōchi prefect Japan
61 P14 Kochinda Okinawa
52 D3 Kochkoma U.S.S.R.
57 H4 Kochkorka U.S.S.R.
52 K2 Kochmes U.S.S.R.
101 O4 Koch Mt Montana
31 K4 Kocie Góry mts Poland
31 N4 Kock Poland
33 O7 Köckte E Germany
48 E4 Kocsola Hungary
52 J3 Kodachdikost U.S.S.R.
76 C5 Kodaikanal India
60 O4 Kodamari misaki C Japan
75 L6 Kodarma India
83 L9 Koddiyar B Sri Lanka
31 O4 Kodeń Poland
116 L8 Kodiak Alaska
116 L8 Kodiak I Alaska
83 K8 Kodikamam Sri Lanka
52 F4 Kodima U.S.S.R.
74 D8 Kodinar India
52 E3 Kodino U.S.S.R.
86 F4 Kodok Sudan
60 O4 Kodomari Japan
48 M2 Kodyma U.S.S.R.
22 D1 Koekelare Belgium
22 J1 Koersel Belgium
87 C11 Koes Namibia
60 P1 Koetoi Japan
103 L8 Kofa Mts Arizona
37 N6 Köfering W Germany
87 E11 Koffiefontein S Africa
71 C3 Kofiau isld W Irian
85 D7 Koforidua Ghana
61 M10 Kōfu Japan
61 N9 Koga Japan
141 K7 Kogan Queensland
28 J6 Køge Denmark
28 K6 Køge Bugt B Denmark
52 J3 Kogel' R U.S.S.R.
48 M4 Kogilnik R U.S.S.R.
116 H6 Kogrukluk R Alaska
60 D11 Kogushi Japan
74 D2 Kohat Pakistan
52 B5 Kohila U.S.S.R.
75 Q6 Kohima India
68 G6 Koh Ker Cambodia
146 H11 Kohler Ra Antarctica
37 O1 Kohren Sahlis E Germany
77 G2 Kohsun Afghanistan
68 F7 Koh Tang isld Cambodia
52 C5 Kohtla-Järve U.S.S.R.
47 K8 Kohu Dağ mt Turkey
145 E3 Kohuratahi New Zealand
61 M8 Koide Japan
114 E5 Koidern Yukon Terr
69 A8 Koihoa Nicobar Is
52 H3 Koin R U.S.S.R.
78 K3 Koi Sanjaq Iraq
29 P8 Koitere L Finland
29 L5 Koivu Finland
65 G7 Kŏje isld S Korea
31 K6 Kojetín Czechoslovakia
60 N4 Ko jima isld Japan
143 B10 Kojonup W Australia
86 G4 Koka Dam Ethiopia
95 S1 Kokadjo Maine
83 L10 Kokagala mt Sri Lanka
55 D6 Kokalaat U.S.S.R.
57 F4 Kokand U.S.S.R.
117 P11 Kokanee Glacier Nat. Park Br Col
57 B2 Kokaral U.S.S.R.
48 F2 Kokava Czechoslovakia
60 J11 Kokawa Japan
57 D5 Kokayty U.S.S.R.
57 F6 Kokcha R Afghanistan
55 E4 Kokchetav U.S.S.R.
29 K10 Kokemäenjoki R Finland
29 J10 Kokemäki Finland
54 A2 Kokhanovo U.S.S.R.
80 B7 Kokhav Israel
29 K8 Kokkola Finland
85 E6 Koko Nigeria
136 K3 Kokoda Papua New Guinea
102 S12 Koko Head Hawaiian Is
116 F2 Kokolik R Alaska
94 A6 Kokomo Indiana
136 H2 Kokonau W Irian
144 C6 Kokonga New Zealand
Koko Nor see Qinghai Hu
52 C4 Kokonselka L Finland
54 F4 Kokorevka U.S.S.R.
69 B11 Kokos isld Indonesia
116 K4 Kokrines Hills Alaska
57 E4 Koksaray U.S.S.R.
66 B3 Kok Shaal Tau mts U.S.S.R.
52 G6 Kokshaga R U.S.S.R.
52 F4 Kokshen'ga R U.S.S.R.
22 D1 Koksijde Belgium
115 N6 Koksoak R Quebec
54 M8 Koksovyy U.S.S.R.
89 F8 Kokstad S Africa
60 D14 Kokubu Japan
60 D12 Kokura Japan
70 G7 Koku, Tg C Sulawesi
116 H7 Kokwok R Alaska
57 G4 Kok-Yangak U.S.S.R.
52 D1 Kola U.S.S.R.
70 G7 Kolaka Sulawesi
71 F6 Kolambugan Mindanao Philippines
139 K1 Kolan Queensland
141 K6 Kolan R Queensland
76 D4 Kolar India
76 D4 Kolar Gold Fields India
29 K4 Kolari Finland
Kolarovgrad Bulgaria see Shumen
48 D3 Kolárovo Czechoslovakia
26 F8 Kolåsen Sweden
46 D2 Kolašin Yugoslavia
27 H12 Kolbäck Sweden
71 M10 Kolbano Timor
Kolberg see Kołobrzeg
38 H8 Kölbnitz Austria
26 D9 Kolbotn Norway
31 N5 Kolbuszowa Poland
28 F5 Kolby Denmark
52 E6 Kol'chugino U.S.S.R.
85 A6 Kolda Senegal
28 B3 Koldby Denmark
28 C6 Kolding Denmark
86 E5 Kole Zaïre
135 T3 Kolekole peak Hawaiian Is
37 P5 Koleveč Czechoslovakia
52 B5 Kolga laht G U.S.S.R.
50 D2 Kolguyev Ostrov isld U.S.S.R.
76 B2 Kolhapur India
29 O8 Koli Finland
48 L5 Kolibash U.S.S.R.
116 J7 Koliganek Alaska
31 J5 Kolín Czechoslovakia
101 Q2 Kolin Montana
28 F4 Kolind Denmark
37 P5 Kolinec Czechoslovakia
28 C4 Kølkær Denmark
33 T7 Kol Kienitz E Germany
121 N7 Kol. Kienitz Ontario
37 L1 Kölleda E Germany
28 N2 Kollefjord Faeroes
76 C4 Kollegal India
46 E7 Kollínai Greece
25 F2 Kollum Netherlands
28 C4 Kollund Ringkøbing Denmark
28 C7 Kollund Sønderjylland Denmark
36 B2 Köln W Germany
31 N2 Kolno Poland
31 L3 Koło Poland
135 O1 Koloa Hawaiian Is
31 J1 Kołobrzeg Poland
33 S9 Kolochau E Germany
54 D2 Kolodnya U.S.S.R.
52 F5 Kologriv U.S.S.R.
71 B3 Kolok Indonesia
85 C6 Kolokani Mali
137 M3 Kolombangara isld Solomon Is
54 K1 Kolomna U.S.S.R.
48 J2 Kolomyya U.S.S.R.
141 K6 Kolonga Queensland
70 G6 Kolono Sulawesi
70 G6 Kolonodale Sulawesi
71 B2 Kolorai isld Halmahera Indonesia
55 F3 Kolosovka U.S.S.R.
Kolozsvar see Cluj
52 E5 Kolp' R U.S.S.R.
56 B2 Kolpashevo U.S.S.R.
33 R6 Kölpin-See L E Germany
33 Q10 Kölsa E Germany
26 G9 Kolsätt Sweden
52 D1 Kol'skiy Poluostrov pen U.S.S.R.
52 D1 Kol'skiy Zaliv gulf U.S.S.R.
28 F6 Kølstrup Denmark
27 H12 Kolsva Sweden
28 N2 Kolter Faeroes
52 A3 Kol'tsovo U.S.S.R.
48 F6 Kolubara R Yugoslavia
145 D1 Koluikohu New Zealand
73 L8 Kolumadulu Atoll Maldives
31 M4 Koluszki Poland
55 E5 Koluton U.S.S.R.
52 J1 Kolva R Komi U.S.S.R.
52 J4 Kolva R Perm U.S.S.R.
26 E7 Kolvereid Norway
26 O1 Kolvik Norway
52 D2 Kolvitsa U.S.S.R.
87 E8 Kolwezi Zaïre
54 K1 Kolyberovo U.S.S.R.
54 H1 Kolyubakino U.S.S.R.
147 P2 Kolyuchinskaya U.S.S.R.
116 A3 Kolyuchinskaya Guba gulf U.S.S.R.
56 B5 Kolyvan' U.S.S.R.
27 G14 Kölzby Sweden
46 F1 Kom mt Bulgaria
68 D5 Koma Burma
86 G4 Koma Ethiopia
61 P6 Kōma Japan
85 G6 Komadugu Gana R Nigeria
61 L10 Komagane Japan
60 O3 Komaga-take mt Hokkaido Japan
61 N8 Komaga-take mt Honshu Japan
26 N1 Komagfjord Norway
26 S1 Komagvaer Norway
48 E3 Komárno Czechoslovakia
119 U8 Komarno Manitoba
48 E3 Komárom Hungary
48 E3 Komárom co Hungary
89 G6 Komati R Swaziland
89 G5 Komati Poort S Africa
103 M8 Komatke Arizona
61 K9 Komatsu Ishikawa Japan
61 O7 Komatsu Yamagata Japan
71 L8 Komba isld Indonesia
46 E5 Kombóti Greece
28 E3 Komdrup Denmark
88 D2 Kome I Uganda
61 O5 Kominato Japan
48 E2 Komjatice Czechoslovakia
48 E4 Komló Hungary
53 E9 Kommunarsk U.S.S.R.
57 F5 Kommunizma, Pik mt U.S.S.R.
71 J9 Komodo isld Indonesia
85 D7 Komoé R Ivory Coast
84 J5 Kôm Ombo Egypt
61 M9 Komoro Japan
47 G3 Komotiní Greece
46 D2 Komovi mt Yugoslavia
89 D8 Kompas Berg mt S Africa
68 G7 Kompong Cham Cambodia
68 G6 Kompong Chhnang Cambodia
68 G6 Kompong Kleang Cambodia
68 F7 Kompong Som Cambodia
68 G7 Kompong Speu Cambodia
68 G6 Kompong Sralao Cambodia
68 G6 Kompong Thom Cambodia
68 G6 Kompong Trabek Cambodia
68 G7 Kompong Trach Cambodia
68 G7 Kompong Tralach Cambodia
71 J4 Kompot Sulawesi
48 M4 Komrat U.S.S.R.
89 B9 Komsbergeskarp mts S Africa
55 D4 Komsomolets U.S.S.R.
51 J1 Komsomolets, Ostrov isld U.S.S.R.
54 E8 Komsomol'sk Ukraine U.S.S.R.
52 F6 Komsomol'sk U.S.S.R.
55 D1 Komsomol'skiy U.S.S.R.
54 K9 Komsomol'skoye U.S.S.R.
59 L1 Komsomol'skoye-na-Amure U.S.S.R.
103 M10 Kom Vo Arizona
52 E6 Konakovo U.S.S.R.
77 B5 Konār Takhteh Iran
109 L1 Konawa Oklahoma
42 H3 Končanica Yugoslavia
71 C3 Konda W Irian

55 E2 **Konda** *R* U.S.S.R.
76 E1 **Kondagaon** India
121 O6 **Kondiaronk, L** Quebec
143 C10 **Kondinin** W Australia
88 E4 **Kondoa** Tanzania
52 D4 **Kondopoga** U.S.S.R.
48 F4 **Kondoros** Hungary
54 G2 **Kondrovo** U.S.S.R.
86 B3 **Konduga** Nigeria
143 B9 **Kondut** W Australia
56 D2 **Konduyak** U.S.S.R.
52 J3 **Konetsbor** U.S.S.R.
52 E4 **Konevo** U.S.S.R.
28 H6 **Køng** Denmark
85 D7 **Kong** Ivory Coast
116 R2 **Kongakut** *R* Alaska
115 Q4 **Kong Christian den IX Land** Greenland
115 R3 **Kong Christian den X Land** Greenland
28 B6 **Kongeå** *R* Denmark
28 K5 **Kongens Lyngby** Denmark
115 P5 **Kong Frederik den VI Kyst** *coast* Greenland
29 M9 **Konginkangas** Finland
68 F7 **Kong Kaôh Kong** Cambodia
50 B1 **Kong Karls Land** *isld* Spitzbergen
70 E4 **Kong Kat** *mt* Kalimantan
70 E4 **Kongkemul** *mt* Kalimantan
70 G6 **Kongkong** *R* Sulawesi
87 D9 **Kongola** Namibia
86 E7 **Kongolo** Zaïre
86 F4 **Kongor** Sudan
147 E10 **Kong Oscars Fj** Greenland
26 J3 **Kongsbakktind** *mt* Norway
27 D12 **Kongsberg** Norway
26 R1 **Kongsfjord** Norway
26 R1 **Kongsfjord** *inlet* Norway
28 B6 **Kongsmark** Denmark
26 F7 **Kongsmoen** Norway
28 J6 **Kongsted** Denmark
27 E11 **Kongsvinger** Norway
66 B4 **Kongur Shan** *mt* China
88 F5 **Kongwa** Tanzania
31 M5 **Koniecpol** Poland
36 H4 **Königheim** W Germany
36 F6 **Königsbach** W Germany
Königsberg *see* **Kaliningrad**
36 D4 **Königsberg** *mt* W Germany
37 J6 **Königsbronn** W Germany
33 T10 **Königsbrück** E Germany
37 K7 **Königsbrunn** W Germany
41 O2 **Königsdorf** W Germany
37 L2 **Königsee** E Germany
37 L4 **Königsfeld** W Germany
Königshofen *see* **Lauda-Königshofen**
36 H4 **Königshofen** W Germany
33 N8 **Königslutter** W Germany
36 F5 **Königsstuhl** *mt* W Germany
36 E3 **Königstein** W Germany
38 L5 **Königswiesen** Austria
36 C2 **Königswinter** W Germany
33 T8 **Königs Wusterhausen** E Germany
31 L3 **Konin** Poland
145 E4 **Konini** New Zealand
46 D5 **Konispol** Albania
42 H5 **Konjic** Yugoslavia
48 E6 **Konjuh** *mt* Yugoslavia
26 M3 **Konkämä Älv** *R* Sweden/Finland
88 A8 **Konkola** Zambia
85 B6 **Konkouré** *R* Guinea
33 P9 **Könnern** E Germany
37 N3 **Konnersreuth** W Germany
29 M9 **Konnevesi** Finland
85 D7 **Konongo** Ghana
88 C5 **Konongo** Tanzania
61 N9 **Kōnosu** Japan
54 E5 **Konotop** U.S.S.R.
66 D3 **Konqi He** *R* China
85 C7 **Konsankoro** Guinea
31 M4 **Końskie** Poland
53 F10 **Konstantinovsk** U.S.S.R.
41 K2 **Konstanz** W Germany
85 F6 **Kontagora** Nigeria
86 B4 **Kontcha** Cameroon
22 G1 **Kontich** Belgium
29 N7 **Kontiomäki** Finland
116 L6 **Kontrashibuna L** Alaska
68 J6 **Kontum, Plat. du** Vietnam
52 F2 **Konushinskaya Korga** *C* U.S.S.R.
78 D3 **Konya** Turkey
36 B4 **Konz** W Germany
88 F2 **Konza** Kenya
37 O5 **Konzell** W Germany
55 C2 **Konzhakovskiy Kamen', G** *mt* U.S.S.R.
25 C4 **Koog** Netherlands
116 C5 **Kookooligit Mts** St Lawrence I, Alaska
143 D8 **Kookynie** W Australia
140 F5 **Koolamarra** Queensland
141 F3 **Koolatah** Queensland
140 D2 **Koolatong** *R* N Terr Australia
102 S11 **Koolauloa** Hawaiian Is
102 S12 **Koolaupoko** Hawaiian Is
141 G3 **Koolburra** Queensland
142 B6 **Kooline** W Australia
140 E6 **Koolivoo,L** Queensland
143 C9 **Koolyanobbing** W Australia
143 G9 **Koonalda** S Australia
141 G3 **Koorboora** Queensland
143 B9 **Koorda** W Australia
142 B5 **Koordarrie** W Australia
144 A7 **Kopeka B** New Zealand
33 T8 **Kopenick** E Germany
26 K8 **Köpmanholmen** Sweden
27 F10 **Kopparberg** *county* Sweden
145 E2 **Kopu** New Zealand
145 E4 **Kopuaranga** New Zealand
77 C4 **Kor** *R* Iran
75 K7 **Korba** India
32 J10 **Korbach** W Germany
100 B9 **Korbel** California
69 E10 **Korbu, G.** *mt* Malaysia
46 D4 **Korcë** Albania
42 H6 **Korčula** Yugoslavia
36 B4 **Kordel** W Germany
77 A2 **Kordestan** Iran
77 D1 **Kord Küv** Iran
Kordofan *prov* Sudan *see* **Northern and Southern Kordofan** *provs*
77 G6 **Kords** *reg* Iran
59 H4 **Korea Bay** China/Korea
65 G4 **Korea, North** *rep* E Asia
65 H6 **Korea, South** *rep* E Asia
52 D2 **Korelaksha** U.S.S.R.
54 F5 **Korenevo** U.S.S.R.
26 G5 **Korgen** Norway
85 C7 **Korhogo** Ivory Coast
60 D14 **Kori** Japan
46 F4 **Korinós** Greece
28 E6 **Korinth** Denmark
46 E6 **Korinthiakós Kólpos** *gulf* Greece
46 F7 **Kórinthos** Greece
46 D2 **Koritnik** *mt* Yugoslavia
Koritsa *see* **Korcë**
61 O8 **Kōriyama** Japan
55 D4 **Korkino** U.S.S.R.
47 L7 **Korkuteli** Turkey
54 B3 **Korma** U.S.S.R.
120 G5 **Kormak** Ontario
48 D3 **Körmend** Hungary
55 F3 **Kormilovka** U.S.S.R.
42 G5 **Kornat** *isld* Yugoslavia
37 L5 **Kornburg** W Germany
25 F7 **Kornelimünster** W Germany
37 K1 **Körner** E Germany
48 L3 **Korneshty** U.S.S.R.
55 E4 **Korneyevka** U.S.S.R.
55 F5 **Korneyevka** U.S.S.R.
27 E13 **Kornsjö** Norway
28 C3 **Kornum** Denmark
36 G6 **Kornwestheim** W Germany
70 G5 **Koro** *R* Sulawesi
55 G6 **Korobovskiy** U.S.S.R.
54 J6 **Korocha** U.S.S.R.
78 C1 **Köroglu D** Turkey
88 G4 **Korogwe** Tanzania
138 F7 **Koroit** Victoria
113 F8 **Korona** Florida
85 E7 **Koronga** *mt* Togo
139 G6 **Korong Vale** Victoria
46 E8 **Koróni** Greece
47 F4 **Korónia, L** Greece
31 K2 **Koronowo** Poland
54 D5 **Korop** U.S.S.R.
48 J2 **Koropets** U.S.S.R.
47 F7 **Koropí** Greece
48 F4 **Körös** *R* Hungary
53 C8 **Korosten** U.S.S.R.
86 C2 **Koro Toro** Chad
54 L6 **Korotoyak** U.S.S.R.
116 G9 **Korovin I** Alaska
29 M9 **Korpilahti** Finland
26 N5 **Korpilombolo** Sweden
29 J11 **Korpo** Finland
59 M2 **Korsakov** U.S.S.R.
27 H14 **Korsberga** Sweden
36 B1 **Korschenbroich** W Germany
28 H5 **Korshage** *C* Denmark
48 J2 **Korshev** U.S.S.R.
28 E3 **Korsholm** *isld* Denmark
27 H11 **Korsnäs** Sweden
26 H3 **Korsnes** Norway
28 G6 **Korsør** Denmark
54 C7 **Korsun' Shevchenkovskiy** U.S.S.R.
22 E1 **Kortemark** Belgium
29 K8 **Kortesjärvi** Finland
22 J2 **Kortessem** Belgium
27 G12 **Kortfors** Sweden
25 A5 **Kortgene** Netherlands
52 H4 **Kortkeros** U.S.S.R.
22 E2 **Kortrijk** Belgium
52 F5 **Kortsovo** U.S.S.R.
47 J5 **Korucu** Turkey
47 H4 **Koru Dağı** *mt* Turkey
139 H7 **Korumburra** Victoria
29 O3 **Korvatunturi** *mt* Finland
29 O4 **Korya** U.S.S.R.
52 G4 **Koryazhma** U.S.S.R.
54 D5 **Koryukovka** U.S.S.R.
47 J8 **Kos** *isld* Greece
52 H5 **Kosa** U.S.S.R.
55 D5 **Kosagal** U.S.S.R.
61 O5 **Kosaka** Japan
73 R7 **Ko Samui** *isld* Thailand
57 D1 **Kosay** U.S.S.R.
54 J2 **Kosaya Gora** U.S.S.R.
56 E2 **Kosaya, Shiv** U.S.S.R.
57 C4 **Kosboget** U.S.S.R.
37 M6 **Kösching** W Germany
31 K3 **Kościan** Poland
31 K1 **Kościerzyna** Poland
111 G8 **Kosciusko** Mississippi
117 G7 **Kosciusko I** Alaska
139 J6 **Kosciusko, Mt** Victoria
33 S10 **Koselitz** E Germany
33 U4 **Koserow** E Germany
56 B1 **Koses** *R* U.S.S.R.
76 C2 **Kosgi** India
56 C6 **Kosh Agach** U.S.S.R.
55 D2 **Koshay** U.S.S.R.
60 S2 **Koshikawa** Japan
60 C14 **Koshiki-kaikyō** *str* Japan
60 C14 **Koshiki-rettō** *islds* Japan
110 E5 **Koshkonong** Missouri
57 B4 **Kosh-Kupyr** U.S.S.R.
61 M9 **Koshoku** Japan
48 G2 **Košice** Czechoslovakia
89 H6 **Kosi L** S Africa
55 C5 **Kos-Istek** U.S.S.R.
48 E5 **Koška** Yugoslavia
123 R6 **Koskaecodde L** Nfld
29 K11 **Koski** Finland
26 M5 **Koskivaara** Sweden
57 D1 **Koskol'** U.S.S.R.
57 H3 **Koskuduk** U.S.S.R.
26 L4 **Koskullskulle** Sweden
52 G3 **Koslan** U.S.S.R.
Köslin *see* **Koszalin**
52 G2 **Kosma** *R* U.S.S.R.
48 J2 **Kosmach** U.S.S.R.
100 C3 **Kosmos** Washington
59 J4 **Kosŏng** N Korea
48 J2 **Kosov** U.S.S.R.
46 E2 **Kosovo** Yugoslavia
46 D2 **Kosovska Mitrovica** Yugoslavia
33 S10 **Kossdorf** E Germany
109 L4 **Kosse** Texas
33 P9 **Kösseln** E Germany
37 O1 **Kössern** E Germany
37 P7 **Kösslarn** W Germany
31 N3 **Kossów** Poland
27 H15 **Kosta** Sweden
52 D3 **Kostamus** U.S.S.R.
33 T9 **Kostebrau** E Germany
28 J7 **Koster** Denmark
54 L1 **Kosterevo** U.S.S.R.
86 F3 **Kosti** Sudan
52 F5 **Kostroma** U.S.S.R.
54 D3 **Kostyukovichi** U.S.S.R.
54 B4 **Kostyukovka** U.S.S.R.
61 L9 **Kosugi** Japan
50 H2 **Kosuno** U.S.S.R.
52 J2 **Kos'yu** U.S.S.R.
52 J2 **Kos'yuvom** U.S.S.R.
31 J1 **Koszalin** Poland
48 D3 **Köszeg** Hungary
75 K7 **Kota** India
70 K8 **Kotaagung** Sumatra
70 B5 **Kotabaharu** Kalimantan
69 F9 **Kota Baharu** Malaysia
69 E13 **Kota Baru** Sumatra
70 E1 **Kota Belud** Sabah
70 K8 **Kotabumi** Sumatra
71 J4 **Kotabunan** Sulawesi
70 E2 **Kota Kinabalu** Sabah
29 O4 **Kotala** Finland
71 J4 **Kotamobagu** Sulawesi
76 F1 **Kotapad** India
69 E12 **Kotapinang Baru** Sumatra
69 E12 **Kotatengah** Sumatra
69 F12 **Kota Tinggi** Malaysia
70 B6 **Kotawaringin** Kalimantan
117 N6 **Kotcho** *R* Br Col
47 H2 **Kotel** Bulgaria
53 F9 **Kotel'nikovo** U.S.S.R.
51 N1 **Kotel'nyy, Ostrov** *isld* U.S.S.R.
145 F3 **Kotemaori** New Zealand
33 P9 **Köthen** E Germany
74 F3 **Kot Kapura** India
52 H2 **Kotkino** U.S.S.R.
55 G2 **Kotkino** U.S.S.R.
52 G4 **Kotlas** U.S.S.R.
29 O11 **Kotlin, O** *isld* U.S.S.R.
52 C5 **Kotly** U.S.S.R.
60 G11 **Kotohira** Japan
60 P2 **Kotoni** Japan
42 J6 **Kotor** Yugoslavia
42 H4 **Kotor Varoš** Yugoslavia
53 C10 **Kotovsk** U.S.S.R.
74 C6 **Kotri** Pakistan
57 A1 **Kotr-Tas** U.S.S.R.
38 H8 **Kötschach** Austria
74 J10 **Kottagudem** India
75 K10 **Kottakota** India
76 C6 **Kottayam** India
83 J11 **Kotte** Sri Lanka
86 D4 **Kotto** *R* Cent Afr Republic
26 H8 **Köttsjön** Sweden
76 C3 **Kotturu** India
51 K1 **Kotuy** *R* U.S.S.R.
48 M3 **Kotyuzhany** U.S.S.R.
116 F3 **Kotzebue** Alaska
116 E3 **Kotzebue Sd** Alaska
37 Q1 **Kötzschenbroda** E Germany
37 O5 **Kötzting** W Germany
85 E6 **Kouandé** Benin
86 D4 **Kouango** Cent Afr Republic
86 C2 **Kouba Modounga** Chad
85 D6 **Koudougou** Upper Volta
89 A9 **Koue Bokkeveld** *reg* S Africa
89 D8 **Koueveld Berge** *mts* S Africa
47 H10 **Koufonísi** *isld* Crete Greece
47 H8 **Koufonísia** *isld* Greece
89 C9 **Kougaberge** *mts* S Africa
7 L9 **Kough** *oil rig* North Sea
86 B6 **Koulamoutou** Gabon
68 G6 **Koulen** Cambodia
85 C6 **Koulikoro** Mali
141 J5 **Koumala** Queensland
86 C4 **Koumra** Chad
86 C3 **Koungouri** Chad
48 C1 **Kounice** Czechoslovakia
47 H8 **Kounoupói** *isld* Greece
57 G2 **Kounradskiy** U.S.S.R.
111 B11 **Kountze** Texas
85 D6 **Koupela** Upper Volta
Kouqian *see* **Yongji**
61 Q12 **Kouri-jima** *isld* Okinawa
84 F5 **Kourizo, Passe de** Chad
129 H2 **Kourou** Fr Guiana
85 C6 **Kouroussa** Guinea
89 B9 **Kousberg** *mt* S Africa
85 C5 **Koussa** Mauritania
86 B3 **Kousséri** Cameroon
85 C6 **Koutiala** Mali
85 C7 **Kouto** Ivory Coast
46 F7 **Koutsopódhi** Greece
29 M11 **Kouvola** Finland
86 C6 **Kouyou** *R* Congo
56 F2 **Kova** *R* U.S.S.R.
48 F5 **Kovačica** Yugoslavia
46 C1 **Kovač Planina** *mt* Yugoslavia
52 D2 **Kovda** U.S.S.R.
52 D2 **Kovdozero, Oz** *L* U.S.S.R.
55 E1 **Kovenskaya** *R* U.S.S.R.
52 F6 **Kovernino** U.S.S.R.
29 P9 **Kovero** Finland
48 F6 **Kovin** Yugoslavia
52 G1 **Kovriga, Gora** *mt* U.S.S.R.
54 N1 **Kovrov** U.S.S.R.
52 E5 **Kovzha** *R* U.S.S.R.
52 E4 **Kovzhskoye, Oz** *L* U.S.S.R.
144 C5 **Kowai Bush** New Zealand
31 L3 **Kowal** Poland
31 L2 **Kowalewo** Poland
144 C5 **Kowhitirangi** New Zealand
120 C2 **Kowkash** Ontario
67 G6 **Kowloon** Hong Kong
55 G6 **Koyandy** U.S.S.R.
61 J11 **Kōyasan** Japan
47 K8 **Koyceğiz** Turkey
47 J8 **Köyceğiz Gölü** *L* Turkey
52 F2 **Koyda** U.S.S.R.
52 H4 **Koygorodok** U.S.S.R.
52 G3 **Koynas** U.S.S.R.
61 O6 **Koyoshi-gawa** *R* Japan
52 J4 **Koyp, Gora** *mt* U.S.S.R.
54 L9 **Koysug** U.S.S.R.
57 D4 **Koytash** U.S.S.R.
116 G4 **Koyuk** Alaska
116 L3 **Koyukuk** *R* Alaska
116 J4 **Koyukuk I** Alaska
78 F1 **Koyulhisar** Turkey
55 C2 **Koyva** *R* U.S.S.R.
29 P7 **Koyvozero** U.S.S.R.
61 P13 **Koza** Okinawa
61 J12 **Koza** *R* Japan
47 J5 **Kozak** Turkey
60 C11 **Kō-zaki** *C* Japan
60 G11 **Kōzan** Japan
78 E3 **Kozan** Turkey
46 E4 **Kozáni** Greece
42 H3 **Kozara Plan** Yugoslavia
48 E2 **Kozárovce** Czechoslovakia
54 C6 **Kozelets** U.S.S.R.
54 E7 **Kozel'shchina** U.S.S.R.
54 G2 **Kozel'sk** U.S.S.R.
55 E5 **Kozhakol', Oz** *L* U.S.S.R.
55 G3 **Kozhevnikovo** U.S.S.R.
52 J2 **Kozhim** U.S.S.R.
52 J3 **Kozhim-Iz, Gora** *mt* U.S.S.R.
52 J2 **Kozhimvom** U.S.S.R.
52 E3 **Kozhozero, Oz** *L* U.S.S.R.
52 E3 **Kozhposelok** U.S.S.R.
55 G3 **Kozhurla** U.S.S.R.
52 J2 **Kozhva** U.S.S.R.
31 M4 **Kozienice** Poland
46 E3 **Kozjak** *mt* Yugoslavia
31 L5 **Koźle** Poland
47 G1 **Kozlovets** Bulgaria
54 M6 **Kozlovka** U.S.S.R.
78 C1 **Kozlu** Turkey
31 K4 **Koźmin** Poland
48 L1 **Kozovo** U.S.S.R.
31 L4 **Kozuchów** Poland
61 M11 **Kōzu-shima** *isld* Japan
85 D7 **Kpandu** Ghana
89 E8 **Kraai** *R* S Africa
33 O6 **Kraak** E Germany
25 B6 **Krabbendijke** Netherlands
69 D8 **Krabi** Thailand
68 D7 **Kra Buri** Thailand
37 M2 **Kraftsdorf** E Germany
70 M9 **Kragan** Java
28 C4 **Kragelund** Denmark
28 G7 **Kragenæs** Denmark
27 D13 **Kragerö** Norway
48 F6 **Kragujevac** Yugoslavia
36 G4 **Krahenberg** W Germany
37 K2 **Krahnberg** *mt* E Germany
36 F5 **Kraich** *R* W Germany
36 F5 **Kraichtal** W Germany
73 C7 **Kra, Isthmus of** Thailand
Krakatau *isld see* **Rakata** *I*
79 G4 **Krak des Chevaliers** Syria
26 A9 **Kråkenes** Norway
68 F3 **Krakor** Cambodia
48 H1 **Krakovets** U.S.S.R.
33 C5 **Krakow** E Germany
31 M5 **Kraków** Poland
68 F3 **Kralanh** Cambodia
48 G2 **Král Chlmec** Czechoslovakia
31 K5 **Králíky** Czechoslovakia
46 D1 **Kraljevo Vrnjacka** Yugoslavia
48 E1 **Kralovany** Czechoslovakia
37 Q4 **Kralovice** Czechoslovakia
37 P3 **Kralupy** Czechoslovakia
98 F1 **Kramer** N Dakota
26 J9 **Kramfors** Sweden
68 E6 **Kram, Ko** *isld* Thailand
26 S1 **Krampenes** Norway
25 F5 **Kranenburg** W Germany
26 H3 **Krångede** Sweden
46 E5 **Kraniá** Greece
37 L2 **Kranichfeld** E Germany
46 F7 **Kranídhion** Greece
42 F2 **Kranj** Yugoslavia
38 J9 **Kranjska-Gord** Yugoslavia
31 K5 **Krapkowice** Poland
28 K4 **Krapperup** Sweden
52 G4 **Krasavino** U.S.S.R.
54 K1 **Krashy Oktyabr'** U.S.S.R.
48 K1 **Krasilov** U.S.S.R.
50 E1 **Krasino** U.S.S.R.
59 K3 **Kraskino** U.S.S.R.
52 C6 **Kráslava** U.S.S.R.
37 O3 **Kraslice** Czechoslovakia
31 N5 **Krasnik** Poland
37 O3 **Krásno** Czechoslovakia
55 E4 **Krasnoarmeyesk** U.S.S.R.
54 J8 **Krasnoarmeysk** U.S.S.R.
54 K1 **Krasnoarmeysk** U.S.S.R.
55 D4 **Krasnoarmeyskiy** Kustanay U.S.S.R.
52 G4 **Krasnoborsk** U.S.S.R.
31 O5 **Krasnobród** Poland
53 E11 **Krasnodar** U.S.S.R.
54 L8 **Krasnodon** U.S.S.R.
48 J1 **Krasnoe** U.S.S.R.
52 D6 **Krasnofarfornyy** U.S.S.R.
52 C6 **Krasnogorodskoye** U.S.S.R.
59 M2 **Krasnogorsk** U.S.S.R.
55 D4 **Krasnogorskiy** Chelyabinsk U.S.S.R.
52 H5 **Krasnogorskoye** U.S.S.R.
54 G7 **Krasnograd** U.S.S.R.
55 D3 **Krasnogvardeyskiy** U.S.S.R.
54 G6 **Krasnokutsk** U.S.S.R.
55 G4 **Krasnokutskoye** Pavlodar U.S.S.R.
54 L5 **Krasnolesniyy** U.S.S.R.
31 N1 **Krasnoles'ye** U.S.S.R.
52 C4 **Krasnoostrovskiy** U.S.S.R.
53 F9 **Krasnoslobodsk** U.S.S.R.
55 D2 **Krasnotur'insk** U.S.S.R.
55 C3 **Krasnoufimsk** U.S.S.R.
55 D2 **Krasnoural'sk** U.S.S.R.
55 C4 **Krasnousol'skiy** U.S.S.R.
52 J4 **Krasnovishersk** U.S.S.R.
50 E4 **Krasnovodsk** U.S.S.R.
55 F3 **Krasnoyarka** Omsk U.S.S.R.
55 D2 **Krasnoyarka** Sverdlovsk U.S.S.R.
56 D3 **Krasnoyarsk** U.S.S.R.
54 M1 **Krasnoye Ekho** U.S.S.R.
57 B6 **Krasnoye Znamya** U.S.S.R.
52 H4 **Krasnozatonskiy** U.S.S.R.
55 G4 **Krasnozerskoye** U.S.S.R.
55 E5 **Krasnoznamenskiy** Atbasar U.S.S.R.
55 C4 **Krasnoznamenskiy** Bashkirskaya U.S.S.R.
52 H6 **Krasny Bor** U.S.S.R.
48 M3 **Krasnye Okny** U.S.S.R.
54 J8 **Krasny Liman** U.S.S.R.
54 K8 **Krasny Luch** U.S.S.R.
54 N1 **Krasny Mayak** U.S.S.R.
31 O5 **Krasnystaw** Poland
54 L1 **Krasny Tkach** U.S.S.R.
54 C2 **Krasnyy** U.S.S.R.
52 G6 **Krasnyye-Baki** U.S.S.R.
52 E5 **Krasnyye Tkachi** U.S.S.R.
52 E5 **Krasnyy Kholm** Kalinin U.S.S.R.
55 B5 **Krasnyy Kholm** Orenburg U.S.S.R.
55 C3 **Krasnyy-Klyuch** U.S.S.R.
55 D3 **Krasnyy Oktyabr** U.S.S.R.
52 E5 **Krasnyy Pereval** U.S.S.R.
55 F3 **Krasnyy Yar** Omsk U.S.S.R.
55 D2 **Krasnyy Yar** Sverdlovsk U.S.S.R.
68 H6 **Kratie** Cambodia
38 L7 **Kraubath** Austria
41 K1 **Krauchenwies** W Germany
115 O3 **Kraulshavn** Greenland
36 H5 **Krautheim** W Germany
32 K5 **Krautsand** W Germany
107 P7 **Krebs** Oklahoma
25 G6 **Krefeld** W Germany
28 J5 **Kregme** Denmark
36 F4 **Krehberg** *mt* W Germany
32 L9 **Kreiensen** W Germany
116 D5 **Krekatok I** Alaska
47 F1 **Kremena** Bulgaria
54 E7 **Kremenchug** U.S.S.R.
54 D7 **Kremenchugskoye Vdkhr** *res* U.S.S.R.
54 K7 **Kremennaya** U.S.S.R.
47 F2 **Kremikovtsi** Bulgaria
101 P1 **Kremlin** Montana
33 N8 **Kremlingen** W Germany
33 S7 **Kremmen** E Germany
106 D1 **Kremmling** Colorado
32 K5 **Krempe** W Germany
38 N5 **Krems** Austria
38 M5 **Krems** *R* Austria
116 D9 **Krenitzin Is** Aleutian Is
33 Q10 **Krensitz** E Germany
48 E7 **Kreševo** Yugoslavia
108 F1 **Kress** Texas
52 D6 **Kresti** U.S.S.R.
52 H2 **Krestovka** U.S.S.R.
51 H1 **Kresty** U.S.S.R.
27 M16 **Kretinga** U.S.S.R.
41 P2 **Kreuth** W Germany
36 B2 **Kreuzau** W Germany
41 O3 **Kreuzeck** *mt* W Germany
38 H8 **Kreuzeck-Gruppe** *mts* Austria
38 L5 **Kreuzen** Austria
38 E7 **Kreuzjoch** *mt* Austria
41 K2 **Kreuzlingen** Switzerland
36 E2 **Kreuztal** W Germany
86 A5 **Kribi** Cameroon
54 C3 **Krichev** U.S.S.R.
28 A3 **Krik** Denmark
28 A3 **Krik Vig** *B* Denmark
38 F7 **Krimml** Austria
38 F7 **Krimmler Fälle** Austria
38 F7 **Krimmler Tal** *R* Austria
26 D10 **Kringen** Norway
46 E6 **Krionéri** Greece
47 F9 **Kriós, Akr** *C* Crete Greece
76 C2 **Krishna** *R* India
76 D4 **Krishnagiri** India
75 N7 **Krishnanagar** India
27 H14 **Kristdala** Sweden
17 G9 **Kristel** Algeria
27 H15 **Kristianopel** Sweden
27 C13 **Kristiansand** Norway
27 G15 **Kristianstad** Sweden
27 F15 **Kristianstad** *county* Sweden
26 C8 **Kristiansund** Norway
29 J9 **Kristiinankaupunki** Finland
27 G12 **Kristinehamn** Sweden
28 E4 **Kristrup** Denmark
47 G9 **Kríti** *isld* Greece
46 E2 **Kriva** *R* Yugoslavia
48 E6 **Krivaja** *R* Yugoslavia
46 E2 **Kriva Palanka** Yugoslavia
48 N3 **Krivoye Ozero** U.S.S.R.
54 E9 **Krivoy Rog** U.S.S.R.
52 G5 **Krivyachka** U.S.S.R.
42 F3 **Krk** Yugoslavia
31 J5 **Krkonoše** *mts* Czechoslovakia
31 K5 **Krnov** Czechoslovakia
31 K4 **Krobia** Poland
27 D11 **Kröderen** Norway
28 B5 **Krogager** Denmark
37 P1 **Krögis** E Germany
28 E5 **Krogsbølle** Denmark
69 E10 **Kroh** Malaysia
37 O6 **Kröhstorf** W Germany
70 M9 **Kroja** Java
27 H13 **Krokek** Sweden
26 G6 **Kroken** Norway
89 E5 **Krokodil** *R* S Africa
26 G8 **Krokom** Sweden
31 L1 **Krokowa** Poland
26 J7 **Kroksjö** Sweden
54 E5 **Krolevets** U.S.S.R.
36 D2 **Krombach** W Germany
48 D1 **Kroměříž** Czechoslovakia
25 D5 **Kromme Rijn** *R* Netherlands
37 L3 **Kronach** W Germany
119 N8 **Kronau** Sask
36 E3 **Kronberg** W Germany
37 P3 **Krondorf** Czechoslovakia
36 B3 **Kronenberg** W Germany
68 H5 **Krong Poko** *R* Vietnam
27 G15 **Kronoberg** *county* Sweden
29 K8 **Kronoby** Finland
146 B10 **Kronprinsesse Märtha Kyst** Antarctica
115 Q4 **Kronprins Frederiks Bjerge** *mts* Greenland
146 A6 **Kronprins Olav Kyst** Antarctica
29 O12 **Kronshtadt** U.S.S.R.
68 D5 **Kronwa** Burma
37 N7 **Kronwinkl** W Germany
89 E6 **Kroonstad** S Africa
55 C3 **Kropachevo** U.S.S.R.
33 P4 **Kröpelin** E Germany
53 F10 **Kropotkin** U.S.S.R.
28 K4 **Kropp** Sweden
33 O9 **Kroppenstedt** E Germany
33 R9 **Kropstädt** E Germany
33 T4 **Kröslin** E Germany
31 L3 **Krośniewice** Poland
37 M2 **Krossen** E Germany
31 K4 **Krotoszyn** Poland
41 O2 **Krotten Kopf** *mt* W Germany
111 E11 **Krotz Springs** Louisiana
46 F3 **Kroúsia** *mt* Greece
46 D2 **Krrab** *mt* Albania
36 C3 **Kruft-Mendig** W Germany
89 G4 **Kruger Nat. Park** S Africa
89 E6 **Krugersdorp** S Africa
70 K8 **Krui** Sumatra
22 F2 **Kruishoutem** Belgium
46 D3 **Krujë** Albania
109 K2 **Krum** Texas
38 O6 **Krumbach** Austria
37 J7 **Krumbach** W Germany
46 D2 **Krume** Albania
36 D1 **Krummenerl** W Germany
32 F6 **Krummhörn** W Germany
33 T4 **Krummin** E Germany
47 H3 **Krumovgrad** Bulgaria
41 O2 **Krün** W Germany
Krungkao *see* **Ayutthaya**
Krung Thep *see* **Bangkok**
68 E6 **Krung Thep** Thailand
48 E6 **Krupanj** Yugoslavia
48 E2 **Krupina** Czechoslovakia
116 F3 **Krusenstern, C** Alaska
46 E1 **Kruševac** Yugoslavia
Krušné Hory *mts see* **Erzgebirge** *Mts*
46 E3 **Krušovo** Yugoslavia
52 C6 **Krustpils** U.S.S.R.
52 H3 **Krutaya** U.S.S.R.
19 K5 **Kruth** France
55 D4 **Krutoyarskiy** U.S.S.R.
117 F7 **Kruzof I** Alaska
118 K6 **Krydor** Sask
27 H11 **Krylbo** Sweden
31 P5 **Krylów** Poland
53 D10 **Krym** *reg* U.S.S.R.
48 F1 **Krynica** Poland
31 O2 **Krynki** Poland
37 P3 **Kryry** Czechoslovakia
54 J1 **Kryukovo** U.S.S.R.
48 M3 **Kryulyany** U.S.S.R.
56 E4 **Kryzhina, Khr** *mts* U.S.S.R.
48 M2 **Kryzhopol** U.S.S.R.
31 L5 **Krzepice** Poland
31 N5 **Krzeszów** Poland
31 M5 **Krzeszowice** Poland
31 K4 **Krzywin** Poland
31 J3 **Krzyż** Poland
85 D3 **Ksabi** Algeria
85 C4 **Ksalb Ounane, El** Mali
85 E1 **Ksar el Boukhari** Algeria
16 D9 **Ksar-el-Kebir** Morocco
16 D9 **Ksar Sghir** Morocco
52 J4 **Ksenofontova** U.S.S.R.
85 E2 **Ksour, Mts. des** Algeria
79 C4 **Ktima** Cyprus
69 D9 **Kuah** Malaysia
67 A4 **Kuaize He** *R* China
69 G11 **Kuala** Indonesia
69 D11 **Kuala** Sumatra
69 F10 **Kuala Dungun** Malaysia
69 E10 **Kuala Kangsar** Malaysia
69 F10 **Kuala Kerai** Malaysia
70 C5 **Kualakurun** Kalimantan
69 C10 **Kualalangsa** Sumatra
69 F10 **Kuala Lipis** Malaysia
69 E11 **Kuala Lumpur** Malaysia
70 C5 **Kualamandjual** Kalimantan
69 E9 **Kuala Nerang** Malaysia
70 C6 **Kualapembuang** Kalimantan
70 D2 **Kuala Penyu** Sabah
69 F11 **Kuala Pilah** Malaysia
135 S2 **Kualapuu** Hawaiian Is
69 E11 **Kuala Selangor** Malaysia
69 F10 **Kuala Terengganu** Malaysia
70 E2 **Kuamut** Sabah
70 E2 **Kuamut** *R* Sabah
65 D4 **Kuancheng** China
71 H4 **Kuandang** Sulawesi
71 H4 **Kuandang, Tk** *B* Sulawesi Indonesia
59 H3 **Kuandian** China
69 F11 **Kuantan** Malaysia
145 E2 **Kuaotunu** New Zealand
87 C10 **Kub** Namibia
53 G12 **Kuba** U.S.S.R.
53 F11 **Kuban'** *R* U.S.S.R.
78 G4 **Kubar, el** Syria
26 K8 **Kubbe** Sweden
86 D3 **Kubbum** Sudan
52 F4 **Kubena** *R* U.S.S.R.
52 E5 **Kubenskoye, Oz** *L* U.S.S.R.
52 G6 **Kubnya** *R* U.S.S.R.
60 G12 **Kubokawa** Japan
79 A8 **Kubra, El** Egypt
47 H1 **Kubrat** Bulgaria
70 P10 **Kubu** Indonesia
58 F1 **Kubukhay** U.S.S.R.
70 D4 **Kubumesaäi** Kalimantan
55 E4 **Kubyshevskiy** U.S.S.R.
48 G6 **Kučevo** Yugoslavia
36 H6 **Kuchen** W Germany
41 M3 **Kuchen Spitze** *mt* Austria
70 B4 **Kuching** Sarawak
60 D13 **Kuchinotsu** Japan
60 F10 **Kuchitagi** Japan
55 G4 **Kuchukskoye, Oz** *L* U.S.S.R.
48 M3 **Kuchurgan** *R* U.S.S.R.
33 N5 **Kücknitz** W Germany
47 J6 **Küçük Menderes** *R* Turkey
83 K11 **Kuda** *R* Sri Lanka
61 P14 **Kudaka-jima** *isld* Okinawa
60 E11 **Kudamatsu** Japan
70 B5 **Kudangan** Kalimantan
69 F12 **Kudap** Sumatra
70 E1 **Kudat** Sabah
68 B1 **Kudaw** Burma
55 C4 **Kudeyevskiy** U.S.S.R.
116 F9 **Kudiakof Is** Alaska
31 O1 **Kudirkos Naumiestis** U.S.S.R.
80 G1 **Kudnah** Syria
116 G8 **Kudobin Is** Alaska
142 F5 **Kuduarra Well** W Australia
57 E5 **Kuduk** U.S.S.R.
70 N9 **Kudus** Java
52 H5 **Kudymkar** U.S.S.R.
Kueiyang *see* **Guiyang**
26 S2 **Kuets'yarv, Oz** *L* U.S.S.R.
80 D4 **Kufairāt** Jordan
47 K6 **Kûfi** *R* Turkey
84 G5 **Kufrah Oasis,Al** Libya
80 F4 **Kufr Alma** Jordan
80 F4 **Kufrinja** Jordan
80 F4 **Kufrinja** *R* Jordan
80 G3 **Kufr Jayiz** Jordan
80 G4 **Kufr Khal** Jordan
80 G3 **Kufr Kifiya** Jordan
80 F4 **Kufr Rakib** Jordan
80 G3 **Kufr Saum** Jordan
38 F6 **Kufstein** Austria
60 F11 **Kuga** Japan
57 D5 **Kugitangtau, Khr** *mts* U.S.S.R.
116 F4 **Kugruk** *R* Alaska
37 L7 **Kühbach** W Germany
33 Q6 **Kuhbier** E Germany
77 A2 **Kūh-e Alvand** Iran
77 C4 **Kūh-e Būl** *mt* Iran
77 B3 **Kūh-e Karkas** Iran
78 L2 **Kuhha-ye Sabalan** *mt* Iran
33 T4 **Kühlenhagen** E Germany
29 L10 **Kuhmalahti** Finland
29 O7 **Kuhmo** Finland
77 F6 **Kūhrān, Kūh-e** *mt* Iran
33 Q5 **Kuhs** E Germany
32 J6 **Kuhstedt** W Germany
87 C11 **Kuibis** Namibia
87 C10 **Kuiseb** *R* Namibia
117 F7 **Kuiu I** Alaska
29 L6 **Kuivajoki** *R* Finland
29 L6 **Kuivaniemi** Finland
59 J4 **Kujang-dong** N Korea
61 O9 **Kuji-gawa** Japan
60 E12 **Kujū-san** *mt* Japan
116 G1 **Kuk** *R* Alaska
116 M7 **Kukak** Alaska
116 K7 **Kukaklek L** Alaska
116 G6 **Kukaklik L** Alaska
120 H4 **Kukatush** Ontario
143 C10 **Kukerin** W Australia
46 D2 **Kukës** Albania
29 L5 **Kukkola** Finland
52 H6 **Kukmor** U.S.S.R.
52 E5 **Kukoboy** U.S.S.R.
116 F2 **Kukpowruk** *R* Alaska
116 E2 **Kukpuk** *R* Alaska
135 U4 **Kukuihaele** Hawaiian Is
135 O1 **Kukuiula** Hawaiian Is
118 K1 **Kukukus L** Ontario
83 K11 **Kukulugala** *mt* Sri Lanka
69 F12 **Kukup** Malaysia
70 D6 **Kukusan, G** *mt* Kalimantan
89 B4 **Kul** Botswana
46 F1 **Kula** Bulgaria
47 K6 **Kula** Turkey
48 F5 **Kula** Yugoslavia
69 D12 **Kulabu, Gunung** *mt* Sumatra
74 D3 **Kulachi** Pakistan
57 A2 **Kulandy, Poluostrov** *pen* U.S.S.R.
57 A2 **Kulanoy** U.S.S.R.
55 F6 **Kulanutpes** *R* U.S.S.R.
71 E7 **Kulassein** *isld* Philippines
47 F3 **Kulata** Bulgaria
27 M15 **Kuldiga** U.S.S.R.
Kuldja *see* **Yining**
117 K8 **Kuldo** Br Col
57 C4 **Kul'dzhuktau, Gory** *mt* U.S.S.R.
52 F6 **Kulebaki** U.S.S.R.
54 G8 **Kulebovka** U.S.S.R.
42 G4 **Kulen Vakuf** Yugoslavia
48 M4 **Kulevcha** U.S.S.R.
55 D4 **Kulevchi** U.S.S.R.
140 C7 **Kulgera** N Terr Aust
71 L10 **Kuli** Indonesia
52 H5 **Kuligi** U.S.S.R.
48 J1 **Kulikov** U.S.S.R.
69 E10 **Kulim** Malaysia
143 C10 **Kulin** W Australia
143 B9 **Kulja** W Australia
139 G4 **Kulkyne** *R* New S Wales
28 K4 **Kulla Gunnarstorp** Sweden
28 K4 **Kullen** *mt* Sweden
32 M10 **Küllstedt** E Germany
98 H3 **Kulm** N Dakota
37 M4 **Kulmain** W Germany
37 L3 **Kulmbach** W Germany
52 F3 **Kuloy** U.S.S.R.
52 F4 **Kuloy** *R* U.S.S.R.
138 E5 **Kulpara** S Australia
95 L6 **Kulpmont** Pennsylvania
38 G7 **Kuls** Austria
50 E4 **Kul'sary** U.S.S.R.
36 H4 **Külsheim** W Germany
29 M3 **Kultala** Finland
75 M7 **Kulti** India
26 H7 **Kultsjöluspen** Sweden
26 G6 **Kultsjön** *L* Sweden
33 R10 **Kültzschau** E Germany
78 D2 **Kulu** Turkey
55 G4 **Kulunda** U.S.S.R.
56 B4 **Kulunda** *R* U.S.S.R.
57 E5 **Kulyab** U.S.S.R.
47 J6 **Kum** *R* Turkey
60 F12 **Kuma** Japan
60 D13 **Kuma** *R* Japan
53 G11 **Kuma** *R* U.S.S.R.
61 N9 **Kumagaya** Japan
70 B6 **Kumai** Kalimantan
70 B6 **Kumai, Teluk** *B* Kalimantan
55 D5 **Kumak** U.S.S.R.
55 C5 **Kumak** *R* U.S.S.R.
60 D13 **Kumamoto** Japan
48 F7 **Kumanica** Yugoslavia
61 K12 **Kumano** Japan
46 E2 **Kumanovo** Yugoslavia
144 C5 **Kumara** New Zealand
51 M3 **Kumara** U.S.S.R.
143 D10 **Kumarl** W Australia
85 D7 **Kumasi** Ghana
74 H3 **Kumaun** *reg* India
86 A5 **Kumba** Cameroon
76 D5 **Kumbakonam** India
141 K7 **Kumbarilla** Queensland
47 L5 **Kümbet** Turkey
83 L11 **Kumbukkan Oya** *R* Sri Lanka
59 J4 **Kŭmch'ŏn** S Korea
50 E3 **Kumertan** U.S.S.R.
55 C4 **Kumertau** U.S.S.R.
86 F5 **Kumi** Uganda
60 H10 **Kumihama** Japan
55 E2 **Kuminskiy** U.S.S.R.
47 H5 **Kumkale** Turkey
27 H12 **Kumla** Sweden
29 H11 **Kumlinge** Finland
116 J8 **Kumliun, C** Alaska
47 L8 **Kumluca** Turkey
33 R5 **Kummerow** E Germany
33 R4 **Kummerow** Rostock E Germany
33 R5 **Kummerower See** *L* E Germany
37 M5 **Kümmersbruck** W Germany
33 S8 **Kummersdorf** E Germany
85 G7 **Kumo** Nigeria
65 G7 **Kŭmo** *isld* S Korea
57 D2 **Kumola** *R* U.S.S.R.
75 R5 **Kumon Range** Burma
68 F4 **Kumphawapi** Thailand
76 B3 **Kumta** India
135 V5 **Kumukahi, C** Hawaiian Is
Kumush *see* **Kümüx**
66 D3 **Kümüx** China
31 O1 **Kumuzovo** U.S.S.R.
68 C3 **Kun** *R* Burma
116 J2 **Kuna** *R* Alaska
143 E6 **Kunanaggi Well** W Australia
74 D1 **Kunar** Afghanistan
55 D3 **Kunashak** U.S.S.R.
60 T1 **Kunashir O** *isld* U.S.S.R.
141 K6 **Kunawarara** Queensland
52 C5 **Kunda** U.S.S.R.
88 A6 **Kundelungu** *mt* Zaïre
86 E3 **Kundi, L** Sudan
143 D10 **Kundip** W Australia
74 D7 **Kundla** India
55 D4 **Kundravy** U.S.S.R.
69 F12 **Kundur** *isld* Indonesia
77 L1 **Kunduz** Afghanistan
66 C3 **Künes He** *R* China
27 E14 **Kungälv** Sweden
Kunges *see* **Künes He**
57 H3 **Kungey Alatau, Khr** *mts* U.S.S.R.
117 H9 **Kunghit I** Br Col
57 K3 **Kung-liu** China
57 A3 **Kungrad** U.S.S.R.
27 F14 **Kungsbacka** Sweden
27 J11 **Kungsgården** Sweden
27 H12 **Kungsör** Sweden
86 C5 **Kungu** Zaïre
55 C2 **Kungur** U.S.S.R.
Kungur *mt see* **Kongur Shan**
141 J5 **Kungurri** Queensland
68 C4 **Kungyangon** Burma
48 F3 **Kunhegyes** Hungary
68 D2 **Kunhing** Burma
61 Q12 **Kunigami** Okinawa
60 E13 **Kunimi-dake** *mt* Japan
70 M9 **Kuningan** Java
67 C5 **Kunlun Guan** *pass* China
48 F4 **Kunmadaras** Hungary
67 A4 **Kunming** China
60 R2 **Kunneppu** Japan
25 E3 **Kunnre** Netherlands
60 O3 **Kunnui** *R* Japan
28 O9 **Kunø** Faeroes
65 G7 **Kunsan** S Korea
67 G1 **Kunshan** China
48 F4 **Kunszentmárton** Hungary
48 E3 **Kunszentmiklós** Hungary
52 E6 **Kuntsevo** U.S.S.R.
143 C9 **Kununoppin** W Australia
142 G3 **Kununurra** W Australia
52 D6 **Kunya** U.S.S.R.
52 J5 **Kun'ya** U.S.S.R.
57 A4 **Kunya Urgench** U.S.S.R.
65 E6 **Kunyu Shan** *mts* China
36 H5 **Künzelsau** W Germany
67 G2 **Kuocang Shan** *mts* China
52 C2 **Kuolayarvi** U.S.S.R.
29 N9 **Kuopio** Finland
29 N2 **Kuorboaivi** *mt* Finland
29 K9 **Kuortane** Finland
29 M10 **Kuortti** Finland
26 L5 **Kuouka** Sweden
26 L3 **Kuoutatjärro** *mt* Sweden
71 L10 **Kupang** Timor Indonesia
71 L10 **Kupang, Tk** *B* Timor Indonesia
116 N1 **Kuparuk** *R* Alaska
37 M3 **Kupferberg** W Germany
36 H5 **Kupferzell** W Germany
55 G4 **Kupino** U.S.S.R.
52 B6 **Kupiškis** U.S.S.R.
36 E6 **Kuppenheim** W Germany
117 G7 **Kupreanof I** Alaska
116 H9 **Kupreanof Pt** Alaska
116 L7 **Kupreanof St** Alaska
37 L3 **Küps** W Germany
42 G3 **Kupu** *R* Yugoslavia
54 J7 **Kupyansk** U.S.S.R.
54 J7 **Kupyansk-Uzlovoy** U.S.S.R.
66 C3 **Kuqa** China
59 L1 **Kur** *R* U.S.S.R.
57 G3 **Kuragaty** U.S.S.R.
60 F11 **Kurahashi-jima** *isld* Japan
53 G12 **Kurakh** *R* U.S.S.R.
57 E4 **Kuramins'kiy Khr** *mts* U.S.S.R.
60 C12 **Kuramoto** Japan
141 H3 **Kuranda** Queensland
55 C5 **Kurashasayskiy** U.S.S.R.
60 G11 **Kurashiki** Japan
142 G4 **Kura Soak** W Australia
60 G10 **Kurayoshi** Japan
56 C5 **Kurayskiy Khr** *mts* U.S.S.R.
47 G3 **Kurazhali Dam** Bulgaria
56 G5 **Kurba** *R* U.S.S.R.
56 B6 **Kurchum** *R* U.S.S.R.
57 H3 **Kurday** U.S.S.R.
78 G2 **Kurdistan** *reg* Turkey/Iraq/Iran
74 F9 **Kurduvadi** India
47 G3 **Kürdzhali** Bulgaria
60 F11 **Kure** Japan
80 F4 **Kureiyima** Jordan
51 H2 **Kureyka** U.S.S.R.
51 J2 **Kureyka** *R* U.S.S.R.
55 F5 **Kurgal'dzhino** U.S.S.R.
55 E3 **Kurgan** U.S.S.R.
50 F3 **Kurganskaya Oblast'** *prov* U.S.S.R.
57 E5 **Kurgan-Tyube** U.S.S.R.
57 D1 **Kurgasyn** U.S.S.R.
137 P1 **Kuria** *isld* Kiribati
83 H3 **Kuria Muria** *isld* Arabian Sea
43 D13 **Kuriate Is.** Tunisia
140 F5 **Kuridala** Queensland
29 J9 **Kurikka** Finland
61 O7 **Kurikoma-yama** *mt* Japan
Kuril Is *see* **Kuril'skiye Ostrova**
52 F5 **Kurilovo** U.S.S.R.
59 N2 **Kuril'sk** U.S.S.R.
51 O4 **Kuril'skiye Ostrova** U.S.S.R.
145 F3 **Kuripapango** New Zealand
60 P2 **Kuriyama** Japan
29 O10 **Kurkieki** U.S.S.R.
84 J5 **Kurkur Oasis** Egypt
52 F6 **Kurlovskiy** U.S.S.R.
86 F3 **Kurmuk** Sudan
36 F5 **Kürnbach** W Germany
76 D3 **Kurnool** India
61 O9 **Kurobane** Japan
61 L9 **Kurobe** Japan
61 O5 **Kuroishi** Japan
61 O9 **Kuroiso** Japan
119 O7 **Kuroki** Sask
60 O3 **Kuromatsunai** Japan
60 G10 **Kurosaka** Japan
54 K1 **Kurovskoye** U.S.S.R.
144 C6 **Kurow** New Zealand
31 N4 **Kurów** Poland
139 K5 **Kurri Kurri** New S Wales
54 H5 **Kursk** U.S.S.R.
27 M16 **Kurškiy Zaliv** U.S.S.R.
46 E1 **Kuršumlija** Yugoslavia
57 A4 **Kurt** U.S.S.R.
55 D4 **Kurtamysh** U.S.S.R.
36 C1 **Kürten** W Germany
47 K8 **Kurtoğlu Burun** *C* Turkey
56 D5 **Kurtushibinskiy, Khr** *mts* U.S.S.R.
29 K10 **Kuru** Finland
78 G2 **Kuruçay** Turkey
57 E6 **Kuruk** U.S.S.R.
66 D3 **Kuruktag** *mts* China
89 C6 **Kuruman** S Africa
60 D12 **Kurume** Japan
58 F1 **Kurumkan** U.S.S.R.
140 C5 **Kurundi** N Terr Aust
83 K10 **Kurunegala** Sri Lanka
116 K2 **Kurupa Lakes** Alaska
61 O10 **Kururi** Japan
52 J4 **Kur'ya** U.S.S.R.
68 G7 **Kus** Cambodia
47 J7 **Kuşadasi** Turkey
70 D6 **Kusan, Peg** *mt* Kalimantan
117 E5 **Kusawa L** Yukon Terr
60 G10 **Kuse** Japan
36 C4 **Kusel** W Germany
33 O7 **Kusey** E Germany
26 L7 **Kusfors** Sweden
47 J4 **Kuş Gölü** *L* Turkey
52 E6 **Kushalino** U.S.S.R.
52 E3 **Kushereka** U.S.S.R.
61 P12 **Kushi** Okinawa
61 K11 **Kushida-gawa** *R* Japan
60 D14 **Kushikino** Japan
60 E14 **Kushima** Japan
61 J12 **Kushimoto** Japan
60 S3 **Kushiro** Japan
60 R2 **Kushiro** *prefect* Japan
57 C6 **Kushka** U.S.S.R.
52 F3 **Kushkushara** U.S.S.R.
48 H2 **Kushnitsa** U.S.S.R.
57 D4 **Kushrabat** U.S.S.R.
116 P6 **Kushtaka L** Alaska
75 N7 **Kushtia** Bangladesh
53 H9 **Kushum** *R* U.S.S.R.
55 C2 **Kushva** U.S.S.R.
116 G6 **Kuskokwim** *R* Alaska
116 F7 **Kuskokwim B** Alaska
116 H6 **Kuskokwim Mts** Alaska
116 F6 **Kuskovak** Alaska
75 K4 **Kusma** Nepal
86 G5 **Kussa** Ethiopia
60 S2 **Kussharo ko** *L* Japan
29 L4 **Küstala** Finland
55 D4 **Kustanay** U.S.S.R.
26 J5 **Kustarakaise** *mt* Sweden
29 J11 **Kustavi** Finland
85 F7 **Kuta** Nigeria
56 G3 **Kuta** *R* U.S.S.R.
69 C11 **Kutabuloh** Sumatra
69 C11 **Kutacane** Sumatra
47 K5 **Kütahya** Turkey
70 E5 **Kutai** *R* Kalimantan
53 F12 **Kutaisi** U.S.S.R.
78 K5 **Kūt, Al** Iraq
69 C11 **Kutanibong** Sumatra
57 E2 **Kutansor, Ozero** *L* U.S.S.R.
145 F3 **Kutarere** New Zealand
56 E5 **Ku Tayga, Khr** *mts* U.S.S.R.
106 G3 **Kutch** Colorado
60 O3 **Kutchan** Japan
74 C7 **Kutch, Gulf of** India
74 C6 **Kutch, Rann of** India
54 K9 **Kuteynikovo** U.S.S.R.
42 H3 **Kutina** Yugoslavia
68 F4 **Kut Khao** Thailand
68 F7 **Kut, Ko** *isld* Thailand
31 J6 **Kutná Hóra** Czechoslovakia
31 L3 **Kutno** Poland
70 M9 **Kutoadjo** Java
76 E1 **Kutru** India
26 N3 **Kuttainen** Sweden
110 H4 **Kuttawa** Kentucky
88 F5 **Kutu** Tanzania
86 C6 **Kutu** Zaïre
56 F4 **Kutulik** U.S.S.R.
86 D3 **Kutum** Sudan
56 D4 **Kuturchinskoye Belog** *mt* U.S.S.R.

48 J2 Kuty U.S.S.R.
37 J3 Kützberg W Germany
95 M6 Kutztown Pennsylvania
29 O6 Kuusamo Finland
29 M11 Kuusankoski Finland
52 H5 Kuva U.S.S.R.
55 C5 Kuvandyk U.S.S.R.
52 D6 Kuvshinovo U.S.S.R.
77 A5 Kuwait Kuwait
77 A5 Kuwait *sheikhdom* The Gulf
61 K10 Kuwana Japan
Kuwayt, Al *see* Kuwait
78 L5 Kuwayt, Al Iraq
52 F2 Kuya U.S.S.R.
53 H7 Kuybyshev U.S.S.R.
57 E5 Kuybyshevskiy U.S.S.R.
53 G7 Kuybyshev-skoye U.S.S.R.
55 C3 Kuyeda U.S.S.R.
65 A5 Kuye He *R* China
66 D3 Kuytun China
55 D5 Kuyukkol', Oz *L* U.S.S.R.
128 G3 Kuyuwini *R* Guyana
56 C3 Kuzbass *basin* U.S.S.R.
116 E4 Kuzitrin *R* Alaska
53 G7 Kuznetsk U.S.S.R.
56 C3 Kuznetskiy Alatau *mt* U.S.S.R.
55 D2 Kuznetsovo U.S.S.R.
52 E2 Kuzomen U.S.S.R.
26 H3 Kvaefjord Norway
26 M2 Kvaenangen Norway
26 M1 Kvaenangen *inlet* Norway
26 M2 Kvaenangsbotn Norway
28 H6 Kværkeby Denmark
28 F6 Kværndrup Denmark
28 C7 Kværs Denmark
28 N3 Kvalbø Faeroes
26 N1 Kvalöya *isld* Norway
26 K1 Kvalöy, N *isld* Norway
26 K2 Kvalöy, S *isld* Norway
26 N1 Kvalsund Norway
28 M2 Kvalvig Faeroes
26 D10 Kvam Norway
28 O9 Kvannesund Faeroes
55 C5 Kvarkeno U.S.S.R.
27 G15 Kvarnamåla Sweden
26 G7 Kvarnbergsvattnet *L* Sweden
42 F4 Kvarner *chan* Yugoslavia
42 F4 Kvarnerić *chan* Yugoslavia
27 J13 Kvarsebo Sweden
27 C11 Kvenna *R* Norway
26 C8 Kvernes Norway
26 L2 Kvesmenas Norway
29 J8 Kvevlax Finland
116 J7 Kvichak Alaska
26 G6 Kvigtind *mt* Norway
26 J5 Kvikkjock Sweden
26 D9 Kvikne Norway
27 B13 Kvina *R* Norway
27 B13 Kvinesdal Norway
27 B12 Kvinnherad Norway
27 G12 Kvistbro Sweden
28 K5 Kvistofta Sweden
26 C8 Kvisvik Norway
27 C12 Kviteseid Norway
26 R1 Kvitnes Norway
147 K11 Kvitöya *isld* Spitzbergen
27 A12 Kvitsöy *isld* Norway
28 M2 Kvivig Faeroes
28 A5 Kvong Denmark
28 D4 Kvorning Denmark
117 L7 Kwadacha Wilderness Prov. Park Br Columbia
134 G7 Kwajalein *atoll* Marshall Is Pacific Oc
129 G2 Kwakoegron Suriname
88 G4 Kwale Kenya
85 F7 Kwale Nigeria
86 C6 Kwamouth Zaïre
Kwangchow *see* Guangzhou
65 G7 Kwangju S Korea
86 C6 Kwango *R* Zaïre
Kwangsi *aut reg see* Guangxi
Kwangtung *prov see* Guangdong
86 F5 Kwania, L Uganda
120 H1 Kwataboahegan *R* Ontario
89 G7 Kwazulu *reg* S Africa
Kweichow *prov see* Guizhou
Kweilin *see* Guilin
89 D5 Kweneng *dist* Botswana
87 C7 Kwenge *R* Zaïre
116 G6 Kwethluk Alaska
31 L2 Kwidzyn Poland
116 D7 Kwigamiuk Alaska
116 F7 Kwigillingok Alaska
116 E5 Kwiguk Alaska
116 E5 Kwikpak Alaska
87 C7 Kwilu *R* Zaïre
142 A4 Kwinana W Australia
31 J4 Kwisa *R* Poland
128 G3 Kwitaro *R* Guyana
143 C10 Kwobrup W Australia
136 G2 Kwoka *mt* W Irian
26 D7 Kya *isld* Norway
86 C4 Kyabé Chad
141 G7 Kyabra Queensland
139 H6 Kyabram Victoria
68 B2 Kyadet Burma
68 B3 Kyagu Burma
68 C4 Kyaikkami Burma
68 B4 Kyaiklat Burma
68 C4 Kyaikto Burma
68 D5 Kya-in Seikkyi Burma
88 C2 Kyaka Tanzania
56 G5 Kyakhta U.S.S.R.
139 G5 Kyalite New S Wales
138 D5 Kyancutta S Australia
52 E3 Kyanda U.S.S.R.
52 D3 Kyargozero U.S.S.R.
68 C3 Kyaukhnyat Burma
68 B3 Kyaukkyi Burma
68 C1 Kyaukme Burma
68 B1 Kyaukmyaung Burma
68 A3 Kyaukpyu Burma
68 C2 Kyaukse Burma
68 A2 Kyauktaw Burma
68 B2 Kyaukyit Burma
68 B4 Kyaunggon Burma
138 F6 Kybybolite S Australia
52 F2 Kychema U.S.S.R.
26 G7 Kycklingvattnet Sweden
68 C3 Kyebogyi Burma
144 C6 Kyeburn New Zealand
68 D5 Kyeikdon Burma
68 D4 Kyeikywa Burma
68 B3 Kyeintali Burma
33 O10 Kyffhäuser *mt* E Germany
143 E7 Kyffin-Thomas Hill W Australia
28 F5 Kyholm *isld* Denmark
68 C3 Kyidaunggan Burma
68 A2 Kyindwe Burma
31 K6 Kyjov Czechoslovakia
118 J8 Kyle Sask
98 D6 Kyle S Dakota
109 K6 Kyle Texas
101 T8 Kyle Wyoming
15 C3 Kyleakin Scotland
87 F10 Kyle Dam Zimbabwe
15 D2 Kyle of Durness Scotland
15 C3 Kyle of Lochalsh Scotland
15 D2 Kyle of Tongue Scotland
12 C2 Kyles of Bute *chan* Scotland
36 B3 Kyll *R* W Germany
36 B3 Kyllburg W Germany
29 N10 Kymi *prov* Finland
29 M11 Kymijoki *R* Finland
55 C2 Kyn U.S.S.R.
139 G6 Kyneton Victoria
37 O3 Kynšperk nad Ohři Czechoslovakia
141 F5 Kynuna Queensland
61 P12 Kyoda Okinawa
86 F5 Kyoga, L Uganda
60 J10 Kyōga-misaki *C* Japan
139 L3 Kyogle New S Wales
65 F5 Kyŏmip'o N Korea
68 D4 Kyondo Burma
68 C2 Kyong Burma
141 H5 Kyong Queensland
62 Kyōto *conurbation* Japan
60 J10 Kyōto *prefect* Japan
55 E6 Kypshak, Oz *L* U.S.S.R.
79 D3 Kyrenia Cyprus
33 Q7 Kyritz E Germany
29 L11 Kyrkslätt Finland
29 J8 Kyröjoki *R* Finland
29 K10 Kyrösjärvi *L* Finland
52 J3 Kyrta U.S.S.R.
55 D2 Kyrtym'ya U.S.S.R.
55 C2 Kyr'ya U.S.S.R.
55 G3 Kyshtovka U.S.S.R.
55 D3 Kyshtym U.S.S.R.
52 G3 Kyssa U.S.S.R.
79 D3 Kythrea Cyprus
55 C2 Kytlym U.S.S.R.
68 D5 Kyungyaung Burma
68 C7 Kyun Pila *islds* Burma
117 K10 Kyuquot Br Col
60 D13 Kyūshū *isld* Japan
60 E13 Kyūshū-sanchi *mts* Japan
46 F2 Kyustendil Bulgaria
51 M1 Kyusyur U.S.S.R.
139 H6 Kywong New S Wales
29 L8 Kyyjärvi Finland
56 D5 Kyzyl U.S.S.R.
57 E1 Kyzyldyykan U.S.S.R.
56 E5 Kyzyl-Khem *R* U.S.S.R.
57 F4 Kyzyl-Kiya U.S.S.R.
57 J2 Kyzylkiya U.S.S.R.
57 E1 Kyzyl-Kommuna U.S.S.R.
57 C4 Kyzylkum, Peski *des* U.S.S.R.
55 F5 Kyzyltas U.S.S.R.
57 H1 Kyzyltu U.S.S.R.
57 D1 Kyzyluy U.S.S.R.
57 C1 Kyzylzhar U.S.S.R.
57 J3 Kyzylzhide U.S.S.R.
57 E1 Kzyl-Dzhar U.S.S.R.
57 D3 Kzyl-Orda U.S.S.R.
55 F4 Kzyltu U.S.S.R.
31 J7 Laa Austria
37 M5 Laaber W Germany
36 C3 Laacher See *L* W Germany
33 Q5 Laage E Germany
25 F4 Laag Keppel Netherlands
124 C4 La Angostura Mexico
29 N3 Laanila Finland
36 E2 Laasphe W Germany
127 N9 La Asunción Venezuela
135 R2 Laau Pt Hawaiian Is
108 E7 La Babia Mexico
110 F3 Labadie Missouri
7 E12 Labadie Bank Atlantic Oc
111 F12 Labadieville Louisiana
71 L9 Labala Indonesia
79 F8 Labān Jordan
16 D2 La Baneza Spain
71 L9 Labao Flores Indonesia
124 H7 La Barca Mexico
101 P7 La Barge Wyoming
21 A8 La Barre-de-Monts France
19 P17 La Bastide-des-Jourdans France
18 G8 Labastide Murat France
19 Q13 La Bathie France
19 Q15 La Bâtie-Neuve France
68 A2 Labawa Burma
52 H2 Labazhskoye U.S.S.R.
26 J5 Labbas Sweden
80 D1 Labbouna Lebanon
26 R3 Labdshy'aur, Oz *L* U.S.S.R.
85 B6 Labé Guinea
31 J5 Labe *R* Czechoslovakia
19 Q17 La Bégude Blanche France
99 P9 La Belle Missouri
121 Q6 Labelle Quebec
71 H6 Labengke *isld* Sulawesi
19 Q15 La Bérarde France
117 F5 Laberge, L Yukon Terr
131 E7 Laberinto, Pta Argentina
21 A7 La Bernerie France
21 J8 La Berthenoux France
37 N6 Laberweinting W Germany
70 D2 Labi Brunei
117 L5 La Biche *R* Yukon Terr/Br Col
42 F3 Labin Yugoslavia
69 F11 Labis Malaysia
127 M9 La Blanquilla, I Venezuela
71 F3 Labo Philippines
71 H5 Labobo *isld* Indonesia
103 J10 La Bomba Mexico
101 U7 Labonte Cr Wyoming
31 N6 Laborec *R* Czechoslovakia
48 G1 Laborec *R* Czechoslovakia
70 G6 Labota Sulawesi
143 C7 Labouchere, Mt W Australia
18 E8 Labouheyre France
133 E4 Laboulaye Argentina
115 N7 Labrador City Labrador
115 O6 Labrador Sea Nfld/Greenland
128 F5 Labrea Brazil
128 B4 La Brea, Cer. de *hill* Peru
124 E5 La Brecha Mexico
18 E8 Labrède France
122 C4 Labrieville Quebec
122 C4 Labrieville, Parc de Quebec
18 E8 Labrit France
118 E1 La Broquerie Manitoba
22 B3 Labroye France
21 C7 La Bruffière France
18 G9 Labruguière France
136 F2 Labuha Moluccas Indonesia
71 J9 Labuhanbadjo Sumba Indonesia
69 E11 Labuhanbatu Sumatra
69 E11 Labuhanbilik Sumatra
69 C11 Labuhanhaji Sumatra
69 D11 Labuhanruku Sumatra
70 K8 Labuhanwaiharu Sumatra
19 P14 La Buisse France
70 E2 Labuk *R* Sabah
70 E1 Labuk B Sabah
68 B4 Labutta Burma
138 D4 Labyrinth, L S Australia
50 F2 Labytnangi U.S.S.R.
46 D3 Laç Albania
124 G5 La Cadena Mexico
118 J8 Lacadena Sask
122 J3 Lac Allard Quebec
111 D10 Lacamp Louisiana
18 E8 Lacanau France
128 F2 La Canoa Venezuela
125 O9 Lacantum *R* Mexico
18 G8 Lacapelle-Marival France
131 B8 Lacar, L Argentina
133 E4 La Carlota Argentina
71 F5 La Carlota Negros Philippines
16 E6 La Carolina Spain
18 G9 Lacaune France
Laccadive Is *see* Lakshadweep
122 B8 Lac-Drolet Quebec
99 R4 Lac du Flambeau Wisconsin
13 H6 Laceby England
125 L2 La Ceiba Honduras
128 D2 La Ceiba Venezuela
21 G7 La Celle St Avant France
138 E6 Lacepede B S Australia
142 D3 Lacepede Is W Australia
21 C8 La Chaize-le-Vicomte France
19 Q14 La Chambre France
52 E4 Lacha, Oz *L* U.S.S.R.
20 J3 Lachapelle-aux-Pots France
21 C7 La Chapelle Basse Mer France
21 G7 La Chapelle-Blanche-St. Martin France
21 B6 La Chapelle-Bouexic France
21 E6 La Chapelle-d'Aligné France
19 O15 La Chapelle-en-Vercors France
21 C6 La Chapelle-Glain France
21 I6 La Chapelle St. Mesmin France
21 I9 La Chapelle-Taillefert France
21 G6 La Chartre France
21 J8 La Châtre France
128 C6 Lachay, Pta *point* Peru
41 J3 Lachen Switzerland
36 E5 Lachen W Germany
21 B7 La Chevroliere France
94 D1 Lachine Michigan
139 H5 Lachlan *R* New S Wales
125 P5 La Chorrera Panama
33 M7 Lachte *R* W Germany
121 Q7 Lachute Quebec
19 P18 La Ciotat France
94 J4 Lackawanna New York
14 E3 Lacken Res Irish Rep
71 M9 Lacla *R* Timor
114 H7 Lac la Biche Alberta
117 N10 Lac La Hache Br Columbia
119 M3 Lac la Ronge Sask
100 J1 Laclede Idaho
99 N10 Laclede Missouri
19 Q13 La Clusaz France
133 D3 La Cocha Argentina
8 D5 Lacock England
121 R7 Lacolle Quebec
124 D3 La Colorada Mexico
118 D6 Lacombe Alberta
111 G11 Lacombe Louisiana
99 R8 Lacon Illinois
99 N8 Lacona Iowa
95 L3 Lacona New York
43 C9 Laconi Sardinia
95 Q3 Laconia New Hampshire
113 E9 Lacoochee Florida
130 B9 La Cordillera *dep* Paraguay
121 N4 Lacorne Quebec
21 D7 La Cornuaille France
16 B1 La Coruña Spain
109 J6 Lacoste Texas
19 O14 La Côte St. André France
127 J2 Lacovia Jamaica
98 K4 Lac Qui Parle Minnesota
98 E6 Lacreek L S Dakota
126 A3 Lacre Pt Bonaire W Indies
99 P6 La Crescent Minnesota
21 H7 La Croix France
99 O1 La Croix,L Ontario
99 U8 La Crosse Indiana
107 L3 La Crosse Kansas
94 J10 La Crosse Virginia
99 P6 La Crosse Wisconsin
133 F3 La Cruz Argentina
125 M4 La Cruz Costa Rica
124 F6 La Cruz Mexico
124 G4 La Cruz Mexico
120 G3 Lac Ste. Thérèse Ontario
133 C5 La Cueva Chile
106 E6 La Cueva New Mexico
119 N6 Lac Vert Sask
107 Q3 La Cygne Kansas
21 E7 La Daguenière France
130 H5 Ladainha Brazil
74 G1 Ladakh Range Kashmir
54 D6 Ladan' U.S.S.R.
69 D9 Ladang, Ko *isld* Thailand
129 G7 Ladário Brazil
70 K9 Lada, Teluk *B* Java
9 E3 Ladbroke England
99 R8 Ladd Illinois
107 J3 Ladder Cr Kansas
110 E2 Laddonia Missouri
111 E8 Ladelle Arkansas
28 C7 Ladelund W Germany
36 F5 Ladenburg W Germany
127 O4 La Désirade *isld* Guadeloupe W I
Lādhiqīya, El *see* Latakia
46 E7 Ládhon *R* Greece
83 J12 La Digue *isld* Seychelles
28 D4 Lading Denmark
89 B9 Ladismith S Africa
77 G5 Ladiz Iran
98 C4 Ladner S Dakota
48 G6 Ladne Vode Yugoslavia
74 F5 Ladnun India
8 B7 Ladock England
110 K2 Ladoga Indiana
Ladoga *L see* Ladozhskoye Oz
109 M2 Ladonia Texas
128 D2 La Dorada Colombia
52 D4 Ladozhskoye Oz *L* U.S.S.R.
106 C7 Ladrones Pk New Mexico
116 R5 Ladue *R* Alaska/Yukon Terr
124 E3 La Dura Mexico
52 D4 Ladva Vetka U.S.S.R.
115 L2 Lady Ann Str N W Terr
15 E4 Ladybank Scotland
139 J8 Lady Barron Tasmania
89 E7 Ladybrand S Africa
142 F5 Lady Edith L W Australia
141 L6 Lady Elliot I Gt Barrier Reef Aust
120 K5 Lady Evelyn L Ontario
146 J6 Lady Newnes Ice Shelf Antarctica
100 B1 Ladysmith Br Columbia
89 F7 Ladysmith S Africa
99 P4 Ladysmith Wisconsin
55 E5 Ladyzhenka U.S.S.R.
136 K3 Lae Papua New Guinea
68 E3 Lae Thailand
71 H7 Laëa Indonesia
28 C5 Læborg Denmark
69 B11 Laehobang Indonesia
22 G2 Laeken Belgium
68 F6 Laem Ngop Thailand
17 G6 La Encina Spain
127 L10 La Encrucijada Venezuela
27 B10 Laerdalsöyri Norway
128 F8 La Esmeralda Paraguay
28 G2 Læsø *isld* Denmark
28 F2 Læsø Rende *str* Denmark
133 D5 La Esperanza Argentina
126 F4 La Esperanza Cuba
16 B2 La Estrada Spain
26 P2 Laevajoki Norway
131 D3 La Falda Argentina
95 M2 La Fargeville New York
19 Q18 La Farlède France
111 L9 Lafayette Alabama
106 E2 Lafayette Colorado
112 B3 Lafayette Georgia
110 K1 Lafayette Indiana
111 E11 Lafayette Louisiana
99 M5 Lafayette Minnesota
94 B10 Lafayette Tennessee
95 Q2 Lafayette, Mt New Hampshire
126 B3 La Fe Cuba
109 K9 La Feria Texas
21 E8 La Ferrière-en-Parthenay France
121 M4 Laferte Quebec
21 I7 La Ferte Imbault France
21 I6 La Ferté-St. Aubin France
21 I6 La Ferté St. Cyr France
85 F7 Lafia Nigeria
85 F7 Lafiagi Nigeria
121 N3 Laflamme *R* Quebec
21 E6 La Flèche France
118 L9 Lafleche Sask
38 O7 Lafnitz *R* Austria
94 C10 La Follette Tennessee
21 F6 La Fontaine-St. Martin France
121 M5 Laforce Quebec
120 J5 Laforest Ontario
18 F8 Lafrançaise France
112 E3 La France S Carolina
36 C6 Lafrimbole France
16 C4 La Fuente de San Esteban Spain
69 A9 Laful Nicobar Is
124 G5 La Gallega Mexico
14 E2 Lagan *R* N Ireland
27 G15 Lagan *R* Sweden
16 B2 La Gañiza Spain
36 B6 Lagarde France
41 N6 Lagarina, Val Italy
106 D4 La Garita Mts Colorado
21 B8 La Garnache France
129 H8 Lagarto, Serra do *mts* Brazil
21 C8 La Gaubretière France
32 J8 Lage W Germany
26 D10 Lågen *R* Norway
32 L5 Lägerdorf W Germany
54 H7 Lagery U.S.S.R.
12 C2 Lagg Scotland
15 D3 Laggan Scotland
12 B2 Laggan B Scotland
77 L2 Laghmān Afghanistan
85 E2 Laghouat Algeria
40 B6 Lagnieu France
16 B7 Lagôa Portugal
130 G6 Lagoa Santa Brazil
130 E4 Lagolândia Brazil
43 G8 Lagonegro Italy
71 F4 Lagonoy Gulf Philippines
133 C7 Lago Posadas Argentina
85 E7 Lagos Nigeria
16 B7 Lagos Portugal
45 M2 Lagosanto Italy
100 G4 La Grande Oregon
115 M7 La Grande-Rivière *R* Quebec
111 L8 La Grange Georgia
94 B5 Lagrange Indiana
94 B8 La Grange Kentucky
99 P9 La Grange Missouri
112 K2 La Grange N Carolina
94 E5 Lagrange Ohio
109 L6 La Grange Texas
142 D4 Lagrange W Australia
98 B8 La Grange Wyoming
128 F2 La Gran Sabana *reg* Venezuela
19 Q14 La Grave France
83 M13 Lagrave *mt* Mauritius
127 J10 La Grita Venezuela
27 L12 Lågskär Finland
29 H11 Lågskär *lt ho* Finland
127 L9 La Guaira Venezuela
133 D3 La Guardia Argentina
16 B3 La Guardia Portugal
17 F2 Laguardia Spain
16 C2 La Gudiña Spain
21 C6 La Guerche de Bretagne France
21 A8 La Guérinière France
18 G8 Laguiole France
133 H3 Laguna Brazil
42 E3 Laguna Italy
106 C6 Laguna New Mexico
141 L7 Laguna B Queensland
102 G8 Laguna Beach California
103 O5 Laguna Cr Arizona
103 K9 Laguna Dam Cal/Ariz
102 H9 Laguna Mts California
128 C5 Lagunas Peru
133 E1 Lagunillas Bolivia
127 J9 Lagunillas Venezuela
65 F4 Lagushao China
70 F2 Lahad Datu Sabah
68 F1 Lahadi China
135 S3 Lahaina Hawaiian Is
70 D4 Laham Kalimantan
99 Q9 La Harpe Illinois
70 K7 Lahat Sumatra
80 C8 Lahav Israel
122 H9 La Have Nova Scotia
80 F1 Lahavot HaBashan Israel
32 J8 Lahde W Germany
124 D4 La Higuera Mexico
77 B1 Lāhījān Iran
102 R12 Lahilahi Pt Hawaiian Is
37 K3 Lahm W Germany
30 D5 Lahn W Germany
36 E2 Lahn *R* W Germany
36 F2 Lahntal W Germany
27 F15 Laholm Sweden
27 F15 Laholmsbukten Sweden
71 F4 Lahong Philippines
102 E2 Lahontan Res Nevada
74 F3 Lahore Pakistan
36 D7 Lahr W Germany
73 L6 Lahshadweep *islds* Indian Oc
32 M8 Lahstedt W Germany
29 M11 Lahti Finland
124 G8 La Huerta Mexico
80 G8 Lahun Jordan
71 F4 Lahuy *isld* Philippines
86 C4 Lai Chad
67 F1 Lai'an China
133 F3 La Iberá *L* Argentina
67 C5 Laibin China
68 F2 Lai Chau Vietnam
36 H7 Laichingen W Germany
139 K3 Laidley Queensland
141 K8 Laidley Queensland
102 S11 Laie Hawaiian Is
67 C2 Laifeng China
22 H4 Laifour France
20 C5 Laignelet France
18 H5 Laignes France
44 D4 Laigueglia Italy
21 C9 L'Aiguillon-sur-Mer France
29 J9 Laihia Finland
68 C2 Lai-Hka Burma
68 C2 Lai-Hsak Burma
70 F7 Laikang, Tk *B* Sulawesi
21 I6 Lailly-en-Val France
71 E1 Lai-Lo Luzon Philippines
47 H3 Lainá Greece
38 L6 Lainbach Austria
94 C4 Laingsburg Michigan
89 B9 Laingsburg S Africa
26 K6 Lainijaur Sweden
26 M4 Lainio Sweden
26 M3 Lainio älv *R* Sweden
98 D9 Laird Colorado
118 L6 Laird Sask
15 D2 Lairg Scotland
71 G7 Lais Mindanao Philippines
70 G4 Lais Sulawesi
126 D3 La Isabela Cuba
86 G5 Laisamis Kenya
52 G6 Laishevo U.S.S.R.
65 C5 Laishui China
20 E3 Laison *R* France
18 G8 Laissac France
26 J5 Laisvall Sweden
26 K4 Laitaure *L* Sweden
29 J11 Laitila Finland
65 D6 Laiwu China
65 E6 Laixi China
71 E4 Laiya Philippines
59 H4 Laiyang China
65 C5 Laiyuan China
20 E3 Laize *R* France
65 D6 Laizhou Wan *B* China
133 C5 Laja, L Chile
131 B6 Laja, L. de Chile
133 D5 La Japonesa Argentina
131 A6 Laja, R Chile
106 E4 La Jara Colorado
70 E7 Lajar, Tg *C* Kalimantan
19 Q16 La Javie France
130 F9 Laje dos Santos *isld* Brazil
71 O8 Lajeni Indonesia
130 E10 Lajes Brazil
108 D6 Lajitas Texas
133 E2 Lajitas, Las Argentina
48 F6 Lajkovac Yugoslavia
102 G9 La Jolla California
119 N8 Lajord Sask
48 F3 Lajosmizse Hungary
124 F4 La Joya Mexico
106 D7 La Joya New Mexico
21 D7 La Jumellière France
128 F7 La Junta Bolivia
106 G4 La Junta Colorado
124 F3 La Junta Mexico
71 K9 Lakahembi Sumba Indonesia
26 J8 Lakasjö Sweden
26 M5 Lakaträsk Sweden
101 O5 Lake Idaho
94 B3 Lake Michigan
100 E6 Lake Oregon
113 F9 Lake Alfred Florida
119 N9 Lake Alma Sask
109 P5 Lake Arthur Louisiana
106 F8 Lake Arthur New Mexico
98 K5 Lake Benton Minnesota
143 C10 Lake Biddy W Australia
98 K1 Lake Bronson Minnesota
143 C9 Lake Brown W Australia
113 E7 Lake Butler Florida
143 C10 Lake Camm W Australia
109 O5 Lake Charles Louisiana
110 F6 Lake City Arkansas
100 E8 Lake City California
106 C3 Lake City Colorado
113 E7 Lake City Florida
99 M7 Lake City Iowa
94 B2 Lake City Michigan
99 O5 Lake City Minnesota
94 G4 Lake City Pennsylvania
112 H4 Lake City S Carolina
98 J4 Lake City S Dakota
94 C10 Lake City Tennessee
144 C5 Lake Coleridge New Zealand
100 J8 Lake Cr Nevada
99 M5 Lake Crystal Minnesota
99 R5 Lake Delton Wisconsin
118 F5 Lake Eliza Alberta
138 D2 Lake Eyre Basin S Australia
99 L6 Lakefield Minnesota
121 M8 Lakefield Ontario
141 G2 Lakefield Queensland
99 T7 Lake Forest Illinois
99 S7 Lake Geneva Wisconsin
106 E3 Lake George Colorado
95 O3 Lake George New York
115 N5 Lake Harbour N W Terr
101 U8 Lake Hattie Res Wyoming
103 K7 Lake Havasu City Arizona
102 F7 Lake Hughes California
95 N6 Lakehurst New Jersey
109 M6 Lake Jackson Texas
142 C10 Lake King W Australia
143 C10 Lake King W Australia
112 D6 Lakeland Georgia
119 N6 Lake Lenore Sask
99 S2 Lake Linden Michigan
117 P10 Lake Louise Alberta
137 R5 Lakemba *isld* Fiji
99 N6 Lake Mills Iowa
94 G5 Lake Milton Ohio
116 L5 Lake Minchumina Alaska
95 S1 Lake Moxie Maine
140 E5 Lake Nash N Terr Aust
37 F5 Laken Berg *mt* W Germany/Czech
9 G3 Lakenheath England
94 B4 Lake Odessa Michigan
99 M1 Lake of the Woods *L* Ontario
94 D4 Lake Orion Michigan
100 C4 Lake Oswego Oregon
107 Q5 Lake O' The Cherokees *L* Oklahoma
109 N3 Lake O'The Pines *L* Texas
101 P5 Lake Outlet Wyoming
144 B5 Lake Paringa New Zealand
113 G11 Lake Park Florida
113 D7 Lake Park Georgia
99 L6 Lake Park Iowa
113 F10 Lake Placid Florida
95 O2 Lake Placid New York
102 B2 Lakeport California
113 F11 Lakeport Florida
94 E3 Lakeport Michigan
98 J5 Lake Preston S Dakota
111 E9 Lake Providence Louisiana
144 C6 Lake Pukaki New Zealand
100 F9 Lake Range *mts* Nevada
115 L7 Lake River Ontario
139 J7 Lakes Entrance Victoria
102 E4 Lakeshore California
103 P7 Lakeside Arizona
102 H9 Lakeside California
98 D7 Lakeside Nebraska
101 N8 Lakeside Utah
120 F5 Lake Superior Prov. Park Ontario
144 C5 Lake Tekapo New Zealand
101 O8 Laketown Utah
121 M7 Lake Traverse Ontario
106 C9 Lake Valley New Mexico
118 L8 Lake Valley Sask
109 J5 Lake Victor Texas
99 L7 Lake View Iowa
94 B3 Lakeview Michigan
101 O5 Lakeview Montana
100 E7 Lakeview Oregon
112 H3 Lake View S Carolina
109 N9 Lakeview Texas
111 E8 Lake Village Arkansas
95 O5 Lakeville Connecticut
94 A5 Lakeville Indiana
99 N5 Lakeville Minnesota
94 K4 Lakeville New York
143 D7 Lake Violet W Australia
113 F10 Lake Wales Florida
98 G2 Lake Williams N Dakota
95 N6 Lakewood New Jersey
106 F9 Lakewood New Mexico
94 H4 Lakewood New York
94 F5 Lakewood Ohio
113 G11 Lake Worth Florida
52 D4 Lakhdenpokh'ya U.S.S.R.
74 J5 Lakhimpur India
80 B6 Lakhish Israel
80 C7 Lakhish Israel
80 C7 Lakhish *R* Israel
74 C7 Lakhpat India
107 J4 Lakin Kansas
54 L1 Lakinskiy U.S.S.R.
74 D2 Lakki Pakistan
28 A6 Lakoik Denmark
46 F8 Lakonikós Kólpos *B* Greece
71 O9 Lakor *isld* Indonesia
99 M6 Lakota Iowa
85 C7 Lakota Ivory Coast
98 H1 Lakota N Dakota
68 G3 Lak Sao Laos
26 P1 Lakse Fjord *inlet* Norway
26 O1 Lakselv Norway
26 F6 Laksfors Norway
76 A5 Lakshadweep *islds terr* India
71 F7 Lala Mindanao Philippines
88 C8 Lala Zambia
87 B7 Lalama Angola
47 H3 Lâlapaşa Turkey
86 B5 Lalare Gabon
87 G8 Lalaúa Mozambique
18 G8 Lalbenque France
77 E5 Lāleh Zar, Kūh-e *mt* Iran
33 Q5 Lalendorf E Germany
70 F5 Lalereh, Tg *C* Sulawesi
77 A3 Lāli Iran
128 B4 La Libertad Ecuador
125 O9 La Libertad Guatemala
133 C4 La Ligua Chile
71 H6 Lalimbuë Sulawesi
65 G2 Lalin China
16 B2 Lalin Spain
18 F8 Lalinde France
71 K10 Lalindi Sumba Indonesia
70 G6 Lalindu *R* Sulawesi
65 G2 Lalin He *R* China
74 H6 Lalitpur India
19 P15 Lalley France
70 G7 Laloa Sulawesi
118 H2 La Loche West Sask
71 A2 Laloda Halmahera Indonesia
52 G4 Lal'sk U.S.S.R.
124 H6 La Luz Mexico
46 C3 Lalzës, Gji i *B* Albania
37 P5 Lam W Germany
52 E6 Lama *R* U.S.S.R.
128 D3 La Macarena Colombia
43 C7 La Maddalena Sardinia
106 D5 La Madera New Mexico
65 D4 Lamadong China
124 J4 Lamadrid Mexico
70 E2 Lamag Sabah
68 C5 Lamaing Burma
85 E7 Lama-Kara Togo
71 L9 Lamakera Indonesia
115 M8 La Malbaie Quebec
123 R7 Lamaline Nfld
45 J3 Lama Mocogno Italy
124 H5 La Mancha Mexico
17 F5 La Mancha *reg* Spain
125 M4 La Mansión Costa Rica
110 C6 Lamar Arkansas
106 H3 Lamar Colorado
110 B4 Lamar Missouri
98 E9 Lamar Nebraska
107 O6 Lamar Oklahoma
112 G3 Lamar S Carolina
101 P5 Lamar *R* Wyoming
40 C1 Lamarche France
40 A2 Lamargelle France
133 D5 Lamarque Argentina
109 N6 La Marque Texas
122 B6 Lamartine Quebec
125 L2 La Masica Honduras
19 N15 Lamastre France
126 G4 La Maya Cuba
18 D4 Lamballe France
86 B6 Lambarene Gabon
130 F7 Lambari Brazil
137 Q5 Lambasa Vanua Levu Fiji
70 G7 Lambasina *isld* Sulawesi
28 O9 Lamba Vig *inlet* Faeroes
128 B5 Lambayeque *dep* Peru
14 E3 Lambay I Irish Rep
9 G5 Lamberhurst England
112 F6 Lambert Georgia
111 F7 Lambert Mississippi
98 B2 Lambert Montana
142 B5 Lambert, C W Australia
146 C5 Lambert Gl Antarctica
99 L5 Lamberton Minnesota
87 C12 Lamberts B S Africa
95 N6 Lambertville New Jersey
19 O17 Lambesc France
120 J10 Lambeth Ontario
73 Q6 Lambi *isld* Burma
46 E7 Lámbia Greece
9 E5 Lambourn England
36 E5 Lambrecht W Germany
41 K7 Lambro *R* Italy
94 G10 Lambsburg Virginia
14 A5 Lambs Hd Irish Rep
36 E4 Lambsheim W Germany
121 T7 Lambton Quebec
114 G3 Lambton, C N W Terr
68 F5 Lam Chi *R* Thailand
68 G5 Lam Dom Noi *R* Thailand
101 T4 Lame Deer Montana
16 B3 Lamego Portugal
21 C6 La Meilleraye-de-Bret France
21 G7 La Membrolle France
21 E7 La Ménitre France
127 N4 Lamentin Guadeloupe W I
122 H6 Lameque New Brunswick
122 H6 Lamèque, Ile New Brunswick
133 D3 La Merced Argentina
138 F6 Lameroo S Australia
102 G9 La Mesa California
106 D9 La Mesa New Mexico
108 F3 Lamesa Texas
43 F7 La Meta *mt* Italy
46 E6 Lamia Greece
127 K10 La Miel Venezuela
71 G7 Lamigan Pt Mindanao Philippines
15 E5 Lamington Scotland
124 D3 La Misa Mexico
71 F7 Lamitan Philippines
109 J4 Lamkin Texas
71 C3 Lamlam Indonesia
15 C5 Lamlash Scotland
144 B6 Lammerlaw Range New Zealand
141 G5 Lammermoor Queensland
15 F5 Lammermuir Hills Scotland
25 F7 Lammersdorf W Germany
69 B10 Lammeulo Sumatra
27 G14 Lammhult Sweden
29 L10 Lammi Finland
20 G5 Lamnay France
21 B7 La Moëre France
99 R8 La Moille Illinois
103 J1 Lamoille Nevada
95 P2 Lamoille *R* Vermont
110 F1 La Moine *R* Illinois
100 G2 Lamona Washington
71 E3 Lamon B Luzon Philippines
42 D4 Lamone *R* Italy
70 O9 Lamongan Java
110 C1 Lamoni Iowa
118 E5 Lamont Alberta
102 F6 Lamont California
113 D7 Lamont Florida
101 O6 Lamont Idaho
99 P7 Lamont Iowa
107 N5 Lamont Oklahoma
101 S7 Lamont Wyoming
124 G3 La Morita Mexico
19 P14 La Morte France
22 J4 Lamorteau Belgium
21 E9 La Mothe St. Hérayé France
121 M4 La Motte Quebec
21 J6 Lamotte-Beuvron France
19 P15 La Motte d'Aveillans France
19 P13 La Motte-Servolex France
98 H3 La Moure N Dakota
68 F4 Lam Pao Res Thailand
109 J4 Lampasas Texas
109 K5 Lampasas *R* Texas
125 K4 Lampazos Mexico
36 E4 Lampertheim W Germany
33 T10 Lampërtswalde E Germany
8 B3 Lampeter Wales
8 B4 Lamphey Wales
47 F5 Lampinoú Greece
43 E13 Lampione *isld* Italy
68 F5 Lam Plai *R* Thailand
119 P9 Lampman Sask
45 J4 Lamporecchio Italy
9 F3 Lamport England
52 F2 Lampozhnya U.S.S.R.
29 O6 Lämpsä Finland
70 D5 Lampung Kalimantan
70 K8 Lampung Teluk *B* Sumatra
68 G5 Lam Si Bai *R* Thailand
32 M9 Lamspringe W Germany
32 K5 Lamstedt W Germany
68 B3 Lamu Burma
86 H6 Lamu Kenya
19 P15 La Mure France
19 N12 Lamure-sur-Azergues France
106 E6 Lamy New Mexico
42 D2 Lana Italy
141 G5 Lana Queensland
135 S3 Lanai *isld* Hawaiian Is
135 S3 Lanai City Hawaiian Is
135 S3 Lanaihale *peak* Hawaiian Is
22 K2 Lanaken Belgium
74 H1 Lanak Pass Kashmir/Xizang Zizhiqu
71 G7 Lanao *L* Mindanao Philippines
113 C8 Lanark Florida
99 R7 Lanark Illinois
121 O7 Lanark Ontario
12 E2 Lanark Scotland
Lanark *co see* Strathclyde *reg*
70 E2 Lanas Sabah
68 C7 Lanbi Kyun *isld* Burma
71 F6 Lanboyan Pt Mindanao Philippines
68 D1 Lancang China
Lancang Jiang *R see* Mekong
13 F6 Lancashire *co* England
102 F7 Lancaster California
13 F5 Lancaster England
110 M4 Lancaster Kentucky
98 K1 Lancaster Minnesota
110 D1 Lancaster Missouri
122 F8 Lancaster New Brunswick
95 Q2 Lancaster New Hampshire
94 J4 Lancaster New York
94 E7 Lancaster Ohio
121 Q7 Lancaster Ontario
95 L6 Lancaster Pennsylvania
112 G3 Lancaster S Carolina
109 L3 Lancaster Texas
95 L9 Lancaster Virginia
99 Q7 Lancaster Wisconsin
115 L3 Lancaster Sd N W Terr
98 B6 Lance Cr Wyoming
143 B9 Lancelin W Australia
143 B9 Lancelin I W Australia
143 E7 Lancelot, Mt W Australia
19 O16 Lance, Mt. de la France
118 J8 Lancer Sask
20 H1 Lanchères France
13 G4 Lanchester England
66 C5 Lan-chia Ts'o *L* China
48 J2 Lanchin U.S.S.R.
Lanchow *see* Lanzhou
42 F6 Lanciano Italy
94 C10 Lancing Tennessee
19 O17 Lançon France
31 N5 Łańcut Poland
27 D11 Land *reg* Norway
98 F1 Landa N Dakota
32 K10 Landau Hessen W Germany
36 E5 Landau Rheinland-Pfalz W Germany
20 C5 Landéan France
41 N3 Landeck Austria
26 G4 Landegode *isld* Norway
20 C4 Landelles-et-Coupigny France
22 J2 Landen Belgium
101 R7 Lander Wyoming
140 C5 Lander *R* N Terr Aust
18 C4 Landerneau France
140 B5 Lander R N Terr Aust
27 F14 Landeryd Sweden
94 H8 Landes W Virginia
18 D5 Landes de Lanvaux *reg* France
18 E8 Landes, Les *reg* France
28 G7 Landet Denmark
17 G5 Landete Spain
68 A6 Landfall I Andaman Is
133 C8 Landfall, I Chile
9 E6 Landford England
146 J9 Land Glacier Antarctica
33 S5 Landgraben *R* E Germany
32 J5 Land Hadeln W Germany
74 D1 Landi Khana Pakistan
77 H4 Landi Md. Amin Khan Afghanistan
119 U3 Landing L Manitoba
112 G2 Landis N Carolina
118 J6 Landis Sask
18 C4 Landivisiau France
20 C5 Landivy France
112 F3 Lando S Carolina
99 R3 Land O Lakes Wisconsin
143 B7 Landor W Australia
26 G8 Landösjön *L* Sweden
22 F3 Landrecies France
22 J5 Landres Ardennes France
22 K5 Landres Meurthe-et-Moselle France
121 N4 Landrienne Quebec
142 F4 Landrigan Cliffs W Australia
38 F8 Landro Italy
112 E2 Landrum S Carolina
40 E6 Landry France
26 M5 Landså Sweden
Landsberg *see* Gorzów Wielkopolski
33 Q9 Landsberg E Germany
41 N1 Landsberg W Germany
141 L7 Landsborough Queensland
144 B5 Landsborough *R* New Zealand
141 G5 Landsborough *R* Queensland
9 F7 Land's End England
114 G2 Lands End *C* N W Terr
37 N6 Landshut W Germany
28 K5 Landskrona Sweden
36 D5 Landstuhl W Germany
101 R2 Landusky Montana
32 L10 Landwehrhagen W Germany
37 N3 Landwüst E Germany
112 H4 Lane S Carolina
98 H5 Lane S Dakota
109 L6 Lane City Texas
22 G3 Laneffe Belgium
99 P6 Lanesboro Minnesota
111 L9 Lanett Alabama
22 D5 Laneuville-Roy France
22 J5 Laneuville-sur-Meuse France
Lanfeng *see* Lankao
118 G7 Lanfine Alberta
119 N9 Lang Sask
28 F6 Langå Denmark
66 C5 La'nga Co *L* China
16 E3 Langa de Duero Spain
47 F4 Langadhás Greece
46 E7 Langádhia Greece
86 G4 Langana, L Ethiopia
71 H7 Langara Sulawesi
117 G8 Langara I Br Columbia
77 A1 Langarūd Iran
119 P8 Langbank Sask
67 B6 Lang Chanh Vietnam
Lang-ch'u Ho *see* Sutlej
111 L9 Langdale Alabama
118 D8 Langdon Alberta
107 M4 Langdon Kansas
98 H1 Langdon N Dakota
13 F4 Langdon Beck England
18 H7 Langeac France
21 F7 Langeais France
89 A9 Langeberg *mts* S Africa
89 C7 Langebergen *mts* S Africa
19 P18 L'Ange, Col de France
28 F7 Langeland *isld* Denmark
29 L10 Längelmäki Finland
29 L10 Längelmävesi *L* Finland
33 M9 Langelsheim W Germany
22 D2 Langemark Belgium
36 F4 Langen Hessen W Germany
32 J5 Langen W Germany
37 P2 Langenau E Germany
37 J7 Langenau W Germany
37 N2 Langenberg Gera W Germany
32 F10 Langenberg W Germany
37 M4 Langenbruck W Germany
119 Q8 Langenburg Sask
36 H5 Langenburg W Germany
26 H2 Langenes *lt ho* Norway
28 B7 Langeness *isld* W Germany
32 L8 Langenhagen W Germany
28 B7 Langenhorn W Germany
37 O6 Langenisarhofen W Germany
38 N5 Langenlois Austria
36 D4 Langenlonsheim W Germany
33 S9 Langennaundorf E Germany
36 G3 Langenselbold W Germany
37 J5 Langensteinach W Germany
36 F6 Langensteinbach W Germany
40 G3 Langenthal Switzerland
38 N6 Langenwang Austria
37 K5 Langenzenn W Germany
32 F5 Langeoog W Germany
28 E2 Lange-Rak *inlet* Denmark
28 F6 Langeskov Denmark
28 H5 Langesø *L* Denmark
27 D12 Langesund Norway
27 D13 Langesundsfjord *inlet* Norway

26 M7 Lövånger Sweden
48 E3 Lovasberény Hungary
48 D3 Lovászpatona Hungary
54 B1 Lovat' R U.S.S.R.
26 K6 Lövberg Sweden
26 H8 Lövberga Sweden
42 J6 Lovćen mt Yugoslavia
28 G5 Løve Denmark
119 N5 Love Sask
68 F6 Lovea Cambodia
47 G1 Lovech Bulgaria
109 O9 Love Field Airport Texas
28 C3 Løvel Denmark
109 M4 Lovelady Texas
98 A9 Loveland Colorado
110 M2 Loveland Ohio
106 E2 Loveland Pass Colorado
101 R5 Lovell Wyoming
94 C2 Lovells Michigan
100 G9 Lovelock Nevada
103 O1 Lovenia, Mt Utah
95 L7 Love Point Maryland
42 C3 Lovere Italy
118 H7 Loverna Sask
140 C6 Loves Creek N Terr Aust
113 D7 Lovett Florida
26 F10 Lövhögen Sweden
26 N4 Lovikka Sweden
106 F9 Loving New Mexico
109 J2 Loving Texas
94 J9 Lovingston Virginia
99 S10 Lovington Illinois
106 G9 Lovington New Mexico
16 B3 Lovios Spain
29 M11 Lovisa Finland
26 J5 Lövnäs Sweden
28 C3 Lovns Bredning B Denmark
30 H5 Lovosice Czechoslovakia
52 E1 Lovozero U.S.S.R.
45 P1 Lovre čica Yugoslavia
48 F5 Lovrin Romania
26 H7 Lövsjön Sweden
26 F5 Lovunden isld Norway
103 L1 Low Utah
86 E6 Lowa Zaïre
144 B6 Lowburn New Zealand
120 K4 Low Bush River Ontario
115 L5 Low, C N W Terr
99 P8 Lowden Iowa
100 E6 Low Desert Oregon
9 F1 Lowdham England
103 P10 Lowell Arizona
110 B5 Lowell Arkansas
100 K3 Lowell Idaho
99 T8 Lowell Indiana
95 Q4 Lowell Massachusetts
94 B4 Lowell Michigan
94 F7 Lowell Ohio
100 C6 Lowell Oregon
100 J6 Lowell, L Idaho
33 S7 Löwenberg E Germany
28 C7 Löwenstedt W Germany
36 G5 Löwenstein W Germany
117 P11 Lower Arrow L Br Col
98 G5 Lower Brule S Dakota
101 P5 Lower Falls Wyoming
119 V8 Lower Ft.Garry Manitoba
103 L6 Lower Granite Gorge Arizona
145 G4 Lower Hutt New Zealand
123 U6 Lower Island Cove Nfld
100 D8 Lower Klamath L California
102 B3 Lower L California
117 F5 Lower Laberge Yukon Terr
115 K4 Lower Macdougall L N W Terr
122 G6 Lower Neguac New Brunswick
122 G10 Lower Ohio Nova Scotia
135 T3 Lower Paia Hawaiian Is
117 J6 Lower Post Br Columbia
99 L2 Lower Red L Minnesota
101 O5 Lower Red Rock L Montana
115 N5 Lower Savage Is N W Terr
122 G10 Lower West Pubnico Nova Scotia
15 F1 Lower Whitehall Scotland
110 H5 Lowes Kentucky
9 H3 Lowestoft England
139 H8 Low Head Tasmania
13 G2 Lowick England
13 E5 Lowick Br England
31 M3 Łowicz Poland
141 H3 Low Is Queensland
110 K5 Lowman Idaho
111 K9 Lowndesboro Alabama
83 M9 Low Pt Christmas I Indian Oc
139 H9 Low Rocky Pt Tasmania
110 C3 Lowry City Missouri
87 H10 Lowry, Iles Madagascar
112 F3 Lowrys S Carolina
13 F4 Lowther England
113 K3 Lowther I N W Terr
121 P9 Lowville New York
15 P9 Loxicha Mexico
111 J11 Loxley Alabama
138 F5 Loxton S Australia
99 Q5 Loyal Wisconsin
121 F7 Loyalist Alberta
94 D10 Loyall Kentucky
95 L5 Loyalsock Cr Pennsylvania
102 D2 Loyalton California
98 G4 Loyalton S Dakota
Loyang see Luoyang
137 O6 Loyauté, Is Pacific Oc
54 B5 Loyev U.S.S.R.
52 G4 Loyma U.S.S.R.
52 H5 Loyno U.S.S.R.
47 H2 Lozarevo Bulgaria
18 H8 Lozère dep France
18 H8 Lozère, Mt France
48 E6 Loznica Yugoslavia
54 H8 Lozovaya U.S.S.R.
50 F2 Lozva R U.S.S.R.
86 C5 Lua R Zaïre
87 D8 Luacano Angola
87 D7 Luachimo Angola
69 D13 Luahasibuka Indonesia
88 F10 Luala R Mozambique
86 E6 Lualaba R Zaïre
86 E6 Luama R Zaïre
87 F8 Luambe Zambia
87 D9 Luampa Zambia
87 D8 Luan Angola
69 G5 Lu'an China
127 J2 Luana Pt Jamaica
68 F2 Luan Chau Vietnam
65 C6 Luancheng China
65 C5 Luancheng China
65 B8 Luanchuan China
87 B8 Luanda Angola
87 C8 Luando R Angola
71 O9 Luang isld Indonesia
69 D8 Luanganga R Angola
69 D8 Luang, Khao mt Thailand
68 F3 Luang Prabang Laos
69 E9 Luang, Thale L Thailand
87 C7 Luangue R Angola
88 C8 Luangwa R Zambia
65 D4 Luan He R China
65 D5 Luannan China
88 B9 Luano Zambia
65 D4 Luanping China
88 B8 Luanshya Zambia
65 D5 Luan Xian China
88 B7 Luapula Zambia
88 B8 Luapula R Zaïre
16 C1 Luarca Spain
69 C4 Luar, D L Kalimantan
27 D8 Luashi Zaïre
87 F8 Luatize R Mozambique
125 P9 Lubaantum Belize
31 O5 Lubaczów Poland
87 C7 Lubalo Angola
31 J4 Lubań Poland
52 C6 Lubāna U.S.S.R.
52 C6 Lubānasezers L U.S.S.R.
71 E4 Lubang Philippines
82 D6 Lubango Angola
88 C7 Lubansenshi R Zambia
33 Q8 Lübars E Germany
31 O4 Lubartów Poland
31 M2 Lubawa Poland
32 J8 Lübbecke W Germany
33 T9 Lübben E Germany
33 T9 Lübbenau E Germany
108 F2 Lubbock Texas
139 G6 Lubeck Victoria
33 N5 Lübeck W Germany
33 O4 Lübecker Bucht W Germany
86 D6 Lubefu Zaïre
37 P3 Lubenec Czechoslovakia
55 B5 Lubenka U.S.S.R.
88 B2 Lubero Zaïre
19 O17 Lubéron, Montagne du mts France
88 C8 Lubi R Zambia
71 E5 Lubic isld Philippines
118 B2 Lubicon L Alberta
31 J2 Lubie, Jezioro L Poland
31 L3 Lubień Poland
87 D7 Lubilash R Zaïre
31 J4 Lubiń Poland
31 O4 Lublin Poland
99 Q4 Lublin Wisconsin
31 L5 Lubliniec Poland
33 T4 Lubmin E Germany
72 E5 Lubnaig, L Scotland
15 D4 Lubny U.S.S.R.
54 D6 Lubok Anto Sarawak
70 B4 Lubosalma U.S.S.R.
29 P8 Lubrín Spain
17 F7 Lubsko Poland
31 H4 Lübtheen E Germany
33 O6 Lubuagan Luzon Philippines
71 E2 Lubudi Zaïre
87 E8 Lubudi R Zaïre
87 D7 Lubukbatang Sumatra
70 K8 Lubukbertubung Sumatra
69 F12 Lubuklinggau Sumatra
69 F14 Lubukpakam Sumatra
69 D11 Lubuksikaping Sumatra
69 E12 Lubule R Zaïre
88 B6 Lubumbashi Zaïre
87 E8 Lubutu Zaïre
86 E6 Lubutu Zaïre
37 N3 Lučany Czechoslovakia
33 Q6 Lübz E Germany
20 E3 Luc France
87 C7 Lucala Angola
14 E3 Lucan Irish Rep
120 J9 Lucan Ontario
68 G1 Luc An Chau Vietnam
116 R6 Lucania, Mt Yukon Terr
43 G8 Lucano, Appennino mts Italy
129 G6 Lucas Brazil
99 N8 Lucas Iowa
107 M2 Lucas Kansas
142 G5 Lucas, L W Australia
126 E1 Lucaya Grand Bahama I
21 H7 Luçay le Mâle France
71 E3 Lucban Luzon Philippines
45 J4 Lucca Italy
98 F1 Lucca N Dakota
129 G3 Luce R Suriname
127 H1 Lucea Jamaica
15 D6 Luce B Scotland
111 H11 Lucedale Mississippi
130 E7 Lucélia Brazil
71 E4 Lucena Philippines
17 G4 Lucena del Cid Spain
16 E7 Lucena, Sa. de mts Spain
31 K7 Lučenec Czechoslovakia
43 G7 Lucera Italy
Lucerne see Luzern
102 B2 Lucerne California
99 N9 Lucerne Missouri
100 E1 Lucerne Washington
101 R6 Lucerne Wyoming
102 H7 Lucerne L California
102 H7 Lucerne Valley California
124 F2 Lucero Mexico
107 P3 Lucerville Quebec
65 B6 Lucheng China
67 B4 Lucheng China
88 E9 Luchenza Malawi
21 F6 Luché-Pringé France
111 F11 Lucher Louisiana
54 B2 Luchesa R U.S.S.R.
20 K1 Lucheux France
33 O7 Lüchow W Germany
68 K1 Luchuan China
20 K2 Luchy France
102 C5 Lucia California
122 J6 Lucie, L Quebec
100 J4 Lucile Idaho
16 C2 Lucillo Spain
101 M8 Lucin Utah
94 H5 Lucinda Pennsylvania
141 H4 Lucinda Queensland
138 F6 Lucindale S Australia
87 B8 Lucira Angola
99 O4 Luck Wisconsin
37 N1 Lucka E Germany
33 T9 Luckau E Germany
33 S8 Luckenwalde E Germany
143 E8 Luck, Mt W Australia
74 J5 Lucknow India
120 J9 Lucknow Ontario
140 F6 Lucknow Queensland
118 K8 Lucky Lake Sask
118 F9 Lucky Peak Res Idaho
118 F9 Lucky Strike Alberta
21 C9 Luçon France
45 O6 Luco ne Marsi Italy
108 A5 Lucero Mexico
22 G4 Lucquy France
126 G4 Lucrecia, C Cuba
87 D8 Lucusse Angola
106 E7 Lucy New Mexico
140 D5 Lucy Creek N Terr Aust
140 C6 Lucy, Mt N Terr Aust
59 H4 Lüda China
13 F6 Ludborough England
98 H3 Ludden N Dakota
107 K2 Ludell Kansas
32 G10 Lüdenscheid W Germany
37 O4 Lüderitz E Germany
87 C11 Lüderitz Namibia
120 K7 Ludgate Ontario
9 E5 Ludgershall England
74 F3 Ludhiana India
32 F9 Lüdinghausen W Germany
99 U6 Ludington Michigan
103 H7 Ludlow California
106 F4 Ludlow Colorado
8 D3 Ludlow England
99 R8 Ludlow Illinois
122 F7 Ludlow New Brunswick
94 J5 Ludlow Pennsylvania
98 C4 Ludlow S Dakota
95 P3 Ludlow Vermont
47 H1 Ludogorie Bulgaria
52 C5 Ludoni U.S.S.R.
112 F6 Ludowici Georgia
36 E5 Ludwigshöhe W Germany
48 J4 Luduş Romania
27 H11 Ludvika Sweden
36 G6 Ludwigsburg W Germany
36 G6 Ludwigsburg W Germany
37 M3 Ludwigschorgast W Germany
36 E5 Ludwigshafen W Germany
37 N2 Ludwigs Kanal canal W Germany
33 O6 Ludwigslust E Germany
37 L3 Ludwigsstadt W Germany
52 C6 Ludza U.S.S.R.
86 D6 Luebo Zaïre
109 H3 Lueders Texas
86 E6 Lueki Zaïre
87 C8 Luena Angola
87 D8 Luena R Angola
88 D10 Luenha R Mozambique
128 F2 Luepa Venezuela
87 D7 Lueta Zaïre
87 D9 Lueti R Zambia
85 F5 Lüeyang China
67 F5 Lufeng China
111 B10 Lufkin Texas
88 C6 Lufubu R Zambia
88 B10 Lufya R Zambia
48 F6 Lug R Yugoslavia
52 C5 Luga U.S.S.R.
52 C5 Luga R U.S.S.R.
88 B4 Lugamba Zaïre
41 J5 Lugano Switzerland
42 B3 Lugano, L. di Italy
Lugansk see Voroshilovgrad
126 F4 Lugareño Cuba
32 K9 Lügde W Germany
88 F10 Lugela Mozambique
88 F10 Lugela R Mozambique
88 F8 Lugenda R Mozambique
144 B6 Luggate New Zealand
8 D3 Lugg, R England
Lugh Ferrandi see Ganane
14 E4 Lugnacuilla mt Irish Rep
41 K4 Lugnezer Tal Switzerland
45 L3 Lugo Italy
16 B1 Lugo Spain
16 B1 Lugo prov Spain
48 G5 Lugoj Romania
55 E1 Lugovoy U.S.S.R.
12 D2 Lugton Scotland
86 E6 Lugulu R Zaïre
71 E8 Lugus isld Philippines
70 G6 Luha isld Celebes
29 M10 Luhanka Finland
72 E5 Luhayyah, Al N Yemen
67 F1 Luhe China
37 N4 Luhe W Germany
32 M6 Luhe R W Germany
65 D1 Luhin Sum China
33 T4 Lühmannsdorf E Germany
87 C7 Lui R Angola
88 D10 Luia R Mozambique
87 D9 Luiana Angola
Luichow Pen see Leizhou Bandao
Luik see Liège
86 D6 Luilaka R Zaïre
20 K4 Luine R France
15 C4 Luing isld Scotland
42 B2 Luino Italy
29 N4 Luira R Finland
124 E4 Luis Mexico
130 E10 Luis Alves Brazil
130 H9 Luis Gomes Brazil
87 E8 Luishia Zaïre
124 H5 Luis Moya Mexico
146 D10 Luitpold Coast Antarctica
87 D7 Luiza Zaïre
88 A5 Luizi R Zaïre
133 D4 Lujan Argentina
131 F5 Luján R Argentina
67 F1 Lujiang China
67 C5 Lujing China
37 P3 Luka Czechoslovakia
87 E8 Lukafu Zaïre
88 A8 Lukanga R Zambia
88 A8 Lukanga Sw Zambia
143 B7 Luke, Mt W Australia
86 C6 Lukenie R Zaïre
52 F6 Lukh U.S.S.R.
54 L2 Lukhovitsy U.S.S.R.
41 J4 Lukmanier Pass Switzerland
86 C6 Lukolela Zaïre
67 D3 Lukou China
46 D3 Lukova Yugoslavia
47 G1 Lukovit Bulgaria
31 N4 Łuków Poland
52 F6 Lukoyanov U.S.S.R.
21 B6 Lukula Zaïre
87 G7 Lukuledi R Tanzania
87 D8 Lukulu Zambia
88 D7 Lukulu R Zambia
87 G7 Lukumburu Tanzania
69 C10 Lukup Sumatra
88 D8 Lukuzye R Zambia
112 D3 Lula Georgia
111 F7 Lula Mississippi
26 M6 Luleå Sweden
26 M6 Lule älv R Sweden
47 J3 Lüleburgaz Turkey
87 D8 Lulembe R Angola
67 A4 Luliang China
65 B6 Lüliang Shan ra China
111 F12 Luling Louisiana
109 K6 Luling Texas
65 D5 Lulong China
65 D5 Lulonga R Zaïre
13 F7 Lulua R Zaïre
86 D7 Lulua R Zaïre
Luluabourg see Kananga
8 D6 Lulworth Cove England
143 C7 Lulworth, Mt W Australia
70 O10 Lumadjang Java
70 D2 Lumaku mt Sabah
87 D8 Lumbala Angola
112 H3 Lumber R N Carolina
112 E6 Lumber City Georgia
94 J6 Lumber City Pennsylvania
94 G7 Lumberport W Virginia
111 G10 Lumberton Mississippi
112 H3 Lumberton N Carolina
106 D5 Lumberton New Mexico
18 E10 Lumbier Spain
70 E2 Lumbis Kalimantan
88 G8 Lumbo Mozambique
52 F1 Lumbovka U.S.S.R.
16 C4 Lumbrales Spain
22 C2 Lumbres France
28 E6 Lumby Denmark
75 P6 Lumding India
27 F5 Lumijoki Finland
87 F8 Lumimba R Zambia
22 J2 Lummen Belgium
29 H11 Lumparland Finland
111 M9 Lumpkin Georgia
28 H5 Lumsås Denmark
144 B6 Lumsden New Zealand
123 T4 Lumsden Nfld
119 N8 Lumsden Sask
15 F3 Lumsden Scotland
70 G4 Lumu Sulawesi
69 E10 Lumut Malaysia
70 D5 Lumut, Bt mt Kalimantan
71 E2 Luna Luzon Philippines
106 B8 Luna New Mexico
131 G2 Luna, L Argentina
67 A4 Lunan China
15 F4 Lunan B Scotland
74 E7 Lunavada India
17 L10 Lund Br Columbia
28 D5 Lund Denmark
103 J3 Lund Nevada
27 F16 Lund Sweden
103 L3 Lund Utah
27 J13 Lunda Sweden
27 J13 Lunda Chishinga Zambia
28 K5 Lundåkrabukten B Sweden
120 F3 Lundar Manitoba
88 D7 Lundazi Zambia
88 B8 Lundazi R Zambia
118 C9 Lundbreck Alberta
28 H6 Lundby Denmark
28 E5 Lunde Denmark
28 F6 Lundeborg Denmark
28 C6 Lunderskov Denmark
27 B13 Lunde-Vatn L Norway
89 G3 Lundi R Zimbabwe
28 C3 Lundø Denmark
28 D3 Lundsgaard Denmark
8 B5 Lundy isld England
33 M6 Lüne W Germany
32 J6 Lüne R W Germany
33 N6 Lüneburg W Germany
33 M6 Lüneburger Heide W Germany
32 M6 Lüneburger Heide reg W Germany
18 H9 Lunel France
32 G9 Lünen W Germany
122 H9 Lunenburg Nova Scotia
95 O2 Lunenburg Vermont
20 K5 Luneray France
22 H5 Lunéville France
41 L3 Lüner See L Austria
19 K4 Lunéville France
88 B7 Lunga R Zambia
68 H1 Lung-chou China
66 C5 Lunggar China
44 G3 Lungo Italy
26 H8 Lungsjön Sweden
27 G12 Lungsund Sweden
88 C6 Lungu Zambia
87 C8 Lungue Bungo R Angola
102 F3 Luning Nevada
71 H9 Lunjuk Sumbawa Indonesia
15 G2 Lunna Scotland
32 F8 Lünne W Germany
85 B7 Lunsar Sierra Leone
88 B8 Lunsemfwa R Zambia
66 C3 Luntai China
38 M6 Lunz am See Austria
37 O2 Lunzenau E Germany
88 D7 Lunzi R Zambia
86 B6 Luobomo Congo
67 C4 Luocheng China
58 E4 Luochuan China
67 B4 Luodian China
67 D3 Luoding China
65 A7 Luo He R China
65 B7 Luo He R China
67 A1 Luojiang China
67 D5 Luojing China
67 B2 Luolong China
65 A7 Luonan China
26 M4 Luongastunturi mt Sweden
88 B7 Luongo R Zambia
67 B4 Luoning China
67 A4 Luoping China
67 D2 Luoqing Jiang R China
67 C4 Luorong China
67 D2 Luoshan China
67 E1 Luoshan China
67 E1 Luotian China
65 E1 Luotuobozi China
67 B1 Luowenba China
65 B7 Luoyang China
67 F3 Luoyuan China
86 B6 Luozi Zaïre
86 D6 Lupa R Tanzania
88 D8 Lupachi R Malawi
89 F2 Lupani R Zimbabwe
70 B4 Lupar R Sarawak
31 K1 Łupawa R Poland
37 M5 Lupburg W Germany
48 H5 Lupeni Romania
127 J5 Luperón Dom Rep
41 J1 Lupfen mt W Germany
87 G8 Lupilichi Mozambique
67 B3 Luping China
87 C8 Lupire Angola
54 B3 Lupolovo U.S.S.R.
71 G7 Lupon Mindanao Philippines
33 R10 Luppa E Germany
110 D3 Lupus Missouri
88 C5 Luque Zaïre
52 H4 Lup'ya R U.S.S.R.
130 B9 Luque Paraguay
107 M2 Luray Kansas
94 J8 Luray Virginia
112 E2 Lure, L N Carolina
19 P16 Lure, Mt de France
14 E2 Lurgan N Ireland
128 E7 Luribay Bolivia
128 C6 Lurín Peru
87 H8 Lurio Mozambique
26 F5 Lurøy Norway
19 P17 Lurs France
110 C6 Lurton Arkansas
21 J7 Lury-sur-Arnon France
88 B9 Lusaka Zambia
86 D6 Lusambo Zaïre
88 C8 Lusangazi R Zambia
21 B6 Lusanger France
117 P9 Luscar Alberta
118 H6 Luseland Sask
75 P7 Lushai Hills India
65 D6 Lu Shan mt China
58 F5 Lushi China
142 F3 Lush, Mt W Australia
88 G4 Lushoto Tanzania
67 F1 Lu Shui R China
65 E5 Lüshun China
67 G1 Lüsi China
70 N9 Lusi R Java
21 F9 Lusignan France
98 B7 Lusk Wyoming
75 P5 Lus-la-Croix Haute France
38 E8 Luson Italy
26 L4 Luspebryggan Sweden
15 D4 Luss Scotland
18 F6 Lussac les Châteaux France
21 H9 Lussac-les-Eglises France
12 C3 Lussa, L Scotland
129 H8 Lussanvira Brazil
78 J6 Lussuf, Al Iraq
141 J7 Lussvale Queensland
36 E5 Lustadt W Germany
41 L3 Lustenau Austria
37 J5 Lustenau W Germany
27 B10 Luster Norway
22 H3 Lustin Belgium
18 I3 Lustre Montana
101 U1 Lusignan see Ninghe
77 E3 Lut, Dasht-e des Iran
87 D8 Lutembo Angola
110 G4 Lutesville Missouri
109 N8 Luther Iowa
107 N6 Luther Oklahoma
108 G1 Lutie Texas
33 N4 Lütjenburg W Germany
9 F4 Luton England
40 E4 Lutry Switzerland
87 C7 Lutshima R Zaïre
32 M9 Lutter am Barenberge W Germany
37 M7 Lutterloh W Germany
9 E3 Lutterworth England
22 G3 Luttre Belgium
112 D1 Luttrell Tennessee
36 C1 Lüttringhausen W Germany
24 E5 Lutz Florida
113 E9 Lützelbourg France
36 C6 Lützelbourg France
36 C6 Lützelhouse France
33 Q10 Lützen E Germany
33 O8 Lützerath W Germany
143 B6 Lützow-Holm Bay Antarctica
146 A6 Lützow-Holmbukta Antarctica
29 N11 Luumäki Finland
71 H8 Luusua Finland
111 K10 Luverne Alabama
99 M7 Luverne Iowa
99 M6 Luverne Minnesota
98 J2 Luverne N Dakota
29 J10 Luvia Finland
26 K5 Luvos Sweden
52 E4 Luvozero U.S.S.R.
29 F7 Luvua R Zaïre
87 D8 Luwingu Zambia
88 E5 Luwegu R Tanzania
88 C8 Luwingu Zambia
71 B2 Luwuk isld Halmahera Indonesia
68 J1 Luwu China
71 H5 Luwuk Sulawesi
88 D7 Luwumbu R Zambia
111 J8 Luxapalila R Alabama
22 L4 Luxembourg Luxembourg
22 L4 Luxembourg, Gd. Duchy of Europe
99 P7 Luxemburg Iowa
40 D2 Luxeuil-les-Bains France
67 A4 Luxi China
67 C2 Luxi China
67 B2 Lu Xian China
84 J4 Luxor Egypt
21 G9 Luy R France
21 G7 Luynes France
18 E10 Luz France
52 G4 Luza U.S.S.R.
52 J2 Luza R Komi U.S.S.R.
20 K3 Luzarches France
18 F8 Luzech France
21 H8 Luzeret France
41 H3 Luzern Switzerland
94 C2 Luzerne Michigan
95 O3 Luzerne New York
67 C4 Luzhai China
67 A4 Luzhi China
67 B3 Luzhou China
130 F5 Luziânia Brazil
21 H7 Luzille-sur-Indre France
31 H6 Lužnice R Czechoslovakia
71 E2 Luzon Philippines
18 H6 Luzy France
45 J2 Luzzara Italy
48 J1 L'vov U.S.S.R.
88 B7 Lwela R Zambia
88 C8 Lwitikila R Zambia
31 J3 Lwówek Poland
31 J4 Lwówek Śląski Poland
52 E4 Lyadiny U.S.S.R.
48 L2 Lyadova R U.S.S.R.
147 Q7 Lyakhovskiye Os isld U.S.S.R.
144 A6 Lyall, Mt New Zealand
Lyallpur see Faisalabad
57 E5 Lyal'-Mikar U.S.S.R.
55 D2 Lyalya R U.S.S.R.
55 F1 Lyamin R U.S.S.R.
57 D4 Lyangar U.S.S.R.
52 D4 Lyaskelya U.S.S.R.
47 H1 Lyaskovets Bulgaria
106 C5 Lybrook New Mexico
15 E2 Lybster Scotland
28 C3 Lyby Denmark
106 H4 Lycan Colorado
33 S6 Lychen E Germany
52 D5 Lychkovo U.S.S.R.
47 K8 Lycia Turkey
Lyck see Ełk
26 K7 Lycksele Sweden
9 G6 Lydd England
Lydda see Lod
119 T3 Lyddal Manitoba
89 G5 Lydenburg S Africa
8 D3 Lydford England
8 B3 Lydham England
112 G3 Lydia S Carolina
119 V3 Lydiatt Manitoba
8 D4 Lydney England
8 B6 Lyd, R England
28 A5 Lydum Denmark
21 H7 Lye France
145 D4 Lyell New Zealand
140 B6 Lyell Brown, Mt N Terr Aust
117 H9 Lyell I Br Col
139 H8 Lyell, Mt Tasmania
111 L7 Lyerly Georgia
26 K2 Lyfjord Norway
109 K9 Lyford Texas
113 K9 Lyford Cay isld New Providence I Bahamas
27 B13 Lygna R Norway
95 L6 Lykens Pennsylvania
52 D5 Lykoshino U.S.S.R.
99 O6 Lyle Minnesota
100 D4 Lyle Washington
110 J6 Lyles Tennessee
119 Q9 Lyleton Manitoba
111 G11 Lyman Mississippi
107 O5 Lyman Oklahoma
112 E3 Lyman S Carolina
101 P8 Lyman Wyoming
117 O8 Lymburn Alberta
95 P3 Lyme New Hampshire
8 D6 Lyme B England
8 D6 Lyme Regis England
8 D6 Lyminge England
9 E6 Lymington England
31 M1 Łyna R Poland
28 H5 Lynæs Denmark
98 H7 Lynch Nebraska
94 D7 Lynchburg Ohio
110 K6 Lynchburg Tennessee
94 H9 Lynchburg Virginia
112 G3 Lynches R S Carolina
95 R2 Lynchville Maine
141 G4 Lynd Queensland
141 G3 Lynd R Queensland
28 H5 Lyndby Denmark
100 C1 Lynden Washington
115 E9 Lyndhurst England
144 C5 Lyndhurst New Zealand
141 G4 Lyndhurst Queensland
138 E4 Lyndhurst S Australia
107 P3 Lyndon Kansas
95 P2 Lyndon Vermont
143 B6 Lyndon W Australia
109 J5 Lyndon B. Johnson, L Texas
143 A6 Lyndon, R W Australia
94 J3 Lyndonville New York
95 P2 Lyndonville Vermont
28 A5 Lyne Denmark
13 E2 Lyne Scotland
28 F4 Lyngby Denmark
28 D4 Lyngbygd Å R Denmark
27 B13 Lyngdal Norway
28 H5 Lynge Denmark
26 L2 Lyngen Norway
26 L2 Lyngør Norway
27 D13 Lyngør Norway
28 A3 Lyngs Denmark
28 F2 Lyngså Denmark
26 F5 Lyngseidet Norway
26 L2 Lyngsfjord inlet Norway
142 D3 Lynher Reef W Australia
8 C5 Lynmouth England
111 J7 Lynn Alabama
94 C6 Lynn Indiana
95 R4 Lynn Massachusetts
101 M8 Lynn Utah
117 F6 Lynn Canal Alaska
103 M2 Lynndyl Utah
111 L11 Lynn Haven Florida
119 Q2 Lynn Lake Manitoba
110 J6 Lynnville Iowa
110 J6 Lynnville Tennessee
15 F5 Lynton England
143 A8 Lynton W Australia
28 E6 Lyø Denmark
40 A6 Lyon France
94 C2 Lyon Manor Michigan
95 O2 Lyon Mountain New York
18 H7 Lyonnais, Mts.du France
Lyons see Lyon
98 A9 Lyons Colorado
112 E5 Lyons Georgia
110 J3 Lyons Indiana
107 M3 Lyons Kansas
94 C4 Lyons Michigan
98 K8 Lyons Nebraska
95 L3 Lyons New York
94 C5 Lyons Ohio
100 C5 Lyons Oregon
98 K6 Lyons S Dakota
109 L6 Lyons Texas
99 S7 Lyons Wisconsin
95 L4 Lyons Falls New York
20 H3 Lyons-la-Forêt France
143 B8 Lyons, R W Australia
137 L2 Lyra Reef Bismarck Arch
22 D2 Lys R France
28 F3 Lys R Italy
31 H5 Lysá Czechoslovakia
27 A13 Lyse Norway
27 B12 Lysefjorden inlet Norway
27 E13 Lysekil Sweden
79 D3 Lysi Cyprus
101 S6 Lysite Wyoming
40 F3 Lyss Switzerland
121 T6 Lyster Quebec
55 C2 Lys'va U.S.S.R.
28 D4 Lysvik Sweden
8 D6 Lytchett England
13 E4 Lytham St.Annes England
109 J6 Lytle Texas
144 B4 Lyttelton New Zealand
117 N10 Lytton Br Columbia
102 B3 Lytton California
121 O6 Lytton Quebec
52 D6 Lyuban' U.S.S.R.
52 E6 Lyubashevka U.S.S.R.
52 E6 Lyubertsu U.S.S.R.
54 J1 Lyubertsy U.S.S.R.
52 H6 Lyubim U.S.S.R.
47 H3 Lyubimets Bulgaria
55 F3 Lyubimovka U.S.S.R.
55 F3 Lyubinskiy U.S.S.R.
54 F3 Lyublino U.S.S.R.
54 F3 Lyubokhna U.S.S.R.
54 F3 Lyubotin U.S.S.R.
54 G7 Lyudinovo U.S.S.R.
52 H6 Lyuk U.S.S.R.
52 G5 Lyunda R U.S.S.R.
52 J2 Lyzha R U.S.S.R.
68 D1 Ma R Burma
80 F3 Ma'ad Jordan
79 B9 Ma'ādi Egypt
80 F3 Ma'agan Israel
80 C3 Ma'agan Mikha'el Israel
87 H8 Maaia Mozambique
135 T3 Maalaea Hawaiian Is
80 E6 Maale Alummin Jordan
73 L7 Maalosmadulu Atoll Maldives
79 F8 Ma'ān Jordan
29 N8 Maaninka Finland
29 O8 Maanselkä Finland
58 G5 Ma'anshan China
71 F5 Ma-ao Negros Philippines
25 E6 Maarheeze Netherlands
79 G3 Ma'arret en Nu'man Syria
25 D4 Maarsbergen Netherlands
25 D4 Maarssen Netherlands
25 D4 Maartensdijk Netherlands
86 A3 Maas Somalia
25 E6 Maas R Netherlands
25 E6 Maasbracht Netherlands
22 K1 Maaseik Belgium
22 K2 Maasmechelen Belgium
25 B5 Maassluis Netherlands
22 K2 Maastricht Belgium
25 E7 Maastricht Netherlands
139 H9 Maatsuyker Is Tasmania
Maba see Qujiang
71 B2 Maba Halmahera Indonesia
87 F10 Mabalane Mozambique
109 L3 Mabank Texas
80 C4 Ma'barot Israel
71 F4 Mabatobato Philippines
70 B6 Mabau Kalimantan
99 P6 Mabel Minnesota
138 C3 Mabel Creek S Australia
142 G3 Mabel Downs W Australia
119 O2 Mabella Ontario
94 F9 Maben W Virginia
121 O8 Maberly Ontario
122 K2 Mabille, L Quebec
28 B4 Mábjerg Denmark
112 G6 Mablethorpe England
9 G1 Mabou C Breton I, N Scotia
123 L7 Mabrouk Mali
85 D5 Mabrouk Mali
84 E5 Mabrous Niger
84 F4 Mabruk Libya
100 E3 Mabton Washington
61 P14 Mabuni Okinawa
133 C7 Maca mt Chile
122 E8 McAdam New Brunswick
143 B7 Macadam Plains W Australia
140 A2 Macadam Ra N Terr Aust
130 H8 Macaé Brazil
130 J8 Macaíba Brazil
71 G6 Macajalar B Philippines
109 M1 McAlester Oklahoma
139 J5 McAlister, Mt New S Wales
109 J9 McAllen Texas
101 O4 McAllister Montana
113 E7 McAlpin Florida
114 J4 McAlpine L N W Terr
121 L4 Macamic Quebec
71 K8 Macan, Pulau Pulau islds Indonesia
Macao see Macau
16 B5 Mação Portugal
128 E5 Macapá Amazonas Brazil
129 H4 Macapá Brazil
127 O10 Macareo R Venezuela
141 F3 Macaroni Queensland
100 D8 McArthur California
94 E7 McArthur Ohio
138 F7 Macarthur Victoria
140 D3 McArthur R N Terr Aust
140 D3 McArthur River N Terr Aust
94 A4 Macatawa Michigan
129 L5 Macau Brazil
67 D5 Macau prov E Asia
99 O8 McAuley Manitoba
137 R8 Macauley I Kermadec Is Pacific Oc
94 B2 McBain Michigan
110 D3 McBaine Missouri
112 F4 McBean Georgia
112 G3 McBee S Carolina
110 F3 McBeth Pt Manitoba
117 N9 McBride Br Col
133 F8 Macbride Hd Falkland Is
100 J5 McCall Idaho
108 E4 McCamey Texas
101 N7 McCammon Idaho
122 H8 McCann Nova Scotia
98 J1 McCanna N Dakota
44 M6 Maccarese Italy
117 H9 McCauley I Br Col
100 B2 McCleary Washington
112 H4 McClellanville S Carolina
113 E7 Macclenny Florida
8 D1 Macclesfield England
123 S5 Macclesfield L Newfoundland
114 J3 McClintock Ch N W Terr
146 H6 McClintock, Mt Antarctica
117 P8 McClintock Ra W Australia
100 C8 McCloud California
140 C1 McCluer I N Terr Aust
94 D5 McClure Ohio
95 K6 McClure Pennsylvania
100 B2 McClure, L California
114 H3 McClure Str N W Terr
98 G1 McClusky N Dakota
118 H3 McClusker R Sask
98 F2 McClusky N Dakota
111 F10 McComb Mississippi
94 D5 McComb Ohio
98 D8 McConaughy, L Nebraska
117 M3 McConnell Range N W Terr
94 J7 McConnellsburg Pennsylvania
98 F9 McCook Nebraska
111 G8 McCool Mississippi
98 J8 McCool Junct Nebraska
118 J9 McCord Sask
112 E4 McCormick S Carolina
106 D2 McCoy Colorado
117 L3 McCracken Kansas
119 S8 McCreary Manitoba
110 E3 McCredie Missouri
110 E6 McCrory Arkansas
115 M3 Macculloch, C N W Terr
103 J6 McCullough Ridge Nevada
110 B6 McCurtain Oklahoma
109 K5 McDade Texas
117 J6 McDame Br Col
94 D8 McDermott Ohio
120 B3 Macdiarmid Ontario
102 C8 Mcdoel California
107 J2 McDonald Kansas
140 D5 McDonald Downs N Terr Aust
81 E10 Macdonald Is Indian Oc
101 M1 McDonald, L Montana
143 G6 Macdonald, L W Australia
100 E9 McDonald Peak mt California
101 M2 McDonald Pk Montana
142 E3 Macdonald Ra W Australia
101 L1 Macdonald Range Br Col
138 E3 McDonnell Range
136 G6 MacDonnell Ranges N Terr Australia
112 C4 McDonough Georgia
138 D3 McDouall Peak S Australia
140 C4 McDouall Ra N Terr Aust
115 K7 McDowell L Ontario
103 N8 McDowell Pk Arizona
15 F3 MacDuff Scotland
16 C3 Macedo de Chavaleiros Portugal
95 K3 Macedon New York
Macedonia see Makedhonia
99 L8 Macedonia Iowa
139 G7 Macedon, Mt Victoria
130 J10 Maceió Alagoas Brazil
87 G8 Macelage Mozambique
85 C7 Macenta Guinea
42 E5 Macerata Italy
100 G5 McEwen Oregon
110 J5 McEwen Tennessee
101 T8 McFadden Wyoming
99 M9 McFall Missouri
107 O2 McFarland Kansas
138 D4 Macfarlane, L S Australia
144 B5 Macfarlane, Mt New Zealand
106 B6 McGaffey New Mexico
118 J7 McGee Sask
111 E8 McGehee Arkansas
103 K2 McGill Nevada
100 K1 McGillivray Range mts Br Col
14 B5 Macgillycuddy's Reeks mts Irish Rep
116 K5 McGrath Alaska
95 L4 McGraw New York
119 T9 McGregor Manitoba
94 E3 McGregor Michigan
99 N3 McGregor Minnesota
109 K4 McGregor Texas
118 E8 McGregor L Alberta
117 N8 McGregor R Br Col
141 F7 McGregor Ra Queensland
138 F2 McGregor Rge Queensland
98 C8 McGrew Nebraska
101 L4 McGuire, Mt Idaho
77 K5 Mach Pakistan
89 F7 Machache Mt Lesotho
128 C4 Machachi Ecuador
130 F7 Machado Brazil
80 F7 Machaerus Jordan
87 F10 Machaila Mozambique
88 F2 Machakos Kenya
128 C4 Machala Ecuador
70 C4 Machan Sarawak
67 B3 Machangping China
133 E2 Macharetí Bolivia
140 E6 Machattie L Queensland
22 G5 Machault France
87 F10 Machaze Mozambique
21 B8 Machecoul France
112 D4 Machen Georgia
67 E1 Macheng China
99 S7 McHenry Illinois
111 G11 McHenry Mississippi
76 D2 Macherla India
33 R10 Machern E Germany
79 F5 Machgharah Lebanon
95 U2 Machias Maine
95 S7 Machias R Maine
17 F1 Machichaco, C Spain
76 E2 Machilipatnam India
127 H9 Machiques Venezuela
12 C2 Machrie Scotland
12 C3 Machrihanish Scotland
8 C2 Machynlleth Wales
87 F10 Macia Mozambique
Macias Nguema Biyogo see Bioko
87 F9 McIlwaine Nat. Park Zimbabwe
141 G2 McIlwraith Ra Queensland
48 L5 Măcin Romania
85 C6 Macina reg Mali
12 J3 Mc. Innes Ontario
99 O6 McIntire Iowa
118 J1 McIntosh Ontario
98 E4 McIntosh S Dakota
98 E3 McIntyre B Ontario
141 K8 McIntyre Brook Queensland
122 K7 McIntyre, R Queensland
106 B2 Mack Colorado
119 O6 McKague Sask
101 M6 Mackay Idaho
141 K5 Mackay Queensland
142 G6 Mackay, L N Terr/W Aust
114 H5 Mackay L N W Terr
120 D3 McKay L Ontario
142 D5 Mackay, Mt W Australia
117 R7 McKay R Alberta
143 D6 McKay Ra W Australia
137 S2 McKean I Phoenix Is Pacific Oc
94 H6 McKeesport Pennsylvania
94 G6 McKees Rocks Pennsylvania
33 T10 Mackenberg E Germany
133 E4 Mackenna Argentina
33 N9 Mackenrode E Germany
111 K10 McKenzie Alabama
98 F3 McKenzie N Dakota
110 H5 McKenzie Tennessee
114 G5 Mackenzie R N W Terr
141 J6 Mackenzie R Queensland
146 C4 Mackenzie B Antarctica
114 F4 Mackenzie B Yukon Terr
100 C5 McKenzie Bridge Oregon
114 H5 Mackenzie, Dist.of N W Terr
114 H2 Mackenzie King I N W Terr
119 N2 McKenzie L Ontario
119 P4 McKenzie L Sask
117 H3 Mackenzie Mts Yukon Terr/N W Terr
100 D5 McKenzie Pass Oregon
144 C6 Mackenzie Plains New Zealand
119 S1 MacKerracher L Manitoba
144 B6 Mackinac Michigan
94 C1 Mackinac Michigan
94 C1 Mackinac, Str. of Michigan
99 R9 Mackinaw Illinois
99 R9 Mackinaw R Illinois
94 C1 Mackinaw City Michigan
141 F5 McKinlay Queensland
141 F5 McKinlay R Queensland
116 M5 McKinley, Mt Alaska
146 J9 McKinley Pk Antarctica
110 M4 McKinney Kentucky
109 L2 McKinney Texas
107 J3 McKinney, L Kansas
144 A6 McKinnon Pass New Zealand
139 H8 Mackintosh L. Tasmania
143 F7 Mackintosh Ra W Australia
120 B3 McKirdy Ontario
102 E6 McKittrick California
118 E6 Macklin Sask
119 Q8 McKnight L Manitoba
119 F6 Macks Inn Idaho
101 O5 Macks Inn Idaho
137 M4 Macksville New S Wales
139 L5 Macksville New S Wales
141 F6 Mackunda R Queensland
116 O5 McLain Mississippi
111 H10 McLain Mississippi
116 M5 Maclaren R Alaska
142 E4 McLarty Hills W Australia
142 E5 McLarty, Mt W Australia
118 D4 McLaughlin Alberta
98 F4 McLaughlin S Dakota
119 U5 McLaughlin R Manitoba
99 S10 McLean Illinois
139 L3 Maclean New S Wales
118 H5 McLean Sask
118 H2 McLean L Sask
118 J5 McLeansboro Illinois
87 E12 Maclear S Africa
88 E8 Maclear, C Malawi
139 L4 Macleay R New S Wales
118 A3 McLennan Alberta
119 M3 McLennan Lake Saskatchewan
98 J3 McLeod N Dakota
114 J5 McLeod B N W Terr
142 A5 McLeod, L W Australia
117 M8 McLeod Lake Br Col
118 B5 McLeod R Alberta
68 C7 McLeods I Burma
110 A2 McLouth Kansas
118 K8 McMahon Sask
94 G7 McMechen W Virginia
83 M9 McMicken Pt Christmas I Indian Oc
99 V3 McMillan Michigan
141 G1 Macmillan R Queensland
117 F4 Macmillan R Yukon Terr
106 F9 McMillan, L New Mexico
140 C6 McMinn Cr N Terr Aust
100 B4 McMinnville Oregon
110 L6 McMinnville Tennessee
118 J7 McMorran Sask
18 F1 McMunn Manitoba

146 H6 McMurdo Sound Antarctica
117 O10 McMurphy Br Col
100 C1 McMurray Washington
111 E10 McNair Mississippi
103 P7 McNary Arizona
108 B4 McNary Texas
100 F4 McNary Dam Oregon
117 O9 McNaughton, L Canada
103 P10 McNeal Arizona
111 C8 McNeil Arkansas
109 K5 McNeil Texas
111 G11 McNeill Mississippi
119 Q7 MacNutt Sask
122 G10 McNutt I Nova Scotia
128 D1 Macollo, Pta C Venezuela
110 F1 Macomb Illinois
107 O6 Macomb Oklahoma
43 B8 Macomer Sardinia
88 H8 Macomia Mozambique
22 G3 Maçon Belgium
19 J6 Mâcon France
112 D5 Macon Georgia
99 S10 Macon Illinois
111 H8 Macon Mississippi
99 O10 Macon Missouri
98 G9 Macon Nebraska
87 D8 Macondo Angola
119 O9 Macoun Sask
107 N3 McPherson Kansas
142 D5 Macpherson, Mt W Australia
141 L8 Macpherson Ra N S W/Qnsld
68 A7 Macpherson's Str Andaman Is
139 J4 MacQuarie R New S Wales
139 H8 Macquarie R Tasmania
139 H8 Macquarie Harbour Tasmania
81 J12 Macquarie I S Pacific Oc
139 K5 Macquarie, L New S Wales
139 J4 Macquarie Marshes New S Wales
139 J5 Macquarie, Mt New S Wales
22 G4 Macquenoise Belgium
117 E4 McQuesten Yukon Terr
117 E4 McQuesten R Yukon Terr
112 E5 McRae Georgia
144 D5 McRae, L New Zealand
142 C5 McRae, Mt W Australia
144 C6 Macraes Flat New Zealand
94 E9 McRoberts Kentucky
146 C5 MacRobertson Land Antarctica
14 C5 Macroom Irish Rep
118 K7 Macrorie Sask
141 H4 Macrossan Queensland
119 N9 McTaggart Sask
71 G5 Mactan isld Philippines
118 D1 McTavish Manitoba
128 D3 Macujer Colombia
71 G4 Maculiv Philippines
138 D2 Macumba R S Australia
95 M6 Macungie Pennsylvania
128 D6 Macusani Peru
87 G9 Macuse Mozambique
125 N9 Macuspana Mexico
124 E4 Macuzari, Presa res Mexico
94 E9 McVeigh Kentucky
119 Q2 McVeigh Manitoba
117 N3 McVicar Arm inlet N W Terr
98 H2 McVille N Dakota
121 M4 McWatters Quebec
111 J10 McWilliams Alabama
86 A4 Mada R Nigeria
80 G7 Madaba Jordan
86 D2 Madadi Chad
87 H11 Madagascar Indian Oc
81 C8 Madagascar Basin Indian Oc
76 C4 Madakasira India
70 E1 Madalon mt Sabah
84 E5 Madama Niger
76 D4 Madanapalle India
136 K3 Madang Papua New Guinea
85 F6 Madaoua Niger
75 O7 Madaripur Bangladesh
85 F6 Madarounfa Niger
95 S6 Madawaska Maine
121 M7 Madawaska Ontario
121 N7 Madawaska R Ontario
122 D6 Madawaska R Quebec
68 C1 Madaya Burma
45 Q7 Maddaloni Italy
143 C10 Madden, Mt W Australia
142 C2 Maddington dist Perth, W Aust
98 G2 Maddock N Dakota
85 A2 Madeira Atlantic Oc
128 F5 Madeira R Brazil
128 F5 Madeirinho R Brazil
41 M3 Madelegabel mt Austria
20 G5 Madeleine Bouvet, la France
123 L6 Madeleine, Iles de la Quebec
18 H6 Madeleine, Mts.de la France
99 M5 Madelia Minnesota
100 E8 Madeline California
99 Q3 Madeline I Wisconsin
57 J1 Madeniyet U.S.S.R.
102 D5 Madera California
124 E3 Madera Mexico
94 J6 Madera Pennsylvania
108 E5 Madera Mt Texas
32 J10 Madfeld W Germany
119 Q7 Madge L Sask
83 J12 Madge Rocks Seychelles
75 M5 Madhubani India
74 G7 Madhya Pradesh prov India
65 H3 Madida China
128 E6 Madidi R Bolivia
70 C4 Madi, Dtt Kalimantan
138 E3 Madigan Gulf S Australia
146 J3 Madigan Nunatak Antarctica
109 L1 Madill Oklahoma
86 C6 Madimba Zaïre
86 H3 Madinat ash Sha'ab S Yemen
81 C5 Madingley Rise Indian Oc
86 B6 Madingo-Kayes Congo
86 B6 Madingou Congo
110 F6 Madison Arkansas
113 D7 Madison Florida
112 D4 Madison Georgia
107 O3 Madison Kansas
98 K4 Madison Minnesota
110 D2 Madison Missouri
112 H1 Madison N Carolina
98 J8 Madison Nebraska
94 F5 Madison Ohio
111 M12 Madison St Louis
118 J7 Madison Sask
98 J5 Madison S Dakota
110 K5 Madison Tennessee
94 J8 Madison Virginia
99 R6 Madison Wisconsin
94 F8 Madison W Virginia
101 O4 Madison R Montana
94 H9 Madison Heights Virginia
101 P5 Madison Junct Wyoming
101 O4 Madison Ra Montana
110 J4 Madisonville Kentucky
111 F11 Madisonville Louisiana
112 C2 Madisonville Tennessee
109 M5 Madisonville Texas
70 N9 Madiun Java
8 D3 Madley England
143 E6 Madley, Mt W Australia
98 A1 Madoc Montana
121 N8 Madoc Ontario
86 G5 Mado Gashi Kenya
52 C6 Madona U.S.S.R.
100 B9 Mad R California
47 J5 Madra Dağı mt Turkey
76 E4 Madras India
100 D5 Madras Oregon
128 D6 Madre de Dios dep Peru
128 E6 Madre de Dios R Bolivia/Peru
133 B8 Madre de Dios, I Chile
125 L5 Madre. Laguna Mexico
109 K9 Madre, Laguna Texas
124 F4 Madre Occidental, Sierra mts Mexico
18 G10 Madrès mt France
71 F2 Madre, Sierra mts Luzon Philippines
99 N8 Madrid Iowa
71 G6 Madrid Mindanao Philippines
98 E9 Madrid Nebraska
106 D6 Madrid New Mexico
95 M2 Madrid New York
16 E4 Madrid Spain
16 E4 Madrid prov Spain
71 F5 Madridejos Philippines
16 E5 Madridejos Spain
16 D3 Madrigal de las Atlas Torres Spain
16 E6 Madrona, Sa mts Spain
128 G4 Madruba, L Brazil
126 D3 Madruga Cuba
79 E11 Madsûs, G mt Egypt
71 K8 Madu isld Indonesia
71 E5 Maducang isld Philippines
28 A4 Madum Denmark
28 D3 Madum Sø Denmark
143 F9 Madura W Australia
70 O9 Madura isld Indonesia
76 D6 Madurai India
70 O9 Madura, Selat str Java
83 L10 Maduru Oya R Sri Lanka
52 H4 Madzha U.S.S.R.
60 D12 Maebaru Japan
61 N9 Maebashi Japan
68 C3 Mae Hong Son Thailand
61 O13 Mae-jima isld Okinawa
68 D5 Mae Khlong R Thailand
69 D8 Mae Kirirath R Thailand
27 C12 Mael Norway
68 D3 Mae Lao R Thailand
68 D3 Mae Li R Thailand
17 H3 Maella Spain
69 D8 Mae Luang R Thailand
68 F4 Mae Nam R Thailand
68 E3 Mae Nam Ing R Thailand
68 F5 Mae Nam Mun R Thailand
68 E3 Mae Nam Nan R Thailand
68 D3 Mae Nam Ping R Thailand
68 E3 Mae Nam Yom R Thailand
68 D3 Mae Rim Thailand
48 K5 Măeruş Romania
103 P1 Maeser Utah
8 C4 Maesteg Wales
45 M2 Maestra, Pta Italy
126 F4 Maestra, Sierra mts Cuba
71 E4 Maestre de Campo isld Philippines
137 O5 Maewo isld New Hebrides
88 H10 Mafameda isld Mozambique
114 J7 Mafeking Manitoba
89 D5 Mafeking S Africa
89 E7 Mafeteng Lesotho
139 H7 Maffra Victoria
88 G5 Mafia Channel Tanzania
88 G5 Mafia,I Tanzania
88 E8 Mafinto Mozambique
67 E1 Ma-fou China
130 E10 Mafra Brazil
16 A6 Mafra Portugal
89 F2 Mafungabusi Plateau Zimbabwe
51 P3 Magadan U.S.S.R.
51 P2 Magadanskaya Oblast' U.S.S.R.
88 F2 Magadi Kenya
88 F2 Magadi L Kenya
122 E8 Magaguadavic L New Brunswick
71 F4 Magallanes Philippines
133 C8 Magallanes prov Chile
133 C8 Magallanes, Estrecho de chan Chile
71 F5 Magallon Negros Philippines
86 H4 Magalo Ethiopia
71 C3 Magamo W Irian
126 G10 Magangué Colombia
128 C2 Magangue Colombia
85 F6 Magaria Niger
61 Q12 Magari-zaki C Okinawa
71 E2 Magat R Luzon Philippines
89 G4 Magato Mts S Africa
110 C6 Magazine Mt Arkansas
85 B7 Magburaka Sierra Leone
59 J1 Magdagachi U.S.S.R.
37 L2 Magdala E Germany
86 G3 Magdala Ethiopia
128 F6 Magdalena Bolivia
106 C7 Magdalena New Mexico
124 D2 Magdalena Sonora Mexico
128 D2 Magdalena div Colombia
128 C3 Magdalena R Colombia
133 C6 Magdalena, I Chile
124 C5 Magdalena, I Mexico
70 E2 Magdalena, Mt Sabah
115 N8 Magdalen Is Quebec
33 P8 Magdeburg E Germany
33 P8 Magdeburg reg E Germany
33 Q8 Magdeburgerforth E Germany
141 K3 Magdelaine Cays islds Gt Barrier Reef Aust
33 O9 Mägdesprung E Germany
80 C5 Magdi'el Israel
111 G10 Magee Mississippi
14 F2 Magee, I N Ireland
116 K7 Mageik Vol Alaska
70 N9 Magelang Java
133 D8 Magellan, Str. of Chile
80 E3 Magen Shaul Israel
41 J7 Magenta Italy
143 C10 Magenta, L W Australia
41 K3 Magereu mt Switzerland
26 P1 Mageröya isld Norway
80 D4 Maggal Israel
41 J5 Maggia, Val Switzerland
44 F2 Maggiorasca mt Italy
41 J6 Maggiore, Lago Italy
43 F7 Maggiore, M mt Italy
127 J2 Maggotty Jamaica
79 A10 Maghâgha Egypt
79 D8 Maghâra, G mt Egypt
14 A4 Magharee Is Irish Rep
14 E2 Maghera N Ireland
14 E2 Magherafelt N Ireland
17 F10 Maghnia Algeria
84 H3 Maghra, El Egypt
13 F6 Maghull England
101 L6 Magic Res Idaho
14 E1 Magilligan Pt N Ireland
16 E7 Mágina mt Spain
56 G3 Magistral'niy U.S.S.R.
48 E6 Maglaj Yugoslavia
40 E5 Magland France
28 K6 Magleby Denmark
28 K7 Magleby isld Denmark
28 G7 Maglehöjstrand Denmark
45 M6 Magliana Italy
45 O5 Magliano de Marsi Italy
48 E7 Maglić mt Yugoslavia
43 J8 Maglie Italy
103 N8 Magma Arizona
21 H9 Magnac-Laval France
21 J10 Magnat-l'Etrange France
98 J7 Magnet Nebraska
121 L7 Magnetawan Ontario
146 A5 Magnet B Antarctica
141 H4 Magnetic I Queensland
55 C3 Magnitka U.S.S.R.
55 C4 Magnitogorsk U.S.S.R.
109 O2 Magnolia Arkansas
111 F10 Magnolia Mississippi
112 J3 Magnolia N Carolina
109 M5 Magnolia Texas
27 F12 Magnor Norway
6 L1 Magnus oil rig North Sea
20 J3 Magny-en-Vexin France
20 E3 Magny-la-Campagne France
88 C9 Magoe Mozambique
121 S7 Magog Quebec
8 D4 Magor Wales
120 F4 Magpie Ontario
122 H3 Magpie Quebec
122 H2 Magpie L Quebec
120 F4 Magpie Mine Ontario
122 H2 Magpie R Quebec
44 G3 Magra, R Italy
118 E9 Magrath Alberta
17 G5 Magro R Spain
102 G4 Magruder Mt Nevada
71 E2 Magsingal Luzon Philippines
28 C6 Magstrup Denmark
67 A5 Maguan China
129 J4 Maguari, C Brazil
89 H5 Magude Mozambique
67 D5 Magui China
86 B3 Magumeri Nigeria
68 B2 Magwe Burma
68 A2 Magyichaung Burma
78 K3 Mahâbâd Iran
74 E10 Mahabaleshwar India
87 G12 Mahabo Madagascar
74 E9 Mahad India
86 A3 Mahaddei Uen Somalia
74 H7 Mahadeo Hills India
94 J6 Mahaffey Penn
86 F5 Mahagi Zaïre
87 H11 Mahajamba, B.de Madagascar
87 H11 Mahajanga Madagascar
70 D4 Mahakam R Kalimantan
89 E4 Mahalapye Botswana
46 E6 Mahalás Greece
79 E8 Mahalla, El Egypt
77 B3 Mahallat Iran
77 E4 Mahân Iran
75 K8 Mahanadi R India
71 G5 Mahanay isld Philippines
95 L6 Mahanoy City Pennsylvania
65 G3 Mahao China
83 J10 Maha Oya R Sri Lanka
74 E9 Maharashtra prov India
75 K8 Mahasamund India
68 F4 Maha Sarakham Thailand
98 J10 Mahaska Kansas
87 H11 Mahavavy R Madagascar
87 H11 Mahavelona Madagascar
83 K10 Mahaweli Ganga R Sri Lanka
68 G4 Mahaxay Laos
74 H10 Mahbubabad India
76 C2 Mahbubnagar India
77 D7 Mahḑah Oman
85 G1 Mahdia Tunisia
76 B5 Mahe India
83 J12 Mahé isld Seychelles
83 M13 Mahebourg Mauritius
88 F6 Mahenge Tanzania
144 C6 Maheno New Zealand
120 J3 Maher Ontario
74 F7 Maheshwar India
145 F3 Mahia New Zealand
74 E9 Mahim India
144 C5 Mahinapua, L New Zealand
144 B6 Mahinerangi, L New Zealand
80 G6 Mahis Jordan
87 F11 Mahlabatini S Africa
68 B2 Mahlaing Burma
33 S8 Mahlow E Germany
33 P8 Mahlwinkel E Germany
75 J5 Mahmudabad India
48 M5 Mahmudia Romania
83 K10 Maho Sri Lanka
74 H6 Mahoba India
145 E3 Mahoenui New Zealand
100 F8 Mahogany Peak mt Nevada
99 S9 Mahomet Illinois
17 K5 Mahón Menorca
122 H9 Mahone Bay Nova Scotia
117 L3 Mahony L N W Terr
17 F5 Mahora Spain
85 G2 Mahrès Tunisia
74 E7 Mahsana India
98 F4 Mahto S Dakota
145 E4 Mahuri New Zealand
74 D8 Mahuva India
137 P1 Maiana atoll Kiribati
71 M9 Maibang Indonesia
61 K10 Maibara Japan
48 L5 Măicănești Romania
19 K5 Maich France
40 E3 Maiche France
68 J2 Maichen China
86 G3 Maichew Ethiopia
68 J2 Mai-ch'u China
129 H3 Maicuru R Brazil
142 C1 Maida Vale W Australia
112 F2 Maiden N Carolina
8 D5 Maiden Bradley England
9 F4 Maidenhead England
8 D6 Maiden Newton England
99 O5 Maiden Rock Wisconsin
12 D3 Maidens Scotland
71 A2 Maidi Halmahera Indonesia
9 G5 Maidstone England
118 H5 Maidstone Sask
86 B3 Maidugun Nigeria
42 E3 Maiella, M.della Italy
41 L3 Maienfeld Switzerland
20 K2 Maignelay France
128 E2 Maigualida, Sierra mts Venezuela
14 C4 Maigue R Irish Rep
74 J8 Maikala Range India
36 E5 Maikammer W Germany
102 R12 Maili Hawaiian Is
20 H4 Maillebois France
20 G3 Mailleraye-sur-Seine, la France
21 D9 Maillezais France
22 D3 Mailly Maillet France
74 E4 Mailsi Pakistan
144 C5 Maimai New Zealand
77 J2 Maimana Afghanistan
127 J5 Maimon, B.de Dom Rep
80 F7 Ma'in Jordan
14 E2 Main R N Ireland
37 K3 Main R W Germany
123 N8 Main-à-Dieu C Breton I, N Scotia
37 J4 Mainbernheim W Germany
123 Q2 Main Brook Nfld
37 M6 Mainburg W Germany
118 K8 Main Centre Sask
120 J7 Main Channel Cave I Ontario
86 C6 Mai Ndombe, L Zaïre Maindong see Coqên
121 O9 Main Duck I Ontario
103 N6 Maine Arizona
95 L4 Maine New York
21 C7 Maine R France
20 F5 Maine reg France
95 R1 Maine state U.S.A.
21 D7 Maine-et-Loire dep France
85 G6 Mainé-Soroa Niger
110 M2 Maineville Ohio
68 D6 Mairgy isld Burma
36 H5 Mair hardt W Germany
71 G6 Mainit, L Mindanao Philippines
15 G2 Mainland Shetland Scotland
140 C2 Mainoru N Terr Aust
74 H5 Mainpuri India
138 F4 Main Range Barrier New S Wales
122 F7 Main S.W. Miramichi R New Brunswick
36 F3 Maintal W Germany
20 J4 Maintenon France
87 G11 Maintirano Madagascar
123 Q4 Main Topsail peak Newfoundland
29 N7 Mainua Finland
74 D2 Mainwali Pakistan
36 E3 Mainz W Germany
45 R8 Maiori Italy
133 D4 Maipo mt Chile/Arg
133 C4 Maipo R Chile
131 B5 Maipo Vol peak Arg/Chile
133 F5 Maipu Argentina
127 L9 Maiquetia Venezuela
44 B3 Maira R Italy
75 P5 Mairabari India
37 L7 Maisach W Germany
21 C7 Maisdon France
126 G4 Maisí Cuba
122 G6 Maisonnette New Brunswick
20 K4 Maisons-Laffitte France
38 N4 Maissau Austria
20 K5 Maisse France
22 J4 Maissin Belgium
86 J3 Mait Somalia
99 L9 Maitland Missouri
139 K5 Maitland New S Wales
122 J8 Maitland Nova Scotia
138 D5 Maitland S Australia
122 G9 Maitland Br Nova Scotia
143 D7 Maitland, L W Australia
143 C7 Maitland, Mt W Australia
142 B5 Maitland, R W Australia
70 E2 Maitland Ra Sabah
140 C2 Maiwok R N Terr Aust
61 P7 Maiya Japan
140 A4 Maiyu, Mt N Terr Aust
75 O4 Maizhokunggar China
36 B6 Maizières-les-Vic France
60 J10 Maizuru Japan
128 D2 Majagual Colombia
128 F3 Majari R Brazil
26 F6 Majavatn L Norway
28 H7 Majbølle Denmark
80 E5 Majdal Bani Fadil Jordan
80 F8 Majdalein Jordan
31 N5 Majdan Poland
48 G6 Majdanpek Yugoslavia
80 D2 Majd el Kurum Israel
130 G8 Majé Brazil
70 F6 Majene Sulawesi
48 E6 Majevica mts Yugoslavia
86 G4 Maji Ethiopia
67 B3 Majiang China
67 D5 Majiang China
67 A4 Majie China
67 F2 Majin China
67 D2 Majitang China
118 H7 Major Sask
Majorca isld see Mallorca
89 F6 Majuba Hill S Africa
Majunga see Mahajanga
85 B6 Maka Senegal
61 P14 Makabe Okinawa
102 R12 Makaha Hawaiian Is
86 G3 Makale Ethiopia
70 F6 Makale Sulawesi
69 E14 Makalo Indonesia
75 M5 Makalu mt Xizang Zizhiqu/Nepal
87 F7 Makambako Tanzania
135 U4 Makapala Hawaiian Is
102 S12 Makapuu Hd Hawaiian Is
145 E2 Makarau New Zealand
144 B7 Makarewa New Zealand
52 G3 Makar-Ib U.S.S.R.
52 J2 Makarikha U.S.S.R.
144 B6 Makarora R New Zealand
59 M2 Makarov U.S.S.R.
42 H5 Makarska Yugoslavia
52 G5 Makar'ye U.S.S.R.
Makassar see Ujung Pandang
70 F5 Makassar Str Indonesia
89 H6 Makatini Flats reg S Africa
135 T3 Makawao Hawaiian Is
71 C3 Makbon W Irian
46 E4 Makedhonia Greece
46 E3 Makedonija Yugoslavia
135 N10 Makemo atoll Pac Oc
85 B7 Makeni Sierra Leone
145 F2 Maketu New Zealand
54 K8 Makeyevka U.S.S.R.
89 D3 Makgadikgadi Pans salt pans Botswana
78 J1 Makharadze U.S.S.R.
16 D9 Makhazen R Morocco
55 D2 Makhnevo U.S.S.R.
55 E4 Makhorovka U.S.S.R.
80 F3 Makhraba Jordan
61 M8 Maki Japan
71 A2 Makian Halmahera Indonesia
144 C6 Makikihi New Zealand
84 G3 Makili Al Libya
119 S8 Makinak Manitoba
55 F4 Makinsk U.S.S.R.
115 M2 Makinson Inlet N W Terr
26 S1 Makkaur Norway
25 F3 Makkinga Netherlands
115 O6 Makkovik Labrador
25 D2 Makkum Netherlands
48 F4 Makó Hungary
120 C1 Makokibatan L Ontario
87 F7 Makongolosi Tanzania
145 F3 Makorako mt New Zealand
98 E2 Makoti N Dakota
145 F4 Makotuku New Zealand
86 C5 Makoua Congo
31 L6 Makov Czechoslovakia
31 M6 Maków Poland
31 N3 Maków Mazowiecki Poland
80 D2 Makr Israel
47 H8 Makrá islo Greece
74 F5 Makrana India
77 J7 Makran Coast Range Pakistan
47 H4 Mákri Greece
76 E1 Makri India
47 G7 Makronisi isld Greece
52 J3 Maksim U.S.S.R.
85 F1 Maktar Tunisia
78 K2 Maku Iran
70 C4 Makup, Bt mt Kalimantan
60 D14 Makurazaki Japan
86 A4 Makurdi Nigeria
55 E3 Makushino U.S.S.R.
116 D10 Makushin Vol Aleutian Is
88 D7 Makutu Mts Zambia
118 H4 Makwa L Sask
89 G1 Makwiro Zimbabwe
128 C6 Mala Peru
71 G7 Malabang Mindanao Philippines
113 G9 Malabar Florida
76 B5 Malabar Coast India
70 L9 Malabar, G mt Java
85 F8 Malabo Bioko Equat Guinea
85 F8 Malabo Fernando Póo Eq Guinea
71 C6 Malabuñgan Palawan Philippines
69 E11 Malacca, Str. of Malaysia
118 H1 Malachi Ontario
31 K7 Malacky Czechoslovakia
101 N7 Malad City Idaho
17 H2 Maladeta Spain
31 L6 Malá Fatra mts Czechoslovakia
16 E8 Málaga Spain
100 E2 Malaga Washington
16 D8 Málaga prov Spain
88 C4 Malagarasi Tanzania
Malagasy Rep see Madagascar
16 E5 Malagón Spain
14 E3 Malahide Irish Rep
87 G12 Malaimbandy Madagascar
137 N3 Malaita isld Solomon Is
71 J9 Malaka mt Sumbawa Indonesia
86 F4 Malakal Sudan
42 G4 Mala Kapela Yugoslavia
109 L3 Malakoff Texas
71 B2 Malaku islds Indonesia
45 L2 Malalbergo Italy
70 G6 Malamala Sulawesi
71 A3 Malamala isld Indonesia
71 E7 Malamaui isld Philippines
45 M1 Malamocco Italy
71 D5 Malampaya Snd Philippines
141 H3 Malanda Queensland
70 O10 Malang Java
88 E6 Malangali Tanzania
70 M9 Malangbong Java
26 K2 Malangen Norway
26 K2 Malangen inlet Norway
26 J2 Malangsgrunnen shoal Norway
75 L5 Malangwa Nepal
48 K3 Mălani Romania
71 F7 Malanipa isld Philippines
87 C7 Malanje Angola
71 D6 Malanut B Philippines
85 E6 Malanville Benin
65 D4 Malanyu China
131 C3 Malanzán, Sa. de mts Argentina
27 J12 Mälaren L Sweden
133 D5 Malargue Argentina
131 B5 Malargue R Argentina
129 H3 Malaripo Brazil
121 M4 Malartic Quebec
70 F7 Malasoro, Tk B Sulawesi
117 C6 Malaspina Gl Alaska
144 A6 Malaspina Reach New Zealand
117 L11 Malaspina Str Br Col
26 K6 Malåtrask Sweden
78 G2 Malatya Turkey
19 O16 Malaucène France
20 H2 Malaunay France
70 E1 Malawali isld Sabah
88 D8 Malawi rep Africa
Malawi, L see Nyasa, L
29 J9 Malax Finland
55 D1 Malaya Sos'va R U.S.S.R.
52 D5 Malaya Vishera U.S.S.R.
77 A2 Malāyer Iran
141 J4 Malay Reef Gt Barrier Reef Aust
69 Malaysia S E Asia
69 E10 Malaysia, Peninsular S E Asia
14 B4 Mal B Irish Rep
122 H5 Mal Baie Quebec
122 B6 Malbaie R Quebec
131 B6 Malbarco, L Argentina
140 F5 Malbon Queensland
138 C4 Malbooma S Australia
38 J9 Malborghetto Italy
31 L1 Malbork Poland
41 N6 Malcesine Italy
33 R5 Malchin E Germany
33 Q6 Malchow E Germany
143 D8 Malcolm W Australia
116 R2 Malcolm R Yukon Terr
68 D7 Malcolm I Burma
143 E10 Malcolm,Pt W Australia
99 O8 Malcom Iowa
22 E1 Maldegem Belgium
95 Q4 Malden Massachusetts
110 G5 Malden Missouri
100 H2 Malden Washington
94 F8 Malden W Virginia
135 M8 Malden I Pacific Oc
73 L8 Maldive Is rep Indian Oc
43 B9 Mal di Ventre isld Sardinia
73 L9 Maldive Ridge Indian Oc
9 G4 Maldon England
131 G5 Maldonado Uruguay
131 G5 Maldonado dep Uruguay
41 N5 Male Italy
73 L8 Male Maldives
47 H5 Maléa, Akr Turkey
47 F8 Maléa, Akr C Greece
74 F8 Malegaon India
48 D2 Male Karpaty Czechoslovakia
137 O5 Malekula isld New Hebrides
121 P4 Mâle, L.du Quebec
88 F9 Malema Mozambique
87 E7 Malemba Nkulu Zaïre
47 F9 Máleme Crete
52 E3 Malen'ga U.S.S.R.
33 N4 Malente W Germany
74 F3 Maler Kotla India
47 H9 Máles Crete Greece
18 G4 Malesherbes France
54 K3 Malevka U.S.S.R.
37 O6 Malgersdorf W Germany
86 E2 Malha Sudan
13 F5 Malham England
100 H5 Malheur Oregon
100 H6 Malheur R Oregon
83 K12 Malheureu, Cap Mahé I Indian Oc
100 G6 Malheur L Oregon
66 F6 Mali P Burma
85 D5 Mali rep W Africa
21 E6 Malicorne-sur-Sarthe France
71 F7 Maligcy B Mindanao Philippines
80 F4 Malih R Jordan
19 Q16 Malijai France
71 H5 Malik Sulawesi
68 D6 Mali Kyun isld Burma
70 G6 Malili Sulawesi
27 H14 Målilla Sweden
88 B5 Malimba mts Zaïre
100 D7 Malin Oregon
71 G5 Malinao Inlet Philippines
70 E3 Malinau Kalimantan
71 F6 Malindang, Mt Mindanao Philippines
88 H3 Malindi Kenya
48 F2 Malinec Czechoslovakia
Malines see Mechelen
70 G4 Maling, G mt Sulawesi
70 L9 Malingping Java
27 H12 Malingsbo Sweden
14 D1 Malin Hd Irish Rep
14 C2 Malin More Irish Rep
70 F7 Malino Sulawesi
54 H7 Malinovka U.S.S.R.
55 G5 Malinovoye Ozero U.S.S.R.
28 M2 Malinstindur mt Faeroes
68 G1 Malipo China
71 G7 Malita Mindanao Philippines
71 G5 Malitbog Leyte Philippines
68 D7 Maliwun Burma
106 G9 Maljamar New Mexico
46 F1 Maljen mt Yugoslavia
80 F3 Malka Jordan
53 F11 Malka R U.S.S.R.
74 G8 Malkapur India
47 H4 Malkara Turkey
56 G5 Malkhanskiy Khr mts U.S.S.R.
31 N3 Malkinia Poland
80 F1 Malkiyya Israel
47 J2 Malko Tŭrnovo Bulgaria
139 J7 Mallacoota Victoria
118 F4 Mallaig Alberta
15 C3 Mallaig Highland Scotland
99 M7 Mallard Iowa
84 J4 Mallawi Egypt
131 A7 Malleco prov Chile
19 O17 Mallemort France
37 N6 Mallersdorf W Germany
41 N4 Malles Venosta Italy
130 E9 Mallet Brazil
142 C5 Mallina W Australia
28 E4 Malling Denmark
38 H8 Mallnitz Austria
17 J5 Mallorca isld Balearic Is
94 F9 Mallory W Virginia
121 P8 Mallorytown Ontario
14 C4 Mallow Irish Rep
142 E5 Mallowa Well W Australia
8 B1 Malltraeth B Môn Wales
22 F5 Malmaison, la France
27 G14 Malmbäck Sweden
26 L4 Malmberget Sweden
22 L3 Malmédy Belgium
8 D4 Malmesbury England
89 A9 Malmesbury S Africa
26 K6 Malmesjaure L Sweden
27 J12 Malmköping Sweden
28 K5 Malmö Sweden
27 F16 Malmöhus county Sweden
126 A2 Malmok pt Bonaire W Indies
52 H6 Malmyzh U.S.S.R.
26 G3 Malnes Norway
137 O5 Malo isld New Hebrides
129 G3 Maloca Amapá Brazil
129 H5 Maloca Pará Brazil
41 L5 Maloggia Switzerland
71 E3 Malolos Luzon Philippines
55 C2 Malomal'sk U.S.S.R.
88 E9 Malombe,L Malawi
47 H2 Malomir Bulgaria
113 B7 Malone Florida
95 N2 Malone New York
121 N8 Malone Ontario
109 L4 Malone Texas
98 F8 Maloney Res Nebraska
67 A4 Malong China
87 D8 Malonga Zaïre
26 N6 Malören Sweden
31 P4 Malorita U.S.S.R.
52 E3 Maloshuyka U.S.S.R.
89 F7 Maloti Mts Lesotho
100 F1 Malott Washington
55 C4 Malouchalinskiy U.S.S.R.
26 A10 Måløy Norway
54 H1 Maloyaroslavets U.S.S.R.
55 E2 Maloye Gorodishche U.S.S.R.
52 H1 Malozemel'skaya Tundra plain U.S.S.R.
106 C10 Malpais New Mexico
8 D1 Malpas England
138 F5 Malpas S Australia
124 H6 Malpaso Mexico
90 A8 Malpelo I Pacific Oc
122 J7 Malpeque B Pr Edward I
16 D5 Malpica Spain
16 B1 Malpica de Bergantiños Spain
131 B4 Malpo R Chile
73 L5 Malprabha R India
74 F5 Malpura India
36 E6 Malsch W Germany
31 H7 Malše R Czechoslovakia
26 K2 Målselv Norway
26 K2 Målselv R Norway
36 H1 Malsfeld W Germany
77 A7 Malsūnīyah, Al Saudi Arabia
38 J8 Malta Austria
106 D2 Malta Colorado
101 M7 Malta Idaho
101 S1 Malta Montana
94 F7 Malta Ohio
43 F13 Malta rep Mediterranean Sea
43 F12 Malta Ch Med Sea
87 C10 Maltahöhe Namibia
38 H7 Maltatal V Austria
9 G1 Maltby Lincs England
13 G6 Maltby S Yorks England
144 C5 Malte Brun mt New Zealand
13 H5 Malton England
121 L9 Malton airport Ontario
48 K6 Malu Romania
71 D5 Malubutglubut isld Philippines
85 F6 Malumfashi Nigeria
70 F6 Malunda Sulawesi
27 G11 Malung Sweden
41 K5 Malvaglia Switzerland
76 A2 Malvan India
109 P1 Malvern Arkansas
99 L9 Malvern Iowa
127 J2 Malvern Jamaica
94 F6 Malvern Ohio
127 J3 Malvern peak Jamaica
141 H6 Malvern Hills Queensland
8 D3 Malvern Wells England
21 B7 Malville France
Malvinas, Is see Falkland Is.
74 F7 Malwa Plateau India
83 K9 Malwatu Oya R Sri Lanka
78 K1 Maly Kavkaz mt U.S.S.R.
55 E1 Malyy Atlym U.S.S.R.
55 F1 Malyy Balyk R U.S.S.R.
55 G4 Malyye Chany, Oz L U.S.S.R.
52 G6 Malyy Kundysh R U.S.S.R.
51 O1 Malyy Lyakhovski,Ostrov isld U.S.S.R.
51 K1 Malyy Taymyr, Ostrov isld U.S.S.R.
55 G2 Malyy Yugan R U.S.S.R.
56 H2 Mama U.S.S.R.
56 H2 Mama R U.S.S.R.
52 H6 Mamadysh U.S.S.R.
48 M6 Mamaia Romania
120 F5 Mamainse Point Ontario
145 F3 Mamaku New Zealand
145 D1 Mamaranui New Zealand
70 F6 Mamasa Sulawesi
71 D7 Mambahenauhan isld Philippines
71 G6 Mambajao Philippines
89 F3 Mambala Cave Zimbabwe
86 E5 Mambasa Zaïre
136 H2 Mamberamo R W Irian
86 C4 Mambéré R Cent Afr Republic
71 E4 Mamburao Philippines
70 D4 Mamehaktebo Kalimantan
118 K1 Mameigwess L Ontario
83 J12 Mamelle isld Seychelles
118 D6 Ma-Me-O Beach Alberta
118 D5 Ma-Me-O Beach Prov. Park Alberta
22 K4 Mamer Luxembourg
20 F5 Mamers France
86 A4 Mamfé Cameroon
128 F4 Mamiá, L Brazil
40 D3 Mamirolle France
55 E4 Mamlyutka U.S.S.R.
120 F2 Mammamattawa Ontario
28 D4 Mammen Denmark
37 L7 Mammendorf W Germany
37 O6 Mamming W Germany
43 G10 Mammola Italy
94 F8 Mammoth W Virginia
110 K4 Mammoth Cave Kentucky
101 P5 Mammoth Hot Springs Wyoming
110 E5 Mammoth Spring Arkansas
126 G9 Mamonal Colombia
130 G4 Mamonas Brazil
31 M1 Mamo-novo U.S.S.R.
128 E6 Mamore R Bolivia/Brazil
128 F4 Mamoré, L Brazil
85 B6 Mamou Guinea
111 D11 Mamou Louisiana
87 H11 Mampikohy Madagascar
16 D1 Mampodre mt Spain
85 D7 Mampong Ghana
83 J9 Mampuri Sri Lanka
31 N1 Mamry,Jezioro L Poland
15 C3 Mam Soul mt Scotland
70 F6 Mamudju Sulawesi
Mamuji see Yucheng
87 D10 Mamuno Botswana
55 C5 Mamyt U.S.S.R.
85 C7 Man Ivory Coast
94 F9 Man W Virginia
135 N1 Mana Hawaiian Is
129 H3 Mana R Fr Guiana
56 D3 Mana R U.S.S.R.
128 B4 Manabi Ecuador
128 F4 Manacapuru Brazil
128 F4 Manacapuru,L.Grande de Brazil
17 K5 Manacor Majorca
71 J4 Manado Sulawesi
71 J4 Manadotua isld Sulawesi
22 G3 Manage Belgium
140 D3 Managoora N Terr Aust
125 L3 Managua Nicaragua
145 E4 Manaia I New Zealand
145 E3 Manaia New Zealand
87 H12 Manakara Madagascar
145 E4 Manakau New Zealand
144 D5 Manakau mt New Zealand
136 K2 Manam isld Papua New Guinea
76 D6 Manamadurai India
77 B6 Manamah,Al Bahrain
87 G11 Manambaho R Madagascar
127 N10 Mánamo R Venezuela
71 E5 Manamoc isld Philippines
102 S12 Manana Hawaiian Is
87 H11 Mananara Madagascar
139 G6 Manangatang Victoria
87 H12 Mananjary Madagascar
128 F2 Manano,Caño creek Venezuela
87 H12 Manantenina Madagascar
144 A6 Manapouri New Zealand
66 D3 Manas China
Manasarowar Lake see Mapam Yumco
66 D3 Manas He R China
75 L4 Manaslu mt Nepal
95 N6 Manasquan New Jersey
106 E4 Manassa Colorado
94 K8 Manassas Virginia
71 M9 Manatang Indonesia
127 L5 Manatí Puerto Rico
128 G4 Manaus Brazil
78 C3 Manavgat Turkey
99 S5 Manawa Wisconsin
119 P3 Manawan L Sask
145 E2 Manawaru New Zealand
145 E4 Manawatu R New Zealand
71 G7 Manay Mindanao Philippines
140 B2 Manbulla N Terr Aust
94 C2 Mancelona Michigan
16 E7 Mancha Real Spain
20 C3 Manche dep France
20 K5 Manchecourt France
Manche,la see English Channel
74 H9 Mancheral India
102 A3 Manchester California
95 P5 Manchester Connecticut
112 C5 Manchester Georgia
110 F2 Manchester Illinois
99 P7 Manchester Iowa
107 N2 Manchester Kansas
110 N4 Manchester Kentucky
94 C4 Manchester Michigan
95 Q4 Manchester New Hampshire
95 K4 Manchester New York
94 D8 Manchester Ohio
107 M5 Manchester Oklahoma
95 L6 Manchester Pennsylvania
110 K6 Manchester Tennessee
95 O3 Manchester Vermont
11 E2 Manchester conurbation England
127 K3 Manchester parish Jamaica
37 M6 Manching W Germany
127 M2 Manchioneal Jamaica
65 E1 Manchuria reg China
42 D6 Manciano Italy
128 B4 Máncora Peru
106 B4 Mancos Colorado
77 B5 Mand R Iran
87 F8 Manda Tanzania
130 D8 Mandaguari Brazil
80 F3 Mandah Jordan
88 D7 Manda Hd Zambia
77 G3 Mandal Afghanistan
58 D2 Mandal Mongolia
27 B13 Mandal Norway
68 C2 Mandalay Burma
78 A3 Mandalaya isld Turkey
58 E2 Mandalgovi Mongolia
78 K5 Mandali Iraq
58 D3 Mandal-Ovoo Mongolia
27 B13 Mandalsåni R Norway
Mandalt see Sonid Zuoqi
47 J7 Mandalya Körfezi B Turkey
98 F3 Mandan N Dakota
36 C5 Mandelbachtal W Germany
127 K2 Mandeville Jamaica
111 F11 Mandeville Louisiana
144 B7 Mandeville New Zealand
146 B10 Mandheim Antarctica
130 B6 Mandioré, Lagoa L Bolivia/Brazil
74 J7 Mandla India
142 D4 Mandora W Australia
47 F6 Mandoúdhion Greece
143 B10 Mandurah W Australia
145 E4 Mangahao New Zealand
145 E3 Mangakino New Zealand
76 E2 Mangalagiri India
76 B4 Mangalore India
141 H7 Mangalore Queensland
145 E4 Mangamahoe New Zealand
145 E3 Mangamahu New Zealand
144 D5 Mangamaunu New Zealand
145 D1 Mangamuka New Zealand
145 E3 Mangapehi New Zealand
145 E4 Mangatainoka New Zealand
145 E3 Mangaweka New Zealand
145 E2 Mangawhai New Zealand
142 A4 Mangles B W Australia
66 E4 Mangnai China
88 E9 Mangoche Malawi
87 G12 Mangoky R Madagascar
145 D1 Mangonui New Zealand
87 H12 Mangoro Madagascar
74 D8 Mangrol India
126 F2 Mangrove Cay Andros Bahamas
113 J11 Mangrove Cay isld Bahamas
71 E4 Mangsoagui Pt Philippines
130 H10 Manguaba,L Brazil
16 B4 Mangualde Portugal
86 D3 Mangueigne Chad
131 H4 Mangueira, L Brazil
130 D9 Mangueirinha Brazil
84 E5 Mangueni,Pl.du Niger
87 G7 Mangula Tanzania
108 E9 Mangum Oklahoma
69 F14 Mangunjaya Sumatra
67 A5 Manhao China
99 T8 Manhattan Illinois
107 O2 Manhattan Kansas
101 O4 Manhattan Montana
102 G3 Manhattan Nevada
22 K3 Manhay Belgium
130 H7 Manhuaçu Brazil
130 H6 Manhuaçu,R Brazil
113 L12 Man I Bahamas
87 E7 Mani Zaïre
87 H11 Mania R Madagascar
42 E2 Maniago Italy
88 E8 Maniamba Mozambique
87 F9 Manica Mozambique
71 G5 Manicani isld Philippines
122 D4 Manic Deux Dam Quebec
128 F5 Manicoré R Brazil
122 D3 Manicouagan Quebec
122 D4 Manicouagan Pen Quebec
122 D4 Manicouagan R Quebec
122 D2 Manicouagan Res. Quebec
141 K6 Manifold, C Queensland
119 V7 Manigotagan Manitoba
110 F6 Manila Arkansas
71 E3 Manila Luzon Philippines
101 O9 Manila Utah
71 E3 Manila B Luzon Philippines
139 J5 Manildra New S Wales
99 L8 Manilla Iowa
139 K4 Manilla New S Wales
70 F5 Manimbaja,Tg C Sulawesi
69 E13 Manindjan,Danau L Sumatra
87 H11 Maningory Madagascar
140 C1 Maningrida N Terr Aust
85 C6 Maninian Ivory Coast
69 E13 Maninjau Danau L Sumatra
75 P6 Manipur prov India
73 P4 Manipur R Burma
47 J6 Manisa Turkey
17 G5 Manises Spain
12 D5 Man,Isle of U.K.
99 U5 Manistee Michigan
94 B2 Manistee R Michigan
99 U4 Manistique Michigan
99 U3 Manistique R Michigan
99 V3 Manistique L Michigan
99 R9 Manito Illinois

119 Manitoba Canada
119 S7 Manitoba, L Manitoba
118 H6 Manito L Sask
119 T9 Manitou Manitoba
109 J1 Manitou Oklahoma
119 M7 Manitou Bch Sask
99 T2 Manitou I Michigan
120 J7 Manitou L Ontario
122 G3 Manitou,L Quebec
120 H7 Manitoulin I Ontario
122 G2 Manitou R Quebec
106 F3 Manitou Springs Colorado
120 E3 Manitouwadge Ontario
120 J7 Manitowaning Ontario
120 F4 Manitowik L Ontario
99 T5 Manitowoc Wisconsin
121 P6 Maniwaki Quebec
128 C2 Manizales Colombia
80 G6 Manja Jordan
87 G12 Manja Madagascar
143 B10 Manjimup W Australia
74 G9 Manjlegaon India
38 M5 Mank Austria
107 M2 Mankato Kansas
99 N5 Mankato Minnesota
86 B5 Mankim Cameroon
109 J2 Mankins Texas
85 C7 Mankono Ivory Coast
118 K9 Mankota Sask
48 N2 Mankovka U.S.S.R.
76 E6 Mankulam Sri Lanka
95 M3 Manlius New York
17 J2 Manlleu Spain
99 N6 Manly Iowa
139 K5 Manly New S Wales
74 F8 Manmad India
140 C2 Mann R N Terr Aust
138 F4 Mannahill S Australia
83 J9 Mannar Sri Lanka
73 M7 Mannar,G.of India/Sri Lanka
76 D5 Mannargudi India
83 J8 Mannar I Sri Lanka
36 F5 Mannheim W Germany
14 A3 Mannin B Irish Rep
117 P7 Manning Alberta
109 P1 Manning Arkansas
99 L8 Manning Iowa
98 D2 Manning N Dakota
112 G4 Manning S Carolina
109 N4 Manning Texas
139 K4 Manning R New S Wales
117 N11 Manning Prov. Park Br Col
94 G7 Mannington W Virginia
9 H4 Manningtree England
140 A7 Mann, Mt N Terr Aust
140 A7 Mann Ranges N Terr/S Aust
112 M2 Manns Harbor N Carolina
95 L3 Mannsville New York
43 C9 Mannu R Sardinia
43 B8 Mannu,C Sardinia
138 E5 Mannum S Australia
118 F5 Mannville Alberta
85 B7 Mano Sierra Leone
128 E5 Manoa Bolivia
80 B8 Manoah R Israel
127 N1 Man of War B Tobago
116 H7 Manokotak Alaska
136 G2 Manokwari W Irian
46 E6 Manolás Greece
87 G12 Manombo Madagascar
88 A5 Manono Zaïre
112 E6 Manor Georgia
119 Q9 Manor Sask
109 K5 Manor Texas
8 B4 Manorbier Wales
144 B6 Manorburn Res New Zealand
14 C2 Manorhamilton Irish Rep
85 B7 Mano River Liberia
68 D7 Manoron Burma
19 P17 Manosque France
21 G10 Manot France
20 G5 Manou France
121 Q5 Manouane Quebec
122 B3 Manouane L Quebec
61 M8 Mano-wan B Japan
68 C1 Man Pan Burma
17 J3 Manresa Spain
88 B7 Mansa Zambia
85 A6 Mansaba Guinea-Bissau
85 A6 Mansa Konko The Gambia
71 E4 Mansalay B Philippines
68 C1 Man Sam Burma
142 G4 Mansbridge, Mt W Australia
115 L5 Mansel I N W Terr
33 O9 Mansfeld E Germany
110 B6 Mansfield Arkansas
9 E1 Mansfield England
112 D4 Mansfield Georgia
99 S9 Mansfield Illinois
109 O3 Mansfield Louisiana
95 Q4 Mansfield Massachusetts
110 D4 Mansfield Missouri
94 E6 Mansfield Ohio
98 H4 Mansfield S Dakota
109 K3 Mansfield Texas
139 H6 Mansfield Victoria
100 F2 Mansfield Washington
95 P2 Mansfield,Mt Vermont
56 D4 Manskoye Belogor'ye mts U.S.S.R.
21 F10 Mansle France
99 M7 Manson Iowa
100 E2 Manson Washington
117 L8 Manson Creek Br Col
130 C4 Manso,R Brazil
8 D6 Manston England
71 C3 Mansuar isld W Irian
111 D10 Mansura Louisiana
79 B7 Mansûra,El Egypt
128 B4 Manta Ecuador
71 C6 Mantalingajan, Mt Palawan Philippines
70 E1 Mantanani Besar isld Sabah
86 D6 Mantantale Zaïre
65 H4 Mantap-san mt N Korea
71 J5 Mantarara Indonesia
118 H7 Mantario Sask
128 C6 Mantaro R Peru
102 C4 Manteca California
111 G8 Mantee Mississippi
37 N4 Mantel W Germany
130 H6 Mantena Brazil
99 T8 Manteno Illinois
112 M2 Manteo N Carolina
107 J4 Manter Kansas
71 J4 Manterawo isld Sulawesi
20 J4 Mantes France
25 E2 Mantgum Netherlands
74 H9 Manthani India
21 G7 Manthelan France
103 N2 Manti Utah
130 F8 Mantiqueira,Serra da mts Brazil
100 D9 Manton California
94 B2 Manton Michigan
65 B5 Mantou Shan mt ra China
45 J1 Mantova Italy
29 L11 Mäntsälä Finland
29 L10 Mänttä Finland
126 B3 Mantua Cuba
Mantua Italy see Mantova
94 F5 Mantua Ohio
141 H6 Mantuan Downs Queensland
52 F5 Manturovo U.S.S.R.
29 J10 Mäntyluoto Finland
128 D6 Manú Peru
Manuan see Manouane
122 B3 Manuanis,L Quebec
71 F6 Manucan Mindanao Philippines
129 J5 Manuel Alves R Brazil
106 B6 Manuelito New Mexico
130 D9 Manuel Ribas Brazil
133 C8 Manuel Rodríguez, I Chile
128 E5 Manuel Urbano Brazil
129 H5 Manuelzinho Brazil
71 H6 Manui isld Indonesia
77 E6 Manūjān Iran
145 G2 Manukau New Zealand
70 F2 Manuk Manka Philippines
138 E4 Manunda R S Australia
145 E3 Manunui New Zealand
71 C3 Manuran isld W Irian
128 E6 Manuripe R Bolivia/Peru
136 K2 Manus isld Bismarck Arch
145 E3 Manutahi New Zealand
138 E3 Manuwalkaninna S Australia
98 J1 Manvel N Dakota
76 C3 Manvi India
98 B7 Manville Wyoming
109 O4 Many Louisiana
52 K4 Man'ya U.S.S.R.
88 B10 Manyangau mt Zimbabwe
88 G3 Manyara,L Tanzania
47 J4 Manyas Turkey
118 G9 Manyberries Alberta
54 M9 Manych R U.S.S.R.
118 G8 Many Island I Alberta
88 E4 Manyoni Tanzania
141 K6 Many Peaks Queensland
143 C10 Many Peaks, Mt W Australia
79 B7 Manzala,El Egypt
84 J3 Manzala, L Egypt
89 E2 Manzamnyama R Zimbabwe
16 E5 Manzanares Spain
127 P2 Manzanilla B Trinidad
126 F4 Manzanillo Cuba
124 G8 Manzanillo Mexico
106 D7 Manzano New Mexico
131 A8 Manzano,B del Chile
106 G3 Manzanola Colorado
106 D7 Manzano Mts New Mexico
58 G2 Manzhouli China
79 G7 Manzil Jordan
89 G6 Manzini Swaziland
Manzovka see Sibirtsevo
86 C3 Mao Chad
65 G2 Mao'ershan China
136 H2 Maoke, Pegunungan ra W Irian
65 F4 Maokui Shan mt China
65 G3 Maolin China
67 C6 Maoming China
67 C1 Maoping China
67 G6 Mao-pi T'ou C Taiwan
67 B3 Maotai China
67 A1 Maowen China
65 F2 Maoxing China
80 F4 Ma'oz Israel
70 F5 Mapaga Sulawesi
87 F10 Mapai Mozambique
66 C5 Mapam Yumco L China
70 B6 Mapan Kalimantan
70 G5 Mapane Sulawesi
70 F5 Mapida Sulawesi
70 F6 Mapili Sulawesi
124 G4 Mapimí, Bolson de dist Mexico
67 D1 Maping China
128 F2 Mapire Venezuela
129 H3 Mapireme Brazil
128 E7 Mapiri R La Paz Bolivia
128 F4 Mapixari, L Brazil
99 L7 Maple R Iowa
94 C3 Maple R Michigan
118 H9 Maple Creek Sask
99 N6 Maple Island Minnesota
111 K9 Maplesville Alabama
99 L7 Mapleton Iowa
95 S7 Mapleton Maine
99 N6 Mapleton Minnesota
122 H8 Mapleton Nova Scotia
100 B5 Mapleton Oregon
100 C2 Maple Valley Washington
95 L3 Maple View New York
141 F1 Mapoon Queensland
144 C5 Mapourika, L New Zealand
13 H6 Mappleton England
129 G4 Mapuera R Brazil
69 G12 Mapur isld Indonesia
89 H5 Maputo Mozambique
89 H6 Maputo R Mozambique
80 F8 Maqam en Nabi Yusha Jordan
78 H6 Maqar an Naam Iraq
46 D3 Maqellarë Albania
65 H2 Maqiaohe China
79 E10 Maqnā Saudi Arabia
66 C6 Maquan He R China
71 G4 Maqueda Chan Philippines
122 H5 Maquereau Pte.au Quebec
133 D6 Maquinchao Argentina
131 B8 Maquinchao, R Argentina
99 Q7 Maquoketa Iowa
99 Q9 Maquon Illinois
70 E3 Mara Kalimantan
127 J9 Mara Venezuela
128 E4 Maraa Brazil
129 J5 Marabá Brazil
70 D6 Marabahan Kalimantan
40 B2 Marac France
127 J9 Maracaibo Venezuela
127 J9 Maracaibo, L. de Venezuela
129 H3 Maracá, Ilha de Amapá Brazil
128 F3 Maracá, Ilha de Roraima Brazil
133 F2 Maracaju Brazil
130 C7 Maracaju,Serra de mts Brazil
129 J4 Maracana Brazil
127 O2 Maracas B Trinidad
127 L9 Maracay Venezuela
84 F4 Maradah Libya
85 F6 Maradi Niger
145 E3 Maraetai New Zealand
78 L3 Marāgheh Iran
130 J10 Maragogi Brazil
128 E3 Marahuaca,Co mt Venezuela
65 E2 Marain Sum China
110 A3 Marais des Cygnes R Kansas/Missouri
20 F3 Marais-Vernier France
129 J4 Marajó,I.de Brazil
86 G5 Maralal Kenya
55 G4 Maraldy U.S.S.R.
86 C4 Marali Cent Afr Republic
137 N3 Maramasike isld Solomon Is
Maramba see Livingstone Zambia
48 H3 Maramures old prov Romania
69 F11 Maran Malaysia
103 N9 Marana Arizona
140 C2 Maranboy N Terr Aust
17 F3 Maranchón Spain
78 K2 Marand Iran
89 G2 Marandellas Zimbabwe
45 J2 Maranello Italy
68 D7 Marang Burma
69 F10 Marang Malaysia
129 L4 Maranguape Brazil
130 E4 Maranhão R Brazil
129 J4 Maranhão state Brazil
141 J7 Maranoa R Queensland
45 Q8 Marano di Napoli Italy
128 D4 Marañón R Peru
21 C9 Marans France
40 A1 Maranville France
16 B3 Marão, Sa do mts Portugal
129 G3 Marapi R Brazil
128 E5 Marari Brazil
144 B6 Mararoa R New Zealand
78 F3 Maras Turkey
70 F7 Marasende isld Indonesia
48 L5 Mărăşeşti Romania
71 C6 Marasi B Palawan Philippines
16 B6 Marateca Portugal
46 D7 Marathiás,Akr C Greece
113 F13 Marathon Florida
47 F6 Marathón Greece
95 L4 Marathon New York
120 D4 Marathon Ontario
141 G5 Marathon Queensland
108 D5 Marathon Texas
99 R5 Marathon Wisconsin
70 F3 Maratua isld Indonesia
129 L6 Maraú Brazil
128 E3 Marauaí R Brazil
127 O2 Maraval Trinidad
108 E6 Maravillas Cr Texas
71 G7 Marawi Mindanao Philippines
38 M5 Marbach Austria
36 F2 Marbach W Germany
22 K4 Marbehan Belgium
106 C2 Marble Colorado
100 H1 Marble Washington
142 C5 Marble Bar W Australia
103 N5 Marble Canyon Arizona
110 B6 Marble City Oklahoma
109 J5 Marble Falls Texas
87 E10 Marble Hall S Africa
99 P10 Marblehead Illinois
95 R4 Marblehead Massachusetts
94 E5 Marblehead Ohio
99 O7 Marble Rock Iowa
121 T7 Marbleton Quebec
101 P7 Marbleton Wyoming
36 F2 Marburg W Germany
95 K8 Marbury Maryland
26 G8 Marby Sweden
48 D3 Marcal R Hungary
47 J7 Marçal Dağ mt Turkey
48 D4 Marcali Hungary
45 J1 Marcaria Italy
21 F9 Marçay France
122 F2 Marceau,L Quebec
118 L6 Marcelin Sask
110 D2 Marceline Missouri
133 G3 Marcelino Ramos Brazil
110 E6 Marcella Arkansas
94 B4 Marcellus Michigan
100 G2 Marcellus Washington
45 O5 Marcetelli Italy
9 G2 March England
20 G4 Marchainville France
118 E2 Marchand Manitoba
138 E4 Marchant Hill S Australia
40 D3 Marchaux France
21 I9 Marche reg France
45 N4 Marche reg Italy
22 J3 Marche-en-Famenne Belgium
16 D7 Marchena Spain
128 A7 Marchena isld Galapagos Is
21 H6 Marchenoir France
70 E1 Marchesa B Sabah
20 C3 Marchésieux France
127 P6 Marchfield Barbados
22 E3 Marchiennes-Ville France
22 J3 Marchin Belgium
140 D1 Marchinbar I N Terr Aust
131 E3 Mar Chiquita, L Córdoba Argentina
45 Q7 Marcianise Italy
18 H6 Marcigny France
18 G8 Marcillac France
20 D5 Marcille-la-Ville France
20 H4 Marcilly France
21 I7 Marcilly-en Gault France
21 J6 Marcilly-en Villette France
40 G1 Marckolsheim France
122 J1 Marc,L Labrador
113 F12 Marco Florida
110 J3 Marco Indiana
43 G9 Marco Argentano, S Italy
22 E3 Marcoing France
100 C5 Marcola Oregon
21 G6 Marçon France
118 C1 Marconi Manitoba
22 K3 Marcourt Belgium
99 L7 Marcus Iowa
100 G1 Marcus Washington
116 O6 Marcus Baker,Mt Alaska
134 G5 Marcus I Pacific Oc
95 M3 Marcy New York
95 O2 Marcy, Mt New York
80 D5 Marda Jordan
74 E1 Mardan Pakistan
131 F6 Mar del Plata Argentina
9 G5 Marden England
142 B5 Mardie W Australia
78 H3 Mardin Turkey
26 M5 Mårdsel Sweden
26 K7 Mårdsele Sweden
26 J7 Mardsjö Sweden
26 H8 Mårdsjön Sweden
70 G7 Mare Sulawesi
71 A2 Mare isld Halmahera Indonesia
137 O6 Maré isld Îles Loyauté Pac Oc
86 G3 Mareb R Ethiopia
45 M3 Marecchia R Italy
130 J10 Marechal Deodoro Brazil
141 H3 Mareeba Queensland
110 K3 Marengo Indiana
99 P8 Marengo Iowa
41 N7 Marengo Italy
94 E6 Marengo Ohio
118 H7 Marengo Sask
100 G2 Marengo Washington
99 Q3 Marengo Wisconsin
99 R3 Marenisco Michigan
21 C10 Marennes France
145 E2 Mareretu New Zealand
86 A2 Marergur Somalia
9 G6 Maresfield England
43 E11 Marettimo isld Sicily
22 E3 Maretz France
21 C8 Mareuil France
21 J8 Mareuil-sur-Arnon France
108 C5 Marfa Texas
66 D4 Margai Caka L China
75 M1 Margai Caka L China
8 C4 Margam Wales
57 D1 Marganets U.S.S.R.
76 A3 Margao India
123 L7 Margaree Harbour C Breton I, N Scotia
123 L7 Margaree I Nova Scotia
123 M7 Margaree Valley C Breton I, N Scotia
108 H1 Margaret Texas
138 D3 Margaret R S Australia
117 K10 Margaret Bay Br Col
141 G1 Margaret Bay Queensland
117 Q6 Margaret L Alberta
117 P3 Margaret L N W Terr
142 C5 Margaret, Mt W Australia
143 B10 Margaret R W Australia
95 N4 Margaretville New York
130 C7 Margarida Brazil
127 N9 Margarita I. de Venezuela
46 D5 Margarítion Greece
9 H5 Margate England
89 G8 Margate S Africa
139 H9 Margate Tasmania
95 N7 Margate City New Jersey
18 H8 Margeride, Mts de la France
Margherita see Giamame Somalia
48 G3 Mărghita Romania
118 F3 Margie Alberta
99 N1 Margie Minnesota
57 F4 Margilan U.S.S.R.
48 G5 Mărgina Romania
48 G5 Margita Yugoslavia
119 O7 Margo Sask
77 H4 Margo, Dasht-i- des Afghanistan
71 F7 Margosatubig Mindanao Philippines
94 C2 Margrethe, L Michigan
117 M9 Marguerite Br Columbia
146 F13 Marguerite B Antarctica
22 J4 Margut France
80 F3 Marhaba Jordan
122 F5 Maria Quebec
124 F7 María Cleofas, I Mexico
28 D3 Mariager Denmark
32 M7 Mariaglück W Germany
68 C7 Maria I Burma
140 D2 Maria I N Terr Aust
139 J8 Maria I Tasmania
36 C3 Maria Laach W Germany
38 G8 Maria Luggau Austria
124 F7 María Madre, I Mexico
124 F7 María Magdalena, I Mexico
103 K8 Maria Mts California
141 J5 Marian Queensland
130 G7 Mariana Brazil
118 E3 Mariana Lake Alberta
126 C3 Marianao Cuba
134 E6 Marianas islds Pacific Oc
75 Q5 Mariani India
117 P4 Marian L N W Terr
110 F7 Marianna Arkansas
113 B7 Marianna Florida
27 H14 Mariannelund Sweden
87 B8 Mariano Machado Angola
37 O4 Marianské Lázně Czechoslovakia
119 T9 Mariapolis Manitoba
101 N1 Marias R Montana
17 F7 Maria,Sierra de mts Spain
101 M1 Marias Pass Montana
38 F6 Mariastein Austria
135 M12 Maria Theresa Reef Pacific Oc
145 D1 Maria van Diemen, C New Zealand
38 M6 Mariazell Austria
99 T5 Maribel Wisconsin
28 G7 Maribo Denmark
Maribo co see Storstrøm
38 N8 Maribor Yugoslavia
71 E4 Maricaban isld Philippines
89 E5 Marico R Botswana
103 M8 Maricopa Arizona
102 E6 Maricopa California
103 M8 Maricopa Mts Arizona
115 M5 Maricourt Quebec
86 E5 Maridi Sudan
128 E4 Marié R Brazil
83 K12 Marie Anne I Seychelles
146 H10 Marie Byrd Land Antarctica
27 H13 Mariedam Sweden
27 J12 Mariefred Sweden
127 N5 Marie Galante isld Guadeloupe W Indies
27 L11 Mariehamn Finland
118 G4 Marie L Alberta
126 C3 Mariel Cuba
Marienbad see Marianské Lázně
37 P2 Marienberg E Germany
25 G3 Marienberg Netherlands
32 L8 Marienberg W Germany
22 H3 Marienbourg Belgium
Marienburg see Malbork
36 C2 Marienburg Nordrhein-Westfalen W Germany
37 N3 Marieney E Germany
32 F5 Marienhafe W Germany
36 C1 Marienheide W Germany
28 G7 Marienleuchte C W Germany
89 A5 Mariental Namibia
107 J3 Marienthal Kansas
94 H5 Marienville Pennsylvania
Marienwerder see Kwidzyn
140 B1 Marie Shoal N Terr Aust
27 G13 Mariestad Sweden
112 C4 Marietta Georgia
94 F7 Marietta Ohio
109 K2 Marietta Oklahoma
112 E2 Marietta S Carolina
121 R7 Marieville Quebec
19 O18 Marignane France
21 F6 Marigné France
20 C3 Marigny France
127 N5 Marigot Saint Martin W I
56 C3 Mariinsk U.S.S.R.
55 D4 Mariinskoye U.S.S.R.
52 G6 Mariinsky Posad U.S.S.R.
71 J5 Marikasu,Tg C Indonesia
130 D8 Marila Brazil
133 H2 Marília Brazil
142 C6 Marillana W Australia
130 E7 Marimbondo Cachoeira rapids Brazil
127 M4 Marin Martinique W I
16 B2 Marín Spain
44 H3 Marina di Carrara Italy
44 H3 Marina di Massa Italy
44 H4 Marina di Pisa Italy
45 M3 Marina di Ravenna Italy
128 G2 Marina Fall Guyana
70 B6 Marindjahan Kalimantan
71 E4 Marinduque isld Philippines
110 G3 Marine Illinois
113 F8 Marineland Florida
20 K3 Marines France
99 T4 Marinette Wisconsin
129 H8 Maringá Brazil
86 D5 Maringa R Zaïre
111 E11 Maringouin Louisiana
87 F9 Maringue Mozambique
16 B5 Marinha Grande Portugal
54 J9 Mar'inka U.S.S.R.
42 E7 Marino Italy
128 E3 Marinuma Colombia
111 J9 Marion Alabama
110 F6 Marion Arkansas
117 Q11 Marion Idaho
110 H4 Marion Illinois
94 B6 Marion Indiana
99 P7 Marion Iowa
107 O3 Marion Kansas
110 H4 Marion Kentucky
111 D9 Marion Louisiana
95 U2 Marion Maine
94 B2 Marion Michigan
111 H9 Marion Mississippi
101 L1 Marion Montana
112 E2 Marion N Carolina
98 H3 Marion N Dakota
98 F9 Marion Nebraska
94 D6 Marion Ohio
112 H3 Marion S Carolina
98 J6 Marion S Dakota
109 J6 Marion Texas
94 F10 Marion Virginia
99 S5 Marion Wisconsin
139 J8 Marion B Tasmania
140 E6 Marion Downs Queensland
111 J9 Marion Junction Alabama
137 L5 Marion Reef Coral Sea
141 K4 Marion Reef Gt Barrier Reef Aust
110 C4 Marionville Missouri
128 E2 Maripa Venezuela
71 G5 Maripipi isld Philippines
102 E4 Mariposa California
102 D4 Mariposa R California
70 G4 Marisa Sulawesi
133 E2 Mariscal Estigarribia Paraguay
110 G3 Marissa Illinois
47 H2 Maritsa Bulgaria
Maritsa R see Évros R
47 G2 Maritsa R Bulgaria
44 B3 Marittime, Alpi mts Italy/France
52 G6 Mari Turek U.S.S.R.
Mariupol see Zhdanov
127 O10 Mariusa R Venezuela
77 J4 Marja Afghanistan
84 G3 Marj, Al Libya
26 N5 Marjärv Sweden
79 F5 Marjayoûn Lebanon
25 C5 Mark R Netherlands
80 G6 Marka Jordan
26 E8 Markabygd Norway
78 H4 Markada Syria
56 C6 Markakal', Oz L U.S.S.R.
52 J4 Markalasta U.S.S.R.
58 C6 Markam China
76 D3 Markapur India
120 K8 Markdale Ontario
41 K2 Markdorf W Germany
110 F6 Marked Tree Arkansas
25 G4 Markelo Netherlands
28 G7 Markelsdorfe Huk C W Germany
25 D4 Marken Netherlands
25 D3 Markerwaard Netherlands
99 S6 Markesan Wisconsin
9 F2 Market Deeping England
8 D2 Market Drayton England
9 F3 Market Harborough England
14 E2 Markethill N Ireland
13 H6 Market Rasen England
9 E1 Market Warsop England
13 H6 Market Weighton England
36 G6 Markgröningen W Germany
121 L9 Markham Ontario
109 L7 Markham Texas
100 B3 Markham Washington
66 C4 Markham Lake China
9 F1 Markham Moor England
146 G7 Markham,Mt Antarctica
119 N8 Markinch Sask
15 E4 Markinch Scotland
33 T8 Märkisch Buchholz E Germany
26 M4 Markitta Sweden
102 E3 Markleeville California
37 O6 Marklkofen W Germany
37 N3 Markneukirchen E Germany
26 J4 Markotjäkko mt Sweden
33 Q10 Markrapstädt E Germany
111 F7 Marks Mississippi
8 D5 Marksbury England
120 K6 Markstay Ontario
9 G4 Marks Tey England
37 J2 Marksuhl E Germany
111 D10 Marksville Louisiana
37 J5 Marktbergel W Germany
37 J4 Markt Bibart W Germany
37 J4 Marktbreit W Germany
37 L3 Marktgraitz W Germany
36 H4 Marktheidenfeld W Germany
37 L7 Markt Indersdorf W Germany
37 O7 Marktl W Germany
37 M3 Marktleugast W Germany
37 J6 Marktoffingen W Germany
37 N3 Marktredwitz W Germany
37 M3 Marktschorgast W Germany
37 J4 Marktsteft W Germany
41 N1 Markt Wald W Germany
37 L3 Marktzeuln W Germany
99 O3 Markville Minnesota
32 F9 Marl W Germany
107 N5 Marland Oklahoma
143 B8 Marlandy Hill W Australia
121 N8 Marlbank Ontario
95 Q4 Marlboro Massachusetts
95 P4 Marlboro New Hampshire
9 E5 Marlborough England
128 G2 Marlborough Guyana
141 J6 Marlborough Queensland
145 D4 Marlborough stat area New Zealand
22 F4 Marle France
33 S8 Marlendorf E Germany
33 S8 Marlenfelde E Germany
94 D3 Marlette Michigan
109 L4 Marlin Texas
94 G8 Marlinton W Virginia
139 J7 Marlo Victoria
22 J3 Marloie Belgium
33 R4 Marlow E Germany
9 F4 Marlow England
95 P3 Marlow New Hampshire
109 K1 Marlow Oklahoma
141 H5 Marlow Queensland
22 F4 Marly France
20 K4 Marly-le-Roi France
27 J10 Marma Sweden
110 F5 Marmaduke Arkansas
18 F8 Marmande France
47 J4 Marmara Turkey
47 J4 Marmaraereğlisi Turkey
47 J6 Marmara Gölü L Turkey
47 J4 Marmara,Sea of Turkey
47 J8 Marmaris Turkey
98 C3 Marmarth N Dakota
26 K3 Mårmatj mt Sweden
94 E4 Marme City Michigan
16 B2 Marmed,Sa des S mts Spain
128 F5 Marmelos R Brazil
94 F8 Marmet W Virginia
121 P4 Marmette,L Quebec
118 L1 Marmion L res Ontario
143 C8 Marmion, Mt W Australia
45 J1 Marmirolo Italy
42 D2 Marmolada mt Italy
16 E6 Marmolejo Spain
116 L7 Marmot B Alaska
125 M9 Mar Muerto B Mexico
19 J5 Marnay France
32 K5 Marne W Germany
18 H4 Marne dep France
40 B1 Marne R France
36 B6 Marne, Canal de la France
36 D4 Marnheim W Germany
33 P6 Marnitz E Germany
139 G6 Marnoo Victoria
99 S9 Maroa Illinois
145 F3 Maroa New Zealand
87 H11 Maroantsetra Madagascar
74 C2 Marobi Pakistan
22 D3 Marœuil France
22 F3 Maroilles France
37 K3 Maroldsweisach W Germany
20 F5 Marolles-les-Braults France
87 H10 Maromandia Madagascar
20 H3 Maromme France
47 H4 Marónia Greece
18 G7 Maronne R France
141 G7 Maroo Queensland
143 B6 Maroonah W Australia
127 J2 Maroon Town Jamaica
70 F7 Maros Sulawesi
70 F7 Maros R Sulawesi
145 E1 Marotiri Is New Zealand
86 B3 Maroua Cameroon
121 L4 Marouf Jct Quebec
129 H3 Marouini R Fr Guiana
87 H11 Marovoay Madagascar
110 F4 Marquano Missouri
135 U13 Marquesas Is Pacific Oc
113 E13 Marquesas Keys islds Florida
130 G8 Marquês de Valença Brazil
99 P6 Marquette Iowa
107 N3 Marquette Kansas
118 D1 Marquette Manitoba
99 T3 Marquette Michigan
98 H8 Marquette Nebraska
99 U6 Marquette R Michigan
106 C6 Marquez New Mexico
109 L4 Marquez Texas
17 F1 Marquina Spain
22 E3 Marquion France
119 M8 Marquis Sask
22 B2 Marquise France
139 G4 Marra New S Wales
139 H4 Marra R New S Wales
89 H5 Marracuene Mozambique
45 L3 Marradi Italy
143 B10 Marradong W Australia
86 D3 Marra, Jebel mts Sudan
140 B2 Marrakai N Terr Aust
85 C2 Marrakech Morocco
85 E2 Marraket, Hassi Algeria
139 H5 Marrar New S Wales
43 B8 Marrargiu, C Sardinia
139 G8 Marrawah Tasmania
28 H7 Marrebæk Denmark
138 E3 Marree S Australia
111 J13 Marrero New Orleans
87 G9 Marromeu Mozambique
16 D8 Marroqui,Pta Spain
88 F8 Marrupa Mozambique
138 C2 Marryat R S Australia
94 G6 Mars Pennsylvania
84 K4 Marsá Alam Egypt
17 F9 Marsa Ben Mehidi Algeria
86 G5 Marsabit Kenya
Marsa Brega see Qasr al Burayqal
21 B6 Marsac-sur-Don France
130 F8 Mar,Sa.do mts Brazil
86 H3 Marsa Fatma Ethiopia
36 B6 Marsal France
43 E11 Marsala Sicily
19 N15 Marsanne France
84 G3 Marsá Sūsah Libya
13 G4 Marsden England
139 J5 Marsden New S Wales
118 H6 Marsden Sask
19 O18 Marseille France
20 J2 Marseille-en-Beauvaisis France
19 N18 Marseille-Rhône, Canal France
Marseilles France see Marseille
99 S8 Marseilles Illinois
94 D6 Marseilles Ohio
98 B3 Marsh Montana
79 E10 Marshah, J mt Saudi Arabia
110 D6 Marshall Arkansas
99 T10 Marshall Illinois
94 C4 Marshall Michigan
99 L5 Marshall Minnesota
110 C2 Marshall Missouri
112 E2 Marshall N Carolina
98 D2 Marshall N Dakota
107 N5 Marshall Oklahoma
118 H5 Marshall Sask
109 N3 Marshall Texas
94 K8 Marshall Virginia
101 U7 Marshall Wyoming
140 D6 Marshall R N Terr Aust
139 J7 Marshall B Tasmania
134 G7 Marshall Is Pacific Oc
120 C2 Marshall L Ontario
99 O7 Marshalltown Iowa
8 D3 Marshbrook England
8 D5 Marshfield England
110 D4 Marshfield Missouri
99 Q5 Marshfield Wisconsin
113 K11 Marsh Harbour Great Abaco I Bahamas
95 L5 Marsh Hill Pennsylvania
95 T7 Mars Hill Maine
111 D12 Marsh Island Louisiana
117 F5 Marsh L Yukon Terr
98 K4 Marsh Lake Minnesota
101 Q9 Marsh Pk Utah
112 G3 Marshville N Carolina
100 J6 Marsing Idaho
98 C7 Marsland Nebraska
19 J3 Mars la Tour France
28 E4 Mårslet Denmark
28 F6 Marslev Denmark
27 J12 Märsta Sweden
28 F7 Marstal Denmark
28 E7 Marstal Bugt B Denmark
101 Q8 Marston Wyoming
27 E14 Marstrand Sweden
28 C6 Marstrup Denmark
25 E2 Marsum Netherlands
55 D1 Marsyaty U.S.S.R.
109 L4 Mart Texas
42 D6 Marta R Italy
68 C4 Martaban Burma
73 Q5 Martaban,G.of Burma
21 F8 Martaizé France
70 D6 Martapura Kalimantan
70 K8 Martapura Sumatra
18 G8 Martel France
22 K4 Martelange Belgium
41 N4 Martello, Val Italy
47 H1 Marten Bulgaria
99 N8 Martensdale Iowa
17 G5 Martés,Sierra mts Spain
139 J4 Marthaguy R New S Wales
110 E3 Marthasville Missouri
95 R5 Marthas Vineyard Massachusetts
36 B6 Marthille France
126 F4 Martí Cuba
45 M5 Martignano,L.di Italy
20 D5 Martigné France
21 E7 Martigné-Briand France
21 C6 Martigné-Ferchaud France
40 F5 Martigny Switzerland
40 C1 Martigny-les-Bains France
19 O18 Martigues France
16 D9 Martil Morocco
116 N4 Martin Alaska
31 L6 Martin Czechoslovakia
94 E9 Martin Kentucky
94 B4 Martin Michigan
98 E6 Martin S Dakota
110 H5 Martin Tennessee
17 G4 Martin R Spain
41 M4 Martina Switzerland
43 H8 Martina Franca Italy
145 E4 Martinborough New Zealand
109 K6 Martindale Texas
102 B3 Martinez California
125 L7 Martínez Mexico
32 M10 Martinfeld E Germany
130 F6 Martinho Campos Brazil
127 L4 Martinique isld Lesser Antilles
111 L9 Martin L Alabama
130 D8 Martinópolis Brazil
146 H11 Martin Pen Antarctica
116 Q1 Martin Pt Alaska
144 A6 Martin's B New Zealand
38 M5 Martinsberg Austria
Martinsbrück see Martina
110 E2 Martinsburg Missouri
95 M3 Martinsburg New York
94 E6 Martinsburg Ohio
94 J6 Martinsburg Pennsylvania
94 K7 Martinsburg W Virginia
101 P3 Martinsdale Montana
94 G6 Martins Ferry Ohio
99 T10 Martinsville Illinois
94 A7 Martinsville Indiana
94 H10 Martinsville Virginia
20 B2 Martinvast France
21 H8 Martizay France
9 H3 Martlesham England
8 D6 Martock England
28 F5 Martofte Denmark
9 F1 Marton England
145 E4 Marton New Zealand
17 J3 Martorell Spain
16 E7 Martos Spain
117 O4 Martre, Lac La N W Terr
29 N4 Martti Finland
29 K11 Marttila Finland
55 C5 Martuk U.S.S.R.
52 J2 Martyn U.S.S.R.
80 G3 Maru Jordan
77 H2 Maruchak Afghanistan
70 D2 Marudi Sarawak
70 E1 Marudu Bay Sabah
77 K4 Maruf Afghanistan
60 G11 Marugame Japan
144 D5 Maruia New Zealand
129 L6 Maruim Brazil
28 J4 Mårum Denmark
25 F2 Marum Netherlands
145 F3 Marumaru New Zealand
140 C2 Marumba Mt N Terr Aust
88 B5 Marungu mts Zaïre
61 K9 Maruoka Japan
77 D4 Marvast Iran
27 C11 Mår-vatn L Norway
18 H8 Marvejols France
111 F7 Marvell Arkansas
143 C9 Marvel Loch W Australia
22 J5 Marville France
98 K4 Marvin S Dakota
106 C1 Marvine Colorado
103 N3 Marvine,Mt Utah
77 H2 Marwa Afghanistan
74 E6 Marwar India
118 G5 Marwayne Alberta
15 E1 Marwick Hd Orkney Scotland
32 G6 Marx W Germany
33 S9 Marxdorf E Germany
37 M3 Marxgrün W Germany
77 G1 Mary U.S.S.R.
142 B5 Mary Ann Pt W Australia
55 F3 Mar'yanovka U.S.S.R.
139 G6 Maryborough New S Wales
141 L7 Maryborough Queensland
87 D11 Marydale S Africa
55 E4 Mar'yevka U.S.S.R.
119 Q9 Maryfield Sask
117 L6 Mary Henry,Mt Br Col
12 D2 Maryhill Scotland
140 F5 Mary Kathleen Queensland
111 E10 Mary,L Mississippi
89 G1 Maryland Zimbabwe
95 K7 Maryland state U.S.A.
108 G3 Maryneal Texas
12 E4 Maryport England
141 K7 Mary R Queensland
123 R1 Mary's Hbr Labrador
100 K8 Marys R Nevada
123 R6 Marystown Newfoundland
103 M3 Marysvale Utah
101 O5 Marysville Idaho
107 O2 Marysville Kansas
94 E4 Marysville Michigan
122 F8 Marysville New Brunswick
94 D6 Marysville Ohio
100 C1 Marysville Washington
141 H4 Maryvale Queensland
141 K8 Maryvale Queensland
99 M9 Maryville Missouri
112 D2 Maryville Tennessee
45 K3 Marzabotto Italy
85 D5 Marzafal Mali
130 E5 Marzagão Brazil
33 R8 Marzahna E Germany
33 R7 Marzahne E Germany
128 C2 Marzo,C Colombia
84 E4 Marzūq Libya
70 O9 Mas R Java
69 D13 Masa isld Indonesia
Masada see Mezada
80 F1 Mas'ada Syria
88 F4 Masai Steppe Tanzania
88 C2 Masaka Uganda
86 C3 Masalasef Chad
70 G6 Masamba Sulawesi
65 G7 Masan S Korea
71 N8 Masapun Indonesia
95 S7 Masardis Maine
113 E9 Masaryktown Florida
88 G7 Masasi Tanzania
Mas Atierra isld see Robinson Crusoe I
71 F4 Masbate isld Philippines
32 F9 Masbeck W Germany
17 H9 Mascara Algeria
81 C7 Mascarene Basin Indian Oc
81 C7 Mascarene I Indian Oc
81 C7 Mascarene Rge Indian Oc
98 G9 Mascot Nebraska
112 D1 Mascot Tennessee
130 H4 Mascote Brazil
110 G3 Mascoutah Illinois
18 F9 Mas d'Azil, le France
118 K9 Masefield Sask
70 E3 Ma Sekatok Kalimantan
71 O9 Masela isld Indonesia
38 N7 Masenberg mt Austria
45 L1 Masera di P Italy
121 P4 Masères,L Quebec
89 E7 Maseru Lesotho
40 E2 Masevaux France
87 F9 Mashabe Zimbabwe
13 G5 Masham England
65 H2 Mashan China
67 C5 Mashan China
80 G1 Masharah Syria
80 E7 Mashash R Jordan
80 F2 Mashfa Syria
77 F1 Mashhad Iran
85 E7 Mashi R Nigeria
60 P2 Mashike Japan
77 E5 Mashīz Iran
77 H6 Mashkel R Pakistan
120 F5 Mashkode Ontario
89 C6 Mashowing watercourse S Africa
95 R5 Mashpee Massachusetts
60 S2 Mashū-ko L Japan
26 N2 Masi Norway
124 E4 Masiáca Mexico
86 C6 Masi-Manimba Zaïre
70 F5 Masimbu Sulawesi
86 F5 Masindi Uganda
71 D3 Masinloc Luzon Philippines
72 H4 Maşirah isld Oman
77 B4 Masiri Iran
89 G5 Masitonto R S Africa
77 A4 Masjed Soleymān Iran
125 P9 Maskall Belize
121 R6 Maskinongé Quebec
14 B3 Mask,L Irish Rep
29 J11 Masku Finland
47 J2 Maslen Nos Bulgaria
55 D1 Maslovo U.S.S.R.
56 B4 Maslyanino U.S.S.R.
55 F3 Maslyanskoye U.S.S.R.
28 H7 Masnedssund Denmark
22 E3 Masnieres France
87 I11 Masoala, C Madagascar
110 H3 Mason Illinois
94 C4 Mason Michigan
102 E3 Mason Nevada
110 M2 Mason Ohio
98 C4 Mason S Dakota
110 G6 Mason Tennessee
109 H5 Mason Texas
99 P3 Mason Wisconsin
101 P7 Mason Wyoming
144 A7 Mason Bay New Zealand
99 R9 Mason City Illinois
99 N6 Mason City Iowa
98 G8 Mason City Nebraska
117 M7 Mason Creek Br Columbia
88 F3 Masongaleni Kenya
71 J5 Masoni isld Indonesia
143 C8 Mason, L W Australia
94 H7 Masontown Pennsylvania
94 H7 Masontown W Virginia
26 O1 Måsöy isld Norway
99 R3 Mass Michigan
44 H3 Massa Italy
95 P4 Massachusetts state U.S.A.
95 R4 Massachusetts B U.S.A.
45 H4 Massaciuccoli,L.di Italy
100 F8 Massacre L Nevada
80 F3 Massada Israel
106 B1 Massadona Colorado
45 M2 Massa Fiscáglia Italy
86 C3 Massaguet Chad
86 C3 Massakoti Chad
45 L3 Massa Lombarda Italy
45 Q8 Massa Lubrense Italy
42 D5 Massa Marittima Italy
87 F10 Massanga Mozambique
87 F10 Massangena Mozambique
94 J8 Massanutten Mt Virginia
129 K4 Massape Brazil
94 K8 Massaponax Virginia
45 H4 Massarosa Italy
18 F10 Massat France
55 D1 Massava U.S.S.R.
86 G2 Massawa Ethiopia
86 H2 Massawa Chan Ethiopia
21 I7 Massay France
37 J3 Massbach W Germany
99 M8 Massena Iowa
95 N2 Massena New York
86 C3 Massénya Chad
117 G9 Masset Br Col
18 F9 Masseube France
120 H6 Massey Ontario
18 H7 Massiac France
45 P7 Massico, M mt Italy
94 H9 Massies Mill Virginia
18 H7 Massif Central plat France
86 B4 Massif de l'Adamaoua mt Cameroon
18 F10 Massif de Néouvieille mt France
86 D4 Massif des Bongos mts Cent Afr Republic
19 Q18 Massif des Maures mts France
85 F4 Massif de Tarazit mts Niger
85 G5 Massif de Termit mts Niger
19 O15 Massif du Diois mts France
19 Q15 Massif du Pelvoux mts France
86 D4 Massif du Tondou mts Cent Afr Republic

94 F6 Massillon Ohio
87 G10 Massinga Mozambique
89 G4 Massingir Mozambique
121 P7 Masson Quebec
80 C7 Massu'a Israel
74 B4 Mastang Pakistan
27 K14 Mästerby Sweden
145 E4 Masterton New Zealand
95 P6 Mastic Beach Long I, N Y
126 E2 Mastic Point Andros Bahamas
47 H3 Mástikho,Akr C Greece
37 P3 Maštov Czechoslovakia
74 E1 Mastuj Pakistan
60 E11 Masuda Japan
79 G3 Masyāf Syria
46 D3 Mat R Albania
68 F5 Mat R Thailand
133 C7 Mata Amarilla Argentina
89 E2 Matabeleland reg Zimbabwe
71 H4 Matabulawa mt Sulawesi
88 F8 Mataca Mozambique
120 K5 Matachewan Ontario
86 B7 Matadi Zaïre
118 K8 Matador Sask
108 G1 Matador Texas
125 M3 Matagalpa Nicaragua
115 M8 Matagami Quebec
109 M7 Matagorda Texas
109 L7 Matagorda I Texas
130 H10 Mata Grande Brazil
126 C3 Matahambre Cuba
145 F3 Matahina New Zealand
134 C12 Mataiea Tahiti I Pac Oc
145 F4 Mataikona New Zealand
145 E3 Mataimoana mt New Zealand
69 H11 Matak isld Indonesia
139 H5 Matakana New S Wales
145 E2 Matakana New Zealand
145 F2 Matakana I New Zealand
145 G2 Matakaoa Pt New Zealand
144 D5 Matakitaki R New Zealand
145 E2 Matakohe New Zealand
87 C8 Matala Angola
85 B5 Matam Senegal
145 E2 Matamata New Zealand
145 F4 Matamau New Zealand
85 F6 Matameye Niger
95 N5 Matamoras Pennsylvania
124 H5 Matamoros Coahuila Mexico
125 L5 Matamoros Tamaulipas Mexico
71 F7 Matanal Pt Philippines
86 D1 Matan as Sarra Libya
84 G5 Ma'tan Bisharah Libya
88 G6 Matandu R Tanzania
115 N8 Matane Quebec
122 F5 Matane,Parc Quebec
122 E5 Matane R Quebec
145 E2 Matangi New Zealand
145 E2 Matangi I New Zealand
113 J10 Matanilla Reef Bahamas
116 O6 Matanuska mt Alaska
126 D3 Matanzas Cuba
113 F8 Matanzas Inlet Florida
131 C6 Matanzilla, Pampa de la plain Argentina
129 H5 Matão, Serra do mts Brazil
Matapán, C Greece see Tainaron, Akr
122 F6 Matapedia Quebec
122 E5 Matapedia L Quebec
122 E5 Matapedia R Quebec
16 D3 Matapozuelos Spain
131 B5 Mataquito R Chile
83 K12 Matara Sri Lanka
70 O10 Mataram Indonesia
128 D7 Matarani Peru
140 C2 Mataranka N Terr Aust
71 H6 Matarape,Tk B Sulawesi
17 J3 Mataró Spain
145 E3 Mataroa New Zealand
71 M9 Mataru Indonesia
17 F3 Mata,Sierra de la mts Spain
145 F2 Matata New Zealand
87 E12 Matatiele S Africa
144 B7 Mataura New Zealand
145 F3 Matawai New Zealand
121 R6 Matawin R Quebec
57 J2 Matay U.S.S.R.
145 E5 Matcha U.S.S.R.
121 N5 Matchi-Manitou, L Quebec
128 F6 Mategua Bolivia
125 J6 Matehuala Mexico
89 G3 Mateke Hills Zimbabwe
127 P1 Matelot Trinidad
145 E3 Matemateaonga Ra New Zealand
88 H8 Matemo isld Mozambique
18 H8 Matera Italy
45 Q7 Matese L Italy
45 Q7 Matese, Monti del mts Italy
48 G3 Mátészalka Hungary
43 C11 Mateur Tunisia
129 L7 Mateus Brazil
129 K7 Mateus R Brazil
94 E9 Matewan W Virginia
107 O3 Matfield Green Kansas
26 J9 Matfors Sweden
21 E10 Matha France
146 F14 Matha Strait Antarctica
102 E4 Mather California
94 G7 Mather Pennsylvania
74 E9 Matheran India
99 Q8 Matherville Illinois
106 G2 Matheson Colorado
120 K4 Matheson Ontario
119 V7 Matheson Island Manitoba
111 K9 Mathews Alabama
95 L9 Mathews Virginia
144 C5 Mathias Pass New Zealand
109 K7 Mathis Texas
108 G4 Mathis Field airport Texas
111 G8 Mathiston Mississippi
80 F8 Mathluthn Jordan
20 H2 Mathonville France
139 G6 Mathoura New S Wales
8 A4 Mathry Wales
66 E5 Mathura India
71 G7 Mati Mindanao Philippines
125 M9 Matías Romero Mexico
145 E3 Matiere New Zealand
22 E4 Matigny France
16 D4 Matilla de los Caños del Rio Spain
120 H6 Matinenda L Ontario
120 D7 Matiairi isld Indonesia
134 C13 Matiti Tahiti I Pac Oc
89 E5 Matlabas R S Africa
119 V8 Matlock Manitoba
102 B2 Matlock Washington
9 E1 Matlock Bath England
94 F9 Matoaka W Virginia
55 F10 Matochkin Shar U.S.S.R.
129 G8 Mato Grosso reg Brazil
130 D4 Mato Grosso,Chapada de hills Brazil
130 C7 Mato Grosso do Sul state Brazil
130 C4 Mato Grosso,Planalto de plat Brazil
122 C2 Matonipi L Quebec
122 C2 Matonipis L Quebec
89 F3 Matope Hills Nat. Park Zimbabwe
87 E10 Matopos Nat. Park Zimbabwe
130 D10 Matos Costa Brazil
16 B3 Matosinhos Portugal
Matou see Qiu Xian
86 B6 Matouti, Pto Gabon
130 G4 Mato Verde Minas Gerais Brazil
48 F3 Mátra mts Hungary
72 H4 Matrah Oman
27 F11 Matrand Norway
83 K13 Mât, R. du Réunion Indian Ocean
27 A11 Matre Norway
41 O3 Matrei am Brenner Austria
89 A9 Matroos Berg mt S Africa
59 M2 Matrosov U.S.S.R.
84 H3 Matrûh Egypt
61 N10 Matsudo Japan
59 K4 Matsue Japan
60 O4 Matsumae Japan
61 L9 Matsumoto Japan
60 G11 Matsunaga Japan
61 M9 Matsushiro Japan
67 G3 Ma-tsu Tao isld Taiwan
61 K9 Matsuto Japan
60 C12 Matsuura Japan
61 P7 Matsuyama Honshu Japan
60 F12 Matsuyama Shikoku Japan
61 K11 Matsuzaka Japan
61 M11 Matsuzaki Japan
120 J4 Mattagami Heights Ontario
120 J5 Mattagami L Ontario
120 H2 Mattagami R Ontario
112 L2 Mattamuskeet L N Carolina
76 C6 Mattancheri India
95 K9 Mattaponi R Virginia
115 M8 Mattawa Ontario
95 T1 Mattawamkeag Maine
89 E3 Mattengwe R Botswana
100 H4 Matterhorn mt Oregon
40 G6 Matterhorn mt Switzerland
48 C3 Mattersburg Austria
137 P6 Matthew isld Pacific Oc
126 H4 Matthew Town Great Inagua I Bahamas
103 M7 Matthie Arizona
120 G3 Matthe Ontario
38 H5 Mattig R Austria
95 P6 Mattituck Long I, N Y
26 G8 Mattmar Sweden
102 A1 Mattole R California
99 S10 Mattoon Illinois
110 H4 Mattoon Kentucky
99 R4 Mattoon Wisconsin
113 E7 Mattox Georgia
115 K4 Matty I N W Terr
70 B3 Matu Sarawak
70 B6 Matua Kalimantan
128 C6 Matucana Peru
144 B6 Matukituki R New Zealand
77 L3 Matūn Afghanistan
145 D1 Matupia I New Zealand
127 P2 Matura Trinidad
127 N10 Maturin Venezuela
55 B4 Matveyevka U.S.S.R.
75 K6 Mau India
87 G8 Maua Mozambique
71 M9 Maubara Timor
18 F10 Mauberme, Pic de mt France/Spain
22 G4 Maubert-Fontaine France
22 F3 Maubeuge France
68 B4 Maubin Burma
18 E9 Maubourguet France
12 D3 Mauchline Scotland
94 A8 Mauckport Indiana
107 O6 Maud Oklahoma
109 N2 Maud Texas
146 B10 Maudheim Vidda Antarctica
101 O3 Maudlow Montana
90 J15 Maud Seamount S Atlantic Oc
87 F10 Mau-é-ele Mozambique
129 G4 Maués Brazil
134 A1 Maugaafi Western Samoa
94 K7 Maugansville Maryland
12 D5 Maughold Hd I of Man U.K.
135 T3 Maui isld Hawaiian Is
36 F6 Maulbronn W Germany
22 E3 Maulde France
20 J4 Maule France
131 A5 Maule prov Chile
131 B5 Maule R Chile
18 E9 Mauléon Licharre France
21 D7 Mauléviier France
14 B2 Maumakeogh mt Irish Rep
94 D5 Maumee Ohio
94 D5 Maumee Bay Michigan/Ohio
110 D7 Maumelle, L Arkansas
71 L9 Maumere Flores Indonesia
14 B3 Maumturk Mts Irish Rep
21 C7 Maumusson France
21 C10 Maumusson, Pertuis de str France
87 D9 Maun Botswana
135 U5 Mauna Kea peak Hawaiian Is
135 R2 Mauna Loa Hawaiian Is
135 U5 Mauna Loa vol Hawaiian Is
102 S12 Maunalua Bay Hawaiian Is
116 K3 Mauneluk R Alaska
145 F3 Maungahaumi mt New Zealand
145 E3 Maungamangero mt New Zealand
145 F3 Maungapohatu New Zealand
145 F3 Maungataniwha mt New Zealand
145 E1 Maungatapere New Zealand
145 E2 Maungaturoto New Zealand
144 B6 Maungawera New Zealand
68 A2 Maungdaw Burma
68 C5 Maungmagan islds Burma
114 G4 Maunoir,L N W Terr
138 D6 Maupertuis B S Australia
100 D4 Maupin Oregon
38 E7 Maurach Austria
19 Q16 Maure,Col de pass France
21 B6 Maure-de-Bretagne France
111 F11 Maurepas,L Louisiana
18 G7 Mauriac France
145 E4 Mauriceville New Zealand
111 C11 Mauriceville Texas
19 Q14 Maurienne dist France
40 D7 Maurienne V France
98 D4 Maurine S Dakota
85 B4 Mauritania rep W Africa
83 L12 Mauritius Indian Oc
18 D4 Mauron France
18 G8 Maurs France
19 N17 Maussane France
99 Q6 Mauston Wisconsin
38 N5 Mautern Austria
38 J7 Mauterndorf Austria
38 L5 Mauthausen Austria
40 B2 Maûtz France
19 N14 Mauves France
18 F9 Mauvezin France
21 D9 Mauzé France
21 E8 Mauzé-Thouarsais France
128 E3 Mavaca R Venezuela
21 H6 Maves-Pontijou France
87 D9 Mavinga Angola
19 H10 Mavipora L India
144 B6 Mavora L N New Zealand
46 F5 Mavrovúni mt Greece
88 D9 Mavudzi R Mozambique
88 C10 Mavuradonha Mts Zimbabwe
70 C4 Mawa, Bt mt Kalimantan
71 H7 Mawasangka Indonesia
68 C3 Mawchi Burma
68 D7 Mawdaung pass Burma/Thailand
119 R4 Mawdesley L Manitoba
118 L8 Mawer Sask
145 E3 Mawheraiti New Zealand
68 D4 Mawkhi Burma
68 C2 Mawkmai Burma
75 Q7 Mawlaik Burma
146 B4 Mawson Coast Antarctica
146 C5 Mawson Escarpment Antarctica
146 K4 Mawson Pen Antarctica
70 L9 Mawuk Java
98 E2 Max N Dakota
98 E9 Max Nebraska
98 E1 Maxbass N Dakota
21 A6 Maxent France
70 D4 Maxeys Georgia
117 M6 Maxhamish L Br Col
37 N5 Maxhütte-Haidof W Germany
36 E5 Maximiliansau W Germany
94 G10 Max Meadows Virginia
29 J8 Maxmo Finland
118 L9 Maxstone Sask
112 H3 Maxton N Carolina
113 E7 Maxville Florida
101 M3 Maxville Montana
121 Q7 Maxville Ontario
102 B2 Maxwell California
99 N8 Maxwell Iowa
98 F8 Maxwell Nebraska
106 F5 Maxwell New Mexico
12 E3 Maxwelltown Scotland
141 G6 Maxwelton Queensland
101 M5 May Idaho
108 E7 May Oklahoma
109 J4 May Texas
59 K1 Maya R U.S.S.R.
55 C4 Mayachnyy U.S.S.R.
126 H3 Mayaguana Passage Bahamas
127 L5 Mayagüez Puerto Rico
85 F6 Mayahi Niger
55 C5 Mayak U.S.S.R.
31 M1 Mayak lt ho U.S.S.R.
17 H3 Mayals Spain
77 D1 Mayamey Iran
80 D3 May 'Ami Israel
125 P9 Maya Mts Belize
67 C3 Mayang China
126 G4 Mayari Cuba
127 P3 Mayaro co Trinidad
94 D4 Maybee Michigan
106 B1 Maybell Colorado
12 D3 Maybole Scotland
77 L2 Maydan Afghanistan
127 K3 May Day Mts Jamaica
109 M4 Maydelle Texas
139 H9 Maydena Tasmania
36 C3 Mayen W Germany
20 D5 Mayenne France
20 D5 Mayenne dep France
103 M7 Mayer Arizona
118 B5 Mayerthorpe Alberta
112 G4 Mayesville S Carolina
21 F5 Mayet France
107 P2 Mayetta Kansas
118 K5 Mayfair Sask
9 G5 Mayfield E Sussex England
100 K3 Mayfield Idaho
110 H5 Mayfield Kentucky
144 C5 Mayfield New Zealand
107 L6 Mayfield Oklahoma
95 M5 Mayfield Pennsylvania
141 G7 Mayfield Queensland
9 E1 Mayfield Staffs England
103 N2 Mayfield Utah
110 D7 Mayflower Arkansas
111 H6 Mayhew Mississippi
106 E9 Mayhill New Mexico
65 G2 Mayi He R China
13 F4 May, I. of Scotland
55 G5 Maykain U.S.S.R.
57 H2 Maykamys U.S.S.R.
53 F11 Maykop U.S.S.R.
52 J5 Maykor U.S.S.R.
110 L5 Mayland Tennessee
142 B1 Maylands dist Perth, W Aust
57 C2 Maylibash U.S.S.R.
57 L2 Mayli, Khrebet mts U.S.S.R.
57 D2 Maylykum U.S.S.R.
57 F3 Maymak U.S.S.R.
118 K6 Maymont Sask
68 C1 Maymyo Burma
99 P7 Maynard Iowa
143 C8 Maynard Hills W Australia
141 F5 Maynard R Queensland
14 E3 Maynooth Irish Rep
121 N7 Maynooth Ontario
51 R2 Maynopilgyn U.S.S.R.
113 D7 Mayo Florida
95 L8 Mayo Maryland
117 F4 Mayo Yukon Terr
14 B3 Mayo co Irish Rep
128 C5 Mayo R Peru
71 G7 Mayo B Mindanao Philippines
86 B4 Mayo Daga Nigeria
94 G10 Mayodan N Carolina
71 G5 Mayon mt Philippines
17 F4 Mayor R Spain
16 D2 Mayorga Spain
145 F2 Mayor I New Zealand
133 E2 Mayor Pablo Lagerenza Paraguay
87 H10 Mayotte isld Comoros
127 K3 May Pen Jamaica
113 F7 Mayport Florida
142 E3 May R W Australia
71 E1 Mayraira Pt Luzon Philippines
38 E7 Mayrhofen Austria
79 F5 Mayrouba Lebanon
55 G3 Maysk U.S.S.R.
59 J1 Mayskiy U.S.S.R.
55 G5 Mayskoye U.S.S.R.
95 N7 Mays Landing New Jersey
112 D3 Maysville Georgia
94 D8 Maysville Kentucky
99 M10 Maysville Missouri
112 K3 Maysville N Carolina
107 N7 Maysville Oklahoma
71 D5 Maytiguid Philippines
141 G5 Maytown Queensland
68 A2 Mayu R Burma
86 B6 Mayumba Gabon
94 D3 Mayville Michigan
98 J2 Mayville N Dakota
94 H4 Mayville New York
100 E4 Mayville Oregon
99 S6 Mayville Wisconsin
98 F9 Maywood Nebraska
133 E5 Maza Argentina
98 G1 Maza N Dakota
88 A9 Mazabuka Zambia
129 H4 Mazagão Brazil
22 F5 Mazagran France
85 F2 Mazalat mt Bulgaria
100 E1 Mazama Washington
18 G9 Mazamet France
77 B1 Mazandaran Iran
124 J5 Mazapil Mexico
79 F7 Mazar Jordan
43 E11 Mazara del Vallo Sicily
16 D9 Mazari,C Morocco
77 K1 Mazar-i-Sharif Afghanistan
133 D7 Mazarredo Argentina
17 G7 Mazarrón Spain
80 F8 Mazar Saiyidna Suleiman Jordan
128 F2 Mazaruni R Guyana
124 F6 Mazatán Mexico
125 C10 Mazatenango Guatemala
124 F6 Mazatlán Mexico
103 N7 Mazatzal Pk Arizona
77 B3 Mazdaj Iran
52 B6 Mažeikiai U.S.S.R.
118 D8 Mazeppa Alberta
21 F7 Mazières France
21 E8 Mazieres-en-Gatine France
52 B5 Mazirbe U.S.S.R.
55 C3 Mazliah Israel
89 G1 Mazoe Zimbabwe
88 C10 Mazoe R Zimbabwe
99 R6 Mazomanie Wisconsin
99 S8 Mazon Illinois
86 E3 Mazrub Sudan
87 E10 Mazunga Zimbabwe
22 H4 Mazures, les France
31 M2 Mazury reg Poland
89 G6 Mbabane Swaziland
86 C5 Mbaéré R Cent Afr Republic
85 D7 Mbahiakro Ivory Coast
86 C4 Mbaïki Cent Afr Republic
88 C6 Mbala Zambia
86 F5 Mbale Uganda
86 B5 Mbalmayo Cameroon
86 B4 Mbam R Cameroon
87 F8 Mbamba B Tanzania
86 C5 Mbandaka Zaïre
85 F8 Mbanga Cameroon
86 B6 M'Banio, L Gabon
86 B7 Mbanza-Ngungu Zaïre
88 C2 Mbarara Uganda
88 F6 Mbarika mt Tanzania
88 G6 Mbemkuru R Tanzania
88 D6 Mbeya Tanzania
88 D6 Mbeya mt Tanzania
85 G8 Mbini prov Eq Guinea
87 F10 Mbizi Zimbabwe
86 C4 Mbo Cent Afr Republic
85 A6 Mbour Senegal
85 B5 Mbout Mauritania
87 B7 M'Bridge R Angola
86 D7 Mbuji Mayi Zaïre
88 C3 Mbulamuti Uganda
88 E3 Mbulu Tanzania
88 F6 Mbungu Tanzania
133 F3 Mburucuyá Argentina
88 G6 Mchinja Tanzania
88 D8 Mchinji Malawi
117 F5 M'Clintock Yukon Terr
115 M1 M'Clintock, C N W Terr
115 L1 M'Clintock Inlet N W Terr
85 C3 Mdakane, Hassi Algeria
43 B12 M'Daourouch Algeria
85 C4 Mdennah Mali/Mauritania
68 J6 Mdrak Vietnam
71 C3 Me isld Indonesia
100 G4 Meacham Oregon
119 M6 Meacham Sask
120 G3 Mead Ontario
100 H2 Mead Washington
107 K4 Meade Kansas
116 K1 Meade R Alaska
101 O7 Meade Pk Idaho
103 K5 Mead,L Nev/Ariz
103 K6 Mead, L. National Recreational Area Arizona
98 D4 Meadow S Dakota
108 E2 Meadow Texas
143 A7 Meadow W Australia
94 G9 Meadow Bridge W Virginia
109 M9 Meadowbrook Texas
94 G9 Meadow Creek W Virginia
98 B7 Meadowdale Wyoming
118 J4 Meadow Lake Sask
99 O2 Meadowlands Minnesota
118 H4 Meadow L. Prov. Park Sask
119 S7 Meadow Portage Manitoba
100 J5 Meadows Idaho
103 K4 Meadow Val.Mts Nevada
103 K5 Meadow Val.Wash R Nevada
110 C2 Meadville Missouri
98 C7 Meadville Nebraska
94 G5 Meadville Pennsylvania
120 K8 Meaford Ontario
122 J9 Meaghers Grant Nova Scotia
60 R2 Me-akan dake mt Japan
16 B4 Mealhada Portugal
13 E4 Mealsgate England
115 N7 Mealy Mts Labrador
141 J7 Meandarra Queensland
117 P6 Meander River Alberta
122 B4 Meares,Cape Oregon
80 C3 Me 'Arot Karmel Israel
99 U6 Mears Michigan
15 C3 Measach Falls Scotland
9 E2 Measham England
14 E3 Meath co Irish Rep
119 M5 Meath Park Sask
19 G7 Meaux France
112 H1 Mebane N Carolina
17 G9 Mebtoub R Algeria
70 P10 Mebulu,Tg C Bali Indonesia
101 S2 Mecaha Montana
123 O3 Mecatina I.,Gt Quebec
123 N3 Mecatina I.,Little Quebec
123 M1 Mecatina,Riv.du Petite Quebec
103 H8 Mecca California
86 G1 Mecca Saudi Arabia
95 R2 Mechanic Falls Maine
94 D6 Mechanicsburg Ohio
95 K6 Mechanicsburg Pennsylvania
95 L8 Mechanicsville Maryland
95 O4 Mechanicville New York
111 F12 Mechant,L Louisiana
22 G1 Mechelen Belgium
36 B4 Mechelen Netherlands
85 D2 Mecheria Algeria
36 B2 Mechernich W Germany
122 F5 Méchins,Les Quebec
37 Q3 Mechoulpy Czechoslovakia
33 M6 Mechtersen W Germany
87 F8 Mecidiye Turkey
37 P5 Měčín Czechoslovakia
41 L2 Meckenbeuren W Germany
36 C2 Meckenheim W Germany
36 E5 Meckenheim W Germany
36 E5 Meckesheim W Germany
33 O5 Mecklenburg E Germany
33 O4 Mecklenburger Bucht B W Germany
88 G9 Meconta Mozambique
94 B3 Mecosta Michigan
48 E3 Mecsek mts Hungary
88 G9 Mecuburi R Mozambique
88 H8 Mecufi Mozambique
87 G8 Mecula Mozambique
16 C4 Meda Portugal
74 H9 Medak India
42 G4 Medak Yugoslavia
69 D11 Medan Sumatra
71 H9 Medang isld Indonesia
124 D4 Médanos Mexico
133 E5 Médanos Argentina
133 D7 Médanos,Pta Argentina
99 U8 Medaryville Indiana
17 K2 Medas isld Spain
83 K9 Medawachchiya Sri Lanka
144 D5 Medbury New Zealand
95 U1 Meddybemps L Maine
85 E1 Médéa Algeria
36 F1 Medebach W Germany
41 J4 Medel mt Switzerland
94 K7 Medelby W Germany
128 C2 Medellín Colombia
86 B5 Medemblik Netherlands
32 J5 Medem R W Germany
25 D3 Medenine Tunisia
85 G2 Mederdra Mauritania
85 A5 Medernach Luxembourg
22 L4 Medford Massachusetts
95 Q4 Medford Oklahoma
107 N5 Medford Oregon
100 C7 Medford Wisconsin
99 Q5 Medfra Alaska
116 K5 Medgidia Romania
48 L6 Medgidia Romania
99 P8 Mediapolis Iowa
48 H4 Medias Romania
100 H2 Medical Lake Washington
45 L3 Medicina Italy
101 T8 Medicine Bow Wyoming
101 T8 Medicine Bow R Wyoming
106 D1 Medicine Bow Mts Wyo/Colo
101 T8 Medicine Bow Pk Wyoming
118 G8 Medicine Hat Alberta
102 C1 Medicine L California
98 B1 Medicine L Montana
107 M4 Medicine Lodge Kansas
101 T8 Medicine Mound Texas
118 C6 Medicine R Alberta
101 O2 Medicine Rocks Montana
130 H5 Medina Brazil
98 G2 Medina N Dakota
94 J3 Medina New York
94 F5 Medina Ohio
72 D4 Medina Saudi Arabia
110 H6 Medina Tennessee
109 H6 Medina Texas
143 B9 Medina W Australia
17 F3 Medinaceli Spain
16 D3 Medina de Campo Spain
16 D3 Medina de Rioseco Spain
131 F2 Medina,L Argentina
16 D8 Medina Sidonia Spain
33 N6 Medingen W Germany
84 F2 Mediterranean Sea Europe/Africa
85 F1 Medjerda R Tunisia
43 B12 Medjerda, Monts de la Algeria/Tunisia
118 G4 Medley Alberta
55 C5 Mednogorsk U.S.S.R.
18 E7 Medoc reg France
45 J1 Médole Italy
110 H6 Medon Tennessee
110 F2 Medora Illinois
107 N3 Medora Kansas
119 R9 Medora Manitoba
98 C3 Medora N Dakota
86 B5 Medouneu Gabon
20 A5 Médréac France
118 J5 Medstead Sask
122 E8 Meductic New Brunswick
Medu Kongkar see Maizhokunggar
46 E2 Medveda Yugoslavia
55 E2 Medvedchikovo U.S.S.R.
52 H6 Medvedok U.S.S.R.
51 J1 Medvezhiy Yar U.S.S.R.
59 L2 Medvezh'ya, Gora mt U.S.S.R.
55 F3 Medvezh'ye U.S.S.R.
52 D3 Medvezh'yegorsk U.S.S.R.
52 E6 Medvyeditsa R U.S.S.R.
95 T1 Medway Maine
9 G5 Medway,R England
83 M9 Medwin Pt Christmas I Indian Oc
54 G2 Medyn U.S.S.R.
48 L1 Medzhibozh U.S.S.R.
31 N6 Medzilaborce Czechoslovakia
141 L1 Meeandah dist Brisbane, Qnsld
143 B7 Meeberrie W Australia
37 K3 Meeder W Germany
143 C7 Meekatharra W Australia
106 C1 Meeker Colorado
107 O6 Meeker Oklahoma
123 Q5 Meelpaeg L Newfoundland
37 N2 Meerane E Germany
36 B3 Meerfeld W Germany
25 F5 Meerlo Netherlands
25 E7 Meerssen Netherlands
74 G4 Meerut India
101 R5 Meeteetse Wyoming
118 E6 Meeting Cr Alberta
14 E4 Meeting of the Waters Irish Rep
118 K5 Meetoos Sask
33 R5 Meetschow E Germany
22 K1 Meeuwen Belgium
80 B7 Mefallesim Israel
86 G5 Mega Ethiopia
71 C3 Mega W Irian
69 E14 Mega isld Indonesia
80 C3 Megadim Israel
18 H7 Megal mt France
47 J8 Megálo Khorió Tílos I Greece
46 F7 Megalópolis Greece
46 D6 Meganísi mt Greece
122 B8 Megantic Quebec
122 B8 Megantic,L Quebec
47 F6 Mégara Greece
109 J2 Megargel Texas
46 E5 Mégdhova R Greece
25 E5 Megen Netherlands
40 E6 Megève France
33 E1 Meggen W Germany
112 G5 Meggett S Carolina
85 F2 Meghaïer, El Algeria
75 O6 Meghalaya prov India
75 O6 Meghna R Bangladesh
121 P4 Mégiscane, L Quebec
100 B3 Megler Washington
52 F2 Megra Arkhangelsk U.S.S.R.
52 E4 Megra Vologda U.S.S.R.
48 G6 Mehadia Romania
70 D6 Mehakit Kalimantan
26 Q1 Mehamn Norway
48 H6 Mehedinti reg Romania
94 J9 Meherrin Virginia
94 J10 Meherrin R Virginia
37 N2 Mehltheuer E Germany
74 G8 Mehkar India
75 K5 Mehndawal India
78 L5 Mehran Iran
36 B3 Mehren W Germany
36 B4 Mehring W Germany
77 D4 Mehriz Iran
21 J7 Mehun sur Yèvre France
130 E5 Meia Ponte,R Brazil
67 D2 Meichengzhen China
67 F1 Meichuan China
8 C2 Meifod Wales
86 B4 Meiganga Cameroon
114 K1 Meighen I N W Terr
112 C6 Meigs Georgia
25 E6 Meijel Netherlands
67 B5 Mei Jiang R China
117 O7 Meikle R Alberta
68 B2 Meiktila Burma
Meilin see Gan Xian
20 B5 Meillac France
117 L5 Meilleur Cr N W Terr
33 N8 Meine W Germany
33 M8 Meinersen W Germany
36 D1 Meinerzhagen W Germany
37 J2 Meiningen E Germany
16 C1 Meira, Sa. de mts Spain
41 H4 Meiringen Switzerland
80 C3 Me'ir Shefeya Israel
33 O10 Meisdorf E Germany
36 G4 Meisenheim W Germany
67 A1 Meishan China
Meishan see Jinzhai
67 E1 Meishan Shuiku res China
37 P1 Meissen E Germany
37 L7 Meissenhoff W Germany
36 H1 Meissner mt W Germany
67 B3 Meitan China
37 K6 Meitingen W Germany
67 E4 Mei Xian China
65 E2 Meiyao China
43 C12 Mejerda R Tunisia
43 C12 Mejez el-Bab Tunisia
133 C2 Mejillones Chile
75 M5 Mejrup Denmark
86 B5 Mekambo Gabon
120 F5 Mekatina Ontario
55 D3 Mekhonoskoye U.S.S.R.
74 C3 Mekhtar Pakistan
98 D1 Mekinock N Dakota
85 C2 Meknès Morocco
68 G6 Mekong R S E Asia
70 G6 Mekongga, G mt Sulawesi
71 H6 Mekongga, Tk B Sulawesi
69 H8 Mekong, Mouths of the Vietnam
116 D6 Mekoryuk Alaska
85 E6 Mekrou R Benin/Niger
69 F11 Melaka Malaysia
47 G9 Melambes Crete Greece
137 O4 Melanesia Pac Oc
137 P4 Melanesian Border Plat Pacific Oc
70 D2 Melapap Sabah
70 D2 Melaut mt Sabah
118 L9 Melaval Sask
70 C5 Melawi R Kalimantan
21 D7 Melay France
100 J6 Melba Idaho
33 M6 Melbeck W Germany
13 G6 Melbourne England
9 E2 Melbourne England
113 G9 Melbourne Florida
99 N8 Melbourne Iowa
138 C7 Melbourne Victoria
113 G9 Melbourne Beach Florida
26 G3 Melbu Norway
26 H8 Melby Denmark
99 N8 Melcher Iowa
120 G7 Melchett L Ontario
124 J5 Melchor Ocampo Coahuila Mexico
124 H8 Melchor Ocampo Michigan Mexico
26 D8 Meldal Norway
26 M6 Meldersteín Sweden
45 M3 Meldola Italy
32 K4 Meldorf W Germany
112 F5 Meldrim Georgia
120 G7 Meldrum Bay Ontario
80 D3 Melea Israel
119 U8 Meleb Manitoba
44 F1 Melegnano Italy
47 G9 Melékhas, Akr C Crete Greece
52 J5 Melekhina U.S.S.R.
87 G9 Melela R Mozambique
70 A10 Meleman Java
52 F6 Melenki U.S.S.R.
55 D3 Melent'yevskoye U.S.S.R.
20 B5 Melesse France
20 F5 Mêle-sur-Sarthe, le France
55 C4 Meleuz U.S.S.R.
95 M9 Melfa Virginia
45 P6 Melfa R Italy
86 C3 Melfi Chad
43 G8 Melfi Italy
114 J7 Melfort Sask
28 E2 Melholt Denmark
26 D8 Melhus Norway
36 F4 Melibocus mt W Germany
20 G4 Melicourt France
130 E9 Mel, I. do Brazil
46 D5 Meligalá Greece
71 H5 Melilis isld Indonesia
85 D1 Melilla Spain exclave Morocco
133 C6 Melimoyu mt Chile
144 B6 Melina, Mt New Zealand
48 J6 Melinești Romania
70 E5 Melintang, D L Kalimantan
133 C4 Melipilla Chile
119 R9 Melita Manitoba
43 G11 Melito di Porto Salvo Italy
54 G10 Melitopol' U.S.S.R.
38 M5 Melk Austria
8 D5 Melksham England
44 H1 Mella R Italy
26 H9 Mellansjö Sweden
22 F2 Melle Belgium
21 E9 Melle France
32 H8 Melle W Germany
43 B12 Mellègue R Tunisia
99 Q3 Mellen Wisconsin
32 L7 Mellendorf W Germany
27 F13 Mellerud Sweden
21 E8 Melle S. Bretonne France
98 H4 Mellette S Dakota
16 B2 Mellid Spain
22 K4 Mellier Belgium
37 L2 Mellingen E Germany
137 M5 Mellish Rise Coral Sea
86 E3 Mellit Sudan
13 F6 Mellor Brook England
32 H5 Mellum isld W Germany
111 E7 Mellwood Arkansas
13 F4 Melmerby England
47 F3 Melnik Bulgaria
31 H5 Mělník Czechoslovakia
48 K2 Melnitsa Podolskaya U.S.S.R.
131 G4 Melo Uruguay
52 G2 Melogorskoye U.S.S.R.
71 K9 Melolo Sumba Indonesia
102 D4 Melones Res California
54 M7 Melovoye U.S.S.R.
26 F5 Meløy Norway
116 K4 Melozitna R Alaska
22 J3 Melreux Belgium
17 G9 Melrir R Algeria
100 J3 Melrose Idaho
99 M4 Melrose Minnesota
101 N4 Melrose Montana
106 G7 Melrose New Mexico
122 K8 Melrose Nova Scotia
100 B6 Melrose Oregon
13 F2 Melrose Scotland
143 D8 Melrose W Australia
99 P5 Melrose Wisconsin
87 F9 Melsetter Zimbabwe
101 S3 Melstone Montana
99 U3 Melstrand Michigan
36 H1 Melsungen W Germany
70 E2 Melta, Mt Sabah
29 L5 Meltaus Finland
13 G6 Meltham England
9 F2 Melton Mowbray England
88 G10 Meluli R Mozambique
68 A2 Melun Burma
18 G4 Melun France
86 F3 Melut Sudan
107 P3 Melvern Kansas
15 E2 Melvich Scotland
111 E11 Melville Louisiana
101 Q3 Melville Montana
98 G2 Melville N Dakota
119 P8 Melville Sask
140 D1 Melville B N Terr Aust
115 N2 Melville Bugt B Greenland
141 G2 Melville, C Queensland
71 C6 Melville, Cape Philippines
114 G4 Melville Hills N W Terr
140 B1 Melville I N Terr Aust
114 H2 Melville I N W Terr
115 L7 Melville, L Labrador
115 O7 Melville Pen N W Terr
142 A1 Melville Water B Perth, W Aust
109 H4 Melvin Texas
14 C2 Melvin, L Irish Rep
119 R1 Melvin L Manitoba
48 E4 Mélykút Hungary
70 C5 Memala Kalimantan
68 H6 Meman Cambodia
88 H9 Memba Mozambique
79 H2 Membij Syria
71 J9 Memboro Sumba Indonesia
22 H4 Membre France
Memel see Klaipeda
32 E5 Memmert isld W Germany
41 M2 Memmingen W Germany
70 E1 Mempakul Sabah
99 O9 Memphis Missouri
110 G6 Memphis Tennessee
108 G1 Memphis Texas
84 J4 Memphis ruins Egypt
121 S8 Memphremagog, L Vermont
122 H7 Memramcook New Brunswick
60 R3 Memuro Japan
110 B7 Mena Arkansas
71 M9 Mena Timor Indonesia
54 D5 Mena U.S.S.R.
80 D4 Menahemya Israel
99 L3 Menahga Minnesota
8 B1 Menai Str Wales
85 E5 Ménaka Mali
101 O4 Menard Montana
108 H5 Menard Texas
99 S5 Menasha Wisconsin
123 L2 Menaskwagama, L Quebec
45 M2 Menate Italy
70 C5 Menate Kalimantan
69 H14 Mendanau isld Indonesia
130 G6 Mendanha Brazil
69 H12 Mendanha Indonesia
70 C6 Mendawai Kalimantan
18 H8 Mende France
86 G4 Mendebo Mts Ethiopia
56 D3 Mendel' R U.S.S.R.
32 G10 Menden W Germany
111 G10 Mendenhall Mississippi
116 D7 Mendenhall, C Alaska
47 K6 Menderes R Turkey
55 E5 Mendesh U.S.S.R.
71 E3 Mendez-Nuñez Luzon Philippines
118 E5 Mendham Sask
136 J3 Mendi Papua New Guinea
9 E5 Mendip Hills England
143 D8 Mendleyarri W Australia
99 P3 Mendocino, C California
135 N4 Mendocino Seascarp Pacific Oc
94 B4 Mendon Michigan
110 M1 Mendon Ohio
139 J4 Mendooran New S Wales
102 D5 Mendota California
99 R8 Mendota Illinois
108 D8 Mendota Texas
99 R6 Mendota, L Wisconsin
131 C4 Mendoza Argentina
128 C5 Mendoza Peru
131 C5 Mendoza prov Argentina
16 B6 Mendro mt Portugal
69 F12 Mendung Sumatra
44 G2 Menegosa mt Italy
127 J10 Mene Grande Venezuela
47 J6 Menemen Turkey
22 E2 Menen Belgium
47 J9 Menetaí Kárpathos I Greece
21 J7 Ménétréol-sous-Sancerre France
43 E11 Menfi Sicily
70 D1 Mengalum isld S China Sea
58 G5 Mengcheng China
65 D5 Mengcun China
41 K1 Mengen W Germany
32 J10 Mengeringhausen W Germany
36 E2 Mengerskirchen W Germany
70 K8 Menggala Sumatra
68 E2 Menghai China
65 H1 Mengjiagang China
65 G3 Mengjiang China
65 A5 Mengjiawan China
65 B7 Mengjin China
70 B4 Mengkiang R Kalimantan
37 N6 Mengkofen W Germany
68 E2 Mengla China
68 D1 Menglian China
68 E1 Meng man China
67 C4 Mengshan China
68 E1 Mengwang China
65 B7 Meng Xian China
65 D7 Mengyin China
68 E2 Mengyuan China
67 A5 Mengzi China
21 E9 Ménigoute France
115 N7 Menihek, Lac Labrador
83 L11 Menik Ganga R Sri Lanka
20 H3 Ménilles France
36 B7 Ménil-sur-Bélvitte France
Menin see Menen
139 G4 Menindee New S Wales
138 E6 Meningie S Australia
70 E4 Menjapa, Gt mt Kalimantan
51 M2 Menkere U.S.S.R.
112 B3 Menlo Georgia
99 M8 Menlo Iowa
107 K2 Menlo Kansas
102 B4 Menlo Pk California
20 K4 Mennecy France
21 I7 Mennetou-sur-Cher France
98 J6 Menno S Dakota
12 E3 Mennock P Scotland
99 T4 Menominee R Michigan
99 S6 Menomonee Falls Wisconsin
99 P5 Menomonie Wisconsin
17 K5 Menorca isld Balearic Is
55 G3 Men'shchikovo U.S.S.R.
66 C5 Men-shih China
32 G7 Menslage W Germany
12 E1 Menstrie Scotland
28 H6 Menstrup Denmark
70 E5 Mentaja R Kalimantan
69 F11 Mentakab Malaysia
45 N5 Mentana Italy
70 E2 Mentapok Sabah
70 E3 Mentarang R Kalimantan
116 C5 Mentasta Mts Alaska
73 Q9 Mentawai, Kep islds Indonesia
69 G14 Mentok Sumatra
44 B4 Menton France
94 A5 Mentone Indiana
108 D4 Mentone Texas
98 K2 Mentor Minnesota
94 F5 Mentor Ohio
70 C5 Mentubar R Kalimantan
70 D9 Mentz, L S Africa
58 E2 Menza R Mongolia
56 G5 Menza R U.S.S.R.
43 C11 Menzel Bourguiba Tunisia
55 H6 Menzelinsk U.S.S.R.
43 D12 Menzel Temime Tunisia
143 D8 Menzies W Australia
146 C5 Menzies, Mt Antarctica
Menzingen see Kraichtal
9 G5 Meopham England
124 G3 Meoqui Mexico
118 J5 Meota Sask
25 F3 Meppel Netherlands
32 F7 Meppen W Germany
17 H3 Mequinenza Spain
21 I6 Mer France
52 F5 Mera R U.S.S.R.
47 H9 Merabéllou, Kólpos B Crete Greece
70 E4 Merah Kalimantan
70 K8 Merak Java
26 E8 Meråker Norway
137 O4 Mera Lava isld New Hebrides
138 B3 Meramangye, L S Australia
110 F3 Meramec Park Missouri
Meran see Merano
41 O4 Merano Italy
70 P9 Merapi, G mt Java
123 S6 Merasheen Newfoundland
70 D5 Meratus, Peg mts Kalimantan
136 J3 Merauke W Irian
69 F12 Merbau Sumatra
138 F5 Merbein Victoria
22 G3 Merbes-le-Château Belgium
70 P10 Merbuk mt Indonesia
86 H5 Merca Somalia
76 B4 Mercara India
45 M4 Mercato Saraceno Italy
102 D4 Merced California
102 C4 Merced R California
131 B3 Mercedario, Cerro mt Chile/Arg
131 D4 Mercedes Argentina
131 F5 Mercedes Buenos Aires Argentina
131 F2 Mercedes Corrientes Argentina
109 K9 Mercedes Texas
131 F4 Mercedes Uruguay
133 C3 Merceditas Chile
99 N9 Mercer Missouri
98 F2 Mercer N Dakota
145 E2 Mercer New Zealand
94 G5 Mercer Pennsylvania
110 H6 Mercer Tennessee
99 Q3 Mercer Wisconsin
94 J7 Mercersburg Pennsylvania
22 G2 Merchtem Belgium
121 O6 Mercier Dam Quebec
117 P9 Mercoal Alberta
45 R8 Mercogliano Italy
103 M1 Mercur Utah
48 H5 Mercurea Romania
109 H4 Mercury Texas
19 Q13 Mercury-Gemilly France
145 E2 Mercury Is New Zealand
114 H3 Mercy B N W Terr
115 N5 Mercy, C N W Terr
20 C3 Merderet R France
21 F10 Merdrignac France
8 D5 Mere England
133 E8 Meredith, C Falkland Is
95 Q3 Meredith Hill New Hampshire
108 C8 Meredith, L Texas
99 Q10 Meredosia Illinois
85 E3 Meredoua Algeria
54 H7 Merefa U.S.S.R.
86 A3 Meregh Somalia
85 C5 Mereié, El reg Mauritania/Mali
36 E3 Merenberg W Germany
20 K5 Méréville France
9 G5 Mereworth England
Merga see Nukheila
68 D6 Mergui Burma
73 Q6 Mergui Arch Burma
138 F5 Meribah S Australia
47 H3 Meriç Turkey
47 H3 Meriç R Greece
118 H7 Merid Sask

130 C10 **Misiones, Sa.de** *ra* Argentina
88 B4 **Misisi** Zaïre
125 N2 **Miskito, Cayos** *islds* Nicaragua
48 F2 **Miskolc** Hungary
60 G10 **Misogu chi** Japan
71 C3 **Misoöl** *isld* W Irian
99 Q2 **Misquah Hills** Minnesota
84 F3 **Misrātah** Libya
120 F4 **Missanabie** Ontario
130 G9 **Missão Velhá** Brazil
21 A7 **Missillac** France
120 G4 **Missinaibi L** Ontario
120 H2 **Missinaibi R** Ontario
100 C1 **Mission** Br Col
98 F6 **Mission** S Dakota
109 J3 **Mission** Texas
117 M11 **Mission City** Br Col
98 J7 **Mission Hill** S Dakota
101 M2 **Mission Range** Montana
121 L1 **Missisicabi** *R* Quebec
120 G6 **Mississagi** *R* Ontario
121 L5 **Mississauga** Ontario
111 E10 **Mississippi** *R* U.S.A.
92 J4 **Mississippi** *state* U.S.A.
111 G12 **Mississippi Delta** Louisiana
121 O7 **Mississippi, L** Ontario
111 H11 **Mississippi Sound** Mississippi
Missolonghi Greece *see* **Mesolóngion**
120 H4 **Missonga** Ontario
101 L3 **Missoula** Montana
110 C2 **Missouri** *R* Missouri
92 H3 **Missouri** *state* U.S.A.
109 O2 **Missouri, Lit** *R* Arkansas
98 F3 **Missouri Res** N Dakota
99 L8 **Missouri Valley** Iowa
141 H5 **Mistake Cr** Queensland
140 A3 **Mistake Creek** N Terr Aust
123 K2 **Mistanipisipou R** Quebec
121 S4 **Mistassini** Quebec
115 M7 **Mistassini, Lac** Quebec
119 O6 **Mistatim** Sask
121 M3 **Mistawak L** Quebec
31 K7 **Mistelbach** Austria
27 J14 **Misterhult** Sweden
126 C5 **Misteriosa Bank** Caribbean
8 D6 **Misterton** England
128 D7 **Misti** *mt* Peru
122 E5 **Mistigougèche L** Quebec
37 P3 **Misto** Czechoslovakia
131 D3 **Mistolar, L** Argentina
26 E10 **Mistra** *R* Norway
43 F11 **Mistretta** Sicily
60 E11 **Misumi** Japan
60 D13 **Misumi-ura** Japan
60 E13 **Mitai** Japan
127 P2 **Mitan** Trinidad
124 G7 **Mita, Pta.de** *C* Mexico
8 D4 **Mitcheldean** England
8 A7 **Mitchell** England
110 K3 **Mitchell** Indiana
98 C8 **Mitchell** Nebraska
120 J9 **Mitchell** Ontario
100 E5 **Mitchell** Oregon
141 J7 **Mitchell** Queensland
98 H6 **Mitchell** S Dakota
139 K3 **Mitchell** *R* New S Wales
111 K9 **Mitchell L** Alabama
94 B2 **Mitchell, L** Michigan
112 E2 **Mitchell, Mt** N Carolina
140 A1 **Mitchell Pt** N Terr Aust
141 F3 **Mitchell River** Queensland
14 C4 **Mitchelstown** Irish Rep
121 Q5 **Mitchinamecus, L** Quebec
74 C6 **Mithi** Pakistan
47 H5 **Míthimna** Greece
71 B2 **Miti** *isld* Halmahera Indonesia
47 H5 **Mitilíni** Greece
52 G2 **Mitina** U.S.S.R.
119 S4 **Mitishto R** Manitoba
117 G7 **Mitkof I** Alaska
79 C8 **Mitla Pass** Egypt
61 O9 **Mito** Japan
86 A5 **Mitra** *mt* Equat Guinea
137 P4 **Mitre** *isld* Santa Cruz Is
145 E4 **Mitre, Mt** New Zealand
144 A6 **Mitre Pk** New Zealand
116 H9 **Mitrofania I** Alaska
52 J3 **Mitrofanovskaya** U.S.S.R.
46 D5 **Mitsikéli** *R* Greece
60 F11 **Mitsu** Japan
60 F12 **Mitsuhama** Japan
60 H11 **Mitsuishi** Japan
60 Q3 **Mitsuishi** Japan
61 N9 **Mitsukaidō** Japan
61 M8 **Mitsuke** Japan
60 R2 **Mitsumata** Japan
139 K5 **Mittagong** New S Wales
141 F4 **Mittagong** Queensland
41 L3 **Mittagspitze** *mt* Austria
139 J6 **Mitta Mitta** Victoria
41 N4 **Mittelberg** Austria
37 J5 **Mittelfranken** *dist* Bayern W Germany
40 F4 **Mittelland** *dist* Switzerland
32 H8 **Mittellandkanal** W Germany
33 R8 **Mittelmark** *reg* E Germany
36 H3 **Mittelsinn** W Germany
41 O3 **Mittenwald** W Germany
33 T8 **Mittenwalde** E Germany
38 M6 **Mitterbach** Austria
37 O6 **Mitterfels** W Germany
38 G7 **Mitter Pinzgau** *V* Austria
36 B6 **Mittersheim** France
37 N4 **Mitterteich** W Germany
140 D4 **Mittiebah** *R* N Terr Aust
37 O2 **Mittweida** E Germany
128 D3 **Mitú** Colombia
88 B3 **Mitumba** *mts* Zaïre
87 E7 **Mitwaba** Zaïre
55 D1 **Mityayevo** U.S.S.R.
86 B5 **Mitzic** Gabon
60 O4 **Miumaya** Japan
61 N10 **Miura** Japan
54 K9 **Mius** *R* U.S.S.R.
54 K9 **Miusskiy Liman** *lagoon* U.S.S.R.
65 B7 **Mi Xian** China
38 M7 **Mixnitz** Austria
61 K11 **Miya-gawa** *R* Japan
61 Q12 **Miyagi** Okinawa
61 O7 **Miyagi** *prefect* Japan
61 P13 **Miyagusuku-jima** *isld* Okinawa
78 G4 **Miyah, Wadi El** Syria
61 N11 **Miyake-jima** *isld* Japan
61 P6 **Miyako** Japan
60 E14 **Miyakonojō** Japan
55 B6 **Miyaly** U.S.S.R.
60 E14 **Miyazaki** Japan
60 E13 **Miyazaki** *prefect* Japan
60 J10 **Miyazu** Japan
60 F11 **Miyoshi** Japan
65 C4 **Miyun** China
65 D4 **Miyun Shuiku** *res* China
86 G4 **Mizan Teferi** Ethiopia
84 E3 **Mizdah** Libya
111 G10 **Mize** Mississippi
14 B5 **Mizen Hd** Cork Irish Rep
14 E4 **Mizen Hd** Wicklow Irish Rep
65 A6 **Mizhi** China
48 K6 **Mizil** Romania
75 P7 **Mizoram** *prov* India
99 M2 **Mizpah** Minnesota
79 E7 **Mizpe Ramon** Israel
146 B6 **Mizuho** Japan
61 P6 **Mizusawa** Japan
88 C1 **Mjanji** Uganda
27 F14 **Mjöbäck** Sweden
27 H13 **Mjölby** Sweden
28 B6 **Mjolden** Denmark
27 D12 **Mjöndalen** Norway
27 F14 **Mjörn** *L* Sweden
27 E11 **Mjösa** *L* Norway
28 O9 **Mjóvanes** *C* Faeroes
88 C9 **Mkokomo** *mt* Zambia
88 G4 **Mkokotoni** Tanzania
88 B8 **Mkuku** Zambia
87 E8 **Mkushi** Zambia
88 B8 **Mkushi** *R* Zambia
31 H5 **Mladá Boleslav** Czechoslovakia
48 F6 **Mladenovac** Yugoslavia
37 P4 **Mladotice** Czechoslovakia
88 C5 **Mlala Hills** Tanzania
48 G6 **Mlava** *R* Yugoslavia
31 M2 **Mława** Poland
88 G10 **M'lela** *R* Mozambique
87 G7 **Mlimba** Tanzania
42 H6 **Mljet** *isld* Yugoslavia
88 E7 **Mlowe** Malawi
37 O3 **Mnichov** Czechoslovakia
31 H5 **Mnichovo Hradiště** Czechoslovakia
48 F2 **Mníšek** Czechoslovakia
26 K8 **Mo** Sweden
71 N9 **Moa** *isld* Indonesia
128 D5 **Moa** *R* Brazil
85 B7 **Moa** *R* Sierra Leone/Guinea
103 P3 **Moab** Utah
119 U3 **Moak L** Manitoba
139 G6 **Moama** New S Wales
89 H5 **Moamba** Mozambique
144 C5 **Moana** New Zealand
145 E3 **Moana** *mt* New Zealand
138 F3 **Moanba, L** S Australia
86 B6 **Moanda** Gabon
86 B7 **Moanda** Zaïre
103 K5 **Moapa** Nevada
71 N8 **Moapora** *isld* Indonesia
14 D3 **Moate** Irish Rep
88 D10 **Moatize** Mozambique
145 E3 **Moawhango** New Zealand
87 E7 **Moba** Zaïre
61 O10 **Mobara** Japan
77 B3 **Mobārakeh** Iran
86 D5 **Mobaye** Cent Afr Republic
86 D5 **Mobayi** Zaïre
138 C4 **Mobella** S Australia
110 D2 **Moberly** Missouri
117 N8 **Moberly Lake** Br Col
120 E4 **Mobert** Ontario
111 H11 **Mobile** Alabama
103 M8 **Mobile** Arizona
111 J11 **Mobile Pt** Alabama
141 G7 **Moble** *R* Queensland
71 F4 **Mobo** Philippines
28 A4 **Møborg** Denmark
98 F4 **Mobridge** S Dakota
Mobutu, L *see* **Albert, L**
127 J5 **Moca** Dom Rep
129 J4 **Mocajuba** Brazil
Moçambique *see* **Mozambique**
88 H9 **Moçambique** *dist* Mozambique
87 B9 **Moçâmedes** Angola
95 L5 **Mocanaqua** Pennsylvania
103 M5 **Moccasin** Arizona
101 Q2 **Moccasin** Montana
68 G2 **Moc Chau** Vietnam
125 Q7 **Mocche** Mexico
Mocha *see* **Mukha, Al**
131 A7 **Mocha** *isld* Chile
124 E5 **Mochicahui** Mexico
127 K2 **Mocho Mts** Jamaica
89 E5 **Mochudi** Botswana
88 H7 **Mocímboa da Praia** Mozambique
48 H4 **Mociu** Romania
27 G15 **Möckeln** *L* Sweden
33 P8 **Möckern** E Germany
95 M9 **Mockhorn** *isld* Virginia
27 J15 **Möckleby, N** Sweden
27 H15 **Möckleby, S** Sweden
36 G5 **Mockmühl** W Germany
33 R9 **Mockrehna** E Germany
112 G2 **Mocksville** N Carolina
100 A2 **Moclips** Washington
128 C3 **Mocoa** Colombia
130 F7 **Mococa** Brazil
131 F3 **Mocoretá** *R* Argentina
124 F5 **Mocorito** Mexico
124 F2 **Moctezuma** Chihuahua Mexico
124 E3 **Moctezuma** Sonora Mexico
88 F10 **Mocuba** Mozambique
40 E7 **Modane** France
83 K9 **Modaragam Aru** *R* Sri Lanka
74 E7 **Modasa** India
22 J3 **Modave** Belgium
8 C7 **Modbury** England
89 D7 **Modder** *R* S Africa
106 F4 **Model** Colorado
45 J2 **Modena** Italy
103 L4 **Modena** Utah
45 J3 **Modena** *prov* Italy
19 L4 **Moder** *R* France
38 K7 **Moderbrugg** Austria
102 C4 **Modesto** California
43 F12 **Modica** Sicily
45 L3 **Modigliana** Italy
80 C6 **Modi'im** Israel
86 D5 **Modjamboli** Zaïre
70 O9 **Modjokerto** Java
94 B6 **Modoc** Indiana
107 J3 **Modoc** Kansas
112 E4 **Modoc** S Carolina
100 D7 **Modoc Point** Oregon
36 B2 **Mödrath** W Germany
48 E6 **Modriča** Yugoslavia
48 E2 **Modrý Kameň** Czechoslovakia
139 H7 **Moe** Victoria
8 B1 **Moelfre** Môn Wales
8 C2 **Moel Sych** *mt* Wales
27 E11 **Moelv** Norway
129 H2 **Moengo** Suriname
103 N5 **Moenkopi** Arizona
144 B5 **Moeraki, L** New Zealand
22 F1 **Moerbeke** Belgium
25 C5 **Moerdijk** Netherlands
22 D1 **Moere** Belgium
145 E1 **Moerewa** New Zealand
145 E3 **Moeroa** New Zealand
Moero, Lac *see* **Mweru, L**
106 E3 **Moffat** Colorado
13 E3 **Moffat** Scotland
144 B6 **Moffat Pk** New Zealand
106 E2 **Moffat Tunnel** Colorado
98 F3 **Moffit** N Dakota
74 F3 **Moga** India
Mogadiscio *see* **Mogadishu**
72 F8 **Mogadishu** Somalia
94 F5 **Mogadore** Ohio
16 C3 **Mogadouro** Portugal
89 F4 **Mogalakwena** *R* S Africa
61 N7 **Mogami-gawa** *R* Japan
67 F1 **Mogan Shan** *mt* China
75 R6 **Mogaung** Burma
28 B7 **Møgeltønder** Denmark
17 G6 **Mogente** Spain
36 H6 **Mögglingen** W Germany
60 C13 **Mogi** Japan
129 J8 **Mogi das Cruzes** Brazil
31 M4 **Mogielnica** Poland
130 F7 **Mogi Guaçu** *R* Brazil
54 H9 **Mogila-Bel'mak Gora** *mt* U.S.S.R.
54 B3 **Mogilev** U.S.S.R.
48 L2 **Mogilev Podolskiy** U.S.S.R.
139 J3 **Mogil-Mogil** New S Wales
31 K3 **Mogilno** Poland
130 F8 **Mogi Mirim** Brazil
88 H9 **Mogincual** Mozambique
45 J2 **Móglia** Italy
42 E3 **Mogliano** Italy
45 M1 **Mogliano Veneto** Italy
46 D4 **Moglicë** Albania
19 N12 **Mogneneins** France
59 G1 **Mogocha** U.S.S.R.
68 C1 **Mogok** Burma
89 E4 **Mogol** *R* S Africa
106 B8 **Mogollon** New Mexico
106 B8 **Mogollon Mts** New Mexico
103 O7 **Mogollon Rim** *tableland* Arizona
106 D4 **Mogote** Colorado
58 C2 **Mogoyn** Mongolia
16 C7 **Moguer** Spain
143 B9 **Mogumber** W Australia
48 E5 **Mohács** Hungary
145 F3 **Mohaka** New Zealand
98 E1 **Mohall** N Dakota
17 H9 **Mohammadia** Algeria
35 C2 **Mohammedia** Morocco
103 K6 **Mohave, L** Nev/Ariz
103 K7 **Mohave Mts** Cal/Ariz
103 L9 **Mohawk** Arizona
99 S2 **Mohawk** Michigan
95 N4 **Mohawk** *R* New York
103 L9 **Mohawk Mts** Arizona
27 G14 **Moheda** Sweden
87 G10 **Mohéli** *isld* Comoros
87 D9 **Mohembo** Botswana
74 C5 **Mohenjo Daro** *anc site* Pakistan
14 B4 **Moher, Cliffs of** Irish Rep
116 D6 **Mohican, C** Alaska
14 D3 **Mohill** Irish Rep
100 J3 **Mohler** Idaho
32 H10 **Möhne** *R* W Germany
32 H10 **Möhnesee** W Germany
32 H10 **Möhnestausee** *L* W Germany
27 G13 **Moholm** Sweden
103 L7 **Mohon Pk** Arizona
70 O10 **Mohoreru, G** *mt* Java
88 G6 **Mohoro** Tanzania
124 H4 **Mohovano Ranch** Mexico
37 J2 **Möhra** E Germany
36 G6 **Möhringen** W Germany
28 D7 **Mohrkirch** W Germany
27 B13 **Moi** Norway
16 B4 **Moimenta da Beira** Portugal
66 C5 **Moincêr** China
57 G2 **Mointy** U.S.S.R.
95 M2 **Moira** New York
26 G5 **Mo i Rana** Norway
19 F14 **Moirans** France
47 G9 **Moíres** Crete Greece
52 C5 **Mõisaküla** U.S.S.R.
21 C8 **Moisdon** France
55 G2 **Moiseyevka** U.S.S.R.
122 F3 **Moisie** Quebec
19 Q17 **Moissac** France
86 C4 **Moissala** Chad
20 J3 **Moisson** France
21 H6 **Moisy** France
27 K12 **Möja** Sweden
17 F7 **Mojácar** Spain
102 F6 **Mojave** California
102 G7 **Mojave** *R* California
102 G6 **Mojave Desert** California
60 E12 **Moji** Japan
130 F8 **Moji das Cruzes** Brazil
120 B2 **Mojikit L** Ontario
86 G4 **Mojjo** Ethiopia
86 F5 **Mojo** Uganda
71 H9 **Mojo** *isld* Indonesia
128 E7 **Mojos, Llanos de** *plain* Bolivia
129 J4 **Moju** *R* Brazil
61 O9 **Mōka** Japan
145 E3 **Mokai** New Zealand
75 L6 **Mokameh** India
110 E3 **Mokane** Missouri
102 S12 **Mokapu Pen** Hawaiian Is
145 E3 **Mokau** New Zealand
102 D3 **Mokelumne** *R* California
89 F7 **Mokhotlong** *mt* Lesotho
55 F3 **Mokhovoy Prival** U.S.S.R.
27 J11 **Möklinta** Sweden
85 G1 **Moknine** Tunisia
145 E1 **Mokohinau Is** New Zealand
145 E3 **Mokoia** New Zealand
75 Q5 **Mokokchung** India
86 B3 **Mokolo** Cameroon
144 B7 **Mokoreta** New Zealand
144 B7 **Mokotua** New Zealand
65 G7 **Mokp'o** S Korea
46 D2 **Mokra Pl** *mt* Yugoslavia
48 F5 **Mokrin** Yugoslavia
55 E3 **Mokrousovo** U.S.S.R.
29 L8 **Möksy** Finland
102 S11 **Mokuauia I** Hawaiian Is
135 U5 **Mokuaweoweo Crater** Hawaiian Is
102 R11 **Mokuleia** Hawaiian Is
102 S12 **Mokulua Is** Hawaiian Is
22 J1 **Mol** Belgium
100 C4 **Molalla** Oregon
125 K7 **Molango** Mexico
46 F8 **Moláoi** Greece
42 F4 **Molat** *isld* Yugoslavia
20 D3 **Molay, la** France
32 G7 **Molbergen** W Germany
28 B5 **Mølby** Denmark
8 C1 **Mold** Wales
48 G2 **Moldava nad Bodvon** Czechoslovakia
48 K4 **Moldavia** *reg* Romania
26 B9 **Molde** Norway
48 K3 **Moldova** *R* Romania
48 J5 **Moldoveanu** *mt* Romania
48 K3 **Moldoviţa** Romania
28 D3 **Møldrup** Denmark
40 D5 **Môle** *mt* France
89 D5 **Molepolole** Botswana
8 C6 **Mole, R** England
9 F5 **Mole, R** England
144 D5 **Molesworth** New Zealand
43 H7 **Molfetta** Italy
133 C5 **Molina** Chile
17 F4 **Molina de Aragón** Spain
17 G6 **Molina de Segura** Spain
99 Q8 **Moline** Illinois
107 O4 **Moline** Kansas
94 B4 **Moline** Michigan
45 L2 **Molinella** Italy
38 E8 **Molini** Italy
111 J11 **Molino** Florida
124 D3 **Molino** Mexico
42 F7 **Molise** *prov* Italy
47 K4 **Mollafeneri** Turkey
40 D2 **Mollans** France
28 K4 **Mölle** Sweden
28 C5 **Mølleberg** *hill* Denmark
33 S6 **Möllenbeck** E Germany
128 D7 **Mollendo** Peru
33 R5 **Möllenhagen** E Germany
143 C9 **Mollerin, L** W Australia
28 D4 **Mollerup** Denmark
17 H3 **Mollerusa** Spain
26 O2 **Mollesjok** Norway
20 K2 **Molliens-Dreuil** France
12 D2 **Mollinsburn** Scotland
26 M2 **Mollius** *mt* Norway
33 S5 **Mölln** E Germany
33 N5 **Mölln** W Germany
38 G8 **Molltal** *V* Austria
27 F14 **Mölndal** Sweden
54 G9 **Molochansk** U.S.S.R.
88 G10 **Molocue** *R* Mozambique
55 F4 **Molodogvardeyskaya** U.S.S.R.
52 D6 **Molodoy-Tud** U.S.S.R.
52 E5 **Mologa** *R* U.S.S.R.
102 V13 **Molokai** *isld* Hawaiian Is
135 S3 **Molokini** *isld* Hawaiian Is
52 E5 **Molokovo** U.S.S.R.
52 G5 **Moloma** *R* U.S.S.R.
139 J5 **Molong** New S Wales
89 B6 **Molopo** *R* S Africa
46 F6 **Mólos** Greece
86 C5 **Moloundou** Cameroon
28 F4 **Mols B** *hill* Denmark
36 D6 **Molsheim** France
118 E1 **Molson** Manitoba
119 V4 **Molson L** Manitoba
101 R4 **Molt** Montana
87 E12 **Molteno** S Africa
Moluccas *see* **Malaku**
88 G10 **Moma** Mozambique
86 D6 **Moma** Zaïre
51 O2 **Moma** *R* U.S.S.R.
139 G4 **Momba** New S Wales
88 D6 **Momba** *R* Tanzania
45 N4 **Mombaroccio** Italy
88 G4 **Mombasa** Kenya
60 Q3 **Mombetsu** Japan
60 R1 **Mombetsu** Japan
130 D6 **Mombuca, Serra da** *mts* Brazil
47 G3 **Momchilgrad** Bulgaria
99 T8 **Momence** Illinois
22 G3 **Momignies** Belgium
36 D6 **Mommenheim** France
71 F4 **Mompog Passage** Philippines
86 D5 **Mompono** Zaïre
126 G10 **Mompós** Colombia
68 C3 **Mon** Burma
28 K7 **Møn** *isld* Denmark
8 B1 **Môn** *isld* Wales
68 B2 **Mon** *R* Burma
127 L2 **Mona** Jamaica
103 N2 **Mona** Utah
94 G6 **Monaca** Pennsylvania
15 A3 **Monach I** Outer Hebrides Scotland
44 B4 **Monaco** *princ*
15 D3 **Monadhliath Mts** Scotland
29 J8 **Monå Fjärd** *inlet* Finland
128 F2 **Monagas** *state* Venezuela
14 E2 **Monaghan** Irish Rep
14 E2 **Monaghan** *co* Irish Rep
108 E4 **Monahans** Texas
127 L5 **Mona, I** Dom Rep
98 H3 **Monango** N Dakota
87 C7 **Mona Quimbundo** Angola
118 D9 **Monarch** Alberta
106 D3 **Monarch** Colorado
101 P2 **Monarch** Montana
117 L10 **Monarch Mt** Br Columbia
103 N2 **Mona Res** Utah
117 O10 **Monashee Mts** Br Col
14 D3 **Monasterevin** Irish Rep
18 H8 **Monastier, le** France
43 D13 **Monastir** Tunisia
48 J1 **Monastyriska** U.S.S.R.
55 D2 **Monastyrskoye** U.S.S.R.
44 C2 **Moncalieri** Italy
16 B2 **Monção** Portugal
17 F3 **Moncayo, Sierra del** Spain
22 F4 **Monceau-le-Neuf** France
38 L5 **Mönchdorf** Austria
52 D1 **Monchegorsk** U.S.S.R.
36 B1 **Mönchengladbach** W Germany
30 H1 **Mönchgut** *pen* E Germany
16 B7 **Monchique** Portugal
112 G4 **Moncks Corner** S Carolina
124 J4 **Monclova** Mexico
21 E8 **Moncontour** France
122 B5 **Moncouche, L** Quebec
122 H7 **Moncton** New Brunswick
130 D10 **Mondai** Brazil
99 L8 **Mondamin** Iowa
45 N4 **Mondavio** Italy
130 C9 **Monday, R** Paraguay
16 B4 **Mondego** *R* Portugal
16 B4 **Mondego, C** Portugal
16 E4 **Mondéjar** Spain
70 G6 **Mondeodo** Sulawesi
20 E3 **Mondeville** France
89 G3 **Mondi** *R* Zimbabwe
86 C3 **Mondo** Chad
45 O4 **Mondolfo** Italy
16 C1 **Mondoñedo** Spain
22 L4 **Mondorf-les-Bains** Luxembourg
20 G6 **Mondoubleau** France
44 C3 **Mondovi** Italy
99 P5 **Mondovi** Wisconsin
19 N16 **Mondragon** France
45 P7 **Mondragone** Italy
143 E10 **Mondrain I** W Australia
41 P3 **Mondschein Spitze** *mt* Austria
38 H6 **Mondsee** Austria
127 K2 **Moneague** Jamaica
44 F3 **Moneglia** Italy
18 E9 **Monein** France
46 F8 **Monemvasía** Greece
94 H9 **Moneta** Virginia
101 S6 **Moneta** Wyoming
110 C5 **Monett** Missouri
110 F6 **Monette** Arkansas
42 F3 **Monfalcone** Italy
68 D3 **Mon Fang** Thailand
44 C2 **Monferrato** *dist* Italy
86 D5 **Monga** Zaïre
95 N5 **Mongaup Vall** New York
68 H2 **Mong Cai** Vietnam
142 A1 **Monger L** Perth, W Aust
143 B8 **Monger, L** W Australia
68 D2 **Mong Hai** Burma
68 D2 **Mong Hang** Burma
45 K3 **Monghidoro** Italy
68 E2 **Mong Hkan** Burma
68 D2 **Mong Hkok** Burma
68 D2 **Mong Hpayak** Burma
68 D2 **Mong Hsat** Burma
68 C2 **Mong Hsawk** Burma
68 D2 **Mong Hsu** Burma
75 M6 **Monghyr** India
44 C3 **Mongioie** *mt* Italy
68 F6 **Mongkol Borey** Cambodia
68 D3 **Mong Kyawt** Burma
68 D2 **Mong La** Burma
68 C2 **Mong Lang** Burma
68 E2 **Mong Lin** Burma
68 E2 **Mong Loi** Burma
68 C1 **Mong Long** Burma
68 C3 **Mong Mau** Burma
68 C2 **Mong Nai** Burma
68 D2 **Mong Nawng** Burma
94 B5 **Mongo** Indiana
17 H6 **Mongo** *mt* Spain
58 C2 **Mongolia** *People's Rep* Asia
85 G8 **Mongomo** Mbini Eq Guinea
86 B3 **Mongonu** Nigeria
68 C3 **Mong Pai** Burma
68 D2 **Mong Pan** Burma
68 D1 **Mong Pat** Burma
68 D1 **Mong Pawk** Burma
68 C2 **Mong Pawn** Burma
68 D2 **Mong Ping** Burma
68 D2 **Mong Pu** Burma
68 D2 **Mong Pu-awn** Burma
124 H9 **Mongrove, Pta** *C* Mexico
68 D2 **Mong Ton** Burma
68 D2 **Mong Tum** Burma
68 C1 **Mong Tung** Burma
87 D9 **Mongu** Zambia
38 F8 **Monguelfo** Italy
68 E2 **Mong Un** Burma
68 D1 **Mong Yai** Burma
68 D2 **Mong Yang** Burma
68 D2 **Mong Yawn** Burma
68 E2 **Mong Yawng** Burma
95 S3 **Monhegan I** Maine
37 K6 **Monheim** Bayern W Germany
36 B1 **Monheim** Nordrhein-Westfalen W Germany
113 E7 **Moniac** Georgia
12 E3 **Moniaive** Scotland
19 O16 **Monieux** France
13 F1 **Monifieth** Scotland
18 H7 **Monistrol-sur-Loire** France
118 G7 **Monitor** Alberta
102 H3 **Monitor** *peak* Nevada
14 C3 **Monivea** Irish Rep
28 B7 **Mönkebüll** W Germany
140 F6 **Monkira** Queensland
86 D6 **Monkoto** Zaïre
120 J9 **Monkton** Ontario
12 D3 **Monkton** Scotland
99 Q9 **Monmouth** Illinois
95 R2 **Monmouth** Maine
8 D4 **Monmouth** Wales
Monmouth *co see* **Gwent**
117 M10 **Monmouth, Mt** Br Col
20 F4 **Monnai** France
21 G7 **Monnaie** France
24 E1 **Monnickendam** Netherlands
85 E7 **Mono** *R* Togo
102 F3 **Mono L** California
47 J8 **Monólithos** Rhodes Greece
95 S5 **Monomoy Pt** Massachusetts
99 U9 **Monon** Indiana
99 P6 **Monona** Iowa
94 G7 **Monongah** W Virginia
94 H6 **Monongahela** Pennsylvania
43 H8 **Monopoli** Italy
48 E3 **Monor** Hungary
127 N1 **Monos I** Trinidad
86 D2 **Monou** Chad
17 G6 **Monóvar** Spain
144 A6 **Monowai** New Zealand
98 H7 **Monowi** Nebraska
18 F8 **Monpont** France
36 C3 **Monreal** W Germany
17 G4 **Monreal del Campo** Spain
43 E10 **Monreale** Sicily
102 A2 **Monroe** California
112 D4 **Monroe** Georgia
94 C6 **Monroe** Indiana
99 N8 **Monroe** Iowa
111 D9 **Monroe** Louisiana
94 D5 **Monroe** Michigan
112 G3 **Monroe** N Carolina
95 N5 **Monroe** New York
100 B5 **Monroe** Oregon
95 L5 **Monroe** Pennsylvania
98 J6 **Monroe** S Dakota
103 M3 **Monroe** Utah
94 H9 **Monroe** Virginia
100 D2 **Monroe** Washington
99 R7 **Monroe** Wisconsin
99 P10 **Monroe City** Missouri
113 F9 **Monroe, L** Florida
110 K2 **Monroe Res** Indiana
111 J10 **Monroeville** Alabama
94 C6 **Monroeville** Indiana
94 E5 **Monroeville** Ohio
102 G7 **Monrovia** California
85 B7 **Monrovia** Liberia
17 G4 **Monroyo** Spain
22 F3 **Mons** Belgium
16 C4 **Monsanto** Portugal
130 H6 **Monsarás, Pta. de** Brazil
22 L2 **Monschau** W Germany
71 H7 **Monse** Indonesia
42 D3 **Monselice** Italy
36 E4 **Monsheim** W Germany
95 P4 **Monson** Massachusetts
28 C4 **Mønsted** Denmark
25 B4 **Monster** Netherlands
27 H14 **Mönsterås** Sweden
45 J4 **Monsummano** Italy
22 K3 **Mont** Belgium
36 D3 **Montabaur** W Germany
41 L3 **Montafon** *V* Austria
45 K1 **Montagnana** Italy
89 B9 **Montagu** S Africa
100 C8 **Montague** California
94 A3 **Montague** Michigan
122 K7 **Montague** Pr Edward I
109 K2 **Montague** Texas
116 O6 **Montague I** Alaska
103 K10 **Montague, I** Mexico
139 K6 **Montague I** New S Wales
143 C7 **Montague Ra** W Australia
142 F2 **Montague Sd** W Australia
116 N7 **Montague Str** Alaska
146 A13 **Montagu I** Antarctica
21 C8 **Montaigu** France
18 F8 **Montaigu-de-Quercy** France
40 D7 **Montaimont** France
45 J4 **Montaione** Italy
70 D5 **Montalat** *R* Kalimantan
17 G4 **Montalbán** Spain
127 K9 **Montalbán** Venezuela
45 K4 **Montale** Italy
16 B3 **Montalegre** Portugal
40 B6 **Montalieu** France
19 O13 **Montalieu Vercieu** France
43 G10 **Montalto** *mt* Italy
21 F8 **Montamise** France
116 N5 **Montana** Alaska
101 P3 **Montana** *state* U.S.A.
40 G7 **Montanaro** Italy
16 C5 **Montánchez** Spain
121 T5 **Mont-Apica** Quebec
18 G5 **Montargis** France
38 H9 **Montasio** *mt* Italy
20 K3 **Montataire** France
18 F9 **Montauban** France
20 A5 **Montauban-de-Bretagne** France
20 D5 **Montaudin** France
18 H5 **Montbard** France
40 C3 **Montbarrey** France
21 G7 **Montbazon** France
40 E2 **Montbéliard** France
109 N6 **Mont Belvieu** Texas
40 D4 **Montbenoit** France
21 C7 **Montbert** France
40 E6 **Mont Blanc** *mt* France
17 H3 **Montblanch** Spain
40 D3 **Montbozon** France
20 C4 **Montbray** France
18 H7 **Montbrison** France
Montcalm, L *see* **Dogai Coring**
18 F10 **Montcalm, Pic** *mt* France
20 D4 **Montchamp** France
22 G4 **Montcornet** France
18 E9 **Mont de Marsan** France
22 D4 **Montdidier** France
43 G9 **Montea** *mt* Italy
110 L6 **Monteagle** Tennessee
129 H4 **Monte Alegre** Brazil
17 G6 **Montealegre del Castillo** Spain
130 E6 **Monte Alegre de Minas** Brazil
130 G4 **Monte Azul** Brazil
121 Q7 **Montebello** Quebec
142 B5 **Monte Bello Is** W Australia
45 K1 **Montebello Vic** Italy
42 E3 **Montebelluna** Italy
20 C3 **Montebourg** France
45 N4 **Montecalvo in Foglia** Italy
45 S7 **Montecalvo Irpino** Italy
133 G3 **Montecarlo** Argentina
44 B4 **Monte-Carlo** Monaco
129 J7 **Monte Carmelo** Brazil
45 O4 **Montecarotto** Italy
131 F3 **Monte Caseros** Argentina
45 J4 **Montecatini Terme** Italy
45 K1 **Montecchio Maggiore** Italy
45 H2 **Montecchio nell'Emilia** Italy
45 N5 **Montecélio** Italy
18 F9 **Montech** France
112 H3 **Monte Clare** S Carolina
45 R8 **Montecorvino Rovella** Italy
45 J3 **Montecreto** Italy
127 J5 **Montecristi** Dom Rep
128 F6 **Monte Cristo** Bolivia
42 C6 **Montecristo** *isld* Italy
41 O4 **Montecroce, Pta di** *mt* Italy
124 H6 **Monte Escobedo** Mexico
45 M4 **Montefeltro** Italy
45 J3 **Montefiorino** Italy
45 R8 **Monteforte Irpina** Italy
16 E7 **Montefrio** Spain
127 J1 **Montego Bay** Jamaica
45 M4 **Monte Grimano** Italy
130 H9 **Monteiro** Brazil
140 B3 **Montejinnie** N Terr Aust
45 O6 **Montelanico** Italy
131 E6 **Monte, L.del** Argentina
19 N15 **Montélimar** France
129 G8 **Monte Lindo** Paraguay
108 G6 **Montell** Texas
45 S8 **Montella** Italy
16 D8 **Montellanto** Spain
101 L8 **Montello** Nevada
99 R6 **Montello** Wisconsin
45 K4 **Montelupo Fiorentino** Italy
45 R8 **Montemárano** Italy
45 O4 **Montemarciano** Italy
133 D6 **Montemayor, Meseta de** *hills* Argentina
21 G10 **Montemboeuf** France
45 L4 **Montemignaio** Italy
45 R7 **Montemiletto** Italy
125 K5 **Montemorelos** Mexico
45 K4 **Montemurio** Italy
20 D5 **Montenay** France
18 E7 **Montendre** France
46 C2 **Montenegro** *hist reg* Yugoslavia
42 D6 **Montepescali** Italy
127 K5 **Monte Plata** Dom Rep
45 O4 **Monteporzio** Italy
88 G8 **Montepuez** Mozambique
42 D5 **Montepulciano** Italy
18 G4 **Montereau** France
45 K3 **Monterenzio** Italy
102 C5 **Monterey** California
99 U8 **Monterey** Indiana
110 L5 **Monterey** Tennessee
94 H8 **Monterey** Virginia
102 B5 **Monterey B** California
126 G10 **Montería** Colombia
128 F7 **Montero** Bolivia
20 H2 **Montérolier** France
45 M5 **Monterosi** Italy
44 M5 **Monterosi, L** Italy
45 N5 **Monterotondo** Italy
125 J5 **Monterrey** Mexico
42 G7 **Monte S. Angelo** Italy
100 B3 **Montesano** Washington
130 G11 **Monte Santo** Brazil
130 F7 **Monte Santo de Minas** Brazil
45 R7 **Montesarchio** Italy
45 O7 **Monte S. Biágio** Italy
129 K7 **Montes Claros** Brazil
45 J3 **Montese** Italy
45 O4 **Montesicuro** Italy
45 K4 **Montespértoli** Italy
18 F9 **Montesquieu-Volvestre** France
18 H6 **Montet, le** France
111 K8 **Montevallo** Alabama
42 D5 **Montevarchi** Italy
45 K3 **Monteveglio** Italy
45 O5 **Monte Velino** Italy
99 L5 **Montevideo** Minnesota
131 G5 **Montevideo** Uruguay
101 N6 **Monteview** Idaho
106 D4 **Monte Vista** Colorado
103 L8 **Montezuma** Arizona
112 C5 **Montezuma** Georgia
99 T10 **Montezuma** Indiana
99 O8 **Montezuma** Iowa
107 K4 **Montezuma** Kansas
103 N7 **Montezuma Castle** Nat.Mon Arizona
102 G4 **Montezuma Pk** Nevada
20 C2 **Montfarville** France
21 C7 **Montfaucon** Maine-et-Loire France
22 J5 **Montfaucon** Meuse France
19 P14 **Montferrat** France
20 J4 **Montfort l'Amaury** France
20 F5 **Montfort-le-Rotrou** France
20 B5 **Montfort-sur-Meu** France
20 G3 **Montfort-sur-Risle** France
19 N17 **Montfrin** France
111 K9 **Montgomery** Alabama
111 D10 **Montgomery** Louisiana
94 C5 **Montgomery** Michigan
99 N5 **Montgomery** Minnesota
109 M5 **Montgomery** Texas
8 C2 **Montgomery** Wales
94 F8 **Montgomery** W Virginia
Montgomery *co see* **Powys**
110 E3 **Montgomery City** Missouri
100 D9 **Montgomery Creek** California
142 E3 **Montgomery I** W Australia
18 E7 **Montguyon** France
22 H4 **Monthermé** France
40 E5 **Monthey** Switzerland
22 H5 **Monthois** France
40 C1 **Monthureux-sur-Saône** France
43 C8 **Monti** Sardinia
111 E8 **Monticello** Arkansas
113 D7 **Monticello** Florida
112 D4 **Monticello** Georgia
110 H1 **Monticello** Illinois
110 K1 **Monticello** Indiana
99 P7 **Monticello** Iowa
110 M5 **Monticello** Kentucky
95 T7 **Monticello** Maine
99 N4 **Monticello** Minnesota
111 F10 **Monticello** Mississippi
110 E1 **Monticello** Missouri
106 C8 **Monticello** New Mexico
95 N5 **Monticello** New York
103 P4 **Monticello** Utah
99 R7 **Monticello** Wisconsin
45 J1 **Montichiari** Italy
43 C8 **Monti del Gennargentu** Sardinia
131 F3 **Montiel, Cuchilla de** *mts* Argentina
19 J4 **Montier en Der** France
22 D5 **Montiers** France
18 F7 **Montignac** France
20 C4 **Montigny** Manche France
36 B6 **Montigny** Meurthe-et-Moselle France
40 B2 **Montigny-le-Roi** France
16 B6 **Montijo** Portugal
16 C6 **Montijo** Spain
125 O6 **Montijo, G.de** Panama
16 D7 **Montilla** Spain
45 N5 **Monti Sabini** Italy
130 D5 **Montividiu** Brazil
20 F2 **Montivilliers** France
21 D7 **Montjean** France
70 F7 **Montjobalang** Sulawesi
20 C4 **Montjoie** France
115 N8 **Mont-Joli** Quebec
70 F7 **Montjonglowe** Sulawesi
138 F2 **Montkeleary** *R* S Australia
20 H5 **Montlandon** France
115 M8 **Mont-Laurier** Quebec
40 E3 **Montlebon** France
20 K4 **Montlhéry** France
18 E7 **Montlieu** France
18 G10 **Mont Louis** France
122 G4 **Mont Louis** Quebec
18 G6 **Montluçon** France
19 O13 **Montluel** France
122 B7 **Montmagny** Quebec
20 B4 **Montmartin-sur-Mer** France
119 O8 **Montmartre** Sask
22 J4 **Montmédy** France
19 Q14 **Montmélian** France
40 A5 **Montmerle** France
19 Q17 **Montmeyan** France
19 N15 **Montmeyran** France
18 H4 **Montmirail** Marne France
20 G5 **Montmirail** Sarthe France
18 F7 **Montmoreau** France
20 K4 **Montmorency** France
121 T6 **Montmorency** Quebec
122 A6 **Montmorency, R** Quebec
21 G9 **Montmorillon** France
19 P16 **Montmorin** France
141 K6 **Monto** Queensland
21 A7 **Montoir de Bretagne** France
21 G6 **Montoire-sur-Loir** France
45 M3 **Montone** *R* Italy
16 E6 **Montoro** Spain
99 O8 **Montour** Iowa
95 L4 **Montour Falls** New York
95 L5 **Montoursville** Pennsylvania
106 F6 **Montoya** New Mexico
101 O7 **Montpelier** Idaho
110 L1 **Montpelier** Indiana
127 J2 **Montpelier** Jamaica
98 H3 **Montpelier** N Dakota
94 C5 **Montpelier** Ohio
95 P2 **Montpelier** Vermont
18 H9 **Montpellier** France
121 P7 **Montpellier** Quebec
40 B4 **Montpont** France
18 G9 **Montréal** France
121 R7 **Montréal** Quebec
99 Q3 **Montreal** Wisconsin
120 K5 **Montreal** *R* Ontario
120 F5 **Montreal I** Ontario
119 M4 **Montreal Lake** Sask
119 M4 **Montreal R** Sask
120 F5 **Montreal River** Ontario
18 G9 **Montredon Labessonié** France
18 F9 **Montrejeau** France
21 H7 **Montrésor** France
22 B3 **Montreuil** France
21 E7 **Montreuil-Bellay** France
20 E5 **Montreuil-le-Chetif** France
20 B5 **Montreuil-sur-Ille** France
40 E5 **Montreux** Switzerland
21 C7 **Montrevault** France
21 H7 **Montrichard** France
111 E8 **Montrose** Arkansas
106 C3 **Montrose** Colorado
110 H2 **Montrose** Illinois
99 P9 **Montrose** Iowa
98 C7 **Montrose** Nebraska
95 L5 **Montrose** Pennsylvania
15 F4 **Montrose** Scotland
98 J6 **Montrose** S Dakota
95 L8 **Montross** Virginia
22 G3 **Mont. St.Christophe** Belgium
22 G2 **Mont-St.Jean** Belgium
22 K4 **Mont St.Martin** France
20 B4 **Mont St.Michel, B.du** France
20 B4 **Mont St. Michel, le** France
20 D4 **Montsecret** France
17 H2 **Montseny** *mt* Spain
17 J3 **Montseny, Sierra de** *mts* Spain
17 J3 **Montserrat** *dist* Spain
127 N6 **Montserrat** *isld* Lesser Antilles
129 H3 **Montsinery** Fr Guiana
21 F7 **Montsoreau** France
20 K3 **Montsoult** France
115 N8 **Monts, Pointe des** Quebec
21 F8 **Monts-sur-Guesnes** France
22 H2 **Mont.St.Guibert** Belgium
20 D5 **Montsûrs** France
121 Q6 **Mont Tremblant** Quebec
20 F4 **Montviette** France
95 P5 **Montville** Connecticut
106 F2 **Monument** Colorado
107 J2 **Monument** Kansas
108 D3 **Monument** New Mexico
100 F5 **Monument** Oregon
116 F4 **Monument Mt** Alaska
103 O4 **Monument V** Utah/Ariz
86 D5 **Monveda** Zaïre
20 H2 **Monville** France
68 B1 **Monywa** Burma
41 K6 **Monza** Italy
87 E9 **Monze** Zambia
17 H3 **Monzón** Spain
45 K3 **Monzuno** Italy
109 K4 **Moody** Texas
95 O2 **Mooers** New York
138 B2 **Moolalpinna Hill** S Australia
138 E3 **Moolawatana** S Australia
138 E2 **Moolionburrinna, L** S Australia
140 B3 **Mooloolоо** N Terr Aust
139 J3 **Moomin** *R* New S Wales
138 D4 **Moonaree** S Australia
120 H3 **Moonbeam** Ontario
140 F7 **Moonda L** Queensland
141 K8 **Moonie** Queensland
141 J8 **Moonie** *R* Queensland
103 O1 **Moon L.Res** Utah
139 K4 **Moonoi Ra** *mts* New S Wales
138 D5 **Moonta** S Australia
143 B9 **Moora** W Australia
140 F7 **Mooraberree** Queensland
98 B5 **Moorcroft** Wyoming
101 M6 **Moore** Idaho
101 Q3 **Moore** Montana
107 N6 **Moore** Oklahoma
109 H6 **Moore** Texas
134 A11 **Moorea** *isld* Society Is Pacific Oc
146 H7 **Moore B** Antarctica
116 J5 **Moore Creek** Alaska
98 F9 **Moorefield** Nebraska
94 J7 **Moorefield** W Virginia
113 F11 **Moore Haven** Florida
143 C8 **Moore, L** W Australia
108 E7 **Mooreland** Oklahoma
140 D2 **Moore, Mt** N Terr Aust
143 C9 **Moore, Mt** W Australia
143 E7 **Moore, Mt** W Australia
143 G7 **Moore, Mt** W Australia
95 Q2 **Moore Res** Vermont
112 J3 **Moores Cr. Nat. Mil. Park** N Carolina
122 E8 **Moore's Mills** New Brunswick
110 K2 **Mooresville** Indiana
112 G2 **Mooresville** N Carolina
98 J3 **Mooreton** N Dakota
127 M2 **Moore Town** Jamaica
13 E2 **Moorfoot Hills** Scotland
98 K3 **Moorhead** Minnesota
111 F8 **Moorhead** Mississippi
101 U4 **Moorhead** Montana
109 O3 **Mooringsport** Louisiana
121 N6 **Moor Lake** Ontario
99 M7 **Moorland** Iowa
110 J4 **Moorman** Kentucky
138 C4 **Moornaba Rock** S Australia
139 G5 **Moornanyah L** New S Wales
87 F7 **Moorokosa** Zambia
141 K2 **Moorooka** *dist* Brisbane, Qnsld
140 D1 **Mooroongga I** N Terr Aust
139 H6 **Mooroopna** Victoria
102 F7 **Moorpark** California
22 G2 **Moorsel** Belgium
22 E2 **Moorslede** Belgium
89 F5 **Moos** *R* S Africa
37 N4 **Moosbach** W Germany
32 L9 **Moosberg** *mt* W Germany
37 M7 **Moosburg** W Germany
101 P6 **Moose** Wyoming
115 L7 **Moose** *R* Ontario
120 K1 **Moose Factory** Ontario
95 S1 **Moosehead L** Maine
119 O2 **Moose Hill** Ontario
119 T7 **Moosehorn** Manitoba
119 U7 **Moose I** Manitoba
119 M8 **Moose Jaw** Sask
119 N8 **Moosejaw Cr** Sask
99 O3 **Moose L** Minnesota
119 R5 **Moose Lake** Manitoba
95 R2 **Mooselookmeguntic L** Maine
119 P9 **Moose Mt. Prov. Park** Sask
119 W2 **Moose Nose L** Manitoba
116 N6 **Moose Pass** Alaska
120 J2 **Moose River** Ontario
37 N6 **Moosham** W Germany
38 M8 **Mooskirchen** Austria
119 Q8 **Moosomin** Sask
120 K1 **Moosonee** Ontario
95 Q5 **Moosup** Connecticut
89 G7 **Moot** *R* S Africa
138 F4 **Mootwingee** New S Wales
87 G9 **Mopeia** Mozambique
85 D6 **Mopti** Mali
99 P3 **Moquah** Wisconsin
128 D7 **Moquegua** Peru
128 D7 **Moquegua** *dep* Peru
48 E3 **Mór** Hungary
86 B3 **Mora** Cameroon
100 J6 **Mora** Idaho
99 N4 **Mora** Minnesota
106 E6 **Mora** New Mexico
16 B6 **Mora** Portugal
16 E5 **Mora** Spain
27 G10 **Mora** Sweden
141 J7 **Moraby** Queensland
46 C2 **Morača** *R* Yugoslavia
131 B5 **Mora, Cerro** *peak* Arg/Chile
74 H4 **Moradabad** India
16 B5 **Moradal, Sa. do** *mts* Portugal
130 F6 **Morada Nova de Minas** Brazil
17 H3 **Mora de Ebro** Spain
17 G4 **Mora de Rubielos** Spain
87 G11 **Morafenobe** Madagascar
31 M2 **Morąg** Poland
83 K11 **Moragala** Sri Lanka
133 C6 **Moraleda, Canal** *str* Chile
109 L6 **Morales** Texas
87 H11 **Moramanga** Madagascar
110 A4 **Moran** Kansas
109 H3 **Moran** Texas

101 P6 **Moran** Wyoming
141 J5 **Moranbah** Queensland
43 G9 **Morano Cal** Italy
126 G6 **Morant Cays** *reefs* W Indies
16 C1 **Morás** *C* Spain
16 E4 **Moras** *R* Spain
16 E4 **Morata de T** Spain
17 F6 **Moratalla** Spain
83 J11 **Moratuwa** Sri Lanka
31 K7 **Morava** *R* Czechoslovakia
48 G6 **Morava** *R* Yugoslavia
48 D1 **Moravia** Czechoslovakia
99 O9 **Moravia** Iowa
95 L4 **Moravia** New York
46 D1 **Moravica** *R* Yugoslavia
31 K6 **Moravice** *R* Czechoslovakia
31 K6 **Moravská Třebová** Czechoslovakia
31 J6 **Moravski Budějovice** Czechoslovakia
143 B8 **Morawa** W Australia
128 G2 **Morawhanna** Guyana
Moray *co see* **Grampian** *reg*
141 H5 **Moray Downs** Queensland
15 E3 **Moray Firth** Scotland
140 B3 **Moray Ra** N Terr Aust
36 C4 **Morbach** W Germany
22 C2 **Morbecque** France
41 L5 **Morbegno** Italy
18 D5 **Morbihan** *dep* France
27 H15 **Mörbylånga** Sweden
18 E8 **Morcenx** France
45 N4 **Morciano di Romagna** Italy
124 G5 **Morcillo** Mexico
45 R7 **Morcone** Italy
9 F2 **Morcott** England
20 B5 **Mordelles** France
98 H1 **Morden** Manitoba
138 F4 **Morden** New S Wales
122 H8 **Morden** Nova Scotia
139 H7 **Mordialloc** Victoria
52 H4 **Mordino** U.S.S.R.
53 F7 **Mordovskaya A.S.S.R** U.S.S.R.
116 E9 **Mordvinof, C** Aleutian Is
31 N3 **Mordy** Poland
98 E4 **Moreau** *R* S Dakota
111 E10 **Moreauville** Louisiana
13 F3 **Morebattle** Scotland
13 F5 **Morecambe** England
16 E7 **Moreda** Spain
21 H6 **Morée** France
139 J3 **Moree** New S Wales
94 D8 **Morehead** Kentucky
141 G2 **Morehead** *R* Queensland
112 L3 **Morehead City** N Carolina
110 G5 **Morehouse** Missouri
128 F4 **Moreira** Brazil
101 N6 **Moreland** Idaho
124 J8 **Morelia** Mexico
141 G6 **Morella** Queensland
124 H6 **Morelos** Mexico
74 H5 **Morena** India
102 H9 **Morena Res** California
16 C7 **Morena, Sa** *mts* Spain
103 P8 **Morenci** Arizona
94 C5 **Morenci** Michigan
48 K6 **Moreni** Romania
124 D3 **Moreno** Mexico
26 C9 **More og Romsdal** *reg* Norway
145 F3 **Morere** New Zealand
12 E4 **Moresby** England
113 K11 **Mores I** Bahamas
22 K2 **Moresnet** Belgium
40 B6 **Morestel** France
18 G4 **Moret** France
141 G1 **Moreton** Queensland
139 L2 **Moreton B** Queensland
8 C6 **Moretonhampstead** England
141 L7 **Moreton I** Queensland
9 E4 **Moreton in Marsh** England
95 P2 **Moretown** Vermont
20 K2 **Moreuil** France
40 D4 **Morez** France
36 F4 **Mörfelden** W Germany
29 M3 **Morgam Viibus** *mt* Finland
112 C6 **Morgan** Georgia
138 E5 **Morgan** S Australia
109 K3 **Morgan** Texas
101 O8 **Morgan** Utah
110 J4 **Morganfield** Kentucky
102 C4 **Morgan Hill** California
109 J3 **Morgan Mill** Texas
102 F4 **Morgan, Mt** California
140 D4 **Morgan, Mt** N Terr Aust
113 K12 **Morgans Bluff** Bahamas
112 F2 **Morganton** N Carolina
110 K2 **Morgantown** Indiana
110 K4 **Morgantown** Kentucky
111 F10 **Morgantown** Mississippi
94 H7 **Morgantown** W Virginia
141 K7 **Morganville** Queensland
111 E11 **Morganza** Louisiana
40 E4 **Morges** Switzerland
40 F6 **Morgex** Italy
20 J3 **Morgny** France
36 B6 **Morhange** France
22 K4 **Morhet** Belgium
122 K2 **Morhiban, L.de** Quebec
66 E3 **Mori** China
41 N6 **Mori** Italy
60 O3 **Mori** Japan
95 O2 **Moriah** New York
127 M2 **Moriah** Tobago
103 K2 **Moriah, Mt** Nevada
22 H3 **Morialme** Belgium
108 A1 **Moriarty** New Mexico
141 H8 **Moriarty's Ra** Queensland
138 D2 **Morice Hill** S Australia
117 K8 **Morice L** Br Col
128 D3 **Morichal** Colombia
45 N5 **Moricone** Italy
118 J4 **Morin Creek** Sask
32 L9 **Moringen** W Germany
52 D5 **Morino** U.S.S.R.
118 D5 **Morinville** Alberta
61 P6 **Morioka** Japan
124 E3 **Moris** Mexico
139 K5 **Morisset** New S Wales
122 B7 **Morisset Sta** Quebec
32 L8 **Moritzberg** W Germany
37 L5 **Moritzberg** *mt* W Germany
61 O6 **Moriyashi-zan** *mt* Japan
138 F5 **Morkalla** Victoria
28 E4 **Mørke** Denmark
52 G6 **Morki** U.S.S.R.
28 G5 **Mørkøv** Denmark
18 C4 **Morlaix** France
107 K2 **Morland** Kansas
36 F4 **Mörlenbach** W Germany
118 C7 **Morley** Alberta
106 F4 **Morley** Colorado
13 G6 **Morley** England
110 G4 **Morley** Missouri
117 G5 **Morley River** Yukon Terr
45 N5 **Morlupe** Italy
43 G9 **Mormanno** Italy
19 O16 **Mormoiron** France
103 N7 **Mormon L** Arizona
101 L4 **Mormon Mt** Idaho
103 K5 **Mormon Mts** Nevada
19 N13 **Mornant** France
19 N16 **Mornas** France
83 M14 **Morne, Pte** Kerguelen Indian Oc
141 F7 **Morney** Queensland
141 F7 **Morney** *R* Queensland
140 F4 **Morning Inlet** *R* Queensland
141 K1 **Morningside** *dist* Brisbane, Qnsld
99 P8 **Morning Sun** Iowa
133 B7 **Mornington, I** Chile
140 E3 **Mornington I** Queensland
140 E3 **Mornington Mission** Queensland
46 E6 **Mórnos** *R* Greece
36 F2 **Mornshausen** W Germany
37 L6 **Mörnsheim** W Germany
110 F7 **Moro** Arkansas
100 E4 **Moro** Oregon
136 K3 **Morobe** Papua New Guinea
99 T9 **Morocco** Indiana
85 B3 **Morocco** *kingdom* N Africa
88 F5 **Morogoro** Tanzania
71 F7 **Moro Gulf** Philippines
89 C6 **Morokweng** S Africa
124 J7 **Moroleón** Mexico
71 J7 **Moromaho** *isld* Indonesia
87 G12 **Morombe** Madagascar
126 E3 **Morón** Cuba
58 D2 **Mörön** Mongolia
127 K9 **Morón** Venezuela
40 F3 **Moron** *mt* Switzerland
128 C4 **Morona** Ecuador
128 C4 **Morona-Santiago** *prov* Ecuador
87 G12 **Morondava** Madagascar
17 F3 **Morón de Almazán** Spain
16 D7 **Morón de la Frontera** Spain
87 G10 **Moroni** Comoros
103 N2 **Moroni** Utah
66 E5 **Moron Us He** *R* China
61 K11 **Morosaki** Japan
71 B1 **Morotai** *isld* Halmahera Indonesia
48 E5 **Morovič** Yugoslavia
70 G5 **Morowali** Sulawesi
55 D2 **Morozkovo** U.S.S.R.
13 G3 **Morpeth** England
120 J10 **Morpeth** Ontario
79 C3 **Morphou B** Cyprus
94 D6 **Morral** Ohio
130 E9 **Morretes** Brazil
99 L10 **Morrill** Kansas
98 C8 **Morrill** Nebraska
110 D6 **Morrilton** Arkansas
118 E7 **Morrin** Alberta
130 E5 **Morrinhos** Brazil
145 E2 **Morrinsville** New Zealand
99 S8 **Morris** Illinois
119 U9 **Morris** Manitoba
99 L4 **Morris** Minnesota
95 M4 **Morris** New York
107 P6 **Morris** Oklahoma
95 K5 **Morris** Pennsylvania
121 P8 **Morrisburg** Ontario
112 H5 **Morris I** S Carolina
138 B2 **Morris, Mt** S Australia
142 D4 **Morris, Mt** W Australia
99 R8 **Morrison** Illinois
107 O5 **Morrison** Oklahoma
110 L6 **Morrison** Tennessee
144 C6 **Morrisons** New Zealand
110 G2 **Morrisonville** Illinois
113 E8 **Morriston** Florida
8 C4 **Morriston** Wales
103 M8 **Morristown** Arizona
99 N5 **Morristown** Minnesota
95 N6 **Morristown** New Jersey
95 M2 **Morristown** New York
98 E4 **Morristown** S Dakota
112 D1 **Morristown** Tennessee
95 M4 **Morrisville** New York
95 N6 **Morrisville** Pennsylvania
95 P2 **Morrisville** Vermont
94 K8 **Morrisville** Virginia
130 G4 **Morro** Brazil
130 E7 **Morro Agudo** Brazil
102 D6 **Morro B** California
131 A7 **Morro Bonifacio** *C* Chile
130 H6 **Morro d'Anta** Brazil
131 A8 **Morro del Compas** *C* Chile
129 G6 **Morro Do Sinal** Brazil
133 C3 **Morro, Pta** Chile
131 D4 **Morro, Sa. del** *peak* Argentina
126 G10 **Morrosquillo, G. de** Colombia
111 D11 **Morrow** Louisiana
110 M2 **Morrow** Ohio
88 E10 **Morrumbala** Mozambique
87 G10 **Morrumbene** Mozambique
28 B3 **Mors** *isld* Denmark
20 C2 **Morsalines** France
36 D2 **Morsbach** W Germany
36 E6 **Mörsch** W Germany
37 M2 **Mörsdorf** E Germany
111 D11 **Morse** Louisiana
118 K8 **Morse** Sask
108 C7 **Morse** Texas
53 F7 **Morshansk** U.S.S.R.
52 D3 **Morskaya Maselga** U.S.S.R.
27 E11 **Morskogen** Norway
33 O8 **Morsleben** E Germany
118 H1 **Morson** Ontario
43 B13 **Morsott** Algeria
140 E4 **Morstone** Queensland
28 A7 **Morsum** W Germany
26 H4 **Morsvik** Norway
140 F5 **Mort** *R* Queensland
36 B7 **Mortagne** *R* France
20 G5 **Mortagne (au Perche)** France
21 D8 **Mortagne-sur-Sèvre** France
16 B4 **Mortágua** Portugal
20 D4 **Mortain** France
138 C5 **Mortana** S Australia
41 J7 **Mortara** Italy
40 E3 **Morteau** France
20 E4 **Morteaux Couliboeuf** France
8 B5 **Mortehoe** England
130 G7 **Mortes** *R* Brazil
129 H6 **Mortes, Rio das** *R* Brazil
22 F4 **Mortiers** France
142 B6 **Mortimer, Mt** W Australia
8 D3 **Mortimers Cross** England
118 L8 **Mortlach** Sask
139 G7 **Mortlake** Victoria
103 J8 **Mortmar** California
99 R9 **Morton** Illinois
99 M5 **Morton** Minnesota
111 G9 **Morton** Mississippi
108 E2 **Morton** Texas
100 C3 **Morton** Washington
110 J4 **Mortons Gap** Kentucky
20 F4 **Mortrée** France
22 G1 **Mortsel** Belgium
28 E6 **Morúd** Denmark
127 O3 **Moruga** Trinidad
139 H5 **Morundah** New S Wales
139 K6 **Moruya** New S Wales
18 H5 **Morvan** *mts* France
113 D7 **Morven** Georgia
112 G3 **Morven** N Carolina
144 C6 **Morven** New Zealand
141 H7 **Morven** Queensland
15 E2 **Morven** *mt* Scotland
15 C4 **Morvern** Scotland
74 D7 **Morvi** India
8 D2 **Morville** England
56 B3 **Moryakovskiy Zaton** U.S.S.R.
52 F2 **Morzhovets, Os** *isld* U.S.S.R.
116 F9 **Morzhovoi B** Alaska
54 F2 **Mosal'sk** U.S.S.R.
28 E2 **Mosbjerg** Denmark
101 S2 **Mosby** Montana
Moscow *see* **Moskva**
100 J3 **Moscow** Idaho
107 J4 **Moscow** Kansas
110 F3 **Moscow** Missouri
110 M3 **Moscow** Ohio
95 M5 **Moscow** Pennsylvania
110 G6 **Moscow** Tennessee
146 H3 **Mose, C** Antarctica
37 N2 **Mosel** E Germany
36 C3 **Mosel** *R* W Germany
94 K9 **Moseley** Virginia
36 C3 **Moselkern** W Germany
111 G10 **Moselle** Mississippi
36 B5 **Moselle** *dep* France
40 E1 **Moselle** *R* France
40 E2 **Moselotte** *R* France
123 K9 **Mosers River** Nova Scotia
106 G5 **Moses** New Mexico
100 F2 **Moses Coulee** *R* Washington
100 H9 **Moses, Mt** Nevada
116 F4 **Moses Point** Alaska
60 P2 **Moseushi** Japan
52 G2 **Moseyevo** U.S.S.R.
144 C6 **Mosgiel** New Zealand
52 D2 **Mosha** U.S.S.R.
52 F4 **Mosha** *R* U.S.S.R.
52 C5 **Moshchnyy, Ostrov** *isld* U.S.S.R.
112 E1 **Mosheim** Tennessee
120 F4 **Mosher** Ontario
88 F3 **Moshi** Tanzania
52 F6 **Moshok** U.S.S.R.
52 H3 **Mosh'yuga** U.S.S.R.
33 Q9 **Mosigkau** E Germany
31 K3 **Mosina** Poland
99 R5 **Mosinee** Wisconsin
26 F6 **Mosjöen** Norway
59 M1 **Moskalvo** U.S.S.R.
98 B5 **Moskee** Wyoming
26 F4 **Moskenes** Norway
26 F4 **Moskenesöy** *isld* Norway
26 F4 **Moskenstraumen** *isld* Norway
26 M4 **Moskijärvi** Sweden
26 L6 **Moskosel** Sweden
29 M4 **Moskuvaara** Finland
49 **Moskva** *conurbation* U.S.S.R.
54 G1 **Moskva** *R* U.S.S.R.
56 D4 **Moskva, Gora** *mt* U.S.S.R.
54 J1 **Moskvy, Kanal Imeni** U.S.S.R.
42 H3 **Moslavacka Gora** *mt* Yugoslavia
21 H7 **Mosnes** France
41 O4 **Moso** Italy
87 E10 **Mosomane** Botswana
48 D3 **Mosonmagyarovar** Hungary
54 K9 **Mospino** U.S.S.R.
128 C3 **Mosquera** Colombia
125 M2 **Mosquitia** *reg* Honduras
130 H4 **Mosquito** *R* Brazil
94 G5 **Mosquito Cr.Res** Ohio
125 N3 **Mosquitos, Costa de** Nicaragua
27 E12 **Moss** Norway
130 E5 **Mossâmedes** Brazil
118 L9 **Mossbank** Sask
15 G2 **Mossbank** Scotland
144 B6 **Mossburn** New Zealand
89 C10 **Mosselbaai** S Africa
86 B6 **Mossendjo** Congo
139 G5 **Mossgiel** New S Wales
36 G7 **Mössingen** W Germany
119 T1 **Moss L** Manitoba
13 F6 **Mossley** England
141 H3 **Mossman** Queensland
28 D4 **Mossø** *L* Denmark
129 L5 **Mossoro** Brazil
13 F3 **Mosspaul** Scotland
111 H11 **Moss Point** Mississippi
88 H9 **Mossuril** Mozambique
139 K5 **Moss Vale** New S Wales
113 A7 **Mossy Head** Florida
119 U6 **Mossy Pt** Manitoba
119 O4 **Mossy R** Sask
100 C3 **Mossyrock** Washington
47 H3 **Most** Bulgaria
30 H5 **Most** Czechoslovakia
17 H9 **Mostaganem** Algeria
42 H5 **Mostar** Yugoslavia
31 O6 **Mostiska** U.S.S.R.
55 C3 **Mostovaya** U.S.S.R.
55 E3 **Mostovskoy** U.S.S.R.
31 P2 **Mosty** U.S.S.R.
70 F2 **Mostyn** Sabah
8 C1 **Mostyn** Wales
78 J3 **Mosul** Iraq
27 C12 **Mös-vatn** *L* Norway
26 E8 **Mosvik** Norway
86 G3 **Mota** Ethiopia
86 C5 **Motaba** *R* Congo
17 F5 **Mota del Cuervo** Spain
16 D3 **Mota del Marqués** Spain
125 O10 **Motagua** *R* Guatemala
27 H13 **Motala** Sweden
127 J10 **Motatán** Venezuela
61 O9 **Motegi** Japan
145 E3 **Motere** *mt* New Zealand
116 J8 **Mother Goose L** Alaska
12 E2 **Motherwell** Scotland
58 D5 **Motian Ling** *mt ra* China
40 F4 **Môtier** Switzerland
75 L5 **Motihari** India
71 A2 **Moti, I** California
17 F5 **Motilla del Palancar** Spain
145 F2 **Motiti I** New Zealand
27 G12 **Motjärnshyttan** Sweden
99 M3 **Motley** Minnesota
89 F3 **Motloutse** *R* Botswana
60 O4 **Motomachi** Japan
52 D1 **Motovskiy Zaliv** *gulf* U.S.S.R.
42 F3 **Motovun** Yugoslavia
60 G12 **Motoyama** Japan
61 N13 **Moto-yama** *peak* Iwo Jima Japan
61 P7 **Motoyoshi** Japan
16 E8 **Motril** Spain
60 N3 **Motsuta misaki** *C* Japan
98 D3 **Mott** N Dakota
45 J1 **Motteggiana** Italy
36 H3 **Motten** W Germany
20 G2 **Motteville** France
145 F3 **Motu** New Zealand
145 G3 **Motu Ahiauru** New Zealand
145 D4 **Motueka** New Zealand
145 F2 **Motuhora I** New Zealand
144 D5 **Motukarara** New Zealand
145 D1 **Motukawanui I** New Zealand
Motukorea I *see* **Browns I**
144 D5 **Motunau I** New Zealand
135 L10 **Motu One** *isld* Society Is Pacific Oc
145 G3 **Motuoroi I** New Zealand
145 D4 **Motupiko** New Zealand
145 F2 **Motu R** New Zealand
145 D1 **Moturoa Is** New Zealand
145 E3 **Motutaiko I** New Zealand
145 D1 **Motutang** New Zealand
145 E2 **Motutapu I** New Zealand
28 E3 **Mou** Denmark
146 K6 **Moubray B** Antarctica
122 C2 **Mouchalagane R.** Quebec
127 J4 **Mouchoir Passage** Caribbean
47 G5 **Moúdhros** Greece
85 B5 **Moudjéria** Mauritania
40 E4 **Moudon** Switzerland
21 E9 **Mougon** France
86 B6 **Mouila** Gabon
86 D4 **Mouka** Cent Afr Republic
139 G6 **Moulamein** New S Wales
16 C10 **Moulay-Bouselham** Morocco
114 H2 **Mould Bay** N W Terr
127 N4 **Moule** Guadeloupe W I
20 G4 **Moulicent** France
21 F7 **Mouliherne** France
18 H6 **Moulins** Allier France
20 E5 **Moulins** Sarthe France
18 H6 **Moulins-Engilbert** France
20 F4 **Moulins-la-Marche** France
21 I7 **Moulins-sur-Cephons** France
68 C4 **Moulmein** Burma
85 D2 **Moulouya** *R* Morocco
111 J7 **Moulton** Alabama
101 M7 **Moulton** Idaho
110 D1 **Moulton** Iowa
109 K6 **Moulton** Texas
112 D6 **Moultrie** Georgia
112 G4 **Moultrie, L** S Carolina
86 B6 **Mounana** Gabon
46 D6 **Moúnda, Akr** *C* Greece
111 F8 **Mound Bayou** Mississippi
110 G4 **Mound City** Illinois
110 B3 **Mound City** Kansas
99 L9 **Mound City** Missouri
98 F4 **Mound City** S Dakota
94 D7 **Mound City Nat.Mon** Ohio
86 C4 **Moundou** Chad
107 N3 **Mound Ridge** Kansas
110 G4 **Mounds** Illinois
107 O6 **Mounds** Oklahoma
94 G7 **Moundsville** W Virginia
110 A4 **Mound Valley** Kansas
111 J9 **Moundville** Alabama
68 F6 **Moung** Cambodia
68 F1 **Moung Hat Hin** Laos
98 J1 **Mountain** N Dakota
94 G7 **Mountain** W Virginia
108 A1 **Mountainair** New Mexico
8 C4 **Mountain Ash** Wales
100 K8 **Mountain City** Nevada
109 N9 **Mountain Cr.L** Texas
109 N1 **Mountain Fork** *R* Oklahoma
110 D4 **Mountain Grove** Missouri
110 D5 **Mountain Home** Arkansas
100 K6 **Mountain Home** Idaho
109 H5 **Mountain Home** Texas
103 O1 **Mountain Home** Utah
112 G2 **Mountain Island L** N Carolina
117 P9 **Mountain Park** Alberta
109 J1 **Mountain Park** Oklahoma
109 O1 **Mountain Pine** Arkansas
118 D9 **Mountain View** Alberta
110 D6 **Mountain View** Arkansas
135 V5 **Mountain View** Hawaiian Is
110 E5 **Mountain View** Missouri
107 M6 **Mountain View** Oklahoma
101 P8 **Mountainview** Wyoming
116 F5 **Mountain Village** Alaska
95 K7 **Mount Airy** Maryland
112 G1 **Mount Airy** N Carolina
99 S4 **Mountan** Wisconsin
100 C4 **Mount Angel** Oregon
144 B6 **Mount Aspiring Nat. Park** New Zealand
118 B8 **Mount Assiniboine Prov Park** Br Col/Alberta
99 R10 **Mount Auburn** Illinois
143 B6 **Mount Augustus** W Australia
89 F8 **Mount Ayliff** S Africa
99 M9 **Mount Ayr** Iowa
138 E6 **Mount Barker** S Australia
143 C10 **Mount Barker** W Australia
142 F3 **Mount Barnett** W Australia
14 C3 **Mount Bellew Br** Irish Rep
138 F3 **Mount Browne** New S Wales
145 E4 **Mount Bruce** New Zealand
140 B2 **Mount Bundey** N Terr Aust
120 J4 **Mount Byers** Ontario
109 L4 **Mount Calm** Texas
141 H3 **Mount Carbine** Queensland
110 J3 **Mount Carmel** Illinois
123 T6 **Mount Carmel** Newfoundland
95 L6 **Mount Carmel** Pennsylvania
99 R7 **Mount Carroll** Illinois
140 C7 **Mount Cavenagh** N Terr Aust
143 D8 **Mount Celia** W Australia
138 C4 **Mount Christie** S Australia
98 H9 **Mount Clare** Nebraska
94 G7 **Mount Clare** W Virginia
143 C7 **Mount Clere** W Australia
141 H5 **Mount Coolon** Queensland
88 C10 **Mount Darwin** Zimbabwe
140 B5 **Mount Denison** N Terr Aust
95 T2 **Mount Desert I** Maine
95 T3 **Mount Desert Rock** Maine
108 A7 **Mount Dora** New Mexico
140 B5 **Mount Doreen** N Terr Aust
141 H5 **Mount Douglas** Queensland
138 D2 **Mount Dutton** S Australia
138 D4 **Mount Eba** S Australia
140 C7 **Mount Ebenezer** N Terr Aust
117 F7 **Mount Edgecumbe** Alaska
117 H7 **Mount Edziza Prov. Park** Br Columbia
101 P9 **Mount Emmons** Utah
141 G5 **Mount Emu Plains** Queensland
109 N4 **Mount Enterprise** Texas
140 C6 **Mount Ertwa** N Terr Aust
89 F8 **Mount Fletcher** S Africa
89 F8 **Mount Frere** S Africa
138 F6 **Mount Gambier** S Australia
141 H4 **Mount Garnet** Queensland
112 H2 **Mount Gilead** N Carolina
94 E6 **Mount Gilead** Ohio
141 L2 **Mount Gravatt** *dist* Brisbane, Qnsld
136 J3 **Mount Hagen** Papua New Guinea
106 C1 **Mount Harris** Colorado
100 C8 **Mount Hebron** California
141 G4 **Mount Hogan** Queensland
95 N6 **Mount Holly** New Jersey
94 K6 **Mount Holly** Pennsylvania
107 N4 **Mount Hope** Kansas
99 R6 **Mount Horeb** Wisconsin
142 F3 **Mount House** W Australia
141 F7 **Mount Howitt** Queensland
144 C5 **Mount Hutt** New Zealand
109 O1 **Mount Ida** Arkansas
143 D8 **Mount Ida** W Australia
100 J4 **Mount Idaho** Idaho
140 E5 **Mount Isa** Queensland
94 J8 **Mount Jackson** Virginia
94 J5 **Mount Jewett** Pennsylvania
120 H6 **Mount L** Ontario
83 J11 **Mount Lavinia** Sri Lanka
142 B1 **Mount Lawley** *dist* Perth, W Aust
141 J5 **Mount Lookout** Queensland
141 H5 **Mount McConnell** Queensland
116 M5 **Mount McKinley Nat. Park** Alaska
143 C8 **Mount Magnet** W Australia
139 G4 **Mount Manara** New S Wales
141 G6 **Mount Marlow** Queensland
145 F2 **Mount Maunganui** New Zealand
100 E9 **Mount Meadows Res** California
14 D3 **Mountmellick** Irish Rep
141 H3 **Mount Molloy** Queensland
102 F4 **Mount Montgomery** Nevada
141 K6 **Mount Morgan** Queensland
110 C1 **Mount Moriah** Missouri
99 R7 **Mount Morris** Illinois
94 K4 **Mount Morris** New York
141 G3 **Mount Mulligan** Queensland
139 G4 **Mount Murchison** New S Wales
140 C1 **Mount Norris B** N Terr Aust
106 D2 **Mount of the Holy Cross** Colorado
110 G2 **Mount Olive** Illinois
111 G10 **Mount Olive** Mississippi
110 M3 **Mount Olivet** Kentucky
110 N2 **Mount Orab** Ohio
121 S7 **Mount Orford, Parc de** Quebec
140 C5 **Mount Peake** N Terr Aust
141 K7 **Mount Perry** Queensland
140 E5 **Mount Philip** Queensland
99 P9 **Mount Pleasant** Iowa
94 C3 **Mount Pleasant** Michigan
94 H6 **Mount Pleasant** Pennsylvania
110 J6 **Mount Pleasant** Tennessee
109 N2 **Mount Pleasant** Texas
103 N2 **Mount Pleasant** Utah
95 M5 **Mount Pocono** Pennsylvania
99 R9 **Mount Pulaski** Illinois
100 D3 **Mount Rainier Nat.Pk** Washington
14 D3 **Mountrath** Irish Rep
117 O10 **Mount Revelstoke Nat. Park** Br Col
106 C10 **Mount Riley** New Mexico
98 C6 **Mount Rushmore Nat.Mem** S Dakota
140 B3 **Mount Sanford** N Terr Aust
94 J7 **Mount Savage** Maryland
9 F7 **Mount's B** England
109 M3 **Mount Selman** Texas
140 C7 **Mount Squires** N Terr Aust
99 Q10 **Mount Sterling** Illinois
110 M3 **Mount Sterling** Kentucky
94 D7 **Mount Sterling** Ohio
122 K7 **Mount Stewart** Pr Edward I
94 H7 **Mount Storm** W Virginia
141 G5 **Mount Sturgeon** Queensland
141 G4 **Mount Surprise** Queensland
140 D6 **Mount Swan** N Terr Aust
103 L5 **Mount Trumbull** Arizona
122 J9 **Mount Uniacke** Nova Scotia
94 K6 **Mount Union** Pennsylvania
111 J10 **Mount Vernon** Alabama
110 D6 **Mount Vernon** Arkansas
112 E5 **Mount Vernon** Georgia
110 H3 **Mount Vernon** Illinois
110 J4 **Mount Vernon** Indiana
99 P8 **Mount Vernon** Iowa
110 M4 **Mount Vernon** Kentucky
110 C4 **Mount Vernon** Missouri
95 O6 **Mount Vernon** New York
94 E6 **Mount Vernon** Ohio
100 F5 **Mount Vernon** Oregon
98 H6 **Mount Vernon** S Dakota
109 M2 **Mount Vernon** Texas
95 K8 **Mount Vernon** Virginia
100 C1 **Mount Vernon** Washington
143 C6 **Mount Vernon** W Australia
94 D6 **Mount Victory** Ohio
138 D5 **Mount Wedge** S Australia
111 K9 **Mount Willing** Alabama
138 C3 **Mount Willoughby** S Australia
142 B1 **Mount Yokine** *dist* Perth, W Aust
110 H2 **Mount Zion** Illinois
99 P9 **Mount Zion** Iowa
16 C6 **Moura** Portugal
141 J6 **Moura** Queensland
128 D5 **Moura** *R* Brazil
85 C6 **Mourdiah** Mali
19 N17 **Mouriès** France
141 H4 **Mourilyan Harbour** Queensland
14 D2 **Mourne** *R* N Ireland
14 E2 **Mourne Mts** N Ireland
15 G2 **Mousa** *isld* Shetland Scotland
22 E2 **Mouscron** Belgium
98 E1 **Mouse** *R* N Dakota
36 B6 **Moussey** Moselle France
36 C7 **Moussey** Vosges France
86 C3 **Moussoro** Chad
19 Q17 **Moustiers** France
12 E3 **Mouswald** Scotland
36 C6 **Mouterhouse** France
40 D4 **Mouthe** France
40 D3 **Mouthier** France
40 F3 **Moutier** Switzerland
40 E7 **Moutiers** France
20 G5 **Moutiers-au-Perche** France
21 C9 **Moutiers les Mauxfaits** France
145 F3 **Moutohora** New Zealand
70 G4 **Moutong** Sulawesi
122 H10 **Mouton I** Nova Scotia
20 K3 **Mouy** France
22 J5 **Mouzay** France
22 J4 **Mouzon** France
124 E3 **Movas** Mexico
99 L7 **Moville** Iowa
14 D1 **Moville** Irish Rep
141 K7 **Mowbullan, Mt** Queensland
99 S10 **Moweaqua** Illinois
145 E3 **Mowhanau** New Zealand
100 D6 **Mowich** Oregon
100 E3 **Moxee City** Washington
130 H10 **Moxotó,R** Brazil
14 B3 **Moy** *R* Irish Rep
17 J3 **Moyá** Spain
106 F6 **Moya** *R* New Mexico
143 C8 **Moyagee** W Australia
124 H7 **Moyahua** Mexico
86 G5 **Moyale** Kenya
85 B7 **Moyamba** Sierra Leone
20 F3 **Moyaux** France
52 F2 **Moyda** U.S.S.R.
22 E4 **Moy-de-l'Aisne** France
65 E6 **Moye Dao** *isld* China
36 B7 **Moyenmoutier** France
83 K12 **Moyenne** *isld* Mahé I Indian Oc
20 J1 **Moyenneville** France
36 B6 **Moyenvic** France
100 K1 **Moyie** Br Col
100 J1 **Moyie Springs** Idaho
86 C4 **Moyo** Chad
128 C5 **Moyobamba** Peru
86 C3 **Moyto** Chad
87 G9 **Mozambique** *state* Africa
81 B9 **Mozambique Ridge** Indian Oc
120 H6 **Mozhabong L** Ontario
52 E6 **Mozhaysk** U.S.S.R.
52 H6 **Mozhga** U.S.S.R.
77 G2 **Mozhnābād** Iran
68 B1 **Mozo** Burma
45 J1 **Mozzecane** Italy
87 E7 **Mpala** Zaïre
88 C7 **Mpika** Zambia
88 C6 **Mporokoso** Zambia
86 C6 **M'Pouya** Congo
85 D7 **Mpraeso** Ghana
87 F7 **Mpulungu** Zambia
87 G7 **Mpwapwa** Tanzania
31 N2 **Mragowo** Poland
55 C4 **Mrakovo** U.S.S.R.
56 C4 **Mras-Su** *R* U.S.S.R.
85 C4 **Mreiti,El** Mauritania
88 C10 **Mrewa** Zimbabwe
42 H4 **Mrkonjič Grad** Yugoslavia
31 J5 **Mrlina** *R* Czechoslovakia
31 J1 **Mrzeźyno** Poland
43 D13 **Msaken** Tunisia
31 H5 **Mšeno** Czechoslovakia
52 D5 **Msta** *R* U.S.S.R.
54 C2 **Mstislavl'** U.S.S.R.
31 M4 **Mszczonów** Poland
88 C5 **Mtakuja** Tanzania
89 G6 **Mtambama Mt** Swaziland
88 C5 **Mtambo** *R* Tanzania
120 J10 **Mt. Brydges** Ontario
103 M4 **Mt Carmel** Utah
144 C5 **Mt Hutt** New Zealand
89 G3 **Mtilikwe** *R* Zimbabwe
141 G6 **Mt Marlow** Queensland
88 D10 **Mtoko** Zimbabwe
144 C5 **Mt Somers** New Zealand
87 F11 **Mtubatuba** S Africa
88 H7 **Mtwara** Tanzania
16 B7 **Mu** *mt* Portugal
70 D5 **Muakateweh** Kalimantan
70 B4 **Mualang** Kalimantan
88 G7 **Mualo** *R* Mozambique
88 C8 **Muamadzi** *R* Zambia
20 E3 **Muance** *R* France
68 F6 **Muang** Cambodia
68 E4 **Muang Botene** Thailand
68 G5 **Muang Bua** Thailand
68 E5 **Muang Chainat** Thailand
68 E3 **Muang Chaiyaphum** Thailand
68 F5 **Muang Cha Tao** Thailand
68 E4 **Muang Chiang Khan** Thailand
68 D3 **Muang Chiang Rai** Thailand
68 F4 **Muang Kalasin** Thailand
68 D4 **Muang Kosamphi** Thailand
68 F4 **Muang Kuk** Thailand
68 D3 **Muang Lampang** Thailand
68 D3 **Muang Lamphun** Thailand
68 E4 **Muang Loei** Thailand
68 E4 **Muang Lom Sak** Thailand
68 D3 **Muang Long** Thailand
68 G5 **Muang Mai** Thailand
68 G4 **Muang Nakhon Phanom** Thailand
68 D5 **Muang Nakhon Sawan** Thailand
68 E3 **Muang Nan** Thailand
68 D3 **Muang Ngao** Thailand
68 E3 **Muang Oi** Thailand
68 G4 **Muang Phaluka** Thailand
68 D3 **Muang Phan** Thailand
68 F4 **Muang Phannanikhom** Thailand
68 D3 **Muang Phayao** Thailand
68 E4 **Muang Phetchabun** Thailand
68 E4 **Muang Phichai** Thailand
68 E4 **Muang Phichit** Thailand
68 E4 **Muang Phitsanulok** Thailand
68 E3 **Muang Phrae** Thailand
68 G4 **Muang Renu Nakhon** Thailand
68 F5 **Muang Roi Et** Thailand
68 F4 **Muang Sakon Nakhon** Thailand
68 G5 **Muang Sam Sip** Thailand
68 E6 **Muang Samut Prakan** Thailand
68 G5 **Muang Si Chalalai** Thailand
68 F4 **Muang Song** Thailand
68 D4 **Muang Thoen** Thailand
68 D5 **Muang Uthai Thani** Thailand
68 G5 **Muang Yasothon** Thailand
69 F11 **Muar** Malaysia
69 F11 **Muar** *R* Malaysia
70 D2 **Muara** Brunei
69 F14 **Muaraäman** Sumatra
70 E4 **Muara Antjalung** Kalimantan
70 E4 **Muaraätan** Kalimantan
70 D5 **Muarabenangin** Kalimantan
70 K9 **Muarabinuangeun** Java
69 E13 **Muarabungo** Sumatra
70 D5 **Muaradjuloi** Kalimantan
70 K8 **Muaradua** Sumatra
69 F14 **Muaraenim** Sumatra
70 E4 **Muaragusung** Kalimantan
70 E5 **Muarakaman** Kalimantan
69 G13 **Muarakumpe** Sumatra
69 E13 **Muaralabuh** Sumatra
69 F14 **Muaralakitan** Sumatra
70 E4 **Muaralasan** Kalimantan
70 E4 **Muaramawai** Kalimantan
70 E5 **Muarantunan** Kalimantan
70 D5 **Muarapajang** Kalimantan
70 E3 **Muarapangean** Kalimantan
70 D6 **Muarapulau** Kalimantan
69 F14 **Muararupit** Sumatra
69 F13 **Muarasabak** Sumatra
69 D13 **Muarasiberut** Indonesia
69 D12 **Muarasipongi** Sumatra
69 D12 **Muarasoma** Sumatra
70 F4 **Muaras Rf** Indonesia
69 C11 **Muarasukon** Sumatra
69 F13 **Muaratebo** Sumatra
69 F13 **Muaratembesi** Sumatra
70 D5 **Muaratuhup** Kalimantan
69 F13 **Muaratungkal** Sumatra
70 E4 **Muarawahau** Kalimantan
71 A3 **Muari** Halmahera Indonesia
77 A7 **Mubarraz,Al** Saudi Arabia
88 C1 **Mubende** Uganda
80 G5 **Mubis** Jordan
79 F8 **Mubrak, J** *mt* Jordan
69 H11 **Mubur** *isld* Indonesia
142 C5 **Muccan** W Australia
36 C2 **Much** W Germany
117 K11 **Muchalat** Br Col
15 F3 **Muchalls** Scotland
143 B9 **Muchea** W Australia
33 P10 **Mücheln** E Germany
88 C8 **Muchinga Escarp't** Zambia
52 G3 **Muchkas** U.S.S.R.
67 A2 **Muchuan** China
8 D2 **Much Wenlock** England
15 B4 **Muck** *isld* Inner Hebrides Scotland
141 J7 **Muckadilla** Queensland
14 D1 **Muckish Mt** Irish Rep
15 G1 **Muckle Flugga** *isld* Shetland Scotland
15 G2 **Muckle Roe** *isld* Shetland Scotland
9 E2 **Muckley Corner** England
14 C2 **Muckros Hd** Irish Rep
88 H8 **Mucojo** Mozambique
130 H6 **Mucuri** Brazil
130 H5 **Mucuri,R** Brazil
87 D9 **Mucusso** Angola
69 E10 **Muda** *R* Malaysia
80 G7 **Mudaiyina** Jordan
65 H2 **Mudanjiang** China
65 H2 **Mudan Jiang** *R* China
47 K4 **Mudanya** Turkey
36 G4 **Mudau** W Germany
98 D4 **Mud Butte** S Dakota
98 G8 **Mud Cr** Nebraska
76 C2 **Muddebinal** India
26 L5 **Muddus Nat. Park** Sweden
107 O7 **Muddy Boggy Cr** Oklahoma
103 N3 **Muddy Cr** Utah
101 P8 **Muddy Cr** Wyoming
101 S8 **Muddy Cr** Wyoming
101 T7 **Muddy Cr** Wyoming
101 S7 **Muddy Gap** *pass* Wyoming
118 H6 **Muddy L** Sask
103 K5 **Muddy Pk** Nevada
33 M7 **Müden** W Germany
139 J4 **Mudgee** New S Wales
141 H6 **Mudge, Mt** Queensland
74 G9 **Mudhol** Andhra Pradesh India
76 B2 **Mudhol** India
101 N6 **Mud L** Idaho
101 Q1 **Mud L** Montana
102 G4 **Mud L** Nevada
98 H4 **Mud L.Res** S Dakota
68 C4 **Mudon** Burma
47 L4 **Mudurnu** *R* Turkey
52 E3 **Mud'yuga** U.S.S.R.
88 D10 **Mudzi** *R* Zimbabwe
20 E3 **Mue** *R* France
88 G7 **Mueda** Mozambique
20 A5 **Muel** France
17 G4 **Muela de Ares** *mt* Spain
17 G3 **Muela,Sierra de la** Spain
142 G4 **Mueller, Mt** W Australia
142 F4 **Mueller Ra** W Australia
141 F6 **Muellers Ra** Queensland
119 N6 **Muenster** Sask
109 K2 **Muenster** Texas
125 N2 **Muerto,Cayo** *isld* Nicaragua
126 D2 **Muertos Cays** *reefs* Bahamas
52 G3 **Muftyuga** U.S.S.R.
88 B8 **Mufulira** Zambia
67 E2 **Mufu Shan** *mts* Jiangxi/Hubei China
16 A1 **Mugá** Spain
67 B5 **Mugang** China
16 B5 **Muge** Portugal
87 G9 **Mugeba** Mozambique
45 K4 **Mugello** Italy
33 S10 **Mügeln** E Germany
37 L4 **Muggendorf** W Germany
59 K5 **Mugi** Japan
88 B5 **Mugila** *mts* Zaïre
47 J7 **Muğla** Turkey
57 A1 **Mugodzhary** *mts* U.S.S.R.
18 E9 **Mugron** France
75 K4 **Mugu** Nepal
86 G1 **Muhammad Qol** Sudan
77 B6 **Muharraq,Al** Bahrain
36 F6 **Mühlacker** W Germany
36 H2 **Mühlbach** W Germany
33 S10 **Mühlberg** Cottbus E Germany
37 K2 **Mühlberg** Erfurt E Germany
38 G5 **Mühldorf** W Germany
41 K3 **Mühlehorn** Switzerland
33 S7 **Mühlenbeck** E Germany
33 O5 **Mühlen Eichsen** E Germany
37 J1 **Mühlhausen** E Germany
37 K4 **Mühlhausen** W Germany
36 C4 **Mühlheim** W Germany
37 M2 **Mühltroff** E Germany
29 M7 **Muhos** Finland
38 H7 **Muhr** Austria
80 D3 **Muhraqa** Israel
36 F7 **Mühringen** W Germany
52 B5 **Muhu** U.S.S.R.
88 C2 **Muhutwe** Tanzania
88 F7 **Muhuwesi** *R* Tanzania
69 G8 **Mui Bai Bung** Vietnam
68 J4 **Mui Chon May Dong** *C* Vietnam
68 J7 **Mui da Vaich** *C* Vietnam
25 D4 **Muiden** Netherlands
21 I6 **Muides-sur-Loire** France
68 J7 **Mui Dinh** *C* Vietnam
20 H3 **Muids** France
61 M8 **Muikamachi** Japan
71 B3 **Muilijk** *isld* Indonesia
68 J7 **Mui Ne** Vietnam
14 E4 **Muine Bheag** Irish Rep
94 C3 **Muir** Michigan
88 D10 **Muira** *R* Mozambique
13 F1 **Muirdrum** Scotland
117 E6 **Muir Gl** Alaska
13 E1 **Muirhead** Scotland
12 D3 **Muirkirk** Scotland
143 B10 **Muir, L** W Australia
143 G7 **Muir, Mt** W Australia
142 A5 **Muiron I., N** W Australia
102 B4 **Muir Woods Nat.Mon** California
87 G8 **Muite** Mozambique
42 G5 **Muiter** *isld* Yugoslavia
68 J6 **Mui Yen** *C* Vietnam
125 Q7 **Mujeres, I** Mexico
80 F8 **Mujib** *R* Jordan
87 D8 **Mujimbeji** Zambia
70 C3 **Mujong** *R* Sarawak
48 H2 **Mukachevo** U.S.S.R.
70 C3 **Mukah** Sarawak
72 F6 **Mukallā, Al** S Yemen
80 E6 **Mukallik** *R* Jordan
60 P3 **Mukawa** Japan
60 Q3 **Mu-kawa** *R* Japan
80 F7 **Mukawir** Jordan
86 G1 **Mukawwar I** Sudan
68 G4 **Mukdahan** Thailand
Mukden *see* **Shenyang**
13 F5 **Muker** England
72 E6 **Mukha, Al** N Yemen
74 G9 **Mukher** India
80 E6 **Mukhmas** Jordan
58 F1 **Mukhor-Konduy** U.S.S.R.
143 C9 **Mukinbudin** W Australia
69 D9 **Muk,Ko** *isld* Thailand
69 E14 **Mukomuko** Sumatra
33 P9 **Mukrena** E Germany
57 D5 **Mukry** U.S.S.R.
75 K4 **Muktinath** Nepal
86 D7 **Mukumbi** Zaïre
77 K3 **Mukur** Afghanistan
86 G5 **Mukutan** Kenya
119 U5 **Mukutawa R** Manitoba
99 S7 **Mukwonago** Wisconsin
17 G6 **Mula** Spain
73 K8 **Mulaku Atoll** Maldives
57 J2 **Mulaly** U.S.S.R.
65 G2 **Mulan** China
71 F4 **Mulanay** Philippines
88 E10 **Mulanje** Malawi
88 E9 **Mulanje** *mt* Malawi
129 H4 **Mulata** Brazil
124 E3 **Mulatos** Mexico
125 Q5 **Mulatupo Sasardi** Panama
110 B6 **Mulberry** Arkansas
113 F10 **Mulberry** Florida
110 K1 **Mulberry** Indiana
107 Q4 **Mulberry** Kansas
110 B4 **Mulberry** Missouri
110 C6 **Mulberry** *R* Arkansas
111 K8 **Mulberry Fork** *R* Alabama
110 G3 **Mulberry Grove** Illinois
116 K6 **Mulchatna** *R* Alaska
133 C5 **Mulchen** Chile
37 P2 **Mulda** E Germany
28 E3 **Muldbjerge** *hill* Denmark
33 Q9 **Mulde** *R* E Germany
101 M6 **Muldoon** Idaho
28 O9 **Mule** Faeroes
108 E5 **Mule Cr** Texas
98 B6 **Mule Cr** Wyoming
106 B8 **Mule Creek** New Mexico
124 C4 **Mulegé** Mexico
80 G7 **Muleih** Jordan
88 C8 **Mulembo** *R* Zambia
86 D6 **Mulenda** Zaïre
71 K9 **Mules** *isld* Flores Indonesia
108 E1 **Muleshoe** Texas
87 G9 **Mulevala** Mozambique
36 H5 **Mulfingen** W Germany
142 C5 **Mulga Downs** W Australia
140 B7 **Mulga Park** N Terr Aust
143 C8 **Mulgar Pk** W Australia
138 C4 **Mulgathing** S Australia
138 C4 **Mulgathing Rocks** *mt* S Australia
141 K6 **Mulgildie** Queensland
123 L8 **Mulgrave** Nova Scotia
116 F3 **Mulgrave Hills** Alaska
141 F1 **Mulgrave I** Queensland
143 C6 **Mulgul** W Australia
16 E7 **Mulhacén** *mt* Spain
107 N5 **Mulhall** Oklahoma
32 E10 **Mülheim** W Germany
40 F2 **Mulhouse** France
65 H2 **Muling** China
65 D6 **Muling Guan** *pass* China
65 H2 **Muling He** *R* China
65 J2 **Muling He** *R* China
76 B4 **Mulki** India
15 C4 **Mull** *isld* Scotland
14 B4 **Mullaghareirk Mts** Irish Rep
76 E6 **Mullaittivu** Sri Lanka
139 J4 **Mullaley** New S Wales
100 K2 **Mullan** Idaho
98 E7 **Mullen** Nebraska
109 J4 **Mullen** Texas
139 H4 **Mullengudgery** New S Wales
94 F9 **Mullens** W Virginia
140 C6 **Muller** *R* N Terr Aust
70 C4 **Muller,Peg** *mts* Kalimantan
113 E10 **Mullet Key** *isld* Florida
94 C1 **Mullett L** Michigan
143 B8 **Mullewa** W Australia
15 F1 **Mull Head** Orkney Scotland
40 G2 **Müllheim** W Germany
95 N7 **Mullica** *R* New Jersey
140 E6 **Mulligan** *R* Queensland
14 D3 **Mullingar** Irish Rep
112 H3 **Mullins** S Carolina
107 L4 **Mullinville** Kansas
139 J5 **Mullion Creek** New S Wales
83 K8 **Mulliyavalai** Sri Lanka
15 D6 **Mull of Galloway** Scotland
15 C5 **Mull of Kintyre** Scotland
12 B2 **Mull of Oa** Scotland
27 G14 **Mullsjö** Sweden
15 C4 **Mull, Sound of** Scotland
139 L3 **Mullumbimby** New S Wales
87 E9 **Mulobezi** Zambia
87 C9 **Mulondo** Angola
87 E7 **Mulongo** Zaïre
138 E3 **Muloorina** S Australia
14 D1 **Mulroy B** Irish Rep
21 F6 **Mulsanne** France
33 P5 **Mulsow** E Germany
74 D3 **Multan** Pakistan
55 F1 **Multanovy** U.S.S.R.
29 L9 **Multia** Finland
26 J8 **Multrå** Sweden
70 D2 **Mulu, G** *mt* Sarawak
130 J9 **Mulungu** Brazil
107 N4 **Mulvane** Kansas
119 T8 **Mulvihill** Manitoba

139 G4 **Mulyah,Mt** New S Wales
55 D1 **Mulym'ya** U.S.S.R.
55 E1 **Mulym'ya** *R* U.S.S.R.
138 F4 **Mulyungarie** S Australia
8 C4 **Mumbles Wales**
87 B3 **Mumbondo Angola**
87 C8 **Mumbué Angola**
87 E8 **Mumbwa Zambia**
87 E8 **Mumena Zaïre**
109 L5 **Mumford** Texas
69 D9 **Mum Nauk,Laem** *C* Thailand
125 P7 **Muna Mexico**
71 H7 **Muna** *isld* Indonesia
67 B5 **Munankwan Lin** *pass* Vietnam/China
143 B8 **Munbinia** W Australia
141 G2 **Munburra** Queensland
37 M3 **Münchberg W Germany**
30 H3 **Müncheberg** E Germany
39 **München** *conurbation* W Germany
37 M2 **Münchenbernsdorf** E Germany
36 F2 **Münchhausen W Germany**
117 L6 **Muncho Lake** Br Col
37 N5 **Münchshofen W Germany**
37 O6 **Münchshofen W Germany**
37 M6 **Münchsmünster** W Germany
110 L1 **Muncie** Indiana
140 E7 **Muncoonie, L** Queensland
95 L5 **Muncy** Pennsylvania
118 E5 **Mundare** Alberta
109 H2 **Munday** Texas
99 S7 **Mundelein** Illinois
83 J10 **Mundel L Sri Lanka**
98 J10 **Munden** Kansas
32 L10 **Münden W Germany**
36 H7 **Munderkingen** W Germany
9 H2 **Mundesley England**
9 G2 **Mundford England**
143 D6 **Mundiwindi** W Australia
141 F4 **Mundjuro** *R* Queensland
17 F6 **Mundo** *R* **Spain**
129 K6 **Mundo Nôvo Brazil**
143 G9 **Mundrabilla** W Australia
141 K7 **Mundubbera** Queensland
56 C4 **Mundybash U.S.S.R.**
46 D3 **Munella** *mt* **Albania**
17 F5 **Munera Spain**
110 L4 **Munfordville** Kentucky
141 J7 **Mungallala** Queensland
141 H8 **Mungallala** *R* Queensland
141 G3 **Mungana** Queensland
141 L7 **Mungar** Queensland
87 F9 **Mungari Mozambique**
142 C5 **Mungaroona Ra** W Australia
56 D5 **Mungash-Kul', Gora** *mt* U.S.S.R.
86 E5 **Mungbere Zaïre**
75 J7 **Mungeli India**
94 D3 **Munger** Michigan
138 E3 **Mungerannie** S Australia
141 J8 **Mungindi** Queensland
87 C8 **Munhango Angola**
98 H1 **Munich** N Dakota
Munich W Germany *see* **München**
88 B8 **Muniengashi** *R* **Zaïre**
17 G3 **Muniesa Spain**
130 H7 **Muniz Freire Brazil**
28 H5 **Munke Bjergby Denmark**
28 F6 **Munkebo Denmark**
27 E13 **Munkedal Sweden**
26 G8 **Munkflohögen Sweden**
27 G12 **Munkfors Sweden**
28 A7 **Munkmarsch W Germany**
26 M6 **Munksund Sweden**
56 F5 **Munku-Sardyk,Gora** *mt* Mongolia/U.S.S.R.
37 J3 **Münnerstadt W Germany**
22 J4 **Muno Belgium**
71 E3 **Muñoz** Luzon **Philippines**
133 C8 **Muñoz Gamero, Pen Chile**
139 J8 **Munro,Mt** Tasmania
36 H7 **Münsingen W Germany**
118 E7 **Munson** Alberta
111 K11 **Munson** Florida
40 F1 **Munster France**
32 M7 **Münster** Niedersachsen W Germany
32 G9 **Münster** Nordrhein-Westfalen W Germany
41 H5 **Münster Switzerland**
14 B4 **Munster** *prov* **Irish Rep**
36 C3 **Münstermaifeld** W Germany
143 C9 **Muntadgin** W Australia
70 F4 **Munte** Sulawesi
48 H4 **Muntelui Mare** *mt* Romania
70 P10 **Muntjar** Java
36 F3 **Münzenberg W Germany**
29 O6 **Muojärvi** *L* Finland
68 F1 **Muong Boum** Vietnam
68 F2 **Muong Hiem** Laos
68 F2 **Muong Hun Xieng Hung** Laos
68 F3 **Muong Khao** Laos
68 F2 **Muong Khoua** Laos
68 G1 **Muong Khuong** Vietnam
68 E3 **Muong Ki** Laos
68 G3 **Muong Lam** Vietnam
68 E3 **Muong Liep** Laos
68 E2 **Muong Luong Nam Tha** Laos
68 H7 **Muong Man** Vietnam
68 F3 **Muong May** Laos
68 F3 **Muong Moc** Laos
68 F2 **Muong Ngoi** Laos
68 F1 **Muong Nhie** Vietnam
68 H4 **Muong Nong** Laos
68 E3 **Muong Oua** Laos
68 E1 **Muong ou Neua** Laos
68 E1 **Muong ou Tay** Laos
68 E3 **Muong Pa** Laos
68 G4 **Muong Phalane** Laos
68 E3 **Muong Phieng** Laos
68 E2 **Muong Sai** Laos
68 E3 **Muong Saiapoun** Laos
68 G3 **Muong Sen** Vietnam
68 E2 **Muong Sing** Laos
68 F2 **Muong Son** Laos
68 G4 **Muong Song Khone** Laos
68 F3 **Muong Soui** Laos
68 F3 **Muong Soum** Laos
68 F1 **Muong Te** Vietnam
68 E3 **Muong Tha Deua** Laos
68 E3 **Muong Thong** Laos
68 F2 **Muong Va** Laos
29 K4 **Muonio Finland**
26 N3 **Muonio älv** *R* Sweden/Finland
29 K4 **Muoniojoki** *R* Finland
26 N4 **Muonionalusta Sweden**
71 B2 **Muor** *isld* Halmahera Indonesia
41 J4 **Muotathal Switzerland**
88 B9 **Mupata Gorge Zambia**
65 E6 **Muping China**
80 G4 **Muqbilla Jordan**
130 H7 **Muqui Brazil**
18 D4 **Mûr** France
38 J7 **Mur** *R* **Austria**
56 E2 **Mura** *R* **U.S.S.R.**
48 C4 **Mura** *R* **Yugoslavia**
47 J6 **Muradiye Turkey**
45 L4 **Muraglione,Pso.di** *pass* Italy
61 N7 **Murakami Japan**
48 D4 **Murakeresztúr Hungary**
133 C7 **Murallón** *mt* **Chile/Arg**
61 N8 **Muramatsu Japan**
88 F2 **Murang'a Kenya**
45 M1 **Murano Italy**
52 G5 **Murashi U.S.S.R.**
18 G7 **Murat France**
78 H2 **Murat** *R* **Turkey**
47 K6 **Murat Dağı Turkey**
47 J3 **Muratlı Turkey**
78 J2 **Murat Suyu** *R* **Turkey**
38 K7 **Murau Austria**
77 C7 **Mur'ban** U.A.E.
16 C3 **Murça** Portugal
77 B3 **Murcheh Khvort** Iran
33 T5 **Murchin** E Germany
145 D4 **Murchison New Zealand**
139 H6 **Murchison** Victoria
6 M1 **Murchison** *oil rig* North Sea
Murchison Falls Uganda *see* **Kabalega Falls**
144 C5 **Murchison, Mt** New Zealand
145 D4 **Murchison, Mt** New Zealand
143 B7 **Murchison, Mt** W Australia
144 A6 **Murchison Mts** New Zealand
143 A8 **Murchison, R** W Australia
140 C5 **Murchison Ra** N Terr **Aust**
89 G4 **Murchison Ra** S **Africa**
88 E9 **Murchison Rapids Malawi**
17 G7 **Murcia Spain**
17 F7 **Murcia** *prov* **Spain**
71 F6 **Murcielagos B** Mindanao Philippines
143 E10 **Murdarbilla** W Australia
18 G8 **Mur-de-Barrez France**
21 I7 **Mur de-Sologne France**
98 F6 **Murdo** S Dakota
141 G2 **Murdoch Pt** Queensland
122 G5 **Murdochville** Quebec
113 E10 **Murdock** Florida
38 N8 **Mureck Austria**
47 J4 **Mürefte Turkey**
61 M9 **Murei Japan**
48 J4 **Muresul** *R* **Romania**
18 F9 **Muret France**
111 C7 **Murfreesboro** Arkansas
95 K10 **Murfreesboro** N Carolina
110 K6 **Murfreesboro** Tennessee
36 E6 **Murg** *R* **W Germany**
57 G5 **Murgab U.S.S.R.**
57 G5 **Murgab** *R* **U.S.S.R.**
46 D5 **Murgána** *mt* **Greece**
47 F2 **Murgash** *mt* **Bulgaria**
140 C1 **Murgenella Cr** N Terr **Aust**
48 L4 **Murgeni Romania**
77 H2 **Murghab** *R* **Afghanistan**
74 C3 **Murgha Kibzai Pakistan**
48 K4 **Murgociu** *mt* **Romania**
141 K7 **Murgon** Queensland
143 B7 **Murgoo** W Australia
75 L7 **Muri India**
130 G7 **Muriaé Brazil**
16 C2 **Murias de Paredes Spain**
87 D7 **Muriege Angola**
118 G4 **Muriel L** Alberta
60 R2 **Murii-dake** *mt* **Japan**
119 O2 **Murill** Ontario
17 G2 **Murillo de Gállego Spain**
33 R6 **Müritz** *L* E Germany
145 F3 **Muriwai New Zealand**
26 L5 **Murjek Sweden**
70 N9 **Murjo, G** *mt* Java
86 G4 **Murle Ethiopia**
36 B3 **Mürlenbach W Germany**
52 D1 **Murmansk U.S.S.R.**
52 D1 **Murmashi U.S.S.R.**
54 M2 **Murmino U.S.S.R.**
41 O2 **Murnau W Germany**
102 G7 **Muroc L** California
52 F6 **Murom U.S.S.R.**
55 G3 **Muromtsevo U.S.S.R.**
21 D9 **Muron France**
60 O3 **Muroran Japan**
16 A2 **Muros Spain**
60 H12 **Muroto Japan**
60 N3 **Murotsu-shima** *isld* **Japan**
48 L2 **Murovano Kurilovtsy** U.S.S.R.
31 K3 **Murowana Goslina Poland**
60 E12 **Murozumi Japan**
100 J6 **Murphy** Idaho
112 C2 **Murphy** N Carolina
100 B7 **Murphy** Oregon
146 H11 **Murphy,Mt Antarctica**
102 D3 **Murphys** California
110 G4 **Murphysboro** Illinois
141 H8 **Murra Murra** Queensland
99 N8 **Murray** Iowa
110 H5 **Murray** Kentucky
99 K9 **Murray** Nebraska
103 N1 **Murray** Utah
139 G6 **Murray** *R* New S Wales
138 E6 **Murray Bridge** S Australia
94 E7 **Murray City** Ohio
135 M5 **Murray Deep Pacific Oc**
140 C5 **Murray Downs** N Terr Aust
122 K7 **Murray Hbr** Pr Edward I
123 K8 **Murray Hd** Pr Edward I
83 M9 **Murray Hill** *peak* Christmas I **Indian Oc**
107 N7 **Murray,L** Oklahoma
112 F3 **Murray, L** S Carolina
146 B4 **Murray Monolith** Antarctica
117 N8 **Murray R** Br Col
143 B10 **Murray, R** W Australia
143 G7 **Murray Ra** W Australia
122 K7 **Murray River** Pr Edward I
89 C8 **Murraysburg** S **Africa**
135 M5 **Murray Seascarp** Pacific Oc
99 Q10 **Murrayville** Illinois
138 F6 **Murrayville** Victoria
112 H4 **Murrells Inlet** S Carolina
40 G4 **Mürren Switzerland**
36 H6 **Murrhardt W Germany**
139 J5 **Murringo** New S Wales
143 D8 **Murrin Murrin** W Australia
14 B3 **Murrisk** *mts* **Irish Rep**
139 G5 **Murrumbidgee** *R* New S Wales
139 J5 **Murrumburrah & Harden** New S Wales
139 K4 **Murrurundi** New S Wales
19 O17 **Murs France**
38 O8 **Murska Sobota Yugoslavia**
38 K7 **Mur Tal** *V* **Austria**
41 M4 **Murtarol,Piz** *mt* **Italy**
101 L7 **Murtaugh** Idaho
74 G8 **Murtazapur India**
139 G4 **Murtee** New S Wales
40 F4 **Murten See** *L* **Switzerland**
138 F3 **Murteree,L** S Australia
117 O9 **Murtle L** Br Col
138 F6 **Murtoa** Victoria
29 O6 **Murtovaara Finland**
74 E9 **Murud India**
70 D3 **Murud** *mt* Kalimantan
65 E3 **Muruin Sum Shuiku** *res* China
70 D5 **Murui,R** Kalimantan
70 D4 **Murung,R** Kalimantan
145 F3 **Murupara New Zealand**
128 F3 **Murupu Brazil**
109 N3 **Murvaul Res** Texas
22 K5 **Murville France**
74 J7 **Murwara India**
139 L3 **Murwillumbah** New S Wales
52 G5 **Murygino U.S.S.R.**
38 M6 **Mürzsteg Austria**
38 M7 **Murz Tal** *V* **Austria**
38 N6 **Mürzzuchlag Austria**
78 H2 **Muş Turkey**
86 D6 **Musadi Zaïre**
79 D10 **Mûsa, G** *mt* **Egypt**
74 C3 **Musa Khel Bazar Pakistan**
69 D12 **Musala** *isld* Sumatra
47 F2 **Musala** *mt* **Bulgaria**
59 J3 **Musan N Korea**
77 E6 **Musandam** *pen* **Oman**
77 J3 **Musa Qala Afghanistan**
77 F7 **Muscat Oman**
99 P8 **Muscatine** Iowa
Muscat & Oman *sultanate see* **Oman**
99 Q6 **Muscoda** Wisconsin
95 S3 **Muscongus B** Maine
88 C9 **Muse** *R* **Mozambique**
80 G8 **Museitiba Jordan**
141 G2 **Musgrave** Queensland
138 B2 **Musgrave Ranges** S Australia
123 S5 **Musgravetown** Newfoundland
89 G3 **Mushandike Dam** Zimbabwe
80 G8 **Musheirifa Jordan**
14 C5 **Musheramore** *mt* **Irish Rep**
86 C6 **Mushie Zaïre**
28 G6 **Musholm** *isld* **Denmark**
103 L6 **Music Mt** Arizona
103 N2 **Musinia Pk** Utah
117 M5 **Muskeg** *R* N W Terr
99 L1 **Muskeg B** Minnesota
95 R5 **Muskeget Chan** Massachusetts
119 O1 **Muskeg L** Ontario
94 A3 **Muskegon** Michigan
94 A3 **Muskegon** *R* Michigan
94 A3 **Muskegon Heights** Michigan
26 H4 **Musken Norway**
94 F7 **Muskingum** *R* Ohio
27 K13 **Muskö Sweden**
110 A6 **Muskogee** Oklahoma
121 L7 **Muskoka,L** Ontario
101 S6 **Muskrat Cr** Wyoming
77 F6 **Müskutān Iran**
118 C2 **Muskwa R** Alberta
52 H6 **Muslyumovo U.S.S.R.**
86 G2 **Musmar Sudan**
80 D3 **Musmus Israel**
88 D2 **Musoma Tanzania**
45 O4 **Musone Italy**
45 M1 **Musone** *R* **Italy**
123 L3 **Musquanus L** Quebec
123 L3 **Musquaro** Quebec
122 F8 **Musquash** New Brunswick
122 J8 **Musquodoboit** Nova Scotia
122 J9 **Musquodoboit Hbr** Nova Scotia
28 H7 **Musse Denmark**
25 H3 **Mussel Aa** *R* **Netherlands**
13 E2 **Musselburgh Scotland**
101 R3 **Musselshell** Montana
101 S3 **Musselshell** *R* Montana
87 C8 **Mussende Angola**
18 F7 **Mussidan France**
43 F11 **Mussomeli** Sicily
47 K4 **Mustafa Kemalpaşa** Turkey
86 H4 **Mustahil Ethiopia**
75 K4 **Mustang Nepal**
107 N6 **Mustang** Oklahoma
108 E3 **Mustang Cr** Texas
109 K8 **Mustang I** Texas
55 B5 **Mustayevo U.S.S.R.**
133 D7 **Muster,L Argentina**
98 K4 **Mustinka** *R* Minnesota
127 O8 **Mustique** *isld* Lesser Antilles
27 M13 **Mustjala** Estonia **U.S.S.R.**
52 C5 **Mustla U.S.S.R.**
29 N3 **Mustola Finland**
13 H5 **Muston England**
52 C5 **Mustvee U.S.S.R.**
65 H4 **Musu-dan** *C* **N Korea**
139 K4 **Muswellbrook** New S Wales
48 F1 **Muszyna Poland**
84 H4 **Mut Egypt**
78 D3 **Mut Turkey**
38 M8 **Muta Yugoslavia**
88 C1 **Mutai Uganda**
89 G4 **Mutale** *R* **S Africa**
87 E8 **Mutanda Zambia**
Mutankiang *see* **Mudanjiang**
88 E10 **Mutarara Mozambique**
37 O4 **Mutěnín Czechoslovakia**
12 E1 **Muthill Scotland**
71 M9 **Mutis** *mt* Timor **Indonesia**
52 J2 **Mutnyy-Materik U.S.S.R.**
87 D7 **Mutombo Mukulu Zaïre**
138 F4 **Mutooroo** S Australia
65 D4 **Mutoudeng China**
65 D3 **Mutougou China**
45 R7 **Mutria, M** *mt* **Italy**
87 G10 **Mutsamudu Comoros**
87 D8 **Mutshatsha Zaïre**
60 P4 **Mutsu Japan**
61 O5 **Mutsu-wan** *B* **Japan**
141 G6 **Muttaburra** Queensland
40 G1 **Muttersholtz France**
36 E5 **Mutterstadt W Germany**
41 M4 **Muttler** *mt* **Switzerland**
123 O3 **Mutton Bay** Quebec
144 B7 **Muttonbird Is.** New Zealand
14 B4 **Mutton I Irish Rep**
107 L5 **Mutual** Oklahoma
87 G8 **Mutuala Mozambique**
129 H7 **Mutum** Mato Grosso **Brazil**
130 H6 **Mutum** Minas Gerais **Brazil**
128 F5 **Mutumparaná Brazil**
83 L9 **Mutur Sri Lanka**
36 C6 **Mutzig France**
33 R10 **Mutzschen E Germany**
29 M9 **Muurame Finland**
29 L5 **Muurola Finland**
58 F1 **Muya** *R* **U.S.S.R.**
88 C3 **Muyinga Burundi**
125 M3 **Muy Muy Nicaragua**
57 A3 **Muynak U.S.S.R.**
87 E7 **Muyumba Zaïre**
67 C1 **Muyuping China**
74 E1 **Muzaffarabad** Kashmir
74 D3 **Muzaffargarh Pakistan**
74 G4 **Muzaffarnagar India**
75 L5 **Muzaffarpur India**
130 F7 **Muzambinho Brazil**
57 K4 **Muzat He** *R* **China**
50 F2 **Muzhi U.S.S.R.**
18 D5 **Muzillac France**
40 A3 **Muzin** *R* **France**
117 G8 **Muzon, C** Alaska
108 F8 **Múzquiz Mexico**
66 D4 **Muztag China**
66 C4 **Muztag** *mt* **China**
66 B4 **Muztagata** *mt* **China**
88 E8 **Mvera Malawi**
86 E4 **Mvolo Sudan**
87 G7 **Mvomero Tanzania**
86 B6 **M'Vouti Congo**
88 D7 **Mwambwa** *R* **Zambia**
88 D3 **Mwanza Tanzania**
88 D6 **Mwaya Tanzania**
14 B3 **Mweelrea** *mts* **Irish Rep**
86 D6 **Mweka Zaïre**
87 D7 **Mwene Ditu Zaïre**
88 B3 **Mwenga Zaïre**
88 G6 **Mwera Tanzania**
89 G2 **Mwerihari** *R* **Zimbabwe**
88 B6 **Mweru, L Zaire/Zambia**
88 B6 **Mweru Wantipa Zambia**
89 F3 **Mwewe** *R* **Zimbabwe**
87 D7 **Mwimba Zaïre**
87 D8 **Mwinilunga Zambia**
68 B2 **Myaing Burma**
113 E10 **Myakka** Florida
113 E10 **Myakka City** Florida
52 E5 **Myaksa U.S.S.R.**
31 H3 **Myálibórz Poland**
139 K4 **Myall L** New S Wales
68 B3 **Myanaung Burma**
52 D3 **Myanduselga U.S.S.R.**
54 G2 **Myatlevo U.S.S.R.**
68 A2 **Myaungbwe Burma**
68 B4 **Myaungmya Burma**
68 D4 **Myawadi Burma**
46 F7 **Mycenae Greece**
68 A2 **Myebon Burma**
95 L6 **Myerstown** Pennsylvania
28 L1 **Myggenæs** Faeroes
28 N1 **Mygledal** Faeroes
68 B2 **Myingyan Burma**
68 C2 **Myinkyado Burma**
68 D6 **Myinmoletkat** *mt* **Burma**
68 B2 **Myinmu Burma**
68 B2 **Myitche Burma**
68 D5 **Myitta Burma**
68 C2 **Myittha Burma**
48 D2 **Myjava Czechoslovakia**
26 F5 **Myken** *lt ho* **Norway**
52 H2 **Myla U.S.S.R.**
37 N2 **Mylau E Germany**
29 M11 **Myllykoski Finland**
98 G1 **Mylo** N Dakota
75 O6 **Mymensingh** Bangladesh
29 J11 **Mynämäki Finland**
57 G2 **Mynaral U.S.S.R.**
57 C4 **Mynbulak U.S.S.R.**
8 B3 **Mynydd Bach** *hills* **Wales**
8 C3 **Mynydd Eppynt** *mts* **Wales**
68 A2 **Myohaung Burma**
68 B2 **Myohla Burma**
68 B2 **Myotha Burma**
68 B2 **Myothit Burma**
109 K2 **Myra** Texas
47 K8 **Myra Turkey**
141 F3 **Myra Vale** Queensland
27 B11 **Myrdal Norway**
26 H3 **Myre Norway**
27 G14 **Myresjö Sweden**
26 L6 **Myrheden Sweden**
118 F5 **Myrnam** Alberta
100 J3 **Myrtle** Idaho
119 U9 **Myrtle** Manitoba
111 G7 **Myrtle** Mississippi
121 M8 **Myrtle** Ontario
112 J4 **Myrtle Beach** S Carolina
100 B6 **Myrtle Cr** Oregon
139 H6 **Myrtleford** Victoria
100 A6 **Myrtle Point** Oregon
138 E4 **Myrtle Springs** S Australia
141 L1 **Myrtletown** Queensland
65 H3 **Mys Gamova** *lt ho* **U.S.S.R.**
52 E5 **Myshkino U.S.S.R.**
56 C4 **Myski U.S.S.R.**
31 M6 **Myslenice Poland**
76 C4 **Mysore India**
26 G9 **Myssjo Sweden**
119 U3 **Mystery L** Manitoba
112 D6 **Mystic** Georgia
99 O9 **Mystic** Iowa
98 C5 **Mystic** S Dakota
52 H4 **Mysy** Perm **U.S.S.R.**
31 N2 **Myszyniec Poland**
52 F6 **Myt U.S.S.R.**
68 H7 **My Tho Vietnam**
54 J1 **Mytishchi U.S.S.R.**
101 P9 **Myton** Utah
68 J6 **My Trach Vietnam**
57 H1 **Myylybulak U.S.S.R.**
37 O4 **Mže** *R* **Czechoslovakia**
85 C4 **Mzereb,El Mali**
88 D7 **Mzimba Malawi**
88 E7 **Mzuzu Malawi**
37 M5 **Naab** *R* **W Germany**
25 B5 **Naaldwijk Netherlands**
135 U6 **Naalehu** Hawaiian Is
80 C6 **Na'an Israel**
86 E4 **Naandi Sudan**
29 J11 **Naantali Finland**
25 D4 **Naarden Netherlands**
14 E3 **Naas Irish Rep**
29 N2 **Näätämönjoki** *R* **Finland**
16 B5 **Nabaõ** *R* **Portugal**
61 K11 **Nabari Japan**
71 F5 **Nabas** Panay **Philippines**
79 F5 **Nabatīyet Ett Tahta** Lebanon
143 D7 **Nabberu, L** W Australia
71 E2 **Nabbuan** Luzon **Philippines**
37 N5 **Nabburg W Germany**
52 H6 **Naberezhnyye Chelny** U.S.S.R.
116 Q5 **Nabesna Gl** Alaska
43 D12 **Nabeul Tunisia**
139 K4 **Nabiac** New S Wales
130 B7 **Nabileque,R Brazil**
123 K3 **Nabisipi R** Quebec
80 E5 **Nablus Jordan**
79 E10 **Nabq Egypt**
71 F6 **Nabulao B** Negros Philippines
68 D5 **Nabule Burma**
88 H9 **Nacala Mozambique**
125 L3 **Nacaome Honduras**
67 B5 **Nacham Vietnam**
74 D5 **Nachana India**
100 E3 **Naches** Washington
100 D2 **Naches Pass** Washington
87 G8 **Nachingwea Tanzania**
66 E5 **Na Ch'u** *R* **China**
68 A7 **Nachuge** Andaman Is
102 C6 **Nacimiento** *R* California
102 C6 **Nacimiento Res** California
138 E4 **Nackara** S Australia
33 R7 **Nackel E Germany**
103 P10 **Naco Mexico**
111 B10 **Nacogdoches** Texas
68 B6 **Nacondam I** Andaman Is
124 E2 **Nacozari de García Mexico**
20 B2 **Nacqueville France**
Nada *see* **Dan Xian**
103 L3 **Nada** Utah
61 M8 **Nadachi Japan**
124 J4 **Nadadores Mexico**
67 B6 **Nadang China**
99 T4 **Nadeau** Michigan
Nådendal *see* **Naantali**
55 D4 **Nadezhdinskiy U.S.S.R.**
137 Q5 **Nadi** Viti Levu **Fiji**
74 E7 **Nadiad India**
48 F4 **Nădlac Romania**
85 D1 **Nador Morocco**
48 G3 **Nádudvar Hungary**
77 C3 **Nadūshan Iran**
52 D3 **Nadvoitsy U.S.S.R.**
48 J2 **Nadvornaya U.S.S.R.**
50 G2 **Nadym U.S.S.R.**
27 A13 **Naerbö Norway**
26 E7 **Naeröy Norway**
28 K5 **Nærum Denmark**
28 N9 **Næs** Faeroes
28 N10 **Næs** Faeroes
28 B5 **Næsbjerg Denmark**
28 C3 **Næsborg Denmark**
28 H6 **Næsby Denmark**
28 E6 **Næsbyhoved Denmark**
28 A3 **Næs Sund** *inlet* **Denmark**
28 H6 **Næstelsø Denmark**
28 H6 **Næstved Denmark**
101 M7 **Naf** Idaho
68 A2 **Naf** *R* **Burma**
85 G6 **Nafada Nigeria**
84 G4 **Nafoora Libya**
77 A4 **Naft-e Safīd Iran**
78 K4 **Naft-e Shāh Iran**
71 F4 **Naga Philippines**
120 F3 **Nagagami** Ontario
120 F3 **Nagagamisis L** Ontario
60 F12 **Nagahama Japan**
75 Q5 **Nagaland** *prov* **India**
139 H6 **Nagambie** Victoria
61 O13 **Nagannu-jima** *isld* **Okinawa**
61 M9 **Nagano Japan**
61 L9 **Nagano** *prefect* **Japan**
61 M9 **Naganohara Japan**
61 M8 **Nagaoka Japan**
76 D5 **Nagappattinam India**
76 D2 **Nagar Karnul India**
74 D6 **Nagar Parkar Pakistan**
60 C13 **Nagasaki Japan**
60 C12 **Nagasaki** *prefect* **Japan**
60 D14 **Nagasaki-bana Japan**
60 D13 **Naga shima** *isld* **Japan**
60 F12 **Naga-shima** *isld* **Japan**
60 E12 **Nagasu Japan**
60 E11 **Nagato Japan**
74 E5 **Nagaur India**
Nagchu Dzong *see* **Nagqu**
76 C6 **Nagercoil India**
26 H9 **Naggen Sweden**
74 H4 **Nagina India**
61 P12 **Nago** Okinawa
74 J6 **Nagod India**
36 F6 **Nagold W Germany**
36 F6 **Nagold** *R* **W Germany**
52 H5 **Nagorsk U.S.S.R.**
61 P13 **Nago-wan** *B* **Okinawa**
61 K10 **Nagoya Japan**
74 H8 **Nagpur India**
66 E5 **Nagqu China**
29 J11 **Nagu Finland**
127 K5 **Nagua Dom Rep**
71 E2 **Naguilian** Luzon Philippines
71 G4 **Nagumbuaya Pt** Philippines
48 D4 **Nagybajom Hungary**
48 G3 **Nagyecsed Hungary**
48 G3 **Nagykálló Hungary**
48 D4 **Nagykanizsa Hungary**
48 F3 **Nagykáta Hungary**
48 F3 **Nagykörös Hungary**
48 G3 **Nagyléta Hungary**
Nagyvárad *see* **Oradea**
61 P13 **Naha** Okinawa
70 D4 **Nahabuan** Kalimantan
80 D3 **Nahalal Israel**
80 C7 **Nahalat Israel**
74 G3 **Nahan India**
114 G5 **Nahanni Butte** N W Terr
117 M5 **Nahanni Butte** N W Terr
117 L5 **Nahanni Nat. Park** N W Terr
80 D1 **Nahariyya Israel**
77 A2 **Nahāvand Iran**
36 C4 **Nahbollenbach** W Germany
36 C4 **Nahe** *R* **W Germany**
80 G4 **Nahla Jordan**
21 I7 **Nahon** *R* **France**
80 C3 **Nahsholim Israel**
131 B8 **Nahuel Huapi, L Argentina**
133 D6 **Nahuel Niyeu Argentina**
112 E6 **Nahunta** Georgia
71 E3 **Naic** Luzon **Philippines**
124 G4 **Naica Mexico**
119 N6 **Naicam** Sask
66 E4 **Naij Tal China**
71 L9 **Naikliu** Timor **Indonesia**
37 M3 **Naila W Germany**
65 D4 **Nailin China**
8 D4 **Nailsworth England**
65 E3 **Naiman Qi China**
77 C3 **Na'in Iran**
115 N6 **Nain** Labrador
74 J7 **Nainpur India**
21 F8 **Naintré France**
120 J6 **Nairn** Ontario
15 E3 **Nairn Scotland**
Nairn *co see* **Highland** *reg*
143 B7 **Nairn, Mt** W Australia
15 D3 **Nairn,R Scotland**
88 F2 **Nairobi Kenya**
52 B5 **Naissaar** *isld* **U.S.S.R.**
88 F2 **Naivasha Kenya**
77 B3 **Najafābād Iran**
78 K6 **Najaf, An Iraq**
126 F4 **Najasa** *R* **Cuba**
17 F2 **Nájera Spain**
17 F2 **Najerilla** *R* **Spain**
65 H3 **Najin N Korea**
77 B2 **Najmabad Iran**
72 F5 **Najran Saudi Arabia**
60 H12 **Naka** *R* **Japan**
60 C13 **Nakadōri shima** *isld* **Japan**
60 C12 **Nakagumi Japan**
61 P13 **Nakagusuku-wan** *B* Okinawa
61 N7 **Nakajō Japan**
60 C14 **Naka koshiki jima** *isld* Japan
60 D12 **Nakama Japan**
61 P13 **Nakama** Okinawa
61 O9 **Nakaminato Japan**
Nakamti *see* **Lekemti** Ethiopia
60 E14 **Nakamura Japan**
60 F13 **Nakamura Japan**
61 M9 **Nakano Japan**
61 M9 **Nakanojō Japan**
60 G9 **Nakano-shima** *isld* **Japan**
67 H4 **Nakanougan-jima** *isld* Japan
61 Q12 **Nakaoshi** Okinawa
77 L3 **Naka Pass Afghanistan**
61 O5 **Nakasato Japan**
60 R3 **Nakasatsunai Japan**
60 T2 **Naka-shibetsu Japan**
55 D2 **Nakatay U.S.S.R.**
60 Q1 **Naka-Tombetsu Japan**
60 E12 **Nakatsu Japan**
61 L10 **Nakatsugawa Japan**
60 G10 **Naka-umi Japan**
116 J8 **Nakchamik I** Alaska
116 O6 **Naked I** Alaska
86 G2 **Nakfa Ethiopia**
78 K2 **Nakhichevan U.S.S.R.**
84 J4 **Nakhl Egypt**
65 J3 **Nakhodka U.S.S.R.**
68 E5 **Nakhon Nayok Thailand**
68 D6 **Nakhon Pathom Thailand**
68 F5 **Nakhon Ratchasima** Thailand
69 E8 **Nakhon Si Thammarat** Thailand
68 E4 **Nakhon Thai Thailand**
59 L2 **Nakhtakhe U.S.S.R.**
61 P12 **Nakijin** Okinawa
117 G6 **Nakina** Br Col
115 L7 **Nakina** Ontario
29 K3 **Näkkälä Finland**
29 J10 **Nakkila Finland**
28 O10 **Nakkur Fjord** *inlet* Faeroes
31 K2 **Nakło Poland**
116 J7 **Naknek** Alaska
61 O9 **Nakoso Japan**
67 F3 **Nakou China**
Naksho Biru *see* **Biru**
28 G7 **Nakskov Denmark**
26 G9 **Näkten** *L* **Sweden**
65 G7 **Naktong** *R* **S Korea**
88 F2 **Nakuru Kenya**
88 E2 **Nakuru, L Kenya**
117 P10 **Nakusp** Br Col
68 C1 **Na-lang Burma**
58 E2 **Nalayh Mongolia**
53 F11 **Nal'chik U.S.S.R.**
74 G10 **Naldrug India**
76 D2 **Nalgonda India**
22 G3 **Nalinnes Belgium**
76 D3 **Nallamala Hills India**
94 G8 **Nallen** W Virginia
78 C1 **Nallihan Turkey**
87 D9 **Nalolo Zambia**
68 C1 **Nam** *R* **Burma**
68 F3 **Nam** *R* **Laos**
65 G5 **Nam** *R* **N Korea**
60 C12 **Nama Japan**
87 C9 **Namacunde Angola**
88 F10 **Namacurra Mozambique**
118 D8 **Namaka** Alberta
118 K2 **Namakan L** Minn/Ontario
77 F4 **Namakiār-e Shadād** *salt lake* Iran
77 E2 **Namak, Kavīr-e** *salt waste* Iran
69 H14 **Namang Indonesia**
57 F4 **Namangan U.S.S.R.**
88 G8 **Namapa Mozambique**
88 G9 **Namaponda Mozambique**
87 C12 **Namaqualand** *dist* **S Africa**
88 F9 **Namarroi Mozambique**
86 F5 **Namasagali Uganda**
87 E9 **Nambala Zambia**
142 D4 **Nambeet Well** W Australia
68 E2 **Nam Beng** *R* **Laos**
141 L7 **Nambour** Queensland
139 L4 **Nambucca Heads** New S Wales
68 G3 **Nam Ca Dinh** *R* **Laos**
69 G8 **Nam Can Vietnam**
66 E6 **Namcha Barwa** *mt* **China**
66 E5 **Nam Co** *L* **China**
26 F7 **Namdalen** *V* **Norway**
26 E7 **Namdalseid Norway**
68 H2 **Nam Dinh Vietnam**
88 G8 **Namecala Mozambique**
70 E3 **Nameh** Kalimantan
99 P3 **Namekagon** *R* Wisconsin
61 L9 **Namerikawa Japan**
48 E1 **Námestovo Czechoslovakia**
88 G9 **Nametil Mozambique**
119 P4 **Namew L** Sask
68 F2 **Nam Het** *R* **Laos**
68 D2 **Nam Hsin** *R* **Burma**
87 B10 **Namib Des Namibia**
87 C10 **Namibia** *terr* **Africa**
88 F9 **Namicunde Mozambique**
61 O8 **Namie Japan**
61 O5 **Namioka Japan**
87 C11 **Namiziz** *mt* **Namibia**
68 F3 **Nam Khan** *R* **Laos**
68 D2 **Nam Kok** *R* **Thailand**
68 C1 **Namlan Burma**
68 C2 **Namlang** *R* **Burma**
68 E2 **Nam Loi** *R* **Burma**
68 E2 **Nam Ma** *R* **Laos**
68 C3 **Nammekon Burma**
68 G3 **Nam Muone** *R* **Laos**
68 F1 **Nam Na** *R* **Vietnam**
68 G4 **Nam One** *R* **Laos**
68 E2 **Nam Ngaou** *R* **Laos**
68 F2 **Nam Noud** *R* **Vietnam**
70 F5 **Namo** Sulawesi **Indonesia**
139 J4 **Namoi** *R* New S Wales
68 E1 **Nam Ou** *R* **Laos**
85 D2 **Namous** *watercourse* Algeria
118 A2 **Nampa** Alberta
29 M5 **Nampa Finland**
100 J6 **Nampa** Idaho
85 C5 **Nampala Mali**
68 E4 **Nam Pa Sak** *R* **Thailand**
68 E4 **Nam Pat Thailand**
68 F4 **Nam Phong Thailand**
22 B3 **Nampont France**
88 G9 **Nampula Mozambique**
68 G4 **Nam Pung Res Thailand**
68 C2 **Namsang Burma**
26 F7 **Namsen** *R* **Norway**
68 F2 **Nam Seng** *R* **Laos**
26 E7 **Namsos Norway**
68 F2 **Nam Suong** *R* **Laos**
26 G7 **Namsvatn** *L* **Norway**
68 C2 **Nam Teng Burma**
68 E2 **Nam Tha Laos**
68 G4 **Nam Theun** *R* **Laos**
68 C2 **Namtok Burma**
68 D5 **Nam Tok Thailand**
68 D1 **Namton Burma**
51 M2 **Namtsy U.S.S.R.**
88 F9 **Namuli** *mt* **Mozambique**
83 L11 **Namunakuli** *mt* **Sri Lanka**
87 G8 **Namuno Mozambique**
22 H3 **Namur Belgium**
121 Q7 **Namur** Quebec
117 R7 **Namur L** Alberta
87 C9 **Namutoni Namibia**
87 E9 **Namwala Zambia**
68 D4 **Nam Wang** *R* **Thailand**
88 E9 **Namwera Malawi**
31 L4 **Namysłaki Poland**
31 K4 **Namysłów Poland**
87 D8 **Nana Candundo Angola**
100 B1 **Nanaimo** Br Col
102 R12 **Nanakuli** Hawaiian Is
65 H4 **Nanam N Korea**
143 E10 **Nanambinia** W Australia
67 B6 **Nanan China**
67 F4 **Nan'an China**
141 K7 **Nanango** Queensland
67 F5 **Nan'ao China**
61 K8 **Nanao Japan**
67 F5 **Nan'ao Dao** *isld* **China**
61 L8 **Nanao wan** *B* **Japan**
61 K8 **Nanatsu-jima** *isld* **Japan**
67 B3 **Nanbai China**
67 B1 **Nanbazhen China**
67 B1 **Nanbu China**
21 J7 **Nançay France**
59 J2 **Nancha China**
67 E2 **Nanchang China**
65 E6 **Nanchangshan Dao** *isld* China
67 E3 **Nancheng China**
67 B1 **Nanchong China**
69 A9 **Nancowry** *isld* **Nicobar Is**
19 K4 **Nancy France**
144 A6 **Nancy Sd New Zealand**
74 H3 **Nanda Devi** *mt* **India**
67 B4 **Nandan China**
74 G9 **Nander India**
139 K4 **Nandewar Ra** *mts* New S Wales
37 M6 **Nandlstadt W Germany**
22 J3 **Nandrin Belgium**
67 C7 **Nandu Jiang** *R* **China**
74 F8 **Nandurbar India**
76 D3 **Nandyal India**
36 D4 **Nane** *R* **W Germany**
65 F4 **Nanfen China**
67 D5 **Nanfeng China**
67 E3 **Nanfeng China**
75 P4 **Nang China**
70 C4 **Nangabadau** Kalimantan
86 B5 **Nanga Eboko Cameroon**
71 L9 **Nangahale** Flores Indonesia
70 C4 **Nangakelawit** Kalimantan
74 G3 **Nangal India**
70 B5 **Nangalanki** Kalimantan
71 E5 **Nangalao** *isld* **Philippines**
70 B5 **Nangamau** Kalimantan
70 C5 **Nangamuntatai** Kalimantan
70 C4 **Nangaobat** Kalimantan
74 F1 **Nanga Parbat** *mt* Kashmir
70 B5 **Nangapinoh** Kalimantan
70 C4 **Nangaraun** Kalimantan
77 L2 **Nangarhār Afghanistan**
70 C4 **Nangasuruk** Kalimantan
69 K13 **Nangatayap Indonesia**
68 D7 **Nangin Burma**
18 G4 **Nangis France**
65 G5 **Nangnim Sanmaek** *mts* N Korea
65 C6 **Nangong China**
76 C6 **Nanguneri India**
87 D9 **Nangweshi Zambia**
67 D5 **Nanhai China**
Nanhaoqian *see* **Shangyi**
65 C6 **Nanhe China**
67 D1 **Nan He** *R* **China**
67 G1 **Nanhui China**
76 C4 **Nanjangud India**
58 E5 **Nanjiang China**
67 D2 **Nanjiangqiao China**
Nanjie *see* **Guangning**
67 F1 **Nanjing China**
67 F4 **Nanjing China**
67 C6 **Nankang China**
67 E4 **Nankang China**
Nanking *see* **Nanjing**
65 C4 **Nankouzhen China**
65 C6 **Nanle China**
67 F1 **Nanling China**
67 C4 **Nan Ling** *mts* **China**
Nanma *see* **Yiyuan**
67 G2 **Nanma China**
67 E3 **Nanmiao** Jiangxi **China**
37 L7 **Nannhofen W Germany**
143 C7 **Nannine** W Australia
67 C5 **Nanning China**
143 B10 **Nannup** W Australia
137 Q3 **Nanomana** *isld* **Tuvalu**
137 Q3 **Nanomea** *isld* **Tuvalu**
115 P5 **Nanortalik Greenland**
67 A4 **Nanpan Jiang** *R* **China**
75 J5 **Nanpara India**
67 F5 **Nanpeng Liedao** *islds* China
65 C5 **Nanpi China**
65 H3 **Nanping China**
68 E3 **Nan Poui** *R* **Laos**
65 D5 **Nanpu China**
67 F3 **Nanpu Xi** *R* **China**
Nanqiao *see* **Fengxian**
67 F4 **Nanri Dao** *isld* **China**
51 J5 **Nan Shan** *mt ra* **China**
88 D3 **Nansio Tanzania**
143 A8 **Nanson** W Australia
18 H8 **Nant France**
112 D2 **Nantahala L** N Carolina
115 M5 **Nantais,L** Quebec
75 K5 **Nantanwa India**
21 B7 **Nantes France**
122 A8 **Nantes** Quebec
8 C4 **Nant-garw Wales**
70 K8 **Nanti** *mt* Sumatra
67 G2 **Nantian China**
18 F6 **Nantiat France**
95 L5 **Nanticoke** Pennsylvania
95 M8 **Nanticoke** *R* Delaware/Maryland
8 C4 **Nant Moel Wales**
118 D8 **Nanton** Alberta
67 G1 **Nantong China**
40 C5 **Nantua France**
95 R5 **Nantucket I** Massachusetts
146 E12 **Nantucket Inlet Antarctica**
88 G8 **Nantulo Mozambique**
8 D1 **Nantwich England**
94 J6 **Nanty Glo** Pennsylvania
130 H5 **Nanuque Brazil**
116 M2 **Nanushuk** *R* Alaska
65 B6 **Nanweiquan China**
67 A2 **Nanxi China**
67 D2 **Nan Xian China**
67 C5 **Nanxiang China**
67 E4 **Nanxiong China**
141 J6 **Nanya** Queensland
58 F5 **Nanyang China**
67 C2 **Nanyaojie China**
65 C7 **Nanyi China**
67 F1 **Nanyi Hu China**
61 O7 **Nanyō Japan**
65 C5 **Nanyuan China**
88 F1 **Nanyuki Kenya**
65 F4 **Nanzamu China**
67 D1 **Nanzhang China**
67 G3 **Nanzhen China**
17 H6 **Nao,C.de la Spain**
115 M7 **Naococane,L** Quebec
61 M8 **Naoetsu Japan**
75 N6 **Naogaon Bangladesh**
74 C6 **Naokot Pakistan**
59 K2 **Naol He** *R* **China**
77 G3 **Naomid, Dasht-e** *des* **Iran**
101 O8 **Naomi Pk** Utah
46 E4 **Náousa Greece**
67 C6 **Naozhou Dao** *isld* **China**
102 B3 **Napa** California
71 H7 **Napabalana Indonesia**
122 F7 **Napadogan** New Brunswick
70 D3 **Napaku** Kalimantan
121 O8 **Napanee** Ontario
115 O4 **Napassoq Greenland**
100 C3 **Napavine** Washington
71 F4 **Napayauan Philippines**
68 G3 **Nape Laos**
99 S8 **Naperville** Illinois
123 O2 **Napetipi R** Quebec
40 G4 **Napf** *mt* **Switzerland**
99 L9 **Napier** Missouri
145 F3 **Napier New Zealand**
142 F2 **Napier Broome B** W Australia
140 A4 **Napier, Mt** N Terr **Aust**
146 A5 **Napier Mts Antarctica**
140 D1 **Napier Pen** N Terr **Aust**
142 E3 **Napier Ra** W Australia
121 R7 **Napierville** Quebec
119 R9 **Napinka** Manitoba
Naples *see* **Napoli Italy**
113 F11 **Naples** Florida
95 K4 **Naples** New York
109 N2 **Naples** Texas
67 B5 **Napo China**
68 G1 **Napo China**
128 C4 **Napo** *R* **Peru/Ecuador**
94 B7 **Napoleon** Indiana
98 G3 **Napoleon** N Dakota
94 C5 **Napoleon** Ohio
111 E12 **Napoleonville** Louisiana
43 G7 **Napoletano, Appennino** *mts* Italy
45 Q8 **Napoli Italy**
98 G9 **Naponee** Nebraska
135 U5 **Napoopoo** Hawaiian Is
131 E7 **Naposta** *R* **Argentina**
141 F8 **Nappamerry** Queensland
94 A5 **Nappanee** Indiana
140 C6 **Napperby** N Terr **Aust**
110 C2 **Napton** Missouri
78 K3 **Naqadeh Iran**
79 F8 **Naqb Ishtar Jordan**
79 C9 **Naqb Malba** *mt* **Egypt**
61 J11 **Nara Japan**
85 C5 **Nara Mali**
139 G7 **Naracoopa** Tasmania
138 F6 **Naracoorte** S Australia
139 H5 **Naradhan** New S Wales
143 A8 **Naraling** W Australia
117 O11 **Naramata** Br Col
65 C2 **Naran Bulag China**
113 G12 **Naranja** Florida
124 E5 **Naranjo Mexico**
76 E2 **Naraspur India**
69 E9 **Narathiwat Thailand**
106 G6 **Nara Visa** New Mexico
75 O7 **Narayanganj Bangladesh**
76 C2 **Narayanpet India**
Narbada *R see* **Narmada** *R*
18 H9 **Narbonne France**
9 G2 **Narborough England**
16 C1 **Narcea** *R* **Spain**
43 J8 **Nardò Italy**
8 B7 **Nare Head England**
143 C9 **Narembeen** W Australia
74 H3 **Narendranagar India**
90 D6 **Nares Deep Atlantic Oc**
115 M2 **Nares Str** Canada/Greenland
143 E9 **Naretha** W Australia
31 O3 **Narew Poland**
65 G3 **Narhong China**
65 A5 **Narin China**
66 E4 **Narin Gol** *R* **China**
128 C3 **Nariño** *div* **Colombia**
61 O10 **Narita Japan**
127 P2 **Nariva** *co* **Trinidad**
127 P2 **Nariva Swamp Trinidad**
60 G11 **Nariwa Japan**
124 D4 **Narizon** *pt* **Mexico**
107 N2 **Narka** Kansas
26 N5 **Narken Sweden**
74 F7 **Narmada** *R* **India**
42 E6 **Narni Italy**
71 F5 **Naro** *isld* **Philippines**
52 K2 **Narodnaya, Gora** *mt* U.S.S.R.
54 H1 **Naro-Fominsk U.S.S.R.**
88 E2 **Narok Kenya**
16 B1 **Naron Spain**
139 K6 **Narooma** New S Wales
74 F2 **Narowal Pakistan**
29 J9 **Närpes Finland**
139 K4 **Narrabri** New S Wales
139 J4 **Narrabri West** New S Wales
95 Q5 **Narragansett** Rhode I
139 J3 **Narran** *R* New S Wales
139 H5 **Narrandera** New S Wales
139 H3 **Narran,L** New S Wales
143 E8 **Narra Spring** W Australia
117 N8 **Narraway** *R* Br Col
141 H6 **Narrien Ra** Queensland
143 B10 **Narrogin** W Australia
139 J4 **Narromine** New S Wales
100 G6 **Narrows** Oregon
94 G9 **Narrows** Virginia
95 M5 **Narrowsburg** New York
127 P4 **Narrows,The** *chan* St Kitts W I
142 B1 **Narrows, The** *str* Perth, W Aust
143 B7 **Narryer, Mt** W Australia
37 O1 **Narsdorf** E Germany
74 G7 **Narsinghgarh India**
75 K10 **Narsipatnam India**
115 P5 **Narssalik Greenland**
115 O5 **Narssaq Greenland**
115 P5 **Narssarssuaq Greenland**
65 C3 **Nart China**
46 C4 **Nartës,Gjol i** *isld* **Albania**
61 O7 **Naruko Japan**
131 F2 **Narunjito, L Argentina**
60 B13 **Naru-shima** *isld* **Japan**
61 O10 **Narutō Japan**
60 H11 **Naruto-kaikyō** *str* **Japan**
52 C5 **Narva U.S.S.R.**
71 E2 **Narvacan** Luzon Philippines
52 C5 **Narva-Jõesuu U.S.S.R.**
26 J3 **Narvik Norway**

52 C5 Narvskiy Zaliv gulf U.S.S.R.
74 G4 Narwana India
74 G6 Narwar India
140 C6 Narwietooma N Terr Aust
52 H1 Nar'yan Mar U.S.S.R.
141 F8 Naryilco Queensland
56 B6 Narymskiy Khrebet mts U.S.S.R.
57 H4 Naryn U.S.S.R.
57 G4 Naryn Ugyut R U.S.S.R.
54 G4 Naryshkino U.S.S.R.
27 G11 Nås Sweden
85 F7 Nasarawa Nigeria
48 J3 Năsăud Romania
26 M5 Näsberg Sweden
18 H8 Nasbinals France
144 C6 Naseby New Zealand
107 M5 Nash Oklahoma
8 C5 Nash Wales
122 F6 Nash Cr New Brunswick
116 D6 Nash Harbor Alaska
140 E5 Nash, L Queensland
8 C5 Nash Pt Wales
99 O7 Nashua Iowa
101 T1 Nashua Montana
95 Q4 Nashua New Hampshire
111 C8 Nashville Arkansas
112 D6 Nashville Georgia
110 G3 Nashville Illinois
94 A7 Nashville Indiana
107 M4 Nashville Kansas
94 B4 Nashville Michigan
112 J2 Nashville N Carolina
94 E6 Nashville Ohio
110 K5 Nashville Tennessee
99 N2 Nashwauk Minnesota
48 E5 Našice Yugoslavia
29 K10 Näsijärvi L Finland
74 E8 Nasik India
86 F4 Nasir Sudan
79 A8 Nasr Egypt
79 H4 Naṣrānī, Jebel an mts Syria
117 J8 Nass R Br Col
98 K4 Nassau Minnesota
113 L9 Nassau New Providence I Bahamas
95 O4 Nassau New York
36 D3 Nassau W Germany
141 F3 Nassau R Queensland
133 D9 Nassau,B.de Chile
113 F7 Nassau Sd Florida
95 M9 Nassawadox Virginia
33 T10 Nasseböhla E Germany
37 L6 Nassenfels W Germany
33 S7 Nassenheide E Germany
84 J5 Nasser, L Egypt
27 G14 Nässjö Sweden
22 J3 Nassogne Belgium
38 N6 Nasswald Austria
115 M6 Nastapoka Is N W Terr
36 D3 Nastätten W Germany
71 E3 Nasugbu Luzon Philippines
61 N8 Nasu-Yumoto Japan
52 D6 Nasva U.S.S.R.
26 J10 Näsviken Sweden
87 E10 Nata Botswana
89 E3 Nata R Botswana
128 F5 Natal Brazil
118 C9 Natal Br Col
69 D12 Natal Sumatra
89 F7 Natal prov S Africa
141 H5 Natal R Queensland
90 M13 Natal Basin Indian Oc
141 H5 Natal Downs Queensland
109 J6 Natalia Texas
55 C3 Natalinsk U.S.S.R.
77 B3 Naṭanz Iran
123 L3 Natashquan Quebec
123 L3 Natashquan R Quebec/Labrador
116 K3 Natavukti L Alaska
116 R6 Natazhat Mt Alaska
111 E10 Natchez Mississippi
111 C10 Natchitoches Louisiana
139 H6 Nathalia Victoria
115 R3 Nathorsts Land Greenland
106 D3 Nathrop Colorado
124 J5 Natillas Mexico
138 F6 Natimuk Victoria
116 R4 Nation Alaska
101 L2 National Bison Ra Montana
102 G9 National City California
86 C3 National Park Chad
117 L8 Nation R Br Col
123 K4 Natiskotek B Anticosti I, Quebec
141 H6 Native Companion Cr Queensland
124 B4 Natividad isld Mexico
129 J6 Natividade Brazil
68 C5 Natkyizin Burma
107 M2 Natoma Kansas
124 E3 Nátora Mexico
61 O7 Natori Japan
22 J3 Natoye Belgium
101 T6 Natrona Wyoming
88 F3 Natron L Tanzania
68 B3 Nattalin Burma
83 J10 Nattandiya Sri Lanka
29 N3 Nattaset mt Finland
68 C3 Nattaung mt Burma
26 L5 Nattavaara Sweden
37 O6 Natternberg W Germany
37 J6 Nattheim W Germany
27 H15 Nättraby Sweden
Natuna Besar see Bunguran Utara, Kep. /
Natuna Selatan see Bunguran Selatan Kep /
69 H10 Natuna Utara Indonesia
95 M2 Natural Bridge New York
94 H9 Natural Bridge Virginia
103 O4 Natural Br.Nat.Mon Utah
108 F3 Natural Dam L Texas
143 B10 Naturaliste, C W Australia
143 A7 Naturaliste Chan W Australia
81 H9 Naturaliste Plateau Indian Oc
106 B3 Naturita Colorado
99 V3 Naubinway Michigan
87 C10 Nauchas Namibia
121 T4 Naudville Quebec
33 R7 Nauen E Germany
130 E10 Naufragados, Pta Dos C Brazil
95 O5 Naugatuck Connecticut
71 E4 Naujan Philippines
29 N8 Naulavaara mt Finland
87 B9 Naulila Angola
37 M1 Naumburg E Germany
36 G1 Naumburg W Germany
68 C4 Naunglon Burma
68 C3 Naungpale Burma
33 R10 Naunhof E Germany
80 G6 Na'ur Jordan
36 D2 Nauroth W Germany
137 O2 Nauru rep Pacific Oc
55 D5 Naurzum U.S.S.R.
26 A10 Naustdal Norway
26 C9 Nauste Norway
128 D4 Nauta Peru
26 R3 Nautsi U.S.S.R.
111 J8 Nauvoo Alabama
99 P9 Nauvoo Illinois
108 G7 Nava Mexico
16 D3 Nava de Rey Spain
16 E5 Navahermosa Spain
103 P6 Navajo Arizona
103 M4 Navajo L Utah
103 O4 Navajo Mt Utah
103 O5 Navajo Nat.Mon Arizona
103 N5 Navajo Pt Arizona
106 C5 Navajo Res Colo/New Mex
16 E4 Navalcarnero Spain
16 D5 Navalmoral de la Mata Spain
86 E5 Nava R Zaïre
133 D9 Navarino, I Chile
17 F2 Navarra prov Spain
94 F6 Navarre Ohio
139 G6 Navarre Victoria
102 A2 Navarro California
102 A2 Navarro R California
109 L4 Navarro Mills Res Texas
109 L5 Navasota Texas
126 G5 Navassa I Caribbean
45 P5 Navelli Italy
9 F1 Navenby England
16 C1 Navia Spain
16 C1 Navia R Spain
109 L6 Navidad R Texas
127 K4 Navidad Bank Caribbean
130 H10 Navio R Brazil
54 F4 Navlya U.S.S.R.
54 F4 Navlya R U.S.S.R.
57 D4 Navoi U.S.S.R.
124 E4 Navojoa Mexico
124 F5 Navolato Mexico
52 E3 Navolok U.S.S.R.
52 F5 Navoloki U.S.S.R.
46 E6 Návpaktos Greece
46 F7 Návplion Greece
28 B4 Navr Denmark
85 D6 Navrongo Ghana
74 E8 Navsari India
75 N6 Nawabganj Bangladesh
75 J5 Nawabganj India
74 C5 Nawabshah Pakistan
75 L6 Nawada India
77 K3 Nāwah Afghanistan
83 K10 Nawalapitiya Sri Lanka
84 F3 Nawfaliyah,an Libya
138 F5 Nawingi Victoria
68 D1 Nawng-Hpa Burma
68 C1 Nawngkio Burma
68 D1 Nawngleng Burma
67 B2 Naxi China
47 G7 Náxos Greece
47 H7 Náxos isld Greece
18 E9 Nay France
69 J12 Naya Indonesia
16 E4 Nayacerrada, Pto. de peak Spain
75 L8 Nayagarh India
124 G6 Nayar Mexico
124 G7 Nayarit state Mexico
77 E3 Nay Band Iran
9 G4 Nayland England
113 D7 Naylor Georgia
110 F5 Naylor Missouri
67 B3 Nayong China
59 M3 Nayoro Japan
129 L6 Nazaré Brazil
16 A5 Nazaré Portugal
130 J9 Nazaré da Mata Brazil
22 F2 Nazareth Belgium
Nazareth Ethiopia see Adama
76 C6 Nazareth India
80 E3 Nazareth Israel
95 M6 Nazareth Pennsylvania
130 E5 Nazário Brazil
54 N2 Nazarovka U.S.S.R.
56 D3 Nazarovo Krasnoyarskiy Kray U.S.S.R.
55 F3 Nazarovo Tyumenskaya U.S.S.R.
124 G5 Nazas Mexico
128 D6 Nazca Peru
59 J6 Naze Japan
9 H4 Naze,The C England
47 J7 Nazilli Turkey
56 A1 Nazinskaya R U.S.S.R.
75 Q5 Nazira India
75 O7 Nazir Hat Bangladesh
117 M9 Nazko Br Col
80 A7 Nazla Israel
80 D4 Nazlat Jordan
86 G4 Nazret Ethiopia
67 B4 Nazuo China
55 E1 Nazym R U.S.S.R.
55 F3 Nazyvayevsk U.S.S.R.
37 J1 Nazza E Germany
89 F3 Ncema Dam Zimbabwe
88 A8 Nchanga Zambia
88 E9 Ncheu Malawi
87 B7 Ndalakanda Angola
85 E6 Ndali Benin
71 L10 Ndao isld Indonesia
86 D4 Ndele Cent Afr Republic
86 B6 Ndendé Gabon
137 O4 Ndeni isld Santa Cruz Is
86 B5 Ndikiniméki Cameroon
86 B6 Ndindi Gabon
86 C3 N'Djamena Chad
86 B6 Ndjolé Gabon
86 B6 N'Dogou, L Gabon
88 B8 Ndola Zambia
71 K9 Ndona Flores Indonesia
86 B6 N'Dongo Congo
26 E8 Nea Norway
139 J3 Neabul R Queensland
46 D5 Néa Filippías Greece
14 E2 Neagh,L N Ireland
107 O4 Neal Kansas
140 B6 Neale,L N Terr Aust
138 D3 Neales R S Australia
47 F4 Neá Moudhaniá Greece
21 I6 Néant R France
15 G2 Neap Shetland Scotland
47 H9 Néapolis Crete Greece
46 E4 Neápolis Makedhonia Greece
46 F8 Neápolis Pelopónnisos Greece
47 F6 Néa Psará Greece
116 J9 Near Is Aleutian Is
8 C4 Neath Wales
20 J4 Neauphle-le-Château France
47 H3 Néa Víssi Greece
85 D6 Nebbou Upper Volta
52 G3 Nebdino U.S.S.R.
28 A7 Nebel W Germany
33 Q5 Nebel R E Germany
41 M3 Nebelhorn mt W Germany
43 B12 Nebeur Tunisia
43 C12 Nebhana R Tunisia
141 H8 Nebine R Queensland
50 E5 Nebit-Dag U.S.S.R.
141 J5 Nebo Queensland
52 D5 Nebolchi U.S.S.R.
80 F6 Nebo, Mt Jordan
103 N2 Nebo,Mt Utah
33 P10 Nebra E Germany
98 G8 Nebraska state U.S.A.
99 L9 Nebraska City Nebraska
43 F11 Nebrodi,Monti Sicily
99 Q5 Necedah Wisconsin
117 L9 Nechako R Br Col
98 J1 Neche N Dakota
109 M4 Neches R Texas
128 D2 Nechi R Colombia
33 T6 Nechlin E Germany
36 F7 Neckar R W Germany
36 F5 Neckarbischofsheim W Germany
36 G5 Neckarelz W Germany
36 F5 Neckargemünd W Germany
36 F5 Neckarsteinach W Germany
36 G5 Neckarsulm W Germany
102 U13 Necker I Hawaiian Is
144 B7 Neck, The New Zealand
131 F7 Necochea Argentina
37 P4 Nečtiny Czechoslovakia
86 B6 Necuto Angola
20 E4 Nécy France
16 B1 Neda Spain
33 S5 Neddemin E Germany
121 L5 Nedelec Quebec
106 E2 Nederland Colorado
109 N6 Nederland Texas
25 E5 Neder Rijn R Netherlands
25 E6 Nederweert Netherlands
142 A2 Nedlands dist Perth, W Aust
33 Q8 Nedlitz E Germany
17 F9 Nedroma Algeria
31 L5 Nedza Poland
25 G4 Neede Netherlands
9 H3 Needham Market England
101 Q5 Needle Mt Wyoming
144 A6 Needle Pk New Zealand
103 K7 Needles California
145 E2 Needles Pt New Zealand
9 E6 Needles, The rocks England
109 M6 Needville Texas
119 S9 Neelin Manitoba
101 N7 Neely Idaho
110 F5 Neelyville Missouri
130 B10 Neembucú dep Paraguay
99 S5 Neenah Wisconsin
119 S8 Neepawa Manitoba
25 E6 Neer Netherlands
143 B8 Neereno hill W Australia
106 H3 Nee Res Colorado
115 M3 Neergaard L N W Terr
22 J1 Neerpelt Belgium
22 J2 Neerwinden Belgium
28 A4 Nees Denmark
112 F4 Neeses S Carolina
55 F2 Nefedovo U.S.S.R.
85 F2 Nefta Tunisia
57 F4 Nefteabad U.S.S.R.
8 B2 Nefyn Wales
43 C12 Nefza Tunisia
87 C7 Negage Angola
85 C6 Negala Mali
83 K10 Negama Sri Lanka
70 P10 Negara Bali Indonesia
70 D6 Negara Kalimantan
70 D6 Negara R Kalimantan
99 T3 Negaunee Michigan
80 B7 Negba Israel
86 G4 Negelli Ethiopia
69 F11 Negeri Sembilan Malaysia
79 E8 Negev mt reg Israel
130 C8 Negla R Paraguay
48 J5 Negoiu mt Romania
87 G8 Negomano Mozambique
83 J10 Negombo Sri Lanka
48 H6 Negotin Yugoslavia
46 E3 Negotino Yugoslavia
73 P5 Negrais,C Burma
143 D7 Negrara,R W Australia
130 G6 Negra,Serra mts Brazil
16 B2 Negreira Spain
48 J6 Negreni Romania
18 G8 Nègrepelisse France
48 L4 Negreşti Romania
127 H1 Negril Pt.N Jamaica
141 F7 Negri Mts Queensland
16 E9 Negri,Pta Morocco
128 F4 Negro R Brazil
16 D9 Negro,C Morocco
94 H7 Negro Mt Penn/Maryland
131 C7 Negro,R Argentina
130 B9 Negro,R Paraguay
131 F4 Negro,R Uruguay
71 F5 Negros isld Philippines
47 J1 Negru Vodă Romania
100 B4 Nehalem Oregon
80 C5 Nehalim Israel
77 G4 Nehbandān Iran
59 H2 Nehe China
32 G10 Neheim-Hüsten W Germany
48 K5 Nehoiaşu Romania
20 B3 Néhou France
33 R4 Nehringen E Germany
137 S5 Neiafu Tonga
127 J5 Neiba Dom Rep
33 R10 Neichen E Germany
52 C1 Neiden Norway
118 K8 Neidpath Sask
101 P3 Neihart Montana
65 C7 Neihuang China
67 B2 Neijiang China
Neikiang see Neijiang
16 E2 Neila,Sa.de mts Spain
118 H6 Neilburg Sask
68 A7 Neill I Andaman Is
99 Q5 Neillsville Wisconsin
123 M7 Neil's Harbour C Breton I, N Scotia
100 B2 Neilton Washington
58 E3 Nei Monggol Zizhiqu aut reg China
33 N8 Neindorf W Germany
36 G5 Neipperg W Germany
65 C6 Neiqiu China
Neisse see Nysa
31 H4 Neisse R E Ger/Poland
128 C3 Neiva Colombia
37 O3 Nejdek Czechoslovakia
86 G4 Nejo Ethiopia
98 H1 Nekoma N Dakota
99 R5 Nekoosa Wisconsin
28 G5 Nekselø isld Denmark
51 O2 Neksikan U.S.S.R.
27 H16 Neksø Denmark
27 C13 Nelaug Norway
141 F5 Nelia Queensland
52 D6 Nelidovo U.S.S.R.
54 D1 Nelidovo U.S.S.R.
98 J7 Neligh Nebraska
142 E3 Nellie,Mt W Australia
139 K6 Nelligen New S Wales
76 D3 Nellore India
59 L2 Nel'ma U.S.S.R.
52 F5 Nel'sha U.S.S.R.
103 L6 Nelson Arizona
117 P11 Nelson Br Col
102 C2 Nelson California
13 F6 Nelson England
112 J2 Nelson N Carolina
98 H9 Nelson Nebraska
103 K6 Nelson Nevada
145 D4 Nelson New Zealand
95 K5 Nelson Pennsylvania
138 F7 Nelson Victoria
8 C4 Nelson Wales
99 P5 Nelson Wisconsin
144 C4 Nelson stat area New Zealand
138 F7 Nelson,C Victoria
144 C5 Nelson Cr New Zealand
133 C8 Nelson,Estrecho chan Chile
117 M6 Nelson Forks Br Col
119 T3 Nelson House Manitoba
116 E6 Nelson I Alaska
146 E15 Nelson I S Shetland Is
145 D4 Nelson Lakes Nat. Park New Zealand
119 V3 Nelson R Manitoba
101 S1 Nelson Res Montana
94 E7 Nelsonville Ohio
89 G5 Nelspruit S Africa
52 J4 Nem R U.S.S.R.
85 C5 Néma Mauritania
52 H5 Nema U.S.S.R.
99 O3 Nemadji R Minnesota
99 L9 Nemaha Nebraska
76 C6 Nemam India
31 O2 Neman R U.S.S.R.
71 L10 Nembrala Indonesia
52 F5 Nemda R U.S.S.R.
52 H3 Nemed U.S.S.R.
120 G5 Nemegos Ontario
120 G4 Nemegosenda L Ontario
119 M3 Nemeiban Sask
46 D4 Nëmerçkë Albania
45 N6 Nemi L Italy
48 K4 Nemira mt Romania
48 M2 Nemirov U.S.S.R.
115 M7 Nemiscau Quebec
18 G4 Nemours France
60 T2 Nemuro Japan
60 S2 Nemuro prefect Japan
60 T1 Nemuro-kaikyō str Japan/Kuril Is
14 C4 Nenagh Irish Rep
116 N4 Nenana Alaska
41 L3 Nendeln Liechtenstein
9 F2 Nene, R England
59 J2 Nenjiang China
59 H2 Nen Jiang R China
36 B4 Nennig W Germany
36 H1 Nentershausen W Germany
13 F4 Nenthead England
98 E7 Nenzel Nebraska
41 L3 Nenzing Austria
107 P4 Neodesha Kansas
99 S10 Neoga Illinois
99 L8 Neola Iowa
103 O1 Neola Utah
47 H7 Néon Karlóvasi Greece
99 S5 Neopit Wisconsin
130 H11 Neópolis Brazil
99 S6 Neosho Wisconsin
107 P4 Neosho R Kansas/Okla
80 D3 Neot Golan Israel
80 F1 Ne'ot Mordekhay Israel
56 G2 Nepa R U.S.S.R.
75 K4 Nepal kingdom S Asia
75 J5 Nepalganj India
103 N2 Nephi Utah
14 B2 Nephin mt Irish Rep
14 B2 Nephin Beg mt Irish Rep
121 N8 Nephton Ontario
45 M5 Nepi Italy
37 P3 Nepomyšl Czechoslovakia
119 N9 Neptune Sask
113 F7 Neptune Beach Florida
138 D6 Neptune Is S Australia
146 F10 Neptune Rge Antarctica
52 F6 Ner' U.S.S.R.
31 L4 Ner R Poland
42 E6 Nera R Italy
48 G6 Nera R Romania
18 F8 Nérac France
116 D6 Neragon I Alaska
58 G1 Nercha R U.S.S.R.
33 R10 Nerchau E Germany
58 G1 Nerchinsk U.S.S.R.
59 G1 Nerchinsky Zavod U.S.S.R.
68 C7 Nerchus Passage Burma
52 J5 Nerdva U.S.S.R.
21 E10 Néré France
52 F5 Nerekhta U.S.S.R.
37 J6 Neresheim W Germany
42 H5 Neretva R Yugoslavia
87 D9 Neriquinha Angola
116 H7 Nerka,L Alaska
52 E6 Nerl' U.S.S.R.
45 N5 Nerola Italy
18 G5 Nerondes France
45 N4 Nerone, M mt Italy
130 E5 Nerópolis Brazil
52 J3 Neroyka, Gora mt U.S.S.R.
17 F6 Nerpio Spain
139 K6 Nerriga New S Wales
142 E4 Nerrima W Australia
54 E4 Nerussa R U.S.S.R.
16 C7 Nerva Spain
44 F3 Nervi Italy
52 K2 Ner'yuvom U.S.S.R.
25 E2 Nes Netherlands
27 D11 Nesbyen Norway
95 L5 Nescopeck Pennsylvania
47 J2 Nesebŭr Bulgaria
52 C6 Neshcherdo Oz L U.S.S.R.
80 D2 Nesher Israel
116 A3 Neshkan Alaska
99 R6 Neshkoro Wisconsin
111 G9 Neshoba Mississippi
27 D13 Neslandsvatn Norway
22 D4 Nesle France
123 N3 Nesle,L Quebec
26 F5 Nesna Norway
26 F5 Nesöy isld Norway
100 G1 Nespelem Washington
45 O5 Nespolo Italy
19 O16 Nesque R France
107 L3 Ness City Kansas
37 K1 Nesse R E Germany
26 R1 Nesseby Norway
117 F6 Nesselrode,Mt Br Col/Alaska
18 F10 Neste R France
31 O1 Nesterov U.S.S.R.
120 G6 Nesterville Ontario
52 G6 Nestiary U.S.S.R.
127 P2 Nestor Trinidad
118 J1 Nestor Falls Ontario
99 S3 Nestoria Michigan
46 E4 Nestórion Greece
47 G3 Néstos R Greece
27 A11 Nesttun Norway
80 C6 Nes Ziyyona Israel
80 C4 Netanya Israel
107 P2 Netawaka Kansas
95 N6 Netcong New Jersey
32 K9 Nethe R W Germany
141 J5 Netherdale Queensland
118 H7 Netherhill Sask
25 Netherlands kingdom Europe
8 C5 Nether Stowey England
145 E2 Netherton New Zealand
15 E3 Nethy Bridge Scotland
80 C6 Netiva Israel
80 C7 Netiv HaLamed Israel
80 B8 Netivot Israel
43 H9 Neto R Italy
36 E2 Netphen W Germany
37 J1 Netra W Germany
75 O6 Netrakona Bangladesh
36 C3 Nette R W Germany
36 B3 Nettersheim W Germany
25 F6 Nettetal W Germany
115 M4 Nettilling L N W Terr
99 N1 Nett L Minnesota
9 F4 Nettlebed England
120 K4 Nettle Lakes Prov. Park Ontario
110 F6 Nettleton Arkansas
111 H7 Nettleton Mississippi
45 N7 Nettuno Italy
125 N9 Netzahaulcoyotl, Presa res Mexico
37 N2 Netzschkau E Germany
36 H1 Neu W Germany
32 G7 Neu Arenberg W Germany
37 N5 Neubäu W Germany
32 H9 Neubeckum W Germany
20 G3 Neubourg,le France
33 S5 Neubrandenburg E Germany
33 R5 Neubrandenburg reg E Germany
32 J7 Neubruchhausen W Germany
36 H4 Neubrunn W Germany
33 P4 Neubukow E Germany
33 P5 Neuburg E Germany
37 L6 Neuburg W Germany
40 E3 Neuchâtel canton Switzerland
40 E4 Neuchâtel, Lac de Switzerland
32 M9 Neuckrug W Germany
119 P8 Neudorf Sask
37 M3 Neudrossenfeld W Germany
32 L10 Neu-Eichenberg W Germany
36 F6 Neuenburg Baden-Württemberg W Germany
32 G6 Neuenburg Niedersachsen W Germany
32 E7 Neuenhaus W Germany
32 J6 Neuenkirchen Niedersachsen W Germany
32 F8 Neuenkirchen Nordrhein-Westfalen W Germany
32 G10 Neuenrade W Germany
36 G5 Neuenstadt W Germany
36 H5 Neuenstein W Germany
36 G2 Neuental W Germany
32 J5 Neuenwalde W Germany
37 M7 Neufahrn W Germany
40 G1 Neuf Brisach France
22 J4 Neufchateau Belgium
19 J4 Neufchâteau France
20 F5 Neufchâtel France
20 H2 Neufchâtel-en-Bray France
22 B2 Neufchâtel-Hardelot France
22 F5 Neufchâtel-sur-Aisne France
38 K5 Neufelden Austria
36 G6 Neuffen W Germany
20 J3 Neufmarche France
36 G7 Neufra W Germany
41 N2 Neugablonz W Germany
33 S6 Neuglobsow E Germany
32 G5 Neuharlingersiel W Germany
37 M4 Neuhaus Bayern W Germany
33 N6 Neuhaus E Germany
32 K5 Neuhaus Niedersachsen W Germany
37 P2 Neuhausen E Germany
36 G6 Neuhausen W Germany
33 S8 Neuhof E Germany
38 K5 Neuhofen Austria
36 G5 Neuhütten W Germany
21 G6 Neuillé-Pt. Pierre France
20 G4 Neuilly France
20 K3 Neuilly-en-Thelle France
20 C3 Neuilly-la-Fôret France
36 F3 Neu-Isenburg W Germany
33 R5 Neukalen E Germany
33 O6 Neu Kaliss E Germany
38 F7 Neukirchen Austria
37 O2 Neukirchen E Germany
33 O4 Neukirchen Schleswig-Holstein W Germany
37 N5 Neukirchen Balbini W Germany
33 P5 Neukloster E Germany
32 L6 Neukloster W Germany
37 N2 Neumark E Germany
38 H6 Neumarkt Salzburg Austria
38 K7 Neumarkt Steiermark Austria
37 L5 Neumarkt W Germany
37 O7 Neumarkt-St Veit W Germany
32 L4 Neumünster W Germany
37 N5 Neunburg W Germany
21 I6 Neung sur-Beuvron France
38 O6 Neunkirchen Austria
36 D2 Neunkirchen Nordrhein-Westfalen W Germany
36 E2 Neunkirchen Rheinland-Pfalz W Germany
36 C5 Neunkirchen Saarland W Germany
36 C2 Neunkirchen W Germany
37 O7 Neuötting W Germany
131 C7 Neuquén Argentina
131 B7 Neuquén terr Argentina
131 B7 Neuquén, R Argentina
33 R7 Neuruppin E Germany
37 K7 Neusäss W Germany
112 L3 Neuse R N Carolina
48 D3 Neusiedla Austria
48 D3 Neusiedler See Austria
36 B1 Neuss W Germany
18 H7 Neussargues France
48 C3 Neustadt Austria
37 M2 Neustadt Gera E Germany
36 G2 Neustadt Hessen W Germany
36 G4 Neustadt Hessen W Germany
36 H3 Neustadt Hessen W Germany
33 Q7 Neustadt Potsdam E Germany
36 E5 Neustadt Rheinland-Pfalz W Germany
37 K2 Neustadt Suhl E Germany
37 K4 Neustadt an der Aisch W Germany
37 N4 Neustadt an der Waldnaab W Germany
37 L3 Neustadt bei Coburg W Germany
33 P6 Neustadt-Glewe E Germany
32 G6 Neustadt-gödens W Germany
Neustettin see Szczecinek
37 M7 Neustift W Germany
33 S6 Neustrelitz E Germany
37 J7 Neu Ulm W Germany
22 D2 Neuve Chapelle France
20 G4 Neuve-Lyre, la France
40 F3 Neuveville Switzerland
18 G7 Neuvic France
109 N4 Neuville Texas
20 K5 Neuville-aux-Bois France
21 F8 Neuville-de-Poitou France
22 G5 Neuville-en-Tourne-à-Fuy France
19 O12 Neuville-les-Dames France
20 H2 Neuville-lès-Dieppe France
21 I8 Neuvy-St. Sépulchre France
21 J7 Neuvy sur Barangeon France
33 O8 Neuwegersleben E Germany
36 E6 Neuweier W Germany
32 H5 Neuwerk isld W Germany
36 C3 Neuwied W Germany
36 C6 Neuwiller France
32 L6 Neu-Wulmstorf W Germany
27 G11 Neva Sweden
99 R4 Neva Wisconsin
52 D5 Neva R U.S.S.R.
99 N7 Nevada Iowa
110 B4 Nevada Missouri
109 L2 Nevada Texas
92 C3 Nevada state U.S.A.
102 C2 Nevada City California
128 D2 Nevada de Cocuy,Sa mts Colombia
124 H8 Nevada de Colima Mexico
16 E7 Nevada, Sierra mts Spain
131 C5 Nevado, Cerro peak Argentina
131 B6 Nevados Chillán mt Chile
131 C5 Nevado, Sierra del ra Argentina
54 A1 Nevel' U.S.S.R.
59 M2 Nevel'sk U.S.S.R.
59 H1 Never U.S.S.R.
8 B3 Nevern Wales
26 F6 Nevernes Norway
18 H5 Nevers France
139 J4 Nevertire New S Wales
48 E7 Nevesinje Yugoslavia
45 H2 Neviano d'Arduini Italy
32 F10 Neviges W Germany
20 G2 Neville France
118 K9 Neville Sask
112 F5 Nevils Georgia
53 F11 Nevinnomyssk U.S.S.R.
79 E9 Neviot Egypt
118 D6 Nevis Alberta
99 M3 Nevis Minnesota
127 P4 Nevis isld Lesser Antilles
127 P4 Nevis Pk Nevis W I
80 E6 Nevit HaGedud Jordan
78 E2 Nevşehir Turkey
65 J2 Nevskoye U.S.S.R.
55 D2 Nev'yansk U.S.S.R.
103 J9 New R California
112 F1 New R N Carolina
94 F9 New R Virginia/W Virginia
12 E4 New Abbey Scotland
95 S3 Newagen Maine
87 G8 Newala Tanzania
94 B8 New Albany Indiana
111 G7 New Albany Mississippi
95 L5 New Albany Pennsylvania
99 P6 New Albin Iowa
99 S4 Newald Wisconsin
141 J8 New Angledool New S Wales
110 E6 Newark Arkansas
102 B4 Newark California
95 M7 Newark Delaware
9 F1 Newark England
99 S8 Newark Illinois
98 G9 Newark Nebraska
95 N6 Newark New Jersey
95 K3 Newark New York
94 E6 Newark Ohio
95 L4 Newark Valley New York
110 G3 New Athens Illinois
99 P4 New Auburn Wisconsin
111 G10 New Augusta Mississippi
94 E4 New Baltimore Michigan
94 J7 New Baltimore Pennsylvania
95 R5 New Bedford Massachusetts
146 E12 New Bedford Inlet Antarctica
100 C4 Newberg Oregon
99 Q10 New Berlin Illinois
95 M4 New Berlin New York
111 J9 Newbern Alabama
112 K2 New Bern N Carolina
110 G5 Newbern Tennessee
102 H7 Newberry California
113 E8 Newberry Florida
110 J3 Newberry Indiana
99 V3 Newberry Michigan
112 F3 Newberry S Carolina
94 H5 New Bethlehem Pennsylvania
13 G3 Newbiggin by-the-Sea England
13 E3 Newbigging Scotland
110 D3 New Bloomfield Missouri
99 R4 Newbold Wisconsin
121 O8 Newboro Ontario
8 B1 Newborough Môn Wales
99 Q8 New Boston Illinois
109 N2 New Boston Texas
109 J6 New Braunfels Texas
94 C6 New Bremen Ohio
12 E3 New Bridge Scotland
8 C3 Newbridge Wales
118 G7 New Brigden Alberta
95 P5 New Britain Connecticut
111 L10 New Brockton Alabama
95 N6 New Brunswick New Jersey
115 N8 New Brunswick prov Canada
9 H3 New Buckenham England
99 U8 New Buffalo Michigan
99 O8 Newburg Iowa
110 E4 Newburg Missouri
94 K6 Newburg Pennsylvania
94 H7 Newburg W Virginia
15 E4 Newburgh Fife Scotland
15 F3 Newburgh Grampian Scotland
110 J4 Newburgh Indiana
95 N5 Newburgh New York
121 O8 Newburgh Ontario
123 T5 New Burnt Cove Nfld
9 E5 Newbury England
95 R4 Newburyport Massachusetts
85 E6 New Bussa Nigeria
137 N6 New Caledonia isld Pacific Oc
95 O5 New Canaan Connecticut
99 P10 New Canton Illinois
94 C7 New Carlisle Ohio
122 G5 New Carlisle Quebec
102 C3 Newcastle California
106 C2 New Castle Colorado
94 B7 New Castle Indiana
14 E3 Newcastle Irish Rep
127 L2 Newcastle Jamaica
110 L3 New Castle Kentucky
98 K7 Newcastle Nebraska
127 P4 Newcastle Nevis W I
122 G6 Newcastle New Brunswick
95 M7 New Castle New Jersey
139 K5 Newcastle New S Wales
14 F2 Newcastle N Ireland
107 N6 Newcastle Oklahoma
121 M9 Newcastle Ontario
94 G6 New Castle Pennsylvania
89 F6 Newcastle S Africa
109 J2 Newcastle Texas
103 L4 Newcastle Utah
94 G9 New Castle Virginia
98 B6 Newcastle Wyoming
141 G1 Newcastle B Queensland
122 F7 Newcastle Br New Brunswick
8 B3 Newcastle Emlyn Wales
118 E7 Newcastle Mine Alberta
141 G4 Newcastle Ra Queensland
15 F5 Newcastleton Scotland
8 D1 Newcastle Under Lyme England
13 G4 Newcastle-upon-Tyne England
140 C3 Newcastle Waters N Terr Aust
14 B4 Newcastle West Irish Rep
9 F5 New Chapel England
106 B5 Newcomb New Mexico
94 F6 Newcomerstown Ohio
94 F7 New Concord Ohio
12 D3 New Cumnock Scotland
12 D3 New Dailly Scotland
101 O6 Newdale Idaho
119 R8 Newdale Manitoba
118 E9 New Dayton Alberta
15 F3 New Deer Scotland
143 C10 Newdegate W Australia
76 New Delhi India
117 P11 New Denver Br Col
111 M7 New Echota Nat.Mon Georgia
111 D8 New Edinburg Arkansas
113 E7 Newell Georgia
99 L7 Newell Iowa
112 G2 Newell N Carolina
98 C5 Newell S Dakota
112 F4 New Ellenton S Carolina
118 E8 Newell L Alberta
143 F6 Newell,L W Australia
111 E9 Newellton Louisiana
98 D3 New England N Dakota
139 K4 New England Ra mts New S Wales
90 D4 New England Seamount Chain Atlantic Oc
116 F7 Newenham,C Alaska
8 D4 Newent England
94 A3 New Era Michigan
80 F3 Newe Ur Israel
80 C3 Newe Yam Israel
94 J3 Newfane New York
95 P3 Newfane Vermont
141 K1 New Farm dist Brisbane, Qnsld
95 R3 Newfield Maine
95 M7 Newfield New Jersey
117 P8 New Fish Creek Alberta
110 E3 New Florence Missouri
98 K1 Newfolden Minnesota
9 E6 New Forest England
95 Q3 Newfound L New Hampshire
95 M5 Newfoundland Pennsylvania
123 P1 Newfoundland prov Canada
90 F5 Newfoundland Basin Atlantic Oc
90 E4 Newfoundland Rise Atlantic Oc
110 D2 New Franklin Missouri
95 L7 New Freedom Pennsylvania
8 A4 Newgale Wales
12 D3 New Galloway Scotland
118 B9 Newgate Br Col
137 M3 New Georgia isld Solomon Is
122 H9 New Germany Nova Scotia
99 R7 New Glarus Wisconsin
122 K8 New Glasgow Nova Scotia
95 R3 New Gloucester Maine
127 O3 New Grant Trinidad
136 J3 New Guinea isld S E Asia
109 M6 Newgulf Texas
100 D1 Newhalem Washington
116 K7 Newhalen Alaska
102 F7 Newhall California
116 F5 New Hamilton Alaska
95 Q4 New Hampshire state U.S.A.
99 O6 New Hampton Iowa
99 M9 New Hampton Missouri
95 S3 New Harbor Maine
110 J3 New Harmony Indiana
95 O5 New Hartford Connecticut
95 P5 New Haven Connecticut
9 G6 Newhaven England
94 B5 New Haven Indiana
110 E3 New Haven Missouri
94 F8 New Haven W Virginia
98 B5 New Haven Wyoming
117 K8 New Hazelton Br Col
137 O5 New Hebrides islds Pacific Oc
13 F6 New Hey England
13 H6 New Holland England
99 R9 New Holland Illinois
99 S6 New Holstein Wisconsin
109 O1 Newhope Arkansas
12 E2 Newhouse Scotland
111 E12 New Iberia Louisiana
9 H5 Newington England
112 F5 Newington Georgia
137 L2 New Ireland isld Bismarck Arch
95 N7 New Jersey state U.S.A.
94 H6 New Kensington Pennsylvania
95 L9 New Kent Virginia
106 F6 Newkirk New Mexico
107 N5 Newkirk Oklahoma
143 E8 Newland Ra W Australia
98 E3 New Leipzig N Dakota
94 E7 New Lexington Ohio
99 Q6 New Lisbon Wisconsin
121 L5 New Liskeard Ontario
99 P9 New London Iowa
99 M4 New London Minnesota
99 P10 New London Missouri
94 E5 New London Ohio
99 S5 New London Wisconsin
12 D4 New Luce Scotland
110 G5 New Madrid Missouri
12 E2 Newmains Scotland
102 C4 Newman California
99 T10 Newman Illinois
106 D9 Newman New Mexico
145 E4 Newman New Zealand
143 C6 Newman W Australia
98 J8 Newman Gr Nebraska
142 C6 Newman,Mt W Australia
123 T5 Newman's Cove Nfld
9 G3 Newmarket England
99 M9 New Market Iowa
14 B4 Newmarket Irish Rep
127 J2 Newmarket Jamaica
95 Q3 Newmarket New Hampshire
139 G5 Newmarket New S Wales
121 L8 Newmarket Ontario
94 J8 New Market Virginia
141 K1 Newmarket dist Brisbane, Qnsld
94 E7 New Marshfield Ohio
94 G7 New Martinsville W Virginia
94 F7 New Matamoras Ohio
100 J5 New Meadows Idaho
106 D6 New Mexico state U.S.A.
94 C7 New Miami Ohio
95 O5 New Milford Connecticut
95 M5 New Milford Pennsylvania
12 D2 Newmilns Scotland
108 E2 New Moore Texas
111 M8 Newnan Georgia
113 E8 Newnan L Florida
139 K5 Newnes New S Wales
8 D4 Newnham England
143 B9 New Norcia W Australia
139 H8 New Norfolk Tasmania
118 E6 New Norway Alberta
111 F11 New Orleans Louisiana
119 O6 New Osgoode Sask
95 K7 New Oxford Pennsylvania
95 N5 New Paltz New York
94 C7 New Paris Ohio
94 A8 New Pekin Indiana
94 F6 New Philadelphia Ohio
100 E7 New Pine Creek Oregon
15 F3 New Pitsligo Scotland
100 J6 New Plymouth Idaho
145 E3 New Plymouth New Zealand
110 E6 Newport Arkansas
126 B2 New Port Curaçao
8 B3 Newport Dyfed Wales
9 G4 Newport Essex England
8 D4 Newport Gwent Wales
99 T10 Newport Indiana
9 E6 Newport I of Wight England
14 B3 Newport Irish Rep
127 K3 Newport Jamaica
110 M2 Newport Kentucky
94 D5 Newport Michigan
99 O5 Newport Minnesota
112 L3 Newport N Carolina
98 G7 Newport Nebraska
95 P3 Newport New Hampshire
95 M7 Newport New Jersey
100 A5 Newport Oregon
95 K6 Newport Pennsylvania
122 H5 Newport Quebec
95 Q5 Newport Rhode I
8 D2 Newport Salop England
112 D2 Newport Tennessee
109 J2 Newport Texas
95 P2 Newport Vermont
100 H1 Newport Washington
102 G8 Newport Beach California
95 L10 Newport News Virginia
13 F1 Newport-on-Tay Scotland
9 F3 Newport Pagnell England
113 E9 New Port Richey Florida
112 D1 New Powell Tennessee
99 N5 New Prague Minnesota
113 L9 New Providence isld Bahamas
8 A7 Newquay England
8 B3 New Quay Wales
113 E8 New R Florida
8 C3 New Radnor Wales
106 G1 New Raymer Colorado
99 N6 New Richland Minnesota
94 C8 New Richmond Ohio
122 G5 New Richmond Quebec
99 O4 New Richmond Wisconsin
110 M5 New River Tennessee
112 K3 New River Inlet N Carolina
111 E11 New Roads Louisiana
98 G2 New Rockford N Dakota
9 G6 New Romney England
110 K2 New Ross Indiana
14 E4 New Ross Irish Rep
95 R2 Newry Maine
14 E2 Newry N Ireland
140 A3 Newry N Terr Aust
94 J6 Newry Pennsylvania
14 E2 Newry Canal N Ireland
98 E3 New Salem N Dakota
94 H7 New Salem Pennsylvania
13 E1 New Scone Scotland
99 O8 New Sharon Iowa
New Siberian Is see Novosibirskiye Os
113 G8 New Smyrna Beach Florida
139 New South Wales state Australia
141 J5 Newstead Queensland
94 E7 New Straitsville Ohio
85 D7 New Tamale Ghana
94 D10 New Tazewell Tennessee
116 E6 Newtok Alaska
111 L10 Newton Alabama
9 G2 Newton England
110 H3 Newton Illinois
99 N8 Newton Iowa
107 N3 Newton Kansas
95 Q4 Newton Massachusetts
111 G9 Newton Mississippi
112 F2 Newton N Carolina
13 E3 Newton Scotland
109 O5 Newton Texas
8 C6 Newton Abbot England
13 E4 Newton Arlosh England
95 M2 Newton Falls New York
94 G5 Newton Falls Ohio
8 B7 Newton Ferrers England
112 J2 Newton Grove N Carolina
94 K6 Newton Hamilton Pennsylvania
13 F6 Newton-le-Willows England
12 D2 Newton Mearns Scotland
15 D3 Newtonmore Scotland
101 O8 Newton Res Utah
12 D4 Newton Stewart Scotland

110 C1 Newtown Missouri
123 T4 Newtown Nfld
95 K9 Newtown Virginia
8 C3 Newtown Wales
14 E2 Newtownabbey N Ireland
14 F2 Newtownards N Ireland
14 D2 Newtown Butler N Ireland
14 E2 Newtownhamilton N Ireland
14 E3 Newtown Mt.Kennedy Irish Rep
98 D2 New Town Sanish N Dakota
14 D2 Newtown Stewart N Ireland
99 M5 New Ulm Minnesota
109 L6 New Ulm Texas
98 D5 New Underwood S Dakota
111 L10 Newville Alabama
102 B2 Newville California
94 K6 Newville Pennsylvania
99 N8 New Virginia Iowa
94 E6 New Washington Ohio
123 M7 New Waterford C Breton I, N S
109 M5 New Waverly Texas
117 J11 New Westminster Br Col
95 K7 New Windsor Maryland
123 S4 New World I Nfld
100 F8 New Year L Nevada
96 New York conurbation
95 K4 New York state U.S.A.
103 J6 New York Mts California
144 New Zealand state S W Pacific
21 H10 Nexon France
94 C5 Ney Ohio
52 F5 Neya U.S.S.R.
8 B4 Neyland Wales
77 D5 Neyrīz Iran
77 F1 Neyshābūr Iran
55 D2 Neyvo Shaytanskiy U.S.S.R.
31 H6 Nežárka R Czechoslovakia
54 C5 Nezhin U.S.S.R.
100 J3 Nezperce Idaho
61 N7 Nezugaseki Japan
86 C6 N'Gabé Congo
68 D5 Nga Chong,Khao mt Burma/Thailand
68 H5 Ngac Linh mt Vietnam
68 A2 Ngahan Burma
144 C5 Ngahere New Zealand
145 F3 Ngamatea Swamp New Zealand
66 F5 Ngamda China
87 D10 Ngami, L Botswana
70 N9 Ngandjuk Java
66 C5 Ngangla Ringco L China
Nganglaring Tso see Ngangla Ringco
66 C5 Nganglong Kangri China
74 J2 Nganglong Kangri mt ra China
75 M3 Ngangzê Co L China
68 G3 Ngan Pha R Vietnam
68 G3 Ngan Sau R Vietnam
68 G1 Ngan Son Vietnam
86 C6 N'Gao Congo
86 B4 Ngaoundére Cameroon
144 C6 Ngapara New Zealand
68 B2 Ngape Burma
145 F3 Ngapuketurua mt New Zealand
144 C6 Ngapuna New Zealand
145 E3 Ngaroma New Zealand
145 E2 Ngaruawahia New Zealand
145 F3 Ngaruroro R New Zealand
145 D1 Ngataki New Zealand
145 F3 Ngatapo New Zealand
145 E2 Ngatea New Zealand
68 B4 Ngathainggyaung Burma
145 E3 Ngatira New Zealand
145 E3 Ngauruhoe vol New Zealand
68 D7 Ngawan Chaung R Burma
145 F2 Ngawaro New Zealand
70 N9 Ngawi Java
68 B4 Ngayok B Burma
Ngemda see Ngamda
89 G2 Ngezi R Zimbabwe
89 G2 Ngezi Dam Zimbabwe
Nghia Hung see Phu Qui
70 O9 Ngimbang Java
88 F6 Ngindo Tanzania
87 C9 N'Giva Angola
86 C5 Ngoko R Congo
87 E9 Ngoma Zambia
88 F2 Ngong Kenya
145 F3 Ngongotaha New Zealand
88 D7 Ngoni Malawi
66 F5 Ngoring Hu L China
88 E3 Ngorongoro Crater Tanzania
71 A2 Ngotakiaha Halmahera Indonesia
86 B6 N'Gounie R Gabon
86 B2 N'Gourti Niger
88 B3 Ngozi Burundi
86 B3 N'Guigmi Niger
68 F3 Ngum R Laos
71 K10 Ngundju,Tg C Sumba Indonesia
145 E1 Ngunguru New Zealand
88 E7 Nguni Tanzania
70 O10 Ngunut Java
85 G6 Nguru Nigeria
67 B5 Nguyen Binh Vietnam
89 D5 Ngwaketse dist Botswana
87 G10 Nhachengue Mozambique
128 G6 Nhambiquara Brazil
129 G4 Nhamunda Brazil
67 A6 Nhan Nghia Vietnam
68 J6 Nha Trang Vietnam
130 C6 Nhecolândia Brazil
68 F3 Nhiep R Laos
138 F6 Nhill Victoria
68 G4 Nhommarath Laos
140 D1 Nhulunbuy N Terr Aust
68 G3 Nhu Xuan Vietnam
98 H1 Niagara N Dakota
144 B7 Niagara New Zealand
99 S4 Niagara Wisconsin
94 J3 Niagara Falls New York
121 L9 Niagara Falls Ontario
121 L9 Niagara-on-the-Lake Ontario
70 C3 Niah Sarawak
85 C7 Niakaramandougou Ivory Coast
85 E6 Niamey Niger
86 E5 Niangara Zaïre
85 D5 Niangaye,L Mali
85 C7 Niangbo,Pic de mt Ivory Coast
85 D6 Niangoloko Upper Volta
110 D4 Niangua R Missouri
Niangxi see Xinshao
86 E5 Nia Nia Zaïre
95 P5 Niantic Connecticut
65 E1 Nianzishan China
70 E4 Niapa, G mt Kalimantan
101 L2 Niarada Montana
86 B6 Niari R Congo
69 C12 Nias isld Indonesia
88 F8 Niassa Mozambique
46 F8 Niata Greece
101 R4 Nibbe Montana
28 D3 Nibe Denmark
28 D2 Nibe Bredning B Denmark
142 E5 Nibil Well W Australia
121 R3 Nicabau Quebec
125 L3 Nicaragua rep Cent America
95 T1 Nicatous L
102 B2 Nice California
44 B4 Nice France
111 K11 Niceville Florida
115 M7 Nichicun, L Quebec
60 E11 Nichihara Japan
112 E6 Nicholls Georgia
99 P8 Nichols Iowa
95 L4 Nichols New York
142 G4 Nicholson W Australia
140 E4 Nicholson R Queensland
143 B7 Nicholson Ra W Australia
95 N2 Nicholville New York
99 O1 Nickel L Ontario
129 G2 Nickerie R Suriname
107 M3 Nickerson Kansas
142 B5 Nickol B W Australia
122 F3 Nicman Quebec
69 A8 Nicobar Is Bay of Bengal
117 N10 Nicola Br Col
121 S6 Nicolet Quebec
99 M5 Nicollet Minnesota
78 D4 Nicosia Cyprus
43 F11 Nicosia Sicily
43 G10 Nicotera Italy
125 M4 Nicoya Costa Rica
125 M5 Nicoya,Pen.de Costa Rica
122 E6 Nictau New Brunswick
31 M5 Nida R Poland
123 Q6 Nid á L'Aigle,C.du Miquelon I Atlantic Oc
40 F3 Nidau Switzerland
36 G3 Nidda W Germany
36 F3 Nidda R W Germany
36 F3 Niddatal W Germany
36 B2 Nideggen W Germany
27 C13 Nidelv R Norway
41 H4 Nidwalden canton Switzerland
31 M2 Nidzica Poland
30 D1 Niebüll W Germany
36 G1 Niedenstein W Germany
37 N6 Niederaichbach W Germany
37 L6 Niederarnbach W Germany
36 H2 Nieder Aula W Germany
37 N6 Niederbayern dist W Germany
36 C3 Niederbieber Germany
19 L4 Niederbronn France
33 O6 Nieder Elde R E Germany
36 G2 Nieder Gemünden W Germany
33 R9 Niedergörsdorf E Germany
25 F6 Niederkrüchten W Germany
36 D3 Nieder Lahnstein W Germany
32 J10 Nieder Marsberg W Germany
33 M6 Nieder Marschacht W Germany
36 H5 Niedernhall W Germany
36 E3 Niedernhausen W Germany
36 E4 Nieder Olm W Germany
36 E3 Nieder Ouembach W Germany
32 J7 Niedersachsen land W Germany
36 D2 Nieder Schelden W Germany
36 E3 Niederselters W Germany
32 J10 Niedersfeld W Germany
36 H5 Niederstetten W Germany
37 J6 Niederstotzingen W Germany
36 D4 Niederwald W Germany
36 E2 Nieder Weidbach W Germany
36 F2 Nieder Weimar W Germany
37 P2 Niederwiesa E Germany
36 F3 Nieder Wöllstadt W Germany
36 C3 Nieder Zissen W Germany
33 T8 Nieder Zittau E Germany
32 K9 Nieheim W Germany
98 K2 Nielsville Minnesota
88 B4 Niemba Zaïre
88 B5 Niemba R Zaïre
33 Q9 Niemberg E Germany
31 K5 Niemcza Poland
33 R8 Niemegk E Germany
26 N5 Niemis Sweden
31 K5 Niemodlin Poland
33 N7 Nienbergen W Germany
32 F8 Nienborg W Germany
33 P9 Nienburg E Germany
32 K7 Nienburg W Germany
33 N5 Niendorf W Germany
31 M5 Niepołomice Poland
22 D2 Nieppe France
25 F5 Niers R W Germany
36 E4 Nierstein W Germany
31 L3 Nieszawa Poland
85 C7 Niete, Mt Liberia
33 P10 Nietleben E Germany
21 H10 Nieul France
129 G2 Nieuw Amsterdam Suriname
25 B5 Nieuwe Maas Netherlands
25 C5 Nieuwendijk Netherlands
25 D4 Nieuwersluis Netherlands
25 H2 Nieuweschans Netherlands
32 F6 Nieuweschans W Germany
22 D2 Nieuwkerke Belgium
25 C4 Nieuwkoop Netherlands
129 G2 Nieuw Nickerie Suriname
25 G2 Nieuwolda Netherlands
22 D1 Nieuwpoort Belgium
25 C5 Nieuwpoort Netherlands
25 E6 Nieuwstadt Netherlands
25 C4 Nieuw-Vennep Netherlands
18 H5 Nièvre dep France
122 G6 Nigadoo New Brunswick
78 E3 Niğde Turkey
85 B6 Niger R W Africa
85 F5 Niger rep W Africa
85 F7 Nigeria rep W Africa
85 F8 Niger,Mouths of the Nigeria
144 B6 Nightcaps New Zealand
100 F1 Nighthawk Washington
141 G2 Night I Great Barrier Reef Aust
Nightingale I see Dao Bach Long Vi
90 B16 Nightingale I Atlantic Oc
116 K2 Nigu R Alaska
102 U13 Nihoa Hawaiian Is
131 C5 Nihuili, Embalse del res Argentina
61 N8 Niigata Japan
60 G12 Niihama Japan
135 N1 Niihau isld Hawaiian Is
61 N11 Nii-jima isld Japan
60 Q3 Niikappu R Japan
60 G10 Niimi Japan
60 D4 Niitomi Japan
61 N8 Niitsu Japan
17 F8 Níjar Spain
25 F2 Nijega Netherlands
60 S2 Nijibetsu Japan
79 F8 Nijil Jordan
25 D4 Nijkerk Netherlands
25 E5 Nijmegen Netherlands
25 F4 Nijverdal Netherlands
116 K6 Nikabuna Lakes Alaska
Nikaria isld see Ikaría I Greece
26 S2 Nikel U.S.S.R.
55 C5 Nikel'tau U.S.S.R.
71 M9 Nikiniki Timor Indonesia
47 F4 Nikitas Greece
52 D6 Nikitinka U.S.S.R.
54 K8 Nikitovka U.S.S.R.
85 E7 Nikki Benin
61 N9 Nikkō Japan
61 N9 Nikkō Nat. Park Japan
40 G5 Niklaus Switzerland
48 H1 Nikolaev U.S.S.R.
116 K5 Nikolai Alaska
54 D10 Nikolayev U.S.S.R.
55 E4 Nikolayevka U.S.S.R.
53 G8 Nikolayevsk U.S.S.R.
55 D4 Nikolayevskiy U.S.S.R.
59 M1 Nikolayevsk-na-Amure U.S.S.R.
52 G5 Nikol'sk U.S.S.R.
52 F5 Nikolskoye U.S.S.R.
55 C5 Nikol'skoye U.S.S.R.
88 C3 Nikonga R Tanzania
47 G1 Nikopol Bulgaria
54 F9 Nikopol U.S.S.R.
77 G6 Nīkshahr Iran
42 J6 Nikšić Yugoslavia
78 F1 Niksir Turkey
71 O8 Nila isld Indonesia
103 J8 Niland California
73 L8 Nilande Atoll Maldives
83 L9 Nilaveli Sri Lanka
86 F2 Nile prov Sudan
84 J4 Nile R N E Africa
102 B4 Niles California
107 N3 Niles Kansas
94 A5 Niles Michigan
94 G5 Niles Ohio
121 N6 Nilgaut, L Quebec
76 C5 Nilgiri Hills India
116 E6 Nilikluguk Alaska
57 K3 Nilka China
146 B4 Nilsen B Antarctica
29 N8 Nilsiä Finland
47 K4 Nilüfer R Turkey
83 K11 Nilwala R Sri Lanka
28 D5 Nim Denmark
74 F3 Nimach India
85 C7 Nimba, Mts Guinea/Liberia/Ivory Co
142 E6 Nimberra Well W Australia
139 L3 Nimbin New S Wales
18 H9 Nîmes France
74 F5 Nimka Thana India
139 J6 Nimmitabel New S Wales
101 M3 Nimrod Montana
Nimrod Bay see Xiangshan Gang
146 G7 Nimrod Gl Antarctica
110 C7 Nimrod L Arkansas
144 C6 Nimrod, Mt New Zealand
109 O1 Nimrod Res Arkansas
77 H4 Nimrūz reg Afghanistan
28 F4 Nimtofte Denmark
42 G4 Nin Yugoslavia
71 F4 Nin Bay Philippines
87 D8 Ninda Angola
139 J3 Nindigully Queensland
141 J8 Nindigully Queensland
73 L7 Nine Degree Chan Lakshadweep Indian Ocean
13 E2 Nine Mile Burn Scotland
139 G4 Nine Mile L New S Wales
103 H2 Ninemile Pk Nevada
108 D6 Nine Point Mesa mt Texas
119 S9 Ninette Manitoba
145 D1 Ninety Mile Beach New Zealand
139 J7 Ninety Mile Beach Victoria
112 E3 Ninety Six S Carolina
94 G7 Ninevah Pennsylvania
133 E6 Ninfas,Pta Argentina
9 G6 Ninfield England
143 A6 Ningaloo W Australia
59 J3 Ning'an China
67 G2 Ningbo China
65 D4 Ningcheng China
67 F3 Ningde China
67 E3 Ningdu China
67 D3 Ninggang China
67 F1 Ningguo China
67 G2 Ninghai China
Ninghan mt see Singleton,Mt
65 D5 Ninghe China
Ning-hsia see Yinchuan
67 E3 Ninghua China
58 F4 Ningjin China
65 C6 Ningjin China
66 F5 Ningjing Shan ra China
65 C7 Ningling China
67 B5 Ningming China
Ningpo see Ningpo
Ningsia aut reg see Ningxia
58 E4 Ningxia Hui Aut Reg China
58 D4 Ningxia aut reg China
67 D2 Ningxiang China
65 C7 Ningyang China
67 D4 Ningyuan China
67 B6 Ninh Binh Vietnam
68 J6 Ninh Hoa Vietnam
116 M6 Ninilchik Alaska
142 C5 Niningarra W Australia
107 N7 Ninnekah Oklahoma
107 N4 Ninnescah R Kansas
146 J4 Ninnis Gl Antarctica
111 C9 Ninock Louisiana
60 E14 Ninokata Japan
22 G2 Ninove Belgium
130 C7 Nioaque Brazil
94 H4 Niobe New York
98 J7 Niobrara Nebraska
98 E7 Niobrara R Nebraska
86 C6 Nioki Zaïre
85 B6 Niokolo-koba,Parc Nat.du Senegal
85 A6 Nioro du Rip Senegal
85 C5 Nioro du Sahel Mali
18 E6 Niort France
21 D9 Niortaise R France
21 E9 Niort St.Florent France
Nios isld see Íos I Greece
99 P9 Niota Illinois
112 C2 Niota Tennessee
85 C5 Niout Mauritania
139 K1 Nipan Queensland
76 B2 Nipani India
71 H6 Nipanipa,Tg C Sulawesi
119 N5 Nipawin Sask
119 N4 Nipawin Prov.Park Sask
120 B3 Nipigon Ontario
120 C4 Nipigon B Ontario
120 B3 Nipigon Lake Ontario
118 H3 Nipin R Sask
118 C3 Nipisi R Alberta
122 G6 Nipisquit,B New Brunswick
121 L6 Nipissing Junc Ontario
115 L8 Nipissing,L Ontario
122 F3 Nipissis L Quebec
122 F3 Nipissis R Quebec
122 G3 Nipisso L Quebec
102 D6 Nipomo California
103 J6 Nipton California
84 J5 Niqrûb el Fuqâni, Gebel mt Egypt
126 F4 Niquero Cuba
61 M10 Nirasaki Japan
80 C3 Nir 'Ezyon Israel
80 B6 Nir Gallim Israel
80 B7 Nir Ḥen Israel
74 H9 Nirmal India
75 M5 Nirmali India
80 B8 Nir Moshe Israel
94 B3 Nirvana Michigan
80 C6 Nir Zevi Israel
46 E1 Niš Yugoslavia
16 B5 Nisa Portugal
72 F6 Niṣāb S Yemen
46 F1 Nisava R Yugoslavia
95 K5 Nisbet Pennsylvania
60 O3 Niseko Japan
67 C2 Nishi China
61 P5 Nishi-Hōji Japan
60 J11 Nishinomiya Japan
60 F9 Nishino-shima isld Japan
61 L11 Nishio Japan
60 C13 Nishi-Sonogi-hantō pen Japan
60 C11 Nishi-suidō str Japan
60 H10 Nishiwaki Japan
116 H6 Nishlik L Alaska
99 L8 Nishnabotna, E R Iowa
99 L8 Nishnabotna, W R Iowa
130 J9 Nísia Floresta Brazil
48 J3 Nisipitul Romania
47 J8 Nísíros isld Greece
31 N5 Nisko Poland
98 C5 Nisland S Dakota
117 D4 Nisling R Yukon Terr
48 L3 Nisporeny U.S.S.R.
100 C3 Nisqually R Washington
27 F15 Nissan R Sweden
27 C12 Nissedal Norway
27 C12 Nisserv L Norway
28 A3 Nissum Bredning B Denmark
28 A4 Nissum Fjord inlet Denmark
117 G5 Nisutlin R Yukon Terr
115 M7 Nitchequon Quebec
130 G8 Niterói Brazil
15 E5 Nith,R Scotland
15 E5 Nithsdale* Scotland
71 M9 Nitibe Timor
80 G7 Nitil Jordan
100 A1 Nitinat L Br Col
9 E6 Niton England
48 E2 Nitra Czechoslovakia
31 L7 Nitra R Czechoslovakia
94 F8 Nitro W Virginia
55 D2 Nitsa R U.S.S.R.
29 N2 Nitsjärvi L Finland
37 N5 Nittenau W Germany
37 M5 Nittendorf W Germany
29 P11 Nityuyarvi U.S.S.R.
137 R5 Niuafo'ou isld Pacific Oc
137 S5 Niuatoputapu isld Pacific Oc
137 T5 Niue isld Pacific Oc
137 Q4 Niulakita isld Tuvalu
65 F4 Niumaowu China
Niushan see Donghai
137 Q3 Niutao isld Tuvalu
65 E4 Niuzhuang China
28 K5 Nivå Denmark
29 L8 Nivala Finland
18 E9 Nive R France
139 H2 Nive R Queensland
139 H2 Nive Downs Queensland
141 H7 Nive Downs Queensland
22 G2 Nivelles Belgium
18 H5 Nivernais prov France
118 D1 Niverville Manitoba
20 K3 Nivillers France
102 G4 Nivloc Nevada
40 B6 Nivolas-Vermelle France
52 D2 Nivskiy U.S.S.R.
74 J7 Niwas India
102 E2 Nixon Nevada
109 K6 Nixon Texas
74 H9 Nizamabad India
52 E3 Nizhmozero U.S.S.R.
56 G3 Nizhneangarsk U.S.S.R.
52 H2 Nizhne Bugayevo U.S.S.R.
54 L9 Nizhne Gnilovskoy U.S.S.R.
50 H2 Nizhneimbatskoye U.S.S.R.
52 H1 Nizhne Kamenka U.S.S.R.
55 B4 Nizhne-troitskiy U.S.S.R.
56 E4 Nizhneudinsk U.S.S.R.
50 G2 Nizhnevartovsk U.S.S.R.
55 B4 Nizhneye Il'yasovo U.S.S.R.
52 D2 Nizhneye Kuyto, Oz L U.S.S.R.
55 C3 Nizhni Irginski U.S.S.R.
Nizhniy Novgorod see Gor'kiy
55 C2 Nizhniy Tagil U.S.S.R.
52 E2 Nizhniy Vyalozerskiy U.S.S.R.
52 G4 Nizhniy Yenangsk U.S.S.R.
55 E2 Nizhnyaya Aremzyan U.S.S.R.
55 F3 Nizhnyaya Omka U.S.S.R.
52 J3 Nizhnyaya-Omra U.S.S.R.
52 G2 Nizhnyaya Pesha U.S.S.R.
56 E3 Nizhnyaya Pomya U.S.S.R.
55 D2 Nizhnyaya Salda U.S.S.R.
55 G4 Nizhnyaya Suyetka U.S.S.R.
55 E2 Nizhnyaya Tavda U.S.S.R.
52 F3 Nizhnyaya Toyma R U.S.S.R.
56 G1 Nizhnyaya Tunguska R U.S.S.R.
55 C2 Nizhnyaya Tura U.S.S.R.
52 H4 Nizhnyaya Voch' U.S.S.R.
52 F2 Nizhnyaya Zolotitsa U.S.S.R.
29 Q4 Nizh Pirengskoye Ozero L U.S.S.R.
56 G2 Nizh Tunguska R U.S.S.R.
116 Q6 Nizina Alaska
78 F3 Nizip Turkey
31 L7 Nízké Tatry mts Czechoslovakia
48 F2 Nižm Medzev Czechoslovakia
72 H4 Nizwa Oman
22 G4 Nizy-le-Comte France
44 D2 Nizza Italy
80 C4 Nizzane 'Oz Israel
80 B7 Nizzanim Israel
70 D4 Njaān mt Kalimantan
42 J6 Njegoš mt Yugoslavia
87 G7 Njinjo Tanzania
87 D9 Njoko R Zambia
88 E6 Njombe Tanzania
88 E5 Njombe R Tanzania
88 G10 Njoro isld Mozambique
26 J9 Njurundabommen Sweden
27 J10 Njutånger Sweden
88 D7 Nkanka R Zambia
88 E7 Nkhata B Malawi
88 E8 Nkhotakota Malawi
86 A6 N'komi L Gabon
86 B5 N'kongsamba Cameroon
88 D5 Nkululu R Tanzania
28 A4 No Denmark
20 K3 Noailles France
75 O7 Noakhali Bangladesh
45 M1 Noale Italy
128 C3 Noanama Colombia
95 Q5 Noank Connecticut
26 O3 Noarvas mt Norway
40 F7 Noasca Italy
116 F3 Noatak Alaska
14 E3 Nobber Irish Rep
120 K7 Nobel Ontario
60 E13 Nobeoka Japan
110 H3 Noble Illinois
107 N6 Noble Oklahoma
118 D9 Nobleford Alberta
111 E7 Noble Lake Arkansas
94 A6 Noblesville Indiana
71 L9 Nobo Flores Indonesia
60 P3 Noboribetsu Japan
130 C4 Nobres Brazil
141 G8 Noccundra Queensland
20 G5 Noce France
41 O5 Noce R Italy
45 R8 Nocera Inferiore Italy
44 H2 Noceto Italy
124 H7 Nochistlán Mexico
141 G8 Nockatunga Queensland
109 K2 Nocona Texas
48 J5 Nocrich Romania
61 P5 Noda Japan
133 D7 Nodales,B.de los Argentina
99 M9 Nodaway Iowa
99 M8 Nodaway R Iowa
98 B7 Node Wyoming
21 B6 Noé Blanche France
130 D4 Noedori R Brazil
110 B5 Noel Missouri
123 Q5 Noel Paul's Brook Nfld
120 K6 Noelville Ontario
22 D3 Noeux les Mines France
103 O10 Nogales Arizona
124 D2 Nogales Sonora Mexico
125 L8 Nogales Vera Cruz Mexico
86 A2 Nogal Valley Somalia
116 J6 Nogamut Alaska
45 K1 Nogara Italy
18 E9 Nogaro France
31 L1 Nogat R Poland
60 D12 Nōgata Japan
40 B1 Nogent en Bassigny France
20 F5 Nogent-le-Bernard France
20 J4 Nogent-le-Roi France
20 G5 Nogent le Rotrou France
20 K3 Nogent-sur-Oise France
18 H4 Nogent-sur-Seine France
54 K1 Noginsk U.S.S.R.
59 M1 Nogliki U.S.S.R.
40 C4 Nogno France
141 K7 Nogo R Queensland
141 J6 Nogoa R Queensland
61 K10 Nōgōhaku san mt Japan
131 F4 Nogoya R Argentina
48 E3 Nograd co Hungary
16 C3 Nogueira mt Portugal
17 H2 Noguera Pallarésa R Spain
17 H2 Noguera Ribagorzana R Spain
74 F4 Nohar India
61 P5 Noheji Japan
36 C4 Nohfelden W Germany
36 B3 Nohn W Germany
121 N6 Noire R Quebec
67 A6 Noire R Vietnam
86 B6 Noire,Pte Congo
18 C4 Noires, Mgnes mts France
18 D6 Noirmoutier Île de France
17 H9 Noisy les Bains Algeria
61 N11 Nojima-zaki C Japan
61 M9 Nojiri-ko L Japan
87 D9 Nokaneng Botswana
29 K10 Nokia Finland
74 B8 Nok Kundi Pakistan
144 B6 Nokomai New Zealand
110 G2 Nokomis Illinois
119 N7 Nokomis Sask
86 C5 Nola Cent Afr Republic
45 R8 Nola Italy
119 O2 Nolalu Ontario
98 J2 Nolan N Dakota
108 G3 Nolan Texas
28 E5 Nølev Denmark
44 D3 Noli Italy
112 E1 Nolichucky R Tennessee
112 E1 Nolichucky Dam Tennessee
52 G5 Nolinsk U.S.S.R.
20 H3 Nolléval France
28 O10 Nølsø isld Faeroes
69 E9 Noi,Thale L Thailand
111 L11 Noma Florida
60 D14 Noma-misaki C Japan
95 R5 No Mans Land isld Massachusetts
116 E4 Nome Alaska
98 J3 Nome N Dakota
116 E4 Nome C Alaska
19 K4 Nomeny France
121 P6 Nominingue Quebec
60 C13 Nomo-zaki C Japan
87 C10 Nomtsas Namibia
137 S6 Nomuka isld Tonga
114 J5 Nonacho L N W Terr
20 H4 Nonancourt France
20 D3 Nonant France
20 F4 Nonant-le-Pin France
45 K2 Nonantola Italy
52 H2 Nonburg U.S.S.R.
65 F2 Nong'an China
68 F3 Nong Het Laos
68 F5 Nong Hong Thailand
68 F4 Nong Khai Thailand
87 F11 Nongoma S Africa
19 N15 Nonières France
Nonni R see Nen Jiang R
138 D4 Nonning S Australia
138 D4 Nonning,Mt S Australia
36 B4 Nonnweiler W Germany
130 D10 Nonoai Brazil
124 F4 Nonoava Mexico
71 G6 Nonoc isld Philippines
137 P2 Nonouti atoll Kiribati
119 W2 Nonsuch Manitoba
68 E6 Nonthaburi Thailand
18 F7 Nontron France
116 K7 Nonvianuk L Alaska
139 H7 Noojee Victoria
143 B7 Nookawarra W Australia
138 D2 Noolyeanna,L S Australia
98 C1 Noonan N Dakota
143 C9 Noongaar W Australia
143 B8 Noongal W Australia
142 E4 Noonkanbah W Australia
139 H3 Noorama R Queensland
25 A5 Noord-Beveland Netherlands
25 D5 Noord Brabant Netherlands
25 C5 Noordeloos Netherlands
25 C3 Noord-Holland Netherlands
25 E3 Noordoost Polder Netherlands
126 A1 Noord Pt Curaçao
25 B4 Noordwijk aan zee Netherlands
7 N9 Noordwinning oil rig North Sea
25 F3 Noordwolde Netherlands
25 C4 Noordzee-Kanaal Netherlands
29 J10 Noormarkku Finland
116 G3 Noorvik Alaska
139 L2 Noosa Head Queensland
141 L7 Noosaville Queensland
117 K11 Nootka Br Col
117 K11 Nootka I Br Col
103 H5 Nopah Ra California
99 T4 Noquebay,L Wisconsin
98 J9 Nora Nebraska
119 O6 Nora Sask
27 H12 Nora Sweden
27 J11 Nora Sweden
59 J1 Nora R U.S.S.R.
28 D3 Nørager Denmark
86 G2 Nora I Ethiopia
71 G7 Norala Mindanao Philippines
121 L4 Noranda Quebec
140 F5 Noranside Queensland
99 O6 Nora Springs Iowa
98 G4 Norbeck S Dakota
27 H11 Norberg Sweden
110 C2 Norborne Missouri
107 K2 Norcatur Kansas
42 E6 Norcia Italy
143 D9 Norcott,Mt W Australia
111 M8 Norcross Georgia
27 D12 Nordaguta Norway
26 K7 Nordanås Sweden
27 D11 Nord-Aurdal Norway
50 B1 Nordaustlandet isld Spitzbergen
28 D6 Nordborg Denmark
28 A6 Nordby Denmark
26 B9 Norddal Norway
28 O9 Norddeble Faeroes
32 F5 Norddeich W Germany
28 A7 Norddorf W Germany
32 L7 Norddrebber W Germany
118 B6 Nordegg R Alberta
9 G2 Nordelph England
32 F5 Norden W Germany
37 K6 Nordendorf W Germany
32 H5 Nordenham W Germany
51 J1 Nordenshel'da Arkhipelag U.S.S.R.
117 E5 Nordenskiold R Yukon Terr
28 A7 Norder Aue chan W Germany
32 J5 Nordergründe sandbank W Germany
32 F5 Norderney W Germany
32 F5 Norderney isld W Germany
26 A10 Nordfjord inlet Norway
26 A10 Nordfjord reg Norway
26 B10 Nordfjordeid Norway
26 H4 Nordfold Norway
28 B7 Nordfriesand reg W Germany
30 D1 Nord-friesische Inseln islds W Germany
37 M3 Nordhalben W Germany
33 N10 Nordhausen E Germany
109 K7 Nordheim Texas
32 J5 Nordholz W Germany
27 A11 Nordhordland reg Norway
32 F8 Nordhorn W Germany
26 K9 Nordingrå Sweden
80 C4 Nordiyya Israel
28 C3 Nordjylland co Denmark
26 P1 Nordkapp C Norway
26 Q1 Nordkinn Norway
26 L2 Nordkjosbotn Norway
26 F6 Nordland Fylker Norway
26 G7 Nordli Norway
37 K6 Nördlingen W Germany
26 K8 Nordmaling Sweden
100 J1 Nordman Idaho
27 G12 Nordmark Sweden
27 D11 Nordmarka reg Norway
26 B9 Nordmöre reg Norway
98 F7 Nordon Nebraska
28 O9 Nordöre Faeroes
32 K4 Nord-Ostsee Kanal W Germany
28 F2 Nordre Rønner isld Denmark
115 O4 Nordre Strömfjord inlet Greenland
32 E9 Nordrhein Westfalen land W Germany
28 C7 Nord Schleswig W Germany
28 B6 Nord Slesvig reg Denmark
32 L8 Nord-Stemmen W Germany
30 D1 Nordstrand isld W Germany
26 E7 Nord-Tröndelag Fylker Norway
51 L1 Nordvik U.S.S.R.
32 F8 Nordwalde W Germany
27 C11 Nore Norway
14 D4 Nore R Irish Rep
27 D11 Norefjell mt Norway
122 E1 Nore,L Quebec
120 K4 Norembego Ontario
17 K2 Norfeo,C Spain
110 D5 Norfolk Arkansas
95 O5 Norfolk Connecticut
98 J7 Norfolk Nebraska
95 L10 Norfolk Virginia
9 H2 Norfolk co England
137 O7 Norfolk I Pacific Oc
110 D5 Norfolk L Arkansas
25 F2 Norg Netherlands
13 F2 Norham England
109 K9 Norias Texas
61 L9 Norikura-dake mt Japan
51 H2 Noril'sk U.S.S.R.
141 G8 Norley Queensland
112 J1 Norlina N Carolina
45 N6 Norma Italy
111 C7 Norman Arkansas
98 H9 Norman Nebraska
107 N6 Norman Oklahoma
141 F4 Norman R Queensland
13 H5 Normanby England
145 E3 Normanby New Zealand
141 G2 Normanby R Queensland
141 K5 Normanby Ra Queensland
20 F4 Normandie reg France
121 S4 Normandin Quebec
110 K6 Normandy Tennessee
109 L4 Normangee Texas
143 E7 Norman Hurst,Mt W Australia
112 F2 Norman, L N Carolina
109 K7 Normanna Texas
141 K2 Norman Park dist Brisbane, Qnsld
141 F4 Normanton Queensland
114 G4 Norman Wells N W Terr
121 L4 Normetal Quebec
143 B10 Nornalup W Australia
124 F4 Norogachic Mexico
111 D8 Norphlet Arkansas
119 Q7 Norquay Sask
133 C5 Norquin Argentina
133 C6 Norquinco Argentina
29 J8 Norra Kvarken chan Finland/Sweden
27 J10 Norrala Sweden
27 G15 Norraryd Sweden
26 J4 Norrbotten reg Sweden
28 D4 Nørreå R Denmark
28 C5 Nørre Bramdrup Denmark
28 A5 Nørre Nebel Denmark
22 C2 Norrent-Fontès France
28 D2 Nørre Saltum Denmark
28 D2 Nørresundby Denmark
26 M6 Norrfjärden Sweden
26 K8 Norrfors Sweden
26 J9 Norrhassel Sweden
95 S2 Norridgewock Maine
99 Q9 Norris Illinois
101 O4 Norris Montana
98 E6 Norris S Dakota
112 C1 Norris Tennessee
101 P5 Norris Wyoming
123 R4 Norris Arm Nfld
110 H4 Norris City Illinois
112 C1 Norris Dam Tennessee
112 D1 Norris Lake Tennessee
123 P4 Norris Point Newfoundland
95 M6 Norristown Pennsylvania
27 H13 Norrköping Sweden
29 H8 Norrskär lt ho Finland
27 J11 Norrsundet Sweden
27 K12 Norrtälje Sweden
26 H6 Norrvik Sweden
28 B2 Nors Denmark
27 F12 Norsä R Sweden
143 D9 Norseman W Australia
145 F4 Norsewood New Zealand
27 H13 Norsholm Sweden
26 K7 Norsjö Sweden
27 D12 Norsjö L Norway
26 Q1 Norskholmen Norway
21 B7 Nort France
129 H3 Norte,C Brazil
128 D2 Norte de Santander div Colombia
32 L9 Nörten Hardenburg W Germany
133 E6 Norte,Pta Argentina
131 D3 Norte,Sa de ra Argentina
128 G6 Norte,Serra do mts Brazil
112 F4 North S Carolina
111 J8 North R Alabama
94 C5 North Adams Michigan
13 G5 Northallerton England
143 B9 Northam W Australia
98 F1 North America, Center of N Dakota
90 C6 North American Basin Atlantic Oc
9 F3 Northampton England
95 P4 Northampton Massachusetts
143 A8 Northampton W Australia
141 H6 Northampton Downs Queensland
9 F3 Northamptonshire co England
68 A6 North Andaman isld Andaman Is
94 K8 North Anna R Virginia
95 S2 North Anson Maine
Northants co see Northamptonshire co
117 Q4 North Arm inlet N W Terr
112 E4 North Augusta Georgia
115 N6 North Aulatsivik I Labrador
94 D5 North Baltimore Ohio
118 J6 North Battleford Sask
123 O6 North Bay Nfld
121 L6 North Bay Ontario
98 K8 North Bend Nebraska
100 A6 North Bend Oregon
13 F1 North Berwick Scotland
99 L9 Northboro Iowa
139 H4 North Bourke New S Wales
94 D3 North Branch Michigan
99 O4 North Branch Minnesota
118 H2 North Branch Ontario
121 N8 North Brook Ontario
13 H5 North Burton England
123 M6 North,C C Breton I, N Scotia
108 B7 North Canadian R Oklahoma etc
145 D1 North Cape New Zealand
137 P8 North Cape Rise sea feature Pacific Oc
115 L7 North Caribou L Ontario
112 E2 North Carolina state U.S.A.
100 D1 North Cascades Nat. Park Washington
113 H12 North Cat Cay isld Bahamas
14 F1 North Chan N Ireland/Scotland
120 G6 North Channel Ontario
112 H5 North Charleston S Carolina
13 G2 North Charlton England
99 T7 North Chicago Illinois
143 B10 Northcliffe W Australia
108 F4 North Concho R Texas
100 A3 North Cove Washington
95 N3 North Creek New York
98 F2 North Dakota state U.S.A.
122 F8 North Devon New Brunswick
9 F5 North Downs England
94 H4 North East Pennsylvania
95 R8 North East Carry Maine
141 L5 North-East Cay isld Gt Barrier Reef Aust
90 G3 North Eastern Atlantic Basin Atlantic Oc
122 A3 Northeast Mistassibi R Quebec
126 F2 Northeast Providence Chan Bahamas
123 R1 Northeast Pt Belle Isle, Nfld
83 M9 North East Pt C Christmas I Indian Oc
32 L9 Northeim W Germany
99 O8 North English Iowa
123 T5 Northern Bight Nfld
86 E2 Northern Darfur prov Sudan
113 L12 Northern Eleuthera dist Bahamas
122 F9 Northern Hd New Brunswick
119 U1 Northern Indian L Manitoba
12 A4 Northern Ireland U.K.
86 E2 Northern Kordofan prov Sudan
99 Q1 Northern Light L Ontario
83 M9 Northern Plateau Christmas I Indian Oc
127 O2 Northern Range Trinidad
Northern Sporades islds see Voríai Sporádhes Is
138 B1 Northern Territory Australia
139 H8 North Esk R Tasmania
9 E3 Northfield England
95 P4 Northfield Massachusetts
99 N5 Northfield Minnesota
95 P2 Northfield Vermont
144 A6 North Fiord New Zealand
99 S6 North Fond du Lac Wisconsin
9 H5 North Foreland head England
102 E4 North Fork California
101 M4 North Fork Idaho
100 K8 North Fork Nevada
94 B1 North Fox I Michigan
99 R6 North Freedom Wisconsin
120 J2 North French R Ontario
13 H6 North Frodingham England
13 G3 Northgate England
119 P9 Northgate Sask
141 K1 Northgate dist Brisbane, Qnsld
North Girard see Lake City
95 P5 North Haven Connecticut
144 D5 North Hd. New Zealand
122 F9 North Head New Brunswick
123 O4 North Head Nfld
141 H2 North Horn C Gt Barrier Reef Aust
86 G5 North Horr Kenya
112 H4 North I S Carolina
83 J12 North I Seychelles
9 G6 Northiam England
145 E3 North Island New Zealand
71 E6 North Islet Philippines
103 O6 North Jadito Canyon R Arizona
83 M8 North Keeling I Cocos Is Indian Oc
115 L2 North Kent I N W Terr
94 G5 North Kingsville Ohio
119 V1 North Knife L Manitoba
59 J3 North Korea People's Rep E Asia
North Land see Severnaya Zemlya
99 T3 Northland Michigan
145 D1 Northland stat area New Zealand
9 E4 Northleach England
99 U8 North Liberty Indiana
110 D7 North Little Rock Arkansas
98 H8 North Loup Nebraska
98 H8 North Loup R Nebraska
88 D7 North Luangwa Nat. Park Zambia
70 C2 North Luconia Shoals S China Sea
106 C2 North Mam Pk Colorado
94 B5 North Manchester Indiana
99 U4 North Manitou I Michigan
88 C10 North Mashonaland Zimbabwe
113 G12 North Miami Florida
15 B2 North Minch Scotland
142 E4 North, Mt W Australia
94 A3 North Muskegon Michigan
117 L4 North Nahanni R N W Terr
113 G11 North New River Can Florida
99 M2 Northome Minnesota
8 C1 Northop Wales
102 F4 North Palisade peak California
98 F8 North Platte Nebraska
98 D8 North Platte R Nebraska
101 T8 North Platte R Wyoming
111 J8 Northport Alabama
99 V4 Northport Michigan
98 C8 Northport Nebraska
122 J8 Northport Nova Scotia
100 H1 Northport Washington
100 H4 North Powder Oregon
99 S7 North Prairie Wisconsin
139 J7 North Pt Flinders I, Tasmania
83 J12 North Pt Mahé I Indian Oc
94 D1 North Pt Michigan
122 H6 North Pt Pr Edward I
100 B3 North R Washington
68 A6 North Reef I Andaman Is
109 M9 North Richland Hills Texas
123 M7 North River Bridge C Breton I, N Scotia
15 C1 North Rona Scotland
15 F1 North Ronaldsay Orkney Scotland
15 F1 North Ronaldsay Firth Orkney Scotland
122 J7 North Rustico Pr Edward I
102 C2 North San Juan California
100 C5 North Santiam R Oregon
118 B6 North Sask R Alberta
90 J3 North Sea W Europe
68 A7 North Sentinel I Andaman Is
13 G3 North Shields England
102 G2 North Shoshone Pk Nevada
99 O8 North Skunk R Iowa
116 M1 North Slope Alaska
117 P7 North Star Alberta
110 M1 North Star Ohio
141 L8 North Stradbroke I Queensland
109 M2 North Sulphur R Texas
123 M7 North Sydney C Breton I, N Scotia
8 C6 North Tawton England
144 A7 North Trap islds New Zealand
71 E7 North Ubian isld Philippines
15 A3 North Uist isld Scotland

13 F3 **Northumberland** *co* England
141 J5 **Northumberland** *islds* Queensland
138 F7 **Northumberland,C** S Australia
115 N8 **Northumberland Str** Nova Scotia
117 G10 **North Vancouver** Br Col
71 D5 **North Verde** Philippines
117 P6 **North Vermilion** Alberta
94 B7 **North Vernon** Indiana
95 N3 **Northville** New York
98 H4 **Northville** S Dakota
9 H2 **North Walsham** England
116 R5 **Northway Junc** Alaska
116 B5 **Northwest C.** St Lawrence I, Alaska
113 K11 **Northwest Cay** *isld* Bahamas
74 D2 **North West Frontier Prov** Pakistan
126 E1 **Northwest Providence Chan** Bahamas
83 M9 **North-West Pt** *C* Christmas I Indian Oc
115 N7 **North West River** Labrador
123 N2 **Northwest St.Augustin R** Quebec
114 H4 **North West Territories** *prov* Canada
8 D1 **Northwich** England
112 F1 **North Wilkesboro** N Carolina
99 N6 **Northwood** Iowa
98 J2 **Northwood** N Dakota
72 E5 **North Yemen** *rep* Arabia
13 G5 **North Yorkshire** *co* England
109 L5 **North Zulch** Texas
32 G6 **Nortmoor** W Germany
122 G8 **Norton** New Brunswick
94 E10 **Norton** Virginia
89 G1 **Norton** Zimbabwe
116 G4 **Norton B** Alaska
87 B8 **Norton de Matos** Angola
142 C5 **Norton Plains** W Australia
116 E5 **Norton Sound** Alaska
107 P2 **Nortonville** Kansas
98 H3 **Nortonville** N Dakota
32 L4 **Nortorf** W Germany
32 G7 **Nortrup** W Germany
28 E5 **Norup** Denmark
116 K3 **Norutak L** Alaska
36 B2 **Nörvenich** W Germany
102 F8 **Norwalk** California
95 O5 **Norwalk** Connecticut
99 N8 **Norwalk** Iowa
99 U5 **Norwalk** Michigan
94 E5 **Norwalk** Ohio
99 Q6 **Norwalk** Wisconsin
99 P8 **Norway** Iowa
95 R2 **Norway** Maine
99 T4 **Norway** Michigan
112 F4 **Norway** S Carolina
68 H2 **Norway** *isld* Vietnam
26 **Norway** *kingdom* W Europe
119 U5 **Norway House** Manitoba
115 K2 **Norwegian B** N W Terr
147 E13 **Norwegian Basin** Arctic Oc
147 F12 **Norwegian Sea** Arctic Oc
95 P5 **Norwich** Connecticut
9 H2 **Norwich** England
107 N4 **Norwich** Kansas
95 M4 **Norwich** New York
120 K10 **Norwich** Ontario
141 J6 **Norwich Park** Queensland
15 G1 **Norwick** Scotland
95 Q4 **Norwood** Massachusetts
112 G2 **Norwood** N Carolina
95 N2 **Norwood** New York
121 N8 **Norwood** Ontario
71 E3 **Norzagaray** Luzon Philippines
60 T2 **Nosappu-misaki** *C* Japan
36 G2 **Nösberts** W Germany
61 N5 **Noshiro** Japan
52 G4 **Noshul'** U.S.S.R.
55 E2 **Noska** *R* U.S.S.R.
52 E3 **Nosovshchina** U.S.S.R.
77 F5 **Nosratābād** Iran
130 H11 **Nossa Senhora das Dores** Brazil
130 C4 **Nossa Senhora do Livramento** Brazil
27 F13 **Nossebro** Sweden
22 H2 **Nossegem** Belgium
37 P1 **Nossen** E Germany
33 Q5 **Nossentin** E Germany
87 H10 **Nossi-Bé** *isld* Madagascar
89 B5 **Nossop** *R* Botswana
87 G11 **Nosy Barren** Madagascar
87 H10 **Nosy Lava** Madagascar
87 H10 **Nosy Mitsio** *isld* Madagascar
87 H10 **Nosy Radamà** Madagascar
87 H11 **Nosy Radamà** Madagascar
87 H12 **Nosy Varika** Madagascar
111 L9 **Notasulga** Alabama
103 L2 **Notch Pk** Utah
141 J5 **Notch Pt** Queensland
31 K2 **Noteć** *R* Poland
80 F1 **Notera** Israel
21 I9 **Noth** France
100 B5 **Noti** Oregon
46 E3 **Notia** Greece
114 H6 **Notikewin** Alberta
117 O7 **Notikewin** *R* Alberta
43 G12 **Noto** Sicily
27 D12 **Notodden** Norway
43 G12 **Noto, Golfo di** Sicily
61 K8 **Noto-hantō** *pen* Japan
61 L8 **Noto-jima** *isld* Japan
60 S1 **Notoro-ko** *L* Japan
60 S1 **Notoro-misaki** *C* Japan
Notozero, Oz. *see* **Padunskoye More**
122 H7 **Notre Dame** New Brunswick
122 A8 **Notre Dame** Quebec
123 R4 **Notre Dame B** Nfld
20 F4 **Notre Dame-de Courson** France
115 M5 **Notre Dame de Koartáo** Quebec
121 S4 **Notre-Dame-de-la-Doré** Quebec
119 T9 **Notre Dame de Lourdes** Manitoba
121 P6 **Notre Dame du Laus** Quebec
121 L5 **Notre Dame du-Nord** Quebec
122 A5 **Notre Dame du Rosaire** Quebec
60 T2 **Notsuke-saki** *C* Japan
60 T2 **Notsuke-suidō** *str* Japan/Kuril Is
120 K8 **Nottawasaga Bay** Ontario
121 M2 **Nottaway R** Quebec
27 H14 **Nottebäck** Sweden
112 C3 **Nottely L** Georgia
27 E12 **Nötteröy** *isld* Norway
9 E2 **Nottingham** England
9 E1 **Nottingham** *co* England
115 M5 **Nottingham Island** N W Terr
27 G15 **Nöttja** Sweden
37 K2 **Nottleben** E Germany
94 K10 **Nottoway** *R* Virginia
100 J6 **Notus** Idaho
85 A4 **Nouadhibou** Mauritania
85 A5 **Nouakchott** Mauritania
21 H7 **Nouans-les-Fontaines** France
21 I6 **Nouan sur-Loire** France
22 J5 **Nouart** France
137 O6 **Nouméa** New Caledonia
85 D6 **Nouna** Upper Volta
89 D8 **Noupoort** S Africa
115 M7 **Nouveau-Comptoir** Quebec
115 M5 **Nouveau Québec, Cratèr du** Quebec
122 D4 **Nouvel,L** Quebec
86 C5 **Nouvelle Anvers** Zaïre
Nouvelle Calédonie *isld* *see* **New Caledonia**
115 M5 **Nouvelle-France,Cap de** Quebec
18 H9 **Nouvelle, la** France
122 F5 **Nouvelle,R** Quebec
Nouvelles Hébrides *islds* *see* **New Hebrides**
20 J1 **Nouvion-en-Ponthieu** France
22 F3 **Nouvion-en-Thiérache,Le** France
21 G6 **Nouzilly** France
22 H4 **Nouzonville** France
71 M9 **Nova Anadia** Timor
57 E5 **Novabad** U.S.S.R.
48 E2 **Nová Baňa** Czechoslovakia
87 B7 **Nova Caipemba** Angola
87 D8 **Nova Chaves** Angola
45 M4 **Novafeltria** Italy
130 G8 **Nova Friburgo** Brazil
87 C8 **Nova Gaia** Angola
42 H3 **Nova Gradiška** Yugoslavia
130 G8 **Nova Iguaçu** Brazil
129 K5 **Nova Iorque** Brazil
130 G6 **Nova Lima** Brazil
87 C8 **Nova Lisboa** Angola
87 F10 **Nova Mambone** Mozambique
128 G4 **Nova Olinda do Norte** Brazil
41 J7 **Novara** Italy
129 K4 **Nova Russas** Brazil
71 N9 **Nova Sagres** Timor
122 G9 **Nova Scotia** *prov* Canada
41 K5 **Novate** Italy
102 B3 **Novato** California
130 E10 **Nova Trento** Brazil
48 F7 **Nova Varš** Yugoslavia
128 F6 **Nova Vida** Brazil
55 C5 **Novaya Akkermanovka** U.S.S.R.
55 E3 **Novaya Aptula** U.S.S.R.
54 E10 **Novaya Kakhovka** U.S.S.R.
55 D2 **Novaya Lyala** U.S.S.R.
51 O1 **Novaya Sibir,Ostrov** *isld* U.S.S.R.
50 E1 **Novaya Zemlya** *isld* U.S.S.R.
47 H2 **Nova Zagora** Bulgaria
45 J2 **Novellara** Italy
110 D1 **Novelty** Missouri
45 L1 **Noventa V** Italy
33 N7 **Növenthien** W Germany
48 E3 **Nové Zámky** Czechoslovakia
52 D5 **Novgorod** U.S.S.R.
54 E5 **Novgorod Severskiy** U.S.S.R.
47 J1 **Novgradets** Bulgaria
44 E2 **Novi** Italy
42 F3 **Novi** Yugoslavia
109 H4 **Novice** Texas
45 J2 **Novi di Modena** Italy
42 F3 **Novigrad** Yugoslavia
42 G4 **Novigrad** Yugoslavia
48 F4 **Novi Kneževac** Yugoslavia
59 M2 **Novikovo** U.S.S.R.
45 N4 **Novilara** Italy
124 G6 **Novillero** Mexico
99 O9 **Novinger** Missouri
22 G4 **Novion-Porcien** France
47 J1 **Novi Pazar** Bulgaria
46 D1 **Novi Pazar** Yugoslavia
48 F5 **Novi Sad** Yugoslavia
54 N1 **Novki** U.S.S.R.
129 H4 **Nôvo Acôrdo** Brazil
53 F10 **Novoaleksandrovsk** U.S.S.R.
55 C5 **Novoalekseyevka** U.S.S.R.
56 B4 **Novoaltaysk** U.S.S.R.
128 F5 **Novo Aripuana** Brazil
53 D9 **Novo Arkhangelsk** U.S.S.R.
55 D2 **Novoasbest** U.S.S.R.
54 K9 **Novoazovsk** U.S.S.R.
54 C4 **Novobelitsa** U.S.S.R.
55 C3 **Novobelokatay** U.S.S.R.
55 E3 **Novoberezovka** U.S.S.R.
54 M9 **Novocherkassk** U.S.S.R.
55 F5 **Novodolinka** U.S.S.R.
52 D6 **Novo Dugino** U.S.S.R.
52 F3 **Novodvinsk** Arkhangelsk U.S.S.R.
53 C7 **Novogrudok** U.S.S.R.
131 H2 **Novo Hamburgo** Brazil
59 L1 **Novoilinovka** U.S.S.R.
55 F5 **Novoishimskiy** U.S.S.R.
57 B2 **Novokazalinsk** U.S.S.R.
59 J1 **Novokiyevskiy Uval** U.S.S.R.
55 D4 **Novokocherdyk** U.S.S.R.
56 C4 **Novokuznetsk** U.S.S.R.
129 H3 **Novo, L** Brazil
43 J8 **Novoli** Italy
71 M9 **Novo Luso** Timor
53 E11 **Novomikhaylovskiy** U.S.S.R.
54 C8 **Novomirgorod** U.S.S.R.
54 G8 **Novomoskovsk** U.S.S.R.
54 K2 **Novomoskovsk** U.S.S.R.
55 E3 **Novonikolskoye** U.S.S.R.
55 C5 **Novoorsk** U.S.S.R.
52 C6 **Novopolotsk** U.S.S.R.
87 B8 **Novo Redondo** Angola
53 E11 **Novorossiysk** U.S.S.R.
55 C5 **Novorossiyskiy** U.S.S.R.
54 M3 **Novoryazhsk** U.S.S.R.
55 F5 **Novorybinka** U.S.S.R.
51 K1 **Novorybnoye** U.S.S.R.
52 C6 **Novorzhev** U.S.S.R.
52 H7 **Novo Sakhcha** U.S.S.R.
48 K2 **Novoselitsa** U.S.S.R.
55 B5 **Novosergiyevka** U.S.S.R.
54 L9 **Novoshakhtinsk** U.S.S.R.
52 H6 **Novo Sheshminsk** U.S.S.R.
56 B4 **Novosibirsk** U.S.S.R.
50 G3 **Novosibirskaya Oblast'** *prov* U.S.S.R.
51 O1 **Novosibirskiye Ostrova** *islds* U.S.S.R.
54 J4 **Novosil'** U.S.S.R.
55 D3 **Novosineglazovskiy** U.S.S.R.
52 D6 **Novosokol'niki** U.S.S.R.
55 C5 **Novotroitsk** U.S.S.R.
57 G3 **Novotroitskoye** Kazakhstan U.S.S.R.
55 G3 **Novotroitskoye** Novosibirsk U.S.S.R.
54 K2 **Novougol'nyy** U.S.S.R.
54 C8 **Novoukrainka** U.S.S.R.
55 C5 **Novoursal'sk** U.S.S.R.
48 L2 **Novo Ushitsa** U.S.S.R.
53 G8 **Novo Uzensk** U.S.S.R.
55 F4 **Novovarshavka** U.S.S.R.
55 G2 **Novovaya Vasyugan** U.S.S.R.
52 G5 **Novo-Vyatsk** U.S.S.R.
56 D2 **Novoyeniseysk** U.S.S.R.
55 E3 **Novozaimka** U.S.S.R.
52 E6 **Novozavidovskiy** U.S.S.R.
52 H3 **Novozhilovskaya** U.S.S.R.
42 H3 **Novska** Yugoslavia
31 L6 **Novy Bohumin** Czechoslovakia
31 J5 **Nový Bydžov** Czechoslovakia
22 G4 **Novy-Chevrières** France
54 K8 **Novy Donbass** U.S.S.R.
54 F7 **Novye Senzhary** U.S.S.R.
48 J1 **Novye Strelishcha** U.S.S.R.
48 D1 **Nový Jičin** Czechoslovakia
54 J6 **Novy Oskol** U.S.S.R.
52 D1 **Novyy** U.S.S.R.
52 H2 **Novyy Bor** U.S.S.R.
54 D9 **Novyy Bug** U.S.S.R.
55 E1 **Novyy Karymkary** U.S.S.R.
55 E2 **Novyy Katysh** U.S.S.R.
50 G2 **Novyy Port** U.S.S.R.
52 G6 **Novyy Tor'yal** U.S.S.R.
31 J5 **Nowa Ruda** Poland
31 J4 **Nowa Sól** Poland
107 P5 **Nowata** Oklahoma
77 A2 **Nowbarān** Iran
31 L2 **Nowe** Poland
31 M2 **Nowe Miasto** Poland
139 K4 **Nowendoc** New S Wales
75 P5 **Nowgong** India
116 K4 **Nowitna** *R* Alaska
98 E5 **Nowlin** S Dakota
31 J2 **Nowógard** Poland
31 N2 **Nowogród** Poland
31 J4 **Nowogrodziec** Poland
101 S5 **Nowood Cr** Wyoming
139 K5 **Nowra** New S Wales
75 K9 **Nowrangapur** India
77 B1 **Now Shahr** Iran
74 E1 **Nowshera** Pakistan
31 M3 **Nowy Dwor** Poland
31 O2 **Nowy Dwór** Poland
31 L1 **Nowy Dwór Gdański** Poland
31 M5 **Nowy Korczyn** Poland
48 F1 **Nowy Sącz** Poland
48 F1 **Nowy Targ** Poland
31 J3 **Nowy Tomysl** Poland
111 G9 **Noxapater** Mississippi
95 L5 **Noxen** Pennsylvania
100 K2 **Noxon** Montana
111 H8 **Noxubee** *R* Mississippi
16 B2 **Noya** Spain
17 J3 **Noya** *R* Spain
20 B5 **Noyal-sur-Vilaine** France
21 C6 **Noyant la Gravoyère** France
21 E7 **Noyant-la-Plaine** France
21 F7 **Noyant sur-le Lude** France
20 K2 **Noye** *R* France
20 J1 **Noyelles-sur-Mer** France
21 E6 **Noyen** France
21 H7 **Noyers-sur-Cher** France
117 G8 **Noyes I** Alaska
102 A2 **Noyo** California
22 E4 **Noyon** France
58 D3 **Noyon** Mongolia
123 O2 **Noyrot,L** Quebec
21 B6 **Nozay** France
86 C6 **N'Sah** Congo
88 E10 **Nsanje** Malawi
85 D7 **Nsawam** Ghana
88 C9 **Nsenga** Zambia
86 B5 **Ntem** *R* Cameroon
83 L13 **Nuageuses** *isld* Kerguelen Indian Ocean
21 D7 **Nuaillé** France
21 D9 **Nuaillé-d'Aunis** France
87 F10 **Nuanetsi** Zimbabwe
89 G3 **Nuanetsi** *R* Zimbabwe
52 C3 **Nuasjärvi** *L* Finland
85 E7 **Nuatja** Togo
84 J5 **Nuba, L** Sudan
86 F3 **Nuba Mts** Sudan
84 J5 **Nubian Des** Sudan
100 D8 **Nubieber** California
131 B6 **Nuble** *prov* Chile
131 B6 **Nuble** *R* Chile
48 H4 **Nucet** Romania
65 D2 **Nudam** China
141 K1 **Nudgee** *dist* Brisbane, Qnsld
109 J7 **Nueces** *R* Texas
21 E7 **Nueil** France
115 K5 **Nueltin L** N W Terr
65 E4 **Nü'erhe** China
128 F8 **Nueva Asunción** *dep* Paraguay
124 F2 **Nueva Casas Grandes** Mexico
128 F1 **Nueva Esparta** *state* Venezuela
128 F7 **Nueva Esperanza** Bolivia
130 C8 **Nueva Germania** Paraguay
126 C4 **Nueva Gerona** Cuba
133 D9 **Nueva, I** Chile/Arg
133 C5 **Nueva Imperial** Chile
133 C6 **Nueva Lubecka** Argentina
124 J4 **Nueva Rosita** Mexico
133 E5 **Nueve de Julio** Argentina
126 F4 **Nuevitas** Cuba
71 F5 **Nuevo** Cebu Philippines
133 E6 **Nuevo,G** Argentina
109 H9 **Nuevo Guerrero** Mexico
124 G5 **Nuevo Ideal** Mexico
125 K4 **Nuevo Laredo** Mexico
125 J5 **Nuevo Leon** *state* Mexico
128 C4 **Nuevo Rocafuerte** Ecuador
141 J6 **Nuga Nuga, L** Queensland
84 J5 **Nugrus,Gebel** *mt* Egypt
115 O3 **Nûgssuaq** Greenland
137 L2 **Nuguria Is** Bismarck Arch
145 F3 **Nuhaka** New Zealand
137 Q3 **Nui** *atoll* Tuvalu
68 H5 **Nui Ti On** *mt* Vietnam
18 H5 **Nuits** France
19 J5 **Nuits St.Georges** France
66 E5 **Nu Jiang** *R* China
116 M7 **Nuka I** Alaska
138 D4 **Nukey Bluff** S Australia
84 H6 **Nukheila** Sudan
80 G8 **Nukheila** *R* Jordan
137 R6 **Nuku'alofa** *isld* Tonga
137 Q3 **Nukufetau** *atoll* Tuvalu
135 N9 **Nuku Hiva** *isld* Marquesas Is Pacific Oc
137 Q3 **Nukulaelae** *atoll* Tuvalu
137 M2 **Nukumanu Is** Solomon Is
137 Q2 **Nukunau** *isld* Kiribati
57 A4 **Nukus** U.S.S.R.
17 G5 **Nules** Spain
142 D5 **Nullagine** W Australia
142 D5 **Nullagine R** W Australia
138 B4 **Nullarbor** S Australia
143 F9 **Nullarbor Plain** S/W Australia
141 F5 **Nulloocha** Queensland
65 D4 **Nulu'erhu Shan** *mt ra* China
43 B8 **Nulvi** Sardinia
61 L8 **Numaho** Japan
61 P6 **Numakunai** Japan
141 G8 **Numalla, L** Queensland
86 B4 **Numan** Nigeria
45 O4 **Numana** Italy
17 F3 **Numancia** Spain
25 B5 **Numansdorp** Netherlands
60 P2 **Numata** Japan
86 E4 **Numatinna** *R* Sudan
61 M10 **Numazu** Japan
36 D2 **Nümbrecht** Nordrhein-Westfalen W Germany
140 D2 **Numbulwar Mission** N Terr Aust
27 D11 **Numedal** *V* Norway
27 D12 **Numedalsågen** *R* Norway
29 K11 **Nummi** Finland
139 H6 **Numurkah** Victoria
116 J7 **Nunachuak** Alaska
116 F6 **Nunapitchuk** Alaska
116 E6 **Nunavakanuk L** Alaska
94 K4 **Nunda** New York
141 K1 **Nundah** *dist* Brisbane, Qnsld
139 K4 **Nundle** New S Wales
9 E2 **Nuneaton** England
143 C9 **Nungarin** W Australia
65 D2 **Nungnain Sum** China
87 G8 **Nungo** Mozambique
116 E7 **Nunivak I** Alaska
106 F1 **Nunn** Colorado
110 J6 **Nunnelly** Tennessee
8 D5 **Nunney** England
25 E4 **Nunspeet** Netherlands
138 F4 **Nuntherungie** New S Wales
70 E3 **Nunukan Timur** Kalimantan
59 H2 **Nuomin He** *R* China
43 C8 **Nuoro** Sardinia
26 L5 **Nuortikon** Sweden
137 O4 **Nupani** Santa Cruz Is
128 C2 **Nuquí** Colombia
57 G1 **Nura** U.S.S.R.
57 G1 **Nura** *R* U.S.S.R.
57 D5 **Nuratau, Khr** *mts* U.S.S.R.
36 B3 **Nürburg** W Germany
44 G2 **Nure** *R* Italy
57 E5 **Nurek Vdkhr.** U.S.S.R.
Nuremberg *see* **Nürnberg**
95 L6 **Nuremburg** Pennsylvania
124 E3 **Nuri** Mexico
138 E5 **Nuriootpa** S Australia
74 D1 **Nuristan** *reg* Afghanistan
52 H7 **Nurlat** U.S.S.R.
52 G6 **Nurlaty** U.S.S.R.
29 O8 **Nurmes** Finland
29 K9 **Nurmo** Finland
37 L5 **Nürnberg** W Germany
71 G7 **Nuro** Mindanao Philippines
138 A3 **Nurrari Lakes** S Australia
43 C9 **Nurri** Sardinia
36 G6 **Nürtingen** W Germany
31 O3 **Nurzec** *R* Poland
71 K9 **Nusa Tenggara Timur** Indonesia
78 H3 **Nusaybin** Turkey
116 J6 **Nushagak** *R* Alaska
116 H7 **Nushagak B** Alaska
116 H7 **Nushagak Pen** Alaska
66 F6 **Nu Shan** *mt ra* China
74 B4 **Nushki** Pakistan
33 N5 **Nusse** W Germany
115 N6 **Nutak** Labrador
33 S8 **Nuthe** *R* E Germany
119 O6 **Nut L** Sask
9 G5 **Nutley** England
128 E2 **Nutrias** Venezuela
106 C9 **Nutt** New Mexico
14 E2 **Nutts Corner** N Ireland
140 C3 **Nutwood Downs** N Terr Aust
116 Q5 **Nutzotin Mts** Alaska
135 T3 **Nuu** Hawaiian Is
29 M5 **Nuupas** Finland
75 K4 **Nuwakot** Nepal
83 K11 **Nuwara Eliya** Sri Lanka
89 B9 **Nuweveldreeks** *mts* S Africa
116 J7 **Nuyakuk** *R* Alaska
116 H7 **Nuyakuk,L** Alaska
138 C4 **Nuyts Arch** S Australia
138 B4 **Nuyts,C** S Australia
143 B11 **Nuyts, Pt** W Australia
122 F6 **N.W. Miramichi R** New Brunswick
143 C10 **Nyabing** W Australia
88 B3 **Nyabisindu** Rwanda
101 M1 **Nyack** Montana
88 D10 **Nyaderi** *R* Zimbabwe
88 D10 **Nyagadsi** *R* Zimbabwe
139 G6 **Nyah** Victoria
88 F1 **Nyahururu Falls** Kenya
66 D6 **Nyainqêntanglha Shan** *ra* China
88 D3 **Nyakabindi** Tanzania
26 K8 **Nyåker** Sweden
55 D1 **Nyaksimvol'** U.S.S.R.
86 D3 **Nyala** Sudan
66 D6 **Nyalam** China
88 D3 **Nyalikungu** Tanzania
55 E1 **Nyalino** U.S.S.R.
87 E9 **Nyamandhlovu** Zimbabwe
88 C10 **Nyamanji** *mt* Zimbabwe
87 D8 **Nyamboma Falls** Zambia
86 E4 **Nyamlell** Sudan
87 G8 **Nyamtumba** Tanzania
52 F4 **Nyandoma** U.S.S.R.
143 F8 **Nyanga, L** W Australia
88 E10 **Nyanja** Malawi
87 F8 **Nyanji** Zambia
52 H4 **Nyanyayel'** U.S.S.R.
117 R5 **Nyarling** *R* N W Terr
88 E7 **Nyasa** *tribe* Tanzania
88 E7 **Nyasa,L** Malawi/Moz
Nyasaland *see* **Malawi**
52 H2 **Nyashabozh** U.S.S.R.
68 B3 **Nyaungbinzeik** Burma
68 C4 **Nyaunglebin** Burma
68 B2 **Nyaungu** Burma
55 C3 **Nyazepetrovsk** U.S.S.R.
89 G2 **Nyazvidzi** *R* Zimbabwe
28 F6 **Nyborg** Denmark
26 R1 **Nyborg** Norway
27 H15 **Nybro** Sweden
50 G2 **Nyda** U.S.S.R.
27 G14 **Nydala** Sweden
115 O1 **Nyeboes Land** Greenland
Nyenchen Tanglha Range *see* **Nyainqêntanglha Shan**
86 F4 **Nyerol** Sudan
27 G11 **Nyhammar** Sweden
28 K4 **Nyhamn** Sweden
26 H9 **Nyhem** Sweden
88 D6 **Nyiha** Tanzania
66 D5 **Nyima** China
87 F8 **Nyimba** Zambia
66 E6 **Nyingchi** China
48 G3 **Nyíradony** Hungary
48 G3 **Nyírbátor** Hungary
48 G3 **Nyíregyháza** Hungary
88 F3 **Nyiri Desert** Kenya
86 G5 **Nyiru** *mt* Kenya
29 K8 **Nykarleby** Finland
27 H13 **Nykil** Sweden
28 J5 **Nykøbing** Denmark
28 H7 **Nykøbing** Falster Denmark
28 B3 **Nykøbing** Mors Denmark
27 J13 **Nyköping** Sweden
27 G12 **Nykroppa** Sweden
89 F5 **Nyl** *R* S Africa
26 J8 **Nyland** Sweden
89 F5 **Nylstroom** S Africa
26 K6 **Nylund** Sweden
139 H4 **Nymagee** New S Wales
139 L3 **Nymboida** New S Wales
139 L3 **Nymborda** *R* New S Wales
31 J5 **Nymburk** Czechoslovakia
7 F11 **Nymphe Bank** Atlantic Oc
27 J13 **Nynäshamn** Sweden
139 H4 **Nyngan** New S Wales
139 G4 **Nyngynderry** New S Wales
21 D6 **Nyoiseau** France
86 B5 **Nyong** *R* Cameroon
19 O16 **Nyons** France
37 P4 **Nýřany** Czechoslovakia
52 J4 **Nyrob** U.S.S.R.
37 P5 **Nýrsko** Czechoslovakia
31 K5 **Nysa** Poland
27 F11 **Nyskoga** Sweden
100 H6 **Nyssa** Oregon
Nystad *see* **Uusikaupunki**
61 N5 **Nyūdō zaki** *C* Japan
52 G3 **Nyukhcha** Arkhangelsk U.S.S.R.
52 E3 **Nyukhcha** Karelskaya A.S.S.R. U.S.S.R.
52 D3 **Nyuk, Oz** *L* U.S.S.R.
52 F4 **Nyuksenitsa** U.S.S.R.
59 H1 **Nyukzha** *R* U.S.S.R.
51 L2 **Nyurba** U.S.S.R.
55 E1 **Nyurkoy** U.S.S.R.
52 H4 **Nyuvchim** U.S.S.R.
56 H1 **Nyuya** *R* U.S.S.R.
88 D4 **Nzega** Tanzania
85 C7 **Nzerékore** Guinea
87 B7 **N'Zeto** Angola
98 G6 **Oacoma** S Dakota
98 F4 **Oahe, L** S Dakota
114 J8 **Oahe Res** S Dakota
102 S11 **Oahu** *isld* Hawaiian Is
103 N7 **Oak** *R* Arizona
60 S2 **O-akan-dake** *mt* Japan
122 E8 **Oak B** New Brunswick
138 F5 **Oakbank** S Australia
95 R5 **Oak Bluffs** Massachusetts
112 G2 **Oakboro** N Carolina
119 R8 **Oakburn** Manitoba
112 K2 **Oak City** N Carolina
103 M2 **Oak City** Utah
109 N9 **Oak Cliff** Texas
101 T9 **Oak Creek** Colorado
102 D4 **Oakdale** California
111 D11 **Oakdale** Louisiana
98 J7 **Oakdale** Nebraska
98 H3 **Oakes** N Dakota
100 H2 **Oakesdale** Washington
140 F7 **Oakes, Mt** Queensland
141 K7 **Oakey** Queensland
99 S6 **Oakfield** Wisconsin
99 R9 **Oakford** Illinois
111 E9 **Oak Grove** Louisiana
9 F2 **Oakham** England
94 D5 **Oak Harbor** Ohio
113 G9 **Oak Hill** Florida
107 N2 **Oak Hill** Kansas
94 E8 **Oak Hill** Ohio
94 F9 **Oak Hill** W Virginia
141 H4 **Oak Hills** Queensland
119 R9 **Oak Lake** Manitoba
102 B4 **Oakland** California
99 S10 **Oakland** Illinois
99 L8 **Oakland** Iowa
95 S2 **Oakland** Maine
94 H7 **Oakland** Maryland
111 G7 **Oakland** Mississippi
98 K8 **Oakland** Nebraska
100 B6 **Oakland** Oregon
95 M5 **Oakland** Pennsylvania
110 G6 **Oakland** Tennessee
109 L6 **Oakland** Texas
110 J3 **Oakland City** Indiana
113 G11 **Oakland Park** Florida
139 H6 **Oaklands** New S Wales
145 E1 **Oakleigh** New Zealand
102 C4 **Oakley** California
101 M7 **Oakley** Idaho
107 K2 **Oakley** Kansas
94 C3 **Oakley** Michigan
112 C3 **Oakman** Georgia
94 H6 **Oakmont** Penn
119 R8 **Oakner** Manitoba
142 D5 **Oakover, R** W Australia
112 E5 **Oakpark** Georgia
141 G4 **Oak Park** Queensland
119 T8 **Oak Pt** Manitoba
111 E9 **Oak Ridge** Louisiana
110 G4 **Oak Ridge** Missouri
100 C6 **Oakridge** Oregon
112 C1 **Oak Ridge** Tennessee
119 R8 **Oak River** Manitoba
145 D3 **Oakura** New Zealand
138 F5 **Oakvale** S Australia
119 T9 **Oakville** Manitoba
121 L9 **Oakville** Ontario
109 J7 **Oakville** Texas
110 J1 **Oakwood** Illinois
110 E2 **Oakwood** Missouri
94 C5 **Oakwood** Ohio
107 M6 **Oakwood** Oklahoma
141 H7 **Oakwood** Queensland
144 C6 **Oamaru** New Zealand
61 O10 **Ōami** Japan
71 F4 **Oas** Philippines
60 F11 **Ōasa** Japan
102 G4 **Oasis** California
101 L8 **Oasis** Nevada
146 J5 **Oates Land** Antarctica
139 H8 **Oatlands** Tasmania
103 K6 **Oatman** Arizona
125 L9 **Oaxaca de Juárez** Mexico
56 B4 **Ob'** *R* U.S.S.R.
120 F3 **Oba** Ontario
137 O5 **Oba** *isld* New Hebrides
120 E3 **Obakamiga L** Ontario
120 F4 **Oba L** Ontario
86 B5 **Obala** Cameroon
121 Q3 **Obalski** Quebec
61 J10 **Obama** Japan
144 B7 **Oban** New Zealand
118 J6 **Oban** Sask
15 C4 **Oban** Scotland
61 O7 **Obanazawa** Japan
106 G6 **Obar** New Mexico
120 E4 **Obatanga Prov. Park** Ontario
121 Q3 **Obatogamau L** Quebec
38 L7 **Obdach** Austria
117 P9 **Obed** Alberta
38 J5 **Ober** *dist* Austria
40 G3 **Ober Aargau** *dist* Switzerland
30 F8 **Oberammergau** W Germany
37 Q1 **Oberau** E Germany
41 O2 **Oberau** W Germany
36 H2 **Oberaula** W Germany
36 H3 **Oberbach** W Germany
38 E5 **Oberbayern** *dist* W Germany
25 F6 **Oberbruch-Dremmen** W Germany
39 C2 **Oberbrunn** W Germany
36 H7 **Oberdischingen** W Germany
38 H8 **Ober-Drau-Tal** *V* Austria
37 J4 **Obereisenheim** W Germany
37 J2 **Oberellen** E Germany
41 L4 **Oberengadin** *dist* Switzerland
38 K7 **Oberenns Tal** Austria
37 K3 **Oberessfeld** W Germany
37 P1 **Ober Eula** E Germany
37 L4 **Oberfranken** *dist* W Germany
Oberfrohna *see* **Limbach-Oberfrohna**
38 H8 **Obergailtal** *V* Austria
41 O4 **Obergurgl** Austria
41 L4 **Oberhalbstein** *R* Switzerland
36 E7 **Oberharmersbach** W Germany
36 C6 **Oberhaslach** France
32 E10 **Oberhausen** W Germany
36 E4 **Ober Hilbersheim** W Germany
37 K2 **Oberhof** E Germany
36 E6 **Oberkirch** W Germany
36 F3 **Oberkleen** W Germany
37 J6 **Ober-Kochen** W Germany
37 M3 **Ober Kotzau** W Germany
37 J3 **Ober Lauringen** W Germany
36 H6 **Oberlenningen** W Germany
107 K2 **Oberlin** Kansas
111 D11 **Oberlin** Louisiana
94 E5 **Oberlin** Ohio
36 H7 **Ober Marchthal** W Germany
32 J10 **Ober Marsberg** W Germany
36 D4 **Ober Moschel** W Germany
36 C7 **Obernai** France
36 G4 **Obernburg** W Germany
32 K8 **Obernkirchen** W Germany
98 G2 **Oberon** N Dakota
139 J5 **Oberon** New S Wales
39 C2 **Oberpfaffenhofen** W Germany
37 M5 **Oberpfalz** *dist* W Germany
37 N4 **Oberpfalzer Wald** *mts* W Germany
36 C2 **Oberpleis** W Germany
36 F4 **Ober Ramstadt** W Germany
41 K3 **Oberri** Switzerland
37 O3 **Ober Rittersgrün** E Germany
33 P10 **Ober Röblingen** E Germany
36 F4 **Ober-Roden** W Germany
36 F3 **Ober Rosbach** W Germany
36 G5 **Ober Schefflenz** W Germany
40 F4 **Ober Simmen Tal** Switzerland
36 H5 **Obersontheim** W Germany
33 N10 **Oberspier** E Germany
41 M3 **Oberstdorf** W Germany
36 D5 **Obersteinbach** France
37 J3 **Obertheres** W Germany
37 N6 **Obertraubling** W Germany
37 O7 **Ober Trennbach** W Germany
33 T6 **Oberueckersee** *L* E Germany
36 F3 **Oberursel** W Germany
37 N5 **Oberviechtach** W Germany
41 H4 **Oberwald** Switzerland
38 O7 **Oberwart** Austria
36 D3 **Oberwesel** W Germany
37 O3 **Oberwiesenthal** E Germany
36 C2 **Oberwinter** W Germany
38 K7 **Oberwölz** Austria
60 E14 **Obi** Japan
71 A3 **Obi** *isld* Indonesia
129 G4 **Obidos** Brazil
16 A5 **Obidos** Portugal
60 R3 **Obihiro** Japan
71 A3 **Obi,Kep** *isld* Indonesia
71 A3 **Obilatu** *isld* Indonesia
38 F5 **Obing** W Germany
110 G5 **Obion** Tennessee
110 J3 **Oblong** Illinois
59 K2 **Obluch'ye** U.S.S.R.
54 H1 **Obninsk** U.S.S.R.
86 H3 **Obock** Djibouti
54 A1 **Obol'** *R* U.S.S.R.
120 A3 **Obonga L** Ontario
70 D2 **Obong, G** *mt* Sarawak
31 K3 **Oborniki** Poland
52 F1 **Obornyy, Mys** *C* U.S.S.R.
86 C6 **Obouya Mossaka** Congo
54 H5 **Oboyan'** U.S.S.R.
52 F3 **Obozerskiy** U.S.S.R.
124 E4 **Obregón, Presa** *res* Mexico
120 K5 **O'Brien** Ontario
33 Q8 **Oobritz** E Germany
42 G4 **Obrovac** Yugoslavia
57 E4 **Obruchevo** U.S.S.R.
137 M6 **Observatoire, Caye de l'** *islds* Coral Sea
117 H8 **Observatory Inlet** Br Col
54 D1 **Obsha** *R* U.S.S.R.
55 B5 **Obshciy Syrt** *reg* U.S.S.R.
101 L5 **Obsidian** Idaho
50 G2 **Obskaya Guba** *gulf* U.S.S.R.
85 D7 **Obuasi** Ghana
52 J5 **Obva** *R* U.S.S.R.
41 H4 **Obwalden** *canton* Switzerland
52 G4 **Ob'yachevo** U.S.S.R.
16 E2 **Oca** *R* Spain
113 E8 **Ocala** Florida
124 E3 **Ocampo** Chihuahua Mexico
124 H4 **Ocampo** Coahuila Mexico
16 E2 **Oca,Mt.de** Spain
126 H10 **Ocaña** Colombia
16 E5 **Ocaña** Spain
106 E5 **Ocate** New Mexico
45 L2 **Occhiobello** Italy
95 M8 **Ocean City** Maryland
95 N7 **Ocean City** New Jersey
100 A2 **Ocean City** Washington
117 K9 **Ocean Falls** Br Columbia
95 N7 **Ocean Gate** New Jersey
Ocean Is. *see* **Banaba**
101 R6 **Ocean L** Wyoming
102 D6 **Oceano** California
90 F5 **Oceanographer Fracture** Atlantic Oc
100 A3 **Ocean Park** Washington
102 G8 **Oceanside** California
100 B4 **Oceanside** Oregon
111 H11 **Ocean Springs** Mississippi
95 M8 **Ocean View** Delaware
16 E3 **Ocejón,Pass** Spain
54 C10 **Ochakov** U.S.S.R.
56 H1 **Ochchuguy Botuobuya** *R* U.S.S.R.
52 H5 **Ocher** U.S.S.R.
60 C12 **Ōchi** Japan
60 G10 **Ochiai** Japan
60 T2 **Ochiishi-misaki** *C* Japan
15 E4 **Ochil Hills** Scotland
15 D5 **Ochiltree** Scotland
113 C7 **Ochlocknee** Georgia
111 M11 **Ochlockonee** *R* Florida
100 E5 **Ochoco Res** Oregon
32 G6 **Ocholt** W Germany
113 F12 **Ochopee** Florida
127 K2 **Ocho Rios** Jamaica
119 S7 **Ochre River** Manitoba
40 F4 **Ochsen** *mt* Switzerland
37 J4 **Ochsenfurt** W Germany
41 L1 **Ochsenhausen** W Germany
37 M3 **Ochsenkopf** *mt* W Germany
32 L5 **Ochsenzoll** W Germany
36 C3 **Ochtendung** W Germany
33 O8 **Ochtmersleben** E Germany
32 F8 **Ochtrup** W Germany
112 D6 **Ocilla** Georgia
27 J11 **Ockelbo** Sweden
28 B7 **Ockholm** W Germany
9 F5 **Ockley** England
48 J4 **Ocland** Romania
112 D4 **Ocmulgee** *R* Georgia
112 D5 **Ocmulgee Nat Mon** Georgia
48 J5 **Ocna Sibiului** Romania
48 H3 **Ocna Sugătag** Romania
48 J5 **Ocnele Mari** Romania
113 F9 **Ocoee** Florida
112 C2 **Ocoee** Tennessee
128 D7 **Ocoña** Peru
110 G2 **Oconee** Illinois
98 J8 **Oconee** Nebraska
112 E5 **Oconee** *R* Georgia
141 G5 **O'Connell** *R* Queensland
98 G8 **Oconto** Nebraska
99 T5 **Oconto** Wisconsin
99 S5 **Oconto Falls** Wisconsin
124 E5 **Ocoroni** Mexico
125 M3 **Ocotal** Nicaragua
124 H7 **Ocotlán** Mexico
125 N9 **Ocozocoautla** Mexico
22 J3 **Ocquier** Belgium
112 M2 **Ocracoke** N Carolina
48 E3 **Ocsa** Hungary
48 F4 **Öcsöd** Hungary
20 B2 **Octeville** France
120 D3 **Octopus** Ontario
127 L9 **Ocumare del Tuy** Venezuela
71 M9 **Ocussi Ambeno** Timor
27 F14 **Od** Sweden
85 D7 **Oda** Ghana
60 F10 **Ōda** Japan
61 K11 **Odaigahara-zan** *mt* Japan
61 O8 **Odaka** Japan
27 E11 **Odal,N** Norway
27 E11 **Odal,S** Norway
99 Q3 **Odanah** Wisconsin
61 O5 **Ōdate** Japan
61 N10 **Odawara** Japan
27 B11 **Odda** Norway
86 G1 **Odda,Jebel** *mt* Sudan
28 E5 **Odder** Denmark
27 C13 **Oddernes** Norway
86 H5 **Oddur** Somalia
99 L7 **Odebolt** Iowa
16 B7 **Odeleite** Portugal
99 S8 **Odell** Illinois
98 K9 **Odell** Nebraska
109 H1 **Odell** Texas
37 L7 **Odelzhausen** W Germany
109 K8 **Odem** Texas
16 B7 **Odemira** Portugal
47 J6 **Ödemis** Turkey
110 C7 **Oden** Arkansas
36 D4 **Odenbach** W Germany
89 E6 **Odendaalsrus** S Africa
36 F5 **Odenheim** W Germany
36 B1 **Odenkirchen** W Germany
28 E6 **Odense** Denmark
Odense *co* *see* **Fyn**
28 F5 **Odense Fjord** *inlet* Denmark
36 G4 **Odenwald** *mts* W Germany
Oder *R* *see* **Odra R**
33 U7 **Oderberg** E Germany
33 T8 **Oderin** E Germany
36 E4 **Odernheim** W Germany
33 T8 **Oder-Spree-Kanal** E Germany
42 E3 **Oderzo** Italy
27 G13 **Ödeshög** Sweden
110 C3 **Odessa** Missouri
95 L4 **Odessa** New York
121 O8 **Odessa** Ontario
119 O8 **Odessa** Sask
108 E4 **Odessa** Texas
48 N4 **Odessa** U.S.S.R.
100 G2 **Odessa** Washington
55 F4 **Odesskoye** U.S.S.R.
18 C4 **Odet** *R* France
119 T3 **Odhill** Manitoba
87 E10 **Odiakwe** Botswana
85 C7 **Odiénné** Ivory Coast
9 F5 **Odiham** England
110 G3 **Odin** Illinois
32 E9 **Öding** W Germany
54 J1 **Odintsovo** U.S.S.R.
48 L5 **Odobeşti** Romania
31 K4 **Odolanów** Poland
146 E12 **Odom Inlet** Antarctica
110 K3 **Odon** Indiana
20 D3 **Odon** *R* France
108 F3 **O'Donnell** Texas
25 G3 **Odoorn** Netherlands
48 J4 **Odorhei** Romania
31 J4 **Odra** *R* Poland
16 E2 **Odra** *R* Spain
25 F6 **Odt** W Germany
112 E6 **Odum** Georgia
48 E5 **Odžaci** Yugoslavia
33 O8 **Oebisfelde** E Germany
37 J2 **Oechsen** E Germany
22 E1 **Oedelem** Belgium
37 P2 **Oederan** E Germany
36 E1 **Oedingen** W Germany
129 K5 **Oeiras** Brazil
16 A6 **Oeiras** Portugal
16 B7 **Oeiras** *R* Portugal
32 H9 **Oelde** W Germany
98 C6 **Oelrichs** S Dakota
37 N3 **Oelsnitz** E Germany
99 P7 **Oelwein** Iowa
37 L2 **Oelze** E Germany
135 O11 **Oeno** *atoll* Pacific Oc
140 C1 **Oenpelli** N Terr Aust
32 J9 **Oerlinghausen** W Germany
37 L3 **Oeslau** W Germany
71 M9 **Oessilo** Timor
36 E3 **Oestrich-Winkel** W Germany
133 E3 **Oetling** Argentina
37 K6 **Oettingen** W Germany
32 H10 **Oeventrop** W Germany
111 G9 **Ofahoma** Mississippi
43 G7 **Ofanto** *R* Italy
80 B8 **Ofaqim** Israel
80 C3 **Ofer** Israel
14 D3 **Offaly** *co* Irish Rep
36 F3 **Offenbach am Main** W Germany
36 D7 **Offenburg** W Germany
26 G8 **Offerdal** Sweden
112 E6 **Offerman** Georgia
138 B2 **Officer Cr.,The** S Australia
37 J7 **Offingen** W Germany
20 H2 **Offranville** France
36 E4 **Offstein** W Germany
47 H8 **Ofidhoúsa** *isld* Greece
79 E11 **Ofira** Egypt
26 J3 **Ofotfjord** *inlet* Norway
80 D6 **Ofra** Jordan
61 N6 **Oga** Japan
86 J4 **Ogaden** *reg* Ethiopia
120 E2 **Ogahalla** Ontario
61 N6 **Oga-hantō** *pen* Japan
61 K10 **Ōgaki** Japan
107 L3 **Ogallah** Kansas
98 E8 **Ogallala** Nebraska
54 J3 **Ogarevka** U.S.S.R.
59 M6 **Ogasawara-shoto** Japan
121 M5 **Ogascanan, L** Quebec
61 P5 **Ogawara ko** *L* Japan
85 E7 **Ogbomosho** Nigeria
9 E5 **Ogbourne St.George** England
110 J1 **Ogden** Illinois
99 M7 **Ogden** Iowa
107 O2 **Ogden** Kansas
123 L8 **Ogden** Nova Scotia
101 O8 **Ogden** Utah
117 G6 **Ogden,Mt** Br Col/Alaska
95 M2 **Ogdensburg** New York
115 M9 **Ogdensburg** Ontario
112 F5 **Ogeechee** *R* Georgia
98 K2 **Ogema** Minnesota
119 N9 **Ogema** Sask
32 G5 **Ogenbargen** W Germany
36 B6 **Ogéviller** France
41 K6 **Oggiono** Italy
61 M8 **Ogi** Japan
120 F6 **Ogidaki** Ontario
103 K9 **Ogilby** California
99 N4 **Ogilvie** Minnesota
143 A8 **Ogilvie** W Australia
114 F5 **Ogilvie Mts** Yukon Terr
61 Q12 **Ōgimi** Japan
98 D6 **Oglala** S Dakota
99 R8 **Oglesby** Illinois
109 K4 **Oglesby** Texas
112 C5 **Oglethorpe** Georgia
55 F3 **Oglukhino** U.S.S.R.
141 J6 **Ogmore** Queensland
55 G2 **Ognev Yar** U.S.S.R.
19 J5 **Ognon** *R* France
70 G4 **Ogoamas, G** *mt* Celebes
85 F7 **Ogoja** Nigeria
120 C2 **Ogoki L** Ontario
120 D2 **Ogoki R** Ontario
120 B2 **Ogoki Res** Ontario
86 A6 **Ogooué** *R* Gabon
47 F1 **Ogosta** *R* Bulgaria
70 G4 **Ogotomubu** Sulawesi
61 K9 **Ogoya** Japan
46 F3 **Ograzden Planina** *mt* Yugoslavia
52 B6 **Ogre** U.S.S.R.
28 N3 **Øgrum** Faeroes
61 N10 **Oguchi Dam** Japan
85 D4 **Oguilet Khenachich** Mali
124 F4 **Oguivo** Mexico
85 E7 **Ogun** *R* Nigeria
60 E12 **Oguni** Japan
95 R3 **Ogunquit** Maine
85 F7 **Ogwashi-Uku** Nigeria
145 D1 **Ohaeawai** New Zealand
144 A6 **Ohai** New Zealand
145 E3 **Ohakune** New Zealand
85 F3 **Ohanet** Algeria
86 D2 **O Haouach** *dist* Chad
61 O10 **Ōhara** Japan
60 P4 **Ōhata** Japan
118 E6 **Ohaton** Alberta
145 E4 **Ohau** New Zealand
144 B6 **Ohau, L** New Zealand
145 E2 **Ohaupo** New Zealand
61 P6 **Ōhazama** *R* Japan
32 G7 **Ohe** *R* W Germany
145 E2 **Ohena I** New Zealand
22 J3 **Ohey** Belgium
133 C4 **O'Higgins** *prov* Chile
133 C7 **O'Higgins, L** Chile/Arg
133 C7 **O'Higgins Pirámide** *mt* Chile
145 E2 **Ohinewai** New Zealand
145 E3 **Ohingaiti** New Zealand
99 R8 **Ohio** Illinois
94 C8 **Ohio** *R* Indiana
110 H4 **Ohio** *R* U.S.A.
94 C6 **Ohio** *state* U.S.A.
94 C6 **Ohio City** Ohio
32 G10 **Ohle** W Germany
36 F2 **Ohm** *R* W Germany
33 M8 **Ohof** W Germany
116 G6 **Ohogamiut** Alaska
112 E5 **Ohoopee** *R* Georgia
87 B9 **Ohopoho** Namibia
33 N7 **Ohrdorf** W Germany
37 K2 **Ohrdruf** E Germany
37 O3 **Ohře** *R* Czechoslovakia
33 O8 **Ohre** *R* E Germany
46 D3 **Ohrid** Yugoslavia
46 D3 **Ohridsko Jez** *L* Yugoslavia
36 H5 **Öhringen** W Germany
36 G5 **Ohrnberg** W Germany
26 N5 **Ohtanajärvi** Sweden
145 E3 **Ohura** New Zealand
129 H3 **Oiapoque** Fr Guiana
22 H3 **Oignies** Belgium
29 M6 **Oijärvi** Finland
106 G9 **Oil Center** New Mexico
102 F6 **Oil City** California

111 C9 **Oil City** Louisiana
94 H5 **Oil City** Pennsylvania
120 H10 **Oil Springs** Ontario
107 O5 **Oilton** Oklahoma
109 J8 **Oilton** Texas
94 K9 **Oilville** Virginia
47 H6 **Oinoúsa** *isld* Greece
58 C6 **Oi Qu** *R* China
61 P5 **Oirase-gawa** *R* Japan
21 E8 **Oiron** France
25 D5 **Oirschot** Netherlands
19 Q14 **Oisans** *dist* France
71 L10 **Oisau** Timor Indonesia
20 K3 **Oise** *dep* France
20 K3 **Oise** *R* France
20 J2 **Oisemont** France
20 D5 **Oisseau** France
20 H3 **Oissel** France
25 D5 **Oisterwijk** Netherlands
127 P6 **Oistins** Barbados
22 E3 **Oisy-le-Verger** France
60 E12 **Ōita** Japan
46 E6 **Oíti** *mt* Greece
48 K4 **Oituz** *pass* Romania
60 P3 **Oiwake** Japan
102 E7 **Ojai** California
27 G11 **Öje** Sweden
61 J11 **Ōji** Japan
60 B12 **Ojika-jima** *isld* Japan
124 G3 **Ojinaga** Mexico
61 M8 **Ojiya** Japan
124 H6 **Ojocaliente** Mexico
106 B7 **Ojo Caliente** New Mexico
133 E3 **Ojo de Agua** Argentina
124 F3 **Ojo de Laguna** Mexico
124 C4 **Ojo de Liebre** Mexico
16 E5 **Ojos del Guadiana** *mt* Spain
133 D3 **Ojos del Salado, Nev** *mt* Chile/Arg
17 F4 **Ojos Negros** Spain
113 G12 **Ojus** Florida
27 F10 **Öjvallberget** Sweden
121 Q7 **Oka** Quebec
54 G4 **Oka** *R* U.S.S.R.
56 F4 **Oka** *R* U.S.S.R.
87 C10 **Okahandja** Namibia
145 E1 **Okahu** New Zealand
145 E3 **Okahukura** New Zealand
145 E3 **Okaiawa** *R* New Zealand
145 D1 **Okaihau** New Zealand
115 N6 **Okak Is** Labrador
113 F11 **Okaloacoochee Slough** *swamp* Florida
117 O10 **Okanagan Centre** Br Col
117 O11 **Okanagan Falls** Br Col
86 B6 **Okanda Nat. Park** Gabon
100 F1 **Okanogan** Washington
100 F1 **Okanogan Range** Wash/Br Col
74 E3 **Okara** Pakistan
107 N6 **Okarche** Oklahoma
144 C5 **Okarito** New Zealand
60 D14 **Okasaki** Japan
145 F3 **Okataina L** New Zealand
145 D3 **Okato** New Zealand
111 G10 **Okatoma** *R* Mississippi
87 C9 **Okaukuejo** Namibia
87 C9 **Okavango** *R* Namibia
87 D9 **Okavango Basin** Botswana
60 D12 **Ōkawa** Japan
61 N8 **Ō-kawa** *R* Japan
61 O7 **Okawara** Japan
110 G3 **Okawville** Illinois
107 P6 **Okay** Oklahoma
61 L9 **Okaya** Japan
60 G11 **Okayama** Japan
60 G11 **Okayama** *prefect* Japan
61 L11 **Okazaki** Japan
113 G10 **Okeechobee** Florida
113 G11 **Okeechobee,L** Florida
107 M5 **Okeene** Oklahoma
113 E7 **Okefenokee Swamp** Georgia
8 B6 **Okehampton** England
107 O6 **Okemah** Oklahoma
85 F7 **Okene** Nigeria
33 M9 **Oker** W Germany
33 N8 **Oker** *R* W Germany
60 R2 **Oketo** Japan
98 K10 **Oketo** Kansas
74 C7 **Okha** India
59 M1 **Okha** U.S.S.R.
75 M5 **Okhalchunga** Nepal
47 G6 **Ókhi** *mt* Greece
51 O3 **Okhotsk** U.S.S.R.
59 N1 **Okhotskoye More** *sea* E Asia
Okhotsk,Sea of *see* **Okhotskoye More**
85 F7 **Okigwi** Nigeria
61 P13 **Okinawa** *isld* Japan
60 F13 **Okino-shima** Japan
60 D11 **Okino-shima** *isld* Japan
56 E4 **Okinskiy Khrebet** *mts* U.S.S.R.
60 G9 **Oki shotō** *islds* Japan
85 E7 **Okitipupa** Nigeria
68 B4 **Okkan** Burma
107 N6 **Oklahoma** *state* U.S.A.
107 N6 **Oklahoma City** Oklahoma
109 H1 **Oklaunion** Texas
113 F8 **Oklawaha** *R* Florida
107 P6 **Okmulgee** Oklahoma
48 K2 **Okna** U.S.S.R.
48 L2 **Oknitsa** U.S.S.R.
99 L6 **Okoboji L** Iowa
98 F5 **Okobojo** S Dakota
145 E3 **Okoia** New Zealand
111 H7 **Okolona** Mississippi
86 B6 **Okondja** Gabon
31 K2 **Okonek** Poland
60 R1 **Okoppe** Japan
145 E2 **Okoroire** New Zealand
118 D8 **Okotoks** Alberta
86 B6 **Okoyo** Congo
85 E7 **Okpara** *R* Benin/Nigeria
98 F6 **Okreek** S Dakota
26 C9 **Oksendal** Norway
26 M1 **Öksfjord** Norway
26 M1 **Öksfjord-jökel** *mt* Norway
52 H1 **Oksino** U.S.S.R.
54 M3 **Oksko-Donskaya Ravnina** *plain* U.S.S.R.
26 G3 **Öksnes** Norway
26 G5 **Okstinderne** *mt* Norway
107 P6 **Oktaha** Oklahoma
68 C3 **Oktwin** Burma
55 C6 **Oktyabr'sk** U.S.S.R.
55 D3 **Oktyabr'skiy** Chelyabinsk U.S.S.R.
52 F5 **Oktyabr'skiy** Kostroma U.S.S.R.
55 E5 **Oktyabr'skiy** Kushmurun U.S.S.R.
55 D4 **Oktyabr'skiy** Kustanay U.S.S.R.
55 E2 **Oktyabr'skiy** Tobol'sk U.S.S.R.
55 D4 **Oktyabr'skoye** Chelyabinsk U.S.S.R.
55 E1 **Oktyabr'skoye** Khanty-Mansiysk U.S.S.R.
55 C4 **Oktyabr'skoye** Orenburg U.S.S.R.
54 D10 **Oktyabr'skoye** Ukraine U.S.S.R.
51 J1 **Oktyabr'skoy Revolyutsii, Os** *isld* U.S.S.R.
61 Q12 **Oku** Okinawa
60 D13 **Ōkuchi** Japan
144 D5 **Okuku** *R* New Zealand
52 D5 **Okulovka** U.S.S.R.
146 J8 **Okuma Bay** Antarctica
144 B5 **Okuru** New Zealand
60 N3 **Okushiri-kaikyō** *str* Japan
60 N3 **Okushiri-tō** *isld* Japan
60 J10 **Okutango-hantō** *pen* Japan
89 B4 **Okwa** *watercourse* Botswana
110 C6 **Ola** Arkansas
100 J5 **Ola** Idaho
16 C7 **Olalla de Cala, Sta** Spain
95 T1 **Olamon** Maine
27 J15 **Öland** *isld* Sweden
28 D2 **Øland** *reg* Denmark
52 D2 **Olanga** U.S.S.R.
29 P5 **Olanga** *R* U.S.S.R.
112 H4 **Olanta** S Carolina
18 G9 **Olargues** France
138 C2 **Olarinna** *R* S Australia
138 F4 **Olary** S Australia
107 Q3 **Olathe** Kansas
131 E6 **Olavarría** Argentina
31 K5 **Oława** Poland
103 N8 **Olberg** Arizona
37 P2 **Olbernhau** E Germany
37 L1 **Olbersleben** E Germany
43 C8 **Olbia** Sardinia
37 L7 **Olching** W Germany
94 J3 **Olcott** New York
126 E3 **Old Bahama Chan** Caribbean
14 D3 **Oldcastle** Irish Rep
142 F4 **Old Cherrabun** W Australia
141 F6 **Old Cork** Queensland
114 F4 **Old Crow** Yukon Terr
116 R2 **Old Crow** *R* Alaska/Yukon Terr
88 E3 **Oldeani** Tanzania
109 J3 **Olden** Texas
32 H6 **Oldenbrok** W Germany
33 N4 **Oldenburg** W Germany
33 N6 **Oldendorf** W Germany
33 N7 **Oldenstadt** W Germany
25 G4 **Oldenzaal** Netherlands
32 F6 **Oldersum** W Germany
26 B10 **Oldevatn** *L* Norway
101 P5 **Old Faithful** Wyoming
95 M3 **Old Forge** New York
95 M5 **Old Forge** Pennsylvania
112 E2 **Old Fort** N Carolina
123 O2 **Old Fort Bay** Quebec
143 C8 **Old Gidgee** W Australia
108 G2 **Old Glory** Texas
13 F6 **Oldham** England
98 J5 **Oldham** S Dakota
127 K3 **Old Harbour** Jamaica
110 K5 **Old Hickory** Tennessee
117 L8 **Old Hogem** Br Columbia
9 F3 **Old Hurst** England
33 O10 **Oldisleben** E Germany
51 P2 **Old John L** Alaska
95 P5 **Old Lyme** Connecticut
15 F3 **Oldmeldrum** Scotland
110 F3 **Old Monroe** Missouri
95 R3 **Old Orchard Beach** Maine
123 T5 **Old Perlican** Newfoundland
123 L3 **Old Post Pt** Quebec
116 R3 **Old Rampart** Alaska
113 G12 **Old Rhodes Key** *isld* Florida
127 O5 **Old Road** Antigua W I
127 P4 **Old Road Town** St Kitts W I
118 C7 **Olds** Alberta
95 R2 **Old Speckle Mt** Maine
9 F3 **Old Stratford** England
28 A7 **Oldsum** W Germany
113 E10 **Old Tampa B** Florida
138 E4 **Old Telichie** S Australia
113 D8 **Old Town** Florida
95 T2 **Old Town** Maine
88 E3 **Olduvai Gorge** Tanzania
Old Viking Bank *see* **Bergen Bank**
118 L8 **Old Wives L** Sask
116 H5 **Old Woman** *R* Alaska
103 J7 **Old Woman Mts** California
94 J4 **Olean** New York
122 H7 **O'Leary** Pr Edward I
31 N1 **Olecko** Poland
69 B10 **Oleeheue** Sumatra
16 B5 **Oleiros** Portugal
59 G1 **Olekminski Stanovik** *mt ra* U.S.S.R.
52 G3 **Olema** U.S.S.R.
27 A12 **Ölen** Norway
100 D7 **Olene** Oregon
52 D1 **Olenegorsk** U.S.S.R.
51 L2 **Olenek** *R* U.S.S.R.
52 D6 **Olenino** U.S.S.R.
52 E2 **Olenitsa** U.S.S.R.
55 B5 **Olenty** *R* U.S.S.R.
18 E7 **Oléron,Ile d'** France
48 J1 **Olesko** U.S.S.R.
31 K4 **Oleśnica** Poland
31 L5 **Olesno** Poland
45 O6 **Olevano Romano** Italy
100 E4 **Olex** Oregon
32 F9 **Olfen** W Germany
113 F11 **Olga** Florida
98 H1 **Olga** N Dakota
59 L3 **Ol'ga** U.S.S.R.
116 K8 **Olga B** Alaska
121 N3 **Olga,L** Quebec
140 B7 **Olga, Mt** N Terr Aust
54 J9 **Ol'ginka** U.S.S.R.
55 F3 **Ol'gino** U.S.S.R.
66 D2 **Ölgiy** Mongolia
28 B5 **Ølgod** Denmark
48 M2 **Olgopol** U.S.S.R.
16 B7 **Olhão** Portugal
29 L6 **Olhava** Finland
85 E7 **Oli** *R* Benin/Nigeria
140 A7 **Olia Chain** *mts* N Terr Aust
138 A2 **Olia Chain** *mts* N Terr Australia
17 H2 **Oliana** Spain
42 F4 **Olib** *isld* Yugoslavia
17 G4 **Oliete** Spain
89 A8 **Olifants** S Africa
87 C10 **Olifants** *R* Namibia
89 G5 **Olifants** *R* S Africa
89 A5 **Olifants** *watercourse* Namibia
87 D11 **Olifantshoek** S Africa
89 A9 **Olifants R. Berge** *mts* S Africa
131 G4 **Olimar** *R* Uruguay
46 E7 **Olimbía** Greece
46 E4 **Ólimbos** *mt* Greece
133 F2 **Olimpo** Paraguay
99 P7 **Olin** Iowa
100 C9 **Olinda** California
141 G1 **Olinda Ent** Gt Barrier Reef Aust
129 L6 **Olindina** Brazil
141 G5 **Olio** Queensland
17 F2 **Olite** Spain
17 G6 **Oliva** Spain
131 B2 **Oliva, Cord. de** *mt ra* Arg/Chile
16 C6 **Oliva de Mérida** Spain
131 B3 **Olivares,Cerro del** *peak* Arg/Chile
17 F5 **Olivares de Júcar** Spain
98 A4 **Olive** Montana
94 D8 **Olive Hill** Kentucky
130 G7 **Oliveira** Brazil
16 B4 **Oliveira de Azemeis** Portugal
16 B4 **Oliveira do Hospital** Portugal
112 J2 **Olive, Mt** N Carolina
Olivenca *see* **Lupilichi**
16 C6 **Olivenza** Spain
117 O11 **Oliver** Br Col
112 F5 **Oliver** Georgia
21 I6 **Olivet** France
94 C4 **Olivet** Michigan
98 J6 **Olivet** S Dakota
99 M5 **Olivia** Minnesota
109 L7 **Olivia** Texas
144 B6 **Olivine Range** New Zealand
41 J5 **Olivone** Switzerland
31 L1 **Oliwa** Poland
65 D3 **Olji Moron He** *R* China
54 L6 **Ol'khovatka** U.S.S.R.
55 D3 **Ol'khovka** U.S.S.R.
31 M5 **Olkusz** Poland
111 D10 **Olla** Louisiana
133 D2 **Ollague** *vol* Bolivia/Chile
9 E1 **Ollerton** England
98 B3 **Ollie** Montana
29 N2 **Ollila** Finland
131 B3 **Ollita, Cord. de** *ra* Arg/Chile
131 B3 **Ollitas** *peak* Argentina
27 G12 **Ölme** Sweden
16 D3 **Olmeda** Spain
131 D4 **Olmos,L** Argentina
9 F3 **Olney** England
110 H3 **Olney** Illinois
101 L1 **Olney** Montana
109 J2 **Olney** Texas
106 G3 **Olney Springs** Colorado
26 K8 **Olofsfors** Sweden
27 G15 **Olofström** Sweden
123 M3 **Olomane R** Quebec
86 C6 **Olombo** Congo
48 D1 **Olomouc** Czechoslovakia
41 K7 **Olona** *R* Italy
48 M4 **Oloneshty** U.S.S.R.
52 D4 **Olonets** U.S.S.R.
71 E3 **Olongapo** Luzon Philippines
18 G9 **Olonzac** France
18 E9 **Oloron-St.Marie** France
17 J2 **Olot** Spain
37 O3 **Olovi** Czechoslovakia
48 E6 **Olovo** Yugoslavia
58 G1 **Olovyannaya** U.S.S.R.
107 O3 **Olpe** Kansas
36 D1 **Olpe** W Germany
41 P3 **Olperer** *mt* Austria
107 O2 **Olsburg** Kansas
31 L6 **Olše** *R* Czechoslovakia
54 G3 **Ol'shany** U.S.S.R.
25 F4 **Olst** Netherlands
31 M2 **Olsztyn** Poland
31 M2 **Olsztynek** Poland
40 G3 **Olten** Switzerland
48 K6 **Olteniţa** Romania
133 D6 **Olte,Sa.de** *mts* Argentina
48 H6 **Olteţul** *R* Romania
108 E1 **Olton** Texas
78 H1 **Oltu** Turkey
48 K4 **Oltul** *R* Romania
67 G6 **O-luan-pi** *C* Taiwan
113 E7 **Olustee** Florida
107 L7 **Olustee** Oklahoma
71 F7 **Olutanga** *isld* Philippines
33 P8 **Olvenstedt** E Germany
16 D8 **Olvera** Spain
46 E7 **Olympia** Greece
100 C2 **Olympia** Washington
100 B2 **Olympic Mts** Washington
100 B2 **Olympic Nat. Park** Washington
Olympus *mt* Cyprus *see* **Troödos** *Mt*
Olympus *mt* Greece *see* **Ólimbos** *Mt*
100 B2 **Olympus,Mt** Washington
95 M5 **Olyphant** Pennsylvania
51 R2 **Olyutorskiy** U.S.S.R.
36 B3 **Olzheim** W Germany
56 B3 **Om'** *R* U.S.S.R.
60 O4 **Ōma** Japan
111 F10 **Oma** Mississippi
52 G2 **Oma** U.S.S.R.
61 L9 **Ōmachi** Japan
61 M11 **Omae zaki** *C* Japan
14 D2 **Omagh** N Ireland
128 D4 **Omaguas** Peru
110 C5 **Omaha** Arkansas
99 L8 **Omaha** Nebraska
109 N2 **Omaha** Texas
126 F4 **Omaja** Cuba
100 F1 **Omak** Washington
144 B6 **Omakau** New Zealand
145 F4 **Omakere** New Zealand
72 H5 **Oman** *sultanate* Arabian Pen
77 F7 **Oman, Gulf of** Iran/Oman
145 D1 **Omapere, L** New Zealand
94 E9 **Omar** W Virginia
144 B6 **Omarama** New Zealand
87 C10 **Omaruru** Namibia
128 D7 **Omate** Peru
60 O4 **Ōma-zaki** *C* Japan
120 C2 **Ombabika** Ontario
120 B2 **Ombabika B** Ontario
71 M9 **Ombai,Selat** *str* Indonesia
69 C12 **Ombalata** Indonesia
61 N11 **Ombase-jima** *isld* Japan
8 D3 **Ombersley** England
86 A6 **Omboue** Gabon
45 J4 **Ombrone** *R* Italy
66 D5 **Ombu** China
86 F2 **Omdurman** Sudan
61 N10 **Ome** Japan
111 L10 **Omega** Alabama
112 D6 **Omega** Georgia
107 M6 **Omega** Oklahoma
98 F1 **Omemee** N Dakota
121 M8 **Omemee** Ontario
94 B1 **Omena** Michigan
80 C8 **'Omer** Israel
94 D2 **Omer** Michigan
47 J5 **Ömerköy** Turkey
14 A3 **Omey I** Irish Rep
61 L8 **Ōmi** Japan
22 D4 **Omiecourt** France
144 D5 **Omihi** New Zealand
57 L2 **O-min** U.S.S.R.
60 P4 **Ōminato** Japan
117 L8 **Omineca** *R* Br Col
114 G6 **Omineca Mts** Br Col
117 K7 **Omineca Mts** Br Col
61 J11 **Ōmine San** *mt* Japan
42 H5 **Omis** Yugoslavia
60 E11 **Ōmi-shima** *isld* Japan
60 F11 **Ōmi-shima** *isld* Japan
61 N10 **Ōmiya** Japan
117 F7 **Ommaney,C** Alaska
114 J3 **Ommanney B** N W Terr
28 B5 **Omme Å** *R* Denmark
25 F3 **Ommen** Netherlands
28 G6 **Omø** Denmark
86 G4 **Omo** *R* Ethiopia
51 P2 **Omolon** *R* U.S.S.R.
51 N2 **Omolov** *R* U.S.S.R.
61 O6 **Omono-gawa** *R* Japan
22 H4 **Omont** France
20 B2 **Omonville-la Rogue** France
61 O6 **Omori** Japan
61 P6 **Omoto** Japan
61 P6 **Omoto-gawa** *R* Japan
99 S5 **Omro** Wisconsin
55 F3 **Omsk** U.S.S.R.
50 G3 **Omskaya Oblast'** *prov* U.S.S.R.
68 D1 **O-mu** Burma
60 Q1 **Ōmu** Japan
31 N2 **Omulew** *R* Poland
83 L10 **Omuna** Sri Lanka
60 C13 **Ōmura** Japan
60 C13 **Ōmura wan** *B* Japan
47 H1 **Omurtag** Bulgaria
60 D12 **Ōmuta** Japan
55 E3 **Omutinskiy** U.S.S.R.
52 H5 **Omutninsk** U.S.S.R.
113 F10 **Ona** Florida
26 B9 **Ona** Norway
16 E2 **Oña** Spain
56 C5 **Ona** *R* U.S.S.R.
107 O2 **Onaga** Kansas
61 P7 **Onagawahama** Japan
61 P7 **Onagawa-wan** *B* Japan
61 O9 **Onahama** Japan
98 G4 **Onaka** S Dakota
120 J2 **Onakawana** Ontario
120 J1 **Onakwehegan** *R* Ontario
100 C3 **Onalaska** Washington
99 P6 **Onalaska** Wisconsin
120 C2 **Onaman L** Ontario
99 N3 **Onamia** Minnesota
70 F6 **Onan** Sulawesi
95 M9 **Onancock** Virginia
86 B6 **Onangue, L** Gabon
120 J5 **Onaping L** Ontario
110 H1 **Onarga** Illinois
121 U3 **Onatchiway,L** Quebec
124 F2 **Oñate** Mexico
124 E3 **Onavas** Mexico
98 K7 **Onawa** Iowa
94 C1 **Onaway** Michigan
68 C5 **Onbingwin** Burma
87 B9 **Oncocua** Angola
17 G5 **Onda** Spain
87 C9 **Ondangua** Namibia
31 N6 **Ondava** *R* Czechoslovakia
25 G2 **Onderdendam** Netherlands
85 E7 **Ondo** Nigeria
58 F2 **Öndörhaan** Mongolia
65 E2 **Ondor Had** China
73 L8 **One and Half Degree Chan** Indian Ocean
113 E10 **Oneco** Florida
52 E3 **Onega** U.S.S.R.
Onega *L see* **Onezhskoye, Oz**
52 E4 **Onega** *R* U.S.S.R.
44 D4 **Oneglia** Italy
141 H2 **One & Half Mile Opening** *str* Gt Barrier Reef **Aust**
99 Q8 **Oneida** Illinois
99 P7 **Oneida** Iowa
94 D9 **Oneida** Kentucky
95 M3 **Oneida** New York
110 M5 **Oneida** Tennessee
95 L3 **Oneida L** New York
98 H7 **O'Neill** Nebraska
145 D4 **Onekaka** New Zealand
94 A2 **Onekama** Michigan
86 D6 **Onema** Zaïre
111 K8 **Oneonta** Alabama
95 M4 **Oneonta** New York
145 F3 **Onepoto** New Zealand
145 E1 **Onerahi** New Zealand
118 J1 **One Sided Lake** Ontario
52 E4 **Onezhskoye,Oz** *L* U.S.S.R.
145 F3 **Ongaonga** New Zealand
9 G4 **Ongar** England
145 E3 **Ongarue** New Zealand
89 C8 **Ongers** *watercourse* S Africa
143 C10 **Ongerup** W Australia
65 B3 **Onggon Ul** China
19 P16 **Ongles** France
65 D3 **Ongniud Qi** China
76 E3 **Ongole** India
15 C4 **Onich** Scotland
98 G5 **Onida** S Dakota
87 G12 **Onilahy** *R* Madagascar
118 H5 **Onion Lake** Sask
60 P1 **Onishika** Japan
122 A3 **Onistagan L** Quebec
85 F7 **Onitsha** Nigeria
20 H1 **Onival** France
29 N8 **Onkivesi** *L* Finland
95 M9 **Onley** Virginia
61 P13 **Onna** Okinawa
61 P13 **Onna-dake** *mt* Okinawa
22 F3 **Onnaing** France
60 O4 **Ōno** Japan
60 E11 **Onoda** Japan
61 N11 **Ōnohara-jima** *isld* Japan
137 R6 **Ono-i-lau** *isld* Pacific Oc
145 E4 **Onoke, L** New Zealand
69 C12 **Onolimbu** Indonesia
60 G11 **Onomichi** Japan
58 G1 **Onon** *R* U.S.S.R.
94 C4 **Onondaga** Michigan
58 F2 **Onon Gol** *R* Mongolia
61 O8 **Ono-Niimachi** Japan
59 M1 **Onor** U.S.S.R.
128 E2 **Onoto** Venezuela
137 Q2 **Onotoa** *atoll* Kiribati
118 C5 **Onoway** Alberta
28 F5 **Onsbjerg** Denmark
16 B2 **Ons., I.de** Spain
28 H7 **Ønslev** Denmark
142 B5 **Onslow** W Australia
112 K3 **Onslow B** N Carolina
144 B6 **Onslow, L** New Zealand
94 C4 **Onsted** Michigan
36 G7 **Onstmettingen** W Germany
25 H2 **Onstwedde** Netherlands
61 L10 **Ontake-san** *mt* Japan
102 G7 **Ontario** California
100 J5 **Ontario** Oregon
99 Q6 **Ontario** Wisconsin
120 E3 **Ontario** *prov* Canada
94 J3 **Ontario,L** U.S.A./Canada
17 G6 **Onteniente** Spain
99 R3 **Ontonagon** Michigan
137 M3 **Ontong Java Is** Solomon Is
17 G6 **Ontur** Spain
60 O4 **Onuma** Japan
111 F9 **Onward** Mississippi
102 F6 **Onyx** California
21 H7 **Onzain** France
138 D2 **Oodnadatta** S Australia
135 V4 **Ookala** Hawaiian Is
107 P5 **Oolagah** Oklahoma
138 B4 **Ooldea** S Australia
138 B4 **Ooldea Ra** S Australia
110 K3 **Oolitic** Indiana
107 P5 **Oologah Res** Oklahoma
25 B5 **Ooltgensplaat** Netherlands
141 G5 **Oondooroo** Queensland
140 C6 **Ooraminna Ra** N Terr Aust
140 D5 **Ooratippra** *R* N Terr Aust
141 F5 **Oorindi** Queensland
111 L7 **Oostanaula** *R* Georgia
25 A6 **Oostburg** Netherlands
22 D2 **Oost Cappel** France
22 D1 **Oostduinkerke** Belgium
22 D1 **Oostende** Belgium
25 E5 **Oosterbeër** Netherlands
25 D2 **Oosterend** Netherlands
25 C5 **Oosterhout** Netherlands
25 A5 **Oosterschelde** Netherlands
25 F3 **Oosterwolde** Netherlands
22 F2 **Oosterzele** Belgium
25 D3 **Oosthuizen** Netherlands
25 E4 **Oostlijk-Flevoland** Netherlands
25 F2 **Oostmahoorn** Netherlands
22 H1 **Oostmalle** Belgium
22 F1 **Oost Vlaanderen** Belgium
25 D2 **Oost Vlieland** Netherlands
25 B5 **Oostvoorne** Netherlands
76 C5 **Ootacamund** India
25 G4 **Ootmarsum** Netherlands
117 L9 **Ootsa Lake** Br Col
119 S2 **Opachuanau L** Manitoba
102 R11 **Opaeula** *R* Hawaiian Is
47 H1 **Opaka** Bulgaria
145 E4 **Opaki** New Zealand
118 D5 **Opal** Alberta
124 H5 **Opal** Mexico
101 P8 **Opal** Wyoming
51 P3 **Opala** U.S.S.R.
86 D6 **Opala** Zaïre
31 J3 **Opalenica** Poland
113 G12 **Opa-Locka** Florida
141 G6 **Opalton** Queensland
141 G6 **Opalville** Queensland
76 E7 **Opanake** Sri Lanka
86 F5 **Opari** Sudan
52 G5 **Oparino** U.S.S.R.
120 H3 **Opasatika** Ontario
120 G3 **Opasatika L** Ontario
42 F3 **Opatija** Yugoslavia
31 N5 **Opatów** Poland
31 L4 **Opatówek** Poland
31 K6 **Opava** Czechoslovakia
31 K5 **Opava** *R* Czechoslovakia
121 P3 **Opawica, L** Quebec
111 L9 **Opelika** Alabama
111 D11 **Opelousas** Louisiana
120 D2 **Opemisha** Ontario
144 B5 **Open Bay Is** New Zealand
143 D8 **Open L** W Australia
121 M7 **Opeongo L** Ontario
22 F2 **Ophasselt** Belgium
101 T1 **Opheim** Montana
100 A7 **Ophir** Oregon
101 N9 **Ophir** Utah
22 K1 **Ophoven** Belgium
142 C6 **Ophthalmia Ra** W Australia
45 P6 **Opi** Italy
86 E5 **Opienge** Zaïre
144 C6 **Opihi R** New Zealand
36 B1 **Opladen** W Germany
85 F8 **Opobo** Nigeria
52 C6 **Opochka** U.S.S.R.
122 F1 **Opocopa L** Quebec
31 M4 **Opoczno** Poland
124 D3 **Opodepe** Mexico
31 K5 **Opole** Poland
145 F3 **Oponae** New Zealand
145 D1 **Opononi** New Zealand
Oporto *see* **Porto**
54 F7 **Oposhnya** U.S.S.R.
145 F3 **Opotiki** New Zealand
145 E2 **Opoutere** New Zealand
111 K10 **Opp** Alabama
61 P7 **Oppa-gawa** *R* Japan
61 P7 **Oppa-wan** *B* Japan
26 D9 **Oppdal** Norway
45 K1 **Oppeano** Italy
33 T9 **Oppelhaun** E Germany
Oppeln *see* **Opole**
36 E7 **Oppenau** W Germany
36 E4 **Oppenheim** W Germany
36 G6 **Oppenweiler** W Germany
28 J5 **Oppe Sundby** Denmark
27 D10 **Oppland** *county* Norway
119 Q4 **Optic Lake** Manitoba
107 J5 **Optima** Oklahoma
106 F6 **Optimo** New Mexico
145 E1 **Opua** New Zealand
145 E1 **Opuawhanga** New Zealand
145 D3 **Opunake** New Zealand
124 E2 **Oputo** Mexico
22 G2 **Opwijk** Belgium
99 Q9 **Oquawka** Illinois
124 D2 **Oquitoa** Mexico
95 R2 **Oquossoc** Maine
27 G15 **Ör** Sweden
55 C5 **Or'** *R* U.S.S.R.
41 O5 **Ora** Italy
84 F4 **Ora** Libya
143 D9 **Ora Banda** W Australia
127 L2 **Oracabessa** Jamaica
103 O9 **Oracle** Arizona
48 G3 **Oradea** Romania
74 H6 **Orai** India
103 O6 **Oraibi** Arizona
103 O5 **Oraibi Wash** *creek* Arizona
29 L5 **Orajärvi** Finland
29 M4 **Orajärvi** *L* Finland
98 C6 **Oral** S Dakota
85 D1 **Oran** Algeria
110 G4 **Oran** Missouri
19 N16 **Orange** France
95 P4 **Orange** Massachusetts
139 J5 **Orange** New S Wales
109 O5 **Orange** Texas
94 J8 **Orange** Virginia
87 C11 **Orange** *R* S Africa/Namibia
111 J11 **Orange Beach** Alabama
112 G4 **Orangeburg** S Carolina
129 H3 **Orange,C** Brazil
126 E2 **Orange Cay** *isld* Bahamas
113 F9 **Orange City** Florida
116 Q3 **Orange Cr** Alaska
123 L8 **Orangedale** C Breton I, N Scotia
113 F7 **Orangedale** Florida
95 N6 **Orange, E** New Jersey
89 D7 **Orange Free State** *prov* S Africa
129 G3 **Orange Gebergte** *mts* Suriname
109 K8 **Orange Grove** Texas
113 E8 **Orange L** Florida
113 F7 **Orange Park** Florida
99 R7 **Orangeville** Illinois
103 N2 **Orangeville** Utah
145 E3 **Orangimea** New Zealand
71 E3 **Orani** Luzon Philippines
43 C8 **Orani** Sardinia
33 Q9 **Oranienbaum** E Germany
33 S7 **Oranienburg** E Germany
80 D3 **Oranim** Israel
87 C11 **Oranjemund** Namibia
126 A1 **Oranjestad** Aruba W I
127 N6 **Oranjestad** St Eustatius W I
14 C3 **Oranmore** Irish Rep
133 E2 **Orán, N** Argentina
Orantes *R see* **'Āsi** *R*
143 G6 **Orantjugurr,L** W Australia
80 C3 **Or'Aqiva** Israel
144 C6 **Orari** New Zealand
71 G4 **Oras** Philippines
71 G4 **Oras B** Philippines
48 E5 **Orašje** Yugoslavia
48 H5 **Orăstie** Romania
48 H3 **Oraşu Nou** Romania
124 H5 **Oratario** Mexico
48 M1 **Oratovo** U.S.S.R.
31 L6 **Orava** *R* Czechoslovakia
29 J8 **Oravais** Finland
48 G5 **Oraviţa** Romania
31 L6 **Oravská Magura** *mts* Czechoslovakia
144 A7 **Orawia** New Zealand
18 H9 **Orb** *R* France
44 E2 **Orba** *R* Italy
20 F3 **Orbec** France
42 D6 **Orbetello** Italy
21 H7 **Orbigny** France
16 D2 **Orbigo** *R* Spain
94 K6 **Orbisonia** Pennsylvania
139 J7 **Orbost** Victoria
27 F14 **Örby** Sweden
27 J11 **Örbyhus** Sweden
116 O6 **Orca B** Alaska
128 E1 **Orchila, La** *isld* Venezuela
16 B1 **Ordenes** Spain
103 M4 **Orderville** Utah
28 B3 **Ørding** Denmark
102 H7 **Ord Mt** California
142 F3 **Ord,Mt** W Australia
52 D3 **Ordozero** U.S.S.R.
142 G3 **Ord River** W Australia
78 F1 **Ordu** Turkey
78 K2 **Ordubail** U.S.S.R.
16 E2 **Orduña** Spain
106 G3 **Ordway** Colorado
98 H4 **Ordway** S Dakota
53 F11 **Ordzhonikidze** U.S.S.R.
56 C4 **Ordzhonikidzevskiy** U.S.S.R.
28 E5 **Ore** Denmark
26 C9 **Öre** Norway
26 K7 **Oreälv** *R* Sweden
100 J6 **Oreana** Idaho
102 F1 **Oreana** Nevada
27 H12 **Örebro** Sweden
27 G12 **Örebro** *county* Sweden
109 N3 **Ore City** Texas
99 R7 **Oregon** Illinois
110 A2 **Oregon** Missouri
99 R7 **Oregon** Wisconsin
100 E6 **Oregon** *state* U.S.A.
100 B7 **Oregon Caves Nat. Mon** Oregon
100 C4 **Oregon City** Oregon
112 M2 **Oregon Inlet** N Carolina
27 K11 **Öregrund** Sweden
54 G9 **Orekhov** U.S.S.R.
47 G1 **Orekhovitsa** Bulgaria
47 F1 **Orekhovo** Bulgaria
52 E6 **Orekhovo Zuyevo** U.S.S.R.
54 B2 **Orekhovsk** U.S.S.R.
54 H4 **Orël** Orlov U.S.S.R.
52 J5 **Orël** Perm U.S.S.R.
54 F8 **Orel'** *R* U.S.S.R.
98 C7 **Orella** Nebraska
128 C5 **Orellana** Peru
16 D5 **Orellana, Embalse de** *res* Spain
59 L1 **Orel, Oz** *L* U.S.S.R.
103 N1 **Orem** Utah
47 J7 **Ören** Turkey
55 C5 **Orenburg** U.S.S.R.
50 E3 **Orenburgskaya Oblast'** *prov* U.S.S.R.
16 B2 **Orense** Spain
16 B2 **Orense** *prov* Spain
46 F6 **Oreoí** Greece
144 A7 **Orepuki** New Zealand
47 H3 **Orestiás** Greece
28 K5 **Öresund** *str* Sweden/Denmark
144 B7 **Oreti R** New Zealand
145 E2 **Orewa** New Zealand
22 J2 **Oreye** Belgium
9 H3 **Orford** England
95 P3 **Orford** New Hampshire
139 J8 **Orford** Tasmania
9 H3 **Orford Ness** England
141 G1 **Orfordness** Queensland
106 D9 **Organ** New Mexico
126 C3 **Organos, Sa. de los** *hills* Cuba
103 M9 **Organ Pipe Cactus Nat. Mon** Arizona
16 E5 **Orgaz** Spain
20 K4 **Orge** *R* France
40 C4 **Orgelet** France
20 J5 **Orgères-en-Beauce** France
20 J4 **Orgeval** France
48 M3 **Orgeyev** U.S.S.R.
45 K1 **Orgiano** Italy
16 E8 **Orgiva** Spain
65 B3 **Orgon Tal** China
52 F6 **Orgtrud** U.S.S.R.
47 K5 **Orhaneli** Turkey
47 K5 **Orhaneli** *R* Turkey
47 K4 **Orhangazi** Turkey
Orhanie *see* **Botevgrad**
47 J5 **Orhanlar** Turkey
58 D2 **Orhon Gol** *R* Mongolia
17 F7 **Oria** Spain
17 F1 **Oria** *R* Spain
52 G5 **Orichi** U.S.S.R.
100 A8 **Orick** California
106 E3 **Orient** Colorado
99 M8 **Orient** Iowa
141 G8 **Orient** Queensland
98 G5 **Orient** S Dakota
108 G4 **Orient** Texas
100 G1 **Orient** Washington
112 L2 **Oriental** N Carolina
120 B3 **Orient Bay** Ontario
95 P5 **Orient I** New York
138 F3 **Orientos** New S Wales
141 F8 **Orientos** Queensland
22 G4 **Origny-en-Thiérache** France
22 E4 **Origny-St.-Benoîte** France
17 G6 **Orihuela** Spain
121 L8 **Orillia** Ontario
29 M11 **Orimattila** Finland
98 A7 **Orin** Wyoming
128 F2 **Orinoco** *R* Venezuela
128 F2 **Orinoco, Mouths of the** Venezuela
43 G8 **Oriolo** Italy
118 G9 **Orion** Alberta
99 Q8 **Orion** Illinois
98 J3 **Oriska** N Dakota
95 M4 **Oriskany Falls** New York
75 K8 **Orissa** *prov* India
43 B9 **Oristano** Sardinia
43 B9 **Oristano, G. di** Sardinia
128 E2 **Orituco** *R* Venezuela
29 O9 **Orivesi** *L* Finland
129 G4 **Oriximiná** Brazil
52 D2 **Oriyarvi, Oz** *L* U.S.S.R.
125 L8 **Orizaba** Mexico
47 J2 **Orizare** Bulgaria
42 J6 **Orjen** *mt* Yugoslavia
26 D8 **Orkdalen** *V* Norway
27 F15 **Örkelljunga** Sweden
27 G15 **Örkened** Sweden
26 D9 **Orkla** *R* Norway
87 E11 **Orkney** S Africa
118 K9 **Orkney** Sask
15 F1 **Orkney** *isld* Scotland
108 D4 **Orla** Texas
37 M2 **Orla** *R* E Germany
31 K4 **Orla** *R* Poland
37 M2 **Orlamünde** E Germany
102 B2 **Orland** California
94 B5 **Orland** Indiana
95 T2 **Orland** Maine
113 F9 **Orlando** Florida
107 N5 **Orlando** Oklahoma
43 F10 **Orlando, C.d'** Sicily
20 J5 **Orleanais** *reg* France
100 B8 **Orleans** California
21 I6 **Orleans** France
110 K3 **Orleans** Indiana
95 S5 **Orleans** Massachusetts
98 K1 **Orleans** Minnesota
98 G9 **Orleans** Nebraska
95 P2 **Orleans** Vermont
121 U6 **Orleans, Île d'** Quebec
Orléansville *see* **Asnam, El**
31 J5 **Orlice** *R* Czechoslovakia
56 E5 **Orlik** U.S.S.R.
31 L6 **Orlová** Czechoslovakia
56 C2 **Orlovka** *R* U.S.S.R.
52 F2 **Orlov, Mys** *C* U.S.S.R.
55 F3 **Orlovo** U.S.S.R.
74 C10 **Ormara** Pakistan
13 G4 **Ormesby** England
36 C5 **Ormesheim** W Germany
119 M9 **Ormiston** Sask
71 G5 **Ormoc** Philippines
113 F8 **Ormond** Florida
145 F3 **Ormond** New Zealand
113 F8 **Ormond Beach** Florida
145 F4 **Ormondville** New Zealand
38 O9 **Ormoz** Yugoslavia
99 M6 **Ormsby** Minnesota
99 R4 **Ormsby** Wisconsin
26 H7 **Ormsjö** Sweden
13 F6 **Ormskirk** England
121 R7 **Ormstown** Quebec
19 J4 **Ornain** *R* France
19 K5 **Ornans** France
41 H6 **Ornavasso** Italy
37 K5 **Ornbau** W Germany
20 F4 **Orne** *dep* France
20 F5 **Orne** *R* France
31 M1 **Orneta** Poland
27 K12 **Orno** Sweden
26 K8 **Örnsköldsvik** Sweden
28 H5 **Orø** Denmark
41 L5 **Orobie, Alpi** *mt* Italy
51 M3 **Orochen** U.S.S.R.
128 D3 **Orocué** Colombia
85 D6 **Orodara** Upper Volta
100 J3 **Orofino** Idaho
102 G7 **Oro Grande** California
100 K4 **Orogrande** Idaho
106 D9 **Orogrande** New Mexico
61 P13 **Oroku** Okinawa
122 F8 **Oromocto** New Brunswick
122 F8 **Oromocto L** New Brunswick
79 F8 **Oron** Israel
95 T2 **Orono** Maine
121 M9 **Orono** Ontario
110 B4 **Oronogo** Missouri
12 B1 **Oronsay** *isld* Scotland
16 D5 **Oropesa** Spain
89 H6 **Oro Pt** S Africa
127 P2 **Oropuche** *R* Trinidad
59 H1 **Oroqen Zizhiqi** China
71 F6 **Oroquieta** Mindanao
129 L5 **Orós, Açude** *res* Brazil
43 C8 **Orosei** Sardinia
43 C8 **Orosei, G.di** Sardinia
48 F4 **Orosháza** Hungary
48 E3 **Oroszlany** Hungary
51 P2 **Orotukan** U.S.S.R.
145 E4 **Oroua R** New Zealand
100 H8 **Orovada** Nevada
102 C2 **Oroville** California
100 F1 **Oroville** Washington
101 U7 **Orpha** Wyoming
141 H4 **Orpheus I** Queensland
20 J4 **Orphin** France
19 P16 **Orpierre** France
98 J1 **Orr** N Dakota
107 N7 **Orr** Oklahoma
27 H15 **Orrefors** Sweden
98 F1 **Orrin** N Dakota
15 D3 **Orrin** *R* Scotland
119 U2 **Orr L** Manitoba
26 G10 **Orrmosjön** *L* Sweden
138 E4 **Orroroo** S Australia
27 J11 **Orrskog** Sweden
94 K6 **Orrstown** Pennsylvania
94 F6 **Orrville** Ohio
27 G10 **Orsa** Sweden
44 H3 **Orsaro** *mt* Italy
9 G5 **Orsett** England
54 B2 **Orsha** U.S.S.R.
52 G6 **Orshanka** U.S.S.R.
27 H15 **Örsjö** Sweden
55 C5 **Orsk** U.S.S.R.
27 F13 **Örslösa** Sweden
28 E2 **Ørsø** Denmark
48 G6 **Orşova** Romania
32 E9 **Orsoy** W Germany
26 B9 **Örsta** Norway
27 J12 **Örsundsbro** Sweden
47 K8 **Ortaca** Turkey
47 J7 **Ortaklar** Turkey
80 G1 **Or Tal** Syria
41 H6 **Orta, L. d'** Italy
26 K7 **Örtäsk** Sweden
42 E6 **Orte** Italy
16 B1 **Ortegal, C** Spain
Ortelsburg *see* **Szczytno**
36 G3 **Ortenberg** W Germany
37 P6 **Ortenburg** W Germany
30 F1 **Orth** W Germany
18 E9 **Orthez** France
45 L4 **Ortignano Raggiolo** Italy
16 B1 **Ortigueira** Spain
100 C2 **Orting** Washington
106 D4 **Ortiz** Colorado
124 D3 **Ortiz** Mexico
128 E2 **Ortiz** Venezuela
41 N4 **Ortles** *mt* Italy
37 O2 **Ortmannsdorf** E Germany
127 P3 **Ortoire R** Trinidad
13 F5 **Orton** England
128 E6 **Orton** *R* Bolivia
42 F6 **Ortona** Italy
98 K4 **Ortonville** Minnesota
57 H4 **Orto-Tokoy** U.S.S.R.
33 T10 **Ortrand** E Germany
32 M7 **Ortze** *R* W Germany
145 F3 **Oruanui** New Zealand
51 M2 **Orulgan, Khrebet** *mt* U.S.S.R.
28 D4 **Ørum** Denmark
28 E2 **Ørum** Denmark
133 D1 **Oruro** Bolivia
145 D1 **Oruru** New Zealand
27 E13 **Orust** *isld* Sweden
21 B7 **Orvault** France
42 E6 **Orvieto** Italy
20 J4 **Orvilliers** France
45 N5 **Orvinio** Italy
94 K5 **Orviston** Pennsylvania
95 L3 **Orwell** New York
94 G5 **Orwell** Ohio
95 O3 **Orwell** Vermont
58 G2 **Orxon Gol** *R* China
41 L7 **Orzinuovi** Italy
31 M2 **Orzyc** *R* Poland
31 N2 **Orzysz** Poland
26 E9 **Os** Norway
27 E10 **Osa** *R* Norway
99 O6 **Osage** Iowa
107 O5 **Osage** Oklahoma
119 O9 **Osage** Sask
98 B6 **Osage** Wyoming
107 P3 **Osage City** Kansas
110 D4 **Osage Fork** *R* Missouri
62 **Ōsaka** *conurbation* Japan
55 F5 **Osakarovka** U.S.S.R.
99 L4 **Osakis** Minnesota
99 L4 **Osakis L** Minnesota
107 Q3 **Osawatomie** Kansas
120 E3 **Osawin** *R* Ontario
142 F2 **Osborne Is** W Australia
27 G14 **Os bruk** Sweden
27 G15 **Osby** Sweden
142 F4 **Oscar Ra** W Australia
110 G6 **Osceola** Arkansas
99 N8 **Osceola** Iowa
110 C3 **Osceola** Missouri
98 J8 **Osceola** Nebraska
94 J6 **Osceola** Pennsylvania
99 O4 **Osceola** Wisconsin
33 S10 **Oschatz** E Germany
33 O8 **Oschersleben** E Germany
94 D2 **Oscoda** Michigan
106 D8 **Oscura** New Mexico
26 E7 **Osen** Norway
54 K2 **Osetr** *R* U.S.S.R.
60 B13 **Ōse-zaki** *C* Japan
94 B7 **Osgood** Indiana
110 C1 **Osgood** Missouri
121 P7 **Osgoode Station** Ontario
100 H8 **Osgood Mts** Nevada
57 G4 **Osh** U.S.S.R.
55 F3 **Osha** *R* U.S.S.R.
60 O3 **Oshamanbe** Japan
121 M9 **Oshawa** Ontario
60 P1 **Oshidomari** Japan
61 P7 **Oshika-Hantō** *pen* Japan
59 J6 **O-shima** *isld* Japan
61 N11 **Ō-shima** *isld* Japan
98 D8 **Oshkosh** Nebraska
99 S6 **Oshkosh** Wisconsin
52 J2 **Oshkur'ya** U.S.S.R.
55 D1 **Oshmar'ye** U.S.S.R.
78 K3 **Oshnoviyeh** Iran
85 E7 **Oshogbo** Nigeria
98 B5 **Oshoto** Wyoming
77 A3 **Oshtorān Kūh** *mt* Iran
52 K2 **Oshvor** U.S.S.R.
86 C6 **Oshwe** Zaïre
74 E5 **Osian** India
47 G1 **Osica** Romania
48 J6 **Osica de Jos** Romania
48 E5 **Osijek** Yugoslavia
45 O4 **Osimo** Italy
56 C4 **Osinniki** U.S.S.R.
54 B2 **Osintorf** U.S.S.R.
26 N3 **Oskal** Norway
99 O8 **Oskaloosa** Iowa
107 P2 **Oskaloosa** Kansas
27 H14 **Oskarshamn** Sweden
27 F15 **Oskarström** Sweden
121 P4 **Oskelaneo** Quebec
54 J7 **Oskol** *R* U.S.S.R.
31 J6 **Oslava** *R* Czechoslovakia
118 L6 **Osler** Sask
98 J1 **Oslo** Minnesota
27 E12 **Oslo** Norway
71 F6 **Oslob** Cebu Philippines
27 E13 **Oslofjord** *inlet* Norway
28 C2 **Øsløs** Denmark
54 E2 **Os'ma** *R* U.S.S.R.
74 G9 **Osmanabad** India
78 E1 **Osmancik** Turkey
47 K4 **Osmaneli** Turkey
52 C5 **Osmino** U.S.S.R.
27 J13 **Ösmo** Sweden
98 J7 **Osmond** Nebraska
98 H1 **Osnabrock** N Dakota
32 H8 **Osnabrück** W Germany
31 H3 **Ośno** Poland
46 E2 **Osogovska Planina** *mt* Yugoslavia
41 N7 **Osone** *R* Italy
60 O4 **Osore yama** *mt* Japan
131 A8 **Osorno** Chile
16 E2 **Osorno** Spain
131 A8 **Osorno** *prov* Chile
131 A8 **Osorno, Vol** *peak* Chile
133 C6 **Osorro** *mt* Chile
100 F1 **Osoyoos** Br Col
44 C4 **Ospedaletti** Italy
117 M7 **Ospika** *R* Br Col
113 E10 **Osprey** Florida
141 H2 **Osprey Reef** Gt Barrier Reef **Aust**
9 G5 **Ospringe** England
25 E5 **Oss** Netherlands
46 F5 **Óssa** *mt* Greece
112 F6 **Ossabaw I** Georgia
139 H8 **Ossa, Mt** Tasmania
16 B6 **Ossa, Sa. d'** *mts* Portugal
85 F7 **Osse** *R* Nigeria
27 K12 **Össeby-Garn** Sweden
99 P5 **Osseo** Wisconsin
38 J8 **Ossiach** Austria
99 P6 **Ossian** Iowa
94 D2 **Ossineke** Michigan
95 O5 **Ossining** New York
95 Q3 **Ossipee L** New Hampshire
27 E10 **Os-sjöen** *L* Norway
32 J8 **Ossning** *hills* W Germany
41 H5 **Ossola, Val d'** Italy
51 Q3 **Ossora** U.S.S.R.
121 M5 **Ostaboningue, L** Quebec
77 A2 **Ostan-e Markazi** Iran
52 E6 **Ostashevo** U.S.S.R.
52 D6 **Ostashkov** U.S.S.R.
26 H9 **Östavall** Sweden
32 G8 **Ostbevern** W Germany
32 K5 **Oste** *R* W Germany
113 F9 **Osteen** Florida
45 L2 **Ostellato** Italy
32 K5 **Osten** W Germany
Ostend *see* **Oostende**

32 L7 **Ostenholz** W Germany
41 K6 **Osteno** Italy
54 D3 **Oster** *R* U.S.S.R.
33 P7 **Osterburg** E Germany
94 J6 **Osterburg** Pennsylvania
36 G5 **Osterburken** W Germany
27 J11 **Österby** Sweden
27 H14 **Österbymo** Sweden
32 H8 **Ostercappeln** W Germany
27 G10 **Osterdalälven** *R* Sweden
32 E5 **Osterems** *est* W Germany
27 H13 **Östergotland** *county* Sweden
37 P6 **Osterhofen** W Germany
32 J6 **Osterholz-Scharmbeck** W Germany
38 H6 **Osterhorn Gruppe** *mts* Austria
32 E8 **Øster Hornum** Nordjylland Denmark
27 J11 **Österlövsta** Sweden
26 J7 **Östernoret** Sweden
28 N2 **Østerø** *isld* Faeroes
Osterode Poland *see* **Ostróda**
32 M9 **Osterode** W Germany
27 A11 **Osteröy** *isld* Norway
38 H5 **Osterreich** *dist* Austria
26 G8 **Östersund** Sweden
28 H7 **Øster Ulslev** Denmark
27 J11 **Östervåla** Sweden
33 N9 **Osterwieck** E Germany
36 G6 **Ostfildern** W Germany
27 E12 **Østfold** *reg* Norway
32 F5 **Ostfriesische Inseln** *islds* W Germany
32 F6 **Ostfriesland** *reg* W Germany
32 G6 **Ostgrossefehn** W Germany
27 K11 **Östhammar** Sweden
36 C7 **Ostheim** France
37 J3 **Ostheim** W Germany
45 M6 **Ostia** Italy
42 D5 **Ostiglia** Italy
27 F11 **Östmark** Sweden
33 R5 **Ost Peene** *R* E Germany
45 O4 **Ostra** Italy
94 D6 **Ostrander** Ohio
37 P1 **Ostrau** E Germany
31 L6 **Ostrava** Czechoslovakia
45 O4 **Ostra Vetere** Italy
31 M2 **Ostróda** Poland
31 N2 **Ostrołęka** Poland
120 J5 **Ostrom** Ontario
37 O3 **Ostrov** Czechoslovakia
48 L6 **Ostrov** Romania
52 C6 **Ostrov** U.S.S.R.
55 F3 **Ostrovnaya** U.S.S.R.
51 Q2 **Ostrovnoye** U.S.S.R.
65 J3 **Ostrov Russkiy** *isld* U.S.S.R.
31 K4 **Ostrów** Poland
31 N5 **Ostrowiec** Poland
31 O4 **Ostrów Lubelski** Poland
31 N3 **Ostrów Mazowiecka** Poland
28 C3 **Østrup** Denmark
37 P5 **Ostrý** *mt* Czechoslovakia
31 K4 **Ostrzeszów** Poland
33 O5 **Ostseebad Boltenhagen** E Germany
33 Q4 **Ostseebad Graal-Müritz** E Germany
33 P4 **Ostseebad Kühlungsborn** E Germany
33 P4 **Ostseebad Nienhagen** E Germany
33 P4 **Ostseebad Rerik** E Germany
43 H8 **Ostuni** Italy
52 D6 **Osuga** *R* U.S.S.R.
100 F3 **O'Sullivan Dam** Washington
120 D2 **O'Sullivan, L** Ontario
121 P5 **O'Sullivan, L** Quebec
46 D4 **Osum** *R* Albania
43 G1 **Osum** *R* Bulgaria
60 D14 **Ōsumi-hantō** *pen* Japan
16 D7 **Osuna** Spain
52 J2 **Os'van'** U.S.S.R.
52 C6 **Osveya** U.S.S.R.
13 G5 **Oswaldkirk** England
94 J5 **Oswayo** Pennsylvania
95 M2 **Oswegatchie** *R* New York
99 S8 **Oswego** Illinois
107 P4 **Oswego** Kansas
101 U1 **Oswego** Montana
95 L3 **Oswego** New York
8 C2 **Oswestry** England
31 L5 **Oświęcim** Poland
111 F10 **Osyka** Mississippi
61 N9 **Ōta** Japan
60 F11 **Ōta** *R* Japan
144 B6 **Otago** *stat area* New Zealand
144 D7 **Otago Peninsula** New Zealand
144 C6 **Otaio** New Zealand
60 F11 **Ōtake** Japan
145 E3 **Otakeho** New Zealand
61 M10 **Ōtaki** Japan
145 E4 **Otaki** New Zealand
61 O8 **Ōtakine-yama** *mt* Japan
145 F3 **Otane** New Zealand
145 F2 **Otanewainuku** New Zealand
29 N7 **Otanmäki** Finland
83 K9 **Otappuwa** Sri Lanka
57 H3 **Otar** U.S.S.R.
60 O2 **Otaru** Japan
144 B7 **Otatara** New Zealand
144 B7 **Otautau** New Zealand
30 H6 **Otava** *R* Czechoslovakia
128 C3 **Otavalo** Ecuador
87 C9 **Otavi** Namibia
87 B9 **Otchinjau** Angola
95 M4 **Otego** New York
144 C6 **Otekaieke** New Zealand
48 F5 **Oteleo** Romania
144 C6 **Otematata** New Zealand
52 G5 **Otepää** U.S.S.R.
58 C2 **Otgon** Mongolia
22 K5 **Othain** *R* France
22 J2 **Othée** Belgium
18 H4 **Othe, Forêt d'** France
100 F3 **Othello** Washington
27 K14 **Othem** Sweden
8 D5 **Othery** England
46 C5 **Othonoi** *isld* Greece
46 F5 **Othris** *mt* Greece
70 F5 **Oti** Sulawesi
85 E7 **Oti** *R* W Africa
124 G5 **Otinapa** Mexico
144 C5 **Otira** New Zealand
106 H1 **Otis** Colorado
107 L3 **Otis** Kansas
95 O4 **Otis** Massachusetts
95 L4 **Otisco L** New York
122 B1 **Otish Mts** Quebec
95 N5 **Otisville** New York
87 C10 **Otjiwarongo** Namibia
60 O3 **Otobe-dake** *mt* Japan
42 G4 **Otočac** Yugoslavia
99 K9 **Otoe** Nebraska
60 R2 **Otofuke** Japan
60 Q1 **Otoineppu** Japan
145 F3 **Otoko** New Zealand
145 E3 **Otorohanga** New Zealand
119 P5 **Otosquen** Sask
27 C13 **Otra** *R* Norway
126 B1 **Otrabanda** Curaçao
43 J8 **Otranto** Italy
43 J8 **Otranto, C.d'** Italy
46 C4 **Otranto, Str of** Adriatic Sea
94 C2 **Otsego** Michigan
95 N4 **Otsego L** New York
94 C2 **Otsego Lake** Michigan
95 M4 **Otselic, South** New York
60 R3 **Ōtsu** Hokkaido Japan
61 J10 **Ōtsu** Honshu Japan
61 P6 **Ōtsuchi-wan** *B* Japan
61 M10 **Otsuki** Japan
26 D10 **Otta** Norway
26 C10 **Otta** *R* Norway
22 L5 **Ottange** France
27 F16 **Ottarp** Sweden
45 Q8 **Ottaviano** Italy
99 S8 **Ottawa** Illinois
107 P3 **Ottawa** Kansas
94 C5 **Ottawa** Ohio
120 D9 **Ottawa** Ontario
115 L6 **Ottawa Is** N W Terr
121 M6 **Ottawa, R** Quebec
32 K9 **Ottbergen** W Germany
27 H15 **Ottenby** Sweden
36 H5 **Ottendorf** W Germany
37 M2 **Ottendorf-Okrilla** E Germany
36 E6 **Ottenhöfen** W Germany
38 M5 **Ottenshlag** Austria
32 K9 **Ottenstein** Niedersachsen W Germany
32 E8 **Ottenstein** Nordrhein-Westfalen W Germany
101 T4 **Otter** Montana
110 J1 **Otterbein** Indiana
36 D4 **Otterberg** W Germany
13 F3 **Otterburn** England
118 D1 **Otterburne** Manitoba
113 E8 **Otter Creek** Florida
103 N3 **Otter Cr Res** Utah
38 E6 **Otterfing** W Germany
120 D4 **Otter I** Ontario
116 D8 **Otter I** Pribilof Is Bering Sea
119 N3 **Otter L** Sask
94 D3 **Otter Lake** Michigan
25 E4 **Otterlo** Netherlands
32 J5 **Otterndorf** W Germany
26 E7 **Otteröy** Norway
26 B9 **Otteröy** *isld* Norway
32 K6 **Ottersberg** W Germany
9 F5 **Ottershaw** England
33 P8 **Ottersleben** E Germany
15 G1 **Otterswick** Scotland
98 K3 **Otter Tail** *R* Minnesota
99 L3 **Otter Tail L** Minnesota
28 E5 **Otterup** Denmark
8 B6 **Ottery, R** England
8 C6 **Ottery St. Mary** England
119 P7 **Otthon** Sask
22 H2 **Ottignies** Belgium
109 L4 **Otto** Texas
101 R5 **Otto** Wyoming
37 M7 **Ottobrunn** W Germany
115 L1 **Otto Fiord** N W Terr
94 C6 **Ottoville** Ohio
36 C7 **Ottrott** France
99 O8 **Ottumwa** Iowa
98 E5 **Ottumwa** S Dakota
36 C5 **Ottweiler** W Germany
118 K2 **Otukamamoan L** Ontario
144 B6 **Oturehua** New Zealand
85 F7 **Oturkpo** Nigeria
94 D8 **Otway** Ohio
133 C8 **Otway, B** Chile
139 G7 **Otway, C** Victoria
31 N3 **Otwock** Poland
48 J2 **Otynya** U.S.S.R.
41 N3 **Ötz** Austria
36 B1 **Otzenrath** W Germany
41 N3 **Ötztal** Austria
41 N4 **Ötztaler Alpen** *mt* Austria
111 D8 **Ouachita** *R* Arkansas
110 C7 **Ouachita, L** Arkansas
109 N1 **Ouachita Mts** Ark/Okla
86 D3 **Ouadai** *dist* Chad
85 B4 **Ouadane** Mauritania
86 D4 **Ouadda** Cent Afr Republic
85 D6 **Ouagadougou** Upper Volta
85 D6 **Ouahigouya** Upper Volta
86 D4 **Ouaka** *R* Cent Afr Republic
85 C5 **Oualata** Mauritania
85 E4 **Ouallen** Algeria
86 D5 **Ouango** Cent Afr Republic
85 C7 **Ouangolodougou** Ivory Coast
18 H5 **Ouanne** *R* France
85 F3 **Ouan Taredert** Algeria
129 H3 **Ouaqui** Fr Guiana
85 C4 **Ouarane** *reg* Mauritania
121 Q6 **Ouareau, L** Quebec
85 F2 **Ouargla** Algeria
85 C3 **Ouarkziz, Jbel** *mt reg* Morocco/Algeria
20 J5 **Ouarville** France
85 C2 **Ouarzazate** Morocco
86 D5 **Oubangui** *R* Cent Afr Republic/Zaire
40 B3 **Ouche** *R* France
21 H6 **Oucques** France
25 A5 **Ouddorp** Netherlands
25 B5 **Oude** *R* Netherlands
25 F5 **Oude Ijssel** *R* Netherlands
22 D1 **Oudekapelle** Belgium
22 F2 **Oudenaarde** Belgium
25 C5 **Oudenbosch** Netherlands
25 H2 **Oude Pekela** Netherlands
25 C4 **Oude Rijn** Netherlands
25 C2 **Oudeschild** Netherlands
25 F3 **Oude Smildervaart** *R* Netherlands
25 C4 **Oudewater** Netherlands
22 L3 **Oudler** Belgium
21 C7 **Oudon** France
21 D6 **Oudon** *R* France
68 G7 **Oudong** Cambodia
89 C9 **Oudtshoorn** S Africa
85 F2 **Oued, El** Algeria
16 D9 **Oued Laou** Morocco
17 H9 **Oued Taria** Algeria
85 C2 **Oued Zem** Morocco
85 E7 **Ouémé** *R* Benin
18 B4 **Ouessant, I. d'** France
86 C5 **Ouesso** Congo
83 L14 **Ouest, I de l'** Kerguelen Indian Oc
123 Q7 **Ouest, Pte du** Miquelon I Atlantic Oc
71 F5 **Ouezon** Negros Philippines
85 C2 **Ouezzane** Morocco
22 J3 **Ouffet** Belgium
14 B3 **Oughterard** Irish Rep
40 C3 **Ougney** France
86 C4 **Ouham** *R* Cent Afr Republic
85 E7 **Ouidah** Benin
119 P2 **Ouimet** Ontario
124 E4 **Ouiriego** Mexico
18 H9 **Ouissac** France
20 E3 **Ouistreham** France
85 C5 **Oujaf** Mauritania
85 D2 **Oujda** Morocco
29 L7 **Oulainen** Finland
85 E2 **Ouled-Nail, Mts. des** Algeria
85 C2 **Oulmès** Morocco
13 G6 **Oulton** England
29 L6 **Oulu** Finland
29 M7 **Oulujoki** *R* Finland
86 D2 **Oum Chalouba** Chad
85 C3 **Oum el Guebor** Algeria
85 C2 **Oum er Rbia** *R* Morocco
86 C3 **Oum Hadjer** Chad
29 K3 **Ounasjärvi** *L* Finland
29 L4 **Ounasjoki** *R* Finland
29 K3 **Ounastunturi** *mt* Finland
9 F3 **Oundle** England
98 C1 **Oungre** Sask
84 G6 **Ounianga Kébir** Chad
84 G6 **Ounianga Sérir** Chad
85 C6 **Ouolodo** Mali
61 Q12 **Ōura-wan** *B* Okinawa
106 C3 **Ouray** Colorado
103 P1 **Ouray** Utah
28 F6 **Oure** Denmark
84 F5 **Ouri** Chad
129 K5 **Ouricuri** Brazil
130 H9 **Ouricuri, R** Brazil
130 E8 **Ourinhos** Brazil
16 B7 **Ourique** Portugal
130 F8 **Ouro Fino** Brazil
130 G7 **Ouro Prêto** Brazil
22 K3 **Ourthe** *R* Belgium
20 G2 **Ourville** France
139 H8 **Ouse** Tasmania
9 G2 **Ouse, R** Norfolk England
13 G6 **Ouse, R** N Yorks England
18 D5 **Oust** *R* France
122 D4 **Outardes, R. aux** Quebec
122 D4 **Outardes Trois Dam** Quebec
20 K5 **Outarville** France
85 D2 **Outat-Oulad-El-Haj** Morocco
6 B2 **Outer Bailey** N Atlantic Oc
15 A3 **Outer Hebrides** Scotland
102 F8 **Outer Santa Barbara Chan** California
13 F5 **Outhgill** England
87 C10 **Outjo** Namibia
101 V1 **Outlook** Montana
118 K7 **Outlook** Sask
29 O9 **Outokumpu** Finland
144 C6 **Outram** New Zealand
22 B2 **Outreau** France
15 G2 **Out Skerries** *isld* Scotland
19 O16 **Ouveze** *R* France
138 F6 **Ouyen** New S Wales
21 I6 **Ouzouer-le-Marché** France
44 E2 **Ovada** Italy
131 B3 **Ovalle** Chile
108 H3 **Ovalo** Texas
101 M2 **Ovando** Montana
16 B4 **Ovar** Portugal
38 G9 **Ovaro** Italy
32 H6 **Ovelgönne** W Germany
139 H6 **Ovens** *R* Victoria
36 C2 **Overath** W Germany
107 P3 **Overbrook** Kansas
25 B5 **Overflakkee** Netherlands
119 Q5 **Overflowing R** Manitoba
26 G9 **Överhogdal** Sweden
22 H2 **Overijse** Belgium
26 N5 **Överkalix** Sweden
107 Q3 **Overland Park** Kansas
98 F1 **Overly** N Dakota
29 J9 **Övermark** Finland
131 B5 **Overo, Vol** Argentina
22 J1 **Overpelt** Belgium
9 E5 **Overton** England
98 G9 **Overton** Nebraska
103 K5 **Overton** Nevada
109 N3 **Overton** Texas
8 D2 **Overton** Wales
26 N5 **Övertorneå** Sweden
27 H14 **Överum** Sweden
26 G5 **Over-uman** *L* Sweden
111 G10 **Ovett** Mississippi
106 H1 **Ovid** Colorado
101 O7 **Ovid** Idaho
94 C3 **Ovid** Michigan
95 L4 **Ovid** New York
113 F9 **Oviedo** Florida
16 D1 **Oviedo** Spain
16 C1 **Oviedo** *prov* Spain
26 G9 **Oviken** Sweden
45 P5 **Ovindoli** Italy
52 E5 **Ov'nishche** U.S.S.R.
26 K8 **Öv Nyland** Sweden
27 B13 **Övrebygd** Norway
26 L6 **Övre Grundsel** Sweden
25 F4 **Ovreijssel** *prov* Netherlands
27 B13 **Öv-Sirdal** Norway
26 H8 **Övsjö** Sweden
145 F4 **Owahanga** New Zealand
144 B7 **Owaka** New Zealand
61 O5 **Owani** Japan
95 L4 **Owasco L** New York
61 K11 **Owase** Japan
107 P5 **Owasso** Oklahoma
99 N5 **Owatonna** Minnesota
95 L4 **Owego** New York
14 B2 **Owemore** *R* Irish Rep
36 G6 **Owen** W Germany
99 Q5 **Owen** Wisconsin
142 A3 **Owen Anchorage** W Australia
86 F5 **Owen Falls D** Uganda
68 C7 **Owen I** Burma
145 D4 **Owen, Mt** New Zealand
145 D4 **Owen River** New Zealand
94 F8 **Owens** W Virginia
102 F4 **Owens** *R* California
110 J4 **Owensboro** Kentucky
102 G5 **Owens L** California
120 K8 **Owen Sound** Ontario
140 C6 **Owen Springs** N Terr Aust
136 K3 **Owen Stanley Ra** Papua New Guinea
110 J3 **Owensville** Indiana
110 E3 **Owensville** Missouri
110 M3 **Owenton** Kentucky
102 F5 **Owenyo** California
9 E6 **Ower** England
85 F7 **Owerri** Nigeria
145 E3 **Owhango** New Zealand
117 K10 **Owikeno L** Br Col
94 D8 **Owingsville** Kentucky
36 F5 **Öwisheim** W Germany
106 E1 **Owl Canyon** Colorado
101 R6 **Owl Cr** Wyoming
101 R6 **Owl-Creek Mts** Wyoming
118 F4 **Owl R** Alberta
85 F7 **Owo** Nigeria
94 C3 **Owosso** Michigan
100 J8 **Owyhee** Nevada
100 H6 **Owyhee** Oregon
27 G10 **Oxberg** Sweden
119 P9 **Oxbow** Sask
100 J5 **Oxbow Dam** Oregon
111 F7 **Oxbow L** Mississippi
118 K1 **Oxdrift** Ontario
27 J13 **Oxelösund** Sweden
111 L8 **Oxford** Alabama
9 E4 **Oxford** England
101 N7 **Oxford** Idaho
110 J1 **Oxford** Indiana
99 P8 **Oxford** Iowa
107 N4 **Oxford** Kansas
95 R2 **Oxford** Maine
95 L8 **Oxford** Maryland
95 Q4 **Oxford** Massachusetts
94 D4 **Oxford** Michigan
111 G7 **Oxford** Mississippi
112 J1 **Oxford** N Carolina
98 G9 **Oxford** Nebraska
95 M4 **Oxford** New York
144 D5 **Oxford** New Zealand
122 J8 **Oxford** Nova Scotia
94 C7 **Oxford** Ohio
99 R6 **Oxford** Wisconsin
141 J5 **Oxford Downs** Queensland
119 W4 **Oxford House** Manitoba
119 W3 **Oxford L** Manitoba
101 N7 **Oxford Pk** Idaho
9 E4 **Oxfordshire** *co* England
46 E5 **Oxiá** *mt* Greece
140 E4 **Oxide, Mt** Queensland
47 G6 **Oxílithos** Greece
125 P7 **Oxkutzcab** Mexico
139 G5 **Oxley** New S Wales
141 K2 **Oxley** *sub* Brisbane, Qnsld
139 K4 **Oxleys Pk** New S Wales
14 C2 **Ox Mts** Irish Rep
102 E7 **Oxnard** California
Oxon *co see* **Oxfordshire**
9 E1 **Oxton** England
8 B4 **Oxwich** Wales
70 B3 **Oya** Sarawak
70 C3 **Oya** *R* Sarawak
56 D4 **Oya** *R* U.S.S.R.
61 K9 **Oyabe** Japan
61 M10 **Oyama** Shizuoka Japan
61 N9 **Oyama** Tochigi Japan
61 N7 **Ōyama** Yamagata Japan
60 D13 **Ōyano shima** *isld* Japan
129 H3 **Oyapock, B. d'** Fr Guiana
86 B5 **Oyem** Gabon
118 G7 **Oyen** Alberta
22 C2 **Oye Plage** France
27 E12 **Oyeren** *L* Norway
56 B3 **Oyesh** *R* U.S.S.R.
26 J3 **Öyjord** Norway
15 D3 **Oykel** *R* Scotland
51 O2 **Oymyakon** U.S.S.R.
85 E7 **Oyo** Nigeria
128 C6 **Oyón** Peru
40 C5 **Oyonnax** France
21 G8 **Oyré** France
109 M8 **Oyster Cr** Texas
68 A2 **Oyster I** Burma
142 A3 **Oyster Inlet** W Australia
100 A3 **Oysterville** Washington
57 G3 **Oytal** U.S.S.R.
32 K6 **Oyten** W Germany
51 N2 **Oyun Khomoto** U.S.S.R.
71 F6 **Ozamiz** Mindanao Philippines
111 L10 **Ozark** Alabama
110 C6 **Ozark** Arkansas
110 C4 **Ozark** Missouri
110 C5 **Ozark Plateau** Missouri
110 C3 **Ozarks, L. of the** Missouri
48 F2 **Ozd** Hungary
80 B7 **Ozem** Israel
55 F3 **Ozernoye** U.S.S.R.
55 D4 **Ozernyy** Kustanay U.S.S.R.
54 D1 **Ozernyy** Smolensk U.S.S.R.
55 D3 **Ozernyy** Sverdlovsk U.S.S.R.
55 G3 **Ozero Karachi** U.S.S.R.
65 J2 **Ozero Khanka** *L* China/U.S.S.R.
46 E6 **Ozerós, L** Greece
31 N1 **Ozersk** U.S.S.R.
54 K2 **Ozery** U.S.S.R.
100 A1 **Ozette L** Washington
54 K2 **Ozherel'ye** U.S.S.R.
51 O2 **Ozhogino** U.S.S.R.
43 C8 **Ozieri** Sardinia
31 L5 **Ozimek** Poland
108 F5 **Ozona** Texas
48 E4 **Ozora** Hungary
31 L4 **Ozorków** Poland
55 C5 **Ozorodnyy** U.S.S.R.
86 A6 **Ozouri** Gabon
60 F12 **Ōzu** Japan
60 D13 **Ōzu** *R* Japan
60 E11 **Ozuki** Japan
48 K5 **Ozun** Romania
45 K3 **Ozzano dell'Emilia** Italy
80 B8 **Pa'ame Tashaz** Israel
68 C4 **Pa-an** Burma
37 L6 **Paar** *R* W Germany
33 R7 **Paaren** E Germany
89 A9 **Paarl** S Africa
29 O3 **Paatsjoki** *R* Finland
135 U4 **Paauilo** Hawaiian Is
29 L7 **Paavola** Finland
15 A3 **Pabbay** *isld* Outer Hebrides Scotland
70 P9 **Pabean** Indonesia
31 L4 **Pabjanice** Poland
77 K6 **Pab Range** Pakistan
128 F6 **Pacaás Novos, Sa. dos** *mts* Brazil
129 H4 **Pacajá** *R* Brazil
128 F3 **Pacaraima, Sa** *mts* Brazil/Venezuela
128 C5 **Pacasmayo** Peru
111 F8 **Pace** Mississippi
67 F5 **Pa'-chao Hsü** *isld* Taiwan
124 E2 **Pacheco** Chihuahua Mexico
124 H5 **Pacheco** Zacatecas Mexico
100 A1 **Pachena Pt** Br Col
124 F3 **Pachera** Mexico
43 G12 **Pachino** Sicily
128 D5 **Pachitea** *R* Peru
125 K7 **Pachuca** Mexico
111 H9 **Pachuta** Mississippi
102 D3 **Pacific** California
110 F3 **Pacific** Missouri
135 L14 **Pacific Antarctic Ridge** Pac Oc
100 A2 **Pacific Beach** Washington
100 B4 **Pacific City** Oregon
101 Q7 **Pacific Cr** Wyoming
102 C5 **Pacific Grove** California
135 **Pacific Ocean**
71 G5 **Pacijan** *isld* Philippines
145 E4 **Packakariki** New Zealand
38 L7 **Pack Alpe** *mts* Austria
111 D10 **Packton** Louisiana
99 O8 **Packwood** Iowa
100 D3 **Packwood** Washington
112 E2 **Pacolet** *R* S Carolina
112 F3 **Pacolet Mills** S Carolina
31 J6 **Pacov** Czechoslovakia
123 R4 **Pacquet** Newfoundland
98 C5 **Pactola** S Dakota
135 Q15 **Pactolus Bank** Pacific Oc
130 G5 **Pacui** *R* Brazil
20 H3 **Pacy** France
31 K5 **Paczków** Poland
71 H6 **Padabale** *isld* Sulawesi
71 G7 **Padada** Mindanao Philippines
70 G7 **Padamarang** *isld* Sulawesi
69 G11 **Padang** Indonesia
69 F12 **Padang** Riau Arch Indonesia
69 E13 **Padang** Sumatra
69 E13 **Padangpanjang** Sumatra
69 D12 **Padangsidimpuan** Sumatra
69 B10 **Padangtiji** Sumatra
52 D3 **Padany** U.S.S.R.
70 D2 **Padas** *R* Sabah
29 L10 **Padasjoki** Finland
128 F3 **Padauiri** *R* Brazil
68 B3 **Padaung** Burma
83 K9 **Padawiya Tank** Sri Lanka
141 K1 **Paddington** *dist* Brisbane, Qnsld
117 P7 **Paddle Prairie** Alberta
119 M5 **Paddockwood** Sask
71 H6 **Padea** *isld* Indonesia
94 G7 **Paden City** W Virginia
32 J9 **Paderborn** W Germany
70 D3 **Paderongan** Kalimantan
48 G5 **Padeşu** *mt* Romania
13 F6 **Padiham** England
128 F7 **Padilla** Bolivia
48 L6 **Padina** Romania
26 J4 **Padjelanta Nat. Park** Sweden
115 K5 **Padlei** N W Terr
115 N4 **Padloping Island** N W Terr
122 E5 **Padoue** Quebec
36 B7 **Padoux** France
45 L1 **Padova** Italy
109 K9 **Padre I** Texas
16 B2 **Padrón** Spain
8 B6 **Padstow** England
138 F6 **Padthaway** S Australia
Padua *see* **Padova**
110 H4 **Paducah** Kentucky
108 G1 **Paducah** Texas
45 R7 **Paduli** Italy
52 D1 **Padunskoye More** *L* U.S.S.R.
145 F2 **Paengaroa** New Zealand
65 F6 **Paengnyŏng-do** *isld* S Korea
145 E2 **Paeroa** New Zealand
44 B2 **Paesana** Italy
45 R8 **Paestum** Italy
71 E3 **Paete** Luzon Philippines
87 F10 **Pafuri** Mozambique
42 G4 **Pag** Yugoslavia
42 F4 **Pag** *isld* Yugoslavia
71 L9 **Paga** Flores Indonesia
129 H4 **Paga Centa** Brazil
71 F7 **Pagadian** Mindanao Philippines
69 E14 **Pagai, Pulau** *isld* Indonesia
90 L9 **Pagalu** *isld* Equat Guinea
68 B2 **Pagan** Burma
45 R8 **Pagani** Italy
70 K7 **Pagaralam** Sumatra
46 F5 **Pagasitikós, Kólpos** *B* Greece
70 D6 **Pagatan** Kalimantan
119 P2 **Pagato R** Sask
71 F4 **Pagbulungan Pt** Philippines
103 N5 **Page** Arizona
98 J2 **Page** N Dakota
98 H7 **Page** Nebraska
107 Q7 **Page** Oklahoma
52 B6 **Pagėgiai** U.S.S.R.
112 G3 **Pageland** S Carolina
142 E3 **Page, Mt** W Australia
69 G14 **Pagerdewa** Sumatra
141 K4 **Paget Cay** *isld* Gt Barrier Reef Australia
68 A6 **Paget I** Andaman Is
133 J8 **Paget, Mt** S Georgia
77 L2 **Paghman** Afghanistan
42 D6 **Paglia** *R* Italy
101 S9 **Pagoda Pk** Colorado
142 F2 **Pago Mission** W Australia
47 H7 **Pagóndhas** Greece
70 D2 **Pagonprick, G** *mt* Sarawak
137 S4 **Pago Pago** Amer Samoa
106 C4 **Pagosa Springs** Colorado
106 C6 **Paguate** New Mexico
71 H4 **Pagujaman** *R* Sulawesi
120 D3 **Pagwachuan** Ontario
120 E3 **Pagwachuan** *R* Ontario
120 E2 **Pagwa River** Ontario
116 K3 **Pah** *R* Alaska
102 V14 **Pahala** Hawaiian Is
70 C6 **Pahandut** Kalimantan
73 R8 **Pahang** *R* Malaysia
69 F11 **Pahang, S** *R* Malaysia
145 E4 **Pahaoa R** New Zealand
144 A7 **Pahia Pt** New Zealand
145 E4 **Pahiatua** New Zealand
135 V5 **Pahoa** Hawaiian Is
77 G2 **Pahra** Afghanistan
103 J4 **Pahranagat L** Nevada
103 J4 **Pahranagat Ra** Nevada
103 K4 **Pahrock Ra** Nevada
103 J5 **Pahrump** Nevada
101 M5 **Pahsimeroi** *R* Idaho
102 H4 **Pahute Mesa** Nevada
100 F8 **Pahute Peak** *mt* Nevada
135 T3 **Paia** Hawaiian Is
130 B6 **Paiaguás** Brazil
52 C5 **Paide** U.S.S.R.
109 K5 **Paige** Texas
8 C7 **Paignton** England
145 E1 **Paihia** New Zealand
29 M10 **Päijänne** *reg* Finland
68 F6 **Pailin** Cambodia
Pailing *see* **Chun'an**
135 S3 **Pailolo Ch** Hawaiian Is
9 E3 **Pailton** England
21 A7 **Paimboeuf** France
116 G5 **Paimiut** Alaska
18 C4 **Paimpol** France
69 E13 **Painan** Sumatra
120 H10 **Paincourt** Ontario
133 C8 **Paine** *mt* Chile
99 S2 **Painesdale** Michigan
94 F5 **Painesville** Ohio
103 N5 **Painted Des** Arizona
103 L8 **Painted Rock Res** Arizona
37 M6 **Painten** W Germany
138 E4 **Painter, Mt** S Australia
119 T3 **Paint L** Manitoba
120 J8 **Paisley** Ontario
100 E7 **Paisley** Oregon
12 D2 **Paisley** Scotland
29 M2 **Paistunturit** *mt* Finland
128 B5 **Paita** Peru
67 G4 **Pai-tai Lieh-tao** *islds* Taiwan
70 E1 **Paitan B** Sabah
70 O9 **Paiton** Java
26 K4 **Paittasjärbi** *L* Sweden
16 B4 **Paiva** *R* Portugal
87 B8 **Paiva Couceiro** Angola
21 G8 **Paizay le-Sec** France
69 E13 **Pajakumbuh** Sumatra
26 N4 **Pajala** Sweden
16 D1 **Pajares, Pto. de** Spain
106 D7 **Pajarito** New Mexico
131 B2 **Pajaros** *isld* Chile
71 K9 **Pajeti** Sumba Indonesia
129 L5 **Pajeu** Brazil
130 H10 **Pajeú, R** Brazil
48 D4 **Páka** Hungary
69 F10 **Paka** Malaysia
69 E12 **Pakanbaru** Sumatra
68 B2 **Pakangyi** Burma
128 F2 **Pakaraima Mts** Guyana
119 N1 **Pakashkhan L** *isld* Ontario
68 E3 **Pak Beng** Laos
121 O7 **Pakenham** Ontario
145 D1 **Pakenui** New Zealand
70 E3 **Pakerajan** *R* Kalimantan
68 G4 **Pak Hin Boun** Laos
57 D4 **Pakhtakor** U.S.S.R.
85 F6 **Paki** Nigeria
74 A4 **Pakistan** *rep* Asia
68 E3 **Pak Khop** Laos
68 E3 **Pak Lay** Laos
Paknampho *see* **Muang Nakhon Sawan**
68 E3 **Pak Niam** Laos
68 B2 **Pakokku** Burma
145 D1 **Pakotai** New Zealand
69 E9 **Pak Phayun** Thailand
42 H3 **Pakrac** Yugoslavia
48 E4 **Paks** Hungary
68 F3 **Pak Sane** Laos
68 G5 **Pakse** Laos
68 E2 **Pak Tha** Laos
77 L3 **Paktiā** Afghanistan
70 C3 **Paku** *R* Sarawak
119 T4 **Pakwa L** Manitoba
89 F4 **Pakwe** *R* Botswana
86 F5 **Pakwich** Uganda
68 D6 **Pala** Burma
102 G8 **Pala** California
86 C4 **Pala** Chad
109 L7 **Palacios** Texas
127 L10 **Palacios** Venezuela
133 D6 **Palacios, L** Argentina
17 K3 **Palafrugell** Spain
42 G6 **Palagruža** *isld* Yugoslavia
46 F7 **Palaiá** Greece
45 J4 **Paláia** Italy
47 H9 **Palaiókastron** Crete Greece
47 F9 **Palaiokhóra** Crete Greece
46 D6 **Pálairos** Greece
20 K4 **Palaiseau** France
18 C5 **Palais, le** France
89 F4 **Palala** *R* S Africa
68 A7 **Palalankwe** Andaman Is
46 E5 **Palamás** Greece
71 J9 **Palamedo** Sumba Indonesia
17 K3 **Palamós** Spain
47 J6 **Palamut** Turkey
71 F2 **Palanan** Luzon Philippines
17 G5 **Palancia** *R* Spain
52 B6 **Palanga** U.S.S.R.
77 G4 **Palangān, Kūh-e-** *mts* Iran
70 C6 **Palangka Raya** Kalimantan
16 D2 **Palanquinos** Spain
70 F7 **Palanro** Sulawesi
135 S3 **Palaoa Pt** Hawaiian Is
71 G4 **Palapag** Philippines
89 E4 **Palapye** Botswana
16 B2 **Palas de Rey** Spain
113 F8 **Palatka** Florida
56 B6 **Palattsy** U.S.S.R.
108 F8 **Palau** Mexico
43 C7 **Palau** Sardinia
71 F1 **Palaui** *isld* Luzon Philippines
71 D3 **Palauig** Luzon Philippines
68 D6 **Palauk** Burma
83 J10 **Palavi** Sri Lanka
68 D6 **Palaw** Burma
71 D6 **Palawan** *isld* Philippines
71 C6 **Palawan Passage** Philippines
41 L6 **Palazzolo** Italy
43 F11 **Palazzolo Acreide** Sicily
45 L3 **Palazzuolo** Italy
133 D1 **Palca** Chile
52 B5 **Paldiski** U.S.S.R.
68 B2 **Pale** Burma
70 G4 **Paleleh** Sulawesi
69 G14 **Palembang** Sumatra
38 K6 **Palen** *R* Austria
16 D2 **Palencia** *prov* Spain
103 J8 **Palen L** California
79 D4 **Paleokhorio** Cyprus
102 C2 **Palermo** California
98 D1 **Palermo** N Dakota
43 E10 **Palermo** Sicily
128 E8 **Palestina** Chile
110 J3 **Palestine** Illinois
109 M4 **Palestine** Texas
110 M1 **Palestine Hill** Ohio
109 M3 **Palestine, L** Texas
45 N6 **Palestrina** Italy
68 A2 **Paletwa** Burma
143 B6 **Palgrave, Mt** W Australia
45 O6 **Paliano** Italy
83 K8 **Pali Aru** *R* Sri Lanka
70 P9 **Paliat** *isld* Indonesia
71 G7 **Palimbang** Mindanao Philippines
85 E7 **Palime** Togo
70 E1 **Palin, Mt** Sabah
43 G8 **Palinuro, C** Italy
106 B2 **Palisade** Colorado
98 E9 **Palisade** Nebraska
103 H1 **Palisade** Nevada
101 O6 **Palisades Res** Idaho
127 L3 **Palisadoes** *airport* Jamaica
22 J4 **Paliseul** Belgium
109 J8 **Palito Blanco** Texas
26 K5 **Paljaape** *mt* Sweden
29 L10 **Pälkäne** Finland
83 J8 **Palk Bay** Sri Lanka
52 F5 **Palkino** U.S.S.R.
83 J8 **Palk Str** India/Sri Lanka
83 K8 **Pallai** Sri Lanka
Pallanza *see* **Verbania**
Palla Rd *see* **Dinokwe** Botswana
18 F10 **Pallaresa** *R* Spain
29 L3 **Pallastunturi** *mt* Finland
83 K10 **Pallegama** Sri Lanka
26 K3 **Pallemtjåkko** *mt* Sweden
18 E6 **Pallice, la** France
36 B4 **Pallien** W Germany
70 G7 **Pallima** Sulawesi
9 H2 **Palling** England
Pallíni Greece *see* **Kassándra**
143 C10 **Pallinup, R** W Australia
145 E4 **Palliser Bay** New Zealand
21 H8 **Palluau-sur-Indre** France
88 H7 **Palma** Mozambique
106 E6 **Palma** New Mexico
17 J5 **Palma, B. de** Majorca
45 R8 **Palma Camp** Italy
17 J5 **Palma de Mallorca** Majorca
43 F11 **Palma di Montechiaro** Sicily
80 B6 **Palmaḥim** Israel
127 H9 **Palmar** *R* Venezuela
133 G4 **Palmares do Sul** Brazil
126 G4 **Palmarito** Cuba
43 E8 **Palmarola** *isld* Italy
85 C8 **Palmas, C** Liberia
43 B10 **Palmas, G. di** Sardinia
128 E1 **Palma Sola** Venezuela
126 G4 **Palma Soriano** Cuba
87 B7 **Palmas, Pta. das** Angola
113 G11 **Palm Beach** Florida
142 A4 **Palm Beach** W Australia
102 H8 **Palm Canyon Nat. Mon** California
102 F7 **Palmdale** California
113 F11 **Palmdale** Florida
133 G3 **Palmeira** Brazil
116 N6 **Palmer** Alaska
99 R10 **Palmer** Illinois
99 M7 **Palmer** Iowa
99 T3 **Palmer** Michigan
98 H8 **Palmer** Nebraska
118 L9 **Palmer** Sask
110 L6 **Palmer** Tennessee
109 L3 **Palmer** Texas
141 G3 **Palmer** *R* Queensland
146 F14 **Palmer Arch** Antarctica
146 H12 **Palmer, C** Antarctica
140 C6 **Palmer R** N Terr Aust
144 C6 **Palmerston** New Zealand
141 J5 **Palmerston, C** Queensland
145 E4 **Palmerston North** New Zealand
95 M6 **Palmerton** Pennsylvania
140 C6 **Palmer Valley** N Terr Aust
141 G3 **Palmerville** Queensland
113 E10 **Palmetto** Florida
112 C4 **Palmetto** Georgia
127 N6 **Palmetto Pt** Barbuda W I
126 F2 **Palmetto Pt** Eleuthera Bahamas
113 E9 **Palm Harbor** Florida
43 G10 **Palmi** Italy
128 C3 **Palmira** Colombia
126 D3 **Palmira** Cuba
141 H4 **Palm Is** Queensland
124 G6 **Palmito del Verde, I** Mexico
94 E3 **Palms** Michigan
102 H8 **Palm Springs** California
141 J7 **Palm Tree Cr** Queensland
140 C6 **Palm Valley** N Terr Aust
110 G2 **Palmyra** Illinois
99 P10 **Palmyra** Missouri
98 K9 **Palmyra** Nebraska
95 N7 **Palmyra** New Jersey
95 K3 **Palmyra** New York
95 L6 **Palmyra** Pennsylvania
72 D2 **Palmyra** Syria
110 J5 **Palmyra** Tennessee
94 J9 **Palmyra** Virginia
99 S7 **Palmyra** Wisconsin
135 U7 **Palmyra I** *atoll* Pacific Oc
12 E4 **Palnackie** Scotland
52 J4 **Pal'niki** U.S.S.R.
99 P7 **Palo** Iowa
42 E7 **Palo** Italy
71 G5 **Palo** Leyte Philippines
70 F5 **Palo** Sulawesi
102 B4 **Palo Alto** California
108 B8 **Palo Duro Cr** Texas
108 C7 **Paloduro Cr** Texas/Okla
71 K9 **Paloe** *isld* Flores Indonesia
70 B3 **Paloh** Sarawak
86 F3 **Paloich** Sudan
29 K3 **Palojärvi** Finland
29 K3 **Palojoensuu** Finland
29 K3 **Palojoki** *R* Finland
102 H8 **Palomar Mt** California
103 L9 **Palomas** Arizona
45 N5 **Palombara Sabina** Italy
17 G4 **Palomera, Sa** *mts* Spain
109 J3 **Palo Pinto** Texas
70 G6 **Palopo** Sulawesi
133 F3 **Palo Santo** Argentina
17 G7 **Palos, C. de** Spain
127 O3 **Palo Seco** Trinidad
100 H3 **Palouse** Washington
103 M8 **Palo Verde** Arizona
103 K8 **Palo Verde** California
141 F6 **Palparara** Queensland
27 H12 **Pålsboda** Sweden
29 N7 **Paltamo** Finland
38 H5 **Palting** Austria
70 F5 **Palu** *R* Sulawesi
127 N10 **Palúa** Venezuela
71 E4 **Paluan** Philippines
83 K9 **Palugassegama** Sri Lanka
57 C5 **Pal'vart** U.S.S.R.
85 E6 **Pama** Upper Volta
70 E5 **Pamaluan** Kalimantan
70 L9 **Pamanukan** Java
83 J8 **Pamban** *isld* India
70 F4 **Pambero** Sulawesi
118 K9 **Pambrun** Sask
139 J6 **Pambula** New S Wales
38 M8 **Pameče** Yugoslavia
70 O9 **Pamekasan** Java
70 L9 **Pameungpeuk** Java
18 G9 **Pamiers** France
46 E7 **Pámisos** *R* Greece
112 L2 **Pamlico R** N Carolina
68 E4 **Pamong D.Site** Thailand
133 D4 **Pampa de las Salinas** Argentina
70 G7 **Pampanua** Sulawesi
128 D6 **Pampas** Peru
133 E5 **Pampas, Plains** Argentina
16 B4 **Pampilhosa da Serra** Portugal
16 B4 **Pampilhosa do Botão** Portugal
94 J9 **Pamplin City** Virginia
128 D2 **Pamplona** Colombia
71 F6 **Pamplona** Negros Philippines
17 F2 **Pamplona** Spain
33 O5 **Pampow** E Germany
70 E6 **Pamukan, Teluk** *B* Kalimantan
47 K7 **Pamukkale** Turkey
47 L4 **Pamukova** Turkey
95 K9 **Pamunkey** *R* Virginia
99 R10 **Pana** Illinois
71 F7 **Panabutan B** Mindanao Philippines
103 K4 **Panaca** Nevada
120 J6 **Panache, L** Ontario
83 J11 **Panadura** Sri Lanka
71 D6 **Panagtaran** *point* Palawan Philippines
47 G2 **Panagyurishte** Bulgaria
70 B5 **Panahan** Kalimantan
70 K9 **Panaitan** *isld* Java
76 A3 **Panaji** India
46 E6 **Panakhaíkón** *mt* Greece
94 H4 **Panama** New York
107 Q6 **Panama** Oklahoma
125 P5 **Panamá** Panama
125 O5 **Panama** *rep* Cent America
124 E10 **Panama Canal** Cent America
124 E9 **Panama Canal Zone** Central America
113 B7 **Panama City** Florida
125 P5 **Panamá, Golfo de** Panama
102 G5 **Panamint V** California
71 G6 **Panaon** *isld* Philippines
43 G10 **Panarea** *isld* Italy
45 K2 **Panaro** *R* Italy
70 O9 **Panarukan** Java
71 G4 **Panay** Philippines
71 F5 **Panay** *isld* Philippines
71 F5 **Panay Gulf** Philippines
47 G4 **Panayía** Greece
103 J3 **Pancake Ra** Nevada
21 B6 **Pancé** France
48 F6 **Pančevo** Yugoslavia
48 L5 **Panciu** Romania
69 D11 **Pancurbatu** Sumatra
87 F10 **Panda** Mozambique
108 F5 **Pandale** Texas
71 G3 **Pandan** Catanduanes Philippines
71 F5 **Pandan** Panay Philippines
70 C3 **Pandan** Sarawak
71 C6 **Pandanan** *isld* Palawan Philippines
71 F5 **Pandan Bay** Panay Philippines
70 K8 **Pandan, Bt** *mt* Sumatra
141 F3 **Pandanus** *R* Queensland
87 F10 **Pande** Mozambique
133 C3 **Pan de Azúcar** Chile
71 F5 **Pan de Azucar** Philippines
70 L9 **Pandeglang** Java
130 G4 **Pandeiros** *R* Brazil
138 E2 **Pandie Pandie** S Australia
70 F3 **Pandjang** *isld* Kalimantan
70 G4 **Pandjang, Tg** *C* Sulawesi
133 F4 **Pando** Uruguay
128 E6 **Pando** *dep* Bolivia
125 N5 **Pandora** Costa Rica
141 G1 **Pandora Ent** Gt Barrier Reef Aust
71 E7 **Panducan** *isld* Philippines
8 D4 **Pandy** Wales
52 B6 **Panevėžys** U.S.S.R.
138 D4 **Paney** S Australia
66 C3 **Panfilov** U.S.S.R.
57 H3 **Panfilova, Imeni** U.S.S.R.
86 E5 **Panga** Zaïre
47 F4 **Pangaion** *mt* Greece
70 M9 **Pangandaran** Java
88 G4 **Pangani** Tanzania
88 F4 **Pangani** *R* Tanzania
71 F4 **Panganiran** Philippines
69 J12 **Pangaujalayan** Indonesia
9 E5 **Pangbourne** England
110 E6 **Pangburn** Arkansas
70 F5 **Pangean** Sulawesi
70 N10 **Panggul** Java
68 D1 **Panghsang** Burma
86 E6 **Pangi** Zaïre
70 F7 **Pangkadjene** Sulawesi
70 O9 **Pangkah, Tg** *C* Java
70 B6 **Pangkalanbuun** Kalimantan
69 D10 **Pangkalansusu** Sumatra
69 H14 **Pangkalpinang** Sumatra
71 H5 **Pangkalsiang, Tg** *C* Sulawesi
71 F6 **Panglao** *isld* Philippines
68 C2 **Panglong** Burma
119 N9 **Pangman** Sask
115 N4 **Pangnirtung** N W Terr
70 L9 **Pangrongo, G** *mt* Java
68 C2 **Pangtara** Burma
133 C5 **Panguipulli** *mt* Chile
131 A7 **Panguipulli, L** Chile
103 M4 **Panguitch** Utah
71 E7 **Pangutaran** *isld* Philippines
71 E7 **Pangutaran Group** *islds* Philippines
88 E7 **Pangwa** Tanzania
68 D1 **Pang Yang** Burma
87 F9 **Panhalonga** Zimbabwe
108 C8 **Panhandle** Texas
65 A7 **Panhe** China
86 D7 **Pania Mutembo** Zaïre
137 N6 **Panié, Mt** New Caledonia
71 G5 **Paninihian Pt** Samar Philippines
71 D6 **Panitan** Palawan Philippines
69 D10 **Panjang** Sumatra
Panjang *isld* Cocos Is *see* **West I**
69 J11 **Panjang** *isld* Indonesia
69 F8 **Panjang, Hon** *isld* G of Thailand
77 H6 **Panjgur** *reg* Pakistan
69 C11 **Panji** Sumatra
77 L2 **Panjshir** *reg* Afghanistan
60 Q1 **Panke-zan** *mt* Japan
116 F9 **Pankof, C** Aleutian Is
33 S7 **Pankow** E Germany
85 F7 **Pankshin** Nigeria
65 H3 **Pan Ling** *mts* China
25 F5 **Pannerden** Netherlands
102 D5 **Panoche** California
70 B5 **Panopah** Kalimantan
99 M8 **Panora** Iowa
133 G2 **Panorama** Brazil
141 J6 **Panorama, Mt** Queensland
55 F3 **Panovo** U.S.S.R.
52 D2 **Panozero** U.S.S.R.
65 E4 **Panshan** China
65 G3 **Panshi** China
70 E6 **Pantai** Kalimantan
129 G7 **Pantanal de São Lourénço** *swamp* Brazil
68 B4 **Pantanaw** Burma
103 O9 **Pantano** Arizona
18 F10 **Pantano de Tremp** *L* Spain
71 M9 **Pantar** *isld* Indonesia
112 L2 **Pantego** N Carolina
109 M9 **Pantego** Texas
43 E12 **Pantelleria** *isld* Italy
41 N6 **Pantena, Val** Italy
110 J4 **Panther** *R* Kentucky
71 J9 **Pantjo** Sumbawa Indonesia
70 D4 **Pantjungapang, Bt** *mt* Kalimantan
128 C4 **Pantoja** Peru
69 C10 **Pantonlabu** Sumatra
125 K6 **Pánuco** Mexico
67 A4 **Pan Xian** China
67 D5 **Panyu** China
54 H8 **Panyutino** U.S.S.R.
87 C7 **Panzi** Zaïre
Paoki *see* **Baoji**
43 G9 **Paola** Italy
107 Q3 **Paola** Kansas
98 D9 **Paoli** Colorado
110 K3 **Paoli** Indiana
107 N7 **Paoli** Oklahoma

106 C3 **Paonia** Colorado
134 A11 **Paopao** Tahiti Pacific Ocean
Paotow *see* **Baotou**
135 U6 **Papa** Hawaiian Is
48 D3 **Pápa** Hungary
135 V4 **Papaaloa** Hawaiian Is
46 F8 **Papadhiánika** Greece
125 M4 **Papagayo, Golfo de** Costa Rica
135 V5 **Papaikou** Hawaiian Is
144 C6 **Papakaio** New Zealand
145 E2 **Papakura** New Zealand
71 H7 **Papalia** Indonesia
43 G8 **Papa, Monte del** Italy
125 L7 **Papantla** Mexico
70 D2 **Papar** Sabah
145 F3 **Paparatu** New Zealand
145 E2 **Paparoa** New Zealand
144 C5 **Paparoa Range** New Zealand
46 E6 **Pápas, Akr** Greece
15 G2 **Papa Stour** *isld* Scotland
145 G2 **Papatoetoe** New Zealand
15 F1 **Papa Westray** Orkney Scotland
135 M10 **Papeete** Tahiti I Pac Oc
32 F6 **Papenburg** W Germany
25 C5 **Papendrecht** Netherlands
79 C4 **Paphos** Cyprus
124 E3 **Papigochic** *R* Mexico
121 P7 **Papineauville** Quebec
133 C3 **Paposo** Chile
45 M2 **Papozze** Italy
37 J2 **Pappenheim** E Germany
37 K6 **Pappenheim** W Germany
15 C5 **Paps of Jura** *mt* Scotland
136 K3 **Papua** *terr* Papua New Guinea
136 J3 **Papua, G. of** Papua New Guinea
136 K3 **Papua New Guinea** *state* S W Pacific
141 H3 **Papuan Passage** Gt Barrier Reef **Aust**
42 H3 **Papuk** *mt* Yugoslavia
68 C3 **Papun** Burma
140 B6 **Papunya** N Terr **Aust**
128 E3 **Papuri** *R* Brazil/Colombia
48 J5 **Papusa** *mt* Romania
8 B7 **Par** England
145 D4 **Para** New Zealand
129 J4 **Pará** *R* Brazil
129 H4 **Para** *state* Brazil
56 B2 **Parabel'** *R* U.S.S.R.
143 B6 **Paraburdoo** W Australia
71 F3 **Paracale** Philippines
128 C6 **Paracas, Pena de** *pen* Peru
130 F5 **Paracatu** Brazil
138 E4 **Parachilna** S Australia
46 E1 **Paraćin** Yugoslavia
98 E4 **Parade** S Dakota
130 G6 **Pará de Minas** Brazil
126 A1 **Paradera** Aruba **W Indies**
121 O4 **Paradis** Quebec
102 C2 **Paradise** California
107 M2 **Paradise** Kansas
101 L2 **Paradise** Montana
144 B6 **Paradise New Zealand**
109 K2 **Paradise** Texas
101 O8 **Paradise** Utah
116 H5 **Paradise Hill** Alaska
118 H5 **Paradise Hill** Sask
113 L9 **Paradise I.** New Providence I **Bahamas**
102 G3 **Paradise Pk** Nevada
118 G5 **Paradise Valley** Alberta
100 H8 **Paradise Valley** Nevada
71 J9 **Parado** Sumbawa **Indonesia**
110 K2 **Paragon** Indiana
103 M4 **Paragonah** Utah
110 F5 **Paragould** Arkansas
128 F6 **Paraguá** *R* Bolivia
128 F2 **Paragua** *R* Venezuela
130 E8 **Paraguaca Paulista** Brazil
129 L6 **Paraguaçu** *R* Brazil
133 F2 **Paraguai** *R* Paraguay etc
127 J9 **Paraguaipoa** Venezuela
127 J9 **Paraguaná, Pen. de** Venezuela
130 B10 **Paraguari** *dep* Paraguay
133 F3 **Paraguay** *R* Paraguay
133 F2 **Paraguay** *rep* S America
130 H9 **Paraiba** *state* Brazil
130 G8 **Paraiba do Sul** Brazil
130 H7 **Paraíba, R** Brazil
Parainen *see* **Pargas**
71 K10 **Paraingkareha** Sumba Indonesia
133 G1 **Paraísa** Brazil
85 E7 **Parakou** Benin
138 D4 **Parakylia** S Australia
129 G2 **Paramaribo** Suriname
20 B4 **Paramé** France
131 B4 **Paramillos, Sa. de los** *mts* Argentina
129 K6 **Paramirim** Brazil
46 D5 **Paramithiá** Greece
128 C6 **Paramonga** Peru
133 E4 **Paraná** Argentina
133 G2 **Paraná** *R* Brazil
130 D9 **Paraná** *state* Brazil
130 E9 **Paranaguá** Brazil
133 G1 **Paranaíba** Brazil
130 E6 **Paranaiba, R** Brazil
131 F4 **Paraná Ibicuy** *R* Argentina
131 F2 **Paraná, L** Argentina
129 G2 **Paranam** Suriname
129 H8 **Paranapanema** *R* Brazil
133 G2 **Paranapanema** *R* Brazil
131 F3 **Paraná, R** Argentina
133 G2 **Paranaval** Brazil
47 G3 **Paranéstion** Greece
71 E8 **Parang** Philippines
70 N8 **Parang** *isld* Indonesia
86 F5 **Paranga** Uganda
83 K8 **Parangi Aru** *R* Sri Lanka
130 G6 **Paraopeba** Brazil
145 E4 **Paraparaumu** New Zealand
128 F8 **Parapeti** *R* Bolivia
47 F8 **Parapóla** *isld* Greece
128 E2 **Paraque, Cerro** *mt* Venezuela
70 G6 **Parara** Sulawesi
71 G5 **Parasan** *isld* Philippines
138 E4 **Paratoo** S Australia
139 H8 **Parattah** Tasmania
129 H5 **Parauapebas** *R* Brazil
18 H6 **Paray-le-Monial** France
56 B3 **Parbig** *R* U.S.S.R.
21 F7 **Parçay-les-Pins** France
20 C5 **Parcé** France
55 E5 **Parchevka** U.S.S.R.
33 P6 **Parchim** E Germany
45 O7 **Parco Naz. del Circeo** Italy
22 C3 **Parcq, le** France
31 O4 **Parczew** Poland
102 D3 **Pardee Res** California
99 R6 **Pardeeville** Wisconsin
80 C4 **Pardes Hanna-Karkur** Israel
129 H8 **Pardo** *R* Brazil
130 F4 **Pardo** *R* Minas Gerais **Brazil**
131 H2 **Pardo** *R* Rio Grande do Sul Brazil
142 C5 **Pardoo** W Australia
130 D7 **Pardo, R** Mato Grosso Brazil
31 J5 **Pardubice** Czechoslovakia
70 O9 **Pare** Java
129 G6 **Parecis** Brazil
128 F6 **Parecis, Sa. dos** *mts* Brazil
133 D3 **Pareditas** Argentina
145 D1 **Parengarenga Harbour** New Zealand
20 E5 **Parennes** France
121 Q5 **Parent** Quebec
18 E8 **Parentis en Born** France
121 O4 **Parent L** Quebec
144 C6 **Pareora** New Zealand
70 F7 **Parepare** Sulawesi
33 P8 **Parey** E Germany
52 F5 **Parfen'yevo** U.S.S.R.
46 D5 **Párga** Greece
29 J11 **Pargas** Finland
52 D4 **Pargolovo** U.S.S.R.
127 P4 **Parham** Antigua **W Indies**
103 N4 **Paria** *R* Utah
128 F1 **Paria, G. de** Venezuela/Trinidad
128 F2 **Pariaguán** Venezuela
69 E13 **Pariaman** Sumatra
128 F1 **Paria, Pen. de** Venezuela
103 N5 **Paria Plat** Arizona
128 E4 **Paricá, L** Brazil
70 G5 **Parigi** Sulawesi
21 F6 **Parigné-l'Evêque** France
128 G2 **Parika** Guyana
144 D5 **Parikawa** New Zealand
145 E3 **Parikino** New Zealand
29 O10 **Parikkala** Finland
128 F3 **Parima, Sa** *mts* Brazil/Venezuela
128 D7 **Parinacocha, L** Peru
128 D4 **Parinari** Peru
128 B4 **Pariñas, Pta** Peru
48 L4 **Pårincea** Romania
138 F5 **Paringa** S Australia
129 G4 **Parintins** Brazil
110 C6 **Paris** Arkansas
101 O7 **Paris** Idaho
99 T10 **Paris** Illinois
110 M3 **Paris** Kentucky
110 E2 **Paris** Missouri
110 H5 **Paris** Tennessee
109 M2 **Paris** Texas
23 **Paris** *conurbation* France
95 L3 **Parish** New York
99 W3 **Parisienne, Ile** Ontario
69 E10 **Parit Buntar** Malaysia
71 L10 **Pariti** Timor Indonesia
55 D4 **Parizhskiy** U.S.S.R.
26 N4 **Parkajoki** Sweden
29 K9 **Parkano** Finland
118 L8 **Parkbeg** Sask
110 K4 **Park City** Kentucky
101 R4 **Park City** Montana
103 N1 **Park City** Utah
106 E3 **Parkdale** Colorado
100 D4 **Parkdale** Oregon
103 K7 **Parker** Arizona
106 F2 **Parker** Colorado
101 O6 **Parker** Idaho
107 Q3 **Parker** Kansas
98 J6 **Parker** S Dakota
110 L1 **Parker City** Indiana
94 H5 **Parker City** Pennsylvania
103 K7 **Parker Dam** California
143 D9 **Parker Hill** W Australia
140 E3 **Parker Pt** Queensland
143 C9 **Parker Range** W Australia
99 O7 **Parkersburg** Iowa
94 F7 **Parkersburg** W Virginia
99 L3 **Parkers Prairie** Minnesota
119 O7 **Parkerview** Sask
139 J5 **Parkes** New S Wales
95 M6 **Parkesburg** Pennsylvania
99 Q4 **Park Falls** Wisconsin
102 D6 **Parkfield** California
12 E3 **Parkgate Scotland**
95 L8 **Park Hall** Maryland
57 E5 **Parkhar** U.S.S.R.
120 J9 **Parkhill** Ontario
26 K5 **Parkijaur** *L* Sweden
110 F6 **Parkin** Arkansas
118 E9 **Park Lake Prov. Park** Alberta
118 D8 **Parkland** Alberta
119 Q9 **Parkman** Sask
101 S5 **Parkman** Wyoming
101 T9 **Park Ra** Colorado
99 L3 **Park Rapids** Minnesota
99 T8 **Park Ridge** Illinois
98 J1 **Park River** N Dakota
103 N6 **Parks** Arizona
98 E9 **Parks** Nebraska
111 L13 **Parks Airport** St Louis
118 L5 **Parkside** Sask
95 M9 **Parksley** Virginia
140 C6 **Parks, Mt** N Terr **Aust**
109 K2 **Park Springs** Texas
37 N4 **Parkstein W Germany**
98 J6 **Parkston** S Dakota
95 L7 **Parkton** Maryland
112 H3 **Parkton** N Carolina
101 M8 **Park Valley** Utah
106 D5 **Park View** New Mexico
106 D1 **Park View Mt** Colorado
100 D3 **Parkway** Washington
26 K5 **Pärlälven** *R* Sweden
127 M1 **Parlatuvier Tobago**
100 J6 **Parma** Idaho
45 H2 **Parma** Italy
94 C4 **Parma** Michigan
110 G5 **Parma** Missouri
94 F5 **Parma** Ohio
45 H2 **Parma** *R* Italy
21 H9 **Parnac** France
129 K6 **Parnaguá** Brazil
129 K4 **Parnaiba** Brazil
129 J5 **Parnaíba** *R* Brazil
46 F6 **Parnassós** *mt* Greece
144 D5 **Parnassus New Zealand**
99 O8 **Parnell** Iowa
99 M9 **Parnell** Missouri
108 G1 **Parnell** Texas
47 F6 **Párnis** *mt* Greece
46 F7 **Párnon Óros** *mts* Greece
52 B5 **Pärnu** U.S.S.R.
52 B5 **Pärnu laht** *G* U.S.S.R.
144 C5 **Paroa** New Zealand
59 M1 **Paromay** U.S.S.R.
110 D7 **Paron** Arkansas
141 G8 **Paroo** *R* Queensland
139 G4 **Paroo Chan** New S Wales
77 G2 **Paropamisus** *mts* Afghanistan
70 F6 **Paroreang, Bk** *mt* Sulawesi
47 G7 **Páros** *isld* Greece
127 J3 **Parottee Pt** Jamaica
103 M4 **Parowan** Utah
99 T8 **Parr** Indiana
112 F3 **Parr** S Carolina
8 C5 **Parracombe** England
133 C5 **Parral** Chile
139 K5 **Parramatta** New S Wales
95 M9 **Parramore I** Virginia
124 H5 **Parras de la Fuente** Mexico
8 D5 **Parrett, R** England
111 J8 **Parrish** Alabama
113 E10 **Parrish** Florida
111 M10 **Parrott** Georgia
112 C6 **Parrott** Georgia
94 G9 **Parrott** Virginia
122 H8 **Parrsboro** Nova Scotia
119 N9 **Parry** Sask
115 L4 **Parry B** N W Terr
120 K7 **Parry I** Ontario
114 H2 **Parry Is** N W Terr
115 M2 **Parry, Kap** Greenland
127 N3 **Parrylands** Trinidad
142 B5 **Parry Ra** W Australia
33 N7 **Parsau W Germany**
37 M5 **Parsberg W Germany**
41 M3 **Parseier Spitze** *mt* Austria
98 D2 **Parshall** N Dakota
103 K3 **Parsnip Pk** Nevada
107 P4 **Parsons** Kansas
110 H6 **Parsons** Tennessee
94 H7 **Parsons** W Virginia
123 P3 **Parson's Pond** Nfld
43 E11 **Partanna** Sicily
26 J4 **Pårtefjället** *mt* Sweden
36 E4 **Partenheim** W Germany
21 E8 **Parthenay** France
46 F7 **Parthénion** Greece
124 D5 **Partida** *isld* Mexico
43 E10 **Partinico** Sicily
59 K3 **Partizansk** U.S.S.R.
107 M4 **Partridge** Kansas
120 K2 **Partridge** *R* Ontario
123 R5 **Partridgeberry Hills** Newfoundland
119 U1 **Partridge Breast L** Manitoba
123 Q3 **Partridge Pt** Newfoundland
129 H4 **Paru** *R* Brazil
145 E1 **Parua Bay New Zealand**
77 L2 **Parwān** Afghanistan
66 C6 **Paryang** China
27 H15 **Påryd** Sweden
89 E6 **Parys** S Africa
102 G7 **Pasadena** California
109 G9 **Pasadena** Texas
128 B4 **Pasado, C** Ecuador
124 H5 **Pasaje** Mexico
133 E3 **Pasaje** *R* Argentina
106 G5 **Pasamonte** New Mexico
70 F5 **Pasangkaiu** Sulawesi
77 C4 **Pasargadae** Iran
71 H7 **Pasarwadjo** Indonesia
68 C3 **Pasawng** Burma
111 H11 **Pascagoula** *R* Mississippi
121 N4 **Pascalis** Quebec
48 K3 **Paşcani** Romania
100 F3 **Pasco** Washington
128 C6 **Pasco** *dep* Peru
95 Q5 **Pascoag** Rhode I
130 H5 **Pascoal, Mte** Brazil
140 E3 **Pascoe Inlet** Queensland
141 G2 **Pascoe, R** Queensland
142 B5 **Pasco I** W Australia
120 A2 **Pascopee** Ontario
133 C7 **Pascua** *R* Chile
22 C3 **Pas en Artois** France
33 T5 **Pasewalk** E Germany
52 J3 **Pashnya** U.S.S.R.
52 D4 **Pashskiy-Perevoz** U.S.S.R.
71 E3 **Pasig** Luzon **Philippines**
71 J4 **Pasige** *isld* Indonesia
78 H1 **Pasinler** Turkey
69 C11 **Pasiputih** Sumatra
70 O10 **Pasirian** Java
69 E12 **Pasirpengarayan** Sumatra
69 F10 **Pasir Puteh** Malaysia
27 H14 **Påskallavik** Sweden
102 B2 **Paskenta** California
57 B2 **Paskevicha, Zaliv** *gulf* U.S.S.R.
31 M1 **Pasłęk** Poland
143 E10 **Pasley, C** W Australia
29 L4 **Pasmajärvi** Finland
42 G5 **Pasman** *isld* Yugoslavia
138 E4 **Pasmore** *R* S Australia
77 H7 **Pasni** Pakistan
133 D6 **Paso de Indios** Argentina
125 M4 **Paso del Cascal** *mt* Nicaragua
133 F3 **Paso de los Libres** Argentina
133 F4 **Paso de los Toros** Uruguay
130 B10 **Paso de Patria** Paraguay
68 B2 **Pasok** Burma
133 C6 **Paso Limay** Argentina
125 M2 **Paso Reál** Honduras
133 C7 **Paso Rio Mayo** Argentina
102 D6 **Paso Robles** California
122 G5 **Paspébiac** Quebec
119 M8 **Pasqua** Sask
119 O5 **Pasquia Hills** Sask
119 Q5 **Pasquia R** Manitoba
112 L1 **Pasquotank R** N Carolina
77 C5 **Pas Rūdak** Iran
95 T1 **Passadumkeag** Maine
9 H7 **Passage de la Déroute** Channel Is
99 S1 **Passage I** Michigan
120 B4 **Passage I** Ontario
113 E10 **Pass-a-Grille Beach** Florida
95 N6 **Passaic** New Jersey
20 D5 **Passais** France
38 H4 **Passau** W Germany
40 D2 **Passavant** France
111 G11 **Pass Christian** Mississippi
101 T8 **Pass Cr** Wyoming
22 E2 **Passendale** Belgium
43 G12 **Passero, C** Sicily
123 Q6 **Pass I** Newfoundland
71 F5 **Passi** Philippines
41 O4 **Passiria, Val** Italy
99 S1 **Pass L** Ontario
120 B4 **Pass Lake** Ontario
15 C4 **Pass of Brander** Scotland
133 H2 **Passos** Brazil
128 C4 **Pastaza** *prov* Ecuador
122 F3 **Pasteur, L** Quebec
128 C3 **Pasto** Colombia
116 F5 **Pastol B** Alaska
9 H2 **Paston** England
103 P5 **Pastora Pk** Arizona
129 K5 **Pastos Bons** Brazil
71 E1 **Pasuquin** Luzon **Philippines**
70 O9 **Pasuruan** Java
52 B6 **Pasvalys** U.S.S.R.
52 C1 **Pasvikelv** *R* Norway
119 O6 **Paswegin** Sask
31 M2 **Pasym** Poland
48 F3 **Pásztó** Hungary
86 D4 **Pata** Cent Afr Republic
71 E8 **Pata** *isld* Philippines
103 O10 **Patagonia** Arizona
133 C7 **Patagonia** *terr* Chile/Arg
100 H3 **Pataha** *R* Washington
77 K1 **Pata Kesar** Afghanistan
130 G10 **Patamuté** Brazil
75 L5 **Patan** Nepal
71 B2 **Patani** Indonesia
95 L7 **Patapsco** *R* Maryland
20 J5 **Patay** France
138 F6 **Patchewollock** Victoria
95 P6 **Patchogue** Long I, N Y
145 E3 **Patea** New Zealand
144 C6 **Patearoa** New Zealand
70 G6 **Patedong** Sulawesi
85 F7 **Pategi** Nigeria
43 F11 **Paternò** Sicily
45 R8 **Paternopoli** Italy
100 F1 **Pateros** Washington
95 N6 **Paterson** New Jersey
100 F4 **Paterson** Washington
141 H8 **Paterson** *R* Queensland
144 B7 **Paterson Inlet** New Zealand
142 D5 **Paterson Ra** W Australia
25 G2 **Paterswolde** Netherlands
74 F2 **Pathankot** India
74 F9 **Pathardi** India
101 T7 **Pathfinder Res** Wyoming
13 F2 **Pathhead** Lothian Scotland
12 D3 **Pathhead** Strathclyde Scotland
68 D7 **Pathiu** Thailand
119 N6 **Pathlow** Sask
74 G9 **Pathri** India
68 E5 **Pathum Thani** Thailand
71 N9 **Pati** Indonesia
70 N9 **Pati** Java
70 B5 **Pati** Kalimantan
128 C3 **Patia** *R* Colombia
74 G3 **Patiala** India
143 F6 **Patience Well** W Australia
70 G7 **Patiro Tg** *C* Sulawesi
128 C6 **Pativilca** Peru
70 P9 **Patjinan Tg** *C* Java
70 N10 **Patjitan** Java
75 Q5 **Patkai Bum** *reg* India
111 C8 **Patmos** Arkansas
47 H7 **Pátmos** *isld* Greece
75 L6 **Patna** India
12 D3 **Patna** Scotland
75 K8 **Patnagarh** India
71 F3 **Patnanongan** *isld* Luzon Philippines
78 J2 **Patnos** Turkey
110 G3 **Patoka** Illinois
145 F3 **Patoka** New Zealand
110 K3 **Patoka** *R* Indiana
99 M7 **Paton** Iowa
130 H9 **Patos** Brazil
129 J7 **Patos de Minas** Brazil
127 N1 **Patos, I** Trinidad
100 C1 **Patos I** Washington
131 H3 **Patos, Lagoa dos** Brazil
108 A5 **Patos, Laguna de** Mexico
131 E3 **Patos, L. de los** Santa Fé Argentina
131 B3 **Patos, R. de los** Argentina
133 D4 **Patquía** Argentina
46 E6 **Pátrai** Greece
Patras Greece *see* **Pátrai**
118 F8 **Patricia** Alberta
98 E6 **Patricia** S Dakota
140 B5 **Patricia, Mt** N Terr Aust
133 B7 **Patricio Lynch, I** Chile
13 G5 **Patrick Brompton** England
121 T7 **Patrie, La** Quebec
110 M3 **Patriot** Indiana
133 H1 **Patrocinio** Brazil
111 K10 **Patsaliga** *R* Alabama
41 O3 **Patscherkofel** *mt* Austria
52 C1 **Patsoyoki** *R* U.S.S.R.
86 H6 **Patta** *isld* Kenya
43 C8 **Pattada** Sardinia
70 F7 **Pattallassang** Sulawesi Indonesia
76 C6 **Pattanapuram** India
69 E9 **Pattani** Thailand
69 E9 **Pattani** *R* Thailand
95 S7 **Patten** Maine
32 L8 **Pattensen** W Germany
13 F5 **Patterdale** England
102 C4 **Patterson** California
112 E6 **Patterson** Georgia
101 M5 **Patterson** Idaho
111 E12 **Patterson** Louisiana
94 H7 **Patterson Cr** W Virginia
102 E5 **Patterson Mt** California
117 F3 **Patterson, Mt** Yukon Terr
99 V4 **Patterson, Pt** Michigan
43 F10 **Patti** Sicily
140 B4 **Pattie Cr** N Terr **Aust**
43 G10 **Patti, G. di** Sicily
80 B8 **Pattish** *R* Israel
111 F10 **Pattison** Mississippi
94 J6 **Patton** Pennsylvania
99 M9 **Pattonsburg** Missouri
130 H9 **Patu** Brazil
78 H2 **Patu** Turkey
75 O7 **Patuakhali** Bangladesh
118 K3 **Patuanak** Sask
48 H6 **Pătuele** Romania
70 L9 **Patuha, G** *mt* Java
117 J7 **Patullo, Mt** Br Col
144 D4 **Paturau River** New Zealand
145 F3 **Patutahi** New Zealand
145 E3 **Patutu** *mt* New Zealand
95 L8 **Patuxent** *R* Maryland
18 E9 **Pau** France
145 D1 **Paua** New Zealand
129 J5 **Pau D'Arco** Brazil
121 O7 **Paugan Falls** Quebec
18 E7 **Pauillac** France
128 E5 **Pauini** Brazil
68 B2 **Pauk** Burma
68 A2 **Pauktaw** Burma
101 M7 **Paul** Idaho
38 H8 **Paularo** Italy
114 G4 **Paulatuk** N W Terr
103 M7 **Paulden** Arizona
94 C5 **Paulding** Ohio
146 G2 **Paulding B** Antarctica
18 H9 **Paulhan** France
116 H9 **Paul I** Alaska
115 N6 **Paul I** Labrador
100 F5 **Paulina** Oregon
33 R7 **Paulinenaue** E Germany
Paulis *see* **Isiro**
130 J9 **Paulista** Brazil
129 K5 **Paulistana** Brazil
99 L7 **Paullina** Iowa
41 K7 **Paullo** Italy
21 H8 **Paulnay** France
130 H10 **Paulo Alfonso, Cachoeira de** *falls* Brazil
25 C3 **Paulowna** Netherlands
107 N7 **Pauls Valley** Oklahoma
37 M5 **Paulushofen** W Germany
21 B8 **Paulx** France
68 C4 **Paung** Burma
68 B3 **Paungde** Burma
74 H8 **Pauni** India
74 H3 **Pauri** India
37 M2 **Pausa** E Germany
128 D7 **Pausa** Peru
33 S7 **Pausin** E Germany
128 D2 **Pauto** *R* Colombia
26 J7 **Pauträsk** Sweden
22 G5 **Pauvres** France
135 T3 **Pauwela** Hawaiian Is
103 M3 **Pavant Ra** Utah
55 C2 **Pavda** U.S.S.R.
54 L3 **Pavelets** U.S.S.R.
44 F1 **Pavia** Italy
117 N10 **Pavilion** Br Col
94 K4 **Pavilion** New York
101 R6 **Pavillion** Wyoming
20 G2 **Pavilly** France
27 M15 **Pāvilosta** U.S.S.R.
52 G5 **Pavino** U.S.S.R.
47 G1 **Pavlikeni** Bulgaria
55 G4 **Pavlodar** U.S.S.R.
116 G9 **Pavlof** Alaska
116 F9 **Pavlof Harbour** Aleutian Is
116 G9 **Pavlof Vol** Alaska
54 G8 **Pavlograd** U.S.S.R.
55 F4 **Pavlogradka** U.S.S.R.
54 G8 **Pavlogradskiye Khutora I-ye** U.S.S.R.
55 C3 **Pavlovka** Bashkirskaya U.S.S.R.
55 F5 **Pavlovka** Kazakhstan U.S.S.R.
52 F6 **Pavlovo** U.S.S.R.
56 B4 **Pavlovsk** Altay U.S.S.R.
52 D5 **Pavlovsk** Leningrad U.S.S.R.
55 D4 **Pavlovskiy** Kazakhstan U.S.S.R.
52 H5 **Pavlovskiy** Perm U.S.S.R.
113 D7 **Pavo** Georgia
45 J3 **Pavullo nel Frignano** Italy
107 O5 **Pawhuska** Oklahoma
119 Q3 **Pawistik** Manitoba
95 O3 **Pawlet** Vermont
8 D5 **Pawlett** England
112 H4 **Pawleys Island** S Carolina
68 C3 **Pawn** *R* Burma
99 R10 **Pawnee** Illinois
107 O5 **Pawnee** Oklahoma
109 K7 **Pawnee** Texas
99 L9 **Pawnee City** Nebraska
98 C9 **Pawnee Cr** Colorado
107 L3 **Pawnee Rock** Kansas
94 B4 **Paw Paw** Michigan
94 J7 **Paw Paw** W Virginia
95 Q5 **Pawtucket** Rhode I
47 G9 **Paximádhia** *isld* Crete Greece
46 D5 **Paxoi** *isld* Greece
116 P5 **Paxson** Alaska
116 P5 **Paxson L** Alaska
99 S9 **Paxton** Illinois
98 E8 **Paxton** Nebraska
68 C4 **Payagyi** Burma
58 E3 **Pa-yen-kao-le** China
40 E4 **Payerne** Switzerland
100 J5 **Payette** Idaho
100 J5 **Payette** *R* Idaho
109 L3 **Pay Hubbard, L** Texas
50 F2 **Pay-Khoy, Khrebet** *mt* U.S.S.R.
112 D5 **Payne** Georgia
94 C5 **Payne** Ohio
115 M6 **Payne, L** Quebec
102 C1 **Paynes Cr** California
143 C8 **Payne's Find** W Australia
99 M4 **Paynesville** Minnesota
143 C8 **Paynesville** W Australia
118 J5 **Paynton** Sask
70 C3 **Payong Tg** *C* Sarawak
131 F4 **Paysandu** Uruguay
20 F3 **Pays d'Auge** *reg* France
20 J3 **Pays de Bray** *reg* France
19 N13 **Pays de Dombes** *reg* France
40 F5 **Pays d'Enhaut** Switzerland
103 N7 **Payson** Arizona
103 N1 **Payson** Utah
131 B6 **Payún** *vol* Argentina
131 B6 **Payún Matru, Cerros** *hills* Argentina
77 A4 **Pāzanūn** Iran
47 G2 **Pazardzhik** Bulgaria
47 J5 **Pazarköy** Turkey
124 D5 **Paz, B. de la** Mexico
128 D2 **Paz de Rio** Colombia
42 F3 **Pazin** Yugoslavia
41 M3 **Paznauntal** Austria
52 D5 **Pchevzha** U.S.S.R.
31 M6 **Pcim** Poland
46 E2 **Pčinja** *R* Yugoslavia
68 D6 **Pe** Burma
111 L10 **Pea** *R* Alabama
117 R6 **Peace Point** Alberta
118 A2 **Peace R** Alberta
117 M7 **Peace R** Br Col/Alberta
113 F10 **Peace R** Florida
114 H6 **Peace River** Alberta
117 O11 **Peachland** Br Col
103 L6 **Peach Sp** Arizona
94 B2 **Peacock** Michigan
141 J5 **Peak Downs** Queensland
138 D3 **Peake** *R* S Australia
71 D5 **Peaked Pt** Philippines
140 B3 **Peake, Mt** N Terr **Aust**
143 C7 **Peak Hill** W Australia
102 E7 **Peak Mt** California
141 J6 **Peak Ra** Queensland
146 H12 **Peale Inlet** Antarctica
103 P3 **Peale, Mt** Utah
100 B9 **Peanut** California
118 D9 **Pearce** Alberta
103 P10 **Pearce** Arizona
140 A2 **Pearce Pt** N Terr **Aust**
111 C7 **Pearcy** Arkansas
116 H1 **Peard B** Alaska
110 F2 **Pearl** Illinois
119 P2 **Pearl** Ontario
111 G11 **Pearl** *R* Miss/Louisiana
109 G10 **Pearland** Texas
102 S12 **Pearl City** Hawaiian Is
99 R7 **Pearl City** Illinois
102 S12 **Pearl Hbr** Hawaiian Is
144 A7 **Pearl I New Zealand**
109 H7 **Pearsall** Texas
112 E6 **Pearson** Georgia
138 C5 **Pearson Is** S Australia
119 V2 **Pearson L** Manitoba
114 J2 **Peary Ch** N W Terr
109 H1 **Pease** *R* Texas
47 G5 **Peathoúra** *isld* Greece
21 A6 **Péaule** France
99 S3 **Peavy Falls Res** Michigan
142 C5 **Peawah, R** W Australia
88 G10 **Pebane** Mozambique
128 D4 **Pebas** Peru
133 F8 **Pebble I** Falkland Is
46 D2 **Peć** Yugoslavia
111 D12 **Pecan Island** Louisiana
130 E9 **Peças, I. das** Brazil
99 R7 **Pecatonica** Illinois
99 R7 **Pecatonica** *R* Illinois
45 J4 **Péccioli** Italy
48 L5 **Pechea** Romania
48 J2 **Pechenezhin** U.S.S.R.
29 P2 **Pechenga** U.S.S.R.
55 D1 **Pecherakh** U.S.S.R.
52 J2 **Pechora** U.S.S.R.
52 J3 **Pechora** *R* U.S.S.R.
50 E2 **Pechorskoy More** *sea* U.S.S.R.
52 C5 **Pechory** U.S.S.R.
48 G4 **Pecica** Romania
100 B7 **Peck** Oregon
33 S5 **Peckatel** E Germany
32 K9 **Peckelsheim W Germany**
144 C5 **Pecksniff, Mt** New Zealand
43 B9 **Pecora, C** Sardinia
43 G10 **Pecoraro, M** *mt* Italy
106 E6 **Pecos** New Mexico
108 D4 **Pecos** Texas
106 F6 **Pecos** *R* New Mexico
108 F5 **Pecos** *R* Texas/Mexico
48 E4 **Pécs** Hungary
48 E4 **Pécsvárad** Hungary
110 B3 **Peculiar** Missouri
125 O6 **Pedasí** Panama
139 H9 **Pedder, L** Tasmania
100 B5 **Pedee** Oregon
127 J5 **Pedernales** Dom Rep
124 F3 **Pedernales** Mexico
127 N10 **Pedernales** Venezuela
28 H6 **Pedersborg** Denmark
79 C4 **Pedhoulas** Cyprus
138 D2 **Pedirka** S Australia
129 K7 **Pedra Azul** Brazil
130 J9 **Pedra, Pta. de** *C* Brazil
128 F6 **Pedras Negras** Brazil
124 H5 **Pedriceña** Mexico
129 J5 **Pedro Afonso** Brazil
126 E6 **Pedro Bank** Caribbean
116 K7 **Pedro Bay** Alaska
126 F6 **Pedro Cays** *reefs* Caribbean
Peebles *co see* **Borders** *reg*
140 D7 **Peebles, Mt** N Terr **Aust**
142 B5 **Peedamulla** W Australia
144 C5 **Peel, Mt New Zealand**
103 M7 **Peeples Valley** Arizona
117 Q7 **Peerless L** Alberta
118 A5 **Peers** Alberta
139 G4 **Peery, L** New S Wales
106 G1 **Peetz** Colorado
98 K4 **Peever** S Dakota
144 D5 **Pegasus Bay New Zealand**
37 N1 **Pegau** E Germany
38 M7 **Peggau** Austria
44 E3 **Pegli** Italy
37 M4 **Pegnitz** W Germany
17 G6 **Pego** Spain
45 J2 **Pegognaga** Italy
101 O7 **Pegram** Idaho
13 G3 **Pegswood** England
69 F13 **Peg Tigabuluh** *mt* Sumatra
68 C4 **Pegu** Burma
69 E13 **Pegunungan Barisan** *mt* Sumatra
69 K12 **Pegunungan Bayang** *mt* Indonesia
68 B3 **Pegu Yoma** *ra* Burma
9 H5 **Pegwell B** England
52 H3 **Pegysh** U.S.S.R.
46 F3 **Pehčevo** Yugoslavia
67 B1 **Peijiangchang** China
67 G3 **Pei-Kan-t'ang Tao** *isld* Taiwan
38 M5 **Peilstein** *mt* Austria
32 M8 **Peine** W Germany
133 C8 **Peineta** *mt* Chile
68 B2 **Peinwa** Burma
19 P16 **Peipin** France
Peipus, L *see* **Chudskoye, Ozero**
41 N2 **Peiting** W Germany
133 G2 **Peixe** *R* Brazil
130 C5 **Peixe de Couro, R** Brazil
65 C7 **Pei Xian** China
65 D7 **Pei Xian** China
69 H12 **Pejantan** *isld* Indonesia
48 G6 **Pek** *R* Yugoslavia
70 M9 **Pekalongan** Java
69 F11 **Pekan** Malaysia
99 R9 **Pekin** Illinois
110 G1 **Pekin** Illinois
98 H2 **Pekin** N Dakota
Peking *see* **Beijing**
117 Q10 **Pekisko** Alberta
29 M5 **Pekkala** Finland
68 C3 **Pekon** Burma
69 E11 **Pelabohan Kelang** Malaysia
70 L9 **Pelabuanratu** Java
43 E13 **Pelagie, Isole** Italy
45 L4 **Pelago** Italy
47 G5 **Pélagos** *isld* Greece
111 G9 **Pelahatchee** Mississippi
69 F12 **Pelalawan** Sumatra
70 D6 **Pelampai** Kalimantan
17 G4 **Pelarda, Sa** *mts* Spain
46 F6 **Pelasyía** Greece
89 F7 **Pelatsoeu** *mt* Lesotho
31 J2 **Pełczyce** Poland
48 H5 **Peleaga** *mt* Romania
56 H2 **Peleduy** *R* U.S.S.R.
120 H10 **Pelee Island** Ontario
127 L4 **Pelée, Mt** Martinique W I
48 L3 **Peleney** U.S.S.R.
71 H5 **Peleng** *isld* Indonesia
71 H5 **Peleng, Selat** *str* Sulawesi
71 H5 **Peleng, Tk** *B* Indonesia
112 C6 **Pelham** Georgia
31 J6 **Pelhřimov** Czechoslovakia
119 R6 **Pelican B** Manitoba
113 L11 **Pelican Harbour** Bahamas
118 D3 **Pelican L** Alberta
119 S9 **Pelican L** Manitoba
99 O1 **Pelican L** Minnesota
119 O3 **Pelican L** Sask
99 R4 **Pelican L** Wisconsin
118 E3 **Pelican Portage** Alberta
141 G3 **Pelican R** Queensland
119 R6 **Pelican Rapids** Manitoba
98 K3 **Pelican Rapids** Minnesota
59 L1 **Peliny Osipenko, imeni** U.S.S.R.
112 F4 **Pelion** S Carolina
26 J5 **Peljekaise Nat. Park** Sweden
42 H6 **Pelješac** *pen* Yugoslavia
29 N4 **Pelkosenniemi** Finland
52 D3 **Pelkula** U.S.S.R.
32 G9 **Pelkum** W Germany
99 O8 **Pella** Iowa
43 G8 **Pella** Italy
80 F4 **Pella** Jordan
111 K8 **Pell City** Alabama
133 E5 **Pellegrini** Argentina
133 D5 **Pellegrini, L** Argentina
20 C5 **Pellerine, la** France
45 M1 **Pellestrina** Italy
119 U2 **Pelletier L** Manitoba
140 D3 **Pellew C** N Terr **Aust**
36 B4 **Pellingen** W Germany
29 L5 **Pello** Finland
21 E7 **Pellouailles** France
94 C1 **Pellston** Michigan
30 D1 **Pellworm** *isld* **W Germany**
119 Q7 **Pelly** Sask
117 E4 **Pelly** *R* Yukon Terr
115 L4 **Pelly Bay** N W Terr
117 E4 **Pelly Crossing** Yukon Terr
114 J4 **Pelly L** N W Terr
117 G5 **Pelly Mts** Yukon Terr
71 J8 **Pelokang** *isld* Indonesia
46 E7 **Pelopónnisos** Greece
43 G11 **Peloritani, Mi** *mts* Sicily
145 D4 **Pelorus Sound** New Zealand
131 H3 **Pelotas** Brazil
130 D10 **Pelotas, R.das** Brazil
47 G1 **Pelovo** Bulgaria
31 L2 **Pelplin** Poland
143 A8 **Pelsart Group** *islds* W Australia
33 T5 **Pelsin** E Germany
110 C6 **Pelsor** Arkansas
29 L3 **Peltovuoma** Finland
44 B2 **Pelvo d'Elva** *mt* Italy
19 Q15 **Pelvoux, Mt** France
55 D2 **Pelym** U.S.S.R.
55 D1 **Pelym** *R* U.S.S.R.
55 D1 **Pelymskiy Tuman, Oz** *L* U.S.S.R.
8 B7 **Pelynt** England
112 E3 **Pelzer** S Carolina
33 N4 **Pelzerhaken W Germany**
120 G5 **Pemache, R** Ontario
95 S1 **Pemadumcook L** Maine
70 M9 **Pemalang** Java
70 M9 **Pemalang, Tg** *C* Java
71 H5 **Pemali, Tg** *C* Sulawesi
70 C5 **Pemarunan** Kalimantan
70 E5 **Pemarung, P** Kalimantan
69 D11 **Pematangsiantar** Sumatra
88 H8 **Pemba** Mozambique
87 E9 **Pemba** Zambia
87 H8 **Pemba, B.de** Mozambique
88 G4 **Pemba I** Tanzania
117 M10 **Pemberton** Br Col
143 B10 **Pemberton** W Australia
119 U10 **Pembina** N Dakota
98 H1 **Pembina** *R* Manitoba
118 B5 **Pembina Oil Fields** Alberta
119 T9 **Pembina Mt** Manitoba
118 C5 **Pembina Prov. Park** Alberta
118 C4 **Pembina R** Alberta
99 T4 **Pembine** Wisconsin
112 F5 **Pembroke** Georgia
110 J5 **Pembroke** Kentucky
112 H3 **Pembroke** N Carolina
121 N7 **Pembroke** Ontario
94 G9 **Pembroke** Virginia
8 B4 **Pembroke Wales**
Pembroke *co see* **Dyfed**
133 F8 **Pembroke, C** Falkland Is
144 A6 **Pembroke, Mt** New Zealand
9 G5 **Pembury** England
127 J5 **Peña** Dom Rep
106 D6 **Penablanca** New Mexico
95 Q3 **Penacook** New Hampshire
17 G2 **Peña de Oroel** *mt* Spain
16 B3 **Penafiel** Portugal
16 E3 **Peñafiel** Spain
17 G4 **Peñagolosa** *mt* Spain
127 O3 **Penal** Trinidad
8 B4 **Penally Wales**
70 D3 **Penambo Ra** Kalimantan
16 C3 **Peña Mira** *mt* Spain
70 E2 **Penampang** Sabah
131 B2 **Peña Negra, Pasco de** Arg/Chile
125 K6 **Peña Nevada, Cerro** *mt* Mexico
Penang *see* **Pinang** *I*
130 E7 **Penápolis** Brazil
16 D1 **Peña Prieta** *mt* Spain
16 D4 **Peñaranda de Bracamonte** Spain
95 M6 **Pen Argyl** Pennsylvania
139 G5 **Penarie** New S Wales
17 G4 **Peñarroya** *mt* Spain
16 D6 **Peñarroya-Pueblonuevo** Spain
8 C5 **Penarth Wales**
16 C1 **Peña Rubia** *mt* Spain
17 G2 **Peña, Sa. de la** *mts* Spain
124 M4 **Peñas Blancas** Nicaragua
16 D1 **Peñas, C. de** Spain
106 E5 **Penasco** New Mexico
108 C3 **Penasco, Rio** *R* New Mexico
16 E3 **Peñas de Cervera** Spain
17 F6 **Peñas de San Pedro** Spain
133 C7 **Penas, G.de** Chile
127 N9 **Peñas, Pta** Venezuela
16 C2 **Peña Trevinca** *mt* Spain
16 D1 **Peña Vieja** *mt* Spain
100 H3 **Penawawa** Washington
65 F4 **Pen-ch'i** China
146 D3 **Penck, C** Antarctica
131 C4 **Pencoso, Alto de** *mt* Argentina
46 E4 **Pendálofon** Greece
118 F9 **Pendant d'Oreille** Alberta
86 C4 **Pende** *R* Cent Afr Republic
47 F6 **Pendelikón** *mt* Greece
85 B7 **Pendembu** Sierra Leone
130 H8 **Pendencia** Brazil
98 K7 **Pender** Nebraska
142 E3 **Pender** W Australia
142 E3 **Pender Bay** W Australia
144 A6 **Pender, Mt** New Zealand
8 B4 **Pendine Wales**
13 F6 **Pendlebury** England
13 F6 **Pendle Hill** England
94 B7 **Pendleton** Indiana
100 G4 **Pendleton** Oregon
112 E3 **Pendleton** S Carolina
117 J6 **Pendleton, Mt** Br Col
100 H1 **Pend Oreille** *R* Washington
117 P11 **Pend Oreille L** Idaho
101 N1 **Pendroy** Montana
16 B3 **Peneda** *mt* Portugal
129 L6 **Penedo** Brazil
94 J5 **Penfield** Pennsylvania
70 L9 **Pengalengan** Java
67 B1 **Peng'an** China
67 G4 **P'eng-chia Hsü** *isld* Taiwan
86 D7 **Penge** Zaïre
67 F5 **P'eng-hu Lieh-tao** *isld* Taiwan
67 F5 **P'eng-hu Tao** *isld* Taiwan
69 J12 **Pengiki** *isld* Indonesia
67 E4 **Pengkou** China
65 E6 **Penglai** China
58 G5 **Peng-pu** China
67 A1 **Pengshan** China
67 C2 **Pengshui** China
70 B6 **Pengudjan, Tg** *C* Kalimantan
139 H8 **Penguin** Tasmania
142 F2 **Penguin Deeps** Timor Sea
67 B1 **Pengxi** China
67 A1 **Peng Xian** China
67 E2 **Pengze** China
130 E10 **Penha** Brazil
118 D6 **Penhold** Alberta
8 D4 **Penhow Wales**
120 F3 **Penhurst** Ontario
44 F2 **Penice** *mt* Italy
16 A5 **Peniche** Portugal
13 E2 **Penicuik** Scotland
70 P10 **Penida** *isld* Indonesia
37 O2 **Penig** E Germany
71 G5 **Peninsula Pt** Philippines
69 E10 **Peninsular Malaysia** S E Asia
17 H4 **Peñíscola** Spain
13 G6 **Penistone** England
70 M9 **Penju, Teluk** *B* Java
78 K4 **Penjwin** Iran
38 H8 **Penk** Austria
Penki *see* **Benxi**
8 D2 **Penkridge** England
18 C5 **Penmarch, Pte.de** *C* France
118 K5 **Penn** Sask
45 M4 **Pennabilli** Italy
45 L4 **Penna, M** *mt* Italy
118 J8 **Pennant** Sask
122 J9 **Pennant Pt** Nova Scotia
42 F6 **Penna, Pta. della** Italy
42 F6 **Penne** Italy
18 F8 **Penne d'Agenais** France
146 J7 **Pennell Bank** Antarctica
138 E6 **Penneshaw** S Australia
122 F8 **Pennfield** New Brunswick
40 G5 **Pennine, Alpi** *mts* Switzerland
7 J8 **Pennine Chain** *mts* England
26 G7 **Penningkejsen** *mt* Norway/Sweden
95 N6 **Pennington** New Jersey
109 M4 **Pennington** Texas
94 D10 **Pennington Gap** Virginia
42 E5 **Pennino, M** *mt* Italy
95 M6 **Pennsburg** Pennsylvania
95 M7 **Penns Grove** New Jersey
94 H6 **Pennsylvania** *state* **U.S.A.**
95 K4 **Penn Yan** New York
12 B1 **Pennyghael** Scotland
115 N4 **Penny Ice Cap** N W Terr
115 K2 **Penny Str** N W Terr
52 D6 **Peno** U.S.S.R.
95 T1 **Penobscot** *R* Maine
95 T2 **Penobscot B** Maine
122 G8 **Penobsquis** New Brunswick
138 F6 **Penola** S Australia
124 G5 **Peñón Blanco Mexico**
138 C4 **Penong** S Australia
125 O5 **Penonomé** Panama
100 C8 **Penoyar** California
8 B2 **Penrhyndeudraeth Wales**
13 F4 **Penrith** England
139 K5 **Penrith** New S Wales
8 A7 **Penryn** England
111 J11 **Pensacola** Florida
113 K10 **Pensacola Cay** Bahamas
146 E10 **Pensacola Mts** Antarctica
119 N8 **Pense** Sask
8 D5 **Pensford** England
9 G5 **Penshurst** England
138 F7 **Penshurst** Victoria
70 E2 **Pensiangan** Sabah
137 O5 **Pentecost I** New Hebrides
142 G3 **Pentecost, R** W Australia
122 E4 **Pentecôte, L** Quebec
48 K5 **Penteleu** *mt* Romania
117 O11 **Penticton** Br Col
141 H5 **Pentland** Queensland
15 E2 **Pentland Firth** Scotland
13 E2 **Pentland Hills** Scotland
15 F2 **Pentland Skerries** Orkney Scotland
8 C1 **Pentre-Foelas** Wales
94 A3 **Pentwater** Michigan
131 E5 **Penuajo** Argentina
69 G13 **Penuba** Indonesia
69 G14 **Penuguan** Sumatra
68 C3 **Penwegon** Burma
8 C3 **Penybont** Wales
53 F7 **Penza** U.S.S.R.
9 F6 **Penzance** England
119 M7 **Penzance** Sask
41 O2 **Penzberg** W Germany
51 Q2 **Penzhino** U.S.S.R.
51 Q2 **Penzhinskaya Guba** *gulf* U.S.S.R.
33 S6 **Penzlin** E Germany
100 H3 **Peola** Washington
101 R1 **Peoples Cr** Montana
103 M8 **Peoria** Arizona
99 R9 **Peoria** Illinois
99 T8 **Peotone** Illinois
89 C6 **Pepani** *watercourse* S Africa
85 B7 **Pepel** Sierra Leone
25 F3 **Peperga** Netherlands
145 D4 **Pepin I** New Zealand
99 O5 **Pepin, L** Wisconsin
22 K2 **Pepinster** Belgium
130 D10 **Pepiri Guaçu. R** Brazil
44 B3 **Pepouiri, Mt** Italy
46 D3 **Peqin** Albania
131 H3 **Pequena, L** Brazil
124 C4 **Pequeña, Pta** *C* Mexico
103 K1 **Pequop Mts** Nevada
99 M3 **Pequot Lakes** Minnesota
37 O7 **Perach** W Germany
141 F2 **Pera Hd** Queensland
69 E10 **Perai** Malaysia
69 D10 **Perak** *isld* Malaysia
69 E10 **Perak** *prov* Malaysia
46 F6 **Perakhóra** Greece
38 G8 **Peralba** *mt* Italy
106 D7 **Peralta** New Mexico
47 G9 **Pérama** Crete Greece
29 K9 **Peräseinäjoki** Finland
69 E12 **Perawang** Sumatra
80 E3 **Perazon** Israel
122 H5 **Percé** Quebec
20 D3 **Pércée, Pte de la** France
18 G10 **Perche, Col de la** *pass* France
45 N5 **Percile** Italy
99 L9 **Percival** Iowa
142 E5 **Percival Ls** W Australia
20 C4 **Percy** France
110 G3 **Percy** Illinois
99 N8 **Percy** Iowa
141 K5 **Percy Is** Queensland
143 D9 **Percy, L** W Australia
141 G4 **Percyville** Queensland
17 H2 **Perdido** *mt* Spain
111 J11 **Perdido** *R* Alabama/Florida
133 D6 **Perdido** *R* Argentina
18 F10 **Perdido, M** *mt* Spain
130 B7 **Perdido, R** Brazil
118 K6 **Perdue** Sask
122 B3 **Perdu, L** Quebec
99 U6 **Pere** *R* Michigan
48 G2 **Perechin** U.S.S.R.
48 J2 **Pereginsko** U.S.S.R.
50 F2 **Peregrebnoye** U.S.S.R.
128 C3 **Pereira** Colombia
130 D7 **Pereira Barreto** Brazil
Pereira de Eça *see* **N'Giva**
129 G5 **Pereirinha** Brazil
17 H4 **Perello** Spain
94 A3 **Pere Marquette** *R* Michigan
146 E2 **Peremennyy, C** Antarctica
48 J1 **Peremyshlyany** U.S.S.R.
143 B8 **Perenjori** W Australia
116 L7 **Perenosa B** Alaska
52 E6 **Pereslavl' Zalesskiy** U.S.S.R.
45 O5 **Pereto** Italy
48 H2 **Pereval Veretski** *mt* U.S.S.R.
55 B5 **Perevolotskiy** U.S.S.R.
54 C6 **Pereyaslav Khmel'nitskiy** U.S.S.R.
100 D8 **Perez** California
133 D3 **Pérez** Chile

69 C8 Perforated I Thailand
131 E4 Pergamino Argentina
Pergamum see Bergama
45 N4 Pergola Italy
52 E4 Perguba U.S.S.R.
99 L3 Perham Minnesota
69 F10 Perhentian Besar isld Malaysia
29 L8 Perho Finland
29 L8 Perhojoki R Finland
48 F4 Periam Romania
121 S4 Péribonca Quebec
121 T3 Péribonca R Quebec
122 A3 Péribonca L Quebec
133 D2 Perico Argentina
124 F5 Pericos Mexico
20 C3 Périers France
21 E9 Périgne France
129 J3 Perigoso, Can Brazil
18 F7 Périgueux France
127 H9 Perijá, Sa. de mts Colombia/Venezuela
123 P2 Peril Rock Quebec
117 F7 Peril Str Alaska
72 E6 Perim isld S Yemen
118 C2 Perimeter Highway Manitoba
130 H10 Periquito, Sa do mts Brazil
48 K6 Periş Romania
46 E5 Peristéri mt Greece
133 C7 Perito Moreno Argentina
76 C5 Periyakulam India
95 M6 Perkasie Pennsylvania
112 F5 Perkins Georgia
111 C11 Perkins Louisiana
99 T4 Perkins Michigan
111 G11 Perkinston Mississippi
103 M7 Perkinsville Arizona
22 L5 Perl W Germany
41 P1 Perlach W Germany
125 P5 Perlas, Arch. de las islds Panama
33 P6 Perleberg E Germany
37 P6 Perlesreut W Germany
54 K5 Perlevka U.S.S.R.
98 K2 Perley Minnesota
48 F5 Perlez Yugoslavia
69 E9 Perlis prov Malaysia
52 J5 Perm' U.S.S.R.
101 L2 Perma Montana
52 G5 Permas U.S.S.R.
46 D4 Përmet Albania
Pernambuco see Recife
130 H9 Pernambuco state Brazil
138 D4 Pernatty Lagoon S Australia
107 N7 Pernell Oklahoma
46 F2 Pernik Bulgaria
29 K11 Perniö Finland
25 B5 Pernis Netherlands
40 C5 Peron France
143 A7 Peron, C W Australia
140 B2 Peron Is N Terr Aust
22 D4 Péronne France
22 G3 Peronnes Belgium
143 A7 Peron Pen W Australia
143 B9 Peron, Pt W Australia
20 J5 Péronville France
18 G10 Perpignan France
112 L1 Perquimans R N Carolina
8 A7 Perranporth England
20 J4 Perray-en-Yvelines, le France
109 J2 Perrin Texas
113 G12 Perrine Florida
102 G8 Perris California
40 B2 Perrogney France
108 B1 Perro, Laguna del New Mexico
121 N4 Perron Quebec
18 C4 Perros Guirec France
110 D6 Perry Arkansas
113 D7 Perry Florida
112 D5 Perry Georgia
110 F2 Perry Illinois
99 M8 Perry Iowa
94 C4 Perry Michigan
110 E2 Perry Missouri
94 K4 Perry New York
107 N5 Perry Oklahoma
120 F5 Perry Ontario
116 O6 Perry I Alaska
120 D2 Perry L Ontario
95 L7 Perryman Maryland
110 A2 Perry Res Kansas
94 D5 Perrysburg Ohio
108 D7 Perryton Texas
118 D4 Perryvale Alberta
110 D6 Perryville Arkansas
110 G4 Perryville Missouri
20 K3 Persan France
Persepolis see Takht-e Jamshid
128 F6 Perseverancia Bolivia
121 O4 Pershing Quebec
8 D3 Pershore England
Persia see Iran
99 L8 Persia Iowa
Persian Gulf see Gulf, The
27 J14 Persnäs Sweden
107 N4 Perth Kansas
98 G1 Perth N Dakota
122 E7 Perth New Brunswick
121 O8 Perth Ontario
12 E1 Perth Scotland
139 H8 Perth Tasmania
143 B9 Perth W Australia
Perth co see Central and Tayside regions
95 N6 Perth Amboy New Jersey
38 L4 Pertholz Austria
41 P3 Pertisau Austria
52 E3 Pertominsk U.S.S.R.
42 J6 Pertovac Yugoslavia
20 C5 Pertre, le France
29 M10 Pertunmaa Finland
52 G5 Pertyugskiy U.S.S.R.
99 R8 Peru Illinois
94 A6 Peru Indiana
99 L9 Peru Nebraska
95 O2 Peru New York
128 D6 Peru rep S America
135 S12 Peru-Chile Trench Pacific Oc
42 E5 Perugia Italy
129 J8 Peruibe Brazil
42 G4 Perušić Yugoslavia
22 G3 Peruwelz Belgium
78 J3 Pervari Turkey
20 F5 Pervencheres France
54 G4 Pervoavgustovskiy U.S.S.R.
55 F5 Pervomayka U.S.S.R.
54 K8 Pervomaysk U.S.S.R.
52 H4 Pervomayskaya U.S.S.R.
55 H4 Pervomayskiy Orenburg U.S.S.R.
55 D2 Pervomayskiy Serov U.S.S.R.
55 C4 Pervomayskiy Ufa U.S.S.R.
55 C3 Pervoural'sk U.S.S.R.
22 H2 Perwez Belgium
52 D5 Pes' R U.S.S.R.
45 K4 Pesa R Italy
45 N4 Pesaro Italy
102 B4 Pescadero California
Pescadores islds see P'eng-hu Lieh-tao
128 D7 Pescadores, Pta C Peru
45 H4 Pescaglia Italy
42 F6 Pescara Italy
42 F6 Pescara R Italy
45 P6 Pescasseroli Italy
42 G7 Peschici Italy
45 J1 Peschiera Italy
45 J4 Pescia Italy
45 P5 Pescina Italy
45 R7 Pesco Sannita Italy
45 P6 Pescosolido Italy
52 G2 Pesha R U.S.S.R.
74 D1 Peshawar Pakistan
46 D3 Peshkopi Albania
47 G2 Peshtera Bulgaria
99 T4 Peshtigo Wisconsin
99 S4 Peshtigo R Wisconsin
26 J5 Peskehaure Sweden
50 E5 Peski Karakumy U.S.S.R.
57 B2 Peski Priaral'skiye Karkumy U.S.S.R.
57 C5 Peski Sundukli U.S.S.R.
52 H5 Peskovka U.S.S.R.
38 N8 Pesnica R Yugoslavia
16 B3 Péso de Regua Portugal
110 H2 Pesotum Illinois
129 L5 Pesqueira Brazil
18 E8 Pessac France
33 R7 Pessin E Germany
48 E3 Pest co Hungary
48 H6 Peşteana Jiu Romania
52 E5 Pestovo U.S.S.R.
52 F6 Pestyaki U.S.S.R.
46 E5 Péta Greece
80 C5 Petaḥ Tiqwa Israel
29 L9 Petäjävesi Finland
71 B2 Petak, Tg C Halmahera Indonesia
111 G10 Petal Mississippi
29 J9 Petalax Finland
69 G14 Petaling Sumatra
47 G7 Petalioí isld Greece
47 G7 Petalión Kólpos gulf Greece
102 B3 Petaluma California
22 K4 Petange Luxembourg
127 L9 Petare Venezuela
88 C9 Petauke Zambia
121 P6 Petawaga, L Quebec
121 N7 Petawawa Ontario
125 P9 Petén Itzá, L Guatemala
99 R5 Petenwell Res Wisconsin
120 G4 Peterbell Ontario
9 F2 Peterborough England
95 Q4 Peterborough New Hampshire
121 M8 Peterborough Ontario
138 E5 Peterborough S Australia
15 F3 Peterculter Scotland
15 G3 Peterhead Scotland
135 O16 Peter I. Øy Antarctica
13 G4 Peterlee England
115 O1 Petermann Gletscher gla Greenland
143 G6 Petermann Ra N Terr/W Aust
131 B5 Peteroa, Vol peak Arg/Chile
118 H2 Peter Pond L Sask
36 H2 Petersberg W Germany
117 G7 Petersburg Alaska
110 G1 Petersburg Illinois
110 J3 Petersburg Indiana
94 D5 Petersburg Michigan
98 H1 Petersburg N Dakota
98 H8 Petersburg Nebraska
94 J6 Petersburg Pennsylvania
110 K6 Petersburg Tennessee
108 F2 Petersburg Texas
94 K9 Petersburg Virginia
94 H7 Petersburg W Virginia
116 M5 Peters Creek Alaska
9 F5 Petersfield England
119 V8 Petersfield Manitoba
33 T7 Petershagen E Germany
32 J8 Petershagen W Germany
37 L7 Petershausen W Germany
99 L7 Peterson Iowa
90 D16 Peter 1st I Antarctica
116 M5 Petersville Alaska
143 E7 Peterswald Hill W Australia
123 R4 Peterview Nfld
43 H9 Petilia Policastro Italy
17 G2 Petilla de Aragón Spain
111 H11 Petit Bois I Mississippi
127 N4 Petit Bourg Guadeloupe W I
127 N4 Petit Canal Guadeloupe W I
122 G8 Petitcodiac New Brunswick
127 N4 Petit Cul de Sac Marin B Guadeloupe W I
122 G5 Petite Cascapedia, Parc de la Quebec
122 E5 Petite Matane Quebec
121 Q7 Petite-Nation, Parc Quebec
122 B6 Petite Rivière Quebec
122 H9 Petite Rivière Bridge Nova Scotia
127 H5 Petite Rivière de l'Artibonite Haiti
21 J7 Petite Sauldre R France
20 G2 Petites Dalles, les France
123 M7 Petit Etang C Breton I, N Scotia
127 O4 Petite Terre, Îles de la Guadeloupe W I
122 G4 Petite Vallèe Quebec
127 H5 Petit Goâve Haiti
123 N5 Petit Jardin Nfld
110 C6 Petit Jean R Arkansas
95 U2 Petit Manan Pt Maine
36 B6 Petitmont France
117 N6 Petitot R Br Col
122 G6 Petit Rocher New Brunswick
29 M4 Petkula Finland
74 E7 Petlad India
125 P7 Peto Mexico
145 G4 Petone New Zealand
133 C4 Petorca Chile
94 C1 Petoskey Michigan
52 G4 Petrakovo U.S.S.R.
43 F11 Petralia Sicily
51 L1 Petra, Ostrov isld U.S.S.R.
65 H3 Petra Velikogo, Zaliv B U.S.S.R.
45 P7 Petrella, M mt Italy
121 N9 Petre, Pt Ontario
52 J4 Petretsovo U.S.S.R.
45 N4 Petriano Italy
47 F3 Petrich Bulgaria
141 L2 Petrie, Mt Brisbane, Qnsld
103 O6 Petrified Forest Nat Mon Arizona
54 F8 Petrikovka U.S.S.R.
48 H5 Petrila Romania
8 B6 Petrockstow England
52 C5 Petrodvorets U.S.S.R.
47 F1 Petrokhanski P Bulgaria
52 D5 Petrokrepost' U.S.S.R.
129 L5 Petrolândia Brazil
109 J8 Petroleum Texas
100 A9 Petrolia California
120 H10 Petrolia Ontario
109 J2 Petrolia Texas
129 K5 Petrolina Brazil
46 F6 Petromagoúla Greece
55 E3 Petropavlosk U.S.S.R.
56 G5 Petropavlovka U.S.S.R.
51 P3 Petropavlovsk-Kamchatskiy U.S.S.R.
129 K8 Petrópolis Brazil
112 C1 Petros Tennessee
48 H5 Petroseni Romania
48 G6 Petrovac Yugoslavia
48 F5 Petrovaradin Yugoslavia
55 E4 Petrovka U.S.S.R.
52 E3 Petrovskiy Yam U.S.S.R.
55 C4 Petrovskoye Bashkirskaya U.S.S.R.
52 E6 Petrovskoye Yaroslavl' U.S.S.R.
56 G5 Petrovsk-Zabaykal'skiy U.S.S.R.
52 D4 Petrozavodsk U.S.S.R.
52 K2 Petrun' U.S.S.R.
Petsamo see Pechenga
29 N2 Petsikko mt Finland
25 C3 Petten Netherlands
38 K6 Pettenbach Austria
14 D2 Pettigoe Irish Rep
110 C6 Pettigrew Arkansas
109 K7 Pettus Texas
123 U6 Petty Hbr Nfld
55 E3 Petukhovo U.S.S.R.
9 F6 Petworth England
38 L8 Petzen mt Austria
38 J5 Peuerbach Austria
69 C10 Peuetsagu, Gunung mt Sumatra
69 C10 Peukankuala Sumatra
116 J8 Peulik, Mt Alaska
69 B10 Peunasu isld Sumatra
29 M4 Peurasuvanto Finland
26 J5 Peuraure Sweden
69 C10 Peureulak Sumatra
9 G6 Pevensey England
94 C3 Pewamo Michigan
99 S6 Pewaukee Wisconsin
9 E5 Pewsey England
32 F6 Pewsum W Germany
36 B7 Pexonne France
19 P18 Peynier France
19 P18 Peypin France
21 I10 Peyrat-le Chateau France
18 E9 Peyrehorade France
18 H8 Peyreleau France
19 P17 Peyrolles-en-Provence France
19 P16 Peyruis France
106 F2 Peyton Colorado
52 G2 Peza R U.S.S.R.
18 H9 Pézenas France
31 K7 Pezinok Czechoslovakia
52 H4 Pezmog U.S.S.R.
37 N6 Pfaffenberg W Germany
37 L6 Pfaffenhofen an der Ilm W Germany
36 D6 Pfaffenhoffen France
41 J3 Pfäffikon Switzerland
37 P2 Pfaffroda E Germany
36 C4 Pfälzer Bergland reg W Germany
36 D5 Pfalzer Wald mts W Germany
36 D3 Pfalzfeld W Germany
36 F6 Pfalzgrafenweiler W Germany
37 L6 Pfalzpaint W Germany
37 O7 Pfarrkirchen W Germany
37 K3 Pfarrweisach W Germany
37 N6 Pfatter W Germany
36 E4 Pfeddersheim W Germany
37 M6 Pfeffenhausen W Germany
36 F6 Pfinztal W Germany
140 C6 Pfitzner, Mt N Terr Aust
41 N2 Pflach Austria
37 M6 Pförring W Germany
36 F6 Pforzheim W Germany
37 N5 Pfreimd W Germany
36 D4 Pfrimm R W Germany
41 K2 Pfullendorf W Germany
36 G7 Pfullingen W Germany
41 N4 Pfunds Austria
36 F4 Pfungstadt W Germany
37 L6 Pfünz W Germany
74 F3 Phagwara India
95 T7 Phair Maine
74 E5 Phalodi India
88 E9 Phalombe Malawi
36 C6 Phalsbourg France
76 B2 Phaltan India
69 D8 Pha Luai, Ko isld Thailand
69 E8 Phangan, Ko isld Thailand
69 D8 Phangnga Thailand
68 G5 Phanom Dang Raek mt Thailand
68 D5 Phanom Thuan Thailand
68 J7 Phan Rang Vietnam
68 J7 Phan Thiet Vietnam
103 M5 Phantom Ranch Arizona
109 J9 Pharr Texas
68 H2 Phat Diem Vietnam
69 D9 Phatthalung Thailand
69 D8 Phayam, Ko isld Thailand
68 E5 Phayuhakhiri Thailand
140 D2 Phelp R N Terr Aust
94 E9 Phelps Kentucky
95 K4 Phelps New York
109 M5 Phelps Texas
99 R3 Phelps Wisconsin
112 L2 Phelps L N Carolina
68 F4 Phen Thailand
94 J9 Phenix Virginia
111 L9 Phenix City Alabama
68 D6 Phet Buri Thailand
68 H5 Phiafay Laos
111 G9 Philadelphia Mississippi
99 P10 Philadelphia Missouri
95 M2 Philadelphia New York
97 Philadelphia conurbation Pennsylvania
84 J5 Philae ruins Egypt
111 J7 Phil Campbell Alabama
98 E5 Philip S Dakota
137 O7 Philip I Pacific Oc
111 F8 Philipp Mississippi
Philippeville see Skikda
22 G3 Philippeville Belgium
94 G7 Philippi W Virginia
140 E6 Philippi, L Queensland
25 A6 Philippine Netherlands
71 Philippines rep E Indies
89 D8 Philippolis S Africa
Philippopolis Bulgaria see Plovdiv
36 E5 Philippsburg W Germany
101 M3 Philipsburg Montana
94 J6 Philipsburg Pennsylvania
121 R7 Philipsburg Quebec
116 O2 Philip Smith Mts Alaska
139 H7 Phillip I Victoria
95 R2 Phillips Maine
101 R1 Phillips Montana
98 H9 Phillips Nebraska
108 C8 Phillips Texas
99 Q4 Phillips Wisconsin
107 L2 Phillipsburg Kansas
115 L1 Phillips Inlet N W Terr
143 B6 Phillips, Mt W Australia
138 C3 Phillipson, L S Australia
142 G5 Phillipson Ra W Australia
142 F3 Phillips Ra W Australia
95 O4 Philmont New York
102 A2 Philo California
100 B5 Philomath Oregon
118 F3 Philomena Alberta
115 M3 Philpots Island N W Terr
94 G10 Philpott Dam Virginia
68 G5 Phimun Mangsahan Thailand
118 J6 Phippen Sask
106 D1 Phippsburg Colorado
68 G7 Phnom Penh Cambodia
67 B6 Pho Binh Gia Vietnam
144 D5 Phoebe New Zealand
95 N4 Phoenicia New York
103 M8 Phoenix Arizona
111 G12 Phoenix Louisiana
95 L3 Phoenix New York
134 K8 Phoenix Is Pacific Oc
95 M6 Phoenixville Pennsylvania
68 G1 Pho Lu Vietnam
68 H4 Phong Nha Vietnam
68 F2 Phong Saly Laos
73 R4 Phong Saly Thailand
68 F1 Phong Tho Vietnam
68 F3 Phon Phisai Thailand
139 G7 Phoques B Tasmania
68 H7 Phouc Le Vietnam
68 D3 Phrao Thailand
68 E5 Phra Phutthabat Thailand
69 D8 Phra Saeng Thailand
69 C8 Phra Thong, Ko isld Thailand
68 E5 Phrom Buri Thailand
47 L6 Phrygia Turkey
68 H7 Phu Cuong Vietnam
68 G2 Phuc Yen Vietnam
67 B7 Phu Dien Vietnam
68 G3 Phu Dien Chau Vietnam
69 D9 Phuket, Ko isld Thailand
68 F4 Phu Khieo Thailand
67 B6 Phulang Thuong Vietnam
75 L8 Phulbani India
68 H4 Phu Loc Vietnam
68 G2 Phu Ly Vietnam
68 F6 Phum Bavel Cambodia
68 G7 Phum Hay Cambodia
68 G6 Phum Khvao Cambodia
68 F6 Phum Siem Cambodia
68 F6 Phum Svai Cambodia
68 F6 Phum Treng Cambodia
68 F6 Phum Troy Toch Cambodia
68 J5 Phu My Vietnam
68 G2 Phu Nho Quan Vietnam
75 N5 Phuntsholing Bhutan
69 G8 Phuoc Long Vietnam
68 G3 Phu Qui Vietnam
68 G2 Phu Tho Vietnam
129 J5 Piaca Brazil
44 G1 Piacenza Italy
44 F2 Piacenza prov Italy
45 L1 Piacenza d'Adige Italy
45 J1 Piadena Italy
122 B2 Piakoudie L Quebec
141 L7 Pialba Queensland
139 J4 Pian R New S Wales
41 K5 Pianazzo Italy
130 H9 Piancó R Brazil
45 L4 Pian de Sco Italy
45 M4 Pian di Meleto Italy
45 N4 Pianello Italy
139 G6 Piangil Victoria
45 M1 Pianiga Italy
45 K3 Piano del Voglio Italy
42 G6 Pianosa isld Adriatic Sea
42 C6 Pianosa isld Italy
65 B5 Pianquan China
118 H9 Piapot Sask
127 O2 Piarco airport Trinidad
31 M3 Piaseczno Poland
122 K3 Piashti, L Quebec
31 O4 Piaski Poland
31 L3 Piątek Poland
48 K4 Piatra Neamt Romania
129 K5 Piauí state Brazil
129 K5 Piauí, Sa. do mts Brazil
42 E2 Piave R Italy
143 B9 Piawaning W Australia
45 H3 Piazza al Serchio Italy
43 F11 Piazza Armerina Sicily
133 C8 Piazzi isld Chile
45 L1 Piazzolas B Italy
86 F4 Pibor Post Sudan
118 D4 Pibroch Alberta
103 L6 Pica Arizona
101 L6 Picabo Idaho
103 N9 Picacho Arizona
103 K8 Picacho California
106 E8 Picacho New Mexico
103 N9 Picacho Res Arizona
124 B3 Picachos, Cerro dos mt Mexico
22 D4 Picardie France
20 K1 Picardie reg
20 C3 Picauville France
111 G11 Picayune Mississippi
123 O5 Piccadilly Nfld
106 B2 Piceance Cr Colorado
45 R8 Picentini, Mti mt Italy
124 F3 Picháchic Mexico
133 E2 Pichanal Argentina
131 B4 Pichidangul, B Chile
133 C4 Pichilemu Chile
128 C4 Pichincha prov Ecuador
52 G6 Pichkasy U.S.S.R.
118 D4 Pickardville Alberta
111 F9 Pickens Mississippi
112 E3 Pickens S Carolina
94 G8 Pickens W Virginia
120 K7 Pickerel Ontario
99 P1 Pickerel L Ontario
13 H5 Pickering England
110 B1 Pickering Missouri
143 D8 Pickering, Mt W Australia
126 D4 Pickle Bank Caribbean
115 K7 Pickle Lake Ontario
98 H6 Pickstown S Dakota
109 M2 Pickton Texas
110 H6 Pickwick L Tennessee
45 P7 Pico Italy
16 D4 Pico de Almanzor mt Spain
16 E4 Pico Penalara mt Spain
129 K5 Picos Brazil
16 C2 Picos de Ancares, Sa. de mts Spain
16 C6 Picos de Aroche mt Spain
20 K2 Picquigny France
120 D4 Pic R Ontario
139 K5 Picton New S Wales
145 E4 Picton New Zealand
121 N8 Picton Ontario
139 H9 Picton, Mt Tasmania
122 K8 Pictou Nova Scotia
122 K8 Pictou I Nova Scotia
118 E9 Picture Butte Alberta
95 L5 Picture Rocks Pennsylvania
130 H9 Picuí Brazil
131 B7 Picún Leufú Argentina
138 B4 Pidinga S Australia
45 Q7 Piedimonte d'Alife Italy
111 L8 Piedmont Alabama
110 F4 Piedmont Missouri
112 E3 Piedmont S Carolina
98 C5 Piedmont S Dakota
94 F6 Piedmont Res Ohio
102 E5 Piedra California
106 C4 Piedra R Colorado
17 F3 Piedra R Spain
16 E5 Piedrabuena Spain
16 C2 Piedrafita, Pto. de pass Spain
16 D4 Piedrahita Spain
131 B3 Piedra Lobos, Pta Chile
125 J3 Piedras Negras Mexico
71 D5 Piedras Point Philippines
133 F5 Piedras, Pta Argentina
128 D6 Piedras, R.de las R Peru
99 R1 Pie I Ontario
29 N9 Pieksämäki Finland
38 M5 Pielach R Austria
29 M8 Pielavesi L Finland
29 O8 Pielinen L Finland
29 O9 Pielisjoki R Finland
139 H8 Pieman R Tasmania
31 M1 Pieniężno Poland
22 K5 Piennes France
36 B2 Pier W Germany
106 F1 Pierce Colorado
113 F10 Pierce Florida
100 K3 Pierce Idaho
98 J7 Pierce Nebraska
13 G4 Piercebridge England
110 B5 Pierce City Missouri
94 B5 Pierceton Indiana
107 K4 Pierceville Kansas
102 A2 Piercy California
46 E4 Piéria Óri Greece
15 F1 Pierowall Orkney Scotland
98 J4 Pierpont S Dakota
19 J6 Pierre France
98 F5 Pierre S Dakota
21 H10 Pierre-Buffiere France
19 P15 Pierre-Châtel France
22 D5 Pierrefonds France
120 K3 Pierre L Ontario
19 N16 Pierrelatte France
22 K5 Pierrepont France
121 S6 Pierreville Quebec
127 P3 Pierreville Trinidad
113 F8 Pierson Florida
119 Q9 Pierson Manitoba
36 B4 Piesport W Germany
143 B10 Piesseville W Australia
31 K7 Piešt'any Czechoslovakia
Pietarsaari see Jakobstad
89 G7 Pietermaritzburg S Africa
89 F4 Pietersburg S Africa
22 G3 Piéton Belgium
106 B7 Pie Town New Mexico
44 D3 Pietra Ligure Italy
45 Q7 Pietramelara Italy
44 H4 Pietrasanta Italy
45 Q7 Pietravairano Italy
87 F11 Piet Retief S Africa
43 B9 Pietro, S isld Sardinia
48 J5 Pietroşiţa Romania
48 J3 Pietrosu mt Romania
48 J3 Pietrosul mt Romania
29 P2 Piets'yarvi, Oz L U.S.S.R.
20 B2 Pieux, les France
38 F9 Pieve Italy
42 E2 Pieve di Cadore Italy
45 K2 Pieve di Cento Italy
45 J3 Pievepelago Italy
45 M4 Pieve S. Stefano Italy
47 J9 Pigádhia Kárpathos I Greece
94 D3 Pigeon Michigan
94 C1 Pigeon R Michigan
120 H10 Pigeon B Ontario
111 K10 Pigeon Cr Alabama
140 B3 Pigeon Hole N Terr Aust
127 K3 Pigeon I Jamaica
118 C5 Pigeon L Alberta
121 M8 Pigeon L Ontario
102 B4 Pigeon Pt California
127 M2 Pigeon Pt Tobago
119 V6 Pigeon R Manitoba
119 O2 Pigeon River Ontario
143 C8 Pigeon Rocks W Australia
94 H10 Pigg R Virginia
110 F5 Piggott Arkansas
89 G8 Pigg's Peak Swaziland
19 Q18 Pignans France
45 P7 Pignataro Interamna Italy
45 Q7 Pignatoro Maggiore Italy
133 E5 Pigüe Argentina
145 D3 Pihaina New Zealand
67 E1 Pi He R China
29 L9 Pihlajavesi Finland
56 E4 Pik Grandioznyy mt U.S.S.R.
31 K2 Piła Poland
129 K6 Pilao Arcado Brazil
19 N14 Pilat, Mt France
142 C5 Pilbara W Australia
48 F3 Pilis Hungary
48 E3 Pilisvörösvár Hungary
144 A6 Pillans Pass New Zealand
98 J2 Pillsbury N Dakota
102 B2 Pillsbury, L California
52 G6 Pil'na U.S.S.R.
8 D4 Pilning England
130 F5 Pilões, Sa. dos mts Brazil
46 E8 Pílos Greece
119 N8 Pilot Butte Sask
110 D3 Pilot Grove Missouri
119 T9 Pilot Mound Manitoba
112 G1 Pilot Mountain N Carolina
102 G3 Pilot Pk Nevada
101 Q5 Pilot Pk Wyoming
116 J8 Pilot Point Alaska
109 L2 Pilot Point Texas
100 G4 Pilot Rock Oregon
116 F5 Pilot Station Alaska
139 J6 Pilot, The mt New S Wales
133 E2 Piloya R Bolivia
37 M5 Pilsach W Germany
Pilsen see Plzeň
99 T5 Pilsen Wisconsin
41 O1 Pilsen See L W Germany
37 O6 Pilsting W Germany
55 F1 Pil'tan-Lor, Oz L U.S.S.R.
27 M14 Piltene U.S.S.R.
8 D5 Pilton England
52 J4 Pil'va R U.S.S.R.
31 N6 Pilzno Poland
55 F1 Pim U.S.S.R.
103 P9 Pima Arizona
129 G4 Pimenta Brazil
128 F6 Pimenta Bueno Brazil
127 J5 Pimental Dom Rep
128 C5 Pimentel Peru
113 L12 Pimlico I Bahamas
71 H4 Pimpi Sulawesi
86 D5 Pimu Zaïre
17 G3 Pina Spain
103 L10 Pinacate, Cerro peak Mexico
124 C2 Pinacate, Sa. del mt Mexico
103 O9 Pinaleno Mts Arizona
71 E4 Pinamalayan Philippines
69 E10 Pinang isld Malaysia
70 E2 Pinangah Sabah
78 F2 Pinarbaşi Turkey
126 C3 Pinar del Río Cuba
47 J3 Pinarhisar Turkey
138 F3 Pinaroo, L New S Wales
133 D4 Piñas Argentina
45 L2 Pincara Italy
9 F2 Pinchbeck England
118 D9 Pincher Creek Alberta
117 L8 Pinchi Br Col
128 C4 Pinchincha mt Ecuador
94 D4 Pinckney Michigan
110 G3 Pinckneyville Illinois
20 D4 Pinçon, Mt France
94 C3 Pinconning Michigan
48 G4 Pîncota Romania
31 M5 Pińczów Poland
129 H6 Pindaiba Brazil
110 D5 Pindall Arkansas
143 B8 Pindar W Australia
129 J4 Pindaré R Brazil
70 G4 Pindjang Sulawesi
28 E4 Pindstrup Denmark
103 N7 Pine Arizona
100 K6 Pine Idaho
94 B2 Pine R Michigan
138 F4 Pine R New S Wales
99 Q6 Pine R Wisconsin
111 K10 Pine Apple Alabama
111 D7 Pine Bluff Arkansas
119 P4 Pinebluff L Sask
98 B8 Pine Bluffs Wyoming
123 T7 Pine, C Nfld
113 F9 Pinecastle Florida
126 E2 Pine Cay isld Bahamas
111 E7 Pine City Arkansas
99 O4 Pine City Minnesota
103 H1 Pine Cr Nevada
94 K5 Pine Cr Pennsylvania
140 B2 Pine Creek N Terr Aust
102 E3 Pinecrest California
107 P7 Pine Cr. Res Oklahoma
16 E2 Pineda de la S Spain
117 P9 Pinedale Alberta
102 E5 Pinedale California
101 Q7 Pinedale Wyoming
102 E5 Pine Flat Res California
100 G8 Pine Forest Range Nevada
52 F3 Pinega U.S.S.R.
52 G3 Pinega R U.S.S.R.
95 L6 Pine Grove Pennsylvania
143 B8 Pinegrove W Australia
140 C5 Pine Hill N Terr Aust
141 H6 Pinehill Queensland
114 J6 Pine House Saskatchewan
118 L3 Pine House L Sask
112 H2 Pinehurst N Carolina
100 C2 Pinehurst Washington
118 F4 Pinehurst L Alberta
113 E11 Pine I Florida
99 O5 Pine Island Minnesota
99 S4 Pine L Wisconsin
109 O4 Pineland Texas
146 H11 Pinel B Antarctica
144 B6 Pinelheugh mt New Zealand
113 E10 Pinellas airport Florida
102 C6 Pine Mt California
107 P7 Pine Mt Oklahoma
103 L7 Pine Pk Arizona
117 Q5 Pine Point N W Terr
119 P1 Pine Portage Ontario
113 D8 Pine Pt Florida
114 H5 Pine Pt N W Terr
118 D4 Pine R Alberta
117 M8 Pine R Br Col
98 D6 Pine Ridge S Dakota
119 R7 Pine River Manitoba
99 M3 Pine River Minnesota
118 K3 Pine River Sask
44 B2 Pinerolo Italy
120 J9 Pinery Prov. Park Ontario
111 B9 Pines, L. O'The Texas
108 C4 Pine Springs Texas
89 G7 Pinetown S Africa
110 B7 Pine Valley Oklahoma
103 L4 Pine Valley Utah
103 L4 Pine Valley Mts Utah
94 D10 Pineville Kentucky
111 D10 Pineville Louisiana
110 B5 Pineville Missouri
112 G2 Pineville N Carolina
94 F9 Pineville W Virginia
99 L2 Pinewood Minnesota
99 M1 Pinewood Ontario
112 G4 Pinewood S Carolina
98 K1 Piney Manitoba
101 T2 Piney Buttes hills Montana
110 C6 Piney Cr Arkansas
113 D8 Piney Pt Florida
65 F2 Ping'an China
143 C10 Pingaring W Australia
67 A5 Pingbian China
67 B1 Pingchang China
65 D7 Ping Dao isld China
67 C3 Pingdeng China
65 B6 Pingding China
Pingdingbu see Guyan
58 F5 Pingdingshan China
65 F4 Pingdingshan China
65 G1 Pingding Shan mt China
65 D6 Pingdu China
143 B10 Pingelly W Australia
65 C7 Pinggang China
65 F3 Pinggang China
65 D4 Pinggu China
67 B5 Pingguo China
67 F4 Pinghai China
67 F4 Pinghe China
Pinghu see Pingtang
67 G1 Pinghu China
67 D2 Pingjiang China
67 C4 Pingle China
58 E4 Pingliang China
67 D1 Pinglin China
65 B5 Pinglu China
65 B7 Pinglu China
58 E4 Pingluo China
Pingma see Tiandong
75 N6 Pingna Bangladesh
67 C5 Pingnan China
67 F3 Pingnan China
Pingqiao see Xinyang
65 D4 Pingquan China
101 N6 Pingree Idaho
98 G2 Pingree N Dakota
143 C10 Pingrup W Australia
65 C5 Pingshan China
67 A2 Pingshan China
65 D7 Pingshang China
67 D4 Pingshi China
67 E4 Pingshi China
65 B6 Pingshun China
67 F4 Pingtan China
67 F4 Pingtan Dao isld China
67 B4 Pingtang China
67 G5 P'ing-tung Taiwan
67 B5 Pingxiang China
67 D3 Pingxiang China
65 F1 Pingyang China
67 G3 Pingyang China
65 B6 Pingyao China
65 D7 Pingyi China
65 C6 Pingyin China
67 C3 Pingyong China
65 C6 Pingyuan China
67 E4 Pingyuan China
67 A5 Pingyuanjie China
130 F8 Pinhal Brazil
16 B3 Pinhão Portugal
129 J4 Pinheiro Brazil
16 C4 Pinhel Portugal
69 D12 Pini isld Indonesia
46 E5 Piniós R Greece
46 E7 Piniós R Greece
143 B10 Pinjarra W Australia
143 E9 Pinjin W Australia
38 O7 Pinka R Austria
38 O7 Pinkafeld Austria
141 K1 Pinkenba dist Brisbane, Qnsld
118 H7 Pinkham Sask
112 K2 Pink Hill N Carolina
117 M7 Pink Mountain Br Col
20 G5 Pin la Garenne, le France
68 C2 Pinlaung Burma
145 D4 Pinnacle mt New Zealand
116 C6 Pinnacle I Bering Sea
102 C5 Pinnacles Nat. Mon California
138 F6 Pinnaroo S Australia
32 L5 Pinn Au R W Germany
32 L5 Pinneberg W Germany
106 G1 Pinneo Colorado
9 F4 Pinner England
33 T5 Pinnow E Germany
70 B5 Pinoh R Kalimantan
111 F10 Pinola Mississippi
106 F3 Pinon Colorado
106 E9 Pinon New Mexico
112 H4 Pinopolis Dam S Carolina
126 C4 Pinos, I. de Cuba
102 E7 Pinos, Mt California
17 G6 Pinoso Spain
125 K9 Pinotepa Nacional Mexico
70 F6 Pinrang Sulawesi
137 O6 Pins, Île Des New Caledonia
53 C8 Pinsk U.S.S.R.
111 K8 Pinson Alabama
110 H6 Pinson Tennessee
120 J10 Pins, Pte. aux Ontario
103 P6 Pinta Arizona
128 A7 Pinta isld Galapagos Is
133 D2 Pintados Chile
103 L9 Pinta, Sa Arizona
70 E2 Pintasan Sabah
133 E3 Pinto Argentina
118 K9 Pinto Butte peak Sask
103 J8 Pinto Mts California
138 B4 Pintumba S Australia
103 L4 Pintura Utah
103 J5 Pintwater Ra Nevada
123 Q2 Pinware R Labrador
12 D3 Pinwherry Scotland
143 B8 Pinyalling mt W Australia
52 G4 Pinyug U.S.S.R.
41 N5 Pinzolo Italy
45 M4 Pióbbico Italy
103 K4 Pioche Nevada
19 N16 Piolenc France
42 D6 Piombino Italy
94 C5 Pioneer Ohio
109 H3 Pioneer Texas
101 M4 Pioneer Mts Montana
56 C3 Pioner U.S.S.R.
51 J1 Pioner, Ostrova islds U.S.S.R.
55 D1 Pionerskiy U.S.S.R.
145 E3 Piopio New Zealand
128 F4 Piorini L Brazil
31 L3 Piotrków Bydgoszcz Poland
31 M4 Piotrków Trybunalski Łódź Poland
45 M1 Piove di Sacco Italy
65 G3 Pipa Dingzi mt China
74 E5 Pipar India
102 G4 Piper Pk Nevada
103 M5 Pipe Sp. Nat. Mon Arizona
119 R9 Pipestone Manitoba
98 K6 Pipestone Minnesota
119 Q9 Pipestone Cr Manitoba
98 K5 Pipestone Nat. Mon Minnesota
145 E3 Pipipi mt New Zealand
145 E3 Pipiriki New Zealand
121 U3 Pipmuacan, Rés Quebec
122 B4 Pipmuacan, Res Quebec
60 Q2 Pippu Japan
21 B6 Pipriac France
107 P4 Piqua Kansas
110 M1 Piqua Ohio
17 F2 Piqueras, Pto. de Spain
130 C5 Piquiri, R Mato Grosso Brazil
130 D9 Piquiri, R Paraná Brazil
85 E7 Pira Benin
130 E5 Piracanjuba Brazil
129 J7 Piracanjuba R Brazil
129 J8 Piracicaba Brazil
130 G6 Piracicaba R Brazil
133 F3 Piracuacito Argentina
130 F7 Piraçununga Brazil
129 K4 Piraeuruca Brazil
47 F7 Piraiévs Greece
56 E4 Piramida, G mt U.S.S.R.
42 F3 Piran Yugoslavia
129 L5 Piranhas Alagoas Brazil
129 H7 Piranhas Goiás Brazil
130 D5 Piranhas Goiás Brazil
130 D8 Pirapó, R Brazil
129 K7 Pirapora Brazil
122 A3 Piraube, L Quebec
130 C10 Piray R Argentina
128 F7 Piray R Bolivia
9 F5 Pirbright England
47 G2 Pirdop Bulgaria
20 C5 Piré France
129 J7 Pires do Rio Brazil
47 G9 Pírgos Crete Greece
46 E7 Pírgos Greece
130 B9 Piribebuy Paraguay
17 G2 Pirineos mt Spain
145 E4 Pirinoa New Zealand
145 F3 Piripaua New Zealand
129 K4 Piripiri Brazil
127 M9 Píritu Anzoátegui Venezuela
127 K10 Piritu Miranda Venezuela
37 N3 Pirk E Germany
29 K10 Pirkkala Finland
36 D5 Pirmasens W Germany
30 H5 Pirna E Germany
12 C2 Pirnmill Scotland
145 E2 Pirongia New Zealand
46 F1 Pirot Yugoslavia
20 B3 Pirou France
74 F2 Pir Panjal Rge Kashmir
102 F7 Piru California
136 F2 Piru Moluccas Indonesia
54 D6 Piryatin U.S.S.R.
47 H6 Piryí Greece
77 J4 Pirzada Afghanistan
45 H4 Pisa Italy
133 C1 Pisagua Chile
71 B3 Pisang isld Indonesia
44 H3 Pisanino mt Italy
21 D10 Pisany France
144 B6 Pisa Range New Zealand
70 F1 Pisau, Tg C Sabah
43 G8 Pisciotta Italy
128 C6 Pisco Peru
Piscopi isld see Tílos
95 N3 Piseco New York
30 H6 Písek Czechoslovakia
98 J1 Pisek N Dakota
80 F6 Pisga Jordan
99 L8 Pisgah Iowa
112 E2 Pisgah, Mt N Carolina
144 C6 Pisgah, Mt New Zealand
77 G6 Pishīn Iran
74 B3 Pishin Pakistan
29 P6 Pishta R U.S.S.R.
70 G7 Pising Sulawesi
103 M9 Pisinimo Arizona
102 D6 Pismo Bch California
128 F6 Piso Firme Bolivia
41 M6 Pisogne Italy
85 D6 Pissila Upper Volta
29 P6 Pistayarvi L U.S.S.R.
43 H8 Pisticci Italy
45 J4 Pistoia Italy
123 R2 Pistolet B Nfld
100 A7 Pistol River Oregon
52 F6 Pistsovo U.S.S.R.
8 C2 Pistyll Rhaeadr mt Wales
16 E3 Pisuerga R Spain
31 N2 Pisz Poland
100 D8 Pit R California
85 B6 Pita Guinea
122 G1 Pitaga Labrador
70 D6 Pitap, R Kalimantan
139 G5 Pitarpunga L New S Wales
71 G7 Pitas Pt Mindanao Philippines
135 U11 Pitcairn I Pacific Oc
101 Q5 Pitchfork Wyoming
127 O3 Pitch L Trinidad
26 M6 Piteå Sweden
26 L6 Piteälv R Sweden
45 J3 Piteglio Italy
48 J6 Piteşti Romania
143 B9 Pithara W Australia
20 K5 Pithiviers France
42 D6 Pitigliano Italy
124 C2 Pitiquito Mexico
106 D3 Pitkin Colorado
111 D11 Pitkin Louisiana
52 D1 Pitkul' U.S.S.R.
52 D4 Pitkyaranta U.S.S.R.
15 E4 Pitlochry Scotland
95 M7 Pitman New Jersey
87 G12 Piton des Neiges mt Réunion
111 G11 Pitre, I. au Louisiana
13 F1 Pitscottie Scotland
9 G4 Pitsea England
13 F1 Pittenweem Scotland
117 J9 Pitt I Br Col
137 R10 Pitt I Chatham Is Pacific Oc
112 H2 Pittsboro N Carolina
102 C3 Pittsburg California
110 B4 Pittsburg Kansas
110 M4 Pittsburg Kentucky
121 T7 Pittsburg New Hampshire
107 P7 Pittsburg Oklahoma
109 N3 Pittsburg Texas
94 H6 Pittsburgh Pennsylvania
110 E2 Pittsfield Illinois
95 S2 Pittsfield Maine
95 O4 Pittsfield Massachusetts
95 Q3 Pittsfield New Hampshire
94 C5 Pittsford Michigan
94 K3 Pittsford New York
95 O3 Pittsford Vermont
95 M5 Pittston Pennsylvania
111 L9 Pittsview Alabama
95 M8 Pittsville Maryland
110 C3 Pittsville Missouri
99 Q5 Pittsville Wisconsin
141 K8 Pittsworth Queensland
100 D8 Pittville California
71 B1 Pitu Halmahera Indonesia
88 E6 Pitu R Tanzania
140 E6 Pituri R Queensland
41 N3 Pitz Tal Austria
45 J1 Piú bega Italy
19 Q17 Piumoisson France
128 B5 Piura Peru
128 B4 Piura dep Peru
103 J7 Piute Mts California
102 F6 Piute Pk California
103 M3 Piute Res Utah
75 K4 Piuthan Nepal
42 J5 Piva R Yugoslavia
120 G2 Pivabiska R Ontario
126 G9 Pivijay Colombia
31 M6 Piwniczna Poland
102 E6 Pixley California
46 E5 Piyaí Greece
60 Q1 Piyashiri yama mt Japan
128 E7 Pizacoma Peru
52 G5 Pizhanka U.S.S.R.
52 G5 Pizhma U.S.S.R.
41 K4 Pizol mt Switzerland
43 G10 Pizzo Italy
45 O6 Pizzodeta, M mt Italy
33 Q5 Plaaz E Germany
109 L7 Placedo Texas
123 T6 Placentia Nfld
71 G6 Placer Mindanao Philippines
102 F1 Placeritos Nevada
102 D3 Placerville California
106 B3 Placerville Colorado
126 E3 Placetas Cuba
113 E11 Placida Florida
113 F10 Placid, L Florida
106 D6 Placitas New Mexico
46 E3 Plačkovica mt Yugoslavia
12 C3 Pladda I Scotland
15 C5 Pladda Lt. Ho Scotland
40 F4 Plaffeien Switzerland
99 Q6 Plain Wisconsin
94 D6 Plain City Ohio
101 N8 Plain City Utah
111 C9 Plain Dealing Louisiana
20 J3 Plaine et Collines reg France
94 A7 Plainfield Indiana
99 O7 Plainfield Iowa
95 N6 Plainfield New Jersey
99 R5 Plainfield Wisconsin
112 C5 Plains Georgia
101 L2 Plains Montana
108 E2 Plains Texas
94 K8 Plains, The Virginia
110 C6 Plainview Arkansas
99 O5 Plainview Minnesota
98 J7 Plainview Nebraska
108 F1 Plainview Texas

95 P5 Plainville Connecticut
110 E2 Plainville Illinois
107 L2 Plainville Kansas
94 B4 Plainwell Michigan
18 F9 Plaisance France
127 H5 Plaisance Haiti
69 G14 Plaju Sumatra
47 G4 Pláka, Akr C Greece
47 H9 Pláka, Akra C Crete Greece
46 D3 Plakenska Pl mt Yugoslavia
118 E4 Plamondon Alberta
71 H9 Plampang Indonesia
37 O4 Planá Czechoslovakia
102 D4 Planada California
129 L5 Planalto da Borborema plat Brazil
129 H7 Planalto de Mato Grosso plat Brazil
17 G6 Plana Ó Nueva Tabarca isld Spain
40 E2 Plancher les Mines France
40 D4 Planches-en-Montagne, Les France
131 B5 Planchon, Paso de Chile/Arg
18 D4 Plancoët France
19 O15 Plan-de-Baix France
19 N17 Plan d'Orgon France
17 G9 Plane isld Algeria
33 R8 Plane, R E Germany
126 G10 Planeta Rica Colombia
137 L3 Planet Deep Solomon Sea
37 P5 Plánice Czechoslovakia
37 L4 Plankenfels W Germany
98 H6 Plankinton S Dakota
109 L2 Plano Texas
127 M3 Plantain Garden R Jamaica
113 E9 Plant City Florida
111 K9 Plantersville Alabama
111 E11 Plaquemine Louisiana
16 C4 Plasencia Spain
27 F10 Plassen Norway
55 D4 Plast U.S.S.R.
33 R5 Plasten E Germany
103 J9 Plaster City California
37 P4 Plasy Czechoslovakia
43 E11 Platani R Sicily
133 C2 Plata, Puerta Chile
131 G5 Plata, Rio de la Arg/Uruguay
19 O14 Plateau de Chambarand France
19 J15 Plateau de Langres France
21 K10 Plateau de Peyrelevade France
19 P16 Plateau de St. Etienne France
86 B1 Plateau du Tchigaï Niger
85 C3 Plateau du Tinrhert stony des Algeria
Plateau of Tibet see Xizang Gaoyuan
21 H9 Plateaux de la Marche France
123 T5 Plate Cove Nfld
124 H6 Plateros Mexico
46 F4 Platí Greece
47 G4 Platí Ákra C Greece
46 F5 Platíkambos Greece
102 B1 Platina California
116 G7 Platinum Alaska
126 G10 Plato Colombia
110 D4 Plato Missouri
118 J7 Plato Sask
56 D5 Plato Alash U.S.S.R.
79 C4 Platres Cyprus
98 H6 Platte S Dakota
37 N4 Platte mt W Germany
99 M9 Platte R Missouri
98 G9 Platte R Nebraska
98 J8 Platte Center Nebraska
110 B2 Platte City Missouri
106 E2 Platte Mt Colorado
98 B9 Platteville Colorado
99 Q7 Platteville Wisconsin
36 E6 Plättig W Germany
37 O6 Plattling W Germany
107 O7 Platt Nat. Park Oklahoma
110 B2 Plattsburg Missouri
95 O2 Plattsburg New York
99 K8 Plattsmouth Nebraska
33 Q6 Plau E Germany
33 Q8 Plaue E Germany
37 K2 Plaue Erfurt E Germany
37 N3 Plauen E Germany
46 D2 Plav Yugoslavia
52 C6 Pļaviņas U.S.S.R.
42 J6 Plavnica Yugoslavia
54 J3 Plavsk U.S.S.R.
128 B4 Playas Ecuador
106 B10 Playas L New Mexico
140 D4 Playford R N Terr Aust
140 D6 Playford Mt N Terr Aust
119 U4 Playgreen L Manitoba
124 E5 Playón Mexico
98 E1 Plaza N Dakota
133 D5 Plaza Huincul Argentina
12 E1 Plean Scotland
110 M1 Pleasant Ohio
95 S5 Pleasant B Massachusetts
123 M7 Pleasant Bay C Breton I, N S
94 F7 Pleasant City Ohio
119 N6 Pleasantdale Sask
94 K6 Pleasant Gap Pennsylvania
101 O9 Pleasant Grove Utah
110 F2 Pleasant Hill Illinois
111 C10 Pleasant Hill Louisiana
110 B3 Pleasant Hill Missouri
94 E6 Pleasant Hill Res Ohio
103 M8 Pleasant, L Arizona
122 F8 Pleasant, Mt New Brunswick
112 H5 Pleasant, Mt S Carolina
102 C4 Pleasanton California
110 B3 Pleasanton Kansas
98 G9 Pleasanton Nebraska
109 J7 Pleasanton Texas
110 E6 Pleasant Plains Arkansas
119 S9 Pleasant Pt Manitoba
144 C6 Pleasant Pt New Zealand
100 H5 Pleasant Valley Oregon
100 G3 Pleasant View Washington
99 N8 Pleasantville Iowa
95 N7 Pleasantville New Jersey
94 H5 Pleasantville Pennsylvania
9 E1 Pleasley England
110 L3 Pleasureville Kentucky
18 G7 Pleaux France
37 L4 Plech W Germany
120 G2 Pledger L Ontario
133 F4 Piedra Sola Uruguay
70 D3 Pleieran R Sarawak
70 D6 Pleihari Kalimantan
68 J5 Plei Herel Vietnam
68 J6 Plei Kly Vietnam
68 J6 Pleiku Vietnam
20 B4 Pleine Fougères France
37 L5 Pleinfeld W Germany
9 G6 Pleinmont Pt Channel Is
37 P6 Pleinting W Germany
37 N1 Pleisse R E Germany
68 H5 Plei Ta Uan Vietnam
20 A5 Plélan-le-Grand France
17 F1 Plencia Spain
18 D4 Pléneuf France
48 H6 Plenţiţa Romania
118 J7 Plenty Sask
145 F2 Plenty, Bay of New Zealand
140 D6 Plenty R N Terr Aust
98 B1 Plentywood Montana
20 B4 Plerguer France
52 F3 Plesetsk U.S.S.R.
55 E3 Pleshkova U.S.S.R.
48 F2 Plešivec Czechoslovakia
20 A4 Pleslin France
21 B6 Plessé France
121 T6 Plessisville Quebec
122 B2 Pletipi L Quebec
36 D1 Plettenberg W Germany
89 C10 Plettenberg B S Africa
20 B4 Pleudihen France
20 B5 Pleugueneuc France
20 A4 Pleurtuit France
47 G1 Pleven Bulgaria
98 B3 Plevna Montana
18 C4 Pleyben France
37 N4 Pleystein W Germany
145 E4 Plimmerton New Zealand
48 M1 Pliskov U.S.S.R.
42 G4 Pljesivica dist Yugoslavia
48 E7 Pljevlja Yugoslavia
43 B8 Ploaghe Sardinia
36 D7 Plobsheim France
42 H5 Ploča lt ho Yugoslavia
42 H5 Ploče Yugoslavia
36 G6 Plochingen W Germany
31 M3 Płock Poland
30 H7 Plöckenstein mt Czechoslovakia
22 D2 Ploegsteert Belgium
18 D5 Ploërmel France
48 K6 Ploieşti Romania
47 H6 Plomárion Greece
18 G7 Plomb du Cantal mt France
40 A3 Plombières France
19 K5 Plombières-les-Bains France
22 G4 Plomion France
33 M4 Plön W Germany
31 J2 Płona R Poland
31 M3 Płońsk Poland
48 H6 Plopi Romania
52 D6 Ploskosh' U.S.S.R.
37 N4 Plössberg W Germany
31 J2 Płoty Poland
18 C4 Plouaret France
18 C5 Plouay France
20 A4 Ploubalay France
31 H5 Ploučnice R Czechoslovakia
18 B4 Ploudalmezeau France
20 B4 Plouer France
18 D4 Plouguenast France
18 D4 Plouha France
47 G2 Plovdiv Bulgaria
99 M7 Plover Iowa
99 R5 Plover Wisconsin
99 R5 Plover R Wisconsin
116 K1 Plover Is Alaska
36 H6 Plüderhausen W Germany
119 S8 Plumas Manitoba
99 O5 Plum City Wisconsin
118 D1 Plum Coulee Manitoba
139 L4 Plumer, Pt New S Wales
95 P5 Plum I New York
100 J2 Plummer Idaho
116 H6 Plummer, Mt Alaska
110 D6 Plummerville Arkansas
13 F4 Plumpton Hd England
143 F8 Plumridge Lakes W Australia
87 E10 Plumtree Zimbabwe
52 B6 Plunge U.S.S.R.
119 M7 Plunkett Sask
100 F7 Plush Oregon
18 D5 Pluvigner France
36 B4 Pluwig W Germany
102 D3 Plymouth California
8 B7 Plymouth England
94 A5 Plymouth Indiana
99 N6 Plymouth Iowa
95 R5 Plymouth Massachusetts
127 O6 Plymouth Montserrat W Indies
98 K9 Plymouth Nebraska
95 Q3 Plymouth New Hampshire
94 E6 Plymouth Ohio
95 M5 Plymouth Pennsylvania
127 M2 Plymouth Tobago
101 N8 Plymouth Utah
95 P3 Plymouth Vermont
99 T6 Plymouth Wisconsin
8 B7 Plympton England
122 G9 Plympton Nova Scotia
8 C3 Plynlimon Fawr mt Wales
52 C5 Plyusa U.S.S.R.
52 C5 Plyussa R U.S.S.R.
37 P4 Plzeň Czechoslovakia
31 J3 Pniewy Poland
85 D6 Po Upper Volta
44 C1 Po R Italy
45 J2 Po R Italy
139 H8 Poatina Tasmania
85 E7 Pobé Benin
66 C3 Pobedy, Pik mt U.S.S.R./China
37 O5 Poběžovice Czechoslovakia
31 K3 Pobiedziska Poland
17 J2 Pobla de Lilleta, L Spain
17 H2 Pobla de Segur Spain
110 F5 Pocahontas Arkansas
99 M7 Pocahontas Iowa
94 F9 Pocahontas Virginia
107 N6 Pocasse Oklahoma
94 F8 Pocatalico R W Virginia
101 N7 Pocatello Idaho
31 J6 Počátky Czechoslovakia
131 D3 Pocha, Sa. de mts Argentina
54 E4 Pochep U.S.S.R.
54 D2 Pochinok U.S.S.R.
38 M5 Pochlarn Austria
125 L10 Pochutla Mexico
37 P5 Pocinovice Czechoslovakia
37 P2 Pockau E Germany
37 P7 Pocking W Germany
13 H6 Pocklington England
70 F2 Pock, Mt Sabah
128 D7 Pocoma Peru
95 M8 Pocomoke City Maryland
95 M9 Pocomoke Sd Virginia
129 G7 Poconé Brazil
95 M6 Pocono Mts Pennsylvania
95 M5 Pocono Pines Pennsylvania
129 J8 Pocos de Caldas Brazil
125 O6 Pocrí Panama
125 P9 Poctún Guatemala
103 L5 Pocum Wash creek Arizona
138 F4 Podamacca New S Wales
37 P3 Podbořany Czechoslovakia
52 J3 Podcher'ye U.S.S.R.
31 L4 Poddębice Poland
118 C4 Poddle R Alberta
52 D5 Poddor'ye U.S.S.R.
31 J5 Poděbrady Czechoslovakia
45 M2 Po delle Tolle R Italy
18 E8 Podensac France
48 J1 Podgaits U.S.S.R.
Podgorica see Titograd
54 G8 Podgorodnoye U.S.S.R.
45 M2 Po di Goro R Italy
76 D3 Podile India
45 L2 Po di Volano R Italy
51 Q2 Podkagernoye U.S.S.R.
56 D1 Podkamennay R U.S.S.R.
38 J9 Podkoren Yugoslavia
47 G3 Podkova Bulgaria
55 C5 Podnikovskiy U.S.S.R.
48 F1 Podolinec Czechoslovakia
54 J1 Podolsk U.S.S.R.
85 B5 Podor Senegal
52 G4 Podosinovets U.S.S.R.
42 H4 Podovi Yugoslavia
52 D4 Podporozh'ye U.S.S.R.
55 E2 Podrezovo U.S.S.R.
56 D2 Podtesovo U.S.S.R.
48 L3 Podu Iloaiei Romania
46 E2 Podujevo Yugoslavia
48 L4 Podu Turcului Romania
52 F4 Podyuga U.S.S.R.
33 O4 Poel isld E Germany
22 D2 Poelkapelle Belgium
94 C1 Poe Reef Lt. Ho Michigan
144 C5 Poerua New Zealand
87 C11 Pofadder S Africa
45 O6 Pofi Italy
120 J6 Pogamasing Ontario
54 E4 Pogar U.S.S.R.
33 S4 Poggendorf E Germany
42 D5 Poggibonsi Italy
45 K4 Poggio a Caiano Italy
45 N5 Poggio Moiano Italy
45 K2 Póggio Renatico Italy
45 K2 Póggio Rusco Italy
59 M1 Pogibi U.S.S.R.
48 L6 Pogoanele Romania
46 D4 Pogradec Albania
45 M2 Po Grande R Italy
59 K3 Pogranichnyy U.S.S.R.
48 M1 Pogrebishchenskiy U.S.S.R.
116 E9 Pogromni Vol Aleutian Is
32 F6 Pogum W Germany
71 H5 Poh Sulawesi
135 U5 Pohakuloa Hawaiian Is
59 J4 Pohang S Korea
145 E4 Pohangina New Zealand
145 D4 Pohara New Zealand
29 K11 Pohja Finland
29 O8 Pohjois-Karjala prov Finland
36 F3 Pohl-Göns W Germany
36 F2 Pohlheim W Germany
145 E3 Pohokura New Zealand
145 F3 Pohokura mt New Zealand
48 F2 Pohorelá Czechoslovakia
31 K7 Pohořelice Czechoslovakia
38 M9 Pohorje mt Yugoslavia
102 V14 Pohue B Hawaiian Is
45 K1 Poiana Magg Italy
46 F1 Poiana Mare Romania
48 K3 Poiana Teiului Romania
71 J4 Poigar Sulawesi
29 M4 Poikela Finland
123 O2 Poincaré, L Quebec
146 F2 Poinsett, C Antarctica
113 G9 Poinsett, L Florida
102 D7 Point Arguello California
109 M5 Pointblank Texas
138 E5 Point Broughton S Australia
102 D6 Point Buchon California
139 G7 Point Campbell Victoria
109 L7 Point Comfort Texas
102 D7 Point Conception California
123 N3 Pointe-à Maurier Quebec
127 O3 Pointe-á-Pierre Trinidad
127 N4 Pointe-á-Pitre Guadeloupe W I
120 K7 Pointe au Baril Station Ontario
122 E4 Pointe aux Anglais Quebec
121 R7 Pointe aux Trembles Quebec
121 S4 Pointe Bleue Quebec
122 H7 Pointe du Chêne New Brunswick
120 H9 Point Edward Ontario
122 D4 Pointe le Bel Quebec
127 M4 Pointe Noire Guadeloupe W I
22 C1 Pointe Synthe France
122 G6 Pointe Verte New Brunswick
138 F7 Point Fairy S Australia
127 N3 Point Fortin Trinidad
112 M1 Point Harbor N Carolina
139 H8 Point Hills Tasmania
116 D2 Point Hope Alaska
117 R3 Point L N W Terr
116 F2 Point Lay Alaska
95 L8 Point Lookout Maryland
139 L4 Point Lookout mt New S Wales
94 H7 Point Marion Pennsylvania
94 K7 Point of Rocks Maryland
101 R8 Point of Rocks Wyoming
120 H10 Point Pelee Nat Park Ontario
102 C6 Point Piedras Blancas California
95 N6 Point Pleasant New Jersey
94 E8 Point Pleasant W Virginia
142 B5 Point Samson W Australia
140 B1 Point Stuart N Terr Aust
102 C5 Point Sur California
138 D5 Point Turton S Australia
145 E2 Point Waikato New Zealand
68 F6 Poipet Cambodia
52 H6 Poisevo U.S.S.R.
101 S6 Poison Cr Wyoming
142 B1 Poison Gully R Perth, W Aust
121 P6 Poisson Blanc, L Quebec
142 C5 Poissonnier Pt W Australia
20 K4 Poissy France
21 F8 Poitiers France
21 D8 Poitou reg France
142 B5 Poivre, C W Australia
20 J2 Foix France
22 J3 Foix St. Hubert Belgium
22 H4 Poix-Terron France
46 D4 Pojan Albania
106 D6 Pojoaque New Mexico
102 R12 Pokai Bay Hawaiian Is
145 E3 Pokaka New Zealand
74 D5 Pokaran India
139 J3 Pokataroo New S Wales
52 J3 Pekcha U.S.S.R.
145 E2 Pekeno New Zealand
75 L4 Pokhara Nepal
29 M3 Pokka Finland
86 E5 Poko Zaïre
31 K5 Pokój Poland
116 F2 Poko Mt Alaska
54 L1 Pokrov U.S.S.R.
55 E5 Pokrovka Atbasar U.S.S.R.
55 G3 Pokrovka Novosibirsk U.S.S.R.
55 B5 Pokrovka Orenburg U.S.S.R.
55 E3 Pokrovskoye U.S.S.R.
52 F3 Pokshen'ga R U.S.S.R.
71 E4 Pola Philippines
71 E4 Pola B Philippines
103 O6 Polacca Arizona
103 O6 Polacca Wasa R Arizona
16 D1 Pola de Laviana Spain
16 D1 Pola de Lena Spain
16 D1 Pola de Siero Spain
95 M3 Poland New York
31 K4 Poland rep Europe
31 K1 Polanow Poland
99 S4 Polar Wisconsin
101 M4 Polaris Montana
78 D2 Polatli Turkey
8 B7 Polbathick England
36 C3 Polch W Germany
133 C5 Polcura Chile
31 J2 Połczyn Zdrój Poland
138 D5 Polda S Australia
52 E3 Pole U.S.S.R.
70 G7 Poleang Sulawesi
37 P5 Polecník mt Czechoslovakia
80 C5 Poleg R Israel
9 G6 Polegate England
68 H5 Polei Monu Vietnam
37 P5 Poleň Czechoslovakia
146 D7 Pole of Inaccessibility Antarctica
45 L2 Polesella Italy
31 N1 Polessk U.S.S.R.
53 C8 Polesye marsh U.S.S.R.
55 D3 Polevskoy U.S.S.R.
70 F6 Polewali Sulawesi
48 G3 Polgár Hungary
48 E3 Polgárdi Hungary
55 E3 Polgovskoye U.S.S.R.
86 B4 Poli Cameroon
47 G8 Políaigos isld Greece
43 G8 Policastro, G. di Italy
31 H2 Police Poland
31 J6 Polička Czechoslovakia
85 F3 Polignac Algeria
19 J6 Poligny France
46 F3 Políkastron Greece
47 H5 Polikhnitos Greece
71 E3 Polillo isld Luzon Philippines
45 J3 Polinago Italy
38 H8 Polinik mt Austria
127 L3 Polink Pt Jamaica
79 C3 Polis Cyprus
52 D5 Polist' R U.S.S.R.
52 G3 Politovo U.S.S.R.
98 J8 Polk Nebraska
94 H5 Polk Pennsylvania
56 D1 Polkan, Gora mt U.S.S.R.
113 F9 Polk City Florida
33 P7 Polkritz E Germany
76 C5 Pollachi India
37 L5 Pollanten W Germany
110 F5 Pollard Arkansas
38 N7 Pöllau Austria
32 K9 Polle W Germany
122 A1 Pollet, L Quebec
43 G9 Pollino, M mt Italy
33 P7 Pollitz E Germany
100 J4 Pollock Idaho
111 D10 Pollock Louisiana
98 F4 Pollock S Dakota
143 E10 Pollock Reef W Australia
112 K3 Pollocksville N Carolina
118 F7 Pollockville Alberta
144 B6 Pollux mt New Zealand
29 N2 Polmak Finland
26 Q1 Polmak Norway
12 E2 Polmont Scotland
31 J6 Polná Czechoslovakia
52 C5 Polna U.S.S.R.
99 R8 Polo Illinois
110 B2 Polo Missouri
54 H9 Pologi U.S.S.R.
71 G7 Polomoloc Mindanao Philippines
47 J3 Polos Turkey
54 G2 Polotnanyy U.S.S.R.
52 C6 Polotsk U.S.S.R.
55 E4 Polovinnoye U.S.S.R.
52 H3 Polovniki U.S.S.R.
8 B7 Polperro England
83 K10 Polpitigama Sri Lanka
38 L7 Pöls R Austria
101 L2 Polson Montana
38 K7 Pöls-Tal V Austria
52 F2 Polta R U.S.S.R.
48 F2 Poltár Czechoslovakia
54 F7 Poltava U.S.S.R.
55 F4 Poltavka U.S.S.R.
121 P7 Poltimore Quebec
52 C5 Põltsamaa U.S.S.R.
55 E4 Poludino U.S.S.R.
55 D1 Polunochnoye U.S.S.R.
50 E4 Poluostrov Buzachi pen U.S.S.R.
106 D7 Polvadera New Mexico
29 O9 Polvijärvi Finland
118 L5 Polwarth Sask
31 L1 Półwysep Hel pen Poland
55 E1 Pol'yanovo U.S.S.R.
52 D1 Polyarnyy U.S.S.R.
116 N5 Polychrome Pass Alaska
47 F4 Políyros Greece
56 C4 Polysayevo U.S.S.R.
37 N2 Pölzig E Germany
133 D2 Poma Argentina
144 B6 Pomahaka R New Zealand
133 D3 Poman Argentina
71 L9 Pomana Besar isld Flores Indonesia
16 B7 Pomarão Portugal
112 F3 Pomaria S Carolina
29 J10 Pomarkku Finland
130 G7 Pomba R Brazil
129 L5 Pombal Brazil
16 B5 Pombal Portugal
130 D7 Pombo, R Brazil
19 O18 Pomègues, Île France
31 G2 Pomerania reg E Germany/Poland
99 M7 Pomercy Iowa
103 O9 Pomerene Arizona
14 E2 Pomeroy N Ireland
94 E7 Pomeroy Ohio
100 H3 Pomeroy Washington
45 M6 Pomezia Italy
95 P5 Pomfret Connecticut
45 Q8 Pomigliano d'Arco Italy
110 C4 Pomme de Terre R Missouri
37 M5 Pommelsbrunn W Germany
107 P3 Pomoma Kansas
125 P9 Pomona Belize
102 G7 Pomona California
110 E5 Pomona Missouri
87 C11 Pomona Namibia
141 L7 Pomona Queensland
47 J2 Pomorie Bulgaria
52 E3 Pomorskiy Bereg coast U.S.S.R.
48 J1 Pomoryany U.S.S.R.
54 C8 Pomoshnaya U.S.S.R.
21 E8 Pompaire France
113 G11 Pompano Beach Florida
45 Q8 Pompei Italy
95 L4 Pompey New York
101 S4 Pompeys Pillar Montana
95 N5 Pompton Lakes New Jersey
88 D10 Pompué R Mozambique
123 L8 Pomquet Nova Scotia
33 R10 Pomssen E Germany
119 N6 Ponass L Sask
98 K7 Ponca Nebraska
107 N5 Ponca City Oklahoma
127 L5 Ponce Puerto Rico
111 L11 Ponce de Leon Florida
113 F12 Ponce de Leon B Florida
113 F8 Ponce de Leon Inlet Florida
111 F11 Ponchatoula Louisiana
124 H7 Poncitlán Mexico
107 N5 Pond Creek Oklahoma
109 K2 Ponder Texas
76 D5 Pondicherry India
115 M3 Pond Inlet N W Terr
89 F8 Pondoland reg S Africa
100 D8 Pondosa California
100 H4 Pondosa Oregon
99 M1 Ponemah Minnesota
44 E3 Ponente Italy
94 B6 Poneto Indiana
16 C2 Ponferrada Spain
86 A5 Pongara, Pte Gabon
145 F4 Pongaroa New Zealand
38 H7 Pongau reg Austria
70 G7 Pongkolaero Sulawesi
52 D2 Pon'goma U.S.S.R.
122 H9 Ponhook L Nova Scotia
33 T10 Ponickau E Germany
31 K4 Poniec Poland
71 H4 Poniki, Mt Sulawesi
70 G5 Ponindilisa, Tg C Sulawesi
68 A2 Ponnagyun Burma
68 B1 Ponnyadaung ra Burma
118 D6 Ponoka Alberta
55 B4 Ponomarevka U.S.S.R.
70 N9 Ponorogo Java
52 F2 Ponoy U.S.S.R.
52 E2 Ponoy R U.S.S.R.
18 E7 Pons France
17 H3 Pons Spain
45 J4 Ponsacco Italy
71 G5 Ponson isld Philippines
18 E9 Pontacq France
130 E9 Ponta Grossa Brazil
40 B3 Pontailler France
19 J5 Pontailler-sur-Saône France
19 O15 Pontaix France
22 E3 Pont-à-Marcq France
19 J4 Pont à Mousson France
129 G8 Ponta Porá Brazil
8 C4 Pontardawe Wales
8 B4 Pontarddulais Wales
19 K6 Pontarlier France
45 K4 Pontassieve Italy
20 C4 Pontaubault France
20 G3 Pont Audemer France
18 G7 Pontaumur France
22 F5 Pontavert France
121 M1 Pontax R Quebec
122 K3 Pontbriand B Quebec
40 G7 Pont-Canav Italy
19 Q14 Pontcharra France
21 J10 Pontcharraud France
111 F11 Pontchartrain, L Louisiana
21 A7 Pontchâteau France
19 O12 Pont d'Ain France
19 O15 Pont-de-Barret France
40 C4 Pont-de-Poitte France
19 J6 Pont de Vaux France
19 J6 Pont de Veyle France
20 E4 Pont d'Ouilly France
129 J6 Ponte Alta do Norte Brazil
42 E2 Pontebba Italy
45 R8 Pontecagnano Italy
45 P7 Pontecorvo Italy
20 E4 Pont-Ecrepin Fromentel France
16 B3 Ponte da Barca Portugal
129 G6 Ponte de Pedra Brazil
45 J4 Pontedera Italy
16 B5 Ponte de Sor Portugal
16 B3 Ponte do Lima Portugal
13 G6 Pontefract England
118 K9 Ponteix Sask
45 L2 Pontelagoscuro Italy
13 G3 Ponteland England
45 R7 Pontelandolfo Italy
45 M1 Pontelongo Italy
130 G7 Ponte Nova Brazil
18 E8 Pontenx les Forges France
16 B2 Pontevedra Spain
16 B2 Pontevedra prov Spain
113 F7 Ponte Vedra Beach Florida
41 M7 Pontevico Italy
20 C4 Pontfarcy France
22 G5 Pont Faverger France
20 H5 Pontgouin France
99 S9 Pontiac Illinois
94 D4 Pontiac Michigan
70 A5 Pontianak Kalimantan
43 E7 Pontinia Italy
18 D4 Pontivy France
18 C5 Pont l'Abbé France
122 H6 Pont Lafrance New Brunswick
40 A1 Pont la Ville France
20 F3 Pont-l'Evêque France
21 H7 Pontlevoy France
60 S2 Pōnto Japan
119 S4 Ponton Manitoba
20 B4 Pontorson France
111 G7 Pontotoc Mississippi
109 J5 Pontotoc Texas
44 G3 Pontremoli Italy
41 L4 Pontresina Switzerland
8 C3 Pontrhydfendigaid Wales
18 C4 Pontrieux France
8 D4 Pontrilas England
119 N5 Pontrilas Sask
121 T6 Pont Rouge Quebec
19 N16 Pont-St. Esprit France
22 D5 Pont-Ste. Maxence France
22 F3 Pont-sur-Sambre France
18 H4 Pont-sur-Yonne France
21 F6 Pontvallain France
121 M8 Pontypool Ontario
8 C4 Pontypool Wales
8 C4 Pontypridd Wales
145 E2 Ponui I New Zealand
101 O4 Pony Montana
43 E8 Ponza lt ho Italy
43 E8 Ponziane, Isole isld Italy
138 C4 Poochera S Australia
13 G6 Pool England
138 D2 Poolawanna L S Australia
144 B6 Poolburn Dam New Zealand
9 E6 Poole England
138 F3 Poole, Mt New S Wales
112 F5 Pooler Georgia
95 K7 Poolesville Maryland
15 C3 Poolewe Scotland
12 E1 Pool of Muckart Scotland
109 K3 Poolville Texas
76 A1 Poona India
139 G5 Pooncarie New S Wales
143 B8 Poondarrie,Mt W Australia
139 G4 Poopelloe, L New S Wales
128 E7 Poopó Bolivia
145 E1 Poor Knights Is New Zealand
116 K4 Poorman Alaska
86 C7 Popakabaka Zaïre
129 G3 Popakai Suriname
54 K8 Popasnaya U.S.S.R.
128 C3 Popayan Colombia
103 J8 Pope California
111 G7 Pope Mississippi
27 M14 Pope U.S.S.R.
99 N7 Popejoy Iowa
58 F1 Poperechnoye U.S.S.R.
22 D2 Poperinge Belgium
95 L8 Popes Creek Maryland
95 S3 Popham Beach Maine
51 K1 Popigay R U.S.S.R.
138 F5 Popiltah New S Wales
98 A1 Poplar Montana
99 P3 Poplar Wisconsin
110 F5 Poplar Bluff Missouri
101 U1 Poplar Cr Montana
119 U6 Poplar Pt Manitoba
111 G11 Poplarville Mississippi
125 K8 Popocatepetl vol Mexico
116 G9 Popof I Alaska
70 N10 Popoh Java
45 P5 Popoli Italy
136 K3 Popondetta Papua New Guinea
47 H1 Popovo Bulgaria
37 M5 Poppberg mt W Germany
25 H4 Poppe Netherlands
22 J1 Poppel Belgium
37 J3 Poppenhausen W Germany
45 L4 Poppi Italy
31 M6 Poprad Czechoslovakia
48 F1 Poprad R Czechoslovakia
128 E8 Poquis mt Chile/Arg
95 L9 Poquoson Virginia
145 F4 Porangahau New Zealand
74 C8 Porbandar India
117 H9 Porcher I Br Col
133 D1 Porco Bolivia
16 E7 Porcuna Spain
116 R3 Porcupine R Alaska/Yukon Terr
141 G5 Porcupine R Queensland
90 H3 Porcupine Bank Atlantic Oc
101 T1 Porcupine Cr Montana
118 C8 Porcupine Hills Alberta
119 Q6 Porcupine Hills Man/Sask
99 R3 Porcupine Mts Michigan
119 O6 Porcupine Plain Sask
42 E3 Pordenoné Italy
47 G1 Pordim Bulgaria
42 F3 Poreč Yugoslavia
130 D8 Porecatu Brazil
55 D2 Porech'ye U.S.S.R.
52 G6 Poretskoye U.S.S.R.
145 E4 Porewa New Zealand
85 E6 Porga Benin
29 J10 Pori Finland
145 F4 Porirua New Zealand
80 F3 Poriyya Israel
26 L5 Porjus Sweden
29 L12 Porkala Finland
28 N3 Porkere Faeroes
52 C5 Porkhov U.S.S.R.
128 F1 Porlamar Venezuela
41 K5 Porlezza Italy
8 C5 Porlock England
37 L6 Pörnbach W Germany
21 A7 Pornic France
71 G5 Poro isld Philippines
52 E3 Porog Arkhangelsk U.S.S.R.
52 J4 Porog Komi U.S.S.R.
59 M2 Poronaysk U.S.S.R.
68 G6 Porong R Cambodia
60 Q1 Poronupuri yama mt Japan
145 E3 Porootarao New Zealand
47 F7 Póros isld Greece
60 Q1 Poroshiri yama mt Japan
52 D3 Porosozero U.S.S.R.
52 H3 Porozhsk U.S.S.R.
56 F3 Porozhskiy U.S.S.R.
146 H3 Porpoise B Antarctica
19 Q18 Porquerolles, I. de France
120 K4 Porquis Junct Ontario
40 F3 Pörrentruy Switzerland
45 J3 Porretta Terme Italy
16 B2 Porriño Spain
26 N1 Porsa Norway
26 O1 Pörsangen inlet Norway
27 D12 Porsgrunn Norway
33 Q9 Porst E Germany
47 L5 Porsük R Turkey
78 C2 Porsuk R Turkey
128 F7 Portachuelo Bolivia
138 E5 Port Adelaide S Australia
14 E2 Portadown N Ireland
144 B7 Port Adventure New Zealand
14 F2 Portaferry N Ireland
116 N6 Portage Alaska
95 S7 Portage Maine
101 O2 Portage Montana
94 J6 Portage Pennsylvania
122 H7 Portage Pr Edward I
101 N8 Portage Utah
94 D5 Portage R Ohio
110 F3 Portage des Sioux Missouri
122 G6 Portage I New Brunswick
119 T9 Portage la Prairie Manitoba
110 G5 Portageville Missouri
94 J4 Portageville New York
103 P10 Portal Arizona
112 F5 Portal Georgia
98 D1 Portal N Dakota
14 D3 Portalaoise Irish Rep
117 L11 Port Alberni Br Col
145 E2 Port Albert New Zealand
120 J9 Port Albert Ontario
139 H7 Port Albert Victoria
16 C5 Portalegre Portugal
106 G7 Portales New Mexico
117 F7 Port Alexander Alaska
121 U4 Port Alfred Quebec
89 E9 Port Alfred S Africa
117 K10 Port Alice Br Col
94 J5 Port Allegany Pennsylvania
111 E11 Port Allen Louisiana
141 K6 Port Alma Queensland
117 M11 Port Angeles Washington
109 K8 Port Aransas Texas
102 A3 Port Arena California
14 D3 Portarlington Irish Rep
Port Arthur see Lüshun
139 J9 Port Arthur Tasmania
109 N6 Port Arthur Texas
12 B2 Port Askaig Scotland
138 D4 Port Augusta S Australia
123 O5 Port-au-Port Nfld
123 N5 Port-au-Port pen Nfld
127 H5 Port-au-Prince Haiti
94 D2 Port Austin Michigan
32 J8 Porta Westfalica W Germany
20 B3 Portbail France
12 C2 Port Bannatyne Scotland
111 E11 Port Barre Louisiana
71 D5 Port Barton Palawan Philippines
87 H11 Port Bergé Madagascar
123 L8 Port Bickerton Nova Scotia
68 A7 Port Blair Andaman Is
109 N6 Port Bolivar Texas
17 K2 Port Bou Spain/France
85 D8 Port Bouet Ivory Coast
140 D2 Port Bradshaw inlet N Terr Aust
140 B1 Port Bremer inlet N Terr Aust
20 D5 Port Brillet France
120 J10 Port Bruce Ontario
120 K10 Port Burwell Ontario
99 Q8 Port Byron Illinois
95 L3 Port Byron New York
75 N7 Port Canning India
121 L7 Port Carling Ontario
13 E4 Port Carlisle England
122 F3 Port Cartier Quebec
144 D7 Port Chalmers New Zealand
145 E2 Port Charles New Zealand
15 B5 Port Charlotte Scotland
95 O6 Port Chester New York
111 G12 Port Chicot I Louisiana
116 D4 Port Clarence hbr Alaska
117 G9 Port Clements Br Col
94 E5 Port Clinton Ohio
141 K5 Port Clinton inlet Queensland
95 S3 Port Clyde Maine
121 L10 Port Colborne Ontario
117 M11 Port Coquitlam Br Col
68 A6 Port Cornwallis Andaman Is
121 L9 Port Credit Ontario
19 Q18 Port Cros, I. de France
141 K6 Port Curtis inlet Queensland
121 L9 Port Dalhousie Ontario
122 H5 Port Daniel Quebec
133 F8 Port Darwin Falkland Is
139 H9 Port Davey Tasmania
19 N18 Port de Bouc France
102 A1 Port Delgada California
127 H5 Port-de-Paix Haiti
21 G7 Port-de-Piles France
69 E11 Port Dickson Malaysia
141 H3 Port Douglas Queensland
120 K10 Port Dover Ontario
123 K9 Port Dufferin Nova Scotia
111 G12 Porte a la Hache Louisiana
99 U4 Porte des Morts Wisconsin
117 H8 Port Edward Br Col
89 G8 Port Edward S Africa
130 G4 Porteirinha Brazil
129 H4 Portel Brazil
16 B6 Portel Portugal
130 H7 Portela Brazil
122 H7 Port Elgin New Brunswick
120 J8 Port Elgin Ontario
127 O8 Port Elizabeth Lesser Antilles
89 D9 Port Elizabeth S Africa
22 B2 Portel, le France
12 B2 Port Ellen Scotland
130 B9 Porteña R Argentina
20 D3 Port-en-Bessin France
98 K5 Porter Minnesota
98 C7 Porter Nebraska
107 P6 Porter Oklahoma
112 D4 Porterdale Georgia
99 T4 Porterfield Wisconsin
12 D5 Port Erin I of Man U.K.
117 H6 Porter Landing Br Col
15 G3 Port Errol Scotland
102 E5 Porterville California
87 C12 Porterville S Africa
127 K3 Port Esquivel Jamaica
140 B1 Port Essington inlet N Terr Aust
8 B4 Port Eynon Wales
123 L8 Port Felix Nova Scotia
145 E2 Port Fitzroy New Zealand
Port Francqui see Ilebo
86 A6 Port Gentil Gabon
122 G9 Port George Nova Scotia
111 E10 Port Gibson Mississippi
12 D2 Port Glasgow Scotland
14 E2 Portglenone N Ireland
15 E3 Portgordon Grampian Scotland
145 E4 Port Gore New Zealand
116 M7 Port Graham Alaska
143 A8 Port Gregory B W Australia
122 H8 Port Greville Nova Scotia
8 C4 Porth Wales
85 F8 Port Harcourt Nigeria
117 K10 Port Hardy Br Col
145 D4 Port Hardy New Zealand
123 L8 Port Hastings C Breton I, N Scotia
123 L8 Port Hawkesbury C Breton I, N Scotia
8 C5 Porthcawl Wales
142 C5 Port Hedland W Australia
127 L3 Port Henderson Jamaica
95 O3 Port Henry New York
Port Herald see Nsanje
100 J1 Porthill Idaho
8 B2 Porth Neigwl Wales
123 L8 Port Hood C Breton I, N Scotia
94 E3 Port Hope Michigan
121 M9 Port Hope Ontario
123 Q1 Port Hope Simpson Labrador
102 E7 Port Hueneme California
94 E4 Port Huron Michigan
120 H10 Port Huron Ontario
45 Q8 Portici Italy
16 B7 Portimão Portugal
29 M5 Portimo Finland
12 C1 Portinnisherrich Scotland
107 M2 Portis Kansas
8 B6 Port Isaac England
109 K9 Port Isabel Texas
99 T2 Port Isabelle Michigan
8 D5 Portishead England
139 K5 Port Jackson New S Wales
145 E2 Port Jackson New Zealand
95 O6 Port Jefferson Long I, N Y
95 N5 Port Jervis New York
127 J3 Port Kaiser Jamaica
140 A2 Port Keats N Terr Aust
139 K5 Port Kembla New S Wales
127 P6 Portland Barbados
106 E3 Portland Colorado
94 C6 Portland Indiana
95 R3 Portland Maine
94 C4 Portland Michigan
98 J2 Portland N Dakota
139 J5 Portland New S Wales
145 E1 Portland New Zealand
121 O8 Portland Ontario
100 C4 Portland Oregon
110 K5 Portland Tennessee
109 K8 Portland Texas
138 F7 Portland Victoria
127 M2 Portland parish Jamaica
127 K3 Portland Bight Jamaica
8 D7 Portland, Bill of head England
139 J8 Portland, C Tasmania
117 H8 Portland Canal Br Col/Alaska
123 P3 Portland Cr. Pond Nfld
141 G6 Portland Downs Queensland
8 D6 Portland Hbr England
145 F3 Portland I New Zealand
117 H8 Portland Inlet Br Col
127 K3 Portland Ridge Jamaica
141 G2 Portland Roads Queensland
126 F6 Portland Rock Caribbean
71 E8 Port Languyan Philippines
139 H8 Port Latta Tasmania
109 L7 Port Lavaca Texas
14 D4 Portlaw Irish Rep
144 B4 Port Levy New Zealand
95 M3 Port Leyden New York
138 D5 Port Lincoln S Australia
12 D4 Port Logan Scotland
120 K7 Port Loring Ontario
18 C5 Port Louis France
127 N4 Port Louis Guadeloupe W I
83 L14 Port Louis Kerguelen
83 L12 Port Louis Mauritius
140 D3 Port McArthur B N Terr Aust
138 F7 Port MacDonnell S Australia
121 L8 Port McNicoll Ontario
139 L4 Port Macquarie New S Wales
8 B2 Portmadog Wales
122 F10 Port Maitland Nova Scotia
121 L10 Port Maitland Ontario
109 K9 Port Mansfield Texas
115 N6 Port Manvers Labrador
127 L2 Port Maria Jamaica
146 J3 Port Martin Antarctica
94 J6 Port Matilda Pennsylvania
113 G11 Port Mayaca Florida
122 H9 Port Medway Nova Scotia
117 M11 Port Mellon Br Col
122 H4 Port Menier Quebec
116 G8 Port Moller Alaska
117 M11 Port Moody Br Col
127 M3 Port Morant Jamaica
136 K3 Port Moresby Papua New Guinea
123 N7 Port Morien C Breton I, N Scotia
20 H3 Port Mort France
122 H10 Port Mouton Nova Scotia
141 F1 Port Musgrave inlet Queensland
15 C4 Portnacroish Scotland
12 B2 Portnahaven Scotland
109 O6 Port Neches Texas
138 D5 Port Neill S Australia
126 G3 Port Nelson Bahamas
101 N7 Portneuf Idaho
121 S5 Portneuf, Parc Quebec
122 C5 Portneuf, R Quebec
145 G4 Port Nicholson New Zealand
138 E6 Port Noarlunga S Australia
87 C11 Port Nolloth S Africa
95 M7 Port Norris New Jersey
115 N6 Port-Nouveau Québec Quebec
129 K4 Pôrto Brazil
16 B3 Porto Portugal
128 E5 Pôrto Acre Brazil
130 D7 Pôrto Alegre Mato Grosso Brazil
131 H3 Pôrto Alegre Rio Grande do Sul Brazil
87 B9 Porto Alexandre Angola
87 B8 Porto Amboim Angola
Porto Amelia see Pemba Mozambique
129 G6 Porto Artur Brazil
144 D7 Portobello New Zealand
13 E2 Portobello Scotland
130 E10 Pôrto Belo Brazil
116 L8 Port O'Brian Alaska
130 C9 Pôrto Britânia Brazil
43 C7 Porto Cervo Sardinia
109 L7 Port O'Connor Texas
16 B3 Porto de Leixões Portugal
129 H4 Pôrto de Mos Brazil
129 H6 Pôrto dos Meinacos Brazil
43 F11 Porto Empedocle Sicily
128 G7 Pôrto Espiridião Brazil
42 C6 Portoferraio Elba Italy
44 F3 Portofino Italy
12 D1 Port of Menteith Scotland
15 B2 Port of Ness Scotland
127 O2 Port of Spain Trinidad
45 M2 Porto Garibaldi Italy
129 H3 Pôrto Grande Brazil
42 E3 Portogruaro Italy
129 G7 Pôrto Jofre Brazil
102 D2 Portola California
29 J9 Pörtom Finland
45 L2 Portomaggiore Italy
44 D4 Porto Maurizio Italy
88 H9 Porto Mocambo Mozambique
129 G8 Pôrto Murtinho Brazil
129 J6 Pôrto Nacional Brazil
85 E7 Porto Novo Benin
113 G8 Port Orange Florida
117 M12 Port Orchard Washington
42 F5 Porto Recanati Italy
100 A7 Port Orford Oregon
133 G2 Pôrto San José Brazil
42 D6 Porto San Stefano Italy
85 A2 Pôrto Santo isld Madeira
129 H8 Pôrto São José Brazil
130 H5 Pôrto Seguro Brazil
45 M2 Porto Tolle Italy
43 B8 Porto Torres Sardinia
133 G3 Pôrto União Brazil
128 F5 Pôrto Velho Brazil
44 G3 Portovenere Italy
128 B4 Portoviejo Ecuador
12 C4 Portpatrick Scotland
140 B2 Port Patterson inlet N Terr Aust
144 A7 Port Pegasus New Zealand
121 M8 Port Perry Ontario
139 G7 Port Phillip B Victoria
138 E5 Port Pirie S Australia
114 H4 Port Radium N W Terr
8 A7 Portreath England
15 B3 Portree Scotland

118 J8 **Portreeve** Sask
83 M8 **Port Refuge** Cocos Is Indian Oc
100 A1 **Port Renfrew** Br Col
123 T5 **Port Rexton** Nfld
102 A4 **Port Reyes** California
100 B1 **Port Roberts** Washington
144 D5 **Port Robinson** New Zealand
140 D2 **Port Roper** *inlet* N Terr Aust
120 K10 **Port Rowan** Ontario
127 L3 **Port Royal** Jamaica
112 G5 **Port Royal** S Carolina
95 K8 **Port Royal** Virginia
122 G9 **Port Royal Nat. Hist. Park** Ontario
14 E1 **Portrush** N Ireland
79 C7 **Port Said** Egypt
113 B8 **Port St. Joe** Florida
89 F8 **Port St Johns** S Africa
19 N18 **Port St. Louis** France
18 F8 **Port St. Marie** France
21 B7 **Port St. Père** France
14 D1 **Portsalon** Irish Rep
94 E3 **Port Sanilac** Michigan
102 D6 **Port San Luis** California
123 P3 **Port Saunders** Nfld
38 K8 **Pörtschach** Austria
89 G8 **Port Shepstone** S Africa
117 H8 **Port Simpson** Br Col
142 D4 **Port Smith** *B* W Australia
127 O7 **Portsmouth** Dominica
9 E6 **Portsmouth** England
99 L8 **Portsmouth** Iowa
112 L2 **Portsmouth** N Carolina
95 R3 **Portsmouth** New Hampshire
94 E8 **Portsmouth** Ohio
121 O8 **Portsmouth** Ontario
95 Q5 **Portsmouth** Rhode I
95 L10 **Portsmouth** Virginia
12 C1 **Portsonachan** Scotland
15 F3 **Portsoy** Scotland
120 J10 **Port Stanley** Ontario
139 K5 **Port Stephens** New S Wales
14 E1 **Port Stewart** N Ireland
141 G2 **Port Stewart** *inlet* Queensland
86 G2 **Port Sudan** Sudan
8 C4 **Port Talbot** Wales
71 F4 **Port Tambang** Philippines
79 C9 **Port Taufiq** Egypt
127 O2 **Port Tembladora** Trinidad
29 M3 **Porttipahdan tekojärvi** *L* Finland
114 G8 **Port Tofino** Br Col
117 M11 **Port Townsend** Washington
16 B7 **Portugal** *rep*
83 J9 **Portugal B** Sri Lanka
123 U6 **Portugal Cove** Nfld
17 F1 **Portugalete** Spain
128 E2 **Portuguesa** *state* Venezuela
Portuguese Guinea *see* **Guinea-Bissau** *rep*
14 C3 **Portumna** Irish Rep
123 T5 **Port Union** Nfld
18 H10 **Port Vendres** France
102 F8 **Port Vicente** California
88 D1 **Port Victoria** Kenya
94 J4 **Portville** New York
138 E5 **Port Vincent** S Australia
52 D1 **Port Vladimir** U.S.S.R.
138 E5 **Port Wakefield** S Australia
142 F2 **Port Warrender** *inlet* W Australia
99 T6 **Port Washington** Wisconsin
142 B5 **Port Weld** *B* W Australia
116 N6 **Port Wells** *inlet* Alaska
112 F5 **Port Wentworth** Georgia
12 D4 **Port William** Scotland
122 H8 **Port Williams** Nova Scotia
99 P3 **Port Wing** Wisconsin
107 P6 **Porum** Oklahoma
127 K2 **Porus** Jamaica
133 C8 **Porvenir** Chile
108 C5 **Porvenir** Texas
52 D2 **Por'ya Guba** U.S.S.R.
36 C2 **Porz** W Germany
16 E5 **Porzuna** Spain
16 E5 **Porzuna, Sa. de** *mts* Spain
43 C8 **Posada** *R* Sardinia
133 F3 **Posadas** Argentina
16 D7 **Posadas** Spain
41 M5 **Poschiavo** Switzerland
141 H7 **Poseidon** Queensland
94 D1 **Posen** Michigan
110 J3 **Poseyville** Indiana
52 E5 **Poshekhonye** U.S.S.R.
119 O1 **Poshkokagan L** Ontario
47 F5 **Posídhion, Ákr** *C* Greece
41 O6 **Posina** *R* Italy
37 O5 **Pösing** W Germany
29 N5 **Posio** Finland
45 Q8 **Positano** Italy
70 G5 **Poso** Sulawesi
78 J1 **Posof** Turkey
129 J6 **Posse** Brazil
37 N3 **Posseck** E Germany
146 K6 **Possession I** Antarctica
37 M2 **Pössneck** E Germany
38 M8 **Possruck** Yugoslavia
109 J3 **Possum Kingdom L** Texas
100 E5 **Post** Oregon
37 N6 **Postau** W Germany
37 L5 **Postbauer-Heng** W Germany
8 C6 **Postbridge** England
115 M6 **Poste-de-la-Baleine** Quebec
68 H6 **Poste Deshayes** Cambodia
83 M12 **Poste, R du** Mauritius
85 E4 **Poste Weygand** Algeria
100 J2 **Post Falls** Idaho
114 J7 **Posthern** Sask
71 J8 **Postiljon Pulau** *isld* Indonesia
89 C7 **Postmasburg** S Africa
129 H6 **Pôsto Alto Manissaua** Brazil
128 C4 **Posto Bobonazo** Peru
42 F3 **Postojna** Yugoslavia
99 P6 **Postville** Iowa
42 H5 **Posušje** Yugoslavia
71 K9 **Pota** Indonesia
124 D4 **Pótam** Mexico
47 G3 **Potamoí** Greece
46 F8 **Potamós** Greece
50 H2 **Potapovo** U.S.S.R.
128 G2 **Potaro** *R* Guyana
89 E6 **Potchefstroom** S Africa
48 J6 **Potcoava** Romania
130 H5 **Poté** Brazil
107 Q6 **Poteau** Oklahoma
107 Q7 **Poteau** *R* Okla/Ark
109 J6 **Poteet** Texas
47 G1 **Potelu Lacul** *L* Romania
130 J8 **Potengi** *R* Brazil
43 G8 **Potenza** Italy
144 A7 **Poteriteri, L** New Zealand
16 D1 **Potes** Spain
89 F5 **Potgietersrus** S Africa
109 J6 **Poth** Texas
100 F2 **Potholes Res** Washington
129 K5 **Poti** *R* Brazil
20 E4 **Potigny** France
85 G6 **Potiskum** Nigeria
71 K9 **Potjo Mandasawu** *mt* Indonesia
100 J3 **Potlatch** Idaho
89 B8 **Potloer** *mt* S Africa
48 K6 **Potlogi** Romania
101 M3 **Potomac** Montana
94 J7 **Potomac S. Branch** *R* W Virginia
133 D1 **Potosí** Bolivia
110 F4 **Potosi** Missouri
133 D2 **Potosí** *dep* Bolivia
103 J6 **Potosi Mt** Nevada
71 F5 **Pototan** Panay Philippines
133 D3 **Potrerillos** Chile
131 B2 **Potro, Cerro de** *peak* Chile
33 S8 **Potsdam** E Germany
95 N2 **Potsdam** New York
33 R7 **Potsdam** *reg* E Germany
141 G3 **Pottalah Cr** Queensland
37 L4 **Pottenstein** W Germany
98 C8 **Potter** Nebraska
120 K4 **Potter** Ontario
9 E5 **Potterne** England
9 F4 **Potter's Bar** England
102 A2 **Potter Valley** California
94 C4 **Potterville** Michigan
37 L6 **Pottmes** W Germany
9 F3 **Potton** England
109 L2 **Pottsboro** Texas
111 G7 **Potts Camp** Mississippi
95 M6 **Pottstown** Pennsylvania
95 L6 **Pottsville** Pennsylvania
109 J4 **Pottsville** Texas
83 L11 **Pottuvil** Sri Lanka
107 N4 **Potwin** Kansas
21 C6 **Pouancé** France
68 F3 **Pou Bia** *mt* Laos
117 N8 **Pouce Coupé** Br Col
123 U6 **Pouch Cove** Nfld
95 O5 **Poughkeepsie** New York
18 H5 **Pougues les Eaux** France
21 H7 **Pouillé** France
18 E9 **Pouillon** France
18 J5 **Pouilly en Auxois** France
21 I7 **Poulaines** France
122 B5 **Poulin de Courval, L** Quebec
68 J5 **Poulo Canton, Is de** Vietnam
69 G8 **Poulo Dama, Iles** Vietnam
68 J6 **Poulo Gambir, Cu Lao** *isld* Vietnam
95 O3 **Poultney** Vermont
13 E6 **Poulton-le-Fylde** England
68 E4 **Pou Miang** *mt* Thailand
99 S4 **Pound** Wisconsin
9 F5 **Pound Hill** England
19 P18 **Pourcieux** France
145 F4 **Pourerere** New Zealand
145 G3 **Pourewa I** New Zealand
146 F13 **Pourquoi Pas I** Antarctica
40 E6 **Pourri, Mont** France
20 G2 **Pourville** France
68 F3 **Pou San** *mt* Laos
68 F3 **Pou Sao** *mt* Laos
68 H5 **Pou Set** *mt* Laos
129 G6 **Pouso Alegre** Mato Grosso Brazil
130 F8 **Pouso Alegre** Minas Gerais Brazil
29 O6 **Poussu** Finland
144 A7 **Poutama I** New Zealand
145 E2 **Pouto** New Zealand
121 Q3 **Poutrincourt, L** Quebec
40 D1 **Pouxeux** France
21 D8 **Pouzauges** France
48 E1 **Pov Bystrica** Czechoslovakia
52 D3 **Povenets** U.S.S.R.
145 F3 **Poverty Bay** New Zealand
9 F5 **Povey Cross** England
45 J2 **Poviglio** Italy
48 F6 **Povlen** *mt* Yugoslavia
16 B3 **Póvoa de Varzim** Portugal
65 J3 **Povorotnyy, Mys** *C* U.S.S.R.
115 M5 **Povungnituk** Quebec
121 L6 **Powassan** Ontario
101 T5 **Powder** *R* Wyo/Mont
106 C3 **Powderhorn** Colorado
100 H5 **Powder R** Oregon
98 A4 **Powderville** Montana
113 K11 **Powel Cay** *isld* Bahamas
103 K7 **Powell** Arizona
98 E5 **Powell** S Dakota
99 R3 **Powell** Wisconsin
101 R5 **Powell** Wyoming
139 G2 **Powell** *R* Queensland
94 D10 **Powell** *R* Tenn/Virg
100 D5 **Powell Butte** Oregon
140 C4 **Powell Creek** N Terr Aust
146 C14 **Powell I** S Orkney Is
103 O4 **Powell, L** Ariz/Utah
106 D2 **Powell, Mt** Colorado
102 F3 **Powell Mt** Nevada
126 F2 **Powell Pt** Eleuthera Bahamas
117 L10 **Powell River** Br Col
94 F8 **Powellton** W Virginia
101 O2 **Power** Montana
99 T4 **Powers** Michigan
100 A7 **Powers** Oregon
98 D1 **Powers L** N Dakota
110 C1 **Powersville** Missouri
111 C10 **Powhatan** Louisiana
94 K9 **Powhatan** Virginia
107 P2 **Powhattan** Kansas
8 D3 **Powick** England
141 H5 **Powlathanga** Queensland
95 O4 **Pownal** Vermont
8 C3 **Powys** *co* Wales
130 C5 **Poxoreu** *R* Brazil
67 E2 **Poyang Hu** *L* China
111 D7 **Poyen** Arkansas
99 S5 **Poygan, L** Wisconsin
31 K7 **Poysdorf** Austria
124 C5 **Poza Grande** Mexico
78 E3 **Pozanti** Turkey
48 G6 **Požarevac** Yugoslavia
125 L7 **Poza Rica** Mexico
59 K2 **Pozharskoye** U.S.S.R.
52 J5 **Pozhva** U.S.S.R.
22 D3 **Pozières** France
140 D5 **Pozieres,Mt** N Terr Aust
31 K3 **Poznań** Poland
102 D6 **Pozo** California
17 F7 **Pozo Alcón** Spain
133 D2 **Pozo Almonte** Chile
16 D6 **Pozoblanco** Spain
103 J9 **Pozo Cenizo** Mexico
17 F6 **Pozohondo** Spain
103 J9 **Pozo Salado** Mexico
103 N10 **Pozo Verde** Mexico
52 H4 **Poztykeros** U.S.S.R.
133 D2 **Pozuelos, L. de** Argentina
45 J1 **Pozzolengo** Italy
45 L1 **Pozzonuovo** Italy
45 Q8 **Pozzuoli** Italy
68 F2 **P. Phac Mo** *mt* Vietnam
85 D7 **Pra** *R* Ghana
31 L2 **Prabuty** Poland
45 J3 **Pracchia** Italy
68 D7 **Pracham Hiang, Laem** Thailand
30 H7 **Prachatice** Czechoslovakia
68 E5 **Prachin Buri** Thailand
68 D7 **Prachuap Khiri Khan** Thailand
16 C1 **Pradairo** Spain
31 K5 **Praděd** *mt* Czechoslovakia
18 G10 **Prades** France
70 P9 **Pradjekan** Java
28 E2 **Præstbro** Denmark
28 J6 **Præsto** Denmark
Præstø *co see* **Storstrøm and Roskilde** *counties*
38 N9 **Pragersk** Yugoslavia
38 F7 **Prägraten** Austria
Prague *see* **Praha**
107 O6 **Prague** Oklahoma
31 H5 **Praha** Czechoslovakia
21 E9 **Prahecq** France
48 K5 **Prahova** Romania
48 H6 **Prahova** Yugoslavia
48 K6 **Prahova** *R* Romania
133 G4 **Praia Albardão** *beach* Brazil
48 J4 **Praid** Romania
129 H4 **Prainha** Brazil
122 B3 **Praires, L. des** Quebec
109 K6 **Prairia Lea** Texas
100 K6 **Prairie** Idaho
141 G5 **Prairie** Queensland
110 F1 **Prairie City** Illinois
100 G5 **Prairie City** Oregon
107 K2 **Prairie Dog Cr** Kansas
108 F1 **Prairie Dog Town Fork** *R* Texas
99 P6 **Prairie du Chien** Wisconsin
99 R6 **Prairie du Sac** Wisconsin
110 B6 **Prairie Grove** Arkansas
109 L4 **Prairie Hill** Texas
119 P6 **Prairie River** Sask
110 J2 **Prairieton** Indiana
107 L2 **Prairie View** Kansas
111 F11 **Prairieville** Louisiana
94 E9 **Praise** Kentucky
70 Q10 **Praja** Indonesia
68 F5 **Prakhon Chai** Thailand
40 E7 **Pralognan** France
42 E2 **Pramaggiore** *mt* Italy
70 N9 **Prambanan** Java
37 O3 **Prameny** Czechoslovakia
69 D8 **Pram, Khao** *mt* Thailand
68 D6 **Pran** *R* Thailand
68 D6 **Pran Buri** Thailand
38 K7 **Prankerhöhe** *mt* Austria
69 D11 **Prapat** Sumatra
40 B2 **Praslay** France
83 J12 **Praslin** *isld* Seychelles
47 J9 **Prasonísi, Akr** *C* Rhodes Greece
31 L4 **Praszka** Poland
129 J7 **Prata** *R* Brazil
Pratas *isld see* **Dongsha Qundao**
33 R9 **Pratau** E Germany
17 J3 **Prat de Llobregat** Spain
41 L4 **Prätigau** *V* Switzerland
45 K4 **Prato** Italy
45 R8 **Prátola Serra** Italy
45 L4 **Pratomagno** Italy
42 D5 **Pratomagno** *mt* Italy
45 H3 **Prato, Mt** Italy
45 L4 **Pratovecchio** Italy
18 G10 **Prats-de-Mollo** France
107 M4 **Pratt** Kansas
119 T9 **Pratt** Manitoba
95 N4 **Prattsville** New York
111 K9 **Prattville** Alabama
40 B2 **Prauthoy** France
31 N1 **Pravdinsk** U.S.S.R.
54 J1 **Pravdinskiy** U.S.S.R.
70 M9 **Prav, G** *mt* Java
16 C1 **Pravia** Spain
8 C7 **Prawle Pt** England
21 H7 **Préaux** France
37 O3 **Přebuz** Czechoslovakia
20 C4 **Precey** France
52 D6 **Prechistoye** U.S.S.R.
20 K3 **Précy-sur-Oise** France
45 L3 **Predappio** Italy
42 D2 **Predazzo** Italy
37 O5 **Predigtstuhl** *mt* W Germany
38 M8 **Preding** Austria
38 J7 **Predlitz** Austria
38 F7 **Predoi** Italy
44 E2 **Predosa** Italy
51 O2 **Predporozhnyy** U.S.S.R.
119 P7 **Preeceville** Sask
20 E5 **Pré-en-Pail** France
33 M4 **Preetz** W Germany
31 M1 **Pregolya** *R* U.S.S.R.
127 J10 **Pregonero** Venezuela
18 E8 **Preignac** France
52 C6 **Preiļi** U.S.S.R.
121 M4 **Preissac** Quebec
68 G6 **Prek Kak** Cambodia
68 H6 **Prek Preas** *R* Cambodia
68 G7 **Prek Sandek** Cambodia
68 F7 **Prek Taley** *R* Cambodia
143 F9 **Premier Downs** W Australia
8 B3 **Pren-gwyn** Wales
46 D4 **Prenjas** Albania
33 T6 **Prenzlau** E Germany
144 A7 **Preservation Inlet** New Zealand
130 D8 **Presidente Prudente** Brazil
108 C6 **Presidio** Texas
13 F6 **Preston** England
101 O7 **Preston** Idaho
95 M8 **Preston** Maryland
99 O6 **Preston** Minnesota
110 C4 **Preston** Missouri
103 J3 **Preston** Nevada
107 P6 **Preston** Oklahoma
9 E5 **Preston Candover** England
109 O9 **Preston Hollow** Texas
13 F2 **Prestonpans** Scotland
94 E9 **Prestonsburg** Kentucky
13 F6 **Prestwich** England
12 D3 **Prestwick** Scotland
129 K6 **Preto** *R* Bahia Brazil
129 J7 **Prêto** *R* Minas Gerais Brazil
128 F4 **Prêto do Igapó Açu** *R* Brazil
89 F5 **Pretoria** S Africa
33 R9 **Prettin** E Germany
95 L7 **Prettyboy Res** Maryland
107 M4 **Pretty Prairie** Kansas
33 O7 **Pretzier** E Germany
33 R9 **Pretzsch** E Germany
21 G8 **Preuilly-sur-Claise** France
38 L8 **Prevalje** Yugoslavia
46 D6 **Préveza** Greece
106 B6 **Prewitt** New Mexico
106 G1 **Prewitt Res** Colorado
20 H4 **Prey** France
68 G7 **Prey Lovea** Cambodia
68 G7 **Prey Veng** Cambodia
45 P5 **Prezza** Italy
54 H9 **Priazovskaya Vozvyshenost'** *uplands* U.S.S.R.
116 D8 **Pribilof Is** Bering Sea
30 H6 **Příbram** Czechoslovakia
95 M7 **Price** Maryland
98 F2 **Price** N Dakota
122 D5 **Price** Quebec
103 O2 **Price** Utah
103 O2 **Price** *R* Utah
68 A6 **Price, C** Andaman Is
106 B1 **Price Creek** Colorado
117 J9 **Price I** Br Col
111 H11 **Prichard** Alabama
100 K2 **Prichard** Idaho
54 E9 **Prichernomorskaya Nizmennost'** *lowland* U.S.S.R.
37 J4 **Prichsenstadt** W Germany
127 P5 **Prickly Pt** Grenada
109 J4 **Priddy** Texas
54 D7 **Pridneprovskaya Nizmennost'** *lowland* U.S.S.R.
54 C8 **Pridneprovskaya Vozvyshennost'** *uplands* U.S.S.R.
17 F4 **Priego** Spain
16 E7 **Priego de C** Spain
27 M15 **Priekule** Latvia U.S.S.R.
27 M16 **Priekulė** Lithuania U.S.S.R.
33 Q5 **Priemerburg** E Germany
89 C7 **Prieska** S Africa
37 M1 **Priessnitz** E Germany
33 T10 **Priestewitz** E Germany
100 J1 **Priest L** Idaho
127 M2 **Priestman's River** Jamaica
100 F3 **Priest Rapids** Washington
100 J1 **Priest River** Idaho
117 P11 **Priest River** Idaho
31 L7 **Prievidza** Czechoslovakia
33 Q6 **Prignitz** *reg* E Germany
56 C4 **Priiskovyy** U.S.S.R.
42 H4 **Prijedor** Yugoslavia
53 G9 **Prikaspiyskaya Nizmennost** *lowlands* U.S.S.R.
46 E3 **Prilep** Yugoslavia
54 D6 **Priluki** U.S.S.R.
40 B7 **Primarette** France
118 H6 **Primate** Sask
37 O4 **Přimda** Czechoslovakia
131 D3 **Primero, R** Argentina
139 J8 **Prime Seal I** Tasmania
99 L6 **Primghar** Iowa
52 C4 **Primorsk** U.S.S.R.
59 K3 **Primorskiy** U.S.S.R.
56 F5 **Primorskiy Khrebet** *mts* U.S.S.R.
59 K2 **Primorskiy Kray** *reg* U.S.S.R.
47 J2 **Primorsko** Bulgaria
54 J9 **Primorskoye** U.S.S.R.
122 J7 **Prim, Pt** Pr Edward I
117 F5 **Primrose** *R* Br Col/Yukon Terr
118 H4 **Primrose L** Sask
36 B5 **Prims** *R* W Germany
36 C4 **Primstal** W Germany
118 J6 **Prince** Sask
89 C9 **Prince Albert** S Africa
119 M5 **Prince Albert** Sask
118 L5 **Prince Albert Nat. Park** Sask
114 H3 **Prince Albert Pen** N W Terr
114 G3 **Prince Alfred, C** N W Terr
115 M4 **Prince Charles I** N W Terr
146 C5 **Prince Charles Mts** Antarctica
146 D15 **Prince Charles Str** S Shetland Is
121 O9 **Prince Edward B** Ontario
90 M14 **Prince Edward I** Indian Oc
115 N8 **Prince Edward I** *prov* Canada
122 J7 **Prince Edward I. Nat. Park** Canada
95 L8 **Prince Frederick** Maryland
142 F3 **Prince Frederick Harb** W Australia
117 M9 **Prince George** Br Col
114 J2 **Prince Gustaf Adolf Sea** N W Terr
116 C4 **Prince of Wales, C** Alaska
117 G8 **Prince of Wales I** Alaska
115 J3 **Prince of Wales I** N W Terr
141 F1 **Prince of Wales I** Queensland
114 H3 **Prince of Wales Str** N W Terr
146 G8 **Prince Olav Mts** Antarctica
114 H2 **Prince Patrick I** N W Terr
115 K3 **Prince Regent Inlet** N W Terr
142 F3 **Prince Regent R** W Australia
117 H8 **Prince Rupert** Br Col
130 H9 **Princesa Isabel** Brazil
Princes Is *see* **Kızıl Adalar**
Princes Lake Ontario *see* **Wallace**
9 F4 **Princes Risborough** England
95 M8 **Princess Anne** Maryland
141 G2 **Princess Charlotte B** Queensland
146 D4 **Princess Elizabeth Land** Antarctica
142 F3 **Princess May Ra** W Australia
144 A6 **Princess Mts** New Zealand
143 D7 **Princess Ra** W Australia
117 J9 **Princess Royal I** Br Col
127 O3 **Prince's Town** Trinidad
9 E3 **Princethorpe** England
117 N11 **Princeton** Br Col
102 B2 **Princeton** California
99 R8 **Princeton** Illinois
110 J3 **Princeton** Indiana
110 J4 **Princeton** Kentucky
95 U1 **Princeton** Maine
99 T3 **Princeton** Michigan
99 N4 **Princeton** Minnesota
99 N9 **Princeton** Missouri
112 J2 **Princeton** N Carolina
95 N6 **Princeton** New Jersey
99 R6 **Princeton** Wisconsin
94 F9 **Princeton** W Virginia
8 C6 **Princetown** England
99 R9 **Princeville** Illinois
121 T6 **Princeville** Quebec
116 O6 **Prince William Sound** Alaska
141 J6 **Princhester** Queensland
86 A5 **Príncipe** *isld* G of Guinea
128 F6 **Principe da Beira** Brazil
100 E5 **Prineville** Oregon
98 C6 **Pringle** S Dakota
108 C8 **Pringle** Texas
19 Q13 **Pringy** France
115 P5 **Prins Christians Sund** Greenland
25 C5 **Prinsenhage** Netherlands
68 C6 **Prinsep I** Burma
146 A9 **Prinsesse Astrid Kyst** Antarctica
146 A8 **Prinsesse Ragnhild Kyst** Antarctica
146 A7 **Prins Harald Kyst** Antarctica
50 A1 **Prins Karls Forland** Spitzbergen
123 L4 **Prinsta B** Anticosti I, Quebec
125 N3 **Prinzapolca** Nicaragua
54 L2 **Priokskiy** U.S.S.R.
16 B1 **Prior, C** Spain
52 D4 **Priozersk** U.S.S.R.
52 K3 **Pripolyarnyy Ural** *mts* U.S.S.R.
53 C8 **Pripyat** *R* U.S.S.R.
29 P3 **Prirechnyy** U.S.S.R.
37 P3 **Přísečnice** Czechoslovakia
48 J3 **Prislop Pass** Romania
46 E2 **Priština** Yugoslavia
106 H4 **Pritchett** Colorado
33 Q8 **Pritzerbe** E Germany
33 O6 **Pritzier** E Germany
33 Q6 **Pritzwalk** E Germany
19 N15 **Privas** France
45 O7 **Priverno** Italy
45 O6 **Privernum** Italy
42 F3 **Privka** Yugoslavia
52 F6 **Privolzhsk** U.S.S.R.
53 G7 **Privolzhskaya Vozvyshennost** *uplands* U.S.S.R.
46 D2 **Prizren** Yugoslavia
43 E11 **Prizzi** Sicily
70 O9 **Probolinnggo** Java
37 L2 **Probstzella** E Germany
8 B7 **Probus** England
31 J4 **Prochowice** Poland
45 Q8 **Procida** Italy
43 F8 **Procida** *isld* Italy
106 H1 **Proctor** Colorado
109 J4 **Proctor** Texas
95 O3 **Proctor** Vermont
109 J3 **Proctor Res** Texas
95 P3 **Proctorsville** Vermont
16 B5 **Proènca a Nova** Portugal
37 N1 **Profen** E Germany
22 H3 **Profondeville** Belgium
125 L2 **Progreso** Honduras
125 P7 **Progreso** Mexico
106 E7 **Progresso** New Mexico
56 B6 **Prokhladnoye** U.S.S.R.
46 D2 **Prokletije** Yugoslavia
56 C4 **Prokop'yevsk** U.S.S.R.
46 E1 **Prokuplje** Yugoslavia
52 D5 **Proletariy** U.S.S.R.
54 K8 **Proletarsk** U.S.S.R.
54 G6 **Proletarskiy** U.S.S.R.
54 J1 **Proletarskiy** U.S.S.R.
59 N2 **Proliv Frizi** *str* U.S.S.R.
37 K4 **Prolsdorf** W Germany
68 B3 **Prome** Burma
99 N9 **Promise City** Iowa
101 N8 **Promontory** Utah
56 C3 **Promyshlennaya** U.S.S.R.
52 F5 **Pronino** U.S.S.R.
100 G9 **Pronto** Nevada
54 M2 **Pronya** *R* U.S.S.R.
117 M6 **Prophet River** Br Col
99 R8 **Prophetstown** Illinois
130 H11 **Propriá** Brazil
46 D3 **Prosek** Albania
33 S10 **Prösen** E Germany
141 J5 **Proserpine** Queensland
33 Q9 **Prosigk** E Germany
31 K3 **Prosna** *R* Poland
52 H5 **Prosnitsa** U.S.S.R.
47 F3 **Prosotsáni** Greece
95 M3 **Prospect** New York
94 D6 **Prospect** Ohio
100 C7 **Prospect** Oregon
94 G6 **Prospect** Pennsylvania
127 M3 **Prospect Pt** Jamaica
100 A6 **Prosper** Oregon
112 F3 **Prosperity** S Carolina
98 H9 **Prosser** Nebraska
100 F3 **Prosser** Washington
48 D1 **Prostějov** Czechoslovakia
141 K7 **Proston** Queensland
52 H2 **Prosunduy** U.S.S.R.
54 H8 **Prosyanaya** U.S.S.R.
31 M5 **Proszowice** Poland
107 L4 **Protection** Kansas
99 O6 **Protivin** Iowa
54 J2 **Protva** *R* U.S.S.R.
33 T7 **Prötzel** E Germany
47 J1 **Provadiya** Bulgaria
115 O3 **Prøven** Greenland
111 C10 **Provencal** Louisiana
19 O17 **Provence** *prov* France
36 C7 **Provenchères-sur-Fave** France
127 P5 **Providence** Grenada
110 J4 **Providence** Kentucky
112 J1 **Providence** N Carolina
95 Q5 **Providence** Rhode I
101 O8 **Providence** Utah
120 H7 **Providence Bay** Ontario
116 J8 **Providence, C** Alaska
144 A7 **Providence, C** New Zealand
87 J9 **Providence I** Br Indian Oc Terr
103 J7 **Providence Mts** California
127 H4 **Providenciales** *isld* Turks & Caicos Is
128 F6 **Providencia, Sa. da** *mts* Brazil
116 A4 **Provideniya** U.S.S.R.
141 G2 **Providential Chan** Gt Barrier Reef Aust
95 R4 **Provincetown** Massachusetts
18 H4 **Provins** France
98 C6 **Provo** S Dakota
103 N1 **Provo** Utah
118 G6 **Provost** Alberta
22 D4 **Proyart** France
42 H5 **Prozor** Yugoslavia
52 H4 **Prub** *R* U.S.S.R.
130 E9 **Prudentópolis** Brazil
94 C2 **Prudenville** Michigan
13 G4 **Prudhoe** England
116 O1 **Prudhoe Bay** Alaska
141 J5 **Prudhoe I** Queensland
115 N2 **Prudhoe Land** Greenland
119 M6 **Prud'homme** Sask
31 K5 **Prudnik** Poland
54 H6 **Prudyanka** U.S.S.R.
36 B3 **Prüm** W Germany
21 G6 **Prunay** France
45 J3 **Prunetta** Italy
19 Q15 **Prunières** France
21 I7 **Pruniers** Cher France
21 J8 **Pruniers** Indre France
31 K2 **Pruszcz** Poland
31 M3 **Pruszków** Poland
48 L4 **Prut** *R* U.S.S.R.
48 L3 **Prutul** *R* Romania
41 N3 **Prutz** Austria
52 D4 **Pryazha** U.S.S.R.
31 L6 **Prýdek Mistek** Czechoslovakia
146 C4 **Prydz B** Antarctica
101 R4 **Pryor** Montana
107 P5 **Pryor** Oklahoma
31 M2 **Przasnysz** Poland
31 K2 **Przechlewo** Poland
31 M4 **Przedbórz** Poland
31 O6 **Przemyśl** Poland
31 N5 **Przeworsk** Poland
31 H4 **Przewóz** Poland
57 J4 **Przheval'sk** U.S.S.R.
31 M4 **Przysucha** Poland
47 F6 **Psakhná** Greece
47 H6 **Psará** *isld* Greece
31 K4 **Psie Pole** Poland
47 H9 **Psíra** *isld* Greece
52 C5 **Pskov** U.S.S.R.
52 C5 **Pskovskoye, Ozero** *L* U.S.S.R.
42 H3 **Psunj** *mt* Yugoslavia
31 L1 **Pszczółki** Poland
31 L6 **Pszczyna** Poland
53 C7 **Ptich'** *R* U.S.S.R.
46 E4 **Ptolemaïs** Greece
38 N9 **Ptuj** Yugoslavia
71 H5 **Puah** *isld* Sulawesi
135 U4 **Puako** Hawaiian Is
116 K8 **Puale B** Alaska
133 E5 **Puán** Argentina
67 C5 **Pubei** China
122 G10 **Pubnico** Nova Scotia
128 C5 **Pucacaca** Peru
128 D5 **Pucallpa** Peru
20 J3 **Puchay** France
38 N6 **Puchberg** Austria
65 A7 **Pucheng** China
65 C7 **Pucheng** China
67 F3 **Pucheng** China
52 F6 **Puchezh** U.S.S.R.
31 L6 **Puchov** Czechoslovakia
71 E5 **Pucio Pt** Panay Philippines
31 L1 **Puck** Poland
99 R6 **Puckaway L** Wisconsin
9 G4 **Puckeridge** England
111 G9 **Puckett** Mississippi
143 B7 **Puckford,Mt** W Australia
29 M6 **Pudasjärvi** Finland
8 D6 **Puddletown** England
52 H5 **Pudem** U.S.S.R.
67 B3 **Puding** China
123 Q5 **Pudops L** Nfld
52 E4 **Pudozh** U.S.S.R.
52 E4 **Pudozhgora** U.S.S.R.
13 G6 **Pudsey** England
125 K8 **Puebla** Mexico
16 D5 **Puebla de Alcocer** Spain
17 F7 **Puebla de Don Fadrique** Spain
16 D5 **Puebla de Don Rodrigo** Spain
16 C2 **Puebla de Sanabria** Spain
16 C2 **Puebla de Trives** Spain
106 F3 **Pueblo** Colorado
106 C5 **Pueblo Bonito** New Mexico
133 C3 **Pueblo Hundido** Chile
100 G7 **Pueblo Mts** Oregon
124 G6 **Pueblo Nuevo** Mexico
125 N9 **Pueblo Viejo** Mexico
125 L6 **Pueblo Viejo, L. de** Mexico
133 D5 **Puelches** Argentina
133 D5 **Puelén** Argentina
16 B2 **Puenteareas** Spain
16 B2 **Puente Caldelas** Spain
16 D7 **Puente Genil** Spain
103 P7 **Puerco** *R* Arizona
106 C6 **Puerco, R** New Mexico
128 C2 **Puerta Mutis** Colombia
133 C7 **Puerto Aisén** Chile
125 N5 **Puerto Armuelles** Panama
128 C3 **Puerto Asis** Colombia
128 E2 **Puerto Ayacucho** Venezuela
125 P10 **Puerto Barrios** Guatemala
128 D6 **Puerto Bermúdez** Peru
128 D2 **Puerto Berrio** Colombia
133 C7 **Puerto Bertrand** Chile
128 C6 **Puerto Caballas** Peru
128 E1 **Puerto Cabello** Venezuela
125 N2 **Puerto Cabezas** Nicaragua
Puerto Capaz Morocco *see* **El Jebha**
128 E2 **Puerto Carreño** Colombia
130 B8 **Puerto Casado** Paraguay
128 C5 **Puerto Chicama** Peru
124 G3 **Puerto Chilicote** Mexico
133 C6 **Puerto Cisnes** Chile
133 D8 **Puerto Coig** Argentina
128 D1 **Puerto Colombia** Colombia
125 Q10 **Puerto Cortés** Honduras
128 E1 **Puerto Cumarebo** Venezuela
127 J8 **Puerto Estrella** Colombia
128 C5 **Puerto Eten** Peru
133 C5 **Puerto Fuy** Chile
128 F7 **Puerto Grether** Bolivia
133 D8 **Puerto Harberton** Argentina
128 E6 **Puerto Heath** Bolivia
128 D3 **Puerto Huitoto** Colombia
133 E5 **Puerto Ingeniero White** Argentina
127 M9 **Puerto La Cruz** Venezuela
128 D4 **Puerto Leguizamo** Colombia
125 N2 **Puerto Lempira** Honduras
16 E6 **Puertollano** Spain
128 D7 **Puerto Lomas** Peru
127 J9 **Puerto López** Colombia
17 F7 **Puerto Lumbreras** Spain
133 D6 **Puerto Madryn** Argentina
128 E6 **Puerto Maldonado** Peru
126 F4 **Puerto Manatí** Cuba
128 D4 **Puerto Miraña** Colombia
133 C6 **Puerto Montt** Chile
133 C8 **Puerto Natales** Chile
128 E2 **Puerto Nuevo** Colombia
133 F3 **Puerto Ocampo** Argentina
128 F2 **Puerto Ordaz** Venezuela
126 F4 **Puerto Padre** Cuba
133 C2 **Puerto Patillos** Chile
124 C2 **Puerto Penasco** Mexico
133 F2 **Puerto Pinasco** Paraguay
133 E6 **Puerto Pirámides** Argentina
128 F1 **Puerto Piritu** Venezuela
127 J5 **Puerto Plata** Dom Rep
128 D5 **Puerto Portillo** Peru
71 D6 **Puerto Princesa** Palawan Philippines
125 M5 **Puerto Quepos** Costa Rica
128 E6 **Puerto Rico** Bolivia
113 J7 **Puerto Rico** *terr* Caribbean
127 L5 **Puerto Rico Trench** Caribbean
126 G4 **Puerto Samá** Cuba
130 B8 **Puerto Sastre** Paraguay
128 E6 **Puerto Siles** Bolivia
130 C9 **Puerto Strossner** Paraguay
130 B6 **Puerto Suárez** Bolivia
124 G7 **Puerto Vallarta** Mexico
133 C6 **Puerto Varas** Chile
128 F7 **Puerto Velarde** Bolivia
128 D5 **Puerto Victoria** Peru
128 D2 **Puerto Villamizar** Colombia
133 D7 **Puerto Visser** Argentina
128 D2 **Puerto Wilches** Colombia
133 C7 **Pueyrredón, L** Chile/Arg
25 F7 **Puffendorf** W Germany
124 G7 **Puga** Mexico
52 H6 **Pugachevo** U.S.S.R.
74 E4 **Pugal** India
88 G10 **Puga Puga** *isld* Mozambique
70 O10 **Puger** Java
100 C2 **Puget Sound** Washington
19 P13 **Pugieu** France
43 G8 **Puglia** *prov* Italy
71 K9 **Pugubengo** Flores Indonesia
70 K8 **Pugung, G** *mt* Sumatra
122 J8 **Pugwash** Nova Scotia
145 F3 **Puha** New Zealand
135 O1 **Puhi** Hawaiian Is
145 E2 **Puhoi** New Zealand
48 H5 **Pui** Romania
48 L4 **Puieşti** Romania
17 J2 **Puigcerda** Spain
71 G7 **Pujada B** Mindanao Philippines
65 G4 **Pujan Res** N Korea
19 N16 **Pujaut** France
67 A1 **Pujiang** China
67 F2 **Pujiang** China
119 Q3 **Pukatawagan** Manitoba
46 D2 **Pukë** Albania
145 G2 **Pukeamaru** *mt* New Zealand
145 E3 **Pukearuhe** New Zealand
145 F3 **Pukehou** New Zealand
145 E2 **Pukekawa** New Zealand
145 E2 **Pukekohe** New Zealand
144 C5 **Pukekura** New Zealand
145 E2 **Pukemiro** New Zealand
145 D1 **Pukenui** New Zealand
145 F3 **Pukeokahu** New Zealand
144 C6 **Pukerangi** New Zealand
144 B7 **Pukerau** New Zealand
145 E3 **Pukeroa** New Zealand
145 G3 **Puketawai** New Zealand
144 D5 **Puketeraki Range** New Zealand
145 F3 **Puketitiri** New Zealand
145 F2 **Puketoetoe** *mt* New Zealand
145 F4 **Puketoi Range** New Zealand
145 E3 **Puketutu** New Zealand
145 F2 **Puketutu I** New Zealand
144 C6 **Pukeuri Junction** New Zealand
29 M11 **Pukkila** Finland
67 F1 **Pukou** China
52 F3 **Puksa** U.S.S.R.
52 F3 **Puksoozero** U.S.S.R.
52 H5 **Puksub** U.S.S.R.
98 G6 **Pukwana** S Dakota
42 F4 **Pula** Yugoslavia
128 E8 **Pulacayo** Bolivia
43 C9 **Pula, C. di** Sardinia
Pulandian *see* **Xinjin**
71 G6 **Pulangi** *R* Mindanao Philippines
70 D6 **Pulangpisau** Kalimantan
70 K8 **Pulao Seribu** *isld* Sumatra
70 K9 **Pulasari** *mt* Java
99 O9 **Pulaski** Iowa
95 L3 **Pulaski** New York
110 J6 **Pulaski** Tennessee
94 G9 **Pulaski** Virginia
99 S5 **Pulaski** Wisconsin
69 F13 **Pulaukidjang** Sumatra
70 B4 **Pulaumadjang** Kalimantan
69 D13 **Pulautelo** Indonesia
31 N4 **Puławy** Poland
9 F6 **Pulborough** England
77 L2 **Pul-i-Khumri** Afghanistan
76 D3 **Pulivendla** India
76 C6 **Puliyangudi** India
83 K9 **Puliyankulam** Sri Lanka
29 M7 **Pulkkila** Finland
100 H3 **Pullman** Washington
71 E2 **Pulog, Mt** Luzon Philippines
83 K8 **Puloli** Sri Lanka
52 F2 **Pulonga** U.S.S.R.
52 D1 **Pulozero** U.S.S.R.
124 D4 **Púlpito, Pta** *C* Mexico
33 T10 **Pulsnitz** *R* E Germany
31 M3 **Pułtusk** Poland
66 C4 **Pulu** China
70 P10 **Pulukan** Bali Indonesia
66 E6 **Puma Yumco** *L* China
Pumiao *see* **Yongning**
98 A4 **Pumpkin Cr** Montana
98 C8 **Pumpkin Cr** Nebraska
108 F6 **Pumpville** Texas
8 C3 **Pumsaint** Wales
128 B4 **Puná** *isld* Ecuador
70 G5 **Puna** *R* Sulawesi
144 C5 **Punakaiki** New Zealand
145 D1 **Punakitere R** New Zealand
70 D4 **Punan** Kalimantan
74 F2 **Punch** Kashmir
117 M9 **Punchaw** Br Col
70 C6 **Pundu** Kalimantan
52 F4 **Punduga** U.S.S.R.
55 D1 **Punga** *R* U.S.S.R.
112 L2 **Pungo** N Carolina
59 J3 **Pungsan** N Korea
86 E6 **Punia** Zaïre
70 Q10 **Punikan, G** *mt* Indonesia
131 B2 **Punilla, Sa. de la** *mts* Chile
74 F3 **Punjab** *prov* India
74 D3 **Punjab, The** *prov* Pakistan
140 E4 **Punjaub** Queensland
29 O10 **Punkaharju** Finland
29 K10 **Punkalaidun** Finland
119 N7 **Punnichy** Sask
128 D7 **Puno** Peru
128 D6 **Puno** *dep* Peru
106 D7 **Punta** New Mexico
131 E7 **Punta Alta** Argentina
133 C8 **Punta Arenas** Chile
43 C7 **Puntaccia** *mt* Sardinia
133 C3 **Punta Colorada** Chile
108 B8 **Punta de Agua Cr.** *R* Texas/New Mex
17 H4 **Punta de la Baña** Spain
125 P9 **Punta Gorda** Belize
100 A9 **Punta Gorda** California
113 E11 **Punta Gorda** Florida
125 N4 **Punta Gorda** Nicaragua
131 G6 **Punta Norte** Argentina
127 J5 **Punta Palenque** Dom Rep
124 B3 **Punta Prieta** Mexico
125 M5 **Puntarenas** Costa Rica
128 G8 **Punta Rieles** Paraguay
125 N5 **Punta San Pedrillo** Costa Rica
127 M5 **Punta Tuna** Puerto Rico
128 D1 **Punto Fijo** Venezuela
47 G4 **Punto Lágo** Greece
133 D7 **Puntudo, Cerro** *mt* Argentina
116 C5 **Punuk Is** Bering Sea
94 J6 **Punxsutawney** Pennsylvania
68 F6 **Puok** Cambodia
29 N7 **Puolanka** Finland
26 L5 **Puottaure** Sweden
128 E6 **Puoya** *mt* Bolivia
145 D4 **Puponga** New Zealand
58 F6 **Puqi** China
128 D6 **Puquio** Peru
133 D3 **Puquios** Chile
50 G2 **Pur** *R* U.S.S.R.
128 C3 **Puracé** *vol* Colombia
70 M9 **Purbolinggo** Java
107 N7 **Purcell** Oklahoma
116 J3 **Purcell Mt** Alaska
117 P10 **Purcell Mts** Br Col
100 K1 **Purcell Range** Montana
94 K7 **Purcellville** Virginia
17 F7 **Purchena** Spain
99 N10 **Purdin** Missouri
98 F7 **Purdum** Nebraska
110 C5 **Purdy** Missouri
145 E3 **Pureora** *mt* New Zealand
124 H8 **Purépero** Mexico
145 E1 **Purerua** New Zealand
9 E6 **Purewell** England
106 G4 **Purgatoire** *R* Colorado
116 N3 **Purgatory** Alaska
38 M5 **Purgstall** Austria
75 L9 **Puri** India
128 D3 **Purificación** Colombia
145 E2 **Puriri** New Zealand
9 F5 **Purley** England
25 C3 **Purmerend** Netherlands
74 G9 **Purna** India
138 B2 **Purndu Saltpan** S Australia
75 M6 **Purnea** India
52 E3 **Purnema** U.S.S.R.
118 F9 **Purple Springs** Alberta
68 F6 **Pursat** Cambodia
128 E4 **Purué** *R* Brazil
70 D5 **Puruktjahu** Kalimantan
128 F4 **Purus** *R* Brazil
29 O10 **Puruvesi** *L* Finland
111 G10 **Purvis** Mississippi
47 G2 **Pŭrvomay** Bulgaria
70 N9 **Purwodadi** Java
70 M9 **Purwokerto** Java
70 M9 **Purworedjo** Java
110 H5 **Puryear** Tennessee
66 B4 **Pusa** China
70 B4 **Pusa** Sarawak
52 C6 **Puša** U.S.S.R.
74 G9 **Pusad** India
52 B6 **Pušalotas** U.S.S.R.
65 H7 **Pusan** S Korea
71 G7 **Pusan Pt** Mindanao Philippines
65 D6 **Pushang** China
95 T2 **Pushaw L** Maine
52 D5 **Pushkin** U.S.S.R.
54 J1 **Pushkino** U.S.S.R.
52 E3 **Pushlakhta** U.S.S.R.
123 Q6 **Pushthrough** Nfld
77 H4 **Pusht-i-Rud** *reg* Afghanistan
120 E4 **Puskaskwa Nat. Park** Ontario
121 O3 **Puskitamika L** Quebec
48 G3 **Püspökladány** Hungary
20 J5 **Pussay** France
22 H4 **Pussemange** Belgium
38 K7 **Pusterwald** Austria
52 C6 **Pustoshka** U.S.S.R.
102 B3 **Putah Cr** California
67 G5 **Pu-tai** Taiwan
71 M9 **Putain** Timor Indonesia
20 E4 **Putanges** France
75 R5 **Putao** Burma
145 E3 **Putaruru** New Zealand
30 G1 **Putbus** E Germany
70 P9 **Puteran** *isld* Indonesia
67 F4 **Putian** China
43 H8 **Putignano** Italy
48 J3 **Putila** U.S.S.R.
52 F5 **Putilovo** U.S.S.R.
70 B6 **Puting Tg** *C* Kalimantan
54 E5 **Putivl'** U.S.S.R.
33 Q6 **Putlitz** E Germany
48 K3 **Putna** Romania
95 Q5 **Putnam** Connecticut
108 E8 **Putnam** Oklahoma
109 H3 **Putnam** Texas
112 C6 **Putney** Georgia
98 H4 **Putney** S Dakota
95 P4 **Putney** Vermont
51 J2 **Putorana, Gory** *mt* U.S.S.R.
145 F3 **Putorino** New Zealand
83 J9 **Puttalam** Sri Lanka
83 J9 **Puttalam Lag** Sri Lanka
22 G1 **Putte** Belgium
36 B5 **Puttelange** France
33 O5 **Püttelkow** E Germany
25 E4 **Putten** Netherlands
28 G7 **Puttgarden** W Germany
36 B5 **Püttlingen** W Germany
54 L8 **Putugino** U.S.S.R.
83 K8 **Putukkudiyirippu** Sri Lanka
128 C3 **Putumayo** *div* Colombia
128 D4 **Putumayo** *R* Peru/Colombia
67 G1 **Putuo Shan** *isld* China
70 C4 **Putussibau** Kalimantan
33 T5 **Putzar** E Germany
135 U5 **Puuanahulu** Hawaiian Is
135 U5 **Puu Hualalei** *crater* Hawaiian Is
135 S3 **Puukoli** Hawaiian Is
29 M10 **Puulavesi** *L* Finland
29 N10 **Puumala** Finland
22 G1 **Puurs** Belgium
135 N1 **Puuwai** Hawaiian Is
Puxian *see* **Pucheng**
65 A6 **Pu Xian** China
117 M12 **Puyallup** Washington
65 C7 **Puyang** China
18 G7 **Puy de Dôme** *dep* France
18 G7 **Puy-de-Sancy** *mt* France
131 A8 **Puyehue, L de** Chile
131 B8 **Puyehue, P. de** Argentina
131 A8 **Puyehue, V** Chile
19 Q14 **Puy Gris** *mt* France
18 G9 **Puylaurens** France
18 H7 **Puy, le** France
18 F8 **Puy l'Evêque** France
18 G7 **Puy Mary** *mt* France
20 H2 **Puys** France
52 H4 **Puzla** U.S.S.R.
88 B6 **Pweto** Zaïre
68 B2 **Pwinbyu** Burma
8 B2 **Pwllheli** Wales
52 E2 **Pyalitsa** U.S.S.R.
52 E4 **Pyal'ma** U.S.S.R.
68 B3 **Pyalo** Burma
68 B5 **Pyamalaw** *R* Burma
52 F6 **Pyana** *R* U.S.S.R.
57 E6 **Pyandzh** *R* U.S.S.R./Afghanistan
52 J4 **Pyanteg** U.S.S.R.
52 D2 **Pyaozero, Oz** *L* U.S.S.R.

76 C3 Pyapalli India
68 B4 Pyapon Burma
51 H1 Pyasina R U.S.S.R.
53 F11 Pyatigorsk U.S.S.R.
54 E6 Pyatikhatki U.S.S.R.
52 H4 Pyatigory U.S.S.R.
110 D5 Pyatt Arkansas
52 H6 Pychas U.S.S.R.
116 M7 Pye Is Alaska
29 M8 Pyhäjärvi Finland
27 M11 Pyhäjärvi L Finland
29 L7 Pyhäjoki Finland
29 J11 Pyhäranta Finland
29 O9 Pyhäselkä Finland
38 N5 Pyhra Austria
68 C3 Pyinmana Burma
8 C4 Pyle Wales
29 L9 Pylkönmäki Finland
94 G5 Pymatuning Res Ohio/Penn
69 A9 Pygmalion Pt Nicobar Is
59 J3 Pyŏktong N Korea
65 F5 Pyŏngyang N Korea
100 F9 Pyramid Nevada
103 K6 Pyramid Canyon Ariz/Nev
139 G6 Pyramid Hill Victoria
106 C1 Pyramid Pk Colorado
94 A2 Pyramid Pt Michigan
102 E2 Pyramid Rge Nevada
18 F9 Pyrénées mts France/Spain
18 E9 Pyrénées Atlantiques dep France
18 G10 Pyrénées-Orientales dep France
142 B5 Pyrton,Mt W Australia
31 H2 Pyrzyce Poland
52 G5 Pyshchug U.S.S.R.
55 D3 Pyshma U.S.S.R.
56 C6 Pytalovo U.S.S.R.
121 O6 Pythonga, L Quebec
68 C3 Pyu Burma
68 C3 Pyu R Burma
68 C4 Pyuntaza Burma
31 K3 Pyzdry Poland

84 E3 Qaddāhiyah, Al Libya
74 F3 Qadian India
80 G4 Qafqafa Jordan
58 G2 Qagan China
Qagan Nur see Zhengxiangbai Qi
65 B3 Qagan Nur China
65 B4 Qagan Nur L China
65 C3 Qagan Nur L China
65 F2 Qagan Nur L China
65 D1 Qagan Qulut China
65 D3 Qagan Us China
115 P5 Qagssimiut Greenland
65 B4 Qahar Youyi Houqi China
65 B4 Qahar Youyi Qianqi China
65 B4 Qahar Youyi Zhongqi China
Câhira, El see Cairo
66 E4 Qaidam Pendi reg China
77 J4 Qala Bist Afghanistan
86 G3 Qala'en Nahl Sudan
77 J3 Qala-i-Ghor Afghanistan
77 H3 Qala-i-Kāl Afghanistan
77 K3 Qalāt Afghanistan
79 F3 Qal'at el Marqab Syria
80 F4 Qal'at er Rabad Jordan
78 L6 Qal'at Sālih Iraq
80 C5 Qalqiliya Israel
80 E6 Qalya Jordan
79 B8 Qalyūb Egypt
80 G3 Qam Jordan
74 C5 Qambar Pakistan
66 F5 Qamdo reg China
84 F3 Qaminis Libya
79 H3 Qamishliye, El Syria
74 C3 Qamruddin Karez Pakistan
80 D5 Qana Jordan
65 C3 Qangdin Gol China
65 C3 Qangdin Sum China
79 C8 Qantara, El Egypt
84 H4 Qara Egypt
80 D5 Qarawat Bani Hassan Jordan
79 G3 Qardāha Syria
78 L2 Qareh Su R Iran
79 C10 Qarn el Kabsh, G mt Egypt
66 D4 Qargan He R China
84 E3 Qaryahash Sharqiyah Libya
79 H4 Qaryatein, El Syria
80 G7 Qaryat Falha Jordan
77 H2 Qasa Murg Afghanistan
80 F8 Qasr Jordan
84 G3 Qasr el Burayqal Libya
79 F8 Qasr ed Deir, J mt Jordan
84 H4 Qasr, El Egypt
79 H4 Qasr el Hayr Syria
78 K4 Qasr-e-Shirin Iran
80 G8 Qasr eth Thuraiyat Jordan
84 H4 Qasr Farâfra Egypt
79 G5 Qatana Syria
77 B7 Qatar sheikhdom The Gulf
77 B6 Qatīf, Al Saudi Arabia
79 G8 Qatrāna Jordan
84 E5 Qatrūn, Al Libya
84 H4 Qattara Depression Egypt
77 F3 Qāyen Iran
78 J4 Qayyarah Iraq
77 A1 Qazvin Iran
84 J4 Qena Egypt
77 E6 Qeshm Iran
77 C6 Qeydār Iran
77 C6 Qeys isld Iran
77 A1 Qezel Owzan R Iran
65 D4 Qian'an China
65 F2 Qian'an China
67 C3 Qiancheng China
67 C3 Qian Gorlos China
67 C3 Qiangu'ao China
Qianguozhen see Qian Gorlos
65 D7 Qiangwei He R China
67 C5 Qianjiang China
67 D1 Qianjiang China
67 C2 Qianjiang R China
67 E1 Qianshan China
67 E5 Qian Shan mt ra China
65 E4 Qianwei China
67 A2 Qianwei China
65 D4 Qianxi China
67 B3 Qianxi China
67 C3 Qianyang China
65 D3 Qiaotou China
67 E3 Qiaotou China
67 E1 Qichun China
67 D3 Qidong China
67 G1 Qidong China
66 D4 Qiemo China
67 C2 Qifeng Guan pass China
65 C6 Qihe China
65 B3 Qihreg China
67 B4 Qijiang China
66 E3 Qijiaojing China
Qike see Xunke
65 D5 Qikou China
74 B9 Qila Ladgasht Pakistan
74 D4 Qilaotu Shan mt ra China
74 A8 Qila Safed Pakistan
74 C3 Qila Saifullah Pakistan
Qili see Shitai
66 F4 Qilian Shan mt ra China
65 E4 Qilihe China
67 F2 Qimen China
65 D6 Qingcheng China
65 E6 Qingdao China
65 E5 Qingduizi China
65 C7 Qingfeng China
67 A2 Qingfu China
65 G1 Qinggang China
66 E4 Qinghai prov China
58 D4 Qinghai Hu L China
65 C6 Qinghe China
65 H1 Qinghe China
65 F4 Qinghecheng China
65 E4 Qinghemen China
65 F3 Qinghe Shuiku res China
67 F2 Qinghu China
65 A6 Qingjian China
59 G5 Qingjiang China
67 E2 Qingjiang China
67 C1 Qing Jiang R China
65 A6 Qingjian He R China
Qingkou see Ganyu
67 C7 Qinglan China
67 D7 Qinglan Gang inlet China
67 D4 Qinglian China
67 E3 Qingliu China
65 D4 Qinglong China
67 B4 Qinglong China
65 D4 Qinglong He R China
65 C6 Qingping China
65 J2 Qingping China
67 G1 Qingpu China
67 A2 Qingshen China
65 B5 Qingshuihe China
58 E4 Qingshui He R China
67 C3 Qingshui Jiang R China
67 G2 Qingtian China
65 C5 Qing Xian China
65 B6 Qingxu China
Qingyang see Jinjiang
58 E4 Qingyang China
67 F1 Qingyang China
Qingyuan see Yishan
59 J3 Qingyuan China
67 D5 Qingyuan China
67 F3 Qingyuan China
65 D6 Qingyun China
65 B7 Qin He R China
65 D5 Qinhuangdao China
67 C6 Qin Jiang R China
65 E5 Qin Ling mt ra China
65 B7 Qinshui China
67 C5 Qintang China
58 F4 Qin Xian China
58 F4 Qinyang China
67 G3 Qinyu China
65 B6 Qinyuan China
67 C6 Qinzhou China
68 J2 Qinzhou Wan B China
68 K3 Qionghai China
58 D5 Qionglai China
58 D5 Qionglai Shan mt ra China
68 K3 Qiongshan China
67 C7 Qiongzhong China
Qiongzhou see Qiongshan
68 J2 Qiongzhou Haixia China
67 B1 Qiping China
59 H2 Qiqihar China
77 C5 Qir Iran
80 D7 Qiryat Arba' Jordan
80 D2 Qiryat Ata Israel
80 D3 Qiryat Bialik Israel
80 C7 Qiryat Gat Israel
80 D2 Qiryat Motzkin Israel
80 D3 Qiryat Tiv'on Israel
80 D2 Qiryat Yam Israel
80 D6 Qiryat Yearim Israel
67 E6 Qisha China
80 D3 Qishon 'Emeq Yizre'el Israel
68 J2 Qishui China
66 D3 Qitai China
65 H2 Qitaihe China
67 A4 Qiubei China
65 C6 Qiu Xian China
65 E6 Qixia China
65 B6 Qi Xian China
65 C7 Qi Xian China
65 B4 Qixiaying China
65 J1 Qixing He R China
65 H1 Qixingpao China
67 D3 Qiyang China
67 E1 Qizhou China
65 C2 Qog Ul China
Qogur Feng mt see K2
77 B2 Qom Iran
Qomolangma Feng mt see Everest, Mt
66 D3 Qongkol China
115 O5 Qôrnoq Greenland
77 A2 Qorveh Iran
79 G4 Qoubayat Lebanon
95 P4 Quabbin Res Massachusetts
122 G8 Quaco Hd New Brunswick
74 D2 Quaidabad Pakistan
102 H6 Quail Mts California
143 B9 Quairading W Australia
32 G7 Quakenbrück W Germany
95 M6 Quakertown Pennsylvania
45 Q8 Qualiano Italy
85 E6 Quallam Niger
139 G6 Quambatook Victoria
139 J4 Quambone New S Wales
141 F5 Quamby Queensland
115 N5 Quanah Texas
128 F4 Quanaru, Ilha Brazil
68 J5 Quang Nam Vietnam
68 J5 Quang Ngai Vietnam
68 B4 Quang Tri Vietnam
67 B6 Quang Yen Vietnam
67 D5 Quanjiao China
69 G8 Quan Long Vietnam
67 E4 Quannan China
68 F7 Quan Phu Quoc isld Vietnam
94 K8 Quantico Virginia
120 E1 Quantz L Ontario
67 F2 Quanzhou China
119 O8 Qu'Appelle Sask
119 P8 Qu'Appelle R Sask
118 L7 Qu'Appelle R. Dam Sask
133 F4 Quaraí Brazil
131 G3 Quarai, R Brazil
32 L4 Quarnbek W Germany
122 G7 Quarryville New Brunswick
95 L7 Quarryville Pennsylvania
40 F6 Quart Italy
45 L2 Quartesana Italy
45 M5 Quartière Mt. Sacro Italy
43 C9 Quartu S. Elena Sardinia
102 H4 Quartzite Mt Nevada
102 G4 Quartz Mt Nevada
100 G1 Quartz Mt Washington
103 K8 Quartzsite Arizona
99 P7 Quasqueton Iowa
22 H5 Quatre-Champs France
117 K10 Quatsino Br Columbia
45 H2 Quattro Castella Italy
106 G7 Quay New Mexico
77 F1 Quchān Iran
101 P8 Quealy Wyoming
139 J6 Queanbeyan New S Wales
121 T6 Québec Quebec
130 F6 Quebra Anzol R Brazil
88 D9 Quebrabasa Rapids Mozambique
133 E3 Quebracho Coto Argentina
131 A8 Quedal, C. de Chile
133 G3 Quedas do Iguaçu falls Brazil
33 O9 Quedlinburg E Germany
17 G9 Qued Tlélat Algeria
95 L8 Queen Anne Maryland
117 L10 Queen Bess, Mt Br Columbia
8 G5 Queenborough England
115 M5 Queen, C N W Terr
133 E8 Queen Charlotte B Falkland Is
117 G9 Queen Charlotte Is Br Columbia
117 J10 Queen Charlotte Sd Br Columbia
145 E4 Queen Charlotte Sound New Zealand
117 K10 Queen Charlotte Str Br Columbia
99 O9 Queen City Missouri
109 N2 Queen City Texas
115 K2 Queen Elizabeth Is N W Terr
146 D3 Queen Mary Land Antarctica
117 D5 Queen Mary, Mt Yukon Terr
114 J4 Queen Maud Gulf N W Terr
146 G8 Queen Maud Ra Antarctica
13 G6 Queensbury England
140 A2 Queens Chan N Terr Australia
115 K2 Queens Chan N W Terr
139 G7 Queenscliff Victoria
13 E2 Queensferry Scotland
139 Queensland state Australia
142 B2 Queens Park dist Perth, W Aust
123 L8 Queensport Nova Scotia
118 E8 Queenstown Alberta
95 L8 Queenstown Maryland
144 B6 Queenstown New Zealand
89 E8 Queenstown S Africa
139 H8 Queenstown Tasmania
143 E9 Queen Victoria Spring W Australia
100 A2 Queets Washington
131 F4 Queguay Grande R Uruguay
36 E5 Queich R W Germany
16 C2 Queija, S. de mts Spain
129 L6 Queimadas Brazil
87 C7 Quela Angola
21 D6 Quelaines France
87 E7 Quele Angola
88 F10 Quelimane Mozambique
124 F6 Quelite Mexico
133 C6 Quellen Chile
106 B7 Quemado New Mexico
108 G7 Quemado Texas
Quemoy see Chin-men
133 E5 Quemu Quemu Argentina
22 B3 Quend France
9 G4 Quendon England
22 B3 Quend Plage France
107 P3 Quenemo Kansas
111 F10 Quentin Mississippi
89 F2 Que Que Zimbabwe
133 F5 Quequén Argentina
22 C2 Quercamps France
130 D8 Querência do Norte Brazil
125 J7 Querétaro Mexico
33 P10 Querfurt E Germany
124 D2 Querobabi Mexico
20 K2 Querqueville France
20 K2 Querrieu France
117 M9 Quesnel Br Columbia
117 N9 Quesnel L Br Columbia
22 D4 Quesnoy France
22 F3 Quesnoy, le France
22 E2 Quesnoy-sur-Deule, le France
106 E5 Questa New Mexico
18 D5 Questembert France
133 D2 Quetena Bolivia
99 Q1 Quetico Ontario
118 L2 Quetico L Ontario
99 P1 Quetico Provincial Park Ontario
74 B3 Quetta Pakistan
20 C2 Quettehou France
20 F3 Quetteville France
20 C4 Quettreville France
111 D11 Queue de Tortue R Louisiana
20 J4 Queue-lez-Yvelines, la France
20 K2 Quevauvillers France
121 O3 Quévillon Quebec
70 P9 Quezaltenango Guatemala
79 E8 Queziot Israel
71 C6 Quezon Palawan Philippines
71 E3 Quezon City Luzon Philippines
65 D7 Qufu China
87 B8 Quibala Angola
87 B7 Quibaxe Angola
128 C2 Quibdó Colombia
118 J1 Quibell Ontario
18 C5 Quiberon France
20 G2 Quiberville France
127 K10 Quibor Venezuela
87 B7 Quicama Nat. Park Angola
68 G3 Qui Chau Vietnam
32 L5 Quickborn W Germany
36 C5 Quierschied W Germany
117 F5 Quiet L Yukon Terr
22 F3 Quiévrain Belgium
22 E3 Quiévy France
118 G2 Quigley Alberta
133 F3 Quiindy Paraguay
103 M9 Quijotoa Arizona
124 F5 Quila Mexico
133 C6 Quilán, C Chile
16 E9 Quilates, C Morocco
141 H7 Quilberry Queensland
127 O1 Quilca Peru
100 C2 Quilcene Washington
87 B8 Quilengues Angola
133 E4 Quilino Argentina
128 D6 Quillabamba Peru
128 E7 Quillacollo Bolivia
18 G10 Quillan France
20 G3 Quillebeuf France
131 B7 Quillén, L Argentina
119 N6 Quill Lake Sask
131 B4 Quillota Chile
119 N7 Quill Lakes L Sask
21 B7 Quilly France
141 G7 Quilpie Queensland
87 C8 Quimbango Angola
18 C5 Quimper France
18 C5 Quimperlé France
71 F3 Quinabucasan Pt Philippines
71 F4 Quinalasag isld Philippines
100 B2 Quinault Washington
100 B2 Quinault R Washington
20 H2 Quincampoix France
126 D2 Quince Mil Peru
102 C2 Quincy California
113 E7 Quincy Florida
99 P10 Quincy Illinois
95 R4 Quincy Massachusetts
110 N1 Quincy Ohio
100 B3 Quincy Oregon
100 E2 Quincy Washington
20 C2 Quinéville France
68 F2 Quinh Nhai Vietnam
68 J6 Qui Nhon Vietnam
128 E3 Quiniguа, Cerro mts Venezuela
71 E5 Quiniluban isld Philippines
109 L3 Quinlan Texas
98 G4 Quinn S Dakota
103 J4 Quinn Canyon Ra Nevada
140 C6 Quinn, Mt N Terr Aust
100 G8 Quinn River Crossing Nevada
19 Q17 Quinson France
15 E5 Quintanar de la Orden Spain
125 P8 Quintana Roo terr Mexico
107 K2 Quinter Kansas
18 D4 Quintin France
17 G3 Quinto Spain
131 D5 Quinto R Argentina
107 P6 Quinton Oklahoma
119 N7 Quinton Sask
45 L1 Quinto Vicentino Italy
8 A7 Quintrel Downs England
94 G8 Quinwood W Virginia
88 H7 Quionga Mozambique
130 J10 Quipapá Brazil
15 B3 Quiraing Scotland
87 C8 Quirima Angola
139 K4 Quirindi New S Wales
131 B4 Quiriquina isld Chile
127 N10 Quiriquire Venezuela
121 L6 Quirke L Ontario
36 C5 Quirnbach W Germany
16 C2 Quiroga Spain
123 R2 Quirpon Nfld
88 H8 Quissanga Mozambique
87 F10 Quissico Mozambique
45 J1 Quistello Italy
87 C8 Quitapa Angola
126 D7 Quita Sueño Bank Caribbean
130 D6 Quitéria R Brazil
87 B7 Quitexe Angola
110 D6 Quitman Arkansas
113 D7 Quitman Georgia
109 P3 Quitman Louisiana
111 H9 Quitman Mississippi
109 M3 Quitman Texas
128 C4 Quito Ecuador
103 M10 Quitovac Mexico
20 H3 Quittebeuf France
103 M8 Quivero Arizona
128 C5 Quivilla Peru
129 L4 Quixadá Brazil
67 D4 Qujiang China
67 B1 Qu Jiang R China
67 C6 Qujie China
67 A4 Qujing China
46 D3 Qukës-Shkumbin Albania
80 G6 Quleib R Jordan
66 E4 Qumar He R China
58 C5 Qumarlêb China
89 F8 Qumbu S Africa
84 G4 Qunayyin, S. el Libya
80 G1 Quneitra Syria
72 E5 Qunfidhah, Al Saudi Arabia
66 D5 Qungtag China
83 M12 Quoin Chan Mauritius
140 A2 Quoin I N Terr Aust
141 K6 Quoin I Queensland
89 A10 Quoin Pt S Africa
119 N1 Quorn Ontario
138 E4 Quorn S Australia
129 J4 Quram Brazil
84 J4 Qus Egypt
84 J4 Quseir Egypt
77 G6 Qush-e-Qand Iran
67 C1 Qutang Xia Wu Xia China
87 E12 Quthing Lesotho
79 H2 Quweiq R Syria
79 B8 Quweisna Egypt
65 B7 Quwo China
58 E4 Quwu Shan mt ra China
67 A5 Quxi China
67 B1 Qu Xian China
67 F2 Qu Xian China
75 O4 Qüxü China
65 C5 Quyang China
67 E3 Quyang China
67 B7 Quynh Luu Vietnam
121 O7 Quyon Quebec
65 C6 Quzhou China

28 K5 Rå Sweden
27 F16 Råå Sweden
Raab see Györ
31 J7 Raabs Austria
38 N7 Raab Tal V Austria
29 L7 Raahe Finland
29 O9 Rääl-kylä Finland
25 F4 Raalte Netherlands
115 L2 Raanes Pen N W Terr
29 L5 Raanujärvi Finland
70 P9 Raas isld Indonesia
77 A5 Ra'as Al Khafti Saudi Arabia
15 B3 Raasay, Sd of Scotland
42 F4 Rab isld Yugoslavia
80 E4 Raba Jordan
71 J9 Raba Sumbawa Indonesia
48 D3 Rába R Hungary
48 F1 Raba R Poland
16 C3 Rabaçal R Portugal
18 F9 Rabastens de Bigorre Hautes-Pyrénées France
85 C2 Rabat Morocco
137 L2 Rabaul New Britain
Rabbah see 'Amman
117 K6 Rabbit R Br Columbia
98 D4 Rabbit Cr S Dakota
106 D1 Rabbit Ears Pass Colorado
145 D4 Rabbit I New Zealand
118 K5 Rabbit Lake Sask
117 N5 Rabbitskin R N W Terr
28 D7 Rabel W Germany
36 F2 Rabenau W Germany
77 E5 Rābor Iran
52 F6 Rabotki U.S.S.R.
37 P3 Rabštejn Czechoslovakia
112 D3 Rabun, L Georgia
46 D1 Rača Yugoslavia
44 C2 Racconigi Italy
99 M8 Raccoon R Iowa
126 G3 Raccoon Cay Bahamas
94 E8 Raccoon Cr Ohio
38 N9 Rače Yugoslavia
115 O8 Race, C Nfld
94 E8 Raceland Kentucky
111 F12 Raceland Louisiana
95 R4 Race Pt Massachusetts
100 B1 Race Rocks Br Columbia
101 N3 Race Track Montana
109 J9 Rachal Texas
69 D9 Racha Noi, Ko isld Thailand
79 F5 Râchaya Lebanon
69 D9 Racha Yai, Ko isld Thailand
68 G8 Rach Gia Vietnam
31 L5 Racibórz Poland
37 P3 Račic Czechoslovakia
94 F8 Racine Ohio
99 T7 Racine Wisconsin
122 D1 Racine-de-Bouleau, R Quebec
120 G4 Racine L Ontario
33 Q10 Rackwitz E Germany
37 O4 Racovský mt Czechoslovakia
46 E1 Radan mt Yugoslavia
48 K3 Rădăuţi Romania
37 P4 Radbuza R Czechoslovakia
13 F6 Radcliffe England
99 N7 Radcliffe Iowa
27 E12 Råde Norway
30 H4 Radeberg E Germany
37 Q1 Radebeul E Germany
33 T10 Radeburg E Germany
19 Q18 Rade d'Hyères B France
33 Q9 Radegast E Germany
38 M8 Radel Pass Austria
36 C1 Radevormwald W Germany
94 G9 Radford Virginia
140 B1 Radford Pt N Terr Australia
74 D7 Radhanpur India
142 D4 Radi Hills W Australia
118 K6 Radisson Sask
99 P4 Radisson Wisconsin
101 T10 Radium Colorado
98 K1 Radium Minnesota
37 N3 Radium-Brambach E Germany
138 F4 Radium Hill peak S Australia
117 P10 Radium Hot Springs Br Columbia
106 D9 Radium Springs New Mexico
70 K8 Radjabasa Sumatra
70 O9 Radja, I Indonesia
77 F1 Rādkān Iran
Radldorf see Bergsdorf
38 L6 Radmer-an-dem-Hasel Austria
47 H2 Radnevo Bulgaria
30 H6 Radnice Czechoslovakia
Radnor co see Powys
41 J2 Radolfzell W Germany
31 N4 Radom Poland
86 D4 Radom Sudan
46 F2 Radomir Bulgaria
31 L4 Radomsko Poland
37 P3 Radonice Czechoslovakia
31 K7 Radošina Czechoslovakia
31 M4 Radoszyce Poland
46 E3 Radoviš Yugoslavia
42 F2 Radovljica Yugoslavia
38 H7 Radstadt Austria
8 D5 Radstock England
38 L9 Raduha mt Yugoslavia
42 H5 Radusa mt Yugoslavia
52 B6 Radviliškis U.S.S.R.
119 N9 Radville Sask
118 E4 Radway Alberta
31 O6 Radymno Poland
31 M3 Radzanów Poland
31 L3 Radziejów Poland
31 N3 Radzymin Poland
31 O4 Radzyń Podlaski Poland
117 P4 Rae N W Terr
75 J5 Rae Bareli India
112 H3 Raeford N Carolina
115 L4 Rae Isthmus N W Terr
114 H5 Rae L N W Terr
118 B8 Rae, Mt Br Columbia
22 L2 Raeren Belgium
32 E9 Raesfeld W Germany
143 D8 Raeside, L W Australia
115 K4 Rae Str N W Terr
145 D1 Raetea mt New Zealand
145 E3 Raetihi New Zealand
131 E3 Rafaela Argentina
79 E7 Rafah Egypt
86 D5 Rafai Cent Afr Republic
80 D5 Rafat Jordan
17 G5 Rafelbûnol Spain
78 J7 Rafha Saudi Arabia
77 E4 Rafsanjān Iran
101 M7 Raft R Idaho
119 Q3 Rafter Manitoba
101 M8 Raft R. Mts Utah
26 H3 Raftsund Norway
86 E4 Raga Sudan
71 G7 Ragang, Mt Philippines
71 F4 Ragay G Philippines
28 J4 Rågeleje Denmark
33 R6 Rägelin E Germany
126 G3 Ragged I Bahamas
143 E10 Ragged,Mt W Australia
127 P6 Ragged Pt Barbados
145 E2 Raglan New Zealand
8 D4 Raglan Wales
111 K8 Ragland Alabama
108 D1 Ragland New Mexico
145 D4 Raglan Range New Zealand
107 M4 Rago Kansas
44 G2 Ragola Monte Italy
33 R8 Ragösen E Germany
28 G7 Rågø Sund chan Denmark
84 F4 Raguba Libya
33 Q9 Raguhn E Germany
26 H8 Ragunda Sweden
Ragusa see Dubrovnik
43 F12 Ragusa Sicily
71 H7 Raha Indonesia
86 G3 Rahad R Sudan
86 D3 Rahad el Berdi Sudan
Rahaeng see Tak
80 E8 Rahaf Israel
27 J11 Råhällan Sweden
47 K7 Rahat Dağ mt Turkey
32 J8 Rahden W Germany
86 H3 Raheita Ethiopia
86 E2 Rahib Sudan
80 D8 Rahiya Jordan
145 D3 Raholu New Zealand
74 F9 Rahuri India
16 B6 Raia R Portugal
45 P5 Raiano Italy
76 C2 Raichur India
71 K10 Raidjua isld Indonesia
75 K8 Raigarh India
102 G2 Railroad Pass Nevada
103 J3 Railroad Valley Nevada
139 H8 Railton Tasmania
37 K6 Rain W Germany
37 N6 Rain W Germany
37 J6 Rainau W Germany
138 F6 Rainbow Victoria
103 O4 Rainbow Br. Nat. Mon Utah
124 E9 Rainbow City Panama Canal Zone
141 G1 Raine I Gt Barrier Reef Aust
9 G4 Rainham England
100 C3 Rainier Oregon
100 C3 Rainier Washington
100 D3 Rainier, Mt Washington
100 B5 Rainrock Oregon
94 J7 Rainsburg Pennsylvania
94 C1 Rainy R Michigan
99 M1 Rainy R Minnesota
118 J2 Rainy L Minn/Ontario
99 N1 Rainy Lake Ontario
100 E1 Rainy Pass Washington
116 L5 Rainy Pass Lodge Alaska
118 H2 Rainy R Ontario
115 K8 Rainy River Manitoba
29 J8 Raippaluoto isld Finland
75 J8 Raipur India
74 G7 Raisen India
27 M11 Raisio Finland
22 E3 Raismes France
29 N5 Raistakka Finland
119 O2 Raith Ontario
145 D4 Rai Valley New Zealand
70 F4 Raja Kalimantan
70 B5 Raja, Bt mt Kalimantan
70 C5 Raja, Bt mt Kalimantan
76 E2 Rajahmundry India
76 D3 Rajampet India
70 B3 Rajang Sarawak
74 D4 Rajanpur Pakistan
76 C6 Rajapalaiyam India
74 D5 Rajasthan prov India
69 C11 Raja, Ujung C Sumatra
46 D2 Rajë Albania
75 L6 Rajgir India
31 O2 Rajgród Poland
80 F5 Rajib Jordan
80 F5 Rajib R Jordan
69 G14 Rajik Bangka Indonesia
75 J8 Rajim India
42 F4 Rajinac mt Yugoslavia
74 D7 Rajkot India
75 J8 Raj Nandgaon India
74 E8 Rajpipla India
75 N6 Rajshahi Bangladesh
76 D1 Rajura India
88 C2 Rakai Uganda
144 D5 Rakaia New Zealand
70 K9 Rakata isld Sumatra
145 F3 Rakauroa New Zealand
99 N6 Rake Iowa
144 A7 Rakeahua mt New Zealand
56 C6 Rakhmanoviskoye U.S.S.R.
77 J6 Rakhshan R Pakistan
145 E2 Rakino I New Zealand
26 L3 Rakisvaara mt Sweden
70 M8 Rakit isld Indonesia
145 E2 Rakitu I New Zealand
55 C5 Rakityanka U.S.S.R.
Raki-ura isld see Stewart I
27 E12 Rakkestad Norway
69 D8 Ra, Ko isld Thailand
31 J3 Rakoniewice Poland
87 D10 Rakops Botswana
30 H5 Rakovník Czechoslovakia
46 F2 Rakovo Bulgaria
33 S4 Rakow E Germany
52 F3 Rakula U.S.S.R.
52 G4 Rakulka U.S.S.R.
52 B5 Rakvere Estonia U.S.S.R.
111 G9 Raleigh Mississippi
112 J2 Raleigh N Carolina
98 E3 Raleigh N Dakota
112 L3 Raleigh B N Carolina
101 M1 Raley Alberta
108 F2 Ralls Texas
99 T3 Ralph Michigan
98 C4 Ralph S Dakota
107 O5 Ralston Oklahoma
95 L5 Ralston Pennsylvania
100 G3 Ralston Washington
101 R5 Ralston Wyoming
79 F9 Ram Jordan
117 M5 Ram R N W Terr
80 D4 Râma Jordan
125 M3 Rama Nicaragua
119 P7 Rama Sask
72 E2 Ramādi Iraq
106 F2 Ramah Colorado
106 B6 Ramah New Mexico
16 E1 Ramales de la Victoria Spain
129 K6 Ramalho, Sa. do mts Brazil
133 E4 Ramalio Argentina
80 D6 Ramallah Jordan
76 D6 Ramanathapuram India
89 E3 Ramaquabane R Zimbabwe
54 E4 Ramasukha U.S.S.R.
80 C5 Ramatayim Israel
80 C5 Ramat Gan Israel
80 C5 Ramat Ha Kovesh Israel
80 C5 Ramat Ha Sharon Israel
80 D3 Ramat HaShofet Israel
80 D2 Ramat Yohanan Israel
83 K10 Rambe Sri Lanka
36 E5 Ramberg W Germany
36 B7 Rambervillers France
83 K9 Rambewa Sri Lanka
127 J2 Ramble Jamaica
133 D4 Ramblon Argentina
20 J4 Rambouillet France
33 P6 Rambow E Germany
76 B3 Ramdurg India
123 P6 Ramea Nfld
52 E6 Ramenskoye U.S.S.R.
111 K9 Ramer Alabama
52 E6 Rameshki U.S.S.R.
83 J8 Rameswaram India
75 L7 Ramgarh India
139 J7 Ram Hd Victoria
77 A4 Rāmhormoz Iran
44 B2 Ramière, Punta mt Italy/France
22 H2 Ramillies-Offus Belgium
109 K10 Ramirez Mexico
109 J8 Ramirez Texas
109 J9 Ramirito Texas
86 H4 Ramis R Ethiopia
80 E1 Râmîye Lebanon
27 G14 Ramkvilla Sweden
80 C6 Ramla Israel
80 C6 Ramle Israel
27 G11 Rämmen Sweden
75 K6 Ramnagar India
27 H12 Ramnäs Sweden
48 J5 Râmnicu Vâlcea Romania
89 E3 Ramokgwebana Botswana
80 E3 Ram On Israel
54 L5 Ramon' U.S.S.R.
102 H8 Ramona California
94 B3 Ramona Michigan
107 P5 Ramona Oklahoma
98 J5 Ramona S Dakota
120 K4 Ramore Ontario
124 G5 Ramos Mexico
71 C6 Ramos isld Philippines
80 F1 Ramot Naftali Israel
87 E10 Ramotsua Botswana
116 M4 Rampart Alaska
116 R3 Rampart House Yukon Terr
13 E5 Rampside England
74 H4 Rampur India
75 L8 Rampur India
74 F6 Rampura India
68 A3 Ramree Burma
77 B1 Rāmsar Iran
142 F4 Ramsay Ra W Australia
32 H10 Ramsbeck W Germany
27 H12 Ramsberg Sweden
13 F6 Ramsbottom England
32 E9 Ramsdorf W Germany
32 F7 Ramsel W Germany
26 H8 Ramsele Sweden
112 H2 Ramseur N Carolina
9 F3 Ramsey England
110 G2 Ramsey Illinois
12 D5 Ramsey I of Man U.K.
95 N5 Ramsey New Jersey
120 H5 Ramsey Ontario
8 A4 Ramsey I Wales
9 H5 Ramsgate England
13 G5 Ramsgill England
28 B3 Ramsing Denmark
26 H9 Ramsjö Sweden
22 D1 Ramskapelle Belgium
74 H8 Ramtek India
79 G6 Ramtha Jordan
71 J9 Ramu mt Sumbawa Indonesia
136 K3 Ramu R Papua New Guinea
52 B6 Ramygala U.S.S.R.
26 G5 Rana inlet Norway
16 C1 Rañadoiro, Sa. de mts Spain
26 F5 Ranafjord inlet Norway
75 N7 Ranaghat India
69 J10 Ranai Indonesia
27 K12 Rånäs Sweden
27 E11 Rånåsfoss Norway
70 K8 Ranau, D L Sumatra
131 B5 Rancagua Chile
22 G3 Rance Belgium
20 A5 Rance R France
133 G2 Rancharia Brazil
117 F5 Rancheria Yukon Terr
101 S5 Ranchester Wyoming
75 L7 Ranchi India
129 G6 Rancho de Caça dos Tapiúnas Brazil
124 H6 Rancho Grande Mexico
106 E5 Ranchos de Taos New Mexico
126 D3 Rancho Veloz Cuba
131 A8 Ranco, L. de Chile
106 D1 Rand Colorado
109 J8 Randado Texas
99 N7 Randall Iowa
107 M2 Randall Kansas
99 M3 Randall Minnesota
14 E2 Randalstown N Ireland
43 F11 Randazzo Sicily
28 E4 Randers Denmark
Randers co see Århus
37 J4 Randersacker W Germany
26 L5 Randijaur L Sweden
100 D3 Randle Washington
112 H2 Randleman N Carolina
109 J1 Randlett Oklahoma
103 P1 Randlett Utah
28 E5 Randlev Denmark
99 L9 Randolph Iowa
107 O2 Randolph Kansas
95 S2 Randolph Maine
111 G7 Randolph Mississippi
98 J7 Randolph Nebraska
94 J4 Randolph New York
101 O8 Randolph Utah
95 P3 Randolph Vermont
99 S6 Randolph Wisconsin
123 T5 Random I Nfld
99 T6 Random Lake Wisconsin
20 G4 Randonnai France
102 G6 Randsburg California
27 D11 Randsfjord Norway
32 E5 Randzel sandbank W Germany
26 N6 Råneå Norway
20 E4 Rânes France
118 F5 Ranfurly Alberta
144 C6 Ranfurly New Zealand
69 E9 Rangae Thailand
70 C5 Rangantamiang Kalimantan
70 F6 Rangasa, Tg C Sulawesi
145 E3 Rangataua New Zealand
145 D1 Rangaunu Harbour New Zealand
111 J10 Range Alabama
95 R2 Rangeley Maine
101 R9 Rangely Colorado
109 J3 Ranger Texas
94 E8 Ranger W Virginia
120 G6 Ranger L Ontario
75 O5 Rangia India
145 E3 Ranginui mt New Zealand
144 D5 Rangiora New Zealand
145 F3 Rangitaiki New Zealand
145 F3 Rangitaiki R New Zealand
144 C6 Rangitata New Zealand
145 E4 Rangitikei R New Zealand
145 E2 Rangitoto I New Zealand
145 E3 Rangitoto Ra New Zealand
145 G2 Rangitukia New Zealand
69 D10 Rangkalanberandan Sumatra
70 L9 Rangkasbitung Java
68 C4 Rangoon Burma
68 C4 Rangoon R Burma
75 N6 Rangpur Bangladesh
69 F12 Rangsang isld Sumatra
33 S8 Rangsdorf W Germany
28 C6 Rangstrup Denmark
76 B3 Ranibennur India
99 N1 Ranier Minnesota
75 M7 Raniganj India
37 M2 Ranis E Germany
74 E6 Raniwara India
140 D5 Ranken R N Terr Aust
140 D4 Ranken Store N Terr Aust
110 J1 Rankin Illinois
108 F4 Rankin Texas
115 K5 Rankin Inlet N W Terr
139 H5 Rankin's Springs New S Wales
80 B8 Rannen Israel
141 K6 Rannes Queensland
55 B5 Ranniy U.S.S.R.
15 D4 Rannoch Moor Scotland
87 H12 Ranohira Madagascar
120 J2 Ranoke Ontario
68 D7 Ranong Thailand
69 E9 Ranot Thailand
26 G6 Ransaren L Sweden
36 D3 Ransel W Germany
99 S8 Ransom Illinois
107 L3 Ransom Kansas
94 K7 Ranson W Virginia
36 G3 Ranstadt W Germany
29 N9 Rantasalmi Finland
70 D6 Rantau Kalimantan
69 E12 Rantaukampar Sumatra
70 E3 Rantaupandjang Kalimantan
69 D11 Rantauparapat Sumatra
70 F6 Rantekombola, Bk mt Sulawesi
70 F6 Rantepao Sulawesi
20 K3 Rantigny France
110 H1 Rantoul Illinois
102 H1 Rant Pass Nevada
29 M7 Rantsila Finland
29 M6 Ranua Finland
131 A8 Ranue, R Chile
28 C3 Ranum Denmark
78 K3 Ranya Iraq
68 G3 Rao Go mt Laos
65 J1 Raohe China
36 B7 Raon-l'Etape France
36 C6 Raon-sur-Plaine France
67 E5 Raoping China
41 O6 Raossi Italy
137 R7 Raoul isld Kermadec Is Pacific Oc
65 C5 Raoyang China
144 C5 Rapahoe New Zealand
44 F3 Rapallo Italy
131 B4 Rapel R Chile
101 Q4 Rapelje Montana
115 N4 Raper, C N W Terr
94 H9 Raphine Virginia
14 D2 Raphoe Irish Rep
116 R3 Rapid R Alaska
99 M1 Rapid R Minnesota
94 J8 Rapidan Virginia
94 K8 Rapidan R Virginia
138 E6 Rapid B S Australia
119 R8 Rapid City Manitoba
98 C5 Rapid City S Dakota
121 R5 Rapide Blanc Quebec
121 N6 Rapides des Joachims Quebec
141 H2 Rapid Horn C Gt Barrier Reef Aust
99 U4 Rapid River Michigan
118 H4 Rapid View Sask
52 C5 Räpina U.S.S.R.
52 B5 Rapla U.S.S.R.
95 K8 Rappahannock R Virginia
70 F6 Rappang Sulawesi
41 J3 Rapperswil Switzerland
46 F5 Rapsáni Greece
128 E6 Rapulo R Bolivia
71 G4 Rapu Rapu Philippines
78 G4 Raqqa Syria
95 N2 Raquette R New York
95 N3 Raquette Lake New York
140 D1 Raragala I N Terr Aust
71 K9 Rarakah mt Flores Indonesia
95 N6 Raritan B New Jersey
40 G5 Raron Switzerland
134 A10 Rarotonga isld Pacific Oc
42 F3 Raša Yugoslavia
71 D6 Rasa isld Palawan Philippines
77 D7 Ra's al Khaymah U.A.E.
86 H2 Ras Andadda C Ethiopia
133 E6 Rasa, Pta Argentina
131 E8 Rasa, Pta C Argentina
86 G3 Ras Dashan mt Ethiopia
52 B6 Raseiniai U.S.S.R.
80 G4 Ras el Aqra Jordan
86 A2 Ras el Cheil Somalia
80 F8 Ras el Ghor Jordan
84 H3 Râs el Kenâyis C Egypt
85 D5 Ras el Ma Mali
72 G5 Ra's Fartak C S Yemen
79 D10 Râs Ghârib Egypt
86 F3 Rashad Sudan
86 G1 Râs Hadarba C Egypt
79 F8 Rashādīya Jordan
86 B1 Ras Hafun Somalia
79 A7 Rashîd Egypt
77 A1 Rasht Iran
76 D5 Rasipuram India
77 G6 Rāsk Iran
46 D1 Raška Yugoslavia
86 G2 Râs Kasar C Sudan
86 A1 Ras Khanzira Somalia
28 D5 Raskmølle Denmark
77 J5 Raskoh reg Pakistan
31 N6 Raslavice Czechoslovakia
72 H5 Ra's Madrakah C Oman
79 C9 Râs Matarma Egypt
84 J4 Ras Muhammad C Egypt
85 A4 Ras Nouadhibou Western Sahara
133 D6 Raso, C Argentina
130 H10 Raso da Catarina Brazil
143 E8 Rason,L W Australia
47 F1 Rasovo Bulgaria
116 L7 Raspberry I Alaska
79 D10 Râs Shukheir Egypt
53 F7 Rasskazov U.S.S.R.
77 B6 Ras Tannurah Saudi Arabia
16 D9 Ras Targa Morocco
36 E6 Rastatt W Germany
28 A4 Råsted Denmark
32 H6 Rastede W Germany
Rastenburg see Kętrzyn
38 M4 Rastenfeld Austria
26 P1 Rastigaissa mt Norway
38 E7 Rastkogel mt Austria
26 M3 Råsto Sweden
26 M3 Råstoätno R Sweden
43 B8 Rasu, M mt Sardinia
80 G4 Rasun Jordan
145 E3 Rata New Zealand
71 J4 Ratahan Sulawesi
31 H6 Rataje Czechoslovakia
53 C8 Ratalovka U.S.S.R.
26 G9 Rätan Sweden
26 L8 Ratan Sweden
74 F4 Ratangarh India
68 D6 Ratchaburi Thailand
55 B4 Ratchino U.S.S.R.
110 C6 Ratcliff Arkansas
109 M4 Ratcliff Texas
143 B10 Ratcliff B W Australia
33 N5 Ratekau W Germany
74 H6 Rath India

100 J2 Rathdrum Idaho
14 E4 Rathdrum Irish Rep
68 A2 Rathedaung Burma
33 Q7 Rathenow E Germany
14 E2 Rathfriland N Ireland
14 C4 Ráth Luirc Irish Rep
14 D1 Rathmelton Irish Rep
14 E4 Rathnew Irish Rep
119 T9 Rathwell Manitoba
Ratibor see Racibórz
32 E10 Ratingen W Germany
116 L10 Rat Is Aleutian Is
Ratisbon see Regensburg
119 S2 Rat L Manitoba
74 F7 Ratlam India
116 C4 Ratmanova, Ostrov isld U.S.S.R.
76 A2 Ratnagiri India
83 K11 Ratnapura Sri Lanka
119 N5 Ratner Sask
106 F5 Raton New Mexico
19 O18 Ratonneau, I France
106 F4 Raton Pass Colorado
115 K7 Rat Rapids Ontario
117 R5 Rat River N W Terr
109 M1 Rattan Oklahoma
37 K3 Rattelsdorf W Germany
38 N7 Ratten Austria
38 E7 Rattenberg Austria
106 F4 Rattlesnake Buttes mts Colorado
107 L4 Rattlesnake Cr Kansas
100 H7 Rattlesnake Cr Oregon
101 S7 Rattlesnake Ra Wyoming
123 Q4 Rattling Brook Nfld
15 G3 Rattray Head Scotland
27 H11 Rättvik Sweden
33 N5 Ratzeburg W Germany
33 N5 Ratzeburger See L W Germany
71 B1 Rau Halmahera Indonesia
69 E11 Raub Malaysia
133 F5 Rauch Argentina
22 H4 Raucourt France
29 M5 Raudanjoki R Finland
115 S4 Raufarhöfn Iceland
27 E11 Raufoss Norway
36 G7 Rauhe Alb mts W Germany
37 K4 Rauhe Ebrach R W Germany
37 K4 Rauhenebrach W Germany
145 F2 Raukokore New Zealand
145 G2 Raukumara New Zealand
145 F3 Raukumara Range New Zealand
27 C12 Rauland Norway
27 M10 Rauma Finland
26 C9 Rauma R Norway
145 E4 Raumati New Zealand
36 E6 Raumünzach W Germany
52 C6 Rauna U.S.S.R.
27 B11 Raundal R Norway
70 P10 Raung, G mt Java
145 E3 Raurimu New Zealand
28 K4 Raus Sweden
36 F2 Rauschenberg W Germany
60 T1 Rausu Japan
29 M9 Rautalampi Finland
26 K3 Rautasjaure L Sweden
29 N8 Rautavaara Finland
29 O10 Rautjärvi Finland
101 L2 Ravalli Montana
31 O5 Rava Russkaya U.S.S.R.
45 R8 Ravello Italy
94 F9 Raven Virginia
95 O4 Ravena New York
119 O5 Ravendal Sask
102 D1 Ravendale California
22 C4 Ravenel France
13 E5 Ravenglass England
102 F7 Ravenna California
45 M3 Ravenna Italy
110 N4 Ravenna Kentucky
98 H8 Ravenna Nebraska
94 F5 Ravenna Ohio
45 L3 Ravenna reg Italy
20 C3 Ravenoville France
141 H6 Ravensbourne R Queensland
33 S6 Ravensbrück E Germany
41 L2 Ravensburg W Germany
13 H5 Ravenscar England
118 H9 Ravenscrag Sask
141 H4 Ravenshoe Queensland
25 E5 Ravenstein Netherlands
143 D10 Ravensthorpe W Australia
141 H5 Ravenswood Queensland
94 F8 Ravenswood W Virginia
121 L7 Ravensworth Ontario
74 E3 Ravi R Pakistan
109 L1 Ravia Oklahoma
18 H5 Ravières France
46 E1 Ravna Reka Yugoslavia
38 L8 Ravne Na Koroškem Yugoslavia
57 C2 Ravnina Dar'yalytakyr U.S.S.R.
115 K4 Ravn, Kap Greenland
28 D3 Ravnkilde Denmark
42 H6 Ravno Yugoslavia
48 E6 Ravno mt Yugoslavia
74 E2 Rawalpindi Pakistan
117 Q3 Rawalpindi L N W Terr
31 M4 Rawa Mazowiecka Poland
78 K3 Rawandiz Iraq
70 L9 Rawauntjal Java
121 R6 Rawdon Quebec
119 R4 Rawebb Manitoba
145 D1 Rawene New Zealand
98 B7 Rawhide Cr Wyoming
31 K4 Rawicz Poland
69 D9 Rawi, Ko isld Thailand
143 F9 Rawlinna W Australia
101 S8 Rawlins Wyoming
143 F7 Rawlinson, Mt W Australia
143 G7 Rawlinson Ra W Australia
133 D6 Rawson Argentina
94 D6 Rawson Ohio
38 N6 Raxalpe mts Austria
103 O8 Ray Arizona
99 N1 Ray Minnesota
98 C1 Ray N Dakota
116 M4 Ray R Alaska
76 D3 Rayachoti India
76 C3 Rayadrug India
75 K9 Rayagada India
79 G5 Rayak Lebanon
115 O8 Ray, C Nfld
59 J2 Raychikhinsk U.S.S.R.
112 D6 Ray City Georgia
77 E5 Rāyen Iran
55 B4 Rayevskiy U.S.S.R.
54 J8 Raygorodok U.S.S.R.
9 G4 Rayleigh England
118 E9 Raymond Alberta
102 E4 Raymond California
110 G2 Raymond Illinois
111 F9 Raymond Mississippi
98 B1 Raymond Montana
98 J5 Raymond S Dakota
109 N3 Raymond Texas
100 B3 Raymond Washington
139 K5 Raymond Terrace New S Wales
109 K9 Raymondville Texas
119 N7 Raymore Sask
116 L4 Ray Mts Alaska
111 D11 Rayne Louisiana
101 P2 Raynesford Montana
108 A1 Rayo New Mexico
68 E6 Rayong Thailand
111 E9 Rayville Louisiana
77 A2 Razan Iran
56 D2 Razdolinsk U.S.S.R.
48 M6 Razelm, L Romania
21 H9 Razès France
47 H1 Razgrad Bulgaria
47 F3 Razlog Bulgaria
18 B4 Raz, Pte. du France
110 B1 Rea Missouri
142 A1 Reabold Hill W Australia
117 D6 Reaburn, Mt Alaska
109 O2 Reader Arkansas
119 Q5 Reader L Manitoba
9 F5 Reading England
127 J2 Reading Jamaica
94 C5 Reading Michigan
99 L6 Reading Minnesota
95 M6 Reading Pennsylvania
119 M9 Readlyn Sask
95 P4 Readsboro Vermont
99 Q6 Readstown Wisconsin
109 L4 Reagan Texas
128 E7 Real, Cord mts Bolivia
128 C4 Real, Cord mts Ecuador
44 C1 Reale Italy
133 E5 Realico Argentina
109 J8 Realitos Texas
68 F7 Ream Cambodia
100 H2 Reardan Washington
15 G2 Reawick Scotland
112 D6 Rebecca Georgia
143 D9 Rebecca, L W Australia
100 H8 Rebel Creek Nevada
33 T5 Rebelow E Germany
117 P3 Rebesca L N W Terr
84 G5 Rebiana Libya
28 D3 Rebild Denmark
26 J5 Rebnesjaure L Sweden
128 G5 Reboja, Cachoeira de Brazil
29 P8 Reboly U.S.S.R.
47 F2 Rebrovo Bulgaria
60 P1 Rebun-suidō str Japan
60 P1 Rebun-tō isld Japan
133 E5 Recalde Argentina
48 G5 Recaş Romania
44 F3 Recco Italy
40 A2 Recey France
19 J5 Recey-sur-Ource France
143 D10 Recherche, Arch.of the W Australia
36 B6 Réchicourt le Château France
54 B4 Rechitsa U.S.S.R.
33 R6 Rechlin E Germany
22 L3 Recht Belgium
130 J10 Recife Brazil
89 D10 Recife, C S Africa
83 J12 Recif I Seychelles
32 G8 Recke W Germany
32 F9 Recklinghausen W Germany
101 U5 Recluse Wyoming
22 J4 Recogne Belgium
131 F2 Reconquista Argentina
19 O15 Recoubeau France
146 E10 Recovery Gl Antarctica
133 D3 Recreo Argentina
143 C8 Recruit Flats salt pan W Aust
31 J2 Recz Poland
110 E6 Red R Arkansas
98 K2 Red R Minnesota
69 F10 Redang isld Malaysia
22 K4 Redange Luxembourg
122 G7 Red Bank New Brunswick
95 N6 Red Bank New Jersey
141 K7 Redbank Queensland
Red Basin see Sichuan Pendi
111 H7 Red Bay Alabama
113 B7 Redbay Florida
123 Q2 Red Bay Labrador
120 J8 Red Bay Ontario
118 K6 Redberry L Sask
109 N10 Red Bird Airfield Texas
102 B1 Red Bluff California
141 G3 Red Bluff Queensland
143 C6 Red Bluff mt W Australia
108 D4 Red Bluff Res Texas/New Mex
9 F4 Redbourn England
110 G3 Red Bud Illinois
103 M6 Red Butte mt Arizona
98 A8 Red Buttes Wyoming
99 M2 Redby Minnesota
13 G4 Redcar England
106 D2 Red Cliff Colorado
141 L7 Redcliffe Queensland
89 F2 Redcliffe Zimbabwe
143 D8 Redcliffe, Mt W Australia
138 F5 Red Cliffs Victoria
111 H11 Red Cr Mississippi
101 R8 Red Cr Wyoming
95 L3 Red Creek New York
118 D6 Red Deer Alberta
119 Q6 Red Deer L Manitoba
119 P6 Red Deer R Sask
111 D11 Reddell Louisiana
13 E4 Red Dial England
113 E8 Reddick Florida
102 B1 Redding California
118 H1 Reddit Ontario
9 E3 Redditch England
33 O6 Redefin E Germany
98 E4 Red Elm S Dakota
129 K5 Redenção Brazil
85 F2 Redeyef Tunisia
111 D7 Redfield Arkansas
99 M8 Redfield Iowa
98 H5 Redfield S Dakota
101 L5 Redfish L Idaho
108 C6 Redford Texas
99 R5 Redgranite Wisconsin
9 F5 Redhill England
145 D4 Red Hill mt New Zealand
143 B7 Red Hill peak W Australia
111 K10 Red Hills Alabama
95 O5 Red Hook New York
100 H8 Red House Nevada
123 S6 Red I Nfld
98 C4 Redig S Dakota
123 Q5 Red Indian L Nfld
103 O9 Redington Arizona
98 C8 Redington Nebraska
110 L1 Red Key Indiana
52 E6 Redkino U.S.S.R.
117 O5 Redknife R N W Terr
103 K6 Red L Arizona
138 D4 Red L S Australia
103 M6 Red Lake Arizona
115 K7 Red Lake Ontario
143 D10 Red Lake W Australia
102 G7 Redlands California
98 K2 Red L. Falls Minnesota
95 L7 Red Lion Pennsylvania
101 Q4 Red Lodge Montana
118 C7 Red Lodge Prov. Park Alberta
145 E2 Red Mercury I New Zealand
13 G5 Redmire England
110 J2 Redmon Illinois
100 D5 Redmond Oregon
103 N2 Redmond Utah
102 G6 Red Mt California
112 C1 Red Mt Tennessee
37 L5 Rednitz R W Germany
99 L8 Red Oak Iowa
110 A7 Red Oak Oklahoma
109 L3 Red Oak Texas
21 A6 Redon France
16 B2 Redondela Spain
16 B6 Redondo Portugal
102 F8 Redondo Beach California
128 F3 Redondo, Pico mt Brazil
116 L6 Redoubt Vol Alaska
117 O9 Red Pass Br Columbia
118 J6 Red Pheasant Sask
141 G2 Red Pt Queensland
117 J6 Red R Br Columbia
111 D10 Red R Louisiana
119 U9 Red R Manitoba
109 J1 Red R Texas
Red R Vietnam see Song-koi
122 E7 Red Rapids New Brunswick
101 K4 Red R. Hot Springs Idaho
103 N9 Redrock Arizona
106 B9 Red Rock New Mexico
107 N5 Red Rock Oklahoma
119 P2 Red Rock Ontario
109 K6 Red Rock Texas
117 Q3 Redrock L N W Terr
99 N8 Red Rock Res Iowa
143 G9 Red Rocks Pt W Australia
8 A7 Redruth England
86 G1 Red Sea Africa/Arabian Pen
112 H3 Red Springs N Carolina
117 M9 Redstone Br Columbia
101 V1 Redstone Montana
117 K4 Redstone R N W Terr
120 J4 Redstone R Ontario
124 E9 Red Tank Panama Canal Zone
22 J4 Redu Belgium
119 Q9 Redvers Sask
118 D5 Redwater Alberta
121 L6 Redwater Ontario
109 N2 Redwater Texas
98 A2 Redwater R Montana
143 C7 Red Well W Australia
8 B1 Red Wharf B Wales
118 E6 Red Willow Alberta
98 E9 Red Willow Cr Nebraska
99 O5 Red Wing Minnesota
102 B4 Redwood City California
99 L5 Redwood Falls Minnesota
102 A2 Redwood Valley California
71 C5 Reed Bank S China Sea
94 B3 Reed City Michigan
98 D3 Reeder N Dakota
102 E5 Reedley California
101 Q4 Reedpoint Montana
106 C8 Reeds Pk New Mexico
100 A6 Reedsport Oregon
94 F8 Reedy W Virginia
112 E3 Reedy R S Carolina
138 D4 Reedy Lagoon S Australia
141 G4 Reedy Springs Queensland
144 C5 Reefton New Zealand
98 G5 Ree Heights S Dakota
14 C3 Ree, L Irish Rep
110 G5 Reelfoot L Tennessee
32 G6 Reepsholt W Germany
28 G5 Reersø Denmark
25 F5 Rees W Germany
94 D3 Reese Michigan
100 H9 Reese R Nevada
120 G3 Reesor Ontario
33 P6 Reetz E Germany
146 J6 Reeves Gl Antarctica
78 G2 Refahiye Turkey
111 J8 Reform Alabama
133 D3 Refresco Chile
28 F6 Refs Denmark
27 G14 Reftele Sweden
109 K7 Refugio Texas
31 J2 Rega R Poland
120 E4 Regan Ontario
80 D3 Regavim Israel
37 N5 Regen R W Germany
37 N5 Regensburg W Germany
37 N5 Regenstauf W Germany
119 R9 Regent Manitoba
120 F5 Regent Ontario
85 E3 Reggane Algeria
45 L4 Reggello Italy
43 G10 Reggio di Calabria Italy
45 J2 Reggiolo Italy
45 J2 Reggio nell Emilia Italy
129 H3 Regina Brazil
119 N8 Regina Sask
37 N1 Regis E Germany
77 J4 Registan Afghanistan
22 G4 Régniowez France
37 K4 Regnitz R W Germany
16 B6 Reguengos de Monsaraz Portugal
37 N3 Rehau W Germany
36 D5 Rehberg mt W Germany
32 H7 Rehden W Germany
33 Q7 Rehfeld E Germany
74 H7 Rehli India
32 J8 Rehme W Germany
33 O5 Rehna E Germany
87 C10 Rehoboth Namibia
95 M8 Rehoboth Beach Delaware
80 C6 Rehovot Israel
36 F3 Reichelshausen W Germany
37 N2 Reichenbach E Germany
38 L7 Reichenfels Austria
37 J1 Reichensachsen W Germany
38 F5 Reichertsheim W Germany
37 L6 Reichertshofen W Germany
101 N4 Reichle Montana
36 D2 Reichshof W Germany
36 D6 Reichshoffen France
143 G9 Reid W Australia
118 J8 Reid L Saskatchewan
140 B4 Reid, Mt N Terr Aust
141 H4 Reid R Queensland
112 E5 Reidsville Georgia
112 H1 Reidsville N Carolina
9 F5 Reigate England
27 N13 Reigi U.S.S.R.
25 C5 Reijen Netherlands
21 C9 Ré, Ile de France
103 O9 Reiley Pk Arizona
36 F5 Reilingen W Germany
19 P17 Reillanne France
80 A8 Re'im Israel
22 G5 Reims France
18 H3 Reims, Mt de France
133 C8 Reina Adelaida, Arch. de la islds Chile
99 O7 Reinbeck Iowa
32 M5 Reinbek W Germany
33 S4 Reinberg E Germany
119 U6 Reindeer I Manitoba
119 Q1 Reindeer L Man/Sask
26 F4 Reine Norway
140 D6 Reinecke, Mt N Terr Aust
27 C11 Reineskarvet mt Norway
33 M5 Reinfeld W Germany
145 D1 Reinga, C New Zealand
32 L10 Reinhausen W Germany
36 C5 Reinheim W Germany
33 S7 Reinickendorf E Germany
33 T7 Reinickendorf W Germany
16 E1 Reinosa Spain
26 L2 Reinöy isld Norway
37 P1 Reinsberg E Germany
36 B4 Reinsfeld W Germany
33 P5 Reinstorf E Germany
26 M2 Reisa R Norway
37 O6 Reisbach W Germany
29 L8 Reisjärvi Finland
38 H8 Reisseck mt Austria
25 F2 Reitdiep R Netherlands
38 G6 Reiter Alpen mt Austria
38 J7 Reitereck mt Austria
87 E11 Reitz S Africa
37 P2 Reitzenhain E Germany
27 H13 Rejmyra Sweden
31 O4 Rejowiec Poland
28 B6 Rejsby Denmark
27 H12 Rekarne Sweden
32 F9 Reken W Germany
60 R3 Rekifune-gawa R Japan
109 N4 Reklaw Texas
46 E1 Rekovac Yugoslavia
112 E6 Relee Georgia
98 G6 Reliance S Dakota
101 Q8 Reliance Wyoming
85 E1 Relizane Algeria
124 G4 Rellano Mexico
36 C2 Remagen W Germany
20 G5 Rémalard France
129 K5 Remanso Brazil
138 E4 Remarkable, Mt S Australia
70 N9 Rembang Java
36 F6 Remchingen W Germany
37 L2 Remda E Germany
126 E3 Remedios Cuba
124 F5 Remedios Mexico
32 G6 Remels W Germany
77 F6 Remeshk Iran
22 L4 Remich Luxembourg
121 L5 Rémigny Quebec
120 H3 Remi L Ontario
22 J4 Remilly-Allicourt France
99 T9 Remington Indiana
94 K8 Remington Virginia
40 E1 Remiremont France
33 N8 Remlingen W Germany
100 B6 Remote Oregon
22 K3 Remouchamps Belgium
19 N17 Remoulins France
83 K14 Remparts, R. des Réunion Indian Oc
36 H6 Rems R W Germany
36 C1 Remscheid W Germany
99 L7 Remsen Iowa
121 P9 Remsen New York
94 B3 Remus Michigan
19 O16 Rémuzat France
27 E10 Rena Norway
120 G4 Renabie Ontario
21 B6 Renac France
Renaix see Ronse
71 D2 Rena Pt Luzon Philippines
128 E4 Renascenca Brazil
21 C6 Renazé France
36 E6 Renchen W Germany
26 E10 Rendal Norway
28 A5 Renderne Denmark
32 L4 Rendsburg W Germany
121 L4 Reneault Quebec
123 U7 Renews Nfld
121 O7 Renfrew Ontario
12 D2 Renfrew Scotland
Renfrew co see Strathclyde reg
69 F13 Rengat Sumatra
67 C1 Ren He R China
67 D4 Renhua China
67 B3 Renhuai China
48 L5 Reni U.S.S.R.
94 G9 Renick W Virginia
120 J2 Renison Ontario
139 H8 Renison Bell Tasmania
86 F3 Renk Sudan
29 L11 Renko Finland
25 E5 Renkum Netherlands
115 R3 Renland reg Greenland
138 F5 Renmark S Australia
65 F1 Renmin China
26 D9 Rennebu Norway
137 N4 Rennell isld Solomon Is
36 E2 Rennerod W Germany
140 C4 Renner Springs N Terr Aust
37 L6 Rennertshafen W Germany
20 B5 Rennes France
27 A12 Rennesöy isld Norway
118 F1 Rennie Manitoba
38 J7 Rennweg Austria
102 E2 Reno Nevada
45 K3 Reno R Italy
99 L4 Reno, L Minnesota
122 G7 Renous New Brunswick
94 K5 Renovo Pennsylvania
119 M7 Renown Sask
65 C5 Renqiu China
28 C7 Rens Denmark
67 E5 Renshan China
67 A2 Renshou China
99 T9 Rensselaer Indiana
95 O4 Rensselaer New York
95 N4 Rensselaerville New York
25 E4 Renswoude Netherlands
100 C2 Renton Washington
37 K3 Rentweinsdorf W Germany
37 J3 Rentwertshausen E Germany
99 L5 Renville Minnesota
119 R6 Renwer Manitoba
22 H4 Renwez France
99 N7 Renwick Iowa
145 D4 Renwick New Zealand
65 C6 Ren Xian China
67 D7 Renxing China
18 E8 Réole, la France
76 E2 Repalle India
129 G4 Repartição Brazil
129 G4 Repartimento Brazil
40 E3 Repentis, Mt France
29 J8 Replot Finland
55 E1 Repolovo U.S.S.R.
145 F3 Reporoa New Zealand
40 E6 Reposoir, Chaine de mt France
26 J5 Reppentjåkko mt Sweden
111 J10 Repton Alabama
107 N2 Republic Kansas
94 D5 Republic Ohio
100 G1 Republic Washington
98 H9 Republican R Nebraska/Kansas
115 L4 Repulse Bay N W Terr
141 J5 Repulse Bay Queensland
26 P1 Repvåg Norway
98 F2 Reqan N Dakota
130 H6 Reqência Brazil
98 D3 Reqent N Dakota
20 B3 Reqnéville France
25 G4 Reqqe R Netherlands
100 A8 Requa California
128 D5 Requena Peru
17 G5 Requena Spain
18 G8 Réquista France
21 J7 Rère R France
145 F3 Rerewhakaaitu L New Zealand
15 G2 Rerwick Scotland
70 K8 Resag, G mt Sumatra
102 F7 Reseda California
26 J8 Resele Sweden
28 C3 Resen Denmark
28 C4 Resen Denmark
46 E3 Resen Yugoslavia
111 F11 Reserve Louisiana
98 B1 Reserve Montana
106 B8 Reserve New Mexico
119 P6 Reserve Sask
54 F7 Reshetilovka U.S.S.R.
41 N4 Resia Italy
133 F3 Resistencia Argentina
48 G5 Reşiţa Romania
122 E6 Resitgouche R New Brunswick
115 K3 Resolute N W Terr
144 A6 Resolution I New Zealand
115 N5 Resolution Island N W Terr
115 N6 Resolution L Quebec
32 L7 Resse W Germany
20 K3 Ressons France
22 D4 Ressons-sur-Matz France
127 K3 Rest Jamaica
12 D1 Rest and be Thankful hill Scotland
122 F5 Restigouche Quebec
119 Q9 Reston Manitoba
13 F2 Reston Scotland
121 L6 Restoule Ontario
31 N1 Reszel Poland
48 H5 Retezatului, Munti mts Romania
22 G5 Rethel France
32 K7 Rethem W Germany
32 L8 Rethen W Germany
47 G9 Réthimnon Crete Greece
42 C2 Retiche, Alpi mts Italy
22 J1 Retie Belgium
21 C6 Retiers France
118 E8 Retlaw Alberta
141 G7 Retreat Queensland
108 E8 Retrop Oklahoma
9 G4 Rettendon England
36 D3 Rettert W Germany
31 J7 Retz Austria
21 B7 Retz reg France
36 H4 Retzbach W Germany
21 G7 Reugny France
22 L3 Reuland Belgium
83 K13 Réunion isld Indian Oc
17 H3 Reus Spain
25 D6 Reusel Netherlands
41 J4 Reuss R Switzerland
33 Q10 Reussen E Germany
48 L3 Reut R U.S.S.R.
33 R5 Reuterstadt Stavenhagen E Germany
37 M3 Reuth E Germany
37 N4 Reuth W Germany
36 G7 Reutlingen W Germany
41 N3 Reutte Austria
98 C4 Reva S Dakota
80 C6 Revadim Israel
40 C6 Revard mt France
103 H4 Reveille Pk Nevada
18 G9 Revel France
142 G2 Reveley I W Australia
117 O10 Revelstoke Br Columbia
118 J6 Revenue Sask
45 K1 Revere Italy
9 F1 Revesby England
19 J4 Revigny France
117 H8 Revillagigedo I Alaska
20 C2 Réville France
98 K5 Revillo S Dakota
22 H4 Revin France
79 E7 Revivim Israel
28 F6 Revninge Denmark
26 O1 Revsbotn Norway
26 H9 Revsund Sweden
88 D9 Revubué R Mozambique
94 J5 Rew Pennsylvania
75 J6 Rewa India
145 E4 Rewa mt New Zealand
80 B7 Rewaha Israel
118 H6 Reward Sask
74 G4 Rewari India
99 Q7 Rewey Wisconsin
101 O6 Rexburg Idaho
107 K2 Rexford Kansas
100 K1 Rexford Montana
22 D2 Rexpoede France
122 H7 Rexton New Brunswick
80 D2 Reyba Israel
86 B4 Rey-Bouba Cameroon
28 N2 Reydhafells Tindur mt Faeroes
107 L6 Reydon Oklahoma
102 E7 Reyes Pk California
115 R5 Reykjavík Iceland
119 T7 Reykjavik Manitoba
119 M6 Reynaud Sask
112 C5 Reynolds Georgia
100 J6 Reynolds Idaho
99 Q8 Reynolds Illinois
110 K1 Reynolds Indiana
98 J9 Reynolds Nebraska
140 B2 Reynolds R N Terr Aust
138 D4 Reynolds, L S Australia
140 C5 Reynolds Ra N Terr Aust
94 J5 Reynoldsville Pennsylvania
109 J9 Reynosa Mexico
40 B5 Reyssouze R France
78 K3 Rezaiyeh Iran
37 K5 Rezat R W Germany
52 C6 Rēzekne U.S.S.R.
55 D3 Rezh U.S.S.R.
48 M3 Rezina U.S.S.R.
47 J3 Rezvaya R Turkey
41 K5 Rezzonico Italy
32 K6 Rhade W Germany
93 C3 Rhame N Dakota
41 L3 Rhätikon mt Switzerland
36 C4 Rhaunen W Germany
8 C3 Rhayader Wales
79 F4 Rhazir Lebanon
32 H9 Rheda-Wiedenbrück W Germany
32 F6 Rhede Niedersachsen W Germany
32 E9 Rhede Nordrhein-Westfalen W Germany
25 F4 Rheden Netherlands
9 F3 Rhee, R England
119 P7 Rhein Sask
36 E6 Rhein R W Europe
36 D6 Rheinau W Germany
36 B2 Rheinbach W Germany
36 D3 Rheinböllen W Germany
36 C3 Rheinbrohl W Germany
25 F6 Rheindahlen W Germany
32 F8 Rheine W Germany
41 J2 Rheinfall Switzerland
40 G2 Rheinfeldon Switzerland
32 E10 Rheinhausen W Germany
36 B3 Rheinland-Pfalz land W Germany
36 E6 Rheinmünster W Germany
33 R6 Rheinsberg E Germany
36 E6 Rheinstetten W Germany
41 L3 Rhein Tal V Switzerland
36 E5 Rheinzabern W Germany
40 F6 Rhêmes, Val de Italy
85 D3 Rhemilès Algeria
32 J10 Rhena W Germany
25 E5 Rhenen Netherlands
36 D3 Rhens W Germany
36 B1 Rheydt W Germany
33 R6 Rhin R E Germany
40 G2 Rhin R France
36 D7 Rhinau France
112 D6 Rhine Georgia
Rhine R France see Rhin R
Rhine R Germany/Switzerland see Rhein R
95 O5 Rhinebeck New York
99 R4 Rhinelander Wisconsin
33 R7 Rhinkanal E Germany
33 Q7 Rhinow E Germany
16 E10 Rhis R Morocco
41 K6 Rho Italy
127 K1 Rhoades, Pt Jamaica
95 Q5 Rhode I state U.S.A.
94 F9 Rhodell W Virginia
32 K10 Rhoden W Germany
94 C3 Rhodes Michigan
83 L13 Rhodes B Kerguelen Indian Oc
Rhodes isld see Ródhos
Rhodesia see Zimbabwe
112 F2 Rhodhiss L N Carolina
109 K2 Rhome Texas
8 C4 Rhondda Wales
19 O13 Rhône R France
41 H5 Rhône R Switzerland
19 N18 Rhône, Grand R France
19 Rhône Valley France
8 B4 Rhosili Wales
8 B1 Rhosneigr Môn Wales
8 C1 Rhos-on-Sea Wales
85 F2 Rhourd El Baguel Algeria
18 G7 Rhue R France
32 M9 Rhume R W Germany
18 D9 Rhune, la mt France/Spain
8 C1 Rhyl Wales
32 G9 Rhynern W Germany
15 F3 Rhynie Scotland
131 E8 Riachos, I de los Argentina
16 B2 Ría de Arosa Spain
16 A2 Ría de Corcubion Spain
16 A1 Ria de Lage Spain
16 A2 Ría de Murosa y Noya Spain
16 B2 Ría de Pontevedra Spain
16 B1 Ria de Sta. Marta Spain
16 B2 Ría de Vigo Spain
21 C7 Riaillé France
70 B5 Riam Kalimantan
45 N5 Riano Italy
16 D2 Riaño Spain
19 P17 Rians France
16 E5 Riansares R Spain
74 F2 Riasi Kashmir
69 F12 Riau, Kep islds Indonesia
16 E3 Riaza Spain
16 B2 Ribadavia Spain
16 C1 Ribadeo Spain
16 D1 Ribadesella Spain
17 H2 Ribagorza dist Spain
129 K4 Ribamar Brazil
17 H3 Ribarroja, Emb. de res Spain
17 J2 Ribas de Fresser Spain
130 D7 Ribas do Rio Pardo Brazil
16 B5 Ribatejo prov Portugal
88 G9 Ribauè Mozambique
26 K1 Ribbenesöy isld Norway
13 F6 Ribble, R England
28 B6 Ribe Denmark
28 B6 Ribe Å R Denmark
40 F1 Ribeauville France
22 D4 Ribécourt France
133 H2 Ribeira R Brazil
133 H2 Ribeirão Prêto Brazil
129 J5 Ribeiro Gonçalves Brazil
22 E4 Ribemont France
43 E11 Ribera Sicily
18 F7 Ribérac France
128 E6 Riberalta Bolivia
19 P16 Ribiers France
121 L5 Rib Lake Ontario
99 Q4 Rib Lake Wisconsin
99 R5 Rib Mt Wisconsin
42 F3 Ribnica Yugoslavia
33 Q4 Ribnitz-Damgarten E Germany
118 G6 Ribstone Alberta
118 F6 Ribstone Cr Alberta
109 K8 Ricardo Texas
45 M3 Riccione Italy
103 K7 Rice California
109 L3 Rice Texas
112 F6 Riceboro Georgia
99 N3 Rice L Minnesota
121 M8 Rice L Ontario
120 H5 Rice Lake Ontario
99 P4 Rice Lake Wisconsin
119 N8 Riceton Sask
99 O6 Riceville Iowa
18 H5 Riceys, les France
118 K6 Richard Sask
114 H3 Richard Collinson Inlet N W Terr
89 H7 Richards B S Africa
114 F4 Richards I N W Terr
144 A6 Richards, Mt New Zealand
116 N6 Richardson Alaska
109 O8 Richardson Texas
117 O3 Richardson I N W Terr
95 R2 Richardson Lakes Maine
143 C8 Richardson, Mt W Australia
144 B6 Richardson Mts New Zealand
114 F4 Richardson Mts Yukon Terr/N W Terr
119 N8 Richardson Sta Sask
85 A5 Richard Toll Senegal
98 D3 Richardton N Dakota
94 J4 Richburg New York
118 F7 Richdale Alberta
143 C10 Riche, C W Australia
21 F7 Richelieu France
121 R7 Richelieu R Quebec
20 J2 Richemont France
123 P3 Riche Pt Nfld
101 U2 Richey Montana
101 L6 Richfield Idaho
107 J4 Richfield Kansas
103 M3 Richfield Utah
95 L4 Richford New York
121 S8 Richford Vermont
102 E6 Richgrove California
110 B3 Rich Hill Missouri
122 H7 Richibucto New Brunswick
118 F4 Rich Lake Alberta
112 C5 Richland Georgia
94 B4 Richland Michigan
110 D4 Richland Missouri
101 T1 Richland Montana
95 N7 Richland New Jersey
100 H5 Richland Oregon
100 F3 Richland Washington
99 Q6 Richland Center Wisconsin
109 L4 Richland Cr Texas
112 K3 Richlands N Carolina
94 F9 Richlands Virginia
109 J4 Richland Springs Texas
118 J7 Richlea Sask
102 B4 Richmond California
9 F5 Richmond Greater London England
110 M2 Richmond Indiana
127 L2 Richmond Jamaica
110 M4 Richmond Kentucky
95 S2 Richmond Maine
99 M4 Richmond Minnesota
139 K5 Richmond New S Wales
145 D4 Richmond New Zealand
13 G5 Richmond North Yorkshire England
121 P7 Richmond Ontario
100 F5 Richmond Oregon
122 H7 Richmond Pr Edward I
121 S7 Richmond Quebec
141 G5 Richmond Queensland
89 C8 Richmond S Africa
139 H8 Richmond Tasmania
109 M6 Richmond Texas
101 O8 Richmond Utah
94 K9 Richmond Virginia
112 F6 Richmond Hill Georgia
121 L9 Richmond Hill Ontario
142 A4 Richmond, L W Australia
139 L3 Richmond R New S Wales
139 L3 Richmond Ra mts New S Wales
95 N4 Richmondville New York
118 H8 Richmound Sask
110 B7 Rich Mt Arkansas
33 R4 Richtenberg E Germany
111 H10 Richton Mississippi
99 L3 Richville Minnesota
94 D6 Richwood Ohio
99 S6 Richwood Wisconsin
94 G8 Richwood W Virginia
110 F3 Richwoods Missouri
32 M4 Rickling W Germany
9 F4 Rickmansworth England
17 G3 Ricla Spain
106 B4 Rico Colorado
40 F5 Riddes Switzerland
100 J7 Riddle Idaho
100 B7 Riddle Oregon
140 C6 Riddock, Mt N Terr Aust
121 P7 Rideau R Ontario
121 P8 Rideau Canal Ontario
121 O8 Rideau, L Ontario
98 B4 Ridge Montana
120 F2 Ridge R Ontario
101 N7 Ridgedale Idaho
119 N5 Ridgedale Sask
99 T10 Ridge Farm Illinois
95 O5 Ridgefield Connecticut
111 F9 Ridgeland Mississippi
112 F5 Ridgeland S Carolina
99 P4 Ridgeland Wisconsin
141 K6 Ridgelands Queensland
94 J7 Ridgeley W Virginia
95 M8 Ridgely Maryland
112 F4 Ridge Spring S Carolina
120 J10 Ridgetown Ontario
110 L1 Ridgeville Indiana
118 E1 Ridgeville Manitoba
112 G4 Ridgeville S Carolina
110 C1 Ridgeway Missouri
112 G3 Ridgeway S Carolina
99 Q6 Ridgeway Wisconsin
110 G5 Ridgley Tennessee
106 C3 Ridgway Colorado
110 H4 Ridgway Illinois
98 B4 Ridgway Montana
94 J5 Ridgway Pennsylvania
119 R8 Riding Mt Manitoba
143 D10 Ridley, Mt W Australia
142 C5 Ridley, R W Australia
118 J7 Ridpath Sask
98 F4 Ridqeview S Dakota
13 F3 Ridsdale England
38 H5 Ried Austria
37 M5 Rieden W Germany
37 M6 Riedenburg W Germany
36 D5 Riedseltz France
40 G2 Riehen Switzerland
118 B2 Riel Manitoba
32 H8 Riemsloh W Germany
36 H3 Rieneck W Germany
33 S10 Riesa E Germany
133 C8 Riesco, I Chile
43 F11 Riesi Sicily
33 O10 Riestedt E Germany
89 D7 Riet R S Africa
52 B6 Rietavas U.S.S.R.
32 H9 Rietberg W Germany
89 B3 Rietfontein Botswana
42 E6 Rieti Italy
41 O3 Rietzer Grieskogel mt Austria
18 G8 Rieupeyroux France
19 Q17 Riez France
22 G4 Riezes Belgium
16 E10 Rif dist Morocco
106 C2 Rifle Colorado
94 C2 Rifle R Michigan
52 B5 Riga, G of U.S.S.R.
142 B5 Riga, Mt W Australia
77 F5 Rigān Iran
121 Q7 Rigaud Quebec
19 J6 Rigaud, Mt France
101 O6 Rigby Idaho
110 F2 Riggston Illinois
37 M4 Riglasreuth W Germany
45 K4 Rignano sull'Arno Italy
21 F7 Rigny-Ussé France
115 O7 Rigolet Labrador
80 G4 Rihaba Jordan
29 M4 Riipi Finland
146 A7 Riiser-Larsenhalvøya pen Antarctica
42 F3 Rijeka Yugoslavia
25 C5 Rijsbergen Netherlands
25 G4 Rijssen Netherlands
25 R4 Rijswijk Netherlands
48 H2 Rika R U.S.S.R.
60 R2 Rikubetsu Japan
61 Q6 Rikuchū Kaigan Nat. Park Japan
61 P6 Rikuzen Takata Japan
110 J2 Riley Indiana
107 O2 Riley Kansas
106 C7 Riley New Mexico
100 F6 Riley Oregon
21 F7 Rillé France
47 F2 Rilski Manastir Bulgaria
128 C4 Rimachi, L Peru
145 E1 Rimariki I New Zealand
40 B1 Rimaucourt France
48 F2 Rimava R Czechoslovakia
118 C6 Rimbey Alberta
27 K12 Rimbo Sweden
94 H5 Rimersburg Pennsylvania
27 H13 Rimforsa Sweden
45 N3 Rimini Italy
80 E2 Rimmon Israel
48 K5 Rîmnicul R Romania
22 H4 Rimoqne France
122 D5 Rimouski R Quebec
36 H4 Rimpar W Germany
40 G5 Rimpfischhorn mt Switzerland
75 N4 Rinbung China
37 P6 Rinchnach W Germany
126 A2 Rincon Bonaire W Indies
106 C9 Rincon New Mexico
133 D2 Rinconada Argentina
124 H6 Rincón de Romos Mexico
28 A6 Rindby Denmark
70 K8 Rindingan, Bt mt Sumatra
71 J9 Rindja isld Indonesia
70 Q10 Rindjani,G mt Indonesia
28 B4 Rind Kirke Denmark
139 J8 Ringarooma Tasmania
28 E6 Ringe Denmark
27 D10 Ringebu Norway
41 K4 Ringelspitz mt Switzerland
32 E9 Ringenberg W Germany
33 T6 Ringenwalde E Germany
27 D11 Ringerike L Norway
12 D4 Ringford Scotland
37 J1 Ringgau W Germany
109 O3 Ringgold Louisiana
109 K2 Ringgold Texas
28 C5 Ringive Denmark
28 A4 Ringkøbing Denmark
101 P3 Ringling Montana
109 K1 Ringling Oklahoma
9 G6 Ringmer England
109 M1 Ringold Oklahoma
27 E11 Ringsaker Norway
28 H6 Ringsted Denmark
99 M6 Ringsted Iowa
27 H13 Ringstorp Sweden
74 F5 Ringus India
26 K2 Ringvassöy isld Norway
9 E6 Ringwood England
140 C6 Ringwood N Terr Aust
107 M5 Ringwood Oklahoma
139 H7 Ringwood Victoria
47 G7 Rinía isld Greece
133 C5 Rinihue Chile
131 A7 Riñihue, L Chile
28 D7 Rinkenæs Denmark
41 O3 Rinn Austria
12 B2 Rinns Pt Scotland
27 G16 Rinqsjön L Sweden
32 K8 Rinteln W Germany
22 B2 Rinxent France
99 Q8 Rio Illinois
111 G11 Rio Louisiana
99 R6 Rio Wisconsin
125 P5 Río Abajo Panama
130 C5 Rio Aleqre Brazil
124 G4 Rio Arreola Mexico
128 C4 Riobamba Ecuador
85 F8 Rio Benito Mbini Eq Guinea
128 E5 Rio Branco Brazil
133 G4 Rio Branco Uruguay
130 E9 Rio Branco do Sul Brazil
109 J10 Río Bravo Mexico
108 B5 Rio Bravo del Norte R Mexico
133 C6 Rio Bueno Chile
127 K1 Rio Bueno Jamaica
127 N9 Río Caribe Venezuela
133 D7 Río Chico Argentina
127 M9 Río Chico Venezuela
130 F8 Rio Claro Brazil
127 P3 Rio Claro Trinidad
127 K10 Rio Claro Venezuela
131 D4 Río Cuarto Argentina
132 Rio de Janeiro conurbation Brazil
100 A9 Rio Dell Scotia California
128 D2 Rio de Oro Colombia
85 B4 Rio de Oro terr Mauritania/Morocco
85 A4 Rio de Oro, B. de Mauritania
131 E2 Rio Dulce Argentina
133 D8 Río Gallegos Argentina
131 H4 Rio Grande Brazil
124 H6 Río Grande Mexico
131 B6 Rio Grande R Argentina
125 M3 Rio Grande R Nicaragua
106 D4 Rio Grande R U.S.A./Mexico
109 J9 Rio Grande City Texas
130 H8 Rio Grande do Norte Brazil
131 G2 Rio Grande do Sul state Brazil
106 C4 Rio Grande Res Colorado
90 F12 Rio Grande Rise Atlantic Oc
109 K10 Rio Grande Valley airport Texas
127 H9 Ríohacha Colombia
109 K9 Rio Hondo Texas
108 B2 Rio Hondo R New Mexico
128 C5 Rioja Peru
102 C3 Rio Landa California
130 J10 Rio Largo Brazil
102 C3 Rio Linda California
16 B5 Rio Maior Portugal
109 J6 Riomedina Texas
18 G7 Riom ès Montagne France
133 E3 Río Muerto Argentina
133 D1 Ríos Mulatos Bolivia
Rio Muni see Mbini
130 E10 Rio Negro Brazil
131 F4 Rio Negro dep Uruguay
131 C8 Rio Negro prov Argentina
131 G4 Rio Negro, Embalse del res Uruguay
130 C6 Rio Negro, Pantanal do swamp Brazil
43 G8 Rionero in Vulture Italy
124 F3 Rio Palacio Mexico
17 F6 Riópar Spain
133 G4 Rio Pardo Brazil
127 M5 Rio Piedras Puerto Rico
130 F5 Rio Prêto, Sa. do mts Brazil
128 E8 Rio Quetena R Bolivia
129 L6 Rio Real Brazil
45 J2 Rio Saliceto Italy
130 J9 Rio Tinto Brazil
100 K8 Rio Tinto Nevada
71 C6 Rio Tuba Philippines
133 C8 Río Turbio Mines Argentina
19 O18 Riou, I. de France
128 C3 Rioverde Ecuador
125 J7 Río Verde Mexico
130 C6 Rio Verdi de Mato Grosso Brazil

87 G8 Rovuma R Mozambique
99 N7 Rowan Iowa
118 J1 Rowan L Ontario
106 E6 Rowe New Mexico
139 J3 Rowena New S Wales
108 G4 Rowena Texas
112 G4 Rowesville S Carolina
100 K8 Rowland Nevada
94 H7 Rowlesburg W Virginia
118 E7 Rowley Alberta
115 M4 Rowley I N W Terr
142 C3 Rowley Shoals W Australia
103 M9 Rowood Arizona
9 E1 Rowsley England
103 K5 Rox Nevada
71 E2 Roxas Luzon Philippines
71 E4 Roxas Mindoro Philippines
71 D5 Roxas Palawan Philippines
71 F5 Roxas Panay Philippines
112 H1 Roxboro N Carolina
127 N2 Roxborough Tobago
140 E6 Roxborough Downs Queensland
144 B6 Roxburgh New Zealand
Roxburgh co see Borders reg
95 N4 Roxbury New York
95 P2 Roxbury Vermont
27 H13 Roxen L Sweden
111 E10 Roxie Mississippi
121 S7 Roxton Quebec
109 M2 Roxton Texas
101 N7 Roy Idaho
101 R2 Roy Montana
106 F6 Roy New Mexico
100 C2 Roy Washington
98 H7 Royal Nebraska
14 E3 Royal Canal Irish Rep
99 U9 Royal Center Indiana
70 C1 Royal Charlotte Reef S China Sea
113 L12 Royal I Bahamas
120 B3 Royal, Mount Ontario
119 P1 Royal, Mt Ontario
89 F7 Royal Natal Nat. Park S Africa
94 D4 Royal Oak Michigan
113 F12 Royal Palm Hammock Florida
113 G12 Royal Palm Ranger Sta Florida
146 H6 Royal Society Rge Antarctica
118 C8 Royalties Alberta
18 E7 Royan France
19 O14 Roybon France
22 D4 Roye France
95 M6 Royersford Pennsylvania
142 C6 Roy Hill W Australia
27 D11 Röykenvik Norway
122 C4 Roy, L Quebec
26 G7 Röyrvik Norway
109 L3 Royse City Texas
26 C10 Röysheim Norway
9 F3 Royston England
112 D3 Royston Georgia
29 L6 Röytta Finland
31 N3 Różan Poland
46 E3 Rožden Yugoslavia
20 A3 Rozel Jersey, Channel Is
107 L3 Rozel Kansas
20 B3 Rozel, Pte.du France
98 A5 Rozet Wyoming
31 L1 Rozewie C Poland
55 F5 Rozhdestvenka U.S.S.R.
52 G5 Rozhdestvenskoye U.S.S.R.
22 G4 Rozoy France
31 M4 Rozprza Poland
31 N5 Rozwadów Poland
46 E1 Rtanj mt Yugoslavia
87 G7 Ruaha, Gt R Tanzania
88 E5 Ruaha Nat. Park Tanzania
145 F4 Ruahine Range New Zealand
145 E1 Ruakaka New Zealand
145 E2 Ruakura Jun New Zealand
71 J4 Ruang isld Indonesia
145 E3 Ruapehu vol New Zealand
144 B7 Ruapuke I New Zealand
145 F3 Ruatahuna New Zealand
144 C5 Ruatapu New Zealand
71 J9 Rua, Tg C Sumba Indonesia
145 F3 Ruatoki New Zealand
145 G2 Ruatoria New Zealand
145 E2 Ruawai New Zealand
77 C7 Ru'ays U.A.E.
83 G3 Rub al Khali des Saudi Arabia
33 N9 Rübeland E Germany
60 R2 Rubeshibe Japan
54 K7 Rubezhnoye U.S.S.R.
15 C2 Rubha Coigeach Scotland
15 B3 Rubha Hunish Scotland
15 C3 Rubha Reidh Scotland
86 E5 Rubi R Zaïre
102 D3 Rubicon R California
45 J2 Rubiera Italy
133 G2 Rubinéia Brazil
124 F3 Rubio Mexico
16 E3 Rubio mt Spain
28 D2 Rubjerg Knude hill Denmark
56 B5 Rubtsovsk U.S.S.R.
116 K4 Ruby Alaska
103 N10 Ruby Arizona
100 H1 Ruby Washington
101 N4 Ruby R Montana
103 J1 Ruby Dome peak Nevada
103 J1 Ruby L Nevada
103 J1 Ruby Mts Nevada
103 J1 Ruby Valley Nevada
100 B7 Ruch Oregon
52 H4 Ruch' U.S.S.R.
67 D4 Rucheng China
52 F2 Ruch'i U.S.S.R.
Ruchugi see Uvinza
27 H14 Ruda Sweden
143 E6 Rudall, R W Australia
140 B6 Rudalls R N Terr Aust
77 E6 Rudan Iran
75 J5 Rudauli India
77 H4 Rudbar Afghanistan
77 A1 Rudbār Iran
28 B7 Rudbøl Denmark
118 K6 Ruddell Sask
22 E1 Ruddervoorde Belgium
119 R3 Ruddock Manitoba
116 P6 Rude R Alaska
38 L8 Ruden Austria
33 T4 Ruden isld E Germany
36 H6 Rudersberg W Germany
33 T8 Rudersdorf E Germany
36 D4 Rüdesheim W Germany
31 O6 Rudki U.S.S.R.
28 F7 Rudkøbing Denmark
31 J4 Rudna Poland
59 L3 Rudnaya Pristan' U.S.S.R.
52 H5 Rudnichnyy U.S.S.R.
47 J2 Rudnik Bulgaria
31 N5 Rudnik Poland
54 C2 Rudnya U.S.S.R.
55 D4 Rudnyy U.S.S.R.
Rudok see Rutog
46 D3 Rudoka Planina mt Yugoslavia
50 E1 Rudol'fa, O isld U.S.S.R.
86 G5 Rudolf, L Kenya
37 L2 Rudolstadt E Germany
67 G1 Rudong China
77 B1 Rūd Sar Iran
28 G5 Ruds Vedby Denmark
101 P1 Rudyard Montana
22 B3 Rue France
120 J5 Ruel Ontario
20 K3 Rue St. Pierre, la France
86 F3 Rufa'a Sudan
21 F9 Ruffec Charente France
21 H8 Ruffec Indre France
21 C6 Ruffigne France
112 G4 Ruffin S Carolina
88 F6 Rufiji R Tanzania
45 K4 Rufina Italy
131 E5 Rufino Argentina
85 A6 Rufisque Senegal
88 C9 Rufunsa R Zambia
100 F1 Rufus Woods L Washington
67 G1 Rugao China
9 E3 Rugby England
98 G1 Rugby N Dakota
9 E2 Rugeley England
30 H1 Rügen isld E Germany
144 A7 Rugged Is New Zealand
37 K5 Rügland W Germany
20 G4 Rugles France
29 P5 Rug Oz L U.S.S.R.
52 D3 Rugozero U.S.S.R.
80 B7 Ruhama Israel
75 N5 Ruhea Bangladesh
33 N7 Rühen W Germany
29 L11 Rühimäki Finland
37 J2 Ruhla E Germany
33 T10 Ruhland E Germany
33 S7 Ruhleben E Germany
37 O6 Ruhmannsfelden W Germany
33 P5 Rühn E Germany
33 P6 Ruhner Bge mt E Germany
32 F10 Ruhr R W Germany
35 Ruhr, The reg W Germany
88 E6 Ruhudji R Tanzania
88 E7 Ruhuhu R Tanzania
88 C10 Ruia R Zimbabwe
67 G3 Rui'an China
67 E2 Ruichang China
65 A7 Ruicheng China
108 C6 Ruidosa Texas
106 E8 Ruidoso New Mexico
108 B2 Ruidoso New Mexico
67 E4 Ruijin China
80 G7 Ruim el Hiri Jordan
22 E1 Ruiselede Belgium
9 F4 Ruislip England
25 H3 Ruiten Aa R Netherlands
124 G7 Ruiz Mexico
80 G7 Rujeim Salim Jordan
46 E2 Rujen mt Yugoslavia
52 C5 Rūjiena U.S.S.R.
29 O5 Rukatunturi mt U.S.S.R.
88 C10 Rukovakuona Mts Zimbabwe
88 D7 Rukuru R Malawi
88 C5 Rukwa reg Tanzania
88 D5 Rukwa, L Tanzania
107 J2 Ruleton Kansas
111 F8 Ruleville Mississippi
26 G10 Rullbo Sweden
99 L9 Rulo Nebraska
36 E5 Rülzheim W Germany
15 B3 Rum isld Scotland
48 F5 Ruma Yugoslavia
Rumania see Romania
140 C7 Rumbalara N Terr Aust
86 E4 Rumbek Sudan
71 J4 Rumbiä Sulawesi
31 H5 Rumburk Czechoslovakia
126 G3 Rum Cay isld Bahamas
22 E3 Rumegies France
22 L5 Rumelange Luxembourg
95 R2 Rumford Maine
22 G4 Rumigny France
22 E2 Rumillies Belgium
140 B2 Rum Jungle N Terr Aust
80 E2 Rummāna Israel
Rummelsburg see Miastko
60 P2 Rumoi Japan
88 D7 Rumphi Malawi
118 E7 Rumsey Alberta
95 N6 Rumson New Jersey
144 C5 Rumu New Zealand
141 H3 Rumula Queensland
144 C5 Runanga New Zealand
127 K1 Runaway Bay Jamaica
8 D1 Runcorn England
69 C11 Rundeng Sumatra
36 C1 Ründeroth W Germany
28 D7 Rundhof W Germany
26 A9 Rundöy Norway
71 J7 Runduma isld Indonesia
29 G8 Rundvik Sweden
71 M8 Rung isld Indonesia
70 C6 Rungan R Kalimantan
109 K7 Runge Texas
28 K5 Rungsted Denmark
88 D5 Rungwa R Tanzania
88 D6 Rungwe peak Tanzania
27 J11 Runhällen Sweden
36 E3 Runkel W Germany
27 H11 Runn L Sweden
99 N8 Runnells Iowa
108 E1 Running Water Cr Texas/Okla
119 Q7 Runnymede Sask
143 E6 Runton Ra W Australia
87 C9 Runtu Namibia
29 O10 Ruokolahti Finland
66 D4 Ruoqiang China
58 D3 Ruo Shui R China
29 L10 Ruovesi Finland
131 A8 Rupanco, L Chile
139 G6 Rupanyup Victoria
69 E12 Rupat isld Sumatra
101 M7 Rupert Idaho
95 O3 Rupert Vermont
94 G9 Rupert W Virginia
141 F5 Rupert R Queensland
121 L1 Rupert B Quebec
121 N1 Rupert, R Quebec
37 L6 Rupertsbuch W Germany
146 J9 Ruppert Coast Antarctica
36 G2 Ruppertenrod W Germany
36 F2 Ruppertsberg W Germany
36 C2 Ruppichteroth W Germany
33 S7 Ruppiner Kanal E Germany
128 G3 Rupununi R Guyana
80 G2 Ruqqād R Syria
80 G1 Ruqqād Sakhr Syria
25 F6 Rur R W Germany
112 G1 Rural Hall N Carolina
94 F10 Rural Retreat Virginia
128 E6 Rurrenabaque Bolivia
28 C6 Rurup Denmark
17 F5 Rus R Spain
87 F9 Rusape Zimbabwe
Ruschuk see Ruse Bulgaria
47 H1 Ruse Bulgaria
38 M8 Ruše Yugoslavia
37 P6 Rusel W Germany
106 F3 Rush Colorado
14 E3 Rush Irish Rep
9 E5 Rushall England
65 E6 Rushan China
57 F5 Rushanskiy Khrebet mts U.S.S.R.
107 L3 Rush Center Kansas
99 O4 Rush City Minnesota
106 G3 Rush Cr Colorado
9 F3 Rushden England
99 P6 Rushford Minnesota
94 J4 Rushford New York
118 K8 Rush Lake Sask
107 N7 Rush Springs Oklahoma
110 F1 Rushville Illinois
110 L2 Rushville Indiana
98 D7 Rushville Nebraska
139 H6 Rushworth Victoria
109 M4 Rusk Texas
113 E10 Ruskin Florida
26 K7 Rusksele Sweden
26 K7 Ruskträsk Sweden
98 F2 Ruso N Dakota
129 L4 Russas Brazil
38 H6 Russbachsaag Austria
113 L12 Russel I Bahamas
99 N9 Russell Iowa
107 M3 Russell Kansas
94 E8 Russell Kentucky
119 Q8 Russell Manitoba
99 L5 Russell Minnesota
95 M2 Russell New York
145 E1 Russell New Zealand
121 P7 Russell Ontario
94 H5 Russell Pennsylvania
143 E6 Russell Headland mt W Aust
115 K3 Russell I N W Terr
137 M3 Russell Is Solomon Is
119 Q2 Russell L Manitoba
117 Q4 Russell L N W Terr
116 M5 Russell, Mt Alaska
143 C7 Russell,Mt W Australia
143 E10 Russell Ra W Australia
110 L4 Russell Springs Kentucky
110 N1 Russells Pt Ohio
111 J7 Russellville Alabama
110 D6 Russellville Arkansas
110 K5 Russellville Kentucky
110 D3 Russellville Missouri
94 D8 Russellville Ohio
45 M3 Russi Italy
116 G6 Russian Mission Alaska
116 H6 Russian Mts Alaska
Russian Soviet Federated Socialist Republic see Rossiyskaya SFSR
50 F1 Russkaya Gavan' U.S.S.R.
55 F4 Russkaya-Polyana U.S.S.R.
55 D3 Russkaya-Techa U.S.S.R.
54 M6 Russkaya-Zhuravka U.S.S.R.
51 J1 Russkiy, Ostrova islds U.S.S.R.
77 L1 Rustak Afghanistan
78 K1 Rustavi U.S.S.R.
94 H9 Rustburg Virginia
89 E5 Rustenburg S Africa
32 H5 Rustersiel W Germany
109 P3 Ruston Louisiana
88 C3 Rutana Burundi
16 E7 Rute Spain
27 K14 Rute Sweden
33 S6 Rutenberg E Germany
32 F7 Rütenbrock W Germany
71 K9 Ruteng Flores Indonesia
102 A1 Ruth California
103 K2 Ruth Nevada
32 H10 Rüthen W Germany
112 F2 Rutherfordton N Carolina
121 L6 Rutherglen Ontario
12 D2 Rutherglen Scotland
94 K9 Ruther Glen Virginia
116 M5 Ruth Glacier Alaska
118 J7 Ruthilda Sask
8 C1 Ruthin Wales
98 K5 Ruthton Minnesota
99 M6 Ruthven Iowa
141 G6 Ruthven Queensland
88 E7 Rutikira R Tanzania
52 G6 Rutka R U.S.S.R.
99 R9 Rutland Illinois
98 J3 Rutland N Dakota
94 E7 Rutland Ohio
95 P3 Rutland Vermont
Rutland co see Leicestershire
68 A7 Rutland I Andaman Is
141 F3 Rutland Plains Queensland
118 H6 Rutland Station Sask
9 F2 Rutland Water L England
99 O3 Rutledge Minnesota
110 D1 Rutledge Missouri
66 B5 Rutog China
25 E3 Rutten Netherlands
120 K6 Rutter Ontario
25 F4 Ruurlo Netherlands
87 G7 Ruvu Tanzania
88 G5 Ruvu R Tanzania
88 E7 Ruvuma Tanzania
88 G7 Ruvuma R Tanzania
86 E2 Ruweiba Sudan
88 C1 Ruwenzori Rge mts Uganda
36 B4 Ruwer W Germany
65 B7 Ruyang China
67 D4 Ruyuan China
55 E4 Ruzayevka U.S.S.R.
48 M1 Ruzhin U.S.S.R.
48 E1 Ružomberok Czechoslovakia
88 B2 Rwanda rep Cent Africa
28 D4 Ry Denmark
28 D2 Ryå Denmark
47 H1 Ryakhovo Bulgaria
99 P7 Ryan Iowa
109 K1 Ryan Oklahoma
12 C4 Ryan, Loch Scotland
101 T8 Ryan Park Wyoming
101 L6 Ryan Pk Idaho
53 E7 Ryazan' U.S.S.R.
54 M3 Ryazhsk U.S.S.R.
57 H4 Rybach'ye U.S.S.R.
37 O3 Rybáře Czechoslovakia
52 E5 Rybinsk U.S.S.R.
52 E5 Rybinskoye Vdkhr res U.S.S.R.
31 L5 Rybnik Poland
48 M3 Rybnitsa U.S.S.R.
54 L2 Rybnoye U.S.S.R.
55 D2 Rychkovo U.S.S.R.
31 J5 Rychnov Czechoslovakia
31 L3 Rychwał Poland
33 S4 Ryckgraben R E Germany
117 O8 Rycroft Alberta
120 G6 Rydal Bank Ontario
28 B4 Ryde Denmark
28 G7 Ryde Denmark
9 E6 Ryde England
98 E2 Ryder N Dakota
100 B3 Ryderwood Washington
27 H14 Ryd, V Sweden
106 F4 Rye Colorado
28 D4 Rye Denmark
28 H5 Rye Denmark
9 G6 Rye England
95 R3 Rye New Hampshire
109 N5 Rye Texas
77 B5 R-ye Dalaki R Iran
101 Q3 Ryegate Montana
100 G9 Rye Patch Nevada
102 F1 Rye Patch Res Nevada
119 Q9 Ryerson Sask
20 D3 Ryes France
27 A12 Ryfylke Norway
13 G4 Ryhope England
31 N4 Ryki Poland
120 G3 Ryland Ontario
118 E5 Ryley Alberta
54 F5 Ryl'sk U.S.S.R.
139 J5 Rylstone New S Wales
31 N6 Rymanow Poland
31 K6 Rýmařov Czechoslovakia
55 F1 Rymovy U.S.S.R.
31 N2 Ryn Poland
52 E1 Rynda U.S.S.R.
53 G9 Ryn Peski des U.S.S.R.
28 F4 Ryomgard Denmark
61 P7 Ryōri-zaki C Japan
61 M7 Ryōtsu Japan
31 L2 Rypin Poland
48 L3 Ryshkany U.S.S.R.
28 F6 Ryslinge Denmark
32 F6 Rysum W Germany
61 O10 Ryūgasaki Japan
134 D4 Ryukyu Ridge Pac Oc
134 D5 Ryukyu Tr Pac Oc
31 H3 Rzepin Poland
31 N5 Rzeszów Poland
52 D6 Rzhev U.S.S.R.
77 C4 Sa'ādatābād Iran
33 R4 Saal E Germany
37 J3 Saal W Germany
36 F5 Saal R W Germany
38 G7 Saalach R Austria
37 M3 Saalburg E Germany
36 F3 Saalburg W Germany
33 P9 Saale R E Germany
37 M3 Saale R W Germany
36 C7 Saales France
37 L2 Saalfeld E Germany
40 F5 Saanen Switzerland
117 M11 Saanich Br Col
36 B5 Saar R W Germany
19 K3 Saarbrücken France
36 B5 Saarbrücken W Germany
36 B4 Saarburg W Germany
27 M14 Sääre U.S.S.R.
27 M13 Saaremaa U.S.S.R.
29 M5 Saarenkylä Finland
29 O10 Saari Finland
29 L9 Saarijärvi Finland
29 N3 Saariselkä mts Finland
36 B5 Saarland land W Germany
36 B5 Saarlouis W Germany
33 S8 Saarmund E Germany
36 B5 Saar-Wellingen W Germany
36 D7 Saasenheim France
40 G5 Saas Tal Switzerland
70 E3 Saätan Kalimantan
133 E5 Saavedra Argentina
131 A7 Saavedra, Pto Chile
125 L2 Sabá Honduras
127 N6 Saba isld Lesser Antilles
32 L9 Sababurg W Germany
48 F6 Sabac Yugoslavia
17 J3 Sabadell Spain
70 E2 Sabah state Borneo
69 E11 Sabak Malaysia
71 H5 Sabal Sulawesi
71 J8 Sabalana isld Indonesia
44 M5 Saba, Mt Italy
126 D3 Sabana, Arch. de islds Cuba
127 K5 Sabana de la Mar Dominican Rep
127 J10 Sabana de Mendoza Venezuela
128 D1 Sabanalarga Colombia
127 K9 Sabaneta Venezuela
70 F4 Sabang Sulawesi
69 B10 Sabang Sumatra
70 C6 Sabangan Teluk B Kalimantan
83 K11 Sabaragamuwa reg Sri Lanka
71 J8 Sabaru isld Indonesia
80 D4 Sabastiya Jordan
45 O7 Sabaudia Italy
128 E7 Sabaya Bolivia
41 M6 Sabbia, V Italy
45 H2 Sabbioneta Italy
77 G4 Şāberi, Hāmūn-e L Iran
107 P2 Sabetha Kansas
84 E4 Sabhah Libya
87 F10 Sabi R Zimbabwe
89 G5 Sabie R S Africa
52 B6 Sabile U.S.S.R.
45 N5 Sabina Italy
94 D7 Sabina Ohio
124 F2 Sabinal Mexico
109 H6 Sabinal Texas
17 G2 Sabiñánigo Spain
108 F8 Sabinas Mexico
125 J4 Sabinas Hidalgo Mexico
111 C11 Sabine R Louisiana/Texas
146 K6 Sabine, Mt Antarctica
42 E6 Sabini, Monti Italy
79 H2 Sabkhat al Jabbūl Syria
79 D7 Sabkhet el Bardawîl Egypt
71 E4 Sablayan Philippines
137 M5 Sable isld Coral Sea
115 N9 Sable, C Nova Scotia
123 N10 Sable I Nova Scotia
122 G10 Sable River Nova Scotia
120 H6 Sables, L. aux Ontario
120 H6 Sables, River Aux Ontario
19 O16 Sablet France
19 N18 Sablon, Pte. du France
19 N14 Sablons France
16 C3 Sabor R Portugal
131 G2 Sā Borja Brazil
94 H7 Sabraton W Virginia
18 E8 Sabres France
146 G3 Sabrina Coast Antarctica
28 E4 Sabro Denmark
16 C4 Sabugal Portugal
99 Q7 Sabula Iowa
47 L5 Sabuncu Turkey
70 P9 Sabunting isld Indonesia
77 E1 Sabzevār Iran
110 C4 Sac R Missouri
128 E7 Sacaca Bolivia
95 N3 Sacandaga Res New York
103 N8 Sacaton Arizona
99 L7 Sac City Iowa
43 E7 Sacco R Italy
45 L1 Saccolongo Italy
17 F4 Sacedón Spain
115 K7 Sachigo R Ontario
109 O8 Sachse Texas
36 F1 Sachsenberg W Germany
38 H8 Sachsenburg Austria
33 O10 Sachsenburg E Germany
32 K8 Sachsenhagen W Germany
32 K10 Sachsenhausen W Germany
114 G3 Sachs Harbour N W Terr
42 E3 Sacile Italy
95 L3 Sackets Harbor New York
122 H8 Sackville New Brunswick
110 B3 Sac, L Missouri
20 K5 Saclas France
95 R3 Saco Maine
101 S1 Saco Montana
71 F7 Sacol isld Philippines
40 B2 Sacquenay France
102 C3 Sacramento California
102 B2 Sacramento R California
108 B3 Sacramento Mts New Mexico
102 B1 Sacramento V California
103 K6 Sacramento Wash R Arizona
16 E8 Sacratif, C Spain
122 D5 Sacré Coeur Quebec
122 C5 Sacré-Coeur Saguenay Quebec
130 F6 Sacremento Brazil
48 G3 Săcueni Romania
18 E10 Sadaba Spain
77 B5 Sa'dabad Iran
72 E5 Şa'dah N Yemen
60 F12 Sada-misaki Japan
69 E9 Sadao Thailand
13 G4 Sadberge England
74 D2 Sadda Pakistan
141 G2 Saddle Hill Queensland
142 D4 Saddle Hill W Australia
100 A7 Saddle Mt Oregon
101 Q5 Saddle Mt Wyoming
68 A6 Saddle Pk Andaman Is
68 G7 Sa Dec Vietnam
48 K2 Sadgora U.S.S.R.
127 O3 Sadhoowa Trinidad
94 C8 Sadieville Kentucky
85 B6 Sadiola Mali
74 D4 Sadiqabad Pakistan
16 B6 Sado R Portugal
61 M7 Sado-shima isld Japan
74 E6 Sadri India
26 H5 Sadvajaur L Sweden
28 F2 Sæby Nordjylland Denmark
28 G5 Sæby Vestjælland Denmark
28 J6 Sædder Denmark
28 B4 Sædding Denmark
60 E13 Saeki Japan
60 E13 Saeki-wan B Japan
17 F5 Saelices Spain
32 G8 Saerbeck W Germany
28 E5 Særslev Denmark
22 K4 Saeul Luxembourg
Safad see Zefat
55 D4 Safakulevo U.S.S.R.
48 F2 Sáfárikovo Czechoslovakia
57 F5 Safed Khirs reg Afghanistan
77 L2 Safed Koh mt Afghanistan
38 O7 Safen R Austria
77 J4 Safer Afghanistan
142 A4 Safety Bay dist W Aust
80 D5 Saffārin Jordan
79 B9 Şaff, El Egypt
27 F12 Säffle Sweden
111 J9 Safford Alabama
103 P9 Safford Arizona
21 B7 Saffré France
9 G3 Saffron Walden England
85 C2 Safi Morocco
77 G4 Safidabeh Iran
77 A1 Safid Rud R Iran
41 K4 Safier Tal Switzerland
130 H6 Safiras, Sa. das mts Brazil
79 G4 Sāfita Syria
54 K3 Safonovka U.S.S.R.
52 G2 Safonovo U.S.S.R.
78 D1 Safronbolu Turkey
27 G11 Säfsnäs Sweden
80 G5 Safut Jordan
66 D6 Saga China
60 D12 Saga Kyūshū Japan
60 G12 Saga Shikoku Japan
60 C11 Saga Tsushima Japan
57 C1 Saga U.S.S.R.
60 D12 Saga prefect Japan
61 O7 Sagae Japan
68 B2 Sagaing Burma
59 L5 Sagami-nada B Japan
61 N10 Sagami-wan B Japan
94 H6 Sagamore Pennsylvania
86 G4 Sagan watercourse Ethiopia
119 N2 Saganaga L Ontario
120 H3 Saganash L Ontario
60 E12 Saganoseki Japan
68 D6 Saganthit Kyun isld Burma
76 C2 Sagar India
61 M11 Sagara Japan
88 F5 Sagara Tanzania
57 B5 Sagar-Chaga U.S.S.R.
116 N2 Sagavanirkok R Alaska
32 H7 Sage W Germany
101 P8 Sage Wyoming
101 P1 Sage Cr Montana
101 S8 Sage Cr Wyoming
27 G11 Sågen Sweden
26 H4 Sagfjord Norway
26 J5 Saggat L Sweden
95 P6 Sag Harbor Long I, N Y
94 D3 Saginaw Michigan
109 L9 Saginaw Texas
94 D3 Saginaw Bay Michigan
88 D2 Sagitu isld Uganda
115 N6 Saglek B Labrador
71 H6 Sago isld Indonesia
99 S3 Sagola Michigan
17 F7 Sagra, La mt Spain
85 F8 Sagre, Pto.de Bioko Eq Guinea
16 B7 Sagres Portugal
71 L9 Sagu Indonesia
106 D3 Saguache Colorado
126 G4 Sagua de Tánamo Cuba
126 D3 Sagua la Grande Cuba
103 N8 Saguaro L Arizona
103 O9 Saguaro Nat.Mon Arizona
115 M8 Saguenay R Quebec
85 B3 Saguia el Hamra terr Morocco
17 G5 Sagunto Spain
114 E4 Sagwan Alaska
80 G3 Saham Jordan
85 C4 Sahara des N Africa
79 E10 Sahara, G mt Egypt
74 G4 Saharanpur India
142 E5 Sahara Well W Australia
75 L5 Sahibganj India
28 D4 Sahl Denmark
71 A2 Sahu Halmahera Indonesia
124 E3 Sahuaripa Mexico
103 O10 Sahuarita Arizona
124 H7 Sahuayo Mexico
135 F4 Sahul Shelf Timor Sea
13 O16 Sahune France
68 J5 Sa Huynh Vietnam
61 L9 Sai R Japan
136 J3 Saibai I Papua New Guinea
69 D13 Saibi Indonesia
69 E9 Sai Buri Thailand
69 E9 Sai Buri R Thailand
85 E2 Saïda Algeria
79 F5 Saïda Lebanon
77 D5 Sa'īdābād Iran
68 F6 Sai Dao Tai, Khao mt Thailand
86 D4 Said Bundas Sudan
75 N6 Saidpur Bangladesh
74 E1 Saidu Pakistan
40 E3 Saignelégier Switzerland
60 G9 Saigō Japan
Saigon see Ho Chi Minh
68 H7 Saigon R Vietnam
29 O4 Saija Finland
60 G12 Saijō Japan
60 C13 Saikai Nat. Park Japan
71 C3 Saileen W Irian
19 O15 Saillans France
71 C3 Sailolof W Irian
100 K7 Sailor Cr Idaho
76 C1 Sailu India
65 F4 Saima China
29 N10 Saimaa L Finland
29 N11 Saimaa Canal Finland/U.S.S.R.
124 H6 Sain Alto Mexico
74 A8 Saindak Pakistan
22 D2 Sainghin-en-Weppes France
22 G3 Sains-du-Nord France
22 F4 Sains-Richaumont France
15 F5 St. Abb's Head Scotland
122 H5 Ste. Adelaide Quebec
121 Q7 Ste.Adèle Quebec
20 F3 Ste.Adresse France
38 N6 St.Aegyd Austria
18 G9 St.Affrique France
121 T6 St.Agapit Quebec
119 U9 Ste.Agathe Manitoba
121 Q6 Ste.Agathe des Monts Quebec
20 G5 St.Agil France
8 A7 St.Agnes England
121 L4 Ste.Agnes Quebec
9 F7 St.Agnes isld Isles of Scilly England
21 H7 St.Aignan-la-Ronde France
21 C6 St. Aignan sur Roë France
28 D3 Ste. Ajstrup Denmark
9 F4 St.Albans England
123 R6 St.Alban's Nfld
95 P2 St.Albans Vermont
94 F8 St.Albans W Virginia
118 D5 St.Albert Alberta
122 C6 St.Alexandre Quebec
121 R6 St.Alexis des Monts Quebec
22 E3 St.Amand-les-Eaux France
21 H6 St.Amand-Longpre France
18 G6 St. Amand Mont Rond France
21 D8 St.Amand-sur-Sevre France
21 F10 St. Amant de Boixe France
40 F2 St.Amarin France
121 T4 St.-Ambroise Quebec
21 J8 St.Ambroix France
122 D5 St.Anaclet Quebec
38 L8 St. Andra-im-Lavanttal Austria
83 K13 St.André Réunion Indian Oc
33 M9 St. Andreasberg W Germany
87 G11 St.André, C Madagascar
19 N13 St.Andre-de-Corcy France
18 E8 St.André-de-Cubzac France
20 H4 St.André-de-l'Eure France
20 H4 St.André, Plaine de France
111 L11 St.Andrew Florida
127 P2 St.Andrew co Trinidad
127 L2 St.Andrew parish Jamaica
144 C6 St. Andrews New Zealand
123 N6 St.Andrew's Nfld
13 F1 St.Andrews Scotland
123 M7 St.Andrew's Chan Nova Scotia
113 F7 St.Andrew Sd Georgia
21 F10 St.Angeau France
98 F9 St.Ann Nebraska
127 K2 St.Ann parish Jamaica
126 B2 St. Anna-Baai B Curaçao
9 H6 St.Anne Channel Is
20 G4 Ste.Anne France
127 N4 Ste.Anne Guadeloupe W Indies
99 T8 St.Anne Illinois
119 V9 Ste.Anne Manitoba
127 L4 Ste.Anne Martinique W Indies
121 U5 Ste.-Anne-de-Beaupré Quebec
121 S6 Ste. Anne de la Pérade Quebec
122 B6 Ste.Anne de la Pocatière Quebec
122 F4 Ste.Anne des Monts Quebec
121 P6 Ste.Anne du Lac Quebec
122 E3 Ste.Anne, L Quebec
118 C5 Ste. Anne, Lac Alberta
122 B6 Ste.Anne, R Quebec
20 A2 St.Annes Alderney, Channel Is
117 Q9 St.Ann, L Alberta
123 M7 St. Anns Nova Scotia
141 H5 St.Anns Queensland
127 K2 St. Ann's Bay Jamaica
12 E3 St Ann's Bridge Scotland
99 O6 St.Ansgar Iowa
25 E5 St.Anthonis Netherlands
101 O6 St.Anthony Idaho
115 O7 St.Anthony Nfld
19 O18 St.Antoine France
41 M3 St.Anton Austria
18 G8 St.Antonin France
122 C6 St.Antonin Quebec
21 I8 St.Août France
20 H3 St.Aquilin-de-Pacy France
145 D4 St. Arnaud New Zealand
139 G6 St.Arnaud Victoria
20 J4 St.Arnoux France
122 C6 St.Arsène Quebec
140 B1 St.Asaph B N Terr Aust
18 F7 St.Astier France
122 C6 St.Athanase Quebec
122 B6 St.Aubert Quebec
20 E3 St.Aubin France
20 A3 St.Aubin Jersey, Channel Is
20 B5 St. Aubin-d'Aubigné France
20 C4 St.Aubin-de-Terregatte France
20 C5 St.Aubin-du-Cormier France
20 H2 St.Aubin-le-Cauf France
123 O2 St.Augustin Quebec
36 C2 St. Augustin W Germany
123 O2 St.Augustin B Quebec
87 G12 St.Augustin, B.de Madagascar
21 D7 St.Augustin-des-Bois France
113 F8 St.Augustine Florida
127 O2 St.Augustine Trinidad
123 N2 St.Augustin R Quebec
18 F7 St.Aulaye France
8 B7 St. Austell England
19 K3 St.Avold France
121 S6 St.Barnabé Nord Quebec
121 R6 St.Barthélémi Quebec
18 G10 St.Barthélemy France
127 N5 St. Barthélemy isld Lesser Antilles
144 B6 St. Bathans New Zealand
19 P18 Ste.Baume France
18 F10 St. Béat France
12 E5 St.Bees England
99 M6 St.Benedict Iowa
119 M6 St.Benedict Sask
21 H9 St.Benoit-du-Sault France
122 B7 St.Benoit Labre Quebec
122 H5 Ste.Bernadette Quebec
121 T6 St.Bernard Quebec
144 D5 St. Bernard mt New Zealand
40 F6 St. Bernard, Col du Gd. Switz/Italy
42 A3 St. Bernard, Petit pass Italy/France
110 J2 St.Bernice Indiana
19 P13 St.Beron France
20 D5 St.Berthevin France
36 C7 St.Blaise France
122 D5 Ste.Blandine Quebec
8 B7 St.Blazey England
118 D1 St.Boniface Manitoba
21 H10 St. Bonnet-Briance France
118 L8 St.Boswells Sask
13 F2 St. Boswells Scotland
21 G7 St.Branchs France
123 T5 St.Brendan's Nfld
21 A7 St. Brévin les Pins France
20 A4 St.Briac France
20 C5 St.Brice-en-Cogles France
118 B7 St.Bride, Mt Alberta
123 S7 St.Bride's Nfld
8 A4 St. Bride's Wales
18 D4 St. Brieuc France
119 N6 St.Brieux Sask
20 B4 St.Broladre France
121 L5 St. Bruno de Guiques Quebec
21 G6 St.Calais France
119 T9 St.Calude Manitoba
122 B7 St.Camille Quebec
121 S6 St.Casimir Quebec
18 D4 St.Cast France
115 M9 St. Catharines Ontario
127 K2 St. Catherine parish Jamaica
127 P5 St.Catherine, Mt Grenada
112 F6 St.Catherines I Georgia
9 E6 St.Catherines Pt England
122 B8 Ste.Cécile Quebec
18 G8 St. Céré France
18 G7 St.Cernin France
121 R7 St.Césaire Quebec
18 H7 St.Chamond France
101 O7 St.Charles Idaho
99 S8 St.Charles Illinois
118 A1 St.Charles Manitoba
94 C3 St.Charles Michigan
99 O6 St.Charles Minnesota
110 F3 St.Charles Missouri
18 H8 St. Chély l'Apcher France
20 K4 St.Chéron France
18 G9 St.Chinian France
126 A1 St.Christoffel Berg mt Curaçao
19 Q15 St.Christophe d'Oisans France
St. Christopher isld see St Kitts
121 T4 St.-Cîour-de-Marie Quebec
20 C3 St. Clair France
94 E4 St.Clair Michigan
99 N5 St.Clair Minnesota
110 F3 St.Clair Missouri
94 E4 St. Clair, L U.S.A./Canada
120 H9 St.Clair R Ontario/Mich
20 J3 St.Clair-sur-Epte France
19 J6 St.Claude France
127 N4 St.Claude Guadeloupe W I
8 B4 St.Clears Wales
122 C6 St.Clement Quebec
21 D7 St. Clement-de-la-Place France
121 S7 Ste.Clothilde Quebec
113 F9 St.Cloud Florida
20 K4 St.Cloud France
99 M4 St.Cloud Minnesota
8 B7 St.Columb England
121 R6 St.Côme Quebec
20 C3 St.Côme-du-Mont France
20 F5 St.Cosme-de-Vair France
122 E8 Ste.Croix New Brunswick
40 D4 Ste.Croix Switzerland
95 T8 St. Croix R Maine/New Brunswick
99 O4 St. Croix R Wisconsin
36 C7 Ste.Croix aux Mines France
113 L8 St.Croix I Virgin Is
18 E7 St. Cybard Chalais France
18 F8 St.Cyprien France
122 C6 St.Cyprien Quebec
19 P18 St.Cyr France
20 D4 St.Cyr-du-Bailleul France
21 I6 St. Cyr-en Val France
121 S7 St.Cyrille Quebec
121 P4 St.Cyr, L Quebec
118 J4 St. Cyr Lake Sask
122 B7 St.Damien Quebec
110 F1 St.David Illinois
127 P1 St.David co Trinidad
122 A5 St.David-de-Falardeau Quebec
123 O5 St. David's Nfld
8 A4 St. David's Wales
90 D1 St.Davids I Bermuda
22 G3 St.Denis Belgium
20 K4 St. Denis France
121 R7 St.Denis Quebec
83 J13 St.Denis Réunion Indian Oc
21 E6 St.Denis d'Anjou France
20 D5 St.Denis-de-Gastines France
21 C9 St.Denis-d'Oléron France
20 E5 St. Denis-d'Orques France
20 E5 St.Denis-sur-Sarthon France
19 O16 St.Didier France
36 B7 St. Dié France
19 J4 St.Dizier France
20 B5 St. Domineuc France
19 N14 St.Donat sur l'Herbasse France
98 J8 St.Edward Nebraska
116 P7 St.Elias, C Alaska
117 D5 St. Elias Mts Alaska/Yukon Terr
121 S4 Ste.Elisabeth Quebec
127 J2 St.Elizabeth parish Jamaica
110 H2 St.Elmo Illinois
122 C5 St.Eloi Quebec
18 G6 St Éloy-les-Mines France
121 R6 Ste.Emélie Quebec
18 H8 Ste.Enimie France
20 C3 Sainteny France
21 G7 St.Epain France
122 B7 St.Ephrem Quebec
121 L3 St.Ephrem de Paradis Quebec
122 C6 St.-Epiphane Quebec
20 B5 St.Erblon France
22 F5 St.Erme-Outre-et-Ramecourt France
21 D10 Saintes France
127 L4 St. Ésprit, Le Martinique W Indies
22 B2 St.Étienne-au-Mont France
18 E9 St. Étienne de Baïgorry France
19 O14 St.Étienne de St.Geoirs France
20 H3 St.Étienne-du-Rouvray France
121 M4 St. Eugène Quebec
121 S4 St.-Eugène Quebec
122 D6 St.Eusèbe Quebec
121 R7 St.Eustache Quebec
20 F4 St.Evroult Notre Dame-du-Bois France
122 D5 St.Fabien Quebec
122 B7 Ste.Familie Quebec
121 P6 Ste.Famille d'Aumond Quebec
18 H5 St.Fargeau France
121 S4 St.Félicien Quebec
122 E5 Ste.Félicité Quebec
121 R6 St. Félix de Valois Quebec
12 D1 St.Fillans Scotland
14 A5 St. Finan's B Irish Rep
123 O5 St.Fintan's Nfld
121 T6 St.Flavien Quebec
122 E5 Ste.Florence Quebec
21 C8 St.Florent-des-Bois France
18 H4 St.Florentin France
18 G6 St.Florent-sur-Cher France
18 H7 St.Flour France
21 H8 St.Flovier France
19 N15 St.Fortunat France
121 T7 St.Fortunat Quebec
18 F8 Ste.Foy-la-Grande France
107 J2 St.Francis Kansas
95 R6 St. Francis R Maine/New Brunswick
110 F5 St. Francis R Missouri/Ark
89 D10 St. Francis B S Africa
123 U6 St.Francis, C Nfld
89 D10 St. Francis C S Africa
138 C4 St.Francis, I.of S Australia
110 J3 St. Francisville Illinois
111 E11 St.Francisville Louisiana
127 N4 St.François Guadeloupe W Indies
121 S7 St. François R Quebec
121 T7 St. François, L Quebec
110 F4 St. Francois Mts Missouri
121 S7 St.François Xavier Quebec
95 S7 St.Froid L Maine
21 C8 St.Fulgent France
111 E11 St.Gabriel Louisiana
121 R6 St.Gabriel de Brandon Quebec
122 H5 St.Gabriel de Gaspé Quebec
41 K3 St. Gallen Switzerland
20 F4 Ste.Gauburge-Ste. Colombe France
18 F9 St.Gaudens France
21 H8 St.Gaultier France
122 B8 St.Gédéon Quebec
20 K3 St. Genevieve France
110 F4 Ste.Genevieve Missouri
123 P2 St.Genevieve B Quebec
18 G8 St.Geniez France
19 P14 St Geoire-en-Valdaine France
90 C1 St.George Bermuda
113 E7 St.George Georgia
122 F8 St.George New Brunswick
141 J8 St.George Queensland
112 G4 St.George S Carolina
103 L4 St.George Utah
127 O2 St.George co Trinidad
127 P6 St.George parish Barbados
141 G3 St. George R Queensland
123 N5 St.George, C Nfld
139 K6 St.George Hd New S Wales
113 C8 St.George I Florida
116 D8 St. George I Pribilof Is Bering Sea
41 H1 St.Georgen W Germany
100 A8 St.George, Pt California
142 E4 St.George Ra W Australia
36 B6 St.Georges France
129 H3 St.Georges Fr Guiana
127 P5 St.George's Grenada
123 O5 St.George's Nfld
122 B7 St.Georges Quebec
123 N5 St.George's B Nfld
125 P9 St. Georges Cay isld Belize
7 F11 St Georges Chan U.K.
137 L2 St.George's Channel Bismarck Arch
14 E5 St. Georges Channel Ireland/U.K.
69 A9 St.George's Channel Nicobar Is
20 C5 St. Georges-de-Reintembault France
21 C10 St. Georges-d'Oléron France
20 G3 St.Georges-du-Mesnil France
20 G3 St.Georges-du-Vièvre France
90 C1 St.George's, I Bermuda
21 F8 St. Georges-les-Baillargeaux France
20 H4 St.Georges Motel France
20 H5 St.Georges-sur-Eure France
21 I7 St. Georges-sur-la Prée France
21 D7 St.Georges-sur-Loire France
22 H3 St.Gérard Belgium
121 M4 St. Gerard-Centre Quebec
19 N13 St. Germain au Mt D'Or France

20 D5 **St.Germain d'Anxure** France
20 G5 **St. Germain-de-la-Coudre** France
18 H6 **St.Germain-des-Fosses** France
19 J6 **St.Germain du Bois** France
122 B7 **Ste.Germaine** Quebec
20 K4 **St.Germain-en-Laye** France
20 B3 **St.Germain, Hâvre de** France
20 F3 **St. Germain-la Campagne** France
18 G7 **St.Germain-les-Belles** France
20 B3 **St.Germain-sur-Ay** France
8 B7 **St.Germans** England
20 J3 **St.Germer-de-Fly** France
22 F3 **St.Ghislain** Belgium
21 B6 **St.Gildas des Bois** France
18 D5 **St.Gildas, Pte.de** *C* France
121 T6 **St.Giles** Quebec
127 N1 **St. Giles Is** Tobago
22 G1 **St. Gillis-bij-Dendermonde** Belgium
22 G1 **St.Gillis-Waas** Belgium
18 F10 **St.Girons** France
27 F12 **St.Gla** *L* Sweden
36 D3 **St.Goar** W Germany
22 E4 **St.Gobain** France
122 G5 **St.Godefroi** Quebec
41 J4 **St.Gotthard** *P* Switzerland
8 B4 **St.Govan's Hd** Wales
119 N6 **St.Gregor** Sask
123 O4 **St.Gregory, Mt** Nfld
121 S7 **St. Guillaume** Quebec
19 Q15 **St. Guillaume, Mt** France
94 C2 **St.Helen** Michigan
102 B3 **St.Helena** California
90 B14 **St. Helena** *isld* Atlantic Oc
89 A9 **St.Helena B** S Africa
90 J10 **St. Helena Fracture** Atlantic Oc
94 B1 **St.Helena I** Michigan
112 G5 **St.Helena Sd** S Carolina
18 E8 **Ste.Hélène** France
122 B6 **Ste.Hélène** Quebec
13 F6 **St.Helens** England
100 C4 **St.Helens** Oregon
139 J8 **St.Helens** Tasmania
100 C3 **St.Helens, Mt** Washington
139 J8 **St.Helens Pt** Tasmania
20 A3 **St.Hélier** Jersey, Channel Is
122 H4 **St.Hélier** Quebec
121 U6 **Ste.Hénédine** Quebec
121 T6 **St.Henri** Quebec
121 T7 **St.Herménégilde** Quebec
18 G9 **St.Hilaire** France
98 K1 **St.Hilaire** Minnesota
21 B7 **St. Hilaire-de-Chaleons** France
21 C7 **St.Hilaire de Loulay** France
21 D9 **St.Hilaire-des-Loges** France
20 C4 **St. Hilaire du-Harcouet** France
21 I10 **St. Hilaire-le Château** France
21 E7 **St. Hilaire-St. Florent** France
140 D6 **Sainthill,Mt** N Terr Aust
19 K5 **St.Hippolyte** Doubs France
21 H7 **St.Hippolyte** Indre-et-Loire France
18 H9 **St.Hippolyte du Fort** France
122 A5 **St.Honoré** Quebec
122 C6 **St.Honoré** Quebec
20 D3 **Ste.Honorine** France
20 E3 **Ste.Honorine-du-Fay** France
22 J3 **St.Hubert** Belgium
25 F6 **St.Hubert** W Germany
115 M8 **St-Hyacinthe** Quebec
28 K5 **St.Ibb** Sweden
94 C1 **St.Ignace** Michigan
121 R6 **St.Ignace du Lac** Quebec
120 C4 **St. Ignace, Isle** Ontario
101 L2 **St.Ignatius** Montana
40 E3 **St.Imier** Switzerland
36 D4 **St.Ingbert** W Germany
122 B6 **St.Irénée** Quebec
121 S5 **St.Isidore** Quebec
121 T7 **St.Isidore** Quebec
26 K3 **St.Istind** *mt* Norway
9 F3 **St.Ives** Cambridge England
8 A7 **St.Ives** Cornwall England
25 E2 **St.Jacobi Parochie** Netherlands
122 D6 **St.Jacques** New Brunswick
20 B5 **St.Jacques-de-la-Lande** France
38 F8 **St.Jakob** Austria
20 C4 **St.James** France
118 A1 **St.James** Manitoba
99 V4 **St.James** Michigan
99 M5 **St.James** Minnesota
110 E3 **St.James** Missouri
127 J2 **St.James** *parish* Jamaica
117 H10 **St.James, C** Br Columbia
113 E11 **St.James City** Florida
121 L4 **St.Janvier** Quebec
20 E5 **St.Jean** France
121 R7 **St.Jean** Quebec
119 U9 **St.Jean Baptiste** Manitoba
121 S5 **St.Jean Bosco** Quebec
21 E10 **St. Jean d'Angély** France
21 D10 **St. Jean-d'Angle** France
20 F5 **St.Jean-d'Asse** France
19 O13 **St.Jean-de-Bournay** France
20 C3 **St.Jean-de-Daye** France
122 C5 **St.Jean de Dieu** Quebec
19 J5 **St.Jean de Losne** France
18 D9 **St.Jean-de-Luz** France
121 R6 **St. Jean-de-Matha** Quebec
19 Q14 **St.Jean-de-Maurienne** France
21 A8 **St.Jean-de-Monts** France
21 F8 **St.Jean-de-Sauves** France
18 H8 **St.Jean du Gard** France
19 O14 **St.Jean-en-Royans** France
115 M8 **Saint-Jean, Lac** Quebec
20 B4 **St.Jean-la-Thomas** France
18 E9 **St.Jean Pied de Port** France
122 B6 **St.Jean Port Joli** Quebec
122 H3 **St.Jean, R** Quebec
36 B5 **St.Jean Rohrbach** France
20 C5 **St.Jean-sur-Couesnon** France
121 Q7 **St.Jérôme** Quebec
19 N14 **St. Jeure D'Ay** France
109 K2 **St.Jo** Texas
21 A7 **St.Joachim** France
122 B6 **St.Joachim** Quebec
41 O3 **St.Jodok** Austria
110 D5 **St.Joe** Arkansas
100 J2 **St.Joe** Idaho
94 C5 **St.Joe** Indiana
36 E4 **St.Johann** W Germany
38 G8 **St. Johann-im-Walde** Austria
107 M3 **St.John** Kansas
119 S10 **St.John** N Dakota
115 N8 **St.John** New Brunswick
103 M1 **St.John** Utah
100 H2 **St.John** Washington
127 P6 **St.John** *parish* Barbados
95 R7 **St. John** *R* Maine
123 P3 **St John B** Nfld
123 R3 **St.John, C** Nfld
113 L7 **St.John I** Virgin Is
123 S5 **St.John, L** Nfld
122 E7 **St. John R** New Brunswick
122 G5 **St. John R** Quebec
127 P4 **St.John's** Artigua W Indies
103 P7 **St.Johns** Arizona
94 C3 **St.Johns** Michigan
115 O8 **St. John's** Nfld
95 P2 **St.Johnsbury** Vermont
13 F4 **St.John's Chapel** England
14 C2 **St.John's Pt** Irish Rep
113 F7 **St.Johns R** Florida
95 N3 **St.Johnsville** New York
20 C3 **St.Jores** France
22 H2 **St.Joris-Winge** Belgium
111 E10 **St.Joseph** Louisiana
127 L4 **St.Joseph** Martinique W Indies
127 P2 **St.Joseph** Mayoro Trinidad
99 U7 **St.Joseph** Michigan
99 M10 **St.Joseph** Missouri
121 U6 **St.Joseph** Quebec
83 K14 **St.Joseph** Réunion Indian Oc
127 O2 **St.Joseph** St George Trinidad
127 P6 **St.Joseph** *parish* Barbados
94 A5 **St. Joseph** *R* Michigan
113 B8 **St. Joseph Bay** Florida
120 G6 **St. Joseph I** Ontario
109 L8 **St. Joseph I** Texas
115 K7 **St. Joseph, L** Ontario
123 T6 **St.Joseph's** Nfld
22 B3 **St.Josse** France
20 A5 **St. Jouan-de-l'Isle** France
20 A4 **St. Jouan des-Guerets** France
20 F2 **St.Jouin** France
121 Q6 **St. Jovite** Quebec
126 A1 **St. Jozefsdal** Curaçao
19 N14 **St.Julian Molin-Molette** France
40 D5 **St.Julien** France
21 C7 **St. Julien-de-Concelles** France
21 C6 **St. Julien de-Vouvantes** France
19 O15 **St.Julien en Quint** France
20 F3 **St. Julien-le-Faucon** France
18 F7 **St.Junien** France
9 F7 **St.Just** England
20 K2 **St.Just-en-Chausée** France
18 H7 **St.Just-en-Chevalet** France
38 M7 **St.Katherein** Austria
127 P3 **St.Kitts** *isld* Lesser Antilles
126 A1 **St.Kruis** Curaçao
21 R7 **St.Lambert** Quebec
121 T6 **St.Lambert** Quebec
142 G2 **St.Lambert,C** W Australia
21 E7 **St. Lambert-des-Levées** France
21 D7 **St. Lambert-du-Lattay** France
111 D11 **St.Landry** Louisiana
19 J6 **St. Laurent** France
129 H2 **St.Laurent** Fr Guiana
119 U8 **St.Laurent** Manitoba
121 L4 **Saint-Laurent** Quebec
18 G10 **St.Laurent de la Salanque** France
19 O13 **St.Laurent-de-Mûre** France
21 I6 **St. Laurent-des Eaux** France
19 P14 **St.Laurent-du-Pont** France
20 G2 **St. Laurent-en-Caux** France
21 G6 **St. Laurent-en-Gâtines** France
18 E7 **St.Laurent-et-Benon** France
121 U5 **St.Laurent, R** Quebec
21 G10 **St.Laurent-sur-Gorre** France
20 D3 **St.Laurent-sur-Mer** France
22 K5 **St.Laurent-sur-Othain** France
123 R7 **St.Lawrence** Nfld
141 J5 **St.Lawrence** Queensland
95 M2 **St. Lawrence** *R* Canada/U.S.A.
115 N8 **St.Lawrence, G.of** Canada
116 B5 **St.Lawrence I** Bering Sea
121 O8 **St. Lawrence I Nat. Park** Ontario
121 P8 **St.Lawrence Seaway** Canada/U.S.A.
119 Q8 **St.Lazare** Manitoba
22 K4 **St.Léger** Belgium
20 J4 **St. Léger-en-Yvelines** France
22 H1 **St. Lenaarts** Belgium
122 E5 **St.Léon** Quebec
36 B7 **St. Léonard** France
122 E6 **St.-Léonard** New Brunswick
121 S6 **St.Léonard** Quebec
21 I10 **St. Léonard-de-Noblat** France
9 G6 **St.Leonards** England
121 T4 **St.-Léon-de-Chicoutimi** Quebec
122 B7 **St.Léon de Standon** Quebec
38 L8 **St.Leonhard** Kärnten Austria
38 N4 **St.Leonhard** Nieder Österreich **Austria**
20 K3 **St.Leu-la-Forêt** France
123 Q1 **St.Lewis R** Labrador
121 S7 **St.Liboire** Quebec
18 F8 **Ste. Livrade** France
18 F9 **St.Lizier** France
20 C3 **St.Lô** France
127 N4 **St.Louis** Marie Galante W Indies
85 A5 **St.Louis** Mauritania
94 C3 **St.Louis** Michigan
122 H7 **St.Louis** Pr Edward I
83 J14 **St.Louis** Réunion **Indian Oc**
119 M6 **St.Louis** Sask
105 **St.Louis** *conurbation* Missouri
99 O2 **St. Louis** *R* Minnesota
122 H7 **St.Louis de Kent** New Brunswick
122 D6 **St.Louis du Ha Ha** Quebec
126 H5 **St.Louis du Sud** Haiti
122 B6 **Ste.Louise** Quebec
121 R7 **St.Louis, L** Quebec
36 C5 **St. Louis-lès-Bitche** France
94 E6 **St.Louisville** Ohio
40 D2 **St. Loup-sur-Semoise** France
19 K5 **St.Loup-sur-Semouse** France
20 H4 **St.Lubin-des-Joncherets** France
127 L4 **Ste.Luce** Martinique W Indies
141 K2 **St.Lucia** *dist* Brisbane, Qnsld
127 O8 **St. Lucia** *isld* Lesser Antilles
87 F11 **St. Lucia, C** S Africa
121 Q6 **Ste.Lucie** Quebec
113 G10 **St. Lucie Canal** Florida
127 P6 **St.Lucy** *parish* Barbados
122 B8 **St.Ludger** Quebec
127 H5 **St.Luis du Nord** Haiti
20 A4 **St.Lunaire** France
123 R2 **St Lunaire** Nfld
21 A7 **St. Lyphard** France
25 B5 **St.Maartens-dijk** Netherlands
18 E8 **St. Macaire** Gironde France
21 D7 **St.Macaire** Maine-et-Loire France
15 G2 **St.Magnus B** Scotland
21 E9 **St.Maixent-l'Ecole** France
122 B7 **St.Malachie** Quebec
20 A4 **St.Malo** France
20 B3 **St. Mâlo-de-la-Lande** France
20 B4 **St.Malo, G.de** France
20 A5 **St.Malon-sur-Mel** France
19 P18 **St.Mandrier** France
127 H5 **St.Marc** Haiti
121 S6 **St.Marc des Carrières** Quebec
122 B7 **St.Marcel** Quebec
19 O14 **St.Marcellin** France
20 C3 **St. Marcouf, I** France
20 C5 **St.Marc-sur-Couesnon** France
22 K4 **St.Mard** Belgium
123 P2 **St.Margaret B** Nfld
122 J9 **St.Margaret B** Nova Scotia
38 K8 **St.Margarethen** Austria
32 K5 **St.Margarethen** W Germany
15 F2 **St.Margarets Hope** Scotland
122 B5 **Ste.Marguerite, R** Quebec
122 F3 **Ste.Marguerite, R** Quebec
110 H3 **Ste.Marie** Illinois
127 L4 **Ste.Marie** Martinique W Indies
121 T6 **Ste.Marie** Quebec
83 K13 **Ste.Marie** Réunion Indian Oc
19 K4 **Ste.Marie aux Mines** France
36 C7 **Ste. Marie, Col de** *pass* France
20 C3 **Ste.Marie-du-Mont** France
19 Q17 **St Marie Mourre de Chanier** *mt* France
100 L2 **St.Maries** Idaho
113 C7 **St.Marks** Florida
21 F6 **St. Mars-d'Outillé** France
21 C7 **St. Mars-du-Désert** France
20 F5 **St.Mars-la-Brière** France
21 C7 **St.Mars la Jaille** France
20 C5 **St.Mars-sur-la-Futaie** France
122 F4 **Ste.Marthe de Gaspé** Quebec
18 E6 **St.Martin** France
127 N3 **St.Martin** *isld* Lesser Antilles
22 B2 **St.Martin-Boulogne** France
127 L4 **St. Martin, C** Martinique W Indies
89 A9 **St.Martin, C** S Africa
20 J5 **St.Martin-de-Bretencourt** France
19 N17 **St.Martin-de-Crau** France
20 C4 **St.Martin-de-Landelle** France
21 C9 **St.Martin-de-Ré** France
20 D3 **St.Martin-des-Besaces** France
16 E4 **St.Martin de Valdeiglesias** Spain
19 P12 **St.Martin-du-Fresne** France
19 O12 **St.Martin-du-Mont** France
40 B4 **St.Martin en Bresse** France
20 H2 **St.Martin-en-Campagne** France
99 U4 **St.Martin I** Michigan
119 T7 **St. Martin, L** Manitoba
122 G8 **St. Martin's** New Brunswick
9 F7 **St. Martin's** *isld* Isles of Scilly England
68 A2 **St.Martin's I** Burma
119 T7 **St. Martin Station** Manitoba
111 E11 **St.Martinville** Louisiana
9 H7 **St.Mary** Channel Is
127 L2 **St.Mary** *parish* Jamaica
101 M1 **St. Mary** *R* Mont/Alberta
123 N3 **St. Mary Is** Quebec
101 M1 **St.Mary L** Montana
117 P11 **St. Mary, Mt** Br Columbia
144 B6 **St. Mary, Mt** New Zealand
123 N3 **St.Mary Reefs** Quebec
118 D9 **St.Mary Res** Alberta
113 F7 **St.Marys** Georgia
107 O2 **St.Marys** Kansas
110 G4 **St.Marys** Missouri
123 T7 **St.Marys** Nfld
94 C6 **St.Marys** Ohio
94 J5 **St.Marys** Pennsylvania
15 F2 **St. Marys** Scotland
139 J8 **St.Marys** Tasmania
127 O3 **St. Mary's** Trinidad
94 F7 **St. Marys** W Virginia
9 F7 **St.Mary's** *isld* Isles of Scilly England
94 B6 **St. Mary's** *R* Indiana
123 T7 **St.Mary's B** Nfld
122 F9 **St.Mary's B** Nova Scotia
95 L8 **St. Marys City** Maryland
89 H6 **St.Mary's Hill** S Africa
15 E5 **St. Marys Loch** Scotland
113 F7 **St.Marys R** Florida/Georgia
123 K8 **St.Mary's, R** Nova Scotia
112 G4 **St. Mathews** S Carolina
21 G10 **St.Mathieu** France
121 M4 **St.Mathieu** Quebec
18 B4 **St. Mathieu, Pte** France
116 C6 **St.Matthew I** Bering Sea
136 K2 **St. Matthias Group** *islds* Bismarck Arch
21 G7 **Ste. Maure de-Touraine** France
40 E2 **St.Maurice** France
21 D7 **St.Maurice-la-Fougereuse** France
20 G4 **St. Maurice-les-Charencey** France
121 R5 **St.Maurice, Parc** Quebec
8 A7 **St. Mawes** England
122 B7 **St. Maxime** Quebec
19 P18 **St.Maximin** France
22 J4 **St. Médard** Belgium
18 E8 **St Médard en Jalles** France
110 K3 **St.Meinrad** Indiana
8 C4 **St.Mellons** Wales
20 B4 **St. Meloir-des-Ondes** France
19 J3 **St. Menehould** France
22 H4 **St.Menges** France
20 C3 **Ste. Mère-Eglise** France
98 H8 **St.Michael** Nebraska
127 P6 **St.Michael** *parish* Barbados
32 K5 **St.Michaelisdonn** W Germany
103 P6 **St.Michaels** Arizona
95 L8 **St.Michaels** Maryland
22 G4 **St.Michel** Aisne France
21 C6 **St.Michel** Maine-et-Loire France
127 H5 **St.Michel de L'Atalaye** Haiti
121 R6 **St.Michel des Saints** Quebec
36 B7 **St.Michel-sur-Meurthe** France
126 B1 **St.Michiel** Curaçao
19 J4 **St Mihiel** France
22 C2 **St.Momelin** France
13 F1 **St.Monance** Scotland
41 L5 **St.Moritz** Switzerland
21 A7 **St.Nazaire** France
19 O14 **St.Nazaire-en-Royans** France
9 F3 **St.Neots** England
St.Nicolas *see* **St.Niklaas**
20 H2 **St.Nicolas-d'Aliermont** France
22 G1 **St.Niklaas** Belgium
119 U9 **St.Norbert** Manitoba
25 F6 **St.Odilienberg** Netherlands
25 D5 **St.Oedenrode** Netherlands
22 C2 **St.Omer** France
145 D4 **St. Omer** New Zealand
122 F5 **St.Omer** Quebec
98 C5 **St.Onge** S Dakota
18 E7 **Saintonge** *prov* France
20 C4 **St.Osvin** France
20 D5 **St.Ouen-des-Toits** France
20 K3 **St.Ouen-l'Aumône** France
121 R7 **St.Ours** Quebec
122 C6 **St.Pacôme** Quebec
20 B4 **St.Pair** France
18 E9 **St.Palais** France
122 C7 **St.Pamphile** Quebec
18 F7 **St.Pardoux la Rivière** France
94 D6 **St.Paris** Ohio
122 C6 **St.Pascal** Quebec
20 F5 **St.Paterne** France
121 N6 **St.Patrice, L** Quebec
127 O3 **St.Patrick** *co* Trinidad
114 H7 **St.Paul** Alberta
110 C6 **St.Paul** Arkansas
38 L8 **St.Paul** Austria
18 E9 **St.Paul** France
94 B7 **St.Paul** Indiana
107 P4 **St.Paul** Kansas
99 N4 **St.Paul** Minnesota
98 H8 **St.Paul** Nebraska
83 J13 **St.Paul** Réunion **Indian Oc**
112 G4 **St.Paul** S Carolina
94 E10 **St.Paul** Virginia
85 C7 **St. Paul** *R* Guinea/Liberia
18 G10 **St. Paul de Fenouillet** France
122 C6 **St.-Paul-de-la-Croix** Quebec
122 B7 **St.Paul de Montminy** Quebec
122 C5 **St.Paul du Nord** Quebec
123 M6 **St.Paul I** C Breton I, N S
81 E9 **St. Paul, Î** Indian Oc
116 D8 **St.Paul I** Pribilof Is Bering Sea
18 H7 **St.Paulien** France
121 R6 **St.Paulin** Quebec
19 P17 **St.Paul-les-Durance** France
123 P2 **St.Paul R** Quebec
90 G8 **St.Paul Rocks** Atlantic Oc
112 H3 **St.Pauls** N Carolina
127 P4 **St.Pauls** St Kitts W Indies
123 P4 **St.Paul's Inlet** Nfld
19 N16 **St Paul-Trois-Châteaux** France
18 E9 **St.Pé de B** France
20 J5 **St. Peravy-la-Colombe** France
21 A7 **St. Père-en-Retz** France
122 C6 **Ste.Perpétue** Quebec
110 H3 **St.Peter** Illinois
38 K7 **St.Peter-am-Kammersberg** Austria
123 R1 **St.Peter B** Labrador
32 J4 **St Peter-Ording** W Germany
9 G6 **St.Peter Port** Channel Is
122 H5 **St.Peter, Pt** Quebec
123 M8 **St.Peters** C Breton I, N S
122 K7 **St.Peters** Pr Edward I
St.Petersburg *see* **Leningrad**
113 E10 **St.Petersburg** Florida
69 J12 **St.Petrus** *isld* Indonesia
21 B7 **St.Philbert de Grandlieu** France
122 B7 **St.Philémon** Quebec
127 P6 **St. Philip** *parish* Barbados
25 B5 **St.Philipsland** Netherlands
121 S7 **St.Pie** Quebec
123 Q7 **St. Pierre** Atlantic Oc
119 V9 **St.Pierre** Manitoba
127 L4 **St.Pierre** Martinique W Indies
83 J14 **St.Pierre** Réunion Indian Oc
19 Q13 **St Pierre d'Albigny** France
20 H3 **St.Pierre-d'Autils** France
20 B5 **St.Pierre-de-Plesguen** France
21 D8 **St.Pierre-des-Echaubrognes** France
20 E5 **St. Pierre-des-Nids** France
21 C10 **St. Pierre-d'Oléron** France
20 H3 **St.Pierre-du-Vauvray** France
20 C2 **St. Pierre Eglise** France
20 F2 **St.Pierre-en-Port** France
81 C6 **St.Pierre I** Indian Oc
121 S6 **St.Pierre, L** Quebec
20 C5 **St.Pierre-la-Cour** France
20 B4 **St.Pierre-Langers** France
18 H6 **St. Pierre le Moûtier** France
20 H3 **St. Pierre-les-Elbeuf** France
20 E3 **St.Pierre-sur-Dives** France
20 E5 **St.Pierre-sur-Orthe** France
20 C4 **St.Pois** France
21 C6 **St.Poix** France
22 C1 **St.Pol** France
22 C3 **St.Pol** France
18 C4 **St.Pol-de-Léon** France
38 N5 **St.Pölten** Austria
19 K6 **St.Pon, L.de** France
18 G9 **St Pons** France
18 H6 **St.Pourcain-sur-Sioule** France
121 S4 **St.-Prime** Quebec
22 E4 **St.Quentin** Aisne France
21 D6 **St.Quentin** Maine-et-Loire France
122 E6 **St.Quentin** New Brunswick
20 K4 **St. Quentin-en-Yvelines** France
22 B3 **St.Quentin, Pte.de** France
36 C6 **St.Quirin** France
18 H7 **St.Rambert** France
122 B7 **St.Raphaël** Quebec
121 T6 **St.Raymond** Quebec
101 L2 **St.Regis** Montana
95 N2 **St. Regis Falls** New York
121 R7 **St.Rémi** Quebec
19 N17 **St. Rémy** Bouches du Rhône France
20 E4 **St.Rémy** Calvados France
20 F5 **St.Rémy-des-Monts** France
20 F5 **St.Rémy-du-Plain** France
20 B5 **St. Remy-du-Plein** France
20 H4 **St. Remy-sur-Avre** France
18 H7 **St. Rémy-sur-Durolle** France
40 F6 **St.Rhémy** Italy
20 J1 **St.Riquier** France
121 R7 **St.Robert** Quebec
122 A8 **St.Romain** Quebec
20 F2 **St.Romain-de-Colbosc** France
21 H7 **St.Romain-sur-Cher** France
121 T6 **St.Romuald** Quebec
141 G4 **St. Ronans** Queensland
127 N4 **Ste.Rose** Guadeloupe W Indies
121 R7 **Ste.Rose** Quebec
119 S7 **Ste.Rose de Lac** Manitoba
122 D6 **Ste.Rose du Dégelé** Quebec
38 N7 **St.Ruprecht-an-der-Raab** Austria
20 H2 **St.Saëns** France
31 O6 **St.Sambor** U.S.S.R.
9 G6 **St.Sampson** Channel Is
19 O17 **St.Saturnin d'Apt** France
19 N17 **St Saturnin-lès-Avig-non** France
20 K2 **St.Saufiieu** France
20 E4 **St.Sauveur** France
121 Q7 **St.Sauveur** Quebec
20 C3 **St. Sauveur Lendelin** France
20 B3 **St.Sauveur-le-Vicomte** France
18 E7 **St.Savin** France
21 D10 **St.Savinien** France
20 F4 **Ste.Scolasse** France
87 H10 **St.Sebastien, C** Madagascar
18 G9 **St.Sernin-sur-Rance** France
20 A4 **St.Servan** France
18 E9 **St.Sever** France
20 C4 **St.Sever-Calyados** France
21 E10 **Ste Sévère** France
123 T7 **St.Shott's** Nfld
22 E4 **St.Simon** France
122 C5 **St.Simon** Quebec
112 F6 **St. Simons** Georgia
26 J4 **St. Sjöfallets Nat. Park** Sweden
115 N8 **St.Stephen** New Brunswick
112 H4 **St.Stephen** S Carolina
101 R7 **St.Stephens** Wyoming
18 G9 **St.Sulpice** France
20 G4 **St.Sulpice** France
21 B6 **St.Sulpice des Landes** France
18 G6 **St. Sulpice Laurière** France
21 H9 **St.Sulpice les Feuilles** France
20 E5 **Ste.Suzanne** France
83 K13 **Ste.Suzanne** Réunion Indian Oc
20 E3 **St.Sylvain** France
121 T6 **St.-Sylvestre** Quebec
18 E8 **St.Symphorien** France
117 F6 **St. Terese** Alaska
122 E5 **St.Tharsicius** Quebec
121 S6 **Ste.Thècle** Quebec
122 B8 **St. Théophile** Quebec
121 R7 **Ste.Thérèse** Quebec
117 N3 **Ste. Thérèse, Lac** N W Terr
40 C1 **St.Thiébault** France
98 J1 **St.Thomas** N Dakota
120 J10 **St.Thomas** Ontario
127 P6 **St.Thomas** *parish* Barbados
127 M3 **St.Thomas** *parish* Jamaica
113 K7 **St.Thomas I** Virgin Is
121 S6 **St.Tite** Quebec
122 B6 **St.Tite des Caps** Quebec
40 B5 **St.Trivier de Courtes** France
19 N12 **St. Trivier-Moignans** France
St.Trond *see* **St.Truiden**
22 J2 **St.Truiden** Belgium
8 B2 **St. Tudwal's Is** Wales
27 H11 **St.Tuna** Sweden
122 E5 **St.Ulric** Quebec
122 B6 **St.Urbain** Quebec
20 G2 **St.Vaast** France
20 C2 **St.Vaast-la-Hougue** France
20 G2 **St.Valery-en-Caux** France
20 J1 **St. Valéry-sur-Somme** France
122 B7 **St.Vallier** Quebec
38 H7 **St.Veit** Austria
38 K8 **St.Veit-an-der-Glan** Austria
22 D2 **St.Venant** France
121 Q6 **Ste.Véronique** Quebec
21 I6 **St. Viâtre** France
19 P17 **Ste Victoire, Mt** France
21 A6 **St.Vincent** France
127 O8 **St. Vincent** *isld* Lesser Antilles
87 G12 **St.Vincent, C** Madagascar
139 H9 **St.Vincent, C** Tasmania
18 E9 **St.Vincent-de-Tyrosse** France
133 E5 **St.Vincent, G** S Australia
113 B8 **St. Vincent I** Florida
123 T7 **St.Vincent's** Nfld
21 B9 **St.Vincent-sur-Jard** France
118 A2 **St.Vital** Manitoba
94 C1 **St. Vital Pt** Michigan
22 L3 **St.Vith** Belgium
18 E7 **St.Vivien-de-Médoc** France
106 G7 **St.Vrain** New Mexico
118 H5 **St.Walburg** Sask
20 G2 **St.Wandrille** France
36 C5 **St.Wendel** W Germany
126 A1 **St. Willebrordus** Curaçao
120 K10 **St.Williams** Ontario
101 S4 **St.Xavier** Montana
18 F7 **St. Yrieix** France
122 H4 **St.Yvon** Quebec
19 P18 **St.Zacharie** France
20 J5 **Sainville** France
134 E6 **Saipan** *isld* Mariana Is Pacific Oc
20 C2 **Saire** *R* France
20 C2 **Saire, Pte. de** France
18 E9 **Saison** *R* France
61 M10 **Saitama** *prefect* Japan
68 A1 **Saitlai** Burma
60 E13 **Saito** Japan
26 N3 **Saivomuotka** Sweden
21 E9 **Saivres** France
77 L2 **Saiydabad** Afghanistan
77 L1 **Saiyid** Afghanistan
74 E3 **Saiyidwala** Pakistan
71 B2 **Sajafi** *isld* Indonesia
128 E7 **Sajama** Bolivia
71 B2 **Sajang** *isld* Indonesia
48 F2 **Sajó** *R* Hungary
89 B7 **Sak** *watercourse* S Africa
88 G2 **Saka** Kenya
Saka Dzong *see* **Saga**
59 L5 **Sakai** Japan
60 G11 **Sakaide** Japan
60 G10 **Sakai Minato** Japan
72 E2 **Sakākah** Saudi Arabia
78 H7 **Sakakah** Saudi Arabia
98 E2 **Sakakawea, L** N Dakota
70 Q9 **Sakala** *isld* Indonesia
61 N7 **Sakamachi** Japan
115 M7 **Sakami L** Quebec
88 B8 **Sakania** Zaïre
Sakar *see* **Brannitsa** Bulgaria
57 C5 **Sakar** U.S.S.R.
87 G12 **Sakaraha** Madagascar
78 C1 **Sakarya** *R* Turkey
78 C2 **Sakarya** *R* Turkey
59 L4 **Sakata** Japan
111 H8 **Sakatonchee** *R* Mississippi
85 E7 **Sakete** Benin
51 O3 **Sakhalin** *isld* U.S.S.R.
51 O4 **Sakhalinskaya Oblast'** U.S.S.R.
51 O3 **Sakhalinskiy Zaliv** *B* U.S.S.R.
54 G7 **Sakhnovshchina** U.S.S.R.
52 B7 **Šakiai** U.S.S.R.
80 G4 **Sakib** Jordan
60 H12 **Sakihama** Japan
67 H4 **Sakishima-guntō** *islds* Japan
55 C5 **Sakmara** U.S.S.R.
68 C3 **Sa-koi** Burma
95 Q5 **Sakonnet R** Rhode I
86 G3 **Sakota** Ethiopia
87 D12 **Sakrivier** S Africa
28 E5 **Saksild** Denmark
28 H7 **Sakskøbing** Denmark
75 K7 **Sakti** India
51 M1 **Saktyakh** U.S.S.R.
61 M9 **Saku** Japan
61 L10 **Sakuma** Japan
61 J11 **Sakurai** Japan
60 D14 **Sakura jima** *isld* Japan
27 M10 **Säkylä** Finland
80 G3 **Sal** Jordan
53 F9 **Sal** *R* U.S.S.R.
48 D2 **Šala** Czechoslovakia
27 J12 **Sala** Sweden
68 F7 **Sala Andong Tuk** Cambodia
71 H6 **Salabangka** *isld* Sulawesi
52 B5 **Salacgriva** U.S.S.R.
43 G8 **Sala Consilina** Italy
109 K5 **Salad** Texas
133 C3 **Salada, B** Chile
131 G6 **Salada, L** Buenos Aires Argentina
131 F2 **Salada, L** Corrientes Argentina
124 B1 **Salada, L** Mexico
103 J9 **Salada, Laguna** *L* Mexico
131 E4 **Saladillo** *R* Argentina
131 B2 **Salado** *R* La Rioja Argentina
106 C7 **Salado, R** New Mexico
131 E2 **Salado, R** Santa Fé Argentina
85 D7 **Salaga** Ghana
68 F7 **Sala Hintoun** Cambodia
78 H4 **Salahiye** Syria
56 C4 **Salair** U.S.S.R
56 C4 **Salairskiy Kryazh** *ridge* U.S.S.R.
48 H3 **Šalaj** *prov* Romania
71 K8 **Salajar** Indonesia
70 G7 **Salajar, Selat** *str* Sulawesi
70 L9 **Salak, G** *mt* Java
86 C3 **Salal** Chad
72 G5 **Salālah** Oman
125 O10 **Salamá** Guatemala
94 J4 **Salamanca** New York
16 D4 **Salamanca** Spain
16 C4 **Salamanca** *prov* Spain
86 C4 **Salamat** *R* Chad
128 C2 **Salamina** Colombia
79 D3 **Salamis** Cyprus
47 F7 **Salamís** Greece
94 B6 **Salamonie** *R* Indiana
70 E2 **Salang** Kalimantan
26 J3 **Salangen** Norway
52 B6 **Salantai** U.S.S.R.
45 K2 **Salara** Italy
48 G3 **Sălard** Romania
133 D2 **Salar de Arizaro** *salt pan* Argentina
133 D2 **Salar de Atacama** *salt pan* Chile
133 D2 **Salar de Cauchari** *salt pan* Argentina
133 D1 **Salar de Coipasa** *salt pan* Bolivia
133 D3 **Salar del Hombre Muerto** *salt pan* Argentina
133 D2 **Salar de Uyuni** *salt pan* Bolivia
16 C1 **Salas** Spain
46 E1 **Salaš** Yugoslavia
16 E2 **Salas de los Infantes** Spain
18 F9 **Salat** *R* France
70 N9 **Salatiga** Java
18 F10 **Salau, Pont de** *pass* France/Spain
52 H6 **Salaushi** U.S.S.R.
55 C4 **Salavat** U.S.S.R.
128 C5 **Salaverry** Peru
133 E3 **Salavina** Argentina
71 C3 **Salawati** *isld* W Irian
71 G6 **Salay** Mindanao **Philippines**
135 Q11 **Sala y Gómez** *isld* Pacific Oc
Salazar *see* **Ndalatanda**
21 J7 **Salbris** France
126 D3 **Sal, Cay** *isld* Bahamas
127 J5 **Salcedo** Dominican Rep
116 P4 **Salcha** *R* Alaska
116 O4 **Salchaket** Alaska
33 P8 **Salchau** E Germany
37 O6 **Salching** W Germany
47 G1 **Salcia** Romania
8 C7 **Salcombe** England
47 K7 **Salda Gölü** *L* Turkey
16 D2 **Saldaña** Spain
87 C12 **Saldanha** S Africa
41 N4 **Saldura, Pta** *mt* Italy
52 B6 **Saldus** U.S.S.R.
68 B2 **Sale** Burma
8 D1 **Sale** England
85 C2 **Sale** Morocco
139 H7 **Sale** Victoria
112 C6 **Sale City** Georgia
112 B2 **Sale Creek** Tennessee
77 A2 **Sālehābad** Iran
71 H9 **Saleh, Teluk** *B* Indonesia
147 N15 **Salekhard** U.S.S.R.
111 L9 **Salem** Alabama
110 E5 **Salem** Arkansas
113 D8 **Salem** Florida
110 H3 **Salem** Illinois
76 D5 **Salem** India
110 K3 **Salem** Indiana
95 R4 **Salem** Massachusetts
110 E4 **Salem** Missouri
95 Q4 **Salem** New Hampshire
95 M7 **Salem** New Jersey
106 C9 **Salem** New Mexico
95 O3 **Salem** New York
94 G6 **Salem** Ohio
100 B5 **Salem** Oregon
112 E3 **Salem** S Carolina
98 J6 **Salem** S Dakota
94 G9 **Salem** Virginia
99 S7 **Salem** Wisconsin
70 D7 **Salembu Besar** *isld* Indonesia
43 E11 **Salemi** Sicily
15 C4 **Salen** Scotland
27 F10 **Sälen** Sweden
142 E3 **Sale, R** W Australia
19 Q17 **Salernes** France
113 G10 **Salerno** Florida
43 F8 **Salerno** Italy
43 F8 **Salerno, Golfo di** Italy
45 L1 **Saletto** Italy
20 K2 **Saleux** France
19 Q12 **Salève, Mt** France
13 F6 **Salford** England
130 H9 **Salgado** *R* Brazil
131 H2 **Salgado Filho** *airport* Brazil
48 F2 **Salgótarján** Hungary
130 G10 **Salgueiro** Brazil
79 C8 **Sâlhîya, El** Egypt
127 P2 **Salibea** Trinidad
106 D3 **Salida** Colorado
18 E9 **Salies de Béarn** France
18 F9 **Salies du Salat** France
47 J6 **Salihli** Turkey
87 F8 **Salima** Malawi
70 E3 **Salimbatu** Kalimantan
68 B2 **Salin** Burma
68 B2 **Salin** *R* Burma
107 N3 **Salina** Kansas
110 A5 **Salina** Oklahoma
103 N3 **Salina** Utah
43 F10 **Salina** *isld* Italy
125 M9 **Salina Cruz** Mexico
133 D4 **Salina La Antigua** *salt pan* Argentina
126 G3 **Salina Pt** Acklins I Bahamas
129 K7 **Salinas** Brazil
102 C5 **Salinas** California
128 B4 **Salinas** Ecuador
128 C6 **Salinas** Peru
102 C5 **Salinas** *R* California
133 D4 **Salinas Grandes** Argentina
131 C3 **Salinas, Pampa de la** Argentina
106 D8 **Salinas Pk** New Mexico
87 B8 **Salinas, Pte. das** Angola
94 D4 **Saline** Michigan
12 E1 **Saline** Scotland
111 D8 **Saline** *R* Arkansas
110 H4 **Saline** *R* Illinois
107 L2 **Saline** *R* Kansas
127 P2 **Saline B** Trinidad
109 P3 **Saline Bayou** *R* Louisiana
109 P4 **Saline L** Louisiana
127 P5 **Salines, Pt** Grenada
102 G5 **Saline V** California
94 G6 **Salineville** Ohio
68 B1 **Salingyi** Burma
133 C3 **Salinitas** Chile
129 J4 **Salinópolis** Brazil
70 F6 **Salipolo** Sulawesi
95 O4 **Salisbury** Connecticut
9 E5 **Salisbury** England
95 M8 **Salisbury** Maryland
110 D2 **Salisbury** Missouri
112 G2 **Salisbury** N Carolina
122 G7 **Salisbury** New Brunswick
94 H7 **Salisbury** Pennsylvania
138 E5 **Salisbury** S Australia
95 O3 **Salisbury** Vermont
88 C10 **Salisbury** Zimbabwe
141 K2 **Salisbury** *dist* Brisbane, Qnsld
115 M5 **Salisbury I** N W Terr
86 F5 **Salisbury, L** Uganda
116 O2 **Salisbury, Mt** Alaska
9 E5 **Salisbury Plain** England
48 H5 **Săliste** Romania
129 K6 **Salitre** *R* Brazil
80 G8 **Saliya** Jordan
45 K1 **Salizzole** Italy
112 F4 **Salkehatchie** *R* S Carolina
79 G6 **Salkhad** Syria
28 D4 **Sall** Denmark
38 L7 **Salla** Austria
29 O5 **Salla** Finland
17 G2 **Sallent de G** Spain
19 N16 **Salles** France
18 G8 **Salles-Curan** France
112 F4 **Salley** S Carolina
33 T9 **Sallgast** E Germany
28 B3 **Salling** *reg* Denmark
107 Q6 **Sallisaw** Oklahoma
86 G2 **Sallom** Sudan
78 K6 **Salman, As** Iraq
78 K2 **Salmas** Iran
17 F4 **Salmerón** Spain
29 N5 **Salmivaara** Finland
100 H1 **Salmo** Br Columbia
116 Q3 **Salmon** Alaska
101 M4 **Salmon** Idaho
117 M8 **Salmon** *R* Br Columbia
114 H7 **Salmon Arm** Br Columbia
123 P2 **Salmon Bay** Quebec
101 L7 **Salmon Cr.Res** Idaho
142 F3 **Salmond R** W Australia
101 L7 **Salmon Falls** Idaho
116 R4 **Salmon Fork** *R* Alaska
143 D10 **Salmon Gums** W Australia
123 T6 **Salmonier** Nfld
100 B8 **Salmon Mt** California
122 G7 **Salmon R** New Brunswick
122 K4 **Salmon, R** Quebec
95 M3 **Salmon Res** New York
114 H9 **Salmon River Mts** Idaho
36 G3 **Salmünster** W Germany
52 E2 **Sal'nitsa** U.S.S.R.
42 D3 **Salò** Italy
52 G6 **Salobelyak** U.S.S.R.
130 C7 **Salobra, R** Brazil
29 L7 **Saloinen** Finland
99 L1 **Salol** Minnesota
103 L8 **Salome** Arizona
127 L4 **Salomon, C** Martinique W Indies
40 C2 **Salon** *R* France
19 O17 **Salon-de-Provence** France
Salonica *see* **Thessaloníki**
48 G4 **Salonta** Romania
8 D2 **Salop** *co* England
17 H3 **Salou, C** Spain
29 M11 **Salpausselkä** *reg* Finland
26 K9 **Salsåker** Sweden
53 F10 **Sal'sk** U.S.S.R.
43 F11 **Salso** *R* Sicily
44 G2 **Salsomaggiore Terme** Italy
80 F5 **Salt** Jordan
103 N8 **Salt** *R* Arizona
110 L3 **Salt** *R* Kentucky
110 E2 **Salt** *R* Missouri
133 D2 **Salta** Argentina
55 F3 **Saltaim, Oz** *L* U.S.S.R.
8 B7 **Saltash** England
28 G5 **Saltbæk Vig** *lagoon* Denmark
108 B4 **Salt Basin** Texas
13 H4 **Saltburn** England
119 P7 **Saltcoats** Sask
12 D2 **Saltcoats** Scotland
110 G1 **Salt Cr** Illinois
94 E7 **Salt Cr** Ohio
101 T6 **Salt Cr** Wyoming
99 R9 **Salt Cr** *R* Illinois
26 H4 **Saltdal** Norway
108 C4 **Salt Draw** *R* Texas
14 E4 **Saltee Is** Irish Rep
26 H5 **Saltelv** *R* Norway
26 G4 **Salten** *reg* Norway
28 D4 **Salten Langsø** *L* Denmark
26 G4 **Saltfjord** *inlet* Norway
108 B4 **Salt Flat** Texas
13 J6 **Saltfleet** England
107 M5 **Salt Fork** *R* Oklahoma
108 F2 **Salt Fork** *R* Texas
109 H4 **Salt Gap** Texas
28 K5 **Saltholm** *isld* Denmark
125 J5 **Saltillo** Mexico
94 J6 **Saltillo** Pennsylvania
110 H6 **Saltillo** Tennessee
106 G9 **Salt L** New Mexico
108 C4 **Salt L** Texas
140 E6 **Salt Lake** Queensland
101 O9 **Salt Lake City** Utah
143 C8 **Salt Lakes** W Australia
94 D8 **Salt Lick** Kentucky
143 D6 **Salt Ls** W Australia
133 E4 **Salto** Argentina
130 F8 **Salto** Brazil
131 F3 **Salto** Uruguay
131 F3 **Salto** *dep* Uruguay
42 E6 **Salto** *R* Italy
130 C9 **Salto das Sete Quedas** *falls* Paraguay
130 D7 **Salto do Urubupungá** *falls* Brazil
45 O5 **Salto, L. del** Italy
26 K4 **Saltoluokta** Sweden
103 J8 **Salton** California
103 J8 **Salton Sea** California
127 L3 **Salt Ponds, The** Jamaica
74 E2 **Salt Range** Pakistan
127 K3 **Salt River** Jamaica
127 H5 **Saltrou** Haiti
101 P7 **Salt R. Ra** Wyoming
27 K12 **Saltsjöbaden** Sweden
27 L11 **Saltvik** Finland
94 F10 **Saltville** Virginia
102 F2 **Salt Wells** Nevada
112 F3 **Saluda** S Carolina
112 E3 **Saluda** *R* S Carolina
71 H5 **Salue** *isld* Indonesia
71 H5 **Salue Timpaus, Selat** *str* Indonesia
84 H3 **Salûm** Egypt
45 N4 **Saluoecio** Italy
71 F7 **Saluping** *isld* Philippines
76 F1 **Salur** India
110 C6 **Salus** Arkansas
129 H2 **Salut, I.du** Fr Guiana
44 B2 **Saluzzo** Italy
129 L6 **Salvador** Brazil
84 E5 **Salvador** Niger
118 H6 **Salvador** Sask
111 F12 **Salvador, L** Louisiana
123 T5 **Salvage** Nfld
16 B5 **Salvaterra de Magos** Portugal
125 J7 **Salvatierra** Mexico
103 N3 **Salvation Cr** Utah
141 H6 **Salvator, L** Queensland
18 G8 **Salvetat, la** Aveyron France
18 G9 **Salvetat, la** Hérault France
117 J8 **Salvus** Br Columbia
73 Q5 **Salween** *R* Burma/Thailand
75 K4 **Salyan** Nepal
94 D9 **Salyersville** Kentucky
38 L6 **Salza** *R* Austria
32 F8 **Salzbergen** W Germany
38 H6 **Salzburg** Austria
38 H7 **Salzburg** *prov* Austria
32 L9 **Salzderhelden** W Germany
33 M8 **Salzgitter** W Germany
33 M8 **Salzgitter-Bad** W Germany
38 J6 **Salzkammer-gut** *res* Austria
32 J9 **Salzkotten** W Germany
33 P9 **Salzmünde** E Germany
33 O7 **Salzwedel** E Germany
101 O6 **Sam** Idaho
80 G3 **Sama** Jordan
80 G4 **Samad** Jordan
71 J5 **Samada** *isld* Indonesia
16 D1 **Sama de Langreo** Spain
56 E5 **Samagaltay** U.S.S.R.
80 F2 **Samak** Syria
71 G7 **Samal** *isld* Mindanao Philippines
69 C10 **Samalanga** Sumatra
108 A4 **Samalayuca** Mexico
71 E7 **Samales Group** *islds* Philippines
76 F2 **Samalkot** India
84 J4 **Samâlût** Egypt
127 K5 **Samaná** Dominican Rep
126 H3 **Samana Cay** *isld* Bahamas
78 E3 **Samandag** Turkey
60 Q3 **Samani** Japan
121 S3 **Samaqua** *R* Quebec
80 G3 **Samar** Jordan
71 G5 **Samar** *isld* Philippines
53 H7 **Samara** *R* U.S.S.R.
136 L4 **Samarai** Papua New Guinea
101 N7 **Samaria** Idaho
80 D4 **Samaria** Jordan
46 E4 **Samarína** Greece
70 E5 **Samarinda** Kalimantan
57 D5 **Samarkand** U.S.S.R.
78 J4 **Sāmarrā'** Iraq
71 G5 **Samar Sea** Philippines
71 C3 **Samate** W Irian
78 K6 **Samāwah, Aq** Iraq
86 D5 **Samba** Equateur Zaïre
86 E6 **Samba** Kasai Oriental Zaïre
70 C5 **Samba** *R* Kalimantan
87 C7 **Samba Caju** Angola
71 A3 **Sambaki, Selat** Indonesia
70 F4 **Sambaliung** *mts* Kalimantan
75 L8 **Sambalpur** India
70 G7 **Sambapolulu, G** *mt* Sulawesi

87 J10 Sambava Madagascar
25 E5 Sambeek Netherlands
74 H4 Sambhal India
21 H7 Sambin France
70 F4 Sambit isld Kalimantan
129 K5 Sambito R Brazil
70 E5 Sambodja Kalimantan
68 H6 Sambor Cambodia
48 H1 Sambor U.S.S.R.
131 G6 Samborombón, B Argentina
22 H3 Sambre R Belgium
69 F12 Sambu Indonesia
70 D5 Sambuan Kalimantan
45 J3 Sambuca Pistojese Italy
59 J4 Samchŏk S Korea
68 D6 Same Burma
88 F4 Same Tanzania
22 B2 Samer France
68 E6 Samet, Ko isld Thailand
87 E8 Samfya Zambia
68 A2 Sami Burma
46 D6 Sámi Greece
71 H4 Samia, Tg C Sulawesi Indonesia
128 D5 Samiria R Peru
85 E5 Samit Mali
68 C2 Samka Burma
29 K11 Sammatti Finland
80 F3 Sammu' Jordan
68 F5 Samnak Kado Thailand
41 M3 Samnaun Gruppe mt Austria
68 F2 Sam Neua Laos
80 E6 Samniya Auja R Jordan
84 F4 Samnū Libya
100 A9 Samoa California
Samoa i Sisifo islds see Western Samoa
52 F3 Samoded U.S.S.R.
40 E5 Samoëns France
47 F2 Samokov Bulgaria
68 C2 Samon R Burma
92 C4 Samora Desert Cal/Ariz
47 H7 Sámos isld Greece
46 D5 Samothráki isld Ionian Is Greece
47 H4 Samothráki isld Thraki Greece
133 E4 Sampacho Argentina
70 F6 Sampaga Sulawesi
71 E3 Sampaloc Pt Luzon Philippines
70 O9 Sampang Indonesia
17 G3 Samper de Calanda Spain
113 L12 Samphire Cay isld Bahamas
70 C6 Sampit Kalimantan
70 C6 Sampit, Teluk B Kalimantan
71 H7 Sampolawa Indonesia
87 E7 Sampwe Zaïre
80 F8 Samra Jordan
111 B10 Sam Rayburn Res Texas
22 K3 Samrée Belgium
68 F6 Samrong R Cambodia
78 G3 Samsat Turkey
28 F5 Samsø isld Denmark
111 K10 Samson Alabama
68 G3 Sam Son Vietnam
78 F1 Samsun Turkey
47 J7 Samsun Dağ mt Turkey
67 A6 Sam Teu Laos
140 C4 Samuel, Mt N Terr Aust
47 H1 Samuil Bulgaria
56 B3 Samus' U.S.S.R.
68 E6 Samut Sakhon Thailand
68 E6 Samut Songkhram Thailand
85 D6 San Mali
31 N6 San R Poland
72 E5 San'ā' N Yemen
42 H4 Sana R Yugoslavia
106 D7 San Acacia New Mexico
86 B5 Sanaga R Cameroon
106 D10 San Agustin Mexico
71 G7 San Agustin, C Mindanao Philippines
133 D4 San Agustín de Valle Fértil Argentina
116 F9 Sanak I Aleutian Is
45 M2 San Alberto Italy
135 S12 San Ambrosio isld Pacific Oc
102 D3 San Andreas California
125 P9 San Andrés Guatemala
106 D9 San Andres Mts New Mexico
125 M8 San Andrés Tuxtla Mexico
41 K7 San Angelo Italy
108 G4 San Angelo Texas
126 C3 San Anton de los Baños Cuba
125 P9 San Antonio Belize
131 B4 San Antonio Chile
113 E9 San Antonio Florida
125 L2 San Antonio Honduras
71 E2 San Antonio Luzon Philippines
124 E6 San Antonio Mexico
106 D8 San Antonio New Mexico
109 J6 San Antonio Texas
128 E3 San Antonio Venezuela
109 K7 San Antonio R Texas
17 H6 San Antonio Abad Ibiza
71 C6 San Antonio B Palawan Philippines
109 L7 San Antonio B Texas
133 F5 San Antonio, C Argentina
126 B4 San Antonio, C Cuba
17 H6 San Antonio, C Spain
133 D2 San Antonio de los Cobres Argentina
124 E3 San Antonio del Rio Mexico
127 N9 San Antonio de Maturín Venezuela
127 L10 San Antonio de Tamanaco Venezuela
102 G7 San Antonio, Mt California
108 B4 San Antonio Mt Texas
133 E6 San Antonio Oeste Argentina
130 J9 San Antonio, Pta. de C Brazil
128 E2 Sanariapo Venezuela
19 P18 Sanary France
111 B10 San Augustine Texas
74 G7 Sanawad India
16 B7 San Bartolómeu de Messines Portugal
45 R7 San Bartolomew in Galdo Italy
42 F6 San Benedetto del Tronto Italy
45 J1 San Benedetto Po Italy
125 P9 San Benito Guatemala
109 K9 San Benito Texas
102 C5 San Benito R California
102 D5 San Benito Mt California
71 G4 San Bernadino Str Philippines
109 M6 San Bernard R Texas
102 G7 San Bernardino California
130 B9 San Bernardino Paraguay
103 J8 San Bernardino Mts California
41 K5 San Bernardino P Switzerland
131 B4 San Bernardo Chile
124 G4 San Bernardo Mexico
128 C2 San Bernardo, I.de Colombia
60 F10 Sanbe-san mt Japan
45 L2 San Biagio Italy
113 B7 San Blas Florida
124 G7 San Blas Nayarit Mexico
124 E4 San Blas Sonora Mexico
125 P5 San Blas, Archipélago de islds Panama
113 B8 San Blas, C Florida
125 P5 San Blas, Serrania de mts Panama
41 O7 San Bonifacio Italy
128 E6 San Borja Bolivia
124 C3 San Borja Mexico
99 L6 Sanborn Iowa
99 L5 Sanborn Minnesota
98 H3 Sanborn N Dakota
95 Q3 Sanbornville New Hampshire
124 J4 San Buenaventura Mexico
68 E5 San Buri Thailand
128 F8 San Camilo Argentina
133 D4 San Carlos Argentina
103 O8 San Carlos Arizona
124 C4 San Carlos Baja Calif Sur Mexico
131 B6 San Carlos Chile
124 H5 San Carlos Coahuila Mexico
71 E3 San Carlos Luzon Philippines
71 F5 San Carlos Negros Philippines
133 G4 San Carlos Uruguay
127 K10 San Carlos Venezuela
131 B8 San Carlos de Bariloche Argentina
17 H4 San Carlos de la Rápita Spain
128 D2 San Carlos del Zulia Venezuela
128 E3 San Carlos de Rio Negro Venezuela
103 O8 San Carlos L Arizona
124 B3 San Carlos, Mesa de mt Mexico
45 K4 San Casciano in Valdi Pesa Italy
17 J3 San Celoní Spain
18 G5 Sancergues France
18 G5 Sancerre France
45 K2 San Cesario sul Panaro Italy
20 J5 Sancheville France
127 K5 Sánchez Dominican Rep
106 E4 Sanchez Res Colorado
52 G6 Sanchursk U.S.S.R.
125 K7 San Ciro de Acosta Mexico
102 G8 San Clemente California
17 F5 San Clemente Spain
102 F9 San Clemente isld California
18 G6 Sancoins France
71 G6 Sanco Pt Mindanao Philippines
130 B10 San Cosme Argentina
133 F3 San Cosme Paraguay
45 O4 San Costanzo Italy
131 E3 San Cristóbal Argentina
127 J5 San Cristóbal Dom Rep
137 N4 San Cristobal Solomon Is
128 D2 San Cristóbal Venezuela
128 B8 San Cristóbal isld Galapagos Is
125 N9 San Cristóbal de las Casas Mexico
103 L9 San Cristobal Wash R Arizona
45 J4 San Croce sulee Arno Italy
133 C4 San Cruz Chile
126 E4 Sancti Spíritus Cuba
118 J7 Sanctuary Sask
22 K5 Sancy France
28 N2 Sand Faeroes
27 B12 Sand Norway
89 E7 Sand R Orange Free State S Africa
89 F4 Sand R Transvaal S Africa
60 J11 Sanda Japan
15 C5 Sanda isld Scotland
28 D6 Sandager Denmark
70 F2 Sandakan Sabah
68 H6 Sandan Cambodia
26 B10 Sandane Norway
47 F3 Sandanski Bulgaria
65 H2 Sandaotong China
65 G1 Sandaozhen China
85 B6 Sandare Mali
27 J10 Sandarne Sweden
106 H4 Sand Arroyo R Colo/Kansas
33 Q7 Sandau E Germany
15 F1 Sanday Scotland
8 D1 Sandbach England
37 P6 Sandbach W Germany
27 G15 Sandbäck Sweden
12 D2 Sandbank Scotland
120 H1 Sandbank L Ontario
28 G7 Sandby Denmark
26 F7 Sanddöla R Norway
26 A9 Sande Norway
27 A10 Sande Norway
32 H5 Sande W Germany
27 D12 Sandefj Norway
103 P6 Sanders Arizona
100 J2 Sanders Idaho
37 M6 Sandersdorf W Germany
33 P9 Sandersleben E Germany
113 E7 Sanderson Florida
108 E5 Sanderson Texas
112 E5 Sandersville Georgia
111 H10 Sandersville Mississippi
33 M5 Sandesneben W Germany
28 B5 Sandet Denmark
28 M2 Sandevåg Faeroes
118 L3 Sandfly L Sask
94 G8 Sand Fork W Virginia
9 H5 Sandgate England
141 L7 Sandgate Queensland
36 F5 Sandhausen W Germany
12 D4 Sandhead Scotland
26 G4 Sandhornöy isld Norway
99 Q3 Sand I Wisconsin
109 K7 Sandia Texas
106 D6 Sandia Pk New Mexico
102 G9 San Diego California
124 G3 San Diego Mexico
109 J8 San Diego Texas
102 G8 San Diego Aqueduct California
133 D8 San Diego, C Argentina
128 F2 San Diego de Cabrutica Venezuela
47 L6 Sandıklı Turkey
74 J5 Sandila India
118 E1 Sandilands Manitoba
113 M9 Sandilands Village New Providence I Bahamas
143 B6 Sandiman, Mt W Australia
124 G5 San Dimas Mexico
69 E14 Sanding isld Indonesia
116 D5 Sand Is Alaska
52 J2 Sandivey R U.S.S.R.
32 H6 Sandkrug W Germany
38 L4 Sandl Austria
120 F5 Sand Lake Ontario
27 C13 Sandnes Aust Agder Norway
27 A13 Sandnes Rogaland Norway
15 G2 Sandness Scotland
26 F5 Sandnessjöen Norway
28 N2 Sandø isld Faeroes
87 D7 Sandoa Zaïre
31 N5 Sandomierz Poland
45 P6 San Donato Val di Comino Italy
110 G3 Sandoval Illinois
106 D6 Sandoval New Mexico
140 D5 Sandover R N Terr Aust
52 E5 Sandovo U.S.S.R.
68 B3 Sandoway Burma
9 E6 Sandown England
89 A10 Sandown B S Africa
Sandoy isld see Sandø
116 G9 Sand Point Alaska
117 P11 Sandpoint Idaho
118 F4 Sand R Alberta
47 K7 Sandras Dağı mt Turkey
9 G2 Sandringham England
140 E6 Sandringham Queensland
99 T3 Sands Michigan
27 G14 Sandsjö, N Sweden
113 G12 Sands Key isld Florida
117 H9 Sandspit Br Columbia
38 G8 Sandspitze mt Austria
101 S2 Sand Springs Montana
107 O5 Sand Springs Oklahoma
102 F2 Sand Springs Salt Flat Nevada
26 D8 Sandstad Norway
32 J6 Sandstedt W Germany
95 K9 Sandston Virginia
99 O3 Sandstone Minnesota
143 C8 Sandstone W Australia
103 M9 Sand Tanks Mts Arizona
123 L4 Sandtop, C Anticosti I, Quebec
67 B3 Sandu China
67 B4 Sandu Guizhou China
67 E2 Sandu Jiangxi China
94 E3 Sandusky Michigan
94 E5 Sandusky Ohio
94 D5 Sandusky R Ohio
28 H6 Sandved Denmark
87 C11 Sandverhaar Namibia
27 G16 Sandvig Denmark
27 D12 Sandvika Norway
27 J11 Sandviken Sweden
9 H5 Sandwich England
99 S8 Sandwich Illinois
95 R5 Sandwich Massachusetts
115 O7 Sandwich B Labrador
141 H4 Sandwich, C Queensland
15 G2 Sandwick Scotland
118 J5 Sandwith Sask
103 J6 Sandy Nevada
100 C4 Sandy Oregon
103 N1 Sandy Utah
95 R2 Sandy R Maine
127 H1 Sandy Bay Jamaica
119 P3 Sandy Bay Saskatchewan
118 K1 Sandybeach L Ontario
141 L6 Sandy C Queensland
139 G8 Sandy C Tasmania
101 O9 Sandy City Utah
109 L6 Sandy Cr Texas
101 Q7 Sandy Cr Wyoming
95 L3 Sandy Creek New York
121 O7 Sandy Creek Quebec
95 O5 Sandy Hook Connecticut
94 D8 Sandy Hook Kentucky
111 G10 Sandy Hook Mississippi
95 N6 Sandy Hook point New Jersey
57 C6 Sandykachi U.S.S.R.
123 Q4 Sandy L Nfld
115 K7 Sandy L Ontario
119 R8 Sandy Lake Manitoba
119 O3 Sandy Narrows Sask
112 L2 Sandy Pt N Carolina
127 P4 Sandy Pt St Kitts W Indies
126 G9 San Estanislao Colombia
129 G8 San Estanislao Paraguay
71 E2 San Fabian Luzon Philippines
45 O7 San Felice Circeo Italy
45 K2 San Felice sul Panaro Italy
124 B2 San Felipe Baja California Mexico
124 F4 San Felipe Chihuahua Mexico
131 B4 San Felipe Chile
128 E3 San Felipe Colombia
127 K9 San Felipe Venezuela
126 C4 San Felipe, Cayos de islds Cuba
17 F4 San Felipe, Cerro de peak Spain
103 H8 San Felipe Cr California
106 D6 San Felipe Pueblo New Mexico
17 K3 San Feliú de Guixols Spain
17 J3 San Felíu de Llobregat Spain
135 S12 San Félix isld Pacific Oc
102 F7 San Fernando California
131 B5 San Fernando Chile
71 E2 San Fernando Luzon Philippines
124 B3 San Fernando Mexico
16 C8 San Fernando Spain
127 O3 San Fernando Trinidad
128 E2 San Fernando de Apure Venezuela
128 E3 San Fernando de Atabape Venezuela
26 G9 Sånfjället mt Sweden
106 E4 Sanford Colorado
113 F9 Sanford Florida
95 R3 Sanford Maine
118 D1 Sanford Manitoba
112 H2 Sanford N Carolina
108 C8 Sanford Texas
94 C3 Sanford L Michigan
116 Q5 Sanford, Mt Alaska
143 B7 Sanford, R W Australia
127 N3 San Francique Trinidad
131 E3 San Francisco Argentina
127 J9 San Francisco Venezuela
104 San Francisco conurbation California
106 B8 San Francisco R Ariz/New Mex
102 B4 San Francisco Bay California
108 E6 San Francisco Cr Texas
124 G4 San Francisco de Conchos Mexico
133 E3 San Francisco del Chanar Argentina
133 D4 San Francisco del Monte de Oro Argentina
124 G4 San Francisco del Oro Mexico
124 H7 San Francisco del Rincón Mexico
127 J5 San Francisco de Macoris Dominican Rep
133 D7 San Francisco de Paula, C Argentina
133 G4 San Gabriel Brazil
102 G7 San Gabriel Mts California
124 C3 San Gabriel, Pta C Mexico
76 B1 Sangammer India
99 R10 Sangamon R Illinois
77 J3 Sangan, Koh-i mt Afghanistan
51 M2 Sangar U.S.S.R.
70 E5 Sangasanga Kalimantan
70 F2 Sanga Sanga isld Philippines
85 C6 Sangasso Mali
22 B2 Sangatte France
128 C4 Sangay vol Ecuador
71 E7 Sangboy Island Philippines
71 J9 Sangeang isld Indonesia
102 E5 Sanger California
98 E2 Sanger N Dakota
109 K2 Sanger Texas
33 O10 Sangerhausen E Germany
127 L5 San Germán Puerto Rico
65 C4 Sanggan He R China
71 J9 Sanggar Sumbawa Indonesia
71 J9 Sanggar, Teluk B Indonesia
70 G6 Sanggona Sulawesi
65 E6 Sanggou Wan B China
86 C5 Sangha R Congo
56 B1 Sangil'ka R U.S.S.R.
45 R7 San Giorgio del Sannio Italy
42 E3 San Giorgio di N Italy
45 K2 San Giorgio di Piano Italy
45 R7 San Giorgio la Molara Italy
38 E8 San Giovanni Italy
45 Q8 San Giovanni a Teducio Italy
45 J1 San Giovanni in Croce Italy
45 K2 San Giovanni in Persiceto Italy
43 G10 San Giovanni, V Italy
45 L4 San Giovanni Valdarno Italy
71 E3 Sangitan Luzon Philippines
45 M1 San Giuliano Italy
45 H4 San Giuliano Terme Italy
45 R8 San Giuseppe Vesuviano Italy
45 M4 San Giustino Italy
65 G6 Sangju S Korea
70 C7 Sangkadura Indonesia
70 F7 Sangkarang, Kep isld Sulawesi
68 D5 Sangkhla Buri Thailand
70 E4 Sangkulirang Kalimantan
70 F4 Sangkulirang, Teluk B Kalimantan
74 E3 Sangla Pakistan
76 B2 Sangli India
86 B5 Sangmélima Cameroon
45 L4 San Godenzo Italy
17 G7 Sangonera R Spain
102 H7 San Gorgonio Mt California
71 B1 Sangowo Halmahera Indonesia
106 E5 Sangre de Cristo Mts New Mex/Colo
102 B4 San Gregorio California
127 P2 Sangre Grande Trinidad
42 F6 Sangro R Italy
74 F3 Sangrur India
88 E5 Sangu Tanzania
118 C5 Sangudo Alberta
129 G6 Sangue R Brazil
18 E10 Sangüesa Spain
41 O7 Sanguinetto Italy
Sangyuan see Wuqiao
67 C2 Sangzhi China
Sanhe see Sandu
59 H1 Sanhe China
65 D4 Sanhe China
67 D1 Sanhedian China
59 J1 Sanhezhan China
124 D5 San Hilario Mexico
59 H1 San he China
67 D1 San Hu L China
67 B1 Sanhuizhen China
113 E11 Sanibel I Florida
130 C10 San Ignacio Argentina
128 E6 San Ignacio Beni Bolivia
124 D2 San Ignacio Mexico
128 F7 San Ignacio Santa Cruz Bolivia
124 C4 San Ignacio, Laguna Mexico
106 D6 San Ildefonso New Mexico
16 E4 San Ildefonso Spain
71 F2 San Ildefonso, C Luzon Philippines
79 H3 Sanime, Wādī watercourse Syria
60 H10 San'in Japan
106 E4 San Isabel Colorado
133 F4 San Isidro Argentina
71 G5 San Isidro Leyte Philippines
124 H5 San Isidro Mexico
33 Q4 Sanitz E Germany
102 H8 San Jacinto California
126 G10 San Jacinto Colombia
101 L8 San Jacinto Nevada
71 F4 San Jacinto Philippines
102 H8 San Jacinto Mts California
133 F4 San Javier Argentina
124 F4 San Javier Mexico
131 F2 San Javier, R Argentina
125 J9 San Jerónimo Mexico
Sanjiang see Liannan
67 C4 Sanjiang China
65 F3 Sanjiangkou China
65 F3 Sanjiazi China
61 M8 Sanjō Japan
128 F6 San Joaquin Bolivia
102 D5 San Joaquin California
130 C9 San Joaquin Paraguay
102 D4 San Joaquin R California
102 D5 San Joaquin Valley California
108 A8 San Jon New Mexico
128 C2 San Jorge R Colombia
133 D7 San Jorge, G Argentina
17 H4 San Jorge, G.de Spain
102 C4 San Jose California
125 M5 San José Costa Rica
99 R9 San Jose Illinois
106 E6 San Jose New Mexico
71 E4 San Jose Philippines
131 G5 San José Uruguay
131 G5 San José dep Uruguay
124 D5 San José isld Mexico
131 B4 San Jose vol Chile
131 F3 San José, Cuchilla de mts Uruguay
128 F2 San José de Amacuro Venezuela
128 F7 San José de Chiquitos Bolivia
124 D3 San José de Dimas Mexico
133 F4 San José de Feliciano Argentina
124 F4 San José de Gracia Sinaloa Mexico
127 M10 San José de Guaribe Venezuela
127 J5 San José de las Matas Dominican Rep
124 E6 San José del Cabo Mexico
128 D3 San José del Gauviare Colombia
127 J5 San José de Ocoa Dominican Rep
128 D3 San José de Ocuné Colombia
106 C6 San Jose, R New Mexico
131 C3 San Juan Argentina
128 F7 San Juan Bolivia
124 F4 San Juan Chihuahua Mexico
124 J4 San Juan Coahuila Mexico
127 J5 San Juan Dominican Rep
71 G6 San Juan Mindanao Philippines
128 D7 San Juan Peru
127 L5 San Juan Puerto Rico
109 J9 San Juan Texas
128 E2 San Juan Venezuela
126 D4 San Juan mt Cuba
131 B3 San Juan prov Argentina
102 D6 San Juan R California
128 C3 San Juan R Colombia
125 M4 San Juan R Costa Rica
103 P4 San Juan R Utah
102 C5 San Juan Bautista California
128 C7 San Juan, B. de B Peru
133 E8 San Juan, C Argentina
102 G8 San Juan Capistrano California
124 H5 San Juan de Guadalupe Mexico
18 G10 San Juan de las Abadesas Spain
124 H8 San Juan de Lima, Pta C Mexico
125 N4 San Juan del Norte Nicaragua
127 K9 San Juan de los Cayos Venezuela
124 H7 San Juan de los Lagos Mexico
127 L10 San Juan de los Morros Venezuela
125 J7 San Juan del Río Mexico
100 C1 San Juan Is Washington
124 F7 San Juanito, I Mexico
106 C4 San Juan Mts Colo/New Mex
125 L9 San Juan Quiotepec Mexico
131 C3 San Juan, R Argentina
126 C3 San Juan y Martínez Cuba
133 D7 San Julián Argentina
133 E4 San Justo Argentina
17 G4 San Just, Sa. de mts Spain
85 C6 Sankarani R Guinea/Mali
76 B2 Sankeshwar India
32 J4 Sankt Peter W Germany
86 D6 Sankuru R Zaïre
45 H2 San Lazzaro Italy
45 M4 San Leo Italy
124 C3 San Lino, Sa mt Mexico
133 E4 San Lorenzo Argentina
128 E6 San Lorenzo Bolivia
128 C3 San Lorenzo Ecuador
125 P9 San Lorenzo Guatemala
124 F3 San Lorenzo Mexico
106 C9 San Lorenzo New Mexico
128 E6 San Lorenzo Peru
127 J10 San Lorenzo Venezuela
124 C3 San Lorenzo isld Mexico
133 C7 San Lorenzo mt Chile/Arg
44 C4 San Lorenzo al Mare Italy
128 B4 San Lorenzo, C Ecuador
17 F5 San Lorenzo de la Parrilla Spain
17 J2 San Lorenzo de Morunys Spain
128 C6 San Lorenzo, I Peru
45 N4 San Lorenzo in Campo Italy
16 C8 Sanlúcar de Barrameda Spain
16 C7 Sanlúcar la Mayor Spain
128 E8 San Lucas Bolivia
102 C5 San Lucas California
124 E6 San Lucas Mexico
131 C4 San Luis Argentina
103 K9 San Luis Arizona
124 F4 San Luis Chihuahua Mexico
106 E4 San Luis Colorado
126 G4 San Luis Cuba
125 P9 San Luís Guatemala
71 E2 San Luis Luzon Philippines
125 J9 San Luis Mexico
124 D3 San Luís Sonora Mexico
127 K9 San Luis Venezuela
131 C4 San Luis prov Argentina
124 E4 San Luis Babarocos Mexico
125 J7 San Luis de la Paz Mexico
128 F6 San Luis, L Bolivia
103 K9 San Luis, Mesa de Mexico
102 D6 San Luis Obispo California
109 M6 San Luis Pass Texas
106 D3 San Luis Pk Colorado
125 J6 San Luis Potosí Mexico
102 G8 San Luis Rey R California
124 B1 San Luis Rio Colorado Mexico
131 C4 San Luis, Sa. de mts Argentina
71 E3 San Marcelino Luzon Philippines
124 D3 San Marcial Mexico
106 C8 San Marcial New Mexico
124 D5 San Marcial, Pta C Mexico
43 B9 San Marco, C Sardinia
126 G10 San Marcos Colombia
124 G7 San Marcos Mexico
109 K6 San Marcos Texas
124 C4 San Marcos isld Mexico
42 E5 San Marino rep S Europe
128 D3 San Martín Colombia
128 C5 San Martin dep Peru
128 F6 San Martin R Bolivia
133 C6 San Martín de los Andes Argentina
133 C7 San Martin, L Chile/Arg
45 L2 San Martino in Argine Italy
38 E8 San Martino in Badia Italy
45 J2 San Martino in Rio Italy
45 K2 San Martino in Spino Italy
102 B4 San Mateo California
125 M5 San Mateo Costa Rica
106 C6 San Mateo New Mexico
17 H4 San Mateo Spain
127 M10 San Mateo Venezuela
106 C8 San Mateo Pk New Mexico
128 G7 San Matías Bolivia
131 D8 San Matias, G Argentina
121 R5 Sanmaur Quebec
127 L10 San Mauricio Venezuela
67 G2 Sanmen China
67 G2 Sanmen Wan B China
65 B7 Sanmenxia China
103 N10 San Miguel Arizona
102 D6 San Miguel California
125 Q11 San Miguel Honduras
124 J5 San Miguel Mexico
128 D6 San Miguel Peru
71 D6 San Miguel islds Philippines
106 B3 San Miguel R Colorado
128 C3 San Miguel R Ecuador
124 D3 San Miguel R Mexico
71 F4 San Miguel B Philippines
109 J9 San Miguel Camargo Mexico
109 J7 San Miguel Cr Texas
125 J7 San Miguel de Allende Mexico
128 E7 San Miguel de Huachi Bolivia
133 D3 San Miguel de Tucumán Argentina
102 D7 San Miguel I California
67 F3 Sanming China
45 J4 San Miniato Italy
71 E3 San Narciso Luzon Philippines
42 G7 Sannicandro Garganico Italy
131 E4 San Nicolas Argentina
71 E1 San Nicolas Luzon Philippines
71 E2 San Nicolas Luzon Philippines
124 G5 San Nicolás Mexico
102 E8 San Nicolas I California
45 L2 San Nicolo Ferrarese Italy
27 D13 Sannidal Norway
51 O1 Sannikoya, Proliv str U.S.S.R.
45 R7 Sannio mts Italy
61 N9 Sano Japan
31 N6 Sanok Poland
102 G8 San Onofre California
133 D8 San Pablo Argentina
128 F7 San Pablo Bolivia
133 D2 San Pablo Bolivia
71 E3 San Pablo Luzon Philippines
124 F4 San Pablo Balleza Mexico
124 B4 San Pablo, Pta C Mexico
124 H6 San Pascual Mexico
131 F4 San Pedro Buenos Aires Argentina
102 F8 San Pedro California
128 F8 San Pedro Jujuy Argentina
124 E4 San Pedro Mexico
130 C10 San Pedro Misiones Argentina
130 B9 San Pedro Paraguay
128 F2 San Pedro Venezuela
103 O9 San Pedro R Arizona
71 G5 San Pedro B Philippines
131 A8 San Pedro, B.de Chile
102 F8 San Pedro Chan California
128 D3 San Pedro de Arimena Colombia
124 E3 San Pedro de la Cueva Mexico
124 H5 San Pedro de las Colonias Mexico
128 C5 San Pedro de Lloc Peru
17 G7 San Pedro del Pinatar Spain
127 K5 San Pedro de Macoris Dominican Rep
133 C3 San Pedro, Pta C Chile
16 C5 San Pedro, Sa. de mts Spain
125 P10 San Pedro Sula Honduras
44 E3 San Pier d'Arena Italy
45 K4 San Piero a Sieve Italy
99 U8 San Pierre Indiana
45 K1 San Pietro di Morubio Italy
45 K2 San Pietro di Piano Italy
43 H8 San Pietro, I Italy
42 C3 San Pietro, Pte Italy
100 G1 Sanpoil R Washington
45 H2 San Polo d'Enza in Caviano Italy
45 J2 San Possidónio Italy
45 K2 San Prospero Italy
15 E5 Sanquhar Scotland
124 A2 San Quintín Mexico
131 C5 San Rafael Argentina
128 F7 San Rafael Bolivia
102 B4 San Rafael California
106 C6 San Rafael New Mexico
127 K10 San Rafael Venezuela
103 O2 San Rafael R Utah
127 K5 San Rafael, C Dominican Rep
127 K5 San Rafael del Yuma Dominican Rep
103 O3 San Rafael Knob mt Utah
102 E7 San Rafael Mts California
125 M3 San Ramón Nicaragua
128 C6 San Ramón Peru
67 E5 Sanrao China
44 C4 Sanremo Italy
108 F7 San Rodrigo R Mexico
127 J8 San Román, C Venezuela
16 D8 San Roque Spain
109 J4 San Saba Texas
108 G5 San Saba R Texas
21 D9 Sansais France
125 P11 San Salvador El Salvador
126 A3 San Salvador isld Bahamas
128 A8 San Salvador isld Galapagos Is
131 F4 San Salvador R Uruguay
133 D2 San Salvador de Jujuy Argentina
85 E6 Sansanne-Mango Togo
133 D8 San Sebastián Argentina
85 A3 San Sebastian Canary Is
17 F1 San Sebastian Spain
127 L10 San Sebastián Venezuela
124 C3 San Sebastián isld Mexico
129 J8 San Sebastião Brazil
42 E5 Sansepolcro Italy
42 G7 San Severo Italy
67 G3 Sansha China
128 E6 San Silvestre Bolivia
127 J10 San Silvestre Venezuela
102 C6 San Simeon California
103 P9 San Simon Arizona
103 P9 San Simon Cr Arizona
42 H4 Sanski Most Yugoslavia
145 E4 Sanson New Zealand
108 B6 San Sostenes Mexico
44 C4 San Stefano al Mare Italy
127 N4 Sans Toucher mt Guadeloupe W Indies
67 C3 Sansui China
128 C5 Santa Peru
125 O9 Santa Amelia Guatemala
128 E6 Santa Ana Bolivia
102 G8 Santa Ana California
128 B4 Santa Ana Ecuador
125 P11 Santa Ana El Salvador
124 D2 Santa Ana Mexico
127 M10 Santa Ana Venezuela
102 G8 Santa Ana R California
124 F3 Santa Ana Babicora Mexico
102 G8 Santa Ana Mts California
44 F1 Santa Angelo Italy
109 H4 Santa Anna Texas
130 G6 Santa Bárbara Brazil
102 E7 Santa Barbara California
126 C4 Santa Bárbara Cuba
124 G4 Santa Bárbara Mexico
127 N10 Santa Bárbara Venezuela
102 D7 Santa Barbara Ch California
102 E8 Santa Barbara I California
102 E7 Santa Barbara Res California
130 D7 Santa Barbara, Sa de mts Brazil
128 E8 Santa Catalina Argentina
133 D3 Santa Catalina Chile
124 D5 Santa Catalina isld Mexico
102 G8 Santa Catalina, G.of California
102 F8 Santa Catalina, I California
124 B3 Santa Catarina Mexico
133 G3 Santa Catarina state Brazil
124 G5 Santa Catarina de Tepehuanes Mexico
126 B1 Santa Catharina Curaçao
102 B4 Santa Clara California
128 E4 Santa Clara Colombia
126 E3 Santa Clara Cuba
103 K10 Santa Clara Mexico
95 N2 Santa Clara New York
103 L4 Santa Clara Utah
133 B9 Santa Clara isld Juan Fernández Is Pacific Oc
102 E7 Santa Clara R California
110 K3 Santa Claus Indiana
17 J3 Santa Coloma de Farnés Spain
87 C8 Santa Comba Angola
16 B1 Santa Comba Spain
128 D5 Santa Cruz Amazonas Brazil
126 A1 Santa Cruz Aruba W I
128 F7 Santa Cruz Bolivia
102 B5 Santa Cruz California
71 D3 Santa Cruz Luzon Philippines
71 E2 Santa Cruz Luzon Philippines
71 E3 Santa Cruz Luzon Philippines
71 F6 Santa Cruz Negros Philippines
106 D6 Santa Cruz New Mexico
128 C5 Santa Cruz Peru
130 J9 Santa Cruz Rio Grande do Norte Brazil
128 A8 Santa Cruz isld Galapagos Is
124 D5 Santa Cruz isld Mexico
133 C7 Santa Cruz prov Argentina
130 H5 Santa Cruz Cabralia Brazil
85 A3 Santa Cruz de la Palma Canary Is
16 E5 Santa Cruz de la Zarza Spain
126 F4 Santa Cruz del Sur Cuba
16 E6 Santa Cruz de Mudela Spain
85 A3 Santa Cruz de Tenerife Canary Is
133 G3 Santa Cruz do Sul Brazil
137 O4 Santa Cruz Is Solomon Is
102 B4 Santa Cruz Mts California
127 J2 Santa Cruz Mts Jamaica
17 F3 Santa Cruz, Sa. de mts Spain
79 B8 Santa, El Egypt
128 B4 Santa Elena Ecuador
109 J9 Santa Elena Texas
128 F3 Santa Elena Venezuela
128 B4 Santa Elena, B. de Ecuador
125 M4 Santa Elena, C Costa Rica
100 J2 Santa Emida Idaho
16 A2 Santa Eugenia de Ribeira Spain
17 G4 Santa Eulalia Spain
17 J6 Santa Eulalia del Rio Ibiza
131 E3 Santa Fe Argentina
126 C4 Santa Fé Cuba
106 E6 Santa Fe New Mexico
71 F4 Santa Fe Philippines
16 E7 Santafé Spain
128 A8 Santa Fe isld Galapagos Is
133 E4 Santa Fe prov Argentina
113 E8 Santa Fe R Florida
129 J5 Santa Filomena Brazil
124 E6 Santa Genovéva mt Mexico
124 G4 Santa Gertrudis Mexico
129 J4 Santa Helena Brazil
58 E5 Santai China
133 C8 Santa Ines, I Chile
133 D5 Santa Isabel Argentina
128 G5 Santa Isabel Brazil
Santa Isabel Fernando Póo see Malabo Macias Nguema Biyogo
137 M3 Santa Isabel isld Solomon Is
124 B2 Santa Isabel, Sa mts Mexico
129 J5 Santa Isobel do Araguaia Brazil
129 G5 Santa Julía Brazil
130 F6 Santa Juliana Brazil
126 B3 Santa Lucía Cuba
124 G5 Santa Lucía Mexico
131 F2 Santa Lucia, R Argentina
131 G5 Santa Lucia, R Uruguay
102 C5 Santa Lucia Rge California
130 C6 Santa Luisa, Sa. de mts Brazil
130 H9 Santa Luzia Brazil
102 D6 Santa Margarita California
124 D5 Santa Margarita isld Mexico
102 G8 Santa Margarita R California
44 F3 Santa Margherita Italy
128 G4 Santa Maria Amazonas Brazil
133 D3 Santa María Argentina
102 D7 Santa Maria California
131 H2 Santa Maria Rio Grande do Sul Brazil
87 E8 Santa Maria Zambia
128 A8 Santa María isld Galapagos Is
137 O4 Santa Maria isld New Hebrides
133 D5 Santa María mt Argentina
103 L7 Santa Maria R Arizona
131 G3 Santa Maria R Brazil
124 F2 Santa María R Mexico
131 G5 Santa Maria, C Uruguay
43 F7 Santa Maria Capua Vetere Italy
16 B7 Santa Maria, C. de Portugal
130 F4 Santa Maria, Chapadão de hills Brazil
124 F4 Santa María de Cuevas Mexico
127 M10 Santa Maria de Ipire Venezuela
124 G5 Santa María del Oro Mexico
43 J9 Santa Maria di Leuca, C Italy
131 A6 Santa María, I Chile
103 M7 Santa Maria Mts Arizona
128 C6 Santa María, Pta C Peru
130 C7 Santa Maria, R Brazil
130 F4 Santa Maria, Sa. de mts Brazil
131 B6 Santa Mariá, Vol Argentina
126 G3 Santa Marie, C Long I Bahamas
126 G9 Santa Marta Colombia
87 B8 Santa Marta, C Angola
126 H9 Santa Marta, Sa. Nevada de mts Colombia
130 D6 Santa Martha, Sa. de mts Brazil
Santa Maura isld see Levkás Greece
102 F7 Santa Monica California
108 G7 Santa Mónica Mexico
109 K9 Santa Monica Texas
102 F8 Santa Monica B California
102 H8 Santa Mts California
70 E5 Santan Kalimantan
129 K6 Santana Brazil
131 G3 Santana, Coxilha de mt Brazil/Uruguay
131 G3 Santana do Livramento Brazil
128 C3 Santander Colombia
16 E1 Santander Spain
16 E1 Santander prov Spain
66 E3 Santanghu China
71 G5 Santa Niño Samar Philippines
103 N8 Santan Mt Arizona
102 E7 Santa Paula California
109 K9 Santa Perlita Texas
17 G6 Santa Pola, C. de Spain
101 O10 Santaquin Utah
16 B5 Santarem Portugal
130 J9 Santa Rita Brazil
101 N1 Santa Rita Montana
127 J9 Santa Rita Venezuela
131 D6 Santa Rosa Argentina
102 B3 Santa Rosa California
128 E3 Santa Rosa Colombia
108 C1 Santa Rosa New Mexico
130 C10 Santa Rosa Paraguay
125 M2 Santa Rosa de Aguán Honduras
128 F7 Santa Rosa de la Roca Bolivia
125 L3 Santa Rosa de Lima El Salvador
111 J11 Santa Rosa I Florida
109 H2 Santa Rosa L Texas
124 C4 Santa Rosalía Mexico
130 C10 Santa Rosa, R Brazil
100 H8 Santa Rosa Range Nevada
103 N9 Santa Rosa Wash R Arizona
133 E3 Santa Sylvina Argentina
124 G6 Santa Teresa Mexico
129 J6 Santa Teresa R Brazil
43 C7 Santa Teresa Gallura Sardinia
129 H6 Santa Teresinha Brazil
140 C6 Santa Theresa Mission N Terr Aust
133 G4 Santa Vitória do Palmar Brazil
102 D7 Santa Ynez California
102 D7 Santa Ynez Mts California
102 H8 Santa Ysabel California
112 H4 Santee R S Carolina
112 H4 Santee Pt S Carolina
112 D2 Santeetlah, L N Carolina
124 A2 San Telmo Mexico
124 H8 San Telmo, Pta C Mexico
45 O5 Sante Marie Italy
21 H6 Santenay France
42 D4 Santerno R Italy
20 J5 Santeuil France
44 D1 Santhià Italy
124 D6 Santiago Baja California Mexico
131 B4 Santiago Chile
133 C4 Santiago Chile
124 G8 Santiago Colima Mexico
127 J5 Santiago Dominican Rep
125 O5 Santiago Panama
130 C10 Santiago Paraguay
131 B4 Santiago prov Chile
128 C4 Santiago R Peru
16 B2 Santiago de Compostela Spain
126 G4 Santiago de Cuba Cuba
17 F6 Santiago de la Espana Spain
133 E3 Santiago del Estero prov Argentina
16 B6 Santiago do Cacem Portugal
124 G7 Santiago Ixcuintla Mexico
108 D6 Santiago Mts Texas
124 G5 Santiago Papasquiaro Mexico
102 G8 Santiago Pk California
124 H7 Santiago, Rio Grande de Mexico
128 G7 Santiago, Serrania de mts Bolivia
124 G5 Santiaguillo, L. de Mexico
70 G4 Santigi Sulawesi
16 E1 Santillana Spain
16 E6 Santisteban del Puerto Spain
109 J3 Santo Texas
130 F8 Santo Amaro, I. de Brazil
130 G6 Santo Antônia Brazil
128 F5 Santo Antonio Brazil
129 K6 Santo Antônio de Jesus Brazil
128 E4 Santo Antônio do Içá Brazil
86 B7 Santo Antonio do Zaire Angola

130 C10 Santo Cristo R Brazil
87 D9 Santo Cruz do Cuando Angola
124 B3 Santo Domingo Baja California Mexico
124 H3 Santo Domingo Coahuila Mexico
126 D3 Santo Domingo Cuba
127 K5 Santo Domingo Dominican Rep
126 G4 Santo Domingo, Cay isld Bahamas
17 F2 Santo Domingo de la Calza Spain
124 C5 Santo Domingo del Pacifico Mexico
130 G6 Santo Maria do Suaçuí Brazil
127 M10 San Tomé Venezuela
128 F2 San Tome de Guayana Venezuela
16 E1 Santoña Spain
65 G3 Santong He R China
Santorini isld see Thíra I Greece
130 F8 Santos Brazil
128 E5 Santos Dumont Amazonas Brazil
130 G7 Santos Dumont Minas Gerais Brazil
16 D6 Santos, Sa. de los mts Spain
16 B3 Santo Tirso Portugal
124 F3 Santo Tomás Mexico
128 D6 Santo Tomás Peru
133 F3 Santo Tomé Argentina
43 C8 Santu, C. di M mt Sardinia
65 D4 Santunying China
103 L6 Sanup Plat Arizona
133 C7 San Valentin mt Chile
20 F3 Sanvic France
71 F1 San Vicente Luzon Philippines
124 A2 San Vicente Mexico
128 C6 San Vicente de Cañete Peru
16 E1 San Vicente de la Barquera Spain
45 P6 San Vicenze Falle Roveto Italy
42 E3 San Vito al Tag Italy
43 E10 San Vito, C Sicily
38 F9 San Vito di Cadore-Antelao Italy
45 N6 San Vito Romano Italy
Sanya see Ya Xian
109 H8 San Ygnacio Texas
102 G9 San Ysidro California
106 D6 San Ysidro New Mexico
58 E5 Sanyuan China
65 F3 Sanyuanpu China
87 C7 Sanza Pomba Angola
65 F2 Sanzhan China
130 F8 São Bernardo do Campo Brazil
130 F8 São Carlos Brazil
129 L6 São Cristóvão Brazil
129 J6 São Domingos Brazil
130 D6 São Domingos, R Brazil
129 K7 São Felippe, Serra de mts Brazil
129 H5 São Felix do Xingu Brazil
129 K7 São Francisco Brazil
130 F6 São Francisco R Brazil
130 E10 São Francisco do Sul Brazil
130 E10 Sao Francisco, I.de Brazil
129 J7 São Gabriel de Goias Brazil
87 G7 Sao Hill Tanzania
130 D8 São João R Brazil
129 J6 São João da Alianca Brazil
130 F7 São João da Boa Vista Brazil
130 G7 São João del Rei Brazil
129 K5 São João do Piauí Brazil
129 J5 São João du Araguaia Brazil
129 K4 São João, I. de Brazil
128 F5 São João, Sa. de mts Brazil
128 E4 São Joaquim Brazil
128 E4 São José Brazil
128 F3 São José do Anauá Brazil
133 G4 São José do Norte Brazil
130 E7 São José do Rio Prêto Brazil
130 F8 São José dos Campos Brazil
130 E9 São José dos Pinhais Brazil
71 A2 Saolat, Bukit mt Halmahera Indonesia
133 G3 São Leopoldo Brazil
130 C5 São Lourenço Brazil
133 G4 São Lourenço do Sul Brazil
130 C5 São Lourenço, Pantanal de swamp Brazil
129 J4 São Luís Brazil
128 F5 São Luis de Cassianá Brazil
133 G3 São Luis Gonzaga Brazil
128 E3 São Marcelino Brazil
129 K4 São Marco, B. de Brazil
130 F5 São Marcos, R Brazil
130 H6 São Mateus Brazil
130 F4 São Miguel R Brazil
127 K5 Saona, I Dominican Rep
19 N12 Saône R France
71 C3 Saonek W Irian
130 F8 São Paulo Brazil
128 E4 São Paulo de Olivença Brazil
128 F5 São Pedro Brazil
129 L5 São Rafael Brazil
129 J5 São Raimundo das Mangabeiras Brazil
129 K5 São Raimundo Nonato Brazil
128 E5 São Romão Brazil
129 H5 São Sebastião Brazil
130 F7 São Sebastião do Paraíso Brazil
130 F8 São Sebastião, I. de Brazil
128 F6 São Simão R Brazil
86 A5 Sao Tome and Principe islds, rep West Africa
130 H7 São Tomé, C. de Brazil
68 F7 Sa Oui Cambodia
85 D3 Saoura watercourse Algeria
129 J8 Sao Vicente Brazil
47 H3 Sápai Greece
47 L4 Sapanca Turkey
71 E3 Sapangbato Luzon Philippines
85 F7 Sapele Nigeria
106 E6 Sapello New Mexico
112 F6 Sapelo I Georgia
16 C4 Sa. Peña de Francia mt Spain
71 J9 Sape Selat Indonesia
71 J9 Sape Teluk B Indonesia
47 K5 Şaphane Turkey
68 G2 Sa Phin, Pou mt Vietnam
46 E8 Sapiéntza isld Greece
106 C3 Sapinero Colorado
20 F4 Sap, le France
71 E2 Sapocoy, Mt Luzon Philippines
125 P6 Sapo, Serranía del ra Panama
128 C5 Saposoa Peru
54 M3 Sapozhok U.S.S.R.
98 F10 Sappa Cr Kansas
38 G8 Sappada Italy
101 M3 Sapphire Mts Montana
26 M4 Sappisaasi Sweden
59 M3 Sapporo Japan
43 G8 Sapri Italy
129 G4 Sapucua, L. de Brazil
70 P9 Sapudi isld Indonesia
70 E2 Sapulot Sabah
107 O5 Sapulpa Oklahoma
78 L3 Saqqez Iran
78 L3 Sarab Iran
68 E5 Sara Buri Thailand
106 E6 Sarafina New Mexico
108 D4 Saragosa Texas
Saragossa see Zaragoza
128 C4 Saraguro Ecuador
29 M7 Säräisniemi Finland
48 E7 Sarajevo Yugoslavia
140 J5 Saraji Queensland
77 G1 Sarakhs Iran
46 F4 Saraklí Greece
55 C5 Saraktash U.S.S.R.
129 G2 Saramacca R Suriname
18 F9 Saramon France
138 D2 Sara, Mt S Australia
57 G1 Saran' U.S.S.R.
94 B4 Saranac Michigan
95 N2 Saranac Lake New York
46 D5 Sarandë Albania
130 D10 Sarandi Brazil
133 F4 Sarandi del Yi Uruguay
70 B5 Saran, G mt Kalimantan
71 G8 Sarangani isld Mindanao Philippines
75 K8 Sarangarh India
53 G7 Saransk U.S.S.R.
59 L2 Sarapul'skoye U.S.S.R.
113 E10 Sarasota Florida
113 E10 Sarasota Key isld Florida
111 B11 Saratoga Texas
101 T8 Saratoga Wyoming
95 O3 Saratoga Springs New York
70 B4 Saratok Sarawak
53 G8 Saratov U.S.S.R.
77 H6 Saravan Iran
68 H5 Saravane Laos
68 D6 Sarawa R Burma
70 Sarawak state Malaysia
47 J3 Saray Turkey
47 K7 Sarayköy Turkey
77 G6 Sarbāz Iran
42 D3 Sarca R Italy
33 T9 Särchen E Germany
133 C3 Sarco Chile
110 B4 Sarcoxie Missouri
85 G3 Sardalas Libya
74 F4 Sardarshahr India
86 G5 Sardindida Plain Kenya
Sardinia see Sardegna
94 D7 Sardinia Ohio
43 B8 Sardinia isld Italy
112 F5 Sardis Georgia
111 G7 Sardis Mississippi
110 H6 Sardis Tennessee
47 J6 Sardis Turkey
115 P5 Sârdloq Greenland
86 H3 Sardo Ethiopia
71 J8 Sarege isld Indonesia
45 K1 Sarego Italy
26 J4 Sarektjåkko mt Sweden
70 D5 Sarempaka mt Kalimantan
86 G3 Sarenga mt Ethiopia
41 O4 Sarentina, V Italy
42 D2 Sarentine, Alpi mts Italy
41 O4 Sarentino Italy
111 C9 Sarepta Louisiana
77 D4 Sar e Yazd Iran
41 K3 Sargans Switzerland
90 C6 Sargasso Sea Atlantic Oc
55 F3 Sargatskoye U.S.S.R.
20 F5 Sargé France
102 C5 Sargent California
98 G8 Sargent Nebraska
116 N6 Sargent Icefield Alaska
106 D3 Sargents Colorado
21 G6 Sargé-sur-Braye France
74 E2 Sargodha Pakistan
86 C4 Sarh Chad
85 C2 Sarhro, Jbel mts Morocco
77 C1 Sari Iran
47 J9 Sária isld Greece
124 D2 Sáric Mexico
116 E9 Sarichef, C Aleutian Is
80 D3 Sarid Israel
47 K6 Sarigöl Turkey
78 J1 Sarikamis Turkey
70 B3 Sarikei Sarawak
141 J5 Sarina Queensland
17 G3 Sariñena Spain
77 J1 Sar-i-Pul Afghanistan
77 K2 Sar-i-Pul Afghanistan
84 G4 Sarir Libya
109 K8 Sarita Texas
59 J4 Sariwŏn N Korea
47 K3 Sarıyer Turkey
29 L7 Sarjakylä Finland
9 H6 Sark isld Channel Is
57 J2 Sarkand U.S.S.R.
78 F2 Sarkisla Turkey
47 J4 Şarköy Turkey
18 F8 Sarlat France
77 K4 Sarlath Range Afghanistan/Pakistan
98 H1 Sarles N Dakota
119 T10 Sarles N Dakota
52 H6 Sarmany U.S.S.R.
48 J4 Sărmaşu Romania
136 H2 Sarmi W Irian
133 D7 Sarmiento Argentina
133 C8 Sarmiento mt Chile
27 F10 Särna Sweden
27 M14 Särnate U.S.S.R.
41 H4 Sarnen Switzerland
115 L9 Sarnia Ontario
41 L6 Sarnico Italy
43 F8 Sarno Italy
27 E14 Särö Sweden
70 G6 Saroako Sulawesi
77 L2 Sarobi Afghanistan
69 F14 Sarolangun Sumatra
60 R1 Saroma-ko L Japan
47 F7 Saronikós Kólpos B Greece
42 C3 Saronno Italy
47 H4 Saros Körfezi B Turkey
46 D2 Šar Planina mt Yugoslavia
27 E12 Sarpsborg Norway
101 T4 Sarpy Montana
115 O3 Sarqaq Greenland
36 C6 Sarralbe France
36 C6 Sarraltroff France
19 N14 Sarras France
36 C6 Sarrebourg France
19 K3 Sarreguemines France
16 C2 Sarria Spain
19 N16 Sarrians France
17 G4 Sarrión Spain
80 G5 Sarrut Jordan
55 C3 Sars U.S.S.R.
52 H6 Sarsak Omga U.S.S.R.
45 M4 Sarsina Italy
22 D3 Sars, le France
22 G3 Sars-Poteries France
81 C16 Sars Seamount S Pacific Oc
32 L8 Sarstedt W Germany
22 K2 Sart Belgium
74 D5 Sartanahu Pakistan
51 N2 Sartang R U.S.S.R.
21 F6 Sarthe dep France
20 E5 Sarthe R France
20 C4 Sartilly France
Sartu see Anda
60 R3 Sarubetsu R Japan
60 F10 Sarumasay Japan
75 O5 Sarupeta India
79 G3 Sarūt R Syria
78 L4 Sarvabad Iran
48 E4 Sarviz R Hungary
26 F9 Särvsjö Sweden
57 B2 Sarychoganak, Zaliv gulf U.S.S.R.
57 H2 Saryishikotrau, Peski des U.S.S.R.
57 G2 Sarykomey U.S.S.R.
55 D5 Sarykopa, Oz L U.S.S.R.
55 D5 Sarymoin, Oz L U.S.S.R.
57 J3 Sary-Ozek U.S.S.R.
57 G2 Sary-Shagan U.S.S.R.
57 E2 Sarysu R U.S.S.R.
57 G5 Sary-Tash U.S.S.R.
52 J3 Sar'yudin U.S.S.R.
57 B6 Sary-Yazikskoye Vdkhr res U.S.S.R.
44 G3 Sarzana Italy
18 D5 Sarzeau France
86 H4 Sasa Baneh Ethiopia
103 N10 Sasabe Arizona
124 D2 Sásabe Mexico
69 D12 Sasak Sumatra
75 L6 Sasaram India
71 J9 Sasar Tg C Sumba Indonesia
60 J10 Sasayama Japan
40 G1 Sasbach W Germany
60 C12 Sasebo Japan
118 H5 Saskatchewan prov Canada
118 L6 Saskatoon Sask
119 Q5 Saskeram L Manitoba
51 L1 Saskylakh U.S.S.R.
125 M3 Saslaya mt Nicaragua
109 J6 Saspamco Texas
112 E2 Sassafras Mt S Carolina
85 C8 Sassandra Ivory Coast
85 C7 Sassandra R Ivory Coast
37 K4 Sassanfahr W Germany
43 B8 Sassari Sardinia
33 S4 Sassen E Germany
19 F14 Sassenage France
32 H9 Sassenberg W Germany
33 N7 Sassenburg W Germany
25 C4 Sassenheim Netherlands
20 G2 Sassetot France
30 H1 Sassnitz E Germany
45 N4 Sassocorvaro Italy
45 K3 Sasso Marconi Italy
38 E8 Sass Rigais mt Italy
45 J2 Sassuolo Italy
17 G3 Sástago Spain
133 E4 Sastre Argentina
60 C11 Sasuna Japan
25 A6 Sas-van Gent Netherlands
57 K2 Sasykkol', Ozero L U.S.S.R.
48 M5 Sasyk, Oz L U.S.S.R.
85 B6 Satadougou Mali
60 D14 Sata-misaki C Japan
106 B6 Satan Pass New Mexico
107 K4 Satanta Kansas
76 A2 Satara India
114 H2 Satellite B N W Terr
71 H8 Satengar isld Indonesia
27 H11 Säter Sweden
32 G6 Saterland reg W Germany
112 E6 Satilla R Georgia
19 N14 Satillieu France
128 D6 Satipo Peru
26 K4 Satisjaure L Sweden
55 C4 Satka U.S.S.R.
13 G4 Satley England
74 F8 Satmala Hills India
71 H9 Satonda isld Indonesia
86 D6 Satonga R Zaïre
42 H4 Šator mt Yugoslavia
48 G2 Sátoraljaújhely Hungary
33 P5 Satow E Germany
74 F8 Satpura Range India
28 D7 Satrup W Germany
60 D14 Satsuma-hantō pen Japan
26 N4 Sattajärvi Sweden
29 M4 Sattanen Finland
41 J3 Sattel Switzerland
76 E2 Sattenapalle India
68 B3 Satthwa Burma
26 J9 Sättna Sweden
38 K8 Sattnitz reg Austria
70 D6 Satui Kalimantan
48 H3 Satu Mare Romania
69 D9 Satun Thailand
100 B1 Saturna I Br Col
100 E3 Satus Washington
76 C5 Satyamangalam India
55 D2 Satyga U.S.S.R.
38 L8 Saualpe mts Austria
70 P9 Saubi isld Indonesia
20 F3 S.Aubin-de-Scellon France
122 H2 Saubosq, L Quebec
124 J5 Sauceda Mexico
103 M9 Sauceda Mts Arizona
131 E7 Sauce, R Argentina
124 G4 Sauces Mexico
111 G11 Saucier Mississippi
124 G3 Saucillo Mexico
27 B12 Sauda Norway
128 F5 Saudade Brazil
72 E4 Saudi Arabia kingdom
36 D1 Sauerland reg W Germany
129 G6 Saueruina R Brazil
71 G7 Saug R Mindanao Philippines
99 U7 Saugatuck Michigan
120 J8 Saugeen R Ontario
117 K9 Saugstad, Mt Br Col
18 H8 Saugues France
129 G4 Sauiá Brazil
18 E7 Saujon France
99 M4 Sauk R Minnesota
100 D1 Sauk R Washington
99 M4 Sauk Center Minnesota
99 R6 Sauk City Wisconsin
52 B6 Šaukenai U.S.S.R.
22 G4 Saulces-Monclin France
18 G5 Sauldre R France
20 E5 Saule, Mt.du France
41 L1 Saulgau W Germany
41 O2 Saulgrub W Germany
18 H5 Saulieu France
52 B6 Saulkrasti U.S.S.R.
122 F9 Saulnierville Nova Scotia
19 O16 Sault France
122 C5 Sault au Mouton Quebec
122 C5 Sault-aux-Cochons, R Quebec
115 L8 Sault Ste. Marie Ontario
36 C7 Saulxures France
80 G3 Saum Jordan
141 L5 Saumarez Reef Gt Barrier Reef Aust
127 J5 Saumâtre, Etang L Haiti
20 H5 Saumeray France
136 G3 Saumlaki Moluccas Indonesia
21 E7 Saumur France
122 K2 Saumur, L Quebec
29 N4 Saunavaara Finland
118 B6 Saunders Alberta
8 B4 Saundersfoot Wales
146 A14 Saunders I Falkland Is
140 B2 Saunders, Mt N Terr Aust
143 F8 Saunders Ra W Australia
8 B5 Saunton England
57 L2 Saur, Khrebet mts U.S.S.R.
41 K4 Sauronstock mt Switzerland
38 M8 Sausal reg Austria
102 B4 Sausalito California
71 C3 Sausapor W Irian
20 C2 Saussemesnil France
19 O18 Sausset-les-Pins France
40 A3 Saussy France
70 G5 Sausu Sulawesi
87 C8 Sautar Angola
122 H2 Sauterelles, Lac aux Quebec
127 P5 Sauteurs Grenada
21 B7 Sautron France
18 E9 Sauveterre France
18 F8 Sauveterre-de-Guyenne France
21 I10 Sauviat-sur-Vige France
29 K11 Sauvo Finland
25 G2 Sauwerd Netherlands
42 H3 Sava R Yugoslavia
95 L7 Savage Maryland
111 F7 Savage Mississippi
98 B2 Savage Montana
101 U6 Savageton Wyoming
137 S4 Savaii isld W Samoa
85 E7 Savalou Benin
122 A2 Savane, R Quebec
126 A2 Savaneta Aruba W I
99 Q7 Savanna Illinois
107 P7 Savanna Oklahoma
112 F5 Savannah Georgia
110 B2 Savannah Missouri
94 E6 Savannah Ohio
110 H6 Savannah Tennessee
112 E3 Savannah R S Carolina
112 F6 Savannah Beach Georgia
141 F4 Savannah Downs Queensland
126 F2 Savannah Sound Eleuthera Bahamas
68 G4 Savannakhet Laos
127 H2 Savanna la Mar Jamaica
76 A3 Savantvadi India
76 B3 Savanur India
26 L8 Sävar Sweden
26 L7 Sävarån R Sweden
40 F6 Savaranche, V Italy
26 M6 Sävast Sweden
47 J5 Savaştepe Turkey
85 E7 Savé Benin
18 F9 Save R France
87 F10 Save R Mozambique
77 B2 Sāveh Iran
85 D7 Savelugu Ghana
45 K3 Savena R Italy
21 B7 Savenay France
18 G9 Saverdun France
36 C6 Saverne France
101 S8 Savery Wyoming
44 C2 Savigliano Italy
45 M3 Savignano Italy
21 F6 Savigne France
20 F5 Savigné-l'Evêque France
45 K3 Savigno Italy
21 F7 Savigny-en-Véron France
21 G6 Savigny-sur-Braye France
19 Q15 Savines France
42 F2 Savinja R Yugoslavia
52 H2 Savino U.S.S.R.
52 J3 Savinobor U.S.S.R.
45 M3 Savio Italy
45 M4 Sâvio R Italy
29 N10 Savitaipale Finland
42 J6 Šavnik Yugoslavia
120 F3 Savoff Ontario
117 N10 Savona Br Columbia
44 D3 Savona Italy
95 K4 Savona New York
29 O10 Savonlinna Finland
29 O9 Savonranta Finland
116 B5 Savoonga St Lawrence I, Alaska
111 H9 Savoy Mississippi
101 R1 Savoy Montana
27 G14 Sävsjö Sweden
27 H15 Sävsjöström Sweden
42 F3 Savudrija Rtič C Yugoslavia
29 N4 Savukoski Finland
78 H3 Savur Turkey
71 K9 Savu Sea Indonesia
80 C5 Savyon Israel
68 B2 Saw Burma
70 D3 Sawah Kalimantan
69 E13 Sawahlunto Sumatra
74 G6 Sawai Madhopur India
70 M9 Sawall, G mt Java
69 F12 Sawang Indonesia
68 D4 Sawankhalok Thailand
60 O3 Sawara Hokkaido Japan
61 O10 Sawara Honshu Japan
61 M8 Sawasaki-bana C Japan
106 D2 Sawatch Ra Colorado
121 L1 Sawayan Pt Quebec
119 Q1 Sawbill Manitoba
84 E4 Sawda, Jabal as Libya
118 D4 Sawdy Alberta
14 D2 Sawel mt N Ireland
84 E3 Sawfajjin Libya
69 A8 Sawi B Nicobar Is
84 E4 Sawknah Libya
107 L4 Sawlog Cr Kansas
117 O3 Sawmill Bay N W Terr
9 G3 Sawston England
116 N4 Sawtooth Mt Alaska
99 P2 Sawtooth Mts Minnesota
101 L6 Sawtooth Range Idaho
100 E1 Sawtooth Range Washington
71 K10 Sawu isld Indonesia
107 M4 Sawyer Kansas
98 E1 Sawyer N Dakota
99 T5 Sawyer Wisconsin
100 B8 Sawyers Bar California
121 T7 Sawyerville Quebec
141 F4 Saxby R Queensland
141 G5 Saxby Downs Queensland
9 F1 Saxilby England
9 H3 Saxmundham England
26 H7 Saxnäs Sweden
99 Q3 Saxon Wisconsin
94 J6 Saxton Pennsylvania
144 D5 Saxton Pass New Zealand
85 E6 Say Niger
79 F3 Saya Syria
68 E3 Sayaboury Laos
81 C7 Saya de Malha Bank Indian Oc
57 H2 Sayak Pervyy U.S.S.R.
128 C6 Sayán Peru
56 D5 Sayanskiy Khrebet mt U.S.S.R.
57 C5 Sayat U.S.S.R.
125 O9 Sayaxché Guatemala
37 P2 Sayda E Germany
69 C8 Sayer I Thailand
139 G5 Sayers Lake New S Wales
72 G5 Sayhūt S Yemen
56 C6 Saylyugem, Khrebet mts U.S.S.R.
29 M9 Säynätsalo Finland
58 F3 Saynshand Mongolia
108 E8 Sayre Oklahoma
95 L5 Sayre Pennsylvania
124 H8 Sayula Mexico
117 L10 Sayward Br Col
72 F5 Saywūn S Yemen
46 C4 Sazan isld Albania
31 J6 Sázava R Czechoslovakia
55 C3 Sazhino U.S.S.R.
85 D3 Sbaa Algeria
85 F1 Sbeitla Tunisia
143 D10 Scaddan W Australia
18 C4 Scaër France
45 R8 Scafati Italy
13 E5 Scafell Pikes mt England
13 H5 Scalby England
43 G9 Scalea Italy
99 Q7 Scales Mound Illinois
15 G2 Scalloway Shetland Scotland
15 C3 Scalpay isld Scotland
116 E6 Scammon Bay Alaska
9 F1 Scampton England
118 F8 Scandia Alberta
107 N2 Scandia Kansas
45 J2 Scandiano Italy
45 N5 Scandriglia Italy
119 V8 Scanterbury Manitoba
118 F7 Scapa Alberta
15 E2 Scapa Flow Orkney Scotland
100 C4 Scappoose Oregon
43 F12 Scaramia, C Sicily
15 C4 Scarba isld Scotland
13 H5 Scarborough England
127 M2 Scarborough Tobago
142 A1 Scarborough dist Perth, W Aust
144 D5 Scargill New Zealand
14 A5 Scariff isld Irish Rep
15 A2 Scarp isld Lewis Scotland
Scarpanto isld see Karpathos Greece
22 D3 Scarpe R France
45 K4 Scarperia Italy
119 R9 Scarth Manitoba
123 N7 Scaterie I C Breton I, N Scotia
15 B3 Scavaig, L Scotland
138 C5 Sceale B S Australia
20 K4 Sceaux Paris France
20 G5 Sceaux Sarthe France
42 G5 Šćedro isld Yugoslavia
98 D6 Scenic S Dakota
118 H8 Sceptre Sask
33 N6 Schaale R E Germany
33 N5 Schaalsee L Germany
38 H6 Schafberg mt Austria
99 T4 Schaffer Michigan
41 J2 Schaffhausen Switzerland
28 C7 Schaffland W Germany
33 P10 Schafstädt E Germany
25 C3 Schagen Netherlands
36 C6 Schalbach France
37 P6 Schalding W Germany
32 G8 Schale W Germany
37 L3 Schalkau E Germany
32 G10 Schalksmühle W Germany
99 L7 Schaller Iowa
41 K4 Schams R Switzerland
32 G8 Schapen W Germany
38 H5 Schärding Austria
32 H5 Scharhörn isld W Germany
33 M6 Scharnebeck W Germany
41 O3 Scharnitz Austria
32 G6 Scharrel W Germany
36 G1 Schauenburg W Germany
37 M3 Schauenstein W Germany
32 K8 Schaumburg W Germany
36 H6 Schechingen W Germany
25 G2 Scheemda Netherlands
41 K1 Scheer W Germany
32 K6 Scheessel W Germany
115 N7 Schefferville Quebec
38 M6 Scheibbs Austria
37 K4 Scheinfeld W Germany
22 G1 Schelde R Belgium
36 H7 Schelklingen W Germany
103 K2 Schell Creek Ra Nevada
95 O4 Schenectady New York
32 K4 Schenefeld W Germany
32 L5 Schenefeld W Germany
36 H2 Schenklengsfeld W Germany
32 K9 Scherfede W Germany
32 E9 Schermbeck W Germany
25 C3 Schermerhorn Netherlands
33 N10 Schernberg E Germany
22 H2 Scherpen Heuvel Belgium
28 D7 Schersberg hill W Germany
109 J6 Schertz Texas
41 L3 Schesaplana mt Austria
37 L4 Schesslitz W Germany
25 B4 Scheveningen Netherlands
38 J7 Schiadming Austria
25 B5 Schiedam Netherlands
32 K9 Schieder W Germany
15 D4 Schiehallion mt Scotland
33 N6 Schierling W Germany
25 F2 Schiermonnikoog Netherlands
25 F2 Schiermonnokoog isld Netherlands
33 S8 Schiessplatz E Germany
36 F2 Schiffenberg W Germany
36 E5 Schifferstadt W Germany
36 C5 Schiffweiler W Germany
25 D5 Schijndel Netherlands
33 R10 Schildau E Germany
33 N6 Schilde R E Germany
33 R6 Schillersdorf E Germany
32 L8 Schillerslage W Germany
32 H5 Schillighörn point W Germany
37 J5 Schillingsfürst W Germany
41 M5 Schilpario Italy
36 E7 Schiltach W Germany
38 N4 Schiltern Austria
41 O6 Schio Italy
25 F4 Schipbeek R Netherlands
25 C4 Schiphol Netherlands
19 K4 Schirmeck France
33 Q10 Schkeuditz E Germany
37 M1 Schkölen E Germany
33 T9 Schlabendorf E Germany
38 J7 Schladminger Tauern mts Austria
36 E3 Schlangenbad W Germany
36 C1 Schlebusch W Germany
30 E1 Schlei R W Germany
36 B2 Schleiden W Germany
36 E6 Schleithal France
37 M2 Schleiz E Germany
33 P5 Schlemmin E Germany
99 L7 Schleswig Iowa
30 E1 Schleswig W Germany
32 K4 Schleswig Holstein land W Germany
37 O2 Schlettau E Germany
37 K2 Schleusinger-Neundorf E Germany
37 M4 Schlicht W Germany
33 S9 Schlieben E Germany
40 G2 Schliengen W Germany
36 H3 Schlüchtern W Germany
36 H2 Schlitz W Germany
32 J9 Schloss-Holte W Germany
37 L1 Schlossvippach E Germany
37 K1 Schlotheim E Germany
40 H2 Schluchsee W Germany
40 F1 Schlucht, Col de la pass France
32 K8 Schlüsselburg W Germany
33 N5 Schlutup W Germany
36 E1 Schmallenberg W Germany
33 O7 Schmarsau W Germany
36 B5 Schmelz W Germany
37 M5 Schmidmühlen W Germany
36 B3 Schmidthein W Germany
37 K2 Schmiedefeld E Germany
36 F1 Schmittlotheim W Germany
81 A10 Schmitt-Ott Seamount Atlantic Oc
37 N2 Schmölln E Germany
37 K7 Schmutter R W Germany
37 M4 Schnabelwaid W Germany
33 P6 Schnackenburg W Germany
37 N4 Schnaittenbach W Germany
37 O2 Schneeberg E Germany
36 C6 Schnee Berg mt France
37 M3 Schneeberg mt W Germany
32 K7 Schneeren W Germany
Schneidemühl see Piła
33 O9 Schneidlingen E Germany
37 J5 Schnelldorf W Germany
32 L6 Schneverdingen W Germany
38 K7 Schöder Austria
127 L4 Schœlcher Martinique W I
40 G1 Schöenau France
99 R5 Schofield Wisconsin
135 Q2 Schofield Barracks Hawaiian Is
95 N4 Schoharie New York
41 P3 Scholastika Austria
33 Q7 Schollene E Germany
36 G3 Schöllkrippen W Germany
89 D7 Scholtzkop mt S Africa
36 F7 Schömberg W Germany
38 J6 Schön mt Austria
36 G6 Schönaich W Germany
37 J2 Schönau E Germany
36 B3 Schönau Nordrhein-Westfalen W Germany
36 F5 Schönau W Germany
22 L3 Schonberg Belgium
33 R7 Schönberg E Germany
30 E1 Schönberg W Germany
36 H3 Schondra W Germany
33 P8 Schönebeck E Germany
33 S8 Schöneberg E Germany
37 N3 Schöneck E Germany
36 B3 Schönecker-Wetteldorf W Germany
33 S8 Schönefeld airport E Germany
36 C5 Schönenberg-Kubelberg W Germany
33 S9 Schönewalde E Germany
36 B3 Schönfeld W Germany
41 N2 Schongau W Germany
32 L9 Schönhagen W Germany
33 Q7 Schönhausen E Germany
37 O3 Schönheide E Germany
33 N8 Schöningen W Germany
37 O4 Schönsee W Germany
36 H5 Schöntal W Germany
37 O5 Schönthal W Germany
37 J3 Schonungen W Germany
33 S7 Schönwalde E Germany
33 N4 Schönwalde am Bungsberg W Germany
95 S1 Schoodic L Maine
94 B4 Schoolcraft Michigan
25 C5 Schoonhoven Netherlands
25 C3 Schoorl Netherlands
40 G2 Schopfheim W Germany
33 T7 Schopfurch E Germany
33 N8 Schöppenstedt W Germany
32 F8 Schöppingen W Germany
36 C5 Schorbach France
36 H6 Schorndorf W Germany
32 G5 Schortens W Germany
36 G3 Schotten W Germany
139 J8 Schouten I Tasmania
25 A5 Schouwen Netherlands
100 G2 Schrag Washington
36 E7 Schramberg W Germany
33 P10 Schraplau E Germany
40 H4 Schreckhorn mt Switzerland
36 G2 Schrecksbach W Germany
115 L8 Schreiber Ontario
33 Q6 Schrepkow E Germany
33 N5 Schretstaken W Germany
36 F5 Schriesheim W Germany
37 L6 Schrobenhausen W Germany
95 O3 Schroon Lake New York
36 H5 Schrozberg W Germany
41 L3 Schruns Austria
103 M9 Schuchuli Arizona
109 L6 Schulenburg Texas
32 L8 Schulenburg W Germany
118 G8 Schuler Alberta
14 B5 Schull Irish Rep
37 M1 Schulpforta E Germany
107 P6 Schulter Oklahoma
141 K1 Schultz Can Brisbane, Qnsld
115 K5 Schultz L N W Terr
33 T8 Schulzendorf E Germany
120 J4 Schumacher Ontario
33 N8 Schunter R W Germany
40 H4 Schüpfheim Switzerland
102 F3 Schurz Nevada
41 L2 Schussen R W Germany
36 D7 Schutterwald W Germany
32 F8 Schüttorf W Germany
98 J8 Schuyler Nebraska
94 J9 Schuyler Virginia
95 L6 Schuylkill Haven Pennsylvania
33 Q5 Schwaan E Germany
37 L5 Schwabach W Germany
37 J7 Schwaben reg W Germany
37 L7 Schwabhausen W Germany
36 G7 Schwäbische Alb mts W Germany
36 H6 Schwäbisch Gmünd W Germany
36 H5 Schwäbisch Hall W Germany
41 K3 Schwägalp Switzerland
37 M7 Schwaig W Germany
36 G5 Schwaigern W Germany
32 K9 Schwalenberg W Germany
36 G2 Schwalm R W Germany
38 M8 Schwanberg Austria
37 L5 Schwand W Germany
41 K3 Schwanden Switzerland
37 N5 Schwandorf W Germany
33 O9 Schwanebeck E Germany
70 C5 Schwaner Peg mts Kalimantan
32 J6 Schwanewede W Germany
32 L7 Schwarmstedt W Germany
146 A5 Schwartz Rge Antarctica
33 R6 Schwarz E Germany
37 L2 Schwarza E Germany
38 H7 Schwarzach Austria
37 N5 Schwarzach R W Germany
37 L2 Schwarzburg E Germany
33 S9 Schwarze Elster R E Germany
37 M3 Schwarzenbach W Germany
33 M6 Schwarzenbek W Germany
37 K4 Schwarzenberg W Germany
36 G2 Schwarzenborn Hessen W Germany
36 B3 Schwarzenborn Rheinland-Pfalz W Germany
40 F4 Schwarzenburg Switzerland
37 N5 Schwarzenfeld W Germany
36 H3 Schwarzenfels W Germany
36 B3 Schwarzer Mann mt W Germany
37 O5 Schwarzer Regen R W Germany
37 N5 Schwarzhofen W Germany
40 G5 Schwarzhorn mt Switzerland
36 E7 Schwarzwald mts W Germany
36 B4 Schwarzwälder Hochwald mts W Germany
116 J3 Schwatka Mts Alaska
41 P3 Schwaz Austria
31 H2 Schwedt E Germany
40 F4 Schwefelberg Switzerland
36 B4 Schweich W Germany
36 D7 Schweighausen W Germany
37 J2 Schweina E Germany
33 M7 Schweinau W Germany
37 J3 Schweinfurt W Germany
33 S9 Schweinitz E Germany
32 F10 Schwelm W Germany
Schwenningen see Villingen-Schwenningen
33 O5 Schwerin E Germany
33 O6 Schwerin reg E Germany
33 O5 Schweriner See L E Germany
32 G10 Schwerte W Germany
36 F5 Schwetzingen W Germany
33 T5 Schwichtenberg E Germany
31 H3 Schwielochsee L E Germany
33 R8 Schwielowsee L E Germany
32 K5 Schwinge R W Germany
33 R5 Schwinkendorf E Germany
33 P9 Schwittersaf E Germany
41 J3 Schwyz Switzerland
43 E11 Sciacca Sicily
43 F12 Scicli Sicily
20 H2 Scie R France
9 F7 Scilly, Isles of England
31 J4 Ścinawa Poland
94 K4 Scio New York
94 F6 Scio Ohio
94 D8 Scioto R Ohio
94 E8 Sciotoville Ohio
103 M2 Scipio Utah
119 R7 Sclater Manitoba
8 B4 Scleddau Wales
48 H5 Scoarţa Romania
98 A1 Scobey Montana
103 N2 Scofield Res Utah
118 E7 Scollard Alberta
139 K4 Scone New S Wales
15 E4 Scone Scotland
111 H9 Scooba Mississippi
115 R3 Scoresby Land Greenland
115 R3 Scoresbysund Greenland
100 G9 Scossa Nevada
102 A1 Scotia California
98 H8 Scotia Nebraska
121 L7 Scotia Ontario
100 H1 Scotia Washington
117 G6 Scotia Bay Br Col
81 A14 Scotia Ridge Antarctica
81 A15 Scotia Sea Antarctica
98 J6 Scotland S Dakota
109 J2 Scotland Texas
15 Scotland U.K.
112 K1 Scotland Neck N Carolina
111 E11 Scotlandville Louisiana
122 H8 Scots B Nova Scotia
122 K8 Scotsburn Nova Scotia
118 J9 Scotsguard Sask
121 T7 Scotstown Quebec
112 E5 Scott Georgia
111 E8 Scott Mississippi
94 C6 Scott Ohio
118 J6 Scott Sask
100 C8 Scott R California
138 E4 Scott R S Australia
100 C8 Scott Bar California
89 G8 Scottburgh S Africa
117 J10 Scott, C Vancouver I, Br Col
140 A2 Scott, Cape N Terr Aust
107 K3 Scott City Kansas
146 H6 Scott Coast Antarctica
94 H6 Scottdale Pennsylvania
146 E3 Scott Gl Antarctica
142 E4 Scott Headland mt W Australia
115 M3 Scott Inlet N W Terr
117 J10 Scott, Is Br Col
100 C7 Scott, Mt Oregon
146 A5 Scott Mts Antarctica
142 D2 Scott Reef Indian Oc
94 B4 Scotts Michigan
98 C8 Scottsbluff Nebraska
98 C8 Scotts Bluff Nat. Mon Nebraska
94 B8 Scottsburg Indiana
100 B6 Scottsburg Oregon
94 J10 Scottsburg Virginia
103 N8 Scottsdale Arizona
139 J8 Scottsdale Tasmania
111 L11 Scotts Ferry Florida
127 O7 Scotts Head Dominica
123 L7 Scottsville C Breton I, N Scotia
107 N2 Scottsville Kansas
110 K5 Scottsville Kentucky
94 J9 Scottsville Virginia
94 A3 Scottville Michigan
141 J5 Scottville Queensland
102 G4 Scottys Castle California
102 G4 Scottys Junct Nevada
15 C2 Scourie Scotland
118 L9 Scout Lake Sask
15 E2 Scrabster Scotland
110 C6 Scranton Arkansas
107 P3 Scranton Kansas
98 C3 Scranton N Dakota
95 M5 Scranton Pennsylvania
95 L3 Scriba New York
98 K8 Scribner Nebraska
15 B4 Scridain, Loch Scotland
44 E2 Scrivia R Italy
120 H10 Scudder Ontario
121 M8 Scugog, L Ontario
13 H6 Scunthorpe England
45 O5 Scurcola Marsicana Italy
Scutari Albania see Shkodër
Scutari Turkey see Üsküdar
112 K1 Seaboard N Carolina
109 M6 Seabrook Texas
143 C9 Seabrook, L W Australia
143 C7 Seabrook, Mt W Australia
144 C6 Seacliff New Zealand
89 D8 Seacow R S Africa
109 L7 Seadrift Texas
139 G7 Sea Elephant B Tasmania
95 M8 Seaford Delaware
9 G6 Seaford England
127 M3 Seaforth Jamaica
120 J9 Seaforth Ontario
142 C3 Seaforth W Australia
119 O4 Seager Wheeler L Sask
108 E3 Seagraves Texas
112 H2 Seagrove N Carolina
13 G4 Seaham England
122 G1 Seahorse Labrador
115 L5 Seahorse Pt N W Terr
70 C2 Seahorse Shoal S China Sea
13 G2 Seahouses England
112 F6 Sea Island Georgia
95 N7 Sea Isle City New Jersey
115 K6 Seal R Manitoba
139 G6 Sea Lake Victoria
123 R1 Seal Bight Labrador
116 H9 Seal C Alaska
89 C10 Seal C S Africa
127 J4 Seal Cays islds Turks & Caicos Is
122 F9 Seal Cove New Brunswick
123 Q4 Seal Cove Nfld
111 L9 Seale Alabama
144 C5 Seal I New Zealand
133 F8 Sea Lion Is Falkland Is
139 H7 Seal Is Victoria
115 M6 Seal Lakes Quebec
144 A7 Seal Pt New Zealand
100 A5 Seal Rock Oregon
109 L6 Sealy Texas
144 C5 Sealy, Mt New Zealand
144 C5 Sealy Pass New Zealand
103 J4 Seaman Ra Nevada
13 H5 Seamer England
103 K6 Searchlight Nevada
120 F6 Searchmont Ontario
110 E6 Searcy Arkansas
102 G6 Searles California
102 G6 Searles Lake California
95 T2 Searsport Maine
123 N6 Searston Nfld
12 E5 Seascale England
102 C5 Seaside California
100 B4 Seaside Oregon
95 N7 Seaside Heights New Jersey
8 C6 Seaton England
100 C2 Seattle Washington
117 D5 Seattle, Mt Alaska/Yukon Terr
141 H4 Seaview Ra Queensland
95 N7 Seaville, S New Jersey
144 D5 Seaward Kaikoura Range New Zealand
127 P6 Seawell airport Barbados
71 K10 Seba Indonesia
118 C5 Seba Beach Alberta
95 R3 Sebago L Maine
70 B5 Sebajan mt Kalimantan
70 E5 Sebakung Kalimantan
89 G2 Sebakwe R Zimbabwe
69 E12 Sebanga Sumatra
68 G4 Se Bang Fai R Laos
69 G12 Sebangka isld Indonesia
113 G10 Sebastian Florida
109 K9 Sebastian Texas
124 B3 Sebastián Vizcaino, B Mexico
95 S2 Sebasticook L Maine
102 B3 Sebastopol California
111 G9 Sebastopol Mississippi
70 E2 Sebatik isld Borneo
70 C3 Sebauh Sarawak
28 D3 Sebbersund Denmark
99 L3 Sebeka Minnesota
78 C1 Seben Turkey
124 D4 Seberi, Cerro mt Mexico
70 K8 Sebesi isld Sumatra
48 H5 Sebesul R Romania
48 H5 Sebesului Muntii mts Romania
94 D3 Sebewaing Michigan
52 C6 Sebezh U.S.S.R.
78 G1 Şebinkarahisar Turkey
48 G4 Sebis Romania
85 B4 Sebjet Agsumal Morocco
85 B4 Sebkha de Chinchane Mauritania
85 B4 Sebkha Oum el Drouss Guebli Morocco
85 B4 Sebkha Oum el Drouss Telli Mauritania
43 C13 Sebkhet Kelbia L Tunisia
84 F3 Sebkhet Taworgha Libya
85 B4 Sebkhet Idjil Mauritania

85 E3 **Sebkra Azzel Matti** *salt flats* Algeria
85 C3 **Sebkra de Tindouf** *salt flats* Algeria
17 G9 **Sebkra d'Oran** Algeria
85 E3 **Sebkra Mekerrhane** *salt flats* Algeria
69 E14 **Seblat** Sumatra
31 H5 **Sebnitz** E Germany
95 T1 **Seboeis L** Maine
95 R8 **Seboomook L** Maine
85 C2 **Sebou** *R* Morocco
110 J4 **Sebree** Kentucky
95 K10 **Sebrell** Virginia
113 F10 **Sebring** Florida
94 F6 **Sebring** Ohio
70 E2 **Sebuku** Kalimantan
70 E6 **Sebuku** *isld* Kalimantan
70 B4 **Sebuyau** Sarawak
37 O4 **Seč** Czechoslovakia
42 C4 **Secchia** *R* Italy
112 E3 **Secession L** S Carolina
68 G4 **Se Cham** *R* Laos
122 C1 **Séchelles, L** Quebec
128 B5 **Sechura, B. de** Peru
128 B5 **Sechura, Des. de** *des* Peru
38 L7 **Seckau** Austria
38 L7 **Seckauer Alpen** *mts* Austria
22 E2 **Seclin** France
133 D7 **Seco** *R* Argentina
17 H4 **Seco** *R* Spain
21 E8 **Secondigny** France
118 L8 **Secretan** Sask
144 A6 **Secretary I** New Zealand
76 D2 **Secunderabad** India
128 E7 **Sécure** *R* Bolivia
48 E3 **Séd** *R* Hungary
52 B6 **Seda** U.S.S.R.
16 B5 **Seda** *R* Portugal
71 L10 **Sedah** Indonesia
118 G7 **Sedalia** Alberta
106 F2 **Sedalia** Colorado
94 D7 **Sedalia** Ohio
19 J3 **Sedan** France
107 O4 **Sedan** Kansas
106 G5 **Sedan** New Mexico
138 E5 **Sedan** S Australia
56 F3 **Sedannavskaya, Shiver** *falls* U.S.S.R.
16 E2 **Sedano** Spain
13 F5 **Sedbergh** England
145 E4 **Seddon** New Zealand
115 O2 **Seddon, Kap** *C* Greenland
144 C4 **Seddonville** New Zealand
47 H4 **Seddülbahir** Turkey
79 E8 **Sede Boqer** Israel
80 B7 **Sede Dawid** Israel
80 F1 **Sede Eli'ezer** Israel
80 F4 **Sede Eliyyahu** Israel
55 G3 **Sedel'nikovo** U.S.S.R.
80 C7 **Sede Moshe** Israel
80 F1 **Sede Neḥemya** Israel
19 P16 **Séderon** France
80 B7 **Sederot** Israel
80 G2 **Sede Yaaqov** Syria
80 B8 **Sede Zevi** Israel
9 E3 **Sedgeberrow** England
13 G4 **Sedgefield** England
8 D2 **Sedgley** England
106 H1 **Sedgwick** Colorado
107 N4 **Sedgwick** Kansas
95 T2 **Sedgwick** Maine
70 E6 **Sedjaka** Kalimantan
31 H6 **Sedlčany** Czechoslovakia
9 G6 **Sedlescombe** England
119 O8 **Sedley** Sask
79 F7 **Sedom** Israel
103 N7 **Sedona** Arizona
68 G5 **Se Done** *R* Laos
80 C7 **Sedot Mikha** Israel
80 C4 **Sedot Yam** Israel
100 C1 **Sedro Woolley** Washington
52 B6 **Šeduva** U.S.S.R.
20 C4 **See** *R* France
33 O4 **Seebad Heringsdorf** W Germany
118 C7 **Seebe** Alberta
37 K2 **Seebergen** E Germany
33 P10 **Seeburg** E Germany
41 O3 **Seefeld** Austria
33 T7 **Seefeld** E Germany
40 G2 **Seefelden** W Germany
33 O8 **Seehausen** E Germany
87 C11 **Seeheim** Namibia
36 F4 **Seeheim** W Germany
36 D7 **Seelbach** W Germany
101 M2 **Seeley Lake** Montana
121 O8 **Seeleys Bay** Ontario
146 G10 **Seelig, Mt** Antarctica
33 R10 **Seelingstädt** E Germany
36 C2 **Seelscheid** W Germany
70 P10 **Seemanandjung** Java
33 S10 **Seerhausen** E Germany
41 J2 **Seerücken** *mt* Switzerland
20 F4 **Sées** France
32 M9 **Seesen** W Germany
41 O2 **Seeshaupt** W Germany
38 L7 **Seetaler Alpen** *mts* Austria
41 K3 **Seez** *R* Switzerland
47 H6 **Seferihisar** Turkey
17 G9 **Sefioun** *R* Algeria
85 D2 **Sefrou** Morocco
144 D5 **Sefton** New Zealand
144 C5 **Sefton, Mt** New Zealand
70 F2 **Segama** *R* Sabah
69 F11 **Segamat** Malaysia
70 M9 **Segara Anakan** Java
47 F1 **Segarcea** Romania
70 F7 **Segeri** Sulawesi
43 E11 **Segesta** Sicily
71 C3 **Seget** W Irian
52 D3 **Segezha** U.S.S.R.
57 D3 **Segiz, Ozero** *L* U.S.S.R.
41 K4 **Segnes Pass** Switzerland
45 O6 **Segni** Italy
103 P2 **Sego** Utah
17 G5 **Segorbe** Spain
85 C6 **Segou** Mali
16 E4 **Segovia** Spain
108 H5 **Segovia** Texas
16 E3 **Segovia** *prov* Spain
52 D3 **Segozero, Oz** *L* U.S.S.R.
21 D6 **Segré** France
17 H2 **Segre** *R* Spain
84 E5 **Séguedine** Niger
85 C7 **Séguéla** Ivory Coast
107 K2 **Seguin** Kansas
124 J5 **Seguín** Mexico
109 K6 **Seguin** Texas
106 F4 **Segundo** Colorado
133 E4 **Segundo** *R* Argentina
70 E4 **Seguntur** Kalimantan
17 F6 **Segura** *R* Spain
17 F6 **Segura, Sa de** *mts* Spain
32 L8 **Sehnde** W Germany
71 J5 **Seho** *isld* Indonesia
74 B5 **Sehwan** Pakistan
100 B8 **Seiad Valley** California
37 L3 **Seibelsdorf** W Germany
106 H2 **Seibert** Colorado
127 K5 **Seibo** Dom Rep
21 C6 **Seiche** *R* France
21 E6 **Seiches** France
80 D4 **Seidā** Jordan
80 F3 **Seidur** Jordan
140 E4 **Seigals Creek** N Terr Aust
122 C1 **Seignelay, R** Quebec
68 B2 **Seikpyu** Burma
68 B2 **Seiktein** Burma
12 C1 **Seil** *isld* Scotland
26 N1 **Seiland** *isld* Norway
18 G7 **Seilhac** France
107 M5 **Seiling** Oklahoma
19 K4 **Seille** *R* France
29 K9 **Seinäjoki** Finland
20 H3 **Seine** *R* France
20 D2 **Seine, B. de la** France
18 H4 **Seine-et-Marne** *dep* France
20 G2 **Seine-Maritime** *dep* France
18 B4 **Sein, I. de** France
69 J12 **Seipenyu** Indonesia
38 L5 **Seitenstetten** Austria
18 F10 **Seix** France
28 G5 **Sejerø** *isld* Denmark
28 B3 **Sejerslev** Denmark
28 E3 **Sejflod** Denmark
31 O1 **Sejny** Poland
28 D4 **Sejs** Denmark
28 B6 **Sejstrup** Denmark
70 B5 **Sekadau** Kalimantan
69 G13 **Sekanak, Teluk** *B* Sumatra
69 F14 **Sekayu** Sumatra
88 E4 **Sekenke** Tanzania
61 K10 **Seki** Japan
70 B5 **Sekima** Kalimantan
70 K8 **Sekintjau** *mt* Sumatra
85 D7 **Sekondi** Ghana
68 H6 **Se Kong** *R* Laos/Cambodia
77 G4 **Sekuheh** Iran
69 E14 **Selagan** *R* Sumatra
100 E3 **Selah** Washington
70 B4 **Selalang** Sarawak
69 E10 **Selama** Malaysia
69 E11 **Selangor** Malaysia
68 H4 **Se La Nong** *R* Laos
29 M10 **Selänpää** Finland
69 F14 **Selara Ladangpait** Sumatra
70 D7 **Selatan, Tg** *C* Kalimantan
69 F12 **Selatpanjang** Sumatra
69 F12 **Selat Panjang** *R* Sumatra
69 D13 **Selat Siberut** *str* Sumatra
69 D14 **Selat Sipora** *str* Indonesia
116 H3 **Selawik** Alaska
116 G3 **Selawik L** Alaska
37 N3 **Selb** W Germany
37 M3 **Selbitz** W Germany
27 A12 **Selbjörnfj** *inlet* Norway
26 E8 **Selbusjö** *L* Norway
13 G6 **Selby** England
98 F4 **Selby** S Dakota
116 K3 **Selby, L** Alaska
95 M8 **Selbyville** Delaware
28 C3 **Selde** Denmark
107 K2 **Selden** Kansas
123 S4 **Seldom** Nfld
116 M7 **Seldovia** Alaska
71 C3 **Sele** W Irian
43 G8 **Sele** *R* Italy
87 E10 **Selebi-Pikwe** Botswana
59 K1 **Selemdzha** *R* U.S.S.R.
79 H3 **Selemiya** Syria
47 K6 **Selendi** Turkey
56 G5 **Selenga** *R* U.S.S.R.
86 C6 **Selenge** Zaïre
58 E2 **Selenge Mörön** *R* Mongolia
46 D4 **Selenicë** Albania
51 O2 **Selennyakh** *R* U.S.S.R.
33 M4 **Selent** W Germany
33 M4 **Selenter See** *L* W Germany
71 C3 **Sele, Selat** *str* W Irian
40 F1 **Sélestat** France
55 F4 **Selety** *R* U.S.S.R.
50 G3 **Seletyteniz, Ozero** *L* U.S.S.R.
115 R5 **Selfoss** Iceland
98 F3 **Selfridge** N Dakota
52 G3 **Selib** U.S.S.R.
85 B5 **Selibaby** Mauritania
36 F3 **Seligenstadt** W Germany
52 D6 **Seliger, Oz** *L* U.S.S.R.
103 M6 **Seligman** Arizona
110 C5 **Seligman** Missouri
84 H5 **Selima Oasis** Sudan
70 C4 **Selimbau** Kalimantan
47 J7 **Selimiye** Turkey
46 E7 **Selinoús** Greece
95 L6 **Selinsgrove** Pennsylvania
55 F1 **Seliyarovo** U.S.S.R.
52 D6 **Selizharovo** U.S.S.R.
33 O9 **Selke** *R* E Germany
107 J3 **Selkirk** Kansas
115 K7 **Selkirk** Manitoba
94 C2 **Selkirk** Michigan
13 F2 **Selkirk** Scotland
Selkirk *co see* **Borders** *reg*
114 H7 **Selkirk Mts** Br Col/Idaho
119 S5 **Selkirk T** Manitoba
20 K2 **Selle** *R* France
100 D2 **Selleck** Washington
94 B8 **Sellersburg** Indiana
21 I7 **Selles-St Denis** France
21 I7 **Selles-sur-Cher** France
141 H5 **Sellheim** *R* Queensland
40 C4 **Sellières** France
9 G5 **Sellindge** England
41 O3 **Sellrain** Austria
103 N10 **Sells** Arizona
32 F9 **Selm** W Germany
111 J9 **Selma** Alabama
111 D10 **Selma** Louisiana
112 J2 **Selma** N Carolina
100 B7 **Selma** Oregon
110 H6 **Selmer** Tennessee
33 N5 **Selmsdorf** E Germany
21 H6 **Selommes** France
70 Q10 **Selong** Indonesia
40 B2 **Selongey** France
88 F6 **Selous Game Res** Tanzania
117 G4 **Selous, Mt** Yukon Terr
71 C3 **Selpele** Indonesia
83 K12 **Sel Pt** Mahé I Indian Ocean
9 F6 **Selsey** England
32 K6 **Selsingen** W Germany
36 D2 **Selters** W Germany
54 F3 **Sel'tso** U.S.S.R.
52 H6 **Selty** U.S.S.R.
33 S5 **Seltz** E Germany
36 E6 **Seltz** France
69 H10 **Seluan** *isld* Indonesia
87 E9 **Selukwe** Zimbabwe
20 C4 **Selune** *R* France
133 E3 **Selva** Argentina
38 E8 **Selva** Italy
128 D5 **Selvas** *forests* Brazil
140 F5 **Selwyn** Queensland
117 H4 **Selwyn Mts** Yukon Terr
140 F5 **Selwyn Ra** Queensland
98 G2 **Selz** N Dakota
36 E4 **Selz** *R* W Germany
40 F3 **Selzach** Switzerland
38 K6 **Selzthal** Austria
70 E5 **Semajang, D** *L* Kalimantan
20 F5 **Semallé** France
46 D4 **Seman** *R* Albania
70 K8 **Semang Ka, Teluk** *B* Sumatra
79 G2 **Semán, Jebel** *mts* Syria
119 N7 **Semans** Sask
70 N10 **Semanu** Java
85 B3 **Semara** Morocco
70 N9 **Semarang** Java
71 L10 **Semau** *isld* Timor Indonesia
88 C2 **Sembabule** Uganda
70 E3 **Sembakung** *R* Kalimantan
86 B5 **Sembé** Congo
21 G7 **Semblancay** France
52 F6 **Semenov** U.S.S.R.
54 D4 **Semenovka** Chernigov U.S.S.R.
54 E7 **Semenovka** Poltava U.S.S.R.
52 G6 **Semenovo** U.S.S.R.
52 F5 **Semenovskoye** Kostroma U.S.S.R.
52 F5 **Sementsovo** U.S.S.R.
70 O10 **Semeru** Java
116 J8 **Semidi Is** Alaska
52 F5 **Semigorodnyaya** U.S.S.R.
31 J5 **Semily** Czechoslovakia
111 G10 **Seminary** Mississippi
101 T7 **Seminoe Dam** Wyoming
101 T7 **Seminoe Res** Wyoming
107 O6 **Seminole** Oklahoma
108 E3 **Seminole** Texas
111 M11 **Seminole, L** Georgia
56 C5 **Seminsky Khrebet** *mts* U.S.S.R.
55 D4 **Semiozernoye** U.S.S.R.
56 B5 **Semipalatinsk** U.S.S.R.
55 E4 **Semipolka** U.S.S.R.
71 E5 **Semirara** *isld* Philippines
77 B4 **Semirom** Iran
70 C4 **Semitau** Kalimantan
69 H10 **Semium** *isld* Indonesia
55 G5 **Semiyarka** U.S.S.R.
55 F5 **Semiz-Bugu** U.S.S.R.
33 R4 **Semlow** E Germany
33 T7 **Semmelberg** *mt* E Germany
38 N6 **Semmering** Austria
84 J5 **Semna** Sudan
86 F1 **Semna** Sudan
77 C2 **Semnān** Iran
71 A3 **Semo** Indonesia
22 J4 **Semois** *R* Belgium
89 F3 **Semokwe** *R* Zimbabwe
70 E1 **Sempang Mangayau, Tg** *C* Sabah
70 F2 **Semporna** Sabah
45 O6 **Semprevisa** *mt* Italy
70 O10 **Sempu** *isld* Java
26 H5 **Semskefjell** *mt* Norway
129 H4 **Sem Tripa** Brazil
88 E3 **Semu** *R* Tanzania
70 C6 **Semuda** Kalimantan
18 H5 **Semur-en-Auxois** France
89 F2 **Semwe** *R* Zimbabwe
52 F2 **Semzha** U.S.S.R.
128 E6 **Sena** Bolivia
88 E10 **Sena** Mozambique
129 L5 **Senador Pompeu** Brazil
70 E1 **Senaja** Sabah
128 E5 **Sena Madureira** Brazil
87 D9 **Senango** Zambia
20 J2 **Sénarpont** France
19 O17 **Sénas** France
118 H9 **Senate** Sask
110 F5 **Senath** Missouri
111 G7 **Senatobia** Mississippi
61 O7 **Sendai** Honshu Japan
60 D14 **Sendai** Kyūshū Japan
87 C11 **Sendeling's Drift** Namibia
37 J7 **Senden** W Germany
32 G9 **Sendenhorst** W Germany
16 C3 **Sendim** Portugal
70 B5 **Senduruhan** Kalimantan
74 F8 **Sendwha** India
69 E11 **Senebui, Tg** *C* Sumatra
99 S8 **Seneca** Illinois
107 O2 **Seneca** Kansas
110 B5 **Seneca** Missouri
98 F7 **Seneca** Nebraska
100 G5 **Seneca** Oregon
112 E3 **Seneca** S Carolina
98 G4 **Seneca** S Dakota
95 L4 **Seneca L** New York
94 F7 **Seneca Lake** Ohio
94 F7 **Senecaville** Ohio
22 G2 **Seneffe** Belgium
85 B5 **Sénégal** *R* W Africa
85 B6 **Senegal** *rep* W Africa
87 E11 **Senekal** S Africa
99 V3 **Seney** Michigan
30 H4 **Senftenberg** E Germany
87 F7 **Senga Hill** Zambia
52 H1 **Sengeyskiy, Ostrov** *isld* U.S.S.R.
70 G7 **Sengkang** Sulawesi
38 K6 **Sengsengebirge** *mts* Austria
133 C7 **Senguerr** *R* Argentina
88 B10 **Sengwa** *R* Zimbabwe
32 H5 **Sengwarden** W Germany
87 E9 **Sengwe** *R* Zimbabwe
129 K6 **Senhor do Bonfim** Brazil
45 O4 **Senigallia** Italy
45 L3 **Senio** *R* Italy
80 F1 **Senir** Israel
43 G8 **Senise** Italy
42 F4 **Senj** Yugoslavia
26 J2 **Senja** *isld* Norway
67 H4 **Senkaku-shotō** *isld* Japan
52 H2 **Sen'kina** U.S.S.R.
118 H6 **Senlac** Sask
65 H3 **Senlin Shan** *mt* China
68 H6 **Senmonorom** Cambodia
86 F3 **Sennar** Sudan
32 J9 **Senne** *reg* W Germany
40 A4 **Sennecey le Grand** France
32 J9 **Sennelager** W Germany
28 B3 **Sennels** Denmark
115 M8 **Senneterre** Quebec
20 F2 **Senneville** France
54 A2 **Senno** U.S.S.R.
8 C4 **Sennybridge** Wales
133 C8 **Seno Almirantazgo** *gulf* Chile
68 G4 **Se Noi** *R* Laos
111 M8 **Senoia** Georgia
20 H4 **Senonches** France
19 K4 **Senones** France
133 C8 **Seno Otway** *gulf* Chile
133 C8 **Seno Skyring** *gulf* Chile
18 H4 **Sens** France
20 B5 **Sens-de-Bretagne** France
40 F4 **Sense R** Switzerland
48 F5 **Senta** Yugoslavia
70 B4 **Sentarum** *L* Kalimantan
18 F10 **Sentem** France
86 E7 **Sentery** Zaïre
103 L9 **Sentinel** Arizona
109 H1 **Sentinel** Oklahoma
98 C3 **Sentinel Butte** N Dakota
117 N8 **Sentinel Pk** Br Columbia
146 G11 **Sentinel Rge** Antarctica
124 G7 **Sentispac** Mexico
129 K5 **Sento Sé** Brazil
22 H5 **Senuc** France
78 H3 **Şenyurt** Turkey
33 R7 **Senzke** E Germany
74 H7 **Seoni** India
Seoul *see* **Sŏul**
70 C5 **Sepandan** Kalimantan
70 P9 **Sepandjang** Indonesia
70 C5 **Sepang** Kalimantan
106 B9 **Separ** New Mexico
142 E6 **Separation Well** W Australia
70 E4 **Sepasu** Kalimantan
130 G8 **Sepetiba, B. de** Brazil
70 D3 **Seping** *R* Sarawak
45 R7 **Sepino** Italy
21 G7 **Sepmes** France
31 K2 **Sępolno** Poland
68 H4 **Sepone** Laos
31 N1 **Sępopol** Poland
130 B4 **Sepotuba** *R* Brazil
32 F9 **Seppenrade** W Germany
19 O18 **Septêmes les Valdonne** France
47 G2 **Septemvri** Bulgaria
20 J4 **Septeuil** France
20 D5 **Sept Forges** France
122 F3 **Sept Îles** Quebec
18 C4 **Sept Iles, les** France
141 J5 **Septimus** Queensland
122 B2 **Sept-Milles, L** Quebec
70 O9 **Sepulu** Java
16 E3 **Sepúlveda** Spain
70 K8 **Seputih** *R* Sumatra
112 B2 **Sequatchie** *R* Tennessee
16 D3 **Sequillo** *R* Spain
100 B1 **Sequim** Washington
102 F5 **Sequoia Nat. Park** California
79 F3 **Serai** Syria
22 G4 **Seraincourt** France
22 K2 **Seraing** Belgium
71 J9 **Seraja** *isld* Indonesia
70 P10 **Seraja, G** *mt* Indonesia
70 M9 **Seraju** *R* Java
57 B6 **Serakhs** U.S.S.R.
76 C2 **Seram** India
136 F2 **Seram** *isld* Moluccas Indonesia
70 L9 **Serang** Java
69 J11 **Serasan** *isld* Indonesia
69 J11 **Seraya** Indonesia
46 D1 **Serbia** *hist reg* Yugoslavia
45 H4 **Serchio** *R* Italy
70 K8 **Serdang, Tg** *C* Sumatra
53 F7 **Serdobsk** U.S.S.R.
55 F3 **Serebryanoye** U.S.S.R.
56 B6 **Serebryansk** U.S.S.R.
88 F5 **Serebu** *mt* Tanzania
52 F5 **Sereda** U.S.S.R.
52 C5 **Seredka** U.S.S.R.
78 D2 **Şereflikoçhisar** Turkey
18 H5 **Serein** *R* France
69 E11 **Seremban** Malaysia
71 C3 **Seremuk** *R* W Irian
88 E3 **Serengeti Nat. Park** Tanzania
88 C8 **Serenje** Zambia
86 H5 **Serenli** Somalia
48 K1 **Seret** *R* U.S.S.R.
52 F6 **Serezha** *R* U.S.S.R.
47 G7 **Serfopoúla** *isld* Greece
52 G6 **Sergach** U.S.S.R.
98 K7 **Sergeant Bluff** Iowa
58 E2 **Sergelen** Mongolia
87 E7 **Serge Tshimbo** Zaïre
55 E4 **Sergeyevka** Kokchetav U.S.S.R.
55 G3 **Sergeyevka** Novosibirsk U.S.S.R.
50 F2 **Sergino** U.S.S.R.
129 L6 **Sergipe** *state* Brazil
52 E2 **Sergozero, Oz** *L* U.S.S.R.
70 D2 **Seria** Brunei
41 L6 **Seriana, Val** Italy
69 D11 **Seribudolok** Sumatra
130 H9 **Seridó** *R* Brazil
20 J3 **Sérifontaine** France
47 G7 **Sérifos** *isld* Greece
19 N16 **Sérignan** France
68 D5 **Serim** Burma
142 D2 **Seringapatam Reef** Indian Oc
129 H5 **Seringa, Serra da** *mts* Brazil
45 R8 **Serino** Italy
41 L7 **Serio** *R* Italy
85 F4 **Serkout, Dj** *mt* Algeria
138 E4 **Serle, Mt** S Australia
20 K5 **Sermaises** France
71 O9 **Sermata** *isld* Indonesia
45 K1 **Sermide** Italy
45 N6 **Sermoneta** Italy
38 H9 **Sernio** *mt* Italy
33 U6 **Sernitz** *R* E Germany
33 Q8 **Serno** E Germany
60 T2 **Sernovodsk** U.S.S.R.
57 A5 **Sernyy-Zavod** U.S.S.R.
31 N3 **Serock** Poland
126 A2 **Seroe Colorado** Aruba W I
17 F7 **Serón** Spain
85 F4 **Serouenout** Algeria
55 D2 **Serov** U.S.S.R.
89 E4 **Serowe** Botswana
16 B7 **Serpa** Portugal
87 C8 **Serpa Pinto** Angola
43 C9 **Serpeddi, Pta** *mt* Sardinia
116 E4 **Serpentine Hot Springs** Alaska
138 A3 **Serpentine Lakes** S Australia
143 B9 **Serpentine, R** W Australia
122 A3 **Serpent, R. au** Quebec
128 F1 **Serpents Mouth** *str* Venezuela
17 G6 **Serpis** *R* Spain
54 J2 **Serpukhov** U.S.S.R.
20 J2 **Serqueux** France
20 G3 **Serquigny** France
130 H7 **Serra** Brazil
45 L4 **Serra, Alpe di** *mts* Italy
130 E10 **Serra Alta** Brazil
130 F4 **Serra Bonita** Brazil
130 F4 **Serra das Araras** Brazil
129 H3 **Serra do Navio** Brazil
33 Q5 **Serrahn** E Germany
47 F3 **Sérrai** Greece
45 J3 **Serramazzoni** Italy
125 O2 **Serrana Bank** Caribbean
125 P2 **Serranilla Bank** Caribbean
43 G10 **Serra San Bruno** Italy
43 C11 **Serrat, Cape** *C* Tunisia
45 J4 **Serravalle Pistojese** Italy
22 F4 **Serre** *R* France
18 G10 **Serrère, Pic de** *mt* France
19 P16 **Serres** France
133 D4 **Serrezuela** Argentina
129 L6 **Serrinha** Brazil
45 M4 **Serriola, Bocca** *pass* Italy
43 B12 **Sers** Tunisia
16 B5 **Sertã** Portugal
130 F7 **Sertãozinho** Brazil
70 K9 **Sertung** *isld* Sumatra
70 C6 **Serujan** *R* Kalimantan
89 E3 **Serule** Botswana
69 D10 **Seruwai** Sumatra
40 E2 **Servance** France
46 E4 **Sérvia** Greece
100 E5 **Service Creek** Oregon
138 F6 **Serviceton** Victoria
106 E5 **Servilleta** New Mexico
71 N9 **Serwaro** Indonesia
66 F5 **Sêrxü** China
22 G4 **Séry** France
22 E4 **Séry-les-Mezières** France
68 G4 **Se Sang Soi** *R* Laos
70 E3 **Sesatap** Kalimantan
88 D2 **Sese Is** Uganda
120 K4 **Sesekinika** Ontario
71 A3 **Sesepe** Indonesia
87 B9 **Sesfontein** Namibia
87 D9 **Sesheka** Zambia
41 H7 **Sesia R** Italy
70 E2 **Sesibu** Kalimantan
26 N6 **Seskarön** *isld* Sweden
61 P12 **Sesoko-jima** *isld* Okinawa
43 F7 **Sessa Aurunca** Italy
36 D6 **Sessenheim** France
110 G3 **Sesser** Illinois
37 K3 **Sesslach** W Germany
71 K9 **Sessok** Flores Indonesia
45 M4 **Sestino** Italy
45 K4 **Sesto Fiorentino** Italy
31 O1 **Seštokai** U.S.S.R.
45 J3 **Sestola** Italy
52 E6 **Sestra** *R* U.S.S.R.
44 E3 **Sestri** Italy
44 F3 **Sestri Levante** Italy
29 O11 **Sestroretsk** U.S.S.R.
60 D12 **Setaka** Japan
60 N3 **Setana** Japan
9 G2 **Setchey** England
18 H9 **Sète** France
130 G6 **Sete Lagoas** Brazil
130 D8 **Sete Quedas, Ilha Grande ou** *isld* Brazil
27 B12 **Setesdal** Norway
94 F8 **Seth** W Virginia
85 F1 **Sétif** Algeria
60 C13 **Seto** Japan
59 K5 **Seto-naika** *sea* Japan
60 G11 **Seto Naikai** *str* Japan
68 B4 **Setsan** Burma
85 C2 **Settat** Morocco
86 A6 **Sette Cama** Gabon
119 U1 **Settee L** Manitoba
119 T3 **Setting L** Manitoba
13 F5 **Settle** England
140 E3 **Settlement Cr** Queensland
90 C15 **Settlement of Edinburgh** Tristan da Cunha
113 H11 **Settlement Pt** Bahamas
16 B6 **Setúbal** Portugal
37 M5 **Seubersdorf** W Germany
37 K5 **Seukendorf** W Germany
55 E1 **Seul'** *R* U.S.S.R.
99 V4 **Seul Choix Pt** Michigan
69 B10 **Seulimeum** Sumatra
115 K7 **Seul, Lac** Ontario
20 D3 **Seulles** *R* France
69 C11 **Seumanyam** Sumatra
40 B3 **Seurre** France
78 K1 **Sevan, Ozero** U.S.S.R.
53 D11 **Sevastopol'** U.S.S.R.
54 H6 **Sev Donets** *R* U.S.S.R.
28 B4 **Sevel** Denmark
100 J4 **Seven Devils Mts** Idaho
140 D3 **Seven Emu** N Terr Aust
14 C5 **Seven Hd** Irish Rep
122 F3 **Seven Is. Bay** Quebec
106 C6 **Seven Lakes** New Mexico
9 G5 **Sevenoaks** England
118 G9 **Seven Persons** Alberta
109 J7 **Seven Sisters** Texas
112 K2 **Seven Springs** N Carolina
102 F1 **Seven Troughs** Nevada
117 N10 **Seventy Mile House** Br Columbia
25 F6 **Sevenum** Netherlands
18 H8 **Séverac-le-Château** France
107 P2 **Severance** Kansas
139 K3 **Severn** *R* New S Wales
121 L8 **Severn** *R* Ontario
52 J4 **Severnaya Mylva** *R* U.S.S.R.
51 K1 **Severnaya Zemlya** *arch* Arctic Oc
55 G3 **Severnoye** U.S.S.R.
8 D4 **Severn, R** England
55 D3 **Severnyy** U.S.S.R.
52 J3 **Severnyy Ural** *mts* U.S.S.R.
51 L3 **Severo-Baykal'skoye Nagor'ye** *uplands* U.S.S.R.
37 P3 **Severocesky Kraj** *reg* Czechoslovakia
52 E3 **Severodvinsk** U.S.S.R.
31 K6 **Severomoravský** *reg* Czechoslovakia
52 D1 **Severomorsk** U.S.S.R.
55 C1 **Severouralsk** U.S.S.R.
54 K2 **Severo Zadonsk** U.S.S.R.
107 O4 **Severy** Kansas
29 O2 **Sevettijarvi** Finland
103 M3 **Sevier** Utah
103 M2 **Sevier** *R* Utah
103 M2 **Sevier Bridge Res** Utah
103 M2 **Sevier Des** Utah
112 D2 **Sevierville** Tennessee
22 G4 **Sevigny** France
16 D7 **Sevilla** Spain
16 D7 **Sevilla** *prov* Spain
126 F4 **Sevilla** *R* Cuba
Seville *see* **Sevilla**
47 G2 **Sevlievo** Bulgaria
48 J2 **Sevola** *mt* U.S.S.R.
53 F11 **Sev. Osetinsk. A.S.S.R** U.S.S.R.
18 E6 **Sèvre-Niortaise** *R* France
20 K4 **Sevres** France
40 B5 **Sevron** *R* France
54 F4 **Sevsk** U.S.S.R.
85 B7 **Sewa** *R* Sierra Leone
110 L6 **Sewanee** Tennessee
116 N6 **Seward** Alaska
107 M3 **Seward** Kansas
98 J9 **Seward** Nebraska
107 N6 **Seward** Oklahoma
94 H6 **Seward** Pennsylvania
116 R6 **Seward Glacier** Yukon Terr/Alaska
146 F12 **Seward Mts** Antarctica
116 E4 **Seward Pen** Alaska
133 C4 **Sewell** Chile
40 E2 **Sewen** France
94 G6 **Sewickley** Pennsylvania
117 O8 **Sexsmith** Alberta
124 G4 **Sextín** Mexico
77 H3 **Seyah Band Koh** *mts* Afghanistan
43 B12 **Seybouse** *R* Algeria
83 J12 **Seychelles** *islds, rep* Indian Oc
33 R9 **Seyda** E Germany
52 K2 **Seyda** U.S.S.R.
115 S4 **Seydhisfjördhur** Iceland
28 O9 **Seydhtorva** *C* Faeroes
78 C3 **Seydişehir** Turkey
20 B3 **Seye** *R* France
78 E3 **Seyhan** *R* Turkey
47 L5 **Seyit** *R* Turkey
47 L5 **Seyitgazi** Turkey
54 D5 **Seym** *R* U.S.S.R.
95 O5 **Seymour** Connecticut
94 B8 **Seymour** Indiana
110 C1 **Seymour** Iowa
110 D4 **Seymour** Missouri
109 H2 **Seymour** Texas
139 H6 **Seymour** Victoria
99 S5 **Seymour** Wisconsin
140 C6 **Seymour Ra** N Terr Aust
19 Q16 **Seyne-les-Alpes** France
42 F3 **Sežana** Yugoslavia
18 H4 **Sezanne** France
52 D6 **Sezha** *R* U.S.S.R.
16 A6 **Sezimbra** Portugal
45 O6 **Sezze** Italy
85 G2 **Sfax** Tunisia
47 F9 **Sfinári** Crete Greece
48 K5 **Sfîntu Gheorghe** Romania
48 M6 **Sfîntu Gheorghe** *R* Romania
79 H2 **Sfira** Syria
's-Gravenhage *see* **Den Haag**
25 B5 **'s-Gravenzande** Netherlands
15 D3 **Sgurr Mor** *mt* Scotland
58 **Shaanxi** *prov* China
80 F3 **Sha'ar** Israel
79 H4 **Sha'ar, Jebel** *mts* Syria
Sha'av *see* **Sha'ab**
87 E7 **Shaba** *reg* Zaïre
89 G3 **Shabani** Zimbabwe
119 O2 **Shabaqua** Ontario
99 S8 **Shabbona** Illinois
84 H5 **Shab, El** Egypt
78 K2 **Shabestar** Iran
79 F9 **Shabibī, J. esh** *mt* Jordan
47 J1 **Shabla** Bulgaria
86 E6 **Shabunda** Zaïre
55 D2 **Shaburovo** U.S.S.R.
67 B3 **Shachang** China
66 B4 **Shache** China
118 J8 **Shackleton** Sask
146 G7 **Shackleton Coast** Antarctica
146 G8 **Shackleton Glacier** Antarctica
146 D2 **Shackleton Ice Shelf** Antarctica
146 H7 **Shackleton Inlet** Antarctica
146 D10 **Shackleton Rge** Antarctica
74 B5 **Shadadkot** Pakistan
98 D4 **Shadehill Res** S Dakota
67 E3 **Shadi** China
55 D3 **Shadrinsk** U.S.S.R.
111 K10 **Shady Grove** Alabama
113 D7 **Shady Grove** Florida
55 C4 **Shafranovo** U.S.S.R.
102 E6 **Shafter** California
101 L9 **Shafter** Nevada
108 C6 **Shafter** Texas
8 D5 **Shaftesbury** England
55 G5 **Shagan** *R* U.S.S.R.
65 E4 **Shagang** China
48 M5 **Shagany, Oz** *L* U.S.S.R.
Shagedu *see* **Jungar Qi**
55 F4 **Shaglyteniz, Oz** *L* U.S.S.R.
56 D5 **Shagonar** U.S.S.R.
144 C6 **Shag R** New Zealand
133 H8 **Shag Rocks** S Georgia
76 C2 **Shahabad** India
78 L4 **Shahabad** Iran
76 B3 **Shahapur** India
80 B7 **Shaḥar** Israel
74 C6 **Shahbadpur** Pakistan
74 B6 **Shahbandar** Pakistan
75 J7 **Shahdol** India
65 C6 **Shahe** China
65 D6 **Shahe** China
67 E2 **Shahezhen** China
Shahezi *see* **Wan Xian**
77 K2 **Shah Fuladi** *mt* Afghanistan
84 G3 **Shahhāt** Libya
78 L3 **Shahin Dezh** Iran
74 H5 **Shahjahanpur** India
77 E1 **Shāh Jehān, Kuh-e** *mts* Iran
77 K3 **Shahjui** Afghanistan
65 E4 **Shahousuo** China
74 G7 **Shahpur** India
74 F6 **Shahpura** India
77 J2 **Shahrak** Afghanistan
77 G3 **Shāhrakht** Iran
77 D4 **Shahr-e Bābak** Iran
77 B3 **Shahr Kord** Iran
77 B2 **Shahr Rey** Iran
77 D2 **Shahrud Bustam** Iran
77 B1 **Shahsavār** Iran
77 F5 **Shāh Savāran, Kūh-e** *mts* Iran
50 F2 **Shaim** U.S.S.R.
80 G3 **Shajara** Jordan
65 F4 **Shajianzi** China
52 E6 **Shakhovskaya** U.S.S.R.
59 M2 **Shakhtersk** U.S.S.R.
54 M9 **Shakhty** U.S.S.R.
52 G5 **Shakhun'ya** U.S.S.R.
85 E7 **Shaki** Nigeria
84 J4 **Shâkir** *isld* Egypt
99 N5 **Shakopee** Minnesota
60 O2 **Shakotan dake** *mt* Japan
59 L3 **Shakotan misaki** *C* Japan
55 C4 **Shaksha** U.S.S.R.
116 G4 **Shaktolik** Alaska
52 F4 **Shalakusha** U.S.S.R.
86 G4 **Shala, L** Ethiopia
117 M10 **Shalalth** Br Columbia
65 G2 **Shalan** China
67 D6 **Shalang** China
55 G4 **Shalday** U.S.S.R.
52 F6 **Shaldezh** U.S.S.R.
9 F5 **Shalford** England
52 E4 **Shalgachëva** U.S.S.R.
57 F2 **Shalgiya** U.S.S.R.
77 E4 **Shalidab** Iran
55 D5 **Shalkar Karashatau** *L* U.S.S.R.
55 D5 **Shalkar-Yega-Kara** *L* U.S.S.R.
80 G3 **Shallala** Jordan
112 J4 **Shallotte** N Carolina
108 E2 **Shallowater** Texas
120 J8 **Shallow Lake** Ontario
80 C7 **Shalwa** Israel
55 C3 **Shalya** U.S.S.R.
56 C4 **Shalym** U.S.S.R.
88 D5 **Shama** *R* Tanzania
56 G5 **Shaman, Khrebet** *mts* U.S.S.R.
55 C3 **Shamary** U.S.S.R.
86 F4 **Shambe** Sudan
80 D2 **Shamerat** Israel
75 O5 **Shamgong** Bhutan
77 E6 **Shamīl** Iran
80 F1 **Shamir** Israel
78 K6 **Shamiya Des** Iraq
95 L6 **Shamokin** Pennsylvania
113 D8 **Shamrock** Florida
107 O6 **Shamrock** Oklahoma
118 L8 **Shamrock** Sask
108 D8 **Shamrock** Texas
88 C10 **Shamva** Zimbabwe
68 C2 **Shan** *prov* Burma
80 G6 **Sha'nab** Jordan
Shanchengzhen *see* **Nanjing**
77 G5 **Shāndak** Iran
58 D4 **Shandan** China
65 C3 **Shandian He** *R* China
102 D6 **Shandon** California
12 D1 **Shandon** Scotland
65 C6 **Shandong** *prov* China
67 E6 **Shandong Bandao** *pen* China
52 F4 **Shangaly** U.S.S.R.
87 E9 **Shangani** *R* Zimbabwe
65 D4 **Shangbancheng** China
67 E1 **Shangcheng** China
65 F3 **Shangchengzhen** China
67 D6 **Shangchuan Dao** *isld* China
65 B4 **Shangdu** China
Shangdundu *see* **Linchuan**
67 E2 **Shangfu** China
67 E2 **Shanggao** China
67 G1 **Shanghai** China
63 **Shanghai** *conurbation* China
67 E4 **Shanghang** China
65 D6 **Shanghe**
65 C4 **Shanghuangqi** China
67 C1 **Shangkan** China
67 C5 **Shanglin** China
87 D9 **Shangombo** Zambia
Shangpaihe *see* **Feixi**
58 G5 **Shangqiu** China
67 F2 **Shangrao** China
67 B5 **Shangsi** China
58 E5 **Shang Xian** China
65 B5 **Shangyangwu** China
65 C4 **Shangyi** China
67 E4 **Shangyou** China
67 G1 **Shangyu** China
59 J2 **Shangzhi** China
65 D5 **Shanhaiguan** China
65 G2 **Shanhetun** China
100 E4 **Shaniko** Oregon
9 E6 **Shanklin** England
67 E2 **Shankou** China
94 J6 **Shanksville** Penn
112 B3 **Shannon** Georgia
99 R7 **Shannon** Illinois
111 H7 **Shannon** Mississippi
145 E4 **Shannon** New Zealand
14 C4 **Shannon Airport** Irish Rep
99 M9 **Shannon City** Iowa
14 D2 **Shannon Pot** Irish Rep
14 C2 **Shannon R** Irish Rep
Shansi *prov see* **Shanxi**
65 G3 **Shansonggang** China
80 G4 **Shantana** Jordan
51 N3 **Shantarskiye, Ostrova** *islds* U.S.S.R.
67 E5 **Shantou** China
Shantung *prov see* **Shandong**
Shantung Peninsula *see* **Shandong Bandao**
58 F4 **Shanxi** *prov* China
65 C7 **Shan Xian** China
67 F4 **Shanyao** China
58 F4 **Shanyin** China
67 F1 **Shaobo** China
67 D3 **Shaodong** China
67 D3 **Shaoshan** China
67 F3 **Shaowu** China
59 H5 **Shaoxing** China
67 D3 **Shaoyang** China
15 F1 **Shapinsay** Scotland
52 H2 **Shapkina** *R* U.S.S.R.
56 C5 **Shapshal'skiy Khrebet** *mts* U.S.S.R.
Shara Gol *see* **Dang He**
52 H7 **Sharan** U.S.S.R.
52 G6 **Sharanga** U.S.S.R.
121 O8 **Sharbot Lake** Ontario
48 L2 **Shargorodo** U.S.S.R.
60 S2 **Shari** Japan
77 D7 **Sharjah** U.A.E.
52 H6 **Sharkan** U.S.S.R.
71 D5 **Shark Fin B** Philippines
52 C6 **Sharkovshchina** U.S.S.R.
141 H2 **Shark Reef** Gt Barrier Reef Aust
55 B4 **Sharlyk** U.S.S.R.
95 O5 **Sharon** Connecticut
112 E4 **Sharon** Georgia
107 M4 **Sharon** Kansas
94 B2 **Sharon** Michigan
98 J2 **Sharon** N Dakota
108 E7 **Sharon** Oklahoma
110 H5 **Sharon** Tennessee
95 P3 **Sharon** Vermont
99 S7 **Sharon** Wisconsin
80 C5 **Sharon, Plain of** Israel
107 J3 **Sharon Springs** Kansas
54 G6 **Sharovka** U.S.S.R.
98 F5 **Sharpe, L** S Dakota
95 L9 **Sharps** Virginia
99 M9 **Sharpsburg** Iowa
94 K7 **Sharpsburg** Maryland
94 A6 **Sharpsville** Indiana
79 F5 **Sharqi, Jebel esh** *mts* Lebanon
52 G5 **Shar'ya** U.S.S.R.
86 G4 **Shashamanna** Ethiopia
89 F3 **Shashani** *R* Zimbabwe
89 E3 **Shashe** Botswana
89 G2 **Shashe** *R* Zimbabwe
87 E10 **Shashe** *R* Zimbabwe/Botswana
67 D1 **Shashi** China
100 C9 **Shasta L** California
100 C8 **Shasta, Mt** California
67 D4 **Shatian** China
52 F6 **Shatki** U.S.S.R.
55 D3 **Shatrovo** U.S.S.R.
108 E7 **Shattuck** Oklahoma
54 L1 **Shatura** U.S.S.R.
79 F8 **Shaubak** Jordan
80 G3 **Shaumar** Jordan
118 J9 **Shaunavon** Sask
52 D3 **Shaverki** U.S.S.R.
102 E4 **Shaver L** California
94 H8 **Shavers Fork** *R* W Virginia
80 D2 **Shave Ẓiyyon** Israel
111 F8 **Shaw** Mississippi
120 K7 **Shawanaga** Ontario
95 N5 **Shawangunk Mts** New York
99 S5 **Shawano** Wisconsin
99 S5 **Shawano L** Wisconsin
121 R7 **Shawbridge** Quebec
8 D2 **Shawbury** England
141 J5 **Shaw I** Queensland
115 M8 **Shawinigan** Quebec
101 Q3 **Shawmut** Montana
94 E7 **Shawnee** Ohio
107 O6 **Shawnee** Oklahoma
98 A7 **Shawnee** Wyoming
110 H4 **Shawneetown** Illinois
121 O7 **Shawville** Quebec
67 F3 **Sha Xi** *R* China
67 F3 **Sha Xian** China
67 D1 **Shayang** China
84 J4 **Shayib el Banât, Gebel** *mt* Egypt
72 F6 **Shaykh' Uthmān** S Yemen
52 J4 **Shaytanovka** U.S.S.R.
67 G1 **Shazhou** China
54 J3 **Shchekino** U.S.S.R.
54 K1 **Shchelkovo** U.S.S.R.
52 H2 **Shchel'yayur** U.S.S.R.
55 G4 **Shcherbakty** U.S.S.R.
54 J1 **Shcherbinka** U.S.S.R.
54 H5 **Shchigry** U.S.S.R.
54 C5 **Shchors** U.S.S.R.
54 F8 **Shchorsk** U.S.S.R.
50 G3 **Shchuchinsk** U.S.S.R.
55 D3 **Shchuch'ye** U.S.S.R.
55 C3 **Shchuch'ye Ozero** U.S.S.R.
54 K1 **Shchurovo** U.S.S.R.
128 G3 **Shea** Guyana
86 G4 **Shea Ghimirri** Ethiopia
100 H6 **Sheaville** Oregon
119 O2 **Shebandowan L** Ontario
54 H6 **Shebekino** U.S.S.R.
99 T6 **Sheboygan** Wisconsin
86 B4 **Shebshi Mts** Nigeria
80 E5 **Shechem** Jordan
78 H3 **Shedadi** Syria
100 B5 **Shedd** Oregon
120 J10 **Shedden** Ontario
122 H7 **Shediac** New Brunswick
14 D3 **Sheelin, L** Irish Rep
121 N7 **Sheenboro** Quebec
116 Q2 **Sheenjek** *R* Alaska
117 O9 **Sheep Cr** Alberta
101 U7 **Sheep Cr** Wyoming
14 D1 **Sheep Haven** Irish Rep
101 T10 **Sheephorn** Colorado
106 C2 **Sheep Mt** Colorado
103 J5 **Sheep Pk** Nevada
103 J5 **Sheep Ra** Nevada
14 B5 **Sheep's Hd** Irish Rep
118 F7 **Sheerness** Alberta
9 G5 **Sheerness** England
115 N9 **Sheet Harbour** Nova Scotia
80 D2 **Shefar'am** Israel
80 C7 **Shefela** Israel
13 G6 **Sheffield** England
99 R8 **Sheffield** Illinois
99 N7 **Sheffield** Iowa
95 O4 **Sheffield** Massachusetts
144 D5 **Sheffield** New Zealand
94 H5 **Sheffield** Pennsylvania
139 H8 **Sheffield** Tasmania
108 F5 **Sheffield** Texas
94 E5 **Sheffield Lake** Ohio
56 B3 **Shegarka** *R* U.S.S.R.
52 G3 **Shegmas** U.S.S.R.
120 J7 **Sheguiandah** Ontario
119 O7 **Sheho** Sask
67 B1 **Shehong** China
133 C7 **Shehuén** *R* Argentina
86 J4 **Sheikh** Somalia
79 F5 **Sheikh, J. esh** *mt* Lebanon/Syria
120 F3 **Shekak** *R* Ontario
Shekar Dzong *see* **Tingri**
74 F3 **Shekhupura** Pakistan
53 G12 **Sheki** U.S.S.R.
52 E5 **Sheksna** *R* U.S.S.R.
94 E9 **Shelbiana** Kentucky
110 D2 **Shelbina** Missouri
110 J2 **Shelburn** Indiana
115 N9 **Shelburne** Nova Scotia
120 K8 **Shelburne** Ontario
95 O2 **Shelburne** Vermont
141 G1 **Shelburne B** Queensland
95 P4 **Shelburne Falls** Massachusetts
99 T8 **Shelby** Indiana
99 L8 **Shelby** Iowa
99 U6 **Shelby** Michigan
111 F8 **Shelby** Mississippi
101 O1 **Shelby** Montana
112 F2 **Shelby** N Carolina
98 J8 **Shelby** Nebraska
94 E6 **Shelby** Ohio
110 H2 **Shelbyville** Illinois
110 L2 **Shelbyville** Indiana
110 L3 **Shelbyville** Kentucky
110 E2 **Shelbyville** Missouri
110 K6 **Shelbyville** Tennessee
109 N4 **Shelbyville** Texas
99 T9 **Sheldon** Illinois
99 L6 **Sheldon** Iowa
110 B4 **Sheldon** Missouri
98 J3 **Sheldon** N Dakota
117 H4 **Sheldon, Mt** Yukon Terr
95 P2 **Sheldon Springs** Vermont
122 H3 **Sheldrake** Quebec
56 F5 **Shelekhov** U.S.S.R.
90 F16 **Shelf Ice** Antarctica
116 K8 **Shelikof Str** Alaska
101 S5 **Shell** Wyoming
99 L3 **Shell** *R* Minnesota
111 G12 **Shell Beach** Louisiana
118 L5 **Shellbrook** Sask
101 R8 **Shell Cr** Wyoming
101 N6 **Shelley** Idaho
139 K5 **Shellharbour** New S Wales
99 P4 **Shell L** Wisconsin
118 K5 **Shell Lake** Sask
143 F8 **Shell Lakes** W Australia
111 M10 **Shellman** Georgia
119 Q8 **Shellmouth** Manitoba
102 A1 **Shell Mt** California
99 O7 **Shell Rock** Iowa
99 O7 **Shellrock** *R* Iowa
99 P7 **Shellsburg** Iowa
80 D1 **Shelomi** Israel
58 G1 **Shelopugino** U.S.S.R.
102 A1 **Shelter Cove** California
95 P5 **Shelter I** Long I, New York
144 B7 **Shelter Pt** New Zealand
95 O5 **Shelton** Connecticut
98 H9 **Shelton** Nebraska
117 M12 **Shelton** Washington
52 E4 **Sheltozero** U.S.S.R.
78 M1 **Shemakha** U.S.S.R.
56 B5 **Shemonaikha** U.S.S.R.
52 H6 **Shemordan** U.S.S.R.
52 G6 **Shemursha** U.S.S.R.
99 L9 **Shenandoah** Iowa
95 L6 **Shenandoah** Pennsylvania
94 J8 **Shenandoah** Virginia
94 K7 **Shenandoah Junc** W Virginia
94 H8 **Shenandoah Mts** W Virginia/Virginia
94 J8 **Shenandoah Nat. Park** Virginia
94 G5 **Shenango Res** Ohio/Penn
57 D1 **Shenber** U.S.S.R.
65 B5 **Shenchi** China
86 A4 **Shendam** Nigeria
86 F2 **Shendi** Sudan
65 J1 **Shending Shan** *mt* China
46 D3 **Shëngjin** Albania
65 F1 **Shengping** China
67 G1 **Shengsi** China
67 G1 **Shengsi Liedao** *islds* China
67 G2 **Sheng Xian** China
52 F4 **Shenkursk** U.S.S.R.
65 A5 **Shenmu** China

141 K1 South Brisbane dist Brisbane, Qnsld
144 D5 Southbrook New Zealand
123 Q4 South Brook Nfld
122 H9 South Brookfield Nova Scotia
144 C6 Southburn New Zealand
112 F3 South Carolina state U.S.A.
13 H6 South Cave England
94 C1 South Chan Michigan
94 D7 South Charleston Ohio
94 F8 South Charleston W Virginia
67 E6 South China Sea
95 N2 South Colton New York
98 F5 South Dakota state U.S.A.
94 H4 South Dayton New York
13 F3 Southdean Scotland
95 P4 South Deerfield Massachusetts
9 F6 South Downs England
139 H9 South East C Tasmania
139 H7 South East C Victoria
83 K12 South East I Mahé I Indian Oc
135 N15 Southeast Pacific Basin Pac Oc
9 G4 Southend England
114 J6 Southend Sask
12 C3 Southend Scotland
99 O8 South English Iowa
144 C5 Southern Alps mts New Zealand
101 M3 Southern Cross Montana
141 H5 Southern Cross Queensland
143 C9 Southern Cross W Australia
86 D3 Southern Darfur prov Sudan
8 C5 Southerndown Wales
123 T6 Southern Harbour Nfld
119 S2 Southern Indian L Manitoba
86 E3 Southern Kordofan prov Sudan
81 Southern Ocean
111 G10 Southern Pine Hills Miss/Ala
112 H2 Southern Pines N Carolina
142 B2 Southern R Perth, W Aust
142 F5 South Esk Tableland W Australia
119 N8 Southey Sask
110 E2 South Fabius R Missouri
13 H6 South Ferriby England
144 A6 South Fiord New Zealand
100 B9 South Fork California
106 D4 South Fork Colorado
94 J6 South Fork Pennsylvania
118 J9 South Fork Sask
112 F1 South Fork R N Carolina
110 G6 South Fork R Tennessee
98 D4 South Fork R S Dakota
99 V4 South Fox I Michigan
110 H5 South Fulton Tennessee
146 F5 South Geomagnetic Pole (1975) Antarctica
131 H5 South Georgia S Atlantic Oc
99 O9 South Gifford Missouri
8 C4 South Glamorgan co Wales
110 B3 South Grand R Missouri
123 M7 South Harbour Nova Scotia
107 N4 South Haven Kansas
99 U7 South Haven Michigan
115 K5 South Henik L N W Terr
94 J10 South Hill Virginia
94 F10 South Holston L Tenn/Virg
83 M8 South I Cocos Is Indian Oc
140 C1 South I N Terr Aust
115 T2 South Indian L Manitoba
95 P5 Southington Connecticut
144 B5 South Island New Zealand
71 D6 South Islet Sulu Sea
118 F1 South Junc Manitoba
99 T7 South Kenosha Wisconsin
59 J4 South Korea rep Asia
109 M8 Southlake Texas
144 A6 Southland stat area New Zealand
123 K9 South Lochaber Nova Scotia
98 G8 South Loup R Nebraska
88 C8 South Luangwa Nat. Park Zambia
70 C2 South Luconia Shoals S China Sea
94 D4 South Lyon Michigan
120 K7 Southmag Ontario
146 J3 South Magnetic Pole (1975) Antarctica
99 U4 South Manitou I Michigan
95 L10 South Mills N Carolina
99 T7 South Milwaukee Wisconsin
9 G4 Southminster England
141 J5 South Molle I Queensland
8 C5 South Molton England
109 K10 Southmost Texas
95 K6 South Mt Pennsylvania
116 J7 South Naknek Alaska
122 G7 South Nelson New Brunswick
112 F6 South Newport Georgia
95 P5 Southold Long I, New York
90 F15 South Orkney isld S Atlantic Oc
102 B3 South Pablo B California
95 R2 South Paris Maine
94 F7 South Parkersburg W Virginia
101 R7 South Pass Wyoming
101 R7 South Pass City Wyoming
99 R9 South Pekin Illinois
110 L6 South Pittsburg Tennessee
106 E2 South Platte Colorado
146 F8 South Polar Plat Antarctica
146 F8 South Pole Antarctica
120 J4 South Porcupine Ontario
13 E6 Southport England
94 A7 Southport Indiana
112 J4 Southport N Carolina
123 T5 Southport Nfld
139 H9 Southport Tasmania
123 K4 South Pt Anticosti I, Quebec
83 M9 South Pt Christmas I Indian Oc
112 J3 South R N Carolina
99 S2 South Range Michigan
144 A7 South Red Head Pt. New Zealand
113 H12 South Riding Rock Bahamas
95 N6 South River New Jersey
121 L7 South River Ontario
15 F2 South Ronaldsay Scotland
131 J7 South Sandwich Is S Atlantic Oc
102 B4 South San Francisco California
118 J8 South Sask R Sask
9 E6 Southsea England
119 S1 South Seal R Manitoba
146 E15 South Shetland Is Antarctica
13 G3 South Shields England
98 K7 South Sioux City Nebraska
98 K6 South Sioux Falls S Dakota
117 P11 South Slocan Br Columbia
103 N2 South Tent peak Utah
15 A3 South Uist Scotland
9 F1 Southwell England
South West Africa terr see Namibia
113 K9 South West B New Providence I Bahamas
123 K6 Southwest C Madeleine Is, Quebec
139 H9 South West C Tasmania
144 A7 Southwest Cape New Zealand
139 H7 South West I Tasmania
81 C9 South-West Indian Ridge Indian Oc
135 M12 South-West Pacific Basin Pac Oc
113 K12 Southwest Pt Bahamas
118 K7 Southwest Pt Quebec
126 E6 Southwest Rock Caribbean
99 S8 South Wilmington Illinois
9 H3 Southwold England
9 G2 South Wootton England
72 F5 South Yemen rep Arabia
13 G6 South Yorkshire co England
89 F4 Soutpansberg mts S Africa
144 B6 Soutra Hill New Zealand
18 H6 Souvigny France
16 B6 Souzel Portugal
48 J4 Sovata Romania
118 K7 Sovereign Sask
52 B6 Sovetsk U.S.S.R.
52 G5 Sovetsk U.S.S.R.
51 N4 Sovetskaya Gavan U.S.S.R.
52 C4 Sovetskiy Leningrad U.S.S.R.
55 D1 Sovetskiy Tyumenskaya U.S.S.R.
28 E5 Søvind Denmark
52 F2 Sovpol'ye U.S.S.R.
119 N1 Sowden L Ontario
13 G6 Sowerby Br England
60 P1 Sōya Japan
60 P1 Sōya-misaki C Japan
52 F2 Soyana R U.S.S.R.
60 P1 Sōya wan B Japan
38 F5 Soyen W Germany
19 N15 Soyons France
124 E3 Soyopa Mexico
54 B4 Sozh R U.S.S.R.
52 H5 Sozimskiy U.S.S.R.
47 J2 Sozopol Bulgaria
22 K3 Spa Belgium
126 B2 Spaanse Baai B Curaçao
16 Spain rep W Europe
31 M4 Spała Poland
Spalato see Split
9 F2 Spalding England
100 J3 Spalding Idaho
98 H8 Spalding Nebraska
119 N6 Spalding Sask
138 E5 Spalding S Australia
37 K5 Spalt W Germany
25 C3 Spanbroek Netherlands
33 S7 Spandau W Berlin
28 B6 Spandet Denmark
27 H14 Spångenäs Sweden
36 H1 Spangenberg W Germany
100 H2 Spangle Washington
94 J6 Spangler Pennsylvania
123 T6 Spaniard's B Nfld
120 H6 Spanish Ontario
101 O9 Spanish Fork City Utah
106 F4 Spanish Pks Colorado
127 L3 Spanish Town Jamaica
113 L12 Spanish Wells Eleuthera Bahamas
45 Q7 Sparanise Italy
26 E8 Sparbu Norway
28 C4 Sparkær Denmark
111 D8 Sparkman Arkansas
102 D6 Sparks Georgia
111 B3 Sparks Nebraska
102 E2 Sparks Nevada
107 O6 Sparks Oklahoma
99 R8 Sparland Illinois
37 M3 Sparnberg E Germany
94 C1 Sparr Michigan
112 E4 Sparta Georgia
110 G3 Sparta Illinois
94 B3 Sparta Michigan
110 C4 Sparta Missouri
112 G1 Sparta N Carolina
100 H5 Sparta Oregon
110 L6 Sparta Tennessee
99 Q6 Sparta Wisconsin
112 F3 Spartanburg S Carolina
94 H5 Spartansburg Pennsylvania
16 D9 Spartel, C Morocco
43 C10 Spartivento, C Italy
43 B10 Spartivento, C Sardinia
54 M1 Spas-Klepiki U.S.S.R.
56 C4 Spassk U.S.S.R.
52 D4 Spasskaya Guba U.S.S.R.
59 K3 Spassk Dal'niy U.S.S.R.
55 E5 Spasskoye U.S.S.R.
54 M2 Spassk-Ryazanskiy U.S.S.R.
47 F9 Spátha, Akr C Crete Greece
117 J7 Spatsizi Plat. Wilderness Prov. Pk Br Columbia
110 A5 Spavinaw, L Oklahoma
36 D3 Spay W Germany
109 L6 Speaks Texas
15 D4 Spean Bridge Scotland
98 C5 Spearfish S Dakota
119 T7 Spearhill Manitoba
143 D6 Spear Hill W Australia
108 C7 Spearman Texas
107 L4 Spearville Kansas
142 A3 Spearwood dist Perth, W Aust
33 R6 Specker-See L E Germany
95 N3 Speculator New York
118 F4 Spedden Alberta
109 M1 Speer Oklahoma
98 B8 Speer Wyoming
118 K6 Speers Sask
36 B4 Speicher W Germany
37 M4 Speichersdorf W Germany
37 M7 Speichersee L W Germany
127 P6 Speightstown Barbados
116 M6 Spenard Alaska
115 K4 Spence Bay N W Terr
101 N5 Spencer Idaho
110 K2 Spencer Indiana
99 L6 Spencer Iowa
95 P4 Spencer Massachusetts
98 H7 Spencer Nebraska
95 L4 Spencer New York
98 J6 Spencer S Dakota
99 Q5 Spencer Wisconsin
94 F8 Spencer W Virginia
117 E6 Spencer, C Alaska
138 D6 Spencer, C S Australia
138 D5 Spencer Gulf S Australia
95 R1 Spencer L Maine
94 K3 Spencerport New York
116 D4 Spencer, Pt Alaska
140 A3 Spencer Ra N Terr Aust
140 C1 Spencer Ra N Terr Aust
94 C6 Spencerville Ohio
117 N10 Spences Bridge Br Columbia
32 H8 Spenge W Germany
13 G4 Spennymoor England
144 D5 Spenser Mts New Zealand
33 S8 Sperenberg E Germany
27 D11 Sperillen Norway
46 E6 Sperkhiós R Greece
118 D1 Sperling Manitoba
45 O7 Sperlonga Italy
43 B10 Sperone, C Sardinia
14 D2 Sperrin Mts N Ireland
94 J8 Sperryville Virginia
36 G3 Spessart mts W Germany
46 F7 Spétsai isld Greece
15 E3 Spey R Scotland
36 E5 Speyer W Germany
127 N1 Speyside Tobago
44 G3 Spezia, La Italy
115 M4 Spicer Is N W Terr
99 N9 Spickardsville Missouri
32 G5 Spiekeroog W Germany
38 N8 Spielfeld Austria
36 C5 Spiesen-Elversberg W Germany
44 D2 Spigno R Italy
25 G2 Spijk Netherlands
110 C1 Spikard Missouri
116 R3 Spike Mt Alaska
45 K2 Spilamberto Italy
47 G9 Spíli Crete Greece
42 E2 Spilimbergo Italy
9 G1 Spilsby England
28 N3 Spinarnir mt Faeroes
43 G8 Spinazzola Italy
77 K4 Spin Būldak Afghanistan
22 K5 Spincourt France
112 F2 Spindale N Carolina
45 M1 Spinea Italy
143 F7 Spinifex Ra W Australia
89 B8 Spioenberg I mt S Africa
89 A8 Spioenberg II mt S Africa
89 F7 Spioen Kop mt S Africa
144 A6 Spire Pk New Zealand
99 L6 Spirit L Iowa
100 J2 Spirit Lake Idaho
100 C3 Spirit Lake Washington
117 O8 Spirit River Alberta
145 D1 Spirits B New Zealand
98 H3 Spiritwood N Dakota
118 K5 Spiritwood Sask
107 Q6 Spiro Oklahoma
52 D6 Spirovo U.S.S.R.
48 F1 Spišská Belá Czechoslovakia
48 F2 Spišská Nová Ves Czechoslovakia
31 M6 Spišské Podhradie Czechoslovakia
50 A1 Spitsbergen arch Arctic Oc
38 H3 Spittal-an-der-Drau Austria
38 M5 Spitz Austria
28 A4 Spjald Denmark
109 M5 Splendora Texas
42 H5 Split Yugoslavia
122 H8 Split, C Nova Scotia
119 V2 Split L Manitoba
100 G8 Split Pk mt Nevada
38 N9 Spodnje Hoče Yugoslavia
28 F7 Spodsbjerg Denmark
108 G6 Spofford Texas
13 G6 Spofforth England
100 H2 Spokane Washington
41 M4 Spöl R Italy
42 E6 Spoleto Italy
118 F7 Spondin Alberta
68 G6 Spong Cambodia
33 S5 Sponholz E Germany
22 J3 Spontin Belgium
99 Q9 Spoon R Illinois
99 P4 Spooner Wisconsin
100 E8 Spooner Res California
47 H8 Sporádhes islds Greece
33 P6 Spornitz E Germany
28 E4 Spørring Denmark
44 D3 Spotorno Italy
101 U5 Spotted Horse Wyoming
103 J5 Spotted Ra Nevada
111 K9 Sprague Alabama
118 F1 Sprague Manitoba
100 H2 Sprague Washington
99 Q5 Sprague Wisconsin
100 D7 Sprague River Oregon
36 H6 Spraitbach W Germany
33 M7 Sprakensehl W Germany
100 F5 Spray Oregon
48 E6 Spreča R Yugoslavia
54 J4 Spredne Russkaya Vozvyshennost' uplands U.S.S.R.
31 H4 Spree R E Germany
33 T9 Spreewald E Germany
31 H4 Spremberg E Germany
36 F3 Sprendlingen Hessen W Germany
36 E4 Sprendlingen Rheinland-Pfalz W Germany
22 K3 Sprimont Belgium
109 M5 Spring Texas
110 E5 Spring R Arkansas
110 B5 Spring R Oklahoma
101 N8 Spring B Utah
89 A7 Springbok S Africa
94 G5 Springboro Pennsylvania
109 J6 Spring Branch Texas
98 C1 Spring Brook N Dakota
118 A3 Springburn Alberta
144 C5 Springburn New Zealand
95 M6 Spring City Pennsylvania
112 C2 Spring City Tennessee
103 N2 Spring City Utah
118 D9 Spring Coulee Alberta
98 E9 Spring Cr Nebraska
101 L8 Spring Cr Nevada
145 D4 Spring Cr New Zealand
140 E4 Spring Cr N Terr Aust
140 F6 Spring Cr Queensland
110 B5 Springdale Arkansas
101 P4 Springdale Montana
102 H4 Springdale Nevada
123 Q4 Springdale Nfld
103 M4 Springdale Utah
100 H1 Springdale Washington
32 L8 Springe W Germany
106 F5 Springer New Mexico
109 K1 Springer Oklahoma
121 Q3 Springer, Mt Quebec
103 P7 Springerville Arizona
106 H4 Springfield Colorado
112 F5 Springfield Georgia
101 N6 Springfield Idaho
110 G2 Springfield Illinois
94 B9 Springfield Kentucky
95 P4 Springfield Massachusetts
110 C4 Springfield Missouri
122 G8 Springfield New Brunswick
144 C5 Springfield New Zealand
122 H9 Springfield Nova Scotia
94 D7 Springfield Ohio
114 G9 Springfield Oregon
141 G7 Springfield Queensland
112 F4 Springfield S Carolina
98 J7 Springfield S Dakota
110 K5 Springfield Tennessee
95 P3 Springfield Vermont
89 D8 Springfontein S Africa
99 Q6 Spring Green Wisconsin
99 P6 Spring Grove Minnesota
95 L7 Spring Grove Pennsylvania
111 C9 Springhill Louisiana
122 H8 Springhill Nova Scotia
110 K6 Spring Hill Tennessee
112 J2 Spring Hope N Carolina
99 U6 Spring Lake Michigan
95 N6 Spring Lake New Jersey
108 E1 Springlake Texas
103 J5 Spring Mts Nevada
126 H3 Spring Point Acklins I Bahamas
95 K6 Springs Pennsylvania
89 F6 Springs S Africa
119 P7 Springside Sask
144 D5 Springs Junction New Zealand
144 D5 Springston New Zealand
141 J6 Springsure Queensland
109 K3 Springtown Texas
95 R3 Springvale Maine
140 F6 Springvale Queensland
141 G3 Springvale Queensland
142 G4 Springvale W Australia
99 O6 Spring Valley Minnesota
119 M9 Spring Valley Sask
98 G7 Springview Nebraska
111 K8 Springville Alabama
94 J4 Springville New York
101 O9 Springville Utah
118 J7 Springwater Sask
13 H6 Sproatley England
28 F6 Sprogø isld Denmark
32 L6 Sprötze W Germany
94 D2 Spruce Michigan
123 O5 Spruce Brook Nfld
121 L7 Sprucedale Ontario
94 H8 Spruce Knob mt W Virginia
118 H5 Spruce Lake Sask
101 L9 Spruce Mt Nevada
112 E2 Spruce Pine N Carolina
103 M4 Spry Utah
25 B5 Spui R Netherlands
43 H9 Spulico, C Italy
108 G2 Spur Texas
118 C3 Spurfield Alberta
111 B11 Spurger Texas
106 B8 Spur Lake New Mexico
116 L6 Spurr, Mt Alaska
46 C2 Spuž Yugoslavia
22 H3 Spy Belgium
119 Q8 Spy Hill Sask
117 M11 Squamish Br Columbia
95 Q3 Squam L New Hampshire
95 S7 Squapan L Maine
101 P2 Square Butte Montana
95 S6 Square L Maine
122 D6 Squattack Quebec
99 M2 Squaw L Minnesota
123 L3 Squaw L Quebec
119 O5 Squaw Rapids Sask
43 H10 Squillace, Golfo di Italy
43 J8 Squinzano Italy
138 C2 Squires, Mt N Terr Australia
143 G7 Squires,Mt W Australia
116 G3 Squirrel R Alaska
120 F2 Squirrel R Ontario
70 N9 Sragen Java
46 D2 Srbica Yugoslavia
46 D1 Srbija Yugoslavia
48 F5 Srbobran Yugoslavia
68 F7 Srê Âmbêl Cambodia
46 C1 Srebrnica Yugoslavia
47 J2 Sredetska R Bulgaria
47 G2 Sredna Gora Bulgaria
51 K2 Sredne-Sibirskoye Ploskogor'ye tableland U.S.S.R.
52 D2 Sredneye Kuyto, Oz L U.S.S.R.
47 G3 Sredni Rodopi Bulgaria
58 G1 Sredniy Kalar U.S.S.R.
55 C3 Sredniy Ural ra U.S.S.R.
68 H6 Sre Khtum Cambodia
31 K3 Śrem Poland
48 F6 Srem Mitrovica Yugoslavia
48 E6 Srem Raca Yugoslavia
48 F5 Sremski Karlovci Yugoslavia
58 G1 Sretensk U.S.S.R.
76 F1 Srikakulam India
83 Sri Lanka rep S Asia
74 F1 Srinagar Kashmir
76 B4 Sringeri India
76 C6 Srivilliputtur India
42 H4 Srnetica Yugoslavia
31 K3 Środa Poland
31 K4 Środa Śląska Poland
76 F1 Srungavarapukota India
141 F3 Staaten R Queensland
26 O1 Stabburselv R Norway
33 Q4 Stäbelow E Germany
100 D4 Stabler Washington
28 A4 Staby Denmark
120 J5 Stackpool Ontario
15 D1 Stack Skerry isld Scotland
14 B4 Stack's Mts Irish Rep
16 E4 Sta. Cruz del Retamar Spain
100 E9 Stacy California
112 L3 Stacy N Carolina
32 K5 Stade W Germany
22 E2 Staden Belgium
36 F3 Staden W Germany
9 E4 Stadhampton England
28 A4 Stadil Denmark
28 A4 Stadil Fjord inlet Denmark
26 A9 Stadlandet Norway
25 G2 Stadskanaal Netherlands
36 F2 Stadt Allendorf W Germany
37 N5 Stadtamhof W Germany
37 K7 Stadtbergen W Germany
32 K8 Stadthagen W Germany
37 L2 Stadtilm E Germany
36 B3 Stadtkyll W Germany
32 H6 Stadtland W Germany
37 J3 Stadtlauringen W Germany
37 J2 Stadtlengsfeld E Germany
32 E8 Stadtlohn W Germany
32 L9 Stadtoldendorf W Germany
36 G4 Stadtprozelten W Germany
37 M2 Stadtroda E Germany
37 J4 Stadt Schwarzach W Germany
37 M3 Stadtsteinach W Germany
15 B4 Staffa isld Scotland
33 R7 Staffelde E Germany
37 L3 Staffelstein W Germany
44 F2 Staffora R Italy
8 D2 Stafford England
107 M4 Stafford Kansas
98 H7 Stafford Nebraska
94 K8 Stafford Virginia
141 K1 Stafford dist Brisbane, Qnsld
8 D2 Staffordshire co England
95 P5 Stafford Springs Connecticut
117 Q4 Stagg L N W Terr
45 H4 Stagno Italy
9 F3 Stagsden England
33 S4 Stahlbrode E Germany
33 S8 Stahnsdorf E Germany
52 B5 Staicele U.S.S.R.
38 K6 Stainach Austria
9 F5 Staines England
12 D3 Stair Scotland
13 H4 Staithes England
48 G2 Stakčín Czechoslovakia
53 E9 Stakhanov U.S.S.R.
28 B5 Stakroge Denmark
46 E1 Stalać Yugoslavia
27 J12 Stålboga Sweden
8 D6 Stalbridge England
9 H2 Stalham England
27 B11 Stalheim Norway
52 D3 Stalina Kanal U.S.S.R.
Stalingrad see Volgograd
117 L6 Stalin, Mt Br Columbia
Stalino see Donetsk
38 H8 Stall Austria
37 O5 Stallwang W Germany
48 J5 Stâlpeni Romania
119 M7 Stalwart Sask
13 F6 Stalybridge England
47 G1 Stamboliyski Dam Bulgaria
95 O5 Stamford Connecticut
9 F2 Stamford England
95 N4 Stamford New York
141 G5 Stamford Queensland
98 E6 Stamford S Dakota
108 H3 Stamford Texas
37 L6 Stammham W Germany
27 A11 Stamnes Norway
Stampalia isld see Astipálaia / Greece
100 D2 Stampede Washington
94 C8 Stamping Ground Kentucky
87 C10 Stampriet Namibia
25 E6 Stamproij Netherlands
109 O2 Stamps Arkansas
37 O5 Stamsried W Germany
26 G3 Stamsund Norway
94 J8 Stanadsville Virginia
99 M9 Stanberry Missouri
147 Q6 Stanchik U.S.S.R.
118 E7 Standard Alberta
103 O7 Standard Arizona
87 E11 Standerton S Africa
94 D3 Standish Michigan
101 M8 Standrod Utah
100 F4 Stanfield Oregon
110 K2 Stanford Indiana
110 M4 Stanford Kentucky
101 P2 Stanford Montana
9 G4 Stanford-le-Hope England
8 D3 Stanford on Teme England
27 K14 Stånga Sweden
27 E11 Stange Norway
87 F11 Stanger S Africa
45 L1 Stanghella Italy
26 C9 Stangvik Norway
126 F2 Staniard Cr Andros Bahamas
102 D4 Stanislaus R California
Stanislav see Ivano-Frankovsk
46 F2 Stanke Dimitrov Bulgaria
37 P4 Staňkov Czechoslovakia
131 G8 Stanley Falkland Is
101 L5 Stanley Idaho
112 F2 Stanley N Carolina
98 D1 Stanley N Dakota
122 F7 Stanley New Brunswick
106 E6 Stanley New Mexico
109 M1 Stanley Oklahoma
15 E4 Stanley Scotland
139 H8 Stanley Tasmania
94 J8 Stanley Virginia
99 Q5 Stanley Wisconsin
119 M3 Stanley Mission Sask
144 D5 Stanley, Mt New Zealand
140 B6 Stanley,Mt N Terr Aust
139 G8 Stanley, Mt Tasmania
86 C6 Stanley Pool Zaïre
Stanleyville see Kisangani
118 F7 Stanmore Alberta
99 T2 Stannard Rock Michigan
125 P9 Stann Creek Belize
13 G3 Stannington England
55 F3 Stanovka U.S.S.R.
55 D2 Stanovoy U.S.S.R.
51 M3 Stanovoy Khrebet mts U.S.S.R.
41 P3 Stans Austria
138 E5 Stansbury S Australia
136 F6 Stansmore Ra W Australia
142 G5 Stansmore Ra W Australia
9 G4 Stansted England
141 K8 Stanthorpe Queensland
99 L9 Stanton Iowa
94 D9 Stanton Kentucky
94 B3 Stanton Michigan
98 E2 Stanton N Dakota
98 J8 Stanton Nebraska
147 J1 Stanton N W Terr
110 G6 Stanton Tennessee
108 F3 Stanton Texas
6 E6 Stanton Banks Atlantic Oc
94 B3 Stanwood Michigan
117 M11 Stanwood Washington
41 N3 Stanzach Austria
33 N9 Stapelburg E Germany
25 F3 Staphorst Netherlands
9 E5 Stapleford England
111 J11 Stapleton Alabama
112 E4 Stapleton Georgia
111 F9 Star Mississippi
112 H2 Star N Carolina
109 J4 Star Texas
54 F3 Star' U.S.S.R.
48 F1 Stara L'ubovňa Czechoslovakia
37 O3 Stará-Role Czechoslovakia
52 D5 Staraya Russa U.S.S.R.
55 E1 Staraya Vorpavla U.S.S.R.
47 H2 Stara Zagora Bulgaria
119 U9 Starbuck Manitoba
99 L4 Starbuck Minnesota
100 G3 Starbuck Washington
135 L9 Starbuck I Pacific Oc
111 E8 Star City Arkansas
94 A6 Star City Indiana
119 N6 Star City Sask
94 H7 Star City W Virginia
141 G2 Starcke Queensland
8 C6 Starcross England
37 O4 Staré Sedliště Czechoslovakia
31 J2 Stargard Poland
42 H4 Stari Majdan Yugoslavia
31 N6 Starina Czechoslovakia
52 D6 Staritsa U.S.S.R.
103 O10 Stark Arizona
101 L2 Stark Montana
95 Q2 Stark New Hampshire
55 C6 Star Karabutak U.S.S.R.
113 E8 Starke Florida
100 J5 Starkey Idaho
100 G4 Starkey Oregon
109 O5 Starks Louisiana
106 F4 Starkville Colorado
111 H8 Starkville Mississippi
98 H1 Starkweather N Dakota
99 R3 Starlake Wisconsin
41 O1 Starnberg W Germany
54 K7 Star'obel'sk U.S.S.R.
54 D4 Starodub U.S.S.R.
31 L2 Starogard Poland
48 M4 Starokazache U.S.S.R.
48 L1 Staro Konstantinov U.S.S.R.
47 J2 Staro Oryakhovo Bulgaria
31 O2 Starosielce Poland
55 F3 Starosoldatskoye U.S.S.R.
55 C4 Starosubkhangulovo U.S.S.R.
55 C3 Staroutkinsk U.S.S.R.
52 G5 Starovercheskaya U.S.S.R.
52 H6 Staroye Baysarovo U.S.S.R.
102 F1 Star Pk Nevada
8 C7 Start Pt England
15 F1 Start Pt Scotland
48 F1 Stary Sącz Poland
48 H1 Stary Sambor U.S.S.R.
52 H6 Staryye Zyattsy U.S.S.R.
52 H6 Staryy Menzelyabash U.S.S.R.
54 J5 Staryy Oskol U.S.S.R.
52 D5 Staryy Ryad U.S.S.R.
33 P9 Stassfurt E Germany
31 N5 Staszów Poland
99 N7 State Center Iowa
94 K6 State College Pennsylvania
111 H10 State Line Mississippi
Staten I Argentina see Estados, I de los
95 N6 Staten I New York
112 F5 Statesboro Georgia
112 G2 Statesville N Carolina
27 D12 Stathelle Norway
33 S10 Stauchitz E Germany
36 F2 Staufenberg W Germany
100 E6 Stauffer Oregon
8 D4 Staunton England
110 G2 Staunton Illinois
94 H8 Staunton Virginia
27 A13 Stavanger Norway
22 H3 Stave Belgium
117 M11 Stave L Br Columbia
13 F5 Staveley Cumbria England
9 E1 Staveley Derby England
22 K3 Stavelot Belgium
118 D8 Stavely Alberta
33 S5 Staven E Germany
25 B5 Stavenisse Netherlands
25 D3 Staveren Netherlands
28 A5 Stavning Denmark
28 F3 Stavnshoved C Denmark
28 J6 Stavreby Denmark
28 F6 Stavreshoved C Denmark
53 F10 Stavropol' U.S.S.R.
55 E4 Stavropolka U.S.S.R.
53 F10 Stavropol'skaya Vozvyshennost' uplands U.S.S.R.
46 E5 Stavrós Greece
47 G9 Stavrós, Akra C Crete Greece
47 G3 Stavroúpolis Greece
139 G6 Stawell Victoria
31 N2 Stawiski Poland
31 L4 Stawiszyn Poland
120 K8 Stayner Ontario
100 C5 Stayton Oregon
45 H4 Stazzema Italy
102 E2 Steamboat Nevada
106 D1 Steamboat Springs Colorado
94 C10 Stearns Kentucky
31 M2 Stębark Poland
116 F5 Stebbins Alaska
33 Q7 Stechow E Germany
41 J2 Steckborn Switzerland
28 B7 Stedesand W Germany
116 R4 Steel Creek Alaska
111 K8 Steele Alabama
110 G5 Steele Missouri
98 G3 Steele N Dakota
98 K9 Steele City Nebraska
146 E13 Steele I Antarctica
117 C5 Steele,Mt Yukon Terr
110 G3 Steeleville Illinois
120 D4 Steel R Ontario
95 L6 Steelton Pennsylvania
110 E4 Steelville Missouri
25 B5 Steenbergen Netherlands
89 G5 Steenkamps Berg mts S Africa
22 G2 Steenkerque Belgium
117 P6 Steen River Alberta
25 D6 Steensel Netherlands
100 G7 Steens Mt Oregon
115 O2 Steenstrups Gletscher gla Greenland
22 D2 Steenvoorde France
22 D2 Steenwerck France
25 F3 Steenwijk Netherlands
119 M5 Steep Cr Sask
119 O3 Steephill L Sask
71 D6 Steep Pt Philippines
115 K7 Steep Rock Manitoba
118 K2 Steep Rock Ontario
143 B6 Steere, Mt W Australia
13 G6 Steeton England
48 L3 Stefanești Romania
86 G5 Stefanie, L Ethiopia
43 F10 Stefano di Cam., S Sicily
146 A4 Stefansson B Antarctica
147 H3 Stefansson I N W Terr
133 C6 Steffen mt Chile/Arg
36 F2 Steffenberg W Germany
98 C8 Stegall Nebraska
28 J7 Stege Denmark
28 J6 Stege Bugt B Denmark
33 P8 Stegelitz E Germany
99 T8 Steger Illinois
87 F11 Stegi Swaziland
33 S8 Steglitz W Berlin
100 E1 Stehekin Washington
38 L7 Steiermark prov Austria
37 J4 Steigerwald hills W Germany
37 L5 Stein W Germany
37 L3 Steinach E Germany
37 J5 Steinach W Germany
36 H3 Steinau W Germany
99 K9 Steinauer Nebraska
37 J2 Steinbach E Germany
118 E1 Steinbach Manitoba
36 E6 Steinbach W Germany
37 K2 Steinbach Hallenberg E Germany
28 D7 Steinberg W Germany
38 G6 Steinberge Austria
36 C6 Steinbourg France
129 H6 Steinen R Brazil
38 G7 Steinernes Meer mts Austria
32 H7 Steinfeld W Germany
22 K4 Steinfort Luxembourg
32 H8 Steinhagen W Germany
113 D8 Steinhatchee Florida
87 C10 Steinhausen Namibia
37 L3 Steinheid E Germany
36 F3 Steinheim W Germany
33 M5 Steinhorst W Germany
32 K8 Steinhuder Meer L W Germany
32 L5 Steinkirchen W Germany
26 E8 Steinkjer Norway
87 C11 Steinkopf S Africa
38 L7 Steinplan mt Austria
106 B9 Steins New Mexico
36 F5 Steinsfurt W Germany
37 L3 Steinwiesen W Germany
22 G1 Stekene Belgium
112 K3 Stella N Carolina
99 L9 Stella Nebraska
122 K8 Stellarton Nova Scotia
45 K2 Stellata Italy
32 M6 Stelle W Germany
87 C12 Stellenbosch S Africa
116 Q6 Steller, Mt Alaska
42 D2 Stelvio, Passo di Italy
112 J1 Stem N Carolina
32 K7 Stemmen W Germany
26 C8 Stemshaug Norway
32 H8 Stemwede W Germany
22 J5 Stenay France
28 A3 Stenbjerg Denmark
33 P7 Stendal E Germany
52 B6 Stende U.S.S.R.
28 D5 Stenderup Denmark
28 D7 Stenderup W Germany
119 P7 Stenen Sask
28 E2 Stenhöj Denmark
138 D6 Stenhouse B S Australia
28 D3 Stenild Denmark
28 H5 Stenlille Denmark
28 J5 Stenløse Denmark
15 G2 Stenness Shetland Scotland
15 E1 Stenness,L.of Orkney Scotland
26 J6 Stensele Sweden
27 G14 Stensjön Sweden
27 G13 Stenstorp Sweden
28 E6 Stenstrup Denmark
26 L5 Stenträsk Sweden
27 E13 Stenungsund Sweden
28 F4 Stenvad Denmark
78 K1 Stepanavan U.S.S.R.
78 L2 Stepankert U.S.S.R.
55 C5 Stepanovka U.S.S.R.
33 O5 Stepenitz R E Germany
33 P6 Stepenitz R E Germany
37 O6 Stephansposching W Germany
98 K1 Stephen Minnesota
109 O2 Stephens Arkansas
94 J7 Stephens City Virginia
138 F4 Stephens Creek New S Wales
117 H8 Stephens I Br Col
99 T4 Stephenson Michigan
145 D1 Stephenson I New Zealand
117 G7 Stephens Pass Alaska
115 O8 Stephenville Nfld
109 J3 Stephenville Texas
123 O5 Stephenville Crossing Nfld
57 D5 Step' Karnabchul' U.S.S.R.
55 F5 Stepnogorsk U.S.S.R.
57 G3 Stepnoye U.S.S.R.
55 F4 Stepnyak U.S.S.R.
116 G9 Stepovak B Alaska
28 C6 Stepping Denmark
103 K2 Steptoe Nevada
36 H3 Sterbfritz W Germany
87 E12 Sterkstroom S Africa
108 F1 Sterley Texas
55 C4 Sterlibashevo U.S.S.R.
106 G1 Sterling Colorado
99 R8 Sterling Illinois
107 M3 Sterling Kansas
94 C2 Sterling Michigan
98 F3 Sterling N Dakota
98 K9 Sterling Nebraska
109 J1 Sterling Oklahoma
103 N2 Sterling Utah
108 G4 Sterling City Texas
55 C4 Sterlitamak U.S.S.R.
33 P5 Sternberg E Germany
31 K6 Šternberk Czechoslovakia
22 H2 Sterrebeek Belgium
52 E4 Steshevskaya U.S.S.R.
31 K3 Stęszew Poland
46 D1 Stet Yugoslavia
41 K1 Stetten W Germany
Stettin see Szczecin
33 U5 Stettiner Haff E Germany
118 E6 Stettler Alberta
99 U3 Steuben Michigan
99 Q6 Steuben Wisconsin
94 G6 Steubenville Ohio
33 Q9 Steutz E Germany
9 F4 Stevenage England
120 E3 Stevens Ontario
145 D4 Stevens, Mt New Zealand
119 U9 Stevenson Manitoba
100 D4 Stevenson Washington
138 C2 Stevenson R S Australia
119 W5 Stevenson L Manitoba
143 D10 Stevenson's L W Australia
99 R5 Stevens Pt Wisconsin
12 D2 Stevenston Scotland
116 N4 Stevens Village Alaska
94 A4 Stevensville Michigan
32 F9 Stever R W Germany
118 F8 Steveville Prov.Pk Alberta
28 K6 Stevns isld Denmark
22 J2 Stevoort Belgium
99 S8 Steward Illinois
110 H2 Stewardson Illinois
117 H8 Stewart Br Col
99 M5 Stewart Minnesota
102 E2 Stewart Nevada
117 D4 Stewart Yukon Terr
141 G2 Stewart R Queensland
140 C1 Stewart, C N Terr Aust
144 A7 Stewart I New Zealand
137 N3 Stewart Is Pacific Oc
143 C10 Stewart, Mt W Australia
15 D5 Stewarton Scotland
95 L7 Stewartstown Pennsylvania
110 B2 Stewartsville Missouri
127 K2 Stewart Town Jamaica
118 K8 Stewart Valley Sask
99 O6 Stewartville Minnesota
122 J8 Stewiacke Nova Scotia
32 K7 Steyerberg W Germany
9 F6 Steyning England
8 A4 Steynton Wales
38 K5 Steyr Austria
45 L4 Stia Italy
8 B6 Stibb Cross England
100 K5 Stibnite Idaho
9 G1 Stickford England
32 G6 Stickhausen W Germany
9 G1 Stickney England
98 H6 Stickney S Dakota
33 N9 Stiege E Germany
25 E2 Stiens Netherlands
45 L2 Stienta Italy
107 P6 Stigler Oklahoma
43 G8 Stigliano Italy
26 J9 Stigsjö Sweden
114 G6 Stikine R Alaska/Br Col
117 H6 Stikine Ranges Br Col
117 G7 Stikine Str Alaska
108 F4 Stiles Texas
110 K2 Stilesville Indiana
46 F6 Stilís Greece
28 D4 Stilling Denmark
13 G5 Stillington England
99 R7 Stillman Valley Illinois
99 O4 Stillwater Minnesota
102 F2 Stillwater Nevada
107 N5 Stillwater Oklahoma
101 L1 Stillwater R Montana
102 F2 Stillwater Ra Nevada
43 H10 Stilo, Pta Italy
110 B6 Stilwell Oklahoma
46 E7 Stimfalías, L Greece
101 M1 Stimson,Mt Montana
12 D3 Stinchar,R Scotland
98 E9 Stinking Water Cr Nebraska
46 E3 Štip Yugoslavia
47 G6 Stíra Greece
118 E9 Stirling Alberta
144 B7 Stirling New Zealand
140 C5 Stirling N Terr Aust
121 N8 Stirling Ontario
138 E5 Stirling S Australia
12 E1 Stirling Scotland
Stirling co see Strathclyde and Central regions
100 D10 Stirling City California
143 C9 Stirling, Mt W Australia
143 D8 Stirling, Mt W Australia
143 C10 Stirling Ra W Australia
44 H2 Stirone R Italy
98 J3 Stirum N Dakota
100 K3 Stites Idaho
119 V3 Stitt Manitoba
99 Q7 Stitzer Wisconsin
27 K14 Stjärnarve Sweden
26 N1 Stjernöya isld Norway
26 E8 Stjördalselv R Norway
26 E8 Stjördalshalsen Norway
13 E2 Stobo Scotland
41 K2 Stockach W Germany
27 G14 Stockaryd Sweden
9 E5 Stockbridge England
95 O4 Stockbridge Massachusetts
94 C4 Stockbridge Michigan
94 E8 Stockdale Ohio
109 K6 Stockdale Texas
33 N5 Stockelsdorf W Germany
48 C2 Stockerau Austria
36 B6 Stock,Etang du L France
101 O2 Stockett Montana
98 J9 Stockham Nebraska
37 L3 Stockheim W Germany
95 S6 Stockholm Maine
119 P8 Stockholm Sask
27 K12 Stockholm Sweden
27 J12 Stockholm county Sweden
40 G4 Stockhorn mt Switzerland
139 J5 Stockinbingal New S Wales
13 F6 Stockport England
94 F7 Stockport Ohio
111 J10 Stockton Alabama
102 C4 Stockton California
99 Q7 Stockton Illinois
107 L2 Stockton Kansas
119 S9 Stockton Manitoba
95 M8 Stockton Maryland
110 C4 Stockton Missouri
139 K5 Stockton New S Wales
144 C4 Stockton New Zealand
101 N9 Stockton Utah
99 Q3 Stockton I Wisconsin
116 O1 Stockton Is Alaska
13 G4 Stockton-on-Tees England
95 T2 Stockton Springs Maine
98 F9 Stockville Nebraska
31 N4 Stoczek Łukowski Poland
37 P4 Stod Czechoslovakia
26 E7 Stod Norway
99 P6 Stoddard Wisconsin
26 J9 Stöde Sweden
15 C2 Stoer,Pt of Scotland
28 C4 Stoholm Denmark
145 D4 Stoke New Zealand
9 G2 Stoke Ferry England
8 C7 Stoke Fleming England
9 F4 Stokenchurch England
8 D1 Stoke-on-Trent England
120 J7 Stokes Bay Ontario
112 H1 Stokesdale N Carolina
143 D10 Stokes Inlet W Australia
145 E4 Stokes, Mt New Zealand
139 G8 Stokes Pt Tasmania
140 B3 Stokes Ra N Terr Aust
53 C8 Stokhod R U.S.S.R.
28 G7 Stokkemarke Denmark
26 D7 Stokksund Norway
26 G3 Stokmarknes Norway
42 H5 Stolac Yugoslavia
33 N9 Stolberg E Germany
25 F7 Stolberg W Germany
147 Q8 Stolbovoy,Ostrov U.S.S.R.
48 F2 Stolica mt Czechoslovakia
37 O2 Stollberg E Germany
32 H5 Stollhamm W Germany
Stolp see Słupsk
90 A16 Stoltenhoff I Tristan da Cunha
32 K7 Stolzenau W Germany
36 D3 Stolzenfels W Germany
46 F5 Stómion Greece
36 B1 Stommeln W Germany
8 D2 Stone England
94 G5 Stoneboro Pennsylvania
9 E3 Stonebridge England
106 F3 Stone City Colorado
121 N6 Stonecliffe Ontario
100 F7 Stone Corral L Oregon
98 C9 Stoneham Colorado
122 A7 Stoneham Quebec
95 N7 Stone Harbor New Jersey
15 F4 Stonehaven Scotland
141 G6 Stonehenge Queensland
9 E5 Stonehenge anc mon England
8 D4 Stonehouse England
99 P4 Stone L Wisconsin
112 C4 Stone Mt Georgia
117 L6 Stone Mt. Prov. Park Br Col

76 B4 **Tarikere** India
145 E3 **Tariki** New Zealand
72 F5 **Tarim** S Yemen
Tarim Basin *see* **Tarim Pendi**
88 F6 **Tarime** Tanzania
66 D3 **Tarim He** *R* China
66 C3 **Tarim Pendi** *basin* China
69 C11 **Taring** Sumatra
Tari Nor *see* **Dalai Nur**
70 E1 **Taritipan** Sabah
89 D9 **Tarka** *R* S Africa
87 E12 **Tarkastad** S Africa
110 A1 **Tarkio** Missouri
101 L2 **Tarkio** Montana
50 G2 **Tarko-Sale** U.S.S.R.
85 D7 **Tarkwa** Ghana
133 C7 **Tar,L** Argentina
71 E3 **Tarlac** Philippines
15 F3 **Tarland** Scotland
13 F6 **Tarleton** England
28 B5 **Tarm** Denmark
128 C6 **Tarma** Peru
32 K6 **Tarmstedt** W Germany
18 G9 **Tarn** *dep* France
18 F9 **Tarn** *R* France
48 F3 **Tarna** *R* Hungary
26 H6 **Tärnaby** Sweden
77 K3 **Tarnak** *R* Afghanistan
18 F8 **Tarn-et-Garonne** *dep* France
18 H8 **Tarn,Gorges du** France
31 N5 **Tarnobrzeg** Poland
52 F4 **Tarnogskiy Gorodok** U.S.S.R.
119 M6 **Tarnopo** Sask
33 Q5 **Tarnow** E Germany
31 M5 **Tarnow** Poland
31 L5 **Tarnowskie Gory** Poland
44 H2 **Taro** *R* Italy
141 K7 **Tarong** Queensland
141 J7 **Taroom** Queensland
85 C2 **Taroudannt** Morocco
28 C7 **Tarp** W Germany
140 D4 **Tarpaulin Swamp** N Terr Aust
109 H6 **Tarpley** Texas
113 E9 **Tarpon Springs** Florida
113 L12 **Tarpum Bay** Eleuthera Bahamas
44 L5 **Tarquinia** Italy
80 D7 **Tarqumiya** Jordan
17 H3 **Tarragona** Spain
17 H3 **Tarragona** *prov* Spain
139 H8 **Tarraleah** Tasmania
139 H4 **Tarran Hills** New S Wales
111 K8 **Tarrant City** Alabama
8 D6 **Tarrant Hinton** England
140 E3 **Tarrant,Pt** Queensland
144 B6 **Tarras** New Zealand
17 J3 **Tarrasa** Spain
26 J4 **Tarrekaise** *mt* Sweden
41 N3 **Tarrenz** Austria
141 K8 **Tarrewinna** Queensland
106 E2 **Tarryall** Colorado
112 E5 **Tarrytown** Georgia
95 O5 **Tarrytown** New York
17 F9 **Tarsa,C** Algeria
45 P1 **Tarski Zaliv** *B* Yugoslavia
84 F5 **Tarso Taro** *mt* Chad
86 C1 **Tarso Tieroko** *mt* Chad
78 E3 **Tarsus** Turkey
133 E2 **Tartagal** Argentina
6 L4 **Tartan** *oil rig* North Sea
45 J1 **Tártaro** *R* Italy
18 E9 **Tartas** France
56 A3 **Tartas** *R* U.S.S.R.
52 C5 **Tartu** U.S.S.R.
79 F4 **Tartūs** Syria
80 C6 **Tarum** Israel
60 P3 **Tarumae yama** *mt* Japan
130 H6 **Tarumirim** Brazil
60 D14 **Tarumizu** Japan
54 J2 **Tarusa** U.S.S.R.
69 D9 **Tarutao,Ko** *isld* Thailand
48 M4 **Tarutino** U.S.S.R.
69 D11 **Tarutung** Sumatra
26 D8 **Tarva** *isld* Norway
38 J9 **Tarvisio** Italy
120 K5 **Tarzwell** Ontario
108 B6 **Tasajera, Sa** *mts* Mexico
57 G2 **Tasaral** U.S.S.R.
84 E4 **Tasāwah** Libya
57 D3 **Tas Buget** U.S.S.R.
121 M4 **Taschereau** Quebec
107 K2 **Tasco** Kansas
69 F11 **Tasek Dampar** Malaysia
117 M10 **Taseko, Mt** Br Col
56 D2 **Taseyeva** *R* U.S.S.R.
76 B2 **Tasgaon** India
58 A2 **Tashanta** U.S.S.R.
57 A4 **Tashauz** U.S.S.R.
75 O5 **Tashigang** Bhutan
57 E4 **Tashkent** U.S.S.R.
57 C6 **Tashkepri** U.S.S.R.
57 F4 **Tash-Kumyr** U.S.S.R.
55 B5 **Tashla** U.S.S.R.
120 C2 **Tashota** Ontario
56 C4 **Tashtagol** U.S.S.R.
56 C4 **Tashtyp** U.S.S.R.
70 M9 **Tasikmalaja** Java
80 G2 **Tasil** Syria
28 F7 **Tåsinge** *isld* Denmark
115 O3 **Tasiussaq** Greenland
26 H7 **Tåsjö** Sweden
26 H7 **Tåsjön** *L* Sweden
85 G5 **Tasker** Niger
56 E5 **Taskyl,Khrebet** *mts* U.S.S.R.
145 D4 **Tasman Bay** New Zealand
139 H9 **Tasman Hd** Tasmania
139 H8 **Tasmania** *state* Australia
145 D4 **Tasman Mountains** New Zealand
144 C5 **Tasman, Mt** New Zealand
139 J9 **Tasman Pen** Tasmania
134 G13 **Tasman Plateau** Pac Oc
137 M9 **Tasman Sea** Pacific Oc
48 H3 **Tăşnad** Romania
85 F5 **Tassara** Niger
19 J5 **Tasselot, Mt** France
115 M6 **Tassialouc,L** Quebec
85 E5 **Tassili du Hoggar** *plat* Algeria
85 F3 **Tassili-n'-Ajjer** *plat* Algeria
28 J5 **Tåstrup** Denmark
51 M2 **Tas Tumus** U.S.S.R.
57 E3 **Tasty** U.S.S.R.
85 C3 **Tata** Morocco
48 E3 **Tatabanya** Hungary
71 E7 **Tatalan** *isld* Philippines
71 B2 **Tatam** Halmahera Indonesia
122 J8 **Tatamagouche** Nova Scotia
85 G2 **Tataouine** Tunisia
145 E3 **Tatara** *mt* New Zealand
48 M5 **Tatarbunary** U.S.S.R.
47 H3 **Tatarlar** Turkey
55 G3 **Tatarsk** U.S.S.R.
59 M1 **Tatarskiy Proliv** *str* U.S.S.R.
70 C3 **Tatau** Sarawak
112 C3 **Tate** Georgia
119 N7 **Tate** Sask
89 E3 **Tate** *R* Botswana
141 G3 **Tate** *R* Queensland
61 O6 **Tateai** Japan
140 C2 **Tate Bluff** *hill* N Terr Aust
60 O4 **Tateura** Japan
61 N11 **Tateyama** Japan
61 L9 **Tate yama** *mt* Japan
117 P5 **Tathlina L** N W Terr
139 K6 **Tathra** New S Wales
116 O6 **Tatitlek** Alaska
117 L10 **Tatla Lake** Br Col
117 K7 **Tatlatui Prov. Park** Br Columbia
116 K5 **Tatlawiksuk** *R* Alaska
117 L10 **Tatlayoko Lake** Br Col
117 M10 **Tatlow, Mt** Br Col
101 R5 **Tatman Mt** Wyoming
116 K6 **Tatna L** Alaska
115 K6 **Tatnam,C** Manitoba
139 H6 **Tatong** Victoria
66 D4 **Tatrang** China
31 M6 **Tatry** *mts* Czech/Poland
117 E6 **Tatshenshini** *R* Br Col
61 K8 **Tatsuruhama** Japan
77 K7 **Tatta** Pakistan
9 F1 **Tattershall** England
57 G3 **Tatty** U.S.S.R.
130 F8 **Tatuí** Brazil
131 B2 **Tatul,Sa de** *mts* Chile
108 D2 **Tatum** New Mexico
109 N3 **Tatum** Texas
107 N7 **Tatums** Oklahoma
Tatung *see* **Datong**
139 H6 **Tatura** Victoria
129 K5 **Tauá** Brazil
128 F4 **Tauapeçaçu** Brazil
37 L2 **Taubach** E Germany
130 F8 **Taubaté** Brazil
36 H5 **Tauber** *R* W Germany
33 R10 **Taucha** E Germany
38 H7 **Tauerin Tunnel** Austria
37 N7 **Taufkirchen** W Germany
36 G2 **Taufstein** *mt* W Germany
128 G3 **Tauini** *R* Brazil
145 E2 **Taukoa** New Zealand
19 N16 **Taulignan** France
28 D5 **Taulov** Denmark
145 E3 **Taumarunui** New Zealand
128 D5 **Taumaturgo** Brazil
110 F4 **Taum Sauk Mt** Missouri
130 C7 **Taunay** Brazil
89 D6 **Taung** S Africa
68 C5 **Taungbon** Burma
68 B2 **Taungdwingyi** Burma
68 C2 **Taung-Gyi** Burma
68 D3 **Taunggyi** *mt* Burma/Thailand
68 C2 **Taunglau** Burma
68 C4 **Taungnyo A** *ra* Burma
68 B2 **Taungtha** Burma
68 B3 **Taungup** Burma
74 D3 **Taunsa** Pakistan
8 C5 **Taunton** England
95 Q5 **Taunton** Massachusetts
95 R5 **Taunton,E** Massachusetts
36 E3 **Taunus** *mts* W Germany
145 E2 **Taupiri** New Zealand
145 F3 **Taupo** New Zealand
52 B6 **Taurage** U.S.S.R.
145 E3 **Taurakawa** *mt* New Zealand
145 F2 **Tauranga** New Zealand
121 R6 **Taureau, L** Quebec
21 H10 **Taurion** *R* France
145 D1 **Tauroa Pt** New Zealand
55 F2 **Taurovy** U.S.S.R.
Taurus Mts *see* **Toros Dağlari**
17 G3 **Tauste** Spain
144 B7 **Tautuku Peninsula** New Zealand
137 M2 **Tauu Is** Solomon Is
115 K5 **Tavani** N W Terr
40 F3 **Tavannes** Switzerland
113 F9 **Tavares** Florida
45 K4 **Tavarnelles Val di Pesa** Italy
47 K7 **Tavas** Turkey
26 L3 **Tavätno** *R* Sweden
22 F4 **Tavaux** France
55 E2 **Tavda** U.S.S.R.
50 F3 **Tavda** *R* U.S.S.R.
26 L7 **Tavelsjö** Sweden
41 J5 **Taverne** Switzerland
45 K1 **Tavernelle** Italy
115 M4 **Taverner B** N W Terr
19 Q17 **Tavernes** France
113 G12 **Tavernier** Florida
20 K3 **Taverny** France
88 F3 **Taveta** Kenya
137 R5 **Taveuni** *isld* Fiji
16 B7 **Tavira** Portugal
8 B6 **Tavistock** England
43 C8 **Tavolara** *isld* Sardinia
55 G4 **Tavolzhan** U.S.S.R.
16 B4 **Távora** *R* Portugal
68 D5 **Tavoy** Burma
68 D6 **Tavoy Pt** Burma
65 H3 **Tavrichanka** U.S.S.R.
55 F4 **Tavricheskoye** U.S.S.R.
47 K4 **Tavşancıl** Turkey
47 K5 **Tavşanlı** Turkey
145 G4 **Tawa** New Zealand
109 M3 **Tawakoni, L** Texas
69 C10 **Tawar,Danau** *L* Sumatra
94 D2 **Tawas City** Michigan
118 D4 **Tawatinaw** Alberta
70 E2 **Tawau** Sabah
86 E3 **Taweisha** Sudan
8 C4 **Tawe,R** Wales
145 E1 **Tawhiti Rahi I** New Zealand
70 F2 **Tawitawi** Philippines
8 B5 **Taw,R** England
67 G5 **Ta-wu** Taiwan
38 G7 **Taxenbach** Austria
27 J12 **Taxinge** Sweden
66 B4 **Taxkorgan** China
128 C5 **Tayabamba** Peru
71 E4 **Tayabas B** Philippines
69 K13 **Tayan** Indonesia
52 D1 **Taybola** U.S.S.R.
13 E1 **Tay,Firth of** Scotland
56 C3 **Tayga** U.S.S.R.
12 C2 **Tayinloan** Scotland
143 D10 **Tay,L** W Australia
103 O7 **Taylor** Arizona
109 O2 **Taylor** Arkansas
117 N7 **Taylor** Br Col
111 G7 **Taylor** Mississippi
110 E2 **Taylor** Missouri
98 G8 **Taylor** Nebraska
109 K5 **Taylor** Texas
100 D2 **Taylor** Washington
99 P5 **Taylor** Wisconsin
140 C5 **Taylor** *R* N Terr Aust
106 C6 **Taylor, Mt** New Mexico
144 C5 **Taylor, Mt** New Zealand
116 J6 **Taylor Mts** Alaska
106 D3 **Taylor Park Res** Colorado
112 B3 **Taylor Ridge** Georgia
112 E3 **Taylors** S Carolina
142 B3 **Taylors Crossing** W Australia
106 F5 **Taylor Springs** New Mexico
94 B8 **Taylorsville** Kentucky
111 G10 **Taylorsville** Mississippi
112 F2 **Taylorsville** N Carolina
94 F7 **Taylorsville** Ohio
110 G2 **Taylorville** Illinois
122 F7 **Taymouth** New Brunswick
51 K2 **Taymura** *R* U.S.S.R.
51 K1 **Taymyr,Ozero** *L* U.S.S.R.
51 J1 **Taymyr,Poluostrov** *pen* U.S.S.R.
55 E4 **Tayncha** U.S.S.R.
68 H7 **Tay Ninh** Vietnam
12 C1 **Taynuilt** Scotland
71 G6 **Tayoloan** *R* Mindanao Philippines
13 F1 **Tayport** Scotland
15 E4 **Tay,R** Scotland
56 E3 **Tayshet** U.S.S.R.
58 C2 **Tayshir** Mongolia
15 E4 **Tayside** *reg* Scotland
71 E3 **Taytay** Luzon Philippines
71 D5 **Taytay** Palawan Philippines
71 G5 **Taytay Pt** Philippines
77 G2 **Tayyebāt** Iran
79 E10 **Ţayyib al Ism** Saudi Arabia
50 H2 **Taz** *R* U.S.S.R.
85 D2 **Taza** Morocco
85 F5 **Tazalc** Niger
61 O6 **Tazawa ko** *L* Japan
84 G4 **Tazerbo Oasis** Libya
112 D1 **Tazewell** Tennessee
94 F9 **Tazewell** Virginia
48 K4 **Taziăul** *R* Romania
65 F1 **Tazicheng** China
116 K7 **Tazimina Lakes** Alaska
116 O6 **Tazlina L** Alaska
50 G2 **Tazovskaya Guba** *gulf* U.S.S.R.
50 G2 **Tazovskoye** U.S.S.R.
66 F6 **Tazungdam** Burma
78 K1 **Tbilisi** U.S.S.R.
85 E7 **Tchaourou** Benin
86 B6 **Tchibanga** Gabon
84 E5 **Tchigaï, Plat. du** Chad/Niger
68 J2 **Tching Lan Xan** *isld* Vietnam
85 F5 **Tchin-Tabaradene** Niger
86 B4 **Tcholliré** Cameroon
111 F8 **Tchula** Mississippi
31 L1 **Tczew** Poland
98 K6 **Tea** S Dakota
128 E4 **Tea** *R* Brazil
48 J4 **Teaca** Romania
124 G6 **Teacapán** Mexico
108 D3 **Teague** New Mexico
109 L4 **Teague** Texas
143 D7 **Teague,L** W Australia
13 G4 **Team Valley** England
144 A6 **Te Anau** New Zealand
145 E3 **Te Anga** New Zealand
45 Q7 **Teano** Italy
143 C6 **Teano Ra** W Australia
101 T6 **Teapot Dome** *hill* Wyoming
145 G2 **Te Araroa** New Zealand
145 E2 **Te Aroha** New Zealand
140 C5 **Tea Tree** N Terr Aust
145 E4 **Te Awaiti** New Zealand
145 E3 **Te Awamutu** New Zealand
16 D8 **Teba** Spain
70 K8 **Tebak, G** *mt* Sumatra
85 F1 **Tebessa** Algeria
130 B10 **Tebicuary** Paraguay
69 D11 **Tebingtinggi** Sumatra
69 F12 **Tebingtinggi** *isld* Sumatra
69 E13 **Tebo** *R* Sumatra
43 C12 **Tebourba** Tunisia
43 C12 **Teboursouk** Tunisia
69 F12 **Tebrau** Malaysia
18 G10 **Tech** *R* France
55 D3 **Techa** *R* U.S.S.R.
85 D7 **Techiman** Ghana
47 J1 **Techirghiol** Romania
144 D5 **Technical, Mt** New Zealand
33 Q6 **Techow** E Germany
36 G6 **Teck** W Germany
133 C6 **Tecka** Argentina
32 G8 **Tecklenburg** W Germany
27 F16 **Teckomatorp** Sweden
106 E7 **Tecolote** New Mexico
124 G7 **Tecolotlán** Mexico
101 L8 **Tecoma** Nevada
124 H8 **Tecomán** Mexico
103 H6 **Tecopa** California
124 F4 **Tecorichic** Mexico
124 E3 **Tecoripa** Mexico
125 J9 **Tecpan** Mexico
124 G6 **Tecuala** Mexico
48 L5 **Tecuci** Romania
94 D4 **Tecumseh** Michigan
110 D5 **Tecumseh** Missouri
98 K9 **Tecumseh** Nebraska
107 O6 **Tecumseh** Oklahoma
120 H10 **Tecumseh** Ontario
8 C6 **Tedburn St Mary** England
70 P16 **Tedjakula** Indonesia
57 B5 **Tedzhen** U.S.S.R.
77 G1 **Tedzhen** U.S.S.R.
118 D6 **Tees** Alberta
13 G5 **Tees,R** England
120 J9 **Teeswater** Ontario
71 D6 **Teeth,The** *mt* Palawan Philippines
128 F4 **Tefe** Brazil
47 K7 **Tefenni** Turkey
26 L8 **Teg** Sweden
70 M9 **Tegal** Java
33 S7 **Tegel** E Germany
25 F6 **Tegelen** Netherlands
41 P2 **Tegernsee** *L* W Germany
85 F6 **Tegina** Nigeria
70 K8 **Tegineneng** Sumatra
139 H3 **Tego** Queensland
86 H3 **Tegre** *prov* Ethiopia
125 L2 **Tegucigalpa** Honduras
85 F5 **Teguiddan Tessoum** Niger
89 E3 **Tegwani** *R* Zimbabwe
102 F6 **Tehachapi** California
102 F7 **Tehachapi Mts** California
102 B1 **Tehama** California
145 E2 **Te Hana** New Zealand
145 D1 **Te Hapua** New Zealand
145 F3 **Te Haroto** New Zealand
145 F3 **Te Hauke** New Zealand
115 K4 **Tehek L** N W Terr
69 C12 **Tehemberau** Indonesia
77 B2 **Tehrān** Iran
125 L8 **Tehuacán** Mexico
125 M9 **Tehuantepec** Mexico
37 L2 **Teichel** E Germany
8 C3 **Teifi** *R* Wales
8 C6 **Teignmouth** England
8 C6 **Teign,R** England
21 B6 **Teillay** France
21 C7 **Teille** France
61 Q12 **Teima** Okinawa
Teinach *see* **Bad Teinach-Zavelstein**
36 F6 **Teinach** W Germany
145 F3 **Te Iringa Ahimanawa Range** New Zealand
37 N6 **Teisbach** W Germany
29 K10 **Teisko** Finland
88 G3 **Teita Hills** Kenya
12 D1 **Teith,R** Scotland
48 H4 **Teius** Romania
130 H9 **Teixeira** Brazil
87 C8 **Teixeira da Silva** Angola
Teixeira de Sousa *see* **Luan**
130 G7 **Teixeiras** Brazil
130 E9 **Teixeira Soares** Brazil
16 E8 **Tejeda,Sa** *mts* Spain
16 B5 **Tejo** *R* Portugal
124 F3 **Tejolocachic** Mexico
102 F7 **Tejon Pk** California
130 E6 **Tejuco,R** Brazil
125 J8 **Tejupilco** Mexico
145 F2 **Te Kaha** New Zealand
98 K8 **Tekamah** Nebraska
145 F3 **Te Karaka** New Zealand
145 E2 **Te Kauwhata** New Zealand
145 E3 **Te Kawa** New Zealand
57 J3 **Tekeli** U.S.S.R.
55 F4 **Teke, Oz** *L* U.S.S.R.
57 K3 **Tekes** China
66 C3 **Tekes** *R* U.S.S.R.
57 K3 **Tekes He** *R* China
144 C5 **Te Kinga** New Zealand
47 J4 **Tekirdağ** Turkey
47 J4 **Tekir Dağları** *mts* Turkey
145 D3 **Te Kiri** New Zealand
68 A2 **Teknaf** Burma
100 H2 **Tekoa** Washington
144 D5 **Tekoa, Mt** New Zealand
94 C4 **Tekonsha** Michigan
145 D2 **Te Kopuru** New Zealand
86 D2 **Tekro** Chad
71 H5 **Teku** Sulawesi
145 E3 **Te Kuiti** New Zealand
125 Q10 **Tela** Honduras
80 E3 **Tel 'Adashim** Israel
69 H11 **Telaga** *isld* Indonesia
17 G10 **Télagh** Algeria
80 B7 **Telamim** Israel
69 G12 **Telan** *isld* Indonesia
69 F13 **Telanaipura** Sumatra
116 L6 **Telaquana,L** Alaska
80 B6 **Tel Ashdod** Israel
80 B7 **Tel Ashqelon** Israel
53 G12 **Telavi** U.S.S.R.
80 C5 **Tel Aviv** Israel
80 C7 **Tel Azeqa** Israel
56 C4 **Tel'bes** U.S.S.R.
80 F3 **Tel Bet She'an** Israel
80 C7 **Tel Bet Shemesh** Israel
80 F3 **Tel Bet Yerah** Israel
31 J6 **Telč** Czechoslovakia
48 J3 **Telciu** Romania
80 C8 **Tel Devir** Israel
70 C6 **Telegapulang** Kalimantan
117 H7 **Telegraph Creek** Br Col
80 F6 **Teleilet el Ghassul** Jordan
27 C12 **Telemark** *prov* Norway
70 E4 **Telen** *R* Kalimantan
48 L3 **Teleneshty** U.S.S.R.
48 J6 **Teleormanul** *R* Romania
109 L2 **Telephone** Texas
102 G5 **Telescope Pk** California
127 P5 **Telescope Pt** Grenada
129 G5 **Teles Pires** *R* Brazil
56 C5 **Teletskoye, Oz** *L* U.S.S.R.
80 C8 **Tel Eyton** Israel
80 D4 **Tel Gat** Israel
32 G9 **Telgte** W Germany
85 B6 **Telimele** Guinea
80 F2 **Tel Kinnerot** Israel
78 J3 **Tel Kotchek** Syria
117 K8 **Telkwa** Br Col
108 G1 **Tell** Texas
80 C7 **Tel Lakhish** Israel
22 K5 **Tellancourt Villers** France
79 G4 **Tell Bisa** Syria
110 K4 **Tell City** Indiana
80 F5 **Tell Deir'Alla** Jordan
26 L5 **Tellejokk** Sweden
116 D4 **Teller** Alaska
76 B5 **Tellicherry** India
112 C2 **Tellico Plains** Tennessee
122 F3 **Tellier** Quebec
22 J3 **Tellin** Belgium
32 K4 **Tellingstedt** W Germany
80 C5 **Tel Litwinsky** Israel
80 F6 **Tell Nimrin** Jordan
106 C4 **Telluride** Colorado
57 B4 **Tel'mansk** U.S.S.R.
80 C7 **Tel Maresha** Israel
58 C2 **Telmen Nuur** *L* Mongolia
80 B8 **Tel Mifsah** Israel
80 C4 **Tel Mond** Israel
100 H4 **Telocaset** Oregon
69 E10 **Telok Anson** Malaysia
125 K8 **Teloloapán** Mexico
52 J3 **Tel'pos-Iz, Gora** *mt* U.S.S.R.
80 F1 **Tel Qedesh** Israel
133 D6 **Telsen** Argentina
80 C2 **Tel Shiqmona** Israel
80 C8 **Tel Shoqet** Israel
52 B6 **Telšiai** U.S.S.R.
120 E3 **Teltaka** Ontario
33 S8 **Teltow** E Germany
70 E3 **Telukbajur** Kalimantan
69 E13 **Telukbayur** Sumatra
70 K8 **Telukbetung** Sumatra
69 J10 **Telukbutun** Indonesia
69 C12 **Telukdalam** Indonesia
69 F12 **Teluklanjut** Sumatra
85 F5 **Telwes** Niger
80 C8 **Tel Ziqlag** Israel
85 E7 **Tema** Ghana
69 J12 **Temaju** *isld* Indonesia
94 K9 **Teman** Virginia
70 B4 **Temangga** Kalimantan
70 N9 **Temanggung** Java
85 F4 **Temasint** Algeria
69 E14 **Tembesi** *R* Sumatra
69 F13 **Tembilahan** Sumatra
102 D6 **Temblor Rge** California
87 C7 **Tembo Aluma** Angola
89 E8 **Tembuland** *dist* S Africa
102 G8 **Temecula** California
56 E5 **Temenchulu,Gora** *mt* U.S.S.R.
8 D3 **Teme,R** England
48 F5 **Temerin** Yugoslavia
69 F11 **Temerloh** Malaysia
69 G12 **Temiang** *isld* Indonesia
71 C3 **Teminabuan** W Irian
57 A1 **Temir** U.S.S.R.
56 C4 **Temirtau** U.S.S.R.
122 A2 **Temiscamie L** Quebec
122 A2 **Temiscamie R** Quebec
115 M8 **Témiscaming** Quebec
122 D6 **Temiscouata L** Quebec
121 L6 **Témiskaming** Quebec
139 G8 **Temma** Tasmania
56 F5 **Temnik** *R* U.S.S.R.
139 J5 **Temora** New S Wales
124 F3 **Temósachic** Mexico
103 N8 **Tempe** Arizona
70 F7 **Tempe, L** *isld* Sulawesi
33 S8 **Tempelhof** E Germany
94 D5 **Temperance** Michigan
69 F13 **Temping** Sumatra
43 C8 **Tempio Paus** Sardinia
95 R2 **Temple** Maine
94 C2 **Temple** Michigan
109 J1 **Temple** Oklahoma
95 M6 **Temple** Pennsylvania
109 K4 **Temple** Texas
141 G1 **Temple B** Queensland
8 B3 **Temple Bar** Wales
140 B6 **Temple Downs** N Terr Aust
9 H5 **Temple Ewell** England
14 D4 **Templemore** Irish Rep
13 F4 **Temple Sowerby** England
102 D6 **Templeton** California
94 H6 **Templeton** Pennsylvania
8 B4 **Templeton** Wales
140 E5 **Templeton** *R* Queensland
22 E2 **Templeuve** Belgium
33 T6 **Templin** E Germany
87 C8 **Tempué** Angola
33 P5 **Tempzin** E Germany
55 E2 **Temryak, Oz** *L* U.S.S.R.
22 G1 **Temse** Belgium
131 A7 **Temuco** Chile
144 C6 **Temuka** New Zealand
98 F3 **Temvik** N Dakota
55 C4 **Temyasovo** U.S.S.R.
128 C4 **Tena** Ecuador
102 H1 **Tenabo** Nevada
124 G8 **Tenacatita** Mexico
109 N4 **Tenaha** Texas
117 F7 **Tenakee Springs** Alaska
29 K11 **Tenala** Finland
76 E2 **Tenali** India
124 G7 **Tenamaxtlán** Mexico
145 D4 **Te Namu** New Zealand
68 D6 **Tenasserim** Burma
73 Q6 **Tenasserim** *R* Burma
68 C6 **Tenasserim I** Burma
19 P13 **Tenay** France
8 D3 **Tenbury Wells** England
8 B4 **Tenby** Wales
120 G6 **Tenby Bay** Ontario
18 H7 **Tence** France
73 P7 **Ten Degree Ch** Andaman/Nicobar Is
86 F3 **Tendelti** Sudan
61 O7 **Tendō** Japan
101 M5 **Tendoy** Idaho
85 D2 **Tendrara** Morocco
40 D4 **Tendre, Mt** Switzerland
9 H4 **Tendring** England
85 G4 **Ténéré du Tafassasset** *reg* Niger
85 A3 **Tenerife** *isld* Canary Is
85 E1 **Ténès** Algeria
47 H2 **Tenevo** Bulgaria
70 N9 **Tengah, Jawa** *prov* Java
Tengchow *see* **Penglai**
70 E5 **Tenggarong** Kalimantan
70 O9 **Tengger** Java
69 F10 **Tenggol** *isld* Malaysia
70 E1 **Tenghilan** Sabah
55 E5 **Tengiz, Oz** *L* U.S.S.R.
71 E7 **Tengolan** *isld* Philippines
67 C7 **Tengqiao** China
65 D7 **Teng Xian** China
67 C5 **Teng Xian** China
141 G7 **Tenham** Queensland
27 G14 **Tenhult** Sweden
44 B3 **Tenibres** *mt* Italy/France
85 B3 **Teniegrad** Morocco
100 C3 **Tenino** Washington
55 F3 **Tenis, Oz** *L* U.S.S.R.
55 D4 **Teniz, Oz** *L* U.S.S.R.
76 C6 **Tenkasi** India
52 G6 **Ten'ki** U.S.S.R.
110 B6 **Tenkiller Ferry Res** Oklahoma
85 D6 **Tenkodogo** Upper Volta
69 A9 **Tenlaa** Nicobar Is
123 Q2 **Ten Mile L** Nfld
42 F5 **Tenna** *R* Italy
100 D8 **Tennant** California
140 C4 **Tennant Creek** N Terr Aust
38 H6 **Tennen-Geb** *mts* Austria
110 H6 **Tennessee** *state* U.S.A.
106 D2 **Tennessee Pass** Colorado
110 J6 **Tennessee R** Tennessee
26 F4 **Tennholmen** Norway
112 E5 **Tennille** Georgia
29 O4 **Tenniöjoki** *R* Finland
144 D5 **Tennyson, L** New Zealand
131 B5 **Teno** *R* Chile
29 M2 **Tenojoki** *R* Finland
70 D2 **Tenom** Sabah
125 O9 **Tenosique** Mexico
61 J11 **Tenri** Japan
61 L11 **Tenryū** Japan
111 E9 **Tensas** *R* Louisiana
111 J11 **Tensaw** *R* Alabama
100 J2 **Tensed** Idaho
85 C2 **Tensift** *R* Morocco
99 M2 **Tenstrike** Minnesota
70 G5 **Tentena** Sulawesi
9 G5 **Tenterden** England
143 B10 **Tenterden** W Australia
139 K3 **Tenterfield** New S Wales
113 F12 **Ten Thousand Is** Florida
70 G4 **Tentolomatinan** *mt* Sulawesi
124 H7 **Teocalitche** Mexico
45 M3 **Teodorano** Italy
130 H5 **Teófilo Otôni** Brazil
43 K1 **Teofipol** U.S.S.R.
71 E7 **Teomabal** *isld* Philippines
125 L8 **Teotitlan** Mexico
71 O8 **Tepa** Indonesia
124 E3 **Tepache** Mexico
124 H7 **Tepatitlán de Morelos** Mexico
46 E2 **Tepe** *mt* Yugoslavia
125 K8 **Tepeji** Mexico
57 B3 **Tepekul'** U.S.S.R.
46 D4 **Tepelenë** Albania
37 O4 **Tepelská Plošina** *mts* Czechoslovakia
124 G7 **Tepic** Mexico
37 O4 **Teplá** Czechoslovakia
30 H5 **Teplice** Czechoslovakia
37 O3 **Teplička** Czechoslovakia
48 M2 **Teplik** U.S.S.R.
52 H4 **Teplogorka** U.S.S.R.
54 K8 **Teplogorsk** U.S.S.R.
124 C2 **Tepoca, C** Mexico
145 F3 **Te Pohue** New Zealand
145 G3 **Te Puia** New Zealand
145 F2 **Te Puke** New Zealand
80 D7 **Teqoa** Jordan
124 H7 **Tequila** Mexico
17 J3 **Ter** *R* Spain
85 E6 **Téra** Niger
16 B6 **Tera** *R* Portugal
16 C3 **Tera** *R* Spain
25 C4 **Ter Aar** Netherlands
61 M8 **Teradomari** Japan
61 P7 **Teraike** Japan
42 F6 **Teramo** Italy
139 G7 **Terang** Victoria
25 H3 **Ter Ape** Netherlands
77 L5 **Teratani** *R* Pakistan
70 P10 **Terawangan** Indonesia
71 O8 **Terbang Selatan** Indonesia
71 O8 **Terbang Utara** *isld* Indonesia
25 F5 **Terborg** Netherlands
78 H2 **Tercan** Turkey
133 E4 **Tercero** *R* Argentina
106 E4 **Tercio** Colorado
48 K1 **Terebovlya** U.S.S.R.
48 G5 **Teregova** Romania
53 G11 **Terek** *R* U.S.S.R.
56 E5 **Tere-Khol',Oz** *L* U.S.S.R.
54 C4 **Terekhovka** U.S.S.R.
56 C5 **Terektinskiy Khrebet** *mts* U.S.S.R.
69 H11 **Terempa** Indonesia
122 J9 **Terence B** Nova Scotia
69 F10 **Terengganu** *R* Malaysia
69 F10 **Terengganu** *state* Malaysia
130 C7 **Terenos** Brazil
55 C5 **Terensay** U.S.S.R.
70 E5 **Terentang,P** Kalimantan
57 C2 **Teren Uzyak** U.S.S.R.
130 D9 **Teresa Cristina** Brazil
53 G8 **Tereshka** *R* Penza U.S.S.R.
48 H2 **Tereshva** *R* Ukraine U.S.S.R.
129 K5 **Teresina** Brazil
129 H3 **Teresinha** Brazil
128 E3 **Teresita** Colombia
130 G8 **Teresópolis** Brazil
31 O3 **Terespol** Poland
69 A8 **Teressa I** Nicobar Is
139 J3 **Terewah I** New S Wales
16 B7 **Terge** *R* Portugal
22 E4 **Tergnier** France
85 C4 **Terhazza** Mali
52 E1 **Teriberka** U.S.S.R.
69 C10 **Teripa** *R* Sumatra
47 K3 **Terkos Gölü** *L* Turkey
108 D6 **Terlingua** Texas
78 F1 **Terme** Turkey
77 K1 **Termez** U.S.S.R.
40 E7 **Termignon** France
143 D10 **Termination I** W Australia
20 J5 **Terminiers** France
43 F11 **Termini Imerese** Sicily
42 E6 **Terminillo** *mt* Italy
45 R8 **Terminio, M** *mt* Italy
125 O8 **Términos,L.de** Mexico
100 E9 **Termo** California
42 F7 **Termoli** Italy
Termonde *see* **Dendermonde**
71 A2 **Ternate** Halmahera Indonesia
83 J12 **Ternay,C** Mahé I Indian Oc
83 K12 **Ternay Pass** Mahé I Indian Oc
38 K6 **Ternberg** Austria
28 E3 **Terndrup** Denmark
25 A6 **Terneuzen** Netherlands
59 L2 **Terney** U.S.S.R.
102 T13 **Tern I** Hawaiian Is
42 E6 **Terni** Italy
48 K1 **Ternopol** U.S.S.R.
54 D9 **Ternovka** U.S.S.R.
145 E3 **Te Roti** New Zealand
16 D10 **Teroual** Morocco
138 E5 **Terowie** S Australia
59 M2 **Terpeniya,Mys** *C* U.S.S.R.
55 E3 **Terpugovo** U.S.S.R.
94 H7 **Terra Alta** W Virginia
102 E6 **Terra Bella** California
117 J8 **Terrace** Br Col
120 C4 **Terrace Bay** Ontario
143 D8 **Terraces, The** *hills* W Australia
45 O7 **Terracina** Italy
87 D11 **Terra Firma** S Africa
109 K2 **Terral** Oklahoma
43 B9 **Terralba** Sardinia
123 S5 **Terra Nova** Nfld
146 J6 **Terra Nova B** Antarctica
45 L4 **Terranuova Bracc** Italy
18 F7 **Terrasson** France
124 F3 **Terrazas** Mexico
146 H3 **Terre Adélie** Antarctica
100 D5 **Terrebonne** Oregon
111 F12 **Terrebonne B** Louisiana
127 N5 **Terre de Bas** *isld* Guadeloupe W Indies
127 N5 **Terre de Haut** *isld* Guadeloupe W I
110 J2 **Terre Haute** Indiana
109 L3 **Terrell** Texas
123 S6 **Terrenceville** Nfld
101 N6 **Terreton** Idaho
20 C3 **Terrette** *R* France
40 F3 **Terri, Mt** Switzerland
111 F9 **Terry** Mississippi
101 U3 **Terry** Montana
55 E6 **Tersakkan** *R* U.S.S.R.
25 D2 **Terschelling** *isld* Netherlands
25 D2 **Terschellinger Wad** Netherlands
86 C3 **Tersef** Chad
57 H4 **Terskey Alatau, Khrebet** *mts* U.S.S.R.
52 E2 **Terskiy Bereg** *coast* U.S.S.R.
43 C9 **Tertenia** Sardinia
17 G4 **Teruel** *prov* Spain
47 J1 **Tervel** Bulgaria
29 M9 **Tervo** Finland
29 L5 **Tervola** Finland
22 H2 **Tervuren** Belgium
42 H4 **Tešanj** Yugoslavia
107 N2 **Tescott** Kansas
52 F6 **Tesha** *R* U.S.S.R.
116 L1 **Teshekpuk L** Alaska
60 S2 **Teshikaga** Japan
60 H11 **Te-shima** *isld* Japan
60 Q1 **Teshio** *R* Japan
60 Q2 **Teshio dake** *mt* Japan
60 P1 **Teshio-sanchi** *mts* Japan
46 E1 **Tešica** Yugoslavia
117 F5 **Teslin** *R* Yukon Terr
117 G5 **Teslin L** Br Col/Yukon Terr
130 E4 **Tesouras, R** Brazil
130 D5 **Tesouro** Brazil
52 D5 **Tesovo Netyl'skiy** U.S.S.R.
17 G9 **Tessala, Mt.du** Algeria
85 E4 **Tessalit** Mali
85 F6 **Tessaoua** Niger
86 G2 **Tessenei** Ethiopia
118 K7 **Tessier** Sask
33 Q4 **Tessin** E Germany
20 C4 **Tessy** France
43 C7 **Testa, C** Sardinia
42 G7 **Testa del Gargano** Italy
18 E8 **Teste-de-Buch, la** France
32 L6 **Testedt** W Germany
43 C12 **Testour** Tunisia
9 E5 **Test, R** England
106 E6 **Tesuque** New Mexico
48 D3 **Tét** Hungary
18 G10 **Tet** *R* France
117 L9 **Tetachuck L** Br Col
122 F6 **Tetagouche R** New Brunswick
125 J9 **Tetala** Mexico
17 F4 **Tetas de Viana** *mt* Spain
133 C2 **Tetas, Pta** Chile
8 D4 **Tetbury** England
88 D10 **Tete** Mozambique
123 N3 **Tete à la Baleine** Quebec
117 O9 **Tete Jaune Cache** Br Col
145 F3 **Te Teko** New Zealand
36 B5 **Téterchen** France
56 F1 **Tetere** *R* U.S.S.R.
33 R5 **Teterow** E Germany
47 G2 **Teteven** Bulgaria
48 M1 **Tetiyev** U.S.S.R.
116 Q5 **Tetlin** Alaska
101 O2 **Teton** *R* Montana
101 O6 **Tetonia** Idaho
101 P6 **Teton Ra** Wyoming
16 D9 **Tetouan** Morocco
46 E7 **Tetráyi** *mt* Greece
37 L3 **Tettau** W Germany
32 G5 **Tettens** W Germany
Tetyukhe *see* **Dal'negorsk**
Tetyukhe Pristan' *see* **Rudnaya Pristan'**
52 G7 **Tetyushi** U.S.S.R.
37 N1 **Teuchern** E Germany
133 E3 **Teuco** *R* Argentina
38 N7 **Teufelstein** *mt* Austria
128 E5 **Teuini** Brazil
43 B10 **Teulada** Sardinia
124 H7 **Teul de G. Ortega** Mexico
119 U8 **Teulon** Manitoba
71 O8 **Teun** *isld* Indonesia
69 B10 **Teunom** *R* Sumatra
33 T8 **Teupitz** E Germany
60 P1 **Teuri-tō** *isld* Japan
37 L3 **Teuschnitz** W Germany
32 H8 **Teutoburger Wald** W Germany
29 J9 **Teuva** Finland
26 H9 **Tevansjö** Sweden
45 M6 **Tevere** *R* Italy
144 B6 **Teviot** New Zealand
15 F5 **Teviotdale V** Scotland
13 F3 **Teviot, R** Scotland
50 G3 **Tevriz** U.S.S.R.
144 A7 **Te Waewae Bay** New Zealand
70 C5 **Tewah** Kalimantan
70 D5 **Teweh** *R* Kalimantan
145 E3 **Te Wera** New Zealand
145 F3 **Te Whaiti** New Zealand
145 E4 **Te Wharau** New Zealand
8 D4 **Tewkesbury** England
117 L11 **Texada I** Br Col
12 B2 **Texa I** Scotland
109 O2 **Texarkana** Texas/Ark
109 N2 **Texarkana, L** Texas
141 K8 **Texas** Queensland
109 **Texas** *state* U.S.A.
109 N6 **Texas City** Texas
25 C2 **Texel** *isld* Netherlands
25 C2 **Texelstroom** Netherlands
108 C7 **Texhoma** Texas/Okla
108 D1 **Texico** New Mexico
108 B7 **Texline** Texas
125 K8 **Texmelucan** Mexico
109 L2 **Texoma, L** Oklahoma
108 F4 **Texon** Texas
67 A1 **Te-yang** China
52 F6 **Teykovo** U.S.S.R.
77 J3 **Teyvareh** Afghanistan
52 F6 **Teza** *R* U.S.S.R.
125 L8 **Teziutlán** Mexico
75 P5 **Tezpur** India
87 E11 **Thabana Ntlenyana** *mt* Lesotho
89 E7 **Thaba Putsoa** *mt* Lesotho
68 B4 **Thabaung** Burma
87 E10 **Thabazimbi** S Africa
68 C1 **Thabeikkyin** Burma
79 E10 **Thabt, G. el** *mt* Egypt
68 C2 **Thabyedaung** Burma
109 K2 **Thackerville** Oklahoma
68 D6 **Thagyettaw** Burma
Tha Hin *see* **Lop Buri**
67 B6 **Thai Binh** Vietnam
68 H4 **Thai Duong Thung** Vietnam
68 E5 **Thailand** *kingdom* S E Asia
73 R6 **Thailand, G. of** Thailand
67 B6 **Thai Nguyen** Vietnam
69 D8 **Tha Khanon** Thailand
68 G4 **Thakhek** Laos
38 G8 **Thal** Austria
37 J2 **Thal** E Germany
74 D2 **Thal** Pakistan
85 F1 **Thala** Tunisia
69 D8 **Thalang** Thailand
66 F6 **Thala Pass** China/Burma
33 O9 **Thale** E Germany
73 R7 **Thale Luang** Thailand
36 B4 **Thalfang** W Germany
38 H6 **Thalgau** Austria
37 O2 **Thalheim** E Germany
41 K4 **Thalkirch** Switzerland
141 J8 **Thallon** Queensland
112 F6 **Thalmann** Georgia
37 L5 **Thalmässing** W Germany
84 F4 **Thamad Bu, Hashishah** Libya
9 F4 **Thame** England
145 E2 **Thames** New Zealand
120 H10 **Thames** *R* Ontario
120 J9 **Thamesford** Ontario
9 G4 **Thames, R** England
120 J10 **Thamesville** Ontario
68 D6 **Thamihla Kyun** *isld* Burma
84 F3 **Thāmit, Wadi** Libya
37 K1 **Thamsbrück** E Germany
26 D8 **Thamshamn** Norway
76 A1 **Thana** India
68 C4 **Thanatpin** Burma
68 C5 **Thanbyuzayat** Burma
141 K8 **Thane** Queensland
68 J5 **Thang Binh** Vietnam
142 D4 **Thangoo** W Australia
141 K6 **Thangool** Queensland
68 G3 **Thanh Hoa** Vietnam
68 H2 **Thanh Moi** Vietnam
68 G1 **Thanh Thuy** Vietnam
76 D5 **Thanjavur** India
40 F2 **Thann** France
38 F5 **Thann** W Germany
37 J7 **Thannhausen** W Germany
77 K7 **Thano Bula Khan** Pakistan
36 C7 **Thanville** France
40 D1 **Thaon** France
19 K4 **Thaon les Vosages** France
68 E4 **Tha Pla** Thailand
69 D8 **Thap Put** Thailand
68 D7 **Thap Sakae** Thailand
73 L3 **Thar** *des* India
68 D6 **Tharabwin** Burma
37 Q2 **Tharandt** E Germany
74 D5 **Thar Desert** India
141 G8 **Thargomindah** Queensland
68 B4 **Tharrawaddy** Burma
68 B4 **Tharrawaw** Burma
78 J5 **Tharthar Basin** Iraq
47 G4 **Thásos** *isld* Greece
9 E5 **Thatcham** England
103 P9 **Thatcher** Arizona
106 F4 **Thatcher** Colorado
101 O7 **Thatcher** Idaho
67 B5 **That Khe** Vietnam
68 C4 **Thaton** Burma
18 H9 **Thau, Étang de** *L* France
68 D4 **Thaungyin** *R* Thailand
68 C6 **Thayawthadang-yi Kyun** *isld* Burma
110 E5 **Thayer** Missouri
68 D6 **Thayetchaung** Burma
68 B3 **Thayetmyo** Burma
101 P7 **Thayne** Wyoming
68 A3 **Thazi** Arakan Burma
68 B2 **Thazi** Magwe Burma
68 C2 **Thazi** Mandalay Burma
9 E5 **Theale** England
103 M9 **Theba** Arizona
Thebes *see* **Thívai**
110 G4 **Thebes** Illinois
84 J4 **Thebes** *ruins* Egypt
98 F7 **Thedford** Nebraska
120 J9 **Thedford** Ontario
32 K7 **Thedinghausen** W Germany
141 L7 **Theebine** Queensland
68 B3 **Thegon** Burma
98 K1 **Theif River Falls** Minnesota
20 G5 **Theil, le** France
20 G3 **Theil, le Gros** France
68 D7 **Theinkun** Burma
68 C4 **Theinzeik** Burma
37 N1 **Theissen** E Germany
114 J5 **Thekulthili L** N W Terr
8 C6 **Thelbridge** England
113 E7 **Thelma** Georgia
114 J5 **Thelon** *R* N W Terr
28 D4 **Them** Denmark
37 K3 **Themar** E Germany
21 H7 **Thenay** France
18 F7 **Thenon** France
111 H11 **Theodore** Alabama
141 K7 **Theodore** Queensland
119 P7 **Theodore** Sask
128 F6 **Theodore Roosevelt** *R* Brazil
103 N8 **Theodore Roosevelt L** Arizona
98 C2 **Theodore Roosevelt Nat. Mem. Park** N Dakota
140 B5 **Theo, Mt** N Terr Aust
20 K3 **Therain** *R* France
95 M2 **Theresa** New York
99 S6 **Theresa** Wisconsin
141 J6 **Theresa** *R* Queensland
83 K12 **Thérèse** *isld* Mahé I Indian Oc
118 F4 **Therien** Alberta
111 F12 **Theriot** Louisiana
46 F4 **Thermaïkós, Kólpos** *B* Greece
103 L3 **Thermo** Utah
46 E6 **Thérmon** Greece
101 R6 **Thermopolis** Wyoming
46 F6 **Thermopylai** Greece
139 H6 **The Rock** New S Wales
146 D10 **Theron Mts** Antarctica
22 C2 **Thérouanne** France
21 H7 **Thésée** France
114 G3 **Thesiger B** N W Terr
46 E5 **Thessalía** Greece
120 G6 **Thessalon** Ontario
46 F4 **Thessaloníki** Greece
9 G3 **Thetford** England
121 T6 **Thetford Mines** Quebec
68 B5 **Thetkethaung** *R* Burma
119 P3 **The Two Rivers** Sask
20 J5 **Theuville** France
22 K2 **Theux** Belgium
138 C4 **Thevenard** S Australia
142 A5 **Thevenard I** W Australia
19 P16 **Thèze** France
46 D5 **Thiamis** *R* Greece
111 F12 **Thibodaux** Louisiana
20 G3 **Thibouville** France
119 T3 **Thicket Portage** Manitoba
8 D6 **Thickthorn** England
118 E2 **Thickwood Hills** Alberta
100 H4 **Thief V.Res** Oregon
146 F9 **Thiel Mts** Antarctica
100 C6 **Thielsen, Mt** Oregon
Thielt *see* **Tielt**
99 T6 **Thiensville** Wisconsin
22 F4 **Thiérache** France
18 H7 **Thiers** France
37 N3 **Thiersheim** W Germany
85 A6 **Thies** Senegal
43 B8 **Thiesi** Sardinia
33 T4 **Thiessow** E Germany
88 F2 **Thika** Kenya
73 L7 **Thiladunmathi Atoll** Maldives
20 J3 **Thilliers-en-Vexin, les** France
40 E2 **Thillot, le** France
75 N5 **Thimbu** Bhutan
20 H4 **Thimert** France
22 H4 **Thin le-Moutier** France
86 H3 **Thio** Ethiopia
137 O6 **Thio** New Caledonia
19 K3 **Thionville** France
85 D6 **Thiou** Upper Volta
47 G8 **Thíra** *isld* Greece
47 G8 **Thirasía** *isld* Greece
20 H5 **Thiron-Gardais** France
13 G5 **Thirsk** England
13 G3 **Thirston** England
143 D9 **Thirsty, Mt** W Australia
120 K7 **Thirty Thousand Is** Ontario
28 B3 **Thisted** Denmark
Thisted *co see* **Viborg**
101 O10 **Thistle** Utah
138 D5 **Thistle I** S Australia
68 B1 **Thitseingyi** Burma
47 F6 **Thívai** Greece
20 H5 **Thivars** France
18 F7 **Thiviers** France
18 H6 **Thizy** France
115 S5 **Thjorsá** *R* Iceland
19 Q16 **Thoard** France
68 E3 **Thoeng** Thailand
20 J4 **Thoiry** France
25 B5 **Tholen** Netherlands
36 C5 **Tholey** W Germany
19 P18 **Tholonet** France
107 M6 **Thomas** Oklahoma
94 H7 **Thomas** W Virginia
102 E4 **Thomas A Edison, L** California
113 K11 **Thomas B** Bahamas
115 K1 **Thomas Hubbard, C** N W Terr
108 F3 **Thomas, J.B., L** Texas
138 E2 **Thomas, L** S Australia
102 H8 **Thomas Mt** California
144 D5 **Thomas, Mt** New Zealand
140 B6 **Thomas Res** N Terr Aust
111 J9 **Thomaston** Alabama
112 C5 **Thomaston** Georgia
95 S2 **Thomaston** Maine
109 K7 **Thomaston** Texas
14 D4 **Thomastown** Irish Rep
111 G9 **Thomastown** Mississippi
111 J10 **Thomasville** Alabama
113 D7 **Thomasville** Georgia
110 E5 **Thomasville** Missouri
112 G2 **Thomasville** N Carolina
20 H4 **Thomer-la-Sogne** France
127 J5 **Thomonde** Haiti
95 Q5 **Thompson** Connecticut

99 N6 Thompson Iowa
119 U3 Thompson Manitoba
99 U4 Thompson Michigan
98 J2 Thompson N Dakota
95 M5 Thompson Pennsylvania
103 P3 Thompson Utah
117 N10 Thompson *R* Br Col
110 C1 Thompson *R* Missouri
100 K2 Thompson Falls Montana
142 B3 Thompson L W Australia
117 R4 Thompson Lake N W Terr
114 H5 Thompson Landing N W Terr
140 B6 Thompson, Mt N Terr Aust
138 B1 Thompson, Mt N Terr Australia
116 P6 Thompson Pass Alaska
109 M6 Thompsons Texas
144 A6 Thompson Sd New Zealand
Thompson's Falls *see* Nyahururu Falls
95 P4 Thompsonville Connecticut
99 V5 Thompsonville Michigan
99 Q8 Thomson Illinois
141 G6 Thomson *R* Queensland
143 B6 Thomson, Mt W Australia
144 B6 Thomson Mts New Zealand
68 E6 Thon Buri Thailand
40 D6 Thônes France
68 C4 Thongwa Burma
40 D5 Thonon France
21 G6 Thore France
18 G9 Thoré *R* France
106 B6 Thoreau New Mexico
21 F6 Thorée France
40 D5 Thorens les Glières France
Thorez *see* Torez
118 D4 Thorhild Alberta
141 G8 Thorlindah, L Queensland
13 G4 Thornaby England
9 H2 Thornage England
94 B4 Thornapple *R* Michigan
94 K8 Thornburg Virginia
8 D4 Thornbury England
144 B7 Thornbury New Zealand
120 K8 Thornbury Ontario
109 K5 Thorndale Texas
13 H6 Thorne England
102 F3 Thorne Nevada
9 F2 Thorney England
12 D1 Thornhill Central Scotland
12 E3 Thornhill Dumfries & Galloway Scotland
121 L9 Thornhill Ontario
109 P2 Thornton Arkansas
99 N7 Thornton Iowa
13 E1 Thornton Scotland
109 L4 Thornton Texas
100 H2 Thornton Washington
141 F4 Thorntonia Queensland
110 K1 Thorntown Indiana
121 L9 Thorold Ontario
Thorout *see* Torhout
100 E2 Thorp Washington
99 Q5 Thorp Wisconsin
145 D4 Thorpe New Zealand
9 H3 Thorpeness England
28 E4 Thorsager Denmark
118 C5 Thorsby Alberta
28 N2 Thorshavn Faeroes
146 A7 Thorshavnfjella Antarctica
28 D4 Thorsø Denmark
119 U1 Thorsteinson L Manitoba
146 G8 Thorvald Nilsen Mts Antarctica
8 C6 Thorverton England
68 G7 Thot Not Vietnam
21 E8 Thouars France
142 C5 Thouin Pt W Australia
46 E7 Thouría Greece
21 C6 Thourie France
22 D5 Thourotte France
95 L2 Thousand Is Ontario/New York
103 N3 Thousand Lake Mt Utah
101 L8 Thousand Spring Cr Nevada
101 L7 Thousand Springs Idaho
47 H3 Thrace Turkey
109 K5 Thrall Texas
100 E3 Thrall Washington
9 F3 Thrapston England
139 J6 Thredbo New S Wales
8 C3 Three Cocks Wales
101 K7 Three Creek Idaho
101 O4 Three Forks Montana
118 D7 Three Hills Alberta
139 G8 Three Hummock I Tasmania
110 J5 Three I.Res Tennessee
9 F2 Threekingham England
137 O8 Three Kings Basin Pacific Oc
145 D1 Three Kings Is New Zealand
140 D3 Three Knobs *mt* N Terr Aust
99 R4 Three Lakes Wisconsin
141 G2 Three Mile Opening, First & Second *straits* Gt Barrier Reef Aust
99 U8 Three Oaks Michigan
68 D5 Three Pagodas Pass Burma/Thailand
119 T3 Threepoint L Manitoba
85 D8 Three Points, C Ghana
102 F5 Three Rivers California
94 B5 Three Rivers Michigan
106 D8 Three Rivers New Mexico
109 J7 Three Rivers Texas
123 N5 Three Rock Cove Nfld
141 G1 Three Sisters *islds* Queensland
100 D5 Three Sisters *mts* Oregon
143 B8 Three Springs W Australia
13 E4 Threlkeld England
109 H2 Throckmorton Texas
68 F5 Throm Cambodia
143 E8 Throssell, L W Australia
143 E7 Throssell, Mt W Australia
142 D5 Throssel Ra W Australia
68 J5 Thu Bon *R* Vietnam
139 J5 Thuddungra New S Wales
18 H8 Thueyts France
40 E6 Thuile, la Italy
22 G3 Thuin Belgium
115 N2 Thule Greenland
146 A13 Thule I Antarctica
37 O2 Thum E Germany
101 P5 Thumb Wyoming
144 C5 Thumbs, The *mt* New Zealand
40 G4 Thun Switzerland
141 G7 Thunda Queensland
119 O2 Thunder Ontario
94 D2 Thunder B Michigan
99 R1 Thunder Bay Ontario
98 D4 Thunder Butte Cr S Dakota
120 G2 Thunderhouse Falls Ontario
126 D6 Thunder Knoll Caribbean
118 C4 Thunder L. Prov. Park Alberta
116 G2 Thunder Mt Alaska
36 H4 Thüngen W Germany
69 D8 Thung Maphrao Thailand
69 D8 Thung Song Thailand
69 D9 Thung Wa Thailand
75 O5 Thunkar Bhutan
40 B4 Thurey France
33 R5 Thürikow E Germany
41 L3 Thüringen Austria
37 J2 Thüringer Wald *mts* E Germany
19 N13 Thurins France
14 D4 Thurles Irish Rep
8 C7 Thurlestone England
139 G3 Thurloo Downs New S Wales
101 T3 Thurlow Montana
37 L3 Thurnau W Germany
28 F6 Thurø Denmark
13 E4 Thursby England
141 F1 Thursday I Queensland
121 P7 Thurso Quebec
15 E2 Thurso Scotland
15 E2 Thurso *R* Scotland
20 E4 Thury-Harcourt France
117 K7 Thutade L Br Col
28 A3 Thy *reg* Denmark
141 G7 Thylungra Queensland
87 G9 Thyolo Malawi
139 K4 Tia New S Wales
127 J9 Tía Juana Venezuela
65 G3 Tianboashan China
67 B5 Tiandeng China
67 B5 Tiandong China
67 B4 Tian'e China
67 C4 Tianhe China
65 D5 Tianjin China
67 D1 Tianmen China
65 H3 Tianqiaoling China
Tianshan *see* Ar Horquin Qi
65 G1 Tiansheng China
58 E5 Tianshui China
67 G2 Tiantai China
67 B5 Tianyang China
Tianyi *see* Ningcheng
Tianzhen *see* Gaoqing
65 C4 Tianzhen China
67 C3 Tianzhu China
134 C11 Tiarel Tahiti I Pac Oc
85 E1 Tiaret Algeria
141 L7 Tiaro Queensland
85 D7 Tiassalé Ivory Coast
130 E9 Tibagi Brazil
86 B4 Tibati Cameroon
Tiber *R see* Tevere *R*
80 F2 Tiberias Israel
80 F2 Tiberias, L Israel
101 O1 Tiber Res Montana
86 C1 Tibesti *reg* Chad
84 F5 Tibesti, Sarīr Libya
Tibet *aut reg see* Xizang Zizhiqu
66 C5 Tibet *aut reg* China
121 N4 Tiblemont Quebec
48 J3 Tiblesului Muntii Romania
138 F3 Tibooburra New S Wales
75 K4 Tibrikot Nepal
124 C3 Tiburón *isld* Mexico
71 F4 Ticao *isld* Philippines
9 G5 Ticehurst England
121 O8 Tichborne Ontario
85 C5 Tichitt Mauritania
85 B4 Tichla Mauritania
41 J5 Ticino *canton* Switzerland
44 E1 Ticino *R* Italy
13 G6 Tickhill England
9 E2 Ticknall England
95 O3 Ticonderoga New York
27 G13 Tidaholm Sweden
122 F6 Tide Hd New Brunswick
118 F8 Tide L Alberta
69 A9 Tiden Nicobar Is
100 B5 Tidewater Oregon
85 E3 Tidikelt *reg* Algeria
94 H5 Tidioute Pennsylvania
85 B5 Tidjikja Mauritania
138 E2 Tidna Hill S Australia
122 H8 Tidnish Nova Scotia
44 F2 Tidone *R* Italy
71 A2 Tidore Halmahera Indonesia
85 A5 Tidra, I Mauritania
9 E5 Tidworth England
85 C7 Tiébissou Ivory Coast
33 T7 Tiefensee E Germany
36 C6 Tieffenbach France
116 P6 Tiekel Alaska
25 D5 Tiel Netherlands
65 G1 Tieli China
65 F3 Tieling China
22 E1 Tielt Belgium
85 C7 Tiéme Ivory Coast
22 H2 Tienen Belgium
66 C3 Tien Shan *ra* China/U.S.S.R.
Tientsin *see* Tianjin
67 B6 Tien Yen Vietnam
89 D9 Tier Berg *mt* S Africa
27 J11 Tierp Sweden
106 D5 Tierra New Mexico
125 L8 Tierra Blanca Mexico
133 D8 Tierra del Fuego, I.Grande de Arg/Chile
101 U8 Tie Siding Wyoming
16 D4 Tiétar *R* Spain
130 F8 Tietê Brazil
130 E7 Tietê *R* Brazil
138 B2 Tietkens, Mt S Australia
100 E3 Tieton Washington
100 D3 Tieton Res Washington
138 C2 Tieyon S Australia
45 Q7 Tifata, M *mt* Italy
100 F1 Tiffany Mt Washington
86 G4 Tiffi Ethiopia
99 P8 Tiffin Iowa
94 D5 Tiffin Ohio
17 H10 Tiffrit Algeria
16 E9 Tifriste Morocco
112 D6 Tifton Georgia
70 D2 Tiga *isld* Sabah
116 E9 Tigalda I Aleutian Is
100 C4 Tigard Oregon
100 H1 Tiger Washington
112 F3 Tiger *R* S Carolina
99 R5 Tigerton Wisconsin
15 C5 Tighnabruaich Scotland
86 H5 Tigieglo Somalia
51 P3 Tigil U.S.S.R.
56 B5 Tigiretskiy Khrebet *mts* U.S.S.R.
112 E4 Tignall Georgia
86 B4 Tigneré Cameroon
42 A3 Tignes, Bge. de France
122 H7 Tignish Pr Edward I
128 C4 Tigre *R* Peru
127 N10 Tigre *R* Venezuela
125 K6 Tigre, Cerro del *mt* Mexico
131 B3 Tigre, Sa *ra* Argentina
78 J4 Tigris *R* Iraq
57 A3 Tigrovyy Khvost, Mys *C* U.S.S.R.
85 F3 Tiguentourine Algeria
86 C2 Tigui Chad
16 D9 Tiguisas Morocco
21 J6 Tigy France
79 D9 Tîh, Gebel el *plat* Egypt
145 E3 Tihoi New Zealand
28 B4 Tihøje *hill* Denmark
70 G6 Tiinampuu Sulawesi
106 D6 Tijeras New Mexico
124 A1 Tijuana Mexico
130 E10 Tijucas Brazil
122 G3 Tika Quebec
125 P9 Tikal *anc site* Guatemala
74 H6 Tikamgarh India
116 H6 Tikchik L Alaska
53 F10 Tikhoretsk U.S.S.R.
52 D5 Tikhvin U.S.S.R.
145 G2 Tikitiki New Zealand
145 F3 Tikokino New Zealand
137 O4 Tikopia *isld* Santa Cruz Is
78 J4 Tikrit Iraq
52 D3 Tiksha U.S.S.R.
52 D2 Tikshozero, Oz *L* U.S.S.R.
51 M1 Tiksi U.S.S.R.
71 H4 Tilamuta Sulawesi
141 H8 Tilbooroo Queensland
25 D5 Tilburg Netherlands
9 G5 Tilbury England
120 H10 Tilbury Ontario
133 D2 Tilcara Argentina
138 F3 Tilcha S Australia
110 G3 Tilden Illinois
98 J7 Tilden Nebraska
109 J7 Tilden Texas
48 G3 Tileagd Romania
85 D3 Tilemsï el Fasi Algeria
85 E5 Tilemsi, Vallée du Mali
98 C5 Tilford S Dakota
74 H5 Tilhar India
51 Q2 Tilichiki U.S.S.R.
68 B2 Tilin Burma
85 E6 Tillabéri Niger
100 B4 Tillamook Oregon
100 A4 Tillamook Rock Oregon
69 A8 Tillanchong I Nicobar Is
20 J5 Tillay-le-Peneux France
27 J12 Tillberge Sweden
40 E3 Tille *R* France
112 G2 Tillery, L N Carolina
118 F8 Tilley Alberta
85 E5 Tillia Niger
12 E1 Tillicoultry Scotland
20 H4 Tillières-sur-Avre France
28 G7 Tillitse Denmark
112 F5 Tillman S Carolina
113 L11 Tilloo Cay *isld* Bahamas
13 G2 Till, R England
120 K10 Tillsonburg Ontario
21 H3 Tilly France
20 D3 Tilly-sur-Seulles France
71 M9 Tilomar Timor
47 J8 Tílos *isld* Greece
139 G4 Tilpa New S Wales
85 E2 Tilrhemt Algeria
9 E5 Tilshead England
119 Q9 Tilston Manitoba
123 S4 Tilting Nfld
110 J1 Tilton Illinois
95 Q3 Tilton New Hampshire
70 G5 Tily *mt* Sulawesi
28 A4 Tim Denmark
54 J5 Tim U.S.S.R.
121 L5 Timagami Ontario
52 G2 Timanskiy Kryazh *ra* U.S.S.R.
144 C6 Timaru New Zealand
47 G9 Timbákion Crete Greece
111 F12 Timbalier I Louisiana
70 F2 Timbang *isld* Sabah
130 J9 Timbaúba Brazil
85 C5 Timbédra Mauritania
100 B4 Timber Oregon
140 B3 Timber Creek N Terr Aust
98 E4 Timber L S Dakota
112 J1 Timberlake N Carolina
102 H4 Timber Mt Nevada
139 G7 Timboon Victoria
130 E10 Timbo, R Brazil
Timbuktu *see* Tombouctou
70 F2 Timbun Mata Sabah
85 F3 Timellouline Algeria
85 D5 Timetrine Mts Mali
46 D5 Tímfi, Óros *mt* Greece
46 E6 Timfristós *mt* Greece
85 F5 Timia Niger
85 E3 Timimoun Algeria
Timiris, C *see* Mirik, C
56 B3 Timiryazevskiy U.S.S.R.
121 L5 Timiskaming, L Quebec
48 G5 Timişoara Romania
48 G5 Timişul *R* Romania
55 D1 Timkapaul' U.S.S.R.
33 N5 Timmendorfer Strand W Germany
27 G13 Timmersdala Sweden
85 F5 Timmersoi *watercourse* Niger
120 J4 Timmins Ontario
112 H3 Timmonsville S Carolina
46 E1 Timok *R* Yugoslavia
129 K5 Timon Brazil
71 M9 Timor *isld* E Indies
136 E4 Timor Trough Timor Sea
52 E4 Timoshino U.S.S.R.
133 E5 Timote Argentina
127 J10 Timotes Venezuela
70 D5 Timpah Kalimantan
103 J4 Timpahute Ra Nevada
101 O9 Timpanogos Cave Nat. Mon Utah
143 E7 Timperley Ra W Australia
101 N9 Timpie Utah
109 N4 Timpson Texas
26 J9 Timrå Sweden
28 B4 Timring Denmark
112 A2 Tims Ford L Tennessee
52 H4 Timsher U.S.S.R.
57 E3 Timur U.S.S.R.
70 O9 Timur, Jawa *prov* Java
144 D5 Timutimu Headland New Zealand
89 F8 Tina *R* S Africa
71 G8 Tinaca Pt Mindanao Philippines
127 K10 Tinaco Venezuela
71 F3 Tinaga *isld* Philippines
71 G5 Tinago Leyte Philippines
14 E4 Tinahely Irish Rep
124 J5 Tinaja Mexico
137 O4 Tinakula *isld* Santa Cruz Is
85 G4 Tin Alkoum Algeria
70 F6 Tinambung Sulawesi
127 K10 Tinaquillo Venezuela
48 G4 Tinca Romania
20 D4 Tinchebray France
22 C3 Tincques France
100 K7 Tindall Idaho
76 D4 Tindivanam India
70 K9 Tindjil *isld* Java
85 C3 Tindouf Algeria
28 N2 Tindur *mt* Faeroes
86 D2 Tine Sudan
85 E4 Tinef Algeria
102 F4 Tinemaha Res California
16 C1 Tineo Spain
85 C3 Tinfouchy Algeria
85 F3 Tin Fouye Algeria
141 L1 Tingalpa *dist* Brisbane, Qnsld
69 G11 Tinggi *isld* Malaysia
139 K3 Tingha New S Wales
75 K4 Tingjegaon Nepal
28 C7 Tinglev Denmark
99 M9 Tingley Iowa
115 P5 Tingmiarmiut Greenland
128 C5 Tingo María Peru
67 C3 Tingping China
85 C6 Tingrela Ivory Coast
66 D6 Tingri China
67 E2 Tingsiqiao China
27 G15 Tingsryd Sweden
133 D4 Tinguiririca *mt* Chile/Arg
26 C9 Tingvoll Norway
121 T7 Tingwick Quebec
Tingzhou *see* Changting
129 L6 Tinharé, I.de Brazil
67 B7 Tinh Gia Vietnam
145 F3 Tiniroto New Zealand
70 D3 Tinjar *R* Sarawak
144 D5 Tinline, Mt New Zealand
27 C11 Tinn Norway
141 H8 Tinnenburra Queensland
27 D12 Tinnoset Norway
27 D12 Tinnsjö *L* Norway
44 G3 Tino, I.di Italy
70 G4 Tinombo Sulawesi
69 E14 Tinopo *isld* Indonesia
47 G7 Tínos *isld* Greece
85 E4 Ti-n Rerhoh Algeria
111 D8 Tinsman Arkansas
142 C5 Tinstane, Mt W Australia
75 Q5 Tinsukia India
8 B6 Tintagel England
98 K3 Tintah Minnesota
85 F4 Tin Tarabine *watercourse* Algeria
20 B5 Tinténiac France
8 D4 Tintern England
22 K4 Tintigny Belgium
133 E3 Tintina Argentina
138 F6 Tintinara S Australia
16 C7 Tinto *R* Spain
15 E5 Tinto, Mt Scotland
145 F4 Tinui New Zealand
144 C5 Tinwald New Zealand
85 E4 Tin Zaouaten Algeria
111 D10 Tioga Louisiana
98 D1 Tioga N Dakota
95 K5 Tioga Pennsylvania
109 L2 Tioga Texas
94 G8 Tioga W Virginia
69 G11 Tioman *isld* Malaysia
120 H4 Tionaga Ontario
41 N5 Tione Italy
42 D2 Tione di Trento Italy
100 D8 Tionesta California
94 H5 Tionesta Pennsylvania
71 H7 Tioro Indonesia
71 C3 Tipin W Irian
94 A5 Tippecanoe Indiana
99 U9 Tippecanoe *R* Indiana
14 C4 Tipperary Irish Rep
14 D4 Tipperary *co* Irish Rep
111 F8 Tippo Mississippi
102 E5 Tipton California
110 K1 Tipton Indiana
107 M2 Tipton Kansas
110 D3 Tipton Missouri
109 H1 Tipton Oklahoma
103 K6 Tipton, Mt Arizona
110 G5 Tiptonville Tennessee
120 D4 Tip Top Hill Ontario
9 G4 Tiptree England
76 C4 Tiptur India
128 E3 Tiquié *R* Brazil
80 C5 Tira Israel
129 J4 Tiracambu, Sa.do *mts* Brazil
79 E11 Tirān *isld* Saudi Arabia
46 D3 Tiranë Albania
41 M5 Tirano Italy
83 K9 Tirappane Sri Lanka
53 C10 Tiraspol' U.S.S.R.
80 C2 Tirat Karmel Israel
80 F4 Tirat Zevi Israel
145 E2 Tirau New Zealand
145 F4 Tiraumea New Zealand
47 J6 Tire Turkey
78 G1 Tirebolu Turkey
15 B4 Tiree *isld* Scotland
48 J6 Tîrgovişte Romania
48 L3 Tîrgu Frumos Romania
48 H5 Tîrgu Jiu Romania
48 J4 Tîrgu Mures Romania
48 K3 Tîrgu Neamt Romania
48 K4 Tîrgu Ocna Romania
48 K4 Tîrgu Secuesc Romania
47 K4 Tirilye Turkey
85 B4 Tiris *reg* Mauritania
145 E2 Tiritiri New Zealand
Tirlemont *see* Tienen
55 C4 Tirlyanskiy U.S.S.R.
48 J4 Tîrnava Mare *R* Romania
48 J4 Tîrnava Mică *R* Romania
48 J4 Tîrnăveni Romania
46 E5 Tírnavos Greece
94 E6 Tiro Ohio
70 G7 Tiro Sulawesi
38 F8 Tirol *prov* Austria
41 O4 Tirolo Italy
80 C6 Tirosh Israel
86 D4 Tiroungoulou Cent Afr Republic
45 H4 Tirrenia Italy
138 D3 Tirret Ra S Australia
37 N4 Tirschenreuth W Germany
43 B8 Tirso *R* Sardinia
43 B8 Tirso, L. del Sardinia
28 G7 Tirsted Denmark
131 A7 Tirua, Pta Chile
76 D6 Tiruchchendur India
76 D5 Tiruchirappalli India
76 C6 Tirunelveli India
128 D5 Tiruntán Peru
76 D4 Tirupati India
76 D4 Tiruppattur India
76 C5 Tiruppur India
76 D4 Tiruvannamalai India
142 F5 Tiru Well W Australia
119 N6 Tisdale Sask
111 H7 Tishomingo Mississippi
109 L1 Tishomingo Oklahoma
99 R8 Tiskilwa Illinois
28 C6 Tislund Denmark
27 H13 Tisnaren *L* Sweden
31 J6 Tišnov Czechoslovakia
48 F2 Tisovec Czechoslovakia
48 H2 Tissa *R* U.S.S.R.
83 L11 Tissamaharama Sri Lanka
9 E1 Tissington England
27 E12 Tistedal Norway
48 F3 Tisza *R* Hungary
31 N8 Tiszavasvari Hungary
85 E3 Tit Algeria
116 K2 Titaluk *R* Alaska
9 E6 Titchfield England
128 E7 Titicaca, L Peru/Bolivia
116 L4 Titna *R* Alaska
42 J6 Titograd Yugoslavia
99 M6 Titonka Iowa
48 F7 Titova Užice Yugoslavia
52 D1 Titovka *R* U.S.S.R.
46 E3 Titov Veles Yugoslavia
26 C8 Titran Norway
94 C3 Tittabawassee *R* Michigan
37 L6 Titting W Germany
38 G5 Tittmoning W Germany
48 K6 Titu Romania
86 E5 Titule Zaïre
113 G9 Titusville Florida
94 H5 Titusville Pennsylvania
85 A6 Tivaouane Senegal
27 G13 Tived Sweden
8 C6 Tiverton England
122 F9 Tiverton Nova Scotia
120 J8 Tiverton Ontario
95 Q5 Tiverton Rhode I
45 N6 Tivoli Italy
95 O4 Tivoli New York
109 L7 Tivoli Texas
144 B7 Tiwai Pt New Zealand
68 D6 Ti-ywa Burma
124 H7 Tizapán el Alto Mexico
17 H9 Tizi Algeria
16 E10 Tizi-Ifri Morocco
125 P7 Tizimín Mexico
85 C3 Tiznit Morocco
124 J5 Tizoc Mexico
16 E10 Tiztoutine Morocco
28 B6 Tjæreborg Denmark
28 G6 Tjæreby Denmark
27 H13 Tjällmo Sweden
70 L9 Tjamara Java
26 K5 Tjåmotis Sweden
71 L10 Tjamplong Timor Indonesia
70 K9 Tjankuang Tg *C* Java
26 L4 Tjårro Keble *mt* Sweden
26 J5 Tjeggelvas *L* Sweden
26 H3 Tjeldöy *isld* Norway
28 D3 Tjele Denmark
70 D4 Tjemaru, G *mt* Kalimantan
71 J9 Tjempi, Teluk *B* Sumbawa Indonesia
70 F6 Tjenrana Sulawesi
70 N9 Tjepu Java
70 M9 Tjereme *mt* Java
25 E3 Tjeuke Meer Netherlands
70 L9 Tjiandjur Java
70 L9 Tjibadak Java
70 L9 Tjibatu Java
70 L9 Tjibuni *R* Java
70 M9 Tjidjulang Java
70 L9 Tjidua Java
70 L9 Tjihara Java
70 L9 Tjikadjang Java
70 L9 Tjikampek Java
70 M9 Tjilatjap Java
70 M9 Tjiledug Java
70 L9 Tjimahi Java
70 G6 Tjimpu Sulawesi
70 K8 Tjina, Tg *C* Sumatra
70 M9 Tjipatudjah Java
70 M9 Tjirebon Java
70 L9 Tjitarum *R* Java
27 E12 Tjöme *isld* Norway
27 E13 Tjörn *isld* Sweden
28 M1 Tjørnevig Faeroes
28 B4 Tjørring Denmark
26 F6 Tjötta Norway
69 F14 Tjurup Sumatra
53 F11 Tkvarcheli U.S.S.R.
125 L9 Tlacolula de Matamoros Mexico
125 M8 Tlacotalpan Mexico
125 K8 Tlalnepantla Mexico
125 K8 Tlálpam Mexico
125 L8 Tlapacoyán Mexico
124 H7 Tlaquepaque Mexico
125 K8 Tlaxcala Mexico
85 D2 Tlemcen Algeria
85 E5 Tlemcès Niger
48 J2 Tlumach U.S.S.R.
31 N3 Tłuszcz Poland
52 E6 T'ma *R* U.S.S.R.
84 F4 Tmassah Libya
85 D4 Tni Haïa Algeria
68 C4 To *R* Burma
126 G4 Toa *R* Cuba
117 L6 Toad River Br Col
87 H11 Toamasina Madagascar
45 J3 Toano Italy
95 L9 Toano Virginia
101 L9 Toano *mt ra* Nevada
145 F3 Toatoa New Zealand
133 E5 Toay Argentina
61 K11 Toba Japan
69 D11 Toba, Danau *L* Sumatra
127 M1 Tobago *isld* W Indies
117 L10 Toba Inlet Br Col
77 K4 Toba & Kakar Ranges Pakistan
101 L9 Tobar Nevada
17 F6 Tobarra Spain
60 D12 Tobata Japan
14 C2 Tobbercurry Irish Rep
71 H7 Tobea *isld* Indonesia
140 E5 Tobermorey N Terr Aust
120 J7 Tobermory Ontario
141 G7 Tobermory Queensland
15 B4 Tobermory Scotland
60 P2 Tobetsu Japan
98 J9 Tobias Nebraska
61 N14 Tobiishi-hana *C* Iwo Jima Japan
115 R3 Tobin, Kap *C* Greenland
119 O5 Tobin L Sask
142 F5 Tobin,L W Australia
102 G1 Tobin, Mt Nevada
122 E6 Tobique R New Brunswick
61 N6 Tobi-shima *isld* Japan
69 H14 Toboali Indonesia
55 D4 Tobol U.S.S.R.
70 G5 Toboli Sulawesi
55 E2 Tobol'sk U.S.S.R.
68 J6 To Bong Vietnam
71 F5 Toboso Negros Philippines
Tobruk *see* Tubruq
95 M5 Tobyhanna Pennsylvania
52 H3 Tobysh U.S.S.R.
52 H2 Tobysh *R* U.S.S.R.
141 G6 Tocal Queensland
129 J5 Tocantínia Brazil
129 J5 Tocantinópolis Brazil
129 J4 Tocantins *R* Brazil
112 D3 Toccoa Georgia
41 H5 Toce *R* Italy
61 N9 Tochigi Japan
61 M8 Tochio Japan
133 D2 Toco Chile
133 C2 Tocopilla Chile
133 D2 Tocorpuri *mt* Chile/Bolivia
139 H6 Tocumwal New S Wales
127 K9 Tocuyo *R* Venezuela
127 K9 Tocuyo de la Costa Venezuela
74 F5 Toda India
26 C9 Todal Norway
116 L3 Todatonten Alaska
122 F7 Todd Mt New Brunswick
140 B2 Todd,Mt N Terr Aust
140 C6 Todd R N Terr Aust
143 F7 Todd Ra W Australia
47 J1 Toder Ikonomovo Bulgaria
32 M5 Todesfelde W Germany
13 F1 Todhills Scotland
42 E6 Todi Italy
41 J4 Tödi *mt* Switzerland
70 G5 Todjo Sulawesi
13 F6 Todmorden England
138 C2 Todmorden S Australia
61 Q6 Todoga-saki *C* Japan
60 P4 Todohokke Japan
131 A8 Todos los Santos, L Chile
129 L6 Todos os Santos, B. de Brazil
124 D6 Todos Santos Mexico
56 E5 Todzha, Oz *L* U.S.S.R.
14 B5 Toe Hd Irish Rep
68 D5 Toe Jaga, Khao *mt* Burma/Thailand
144 B7 Toetoes B New Zealand
118 E5 Tofield Alberta
117 L11 Tofino Br Col
27 F14 Tofta Sweden
27 E12 Tofte Norway
28 C6 Toftlund Denmark
116 M4 Tofty Alaska
137 R5 Tofua *isld* Tonga
Tōfutsu *see* Sernovodsk
61 O10 Tōgane Japan
41 H5 Togano, Monte Italy
41 K3 Toggenburg *mt* Switzerland
61 K8 Togi Japan
116 G7 Togiak Alaska
70 G5 Togian Kep *isld* Sulawesi
37 O7 Töging W Germany
86 G2 Togni Sudan
119 Q7 Togo Sask
85 E7 Togo *rep* W Africa
Togrog Ul *see* Qahar Youyi Qianqi
65 B4 Togtoh China
61 P12 Toguchi Okinawa
56 B3 Toguchin U.S.S.R.
56 E4 Togul'skiy Khrebet *mts* U.S.S.R.
57 B2 Togyz U.S.S.R.
102 E1 Tohakum Pk Nevada
74 F4 Tohana India
106 B6 Tohatchi New Mexico
70 C4 Tohenbatu *mt* Sarawak
134 A11 Tohiea Tahiti I Pac Oc
29 P9 Tohmajärvi Finland
29 L8 Toholampi Finland
113 F9 Tohopekaliga, L Florida
61 M11 Toi Japan
68 A7 Toibalewe Andaman Is
29 K10 Toijala Finland
71 H5 Toili Sulawesi
99 P2 Toimi Minnesota
60 E14 Toi-misaki Japan
29 K9 Toisvesi *L* Finland
29 M9 Toivakka Finland
99 S3 Toivola Michigan
102 G2 Toiyabe Ra Nevada
60 G11 Tōjō Japan
30 H6 Tok *mt* Czechoslovakia
145 E3 Tokaanu New Zealand
60 R2 Tokachi *prefect* Japan
60 Q2 Tokachi dake *mt* Japan
48 G2 Tokajo Hungary
70 G5 Tokala, G *mt* Sulawesi
61 M8 Tōkamachi Japan
144 B7 Tokanui New Zealand
86 G2 Tokar Sudan
59 J5 Tokara-retto *islds* Japan
55 F5 Tokarevka U.S.S.R.
52 D4 Tokari U.S.S.R.
52 G5 Tokarikha U.S.S.R.
78 F1 Tokat Turkey
145 D2 Tokatoka New Zealand
65 F6 Tŏkchŏk-kundo *B* S Korea
59 K4 Tok-do *isld* Japan/Korea
70 G6 Toke Sulawesi
134 K9 Tokelau Is Pacific Oc
101 P9 Tokewanna Pk Utah
56 E1 Tokhoma *R* U.S.S.R.
57 G5 Tokhtamysh U.S.S.R.
61 L10 Toki Japan
98 H2 Tokio N Dakota
116 Q5 Tok Junc Alaska
27 D12 Tokke-Vatn *L* Norway
116 M4 Toklat Alaska
Tokmak *see* Esme
57 H3 Tokmak U.S.S.R.
145 E3 Toko New Zealand
70 G6 Tokolimbu Sulawesi
145 E4 Tokomaru New Zealand
145 G3 Tokomaru Bay New Zealand
60 S1 Tokoro Japan
145 E3 Tokoroa New Zealand
57 H1 Tokrau *R* U.S.S.R.
52 E3 Toksha-Kuznetsova U.S.S.R.
66 D3 Toksun China
57 G4 Toktogul Vdkhr U.S.S.R.
57 K2 Tokty U.S.S.R.
70 D5 Tokung Kalimantan
59 K1 Tokur U.S.S.R.
60 H11 Tokushima Japan
60 E11 Tokuyama Japan
89 G3 Tokwe *R* Zimbabwe
62 Tōkyō *conurbation* Japan
61 N10 Tōkyō-wan *B* Japan
145 G3 Tolaga Bay New Zealand
106 G7 Tolar New Mexico
109 K3 Tolar Texas
78 K1 Tolavi U.S.S.R.
55 C4 Tolbazy U.S.S.R.
47 J1 Tolbukhin Bulgaria
130 D9 Toledo Brazil
133 C3 Toledo Chile
110 H2 Toledo Illinois
99 O7 Toledo Iowa
94 D5 Toledo Ohio
100 B5 Toledo Oregon
16 E5 Toledo Spain
100 C3 Toledo Washington
16 E5 Toledo *prov* Spain
109 O4 Toledo Bend Res Louisiana
16 D5 Toledo, Montes de *mts* Spain
42 E5 Tolentino Italy
44 L5 Tolfa, Mt.della Italy
27 G14 Tolg Sweden
26 E9 Tolga Norway
87 G12 Toliara Madagascar
128 C3 Tolima *div* Colombia
70 G4 Tolitoli Sulawesi
27 G16 Tollarp Sweden
33 S5 Tollense *R* E Germany
33 S5 Tollensesee *L* E Germany
103 M8 Tolleson Arizona
98 E1 Tolley N Dakota
102 E4 Tollhouse California
28 H5 Tølløse Denmark
57 B3 Tolmacheva, Ozero *L* U.S.S.R.
52 C5 Tolmachevo U.S.S.R.
42 E2 Tolmezzo Italy
42 F2 Tolmin Yugoslavia
48 E4 Tolna Hungary
48 E4 Tolna *co* Hungary
28 E2 Tolne Denmark
86 C6 Tolo Zaïre
54 A2 Tolochin U.S.S.R.
110 H2 Tolono Illinois
17 F1 Tolosa Spain
70 G6 Tolo, Teluk *B* Sulawesi
116 N4 Tolovana *R* Alaska
65 G7 Tolsan *isld* S Korea
15 B2 Tolsta Head Scotland
48 K2 Tolstoe U.S.S.R.
103 N9 Toltec Arizona
133 C5 Toltén Chile
131 A7 Toltén, R Chile
126 G10 Tolú Colombia
99 R8 Toluca Illinois
125 K8 Toluca Mexico
29 P5 Tolvant, Oz *L* U.S.S.R.
52 D4 Tolvayarvi U.S.S.R.
52 E4 Tolvuya U.S.S.R.
55 A4 Tol'yatti U.S.S.R.
55 D5 Tolybay U.S.S.R.
56 B3 Tom' *R* U.S.S.R.
99 Q6 Tomah Wisconsin
99 R4 Tomahawk Wisconsin
60 P3 Tomakomai Japan
60 P1 Tomamae Japan
128 F4 Tomar Brazil
16 B5 Tomar Portugal
57 H2 Tomar U.S.S.R.
Tomari *see* Golovnino
60 N3 Tomari Japan
59 M2 Tomari U.S.S.R.
31 O4 Tomashevka U.S.S.R.
48 M2 Tomashpol U.S.S.R.
130 E8 Tomasina Brazil
31 O5 Tomaszów Lubelski Poland
31 M4 Tomaszów Mazowiecka Poland
15 D3 Tomatin Scotland
124 G8 Tomatlán Mexico
38 O9 Tomaz Yugoslavia
109 M5 Tomball Texas
60 F10 Tombara Japan
86 F4 Tombe Sudan
111 H8 Tombigbee *R* Mississippi
71 H5 Tombila *mt* Sulawesi
87 B7 Tomboco Angola
70 G6 Tomboli Sulawesi
130 G7 Tombos Brazil
85 D5 Tombouctou Mali
103 O10 Tombstone Arizona
131 A6 Tome Chile
71 J7 Tomea *isld* Indonesia
27 G16 Tomelilla Sweden
121 L6 Tomiko Ontario
139 J4 Tomingley New S Wales
70 G4 Tomini Sulawesi
70 G5 Tomini, Teluk *B* Sulawesi
15 E3 Tomintoul Scotland
61 O8 Tomioka Japan
143 G7 Tomkinson Ras S/W Australia
26 F5 Tomma *isld* Norway
28 C2 Tømmerby Denmark
28 E6 Tommerup Denmark
51 M3 Tommot U.S.S.R.
60 G11 Tomo Japan
128 E2 Tomo *R* Colombia
124 F3 Tomóchic Mexico
60 H11 Tomogashima-suidō *str* Japan
71 J4 Tomohon Sulawesi
70 G6 Tomori Tk *B* Sulawesi
118 J8 Tompkins Sask
94 C4 Tompkins Center Michigan
110 L5 Tompkinsville Kentucky
70 G4 Tompo Sulawesi
143 C6 Tom Price W Australia
142 C6 Tom Price,Mt W Australia
66 D5 Tomra China
86 H4 Tomsa Ethiopia
56 C3 Tomsk U.S.S.R.
56 B2 Tomskaya Oblast *prov* U.S.S.R.
83 M9 Tom's Ridge Christmas I Indian Oc
95 N6 Toms River New Jersey
60 Q2 Tomuraushi yama *mt* Japan
Tomur Feng *see* Pobedy, Pik
116 Q6 Tom White, Mt Alaska
124 F4 Tónachic Mexico
125 N9 Tonalá Mexico
103 O5 Tonalea Arizona
42 D2 Tonale, Pso. di Italy
61 K9 Tonami Japan
128 E4 Tonantins Brazil
100 F1 Tonasket Washington
121 M9 Tonawanda New York
9 G5 Tonbridge England
60 J12 Tonda Japan
71 J4 Tondano Sulawesi
16 B4 Tondela Portugal
28 B7 Tønder Denmark
Tønder *co see* Sønderjylland
120 E3 Tondern Ontario
85 E4 Tondjara *watercourse* Algeria
88 C10 Tondongwe *mt* Zimbabwe
36 B3 Tondorf W Germany
61 N9 Tone *R* Japan
61 O10 Tone-gawa *R* Japan
8 C5 Tone, R England
139 G4 Tonga New S Wales
86 F4 Tonga Sudan
88 B10 Tonga Zambia
137 S6 Tonga *island kingdom* Pacific Oc
89 G7 Tongaat S Africa
145 D4 Tonga I New Zealand
139 G4 Tonga L New S Wales
139 G6 Tongala Victoria
67 F4 Tong'an China
110 A2 Tonganoxie Kansas
145 E3 Tongaporutu New Zealand
145 E3 Tongariro *mt* New Zealand
137 R6 Tongatapu Group Tonga
58 F5 Tongbai Shan *mt ra* China
Tongcheng *see* Dong'e
58 G5 Tongcheng China
67 D2 Tongcheng China
67 E1 Tongcheng China
58 E4 Tongchuan China
67 C3 Tongdao China
22 J2 Tongeren Belgium
67 E2 Tonggu China
65 A7 Tongguan China
67 A4 Tonghai China
59 J2 Tonghe China
59 J3 Tonghua China
59 K2 Tongjiang China
67 B1 Tongjiang China
59 J2 Tongken He *R* China
67 B6 Tong King, G. of Vietnam
12 D4 Tongland Scotland
67 B2 Tongliang China
59 H3 Tongliao China
67 F1 Tongling China
67 F2 Tonglu China
67 B1 Tongnan China
68 H6 Tong Noy Cambodia
87 G12 Tongobory Madagascar
131 B3 Tongoi, Bahia Chile
133 C4 Tongoy Chile
Tongquan *see* Malong
71 E7 Tongquil *isld* Philippines
67 C3 Tongren China
Tongres *see* Tongeren
Tongshan *see* Xuzhou
67 E2 Tongshan China
68 D2 Tongta Burma
58 C5 Tongtian He *R* China
15 D2 Tongue Scotland
101 U3 Tongue *R* Montana
126 F2 Tongue of the Ocean *chan* Bahamas
101 T4 Tongue R.Res Montana
65 C5 Tong Xian China
67 G1 Tongxiang China
65 D3 Tongxing China
65 C7 Tongxu China
65 F2 Tongyu China
65 F4 Tongyuanpu China
67 B4 Tongzhou China
67 B2 Tongzi China
58 B2 Tonhil Mongolia
99 R8 Tonica Illinois
124 E3 Tónichi Mexico
124 H8 Tonila Mexico
86 E4 Tonj Sudan
74 F5 Tonk India
107 N5 Tonkawa Oklahoma
52 G6 Tonkino U.S.S.R.
68 G7 Tonle Sap *R* Cambodia
21 D10 Tonnay-Charente France
18 F8 Tonneins France
28 D5 Tønning Denmark
32 J4 Tönning W Germany
102 G3 Tonopah Nevada
60 H11 Tonoshō Japan
27 D12 Tönsberg Norway
27 B13 Tonstad Norway
131 B3 Tontal, Sa *ra* Argentina
103 N8 Tonto Basin Arizona
103 O8 Tonto Nat.Mon Arizona
116 L5 Tonzona *R* Alaska
141 J8 Toobeah Queensland
143 B9 Toodyay W Australia
101 N9 Tooele Utah
141 K7 Toogoolawah Queensland
139 G6 Tooleyone New S Wales
143 G9 Toolgana W Australia
138 D5 Tooligie S Australia
116 N2 Toolik *R* Alaska
138 F6 Toolondo Victoria
139 J6 Tooma *R* New S Wales
141 G7 Toompine Queensland
141 F5 Toorak Queensland
141 K2 Toowong *dist* Brisbane, Qnsld
141 K8 Toowoomba Queensland
116 J1 Topagoruk *R* Alaska
48 L6 Topalu Romania
17 F7 Topares, Sa.de *mts* Spain
103 N10 Topawa Arizona
102 E3 Topaz L California
33 T8 Töpchin E Germany
13 G5 Topcliffe England
94 B5 Topeka Indiana
107 P2 Topeka Kansas
124 F5 Topia Mexico
56 C3 Topki U.S.S.R.
48 G1 Topl'a *R* Czechoslovakia
118 C4 Topland Alberta
117 K8 Topley Lodge Br Col
46 E1 Toplica *R* Yugoslavia
42 G3 Toplice Yugoslavia
48 J4 Topliţa Romania
131 A5 Topocalma, Pta Chile
103 K7 Topock Arizona
48 F6 Topola Yugoslavia
46 E3 Topolčane Yugoslavia
48 E2 Topol'čany Czechoslovakia
29 O10 Topol'ki U.S.S.R.
47 G2 Topolnitsa *R* Bulgaria
124 E5 Topolobampo Mexico
48 J6 Topoloveni Romania
47 H2 Topolovgrad Bulgaria
38 L9 Topolšica Yugoslavia
106 D1 Toponas Colorado
52 E5 Topornya U.S.S.R.
100 E3 Toppenish Washington
47 J1 Topraisar Romania
57 B4 Toprak-kala U.S.S.R.
52 F3 Topsa U.S.S.R.
95 U1 Topsfield Maine
8 C6 Topsham England
95 R3 Topsham Maine
95 M6 Topton Pennsylvania
103 L4 Toquerville Utah
102 G3 Toquima Ra Nevada
17 H3 Torá Spain
71 J4 Torawitan, Tg *B* Sulawesi
123 L8 Tor B Nova Scotia
143 C11 Tor B W Australia
47 J6 Torbalı Turkey
77 F2 Torbat-e-Heydarīyeh Iran
77 G2 Torbat-e Jām Iran
8 C7 Torbay England
123 U6 Torbay Nfld
123 L8 Torbay Nova Scotia
27 F10 Torberget Norway
116 L6 Torbert, Mt Alaska
52 D5 Torbino U.S.S.R.
94 B1 Torch L Michigan
8 C7 Torcross England
20 H2 Torcy-le-Grand France
16 D3 Tordesillas Spain
138 F5 Tor Downs New S Wales
26 N6 Töre Sweden
27 G13 Töreboda Sweden
28 H7 Toreby Denmark
28 K4 Torekov Sweden
145 F2 Torere New Zealand
27 J12 Toresund Sweden
17 F3 Torete *R* Spain
54 K8 Torez U.S.S.R.
21 C7 Torfou France
33 S9 Torgau E Germany
33 U5 Torgelow E Germany
26 F6 Torghatten *isld* Norway
53 G8 Torgun *R* U.S.S.R.
27 H15 Torhamn Sweden
22 E1 Torhout Belgium
86 F4 Tori Ethiopia
70 G5 Toribulu Sulawesi
61 O10 Toride Japan
20 D3 Torigny-sur-Vire France
44 C1 Torino Italy
86 F5 Torit Sudan
130 D5 Torixoreu Brazil
52 D5 Torkovichi U.S.S.R.
29 N3 Törmänen Finland
8 D5 Tormarton England
142 E3 Torment, Pt W Australia
16 D4 Tormes *R* Spain
117 Q11 Tornado Mt Alberta/Br Col
28 D1 Tornby Denmark
26 M4 Torne älv *R* Sweden
32 L5 Tornesch W Germany
26 L3 Torneträsk Sweden
26 K3 Torneträsk *L* Sweden
115 N6 Torngat Mts Quebec/Labrador
48 F7 Tornik *mt* Yugoslavia

Urumchi see Ürümqi
79 G2 Urum es Sughra Syria
66 D3 Ürümqi China
69 C11 Urung Indonesia
139 L4 Urunga New S Wales
88 B10 Urungwe Zimbabwe
128 F6 Urupa R Brazil
52 H6 Urussu U.S.S.R.
130 F4 Urutágua Brazil
130 E5 Urutaí Brazil
145 E3 Uruti New Zealand
77 K3 Uruzgan Afghanistan
77 J3 Urüzgān reg Afghanistan
20 B2 Urville France
136 H2 Urville, Tg. D' C W Irian
89 B4 Urwi Botswana
60 Q2 Uryū R Japan
60 Q1 Uryū-ko L Japan
58 G1 Uryum R U.S.S.R.
56 C3 Uryup R U.S.S.R.
53 F8 Uryupinsk U.S.S.R.
52 G6 Urzhum U.S.S.R.
48 K6 Urziceni Romania
36 B4 Urzig W Germany
60 E12 Usa Japan
71 E7 Usada isld Philippines
47 K6 Uşak Turkey
87 C10 Usakos Namibia
80 E5 Usarin Jordan
133 F8 Usborne hill Falkland Is
33 T5 Usedom E Germany
80 D2 Usha Israel
116 L7 Ushagat I Alaska
50 G1 Ushakova, Ostrova islds U.S.S.R.
55 E3 Ushakovo U.S.S.R.
Ushant see Ouessant, I. d'
60 D13 Ushibuka Japan
61 L8 Ushitsu Japan
60 D12 Ushizu Japan
57 J2 Ush-Tobe U.S.S.R.
133 D8 Ushuaia airport Argentina
129 H5 Usina Brazil
36 F3 Usingen W Germany
8 D4 Usk Wales
27 A12 Uskedal Norway
8 C4 Usk,R Wales
Üskub see Skopje
47 K3 Üsküdar Turkey
47 J3 Üsküp Turkey
32 L9 Uslar W Germany
54 L4 Usman U.S.S.R.
56 D3 Usolka R U.S.S.R.
52 J5 Usol'ye U.S.S.R.
55 G4 Uspenka U.S.S.R.
57 G1 Uspenskiy U.S.S.R.
40 F7 Usseglio Italy
18 G7 Ussel France
13 H6 Usselby England
32 J10 Usseln W Germany
28 K5 Usserød Denmark
18 F6 Usson du Poitou France
59 K2 Ussuri R U.S.S.R.
59 K3 Ussuriysk U.S.S.R.
20 E4 Ussy France
52 G6 Usta R U.S.S.R.
56 D5 Ust'-Abakan U.S.S.R.
52 G4 Ust' Alekseyevo U.S.S.R.
27 C11 Ustaoset Norway
55 D3 Ust-Bagaryak U.S.S.R.
52 H4 Ust' Chernaya U.S.S.R.
48 H2 Ustchorna U.S.S.R.
52 J5 Ust' Dolgaya U.S.S.R.
41 J3 Uster Switzerland
43 E10 Ustica isld Italy
56 F3 Ust'-Ilimskiy Vdkhr U.S.S.R.
52 J3 Ust'-Ilych U.S.S.R.
30 H5 Ústi'nad Czechoslovakia
55 F2 Ust'Ishim U.S.S.R.
55 G3 Ust'Izes U.S.S.R.
31 K1 Ustka Poland
56 B6 Ust'-Kamenogorsk U.S.S.R.
58 G1 Ust'Karenga U.S.S.R.
55 C4 Ust'Katav U.S.S.R.
55 C3 Ust Kishert U.S.S.R.
52 H3 Ust'Koin U.S.S.R.
52 H4 Ust'Kulom U.S.S.R.
56 G3 Ust'-Kut U.S.S.R.
55 D2 Ust' Loz'va U.S.S.R.
52 C5 Ust' Luga U.S.S.R.
52 J2 Ust' Lyzha U.S.S.R.
51 N2 Ust'Maya U.S.S.R.
51 L3 Ust'-Muya U.S.S.R.
52 H4 Ust'Nem U.S.S.R.
59 K1 Ust'Niman U.S.S.R.
56 F4 Ust'-Ordynskiy U.S.S.R.
56 F4 Ust'Ordynskiy Buryat Nats Okr dist U.S.S.R.
47 G3 Ustovo Bulgaria
52 F4 Ust' Paden'ga U.S.S.R.
52 F3 Ust' Pinega U.S.S.R.
50 H2 Ust'-Port U.S.S.R.
52 F4 Ust' Puya U.S.S.R.
52 G4 Ust' Reka U.S.S.R.
31 O6 Ustrzyki Dolne Poland
52 D4 Ust'Sara U.S.S.R.
52 J3 Ust'-Shchugor U.S.S.R.
55 D1 Ust'-Tapsuy U.S.S.R.
55 F3 Ust'Tara U.S.S.R.
55 G3 Ust'Tarka U.S.S.R.
55 F3 Ust' Tava U.S.S.R.
52 H2 Ust' Tsil'ma U.S.S.R.
59 K1 Ust'Tyrma U.S.S.R.
52 J4 Ust' Un'ya U.S.S.R.
52 F3 Ust'ura U.S.S.R.
59 H1 Ust'urov U.S.S.R.
52 J2 Ust' Usa U.S.S.R.
55 D4 Ust'-Uyskoye U.S.S.R.
52 G3 Ust' Vacherga U.S.S.R.
52 J3 Ust'-Voya U.S.S.R.
52 G3 Ust' Vyyskaya U.S.S.R.
52 F4 Ust'ya R U.S.S.R.
52 E5 Ust'ye U.S.S.R.
52 E6 Ust'ye R U.S.S.R.
50 E4 Ustyurt,Plato U.S.S.R.
52 E5 Ustyuzhna U.S.S.R.
66 C3 Usu China
71 L10 Usu isld Indonesia
60 E12 Usuki Japan
125 P11 Usulután El Salvador
125 O9 Usumacinta R Mexico
70 D3 Usun Apau Plateau Sarawak
89 G6 Usutu R Swaziland
52 D6 Usvyaty U.S.S.R.
71 B2 Uta isld Indonesia
103 N2 Utah state U.S.A.
103 N1 Utah L Utah
29 M7 Utajärvi Finland
60 Q2 Utashinai Japan
99 L7 Ute Iowa
17 G3 Utebo Spain
106 G6 Ute Cr New Mexico
88 G6 Utenge,L Tanzania
106 E5 Ute Park New Mexico
37 P4 Uterý Czechoslovakia
55 G4 Utes U.S.S.R.
88 G6 Utete Tanzania
77 K7 Uthal Pakistan
32 J6 Uthlede W Germany
68 G5 Uthumphon Phisai Thailand
129 G6 Utiariti Brazil
107 K3 Utica Kansas
94 D4 Utica Michigan
99 P6 Utica Minnesota
111 F9 Utica Mississippi
110 C2 Utica Missouri
101 P3 Utica Montana
98 J9 Utica Nebraska
95 M3 Utica New York
94 E6 Utica Ohio
17 G5 Utiel Spain
26 K7 Utifällan Sweden
119 W3 Utik L Manitoba
145 E3 Utiku New Zealand
118 B3 Utikuma L Alberta
27 H16 Utklippan isld Sweden
27 C10 Utla R Norway
27 H15 Utlängan isld Sweden
109 K5 Utley Texas
106 G4 Utleyville Colorado
74 D1 Utmanzai Pakistan
27 K13 Utö Sweden
27 M12 Utö lt ho Finland
140 C5 Utopia N Terr Aust
109 H6 Utopia Texas
75 K5 Utraula India
25 D4 Utrecht Netherlands
89 G6 Utrecht S Africa
16 D7 Utrera Spain
27 A12 Utsira lt ho Norway
29 N2 Utsjoki Finland
61 N9 Utsunomiya Japan
53 G10 Utta U.S.S.R.
68 E4 Uttaradit Thailand
74 H4 Uttar Pradesh prov India
27 H12 Uttersberg Sweden
28 G7 Utterslev Denmark
36 H4 Üttingen W Germany
9 E2 Uttoxeter England
116 G2 Utukok R Alaska
137 O4 Utupua isld Santa Cruz Is
55 B5 Utva R U.S.S.R.
37 O3 Útvina Czechoslovakia
52 H6 Utyashkino U.S.S.R.
32 M8 Utze W Germany
33 S5 Utzedel E Germany
17 G3 uuadalope R Spain
29 O10 Uukuniem Finland
58 F2 Uuldza R Mongolia
29 L9 Uurainen Finland
Uusikaarlepyy see Nykarleby
29 J11 Uusikaupunki Finland
29 L11 Uusimaa prov Finland
52 H6 Uva U.S.S.R.
48 F7 Uvac R Yugoslavia
103 K2 Uvada Nevada
128 D3 Uva, L Colombia
112 E5 Uvalda Georgia
108 H6 Uvalde Texas
54 B4 Uvarovichi U.S.S.R.
52 E6 Uvarovka U.S.S.R.
55 E2 Uvat U.S.S.R.
137 O6 Uvéa isld Îles Loyauté Pacific Oc
137 R4 Uvea isld Îles Wallis Pacific Oc
55 D4 Uvel'skiy U.S.S.R.
55 D3 Uvil'dy, Oz L U.S.S.R.
88 C4 Uvinza Tanzania
88 B3 Uvira Zaïre
115 O3 Uvkusigssat Greenland
60 E13 Uwae Japan
60 F12 Uwajima Japan
84 H5 Uweinat,Jebel mt Sudan
135 V5 Uwekahuna Hawaiian Is
69 H12 Uwi isld Indonesia
9 F4 Uxbridge England
121 L8 Uxbridge Ontario
65 A5 Uxin Ju China
125 P7 Uxmal Mexico
55 D4 Uy R U.S.S.R.
116 K8 Uyak B Alaska
57 B3 Uyaly, Ozero L U.S.S.R.
51 O2 Uyandina R U.S.S.R.
56 D3 Uyar U.S.S.R.
15 G1 Uyea isld Scotland
15 G1 Uyeasound Scotland
50 H1 Uyedineniya,Ostrov isld U.S.S.R.
52 H2 Uyeg U.S.S.R.
85 F7 Uyo Nigeria
47 K6 Uysal Dağ mt Turkey
55 D4 Uyskoye U.S.S.R.
57 F3 Uyuk U.S.S.R.
133 D2 Uyuni Bolivia
48 G2 Uz R Czechoslovakia
57 B3 Uzbekistan S.S.R rep U.S.S.R.
48 F5 Uzdin Yugoslavia
53 G8 Uzen', Malyy R U.S.S.R.
57 G4 Uzgen U.S.S.R.
48 G2 Uzhgorod U.S.S.R.
48 H2 Uzhok U.S.S.R.
56 C3 Uzhur U.S.S.R.
48 F7 Užicka Požega Yugoslavia
41 J3 Uznach Switzerland
52 F6 Uzola R U.S.S.R.
47 K8 Üzümlü Turkey
47 H6 Uzun isld Turkey
88 E6 Uzungwa Tanzania
47 H3 Uzunköprü Turkey
57 B3 Uzynkair U.S.S.R.
29 M9 Vaajakoski Finland
89 E6 Vaal R S Africa
29 M7 Vaala Finland
89 F6 Vaal Dam S Africa
29 N11 Vaalimaa Finland
87 E10 Vaalwater S Africa
29 M8 Vaaraslahti Finland
21 F6 Vaas France
29 J8 Vaasa Finland
25 E4 Vaassen Netherlands
29 L4 Vaattojärvi Finland
28 H7 Våbensted Denmark
57 C5 Vabkent U.S.S.R.
130 C7 Vacaria,R Brazil
130 C7 Vacaria,Sa mts Brazil
131 B4 Vacas,Pta De Argentina
102 B3 Vacaville California
19 N17 Vaccarès, Etang de L France
52 F6 Vacha U.S.S.R.
126 H5 Vache, Île-à- Haiti
40 E5 Vacheresse France
19 N16 Vacqueyras France
52 F6 Vad U.S.S.R.
100 C3 Vader Washington
27 A10 Vadheim Norway
106 E5 Vadito New Mexico
27 B12 Vadla Norway
44 D3 Vado Italy
74 E7 Vadodara India
124 F2 Vado de Santa María Mexico
52 D1 Vadozero, Oz L U.S.S.R.
26 R1 Vadsö Norway
27 G13 Vadstenna Sweden
48 M6 Vadu Romania
28 D2 Vadum Denmark
41 L3 Vaduz Liechtenstein
28 H7 Væggerløse Denmark
28 K5 Værløsa Denmark
26 F4 Vaeröy Norway
28 G5 Værslev Denmark
28 N3 Våg Faeroes
26 J9 Vaga Sweden
52 F4 Vaga R U.S.S.R.
26 D10 Vågåmo Norway
26 G3 Vagan Norway
42 G4 Vaganski mt Yugoslavia
55 E2 Vagay U.S.S.R.
29 O2 Vaggetem U.S.S.R.
26 R2 Vaggetem-javrre L Norway
45 K4 Vaglia Italy
27 J13 Vagnahärad Sweden
28 M2 Vågø isld Faeroes
16 B4 Vagos Portugal
27 F11 Vägsjöfors Sweden
26 A10 Vågsöy isld Norway
31 L6 Váh R Czechoslovakia
29 J8 Vähäkyrö Finland
79 F8 Vahal Israel
146 D11 Vahsel B Antarctica
111 G8 Vaiden Mississippi
20 E5 Vaiges France
36 F6 Vaihingen W Germany
76 B1 Vaijapur India
52 C5 Väike-Maarja U.S.S.R.
26 L5 Vaikijaur Sweden
103 O9 Vail Arizona
15 G2 Vaila isld Scotland
22 F5 Vailly-sur-Aisne France
134 B1 Vailoa W Samoa
29 N11 Vainikkala Finland
45 Q7 Vairano Patenora Italy
21 B8 Vairé France
137 Q3 Vaitupu isld Tuvalu
47 F2 Vakarel Bulgaria
27 G11 Vakern Sweden
56 B1 Vakh R U.S.S.R.
57 F6 Vakhanskiy Khrebet mts U.S.S.R.
73 K1 Vakhsh R U.S.S.R.
57 E5 Vakhshstroy U.S.S.R.
52 G5 Vakhtan U.S.S.R.
52 D3 Vaknavolok U.S.S.R.
27 A11 Vaksdal Norway
26 F8 Vålådalen Sweden
76 E7 Valaichchenai Sri Lanka
40 F5 Valais canton Switzerland
52 H5 Valamaz U.S.S.R.
46 F3 Valandovo Yugoslavia
27 G12 Valåsen Sweden
95 O4 Valatie New York
47 G6 Valáxa isld Greece
38 E8 Val Badia Italy
121 P6 Val Barrette Quebec
26 G3 Valberg Norway
19 P15 Valbonnais France
122 E5 Val Brilliant Quebec
25 E5 Valburg Netherlands
133 D6 Valcheta Argentina
121 S7 Valcourt Quebec
41 O6 Valdagno Italy
16 D2 Valdavia R Spain
52 D5 Valday U.S.S.R.
52 D6 Valdayskaya Vozvyshennost' uplands U.S.S.R.
17 G4 Valde Algorfa Spain
16 D5 Valdecañas, Embalse de res Spain
17 F5 Valdeganga Spain
52 B6 Valdemārpils U.S.S.R.
27 J13 Valdemarsvik Sweden
16 E4 Valdemoro Spain
17 F4 Valdemoro-Sierra Spain
16 E6 Valdepeñas Spain
16 D3 Valderaduey R Spain
17 H4 Valderrobres Spain
99 T5 Valders Wisconsin
121 P7 Val des Bois Quebec
112 F2 Valdese N Carolina
133 E6 Valdés, Pen Argentina
116 O6 Valdez Alaska
106 F4 Valdez Colorado
131 A7 Valdivia Chile
131 A8 Valdivia prov Chile
20 C5 Val d'Izé France
20 K3 Val-d'Oise dep France
121 N4 Val-d'Or Quebec
113 D7 Valdosta Georgia
27 D11 Valdres plat Norway
19 P16 Valdrome France
9 G6 Vale Channel Is
100 H6 Vale Oregon
98 C5 Vale S Dakota
48 G3 Valea Lui Mihai Romania
48 J3 Valea Vişeului Romania
37 P3 Valeč Czechoslovakia
45 J1 Valéggio Italy
129 L6 Valença Brazil
21 I7 Valençay France
19 N15 Valence France
18 F8 Valence d'Agen France
18 F9 Valence-sur-Baïse France
17 G5 Valencia Spain
127 K9 Valencia Venezuela
17 G5 Valencia prov Spain
16 C5 Valência de Alcantara Spain
16 D2 Valencia de Don Juan Spain
16 B3 Valençia do Minho Portugal
17 H5 Valencia,G de Spain
14 A5 Valencia I Irish Rep
127 L9 Valencia,L.de Venezuela
22 F3 Valenciennes France
48 K5 Vălenii de Munte Romania
19 P17 Valensole France
59 K3 Valentin U.S.S.R.
103 L6 Valentine Arizona
111 F12 Valentine Louisiana
101 R2 Valentine Montana
98 F7 Valentine Nebraska
108 C5 Valentine Texas
44 E1 Valenza Italy
27 E11 Våler Norway
109 H4 Valera Texas
127 J10 Valera Venezuela
27 A12 Valestrand Norway
130 H5 Vale Verde Brazil
41 M4 Valfurva R Italy
52 C5 Valga U.S.S.R.
120 K4 Val Gagné Ontario
43 F11 Valguarnera Caropepe Sicily
101 N1 Valier Montana
28 K4 Välinge Sweden
48 F6 Valjevo Yugoslavia
26 P2 Valjok Norway
19 Q15 Valjouffrey France
29 L10 Valkeakoski Finland
29 M11 Valkeala Finland
29 L5 Valkeavaara mt Finland
25 E7 Valkenburg Netherlands
25 D6 Valkenswaard Netherlands
54 G7 Valki U.S.S.R.
29 M11 Valkom Finland
19 N17 Vallabrègues France
16 D3 Valladolid Spain
16 D3 Valladolid prov Spain
121 N4 Val Laflamme Quebec
41 P4 Vallarga Italy
41 O6 Vallarsa R Italy
103 M6 Valle Arizona
27 C12 Valle Norway
38 E7 Valle Aurina Italy
106 C4 Vallecito Res Colorado
106 D5 Vallecitos New Mexico
45 O7 Vallecorsa Italy
131 B2 Valle Cura,Rio Del Argentina
42 A3 Valle d'Aosta Italy
40 G6 Valle d'Aosta aut reg Italy
124 G7 Valle de Banderas Mexico
16 E1 Valle de Cabuérniga Spain
127 M10 Valle de la Pascua Venezuela
128 C3 Valle del Cauca div Colombia
124 F4 Valle de Olivos Mexico
124 F4 Valle de Rosario Mexico
124 G4 Valle de Zaragoza Mexico
126 H9 Valledupar Colombia
85 E5 Vallée de Zgarat Mali
122 B7 Vallée Jonction Quebec
85 E5 Vallée L'Azawak Mali/Niger
131 C3 Valle Fértil, Sa. de mts Argentina
128 F7 Valle Grande Bolivia
40 C5 Valleiry France
102 B3 Vallejo California
45 P7 Vallemaio Italy
26 M7 Vallen Västerbotten Sweden
26 J8 Vallen Väster Norrland Sweden
131 B2 Vallenar Chile
36 D3 Vallendar W Germany
28 H6 Vallensved Denmark
45 O6 Vallepretra Italy
133 E2 Valle,R.del Argentina
21 C7 Vallet France
43 F13 Valletta Malta
111 F9 Valley Mississippi
98 K8 Valley Nebraska
122 J8 Valley Nova Scotia
8 B1 Valley Wales
100 H1 Valley Washington
101 Q5 Valley Wyoming
107 N4 Valley Center Kansas
118 K7 Valley Centre Sask
98 J3 Valley City N Dakota
107 P2 Valley Falls Kansas
100 E7 Valley Falls Oregon
121 Q7 Valleyfield Quebec
111 L7 Valley Head Alabama
94 G8 Valley Head W Virginia
109 K4 Valley Mills Texas
116 K7 Valley of Ten Thousand Smokes Alaska
110 F3 Valley Park Missouri
101 L8 Valley Pass Nevada
94 B8 Valley Sta Kentucky
117 P8 Valleyview Alberta
109 K2 Valley View Texas
Vallgrund isld see Rappaluolo
109 M2 Valliant Oklahoma
45 M2 Valli di Comacchio reg Italy
21 J10 Vallières France
18 F10 Vallier, Mt France
121 P6 Val Limoges Quebec
20 G2 Valliquerville France
28 J6 Valløby Denmark
43 G8 Vallo di Diano Italy
43 G8 Vallo di Lucania Italy
45 L4 Vallombrosa Italy
94 A8 Vallonia Indiana
21 E6 Vallon-sur-Gée France
40 D4 Vallorbe Switzerland
27 D12 Vallöy Norway
17 H3 Valls Spain
27 H10 Vallsta Sweden
41 M3 Valluga mt Austria
27 J10 Vallvik Sweden
118 K9 Val Marie Sask
16 E1 Valmaseda Spain
31 K6 Val. Meziříčí Czechoslovakia
52 C5 Valmiera U.S.S.R.
20 K3 Valmondois France
20 G2 Valmont France
106 E9 Valmont New Mexico
45 N6 Valmontone Italy
100 H9 Valmy Nevada
16 E1 Valnera mt Spain
20 C3 Valognes France
Valona see Vlorë
16 D3 Valoria la Buena Spain
16 C3 Valpaços Portugal
76 C5 Valparai India
131 B4 Valparaíso Chile
111 K11 Valparaiso Florida
99 T8 Valparaiso Indiana
124 H6 Valparaíso Mexico
98 K8 Valparaiso Nebraska
119 N6 Valparaiso Sask
131 B4 Valparaiso prov Chile
40 F6 Valpelline V Italy
48 E5 Valpovo Yugoslavia
40 G7 Valprato Soana Italy
122 A8 Val-Racine Quebec
19 N16 Valréas France
89 E6 Vals R S Africa
28 H7 Vålse Denmark
100 B5 Valsetz Oregon
28 D3 Valsgård Denmark
26 G7 Valsjö Sweden
27 H12 Valskog Sweden
29 J8 Valsörarna lt ho Finland
41 L5 Valtellina V Italy
45 M4 Val Tiberina Italy
29 O8 Valtimo Finland
54 K6 Valuyki U.S.S.R.
85 A3 Valverde Canary Is
127 J5 Valverde Dom Rep
17 F5 Valverde de Júcar Spain
16 C7 Valverde del Camino Spain
26 M5 Valvträsk Sweden
48 K3 Vama Romania
28 C6 Vamdrup Denmark
27 G10 Våmhus Sweden
88 H7 Vamizi isld Mozambique
27 E12 Vamma Norway
29 K10 Vammala Finland
47 G9 Vámos Crete Greece
48 G3 Vámospéros Hungary
109 M3 Van Texas
78 J2 Van Turkey
29 L10 Vanajanselka L Finland
109 L2 Van Alstyne Texas
101 S3 Vananda Montana
56 F1 Vanavara U.S.S.R.
68 G1 Van-Ban Vietnam
121 S5 Van Bruyssel Quebec
110 B6 Van Buren Arkansas
94 B6 Van Buren Indiana
95 T6 Van Buren Maine
110 F5 Van Buren Missouri
68 J6 Van Canh Vietnam
22 K4 Vance Belgium
21 G6 Vancé France
112 K2 Vanceboro N Carolina
94 D8 Vanceburg Kentucky
68 G2 Van Chan Vietnam
57 F5 Vanchskiy Khrebet mts U.S.S.R.
117 G11 Vancouver Br Col
100 C4 Vancouver Washington
116 E6 Vancouver, C Alaska
143 C10 Vancouver,C W Australia
117 K10 Vancouver I Br Col
117 D5 Vancouver, Mt Alaska/Yukon Terr
110 G3 Vandalia Illinois
110 E2 Vandalia Missouri
41 L3 Vandans Austria
28 A3 Vandborg Denmark
119 Q1 Vandekerckhove Sask
28 C5 Vandel Denmark
112 L2 Vandemere N Carolina
89 E6 Vanderbijl Pk S Africa
94 C1 Vanderbilt Michigan
109 L7 Vanderbilt Texas
94 H6 Vandergrift Pennsylvania
117 M8 Vanderhoof Br Columbia
140 D3 Vanderlin I N Terr Aust
109 N1 Vandervoort Arkansas
28 B2 Vandet Sø Denmark
136 G4 Van Diemen N Terr Australia
140 E3 Van Diemen,C Queensland
140 B1 Van Diemen G N Terr Aust
140 F3 Van Diemen R Queensland
55 E1 Vandmtor, Oz L U.S.S.R.
121 R5 Vandry Quebec
110 G5 Vanduser Missouri
100 A9 Van Duzen R California
27 F13 Vänern L Sweden
27 F13 Vänersborg Sweden
95 L4 Van Etten New York
27 C10 Vang Norway
88 G4 Vanga Tanzania
87 H12 Vangaindrano Madagascar
27 F13 Vanga,N Sweden
78 J2 Van Gölü L Turkey
27 C10 Vangsmjösa Norway
118 K9 Vanguard Sask
70 A1 Vanguard Bank S China Sea
137 M3 Vangunu isld Solomon Is
68 F3 Vang Vieng Laos
26 S2 Vanhakylä U.S.S.R.
98 D2 Van Hook N Dakota
108 C4 Van Horn Texas
106 F5 Van Houten New Mexico
137 O4 Vanikoro Is Santa Cruz Is
26 K7 Vänjaurbäck Sweden
26 K7 Vänjaurträsk Sweden
51 S2 Vankarem U.S.S.R.
121 Q7 Vankleek Hill Ontario
98 F5 Van Metre S Dakota
26 L1 Vanna isld Norway
26 L8 Vännäs Sweden
83 J9 Vannativillu Sri Lanka
18 D5 Vannes France
21 J6 Vannes sur-Cosson France
68 J6 Van Ninh Vietnam
107 O7 Vanoss Oklahoma
87 C12 Vanrhynsdorp S Africa
141 F3 Vanrook Queensland
94 E9 Vansant Virginia
27 G11 Vansbro Sweden
118 L6 Vanscoy Sask
142 F2 Vansittart B W Australia
115 L4 Vansittart I N W Terr
18 H8 Vans, les France
29 L11 Vantaa Finland
29 L11 Vantaa R Finland
118 L9 Vantage Sask
100 F3 Vantage Washington
98 B7 Van Tassell Wyoming
137 O3 Vanua Lava isld New Hebrides
137 Q5 Vanua Levu isld Fiji
99 N9 Van Wert Iowa
94 C6 Van Wert Ohio
87 D12 Vanwyksvlei S Africa
67 A6 Van Yen Vietnam
26 A9 Vanylven Norway
26 A9 Vanylvsgapet B Norway
110 D5 Vanzant Missouri
48 M2 Vapnyarka U.S.S.R.
19 Q18 Var dep France
44 B4 Var R France
27 F13 Vara Sweden
44 G3 Vara R Italy
126 D3 Varadero Cuba
21 C7 Varades France
19 P17 Varages France
44 B2 Varaita R Italy
41 H6 Varallo Italy
42 B3 Varallo Italy
77 B2 Varamin Iran
75 K6 Varanasi India
26 R1 Varangerfjorden inlet Norway
26 R1 Varangerhalvöya mt Norway
42 G7 Varano, L. di Italy
131 A8 Varas,Pto Chile
16 D6 Varas,R Spain
20 E3 Varaville France
44 E3 Varazze Italy
27 F14 Varberg Sweden
111 G8 Vardaman Mississippi
46 E6 Vardhoúsia Óri mt Greece
27 L11 Vårdö Finland
26 S1 Vardö Norway
52 E5 Varegovo U.S.S.R.
32 H6 Varel W Germany
20 G2 Varengeville France
20 B3 Varenguebec France
20 D5 Varenne R France
21 I7 Varennes France
19 J3 Varennes en Argonne France
40 B5 Varennes St.Sauveur France
48 E6 Vareš Yugoslavia
41 J6 Varese Italy
40 A7 Vareze R France
27 F13 Vårgårda Sweden
55 E3 Vargashi U.S.S.R.
130 G10 Vargem R Brazil
130 F7 Varginha Brazil
18 G9 Varilhes France
112 J2 Varina N Carolina
27 G13 Väring Sweden
20 J5 Varize France
26 K5 Varjisträsk Sweden
29 N9 Varkaus Finland
143 C10 Varley,L W Australia
27 F12 Varmland reg Sweden
47 J1 Varna Bulgaria
55 D4 Varna U.S.S.R.
111 G11 Varnado Louisiana
28 D6 Varnæs Denmark
27 G14 Värnamo Sweden
27 F11 Värnäs Sweden
52 F5 Varnavino U.S.S.R.
108 B1 Varney New Mexico
31 H5 Varnsdorf Czechoslovakia
27 F14 Varnum Sweden
112 F5 Varnville S Carolina
79 D3 Varosha Cyprus
48 D3 Városlöd Hungary
48 E3 Várpalota Hungary
18 F7 Vars France
52 G2 Varsh, Oz L U.S.S.R.
28 E3 Vårst Denmark
78 H2 Varto Turkey
27 G13 Vartofta Sweden
76 E6 Varuniya Sri Lanka
46 E7 Varvára mt Greece
46 E1 Varvarin Yugoslavia
54 C10 Varvarovka U.S.S.R.
130 G9 Várzea Alegre Brazil
130 G5 Várzea da Palma Brazil
129 G7 Várzea Grande Brazil
130 E9 Várzea,R Brazil
52 E1 Varzino U.S.S.R.
52 E2 Varzuga U.S.S.R.
52 E2 Varzuga R U.S.S.R.
18 H5 Varzy France
48 D3 Vas co Hungary
130 H11 Vasa Barris,R Brazil
52 B5 Vasalemma U.S.S.R.
48 G2 Vásárosnamény Hungary
28 K4 Väsby Sweden
16 B7 Vascâo R Portugal
48 G4 Vaşcau Romania
20 H3 Vascoeuil France
17 F2 Vascongadas reg Spain
52 G3 Vashka R U.S.S.R.
48 K2 Vashkovtsy U.S.S.R.
100 C2 Vashon I Washington
98 G2 Vashti N Dakota
109 J2 Vashti Texas
52 G3 Vasil'evo U.S.S.R.
54 H8 Vasil'kovka U.S.S.R.
55 F2 Vasiss U.S.S.R.
52 C5 Vasknarva U.S.S.R.
29 M3 Vaskojoki R Finland
48 E4 Vaskút Hungary
21 E8 Vasles France
48 L4 Vaslui Romania
112 H2 Vass N Carolina
118 F1 Vassar Manitoba
94 D3 Vassar Michigan
27 B12 Vassdalseggja mt Norway
26 K3 Vassijuare Sweden
20 D4 Vassy France
26 J4 Vastenjaure L Sweden
27 J12 Västerås Sweden
26 H7 Västerbotten reg Sweden
27 F11 Vasterdalälven R Sweden
26 J5 Västerfjäll Sweden
27 K12 Västerhaninge Sweden
27 H12 Västermo Sweden
26 J7 Vastermyrriset Sweden
26 J8 Väster Norr Land Sweden
27 J14 Västervik Sweden
27 J11 Västland Sweden
27 H12 Västmanland reg Sweden
42 F6 Vasto Italy
33 N6 Vastorf W Germany
26 L8 Vastra Kvarken chan Sweden
48 D3 Vasvár Hungary
55 G2 Vasyugan R U.S.S.R.
21 I7 Vatan France
137 O4 Vatganai isld New Hebrides
33 P8 Väthen E Germany
47 H7 Vathí Greece
46 E8 Váthia Greece
45 M6 Vaticano, Citta del Italy
115 S5 Vatnajökull ice cap Iceland
26 B9 Vatne Norway
115 R4 Vatneyri Iceland
27 K12 Vätö Sweden
137 R5 Vatoa isld Fiji
87 H11 Vatomandry Madagascar
48 J3 Vatra Dornei Romania
27 G13 Vättern L Sweden
41 K4 Vättis Switzerland
26 J10 Vattrång Sweden
40 C5 Vauche Marlioz,Mt.De France
127 M4 Vauclin Martinique W Indies
112 F4 Vaucluse S Carolina
19 O17 Vaucluse dep France
40 C2 Vauconcourt France
20 F2 Vaucottes France
19 J4 Vaucouleurs France
36 B6 Vaucourt France
40 D4 Vaud canton Switzerland
20 H3 Vaudreuil, Le France
122 H9 Vaughan Nova Scotia
140 B5 Vaughan Springs N Terr Aust
101 O2 Vaughn Montana
108 B1 Vaughn New Mexico
128 D3 Vaupés div Colombia
18 H9 Vauvert France
20 B2 Vauville France
40 D2 Vauvillers France
118 E8 Vauxhall Alberta
87 J11 Vavatenina Madagascar
137 S5 Vava'u Group islds Tonga
52 H6 Vavozh U.S.S.R.
83 K9 Vavuniya Sri Lanka
118 J5 Vawn Sask
27 K12 Vaxholm Sweden
27 G15 Växjö Sweden
76 D4 Vayalpod India
50 F1 Vaygach, Ostrov isld U.S.S.R.
52 F3 Vaymuga R U.S.S.R.
129 L5 Vaza R Brazil
130 F5 Vazante Brazil
52 G3 Vazhgort U.S.S.R.
47 G2 Vazovgrad Bulgaria
129 J6 Veadeiras Brazil
68 F7 Veal Renh Cambodia
28 D3 Vebbestrup Denmark
98 J4 Veblen S Dakota
26 M7 Vebomark Sweden
33 M8 Vechelde W Germany
25 F3 Vecht R Netherlands
32 H7 Vechta W Germany
32 H7 Vechta R W Germany
32 L10 Veckerhagen W Germany
27 J12 Veckholm Sweden
28 K5 Vedbæk Denmark
27 F14 Veddige Sweden
28 E3 Veddum Denmark
48 J6 Vedea Romania
28 A4 Vedersø Denmark
27 H12 Vedevåg Sweden
133 E4 Vedia Argentina
17 H6 Vedra isld Balearic Is
22 H3 Vedrin Belgium
28 E5 Vedslet Denmark
28 C6 Vedsted Denmark
28 G6 Ved Stranden Denmark
27 F13 Vedum Sweden
110 J1 Veedersburg Indiana
25 G2 Veendam Netherlands
25 E4 Veenendaal Netherlands
25 F2 Veenhuizen Netherlands
25 E2 Veenwouden Netherlands
25 A5 Veere Netherlands
25 A5 Veerse Meer Netherlands
33 N7 Veerssen W Germany
28 E6 Veflinge Denmark
26 E6 Vega isld Norway
16 C2 Vega de Tera Spain
27 D13 Vegårs Vatn L Norway
28 K4 Vegeån R Sweden
32 J6 Vegesack W Germany
28 D3 Veggerby Denmark
27 D11 Veggli Norway
46 E4 Vegorrítis, L Greece
118 F5 Vegreville Alberta
108 A1 Veguita New Mexico
33 Q6 Vehlow E Germany
27 M11 Vehmaa Finland
52 E4 Veilikaya Guba U.S.S.R.
26 P1 Veines Norway
27 F15 Veinge Sweden
120 D3 Vein L Ontario
133 D5 Veinticinco de Mayo Argentina
45 M5 Veio Italy
36 H4 Veitshöchheim W Germany
28 J4 Vejby Denmark
28 C6 Vejen Denmark
28 A5 Vejers Denmark
28 D4 Vejerslev Denmark
28 E2 Vejgård Denmark
28 E4 Vejlby Århus Denmark
28 D5 Vejlby Vejle Denmark
28 D5 Vejle Denmark
28 C5 Vejle co Denmark
28 D5 Vejle Fjord inlet Denmark
28 H6 Vejlø Denmark
28 E7 Vejnæs Nokke C Denmark
37 P3 Vejprty Czechoslovakia
28 G5 Vejrhøj hill Denmark
28 F5 Vejrø isld Århus Denmark
28 G6 Vejrø isld Storstrøm Denmark
28 B5 Vejrup Denmark
28 F6 Vejstrup Denmark
28 J5 Veksø Denmark
52 F4 Vel R U.S.S.R.
127 H8 Vela, C. de la Colombia
22 E2 Velaines Belgium
46 E5 Velaóra Greece
106 E5 Velarde New Mexico
124 H5 Velardeña Mexico
16 C7 Vela Real de Sto António Portugal
109 M7 Velasco Texas
18 H7 Velay, Mts du France
32 F10 Velbert W Germany
37 M5 Velburg W Germany
37 M4 Velden W Germany
25 D6 Veldhoven Netherlands
47 J2 Veleka R Bulgaria
32 E9 Velen W Germany
48 E3 Velencei Tó L Hungary
46 F5 Velestínon Greece
17 F7 Vélez Bianco Spain
16 E8 Vélez Málaga Spain
17 F7 Vélez Rubio Spain
26 F6 Velfjord Norway
33 R4 Velgast E Germany
130 G6 Velhas,R Brazil
42 H3 Velika Yugoslavia
48 G6 Velika Gradište Yugoslavia
42 F3 Velika Kapela dist Yugoslavia
48 G6 Velika Plana Yugoslavia
52 G2 Velikaya U.S.S.R.
52 C6 Velikaya R U.S.S.R.
52 G5 Velikaya R U.S.S.R.
48 K1 Veliki Borki U.S.S.R.
48 K1 Veliki Glubochek U.S.S.R.
52 D6 Velikiye-Luki U.S.S.R.
52 G4 Velikiy Ustyug U.S.S.R.
54 M1 Velikodvorskiy U.S.S.R.
47 H1 Veliko Turnovo Bulgaria
52 H2 Velikovisochnoye U.S.S.R.
52 F5 Velikovo U.S.S.R.
54 M1 Velikoye, Oz L U.S.S.R.
85 B6 Velingara Senegal
47 F2 Velingrad Bulgaria
42 E6 Velino R Italy
42 E6 Velino, M mt Italy
54 C1 Velizh U.S.S.R.
48 E2 Velká Fatra mt Czechoslovakia
48 E1 Vel Karlovice Czechoslovakia
48 G2 Vel'ké Kapušány Czechoslovakia
31 L6 Velké Karlovice Czechoslovakia
48 G2 Velki Berezny U.S.S.R.
48 D3 Velký ŽitnÝ Ostrov' reg Czechoslovakia
38 L8 Vellach Austria
33 N6 Vellahn E Germany
137 M3 Vella Lavella isld Solomon Is
45 J4 Vellano Italy
36 H5 Vellberg W Germany
45 N6 Velletri Italy
28 D4 Vellev Denmark
28 A4 Velling Denmark
27 F16 Vellinge Sweden
45 O5 Vellino, M mt Italy
76 D4 Vellore India
56 D1 Vel'mo R U.S.S.R.
22 J5 Velosnes France
25 E4 Velp Netherlands
25 C4 Velsen Netherlands
52 F4 Vel'sk U.S.S.R.
52 H1 Vel't U.S.S.R.
33 S7 Velten E Germany
25 E4 Veluwe Netherlands
25 E4 Veluwemeer Netherlands
98 F1 Velva N Dakota
90 E7 Vema Fracture Atlantic Oc
28 A4 Vemb Denmark
26 G9 Vemdalen Sweden
28 G6 Vemmelev Denmark
28 F7 Vemmenæs Denmark
59 M2 Vemor'Ye U.S.S.R.
28 K5 Ven isld Sweden
27 H14 Vena Sweden
27 D10 Venabygd Norway
12 D1 Venachar,L Scotland
131 E4 Venado Tuerto Argentina
45 Q7 Venafro Italy
128 F2 Venamo,Cerro mt Venezuela/Guyana
98 E9 Venango Nebraska
141 F4 Vena Park Queensland
44 C1 Venaria Italy
100 G6 Venator Oregon
130 E8 Venceslau Bráz Brazil
Venda see Vantaa
45 L1 Venda mt Italy
16 B6 Vendas Novas Portugal
21 C8 Vendée dep France
36 D6 Vendenheim France
22 D3 Vendin-le-Viel France
21 H6 Vendôme France
17 H3 Vendrell Spain
22 H4 Vendresse France
28 D2 Vendsyssel reg Denmark
45 M1 Veneta, Laguna Italy
116 P3 Venetie Landing Alaska
45 K1 Veneto reg Italy
52 F6 Venets U.S.S.R.
54 K2 Venev U.S.S.R.
45 M1 Venezia Italy
42 D3 Venezia-Euganea prov Italy
42 E3 Venezia,G.di Italy
128 E2 Venezuela rep S America
127 J9 Venezuela,G.de Venezuela
28 D4 Veng Denmark
55 G3 Vengerovo U.S.S.R.
76 A3 Vengurla India
16 D3 Venialbo Spain
116 H8 Veniaminof Vol Alaska
118 E4 Venice Alberta
113 E10 Venice Florida
Venice Italy see Venezia
111 G12 Venice Louisiana
111 M12 Venice St Louis
19 N13 Vénissieux France
27 G11 Venjan Sweden
76 D4 Venkataguri India
76 E1 Venkatapuram India
98 J3 Venlo N Dakota
25 F6 Venlo Netherlands
119 M7 Venn Sask
28 D2 Vennebjerg Denmark
32 E7 Vennebrügge W Germany
27 C13 Vennesla Norway
28 B3 Venø Denmark
28 B3 Venø Bugt B Denmark
19 Q15 Venosc France
121 O7 Venosta Quebec
41 N4 Venosta, Val Italy
41 N4 Venostie, Alpi Italy
25 E5 Venray Netherlands
27 M14 Venta R U.S.S.R.
124 E5 Ventana,Pta de la C Mexico
133 E5 Ventana,Sa ra Argentina
16 E8 Ventas de Zafarraya Spain
28 H5 Vented Denmark
44 C4 Ventimiglia Italy
9 E6 Ventnor England
43 E8 Ventotene isld Italy
19 O16 Ventoux, Mt France
33 P5 Ventschow E Germany
27 M14 Ventspils U.S.S.R.
128 E3 Ventuari R Venezuela
102 E7 Ventura California
98 G3 Venturia N Dakota
113 F10 Venus Florida
109 K3 Venus Texas
138 C5 Venus B S Australia
124 H8 Venustiano Carranza Mexico
52 D4 Vepsovskaya Vozvyshennost' uplands U.S.S.R.
133 E3 Vera Argentina
17 F7 Vera Spain
109 H2 Vera Texas
133 D6 Vera, B Argentina
130 E8 Vera Cruz Brazil
125 L8 Veracruz Mexico
74 D8 Veraval India
42 B3 Verbania Italy
111 K9 Verbena Alabama
22 D5 Verberie France
52 E6 Verbilki U.S.S.R.
41 H7 Vercelli Italy
33 R5 Verchen E Germany
19 O15 Vercors reg France
19 Q16 Verdaches France
26 E8 Verdal Norway
26 E8 Verdalsöra Norway
71 E4 Verde isld Philippines
133 D6 Verde R Argentina
103 N7 Verde R Arizona
130 E4 Verde R Brazil
133 F2 Verde R Paraguay
85 A6 Verde, C Senegal
126 G3 Verde, Cay isld Bahamas
130 G4 Verde Grande R Brazil
98 H7 Verdel Nebraska
109 J1 Verden Oklahoma
32 K7 Verden W Germany
131 E7 Verde,Pen Argentina
130 G4 Verde Pequeno, R Brazil
130 D7 Verde,R Brazil
21 H6 Verdes France
98 H7 Verdigre Nebraska
107 O3 Verdigris R Okla/Kansas
118 F9 Verdigris L Alberta
130 D5 Verdinho,Sa.do mts Brazil
99 L9 Verdon Nebraska
19 Q17 Verdon R France
18 E7 Verdon, le France
19 J3 Verdun France
18 F9 Verdun-sur-Garonne France
19 J6 Verdun-sur-le-Doubs France
124 E5 Verdura Mexico
52 D6 Vereche U.S.S.R.
89 E6 Vereeniging S Africa
119 P7 Veregin Sask
98 D2 Verendrye Nat.Mon N Dakota
121 N5 Vérendrye, Parc Prov. de la Quebec
52 H5 Vereshchagino U.S.S.R.
52 E5 Verestovo, Oz L U.S.S.R.
54 H1 Vereya U.S.S.R.
85 B6 Verga,C Guinea
17 F1 Vergara Spain
133 G4 Vergara Uruguay
45 K3 Vergato Italy
36 B6 Vergaville France
141 G6 Vergemont Queensland
141 G6 Vergemont R Queensland
95 O2 Vergennes Vermont
45 L4 Verghereto Italy
45 R8 Vérgine, M mt Italy
16 C3 Verín Spain
41 K1 Veringenstadt W Germany
87 D7 Verissimo Sarmento Angola
56 H3 Verkh Angara R U.S.S.R.
55 C3 Verkhiye Kigi U.S.S.R.
52 J5 Verkhnaya Yarva U.S.S.R.
56 H3 Verkhneangarskiy Khrebet mts U.S.S.R.
55 C4 Verkhnearshinskiy U.S.S.R.
55 C4 Verkhne-Avzyan U.S.S.R.
54 F8 Verkhnedneprovsk U.S.S.R.
54 E2 Verkhnedneprovskiy U.S.S.R.
55 D4 Verkhnesanarskiy U.S.S.R.
52 E4 Verkhne Svirskoye Vod res U.S.S.R.
29 Q3 Verkhnetulomskiy U.S.S.R.
55 C4 Verkhneural'sk U.S.S.R.
52 H6 Verkhne Yarkeyevo U.S.S.R.
54 K8 Verkhneye U.S.S.R.
55 G3 Verkhneye Krasnoyarka U.S.S.R.
52 D2 Verkhneye Kuyto, Oz L U.S.S.R.

130 H10 **Volta** Brazil
41 N7 **Volta** Italy
85 E7 **Volta** *R* Ghana
85 D6 **Volta Blanche** *R* Upper Volta/Ghana
98 F1 **Voltaire** N Dakota
142 F2 **Voltaire, C** W Australia
85 D7 **Volta,L** Ghana
85 D6 **Volta Noire** *R* Upper Volta
130 G8 **Volta Redonda** Brazil
85 D6 **Volta Rouge** *R* Upper Volta/Ghana
42 D5 **Volterra** Italy
52 F3 **Volteva** U.S.S.R.
44 E3 **Voltri** Italy
45 R8 **Volturara Irpina** Italy
45 Q7 **Volturno** *R* Italy
47 F4 **Vólvi, L** Greece
19 P17 **Volx** France
52 G6 **Volzhsk** U.S.S.R.
53 F9 **Volzhskiy** U.S.S.R.
42 F6 **Vomano** *R* Italy
106 H2 **Vona** Colorado
118 L6 **Vonda** Sask
87 H12 **Vondrozo** Madagascar
22 J3 **Vonêche** Belgium
116 K5 **Von Frank Mt** Alaska
52 F3 **Vonga** U.S.S.R.
28 C5 **Vonge** Denmark
40 B3 **Vonges** France
46 D6 **Vónitsa** Greece
129 H5 **Von Martius,Cachoeira** *rapids* Brazil
21 F9 **Vonne** *R* France
28 D6 **Vonsbæk** Denmark
28 C6 **Vonsild** Denmark
25 B4 **Voorburg** Netherlands
25 B5 **Voorne** Netherlands
25 B4 **Voorschoten** Netherlands
25 F4 **Voorst** Netherlands
25 E4 **Voorthuizen** Netherlands
115 S4 **Vopnafjördhur** Iceland
25 F6 **Vopst** W Germany
29 J8 **Vörå** Finland
41 K4 **Vorab** *mt* Switzerland
41 L3 **Vorarlberg** *prov* Austria
38 N7 **Vorau** Austria
28 C5 **Vorbasse** Denmark
25 F4 **Vorden** Netherlands
32 H8 **Vörden** W Germany
38 L7 **Vordernberg** Austria
41 J4 **Vorder Rhein** *R* Switzerland
28 H6 **Vordingborg** Denmark
19 P14 **Voreppe** France
54 D3 **Vorga** U.S.S.R.
28 B4 **Vorgod** Denmark
47 G5 **Voríai Sporádhes** *islds* Greece
50 F2 **Vorkuta** U.S.S.R.
27 E11 **Vorma** *R* Norway
28 D3 **Vorning** Denmark
55 G3 **Vorob'yevo** U.S.S.R.
53 F8 **Vorona** *R* U.S.S.R.
54 C3 **Voronevo** U.S.S.R.
54 E5 **Voronezh** Ukraine U.S.S.R.
54 L5 **Voronezh** Voronezh U.S.S.R.
54 L4 **Voronezh** *R* U.S.S.R.
48 M1 **Voronovitsa** U.S.S.R.
52 F2 **Voronov, Mys** *C* U.S.S.R.
55 D2 **Vorontsovka** U.S.S.R.
52 C6 **Vorontsovo** U.S.S.R.
52 E1 **Voron'ya** *R* U.S.S.R.
52 F5 **Voron'ye** U.S.S.R.
54 L8 **Voroshilovgrad** U.S.S.R.
52 G5 **Voroshno** U.S.S.R.
54 N1 **Vorovskogo, im** U.S.S.R.
54 F5 **Vorozhba** U.S.S.R.
33 S5 **Vorpommern** *reg* E Germany
33 N8 **Vorsfelde** W Germany
54 G6 **Vorskala** *R* U.S.S.R.
52 F6 **Vorsma** U.S.S.R.
52 C5 **Vörtsjäry** U.S.S.R.
52 C5 **Võru** U.S.S.R.
28 E4 **Vorup** Denmark
55 D1 **Vor'ya** *R* U.S.S.R.
55 D1 **Vor'yapaul'** U.S.S.R.
52 H3 **Vorykva** *R* U.S.S.R.
36 B7 **Vosges** *dep* France
40 E2 **Vosges** *mt* France
55 C4 **Voskresenskoye** Bashkirskaya U.S.S.R.
52 G6 **Voskresenskoye** Gor'ki U.S.S.R.
52 E5 **Voskresenskoye** Vologda U.S.S.R.
55 F4 **Vosnesenka** U.S.S.R.
27 B11 **Voss** Norway
56 B6 **Vost Kazakhstanskaya Oblast'** *prov* U.S.S.R.
52 E1 **Vostochnaya Litsa** U.S.S.R.
57 H2 **Vostochno-Kounradskiy** U.S.S.R.
56 E4 **Vostochnyy Sayan** *mts* U.S.S.R.
146 F13 **Vostok,C** Antarctica
135 M9 **Vostok I** Pacific Oc
55 E1 **Vostykhoy** U.S.S.R.
109 N5 **Votaw** Texas
109 N5 **Voth** Texas
31 H6 **Votice** Czechoslovakia
52 H6 **Votkinsk** U.S.S.R.
130 E7 **Votuporanga** Brazil
16 B4 **Vouga** *R* Portugal
46 E5 **Voulgára** *mt* Greece
46 E5 **Voulgarélion** Greece
19 N15 **Voulte, la** France
46 E4 **Voúrinos** *mt* Greece
20 E5 **Voutré** France
21 G7 **Vouvray** France
21 J7 **Vouzeron** France
22 G5 **Vouziers** France
21 J6 **Vouzon** France
20 J5 **Voves** France
27 H10 **Voxna** Sweden
27 H10 **Voxnan** Sweden
27 G14 **Voxtorp** Sweden
52 H5 **Voya** *R* U.S.S.R.
146 G2 **Voyeykov Ice Shelf** Antarctica
52 D2 **Voynitsa** U.S.S.R.
52 H3 **Voy Vozh** U.S.S.R.
52 J3 **Voyvozh** U.S.S.R.
52 G3 **Vozhayel'** U.S.S.R.
52 F4 **Vozhega** U.S.S.R.
52 E4 **Vozhe, Oz** *L* U.S.S.R.
52 H5 **Vozhgaly** U.S.S.R.
52 G3 **Vozhgora** U.S.S.R.
54 C9 **Voznesensk** U.S.S.R.
52 E4 **Voznesenye** U.S.S.R.
55 F4 **Vozvyshenskiy** U.S.S.R.
28 D2 **Vrå** Denmark
48 E2 **Vráble** Czechoslovakia
27 C12 **Vrådalsv** *L* Norway
28 C4 **Vrads** Denmark
46 E6 **Vrakhnéïka** Greece
42 H5 **Vran** *mt* Yugoslavia
48 K5 **Vrancea** *reg* Romania
48 K5 **Vrancei, Muntii** *mts* Romania
147 P3 **Vrangelya, Os** *isld* U.S.S.R.
42 H5 **Vranica** *mt* Yugoslavia
46 E2 **Vranje** Yugoslavia
48 G2 **Vranov** Czechoslovakia
22 G1 **Vrasene** Belgium
47 F1 **Vratsa** Bulgaria
42 H4 **Vrbas** *R* Yugoslavia
31 K5 **Vrbno** Czechoslovakia
31 J5 **Vrchlabí** Czechoslovakia
48 F5 **Vrdnik** Yugoslavia
89 F6 **Vrede** S Africa
32 E8 **Vreden** W Germany
32 G7 **Vrees** W Germany
25 D4 **Vreeswijk** Netherlands
28 D2 **Vrensted** Denmark
28 F6 **Vresen** *isld* Denmark
22 H4 **Vress** France
20 B3 **Vrétot, le** France
27 G12 **Vretstorp** Sweden
42 H5 **Vrgorac** Yugoslavia
76 D5 **Vriddhachalam** India
28 C4 **Vridsted** Denmark
25 G2 **Vries** Netherlands
25 G4 **Vriezenveen** Netherlands
27 G14 **Vrigstad** Sweden
41 K4 **Vrin** Switzerland
22 H4 **Vringe-aux-Bois** France
28 A3 **Vrist** Denmark
22 F3 **Vrith-St.Léger** France
22 H5 **Vrizy** France
28 A5 **Vrøgum** Denmark
22 B3 **Vron** France
47 H6 **Vrondádhes** Greece
46 F8 **Vrondamás** Greece
25 G4 **Vroomshoop** Netherlands
28 C4 **Vroue** Denmark
48 G5 **Vršac** Yugoslavia
45 P1 **Vrsar** Yugoslavia
48 E1 **Vrútky** Czechoslovakia
89 D6 **Vryburg** S Africa
89 G6 **Vryheid** S Africa
37 O5 **Všeruby** Czechoslovakia
37 P4 **Všeruby** Czechoslovakia
31 K6 **Vsetín** Czechoslovakia
55 C1 **Vsevolodo Blagodatskiy** U.S.S.R.
48 E2 **Vtáčnik** *mt* Czechoslovakia
19 P12 **Vuache, Mt de** France
68 G2 **Vu Ban** Vietnam
47 G3 **Vŭcha** *R* Bulgaria
46 D2 **Vučitrn** Yugoslavia
21 B7 **Vue** France
25 D5 **Vught** Netherlands
48 E5 **Vuka** *R* Yugoslavia
48 E5 **Vukovar** Yugoslavia
118 D8 **Vulcan** Alberta
48 H5 **Vulcan** Romania
43 F10 **Vulcano** *isld* Italy
67 B7 **Vu Liet** Vietnam
43 G8 **Vulture** *mt* Italy
103 M8 **Vulture Mts** Arizona
68 J4 **Vung Da Nang** *B* Vietnam
68 J7 **Vung Phan Thiet** *B* Vietnam
68 H7 **Vung Tau** Vietnam
89 F2 **Vungu** *R* Zimbabwe
26 M5 **Vuodas** Sweden
29 N7 **Vuokatti** Finland
29 O11 **Vuoksa** *L* U.S.S.R.
29 O10 **Vuoksenniska** Finland
29 N7 **Vuolijoki** Finland
26 L5 **Vuollerim** Sweden
29 N5 **Vuostimo** Finland
29 N3 **Vuotso** Finland
26 N2 **Vuovdasoaivve** *mt* Norway
47 H2 **Vŭrbitsa** Bulgaria
28 C2 **Vust** Denmark
48 L4 **Vutcani** Romania
55 D4 **Vvedenka** U.S.S.R.
100 F8 **Vya** Nevada
52 E2 **Vyalozero, Oz** *L* U.S.S.R.
52 F5 **Vyaltsevo** U.S.S.R.
29 P9 **Vyartsilya** U.S.S.R.
52 G5 **Vyatka** *R* U.S.S.R.
52 H6 **Vyatskiye Polyany** U.S.S.R.
59 K2 **Vyazemskiy** U.S.S.R.
54 F1 **Vyaz'ma** U.S.S.R.
54 E1 **Vyazma** *R* U.S.S.R.
52 F6 **Vyazniki** U.S.S.R.
52 C6 **Vybor** U.S.S.R.
29 O11 **Vyborg** U.S.S.R.
29 N11 **Vyborgskiy Zaliv** *gulf* U.S.S.R.
52 H4 **Vychegda** *R* U.S.S.R.
31 J5 **Vychodočeský** *reg* Czechoslovakia
52 E3 **Vyg** *R* U.S.S.R.
48 N4 **Vygoda** U.S.S.R.
52 D3 **Vygozero, Oz** *L* U.S.S.R.
48 G2 **Vyhorlát** *mt* Czechoslovakia
52 F6 **Vyksa** U.S.S.R.
52 H3 **Vym'** *R* U.S.S.R.
52 G4 **Vymsk** U.S.S.R.
52 C5 **Vyra** U.S.S.R.
52 D5 **Vyritsa** U.S.S.R.
8 C2 **Vyrnwy, L** Wales
31 K6 **Vyškov** Czechoslovakia
31 L6 **Vysoká** *mt* Czechoslovakia
52 G6 **Vysokaya Gora** U.S.S.R.
52 J4 **Vysokaya Parma** *plat* U.S.S.R.
31 J6 **Vysoké Mýto** Czechoslovakia
59 L1 **Vysokogornyy** U.S.S.R.
52 E6 **Vysokovsk** U.S.S.R.
31 O3 **Vysokoye** U.S.S.R.
29 O11 **Vysotsk** U.S.S.R.
38 K4 **Vyšši Brod** Czechoslovakia
52 E4 **Vytegra** U.S.S.R.
52 G3 **Vyya** *R* U.S.S.R.
85 D6 **Wa** Ghana
25 D5 **Waal** *R* Netherlands
25 B5 **Waalhaven** Netherlands
25 D5 **Waalwijk** Netherlands
25 D2 **Waardgronden** Netherlands
22 E1 **Waarschoot** Belgium
120 D2 **Wababimiga L** Ontario
118 C5 **Wabamun** Alberta
123 U6 **Wabana** Nfld
118 D3 **Wabasca** Alberta
117 Q7 **Wabasca** *R* Alberta
111 F7 **Wabash** Arkansas
94 B6 **Wabash** Indiana
110 J3 **Wabash** *R* U.S.A.
99 O5 **Wabasha** Minnesota
113 G10 **Wabasso** Florida
99 L5 **Wabasso** Minnesota
120 F4 **Wabatongushi L** Ontario
99 S4 **Wabeno** Wisconsin
Wabern *see* **Egling**
118 K1 **Wabigoon** Ontario
121 R4 **Wabino** *R* Quebec
120 A2 **Wabinosh L** Ontario
120 C2 **Waboose Dam** Ontario
120 F6 **Wabos** Ontario
119 T4 **Wabowden** Manitoba
31 L2 **Wąbrzezno** Poland
58 G5 **Wabu Hu** *L* China
115 N7 **Wabush** Labrador
102 E2 **Wabuska** Nevada
112 H4 **Waccamaw** *R* S Carolina
112 J3 **Waccamaw, L** N Carolina
113 D8 **Waccasassa B** Florida
95 M9 **Wachapreague** Virginia
36 H5 **Wachbach** W Germany
36 E5 **Wachenheim** W Germany
37 K4 **Wachenroth** W Germany
33 R7 **Wachow** E Germany
22 F1 **Wachtbeke** Belgium
25 F6 **Wachtendonk** W Germany
36 G3 **Wächtersbach** W Germany
32 G7 **Wachtum** W Germany
95 Q4 **Wachusett Res** Massachusetts
135 M11 **Wachusett Shoal** Pacific Oc
32 K4 **Wacken** W Germany
98 J9 **Waco** Nebraska
122 G2 **Waco** Quebec
109 K4 **Waco** Texas
99 N5 **Waconia** Minnesota
122 G2 **Wacouno R** Quebec
77 K6 **Wad** Pakistan
142 D6 **Wadara Hills** W Australia
60 H10 **Wadayama** Japan
86 E3 **Wad Banda** Sudan
139 H8 **Waddamana** Tasmania
84 F4 **Waddān** Libya
25 D2 **Waddenzee** Netherlands
143 C9 **Wadderin** W Australia
9 F4 **Waddesdon** England
9 F1 **Waddington** England
95 M2 **Waddington** New York
117 L10 **Waddington, Mt** Br Col
94 B8 **Waddy** Kentucky
112 J2 **Wade** N Carolina
8 B7 **Wadebridge** England
99 L3 **Wadena** Minnesota
119 O7 **Wadena** Sask
36 B4 **Wadern** W Germany
32 H9 **Wadersloh** W Germany
112 G3 **Wadesboro** N Carolina
123 T4 **Wadham Is** Nfld
117 K10 **Wadhams** Br Columbia
9 G5 **Wadhurst** England
80 G6 **Wadi es Sir** Jordan
84 K5 **Wâdi Gimâl I** Egypt
86 F1 **Wadi Halfa** Sudan
138 D5 **Wadikee** S Australia
79 F8 **Wādi Mūsā** Jordan
111 L8 **Wadley** Alabama
112 E5 **Wadley** Georgia
86 F3 **Wad Medani** Sudan
31 L6 **Wadowice** Poland
102 E2 **Wadsworth** Nevada
94 F5 **Wadsworth** Ohio
13 G6 **Wadworth** England
65 G7 **Waegwan** S Korea
109 K6 **Waelder** Texas
68 F4 **Waeng** Thailand
65 E2 **Wafang** China
Wafangdian *see* **Fu Xian**
77 A5 **Wafra** Iran
61 O6 **Waga-gawa** *R* Japan
120 B2 **Wagaming** Ontario
111 H10 **Wagarville** Alabama
32 J7 **Wagenfeld** W Germany
25 E5 **Wageningen** Netherlands
140 E4 **Waggabundi** Queensland
139 H6 **Wagga Wagga** New S Wales
74 E8 **Waghai** India
36 F5 **Waghäusel** W Germany
143 B10 **Wagin** W Australia
101 R1 **Wagner** Montana
98 H6 **Wagner** S Dakota
107 P6 **Wagoner** Oklahoma
106 F5 **Wagon Mound** New Mexico
100 F6 **Wagontire** Oregon
106 D4 **Wagon Wheel Gap** Colorado
112 H3 **Wagram** N Carolina
31 K3 **Wągrowiec** Poland
100 J3 **Waha** Idaho
84 G4 **Waha** Libya
83 K9 **Wahalkada Tank** Sri Lanka
145 E2 **Waharoa** New Zealand
84 G4 **Waḥat Jālu** Libya
102 R12 **Wahiawa** Hawaiian Is
145 E2 **Wahi L** New Zealand
36 F4 **Wahlen** W Germany
36 C2 **Wahn** W Germany
32 K7 **Wahnebergen** W Germany
98 K8 **Wahoo** Nebraska
98 K3 **Wahpeton** N Dakota
33 S9 **Wahrenbrück** E Germany
33 N7 **Wahrenholz** W Germany
103 L3 **Wah Wah Mts** Utah
76 A2 **Wai** India
135 U6 **Waiahukini** Hawaiian Is
135 T3 **Waiakoa** Hawaiian Is
135 O1 **Waialeale** *peak* Hawaiian Is
102 R11 **Waialee** Hawaiian Is
102 R11 **Waialua** Hawaiian Is
102 R12 **Waianae** Hawaiian Is
102 R12 **Waianae Ra** Hawaiian Is
144 C6 **Waianakarua** New Zealand
144 B7 **Waianiwa** New Zealand
144 B6 **Waiatoto R** New Zealand
144 D5 **Waiau** New Zealand
144 A6 **Waiau** *R* New Zealand
145 F3 **Waiau R** New Zealand
36 G6 **Waiblingen** W Germany
37 N4 **Waidhaus** W Germany
31 J7 **Waidhofen** Austria
38 L6 **Waidhofen an der Ybbs** Austria
71 B3 **Waigama** Indonesia
143 G8 **Waigen Lakes** W Australia
71 C3 **Waigeo** *isld* W Irian
37 J4 **Waigolshausen** W Germany
144 C6 **Waihao Forks** New Zealand
145 D1 **Waiharara** New Zealand
145 E2 **Waiheke I** New Zealand
145 E2 **Waihi** New Zealand
144 A7 **Waihoaka** New Zealand
144 C7 **Waihola** New Zealand
145 D4 **Waihopai** *R* New Zealand
145 D1 **Waihopo** New Zealand
144 C5 **Waiho R** New Zealand
145 E2 **Waihou** New Zealand
145 E2 **Waihou R** New Zealand
145 F3 **Waihua** New Zealand
71 J9 **Waikabubak** Sumba Indonesia
144 B6 **Waikaia** New Zealand
144 B6 **Waikaia Plain** New Zealand
144 B6 **Waikaka** New Zealand
145 E4 **Waikanae** New Zealand
102 S12 **Waikane** Hawaiian Is
145 F3 **Waikareiti, L** New Zealand
145 E2 **Waikare, L** New Zealand
145 F3 **Waikaremoana, L** New Zealand
145 E2 **Waikaretu** New Zealand
144 D5 **Waikari** New Zealand
145 E3 **Waikato** New Zealand
144 B7 **Waikawa** New Zealand
145 E4 **Waikawa** New Zealand
71 J9 **Waikelo Teluk** *B* Sumba Indonesia
138 E5 **Waikerie** S Australia
135 U5 **Waikii** Hawaiian Is
142 A4 **Waikiki** W Aust
102 S12 **Waikiki Beach** Hawaiian Is
145 F3 **Waikohu** New Zealand
145 F3 **Waikokopu** New Zealand
144 B7 **Waikotkoi** New Zealand
144 C6 **Waikouaiti** New Zealand
144 A7 **Waikouro** New Zealand
102 V13 **Wailuku** Hawaiian Is
144 B7 **Waimahaka** New Zealand
144 A4 **Waimakariri R** New Zealand
145 D1 **Waimamaka** New Zealand
145 F3 **Waimana** New Zealand
102 S12 **Waimanalo** Hawaiian Is
144 C4 **Waimangaroa** New Zealand
145 F3 **Waimarama** New Zealand
144 C4 **Waimarie** New Zealand
144 C6 **Waimate** New Zealand
145 E2 **Waimauku** New Zealand
135 U4 **Waimea** Hawaiian Is
135 Q2 **Waimea** Hawaiin Is Pac Oc
102 R11 **Waimea B** Hawaiian Is
22 L3 **Waimes** Belgium
145 E3 **Waimiha** New Zealand
9 G1 **Wainfleet** England
71 K9 **Waingapu** Sumba Indonesia
145 E4 **Waingawa** New Zealand
135 O1 **Wainiha** Hawaiian Is
144 C5 **Wainihinihi** New Zealand
99 S3 **Wainola** Michigan
116 G1 **Wainwright** Alaska
118 G6 **Wainwright** Alberta
145 F3 **Waioeka R** New Zealand
135 U6 **Waiohinu** Hawaiian Is
145 E1 **Waiolira** New Zealand
145 F3 **Waiotapu** New Zealand
145 E3 **Waiouru** New Zealand
144 B7 **Waipahi** New Zealand
102 R12 **Waipahu** Hawaiian Is
145 F3 **Waipaoa** New Zealand
145 D1 **Waipapakauri** New Zealand
145 E2 **Waipa R** New Zealand
144 D5 **Waipara** New Zealand
145 F3 **Waipawa** New Zealand
144 C6 **Waipiata** New Zealand
135 U4 **Waipio** Hawaiian Is
145 E2 **Waipipi** New Zealand
145 G3 **Waipiro Bay** New Zealand
144 C6 **Waipori, L** New Zealand
145 E1 **Waipu** New Zealand
145 F3 **Waipukurau** New Zealand
145 G2 **Waipu R** New Zealand
145 F3 **Wairakei** New Zealand
145 E4 **Wairarapa, L** New Zealand
145 D4 **Wairau Valley** New Zealand
144 B7 **Wairio** New Zealand
145 F3 **Wairoa** New Zealand
145 E2 **Wairoa R** New Zealand
145 E1 **Wairua** *R* New Zealand
144 B7 **Wairuna** New Zealand
71 C3 **Waisai** W Irian
37 L4 **Waischenfeld** W Germany
145 F3 **Waitahanui** New Zealand
144 C5 **Waitaha R** New Zealand
144 B6 **Waitahuna** New Zealand
145 E2 **Waitakaruru** New Zealand
144 C6 **Waitaki L** New Zealand
145 E1 **Waitangi** New Zealand
145 E3 **Waitara** New Zealand
145 E4 **Waitarere** New Zealand
144 D6 **Waitati** New Zealand
140 B5 **Waite** *R* N Terr Aust
145 F1 **Waitemata Harb** New Zealand
143 D8 **Waite, Mt** W Australia
145 E2 **Waitoa** New Zealand
145 E3 **Waitomo** New Zealand
145 E3 **Waitotara** New Zealand
145 E3 **Waitotara** *R* New Zealand
100 G3 **Waitsburg** Washington
119 M6 **Waitville** Sask
145 E2 **Waiuku** New Zealand
144 C5 **Waiuta** New Zealand
145 E2 **Waiwera** New Zealand
144 B7 **Waiwera South** New Zealand
71 B1 **Wajabula** Halmahera Indonesia
71 C2 **Wajag** *isld* Indonesia
71 B2 **Wajamli** Indonesia
60 H12 **Wajiki** Japan
61 K8 **Wajima** Japan
86 H5 **Wajir** Kenya
69 C10 **Wak** Sumatra
86 D5 **Waka** Zaïre
60 D12 **Wakamatsu** Japan
60 B12 **Wakamatsu-jima** *isld* Japan
120 H5 **Wakami L** Ontario
144 C5 **Wakanui** New Zealand
145 F3 **Wakarara Range** New Zealand
94 A5 **Wakarusa** Indiana
61 J10 **Wakasa-wan** *B* Japan
144 B6 **Wakatipu, L** New Zealand
119 M6 **Wakaw** Sask
60 J11 **Wakayama** Japan
60 J12 **Wakayama** *prefect* Japan
61 P7 **Wakayanagi** Japan
107 L2 **Wa Keeney** Kansas
13 G6 **Wakefield** England
127 J2 **Wakefield** Jamaica
107 O2 **Wakefield** Kansas
99 R3 **Wakefield** Michigan
98 K7 **Wakefield** Nebraska
145 D4 **Wakefield** New Zealand
121 P7 **Wakefield** Quebec
95 Q5 **Wakefield** Rhode I
95 K10 **Wakefield** Virginia
112 J2 **Wake Forest** N Carolina
134 H6 **Wake Island** Pacific Oc
68 B4 **Wakema** Burma
122 H5 **Wakenam** Quebec
94 A5 **Wakerton** Indiana
74 E1 **Wakhan** *reg* Afghanistan
60 H11 **Waki** Japan
60 O4 **Wakinosawa** Japan
107 N5 **Wakita** Oklahoma
60 P1 **Wakkanai** Japan
87 F11 **Wakkerstroom** S Africa
Wako *see* **Watcomb**
120 G6 **Wakomata L** Ontario
139 G6 **Wakool** New S Wales
119 S9 **Wakopa** Manitoba
98 F4 **Wakpala** S Dakota
71 C3 **Wakre** W Irian
113 C7 **Wakulla** Florida
120 K2 **Wakwayowkastic** *R* Ontario
86 G4 **Walaga** *prov* Ethiopia
103 L6 **Walapai** Arizona
83 K11 **Walawe Ganga** *R* Sri Lanka
33 O8 **Walbeck** E Germany
36 D6 **Walbourg** France
94 D5 **Walbridge** Ohio
31 J5 **Wałbrzych** Poland
36 H1 **Walburg** W Germany
139 K4 **Walcha** New S Wales
38 G7 **Walchen** Austria
41 O2 **Walchensee** *L* W Germany
25 A5 **Walcheren** Netherlands
38 F6 **Walchsee** Austria
117 K8 **Walcott** Br Columbia
98 K3 **Walcott** N Dakota
101 T8 **Walcott** Wyoming
142 E3 **Walcott Inlet** W Australia
101 M7 **Walcott, L., Res** Idaho
146 F9 **Walcott,Mt** Antarctica
22 G3 **Walcourt** Belgium
31 J2 **Wałcz** Poland
38 L5 **Wald Aist** *R* Austria
36 F5 **Waldangeloch** W Germany
36 D4 **Waldböckelheim** W Germany
36 C2 **Waldbreitbach** W Germany
36 D2 **Waldbröl** W Germany
36 G5 **Waldbrunn** Baden-Württemberg W Germany
36 G5 **Waldbrunn** Hessen W Germany
143 B6 **Waldburg Ra** W Australia
33 T9 **Walddrehna** E Germany
118 K8 **Waldeck** Sask
36 G1 **Waldeck** W Germany
101 T9 **Walden** Colorado
95 N5 **Walden** New York
37 O2 **Waldenberg** E Germany
36 G6 **Waldenbuch** W Germany
Waldenburg *see* **Wałbrzych**
110 F6 **Waldenburg** Arkansas
36 H5 **Waldenburg** W Germany
37 N4 **Waldershof** W Germany
36 D5 **Waldfischbach** W Germany
37 P1 **Waldheim** E Germany
118 L6 **Waldheim** Sask
86 G3 **Waldia** Ethiopia
36 H1 **Waldkappel** W Germany
40 G1 **Waldkirch** W Germany
30 H7 **Waldkirchen** W Germany
36 F4 **Waldmichelbach** W Germany
37 O5 **Waldmünchen** W Germany
37 N4 **Wald Naab** *R* W Germany
25 F6 **Waldniel** W Germany
109 O2 **Waldo** Arkansas
118 B9 **Waldo** Br Columbia
113 E8 **Waldo** Florida
107 M2 **Waldo** Kansas
94 D6 **Waldo** Ohio
99 T6 **Waldo** Wisconsin
100 C6 **Waldo L** Oregon
95 L8 **Waldorf** Maryland
99 N6 **Waldorf** Minnesota
100 A5 **Waldport** Oregon
109 N1 **Waldron** Arkansas
119 P8 **Waldron** Sask
146 G2 **Waldron,C** Antarctica
37 N3 **Waldsassen** W Germany
41 H2 **Waldshut** W Germany
37 J7 **Waldstetten** W Germany
37 N4 **Waldthurn** W Germany
36 B5 **Waldwisse** France
71 H5 **Waleabahi** *isld* Sulawesi
71 H5 **Waleakodi** *isld* Sulawesi
71 H5 **Walea,Selat** *str* Sulawesi
116 C4 **Wales** Alaska
99 P2 **Wales** Minnesota
98 H1 **Wales** N Dakota
103 N2 **Wales** Utah
8 C3 **Wales** *princ* U.K.
115 L4 **Wales I** N W Terr
85 D6 **Walewale** Ghana
33 O5 **Walfisch** E Germany
139 J4 **Walgett** New S Wales
146 H11 **Walgreen Coast** Antarctica
98 J1 **Walhalla** N Dakota
112 D3 **Walhalla** S Carolina
37 N5 **Walhalla** *mt* W Germany
70 N9 **Walikukun** Java
143 A8 **Walkaway** W Australia
33 R5 **Walkendorf** E Germany
33 N9 **Walkenried** W Germany
100 C8 **Walker** California
99 P7 **Walker** Iowa
107 L3 **Walker** Kansas
111 F11 **Walker** Louisiana
99 M2 **Walker** Minnesota
110 B4 **Walker** Missouri
98 E4 **Walker** S Dakota
102 E2 **Walker** *R* Nevada
140 B6 **Walker** *R* N Terr Aust
141 F3 **Walker** *R* Queensland
89 A10 **Walker B** S Africa
13 E2 **Walkerburn** Scotland
113 J10 **Walker Cay** *isld* Bahamas
116 K3 **Walker L** Alaska
119 V4 **Walker L** Manitoba
102 F3 **Walker L** Nevada
122 E3 **Walker L** Quebec
146 H12 **Walker Mts** Antarctica
102 G6 **Walker Pk** California
140 D2 **Walker R** N Terr Aust
70 D2 **Walker Ra** Sabah
94 G8 **Walkersville** W Virginia
120 J8 **Walkerton** Ontario
112 G1 **Walkertown** N Carolina
99 U6 **Walkerville** Michigan
101 N3 **Walkerville** Montana
98 D5 **Wall** S Dakota
143 A8 **Wallabi Group** *islds* W Australia
140 E3 **Wallaby I** Queensland
141 F3 **Wallaby I** Queensland
138 C4 **Wallaby,Mt** S Australia
114 H8 **Wallace** Idaho
107 J3 **Wallace** Kansas
99 T4 **Wallace** Michigan
112 J3 **Wallace** N Carolina
98 E9 **Wallace** Nebraska
122 J8 **Wallace** Nova Scotia
121 M7 **Wallace** Ontario
98 J4 **Wallace** S Dakota
94 G7 **Wallace** W Virginia
120 H10 **Wallaceburg** Ontario
109 O3 **Wallace L** Louisiana
118 B3 **Wallace Mt** Alberta
120 J10 **Wallacetown** Ontario
141 H7 **Wallal** Queensland
142 D4 **Wallal Downs** W Australia
143 C9 **Wallambin, L** W Australia
141 K8 **Wallangarra** Queensland
142 D5 **Wallani Well** W Australia
141 H8 **Wallan, R** Queensland
138 D5 **Wallaroo** S Australia
8 C1 **Wallasey** England
140 B3 **Wallaston, Mt** N Terr Aust
36 E2 **Wallau** W Germany
139 H6 **Walla Walla** New S Wales
114 H8 **Walla Walla** Washington
100 G4 **Walla Walla** *R* Oregon
138 C2 **Wall Cr** N Terr Australia
140 C7 **Wall Creek** N Terr Aust
37 J2 **Walldorf** E Germany
36 F5 **Walldorf** W Germany
37 L2 **Wallendorf** E Germany
37 L3 **Wallenfels** W Germany
32 H8 **Wallenhorst** W Germany
95 M5 **Wallenpaupack, L** Pennsylvania
41 K3 **Wallen See** *L* Switzerland
32 L8 **Wallensen** W Germany
37 O6 **Wallersdorf** W Germany
36 F1 **Wallershöhe** *mt* W Germany
37 J6 **Wallerstein** W Germany
33 O10 **Wallhausen** E Germany
142 B3 **Walliabup** W Australia
95 P5 **Wallingford** Connecticut
9 E4 **Wallingford** England
145 F4 **Wallingford** New Zealand
95 P3 **Wallingford** Vermont
109 L6 **Wallis** Texas
137 R4 **Wallis, Îles** Pacific Oc
139 L4 **Wallis L** New S Wales
99 L7 **Wall L** Iowa
36 D3 **Wallmerod** W Germany
142 B6 **Wall, Mt** W Australia
86 G3 **Wallo** *prov* Ethiopia
141 K6 **Walloon** Queensland
94 C1 **Walloon L** Michigan
95 M9 **Wallops I** Virginia
100 H4 **Wallowa** Oregon
100 H4 **Wallowa Mts** Oregon
15 G2 **Walls** Scotland
28 C7 **Wallsbüll** W Germany
139 K5 **Wallsend** New S Wales
33 O7 **Wallstawe** E Germany
32 J8 **Wallucke** W Germany
100 G3 **Wallula** Washington
141 J7 **Wallumbilla** Queensland
33 Q9 **Wallwitzhafen** E Germany
9 H5 **Walmer** England
13 E5 **Walney I** England
99 R8 **Walnut** Illinois
107 P4 **Walnut** Kansas
107 K3 **Walnut** *R* Kansas
103 N6 **Walnut Canyon Nat.Mon** Arizona
112 G1 **Walnut Cove** N Carolina
111 G9 **Walnut Grove** Mississippi
110 C4 **Walnut Grove** Missouri
109 O9 **Walnut Hills** Texas
110 F5 **Walnut Ridge** Arkansas
109 K3 **Walnut Springs** Texas
125 M2 **Walpatanta** Honduras
138 F6 **Walpeup** Victoria
95 P3 **Walpole** New Hampshire
137 O6 **Walpole** *isld* Pacific Oc
116 D8 **Walrus I** Pribilof Is Bering Sea
116 G7 **Walrus Is** Alaska
9 E2 **Walsall** England
37 K1 **Walschleben** E Germany
36 E3 **Walsdorf** W Germany
106 F4 **Walsenburg** Colorado
118 G9 **Walsh** Alberta
106 H4 **Walsh** Colorado
141 G3 **Walsh** Queensland
141 G3 **Walsh** *R* Queensland
117 D5 **Walsh, Mt** Yukon Terr
22 J2 **Walshoutem** Belgium
25 B6 **Walsoorden** Netherlands
32 L7 **Walsrode** W Germany
32 E9 **Walsum** W Germany
112 G5 **Walterboro** S Carolina
109 J1 **Walters** Oklahoma
37 K2 **Waltershausen** E Germany
141 G8 **Walter's Ra** Queensland
111 G8 **Walthall** Mississippi
9 F2 **Waltham** England
101 P2 **Waltham** Montana
121 O7 **Waltham** Quebec
9 G4 **Waltham Abbey** England
9 F4 **Waltham Cross** England
98 K7 **Walthill** Nebraska
101 S6 **Waltman** Wyoming
9 F5 **Walton** England
94 A6 **Walton** Indiana
94 C8 **Walton** Kentucky
95 M4 **Walton** New York
145 E2 **Walton** New Zealand
122 J8 **Walton** Nova Scotia
120 J9 **Walton** Ontario
94 F8 **Walton** W Virginia
126 E6 **Walton Bank** Caribbean
94 B2 **Walton Junc** Michigan
9 H4 **Walton on the Naze** England
110 G3 **Waltonville** Illinois
32 F9 **Waltrop** W Germany
87 B10 **Walvis Bay** S Africa
90 J12 **Walvis Ridge** Atlantic Oc
99 S7 **Walworth** Wisconsin
143 C9 **Walyahmoing** *hill* W Australia
36 F5 **Walzbuchtal** W Germany
86 A4 **Wamba** Nigeria
86 E5 **Wamba** Zaïre
87 C7 **Wamba** *R* Zaïre
139 H5 **Wamboyne** New S Wales
107 O2 **Wamego** Kansas
25 D5 **Wamel** Netherlands
100 D4 **Wamic** Oregon
94 G6 **Wampum** Pennsylvania
101 R8 **Wamsutter** Wyoming
77 L3 **Wana** Pakistan
139 G3 **Wanaaring** New S Wales
144 B6 **Wanaka** New Zealand
67 E3 **Wan'an** China
126 A2 **Wanapa** Bonaire W Indies
120 K6 **Wanapitei L** Ontario
95 N5 **Wanaque Res** New Jersey
99 U8 **Wanatah** Indiana
138 F5 **Wanbi** S Australia
98 E6 **Wanblee** S Dakota
112 M2 **Wanchese** N Carolina
138 E3 **Wancoocha, L** S Australia
130 C10 **Wanda** Argentina
138 C4 **Wandana** S Australia
59 K2 **Wanda Shan** *mt ra* China
118 E3 **Wandering River** Alberta
37 K2 **Wandersleben** E Germany
28 C7 **Wanderup** W Germany
33 S7 **Wandlitz** E Germany
141 J7 **Wandoan** Queensland
141 G4 **Wando Vale** Queensland
22 K2 **Wandre** Belgium
109 K1 **Wanette** Oklahoma
65 E4 **Wanfu** China
65 C7 **Wanfu He** *R* China
141 G8 **Wangamurra** *R* Queensland
145 E3 **Wanganui** New Zealand
144 C5 **Wanganui R** New Zealand
139 G6 **Wangaratta** Victoria
138 D5 **Wangary** S Australia
67 B2 **Wangcaoba** China
65 B5 **Wangcun** China
67 C2 **Wangcun** China
67 B4 **Wangdian** China
65 C5 **Wangdu** China
33 N4 **Wangels** W Germany
41 L2 **Wangen** W Germany
32 G5 **Wangerland** *reg* W Germany
32 G5 **Wangerooge** W Germany
9 H3 **Wangford** England
71 K10 **Wanggameti** *mt* Sumba Indonesia
67 D4 **Wanggao** China
Wanggezhuang *see* **Jiaonan**
138 E3 **Wangianna** S Australia
71 H7 **Wangiwangi** *isld* Indonesia
67 D2 **Wangjiachang** China
67 E1 **Wangjiadian** China
67 E1 **Wangjiang** China
68 D5 **Wangka** Thailand
65 G1 **Wangkui** China
Wang Mai Khon *see* **Sawankhalok**
67 C5 **Wangmao** China
67 B4 **Wangmo** China
65 H3 **Wangqing** China
68 D2 **Wan hsa-la** Burma
71 H7 **Wani** *mt* Indonesia
86 E5 **Wanie Rukula** Zaïre
111 F10 **Wanilla** Mississippi
65 E5 **Wanjialing** China
74 D7 **Wankaner** India
32 M4 **Wankendorf** W Germany
89 E2 **Wankie** Zimbabwe
87 E9 **Wankie Nat. Park** Zimbabwe
119 Q4 **Wanless** Manitoba
12 E3 **Wanlockhead** Scotland
143 G8 **Wanna Lakes** W Australia
32 F9 **Wanne-Eickel** W Germany
143 B9 **Wanneroo** W Australia
67 F2 **Wannian** China
68 K3 **Wanning** China
33 S8 **Wannsee** E Germany
76 D2 **Wanparti** India
65 C4 **Wanquan** China
125 M2 **Wanquibila** Honduras
65 A7 **Wanrong** China
13 G3 **Wansbeck, R** England
9 F2 **Wansford** England
67 C3 **Wanshan** China
67 D6 **Wanshan Qundao** *islds* China
145 F4 **Wanstead** New Zealand
9 E4 **Wantage** England
36 D6 **Wantzenau** France
120 K6 **Wanup** Ontario
67 C1 **Wanxian** China
58 E5 **Wanyuan** China
67 E2 **Wanzai** China
Wanzhi *see* **Wuhu**
33 O8 **Wanzleben** E Germany
145 E3 **Waotu** New Zealand
94 C6 **Wapakoneta** Ohio
109 L1 **Wapanucka** Oklahoma
100 E3 **Wapato** Washington
119 N4 **Wapawekka Hills** Sask
119 Q8 **Wapella** Sask
101 N6 **Wapello** Idaho
99 P8 **Wapello** Iowa
119 S3 **Wapisu L** Manitoba
117 O8 **Wapiti** *R* Alberta
101 Q5 **Wapiti Ra** Wyoming
110 F4 **Wappapello Res** Missouri
95 O5 **Wappingers Falls** New York
99 O7 **Wapsipinicon** *R* Iowa
119 P2 **Wapus L** Sask
123 N2 **Wapustagamau L** Quebec
94 F9 **War** W Virginia
86 H4 **Warandab** Ethiopia
76 D1 **Warangal** India
139 H6 **Waranga Res** Victoria
139 H8 **Waratah** Tasmania
139 H7 **Waratah B** Victoria
99 N2 **Warba** Minnesota
9 F3 **Warboys** England
141 G6 **Warbreccan** Queensland
118 C5 **Warburg** Alberta
32 K10 **Warburg** W Germany
139 H7 **Warburton** Victoria
138 E2 **Warburton** *R* S Australia
143 F7 **Warburton Mission** W Australia
143 F7 **Warburton Ra** W Australia
138 C4 **Warburton Rge** S Australia
111 H9 **Ward** Alabama
145 E4 **Ward** New Zealand
141 H7 **Ward** *R* Queensland
138 D5 **Wardang I** S Australia
87 E11 **Warden** S Africa
100 F3 **Warden** Washington
32 H6 **Wardenburg** W Germany
118 E6 **Warden Junc** Alberta
94 J7 **Wardensville** W Virginia
74 H8 **Wardha** India
115 M1 **Ward Hunt I** N W Terr
118 F8 **Wardlow** Alberta
144 A6 **Ward, Mt** New Zealand
144 B5 **Ward, Mt** New Zealand
118 B9 **Wardner** Br Col
13 F5 **Wards Stone** *mt* England
117 L7 **Ware** Br Col
9 F4 **Ware** England
95 P4 **Ware** Massachusetts
145 D3 **Warea** New Zealand
22 E2 **Waregem** Belgium
8 D6 **Wareham** England
22 J2 **Waremme** Belgium
33 R5 **Waren** E Germany
140 F6 **Warenda** Queensland
32 G9 **Warendorf** W Germany
144 B7 **Warepa** New Zealand
140 B4 **Ware Ra** N Terr Aust
112 E6 **Waresboro** Georgia
112 E3 **Ware Shoals** S Carolina
95 N7 **Waretown** New Jersey
25 G2 **Warfum** Netherlands
9 F5 **Wargrave** England
139 K3 **Warialda** New S Wales
33 P5 **Warin** E Germany
68 G5 **Warin Chamrap** Thailand
109 J6 **Waring** Texas
116 H3 **Waring Mts** Alaska
13 F2 **Wark** England
31 N4 **Warka** Poland
13 G3 **Warkworth** England
145 E2 **Warkworth** New Zealand
121 N8 **Warkworth** Ontario
8 D3 **Warley** England
9 F5 **Warlingham** England
20 K2 **Warloy Baillon** France
89 A7 **Warmbad** Namibia
117 G6 **Warm Bay Hotsprings** Br Columbia
32 L8 **Warmbüchen** W Germany
37 M4 **Warmensteinach** W Germany
22 G5 **Warmeriville** France
9 E3 **Warmington** England
8 D5 **Warminster** England
25 C4 **Warmond** Netherlands
32 J8 **Warmsen** W Germany
112 C5 **Warm Springs** Georgia
101 N3 **Warmsprings** Montana
102 H3 **Warm Springs** Nevada
100 D5 **Warm Springs** Oregon
94 H8 **Warm Springs** Virginia
100 G6 **Warm Springs Res** Oregon
89 B9 **Warmwaters Berg** *mt* S Africa
8 D6 **Warmwell** England
22 J2 **Warnant-Dreye** Belgium
120 B3 **Warneford** Ontario
33 Q4 **Warnemünde** E Germany
101 N1 **Warner** Alberta
95 Q3 **Warner** New Hampshire
107 P6 **Warner** Oklahoma
98 H4 **Warner** S Dakota
100 F7 **Warner Lakes** Oregon
100 E8 **Warner Mts** California
112 D5 **Warner Robins** Georgia
102 H8 **Warner Springs** California
22 D2 **Warneton** Belgium
139 L3 **Warning,Mt** New S Wales
33 Q5 **Warnow** *R* E Germany
143 B10 **Waroona** W Australia
74 H8 **Warora** India
141 K7 **Warra** Queensland
142 F5 **Warrabuda Well** W Australia
138 F6 **Warracknabeal** Victoria
139 K5 **Warragamba Res** New S Wales
139 H7 **Warragul** Victoria
138 E3 **Warrakalanna,L** S Australia
138 D5 **Warramboo** S Australia
143 C8 **Warramboo** *mt* W Australia
139 J3 **Warrambool** *R* New S Wales
80 G4 **Warran** *R* Jordan
138 E2 **Warrandininna,L** S Australia
142 D5 **Warrawagine** W Australia
139 H2 **Warrego** *R* Queensland
141 H6 **Warrego Ra** Queensland
103 P10 **Warren** Arizona
111 D8 **Warren** Arkansas
100 K4 **Warren** Idaho
99 R7 **Warren** Illinois
94 B6 **Warren** Indiana
98 K1 **Warren** Minnesota
101 R4 **Warren** Montana
95 Q3 **Warren** New Hampshire
139 J4 **Warren** New S Wales
94 G5 **Warren** Ohio
120 K6 **Warren** Ontario
94 H5 **Warren** Pennsylvania
95 Q5 **Warren** Rhode I
109 N5 **Warren** Texas
94 J9 **Warren** Virginia
115 L3 **Warrender,C** N W Terr
119 U5 **Warren Landing** Manitoba
143 E8 **Warren, Mt** W Australia
14 E2 **Warrenpoint** N Ireland
99 Q5 **Warrens** Wisconsin
99 R10 **Warrensburg** Illinois
110 C3 **Warrensburg** Missouri
95 O3 **Warrensburg** New York
112 E4 **Warrenton** Georgia
110 E3 **Warrenton** Missouri
112 J1 **Warrenton** N Carolina
100 B3 **Warrenton** Oregon
89 D7 **Warrenton** S Africa
94 K8 **Warrenton** Virginia
101 Q1 **Warrick** Montana
143 B8 **Warriedar** *mt* W Australia
141 H5 **Warrigal** Queensland
138 F3 **Warri House** New S Wales
138 D3 **Warrina** S Australia
138 D3 **Warriners Cr** S Australia
13 F6 **Warrington** England
111 J11 **Warrington** Florida
144 D6 **Warrington** New Zealand
111 K8 **Warrior** Alabama
138 E4 **Warriota** *R* S Australia
138 F7 **Warrnambool** Victoria
99 L1 **Warroad** Minnesota
139 J2 **Warrong** Queensland
138 D5 **Warrow** S Australia
139 J4 **Warrumbungle Ra** New S Wales
141 F8 **Warry Warry** *R* Queensland
Warsaw *see* **Warszawa**
99 P9 **Warsaw** Illinois
94 B5 **Warsaw** Indiana
94 C8 **Warsaw** Kentucky
110 C3 **Warsaw** Missouri
112 J2 **Warsaw** N Carolina
94 J4 **Warsaw** New York
95 L9 **Warsaw** Virginia
38 K6 **Warscheneck** *mt* Austria
118 E4 **Warspite** Alberta
32 H10 **Warstein** W Germany
31 M3 **Warszawa** Poland
31 H2 **Warszów** Poland
31 J3 **Warta** *R* Poland
38 N6 **Wartberg** Austria
37 J2 **Wartburg** E Germany
37 M7 **Wartenberg** W Germany
13 H6 **Warter** England
41 M3 **Warth** Austria
118 J7 **Wartime** Sask
13 F6 **Warton** England
142 F3 **Warton Ra** W Australia
110 K6 **Wartrace** Tennessee
13 F4 **Warwick** Cumbria England
112 D6 **Warwick** Georgia
98 H2 **Warwick** N Dakota
95 N5 **Warwick** New York
121 T7 **Warwick** Quebec
141 K8 **Warwick** Queensland
95 Q5 **Warwick** Rhode I
9 E3 **Warwick** Warwicks England
140 D2 **Warwick Chan** N Terr Aust
9 E3 **Warwickshire** England
117 Q11 **Wasa** Br Col
120 K8 **Wasaga Beach** Ontario
85 F6 **Wasagu** Nigeria
103 N2 **Wasatch Ra** Utah
102 E6 **Wasco** California
100 E4 **Wasco** Oregon
99 P3 **Wascott** Wisconsin
99 N5 **Waseca** Minnesota
118 H5 **Waseca** Sask
121 L8 **Washago** Ontario
101 Q6 **Washakie Needles** *mts* Wyoming
9 H3 **Washbrook** England
99 R9 **Washburn** Illinois
95 S7 **Washburn** Maine
98 E2 **Washburn** N Dakota
108 C8 **Washburn** Texas
114 J3 **Washburn L** N W Terr
101 P5 **Washburn,Mt** Wyoming
144 C6 **Washdyke** New Zealand
8 C5 **Washford** England
123 M3 **Washikuti** Quebec
74 G8 **Washim** India
121 S3 **Washimeska** *R* Quebec
109 O2 **Washington** Arkansas
112 E4 **Washington** Georgia
99 R9 **Washington** Illinois
110 J3 **Washington** Indiana
99 P8 **Washington** Iowa

142 G5 White, L W Australia
99 S4 White Lake Wisconsin
94 A7 Whiteland Indiana
139 J8 Whitemark Tasmania
116 F4 White Mountain Alaska
14 E4 White Mt Irish Rep
116 O4 White Mts Alaska
102 F4 White Mts California
95 Q2 White Mts New Hampshire
117 P7 Whitemud *R* Alberta
86 F3 White Nile *prov* Sudan
86 F3 White Nile *R* Sudan
86 F2 White Nile Dam Sudan
112 K3 White Oak N Carolina
109 M2 White Oak Cr Texas
109 O2 White Oak L Arkansas
118 K1 White Otter L Ontario
98 D5 White Owl S Dakota
9 E5 Whiteparish England
117 F6 White Pass Br Col/Alaska
100 D3 White Pass Washington
94 B5 White Pigeon Michigan
99 R3 White Pine Michigan
100 K2 Whitepine Montana
112 D1 White Pine Tennessee
103 J2 White Pine Ra Nevada
112 G1 White Plains N Carolina
95 N5 White Plains New York
123 R2 White Pt Belle I, Nfld
140 D6 White Quartz Hill *mt* N Terr Aust
118 B8 White R Br Col
94 B8 White R Indiana
127 L2 White R Jamaica
98 F6 White R S Dakota
120 E4 White River Ontario
95 P3 White River Junc Vermont
103 J3 White River Valley Nevada
100 J8 White Rock Nevada
109 O9 White Rock Texas
107 M2 White Rock Cr Kansas
103 K3 White Rock Peak Nevada
White Russia *see* Belorussiya S.S.R.
117 K9 Whitesail L Br Col
100 D4 White Salmon Washington
117 P6 Whitesand *R* Alberta
8 B7 Whitesand B England
119 P7 Whitesand R Sask
108 A3 White Sands Missile Ra New Mexico
108 A3 White Sands Nat. Mon New Mexico
95 M3 Whitesboro New York
109 L2 Whitesboro Texas
112 C4 Whitesburg Georgia
94 E9 Whitesburg Kentucky
White Sea *see* Beloye More
109 L9 White Settlement Texas
118 F1 Whiteshell Manitoba
100 B4 Whiteson Oregon
119 U2 Whitestone L Manitoba
101 P3 White Sulphur Springs Montana
110 K4 Whitesville Kentucky
94 K4 Whitesville New York
94 F9 Whitesville W Virginia
100 E3 White Swan Washington
119 M4 Whiteswan L Sask
98 A1 Whitetail Montana
112 J3 Whiteville N Carolina
110 G6 Whiteville Tennessee
85 D7 White Volta *R* Ghana
101 S1 Whitewater Montana
106 B9 Whitewater New Mexico
99 S7 Whitewater Wisconsin
94 B7 Whitewater *R* Indiana
113 F12 Whitewater B Florida
120 A2 Whitewater L Ontario
138 B4 White Well S Australia
141 G5 Whitewood Queensland
119 P8 Whitewood Sask
98 C5 Whitewood S Dakota
98 J5 Whitewood, L S Dakota
109 L2 Whitewright Texas
139 H6 Whitfield Victoria
13 F4 Whitfield Hall England
127 H2 Whithorn Jamaica
12 D4 Whithorn Scotland
145 E2 Whitianga New Zealand
107 P2 Whiting Kansas
95 N7 Whiting New Jersey
117 G6 Whiting *R* Br Col/Alaska
12 C3 Whiting B Scotland
95 P4 Whitingham Res Vermont
118 K6 Whitkow Sask
118 F9 Whitla Alberta
8 B4 Whitland Wales
101 O1 Whitlash Montana
13 G3 Whitley Bay England
94 C10 Whitley City Kentucky
98 F4 Whitlocks Crossing S Dakota
95 R4 Whitman Massachusetts
98 H1 Whitman N Dakota
98 E7 Whitman Nebraska
100 G3 Whitman Nat. Mon Washington
112 F3 Whitmire S Carolina
8 C3 Whitney England
98 C7 Whitney Nebraska
103 J5 Whitney Nevada
121 M7 Whitney Ontario
100 G5 Whitney Oregon
109 K4 Whitney, L Texas
102 F5 Whitney, Mt California
109 J7 Whitsett Texas
9 H5 Whitstable England
141 J5 Whitsunday I Queensland
109 J3 Whitt Texas
94 G7 Whittaker W Virginia
99 M6 Whittemore Iowa
94 D2 Whittemore Michigan
116 N6 Whittier Alaska
102 F8 Whittier California
13 G3 Whittingham England
139 H7 Whittlesea Victoria
9 F2 Whittlesey England
139 H5 Whitton New S Wales
8 C3 Whitton Wales
13 G4 Whittonstall England
141 F7 Whitula *R* Queensland
9 E1 Whitwell England
112 B2 Whitwell Tennessee
114 J5 Wholdaia L N W Terr
138 D5 Whyalla S Australia
123 L8 Whycocomagh Nova Scotia
139 G3 Whyjonta New S Wales
68 D3 Wiang Pa Pao Thailand
68 D2 Wiang Phrao Thailand
120 J8 Wiarton Ontario
31 K5 Wiązów Poland
98 B2 Wibaux Montana
13 G6 Wibsey England
107 N4 Wichita Kansas
109 J1 Wichita *R* Texas
109 J2 Wichita Falls Texas
109 J1 Wichita Mts Oklahoma
15 E2 Wick Scotland
32 G10 Wickede W Germany
103 M8 Wickenburg Arizona
122 J4 Wickenden L Quebec
143 C10 Wickepin W Australia
100 C1 Wickersham Washington
108 D4 Wickett Texas
9 G4 Wickford England
95 Q5 Wickford Rhode I
9 E6 Wickham England
139 G7 Wickham, C Tasmania
140 A3 Wickham Mt N Terr Aust
121 S7 Wickham West Quebec
100 D6 Wickiup Res Oregon
110 G5 Wickliffe Kentucky
14 E4 Wicklow Irish Rep
14 E4 Wicklow *co* Irish Rep
8 D4 Wickwar England
31 L4 Widawka *R* Poland
36 G5 Widdern W Germany
121 L6 Widdifield Ontario
90 A11 Wideawake Ascension I
116 J8 Wide B Alaska
141 L7 Wide B Queensland
8 C6 Widecombe-in-the-Moor England
138 B2 Wide Gum *R* S Australia
94 G8 Widen W Virginia
141 H8 Widgeegoara *R* Queensland
143 D9 Widgiemooltha W Australia
71 B3 Widi, Pulau Pulau *islds* Indonesia
36 F4 Wiebelsbach W Germany
36 C5 Wiebelskirchen W Germany
31 K2 Więcbork Poland
36 C2 Wied W Germany
Wiedenbrück *see* Rheda-Wiedenbrück
32 H6 Wiefelstede W Germany
33 O10 Wiehe E Germany
32 J8 Wiehengebirge *hills* W Germany
36 D2 Wiehl W Germany
31 M2 Wielbark Poland
31 J3 Wieleń Poland
31 M6 Wieliczka Poland
31 L4 Wieluń Poland
38 O5 Wien Austria
38 O6 Wiener Neustadt Austria
32 M7 Wienhausen W Germany
116 M4 Wien L Alaska
33 O7 Wiepke E Germany
31 O5 Wieprz *R* Poland
33 N7 Wieren W Germany
109 O4 Wiergate Texas
25 D3 Wieringen Netherlands
25 C3 Wieringermeer Netherlands
31 L4 Wieruszów Poland
31 N4 Wierzbnik Poland
31 L2 Wierzchucin Poland
31 L2 Wierzyca *R* Poland
38 M8 Wies Austria
37 N4 Wiesau W Germany
36 E3 Wiesbaden W Germany
40 G2 Wiese *R* W Germany
33 Q8 Wiesenburg E Germany
36 H6 Wiesensteig W Germany
37 L4 Wiesent *R* W Germany
37 J4 Wiesentherd W Germany
37 L4 Wiesenttal W Germany
36 F5 Wiesloch W Germany
32 G6 Wiesmoor W Germany
32 F7 Wietmarschen W Germany
32 L7 Wietz W Germany
32 K7 Wietzen W Germany
32 L7 Wietzendorf W Germany
13 F6 Wigan England
98 B9 Wiggins Colorado
111 G11 Wiggins Mississippi
9 E6 Wight, I. of England
8 D3 Wigmore England
31 O2 Wigry, Jezioro *L* Poland
9 E2 Wigston England
13 E4 Wigton England
12 D4 Wigtown Scotland
Wigtown *co see* Dumfries and Galloway *reg*
25 F4 Wijhe Netherlands
25 E7 Wijk Netherlands
25 C4 Wijk aan Zee Netherlands
103 L7 Wikieup Arizona
120 J7 Wikwemikong Ontario
41 K3 Wil Switzerland
83 L11 Wila Oya *R* Sri Lanka
98 K9 Wilber Nebraska
121 M7 Wilberforce Ontario
140 D1 Wilberforce,C N Terr Aust
144 C5 Wilberforce R New Zealand
101 N3 Wilborn Montana
100 B6 Wilbur Oregon
100 G2 Wilbur Washington
94 E10 Wilbur Dam Tennessee
110 A7 Wilburton Oklahoma
9 F3 Wilby England
139 G4 Wilcannia New S Wales
99 M9 Wilcox Missouri
98 G9 Wilcox Nebraska
94 J5 Wilcox Pennsylvania
119 N8 Wilcox Sask
33 T8 Wildau E Germany
36 F6 Wildbad W Germany
33 R7 Wildberg E Germany
36 F6 Wildberg W Germany
123 Q4 Wild Bight Nfld
102 H2 Wildcat Pk Nevada
119 V3 Wilde Manitoba
37 J2 Wildeck W Germany
37 O2 Wildenfels E Germany
94 B10 Wilder Tennessee
41 O4 Wilder Freiger *mt* Austria
117 O9 Wilderness Prov. Park Alberta
110 H6 Wildersville Tennessee
25 G2 Wildervank Netherlands
32 H7 Wildeshausen W Germany
36 H3 Wildflecken W Germany
120 A4 Wild Goose Ontario
40 F5 Wildhorn *mt* Switzerland
101 P1 Wild Horse Alberta
100 K8 Wildhorse Res Nevada
119 P4 Wildnest L Sask
108 B8 Wildorado Texas
33 R8 Wildpark E Germany
98 K2 Wild Rice *R* Minnesota
98 K3 Wild Rice *R* N Dakota
98 C1 Wildrose N Dakota
99 R5 Wild Rose Wisconsin
40 G5 Wildstrubel *mt* Switzerland
118 B5 Wildwood Alberta
113 E9 Wildwood Florida
95 N8 Wildwood New Jersey
118 B1 Wildwood Pk Manitoba
106 H3 Wiley Colorado
36 F6 Wilferdingen W Germany
120 E2 Wilgar Ontario
89 F6 Wilge *R* S Africa
138 C4 Wilgena S Australia
146 D3 Wilhelm II Land Antarctica
129 G3 Wilhelmina Geb *mts* Suriname
25 D5 Wilhelmina Kanal Netherlands
136 J3 Wilhelm, Mt Papua New Guinea
31 H4 Wilhelm-Pieck-Stadt East Germany
31 H4 Wilhelm Pieck Stadt E Germany
32 H5 Wilhelmshaven W Germany
36 F2 Wilhelmshütte W Germany
33 O5 Wiligrad E Germany
70 N9 Wilis *mt* Java
95 M5 Wilkes Barre Pennsylvania
112 F1 Wilkesboro N Carolina
146 H3 Wilkes Coast Antarctica
146 F3 Wilkes Land Antarctica
37 N2 Wilkhau Hasslau E Germany
118 J6 Wilkie Sask
146 E13 Wilkins Coast Antarctica
146 F13 Wilkins Ice Antarctica
138 C3 Wilkinson L S Australia
112 D6 Willacoochee Georgia
103 M6 Willaha Arizona
100 B4 Willamette *R* Oregon
139 G5 Willangra Billabong *R* New S Wales
100 B3 Willapa *R* Washington
139 G3 Willara New S Wales
138 E2 Willara, L S Australia
98 C9 Willard Colorado
124 D3 Willard Mexico
98 B3 Willard Montana
106 D7 Willard New Mexico
94 E5 Willard Ohio
101 N8 Willard Utah
95 M8 Willards Maryland
139 G4 Willaroy New S Wales
103 P9 Willcox Arizona
32 K9 Willebadessen W Germany
22 G1 Willebroek Belgium
22 E2 Willems France
25 C5 Willemsdorp Netherlands
126 B1 Willemstad Curaçao
25 B5 Willemstad Netherlands
140 B3 Willeroo N Terr Aust
8 D3 Willersley England
22 H4 Willerzie Belgium
9 F4 Willesden England
118 C6 Willesden Green Alberta
120 B2 Willet Ontario
143 B6 Williambury W Australia
138 D3 William Creek S Australia
119 S5 William L Manitoba
138 F6 William, Mt Victoria
143 B10 William,Mt W Australia
103 M6 Williams Arizona
102 B2 Williams California
110 K3 Williams Indiana
99 N7 Williams Iowa
99 L1 Williams Minnesota
143 B10 Williams W Australia
140 F5 Williams *R* Queensland
99 S7 Williams Bay Wisconsin
99 O8 Williamsburg Iowa
94 C10 Williamsburg Kentucky
95 P4 Williamsburg Massachusetts
94 C7 Williamsburg Ohio
94 J6 Williamsburg Pennsylvania
95 L9 Williamsburg Virginia
127 K2 Williamsfield Jamaica
120 K8 Williamsford Ontario
126 E2 Williams I Bahamas
117 M9 Williams Lake Br Columbia
99 N8 Williamson Iowa
95 K3 Williamson New York
94 E9 Williamson W Virginia
146 K3 Williamson Hd Antarctica
99 T9 Williamsport Indiana
94 K7 Williamsport Maryland
123 Q3 Williamsport Nfld
95 K5 Williamsport Pennsylvania
94 C4 Williamston Michigan
112 K2 Williamston N Carolina
112 E3 Williamston S Carolina
94 C8 Williamstown Kentucky
95 O4 Williamstown Massachusetts
95 P2 Williamstown Vermont
94 F7 Williamstown W Virginia
110 F5 Williamsville Missouri
141 G8 Willie's Ra Queensland
127 P4 Willikie's Antigua W Indies
95 P5 Willimantic Connecticut
118 E5 Willingdon Alberta
117 P10 Willingdon, Mt Alberta
32 J10 Willingen W Germany
9 G3 Willingham England
13 G4 Willington England
109 M5 Willis Texas
94 G10 Willis Virginia
40 G3 Willisau Switzerland
141 K3 Willis Grp *islds* Gt Barrier Reef Aust
146 B15 Willis I S Georgia
113 E8 Williston Florida
98 C1 Williston N Dakota
87 D12 Williston S Africa
112 F4 Williston S Carolina
117 M8 Williston L Br Col
110 G4 Willisville Illinois
8 C5 Williton England
102 A2 Willits California
99 L4 Willmar Minnesota
119 P9 Willmar Sask
94 F5 Willoughby Ohio
138 E6 Willoughby, C S Australia
116 M6 Willow Alaska
108 E8 Willow Oklahoma
117 M9 Willow *R* Br Col
119 P7 Willowbrook Sask
119 M9 Willow Bunch L Sask
98 F1 Willow City N Dakota
100 E9 Willow Cr California
100 H5 Willow Cr Oregon
118 D8 Willow Cr. Prov. Park Alberta
117 O4 Willow L N W Terr
98 J5 Willow L S Dakota
117 N4 Willowlake *R* N W Terr
89 C9 Willowmore S Africa
140 C5 Willowra N Terr Aust
100 E8 Willow Ranch California
99 R4 Willow Res Wisconsin
99 O3 Willow River Minnesota
94 D4 Willow Run Michigan
102 B2 Willows California
119 M9 Willows Sask
110 E5 Willow Springs Missouri
139 K4 Willow Tree New S Wales
95 O2 Willsboro New York
142 G5 Wills,L W Australia
109 L3 Wills Point Texas
138 E6 Willunga S Australia
146 B5 Wilma Gl Antarctica
111 H11 Wilmer Alabama
33 T6 Wilmersdorf E Germany
99 T7 Wilmette Illinois
95 M7 Wilmington Delaware
99 S8 Wilmington Illinois
112 K3 Wilmington N Carolina
94 D7 Wilmington Ohio
138 E4 Wilmington S Australia
95 O4 Wilmington Vermont
99 L6 Wilmont Minnesota
107 L4 Wilmore Kansas
94 C9 Wilmore Kentucky
111 E8 Wilmot Arkansas
94 F6 Wilmot Ohio
144 B6 Wilmot, L New Zealand
144 A6 Wilmot Pass New Zealand
25 C4 Wilnis Netherlands
121 N7 Wilno Ontario
36 E2 Wilnsdorf W Germany
83 J9 Wilpattu *game reserve* Sri Lanka
138 E4 Wilpena *R* S Australia
22 G1 Wilrijk Belgium
101 P3 Wilsall Montana
37 Q1 Wilsdruff E Germany
32 L6 Wilseder Berg *hill* W Germany
110 F6 Wilson Arkansas
107 M3 Wilson Kansas
111 E11 Wilson Louisiana
112 K2 Wilson N Carolina
94 J3 Wilson New York
109 K1 Wilson Oklahoma
108 F2 Wilson Texas
101 P6 Wilson Wyoming
139 G3 Wilson *R* Queensland
138 A4 Wilson Bluff S Australia
115 L4 Wilson, C N W Terr
142 F5 Wilson Cliffs *hill* W Australia
100 F2 Wilson Creek Washington
103 K3 Wilson Cr. Ra Nevada
106 H3 Wilson Junc Colorado
138 A2 Wilson, L S Australia
102 G7 Wilson, Mt California
106 C4 Wilson, Mt Colorado
103 K3 Wilson, Mt Nevada
142 G5 Wilson,Mt W Australia
107 M3 Wilson Res Kansas
139 H7 Wilson's Promontory Victoria
12 E2 Wilsontown Scotland
98 F9 Wilsonville Nebraska
32 K6 Wilstedt W Germany
32 K5 Wilster W Germany
109 N2 Wilton Arkansas
9 E5 Wilton England
99 P8 Wilton Iowa
98 F2 Wilton N Dakota
95 Q4 Wilton New Hampshire
99 Q6 Wilton Wisconsin
140 C2 Wilton *R* N Terr Aust
9 E5 Wiltshire *co* England
22 K4 Wiltz Luxembourg
143 D7 Wiluna W Australia
22 L4 Wilwerwiltz Luxembourg
119 S3 Wimapedi L Manitoba
113 E10 Wimauma Florida
9 F5 Wimbledon England
98 H2 Wimbledon N Dakota
145 F4 Wimbledon New Zealand
118 D7 Wimborne Alberta
9 E6 Wimborne England
22 B2 Wimereux France
113 B8 Wimico, L Florida
22 B2 Wimille France
38 K8 Wimitz *R* Austria
36 C6 Wimmenau France
138 F6 Wimmera *R* Victoria
118 A3 Winagami L Alberta
94 A5 Winamac Indiana
88 E2 Winam Gulf Kenya
139 G4 Winbar New S Wales
141 G7 Winbin Queensland
87 E11 Winburg S Africa
8 D5 Wincanton England
12 E2 Winchburgh Scotland
9 E4 Winchcomb England
109 H4 Winchell Texas
9 G6 Winchelsea England
95 P4 Winchendon Massachusetts
9 E5 Winchester England
100 J3 Winchester Idaho
99 Q10 Winchester Illinois
94 C6 Winchester Indiana
94 C9 Winchester Kentucky
95 P4 Winchester New Hampshire
144 C6 Winchester New Zealand
94 D8 Winchester Ohio
121 P7 Winchester Ontario
110 K6 Winchester Tennessee
109 K5 Winchester Texas
101 R6 Winchester Wyoming
100 A6 Winchester Bay Oregon
101 R6 Wind *R* Wyoming
138 D4 Windabout, L S Australia
101 P2 Windam Montana
143 D8 Windarra W Australia
Windau *see* Ventspils
94 J6 Windber Pennsylvania
98 C6 Wind Cave Nat. Park S Dakota
36 F3 Windecken W Germany
36 E5 Winden W Germany
112 D4 Winder Georgia
141 K7 Windera Queensland
113 L12 Windermere Bahamas
13 F5 Windermere England
120 G5 Windermere L Ontario
94 B6 Windfall Indiana
95 M6 Wind Gap Pennsylvania
95 R3 Windham, S Maine
32 K8 Windheim W Germany
87 C10 Windhoek Namibia
143 D7 Windich Springs W Australia
121 R5 Windigo Quebec
107 P7 Winding Stair Mts Oklahoma
37 N4 Windischeschenbach W Germany
38 K6 Windischgarsten Austria
146 F2 Windmill I Antarctica
95 M9 Windmill Pt Virginia
107 N3 Windom Kansas
99 L6 Windom Minnesota
106 C4 Windom Pk Colorado
141 G7 Windorah Queensland
37 P6 Windorf W Germany
99 T7 Wind Point Wisconsin
101 Q7 Wind R. Ra Wyoming
37 K5 Windsbach W Germany
106 F1 Windsor Colorado
95 P5 Windsor Connecticut
9 F5 Windsor England
99 S10 Windsor Illinois
95 P4 Windsor Massachusetts
110 C3 Windsor Missouri
112 L2 Windsor N Carolina
139 K5 Windsor New S Wales
95 M4 Windsor New York
144 C6 Windsor New Zealand
123 R5 Windsor Nfld
122 H9 Windsor Nova Scotia
120 H10 Windsor Ontario
121 T7 Windsor Quebec
112 F4 Windsor S Carolina
95 L10 Windsor Virginia
141 K1 Windsor *dist* Brisbane, Qnsld
94 G6 Windsor Heights W Virginia
126 H4 Windsor L. Great Inagua I Bahamas
95 P5 Windsor Locks Connecticut
109 J2 Windthorst Texas
141 F7 Windula *R* Queensland
127 O7 Windward Is W Indies
126 H5 Windward Passage Cuba/Haiti
116 N5 Windy Alaska
116 K5 Windy Fork *R* Alaska
119 P4 Windy L Sask
117 Q5 Windy Pt N W Terr
118 G3 Winefred L Alberta
99 R3 Winegar Wisconsin
94 C3 Winegars Michigan
100 E2 Winesap Washington
111 J8 Winfield Alabama
118 C6 Winfield Alberta
107 O4 Winfield Kansas
109 M2 Winfield Texas
8 D6 Winfrith England
98 F2 Wing N Dakota
110 J1 Wingate Indiana
106 B6 Wingate New Mexico
140 B2 Wingate Mts N Terr Aust
139 K4 Wingen New S Wales
22 E1 Wingene Belgium
36 C6 Wingen-sur-Moder France
9 H5 Wingham England
139 L4 Wingham New S Wales
120 J9 Wingham Ontario
110 H5 Wingo Kentucky
32 K5 Wingst W Germany
71 M9 Wini Timor Indonesia
101 Q2 Winifred Montana
98 J6 Winifred S Dakota
142 E6 Winifred,L W Australia
115 L6 Winisk Ontario
68 D5 Winkana Burma
25 C3 Winkei Netherlands
103 O9 Winkelman Arizona
9 F5 Winkfield England
37 O5 Winklarn W Germany
8 C6 Winkleigh England
119 U9 Winkler Manitoba
38 G8 Winklern Austria
100 C3 Winlock Washington
95 T1 Winn Maine
94 C3 Winn Michigan
140 B6 Winnalls Ridge N Terr Aust
85 D7 Winneba Ghana
99 M6 Winnebago Minnesota
98 K7 Winnebago Nebraska
99 S5 Winnebago, L Wisconsin
142 G6 Winnecke Hills N Terr/W Aust
140 B4 Winnecke,Mt N Terr Aust
142 E6 Winnecke Rock *hill* W Australia
99 S5 Winneconne Wisconsin
100 H9 Winnemucca Nevada
102 E1 Winnemucca L Nevada
36 G6 Winnenden W Germany
98 G6 Winner S Dakota
99 T7 Winnetka Illinois
98 H7 Winnetoon Nebraska
101 R2 Winnett Montana
109 P4 Winnfield Louisiana
99 M2 Winnibigoshish L Minnesota
109 N6 Winnie Texas
118 F9 Winnifred Alberta
33 O9 Winnigen E Germany
142 A6 Winning W Australia
36 D3 Winningen W Germany
138 E4 Winnininnie S Australia
118 A1 Winnipeg Manitoba
119 V8 Winnipeg Beach Manitoba
119 T5 Winnipeg, L Manitoba
119 S7 Winnipegosis Manitoba
119 R6 Winnipegosis, L Manitoba
95 Q3 Winnipesaukee, L New Hampshire
111 E9 Winnsboro Louisiana
112 F3 Winnsboro S Carolina
109 M3 Winnsboro Texas
112 E6 Winokur Georgia
103 N6 Winona Arizona
107 J2 Winona Kansas
99 S3 Winona Michigan
99 P5 Winona Minnesota
110 E4 Winona Missouri
109 M3 Winona Texas
100 H3 Winona Washington
109 P1 Winona, L Arkansas
95 O2 Winooski Vermont
95 P2 Winooski *R* Vermont
25 H2 Winschoten Netherlands
32 L7 Winsen W Germany
32 M6 Winsen W Germany
8 D1 Winsford England
98 J7 Winside Nebraska
103 O6 Winslow Arizona
110 B6 Winslow Arkansas
9 F4 Winslow England
110 J3 Winslow Indiana
95 S2 Winslow Maine
100 C2 Winslow Washington
137 R2 Winslow Reef Phoenix Is Pacific Oc
101 N5 Winsper Idaho
95 O5 Winsted Connecticut
9 E1 Winster England
13 G4 Winston England
101 O3 Winston Montana
106 C8 Winston New Mexico
112 G1 Winston Salem N Carolina
25 G2 Winsum Netherlands
118 H6 Winter Sask
38 M6 Winterbach Austria
36 D4 Winterberg W Germany
36 F1 Winterberg W Germany
8 D6 Winterbourne Abbas England
9 E5 Winterbourne Stoke England
33 O7 Winterfeld E Germany
113 F9 Winter Garden Florida
114 J3 Winter Harb N W Terr
103 K9 Winterhaven California
113 F9 Winter Haven Florida
119 U3 Wintering L Manitoba
36 G7 Winterlingen W Germany
106 E2 Winter Park Colorado
113 F9 Winter Park Florida
95 T2 Winterport Maine
102 C3 Winters California
108 H4 Winters Texas
103 M8 Wintersburg Arizona
99 M8 Winterset Iowa
22 K2 Winterslag Belgium
25 G5 Winterswijk Netherlands
41 J3 Winterthur Switzerland
13 H6 Winterton England
123 T6 Winterton Nfld
95 S7 Winterville Maine
95 R4 Winthrop Massachusetts
99 M5 Winthrop Minnesota
95 N2 Winthrop New York
100 E1 Winthrop Washington
99 T7 Winthrop Harbor Illinois
138 C2 Wintinna S Australia
99 P2 Winton Minnesota
112 K1 Winton N Carolina
113 M9 Winton New Providence I Bahamas
144 B7 Winton New Zealand
95 M5 Winton Pennsylvania
141 G5 Winton Queensland
100 E2 Winton Washington
101 Q8 Winton Wyoming
40 F1 Wintzenheim France
112 H4 Winyah B S Carolina
37 P6 Winzer W Germany
99 M8 Wiota Iowa
33 N10 Wipper *R* E Germany
36 C1 Wipperfürth W Germany
33 O9 Wippra E Germany
41 O3 Wipp Tal Austria
83 K11 Wiraketiya Sri Lanka
25 E2 Wirdum Netherlands
32 F6 Wirdum W Germany
9 E1 Wirksworth England
145 F2 Wiroa I New Zealand
138 E5 Wirrabara S Australia
138 D4 Wirraminna S Australia
138 D4 Wirrapa S Australia
138 F6 Wirrega S Australia
138 C3 Wirrida, L S Australia
138 C4 Wirrulla S Australia
99 N2 Wirt Minnesota
22 B2 Wirwignes France
9 G2 Wisbech England
9 F5 Wisborough Green England
95 S2 Wiscasset Maine
32 K5 Wischhafen W Germany
99 R4 Wisconsin *R* Wisconsin
99 R5 Wisconsin *state* U.S.A.
99 R6 Wisconsin Dells Wisconsin
99 R6 Wisconsin, L Wisconsin
146 G9 Wisconsin Ra Antarctica
99 R5 Wisconsin Rapids Wisconsin
101 M4 Wisdom Montana
94 E9 Wise Virginia
116 M3 Wiseman Alaska
101 N4 Wise River Montana
118 K7 Wiseton Sask
119 O7 Wishart Sask
12 E2 Wishaw Scotland
98 G3 Wishek N Dakota
100 E4 Wishram Washington
48 E1 Wisla Poland
31 L2 Wisła *R* Poland
31 N6 Wisłok *R* Poland
33 O5 Wismar E Germany
33 O5 Wismarbucht E Germany
111 E10 Wisner Louisiana
98 K8 Wisner Nebraska
22 B2 Wissant France
136 H2 Wissel, Danau D *L* W Irian
36 D5 Wissembourg France
36 D2 Wissen W Germany
9 G2 Wissey, R England
32 H8 Wissingen W Germany
99 P5 Wissota L Wisconsin
31 N4 Wista *R* Poland
117 K9 Wistaria Br Columbia
109 N1 Wister Oklahoma
89 F5 Witbank S Africa
89 E8 Witberge *mts* S Africa
119 U3 Witchai L Manitoba
143 B10 Witchcliffe W Australia
118 K5 Witchekan L Sask
87 D11 Witdrail S Africa
9 G4 Witham England
9 F1 Witham, R England
8 C6 Witheridge England
9 G1 Withern England
13 J6 Withernsea England
141 J6 Withersfield Queensland
106 C8 Withington, Mt New Mexico
113 E9 Withlacoochee *R* Florida
100 F2 Withrow Washington
31 K3 Witkowo Poland
123 U6 Witless B Nfld
9 E4 Witney England
22 K4 Witry Belgium
22 G5 Witry-les-Reims France
22 D2 Witschate Belgium
110 G2 Witt Illinois
28 A7 Wittdün W Germany
37 L7 Wittelsbach W Germany
98 F6 Witten S Dakota
32 F10 Witten W Germany
33 S7 Wittenau E Germany
33 R9 Wittenberg E Germany
99 R5 Wittenberg Wisconsin
33 P7 Wittenberge E Germany
33 O5 Wittenburg E Germany
142 C5 Wittenoom W Australia
142 G4 Wittenoom,Mt W Australia
37 O2 Wittgensdorf E Germany
125 N2 Witties, The *islds* Nicaragua
36 H4 Wittighausen W Germany
33 N7 Wittingen W Germany
70 E2 Witti Ra Sabah
32 H8 Wittlage W Germany
36 B4 Wittlich W Germany
32 K7 Wittlohe W Germany
103 M8 Wittmann Arizona
32 G5 Wittmund W Germany
13 G4 Witton Gilbert England
13 G4 Witton-le-Wear England
30 G1 Wittow *pen* E Germany
33 Q6 Wittstock E Germany
87 C10 Witvlei Namibia
89 E5 Witwatersberg *ridge* S Africa
89 C2 Witwatersrand S Africa
32 L10 Witzenhausen W Germany
8 C5 Wiveliscombe England
119 W2 Wivenhoe Manitoba
118 L8 Wives Sask
9 H4 Wix England
31 O1 Wizajny Poland
22 C2 Wizernes France
31 M3 Wkra *R* Poland
31 L1 Władysławowo Poland
31 J4 Wleń Poland
31 L3 Włocławek Poland
31 O4 Włodawa Poland
31 M5 Włoszczowa Poland
33 O6 Wöbbelin E Germany
9 F4 Woburn England
142 C5 Wodgina W Australia
139 H6 Wodonga Victoria
31 L5 Wodzisław Poland
25 B6 Woensdrecht Netherlands
25 C4 Woerden Netherlands
36 D6 Wœrth France
22 J5 Wœvre, Forêt de France
94 C10 Wofford Kentucky
25 D3 Wognum Netherlands
41 H3 Wohlen Switzerland
33 O5 Wohlenberg E Germany
40 F4 Wohlen See *L* Switzerland
36 F2 Wohratal W Germany
32 J4 Wöhrden W Germany
121 N7 Woito Ontario
143 A8 Wokarina W Australia
65 H1 Woken China
65 H1 Woken He *R* China
117 O8 Woking Alberta
9 F5 Woking England
9 F5 Wokingham England
141 G5 Wokingham *R* Queensland
33 S6 Wokuhl E Germany
31 L4 Wola Poland
98 H8 Wolbach Nebraska
32 G9 Wolbeck W Germany
101 T10 Wolcott Colorado
95 L3 Wolcott New York
32 E2 Woldbrunn W Germany
33 T6 Woldegk E Germany
141 J7 Woleebee Queensland
111 G11 Wolf *R* Mississippi
110 G6 Wolf *R* Tennessee
99 S4 Wolf *R* Wisconsin
117 G5 Wolf *R* Yukon Terr
36 E7 Wolfach W Germany
37 P6 Wolfachau W Germany
123 M3 Wolf Bay Quebec
108 D7 Wolf Cr Texas/Okla
94 B10 Wolf Cr. Dam Kentucky
101 N2 Wolf Creek Montana
100 B7 Wolf Creek Oregon
106 D4 Wolf Cr. Pass Colorado
118 J6 Wolfe Sask
95 Q3 Wolfeboro New Hampshire
109 L2 Wolfe City Texas
121 O8 Wolfe Island Ontario
118 G4 Wolfe L Alberta
33 Q9 Wolfen E Germany
33 N8 Wolfenbüttel W Germany
9 G2 Wolferton England
32 K10 Wolfhagen W Germany
103 L5 Wolf Hole Arizona
123 L6 Wolf I Madeleine Is, Quebec
117 H5 Wolf L Yukon Terr
101 S4 Wolf Mts Wyo/Mont
98 G1 Wolford N Dakota
98 A1 Wolf Pt Montana
140 B2 Wolfram Hill N Terr Aust
37 K5 Wolframs-Eschenbach W Germany
41 O2 Wolfratshausen W Germany
38 L8 Wolfsberg Austria
33 N8 Wolfsburg W Germany
37 N2 Wolfsgefärth E Germany
36 E4 Wolfskehlen W Germany
36 D4 Wolfstein W Germany
122 H8 Wolfville Nova Scotia
33 T4 Wolgast E Germany
33 T4 Wolgaster Fähre E Germany
31 H2 Wolin Poland
37 L3 Wölkendorf W Germany
37 P2 Wolkenstein E Germany
33 N10 Wolkramsh E Germany
114 H3 Wollaston, C N W Terr
133 D9 Wollaston, Is Chile
114 J6 Wollaston Lake Post Sask
114 H4 Wollaston Pen N W Terr
36 B2 Wollersheim W Germany
139 K5 Wollongong New S Wales
36 D4 Wöllstein W Germany
87 E11 Wolmaransstad S Africa
33 O9 Wolmirsleben E Germany
33 P8 Wolmirstedt E Germany
37 M6 Wolnzach W Germany
70 G6 Wolo Sulawesi
31 N3 Wołomin Poland
31 K4 Wołow Poland
71 K9 Wolowaru Flores Indonesia
119 O8 Wolseley Sask
138 F6 Wolseley S Australia
98 H5 Wolsey S Dakota
36 B4 Wolsfeld W Germany
13 G4 Wolsingham England
115 M5 Wolstenholme, C Quebec
31 J3 Wolsztyn Poland
32 L7 Wolthausen W Germany
33 M8 Woltorf W Germany
25 F3 Wolvega Netherlands
8 D2 Wolverhampton England
94 C1 Wolverine Michigan
22 G2 Wolvertem Belgium
9 E5 Wolverton England
98 K3 Wolverton Minnesota
9 E3 Wolvey England
120 H5 Woman River Ontario
141 F7 Wombunderry *R* Queensland
13 G6 Wombwell England
95 L6 Womelsdorf Pennsylvania
138 F3 Wompah New S Wales
140 D4 Wonarah N Terr Aust
143 E10 Wonberna W Australia
141 K7 Wondai Queensland
22 F1 Wondelgem Belgium
100 B7 Wonder Oregon
116 M5 Wonder L Alaska
140 E6 Wonditti,L Queensland
86 G4 Wondo Ethiopia
138 C4 Wondoma, C S Australia
140 F4 Wondoola Queensland
139 G4 Wongalarroo L New S Wales
141 G5 Wongalee Queensland
143 B9 Wongan Hills W Australia
70 G4 Wonggarasi Sulawesi
59 J4 Wŏnju S Korea
70 N9 Wonogiri Java
70 O9 Wonokromo Java
138 F4 Wonominta *R* N S Wales
70 N9 Wonosari Java
70 M9 Wonosobo Java
71 N9 Wonreli Indonesia
59 J4 Wŏnsan N Korea
139 H7 Wonthaggi Victoria
143 C6 Wonyulgunna,Mt W Australia
138 D4 Woocalla S Australia
94 J6 Wood Pennsylvania
98 F6 Wood S Dakota
116 O4 Wood *R* Alaska
140 D2 Woodah I N Terr Aust
146 J6 Wood B Antarctica
113 F7 Woodbine Georgia
99 L8 Woodbine Iowa
107 N3 Woodbine Kansas
94 C10 Woodbine Kentucky
95 N7 Woodbine New Jersey
9 H3 Woodbridge England
121 L9 Woodbridge Ontario
95 K8 Woodbridge Virginia
117 R6 Wood Buffalo Nat. Park Alberta
99 N8 Woodburn Iowa
110 K5 Woodburn Kentucky
139 L3 Woodburn New S Wales
100 C4 Woodburn Oregon
112 C5 Woodbury Georgia
95 M7 Woodbury New Jersey
110 K6 Woodbury Tennessee
112 F5 Woodcliff Georgia
140 C4 Woodcock,Mt N Terr Aust
139 L3 Wooded Bluff New S Wales
139 L3 Woodenbong New S Wales
144 B7 Woodend New Zealand
117 M11 Woodfibre Br Columbia
9 G4 Woodford England
127 P5 Woodford Grenada
14 C3 Woodford Irish Rep
140 C5 Woodforde *R* N Terr Aust
102 E3 Woodfords California
9 F4 Wood Green England
140 C5 Woodgreen N Terr Aust
9 F1 Woodhall Spa England
13 G6 Woodhead England
99 Q8 Woodhull Illinois
95 K4 Woodhull New York
100 C2 Woodinville Washington
122 K8 Wood Is Pr Edward I
119 U1 Wood L Manitoba
98 F7 Wood L Nebraska
119 O3 Wood L Sask
102 E5 Woodlake California
102 C3 Woodland California
110 J1 Woodland Illinois
94 J6 Woodland Pennsylvania
100 C4 Woodland Washington
109 N10 Woodland Hills Texas
106 E3 Woodland Park Colorado
119 U8 Woodlands Manitoba
137 L3 Woodlark *isld* Papua New Guinea
110 G3 Woodlawn Illinois
142 A3 Woodman Pt W Australia
101 Q4 Wood, Mt Montana
118 L9 Wood Mt Sask
117 C5 Wood, Mt Yukon Terr
117 M9 Woodpecker Br Columbia
118 E1 Woodridge Manitoba
140 E6 Woodridge,Mt N Terr Aust
110 F3 Wood River Illinois
98 H9 Wood River Nebraska
140 E5 Woodroffe *R* N Terr/Queensland
138 B2 Woodroffe, Mt S Australia
106 G2 Woodrow Colorado
118 L9 Woodrow Sask
103 O7 Woodruff Arizona
107 L2 Woodruff Kansas
101 O8 Woodruff Utah
101 Q4 Woods *mt* Montana
109 K7 Woodsboro Texas
94 F7 Woodsfield Ohio
122 G10 Woods Harbour Nova Scotia
145 E4 Woodside New Zealand
103 O2 Woodside Utah
139 H7 Woodside Victoria
140 C4 Woods,L N Terr Aust
118 H1 Woods, Lake of the Minn/Ontario
111 D7 Woodson Arkansas
99 Q10 Woodson Illinois
109 H2 Woodson Texas
139 H7 Woods Pt Victoria
9 E4 Woodstock England
99 S7 Woodstock Illinois
122 E7 Woodstock New Brunswick
141 G4 Woodstock Queensland
141 H4 Woodstock Queensland
95 P3 Woodstock Vermont
95 Q2 Woodstock, N New Hampshire
107 M2 Woodston Kansas
95 M7 Woodstown New Jersey
95 Q2 Woodsville New Hampshire
111 M11 Woodville Florida
111 E10 Woodville Mississippi
145 E4 Woodville New Zealand
94 D5 Woodville Ohio
121 M8 Woodville Ontario
109 N5 Woodville Texas
107 L5 Woodward Oklahoma
102 D4 Woodward Res California
122 F9 Woodwards Cove New Brunswick
109 P4 Woodworth Louisiana
98 G2 Woodworth N Dakota
8 C5 Woody B England
116 L8 Woody Island Alaska
123 P4 Woody Point Newfoundland
119 Q6 Woody R Manitoba
8 D3 Woofferton England
71 A3 Wooi Indonesia
8 D6 Wool England
8 B5 Woolacombe England
110 D3 Wooldridge Missouri
13 F3 Wooler England
118 D9 Woolford Prov. Park Alberta
143 D9 Woolgangie W Australia
141 G4 Woolgar Queensland
143 C6 Woolgathara W Australia
139 L4 Woolgoolga New S Wales
143 D9 Woolibar W Australia
140 C5 Woolla Downs N Terr Aust
9 G3 Woolpit England
102 F1 Woolsey Nevada
138 E4 Wooltana S Australia
8 D5 Woolverton England
9 G5 Woolwich England
138 D4 Woomera S Australia
95 Q5 Woonsocket Rhode I
98 H5 Woonsocket S Dakota
13 G3 Wooperton England
141 J6 Woorabinda Queensland
143 A7 Wooramel W Australia
143 A7 Wooramel R W Australia
8 D2 Woore England
138 C3 Woorong, L S Australia
94 F6 Wooster Ohio
9 E4 Wootton Bassett England
38 O6 Wopfing Austria
117 O7 Wor Alberta
71 B2 Wor *isld* Halmahera Indonesia
33 M10 Worbis E Germany
8 D3 Worcester England
95 Q4 Worcester Massachusetts
95 N4 Worcester New York
89 A9 Worcester S Africa
Worcester *co see* Hereford and Worcester *co*
110 G3 Worden Illinois
101 R4 Worden Montana
100 D7 Worden Oregon
146 F13 Wordie Ice Shelf Antarctica
119 P9 Wordsworth Sask
38 F7 Wörgl Austria
12 E4 Workington England
9 E1 Worksop England
25 D3 Workum Netherlands
101 S5 Worland Wyoming
8 D5 Worle England
33 Q9 Wörlitz E Germany
8 D4 Wormbridge England
25 C4 Wormerveer Netherlands
22 C2 Wormhoudt France
13 F1 Wormit Scotland
33 P10 Wormlitz E Germany
36 E4 Worms W Germany
8 B4 Worms Head Wales
37 K6 Wörnitz *R* W Germany
32 J6 Worpswede W Germany
36 B1 Worringen W Germany
36 E4 Wörrstadt W Germany
143 E7 Worsnop,Mt W Australia
38 G7 Wörth Austria

38 O7 Wörth Austria
37 N6 Wörth Bayern W Germany
99 M9 Worth Missouri
36 E5 Wörth Rheinland-Pfalz W Germany
109 L4 Wortham Texas
8 C2 Worthen England
38 K8 Wörther See L Austria
127 P6 Worthing Barbados
9 F6 Worthing England
110 K2 Worthington Indiana
99 L6 Worthington Minnesota
99 O9 Worthington Missouri
94 D6 Worthington Ohio
109 L9 Worth, L Texas
94 B3 Worthville Kentucky
13 G6 Wortley England
71 A3 Wosi Halmahera Indonesia
118 E5 Wostok Alberta
70 G6 Wosu Sulawesi
121 T7 Wotton Quebec
8 D4 Wotton under Edge England
70 G6 Wotu Sulawesi
25 D4 Woudenberg Netherlands
25 C5 Woudrichem Netherlands
98 D6 Wounded Knee S Dakota
25 B5 Wouw Netherlands
141 K6 Wowan Queensland Aust
71 H7 Wowoni isld Indonesia
69 C10 Woyla R Sumatra
31 L5 Woźniki Poland
9 F1 Wragby England
Wrangel I see Vrangelya, Os.
117 G7 Wrangell Alaska
116 Q6 Wrangell Mts Alaska/Yukon Terr
9 G1 Wrangle England
106 H1 Wray Colorado
9 F2 Wreak, R England
141 G1 Wreck B Gt Barrier Reef Aust
32 H5 Wremen W Germany
100 B5 Wren Oregon
112 E4 Wrens Georgia
118 E9 Wrentham Alberta
9 H3 Wrentham England
95 Q4 Wrentham Massachusetts
8 D1 Wrexham Wales
30 H3 Wriezen E Germany
107 L4 Wright Kansas
121 O6 Wright Quebec
71 G5 Wright Samar Philippines
112 M1 Wright Bros. Nat. Mem N Carolina
107 P7 Wright City Oklahoma
138 A3 Wright, L S Australia
138 F4 Wright, Mt N S Wales
68 A7 Wrightmyo Andaman Is
103 O10 Wrightson, Mt Arizona
112 E5 Wrightsville Georgia
95 L6 Wrightsville Pennsylvania
112 K3 Wrightsville Beach N Carolina
139 H4 Wrightville New S Wales
102 G7 Wrightwood California
117 M4 Wrigley N W Terr
146 J10 Wrigley G Antarctica
32 L5 Wrist W Germany
118 F9 Writing-on-Stone Prov. Park Alberta
31 K4 Wrocław Poland
119 V6 Wrong L Manitoba
31 J3 Wronki Poland
9 G5 Wrotham England
8 D2 Wroxeter England
9 H2 Wroxham England
9 E3 Wroxton England
119 Q7 Wroxton Sask
31 J4 Wschowa Poland
65 C6 Wu'an China
143 B9 Wubin W Australia
65 A6 Wubu China
65 E1 Wuchagou China
65 G2 Wuchang China
67 E1 Wuchang China
65 B6 Wucheng China
65 D6 Wucheng China
Wuchow see Wuzhou
65 B4 Wuchuan China
67 C2 Wuchuan China
67 B5 Wucun China
58 E4 Wuda China
65 E5 Wudao China
65 F3 Wudaogou China
67 C2 Wudaoshui China
65 D6 Wudi China
65 A6 Wuding He R China
138 D5 Wudinna S Australia
58 D5 Wudu China
67 A1 Wudu China
67 C1 Wufeng China
67 C3 Wugang China
58 E4 Wuhai China
67 E1 Wuhan China
58 G5 Wuhe China
32 J6 Wuhrden reg W Germany
67 F1 Wuhu China
65 C5 Wuji China
65 G2 Wujia China
67 C6 Wujia China
67 G1 Wujiang China
67 B3 Wu Jiang R China
67 C2 Wu Jiang R China
65 F2 Wujiazhan China
67 F1 Wukang China
85 F7 Wukari Nigeria
65 G2 Wulajie China
33 P9 Wulfen E Germany
32 F9 Wulfen W Germany
33 Q6 Wulfersdorf E Germany
32 F10 Wülfrath W Germany
32 M6 Wulfsen W Germany
32 M9 Wulften W Germany
68 J1 Wuli China
65 D7 Wulian China
67 B1 Wulian China
67 A3 Wulian Feng mts China
65 B8 Wulichuan China
67 C5 Wuli Jiang R China
116 F3 Wulik R Alaska
65 H2 Wulin China
67 C2 Wuling Shan mts China
67 C1 Wulingzhen China
67 B2 Wulong China
71 O8 Wulur Indonesia
37 K5 Wülzburg W Germany
85 G7 Wum Cameroon
139 H5 Wumbulgel New S Wales
67 A3 Wumeng Shan mts China
67 C5 Wuming China
32 K6 Wümme R W Germany
74 H8 Wun India
142 C3 Wungang R W Australia
88 D6 Wungu Tanzania
67 E2 Wuning China
138 F5 Wunkar S Australia
32 J9 Wünnenberg W Germany
33 S8 Wünsdorf East Germany
37 N3 Wunsiedel W Germany
32 K8 Wunstorf W Germany
75 Q7 Wuntho Burma
103 N6 Wupatki Nat. Mon Arizona
67 E4 Wuping China
32 F10 Wuppertal W Germany
66 A4 Wuqia China
65 C5 Wuqiang China
65 C6 Wuqiao China
65 D5 Wuqing China
143 B8 Wurarga W Australia
37 O7 Wurmannsquick W Germany
85 F6 Wurno Nigeria
25 F7 Würselen W Germany
95 N5 Wurtsboro New York
140 F4 Wurung Queensland
37 M3 Wurzbach E Germany
36 H4 Würzburg W Germany
33 R10 Wurzen E Germany
67 C1 Wushan China
67 D1 Wushan China
67 C1 Wu Shan mts China
67 B1 Wusheng China
67 F2 Wusheng China
67 D1 Wusheng Guan pass China
57 J4 Wushi China
68 J2 Wushi China
67 C3 Wu Shui R China
67 G1 Wusong China
36 H3 Wüstensachsen W Germany
33 Q7 Wusterhausen E Germany
33 R7 Wustermark E Germany
32 H6 Wüsting W Germany
33 R7 Wustrau E Germany
33 P4 Wustrow E Germany
33 O7 Wustrow W Germany
59 K2 Wusuli Jiang R China
41 H2 Wutach R W Germany
65 B5 Wutai China
58 F4 Wutai Shan mt ra China
65 D3 Wu-tan China
67 C4 Wutong China
67 A2 Wutongqiao China
22 H1 Wuustwezel Belgium
58 D4 Wuwei China
67 F1 Wuwei China
67 C1 Wuxi China
67 G1 Wuxi China
65 B6 Wuxiang China
67 G1 Wuxing China
67 C5 Wuxuan China
Wuxue see Guangji
Wuyang see Zhenyuan
65 B6 Wuyang China
65 C6 Wuyi China
67 F1 Wuyi China
67 F2 Wuyi China
67 E4 Wuyi Shan mts China
58 E3 Wuyuan China
67 F2 Wuyuan China
Wuyuanzhen see Haiyan
65 B5 Wuzhai China
65 G2 Wuzhan China
65 A6 Wuzhen China
67 D1 Wuzhen China
65 B7 Wuzhi China
67 C7 Wuzhi Shan pk China
58 E4 Wuzhong China
67 D5 Wuzhou China
141 F3 Wyaaba Cr Queensland
99 P9 Wyaconda R Missouri
143 B9 Wyalkatchem W Australia
139 H5 Wyalong New S Wales
94 D4 Wyandotte Michigan
141 H7 Wyandra Queensland
139 J5 Wyangala Res New S Wales
141 G8 Wyara L Queensland
101 T5 Wyarno Wyoming
110 G5 Wyatt Missouri
9 G5 Wych Cross England
139 G6 Wycheproof Victoria
9 G5 Wye England
143 C8 Wyemandoo mt W Australia
8 D4 Wye, R Wales/England
99 Q5 Wyeville Wisconsin
109 L2 Wylie Texas
142 B6 Wyloo W Australia
8 D5 Wylye, R England
95 S1 Wyman Dam Maine
118 K8 Wymark Sask
100 E3 Wymer Washington
9 H2 Wymondham England
98 K9 Wymore Nebraska
138 C4 Wynbring S Australia
144 B7 Wyndham New Zealand
136 F5 Wyndham W Australia
142 G3 Wyndham W Australia
142 E3 Wyndham Ra W Australia
98 J3 Wyndmere N Dakota
110 F6 Wynne Arkansas
142 E4 Wynne,Mt W Australia
107 N7 Wynnewood Oklahoma
114 H3 Wynniatt B N W Terr
141 L7 Wynnum Queensland
107 O5 Wynona Oklahoma
98 J7 Wynot Nebraska
119 N7 Wynyard Sask
139 H8 Wynyard Tasmania
99 R6 Wyocena Wisconsin
98 A5 Wyodak Wyoming
101 S4 Wyola Montana
138 B3 Wyola, L S Australia
95 M7 Wyoming Delaware
99 R8 Wyoming Illinois
99 N4 Wyoming Minnesota
94 J4 Wyoming New York
120 H10 Wyoming Ontario
95 Q5 Wyoming Rhode I
101 R6 Wyoming state U.S.A.
101 P7 Wyoming Pk Wyoming
101 P7 Wyoming Ra Wyoming
139 K5 Wyong New S Wales
13 F6 Wyre, R England
31 K2 Wyrzysk Poland
31 O5 Wysokie Poland
31 N3 Wysokie Mazowieckie Poland
31 N3 Wyszków Poland
31 M3 Wyszogrod Poland
13 E5 Wythburn England
94 F10 Wytheville Virginia
83 M14 Wyville-Thomson mt Kerguelen Indian Oc
66 B4 Xaidulla China
66 D5 Xainza China
87 F11 Xai-Xai Mozambique
125 P7 Xal, Cerro de mt Mexico
Xamba see Hanggin Houqi
129 J5 Xambioa Brazil
65 A3 Xangdin Hural China
66 C5 Xangdoring China
25 F5 Xanten W Germany
47 G3 Xánthi Greece
130 D10 Xanxerê Brazil
128 E6 Xapuri Brazil
65 C2 Xar Hudag China
65 B3 Xar Moron China
59 G3 Xar Moron He R China
65 B3 Xar Moron Sum China
Xauen see Chechaouen
87 D10 Xau, L Botswana
129 J6 Xavantes, Sa. dos mts Brazil
57 L4 Xayar China
Xêgar see Tingri
110 H3 Xenia Illinois
94 D7 Xenia Ohio
128 F4 Xeriuini R Brazil
46 D5 Xerovoúni R Greece
67 F3 Xiabaishi China
Xiabancheng see Chengde
65 D4 Xiabancheng China
65 H2 Xiachengzi China
65 B7 Xiachuan China
67 D6 Xiachuan Dao isld China
Xiacun see Rushan
65 C4 Xiahuayuan China
67 C4 Xiajiang China
67 E3 Xiajiang China
65 C6 Xiajin China
67 F4 Xiamen China
58 E5 Xi'an China
67 C2 Xianfeng China
58 C6 Xiangcheng China
65 B8 Xiangcheng China
67 D3 Xiangdong China
67 B5 Xiangdu China
58 F5 Xiangfan China
65 B7 Xiangfen China
65 D5 Xianghe China
65 B3 Xianghuang Qi China
67 D3 Xiang Jiang R China
65 H1 Xianglan China
65 A7 Xiangning China
66 B5 Xiangquan He R China
67 G2 Xiangshan China
67 G2 Xiangshan Gang B China
65 D7 Xiangshui China
67 D3 Xiangtan China
67 D3 Xiangxiang China
65 G2 Xiangyang China
67 D2 Xiangyin China
65 B6 Xiangyuan China
67 C5 Xiangzhou China
67 G2 Xianju China
58 F6 Xianning China
Xiannumiao see Jiangdu
Xiantaozhen see Mianyang
67 F3 Xianxia Ling mt ra China
58 E5 Xianyang China
67 F4 Xianyou China
65 G1 Xiaobai China
65 G2 Xiaocheng China
65 D3 Xiaochengzi China
65 D4 Xiaochengzi China
68 J1 Xiaodong China
Xiaofan see Wuqiang
67 D1 Xiaogan China
66 C2 Xiaoguai China
67 E1 Xiaohexi China
59 J1 Xiao Hinggan Ling mt ra China
Xiaojiang see Pubei
65 E3 Xiaojieji China
66 F4 Xiao Qaidam China
67 G1 Xiaoshan China
65 A7 Xiao Shan ra China
65 F4 Xiaoshi China
67 D4 Xiao Shui R China
65 A6 Xiaosuan China
65 C5 Xiaowutai Shan mt China
67 F2 Xiao Xi R China
65 D7 Xiao Xian China
Xiaoxita see Yichang
Xiaoyi see Gong Xian
65 B6 Xiaoyi China
67 F3 Xiapu China
Xiashi see Haining
65 B7 Xia Xian China
65 C7 Xiayi China
Xiayingpan see Luzhi
58 D6 Xichang China
67 C6 Xichang China
67 C2 Xiche China
Xicheng see Yangyuan
67 B1 Xichong China
67 A5 Xichou China
65 E2 Xi Dorolj China
67 D3 Xidu China
Xiedian see Wanrong
Xiejiaji see Qingyun
67 D1 Xiemahe China
68 F3 Xieng Khouang Laos
67 C6 Xieyang Dao isld China
65 A7 Xiezian China
65 F3 Xifeng China
67 B3 Xifeng China
65 D4 Xifengkou China
66 D6 Xigazê China
65 E4 Xi He R China
65 G1 Xiji China
67 D5 Xi Jiang R China
65 E1 Xikou China
67 C2 Xikou China
65 B3 Xil China
67 B4 Xilin China
62 C2 Xilin Gol R China
65 H2 Xilinhe China
65 B2 Xilin Qagan Obo China
46 F6 Xilókastron Greece
65 D3 Xiluga He R China
67 B3 Ximahe China
65 E5 Ximayi isld China
58 C3 Ximiao China
65 E4 Ximucheng China
65 B7 Xin'an China
67 F2 Xin'anjiang Shuiku res China
Xin'anzhen see Xinyi
65 F2 Xin'anzhen China
59 H3 Xinbin China
Xin Bulag see Xianghuang Qi
58 G5 Xincai China
67 D2 Xinchang China
59 H6 Xinchang Zhejiang China
65 C5 Xincheng China
65 H1 Xincheng China
67 C4 Xincheng China
65 F3 Xinchengzi China
67 C7 Xincun China
Xindeng see Chengyang
65 G2 Xindian China
67 C1 Xindianzi China
67 A1 Xindu China
67 D4 Xindu China
67 E3 Xinfeng China
67 E4 Xinfeng China
67 C4 Xing'an China
67 E3 Xingan China
67 E4 Xingcheng China
65 C5 Xingchi China
67 E3 Xingguo China
65 B4 Xinghe China
65 G1 Xinghua China
67 F4 Xinghua Wan B China
65 J2 Xingkai Hu L China
65 D4 Xinglong China
65 G1 Xinglongzhen China
67 E4 Xingning China
67 B3 Xingren China
67 B4 Xingren China
65 F1 Xingshan China
67 C1 Xingshan China
58 F4 Xingtai China
65 C5 Xingtang China
67 F3 Xingtian China
129 H4 Xingú R Brazil
67 A2 Xingwen China
65 B5 Xing Xian China
65 B7 Xingyang China
67 A4 Xingyi China
67 E2 Xingzi China
57 L4 Xinhe China
65 C6 Xinhe China
Xin Hot see Abag Qi
67 D3 Xinhua China
67 C3 Xinhuang China
Xinhui see Aohan Qi
67 D5 Xinhui China
46 E5 Xiniás, L Greece
58 D4 Xining China
Xinji see Shulu
67 E2 Xinjian China
65 B7 Xinjiang Shanxi China
67 E2 Xin Jiang R China
Xinjiangkou see Songzi
66 C3 Xinjiang Uygur Zizhiqu China
65 E5 Xinjin China
67 A1 Xinjin China
65 E3 Xinkai He R China
65 C5 Xinle China
65 G2 Xinli China
65 D3 Xinlin China
65 E3 Xinlitun China
65 A5 Xinminzhen China
67 C3 Xinning China
Xinpu see Lianyungang
67 D2 Xinqiang China
67 D3 Xinshao China
65 D7 Xintai China
67 D1 Xintankou China
67 D4 Xintian China
65 D7 Xinwen China
65 B5 Xin Xian China
67 E1 Xin Xian China
65 B7 Xinxiang China
67 D5 Xinxing China
68 J3 Xinxing China
58 F5 Xinyang China
67 E1 Xinyang China
65 D7 Xinyi China
67 C5 Xinyi China
65 D7 Xinyi He R China
67 C7 Xinying China
67 E3 Xinyu China
65 D6 Xinzhai China
65 F2 Xinzhan China
65 G3 Xinzhan China
65 B7 Xinzheng China
58 F5 Xinzhou China
67 E1 Xinzhou China
58 F5 Xiong'er Shan mt ra China
65 C5 Xiong Xian China
65 E4 Xiongyuecheng China
65 B4 Xiping China
58 D4 Xiqing Shan mt ra China
129 K6 Xique-Xique Brazil
Xishuanghe see Kenli
67 B2 Xishui Guizhou China
67 E1 Xishui Hubei China
65 D2 Xi Ujimqin Qi China
67 F2 Xiuning China
58 E6 Xiushan China
67 C2 Xiushan China
67 E2 Xiushui China
67 E2 Xiu Shui R China
65 B7 Xiuwu China
65 F4 Xiuyan China
Xiwanzi see Chongli
66 D6 Xixabangma Feng mt China
65 A6 Xi Xian China
65 B6 Xiyang China
67 F3 Xiyang China
67 G3 Xiyang Dao isld China
67 B5 Xiyang Jiang R China
67 B5 Xiyangjie China
66 C5 Xizang Zizhiqu aut reg China
65 E5 Xizhong Dao isld China
125 K8 Xochimilco Mexico
58 G5 Xuancheng China
67 C1 Xuan'en China
67 B1 Xuanhan China
58 F3 Xuanhua China
67 A3 Xuanwei China
58 F5 Xuchang China
67 G2 Xuedou Shan mt China
67 C3 Xuefeng Shan mts China
65 A7 Xuejiaying China
Xugezhuang see Fengnan
59 H2 Xuguit Qi China
67 E3 Xu Jiang R China
65 E4 Xujiatun China
Xulun Hobot Qagan see Zhengxiangbai Qi
Xulun Hoh see Zhenlan Qi
67 A4 Xundian China
59 J2 Xunhe China
58 E5 Xun He R China
67 E4 Xunwu China
65 C7 Xun Xian China
65 A7 Xunyi China
67 C3 Xupu China
65 C5 Xushui China
67 E3 Xuwan China
67 C6 Xuwen China
68 H7 Xuyen Moc Vietnam
58 E6 Xuyong China
58 G5 Xuzhou China
100 K1 Yaak Montana
141 K6 Yaamba Queensland
67 A2 Ya'an China
138 F6 Yaapeet Victoria
86 B5 Yabassi Cameroon
86 G5 Yabelo Ethiopia
80 F4 Yabis R Jordan
125 N2 Yablis Nicaragua
48 J2 Yablonitse, Pereval pass U.S.S.R.
48 J2 Yablonov U.S.S.R.
51 L3 Yablonovyy, Khrebet mts U.S.S.R.
79 G5 Yabrūd Syria
141 H4 Yabulu Queensland
141 H5 Yacamunda Queensland
Yacha see Baisha
100 A5 Yachats Oregon
67 C7 Yacheng China
60 D14 Yachi Japan
67 B3 Yachi He R China
130 C10 Yaciretá isld Paraguay
139 H6 Yackandandah Victoria
100 C4 Yacolt Washington
133 E2 Yacuiba Bolivia
128 E6 Yacuma R Bolivia
128 E3 Yacurai Venezuela
80 D4 Yad Hanna Israel
112 F1 Yadkin R N Carolina
112 G1 Yadkinville N Carolina
80 B7 Yad Mordekhay Israel
80 C6 Yad Rambam Israel
68 H6 Ya Drang R Cambodia
52 G6 Yadrin U.S.S.R.
80 C5 Yafo Israel
84 E3 Yafran Libya
61 Q12 Yagaji-jima isld Okinawa
60 C13 Yagami Japan
47 J5 Yağcılar Turkey
60 P1 Yagishiri-tō isld Japan
124 G7 Yago Mexico
55 E2 Yagodnyy U.S.S.R.
52 G4 Yagrysh U.S.S.R.
126 E3 Yaguajay Cuba
131 G3 Yaguari R Uruguay
128 D4 Yaguas R Peru
124 E4 Yagui Mexico
80 D3 Yagur Israel
69 E9 Yaha Thailand
61 L10 Yahagi-gawa R Japan
100 J1 Yahk Br Columbia
124 H7 Yahualica Mexico
86 D5 Yahuma Zaïre
78 E2 Yahyali Turkey
68 D6 Yai, Khao mt Burma/Thailand
61 N9 Yaita Japan
61 M11 Yaizu Japan
80 G5 Yajuz Jordan
116 Q6 Yakataga Alaska
Yakeshi see Xuguit Qi
80 B8 Yakhini Israel
54 J1 Yakhroma U.S.S.R.
55 E2 Yakhtur, Oz L U.S.S.R.
100 E3 Yakima Washington
74 C8 Yakmach Pakistan
85 D6 Yako Upper Volta
117 E6 Yakobi I Alaska
86 D5 Yakoma Zaïre
47 F2 Yakoruda Bulgaria
86 D4 Yakossi Cent Afr Republic
57 K4 Yakrik China
52 J4 Yaksha U.S.S.R.
52 G5 Yakshanga U.S.S.R.
52 H6 Yakshur-Bod'ya U.S.S.R.
101 L1 Yakt Montana
60 O3 Yakumo Japan
59 J5 Yaku-shima isld Japan
117 D6 Yakutat Alaska
117 C6 Yakutat B Alaska
51 M2 Yakutsk U.S.S.R.
69 E9 Yala Thailand
83 L11 Yala game reserve Sri Lanka
47 K4 Yalakdere Turkey
144 D5 Yaldhurst New Zealand
117 N11 Yale Br Columbia
110 H2 Yale Illinois
99 M8 Yale Iowa
94 E3 Yale Michigan
107 O5 Yale Oklahoma
98 H5 Yale S Dakota
86 D5 Yaleko Zaïre
100 C4 Yale L Washington
143 B8 Yalgoo W Australia
86 D4 Yalinga Cent Afr Republic
127 L3 Yallahs Jamaica
127 L2 Yallahs R Jamaica
141 H6 Yalleroi Queensland
143 B10 Yallingup W Australia
139 H7 Yallourn Victoria
111 F8 Yalobusha R Mississippi
143 C7 Yaloginda W Australia
86 C4 Yaloké Cent Afr Republic
66 F5 Yalong Jiang R China
47 K4 Yalova Turkey
48 M4 Yalpukh R U.S.S.R.
138 F3 Yalpunga New S Wales Australia
48 L1 Yaltushkov U.S.S.R.
65 E1 Yalu He R China
65 G4 Yalu River China/Korea
55 E4 Yalym U.S.S.R.
60 Q2 Yamabe Karikachi Pass Japan
61 Q6 Yamada wan B Japan
60 D12 Yamaga Japan
61 O7 Yamagata Japan
61 N7 Yamagata prefect Japan
60 D14 Yamagawa Japan
60 E11 Yamaguchi Japan
59 K1 Yam-Alin', Khrebet mt U.S.S.R.
50 F1 Yamal, Poluostrov pen U.S.S.R.
61 M10 Yamanaka ko L Japan
61 M10 Yamanashi prefect Japan
47 J6 Yamanlar Dağı mt Turkey
58 F1 Yamarovka U.S.S.R.
60 H10 Yamasaki Japan
121 S6 Yamaska Quebec
113 G11 Yamato Florida
139 L3 Yamba New S Wales
138 F5 Yamba S Australia
139 G7 Yambacoona Tasmania
86 D4 Yambala Cent Afr Republic
85 B6 Yambering Guinea
128 D3 Yambi, Mesa de Colombia
86 E5 Yambio Sudan
47 H2 Yambol Bulgaria
Yamdrok Tso see Yamzho Yumco
68 C2 Yamethin Burma
80 E8 Yam Hamelah Israel
52 D6 Yami U.S.S.R.
61 O9 Yamizo-san mt Japan
80 F2 Yam Kinneret Israel
52 C5 Yamm U.S.S.R.
141 F7 Yamma Yamma,L Queensland
79 E7 Yammit Israel
85 D7 Yamoussoukro Ivory Coast
101 T9 Yampa Colorado
101 R9 Yampa R Colorado
142 E3 Yampi Sound W Australia
48 L2 Yampol U.S.S.R.
100 D7 Yamsay Mt Oregon
52 G4 Yamskoye U.S.S.R.
73 M3 Yamuna R India
74 G3 Yamunanagar India
55 G4 Yamyshevo U.S.S.R.
66 E6 Yamzho Yumco L China
51 N2 Yana R U.S.S.R.
138 F6 Yanac Victoria
60 D12 Yanagawa Japan
61 O8 Yanagawa Japan
61 P12 Yanaha-jima isld Okinawa
76 F2 Yanam India
65 A6 Yan'an China
128 D6 Yanaoca Peru
56 D2 Yanashimskiy Polkan peak U.S.S.R.
139 G4 Yancannia New S Wales
109 H6 Yancey Texas
112 H1 Yanceyville N Carolina
65 A6 Yanchang China
77 B3 Yanchashmeh Iran
Yancheng see Qihe
59 H5 Yancheng China
67 F1 Yancheng China
143 B9 Yanchep W Australia
65 A6 Yanchuan China
139 H5 Yanco New S Wales
143 D8 Yandal W Australia
138 F3 Yandama R S Australia
65 A4 Yandian China
143 C7 Yandil W Australia
141 L7 Yandina Queensland
68 B4 Yandoon Burma
85 C6 Yanfolila Mali
86 D5 Yangambi Zaïre
66 E5 Yangbajain China
65 B7 Yangcheng China
Yangchuan see Suiyang
67 D5 Yangchun China
Yangcun see Wuqing
67 E5 Yangcun China
65 F3 Yangdachengzi China
142 A3 Yangebup L W Australia
65 J2 Yanggang China
58 F3 Yanggao China
65 C6 Yanggu China
57 F4 Yangibazar U.S.S.R.
77 B2 Yangi Emām Iran
67 D6 Yangjiang China
65 E4 Yangjiazhangzi China
67 F3 Yangkou China
67 A4 Yanglin China
67 D2 Yangloudong China
65 C7 Yangmiao China
67 D3 Yangming Shan mt China
52 E3 Yangory U.S.S.R.
67 D7 Yangpu Gang inlet China
65 B6 Yangquan China
67 D3 Yangquan China
65 C7 Yangshan China
67 D4 Yangshan China
Yangshe see Shazhou
67 C4 Yangshuo China
67 F1 Yangtan China
Yangtze Gorges see Qutang Xia Wu Xia
Yangtze Kiang R see Chang Jiang
67 G1 Yangtze Kiang, Mouths of the China
55 E2 Yangutumskiye U.S.S.R.
68 D6 Yangwa Burma
67 E2 Yangxin China
65 B4 Yangyuan China
67 F1 Yangzhou China
67 C2 Yanhe China
65 A6 Yan He R China
138 D5 Yaninee, L S Australia
52 D4 Yanis'yarvi, Oz L U.S.S.R.
65 H3 Yanji China
65 C7 Yanjin China
67 A2 Yanjin China
67 B2 Yanjing China
139 H6 Yanko R New S Wales
138 F4 Yanko Glen New S Wales
98 J7 Yankton S Dakota
65 C7 Yanling China
Yannina see Ioánnina
54 B1 Yanovichi U.S.S.R.
52 G6 Yanovo U.S.S.R.
83 K9 Yan Oya R Sri Lanka
66 D3 Yanqi China
65 C4 Yanqing China
142 A6 Yanrey W Australia
65 D5 Yanshan China
67 A5 Yanshan China
67 F2 Yanshan China
65 D4 Yan Shan mts China
65 B7 Yanshi China
67 F4 Yanshi China
59 J2 Yanshou China
51 N1 Yanskiy Zaliv B U.S.S.R.
139 H3 Yantabulla New S Wales
59 H4 Yantai China
138 F3 Yantara, L N S Wales
67 B1 Yanting China
65 G3 Yantongshan China
67 G2 Yantou China
47 H1 Yantra R Bulgaria
80 D2 Yanūh Israel
Yanwu see Yuanyang
57 D3 Yany Kurgan U.S.S.R.
65 C7 Yanzhou China
67 B3 Yanzikou China
86 C3 Yao Chad
61 J11 Yao Japan
Yaodu see Dongzhi
65 A6 Yaotou China
86 B5 Yaoundé Cameroon
65 D7 Yaowan China
65 A7 Yao Xian China
69 D9 Yao Yai, Ko isld Thailand
136 H2 Yapen isld W Irian
141 F4 Yappar R Queensland
Yaqian see Yuexi
127 J5 Yaque del Sur R Dom Rep
124 E3 Yaqui R Mexico
100 A5 Yaquina Head Oregon
80 C5 Yaqum Israel
52 H5 Yar U.S.S.R.
126 F4 Yara Cuba
128 E1 Yaracuy state Venezuela
141 G6 Yaraka Queensland
52 G6 Yaransk U.S.S.R.
47 K7 Yaraşlı Gölü L Turkey
47 K6 Yarbasan Turkey
8 C6 Yarcombe England
138 D4 Yardea S Australia
80 F3 Yardena Israel
52 H3 Yarega U.S.S.R.
48 J2 Yaremcha U.S.S.R.
52 G3 Yarenga U.S.S.R.
52 G4 Yarensk U.S.S.R.
9 H2 Yare, R England
128 D3 Yari R Colombia
47 L5 Yarimca Turkey
80 D1 Yârîne Lebanon
140 E5 Yaringa R Queensland
128 E1 Yaritagua Venezuela
Yarkand see Shache
Yarkand R see Yarkant He
66 B4 Yarkant He R China
55 E3 Yarkovo U.S.S.R.
138 B4 Yarle Lakes S Australia
66 D6 Yarlung Zangbo Jiang R China
13 G5 Yarm England
48 K1 Yarmolintsy U.S.S.R.
9 E6 Yarmouth England
95 R3 Yarmouth Maine
95 R5 Yarmouth Massachusetts
122 F10 Yarmouth Nova Scotia
80 F3 Yarmuk R Syria
103 M7 Yarnell Arizona
52 E5 Yaroslavl' U.S.S.R.
80 E1 Yâroûn Lebanon
54 J7 Yarovaya U.S.S.R.
80 C5 Yarqon Israel
139 H7 Yarra R Victoria
141 G2 Yarraden Queensland
142 B5 Yarraloola W Australia
139 H7 Yarram Victoria
141 K7 Yarraman Queensland
140 D4 Yarran Ra N Terr Aust
139 H6 Yarrawonga Victoria
143 B8 Yarra Yarra Ls W Australia
142 D5 Yarrie W Australia
141 H7 Yarronvale Queensland
15 E5 Yarrow R Scotland
141 H5 Yarrowmere Queensland
55 F1 Yarsomovy U.S.S.R.
54 D1 Yartsevo U.S.S.R.
128 C2 Yarumal Colombia
48 L2 Yaryshev U.S.S.R.
86 D5 Yasanyama Zaire
137 Q5 Yasawa Grp islds Fiji
85 F6 Yashi Nigeria
85 E7 Yashikera Nigeria
60 F12 Ya-shima Japan
61 O6 Yashima Japan
60 F12 Yashiro-jima Japan
55 B4 Yashkino U.S.S.R.
54 J8 Yasinovataya U.S.S.R.
48 J2 Yasinya U.S.S.R.
139 J5 Yass New S Wales
60 G12 Yasuda Japan
60 G10 Yasugi Japan
77 B4 Yasuj Iran
128 E6 Yata Bolivia
47 J7 Yatağan Turkey
85 E6 Yatakala Niger
106 G5 Yates New Mexico
94 H6 Yatesboro Pennsylvania
107 P4 Yates Center Kansas
115 K5 Yathkyed L N W Terr
80 D5 Yatma Jordan
86 D5 Yatolema Zaïre
Yatou see Rongcheng
61 M10 Yatsuga take mt Japan
61 L9 Yatsuo Japan
60 D13 Yatsushiro Japan
80 D8 Yatta Jordan
8 D5 Yatton England
141 J6 Yatton Queensland
128 E3 Yatua R Venezuela
128 D7 Yauca Peru
127 L5 Yauco Puerto Rico
112 H4 Yauhannah S Carolina
128 C6 Yauyos Peru
103 M7 Yava Arizona
57 E5 Yavan U.S.S.R.
124 E4 Yavaros Mexico
128 D6 Yavero R Peru
128 E8 Yavi Argentina
128 E2 Yavi, Co mt Venezuela
128 E3 Yavita Venezuela
55 E4 Yavlenka U.S.S.R.
80 B6 Yavne Israel
80 F3 Yavnee Israel
31 O6 Yavorov U.S.S.R.
29 O3 Yavra R U.S.S.R.
68 B2 Yaw R Burma
60 F12 Yawatahama Japan
68 C2 Yawng-hwe Burma
67 B3 Yaxi China
67 C7 Ya Xian China
56 C3 Yaya U.S.S.R.
52 J5 Yayva R U.S.S.R.
77 C3 Yazd Iran
77 C4 Yazd-e Khvāst Iran
57 F5 Yazgulemskiy Khr mts U.S.S.R.
55 C4 Yazikovo U.S.S.R.
111 F9 Yazoo City Mississippi
52 J4 Yaz'va R U.S.S.R.
38 M5 Ybbs Austria
38 L6 Ybbsitz Austria
130 C9 Ybycúi Paraguay
28 A3 Ydby Denmark
28 G5 Yderby Denmark
28 D5 Yding Skovhøj hill Denmark
52 J3 Ydzhid Parma U.S.S.R.
68 C5 Ye Burma
139 H6 Yea Victoria
8 B7 Yealmpton England
Yebaishou see Jianping
86 C1 Yebbi bou Chad
16 D9 Yebel Buhasen mt Morocco
20 G2 Yébleron France
68 D5 Yebyu Burma
66 B4 Yecheng China
17 G6 Yecla Spain
124 E3 Yécora Mexico
68 C3 Yedashe Burma
47 K8 Yedi Burun C Turkey
48 L2 Yedintsy U.S.S.R.
52 F3 Yedoma Arkhangelsk U.S.S.R.
52 H2 Yedoma Komi U.S.S.R.
84 F5 Yédri Chad
142 E4 Yeeda River W Australia
138 D5 Yeelanna S Australia
52 D5 Yefimovskiy U.S.S.R.
54 K3 Yefremov U.S.S.R.
55 G6 Yegendybulak U.S.S.R.
55 E5 Yegindykol' U.S.S.R.
53 F10 Yegorlyk R U.S.S.R.
54 L1 Yegor'yevsk U.S.S.R.
130 C10 Yegros Paraguay
109 K5 Yegua Cr Texas
16 D7 Yeguas, Sa. de mts Spain
131 B5 Yeguas, Vol Chile
50 F2 Yehzarovo U.S.S.R.
86 F5 Yei Sudan
67 E1 Yeji China
85 D7 Yeji Ghana
Yekaterinburg see Sverdlovsk
55 D1 Yekaterininka U.S.S.R.
55 F3 Yekaterininskoye U.S.S.R.
59 J1 Yekaterinoslavka U.S.S.R.
54 K4 Yekaterinovka U.S.S.R.
68 A3 Ye Kyun isld Burma
52 H6 Yelabuga U.S.S.R.
55 D2 Yelan' U.S.S.R.
53 F8 Yelan' R U.S.S.R.
54 N5 Yelan'-Koleno U.S.S.R.
141 K8 Yelarbon Queensland
58 F1 Yeleninskiy U.S.S.R.
54 J9 Yelenovka U.S.S.R.
54 G3 Yelenskiy U.S.S.R.
54 K4 Yelets U.S.S.R.
55 E1 Yelizarovo U.S.S.R.
55 C5 Yelizavetinka U.S.S.R.
59 M1 Yelizavety, Mys C U.S.S.R.
15 G1 Yell isld Scotland
76 E2 Yellandu India
111 K10 Yellow R Alabama
99 Q5 Yellow R Wisconsin
119 M6 Yellow Creek Sask
143 C9 Yellowdine W Australia
119 N9 Yellow Grass Sask
114 H7 Yellowhead Pass Alberta
114 H5 Yellowknife N W Terr
99 L5 Yellow Medicine R Minnesota
139 H4 Yellow Mt New S Wales
100 K5 Yellow Pine Idaho
Yellow R see Huang He
59 H4 Yellow Sea China/Korea
110 N2 Yellow Springs Ohio
98 B2 Yellowstone R Montana
101 P5 Yellowstone L Wyoming
101 P5 Yellowstone Nat. Park Wyoming
15 G1 Yell Sound Scotland
110 D5 Yellville Arkansas
54 E2 Yel'nya U.S.S.R.
56 C1 Yeloguy R U.S.S.R.
55 E3 Yeloshnoye U.S.S.R.
55 C3 Yelovo Barda U.S.S.R.
16 C4 Yeltes R Spain
52 D6 Yel'tsy U.S.S.R.
125 M2 Yelucá mt Nicaragua
52 H3 Yelva R U.S.S.R.
140 E5 Yelvertoft Queensland
8 B7 Yelverton England
115 L1 Yelverton B N W Terr
85 E6 Yelwa Nigeria
55 D4 Yemanzhelinsk U.S.S.R.
112 G5 Yemassee S Carolina
72 E5 Yemen, North rep Arabia
72 F5 Yemen, South rep Arabia
55 E3 Yemets R U.S.S.R.
52 F3 Yemetsk U.S.S.R.
52 F3 Yemtsa U.S.S.R.
52 D1 Yena U.S.S.R.
54 K8 Yenakiyevo U.S.S.R.
68 B2 Yenangyat Burma
68 B2 Yenangyaung Burma
68 B3 Yenanma Burma
67 A6 Yen Bai Vietnam
67 A6 Yen Chau Vietnam
139 H5 Yenda New S Wales
85 E7 Yendi Ghana
58 F1 Yendondin U.S.S.R.
55 E1 Yendra U.S.S.R.
55 E1 Yendyr' U.S.S.R.
68 C2 Yengan Burma
66 B4 Yengisar China
47 J5 Yenice Turkey
47 H6 Yenifoça Turkey
47 J5 Yeniköy Turkey
31 M1 Yenino U.S.S.R.
47 J7 Yenipazar Aydin Turkey
47 L4 Yenipazar Bilecik Turkey
47 K4 Yenişehir Turkey
56 D2 Yenisey R U.S.S.R.
56 D2 Yeniseysk U.S.S.R.
50 H1 Yeniseyskiy Zaliv gulf U.S.S.R.
68 G2 Yen Lap Vietnam
68 G1 Yen Minh Vietnam
19 P13 Yenne France
52 E1 Yenozero, Oz L U.S.S.R.
68 G3 Yen Thanh Vietnam
116 M5 Yentna R Alaska
143 E8 Yeo, L W Australia
74 F8 Yeola India
Yeóryios isld see Áyios I
74 H8 Yeotmal India
139 J5 Yeoval New S Wales
8 D6 Yeovil England
124 E3 Yepachic Mexico
54 K3 Yepifan U.S.S.R.
141 K6 Yeppoon Queensland
46 F7 Yeráki Greece
124 J6 Yerbabuena Mexico
56 G1 Yerbogachen U.S.S.R.
78 E2 Yercöy Turkey
138 C4 Yerda S Australia
20 H2 Yère R France
55 F5 Yerementau, Gy mt U.S.S.R.
78 K1 Yerevan U.S.S.R.
56 D4 Yergak-Targak-Tayga, Khrebet mts U.S.S.R.
53 F9 Yergeni hills U.S.S.R.
143 D8 Yerilla W Australia
102 E3 Yerington Nevada
47 J7 Yerkesik Turkey
55 G4 Yermak U.S.S.R.
55 F1 Yermakovo U.S.S.R.
56 D4 Yermakovskoye U.S.S.R.
55 F5 Yermentau U.S.S.R.
52 H2 Yermitsa U.S.S.R.
102 H7 Yermo California
124 G4 Yermo Mexico
55 C4 Yermolayevo U.S.S.R.
54 H1 Yermolino U.S.S.R.
59 H1 Yerofey Pavlovich U.S.S.R.
79 E8 Yeroham Israel
141 K2 Yeronga dist Brisbane, Qnsld
52 H2 Yersa R U.S.S.R.
25 B6 Yerseke Netherlands
52 F4 Yertsevo U.S.S.R.
128 C6 Yerupaja mt Peru
80 D6 Yerushalayim Israel
20 G2 Yerville France
68 B2 Yesagyo Burma
67 C1 Yesanguan China
52 D6 Yesenovichi U.S.S.R.
55 E5 Yesil' U.S.S.R.
47 K5 Yesil Dağı mt Turkey
47 K7 Yeşilova Turkey
108 C1 Yeso New Mexico
80 C6 Yesodot Israel
51 K2 Yessey U.S.S.R.
17 F6 Yeste Spain
80 F1 Yesud HaMa'ala Israel
13 F3 Yetholm Scotland
139 K3 Yetman New S Wales
68 B1 Yeu Burma
18 D6 Yeu, I d' France
55 F3 Yevgashchino U.S.S.R.
21 J7 Yèvre R France
59 K2 Yevreysk Aut. Oblast reg U.S.S.R.
65 D6 Ye Xian China
78 L1 Yeylakh U.S.S.R.
53 E10 Yeysk U.S.S.R.
52 D6 Yezerishche U.S.S.R.
52 G5 Yezhikha U.S.S.R.
52 G3 Yezhuga R U.S.S.R.
130 C9 Yguazu, R Paraguay
130 C9 Yhú Paraguay
47 J8 Yiali isld Greece
84 J3 Yi' Allaq, Gebel Egypt
79 E3 Yialousa Cyprus
47 H9 Yianisádhes isld Crete Greece
46 E4 Yiannitsá Greece
68 E1 Yibang China
Yibei see Minglun
67 A2 Yibin China
80 B6 Yibna Israel
58 F5 Yichang China
67 D1 Yichang China
65 B7 Yicheng China
65 D7 Yicheng China
67 D1 Yicheng China
65 A6 Yichuan China
65 B7 Yichuan China
59 J2 Yichun China
67 E3 Yichun China
58 F5 Yidu China
65 D6 Yidu China
67 E2 Yifeng China
80 F1 Yiftah Israel
65 B7 Yi He R China
65 D7 Yi He R China

25 D4 **Zuidelijk-Flevoland** Netherlands
Zuider Zee *see* **Ijsselmeer**
25 C4 **Zuid Holland** *prov* Netherlands
25 F2 **Zuidhorn** Netherlands
25 G2 **Zuidlaarder Meer** Netherlands
25 B5 **Zuidland** Netherlands
25 G2 **Zuidlaren** Netherlands
25 F3 **Zuidwolde** Netherlands
17 F7 **Zújar** Spain
16 D6 **Zújar** *R* Spain
16 D6 **Zújar, Embalse de** *res* Spain
86 G2 **Zula** Ethiopia
128 D2 **Zulia** *state* Venezuela
36 B2 **Zülpich** W Germany
87 F9 **Zumbo** Mozambique
99 O5 **Zumbro** *R* Minnesota
99 O5 **Zumbro Falls** Minnesota
99 O5 **Zumbro R** Minnesota
125 K8 **Zumpango** Mexico
100 J4 **Zumwalt** Oregon
25 C6 **Zundert** Netherlands
85 F7 **Zungeru** Nigeria
58 G3 **Zunhua** China
106 B6 **Zuni** New Mexico
67 B3 **Zunyi** China
67 B5 **Zuo Jiang** *R* China
65 B4 **Zuoyun** China
67 B5 **Zuozhou** China
41 J3 **Zürich** Switzerland
41 J3 **Zürich See** *L* Switzerland
25 F4 **Zutphen** Netherlands
56 G3 **Zvezdnyy** U.S.S.R.
36 C5 **Zweibrücken** W Germany
37 N2 **Zwickau** E Germany
25 F3 **Zwolle** Netherlands
56 B6 **Zyryanovsk** U.S.S.R.
79 D4 **Zyyi** Cyprus

THE TRANSCRIPTION OF CHINESE PLACE-NAMES

Chinese is written in Han characters, a system of writing which has remained in use for more than 3,000 years. Its most conspicuous features are the large number of characters and the complexity of most of them. All told, there cannot be fewer than 50,000, of which perhaps 11,000 may be encountered in bibliographic or similar research. Up to 3,000 characters are used in everyday written communication.

Han characters are ideographs but since the language is a spoken language and not just written, each character can be represented by a syllable – a vowel or a vowel with one or more consonants. Because the spoken language evolves with time and pronunciation varies with dialect many different readings of a character are possible.

Compared with English and other European languages, Chinese has few syllables, in Modern Standard Chinese hardly more than 400. With thousands of characters in use, many are equated with the same syllable. The syllable **sên** is represented by only one character. In contrast **yi** can be expressed by over 215. Tone (the modulation of the voice) helps to distinguish meaning, but generally context alone determines what is meant.

So complex a system of writing is not well suited to a modern industrial society but rather to a peasant community where the literate few have unlimited time to study. Printing is a formidable matter compared with European languages. Learning to read and write involves mastery of a large number of characters, imposing a great demand on memory and requiring a considerable amount of time.

There are many romanization systems for Chinese. Four are widely used in English. Of these the Wade-Giles system is most familiar. All British and American official maps have used the system exclusively since 1942, and millions of references exist in Wade-Giles romanizations. The system was first published in 1859 by Sir Thomas Wade and it was the basis, slightly modified, for the Chinese-English Dictionary of H. A. Giles published in 1912.

Of all the dialects of China, Northern Chinese (formerly called Mandarin Chinese) is most widespread. Wade-Giles and all systems since have used the educated Peking dialect of Northern Chinese as the standard language and the preferred readings of characters are given in that dialect which has become the model for Modern Standard Chinese.

Chinese, as distinct from European, interest in romanization was stimulated by the desire to promote a national language as well as to assist in learning to read the characters. Romanization would also serve as a means of writing the non-Chinese languages spoken within China and to help to write them in Chinese. A further aim was to encourage foreigners to learn Chinese.

As a first step towards these goals the most commonly used characters were simplified. Much discussion has centred around the replacement of Han characters by an alphabet, but this can only happen in the very remote future. Romanized Chinese may increasingly exist side-by-side with the characters but that does not mean that the Han characters are about to be dropped from use.

In 1958, the Chinese government approved the system called **Pinyin zimu** (phonetic alphabet) for the romanization of Chinese. Teachers of Chinese prefer Pinyin to Wade-Giles. It is a better source for up-to-date idiom and vocabulary but a great amount of material is not yet available in Pinyin. Students of Chinese, therefore, have to deal with other systems of romanization. For geographical names almost nothing existed in Pinyin for many years. Everything worth considering was in Wade-Giles. Yet in spite of the fact that the letters **c**, **q** and **x** were used in a way totally alien to English usage, Pinyin was neater than Wade-Giles which, for example, produces **Wu-lu-mu-chi** for English conventional **Urumchi** where Pinyin gives **Urumqi**. **Harbin** is so spelled in Pinyin but becomes **Ha-erh-pin** in Wade-Giles.

Ever since Pinyin was launched in 1958, the publishers of *The Times Atlas* have contemplated but, until now, rejected, the adoption of Pinyin for the map plates covering China. Among the factors considered were the availability of sources for Pinyin names, the extent to which Pinyin was used in China and the acceptance and use of Pinyin outside China, particularly for geographical names. In spite of a State Council directive of 1975 that Pinyin would be used as the standard and sole romanization system for geographical and personal names, little was done in China to follow the directive until 1977. Early in 1979 Pinyin was accepted by most nations of the world as the system to be employed officially for romanized Chinese names. Times Books of London, the publishers of the Atlas, therefore decided to adopt Pinyin in place of Wade-Giles for the names of Mainland China and the map plates in this atlas now contain Pinyin names in place of Wade-Giles.

By way of example Peking in conventional English is **Beijing** in Pinyin and appears in that form in this atlas as opposed to **Pei-ching** in Wade-Giles. **Guangzhou** (Canton) in Pinyin was **Kuang-chou** in Wade-Giles. Further examples are: **Chongqing** (Chungking), **Ch'ung-ch'ing**; **Fuzhou** (Foochow), **Fu-chou**; **Jilin** (Kirin), **Chi-lin**; **Xian** (Sian), **Hsi-an**.

In Taiwan, where Pinyin is not used, Wade-Giles has been retained to conform to local practice. In Hong Kong a romanization based on Cantonese is used. Pinyin would be in conflict with official practice in Hong Kong.

In order to facilitate reference to Wade-Giles names, the relationship of consonants and vowels in the two systems is shown on this page.

No attempt has been made in this atlas to fabricate Pinyin names by conversion from Wade-Giles or by other methods: all Pinyin names have been taken from official Chinese sources. There are several reasons why fabrication would be inadmissible. The name itself may have changed; the administrative status of the place may not be known; there may be errors in the Wade-Giles transcription; the reading of the Han character may have changed. In areas where the people are not Chinese, e.g. Sinkiang, Tibet, Inner Mongolia, guessing at the Pinyin spelling could produce nonsensical names. For example, the character **shen** in Chinese is used to produce **xain** in **xainza** but **sên** in **Sêndo**. Likewise, to convert **Pa-yen-wu-la** from Wade-Giles would give **Bayan Wula** for the place in Inner Mongolia which is shown on Plate 23 as **Xi Ujimqin Qi (Bayan Ul Hot)**.

COMPARATIVE TABLES OF PINYIN AND WADE-GILES

VOWELS

Wade-Giles	Pinyin	Approximate pronunciation	Pinyin	Wade-Giles
eh	**e**	**e** as in m**e**t	**e** (after h, g, k)	o
erh	**er**	**er** as in h**er**	**e** (after i, u, y)	eh
i (when initial or standing alone)	**yi**	**yea** as in **yea**st	**er**	erh
			i (after j, q, r, sh)	ih
ieh	**ie**	**ie** as in f**ie**sta	**ian**	ien
ien	**ian**	**ean** as in m**ean**der	**ie**	ieh
ih	**i**	**e** as in h**e**r	**ong**	ung
o (standing alone or after h, k, k')	**e**	**e** as in h**e**r	**ou** (after y)	u
			u (after j, q, x, y)	ü
o (after f, m, p, p', w)	**o**	**o** as in c**o**rn	**ü** (after l, n)	ü
o (after other consonants)	**uo**	**uo** as in d**uo**	**ui** (after g, k')	uei
			uo (after g, h, k, sh)	uo
u (after y)	**ou**	**ou** as in **you**	**uo** (otherwise)	o
ü (after l, n)	**ü**	**u** as in t**u** (French) or **ü** as in d**ü**nn (German)	**yan**	yen
			yi	i
ü (after ch, ch', hs, y)	**u**	**o** as in d**o**		
uei (occurs only after k, k')	**ui**	**uai** as in q**uai**nt	Certain syllables eg Wade-Giles **yai** cannot be converted mechanically from system to system	
ung	**ong**	**ung** as in j**ung** (German)		

Note
In both panels the first column gives the Wade-Giles in alphabetical order; the second gives the Pinyin equivalent; the third, the pronunciation. The fourth and fifth columns give the same information as the first and second, but in Pinyin alphabetical order, to enable the reader to refer back from Pinyin. Unless otherwise stated, consonants are pronounced as in English and vowels as in Italian.

CONSONANTS

Wade-Giles	Pinyin	Approximate pronunciation	Pinyin	Wade-Giles
ch (except when followed by i or ü)	**zh**	**j** as in **j**ump	**b**	p
			c	ts'
ch' (except when followed by i or ü)	**ch**	**ch** as in **ch**urch	**ci**	tz'u
			chi	ch'ih
chi; chü	**ji; ju**	**j** as in **j**am	**ch**	ch'
ch'i; ch'ü	**qi; qu**	**ch** as in church	**d**	t
chih	**zhi**		**g**	k
ch'ih	**chi**		**j**	ch (when followed by i or u)
hs	**x**	**sh** as in **sh**oe		
j	**r**	**r** as in **r**ed or **z** as in a**z**ure	**k**	k'
k	**g**	**g** as in **g**ood	**p**	p
k'	**k**	**k** as in **k**in	**q**	ch' (when followed by i or u)
p	**b**	**b** as in **b**at		
p'	**p**	**p** as in **p**at	**r**	j
ssu (sze)	**si**	**si** as in **si**erra	**si**	ssu (sze)
t	**d**	**d** as in **d**og	**t**	t'
t'	**t**	**t** as in **t**ot	**x**	hs
ts	**z**	**z** as in **z**ulu	**yi**	i
ts'	**c**	**ts** as in si**ts**	**you**	yu
tzu	**zi**	**ze** as in **ze**ro	**z**	ts
tz'u	**ci**	**tsy** as in Be**tsy**	**zi**	tzu
yai	**ya** or **ai**	**yea** as in **yea**	**zh**	ch
			zhi	chih

North America
Key to map plates